BARRON'S

FINANCE & INVESTMENT HANDBOOK

FIFTH EDITION

John Downes
Editor, *Beating the Dow*
Former Vice President, AVCO Financial Services, Inc.
Office for Economic Development, City of New York

Jordan Elliot Goodman
Financial Analyst, *NBC News at Sunrise*
Author, *Everyone's Money Book*
Creator, *The Money Answers Program*
Former Wall Street Correspondent,
MONEY Magazine, Time Warner Incorporated
Former Business News Commentator,
Mutual Broadcasting System

All inquiries should be addressed to:
Barron's Educational Series, Inc.
250 Wireless Boulevard
Hauppauge, New York 11788
http://www.barronseduc.com

Library of Congress Catalog Card No.: 98-36776

International Standard Book No.: 0-7641-5099-5

Library of Congress Cataloging-in-Publication Data
Barron's finance & investment handbook / John Downes, Jordan Elliot
    Goodman. — 5th ed.
      p. cm.
    Includes bibliographical references and index.
    ISBN 0-7641-5099-5
    1. Finance—Handbooks, manuals, etc.   2. Investments—Handbooks,
manuals, etc.   3. Finance—Dictionaries.   4. Investments—Dictionaries.
I. Goodman, Jordan Elliot.   II. Title: Finance & investment handbook.
HG173.D66   1999
332.67'8—dc21   98-36776
                                                                CIP

PRINTED IN THE UNITED STATES OF AMERICA

987654

CONTENTS

Contents

APPENDIX

ACKNOWLEDGMENTS

A project as massive as this *Handbook* is clearly the work of more than two people, and to thank all adequately would add considerably to its bulk. There are several individuals and organizations, however, without whose help the project in its present form would not have been feasible at all.

Following is the list of individuals, companies, and organizations whose help in preparation of this book was invaluable.

Accounting Today
American Association of Individual Investors
American Bankers Association
American Council of Life Insurance
American Express Company
American Institute of Certified Public Accountants
American Society of CLU & ChFC (Chartered Life Underwriters)
American Stock Exchange
Associated Credit Bureaus
Bankers Trust Company
A.M. Best & Company
Board of Trade of The City of New York
The Bond Buyer
Bond Market Association
Boston Stock Exchange
Canadian Consulate General (New York City)
Chase Manhattan Bank NA
Chicago Board of Trade
Chicago Board Options Exchange
Chicago Mercantile Exchange
Cincinnati Stock Exchange
Coffee, Sugar & Cocoa Exchange
Commodity Futures Trading Commission
Dow Jones & Company
Employee Benefit Research Institute
EQUIS International
The European Commission
Fannie Mae
Federal Energy Regulatory Commission
Federal Reserve Bank of New York
Federal Trade Commission
FINEX
Frank Russell Company
Futures Industry Association

Goldman Sachs & Company
Health Insurance Institute of America
Hulbert Financial Digest
IBC Organization
I/B/E/S Incorporated
Insurance Information Institute
Intermarket Management Incorporated
Internal Revenue Service
International Petroleum Exchange
International Swaps and Derivatives Association
Investment Company Institute
Investment Management Consultants Association
Investment Program Association
J. P. Morgan
Kansas City Board of Trade
Richard J. Kittrell, Esq./Kittrell & Kittrell P.C.
Liquidity Financial Corporation
London International Financial Futures Exchange
London Metal Exchange
MATIF, S.A.
Mercer and Company
Merrill Lynch
MidAmerica Commodity Exchange
Minneapolis Grain Exchange
Montreal Exchange/Bourse de Montreal
Morgan Stanley Dean Witter
Morningstar
Mortgage Bankers Association
Municipal Bond Investors Assurance Corporation
NASDAQ Stock Market
National Association of Investors Corporation
National Association of Real Estate Investment Trusts
National Association of Realtors
National Association of Securities Dealers
National Association of Variable Annuities
National Credit Union Administration
New York Cotton Exchange
New York Futures Exchange
New York Life Insurance Company
New York Mercantile Exchange
New York Stock Exchange
Office of Thrift Supervision
Options Clearing Corporation
Options Institute
Pacific Exchange
Pension Benefit Guaranty Corporation
Philadelphia Stock Exchange
Prudential Securities
Salomon Smith Barney
Securities and Exchange Commission
Securities Industry Association
Singapore International Monetary Exchange
Standard & Poor's Corporation

Sydney Futures Exchange
Tokyo Stock Exchange
Toronto Stock Exchange
Trimedia Incorporated
U.S. Department of Commerce
U.S. Department of Labor
Value Line Investment Survey
Visa International
Wall Street & Technology Magazine
WEFA Group
The Weiser Group
Wheat First Butcher Singer Incorporated
Wilshire Associates
Winnipeg Commodity Exchange
World Gold Council
Wrap Industry Association
Zacks Investment Research

Other people made contributions for which the word acknowledgment doesn't do. Thomas F. Hirsch, Barron's editor for the first two editions, was a full partner in the original project and we value his professional guidance and ongoing friendship. Mary Falcon and Lynne Vessie of Barron's handled an unbelievable amount of editorial work with skill and patience and guided this Fifth Edition to print. Roberta Yafie's tireless work in updating and in fact-checking thousands of pieces of information was truly incredible—her efforts and high standards went well beyond the call of duty. Austin Lynas spent several months meticulously updating the data on Publicly Traded Companies and Mutual Funds. We are immensely grateful to them all.

Suzanne and Jason Goodman, Katie Downes and Annie Downes-Whelan, and Nancy Weinberg all sacrificed unselfishly at various stages of the project and are in our debt.

John Downes
Jordan Elliot Goodman

PREFACE TO THE FIFTH EDITION

People retiring in the early years of the 21st century, the so-called baby boom generation, have witnessed a revolution in the world of finance and investment during their working years. The forces of globalization assure that their children, now in their earning years, face a future just as dynamic.

Deregulation of the securities, banking, and savings industries, starting in the 1970s, made a vast range of financial and investment products and services available to people at all economic levels. It also led to abuses and financial losses that required government intervention and a modernization of investor safeguards.

Merger mania in the "roaring 1980s" saw many of America's best-known corporations in hostile takeovers or leveraged buyouts financed by junk bonds, giving rise to defensive tactics known by such colorful names as the "poison pill," the "Pac-Man strategy," or the "white knight." Insider trading scandals were one result, but another was the innovation of investment techniques designed to capitalize on the profit opportunities created by corporate takeovers.

The 1990s brought corporate downsizing and restructuring, massive stock buybacks, strategic mergers on a global scale, and a prolonged bull market fueled by corporate profitability, low inflation, and sustained economic growth.

With globalization, the world's economies, more free of trade and economic barriers, have become more interdependent and in some ways more vulnerable. On the eve of the new millennium, political and economic turmoil in Russia, floundering Asian economies, and a recession in Japan threatened markets in North and South America and challenged the confidence of a new European Monetary Union with its common currency, the Euro, and its promise of expanded financial markets.

The computer and advanced communications systems have created both greater simplicity and greater complexity in the more unified world of finance and investment. By linking markets and processing massive information, these systems have given rise to investment vehicles, transactions, and methods of managing risk not previously imaginable.

The generation produced by the baby boomers must plan its personal finances in an economy offering less assurance of future financial security. The restructurings of the 1990s made corporations more efficient but took their human toll, just as the demographics that earlier created surpluses in the Social Security system became less favorable for future recipients. The enormous growth of 401(k) and individual retirement accounts addresses this problem but also points to its gravity.

The introduction of Roth IRAs, the lowering of long-term capital gains tax rates, and other provisions of the Taxpayer Relief Act of 1997 and the IRS Restructuring and Reform Act of 1998, also recognize the increasing importance of self-reliance in personal financial planning.

This thoroughly revised *Finance and Investment Handbook, Fifth Edition,* begins with a discussion of 30 key investment alternatives—with their many variations—as they have emerged from this period of historic change. Some are new, others are modernized versions of traditional investment vehicles. Each is presented with an introductory overview followed by questions and answers offering concise information on such crucial matters as costs; minimum purchase amounts; risks; liquidity; tax implications; and suitability for tax-deferred retirement plans. The section's purpose is not to offer specific recommendations, but rather to set forth in an easy-to-read format the vital features distinguishing the various investments so you will be able to make better-informed investment decisions.

Corporate annual reports and other communications of publicly held corporations, as an ironic result of stricter disclosure requirements, have become increasingly elaborate and difficult to understand, leaving many investors more befuddled than enlightened. The second section of the *Handbook* explains what corporate reports contain, what to focus on, and how to analyze and interpret the data provided.

You must know how to read and understand financial information in order to make intelligent investment choices and then to follow their progress. Not surprisingly, the proliferation of investment products and the broadening of public participation in the securities markets has fattened the financial sections of daily newspapers and flooded the World Wide Web with information aimed at individual and institutional investors. Also, with the growth of cable television, many investors are getting their financial news from channels displaying a running ticker tape throughout the business day. The third part of the *Handbook* explains how to read the financial news and the ticker tape.

Essential to decision-making in any field is understanding the language in which information is communicated. In a technical, dynamic field like finance and investment, keeping up with changing terminology would be a challenge in any event, but developments of the last decade have added a whole new lexicon of finance and investment terms and largely redefined the traditional vocabulary. The argot of the field has been spiced by a wave of new Wall Street buzzwords, like "chastity bonds," "Goldilocks economy," and "Lady Macbeth strategy." These and over 4000 other key terms are defined clearly and comprehensively, with examples and illustrations, in the *Handbook's* fourth major section, the Dictionary of Finance and Investment.

The fifth section of the *Handbook* presents wide-ranging reference material. The information, arranged in an easily accessible manner, is designed to be *used* by investors—beginners and professionals alike—to locate specific data as well as to gain a broader understanding of finance and investment.

The finance and investment marketplace has not only grown in size but has changed character as a result of diversification, mergers, and the introduction of new firms that exist either to market new investment products or to provide information on them. The regulatory establishment, which consists of federal and state government agencies as well as self-regulatory organizations, and relevant trade association and consumer protection groups have expanded and adapted to an industry and has become more consumer-oriented. The most important of these government and nongovernment organizations—including those of Canada—are listed in the opening portions of the *Handbook's* reference listings.

The growing importance of the individual consumer in the investment community has been a catalyst for the burgeoning financial information industry. The *Handbook* lists the major finance and investment publications from national magazines to specialized newsletters, providing addresses and telephone numbers so they can be contacted easily. The industry also has an important electronic dimension in the form of computer databases and software, and the major sources of these products are presented.

New to the Fifth Edition is a section called Investment Web Sites that list sources of news and analysis, historical information, broad general information on the economy, taxes and portfolio management, and specific information on stocks, bonds, mutual funds, futures and options and technical analysis.

"You can't tell the players without a scorecard" goes an old baseball adage, which certainly applies to today's major leagues of financial services. Despite diversification, financial institutions continue to be discussed mainly in terms of their principal and traditional activities—that is, as commercial banks, thrifts, brokerage firms, and life insurance companies. The *Handbook* lists the 100 largest in each of these categories. Also listed are the Federal Reserve and Federal Home Loan banks and branches, the primary government securities dealers, the 25 largest accounting firms, and the world's major securities and futures and options exchanges.

Highly useful information, including name, address, phone number, and investment objective of both open-end and closed-end mutual funds and fund families is provided for those who would rather leave portfolio decisions to a professional manager.

Increasingly, U.S. and Canadian exchanges, in response to growing investor interest, are listing options and futures on financial instruments, stock indexes, and foreign currencies, as well as traditional stock options and futures on agricultural and other commodities. The *Handbook* provides a complete and detailed summary of contracts of all types on all major U.S., Canadian, European, and Asian exchanges.

No handbook would be complete if it didn't supply the historical framework of the investment markets and the overall economy. This *Handbook* includes easy to understand but telling historical graphs together with background information and related statistical data on the principal stock and bond market indexes, as well as key economic indicators.

To facilitate ordering through brokers, particularly discount brokers, and to help you take advantage of an increasing willingness on the part of corporations to communicate directly with shareholders or potential shareholders, the *Handbook* provides a list—not readily available elsewhere—of the name, stock symbol, address, phone number, and line of business of several thousand public companies in which you can buy shares or American Depositary Receipts on the New York Stock Exchange, the American Stock Exchange, the Toronto Stock Exchange, and the NASDAQ National Market System. In addition, we indicate stocks on which listed options are traded and those offering dividend reinvestment plans. A limited number of companies offer free merchandise or other items or services of value as part of their shareholder relations efforts. You'll find a list of companies providing such "freebies."

The Appendix is an important part of the *Handbook*. In it you will find an annotated bibliography of selected key works on finance and investment. There is also a listing of the currencies of independent countries, which will be helpful in tracking international developments. At the conclusion of the *Handbook* is one of its important assets—the index—which will make is easier to find all the information on a particular topic in the book.

As in the previous edition, this revision recognizes the growing global context in which finance and investment decisions will be made as the 1990s lead into the new millennium.

HOW TO USE THIS *HANDBOOK* EFFECTIVELY

Each section of this *Handbook* is a self-contained entity. At the same time, however, the relevance of the various sections to each other is clear, since the objective of the *Handbook* is to join in one volume the different elements that together make up today's world of finance and investment. Tempting though it was from an editorial standpoint, cross-referencing has been kept to a minimum in the belief that readers would prefer not to be distracted by such editorial devices. At certain points, however, where reliance on the fuller explanation of a term in the *Handbook's* Dictionary of Finance and Investment seemed preferable to a discussion, cross-references to the dictionary are indicated by small capitals (for instance, ABC AGREEMENT). In any case, the dictionary is a source of comprehensive information on terms and concepts used throughout the *Handbook* and should be consulted whenever an aspect of finance and investment is not clear to you. The Table of Contents and especially the Index will also help you locate related information in different part of the *Handbook* and should be consulted regularly.

* * *

Although the *Handbook* was a collaborative effort in every sense of the word, primary responsibility was divided as follows: The sections on investment alternatives and reading financial reports were written by John Downes. The section on reading the financial pages was written by Charles Koshetz and edited by John Downes and Jordan Elliot Goodman. The Dictionary of Finance and Investment was authored coequally by John Downes and Jordan Elliot Goodman. The reference lists and the accompanying explanatory material were compiled, edited, and written by Jordan Elliot Goodman.

John Downes
Jordan Elliot Goodman

PART I

How to Invest Your Money: 30 Key Personal Investment Opportunities

INTRODUCTION

Perhaps the most important benefit of deregulation and other recent landmark changes in the securities and banking industries has been the availability to the average individual of investment alternatives that were formerly reserved for the wealthy. But welcome though this development is, it has brought with it choices that are bewildering both in range and complexity. Traditional investment vehicles have been modernized, new ones have been introduced, and, as the marketing departments of financial services conglomerates have sought to give their products mass appeal, the distinctions between different investment alternatives have become blurred.

This section presents 30 basic investment alternatives as they have emerged from the revolutionary events of the 1970s, 80s, and 90s. It is divided into 30 *basic* alternatives; each discussion, however, includes important variations, which, if counted separately, would more than double the number of alternatives.

The purpose of the section is not to provide advice. Investment decisions must always be made in subjective terms, taking into account one's financial position, risk comfort level, and goals. Rather, the section is designed to set forth in current terms the vital features distinguishing different investments, so you can talk knowledgeably with your investment counselor or, if you are a finance or investment professional, so you can be a better source of advice.

Preceding the discussions of investments is a table showing important characteristics of each investment. The chart is a quick way to learn pertinent facts, but should be used in conjunction with the discussions themselves to make sure you are aware of nuances and exceptions associated with a particular type of investment.

The discussions of investment alternatives begin with short overviews designed to describe the essential features of the investment and, where helpful, provide some historical perspective. These overviews are followed by sections in question-and answer format designed to present concisely and informatively the basic data needed to evaluate investment alternatives. Let's look at the questions and what they mean. (Remember, if you don't understand a finance or investment term, consult the extensive dictionary in this *Handbook*.)

Buying, Selling, and Holding

How do I buy and sell it? A few years ago, things were simpler: you bought your stocks and bonds from a broker, your life insurance from an insurance agent, and went to a bank with your savings or your loan request. The trend today is toward FULL-SERVICE BROKERS and FINANCIAL SUPERMARKETS that offer all these services and more. We have tried to be as helpful as possible, but there is no universality as to what full-service means from one firm to the next. One thing can be said for certain, though: you won't sound foolish these days if you ask a bank or broker if a given investment—no matter how specialized—can be bought or sold through his or her firm. DISCOUNT BROKERS are a special breed. They handle a variety of securities, but as a rule function strictly as brokers; some provide research, but do not look to them for investment guidance.

Is there a minimum purchase amount, and what is the price range? This question is aimed at giving you an idea of what it costs to get in the game, which is often more than just the minimum DENOMINATION or UNIT in which an investment is issued. The question cannot always be answered in absolute terms, since broker policies vary in terms of minimum orders and there may be SUITABILITY RULES requiring that you prove a certain financial capacity to take the risks associated with a particular investment. Certain securities trade in ROUND LOTS (for instance, 100 shares of common stock), though it is usually possible to buy ODD LOT quantities (for instance, 35 shares) at a higher commission per unit. In any event, call the broker and ask; many large firms have special programs that combine small orders from different investors and thereby make it possible to buy and sell modest amounts at modest commissions.

What fees and charges are involved? Again, we have been specific wherever possible, but with some investments, notably common stocks, commissions are sometimes negotiated, based on the size and nature of the transaction. DISCOUNT BROKERS, which as a rule do not give investment advice but execute trades at rates that are roughly half those of most full-service brokers, also have different rates for different transactions. Online brokers, which are becoming more populous as the Internet expands, offer even deeper discounts than traditional discount brokers for bare-bones service. See the entries for SHARE BROKER and VALUE BROKER in this *Handbook's* dictionary for discussions of different categories of discount broker. You will also frequently see references to DEALER spreads. This term refers to the MARKDOWNS and markups that are deducted from your selling price or added to your buying price when a broker-dealer is operating as a DEALER rather than simply as a BROKER.

Does it mature, expire, or otherwise terminate? Some investments are issued with a fixed MATURITY DATE, others are not. But even those with a fixed maturity date may be CALLABLE—that is, bought back at the pleasure of the issuer, or as part of a SINKING FUND provision. Others may have PUT OPTIONS, permitting REDEMPTION by the investor before maturity.

Can I sell it quickly? This question has to do with LIQUIDITY, the ability to convert an investment into cash without significant loss of value. Investments normally enjoying high liquidity are those with an active SECONDARY MARKET, in which they are actively traded among other investors subsequent to their original issue. Shares of LISTED SECURITIES have high liquidity. Liquidity can also be provided in other ways: for example, the SPONSOR of a unit investment trust might offer to MAKE A MARKET— to find a buyer to match you as a seller, should the need arise for you to sell.

How is market value determined and how do I keep track of it? MARKET VALUE is the price your investment would fetch in the open market, assuming that it is traded in a SECONDARY MARKET. In these discussions you will often encounter the word, VOLATILE, referring to the extent to which the market price of an investment fluctuates. Professionals use the term SYSTEMATIC RISK or its synonym market risk when discussing an investment's tendency to rise or fall in price as a result of market forces.

Investment Objectives

Should I buy this if my objective is capital appreciation? The purpose here is to identify investments likely to gain in value—to produce CAPITAL GAINS. Although APPRECIATION does not refer to capital growth due to factors such as reinvested dividends or compound interest, such factors are noted as a matter of relevance where they exist to a substantial degree. In the same category is appreciation due to ORIGINAL ISSUE DISCOUNT on fixed-income securities, which is considered interest. Other fixed-income investments bought in the market at a DISCOUNT from PAR because rising rates (or other factors) caused lower prices, create appreciation in the sense of capital gains either at REDEMPTION or when resold in the market at a higher price. Prices can also be at a PREMIUM, meaning higher than par value, when speaking of fixed-income investments.

Should I buy this if my objective is income? Here the purpose is to identify investments whose primary feature is providing regular income, as distinguished from alternatives primarily featuring capital gains or other potential values.

To what extent does it protect against inflation? If the value of an investment usually rises at the same rate or a higher rate than the rate of INFLATION erodes the value of the dollar, the investment is inflation-sensitive. Investments vary in the degree of protection they provide—some provide no protection. Although it is probably safe to assume that inflation will continue at a controlled rate for the foreseeable future, some economists, for the first time in many years, acknowledge a possibility of deflation. Assets that rise in value during inflation would decline in value during deflation.

Is it suitable for tax-deferred retirement accounts? Such accounts include INDIVIDUAL RETIREMENT ACCOUNTS (IRAs), ROTH IRAS, KEOGH PLANS, 401(K) PLANS, and other pension plans that are TAX-DEFERRED. The question addresses both the legality and, in some cases, the practicality of using a particular investment in such an account. Investments that might be ruled out for an IRA because of the $2000 annual maximum per person might be appropriate for an IRA ROLLOVER.

Can I borrow against it? This question considers the general value of an investment as COLLATERAL at a bank or other lending institution, and also the eligibility of an investment for trading in MARGIN ACCOUNTS with brokers under Federal Reserve Board MARGIN REQUIREMENTS. A key consideration is the concept of LEVERAGE, the ability to control a given amount of value with a smaller amount of cash. Borrowing can also be a way of raising cash when an investment is ILLIQUID.

Risk Considerations

How assured can I be of getting my full investment back? Here the discussion concerns safety of PRINCIPAL, which has mainly to do with two types of risk: (1) market or SYSTEMATIC RISK and (2) financial or CREDIT RISK (risk that an issuer will DEFAULT on a contractual obligation or that an EQUITY investment will lose value because of financial difficulty or BANKRUPTCY of an issuer). Insurance considerations and HEDGING, protecting against loss of value through an offsetting position, are also discussed where appropriate.

How assured is my income? Assuming an investment produces income, this question deals with market risk as it may (or may not) affect income, with an issuer's legal obligation to pay income, and with priority of claim in LIQUIDATION.

Are there any other risks unique to this investment? This question intends only to highlight risks peculiar to a particular investment. It is not meant to imply that any risks not included do not exist.

Is it commercially rated? Commercial RATING agencies, such as MOODY'S INVESTORS SERVICE and STANDARD & POOR'S CORPORATION, analyze and rate certain securities and their issuers on a continuous basis. Most ratings are designed to indicate a company's financial strength and thus guide investors as to the degree of CREDIT RISK a security represents, though sometimes other factors are rated. Rating changes usually affect market values.

Tax Considerations

What tax advantages (or disadvantages) does it offer? This discussion is designed to present the tax considerations associated with an investment. Obviously, each individual's tax situation is unique and each investor should obtain professional advice to determine whether an investment with certain tax features represents an advantage or disadvantage in his or her particular case. Many tax advantages formerly enjoyed by investors disappeared with the landmark Tax Reform Act of 1986 and subsequent tax acts. Instances where investment values have changed are noted.

Economic Considerations

What economic factors most affect buy, hold, and sell decisions? Here again, only the most general economic considerations are covered and what applies in general might not apply to you.

PERSONAL INVESTMENTS AT A GLANCE

The following chart applies nine key investment criteria to the 30 personal investment alternatives discussed in this section. It is designed simply to answer the question: Is this alternative one I might want to learn more about in view of my own investment objectives? A bullet (●) means that a given characteristic is usually associated, to one degree or another, with a particular alternative. A blank means it is not. A V means that variation within the investment category exists to such an extent that even broad classification would be misleading.

Exceptions abound, and in every case there is a question of degree. In the modern universe of investment alternatives, just about nothing is pure; that fact is indeed what this section of the Handbook is all about. So with cognizance of its limitations, use this chart for quick and handy reference and refer to the overviews and questionnaires for more complete understanding.

Investment	Regular Current Income	Capital Appreciation	Tax Benefits	Safety of Principal	Liquidity	Inflation Protection	Leverage*	Future Income or Security	Suitability for IRAs and other Tax-Deferred Accounts
Annuity		●	●	●		V		●	
Bond, Corporate	●	●		●	●				●
Closed-End Fund	●	●		V	●	V			●
Collectible		●				●			
Common Stock	●	●		V	●	●	●		●
Convertible Security	●	●		●	●	●	●		●
Foreign Stocks and Bonds	●	●		V	V	●			●
Futures Contract on a Commodity		●			●		●		
Futures Contract on an Interest Rate		●			●		●		
Futures Contract on a Stock Index		●			●		●		
Government Agency Security	●	●	●	●	●				●
Life Insurance (Cash Value)		●	●	●		V		●	
Limited Partnership	●	●	●	V		V			●

Investment	1	2	3	4	5	6	7	8
Money Market Fund	•			•	•			•
Mortgage-Backed (Pass-Through) Security	•		•	•				•
Municipal Security	•	•	• / >	•				•
Mutual Fund (Open-End)	•			•	>	>		•
Option Contract (Put or Call)	•			•				
Option Contract on a Futures Contract (Futures Option)	•			•		•		
Option Contract on an Interest Rate (Debt Option)	•			•		•		
Option Contract on a Stock Index	•			•		•		
Option Contract or Futures Contract on a Currency	•		>	•		•		
Precious Metals	•		•		•			
Preferred Stock (Nonconvertible)	•		•	•				•
Real Estate Investment Trust (REIT and FREIT)	•	•	>	•	•	>		•
Real Estate, Physical	>	>	>		• / >	•		>
Savings Alternatives	•	>	•	•	>			>
Treasury Securities	•	>	• / >	•	>			•
Unit Investment Trust	•		>	•	>			•
Zero-Coupon Security	•		•	•			•	•

* Refers to margin securities and investments wherein large amounts of value can be controlled with small amounts of cash. The general value of investments as loan collateral is covered in the discussions of each of the investment alternatives.

HOW TO INVEST YOUR MONEY: 30 KEY PERSONAL INVESTMENT OPPORTUNITIES

ANNUITY

After a period of modernization, tax rulings, and the shock of a big insurance company bankruptcy, the time-honored annuity is again gaining popularity as an investment alternative. It comes in several varieties, with two basic attractions: (1) tax-deferred capital growth and (2) the option of income for life or a guaranteed period. Among the drawbacks are high penalties (by insurers and the Internal Revenue Service) on premature withdrawal and lower investment returns than could usually be realized directly.

Traditionally, annuities provided fixed income payments for an individual's remaining lifetime in exchange for a lump-sum cash payment. But inflation's negative impact on fixed-income annuities combined with increased life expectancy gave rise, in the late 1950s, to the variable annuity, invested in assets, like stocks, that rise with inflation, thus preserving some purchasing power, although at the price of some market risk.

In the late 1960s and early 70s came the wraparound annuity, which enabled investors to wrap their own mutual funds, savings accounts, or other investments in the annuity vehicle, thus sheltering them from taxes. In the early 1980s, the IRS blew the whistle, ruling that to qualify for tax deferral, annuity investments had to be managed by insurance companies and be available only to annuity contract holders. The annuity once again became a vehicle largely limited to retirement goals, but it has gained appeal with the modern features acquired along the way.

Annuities are available in two basic types:

Fixed annuities are "fixed" in two ways: (1) The amount you invest earns interest (tax-deferred) at a guaranteed rate (1% to 2% under long-term U.S. government bonds, typically) while your principal is guaranteed not to lose value. (2) When you withdraw or opt to "annuitize" (begin taking monthly income) you receive a guaranteed amount based on your age, sex, and selection of payment options. Inflation protection is, of course, minimal.

Variable annuities, in contrast, are "variable" in two ways: (1) The amount you put in is invested in your choice of a stock, fixed-income bond or money market account, the value and/or earnings of which vary with market conditions. (2) Market value determines the amount available for withdrawals, or (with actuarial factors) the amount the annuitant is paid from one month to the next. Variable annuities thus offer inflation protection in exchange for market risk (minimized somewhat when switching among funds is permitted).

The bankruptcy in the early 1980s of the Baldwin-United Corporation, the biggest name in deferred annuities, shook the confidence of an investor community that had learned to take the financial strength of insurance companies for granted. As it turned out, arrangements were made for investors to regain most of their money, and confidence in the industry, which is heavily regulated and high on any scale of safety, was restored.

In general, annuities, with a variety of optional features for both accumulation and payout, are for long-term investors willing to trade liquidity and some degree of return for safety and tax-deferred capital growth, and whose objective is to defer taxability until later (lower tax-rate) years and/or to guarantee retirement income.

*   *   *

What Is an Annuity?

An annuity is a contract between an insurance company and an annuitant whereby the company, in exchange for a single or flexible premium guarantees a fixed or variable payment to the annuitant at a future time. *Immediate annuities* begin paying out as soon as the premium is paid; *deferred annuities,* which may be paid for in a lump sum or in installments, start paying out at a specified date in the future.

Buying, Selling, and Holding

How do I buy and sell it? Insurance brokers, insurance company sales agents, savings institutions, full-service brokers, commercial banks, and other financial service organizations sell annuities.

Is there a minimum purchase amount, and what is the price range? It varies with the plan, but deferred annuities typically have minimums ranging from $1000 to $5000.

What fees and charges are involved? Fees and charges may include front-end load sales charges ranging from 1% to 10% (although there is a trend toward no initial commissions), premium taxes (imposed on the insurance company by some states and passed on to contract holders), annual fees (typically $15 to $30 per year up to a maximum of $1\frac{1}{2}\%$ of account value), surrender charges or early withdrawal penalties (typically starting at 6% and decreasing to zero over a seven-year period), and other charges. (See Tax Considerations, below, for tax penalties).

Does it mature, expire, or otherwise terminate? Yes; both the accumulation period and the payout period are specified in the contract.

Can I sell it quickly? Accumulated cash value (principal payments plus investment earnings) can always be withdrawn, but there may be substantial withdrawal penalties as well as tax penalties.

How is market value determined and how do I keep track of it? Annuities do not have secondary market value, but information concerning account balances is supplied by the insurance company.

Investment Objectives

Should I buy an annuity if my objective is capital appreciation? Not in the sense that you would buy an investment at one price and hope to sell it at a higher price. But deferred annuities accumulate value through (tax-deferred) compounding, and variable annuities may be invested in stocks or other securities having capital gains potential.

Should I buy this if my objective is income? Annuities are designed to provide income for future guaranteed periods, so you would not buy a deferred annuity for current income needs.

To what extent does it protect against inflation? Fixed annuities provide no inflation protection. Variable annuities provide protection when their portfolios are invested in inflation-sensitive securities.

Is it suitable for tax-deferred retirement accounts? Yes, but since annuities have tax-deferred status themselves, it may be wiser to use them as supplements to IRAs, Keoghs, and other tax-deferred programs.

Can I borrow against it? Yes.

Risk Considerations

How assured can I be of getting back my full investment in an annuity? Insurance companies are heavily regulated and required to maintain reserves, so with established companies there is low risk of loss due to corporate failure. Most annuities permit early withdrawal of principal, but penalties may apply. Once annuitized (i.e., when payments by the insurance company begin) it becomes a question of how long you live. The insurance company (with the odds in its favor) bets you will die before the annuity is fully paid out.

How assured is my income? While variable annuity income can fluctuate, the risk of default is low. (See previous question.)

Are there any other risks unique to this investment? Although heavily regulated, insurance companies are potentially subject to mismanagement and fraud, and policyholders are not themselves covered by federal protection as bank depositors, for example, are covered by the Federal Deposit Insurance Corporation (FDIC).

Is it commercially rated? Yes. Insurance companies are rated by Best's Rating Service.

Tax Considerations

What tax advantages (or disadvantages) does an annuity offer? Earnings on money invested in deferred annuities, including all interest, dividends, and capital gains, accumulate and compound tax-deferred. Portions of payments to annuitants are returns of investor's principal and thus are not subject to income taxes. In variable annuities, you may switch among mutural funds without incurring a capital gains tax liability. Withdrawals of accumulated earnings prior to age 59½ or within 5 years of the purchase date (whichever comes first) are subject to a 10% tax penalty. (An exception is made for life annuities, payable for the lifetimes, or life expectancies, of one or more annuitants.)

Economic Considerations

What economic factors most affect buy, hold, and sell decisions? Although factors such as inflationary expectations and anticipated interest rate movements may guide choices among types of annuities, the decision to buy and hold is based on insurance rather than economic considerations. Annuities are appropriate for people without dependents or heirs, who seek assured income for their remaining lives.

BOND, CORPORATE (INTEREST-BEARING)

The traditional attractions of a corporate bond have been (1) higher yield compared to government bonds and (2) relative safety. Whether secured (usually a mortgage bond) or unsecured (called a debenture), it has a higher claim on earnings than equity investments. If the firm goes out of business, bonds also have a higher claim on the assets of the issuer, whose financial well-being is safeguarded by provisions in bond indentures and is closely monitored by the major bond rating services. Interest on corporates is fully taxable.

Much publicized in the 1980s because of their widespread use in financing corporate takeovers were so-called junk bonds, corporate bonds with lower than investment-grade ratings that pay high yields to compensate for high risk. Although issuers could point to the fact that high-yield bonds in general have had a low default record historically, fears that a prolonged recession would put the more heavily leveraged issuers in trouble have caused depressed prices and poor liquidity in the junk bond market at times when the economic outlook was gloomy.

Bonds are contracts between borrowers and lenders in which the issuer (borrower) promises the bondholder (lender) a specified rate of interest and repayment of principal at maturity.

The face, or par, value of a corporate bond is almost always $1000 (the exceptions being baby bonds with pars of $500 or less), but bonds do not necessarily sell at par value. Particularly in the secondary market, bonds are traded at discounts or premiums relative to par in order to bring their stated (coupon) rates in line with market rates. This inverse relationship between bond prices and interest rate movements causes market risk as the term applies to bonds; when interest rates rise, there is a decline in the price of a bond with a lower fixed interest rate.

Bond prices also vary with the time remaining to maturity. This is because of the time value of money and because time involves risk and risk means higher yield. Bond yields thus normally decrease (and prices increase) as the bond approaches maturity. The concept of yield-to-maturity is basic to bond pricing, and it takes into account the price paid for the bond and all cash inflows and their timing.

The safety and value of corporate bonds are also related to credit risk, quite simply the borrower's ability to pay interest and principal when due. The relative financial strength of the issuer, as reflected in the regularly updated rating assigned to its bonds by the major services, influences yield, which is adjusted by changes in the market price.

Concern that hostile takeovers and recapitalizations would weaken the value of existing holdings has inspired protective provisions in bond indenture agreements. Standard & Poor's publishes "Event Risk Covenant Rankings," a system's supplementing its credit ratings, that evaluates such protection. A common provision is the "poison put," which gives bondholders the right to redeem at par if certain designated events occur, such as a hostile takeover, the purchase of a big block of stock, or an excessive dividend payout.

Other considerations influencing corporate bond prices include the existence of call features, which empower the issuer to redeem prior to maturity, often to the disadvantage of the bondholder; call protection periods, which benefit holders; sinking funds, which require the issuer to set aside funds for the retirement of the bonds at maturity; put options giving the investor the right to redeem at specified times prior to maturity; subordinations, which give issues precedence over other issues in liquidation; and guarantees or insurance.

Variable-rate issues, usually called floating-rate notes even though some issues have terms of 30 years, adjust interest rates periodically in line with market rates. These issues generally have lower yields to compensate for the benefit to the holder, but they enjoy greater price stability to the extent the rate adjustments are responsive to market rate movements.

See also the discussions of Convertible Securities and Zero-Coupon Securities.

* * *

What Is a Corporate Bond?

A corporate bond is a debt security of a corporation requiring the issuer to pay the holder the par value at a specified maturity and to make agreed scheduled interest payments.

Buying, Selling, and Holding

How do I buy and sell a corporate bond? Through a securities broker-dealer.

Is there a minimum purchase amount, and what is the price range? Bonds are normally issued with $1000 par values, with baby bonds in smaller denominations. Issuers often have 5-bond minimums and broker-dealers trade in round lots of 10 or 100 units. Odd lots may be available at higher brokerage commissions or dealer spreads.

What fees and charges are involved? A per-bond commission of $2.50 to $20, depending on the broker and negotiations with the customer. However, a minimum charge of $30 is common. New issues involve no charges to the investor.

Does it mature, expire, or otherwise terminate? All bonds have maturity dates, but may be callable prior to maturity.

Can I sell it quickly? Usually yes. Most major issues are actively traded, but in large amounts. Small lots can be harder to trade and may involve some price sacrifice and higher transaction costs. Some high-yield junk bonds have been hard to sell because of the fear of default.

How is market value determined and how do I keep track of it? The market value of a fixed-income bond is a function of its yield to maturity and prevailing market interest rates. Prices thus decline when interest rates rise and rise when interest rates decline to result in an appropriate competitive yield. A change in the issuer's rating can also cause a change in price as higher (or lower) risk is reflected in the price/yield relationship. Even without a formal rating change, reduced demand can cause lower bond prices; this has been seen in junk bond prices reflecting fears that a recession will cause defaults. Bond prices are quoted in daily newspapers and electronic databases.

Investment Objectives

Should I buy a corporate bond if my objective is capital appreciation? Usually not, although capital appreciation is possible when bonds can be bought at a discount to their par value, bought prior to a drop in market interest rates, or bought at a favorable price because of a decline in the issuer's credit rating.

Should I buy this if my objective is income? Yes; bonds pay interest, usually semiannually. Yields on top-rated bonds are lower than on bonds of less than investment grade, called junk bonds, which pay more and have higher credit risk.

To what extent does it protect against inflation? Although normal inflationary expectations are built into interest rates, fixed-rate bonds offer no protection against high inflation. Variable-rate issues offer some protection.

Is it suitable for tax-deferred retirement accounts? Yes.

Can I borrow against it? Yes, subject to Federal Reserve margin rules (convertible bonds only) and brokerage-firm and lending-institution policies.

Risk Considerations

How assured can I be of getting my full investment back? If you hold to maturity, it will depend on the issuer's credit, which is evaluated regularly by the major investor's rating services and reflected in ratings from AAA down to D. If you plan to sell in the secondary market before maturity, you are subject also to market risk, the risk that bond prices will be down as a result of higher interest rates. Sophisticated investors sometimes protect against loss of value due to market risk by hedging, using options and futures available on long-term Treasury securities which are similarly affected by interest rate changes.

How assured is my income? Uninterrupted payment of interest depends on the issuer's financial strength and stability of earnings, factors reflected in its bond rating. Inflation can erode the dollar value of fixed-interest payments.

Are there any other risks unique to this investment? A callable bond can be redeemed by the issuer after a certain period has elapsed. Issuers normally force redemption when interest rates have declined and financing can be obtained more cheaply. Under just those circumstances, however, the investor finds the holding most attractive; the market price is up and the coupon interest rate is higher than the prevailing market interest rate. Look for bonds with call protection (typically 10 years). Event risk, the risk of a deterioration in credit quality owing to takeover-related changes in capitalization, is another consideration. Although issuers considering themselves vulnerable may have indenture provisions to protect bondholders (rated by Standard & Poor's Event Risk Covenant Rankings), such measures can result in early redemption and deprive the holder of a long-term investment.

Is it commercially rated ? Yes. Duff & Phelps/MCM, Fitch Investors Service, Moody's Investors Service, and Standard & Poor's Corporation are the major rating services.

Tax Considerations

What tax advantages (or disadvantages) does a corporate bond offer? None. Bond interest is taxed as ordinary income and realized gains are subject to capital gains tax, except that appreciation resulting from original issue discounts is taxed (as earned) at ordinary income rates.

Economic Considerations

What economic factors most affect buy, hold, or sell decisions? It is best to buy a corporate bond when interest rates are high and the best yields can be obtained. Holding is most attractive when rates are declining, causing an upward move in the market values of fixed-income securities. High inflation erodes the dollar value of fixed interest payments. Poor business conditions over a prolonged period can cause financial weakness and jeopardize a firm's ability to pay.

CLOSED-END FUND

Closed-end funds, so-called because, unlike open-end mutual funds, their sponsoring investment companies do not stand ready to issue and redeem shares on a continuous basis, have a fixed capitalization represented by publicly traded shares that are often listed on the major stock exchanges. Because the net asset value of a closed-end fund varies independently of its own share price, the investment has been compared to a water bed on a boat.

Closed-end funds tend to have specialized portfolios of stocks, bonds, convertibles, or combinations thereof, and may be oriented toward income, capital gains, or a combination of those objectives. Examples are the Korea Fund, which specializes in the stock of Korean firms and is an example of a "single country fund," and ASA Ltd., which invests in South African gold mining stocks. Both are traded on the New York Stock Exchange.

The attraction of a closed-end fund is twofold: (1) Because management is not concerned with continuous buying and selling to accommodate new investors and redemptions, a responsibility of open-end funds that frequently conflicts with ideal market timing, a well-managed closed-end fund can often buy and sell on more favorable terms. (2) Because the popular investor perception is just the opposite—that closed-end funds have less flexibility than open-end funds—shares of closed-end funds can usually be obtained at a discount from net asset value. As a result of these combined factors, annual earnings of closed-end funds sometimes exceed earnings of open-end funds with comparable portfolios.

A special form of closed-end fund is the *dual-purpose fund.* These hybrids have two classes of stock. Preferred shareholders receive all the income from the portfolio—dividends and interest—while common shareholders receive all capital gains realized on the sale of securities in the fund's portfolio. Dual-purpose funds are set up with a specific expiration date, when preferred shares are redeemed at a predetermined price and common shareholders claim the remaining assets, voting either to liquidate or continue the fund on an open-end basis.

Closed-end funds, of which more than 400 are publicly and actively traded, are regulated by the Securities and Exchange Commission.

See also the discussion of Mutual Funds.

* * *

What Is a Closed-End Fund?

A closed-end fund is a type of mutual fund that invests in diversified holdings and has a fixed number of shares that are publicly traded.

Buying, Selling, and Holding

How do I buy and sell a closed-end fund? Through a securities broker-dealer.

Is there a minimum purchase amount, and what is the price range? Round-lot 100 share purchases save commissions. Prices vary but many funds sell for $25 or less per share.

What fees and charges are involved? Standard brokerage commissions plus an annual management fee averaging $1/2\%$ to 1% of the investment.

Does it mature, expire, or otherwise terminate? Funds can be liquidated or converted to open-end funds or operating companies if a majority of shareholders approve. Dual-purpose funds expire, typically in ten years.

Can I sell it quickly? Usually yes. Most funds offer good liquidity.

How is market value determined and how do I keep track of it? By supply and demand factors affecting shares in the market. Whether shares trade at a premium (rare) or at more or less of a discount (the rule) relative to the net asset value of the fund, can depend on the portfolio, yield, the general market, and factors like year-end tax selling. Some funds have stock buyback programs designed to reduce outstanding shares and increase earnings per share. New issues tend initially to sell at premiums, then to slack off when brokers turn their aggressive sales efforts to other products. *The Wall Street Journal* and *The New York Times* on Monday and the weekly *Barron's,* report the net asset value, price, and discount or premium for the previous week on actively traded funds.

Investment Objectives

Should I buy a closed-end fund if my objective is capital appreciation? Although fund shares rise and fall in the marketplace, influenced, among other factors, by the value of the fund's portfolio, investors seeking to participate in capital gains would select a fund having appreciation as its primary objective—an aggressive stock fund, for example, as opposed to a bond fund, though gains and losses are possible in both. Dual-purpose funds offer two classes of stock, common share-holders benefiting from all the capital gains, preferred shareholders getting all the interest and dividend income. Funds bought at a discount offer the prospect of additional appreciation through increases in fund share prices.

Should I buy this if my objective is income? Yes, especially funds whose objective is income. (See the preceding question.) Some funds offer guaranteed payouts, but it should be recognized that unless the fund generates income equal to the guaranteed payment, it may come out of funds contributed by investors.

To what extent does it protect against inflation? Some portfolios are more sensitive (less vulnerable) to inflation than others, stocks being better than bonds, for example. Of course, increases in the portfolio benefit investors only when passed on in capital gains distributions or reflected in higher fund share values.

Is it suitable for tax-deferred retirement accounts? Yes.

Can I borrow against it? Yes, subject to Federal Reserve margin requirements and individual lender policies.

Risk Considerations

How assured can I be of getting my full investment back? Fund shares can be just as volatile as common stock. Professionals use various techniques to hedge funds selling at discounts or premiums or converting to open-end funds. These techniques include purchasing options and selling short other funds, treasury securities and futures, and stocks in the same fund's portfolio. Some funds have "open-ending" provisions, whereby they guarantee that investors can choose to collect the full net asset value of fund shares on a specified future debt; it is important to note, however, that although the net asset value may be higher than the market price, it can be lower than your original investment.

How assured is my income? It depends on the quality of the portfolio and the risk characteristics of the investments comprising it. Funds offering guaranteed payouts may have to liquidate capital to make good.

Are there any other risks unique to this investment? The risk unique to closed-end funds is that the value of fund shares can move independently of the value of the securities comprising the fund's portfolio. If this causes shares to trade at a discount to net asset values, it is bad for holders, although it can be viewed as a buying opportunity.

Is it commercially rated? Funds are not usually rated, but information helpful to investors is provided by Standard & Poor's Stock Record Sheets, Moody's Finance Manuals, and other sources.

Tax Considerations

What tax advantages (or disadvantages) does a closed-end fund offer? The tax treatment of closed-end fund shares is the same as for common stock except that capital gains distributions enjoy preferential long-term capital gains treatment regardless of how long the fund has been held.

Economic Considerations

What economic factors most affect buy, hold or sell decisions? Most experts say to buy when shares can be obtained at a good discount and the stock market seems poised for a rise. Otherwise, decisions should consider the effects of different economic and market scenarios on various types of portfolios, such as bonds, stocks, or convertibles. It is probably wise to view closed-end funds as long-term investments and to sell when significant appreciation has occurred.

COLLECTIBLES

Collectibles, the name for a diverse range of physical possessions presumed to gain value with time, enjoyed a wave of popularity as a haven for investment money during the inflation-ravaged 1970s. Then the 1981–82 recession revealed how fickle the marketplace can be and how vulnerable collectibles are to adverse economic conditions. When that period was followed by one in which inflation was brought under control and financial investments became attractive again, enthusiasm for collectibles as an investment alternative, exclusive of their utility or personal enjoyment value, waned considerably. Some collectibles continue to perform well, although the frenzied interest of the 1970s never returned.

There is no universal definition of a collectible. Some experts apply the criteria of rarity, quality, uniqueness, and age, while others put commodities with utilitarian value (like gemstones) or intrinsic value (like coins with gold or silver content) in addition to collector's value in separate categories.

In the broadest definition, however, collectibles are physical assets (not financial or real, in the sense of real estate), that have psychic or utilitarian value for their owners, are unique or in limited supply, and can be expected to increase in value with time and demand. The category thus includes stamps, coins, antiques, gemstones, fine art, photographs, and an almost endless list of other groups and subdivisions ranging from folk art and crafts to baseball cards, comic books, antique automobiles, and miscellaneous collectible junk.

While books have been written on the major categories of collectibles, certain common denominators exist to varying degrees from an investment perspective: often high costs to trade and own; high price volatility; no current income; and undependable or poor liquidity.

These factors plus the opportunity cost of an unproductive investment lead to one conclusion: Collectibles, especially when the relevant group of collectors is solidly in place and in good communication, will probably gain value and outstrip inflation over the long term, but the costs and risks of holding collectibles for investment purposes can be justified only when the assets also provide their owners pleasure or utility.

* * *

What Is a Collectible?

A collectible is a physical asset of a non-real estate and nonfinancial nature that exists in limited supply, usually provides enjoyment or utility to its owner, and is expected to increase in value because of inflation or supply and demand factors such as popularity and rarity.

Buying, Selling, and Holding

How do I buy and sell a collectible? Through dealers, galleries, auctions, private owners, flea markets, and catalogs and other collector publications.

Is there a minimum purchase amount, and what is the price range? Minimums and price ranges vary with the collectible and run a gamut from a few pennies to millions of dollars.

What fees and charges are involved? This depends on the collectible, where it is traded, and many other factors, but fees are an important consideration. Costs may include dealer profits (markups), sales taxes, appraisal fees, storage and safe keeping, maintenance, insurance, as well as opportunity cost—the return you would get if your money were invested more productively.

Does it mature, expire, or otherwise terminate? No.

Can I sell it quickly? A collectible varies in liquidity, from one, like a painting or an antique, bought through established dealers standing ready to repurchase at an agreed-on price, to another salable only through consignment to dealers or auction houses.

How is market value determined and how do I keep track of it? Market value is determined by supply and demand. Some collectibles are more vulnerable to fads than others, and the marketplace can be more efficient in one type of collectible than another because it has more dealers and better communication among dealers and collectors. Some major newspapers, like *The New York Times*, carry advertisements for collectibles of various types; most of the main categories of collectibles are served by specialized periodicals or newsletters; and a number of national magazines contain classified sections and even articles aimed at collectors within their fields of interest. Dealers and appraisers are a source of information about market value, but it is important to satisfy oneself as to their objectivity.

Investment Objectives

Should I buy a collectible if my objective is capital appreciation? Yes, but short-term profits depend on a combination of expertise and luck, and long-term appreciation can be affected by fads as well as economic developments.

Should I buy this if my objective is income? No.

To what extent does it protect against inflation? Although there are many risks that can undermine the value of a collectible, if the condition of the collectible remains good and supply and demand factors stay favorable, values will increase with inflation.

Is it suitable for tax-deferred retirement accounts? Collectibles are not legal investments in such accounts unless they are part of portfolios directed by trustees.

Can I borrow against it? Yes; many lenders will accept marketable collectibles as collateral.

Risk Considerations

How assured can I be of getting my full investment back? With most collectibles, this has mainly to do with your level of expertise and the amount of time you hold the asset. In the short term, it is likely that costs and commissions will offset whatever small gain might be realized. In the long run, collectibles become more limited in supply and (assuming good quality and condition) more valuable, but only if the demand has continued strong and economic conditions have not eroded purchasing power. Many collectibles are vulnerable to fads, though some bought from well-established and reputable dealers may be sold back at agreed upon prices.

How assured is my income? Collectibles normally provide no income, and are in fact a drain on cash that might otherwise be invested for income.

Are there any other risks unique to this investment? Collectibles are subject to a wide range of unique risks—forgery and other frauds; physical risk, such as deterioration, fire, and theft; "warehouse finds," where a large supply of a previously limited item is suddenly discovered and becomes a drug on the market; the reverse situation, where a large chunk of a given collectible's supply goes "in collection," leaving so little in circulation that diminished interest reduces demand.

Each category has its own special risks and prospective collectors are advised to research them.

Is it commercially rated? No.

Tax Considerations

What tax advantages (or disadvantages) does it offer? Realized capital gains and capital losses are subject to standard rates for capital assets. Other tax advantages may pertain, depending on whether the collecting is done as a hobby or as a for-profit investment activity. Tax advice should be obtained.

Economic Considerations

What economic factors most affect buy, hold, and sell decisions? Collectibles have traditionally been favored by investors in times of inflation, though the value of this investment category as an inflation hedge is tempered by the many risks. The marketability of collectibles is more dependent on good economic conditions than most other investments.

COMMON STOCK

For total return over the long term, no publicly traded investment alternative offers more potential under normal conditions than common stock.

A share of common stock is the basic unit of equity ownership in a corporation. The shareholder is usually entitled to vote in the election of directors and on other important matters and to share in the wealth created by corporate activities, both through the appreciation of share values and the payment of dividends out of the earnings remaining after debt obligations and holders of preferred stock are satisfied. In the event of liquidation of assets, common shareholders divide the assets remaining after creditors and preferred shareholders have been repaid.

In public corporations, shares have market values primarily based on investor expectations of future earnings and dividends. The relationship of this market price to the actual or expected earnings, called the price-earnings ratio or "multiple," is a measure of these expectations. Stock values are also affected by forecasts of business activity in general and by whatever "investor psychology" is produced by the immediate business and economic environment.

Stocks of young, fast-growing companies, particularly those in industries that are cyclical or high technology-oriented, tend to be volatile, to have high price-earnings ratios, and generally to carry a high degree of risk. Called *growth stocks,* they seldom pay dividends, since earnings are reinvested to finance growth. These stocks are often traded in the over-the-counter market or on the American Stock Exchange.

At the other end of the spectrum, stocks of old, established firms in mature industries and with histories of regular earnings and dividends tend to be characterized by relative price stability and low multiples. These stocks are usually found listed on the New York Stock Exchange (although there are exceptions) and the cream of the crop are known as blue chips. As a general category, these regular dividend payers are called *income stocks.*

Spanning the growth income continuum is a wide range of common stock investment choices that can be made only in terms of one's personal objectives and risk comfort level. To help in the process is a professional establishment comprised of brokers, investment advisers, and financial planners supported by practitioners of various securities analysis approaches—those trained in fundamental analysis, technical analysis, chartists, and others.

Investors with limited means can gain the advantages of common stock ownership together with the benefits of professional management and portfolio diversification through mutual funds, which are discussed elsewhere in this section.

*   *   *

What Is Common Stock?

A common stock represents ownership in a corporation, usually carries voting rights, and often earns dividends (paid out at the discretion of the corporation's board of directors).

Buying, Selling, and Holding

How do I buy and sell common stock? Through a securities broker-dealer. Some companies permit direct purchase of shares as part of their dividend reinvestment plans.

Is there a minimum purchase amount, and what is the price range? There is no minimum, but buying in round lots (usually 100 shares) saves extra odd-lot (under 100 shares) charges. Some brokers offer programs allowing odd-lot purchases at regular rates. Stock prices range widely, with the majority under $50.

What fees and charges are involved? The brokerage commission, the principal charge, varies by the value and/or size of transaction. Discount brokers charge less than full-service brokers. A nominal transfer tax is imposed on sellers by the federal government and several state governments. Interest and other charges may be incurred in margin accounts, in which qualifying stocks can be traded on credit within requirements of the Federal Reserve Board and individual brokerage firms.

Does it mature, expire, or otherwise terminate? No, although tender offers by issuing companies and outside acquirers often give shareholders the opportunity to sell within a set period at a premium over prevailing stock market prices.

Can I sell it quickly? Usually, yes. Shares of publicly held and actively traded companies are highly liquid.

How is market value determined and how do I keep track of it? Market value is basically determined by investor expectations of future earnings and dividend payments, although the value of assets is also important. Prices may also be affected temporarily by large transactions creating bid-offer imbalances, by rumors of various sorts, and by public tender offers. Newspapers and electronic databases show daily prices on stocks traded on exchanges and over the counter.

Investment Objectives

Should I buy common stock if my objective is capital appreciation? Yes, especially growth stocks of younger firms, which tend to reinvest earnings rather than pay dividends as older, established firms do.

Should I buy this if my objective is income? Yes, especially if your objectives also include some capital appreciation and inflation protection. Established companies are more likely to pay dividends regularly than are fast-growing firms that tend to reinvest earnings.

To what extent does it protect against inflation? Over the long run, stocks rise in value and increase dividends with inflation, though they do not protect against hyperinflation.

Is it suitable for tax-deferred retirement accounts? Yes. Stocks are suitable for IRAs, Keoghs, 401(K) plans, and other tax-deferred plans.

Can I borrow against it? Yes, subject to Federal Reserve margin rules and lender policies concerning marketable securities collateral.

Risk Considerations

How assured can I be of getting my full investment back? There is no concrete assurance. There is always the risk that market prices will decline in value, though some stocks are more volatile than others. When a company goes out of business and liquidates its assets, common shareholders are paid last—after preferred stock-holders and creditors.

How assured is my income? Dividends come out of earnings and are declared at the discretion of the board of directors. They can be suspended if profits are off, or if the directors decide reinvestment is preferable. Older, established, blue chip companies are the most dependable dividend payers; young, growth-oriented firms tend to reinvest earnings and thus pay no (or low) dividends.

Are there any other risks unique to this investment? Anything that can affect the fortunes of a company can affect its stock value and dividend payments.

Is it commercially rated? Yes, Moody's, Standard & Poor's, Value Line Investment Survey, and others rate many publicly traded issues.

Tax Considerations

What tax advantages (or disadvantages) does common stock offer? Dividends to individuals are fully taxable in the year they are paid, at the shareholder's tax rate. Gains on the sale of stock held more than one year receive a preferential long-term capital gains rate of 20% (10% for those in the 15% income bracket). After-tax corporate earnings not paid out as dividends accumulate without being taxed. Corporations can exclude 70% of dividends received from other domestic corporations.

Economic Considerations

What economic factors most affect buy, hold, or sell decisions? Stocks are most attractive as holdings when inflation is moderate, interest rates are low, and business conditions are generally favorable to growth and bigger profits.

CONVERTIBLE SECURITY

Convertible securities—bonds (debentures) or preferred stock convertible into common stock (usually of the issuer but, in rare cases. of the issuer's subsidiary or affiliate)—offer both fixed income and appreciation potential but are not quite the best of both worlds. The yield on the convertible bond or preferred is normally less than that of a "straight" bond or preferred, and the potential for capital gain is less than with a common stock investment.

On the other hand, convertibles (sometimes called CVs and identified that way in the newspaper bond tables, but not the stock tables) do offer less credit risk and market risk than common shares while providing an opportunity to share in the future wealth of the corporation for whose shares the convertible can be exchanged.

In terms of priority of claim on earnings and assets, convertible bonds and convertible preferred stock have the same status as regular bonds and preferred. Bonds, whether convertible or straight, receive payments before preferred stock, whatever its type, and both bonds and preferred have precedence over common stock.

From the investor's standpoint, convertibles must be understood in terms of what is called their *investment value* and their *conversion value*. Investment value is the market value the convertible would have if it were not convertible—its value as a straight bond or straight preferred. Conversion value is the market price of the common stock times the number of shares into which the bond or preferred is convertible (called the conversion rate or ratio).

Since convertible owners hope to capitalize on rises in common shares through conversion and therefore value the conversion privilege, CVs begin trading at a premium over conversion value. As the common rises and the CV is viewed more and more as a common stock investment, the CV tends to sell for its common stock equivalent. Conversion is not advisable until the common dividend has more value than the income on the CV and it is normal for the common price to rise beyond the CV price until that equation is reached.

Of course, common-share prices cannot be guaranteed to rise, and in a down market convertible holders look at their investment in terms of its value as a bond or preferred stock. This investment value represents downside risk protection in the sense that the convertible will never be worth less than this value. Investment value is, however, subject to market risk; it can be pushed down by a general rise in interest rates. But should that happen, investors have downside protection in that the CV will never drop significantly below its conversion value.

Conventional wisdom holds that investors should not buy convertibles unless attracted by the soundness of the underlying common stock. They should be wary also of issues selling at high premiums over the value of the common stock or the prices at which they are callable.

See also the discussion of Zero-coupon Securities.

* * *

What Is a Convertible Security?

A convertible security is a preferred stock or debenture (unsecured bond) paying a fixed dividend or rate of interest and convertible into common stock, usually of the issuer, at a specified price or conversion ratio.

Buying, Selling, and Holding

How do I buy and sell a convertible security? Through a securities broker-dealer.

Is there a minimum purchase amount and what is the price range? Convertible preferred stock typically trades in 10-share round lots and has par values ranging from $100 down to $10. Bonds sell in $1000 units but exceptions, called baby bonds, can have lower par values, usually $500 down to $25. Brokers often have minimum orders of 10 bonds or, frequently, 100 bonds. Odd lots involve higher commissions or dealer spreads.

What fees and charges are involved? Standard brokerage commissions or dealer spreads. Bonds usually involve a per-bond commission of $2.50 to $20, depending on the broker and the size of the order. However, a minimum of $30 is common.

Does it mature, expire, or otherwise terminate? Bonds mature; preferred stocks do not. Both may be callable, however, and the regular redemption and retirement of both shares and bonds may be provided for by sinking fund agreements. Of course, once converted to common stock, there are no maturities or calls.

Can I sell it quickly? Most can be readily sold, but trading volume is not ordinarily heavy and prices can fluctuate significantly.

How is market value determined and how do I keep track of it? Market value is influenced both by the market price of the underlying common stock and the investment value of the convertible security—that is, its value as a bond or preferred stock exclusive of the conversion feature. When the conversion premium—the amount by which the price of the convertible security exceeds the price of the underlying common stock—is high, the convertible trades like a bond or preferred stock. When trading like a fixed-income investment, its value fluctuates in inverse relation to interest rates, though it will not decline below its investment value. Once parity has been reached—that is, the price of the convertible and its value assuming conversion are the same—the convertible will rise along with the underlying common stock. Prices of convertibles are reported in the stock or bond tables of daily newspapers and in electronic databases.

Investment Objectives

Should I buy a convertible security if my objective is capital appreciation? Yes; convertibles offer the opportunity to capitalize on growth in common share values while enjoying the greater yield and safety of bonds or preferred.

Should I buy this if my objective is income? Yes; but since growth is a feature, the yield is less than on a straight bond or preferred.

To what extent does it protect against inflation? Convertible prices tend to rise with common share prices, which tend to rise with inflation.

Is it suitable for tax-deferred retirement accounts? Yes, CVs qualify for IRAs, Keoghs, 401(K) plans, and other tax-deferred plans.

Can I borrow against it? Yes, subject to margin rules. CVs are acceptable general collateral, with bonds having more loan value than stock.

Risk Considerations

How assured can I be of getting my full investment back? CVs have downside protection in that their value will not sink below the market value the same investment would have as a straight (nonconvertible) bond or preferred. That "investment value" varies inversely with rates, however, so when rates go up the "floor" goes down. The price of a CV is determined, on the other hand, by the value of its conversion feature, so as long as the common holds up, the CV should not decline to its investment value. Of course, once converted, your investment becomes subject to all the risks of common stock. In liquidation, convertible bonds are paid before convertible preferred stock, and both have precedence over the corporation's common stock.

How assured is my income? The interest on convertible bonds, as a legal obligation of the issuer, has a higher claim on earnings than dividends on convertible preferred stock, which can be omitted if the issuer gets tight for cash. Preferred dividends must be paid before common dividends, however. Assuming the issuer is strong financially and has dependable earnings, there is little to worry about.

Are there any other risks unique to this investment? Dilution—a decrease in the value of common shares into which the CV converts—can happen for many reasons. Provision for such obvious corporate actions as stock splits, new issues, or spinoffs of stock or other properties, is normally made in the bond indenture or preferred stock agreement, but subtle developments, such as small quarterly stock dividends or unplanned events, can be a risk.

Is it commercially rated? Yes, by Moody's, Standard & Poor's, Value Line, and other services.

Tax Considerations

What tax advantages (or disadvantages) does it offer? None, except that gains resulting from conversion to the issuer's common stock are not treated as gains for tax purposes, provided the stock you receive is that of the same corporation that issued the convertible. Corporations can exclude from taxes 70% of preferred dividends.

Economic Considerations

What economic factors most affect buy, hold, or sell decisions? Assuming economic conditions are not threatening the issuer's financial health, convertibles offer holders protection from adverse factors affecting both common stock and fixed-income securities. The CV is thus a security for all seasons, though the price of having it both ways is less appreciation potential than common stock and less yield than straight bonds or preferred stock. It follows that CVs are popular in times of economic and market uncertainty. The ideal time to buy is when rates are high and stocks are low and the best time to hold is in a rising stock market. Stagflation is the worst scenario because stocks are hurt by the stagnation and fixed-income securities are hurt by the inflation; both the conversion and investment values of CVs thus suffer.

FOREIGN STOCKS AND BONDS

Foreign stocks and bonds—those of foreign issuers denominated in foreign currencies—offer opportunities (1) to invest where economies or industry sectors may be faster growing than those at home and (2) to augment total returns through profits on currency movements.

Foreign securities began gaining luster in the 1970s and 1980s, as ways to shift money from sometimes sluggish U.S. markets into more vibrant overseas economies (while gaining an edge on domestic inflation, which was rampant during those years) and as "dollar plays," ways of capitalizing on expected declines in the value of the U.S. dollar vis-a-vis foreign currencies. Generally, foreign investment activity picked up with deregulation of foreign markets, improved communications, and increased internationalization of business.

The mid-1990s, however, brought good news and bad news. What had been hailed as the "Asian miracle," an explosive economic boom in the Asian-Pacific region, suddenly and without warning gave way to economic turmoil and currency collapses that caused investment values to sink not only in that region, but also in Latin America and to some extent in Europe. That, in turn spurred massive capital flows into the U.S. economy, helping to fuel a raging bull market and making the dollar strong.

Approaching the year 2000, the United States is poised for an economic slowdown that is long overdue. At the same time, Western Europe is about to take a giant step into the economic unknown. In 1999 Germany, France, Italy, Spain, and seven smaller European countries will meld their currencies (officially effective in 2002) and economic policies into one. The aim is an economic community where markets, not governments, steer economies and where the Euro will counterbalance the global importance of the dollar. Some say that Europe now is like the United States 15 years ago, poised for a wave of deregulation, innovation, merger mania, and cost cutting—all catnip for stock prices. And the uniting of countries traditionally too small to support corporate bond markets may mean a bonanza in European corporate bond issuance. Exciting as all that sounds, however, Europe has traditionally been conservative and nationalistic, and it remains to be seen what Euroland will mean for international interests.

In Asia, some of the broken economies seem to be mending, but the outlook is far from clear. As this is written in late 1998, some Pacific stock indexes are off 30% from where they were 12 months ago. An opportunity? Perhaps. But fraught with uncertainty.

Problems with foreign investments, depending on the issue and the market, include inadequate financial information and regulation; high minimum purchase requirements; additional transaction costs and risks; taxes; possible illiquidity; political risk; and the possibility of currency losses. Unless you are wealthy, able to take big risks, and sophisticated in the ways of international interest rates and foreign exchange, you are better advised to achieve international diversification through open-end and closed-end funds or other investment pools specializing in foreign securities.

An exception for some investors might be American Depositary Receipts (ADRs). Many foreign stocks can be owned by way of these negotiable receipts, which are issued by United States banks and represent actual shares held in their foreign branches. ADRs are actively traded on the major stock exchanges and in the over-the-counter market. Although currency risks and foreign withholding taxes remain, the depositary pays dividends and capital gains in U.S. dollars and handles rights offerings, splits, stock dividends, and other corporate actions. ADRs eliminate trading inconveniences and custodial problems that otherwise exist with foreign stocks.

Eurobonds—bonds issued by governments and their agencies, banks, international institutions, and corporations (U.S. and foreign) and sold outside their countries through international syndicates for purchase by international investors—also warrant a special word. They may be denominated in foreign currencies, Eurodollars, or composite currency units, such as Special Drawing Rights (SDRs) or European Units of Account (EUAs) whose certificates representing the combined value of two or more currencies are designed to minimize the effects of currency fluctuations. Most are fixed-income obligations, but some Eurodollar issues have floating rates tied to the London Interbank Offered Rate (LIBOR). Eurobonds, which are issued in bearer form, attract upscale personal investors because they are available in a wide range of maturities, are not subject to a withholding tax, and offer good liquidity.

Traditionally, new issues of Eurobonds may not be sold legally to United States investors until a 90-day seasoning period has expired. Actually, most United States broker-dealers extend this rule to include all new issues in foreign currencies; foreign banks and broker-dealers are generally more solicitous of United States investors in selling new issues. Except for Yankee bonds, obligations of foreign borrowers issued in the United States and denominated in dollars, foreign bonds are not subject to Securities and Exchange Commission regulation.

*　*　*

What Are Foreign Stocks and Bonds?

Foreign stocks and bonds are stock of foreign companies listed on foreign exchanges; stock of foreign companies listed on United States exchanges or represented by listed American Depositary Receipts (ADRs); bonds of foreign government entities and corporations, including Eurobonds and nondollar-denominated bonds issued by local syndicates.

Buying, Selling, and Holding

How do I buy and sell foreign stocks and bonds? Through securities broker-dealers with foreign offices or with expertise in foreign markets, and through foreign banks and their American offices. (ADRs and shares traded on U.S. exchanges can be bought and sold through any broker.)

Is there a minimum purchase amount, and what is the price range? ADRs and U.S. exchange-listed foreign stocks trade just like domestic common stock. Minimums on other stocks and bonds vary widely by issue and dealer, but are often high. With the extra risks, diversification is important, which raises the cost even higher. Unless you are wealthy, you should probably opt for one of the mutual funds or other investment vehicles pooling foreign securities.

What fees and charges are involved? Transaction costs can be a significant consideration. They vary depending on many factors, but may include custodial fees, local turnover or transfer taxes, and currency conversion fees, in addition to broker commissions or dealer spreads. Transaction and custodial costs are minimized with ADRs.

Do foreign stocks and bonds mature, expire, or otherwise terminate? Bonds mature, stocks do not. However remote, the risk exists that a sovereign government will confiscate or devalue assets of foreign investors.

Can I sell them quickly? U.S. exchange-listed foreign stocks and ADRs normally enjoy high liquidity. With other foreign securities, illiquidity is often a problem. Even widely held issues are often kept as permanent investments by governments, banks, and other companies and may not trade actively. Canada, England, and Japan have high average turnover on their stock exchanges.

How is market value determined and how do I keep track of it? Economic, market, and monetary (interest-rate) factors affect foreign stock and bond values the same way they do domestic equity and debt securities, though conditions and growth rates differ among countries. Traditionally, foreign stocks, on average, have been less volatile than domestic issues, because issuers tended to be older firms whose stock was held largely by long-term investors. Today, foreign exchanges list a growing number of young, dynamic companies whose shares are actively traded and often quite volatile. *The Wall Street Journal,* the *Financial Times* (London), and other leading newspapers report on major foreign exchanges, as well as ADRs and foreign stocks and bonds traded in domestic markets.

Investment Objectives

Should I buy foreign stocks and bonds if my objective is capital appreciation? Especially in growing economies, stocks offer potential for both capital and currency appreciation. Unless bought at a discount or in a period of declining interest rates, bonds do not appreciate, although gains due to currency movements are possible.

Should I buy them if my objective is income? Yes, but most foreign stocks have lower dividend yields than domestic stocks, and exchange-rate fluctuations are a factor in the expected returns of both stocks and bonds.

To what extent do they protect against inflation? Foreign stocks can hedge inflation to the extent local economies and industry sectors offer better growth prospects than exist in the United States. But gains from dividends and appreciation can be eroded by foreign-exchange losses.

Are they suitable for tax-deferred retirement accounts? Yes.

Can I borrow against them? Yes; quality securities are acceptable collateral at most banks, and banks headquartered in the country of the issuer will often lend higher percentages of value. Foreign stocks listed on American exchanges are subject to Federal Reserve margin requirements.

Risk Considerations

How assured can I be of getting my full investment back? Although more young, growing firms appear every day on foreign exchanges, most shares represent solid issuers and volatility has traditionally been low, so foreign equities, on average, may actually be safer than many domestic issues, assuming no adverse currency fluctuations. Bondholders, who lack regulatory protection and full credit information, have more credit risk than owners of domestic issues, in addition to having political, interest rate, and currency risks. (Foreign exchange risk can be hedged using currency futures and options.)

How assured is my income? Since issuers tend to be established, reputable firms or governments, there have historically been few defaults on payments of interest or instances of omitted dividends. On the other hand, a lack of full financial disclosure and regulatory supervision makes it difficult to anticipate adverse financial developments. Also, many newer companies, whose securities are riskier than those of traditional foreign issuers, are likewise listed on foreign exchanges. Foreign-exchange risk can also affect income.

Are there any other risks unique to this investment? Political or sovereign risk—the risk, for example, that foreign assets might be expropriated or devalued or that local tax policies might adversely affect debt or equity holders; the risk of transactional losses caused by settlement delays or fraud; with stock not registered with the Securities and Exchange Commission, there are legal difficulties for Americans in subscribing to rights offerings, a fact which can also affect the salability of rights (rights problems do not exist with ADRs or U.S. exchange-listed foreign shares).

Are they commercially rated? Some foreign debt issues are rated. Information can be found in a publication called *Credit Week International,* available at some larger brokerage firms.

Tax Considerations

What tax advantages (or disadvantages) do they offer? Some countries impose a withholding tax, typically from 15% to 20%, on dividends and interest (except Eurobonds). U.S. tax treaties can result in partial reclamation of withholdings in some countries, and the tax can be offset to some extent against federal income taxes. There is usually no capital gains tax imposed by foreign governments, though such gains are taxed by the U.S. government. Special rules apply to 10% or more ownership of a foreign corporation.

Economic Considerations

What economic factors most affect buy, hold, or sell decisions? Foreign securities are best bought when the U.S. dollar is strong against the currency of denomination. To profit from currency movements (or, conversely, to avoid losses) it is best to hold when the dollar is declining against the local currency. Foreign equities are attractive relative to American investments when the foreign economy or industrial sector has a better outlook than its domestic counterpart. Foreign bonds rise and fall in inverse relation to market interest rates.

FUTURES CONTRACT ON A COMMODITY

A futures contract is a commitment to buy or sell a specified quantity of a commodity or financial instrument at a specified price during a particular delivery month. Once restricted largely to agricultural commodities and metals, futures contracts have in recent years been extended to include what are broadly termed financial futures—contracts on debt instruments, such as Treasury bonds and Government National Mortgage Association ("Ginnie Mae") certificates and on foreign currencies—and, even more recently, contracts on stock indexes. Contract prices are determined through open outcry—a system of verbal communication between sellers and buyers on the floors of regulated commodities exchanges.

The futures markets are broadly divided into two categories of participants: (1) Hedgers have a position in (i.e., own) the underlying commodity or instrument (such as a farmer in the case of an agricultural commodity or an investor in the case of a financial or index future). Hedgers use futures to create countervailing positions, thus protecting against loss due to price (or rate) changes. (2) Speculators do not own the underlying asset for commercial or investment purposes, but instead aim to capitalize on the ups and downs (the volatility) of the contracts themselves. It is the speculators who provide the liquidity essential to the efficient operation of the futures markets.

As with option contracts, which are also discussed in this section, the great majority of futures contracts are closed out before their expiration—or delivery—date. This is done by buying or selling an offsetting contract. It is vital to note that with futures, in contrast to options (which simply expire), the alternative to an offset is a delivery, though this is done with title documentation or, in the case of index futures, cash, not by the legendary dumping of pork bellies on the front steps of absentminded contract holders. When the future is a contract to buy value, delivery of the future is avoided by buying an offsetting future to sell.

The attraction of futures for speculators, again like options, is the enormous leverage they provide. Although brokers normally require investors to meet substantial net worth and income requirements, it is possible to trade contracts with outlays of cash (or sometimes U.S. Treasury securities) equal to 5% to 10% of contract values. Such "margins" (actually good-faith deposits, more in the nature of performance bonds and required of both buyers and sellers) are set by the exchanges, although brokers normally have their own maintenance requirements. Margin calls are normally made when deposits drop to one half the original percentage value.

The commodity exchanges, with oversight by the Commodities Futures Trading Commission (CFTC), each day set limits, based on the previous day's closing price, to the extent a given contract's trading price may vary. While these trading limits help preclude exaggerated short-term volatility and thus make it possible for margin requirements to be kept low, they can also lock a trader into a losing position, where he must meet a margin call but is prevented from trading out of the position because the contract is either up limit or down limit (as high or as low as the daily limit permits it to be traded).

Speculators in futures contracts fall into three groups: (1) the exchange floor traders (scalpers), who make markets in contracts and turn small profits usually within the trading day; (2) spread traders, who hope to profit from offsetting positions in contracts having different maturities but the same underlying commodity or instrument, similar maturities but different (although usually closely related) underlying commodities, or similar contracts in different markets; and (3) position traders, who have the expertise and financial ability to analyze longer-term factors and ride out shorter term fluctuations in the expectation of ultimate gains.

While speculation in futures contracts is not recommended for the average investor, individuals with the money and risk tolerance may participate by choosing among the following alternatives: trading for one's own account, which involves time and expertise; trading through a managed account or a discretionary account with a commodities broker, which utilizes a professional's time and expertise for a fee or sometimes involves a participation in profits; or mutual funds, which offer both professional management and diversification and are regulated by both the CFTC and the Securities and Exchange Commission.

*   *   *

What Is a Commodity Futures Contract?

A commodity futures contract is an agreement to buy or sell a specific amount of a commodity at a particular price in a stipulated future month.

Buying, Selling, and Holding

How do I buy and sell it? Through a full-service broker or firm specializing in commodities transactions.

Is there a minimum purchase amount, and what is the price range? Contract sizes and unit prices vary widely from commodity to commodity, but the exchanges have liberal margin rules making it possible to trade with as little as 5% to 10% down. In some commodities, that can be $100, but brokers often have minimum deposits of $1000 to $2500. (They may also have strict personal income and net worth rules for investors.) One national exchange, the Mid-America Commodity Exchange, offers minicontracts in a number of commodities, currencies, and instruments; they range from one fifth to one half the size of regular contracts.

What fees and charges are involved? Broker commissions, which vary by contract but average $25 to $50 for a round-turn (buy and sell) trade with lower rates for intraday and spread (e.g., buy soybeans, sell soybean oil) transactions. Managed accounts involve management fees and, sometimes, participation in profits.

Does a commodity futures contract mature, expire, or otherwise terminate? Yes. All contracts have a stipulated expiration date.

Can I sell it quickly? Most established contracts are liquid, though daily price limits can create illiquidity when a commodity is down limit or up limit (as high or as low as the daily trading limit permits).

How is market value determined and how do I keep track of it? By supply and demand, which is affected by natural causes as well as general economic developments. Futures prices are quoted daily in the financial pages of newspapers and electronic databases.

Investment Objectives

Should I buy a commodity futures contract if my objective is capital appreciation? Only if you are expert, wealthy, and have a high tolerance for risk. Then, with the high leverage possible, capital gains (and losses) can be huge.

Should I buy this if my objective is income? No. Contracts pay no income.

To what extent does it protect against inflation ? Forward commodity prices reflect inflation expectations, but since contracts are short-term oriented, inflation protection is a secondary consideration.

Is it suitable for tax-deferred retirement accounts? Although not prohibited by the Internal Revenue Service, most brokerage firms rule out futures contracts as too risky for retirement accounts. They may have a limited role in managed accounts, primarily as a hedging tool. Certain pooled investment vehicles trading in futures may be appropriate in selected situations for people with high risk tolerance.

Can I borrow against it? Futures are not acceptable collateral with most lenders. Of course, they provide leverage inherently because of the relatively small deposits required to control contracts.

Risk Considerations

How assured can I be of getting my full investment back? Commodity futures are inherently speculative and it is actually possible to lose more than your investment (though margin calls would usually limit losses to the amount deposited if the account was sold out—that is, liquidated by the broker to meet the margin call).

How assured is my income? Futures provide no income.

Are there any other risks unique to this investments? The possibility of losses in excess of investment and the risk of illiquidity when a contract is down or up limit (thus making it impossible to trade out of a position) are risks unique to commodity futures trading. Of course, there is the risk (nightmare?) of actual delivery of a commodity if you fail to close out a position prior to expiration of a contract.

Is it commercially rated? No.

Tax Considerations

What tax advantages (or disadvantages) does a commodity futures contract offer? Speculators' open positions are marked to market at year end and paper profits and losses taxed as though realized. Sixty percent of profits are taxed as long-term capital gains and 40% at short-term (ordinary income) rates. Other tax treatments apply to nonspeculative and hedging uses and tax advice is recommended.

Economic Considerations

What economic factors most affect buy, hold, and sell decisions? Anything that affects supply and demand for a commodity makes contract values move up and down.

FUTURES CONTRACT ON AN INTEREST RATE

For a general discussion of a futures contract, see Futures Contract on a Commodity.

*   *   *

What Is a Futures Contract on an Interest Rate?

A futures contract on an interest rate is an agreement to buy or sell a given amount of a fixed-income security, such as a Treasury bill, bond, or note or Government National Mortgage Association security at a particular price in a stipulated future month.

Buying, Selling, and Holding

How do I buy and sell it? Through a full-service broker or firm specializing in commodities transactions.

Is there a minimum purchase amount, and what is the price range? Contract sizes vary with the underlying security and the exchange, but range from $20,000 to $1 million; since exchange margin rules allow trading with as little as 5% deposited, the actual cost of investing can be relatively low.

What fees and charges are involved? Broker commissions averaging $25 to $50 per contract transaction.

Does it mature, expire, or otherwise terminate? Yes; futures contracts have specific expiration dates.

Can I sell it quickly? Yes, except that liquidity may become a problem if the contract reaches the maximum price movement allowable in one day, in effect locking you into a position.

How is market value determined and how do I keep track of it? By market interest rate movements, essentially. When rates go up, the prices of fixed-income securities (and futures related to them) go down, and vice versa. Prices are reported daily in newspapers and electronic databases.

Investment Objectives

Should I buy a futures contract on an interest rate if my objective is capital appreciation? Speculators use the leverage available with futures to capitalize on expected interest rate movements, standing to gain (or lose) substantially more than the amount invested.

Should I buy this if my objective is income? No, though you might use futures to hedge the value of securities bought for income or to lock in the yield on a security to be bought at a later date.

To what extent does it protect against inflation? To the extent inflation expectations are a factor in the volatility of fixed-income investments, futures can offer some protection against loss.

Is it suitable for tax-deferred retirement accounts? Although not prohibited by the Internal Revenue Service, most brokerage firms rule out futures contracts as too risky for retirement accounts. They may have a limited role in managed accounts, primarily as a hedging tool. Certain pooled investment vehicles trading in futures may be appropriate in selected situations for people with high risk tolerance.

Can I borrow against it? No; futures contracts are not acceptable collateral at most lenders. Of course, there is considerable leverage inherent in the small deposit required to control contracts.

Risk Considerations

How assured can I be of getting my full investment back? Just as interest rate movements cannot be predicted with certainty, interest rate futures can result in losses as well as gains; it is in fact possible to lose more than your investment (called open-ended risk) but margin calls would normally limit losses to the amount invested, assuming the account was sold out (liquidated) to meet the call.

How assured is my income? Futures do not provide income.

Are there any other risks unique to this investment? Open-ended risk and the risk of illiquidity when a contract is down limit or up limit, making it impossible to trade out of a position, are risks unique to futures contracts.

Is it commercially rated? No.

Tax Considerations

What tax advantages (or disadvantages) does it offer? Speculators' open positions are marked to market at year end and paper profits and losses taxed as though realized. Sixty percent of profits are taxed as long-term capital gains and 40% at short-term (ordinary income) rates. Other tax treatments apply to nonspeculative and hedging uses and tax advice is recommended.

Economic Considerations

What economic factors most affect buy, hold, and sell decisions? Economic and monetary factors affecting interest rates govern choices having to do with interest rate futures.

FUTURES CONTRACT ON A STOCK INDEX

For a general discussion of a futures contract, see Futures Contract on a Commodity.

* * *

What Is a Futures Contract on a Stock Index?

A futures contract on a stock index is an agreement to buy or sell a stock index at a price based on the index value in a stipulated future month with settlement in cash.

Buying, Selling, and Holding

How do I buy and sell it? Through a full-service broker or firm specializing in commodities transactions.

Is there a minimum purchase amount, and what is the price range? Contracts are priced according to formulas based on index values, and vary in terms both of formulas and index values. For example, the contracts on the New York Stock Exchange Composite Index, the Standard & Poor's 500 Stock Index, and The Value Line Stock Index are priced by multiplying $500 times the index value, which ranges roughly between 100 and 300; if one of those indexes had a value of 200, a contract would cost $100,000, which might require a deposit of 10% or $10,000. To play, though, you would probably have to meet an income and liquid net worth test requiring substantial means.

What fees and charges are involved? Broker commissions.

Does it mature, expire, or otherwise terminate? Yes, all contracts have specific expirations.

Can I sell it quickly? Yes, except that liquidity may become a problem if the contract reaches the maximum price movement allowable in one day (i.e., becomes down limit or up limit).

How is market value determined and how do I keep track of it? By the market performance of the stocks comprising the index as they affect the index value. Index futures are reported with other futures prices in the financial pages of daily newspapers and electronic databases.

Investment Objectives

Should I buy a futures contract on a stock index if my objective is capital appreciation? Speculators use the leverage available with futures to capitalize on expected market movements, standing to gain (or lose) substantially more than the amount invested.

Should I buy this if my objective is income? No, but they are used, mainly by professionals, to hedge the value of income-producing stocks.

To what extent does it protect against inflation? This is not an investment you would hold as an inflation hedge.

Is it suitable for tax-deferred retirement accounts? Although not prohibited by the Internal Revenue Service, most brokerage firms rule out futures contracts as too risky for retirement accounts. They may have a limited role in managed accounts, primarily as a hedging tool. Certain pooled investment vehicles trading in futures may be appropriate in selected situations for people with high risk tolerance.

Can I borrow against it? No; futures are not acceptable collateral at most lenders. Of course, there is considerable leverage inherent in the relatively small deposit required to control contracts.

Risk Considerations

How assured can I be of getting my full investment back? Just as market movements cannot be predicted with certainty, index futures can result in losses as well as gains; in fact, it is quite possible to lose more than your investment (called open-ended risk), although margin calls are a safeguard against losses in excess of investment if an account is sold out (liquidated) to meet the call.

How assured is my income? Index futures do not provide income.

Are there any other risks unique to this investment? Index futures and the individual stocks comprising the index may not move exactly together, so it is not a perfect hedging tool.

Is it commercially rated? No.

Tax Considerations

What tax advantages (or disadvantages) does it offer? Speculators' open positions are marked to market at year end and paper profits and losses taxed as though realized. Sixty percent of profits are taxed as long-term capital gains and 40% at short-term (ordinary income) rates. Other tax treatments apply to nonspeculative and hedging uses and tax advice is recommended.

Economic Considerations

What economic factors most affect buy, hold, and sell decisions? The myriad factors affecting the market outlook affect choices having to do with stock index futures, whether they are used to speculate or as a hedging tool.

GOVERNMENT AGENCY SECURITY

Government agency securities, popularly called agencies, are indirect obligations of the United States government, issued by federal agencies and government-sponsored corporations under authority from the United States Congress, but, with a few exceptions, not backed, as U.S. Treasury securities are, by the full faith and credit of the government.

While it is highly unlikely—even unthinkable—that they could ever be allowed to default on principal or interest, these agency securities cannot be considered absolutely risk-free, and therein lies their attraction—because of the slight difference in safety, they generally yield as much as a half percentage point more than direct obligations.

Agencies are also, like Treasuries, exempt from state and local taxes, although there are exceptions—for example, securities guaranteed by the Government

National Mortgage Association (GNMA), and issues of the Federal National Mortgage Association (FNMA) and the Federal Home Loan Mortgage Corporation (FHLMC), including both mortgage-backed pass-throughs and bonds and notes issued to finance their operations.

Unlike Treasuries, agencies are not sold by auction but rather are marketed at the best yield possible by the Federal Reserve Bank of New York, as fiscal agent, through its network of primary dealers. Information can be obtained from the Federal Reserve Bank of New York, Treasury and Agency Issues Division, from the issuing agencies, or from dealer commercial banks and securities brokers.

Agencies that have issued or guaranteed securities include:

Asian Development Bank

College Construction Loan Insurance Corporation (Connie Lee)

District of Columbia Armory Board (D.C. Stadium)

Export-Import Bank of the United States

Farm Credit Financial Assistance Corporation

Farmers Home Administration

Federal Agricultural Mortgage Corporation (Farmer Mac)

Federal Farm Credit Consolidated System-Wide Securities

Federal Home Loan Bank

Federal Home Loan Mortgage Corporation

Federal Housing Administration (FHA)

Federal National Mortgage Association (FNMA)

Financing Corp. (FICO)

Government National Mortgage Association (GNMA)

Interamerican Development Bank

International Bank for Reconstruction and Development (World Bank)

Maritime Administration

Resolution Funding Corporation (Refcorp.)

Resolution Trust Corporation (RTC)

Small Business Administration (SBA)

Student Loan Marketing Association (SLMA)

Tennessee Valley Authority (TVA)

United States Postal Service

Washington Metropolitan Area Transit Authority

*   *   *

What Is a Government Agency Security?

A government agency security is a negotiable debt obligation of an agency of the United States government, which may be backed by the full faith and credit of the federal government but is more often guaranteed by the sponsoring agency with the implied backing of Congress.

Buying, Selling, and Holding

How do I buy and sell it? Through a securities broker-dealer or at many commercial banks.

Is there a minimum purchase amount, and what is the price range? Denominations and minimums vary widely from $1000 to $25,000 and up, depending on the issue, the issuing agency, and the dealer.

What fees and charges are involved? None in the case of new issues bought from a member of the underwriting group; otherwise a commission or dealer markup.

Does it mature, expire, or otherwise terminate? Yes, maturities range from 30 days to 30 years.

Can I sell it quickly? Yes, but bid and asked spreads tend to be wider than with direct Treasury obligations, which raises the cost of trading in the secondary market. Inflation-indexed bonds may be less liquid.

How is market value determined and how do I keep track of it? Market values of fixed-income securities vary inversely with market interest rate movements. Daily newspapers, brokers, and large banks provide price information.

Investment Objectives

Should I buy a government agency security if my objective is capital appreciation? No, though appreciation is possible when fixed-rate securities are bought prior to a drop in market interest rates.

Should I buy this if my objective is income? Yes. Yields are a bit higher than those of direct government obligations, but lower than those of corporate obligations.

To what extent does it protect against inflation? As fixed-income securities, agencies offer no protection, though shorter-term issues offer less exposure to inflation risk. Some agencies, such as Tennessee Valley Authority and the Federal Home Loan Bank, have begun issuing inflation-indexed securities, which protect against inflation but would be a risk in deflation.

Is it suitable for tax-deferred retirement accounts? Yes.

Can I borrow against it? Yes; lenders will often lend 90% of value.

Risk Considerations

How assured can I be of getting my full investment back? Agencies are second only to Treasury securities as good credit risks. Market prices fall as interest rates rise, however, so you may not get a full return of principal if you sell in the secondary market prior to maturity. Some sophisticated investors hedge market risk using options, futures, and futures options that are available on certain Treasury securities and Government National Mortgage Association securities.

How assured is my income? Very assured. It is highly unlikely the U.S. Treasury, Congress, or a regulatory body like the Federal Reserve Board would allow a government agency to default on interest.

Are there any other risks unique to a government agency security? No, but mortgage-backed pass-through securities issued by government-sponsored entities have different characteristics and are covered separately in this section.

Is it commercially rated? Some issues are rated by major services.

Tax Considerations

What tax advantages (or disadvantages) does it offer? Agencies are fully taxable at the federal level but are exempt from state and local taxes with certain exceptions, such as issues of the Federal National Mortgage Association and the Government National Mortgage Association. With inflation-indexed bonds, the annual inflation adjustment is taxable but not paid out until maturity.

Economic Considerations

What economic factors most affect buy, hold, or sell decisions? It is best to buy when interest rates are high and the best yields can be obtained. Holding is most attractive when rates are declining, causing an upward move in the market values of fixed-income securities, and high inflation is not present to erode the value of fixed returns.

LIFE INSURANCE (CASH VALUE)

For young families as yet without sufficient financial security to provide for expenses in the event of the premature death of the breadwinner or homemaker, life insurance provides essential protection. By far the cheapest and simplest way to obtain that protection is *term life insurance,* a no-frills deal whereby premiums buy insurance but do not create cash value. The alternatives—variously called cash value, straight, whole, permanent, or ordinary life insurance—combine protection with an investment program.

The traditional cash value policy requires a fixed premium for the life of the insured and promises a fixed sum of money on the death of the insured. A portion of the premium covers expenses and actual insurance, the rest earns interest in a tax-deferred savings program, gradually building up a cash value. The latter can be cashed in by canceling the policy (hence the term "cash surrender value"), can be used to buy more protection, or can be borrowed at a below-market or even zero interest rate with the loan balance deducted from the death benefit. On the death of the insured, the beneficiary receives only the death benefit.

Variations called single-premium or limited-payment life policies, have higher up-front premiums so that a policy becomes paid-up—the cash value becomes sufficient to cover the death benefit without further premiums. Later, if the insured is still living, the policy begins paying benefits that can supplement retirement income or be converted to an annuity, thus guaranteeing income for life.

The one serious drawback of cash value policies has been that the interest rate is not competitive with other investments. With soaring interest rates and inflation in the 1970s and in the excitement of new investment products spawned by deregulation in the 1980s, upwardly mobile young investors began questioning the value of insurance policies providing neither competitive investment returns nor the flexibility their dynamic personal financial circumstances required. Faced with cancellations and poor sales, insurers came forth with the following:

> *Universal Life,* which clearly separates the cash value and protection elements of the policy and invests the cash value in a tax-deferred savings program tied to a money market rate. The cost of the insurance is fixed, based on the insured's age and sex, so depending on what the cash value portion earns (it is guaranteed to earn a minimum rate, but can earn more if market rates rise), the premium can vary. The insured may also change the amount of protection at any time. Flexibility is the main feature of this type of policy.

Variable Life, which has a fixed premium like straight life, but the cash value goes into a choice of stock, bond, or money market portfolios, which the investor can alternate. The insurer guarantees a minimum death benefit regardless of portfolio performance, although excess gains buy additional coverage. The attraction here is capital growth opportunity.

Universal Variable Life, a mid-1980s innovation that combines the flexibility of universal life with the growth potential of variable life.

Even with modern policies, however, the question persists: Why sacrifice a portion of income to an insurance company when pure protection can be more cheaply obtained through term insurance and returns as good or better can be obtained by investing directly? The answer depends on an individual's expertise, self-confidence, and willingness to spend time managing investments.

$$* \quad * \quad *$$

What Is Cash Value Life Insurance?

Cash value life insurance is a contract combining payment to beneficiaries, in the event of the insured's premature death, with investment programs.

Buying, Selling, and Holding

How do I buy and sell it? Through insurance brokers, insurance company sales agents, savings institutions, full-service brokers, commercial banks, financial planners, and other financial services organizations.

Is there a minimum purchase amount, and what is the price range? Annual premiums vary widely with the type of policy and such factors as the age and sex of the insured.

What fees and charges are involved? Cost of coverage, sales commissions, and insurance company operating costs are built into premiums. Some policies have penalties for cancellation before specified dates.

Does it mature, expire, or otherwise terminate? Policies mature in 10 years to life, depending on the program.

Can I sell it quickly? Yes. Policies can be canceled and cash values claimed anytime (although actual payment may require several weeks of processing time).

How is market value determined and how do I keep track of it? Policies are not traded in a secondary market. Cash values are determined by accumulated premiums plus investment income and performance.

Investment Objectives

Should I buy cash value life insurance if my objective is capital appreciation? Assuming death benefits are your primary objective, you might buy a variable life insurance policy or a universal variable life insurance policy with investments in a stock fund to gain capital appreciation.

Should I buy this if my objective is income? No, although policies combining annuities provide for income payments on annuitization.

To what extent does it protect against inflation? Universal, variable, and universal variable policies can offer some inflation protection through adjustable death benefits and the investment of cash values in inflation-sensitive securities.

Is it suitable for tax deferred retirement accounts? No; life insurance is not an eligible investment.

Can I borrow against it? Yes. Insurance companies will normally loan cash value at lower-than-market rates and reduce the death benefit by the amount of the loan.

Risk Considerations

How assured can I be of getting my full investment back? Insurance companies are highly regulated and there is little risk they will not meet commitments. However, policies that provide for market returns on cash value investments also carry market risk: e.g., a variable life policy invested in a bond fund would lose cash value if interest rates rose, while one invested in stocks would lose in a down market.

How assured is my income? That depends on how cash values are invested. Policies that invest cash value in money market instruments, for example, are subject to fluctuating income.

Are there any other risks unique to cash value life insurance? Although heavily regulated, insurance companies are potentially subject to mismanagement and fraud and are not themselves covered by federal protection in the sense that banks, for example, are covered by the Federal Deposit Insurance Corporation.

Is it commercially rated? Yes. Insurance companies are rated by A.M. Best Co. or Weiss Research.

Tax Considerations

What tax advantages (or disadvantages) does it offer? Income earned on cash value accumulates and compounds tax-deferred. Though subject to federal estate taxes (after a $1 million exclusion) and local inheritance taxes, life insurance proceeds paid to a named beneficiary avoid probate. Proceeds to beneficiaries are normally not subject to federal income taxes. Single-premium life insurance, which offers tax-free cash value accumulation and tax-free access to funds in the form of policy loans, was one of the few tax shelters to survive the Tax Reform Act of 1986. In 1987, however, tax legislation made tax-free borrowings possible only when a test is met requiring substantial insurance coverage relative to premiums over a lengthy time period.

Economic Considerations

What economic factors most affect buy, hold, and sell decisions? Inflation and volatility of interest rates gave rise to life insurance policies whose cash values vary with market conditions. Investors concerned about such factors can choose among such "new breed" alternatives, rather than buying traditional fixed-rate policies, and make their choices based on their expectations. Thus an investor anticipating high inflation and high interest rates would not choose a variable life policy invested in fixed-income bonds but might choose one with a stock fund or one that is money market-oriented. Variable and universal variable life insurance permit switching between bond, stock, and money market funds to afford maximum market flexibility.

LIMITED PARTNERSHIP (LP)

The unique feature of a limited partnership is that financial and tax events flow directly through to individual investors. Until 1987 this meant that limited partners in real estate ventures, oil and gas projects, and other activities could use liberal tax benefits such as depreciation, depletion, intangible drilling costs, and tax credits, as well as operating losses, as deductions against taxable income from wages and investment income. With aggressive marketing by brokers and financial planners, LPs attracted some $100 billion of funds from 12 million investors in the 1980s.

The Tax Reform Act of 1986 severely curtailed the use of LPs as tax shelters by ruling that losses from "passive" sources, like LPs, could be used only against passive income. And while some "economic programs"—those LPs emphasizing income, appreciation, and safety—have continued to provide attractive returns, their ability to shelter cash flow has been lessened by reduced benefits, notably the elimination of accelerated depreciation of real property and the repeal of the investment credit. In the 1990s, partnerships were offered, but in much lower volumes since the partnership form of ownership had been largely discredited.

A limited partnership is an organization comprising a general partner with unlimited liability, who is both sponsor and manager, and limited partners, who provide most of the capital, have limited liability, and have no active management role. Most LPs aim to sell or refinance their assets within seven to ten years and distribute proceeds to shareholders.

Limited partnerships may be private, which are restricted to small numbers of wealthy investors and not required to register with the Securities and Exchange Commission, or public, which market shares in typical amounts of $1000 to $5000 to as many limited partners as the sponsor desires. Public LPs must register with the SEC and provide investors with a prospectus and other disclosures.

Limited partnerships are also distinguished in terms of their use of leverage to finance assets. *Leveraged programs,* whose assets are financed 50% or more with borrowed money, offer greater tax benefits because (1) with a larger asset base they generate more deductions, such as depreciation, and because (2) the interest is deductible. *Unleveraged programs* are favored by investors seeking maximum income and less risk.

From the investor's standpoint, one drawback of limited partnerships traditionally has been lack of liquidity. Although a growing number of independent investment firms buy and sell partnership shares, they represent more of a distress market than a formal secondary market for shares. While some sponsors offer market-making services to investors under some circumstances, the selling of shares during the life of the partnership is generally discouraged.

Inspired by investor reservations about the future of tax-advantaged partnerships after tax reform, some sponsors in the mid-1980s began marketing programs featuring depositary receipts, which represent unit interests and can be traded in the open marketplace. Liquidity provided this way is a feature of *master limited partnerships,* a mid-1980s innovation in which corporate assets or private partnerships are reorganized as public limited partnerships combining various objectives. Master limited partnerships, however, were deemed taxable as corporations starting in 1998 and most converted to corporate form in advance of that deadline.

*   *   *

What Is a Limited Partnership?

A limited partnership is a form of business organization, having any of a variety of activities and investment objectives, which is made up of a general partner who organizes and manages the partnership and its operations, and limited partners who contribute capital, have limited liability, and assume no active role in day-to-day business affairs.

Buying, Selling, and Holding

How do I buy and sell it? Unit shares are bought through a securities broker-dealer or financial planner. There is no official secondary market, although some sponsors agree to make markets under certain circumstances and a number of firms trade in partnership shares at distress prices.

Is there a minimum purchase amount, and what is the price range? Public limited partnerships usually have a $1000 to $5000 minimum, with a $2000 minimum for IRAs. Private limited partnerships require at least $20,000. Offerings frequently involve suitability rules, requiring that individuals meet minimum net worth, income, and tax bracket criteria.

What fees and charges are involved? Brokerage commissions and other front-end costs, often totaling 20% or more of the amount invested. There may be additional management fees during the partnership's operating phase.

Does it mature, expire, or otherwise terminate? Most partnerships intend to dispose of their holdings within a specified period (7 to 10 years typically) and distribute the proceeds as capital gains to investors.

Can I sell it quickly? Usually not. There is no secondary market for partnership shares, although some sponsors offer to try to make a market to accommodate investors under certain circumstances. Certain private firms buy LP shares from holders, but the price for this kind of marketability can be high. Some partnerships offer liquidity through depositary receipts, which represent shares and are traded in secondary markets.

How is market value determined and how do I keep track of it? There is no active secondary market for limited partnerships shares and independent firms that buy shares pay widely varying and deeply discounted prices.

The 1986 Tax Act required that sponsors provide annual valuation reports for LPs held in IRAs, and some sponsors provide valuations to all shareholders. Valuation standards are not uniform, however. Industry guidelines recommend that interests be valued at cost for the first three years (even if a high percentage of cost is sales charges unrelated to asset values) and at asset values thereafter; asset appraisals however, may be independent or "direct," meaning estimates are made by the sponsor.

In any event, share values to be ultimately realized as capital gains are affected by various factors, depending on the activities of the partnership and assets it holds.

Investment Objectives

Should I buy a share in a limited partnership if my objective is capital appreciation? Certain types of partnerships emphasize capital gains potential; others do not. Those offering the greatest potential are the riskiest.

Should I buy this if my objective is income? Yes, though not all partnerships have income as a primary objective and some emphasize the tax sheltering of income from other passive sources.

To what extent does it protect against inflation? Some, like all-cash equity programs with investments in inflation-sensitive real estate, offer high protection. Others, such as programs specializing in fixed-rate mortgages, suffer.

Is it suitable for tax-deferred retirement accounts? Yes.

Can I borrow against it? Because of their low liquidity, partnership shares may not be acceptable as marketable securities with many lenders.

Risk Considerations

How assured can I be of getting my full investment back? Safety of principal depends on the type of partnership and the quality of its holdings. Insured mortgage programs held for the life of the partnership offer high safety, but no appreciation, while leveraged programs aimed at high capital gains involve commensurate risk.

How assured is my income? Only insured mortgage programs offer any real assurance of income. Other income partnerships vary with the type and quality of their portfolios.

Are there any other risks unique to this investment? Yes, because limited partners have no active role in management, everything depends on the integrity and management ability of the general partner. In fact, some partnerships (such as those in real estate) are sold as blind pools—that is, the general partner has not even made property selections at the time that investment is made. Programs set up primarily as tax shelters run the risk of being declared abusive, subjecting the investor to heavy penalties and interest as well as back taxes. A sponsor may postpone liquidation to "ride out" a soft market, thus delaying the payout to holders. LPs bought in the secondary market may have hidden tax liabilities stemming from deductions taken by previous shareholders.

Is it commercially rated? Yes. Standard & Poor's Corporation rates limited partnerships, and several firms, such as Robert A. Stanger & Co., analyze limited partnerships and rate such factors as offering terms.

Tax Considerations

What tax advantages (or disadvantages) does it offer? Tax benefits flow through to limited partners. Since 1986, however, such "passive" losses have been usable only to offset income from other passive sources and not earned or investment income.Net losses are tax preference items. Unused losses may be carried forward, and after off-setting any gain from the disposition of the passive investment, may be used against any other passive investment. Any excess losses then remaining can be generally applied. At risk rules now include real estate. Master limited partnerships were made taxable as corporations after 1998.

Economic Considerations

What economic factors most affect buy, hold, and sell decisions? Because limited partnership investments are generally held for the life of the partnership, hold and sell decisions have limited applicability. Buy decisions should be guided by the outlook for the type of activity in which the partnership specializes and such factors as the expected life of the program and whether it is leveraged or unleveraged.

MONEY MARKET FUND

This special breed of mutual fund gives personal investors the opportunity to own money market instruments that would otherwise be available only to large institutional investors. The attraction is higher yields than individuals could obtain on their own or from most bank money market deposit accounts, plus a high degree of safety and excellent liquidity, complete with checkwriting.

Money market funds are sponsored by mutual fund organizations (investment companies), brokerage firms, and institutions, like insurance companies, which sell and redeem shares without any sales charges or commissions. The company charges only an annual management fee, usually under 1%, although extra services may entail additional charges. Income earned from interest-bearing investments is credited and reinvested (in effect compounded) for shareholders on a daily basis.

The disadvantage of money market funds over other short-term investment alternatives is that income (although normally paid out monthly) fluctuates daily as investments in the fund's portfolio mature and are replaced with new investments bearing current interest rates. In a declining rate market, this can be a disadvantage as compared, say, to a certificate of deposit, which would continue to pay an above-market rate until maturity. As a general rule, fund dividend rates lag behind money market rate changes by a month or so, depending on the average length of their portfolios, which is controlled to an extent by the manager's expectations as to where rates will go. Major sponsors permit switching among different funds in their families.

The market value of a money market fund investment is normally maintained at a constant figure, usually $1 a share. This means capital gains (and the favorable tax treatment they receive) are not a feature of money market funds, though investors may achieve some growth through compounding by opting to reinvest monthly payments.

Funds may differ in terms of the type of securities comprising their portfolios, some specializing only in U.S. Treasury bills or in tax-exempt municipal securities. A general portfolio, however, would typically be comprised of bank and industrial commercial paper, certificates of deposit, acceptances, repurchase agreements, direct and indirect U.S. government obligations, Eurodollar CDs, and other safe and liquid investments. Bonds and foreign debt securities are sometimes included to lift yields.

Money market funds are not covered by federal insurance the way bank deposits are, although funds sponsored by brokerage firms are insured by the Securities Investor Protection Corporation (SIPC) against losses caused by a failure of the firm. Some funds may also be covered by private insurance.

For longer-term investment purposes, alternative investments offer better yield with comparable safety while also providing growth opportunity, tax advantages, and similar inflation protection. The convenience and income of money market funds, although increasingly challenged by bank deposit products, remain attractive for providing for emergencies and for parking temporarily idle cash.

*   *   *

What Is a Money Market Fund?

A money market fund is a type of mutual fund in which a pool of money is invested in various money market securities (short-term debt instruments) and which compounds interest daily and pays out (or reinvests) dividends to shareholders monthly.

Buying, Selling, and Holding

How do I buy and sell it? Through sponsoring brokerage firms and mutual fund organizations. Accounts are also offered by insurance companies and other financial institutions as a parking place for temporarily idle funds.

Is there a minimum purchase amount, and what is the price range? The minimum investment usually ranges from $500 to $5000. For funds offered through brokers, $1000 is typical; $2500 is a typical minimum investment for funds offered directly by fund sponsors. Additional investment is usually allowed in increments as small as $100.

What fees and charges are involved? Most are no-load (without sales fee), charging only an annual management fee, which is usually less than 1% of the investment. There may be extra fees for special services, such as money transfers.

Does it mature, expire, or otherwise terminate? No.

Can I sell it quickly? Yes. Shares are redeemable anytime and most funds offer checkwriting privileges, though $500 minimums for checks are common.

How is market value determined and how do I keep track of it? Market values of shares are kept constant. Yields change in response to money market conditions as investments turn over and are calculated on a daily basis. Seven and 30-day average yields are reported weekly in the financial pages of newspapers and current information can be obtained directly by calling the sponsoring organizations.

Investment Objectives

Should I buy this if my objective is capital appreciation? No.

Should I buy this if my objective is income? Yes. The attraction of money market funds is that the individuals can earn the same high yields that would otherwise be available only to institutional investors. Of course, income fluctuates and there is little protection against a decline in market rates.

To what extent does it protect against inflation? Because interest rates on newly offered debt instruments rise with inflation, money market funds, being composed of constantly rotating short-term investments, have performed well in inflation and paid dividends that kept pace with rising price levels.

Is it suitable for tax-deferred retirement accounts? Yes.

Can I borrow against it? Yes, banks and brokers will lend a high percentage (often 90%) of the value of your shares.

Risk Considerations

How assured can I be of getting my full investment back? Your investment in a money market fund is quite safe, since portfolios comprise securities of banks, governments, and top corporations. Investors seeking maximum safety can choose funds investing exclusively in U.S. government direct obligations, though at some sacrifice of yield; while this does not mean the fund is guaranteed by Uncle Sam, the fact that its investments are so guaranteed actually does provide a high degree of security. Some funds are privately insured against default.

How assured is my income? While the risk of default is very small, there is no way of preventing fluctuations in money market interest rates. Dividend rates could therefore decline, although the reaction to market rate changes may be more or less delayed, depending on the average maturity of a portfolio. Most fund sponsors permit shifting into other investment vehicles within their families when adverse developments can be foreseen or when better opportunities exist.

Are there any other risks unique to this investment? A fund that invested relatively long-term just prior to a drastic rise in rates could be forced to sell investments at a loss to meet redemptions. Well-managed and established funds are aware of this obvious risk and take measures to avoid it. Overall, the industry, which is regulated by the Securities and Exchange Commission, has enjoyed an excellent safety record.

Is it commercially rated? A number of organizations record past performance and a few predict future yields, but money market funds arc not rated in the sense that bonds and stocks are.

Tax Considerations

What tax advantages (or disadvantages) does it offer? Where portfolios are comprised of tax-exempt securities, investors are exempt from federal taxes and, depending on state laws, possibly state and local taxes. (States may treat tax-exempt funds differently from tax-exempt direct investments.) Otherwise, dividends are fully taxable. Some states that do not tax interest earned on direct investments will tax dividends from funds, even though the fund's income is from interest earned.

Economic Considerations

What economic factors most affect buy, hold and sell decisions? Money market funds are most attractive when short-term interest rates are high and alternative investments are beset with uncertainty. As a rule, investors use money market funds to park cash temporarily, choosing other investments for longer-term purposes.

MORTGAGE-BACKED (PASS-THROUGH) SECURITY

A mortgage-backed (pass-through) security offers one of the best risk/return deals available to investors, plus excellent liquidity. Two drawbacks, though, are that monthly income payments fluctuate and the term of the investment cannot be predicted with certainty.

Pass-through securities represent shares in pools of home mortgages having approximately the same terms and interest rates. They were introduced in the 1960s to make lenders liquid and stimulate home buying.

The process begins when prospective homeowners apply for mortgages to banks, savings and loan associations, and mortgage bankers. The loan paper is sold to intermediaries, such as Freddie Mac or private organizations who repackage it in units represented by certificates, which are marketed to investors. Interest and principal, including prepayments, pass from the homeowner through the intermediary to the investor. When the mortgages mature or are prepaid, the investment expires.

Pass-throughs also enjoy an active secondary market, where securities trade either at discounts or premiums depending on prevailing interest rates. Interestingly, pass-throughs representing pools of low-rate mortgages, when they can be bought favorably to result in attractive yields, are the most desirable holdings because the prepayment risk is low.

The following are principal mortgage-backed securities:

Government National Mortgage Association (GNMA): Ginnie Maes are the most widely held pass-throughs and are backed by Federal Housing Administration (FHA)-insured and Veterans Administration (VA) guaranteed mortgages plus the general guarantee of GNMA, which (by virtue of rulings of the Treasury and Justice departments) brings the full faith and credit of the U.S. government behind these securities. They are as safe as Treasury bonds but typically yield 1% to 2% higher.

Federal Home Loan Mortgage Corporation (FHLMC): Freddie Mac PCs (Participation Certificates) are backed by both FHA and VA mortgages and privately insured conventional mortgages plus the general guarantee of FHLMC, a privately managed public institution owned by the Federal Home Loan Bank Board System members. With less safety, PCs yield 15–40 basis points more than GNMAs.

Federal National Mortgage Association (FNMA): Fannie Mae MBSs (Mortgage-Backed Securities) are issued and guaranteed by FNMA, a government-sponsored, publicly held (NYSE-traded) company, and backed by both conventional and FHA and VA mortgages. They are essentially similar to Freddie Macs and tend to have similar yields.

Private mortgage participation certificates issued by lending institutions or conduit firms have varying characteristics and different ratings, depending on such factors as private mortgage insurance, cash-fund backing, and over-collateralization (the extent to which the market values of underlying properties exceed the mortgages). These include jumbo pools of mortgages from different lenders.

Collateralized mortgage obligations (CMOs), a variation, are instruments, technically mortgage-backed bonds, that break up mortgage pools into separate maturity classes, called tranches. This is accomplished by applying mortgage income first to the bonds with the shortest maturity. Tranches pay different rates of interest and typically mature in 2, 5, 10, and 20 years. Issued by Freddie Mac and private issuers, CMOs are usually backed by government-guaranteed or other top-grade mortgages and most have AAA bond ratings. For a slight sacrifice of yield, CMOs lessen anxiety about the uncertain term of pass-through investments.

Variations exist on CMOs that are really too sophisticated for most individual investors to risk owning. These include Z tranches having characteristics of zero-coupon bonds, multiple Z tranches, Y tranches with sinking fund features, and even equity CMOs representing residual cash flows.

Real estate mortgage investment conduits (REMICs), still another variation, created by the Tax Reform Act of 1986. REMICs offer issuers, who may be government or private entities, more flexibility than CMOs and protection from double taxation, which CMOs have avoided with legal technicalities. They are thus able to separate mortgage pools not only into maturity classes but also into classes of risk. The practical effect of this has been that whereas CMOs have financed top-quality mortgages in order to obtain AAA ratings, REMICs have been used to finance mortgages of lesser quality, even some that are financially distressed. More often than not, a REMIC obligation in the late 1980s was a high-yield, junk mortgage bond.

More exceptions are being created all the time. Fannie Mae routinely issues REMIC-backed Ginnie Mae pass-throughs. They are divided into many parts with many average lives and a wide range of yields.

Strips: Mortgage-backed securities are also stripped and sold as zero-coupon securities. See the section on zero coupon securities for a discussion of this alternative.

*   *   *

What Is a Mortgage-Backed (Pass-Through) Security?

A mortgage-backed security is a share in an organized pool of residential mortgages, the principal and interest payments on which are passed through to shareholders, usually monthly. The category includes collateralized mortgage obligations (CMOs), technically mortgage-backed bonds, which provide for different maturities, and real estate mortgage investment conduits (REMICs), which provide for both separate maturity and separate risk classes. It does not include mortgage-backed securities that are corporate bonds or government agency securities and are covered in those sections.

Buying, Selling, and Holding

Where do I buy and sell it? At a securities broker-dealer.

Is there a minimum purchase amount, and what is the price range? Most new pass-throughs are sold in minimum amounts of $25,000, although some older issues can be bought with less and some private issues and CMOs and REMICs can be bought for as little as $1000. Shares of funds, limited partnerships, and unit investment trusts that buy such securities range from $1000–$5000.

What fees and charges are involved? This varies among vehicles and brokers, but can be either a flat fee or a dealer spread. Sponsors deduct modest fees from passed-through income.

Does it mature, expire, or otherwise terminate? Yes, the life of a pool, and its related securities, ends when the mortgages mature or are prepaid. CMOs and REMICs offer investors a choice of earlier or later payouts.

Can I sell it quickly? Yes, liquidity is very good.

How is market value determined and how do I keep track of it? Market value, to the extent mortgage pools have fixed-rate obligations, goes up when market interest rates go down, and vice versa. On the other hand, prepayments rise when rates decline, shrinking the pool and lowering share values. Daily price and yield information is published in the financial pages of newspapers and in electronic databases.

Investment Objectives

Should I buy this if my objective is capital appreciation? Although most investors plan to hold for the life of the issue, capital appreciation is possible as the result of declining market interest rates.

Should I buy this if my objective is income? Yes; mortgage pass-throughs generally offer good yields. The most conservative, Ginnie Maes, normally yield at least 1% more than U.S. Treasury bonds and have the same safety from default. CMOs and REMICs pay slightly lower yields than straight pass-throughs with comparable risk characteristics.

To what extent does it protect against inflation? Because they are based largely on fixed-income mortgages, pass-throughs suffer in high inflation.

Is it suitable for tax-deferred retirement accounts? Yes; except for rollovers, however, the minimum investments exceed IRA limits.

Can I borrow against it? Yes.

Risk Considerations

How assured can I be of getting my full investment back? Although some issues are safer than others (Ginnie Maes are U.S. government-guaranteed against default on underlying mortgages, for example) most pass-throughs are either government-sponsored or otherwise insured in addition to being over-collateralized (i.e., the market value of the real estate behind the mortgages exceeds the face value of the mortgages). They thus offer a high degree of credit safety, although loss of value due to rising interest rates is a risk if sold in the secondary market. REMICs tend to have riskier backing and should be analyzed.

How assured is my income? Income is safe from the credit standpoint (see the previous question) but can vary from month to month as the result of prepayments and other factors.

Are there any other risks unique to this investment? Prepayments may shorten the life of the investment, although the cash they create is of course passed through to investors.

Is it commercially rated? Yes, Standard & Poor's and other services rate mortgage-backed securities.

Tax Considerations

What tax advantages (or disadvantages) does it offer? None. Interest is taxed as ordinary income and profits or losses from the sale of pass-through securities in the secondary market are taxed as capital gains or losses. But the monthly payment received by an investor in a pass-through is only partly interest. Because payments to the investor are simply pass-throughs of payments by homeowners on their mortgages, and those payments are part interest and part principal, the investor pays taxes only on the portion of his payment representing interest; the rest, as principal, is treated as a nontaxable return of capital. Since home mortgage payments have a higher ratio of interest to principal in the earlier years of the mortgage, it follows that income payments on pass-through securities normally have a higher proportion of taxable interest in the earlier years of the life of the pool.

Economic Considerations

What economic factors most affect buy, hold, and sell decisions? Mortgage-backed pass-throughs are most attractive to hold when general interest rates are low relative to the yield on the mortgage pool. However, this scenario can also cause a high rate of prepayments just when the investment is most attractive. The best holding is a pool of low-rate mortgages whose shares are bought at a good discount; that results in an attractive yield for investors, but since the homeowners are also happy with their low-rate mortgages, the risk of prepayment is much less. Of course, inflation erodes the value of fixed payments, which are the basis of income from pass-throughs.

MUNICIPAL SECURITY

A municipal security, or muni, is a debt obligation of a U.S. state, territory, or political subdivision, such as a county, city, town, village, or authority.

What has historically made munis special has been their exemption from federal income taxes and, frequently, from state and local income taxes as well. Because of this tax-exempt status, munis have traditionally paid lower rates of interest than taxable securities, making their after-tax return more attractive as an individual's income moved into higher brackets.

The Tax Reform Act of 1986 changed the municipal bond investment environment in fundamental ways primarily by dividing obligations into two basic groups:

> *Public purpose bonds,* also called traditional government purpose bonds or essential purpose bonds, continue to be tax-exempt and to be issued without limit.

> *Private purpose bonds,* vaguely defined as a bond involving more than a 10% benefit to private parties, are taxable unless specifically exempted. Such exempted *permitted private purpose bonds* are subject, with exceptions, to caps.

Whether tax-exempt or not, munis are either (1) general obligations, notes or bonds backed by the full faith and credit (including the taxing power) of the issuing entity and used to finance capital expenditures or improvements; or (2) *revenue obligations,* which are used to finance specific projects and are repaid from the revenues of the facilities they finance.

Although munis vary in the degree of credit strength backing them, and although there have been some famous defaults, such as the Washington Public Power Supply System (WHOOPS) in the 1980s and Orange County in 1994, their safety record has generally been excellent, earning them a place between Treasuries and high-grade corporate bonds in terms of investor confidence.

In addition to taxable bonds, recent innovations in the municipal securities field have included *tax-exempt commercial paper,* short-term discounted notes usually backed by bank lines of credit; *bonds with put options* typically exercisable after one to five years, which carry a somewhat lower yield in exchange for the put privilege; *floating (or variable) rate* issues tied to the Treasury bill or another market rate: and *enhanced security issues,* in which the credit of the municipal entity is supplemented by bank lines of credit or other outside resources.

For smaller investors, open and closed-end funds, unit investment trusts, and other pooled vehicles with portfolios of municipal obligations offer diversification and professional management with lower minimums.

Munis are also available as zero-coupon securities and are covered in the section dealing with that investment alternative.

* * *

What Is a Municipal Security?

A municipal security is a negotiable bond or note issued by a U.S. state or subdivision. A muni may be a general obligation backed by the full faith and credit (i.e., the borrowing and taxing power) of a government; a revenue obligation paid out of the cash flow from an income-producing project; or a special assessment obligation paid out of taxes specially levied to finance specific public works. Some municipal bonds, such as those to finance low-income housing, may be backed by a federal government agency.

Buying, Selling, and Holding

How do I buy and sell it? Most securities broker-dealers handle municipal securities.

Is there a minimum purchase amount, and what is the price range? Although munis are issued in units of $5000 or $1000 par value as a rule, with exceptions as low as $100, broker-dealers usually require minimum orders of at least $5000 and often want $10,000, $25,000, or up to $100,000. Odd lots are sometimes available from broker-dealers at extra commissions or spreads. Smaller investments can be made through mutual funds, closed-end funds, unit investment trusts and other pooled vehicles with tax-exempt portfolios.

What fees and charges are involved? Sometimes a commission, but usually a spread (rarely exceeding 5%) between the dealer's buying and selling prices.

Does it mature, expire, or otherwise terminate? Yes. Maturities range from one month (notes) to 30 years (bonds). Serial bonds mature in scheduled stages. Munis may also be callable or have put features.

Can I sell it quickly? Some munis have good liquidity, although issues of obscure municipalities and authorities can have inactive markets and be hard to sell.

How is market value determined and how do I keep track of it? Most munis are fixed-income securities and thus rise and fall in opposite relationship to market interest rates. Variable-rate issues, whose rates are periodically adjusted to reflect changes in U.S. Treasury bill yields or other money market rates, tend to sell at or close to their par values. Muni quotes are not normally published in daily newspapers, but prices published in *The Daily Bond Buyer* (mainly new muni issues) and the *Blue List of Current Municipal Offerings* (a Standard and Poor's publication reporting details of secondary market offerings and their size) are available through brokers or directly by subscription.

Investment Objectives

Should I buy a municipal security if my objective is capital appreciation? No, although appreciation is possible when munis sell at discounts because rates have risen or credit questions arise.

Should I buy this if my objective is income? Yes, but only if the after-tax yield in your tax bracket compares favorably to the yield on a taxable investment of comparable safety.

To what extent does it protect against inflation? Fixed-income munis offer no inflation protection. Variable-rate munis would offer some, if interest rates rose.

Is it suitable for tax-deferred accounts? Tax-exempt issues bearing a lower interest rate than a taxable security are not suitable. Taxable munis are suitable.

Can I borrow against it? You can, but the interest you pay is not tax-deductible if the proceeds are used to buy municipals. With the lower rate you earn on most munis, it would hardly pay. While munis are acceptable collateral for other loans, care must be taken to avoid the appearance of a violation of the rule against deducting interest.

Risk Considerations

How assured can I be of getting my full investment back? In most cases, you can be quite sure of getting your investment back at maturity. Munis generally rank between U.S. government securities and corporate bonds in credit safety. But the risk of default varies with the credit of the issuer and the type of obligation (mainly general obligation or revenue obligations). Some munis are covered for default by private insurers. Of course, prices of all fixed-income securities decline when interest rates go up.

How assured is my income? Munis are relatively safe (see the preceding question) but defaults are possible due to such factors as limited ability to impose taxes, disappointing revenues from the use of facilities, or mismanagement of municipal finances. Issues may also be callable, enabling the issuer to force redemption after specified times.

Are there any other risks unique to this investment? Munis are not subject to Securities and Exchange Commission regulation, so the legality of the issue must be established. Make sure a legal opinion accompanies the issue.

Is it commercially rated? Moody's Investors Service, Standard & Poor's, and others rate credit. White's Tax-Exempt Bond Rating Service rates market risk.

Tax Considerations

What tax advantages (or disadvantages) does it offer? Interest may be exempt from federal income taxes and frequently from state and local income taxes (36 states tax exempt munis of other states but not their own: 5 states tax their own exempt munis and those of other states; 9 states plus the District of Columbia do not tax any exempt munis). Munis issued by Puerto Rico, Guam, and the Virgin Islands (U.S. territories) are tax-exempt in all states. Capital gains are taxable. Permitted private purpose bond interest may be a tax preference item in computing the Alternative Minimum Tax. Up to 85% of Social Security benefits can be taxed if municipal bond interest income plus adjusted gross income plus half the Social Security payments exceeds $32,000 for couples or $25,000 for single taxpayers.

Economic Considerations

What economic factors most affect buy, hold, or sell decisions? Personal tax considerations, of course, then interest rate levels and the inflation rate. Buy when rates are high to get good yields; hold as rates decline to see market values rise. Because tax-exempt munis pay a relatively low interest rate, inflation is especially devastating if the rate is fixed. Prolonged economic downturns can increase the risk of municipal defaults. Special supply and demand factors owing to the uncertain status of tax-exempt issues under tax reform legislation then pending, caused abnormally high municipal yields in the mid-1980s.

MUTUAL FUNDS (OPEN END)

An open-end mutual fund is so named because its sponsoring organization, called an investment company or a management company, stands ready at any time to issue new shares or to redeem existing shares at their daily-computed net asset value. An open-end fund offers investors with moderate means the diversification, professional management (for a fee), economy of scale, and, where it might not otherwise exist, the liquidity available only to large investors.

Mutual funds are available with portfolio compositions designed for an almost infinite variety of investment objectives and risk levels. The following is a partial list of types of funds, with their basic portfolio or mode of operation:

Income Fund (stocks paying dividends, preferred stocks, corporate bonds)

Growth Fund (growth stocks)

Aggressive Growth Fund (smaller, riskier growth stocks)

Balanced Fund (stocks and bonds)

Performance Fund (high-risk stocks, venture capital investments, etc.)

Conservative Balanced Fund (high-grade income and growth securities)

United States Government Bond Fund (U.S. Treasury or agency bonds)

International Fund (foreign stocks or bonds)

Global Fund (foreign and U.S. stocks or bonds)

Domestic Taxable Bond Fund (corporate bonds with investment-grade ratings)

Corporate High-Yield Bond Fund (corporate bonds with ratings below investment grade)

Municipal Bond Fund (tax-exempt municipal securities)

Special Situations Fund (venture capital, debt/equity securities)

Stock Index Fund (replicating or representative of the major stock indexes)

Market Sector Fund or *Specialized Fund* (securities of high-growth industries or specialized industries like gold-mining)

Tax-managed Fund (utility stocks whose dividends are reinvested for long-term capital gains)

Speculative Fund (engages in selling short and leverage)

Commodities Fund (commodity futures contracts)

Option Fund (sells puts and calls for extra income, sometimes speculating by taking positions without owning underlying securities or instruments)

Socially-conscious Fund (excludes investments offensive on moral or ethical grounds)

Fund of Funds (invests in other funds with top performance)

Money Market Fund (short-term, interest-bearing debt instruments)

Tax-exempt Money Market Fund (trades long-term and short-term municipals for best yields and capital gains)

Ginnie-Mae Fund (mortgage-backed pass-through securities guaranteed by Government National Mortgage Association)

Major sponsors allow switching of investments from shares of one fund to another within their fund families. Other services commonly available to investors include term life insurance; automatic reinvestment plans; regular income checks; open account plans allowing fractional share purchases with Social Security or pension checks or other relatively small amounts of cash; loan programs; and toll-free information services.

* * *

What Is an Open-End Mutual Fund?

An open-end mutual fund is an investment company that pools shareholder funds and invests in a diversified securities portfolio having a specified objective. It provides professional management and stands ready to sell new shares and redeem outstanding shares on a continuous (open-end) basis.

Buying, Selling, and Holding

Where do I buy and sell it? Load funds, in which a sales charge is deducted from the amount invested, are bought from securities brokers and financial planners. No-load funds are bought directly from the sponsor. Shares are not sold in the sense that shares of stock are transferred to other owners; rather they are redeemed (by phone, mail, or checkwriting privilege) by the fund at net asset value.

Is there a minimum purchase amount, and what is the price range? Some funds have minimum deposits of $1000–$2500. Others have no minimum. Share prices vary, but a majority are under $20. Many funds offer convenient share accumulation plans for investors of modest means.

What fees and charges are involved? Load funds charge a sales commission, typically 8¹/2% of the amount invested, though with larger purchases the load can go as low as 1¹/2%. No-load funds have no sales commissions. A hybrid, low-load funds, charge commissions of 3% or less. Both load and no-load funds charge annual management fees of from ¹/2% to 1% of the value of the investment. There is usually no redemption charge (back-end load, or exit fee), with load funds; no-loads may or may not have a 1% to 2% redemption fee to discourage short-term trading. Various share accumulation plans may involve extra service charges. Some funds discourage frequent switching by imposing extra charges. 12B-1 mutual funds, a type of fund that covers all or part of its sales and marketing expenses by charging fees to shareholders, may charge ¹/4% or less of assets in the case of no-load funds, ranging to 8¹/2% for load funds.

Does it mature, expire, or otherwise terminate? No.

Can I sell it quickly? Funds stand ready to redeem shares daily. Some managing companies allow switching among different funds they sponsor at either no charge (no-load fund families) or a small transaction fee.

How is market value determined and how do I keep track of it? Market value, called net asset value, depends on the way various economic and market forces affect the type of investments composing a particular fund's portfolio; a given economic or interest-rate scenario will have a different effect on bond fund values than stock fund values. Mutual fund quotations are reported daily in newspapers and a fund management company reports, usually quarterly, on the composition of portfolios and transactions during the reporting period.

Investment Objectives

Should I buy an open-end mutual fund if my objective is capital appreciation? Yes, but you would buy a fund with capital gains as a primary objective, such as a growth stock or special situations fund.

Should I buy this if my objective is income? Yes, but you would buy a fund with income as its primary objective, such as a bond or money market fund or a stock fund investing in high-yield stocks.

To what extent does it protect against inflation? That depends on the type of fund. Equity-oriented funds or money market funds offer more protection than fixed income bond portfolios, which provide little or no protection.

Is it suitable for tax-deferred retirement accounts? Yes, except when the fund is invested in tax-exempt securities, such as municipal bonds.

Can I borrow against it? Yes, subject to Federal Reserve margin rules. Collateral value varies with the type of fund. A lender that might loan 90% of the value of money market fund shares might find a high-risk fund unacceptable as collateral.

Risk Considerations

How assured can I be of getting my full investment back? It depends on the type of fund, the quality of the portfolio, and the adroitness of management in avoiding adverse developments. A money market fund has high safety of principal, whereas a bond fund is vulnerable to interest rate movements and a stock fund is subject to market risk, for example.

How assured is my income? Again, it depends on the type of portfolio, its quality, and the skill of the manager. A fund with AAA bonds will be a safer source of income than one comprised of higher-yielding but riskier junk bonds. Other funds stress capital growth at the expense of income. Money market funds offer assured income at a conservative rate, which goes up and down with market conditions.

Are there any other risks unique to this investment? Except for the fact that funds provide automatic diversification, the same risk considerations apply as affect individual investments.

Is it commercially rated? No, but some funds invest exclusively in securities with given commercial ratings, and a number of organizations rate mutual funds in terms of historical performance.

Tax Considerations

What tax advantages (or disadvantages) does it offer? Income is subject to the same federal income taxes as the investments from which it derives. Thus, a shareholder pays taxes just as if he owned the portfolio directly, except that all capital gains distributions are considered long-term, regardless of the time the fund has been held. Funds invested in tax-exempt municipal securities (some are triple—federal, state, and local—tax-exempt) provide tax-free income, at least at the federal level. States vary in their tax treatment of income from municipal securities (see the discussion of tax considerations in the section on Municipal Securities) and the same rules usually apply to fund income. Some states that would not tax interest will tax dividends from funds, however, even though the fund's income is from interest earned. In such states, dividends from a tax-exempt fund would be taxable.

Economic Considerations

What economic factors most affect buy, hold, or sell decisions? The same economic and market forces that affect individual investments affect funds made up of those investments, so choices should be made in the same terms.

OPTION CONTRACT (PUT OR CALL)

Put and call options are contracts that give holders the right, for a price, called a premium, to sell or buy an underlying stock or financial instrument at a specified price, called the exercise or strike price, before a specified expiration date. Option sellers are called writers—covered writers if they own the underlying security or financial instrument, naked writers if they don't—and buyers of options are called option buyers. A put is an option to sell and a call is an option to buy.

Listed options are options traded (since 1973) on national stock and commodity exchanges and thus have both visibility and liquidity, as opposed to conventional over-the-counter options, which are individually negotiated, more expensive, and less liquid. Listed options are available on stocks, stock indexes, debt instruments, foreign currencies, and futures of different types. The issuance and settlement—all the mechanics of options clearing—are handled by the options clearing corporation (OCC), which is owned by the exchanges.

Options make it possible to control a large amount of value with a much smaller amount of money. Because a small percentage change in the value of a financial instrument can result in a much larger percentage change in the value of an option, large gains (and losses) are possible with the leverage that options provide. Although sometimes options are bought with the idea of holding the underlying security as an investment after the exercise of the option, options are usually bought and sold without ever being exercised and settled. They have a life of their own.

The value of options—that is, the amount of their premiums—is mainly determined by the relationship between the exercise price and the market price of the underlying instrument, by the volatility of the underlying instrument, and by the time remaining before expiration.

When the relationship between an option's strike price (exercise price) and the underlying market price is such that the holder would profit (transaction costs aside) by exercising it, an option has intrinsic value and is said to be in the money. In contrast, there is no intrinsic value in an out-of-the-money option—such as a put whose strike price is below the market price or a call whose strike price is above the market price. A premium will normally trade for at least its intrinsic value, if any. An out-of-the-money option, on the other hand, has obviously more risk and a lower premium than an option that is more likely to become profitable. Options on highly volatile securities and instruments command higher premiums because they are more likely to produce profits when and if they move.

Time value influences premiums because the longer the time remaining, the greater the chance of a favorable movement and the higher the present value of the underlying instrument if exercised. This time value, also called net premium, decreases as the option approaches its expiration. (For this reason, options are called wasting assets.) The value of an out-of-the-money option is all time value; that of an in-the-money option is a combination of time value and intrinsic value. In general, the greater the potential for gain, the greater the risk of not achieving it. The farther from expiration and the greater the volatility, the higher the premium an option will have.

Professional traders have multioption strategies, some quite complex, designed to limit risk while capitalizing on premium movements. Called straddles, combinations, and spreads (which have many varieties), they involve close monitoring, expertise, and sometimes onerous commissions. Options trading is not for the average investor.

Options do have a conservative role, however, for personal as well as institutional investors. Options can be used very much like term life insurance policies to protect investors against losses in investments already owned. Option selling (writing) can be a source of added returns.

The use of options as insurance involves the purchase of a put to limit losses or lock in the profit on a position already owned, or the purchase of a call to limit losses or lock in the profit on a short sale. For example, an individual with 100 shares of XYZ at a market value of $60 who expects the price to rise to $70 might buy, at a premium of $125, a put at $55 expiring in three months. If the stock rises, the insurance would have cost $125 and that amount would have to be subtracted from the capital gain. If the stock dropped, however, the put could be exercised and the stock sold for no lower than $55; that would limit the investor's loss to $625—$60 less $55 (times 100 shares) plus the premium of $125. The investor who thought the stock would drop could have sold it short and bought a call to assure the ability to buy the shares to cover at the call price.

Covered option writing—writing calls on stock or other instruments that are owned—is a safe way to increase the income return on an investment, provided the investor is prepared to sell the underlying holding at the exercise price if the price moves that way. Potential gains are limited to the amount of the premium (a significant drawback if the underlying holding rises in value and the option is exercised).

Calls can be written at, in, deep in, out of, or deep out of the money. The farther out of the money it is, the less the chance of exercise and the lower the premium it will command. The main problem with writing covered calls is that to warrant a premium high enough to offset the commissions, the underlying asset has to be volatile, and the option close to the money; the more volatile it is and the closer the option is to the money, the greater the chance it will be exercised. If it's exercised the writer's profit is limited to the premium, when a greater profit could have been made by holding the investment.

Mutual funds that make their income by writing and trading options are an alternative for small investors.

What are LEAPS? LEAPS are among the most notable innovations of the 1990s. An acronym for Long-Term Equity Anticipation Securities, LEAPS were introduced by the Chicago Board Options Exchange (CBOE) in October 1990. LEAPS are long-term put and call options that by the mid-nineties were being traded (on the NYSE, Amex, Philadelphia, and options exchanges) on about 150 stocks and several stock indexes. LEAPS are presently available with expirations of 1 to 3 years and applications for 5-year LEAPS are pending as this is written. Generally speaking, everything that is said in the following pages about regular puts and calls applies to LEAPS, except, of course, that being longer in term, LEAPS have higher premiums.

* * *

What Is an Option Contract (Put or Call)?

An option contract is a contract that grants the right, in exchange for a price or premium to buy (call) or sell (put) an underlying security at a specified price within a specified period of time.

Buying, Selling, and Holding

Where do I buy and sell it? At a full-service or discount broker.

Is there a minimum purchase amount, and what is the price range? The minimum is one option contract covering 100 shares. Contracts typically cost a few hundred dollars (usually less than $500).

What fees and charges are involved? In addition to the premium, brokerage commissions are charged for buying, selling, and exercising options. The maximum charge is $25 for a transaction covering one option; the average for multiple-contract transactions is about $14.

Does it mature, expire, or otherwise terminate? Yes; options have a specified expiration date, usually within nine months.

Can I sell it quickly? Yes; most options enjoy good liquidity.

How is market value determined and how do I keep track of it? The market value of an option is its premium value, which is determined by a combination of its intrinsic value (the difference between its exercise price and the market value of the underlying stock) and its time value (the value investors place on the amount of time until the expiration of the option). A small change in a stock price can cause a larger percentage change in an option premium; premium changes are reported daily in the financial sections of newspapers.

Investment Objectives

Should I buy an option contract if my objective is capital appreciation? Because a small change in a stock price causes a higher percentage change in a related option premium, speculators gain leverage using options. Of course, if the underlying stock fails to move in the right direction, the speculator is out the cost of the premium. Options are also used as hedging tools to protect the value of shares held for capital gains.

Should I buy this if my objective is income? Although sellers (writers) of options receive income from premiums and thereby augment the income return on the underlying holding, they may be forced to buy or sell the underlying holding if its price moves adversely. Options are not themselves income-producing investments, although speculators and some mutual funds create income through option writing and various spread strategies.

To what extent does it protect against inflation? Puts and calls, as short-term options, are not designed to capitalize on longer-term movements in common stock prices as might be caused by inflationary factors. Of course, LEAPS subscription warrants and employee stock options, which are related to put and call options, could be viewed as inflation protection.

Is it suitable for tax-deferred retirement accounts? Although not prohibited by the Internal Revenue Service, most brokerage firms rule out options contracts as too risky for retirement accounts. They may have a limited role in managed accounts, primarily as a hedging tool. Mutual funds or other pooled investments that generate income by writing and speculating in options may be appropriate investments in selected situations for people with high risk tolerance.

Can I borrow against it? No. Although Federal Reserve margin rules allow options transactions in margin accounts, options cannot be used as part of the borrowing base. Of course, options are themselves a source of considerable leverage.

Risk Considerations

How assured can I be of getting my full investment back? Your investment is the premium plus commissions. It is recovered only if the underlying stock or instrument moves favorably to such an extent that the profit gained from selling or exercising the option exceeds the investment; whether it does or not is pure speculation.

How assured is my income? The only income that options provide is from premiums earned in selling them. That is assured income, but it can be more than offset if the underlying stock moves adversely and the option is exercised by its holder.

Are there any other risks unique to this investment? The risk in options ranges from the simple loss of a premium if the option proves valueless to the risk of a magnified loss in the case of uncovered or naked positions—that is, where a put or call is sold without owning the underlying security or instrument. Upon exercise, the security or instrument must be bought or sold at a market price that may be in wide variance from the exercise price.

Is it commercially rated? No.

Tax Considerations

What tax advantages (or disadvantages) does it offer? Options on stocks are subject to the same capital gains taxation as the stocks themselves. Some traditional uses of options to defer income from one year to another have been curtailed by recent tax legislation and advice should be sought. See also the entry for Tax Straddle in Part IV.

Economic Considerations

What economic factors most affect buy, hold, and sell decisions? The same economic factors that affect stock investments in the short term apply essentially to decisions involving put and call options used in speculation and hedging.

OPTION CONTRACT ON A FUTURES CONTRACT (FUTURES OPTION)

For a general discussion of an option, see Option Contract (Put or Call).

* * *

What Is an Option Contract on a Futures Contract?

A futures option is a contract that grants the right, in exchange for a price (premium) to buy (call) or sell (put) a specified futures contract within a specified period of time.

Buying, Selling, and Holding

How do I buy and sell it? At a full-service or discount broker.

Is there a minimum purchase amount, and what is the price range? The minimum purchase is one option on one futures contract. It can cost several hundred to several thousand dollars, depending on the underlying future.

What fees and charges are involved? In addition to the premium, brokerage commissions are charged for buying, selling, and exercising an option. Generally, the maximum charge is $25, and the average charge for multiple option transactions is around $14, with lower rates for high-volume transactions.

Does it mature, expire, or otherwise terminate? Yes; options have a specified expiration date, usually within one year.

Can I sell it quickly? Yes; most futures options have good liquidity and they are not subject to daily trading limits that can affect the liquidity of futures themselves.

How is market value determined and how do I keep track of it? The same factors that affect the market value of futures affect the premium values of futures options. (See the sections Futures Contract on a Commodity and Futures Contract on an Interest Rate.) Prices are reported daily in newspapers and electronic databases.

Investment Objectives

Should I buy a futures option if my objective is capital appreciation? Only if you are a speculator attracted to the high degree of leverage offered by options, although options on futures are used by investors to hedge the value of other investments held for capital gains.

Should I buy this if my objective is income? Although selling options is a source of income, options are not themselves an income-producing investment. Some mutual funds trade in options for the purpose of generating income, however.

To what extent does it protect against inflation? Only to the limited extent that futures offer the opportunity to capitalize on inflation expectations and their effects on interest rates and commodity prices.

Is it suitable for tax-deferred retirement accounts? Although not prohibited by the Internal Revenue Service, most brokerage firms rule out options contracts as too risky for retirement accounts. They may have a limited role in managed accounts, primarily as a hedging tool. Mutual funds or other pooled investments that generate income by writing and speculating in options may be appropriate investments in selected situations for people with high risk tolerance.

Can I borrow against it? No. Although Federal Reserve margin rules allow options transactions in margin accounts, options cannot be used as part of the borrowing base. Of course, options are themselves a source of significant leverage.

Risk Considerations

How assured can I be of getting my full investment back? Your investment is the premium plus commissions. It is recovered only if the underlying futures contract moves favorably to such an extent that the proceeds realized from selling or exercising the option exceed the amount expended; whether it does or not is pure speculation.

How assured is my income? The only income that options provide is from premiums earned in selling them. That is assured income, but it can be more than offset if the underlying future moves adversely and the option is exercised by the holder.

Are there any other risks unique to this investment? Essentially the same risks apply as are involved with regular options and futures on the same underlying assets. A special positive feature, however, is that futures options, particularly on debt instruments, have better liquidity than either straight options or straight futures; that is because of less restrictive trading limits on futures options than on futures, and because the open interest on futures options tends to be much higher than on regular interest-rate (debt) options.

Is it commercially rated? No.

Tax Considerations

What tax advantages (or disadvantages) does it offer? Options on futures are subject to the same tax treatment as futures are. See the section on a Futures Contract on a Commodity.

Economic Considerations

What economic factors most affect buy, hold, and sell decisions? The same economic forces that affect interest rate and commodity futures affect the options available on those contracts.

OPTION CONTRACT ON AN INTEREST RATE (DEBT OPTION)

For a general discussion of an option, see Option Contract (Put or Call).

* * *

What Is an Option Contract on an Interest Rate?

An interest-rate option is a contract that grants the right, in exchange for a price (premium), to buy (call option) or sell (put option) a certain debt security at a specified price within a specified period of time, thereby producing a particular yield.

Buying, Selling, and Holding

How do I buy and sell it? Through a full-service or discount broker.

Is there a minimum purchase amount, and what is the price range? The minimum purchase is one contract. Premiums, where the underlying security is interest-bearing, are determined as a percentage (in 32nds for Treasury bonds and notes) of par value. Thus a contract on a $100,000 par value U.S. Treasury bond with a premium of 2.50 (2 and $16/32$) would cost $2500, while a $20.000 minicontract with a premium of 1.24 (1 and $24/32$ or $1^3/4$) would cost $350. Where the underlying security is discounted rather than interest-bearing, as with the 13-week Treasury bill, premiums are quoted with reference to basis point (100ths of one percent) differences between prices, expressed as complements of annualized discount rates. For example, with a 9% yield, a 13-week Treasury bill (par value $1 million) would have a price basis of 91 and might have an option trading at 92.20. With a premium thus quoted at 1.20 (120 basis points), it would cost $3000, calculated: $.012 \times 13/52 \times \$1$ million. (A quick way of approximating dollar premiums is to multiply basis points times $25.)

What fees and charges are involved? Brokerage commissions are charged for buying, selling, or exercising options. The maximum charge is $25 for a transaction covering one contract, with reduced rates for larger trades. Margin accounts may entail interest and other added charges. There may also be income and net worth rules to qualify investors.

Does it mature, expire, or otherwise terminate? Yes. All options have expiration dates, usually within nine months.

Can I sell it quickly? Interest rate options have generally good liquidity. Those with the most contracts outstanding (represented by open interest figures in newspapers) are usually easiest to trade.

How is market value determined and how do I keep track of it? Market value, which is premium value, is determined by a combination of intrinsic value (exercise value less market value of the underlying security) and time value (the diminishing value investors place on the time remaining to expiration). Intrinsic value changes with interest rate movements, which are influenced by Federal Reserve Board monetary policy and other economic factors. Option prices are reported daily in newspapers and electronic databases.

Investment Objectives

Should I buy an interest-rate option if my objective is capital appreciation? Speculators use the high leverage possible with options to capitalize on the price volatility resulting from interest rate movements.

Should I buy this if my objective is income? Option writers earn income in addition to the interest they receive on the underlying security, while taking the risk that the option will be exercised if rates move adversely. Investors also use interest rate options to hedge the value of other income-producing investments.

To what extent does it protect against inflation? As short-term instruments, interest-rate options are not designed for dealing with the longer-term effects of inflation on debt securities. However, inflation expectations are a factor in the term structure of interest rates, and it is possible, using options, to capitalize on short-term movements.

Is it suitable for tax-deferred retirement accounts? Although not prohibited by the Internal Revenue Service, most brokerage firms rule out options contracts as too risky for retirement accounts. They may have a limited role in managed accounts, primarily as a hedging tool. Mutual funds or other pooled investments that generate income by writing and speculating in options may be appropriate investments in selected situations for people with high risk tolerance.

Can I borrow against it? No. Although Federal Reserve margin rules allow options transactions in margin accounts, options cannot be used as part of the borrowing base. Of course, options are themselves a source of considerable leverage.

Risk Considerations

How assured can I be of getting my full investment back? Your investment is recovered only if interest rates move favorably to the extent that the proceeds of the sale of the option exceed the premium plus commissions already expended; that is a matter of pure speculation.

How assured is my income? The only income is from premiums earned in selling options and even that can be negated by losses resulting from exercise by the holder.

Are there any other risks unique to this investment? The marketplace of interest-rate options is dominated on one hand by large institutional investors and their portfolio managers and on the other by dealers who handle the large volumes of high-denomination securities that underlie the options. This puts the smaller investor at a disadvantage in terms both of information and transaction cost. Other special risks have to do with the Option Clearing Corporation's power to remedy shortages of underlying securities by permitting substitutions and adjusting strike prices, and with trading hour differences between options and underlying debt instruments. Sellers of options on discount instruments settled in current instruments take a risk to the extent that they cannot hedge perfectly against exercise.

Is it commercially rated? No.

Tax Considerations

What tax advantages (or disadvantages) does it offer? Unlike regular put and call options, traders in interest-rate options are subject to tax rules covering futures trading; this means open positions are marked to market at year-end with paper gains or losses treated as if realized and taxed as net capital gains (see page 31). Tax advice should be sought.

Economic Considerations

What economic factors most affect buy, hold, and sell decisions? Economic and monetary factors affecting interest rates govern choices having to do with interest-rate options.

OPTION CONTRACT ON A STOCK INDEX

For a general discussion of an option, see Option Contract (Put or Call).

* * *

What Is an Option Contract on a Stock Index?

A stock-index option is a contract that grants the right, in exchange for a price (premium), to buy (call option) or sell (put option) the value of an underlying stock index or subindex at a specified price within a specified period of time with settlement in cash.

Buying, Selling, and Holding

How do I buy and sell it? Through a full-service or discount broker.

Is there a minimum purchase amount, and what is the price range? The minimum purchase is one contract. The premium is the difference in index values times $100. A contract based on a 5-point difference between the current (base) value and the exercise value would thus cost $500. Because contracts are settled in cash, margin security in the form of cash or securities is required by brokers, who may also have suitability requirements calling for substantial net worth and income.

What fees and charges are involved? In addition to the premium, brokerage commissions are charged for buying, selling, and exercising options. The maximum charge is $25 for a transaction covering one contract, with reduced rates for large trades. Margin accounts may entail interest and other additional charges.

Does it mature, expire, or otherwise terminate? Yes; options have a specified expiration date.

Can I sell it quickly? Most stock-index options have good liquidity, though newly introduced contracts may have less active markets than contracts that are better established and more popular. Those with many contracts outstanding (represented by large open interest figures in the newspapers) are generally the easiest to trade.

How is market value determined and how do I keep track of it? Premium value is determined by a combination of intrinsic value (exercise price less the index value) and time value (the value investors place on the amount of time remaining to expiration). The intrinsic value is subject to all the forces that make the stock market go up and down; a small movement in the market, as represented by the index, will result in a much larger percentage change in premium value. Indexes are revalued constantly during the trading day and closing prices are published in daily newspapers and electronic databases along with the option values based on them.

Investment Objectives

Should I buy a stock-index option if my objective is capital appreciation? You might if you were a speculator expecting a move in the stock market and were attracted to the high leverage provided by options. You might also use index options to hedge against possible losses in other securities being held for capital gains.

Should I buy this if my objective is income? Although sellers of options receive premium income and thereby increase the income return on their portfolios, options are not themselves income securities.

To what extent does it protect against inflation? Index options are short-term investments and not designed to capitalize on longer-term market movements as might be caused by inflation.

Is it suitable for tax-deferred retirement accounts? Although not prohibited by the Internal Revenue Service, most brokerage firms rule out options contracts as too risky for retirement accounts. They may have a limited role in managed accounts, primarily as a hedging tool. Mutual funds or other pooled investments that generate income by writing and speculating in options may be appropriate investments in selected situations for people with high risk tolerance.

Can I borrow against it? No. Although Federal Reserve margin rules allow options transactions in margin accounts, options cannot be used as part of the borrowing base. Of course, options are themselves a source of significant leverage.

Risk Considerations

How assured can I be of getting my full investment back? Your investment is recovered only if the underlying index value moves favorably to such an extent that the proceeds gained from selling or exercising the option exceed the cost plus commissions; whether it does is pure speculation.

How assured is my income? The only income that options provide is from premiums earned in selling the options. Even that, however, can be negated if the underlying index moves adversely and the option is exercised by the holder.

Are there any other risks unique to this investment? Index options share the same risks as regular puts and calls, but have a few that are unique. These have basically to do with (1) the limitations of index options as a hedging tool (it is impractical to compose a portfolio that duplicates an index exactly and even then there is rarely dollar-for-dollar variation) and with (2) the fact that settlement is made in cash; the settlement figure is the difference between the strike price and the closing value of the index on the day of exercise, and since the seller is not informed of the assignment until the next business day or even later, his hedge position may have lost value. This timing risk must be considered in all multioption strategies using index options. Other risks have to do with trading halts affecting underlying shares (but not the indexes) and causing index values to be based on noncurrent prices, or trading halts in the index options themselves, with the risk that the index value will move adversely before a position can be closed out.

Is it commercially rated? No.

Tax Considerations

What tax advantages (or disadvantages) does it offer? Unlike regular put and call options, index options are subject to tax rules covering futures trading. This means open positions are marked to market at year-end; paper profits or losses are treated as if realized and taxed as net capital gains (see page 31). Tax advice should be sought.

Economic Considerations

What economic factors most affect buy, hold, and sell decisions? Index options are used to make market bets or to protect other holdings against market risk. Any and all economic factors affecting the market become relevant to decisions involving stock options.

OPTION CONTRACT OR FUTURES CONTRACT ON A CURRENCY

For a general discussion of an option, see Option Contract (Put or Call); for a general discussion of a futures contract, see Futures Contract on a Commodity.

*   *   *

What Is a Futures Contract or an Option Contract on a Currency?

They are contracts to buy or sell (futures) or that represent rights (options) to buy or sell a foreign currency at a particular price within a specified period of time.

Buying, Selling, and Holding

How do I buy and sell them? Through a full-service broker or commodities dealer.

Is there a minimum purchase amount, and what is the price range? Contract sizes vary with different currencies and different markets. The minimum purchase is one contract, which, for an option, typically costs a few hundred dollars. Futures contracts tend to be sizable (standard-size contracts are 12.5 million yen and 125,000 Swiss francs, for example, which on one day in the mid-1980s both equalled about $62,500) but they can be bought with small (1.5% to 4.2%) margins. Also, minicontracts are traded in several currencies on the Mid-America Commodity Exchange—6.25 million yen and 62,500 Swiss francs, for example.

What fees and charges are involved? Broker's commissions, typically $25 or less per contract for options; $50 to $80 for a round-trip futures contract transaction (purchase and sale). In the event of actual delivery, other fees, charges, or taxes may be required.

Do they mature, expire, or otherwise terminate? Yes; all contracts have specified expiration dates.

Can I sell them quickly? Yes; option and futures contracts enjoy good liquidity, although daily price limits on futures can create illiquidity when contracts are down limit or up limit and it is impossible to trade out of a position, because maximum allowable price movement has occurred during the trading day.

How is market value determined and how do I keep track of it? Premiums and contract values change as the exchange rate between the dollar and the foreign currency changes. The exchange rate is determined by the relative value of two currencies, which can change as events affect either or both of the underlying currencies. Daily prices are published in newspapers and electronic databases.

Investment Objectives

Should I buy them if my objective is capital appreciation? Speculators use the high leverage afforded by options and futures contracts to seek gains on relative currency values.

Should I buy them if my objective is income? Except for premium income earned from selling (writing) options, contracts do not provide income. Contracts are frequently used in hedging strategies to protect other income-producing securities from losses due to currency values.

To what extent do they protect against inflation? Because they are short-term contracts, currency options and futures are not affected directly by inflation.

Are they suitable for tax-deferred retirement accounts? Although not prohibited by the Internal Revenue Service, most brokerage firms rule out options and futures contracts as too risky for retirement accounts. They may have a limited role in managed accounts, primarily as a hedging tool. Mutual funds or other pooled investments that generate income through options and futures may be appropriate investments in selected situations for people with high risk tolerance.

Can I borrow against them? Options can be traded in margin accounts but cannot be used as collateral. Moreover, since foreign currency does not have borrowing value either for margin purposes, purchases as the result of exercise may require extra cash or securities. Futures cannot be used as collateral, but provide leverage because they can be held with small margins, actually good faith deposits.

Risk Considerations

How assured can I be of getting my full investment back? With options, the only investment is the premium plus commissions and it is recovered only when the underlying rate of exchange moves favorably to such an extent that the proceeds gained from sale or exercise exceed the amount expended. Futures are inherently speculative and it is possible to lose more than your investment, although margin calls would normally limit losses to the amount invested, assuming the account was closed out (liquidated) to meet the call.

How assured is my income? Other than premium income from option writing (selling), options and futures provide no income.

Are there any other risks unique to these investments? Since two currencies are involved, developments in either country can affect the values of options and futures. Risks include general economic factors as well as government actions affecting currency valuation and the movements of currencies from one country to another. The quantities of currency underlying option contracts represent odd lots in a market dominated by transactions between banks; this can mean extra transaction costs upon exercise. The fact that options markets may be closed while round-the-clock interbank currency markets are open can create problems due to price and rate discrepancies. With futures, there is always the risk of actual delivery if a position is not closed out prior to expiration of the contract.

Are they commercially rated? No, neither options nor futures are rated.

Tax Considerations

What tax advantages (or disadvantages) do they offer? Options are subject to the same capital gains rules as the underlying assets. Futures are subject to special rules requiring that open positions be marked to market at year-end and be taxed as realized capital gains (see page 31). Net trading losses can be applied against capital gains on other investments and unused portions carried forward. Other tax treatments may apply where contracts are used for hedging purposes. Tax advice should be sought.

Economic Considerations

What economic factors most affect buy, hold, and sell decisions? All factors that affect either currency affect the values of options and futures contracts.

PRECIOUS METALS

Precious metals—gold, silver, platinum, and palladium—are bought by investors primarily to hedge against inflation, economic uncertainty, and foreign exchange risk, in the belief that these metals are repositories of absolute value, whereas paper currencies and securities denominated in such currencies have relative value and are vulnerable to loss.

The economics of precious metals have less to do with the production process, industrial demand, or their greatly diminished monetary role than with the psychology of the financial marketplace. There, precious metals—gold especially—are perceived to be the best store of value available when anxiety causes the value of other assets to go into a tailspin. Historically, in such scenarios gold and other precious metals have risen.

The most famous example was in January 1980 when high international inflation due to rising oil prices, the American-hostage crisis in Iran, and civil disorder in Saudi Arabia combined to cause abnormally heavy buying of precious metals, which drove gold to a record price of $887.50 per ounce and led silver and platinum to peak levels as well. When calmer times returned, however, prices soon fell and stabilized at lower levels. It was a memorable lesson in how volatile this store of value can be.

Physical ownership is one way of owning precious metals, available in bullion form in units ranging from 400-Troy-ounce gold bars to 1-ounce platinum ingots. These are sold by dealers at markups or premiums that fall as weights and dollar values rise. Gold can also be held in coins, such as the South African Krugerrand, the Canadian Maple Leaf, and the U.S. Eagle series, introduced in 1986. Generally, the more popular the coin, the greater its liquidity and the higher its premium. Silver can be bought in bags containing U.S. coins of $1000 total face value, priced at a discount to the silver value to cover melting and refining costs. The drawbacks of physical ownership are mainly the high premiums, safekeeping and insurance costs, and sales taxes.

Certificates—actually warehouse receipts issued by some banks, dealers, and full-service brokers—represent gold, silver, platinum, or palladium held in safekeeping. Typically, for a fee of 3% or higher, the bank or dealer will buy metals in $1000 units and, for a small annual charge, provide insurance and storage. It will also, for 1% or so, sell the bullion or deliver it without a sales tax. The attraction is the convenience and lower transaction costs compared to physical ownership.

Other alternatives include *securities* of companies engaged in mining or processing, including some exchange-traded South African companies (many represented by American Depositary Receipts) as well as highly speculative penny stocks, traded over-the-counter or on regional or Canadian exchanges. There are also *mutual funds* and *closed-end funds* that specialize in both debt and equity issues of precious metals firms.

Finally, *commodity futures, options,* and *options on futures* are traded on precious metals. They provide leverage and hedging opportunities for well-capitalized investors with high expertise and risk tolerance. Scc separate discussions of these investment vehicles.

$$* \quad * \quad *$$

What Are Investments in Precious Metals?

Investments in precious metals involve gold, silver, platinum, and palladium as commodities (i.e.. not as money), owned by investors, in physical form or through securities, because of their presumed value as stores of wealth and as hedges against inflation and economic uncertainty. Precious metals are traded by speculators who hope to profit from volatility in the financial marketplace.

Buying, Selling, and Holding

How do I buy and sell them? Through various dealers and brokers, depending on the form of ownership. Coins and certificates are bought and sold through major banks.

Is there a minimum purchase amount and what is the price range? Precious metals can be bought with almost any amount of money, depending on the form of investment. Certificates generally have $1000 minimums.

What fees and charges are involved? Bullion involves a dealer markup, varying with quantity. Certificates cost 3% and up, with storage and insurance another 1% or more and sales fees of 1% or higher. Domestic and foreign securities and other forms of investment, like mutual funds, are subject to standard fees and commissions. Depending on the form of ownership, other costs may include sales or transfer taxes, shipping and handling, assay fees, insurance, storage, and safekeeping. Physical ownership involves an opportunity cost as well, since the money tied up could otherwise be invested in assets producing income.

Do they mature, expire, or otherwise terminate? Certain investment vehicles, such as options and futures, have specified expirations.

Can I sell them quickly? Usually yes, though platinum and palladium are less liquid than gold and silver. Larger ingots and less popular gold coins can have uncertain liquidity.

How is market value determined and how do I keep track of it? Market value is a complex affair. While investor demand is highest when inflation and economic uncertainty loom largest, industrial demand depends on economic health and certainty. Other factors, such as interest rates and foreign exchange rates, play a key role, and speculators are active. Different forms of investment may be affected in different ways at different times. Dealers are a source of information concerning physical assets; securities and commodities information is reported in the financial pages of daily newspapers.

Investment Objectives

Should I invest in precious metals if my objective is capital appreciation? Yes, but myriad forces affect market value, and a high degree of expertise is required to achieve short-term gains.

Should I buy them if my objective is income? Some forms of ownership, like stocks and mutual funds, may provide income, while others, like physical ownership, provide none and may involve negative returns. In general, precious metals are not purchased for income.

To what extent do they protect against inflation? Although used by investors primarily to hedge political and economic uncertainty, precious metals over the long term have risen in value with inflation. Investors buying precious metals for inflation protection should be mindful, however, that many factors can cause volatility in the shorter term.

Are they suitable for tax-deferred retirement accounts? Except for American gold and silver coins, physical investment is not permitted. Common stocks and mutual fund shares involving precious metals may be suitable for some accounts.

Can I borrow against them? Yes; depending on the form of investment, there are various ways to leverage investments and use them as loan collateral.

Risk Considerations

How assured can I be of getting my full investment back? Precious metals tend to be volatile and offer no assurance that values will be retained.

How assured is my income? Where such investments provide income at all, such as mining stocks paying dividends, the risk is often great.

Are there any other risks unique to these investments? Many investors in precious metals have lost money doing business with unscrupulous dealer-brokers. Political risks in countries where mining is done and related developments, such as the sentiment in the mid-1980s for divestiture of shares of firms doing business in South Africa, can jeopardize investment values. Inaccurate or misleading estimates of reserves of mining companies is another risk.

Are they commercially rated? Some common stocks are rated by Standard & Poor's and other major services.

Tax Considerations

What tax advantages (or disadvantages) do they offer? Assuming you are not engaged in mining or processing or using gold in a business or profession, dividend income and capital gains and losses are subject to the usual tax treatment. In addition, you may have to pay state sales taxes on physical purchases.

Economic Considerations

What economic factors most affect buy, hold, and sell decisions? Investors favor precious metals to hedge anticipated high inflation; however, many other economic factors can affect the value of precious metals and related investment alternatives, often in different ways.

PREFERRED STOCK (NONCONVERTIBLE)

Preferred stock is a hybrid security that combines features of both common stock and bonds. It is equity, not debt, however, and is thus riskier than bonds. It rarely carries voting rights.

Preferred dividends, like bond interest, are usually a fixed percentage of par value, so share prices, like bond prices, go up when interest rates move down and vice versa. But whereas bond interest is a contractual expense of the issuer, preferred dividends, although payable before common dividends, can be skipped if earnings are low. If the issuer goes out of business, preferred shareholders do not share in assets until bondholders are paid in full, though preferred shareholders rank ahead of common stockholders. Like bonds, preferreds may have sinking funds, be callable, or be redeemable by their holders.

Because preferred issues are designed for insurance companies and other institutional investors which, as corporations, enjoy a 70% tax exclusion on dividends earned, fully taxable yields for individuals are not much better than those on comparable bonds offering more safety. Moreover, trading is often inactive or in big blocks, meaning less liquidity and higher transaction costs for small investors.

Still, personal investors do hold preferred stock. A broker can usually find good buys as investor perceptions of risk in different industrial sectors create yield differences in stocks that are otherwise comparable. Capital appreciation can result from shares bought at a discount from the prices at which a sinking fund will purchase them, or from discounted shares of turnaround firms with dividend arrearages.

Different types of preferred stock include:

> *Convertible preferred,* convertible into common shares and thus offering growth potential plus fixed income; tends to behave differently in the marketplace than straight preferred (see Convertible Security).

> *Noncumulative preferred* is a hangover from the heyday of the railroads and is rare today. Dividends, if unpaid, do not accumulate.

Cumulative preferred is the most common type. Dividends, if skipped, accrue, and common dividends cannot be paid while arrearages exist.

Participating preferred is unusual and typically issued by firms desperate for capital. Holders share in profits with common holders by way of extra dividends declared after regular dividends are paid. This type may have voting rights.

Adjustable (floating or variable) rate preferred adjusts the dividend rate quarterly (usually based on the 3-month U.S. Treasury bill) to reflect money market rates. It is aimed at corporate investors seeking after-tax yields combined with secondary market price stability. Individuals, looking at modest, fully taxable dividends that can go down as well as up, might prefer the safety of a money market fund.

Prior preferred stock (or preference shares) has priority of claim on assets and earnings over other preferred shares.

PIK Preferred Stock—PIK is an acronym for payment in kind—refers to an oddity spawned in the wave of leveraged buyouts in the 1980s. PIK preferred pays its dividend in the form of additional preferred stock. It is highly speculative almost by definition, since it implies a dearth of cash and raises a question about the adequacy of the issuer's working capital.

$$* \quad * \quad *$$

What Is Nonconvertible Preferred Stock?

Nonconvertible preferred is a form of owner's equity, usually nonvoting, paying dividends at a specified rate and having prior claim over common stock on earnings and assets in liquidation.

Buying, Selling, and Holding

How do I buy and sell it? Through a securities broker-dealer.

Is there a minimum purchase amount, and what is the price range? Buying round lots (usually 10 shares) saves commissions. Shares have par (face) values normally ranging from $100 down to $10, and market prices may be higher or lower than par values to bring yields in line with prevailing interest rate levels.

What fees and charges are involved? Standard commissions, with added transaction charges on inactively traded shares.

Does it mature, expire, or otherwise terminate? Preferred stock may be outstanding indefinitely, but many issues have call features or sinking fund provisions, whereby the issuer, usually for a small premium over par value, can require holders to redeem shares. Preferred issues may also have put features, which allow holders to redeem shares.

Can I sell it quickly? In most cases, yes. As a rule, preferreds are less liquid than common stocks and more liquid than bonds. Because large corporate investors dominate, smaller lots can sometimes be difficult for brokers to transact quickly.

How is market value determined and how do I keep track of it? Assuming good financial condition, fixed-income preferreds vary inversely with market interest rates. Adjustable-rate preferreds tend to be less volatile because dividends are adjusted quarterly to reflect money market conditions. Preferred prices are reported daily in the stock tables of newspapers and in databases, identified by the abbreviation "PF" in newspapers and "PR" in most electronic media.

Investment Objectives

Should I buy nonconvertible preferred stock if my objective is capital appreciation? No, although appreciation is possible in shares bought at a discount from par or redemption value or bought prior to a decline in interest rates. Substantial appreciation is possible in turnaround situations where cumulative preferred issues of troubled companies are selling at big discounts and there is a sizable accumulated dividend obligation.

Should I buy this if my objective is income? Yes, but unless you're a corporation or you buy at a discount, your yield won't be much better than that on a comparable corporate bond, and bonds are less risky in terms of both income and principal.

To what extent does it protect against inflation? Fixed-rate preferred offers no protection against inflation. Adjustable-rate preferred offers some.

Is it suitable for tax-deferred retirement accounts? Yes.

Can I borrow against it? Yes, subject to lender policies and Federal Reserve margin requirements.

Risk Considerations

How assured can I be of getting my full investment back? The market value of fixed-rate preferred stock declines as interest rates rise. (Adjustable-rate preferred has greater price stability.) In liquidation, holders of preferred stock are paid after bondholders but before common stockholders.

How assured is my income? Dividends, unlike interest, are not legal obligations and are paid from earnings, so income is as reliable as the issuer's earnings are stable. Established companies, such as utilities, with predictable cash flows are better bets than young firms or firms in cyclical industries, such as housing. Preferred dividends must be paid before common distributions, however; that means common dividends wait until all unpaid preferred dividends of cumulative issues are satisfied.

Are there any other risks unique to this investment? Call features, when present, allow the issuer to force holders to redeem shares, usually at par value plus a small premium. Firms normally call issues when market rates have declined and they can obtain financing more cheaply. But it is exactly under such circumstances that shares are enjoying higher market values and paying higher than market yields to holders who bought before rates declined. So call features represent a risk to investors; indeed the very presence of a call feature can limit upside price potential. Another risk of preferred stock is that should a dividend be omitted, the market may perceive financial weakness and drive down the share values

Is it commercially rated? Yes. Major issues are rated by Moody's, Standard & Poor's, Value Line Investment Survey, and other services.

Tax Considerations

What tax advantages (or disadvantages) does it offer? None for personal investors. Corporations enjoy a 70% exemption from federal income taxes on dividends from other domestic corporations, effectively raising returns.

Economic Considerations

What economic factors most affect buy, hold, or sell decisions? Since most preferred stock pays a fixed dividend, it is best to buy when market rates are high and the issuer is forced to offer a competitive yield. Prices vary inversely with interest rates, so values increase as interest rates decline. Fixed-rate preferred stock loses value in inflation. Poor business conditions may affect profits and threaten dividends.

REAL ESTATE INVESTMENT TRUST (REIT AND FREIT)

If 1986 Tax Reform spoiled the party for "tax-advantaged" real estate limited partnerships, it made real estate investment trusts, or REITs, which are all about income, more popular than ever. The reasons are two:

First, by extending depreciation from 19 to 27.5 years, tax reform removed one the sweetest tax deductions benefiting limited partners, but REITs had always used a mandatory 35-year schedule, and thus were unaffected. Second, the use of writeoffs against salary and other investment income, a major benefit to limited partners before Tax Reform limited passive loss deductions to passive income, was never a benefit of REITs; REITs generate portfolio income, which is now worth relatively more.

The market environment for REITs has also become more favorable. Overbuilding before Tax Reform, then slow construction when tax benefits dried up, caused both depressed prices and a dearth of supply in the commercial market. Following a deep real estate recession in the late 1980s and early 1990s, rising rents and values began driving up the prices of existing REITs and spurred an unprecedented boom in REIT initial public offerings. Helped by low interest rates, the bull market in REITs was still going strong as this was going to press in the late 1990s.

REITs were authorized by Congress in the early 1960s to provide small investors with an opportunity to invest in large-scale real estate. After a tumultuous period in the mid-1970s, when rising interest rates and tight money pressured builders, causing loan defaults and forcing many REITs into financial difficulty, the industry, wiser for the experience, enjoyed a resurgence.

Like shares of stock, REITs trade publicly, and like mutual funds their money is invested in a diverse array of assets, from shopping malls and office buildings to health care facilities, apartment complexes and hotels, usually with geographical diversification as well.

Some REITs, called *equity REITs,* take ownership positions in real estate; shareholders receive income from the rents received from the properties and receive capital gains as properties are sold at a profit. Because both rents and property values rise with inflation, inflation protection is an important benefit of equityoriented real estate investments. Other REITs specialize in lending money to real estate developers. Called *mortgage REITs,* they pass interest income on to shareholders. *Hybrid* or *balanced REITs* feature a mix of equity and debt investments.

By law, REITs must derive 75% of income from rents, dividends, interest, and gains from the sale of real estate properties, and must pay out 95% to shareholders. Companies meeting those requirements are exempt from federal taxation at the corporate level, although dividends are taxable to shareholders. REITs thus allow investors to share, with limited liability, the financial and tax benefits of real estate while avoiding the double taxation of corporate ownership. REITs also offer liquidity, since you can sell your shares on the market any time you wish.

On the negative side, REIT shares can be just as volatile as shares of stock. When conditions are unfavorable, such as when interest rates are high, materials are short, and the real-estate market is overbuilt, share values suffer.

FREITS: A variation of the REIT is the *finite life real estate investment trust,* or FREIT. FREITs, like limited partnerships, are self-liquidating—that is, they aim to sell or finance their holdings by a given date and distribute the proceeds to investors, thereby enabling them to realize capital gains. Investors thus have the choice of (1) selling their FREIT shares in the market (share values tend to more closely reflect market values of property holding than with REITs) or of (2) waiting to receive the full value of their shares when the portfolio is sold and the cash is distributed. Of course, the disadvantages of REITs apply to FREITs as well—the risk of a soft market at the time of sale or liquidation, and the inability to share in tax-deductible losses.

CMO REITs: A recent and popular innovation has been the CMO REIT, a complex and risky investment created when the issuer of a collateralized mortgage obligation—see section on mortgage-backed (pass-through) securities—sells the CMO's residual cash flows (the spread between the rate paid by mortgage holders and the lower, shorter-term rate paid to CMO investors) to the CMO REIT. REIT shareholders benefit when the spread widens and and get lower returns as the spread narrows.

The main variable affecting the spread is the prepayment rate on the mortgages underlying the CMO. Prepayments fall and spreads widen when market interest rates increase; the reverse happens when rates decrease. Because returns rise and fall with interest rates, CMO REIT investors theoretically enjoy an investment that is countercyclical to other equity investments in real estate, which react adversely to rate increases.

CMO REITs may be vulnerable to more than prepayment risk, however. Depending on how they are structured, an increase in short-term versus long-term interest rates can create a rate squeeze. Moreover, spreads tend to narrow as a function of time as normal prepayments are made and as faster-pay, lower-rate CMO components are paid off, leaving the REIT with more costly longer-term bonds.

CMO REITs, which have been marketed aggressively, can seem appealing because of high initial yields and AAA ratings of the underlying CMOs. But at least one CMO REIT has gone bankrupt, and only investors who understand this sophisticated vehicle and can afford high risk should get involved.

*   *   *

What Is a Real Estate Investment Trust (REIT)?

A REIT is a trust that invests in real estate-related assets, such as properties or mortgages, with funds obtained by selling shares, usually publicly traded, to investors.

Buying, Selling, and Holding

How do I buy and sell it? Through a securities broker-dealer.

Is there a minimum purchase amount, and what is the price range? Like common stocks, shares trade in round lots of 100 shares, with odd-lot transactions involving higher commissions. Prices vary, but most shares trade under $50.

What fees and charges are involved? Standard brokerage commissions.

Does it mature, expire, or otherwise terminate? Not normally. A variation, called the finite life real estate investment trust or FREIT, is self-liquidating—that is, the management has an expressed intention to sell all its properties and distribute the proceeds within a specified time frame.

Can I sell it quickly? Yes, good liquidity is a major attraction.

How is market value determined and how do I keep track of it? Shares of equity REITs reflect property values, rent trends, and market sentiment about real estate. Mortgage REITs fluctuate as market interest rates affect profits. Balanced REITs— part equity, part mortgage—tend to have greater price stability. CMO REITs tend to rise in value as interest rates increase, and vice versa. FREITs, because shareholders will sooner or later realize capital gains income, tend to have share values somewhat more reflective of underlying property values. Share prices are reported in the stock tables of daily newspapers and in electronic databases.

Investment Objectives

Should I buy this if my objective is capital appreciation? Yes, but the potential for share value increases is greater with equity REITs than mortgage REITs. Also, automatic reinvestment of dividends increases capital gains potential. FREITs aim to pay out realized capital gains within a targeted period.

Should I buy this if my objective is income? Yes, especially since yields are not reduced by taxation at the corporate level. Mortgage REITs and CMO REITs are more income-oriented than equity REITs.

To what extent does it protect against inflation? Since income from rents and capital gains increases with inflation, equity REITs provide excellent inflation protection. Mortgage REITs provide less.

Is it suitable for tax-deferred retirement accounts? Yes.

Can I borrow against it? Yes, subject to Federal Reserve margin rules and individual lender policies.

Risk Considerations

How assured can I be of getting my full investment back? REITs shares have the same market risks as common stocks plus the risk of a decline in property values. Mortgage REIT shares suffer when rising interest rates squeeze profits, and unless insured, can involve the risk of default on mortgages. CMO REITs are subject to special risks (see overview discussion). You should not buy REITs if safety of principal is a paramount concern.

How assured is my income? Assuming REITs are well managed, income, which derives from rents or mortgage interest primarily, should be relatively secure. Still, real estate is sensitive to economic adversity, and there are many safer ways to invest for income. CMO REITs are subject to special risks (see overview discussion).

Are there any other risks unique to this investment? Much depends on expert management in terms of selecting, diversifying, and managing portfolios. Valuation of real estate is anything but an exact science. Certain types of REIT portfolios are riskier than others, those whose portfolios comprise short-term construction loan paper being the riskiest.

Is it commercially rated? Yes, by Standard & Poor's, Moody's, and others.

Tax Considerations

What tax advantages (or disadvantages) does it offer? REITs are not taxed at the corporate level, so dividends are higher. But shareholders personally are taxed. Unlike real estate limited partnerships, REITs cannot offer flow-through tax benefits, but some trustees pass on tax-sheltered cash flow (in excess of income) as a nontaxable return of capital. When shares are sold, however, the cost basis must be adjusted by such returns of capital in calculating capital gains taxes. To meet Internal Revenue Service tax-exemption requirements, 75% of a REIT's income must be real-estate related and 95% of it must be paid out to shareholders.

Economic Considerations

What economic factors most affect buy, hold, or sell decisions? REITs are most attractive to buy and hold when interest rates are low and supply and demand factors in the real estate industry favor growth in property values. Shares tend to be inflation-sensitive as values increase and dividends rise with higher rentals. Real estate is a cyclical industry and the risk-return relationship is maximized when investments are made over the long term. CMO REITs tend to be countercyclical.

REAL ESTATE, PHYSICAL

No investment alternative has been more ballyhooed as a way to get rich quick than real estate. With inflation a fact of life for half a century, this inflation-sensitive investment, with its high potential for leverage through mortgage financing and its abundant tax benefits, has indeed made many millionaires and provided millions of average home owners with nest eggs in the form of home equity.

Although the most liberal tax benefits of investment property were casualties of Tax Reform in 1986 and the baby boom that kept residential property values ascending for 30 years gave way in the 1990s to the baby bust, physical real estate, as long as the country continues to grow, holds the potential for substantial gain for those who know how to locate the best values and have the patience to endure the inevitable cycles, both regional and national.

Real estate has many drawbacks and risks, however, whether owned as an individual; in one of the several forms of joint ownership, which are distinguished mainly in terms of how an interest can be terminated and what happens to it in death or divorce; or through a corporation, which has the advantage of limited liability and the disadvantage of double taxation.

Among the problems of real estate ownership are high carrying costs in the form of property taxes, insurance, maintenance, and repairs; the risk of illiquidity; the risk of loss of value as the result of deflation or of demographic factors, declining neighborhoods, local economic changes, or government policies (such as a rise in property taxes or the imposition of rent controls); competition from professional and institutional investors affecting local supply and demand factors; changes in federal tax provisions; high costs of selling; and a host of special risks associated with specific types of holdings.

Physical real estate can be categorized as (1) residential, where, because the owner lives there, the utility of shelter or recreational use is an important part of the value but depreciation and maintenance are not allowable tax deductions; (2) rental, where income and tax benefits are primary goals, and appreciation secondary; (3) speculative, where income and utilitarian values are traded off for capital gains potential and losses can result from carrying costs (an example is investment in raw land); and (4) multipurpose, such as a multifamily residence used partly to live in and partly to rent, or a vacation property combining recreational use and rental income (tax implications where the status is not clearly established can be serious).

Properties can also be held in forms of shared ownership, which bring tax advantages and other benefits of home ownership to apartments and town houses. Cooperatives, where owners hold shares in total projects, and condominiums, where apartment units are owned along with a share of commonly shared facilities and amenities, often require a tradeoff of certain lifestyle prerogatives (e.g., a ban on pets) and have eligibility criteria advertising restrictions, or even prohibitions against renting that can severely limit liquidity. Condominium time-shares, where each of two or more owners has exclusive right of occupancy for a defined period, make condominium units much more affordable. The occupancy rights of some time-shared property even trade in a secondary market, not unlike securities.

The inflation protection, tax breaks, and total returns of real estate are also available through limited partnerships and real estate investment trusts (REITs). Such syndications offer diversification (by type of holding and geography), professional management, economies of scale, and limited liability for small investments, along with some risks and costs of their own.

*   *   *

What Is Physical Real Estate?

Physical real estate includes personal residences and investment properties in the form of developed and undeveloped land, established commercial or residential properties, condominiums, and cooperatives.

Buying, Selling, and Holding

How do I buy and sell it? Through a real estate broker or direct negotiation.

Is there a minimum purchase amount, and what is the price range? There is no minimum purchase amount; the price range is limitless. Properties can generally be financed with a down payment of 5% to 50% of value.

What fees and charges are involved? Real estate involves broker commissions and carrying costs in the form of debt interest, real estate taxes, and maintenance costs. Though there are many tax benefits associated with such costs, they can nonetheless be highly burdensome, especially if a property is not producing income.

Does it mature, expire, or otherwise terminate? Not in a financial sense, although related debt instruments have fixed maturities. Physical real estate is, of course, subject to destructive acts of nature, vandalism, and deterioration from use and time.

Can I sell it quickly? Liquidity varies with the type of property and market conditions; as a general rule, real estate is not a liquid investment.

How is market value determined and how do I keep track of it? Although general economic conditions and such factors as money supply and mortgage interest rates have an important effect, real estate is often characterized by independent markets. One segment of the industry (such as residential homes) can be booming, while another (such as office buildings) is depressed, and market conditions can vary widely from one community or geographical area to another. There is no formalized source of information about real estate prices. Trade associations can be a source of national and regional statistics and real estate brokers keep abreast of local values.

Investment Objectives

Should I buy this if my objective is capital appreciation? Yes.

Should I buy this if my objective is income? Yes, but only rental properties provide regular income.

To what extent does it protect against inflation? Real estate is inflation-sensitive, that is, both property values and rental income increase with inflation.

Is it suitable for tax-deferred retirement accounts? Personal residences are not legal investments. Real estate securities, such as real estate investment trusts (REITs) or income-oriented limited partnerships, can be appropriate investments, however.

Can I borrow against it? Yes; first, second, even third mortgages are common ways of borrowing against real estate. Home equity loans, a popular product of banks and other financial services institutions, are a convenient form of borrowing for home owners. On a professional scale, substantial fortunes have been made and lost using the financial leverage provided by real estate.

Risk Considerations

How assured can I be of getting my full investment back? Real estate offers no guarantees that values will not decline.

How assured is my income? A lease assures income for its term, to the extent the tenant is dependable and creditworthy.

Are there any other risks unique to this investment? Yes, many—including some not invented yet. Common risks include shifting population centers, changing local economies (including tax policies and rent control legislation), zoning changes, acts of nature, crimes like vandalism and arson, and physical deterioration.

Is it commercially rated? No.

Tax Considerations

What tax advantages (or disadvantages) does it offer? The main tax benefits are deductibility from federal income taxes of mortgage interest and property taxes, and on investment property, depreciation (which reduces taxable income without affecting cash flow) and deductible maintenance costs. All rental income is passive, but $25,000 of passive activity losses can be offset against nonpassive income (phased out for high-income taxpayers). Owners of personal residences classified as primary may exempt from capital gains taxes every two years, profits up to $500,000 for married couples filing jointly, and up to $250,000 for single taxpayers. Capital gains over $500,000 are subject to a 20% tax. Real estate investors who sell depreciated property owe a maximum 25% capital gains tax for the part of their gain due to depreciation. Unlike other consumer interest, which became nondeductible at the end of 1991, interest on loans secured by home equity is deductible up to $100,000 and on higher amounts if the proceeds are used to purchase investments or for business purposes. The tax code on this has changed several times, however, and you should get up-to-date advice.

Economic Considerations

What economic factors most affect buy, hold, and sell decisions? Real estate values parallel general economic cycles but are also subject to supply and demand conditions in local markets and in segments of the industry (such as commercial, industrial, residential). The most successful real estate investors have diversified portfolios (in terms of geography and type of holding) and stay in an investment until it becomes profitable. These opportunities, together with professional management and economies of scale, are available to individuals through real estate investment trusts (REITs) and limited partnerships.

SAVINGS ALTERNATIVES

For emergencies and for the sake of prudence, every investor should keep a certain amount of money in cash and in risk-free financial assets. Depending on one's need for liquidity, this often means choosing among the deposit accounts and certificates of deposit offered by banks and thrift institutions and U.S. Savings Bonds.

The following are brief descriptions of major savings alternatives:

Deposit accounts Depositors in subscribing banks, savings and loans, and credit unions are insured up to $100,000, respectively, by the Bank Insurance Fund (BIF), the Savings Association Insurance Fund (SAIF), and the National Credit Union Administration (NCUA). (BIF and SAIF are units of the Federal Deposit Insurance Corporation (FDIC) that were created in 1989 as part of the regulatory reform accompanying the federal bailout of failing savings and loan associations). Different accounts have different features, however.

With full deregulation in March 1986, institutions became legally free to pay any rate of interest. Because banks and thrift institutions must keep costly reserves, however, and because their federal insurance gives them a marketing advantage, their best rates tend generally to be a hair below money market mutual funds. The exceptions are the more aggressive money center banks and institutions with riskier (thus higher-yielding) loan portfolios or skimpier services.

Certificates of Deposit   CDs are issued by banks, savings and loan associations (S&Ls), and credit unions, in various denominations and maturities (some institutions offer designer CDs, with maturities to suit the customer) are also federally insured at member institutions. CDs, which can have similar maturities and vary a couple of points between issuers, are issued both in discount and interest-bearing form and sometimes with variable rates. Other variations include split-rate CDs, where a higher rate is paid early in the CD's term than in its later life; convertible-term CDs, which convert from fixed-rate to variable-rate instruments; and expandable CDs, which allow adding to the investment at the original rate. CDs can also be bought from some brokers, who make bulk purchases of high-yielding CDs from issuing institutions around the country and then resell them; since the brokers make markets in such CDs, buyers have liquidity they would not enjoy as direct investors.

Savings Bonds   Savings bonds come with flexible yields (that become more attractive for bonds issued after May 1, 1997) plus deferred federal taxability and exemption from state and local taxes. From 1941 to 1979, the government issued Series E bonds. Since 1980, EE and HH bonds have been issued, and in 1998, inflation-indexed I-Bonds made their debut.

Series EE bonds are issued with 30-year maturities at a discount of half their face values, which range from $50 to $10,000. Interest, posted monthly, is earned at a rate equal to 90% of the average yield on 5-year Treasury notes during the preceding six months. The rate is effective immediately (i.e., there is no longer a minimum holding period), but bonds held for less than five years are subject to a penalty equal to three months interest. Yields are readjusted every six months, on May 1 and November 1. (A guaranteed minimum rate feature was discontinued in 1995.) Taxpayers meeting income qualifications can buy EE bonds to save for higher education expenses and enjoy total or partial federal tax exemption (see Tax Considerations below).

Series HH bonds that were issued after March 1, 1993 are interest-bearing, pay a fixed 4% annual rate in two semi-annual payments, mature in 20 years, and come in denominations ranging from $500 to $10,000. They are available only through an exchange of Series E or EE bonds, but the exchange extends the tax-deferral that would otherwise end when the E and EE bonds mature.

Inflation-indexed savings bonds, introduced in September 1998, are issued at face value with a 30-year maturity in eight denominations ranging from $50 to $10,000. I-Bonds, as they are called, protect investors from rising prices because the payments are adjusted semi-annually to reflect the going inflation rate. The payout, which is not actually paid out but is instead reinvested and compounded semi-annually, is determined by two rates. A fixed rate, that ranged from 3% to 3.5% when the bonds were first introduced, is set by the Treasury Department. A second rate, a rate of inflation, is determined every six months by the Bureau of Labor Statistics to reflect changes in a version of the Consumer Price Index. The second rate is added to (or subtracted from, if there is deflation) the principal at the end of each year, so that the following year, the fixed rate is based on the adjusted principal. Interest is exempt from state and local taxes and federal taxes are deferred until the bonds mature or are cashed in. If the bond is redeemed to pay for college tuition or other college fees, investors may exclude part or all from federal taxes, depending on the holder's income level. In addition, you can't redeem your I-Bonds during the first six months, and you'll lose three months of earnings if you cash them in before the end of the first five years. Some protection against deflation exists in that any decline in the CPI could eat into the fixed rate, but not the principal.

*   *   *

What Are Savings Alternatives?

Savings alternatives include interest-bearing deposit accounts at banks, savings and loans, and credit unions; bank certificates of deposit (CDs); and Series EE, HH, and inflation-indexed U.S. Savings Bonds (I-Bonds).

Buying, Selling, and Holding

How do I buy and sell them? Deposit accounts, CDs, and savings bonds may be transacted at banks or other savings and financial services institutions. Series EE bonds and I-Bonds may also be available through employer-sponsored payroll savings programs. Series HH bonds can be acquired by exchanging Series E, EE, and freedom share bonds at Federal Reserve banks and branches or the Bureau of Public Debt (Parkersburg, West Virginia 26106). The Federal Reserve or BPD will also redeem HH bonds after six months from issue.

Is there a minimum purchase amount, and what is the price range? Deposit accounts are available with no minimum deposits, but interest may vary with balances and some banks impose charges (negative interest) when low balances become an administrative burden. CDs are usually issued for $500 and up, although some $100 CDs are available. Jumbo CDs are issued for $100,000 and up. Series EE bonds sell for $25 ($50 face value) to $5000 ($10,000 face value). I-Bonds sell for face value in denominations from $50 to $10,000. Series HH bonds are issued in $500 to $10,000 denominations.

What fees and charges are involved? Fees and charges on deposit accounts vary with the institution and its product. As a general rule, the higher the balance, the longer the commitment, and the less service, the less the cost to the depositor. Such factors usually are reflected both in rates and in fees and charges. Although CDs involve no fees or charges to buy or to redeem at maturity, the Federal Reserve Board voted in March 1986 to impose a penalty of seven days' interest on amounts withdrawn within the first week from personal CDs. (Institutional CDs were made subject to other penalties for early withdrawal.) Savings bonds involve no fees or charges.

Do they mature, expire, or otherwise terminate? CDs have maturities ranging from 32 days to 10 years. Series EE bonds and I-Bonds have 30-year maturities, but may be redeemed after five years without penalties. Series HH bonds mature in 20 years.

Can I sell them quickly? Certain deposit accounts may require notice of withdrawal. CDs may be subject to early withdrawal penalties or the issuer may refuse withdrawal prior to maturity, except in cases of hardship. (Of course, it is usually possible to borrow against such collateral and interest is tax-deductible.) NOW and other savings accounts offer instant liquidity through checkwriting. CDs bought through brokers can be sold in the secondary market. Savings bonds may be redeemed after 6 months, but there are interest penalties if held for less than five years.

How is market value determined and how do I keep track of it? Large CDs traded by dealers and institutional investors and smaller CDs marketed by brokers have secondary market values that rise and fall in inverse relation to prevailing interest rates. There is no secondary market for consumer-size CDs bought directly from banks and other issuing institutions or for savings bonds and deposit accounts.

Investment Objectives

Should I buy these if my objective is capital appreciation? Other than interest compounding, there is no capital gains opportunity except in CDs traded in the secondary market.

Should I buy these if my objective is income? Deposit accounts provide income, although they vary in terms of how rates are determined, how interest is compounded and credited, and how effective annual yields compare competitively. CDs are used for income, but those due in less than one year and zero-coupon CDs are issued on a discount basis—that is, they are sold at less than face value and redeemed at face value. Series EE bonds and I-Bonds do not pay interest until maturity or redemption, and must be held 5 years to receive the full rate on redemption. Series HH bonds issued after March 1, 1993 pay a fixed rate of 4%.

To what extent do they protect against inflation? To the extent rates move with inflation, deposit accounts offer some protection. Fixed-rate CDs provide none, but short maturities limit risk. Variable-rate CDs provide some protection. Series EE bonds offer some protection because the rate is adjustable. I-Bonds are designed to protect against inflation and there is deflation protection to the extent declines in the Consumer Price Index cannot reduce underlying principal. Series HH bonds have a fixed rate and offer none.

Are they suitable for tax-deferred retirement accounts? Deposit accounts are legally eligible, but CDs are a better choice due to their higher yields. Because savings bonds already offer tax deferral, there would be no advantage in putting them in such accounts.

Can I borrow against them? Yes.

Risk Considerations

How assured can I be of getting my full investment back? Most deposits and CDs are insured to $100,000 per depositor by the Bank Insurance Fund (BIF) and the Savings Association Insurance Fund (SAIF)—both are units of the Federal Deposit Insurance Corporation (FDIC)—and by the National Credit Union Administration (NCUA). The FDIC and NCUA are federally sponsored agencies. (Nonmembers are insured by state-backed or private insurers, but check the exact conditions.) Savings bond are direct obligations of the federal government and are risk-free.

How assured is my income? Although rates may in some cases fluctuate, income is very safe because the agencies that insure principal oversee the financial affairs of the institutions.

Are there any other risks unique to these investments? No.

Are they commercially rated? Moody's and other services rate CDs.

Tax Considerations

What tax advantages (or disadvantages) do they offer? Savings bonds are exempt from state and local taxes. Interest on Series EE bonds and I-Bonds is tax-deferred until cashed in or redeemed at maturity; when exchanged for Series HH bonds, interest on EE bonds is tax-deferred until the HH bonds are redeemed (although interest on the HH bonds, paid semiannually, is taxed in the year received). Individuals with modified adjusted gross incomes between $50,850 and $65,850 and married couples filing jointly with incomes between $76,250 and $106,250 may enjoy total or partial exemption from federal income taxes on income from EE bonds and I-Bonds that is used to finance a child's higher education (tuition and fees, but not room and board).

Economic Considerations

What economic factors most affect buy, hold, and sell decisions? Safety and growth of principal through interest compounding are the main objectives with savings vehicles, although expectations concerning interest rate movements and inflation may guide decisions.

TREASURY SECURITIES (BILLS, BONDS, AND NOTES)

United States Treasury securities, called Treasuries for short. are backed by the full faith and credit of the U.S. government and are issued to finance activities ranging from daily cash management to the refinancing of long-term bonded debt.

Investors seeking income thus have a wide choice of maturities, yields, and denominations along with the utmost safety. The government would have to become insolvent before default could occur, and as long as it has the power to create money, that is not a real possibility.

Treasuries also offer excellent liquidity and exemption from taxation at the state and local (but not federal) levels, an advantage that can add significantly to yield in high-tax states and localities.

Being fixed-income securities, however, Treasuries, unless they are inflation-indexed, are not immune to the ravages of rising prices, nor are they safe from market risk. When general interest rates move up, the prices of fixed-rate Treasuries move down—unluckily for investors forced to sell prior to maturity in the secondary market. On the other hand, Treasuries, unlike many other fixed-income investments, are not usually callable. With the exception of a recent 20-year issue with a 5-year call provision and some 30-year bonds callable 5 years before maturity, the government cannot force redemption when rates move down.

The major categories of Treasury securities are:

> *Treasury bills* Called T-bills for short, they are issued weekly with 13-week and 26-week maturities and monthly with a 52-week maturity, on a discount basis and in denominations beginning at $10,000 with multiples of $5000 thereafter. They are issued through the

Federal Reserve System, and investors may submit tenders either on a competitive basis, specifying terms and risking rejection, or on a noncompetitive basis, in which case the average rate established in the regular auction applies and purchase is assured. T-bills can also be bought for a fee through banks and other dealers.

Treasury bonds and notes   These are interest-bearing, paying semi-annually in most cases, and, like T-bills, sold through Federal Reserve banks and branches on a competitive or noncompetitive basis. Maturities of bonds range from 10 to 30 years, those of notes from 2 to 10 years. Bonds and notes can be bought in denominations as low as $1000. Except for 2-year notes, which are usually sold monthly, bonds and notes are offered as the need arises. Of course, outstanding issues with almost any maturity can be bought in the secondary market.

Inflation-indexed Treasuries, which range from 5-year notes to 30-year bonds, were first introduced in 1997. They offer a fixed rate of return as well as a fluctuating rate of return that matches inflation. The fixed portion is paid out as interest, while the indexed portion is represented by an annual adjustment of principal. In a period of rising inflation, therefore, the fixed rate would be applied each year to a higher amount of principal. With low inflation prevailing in the late 1990s, inflation-indexed Treasuries, which sacrifice some return for the inflation protection, met a lackluster reception, making liquidity (at least initially) a drawback. Other drawbacks are the prospect of deflation and the fact that the inflation adjustment is taxable annually but not paid out until maturity.

Other Treasury securities, covered elsewhere, include savings bond Series EE, HH, and inflation-indexed I-Bonds and zero-coupon products created by separating the principal and interest coupons from Treasury bonds. A special class, known as flower bonds, is discussed under Tax Considerations below.

Investors may also buy shares of mutual funds or unit investment trusts that invest in portfolios of Treasury securities.

*   *   *

What Is a Treasury Security?

A Treasury security is a negotiable debt obligation of the United States government, backed by its full faith and credit, and issued with various maturities.

Buying, Selling, and Holding

How do I buy and sell it? New issues of bills, bonds, and notes may be purchased through competitive or noncompetitive auction at Federal Reserve banks and branches. They can also be bought and sold at commercial banks, securities broker-dealers, and other financial services companies.

Is there a minimum purchase amount, and what is the price range? Treasury bills are issued in minimum denominations of $10,000 and multiples of $5000 thereafter. Notes and bonds are issued in denominations of $1000, $5000, $10,000, $100,000, and $1 million.

What fees and charges are involved? Treasury securities bought and redeemed through Federal Reserve banks and branches are without fees. Purchases and sales through banks or broker-dealers involve modest fees (about $25) and/or markups.

Does it mature, expire, or otherwise terminate? Yes. Maturities range from 23 days (cash management bills) to 30 years (bonds).

Can I sell it quickly? Yes; bills, bonds, and notes enjoy an active secondary market and are highly liquid. Inflation-indexed notes and bonds, being introduced in the late 1990s when inflation was low, were not as widely sold and were less liquid.

How is market value determined and how do I keep track of it? As wholly or partly fixed-income securities, Treasuries rise and fall in price in inverse relation to market interest rates. Because they are risk-free investments, money flows into Treasuries when investors are worried about the credit safety of other debt securities, causing lower yields and higher prices. The financial sections of daily newspapers report new offerings and secondary market yields. The Bureau of Public Debt (Washington, DC 20226) or the Federal Reserve bank or branch in your district will respond to inquiries concerning upcoming offerings.

Investment Objectives

Should I buy this if my objective is capital appreciation? No, but appreciation is possible if market rates decline.

Should I buy this if my objective is income? Yes, particularly Treasuries with longer maturities, but you are sacrificing yield in return for safety. After-tax yields get a boost in high-tax states and localities because interest is not taxed at the state and local levels.

To what extent does it protect against inflation? Fixed-income issues provide no protection, though short maturities offer less exposure to the risk of inflation. Inflation-indexed securities protect against inflation, but deflation is a risk.

Is it suitable for tax-deferred retirement accounts? Yes.

Can I borrow against it? Yes, to 90% at most banks and brokers.

Risk Considerations

How assured can I be of getting my full investment back? From the credit standpoint, Treasuries offer the highest degree of safety available. You can be assured of getting your money back at maturity. Should you wish to sell earlier in the secondary market, you may find market prices have declined because of rising market interest rates. (Experts sometimes hedge this risk using interest-rate options, futures, and futures options.) Inflation, of course, erodes dollar values and inflation-indexed securities have the risk of deflation.

How assured is my income? There is virtually no risk the government will default on interest. Some bonds may be callable, terminating interest prematurely. Inflation, of course, can erode the value of fixed-interest payments, and low-yielding securities, like Treasuries, are especially vulnerable in hyperinflation, where the inflation rate can exceed the interest rate. Inflation-indexed securities would, of course, be an exception.

Are there any other risks unique to this investment? No.

Is it commercially rated? No, since Treasuries are risk-free, there is no need for commercial credit ratings.

Tax Considerations

What tax advantages (or disadvantages) does it offer? Treasuries are fully taxable at the federal level but are exempt from state and local taxes. A special class, called estate tax anticipation bonds or flower bonds, can be used, regardless of cost, at par value in payment of estate taxes, if legally held by the decedent at time of death. With inflation-indexed bonds, the annual inflation adjustment is taxable but not paid out until maturity. Savings bonds, discussed in the section dealing with savings alternatives, are exempt from federal taxes in a specific instance.

Economic Considerations

What economic factors most affect buy, hold, or sell decisions? As with any fixed-income investment, it is best to buy when market rates are high and issues carry a competitive yield. Since prices vary inversely with market interest rates, the holding becomes more attractive as market rates decline. Inflation-indexed bonds and notes, being only partially fixed rate, would be less vulnerable to rate increases accompanied by inflation. As low-yielding, fixed-income securities, treasuries fare poorly in inflation. Because they are virtually default-proof, they are highly desirable holdings when poor business conditions make other investments vulnerable to default, though yields of Treasuries may decline as a result.

UNIT INVESTMENT TRUST

Like a mutual fund, a unit investment trust (UIT) offers to small investors the advantages of a professionally selected and diversified portfolio. Unlike a mutual fund, however, its portfolio is fixed; once structured, it is not actively managed, except for some limited surveillance. It is also self-liquidating, distributing principal as debt securities mature or are redeemed, and paying out the proceeds from equities as they are sold in accordance with predetermined timetables. A onetime sales charge of less than 5% is the only significant cost, and considering this can buy you a share in a "millionaire's portfolio" of municipal bonds, it is one of the attractions.

While sponsors commonly offer instant liquidity as a feature of UITs, liquidity is provided specifically through agreements to make markets in shares or to redeem them; there is not an active secondary market in the public sense, and investors should read the prospectus to determine whether and by what means liquidity provisions exist.

The most time-honored form of UIT is made up of tax-exempt municipal bonds, put together by an investment firm with special expertise in the municipals field. The bonds are deposited with a trustee, usually a bank, which distributes interest and the proceeds from redemptions, calls, and maturities and provides unitholders with audited annual reports. Since unitholders pay taxes as though they were direct investors, portions of income payments representing interest are not taxable, nor are portions representing principal, which are tax-free returns of capital. Capital gains, however, are taxable, technically at the time the trust realizes them, although unit holders commonly recognize them only after their investment in the trust has been recovered from distributions of principal or at the time they sell their shares. It is important to get tax advice on this.

The 1990s saw an explosion in popularity of equity UITS holding as few as 5 or 10 stocks, maturing annually, and following a formula investing approach. The first of these was inspired by the book, *Beating the Dow,* by Michael O'Higgins and John Downes, which introduced a market beating system whereby 5 or 10 of the highest yielding stocks in the Dow Jones Industrial Average were bought in equal dollar amounts and held for a year. This "Dogs of the Dow" concept was adapted to foreign market indexes and other stock categories, and today comprises a list of some 75 trusts offered by major brokers and reported by Barron's in a category called Defined Asset Funds (Equity Investor Funds). The typical equity trust has a total fee of around 2.75%, which is reduced when the trust is renewed.

Unit investment trusts are also available with portfolios of money market securities; corporate bonds of different grades; mortgage-backed securities; U.S. government securities; adjustable and fixed-rate preferred stocks; utility common stocks; foreign bonds; replications of stock indexes; and other investments. New varieties of UITs are being created all the time.

This discussion does not include investments that are legally organized as unit investment trusts, but are exchange listed and traded as common stocks. Examples would be Spiders and Diamonds, which are shares in long-term trusts holding portfolios of stocks that track the S&P 500 Index and the Dow Jones Industrial Average, respectively. Since their characteristics are identical, see Common Stock.

* * *

What Is a Unit Investment Trust?

A unit investment trust (UIT) is a trust that invests in a fixed portfolio of income-producing securities and sells shares to investors.

Buying, Selling, and Holding

How do I buy and sell it? UITs are bought from sponsoring broker-dealers, who usually stand ready to redeem shares.

Is there a minimum purchase amount, and what is the price range? Shares (units) costing $1000 ($250 for IRAs) are typical.

What fees and charges are involved? A sales charge (load) ranging from less than 1% to 5% of your investment (4% is typical, with discounts for volume). An annual fee, usually 0.15%, is factored into the yield. Additional fees (0.30% typically) may apply when the portfolio is insured. Equity trusts, such as the popular Select Ten Portfolios that hold high-yielding Dow Jones Industrial stocks for one year, typically cost 2.75% and offer reduced fees for annual "renewals."

Does it mature, expire, or otherwise terminate? Trusts are self-liquidating. Proceeds are distributed as securities mature or are sold. The life of most municipal UITs is 25 to 30 years, but 10-year trusts are common and some are as short as 6 months. Most equity trusts expire in one year.

Can I sell it quickly? Liquidity is not guaranteed, but it usually exists to some extent because of most sponsors' intentions, once shares are sold, to make markets as an accommodation to holders wishing to sell. Trustees may also redeem shares, but such provisions should be investigated before buying shares. Sponsors may also allow switching into their other investment products at little or no cost.

How is market value determined and how do I keep track of it? Since shares represent units in an investment pool, values are determined by the forces affecting the securities in the pool. Thus trusts composed of fixed-income bonds will increase in value as interest rates decline and vice versa. A trust made up of stocks will be affected by market movements and earnings forecasts for individual stocks, among other factors. Details of a particular trust and its portfolio are set forth in the prospectus that, by law, is provided to investors. The net asset values of equity trusts are shown weekly in Barron's under Defined Asset Funds (Equity Investor Funds).

Investment Objectives

Should I buy this if my objective is capital appreciation? UITs usually are set up to provide income (but even with a fixed portfolio, capital gains and losses can result from interest rate movements and other factors). Stock index trusts and other equity products have capital gains or total returns as a primary goal.

Should I buy this if my objective is income? Yes.

To what extent does it protect against inflation? Bond trusts offer no protection; equity trusts and floating-rate trusts offer some.

Is it suitable for tax-deferred retirement accounts? Yes, except those with portfolios of securities that are already tax-exempt.

Can I borrow against it? Yes, subject to Federal Reserve margin rules. The lack of an active secondary market raises a question about ready marketability and the attractiveness of shares as collateral.

Risk Considerations

How assured can I be of getting my full investment back? This varies with the safety of the investments in the trust, government bonds and common equities being at opposite ends of the spectrum. Interest rates may decrease the value of bonds, and therefore of shares, unless held for the life of the trust; market risk is always a question with equities. A growing number of trusts purchase insurance against credit risk.

How assured is my income? Portfolios are well diversified, making income relatively secure.

Are there any other risks unique to this investment? The lack of active management, once the portfolio is established and the shares sold, limits responsive corrective action in the face of adverse portfolio developments. Diversification provides some protection, however. Trusts holding foreign securities have political and currency risk.

Is it commercially rated? Yes.

Tax Considerations

What tax advantages (or disadvantages) does it offer? None. UITs are subject to the same taxes (or exemptions) as the investments comprising them. But trusts composed of municipal bonds, some specializing in triple-tax-exempt portfolios for qualified residents, are common, and many taxable UITs are designed for tax-deferred retirement programs. Equity trusts expiring in a year technically create a long-term tax event for all the stocks in the trust, but the IRS has made an exception in the case of stocks that remain in the portfolios when the trusts are renewed.

Economic Considerations

What economic factors most affect buy, hold, or sell decisions? Unit investment trusts are bought with the intention of holding until they self-liquidate. The same considerations that would guide an investor in choosing debt, equity, or money market securities would guide the choice of a particular UIT.

ZERO-COUPON SECURITY

Zero-coupon securities don't pay out their fixed rate of interest like other debt securities; they are issued at deep discounts and accumulate and compound the interest, then pay the full face value at maturity. The attractions for the investor are mainly twofold: (1) They can be bought at very low prices because of the deep discount and (2) Their yield to maturity is locked in, which takes the guesswork out of interest reinvestment.

The mathematical effects of a zero-coupon security, unless one is used to thinking in terms of compound interest over long periods, can seem astonishing: $1000 invested today in a 7%, 30-year zero-coupon bond will bring $7878 at maturity! The disadvantages of zeros are that income taxes (unless they are tax-exempt) are payable as interest accrues (and out of cash raised from another source); they are highly volatile; and their value at maturity can erode with inflation. (Of course, the opposites are also true: Higher volatility means advantageously higher capital gains when rates are declining, and in a deflationary environment, value at maturity would be greater.) Credit risk, especially with corporate zeros, can be greater than with a regular bond; if the issuer defaults after a certain amount of time has passed, the investor has more to lose, since nothing has been received along the way.

Not surprisingly, a popular use of taxable zeros, with their low purchase prices and automatic compounding, is tax-deferred retirement accounts, where they are sheltered from taxability on imputed interest.

The following are principal types of zeros:

Corporate zero-coupon securities   These are not usually recommended for individual investors because of credit risk and because the yield tends not to be competitive in relation to the risk. One explanation is that these issues are marketed to investors who do not have to pay taxes on imputed interest such as foreign investors.

Strips and STRIPS   Strips are U.S. Treasury or municipal securities that brokerage firms have separated into principal and interest which, represented by certificates (the actual securities are held in escrow), are marketed as zero-coupon securities under proprietary acronyms like Salomon Brothers' CATS (Certificates of Accrual on Treasury Securities) and M-CATS (Certificates of Accrual on Tax-exempt Securities). Although the obligor is actually the broker, the escrow arrangement assures a high degree of security. Free of risk altogether are STRIPS, Separate Trading of Registered Interest and Principal of Securities, the Treasury's acronym for its own zero-coupon securities. STRIPS are Treasury bonds issued in the traditional way but separated into interest and principal components at the discretion of bondholders using book entry accounts at Federal Reserve banks.

Strips of mortgage-backed securities placed privately or by government agencies are also available. To enter the Federal Reserve's book-entry system, however, federal agency strips must satisfy a technicality requiring a minimum of 1% of the principal of the underlying loans; in other words, they can't be 100% interest.

Municipal zero-coupon securities   These securities are issued by state and local governments and are usually exempt from federal taxes and from state taxes in the state of issue. They provide a convenient way of providing for the future goals of high-bracket investors who get an after-tax benefit from their lower interest rates. One caveat, however: some are issued with call features, which can defeat the purpose of a zero from the investor's standpoint, so avoid those.

Zero-coupon convertibles   Introduced in the mid-1980s, these convertibles come in two varieties: one, issued with a put option, converts into common stock, thus providing growth potential; the other, usually a municipal bond, converts into an interest-paying bond, thus enabling the investor to lock in a rate, then, 15 years later, to begin collecting interest.

*   *   *

What Is a Zero-Coupon Security?

A zero-coupon security is a debt security or instrument that does not pay periodic interest but is issued at a deep discount and redeemed at face value.

Buying, Selling, and Holding

How do I buy and sell it? Through a securities broker-dealer and many banks. Some products are proprietary, available only at the dealers marketing them.

Is there a minimum purchase amount, and what is the price range? Because of their deep discount, zero-coupon securities can be bought quite cheaply; a $1000 20-year bond yielding 6% would cost about $312, for example. Broker-dealer minimums of 10 bonds or more are common.

What fees and charges are involved? A broker commission or a dealer spread.

Does it mature, expire or otherwise terminate? Yes; zero-coupon securities have a specified maturity, although some may have put options or be convertible into common stock or interest-bearing bonds. Some zeros have been issued with call features.

Can I sell it quickly? Investors generally buy zeros intending to hold them until maturity. Should you need to sell, the broker-dealer you bought it from can probably make a market, although you would certainly pay a higher transaction cost. Zeros based on treasury securities are somewhat more liquid than corporate or municipal zeros.

How is market value determined and how do I keep track of it? Zeros, being essentially fixed-rate investments, rise and fall in inverse relation to interest rates and are especially volatile. Zeros are listed along with regular bonds in daily newspapers.

Investment Objectives

Should I buy zeros if my objective is capital appreciation? Investing one sum of money and getting back a larger sum is what zeros are all about, so the answer is really yes. Strictly speaking, however, the appreciation is not a capital gain, but is rather compounded interest. Capital gains are possible from secondary market sales after interest rates have declined.

Should I buy this if my objective is income? No. Zeros pay no periodic income.

To what extent does it protect against inflation? As fixed-rate investments, zeros generally offer no inflation protection. Zeros convertible into common stock offer some.

Is it suitable for tax-deferred retirement accounts? Because zeros are taxed as though annual interest were being paid, they are considered ideal candidates for tax-deferred plans. An exception, of course, would be municipal zeros, which are tax-exempt anyway.

Can I borrow against it? Yes, subject to Federal Reserve margin rules and lender policies.

Risk Considerations

How assured can I be of getting my full investment back? Corporate and municipal issues, unless insured, vary with the credit of the issuer, so credit ratings are important. Treasury issues that are stripped (split into two parts—principal and interest) by brokerage houses and marketed separately as zero-coupon securities represented by receipts or certificates, are highly safe as long as the broker holds the underlying Treasury security in escrow, as is the practice. Some municipal strips issued by brokers (e.g., M-CATS) have indirect U.S. government backing, since they represent prefundings invested in Treasury securities. Direct Treasury zeros (STRIPS) are risk-free. Zeros sold in the secondary market are susceptible to interest rate risk and a wide dealer spread. Of course, full investment, when talking zeros, means face value, not the small amount originally invested, since money is assumed to have a time value

How assured is my income? Zeros do not pay income; the income return is built into the redemption value.

Are there any other risks unique to this investment? Other than the small risk of an issuing firm going bankrupt in the case of receipts and certificates issued by brokerages, the unique risk of zeros has to do with the degree of exposure; should a zero default, there is more to lose compared with an interest-bearing security, where some portion of interest would have been paid out and presumably been reinvested. Some municipal issues may be callable, which largely defeats the purpose for which most investors hold zeros. Mortgage-backed strips respond to the prepayment experience of the underlying loans. If rates fall, prepayments increase. This shortens the life of strips and decreases the amount of interest earned.

Is it commercially rated? Municipal and corporate issues are rated.

Tax Considerations

What tax advantages (or disadvantages) does it offer? Interest is taxable as it accrues each year, just as if it were paid out. An exception, of course, are tax-exempt municipal zeros, which may also be exempt from taxes in the state of issue. U.S. government zeros are taxable at the federal level but exempt from state and local taxes. Savings bonds, a form of U.S. Government zero-coupon bond are another exception. Series EE holders may elect to defer paying taxes until the bonds mature and can then exchange them for Series HH bonds and continue deferring taxation until the HH bonds come due (see Savings Alternatives, page 74).

Economic Considerations

What economic factors most affect buy, hold, and sell decisions? Zeros are purchased based on competitive yield considerations and are normally held until maturity, their appeal being a locked-in interest rate as opposed to a yield that varies with the reinvestment value of periodic interest payments in changing markets. Should it be necessary to sell in the secondary market, lower rates mean higher prices. Considerations governing convertible zeros are complex and vary with the provisions of the issue.

PART II

How to Read an
Annual Report

How to Read a Quarterly Report

HOW TO READ AN ANNUAL REPORT

Weekend sailors know an axiom that if you can understand a dinghy you can sail a yacht. It's all in grasping the fundamentals. Annual reports are the yachts of corporate communications, and in full regalia they can be as formidable as they are majestic. Fashioned by accountants and lawyers as well as marketers and executives, and costing major companies as much as $250,000 to $750,000 to publish, the reports are aimed at a variety of audiences—stockholders, potential stockholders, securities analysts, lenders, customers, and even employees. Essentially, however, they are financial statements, and if you can understand the basics, you will find that the rest is elaboration, much of which is legally required and very helpful. Of course, there are other parts that are simply embellishment, and those you take with a grain of salt. First, let's look at a "dinghy."

Basically, a financial statement comprises a *balance sheet* and an *income statement*. Exhibit 1A illustrates a balance sheet reduced to "bare timbers."

EXHIBIT 1A

BALANCE SHEET
December 31, 20XX

Cash/near cash	**5**	Accounts and notes payable	15
Accounts receivable	**20**	Accrued liabilities	5
Inventory	35	Current portion, long-term debt	5
CURRENT ASSETS	**60**	**CURRENT LIABILITIES**	**25**
		Long-term liabilities	25
		TOTAL LIABILITIES	**50**
Net fixed assets	35		
Other assets	5	Capital stock	10
		Retained earnings	40
		NET WORTH	**50**
TOTAL ASSETS	**$100**	**TOTAL LIABILITIES AND NET WORTH**	**$100**

THE BASIC BALANCE SHEET

A balance sheet (also called a statement of financial position or a statement of condition) is simply the status of a company's accounts at one moment in time, usually the last business day of a quarter or year. It is often compared to a snapshot, in contrast to a motion picture. On one side, it lists what the company owns—its assets. On the other side it lists what the company owes—its liabilities—and its net worth, or owners' equity, which is what investors have put into the firm plus earnings that have been retained in the business rather than paid out in dividends. The two sides are always equal. Even if a firm were insolvent—that is, owed more than it had in assets—the sides would be equalized by showing a negative (or deficit) net worth.

(A minor technical point: Balance sheets can be presented with opposing sides, as just described, which is known as the account form, or with the assets above the liabilities and owners' equity, which is called the report form.)

Exhibit 1B illustrates a very basic income statement.

EXHIBIT 1B
INCOME STATEMENT
for the year ended December 31, 20XX

SALES		**$110**
Cost of goods sold	80	
Depreciation	5	
Selling, general, and administrative expenses	15	
	100	
NET OPERATING PROFIT		**10**
Other income or expense	1	
Interest expense	2	
Income taxes	2	
NET INCOME	5	**5**

THE BASIC INCOME STATEMENT

The income statement, which goes by such other names as statement of profit and loss, operating statement, and earnings statement, reports the results of operations over a specified period of time—12 months in the case of an annual report. As customers are billed, and as the costs and expenses of producing goods, running the business. and creating sales are incurred and recorded, the information summarized in the income statement is accumulated.

The income statement will be discussed below in more detail; it is enough for now to understand that its highlights are sales (or revenues), net operating profit (or operating income), and net income. It is this last amount—popularly called the bottom line because it comes after interest expense, unusual income and charges, and income taxes—that is available to pay dividends to shareholders or to be kept in the business as retained earnings.

A word about one expense item, called depreciation, which is important to understand because it is a major factor in cash flow, the net amount of cash taken into the business during a given period and the cash paid out during that period. Depreciation, which is sometimes combined in the figure for cost of goods sold, is merely a bookkeeping entry that reduces income without reducing cash. In other words, depreciation is a noncash expense, and it is added back to net income to determine a company's cash earnings. Net income plus depreciation equals cash flow from operations. More about depreciation and cash flow later.

BASIC RATIO TESTS

With the foregoing information on balance sheets and income statements, it is possible to look at a firm's year-to-year financial statements and make some tentative judgments about the firm's basic financial health and operating trends, particularly if you can compare the figures with those of other firms in a comparable industry. An in-depth look at important financial ratios is at the end of the discussion of the annual report, but much can be learned at a glance by applying the following basic ratio tests.

Current Ratio The current ratio is current assets divided by current liabilities. Current assets are assets expected to be converted to cash within a normal business cycle (usually one year), and current liabilities are obligations that must be paid during the same short-term period. For a manufacturing company (standards vary from industry to industry), a ratio of between 1.5 to 1 and 2 to 1—$1.50 to $2.00 of current assets for each $1.00 of current liabilities—is generally considered an indication that the firm is sufficiently liquid. In other words, there is enough net working capital (the difference between the two figures) to ensure that the firm can meet its current obligations and operate comfortably.

It is important that a company have this cushion because the liquidity of current assets, with the exception of cash and its equivalents, cannot be taken for granted; receivables can become slow or uncollectible (although a reserve for expected write-offs is normally provided) and inventory can lose value or become unsalable. Such things happen in recessions, and can result from poor credit, purchasing, or marketing decisions. Liabilities, unfortunately, remain constant. Of course, a company can have too much liquidity, suggesting inefficient use of cash resources, shrinking operations, or even vulnerability to a takeover attempt by an outside party. Well-run companies are lean, not fat.

Quick Ratio The quick ratio, which is also known as the acid-test ratio, is the current ratio, with inventory, its least liquid and riskiest component, excluded. It is calculated by adding cash, near-cash (for instance, marketable securities), and accounts receivable (sometimes collectively termed monetary assets), and dividing by current liabilities. Assuming no negative trends are revealed in year-to-year comparisons, a ratio of between .50 to 1 and 1 to 1 generally signifies good health, depending on the quality of the accounts receivable.

Average Collection Period A quick way of testing accounts receivable quality is to divide annual sales by 360 and divide the result into the accounts receivable. That tells you the average number of days it takes to collect an account. Since terms of sale in most industries are 30 days, a figure of 30 to 60 would indicate normal collections and basically sound receivables—at least up to the date of the statement. It may be helpful to compare a company's figure with that of other firms in the same industry.

Inventory Turnover Inventory turnover ratio tells the approximate number of times inventory is sold and replaced over a 12 month period and can be a tipoff, when compared with prior years' figures or comparative industry data, to unhealthy accumulations. Inventory should be kept adequate but trim, because it ties up costly working capital and carries market risks. To calculate turnover, divide the balance sheet inventory into sales. (*Note:* Industry comparative data published by Dun & Bradstreet and other firms providing financial data on companies compute this ratio using sales, not cost of goods sold. While cost of goods sold, because it does not include profit, produces a purer result, it is necessary to use sales for the sake of comparability.) As a general rule, high inventory turnover reflects efficient inventory management, but there are exceptions. A firm may be stockpiling raw materials in anticipation of shortages, for instance, or preparing to meet firm orders not yet reflected as sales. If inventory turnover is falling compared to prior years or is out of line with industry data, you should investigate the reasons. Year-to-year comparisons of inventory turnover are of particular significance in high volume–low profit margin industries such as garment manufacturing and retailing.

Debt-to-Equity Ratio   The debt-to-equity ratio can be figured in several ways, but for our purposes it is total liabilities divided by net worth. It measures reliance on creditors to finance operations and is one of several capitalization ratios summarized below. Although financial leverage—using other people's money to increase earnings per share—is desirable to a point, too much debt can be a danger sign. Debt involves contractual payments that must be made regardless of earnings levels; it must usually be refinanced when it matures at prevailing (perhaps much higher) money costs; and it has a prior claim on assets in the event of liquidation. Moreover, debt can limit a company's ability to finance additional growth and can adversely affect a firm's credit rating, with implications for the market value of shares. What is considered a proper debt-to-equity ratio varies with the type of company. Those with highly stable earnings, such as many utilities, are able to afford higher ratios than companies with volatile or cyclical earnings. For a typical industrial company, a debt-to-equity ratio significantly higher than 1 to 1 should be looked at carefully.

Operating Profit Margin   This figure, obtained by dividing a firm's net operating profit by sales, is a measure of operating efficiency. (Analysts sometimes add depreciation back into net operating profit since it is not a cash expense.) Year-to-year comparisons can be a reflection on cost control or on purchasing and pricing policies. Comparisons with other firms in the same industry provide insight into a company's ability to compete.

Return on Equity   This is the bottom line as a percentage of net worth (net worth is divided into net income), and it tells how much the company is earning on shareholder investment. Compared with the figures of prior years and similar companies, it is a measure of overall efficiency—a reflection on financial as well as operational management. But it can also be affected by factors beyond the control of management, such as general economic conditions or higher tax rates. And be suspicious of a firm with abnormally high returns; it could be in for competition from firms willing to sacrifice returns to gain a larger market share. As a rule of thumb, return on equity should be between 10% and 20%.

By applying the foregoing ratio tests to a company's basic balance sheet and income statement, particularly with the help of data on the company's prior years and on other companies in the same industry, you get a sense of whether the company's financial structure and operational trends are essentially sound. There is, however, a great deal you still don't know, such as:

- How reliable are the numbers?
- Are results affected by changes in accounting methods?
- Have there been changes in the company's top management?
- From what product lines did sales and profits largely derive?
- Did any special events affect last year's results?
- What new products are on the horizon?
- Are there any lawsuits or other contingent liabilities that could affect future results or asset values?
- To what extent are the company's operations multinational, and what is its exposure to foreign exchange fluctuations and/or political risk?
- If the company is labor-intensive, what is the status of its union contracts?
- What is the status of the company's debt? Is any financing or refinancing planned that could affect share values?

- How sensitive is the company to changes in interest rates?
- What were the sources and applications of cash?
- Are any major capital expenditures (for instance, real estate, machinery, equipment) being planned? How are existing fixed assets depreciated?
- How much is allocated to research and development?
- What other operational or financial changes has management planned?
- Does the company have a broad base of customers, or a few major customers?
- To what extent is the company dependent on government contracts?
- What is the company's pension liability, and what are its pension assets? Has it adequately provided for other postretirement employee obligations?
- Does the company have significant financial assets (such as leases or "derivatives") that may represent "off-balance sheet" risk, deferral of losses, or premature recognition of gains?
- If the company has been "downsizing" (a 90s trend), is it clear what impact discontinued operations have had and what the future of continuing operations is likely to be?

WHAT THE ANNUAL REPORT INCLUDES

The majority of annual reports of major public companies include a table of contents on the inside front cover. The following is typical:

Contents
Highlights
Letter to Shareholders
Review of Operations
Financial Statements
    Report of Independent Accountants
    Consolidated Financial Statements
    Statement of Consolidated Cash Flows
    Notes to Financial Statements
    Supplementary Tables
    Management's Discussion and Analysis
Investor's Information
Directors and Officers

Highlights

The highlights greet you at the start of an annual report. Often including charts and other graphics, they present basic information in a clear, comparative way that requires little explanation. At the very least, you should expect to find the company's total sales for the past two years and its net income, expressed both as a total and on a per-share basis. Needless to say, upward trends (usually, but with exceptions) are positive and downward trends negative. But what is most important to understand is that the company and its public relations advisors can include here whatever other information they feel will create the desired impression on the shareholder. That usually means you can expect to find highlights that add up to a positive impression, although it has become lately a matter both of fashion and good business to include a downward trend or two for the sake of credibility. Basically, though, what you can expect to find highlighted, aside from the unavoidable, are the statistics of which the company is most proud. If dividends were up, they will probably be highlighted; if they were down, the same space might be devoted to an increase in research and development (R&D) expenditures, with the implicit promise of a future payoff for shareholders.

Where earnings are presented on a per-share basis, accounting regulations now require that they be reported two ways. The first, called "basic earnings per share," represents earnings per share of stock presently outstanding. The second, called "diluted earnings per share," shows earnings per share assuming the conversion or exercise of all outstanding securities and rights potentially causing the issuance of additional shares. The second figure is normally lower because more shares are competing for the same amount of earnings. Potentially dilutive items would include convertible bonds, convertible preferred stock, warrants, and executive or employee stock options. Under accounting regulations existing prior to December 1997, the terminology used was "primary" and "fully diluted" earnings per share and companies were required to make the distinction only when the effect was deemed significant.

Should you encounter any other unfamiliar figures in the highlights, consult the Ratio Analysis Summary at the end of this discussion of an annual report.

Letter to Shareholders

In the many spoofs that have been written about corporate annual reports and their reputation for obfuscation, the least mercy has been reserved for the letter to shareholders. This review of the year just passed and look at the year ahead leads off the textual part of the report. It is usually signed by the chairperson and president and is often accompanied by a picture of the two together, suggesting amity not always characteristic of their day-to-day relationship.

While it is certainly true that the letter to shareholders is worded to put the best face on the past year's results and to soothe any anxieties that might be aroused by the financial figures to follow, it is nonetheless a statement of management's intentions and, when compared to prior years' messages, a test of management's credibility. Although it is not an audited, formal part of the report, it purports to be a serious comment on the year's results and their financial impact, a report that puts into perspective the major developments affecting shareholders, a statement of management's position on relevant social issues, and an expression of management's plans for the company's future. An impressive letter is one that compares past predictions with actual results and explains in a candid way the disappointments as well as the successes. Be wary of euphemisms (a "challenging" year was probably a bad one) and wording that is vague or qualified, a product area "positioned for growth" may sound promising, but it's not growing yet. If it were, the letter would say so. Much of the meaning of the letter to shareholders is between the lines.

Review of Operations

This review section consists of pictures and prose and often occupies the bulk of the pages of an annual report. Frequently slick, public relations-oriented, and designed to impress a corporation's various publics, the review can nonetheless be a valuable source of information about the company's products, services, facilities, and future direction. Unfortunately, it is also sometimes designed to divert the reader's attention from unpleasant realities. Be suspicious of reviews that stress the future and give the present short shrift or that are built around themes, such as the loyalty of employees or the company's role in building a stronger America. Also, what is not discussed can be more significant that what is discussed. Lack of reference to an aspect of operations described in the preceding year's annual report as an area of rapid growth and expansion may indicate that the company's expectations were not fulfilled and a write-off may be on the horizon. By and large, though, companies are responding to pressures for greater straightforwardness in the way they present themselves. In addition, companies these days are required to provide detailed financial information about the various segments contributing to their sales and profits. Although that information appears later in the supplementary financial data, it allows you to relate the activities being "promoted" to actual results and thus to evaluate the financial significance of different product areas. The Securities and Exchange Commission (SEC) has imposed stricter disclosure requirements in recent years, and these requirements have had a generally positive effect in terms of making annual reports more credible documents.

Financial Statements

Financial statements are, of course, the basic purpose of annual reports, and as the result both of expanded SEC disclosure regulation and companies' own interest in satisfying the information requirements of securities and credit analysts, financial statements have evolved over the years into presentations that elaborate substantially on the basic balance sheet and income statements. Reporting has also become more complex due to the complexity of the companies themselves, which have become diversified in terms both of product lines and geography, with a trend toward multinational operations involving political and currency risks.

Report of Independent Accountants: This report, also known as the auditor's opinion, is sometimes found at the beginning of the financial statement section and sometimes at the end, but it should be the first thing you read. Numbers are only numbers, and the opinion of an independent accounting firm, which is legally required of public companies, certifies that the financial statements were examined and validated. A "clean" or unqualified opinion—we'll get to what a qualified opinion means in a minute—typically reads as shown in Exhibit 2.

EXHIBIT 2

Report of Independent Accountants

To the Shareholders of XYZ Corporation:

We have audited the accompanying consolidated balance sheets of XYZ Corporation and subsidiaries as of December 31, 2001 and 2000 and the related consolidated statements of earnings, shareholders' equity, and cash flows for each of the three years in the period ended December 31, 2001. These financial statements are the responsibility of the Company's management. Our responsibility is to express an opinion on these financial statements based on our audits.

We conducted our audits in accordance with generally accepted auditing standards. Those standards require that we plan and perform the audit to obtain reasonable assurance about whether the financial statements are free of material misstatement. An audit includes examining, on a test basis, evidence supporting the amounts and disclosures in the financial statements. An audit also includes assessing the accounting principles used and significant estimates made by management, as well as evaluating the overall financial statement presentation. We believe that our audits provide a reasonable basis for our opinion.

In our opinion, the financial statements referred to above present fairly, in all material respects, the consolidated financial position of XYZ Corporation and subsidiaries as of 2001 and 2000, and the consolidated results of their operations and their cash flows for each of the three years in the period ended December 31, 2001, in conformity with generally accepted accounting principles.

The above format would explain any exceptions to "present fairly." It is thus possible to have an opinion that is clean but followed by explanations of potential problems.

Such "modified opinions" challenge the reader to understand the issues raised. Explanations are usually found in footnotes to the financial statements and/or the management's discussion and analysis section.

Qualified opinions include a statement that "except for" specified problems or departures from generally accepted accounting principles, the report would present fairly the company's financial position. Such language is rare, since it means the Securities and Exchange Commission will require the company to resolve the problem or make the accounting treatment acceptable.

Even rarer are two other types of auditor's opinion, the disclaimer of opinion and the adverse opinion. A disclaimer of opinion states that an opinion is not possible because of a material restriction on the scope of the audit (for example, an inability to verify inventory quantities) or a material uncertainty about the accounts (for example, doubt about the company's continued existence as a going concern). An adverse opinion states that the company's financial statements do not present fairly the financial position or results of operations in accordance with generally accepted accounting principles. Either type of opinion is cause for concern, but you are unlikely to run into these types of opinions since the company will normally take the auditor's advice and make the necessary corrections.

You should be wary of a company's figures if the company regularly replaces the independent auditors. Such conduct could indicate that the company is opinion shopping— looking for auditors whose approach would produce the most favorable sales and earnings figures for the company and thereby perhaps hide problem areas or potential problem areas.

Report by Management: Usually accompanying the Report of Independent Accountants is a similar Report by Management certifying responsibility for the information examined by the accounting firm. This section attests to the objectivity and integrity of the data, estimates, and judgments on which the financial statements were based. It alludes to the company's internal controls and oversight responsibility of the board of directors for the financial statements as carried out through an audit committee composed of directors who are not employees. It is sometimes signed by the chief financial officer of the company and/or the chief executive officer.

Consolidated Financial Statements—Part 1: The Balance Sheet: In the following pages, we will discuss the financial statement of our hypothetical company, XYZ Corporation. As required, the statement presents comparative balance sheets as of the company's two most recent fiscal year ends and income statements for the past three years. Many variations exist on the accounts discussed below, and there are as many unique items as there are companies. But if you grasp the following, you will understand the basis of the vast majority of balance sheets and income statements.

First, an item-by-item explanation of XYZ's balance sheet (see Exhibit 3).

CURRENT ASSETS

Cash and Cash Equivalents   Cash requires little explanation; it is cash in the bank, on its way to the bank, or in the till. Cash equivalents, sometimes listed separately under cash and called marketable securities, represent idle funds invested in highly safe, highly liquid securities with a maturity, when acquired, of less than 3 months. Examples would be U.S. Treasury bills, certificates of deposit, and commercial paper. They are carried at the lower of their cost or market value. If they are shown at cost, their market value is indicated parenthetically or in a footnote.

Accounts and Notes Receivable   These are customer balances owing. When a company makes a sale, a customer is required either to pay in cash (cash sales) or, as in the majority of cases, within credit terms (credit sales), which tend to be standardized within industries but are typically 30 days and rarely more than 90 days.

Accounts receivable—sometimes called just receivables—are credit accounts that are not yet received. Often there is a reference to a footnote containing an aging schedule, a breakdown of accounts in terms of where they stand in relation to their due dates. This reveals delinquency and trends and is a valuable tool for analysts. Of course, a company expects a certain percentage of uncollectible accounts and, based on its historical experience and current policies (it might, for example decide to liberalize credit policy to boost sales), it sets up a reserve (or allowance) for bad debts, which is deducted from gross receivables to arrive at the balance sheet value. This is either noted on the balance sheet or explained in a footnote. Special attention should be paid to accounts receivable if a company does a significant percentage of its business with a few key customers. If any of these key customers were to have financial problems, the worth of the receivables carried on the company's books would quickly be in jeopardy.

Notes receivable normally account for a small portion of the total and usually represent cases in which special terms were granted and obligations were documented with promissory notes. If a short-term note receivable arose out of a loan or the sale of property or some other nontrade transaction, it would, if material, normally be shown separately or footnoted.

Inventories   This figure, when a company is engaged in manufacturing, is a combination of finished goods, work in process, and raw materials. Conservative accounting practice requires that inventories be carried at the lower of cost or market value, but there are different methods of inventory valuation, principally First In, First Out (FIFO) and Last In, First Out (LIFO).

Under the FIFO method, inventory is assumed to be sold in the chronological order in which it was purchased. Under the LIFO method, the reverse is true: The goods sold in a period are assumed to be those most recently bought. When prices are rising or falling, the difference is reflected in the balance sheet value of inventory. A company using the LIFO method during a period of inflation, because its cost of goods sold reflects the most recent—and higher—prices, will show lower profits on its income statement and a lower balance sheet inventory, since its ending inventory remains valued at older (lower) prices. Because LIFO produces lower taxable income in times of inflation, it is the method adopted by a majority of companies in recent years. Thus, the balance sheet inventories of these companies are undervalued—in other words, they have a "LIFO cushion." It is important to remember that *de* flation would produce the opposite result. An explanation of inventory valuation methods (or, significantly, any change in methods) is provided in the footnotes to the statements, which will also explain adjustments required by the tax law changes.

A company's inventory figure cannot be analyzed in a vacuum. To determine if a company is maintaining adequate inventory control, relate the inventory figure to the growth in sales. Inventory growth should keep pace with sales growth, not exceed it. A buildup of inventory relative to sales should be viewed with skepticism.

Prepaid Expenses   This account represents expenses paid in advance, such as rent, insurance, subscriptions, or utilities, that are capitalized—that is, recognized as asset values, and gradually written off as expenses, as their benefit is realized during the current accounting period. If the amount is important, this account is usually deducted from current assets in computing the current ratio. However, it usually represents an insignificant percentage of current assets and is thus ignored for analytical purposes.

NET FIXED ASSETS

Property, Plant and Equipment   This section of the balance sheet lists the company's fixed assets, sometimes called capital assets or long-term assets. These assets include land, buildings, machinery and equipment, furniture and fixtures, and leasehold improvements—relatively permanent assets that are used in the production of income. The word tangible is sometimes used in describing these assets, to distinguish them from intangible assets (described below), which similarly produce economic benefits for more than a year but which lack physical substance.

Fixed assets are carried—that is, recorded on the books of the company and therefore reported on its balance sheet—at original cost (the cost the company incurred to acquire them) less accumulated depreciation—the cumulative amount of that original cost that the company has written off through annual depreciation expenses charged to income. Land, however, because it is assumed to have unlimited useful life, is not depreciated. (Companies engaged in mining and other extractive industries, whose capital assets represent natural resources, enjoy depletion allowances, a concept similar to depreciation write-offs.) As a result of depreciation writedowns and inflation, it is not unusual for the book value of a company's fixed assets to be considerably lower than their market value. On the other hand, market value is an indication of what it will cost to keep fixed assets up to date and maintain sufficient capacity to support sales growth. The relationship between sales levels and capital expenditures is therefore an important factor in evaluating a firm's viability. However, businesses vary in terms of how capital-intensive they are; manufacturers rely more on fixed assets to produce sales than wholesalers, for example.

The existence of fully depreciated assets on a company's balance sheet may signal that the company is a likely candidate for a takeover attempt or a leveraged buyout. The company's plant, for instance, has most likely appreciated in market value over the years and the depreciated basis on which it is carried on the balance sheet may have no relationship to reality. Thus, new owners could in part finance the purchase of the company by selling some assets at their higher market value.

OTHER ASSETS

This category can include any number of items such as cash surrender value of life insurance policies taken out to insure the lives of key executives; notes receivable after one year; long-term advance payments; small properties not used in daily business operations; and minority stock ownership in other companies or in subsidiaries that for some reason are not consolidated. Additional types of assets, if significant, would be discussed in the footnotes.

Another category of other assets, which is sometimes broken out separately (as in our example), is generally called intangible assets. These are nonphysical rights or resources presumed to represent an advantage to the firm in the marketplace. The most common intangibles are (1) goodwill and (2) a grouping typically labeled patents, trademarks, and copyrights.

Goodwill refers to a company's worth as an operating entity, or going concern— the prestige and visibility of its name, the morale of its employees, the loyalty of its customers, and other going-concern values. These are values beyond the book value of the firm's assets. Thus, when a company is purchased at a price exceeding its book value, the difference—the value of its goodwill—represents a real cost to the acquiring company. Goodwill, though intangible and abstract, *can* be valued. Because it has no liquidation value, however, it is classified as an intangible asset and must be amortized (written off) over time, in accordance with generally accepted accounting principles. As with fixed assets and depreciation, this is done by annual noncash charges to income. Unlike the case of depreciation deductions, however, there has traditionally been no tax benefit to the company when intangibles are written off. However, under the Revenue Reconciliation Act of 1993 (the Clinton tax bill), goodwill and related intangible assets can be deducted ratably over a 15-year period on a straight line basis.

Patents, trademarks and copyrights, the other most common intangible assets, have economic value in the sense that they translate into profits, but their carrying value is based on their cost. Being intangibles, they are written off over what accounting practice deems to be their useful lives.

Other intangible assets might include capitalized advertising costs, organization costs, licenses, permits of various sorts, brand names, and franchises.

EXHIBIT 3

XYZ CORPORATION
Balance Sheet
As of December 31
(Dollars in Millions)

	2001	2000
ASSETS		
Cash and cash equivalents	**7.6**	7.0
Accounts and notes receivable	**10.2**	9.5
Inventories	**23.0**	20.9
Prepaid expenses	**.3**	.2
Total Current Assets	**41.1**	37.6
Property, plant and equipment	**83.3**	79.4
Less: Accumulated Depreciation	**23.5**	21.3
Net Fixed Assets	**59.8**	58.1
Other assets	**3.8**	3.0
Intangible assets	**.9**	.9
TOTAL ASSETS	**105.6**	99.6
LIABILITIES AND SHAREHOLDERS' EQUITY		
Accounts payable	**4.2**	4.3
Notes payable	**.8**	—
Accrued liabilities	**3.2**	2.7
Federal income taxes payable	**8.2**	7.1
Current portion (maturity) of long-term debt	**.7**	.8
Dividends payable	**1.4**	.9
Total Current Liabilities	**18.5**	15.8
Other liabilities	**2.0**	1.4
Long-term debt	**16.2**	17.0
Deferred federal income taxes	**.9**	.7
TOTAL LIABILITIES	**37.6**	34.9
6% cumulative preferred stock ($100 par value; authorized and outstanding: 50,000 shares)	**5.0**	5.0
Common stock ($10 par value; authorized 2,500,000 shares; outstanding 1,555,000 shares)	**15.6**	15.6
Capital surplus	**8.2**	8.2
Retained earnings	**39.2**	35.9
TOTAL STOCKHOLDERS' EQUITY	**68.0**	64.7
TOTAL LIABILITIES AND STOCKHOLDERS' EQUITY	**105.6**	99.6

Because intangible assets are assumed not to have value in liquidation, they are excluded from most ratios used in analyzing values. The term tangible net worth is used to mean shareholder equity less intangible assets.

CURRENT LIABILITIES

Accounts Payable   This account represents amounts owed to suppliers for raw materials and other goods, supplies, and services purchased on credit for use in the normal operating cycle of the business. In other words, one company's account payable is another company's account receivable. As with receivables, conventional credit terms vary from industry to industry, but 30 days is standard and anything over 90 days is the exception (except in highly seasonal industries, such as garment manufacturing, where longer-term dating is commonplace and liquidity is provided by cashing accounts receivable with finance companies known as factors). The level of accounts payable should vary with sales levels, or, more specifically, with the amount of annual purchases—a part of the cost of goods sold. Any bulging of accounts payable in relation to purchases could mean a firm is relying to an unhealthy extent on trade suppliers as a source of working capital.

Notes Payable   These are usually amounts due banks or financial institutions on short-term loans, often under lines of credit. A line of credit is an arrangement by which a company may borrow working capital up to a limit, and details are usually covered in the footnotes. Notes payable may also be due suppliers under special credit arrangements.

Accrued Liabilities   Accrued liabilities arise when an expense is recognized as an obligation but the cash has not yet actually been paid out. Expenses commonly reflected in this account include payroll, commissions, rent, interest, taxes, and other routine expenses.

Federal Income Taxes Payable   This account is similar to accrued liabilities, but is usually broken out in recognition of its importance. (It is to be distinguished from the account called deferred federal income taxes, a noncurrent liability discussed below.)

Current Portion (Maturity) of Long-Term Debt   When a company has a long-term debt obligation that requires regular payments, the amount due in the next 12 months is recorded here as a current liability.

Dividends Payable   These represent dividends that have been declared by the board of directors but have not been paid. Dividends become an obligation when they are declared, and are normally paid quarterly. They include both preferred and common dividends.

LONG-TERM LIABILITIES

These are debt obligations due after one year. Included are term loans from financial institutions, mortgages, and debentures (unsecured bonds), as well as capital lease obligations, pension liabilities, and estimated liabilities under long-term warranties. Details are provided in footnotes.

Depending on a company's accounting practices, long-term liabilities may also include an item called deferred federal income taxes. This is often due to the fact that companies may use different rules for tax purposes and reporting purposes, and this creates timing differences. For example, a company using accelerated depreciation for tax purposes would get large depreciation write-offs in the early years of an asset's life, thus saving taxes, but would have higher taxable income in the later years. For reporting purposes, however, the company might wish to use the straight line method of depreciation, which each year produces equal (and lower) charges, thus resulting in higher reported earnings. The amount of taxes deferred are shown on the statement used for reporting purposes (the annual report) as deferred federal income taxes.

SHAREHOLDERS' EQUITY

This section of the balance sheet represents the owner's interest—the value of assets after creditors, who have a prior legal claim, have all been paid. It includes accounts for preferred stock, common stock, capital surplus, and retained earnings.

Preferred Stock Not all companies issue preferred stock, and it exists in several varieties. Several general characteristics are particularly notable: It usually pays a fixed dividend that must be paid before common dividends can be paid; it has precedence over common stock in the distribution of assets in liquidation; and if it is cumulative, unpaid dividends accumulate and must be paid in full before common dividends can be declared.

In recent years companies have used preferred stock as part of antitakeover programs. Referred to as poison-pill preferreds, these shares are created when a hostile takeover attempt is imminent. The new class of preferred stock is designed to raise the cost of the acquisition to a point where it may be abandoned by the company attempting the takeover. You should check whether a company has issued preferred specifically to fend off a takeover attempt and, if so, try to determine the implications such preferred may have for common shareholders.

Common Stock Shares of common stock are the basic units of ownership in a corporation. Common shareholders follow behind creditors and preferred shareholders in claims on assets and therefore take all the risks inherent in the business. But, with rare exceptions, they vote in elections of directors and on all important matters, and while they may or may not receive dividends, depending on earnings and whether the directors vote to declare dividends, the book value of their shares stands to grow as net worth (shareholders' equity) expands through earnings retained in the business. Common shareholders in publicly traded companies also stand to profit from increases in market prices of shares, which normally reflect expectations of future earnings. But on the balance sheet, common shares are listed either at a par or stated value, an accounting/legal value signifying nothing other than the lowest price at which shares can be initially sold. Sometimes different classes of stock exist and are listed separately, with the privileges or limitations of each indicated parenthetically or in referenced notes.

Capital Surplus Sometimes seen as additional paid-in capital (as preferred stock and common stock are sometimes called paid-in capital), this account reflects proceeds from issuances of stock that were in excess of the par or stated value of shares. For example, XYZ common has a par value of $10 per share; when 100,000 shares were issued at $12 a share, $1,000,000 was added to common stock and $200,000 was added to capital surplus.

Retained Earnings This account is made up of corporate earnings not paid out in dividends and instead retained in the business. Retained earnings are not put in a special bank account or stuffed into a figurative mattress—they are simply absorbed as working capital or to finance fixed assets in order to generate more earnings.

Consolidated Financial Statements—Part 2: The Income Statement: The income statement shows the results of operations over a period of 12 months. Results of the two years prior to the year reported on are included for comparative purposes (see Exhibit 4).

NET SALES

Most income statements (or, more formally, Statements of Income), lead off with Net Sales—the total of cash sales (negligible for most industrial companies) and credit sales for the accounting period (12 months for annual reports). Net simply means after returns of merchandise shipped; freight-out; and allowances for shortages, breakage, and other adjustments having to do with day-to-day commerce. (Note that some service companies, including utilities, and financial organizations use the term revenues instead of sales.) Needless to say, the trend of sales as revealed in the three years' worth of figures is a key indicator of how a company is faring in the marketplace. The figures should of course be adjusted for inflation to give an accurate reading of year-to-year changes.

Changes in the components of a company's sales can be more significant than changes in sales figures. If, for example, a chemical company can shift from marketing bulk chemicals (which have a relatively small profit margin) to marketing specialty chemicals (which have a relatively large profit margin) it will ultimately earn more even without an increase in sales. Changes in sales components can be determined by reviewing the business segment information in the annual report (discussed below.)

COST OF GOODS SOLD

This is the cost of producing inventory and includes raw materials, direct labor, and other overhead that can be directly related to production. It is directly affected by the company's choice of the FIFO or LIFO inventory valuation methods (see Inventories, above). The reason becomes clear when you look at the formula by which cost of goods sold is determined:

Beginning inventory + Purchases during the period − Ending inventory
= Cost of goods sold

When the ending inventory (the balance sheet inventory) is the oldest stock, which is the case when the LIFO method is used, the cost of goods sold, assuming prices are rising with inflation, becomes a higher number than would be the case using FIFO. Of course, the higher the cost of goods sold, the lower will be taxable income, as we will see.

DEPRECIATION

This noncash expense was alluded to at the start of the discussion of an annual report and again under Deferred Federal Income Taxes Payable in the discussion of balance sheet liabilities. To encourage firms to keep facilities modern and thus spur the economy, the U.S. government provides businesses a way to pay less tax and thereby conserve cash. This is accomplished by allowing firms to take an annual percentage (called a depreciation write-off) of what they spent for certain types of fixed assets, such as buildings, machinery, and equipment, and to treat the amount as though it were an actual expense thus reducing taxable income without requiring an outlay of cash.

Depreciation is a highly complex tax accounting concept, and for purposes of reading annual reports it is not necessary to understand it completely. It is enough to know that tax rules make it possible for companies to recover the cost of certain fixed asset investments on an accelerated basis and thus to get the benefit of tax savings sooner than they would using the straight-line method (now required for newly purchased real property). At the same time, companies are allowed, for purposes of annual reports, to reflect depreciation charges based on the straight line method, whereby the estimated useful life of the asset is divided into its cost to get a uniform annual depreciation charge, which is generally much lower than the figure used for tax purposes. Annual reports thus show higher earnings, while the stockholder has the satisfaction of knowing that the company's tax liability has been minimized. It is all spelled out in the footnotes.

What is more important to know is that depreciation charges have a relationship to the age of the assets and vary with the amount of investment in fixed assets. An

EXHIBIT 4

XYZ CORPORATION
Income Statement
Fiscal Year Ended December 31
(Dollars in Millions)

	2001	**2000**	**1999**
Net Sales	98.4	93.5	88.8
Cost of goods sold	64.9	62.2	59.7
Depreciation and amortization	2.2	3.0	2.0
Selling, general, and administrative expenses	12.1	11.1	10.3
	79.2	76.3	72.0
Net Operating Profit	19.2	17.2	16.8
Other Income or (Expenses)			
Income from dividends and interest	.2		
Interest expense	(1.0)	(.9)	(1.0)
Earnings before income taxes	18.4	16.3	15.8
Provision for income taxes	8.3	7.5	7.3
Net Income	10.1	8.8	8.5

Common shares outstanding: 1,555,000
Net earnings per share (after preferred dividend
requirements in 2001 and 2000: 2001: $6.30; 2000: $5.47;
1999: $5.47)

Statement of Retained Earnings

Retained Earnings Beginning of Year	35.9	33.6	31.3
Net Income for Year	10.1	8.8	8.5
Less: Dividends Paid on:			
Preferred stock ($6 per share)	.3	.3	
Common stock (per share): 2001: $4.20; 2000: $4.00;	6.5	6.2	6.2
1999: $4.00			
Retained Earnings End of Year	39.2	35.9	33.6

increase in depreciation usually reflects increases in depreciable assets—fixed assets like plant and equipment. Decreases usually mean fixed assets have been disposed of or have become fully depreciated. Particularly since straight line depreciation is used by most companies for reporting purposes, lower depreciation charges can signal a need for fixed asset expenditures meaning long-term financing, which has implications for shareholders in the form either of dilution of share values or higher interest costs. Of course, increased or modernized plant capacity should also translate eventually into higher sales, greater operating efficiency and higher earnings per share.

SELLING, GENERAL, AND ADMINISTRATIVE (SG&A) EXPENSES

These are all the expenses associated with the normal operations of the business that were not included in cost of goods sold, which represented direct costs of production. Salaries, rent, utilities, advertising, travel and entertainment, commissions, office payroll, office expenses, and other such items are representative of this category, which varies from industry to industry in terms of its composition and the relative importance of selling expenses versus administrative expenses.

A good test of the quality of a company's management is its ability to control selling, general, and administrative expenses. Many companies have fallen into bankruptcy simply because management was unable or unwilling to control expenses and keep them in line with the growth of sales.

NET OPERATING PROFIT

The net operating profit is what is left over after costs of goods sold, depreciation, and SG&A expenses are deducted from sales, and it tells you the company's profit on a normal operating basis—that is, without taking into account unusual items of income or expense or nonoperating expenses such as interest and taxes. As stated above, it is a measure of operating efficiency, and significant variations from year to year or from industry standards should be investigated by looking more closely at the figures behind the totals, many of which are supplied in footnotes or published in the company's form 10-K (see Investor's Information, page 111). Lower than expected profit due to a rise in SG&A expenses as a percentage of sales might be traceable to a single factor, such as a rise in officers' salaries, for example.

OTHER INCOME OR EXPENSES

This category picks up any unusual or nonoperating income or expense items. Examples might include income, gains, or losses from other investments; gains or losses on the sale of fixed assets; or special payments to employees. Nonrecurring items are usually explained in detail in footnotes. In this category is *interest expense,* which, unlike dividends, is a pretax expense. For companies with bonds or other debt outstanding, however, interest expense is a recurring item. Because interest on funded debt is a contractual, fixed expense that, if unpaid, becomes an event of default, analysts follow closely a company's fixed-charge coverage—how many times such fixed charges are covered by pretax annual earnings.

EARNINGS BEFORE INCOME TAXES

This figure nets out all pretax income and expense items, but it would not be accurate to say it is the figure on which federal income taxes are based. That is because tax returns of corporations, as we have seen, use different methods of depreciation for tax purposes than they use for reporting to shareholders and because other factors, such as tax-loss carrybacks and carryforwards, which are not visible on the current year's statement, may affect the company's tax liability.

PROVISION FOR INCOME TAXES

After taking advantage of all available benefits, this is the company's tax liability for the year in question. Note that it is termed a *provision*. Payments based on estimated taxes have been made during the year, and net payments on this liability are payable according to a timetable determined by the Internal Revenue Service. A portion of the liability will be reflected as an accrued liability, as described above.

A company's effective tax rate should be compared with other companies in the same or similar industries. Although many tax loopholes have been ended by recent tax legislation, it may be a mark of smart and aggressive management if a company has a lower effective rate than other companies similarly engaged.

NET INCOME

This is the bottom line, the "after everything except dividends" figure. Dividends, by law, must be paid out of earnings, though not necessarily out of current earnings. Below the bottom line, figures for common shares outstanding and earnings per common share are given. Securities analysts usually focus on earnings per share in assessing a company's status. As a rule, earnings per share are expected to grow from year to year, and it may be a sign of trouble if they do not grow according to predictions or if they do not grow at all.

Consolidated Financial Statements—Part 3: The Statement of Retained Earnings (Shareholders' Equity): What typically follows the Income Statement is an analysis showing retained earnings at the beginning of the period; how net income increased retained earnings; dividends paid on preferred stock and common stock during the period; and the retained earnings account at the end of the fiscal year being reported (see Exhibit 4). The last figure will, of course, be the same as the retained earnings figure in the stockholders' equity section of the balance sheet.

A Statement of Retained Earnings may reflect stock dividends—new shares issued to existing shareholders. Stock dividends are accounted for by decreasing retained earnings and increasing common stock in equal amounts (using par or stated value if the stock dividend represents more than 20 to 25 percent of outstanding shares, and market value if it represents less). Many investors are attracted to companies that regularly declare stock dividends. It should be borne in mind, however, that stock dividends in no way enhance the actual assets of a company.

Statement of Consolidated Cash Flows: By requiring an analysis of changes affecting cash, the Financial Accounting Standards Board (FASB) was recognizing that the viability of a company hinges ultimately on liquidity and that increases in working capital do not necessarily translate into increased cash. For example, a company that relaxed its credit standards to generate increased sales might show higher profits and working capital from one year to another, but it would not be able to meet its obligations unless and until its accounts receivable were collected in cash. Cash means cash and equivalents, defined by the FASB as all highly liquid securities with a known market value and a maturity, when acquired, of less than 3 months.

The statement of cash flows puts operating results on a cash basis while showing balance sheet changes as they affect the cash account. (In order to provide a complete "bridge" between two balance sheets, the statement of cash flows will also show major balance sheet changes not affecting cash, such as an exchange of bonds for stock or the purchase of a fixed asset that is 100% financed by long-term debt.)

The FASB requires that cash flows be analyzed in three separate categories: cash flows from operating activities, cash flows from investing activities, and cash flows from financing activities. The most commonly used format is XYZ Corporation's, illustrated in Exhibit 5.

The operating analysis begins with the net income figure (from the income statement) and follows with the adjustments necessary to convert that figure to a cash basis.

Depreciation and amortization, as earlier discussed, are bookkeeping transactions that reduced the net income figure without any expenditure of cash; this item (found on the income statement) is thus added back to net income. The increase in the (balance sheet liability) account called deferred federal income taxes represents the portion of income tax expense not actually paid in cash and is similarly added back to net income.

Next are adjustments to assets and liabilities that changed because of operating activities and provided or used cash. The increase in the accounts and notes receivable is subtracted because it represents sales revenue included in net income but not collected in cash. The increase in inventories is also subtracted because it represents cash spent for inventory purchases in excess of the expense recognized through cost of goods sold. The increase in prepaid expenses is deducted because it represents cash spent but not charged against income. The decrease in XYZ's accounts payable between 2001 and 2000 is subtracted because the cash paid to vendors in 2001 was greater than the amount of expense recorded. (Cash was paid for some 2000 accounts.) Increases in accrued liabilities and federal income taxes payable were charged to income but not (yet) paid in cash and are thus added back. Other assets and liabilities were either net users (2001) or providers of cash.

(Note: Adjustments to particular asset and liability accounts will not always equal changes in balance sheet figures as they do in the case of XYZ Corporation. In the case of companies with foreign operations, operating assets and liabilities translated from other currencies have been purified of the effects of currency exchange and a separate line is provided to show the effect of exchange rate changes on cash and cash equivalents. Also, the effects of acquisitions, when accounted for by the PURCHASE ACQUISITION method, and divestitures have been excluded from the operating cash flow adjustments although they are reflected in the balance sheet accounts.)

Cash flows from investing activities include changes in the company's investments in property, plant, and equipment; investments in other companies; and loans made and collected. An increase in investment reduces cash and a decrease (sale) increases cash. It is notable that dividends and interest received are typically treated as operating cash flow, although changes in the same investments are analyzed here. In the case of XYZ, the only changes were those affecting fixed assets. XYZ's only other investments are in the securities comprising cash equivalents; since the whole cash flow statement focuses on cash and cash equivalents, it would be redundant to show those changes here. The small amount of income XYZ received on its cash equivalents is reflected in the net income figure above.

Cash flows from financing activities include all changes in cash resulting from financing, such as short- and long-term borrowings, the issuance or repurchase of common and preferred stock, dividends paid, and changes in dividends payable.

To interpret the cash flow statement it is helpful to remember a basic rule of thumb: In a conservatively operated company, *permanent* capital requirements—fixed assets and the portion of working capital that is not seasonal—should be financed through a combination of retained earnings and either long-term debt or equity. *Short-term* requirements should be financed with short-term liabilities in a cycle that begins when accounts payable are created to purchase inventory, which in turn is sold to create accounts receivable, which are collected to produce cash, and so on.

Once that is understood, the statement can be a valuable analytical tool that reveals healthy or unhealthy trends; a company's capacity for future investment; its future cash requirements; its cash position compared to similar companies; and its actual cash flows versus those anticipated.

A look at Exhibit 5 tells us XYZ Corporation has been generating operating cash flows that generally support its steadily increasing sales. Cash flow from operations has been sufficient to finance annual additions and improvements to its plant and equipment and still pay dividends without impairing its working capital. The statement reveals that in 2000 the company, despite profitable operations, would have had a negative cash flow (more cash flowing out than in), after meeting $6.5 million of long-term debt repayments, had management not properly planned for the requirement by issuing $5 million of preferred stock.

Discontinued Operations: One final observation: Discontinued operations, although not a factor in XYZ's case, show up frequently as a separate section of the income statements of large companies. Readers are thus able to distinguish between operating results that can be expected to continue in the future and those that have only historical significance. Discontinued operations are those that have been sold, abandoned, or otherwise disposed of. Any gain or loss from the disposal of a segment must be shown along with the operating results of the discontinued segment.

In their statement of cash flows, however, companies are permitted but not required to separately disclose the flows from discontinued operations and extraordinary items. When companies voluntarily make the separation, they indicate clearly that the analysis of net income and adjustments relates to continuing operations and includes a separate line for net cash provided (or used) by discontinued operations. But when discontinued operations that show up in the income statement are not broken out in the statement of cash flows, it is up to the reader to ascertain if a significant portion of the flows relate to operations that are not ongoing.

Notes to Financial Statements: Footnotes to financial statements, sometimes just called notes, are unfortunately named if there's any implication that they represent superfluous detail. Indeed, the balance sheet, the income statement, and the statement of cash flows contain the sentence: "The Notes to Financial Statements are an integral part of this statement." Footnotes set forth the accounting policies of the business—and provide additional disclosure. They contain information having profound significance for the financial values presented elsewhere in the financial statements.

It would be impossible to list here all the types of information one might find in the notes to financial statements. Here is a sampling, though, and if it succeeds in impressing you with the importance of reading this section of a financial report, it will have accomplished its purpose.

Accounting procedure changes A change in the method of valuing inventory or a change in the company's method of depreciating fixed assets can have significant effects on reported earnings and asset values. You should investigate further if a company frequently changes accounting procedures. The company may, for instance, be trying to hide weak aspects of its operations.

Pension and postretirement benefits In rising securities markets, some companies have used overfunded pension plans to generate cash windfalls, but the reverse also occurs: Some are underfunded, so that the company may be faced with the prospect of cash burdens later on. Pension funding is, at best, an inexact science. Estimates based on a variety of actuarial, personnel, and financial assumptions determine the amount of annual expense required to cover future benefits earned by each year's additional service. Not only are these estimates subject to error, but management has used its discretion over the rate at which pension liabilities are funded to smooth out reported earnings by underfunding in poor years and overfunding in good years. Patterns of underfunding or overfunding can portend future deficiency or surplus, even when estimates are accurate. A liability account termed

EXHIBIT 5

XYZ CORPORATION
Statement of Consolidated Cash Flow
Fiscal Year Ended Decemher 31
(Dollars in Millions)

	2001	2000	1999
CASH FLOWS FROM OPERATING ACTIVITIES			
Net Income	10.1	8.8	8.5
Adjustments to reconcile net income to net cash provided by operating activities:			
Depreciation and amortization	2.2	3.0	2.0
Deferred income taxes	.2	.3	.2
Accounts receivable	(.7)	(.6)	(.8)
Inventories	(2.1)	(1.9)	(1.2)
Prepaid expenses	(.1)	—	(.1)
Accounts payable	(.1)	1.2	.7
Accrued liabilities	.5	.3	.3
Federal income taxes payable	1.1	.8	.6
Other assets and liabilities, net	(.2)	.5	.5
Net cash from operating activities	**10.9**	**12.4**	**10.7**
CASH FLOWS FROM INVESTING ACTIVITIES			
Additions: property, plant, equipment	(3.9)	(4.2)	(2.8)
Net cash used for investing activities	**(3.9)**	**(4.2)**	**(2.8)**
CASH FLOWS FROM FINANCING ACTIVITIES			
Net change in short-term debt	.7	—	—
Repayments of long-term debt	(.8)	(6.5)	(1.0)
Proceeds from sale of preferred stock		5.0	
Payments of dividends	(6.8)	(6.5)	(6.2)
Increase in dividends payable	.5	.3	—
Net cash used for financing activities	**(6.4)**	**(7.7)**	**(7.2)**
NET INCREASE IN CASH AND EQUIVALENTS	.6	.5	.7
Cash and equivalents, beginning of year	7.0	6.5	5.8
Cash and equivalents at end of year	7.6	7.0	6.5

Unfunded Projected Benefit Obligation is another red flag, in this case meaning that the current return on pension fund investments is inadequate to cover projected future benefit payments.

Closely related are Postemployment Benefits Other than Pensions, consisting mainly of health care benefits payable to employees after retirement and before their eligibility for government benefits such as Medicare and Medicaid. The FASB now requires that if funding is elected, companies fund the present value of estimated future benefits earned by employees. Funding forces an estimate of future liability. It should be noted, however, that whereas with pensions, an additional liability has to be recognized if the accumulated benefit obligation is greater than the fair value of the plan assets, no such additional liability is required for postretirement benefits other than pensions.

Long-term debt Detail on debt maturities makes it possible to anticipate refinancing needs, which have implications for investors in terms of the effect of interest costs on profits or potential dilution of common share values. A company's ability to manage its debt structure so as to obtain money at the lowest rate for the longest maturity is viewed by analysts as demonstrating that the company has a capable management team.

Look here (and also in footnotes concerning preferred stock) for information about antitakeover provisions, or "poison pills." The recent wave of hostile takeovers, usually taking the form of leveraged buyouts, has caused many companies to adopt provisions in their indentures or preferred stock agreements designed to make takeovers prohibitively expensive for acquirers or to protect existing holders from the adverse effects of additional debt or liquidation of assets. A common variety is the "poison put," a provision giving bondholders the right to redeem their bonds at par value in the event of a hostile takeover, thus creating an onerous cash requirement for the acquirer. Although generally designed to protect existing investors from unfavorable events, poison pill provisions can have major implications for a company's finances, and it is important to understand them.

Treasury stock By buying their own shares in the market, companies decrease shares outstanding and thus increase earnings per share for existing stockholders. The existence of an active stock purchase program can be viewed as a two-edged sword. On the one hand, such a program provides in effect a support price for the company's shares as well as a buyer with deep pockets—the company itself. On the other hand, a stock purchase program is frequently used as a defense against a hostile takeover attempt and raises the question whether repurchase of stock is the best way to use assets of the company.

Taxes The prospect of an assessment for a prior year's taxes may be disclosed in the footnotes. Of particular significance is any footnote disclosing that a company's tax returns are being audited or that any of the assumptions utilized by the company in determining the taxable basis of its assets are being questioned by the Internal Revenue Service.

Leases One of the most significant of the off-balance sheet liabilities is the long-term noncapital lease. A footnote dealing with a long-term lease should be reviewed carefully.

Financial Assets   With computerization and internationalization have come sophisticated derivative instruments—contracts whose value is related to the value of underlying financial assets, including various financial instruments and securities. They come in different forms, including exotica such as interest rate swaps and caps, collateralized mortgage obligations, and financial futures and forward contracts. Some, having the effect of financial guarantees or loan commitments, may be, like the operating leases discussed above, off-balance sheet. Companies use financial assets for a variety of purposes, including financing, hedging, and investment.

The analytical challenge they present is that they are always complex and sometimes speculative, raising questions about unjustifiable deferral of losses, premature recognition of gains, and inadequate disclosure about risks.

SFAS (Statement of Financial Accounting Standard) No. 105 requires that financial statements provide significant information relating to all financial instruments with or without off-balance sheet risk. SFAS No. 107 requires disclosure about fair value of all financial instruments, assets and liabilities both on and off the balance sheet.

Supplementary Tables: The principal supplementary tables are the following.

SEGMENT REPORTING

The FASB requires companies meeting certain criteria having to do with product and geographical diversification to present certain information in segment form—that is, by product or industry category or markets serviced and by geographical territory. Although this can be done in the body of the financial statement, with supporting footnotes, or in the footnotes section itself, most companies do it in a separate schedule that is an integral part of the financial statements. The information required, which covers the same three-year period as the income statement, includes sales or revenues; operating profit or loss; the book value of identifiable assets; aggregate depreciation, depletion, or amortization; and capital expenditures.

These breakdowns enable shareholders to evaluate a company's exposure to the vagaries of various geographical markets, including political and other risks to a company that has foreign operations. For industry or product-line segments, a stockholder is able to evaluate the company's activities in particular areas in terms of the amount of its investment and the return it is realizing on the investment, as well as the year-to-year trends.

FINANCIAL REPORTING AND CHANGING PRICES

Another ruling of the FASB is aimed at accounting for the effect of inflation or deflation on the inventory, fixed assets, and the income statement values for cost of goods sold and depreciation as they are related to those assets. Thus, companies are encouraged to present the historical figures showing the effects of declines in the purchasing power of the dollar in contrast to the primary values as shown in the financial statements, based on historical cost.

FIVE-YEAR SUMMARY OF OPERATIONS

This required schedule essentially extends the three-year income statement to five years, including preferred and common stock dividend history. It is a useful supplement in terms of permitting analysis of operating trends, and a number of corporations have taken it upon themselves to provide summaries of the last ten years of operations.

This schedule provides a quarterly breakdown of sales, net income, the high and low stock price, and the common dividend. The operating data is most valuable when a company's operations are subject to seasonal factors, as, for example, a retailer is subject to heavy demand during the Christmas season. The market price and dividend data reveal stock price volatility and the regularity with which the company has made dividend payments.

Management's Discussion and Analysis: The general credibility and informational value of annual reports was significantly advanced in the mid-1980s when the Securities and Exchange Commission began requiring and monitoring the section Management's Discussion and Analysis of the Financial Condition and Results of Operations. This is a narrative presentation designed to present management's candid comments on three key areas of a company's business: results of operations, capital resources, and liquidity. Companies are required to address all material developments affecting these three key areas, favorable or unfavorable, including the effects of inflation. In discussing results of operations, companies are required not only to detail operating and unusual events that affected results for the period under discussion, but also any trends or uncertainties that might affect results in the future. The capital resources part involves questions of fixed asset expenditures and considerations of whether it benefits shareholders more to finance such outlays with stock, bonds, or through lease arrangements. Addressing liquidity means discussing anything that affects net working capital, such as the convertibility into cash of accounts receivable or inventory and the availability of bank lines of credit.

When it made this section a requirement, the SEC sought to elicit, in a company's own words, an interpretation of the significance of past and future financial developments.

Investor's Information

This section of the annual report lists the name of the transfer agent, registrar, and trustees; the exchanges on which the company's securities are traded; the date, time, and place of the annual meeting; and a notice as to when proxy materials will be made available to shareholders of record. If the company has an automatic dividend reinvestment plan, the terms and procedures for participating are stated here.

The number of common shareholders (and preferred, if any) as of the fiscal year-end is also usually indicated in this section.

This section may also invite requests for Form 10-K, the annual Securities and Exchange Commission filing corporations are required to make available to shareholders. The 10-K is filed within 90 days of a company's fiscal year-end. It is a thick, drab report containing a mass of detail. Much of what it contains is in the annual report to shareholders or is incorporated by reference to the public annual report, but other information is unique to the 10-K. Such unique information includes historical background; names of principal security holders; security holdings of management; more detailed financial schedules; information about products or services, properties, markets, distribution systems, backlogs, and competitive factors; detail about patents, licenses, or franchises; number of employees; environmental and other regulatory compliances; information concerning amounts paid directors and their share holdings; and background, including employment history, of executives and their relationships to the firm.

Form 10-Q is a shorter, unaudited, update of the 10-K. It must be filed within 45 days of the end of a company's first, second, and third fiscal quarters. It is mainly useful as a source of information about changes in the status of securities outstanding, compliance with debt agreements, and information on matters to be voted on by shareholders, such as the election of directors.

Major corporations commonly provide a variety of financial information, product and company news through the Internet. A home page address is usually found in the Investor's Information section of the annual report.

Directors and Officers

The names of members of the board of directors and their affiliations are listed here as are the names and titles of senior executives. Also usually indicated is the membership of board members on various committees, such as the executive committee, the finance committee, the compensation committee, the committee on corporate responsibility, the research and development committee, and the audit committee. Corporations vary in terms of the use to which they put the backgrounds of their directors—in some cases the role of directors is ceremonial, in others directors are used to advantage—and this section can sometimes provide meaningful insight. The absence of directors unaffiliated with management may indicate a company dominated by senior officers and not responsive to the concerns of outside shareholders. Senior management can also become more entrenched in companies that stagger the terms of directors to help prevent a hostile takeover.

* * *

RATIO ANALYSIS SUMMARY

Ratios are the principal tools of financial statement analysis. By definition, however, ratios indicate relationships, and by excluding considerations such as dollar amounts and the overall size of a company, their meaning in and of themselves can be limited if not misleading. Ratios have their greatest significance when used to make year-to-year comparisons for the purpose of determining trends or when used in comparison with industry data. Composite ratios for different industries are published by Standard & Poor's Corporation, Dun & Bradstreet, Robert Morris Associates, and the Federal Trade Commission. The following is a summary of key ratios and what they signify. Each ratio is computed for XYZ Corporation, whose hypothetical financial statements are shown in the discussion above of the annual report.

Ratios That Measure Liquidity

Ratio	Calculation	XYZ Computation
Current ratio	$\dfrac{\text{Current assets}}{\text{Current liabilities}}$	$\dfrac{41.1}{18.5} = 2.22$

The current ratio measures the extent to which the claims of a firm's short-term creditors are covered by assets expected to be convened to cash within the same short-term period. In XYZ's industry, the standard is 1.9, so its 2.2 ratio indicates comfortable liquidity, although down slightly from last year's ratio of 2.4. In a recession, extra liquidity protection could make a vital difference; slack consumer demand would mean that XYZ's wholesale customers would have lower sales. That would mean less sales and lower inventory turnover for XYZ. As XYZ's customers became tighter for cash and slower paying, or went out of business, XYZ's accounts receivable would become less collectible. Ultimately that could mean insolvency. Hence the importance of this key measure of short-term solvency. Of course, in other types of companies, the current ratio would have less significance. A company whose sales were largely under United States government contracts would have less receivables and inventory risk, for example, and could thus afford a lower current ratio.

Quick ratio $\quad\dfrac{\text{Current assets-inventory}}{\text{Current liabilities}}\quad\dfrac{41.1-23.0}{18.5}=.97$

A refinement of the current ratio, the quick or acid-test ratio answers the question: If sales stopped, could the company meet its current obligations with the readily convertible assets on hand? XYZ has a quick ratio of .97, almost a dollar of quick assets for each dollar of current liabilities, and virtually in line with the industry standard of 1.0. Last year it was slightly better, 1.04 times, but that small a year-to-year difference is probably not enough to signify a negative trend.

Ratios That Measure Activity

Ratio	Calculation	XYZ Computation
Inventory turnover	$\dfrac{\text{Net Sales}}{\text{Inventory}}$	$\dfrac{98.4}{23.0}=4.3$ times

This tells us the number of times inventory is sold in the course of the year. As a general rule, high turnover means efficient inventory management and more marketable inventory with a lower risk of illiquidity. But it could also be a reflection on pricing policies or could reflect shortages and an inability to meet new orders. XYZ's turnover ratio is 4.3 times, down slightly from the prior year's 4.5 times, and the industry standard is 6.7 times. This should be looked into.

Average collection period	$\dfrac{\text{Accounts receivable}}{\text{Annual credit sales/360 days}}$	$\dfrac{10.2}{.270}=37$ days

Assuming a company's terms of sale are standard for its industry, the average collection period—which tells if customers are paying bills on time—can be a reflection on credit policy (a liberal policy, involving relaxed credit standards to generate higher sales volume, will usually result in a longer average collection period); on the diligence of a firm's collection effort; on the attractiveness of discounts offered for prompt payment; or on general economic conditions as they affect the finances of the firm's customers. XYZ's collection period was 38 days this year and 37 days last year compared with an industry average of 37 days. It thus enjoys typical collections, apparently reflecting a sound and competitive credit policy. Of course, there could be potential problems not revealed by this test; for example, a concentration of accounts receivable in one industry or with a few customers, which, if affected by adversity, would have a disproportionate effect on the total receivables portfolio. Footnotes to the financial statements will often contain information concerning the composition of accounts receivable and their age relative to the invoice date.

Fixed assets turnover	$\dfrac{\text{Net sales}}{\text{Net fixed assets}}$	$\dfrac{98.4}{59.8}=1.6$ times

Measured over time and against competitors, this ratio indicates how efficiently a firm is using its property, plant and equipment—its "plant capacity." Increases in fixed assets should produce increases in sales, although the investment will normally lag the sales effect. If, given time, sales fail to increase in relation to plant capacity, it usually reflects poor marketing strategy. XYZ's ratio is low by industry standards. It has recently added to its capacity and has plans to pursue a more aggressive policy aimed at higher sales and increased market share.

Total assets turnover	$\dfrac{\text{Net sales}}{\text{Total assets}}$	$\dfrac{98.4}{105.6} = .93$ times

This ratio measures the amount of sales volume the company is generating on its investment in assets and is thus an indication of the efficiency with which assets are utilized. The relationship between sales and assets is sometimes called operating leverage, since any sales increases that can be generated from the same amount of assets increase profits and return on equity and vice versa. XYZ's turnover of .93, virtually unchanged from the prior year, is considerably under the industry standard of 2.1 meaning XYZ had better increase sales or dispose of some assets. As we observed above, however, it has plans to increase sales and recently added fixed assets in preparation.

Ratios That Measure Profitability

Ratio	**Calculation**	**XYZ Computation**
Operating profit margin	$\dfrac{\text{Net operating profit}}{\text{Net sales}}$	$\dfrac{19.2}{98.4} = 19.5\%$

This ratio is the key to measuring a firm's operating efficiency. It is a reflection on management's purchasing and pricing policies and its success in controlling costs and expenses directly associated with the running of the business and the creation of sales, excluding other income and expenses, interest, and taxes. (Some analysts exclude depreciation from this ratio, but we include it here for the sake of comparability.) XYZ's operating profit margin has been quite consistent over the past three years and is somewhat higher than industry averages. That could mean it is in for some competition or that it is exceptionally good at controlling costs. To zero in on the reasons for XYZ's better-than-average performance, relate cost of goods sold to sales and selling, general, and administrative expenses to sales. The explanation may lie in pricing policy or somewhere in the area of selling, general, and administrative expenses.

Net profit margin	$\dfrac{\text{Net income}}{\text{Net sales}}$	$\dfrac{10.1}{98.4} = 10.3\%$

This measures management's overall efficiency—its success not only in managing operations but in terms of borrowing money at a favorable rate, investing idle cash to produce extra income, and taking advantage of tax benefits. XYZ's ratio of 10.3% compares favorably with industry standards. A company in a field where the emphasis was on high volume—a supermarket, for instance—might show a net profit margin of much less—2% for example.

Return on equity	$\dfrac{\text{Net income}}{\text{Total stockholders' equity}}$	$\dfrac{10.1}{68.0} = 15\%$

This ratio measures the overall return on stockholders' equity. It is the bottom line measured against the money shareholders have invested. XYZ's 15% return is above average for the industry, which is good for shareholders as long as it doesn't invite competition.

Ratios That Measure Capitalization (Leverage)

Ratio	**Calculation**	**XYZ Computation**
Debt to total assets	$\dfrac{\text{Total liabilities}}{\text{Total assets}}$	$\dfrac{37.6}{105.6} = 36\%$

This measures the proportion of assets financed with debt as opposed to equity. Creditors, such as bankers, prefer that this ratio be low, since it means a greater cushion in the event of liquidation. Owners, on the other hand, may seek higher leverage in order to magnify earnings or may prefer to finance the company's activities through debt rather than yield control. XYZ's ratio is about average for its industry.

Ratio	Calculation	XYZ Computation
Long-term debt to total capitalization	$\dfrac{\text{Long-term debt}}{\text{Long-term debt} + \text{stockholders' equity}}$	$\dfrac{16.2}{68.0} = 24\%$

This ratio tells us the proportion of permanent financing that is represented by long-term debt versus equity. XYZ's ratio of 24% (24% of its permanent capital is debt) is low by industry standards, suggesting it might consider increasing its leverage—that is, financing its future growth through bonds rather than stock.

Debt to equity (debt ratio)	$\dfrac{\text{Total liabilities}}{\text{Total stockholders' equity}}$	$\dfrac{37.6}{68.0} = 55\%$

This is the basic ratio. It measures the reliance on creditors—short and long term—to finance total assets and becomes critical in the event of liquidation, when the proceeds from the sale of assets go to creditors before owners. Since assets tend to shrink in liquidation, the lower this ratio the more secure owners can feel. Also, a high debt ratio makes it more difficult to borrow should the need arise. XYZ's debt ratio of 55% is very conservative, and is another indication that its shareholders could safely benefit from greater leverage.

Times interest earned	$\dfrac{\text{Earnings before taxes and interest charges}}{\text{Interest charges}}$	$\dfrac{19.4}{1.0} = 19 \text{ times}$

This ratio measures the number of times fixed interest charges are covered by earnings. Since failure to meet interest payments would be an event of default under the terms of most debenture agreements, this coverage ratio indicates a margin of safety. Put another way, it indicates the extent to which earnings could shrink—in a recession, for example—before the firm became unable to meet its contractual interest charges. XYZ earns 19 times its annual interest payments, which is substantially more than is normally considered conservative. It is another indication that XYZ should consider increasing its leverage.

Fixed charge coverage	$\dfrac{\text{Earnings before taxes and interest charges}}{\text{Interest charges} + \text{lease payments}}$	$\dfrac{19.4}{1.0} = 19 \text{ times}$

This is the times interest earned ratio expanded to include other fixed charges, notably annual lease payments. XYZ has no lease obligations, so the ratio is the same. It is important to note, however, that the extent of this coverage should be sufficient to ensure that a company can meet its fixed contractual obligations in bad times as well as good times.

Ratios That Measure Stock Values

Ratio	Calculation	XYZ Computation
Price-earnings ratio	$\dfrac{\text{Market price of common share}}{\text{Earnings per common share}}$	$\dfrac{63.00}{6.30} = 10 \text{ times}$

This ratio reflects the value the marketplace puts on a company's earnings and the prospect of future earnings. It is important to shareholders because it represents the value of their holdings, and it is also important from the corporate standpoint in that it is an indication of the firm's cost of capital—the price it could expect to receive if it were to issue new shares. XYZs multiple of ten times earnings is about average for an established company.

Ratio	Calculation	XYZ Computation
Market-to-book ratio	$\dfrac{\text{Market price of common share}}{\text{Book value per share (total assets – intangible assets – total liabilities and preferred stock common shares outstanding)}}$	$\dfrac{63.00}{40.00} = 1.58 \text{ times}$

This indicates the value the market places on a firm's expected earnings—its value as a going concern—in relation to the value of its shares if the company were to be liquidated and the proceeds from the sale of assets, after creditor claims were satisfied, were paid to shareholders. XYZ's common shares have a market value that is half again as much as their value in liquidation, assuming its assets could be liquidated at book value.

Dividend payout ratio	$\dfrac{\text{Dividends per common share}}{\text{Earnings per common share}}$	$\dfrac{4.20}{6.30} = 67\%$

This ratio indicates the percentage of common share earnings that are paid out in dividends. As a general rule, young, growing companies tend to reinvest their earnings to finance expansion and thus have low dividend payout ratios or ratios of zero. XYZ's ratio of 67% is higher than most established companies show.

HOW TO READ A QUARTERLY REPORT

In addition to annual reports, publicly held companies issue interim reports usually on a quarterly basis, which update shareholders about sales and earnings and report any material changes in the company's affairs. Companies are also required to file quarterly information with the Securities and Exchange Commission on Form 10-Q within 45 days of the end of the first, second, and third fiscal quarters. These reports, which contain unaudited financial information and news of changes in securities outstanding, compliance with debt agreements, and matters to be voted on by shareholders, may be available from companies directly; or at SEC libraries in Atlanta, Boston, Chicago, Denver, Fort Worth, Los Angeles, New York, Seattle, and the District of Columbia; or through firms that provide all SEC filings (and that advertise in the financial sections of newspapers).

Quarterly shareholder reports vary in comprehensiveness. Some reports provide complete, though usually unaudited, financial statements, but most simply contain summarized updates of the operating highlights of the annual report. Accounting regulations require that companies give at least the following information.

- Sales (or revenues)
- Net income (before and after potential dilution, if pertinent)
- Provision for federal income taxes
- Nonrecurring items of income or expense, with tax implications
- Significant acquisitions or disposals of business segments
- Material contingencies, such as pending lawsuits
- Accounting changes
- Significant changes in financial position, including working capital and capital structure

Accounting regulations require that figures be presented either for the quarter in question or cumulatively for the year-to-date, but prior year data must be included on a comparative basis. That requirement is designed to deal with seasonal factors. For example, the quarterly results of a department store, to cite an industry with marked seasonality (sales bulge at Christmastime), would be meaningless unless compared with the same quarter of the prior year.

The main thing to remember about quarterly reports is that they are designed to update existing shareholders, not to provide prospective shareholders with an overall perspective on the company. They should be read in conjunction with the annual report.

PART III

How to Read the Financial Pages

How to Read Ticker Tapes

HOW TO READ THE FINANCIAL PAGES

Financial news is a swift-running stream that can be harnessed to power your investment decision-making—or drown you in a flood of statistics. Its volume expanded greatly from the 1970s through the 1990s, following deregulation of the financial markets and other developments that increased public participation in a growing investment marketplace, prompting many of us to become our own money managers.

As a result, the financial press has staffed up and daily financial sections have been expanded and redesigned, often along the lines of *The New York Times* free-standing section (whose Sunday edition, in the mid-1990s, was renamed "Money and Business" from just "Business"). *The Wall Street Journal* added a second section and then a third. A relative newcomer, *Investor's Daily,* creates graphs from its computerized data base to show price movements of individual securities. *USA Today* uses innovative graphics to include as much financial information as possible in its pages.

The Financial Times of London responded to the growing appetite for foreign financial news by increasing its international distribution. as did *The Japan Economic Journal* with its weekly English-language edition. *Barron's National Business and Financial Weekly,* long an important weekly source of information for professionals, became more consumer-oriented and added many useful tables and features not found elsewhere.

These and other financial publications have three major goals: (1) To pack as much news as possible into a given space; (2) to attract as many readers as possible; and (3) to allow busy readers to obtain a quick overview and/or easily find whatever specific information they are seeking. These aims are accomplished through packaging the news, and as readers, we must understand how this is done so we can unpackage it to suit ourselves.

THE FIRST PAGE

The outside of the news package—the first page of the financial section of a major daily general-interest newspaper or daily financial newspaper—is aimed at the broadest audience: the consumer, the investor, the civic minded, the curious—all of us, in one way or another. As you move to the inside pages, the information becomes more specific: reports on individual people, companies, markets. The tabular material is the most specific of all, and is included for readers who seek detail—a stock price, currency exchange rates, bond yield, corporate earnings report, or information on a new securities offering, for example. The outside of the package may contain, depending on news developments, one or more of the following elements.

The Digest

The digest presents major stories of the preceding day in summary form, along with summaries of the more important analytical feature stories from that day's newspaper. A good digest also gives you an idea of why an event was important, and what it could lead to. It will also tell you what page to turn to for the full story.

The Economics Story

The fact that a general economics story often appears on the front page of the package is a tribute to the sophistication and interest of the readership. It also reflects the fact that government economic data is scheduled for release well in advance, giving editors and reporters time to reserve space, pull out charts for updating, and line up experts to offer commentary. A monthly cycle of major statistics often starts with the release of data on construction spending and the employment situation (the latter generally is released on the first Friday of the month) and continues with statistics on chain-store sales, crop production, consumer installment credit, industrial production, capacity utilization, housing starts and building permits, producer (wholesale) prices, personal income and outlays, consumer prices, average hourly wages, savings flows, and other matters. The month often ends with a report on the indexes of leading, coincident, and lagging economic indicators. Most of the statistics refer to the previous month, some to two months before. Motor-vehicle manufacturers report on sales every ten days.

Important statistics are also released on a quarterly basis. These statistics include information on U.S. import and export prices, corporate profits, and of particular significance—the gross domestic product (GDP). The GDP (especially its inflation-adjusted version, constant dollar or real GDP) is a measure of the total value of goods and services produced by the United States economy. Of key interest is how the seasonally adjusted annual growth rate of the GDP in a particular quarter compares to the previous quarter and to the same quarter in the previous year. Trends in the GDP are our primary measures of whether the U.S. economy is strong or weak, growing or in recession.

For investment purposes, watch for basic themes in overall stories on the economy. Favorable economic signals bode well for corporate profits, and therefore usually for stock prices, and unfavorable signals can have the opposite effect. A weakening economy can lift bond prices, however, because economic slackness means weaker demand for credit and thus lower rates for new loans, which translates into higher prices for existing bonds and notes. But one monthly figure doesn't make a trend, and other factors, including speculation about Federal Reserve Board monetary policy, also affect securities prices. In any event, between the time economic data is released and its appearance in newspapers, there has been ample opportunity for financial markets to react—to "discount the news," as they say on Wall Street. Most stock markets remained open until 4 P.M. EST the day before (the Pacific Stock Exchange closes 30 minutes later) while the bond market, which is mainly located in brokerage house trading rooms, has no official closing. Thus, the opportunity to react effectively to an economic event may have passed by the time you read of it in the newspaper.

The Interest Rate/Bond Market Story

As market interest rates move up or down, the prices of fixed income securities move in the opposite direction to adjust yields to market levels. Yield determines price, and vice versa. Thus, the daily bond market story is essentially an interest rate story. Major daily newspapers always reserve inside space for this story and move it to the outside of the financial package when warranted by major developments. The event could be a big move in bond values, a new prediction by a widely followed interest-rate forecaster, Congressional testimony or other action by the Federal Reserve Board (especially its chairman), or policy changes by foreign central banks. The bigger the development, the more attention will be focused on its significance to consumers—the prospect of higher or lower mortgage and personal borrowing costs, for instance. A complete story will also explain the significance of such news to investors and include comments by analysts and economists. The Federal Reserve's weekly report on the money supply (usually released on Thursday) provides much of the grist for late-week interest rate stories. If the money supply grows faster than the Federal Reserve had planned, the Fed may be tempted to adopt a restrictive monetary policy. That is, the Federal Reserve may reduce the amount of money in the economy to prevent a rise in inflation. Tighter money means higher interest rates, at least on short-term loans and securities, which usually exerts downward pressure on stock and bond prices. If the Fed thinks the money supply is growing too slowly, especially during an economic slowdown, the Fed could be expected to try to ease monetary policy and stimulate money growth. This often leads to lower interest rates and higher prices for fixed income securities, as well as to optimism and higher prices in the stock markets.

The Commodities Story

The roller coaster action in the prices of oil, gold, and silver in recent years helped make activity in the commodities markets a more frequent front-of-the-package story. When the commodities story gets front-page treatment, the consumer implications—for example, the effects on retail prices of gasoline or orange juice—will usually receive most attention. But there will also be economic and market forecasts and comments by professional analysts and traders, designed to inform investors about commodities futures or futures options contracts. Typical questions answered include: How fast has the price of the commodity futures contract reversed direction in the past? Are there new sources of supply that could affect prices—for example, soybeans from Brazil to replace those from Kansas, or beef from Argentina to replace meat from Texas? Is anything happening that could limit supply? What is the outlook for a political development causing activity in precious metals contracts?

The Takeover or Merger Story

Major takeover bids (called public tender offers) or merger announcements make big news partly because they have important implications for the securities prices of the companies involved. In a takeover or merger story look for (1) the price, total and per share, that's being offered for the target company. Also look at the form of payment cash, securities, or a combination—and how it's being raised. A leveraged buyout, for instance, can sometimes leave the acquired company laden with debt. (2) The reasons for the merger—to combine businesses for greater financial or marketing strength; to avoid an unfriendly takeover; to bail out a troubled corporation, for example. An unfriendly or hostile tender offer could trigger a bidding war which would drive up the price of the target company's stock or prompt legal action. Also, a large-scale takeover or merger runs the risk of antitrust action by the federal government in addition to other impediments. When takeover plans are set back or collapse, the price of the target's stock will most likely drop. (3) Comments by analysts on the acquirer's motives and management skills. A bid substantially above market could mean shares are undervalued or that the acquirer has exciting plans; particularly with reduced float, it might be wiser to hold than tender.

A complete takeover or merger story will also uncover what the risk arbitragers—professional traders who speculate in merger situations—are doing. Heavy buying of the stock of the takeover target combined with short selling of the shares of the acquirer, usually means the professionals think the takeover will succeed.

The Stock Market Story

This daily feature shifts to the front of the financial package when stock indexes undergo an especially big move. Although broader-based and more scientifically weighted indexes exist, the Dow Jones Industrial Average, which tracks 30 blue chip stocks, continues to be the most widely watched barometer and almost invariably is featured in the stock market story. A good roundup should give you the widest possible exploration of factors—the effect of other markets (bonds, commodities, currencies, and to an increased extent, stock options and financial futures), corporate earnings, takeover bids and merger rumors, economic developments, and changing market forecasts. The article should differentiate between different groups of stocks and different markets. The New York Stock Exchange activity often reflects buying and selling by institutional investors while the American Stock Exchange and over the counter (NASDAQ) markets reflect a higher proportion of activity by individual investors interested in less well-known growth stocks. In recent years, market volatility has been intensified by program trading, the computer-driven buying and selling by institutional traders and arbitrage specialists of all stocks in a "basket" or index. Some forms of program trading, particularly index arbitrage, also involve index options, index futures, and stock options, all of which expire together on the third Fridays of March, June, September, and December. Although measures have been instituted to process this extra activity with minimum disruption, expiration dates still cause a surge of trading, and the market closing on those Fridays is known on Wall Street as "the triple witching hour." A complete stock market story will usually include predictions by analysts who engage either in fundamental analysis, which focuses on business conditions and the financial strength of companies, or technical analysis, which concentrates on the conditions of the stock market, such as the supply and demand for shares and the emotional cycles of investors. Technical analysts, including those called chartists, who analyze historical market patterns, are usually more willing than fundamentalists to predict near-term market movements for newspaper stories.

The Company Story

Sometimes company stories are the result of breaking news—a profit report, a takeover attempt, a new product—and sometimes they are features that have been planned, and even written, well in advance of publication. Newspapers often carry a company stock story as part of their regular stock market coverage or because it is an important company to the newspaper's readership (it has a plant in town, for instance). Because stories on publicly owned companies can influence market values, there are laws to prevent capitalizing on advance knowledge of their content.

Among the things that you, as an investor or potential investor in a company, want to learn are: (1) The nature of the company's business, and whether or not it's diversified or a one-product operation; the size of its customer base; whether it does business mainly with the government or with private firms; whether it relies heavily on exports and is therefore sensitive to fluctuations in the dollar's value; whether its sources of supply are secure; and whether it can easily pass costs on to consumers. (2) The amount of debt of the company relative to its overall capital and whether it plans to borrow funds, issue more shares, or pay back loans. Among other things, this financial information will tell you whether the value of shares you may already own will undergo dilution, which could reduce earnings per share and thus reduce the market value of shares. (3) The nature of the company's ownership. Is a substantial proportion of stock held by the company's founders or by its current management? Closely held companies cannot be taken over by unwelcome acquirers as easily as widely held companies, but that can also deprive shareholders of profits they might otherwise gain through public tender offers at premiums to market value. You should also be told if financial institutions own large blocks of shares;

big institutional positions are an indication of how professional investors regard the company. In the case of companies with relatively few shares, however, that can also cause substantial price swings should institutions gobble up or dump large amounts of shares. Trends in insider or institutional ownership can be solid signals as to the prospects of a company—if top management is accumulating shares, they may know before the public about events that might cause the stock to rise. (4) Trends in the company's earnings history. How steady have profits been? Have they been increasing on a per-share basis? Is the company emerging from a period of weakness? Are earnings mainly the result of ongoing operations or of one-time extraordinary items, such as the sale of company property? (5) Trends in dividend payments.

The Industry Story

You'll find many of the same elements of a company story in an industry story, and you will in addition have the opportunity to look at one company in relation to others. These stories are often accompanied by charts comparing companies in an industrial sector (computer chip makers, retailers, or utilities, for instance) according to sales, per-share earnings, stock price range, recent stock price, price-earnings ratio, and other important data.

Advertisements

Throughout the financial pages of most newspapers—even on the front page— you will find advertisements for bank deposit instruments, mutual funds, and other investments. Early in the year many advertisements for individual retirement accounts appear. Some ads include order forms and encourage you to send a check—sometimes for a hefty amount—right away. Mutual funds and sponsors of other publicly offered securities, however, can't accept an investment from you without first sending you a prospectus. A mutual fund sometimes will print the prospectus as part of the advertisement. Never react impulsively to an attractive rate or yield or special deal. It is difficult to compare rates, yields, and terms because each situation is unique and different institutions use various methods to compute yields. Some have withdrawal penalties and other restrictions that might not be obvious in the ad.

You will also find advertisements for financial publications, advisory newsletters, and computer databases and software, among other products. Often these products can be very helpful, but it is usually best to request a sample or a demonstration to make sure the product suits your needs.

SCANNING THE INSIDE FINANCIAL PAGES

You can get a quick picture of current financial events and trends by scanning the financial pages. The news digest, already discussed, is a good starting point. The inside pages are peppered with daily, weekly, or monthly charts and graphs to give you a snapshot of aspects of business and economics. *The Wall Street Journal,* in addition to its news digest, brings such highlights together in its Markets Diary on the front page (C1) of the Money and Investing section. The Markets Diary, which is illustrated below, shows the prior day's change in key prices and rates in the context of the past week and the past 18 months, giving a quick reading of the status quo and trends. The *Journal's* compact summary provides an excellent overview of the financial markets and is an appropriate introduction to the inside financial pages of any newspaper. Let's look at each of its sections in turn:

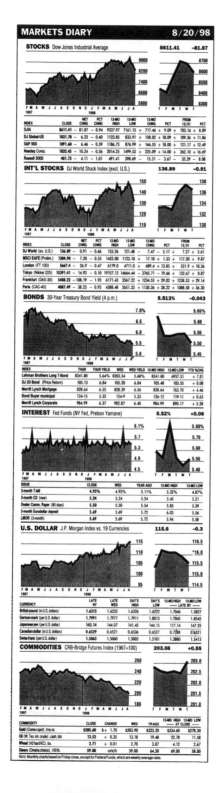

MARKETS DIARY — 8/20/98

STOCKS Dow Jones Industrial Average — 8611.41 −81.87

INDEX	CLOSE	NET CHNG	PCT CHNG	12-MO HIGH	12-MO LOW	12-MO CHNG	PCT	FROM 12/31	PCT
DJIA	8611.41	− 81.87	− 0.94	9337.97	7161.15	+ 717.46	+ 9.09	+ 703.16	+ 8.89
DJ Global-US	1031.70	− 6.23	− 0.60	1123.85	833.91	+ 158.02	+ 18.09	+ 109.36	+ 11.86
S&P 500	1091.60	− 6.46	− 0.59	1186.75	876.99	+ 166.55	+ 18.00	+ 121.17	+ 12.49
Nasdaq Comp.	1822.45	− 10.24	− 0.56	2014.25	1499.53	+ 225.09	+ 14.00	+ 262.10	+ 16.69
Russell 2000	401.73	− 4.11	− 1.01	491.41	398.69	− 15.31	− 3.67	− 35.29	− 8.08

INT'L STOCKS DJ World Stock Index (excl. U.S.) — 136.89 −0.91

INDEX	CLOSE	NET CHNG	PCT CHNG	12-MO HIGH	12-MO LOW	12-MO CHNG	PCT	FROM 12/31	PCT
DJ World (ex. U.S.)	136.89	− 0.91	− 0.66	153.26	121.48	− 7.47	− 5.17	+ 7.27	+ 5.61
MSCI EAFE (Prelim.)	1304.90	− 7.20	− 0.55	1452.00	1123.10	+ 17.10	+ 1.33	+ 117.20	+ 9.87
London (FT 100)	5667.4	− 26.9	− 0.47	6179.0	4711.0	+ 689.4	+ 13.85	+ 531.9	+ 10.36
Tokyo (Nikkei 225)	15391.41	− 14.93	− 0.10	19157.12	14664.44	− 3765.71	− 19.66	+ 132.67	+ 0.87
Frankfurt (DAX-30)	5488.22	−108.19	− 1.93	6171.43	3567.22	+ 1234.55	+ 29.02	+ 1238.53	+ 29.14
Paris (CAC-40)	4087.49	− 38.23	− 0.93	4388.48	2651.33	+ 1130.26	+ 38.22	+ 1088.58	+ 36.30

BONDS 30-Year Treasury Bond Yield (4 p.m.) — 5.513% −0.043

INDEX	THUR	THUR YIELD	WED	WED YIELD	12-MO HIGH	12-MO LOW	YTD %CHG
Lehman Brothers Long T-Bond	8241.80	5.64%	8203.54	5.68%	8241.80	6937.31	+ 7.81
DJ 20 Bond (Price Return)	105.13	6.84	105.20	6.84	105.48	103.55	+ 0.08
Merrill Lynch Mortgage	828.64	6.55	828.39	6.56	828.64	763.70	+ 4.46
Bond Buyer municipal	124-15	5.32	124-9	5.33	126-12	119-11	+ 0.63
Merrill Lynch Corporate	984.99	6.37	982.87	6.40	984.99	890.17	+ 5.28

INTEREST Fed Funds (NY Fed, Prebon Yamane) — 5.52% +0.06

ISSUE	CLOSE	WED	YEAR AGO	12-MO HIGH	12-MO LOW
3-month T-bill	4.92%	4.93%	5.11%	5.32%	4.87%
3-month CD (new)	5.24	5.24	5.24	5.45	5.21
Dealer Comm. Paper (90 days)	5.50	5.50	5.54	5.85	5.39
3-month Eurodollar deposit	5.69	5.69	5.72	6.03	5.56
LIBOR (3-month)	5.69	5.69	5.72	5.94	5.58

U.S. DOLLAR J.P. Morgan Index vs. 19 Currencies — 115.6 −0.3

CURRENCY	LATE NY	LATE WED	DAY'S HIGH	DAY'S LOW	12-MO HIGH	12-MO LOW LATE NY
British pound (in U.S. dollars)	1.6315	1.6235	1.6326	1.6222	1.7046	1.5827
German mark (per U.S. dollar)	1.7991	1.7977	1.7911	1.8013	1.7045	1.8545
Japanese yen (per U.S. dollar)	143.14	144.07	141.45	144.15	117.14	147.25
Canadian dollar (in U.S. dollars)	0.6529	0.6521	0.6536	0.6527	0.7288	0.6521
Swiss franc (per U.S. dollar)	1.5063	1.5060	1.5005	1.5101	1.3880	1.5413

COMMODITIES CRB-Bridge Futures Index (1967=100) — 203.08 +0.55

COMMODITY	CLOSE	CHANGE	WED	YR AGO	12-MO HIGH AT CLOSE	12-MO LOW AT CLOSE
Gold (Comex spot), troy oz.	$285.60	$+ 1.70	$283.90	$323.20	$334.60	$278.30
Oil (W. Tex. int. crude), cash, bbl.	13.53	+ 0.35	13.18	19.48	22.78	11.58
Wheat (#2 hard KC), bu.	2.71	+ 0.01	2.70	3.87	4.12	2.67
Steers (Omaha choice), 100 lb.	59.00	unch	59.00	64.50	69.00	58.00

NOTE: Monthly charts based on Friday close, except for Federal Funds, which are weekly average rates.

Stocks

Stock prices are measured by 11 indexes grouped in two categories: Stocks (meaning U.S. stocks) and International Stocks.

U.S. stocks are represented graphically by the Dow Jones Industrial Average. Although by far the most widely watched stock average in the world, the blue-chip DJIA has its limitations. Being "price-weighted," it can be unduly influenced by major moves in higher-priced components, and since it comprises only 30 large corporations, primarily industrial issues, it is not as representative of the overall market as a broader-based index. Nonetheless, the question "How is the market doing?" is almost universally answered by quoting the Dow, which gives it a unique status not only as a measure of market performance, but as an influential force in market psychology.

Other indexes in the summary include the Dow Jones Global-U.S. Index, formerly the Dow Jones Equity Index, whose 700 stocks measure broader market performance; the Standard & Poor's 500 Stock Index, also a broad-based index and the most widely followed index after the DJIA; the NASDAQ (National Association of Securities Dealers Automated Quotations) Composite Index, which measures a large group of mostly smaller companies traded over-the-counter; and the Russell 2000 Index. The Russell 2000 consists of the 2000 smallest companies in the Russell 3000, which comprises the 3000 largest U.S. companies based on market capitalization (shares outstanding multiplied by the current share price). The 2000 Index has an average market capitalization of $255 million (to put that in perspective, General Electric's market capitalization is $291 billion).

International stocks are represented graphically by the Dow Jones World Stock Index. The information expressed graphically and in the figures shown below it, is derived from the Dow Jones Global Indexes table that appears in the World Stock Markets feature elsewhere in the Money & Investing section of *The Wall Street Journal.* That table compiles 34 company indexes tracking a total of some 3000 companies in Europe, Asia, Africa, and the Americas. It represents about 80% of the equity capital on global markets. The United States is excluded from the compilation to provide a pure indication of international stocks.

The MSCI-EAFE (Prelim.) is a Morgan Stanley (Dean Witter) Capital International group index that measures the performance of stocks in the region known by the acronym EAFE, which stands for Europe and Australasia, Far East. MSCI-EAFE is composed of stocks screened for liquidity, cross-ownership, and industry representation.

The other four indexes track the four most important foreign exchanges: The ISE, formerly call the London stock exchange, which has traditionally been the dominant European market, is tracked by the FT (Financial Times) 100 stock index, popularly called "Footsie;" the Tokyo Stock Exchange, the second largest exchange after the New York Stock Exchange, is tracked by the Nikkei Stock Average of 225 stocks (sometimes called the Nikkei Dow); the Frankfurt-based DAX 30 (stock) index tracks the German market, which acquires new prominence in the new European Community; and the CAC-40 (stock) index tracks the important Paris Bourse. These indexes are widely watched, not only because many people own stocks measured by them, but because of the interdependence of financial markets internationally. In reading the tables, keep in mind that the trading day in the Far East precedes London's, which precedes New York's, and that each market is affected by the others.

In the columns from left to right, the table shows the closing value of each index; the net change over the preceding close expressed in points and then as a percentage; the highest and lowest levels reached in the preceding 12-month period; the change both in points and as a percentage within the preceding 12-month period and for the calendar year to date.

What we can learn from the August 20, 1998 Markets Diary illustrated is that blue chip, broader-based, and smaller capitalization stocks were all down both domestically and abroad for the previous day. The year-to-date comparisons would indicate that for most of the year a different trend existed—both blue chip and broader indexes had year-to-date gains, both in the U.S. and internationally. The only exception was the Russell 2000, which was off for the year to date.

Under normal market conditions, larger stocks tend to outshine smaller stocks in strong economies and vice versa. In slow economies, the greater growth potential of small firms overshadows lower profit margins; thus, their stock prices rise (helped also by the fact that lower-priced stocks tend to register greater percentage changes than higher-priced shares in any market). In contrast, mature companies fare worse in weak economies because their sales and earnings per share tend to go down, taking share prices down with them.

Normally, the 12-month columns would help us detect the trend of stock prices. If, for example, the DJIA outperformed the NASDAQ by a greater amount over a 12-month period than over the shorter period represented by the year-to-date comparisons, one could conclude that smaller stocks were gaining on larger stocks.

At the time of the table illustrated, the record-long bull market in U.S. stocks had, for several days, been showing signs of faltering. Some major corporations had just reported disappointing second-quarterly earnings, the result of an apparent slowing of the American economy in part precipitated by the economic crisis in Southeast Asia, and there was a sell-off of some of the more excessively valued stocks that had been leading the blue chip indexes. This explains the smaller year-to-date gains in the DJIA, the DJ Global, and the S&P 500 when compared to the 12-month changes in those indexes.

Were smaller stocks picking up the slack? The comparisons for the NASDAQ index would suggest they were. It had the lowest percentage loss for the previous day, and its year-to-date gains, the best of any of the indexes reported, were greater than its 12-month gain. But the comparisons for Russell 2000, a purer small stock index than the NASDAQ, which has a lot of smaller companies but some market-leading high-tech names as well—names like Microsoft, and Intel, for example—suggest otherwise. The Russell 2000 not only had the highest loss for the previous day, but its year-to-date loss was almost double its 12-month change.

Looking at international stocks, the European indexes led the previous day's declines, with Frankfurt showing the highest percentage drop. Russia's economic and political turmoil and the devaluation of the ruble that week, had unsettled European markets. Germany, whose banks had an especially large exposure in Russia, was particularly affected. In the preceding year, European stocks had been riding high on European Community excitement, although the Asian crisis had been dampening European economies in recent months. That, in turn, slowed the momentum of stocks somewhat as reflected in the comparisons between 12-month and year-to-date gains. The Tokyo and MSCI-EAFE indexes, whose weight is felt in the DJ World index, had been depressed by Japan's economic crisis and the ongoing economic turmoil in the Pacific Rim. Things had become so bad in those areas that some investors, encouraged by indications that progress was being made, were beginning to look for bargains there, explaining the improvement in year-to-date numbers compared with the past 12 months.

Bonds

As was observed earlier, bond prices move in the opposite direction of interest rates, the market's way of bringing yields in line with prevailing rates. Of course, bond prices and yields are strongly influenced also by risk factors, by inflation expectations, and by supply and demand. Different types of bonds reflect these characteristics to different degrees.

The bond section is highlighted by graphs showing the yield on the 30-year Treasury bond known in Wall Street parlance as "the long bond." Treasury bonds have the "full faith and credit" of the U.S. Government behind them and are free of risks other than those associated with fluctuating interest rates and inflation. And because it is long-term (30 years) and not, like short-term Treasury bills, a direct instrument of Federal Reserve monetary policy, long bond prices and yields reflect more purely than other investments the market's expectations with respect to interest rates and inflation. The 30-year Treasury yield is thus the benchmark for all other rates.

The DJ (Dow Jones) 20 Bond index is an arithmetic average of New York Exchange closing prices of 10 industrial and 10 utility bonds with investment-grade ratings from best to intermediate. (The words "price return" in parentheses tell us that changes in the index are the result purely of market activity as it affects prices and yields; in contrast, the other indexes in the group are based on "total return," meaning they reflect, in addition, changes in value resulting from the assumption that interest is reinvested. Under normal conditions this distinction does not materially affect the value of the indexes as indicators of the fixed-income market's direction.)

The Merrill Lynch mortgage-backed index tracks prices and yields of pass-through securities backed by home mortgages and issued or guaranteed by U.S. Government agencies such as Ginnie Mae, Freddie Mac, and Fannie Mae. Government-backed mortgage securities yield somewhat more than other government-backed bonds because they are subject to the risk that homeowners will prepay their mortgages, thus shortening the life of the investment. The prepayment risk is greatest when market interest rates decline, affording homeowners an opportunity to refinance at lower rates. Rising rates have the reverse effect and increase the demand for mortgage-backed securities.

The Bond Buyer municipal index, compiled by the *Bond Buyer* daily newspaper, tracks the prices and yields of newly issued AA- and A-rated tax-exempt bonds of states and localities. The Tax Reform Act of 1986 imposed certain restrictions on issuers of municipal securities, thus affecting both demand and supply in the tax-exempt market. The result has been that, on an equivalent taxable yield basis, municipals often yield more than taxable bonds of comparable quality and maturity.

The Merrill Lynch corporate index measures prices and yields of nearly 4,000 investment-grade (AAA to BBB) corporate issues. This index provides essentially the same information as the Dow Jones bond index, but differs in its broader base and its total-return method of computation.

Bond information is presented in seven columns. The first four (from left to right) compare the previous day's index value (based on price) and yield with the corresponding figures of the day before. The fifth and sixth columns indicate the range of prices over the past 12 months and the right-hand column tells the percentage change in prices year to date.

It is important to understand that all the bonds covered in the foregoing table are "straight" (not convertible), interest-bearing (not zero-coupon), and fixed-rate (not floating-rate). Such variations would behave differently in the marketplace and not be indicative of fixed-income securities. Also excluded were so-called "junk bonds," whose lower ratings and higher yields reflect their perceived greater risk of default.

The table illustrates that August 20 was a dull day in the bond market, little changed from the previous day except for the bellwether long-bond yield, whose four-basis-point drop (a basis point, the conventional unit by which bond yields are measured, is one 100th of a percentage point) sent prices to a 12-month high. We do see that prices are higher for the year to date and at or close to 12-month highs. This, of course, is a reflection of lower rates, and a glimpse at the 18-month graph indicates that higher prices and lower yields were clearly a trend as 1998 was approaching September.

Interest

Bond prices and yields give an indication of how the market views the future, what existing fixed-income investments might be worth, and what rate of return we could expect from long-term fixed-income investments. Short-term rates, which are highlighted in this section. give an indication as to what the Federal Reserve is doing to regulate the money supply and thereby stimulate or slow down the economy. The Fed's actions, in turn, affect other rates and even the prices of stocks, which generally benefit from low rates. Short-term rate levels also have meaning to us directly, since many of the rates we pay—on credit cards, auto loans, adjustable-rate mortgages, and home-equity loans, for example—are "pegged" to the yields on these key money market instruments. And while high minimum purchase requirements exclude most individuals from participating in the short-term money market directly, these instruments are bought and sold by money market funds and affect the yields we get on those widely popular investments.

The charts here plot the federal funds rate, which is the rate banks with excess reserves charge other banks that need reserves for overnight money. Borrowings are heaviest, and the rate highest, when the Federal Reserve, through its monetary policy, is draining reserves from banks so they will have less money to lend and thus provide less stimulus to the economy. The fed funds rate is the most sensitive of rates—so sensitive, in fact, that daily fluctuations could be misleading. For that reason the graph does not plot daily changes but rather a weekly average. A trend in this rate often signals a change in the Fed's discount rate, and that, in turn, is usually followed by a change in the bank prime rate, the maximum rate banks charge their most creditworthy corporate customers. Other rates generally follow the prime.

Other short-term rates shown in the table increase with different degrees of risk and liquidity. The 3 month Treasury bill yield is established weekly at auction, and the bills are traded actively in the secondary market. Buying (and selling) T-bills, thus putting cash into (or taking cash out of) the economy and increasing (or decreasing) bank reserves, is the Fed's primary instrument of monetary policy, so T-bill yields are widely watched as an indicator of rate trends generally. The 90-day bill is also the benchmark for most floating-rate credit.

New 3-month bank certificates of deposit (CDs) tell us what banks are willing to pay for 3-month money. The rate they offer reflects their consensus that, for 3 months, rates are probably not going to drop significantly lower.

Dealer commercial paper (90 days) represents the IOUs of corporate borrowers. (Dealer means this "paper" is bought and sold through brokerage firms rather than issued and redeemed directly.) Commercial paper is unsecured and marketable only by the most creditworthy organizations, which use this method of borrowing as an alternative to more expensive prime rate bank loans. Commercial paper, which lacks secondary market liquidity, competes with risk-free T-bills for investors' cash and naturally commands a higher rate of interest.

The 3-month Eurodollar deposit rate is the rate paid by borrowers of U.S. dollar deposits held in banks, including U.S. bank subsidiaries, outside the United States, primarily, but not exclusively, in Europe. Whereas domestic short-term rates are directly or indirectly controlled by the monetary policies of central banks (such as the Federal Reserve in the United States and the Bank of England in the United Kingdom), the Eurodollar rate is a pure market rate, free to find its own level through supply and demand. This situation has attracted speculators, who are able to buy futures contracts on Eurodollar time deposit rates. Since overseas banks are relatively free of regulation and can operate on narrower spreads, they are able to compete easily with U.S. instruments for investor's money, although arbitrage keeps Eurodollar rates appropriately in line with rates paid by U.S. banks for deposits of similar maturity.

Eurodollar deposit rates and rates on other Eurodollar transactions and securities are based on the London Interbank Offer Rate (LIBOR), the offer side of quotes among major banks in London that trade deposits with each other in the same fashion that U.S. banks trade federal funds. The rate on 3-month Eurodollar deposits is also watched as a harbinger of changes in the U.S. prime rate, which is listed elsewhere in the financial pages. American banks like to maintain a spread of at least

1.5 percentage points between the prime rate and the Eurodollar rate; thus, whenever the spread is wider than that, conditions may be ripe for a drop in the prime.

The rate tables are straightforward and need little explanation. The previous day's closing rates are compared with those of the prior day, followed by columns showing the year-ago closings and the 12-month highs and lows. In the illustrated example, the tables bear out trends evident in the federal funds graph. Interest rates in general had been declining from their year-ago levels, and many observers believed a lowering of the Fed Funds rate was overdue.

U.S. Dollar

The globalization of consumer, commercial, and financial markets in recent years has made us appreciate more keenly the effect of varying currency exchange rates. When the dollar becomes stronger—that is, when it buys more pounds, marks, yen, or other units of currency—it becomes cheaper in dollar terms for Americans to travel and shop abroad, to import foreign goods, and to buy foreign stocks and bonds. On the other hand, U.S. companies (and their shares) may suffer under such conditions because cheaper imported goods can hurt the sale of those produced domestically. When the dollar becomes weaker—that is, when it buys fewer units of foreign currencies—the cost of foreign travel and imports rise while U.S. exports become more competitive in world markets. Since the prices of foreign securities and the value of their interest and dividends increase as the dollar weakens, investing in foreign stock markets often means tracking the dollar.

The rates at which one currency can be converted to another are established by bid and offer. not unlike stocks, in a world-wide "over-the-counter" market that uses telephones and computers to link the major financial institutions, exchange brokers, and government agencies that dominate the foreign exchange marketplace. The demand for foreign exchange derives from trade, investment, travel and tourism, government needs of various sorts, and from speculators.

Since the exchange market operates 24 hours a day—when it's midnight in New York it's 2:00 P.M. in Tokyo—there are no closing quotes, although rates are reported at regular times late in the business day, making day-to-day comparisons meaningful. Currency rates are, however, highly sensitive to economic, financial, and political news and subject to rapid and pronounced shifts, which governments, except in extreme instances, are reluctant to counteract through market intervention. The exchange rates reported in newspapers can thus vary considerably from the rates prevailing at the time you read them.

The charts in this section show the J. P. Morgan Index of the dollar's value, one of two major U.S. dollar indexes (the other being the Federal Reserve Index, reported in *The New York Times*), compared with an average, weighted by volume of trade, of 19 foreign currencies. It shows a generally strengthening dollar between February 1997 and August 20, 1998.

The tables compare the dollar to five selected major currencies. The British pound and Canadian dollar rates are expressed in U.S. dollars. For example, late on the trading day in New York on Thursday, August 20, it would have cost $1.63 to purchase one British pound and about 65 cents to purchase a Canadian dollar. The other currencies are expressed in units "per U.S. dollar." In other words, on that Thursday the dollar was worth 1.5063 Swiss francs, 143.14 yen, and 1.7991 German marks. (The difference in the methods has to do simply with custom and practicality, and all rates apply to transactions of at least $1 million.)

The data illustrated show very little change between Thursday's exchange rates and the prior Wednesday's. The dollar weakened slightly against the yen, the pound, and the Canadian dollar, and strengthened slightly against the Swiss franc and the mark.

Given the volatility of exchange rates, the two columns showing the high-low range for the trading day can often be more meaningful than the late New York rate by itself. In reading the intraday highs and lows and the 12-month highs and lows, remember that the higher the U.S. dollar figures for the British pound and Canadian dollar, the weaker the dollar, whereas the higher the figure shown for the other currencies, the stronger the dollar.

Thus, consistent with trends revealed by the chart, the dollar on August 20, 1998, was stronger against all the currencies listed in comparison with their 12-month highs but weaker compared to their 12-month lows.

Commodities

The commodities section of the Markets Diary highlights key prices and trends in the raw materials and provisions used by commerce and industry to meet our daily wants and needs.

In these Chicago-dominated markets, commodities are bought and sold on either (1) a "spot" basis, meaning the "actual"—the physical commodities (or warehouse receipts)—are ready for immediate delivery and traded at a "cash price" (for grains) or "spot price" (for other commodities), or (2) a futures basis, meaning a "futures contract" is entered into that provides for delivery and payment in a specified future month at a specified price.

Participants in the market fall into two categories: On one side are businesses buying the commodities for commercial use or using futures contracts to hedge against the risk of loss due to a change in prices. On the other side are traders and speculators who aim to profit from short-term and longer-term price movements.

The average investor may participate in the commodities market through professionally managed pooled investments, or may just be interested in watching commodity price trends for what they reveal about inflationary expectations and the prices of things we eat, drink, wear, or otherwise use in our daily lives.

The Commodity Research Bureau's (CRB) Bridge Futures Index tracks futures prices on 21 commodities, including a diverse range of agricultural contracts, oil, lumber, copper, and precious metals. (This index does not include financial futures traded at commodities exchanges, such as those on interest rates and foreign currencies.) Because commodity prices are direct factors in the cost of living, the CRB Index is a highly sensitive barometer of inflation expectations. Increased inflation, of course, usually means higher interest rates and yields and lower bond prices. The diversity of the CRB Index is important to its value as an indicator of the direction of prices in general, since individual commodity prices are subject not only to supply and demand, but also to all manner of other influences including weather conditions, crop failures, trading cycles, political developments, and government actions.

The tables show spot activity in four of the most economically significant and actively traded commodities. Gold, which receives more daily attention in the press than any other single commodity, is shown in U.S. dollars per troy ounce at the closing price on the Commodity Exchange (Comex) in New York. (The Comex close is actually a settlement price determined shortly after trading ends, and represents the futures contract set to expire soonest, the so-called nearest-month contract. Other reports use the morning and afternoon London gold fixings.) The reasons gold is so widely followed, in addition to its industrial and commercial uses, are primarily three: (1) Gold has historically tended to rise in value when the inflation rate increases, so it is viewed as a measure of inflation expectations. (2) Gold is considered a safe haven when political turmoil threatens the value of financial investments, so the price of gold bullion and bullion futures contracts is a measure of international tensions. (3) Gold is used internationally as an alternative to the U.S. dollar, rising as the dollar weakens and vice versa; thus it is seen as a measure of confidence in the dollar.

The other commodities listed reflect changes in the cash or spot prices of the units in which they are traded. Thus, crude oil is quoted in dollars and cents per barrel, wheat in dollars and cents per bushel, and steers in dollars and cents per hundred pounds.

The rise in gold and oil prices on August 20 was explained in accompanying commodities articles as having to do with increased concerns over financial crises in Latin America and Russia, U.S. military strikes against terrorist targets in Afghanistan and Sudan, and the possibility of action against Iraq.

Earnings Reports

Quarterly profit reports for corporations are carried in major newspapers like *The New York Times, The Wall Street Journal,* and *Investor's Business Daily,* as well as in many other newspapers. In most cases, the abbreviated reports appear in one place, and include the latest sales, net income, net income per share, and shares outstanding, compared with the year-earlier figures. Using year-earlier comparisons rather than comparisons with the previous quarter excludes purely seasonal fluctuations. Department stores, for example, as a rule report the most sales in the fourth quarter, owing to the Christmas season. Comparing the fourth and third quarters, therefore, might give an inaccurate impression of the health of a department-store chain. It is very important also to look at earnings on a per-share basis. Per-share earnings, more than total earnings, are a major determinant of stock prices.

Starting in 1998, companies were required to report earnings per share on two bases: Basic earnings per share is simply the number of shares outstanding divided by a company's net profit. Diluted earnings per share, normally a lower figure, assumes that all potentially dilutive securities, such as convertible bonds and preferred stock, warrants, and options were actually converted or exercised, thus increasing shares outstanding.

By the time you read the brief earnings reports, the stock market usually has had time to react, since the reports are usually released during trading hours. Occasionally, a company releases earnings after the close of trading, and you may see the price of the stock market react to the news when trading resumes. (Some companies release disappointing earnings late Friday in the hope they will be overlooked or their impact lessened because of the two-day break in trading.)

XYZ PRODUCTS (N)

Qtr to March 31	2000	1999
Revenue	$5,600,000	$4,980,000
Net income	463,000	452,000
Share earns—basic	.22	.22
Share earns—diluted	.20	.20
Shares outstanding	2,100,000	2,050,000

Dividend Reports

Lists of quarterly dividends, organized alphabetically by corporation, appear in greater number during the third through fifth weeks of each calendar quarter when earnings reports are most numerous. The dividend reports are generally divided into categories: Irregular, Increased, Reduced, and Regular. The organization of columns looks like this:

DIVIDEND REPORTS

	Regular			
	Period	Rate	Stk of Record	Pay able
XYZ Corp.	Q	.30	4–10	4–30

The table tells you that the regular dividend for the hypothetical XYZ Corporation is paid quarterly, that the dividend is 30 cents per share (which would result in $1.20 per share annually if the rate held steady), that the dividend will be paid to shareowners of record April 10, and that the actual payment will be made on April 30. It's important to remember that stocks go ex-dividend during the interval between the dividend announcement and the actual payment. This means that the dividend isn't payable to investors who buy the stock during that interval. (On the other hand, if you sell the stock during the ex-dividend period, you still collect the dividend.) Shares listed on the NYSE generally go ex-dividend four days before the stockholder of record date. Stocks normally decline by the amount of the dividend when they enter an ex-dividend trading period.

Securities Offerings

Announcements of newly issued or about-to-be issued stocks and bonds come in two forms. Large newspapers include calendars and digests of expected and newly announced securities issues to be distributed by underwriting groups or syndicates. These groups of investment banking houses also place paid advertisements, known as tombstones in the language of Wall Street, which give a very basic summary of the offerings. (Tombstone ads are also used for other purposes, such as announcing major personnel changes or a firm's important role in an acquisition or merger.)

The newspaper listings come under such headings as Finance Briefs (*The New York Times*) or Financing Business (*The Wall Street Journal*). Because a high proportion of the offerings are bonds, these listings can usually be found near the bond tables and the interest rate/bond market news story.

One advantage of buying new issues (which are often reserved for favored customers) over buying existing securities, is that the buyer pays no commission. The broker-dealer is paid out of the underwriting spread, the difference between the price at which the securities are sold to the public and the lower price paid to the issuer by the underwriters. Even if you're not interested in purchasing securities, these notices give you an idea of the prevailing interest rates (in the case of bonds) and the types of companies that are able to attract capital by issuing shares.

In the accompanying illustration of a typical tombstone ad, the boilerplate (standard legal language) advises you to read the prospectus before you buy. Many investors, of course, simply rely on the word of their brokers anyway, but the prospectus is a legally required summary of the facts and risks concerning the issue, and investors are well-advised to read it. The tombstone lists the names of the firms comprising the underwriting group and, by alphabetically organized groups, the relative importance of their participation. The par value of the stock, if any, is usually listed, but has no meaning in terms of market value. The offering price, of course, is included; however, this announcement doesn't tell you anything more, for example, how the proceeds of the sale are to be used.

Tender Offer Announcements

In both friendly and unfriendly takeover situations, the advertisements placed by corporations soliciting your shares may offer the greatest source of practical information regarding what you should or could do with your shares. Among other things,

New Issue   October 2, 20--

750,000 Shares

ABXY Corporation

Common Stock
($.10 par value)

Price $30 per Share

Copies of the Prospectus may be obtained in any State in which this announcement is circulated only
from such of the undersigned as may legally offer these securities in such state.

First XYZ Inc.

MNO Inc.   TUV Securities

ABC Inc.   CDE & Co.   Monopoly Inc.

Ajax Inc.   Dustby Inc.   ZXZ Inc.

HIJ Securities

these comprehensive tombstone type notices identify the company seeking to acquire another company; state the price being offered for your shares and whether payment will be in cash or securities or a combination of the two; inform you of various deadlines to send in your shares or to withdraw your offer; and announce various other conditions, such as the minimum number of shares the acquiring company requires for the deal to be completed. These notices also include the names of companies that act as soliciting and information agents, such as D.F. King & Co., Georgeson & Co., or the Carter Organization, along with their addresses and phone numbers. Such companies have been paid to provide you with information and prospectuses. Of course, these ads can also be biased and are often followed in a few days with ads placed by the target company, citing reasons to reject the bid.

Redemption Notices

Callable bonds and preferred stock can be redeemed by the issuer prior to maturity, and the likelihood of this happening is greatest when the issuer can replace them with new securities providing lower interest rate or dividends. When redemption takes place, issuers often place paid notices in a local newspaper and/or a major publication, such as *The Wall Street Journal*. These notices provide the serial numbers and denominations of the securities being redeemed and the call price of the securities.

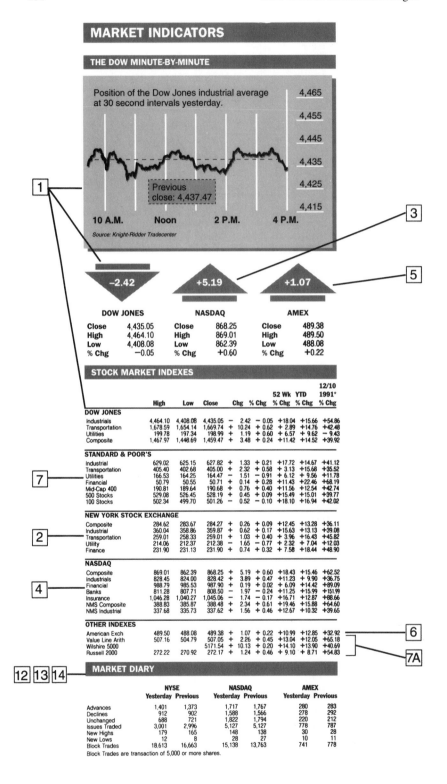

MARKET INDICATORS

THE DOW MINUTE-BY-MINUTE

Position of the Dow Jones industrial average at 30 second intervals yesterday.

4,465
4,455
4,445
4,435
4,425
4,415

Previous close: 4,437.47

10 A.M.   Noon   2 P.M.   4 P.M.

Source: Knight-Ridder Tradecenter

−2.42	+5.19	+1.07
DOW JONES	NASDAQ	AMEX

DOW JONES		NASDAQ		AMEX	
Close	4,435.05	Close	868.25	Close	489.38
High	4,464.10	High	869.01	High	489.50
Low	4,408.08	Low	862.39	Low	488.08
% Chg	−0.05	% Chg	+0.60	% Chg	+0.22

STOCK MARKET INDEXES

	High	Low	Close	Chg	% Chg	52 Wk % Chg	YTD % Chg	12/10 1991* % Chg
DOW JONES								
Industrials	4,464.10	4,408.08	4,435.05	− 2.42	− 0.05	+18.04	+15.66	+54.86
Transportation	1,678.59	1,654.14	1,669.74	+ 10.24	+ 0.62	+ 2.89	+14.76	+42.48
Utilities	199.78	197.34	198.99	+ 1.19	+ 0.60	+ 6.57	+ 9.62	− 9.43
Composite	1,467.97	1,448.69	1,459.47	+ 3.48	+ 0.24	+11.42	+14.52	+39.92
STANDARD & POOR'S								
Industrial	629.02	625.15	627.82	+ 1.33	+ 0.21	+17.72	+14.67	+41.12
Transportation	405.40	402.68	405.00	+ 2.32	+ 0.58	+ 3.13	+15.68	+35.52
Utilities	166.53	164.25	164.47	− 1.51	− 0.91	+ 6.12	+ 9.56	+11.78
Financial	50.79	50.55	50.71	+ 0.14	+ 0.28	+11.43	+22.46	+68.19
Mid-Cap 400	190.81	189.64	190.68	+ 0.76	+ 0.40	+11.56	+12.54	+42.74
500 Stocks	529.08	526.45	528.19	+ 0.45	+ 0.09	+15.49	+15.01	+39.77
100 Stocks	502.34	499.70	501.26	− 0.52	− 0.10	+18.10	+16.94	+42.02
NEW YORK STOCK EXCHANGE								
Composite	284.62	283.67	284.27	+ 0.26	+ 0.09	+12.45	+13.28	+36.11
Industrial	360.04	358.86	359.87	+ 0.62	+ 0.17	+15.63	+13.13	+39.08
Transportation	259.01	258.33	259.01	+ 1.03	+ 0.40	+ 3.96	+16.43	+45.82
Utility	214.06	212.37	212.38	− 1.65	− 0.77	+ 2.32	+ 7.04	+12.03
Finance	231.90	231.13	231.90	+ 0.74	+ 0.32	+ 7.58	+18.44	+48.90
NASDAQ								
Composite	869.01	862.39	868.25	+ 5.19	+ 0.60	+18.43	+15.46	+62.52
Industrials	828.45	824.00	828.42	+ 3.89	+ 0.47	+11.23	+ 9.90	+36.75
Financial	988.79	985.53	987.90	+ 0.19	+ 0.02	+ 6.09	+14.42	+89.09
Banks	811.28	807.71	808.50	− 1.97	− 0.24	+11.25	+15.99	+151.99
Insurance	1,046.28	1,040.27	1,045.06	− 1.74	− 0.17	+16.71	+12.87	+88.66
NMS Composite	388.83	385.87	388.48	+ 2.34	+ 0.61	+19.46	+15.88	+64.60
NMS Industrial	337.68	335.73	337.62	+ 1.56	+ 0.46	+12.67	+10.32	+39.65
OTHER INDEXES								
American Exch	489.50	488.08	489.38	+ 1.07	+ 0.22	+10.99	+12.85	+32.92
Value Line Arith	507.16	504.79	507.05	+ 2.26	+ 0.45	+13.04	+12.05	+65.18
Wilshire 5000			5171.54	+ 10.13	+ 0.20	+14.10	+13.90	+40.69
Russell 2000	272.22	270.92	272.17	+ 1.24	+ 0.46	+ 9.10	+ 8.71	+54.83

MARKET DIARY

	NYSE		NASDAQ		AMEX	
	Yesterday	Previous	Yesterday	Previous	Yesterday	Previous
Advances	1,401	1,373	1,717	1,767	280	283
Declines	912	902	1,588	1,566	278	292
Unchanged	688	721	1,822	1,794	220	212
Issues Traded	3,001	2,996	5,127	5,127	778	787
New Highs	179	165	148	138	30	28
New Lows	12	8	28	27	10	11
Block Trades	18,613	16,663	15,138	13,763	741	778

Block Trades are transaction of 5,000 or more shares.

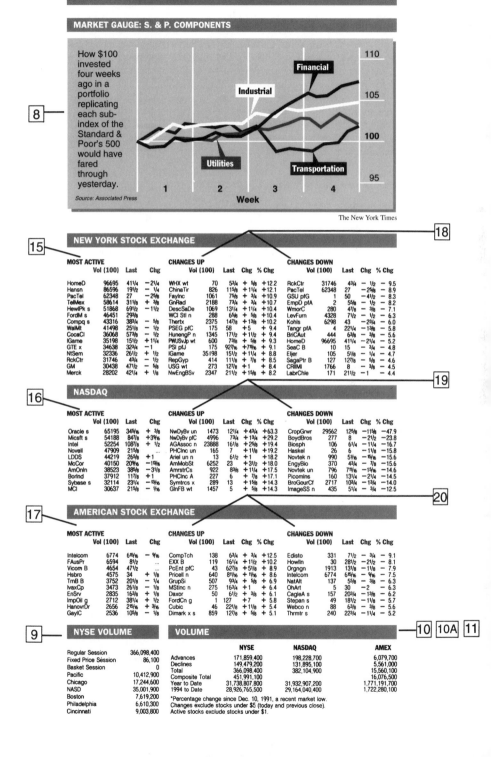

CONSOLIDATED TRADING/TUESDAY, MAY 16, 1995

MARKET GAUGE: S. & P. COMPONENTS

How $100 invested four weeks ago in a portfolio replicating each sub-index of the Standard & Poor's 500 would have fared through yesterday.

Source: Associated Press

Financial
Industrial
Utilities
Transportation

110
105
100
95

1   2   3   4
Week

The New York Times

NEW YORK STOCK EXCHANGE

MOST ACTIVE

	Vol (100)	Last	Chg
HomeD	96695	41¹/₄	−2¹/₄
Hansn	86596	19¹/₂	− ¹/₄
PacTel	62348	27	−2⁵/₈
TelMex	58614	31¹/₈	+ ³/₈
HewlPk s	51868	69¹/₂	−1¹/₂
FordM s	46451	29³/₈	
Compq s	43316	38³/₄	− ⁵/₈
WalMt	41498	25¹/₈	− ¹/₂
CocaCl	36068	57³/₈	+ ⁹/₁₆
IGame	35198	15¹/₂	+1¹/₄
GTE x	34638	32³/₄	−1
NtSem	32336	26¹/₂	+ ¹/₂
RckCtr	31746	43³/₄	− ¹/₂
GM	30438	47¹/₂	− ⁵/₈
Merck	28202	42¹/₄	+ ¹/₈

CHANGES UP

	Vol (100)	Last	Chg	% Chg
WHX wt	70	5³/₄	+ ⁵/₈	+12.2
ChinaTir	826	11⁵/₈	+1¹/₄	+12.1
FayInc	1061	7⁵/₈	+ ³/₄	+10.9
GnRad	2188	7³/₄	+ ³/₄	+10.7
DescSaDe	1069	13¹/₄	+1¹/₄	+10.4
WCl Stl n	288	6⁵/₈	+ ⁵/₈	+10.4
Thertx	2375	14⁷/₈	+1³/₈	+10.2
PSEG pfC	175	58	+5	+ 9.4
HunengP n	1345	17¹/₂	+1¹/₂	+ 9.4
PWUSvJp wt	600	7³/₄	+ ⁵/₈	+ 9.3
PSI pfJ	175	92⁷/₈	+7⁸/₁₆ x	+ 9.1
IGame	35198	15¹/₂	+1¹/₄	+ 8.8
RepGyp	414	11¹/₈	+ ⁷/₈	+ 8.5
USG wt	273	12⁷/₈	+1	+ 8.4
NwEngBSv	2347	21¹/₂	+1⁵/₈	+ 8.2

CHANGES DOWN

	Vol (100)	Last	Chg	% Chg
RckCtr	31746	43³/₄	− ¹/₂	− 9.5
PacTel	62348	27	−2⁵/₈	− 8.9
GSU pfG	1	50	−4¹/₂	− 8.3
EmpD pfA	2	55⁵/₈	− ¹/₂	− 8.2
WmorC	280	47⁵/₈	− ³/₈	− 7.1
LevFurn	4328	7¹/₂	− ¹/₂	− 6.3
Kohls	6298	43	−2³/₄	− 6.0
Tangr pfA	4	22¹/₄	−1³/₈	− 5.8
BriCAut	444	6³/₈	− ³/₈	− 5.6
HomeD	96695	41¹/₄	−2¹/₄	− 5.2
SeaC B	10	15	− ³/₄	− 4.8
Eljer	105	5¹/₈	− ¹/₄	− 4.7
SagaPtr B	127	12⁷/₈	− ⁵/₈	− 4.6
CRIIMI	1766	8	− ³/₈	− 4.5
LabrChle	171	21¹/₂	−1	− 4.4

NASDAQ

MOST ACTIVE

	Vol (100)	Last	Chg
Oracle s	65195	34⁵/₁₆	+ ³/₈
Micsft s	54188	84⁷/₈	+3⁹/₁₆
Intel	52254	108⁷/₈	+ ¹/₂
Novell	47909	21⁵/₈	...
LDDS	44219	26⁵/₈	+1
McCor	40150	20⁹/₁₆	−1⁹/₁₆
AmOnln	38523	38⁵/₈	− ³/₄
Borlnd	37912	11⁷/₈	+1
Sybase s	32114	23¹/₄	− ⁹/₁₆
MCI	30637	21⁵/₈	− ¹/₁₆

CHANGES UP

	Vol (100)	Last	Chg	% Chg
NwDyBv un	1473	12¹/₄	+4³/₄	+63.3
NwDyBv pfC	4996	7³/₄	+1³/₄	+29.2
AGAssoc n	23888	16¹/₈	+2⁵/₈	+19.4
PHCInc un	165	7	+1¹/₈	+19.2
Ariel un n	13	6¹/₂	+1	+18.2
AmMobSt	6252	23	+3¹/₂	+18.0
AmrstrCs	922	8³/₈	+1¹/₄	+17.5
PHCInc A	227	6	+ ⁷/₈	+17.1
Symtrcs x	289	13	+1⁵/₈	+14.3
GlnFB wt	1457	5	+ ⁵/₈	+14.3

CHANGES DOWN

	Vol (100)	Last	Chg	% Chg
CropGrwr	29562	12⁵/₈	−1¹/₈	−47.9
BoydBros	277	8	−2¹/₂	−23.8
Biosph	106	6¹/₄	−1¹/₄	−16.7
Haskel	26	6	−1¹/₈	−15.8
Novtek n	990	5⁹/₁₆	−⁵⁵/₁₆	−15.6
EngyBio	370	4³/₄	− ⁷/₈	−15.6
Novtek un	796	7¹¹/₁₆	−1³/₈	−14.6
Picomlns	160	13¹/₄	−2¹/₄	−14.5
BroGourCf	2717	13¹/₄	−1³/₄	−14.0
ImageSS n	435	5¹/₄	− ³/₄	−12.5

AMERICAN STOCK EXCHANGE

MOST ACTIVE

	Vol (100)	Last	Chg
Intelcom	6774	6¹⁵/₁₆	− ⁹/₁₆
FAusPr	6594	8¹/₂	...
Vicom B	4654	47¹/₂	...
Hsbro	4575	34	+ ¹/₈
TrnB B	3752	20¹/₈	− ¹/₈
IvaxCp	3473	26¹/₈	− ¹/₈
EnSrv	2835	16³/₈	+ ¹/₈
ImpOil g	2712	38¹/₄	+ ¹/₂
HanovrDr	2656	2⁵/₁₆	+ ³/₁₆
GaylC	2536	105/₈	− ¹/₈

CHANGES UP

	Vol (100)	Last	Chg	% Chg
CompTch	138	6³/₄	+ ³/₄	+12.5
EXX B	119	16¹/₄	+1¹/₂	+10.2
PcEnt pfC	43	62⁷/₈	+5¹/₈	+ 8.9
Pricell n	640	8¹¹/₁₆	+ ⁹/₁₆	+ 8.6
GrupSi	507	9³/₄	+ ⁵/₈	+ 6.9
MStinc n	275	16³/₄	+1	+ 6.3
Daxor	50	6¹/₂	+ ³/₈	+ 6.1
FordCn g	1	127	+7	+ 5.8
Cubic	46	22¹/₄	+1¹/₈	+ 5.4
Dimark x s	859	12⁷/₈	+ ⁵/₈	+ 5.1

CHANGES DOWN

	Vol (100)	Last	Chg	% Chg
Edisto	331	7¹/₂	− ³/₄	− 9.1
Howlln	30	28¹/₂	−2¹/₂	− 8.1
Orgngn	1913	13¹/₈	−1¹/₈	− 7.9
Intelcom	6774	6¹⁵/₁₆	− ⁹/₁₆	− 7.5
NatAlt	137	5⁵/₈	− ³/₈	− 6.3
OhArt	5	30	−2	− 6.3
CagleA s	157	20³/₄	−1³/₈	− 6.2
Stepan s	49	18¹/₂	−1¹/₈	− 5.7
Webco n	88	6³/₈	− ³/₈	− 5.6
Thrmtr s	240	22³/₄	−1¹/₄	− 5.2

NYSE VOLUME

Regular Session	366,098,400
Fixed Price Session	86,100
Basket Session	0
Pacific	10,412,900
Chicago	17,244,600
NASD	35,001,900
Boston	7,619,200
Philadelphia	6,610,300
Cincinnati	9,003,800

VOLUME

	NYSE	NASDAQ	AMEX
Advances	171,859,400	198,228,700	6,079,700
Declines	149,479,200	131,895,100	5,561,000
Total	366,098,400	382,104,900	15,560,100
Composite Total	451,991,100		16,076,500
Year to Date	31,738,807,800	31,932,907,200	1,771,191,700
1994 to Date	28,916,765,500	29,164,040,400	1,722,280,100

*Percentage change since Dec. 10, 1991, a recent market low.
Changes exclude stocks under $5 (today and previous close).
Active stocks exclude stocks under $1.

Short Interest

Around the twentieth of each month, the New York and American stock exchanges and NASDAQ release data on short interest—shares sold when they are not actually owned by the seller (usually they are borrowed). The exchanges break down the statistics by individual stocks and also give a total number of shorted shares of their listed companies compared to the total the month before.

Short interest figures generally signify that professional investors anticipate a decline in share prices. However, the figures are somewhat inflated by the inclusion of the short positions of exchange floor specialists; they sell short as part of their stabilizing function as well as for investment purposes. Market analysts also view large short interest positions as potential buying pressure since short positions must ultimately be covered by purchasing shares.

Other Economic and Financial Indicators

Among the more common weekly graphic features relating to business activity, securities prices, and returns on your savings are the following:

Treasury Bill Bar Chart: This appears in many newspapers, usually on Tuesday, following the Treasury bill auction of the preceding day. This table of 3-month Treasury bill yields shows how discount rates have changed on a weekly basis over the past three months, and gives the year-earlier yield as well. This chart gives you an idea of the direction in which rates on adjustable rate mortgages are heading, and whether you'll earn more or less income from a money market fund or an adjustable rate CD.

Money Supply Chart: This type of chart appears on Friday, following the weekly report on the nation's money supply released by the Federal Reserve Board at 4:30 P.M. EST on Thursday. The chart contains a "cone," made up of diverging lines that indicate the upper and lower targets of money supply growth laid down by the Federal Reserve Board. If the line representing M-1 money supply growth moves above the cone, watch out for jittery speculation about tighter monetary policy— speculation that could hurt bond prices. If the M-1 line is below the cone, be prepared for speculation that the Federal Reserve Board intends to loosen monetary policy and push rates lower—speculation that often supports bond prices. M-1, however, fluctuates week to week because it's narrowly based. Broader measures of the money supply, M-2 and M-3, are reported monthly, and articles often include similar charts for these figures.

THE STOCK MARKETS: DAILY SUMMARIES

Key Stock Market Indexes and Charts

It's possible for all but the busiest person to get a quick overview of stock market activity—and even some sense of future market movement—by reviewing the key market indexes and charts clustered at the beginning of the daily stock tables. At first, the mass of figures may overwhelm you. But you can train your eyes and brain to march through such displays, dividing them into mentally digestible components. The principal display of *The Wall Street Journal* appears on the inside front page of the *Money and Investing* (C) section and is headed Stock Market Data Bank. The Market Indicators package of *The New York Times,* shown here, appears at the beginning of its New York Stock Exchange listings. It can be broken down as follows:

Charts 1 to 7A These sets of graphs and tables represent price averages and indexes showing changes in issues listed on the NYSE (1 and 2), NASDAQ (3 and 4), Amex (5 and 6), Standard & Poor's (7), and the (equally weighted) Value Line index, Wilshire 5000 index (the broadest), and Russell 2000 (small companies) index (7A). They simply tell you in which direction the overall group of stocks each covers moved during the most recent trading session. The NYSE receives the most attention, with its list tracked by two families of indexes: the Dow Jones, and the exchange's own NYSE composite. Another important set of indexes, those of Standard & Poor's, are reported separately in *The New York Times* and will be discussed shortly. A composite index includes all the stocks traded on a particular market. A narrower index, such as those that appear here for utilities or transportation shares, tracks relatively few stocks. Utility and financial stocks are sensitive to interest rate changes—and by extension—to the bond market because these industries depend on huge amounts of credit. Therefore, pluses for these indexes immediately indicate the likelihood that the rate situation is stable or improving. Scanning the pluses and minuses in the various markets tells you if the previous day's movements were broadly based or varied from one market to another. The *Times* makes this easy by showing the highlights of the three major indexes in arrow-shaped boxes pointing in the direction the index moved the previous day. Declines for the Amex and NASDAQ next to rising indexes for the NYSE may indicate that institutional investors are more optimistic than individual investors. In the example illustrated, the three indexes all moved in the same direction—down.

Chart 8 This graph varies from day to day and illuminates a relevant aspect of market activity. (*The Wall Street Journal's* counterpart, called *Investment Insight,* appears regularly just below its Markets Diary.) The illustrated example shows how the four subindexes comprising the Standard & Poor's 500 stock index performed relative to each other over a 4-week period. (Current quarterly activity in the S&P 500 is depicted every day in a point-and-figure chart that appears at the beginning of the stock price tables just above another chart showing NYSE volume over the same period.) The S&P 500 is composed mostly of NYSE-listed stocks with some Amex and over-the-counter issues. Although numbers and proportions vary somewhat, its breaks down approximately into 400 industrials, 60 transportation and utility companies, and 40 financial issues. Although broader indexes exist (the Wilshire covers 5,000 stocks and the Value Line about 1,700), the S&P 500 is the most widely followed index of broader market activity and often behaves quite differently than the DJIA index of blue chip stocks. The S&P 100 stock index, which is reported in the table accompanying the graph, has a composition similar to the 500, but it is made up exclusively of stocks for which options are traded.

Charts 9, 10, 10A, and 11 Volume can help you determine in which direction the stock market will continue to move. If stock prices rise amid heavy volume, the indication is that many investors chose to invest heavily in stocks, and they intend to hold out for further price rises. Similarly, a market drop on heavy volume is considered a more serious setback than a drop on light volume. A market rise on light volume will cause the market rise to be questioned. The trick, of course, is to have an idea of what normal volume is for any given exchange during any particular season. Bar charts in *The New York Times* and *The Wall Street Journal* indicate daily volume for the NYSE for the past three months and six months, respectively.

Chart 9   This chart shows how the previous day's volume was distributed among the NYSE and the various regional and electronic exchanges on which NYSE-listed stocks are traded.

Charts 10, 10A, and 11   These tables compare NYSE, NASDAQ, and Amex volume figures. The up and down share volume helps you gauge the daily strength and weakness of the three major markets. The Advanced column presents the number of shares in each market that were rising when they changed hands, while the Declined column indicates the number of shares sold below the price of the previous sale. Shares sold at the same price are not included. These figures can signal an underlying weakness or strength often masked by the indexes. If stocks rose according to the indexes, but were sold on "weakness" (that is, when the shares were dropping) rather than on strength" (that is, on rising prices), this could mean that investors were using an overall price rise to take their profits and get out.

Charts 12, 13, and 14   Called Market Diary here, these figures, like the volume numbers, help you confirm or doubt the validity of changes in the price index. If, for example, the indexes have risen sharply in one of the markets, but the number of issues that advanced are fairly evenly matched with the number of issues that declined, it's possible that the movement of a few stocks was responsible for the rising indexes. Thus, the market isn't as strong as it first appeared. Similarly, the number of stocks that hit 52-week highs during the session indicates how strong the market really was. Major financial sections and publications carry lists of stocks that hit 52-week highs and lows. Obviously, you want to know if any of your stocks are included on these lists. Block trades, defined for this table as 5000 share trades or more, although a significant element in overall trading volume, are less significant as indicators of investor sentiment than aggregate figures for smaller trades. Block activity provides an indication of the portion of total volume transacted by institutional investors. These figures are particularly significant when we know what percentage of block trades was executed above the previous trade (uptick) and below (downtick). When upticks exceed downticks, it is considered a bullish sign and vice versa. This information is provided on Saturdays in *The New York Times* in a section called Tracking the Markets."

Charts 15, 16, and 17   The most active issues—stocks with the heaviest trading volume—are given in the descending order of shares traded for each issue—15 for each market. Sometimes stocks appear on the most active list because of a news item or a rumor regarding profits, mergers, or new products. Some stocks. however, constantly appear because they are actively traded by financial institutions, which often are restricted to buying stocks with large market capitalizations (the number of outstanding shares times the market price).

Charts 18, 19, and 20   Because up and down price changes are expressed in percentage terms, you can get a quick idea of the importance of your gain or loss if one of your stocks appears on this list. Cheaper stocks are more apt to be included on this list, since small point changes translate into bigger percentage changes for cheaper stocks than for expensive ones. The list may also help you find (or avoid) volatile stocks.

New York Stock Exchange and American Stock Exchange Consolidated Tables

You have to reach into stock tables to find specific information. Stock tables remain the heart of daily financial publications and sections, although the commodity, options, and bond tables are becoming increasingly more important as readers become more familiar with other types of investments. The tables for the two major U.S. stock exchanges, the New York and American stock exchanges, and the NASDAQ national market follow the same format. The information encompasses consolidated trading, which also includes trading on regional exchanges and on the over-the-counter market. Starting with the name of each stock, which we'll call Column I, the tables offer:

1. Name It's not always easy to locate a particular stock, because the names are usually radically abbreviated. The abbreviation systems used by the Associated Press and United Press International, which supply most of the tables you see, are different (and not to be confused with stock ticker symbols used on the exchanges); thus, the alphabetical order will differ from one system to the other. Stocks like IBM and AT&T are easy to find; few investors, however, would know immediately that J.P. Morgan is listed under M and Philip Morris is listed under P. Unless otherwise identified, these are names of common stock. Preferred stocks that are convertible to common shares are identified as "pf," but the convertability feature is not indicated in the stock tables as it is in the corporate bond tables. A "v" indicates that trading was suspended in the primary market. Stock tables are usually accompanied by explanatory notes defining any letters that may appear. An "A," "B," or other capital letter differentiates between one class of stock and another. A "wt" identifies the security as a warrant. A "vj" indicates that the company is in bankruptcy proceedings, and "wi" means when issued, signifying that the shares have not yet been issued. If the issuance is canceled, the trades will also be canceled. Also included but not identified are exchange-listed American Depositary Receipts (ADRs), which are negotiable receipts representing shares of foreign issuers.

2. Annual dividend Dividends are listed by dollars and cents per share. Don't confuse this figure with the amount you'll receive in the mail each quarter. The annual dividend is an estimate, based on the most recent quarterly dividend multiplied by four. If a company has a history of steadily rising dividends, consider this a conservative estimate. An "e" in this column indicates that dividends have been irregular, and that the figure represents the amount paid over the past year, rather than an estimate of future dividends. A "g" means dividends are paid in Canadian currency, although the other stock market data is given in terms of U.S. dollars.

3. Yield This is the current dividend divided by the latest closing price, rounded off to the nearest tenth of a percent. A low- or no-yield stock may be a growth stock. which means that profits are reinvested rather than paid out in dividends. Investors purchase growth stocks for capital gains, not for dividends; they hope that stock prices will

NEW YORK STOCK EXCHANGE

⑨		①	②	③	④	⑤	⑥	⑦	⑧
52-Week				**Yid**	**PE**	**Sales**			
High	**Low**	**Stock**	**Div**	**%**	**Ratio**	**100s**	**High**	**Low**	**Last** **Chg.**
25	18	XYZ Corp.	.92	2.0	7	623	17³/₈	17¹/₈	17⁵/₁₆ +¹/₈

increase as profits do. Some investors, however, purchase stocks for dividends, or income. This yield figure allows you to compare the dividend income with the income from other types of investments. Remember, however, that while the yield on a stock represents the potential income, the yield on bonds is a combination of both the annual interest income and the lump-sum capital gain or loss that occurs when the bond is redeemed. In a way, therefore, comparing stock and bond yields is similar to comparing apples and oranges.

4. PE ratio   The price earnings ratio is the latest price divided by the last 12 months' earnings per share, rounded to the nearest whole number. Be sure not to confuse PEs with dividends. PEs are used to compare the perceived value of stocks in the marketplace. PEs indicate how investors view the value of a company's profits. Stocks representing solid, uninflated profits that are expected to grow usually have higher PEs than stocks with questionable profits and profit-growth potential. Growth companies may have PEs of 20 or more. On the other hand, a high PE could be the result of a recent drop in earnings, and the prelude to a drop in the stock's price that will drop the PE to its former, lower level. A start-up or turnaround company could be attractive, but could have no earnings—and therefore no PE. PEs give you a way to calculate per share earnings roughly: divide the stock price by the PE.

5. Sales   This column gives you the trading volume, in hundreds of shares. A "5," in most cases, means 500 shares changed hands; a "1067" means 106,700 shares were traded. A "z," however, indicates that the full figure is being given. Volume measures how liquid a stock is. Stocks that consistently show large volume and small price changes are liquid; it takes a large imbalance between buy and sell orders to move the price much. Stocks with consistently low trading volume may be subject to wide price swings when large orders are finally placed. Sudden surges in volume, accompanied by rising prices, may indicate that an individual or an organization is building up a stake. (If five percent or more of a company's stock is acquired, however, SEC rule 13(d) requires that information, including a statement of intentions, be filed with its offices, with the company, and with the relevant stock exchange.) Volume surges often trigger takeover rumors, which in turn result in even greater volume and price movements. Financial analysts and journalists often ask company executives about the reasons for unusually heavy volume. A response of "no known reason" may cool speculation, while a "no comment" may fuel the guessing game.

An "x" in the volume column means the stock is ex-dividend. During this time buyers do not receive the most recently declared dividend. Stock prices decline by the amount of the dividend when the shares go ex-dividend, and then usually recover gradually.

6. High/Low   These twin columns give the highest and lowest prices during the trading session. A "u" indicates a 52-week high; a "d" indicates a 52-week low.

7. Last sale   The last sale is the closing price. Prices are usually expressed in sixteenths (6.25 cents). Thirty-seconds (3.125 cents) are used infrequently. Tables provided by Associated Press don't indicate the location of the last sale. United Press International does include the location, using "p" for Pacific Stock Exchange, "x" for Philadelphia Stock Exchange, "u" for Midwest Stock Exchange, and "g" for over-the-counter.

8. Change   This figure represents the change in closing price from the previous day.

9. 52-week High-Low   The high-low column gives you the annual trading range, the highest and lowest prices of the previous 52 weeks plus the current trading week, up to, but not through, the last session. A broad range indicates that a stock has demonstrated the potential to make—and lose—money for shareholders. Sometimes, a stock that has traded up and down within a range will meet resistance when it approaches its previous high point, because some investors will use this high point as a benchmark to sell. Similarly, the low point could serve as a buffer against further price drops. At the low point, buyers, hoping history will repeat itself and the stock rise, may purchase shares and thus provide support for the stock's price.

Other Over-the-Counter Stocks Tables

The quantity of information available for over-the-counter stocks has grown dramatically over the years. It's still often necessary, however, to call your broker for a price because many of the lesser-known, less expensive stocks aren't included in the daily tables. Your broker will use the pink sheets published by the National Quotations Bureau, which list bid and asked prices, to give you a price. *Barron's* provides extensive over-the-counter tables on a weekly basis. The *National OTC Stock Journal,* another weekly, carries information about penny stocks, which usually sell for less than $1.00. The daily tables included in large newspapers have expanded, in part because of the efforts of the National Association of Securities Dealers, the umbrella group for over-the-counter dealers. Since the early 1970s, the NASD Automated Quotations, or NASDAQ Stock Market, has allowed dealers using desktop terminals to view each other's bid quotations (the highest prices they're willing to pay), and asked quotations (the lowest prices they'd accept). NASDAQ also passes this and other information on to wire services for use in daily stock tables. Since the early 1980s, the system has been upgraded to allow dealers to enter transaction prices and sizes of trades. As a result, the tables for the more expensive or more heavily traded NASDAQ stocks are identical to the NYSE and Amex tables. Stocks that are subject to this full-line reporting system are included in tables headed NASDAQ National Market Issues.

However, not all the companies meeting NASD criteria to have their shares listed as part of the National Market System are included there. Instead, more limited market information for the shares of these and other NASDAQ-listed companies is included under the heading NASDAQ Small Capitalization Issues. In these tables, you'll mainly find volume figures and closing bid and asked quotations along with the daily change in the bid price from the previous day's closing bid.

The NASDAQ Bid and Asked Quotations table presents the following elements:

1. Name of the stock and its annual dividend, if any.

2. Sales, in hundreds of shares.

3. Last bid of the session, that is, the most a dealer will pay you for a share. You'll note that the spread between bid and asked prices often is considerable.

4. Last asked quotation of the day, that is, the lowest a dealer will accept for a share.

5. Change in the bid from the end of the previous trading day.

NASDAQ NATIONAL LIST

①	②	③	④	⑤
Stock & Div	**Sales 100s**	**Bid**	**Asked**	**Net Chg.**
ABZ Sys	90	$3/8$	$7/8$	$-1/4$
Quiljax	2	6	$6^3/4$	...
Zextap Inc .08	14	$15^1/2$	16	$-1/2$

Many over-the-counter stocks appear on neither the National Market nor the "Small Caps" lists. Some of the larger financial publications and sections include as many of these stocks as they see fit, usually in an abbreviated form that includes only the name, bid, and asked, but no volume or daily change. These stocks are listed under various headings, including Additional OTC Quotes and NASDAQ Supplemental OTC.

Regional and Foreign Stock Market Tables

A relatively small number of stocks are listed only on regional exchanges, such as the Midwest, Pacific, Philadelphia, and Boston stock exchanges. These shares usually aren't very actively traded and attract mainly a regional following. Regional stock trading information in newspapers usually provides daily data on volume; high, low, and closing prices; and change in price. Readers must calculate dividends, yield, the PE ratio, and seek out 52-week high and low prices.

Of increasing importance are stocks traded on foreign markets. Information about the more important stocks are carried in such major newspapers as *The New York Times, Investor's Business Daily,* and *The Wall Street Journal.* The stocks are organized by the exchange on which they're traded. The information carried for the Toronto and Montreal markets in Canada is the same as that carried for the U.S. regional exchange-listed stocks. The data carried for other foreign stocks is more limited: often only the name and the closing price, given in local currency, such as Japanese yen, British pence, French francs, Swiss francs, West German marks, and so on. It's up to the reader to track the daily change, and, if necessary, make use of the foreign exchange tables to translate the price into U.S. dollars and cents. Other tables show foreign securities traded over the counter. The majority of these issues are American Depositary Receipts, representing ownership of securities physically deposited abroad. Where they are not ADRs, the indication "n" is used. Quotes are in U.S. dollars and these tables typically have four columns: sales, bid price, asked price, and net change.

STOCK OPTIONS TABLES

Stock options give you both a conservative way to increase the income on your holdings or insure your portfolio against losses, as well as relatively inexpensive and highly speculative ways to invest in stocks. In any case, don't assume you understand these investment vehicles until you at least understand the stock option tables. Although unheard of a generation ago, these tables now comprise a major portion of the inside of financial news packages. The longest tables are generated by the principal options exchanges, the Chicago Board Options Exchange, the American Stock Exchange, and the Philadelphia Stock Exchange. Shorter tables are included for small options trading operations found on other exchanges.

A 1990s innovation that has rapidly been gaining popularity is LEAPS, a term now used generically but that started as a proprietary acronym of the Chicago Board Options Exchange meaning Long-Term Equity AnticiPation Securities. LEAPS are long-term options expiring in 1 to 3 years (with applications for 5-year expirations pending). Currently being traded on some 150 stocks and several stock indexes, LEAPS are listed separately in the financial pages. Although the following explanations apply to traditional conventional options expiring typically in 9 months or less, LEAPS are essentially no different except that in having longer terms, they logically trade at higher premiums.

Daily Stock Options Tables

Options tables give you the prices of wasting assets. These contracts, which as a rule last no longer than nine months, give the holder the right, but not the obligation, to buy (call) or sell (put) shares of stock at a specified strike price by a specified expiration date. The daily table format, and what it includes, by columns, is as follows.

STOCK OPTIONS

①	②	③			④		
Option & NY Close	**Strike Price**	**Calls—Last**			**Puts—Last**		
		May	**Aug**	**Nov**	**May**	**Aug**	**Nov**
Ⓐ XYZ	35	7	$6^1/2$	$6^3/4$	$3/4$	$1/4$	r
Ⓑ 40	40	2	$1^1/2$	r	1	$1^1/2$	r
Ⓒ 40	45	$3/4$	$1/4$	r	7	$6^1/2$	r

1. Name of the underlying stock and under it, the closing price of the underlying stock, repeated for each row of strike prices. (Since New York Stock Exchange tables now generally include sales of NYSE stocks on other exchanges, the NY Close may differ from the NYSE table, which reports later sales on the Pacific Stock Exchange and elsewhere.) In this example, XYZ Corporation stock closed at 40 on the principal stock exchange on which it's traded, most likely the New York Stock Exchange. Because the stock is worth $40 per share, each 100-share options contract has an exercise value of $4000.

2. The strike price is given in this column. This is the price per share at which the option holder is entitled to buy or sell the stock. The accompanying table includes options series for three strike prices— $35, $40, and $45 per share. Therefore, the values of the 100-share contracts are $3500, $4000, and $4500, respectively.

3. and 4. These figures represent the closing prices, or premiums, that were paid for the various puts and calls. The prices are expressed on a per share basis, meaning that you must multiply by 100 shares to determine the cost of the contract. These prices are given for the different months of expiration, usually spaced three months apart. Each contract has a specific month of expiration, with expiration set at 11:59 A.M. EST on the third Saturday of that month. Whether you gain or lose in options trading usually depends on movements in the premium price. That is because options positions are generally closed out with an offsetting purchase or sale or are allowed to expire. Having to exercise the option, that is, actually buying the stock in the case of calls or coming up with the shares to sell in the case of puts, involves more cash than many options holders want to commit.

Notice how the strike prices of the options series straddle the current market value of the stock. This gives investors a choice of intrinsically worthless—but cheap—options as well as options that have considerable value, but which are expensive to buy. Options exchanges constantly create series with new strike prices to maintain this situation as the price of the underlying stock changes. For stocks selling at $25 to $50 per share, the strike prices are usually set in increments of $5; the increments are $10 on contracts for stocks priced $50 to $200 per share. For options on stocks worth $200 or more per share, strike prices are set $20 apart, and for options on stocks worth less than $25 per share, the increments are $2.50.

Using the Associated Press system of symbols, "r" in the premium column means options for that particular strike price and month of expiration did not trade. An "s" indicates that the Options Clearing Corporation, which guarantees your cash or shares when options are exercised or traded, isn't offering that particular contract. United Press International uses "nt" if an option did not trade, and "no" if the OCC isn't offering an option. Associated Press expresses sixteenths as "¹/₁₆" while United Press uses "1s" to represent that fraction.

The cheapest options are those on which you would lose money (even before considering commission costs) if you exercised them. These are referred to as out-of-the-money options. For example, an XYZ May45 call, giving you the right to pay $45 per share or $4500 per contract for 100 shares of XYZ, costs only ³/₄—75 cents per share or $75 per contract. (See Line C, Column 3.) In other words, someone is willing to pay these prices for the right to later pay out $4500 for a stock currently worth $4000. Of course, the hope is that XYZ stock will rise. For example, if the stock rises to $43 per share (which would still mean that the option is intrinsically worthless and out of the money) another investor may be willing to pay more for that option—perhaps 1¹/₂ or $1.50 a share. The second investor hopes that the stock will rise to the point at which the option would produce a profit if exercised. In any case, the first buyer, who paid $75 for the contract, could get $150 for the contract—doubling his or her money before subtracting commission costs.

Options with intrinsic value, such as the XYZ May35 calls (which give you the right to pay $3500 for something already worth $4000) are naturally more expensive than those with no intrinsic value. In this table, these options finished the previous section at $7 per share (Line C, Column 4), or $700 per contract. The percentage gains or losses on such options are less than the volatile out-of-the-money options, but there is also less chance that these options will have to be allowed to expire worthless.

These tables also indicate how much money you can make by selling options and thus increase the income from your stock portfolio. For example, if you own 100 shares of XYZ, you may decide to sell calls; that is, you may give another person the right to buy your shares. In return, you receive the premium. Assuming the price of options held steady from the previous day's closing levels, you could expect to receive $150 for selling an XYZ Aug40 call (Line B, Column 3). Of course, if the stock price should rise, the call holder could exercise the option, and you would lose the capital gain. Ideally, you would hope that XYZ stock would hold at around 40 until the option you sold expired. In that case, after brokerage commissions were factored into the equation, it would not be worthwhile for another investor to exercise the option you sold.

If you are worried that your XYZ stock might drop, you can lock in a value of $35 a share through most of August by buying an Aug35 put (which gives you the right to get $35 a share) for $25 a contract (Line A, Column 4).

In addition to options on individual stocks, options are traded on debt instruments (interest rate options), foreign currencies, stock indexes, and certain futures contracts. What applies to puts and calls on stocks also applies to options on other instruments, with one major exception—index options. Because they are settled in cash and have other distinct features, they deserve special attention.

Daily Index Options Tables

Index options, which give you the right to buy and sell the dollar value of an index (rather than 100 shares of stock, as with stock options) are relatively few; sometimes, however, they are extremely popular. They often dominate the most-active lists that appear at the head of daily option tables. Index options tables run under their exchange headings: Chicago Board Options Exchange (often referred to in the tables as Chicago Board or just Chicago), the American, Philadelphia, Pacific, and New York stock exchanges, and NASD.

Index options are popular because they allow investors to play the whole market, in the case of broad-based indexes, or segments of the market, in the case of indexes that track technology stocks or gold stocks, among others. An index is assigned a value of a certain number of dollars per point—$100, for example. Standard & Poor's and, more recently, Dow Jones, have allowed their indexes to be used for such purposes, as have the New York Stock Exchange and Value Line. Sometimes indexes are created specifically for trading options on them. Using the usual format, a hypothetical XYZ index option, which for example, tracks hundreds of stocks, would appear like the accompanying example.

INDEX OPTIONS

	①	②			③		
XYZ Index							
Strike Price	**Calls—Last**			**Puts—Last**			
	Feb	**Mar**	**Apr**	**Feb**	**Mar**	**Apr**	
Ⓐ 290	$12^7/8$	$14^1/4$	$14^1/8$	$3/16$	2	$4^1/4$	
Ⓑ 295	$7^5/8$	$10^1/4$	$11^3/8$	$11/16$	$3^1/4$	$6^3/4$	
Ⓒ 300	$3^3/4$	$7^3/4$	$8^1/8$	$1^7/8$	$5^3/8$	$9^1/8$	
Ⓓ 305	$1^3/16$	$4^7/8$	$6^1/2$	$4^3/8$	$10^1/2$	12	
Ⓔ 310	$3/8$	$2^7/8$	$4^1/2$	···	14	···	
Ⓕ Total call volume 27,435 Total call open int. 78,121							
Ⓖ Total put volume 17,477 Total call open int. 75,940							
Ⓗ The index: High 302.55; Low 296.90;							
Close 302.51. + 4.32							

Index option tables have the following components:

1. The strike price is the price you would pay (if you owned a call) or would receive (if you owned a put) if the option were exercised. To compute the dollar value, multiply by $100 per point, because the

XYZ Index has an assigned value of $100 per point. The 290 strike price, for example, would require the payment of $29,000.

2.   Calls-last are the closing prices, or premiums, for calls. Unlike the much longer time periods available for stock options, index options expire in about three months at most. As you can see, investors were paying 12⁷/₈, or $1287.50 per contract,` for the expensive, deep-in-the-money Feb290 calls (Line A, Column 2). That's because the index closed at 302.51—the index's closing level is given on Line H— making its monetary value $30,251. The holder of a call with a strike price of 290, or $29,000, has an option with an intrinsic value of $1251 and hopes the value will rise even higher so the option can be sold or exercised at a profit after commissions.

Meanwhile, the 310 strike price call options have no intrinsic value; they are out of the money and thus, cheap. A Feb310 cost only ³/₈, or $37.50 per contract (Line E, Column 2), because it gives the buyer the right to pay $31,000 for an investment that's currently worth only $30,251.

3.   Premiums on puts move in the opposite direction of calls. The March puts with a 310 strike price (Line E, Column 3) are expensive, ($1400 per contract) because they are deep in the money; they give the holder the right to demand $31,000 for an index that's worth only $30,152.

F.   This line indicates the number of call contracts that were traded during the session and the number of contracts still open (open interest). To some extent, these figures measure investor optimism, because calls are bets that the market index will rise.

G.   This line presents the same type of information given in line F. except that line G deals with puts. These figures reflect investor pessimism, because puts are bets that the market will drop, at least insofar as the group of stocks being tracked by the index is concerned.

H.   This line indicates how the index performed during the session, in terms of its highest, lowest, and closing values, and change from its previous close. The gain shown in this example, 4.32 points, signifies that the value of the XYZ index rose $432.

Weekly Options Tables

Weekly options tables, such as those found in *Barron's* or the Sunday *New York Times,* follow a format different from the daily tables. Calls and puts are stacked rather than placed next to each other. More information is included in these tables. Index options are still run separately.

In the accompanying example of a typical stock-option table, the columns include the following information:

1.   Name of the option, as identified by the underlying stock, the expiration month, and the strike price. The closest expiration months and lowest strike prices appear first. A "p" identifies puts; the other options are calls.

2.   Sales for the week, in terms of the number of contracts that changed hands.

WEEKLY OPTIONS TABLE

① Option	② Sales	③ Open Int.	④ High	⑤ Low	Last	⑥ Net Chg.	⑦ Stock close
ABZ Mar35	1437	10921	$6^1/8$	$3^3/4$	4	$-1^1/8$	39
ABZ Mar35 p	99	5089	$1/16$	$1/16$	$1/16$	$-1/16$	39
ABZ Mar40	5981	7332	$1^{15}/16$	$1/2$	$9/16$	$-1/16$	39
ABZ Mar40 p	237	402	2	1	$1^3/4$	$+^3/8$	39

3. Open interest—the number of contracts in investor and dealer hands that haven't been exercised or closed out yet. Comparing the number of outstanding calls to puts helps you assess the direction speculators expect the price of the stock to take.

4. The highest and lowest premiums, per share, paid for a particular contract during the past week.

5. The closing premium, or price, per share, at the end of the week.

6. Net Change—how much premiums per share rose or fell from the previous weekly close. The $1^1/8$ ($1.125 per share) loss for ABZ Mar35 calls indicates that the contracts lost $112.50 each.

7. The closing price of the underlying shares, which, when multiplied by 100, equals the exercise value of the contracts, $3900.

FUTURES TABLES

Futures tables are grouped by broad categories—agricultural (grains, edible oils, livestock, coffee, sugar, cocoa, orange juice), metals (gold, silver, platinum, palladium, copper), industrials (lumber, cotton, crude oil, heating oil, gasoline), and financial (U.S. Treasury bonds, notes, and bills, foreign currencies, certificates of deposit, stock index futures). About 50 contracts are listed in various futures markets and included in newspaper tables. Commodity contracts are agreements to deliver or take delivery of a commodity in the future. Hence, the "Futures Prices" label for these tables. Most investors in commodities futures contracts are speculators who hope to make big profits by predicting correctly the change in commodity prices. The contracts are identified by their delivery months. A typical table, in this case for cattle. is presented here. The type of contract and the exchange (CME, or Chicago Mercantile Exchange) as well as the size (44,000 pounds) and the units of trade (pennies per pound) are shown in lines B and C.

Other information is presented as follows:

1. The highest and lowest prices paid for a particular delivery month contract since the contract was listed. This indicates the price swings of the contract. The April futures (*Line D*) ranged between 67.07 cents and 55.30 cents per pound, or $29,510 and $24,332 per 44,000-pound contract—a difference of $5178. An investor smart enough or lucky enough to invest $2433 (10% margin when the contract reached its $24,332 low point) and sell when prices peaked would have more than doubled his or her money. On the other hand, someone who invested at the high point could easily have lost all of his or her money. When the loss of a contract's value equals the amount of money that's been invested, brokers will usually demand more margin. If they don't get it, they will sell the contract.

CATTLE FUTURES

	①	②	③		④	⑤	⑥
	...Season...						Open
④	**High**	**Low**	**High**	**Low**	**Close**	**Chg.**	**Int.**
⑧	CATTLE, LIVE BEEF (CME)						
ⓒ	44,000 lb.; ¢ per lb.						
⑩	67.07	55.30 Apr	61.75	60.32	60.40	−.30	29,042
⑥	66.60	56.25 Jun	60.52	59.35	59.47	−.28	17.547
⑥	61.75	55.20 Aug	58.40	57.45	57.47	−.25	5,939
⑥	60.60	55.70 Oct	57.20	56.37	56.50	−.15	2,705
⑥	61.75	57.55 Dec	58.80	58.10	58.35	−.02	612
①	60.20	58.00 Feb	58.90	58.77	58.77	+.07	56
①	Est. sales 21,859. Wed's sales 21.607.						
⑥	Wed.'s open Int 55,901, up 63.						

2. The delivery months differentiate one contract from another. The spacing between delivery months and the length of the longest contract varies from one commodity to the next. Most contracts last no longer than one year.

3. The daily high and low prices.

4. The closing price. At 60.40 cents, the close in the April future made that contract worth $26,576.

5. The change in price—the difference from one close to the next. The .3 cent loss for April cattle signifies a $132 loss for the contract.

6. The open interest—the number of contracts that have not been closed through delivery or offsetting transactions. This indicates which contracts will experience the heaviest trading in the future, as most contracts will be closed out through either a sale or a purchase of an offsetting contract, rather than by the delivery of the commodity.

J. This line estimates the number of contracts that changed hands during the last session, as well as the volume of the previous session.

K. This line presents the total open interest of the two previous days, and the change in the number of open contracts.

A great deal of information is omitted from these tables, including delivery days, delivery specifications (the locations to which the commodities would be sent and how they would arrive), and the daily limits in price changes that exchanges impose on most futures contracts. The contract specifications are available from the exchange on which the commodity is traded. Commodities don't possess the uniform qualities of options contracts; the sequence of delivery months and the maximum length of contracts varies from one commodity to another.

Comprehensive commodities tables also include a listing of cash prices, gathered from various sources each day—exchanges, warehouses, fabricators—which give you the immediate value of many of the commodities for which futures contracts are traded as well as other materials, such as wool and cloth and mercury, which have no formal futures market. In the case of futures-related commodities, remember that the current cash price, while often determining the direction of futures contract prices, is usually different. A glut in grain during the harvest could cause an immediate plunge in prices, while prices in the futures market, which anticipate conditions further down the road, could rise.

CORPORATE BOND TABLES

Although corporate bond tables give you valuable insight into a key financial market, they present only part of the picture. While several thousand corporate bonds are traded on the New York and American stock exchanges, many more that are traded through broker/dealers do not appear in the tables of exchange-listed bonds. In addition, exchange-listed bonds traded in lots of 10 or more are also handled off the exchange. According to the Nine Bond Rule, only lots of nine or fewer must be sent to the exchange floor.

Nevertheless, these tables are important because they (1) give you specific information about bonds you may own or are considering buying and (2) indicate the prevailing yields, which can help you estimate the value of similar bonds that you may have in your portfolio or are considering buying.

The table listings look like this:

CORPORATE BONDS

①	②	③	④	⑤
Bonds	**Current Yield**	**Sales in $1,000**	**Last**	**Net Chg.**
ABZ $10^7/_805$	8.9	20	122	$-^1/_2$
MXY $9^1/_806$	10.0	411	$91^1/_8$	$+^1/_4$
KLO 5.60s99	5.6	7	$99^{21}/_{32}$	$-^3/_{32}$
STU Zr12	...	3	384	...
WVX 8s03	cv	81	41	+1

The accompanying typical bond table presents information as follows:

1. The company abbreviations may vary from the abbreviations used in the stock tables. Also included in this column is the annual interest each bond pays, expressed as a percentage of the par or face value. Most corporate bonds are available in $1000 denominations (though prices are quoted in $100 units), which would mean that ABZ's $10^7/_8$ payout would total $100.875 annually. Where a rate cannot be expressed as a fraction, decimals are used, for example, 5.60 for KLO. The annual interest rate is also referred to as the coupon. Noninterest-paying zero coupon securities are identified by a "zr," as with STU here. The last two numbers in the name cluster represent the year in which the bonds will mature—05 for 2005, 99 for 1999. Among the qualifiers that may also appear after the name is "f," meaning that the bond is trading flat or without accrued interest, and that an interest payment has been missed.

2. The current yield represents the annual interest payment as a percentage of the last closing price. It provides a comparison with yields for other types of investments. In the case of convertible bonds, or convertibles, where prices, and therefore yields, are governed by movements in the underlying shares, no yield is given. Instead, "cv" is inserted in the yield column to indicate that this is a convertible issue. Of course, no yield is given with zero coupon bonds either.

3. This is volume on the exchange, expressed in sales of $1000 bonds, which is the normal corporate bond denomination. Events—

mergers, earnings news, and so on—can cause volume surges, especially in the case of the convertibles. The amount of volume will tell you how liquid the bonds are.

4. The last sale, in terms of $100 units. Multiply by 10 to get the price per $1000 bond. Prices are quoted as a percentage of par value, as though the face value was $100, not $1000. For example, a $1000 face value bond sold at 81 1/4 actually sold at $812.50.

5. The net change indicates the gain or loss since the previous close, expressed as a percentage of par. Therefore, the + 1/4 gain for MXY translates into 25 cents per $100 face value, or $2.50 per $1000 bond. The –1/2 for ABZ indicates a $5 loss for $1000 bond. Price changes reflect changes in interest rates. If bond prices have dropped it means interest rates probably rose, and vice versa.

You should also be familiar with the following information, which is not included in the corporate bond tables:

Ratings   These indicate the risk of default by the issuer on payments of interest or principal. The major bond rating agencies are Duff & Phelps/MCM, Fitch Investor's Service, Moody's Investors Service, and Standard & Poor's Corporation.

Denominations   Not all bonds are available in denominations of $1000. Some, called baby bonds, are denominated in amounts of $500 or less.

Yield to maturity   This represents the return, including both the annual interest payments and the gain or loss realized when the bonds are redeemed, taking into account the timing of payments and the time value of money. Yield to maturity will vary depending on whether you bought the bonds at a discount or a premium in relation to their face value, and with the time remaining to maturity. This type of yield calculation allows you to more easily compare bonds with other types of fixed income investments.

Payment dates   Interest payments on corporate bonds are usually, but not always, made semiannually. In any case, the payment cycles vary.

Callability   If a bond can be redeemed prior to maturity by the issuer, it will most likely be called when rates decline and conditions are favorable to the issuer. For this reason, another yield calculation, yield to call, can have more significance than yield to maturity.

GOVERNMENT SECURITIES TABLES

There's no uniform method of quoting the prices of government securities. In addition, the methods of presenting the values of these bills, notes, and bonds are sometimes as obscure as these markets once were to general investors. Because of the numbers of investors who are now familiar with these markets, however, it's worthwhile for you to know how to extract information from these tables.

Treasury Bills

These obligations—or IOUs—of the U.S. Treasury, are backed by the full faith and credit of the U.S. government. They always mature within one year (3 months, 6 months, 9 months and one year), and are included in many major daily newspapers in the form used in the accompanying table. Information is provided as follows.

TREASURY BILLS

① Date	② Bid	③ Asked	④ Chg	⑤ Ask Yield
Aug 20, 1998	5.02	4.98	+0.01	5.05

1. This is the date on which the bills mature. The maturity date distinguishes one bill from another.

2. The bid is the price dealers were willing to pay late (there is never an official end) in the last trading session. A bid is presented in a way you may find confusing. It's the discount from the face value demanded by dealers, expressed as an annual percentage. The reason for this is that Treasury bills do not pay interest in the usual sense. Instead, you pay less than the face value of the bills, but you receive the full value when the bills mature. The difference equals the interest you would receive. Thus, if you pay $9000 for a one-year $10,000 bill ($10,000 is the minimum size for a Treasury bill), you're paying 10% less than par, or buying the bill at a 10% discount. A bid of 10 would appear in the table. The higher the discount, the lower the price.

3. The asked price is the price the dealer is willing to accept, again expressed as an annualized percentage discount rate. In these tables, the percentages are carried out to the nearest hundredth, or basis point. Note that the dealer demands a smaller discount—a higher price—when he resells the bonds.

4. The change indicates how much the bid discount rate rose or fell during the session. A plus change actually represents a drop in prices, because it indicates an increased discount from par. Just as a larger discount on merchandise in a store window signifies lower prices, so the +0.01, or one basis point, indicates an increase in the discount. A minus change means that Treasury bill prices have risen and that the discount rate—and often other types of yields and rates—has dropped.

5. The yield represents a yield to maturity, based on the price you would actually pay for the Treasury bill, rather than its face value. The 10% discount rate tells you that you would pay 10% less than $10,000—or $9000 for a one year Treasury bill, for a difference—representing interest—of $1000. The actual yield, however, is better expressed in terms of the amount you would really pay for this investment—$9000. In addition, a return of $1000 on a $9000 investment is greater than the 10% discount rate; it's an 11.11% yield. Note that the yield shown in the sample table, 5.05, is higher than the 5.02 discount rate bid shown in column 2.

Treasury Notes and Bonds

Treasury note and bond prices are included in the same tables. The only difference is that the notes, designated by an "n" or a "p," mature in from one to ten years after they are issued, while bonds mature in ten years or longer. These tables present the securities in the order of their maturity dates, with the closest maturity date at the top and the furthest (always the much-quoted government long bond) at the bottom. Notice the increase in yields as the period of maturity increases; this reflects the fact that lenders demand a greater return for locking up their money for longer time periods. As with other government bonds, prices are given as dealer bid and asked quotes, not in terms of last sales. The reason for this is that there is no way for the extensive network of government bond dealers to report transaction prices and amounts in order to register them onto a last-sale "tape." Extra care must be taken in reading the bid and asked quotes because the two digits following the decimal points are 32nds rather than hundredths, reflecting the traditional language of the government bond market.

The information on a typical daily table is as follows:

TREASURY BONDS

①	②	③	④	⑤	⑥
					Ask
Rate	**Date**	**Bid**	**Asked**	**Chg.**	**Yield**
$6^1/4$	Jan 02 n	102:17	102:19	−2	5.41
$12^3/8$	May 04	133:15	133:21	−5	5.46
$7^7/8$	Nov 02–07	109:00	109:02	−4	5.45
$6^1/2$	Nov 26	111:11	111:15	−5	5.68

1. The rate is the coupon rate, or the annual interest rate, expressed as a percentage of the face value ($1000 minimum denominations for bonds and $1000 or $5000 for notes).

2. The date identifies the note or bond by its month and year of maturity; thus an "02" means 2002, a "26" means 2026. In addition, an "n" signifies a note. When the maturity figure consists of two years, such as the 02-07 in this table, the second year (2007 here) represents the maturity, while the first year (2002 here) indicates that the bonds could be repaid early, beginning in 2002. Such capability is rare with Treasury securities; it is found only in the final five years of certain 30-year bond issues.

3. The bid is the price dealers were offering to pay late in the session. It's presented as a percentage of face value. Note, however, that the two digits following the colon are 32nds, not tenths or hundredths. The 102:17 bid for the Jan 02 notes equals $102^{17}/_{32}$. Because 1/32% of $1000 is $31^1/4$ cents, $^{17}/_{32}$ equals $5.31; the total bid, per $1000 of notes, equals 1025.31^1/4$.

4. The asked, the price at which dealers are offering to sell the securities, is calculated similarly to the bid.

5. The daily change from two previous sessions to yesterday's session is based on the rise or fall of the bid price.

6. This figure represents yield to maturity, which combines your current yield (the percentage return in interest based on the price you actually pay) and the difference between the price you paid and the face value at redemption.

Government Agency Bonds

Securities of U.S. agencies such as the Federal Home Loan Bank and Government National Mortgage Association that appear in *The Wall Street Journal* and *The New York Times* use the same type of bid and asked quotes, expressed in 32nds of a percent, as appear in the Treasury note and bond tables.

Municipal Bonds

You probably won't find municipal bond prices in the financial pages. Even major financial publications include only a sampling of revenue bonds—those repaid from the income of a particular project rather than from general tax dollars. Such tables, typically headed Tax-exempt Authority Bonds, include the issuer's name, maturity date, the bid, the asked, and the daily change in the bid. Information on general obligation bonds is even harder to find. One way of approximating the value of your holdings, though, is to look at yields on newly issued bonds as revealed in tombstone ads placed by underwriters or in the short lists of new issues some papers provide. If the yields on new issues are lower than those your municipals are earning, your bonds are probably selling above face value and vice-versa, assuming the bonds are comparable in terms of quality and type of issuer.

MUTUAL FUNDS TABLES

Mutual fund prices are listed several ways in newspapers. Prices of a fund offered by an open-end management company that invests in long-term securities either stocks or bonds—change with changes in market segments or the market as a whole. These funds sell and redeem their own shares. Large newspapers generally list these prices under the heading Mutual Funds.

MUTUAL FUNDS

①	②	③	④
	NAV	**Buy**	**Chg.**
ABZ Grp:			
Genrl Fd	14.38	NL	+ .03
AB Growth	10.50	11.03	+ .01
ABZ Incm	5.22	NL	+ .02
Tax Ex	8.21	NL	− .01

These tables contain the following information, by column:

1. The names of mutual funds are clustered by family of funds— funds sponsored by a particular management company. The names often reflect the type of investments that comprise each fund; for example, a general stock fund, growth stock fund, income fund, or tax-exempt bond fund.

Some fund names are followed by lowercase letters such as "a" (meaning a stock dividend was paid in the past 12 months), "d" (new 52-week low), "f" (quotation refers to previous day), "r" (redemption charge may apply), "u" (new 52-week high), and "x" (fund is trading ex-dividend).

2. NAV stands for net asset value, the per-share value of the fund's assets, minus management costs. This is the amount you would receive, per share, if you redeemed your shares. The numbers indicate dollars and cents per share. Sometimes the column carries the heading

Sell, meaning that you would receive this amount per share if you were the seller.

3. The Buy column may also be headed Offer Price. It tells you, in dollars and cents per share, the price per share, the price you would pay to buy the shares. Funds that carry a sales charge, or front end load, cost more per share than their net asset value. Funds with back end loads discourage withdrawals by charging a fee to redeem your shares. Many funds, however, carry no sales charge; these are no-load funds whose buy-in costs are the same as their net asset values. These funds carry an "NL" or just "n" in the Buy column.

4. Change refers to the daily change in net asset value, determined at the close of each trading day.

Share prices of a fund offered by a closed-end management company, which issues a fixed number of shares that are then traded among investors, are often included in the daily stock tables. Some newspapers also provide weekly tables listing the prices and values of the shares as of the previous day's close-of-the-market.

CLOSED-END FUNDS

①	②	③	④
	N.A. Value	Stk Price	% Diff
Diversified funds			
ABZ Fund	17.55	21¹/₂	+ 3.1
WXY Fund	10.81	11³/₈	− 1.8
ZBF Fund	24.74	20¹/₂	− 5.0
Specialized Equity and Convertible Funds			
ABZ Gold	33.10	33¹/₂	+ 2.2
XYZ Conv	15.77	16	+ 1.6
XYZ Tech	9.97	10¹/₈	− 4.4

1. Fund names are grouped alphabetically by fund type.

2. Net Asset Values, as of the last close (unless otherwise indicated) are listed in terms of dollars and cents per share.

3. Stock prices are the last close.

4. Percent difference represents the weekly rise or fall of the net asset value of the shares.

Listings of shares of dual purpose funds can be found in stock exchange tables. These closed-end funds have two classes of shares. One class entitles shareholders to capital gains based on the market value of the assets. The other class entitles holders to dividend and interest income from the fund. Some major newspapers also carry weekly tables of the per share prices of the capital shares, the net asset value of the capital shares, and the weekly percentage or loss of price of those shares. These tables are useful because the daily stock tables don't include net asset values.

Tables for money market funds appear weekly, usually Thursday, after the release of data by Donoghue's money fund average or the National Association of Securities Dealers. Some newspapers print the tables again on Sunday. If you need information on a money market fund before Thursday, you can call the fund organizations. Many fund groups have toll-free 800 phone numbers for shareholders. Most investors need no more than weekly updates because per share values should remain constant at $1.00. These funds, which invest in short-term debt instruments, often are bought because they are liquid (most allow check-writing) and the yield fluctuates with short-term interest rates. Market movements and the accompanying capital gains and losses don't play a major role in the decision to buy or sell shares. The yield is the main information included in such tables.

MONEY MARKET FUNDS

①	②	③	④	⑤
Fund	**Assets ($ million)**	**Average maturity (days)**	**7-day average yield (%)**	**Effective 7-day average yield (%)**
ABzz Safety Fst	344.7	20	5.61	5.90
Blxx Liquid Secs	1,343.9	26	5.57	5.73
Xymo Govt. Fund	299.0	22	4.11	4.46

The accompanying table includes the following information, by column:

1. Name of the money-market fund.

2. Assets are stated in millions of dollars, to the nearest $100,000. These figures indicate the size of the fund. Investors constantly debate the advantages and disadvantages of size.

3. The average maturity figure represents how long, on average, it takes for the securities in a money fund's portfolio to mature. Shorter average maturities mean that the fund's yield will react more quickly to general interest-rate changes in the fixed-income securities market. This is beneficial when rates are rising, but disadvantageous when rates are dropping. In the latter case, you would want your fund to hold onto higher-yielding securities as long as possible. The move in the average maturity figure is considered by some to be a good predictor of short-term interest rate direction. If a fund's average maturity increases by several days for several weeks, this is an indication that portfolio managers expect short-term rates to drop. If the average maturity decreases, the managers probably expect short-term rates to rise.

4. The 7-day average yield indicates the average daily total return for that period, and is determined largely by subtracting the fund's costs from the investment income. The result is expressed as a percentage of the average share price:

5. The effective 7-day average yield is the 7-day average yield computed after assuming that the rate continues for a year and that dividends are reinvested. This permits comparison with other instruments whose yields are expressed on the same basis, such as bank certificates of deposit.

OTHER TABLES

Interest and currency rates

The key rates highlighted in the Markets Diary discussed earlier are followed
up with more detailed summaries throughout the inside pages.

A complete rate and yield table. for example, would additionally list, with comparisons to the previous day and year ago, the (Federal Reserve) discount rate and
the prime rate, whose significance we have already discussed. It might also list yields
on 7-year Treasury notes, an important benchmark for intermediate-term corporate
and other non-Treasury fixed-income obligations; yields on 30-year Treasury bonds,
the ultimate indicator of the entire bond market and often of the stock market, where
prices normally move inversely to "long bond" yields; and "telephone" bonds,
top-rated obligations of phone companies or other public utilities whose yield is a
direct benchmark for other corporate bonds that are riskier to varying degrees. Major
newspapers also carry additional lists of rates that are mainly of interest to professional traders. Some, like Eurodollar time deposits, the London Interbank Offered
Rate (LIBOR), and commercial paper, were discussed above. Others include
banker's acceptances, which are time drafts created in commerce, accepted (guaranteed, in effect) by major banks, and traded as money market instruments; and the
broker loan rate (or call loan rate), which is the rate banks charge brokers for
overnight loans to cover securities positions of customers. This rate, which usually
hovers just above the rate on (also overnight) federal funds, has meaning to individual investors because it determines what brokers charge on margin loans.

Many financial newspapers and other media now carry weekly listings of the
banks currently offering the highest interest rates on deposit accounts and certificates of deposit.

The meaning and importance of currency exchange rates was discussed earlier.
In addition to highlighting major currency changes, most major financial papers
carry full exchange tables, listed alphabetically by country, which provide the
exchange rates from the previous two days in four columns—two in terms of dollars per unit of foreign currency, two in terms of units of foreign currency per dollar. Major currencies also list 30-, 90-, and 180-day forward rates. These represent
guaranteed future delivery rates offered by banks for customers who must plan
ahead and are willing to pay a premium to eliminate the risk of exchange rates
moving adversely in the interim.

Some papers, including *The Wall Street Journal,* contain a table showing key
currency cross rates. This table lists currencies in terms of each other's value.
Complete currency sections also cover futures, options, and futures options on
leading currencies.

HOW TO READ TICKER TAPES

With the growth of cable television, an increasing number of investors pick up financial news from cablecasters that cover the securities and commodities markets continuously throughout the business day. Like daily newspapers, the purveyors of electronic financial news aim for a broad audience. Through the creative use of graphics and commentary, they manage generally to communicate complex information in a way nonprofessionals can understand.

But unless you work for an investment firm or spend your leisure time sitting around a board room of a brokerage, the figures and symbols that pass constantly—sometimes with maddening rapidity—across the lower portion of the TV screen may require explanation. What you see there is the stock ticker tape, the same report of trading activity displayed on the floors of the major stock exchanges. The only difference is that to give stock exchange members an advantage, it is transmitted with a 15-minute delay.

The most frequently seen display is the consolidated tape, a combination of two networks (not to be confused with television networks): Network A reports all New York Stock Exchange issues traded on the NYSE or other identified markets, which include five regional exchanges, the over-the-counter market, and other markets, such as Instinet, a computerized market in which large institutional blocks are traded. Network B reports all American Stock Exchange issues traded on the Amex or other identified markets. National Association of Securities Dealers (NASDAQ) over-the-counter quotes are presented separately in the lower band.

Elements of the consolidated tape; which reports actual transactions (the term quotes is loosely used to mean trades in ticker tape jargon, although its proper financial meaning refers to bid and asked quotations) are explained as follows:

Stock Symbol The first letters are the stock ticker symbol—XON for Exxon, CCI for Citicorp. IBM for IBM, for example. (There is one exception to this, which is that the prefix Q is used when a company is in receivership or bankruptcy.) The ticker symbol may be followed by an abbreviation designating a type of issue, such as Pr to signify preferred stock, which may, in turn, be followed by a letter indicating a class of preferred. Thus XYZPrE means XYZ Corporation's preferred stock series E. If XYZ's preferred stock series E was convertible, the abbreviation .CV would be added to read XYZPrE.CV. Common stock classes, if any, are indicated by a period plus a letter following the ticker symbol. Thus XYZ's class B common would be designated XYZ.B. (A list of ticker symbols is included at the end of Part V of this book.)

Other abbreviations placed after the ticker symbol as necessary are rt for rights; wi for when issued; .WD for when distributed; .WS for warrants (the abbreviation may be preceded by another period and letter to identify the particular issue of warrant); and .XD for ex-dividend.

Market Identifiers When the information about the stock is followed by an ampersand (&) and a letter, the transaction took place in a market other than the New York Stock Exchange, if you are looking at Network A, or the American Stock Exchange, if you are looking at Network B. The letter identifies the market as follows:

A   American Stock Exchange
B   Boston Stock Exchange
C   Cincinnati Stock Exchange
M   Midwest Stock Exchange
N   New York Stock Exchange
O   Other Markets (mainly Instinet)
P   Pacific Stock Exchange
T   Third market (mainly NASDAQ)
X   Philadelphia Stock Exchange

Volume   The next portion of the transaction information provided on a ticker tape may appear below or to the right of the above stock symbol and market designation. It reports the number of shares traded. However, if the trade is in a round lot of 100 shares, which it usually is, no volume is indicated and the tape simply shows the issue and the price. Thus XYZ 26$^1/_2$ simply means that 100 shares of XYZ were traded at 26.50 a share. Where larger round lot transactions take place, the number of round lots is indicated followed by the letter "s" followed by the price. Thus, XYZ 4 s 26$^1/_2$ means 400 shares were traded at $26.50 a share. Similarly, 1700 shares would be XYZ 17 s 26$^1/_2$ and so on, except that when the volume is 10,000 shares or more the full number is given—XYZ 16,400 s 26$^1/_2$, for example.

Odd lots quantities other than multiples of 100 or whatever other unit represents the round lot—are not printed on the ticker tape unless approved by an exchange official. If approval is given, odd lots of 50 shares and 150 shares of XYZ would be displayed respectively: XYZ 50 SHRS 26$^1/_2$ and XYZ 150 SHRS 26$^1/_2$.

A limited number of issues—mainly inactive stocks or higher priced preferred issues—trade in round lots of less than 100 shares. On the New York Stock Exchange such round lots are always 10 shares, but on the Amex these round lots can be 10, 25, or 50 shares. Transactions in these special round lots are designated by a number indicating how many lots were traded followed by the symbols. Thus, on the New York Stock Exchange, XYZ Pr 3 ^s_s55 means 3 10-share lots (30 shares) of XYZ preferred stock were traded at $55 a share. If XYZ were listed on the Amex, you would not know by looking at the tape whether the lot involved was 10, 25, or 50 shares. For that information, you would have to consult a stock guide.

Active Market Procedures   When trading becomes sufficiently heavy to cause the tape to run more than a minute behind, shortcuts are implemented. The most frequently taken measure to keep up with heavy trading is signified by the tape printout DIGITS AND VOLUME DELETED. This means only the unit price digit and fraction will be printed (for example, 9$^1/_2$ instead of 19$^1/_2$) except when the price ends in zero or is an opening transaction. In addition, volume information will be deleted except when trades are 5000 shares or more (the threshold can be raised if required). Another common procedure is to announce REPEAT PRICES OMITTED, meaning that successive transactions at the same price will not be repeated. A third measure is MINIMUM PRICE CHANGES OMITTED, meaning trades will not be displayed unless the price difference exceeds $^1/_8$ of a point. The second and third measures do not apply to opening transactions or to trades of 5000 shares or more. When activity slackens to a more normal level, the tape will read DIGITS AND VOLUME RESUMED with similar indications for the other measures.

Other Abbreviations   When a transaction is being reported out of its proper order, the letters .SLD will follow the symbol as in XYZ .SLD 3s 26$^1/_2$. SLR followed by a number signifies seller's option and number of days until settlement. This indication is found after the price. CORR indicates that a correction of information follows. ERR or CXL indicates a print is to be ignored. OPD signifies an opening transaction that was delayed or one whose price is significantly changed from the previous day's close.

PART IV

Dictionary of Finance and Investment

HOW TO USE THIS DICTIONARY EFFECTIVELY

Alphabetization: All entries are alphabetized by letter rather than by word so that multiple-word terms are treated as single words. For example, **NET ASSET VALUE** follows **NET ASSETS** as though it were spelled **NETASSETVALUE,** without spacing. Similarly, **ACCOUNT EXECUTIVE** follows **ACCOUNTANT'S OPINION.** In unusual cases, abbreviations or acronyms appear as entries in the main text, in addition to appearing in the back of the book in the separate listing of Abbreviations and Acronyms. This is when the short form, rather than the formal name, predominates in common business usage. For example, NASDAQ is more commonly used in speaking of the National Association of Securities Dealers Automated Quotations system than the name itself, so the entry is at **NASDAQ.** Numbers in entry titles are alphabetized as if they were spelled out.

Abbreviations and Acronyms: A separate list of abbreviations and acronyms follows the Dictionary. It contains shortened versions of terms defined in the book, plus several hundred related business terms.

Cross references: In order to gain a fuller understanding of a term, it will sometimes help to refer to the definition of another term. In these cases the additional term is printed in SMALL CAPITALS. Such cross references appear in the body of the definition or at the end of the entry (or sub-entry). Cross references at the end of an entry (or sub-entry) may refer to related or contrasting concepts rather than give more information about the concept under discussion. As a rule, a term is printed in small capitals only the first time it appears in an entry. Where an entry is fully defined at another entry, a reference rather than a definition is provided; for example, **EITHER-OR ORDER** *see* ALTERNATIVE ORDER.

Italics: Italic type is generally used to indicate that another term has a meaning identical or very closely related to that of the entry. Occasionally, italic type is also used to highlight the fact that a word used is a business term and not just a descriptive phrase. Italics are also used for the titles of publications.

Parentheses: Parentheses are used in entry titles for two reasons. The first is to indicate that an entry's opposite is such an integral part of the concept that only one discussion is necessary; for example, **REALIZED PROFIT (OR LOSS).** The second and more common reason is to indicate that an abbreviation is used with about the same frequency as the term itself; for example, **OVER THE COUNTER (OTC).**

Examples, Illustrations, and Tables: The numerous examples in this Dictionary are designed to help readers gain understanding and to help them relate abstract concepts to the real world of finance and investment. Line drawings are provided in addition to text to clarify concepts best understood visually; for example, technical chart patterns used by securities analysts and graphic concepts used in financial analysis. Tables supplement definitions where essential detail is more effectively condensed and expressed in tabular form; for example, components of the U.S. money supply.

a

ABANDONMENT voluntarily giving up all rights, title, or claims to property that rightfully belongs to the owner. An example of abandoned property would be stocks, bonds, or mutual funds held in a brokerage account for which the firm is unable to locate the listed owner over a specified period of time, usually a few years. If ruled to be abandoned, the property may revert to the state under the laws of ESCHEAT. In addition to financial assets, other kinds of property that are subject to abandonment include patents, inventions, leases, trademarks, contracts, and copyrights.

ABC AGREEMENT agreement between a brokerage firm and one of its employees spelling out the firm's rights when it purchases a New York Stock Exchange membership for the employee. Only individuals can be members of the NYSE, and it is common practice for a firm to finance the purchase of a membership, or SEAT, by one of its employees. The NYSE-approved ABC Agreement contains the following provisions regarding the future disposition of the seat: (1) The employee may retain the membership and buy another seat for an individual designated by the firm. (2) The employee may sell the seat and give the proceeds to the firm. (3) The employee may transfer the seat to another employee of the firm.

ABILITY TO PAY
Finance: borrower's ability to meet principal and interest payments on long-term obligations out of earnings. Also called *ability to service. See also* FIXED-CHARGE COVERAGE.
Industrial relations: ability of an employer, especially a financial organization to meet a union's financial demands from operating income.
Municipal bonds: issuer's present and future ability to generate enough tax revenue to meet its contractual obligations, taking into account all factors concerned with municipal income and property values.
Taxation: the concept that tax rates should vary with levels of wealth or income; for example, the progressive income tax.

ABOVE PAR *see* PAR VALUE.

ABS *see* AUTOMATED BOND SYSTEM.

ABSOLUTE PRIORITY RULE *see* BANKRUPTCY.

ABSORBED
Business: a cost that is treated as an expense rather than passed on to a customer.
Also, a firm merged into an acquiring company.
Cost accounting: indirect manufacturing costs (such as property taxes and insurance) are called absorbed costs. They are differentiated from variable costs (such as direct labor and materials). *See also* DIRECT OVERHEAD.
Finance: an account that has been combined with related accounts in preparing a financial statement and has lost its separate identity. Also called *absorption account* or *adjunct account.*
Securities: issue that an underwriter has completely sold to the public.
Also, in market trading, securities are absorbed as long as there are corresponding orders to buy and sell. The market has reached the *absorption point* when further assimilation is impossible without an adjustment in price. *See also* UNDIGESTED SECURITIES.

ABUSIVE TAX SHELTER LIMITED PARTNERSHIP the Internal Revenue Service deems to be claiming illegal tax deductions—typically, one that inflates the value of acquired property beyond its fair market value. If these writeoffs are denied by the IRS, investors must pay severe penalties and interest charges, on top of back taxes.

ACCELERATED COST RECOVERY SYSTEM (ACRS) provision instituted by the ECONOMIC RECOVERY TAX ACT OF 1981 (ERTA) and modified by the TAX REFORM ACT OF 1986, which established rules for the DEPRECIATION (the recovery of cost through tax deductions) of qualifying assets within a shorter period than the asset's expected useful (economic) life. With certain exceptions, ACRS rules provided for greater acceleration over longer periods of time than ERTA rules, and were effective for property placed in service between 1980 and 1987.
    See also MODIFIED ACCELERATED COST RECOVERY SYSTEM.

ACCELERATED DEPRECIATION Internal Revenue Service-approved methods used in the DEPRECIATION of fixed assets placed in service prior to 1980 when the ACCELERATED COST RECOVERY SYSTEM (ACRS) became mandatory. Such methods provided for faster recovery of cost and earlier tax advantages than traditional STRAIGHT-LINE DEPRECIATION and included such methods as DOUBLE-DECLINING BALANCE METHOD (now used in some ACRS classes) and SUM-OF-THE-YEARS' DIGITS METHOD.

ACCELERATION CLAUSE provision, normally present in an INDENTURE agreement, mortgage, or other contract, that the unpaid balance is to become due and payable if specified events of default should occur. Such events include failure to meet interest, principal, or sinking fund payments; insolvency; and nonpayment of taxes on mortgaged property.

ACCEPTANCE
    In general: agreement created when the drawee of a TIME DRAFT (bill of exchange) writes the word "accepted" above the signature and designates a date of payment. The drawee becomes the acceptor, responsible for payment at maturity.
    Also, paper issued and sold by sales finance companies, such as General Motors Acceptance Corporation.
    Banker's acceptance: time draft drawn on and accepted by a bank, the customary means of effecting payment for merchandise sold in import-export transactions and a source of financing used extensively in international trade. With the credit strength of a bank behind it, the banker's acceptance usually qualifies as a MONEY MARKET instrument. The liability assumed by the bank is called its acceptance liability. *See also* LETTER OF CREDIT.
    Trade acceptance: time draft drawn by the seller of goods on the buyer, who becomes the acceptor, and which is therefore only as good as the buyer's credit.

ACCOMMODATIVE MONETARY POLICY Federal Reserve policy to increase the amount of money available for lending by banks. When the Fed implements an accommodative policy, it is known as easing the money supply. During a period of easing, interest rates fall, making it more attractive for borrowers to borrow, thereby stimulating the economy. The Fed will initiate an accommodative policy when interest rates are high, the economy is weak, and there is little fear of an outbreak of inflation. Once interest rates have been lowered enough to stimulate the economy, the Fed may become concerned about inflation again and switch to a TIGHT MONEY policy. *See also* MONETARY POLICY.

ACCOUNT
    In general: contractual relationship between a buyer and seller under which payment is made at a later time. The term *open account* or *charge account* is used, depending on whether the relationship is commercial or personal.
    Also, the historical record of transactions under the contract, as periodically shown on the *statement of account.*

Banking: relationship under a particular name, usually evidenced by a deposit against which withdrawals can be made. Among them are demand, time, custodial, joint, trustee, corporate, special, and regular accounts. Administrative responsibility is handled by an *account officer.*

Bookkeeping: assets, liabilities, income, and expenses as represented by individual ledger pages to which debit and credit entries are chronologically posted to record changes in value. Examples are cash, accounts receivable, accrued interest, sales, and officers' salaries. The system of recording, verifying, and reporting such information is called accounting. Practitioners of accounting are called *accountants.*

Investment banking: financial and contractual relationship between parties to an underwriting syndicate, or the status of securities owned and sold.

Securities: relationship between a broker-dealer firm and its client wherein the firm, through its registered representatives, acts as agent in buying and selling securities and sees to related administrative matters. *See also* ACCOUNT EXECUTIVE; ACCOUNT STATEMENT.

ACCOUNTANT'S OPINION statement signed by an independent public accountant describing the scope of the examination of an organization's books and records. Because financial reporting involves considerable discretion, the accountant's opinion is an important assurance to a lender or investor. Depending on the scope of an audit and the auditor's confidence in the veracity of the information, the opinion can be unqualified or, to some degree, qualified. Qualified opinions, though not necessarily negative, warrant investigation. Also called *auditor's certificate.*

ACCOUNT BALANCE net of debits and credits at the end of a reporting period. Term applies to a variety of account relationships, such as with banks, credit card companies, brokerage firms, and stores, and to classifications of transactions in a bookkeeping system. The same account may be an asset account balance or a liability account balance, depending on which side of the transaction you are on. For example, your bank balance is an asset account to you and a liability account to the bank. Your credit card (debit) balance is a liability account to you and an asset account (account receivable) to the credit card company.

ACCOUNT EXECUTIVE brokerage firm employee who advises and handles orders for clients and has the legal powers of an AGENT. Every account executive must pass certain tests and be registered with the NATIONAL ASSOCIATION OF SECURITIES DEALERS (NASD) before soliciting orders from customers. Also called *registered representative. See also* BROKER.

ACCOUNTING PRINCIPLES BOARD (APB) board of the American Institute of Certified Public Accountants (AICPA) that issued (1959–73) a series of ACCOUNTANT'S OPINIONS constituting much of what is known as GENERALLY ACCEPTED ACCOUNTING PRINCIPLES. *See also* FINANCIAL ACCOUNTING STANDARDS BOARD (FASB).

ACCOUNT RECONCILIATION the process of adjusting the balance in your checkbook to match your bank statement. Your checkbook balance, plus outstanding checks, less bank charges, plus interest (if any), should equal the balance shown on your bank statement.

ACCOUNTS PAYABLE amounts owing on open account to creditors for goods and services. Analysts look at the relationship of accounts payable to purchases for indications of sound day-to-day financial management. *See also* TRADE CREDIT.

ACCOUNTS RECEIVABLE money owed to a business for merchandise or services sold on open account, a key factor in analyzing a company's LIQUIDITY—

its ability to meet current obligations without additional revenues. *See also* ACCOUNTS RECEIVABLE TURNOVER; AGING SCHEDULE; COLLECTION RATIO.

ACCOUNTS RECEIVABLE FINANCING short-term financing whereby accounts receivable serve as collateral for working capital advances. *See also* FACTORING.

ACCOUNTS RECEIVABLE TURNOVER ratio obtained by dividing total credit sales by accounts receivable. The ratio indicates how many times the receivables portfolio has been collected during the accounting period. *See also* ACCOUNTS RECEIVABLE; AGING SCHEDULE; COLLECTION RATIO.

ACCOUNT STATEMENT
In general: any record of transactions and their effect on charge or open-account balances during a specified period.
Banking: summary of all checks paid, deposits recorded, and resulting balances during a defined period. Also called a *bank statement.*
Securities: statement summarizing all transactions and showing the status of an account with a broker-dealer firm, including long and short positions. Such statements must be issued quarterly, but are generally provided monthly when accounts are active. Also, the OPTION AGREEMENT required when an option account is opened.

ACCREDITED INVESTOR under Securities and Exchange Commission Regulation D, a wealthy investor who does not count as one of the maximum of 35 people allowed to put money into a PRIVATE LIMITED PARTNERSHIP. To be accredited, such an investor must have a net worth of at least $1 million or an annual income of at least $200,000, or must put at least $150,000 into the deal, and the investment must not account for more than 20% of the investor's worth. Private limited partnerships use accredited investors to raise a larger amount of capital than would be possible if only 35 less-wealthy people could contribute.

ACCRETION
1. asset growth through internal expansion, acquisition, or such causes as aging of whisky or growth of timber.
2. adjustment of the difference between the price of a bond bought at an original discount and the par value of the bond.

ACCRUAL BASIS accounting method whereby income and expense items are recognized as they are earned or incurred, even though they may not have been received or actually paid in cash. The alternative is CASH BASIS accounting.

ACCRUAL BONDS bonds that do not make periodic interest payments, but instead accrue interest until the bond matures. Also known as *zero-coupon bonds. See also* ZERO-COUPON SECURITIES.

ACCRUED BENEFITS pension benefits that an employee has earned based on his or her years of service at a company. *See also* VESTING.

ACCRUED INTEREST interest that has accumulated between the most recent payment and the sale of a bond or other fixed-income security. At the time of sale, the buyer pays the seller the bond's price plus accrued interest, calculated by multiplying the coupon rate by the number of days that have elapsed since the last payment.

Accrued interest is also used in a real estate LIMITED PARTNERSHIP when the seller of a building takes a lump sum in cash at the time of sale and gives a second mortgage for the remainder. If the rental income from the building does not cover the mortgage payments, the seller agrees to let the interest accrue until the building is sold to someone else. Accrued interest deals were curtailed by the 1984 tax act.

ACCRUED MARKET DISCOUNT increase in market value of a DISCOUNT BOND that occurs because of its approaching MATURITY DATE (when it is redeemable at PAR) and not because of declining market interest rates.

ACCUMULATED DIVIDEND dividend due, usually to holders of cumulative preferred stock, but not paid. It is carried on the books as a liability until paid. *See also* CUMULATIVE PREFERRED.

ACCUMULATED PROFITS TAX surtax on earnings retained in a business to avoid the higher personal income taxes they would be subject to if paid out as dividends to the owners.

Accumulations above the specified limit, which is set fairly high to benefit small firms, must be justified by the reasonable needs of the business or be subject to the surtax. Because determining the reasonable needs of a business involves considerable judgment, companies have been known to pay excessive dividends or even to make merger decisions out of fear of the accumulated profits tax. Also called *accumulated earnings tax.*

ACCUMULATION
Corporate finance: profits that are not paid out as dividends but are instead added to the company's capital base. *See also* ACCUMULATED PROFITS TAX.
Investments: purchase of a large number of shares in a controlled way so as to avoid driving the price up. An institution's accumulation program, for instance, may take weeks or months to complete.
Mutual funds: investment of a fixed dollar amount regularly and reinvestment of dividends and capital gains.

ACCUMULATION AREA price range within which buyers accumulate shares of a stock. Technical analysts spot accumulation areas when a stock does not drop below a particular price. Technicians who use the ON-BALANCE VOLUME method of analysis advise buying stocks that have hit their accumulation area, because the stocks can be expected to attract more buying interest. *See* chart on next page. *See also* DISTRIBUTION AREA.

ACCUMULATION AREA

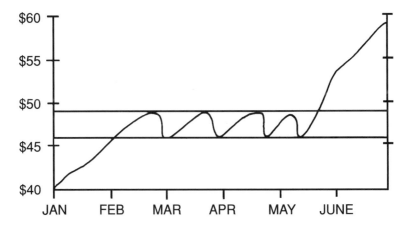

ACES acronym for *Advanced Computerized Execution System,* run by the NASDAQ stock market. ACES automates trades between order-entry and market-maker firms that have established trading relationships with each other, designating securities at specified quantities for automatic execution. Once trading parameters are set, ACES facilitates order entry, best-price order execution and limited-order maintenance, as well as a variety of inventory control capabilities. Trades are then automatically reported for public dissemination and sent for comparison and clearing.

ACID-TEST RATIO *See* QUICK RATIO.

ACKNOWLEDGMENT verification that a signature on a banking or brokerage document is legitimate and has been certified by an authorized person. Acknowledgment is needed when transferring an account from one broker to another, for instance. In banking, an acknowledgment verifies that an item has been received by the paying bank and is or is not available for immediate payment.

ACQUIRED SURPLUS uncapitalized portion of the net worth of a successor company in a POOLING OF INTERESTS combination. In other words, the part of the combined net worth not classified as CAPITAL STOCK.

In a more general sense, the surplus acquired when a company is purchased.

ACQUISITION one company taking over controlling interest in another company. Investors are always looking out for companies that are likely to be acquired, because those who want to acquire such companies are often willing to pay more than the market price for the shares they need to complete the acquisition. *See also* MERGER; POOLING OF INTERESTS; TAKEOVER.

ACQUISITION COST
Finance: price plus CLOSING COSTS to buy a company, real estate or other property.
Investments: SALES CHARGE incurred to buy a LOAD FUND or the original price, plus brokerage commissions, of a security. *See also* TAX BASIS.

ACROSS THE BOARD movement in the stock market that affects almost all stocks in the same direction. When the market moves up across the board, almost every stock gains in price.

An across-the-board pay increase in a company is a raise of a fixed percent or amount for all employees.

ACTING IN CONCERT two or more investors working together to achieve the same investment goal—for example, all buying stock in a company they want to take over. Such investors must inform the Securities and Exchange Commission if they intend to oust the company's top management or acquire control. It is illegal for those acting in concert to manipulate a stock's price for their own gain.

ACTIVE ACCOUNT account at a bank or brokerage firm in which there are many transactions. An active banking account may generate more fees for each check written or ATM transaction completed. An active brokerage account will generate more commission revenue for the brokerage firm than an inactive account. Banks usually impose minimum charges for maintaining a checking and savings account. Many brokerage firms levy a fee if an account does not generate a high enough level of activity. If there is no activity in an account for five years or more, the account may be subject to ESCHEAT procedures in which the account's assets revert to the state.

ACTIVE BOND CROWD members of the bond department of the New York Stock Exchange responsible for the heaviest volume of bond trading. The opposite of the active crowd is the CABINET CROWD, which deals in bonds that are infrequently traded. Investors who buy and sell bonds in the active crowd will tend to get better prices for their securities than in the inactive market, where spreads between bid and asked prices are wider.

ACTIVE BOX collateral available for securing brokers' loans or customers' margin positions in the place—or *box*—where securities are held in safekeeping for clients of a broker-dealer or for the broker-dealer itself. Securities used as collateral must be owned by the firm or hypothecated—that is, pledged or assigned— by the customer to the firm, then by the broker to the lending bank. For margin loans, securities must be hypothecated by the customer to the broker.

ACTIVE MARKET heavy volume of trading in a particular stock, bond, or commodity. The spread between bid and asked prices is usually narrower in an active market than when trading is quiet.

Also, a heavy volume of trading on the exchange as a whole. Institutional money managers prefer such a market because their trades of large blocks of stock tend to have less impact on the movement of prices when trading is generally active.

ACTUALS any physical commodity, such as gold, soybeans, or pork bellies. Trading in actuals ultimately results in delivery of the commodity to the buyer when the contract expires. This contrasts with trading in commodities of, for example, index options, where the contract is settled in cash, and no physical commodity is delivered upon expiration. However, even when trading is in actuals most futures and options contracts are closed out before the contract expires, and so these transactions do not end in delivery.

ACTUARY mathematician employed by an insurance company to calculate premiums, reserves, dividends, and insurance, pension, and annuity rates, using risk factors obtained from experience tables. These tables are based on both the company's history of insurance claims and other industry and general statistical data.

ADDITIONAL BONDS TEST test limiting the amount of new bonds that can be issued. Since bonds are secured by assets or revenues of a corporate or governmental entity, the underwriters of the bond must insure that the bond issuer can meet the debt service requirements of any additional bonds. The test usually sets specific financial benchmarks, such as what portion of an issuer's revenues or cash flow can be devoted to paying interest.

ADDITIONAL PAID-IN CAPITAL see PAID-IN CAPITAL.

ADDITIONAL VOLUNTARY CONTRIBUTIONS contributions made by an employee into a tax-deferred savings account, such as a 401(k) or 403(b), beyond the level at which an employer will match the investment. Depending on the level of contributions, these may be made on a pretax or aftertax basis. Tax law limits the total amount of money that can be contributed to such a tax-deferred account. In any case, all funds so contributed accumulate without taxation until withdrawn at retirement. The employee chooses the investment vehicles in which the money is invested.

ADEQUACY OF COVERAGE test of the extent to which the value of an asset, such as real property, securities, or a contract subject to currency exchange rates, is protected from potential loss either through INSURANCE or HEDGING.

ADJUSTABLE RATE MORTGAGE (ARM) mortgage agreement between a financial institution and a real estate buyer stipulating predetermined adjustments of the interest rate at specified intervals. Mortgage payments are tied to some index outside the control of the bank or savings and loan institution, such as the interest rates on U.S. Treasury bills or the average national mortgage rate. Adjustments are made regularly, usually at intervals of one, three, or five years. In return for taking some of the risk of a rise in interest rates, borrowers get lower rates at the beginning of the ARM than they would if they took out a fixed rate mortgage covering the same term. A homeowner who is worried about sharply rising interest rates should probably choose a fixed rate mortgage, whereas one who thinks rates will rise modestly, stay stable, or fall should choose an adjustable rate mortgage. Critics of ARMs charge that these mortgages entice young homeowners to undertake potentially onerous commitments. Also called a Variable Rate Mortgage (VRM), the ARM should not be confused with the GRADUATED PAYMENT MORTGAGE, which is issued at a fixed rate with monthly payments designed to increase as the borrower's income grows. *See also* CAP; COST OF FUNDS; GROWING EQUITY MORTGAGE; MORTGAGE INTEREST DEDUCTION; SELF-AMORTIZING MORTGAGE; SHARED APPRECIATION MORTGAGE; TEASER RATE.

ADJUSTABLE RATE PREFERRED STOCK (ARPS) PREFERRED STOCK, whose dividend instead of being fixed is adjusted, usually quarterly, based on changes in the Treasury bill rate or other money market rate. The prices of adjustable rate preferreds are less volatile than fixed rate preferreds. Also called *floating rate* or *variable rate* preferred. *See also* CAPS; DUTCH AUCTION PREFERRED STOCK; MANDATORY CONVERTIBLES.

ADJUSTED BALANCE METHOD formula for calculating finance charges based on ACCOUNT BALANCE remaining after adjusting for payments and credits posted during the billing period. Interest charges under this method are lower than those under the AVERAGE DAILY, PREVIOUS BALANCE, and PAST DUE BALANCE METHODS.

ADJUSTED BASIS base price from which to judge capital gains or losses upon sale of an asset like a stock or bond. The cost of commissions in effect is deducted at the time of sale when net proceeds are used for tax purposes. The price must be adjusted to account for any stock splits that have occurred since the initial purchase before arriving at the adjusted basis.

ADJUSTED DEBIT BALANCE (ADB) formula for determining the position of a margin account, as required under Regulation T of the Federal Reserve Board. The ADB is calculated by netting the balance owing the broker with any balance in the SPECIAL MISCELLANEOUS ACCOUNT (SMA), and any paper profits on short accounts. Although changes made in Regulation T in 1982 diminished the significance of ADBs, the formula is still useful in determining whether withdrawals of cash or securities are permissible based on SMA entries.

ADJUSTED EXERCISE PRICE term used in put and call options on Government National Mortgage Association (Ginnie Mae) contracts. To make sure that all contracts trade fairly, the final exercise price of the option is adjusted to take into account the coupon rates carried on all GNMA mortgages. If the standard GNMA mortgage carries an 8% yield, for instance, the price of GNMA pools with 12% mortgages in them are adjusted so that both instruments have the same yield to the investor.

ADJUSTED GROSS INCOME (AGI) income on which an individual or couple computes federal income tax. AGI is determined by subtracting from gross income any unreimbursed business expenses and other allowable adjustments— for example, INDIVIDUAL RETIREMENT ACCOUNTS, SEP and Keogh payments, and alimony payments. Other adjustments include: forfeiture of interest penalties because of premature withdrawals from a certificate of deposit; capital loss deductions up to $3,000; rent and royalty expenses; 50% of self-employed tax liability; health insurance deductions for the self-employed and net operating losses. AGI is the individual's or couple's income before itemized deductions such as medical expenses, state and local income taxes, and real estate taxes. Once AGI exceeds certain income thresholds detailed in the tax code, some itemized deductions are disallowed. For example, for those married couples filing jointly in 1997 with adjusted gross incomes over $121,200, itemized deductions are reduced by 3% of the excess of AGI, over $121,200. These thresholds are adjusted upwards annually.

ADJUSTMENT BOND bond issued in exchange for outstanding bonds when recapitalizing a corporation that faces bankruptcy. Authorization for the exchange comes from the bondholders, who consider adjustment bonds a lesser evil. These bonds promise to pay interest only to the extent earned by the corporation. This gives them one of the characteristics of income bonds, which trade flat—that is, without accrued interest.

ADMINISTRATOR court-appointed individual or bank charged with carrying out the court's decisions with respect to a decedent's estate until it is fully distributed to all claimants. Administrators are appointed when a person dies without having made a will or without having named an executor, or when the named executor cannot or will not serve. The term *administratrix* is sometimes used if the individual appointed is a woman.

In a general sense, an administrator is a person who carries out an organization's policies.

AD VALOREM Latin term meaning "according to value" and referring to a way of assessing duties or taxes on goods or property. As one example, ad valorem DUTY assessment is based on value of the imported item rather than on its weight or quantity. As another example, the city of Englewood, New Jersey, levies an ad valorem property tax based on the assessed value of property rather than its size.

ADVANCE
Employee benefits: cash given to an employee before it is needed or earned. A travel advance is supplied so that an employee has cash to use on an upcoming business trip. A salary advance is provided to help the employee cover emergency expenses.
Securities: increase in the price of stocks, bonds, commodities, or other assets. Often heard when referring to the movement of broad indexes, e.g., "The Dow Jones Industrials advanced 15 points today."
Trade: advance payment for goods or services that will be delivered in the near future. For example, home contractors require an advance from homeowners to pay for building materials.

ADVANCE-DECLINE (A-D) measurement of the number of stocks that have advanced and the number that have declined over a particular period. It is the ratio of one to the other and shows the general direction of the market. It is considered bullish if more stocks advance than decline on any trading day. It is bearish if declines outnumber advances. The steepness of the A-D line graphically shows whether a strong bull or bear market is underway.

ADVANCE-DECLINE LINE

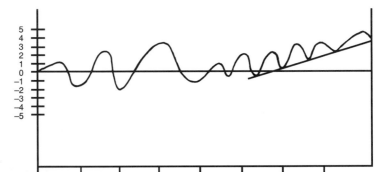

ADVANCED FUNDED PENSION PLAN pension plan under which assets are set aside in amounts and at times approximately coincident with the accruing of benefit rights. In this way, funds are set aside in advance of the date of retirement.

ADVANCE REFUNDING

Government securities: exchange of maturing government securities prior to their due date for issues with a later maturity. It is through advance refunding that the national debt is extended as an alternative to the economic disruptions that would result from eliminating the debt all at once.

Municipal bonds: sale of new bonds (the refunding issue) in advance, usually by some years, of the first call date of the old bonds (the issue to be refunded). The refunding issue would normally have a lower rate than the issue to be refunded, and the proceeds would be invested, usually in government securities, until the higher-rate bonds become callable. This practice, also called *prerefunding*, has been curtailed by several tax acts. *See also* REFUNDING ESCROW DEPOSITS (REDs).

ADVERSE OPINION opinion expressed by a company's independent auditors that the firm's financial statements do not accurately reflect the company's current financial position or operating results. An adverse opinion is a far more serious finding than a QUALIFIED OPINION, in which only some issues are of concern to the auditor. Investors should be extremely cautious about investing in any company with an adverse opinion from its auditors.

ADVERSE SELECTION tendency of people with significant potential to file claims wanting to obtain insurance coverage. For example, those with severe health problems want to buy health insurance, and people going to a dangerous place such as a war zone want to buy more life insurance. Companies employing workers in dangerous occupations want to buy more worker's compensation coverage. In order to combat the problem of adverse selection, insurance companies try to reduce their exposure to large claims by either raising premiums or limiting the availability of coverage to such applicants.

ADVISORY LETTER newsletter aiming to offer financial advice to subscribers. The letter may offer a broad economic and market outlook, or it may focus on a particular sector of the stock, bond, or commodity markets. Some advisory letters specialize in recommending only mutual funds. Some letters also advise their subscribers of new recom-mendations through a toll-free hotline, which can be updated much more quickly than a printed letter. If the advisory letter recommends specific securities, the author usually is registered with the Securities and Exchange Commission as a REGISTERED INVESTMENT ADVISOR. *See also* HULBERT RATING.

AFFIDAVIT written statement made under oath before an authorized person, such as a notary public.

AFFIDAVIT OF DOMICILE AFFIDAVIT made by the executor of an estate that certifies the decedent's place of residence at the time of death. Before securities can be transferred from an estate, it must be verified that no liens exist against them in the home state of the decedent.

AFFILIATE

In general: two companies are affiliated when one owns less than a majority of the voting stock of the other, or when both are subsidiaries of a third company. A SUBSIDIARY is a company of which more than 50% of the voting shares are owned by another corporation, termed the PARENT COMPANY. A subsidiary is always, by definition, an affiliate, but subsidiary is the preferred term when majority control exists. In everyday use, affiliate is the correct word for intercompany relationships, however indirect, where the parent-subsidiary relationship does not apply.

Banking Act of 1933: any organization that a bank owns or controls by stock holdings, or which the bank's shareholders own, or whose officers are also directors of the bank.
Internal Revenue Service: for purposes of consolidated tax returns an affiliated group is composed of companies whose parent or other inclusive corporation owns at least 80% of voting stock.
Interstate Commerce Commission, Account 706: 1. Controlled by the accounting company alone or with others under a joint agreement. **2.** Controlling the accounting company alone or with others under a joint agreement.
Investment Company Act: company in which there is any direct or indirect ownership of 5% or more of the outstanding voting securities.

AFFILIATED CORPORATION corporation that is an AFFILIATE.

AFFILIATED PERSON individual in a position to exert direct influence on the actions of a corporation. Among such persons are owners of 10% or more of the voting shares, directors, and senior elected officers and any persons in a position to exert influence through them—such as members of their immediate family and other close associates. Sometimes called a *control person.*

AFFORDABILITY INDEX standard established by the National Association of Realtors (NAR) to gauge the financial ability of consumers to buy a home. A reading of 100 means a family earning the national median family income (reported by the Census Bureau) can qualify for a mortgage on a typical median-priced existing single-family home. An index above 100 signifies that a family earning the median income more than qualifies for a mortgage loan on a median-priced home, assuming a 20% downpayment. Therefore, an increase in the Affordability Index shows that a family is more able to afford the median priced home. The prevailing mortgage interest rate is the effective rate on loans closed on existing homes from the Federal Housing Finance Board (for the U.S.) and HSH Associates of Butler, NJ (for various regions). The mortgage is based on an 80% loan (20% down payment) and a qualifying ratio of 25%, meaning that 25% of the borrower's gross monthly income will be needed to cover housing costs, including the mortgage. The 25% qualifying ratio covers expected principal and interest payments, but does not cover taxes and insurance.

There are three different types of indices calculated by NAR. The Fixed Rate Index is based on the current effective interest rate on 30-year fixed rate mortgages. The Adjustable Rate Index is calculated using the prevailing effective interest rate on adjustable-rate mortgages. The Composite Index uses a weighted average of the interest rates on fixed and adjustable rate mortgages, weighted by the relative proportion of fixed and adjustable rate loans closed on existing homes.

NAR also calculates a first-time homebuyer Affordability Index, which recognizes the special characteristics of first-time home buyers and the homes they purchase. The group most likely to purchase a first home consists of a young renter family with a head of household aged 25 to 44 and a lower median income than the overall population. This index assumes a 10% downpayment, and adds one quarter of a percentage point to the mortgage rate for the required private mortgage insurance. The first-time home is calculated at 85% of the median price of all existing homes purchased. Some economists maintain that every one-point increase in the home mortgage interest rate results in 300,000 fewer home sales.

AFTER ACQUIRED CLAUSE clause in a mortgage agreement providing that any additional mortgageable property acquired by the borrower after the mortgage is signed will be additional security for the obligation.

While such provisions can help give mortgage bonds a good rating and enable issuing corporations to borrow at favorable rates, by precluding additional first mortgages, they make it difficult to finance growth through new borrowings. This gives rise to various maneuvers to remove after acquired clauses, such as redemption or exchange of bonds or changes in indenture agreements.

AFTER-HOURS DEALING OR TRADING trading of stocks and bonds after regular trading hours on organized exchanges. This may occur when there is a major announcement about positive or negative earnings or a takeover at a particular company. The stock price may therefore soar or plummet from the level at which it closed during regular trading hours. Some brokerage firms specialize in making over-the-counter markets around the clock to accommodate after-hours dealing. *See* MAKE A MARKET.

AFTERMARKET *see* SECONDARY MARKET.

AFTERTAX BASIS basis for comparing the returns on a corporate taxable bond and a municipal tax-free bond. For example, a corporate bond paying 10% would have an aftertax return of 6.4% for someone in the 36% tax bracket. So any municipal bond paying higher than 6.4% would yield a higher aftertax return.

AFTERTAX REAL RATE OF RETURN amount of money, adjusted for inflation, that an investor can keep, out of the income and capital gains earned from investments. Every dollar loses value to inflation, so investors have to keep an eye on the aftertax real rate of return whenever they commit their capital. By and large, investors seek a rate of return that will match if not exceed the rate of inflation.

AGAINST THE BOX SHORT SALE by the holder of a LONG POSITION in the same stock. BOX refers to the physical location of securities held in safekeeping. When a stock is sold against the box, it is sold short, but only in effect. A short sale is usually defined as one where the seller does not own the shares. Here the seller *does* own the shares (holds a long position) but does not wish to disclose ownership; or perhaps the long shares are too inaccessible to deliver in the time required; or, prior to the TAXPAYER RELIEF ACT OF 1997, he may have been holding his existing position to get the benefit of long-term capital gains tax treatment. In any event, when the sale is made against the box, the shares needed to cover are borrowed, probably from a broker. This technique was eliminated as a way to reduce tax liabilities in the TAXPAYER RELIEF ACT OF 1997. *See also* SELLING SHORT AGAINST THE BOX.

AGED FAIL contract between two broker-dealers that is still not settled 30 days after the settlement date. At that point the open balance no longer counts as an asset, and the receiving firm must adjust its capital accordingly.

AGENCY
In general: relationship between two parties, one a principal and the other an AGENT who represents the principal in transactions with a third party.
Finance: certain types of accounts in trust institutions where individuals, usually trust officers, act on behalf of customers. Agency services to corporations are related to stock purchases and sales. Banks also act as agents for individuals.
Government: securities issued by government-sponsored entities and federally related institutions. Agency securities are exempt from Securities and Exchange Commission (SEC) registration requirements. *See also* AGENCY SECURITIES.
Investment: act of buying or selling for the account and risk of a client. Generally, an agent, or broker, acts as intermediary between buyer and seller, taking no financial risk personally or as a firm, and charging a commission for the service.

AGENCY SECURITIES securities issued by U.S. government-sponsored entities (GSEs) and federally related institutions.

GSEs currently issuing securities comprise eight privately owned, publicly chartered entities created to reduce borrowing costs for certain sectors of the economy, such as farmers, homeowners, and students. They include the Federal Farm Credit Bank System, Farm Credit Financial Assistance Corporation, Federal Home Loan Bank, FEDERAL HOME LOAN MORTGAGE CORPORATION, FEDERAL NATIONAL MORTGAGE ASSOCIATION (FNMA), STUDENT LOAN MARKETING ASSOCIATION (SLMA), FINANCING CORPORATION (FICO). GSEs issue discount notes (with maturities ranging from overnight to 360 days) and bonds. With the exception of the Farm Credit Financial Assistance Corporation, GSE securities are not backed by the full faith and credit of the U.S. government. Other GSEs that formerly issued directly now borrow from the FEDERAL FINANCING BANK.

Federally related institutions are arms of the U.S. government and generally have not issued securities directly into the marketplace since the Federal Financing Bank was established to meet their consolidated borrowing needs in 1973. They include the EXPORT-IMPORT BANK (EXIMBANK) of the United States, the Commodity Credit Corporation, the Farmers Housing Administration, the General Services Administration, the GOVERNMENT NATIONAL MORTGAGE ASSOCIATION (GNMA), the Maritime Administration, the Private Export Funding Corporation, the Rural Electrification Administration, the Rural Telephone Bank, the SMALL BUSINESS ADMINISTRATION (SBA), the Tennessee Valley Authority (TVA), and the Washington Metropolitan Area Transit Authority. Except for the Private Export Funding Corporation and the TVA, federally related institution obligations are backed by the full faith and credit of the U.S. government.

Agency securities are exempt from SEC registration and from state and local income taxes.

See also FEDERAL FARM CREDIT SYSTEM; FEDERAL HOME LOAN BANK SYSTEM.

AGENT individual authorized by another person, called the principal, to act in the latter's behalf in transactions involving a third party. Banks are frequently appointed by individuals to be their agents, and so authorize their employees to act on behalf of principals. Agents have three basic characteristics:
1. They act on behalf of and are subject to the control of the principal.
2. They do not have title to the principal's property.
3. They owe the duty of obedience to the principal's orders.
See also ACCOUNT EXECUTIVE; BROKER; TRANSFER AGENT.

AGGREGATE EXERCISE PRICE in stock options trading, the number of shares in a put or call CONTRACT (normally 100) multiplied by the EXERCISE PRICE. The price of the option, called the PREMIUM, is a separate figure not included in the aggregate exercise price. A July call option on 100 XYZ at 70 would, for example, have an aggregate exercise price of 100 (number of shares) times $70 (price per share), or $7000, if exercised on or before the July expiration date.

In options traded on debt instruments, which include GOVERNMENT NATIONAL MORTGAGE ASSOCIATION (GNMA) pass-throughs, Treasury bills, Treasury notes, Treasury bonds, and certain municipal bonds, the aggregate exercise price is determined by multiplying the FACE VALUE of the underlying security by the exercise price. For example, the aggregate exercise price of put option Treasury bond December 90 would be $90,000 if exercised on or before its December expiration date, the calculation being 90% times the $100,000 face value of the underlying bond.

AGGREGATE SUPPLY in MACROECONOMICS, the total amount of goods and services supplied to the market at alternative price levels in a given period of time; also called *total output*. The central concept in SUPPLY-SIDE ECONOMICS, it corresponds with aggregate demand, defined as the total amount of goods and services demanded in the economy at alternative income levels in a given period, including both consumer and producers' goods; aggregate demand is also called *total spending*. The aggregate supply curve describes the relationship between price levels and the quantity of output that firms are willing to provide.

AGGRESSIVE GROWTH MUTUAL FUND mutual fund holding stocks of rapidly growing companies. While these companies may be large or small, they all share histories of and prospects for above-average profit growth. Aggressive growth funds are designed solely for capital appreciation, since they produce little or no income from dividends. This type of mutual fund is typically more volatile than the overall stock market, meaning its shares will rise far more than the average stock during bull markets and will fall much farther than the typical stock in a bear market. Investors in aggressive growth funds must realize that the value of their shares will fluctuate sharply over time. Aggressive growth funds are also called *maximum capital gains funds* or *capital appreciation funds.*

AGING SCHEDULE classification of trade ACCOUNTS RECEIVABLE by date of sale. Usually prepared by a company's auditor, the *aging,* as the schedule is called, is a vital tool in analyzing the quality of a company's receivables investment. It is frequently required by grantors of credit.

The schedule is most often seen as: (1) a list of the amount of receivables by the month in which they were created; (2) a list of receivables by maturity, classified as current or as being in various stages of delinquency. The following is a typical aging schedule.

	dollars (in thousands)	
Current (under 30 days)	$14,065	61%
1–30 days past due	3,725	16
31–60 days past due	2,900	12
61–90 days past due	1,800	8
Over 90 days past due	750	3
	$23,240	100%

The aging schedule reveals patterns of delinquency and shows where collection efforts should be concentrated. It helps in evaluating the adequacy of the reserve for BAD DEBTS, because the longer accounts stretch out the more likely they are to become uncollectible. Using the schedule can help prevent the loss of future sales, since old customers who fall too far behind tend to seek out new sources of supply.

AGREEMENT AMONG UNDERWRITERS contract between participating members of an investment banking SYNDICATE; sometimes called *syndicate contract* or *purchase group agreement*. It is distinguished from the *underwriting agreement,* which is signed by the company issuing the securities and the SYNDICATE MANAGER, acting as agent for the underwriting group.

The agreement among underwriters, (1) appoints the originating investment banker as syndicate manager and agent; (2) appoints additional managers, if considered advisable; (3) defines the members' proportionate liability (usually limited to the amount of their participation) and agrees to pay each member's share on settlement date; (4) authorizes the manager to form and allocate units to a SELLING GROUP, and agrees to abide by the rules of the selling group agreement; (5) states the life of the syndicate, usually running until 30 days after termination of the selling group, or ending earlier by mutual consent.

AIR POCKET STOCK stock that falls sharply, usually in the wake of such negative news as unexpected poor earnings. As shareholders rush to sell, and few buyers can be found, the price plunges dramatically, like an airplane hitting an air pocket.

AIRPORT REVENUE BOND tax-exempt bond issued by a city, county, state, or airport authority to support the expansion and operations of an airport. The repayment of principal and interest is backed by either the general revenues of airport authority or lease payments generated by one or more airlines using the facilities. In some cases, airport revenue bonds are backed directly by the financial strength of the major airline using the airport, which makes the bonds more risky, because airlines are particularly sensitive to economic cycles and could go out of business in a down cycle.

ALIEN CORPORATION company incorporated under the laws of a foreign country regardless of where it operates. "Alien corporation" can be used as a synonym for the term *foreign corporation.* However, "foreign corporation" also is used in U.S. state law to mean a corporation formed in a state other than that in which it does business.

ALIMONY PAYMENT money paid to a separated or divorced spouse as required by a divorce decree or a legal separation agreement. The IRS allows qualifying payments as DEDUCTIONS by the payor and they are taxable income to the payee.

ALLIED MEMBER general partner or voting stockholder of a member firm of the New York Stock Exchange who is not personally a member. Allied members cannot do business on the trading floor. A member firm need have no more than one partner or voting stockholder who owns a membership, so even the chairman of the board of a member firm may be no more than an allied member.

ALLIGATOR SPREAD spread in the options market that "eats the investor alive" with high commission costs. The term is used when a broker arranges a combination of puts and calls that generates so much commission the client is unlikely to turn a profit even if the markets move as anticipated.

ALL IN underwriting shorthand for *all included,* referring to an issuer's interest rate after giving effect to commissions and miscellaneous related expenses.

ALL OR NONE (AON)
Investment banking: an offering giving the issuer the right to cancel the whole issue if the underwriting is not fully subscribed.
Securities: buy or sell order marked to signify that no partial transaction is to be executed. The order will not automatically be canceled, however, if a complete transaction is not executed; to accomplish that, the order entry must be marked FOK, meaning FILL OR KILL.

ALL ORDINARIES INDEX the major index of Australian stocks, representing 330 of the most active listed companies, or the majority of the equity capitalization (excluding foreign companies) listed on the AUSTRALIA STOCK EXCHANGE (ASX). The index is made up of 23 sub-indices representing various industry categories, and it summarizes market price movements by following changes in the aggregate market values of the companies listed.

ALLOTMENT amount of securities assigned to each of the participants in an investment banking SYNDICATE formed to underwrite and distribute a new issue, called *subscribers* or *allottees.* The financial responsibilities of the subscribers are set forth in an allotment notice, which is prepared by the SYNDICATE MANAGER.

ALLOWANCE deduction from the value of an invoice, permitted by a seller of goods to cover damages or shortages. *See also* RESERVE.

ALL-SAVERS CERTIFICATE *see* ECONOMIC RECOVERY TAX ACT OF 1981 (ERTA).

ALPHA

1. coefficient measuring the portion of an investment's RETURN arising from specific (nonmarket) risk. In other words, alpha is a mathematical estimate of the amount of return expected from an investment's inherent values, such as the rate of growth in earnings per share. It is distinct from the amount of return caused by VOLATILITY, which is measured by the BETA coefficient. For example, an alpha of 1.25 indicates that a stock is projected to rise 25% in price in a year when the return on the market and the stock's beta are both zero. An investment whose price is low relative to its alpha is undervalued and considered a good selection.

   In the case of a MUTUAL FUND, alpha measures the relationship between the fund's performance and its beta over a three-year period.

2. on the London Stock Exchange, now called the International Stock Exchange of the United Kingdom and Republic of Ireland (ISE), the designation *alpha stocks* is applied to the largest and most actively traded companies in a classification system that was adopted after the BIG BANG in October 1986 and was replaced in January 1991 with the NORMAL MARKET SIZE (NMS) classification system.

ALPHABET STOCK categories of common stock associated with particular subsidiaries created by acquisitions and restructuring. Examples would be General Motors "E" stock, issued to acquire Electronic Data Systems (EDS), and "H" stock, which was originally issued in the mid-1980s, when GM acquired Hughes Aircraft and combined it with existing electronics operations to form GM Hughes Electronics Corporation. Subsequent to these acquisitions, GM spun off its holdings in EDS so that EDS now trades as a separate company again. General Motors H was recapitalized when Hughes' defense operations were spun off to Raytheon in 1997. The reissued General Motors H (GMH) now tracks the Hughes telecommunications and space businesses that GM retained. The significance of alphabetical categories is that they have different voting rights and pay dividends tied to the operating performance of the particular divisions. Alphabet stock differs from CLASSIFIED STOCK, which is typically designated Class A and Class B, in that classified stock implies a hierarchy of powers and privileges, whereas alphabet stock simply separates differences. *See also* TRACKING STOCKS.

ALTERNATIVE MINIMUM TAX (AMT) federal tax aimed at ensuring that wealthy individuals, trusts, estates, and corporations pay at least some income tax. For individuals, the AMT is computed by adding TAX PREFERENCE ITEMS such as passive losses from tax shelters, accelerated depreciation of property acquired before 1987, and tax-exempt interest on private-purpose bonds issued after August 7, 1986, to adjusted gross income. From this amount, a $45,000 exemption must be subtracted for a married couple filing jointly, $33,750 for a single filer, and $22,500 for a married couple filing separately, or for trusts and estates. (These exemptions are phased out when AMT taxable income exceeds $150,000 for a married couple filing jointly, $112,500 for single filers, and $75,000 for a married couple filing separately.) The remaining amount, up to $175,000 for a married couple filing jointly ($87,500 for a married couple filing separately), is subject to a 26% tax rate. Any amount over $175,000 ($87,500 for couple filing separately) is subject to a 28% tax rate.

   The corporate AMT has the same exemptions but a tax rate of 20%. It is imposed on the amount of money in excess of the alternative minimum taxable income (AMTI) over the exemption amount. In determining the corporate AMT, an adjustment called the adjusted current earnings (ACE) must be made. The ACE adjustment increases a corporation's AMTI by 75% of the amount by which its ACE exceeds its AMTI. This adjustment is designed to eliminate some of the tax savings generated by corporations that have high income for accounting purposes but pay little or no tax as a result of tax benefits. Calculating the correct individual or corporate AMT can be extremely complex and is best left to a professional accountant.

ALTERNATIVE ORDER order giving a broker a choice between two courses of action; also called an *either-or order* or a *one cancels the other order.* Such orders are either to buy or to sell, never both. Execution of one course automatically makes the other course inoperative. An example is a combination buy limit/buy stop order, wherein the buy limit is below the current market and the buy stop is above.

AMBAC Indemnity Corporation *see* MUNICIPAL BOND INSURANCE.

AMENDED TAX RETURN Internal Revenue Service tax return filed on Form 1040X to correct mistakes made on the original return. Amended returns must be filed within three years of the original filing.

AMENDMENT addition to, or change, in a legal document. When properly signed, it has the full legal effect of the original document.

AMERICAN ASSOCIATION OF INDIVIDUAL INVESTORS (AAII) nonprofit organization, based in Chicago, designed to educate individual investors about stocks, bonds, mutual funds, and other financial alternatives through seminars, conferences, and publications. The AAII also evaluates investment-oriented software in a publication called *Computerized Investing.* The AAII web site (www.aaii.org) provides extensive information on the basics of investing, as well as a reference section on a wide variety of topics such as annuities, mutual funds, dividend reinvestment plans and discount brokers. The AAII regularly polls its members for their outlook on the stock market, and the AAII Index of Bullish, Bearish and Neutral Outlook is published weekly in *Barron's* under Investor Sentiment Readings.

AMERICAN DEPOSITARY RECEIPT (ADR) receipt for the shares of a foreign-based corporation held in the vault of a U.S. bank and entitling the shareholder to all dividends and capital gains. Instead of buying shares of foreign-based companies in overseas markets, Americans can buy shares in the U.S. in the form of an ADR. ADRs are available for hundreds of stocks from numerous countries.

AMERICAN DEPOSITARY SHARE (ADS) share issued under a deposit agreement representing the underlying ordinary share which trades in the issuer's home market. The terms ADS and ADR tend to be used interchangeably. Technically, the ADS is the instrument that actually is traded, while the ADR is the certificate that represents a number of ADSs.

AMERICAN STOCK EXCHANGE (AMEX) primary marketplace in the U.S. for equities, bonds, options and derivative securities. Located at 86 Trinity Place in lower Manhattan, AMEX was known as the *Curb Exchange* until 1921. AMEX trades more than 900 issues on its primary list. The two main indices tracking AMEX stocks are the AMEX Composite Index and the AMEX Major Market Index. In the options market, AMEX trades options on 30 broad-based and sector indices and more than 900 stocks and 109 LONG-TERM EQUITY ANTICIPATION SECURITIES (LEAPS). AMEX is a leader in listing warrants on foreign currencies and indices as well as hybrid instruments and other structured products. AMEX trades such derivatives as DIAMONDS (which track the Dow Jones Industrial Average); STANDARD & POOR'S DEPOSITORY RECEIPTS (SPDRS), which track the S&P 500 and are usually called Spiders and WORLD EQUITY BENCHMARK SHARES (WEBS), which track the performance of various countries stock indices.

In 1998, AMEX agreed to merge with the NATIONAL ASSOCIATION OF SECURITIES DEALERS (NASD), making it a subsidiary of NASD. Under terms of the merger, AMEX equity and options markets continue to operate separately from the NASDAQ Stock Market and NASDAQ International, both operated by NASD. The AMEX equity market continues as a centralized, specialist-based auction market with manual and enhanced electronic access. The options structure remains unchanged. Trading hours: 9:30 A.M.–4:00 P.M., Monday through Friday. *See also* EMERGING COMPANY MARKETPLACE (ECM); SECURITIES AND COMMODITIES EXCHANGES; SPDR; STOCK INDICES AND AVERAGES.

AMORTIZATION accounting procedure that gradually reduces the cost value of a limited life or intangible asset through periodic charges to income. For fixed assets the term used is DEPRECIATION, and for wasting assets (natural resources) it is depletion, both terms meaning essentially the same thing as amortization. Most companies follow the conservative practice of writing off, through amortization, INTANGIBLE ASSETS such as goodwill. It is also common practice to amortize any premium over par value paid in the purchase of preferred stock or bond investments. The purpose of amortization is to reflect resale or redemption value.

Amortization also refers to the reduction of debt by regular payments of interest and principal sufficient to pay off a loan by maturity.

Discount and expense on funded debt are amortized by making applicable charges to income in accordance with a predetermined schedule. While this is normally done systematically, charges to profit and loss are permissible at any time in any amount of the remaining discount and expense. Such accounting is detailed in a company's annual report.

AMPS acronym for *Auction Market Preferred Stock,* Merrill Lynch's answer to Salomon Brothers' DARTS and First Boston's STARS. These and other proprietary products are types of DUTCH AUCTION PREFERRED STOCK. Since the auctions take place every 49 days, the shares meet the 46-day holding period required for the 70% dividend exclusion allowed corporations under the tax code.

AMSTERDAM EXCHANGES (AEX) formed by the 1997 merger of the Amsterdam Stock Exchange (ASE), the European Options Exchange (EOE), and Necigef (the Dutch Central Institution for Girosecurities transactions). AEX is a private limited company with shareholders and the central Dutch securities exchanges for stocks, bonds, options and agricultural futures. It is responsible for regulation and control in trading, listing, settlements and safe custody for the exchanges and systems it operates. The stock exchange, founded in 1602, is the oldest in the world. The NEW YORK STOCK EXCHANGE is based on the Dutch system. The majority of domestic shares are bearer shares, while foreign equities generally are in registered form. In February 1997, a market was launched for high-growth, small-cap companies. Trading System Amsterdam (TSA) consists of a wholesale and retail segment; the distinction between the two is determined by the transaction size. The wholesale segment can be traded directly on the screen-based Automatic Interprofessional Dealing System (AIDA). The retail sector has a central market, a floor with specialists. The wholesale sector also may utilize the central market. The Netherlands Central Bureau of Statistics (CBS) All Share Index and the Total Return Index include all ordinary shares of Dutch companies listed on the AEX, except shares of property funds, investment funds, and holding companies. The AEX Index is composed of a weighted average of the 25 most actively-traded Dutch stocks, selected annually. The Amsterdam Midcap Index (AMX) focuses on medium-sized companies.

The AEX-Optiebeurs trades financial futures, stock options, and index options by open outcry and electronically. Futures and options are traded on its EOE Index, as well as the Eurotop 100 Index, the Dutch Top 5 Index and the

U.S. dollar. Futures are traded on the *notional bond*. Options are traded on the Jumbo dollar, gold and silver. The AEX-Agrarische Termijnmarket trades futures on live hogs, piglets, potatoes and wheat by open outcry. Trading hours for all AEX divisions are 9:30 A.M. to 4:30 P.M., Monday through Friday.

ANALYSIS *see* FUNDAMENTAL ANALYSIS; TECHNICAL ANALYSIS.

ANALYST person in a brokerage house, bank trust department, or mutual fund group who studies a number of companies and makes buy or sell recommendations on the securities of particular companies and industry groups. Most analysts specialize in a particular industry, but some investigate any company that interests them, regardless of its line of business. Some analysts have considerable influence, and can therefore affect the price of a company's stock when they issue a buy or sell recommendation. *See also* CREDIT ANALYST.

AND INTEREST phrase used in quoting bond prices to indicate that, in addition to the price quoted, the buyer will receive ACCRUED INTEREST.

ANGEL INVESTMENT GRADE bond, as distinguished from FALLEN ANGEL.

ANKLE BITER stock issue having a MARKET CAPITALIZATION of less than $500 million. Generally speaking, such small-capitalization stocks are more speculative than "high-cap" issues, but their greater growth potential gives them more RELATIVE STRENGTH in recessions. *See also* SMALL FIRM EFFECT.

ANNUAL BASIS statistical technique whereby figures covering a period of less than a year are extended to cover a 12-month period. The procedure, called *annualizing,* must take seasonal variations (if any) into account to be accurate.

ANNUAL EXCLUSION tax rule allowing a taxpayer to exclude certain kinds of income from taxation on a tax return. For example, interest earned from municipal bonds must be reported, even though it is not taxed by the federal government. Proceeds from life insurance policies paid by reason of the death of the insured are not taxable. Gifts received of $10,000 or less are also not taxable, and are therefore subject to the annual exclusion rule. This $10,000 gift tax exclusion limit is subject to upward revision in $1,000 increments tied to the rate of inflation based on the TAXPAYER RELIEF ACT OF 1997.

ANNUALIZE to convert to an annual basis. For example, if a mutual fund earns 1% in a month, it would earn 12% on an annualized basis, by multiplying the monthly return by 12. Many economists annualize a monthly number such as auto sales or housing starts to make it easier to compare to prior years.

ANNUAL MEETING once-a-year meeting when the managers of a company report to stockholders on the year's results, and the board of directors stands for election for the next year. The chief executive officer usually comments on the outlook for the coming year and, with other senior officers, answers questions from shareholders. Stockholders can also request that resolutions on corporate policy be voted on by all those owning stock in the company. Stockholders unable to attend the annual meeting may vote for directors and pass on resolutions through the use of PROXY material, which must legally be mailed to all shareholders of record.

ANNUAL PERCENTAGE RATE (APR) cost of credit that consumers pay, expressed as a simple annual percentage. According to the federal Truth-in-Lending Act, every consumer loan agreement must disclose the APR in large bold type. *See also* CONSUMER CREDIT PROTECTION ACT OF 1968.

ANNUAL RENEWABLE TERM INSURANCE *see* TERM INSURANCE.

ANNUAL REPORT yearly record of a corporation's financial condition that must be distributed to shareholders under SECURITIES AND EXCHANGE COMMISSION regulations. Included in the report is a description of the company's operations as well as its balance sheet and income statement. The long version of the annual report with more detailed financial information—called the 10-K—is available upon request from the corporate secretary.

ANNUAL RETURN TOTAL RETURN per year from an investment, including dividends or interest and capital gains or losses but excluding commissions and other transactions costs and taxes. A *compound annual return* represents the annual rate at which money would have to compound to reach the cumulative figure resulting from annual total returns. It is a discount rate and different from *average annual return,* which is simply an arithmetic mean of annual returns.

ANNUITANT individual receiving benefits from an annuity. The annuity owner can choose to annuitize the policy, meaning that he or she begins to receive regular payments from the annuity.

ANNUITIZE to begin a series of payments from the capital that has built up in an ANNUITY. The payments may be a fixed amount, or for a fixed period of time, or for the lifetimes of one or two *annuitants,* thus guaranteeing income payments that cannot be outlived. *See also* DEFERRED PAYMENT ANNUITY; FIXED ANNUITY; IMMEDIATE PAYMENT ANNUITY; VARIABLE ANNUITY.

ANNUITY form of contract sold by life insurance companies that guarantees a fixed or variable payment to the annuitant at some future time, usually retirement. In a FIXED ANNUITY the amount will ultimately be paid out in regular installments varying only with the payout method elected. In a VARIABLE ANNUITY, the payout is based on a guaranteed number of units; unit values and payments depend on the value of the underlying investments. All capital in the annuity grows TAX-DEFERRED. Key considerations when buying an annuity are the financial soundness of the insurance company *(see* BEST'S RATING), the returns it has paid in the past, and the level of fees and commissions paid to salesmen.

ANNUITY CERTAIN annuity that pays a specified monthly level of income for a predetermined time period, frequently ten years. The annuitant is guaranteed by the insurance company to receive those payments for the agreed upon time period without exception or contingency. If the annuitant dies before the time period expires, the annuity payments are then made to the annuitant's designated beneficiaries. The level of payment in an annuity certain will be higher than for a LIFE ANNUITY because the insurance company knows exactly what its liability will be, whereas with a life annuity, payments depend on how long the annuitant lives.

ANNUITY STARTING DATE date on which an ANNUITANT begins receiving payments from an annuity. Generally, any distributions before age 59½ are subject to a 10% penalty from the IRS, so most annuities start paying after the annuitant has attained that age. The later an annuitant waits to start receiving payments, the higher his or her monthly payments will be under a life annuity, because the insurance company has had more time to invest the money, and the annuitant's remaining life expectancy is shorter.

ANTICIPATED HOLDING PERIOD time during which a limited partnership expects to hold onto an asset. In the prospectus for a real estate limited partnership, for instance, a sponsor will typically say that the anticipated holding period for a particular property is five to seven years. At the end of that time the property is sold, and, usually, the capital received is returned to the limited partners in one distribution.

ANTICIPATION
In general: paying an obligation before it falls due.

Finance: repayment of debt obligations before maturity, usually to save interest. If a formalized discount or rebate is involved, the term used is *anticipation rate.*
Mortgage instrument: when a provision allows prepayment without penalty, the mortgagee is said to have the *right of anticipation.*
Trade payments: bill that is paid before it is due, not discounted.

ANTITRUST LAWS federal legislation designed to prevent monopolies and restraint of trade. Landmark statutes include:
1. the Sherman Antitrust Act of 1890, which prohibited acts or contracts tending to create monopoly and initiated an era of trustbusting.
2. the Clayton Antitrust Act of 1914, which was passed as an amendment to the Sherman Act and dealt with local price discrimination as well as with the INTERLOCKING DIRECTORATES. It went further in the areas of the HOLDING COMPANY and restraint of trade.
3. the Federal Trade Commission Act of 1914, which created the Federal Trade Commission or FTC, with power to conduct investigations and issue orders preventing unfair practices in interstate commerce.

ANY-AND-ALL BID offer to pay an equal price for all shares tendered by a deadline; contrasts with TWO-TIER BID. *See also* TAKEOVER.

ANY-INTEREST-DATE CALL provision found in some municipal bond indentures that gives the issuer the right to redeem on any interest payment due date, with or without a premium (depending on the indenture).

APPRAISAL FEE fee charged by an expert to estimate, but not determine, the market value of property. An appraisal is an opinion of value, and is usually required when real property is sold, financed, condemned, taxed, insured, or partitioned. For example, the appraisal of a work of art done to establish value for the IRS when the art is to be donated to a charity may differ from the appraisal if the piece of art is about to be sold at auction. Similarly, the appraisal of a piece of real estate for insurance purposes may differ from an appraisal for determining property taxes. The appraisal fee is usually a set dollar amount, though in some cases may be calculated as a percentage of the value of the property appraised.

APPRECIATION increase in the value of an asset such as a stock, bond, commodity, or real estate.

APPROVED LIST list of investments that a mutual fund or other financial institution is authorized to make. The approved list may be statutory where a fiduciary responsibility exists. *See also* LEGAL LIST.

APS acronym for *Auction Preferred Stock,* Goldman Sach's DUTCH AUCTION PREFERRED STOCK product.

ARBITRAGE profiting from differences in price when the same security, currency, or commodity is traded on two or more markets. For example, an *arbitrageur* simultaneously buys one contract of gold in the New York market and sells one contract of gold in the Chicago market, locking in a profit because at that moment the price on the two markets is different. (The arbitrageur's selling price is higher than the buying price.) *Index arbitrage* exploits price differences between STOCK INDEX FUTURES and underlying stocks. By taking advantage of momentary disparities in prices between markets, arbitrageurs perform the economic function of making those markets trade more efficiently. *See also* GARBATRAGE; RISK ARBITRAGE.

ARBITRAGE BONDS bonds issued by a municipality in order to gain an interest rate advantage by refunding higher-rate bonds in advance of their call date.

Proceeds from the lower-rate refunding issue are invested in treasuries until the first call date of the higher-rate issue being refunded. Arbitrage bonds, which always raised a question of tax exemption, were further curtailed by the TAX REFORM ACT OF 1986.

ARBITRAGEUR person or firm engaged in ARBITRAGE. Arbitrageurs attempt to profit when the same security or commodity is trading at different prices in two or more markets. Those engaged in RISK ARBITRAGE attempt to profit from buying stocks of announced or potential TAKEOVER targets.

ARBITRATION dispute resolution mechanism designed to help aggrieved parties recover damages. In arbitration, an impartial person or panel hears all sides of the issues as presented by the parties, evaluates the evidence, and decides how the matter should be resolved. Arbitration is final and binding, and is subject to review by a court only on a very limited basis. *See also* ARBITRATION PANEL.

ARBITRATION PANEL each sponsoring organization maintains a roster of individuals whose professional experience qualifies them for service as arbitrators. The arbitrators are not employees of the sponsoring organization and they, not the sponsoring organization, determine the outcome of the dispute. The arbitrators receive an honorarium from the SELF-REGULATORY ORGANIZATIONS.

ARITHMETIC MEAN simple average obtained by dividing the sum of two or more items by the number of items.

ARMS' INDEX better known as TRIN; technical indicator named for *Barron's* writer Richard Arms.

ARM'S LENGTH TRANSACTION transaction that is conducted as though the parties were unrelated, thus avoiding any semblance of conflict of interest. For example, under current law parents may rent real estate to their children and still claim business deductions such as depreciation as long as the parents charge their children what they would charge if someone who is not a relative were to rent the same property.

ARREARAGE
In general: amount of any past-due obligation.
Investments: amount by which interest on bonds or dividends on CUMULATIVE PREFERRED stock is due and unpaid. In the case of cumulative preferred stock, common dividends cannot be paid by a company as long as preferred dividends are in arrears.

ARTICLES OF INCORPORATION document filed with a U.S. state by the founders of a corporation. After approving the articles, the state issues a certificate of incorporation; the two documents together become the CHARTER that gives the corporation its legal existence. The charter embodies such information as the corporation's name, purpose, amount of authorized shares, and number and identity of directors. The corporation's powers thus derive from the laws of the state and from the provisions of the charter. Rules governing its internal management are set forth in the corporation's BYLAWS, which are drawn up by the founders.

ARTIFICIAL CURRENCY *currency substitute,* such as SPECIAL DRAWING RIGHTS (SDRs) and EUROPEAN CURRENCY UNITS (ECUs).

ASCENDING TOPS chart pattern tracing a security's price over a period of time and showing that each peak in a security's price is higher than the preceding peak. This upward movement is considered bullish, meaning that the upward trend is likely to continue. *See also* DESCENDING TOPS.

ASCENDING TOPS

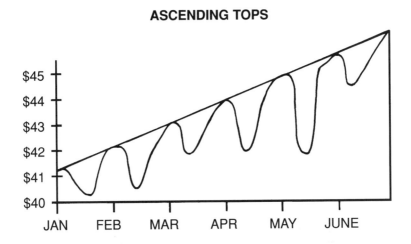

ASKED PRICE
1. price at which a security or commodity is offered for sale on an exchange or in the over-the-counter market. Generally, it is the lowest round lot price at which a dealer will sell. Also called the *ask price, asking price, ask,* or OFFERING PRICE.
2. per-share price at which mutual fund shares are offered to the public, usually the NET ASSET VALUE per share plus a sales charge, if any.

ASPIRIN acronym for *Australian Stock Price Riskless Indexed Notes.* Zero-coupon, four-year bonds guaranteed by the Treasury of New South Wales repayable at face value plus the percentage increase by which the Australian Stock Index of All Ordinaries (common stocks) rises above 1372 points during the period. *See also* ALL ORDINARIES INDEX.

ASSAY test of a metal's purity to verify that it meets the standards for trading on a commodities exchange. For instance, a 100 troy-ounce bar of refined gold must be assayed at a fineness of not less than 995 before the Comex will allow it to be used in settlement of a gold contract.

ASSESSED VALUATION dollar value assigned to property by a municipality for purposes of assessing taxes, which are based on the number of mills per dollar of assessed valuation. If a house is assessed at $100,000 and the tax rate is 50 mills, the tax is $5000. Assessed valuation is important not only to homeowners but also to investors in municipal bonds that are backed by property taxes.

ASSET anything having commercial or exchange value that is owned by a business, institution, or individual. *See also* CAPITAL ASSET; CURRENT ASSETS; DEFERRED CHARGE; FIXED ASSET; INTANGIBLE ASSET; NONCURRENT ASSET.

ASSET ALLOCATION apportioning of investment funds among categories of assets, such as CASH EQUIVALENTS, STOCK, FIXED-INCOME INVESTMENTS, and such tangible assets as real estate, precious metals, and collectibles. Also applies to subcategories such as government, municipal, and corporate bonds, and industry groupings of common stocks. Asset allocation affects both risk and return and is a central concept in personal financial planning and investment management.

ASSET ALLOCATION MUTUAL FUND mutual fund that switches between stocks, bonds, and money market securities to maximize shareholders' returns while minimizing risk. Such funds, which have become extremely popular in recent years, relieve individual shareholders of the responsibility of timing their entry or exit into different markets, since the fund manager is making those decisions. Theoretically, asset allocation funds provide a built-in buffer against declining stock and bond prices because the manager can move all the fund's assets into safe money market instruments. On the other hand, the manager has flexibility to invest aggressively in international and domestic stocks and bonds if he or she sees bull markets ahead for those securities.

ASSET-BACKED SECURITIES bonds or notes backed by loan paper or accounts receivable originated by banks, credit card companies, or other providers of credit and often "enhanced" by a bank LETTER OF CREDIT or by insurance coverage provided by an institution other than the issuer. Typically, the originator of the loan or accounts receivable paper sells it to a specially created trust, which repackages it as securities with a minimum denomination of $1000 and a term of five years or less. The securities are then underwritten by brokerage firms who reoffer them to the public. Examples are CERTIFICATES FOR AUTOMOBILE RECEIVABLES (CARs) and so-called *plastic bonds,* backed by credit card receivables. Because the institution that originated the underlying loans or receivables is neither the obligor nor the guarantor, investors should evaluate the quality of the original paper, the worth of the guarantor or insurer, and the extent of the protection. *See also* PASS-THROUGH SECURITY.

ASSET COVERAGE extent to which a company's net assets cover a particular debt obligation, class of preferred stock, or equity position.

Asset coverage is calculated as follows: from assets at their total book value or liquidation value, subtract intangible assets, current liabilities, and all obligations prior in claim to the issue in question. Divide the result by the dollar amount of the subject issue (or loan) to arrive at the asset coverage ratio. The same information can be expressed as a percentage or, by using units as the divisor, as a dollar figure of coverage per unit. The variation to determine preferred stock coverage treats all liabilities as paid; the variation to arrive at common stock coverage considers both preferred stock and liabilities paid. The term most often used for the common stock calculation is *net book value per share of common stock.*

These calculations reveal *direct* asset coverage. *Overall* asset coverage is obtained by including the subject issue with the total of prior obligations and dividing the aggregate into total tangible assets at liquidating value.

Asset coverage is important as a cushion against losses in the event of liquidation.

ASSET DEPRECIATION RANGE SYSTEM (ADR) range of depreciable lives allowed by the Internal Revenue Service for particular classes of depreciable assets. The ADR system was replaced when the ECONOMIC RECOVERY TAX ACT OF 1981 (ERTA) introduced the ACCELERATED COST RECOVERY SYSTEM (ACRS) but was revived with modifications of ACRS under the TAX REFORM ACT OF 1986. The ADR system assigns an upper and lower limit to the estimated useful lives of asset classes. ACRS classes are based on the mid-points of these ranges. Under the alternative depreciation system, taxpayers may elect STRAIGHT-LINE DEPRECIATION over the applicable ADR-class life.

ASSET FINANCING financing that seeks to convert particular assets into working cash in exchange for a security interest in those assets. The term is replacing *commercial financing* as major banks join commercial finance companies in addressing the financing needs of companies that do not fit the traditional seasonal borrower profile. Although the prevalent form of asset financing continues to be loans against accounts receivable, *inventory loans* are common and *second mortgage loans,* predicated as they usually are on market values containing a high inflation factor, seem to gain popularity by the day. *See also* ACCOUNTS RECEIVABLE FINANCING.

ASSET-LIABILITY MANAGEMENT matching an individual's level of debt and amount of assets. Someone who is planning to buy a new car, for instance, would have to decide whether to pay cash, thus lowering assets, or to take out a loan, thereby increasing debts (or liabilities). Such decisions should be based on interest rates, on earning power, and on the comfort level with debt. Financial institutions carry out asset-liability management when they match the maturity of their deposits with the length of their loan commitments to keep from being adversely affected by rapid changes in interest rates.

ASSET MANAGEMENT ACCOUNT account at a brokerage house, bank, or savings institution that combines banking services like check writing, credit cards, and debit cards; brokerage features like buying securities and making loans on margin; and the convenience of having all financial transactions listed on one monthly statement. Such accounts are also termed *central asset accounts* and are known by such proprietary names as the Cash Management Account (Merrill Lynch), Active Assets Account (Morgan Stanley Dean Witter), or Schwab One Account (Charles Schwab).

ASSET PLAY stock market term for a stock that is attractive because the current price does not reflect the value of the company's assets. For example, an analyst could recommend a hotel chain, not because its hotels are run well but because its real estate is worth far more than is recognized in the stock's current price. Asset play stocks are tempting targets for takeovers because they provide an inexpensive way to buy assets.

ASSET STRIPPER corporate raider who takes over a company planning to sell large assets in order to repay debt. The raider calculates that after selling the assets and paying off the debt, he or she will be left with valuable assets that are worth more than his or her purchase price.

ASSET VALUE net market value of a company's assets on a per-share basis as opposed to the market value of the shares. A company is undervalued by the stock market when asset value exceeds share value.

ASSIGN sign a document transferring ownership from one party to another. Ownership can be in a number of forms, including tangible property, rights (usually arising out of contracts), or the right to transfer ownership at some later time. The party who assigns is called the *assignor* and the party who receives the transfer of title—the assignment—is the *assignee.*

Stocks and registered bonds can be assigned by completing and signing a form printed on the back of the certificate—or, as is sometimes preferred for safety reasons, by executing a separate form, called an *assignment separate from certificate* or *stock/bond power.*

When the OPTIONS CLEARING CORPORATION learns of the exercise of an option, it prepares an assignment form notifying a broker-dealer that an option written by one of its clients has been exercised. The firm in turn assigns the exercise in accordance with its internal procedures.

An assignment for the benefit of creditors, sometimes called simply an *assignment,* is an alternative to bankruptcy, whereby the assets of a company are assigned to the creditors and liquidated for their benefit by a trustee.

ASSIGNED RISK PLANS facilities available in all 50 states in which drivers can obtain auto insurance if they are unable to buy it in the regular or "voluntary" market. Every insurer licensed in the state must participate in these facilities, which are also known as *joint underwriting facilities.* When premiums are too low to cover losses, insurers are usually assessed to make up the difference, and these costs are passed on to all of their customers.

ASSIMILATION absorption of a new issue of stock by the investing public after all shares have been sold by the issue's underwriters. *See also* ABSORBED.

ASSUMED INTEREST RATE rate of interest that an insurance company uses to determine the payout on an ANNUITY contract. The higher the assumed interest rate, the higher the monthly payout will be.

ASSUMPTION act of taking on responsibility for the liabilities of another party, usually documented by an *assumption agreement.* In the case of a MORTGAGE assumption, the seller remains secondarily liable unless released from the obligations by the lender.

ASX DERIVATIVES AND OPTIONS MARKET (ASXD) the world's sixth-largest options market, trading options on more than 50 of Australia's and New Zealand's leading companies. Cash-settled options are traded on three indices—the ALL ORDINARIES INDEX, Twenty Leaders Index, and Gold Index. Formerly known as the Australian Options Market, ASXD was established in 1976 to trade put and call options in the securities of 38 leading Australian companies. Trading is quote driven with liquidity provided by market makers, through open outcry on the Sydney floor of the Australia Stock Exchange, and remote access via the Derivatives Automated Trading System (DATS).

ATP acronym for *arbitrage trading program,* better known as PROGRAM TRADING. Program traders simultaneously place orders for stock index futures and the underlying stocks in an attempt to exploit price variations. Their activity is often blamed for excessive VOLATILITY.

AT PAR at a price equal to the face, or nominal, value of a security. *See also* PAR VALUE.

AT RISK exposed to the danger of loss. Investors in a limited partnership can claim tax deductions only if they can prove that there's a chance of never realizing any profit and of losing their investment as well. Deductions will be disallowed if the limited partners are not exposed to economic risk—if, for example, the general partner guarantees to return all capital to limited partners even if the business venture should lose money.

ATHENS STOCK EXCHANGE (ASE) principal stock exchange in Greece. There are no restrictions on foreign membership on the exchange. Most investors are domestic, private, and institutional; the role of foreign institutional investors is gaining. The ASE General Index represents 75 companies, about 76% of equity market capitalization and turnover. Listings on the Parallel Market Index of companies in northern Greece are promoted by the Thessaloniki Stock Exchange, opened in 1996. The exchange uses an automated trading system, XTS, for all listed companies. Only bonds are traded by open outcry. Equities are traded on account or for cash. Settlement of all transactions is within three days. Trading hours are 10:45 A.M. to 1:30 P.M., Monday through Friday, with a half-hour pre-trading session from 10:15 A.M. to 10:45 A.M.

ATTAINED AGE age at which a person is eligible to receive certain benefits. For example, someone may be eligible to receive the proceeds from a trust when they reach age 21. Or someone who has attained the age of 65 may be eligible for certain pension or other retirement benefits. In some cases, the person may have to take some action when they reach the attained age, such as retire from a company.

AT THE CLOSE ORDER
Securities: market order that is to be executed in its entirety at the closing price on the exchange of the stock named in the order. If it is not so executed, the order is to be treated as canceled.

Futures/Options: in futures and options, a MARKET ON CLOSE ORDER, which is a contract to be executed on some exchanges during the closing period, during which there is a range of prices.

AT THE MARKET *see* MARKET ORDER.

AT THE MONEY at the current price, as an option with an exercise price equal to
or near the current price of the stock or underlying futures contract. *See also* DEEP IN/OUT OF THE MONEY; IN THE MONEY; OUT OF THE MONEY.

AT THE OPENING ORDER
Securities: market or limited price order to be executed on the opening trade of the stock on the exchange. If the order, or any portion of it, is not executed in this manner, it is to be treated as canceled.

Futures/Options: in futures and options, a MARKET ON OPEN ORDER, during which there is a range of prices at the opening.

AUCTION MARKET system by which securities are bought and sold through brokers on the securities exchanges, as distinguished from the over-the-counter market, where trades are negotiated. Best exemplified by the NEW YORK STOCK EXCHANGE, it is a double auction system or TWO-SIDED MARKET. That is because, unlike the conventional auction with one auctioneer and many buyers, here we have many sellers and many buyers. As in any auction, a price is established by competitive bidding between brokers acting as agents for buyers and sellers. That the system functions in an orderly way is the result of several trading rules: (1) The first bid or offer at a given price has priority over any other bid or offer at the same price. (2) The high bid and low offer "have the floor." (3) A new auction begins whenever all the offers or bids at a given price are exhausted. (4) Secret transactions are prohibited. (5) Bids and offers must be made in an audible voice.

Also, the competitive bidding by which Treasury bills are sold. *See also* BILL; DUTCH AUCTION.

AUCTION-RATE PREFERRED STOCK *see* DUTCH AUCTION PREFERRED STOCK.

AUDIT professional examination and verification of a company's accounting documents and supporting data for the purpose of rendering an opinion as to their fairness, consistency, and conformity with GENERALLY ACCEPTED ACCOUNTING PRINCIPLES. *See also* ACCOUNTANT'S OPINION.

AUDITOR'S CERTIFICATE *see* ACCOUNTANT'S OPINION.

AUDITOR'S REPORT public accountant's declaration following the completion of an examination of corporate financial statements. Also called *accountant's opinion.*

AUDIT TRAIL step-by-step record by which accounting data can be traced to their source. Questions as to the validity or accuracy of an accounting figure can be resolved by reviewing the sequence of events from which the figure resulted.

AUNT MILLIE derogatory term for an unsophisticated investor. Wall Street professionals may say that "This investment will interest Aunt Millie," meaning that it is simple to understand. It may also imply that such small investors will not be able to appreciate the amount of risk posed by the investment relative to the opportunity for profit. Brokers and financial advisors, using the KNOW YOUR CUSTOMER rule, should not recommend complex and risky investments to Aunt Millie investors.

AUSTRALIA STOCK EXCHANGE (ASX) six trading floors, formerly independent entities in Adelaide, Brisbane, Hobart (Tasmania), Melbourne, Perth, and Sydney, are wholly owned subsidiaries of the ASX, linked through the Stock Exchange Automated Trading System (SEATS). Administrative headquarters is in Sydney. The resources sector—mining and energy businesses—accounts for one-third of total market capitalization; industrials—including banks, retail, media, transportation—comprise the balance. The most important Australian stocks are tracked by the ALL ORDINARIES INDEX, which consists of 330 of the most active shares and represents the vast majority of equity capitalization, excluding foreign companies. Settlement is three business days after a transaction through the Clearing House Electronic Sub-register System (CHESS). SEATS trading hours are 10 A.M. to 4 P.M. (EST) Monday through Friday; dealings are permitted outside these hours according to the exchange's after-hours trading rules.

AUTEX SYSTEM electronic system for alerting brokers that other brokers want to buy or sell large blocks of stock. Once a match is made, the actual transaction takes place over the counter or on the floor of an exchange.

AUTHENTICATION identification of a bond certificate as having been issued under a specific indenture, thus validating the bond. Also, legal verification of the genuineness of a document, as by the certification and seal of an authorized public official.

AUTHORITY BOND bond issued by and payable from the revenue of a government agency or a corporation formed to administer a revenue producing public enterprise. One such corporation is the Port Authority of New York and New Jersey, which operates bridges and tunnels in the New York City area. Because an authority usually has no source of revenue other than charges for the facilities it operates, its bonds have the characteristics of revenue bonds. The difference is that bondholder protections may be incorporated in the authority bond contract as well as in the legislation that created the authority.

AUTHORIZED SHARES maximum number of shares of any class a company may legally create under the terms of its ARTICLES OF INCORPORATION. Normally, a corporation provides for future increases in authorized stock by vote of the stockholders. The corporation is not required to issue all the shares authorized and may initially keep issued shares at a minimum to hold down taxes and expenses. Also called *authorized stock.*

AUTOMATED BOND SYSTEM (ABS) New York Stock Exchange computerized system that records bids and offers for inactively traded bonds until they are cancelled or executed. Before the ABS, such limit orders were kept in steel cabinets, giving rise to the terms CABINET SECURITY and CABINET CROWD (traders in inactive bonds).

AUTOMATED ORDER ENTRY SYSTEM electronic system that expedites the execution of smaller orders by channeling them directly to the specialist on the exchange floor, bypassing the FLOOR BROKER. The New York Stock Exchange calls its system DOT (Designated Order Turnaround). Other systems include Auto Ex, OSS, PACE, SOES, and SOREX.

AUTOMATIC EXTENSION granting of more time for a taxpayer to file a tax return. By filing an IRS Form 4868 by the original due date of the tax return, a taxpayer can automatically extend his or her filing date by four months, though the tax payment (based on the taxpayer's best estimate) is still due on the original filing date.

AUTOMATIC FUNDS TRANSFER fast and accurate transfer of funds, often internationally, from one account or investment vehicle to another without direct management, using modern electronic and telecommunications technology. A broker's instant transfer of stock sale proceeds to a money market fund is one example.

AUTOMATIC INVESTMENT PROGRAM any program in which an investor can accumulate or withdraw funds automatically. Some of the most popular automatic investment programs include:

• mutual fund debit programs, in which a mutual fund will automatically debit a preset amount from a bank savings or checking account to buy fund shares on a weekly, monthly, quarterly, or annual basis.

• mutual fund reinvestment programs, in which all dividends and capital gains are automatically reinvested in more shares of the fund.

• stock dividend reinvestment plans, in which companies offer their shareholders the opportunity to reinvest their dividends in more shares of the company, and in some cases, buy additional shares at a discount with little or no brokerage commissions.

• defined contribution plans, offered by employers to their employees, which allow automatic investment in several funds through payroll deduction. Corporate plans are called 401(k), nonprofit and educational plans are called 403(b), and federal and municipal government plans are called 457s. To entice employees to participate in these plans, many employers match employee contributions.

• savings bond payroll savings plans, which allow employees to purchase savings bonds through payroll deduction.

In addition to allowing automatic purchases of shares, automatic investment programs also permit participants to withdraw a set amount of money on a regular basis. These are known as AUTOMATIC WITHDRAWAL plans. For example, a retiree may request that a mutual fund automatically sell a fixed dollar amount of shares every month and send him or her a check.

AUTOMATIC REINVESTMENT *see* CONSTANT DOLLAR PLAN; DIVIDEND REINVESTMENT PLAN.

AUTOMATIC WITHDRAWAL mutual fund program that entitles shareholders to a fixed payment each month or each quarter. The payment comes from dividends, including realized capital gains and income on securities held by the fund.

AVERAGE appropriately weighted and adjusted ARITHMETIC MEAN of selected securities designed to represent market behavior generally or important segments of the market. Among the most familiar averages are the Dow Jones industrial and transportation averages.

Because the evaluation of individual securities involves measuring price trends of securities in general or within an industry group, the various averages are important analytical tools.

See also STOCK INDEXES AND AVERAGES.

AVERAGE COST

Investing: average cost of shares of stock or in a fund bought at different prices.
See also AVERAGE DOWN; AVERAGE UP; CONSTANT DOLLAR PLAN.

Manufacturing: total of fixed and variable costs divided by units of production. Companies with relatively low average costs are better able to withstand price-cutting pressures from competition. Term also describes INVENTORY valuation method whereby the cost of goods available for sale is divided by the number of units available for sale.

AVERAGE DAILY BALANCE method for computing interest or finance charges on bank deposit accounts, credit cards, and charge accounts. Deposit accounts use the daily closing balance divided by the number of days in the period and apply the interest rate to that. Credit and charge cards divide the balances owed each day by the number of days and apply the finance charge. The average daily balance method, widely used by department stores, is less favorable to the consumer than the ADJUSTED BALANCE METHOD used for interest earned on bank deposit accounts but more favorable than the PREVIOUS BALANCE METHOD used by most credit cards.

AVERAGE DOWN strategy to lower the average price paid for a company's shares. An investor who wants to buy 1000 shares, for example, could buy 400 at the current market price and three blocks of 200 each as the price fell. The average cost would then be lower than it would have been if all 1000 shares had been bought at once. Investors also average down in order to realize tax losses. Say someone buys shares at $20, then watches them fall to $10. Instead of doing nothing, the investor can buy at $10, then sell the $20 shares at a capital loss, which can be used at tax time to offset other gains. However, the WASH SALE rule says that in order to claim the capital loss, the investor must not sell the $20 stock until at least 30 days after buying the stock at $10. *See also* CONSTANT DOLLAR PLAN.

AVERAGE EQUITY average daily balance in a trading account. Brokerage firms calculate customer equity daily as part of their procedure for keeping track of gains and losses on uncompleted transactions, called MARK TO THE MARKET. When transactions are completed, profits and losses are booked to each customer's account together with brokerage commissions. Even though daily fluctuations in equity are routine, average equity is a useful guide in making trading decisions and ensuring sufficient equity to meet MARGIN REQUIREMENTS.

AVERAGE LIFE average length of time before the principal of a debt issue is scheduled to be repaid through AMORTIZATION or SINKING FUND payments. *See also* HALF-LIFE.

AVERAGE UP buy on a rising market so as to lower the overall cost. Buying an equal number of shares at $50, $52, $54, and $58, for instance, will make the average cost $53.50. This is a mathematical reality, but it does not determine whether the stock is worth buying at any or all of these prices.

AVERAGING *see* CONSTANT DOLLAR PLAN.

AWAY FROM THE MARKET expression used when the bid on a LIMIT ORDER is lower or the offer price is higher than the current market price for the security. Away from the market limit orders are held by the specialist for later execution unless FILL OR KILL (FOK) is stipulated on the order entry.

b

BABY BELLS the seven regional telephone companies created when AT&T was broken up in 1984. The original consent decree creating the Baby Bells gave them a monopoly over local phone service but banned them from participating in the long-distance or equipment manufacturing business. AT&T was excluded from the local phone business in return. Over time, these distinctions eroded. According to the Telecommunications Act of 1996, the Baby Bells can offer long-distance service, AT&T and other long-distance providers like WorldCom-MCI and Sprint can offer local service. The original seven Baby Bells were: NYNEX in the Northeast; Bell Atlantic in the Mid-Atlantic states; BELLSOUTH in the South; SBC (Southwestern Bell Corp.) in the Southwest; Ameritech in the Midwest; U.S. West in the Rocky Mountain States; and Pacific Telesis in the West. Subsequently, Bell Atlantic acquired NYNEX and SBC acquired Pacific Telesis and Ameritech.

BABY BOND convertible or straight debt bond having a par value of less than $1000, usually $500 to $25. Baby bonds bring the bond market within reach of small investors and, by the same token, open a source of funds to corporations that lack entree to the large institutional market. On the negative side, they entail higher administrative costs (relative to the total money raised) for distribution and processing and lack the large and active market that ensures the liquidity of conventional bonds.

BACKDATING
In general: dating any statement, document, check or other instrument earlier than the date drawn.
Mutual funds: feature permitting fundholders to use an earlier date on a promise to invest a specified sum over a specified period in exchange for a reduced sales charge. Backdating, which usually accompanies a large transaction, gives retroactive value to purchases from the earlier date in order to meet the requirements of the promise, or LETTER OF INTENT.

BACK-END LOAD redemption charge an investor pays when withdrawing money from an investment. Most common in mutual funds and annuities, the back-end load is designed to discourage withdrawals. Back-end loads typically decline for each year that a shareholder remains in a fund. For example, if the shareholder sells shares in the first year, a 5% sales charge is levied. The charge is 4% in the second year, 3% in the third year, 2% in the fourth year, 1% in the fifth year, and no fee is charged if shares are sold after the fifth year. Also called *contingent deferred sales load, deferred sales charge, exit fee, redemption charge.*

BACKING AWAY broker-dealer's failure, as market maker in a given security, to make good on a bid for the minimum quantity. This practice is considered unethical under the RULES OF FAIR PRACTICE of the NATIONAL ASSOCIATION OF SECURITIES DEALERS.

BACKLOG value of unfilled orders placed with a manufacturing company. Whether the firm's backlog is rising or falling is a clue to its future sales and earnings.

BACK MONTHS in futures and options trading, the months with the expiration dates furthest out in time. *See also* FURTHEST MONTH.

BACK OFFICE bank or brokerage house departments not directly involved in selling or trading. The back office sees to accounting records, compliance with government regulations, and communication between branches. When stock-market trading is particularly heavy, order processing can be slowed by massive volume; this is called a back office crunch.

BACK TAXES taxes that have not been paid when due. Taxpayers may owe back taxes if they underreported income or overstated deductions, either accidentally, or by design. The Internal Revenue Service and state and local taxing authorities have the right to audit past tax returns and demand payment of back taxes, plus interest and penalties.

BACK-TESTING applying current stock selection criteria to prior periods to create hypothetical PORTFOLIO performance history. A major limitation of back-testing is that it ignores the effect of an investment strategy's popularity on portfolio total returns.

BACK UP turn around; reverse a stock market trend. When prices are moving in one direction, traders would say of a sudden reversal that the market backed up.

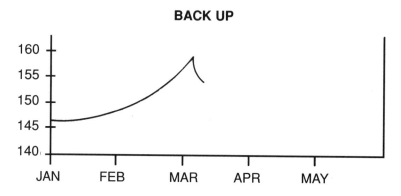

BACK UP

BACKUP LINE BANK LINE of credit in the name of an issuer of commercial paper, covering maturing notes in the event that new notes cannot be marketed to replace them. Ideally, the unused line should always equal the commercial paper outstanding. In practice, something less than total coverage is commonplace, particularly because the compensating balances normally required in support of the line are also available to meet maturing paper.

BACKUP WITHHOLDING system used by the Internal Revenue Service to ensure that taxpayers without Social Security numbers have taxes withheld on earnings. In an instance where a Form 1099 can not be filed by a payor, such as a bank or brokerage, 20% of the interest or dividends is withheld and remitted to the IRS. To avoid backup withholding, you must fill out a federal W-9 form for the financial institution, verifying that your Social Security number is correct.

BACKWARDATION
1. pricing structure in commodities or foreign-exchange trading in which deliveries in the near future have a higher price than those made later on. Backwardation occurs when demand is greater in the near future. *See also* CONTANGO.
2. London Stock Exchange term for the fees and interest due on short sales of stock with delayed delivery.

BAD DEBT
Banks and Corporations: open account balance or loan receivable that has proven uncollectible and is written off. Traditionally, companies and financial institutions have maintained a RESERVE for uncollectible accounts, charging the reserve for actual bad debts and making annual, tax deductible charges to income to replenish or increase the reserve. Companies and large banks ($500 million or more in assets) must generally use the direct charge-off method for tax purposes, although bad debt reserves continue to appear on balance sheets for reporting purposes. Small banks and thrift institutions continue using the reserve method for tax purposes, although with strict limitations. The relationship of bad debt WRITE-OFFS and recoveries to accounts receivable can reveal how liberal or conservative a firm's credit and charge-off policies are.
Individuals: Individuals lending money may deduct bad debts on their tax return when the debtor does not repay the loan. Bad business debts are fully deductible from gross income on Schedule C for self-employed individuals. Nonbusiness bad debts can be deducted as short-term capital losses on Schedule

D. These short-term losses can offset capital gains plus $3,000 of other income. Any excess bad debt losses can be carried forward into future tax years. In order to determine whether a bad debt deduction is legitimate:
1. the debt must be legally valid
2. A debtor-creditor relationship must be formalized at the time the debt arose
3. the funds providing the loan must have previously been reported as income or part of the individual's capital and
4. the individual must prove that the debt became worthless in that tax year.

BAD DELIVERY opposite of GOOD DELIVERY.

BAD TITLE title to property that does not clearly confer ownership. Most frequently applied to real estate, a bad title may prevent a homeowner from selling the property. Title may be clouded by unpaid taxes or other unsatisfied liens, a faulty or incomplete certificate of occupancy, an incorrect survey, or uncorrected building violations, among other causes. Steps must be taken to rectify these problems before title to a property can be legally transferred. Also called *cloud on title.*

BAILING OUT selling a security or commodity quickly without regard to the price received. An investor bails out of a position if losses are mounting quickly and he or she is no longer able to sustain further losses. For example, someone who has sold a stock short may bail out by covering his or her position at a loss if the stock rises sharply.

The term is also used to describe the act of rescuing a person or corporate or government entity in financial distress. For example, the federal government bailed out the Federal Deposit Insurance Corporation with hundreds of billions of dollars when it had to pay for closing down hundreds of bankrupt savings and loans through the Resolution Trust Corporation. When the Chrysler Corporation was teetering near bankruptcy in the early 1980s, the federal government bailed it out by providing loan guarantees.

BAILOUT BOND bond issued by RESOLUTION FUNDING CORPORATION (REFCORP) to finance the rescue or disposition of SAVINGS AND LOAN ASSOCIATIONS that were failing in the 1980s and 1990s. The principal of REFCORP securities is backed by zero-coupon Treasury bonds and the U.S. Treasury guarantees interest payments. Because this is stronger backing than that enjoyed by other GOVERNMENT SECURITIES issued by agencies, bailout bonds yield only slightly more than TREASURIES of comparable maturity. Once the savings and loan crisis ended in the mid-1990s, no more bailout bonds were issued, though existing issues continued to trade in the bond market. See also OFFICE OF THRIFT SUPERVISION (OTS).

BALANCED BUDGET see BUDGET.

BALANCED MUTUAL FUND fund that buys common stock, preferred stock, and bonds in an effort to obtain the highest return consistent with a low-risk strategy. A balanced fund typically offers a higher yield than a pure stock fund and performs better than such a fund when stocks are falling. In a rising market, however, a balanced mutual fund usually will not keep pace with all-equity funds.

BALANCE OF PAYMENTS system of recording all of a country's economic transactions with the rest of the world during a particular time period. Double-entry bookkeeping is used, and there can be no surplus or deficit on the overall balance of payments. The balance of payments is typically divided into three accounts—current, capital, and gold—and these can show a surplus or deficit. The current account covers imports and exports of goods and services; the capital account covers movements of investments; and the gold account covers gold movements. The balance of payments helps a country evaluate its competitive strengths and weaknesses and forecast the strength of its currency. From the standpoint of a national economy, a surplus on a part of the balance of payments is not necessarily good, nor is a deficit necessarily bad; the state of the national economy and the manner of financing the deficit are important considerations. *See also* BALANCE OF TRADE.

BALANCE OF TRADE net difference over a period of time between the value of a country's imports and exports of merchandise. Movable goods such as automobiles, foodstuffs, and apparel are included in the balance of trade; payments abroad for services and for tourism are not. When a country exports more than it imports, it is said to have a favorable balance of trade; when imports predominate the balance is called unfavorable. The balance of trade should be viewed in the context of the country's entire international economic position, however. For example, a country may consistently have an unfavorable balance of trade that is offset by considerable exports of services; this country would be judged to have a good international economic position. *See also* BALANCE OF PAYMENTS.

BALANCE SHEET financial report, also called *statement of condition* or *statement of financial position,* showing the status of a company's assets, liabilities, and owners' equity on a given date, usually the close of a month. One way of looking at a business enterprise is as a mass of capital (ASSETS) arrayed against the sources of that capital (LIABILITIES and EQUITY). Assets are equal to liabilities and equity, and the balance sheet is a listing of the items making up the two sides of the equation. Unlike a PROFIT AND LOSS STATEMENT, which shows the results of operations over a period of time, a balance sheet shows the state of affairs at one point in time. It is a snapshot, not a motion picture, and must be analyzed with reference to comparative prior balance sheets and other operating statements.

BALLOON final payment on a debt that is substantially larger than the preceding payments. Loans or mortgages are structured with balloon payments when some projected event is expected to provide extra cash flow or when refinancing is anticipated. Balloon loans are sometimes called *partially amortized loans.*

BALLOON INTEREST in serial bond issues, the higher COUPON rate on bonds with later maturities.

BALLOON MATURITY bond issue or long-term loan with larger dollar amounts of bonds or payments falling due in the later years of the obligation.

BAN *see* BOND ANTICIPATION NOTE.

BANKER'S ACCEPTANCE *see* ACCEPTANCE.

BANK DISCOUNT BASIS *see* DISCOUNT YIELD.

BANK HOLDING COMPANY company that owns or controls two or more banks or other bank holding companies. As defined in the Bank Holding Company Act of 1956, such companies must register with the BOARD OF GOVERNORS of the FEDERAL RESERVE SYSTEM and hence are called registered bank holding companies. Amendments to the 1956 act set standards for acquisitions (1966) and ended the exemption enjoyed by one-bank holding companies (1970), thus restricting bank holding companies to activities related to banking.

BANK INSURANCE FUND (BIF) FEDERAL DEPOSIT INSURANCE CORPORATION (FDIC) unit providing deposit insurance for banks other than thrifts. BIF was formed as part of the 1989 savings and loan association bailout bill to keep separate the administration of the bank and thrift insurance programs. There are thus two distinct insurance entities under FDIC: BIF and SAVINGS ASSOCIATION INSUR-

ANCE FUND (SAIF). Deposit insurance coverage remains unaffected. *See also* OFFICE OF THRIFT SUPERVISION (OTS).

BANK INVESTMENT CONTRACT (BIC) bank-guaranteed interest in a portfolio providing a specified yield over a specified period. For insurance company equivalent, *see* GUARANTEED INVESTMENT CONTRACT (GIC).

BANK LINE bank's moral commitment, as opposed to its contractual commitment, to make loans to a particular borrower up to a specified maximum during a specified period, usually one year. Because a bank line—also called a *line of credit*—is not a legal commitment, it is not customary to charge a commitment fee. It is common, however, to require that compensating balances be kept on deposit—typically 10% of the line, with an additional 10% of any borrowings under the line. A line about which a customer is officially notified is called an *advised line* or *confirmed line.* A line that is an internal policy guide about which the customer is not informed is termed a *guidance line.*

BANKMAIL bank's agreement with a company involved in a TAKEOVER not to finance another acquirer's bid.

BANK QUALITY *see* INVESTMENT GRADE.

BANKRUPTCY state of insolvency of an individual or an organization—in other words, an inability to pay debts. There are two kinds of legal bankruptcy under U.S. law: involuntary, when one or more creditors petition to have a debtor judged insolvent by a court; and voluntary, when the debtor brings the petition. In both cases, the objective is an orderly and equitable settlement of obligations.

The 1978 Bankruptcy Reform Act removed some of the rigidities of the old law and permitted more flexibility in procedures. The Bankruptcy Reform Act of 1984 curtailed some of the more liberal provisions (mainly affecting consumer bankruptcy) of the 1978 act.

Chapter 7 of the 1978 act, dealing with LIQUIDATION, provides for a court-appointed interim trustee with broad powers and discretion to make management changes, arrange unsecured financing, and generally operate the debtor business in such a way as to prevent loss. Only by filing an appropriate bond is the debtor able to regain possession from the trustee.

Chapter 11, which deals with REORGANIZATION of businesses, provides that, unless the court rules otherwise, the debtor remains in possession of the business and in control of its operation. Debtor and creditors are allowed considerable flexibility in working together.

Chapter 13, which deals with debt adjustment or reorganization for individuals, allows people to put forward a plan to repay creditors over time, usually from future income. Most consumer reorganizations take place under Chapter 13 of the bankruptcy law. A Chapter 13 bankruptcy normally requires monthly payments to the bankruptcy trustee for a period of three to five years. Once payments have been completed under the plan, the debtors are entitled to a discharge. Chapter 13 reorganizations also allow debtors to keep more property than in a Chapter 7 liquidation.

BANK TRUST DEPARTMENT part of a bank engaged in settling estates, administering trusts and guardianships, and performing AGENCY services. As part of its personal trust and ESTATE PLANNING services, it manages investments for large accounts—typically those with at least $50,000 in assets. People who cannot or do not want to make investment decisions are commonly bank trust department clients. Known for their conservative investment philosophy, such departments have custody over billions of dollars, making them a major factor in the movement of stock and bond prices.

Among other things, the departments also act as trustee for corporate bonds, administer pension and profit-sharing plans, and function as TRANSFER AGENTS.

BANK WIRE computerized message system owned and administered by about 250 participating banks in about 75 U.S. cities. Like the FED WIRE, the bank wire transmits large dollar credit transfer information. It also provides information about loan participations, securities transactions, Federal Reserve System funds borrowings, credit history, the payment or nonpayment of "wire fate" items, and other essential matters requiring prompt communication.

BARBELL PORTFOLIO portfolio of bonds distributed like the shape of a barbell, with most of the portfolio in short-term and long-term bonds, but few bonds in intermediate maturities. This portfolio can be adjusted to emphasize short- or long-term bonds, depending on whether the investor thinks interest rates are rising or falling. A portfolio with a higher concentration in medium-term bonds than short- or long-term bonds is called a *bell-shaped curve portfolio*.

BAREFOOT PILGRIM unsophisticated investor who has lost his or her shirt and shoes in securities trading.

BAROMETER selective compilation of economic and market data designed to represent larger trends. Consumer spending, housing starts, and interest rates are barometers used in economic forecasting. The Dow Jones Industrial Average and the Standard & Poor's 500 Stock Index are prominent stock market barometers. The Dow Jones Utility Average is a barometer of market trends in the utility industry.

A *barometer stock* has a price movement pattern that reflects the market as a whole, thus serving as a market indicator. General Motors, for example, is considered a barometer stock.

BARRON'S CONFIDENCE INDEX weekly index of corporate bond yields published by *Barron's*, a Dow Jones financial newspaper. The index shows the ratio of the average yield on 10 top-grade bonds to the average yield on 10 intermediate-grade bonds. People who are worried about the economic outlook tend to seek safety in a FLIGHT TO QUALITY, whereas investors who feel secure about the economy are more likely to buy lower-rated bonds. The spread between high- and low-grade bonds thus reflects investor confidence about the economy. *Barron's* also publishes other confidence indicators, such as the TED SPREAD (the difference between Treasury Bill Futures and Eurodollar Futures contract prices); the Lehman Brothers Treasury Bond Index; the Lehman Brothers Corporate Bond Index; the Ryan Labs Treasury Index; the Bond Buyer 20 Bond Index; the Bond Buyer Municipal Bond Index and the Stock/Bond Yield Gap, which is the difference between the yield on the highest-grade corporate bonds and the yield on the stocks in the Dow Jones Industrial Average.

BARTER trade of goods or services without use of money. When money is involved, whether in such forms as wampum, checks, or bills or coins, a transaction is called a SALE. Although barter is usually associated with undeveloped economies, it occurs in modern complex societies. In conditions of extreme inflation, it can be a preferred mode of commerce. Where a population lacks confidence in its currency or banking system, barter becomes commonplace. In international trade, barter can provide a way of doing business with countries whose soft currencies would otherwise make them unattractive trading partners.

BASE in TECHNICAL ANALYSIS, a chart pattern in which the SUPPORT LEVEL and the RESTRICTED LEVEL come together. During a *basing* period, supply and demand are in relative equilibrium and the stock trades in a narrow range. A positive or negative BREAKOUT from a basing period can be a powerful buy or sell signal.

BASE MARKET VALUE average market price of a group of securities at a given time. It is used as a basis of comparison in plotting dollar or percentage changes for purposes of market INDEXING.

BASE PERIOD particular time in the past used as a yardstick when measuring economic data. A base period is usually a year or an average of years; it can also be a month or other time period. The U.S. rate of INFLATION is determined by measuring current prices against those of a base period; for instance, the CONSUMER PRICE INDEX is determined by comparing current prices with prices in the base reference years of 1982–1984 and the PRODUCER PRICE INDEX is determined by comparing current prices with prices in the base reference year of 1987.

BASE RATE interest rate charged by banks to their best corporate customers in Great Britain. It is the British equivalent of the PRIME RATE in the United States. Many other consumer loan rates are pegged to the base rate in Britain.

BASIC EARNINGS PER SHARE see EARNINGS PER SHARE.

BASIS

In general: original cost plus out-of-pocket expenses that must be reported to the Internal Revenue Service when an investment is sold and must be used in calculating capital gains or losses. If a stock was bought for $1000 two years ago and is sold today for $2000, the basis is $1000 and the profit is a capital gain.

Bonds: an investor's YIELD TO MATURITY at a given bond price. A 10% bond selling at 100 has a 10% basis.

Commodities: the difference between the cash price of a hedged money market instrument and a FUTURES CONTRACT.

BASIS POINT smallest measure used in quoting yields on bills, notes, and bonds. One basis point is .01%, or one one-hundredth of a percent of yield. Thus, 100 basis points equal 1%. A bond's yield that increased from 8.00% to 8.50% would be said to have risen 50 basis points.

BASIS PRICE

In general: price an investor uses to calculate capital gains when selling a stock or bond. *See also* BASIS.

Odd-lot trading: the price arbitrarily established by an exchange floor official at the end of a trading session for a buyer or seller of an odd lot when the market bid and asked prices are more than $2 apart, or if no round-lot transactions have occurred that day. The customer gets the basis price plus or minus the odd-lot differential, if any. This procedure for determining prices is rare, since most odd lots are transacted at the market bid (if a sale) or asked (if a buy) or at prices based on the next round-lot trade.

BASKET
1. unit of 15 or more stocks used in PROGRAM TRADING.
2. program trading vehicles offered by the NEW YORK STOCK EXCHANGE (called *Exchange Stock Portfolio* or *ESP*) and the CHICAGO BOARD OPTIONS EXCHANGE (called *Market Basket*) to institutional investors and index arbitrageurs. Both baskets permit the purchase in one trade of all the stocks making up the STANDARD & POOR'S 500 COMPOSITE INDEX. ESP's design requires a minimum trade of approximately $5 million, and Market Basket's, around $1.7 million. The baskets were introduced in late 1989 to solve problems revealed when institutions tried to negotiate large block trades on BLACK MONDAY and to head off an exodus of program trading business to overseas exchanges. Subsequently, trading in these instruments ceased due to lack of trading volume.

3. informal name for *index participations* (also called *cash index participations* or *CIPS)*, a controversial financial instrument introduced and then withdrawn by the American and Philadelphia stock exchanges in 1989. The product allowed small investors to buy a portfolio position (in the Standard & Poor's index of 500 stocks and in a 25-stock index that has historically correlated with the Dow Jones Industrial Average) without buying individual stocks. It retained advantages of stock ownership by having no expiration date (like a future or an option) and providing for quarterly dividend payments. Originally approved by the SECURITIES AND EXCHANGE COMMISSION as a security, the instrument was challenged by the COMMODITIES FUTURES TRADING COMMISSION, which claimed it was a futures contract. When a federal court ruled against the SEC, the exchanges stopped trading the product.

See also DIAMONDS, SPDR.

BD FORM document that brokerage house must file and keep current with the Securities and Exchange Commission, detailing the firm's finances and officers.

BEACON acronym for the *Boston Exchange Automated Communication Order-routing Network.* This electronic system allows the automatic execution of trades based on the prevailing stock prices on the consolidated market, any of the seven U.S. securities exchanges.

BEAR person with a pessimistic market outlook. Contrast with BULL.

BEARER BOND *see* COUPON BOND.

BEARER FORM security not registered on the books of the issuing corporation and thus payable to the one possessing it. A bearer bond has coupons attached, which the bondholder sends in or presents on the interest date for payment, hence the alternative name COUPON BONDS. Bearer stock certificates are negotiable without endorsement and are transferred by delivery. Dividends are payable by presentation of dividend coupons, which are dated or numbered. Most securities issued today, with the exception of foreign stocks, are in registered form, including municipal bonds issued since 1983.

BEAR HUG TAKEOVER bid so attractive in terms of price and other features that TARGET COMPANY directors, who might be opposed for other reasons, must approve it or risk shareholder protest.

BEAR MARKET prolonged period of falling prices. A bear market in stocks is usually brought on by the anticipation of declining economic activity, and a bear market in bonds is caused by rising interest rates.

BEAR RAID attempt by investors to manipulate the price of a stock by selling large numbers of shares short. The manipulators pocket the difference between the initial price and the new, lower price after this maneuver. Bear raids are illegal under Securities and Exchange Commission rules, which stipulate that every SHORT SALE be executed on an UPTICK (the last price was higher than the price before it) or a ZERO PLUS TICK (the last price was unchanged but higher than the last preceding different price).

BEARS acronym for *Bonds Enabling Annual Retirement Savings* and the flip side of *CUBS*, acronym for *Calls Underwritten By Swanbrook.* Holders of BEARS receive the face value of bonds underlying call options but exercised by CUBS holders. If the calls are exercised, BEARS holders receive the aggregate of the exercise prices.

BEAR SPREAD strategy in the options market designed to take advantage of a fall in the price of a security or commodity. Someone executing a bear spread could buy a combination of calls and puts on the same security at different *strike* *prices* in order to profit as the security's price fell. Or the investor could buy a put of short maturity and a put of long maturity in order to profit from the difference between the two puts as prices fell. *See also* BULL SPREAD.

BEAR TRAP situation confronting short sellers when a bear market reverses itself and turns bullish. Anticipating further declines, the bears continue to sell, and then are forced to buy at higher prices to cover. *See also* SELLING SHORT.

BELL signal that opens and closes trading on major exchanges—sometimes actually a bell but sometimes a buzzer sound.

BELLWETHER security seen as an indicator of a market's direction. In stocks, 3M Company (MMM) is considered both an economic and a market bellwether because it sells to a diverse range of other producers and because so much of its stock is owned by institutional investors who have much control over supply and demand on the stock market. Institutional trading actions tend to influence smaller investors and therefore the market generally. There are bellwethers in specific industries, for example, Microsoft and Intel act as bellwethers for the technology stocks. In bonds, the 30-year U.S. Treasury bond is considered the bellwether, denoting the direction in which all other bonds are likely to move.

BELOW PAR *see* PAR VALUE.

BENEFICIAL OWNER person who enjoys the benefits of ownership even though title is in another name. When shares of a mutual fund are held by a custodian bank or when securities are held by a broker in STREET NAME, the real owner is the beneficial owner, even though, for safety or convenience, the bank or broker holds title.

BENEFICIARY
1. person to whom an inheritance passes as the result of being named in a will.
2. recipient of the proceeds of a life insurance policy.
3. party in whose favor a LETTER OF CREDIT is issued.
4. one to whom the amount of an ANNUITY is payable.
5. party for whose benefit a TRUST exists.

BEQUEST giving of assets, such as stocks, bonds, mutual funds, real estate, and personal property, to beneficiaries through the provisions of a will.

BEST EFFORT arrangement whereby investment bankers, acting as agents, agree to do their best to sell an issue to the public. Instead of buying the securities outright, these agents have an option to buy and an authority to sell the securities. Depending on the contract, the agents exercise their option and buy enough shares to cover their sales to clients, or they cancel the incompletely sold issue altogether and forgo the fee. Best efforts deals, which were common prior to 1900, entailed risks and delays from the issuer's standpoint. What is more, the broadening of the securities markets has made marketing new issues easier, and the practice of outright purchase by investment bankers, called FIRM COMMITMENT underwriting, has become commonplace. For the most part, the best efforts deals we occasionally see today are handled by firms specializing in the more speculative securities of new and unseasoned companies. *See also* BOUGHT DEAL.

BEST'S RATING rating assigned to insurance companies by A.M. Best Co. A Best's Rating is important to buyers of insurance or annuities because it provides an opinion of a company's ability to meet its obligations to policyholders. Best's Ratings are also important to investors in insurance stocks. The top rating is A++. Other companies providing ratings of insurance companies include Duff & Phelps in Chicago, MOODY'S INVESTORS SERVICES in New York, STANDARD & POOR'S in New York and Weiss Research in Palm Beach Gardens, Florida.

BETA

1. coefficient measuring a stock's relative VOLATILITY. The beta is the covariance of a stock in relation to the rest of the stock market. The Standard & Poor's 500 Stock Index has a beta coefficient of 1. Any stock with a higher beta is more volatile than the market, and any with a lower beta can be expected to rise and fall more slowly than the market. A conservative investor whose main concern is preservation of capital should focus on stocks with low betas, whereas one willing to take high risks in an effort to earn high rewards should look for high-beta stocks. *See also* ALPHA.

2. on the London Stock Exchange, the designation *beta stocks* applies to the second tier in a four-level hierarchy introduced with BIG BANG in October 1986 and replaced in January, 1991 with the NORMAL MARKET SIZE (NMS) classification system. With ALPHA stocks representing the equivalent of American BLUE CHIP issues, beta stocks represented smaller issues that were less actively traded. *See also* DELTA (2); GAMMA STOCKS.

BID

1. price a prospective buyer is ready to pay. Term is used by traders who MAKE A MARKET (maintain firm bid and OFFER prices) in a given security by standing ready to buy or sell round lots at publicly quoted prices and by the SPECIALIST in a stock, who performs a similar function on an exchange.

2. TENDER OFFER in a TAKEOVER attempt.

3. any offer to buy at a specified price.

   See also ANY-AND-ALL BID; COMPETITIVE BID; TREASURIES.

BID AND ASKED bid is the highest price a prospective buyer is prepared to pay at a particular time for a trading unit of a given security; asked is the lowest price acceptable to a prospective seller of the same security. Together, the two prices constitute a QUOTATION; the difference between the two prices is the SPREAD. Although the bid and asked dynamic is common to all securities trading, "bid and asked" usually refers to UNLISTED SECURITIES traded OVER THE COUNTER.

BID-ASKED SPREAD difference between BID and offer prices. The term *asked* is usually used in OVER-THE-COUNTER trading; *offered* is used in exchange trading. The bid and asked (or offered) prices together comprise a QUOTATION (or *quote*).

BIDDER party that is ready to buy at a specified price in a TWO-SIDED MARKET or DUTCH AUCTION.

BIDDING UP practice whereby the price bid for a security is successively moved higher lest an upswing in prices leaves orders unexecuted. An example would be an investor wanting to purchase a sizable quantity of shares in a rising market, using buy limit orders (orders to buy at a specified price or lower) to ensure the most favorable price. Since offer prices are moving up with the market, the investor must move his limit buy price upward to continue accumulating shares. To some extent the buyer is contributing to the upward price pressure on the stock, but most of the price rise is out of his control.

BID-TO-COVER RATIO number of bids received in a Treasury security auction compared to the number of bids accepted. A high ratio (over 2.0) is an indication that bidding was aggressive and the auction successful. A low ratio, indicating the government had difficulty selling its securities, is usually accompanied by a long TAIL, a wide spread between the average and high yield (the average and lowest accepted bid).

BID WANTED (BW) announcement that a holder of securities wants to sell and will entertain bids. Because the final price is subject to negotiation, the bid submitted in response to a BW need not be specific. A BW is frequently seen on published market quotation sheets.

BIG BANG deregulation on October 27, 1986, of London-based securities markets, an event comparable to MAY DAY in the United States and marking a major step toward a single world financial market.

BIG BLUE popular name for International Business Machines Corporation (IBM), taken from the color of its logotype.

BIG BOARD popular term for the NEW YORK STOCK EXCHANGE.

BIG FIVE largest U.S. accounting firms as measured by revenue. They do the accounting and auditing for most major corporations, signing the AUDITOR'S REPORT that appears in every annual report. They also offer various consulting services. Over time, there have been several mergers among the top accounting firms, which formerly were called the Big Eight, and until 1998, the Big Six. In alphabetical order they are: Andersen Worldwide; PricewaterhouseCoopers; Deloitte & Touche; Ernst & Young; and KPMG Peat Marwick.

BIG PRODUCER broker who is very successful, and thereby produces a large volume of commission dollars for the brokerage firm he or she represents. Big producers typically will bring in $1 million or more per year in commissions for their firms. In order to retain big producers, many brokerage firms try to tie them to the firm with GOLDEN HANDCUFFS.

BIG THREE the three large automobile companies in America, which are, alphabetically, Chrysler, Ford, and General Motors. Since the automobile business has such a major influence on the direction of the economy, the Big Three's fortunes are closely followed by investors, analysts, and economists. Because auto company profits rise and fall with the economy, they are considered to be CYCLICAL STOCKS. In 1998, Chrysler merged with Daimler-Benz to create DaimlerChrysler AG.

BIG UGLIES stocks that are out of favor with the investing public. These usually are large industrial companies such as steel or chemical firms that are not in glamorous businesses. Because they are unpopular, Big Uglies typically sell at low price/earnings and price/book value ratios.

BILL

In general: (1) short for *bill of exchange,* an order by one person directing a second to pay a third. (2) document evidencing a debtor's obligation to a creditor, the kind of bill we are all familiar with. (3) paper currency, like the $5 bill. (4) *bill of sale,* a document used to transfer the title to certain goods from seller to buyer in the same way a deed to real property passes.

Investments: short for *due bill,* a statement of money owed. Commonly used to adjust a securities transaction when dividends, interest, and other distributions are reflected in a price but have not yet been disbursed. For example, when a stock is sold ex-dividend, but the dividend has not yet been paid, the buyer would sign a due bill stating that the amount of the dividend is payable to the seller.

A due bill may accompany delivered securities to give title to the buyer's broker in exchange for shares or money.

U.S. Treasury bill: commonly called bill or T-bill by money market people, a Treasury bill is a short-term (maturities up to a year), discounted government security sold through competitive bidding at weekly and monthly auctions in denominations from $10,000 to $1 million.

The auction at which bills are sold differs from the two-sided auction used by exchanges. Here, in what is sometimes termed a *Dutch auction,* the Treasury invites anyone interested to submit a bid, called a TENDER, then awards units to the highest bidders going down a list. Three-and six-month bills are auctioned weekly, nine-month and one-year bills monthly. Although the yield on bills may barely top the inflation rate, the high degree of safety together with the liquidity provided by an active SECONDARY MARKET make bills popular with corporate money managers as well as with banks and other government entities.

Individuals may also purchase bills directly, in amounts under $500,000, at no transaction charge, from a Federal Reserve bank, the Bureau of Federal Debt, or certain commercial banks. Bills bought on this basis are priced by noncompetitive bidding, with subscribers paying an average of the accepted bids.

Treasury bills are the most widely used of all government debt securities and are a primary instrument of Federal Reserve monetary policy. *See also* TAX ANTICIPATION BILL; TREASURY DIRECT.

BILLING CYCLE interval between periodic billings for goods sold or services rendered, normally one month, or a system whereby bills or statements are mailed at periodic intervals in the course of a month in order to distribute the clerical workload.

BILL OF EXCHANGE *see* DRAFT.

BINDER sum of money paid to evidence good faith until a transaction is finalized. In insurance, the binder is an agreement executed by an insurer (or sometimes an agent) that puts insurance coverage into force before the contract is signed and the premium paid. In real estate, the binder holds the sale until the closing and is refundable.

BI-WEEKLY MORTGAGE LOAN mortgage loan on which the borrower makes 26 half-month payments a year, resulting in earlier loan retirement and lower total interest costs than with a fully amortized loan with regular monthly payments. For example, a 30-year mortgage may be retired in 20 years if paid bi-weekly. Many bi-weekly plans offer automatic electronic debiting of the borrower's bank account.

BLACK FRIDAY sharp drop in a financial market. The original Black Friday was September 24, 1869, when a group of financiers tried to corner the gold market and precipitated a business panic followed by a depression. The panic of 1873 also began on Friday, and Black Friday has come to apply to any debacle affecting the financial markets.

BLACK MONDAY October 19, 1987, when the Dow Jones Industrial Average plunged a record 508 points following sharp drops the previous week, reflecting investor anxiety about inflated stock price levels, federal budget and trade deficits, and foreign market activity. On Monday, October 27, 1997, the Dow dropped 554 points, precipitated by economic and currency upheaval in Southeast Asia. While the point drop set a new record, the percentage decline based on a higher Dow was far less than in 1987. That 1997 day is also called *Bloody Monday*. Many blamed PROGRAM TRADING for the extreme VOLATILITY.

BLACK-SCHOLES OPTION PRICING MODEL model developed by Fischer Black and Myron Scholes to gauge whether options contracts are fairly valued. The model incorporates such factors as the volatility of a security's return, the level of interest rates, the relationship of the underlying stock's price to the *strike price* of the option, and the time remaining until the option expires. Current valuations using this model are developed by the Options Monitor Service and are available from Standard & Poor's Trading Systems, 11 Broadway, New York, NY 10004.

BLANK CHECK check drawn on a bank account and signed by the maker, but with the amount of the check to be supplied by the drawee. Term is used as a metaphor for any situation where inordinate trust is placed in another person.

BLANK CHECK OFFERING INITIAL PUBLIC OFFERING (IPO) by a company whose business activities have yet to be determined and which is therefore speculative. Similar to the BLIND POOL concept of limited partnerships.

BLANKET CERTIFICATION FORM *see* NASD FORM FR-1.

BLANKET FIDELITY BOND insurance coverage against losses due to employee dishonesty. Brokerage firms are required to carry such protection in proportion to their net capital as defined by the Securities and Exchange Commission. Contingencies covered include securities loss, forgery, and fraudulent trading. Also called *blanket bond.*

BLANKET RECOMMENDATION communication sent to all customers of a brokerage firm recommending that they buy or sell a particular stock or stocks in a particular industry regardless of investment objectives or portfolio size.

BLENDED RATE mortgage financing term used when a lender, to avoid assuming an old mortgage at an obsolitely low rate, offers the incentive to refinance at a rate somewhere between the old rate and the rate on a new loan.

BLIND POOL limited partnership that does not specify the properties the general partner plans to acquire. If, for example, a real estate partnership is offered in the form of a blind pool, investors can evaluate the project only by looking at the general partner's track record. In a *specified pool,* on the other hand, investors can look at the prices paid for property and the amount of rental income the buildings generate, then evaluate the partnership's potential. In general, blind pool partnerships do not perform better or worse than specified pool partnerships.

BLIND TRUST trust in which a fiduciary third party, such as a bank or money management firm, is given complete discretion to make investments on behalf of the trust beneficiaries. The trust is called blind because the beneficiary is not informed about the holdings of the trust. Blind trusts often are set up when there is a potential conflict of interest involving the beneficiary and the investments held in the trust. For example, a politician may be required to place his assets in a blind trust so that his votes are not influenced by his trust's portfolio holdings.

BLITZKREIG TENDER OFFER TAKEOVER jargon for a tender offer that is completed quickly, usually because it was priced attractively. *Blitzkreig* translates from the German as "lightning-like war" and was used to describe World War II bombing raids. Legislation passed in the 1960s was aimed at curtailing surprise takeovers, so the term is relative. *See also* SATURDAY NIGHT SPECIAL.

BLOCK large quantity of stock or large dollar amount of bonds held or traded. As a general guide, 10,000 shares or more of stock and $200,000 or more worth of bonds would be described as a block.

BLOCK POSITIONER dealer who, to accommodate the seller of a block of securities, will take a position in the securities, hoping to gain from a rise in the market price. Block positioners must register with the Securities and Exchange Commission and the New York Stock Exchange (if member firms). Typically they engage in ARBITRAGE, HEDGING, and SELLING SHORT to protect their risk and liquidate their position.

BLOCK TRADE *see* BLOCK.

BLOODY MONDAY *see* BLACK MONDAY.

BLOWOUT quick sale of all shares in a new offering of securities. Corporations like to sell securities in such environments, because they get a high price for their stock. Investors are likely to have a hard time getting the number of shares they want during a blowout. Also called *going away* or *hot issue.*

BLUE CHIP common stock of a nationally known company that has a long record of profit growth and dividend payment and a reputation for quality management, products, and services. Some examples of blue chip stocks: International Business Machines, General Electric, and Du Pont. Blue chip stocks typically are relatively high priced and have moderate dividend yields.

BLUE LIST daily financial publication listing bonds offered for sale by several hundred dealers and banks and representing billions of dollars in par value. The *Blue List,* published by a Standard & Poor's subsidiary, mainly contains data on municipal bonds. With its pertinent price, yield, and other data, the *Blue List* is the most comprehensive source of information on activity and volume in the secondary market for tax-exempt securities. Some corporate bonds offered by the same dealers are also included. Full name, *Blue List of Current Municipal Offerings.* The *Blue List* is also available through an on-line database on the Internet at www.bluelist.com.

BLUE-SKY LAW law of a kind passed by various states to protect investors against securities fraud. These laws require sellers of new stock issues or mutual funds to register their offerings and provide financial details on each issue so that investors can base their judgments on relevant data. The term is said to have originated with a judge who asserted that a particular stock offering had as much value as a patch of blue sky.

BOARD BROKER employee of the CHICAGO BOARD OPTIONS EXCHANGE who handles AWAY FROM THE MARKET orders, which cannot immediately be executed. If board brokers act as agents in executing such orders, they notify the exchange members who entered the orders.

BOARD OF DIRECTORS group of individuals elected, usually at an annual meeting, by the shareholders of a corporation and empowered to carry out certain tasks as spelled out in the corporation's charter. Among such powers are appointing senior management, naming members of executive and finance committees (if any), issuing additional shares, and declaring dividends. Boards normally include the top corporate executives, termed *inside directors,* as well as OUTSIDE DIRECTORS chosen from business and from the community at large to advise on matters of broad policy. Directors meet several times a year and are paid for their services. They are considered control persons under the securities laws, meaning that their shares are restricted. As insiders, they cannot (1) buy and sell the company's stock within a 6-month period; (2) sell short in the company's stock, and if they sell owned shares must deliver in 20 days and/or place certificates in mail within 5 days; (3) effect any foreign or arbitrage transaction in the company's stock; (4) trade on material information not available to the public.

BOARD OF GOVERNORS OF THE FEDERAL RESERVE SYSTEM seven-member managing body of the FEDERAL RESERVE SYSTEM, commonly called the Federal Reserve Board. The board sets policy on issues relating to banking regulations as well as to the MONEY SUPPLY.

BOARD ROOM
Brokerage house: room where customers can watch an electronic board that displays stock prices and transactions.
Corporation: room where the board of directors holds its meetings.

BO DEREK STOCK perfect stock with an exemplary record of earnings growth, product quality, and stock price appreciation. These stocks are named after the movie "10" in which Bo Derek was depicted as the perfect woman.

BOGEY target for purchasing or selling a security or achieving some other objective. An investor's bogey may be a 10% rate of return from a particular stock. Or it may be locking in an 8% yield on a bond. A money manager's bogey may be to beat the Standard & Poor's 500 index.

BOILERPLATE standard legal language, often in fine print, used in most contracts, wills, indentures, prospectuses, and other legal documents. Although what the boilerplate says is important, it rarely is subject to change by the parties to the agreement, since it is the product of years of legal experience.

BOILER ROOM place where high-pressure salespeople use banks of telephones to call lists of potential investors (known in the trade as sucker lists) in order to peddle speculative, even fraudulent, securities. They are called boiler rooms because of the high-pressure selling. Boiler room methods, if not illegal, clearly violate the National Association of Securities Dealers' RULES OF FAIR PRACTICE, particularly those requiring that recommendations be suitable to a customer's account. *See also* BUCKET SHOP.

BOLSA Spanish term for *stock exchange*. There are Bolsas in Spain, Mexico, Chile, Argentina, and many other Spanish-speaking countries. In French, the term is BOURSE; in Italian, Borsa.

BOLSA DE COMMERCIO DE SANTIAGO (SSE) is Chile's dominant stock exchange. SSE publishes three stock indices: the General Price Index (IGPA), a market capitalization weighted index of 161 companies that is rebalanced annually; the Selective Price Index (IPSA), a volume-weighted index 40 stocks most heavily traded in the prior year, that is rebalanced quarterly; and the Inter-10 Index, a volume weighted index of the 10 largest companies with ADRs, revised quarterly. Chile operates three stock exchanges: the Santiago Stock Exchange, the Bolsa Electronica, and the Valparaiso Stock Exchange. SSE, founded in 1893, is the largest, with close to 80% total trading. Bolsa Electronica, established in 1989, is a screen-based electronic stock exchange based in Santiago that accounts for more than 25% of total equity trading in the country. Bolsa de Valparaiso, established in 1892, is Chile's oldest exchange. Settlement usually occurs two days after a transaction, but can be accomplished earlier or by deferred payment on the last Wednesday of every month. Deferred transactions require a deposit and are allowed only in the shares of 124 companies. Open outcry at SSE is in three sessions: 10:30 A.M. to 11:20 A.M.; 12:30 P.M. to 1:20 P.M.; and 4 P.M. to 4:30 P.M. Low-volume shares trade on a computer system from 9:30 A.M. to 4:30 P.M. Shares are traded by auction once a day. There are no market makers, and most brokers trade for their own accounts.

BOLSA DE VALORES DE RIO DE JANIERO (BVRJ) is Brazil's second largest exchange. It calculates the IBV Index, covering the most actively-traded Rio stocks. Trading hours are 10:30 A.M. to 5:30 P.M. All stocks trade simultaneously on the floor and on the electronic system. There is a 30-minute pre-opening session. Physical settlement is on the second business day following the trade, and financial settlement is on the third business day at CLC, an independent clearing house that settles trades entered into the national trading system. The CLC is recognized by the Securities and Exchange Commission as a depository for U.S. institutional investors.

BOLSA DE VALORES DE SAO PAULO (BOVESPA) largest of Brazil's nine stock exchanges, it accounts for two-thirds of all stock transactions. The Bovespa Index is the most widely recognized. The Electric Power Index (IEE) is the first of a series of sector indices. Open outcry sessions are held in two sessions, from 10:30 A.M. to 1:30 P.M., and 2:30 P.M. to 5:30 P.M., Monday through Friday.

Computer assisted trading system (CATS) sessions run simultaneously from 10:30 A.M. to 5:30 P.M. Stock and options of the 22 most actively traded companies are traded in the open outcry session; other stocks and options are traded only on CATS. Stock options and an option with a strike price quoted in points tied to the U.S. dollar are traded on the exchange as well. Physical settlement is on the second business day following the trade, and financial settlement is on the third business day at CALISPA, the exchange's wholly-owned subsidiary.

BOMBAY STOCK EXCHANGE (BSE) see NATIONAL STOCK EXCHANGE; THE STOCK EXCHANGE, MUMBAI (BSE).

BOND any interest-bearing or discounted government or corporate security that obligates the issuer to pay the bondholder a specified sum of money, usually at specific intervals, and to repay the principal amount of the loan at maturity. Bondholders have an IOU from the issuer, but no corporate ownership privileges, as stockholders do.

An owner of *bearer bonds* presents the bond coupons and is paid interest, whereas the owner of *registered bonds* appears on the records of the bond issuer.

A SECURED BOND is backed by collateral which may be sold by the bondholder to satisfy a claim if the bond's issuer fails to pay interest and principal when they are due. An *unsecured bond* or DEBENTURE is backed by the full faith and credit of the issuer, but not by any specific collateral.

A CONVERTIBLE bond gives its owner the privilege of exchange for other securities of the issuing company at some future date and under prescribed conditions.

Also, a bond, in finance, is the obligation of one person to repay a debt taken on by someone else, should that other person default. A bond can also be money or securities deposited as a pledge of good faith.

A surety or PERFORMANCE BOND is an agreement whereby an insurance company becomes liable for the performance of work or services provided by a contractor by an agreed-upon date. If the contractor does not do what was promised, the surety company is financially responsible. *See also* INDENTURE; ZERO-COUPON SECURITY.

BOND ANTICIPATION NOTE (BAN) short-term debt instrument issued by a state or municipality that will be paid off with the proceeds of an upcoming bond issue. To the investor, BANs offer a safe, tax-free yield that may be higher than other tax-exempt debt instruments of the same maturity.

BOND BROKER broker who executes bond trades on the floor of an exchange. Also, one who trades corporate, U.S. government, or municipal debt issues over the counter, mostly for large institutional accounts.

BOND BUYER, THE daily publication containing most of the key statistics and indexes used in the fixed-income markets. *See also* BOND BUYER'S MUNICIPAL BOND INDEX; THIRTY-DAY VISIBLE SUPPLY.

BOND BUYER'S MUNICIPAL BOND INDEX index published daily by the *BOND BUYER,* a newspaper covering the municipal bond market. The index tracks municipal bond prices and is composed of 40 actively traded general obligation and revenue issues rated A or better with a term portion of at least $50 million ($75 million for housing issues); at least 19 years remaining to maturity; a first call date between 7 and 16 years; and at least one call at par before redemption. Starting in July 1, 1995, noncallable bonds became eligible for inclusion in the index. The publication also tracks the Bond Buyer 20 Bond Index, which is an index of yields of 20 general obligation municipal bonds. Investors use the publication's Bond Buyer indices to plot interest rate patterns in the muni market. Traders use the daily Bond Buyer Index to trade municipal bond index futures and futures options at the CHICAGO BOARD OF TRADE.

BOND COUNSEL attorney or law firm that prepares the LEGAL OPINION for a municipal bond issue.

BOND CROWD exchange members who transact bond orders on the floor of the exchange. The work area in which they congregate is separate from the stock traders, hence the term bond crowd.

BOND DISCOUNT amount by which the MARKET PRICE of a bond is lower than its FACE VALUE. Outstanding bonds with fixed COUPONS go to discounts when market interest rates rise. Discounts are also caused when supply exceeds demand and when a bond's CREDIT RATING IS reduced. When opposite conditions exist and market price is higher than face value, the difference is termed a *bond premium.* Premiums also occur when a bond issue with a CALL FEATURE is redeemed prior to maturity and the bondholder is compensated for lost interest. *See also* ORIGINAL ISSUE DISCOUNT.

BOND EQUIVALENT YIELD restatement of a DISCOUNT YIELD as its interest-bearing equivalent.

BONDHOLDER owner of a bond. Bondholders may be individuals or institutions such as corporations, banks, insurance companies, or mutual funds. Bondholders are entitled to regular interest payments as due and return of principal when the bond matures. Bondholders may own corporate, government, or municipal issues. For corporate bonds, bondholders' claims on the assets of the issuing corporation take precedence over claims of stockholders in the event of liquidation. Unlike stockholders, however, straight bondholders do not own an equity interest in the issuing company. Some bonds, such as convertible bonds, do have some claim on the equity of the issuing corporation.

BOND MARKET ASSOCIATION international trade association of banks and broker/dealers in U.S. government and federal agency securities, municipal securities, mortgage-backed securities and money-market securities.

BOND MUTUAL FUND mutual fund holding bonds. Such funds may specialize in a particular kind of bond, such as government, corporate, convertible, high-yield, mortgage-backed, municipal, foreign, or zero-coupon bonds. Other bond mutual funds will buy some or all of these kinds of bonds. Most bond mutual funds are designed to produce current income for shareholders. Bond funds also produce capital gains when interest rates fall and capital losses when interest rates rise. Unlike the bonds in these funds, the funds themselves never mature. There are two types of bond mutual funds: open- and closed-end. *Open-end funds* continually create new shares to accommodate new money as it flows into the funds and they always trade at NET ASSET VALUE. *Closed-end funds* issue a limited number of shares and trade on stock exchanges. Closed-end funds trade at either higher than their net asset value (a premium) or lower than their net asset value (a discount), depending on investor demand for the fund.

BOND PREMIUM *see* BOND DISCOUNT.

BOND POWER form used in the transfer of registered bonds from one owner to another. Sometimes called *assignment separate from certificate,* it accomplishes the same thing as the assignment form on the back of the bond certificate, but has a safety advantage in being separate. Technically, the bond power appoints an attorney-in-fact with the power to make a transfer of ownership on the corporation's books.

BOND RATING method of evaluating the possibility of default by a bond issuer. Duff & Phelps/MCM, Standard & Poor's, Moody's Investors Service, and Fitch's Investors Service analyze the financial strength of each bond's issuer, whether a corporation or a government body. Their ratings range from AAA (highly unlikely to default) to D (in default). Bonds rated BB or below are not INVESTMENT GRADE—in other words, institutions that invest other people's money may not under most state laws buy them. *See also* RATING.

BOND RATIO *leverage* ratio measuring the percentage of a company's capitalization represented by bonds. It is calculated by dividing the total bonds due after one year by the same figure plus all equity. A bond ratio over 33% indicates high leverage—except in utilities, where higher bond ratios are normal. *See also* DEBT-TO-EQUITY RATIO.

BOND SWAP simultaneous sale of one bond issue and purchase of another. The motives for bond swaps vary: *maturity swaps* aim to stretch out maturities but can also produce a profit because of the lower prices on longer bonds; *yield swaps* seek to improve return and *quality swaps* seek to upgrade safety; *tax swaps* create tax-deductible losses through the sale, while the purchase of a substitute bond effectively preserves the investment. *See also* SWAP, SWAP ORDER.

BON VOYAGE BONUS *see* GREENMAIL.

BOOK
1. in an underwriting of securities, (1) preliminary indications of interest rate on the part of prospective buyers of the issue ("What is the book on XYZ Company?") or (2) record of activity in the syndicate account ("Who is managing the book on XYZ?").
2. record maintained by a specialist of buy and sell orders in a given security. The term derives from the notebook that specialists traditionally used for this purpose. Also, the aggregate of sell orders left with the specialist, as in BUY THE BOOK.
3. as a verb, to book is to give accounting recognition to something. ("They booked a profit on the transaction.")
4. collectively, books are the journals, ledgers, and other accounting records of a business.
   See also BOOK VALUE.

BOOK-ENTRY SECURITIES securities that are not represented by a certificate. Purchases and sales of some municipal bonds, for instance, are merely recorded on customers' accounts; no certificates change hands. This is increasingly popular because it cuts down on paperwork for brokers and leaves investors free from worry about their certificates. *See also* CERTIFICATELESS MUNICIPALS.

BOOK PROFIT OR LOSS *see* UNREALIZED PROFIT OR LOSS.

BOOK-TO-BILL RATIO The ratio of orders booked for future delivery to orders being shipped immediately, and therefore billed. The book-to-bill ratio is released on a monthly basis for the semiconductor industry because it provides a very sensitive indicator of whether orders for chips are rising or falling and at what pace. The release of the chip book-to-bill ratio can have a major impact on the stock prices of semiconductor stocks in particular and technology stocks in general.

BOOK VALUE
1. value at which an asset is carried on a balance sheet. For example, a piece of manufacturing equipment is put on the books at its cost when purchased. Its value is then reduced each year as depreciation is charged to income. Thus, its book value at any time is its cost minus accumulated depreciation. However, the primary purpose of accounting for depreciation is to enable a company to

recover its cost, not replace the asset or reflect its declining usefulness. Book value may therefore vary significantly from other objectively determined values, most notably MARKET VALUE.

2. net asset value of a company's securities, calculated by using the following formula:

Total assets *minus* intangible assets (goodwill, patents, etc.) *minus* current liabilities *minus* any long-term liabilities and equity issues that have a prior claim (subtracting them here has the effect of treating them as paid) *equals* total net assets available for payment of the issue under consideration.

The total net asset figure, divided by the number of bonds, shares of preferred stock, or shares of common stock, gives the *net asset value*—or book value—per bond or per share of preferred or common stock.

Book value can be a guide in selecting underpriced stocks and is an indication of the ultimate value of securities in liquidation. *See also* ASSET COVERAGE.

BOOT STRAP to help a company start from scratch. Entrepreneurs founding a company with little capital are said to be boot strapping it in order to become established.

BORROWED RESERVES funds borrowed by member banks from a FEDERAL RESERVE BANK for the purpose of maintaining the required reserve ratios. Actually, the proper term is *net borrowed reserves,* since it refers to the difference between borrowed reserves and excess or free reserves. Such borrowings, usually in the form of advances secured by government securities or eligible paper, are kept on deposit at the Federal Reserve bank in the borrower's region. Net borrowed reserves are an indicator of heavy loan demand and potentially TIGHT MONEY.

BORROWING POWER OF SECURITIES amount of money that customers can invest in securities on MARGIN, as listed every month on their brokerage account statements. This margin limit usually equals 50% of the value of their stocks, 30% of the value of their bonds, and the full value of their CASH EQUIVALENT assets, such as MONEY MARKET account funds. The term also refers to securities pledged (hypothecated) to a bank or other lender as loan COLLATERAL. The loan value in this case depends on lender policy and type of security.

BOSTON STOCK EXCHANGE (BSE) established in 1834, the BSE is the first American exchange to open its membership to foreign brokers. It is the only U.S. exchange with a foreign linkage—to the Montreal Exchange established in 1984—and the only U.S. exchange with an off-site backup trading floor, located in Woburn, Mass. The exchange trades only equities; its more than 2,000 listed securities represent the largest number of New York Stock Exchange listed companies in the U.S. Formerly known as a regional exchange, the BSE is in competition with other national stock exchanges, with 200 member firms and 160 of its own primary listed companies. In 1994, the exchange introduced the Competing Specialists Initiative (CSI) in an auction market environment. It also operates the BEACON automated trading system. The exchange moved to a state-of-the-art facility in downtown Boston in 1999. The BSE uses a three-day settlement. Trading hours are Monday through Friday, 9:30 A.M. to 4 P.M., with a limited crossing network at 5 P.M., matching the New York Stock Exchange's Session No. 1.

BOT

1. stockbroker shorthand for bought, the opposite of SL for sold.
2. in finance, abbreviation for balance of trade.
3. in the mutual savings bank industry, abbreviation for board of trustees.

BOTTOM

In general: support level for market prices of any type. When prices fall below that level and appear to be continuing downward without check, we say that the

bottom dropped out. When prices begin to trend upward again, we say they have *bottomed out.*
Economics: lowest point in an economic cycle.
Securities: lowest market price of a security or commodity during a day, a season, a year, a cycle. Also, lowest level of prices for the market as a whole, as measured by any of the several indexes.

BOTTOM FISHER investor who is on the lookout for stocks that have fallen to their bottom prices before turning up. In extreme cases, bottom fishers buy stocks and bonds of bankrupt or near-bankrupt firms.

BOTTOM-UP APPROACH TO INVESTING search for outstanding performance of individual stocks before considering the impact of economic trends. The companies may be identified from research reports, stock screens, or personal knowledge of the products and services. This approach assumes that individual companies can do well, even in an industry that is not performing well. *See also* TOP-DOWN APPROACH TO INVESTING.

BOUGHT DEAL in securities underwriting, a FIRM COMMITMENT to purchase an entire issue outright from the issuing company. Differs from a STAND-BY COMMITMENT, wherein, with conditions, a SYNDICATE of investment bankers agrees to purchase part of an issue if it is not fully subscribed. Also differs from a BEST EFFORTS commitment, wherein the syndicate agrees to use its best efforts to sell the issue. Most issues in recent years have been bought deals. Typically, the syndicate puts up a portion of its own capital and borrows the rest from commercial banks. Then, perhaps through a selling group, the syndicate resells the issue to the public at slightly more than the purchase price.

BOUNCE return of a check by a bank because it is not payable, usually due to insufficient funds. In securities, the rejection and subsequent RECLAMATION of a security because of *bad delivery.* Term also refers to stock price's sudden decline and recovery.

BOURSE French term for *stock exchange. See* PARIS BOURSE.

BOUTIQUE small, specialized brokerage firm that deals with a limited clientele and offers a limited product line. A highly regarded securities analyst may form a research boutique, which clients use as a resource for buying and selling certain stocks. A boutique is the opposite of a FINANCIAL SUPERMARKET, which offers a wide variety of services to a wide variety of clients.

BOX physical location of securities or other documents held in safekeeping. The term derives from the large metal tin, or tray, in which brokerage firms and banks actually place such valuables. Depending on rules and regulations concerned with the safety and segregation of clients' securities, certificates held in safekeeping may qualify for stock loans or as bank loan collateral.

BRACKET CREEP edging into higher tax brackets as income rises to compensate for inflation.

BRADY BONDS public-issue, U.S. dollar-denominated bonds of developing countries, mainly in Latin America, that were exchanged in a restructuring for commercial bank loans in default. The securities, named for former Bush administration Treasury Secretary Nicholas Brady, are collateralized by U.S. Treasury zero-coupon bonds to ensure principal.

BRANCH OFFICE MANAGER person in charge of a branch of a securities brokerage firm or bank. Branch office managers who oversee the activities of three or more brokers must pass tests administered by various stock exchanges. A customer who is not able to resolve a conflict with a REGISTERED REPRESENTATIVE should bring it to the attention of the branch office manager, who is responsible for resolving such differences.

BREADTH OF THE MARKET percentage of stocks participating in a particular market move. Analysts say there was good breadth if two thirds of the stocks listed on an exchange rose during a trading session. A market trend with good breadth is more significant and probably more long-lasting than one with limited breadth, since more investors are participating. Breadth-of-the-market indexes are alternatively called ADVANCE/DECLINE indexes.

BREAK
Finance: in a pricing structure providing purchasing discounts at different levels of volume, a point at which the price changes—for example, a 10% discount for ten cases.
Investments: (1) sudden, marked drop in the price of a security or in market prices generally; (2) discrepancy in the accounts of brokerage firms; (3) stroke of good luck.

BREAKEVEN POINT
Finance: the point at which sales equal costs. The point is located by breakeven analysis, which determines the volume of sales at which fixed and variable costs will be covered. All sales over the breakeven point produce profits; any drop in sales below that point will produce losses.

Because costs and sales are so complex, breakeven analysis has limitations as a planning tool and is being supplanted by computer based financial planning systems. *See also* LEVERAGE (operating).
Securities: dollar price at which a transaction produces neither a gain nor a loss.

In options strategy the term has the following definitions:
1. long calls and short uncovered calls: strike price plus premium.
2. long puts and short uncovered puts: strike price minus premium.
3. short covered call: purchase price minus premium.
4. short put covered by short stock: short sale price of underlying stock plus premium.

BREAKING THE SYNDICATE terminating the investment banking group formed to underwrite a securities issue. More specifically, terminating the AGREEMENT AMONG UNDERWRITERS, thus leaving the members free to sell remaining holdings without price restrictions. The agreement among underwriters usually terminates the syndicate 30 days after the selling group, but the syndicate can be broken earlier by agreement of the participants.

BREAKOUT rise in a security's price above a resistance level (commonly its previous high price) or drop below a level of support (commonly the former lowest price). A breakout is taken to signify a continuing move in the same direction. *See* chart on next page.

BREAKPOINT SALE in mutual funds, the dollar investment required to make the fundholder eligible for a lower sales charge. *See also* LETTER OF INTENT; RIGHT OF ACCUMULATION.

BREAKUP VALUE *see* PRIVATE MARKET VALUE.

BRETTON WOODS AGREEMENT OF 1944 *see* FIXED EXCHANGE RATE.

BRIDGE LOAN short-term loan, also called a *swing loan,* made in anticipation of intermediate-term or long-term financing.

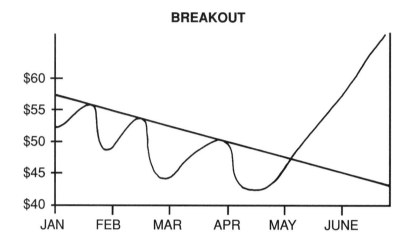

BREAKOUT

BROAD TAPE enlargement of the Dow Jones news ticker tape, projected on a screen in the board room of a brokerage firm. It continually reports major news developments and financial information. The term can also refer to similar information provided by Associated Press, United Press International, Reuters, or Munifacts. The broad tape is not allowed on the exchange floor because it would give floor traders an unfair edge.

BROKER
Insurance: person who finds the best insurance deal for a client and then sells the policy to the client.
Real estate: person who represents the seller and gets a commission when the property is sold.
Securities: person who acts as an intermediary between a buyer and seller, usually charging a commission. A broker who specializes in stocks, bonds, commodities, or options acts as AGENT and must be registered with the exchange where the securities are traded. Hence the term *registered representative. See also* ACCOUNT EXECUTIVE; DEALER; DISCOUNT BROKER.

BROKER-DEALER *see* DEALER.

BROKERED CD CERTIFICATE OF DEPOSIT (CD) issued by a bank or thrift institution but bought in bulk by a brokerage firm and resold to brokerage customers. Brokered CDs pay as much as 1% more than those issued directly by major banks, carry federal deposit insurance up to $100,000, enjoy a liquid secondary market made by the broker, and do not require an investor to pay a commission.

BROKER LOAN RATE interest rate at which brokers borrow from banks to cover the securities positions of their clients. The broker loan rate usually hovers a percentage point or so above such short-term interest rates as the federal funds rate and the Treasury bill rate. Since brokers' loans and their customers' margin accounts are usually covered by the same collateral, the term REHYPOTHECATION is used synonymously with *broker loan borrowing.* Because broker loans are callable on 24-hour notice, the term *call loan rate* is also used, particularly in money rate tables published in newspapers.

BROUGHT OVER THE WALL when somebody in the research department of an investment bank is pressed into the service of the underwriting department in reference to a particular corporate client, the individual has been "brought over the ("Chinese") wall" that legally divides the two functions and, being thus privy to INSIDE INFORMATION, is precluded from providing opinions about the company involved. *See also* CHINESE WALL.

BRUSSELS STOCK EXCHANGE (BSE) was founded by Napoleonic decree in 1801. Tax relief legislation increased growth, and in 1990 BSE was established as a limited liability cooperative. It handles the majority of securities transactions in Belgium. A second exchange is in Antwerp, and it cooperates closely with the BSE. The Belgian market is fully open to foreign investors and can be accessed directly by foreign banks and brokerage firms that register as members. In April 1996, the exchange introduced a decentralized, order-driven trading system called NTS to replace open outcry in the cash market. All forward market stocks were transferred to NTS from the CATS automated trading system. Cash market settlement is on the third trading day following the transaction. For forward transactions, the settlement period is five business days. Cash market trading hours are 11:15 A.M. to 3:15 P.M.; forward market, 10 A.M. to 4:30 P.M. Both trade Monday through Friday.

BUCKET SHOP illegal brokerage firm, of a kind now almost extinct, which accepts customer orders but does not execute them right away as Securities and Exchange Commission regulations require. Bucket-shop brokers confirm the price the customer asked for, but in fact make the trade at a time advantageous to the broker, whose profit is the difference between the two prices. Sometimes bucket shops neglect to fill the customer's order and just pocket the money. *See also* BOILER ROOM.

BUDGET estimate of revenue and expenditure for a specified period. Of the many kinds of budgets, a CASH BUDGET shows cash flow, an expense budget shows projected expenditures, and a CAPITAL BUDGET shows anticipated capital outlays. The term refers to a preliminary financial plan. In a *balanced budget* revenues cover expenditures.

BUDGET DEFICIT excess of spending over income for a government, corporation, or individual over a particular period of time. A budget deficit accumulated by the federal government of the United States must be financed by the issuance of Treasury bonds. Corporate budget deficits must be reduced or eliminated by increasing sales and reducing expenditures, or the company will not survive in the long run. Similarly, individuals who consistently spend more than they earn will accumulate huge debts, which may ultimately force them to declare bankruptcy if the debt cannot be serviced.

BUDGET SURPLUS excess of income over spending for a government, corporation, or individual over a particular period of time. A government with a budget surplus may choose to start new programs or cut taxes. A corporation with a surplus may expand the business through investment or acquisition, or may choose to buy back its own stock. An individual with a budget surplus may choose to pay down debt or increase spending or investment.

BULGE quick, temporary price rise that applies to an entire commodities or stock market, or to an individual commodity or stock.

BULGE BRACKET the group of firms in an underwriting syndicate that share the largest participation. TOMBSTONE ads list the participants alphabetically within in groupings organized by size of participation and presented in tiers. The first and lead grouping is the "bulge bracket." *See also* MEZZANINE BRACKET.

BULL person who thinks prices will rise. One can be bullish on the prospects for an individual stock, bond, or commodity, an industry segment, or the market as a whole. In a more general sense, bullish means optimistic, so a person can be bullish on the economy as a whole.

BULLION COINS coins composed of metal such as gold, silver, platinum, or palladium. Bullion coins provide the purest play on the "up or down" price moves of the underlying metal, and are the most actively traded. These coins trade at a slight premium over their metal content, unlike NUMISMATIC COINS, which trade on their rarity and artistic value. Some of the most popular bullion coins minted by major governments around the world include the American Eagle, the Canadian Maple Leaf, the South African Kruggerand, and the Australian Kangaroo. In addition to trading bullion in coin form, nearly pure precious metals also are available in bar form.

BULL MARKET prolonged rise in the prices of stocks, bonds, or commodities. Bull markets usually last at least a few months and are characterized by high trading volume.

BULL SPREAD option strategy, executed with puts or calls, that will be profitable if the underlying stock rises in value. The following are three varieties of bull spread:
Vertical spread: simultaneous purchase and sale of options of the same class at different strike prices, but with the same expiration date.
Calendar spread: simultaneous purchase and sale of options of the same class and the same price but at different expiration dates.
Diagonal spread: combination of vertical and calendar spreads wherein the investor buys and sells options of the same class at different strike prices and different expiration dates.

An investor who believes, for example, that XYZ stock will rise, perhaps only moderately, buys an XYZ 30 call for 1½ and sells an XYZ 35 call for ½; both options are OUT OF THE MONEY. The 30 and 35 are strike prices and the 1½ and ½ are premiums. The net cost of this spread, or the difference between the premiums, is $1. If the stock rises to 35 just prior to expiration, the 35 call becomes worthless and the 30 call is worth $5. Thus the spread provides a profit of $4 on an investment of $1. If on the other hand the price of the stock goes down, both options expire worthless and the investor loses the entire premium.

BUMP-UP CD certificate of deposit that gives its owner a one-time right to increase its yield for the remaining term of the CD if interest rates have risen from the date of issuance. The CD's yield will not be adjusted downward if rates fall, however. If rates remain stable or decline, the CD will pay its stated rate of interest until maturity.

BUNCHING
1. combining many round-lot orders for execution at the same time on the floor of an exchange. This technique can also be used with odd lot orders, when combining many small orders can save the odd-lot differential for each customer.
2. pattern on the ticker tape when a series of trades in the same security appear consecutively.
3. aggregating income items or deductions in a single year to minimize taxes in that year.

BURNOUT exhaustion of a tax shelter's benefits, when an investor starts to receive income from the investment. This income must be reported to the Internal Revenue Service, and taxes must be paid on it.

BURN RATE in venture capital financing, the rate at which a start-up company spends capital to finance overhead before generating a positive cash flow from operations.

BUSINESS COMBINATION *see* MERGER.

BUSINESS CYCLE recurrence of periods of expansion (RECOVERY) and contraction (RECESSION) in economic activity with effects on inflation, growth, and employment. One cycle extends from a GROSS DOMESTIC PRODUCT (GDP) base line through one rise and one decline and back to the base line, a period typically averaging about 2½ years. The 1990s, however, saw an extended period of expansion. A business cycle affects profitability and CASH FLOW, making it a key consideration in corporate dividend policy, and a factor in the rise and fall of the inflation rate, which in turn affects return on investments. *See also* SOFT LANDING.

BUSINESS DAY

In general: hours when most businesses are in operation. Although individual working hours may differ, and particular firms may choose staggered schedules, the conventional business day is 9 A.M. to 5 P.M.

Finance and investments: day when financial marketplaces are open for trading. In figuring the settlement date on a *regular way* securities transaction—which is the fifth business day after the trade date—Saturday, Sunday, and a legal holiday would not be counted, for example.

BUSINESS SEGMENT REPORTING reporting the results of the divisions, subsidiaries, or other segments of a business separately so that income, sales, and assets can be compared. When not a separate part of the business structure, a segment is generally defined as any grouping of products and services comprising a significant industry, which is one representing 10% or more of total revenues, assets, or income. Allocation of central corporate expenses is not required by the Financial Accounting Standards Board. Also called line of business reporting.

BUSTED CONVERTIBLES CONVERTIBLES that trade like fixed-income investments because the market price of the common stock they convert to has fallen so low as to render the conversion feature valueless.

BUST-UP TAKEOVER LEVERAGED BUYOUT in which TARGET COMPANY assets or activities are sold off to repay the debt that financed the TAKEOVER.

BUTTERFLY SPREAD complex option strategy that involves selling two calls and buying two calls on the same or different markets, with several maturity dates. One of the options has a higher exercise price and the other has a lower exercise price than the other two options. An investor in a butterfly spread will profit if the underlying security makes no dramatic movements because the premium income will be collected when the options are sold.

BUY acquire property in return for money. Buy can be used as a synonym for bargain.

BUY AND HOLD STRATEGY strategy that calls for accumulating shares in a company over the years. This allows the investor to pay favorable long-term capital gains tax on profits and requires far less attention than a more active trading strategy.

BUY AND WRITE STRATEGY conservative options strategy that entails buying stocks and then writing covered call options on them. Investors receive both the dividends from the stock and the premium income from the call options. However, the investor may have to sell the stock below the current market price if the call is exercised.

BUYBACK purchase of a long contract to cover a short position, usually arising out of the short sale of a commodity. Also, purchase of identical securities to cover a short sale. Synonym: *short covering. See also* STOCK BUYBACK.

Bond buyback: corporation's purchase of its own bonds at a discount in the open market. This is done in markets characterized by rapidly rising interest rates and commensurately declining bond prices.

BUY DOWN cash payment by a mortgage lender allowing the borrower to receive a lower rate of interest on a mortgage loan. For example, a home builder having trouble selling homes may offer a buy down with a local lender which will enable home buyers to qualify for mortgages that they would otherwise not qualify for. The buy down may lower the mortgage rate for the life of the loan, or sometimes just for the first few years of the loan.

BUYER'S MARKET market situation that is the opposite of a SELLER'S MARKET. Since there is more supply of a security or product than there is current demand, the prices tend to fall allowing buyers to set both the price and terms of the sale. It contrasts with a seller's market, characterized by excess demand, high prices, and terms suited to seller's desires.

BUY HEDGE *see* LONG HEDGE.

BUY IN
Options trading: procedure whereby the responsibility to deliver or accept stock can be terminated. In a transaction called *buying-in* or CLOSING PURCHASE, the writer buys an identical option (only the premium or price is different). The second of these options offsets the first, and the profit or loss is the difference in premiums.
Securities: transaction between brokers wherein securities are not delivered on time by the broker on the sell side, forcing the buy side broker to obtain shares from other sources.

BUYING CLIMAX rapid rise in the price of a stock or commodity, setting the stage for a quick fall. Such a surge attracts most of the potential buyers of the stock, leaving them with no one to sell their stock to at higher prices. This is what causes the ensuing fall. Technical chartists see a buying climax as a dramatic runup, accompanied by increased trading volume in the stock.

BUYING ON MARGIN buying securities with credit available through a relationship with a broker, called a MARGIN ACCOUNT. Arrangements of this kind are closely regulated by the Federal Reserve Board. *See also* MARGIN.

BUYING POWER amount of money available to buy securities, determined by tabulating the cash held in brokerage accounts, and adding the amount that could be spent if securities were margined to the limit. The market cannot rise beyond the available buying power. *See also* PURCHASING POWER.

BUY MINUS order to buy a stock at a price lower than the current market price. Traders try to execute a buy minus order on a temporary dip in the stock's price.

BUY ON THE BAD NEWS strategy based on the belief that, soon after a company announces bad news, the price of its stock will plummet. Those who buy at this stage assume that the price is about as low as it can go, leaving plenty of room for a rise when the news improves. If the adverse development is indeed temporary, this technique can be quite profitable. *See also* BOTTOM FISHER.

BUY ORDER in securities trading, an order to a broker to purchase a specified quality of a security at the MARKET PRICE or at another stipulated price.

BUYOUT purchase of at least a controlling percentage of a company's stock to take over its assets and operations. A buyout can be accomplished through negotiation or through a tender offer. A LEVERAGED BUYOUT occurs when a small group borrows the money to finance the purchase of the shares. The loan is ultimately repaid out of cash generated from the acquired company's operations or from the sale of its assets. *See also* GOLDEN PARACHUTE.

BUY STOP ORDER BUY ORDER marked to be held until the market price rises to the STOP PRICE, then to be entered as a MARKET ORDER to buy at the best available price. Sometimes called a *suspended market order*, because it remains suspended until a market transaction elects, activates, or triggers the stop. Such an order is not permitted in the over-the-counter market. *See also* STOP ORDER.

BUY THE BOOK order to a broker to buy all the shares available from the specialist in a security and from other brokers and dealers at the current offer price. The book is the notebook in which specialists kept track of buy and sell orders before computers. The most likely source of such an order is a professional trader or a large institutional buyer.

BYLAWS rules governing the internal management of an organization which, in the case of business corporations, are drawn up at the time of incorporation. The charter is concerned with such broad matters as the number of directors and the number of authorized shares; the bylaws, which can usually be amended by the directors themselves, cover such points as the election of directors, the appointment of executive and finance committees, the duties of officers, and how share transfers may be made. Bylaws, which are also prevalent in not-for-profit organizations, cannot countermand laws of the government.

BYPASS TRUST agreement allowing parents to pass assets on to their children to reduce estate taxes. The trust must be made irrevocable, meaning that the terms can never be changed. Assets put in such a trust usually exceed the amount that children and other heirs can receive tax-free at a parent's death. The estate tax exclusion amount was $625,000 in 1998, scheduled to increase gradually to $1 million in 2006 according to the TAXPAYER RELIEF ACT OF 1997. Parents can arrange to receive income from the assets during their lifetimes and may even be able to touch the principal in case of dire need. One variation of a bypass trust is the qualified terminable interest property trust, or Q-TIP TRUST.

C

CABINET CROWD members of the New York Stock Exchange who trade in infrequently traded bonds. Also called *inactive bond crowd* or *book crowd*. Buy and sell LIMIT ORDERS for these bonds are kept in steel racks, called cabinets, at the side of the bond trading floor; hence the name cabinet crowd. *See also* AUTOMATED BOND SYSTEM (ABS).

CABINET SECURITY stock or bond listed on a major exchange but not actively traded. There are a considerable number of such bonds and a limited number of such stocks, mainly those trading in ten-share units. Cabinets are the metal storage racks that LIMIT ORDERS for such securities are filed in pending execution or cancellation. *See also* AUTOMATED BOND SYSTEM (ABS); CABINET CROWD.

CAC 40 INDEX broad-based index of common stocks on the Paris Bourse, based on 40 of the 100 largest companies listed on the forward segment of the official list (reglement menseul); it has a base of 100. It is comparable to the Dow Jones Industrial Average. There are index futures and index options contracts based on the CAC 40 index.

CAFETERIA EMPLOYEE BENEFIT PLAN plan offering employees numerous options among their employee benefits. Each employee is able to pick the benefits that are most valuable in his or her particular situation. For example, a young employee with children may want to receive more life and health insurance than a mid-career employee who is more concerned with building up retirement plan assets.

CAGE section of a brokerage firm's back office where funds are received and disbursed.

Also, the installation where a bank teller works.

CALENDAR list of securities about to be offered for sale. Separate calendars are kept for municipal bonds, corporate bonds, government bonds, and new stock offerings.

CALENDAR SPREAD options strategy that entails buying two options on the same security with different maturities. If the EXERCISE PRICE is the same (a June 50 call and a September 50 call) it is a HORIZONTAL SPREAD. If the exercise prices are different (a June 50 call and a September 45 call), it is a DIAGONAL SPREAD. Investors gain or lose as the difference in price narrows or widens.

CALL

Banking: demand to repay a secured loan usually made when the borrower has failed to meet such contractual obligations as timely payment of interest. When a banker calls a loan, the entire principal amount is due immediately. *See also* BROKER LOAN RATE.

Bonds: right to redeem outstanding bonds before their scheduled maturity. The first dates when an issuer may call bonds are specified in the prospectus of every issue that has a call provision in its indenture. *See also* CALLABLE; CALL PRICE.

Options: right to buy a specific number of shares at a specified price by a fixed date. *See also* CALL OPTION.

CALLABLE redeemable by the issuer before the scheduled maturity. The issuer must pay the holders a premium price if such a security is retired early. Bonds are usually called when interest rates fall so significantly that the issuer can save money by floating new bonds at lower rates. *See also* CALL PRICE; DEMAND LOAN.

CALL DATE date on which a bond may be redeemed before maturity. If called, the bond may be redeemed at PAR or at a slight premium to par. For example, a bond may be scheduled to mature in 20 years but may have a provision that it can be called in 10 years if it is advantageous for the issuer to refinance the issue. The date 10 years from the issue date is the call date. When buying a bond, it is important to know the bond's call date, because you cannot be assured that you will receive interest from that bond beyond the call date.

CALLED AWAY term for a bond redeemed before maturity, or a call or put option exercised against the stockholder, or a delivery required on a short sale.

CALL FEATURE part of the agreement a bond issuer makes with a buyer, called the indenture, describing the schedule and price of redemptions before maturity. Most corporate and municipal bonds have 10-year call features (termed CALL PROTECTION by holders); government securities usually have none. *See also* CALL PRICE.

CALL LOAN any loan repayable on demand, but used in newspaper money rate tables as a synonym for *broker loan* or *broker overnight loan*. *See* BROKER LOAN RATE.

CALL LOAN RATE *see* BROKER LOAN RATE.

CALL OPTION right to buy 100 shares of a particular stock or stock index at a predetermined price before a preset deadline, in exchange for a premium. For buyers who think a stock will go up dramatically, call options permit a profit from a smaller investment than it would take to buy the stock. These options can also produce extra income for the seller, who gives up ownership of the stock if the option is exercised.

CALL PREMIUM amount that the buyer of a call option has to pay to the seller for the right to purchase a stock or stock index at a specified price by a specified date.

In bonds, preferreds, and convertibles, the amount over par that an issuer has to pay to an investor for redeeming the security early.

CALL PRICE price at which a bond or preferred stock with a *call provision* or CALL FEATURE can be redeemed by the issuer; also known as *redemption price*. To compensate the holder for loss of income and ownership, the call price is usually higher than the par value of the security, the difference being the CALL PREMIUM. *See also* CALL PROTECTION.

CALL PROTECTION length of time during which a security cannot be redeemed by the issuer. U.S. government securities are generally not callable, although there is an exception in certain 30-year Treasury bonds, which become callable after 25 years. Corporate and municipal issuers generally provide 10 years of call protection. Investors who plan to live off the income from a bond should be sure they have call protection, because without it the bond could be CALLED AWAY at any time specified in the indenture.

CALL PROVISION clause in a bond's INDENTURE that allows the issuer to redeem the bond before maturity. The call provision will spell out the first CALL DATE and whether the bond will be called at PAR or at a slight premium to par. Some preferred stock issues also have call provisions spelling out the conditions of a redemption.

CALL RISK risk to a bondholder that a bond may be redeemed before scheduled maturity. Bondholders should read the CALL PROVISIONS in a bond's INDENTURE to understand the earliest potential CALL DATE for their bond. The main risk of having a bond called before maturity is that the investor will be unable to replace the bond's yield with another similar-quality bond paying the same yield. The reason the bond issuer will call the bond is that interest rates will have fallen from the time of issuance, and the bond can be refinanced at lower rates.

CAMPS acronym for *Cumulative Auction Market Preferred Stocks,* Oppenheimer & Company's DUTCH AUCTION PREFERRED STOCK product.

CANADIAN DEALING NETWORK, INC. (CDN) the organized over-the-counter stock market of Canada. The CDN became a subsidiary of the TORONTO STOCK EXCHANGE in 1991. Previously, CDN was known as the Canadian Over-the-Counter Automated Trading System (COATS).

CANCEL
In general: void a negotiable instrument by annulling or paying it; also, prematurely terminate a bond or other contract.
Securities trading: void an order to buy or sell. *See also* GOOD-TILL-CANCELED ORDER.

CAP
Bonds: highest level interest rate that can be paid on a floating-rate debt instrument. For example, a variable-rate note might have a cap of 8%, meaning that the yield cannot exceed 8% even if the general level of interest rates goes much higher than 8%.

Mortgages: highest interest rate level that an adjustable-rate mortgage (ARM) can rise to over a particular period of time. For example, an ARM contract may specify that the rate cannot jump more than two points in any year, or a total of six points during the life of the mortgage.

Stocks: short for CAPITALIZATION, or the total current value of a company's outstanding shares in dollars. A stock's capitalization is determined by multiplying the total number of shares outstanding by the stock's price. Analysts also refer to small-, medium- and large-cap stocks as a way of distinguishing the capitalizations of companies they are interested in. Many mutual funds restrict themselves to the small-, medium- or large-cap universes. *See also* COLLAR.

CAPACITY

Debt: ability to repay loans, as measured by credit grantors. Creditors judge an applicant's ability to repay a loan based on assets and income, and assign a certain capacity to service debt. If someone has many credit cards and credit lines outstanding, even if there are no outstanding balances, that is using up that person's debt capacity.

Economics: the amount of productive capacity in the economy is known as *industrial capacity*. This figure is released on a monthly basis by the Federal Reserve to show how much of the nation's factories, mines, and utilities are in use. If more than 85% of industrial capacity is in use, economists worry that production bottlenecks may form and create inflationary pressure. On the other hand, if less than 80% of capacity is in use, industrial production may be slack and inflationary pressures low.

CAPACITY UTILIZATION RATE percentage of production capacity in use by a particular company, an industry, or the entire economy. While in theory a business can operate at 100% of its productive capacity, in practice the maximum output is less than that, because machines need to be repaired, employees take vacations, etc. The operating rate is expressed as a percentage of the potential 100% production output. For example, a company may be producing at an 85% operating rate, meaning its output is 85% of the maximum that could be produced with its existing resources. *See also* CAPACITY.

CAPITAL ASSET long-term asset that is not bought or sold in the normal course of business. Generally speaking, the term includes FIXED ASSETS—land, buildings, equipment, furniture and fixtures, and so on. The Internal Revenue Service definition of capital assets includes security investments.

CAPITAL ASSET PRICING MODEL (CAPM) sophisticated model of the relationship between *expected risk* and *expected return*. The model is grounded in the theory that investors demand higher returns for higher risks. It says that the return on an asset or a security is equal to the risk-free return—such as the return on a short-term Treasury security—plus a risk premium.

CAPITAL BUDGET program for financing long-term outlays such as plant expansion, research and development, and advertising. Among methods used in arriving at a capital budget are NET PRESENT VALUE (NPV), INTERNAL RATE OF RETURN (IRR), and PAYBACK PERIOD.

CAPITAL BUILDER ACCOUNT (CBA) brokerage account offered by Merrill Lynch that allows investors to buy and sell securities. It may be a cash or credit account that allows an investor to access the loan value of his or her eligible securities. Unlike a regular brokerage account, with a CBA one can choose from a money market fund or an insured money market deposit account to have one's idle cash invested or deposited on a regular basis, without losing access to the money.

CAPITAL CONSUMPTION ALLOWANCE amount of depreciation included in the GROSS DOMESTIC PRODUCT (GDP), normally around 11%. This amount is subtracted from GDP, on the theory that it is needed to maintain the productive capacity of the economy, to get net national product (NNP). When adjusted further for indirect taxes, NNP equals national income. Economists use GDP rather than NNP in the analyses we read every day largely because capital consumption allowance figures are not always available or reliable. *See also* DEPRECIATION.

CAPITAL EXPENDITURE outlay of money to acquire or improve CAPITAL ASSETS such as buildings and machinery.

CAPITAL FLIGHT movement of large sums of money from one country to another to escape political or economic turmoil or to seek higher rates of return. For example, periods of high inflation or political revolution have brought about an exodus of capital from many Latin American countries to the United States, which is seen as a safe haven.

CAPITAL FORMATION creation or expansion, through savings, of capital or of *producer's goods*—buildings, machinery, equipment—that produce other goods and services, the result being economic expansion.

CAPITAL GAIN difference between an asset's adjusted purchase price and selling price when the difference is positive. According to the TAXPAYER RELIEF ACT OF 1997, a long-term capital gain is achieved once an asset such as a stock, bond, or mutual fund has been held for at least 12 months. Such long-term gains are taxed at a maximum rate of 20% for taxpayers in the 28% tax bracket or higher. Those in the 15% tax bracket pay a 10% tax on long-term capital gains. Selling assets for a profit after holding them for less than 12 months generates short-term capital gains, which are subject to regular income tax rates. Assets purchased starting January 1, 2000 and held for at least five years qualify for a maximum capital gains tax rate of 18% for those in the 28% tax bracket or higher, and 8% for those in the 15% tax bracket. Capital gains are reported on Schedule D of a tax return.

CAPITAL GAINS DISTRIBUTION mutual fund's distribution to shareholders of the profits derived from the sale of stocks or bonds. Shareholders must pay long-term capital gains tax rates of as much as 20% if the fund held the securities for at least 12 months, no matter how long the shareholder owned shares in the mutual fund. Shareholders must pay short-term capital gains taxes at regular income tax rates on securities sold by the mutual fund that have been held for less than 12 months, no matter how long the shareholder owned shares in the mutual fund. Distributions which are reinvested by shareholders are taxed in the same way as distributions paid to shareholders in cash. If a capital gain distribution is declared in October, November, or December, but paid in January, the fund will still report the distribution as taxable in the year it was declared. Mutual funds report capital gains distributions to shareholders annually on FORM 1099-DIV.

CAPITAL GAINS TAX tax on profits from the sale of CAPITAL ASSETS. Traditionally, the tax law specified a minimum holding period after which a capital gain is taxed at a more favorable rate (recently a maximum of 20% for individuals) than ordinary income. A long-term capital gain is achieved once an asset such as a stock, bond, or mutual fund is held for at least 12 months. Such long-term gains are taxed at a maximum rate of 20% for taxpayers in the 28% tax bracket or higher. Those in the 15% tax bracket pay a 10% tax on long-term capital gains. Assets sold for a profit after having been held for less than 12 months generate short-term capital gains, which are subject to ordinary income tax rates. Assets purchased starting January 1, 2000 and held for at least five years qualify for a maximum capital gains tax rate of 18% for those in the 28% tax bracket or higher, and 8% for those in the 15% tax bracket.

CAPITAL GOODS goods used in the production of other goods—industrial buildings, machinery, equipment—as well as highways, office buildings, government installations. In the aggregate such goods form a country's productive capacity.

CAPITAL-INTENSIVE requiring large investments in CAPITAL ASSETS. Motor vehicle and steel production are capital-intensive industries. To provide an acceptable return on investment, such industries must have a high margin of profit or a low cost of borrowing. Sometimes used to mean a high proportion of fixed assets to labor.

CAPITAL INTERNATIONAL INDEXES indexes maintained by Morgan Stanley's Capital International division which track most major stock markets throughout the world. The Capital International World Index tracks prices of major stocks in all the major markets worldwide. There are also many indexes for European, North American, and Asian markets. Most mutual funds and other institutional investors measure their performance against Capital International indexes.

CAPITAL INVESTMENT see CAPITAL EXPENDITURE.

CAPITALISM economic system in which (1) private ownership of property exists; (2) aggregates of property or capital provide income for the individuals or firms that accumulated it and own it; (3) individuals and firms are relatively free to compete with others for their own economic gain; (4) the profit motive is basic to economic life.

Among the synonyms for capitalism are LAISSEZ-FAIRE economy, private enterprise system, and free-price system. In this context *economy* is interchangeable with *system.*

CAPITALIZATION see CAPITALIZE; CAPITAL STRUCTURE; MARKET CAPITALIZATION.

CAPITALIZATION RATE rate of interest used to convert a series of future payments into a single PRESENT VALUE.

CAPITALIZATION RATIO analysis of a company's capital structure showing what percentage of the total is debt, preferred stock, common stock, and other equity. The ratio is useful in evaluating the relative RISK and leverage that holders of the respective levels of security have. *See also* BOND RATIO.

CAPITALIZE
1. convert a schedule of income into a principal amount, called *capitalized value,* by dividing by a rate of interest.
2. issue securities to finance *capital outlays* (rare).
3. record capital outlays as additions to asset accounts, not as expenses. *See also* CAPITAL EXPENDITURE.
4. convert a lease obligation to an asset/liability form of expression called a *capital lease,* that is, to record a leased asset as an owned asset and the lease obligation as borrowed funds.
5. turn something to one's advantage economically—for example, sell umbrellas on a rainy day.

CAPITAL LEASE lease that under Statement 13 of the Financial Accounting Standards Board must be reflected on a company's balance sheet as an asset and corresponding liability. Generally, this applies to leases where the lessee acquires essentially all of the economic benefits and risks of the leased property.

CAPITAL LOSS amount by which the proceeds from the sale of a CAPITAL ASSET are less than the adjusted cost of acquiring it. Capital losses are deducted first against capital gains, and then against up to $3,000 of other income for married couples filing jointly, and up to $1,500 for married couples filing separately. Any capital losses in excess of $3,000 may be carried over into future tax years. Short-term losses realized on assets sold less than 12 months after purchase are offset against short-term capital gains. Long-term capital losses on assets sold more than 12 months after purchase are offset against long-term capital gains. Capital losses are reported on Schedule D of a tax return. *See also* TAX LOSS CARRYBACK, CARRYFORWARD.

CAPITAL MARKETS markets where capital funds—debt and equity—are traded. Included are private placement sources of debt and equity as well as organized markets and exchanges. *See also* PRIMARY MARKET.

CAPITAL OUTFLOW exodus of capital from a country. A combination of political and economic factors may encourage domestic and foreign owners of assets to sell their holdings and move their money to other countries that offer more political stability and economic growth potential. If a capital outflow becomes large enough, some countries may try to restrict investors' ability to remove money from the country with currency controls or other measures.

CAPITAL OUTLAY *see* CAPITAL EXPENDITURE.

CAPITAL REQUIREMENTS
1. permanent financing needed for the normal operation of a business; that is, the long-term and working capital.
2. appraised investment in fixed assets and normal working capital. Whether patents, rights, and contracts should be included is moot.

CAPITAL SHARES one of the two classes of shares in a dual-purpose investment company. The capital shares entitle the owner to all appreciation (or depreciation) in value in the underlying portfolio in addition to all gains realized by trading in the portfolio. The other class of shares in a dual-purpose investment company are INCOME SHARES, which receive all income generated by the portfolio. If the fund guarantees a minimum level of income payable to the income shareholders, it may be necessary to sell some securities in the portfolio if the existing securities do not provide a high enough level of dividends and interest. In this case, the value of the capital shares will fall.

CAPITAL STOCK stock authorized by a company's charter and having PAR VALUE, STATED VALUE, or NO PAR VALUE. The number and value of issued shares are normally shown, together with the number of shares authorized, in the capital accounts section of the balance sheet.

Informally, a synonym for COMMON STOCK, though capital stock technically also encompasses PREFERRED STOCK.

CAPITAL STRUCTURE corporation's financial framework, including LONG-TERM DEBT, PREFERRED STOCK, and NET WORTH. It is distinguished from FINANCIAL STRUCTURE, which includes additional sources of capital such as short-term debt, accounts payable, and other liabilities. It is synonymous with *capitalization,* although there is some disagreement as to whether capitalization should include long-term loans and mortgages. Analysts look at capital structure in terms of its overall adequacy and its composition as well as in terms of the DEBT-TO-EQUITY RATIO, called *leverage. See also* CAPITALIZATION RATIO; PAR VALUE.

CAPITAL SURPLUS
1. EQUITY—or NET WORTH—not otherwise classifiable as CAPITAL STOCK or RETAINED EARNINGS. Here are five ways of creating surplus:

a. from stock issued at a premium over par or stated value.
b. from the proceeds of stock bought back and then sold again.
c. from a reduction of par or stated value or a reclassification of capital stock.
d. from donated stock.
e. from the acquisition of companies that have capital surplus.
2. common umbrella term for more specific classifications such as ACQUIRED SURPLUS, ADDITIONAL PAID-IN CAPITAL, DONATED SURPLUS, and REEVALUATION SURPLUS (arising from appraisals). Most common synonyms: *paid-in surplus; surplus.*

CAPITAL TURNOVER annual sales divided by average stockholder equity (net worth). When compared over a period, it reveals the extent to which a company is able to grow without additional capital investment. Generally, companies with high profit margins have a low capital turnover and vice versa. Also called *equity turnover.*

CAPS acronym for *convertible adjustable preferred stock,* whose adjustable interest rate is pegged to Treasury security rates and which can be exchanged, during the period after the announcement of each dividend rate for the next period, for common stock (or, usually, cash) with a market value equal to the par value of the CAPS. CAPS solved a problem inherent with DUTCH AUCTION PREFERRED STOCK, which was that the investor could not be certain of the principal value of the preferred. *See also* MANDATORY CONVERTIBLES.

CAPTIVE AGENT insurance agent working exclusively for one company. Such an agent will tend to have more in-depth knowledge of that company's policies than an INDEPENDENT AGENT, who can sell policies from many companies. Captive agents are usually paid on a combination of salary and commissions earned from selling policies, in the first few years they sell policies. Later, they are usually paid exclusively on a commission basis.

CAPTIVE FINANCE COMPANY company, usually a wholly owned subsidiary, that exists primarily to finance consumer purchases from the parent company. Prominent examples are General Motors Acceptance Corporation and Ford Motor Credit Company. Although these subsidiaries stand on their own financially, parent companies frequently make SUBORDINATED LOANS to add to their equity positions. This supports the high leverage on which the subsidiaries operate and assures their active participation in the COMMERCIAL PAPER and bond markets.

CARDS acronym for *Certificates for Amortizing Revolving Debts,* a Salomon Brothers security collaterized by credit card accounts receivable. Also called *plastic bonds. See also* ASSET-BACKED SECURITIES.

CARROT EQUITY British slang for an equity investment with a KICKER in the form of an opportunity to buy more equity if the company meets specified financial goals.

CARRYBACK, CARRYFORWARD *see* TAX LOSS CARRYBACK, CARRYFORWARD.

CARRYING CHARGE
Commodities: charge for carrying the actual commodity, including interest, storage, and insurance costs.
Margin accounts: fee that a broker charges for carrying securities on credit.
Real estate: carrying cost, primarily interest and taxes, of owning land prior to its development and resale.
Retailing: seller's charge for installment credit, which is either added to the purchase price or to unpaid installments.

CARRYOVER *see* TAX LOSS CARRYBACK, CARRYFORWARD.

CARS *see* CERTIFICATE FOR AUTOMOBILE RECEIVABLES.

CARTE BLANCHE full authority to take action. For example, an employee may be given carte blanche to enter into contracts with suppliers. The term also refers to the ability to fill in any amount on a blank check. For example, a father may sign a blank check and give it to his son to fill in when the son makes a major purchase. Carte Blanche is also the brand name of a widely used travel and entertainment card which requires that all balances be paid in full every month.

CARTEL group of businesses or nations that agree to influence prices by regulating production and marketing of a product. The most famous contemporary cartel is the Organization of Petroleum Exporting Countries (OPEC), which, notably in the 1970s, restricted oil production and sales and raised prices. A cartel has less control over an industry than a MONOPOLY. A number of nations, including the United States, have laws prohibiting cartels. TRUST is sometimes used as a synonym for cartel.

CASH asset account on a balance sheet representing paper currency and coins, negotiable money orders and checks, and bank balances. Also, transactions handled in cash. In the financial statements of annual reports, cash is usually grouped with CASH EQUIVALENTS, defined as all highly liquid securities with a known market value and a maturity, when acquirerest rate charged on the cash advance is usually different from the rate charged on purchases made with the same card. Frequently, the cash advance rate is higher. In many cases advance rates are variable, and are usually tied to a certain number of percentage points over the prime rate.

CASH ASSET RATIO balance sheet LIQUIDITY RATIO representing cash (and equivalents) and marketable securities divided by current liabilities. Stricter than the *quick ratio.*

CASH BASIS
Accounting: method that recognizes revenues when cash is received and recognizes expenses when cash is paid out. In contrast, the *accrual method* recognizes revenues when goods or services are sold and recognizes expenses when obligations are incurred. A third method, called *modified cash basis,* uses accrual accounting for long-term assets and is the basis usually referred to when the term cash basis is used.
Series EE Savings Bonds: paying the entire tax on these bonds when they mature. The alternative is to prorate the tax each year until the bonds mature.

CASHBOOK accounting book that combines cash receipts and disbursements. Its balance ties to the cash account in the general ledger on which the balance sheet is based.

CASH BUDGET estimated cash receipts and disbursements for a future period. A comprehensive cash budget schedules daily, weekly, or monthly expenditures together with the anticipated CASH FLOW from collections and other operating sources. Cash flow budgets are essential in establishing credit and purchasing policies, as well as in planning credit line usage and short-term investments in COMMERCIAL PAPER and other securities.

CASH COMMODITY commodity that is owned as the result of a completed contract and must be accepted upon delivery. Contrasts with futures contracts, which are not completed until a specified future date. The cash commodity contract specifications are set by the commodity exchanges.

CASH CONVERSION CYCLE elapsed time, usually expressed in days, from the outlay of cash for raw materials to the receipt of cash after the finished goods have been sold. Because a profit is built into the sales, the term *earnings cycle* is also used. The shorter the cycle, the more WORKING CAPITAL a business generates and the less it has to borrow. This cycle is directly affected by production efficiency, credit policy, and other controllable factors.

CASH COW business that generates a continuing flow of cash. Such a business usually has well-established brand names whose familiarity stimulates repeated buying of the products. For example, a magazine company that has a high rate of subscription renewals would be considered a cash cow. Stocks that are cash cows have dependable dividends.

CASH DISCOUNT TRADE CREDIT feature providing for a deduction if payment is made early. For example: trade terms of "2% 10 days net 30 days" allow a 2% cash discount for payment in 10 days. Term also refers to the lower price some merchants charge customers who pay in cash rather than with credit cards, in which case the merchant is passing on all or part of the merchant fee it would otherwise pay to the credit card company.

CASH DIVIDEND cash payment to a corporation's shareholders, distributed from current earnings or accumulated profits and taxable as income. Cash dividends are distinguished from STOCK DIVIDENDS, which are payments in the form of stock. *See also* YIELD.

INVESTMENT COMPANY cash dividends are usually made up of dividends, interest income, and capital gains received on its investment portfolio.

CASH EARNINGS cash revenues less cash expenses—specifically excluding noncash expenses such as DEPRECIATION.

CASH EQUIVALENTS instruments or investments of such high liquidity and safety that they are virtually as good as cash. Examples are a MONEY MARKET FUND and a TREASURY BILL. The FINANCIAL ACCOUNTING STANDARDS BOARD (FASB) defines cash equivalents for financial reporting purposes as any highly liquid security with a known market value and a maturity, when acquired, of less than three months.

CASH FLOW
1. in a larger financial sense, an analysis of all the changes that affect the cash account during an accounting period. The STATEMENT OF CASH FLOWS included in annual reports analyzes all changes affecting cash in the categories of operations, investments, and financing. For example: net operating income is an increase; the purchase of a new building is a decrease; and the issuance of stock or bonds is an increase. When more cash comes in than goes out, we speak of a *positive cash flow;* the opposite is a *negative cash flow.* Companies with assets well in excess of liabilities may nevertheless go bankrupt because they cannot generate enough cash to meet current obligations.
2. in investments, NET INCOME plus DEPRECIATION and other noncash charges. In this sense, it is synonymous with CASH EARNINGS. Investors focus on cash flow from operations because of their concern with a firm's ability to pay dividends. *See also* CASH BUDGET.

CASHIERING DEPARTMENT *see* CAGE.

CASHIER'S CHECK check that draws directly on a customer's account; the bank becomes the primary obligor. Consumers requiring a cashier's check must pay the amount of the check to the bank. The bank will then issue a check to a third party named by the consumer. Many businesses require that bills be paid by cashier's check instead of personal check, because they are assured that the funds are available with a cashier's check.

CASH INDEX PARTICIPATIONS (CIPS) *see* BASKET.

CASH MANAGEMENT
Corporate finance: efficient mobilization of cash into income-producing applications, using computers, telecommunications technology, innovative investment vehicles, and LOCK BOX arrangements.
Investing: broker's efficient movement of cash to keep it working. Merrill Lynch pioneered its proprietary Cash Management Account to combine securities trading, checking account services, money market investment services, and a debit (Visa) card.

CASH MARKET transactions in the cash or spot markets that are completed; that is, ownership of the commodity is transferred from seller to buyer and payment is given on delivery of the commodity. The cash market contrasts with the futures market, in which contracts are completed at a specified time in the future.

CASH-ON-CASH RETURN method of yield computation used for investments lacking an active secondary market, such as LIMITED PARTNERSHIPS. It simply divides the annual dollar income by the total dollars invested; a $10,000 investment that pays $1000 annually thus has a 10% cash-on-cash return. Investments having a market value and a predictable income stream to a designated maturity or call date, such as bonds, are better measured by CURRENT YIELD or YIELD-TO-MATURITY (or to call).

CASH ON DELIVERY (COD)
Commerce: transaction requiring that goods be paid for in full by cash or certified check or the equivalent at the point of delivery. The term *collect on delivery* has the same abbreviation and same meaning. If the customer refuses delivery, the seller has round-trip shipping costs to absorb or other, perhaps riskier, arrangements to make.
Securities: a requirement that delivery of securities to institutional investors be in exchange for assets of equal value—which, as a practical matter, means cash. Alternatively called *delivery against cost* (DAC) or *delivery versus payment* (DVP). On the other side of the trade, the term is *receive versus payment.*

CASH OR DEFERRED ARRANGEMENT (CODA) *see* 401(K) PLAN.

CASH RATIO ratio of cash and marketable securities to current liabilities; a refinement of the QUICK RATIO. The cash ratio tells the extent to which liabilities could be liquidated immediately. Sometimes called *liquidity ratio.*

CASH SETTLEMENT in the United States, settlement in cash on the TRADE DATE rather than the SETTLEMENT DATE of a securities transaction. In Great Britain, delivery and settlement on the first business day after the trade date.

CASH SURRENDER VALUE in insurance, the amount the insurer will return to a policyholder on cancellation of the policy. Sometimes abbreviated *CSVLI* (cash surrender value of life insurance), it shows up as an asset on the balance sheet of a company that has life insurance on its principals, called *key man insurance.* Insurance companies make loans against the cash value of policies, often at a better-than-market rate.

CASH VALUE INSURANCE life insurance that combines a death benefit with a potential tax-deferred buildup of money (called cash value) in the policy. The three main kinds of cash value insurance are WHOLE LIFE INSURANCE, VARIABLE LIFE INSURANCE, and UNIVERSAL LIFE INSURANCE. In whole life, cash value is accumulated based on the return on the company's investments in stocks, bonds, real estate, and other ventures. In variable life, the policyholder chooses how to allocate the money among stock, bond, and money market options. In universal life, a policyholder's cash value is invested in investments such as money market securities and medium-term Treasury bonds to build cash value. All cash values inside an insurance policy remain untaxed until they are withdrawn from the policy. Unlike cash value insurance, TERM LIFE INSURANCE offers only a death benefit, and no cash value buildup.

CASUALTY INSURANCE insurance that protects a business or homeowner against property loss, damage, and related liability.

CASUALTY LOSS financial loss caused by damage, destruction, or loss of property as the result of an identifiable event that is sudden, unexpected, or unusual. Casualty and theft losses are considered together for tax purposes; are covered by most *casualty insurance* policies; and are tax deductible provided the loss is (1) not covered by insurance or (2) if covered, a claim has been made and denied.

CATASTROPHE CALL premature redemption of a municipal revenue bond because a catastrophe destroyed the source of the revenue backing the bond. For example, a bond backed by toll revenues from a bridge might be called, meaning bondholders will receive their principal back, if a storm destroyed the bridge. Usually, the proceeds for the payment will come from a commercial insurance policy covering the revenue-producing asset such as the bridge. A bond's INDENTURE will spell out the conditions under which a catastrophe call can be implemented.

CATS *see* CERTIFICATE OF ACCRUAL ON TREASURY SECURITIES.

CATS AND DOGS speculative stocks that have short histories of sales, earnings, and dividend payments. In bull markets, analysts say disparagingly that even the cats and dogs are going up.

CAVEAT EMPTOR, CAVEAT SUBSCRIPTOR *buyer beware, seller beware.* A variation on the latter is *caveat venditor.* Good advice when markets are not adequately protected, which was true of the stock market before the watchdog SECURITIES AND EXCHANGE COMMISSION was established in the 1930s.

CBO *see* COLLATERALIZED BOND OBLIGATION (CBO).

CEILING highest level allowable in a financial transaction. For example, someone buying a stock may place a ceiling on the stock's price, meaning they are not willing to pay more than that amount for the shares. The issuer of a bond may place a ceiling on the interest rate it is willing to pay. If market interest rates rise beyond that ceiling, the underwriter must cancel the issue. *See also* CAP.

CENTRAL BANK country's bank that (1) issues currency; (2) administers monetary policy, including OPEN MARKET OPERATIONS; (3) holds deposits representing the reserves of other banks; and (4) engages in transactions designed to facilitate the conduct of business and protect the public interest. In the United States, central banking is a function of the FEDERAL RESERVE SYSTEM.

CERTIFICATE formal declaration that can be used to document a fact, such as a birth certificate.

The following are certificates with particular relevance to finance and investments.

1. auditor's certificate, sometimes called certificate of accounts, or ACCOUNTANT'S OPINION.

2. bond certificate, certificate of indebtedness issued by a corporation containing the terms of the issuer's promise to repay principal and pay interest, and describing collateral, if any. Traditionally, bond certificates had coupons attached, which were exchanged for payment of interest. Now that most bonds are issued in registered form, coupons are less common. The amount of a certificate is the par value of the bond.

3. CERTIFICATE OF DEPOSIT.
4. certificate of INCORPORATION.
5. certificate of indebtedness, government debt obligation having a maturity shorter than a bond and longer than a treasury bill (such as a Treasury Note).
6. PARTNERSHIP certificate, showing the interest of all participants in a business partnership.
7. PROPRIETORSHIP certificate, showing who is legally responsible in an individually owned business.
8. STOCK CERTIFICATE, evidence of ownership of a corporation showing number of shares, name of issuer, amount of par or stated value represented or a declaration of no-par value, and rights of the shareholder. Preferred stock certificates also list the issuer's responsibilities with respect to dividends and voting rights, if any.

CERTIFICATE FOR AUTOMOBILE RECEIVABLES (CARS) PASS-THROUGH SECURITY backed by automobile loan paper of banks and other lenders. *See also* ASSET-BACKED SECURITIES.

CERTIFICATELESS MUNICIPALS MUNICIPAL BONDS that have no certificate of ownership for each bondholder. Instead, one certificate is valid for the entire issue. Certificateless municipals save paperwork for brokers and municipalities and allow investors to trade their bonds without having to transfer certificates. *See also* BOOK ENTRY SECURITIES.

CERTIFICATE OF ACCRUAL ON TREASURY SECURITIES (CATS) U.S. Treasury issues, sold at a deep discount from face value. A ZERO-COUPON security, they pay no interest during their lifetime, but return the full face value at maturity. They are appropriate for retirement or education planning. As TREASURY SECURITIES, CATS cannot be CALLED AWAY.

CERTIFICATE OF DEPOSIT (CD) debt instrument issued by a bank that usually pays interest. Institutional CDs are issued in denominations of $100,000 or more, and individual CDs start as low as $100. Maturities range from a few weeks to several years. Interest rates are set by competitive forces in the marketplace. *See also* BROKERED CD.

CERTIFIED CHECK check for which a bank guarantees payment. It legally becomes an obligation of the bank, and the funds to cover it are immediately withdrawn from the depositor's account.

CERTIFIED FINANCIAL PLANNER (CFP) person who has passed examinations accredited by the Denver-based Certified Financial Planner Board of Standards, testing the ability to coordinate a client's banking, estate, insurance, investment, and tax affairs. Financial planners usually specialize in one or more of these areas and consult outside experts as needed. Some planners charge only fees and make no money on the implementation of their plans. Others charge a commission on each product or service they sell. *See also* FINANCIAL PLANNER.

CERTIFIED FINANCIAL STATEMENTS financial statements accompanied by an ACCOUNTANT'S OPINION.

CERTIFIED PUBLIC ACCOUNTANT (CPA) accountant who has passed certain exams, achieved a certain amount of experience, reached a certain age, and met all other statutory and licensing requirements of the U.S. state where he or she works. In addition to accounting and auditing, CPAs prepare tax returns for corporations and individuals.

CHAIRMAN OF THE BOARD member of a corporation's board of directors who presides over its meetings and who is the highest ranking officer in the corporation. The chairman of the board may or may not have the most actual executive authority in a firm. The additional title of CHIEF EXECUTIVE OFFICER (CEO) is reserved for the principal executive, and depending on the particular firm, that title may be held by the chairman, the president, or even an executive vice president. In some corporations, the position of chairman is either a prestigious reward for a past president or an honorary position for a prominent person, a large stockholder, or a family member; it may carry little or no real power in terms of policy or operating decision making.

CHAPTER 7 *see* BANKRUPTCY.

CHAPTER 10 federal BANKRUPTCY law section providing for reorganization under a court-appointed independent manager (trustee in bankruptcy) rather than under existing management as in the case with Chapter 11.

CHAPTER 11 *see* BANKRUPTCY.

CHAPTER 13 *see* BANKRUPTCY.

CHARGE OFF *see* BAD DEBT.

CHARITABLE LEAD TRUST *see* CHARITABLE REMAINDER TRUST.

CHARITABLE REMAINDER TRUST IRREVOCABLE TRUST that pays income to one or more individuals until the GRANTOR'S death, at which time the balance, which is tax free, passes to a designated charity. It is a popular tax-saving alternative for individuals who have no children or who are wealthy enough to benefit both children and charity.

The charitable remainder trust is the reverse of a *charitable lead trust,* whereby a charity receives income during the grantor's life and the remainder passes to designated family members upon the grantor's death. The latter trust reduces estate taxes while enabling the family to retain control of the assets.

CHARTER *see* ARTICLES OF INCORPORATION.

CHARTERED FINANCIAL ANALYST (CFA) designation awarded by the Institute of Chartered Financial Analysts (ICFA) to experienced financial analysts who pass examinations in economics, financial accounting, portfolio management, security analysis, and standards of conduct.

CHARTERED FINANCIAL CONSULTANT (ChFC) designation awarded by American College, Bryn Mawr, PA, to a professional FINANCIAL PLANNER who completes a four-year program covering economics, insurance, taxation, real estate, and other areas related to finance and investing.

CHARTERED LIFE UNDERWRITER (CLU) designation granted by American College, Bryn Mawr, PA, the insurance and financial service industry's oldest and largest fully accredited institution of higher learning in the United States. Designation requires completion of ten college-level courses, three years of qualifying experience, and adherence to a strict code of ethics. All CLUs may join the American Society of CLU and ChFC, a professional association also headquartered in Bryn Mawr, for continuing education opportunities and other member services. The American Society has chapters in all 50 states.

CHARTIST technical analyst who charts the patterns of stocks, bonds, and commodities to make buy and sell recommendations to clients. Chartists believe recurring patterns of trading can help them forecast future price movements. *See also* TECHNICAL ANALYSIS.

CHASING THE MARKET purchasing a security at a higher price than intended because prices have risen sharply, or selling it at a lower level when prices fall. For example, an investor may want to buy shares of a stock at $20 and place a limit order to do so. But when the shares rise above $25, and then $28, the customer decides to enter a market order and buy the stock before it goes even higher. Investors can also chase the market when selling a stock. For example, if an investor wants to sell a stock at $20 and it declines to $15 and then $12, he may decide to sell it at the market price before it declines even further.

CHASTITY BONDS bonds that become redeemable at par value in the event of a TAKEOVER.

CHATTER *see* WHIPSAWED.

CHECK bill of exchange, or draft on a bank drawn against deposited funds to pay a specified sum of money to a specified person on demand. A check is considered as cash and is NEGOTIABLE when endorsed.

CHECKING THE MARKET canvassing securities market-makers by telephone or other means in search of the best bid or offer price.

CHICAGO BOARD OF TRADE (CBOT) formed in 1848 as a centralized marketplace for the grain trade, CBOT is a pioneer in the development of financial futures and options. Building on its agricultural and precious metals futures and options contracts on grains and silver and gold, CBOT launched GNMA futures in 1975 and grew to become the largest U.S. futures exchange based on volume with the introduction of U.S. Treasury bond and note futures, municipal bond index futures, and catastrophe insurance futures. In 1997, the exchange launched futures and futures options on the Dow Jones Industrial Average. The exchange has an international linkage with the LONDON INTERNATIONAL FINANCIAL FUTURES AND OPTIONS EXCHANGE, providing European markets with access to major U.S. government debt derivatives. Expanded trading sessions accommodate morning trading hours in Hong Kong, Sydney, Tokyo and Singapore. Project A, an electronic order-entry and matching system, enables members to trade futures and options outside of regular pit trading hours, supplementing open outcry. The CBOT Recyclables Exchange, a centralized market for paper, plastics, glass, rubber and other non-hazardous solid waste materials, operates on the Internet at http://cbot-recycle.com. The trading floor is open Monday through Friday, 7:20 A.M. to 2 P.M. Project A hours are Sunday through Thursday, 10:30 P.M. to 4:30 A.M. (agricultural products); and Sunday through Thursday, 10 P.M. to 6:45 A.M. and Monday through Thursday, 2:30 P.M. to 4:30 P.M. (financial products). *See also* SECURITIES AND COMMODITIES EXCHANGES.

CHICAGO BOARD OPTIONS EXCHANGE (CBOE) major U.S. marketplace exclusively for the trading of individual equity, index, and interest rate options. Among the most heavily-traded index options are contracts on the Dow Jones, Standard & Poor's, Russell and NASDAQ indices. CBOE also trades a family of country indices, including those for Japan, Mexico, and Israel. Sector indices cover real estate, technology, energy, metals, gaming and industrials. CBOE trades interest rate options and LEAPS, as well as structured products developed by Merrill Lynch, Bear Stearns, and other investment firms. There is active trading on CBOE Market Volatility Index, known as the VIX Index, which is a measure of the VOLATILITY of four S&P 100 contracts in the two nearby months. In 1998, CBOE consolidated operations with the PACIFIC EXCHANGE (PCX), combining the two exchange's product lines and operating under the CBOE name. Trading hours: Monday through Friday, from 7:20 A.M. to 3:15 P.M. *See also* SECURITIES AND COMMODITIES EXCHANGES.

CHICAGO MERCANTILE EXCHANGE (CME) U.S. derivatives exchange founded in 1874 trading futures and futures options on agriculture products, currencies, indices and interest rates. The CME's Globex automated trading system provides after-hours trading for the exchange's financial futures and options; MATIF and Reuters are the CME's partners in the system. OPEN OUTCRY is in use during regular trading sessions. The CME enjoys a mutual offset arrangement with the Singapore International Monetary Exchange, and with linkages the LONDON INTERNATIONAL FINANCIAL FUTURES AND OPTIONS EXCHANGE to trade short-term European interest rate contract, and with Matif to trade long-term European interest rate contracts. Trading hours: Monday through Friday, 7:20 A.M. to 3:15 P.M. *See also* SECURITIES AND COMMODITIES EXCHANGE.

CHICAGO STOCK EXCHANGE (CHX) founded in 1882, CHX is now a major exchange, particularly in extended trading hours. CHX merged with the stock exchanges in St. Louis, Minneapolis-St. Paul, and Cleveland in 1949 to form the Midwest Stock Exchange. Ten years later, the exchange in New Orleans also joined the Midwest Stock Exchange. The Midwest Stock Exchange changed its name to the Chicago Stock Exchange in 1993. CHX trades only stocks, more than 4,000 of which trade on the New York Stock Exchange, American Stock Exchange and NASDAQ Stock Market. Some issues are traded exclusively on CHX. There are 445 authorized memberships on CHX. The exchange provides retail services through its floor broker community. While trading is conducted on a trading floor, 90% of the trades are executed through the exchange's automated execution system, MAX. CHX is a leading market for executing block trades. Trading hours are 9:30 A.M. to 4:30 P.M.

CHIEF EXECUTIVE OFFICER (CEO) officer of a firm principally responsible for the activities of a company. CEO is usually an additional title held by the CHAIRMAN OF THE BOARD, the president, or another senior officer such as a vice chairman or an executive vice president.

CHIEF FINANCIAL OFFICER (CFO) executive officer who is responsible for handling funds, signing checks, keeping financial records, and financial planning for a corporation. He or she typically has the title of vice president-finance or financial vice president in large corporations, that of treasurer or controller (also spelled comptroller) in smaller companies. Since many state laws require that a corporation have a treasurer, that title is often combined with one or more of the other financial titles.

The controllership function requires an experienced accountant to direct internal accounting programs, including cost accounting, systems and procedures, data processing, acquisitions analysis, and financial planning. The controller may also have internal audit responsibilities.

The treasury function is concerned with the receipt, custody, investment, and disbursement of corporate funds and for borrowings and the maintenance of a market for the company's securities.

CHIEF OPERATING OFFICER (COO) officer of a firm, usually the president or an executive vice president, responsible for day-to-day management. The chief operating officer reports to the CHIEF EXECUTIVE OFFICER and may or may not be on the board of directors (presidents typically serve as board members). *See also* CHAIRMAN OF THE BOARD.

CHINESE WALL imaginary barrier between the investment banking, corporate finance, and research departments of a brokerage house and the sales and trading departments. Since the investment banking side has sensitive knowledge of impending deals such as takeovers, new stock and bond issues, divestitures, spinoffs and the like, it would be unfair to the general investing public if the sales and trading side of the firm had advance knowledge of such transactions. So several SEC and stock exchange rules mandate that a Chinese Wall be erected to prevent premature leakage of this market-moving information. It became law with the passage of SEC Rule 10b-5 of the Securities Exchange Act of 1934. The investment banking department uses code names and logs of the people who have access to key information in an attempt to keep the identities of the parties secret until the deal is publicly announced.

CHUNNEL tunnel crossing the English Channel between Great Britain and France. The Chunnel project took years to build and cost billions of dollars, but was finally opened for passenger and freight traffic in 1994. The Chunnel was built and is operated by Euro-Tunnel PLC.

CHURNING excessive trading of a client's account. Churning increases the broker's commissions, but usually leaves the client worse off or no better off than before. Churning is illegal under SEC and exchange rules, but is difficult to prove.

CINCINNATI STOCK EXCHANGE (CSE) stock exchange established in 1887, the exchange was the first—and still the only—fully automated stock exchange in the U.S., handling members' transactions using computers without a trading floor. CSE created the National Securities Trading System (NSTS), an electronic auction market. Participating brokerage firms enter orders into the NSTS computer system, along with specialists' bids and offers, which matches and clears orders back to brokers. The NSTS contains some of the features envisioned for a national exchange market system. Trading hours are 9:30 A.M. to 4 P.M.

CIRCLE underwriter's way of designating potential purchasers and amounts of a securities issue during the REGISTRATION period, before selling is permitted. Registered representatives canvass prospective buyers and report any interest to the underwriters, who then circle the names on their list.

CIRCUIT BREAKERS measures instituted by the major stock and commodities exchanges to halt trading temporarily in stocks and stock index futures when the market has fallen by an amount based on specified percentage declines in a specified period. For example, circuit breakers instituted at the NEW YORK STOCK EXCHANGE in spring 1998 halt stock trading when the Dow Jones Industrial Average falls 10%, 20%, and 30%, with the point settings revised quarterly on the first day of January, April, July, and October. Circuit breakers were originally instituted after BLACK MONDAY in 1987 and modified following another sharp market drop in October 1989. They are subject to change from time to time, but may include trading halts, curtailment of automated trading systems, and/or price movement limits on index futures. Their purpose is to prevent a market free-fall by permitting a rebalancing of buy and sell orders. *See also* PROGRAM TRADING.

CITIZEN BONDS form of CERTIFICATELESS MUNICIPALS. Citizen bonds may be registered on stock exchanges, in which case their prices are listed in daily newspapers, unlike other municipal bonds. *See also* BOOK-ENTRY SECURITIES.

CITY CODE ON TAKEOVERS AND MERGERS *see* DAWN RAID.

CIVILIAN LABOR FORCE all members of the population aged 16 or over in the United States who are not in the military or institutions such as prisons or mental hospitals and who are either employed or are unemployed and actively seeking and available for work. Every month, the U.S. Department of Labor releases the unemployment rate, which is the percentage of the civilian labor force who are unemployed. The Labor Department also releases the percentage of the civilian non-institutional population who are employed.

CLASS
1. securities having similar features. Stocks and bonds are the two main classes; they are subdivided into various classes—for example, mortgage bonds and debentures, issues with different rates of interest, common and preferred stock, or Class A and Class B common. The different classes in a company's capitalization are itemized on its balance sheet.
2. options of the same type—put or call—with the same underlying security. A class of option having the same expiration date and EXERCISE PRICE is termed a SERIES.

CLASS A/CLASS B SHARES *see* CLASSIFIED STOCK.

CLASS ACTION legal complaint filed on behalf of a group of shareholders having an identical grievance. Shareholders in a class action are typically represented by one lawyer or group of attorneys, who like this kind of business because the awards tend to be proportionate to the number of parties in the class.

CLASSIFIED STOCK separation of equity into more than one CLASS of common, usually designated Class A and Class B. The distinguishing features, set forth in the corporation charter and bylaws, usually give an advantage to the Class A shares in terms of voting power, though dividend and liquidation privileges can also be involved. Classified stock is less prevalent today than in the 1920s, when it was used as a means of preserving minority control.

CLAYTON ANTITRUST ACT *see* ANTITRUST LAWS.

CLEAN
Finance: free of debt, as in a clean balance sheet. In banking, corporate borrowers have traditionally been required to *clean up* for at least 30 days each year to prove their borrowings were seasonal and not required as permanent working capital.
International trade: without documents, as in clean vs. documentary drafts.
Securities: block trade that matches buy or sell orders, sparing the block positioner any inventory risk. If the transaction appears on the exchange tape, it is said to be *clean on the tape.* Sometimes such a trade is called a *natural:* "We did a natural for 80,000 XYZ common."

CLEAR
Banking: COLLECTION of funds on which a check is drawn, and payment of those funds to the holder of the check. *See also* CLEARING HOUSE FUNDS.
Finance: asset not securing a loan and not otherwise encumbered. As a verb, to clear means to make a profit: "After all expenses, we *cleared* $1 million."
Securities: COMPARISON of the details of a transaction between brokers prior to settlement; final exchange of securities for cash on delivery.

CLEARING CORPORATIONS organizations, such as the NATIONAL SECURITIES CLEARING CORPORATION (NSCC), that are exchange-affiliated and facilitate the validation, delivery, and settlement of securities transactions.

CLEARING HOUSE FUNDS funds represented by checks or drafts that pass between banks through the FEDERAL RESERVE SYSTEM. Unlike FEDERAL FUNDS, which are drawn on reserve balances and are good the same day, clearing house funds require three days to clear. Also, funds used to settle transactions on which there is one day's FLOAT.

CLEAR TITLE title that is clear of all claims or disputed interests. It is necessary to have clear title to a piece of real estate before it can be sold by one party to another. In order to obtain a clear title, it is usually necessary to have a title search performed by a title company, which may find various clouds on the title such as an incomplete certificate of occupancy, outstanding building violations, claims by neighbors for pieces of the property, or an inaccurate survey. Once these objections have been resolved, the owner will have a clear and marketable title. *See also* BAD TITLE; CLOUD ON TITLE.

CLIFFORD TRUST trust set up for at least ten years and a day, which made it possible to turn over income-producing assets, then to reclaim the assets when the trust expired. Prior to the TAX REFORM ACT OF 1986, such trusts were popular ways of shifting income-producing assets from parents to children, whose income was taxed at lower rates. However, the 1986 Act made monies put into Clifford trusts after March 1, 1986, subject to taxation at the grantor's tax rate, thus defeating their purpose. For trusts established before that date, taxes are paid at the child's lower tax rate, but only if the child is under the age of 14. Since the Tax Act was implemented, few Clifford trusts are set up. *See also* INTER VIVOS TRUST.

CLONE FUND in a FAMILY OF FUNDS, new fund set up to emulate a successful existing fund.

CLOSE
1. the price of the final trade of a security at the end of a trading day.
2. the last half hour of a trading session on the exchanges.
3. in commodities trading, the period just before the end of the session when trades marked for execution AT THE CLOSE are completed.
4. to consummate a sale or agreement. In a REAL ESTATE closing, for example, rights of ownership are transferred in exchange for monetary and other considerations. At a *loan* closing, notes are signed and checks are exchanged. At the close of an *underwriting* deal, checks and securities are exchanged.
5. in accounting, the transfer of revenue and expense accounts at the end of the period—called *closing the books.*

CLOSE A POSITION to eliminate an investment from one's portfolio. The simplest example is the outright sale of a security and its delivery to the purchaser in exchange for payment. In commodities futures and options trading, traders commonly close out positions through offsetting transactions. Closing a position terminates involvement with the investment; HEDGING, though similar, requires further actions.

CLOSE MARKET market in which there is a narrow spread between BID and OFFER prices. Such a market is characterized by active trading and multiple competing market makers. In general, it is easier for investors to buy and sell securities and get good prices in a close market than in a wide market characterized by wide differences between bid and offer prices.

CLOSED CORPORATION corporation owned by a few people, usually management or family members. Shares have no public market. Also known as *private corporation* or *privately held corporation.*

CLOSED-END FUND type of fund that has a fixed number of shares usually listed on a major stock exchange. Unlike open-end mutual funds, closed end funds do not stand ready to issue and redeem shares on a continuous basis. They tend to have specialized portfolios of stocks, bonds, CONVERTIBLES, or combinations thereof, and may be oriented toward income, capital gains, or a combination of these objectives. Examples are the Korea Fund, which specializes in the stocks of Korean firms, and ASA Ltd., which specializes in South African gold mining stocks. Both are listed on the New York Stock Exchange. Because the managers of closed-end funds are perceived to be less responsive to profit opportunities than open-end fund managers, who must attract and retain shareholders, closed-end fund shares often sell at a discount from net asset value. *See also* DUAL-PURPOSE FUND.

CLOSED-END MANAGEMENT COMPANY INVESTMENT COMPANY that operates a mutual fund with a limited number of shares outstanding. Unlike an OPEN-END MANAGEMENT COMPANY, which creates new shares to meet investor demand, a closed-end fund has a set number of shares. These are often listed on an exchange. *See also* CLOSED-END FUND.

CLOSED-END MORTGAGE mortgage-bond issue with an indenture that prohibits repayment before maturity and the repledging of the same collateral without the permission of the bondholders; also called closed mortgage. It is distinguished from an OPEN-END MORTGAGE, which is reduced by amortization and can be increased to its original amount and secured by the original mortgage.

CLOSED FUND MUTUAL FUND that has become too large and is no longer issuing shares.

CLOSED OUT liquidated the position of a client unable to meet a margin call or cover a short sale. *See also* CLOSE A POSITION.

CLOSELY HELD corporation most of whose voting stock is held by a few shareholders; differs from a CLOSED CORPORATION because enough stock is publicly held to provide a basis for trading. Also, the shares held by the controlling group are not considered likely to be available for purchase.

CLOSING COSTS expenses involved in transferring real estate from a seller to a buyer, among them lawyer's fees, survey charges, title searches and insurance, and fees to file deeds and mortgages.

CLOSING PRICE price of the last transaction completed during a day's trading session on an organized securities exchange. *See also* CLOSING RANGE.

CLOSING PURCHASE option seller's purchase of another option having the same features as an earlier one. The two options cancel each other out and thus liquidate the seller's position.

CLOSING QUOTE last bid and offer prices recorded by a specialist or market maker at the close of a trading day.

CLOSING RANGE range of prices (in commodities trading) within which an order to buy or sell a commodity can be executed during one trading day.

CLOSING SALE sale of an option having the same features (i.e., of the same series) as an option previously purchased. The two have the effect of canceling each other out. Such a transaction demonstrates the intention to liquidate the holder's position in the underlying securities upon exercise of the buy.

CLOSING TICK gauge of stock market strength that nets the number of stocks whose New York Stock Exchange closing prices were higher than their previous trades, called an UPTICK or plus tick, against the number that closed on a DOWNTICK or minus tick. When the closing tick is positive, that is, when more stocks advanced than declined in the last trade, traders say the market closed on an uptick or was "buying at the close," a bullish sign. "Selling at the close," resulting in a minus closing tick or downtick, is bearish. *See also* TRIN.

CLOSING TRIN *see* TRIN.

CLOUD ON TITLE any document, claim, unreleased lien, or encumbrance that may superficially impair or injure the title to a property or make the title doubtful because of its apparent or possible validity. Clouds on title are usually uncovered in a TITLE SEARCH. These clouds range from a recorded mortgage paid in full, but with no satisfaction of mortgage recorded, to a property sold without a spouse's release of interest, to an heir of a prior owner with a questionable claim to the property. The property owner may initiate a quitclaim deed or a quiet title proceeding to remove the cloud on title from the record. Also called *bad title.*

CMO *see* COLLATERALIZED MORTGAGE OBLIGATION (CMO).

CMO REIT specialized type of REAL ESTATE INVESTMENT TRUST (REIT) that invests in the residual cash flows of COLLATERALIZED MORTGAGE OBLIGATIONS (CMOs). CMO cash flows represent the spread (difference) between the rates paid by holders of the underlying mortgage loans and the lower, shorter term rates paid to investors in the CMOs. Spreads are subject to risks associated with interest rate levels and are considered risky investments. Also called *equity CMOs.*

COATTAIL INVESTING following on the coattails of other successful investors, usually institutions, by trading the same stocks when their actions are made public. This risky strategy assumes the research that guided the investor wearing the coat is still relevant by the time the coattail investor reads about it.

COBRA *See* CONSOLIDATED OMNIBUS BUDGET RECONCILIATION ACT (COBRA).

CODE OF PROCEDURE NATIONAL ASSOCIATION OF SECURITIES DEALERS (NASD) guide for its District Business Conduct Committees in hearing and adjudicating complaints filed between or against NASD members under its Rules of Fair Practice.

CODICIL legal document that amends a will.

C.O.D. TRANSACTION *see* DELIVERY VERSUS PAYMENT.

COFFEE, SUGAR AND COCOA EXCHANGE (CSCE) founded in 1882 as the Coffee Exchange of the City of New York. Sugar futures were added in 1914, and in 1979 the Coffee and Sugar Exchange merged with the New York Cocoa Exchange, which was founded in 1925. In 1998, CSCE merged with the NEW YORK COTTON EXCHANGE under an umbrella holding company, the Board of Trade of the City of New York, which provides joint clearing, back-office, and operational functions. The exchange continues to trade its derivative products under its name: futures and options in coffee, sugar, cocoa, basic formula price milk, nonfat dry milk, cheddar cheese and butter. CSCE also offers flexible options, comparable to over-the-counter options, for coffee, sugar, and cocoa. Trading is by open outcry. Contracts trade Monday through Friday, 9 A.M. to 2 P.M. *See also* SECURITIES AND COMMODITIES EXCHANGES.

COINCIDENT INDICATORS economic indicators that coincide with the current pace of economic activity. The Index of Coincident Indicators is published monthly by the Conference Board along with the Index of LEADING INDICATORS and the Index of LAGGING INDICATORS to give the public a reading on whether the economy is expanding or contracting and at what pace. The components of the Index of Coincident Indicators are: non-farm payroll workers, personal income less transfer payments, industrial production, manufacturing, and trade sales.

COINSURANCE sharing of an insurance risk, common when claims could be of such size that it would not be prudent for one company to underwrite the whole risk. Typically, the underwriter is liable up to a stated limit, and the coinsurer's liability is for amounts above that limit.

Policies on hazards such as fire or water damage often require coverage of at least a specified coinsurance percentage of the replacement cost. Such clauses induce the owners of property to carry full coverage or close to it.

COLA acronym for *cost-of-living adjustment,* which is an annual addition to wages or benefits to compensate employees or beneficiaries for the loss of purchasing power due to inflation. Many union contracts contain a COLA providing for salary increases at or above the change in the previous year's CONSUMER PRICE INDEX (CPI). Social Security recipients also have their monthly payments adjusted annually based on a COLA tied to the CPI.

COLD CALLING practice of making unsolicited calls to potential customers by brokers. Brokers hope to interest customers in stocks, bonds, mutual funds, financial planning, or other financial products and services in their cold calls. In some countries, such as Great Britain and parts of Canada, cold calling is severely restricted or even prohibited.

COLLAR
1. in new issue underwriting, the lowest rate acceptable to a buyer of bonds or the lowest price acceptable to the issuer. In an adjustable rate issue, refers to the maximum and minimum rates payable based on par value.
2. in ACQUISITION terminology, feature of an agreement that protects the acquirer from having to put up additional stock or cash in the event the market value of the acquirer falls between the agreement and closing.
3. in options trading, selling an OUT-OF-THE MONEY call and buying an IN-THE-MONEY put, thus limiting both upside and downside.
4. index level at which a CIRCUIT BREAKER is triggered.

COLLATERALIZE *see* ASSIGN; COLLATERAL; HYPOTHECATION.

COLLATERALIZED BOND OBLIGATION (CBO) INVESTMENT-GRADE bond backed by a pool of JUNK BONDS. CBOs are similar in concept to COLLATERALIZED MORTGAGE OBLIGATIONS (CMOs), but differ in that CBOs represent different degrees of credit quality rather than different maturities. Underwriters of CBOs package a large and diversified pool of high-risk, high-yield junk bonds, which is then separated into "tiers." Typically, a top tier represents the higher quality collateral and pays the lowest interest rate; a middle tier is backed by riskier bonds and pays a higher rate; the bottom tier represents the lowest credit quality and instead of receiving a fixed interest rate receives the residual interest payments—money that is left over after the higher tiers have been paid. CBOs, like CMOs, are substantially overcollateralized and this, plus the diversification of the pool backing them, earns them investment-grade bond ratings. Holders of third-tier CBOs stand to earn high yields or less money depending on the rate of defaults in the collateral pool. CBOs provide a way for big holders of junk bonds to reduce their portfolios and for securities firms to tap a new source of buyers in the disenchanted junk bond market of the early 1990s.

COLLATERALIZED MORTGAGE OBLIGATION (CMO) mortgage-backed bond that separates mortgage pools into different maturity classes, called *tranches.* This is accomplished by applying income (payments and prepayments of principal and interest) from mortgages in the pool in the order that the CMOs pay out. Tranches pay different rates of interest and can mature in a few months, or as long as 20 years. Issued by the Federal Home Loan Mortgage Corporation (Freddie Mac) and private issuers, CMOs are usually backed by government-guaranteed or other top-grade mortgages and have AAA ratings. In return for a lower yield, CMOs provide investors with increased security about the life of their investment compared to purchasing a whole mortgage-backed security. Even so, if mortgage rates drop sharply, causing a flood of refinancings, prepayment rates will soar and CMO tranches will be repaid before their expected maturity. CMOs are broken into different classes, called COMPANION BONDS or PLANNED AMORTIZATION CLASS (PAC) bonds.

COLLATERAL TRUST BOND corporate debt security backed by other securities, usually held by a bank or other trustee. Such bonds are backed by collateral trust certificates and are usually issued by parent corporations that are borrowing against the securities of wholly owned subsidiaries.

COLLECTIBLE rare object collected by investors. Examples: stamps, coins, oriental rugs, antiques, baseball cards, photographs. Collectibles typically rise sharply in value during inflationary periods, when people are trying to move their assets from paper currency as an inflation hedge, then drop in value during low inflation. Collectible trading for profit can be quite difficult, because of the limited number of buyers and sellers.

COLLECTION
1. presentation of a negotiable instrument such as a draft or check to the place at which it is payable. The term refers not only to check clearing and payment, but to such special banking services as foreign collections, coupon collection, and collection of returned items (bad checks).
2. referral of a past due account to specialists in collecting loans or accounts receivable, either an internal department or a private collection agency.
3. in a general financial sense, conversion of accounts receivable into cash.

COLLECTION PERIOD *see* COLLECTION RATIO.

COLLECTION RATIO ratio of a company's accounts receivable to its average daily sales. Average daily sales are obtained by dividing sales for an accounting period by the number of days in the accounting period—annual sales divided by 365, if the accounting period is a year. That result, divided into accounts receivable (an average of beginning and ending accounts receivable is more accurate), is the collection ratio—the average number of days it takes the company to convert receivables into cash. It is also called *average collection period. See* ACCOUNTS RECEIVABLE TURNOVER for a discussion of its significance.

COLLECTIVE BARGAINING process by which members of the labor force, operating through authorized union representatives, negotiate with their employers concerning wages, hours, working conditions, and benefits.

COLLEGE CONSTRUCTION LOAN INSURANCE ASSOCIATION federal agency established in 1987 to guarantee loans for college building programs. Informally called *Connie Lee.*

COLTS acronym for *Continuously Offered Longer-term Securities,* 3-year to 30-year fixed rate, variable rate, or zero-coupon bonds offered on an ongoing basis by the INTERNATIONAL BANK FOR RECONSTRUCTION AND DEVELOPMENT (World Bank). Bonds finance general operations of the bank and the terms are determined by bank management at the time of each new offering.

COMBINATION
1. arrangement of options involving two long or two short positions with different expiration dates or strike (exercise) prices. A trader could order a combination with a long call and a long put or a short call and a short put.
2. joining of competing companies in an industry to alter the competitive balance in their favor is called a combination in restraint of trade.
3. joining two or more separate businesses into a single accounting entity; also called *business combination. See also* MERGER.

COMBINATION ANNUITY *see* HYBRID ANNUITY.

COMBINATION BOND bond backed by the full faith and credit of the governmental unit issuing it as well as by revenue from the toll road, bridge, or other project financed by the bond.

COMBINATION ORDER *see* ALTERNATIVE ORDER.

COMBINED FINANCIAL STATEMENT financial statement that brings together the assets, liabilities, net worth, and operating figures of two or more affiliated companies. In its most comprehensive form, called a combining statement, it includes columns showing each affiliate on an "alone" basis; a column "eliminating" offsetting intercompany transactions; and the resultant combined financial statement. A combined statement is distinguished from a CONSOLIDATED FINANCIAL STATEMENT of a company and subsidiaries, which must reconcile investment and capital accounts. Combined financial statements do not necessarily represent combined credit responsibility or investment strength.

COMEX now a division of NEW YORK MERCANTILE EXCHANGE. Formerly known as the Commodity Exchange, it is the leading U.S. market for metals futures and futures options trading. Futures and futures options are traded on aluminum, copper, gold and silver, and the Eurotop 100 Index. Trading is conducted Monday through Friday, 8:10 A.M. to 2:35 P.M. *See also* NEW YORK MERCANTILE EXCHANGE; SECURITIES AND COMMODITIES EXCHANGES.

COMFORT LETTER
1. independent auditor's letter, required in securities underwriting agreements, to assure that information in the registration statement and prospectus is correctly prepared and that no material changes have occurred since its preparation. It is sometimes called *cold comfort letter*—cold because the accountants do not state positively that the information is correct, only that nothing has come to their attention to indicate it is not correct.
2. letter from one to another of the parties to a legal agreement stating that certain actions not clearly covered in the agreement will—or will not—be taken. Such declarations of intent usually deal with matters that are of importance only to the two parties and do not concern other signers of the agreement.

COMMERCIAL HEDGERS companies that take positions in commodities markets in order to lock in prices at which they buy raw materials or sell their products. For instance, Alcoa might hedge its holdings of aluminum with contracts in aluminum futures, or Eastman Kodak, which must buy great quantities of silver for making film, might hedge its holdings in the silver futures market.

COMMERCIAL LOAN short-term (typically 90-day) renewable loan to finance the seasonal WORKING CAPITAL needs of a business, such as purchase of inventory or production and distribution of goods. Commercial loans—shown on the balance sheet as notes payable—rank second only to TRADE CREDIT in importance as a source of short-term financing. Interest is based on the prime rate. *See also* CLEAN.

COMMERCIAL PAPER short-term obligations with maturities ranging from 2 to 270 days issued by banks, corporations, and other borrowers to investors with temporarily idle cash. Such instruments are unsecured and usually discounted, although some are interest-bearing. They can be issued directly—*direct issuers* do it that way—or through brokers equipped to handle the enormous clerical volume involved. Issuers like commercial paper because the maturities are flexible and because the rates are usually marginally lower than bank rates. Investors—actually lenders, since commercial paper is a form of debt—like the flexibility and safety of an instrument that is issued only by top-rated concerns and is nearly always backed by bank lines of credit. Both Moody's and Standard & Poor's assign ratings to commercial paper.

COMMERCIAL PROPERTY real estate that includes income-producing property, such as office buildings, restaurants, shopping centers, hotels, industrial parks, warehouses, and factories. Commercial property usually must be zoned for business purposes. It is possible to invest in commercial property directly, or through REAL ESTATE INVESTMENT TRUSTS or REAL ESTATE LIMITED PARTNERSHIPS. Investors receive income from rents and capital appreciation if the property is sold at a profit. Investing in commercial property also entails large risks, such as nonpayment of rent by tenants or a decline in property values because of over-building or low demand.

COMMERCIAL WELLS oil and gas drilling sites that are productive enough to be commercially viable. A limited partnership usually syndicates a share in a commercial well.

COMMINGLING
Securities: mixing customer-owned securities with those owned by a firm in its proprietary accounts. REHYPOTHECATION—the use of customers' collateral to secure brokers' loans—is permissible with customer consent, but certain securities and collateral must by law be kept separate.
Trust banking: pooling the investment funds of individual accounts, with each customer owning a share of the total fund. Similar to a MUTUAL FUND.

COMMISSION
Real estate: percentage of the selling price of the property, paid by the seller.
Securities: fee paid to a broker for executing a trade based on the number of shares traded or the dollar amount of the trade. Since 1975, when regulation ended, brokers have been free to charge whatever they like.

COMMISSION BROKER broker, usually a floor broker, who executes trades of stocks, bonds, or commodities for a commission.

COMMITMENT FEE lender's charge for contracting to hold credit available. Fee may be replaced by interest when money is borrowed or both fees and interest may be charged, as with a REVOLVING CREDIT.

COMMITTEE ON UNIFORM SECURITIES IDENTIFICATION PROCE-DURES (CUSIP) committee that assigns identifying numbers and codes for all securities. These CUSIP numbers and symbols are used when recording all buy or sell orders. For International Business Machines the CUSIP symbol is IBM and the CUSIP number is 45920010.

COMMODITIES bulk goods such as grains, metals, and foods traded on a commodities exchange or on the SPOT MARKET. *See also* SECURITIES AND COMMODITIES EXCHANGES.

COMMODITIES EXCHANGE CENTER *see* SECURITIES AND COMMODITIES EXCHANGES.

COMMODITY-BACKED BOND bond tied to the price of an underlying commodity. An investor whose bond is tied to the price of silver or gold receives interest pegged to the metal's current price, rather than a fixed dollar amount. Such a bond is meant to be a hedge against inflation, which drives up the prices of most commodities.

COMMODITY FUTURES CONTRACT FUTURES CONTRACT tied to the movement of a particular commodity. This enables contract buyers to buy a specific amount of a commodity at a specified price on a particular date in the future. The price of the contract is determined using the OPEN OUTCRY system on the floor of a commodity exchange such as the Chicago Board of Trade or the Commodity Exchange in New York. There are commodity futures contracts based on meats such as cattle and pork bellies; grains such as corn, oats, soybeans and wheat; metals such as gold, silver, and platinum; and energy products such as heating oil, natural gas, and crude oil. For a complete listing of commodity futures contracts, *see* SECURITIES AND COMMODITIES EXCHANGES.

COMMODITY FUTURES TRADING COMMISSION (CFTC) independent agency created by Congress in 1974 responsible for regulating the U.S. commodity futures and options markets. The CFTC is responsible for insuring market integrity and protecting market participants against manipulation, abusive trade practices, and fraud.

COMMODITY INDICES indices that measure either the price or performance of physical commodities, or the price of commodities as represented by the price of futures contracts that are listed on commodity exchanges. The Journal of Commerce Index, Reuters Index and The Economist Index are three indices that measure industrial performance and raw commodities. Due to the complexities of holding physical commodities, however, investors tend to focus on futures indices that are liquid baskets of commodities. Institutional investors prohibited from investing directly in the futures market can include commodities in their portfolios through these indices. Among the commodity indices that measure futures price performance are:

Bankers Trust Commodity Index (BTCI) is a weighted, composite measure of the values of a basket of five commodities. Energy prices are based on NEW YORK MERCANTILE EXCHANGE contracts. Aluminum is based on the LONDON METAL EXCHANGE contract, while gold and silver are based on London spot fixings. The base prices used are the average prices of each component commodity over the first quarter of 1984. The components are: crude oil—45/$30.191; gold—18/$384.18; aluminum—17/$1,543.67; heating oil—10/$0.8340; silver—10/$9.0043. The value of the index on any given day is calculated by multiplying the current price by the base weight and dividing this figure by the base price.

Chase Physical Commodity Index (CPCI) a value-weighted index of unleveraged physical commodity futures traded on U.S. exchanges. Unleveraged means the CPCI assumes investment in T-bills of a portion of the portfolio's total assets equal to 100% of the notional contract value, effectively collateralizing the long position. Only the risk and return of unleveraged changes in the constituent commodities' prices, augmented by the T-bills' yield, determine investment returns. The index is composed of five commodity categories: Energy (42.9%)—crude oil (19.4%), heating oil (8.02%), unleaded gasoline (5.24%), natural gas (10.24%); Livestock (20.55%)—lean hogs (7.92%), pork bellies (1.66%), live cattle (8.71%), feeder cattle (2.26%); Grain (16.78%)—wheat (6.16%), corn (4.94%), soybeans (3.61%), oats (2.07%); Food/Fiber (11.5%)—cotton (3.58%), coffee (2.59%), sugar (93.3%), cocoa (2.03%); Metals (8.27%)—copper (3%), gold (3.29%), silver (1.98%).

CRB/Bridge Index is made up of 17 commodities whose futures trade on U.S. exchanges. The index is viewed widely as a broad measure of overall commodity price trends. There are five component groups: industrials—crude oil, heating oil, natural gas, copper, cotton; grains—corn, wheat, soybeans; precious metals—gold, silver, platinum; livestock and meats—cattle, hogs; softs—coffee, cocoa, sugar, orange juice. Equal weighting is used for both arithmetic averaging of individual commodity months and for geometric averaging of the 21 commodity averages. As a result, no single month or commodity has undue impact on the index. Futures and options on the CRB/Bridge Index trade on the New York Futures Exchange (NYFE). Futures are settled at contract maturity by cash payment.

Energy and Metals Index (ENMET) is a geometrically weighted index based on the prices of futures contracts and developed by Merrill Lynch. ENMET is comprised of six commodities: crude oil (40%), natural gas (15%), gold (20%), silver (5%), copper (15%), aluminum (5%). The index is weighted to show optimal historic correlation with the CONSUMER PRICE INDEX and the PRODUCER PRICE INDEX. The index is computed daily.

Goldman Sachs Commodity Index (GSCI) consists of 22 commodities. All but the industrials, which trade on the LONDON METAL EXCHANGE, trade on U.S. futures markets. There are five component groups: Energy-crude oil (15.89%), natural gas (15.73%), heating oil (9.94%), unleaded gasoline (9.70%); Agriculture-wheat (8.87%), corn (6.34%), soybeans (2.99%), cotton (2.96%), sugar (2.84%), coffee (1.09%), cocoa (0.29%); Livestock-live cattle (9.35%), live hogs (4.24%); Industrials-aluminum (2.86%), copper (2.07%), zinc (0.77%), nickel (0.48%), lead (0.29%), tin (0.12%); Precious metals-gold (2.53%), platinum (0.40%), silver (0.26%). Each commodity is weighted by quantity of world production as a means of measuring the impact of commodity performance on the global economy. The index includes a rolling yield, achievable by continually rolling forward the futures positions, and it is investable. Price movement reflects spot price changes in the underlying commodities. Commodity yield reflects roll yield and Treasury bill yield. Because delivery of the underlying commodity never occurs, the investor can keep his money invested in Treasury bills. Additionally, there are six sub-indices, representing each of the commodity component groups, calculated daily on real-time prices. Futures and options on the index are traded on the CHICAGO MERCANTILE EXCHANGE. Other investment products based on the GSCI and the GSCI sub-indices include structured notes, swaps, customized over-the-counter options and principal-guaranteed annuity contracts.

Investable Commodity Index (ICI) is a broad-based index of 16 commodities based on exchange-traded commodity futures and developed by Intermarket Management, Inc. The index measures the reinvested total returns of an equally weighted, fully collateralized basket: Grains (19%)—wheat, corn, soybeans; Metals (19%)—gold, silver, copper; Energy (25%)—crude oil, heating oil, gasoline, natural gas; Livestock (12%)—live cattle, live hogs; Food and Fiber (25%)— cocoa, coffee, sugar, cotton. The ICI is a rolling index, and represents the compounded daily percentage change in the geometric mean of the 16 commodities' prices plus 100% of the daily compounded 13-week U.S. Treasury bill returns.

The J. P. Morgan Commodity Index (JPMCI) uses a dollar-weighted arithmetic average of total returns by investment in 11 metals and energy commodities. The index is composed of Base metals (22%)—aluminum (9%), copper (8%), nickel (2%), zinc (3%); Energy (55%)—West Texas Intermediate crude oil (33%), heating oil (10%), natural gas (7%), unleaded gasoline (5%); and Precious metals (23%)—gold (15%), silver (5%), platinum (3%). As a total return index, returns are derived from changes in commodity futures prices, from rolling long futures positions through time along a sloping forward curve, and by full collateralization of the value of the index with Treasury bills. The index has a positive correlation with growth and inflation, and a negative correlation with bond and equity returns. The index is rebalanced monthly to maintain constant dollar weight.

COMMODITY PAPER inventory loans or advances secured by commodities. If the commodities are in transit, a bill of lading is executed by a common carrier. If they are in storage, a trust receipt acknowledges that they are held and that proceeds from their sale will be transmitted to the lender; a warehouse receipt lists the goods.

COMMON MARKET *see* EUROPEAN ECONOMIC COMMUNITY.

COMMON STOCK units of ownership of a public corporation. Owners typically are entitled to vote on the selection of directors and other important matters as well as to receive dividends on their holdings. In the event that a corporation is liquidated, the claims of secured and unsecured creditors and owners of bonds and preferred stock take precedence over the claims of those who own common stock. For the most part, however, common stock has more potential for appreciation. *See also* CAPITAL STOCK.

COMMON STOCK EQUIVALENT preferred stock or bond convertible into common stock, or warrant to purchase common stock at a specified price or discount from market price. Common stock equivalents represent potential dilution of existing common shareholder's equity, and their conversion or exercise is assumed in calculating fully diluted earnings per share. *See also* FULLY DILUTED EARNINGS PER SHARE.

COMMON STOCK FUND MUTUAL FUND that invests only in common stocks.

COMMON STOCK RATIO percentage of total capitalization represented by common stock. From a creditor's standpoint a high ratio represents a margin of safety in the event of LIQUIDATION. From an investor's standpoint, however, a high ratio can mean a lack of *leverage*. What the ratio should be depends largely on the stability of earnings. Electric utilities can operate with low ratios because their earnings are stable. As a general rule, when an industrial company's stock ratio is below 30%, analysts check on earnings stability and fixed charge coverage in bad times as well as good.

COMMUNITY PROPERTY property and income accumulated by a married couple and belonging to them jointly. The two have equal rights to the income from stocks, bonds, and real estate, as well as to the appreciated value of those assets.

COMPANION BONDS one class of a COLLATERALIZED MORTGAGE OBLIGATION (CMO) which is paid off first when the underlying mortgages are prepaid as interest rates fall. When interest rates rise and there are fewer prepayments, the principal on companion bonds will be prepaid more slowly. Companion bonds therefore absorb most of the prepayment risk inherent in a CMO, and are therefore more volatile. In return, they pay higher yields than the other class within a CMO, called PLANNED AMORTIZATION CLASS (PAC) bonds.

COMPANY organization engaged in business as a proprietorship, partnership, corporation, or other form of enterprise. Originally, a firm made up of a group of people as distinguished from a sole proprietorship. However, since few proprietorships owe their existence exclusively to one person, the term now applies to proprietorships as well.

COMPANY DOCTOR executive, usually recruited from the outside, specialized in corporate turnarounds.

COMPARATIVE STATEMENTS financial statements covering different dates but prepared consistently and therefore lending themselves to comparative analysis, as accounting convention requires. Comparative figures reveal trends in a company's financial development and permit insight into the dynamics behind static balance sheet figures.

COMPARISON
1. short for *comparison ticket*, a memorandum exchanged prior to settlement by two brokers in order to confirm the details of a transaction to which they were parties. Also called comparison sheet.
2. verification of collateral held against a loan, by exchange of information between two brokers or between a broker and a bank.

COMPENSATING BALANCE *or* **COMPENSATORY BALANCE** average balance required by a bank for holding credit available. The more or less standard requirement for a bank line of credit, for example, is 10% of the line plus an additional 10% of the borrowings. Compensating balances increase the effective rate of interest on borrowings.

COMPETITIVE BID sealed bid, containing price and terms, submitted by a prospective underwriter to an issuer, who awards the contract to the bidder with the best price and terms. Many municipalities and virtually all railroads and public utilities use this bid system. Industrial corporations generally prefer NEGOTIATED UNDERWRITING on stock issues but do sometimes resort to competitive bidding in selecting underwriters for bond issues.

COMPETITIVE TRADER *see* REGISTERED COMPETITIVE TRADER.

COMPLETE AUDIT usually the same as an unqualified audit, because it is so thoroughly executed that the auditor's only reservations have to do with unobtainable facts. A complete audit examines the system of internal control and the details of the books of account, including subsidiary records and supporting documents. This is done with an eye to locality, mathematical accuracy, accountability, and the application of accepted accounting principles.

COMPLETED CONTRACT METHOD accounting method whereby revenues and expenses (and therefore taxes) on long-term contracts, such as government defense contracts, are recognized in the year the contract is concluded, except that losses are recognized in the year they are forecast. This method differs from the *percentage-of-completion method,* where sales and costs are recognized each year based on the value of the work performed. Under the TAX REFORM ACT OF 1986, manufacturers with long-term contracts must elect either the latter method or the *percentage-of-completion capitalized cost method,* requiring that 40% of the contract be included under the percentage-of-completion method and 60% under the taxpayer's normal accounting method.

COMPLETION PROGRAM oil and gas limited partnership that takes over drilling when oil is known to exist in commercial quantities. A completion program is a conservative way to profit from oil and gas drilling, but without the capital gains potential of exploratory wildcat drilling programs.

COMPLIANCE DEPARTMENT department set up in all organized stock exchanges to oversee market activity and make sure that trading complies with Securities and Exchange Commission and exchange regulations. A company that does not adhere to the rules can be delisted, and a trader or brokerage firm that violates the rules can be barred from trading.

COMPOSITE TAPE *see* TAPE.

COMPOUND ANNUAL RETURN investment return, discounted retroactively from a cumulative figure, at which money, compounded annually, would reach the cumulative total. Also called INTERNAL RATE OF RETURN.

COMPOUND GROWTH RATE rate of growth of a number, compounded over several years. Securities analysts check a company's compound growth rate of profits for five years to see the long-term trend.

COMPOUND INTEREST interest earned on principal plus interest that was earned earlier. If $100 is deposited in a bank account at 10%, the depositor will be credited with $110 at the end of the first year and $121 at the end of the second year. That extra $1, which was earned on the $10 interest from the first year, is the compound interest. This example involves interest compounded annually:

interest can also be compounded on a daily, quarterly, half-yearly, or other basis. *See also* COMPOUND ANNUAL RETURN.

COMPTROLLER OF THE CURRENCY federal official, appointed by the President and confirmed by the Senate, who is responsible for chartering, examining, supervising, and liquidating all national banks. In response to the *comptroller's call,* national banks are required to submit *call reports* of their financial activities at least four times a year and to publish them in local newspapers. National banks can be declared insolvent only by the Comptroller of the Currency.

COMPUTERIZED MARKET TIMING SYSTEM system of picking buy and sell signals that puts together voluminous trading data in search of patterns and trends. Often, changes in the direction of moving average lines form the basis for buy and sell recommendations. These systems, commonly used by commodity funds and by services that switch between mutual funds, tend to work well when markets are moving steadily up or down, but not in trendless markets.

CONCERT PARTY person ACTING IN CONCERT.

CONCESSION
1. selling group's per-share or per-bond compensation in a corporate underwriting.
2. right, usually granted by a government entity, to use property for a specified purpose, such as a service station on a highway.

CONDEMNATION legal seizure of private property by a public authority for public use. Using the powers and legal procedures of EMINENT DOMAIN, a state, city, or town may condemn a property owner's home to make way for a highway, school, park, hospital, public housing project, parking facility, or other public project. The homeowners must give up the property even if they do not want to, and in return they must be compensated at fair market value by the public authority.

CONDITIONAL CALL OPTIONS form of CALL PROTECTION available to holders of some HIGH-YIELD BONDS. In the event the bond is called, the issuing corporation is obligated to substitute a non-callable bond having the same life and terms as the bond that is called.

CONDOMINIUM form of real estate ownership in which individual residents hold a deed and title to their houses or apartments and pay a maintenance fee to a management company for the upkeep of common property such as grounds, lobbies, and elevators as well as for other amenities. Condominium owners pay real estate taxes on their units and can sublet or sell as they wish. Some real estate limited partnerships specialize in converting rental property into condominiums. *See also* COOPERATIVE.

CONDUIT THEORY theory regulating investment companies such as REAL ESTATE INVESTMENT TRUSTS and MUTUAL FUNDS holding that since such companies are pure conduits for all capital gains, dividends, and interest to be passed through to shareholders, the investment company should not be taxed at the corporate level. As long as the investment company adheres to certain regulations, shareholders are therefore taxed only once—at the individual level—on income and capital gains. In contrast, shareholders of corporations are taxed twice: once at the corporate level in the form of corporate income taxes and once at the individual level in the form of individual income taxes on all dividends paid by the corporation.

CONFIRMATION
1. formal memorandum from a broker to a client giving details of a securities transaction. When a broker acts as a dealer, the confirmation must disclose that fact to the customer.
2. document sent by a company's auditor to its customers and suppliers requesting verification of the book amounts of receivables and payables. *Positive confirmations* request that every balance be confirmed, whereas *negative confirmations* request a reply only if an error exists.

CONFORMED COPY copy of an original document with the essential legal features, such as the signature and seal, being typed or indicated in writing.

CONFORMING LOANS mortgage loans that meet the qualifications of FREDDIE MAC or FANNIE MAE, which buy them from lenders and then issue PASS-THROUGH SECURITIES.

CONGLOMERATE corporation composed of companies in a variety of businesses. Conglomerates were popular in the 1960s, when they were thought to provide better management and sounder financial backing, and therefore to generate more profit, than small independent companies. However, some conglomerates became so complex that they were difficult to manage. In the 1980s and 1990s, many conglomerates sold off divisions and concentrated on a few core businesses. Analysts generally consider stocks of conglomerates difficult to evaluate because they are involved in so many unrelated businesses.

CONNIE LEE nickname for COLLEGE CONSTRUCTION LOAN INSURANCE ASSOCIATION.

CONSERVATOR individual appointed by a court to manage the property of a person who lacks the capacity to manage his own property. A conservator may be charged with liquidating the assets of a business in bankruptcy, or may have to take control of the personal finances of an incompetent individual who needs to be protected by the court.

CONSIDERATION something of value that one party gives to another in exchange for a promise or act. In law, a requirement of valid contracts. A consideration can be in the form of money, commodities, or personal services; in many industries the forms have become standardized.

CONSOLIDATED FINANCIAL STATEMENT financial statement that brings together all assets, liabilities, and operating accounts of a parent company and its subsidiaries. *See also* COMBINED FINANCIAL STATEMENT.

CONSOLIDATED MORTGAGE BOND bond issue that covers several units of property and may refinance separate mortgages on these properties. The consolidated mortgage with a single coupon rate is a traditional form of financing for railroads because it is economical to combine many properties in one agreement.

CONSOLIDATED OMNIBUS BUDGET RECONCILIATION ACT (COBRA) federal legislation under which group health plans sponsored by employers with 20 or more employees must offer continuation of coverage to employees who leave their jobs, voluntarily or otherwise, and their dependents. The employee must pay the entire premium up to 102% of the cost of coverage extended by COBRA. Depending on circumstances, COBRA permits employees to extend their coverage for up to 18 months and that of surviving dependents for up to 36 months. COBRA was designed to help former employees maintain health insurance coverage at group rates which may otherwise be unobtainable or unaffordable.

CONSOLIDATED TAPE combined tapes of the New York Stock Exchange and the American Stock Exchange. It became operative in June 1975. Network A covers NYSE-listed securities and identifies the originating market. Network B does the same for Amex-listed securities and also reports on securities listed on regional exchanges.

CONSOLIDATED TAX RETURN return combining the reports of the companies in what the tax law defines as an affiliated group. A firm is part of an affiliated group if it is at least 80% owned by a parent or other inclusive corporation. "Owned" refers to voting stock. (Before the TAX REFORM ACT OF 1986 it also included nonvoting stock.)

CONSOLIDATION LOAN loan that combines and refinances other loans or debt. It is normally an installment loan designed to reduce the dollar amount of an individual's monthly payments.

CONSORTIUM group of companies formed to promote a common objective or engage in a project of benefit to all the members. The relationship normally entails cooperation and a sharing of resources, sometimes even common ownership.

CONSTANT DOLLAR PLAN method of accumulating assets by investing a fixed amount of dollars in securities at set intervals. The investor buys more shares when the price is low and fewer shares when the price is high; the overall cost is lower than it would be if a constant number of shares were bought at set intervals. Also called *dollar cost averaging.*

CONSTANT DOLLARS dollars of a base year, used as a gauge in adjusting the dollars of other years in order to ascertain actual purchasing power. Denoted as C$ by the FINANCIAL ACCOUNTING STANDARDS BOARD (FASB), which defines constant dollars as hypothetical units of general purchasing power.

CONSTANT RATIO PLAN type of FORMULA INVESTING whereby a predetermined ratio is maintained between stock and FIXED-INCOME INVESTMENTS through periodic adjustments. For example, an investor with $200,000 and a 50-50 formula might start out with $100,000 in stock and $100,000 in bonds. If the stock increased in value to $150,000 and the bonds remained unchanged over a given adjustment period, the investor would restore the ratio at $125,000-$125,000 by selling $25,000 of stock and buying $25,000 of bonds.

CONSTANT YIELD METHOD method of allocating annual interest on a ZERO-COUPON SECURITY for income tax purposes. IRS Publication 1212 explains how to figure taxable interest on such ORIGINAL ISSUE DISCOUNT securities.

CONSTRUCTION LOAN short-term real estate loan to finance building costs. The funds are disbursed as needed or in accordance with a prearranged plan, and the money is repaid on completion of the project, usually from the proceeds of a mortgage loan. The rate is normally higher than prime, and there is usually an origination fee. The effective yield on these loans tends to be high, and the lender has a security interest in the real property.

CONSTRUCTION LOAN NOTE (CLN) note issued by a municipality to finance the construction of multi-family housing projects. The notes, which typically mature in three years or less, are normally repaid out of the proceeds of a long-term bond issue.

CONSTRUCTIVE RECEIPT term used by Internal Revenue Service for the date when a taxpayer received dividends or other income. IRS rules say that constructive receipt of income is established if the taxpayer has the right to claim it, whether or not the choice is exercised. For instance, if a bond pays interest on December 29, the taxpayer must report the income in that tax year and not in the following year.

CONSUMER CREDIT debt assumed by consumers for purposes other than home mortgages. Interest on consumer loans had been 100% deductible until the TAX REFORM ACT OF 1986 mandated that the deduction be phased out by 1991. Consumers can borrow through credit cards, lines of credit, loans against insurance policies, and many other methods. The Federal Reserve Board releases the amount of outstanding consumer credit on a monthly basis.

CONSUMER CREDIT PROTECTION ACT OF 1968 landmark federal legislation establishing rules of disclosure that lenders must observe in dealings with borrowers. The act stipulates that consumers be told annual percentage rates, potential total cost, and any special loan terms. The act, enforced by the Federal Reserve Bank, is also known as the *Truth-in-Lending Act.*

CONSUMER DEBENTURE investment note issued by a financial institution and marketed directly to the public. Consumer debentures were a popular means of raising lendable funds for banks during tight money periods prior to deregulation, since these instruments, unlike certificates of deposit, could compete freely with other money-market investments in a high-rate market.

CONSUMER DURABLES products bought by consumers that are expected to last three years or more. These include automobiles, appliances, boats, and furniture. Economists look at the trend in consumer expenditure on durables as an important indicator of the strength of the economy, since consumers need confidence to make such large and expensive purchases. Stock market analysts also classify companies that produce appliances, furniture, cars, and similar items as consumer durables manufacturers, contrasting them with consumer non-durables manufacturers, which make consumable items such as food or drugs.

CONSUMER FINANCE COMPANY *see* FINANCE COMPANY.

CONSUMER GOODS goods bought for personal or household use, as distinguished from CAPITAL GOODS or *producer's goods,* which are used to produce other goods. The general economic meaning of consumer goods encompasses consumer services. Thus the *market basket* on which the CONSUMER PRICE INDEX is based includes clothing, food, and other goods as well as utilities, entertainment, and other services.

CONSUMER INTEREST interest paid on consumer loans. Consumer interest is paid on credit cards, bank lines of credit, retail purchases, car and boat loans, and educational loans. Since the end of 1991, such interest is no longer deductible for tax purposes, based on provisions of the TAX REFORM ACT OF 1986. That tax law distinguished nondeductible consumer interest from other forms of interest which can be deductible, including business interest, investment interest, and mortgage-related interest.

CONSUMER PRICE INDEX (CPI) measures prices of a fixed basket of goods bought by a typical consumer, including food, transportation, shelter, utilities, clothing, medical care, entertainment, and other items. The CPI, published by the Bureau of Labor Statistics in the Department of Labor, is based at 100 in 1982 and is released monthly. It is widely used as a cost-of-living benchmark to adjust Social Security payments and other payment schedules, union contracts, and tax brackets. Also known as the *cost-of-living index.*

CONSUMPTION TAX *see* VALUE-ADDED TAX (VAT).

CONTANGO
1. pricing situation in which futures prices get progressively higher as maturities get progressively longer, creating negative spreads as contracts go farther out.

The increases reflect carrying costs, including storage, financing, and insurance. The reverse condition, an inverted market, is termed BACKWARDATION.
2. in finance, the costs that must be taken into account in analyses involving forecasts.

CONTINGENT BENEFICIARY person named in an insurance policy to receive the policy benefits if the primary beneficiary dies before the benefits become payable.

CONTINGENT DEFERRED SALES LOAD sales charge levied by a mutual fund if a customer sells fund shares within a specified number of years. Instead of charging a traditional FRONT-END LOAD of 5%, for example, a brokerage firm may offer the same fund with a contingent deferred sales load. Customers who sell the fund within the first year pay a 5% load. In the second year, the charge would be 4%. Each year the charge declines by one percentage point until there is no fee for selling fund shares after the fifth year. Also called *back-end load.*

CONTINGENT LIABILITIES
Banking: potential obligation of a guarantor or accommodation endorser; or the position of a customer who opens a letter of credit and whose account will be charged if a draft is presented. The bank's own ultimate responsibility for letters of credit and other commitments, individually and collectively, is its contingent liability.
Corporate reports: pending lawsuits, judgments under appeal, disputed claims, and the like, representing potential financial liability.

CONTINGENT ORDER securities order whose execution depends on the execution of another order; for example, a sell order and a buy order with prices stipulated. Where the purpose is to effect a swap, a price difference might be stipulated as a condition of the order's execution. Generally, brokers discourage these orders, favoring firm instructions.

CONTINUOUS NET SETTLEMENT (CNS) method of securities clearing and settlement that eliminates multiple fails in the same securities. This is accomplished by using a clearing house, such as the National Securities Clearing Corporation, and a depository, such as DEPOSITORY TRUST COMPANY, to match transactions to securities available in the firm's position, resulting in one net receive or deliver position at the end of the day. By including the previous day's fail position in the next day's selling trades, the firm's position is always up-to-date and money settlement or withdrawals can be made at any time with the clearing house. The alternative to CNS is window settlement, where the seller delivers securities to the buyer's cashier and receives payment.

CONTRA BROKER broker on the opposite side—the buy side of a sell order or the sell side of a buy order.

CONTRACT in general, agreement by which rights or acts are exchanged for lawful consideration. To be valid, it must be entered into by competent parties, must cover a legal and moral transaction, must possess mutuality, and must represent a meeting of minds. Countless transactions in finance and investments are covered by contracts.

CONTRACTUAL PLAN plan by which fixed dollar amounts of mutual fund shares are accumulated through periodic investments for 10 or 15 years. The legal vehicle for such investments is the *plan company* or *participating unit investment trust,* a selling organization operating on behalf of the fund's underwriter. The plan company must be registered with the Securities and Exchange Commission, as the underlying fund must be, so the investor receives two prospectuses. Investors in these plans commonly receive other benefits in exchange for their fixed periodic payments, such as decreasing term life insurance. *See also* FRONT-END LOAD.

CONTRARIAN investor who does the opposite of what most investors are doing at any particular time. According to contrarian opinion, if everyone is certain that something is about to happen, it won't. This is because most people who say the market is going up are fully invested and have no additional purchasing power, which means the market is at its peak. When people predict decline they have already sold out, so the market can only go up. Some mutual funds follow a contrarian investment strategy, and some investment advisers suggest only out-of-favor securities, whose price/earnings ratio is lower than the rest of the market or industry.

CONTRIBUTED CAPITAL payments made in cash or property to a corporation by its stockholders either to buy capital stock, to pay an assessment on the capital stock, or as a gift. Also called *paid-in capital.* The contributed or paid-in capital of a corporation is made up of capital stock and capital (or contributed) surplus, which is contributed (or paid-in) capital in excess of PAR value or STATED VALUE. Donated capital and DONATED SURPLUS are freely given forms of contributed (paid-in) capital, but DONATED STOCK refers to fully paid (previously issued) capital stock that is given as a gift to the issuing corporation.

CONTROLLED COMMODITIES commodities regulated by the Commodities Exchange Act of 1936, which set up trading rules for futures in commodities markets in order to prevent fraud and manipulation.

CONTROLLED WILDCAT DRILLING drilling for oil and gas in an area adjacent to but outside the limits of a proven field. Also known as a *field extension.* Limited partnerships drilling in this area take greater risks than those drilling in areas of proven energy reserves, but the rewards can be considerable if oil is found.

CONTROLLER *or* COMPTROLLER chief accountant of a company. In small companies the controller may also serve as treasurer. In a brokerage firm, the controller prepares financial reports, supervises internal audits, and is responsible for compliance with Securities and Exchange Commission regulations.

CONTROLLING INTEREST ownership of more than 50% of a corporation's voting shares. A much smaller interest, owned individually or by a group in combination, can be controlling if the other shares are widely dispersed and not actively voted.

CONTROL PERSON *see* AFFILIATED PERSON.

CONTROL STOCK shares owned by holders who have a CONTROLLING INTEREST.

CONVENTIONAL MORTGAGE residential mortgage loan, usually from a bank or savings and loan association, with a fixed rate and term. It is repayable in fixed monthly payments over a period usually 30 years or less, secured by real property, and not insured by the FEDERAL HOUSING ADMINISTRATION or guaranteed by the Veterans Administration.

CONVENTIONAL OPTION put or call contract arranged off the trading floor of a listed exchange and not traded regularly. It was commonplace when options were banned on certain exchanges, but is now rare.

CONVERGENCE movement of the price of a futures contract toward the price of the underlying CASH COMMODITY. At the start of the contract price is higher because of the time value. But as the contract nears expiration the futures price and the cash price converge.

CONVERSION
1. exchange of a convertible security such as a bond into a fixed number of shares of the issuing corporation's common stock.
2. transfer of mutual-fund shares without charge from one fund to another fund in a single family; also known as fund switching.
3. in insurance, switch from short-term to permanent life insurance.

CONVERSION FEATURE right to convert a particular holding to another form of holding, such as the SWITCHING within a mutual fund family, the right to convert certain preferred stock or bonds to common stock, or the right to switch from one type of insurance policy to another. *See also* CONVERTIBLES.

CONVERSION PARITY common-stock price at which a convertible security can become exchangeable for common shares of equal value.

CONVERSION PREMIUM amount by which the price of a convertible tops the market price of the underlying stock. If a stock is trading at $50 and the bond convertible at $45 is trading at $50, the premium is $5. If the premium is high the bond trades like any fixed income bond. If the premium is low the bond trades like a stock.

CONVERSION PRICE the dollar value at which convertible bonds, debentures, or preferred stock can be converted into common stock, as announced when the convertible is issued.

CONVERSION RATIO relationship that determines how many shares of common stock will be received in exchange for each convertible bond or preferred share when the conversion takes place. It is determined at the time of issue and is expressed either as a ratio or as a conversion price from which the ratio can be figured by dividing the par value of the convertible by the conversion price. The indentures of most convertible securities contain an antidilution clause whereby the conversion ratio may be raised (or the conversion price lowered) by the percentage amount of any stock dividend or split, to protect the convertible holder against dilution.

CONVERSION VALUE
In general: value created by changing from one form to another. For example, converting rental property to condominiums adds to the value of the property.
Convertibles: the price at which the exchange can be made for common stock.

CONVERTIBLE ADJUSTABLE PREFERRED STOCK *see* CAPS.

CONVERTIBLES corporate securities (usually preferred shares or bonds) that are exchangeable for a set number of another form (usually common shares) at a prestated price. Convertibles are appropriate for investors who want higher income than is available from common stock, together with greater appreciation potential than regular bonds offer. From the issuer's standpoint, the convertible feature is usually designed as a sweetener, to enhance the marketability of the stock or preferred.

CONVEXITY mathematical concept that measures sensitivity of the market price of an interest-bearing bond to changes in interest rate levels. *See also* DURATION.

COOK THE BOOKS to falsify the financial statements of a company intentionally. A firm in financial trouble may want to cook the books to prevent investors from pushing down the company's stock price. Companies may also falsify their records to lower their tax liabilities. Whatever the reason, the practice is illegal under SEC, IRS, and stock exchange rules as well as the ethical code of the accounting profession.

COOLING-OFF PERIOD

1. interval (usually 20 days) between the filing of a preliminary prospectus with the Securities and Exchange Commission and the offer of the securities to the public. *See also* REGISTRATION.
2. period during which a union is prohibited from striking, or an employer from locking out employees. The period, typically 30 to 90 days, may be required by law or provided for in a labor agreement.

COOPERATIVE organization owned by its members.

In real estate, a property whose residents own shares in a cooperative giving them exclusive use of their apartments. Decisions about common areas—hallways, elevators, grounds—are made by a vote of members' shares. Members also approve sales of apartments.

Agriculture cooperatives help farmers sell their products more efficiently. Food cooperatives buy food for their members at wholesale prices, but usually require members to help run the organization.

COPENHAGEN STOCK EXCHANGE only securities exchange in Denmark. Stocks, bonds futures and options are traded on ELECTRA, the electronic trading system to which all Danish stock brokerage houses are connected. ELECTRA combines trading, reporting, and information systems. Trading companies using the telephone market are legally obliged to report transactions in all listed securities within 90 seconds, ensuring all market participants the same transparent, real-time market. Transactions in Danish shares are settled three days after trading, and payment is due upon delivery of share certificates. FUTOP, the Danish derivatives market, trades futures and options on the KFX Stock Index, Danish government bonds and equities. FUTOP merged with the exchange in 1997.

CORE CAPITAL thrift institution's bedrock capital, which must be at least 2% of assets to meet proposed rules of the Federal Home Loan Bank. It comprises capital stock and surplus accounts, including perpetual preferred stock, plus minority interests in consolidated subsidiaries.

CORNERING THE MARKET purchasing a security or commodity in such volume that control over its price is achieved. A cornered market in a security would be unhappy news for a short seller, who would have to pay an inflated price to cover. Cornering has been illegal for some years.

CORPORATE BOND debt instrument issued by a private corporation, as distinct from one issued by a government agency or a municipality. Corporates typically have four distinguishing features: (1) they are taxable; (2) they have a par value of $1000; (3) they have a term maturity—which means they come due all at once—and are paid for out of a sinking fund accumulated for that purpose; (4) they are traded on major exchanges, with prices published in newspapers. *See also* BOND; MUNICIPAL BOND.

CORPORATE CHARTER *see* ARTICLES OF INCORPORATION.

CORPORATE EQUIVALENT YIELD comparison that dealers in government bonds include in their offering sheets to show the after-tax yield of government bonds selling at a discount and corporate bonds selling at par.

CORPORATE FINANCING COMMITTEE NATIONAL ASSOCIATION OF SECURITIES DEALERS standing committee that reviews documentation submitted by underwriters in compliance with Securities and Exchange Commission requirements to ensure that proposed markups are fair and in the public interest.

CORPORATE INCOME FUND (CIF) UNIT INVESTMENT TRUST with a fixed portfolio made up of high-grade securities and instruments, similar to a MONEY MARKET FUND. Most CIFs pay out investment income monthly.

CORPORATE INSIDER *see* INSIDER.

CORPORATION legal entity, chartered by a U.S. state or by the federal government, and separate and distinct from the persons who own it, giving rise to a
jurist's remark that it has "neither a soul to damn nor a body to kick."
Nonetheless, it is regarded by the courts as an artificial person; it may own property, incur debts, sue, or be sued. It has three chief distinguishing features:
1. limited liability; owners can lose only what they invest.
2. easy transfer of ownership through the sale of shares of stock.
3. continuity of existence.
    Other factors helping to explain the popularity of the corporate form of
organization are its ability to obtain capital through expanded ownership, and
the shareholders' ability to profit from the growth of the business.

CORPUS Latin for *body*.
1. in trust banking, the property in a trust—real estate, securities and other personal property, cash in bank accounts, and any other items included by the
donor.
2. body of an investment or note, representing the principal or capital as distinct
from the interest or income.

CORRECTION reverse movement, usually downward and exceeding 10%, in the
price of an individual stock, bond, commodity, or index. If prices have been rising
on the market as a whole, then fall dramatically, this is known as a *correction
within an upward trend*. Technical analysts note that markets do not move straight
up or down and that corrections are to be expected during any long-term move.

CORRECTION

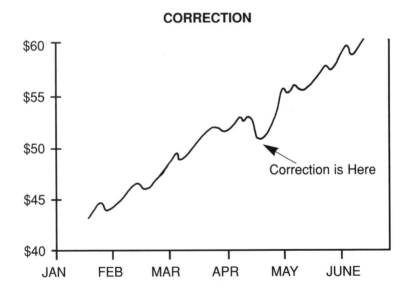

CORRELATION COEFFICIENT statistical measure of the degree to which the
movements of two variables are related.

CORRESPONDENT financial organization that regularly performs services for
another in a market inaccessible to the other. In banking there is usually a depository relationship that compensates for expenses and facilitates transactions.

COST ACCOUNTING branch of accounting concerned with providing the information that enables the management of a firm to evaluate production costs.

COST BASIS original price of an asset, used in determining capital gains. It usually is the purchase price, but in the case of an inheritance it is the appraised value of the asset at the time of the donor's death.

COST-BENEFIT ANALYSIS method of measuring the benefits expected from a decision, calculating the cost of the decision, then determining whether the benefits outweigh the costs. Corporations use this method in deciding whether to buy a piece of equipment, and the government uses it in determining whether federal programs are achieving their goals.

COST OF CAPITAL rate of return that a business could earn if it chose another investment with equivalent risk—in other words, the OPPORTUNITY COST of the funds employed as the result of an investment decision. Cost of capital is also calculated using a weighted average of a firm's costs of debt and classes of equity. This is also called the *composite cost of capital.*

COST OF CARRY out-of-pocket costs incurred while an investor has an investment position, among them interest on long positions in margin accounts, dividends lost on short margin positions, and incidental expenses.

COST OF FUNDS interest cost paid by a financial institution for the use of money. Brokerage firms' cost of funds are comprised of the total interest expense to carry an inventory of stocks and bonds. In the banking and savings and loan industry, the cost of funds is the amount of interest the bank must pay on money market accounts, passbooks, CDs, and other liabilities. Many adjustable rate mortgage loans are tied to a cost-of-funds index, which rises and falls in line with the banks' interest expenses.

COST-OF-FUNDS INDEX (COFI) index used by mortgage lenders on adjustable rate mortgage loans. Borrower's mortgage payments rise or fall based on the widely published COFI, which is based on what financial institutions are paying on money market accounts, passbooks, CDs, and other liabilities. The COFI tends to move far more slowly, both up and down, than other indexes for adjustable rate mortgages, such as one-year Treasuries or the prime rate.

COST OF GOODS SOLD figure representing the cost of buying raw materials and producing finished goods. Depreciation is considered a part of this cost but is usually listed separately. Included in the direct costs are clear-cut factors such as direct factory labor as well as others that are less clear-cut, such as overhead. *Cost of sales* may be used as a synonym or may mean selling expenses. *See also* DIRECT OVERHEAD; FIRST IN, FIRST OUT; LAST IN, FIRST OUT.

COST-OF-LIVING ADJUSTMENT (COLA) adjustment of wages designed to offset changes in the cost of living, usually as measured by the CONSUMER PRICE INDEX. COLAs are key bargaining issues in labor contracts and are politically sensitive elements of Social Security payments and federal pensions because they affect millions of people.

COST-OF-LIVING INDEX *see* CONSUMER PRICE INDEX.

COST OF SALES *see* COST OF GOODS SOLD.

COST-PLUS CONTRACT contract basing the selling price of a product on the total cost incurred in making it plus a stated percentage or a fixed fee—called a *cost-plus-fixed-fee contract.* Cost-plus contracts are common when there is no historical basis for estimating costs and the producer would run a risk of loss—

defense contracts involving sophisticated technology, for example. The alternative is a FIXED PRICE contract.

COST-PUSH INFLATION inflation caused by rising prices, which follow on the heels of rising costs. This is the sequence: When the demand for raw materials exceeds the supply, prices go up. As manufacturers pay more for these raw materials they raise the prices they charge merchants for the finished products, and the merchants in turn raise the prices they charge consumers. *See also* DEMAND-PULL INFLATION; INFLATION.

COST RECORDS
1. investor records of the prices at which securities were purchased, which provide the basis for computing capital gains.
2. in finance, anything that can substantiate the costs incurred in producing goods, providing services, or supporting an activity designed to be productive. Ledgers, schedules, vouchers, and invoices are cost records.

COUNCIL OF ECONOMIC ADVISERS group of economists appointed by the President of the United States to provide counsel on economic policy. The council helps to prepare the President's budget message to Congress, and its chairman frequently speaks for the administration's economic policy.

COUNTERCYCLICAL STOCKS stocks that tend to rise in value when the economy is turning down or is in recession. Traditionally, companies in industries with stable demand, such as drugs and food, are considered countercyclical. Some firms actually do better when the economy or stock market is in turmoil. For example, firms offering money market mutual funds may enjoy an inflow of cash when stock prices fall. Temporary-help firms may benefit if companies are cutting costs by laying off full-time employees and replacing them with temps. Companies that can perform various functions for other companies more efficiently and at lower cost (called *outsourcing firms*) will tend to benefit during economic downturns. *See also* CYCLICAL STOCKS.

COUPON interest rate on a debt security the issuer promises to pay to the holder until maturity, expressed as an annual percentage of face value. For example, a bond with a 10% coupon will pay $10 per $100 of the face amount per year, usually in installments paid every six months. The term derives from the small detachable segment of a bond certificate which, when presented to the bond's issuer, entitles the holder to the interest due on that date. As the REGISTERED BOND becomes more widespread, coupons are gradually disappearing.

COUPON BOND bond issued with detachable coupons that must be presented to a paying agent or the issuer for semiannual interest payment. These are bearer bonds, so whoever presents the coupon is entitled to the interest. Once universal, the coupon bond has been gradually giving way to the REGISTERED BOND, some of which pay interest through electronic transfers. *See also* BOOK-ENTRY SECURITIES; CERTIFICATELESS MUNICIPALS; COUPON.

COUPON COLLECTION *see* COLLECTION.

COUPON-EQUIVALENT RATE same as EQUIVALENT BOND YIELD.

COUPON PASS canvassing by the DESK of the Federal Reserve's Open-Market Committee of PRIMARY DEALERS to determine the inventory and maturities of their Treasury securities. Desk then decides whether to buy or sell specific issues (coupons) to add or withdraw reserves.

COUPON YIELD (OR RATE) *see* COUPON.

COVARIANCE statistical term for the correlation between two variables multiplied by the standard deviation for each of the variables.

COVENANT promise in a trust indenture or other formal debt agreement that certain acts will be performed and others refrained from. Designed to protect the lender's interest, covenants cover such matters as working capital, debt-equity ratios, and dividend payments. Also called *restrictive covenant* or *protective covenant.*

COVER
1. to buy back contracts previously sold; said of an investor who has sold stock or commodities short.
2. in corporate finance, to meet fixed annual charges on bonds, leases, and other obligations, out of earnings.
3. amount of net-asset value underlying a bond or equity security. Coverage is an important aspect of a bond's safety rating.

COVERAGE *see* FIXED-CHARGE COVERAGE.

COVERED OPTION option contract backed by the shares underlying the option. For instance, someone who owns 300 shares of XYZ and sells three XYZ call options is in a covered option position. If the XYZ stock price goes up and the option is exercised, the investor has the stock to deliver to the buyer. Selling a call brings a premium from the buyer. *See also* NAKED OPTION.

COVERED WRITER seller of covered options—in other words, an owner of stock who sells options against it to collect premium income. For example, when writing a CALL OPTION, if a stock price stays stable or drops, the seller will be able to hold onto the stock. If the price rises sharply enough, it will have to be given up to the option buyer.

COVERING SHORT *see* COVER.

CPI *see* CONSUMER PRICE INDEX (CPI).

CRAM-DOWN DEAL merger or leveraged buyout slang for situation in which stockholders are forced, for lack of attractive alternatives, to accept undesirable terms, such as JUNK BONDS instead of cash or equity.

CRASH precipitate drop in stock prices and economic activity, as in the crash of 1929 or BLACK MONDAY in 1987. Crashes are usually brought on by a loss in investor confidence following periods of highly inflated stock prices.

CREDIT
In general: loans, bonds, charge-account obligations, and open-account balances with commercial firms. Also, available but unused bank letters of credit and other standby commitments as well as a variety of consumer credit facilities.
    On another level, discipline in which lending officers and industrial credit people are professionals. At its loftiest it is defined in Dun & Bradstreet's motto: "Credit—Man's Confidence in Man."
Accounting: entry—or the act of making an entry—that increases liabilities, owners' equity, revenue, and gains, and decreases assets and expenses. *See also* CREDIT BALANCE.
Customer's statement of account: adjustment in the customer's favor, or increase in equity.

CREDIT ANALYST person who (1) analyzes the record and financial affairs of an individual or a corporation to ascertain creditworthiness or (2) determines the credit ratings of corporate and municipal bonds by studying the financial condition and trends of the issuers.

CREDIT BALANCE

In general: account balance in the customer's favor. See *also* CREDIT.

Securities: in cash accounts with brokers, money deposited and remaining after purchases have been paid for, plus the uninvested proceeds from securities sold. In margin accounts, (1) proceeds from short sales, held in escrow for the securities borrowed for these sales; (2) free credit balances, or net balances, which can be withdrawn at will. SPECIAL MISCELLANEOUS ACCOUNT balances are not counted as free credit balances.

CREDIT BUREAU agency that gathers information about the credit history of consumers and relays it to credit grantors for a fee. Credit bureaus maintain files on millions of consumers detailing which lines of credit they have applied for and received, and whether they pay their bills in a timely fashion. Bureaus receive this information from credit grantors such as credit card issuers, retail stores, gasoline companies, and others. Credit grantors look at this information, which is constantly being updated, in making their decision as to whether or not to grant credit to a particular consumer, and if so, how much credit is appropriate. Consumers have rights under the FAIR CREDIT REPORTING ACT to see a copy of their credit report and to dispute any item they think is inaccurate. Credit data are maintained by 500 credit bureaus which operate off of three automated systems: Equifax, based in Georgia, Experian, based in California, and Trans Union, based in Illinois.

CREDIT CARD plastic card issued by a bank, savings and loan, retail store, oil company, or other credit grantor giving consumers the right to charge purchases and pay for them later. Most credit cards offer a grace period of about 25 days, during which interest charges do not accrue. After that, consumers pay nondeductible CONSUMER INTEREST on the remaining balance until it is paid off. Some credit cards start charging interest from the day the purchase is registered. Most credit cards also permit consumers to obtain cash on their card in the form of a CASH ADVANCE. *See also* CONSUMER CREDIT PROTECTION ACT OF 1968.

CREDIT ENHANCEMENT techniques used by debt issuers to raise the credit rating of their offering, and thereby lower their interest costs. A municipality may have their bond insured by one of the large insurance companies such as Municipal Bond Investor's Assurance (MBIA) or American Municipal Bond Assurance Corporation (AMBAC), thereby raising the bond's credit rating to AAA. A corporate bond issuer may arrange for a bank letter of credit to back its issue, raising its rating to AAA. While investors in such credit-enhanced issuers feel safer because an insurance company or bank stands ready to step in if there is a default by the underlying issuer, the yield received by the investor is lower than if the bond were uninsured.

CREDIT INSURANCE protection against *abnormal* losses from unpaid accounts receivable, often a requirement of banks lending against accounts receivable.

In consumer credit, life or accident coverage protecting the creditor against loss in the event of death or disability, usually stated as a percentage of the loan balance.

CREDIT LIMIT credit card term, meaning the maximum balance allowed for a particular customer.

CREDITOR party that extends credit, such as a trade supplier, a bank lender, or a bondholder.

CREDITOR'S COMMITTEE group representing firms that have claims on a company in financial difficulty or bankruptcy; sometimes used as an alternative to legal bankruptcy, especially by smaller firms.

CREDIT RATING formal evaluation of an individual's or company's credit history and capability of repaying obligations. Any number of firms investigate, analyze, and maintain records on the credit responsibility of individuals and businesses—Experian (individuals) and Dun & Bradstreet (commercial firms), for example. The bond ratings assigned by Standard & Poor's and Moody's are also a form of credit rating. Most large companies and lending institutions assign credit ratings to existing and potential customers.

CREDIT RISK financial and moral risk that an obligation will not be paid and a loss will result.

CREDIT SCORING objective methodology used by credit grantors to determine how much, if any, credit to grant to an applicant. Credit scoring is devised by three different methods: by a third-party firm, by the credit grantor, or by the credit bureau in cooperation with the credit grantor. Some of the most common factors in scoring are income, assets, length of employment, length of living in one place, and past record of using credit. Any negative events in the past, such as bankruptcies or tax delinquencies, will sharply reduce an applicant's credit score.

CREDIT SPREAD difference in the value of two options, when the value of the one sold exceeds the value of the one bought. The opposite of a DEBIT SPREAD.

CREDIT UNION not-for-profit financial institution typically formed by employees of a company, a labor union, or a religious group and operated as a cooperative. Credit unions may offer a full range of financial services and pay higher rates on deposits and charge lower rates on loans than commercial banks. Federally chartered credit unions are regulated and insured by the National Credit Union Administration.

CREDIT WATCH used by bond RATING agencies to indicate that a company's credit is under review and its rating subject to change. The implication is that if the rating is changed, it will be lowered, usually because of some event that affects the income statement or balance sheet adversely.

CREDITWORTHINESS general eligibility of a person or company to borrow money. *See* CREDIT RATING; CREDIT SCORING.

CREEPING TENDER OFFER strategy whereby individuals ACTING IN CONCERT circumvent WILLIAMS ACT provisions by gradually acquiring TARGET COMPANY shares from arbitrageurs and other sellers in the open market. *See also* TENDER OFFER.

CROSS securities transaction in which the same broker acts as agent in both sides of the trade. The practice—called crossing—is legal only if the broker first offers the securities publicly at a price higher than the bid.

CROSSED MARKET situation in which one broker's bid is higher than another broker's lowest offer, or vice versa. National Association of Securities Dealers (NASD) rules prohibit brokers from crossing the market deliberately.

CROSSED TRADE manipulative practice prohibited on major exchanges whereby buy and sell orders are offset without recording the trade on the exchange, thus perhaps depriving the investor of the chance to trade at a more favorable price. Also called *crossed sale.*

CROWD group of exchange members with a defined area of function tending to congregate around a trading post pending execution of orders. These are specialists, floor traders, odd-lot dealers, and other brokers as well as smaller groups with specialized functions—the INACTIVE BOND CROWD, for example.

CROWDING OUT heavy federal borrowing at a time when businesses and consumers also want to borrow money. Because the government can pay any interest rate it has to and individuals and businesses can't, the latter are crowded out of credit markets by high interest rates. Crowding out can thus cause economic activity to slow.

CROWN JEWELS the most desirable entities within a diversified corporation as measured by asset value, earning power and business prospects. The crown jewels usually figure prominently in takeover attempts; they typically are the main objective of the acquirer and may be sold by a takeover target to make the rest of the company less attractive.

CROWN LOAN demand loan by a high-income individual to a low-income relative, usually a child or elderly parent. This device was named for Chicago industrialist Harry Crown, who first used it. The money would be invested and the income would be taxable at the borrower's lower rates. For years, the crown loan provided a substantial tax benefit for all parties involved, since such loans could be made interest-free. In 1984 the U.S. Supreme Court ruled that such loans had to be made at the market rate of interest or be subject to gift taxes.

CUM DIVIDEND with dividend; said of a stock whose buyer is eligible to receive a declared dividend. Stocks are usually cum dividend for trades made on or before the fifth day preceding the RECORD DATE, when the register of eligible holders is closed for that dividend period. Trades after the fifth day go EX-DIVIDEND.

CUM RIGHTS with rights; said of stocks that entitle the purchaser to buy a specified amount of stock that is yet to be issued. The cut-off date when the stocks go from cum rights to EX-RIGHTS (without rights) is stipulated in the prospectus accompanying the rights distribution.

CUMULATIVE PREFERRED preferred stock whose dividends if omitted because of insufficient earnings or any other reason accumulate until paid out. They have precedence over common dividends, which cannot be paid as long as a cumulative preferred obligation exists. Most preferred stock issued today is cumulative.

CUMULATIVE VOTING voting method that improves minority shareholders' chances of naming representatives on the board of directors. In regular or statutory voting, stockholders must apportion their votes equally among candidates for director. Cumulative voting allows shareholders to cast all their votes for one candidate. Assuming one vote per share, 100 shares owned, and six directors to be elected, the regular method lets the shareholder cast 100 votes for each of six candidates for director, a total of 600 votes. The cumulative method lets the same 600 votes be cast for one candidate or split as the shareholder wishes. Cumulative voting is a popular cause among advocates of corporate democracy, but it remains the exception rather than the rule.

CURB *see* AMERICAN STOCK EXCHANGE.

CURRENCY FUTURES contracts in the futures markets that are for delivery in a major currency such as U.S. dollars, British pounds, French francs, German marks, Swiss francs, or Japanese yen. Corporations that sell products around the world can hedge their currency risk with these futures.

CURRENCY IN CIRCULATION paper money and coins circulating in the economy, counted as part of the total money in circulation, which includes DEMAND DEPOSITS in banks.

CURRENT ACCOUNT (1) an active TRADE CREDIT account; (2) an account with an extender of credit that is up to date; (3) *See* BALANCE OF PAYMENTS.

CURRENT ASSETS cash, accounts receivable, inventory, and other assets that are likely to be converted into cash, sold, exchanged, or expensed in the normal course of business, usually within a year.

CURRENT COUPON BOND corporate, federal, or municipal bond with a coupon within half a percentage point of current market rates. These bonds are less volatile than similarly rated bonds with lower coupons because the interest they pay is competitive with current market instruments.

CURRENT INCOME money that is received on an ongoing basis from investments in the form of dividends, interest, rents, or other income sources.

CURRENT LIABILITY debt or other obligation coming due within a year.

CURRENT MARKET VALUE present worth of a client's portfolio at today's market price, as listed in a brokerage statement every month— or more often if stocks are bought on margin or sold short. For listed stocks and bonds the current market value is determined by closing prices; for over-the-counter securities the bid price is used.

CURRENT MATURITY interval between the present time and the maturity date of a bond issue, as distinguished from original maturity, which is the time difference between the issue date and the maturity date. For example, in 2002 a bond issued in 2000 to mature in 2020 would have an original maturity of 20 years and a current maturity of 18 years.

CURRENT PRODUCTION RATE top interest rate allowed on current GOVERNMENT NATIONAL MORTGAGE ASSOCIATION mortgage-backed securities, usually half a percentage point below the current mortgage rate to defray administrative costs of the mortgage servicing company. For instance, when homeowners are paying 6½% on mortgages, an investor in a GNMA pool including those mortgages will get a current production rate of 6%.

CURRENT RATIO current assets divided by current liabilities. The ratio shows a company's ability to pay its current obligations from current assets. For the most part, a company that has a small inventory and readily collectible accounts receivable can operate safely with a lower current ratio than a company whose cash flow is less dependable. *See also* QUICK RATIO.

CURRENT YIELD annual interest on a bond divided by the market price. It is the actual income rate of return as opposed to the coupon rate (the two would be equal if the bond were bought at par) or the yield to maturity. For example, a 10% (coupon rate) bond with a face (or par) value of $1000 is bought at a market price of $800. The annual income from the bond is $100. But since only $800 was paid for the bond, the current yield is $100 divided by $800, or 12½%.

CUSHION
1. interval between the time a bond is issued and the time it can be called. Also termed CALL PROTECTION.
2. margin of safety for a corporation's financial ratios. For instance, if its DEBT-TO-EQUITY RATIO has a cushion of up to 40% debt, anything over that level might be cause for concern.
3. *see* LAST IN, FIRST OUT.

CUSHION BOND callable bond with a coupon above current market interest rates that is selling for a premium. Cushion bonds lose less of their value as rates rise and gain less in value as rates fall, making them suitable for conservative investors interested in high income.

CUSHION THEORY theory that a stock's price must rise if many investors are taking short positions in it, because those positions must be covered by purchases of the stock. Technical analysts consider it particularly bullish if the short positions in a stock are twice as high as the number of shares traded daily. This is because price rises force short sellers to cover their positions, making the stock rise even more.

CUSIP NUMBER number identifying all stocks and registered bonds, using the COMMITTEE ON UNIFORM SECURITIES IDENTIFICATION PROCEDURES (CUSIP). Brokers will use a security's CUSIP number to look it up on a computer terminal to get further information. The CUSIP number will also be listed on any trading confirmation tickets. The CUSIP system makes it easier to settle and clear trades. Foreign securities use a similar identification system called the CUSIP International Numbering System (CINS).

CUSTODIAL ACCOUNT account that is created for a minor, usually at a bank, brokerage firm, or mutual fund. Minors cannot make securities transactions without the approval of the custodian, who manages cash and other property gifted to minors under the UNIFORM GIFTS TO MINORS ACT or the Uniform Transfers to Minors Act. Any earnings or interest from the account up to $700 are tax-free if the child is under age 14. Earnings from $700 to $1400 are taxed at the child's tax rate. Any earnings over $1400 are taxed at the parents' rate. Once the child turns 14, the earnings are taxed at the child's tax rate. When the child reaches the age of majority, usually 18, they have full discretion over the account, unless the account is set up in a trust controlled by the parent. *See also* CLIFFORD TRUST; CROWN LOAN; UNIFORM GIFTS TO MINORS ACT.

CUSTODIAN bank or other financial institution that keeps custody of stock certificates and other assets of a mutual fund, individual, or corporate client. *See also* CUSTODIAL ACCOUNT.

CUSTODY legal responsibility for someone else's assets or for a child. Term implies management as well as safekeeping. The IRS does not require custodial parents or guardians to declare child support as income, nor is child support deductible by the noncustodial parent.

CUSTOMER'S LOAN CONSENT agreement signed by a margin customer permitting a broker to borrow margined securities to the limit of the customer's debit balance for the purpose of covering other customers' short positions and certain failures to complete delivery.

CUSTOMER'S MAN traditionally a synonym for *registered representative, account executive,* or *account representative.* Now used rarely, as more women work in brokerages.

CUSTOMERS' NET DEBIT BALANCE total credit extended by New York Stock Exchange member firms to finance customer purchases of securities.

CUTOFF POINT in capital budgeting, the minimum rate of return acceptable on investments.

CYCLE *see* BUSINESS CYCLE.

CYCLICAL STOCK stock that tends to rise quickly when the economy turns up and to fall quickly when the economy turns down. Examples are housing, automobiles, and paper. Stocks of noncyclical industries—such as foods, insurance, drugs—are not as directly affected by economic changes.

d

DAILY TRADING LIMIT maximum that many commodities and options markets are allowed to rise or fall in one day. When a market reaches its limit early and stays there all day, it is said to be having an up-limit or down-limit day. Exchanges usually impose a daily trading limit on each contract. For example, the Chicago Board of Trade limit is two points ($2000 per contract) up or down on its treasury bond futures options contract.

DAISY CHAIN trading between market manipulators to create the appearance of active volume as a lure for legitimate investors. When these traders drive the price up, the manipulators unload their holdings, leaving the unwary investors without buyers to trade with in turn.

DATA BASE store of information that is sorted, indexed, and summarized and accessible to people with computers. Data bases containing market and stock histories are available from a number of commercial sources.

DATED DATE date from which accrued interest is calculated on new bonds and other debt instruments. The buyer pays the issuer an amount equal to the interest accrued from the dated date to the issue's settlement date. With the first interest payment on the bond, the buyer is reimbursed.

DATE OF ISSUE
Bonds: date on which a bond is issued and effective. Interest accrues to bondholders from this date.
Insurance: date on which a policy is issued. Normally, the policy is also declared effective on that date, though not in every case.
Stocks: date on which a new stock is publicly issued and begins trading.

DATE OF RECORD date on which a shareholder must officially own shares in order to be entitled to a dividend. For example, the board of directors of a corporation might declare a dividend on November 1 payable on December 1 to stockholders of record on November 15. After the date of record the stock is said to be EX-DIVIDEND. Also called *record date.*

DATING in commercial transactions, extension of credit beyond the supplier's customary terms—for example, 90 days instead of 30 days. In industries marked by high seasonality and long lead time, dating, combined with ACCOUNTS RECEIVABLE FINANCING, makes it possible for manufacturers with lean capital to continue producing goods. Also called *seasonal dating, special dating.*

DAWN RAID British term for a practice whereby a RAIDER instructs brokers to buy all the available shares of another company at the opening of the market, thus giving the acquirer a significant holding before the TARGET COMPANY gets wise to the undertaking. In London-based markets, the practice is restricted by the *City Code on Takeovers and Mergers. See also* SATURDAY NIGHT SPECIAL.

DAY LOAN loan from a bank to a broker for the purchase of securities pending delivery through the afternoon clearing. Once delivered the securities are pledged as collateral and the loan becomes a regular broker's call loan. Also called *morning loan.*

DAY OF DEPOSIT TO DAY OF WITHDRAWAL ACCOUNT bank account that pays interest based on the actual number of days that money is on deposit. Also called *actual balance method.*

DAY ORDER order to buy or sell securities that expires unless executed or canceled the day it is placed. All orders are day orders unless other-wise specified.

The main exception is a GOOD-TILL-CANCELED ORDER, though even it can be executed the same day if conditions are right.

DAY TRADE purchase and sale of a position during the same day.

DEAD CAT BOUNCE sharp rise in stock prices after a severe decline. The saying refers to the fact that a dead cat dropped from a high place will bounce. Often, the bounce is the result of short-sellers covering their positions at a profit.

DEALER
1. individual or firm acting as a PRINCIPAL in a securities transaction. Principals trade for their own account and risk. When buying from a broker acting as a dealer, a customer receives securities from the firm's inventory; the confirmation must disclose this. When specialists trade for their own account, as they must as part of their responsibility for maintaining an orderly market, they act as dealers. Since most brokerage firms operate both as brokers and as principals, the term *broker-dealer* is commonly used.
2. one who purchases goods or services for resale to consumers. The element of inventory risk is what distinguishes a dealer from an agent or sales representative.

DEALER MARKET securities market in which transactions are between principals acting as DEALERS for their own accounts rather than between brokers acting as agents for buyers and sellers. Municipal and U.S. government securities are largely traded in dealer markets. *See also* AUCTION MARKET.

DEALER'S SPREAD *see* MARKDOWN; UNDERWRITING SPREAD.

DEAL FLOW rate of new deals being referred to the investment banking division of a brokerage firm. This might refer to proposals for new stock and bond issues, as well as mergers, acquisitions, and takeovers.

DEAL STOCK stock that may be rumored to be a TAKEOVER target or the party to some other major transaction such as a merger or leveraged buyout. The stock may be subject to a rumor of a prospective deal, or a deal may have been announced that attracts additional bidders and the company is said to be *in play*. Arbitrageurs and other speculators will attempt to buy deal stocks before the deal is finalized or profit when the stock price rises. Of course, if there is no deal, these speculators may lose money if the stock falls back to its pre-rumor price.

DEAR MONEY British equivalent of TIGHT MONEY.

DEATH-BACKED BONDS bonds backed by policyholder loans against life insurance policies. The loans will be repaid either by the policyholder while he or she is alive or from the proceeds of the insurance policy if the policyholder dies. Also called *policyholder loan bonds.*

DEATH BENEFIT amount of money to be paid to beneficiaries when a policyholder dies. The death benefit is the face value of the policy less any unpaid policy loans or other insurance company claims against the policy. Beneficiaries are not taxed on the death benefit when they receive it.

DEATH PLAY stock bought on the expectation that a key executive will die and the shares will gain value as a result. For example, there might be reason to believe that upon the imminent death of a CEO, a company will be broken up and that the shares will be worth more at their PRIVATE MARKET VALUE.

DEATH VALLEY CURVE venture capital term that describes a start-up company's rapid use of capital. When a company begins operations, it uses a great deal of its equity capital to set up its offices, hire personnel, and do research and development. It may be several months or even years before the company has products or services to sell, creating a stream of revenues. The Death Valley Curve is the time period before revenues begin, when it is difficult for the company to raise more equity or issue debt to help it through its cash-flow difficulties.

DEBENTURE general debt obligation backed only by the integrity of the borrower and documented by an agreement called an INDENTURE. An *unsecured bond* is a debenture.

DEBENTURE STOCK stock issued under a contract providing for fixed payments at scheduled intervals and more like preferred stock than a DEBENTURE, since their status in liquidation is equity and not debt.

Also, a type of bond issued by Canadian and British corporations, which refer to debt issues as stock.

DEBIT BALANCE
1. account balance representing money owed to the lender or seller.
2. money a margin customer owes a broker for loans to purchase securities.

DEBIT CARD card issued by a bank to allow customers access to their funds electronically. Debit cards could replace checks as a method of payment for goods and services, and are more convenient because they are more widely accepted than checks. Debit cards can also be used to withdraw cash from automatic teller machines. Unlike credit cards, however, consumers do not have the advantage of the FLOAT on their money since funds are withdrawn immediately.

DEBIT SPREAD difference in the value of two options, when the value of the one bought exceeds the value of the one sold. The opposite of a CREDIT SPREAD.

DEBT
1. money, goods, or services that one party is obligated to pay to another in accordance with an expressed or implied agreement. Debt may or may not be secured.
2. general name for bonds, notes, mortgages, and other forms of paper evidencing amounts owed and payable on specified dates or on demand.

DEBT BOMB situation in which a major financial institution defaults on its obligations, causing major disruption to the financial system of the institution's home country. If a major multinational bank were to run into such trouble, it could have a major negative impact on the global financial system.

DEBT CEILING *see* DEBT LIMIT.

DEBT INSTRUMENT written promise to repay a debt; for instance, a BILL, NOTE, BOND, banker's ACCEPTANCE, CERTIFICATE OF DEPOSIT, or COMMERCIAL PAPER.

DEBTOR any individual or company that owes money. If debt is in the form of a loan from a financial institution, you might use *borrower.* If indebtedness is in the form of securities, such as bonds, you would refer to the *issuer. See also* OBLIGOR.

DEBT LIMIT maximum amount of debt that a municipality can incur. If a municipality wants to issue bonds for an amount greater than its debt limit, it usually requires approval from the voters.

DEBT RETIREMENT repayment of debt. The most common method of retiring corporate debt is to set aside money each year in a SINKING FUND.

Most municipal bonds and some corporates are issued in serial form, meaning different portions of an issue—called series—are retired at different times, usually on an annual or semiannual schedule.

Sinking fund bonds and serial bonds are not classes of bonds, just methods of retiring them that are adaptable to debentures, convertibles, and so on. *See also* REFUNDING.

DEBT SECURITY security representing money borrowed that must be repaid and having a fixed amount, a specific maturity or maturities, and usually a specific rate of interest or an original purchase discount. For instance, a BILL, BOND, COMMERCIAL PAPER, or a NOTE.

DEBT SERVICE cash required in a given period, usually one year, for payments of interest and current maturities of principal on outstanding debt. In corporate bond issues, the annual interest plus annual sinking fund payments; in government bonds, the annual payments into the debt service fund. *See also* ABILITY TO PAY.

DEBT SERVICE COVERAGE
Corporate finance: amount, usually expressed as a ratio, of CASH FLOW available to meet annual interest and principal payments on debt, including SINKING FUND payments.
Government finance: export earnings required to cover annual principal and interest payments on a country's external debts.
Personal finance: ratio of monthly installment debt payments, excluding mortgage loans and rent, to monthly take-home pay.
See also FIXED-CHARGE COVERAGE.

DEBT SWAP exchange, between banks, of a loan, usually to a third-world country in local currency. *See also* SWAP.

DEBT-TO-EQUITY RATIO
1. total liabilities divided by total shareholders' equity. This shows to what extent owner's equity can cushion creditors' claims in the event of liquidation.
2. total long-term debt divided by total shareholders' equity. This is a measure of LEVERAGE—the use of borrowed money to enhance the return on owners' equity.
3. long-term debt and preferred stock divided by common stock equity. This relates securities with fixed charges to those without fixed charges.

DECIMAL TRADING quotation of stock prices in decimals. Several stock markets around the world trade stocks in decimals, and it is anticipated that American markets including the New York and American Exchanges and the NASDAQ Stock Market will convert from quoting stocks in fractions of a dollar to the decimal system sometime early in the 21st century. Proponents of decimal trading maintain that it saves investors money by narrowing the spread between BID AND ASKED prices, and by making stock prices easier to understand. An interim step towards decimal trading was the reduction in the minimum increment in stock prices from one-eighth to one-sixteenth by all the stock exchanges in the late 1990s.

DECLARATION DATE date on which a company announces the amount and date of its next dividend payment. There is normally an interim period of a few days between the declaration date and the EX-STOCK DIVIDEND date which allows people to buy shares and still qualify to receive the upcoming dividend.

DECLARE authorize the payment of a dividend on a specified date, an act of the board of directors of a corporation. Once declared, a dividend becomes an obligation of the issuing corporation.

DECREASING TERM LIFE INSURANCE form of life insurance coverage in which premiums remain constant for the life of the policy while the death benefit declines. Term insurance premiums usually increase every year as the policyholder ages, and the policy is renewed. If there is less need for coverage because, for example, children have become self-sufficient, it may be prudent to decrease the amount of outstanding coverage.

DEDUCTIBLE

Insurance: amount of money that the policyholders must pay out of their pockets before reimbursements from the insurance company begin. The deductible is usually set as a fixed dollar amount, though in some cases it can also be a percentage of the premium paid or some other formula. Some group health insurance plans set the deductible at a set percentage of the employee's salary, for example. In general, the higher a deductible a policyholder will accept, the lower insurance premiums will be. The insurance company is willing to lower its premiums because the company is no longer liable for small claims.

Taxes: *see* TAX DEDUCTIBLE.

DEDUCTION

1. expense allowed by the Internal Revenue Service as a subtraction from adjusted gross income in arriving at a person's taxable income. Such deductions include some interest paid, state and local taxes, charitable contributions.
2. adjustment to an invoice allowed by a seller for a discrepancy, shortage, and so on.

DEED written instrument containing some transfer, bargain, or contract relating to property—most commonly, conveying the legal title to real estate from one party to another.

DEEP DISCOUNT BOND bond selling for a discount of more than about 20% from its face value. Unlike a CURRENT COUPON BOND, which has a higher interest rate, a deep discount bond will appreciate faster as interest rates fall and drop faster as rates rise. Unlike ORIGINAL ISSUE DISCOUNT bonds, deep discounts were issued at a par value of $1000.

DEEP IN/OUT OF THE MONEY CALL OPTION whose exercise price is well below the market price of the underlying stock (deep *in* the money) or well above the market price (deep *out of* the money). The situation would be exactly the opposite for a PUT OPTION. The premium for buying a deep-in-the-money option is high, since the holder has the right to purchase the stock at a striking price considerably below the current price of the stock. The premium for buying a deep-out-of-the-money option is very small, on the other hand, since the option may never be profitable.

DEFAULT failure of a debtor to make timely payments of interest and principal as they come due or to meet some other provision of a bond indenture. In the event of default, bondholders may make claims against the assets of the issuer in order to recoup their principal.

DEFAULT RISK risk that a debtholder will not receive interest and principal when due. One way to gauge default risk is the RATINGS issued by credit rating agencies such as Fitch Investors Service, Moody's, and Standard & Poor's. The higher the rating (AAA or Aaa is highest), the less risk of default. Some issues, such as Treasury bonds backed by the full faith and credit of the U.S. government, are considered free of default risk. Other bonds, such as JUNK BONDS, carry a much higher default risk. One investor defense against default for municipal bonds is MUNICIPAL BOND INSURANCE.

DEFEASANCE

In general: provision found in some debt agreements whereby the contract is nullified if specified acts are performed.

Corporate finance: short for in-substance defeasance, a technique whereby a corporation discharges old, low-rate debt without repaying it prior to maturity. The corporation uses newly purchased securities with a lower face value but paying higher interest or having a higher market value. The objective is a cleaner (more debt free) balance sheet and increased earnings in the amount by which the face amount of the old debt exceeds the cost of the new securities. The use of defeasance in modern corporate finance began in 1982 when Exxon bought and put in an irrevocable trust $312 million of U.S. government securities yielding 14% to provide for the repayment of principal and interest on $515 million of old debt paying 5.8% to 6.7% and maturing in 2009. Exxon removed the defeased debt from its balance sheet and added $132 million—the after-tax difference between $515 million and $312 million—to its earnings that quarter.

In another type of defeasance, a company instructs a broker to buy, for a fee, the outstanding portion of an old bond issue of the company. The broker then exchanges the bond issue for a new issue of the company's stock with an equal market value. The broker subsequently sells the stock at a profit.

DEFENSIVE SECURITIES stocks and bonds that are more stable than average and provide a safe return on an investor's money. When the stock market is weak, defensive securities tend to decline less than the overall market.

DEFERRAL OF TAXES postponement of tax payments from this year to a later year. For instance, an INDIVIDUAL RETIREMENT ACCOUNT (IRA) defers taxes until the money is withdrawn.

DEFERRED ACCOUNT account that postpones taxes until a later date. Some examples: ANNUITY, INDIVIDUAL RETIREMENT ACCOUNT, KEOGH PLAN accounts, PROFIT-SHARING PLAN, SALARY REDUCTION PLAN, SIMPLIFIED EMPLOYEE PENSION (SEP) PLAN.

DEFERRED ANNUITY *see* DEFERRED PAYMENT ANNUITY.

DEFERRED CHARGE expenditure carried forward as an asset until it becomes relevant, such as an advance rent payment or insurance premium. The opposite is *deferred income,* such as advance rent received.

DEFERRED COMPENSATION currently earned compensation that, under the terms of a profit-sharing, pension, or stock option plan, is not actually paid until a later date and is therefore not taxable until that date.

DEFERRED INTEREST BOND bond that pays interest at a later date. A ZERO COUPON BOND, which pays interest and repays principal in one lump sum at maturity, is in this category. In effect, such bonds automatically reinvest the interest at a fixed rate. Prices are more volatile for a deferred interest bond than for a CURRENT COUPON BOND.

DEFERRED PAYMENT ANNUITY ANNUITY whose contract provides that payments to the annuitant be postponed until a number of periods have elapsed—for example, when the annuitant attains a certain age. Also called a *deferred annuity.*

DEFERRED SALES CHARGE *see* BACK-END LOAD.

DEFICIENCY LETTER written notice from the Securities and Exchange Commission to a prospective issuer of securities that the preliminary prospectus needs revision or expansion. Deficiency letters require prompt action; otherwise, the registration period may be prolonged.

DEFICIT
1. excess of liabilities and debts over income and assets. Deficits usually are corrected by borrowing or by selling assets.
2. in finance, an excess of expenditures over budget.

DEFICIT FINANCING borrowing by a government agency to make up for a revenue shortfall. Deficit financing stimulates the economy for a time but eventually can become a drag on the economy by pushing up interest rates. *See also* CROWDING OUT; KEYNESIAN ECONOMICS.

DEFICIT NET WORTH excess of liabilities over assets and capital stock, perhaps as a result of operating losses. Also called *negative net worth.*

DEFICIT SPENDING excess of government expenditures over government revenue, creating a shortfall that must be financed through borrowing. *See also* DEFICIT FINANCING.

DEFINED ASSET FUND a UNIT INVESTMENT TRUST with a fixed portfolio of securities offered by Merrill Lynch, Salomon Smith Barney, Prudential Securities, Morgan Stanley Dean Witter, and Paine Webber. Defined Asset Funds own particular kinds of stocks, such as BLUE CHIPS, REAL ESTATE INVESTMENT TRUSTS, UTILITIES, or the highest yielding stocks in a major index such as the Dow Jones Industrials or the United Kingdom's Footsie Index. There is usually a sales charge to buy shares in one of these trusts. Defined Asset Funds also have a set time period—one to two years, typically—after which they expire. Proceeds can either be taken in cash or rolled over into another Defined Asset Fund. Defined Asset Funds, are also called Equity Investor Funds, and net asset values are available in *Barron's. See also* DOGS OF THE DOW.

DEFINED BENEFIT PENSION PLAN plan that promises to pay a specified amount to each person who retires after a set number of years of service. Such plans pay no taxes on their investments. Employees contribute to them in some cases; in others, all contributions are made by the employer.

DEFINED CONTRIBUTION PENSION PLAN pension plan in which the level of contributions is fixed at a certain level, while benefits vary depending on the return from the investments. In some cases, such as 401(k), 403(b), and 457 plans, employees make voluntary contributions into a tax-deferred account, which may or may not be matched by employers. The level of contribution may be selected by the employee within a range set by the employer, such as between 2% and 10% of annual salary. In other cases, contributions are made by an employer into a profit-sharing account based on each employee's salary level, years of service, age, and other factors. Defined contribution pension plans, unlike DEFINED BENEFIT PENSION PLANS, give the employee options of where to invest the account, usually among stock, bond and money market accounts. Defined contribution plans have become increasingly popular in recent years because they limit a company's pension outlay and shift the liability for investment performance from the company's pension plan to employees.

DEFLATION decline in the prices of goods and services. Deflation is the reverse of INFLATION; it should not be confused with DISINFLATION, which is a slowing down in the rate of price increases. Generally, the economic effects of deflation are the opposite of those produced by inflation, with two notable exceptions: (1) prices that increase with inflation do not necessarily decrease with deflation—union wage rates, for example; (2) while inflation may or may not stimulate output and employment, marked deflation has always affected both negatively.

DEFLATOR statistical factor used to convert current dollar activity into inflation-adjusted activity—in effect, a measure of prices. The change in the gross domestic product (GDP) deflator, for example, is a measure of economy-wide inflation.

DEFLECTION OF TAX LIABILITY legal shift of one person's tax burden to someone else through such methods as the CLIFFORD TRUST, CUSTODIAL ACCOUNTS, and SPOUSAL REMAINDER TRUSTS. Such devices were curtailed but not eliminated by the TAX REFORM ACT OF 1986.

DELAYED DELIVERY delivery of securities later than the scheduled date, which is ordinarily five business days after the trade date. A contract calling for delayed delivery, known as a SELLER'S OPTION, is usually agreed to by both parties to a trade. *See also* DELIVERY DATE.

DELAYED OPENING postponement of the start of trading in a stock until a gross imbalance in buy and sell orders is overcome. Such an imbalance is likely to follow on the heels of a significant event such as a takeover offer.

DELINQUENCY failure to make a payment on an obligation when due. In finance company parlance, the amount of past due balances, determined either on a contractual or recency-of-payment basis.

DELISTING removal of a company's security from an exchange because the firm did not abide by some regulation or the stock does not meet certain financial ratios or sales levels.

DELIVERABLE BILLS financial futures and options trading term meaning Treasury bills that meet all the criteria of the exchange on which they are traded. One such criterion is that the deliverable T-bill is the current bill for the week in which settlement takes place.

DELIVERY *see* DELIVERY DATE; GOOD DELIVERY.

DELIVERY DATE
1. first day of the month in which delivery is to be made under a futures contract. Since sales are on a SELLER'S OPTION basis, delivery can be on any day of the month, as long as proper notice is given.
2. third business day following a REGULAR WAY transaction of stocks or bonds. Seller's option delivery can be anywhere from 3 to 60 days, though there may be a purchase-price adjustment to compensate for DELAYED DELIVERY. The SETTLEMENT DATE was changed from 5 days to 3 days effective June 1, 1995, after approval by the SEC. New deadline is known as *T* (for trade)-*plus-three.*

DELIVERY NOTICE
1. notification from the seller to the buyer of a futures contract indicating the date when the actual commodity is to be delivered.
2. in general business transactions, a formal notice documenting that goods have been delivered or will be delivered on a certain date.

DELIVERY VERSUS PAYMENT securities industry procedure, common with institutional accounts, whereby delivery of securities sold is made to the buying customer's bank in exchange for payment, usually in the form of cash. (Institutions are required by law to require "assets of equal value" in exchange for delivery.) Also called CASH ON DELIVERY, delivery against payment, delivery against cash, or, from the sell side, RECEIVE VERSUS PAYMENT.

DELTA
1. measure of the relationship between an option price and the underlying futures contract or stock price. For a call option, a delta of 0.50 means a

half-point rise in premium for every dollar that the stock goes up. For a put option contract, the premium rises as stock prices fall. As options near expiration, IN-THE-MONEY contracts approach a delta of 1.

2. on the London Stock Exchange, *delta stocks* were the smallest capitalization issues before the system was replaced with today's NORMAL MARKET SIZE.

DELTA HEDGING HEDGING method used in OPTION trading and based on the change in premium (option price) caused by a change in the price of the underlying instrument. The change in the premium for each one-point change in the underlying security is called DELTA and the relationship between the two price movements is called the *hedge ratio*. For example, if a call option has a hedge ratio of 40, the call should rise 40% of the change in the security move if the stock goes down. The delta of a put option, conversely, has a negative value. The value of the delta is usually good the first one-point move in the underlying security over a short time period. When an option has a high hedge ratio, it is usually more profitable to buy the option than to be a WRITER because the greater percentage movement vis-à-vis the underlying security's price and the relatively little time value erosion allow the purchaser greater leverage. The opposite is true for options with a low hedge ratio.

DEMAND DEPOSIT account balance which, without prior notice to the bank, can be drawn on by check, cash withdrawal from an automatic teller machine, or by transfer to other accounts using the telephone or home computers. Demand deposits are the largest component of the U.S. MONEY SUPPLY, and the principal medium through which the Federal Reserve implements monetary policy. *See also* COMPENSATING BALANCE.

DEMAND LOAN loan with no set maturity date that can be called for repayment when the lender chooses. Banks usually bill interest on these loans at fixed intervals.

DEMAND-PULL INFLATION price increases occurring when supply is not adequate to meet demand. *See also* COST-PUSH INFLATION.

DEMONETIZATION withdrawal from circulation of a specified form of currency. For example, the Jamaica Agreement between major INTERNATIONAL MONETARY FUND countries officially demonetized gold starting in 1978, ending its role as the major medium of international settlement.

DENKS acronym for *dual-employed, no kids,* referring to a family unit in which both husband and wife work, and there are no children. Without the expense and responsibility for children, DENKS have a larger disposable income than couples with children, making them a prime target for marketers of luxury goods and services, particularly various types of investments.

DENOMINATION face value of currency units, coins, and securities. *See also* PAR VALUE.

DEPLETION accounting treatment available to companies that extract oil and gas, coal, or other minerals, usually in the form of an allowance that reduces taxable income. Oil and gas limited partnerships pass the allowance on to their limited partners, who can use it to reduce other tax liabilities.

DEPOSIT

1. cash, checks, or drafts placed with a financial institution for credit to a customer's account. Banks broadly differentiate between demand deposits (checking accounts on which the customer may draw at any time) and time deposits, which usually pay interest and have a specified maturity or require 30 days' notice before withdrawal.

2. securities placed with a bank or other institution or with a person for a particular purpose.
3. sums lodged with utilities, landlords, and service companies as security.
4. money put down as evidence of an intention to complete a contract and to protect the other party in the event that the contract is not completed.

DEPOSITARY RECEIPT *see* AMERICAN DEPOSITARY RECEIPT.

DEPOSIT INSURANCE *see* CREDIT UNION; FEDERAL DEPOSIT INSURANCE CORPORATION.

DEPOSITORY INSTITUTIONS DEREGULATION AND MONETARY CONTROL ACT federal legislation of 1980 providing for deregulation of the banking system. The act established the Depository Institutions Deregulation Committee, composed of five voting members, the Secretary of the Treasury and the chair of the Federal Reserve Board, the Federal Home Loan Bank Board, the Federal Deposit Insurance Corporation, and the National Credit Union Administration, and one nonvoting member, the Comptroller of the Currency. The committee was charged with phasing out regulation of interest rates of banks and savings institutions over a six-year period (passbook accounts were deregulated effective April, 1986, under a different federal law). The act authorized interest-bearing NEGOTIABLE ORDER OF WITHDRAWAL (NOW) accounts to be offered anywhere in the country. The act also overruled state usury laws on home mortgages over $25,000 and otherwise modernized mortgages by eliminating dollar limits, permitting second mortgages, and ending territorial restrictions in mortgage lending. Another part of the law permitted stock brokerages to offer checking accounts. *See also* DEREGULATION.

DEPOSITORY TRUST COMPANY (DTC) central securities repository where stock and bond certificates are exchanged. Most of these exchanges now take place electronically, and few paper certificates actually change hands. The DTC is a member of the Federal Reserve System and is owned by most of the brokerage houses on Wall Street and the New York Stock Exchange.

DEPRECIATED COST original cost of a fixed asset less accumulated DEPRECIATION; this is the *net book value* of the asset.

DEPRECIATION
Economics: consumption of capital during production—in other words, wearing out of plant and capital goods, such as machines and equipment.
Finance: amortization of fixed assets, such as plant and equipment, so as to allocate the cost over their depreciable life. Depreciation reduces taxable income but does not reduce cash.
   Among the most commonly used methods are STRAIGHT-LINE DEPRECIATION; ACCELERATED DEPRECIATION; the ACCELERATED COST RECOVERY SYSTEM, and the MODIFIED ACCELERATED COST RECOVERY SYSTEM. Others include the annuity, appraisal, compound interest, production, replacement, retirement, and sinking fund methods.
Foreign exchange: decline in the price of one currency relative to another.

DEPRESSED MARKET market characterized by more supply than demand and therefore weak (depressed) prices. *See also* SYSTEMATIC RISK.

DEPRESSED PRICE price of a product, service, or security that is weak because of a DEPRESSED MARKET. Also refers to the market price of a stock that is low relative to comparable stocks or to its own ASSET VALUE because of perceived or actual risk. Such stocks are identified by high dividend yield, abnormally low PRICE/EARNINGS RATIOS and other such yardsticks. *See also* FUNDAMENTAL ANALYSIS.

DEPRESSION economic condition characterized by falling prices, reduced purchasing power, an excess of supply over demand, rising unemployment, accumulating inventories, deflation, plant contraction, public fear and caution, and a general decrease in business activity. The Great Depression of the 1930s, centered in the United States and Europe, had worldwide repercussions.

DEREGULATION greatly reducing government regulation in order to allow freer markets to create a more efficient marketplace. After the stock-brokerage industry was deregulated in the mid-1970s, commissions were no longer fixed. After the banking industry was deregulated in the early 1980s, banks were given greater freedom in setting interest rates on deposits and loans. Industries such as communications and transportation have also been deregulated, with similar results: increased competition, heightened innovation, and mergers among weaker competitors. Some government oversight usually remains after deregulation.

DERIVATIVE short for *derivative instrument,* a contract whose value is based on the performance of an underlying financial asset, index, or other investment. For example, an ordinary *option* is a derivative because its value changes in relation to the performance of an underlying stock. A more complex example would be an option on a FUTURES CONTRACT, where the option value varies with the value of the futures contract which, in turn, varies with the value of an underlying commodity or security. Derivatives are available based on the performance of assets, interest rates, currency exchange rates, and various domestic and foreign indexes. Derivatives afford leverage and, when used properly by knowledgeable investors, can enhance returns and be useful in HEDGING portfolios. They gained notoriety in the late '80s, however, because of problems involved in PROGRAM TRADING, and in the '90s, when a number of mutual funds, municipalities, corporations, and leading banks suffered large losses because unexpected movements in interest rates adversely affected the value of derivatives. *See also* BEARS; CERTIFICATES OF ACCRUAL ON TREASURY SECURITIES (CATS); COLLATERALIZED BOND OBLIGATION (CBO); COLLATERALIZED MORTGAGE OBLIGATION (CMO); CUBS; DIAMONDS; INDEX OPTIONS; OEX; SPDR; STRIP; SUBSCRIPTION RIGHT; SUBSCRIPTION WARRANT; SWAP; TIGER.

DERIVATIVE INSTRUMENT *see* DERIVATIVE.

DESCENDING TOPS chart pattern wherein each new high price for a security is lower than the preceding high. The trend is considered bearish.

DESIGNATED ORDER TURNAROUND (DOT) electronic system used by the New York Stock Exchange to expedite execution of small MARKET ORDERS by routing them directly from the member firm to the SPECIALIST, thus bypassing the FLOOR BROKER. A related system called *Super DOT* routes LIMIT ORDERS.

DESK trading desk, or Securities Department, at the New York FEDERAL RESERVE BANK, which is the operating arm of the FEDERAL OPEN MARKET COMMITTEE. The Desk executes all transactions undertaken by the FEDERAL RESERVE SYSTEM in the money market or the government securities market, serves as the Treasury Department's eyes and ears in these and related markets, and encompasses a foreign desk which conducts transactions in the FOREIGN EXCHANGE market.

DEUTSCHE BORSE AG operating company for the German securities and derivatives markets. In 1998, it changed its name to Eurex Frankfurt GmbH. It operates the FRANKFURT STOCK EXCHANGE, the country's leading stock exchange, and seven others in Dusseldorf, Munich, Hamburg, Berlin, Stuttgart, Hanover and Bremen. Deutsche Borse also operates DEUTSCHE TERMINBORSE, Germany's only futures exchange, and is responsible for settlement of all securities and futures exchange transactions in Germany. The eight exchanges have different official trading hours. General trading hours are 10:30 A.M. to 1:30 P.M., Monday through Friday. The IBIS system runs from 8:30 A.M. to 5 P.M.

DESCENDING TOPS

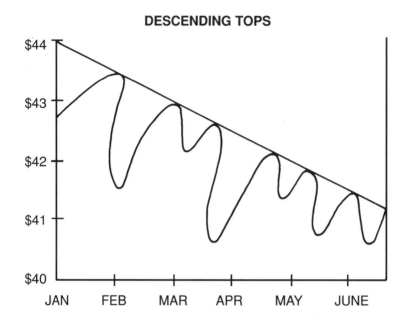

DEUTSCHE TERMINBORSE (DTB) Germany's first fully computerized exchange, and the first German exchange for trading financial futures, opened in January 1990. In January 1994, DTB merged with DEUTSCHE BORSE AG. DTB changed its name to Eurex Deutschland in 1998, when it joined with the SWISS OPTIONS AND FINANCIAL FUTURES EXCHANGE (SOFFEX) to form Eurex. Eurex trades futures and options contracts formerly traded on the two exchanges: futures and options on the DAX Index (the German stock index) and the Swiss Market Index (SMI); futures and future options on the DAX future, BOBL national government bonds (3.3 to 5 years), BUND national government bonds (8.5 to 10 years), Swiss government bonds (Conf), Dow Jones STOXX 50 and Dow Jones Euro STOXX 50; futures on the one-month Euromark, three-month Euromark, Mid-Cap DAX and Jumbo Pfandbrief; stock options on German and Swiss blue chip equities; and U.S. dollar/Deutschemark options.

DEVALUATION lowering of the value of a country's currency relative to gold and/or the currencies of other nations. Devaluation can also result from a rise in value of other currencies relative to the currency of a particular country.

DEVELOPMENTAL DRILLING PROGRAM drilling for oil and gas in an area with proven reserves to a depth known to have been productive in the past. Limited partners in such a program, which is considerably less risky than an EXPLORATORY DRILLING PROGRAM or WILDCAT DRILLING, have a good chance of steady income, but little chance of enormous profits.

DEWKS acronym for *dual-employed, with kids,* referring to a family unit in which both husband and wife work and there are children. Marketers selling products for children, including various investments, target DEWKS.

DIAGONAL SPREAD strategy based on a long and short position in the same class of option (two puts or two calls in the same stock) at different striking prices and different expiration dates. Example: a six-month call sold with a striking price of

40 and a three-month call sold with a striking price of 35. *See also* CALENDAR SPREAD; VERTICAL SPREAD.

DIALING AND SMILING expression for COLD CALLING by securities brokers and other salespeople. Brokers must not only make unsolicited telephone calls to potential customers, but also gain the customer's confidence with their upbeat tone of voice and sense of concern for the customer's financial well-being.

DIALING FOR DOLLARS expression for COLD CALLING in which brokers make unsolicited telephone calls to potential customers, hoping to find people with investable funds. The term has a derogatory implication, and is typically applied to salespeople working in BOILER ROOMS, selling speculative or fraudulent investments such as PENNY STOCKS.

DIAMOND INVESTMENT TRUST unit trust that invests in high-quality diamonds. Begun in the early 1980s by Thomson McKinnon, these trusts let shareholders invest in diamonds without buying and holding a particular stone. Shares in these trusts do not trade actively and are therefore difficult to sell if diamond prices fall, as they did soon after the first trust was set up.

DIAMONDS represent units of beneficial interest in the DIAMONDS Trust, a UNIT INVESTMENT TRUST that holds the 30 component stocks of the Dow Jones Industrial Average. First introduced in January, 1998, DIAMONDS trade under the ticker symbol "DIA" like any other stock on the American Stock Exchange. They are designed to offer investors a low-cost means of tracking the DJIA, the most widely recognized indicator of the American stock market. DIAMONDS pay monthly DIVIDENDS (which can be reinvested into more shares of the trust) that correspond to the dividend yields of the DJIA component stocks and pay capital gains distributions once a year. DIAMONDS are designed to trade at about 1/100 the level of the Dow Jones Industrial Average. So if the DJIA is at 9000, DIAMONDS will trade at about $90 per unit.

For those speculating that stock market prices will fall, it is possible to SELL SHORT using DIAMONDS. Short sellers have an additional advantage: DIAMONDS are not subject to the UPTICK RULE that applies to stocks, meaning they can be sold regardless of which direction the price is moving.

Unlike open-end mutual funds, DIAMONDS trade like stocks, allowing investors to buy or sell at any time during the trading day, whereas index mutual funds are only priced once at the end of each trading day. Like open-end index funds, DIAMONDS charge low management fees because there is little research or trading conducted by the trust's management. There are also no LOADS to buy DIAMONDS, though normal brokerage commissions do apply to trades. Whereas closed-end funds often trade at discounts to their NET ASSET VALUES, investors can create an unlimited number of DIAMONDS trading units, which helps insure they will correlate closely with the performance of the DJIA stocks in the portfolio. *See also* INDEX FUND; SPDR.

DIFF short for *Euro-rate differential,* a futures contract traded on the Chicago Mercantile Exchange that is based on the interest rate spread between the U.S. dollar and the British pound, the German mark, or the Japanese yen.

DIFFERENTIAL small extra charge sometimes called the *odd-lot-differential*—usually $\frac{1}{8}$ of a point—that dealers add to purchases and subtract from sales in quantities less than the standard trading unit or ROUND LOT. Also, the extent to which a dealer widens his round lot quote to compensate for lack of volume.

DIGITS DELETED designation on securities exchange tape meaning that because the tape has been delayed, some digits have been dropped. For example, $26\frac{1}{2}$... $26\frac{5}{8}$... $26\frac{1}{8}$ becomes $6\frac{1}{2}$... $6\frac{5}{8}$... $6\frac{1}{8}$.

DILUTION effect on earnings per share and book value per share if all convertible securities were converted or all warrants or stock options were exercised. *See* FULLY DILUTED EARNINGS PER (COMMON) SHARE.

DINKS acronym for *dual-income, no kids,* referring to a family unit in which there are two incomes and no children. The two incomes may result from both husband and wife working, or one spouse holding down two jobs. Since the couple do not have children, they typically have more disposable income than those with children, and therefore are the prime targets of marketers selling luxury products and services, including various investments. *See also* DENKS; DEWKS.

DIP slight drop in securities prices after a sustained uptrend. Analysts often advise investors to buy on dips, meaning buy when a price is momentarily weak. *See* chart on next page.

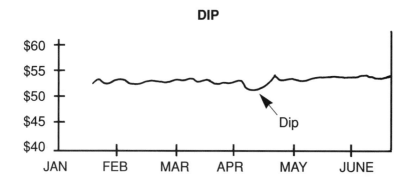

DIRECT INVESTMENT (1) purchase of a controlling interest in a foreign (international) business or subsidiary. (2) in domestic finance, the purchase of a controlling interest or a minority interest of such size and influence that active control is a feasible objective.

DIRECTOR *see* BOARD OF DIRECTORS.

DIRECT OVERHEAD portion of overhead costs—rent, lights, insurance—allocated to manufacturing, by the application of a standard factor termed a *burden rate*. This amount is absorbed as an INVENTORY cost and ultimately reflected as a COST OF GOODS SOLD.

DIRECT PARTICIPATION PROGRAM program letting investors participate directly in the cash flow and tax benefits of the underlying investments. Such programs are usually organized as LIMITED PARTNERSHIPS, although their uses as tax shelters have been severely curtailed by tax legislation affecting PASSIVE investments.

DIRECT PLACEMENT direct sale of securities to one or more professional investors. Such securities may or may not be registered with the SECURITIES AND EXCHANGE COMMISSION. They may be bonds, private issues of stock, limited partnership interests, mortgage-backed securities, venture capital investments, or other sophisticated instruments. These investments typically require large minimum purchases, often in the millions of dollars. Direct placements offer higher potential returns than many publicly offered securities, but also present more risk. Buyers of direct placements are large, sophisticated financial institutions including insurance companies, banks, mutual funds, foundations, and pension funds that are able to evaluate such offerings. Also called *private placement.*

DIRECT PURCHASE purchasing shares in a no-load or low-load OPEN-END MUTUAL FUND directly from the fund company. Investors making direct purchases deal directly with the fund company over the phone, in person at investor centers, or by mail. This contrasts with the method of purchasing shares in a LOAD FUND through a financial intermediary such as a broker or financial planner, who collects a commission for offering advice on which fund is appropriate for the client. Many companies also now allow shareholders to purchase "no-load" stock directly from the company, thereby avoiding brokers and sales commissions. *See also* TREASURY DIRECT.

DIRTY STOCK stock that fails to meet the requirements for GOOD DELIVERY.

DISABILITY INCOME INSURANCE insurance policy that pays benefits to a policyholder when that person becomes incapable of performing one or more occupational duties, either temporarily or on a long-term basis, or totally. The policy is designed to replace a portion of the income lost because of the insured's disability. Payments begin after a specified period, called the *elimination period,* of several weeks or months.

Some policies remain in force until the person is able to return to work, or to return to a similar occupation, or is eligible to receive benefits from another program such as Social Security disability. Disability insurance payments are normally tax-free to beneficiaries as long as they paid the policy premiums. Many employers offer disability income insurance to their employees, though people are able to buy coverage on an individual basis as well.

DISBURSEMENT paying out of money in the discharge of a debt or an expense, as distinguished from a distribution.

DISCHARGE OF BANKRUPTCY order terminating bankruptcy proceedings, ordinarily freeing the debtor of all legal responsibility for specified obligations.

DISCHARGE OF LIEN order removing a lien on property after the originating legal claim has been paid or otherwise satisfied.

DISCLAIMER OF OPINION auditor's statement, sometimes called an *adverse opinion,* that an ACCOUNTANT'S OPINION cannot be provided because of limitations on the examination or because some condition or situation exists, such as pending litigation, that could impair the financial strength or profitability of the client.

DISCLOSURE release by companies of all information, positive or negative, that might bear on an investment decision, as required by the Securities and Exchange Commission and the stock exchanges. *See also* FINANCIAL PUBLIC RELATIONS; INSIDE INFORMATION; INSIDER.

DISCONTINUED OPERATIONS operations of a business that have been sold, abandoned, or otherwise disposed of. Accounting regulations require that continuing operations be reported separately in the income statement from discontinued operations, and that any gain or loss from the disposal of a segment (an entity whose activities represent a separate major line of business or class of customer) be reported along with the operating results of the discontinued segment.

DISCOUNT
1. difference between a bond's current market price and its face or redemption value.
2. manner of selling securities such as treasury bills, which are issued at less than face value and are redeemed at face value.
3. relationship between two currencies. The French franc may sell at a discount to the English pound, for example.

4. to apply all available news about a company in evaluating its current stock price. For instance, taking into account the introduction of an exciting new product.

5. method whereby interest on a bank loan or note is deducted in advance.

6. reduction in the selling price of merchandise or a percentage off the invoice price in exchange for quick payment.

DISCOUNT BOND bond selling below its redemption value. *See also* DEEP DISCOUNT BOND.

DISCOUNT BROKER brokerage house that executes orders to buy and sell securities at commission rates sharply lower than those charged by a FULL SERVICE BROKER.

DISCOUNT DIVIDEND REINVESTMENT PLAN *see* DIVIDEND REINVESTMENT PLAN.

DISCOUNTED CASH FLOW value of future expected cash receipts and expenditures at a common date, which is calculated using NET PRESENT VALUE or INTERNAL RATE OF RETURN and is a factor in analyses of both capital investments and securities investments. The net present value (NPV) method applies a rate of discount (interest rate) based on the marginal cost of capital to future cash flows to bring them back to the present. The internal rate of return (IRR) method finds the average return on investment earned through the life of the investment. It determines the discount rate that equates the present value of future cash flows to the cost of the investment.

DISCOUNTING THE NEWS bidding a firm's stock price up or down in anticipation of good or bad news about the company's prospects.

DISCOUNT POINTS *see* POINT.

DISCOUNT RATE

1. interest rate that the Federal Reserve charges member banks for loans, using government securities or ELIGIBLE PAPER as collateral. This provides a floor on interest rates, since banks set their loan rates a notch above the discount rate.

2. interest rate used in determining the PRESENT VALUE of future CASH FLOWS. *See also* CAPITALIZATION RATE.

DISCOUNT WINDOW place in the Federal Reserve where banks go to borrow money at the DISCOUNT RATE. Borrowing from the Fed is a privilege, not a right, and banks are discouraged from using the privilege except when they are short of reserves.

DISCOUNT YIELD yield on a security sold at a discount—U.S. treasury bills sold at $9750 and maturing at $10,000 in 90 days, for instance. Also called *bank discount basis.* To figure the annual yield, divide the discount ($250) by the face amount ($10,000) and multiply that number by the approximate number of days in the year (360) divided by the number of days to maturity (90). The calculation looks like this:

$$\frac{\$250}{\$10,000} \times \frac{360}{90} = .025 \times 4 = .10 = 10\%.$$

DISCRETIONARY ACCOUNT account empowering a broker or adviser to buy and sell without the client's prior knowledge or consent. Some clients set broad guidelines, such as limiting investments to blue chip stocks.

DISCRETIONARY INCOME amount of a consumer's income spent after essentials like food, housing, and utilities and prior commitments have been covered.

The total amount of discretionary income can be a key economic indicator because spending this money can spur the economy.

DISCRETIONARY ORDER order to buy a particular stock, bond, or commodity that lets the broker decide when to execute the trade and at what price.

DISCRETIONARY TRUST
1. mutual fund or unit trust whose investments are not limited to a certain kind of security. The management decides on the best way to use the assets.
2. personal trust that lets the trustee decide how much income or principal to provide to the beneficiary. This can be used to prevent the beneficiary from dissipating funds.

DISHONOR to refuse to pay, as in the case of a check that is returned by a bank because of insufficient funds.

DISINFLATION slowing down of the rate at which prices increase— usually during a recession, when sales drop and retailers are not always able to pass on higher prices to consumers. Not to be confused with DEFLATION, when prices actually drop.

DISINTERMEDIATION movement of funds from low-yielding accounts at traditional banking institutions to higher-yielding investments in the general market—for example, withdrawal of funds from a passbook savings account paying 5½% to buy a Treasury bill paying 10%. As a counter move, banks may pay higher rates to depositors, then charge higher rates to borrowers, which leads to tight money and reduced economic activity. Since banking DEREGULATION, disintermediation is not the economic problem it once was.

DISINVESTMENT reduction in capital investment either by disposing of capital goods (such as plant and equipment) or by failing to maintain or replace capital assets that are being used up.

DISPOSABLE INCOME personal income remaining after personal taxes and noncommercial government fees have been paid. This money can be spent on essentials or nonessentials or it can be saved. *See also* DISCRETIONARY INCOME.

DISTRESS SALE sale of property under distress conditions. For example, stock, bond, mutual fund or futures positions may have to be sold in a portfolio if there is a MARGIN CALL. Real estate may have to be sold because a bank is in the process of FORECLOSURE on the property. A brokerage firm may be forced to sell securities from its inventory if it has fallen below various capital requirements imposed by stock exchanges and regulators. Because distress sellers are being forced to sell, they usually do not receive as favorable a price as if they were able to wait for ideal selling conditions.

DISTRIBUTING SYNDICATE group of brokerage firms or investment bankers that join forces in order to facilitate the DISTRIBUTION of a large block of securities. A distribution is usually handled over a period of time to avoid upsetting the market price. The term distributing syndicate can refer to a primary distribution or a secondary distribution, but the former is more commonly called simply a syndicate or an underwriting syndicate.

DISTRIBUTION
Corporate finance: allocation of income and expenses to the appropriate subsidiary accounts.
Economics: (1) movement of goods from manufacturers; (2) way in which wealth is shared in any particular economic system.

Estate law: parceling out of assets to the beneficiaries named in a will, as carried out by the executor under the guidance of a court.

Mutual funds and closed-end investment companies: payout of realized capital gains on securities in the portfolio of the fund or closed-end investment company.

Securities: sale of a large block of stock in such manner that the price is not adversely affected. Technical analysts look on a pattern of distribution as a tipoff that the stock will soon fall in price. The opposite of distribution, known as ACCUMULATION, may signal a rise in price.

DISTRIBUTION AREA price range in which a stock trades for a long time. Sellers who want to avoid pushing the price down will be careful not to sell below this range. ACCUMULATION of shares in the same range helps to account for the stock's price stability. Technical analysts consider distribution areas in predicting when stocks may break up or down from that price range. *See also* ACCUMULATION AREA.

DISTRIBUTION PERIOD period of time, usually a few days, between the date a company's board of directors declares a stock dividend, known as the DECLARATION DATE, and the DATE OF RECORD, by which the shareholder must officially own shares to be entitled to the dividend.

DISTRIBUTION PLAN plan adopted by a mutual fund to charge certain distribution costs, such as advertising, promotion and sales incentives, to shareholders. The plan will specify a certain percentage, usually .75% or less, which will be deducted from fund assets annually. *See also* 12b-1 MUTUAL FUND.

DISTRIBUTION STOCK stock part of a block sold over a period of time in order to avoid upsetting the market price. May be part of a primary (underwriting) distribution or a secondary distribution following SHELF REGISTRATION.

DISTRIBUTOR wholesaler of goods to dealers that sell to consumers.

DIVERSIFICATION
1. spreading of risk by putting assets in several categories of investments—stocks, bonds, money market instruments, and precious metals, for instance, or several industries, or a mutual fund, with its broad range of stocks in one portfolio.
2. at the corporate level, entering into different business areas, as a CONGLOMERATE does.

DIVERSIFIED INVESTMENT COMPANY mutual fund or unit trust that invests in a wide range of securities. Under the Investment Company Act of 1940, such a company may not have more than 5 percent of its assets in any one stock, bond, or commodity and may not own more than 10 percent of the voting shares of any one company.

DIVESTITURE disposition of an asset or investment by outright sale, employee purchase, liquidation, and so on.

Also, one corporation's orderly distribution of large blocks of another corporation's stock, which were held as an investment. Du Pont was ordered by the courts to divest itself of General Motors stock, for example.

DIVIDEND distribution of earnings to shareholders, prorated by class of security and paid in the form of money, stock, scrip, or, rarely, company products or property. The amount is decided by the board of directors and is usually paid quarterly. Dividends must be declared as income in the year they are received.

Mutual fund dividends are paid out of income, usually on a quarterly basis from the fund's investments. The tax on such dividends depends on whether the distributions resulted from capital gains, interest income, or dividends received by the fund. *See also* EQUALIZING DIVIDEND; EXTRA DIVIDEND.

DIVIDEND CAPTURE *See* DIVIDEND ROLLOVER PLAN.

DIVIDEND COVER British equivalent of the dividend PAYOUT RATIO.

DIVIDEND DISCOUNT MODEL mathematical model used to determine the price at which a stock should be selling based on the discounted value of projected future dividend payments. It is used to identify undervalued stocks representing capital gains potential.

DIVIDEND EXCLUSION pre-TAX REFORM ACT OF 1986 provision allowing for subtraction from dividends qualifying as taxable income under Internal Revenue Service rules—$100 for individuals and $200 for married couples filing jointly. The 1986 Tax Act eliminated this exclusion effective for the 1987 tax year.

Domestic corporations may exclude from taxable income 70% of dividends received from other domestic corporations. The exclusion was 85% prior to the 1986 Act, which reduced it to 80%.

DIVIDEND IN ARREARS ACCUMULATED DIVIDEND on CUMULATIVE PREFERRED stock, which is payable to the current holder. Preferred stock in a TURNAROUND situation can be an attractive buy when it is selling at a discount and has dividends in arrears.

DIVIDEND PAYOUT RATIO percentage of earnings paid to shareholders in cash. In general, the higher the payout ratio, the more mature the company. Electric and telephone utilities tend to have the highest payout ratios, whereas fast-growing companies usually reinvest all earnings and pay no dividends.

DIVIDEND RECORD publication of Standard & Poor's Corporation that provides information on corporate policies and payment histories.

DIVIDEND REINVESTMENT PLAN automatic reinvestment of shareholder dividends in more shares of the company's stock. Some companies absorb most or all of the applicable brokerage fees, and some also discount the stock price. Dividend reinvestment plans allow shareholders to accumulate capital over the long term using DOLLAR COST AVERAGING. For corporations, dividend reinvestment plans are a means of raising capital funds without the FLOTATION COSTS of a NEW ISSUE.

DIVIDEND REQUIREMENT amount of annual earnings necessary to pay contracted dividends on preferred stock.

DIVIDEND ROLLOVER PLAN method of buying and selling stocks around their EX-DIVIDEND dates so as to collect the dividend and make a small profit on the trade. This entails buying shares about two weeks before a stock goes ex-dividend. After the ex-dividend date the price will drop by the amount of the dividend, then work its way back up to the earlier price. By selling slightly above the purchase price, the investor can cover brokerage costs, collect the dividend, and realize a small capital gain in three or four weeks. Also called *dividend capture. See also* TRADING DIVIDENDS.

DIVIDENDS PAYABLE dollar amount of dividends that are to be paid, as reported in financial statements. These dividends become an obligation once declared by the board of directors and are listed as liabilities in annual and quarterly reports.

DIVIDENDS-RECEIVED DEDUCTION tax deduction allowed to a corporation owning shares in another corporation for the dividends it receives. In most cases, the deduction is 70%, but in some cases it may be as high as 100% depending on the level of ownership the dividend-receiving company has in the dividend-paying entity.

DIVIDEND YIELD annual percentage of return earned by an investor on a common or preferred stock. The yield is determined by dividing the amount of the annual dividends per share by the current market price per share of the stock. For example, a stock paying a $1 dividend per year that sells for $10 a share has a 10% dividend yield. The dividend yields of stocks are listed in the stock tables of most daily newspapers.

DOCUMENTARY DRAFT *see* DRAFT.

DOGS OF THE DOW strategy of buying the 10 high-yielding stocks in the DOW JONES INDUSTRIAL AVERAGE. Over one-year periods, these 10 stocks tend to outperform all 30 Dow stocks because investors are buying them at depressed prices and earning the highest yields, and the stocks tend to bounce back. Investors can execute this strategy by buying all 10 stocks once a year, or by buying DEFINED ASSET FUNDS or other UNIT INVESTMENT TRUSTS specializing in this technique. The strategy of buying the 10 high-yielding stocks in an index has spread far from just the Dow Jones Industrials, as investors now practice it with shares in the United Kingdom, Hong Kong and many other indices. The Dogs of the Dow strategy was popularized by Michael B. O'Higgins and John Downes in their book and newsletter *Beating the Dow*. (Downes is the co-author of this *Dictionary*.)

DOLLAR BEARS traders who think the dollar will fall in value against other foreign currencies. Dollar bears may implement a number of investment strategies to capitalize on a falling dollar, such as buying Japanese yen, Deutsche marks, British pounds or other foreign currencies directly, or buying futures or options contracts on those currencies.

DOLLAR BOND
1. municipal revenue bond quoted and traded on a dollar price basis instead of yield to maturity.
2. bond denominated in U.S. dollars but issued outside the United States, principally in Europe.
3. bond denominated in U.S. dollars and issued in the United States by foreign companies.
   See also EUROBOND; EURODOLLAR BOND.

DOLLAR COST AVERAGING *see* CONSTANT DOLLAR PLAN.

DOLLAR DRAIN amount by which a foreign country's imports from the United States exceed its exports to the United States. As the country spends more dollars to finance the imports than it receives in payment for the exports, its dollar reserves drain away.

DOLLAR PRICE bond price expressed as a percentage of face value (normally $1000) rather than as a yield. Thus a bond quoted at 97½ has a dollar price of $975, which is 97½% of $1000.

DOLLAR SHORTAGE situation in which a country that imports from the United States can no longer pay for its purchases without U.S. gifts or loans to provide the necessary dollars. After World War II a world-wide dollar shortage was alleviated by massive infusions of American money through the European Recovery Program (Marshall Plan) and other grant and loan programs.

DOLLAR-WEIGHTED RETURN portfolio accounting method that measures changes in total dollar value, treating additions and withdrawals of capital as a part of the RETURN along with income and capital gains and losses. For example, a portfolio (or group of portfolios) worth $100 million at the beginning of a reporting period and $120 million at the end would show a return of 20%; this would be true even if the investments lost money, provided enough new money was infused. While dollar weighting enables investors to compare absolute dollars with financial goals, manager-to-manager comparisons are not possible unless performance is isolated from external cash flows; this is accomplished with the TIME-WEIGHTED RETURN method.

DOMESTIC ACCEPTANCE *see* ACCEPTANCE.

DOMESTIC CORPORATION corporation doing business in the U.S. state in which it was incorporated. In all other U.S. states its legal status is that of a FOREIGN CORPORATION.

DOMICILE place where a person has established permanent residence. It is important to establish a domicile for the purpose of filing state and local income taxes, and for filing estate taxes upon death. The domicile is created based on obtaining a driver's license, registering to vote, and having a permanent home to which one returns. Usually, one must be a resident in a state for at least six months of the year to establish a domicile.

DONATED STOCK fully paid capital stock of a corporation contributed without CONSIDERATION to the same issuing corporation. The gift is credited to the DONATED SURPLUS account at PAR VALUE.

DONATED SURPLUS shareholder's equity account that is credited when contributions of cash, property, or the firm's own stock are freely given to the company. Also termed *donated capital*. Not to be confused with contributed surplus or contributed capital, which is the balances in CAPITAL STOCK accounts plus capital contributed in excess of par or STATED VALUE accounts.

DO NOT INCREASE abbreviated *DNI*. Instruction on good-till-canceled buy limit and sell stop orders that prevent the quantity from changing in the event of a stock SPLIT or stock dividend.

DO NOT REDUCE (DNR) instruction on a LIMIT ORDER to buy, or on a STOP ORDER to sell, or on a STOP-LIMIT ORDER to sell, not to reduce the order when the stock goes EX-DIVIDEND and its price is reduced by the amount of the dividend as usually happens. DNRs do not apply to rights or stock dividends.

DONOR individual who donates property to another through a TRUST. Also called a *grantor*. Donors also make tax-deductible charitable contributions of securities or physical property to nonprofit institutions such as schools, philanthropic groups, and religious organizations.

DON'T FIGHT THE TAPE don't trade against the market trend. If stocks are falling, as reported on the BROAD TAPE, some analysts say it would be foolish to buy aggressively. Similarly, it would be fighting the tape to sell short during a market rally.

DON'T KNOW Wall Street slang for a *questioned trade*. Brokers exchange comparison sheets to verify the details of transactions between them. Any discrepancy that turns up is called a don't know or a *QT*.

DOT (and SUPER-DOT) SYSTEM acronym for *Designated Order Turnaround*, New York Stock Exchange AUTOMATED ORDER ENTRY SYSTEMS for expediting small and moderate-sized orders. DOT handles market orders and Super DOT limited price orders. The systems bypass floor brokers and rout orders directly to the SPECIALIST, who executes through a CONTRA BROKER or against the SPECIALIST'S BOOK.

DOUBLE AUCTION SYSTEM *see* AUCTION MARKET.

DOUBLE-BARRELED municipal revenue bond whose principal and interest are guaranteed by a larger municipal entity. For example, a bridge authority might issue revenue bonds payable out of revenue from bridge tolls. If the city or state were to guarantee the bonds, they would be double-barreled, and the investor would be protected against default in the event that bridge usage is disappointing and revenue proves inadequate.

DOUBLE BOTTOM technical chart pattern showing a drop in price, then a rebound, then another drop to the same level. The pattern is usually interpreted to mean the security has much support at that price and should not drop further. However, if the price does fall through that level, it is considered likely to reach a new low. *See also* DOUBLE TOP.

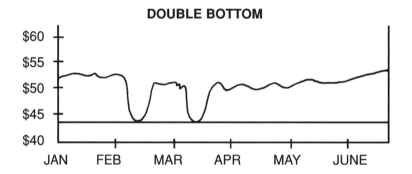

DOUBLE BOTTOM

DOUBLE-DECLINING-BALANCE DEPRECIATION METHOD (DDB) method of accelerated depreciation, approved by the Internal Revenue Service, permitting twice the rate of annual depreciation as the straight-line method. It is also called the 200 percent declining-balance method. The two methods are compared below, assuming an asset with a total cost of $1000, a useful life of four years, and no SALVAGE VALUE.

With STRAIGHT-LINE DEPRECIATION the useful life of the asset is divided into the total cost to arrive at the uniform annual charge of $250, or 25% a year. DDB permits twice the straight-line annual percentage rate—50% in this case— to be applied each year to the undepreciated value of the asset. Hence: 50% × $1000 = $500 the first year, 50% × $500 = $250 the second year, and so on.

YEAR	STRAIGHT-LINE		DOUBLE-DECLINING-BALANCE	
	Expense	Cumulative	Expense	Cumulative
1	$250	$250	$500	$500
2	250	500	250	750
3	250	750	125	875
4	250	1000	63	938
	$1000		$938	

A variation of DDB, called *150 percent declining-balance method,* uses 150% of the straight-line annual percentage rate.

A switch to straight-line from declining balance depreciation is permitted once in the asset's life—logically, at the third year in our example. When the switch is made, however, salvage value must be considered. *See also* MODIFIED ACCELERATED COST RECOVERY SYSTEM; DEPRECIATION.

DOUBLE TAXATION taxation of earnings at the corporate level, then again as stockholder dividends.

DOUBLE TOP technical chart pattern showing a rise to a high price, then a drop, then another rise to the same high price. This means the security is encountering resistance to a move higher. However, if the price does move through that level, the security is expected to go on to a new high. *See also* DOUBLE BOTTOM.

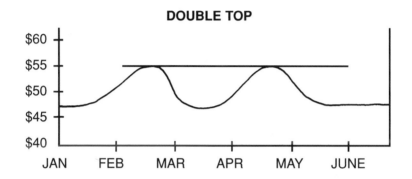

DOUBLE UP sophisticated stock buying (or selling short) strategy that reaffirms the original rationale by doubling the risk when the price goes (temporarily it is hoped) the wrong way. For example, an investor with confidence in XYZ buys 10,000 shares at $40. When the price drops to $35, the investor buys 10,000 additional shares, thus doubling up on a stock he feels will ultimately rise.

DOUBLE WITCHING DAY day when two related classes of options and futures expire. For example, index options and index futures on the same underlying index may expire on the same day, leading to various strategies by ARBITRAGEURS to close out positions. *See also* TRIPLE WITCHING HOUR.

DOW DIVIDEND THEORY *see* DOGS OF THE DOW.

DOW JONES AVERAGES *see* STOCK INDICES AND AVERAGES.

DOW JONES INDUSTRIAL AVERAGE *see* STOCK INDICES AND AVERAGES.

DOWNSIDE RISK estimate that a security will decline in value and the extent of the decline, taking into account the total range of factors affecting market price.

DOWNSIZING term for a corporate strategy popular in the 1990s whereby a company reduces its size and complexity, thereby presumably increasing its efficiency and profitability. Downsizing is typically accomplished through RESTRUCTURING, which means reducing the number of employees and, often, the SPIN-OFF of activities unrelated to the company's core business.

DOWNSTREAM flow of corporate activity from parent to subsidiary. Financially, it usually refers to loans, since dividends and interest generally flow upstream.

DOWNTICK sale of a security at a price below that of the preceding sale. If a stock has been trading at $15 a share, for instance, the next trade is a downtick if it is at 14 ⅞. Also known as MINUS TICK.

DOWNTURN shift of an economic or stock market cycle from rising to falling.

DOW THEORY theory that a major trend in the stock market must be confirmed by a similar movement in the Dow Jones Industrial Average and the Dow Jones Transportation Average. According to Dow Theory, a significant trend is not confirmed until both Dow Jones indexes reach the new highs or lows; if they don't, the market will fall back to its former trading range. Dow Theory proponents often disagree on when a true breakout has occurred and, in any case, miss a major portion of the up or down move while waiting for their signals.

DRAFT signed, written order by which one party (drawer) instructs another party (drawee) to pay a specified sum to a third party (payee). Payee and drawer are usually the same person. In foreign transactions, a draft is usually called a *bill of exchange*. When prepared without supporting papers, it is a *clean draft*. With papers or documents attached, it is a *documentary draft*. A *sight draft* is payable on demand. A *time draft* is payable either on a definite date or at a fixed time after sight or demand.

DRAINING RESERVES actions by the Federal Reserve System to decrease the money supply by curtailing the funds banks have available to lend. The Fed does this in three ways: (1) by raising reserve requirements, forcing banks to keep more funds on deposit with Federal Reserve banks; (2) by increasing the rate at which banks borrow to maintain reserves, thereby making it unattractive to deplete reserves by making loans; and (3) by selling bonds in the open market at such attractive rates that dealers reduce their bank balances to buy them. *See also* MULTIPLIER.

DRAWBACK rebate of taxes or duties paid on imported goods that have been reexported. It is in effect a government subsidy designed to encourage domestic manufacturers to compete overseas.

DRAWER *see* DRAFT.

DRESSING UP A PORTFOLIO practice of money managers to make their portfolio look good at the end of a reporting period. For example, a mutual fund or pension fund manager may sell certain stocks that performed badly during the quarter shortly before the end of that quarter to avoid having to report that holding to shareholders. Or they may buy stocks that have risen during the quarter to show shareholders that they owned winning stocks. Because these portfolio changes are largely cosmetic, they have little effect on portfolio performance except they increase transaction costs. In the final few days of a quarter, market analysts frequently comment that certain stocks rose or fell because of end-of-quarter WINDOW DRESSING.

DRILLING PROGRAM *see* BALANCED DRILLING PROGRAM; COMPLETION PROGRAM; DEVELOPMENTAL DRILLING PROGRAM; EXPLORATORY DRILLING PROGRAM; OIL AND GAS LIMITED PARTNERSHIP.

DRIP *see* DIVIDEND REINVESTMENT PLAN.

DRIP FEED supplying capital to a new company as its growth requires it, rather than in a lump sum at the beginning. *See also* EVERGREEN FUNDING.

DROP-DEAD DAY day on which a deadline, such as the expiration of the national al debt limit, becomes absolutely final.

DROP-DEAD FEE British term meaning a fee paid to a lender only if a deal requiring financing from that lender falls through.

DROPLOCK SECURITY FLOATING RATE NOTE or bond that becomes a FIXED-INCOME INVESTMENT when the rate to which it is pegged drops to a specified level.

DUAL BANKING U.S. system whereby banks are chartered by the state or federal government. This makes for differences in banking regulations, in lending limits, and in services available to customers.

DUAL LISTING listing of a security on more than one exchange, thus increasing the competition for bid and offer prices as well as the liquidity of the securities. Furthermore, being listed on an exchange in the East and another in the West would extend the number of hours when the stock can be traded. Securities may not be listed on both the New York and American stock exchanges.

DUAL PURPOSE FUND exchange-listed CLOSED-END FUND that has two classes of shares. Preferred shareholders receive all the income (dividends and interest) from the portfolio, while common shareholders receive all the capital gains. Such funds are set up with a specific expiration date when preferred shares are redeemed at a predetermined price and common shareholders claim the remaining assets, voting either to liquidate or to continue the fund on an open-end basis. Dual purpose funds are not closely followed on Wall Street, and there is little trading in them.

DUAL TRADING commodities traders' practice of dealing for their own and their clients' accounts at the same time. Reformers favor restricting dual trading to prevent FRONT RUNNING; advocates claim the practice is harmless in itself and economically vital to the industry.

DUE BILL *see* BILL.

DUE DATE date on which a debt-related obligation is required to be paid.

DUE DILIGENCE MEETING meeting conducted by the underwriter of a new offering at which brokers can ask representatives of the issuer questions about the issuer's background and financial reliability and the intended use of the proceeds. Brokers who recommend investment in new offerings without very careful due diligence work may face lawsuits if the investment should go sour later. Although, in itself, the legally required due diligence meeting typically is a perfunctory affair, most companies, recognizing the importance of due diligence, hold informational meetings, often in different regions of the country, at which top management representatives are available to answer questions of securities analysts and institutional investors.

DUE-ON-SALE CLAUSE clause in a mortgage contract requiring the borrower to pay off the full remaining principal outstanding on a mortgage when the mortgaged property is sold, transferred, or in any way encumbered. Due-on-sale clauses prevent the buyer of the property from assuming the mortgage loan.

DUMPING
International finance: selling goods abroad below cost in order to eliminate a surplus or to gain an edge on foreign competition. The U.S. Antidumping Act of 1974 was designed to prevent the sale of imported goods below cost in the United States.
Securities: offering large amounts of stock with little or no concern for price or market effect.

DUN & BRADSTREET (D & B) company that combines credit information obtained directly from commercial firms with data solicited from their creditors, then makes this available to subscribers in reports and a ratings directory. D & B also offers an accounts receivable collection service and publishes financial composite ratios and other financial information. A subsidiary, MOODY'S INVESTOR'S SERVICE, rates bonds and commercial paper.

DUN'S NUMBER short for Dun's Market Identifier. It is published as part of a list of firms giving information such as an identification number, address code, number of employees, corporate affiliations, and trade styles. Full name: Data Universal Numbering System.

DURABLE POWER OF ATTORNEY legal document by which a person with assets (the principal) appoints another person (the agent) to act on the principal's behalf, even if the principal becomes incompetent. If the power of attorney is not "durable," the agent's authority to act ends if the principal becomes incompetent. The agent's power to act for the principal may be broadly stated, allowing the agent to buy and sell securities, or narrowly stated to limit activity to selling a car.

DURATION concept first developed by Frederick Macaulay in 1938 that measures bond price VOLATILITY by measuring the "length" of a bond. It is a weighted-average term-to-maturity of the bond's cash flows, the weights being the present value of each cash flow as a percentage of the bond's full price. A Salomon Smith Barney study compared it to a series of tin cans equally spaced on a seesaw. The size of each can represents the cash flow due, the contents of each can represent the present values of those cash flows, and the intervals between them represent the payment periods. Duration is the distance to the fulcrum that would balance the seesaw. The duration of a zero-coupon security would thus equal its maturity because all the cash flows—all the weights—are at the other end of the seesaw. The greater the duration of a bond, the greater its percentage volatility. In general, duration rises with maturity, falls with the frequency of coupon payments, and falls as the yield rises (the higher yield reduces the present values of the cash flows.) Duration (the term *modified duration* is used in the strict sense because of modifications to Macaulay's formulation) as a measure of percentage of volatility is valid only for small changes in yield. For working purposes, duration can be defined as the approximate percentage change in price for a 100-basis-point change in yield. A duration of 5, for example, means the price of the bond will change by approximately 5% for a 100-basis point change in yield.

For larger yield changes, volatility is measured by a concept called *convexity*. That term derives from the price-yield curve for a normal bond, which is convex. In other words, the price is always falling at a slower rate as the yield increases. The more convexity a bond has, the merrier, because it means the bond's price will fall more slowly and rise more quickly on a given movement in general interest rate levels. As with duration, convexity on straight bonds increases with lower coupon, lower yield, and longer maturity. Convexity measures the rate of change of duration, and for an option-free bond it is always positive because changes in yield do not affect cash flows. When a bond has a call option, however, cash flows are affected. In that case, duration gets smaller as yield decreases, resulting in *negative convexity*.

When the durations of the assets and the liabilities of a portfolio, say that of a pension fund, are the same, the portfolio is inherently protected against interest-rate changes and you have what is called *immunization*. The high volatility and interest rates in the early 1980s caused institutional investors to use duration and convexity as tools in immunizing their portfolios.

DUTCH AUCTION auction system in which the price of an item is gradually lowered until it meets a responsive bid and is sold. U.S. Treasury bills are sold under this system. Contrasting is the two-sided or DOUBLE AUCTION SYSTEM exemplified by the major stock exchanges. *See also* BILL.

DUTCH AUCTION PREFERRED STOCK type of adjustable-rate PREFERRED STOCK whose dividend is determined every seven weeks in a DUTCH AUCTION process by corporate bidders. Shares are bought and sold at FACE VALUES ranging from $100,000 to $500,000 per share. Also known as *auction rate preferred stock, Money Market Preferred Stock* (Lehman Brothers Inc.), and by such proprietary acronyms as DARTS (Salomon Smith Barney Inc.). *See also* AMPS; APS.

DUTY tax imposed on the importation, exportation, or consumption of goods. *See also* TARIFF.

DWARFS pools of mortgage-backed securities, with original maturity of 15 years, issued by the Federal National Mortgage Association (FANNIE MAE).

e

EACH WAY commission made by a broker involved on both the purchase and the sale side of a trade. *See also* CROSSED TRADE.

EAFE acronym for the *Europe and Australasia, Far East Equity* index, calculated by the Morgan Stanley Capital International (MSCI) group. EAFE is composed of stocks screened for liquidity, cross-ownership, and industry representation. Stocks are selected by MSCI's analysts in Geneva. The index acts as a benchmark for managers of international stock portfolios. There are financial futures and options contracts based on EAFE.

EARLY WITHDRAWAL PENALTY charge assessed against holders of fixed-term investments if they withdraw their money before maturity. Such a penalty would be assessed, for instance, if someone who has a six-month certificate of deposit withdrew the money after four months.

EARNED INCOME income (especially wages and salaries) generated by providing goods or services. Also, pension or annuity income.

EARNED INCOME CREDIT TAX CREDIT for qualifying taxpayers with at least one child in residence for more than half the year and incomes below a specified dollar level.

EARNED SURPLUS *see* RETAINED EARNINGS.

EARNEST MONEY good faith deposit given by a buyer to a seller prior to consummation of a transaction. Earnest money is usually forfeited in the event the buyer is unwilling or unable to complete the sale. In real estate, earnest money is the down payment, which is usually put in an escrow account until the closing.

EARNING ASSET income-producing asset. For example, a company's building would not be an earning asset normally, but a financial investment in other property would be if it provided rental income.

EARNINGS BEFORE TAXES corporate profits after interest has been paid to bondholders, but before taxes have been paid.

EARNINGS MOMENTUM pattern of increasing rate of growth in EARNINGS PER SHARE from one period to another, which usually causes a stock price to go up. For example, a company whose earnings per share are up 15% one year and 35% the next has earnings momentum and should see a gain in its stock price.

EARNINGS PER SHARE portion of a company's profit allocated to each outstanding share of common stock. For instance, a corporation that earned $10 million last year and has 10 million shares outstanding would report earnings of $1 per share. The figure is calculated after paying taxes and after paying preferred shareholders and bondholders. Under new accounting rules adopted in 1998, companies must report earnings per share on two bases: BASIC EARNINGS PER SHARE which doesn't count stock options, warrants, and convertible securities, and (fully) *diluted earnings per share,* which includes those securities. *See also* FULLY DILUTED EARNINGS PER (COMMON) SHARE.

EARNINGS/PRICE RATIO relationship of earnings per share to current stock price. Also known as *earnings yield,* it is used in comparing the relative attractiveness of stocks, bonds, and money market instruments. Inverse of PRICE/ EARNINGS RATIO.

EARNINGS REPORT statement issued by a company to its shareholders and the public at large reporting its earnings for the latest period, which is either on a quarterly or annual basis. The report will show revenues, expenses, and net profit for the period. Earnings reports are released to the press and reported in newspapers and electronic media, and are also mailed to shareholders of record. Also called *profit and loss statement* (P&L) or *income statement.*

EARNINGS SURPRISE EARNINGS REPORT that reports a higher or lower profit than analysts have projected. If earnings are higher than expected, a company's stock price will usually rise sharply. If profits are below expectations, the company's stock will often plunge. Many analysts on Wall Street study earnings surprises very carefully on the theory that when a company reports a positive or negative surprise, it is typically followed by another surprise in the same direction. Three firms that follow general trends in earnings surprises are FIRST CALL; I/B/E/S INTERNATIONAL INC; and ZACKS ESTIMATE SYSTEM.

EARNINGS YIELD *see* EARNINGS/PRICE RATIO.

EARN-OUT in mergers and acquisitions, supplementary payments, not part of the original ACQUISITION COST, based on future earnings of the acquired company above a predetermined level.

EASY MONEY *see* TIGHT MONEY.

EATING SOMEONE'S LUNCH expression that an aggressive competitor is beating their rivals. For example, an analyst might say that one retailer is "eating the lunch" of a competitive retailer in the same town if it is gaining market share through an aggressive pricing strategy. The implication of the expression is that the winning competitor is taking food away from the losing company or individual.

EATING STOCK a block positioner or underwriter who can't find buyers may find himself eating stock, that is, buying it for his own account.

ECM *see* EMERGING COMPANY MARKETPLACE (ECM).

ECONOMETRICS use of computer analysis and modeling techniques to describe in mathematical terms the relationship between key economic forces such as labor, capital, interest rates, and government policies, then test the effects of changes in economic scenarios. For instance, an econometric model might show the relationship of housing starts and interest rates.

ECONOMIC GROWTH RATE rate of change in the GROSS NATIONAL PRODUCT, as expressed in an annual percentage. If adjusted for inflation, it is called the *real economic growth rate.* Two consecutive quarterly drops in the growth rate mean recession, and two consecutive advances in the growth rate reflect an expanding economy.

ECONOMIC INDICATORS key statistics showing the direction of the economy. Among them are the unemployment rate, inflation rate, factory utilization rate, and balance of trade. *See also* LEADING INDICATORS.

ECONOMIC RECOVERY TAX ACT OF 1981 (ERTA) tax-cutting legislation. Among the key provisions:
1. across-the-board tax cut, which took effect in three stages ending in 1983.
2. indexing of tax brackets to the inflation rate.
3. lowering of top tax rates on long-term capital gains from 28% to 20%. The top rate on dividends, interest, rents, and royalties income dropped from 70% to 50%.
4. lowering of MARRIAGE PENALTY tax, as families with two working spouses could deduct 10% from the salary of the lower-paid spouse, up to $3000.
5. expansion of INDIVIDUAL RETIREMENT ACCOUNTS to all working people, who can contribute up to $2000 a year, and $250 annually for nonworking spouses. Also, expansion of the amount self-employed people can contribute to KEOGH PLAN account contributions.
6. creation of the *all-savers certificate,* which allowed investors to exempt up to $1000 a year in earned interest. The authority to issue these certificates expired at the end of 1982.
7. deductions for reinvesting public utility dividends.
8. reductions in estate and gift taxes, phased in so that the first $600,000 of property can be given free of estate tax starting in 1987. Annual gifts that can be given free of gift tax were raised from $3000 to $10,000. Unlimited deduction for transfer of property to a spouse at death.
9. lowering of rates on the exercise of stock options.
10. change in rules on DEPRECIATION and INVESTMENT CREDIT.
See also TAX REFORM ACT OF 1986.

ECONOMICS study of the economy. Classic economics concentrates on how the forces of supply and demand allocate scarce product and service resources. MACROECONOMICS studies a nation or the world's economy as a whole, using data about inflation, unemployment and industrial production to understand the past and predict the future. MICROECONOMICS studies the behavior of specific sectors of the economy, such as companies, industries, or households. Over the years, various schools of economic thought have gained prominence, including KEYNESIAN ECONOMICS, MONETARISM and SUPPLY-SIDE ECONOMICS.

ECONOMIES OF SCALE economic principle that as the volume of production increases, the cost of producing each unit decreases. Therefore, building a large factory will be more efficient than a small factory because the large factory will be able to produce more units at a lower cost per unit than the smaller factory. The introduction of mass production techniques in the early twentieth century, such as the assembly line production of Ford Motor Company's Model T, put the theory of economies of scale into action.

ECU *see* EUROPEAN CURRENCY UNIT (ECU).

EDGE ACT banking legislation, passed in 1919, which allows national banks to conduct foreign lending operations through federal or state chartered subsidiaries, called Edge Act corporations. Such corporations can be chartered by other states and are allowed, unlike domestic banks, to own banks in foreign countries and to invest in foreign commercial and industrial firms. The act also permitted the FEDERAL RESERVE SYSTEM to set reserve requirements on foreign banks that do business in America. Edge Act corporations benefited further from the 1978 International Banking Act, which instructs the Fed to strike any regulations putting American banks at a disadvantage compared with U.S. operations of foreign banks.

EDUCATION IRA form of INDIVIDUAL RETIREMENT ACCOUNT created in the TAXPAYER RELIEF ACT OF 1997 allowing parents to contribute up to $500 per year for each child up to the age of 18. This $500 limit is reduced for married couples filing jointly with ADJUSTED GROSS INCOMES between $150,000 and $160,000, or singles reporting incomes between $95,000 and $110,000. Couples with incomes over $160,000 and singles with incomes over $110,000 may not contribute to Education IRAs. Contributions to Education IRAs do not generate tax deductions. However, assets inside the Education IRA grow tax-free and principal and earnings can be withdrawn tax-free as long as the proceeds are used to pay for education expenses at a postsecondary school, including tuition, fees, books, supplies and room and board. In a family with two or more children, Education IRA money not used by the first child can be used by the second or subsequent children if the first child does not attend college. The assets in the Education IRA must be spent on education before the child reaches age 30. If the assets are not used for college expenses, the account must be liquidated and taxes paid on the proceeds at regular income tax rates. Money inside Education IRAs can be invested in stocks, bonds, mutual funds and other investments suitable for regular IRAs.

EEC *see* EUROPEAN ECONOMIC COMMUNITY.

EFFECTIVE DATE
In general: date on which an agreement takes effect.
Securities: date when an offering registered with the Securities and Exchange Commission may commence, usually 20 days after filing the registration statement. *See also* SHELF REGISTRATION.
Banking and insurance: time when an insurance policy goes into effect. From that day forward, the insured party is covered by the contract.

EFFECTIVE DEBT total debt owed by a firm, including the capitalized value of lease payments.

EFFECTIVE NET WORTH net worth plus subordinated debt, as viewed by senior creditors. In small business banking, loans payable to principals are commonly subordinated to bank loans. The loans for principals thus can be regarded as effective net worth as long as a bank loan is outstanding and the subordination agreement is in effect.

EFFECTIVE RATE yield on a debt instrument as calculated from the purchase price. The effective rate on a bond is determined by the price, the coupon rate, the time between interest payments, and the time until maturity. Every bond's effective rate thus depends on when it was bought. The effective rate is a more meaningful yield figure than the coupon rate. *See also* RATE OF RETURN.

EFFECTIVE SALE price of a ROUND LOT that determines the price at which the next ODD LOT will be sold. If the last round-lot price was 15, for instance, the odd-lot price might be 15⅛. The added fraction is the *odd-lot differential*.

EFFECTIVE TAX RATE tax rate paid by a taxpayer. It is determined by dividing the tax paid by the taxable income in a particular year. For example, if a taxpayer with a taxable income of $100,000 owes $30,000 in a year, he has an effective tax rate of 30%. The effective tax rate is useful in tax planning, because it gives a taxpayer a realistic understanding of the amount of taxes he is paying after allowing for all deductions, credits, and other factors affecting tax liability.

EFFICIENT MARKET theory that market prices reflect the knowledge and expectations of all investors. Those who adhere to this theory consider it futile to seek undervalued stocks or to forecast market movements. Any new development is reflected in a firm's stock price, they say, making it impossible to beat the market. This vociferously disputed hypothesis also holds that an investor who throws darts at a newspaper's stock listings has as good a chance to outperform the market as any professional investor.

EFFICIENT PORTFOLIO portfolio that has a maximum expected return for any level of risk or a minimum level of risk for any expected return. It is arrived at mathematically, taking into account the expected return and standard deviation of returns for each security, as well as the covariance of returns between different securities in the portfolio.

EITHER-OR ORDER *see* ALTERNATIVE ORDER.

ELASTICITY OF DEMAND AND SUPPLY
Elasticity of demand: responsiveness of buyers to changes in price. Demand for luxury items may slow dramatically if prices are raised, because these purchases are not essential, and can be postponed. On the other hand, demand for necessities such as food, telephone service, and emergency surgery is said to be inelastic. It remains about the same despite price changes because buyers cannot postpone their purchases without severe adverse consequences.
Elasticity of supply: responsiveness of output to changes in price. As prices move up, the supply normally increases. If it does not, it is said to be inelastic. Supply is said to be elastic if the rise in price means a rise in production.

ELECT
In general: choose a course of action. Someone who decides to incorporate a certain provision in a will elects to do so.
Securities trading: make a conditional order into a market order. If a customer has received a guaranteed buy or sell price from a specialist on the floor of an exchange, the transaction is considered elected when that price is reached. If the guarantee is that a stock will be sold when it reaches 20, and a stop order is put at that price, the sale will be elected at 20.

ELEPHANTS expression describing large institutional investors. The term implies that such investors, including mutual funds, pension funds, banks, and insurance companies, tend to move their billions of dollars in assets in a herd-like manner, driving stock and bond prices up and down in concert. CONTRARIAN investors specialize in doing the opposite of the elephants—buying when institutions are selling and selling when the elephants are buying. The opposite of elephants are SMALL INVESTORS, who buy and sell far smaller quantities of stocks and bonds.

ELEVEN BOND INDEX average yield on a particular day of 11 selected general obligation municipal bonds with an average AA rating, maturing in 20 years. It is comprised of 11 of the 20 bonds in the Twenty Bond Index, also referred to as the BOND BUYER'S MUNICIPAL BOND INDEX, published by the *BOND BUYER* and used as a benchmark in tracking municipal bond yields.

ELIGIBLE PAPER commercial and agricultural paper, drafts, bills of exchange, banker's acceptances, and other negotiable instruments that were acquired by a bank at a discount and that the Federal Reserve Bank will accept for rediscount.

ELIGIBILITY REQUIREMENTS
Insurance: requirements by an insurance company to qualify for coverage. For example, a life insurance company may require that because of a person's health condition, a potential policyholder would need to pay a higher premium to obtain coverage. In this circumstance, the policyholder's ability to pay becomes a primary issue.
For employer group health insurance coverage, an employer may require a person be a full-time employee for coverage of the employee and the employee's dependents.

Pensions: conditions an employee must satisfy to become a participant in a pension plan, such as completing one year of service and reaching the age of 21. Federal pension laws allow plan participants to become VESTED after five years of service. Alternatively, some companies implement a graduated vesting schedule. Public pension plans sponsored by federal, state, and local governments have their own eligibility requirements.

ELVES ten technical analysts who predict the direction of stock prices over the next six months on the "Wall Street Week" television show on the Public Broadcasting System. If five or more analysts are bullish or bearish at one time, the Wall Street Week Elves Index is giving a signal to buy or sell.

EMANCIPATION freedom to assume certain legal responsibilities normally associated only with adults, said of a minor who is granted this freedom by a court. If both parents die in an accident, for instance, the 16-year-old eldest son may be emancipated by a judge to act as guardian for his younger brothers and sisters.

EMBARGO government prohibition against the shipment of certain goods to another country. An embargo is most common during wartime, but is sometimes applied for economic reasons as well. For instance, the Organization of Petroleum Exporting Countries placed an embargo on the shipment of oil to the West in the early 1970s to protest Israeli policies and to raise the price of petroleum.

EMERGENCY FUND cash reserve that is available to meet financial emergencies, such as large medical bills or unexpected auto or home repairs. Most financial planners advocate maintaining an emergency reserve of two to three months' salary in a liquid interest-bearing account such as a money market mutual fund or bank money market deposit account.

EMERGENCY HOME FINANCE ACT OF 1970 act creating the quasigovernmental Federal Home Loan Mortgage Corporation, also known as Freddie Mac, to stimulate the development of a secondary mortgage market. The act authorized Freddie Mac to package and sell Federal Housing Administration- and Veterans Administration-guaranteed mortgage loans. More than half the home mortgages were subsequently packaged and sold to investors in the secondary market in the form of pass-through securities.

EMERGING COMPANY MARKETPLACE (ECM) discontinued service of the AMERICAN STOCK EXCHANGE that focused on the needs of small growth companies meeting special listing requirements. ECM provided matching of public orders, short sale protection, specialist oversight and support, and offered other services and programs designed to promote corporate visibility (through separate listings in newspaper stock tables, for example).

EMERGING MARKETS FREE (EMF) INDEX index developed by Morgan Stanley Capital International to follow stock markets in Mexico, Malaysia, Chile, Jordan, Thailand, the Philippines, and Argentina, countries selected because of their accessibility to foreign investors.

EMINENT DOMAIN right of a government entity to seize private property for the purpose of constructing a public facility. Federal, state, and local governments can seize people's homes under eminent domain laws as long as the homeowner is compensated at fair market value. Some public projects that may necessitate such CONDEMNATION include highways, hospitals, schools, parks, or government office buildings.

EMPLOYEE RETIREMENT INCOME SECURITY ACT (ERISA) 1974 law governing the operation of most private pension and benefit plans, The law eased pension eligibility rules, set up the PENSION BENEFIT GUARANTY CORPORATION, and established guidelines for the management of pension funds.

EMPLOYEE STOCK OWNERSHIP PLAN (ESOP) program encouraging employees to purchase stock in their company. Employees may participate in the management of the company and even take control to rescue the company or a particular plant that would otherwise go out of business. Employees may offer wage and work rule concessions in return for ownership privileges in an attempt to keep a marginal facility operating.

EMPTY HEAD AND PURE HEART TEST SEC Rule 14e-3, subparagraph (b), which, with strict exceptions, prohibits any party other than the bidder in a TENDER OFFER to trade in the stock while having INSIDE INFORMATION.

ENCUMBERED owned by one party but subject to another party's valid claim. A homeowner owns his mortgaged property, for example, but the bank has a security interest in it as long as the mortgage loan is outstanding.

ENDORSE transfer ownership of an asset by signing the back of a negotiable instrument. One can endorse a check to receive payment or endorse a stock or bond certificate to transfer ownership.
    See also QUALIFIED ENDORSEMENT.

ENDOWMENT permanent gift of money or property to a specified institution for a specified purpose. Endowments may finance physical assets or be invested to provide ongoing income to finance operations.

ENERGY MUTUAL FUND mutual fund that invests solely in energy stocks such as oil, oil service, gas, solar energy, and coal companies and makers of energy-saving devices.

ENTERPRISE a business firm. The term often is applied to a newly formed venture.

ENTREPRENEUR person who takes on the risks of starting a new business. Many entrepreneurs have technical knowledge with which to produce a saleable product or to design a needed new service. Often, VENTURE CAPITAL is used to finance the startup in return for a piece of the equity. Once an entrepreneur's business is established, shares may be sold to the public as an INITIAL PUBLIC OFFERING, assuming favorable market conditions.

ENVIRONMENTAL FUND MUTUAL FUND specializing in stocks of companies having a role in the bettering of the environment. Not to be confused with a SOCIALLY CONSCIOUS MUTUAL FUND, which aims in part to satisfy social values, an environmental fund is designed to capitalize on financial opportunities related to the environmental movement.

EOM DATING arrangement—common in the wholesale drug industry, for example—whereby all purchases made through the 25th of one month are payable within 30 days of the end of the following month; EOM means *end of month.* Assuming no prompt payment discount, purchases through the 25th of April, for example, will be payable by the end of June. If a discount exists for payment in ten days, payment would have to be made by June 10th to take advantage of it. End of month dating with a 2% discount for prompt payment (10 days) would be expressed in the trade either as: *2%-10 days, EOM, 30,* or *2/10 prox. net 30,* where prox., or proximo, means "the next."

EPS *see* EARNINGS PER SHARE.

EQUAL CREDIT OPPORTUNITY ACT federal legislation passed in the mid-1970s prohibiting discrimination in granting credit, based on race, religion, sex, ethnic background, or whether a person is receiving public assistance or alimony. The Federal Trade Commission enforces the act.

EQUALIZING DIVIDEND special dividend paid to compensate investors for income lost because a change was made in the quarterly dividend payment schedule.

EQUILIBRIUM PRICE
1. price when the supply of goods in a particular market matches demand.
2. for a manufacturer, the price that maximizes a product's profitability.

EQUILIBRIUM PRICE

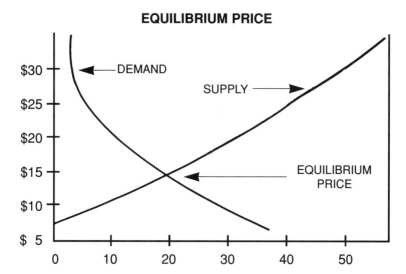

EQUIPMENT LEASING PARTNERSHIP limited partnership that buys equipment such as computers, railroad cars, and airplanes, then leases it to businesses. Limited partners receive income from the lease payments as well as tax benefits such as depreciation. Whether a partnership of this kind works out well depends on the GENERAL PARTNER'S expertise. Failure to lease the equipment can be disastrous, as happened with railroad hopper cars in the mid-1970s.

EQUIPMENT TRUST CERTIFICATE bond, usually issued by a transportation company such as a railroad or shipping line, used to pay for new equipment. The certificate gives the bondholder the first right to the equipment in the event that interest and principal are not paid when due. Title to the equipment is held in the name of the trustee, usually a bank, until the bond is paid off.

EQUITABLE OWNER beneficiary of property held in trust.

EQUITY
In general: fairness. Law courts, for example, try to be equitable in their judgments when splitting up estates or settling divorce cases.
Banking: difference between the amount a property could be sold for and the claims held against it.
Brokerage account: excess of securities over debit balance in a margin account. For instance, equity would be $28,000 in a margin account with stocks and bonds worth $50,000 and a debit balance of $22,000.
Investments: ownership interest possessed by shareholders in a corporation— stock as opposed to bonds.

EQUITY CMO *see* CMO REIT.

EQUITY COMMITMENT NOTES *see* MANDATORY CONVERTIBLES.

EQUITY CONTRACT NOTES *see* MANDATORY CONVERTIBLES.

EQUITY FINANCING raising money by issuing shares of common or preferred stock. Usually done when prices are high and the most capital can be raised for the smallest number of shares.

EQUITY FUNDING type of investment combining a life insurance policy and a mutual fund. The fund shares are used as collateral for a loan to pay the insurance premiums, giving the investor the advantages of insurance protection and investment appreciation potential.

EQUITY KICKER offer of an ownership position in a deal that involves loans. For instance, a mortgage real estate limited partnership that lends to real estate developers might receive as an equity kicker a small ownership position in a building that can appreciate over time. When the building is sold, limited partners receive the appreciation payout. In return for that equity kicker, the lender is likely to charge a lower interest rate on the loan. Convertible features and warrants are offered as equity kickers to make securities attractive to investors.

EQUITY REIT REAL ESTATE INVESTMENT TRUST that takes an ownership position in the real estate it invests in. Stockholders in equity REITs earn dividends on rental income from the buildings and earn appreciation if properties are sold for a profit. The opposite is a MORTGAGE REIT.

EQUIVALENT BOND YIELD comparison of discount yields and yields on bonds with coupons. Also called *coupon-equivalent rate.* For instance, if a 10%, 90-day Treasury bill with a face value of $10,000 cost $9750, the equivalent bond yield would be:

$$\frac{\$250}{\$9750} \times \frac{365}{90} = 10.40\%$$

EQUIVALENT TAXABLE YIELD comparison of the taxable yield on a corporate or government bond and the tax-free yield on a municipal bond. Depending on the tax bracket, an investor's aftertax return may be greater with a municipal bond than with a corporate or government bond offering a highest interest rate. For someone in a 31% federal tax bracket, for instance, a 7% municipal bond would have an equivalent taxable yield of 10.4%. An investor living in a state that levies state income tax should add in the state tax bracket to get a true measure of the equivalent taxable yield. *See* YIELD EQUIVALENCE for method of calculation.

ERISA *see* EMPLOYEE RETIREMENT INCOME SECURITY ACT.

ERM acronym for *exchange rate mechanism,* by which participating member countries agree to maintain the value of their own currencies through intervention.

ERTA *see* ECONOMIC RECOVERY TAX ACT OF 1981.

ESCALATOR CLAUSE provision in a contract allowing cost increases to be passed on. In an employment contract, an escalator clause might call for wage increases to keep employee earnings in line with inflation. In a lease, an escalator clause could obligate the tenant to pay for increases in fuel or other costs.

ESCHEAT return of property (for example, land, bank balances, insurance policies) to the state if abandoned or left by a person who died without making a will. If rightful owners or heirs later appear, they can claim the property.

ESCROW money, securities, or other property or instruments held by a third party until the conditions of a contract are met.

ESCROWED TO MATURITY (ETM) holding proceeds from a new bond issue in a separate escrow account to pay off an existing bond issue when it matures. Bond issuers will implement an ADVANCE REFUNDING when interest rates have fallen significantly, making it advantageous to pay off the existing issue before scheduled maturity at the first CALL DATE. The funds raised by the refunding are invested in government securities in the escrow account until the principal is used to prepay the original bond issue at the first call date. The escrowed funds may also pay some of the interest on the original issue up until the bonds are redeemed.

ESCROW RECEIPT in options trading, a document provided by a bank to guarantee that the UNDERLYING SECURITY is on deposit and available for potential delivery.

ESSENTIAL PURPOSE (or FUNCTION) BOND *see* PUBLIC PURPOSE BOND.

ESTATE all the assets a person possesses at the time of death—such as securities, real estate, interests in business, physical possessions, and cash. The estate is distributed to heirs according to the dictates of the person's will or, if there is no will, a court ruling.

ESTATE PLANNING planning for the orderly handling, disposition, and administration of an estate when the owner dies. Estate planning includes drawing up a will, setting up trusts, and minimizing estate taxes, perhaps by passing property to heirs before death or by setting up a BYPASS TRUST or a TESTAMENTARY TRUST.

ESTATE TAX tax imposed by a state or the federal government on assets left to heirs. Under the ECONOMIC RECOVERY TAX ACT OF 1981, there is no estate tax on transfers of property between spouses, an action known as the MARITAL DEDUCTION. According to the TAXPAYER RELIEF ACT OF 1997, the amount of assets that each person can exclude from federal estate taxes is $625,000 in 1998, rising to $1 million in 2006 and later years. This limit rises to $650,000 in 1999, $675,000 in 2000 and 2001, $700,000 in 2002 and 2003, $850,000 in 2004, $950,000 in 2005 and $1 million in 2006. The law created a special $1.3 million limit for qualifying farmers and small business owners starting January 1, 1998. Any assets passed to beneficiaries over these limits that are not protected by TRUSTS are assessed estate taxes at rates as high as 55%. Many states impose their own estate taxes on top of the federal levies. Careful ESTATE PLANNING, involving the writing of a will and the establishment of trusts, is essential for those wishing to minimize estate taxes.

ESTIMATED TAX amount of estimated tax for the coming year, minus tax credits, based on the higher of regular or ALTERNATIVE MINIMUM TAX (AMT). Corporations, estates and trusts, self-employed persons, and persons for whom less than a fixed percentage of income is withheld by employers must compute estimated tax and make quarterly tax payments to the IRS and state tax authorities, if required. Generally, a taxpayer must pay at least 90% of his or her total tax liability for the year in withholding and/or quarterly estimated tax payments. Alternatively, taxpayers may base their current year's estimated tax on the prior year's income tax. For taxpayers with adjusted gross income (AGI) in the prior tax year of $150,000 or less, estimated taxes must equal 100% of the prior year's tax. For those reporting AGI of more than $150,000, the current year's estimated taxes must be based on 110% of the prior year's tax liability. Thus, for someone reporting an AGI of more than $150,000 who paid $50,000 in taxes in the prior year, estimated taxes of at least $55,000 will be due in the current tax year. Severe penalties are imposed by the IRS and state tax authorities for underpayment of estimated taxes.

ETHICAL FUND *see* SOCIAL CONSCIOUSNESS MUTUAL FUND.

EUREX German-Swiss electronic derivatives exchange. *See* DEUTSCHE TERMIN-BORSE (DTB); SWISS OPTIONS AND FINANCIAL FUTURES EXCHANGE (SOFFEX).

EURO common currency adopted by 11 European nations starting January 1, 1999. The 11 countries are: Austria, Belgium, Finland, France, Germany, Ireland, Italy, Luxembourg, the Netherlands, Portugal and Spain. On that date, the conversion rates of the participating currencies are irrevocably fixed, both among themselves and against the Euro. At first, the Euro will be used in financial markets by companies and governments issuing bonds. Credit cards will also be denominated in Euros. Starting January 1, 2002, the Euro will begin to replace all national currencies as Euro notes and coins are put into circulation. By July 1, 2002, all national notes and coins will be withdrawn from circulation. Euro notes will be issued in denominations of 5, 10, 20, 50, 100, 200 and 500 Euro. There will be eight different coins ranging from one cent (one hundredth of a Euro) to 2 Euro. The Euro replaced the ECU (European Currency Unit) on January 1, 1999.

The EUROPEAN CENTRAL BANK, based in Brussels, started conducting monetary policy for participating European countries starting on January 1, 1999. The bank's role is to protect the value of the Euro and foster economic growth with low inflation. The bank will conduct monetary and foreign-exchange operations in Euros, issue Euro notes and coins, and withdraw national currency from circulation.

The common currency was adopted by the Treaty on European Union, signed in Maastricht, the Netherlands in February 1992 and ratified on behalf of the people by the parliaments of the member states. In some countries, there were direct popular referendums endorsing the single currency. The economic rationale behind the move was that a single, stable currency should make it easier to create a single market for trade among the European states, and between Europe and the rest of the world. The introduction of the Euro is designed to help companies cut their costs because they will not have the expense of conducting business in several currencies. Only Denmark and the United Kingdom opted not to use the Euro as their currencies.

In order for a country to use the Euro, it must meet a series of economic conditions, known as the convergence criteria:
• Its government deficit must equal 3% of its GDP or less, with government debt below the reference value of 60% of GDP.
• Inflation cannot exceed by more than 1.5 percentage points the rate of the three best performing countries.
• The country's currency must have remained within the normal fluctuation margins of the European Monetary System (EMS) for at least two years.
• The country's long-term interest rates should not exceed by more than 2 percentage points the average of the three countries with the lowest inflation rates in the European Union.

The 11 countries that will use the Euro met these conditions, as certified by the European Commission in March 1998. These 11 countries will become known as "Euroland."

EUROBOND bond denominated in U.S. dollars or other currencies and sold to investors outside the country whose currency is used. The bonds are usually issued by large underwriting groups composed of banks and issuing houses from many countries. An example of a Eurobond transaction might be a dollar-denominated debenture issued by a Belgian corporation through an underwriting group comprised of the overseas affiliate of a New York investment banking house, a bank in Holland, and a consortium of British merchant banks; a portion of the issue is sold to French investors through Swiss investment accounts. The Eurobond market is an important source of capital for multinational companies and foreign governments, including Third World governments.

EUROCURRENCY money deposited by corporations and national governments in banks away from their home countries, called *Eurobanks*. The terms

Eurocurrency and Eurobanks do not necessarily mean the currencies or the banks are European, though more often than not, that is the case. For instance, dollars deposited in a British bank or Italian lire deposited in a Japanese bank are considered to be Eurocurrency. The Eurodollar is only one of the Eurocurrencies, though it is the most prevalent. Also known as *Euromoney.*

EURODOLLAR U.S. currency held in banks outside the United States, mainly in Europe, and commonly used for settling international transactions. Some securities are issued in Eurodollars—that is, with a promise to pay interest in dollars deposited in foreign bank accounts.

EURODOLLAR BOND bond that pays interest and principal in Eurodollars, U.S. dollars held in banks outside the United States, primarily in Europe. Such a bond is not registered with the Securities and Exchange Commission, and because there are fewer regulatory delays and costs in the Euromarket, Eurodollar bonds generally can be sold at lower than U.S. interest rates. *See also* EUROBOND.

EURODOLLAR CERTIFICATE OF DEPOSIT CDs issued by banks outside the United States, primarily in Europe, with interest and principal paid in dollars. Such CDs usually have minimum denominations of $100,000 and short-term maturities of less than two years. The interest rate on these CDs is usually pegged to the LONDON INTERBANK OFFERED RATE (LIBOR).

EURO.NM a pan-European network of regulated markets dedicated to growth companies. Formed March 1, 1996, members of this umbrella market include the PARIS BOURSE (Le Nouveau Marche), DEUTSCHE BORSE AG (Neuer Markt), AMSTERDAM EXCHANGES (NMAX) and the BRUSSELS STOCK EXCHANGE (EURO.NM Belgium). The network has hundreds of listings, many of them dually listed on other exchanges such as NASDAQ, the TORONTO STOCK EXCHANGE, and the SWISS ELECTRONIC BOURSE (EBS). The official EURO.NM All-Share Index represents the markets. NASDAQ is the model for EURO.NM, whose objective is to develop a fully integrated, pan-European network of high-growth stock markets providing single points of access for market information and trading across. Convergent regulatory and operational standards have been adopted. EURO.NM provides cross-membership between its markets, and members are linking their existing systems to form a common electronic system for trading and market information.

EUROPEAN CENTRAL BANK (ECB) bank founded to oversee monetary policy for the 11 countries that convert their local currencies into the EURO on January 1, 1999. The 11 countries are: Austria, Belgium, Finland, France, Germany, Ireland, Italy, Luxembourg, the Netherlands, Portugal, and Spain. Based in Brussels, Belgium, the bank's primary mission is to maintain price stability and issue Euro currency. It replaces the Frankfurt-based European Monetary Institute (EMI), which was established in 1994 to prepare the way for a single currency. The economic and monetary policy of Europe is set by the EU Council of Economics and Finance Ministers (known as the Ecofin Council). The European Central Bank's mission is to implement that policy. The bank is run by a Governing Council, which is composed of members of the Executive Board and the Governors of National Central Banks. The Executive Board consists of a president, vice president, and four other members appointed for a non-renewable term of up to eight years.

The Governing Council formulates monetary policy, decisions relating to monetary objectives, key interest rates, and the supply of reserves in the European System of Central Banks (ESCB). The Executive Board implements the policy by instructing the National Central Banks. The National Central Banks will not disappear, but will form, along with the European Central Bank, the ESCB. The ESCB will implement the common European monetary policy, conduct foreign exchange operations, and manage foreign reserves of the member states.

EUROPEAN COMMUNITY (EC) with ratification of the Maastricht Treaty on European Union in November 1993, the former name of European Economic Community was dropped. The EC is part of the EUROPEAN UNION. The EC is an economic and, increasingly, political alliance formed in 1957 by Germany, France, Belgium, Luxembourg, the Netherlands and Italy to foster trade and cooperation among its members and "an ever closer union among the peoples of Europe." Membership was subsequently extended to the UK, Ireland and Denmark (1973); Greece (1981); and Spain and Portugal (1986). Austria, Finland, and Sweden became members in 1995. Norway rejected membership in November 1994. Tariff barriers between the member states have been abolished, and import duties vis-a-vis non-EC countries have been standardized. Many former European dependencies in African, Caribbean, and Pacific countries have preferential trade terms with the EC through the Rome Convention. EC headquarters is in Brussels, administered by the European Commission, the executive arm of the European Union. By December 1992, most remaining non-tariff trade barriers between the member states had been eliminated, and common standards in many industries had been adopted. Also known as the *European Union,* of which it is a part and, anachronistically, the *Common Market.*

EUROPEAN CURRENCY UNIT (ECU) one of two international currency substitutes ("artificial currencies"), the other being the SPECIAL DRAWING RIGHTS (SDRs) of the INTERNATIONAL MONETARY FUND (IMF). Like the SDR, the ECU is a currency basket comprised of a predetermined amount of a number of different currencies. Whereas SDRs represent five currencies, ECUs include all the EUROPEAN ECONOMIC COMMUNITY (EEC) currencies except the Spanish peseta and the Portuguese escudo. Currency substitutes are less volatile than the currencies making them up and are expected to be used increasingly for commercial purposes as the European Community develops.

EUROPEAN OPTIONS EXCHANGE (EOE) the Dutch derivatives exchange merged in 1996 with the Amsterdam Stock Exchange to form the Amsterdam Exchanges. *See also* AMSTERDAM EXCHANGES (AEX).

EUROPEAN-STYLE EXERCISE system of exercising options contracts in which the option buyer can exercise the contract only on the last business day prior to expiration (normally Friday). This system is widely used with index options traded on various U.S. exchanges.

EUROPEAN UNION (EU) umbrella term referring to a "three-pillar" construction comprising the EUROPEAN COMMUNITY (EC) and two new pillars: Common Foreign and Security Policy (including defense) and Justice and Home Affairs (notably cooperation between police and other authorities on crime, terrorism, and immigration issues). The EU is governed by a five-part institutional system, including the European Commission, the EU Council of Ministers, the European Parliament and the European Court of Justice, and the Court of Auditors, which monitors EU budget spending. Under the Maastricht Treaty on European Union of November 1, 1993, the directly elected Parliament gained co-decision powers with the Council and Commission.

EUROYEN BOND EUROCURRENCY deposits in Japanese yen.

EVALUATOR independent expert who appraises the value of property for which there is limited trading—antiques in an estate, perhaps, or rarely traded stocks or bonds. The fee for this service is sometimes a flat amount, sometimes a percentage of the appraised value.

EVENT RISK risk that a bond will suddenly decline in credit quality and warrant a lower RATING because of a TAKEOVER-related development, such as additional debt or a RECAPITALIZATION. Corporations whose INDENTURES include protective COVENANTS, such as POISON PUT provisions, are assigned *Event Risk Covenant Rankings* by Standard & Poor's Corporation. Ratings range from E-1, the highest, to E-5 and supplement basic bond ratings.

EVERGREEN FUNDING similar to DRIP FEED, British term for the gradual infusion of capital into a new or recapitalized enterprise. In the United States, banks use the term *evergreen* to describe short-term loans that are continuously renewed rather than repaid.

EXACT INTEREST interest paid by a bank or other financial institution and calculated on a 365-days-per-year basis, as opposed to a 360-day basis, called ordinary interest. The difference—the ratio is 1.0139—can be material when calculating daily interest on large sums of money.

EX-ALL sale of a security without dividends, rights, warrants, or any other privileges associated with that security.

EXCESS MARGIN equity in a brokerage firm's customer account, expressed in dollars, above the legal minimum for a margin account or the maintenance requirement. For instance, with a margin requirement of $25,000, as set by REGULATION T and a maintenance requirement of $12,500 set by the stock exchange, the client whose equity is $100,000 would have excess margin of $75,000 and $87,500 in terms of the initial and maintenance requirements, respectively.

EXCESS PROFITS TAX extra federal taxes placed on the earnings of a business. Such taxes may be levied during a time of national emergency, such as in wartime, and are designed to increase national revenue. The excess profits tax differs from the WINDFALL PROFITS TAX, designed to prevent excessive corporate profits in special circumstances.

EXCESS RESERVES money a bank holds over and above the RESERVE REQUIREMENT. The money may be on deposit with the Federal Reserve System or with an approved depository bank, or it may be in the bank's possession. For instance, a bank with a reserve requirement of $5 million might have $4 million on deposit with the Fed and $1.5 million in its vaults and as till cash. The $500,000 in excess reserves is available for loans to other banks or customers or for other corporate uses.

EXCHANGE
Barter: to trade goods and services with another individual or company for other goods and services of equal value.
Corporate finance: offer by a corporation to exchange one security for another. For example, a company may want holders of its convertible bonds to exchange their holdings for common stock. Or a company in financial distress may want its bondholders to exchange their bonds for stock in order to reduce or eliminate its debt load. *See also* SWAP.
Currency: trading of one currency for another. Also known as *foreign exchange.*
Mutual funds: process of switching from one mutual fund to another, either within one fund family or between fund families, if executed through a brokerage firm offering funds from several companies. In many cases, fund companies will not charge an additional LOAD if the assets are kept within the same family. If one fund is sold to buy another, a taxable event has occurred, meaning that capital gains or losses have been realized, unless the trade was executed within a tax-deferred account, such as an IRA or Keogh account.

Trading: central location where securities or futures trading takes place. The New York and American Stock Exchanges are the largest centralized place to trade stocks in the United States, for example. Futures exchanges in Chicago, Kansas City, New York, and elsewhere facilitate the trading of futures contracts. *See also* SECURITIES AND COMMODITIES EXCHANGES.

EXCHANGEABLE DEBENTURE like CONVERTIBLES, with the exception that this type of debenture can be converted to the common stock of a SUBSIDIARY or AFFILIATE of the issuer.

EXCHANGE CONTROLS government regulation of foreign exchange (currency trading).

EXCHANGE DISTRIBUTION block trade carried out on the floor of an exchange between customers of a member firm. Someone who wants to sell a large block of stock in a single transaction can get a broker to solicit and bunch a large number of orders. The seller transmits the securities to the buyers all at once, and the trade is announced on the BROAD TAPE as an exchange distribution. The seller, not the buyers, pays a special commission to the broker who executes the trade.

EXCHANGE MEMBERS *see* MEMBER FIRM; SEAT.

EXCHANGE PRIVILEGE right of a shareholder to switch from one mutual fund to another within one fund family—often, at no additional charge. This enables investors to put their money in an aggressive growth-stock fund when they expect the market to turn up strongly, then switch to a money-market fund when they anticipate a downturn. Some discount brokers allow shareholders to switch between fund families in pursuit of the best performance.

EXCHANGE RATE price at which one country's currency can be converted into another's. The exchange rate between the U.S. dollar and the British pound is different from the rate between the dollar and the German mark, for example. A wide range of factors influences exchange rates, which generally change slightly each trading day. Some rates are fixed by agreement; *see* FIXED EXCHANGE RATE.

EXCHANGE STOCK PORTFOLIO (ESP) *see* BASKET.

EXCISE TAX federal or state tax on the sale or manufacture of a commodity, usually a luxury item. Examples: federal and state taxes on alcohol and tobacco.

EXCLUSION
Contracts: item not covered by a contract. For example, an insurance policy may list certain hazards, such as acts of war, that are excluded from coverage.
Taxes: on a tax return, items that must be reported, but not taxed. For example, corporations are allowed to exclude 70% of dividends received from other domestic corporations. Gift tax rules allow DONORS to exclude up to $10,000 worth of gifts to donees annually.

EXCLUSIVE LISTING written listing agreement giving an agent the right to sell a specific property for a period of time with a definite termination date, frequently three months. There are two types of exclusive listings. With the exclusive agency, the owner reserves the right to sell the property himself without owing a commission; the exclusive agent is entitled to a commission if he or she personally sells the property, or if it is sold by anyone other than the seller. Under the exclusive right to sell, a broker is appointed as exclusive agent, entitled to a commission if the property is sold by the owner, the broker, or anyone else. "Right to sell" means the right to find a buyer. Sellers opt for exclusive listings because they think an agent will give their property more attention. An agent with an exclusive listing will not have to share the commission with any other agent as they would under a multiple-listing arrangement. If the property is not sold within the specified time, the seller may expand the selling group through an open, multiple listing.

EX-DIVIDEND interval between the announcement and the payment of the next dividend. An investor who buys shares during that interval is not entitled to the dividend. Typically, a stock's price moves up by the dollar amount of the dividend as the ex-dividend date approaches, then falls by the amount of the dividend after that date. A stock that has gone ex-dividend is marked with an *x* in newspaper listings.

EX-DIVIDEND DATE date on which a stock goes EX-DIVIDEND, typically about three weeks before the dividend is paid to shareholders of record. Shares listed on the New York Stock Exchange go ex-dividend four business days before the RECORD DATE. This NYSE rule is generally followed by the other exchanges.

EXECUTION
Law: the signing, sealing, and delivering of a contract or agreement making it valid.
Securities: carrying out a trade. A broker who buys or sells shares is said to have executed an order.

EXECUTOR/EXECUTRIX administrator of the estate who gathers the estate assets; files the estate tax returns and final personal income tax returns, and administers the estate; pays the debts of and charges against the estate; and distributes the balance in accordance with the terms of the will. The executor's responsibility is relatively short term, one to three years, ending when estate administration is completed. An executor (executrix if a female) may be a bank trust officer, a lawyer, or a family member or trusted friend.

EXEMPTION IRS-allowed direct reductions from gross income. Personal and dependency exemptions are allowed for: individual taxpayers; elderly and disabled taxpayers; dependent children and other dependents more than half of whose support is provided; total or partial blindness; and a taxpayer's spouse.

EXEMPT SECURITIES stocks and bonds exempt from certain Securities and Exchange Commission and Federal Reserve Board rules. For instance, government and municipal bonds are exempt from SEC registration requirements and from Federal Reserve Board margin rules.

EXERCISE make use of a right available in a contract. In options trading a buyer of a call contract may exercise the right to buy underlying shares at a particular price by informing the option seller. A put buyer's right is exercised when the underlying shares are sold at the agreed-upon price.

EXERCISE LIMIT limit on the number of option contracts of any one class that can be exercised in a span of five business days. For options on stocks, the exercise limit is usually 2000 contracts.

EXERCISE NOTICE notification by a broker that a client wants to exercise a right to buy the underlying stock in an option contract. Such notice is transmitted to the option seller through the Options Clearing Corporation, which ensures that stock is delivered as agreed upon.

EXERCISE PRICE price at which the stock or commodity underlying a call or put option can be purchased (call) or sold (put) over the specified period. For instance, a call contract may allow the buyer to purchase 100 shares of XYZ at any time in the next three months at an exercise or STRIKE PRICE of $63.

EXHAUST PRICE price at which broker must liquidate a client's holding in a stock that was bought on margin and has declined, but has not had additional funds put up to meet the MARGIN CALL.

EXIMBANK *see* EXPORT-IMPORT BANK.

EXIT FEE *see* BACK-END LOAD.

EX-LEGAL municipal bond that does not have the legal opinion of a bond law firm printed on it, as most municipal bonds do. When such bonds are traded, buyers must be warned that legal opinion is lacking.

EXPECTED RETURN *see* MEAN RETURN.

EXPENSE RATIO amount, expressed as a percentage of total investment, that shareholders pay annually for mutual fund operating expenses and management fees. These expenses include shareholder service, salaries for money managers and administrative staff, and investor centers, among many others. The expense ratio, which may be as low as 0.2% or as high as 2% of shareholder assets, is taken out of the fund's current income and is disclosed in the prospectus to shareholders.

EXPERIENCE RATING insurance company technique to determine the correct price of a policy premium. The company analyzes past loss experience for others in the insured group to project future claims. The premium is then set at a rate high enough to cover those potential claims and still earn a profit for the insurance company. For example, life insurance companies charge higher premiums to smokers than to non-smokers because smokers' experience rating is higher, meaning their chance of dying is much higher.

EXPIRATION
Banking: date on which a contract or agreement ceases to be effective.
Options trading: last day on which an option can be exercised. If it is not, traders say that the option *expired worthless.*

EXPIRATION CYCLE cycle of expiration dates used in short-term options trading. For example, contracts may be written for one of three cycles: January, April, July, October; February, May, August, November; March, June, September, December. Since options are traded in three-, six-, and nine-month contracts, only three of the four months in the set are traded at once. In our example, when the January contract expires, trading begins on the October contract. Commodities futures expiration cycles follow other schedules.

EX-PIT TRANSACTION purchase of commodities off the floor of the exchange where they are regularly traded and at specified terms.

EXPLORATORY DRILLING PROGRAM search for an undiscovered reservoir of oil or gas—a very risky undertaking. Exploratory wells are called *wildcat* (in an unproven area); *controlled wildcat* (in an area outside the proven limits of an existing field); or *deep test* (within a proven field but to unproven depths). Exploratory drilling programs are usually syndicated, and units are sold to limited partners.

EXPORT-IMPORT BANK (EXIMBANK) bank set up by Congress in 1934 to encourage U.S. trade with foreign countries. Eximbank is an independent entity that borrows from the U.S. Treasury to (1) finance exports and imports; (2) grant direct credit to non-U.S. borrowers; (3) provide export guarantees, insurance against commercial and political risk, and discount loans.

EX-RIGHTS without the RIGHT to buy a company's stock at a discount from the prevailing market price, which was distributed until a particular date. Typically, after that date the rights trade separately from the stock itself. *See also* EX-WARRANTS.

EX-STOCK DIVIDENDS interval between the announcement and payment of a stock dividend. An investor who buys shares during that interval is not entitled to the announced stock dividend; instead, it goes to the seller of the shares, who was the owner on the last recorded date before the books were closed and the stock went EX-DIVIDEND. Stocks cease to be ex-dividend after the payment date.

EXTENDED COVERAGE insurance protection that is extended beyond the original term of the contract. For example, consumers can buy extended warranties when they purchase cars or appliances, which will cover repairs beyond the original warranty period.

EXTENSION OF TIME FOR FILING TAXES time period beyond the original tax filing date. For example, taxpayers who file Form 4868 may get an automatic extension of four months to file their tax returns with the IRS. Though the return will then be due on August 15, the estimated tax is still due on the original filing date of April 15.

EXTERNAL FUNDS funds brought in from outside the corporation, perhaps in the form of a bank loan, or the proceeds from a bond offering, or an infusion of cash from venture capitalists. External funds supplement internally generated CASH FLOW and are used for expansion, as well as for seasonal WORKING CAPITAL needs.

EXTRA DIVIDEND dividend paid to shareholders in addition to the regular dividend. Such a payment is made after a particularly profitable year in order to reward shareholders and engender loyalty.

EXTRAORDINARY CALL early redemption of a revenue bond by the issuer due to elimination of the source of revenue to pay the stipulated interest. For example, a mortgage revenue municipal bond may be subject to an extraordinary call if the issuer is unable to originate mortgages to homeowners because mortgage rates have dropped sharply, making the issuer's normally below-market mortgage interest rate suddenly higher than market rates. In this case, the bond issuer is required to return the money raised from the bond issue to bondholders because the issuer will not be able to realize the expected interest payments from mortgages. Extraordinary calls may also be necessary if another revenue-producing project such as a road or bridge is not able to be built for some reason. Calls are usually made at PAR. Also called a *special call.*

EXTRAORDINARY ITEM nonrecurring occurrence that must be explained to shareholders in an annual or quarterly report. Some examples: writeoff of a division, acquisition of another company, sale of a large amount of real estate, or uncovering of employee fraud that negatively affects the company's financial condition. Earnings are usually reported before and after taking into account the effects of extraordinary items.

EX-WARRANTS stock sold with the buyer no longer entitled to the WARRANT attached to the stock. Warrants allow the holder to buy stock at some future date at a specified price. Someone buying a stock on June 3 that had gone ex-warrants on June 1 would not receive those warrants. They would be the property of the stockholder of record on June 1.

f

FACE-AMOUNT CERTIFICATE debt security issued by face-amount certificate companies, one of three categories of mutual funds defined by the INVESTMENT COMPANY ACT OF 1940. The holder makes periodic payments to the issuer, and the issuer promises to pay the purchaser the face value at maturity or a surrender value if the certificate is presented prior to maturity.

FACE VALUE value of a bond, note, mortgage, or other security as given on the certificate or instrument. Corporate bonds are usually issued with $1000 face values, municipal bonds with $5000 face values, and federal government bonds with $10,000 face values. Although the bonds fluctuate in price from the time they are issued until redemption, they are redeemed at maturity at their face value, unless the issuer defaults. If the bonds are retired before maturity, bondholders normally receive a slight premium over face value. The face value is the amount on which interest payments are calculated. Thus, a 10% bond with a face value of $1000 pays bondholders $100 per year. Face value is also referred to as PAR VALUE or *nominal value.*

FACTORING type of financial service whereby a firm sells or transfers title to its accounts receivable to a factoring company, which then acts as principal, not as agent. The receivables are sold without recourse, meaning that the factor cannot turn to the seller in the event accounts prove uncollectible. Factoring can be done either on a *notification basis,* where the seller's customers remit directly to the factor, or on a *non-notification basis,* where the seller handles the collections and remits to the factor. There are two basic types of factoring:

1. **Discount factoring** arrangement whereby seller receives funds from the factor prior to the average maturity date, based on the invoice amount of the receivable, less cash discounts, less an allowance for estimated claims, returns, etc. Here the factor is compensated by an interest rate based on daily balances and typically 2% to 3% above the bank prime rate.

2. **Maturity factoring** arrangement whereby the factor, who performs the entire credit and collection function, remits to the seller for the receivables sold each month on the average due date of the factored receivables. The factor's commission on this kind of arrangement ranges from 0.75% to 2%, depending on the bad debt risk and the handling costs.

Factors also accommodate clients with "overadvances," loans in anticipation of sales, which permit inventory building prior to peak selling periods. Factoring has traditionally been most closely associated with the garment industry, but is used by companies in other industries as well.

FAIL POSITION securities undelivered due to the failure of selling clients to deliver the securities to their brokers so the latter can deliver them to the buying brokers. Since brokers are constantly buying and selling, receiving and delivering, the term usually refers to a net delivery position—that is, a given broker owes more securities to other brokers on sell transactions than other brokers owe to it on buy transactions. *See also* FAIL TO DELIVER; FAIL TO RECEIVE.

FAIL TO DELIVER situation where the broker-dealer on the sell side of a contract has not delivered securities to the broker-dealer on the buy side. A fail to deliver is usually the result of a broker not receiving delivery from its selling customer. As long as a fail to deliver exists. the seller will not receive payment. *See also* FAIL TO RECEIVE.

FAIL TO RECEIVE situation where the broker-dealer on the buy side of a contract has not received delivery of securities from the broker-dealer on the sell side. As long as a fail to receive exists, the buyer will not make payment for the securities. *See also* FAIL TO DELIVER.

FAIR CREDIT BILLING ACT federal law designed to facilitate the handling of credit complaints and eliminate abusive credit billing practices. For example, the law requires that bills be sent within a prescribed length of time and that consumers' complaints about credit bills be answered promptly.

FAIR CREDIT REPORTING ACT (FCRA) federal law enacted in 1971 giving persons the right to see their credit records at credit reporting bureaus. Designed to improve the confidentiality and accuracy of credit reports, the law is enforced by the FEDERAL TRADE COMMISSION (FTC) and state consumer protection agencies. Individuals may challenge and correct negative aspects of their record if they can prove there is a mistake. Consumers may also submit statements explaining why they received certain negative credit marks. Congress passed amendments to the FCRA that went into effect on October 1, 1997 which augmented consumers' privacy rights and further protected the accuracy of credit report information. For example, the amendments made it a civil law violation for someone to obtain a consumer report without a permissible purpose. Consumers must now give written permission before their credit reports are obtained for employment purposes. Consumers also have the right not to be included in direct mail or telemarketing solicitations based on prescreened lists obtained from credit bureaus. The amendments also state that when a consumer disputes information, the consumer reporting agency and the original furnisher of the information must investigate the claim. Agencies must finish their investigations within 30 days and report their results back to consumers. Consumers can to obtain a copy of their consumer report for a fee not to exceed $8. The law also stipulates that there be a "date certain" for the calculation of the length of time that information can remain in consumer report files in situations involving collections or charge-offs. *See also* CREDIT RATING.

FAIR MARKET VALUE price at which an asset or service passes from a willing seller to a willing buyer. It is assumed that both buyer and seller are rational and have a reasonable knowledge of relevant facts. *See also* MARKET.

FAIRNESS OPINION professional judgment offered for a fee by an investment banker on the fairness of the price being offered in a merger, takeover, or leveraged buyout. For example, if management is trying to take over a company in a leveraged buyout, it will need a fairness opinion from an independent source to verify that the price being offered is adequate and in the best interests of shareholders. If shareholders sue on the grounds that the offer is not adequate, management will rely on the fairness opinion in court to prove its case. Fairness opinions are also obtained when a majority shareholder is trying to buy out the minority shareholders of a company.

FAIR RATE OF RETURN level of profit that a utility is allowed to earn as determined by federal and/or state regulators. Public utility commissions set the fair rate of return based on the utility's needs to maintain service to its customers, pay adequate dividends to shareholders and interest to bondholders, and maintain and expand plant and equipment.

FAIR TRADE ACTS state laws protecting manufacturers from price-cutting by permitting them to establish minimum retail prices for their goods. Fair trade pricing was effectively eliminated in 1975 when Congress repealed the federal laws upholding resale price maintenance.

FALLEN ANGELS bonds that were INVESTMENT GRADE at the time they were issued but have since declined in quality to below investment grade (BB or lower). Fallen angels are a type of JUNK BOND, but the latter term is usually reserved for bonds that are originally issued with ratings of BB or lower.

FALL OUT OF BED sharp drop in a stock's price, usually in response to negative corporate developments. For example, a stock may fall out of bed if a takeover deal falls apart or if profits in the latest period fall far short of expectations.

FAMILY OF FUNDS *see* FUND FAMILY.

FANNIE MAE (FEDERAL NATIONAL MORTGAGE ASSOCIATION) publicly owned, government-sponsored corporation established in 1938 to purchase both government-backed and conventional mortgages from lenders and securitize them. Its objective is to increase the affordability of home mortgage funds for low-, moderate- and middle-income home buyers. Fannie Mae is a congressionally chartered, shareholder-owned company, and the largest source of home mortgage funds in the United States. Fannie Mae is a large issuer of debt securities which are used to finance its activities. Equity shares of Fannie Mae are traded on the New York Stock Exchange.

FARMER MAC see FEDERAL AGRICULTURAL MORTGAGE CORPORATION.

FARMER'S HOME ADMINISTRATION (FHA) federal agency under the Department of Agriculture that makes loans in low-income, rural areas of the United States for farms, homes, and community facilities.

FAR MONTH trading month that is farthest in the future in an options or futures contract. This may be a few months or up to a year or more. Under normal conditions, there is far less trading activity in the far month contracts than in the NEAREST MONTH or SPOT DELIVERY MONTH contracts. Also called *furthest month.*

FARTHER OUT; FARTHER IN relative length of option-contract maturities with reference to the present. For example, an options investor in January would call an option expiring in October farther out than an option expiring in July. The July option is farther in than the October option. *See also* DIAGONAL SPREAD.

FASB see FINANCIAL ACCOUNTING STANDARDS BOARD.

FAT CAT wealthy person who has become lazy living off the dividends and interest from investments. Fat cats also tend to be offered special treatment by brokers and other financial professionals because they have so much money and their accounts can therefore generate large fees and commissions.

FAVORABLE TRADE BALANCE situation that exists when the value of a nation's exports is in excess of the value of its imports. *See* BALANCE OF PAYMENTS; BALANCE OF TRADE.

FAVORITE FIFTY *See* NIFTY FIFTY.

FEDERAL AGENCY SECURITY debt instrument issued by an agency of the federal government such as the Federal National Mortgage Association, Federal Farm Credit Bank, and the Tennessee Valley Authority (TVA). Though not general obligations of the U.S. Treasury, such securities are sponsored by the government and therefore have high safety ratings.

FEDERAL AGRICULTURAL MORTGAGE CORPORATION federal agency established in 1988 to provide a secondary market for farm mortgage loans. Informally called *Farmer Mac.*

FEDERAL DEFICIT (SURPLUS) federal shortfall that results when the government spends more in a fiscal year than it receives in revenue. To cover the shortfall, the government usually borrows from the public by floating long- and short-term debt. Federal deficits, which started to rise in the 1970s, exploded to enormous proportions of hundreds of billions of dollars per year in the 80s and 90s. By the late 90s, revenues from an extended period of strong economic growth and soaring stock prices were applied to eliminate the deficit in accordance with budget balancing legislation which resulted in a *federal surplus.* Though this scenario did not come to pass in the '80s and '90s, some economists think that massive federal deficits can lead to high interest rates and inflation, since they compete with private borrowing by consumers and businesses. Deficits also add to the demand for money from the FEDERAL RESERVE BANK. *See also* CROWDING OUT; NATIONAL DEBT.

FEDERAL DEPOSIT INSURANCE CORPORATION (FDIC) federal agency established in 1933 that guarantees (within limits) funds on deposit in member banks and thrift institutions and performs other functions such as making loans to or buying assets from member institutions to facilitate mergers or prevent failures. In 1989, Congress passed savings and loan association bailout legislation that reorganized FDIC into two insurance units: the BANK INSURANCE FUND (BIF) continues the traditional FDIC functions with respect to banking institutions; the SAVINGS ASSOCIATION INSURANCE FUND (SAIF) insures thrift institution deposits, replacing the FEDERAL SAVINGS AND LOAN INSURANCE CORPORATION (FSLIC), which ceased to exist. *See also* OFFICE OF THRIFT SUPERVISION (OTS).

FEDERAL FARM CREDIT BANK government-sponsored institution that consolidates the financing activities of the Federal Land Banks, the Federal Intermediate Credit Banks, and the Banks for Cooperatives. *See* FEDERAL FARM CREDIT SYSTEM.

FEDERAL FARM CREDIT SYSTEM system established by the Farm Credit Act of 1971 to provide credit services to farmers and farm-related enterprises through a network of 12 Farm Credit districts. Each district has a Federal Land Bank, a Federal Intermediate Credit Bank, and a Bank for Cooperatives to carry out policies of the system. The system sells short-term (5- to 270-day) notes in increments of $50,000 on a discounted basis through a national syndicate of securities dealers. Rates are set by the FEDERAL FARM CREDIT BANK, a unit established to consolidate the financing activities of the various banks. An active secondary market is maintained by several dealers. The system also issues Federal Farm Credit System Consolidated Systemwide Bonds on a monthly basis with 6- and 9-month maturities. The bonds are sold in increments of $5000 with rates set by the system. The bonds enjoy a secondary market even more active than that for the discounted notes. *See also* SECONDARY MARKET.

FEDERAL FINANCING BANK (FFB) U.S. government-owned bank that consolidates financing activities of government AGENCIES in order to reduce borrowing costs.

FEDERAL FUNDS
1. funds deposited by commercial banks at Federal Reserve Banks, including funds in excess of bank reserve requirements. Banks may lend federal funds to each other on an overnight basis at the federal funds rate. Member banks may also transfer funds among themselves or on behalf of customers on a same-day basis by debiting and crediting balances in the various reserve banks. *See* FED WIRE.
2. money used by the Federal Reserve to pay for its purchases of government securities.
3. funds used to settle transactions where there is no FLOAT.

FEDERAL FUNDS RATE interest rate charged by banks with excess reserves at a Federal Reserve district bank to banks needing overnight loans to meet reserve requirements. The federal funds rate is the most sensitive indicator of the direction of interest rates, since it is set daily by the market, unlike the PRIME RATE and the DISCOUNT RATE, which are periodically changed by banks and by the Federal Reserve Board, respectively.

FEDERAL GIFT TAX federal tax imposed on the transfer of securities, property, or other assets. The donor must pay the tax based on the fair market value of the transferred assets. However, federal law allows donors to give up to $10,000 per year to any individual without incurring gift tax liability. So, a husband and wife may gift $20,000 to their child in one year without tax if each parent gives $10,000. This practice is known as GIFT SPLITTING. According to the TAXPAYER RELIEF ACT OF 1997, this gift tax limit is indexed to inflation in $1,000 increments, starting on January 1, 1999. For those making gifts over the limit, a gift tax return using IRS Form 709 must be filed by April 15th of the year following the year of the gift.

FEDERAL HOME LOAN BANK SYSTEM system supplying credit reserves for SAVINGS AND LOANS, cooperative banks, and other mortgage lenders in a manner similar to the Federal Reserve's role with commercial banks. The Federal Home Loan Bank System is made up of 12 regional Federal Home Loan Banks. It raises money by issuing notes and bonds and lends money to savings and loans and other mortgage lenders based on the amount of collateral the institution can provide. The system was established in 1932 after a massive wave of bank failures. In 1989, Congress passed savings and loan bailout legislation revamping the regulatory structure of the industry. The Federal Home Loan Bank Board was dismantled and replaced with the FEDERAL HOUSING FINANCE BOARD, which now oversees the home loan bank system. *See also* OFFICE OF THRIFT SUPERVISION (OTS).

FEDERAL HOME LOAN MORTGAGE CORPORATION (FHLMC) publicly chartered agency that buys qualifying residential mortgages from lenders, packages them into new securities backed by those pooled mortgages, provides certain guarantees, and then resells the securities on the open market. The corporation's stock is owned by savings institutions across the U.S. and is held in trust by the Federal Home Loan Bank System. The corporation, nicknamed Freddie Mac, has created an enormous secondary market, which provides more funds for mortgage lending and allows investors to buy high-yielding securities backed by federal guarantees. Freddie Mac formerly packaged only mortgages backed by the Veteran's Administration or the Federal Housing Administration, but now it also resells nongovernmentally backed mortgages. The corporation was established in 1970. *See also* MORTGAGE BACKED CERTIFICATES.

FEDERAL HOUSING ADMINISTRATION (FHA) federally sponsored agency that insures lenders against loss on residential mortgages. It was founded in 1934 in response to the Great Depression to execute the provisions of the National Housing Act. The FHA was the forerunner of a group of government agencies responsible for the growing secondary market for mortgages, such as the Government National Mortgage Association (Ginnie Mae) and the Federal National Mortgage Association (Fannie Mae).

FEDERAL HOUSING FINANCE BOARD (FHFB) U.S. government agency created by Congress in 1989 to assume oversight of the FEDERAL HOME LOAN BANK SYSTEM from the dismantled Federal Home Loan Bank Board. *See also* OFFICE OF THRIFT SUPERVISION (OTS).

FEDERAL INCOME TAXES *see* INCOME TAXES.

FEDERAL INSURANCE CONTRIBUTIONS ACT (FICA) commonly known as Social Security, the federal law requiring employers to withhold wages and make payments to a government trust fund providing retirement and other benefits. *See also* SOCIAL SECURITY.

FEDERAL INTERMEDIATE CREDIT BANK one of 12 banks that make funds available to production credit associations, commercial banks, agricultural credit corporations, livestock loan companies, and other institutions extending credit to crop farmers and cattle raisers. Their stock is owned by farmers and ranchers, and the banks raise funds largely from the public sale of short-term debentures. *See also* FEDERAL FARM CREDIT BANK; FEDERAL FARM CREDIT SYSTEM.

FEDERAL LAND BANK one of 12 banks under the U.S. Farm Credit Administration that extends long-term mortgage credit to crop farmers and cattle raisers for buying land, refinancing debts, or other agricultural purposes. To obtain a loan, a farmer or rancher must purchase stock equal to 5% of the loan in any one of approximately 500 local land bank associations; these, in turn, purchase an equal amount of stock in the Federal Land Bank. The stock is retired when the loan is repaid. The banks raise funds by issuing Consolidated Systemwide Bonds to the public. *See also* FEDERAL FARM CREDIT BANK; FEDERAL FARM CREDIT SYSTEM.

FEDERAL NATIONAL MORTGAGE ASSOCIATION (FNMA) publicly owned, government-sponsored corporation chartered in 1938 to purchase mortgages from lenders and resell them to investors. The agency, known by the nickname Fannie Mae, mostly packages mortgages backed by the Federal Housing Administration, but also sells some nongovernmentally backed mortgages. Shares of FNMA itself, known as Fannie Maes, are traded on the New York Stock Exchange. The price usually soars when interest rates fall and plummets when interest rates rise, since the mortgage business is so dependent on the direction of interest rates.

FEDERAL OPEN-MARKET COMMITTEE (FOMC) committee that sets interest rate and credit policies for the Federal Reserve System, the United States' central bank. The FOMC has 12 members. Seven are the members of the Federal Reserve Board, appointed by the president of the United States. The other five are presidents of the 12 regional Federal Reserve banks. Of the five, four are picked on a rotating basis; the other is the president of the Federal Reserve Bank of New York, who is a permanent member. The Committee decides whether to increase or decrease interest rates through open-market operations of buying or selling government securities. The Committee's decisions are closely watched and interpreted by economists and stock and bond market analysts, who try to predict whether the Fed is seeking to tighten credit to reduce inflation or to loosen credit to stimulate the economy.

FEDERAL RESERVE BANK one of the 12 banks that, with their branches, make up the FEDERAL RESERVE SYSTEM. These banks are located in Boston, New York, Philadelphia, Cleveland, Richmond, Atlanta, Chicago, St. Louis, Minneapolis, Kansas City, Dallas, and San Francisco. The role of each Federal Reserve Bank is to monitor the commercial and savings banks in its region to ensure that they follow Federal Reserve Board regulations and to provide those banks with access to emergency funds from the DISCOUNT WINDOW. The reserve banks act as depositories for member banks in their regions, providing money transfer and other services. Each of the banks is owned by the member banks in its district.

FEDERAL RESERVE BOARD (FRB) governing board of the FEDERAL RESERVE SYSTEM. Its seven members are appointed by the president of the United States, subject to Senate confirmation, and serve 14-year terms. The Board establishes Federal Reserve System policies on such key matters as reserve requirements and other bank regulations, sets the discount rate, tightens or loosens the availability of credit in the economy, and regulates the purchase of securities on margin.

FEDERAL RESERVE OPEN-MARKET COMMITTEE *see* FEDERAL OPEN-MARKET COMMITTEE.

FEDERAL RESERVE SYSTEM system established by the Federal Reserve Act of 1913 to regulate the U.S. monetary and banking system. The Federal Reserve System (the Fed) is comprised of 12 regional Federal Reserve Banks, their 24 branches, and all national and state banks that are part of the system. National banks are stockholders of the FEDERAL RESERVE BANK in their region.

The Federal Reserve System's main functions are to regulate the national money supply, set reserve requirements for member banks, supervise the printing of currency at the mint, act as clearinghouse for the transfer of funds throughout the banking system, and examine member banks to make sure they meet various Federal Reserve regulations. Although the members of the system's governing board are appointed by the President of the United States and confirmed by the Senate, the Federal Reserve System is considered an independent entity, which is supposed to make its decisions free of political influence. Governors are appointed for terms of 14 years, which further assures their independence. *See also* FEDERAL OPEN-MARKET COMMITTEE; FEDERAL RESERVE BOARD; OPEN-MARKET OPERATIONS.

FEDERAL SAVINGS AND LOAN ASSOCIATION federally chartered institution with a primary responsibility to collect people's savings deposits and to provide mortgage loans for residential housing. Federal Savings and Loans may be owned either by stockholders, who can trade their shares on stock exchanges, or by depositors, in which case the associations are considered mutual organizations. Federal Savings and Loans are members of the Federal Home Loan Bank System. After deregulation, S&Ls expanded into nonhousing-related financial services such as discount stock brokerage, financial planning, credit cards, and consumer loans. *See also* FINANCIAL SUPERMARKET; MUTUAL ASSOCIATION; OFFICE OF THRIFT SUPERVISION (OTS); SAVINGS AND LOAN ASSOCIATION.

FEDERAL SAVINGS AND LOAN INSURANCE CORPORATION (FSLIC) federal agency established in 1934 to insure deposits in member savings institutions. In 1989, Congress passed savings and loan bailout legislation revamping the regulatory structure of the industry. FSLIC was disbanded and its insurance activities were assumed by a new agency, SAVINGS ASSOCIATION INSURANCE FUND (SAIF), a unit of the FEDERAL DEPOSIT INSURANCE CORPORATION (FDIC). Responsibility for insolvent institutions previously under FSLIC's jurisdiction was assumed by another newly created agency, RESOLUTION FUNDING CORPORATION (REFCORP). *See also* OFFICE OF THRIFT SUPERVISION (OTS).

FEDERAL SURPLUS *see* FEDERAL DEFICIT (SURPLUS).

FEDERAL TRADE COMMISSION (FTC) federal agency established in 1914 to foster free and fair business competition and prevent monopolies and activities in restraint of trade. It administers both antitrust and consumer protection legislation.

FEDERAL UNEMPLOYMENT TAX ACT (FUTA) legislation under which federal and state governments require employers (and in some states, such as New Jersey, employees) to contribute to a fund that pays unemployment insurance benefits.

FED PASS move by the Federal Reserve to add reserves to the banking system, thereby making credit more available. The Fed will initiate an open-market operation when it wants to add or subtract reserves in the banking system. It transacts these operations through a group of dealers called PRIMARY DEALERS, banks or security houses with which the Fed has agreed to do business. For example, the buying of securities by the Federal Reserve can be done in such a way that will make reserves more available, thus encouraging banks to lend and making credit easier to obtain by consumer and business borrowers.

FED WIRE high-speed, computerized communications network that connects all 12 Federal Reserve Banks, their 24 branches, the Federal Reserve Board office in Washington, D.C., U.S. Treasury offices in Washington, D.C., and Chicago, and the Washington, D.C. office of the Commodity Credit Corporation; also spelled FedWire and Fedwire. The Fed wire has been called the central nervous system of money transfer in the United States. It enables banks to transfer reserve balances from one to another for immediate available credit and to transfer balances for business customers. Using the Fed wire, Federal Reserve Banks can settle interdistrict transfers resulting from check collections, and the Treasury can shift balances from its accounts in different reserve banks quickly and without cost. It is also possible to transfer bearer short-term government securities within an hour at no cost. This is done through a procedure called CPD (Commissioner of Public Debt of the Treasury) transfers, whereby one Federal Reserve Bank "retires" a seller's security, while another reserve bank makes delivery of a like amount of the same security from its unissued stock to the buyer.

FICA *see* FEDERAL INSURANCE CONTRIBUTIONS ACT.

FICO *see* FINANCING CORPORATION.

FICTITIOUS CREDIT the credit balance in a securities MARGIN ACCOUNT representing the proceeds from a short sale and the margin requirement under Federal Reserve Board REGULATION T (which regulates margin credit). Because the proceeds, which are held as security for the loan of securities made by the broker to effect the short sale, and the margin requirement are both there to protect the broker's position, the money is not available for withdrawal by the customer; hence the term "fictitious" credit. It is in contrast to a free credit balance, which can be withdrawn anytime.

FIDELITY BOND *see* BLANKET FIDELITY BOND.

FIDUCIARY person, company, or association holding assets in trust for a beneficiary. The fiduciary is charged with the responsibility of investing the money wisely for the beneficiary's benefit. Some examples of fiduciaries are executors of wills and estates, receivers in bankruptcy, trustees, and those who administer the assets of underage or incompetent beneficiaries. Most U.S. states have laws about what a fiduciary may or may not do with a beneficiary's assets. For instance, it is illegal for fiduciaries to invest or misappropriate the money for their personal gain. *See also* LEGAL LIST; PRUDENT-MAN RULE.

FIFO *see* FIRST IN, FIRST OUT.

FILING STATUS category a taxpayer chooses in filing a tax return. It determines the filing requirements, standard deduction, eligibility to claim certain deductions and credits, and tax rates. Filing status is determined on the last day of the tax year. The four filing status categories are single, married filing jointly, married filing separately, and head of household. Depending upon the taxpayer's family situation and income, it is more advantageous to file using one category over others. Many accountants figure out a taxpayer's liability using two filing statuses—filing jointly or filing separately—to calculate which one results in the lower tax.

FILL execute a customer's order to buy or sell a stock, bond, or commodity. An order is filled when the amount of the security requested is supplied. When less than the full amount of the order is supplied, it is known as a *partial fill.*

FILL OR KILL (FOK) order to buy or sell a particular security which, if not executed immediately, is canceled. Often, fill or kill orders are placed when a client wants to buy a large quantity of shares of a particular stock at a particular price. If the order is not executed because it will significantly upset the market price for that stock, the order is withdrawn.

FINANCE CHARGE cost of credit, including interest, paid by a customer for a consumer loan. Under the Truth-in-Lending Act, the finance charge must be disclosed to the customer in advance. *See also* CONSUMER CREDIT PROTECTION ACT OF 1968; REGULATION Z.

FINANCE COMPANY company engaged in making loans to individuals or businesses. Unlike a bank, it does not receive deposits but rather obtains its financing from banks, institutions, and other money market sources. Generally, finance companies fall into three categories: (1) consumer finance companies, also known as *small loan* or *direct loan companies,* lend money to individuals under the small loan laws of the individual U.S. states; (2) sales finance companies, also called *acceptance companies,* purchase retail and wholesale paper from automobile and other consumer and capital goods dealers; (3) commercial finance companies, also called *commercial credit companies,* make loans to manufacturers and wholesalers; these loans are secured by accounts receivable, inventories, and equipment. Finance companies typically enjoy high credit ratings and are thus able to borrow at the lowest market rates, enabling them to make loans at rates not much higher than banks. Even though their customers usually do not qualify for bank credit, these companies have experienced a low rate of default. Finance companies in general tend to be interest rate-sensitive—increases and decreases in market interest rates affect their profits directly. For this reason, publicly held finance companies are sometimes referred to as money stocks. *See also* CAPTIVE FINANCE COMPANY.

FINANCIAL ACCOUNTING STANDARDS BOARD (FASB) independent board responsible for establishing and interpreting generally accepted accounting principles. It was formed in 1973 to succeed and continue the activities of the Accounting Principles Board (APB). *See* GENERALLY ACCEPTED ACCOUNTING PRINCIPLES.

FINANCIAL ADVISER professional adviser offering financial counsel. Some financial advisers charge a fee and earn commissions on the products they recommend to implement their advice. Other advisers only charge fees, and do not sell any products or accept commissions. Some financial advisers are generalists, while others specialize in specific areas such as investing, insurance, estate planning, taxes, or other areas.

FINANCIAL ANALYSIS analysis of the FINANCIAL STATEMENT of a company. *See also* FUNDAMENTAL ANALYSIS.

FINANCIAL ASSETS assets in the form of stocks, bonds, rights, certificates, bank balances, etc., as distinguished from tangible, physical assets. For example, real property is a physical asset, but shares in a REAL ESTATE INVESTMENT TRUST (REIT) or the stock or bonds of a company that held property as an investment would be financial assets.

FINANCIAL FUTURE FUTURES CONTRACT based on a financial instrument. Such contracts usually move under the influence of interest rates. As rates rise, contracts fall in value; as rates fall, contracts gain in value. Examples of instruments underlying financial futures contracts: Treasury bills, Treasury notes, Government National Mortgage Association (Ginnie Mae) pass-throughs, foreign currencies, and certificates of deposit. Trading in these contracts is governed by the federal Commodities Futures Trading Commission. Traders use these futures to speculate on the direction of interest rates. Financial institutions (banks, insurance companies, brokerage firms) use them to hedge financial portfolios against adverse fluctuations in interest rates.

FINANCIAL GUARANTEE INSURANCE covers losses from specific financial transactions. The coverage guarantees investors in debt instruments that they will receive timely payment of principal and interest if there is a default on underlying debts. For example, this insurance backs loan portfolios composed of credit card and auto loans.

FINANCIAL INSTITUTION institution that collects funds from the public to place in financial assets such as stocks, bonds, money market instruments, bank deposits, or loans. Depository institutions (banks, savings and loans, savings banks, credit unions) pay interest on deposits and invest the deposit money mostly in loans. Nondepository institutions (insurance companies, pension plans) collect money by selling insurance policies or receiving employer contributions and pay it out for legitimate claims or for retirement benefits. Increasingly, many institutions are performing both depository and nondepository functions. For instance, brokerage firms now place customers' money in certificates of deposit and money market funds and sell insurance. *See* FINANCIAL SUPERMARKET.

FINANCIAL INSTITUTIONS REFORM, RECOVERY AND ENFORCEMENT ACT OF 1989 (FIRREA) legislation enacted into law on August 9, 1989, to resolve the crisis affecting U.S. savings and loan associations. Known as the *bailout bill,* it revamped the regulatory, insurance, and financing structures and established the OFFICE OF THRIFT SUPERVISION. The act created (1) the RESOLUTION TRUST CORPORATION (RTC), which, operating under the management of the FEDERAL DEPOSIT INSURANCE CORPORATION (FDIC), was charged with closing or merging institutions that had become insolvent beginning in 1989; (2) the RESOLUTION FUNDING CORPORATION (REFCORP), charged with borrowing from private capital markets to fund RTC activities and to manage the remaining assets and liabilities taken over by the FEDERAL SAVINGS AND LOAN INSURANCE CORPORATION (FSLIC) prior to 1989; (3) the SAVINGS ASSOCIATION INSURANCE FUND (SAIF) (pronounced "safe"), to replace FSLIC as insurer of thrift deposits and to be administered by the FDIC separately from its bank deposit insurance program, which became the BANK INSURANCE FUND (BIF); and (4) the FEDERAL HOUSING FINANCE BOARD (FHFB), charged with overseeing the FEDERAL HOME LOAN BANKS.

The RTC was authorized to accept additional insolvent institutions through June 1995; after that date, responsibilities for newly failed institutions shifted to the SAIF.

See also BAILOUT BOND.

FINANCIAL INTERMEDIARY commercial bank, savings and loan, mutual savings bank, credit union, or other "middleman" that smooths the flow of funds between "savings surplus units" and "savings deficit units." In an economy viewed as three sectors—households, businesses, and government—a *savings surplus unit* is one where income exceeds consumption; a *savings deficit unit* is one where current expenditures exceed current income and external sources must be called upon to make up the difference. As a whole, households are savings surplus units, whereas businesses and governments are savings deficit units. Financial intermediaries redistribute savings into productive uses and, in the process, serve two other important functions: By making savers infinitesimally small "shareholders" in huge pools of capital, which in turn are loaned out to a wide number and variety of borrowers, the intermediaries provide both diversification of risk and liquidity to the individual saver. *See also* DISINTERMEDIATION; FINDER'S FEE.

FINANCIAL LEASE lease in which the service provided by the lessor to the lessee is limited to financing equipment. All other responsibilities related to the possession of equipment, such as maintenance, insurance, and taxes, are borne by the lessee. A financial lease is usually noncancellable and is fully paid out *(amortized)* over its term.

FINANCIAL LEVERAGE *see* LEVERAGE.

FINANCIAL MARKET market for the exchange of capital and credit in the economy. Money markets concentrate on short-term debt instruments; capital markets trade in long-term debt and equity instruments. Examples of financial markets: stock market, bond market, commodities market, and foreign exchange market.

FINANCIAL NEEDS APPROACH technique to assess the proper amount of life insurance for an individual. The person, either on his or her own or with the help of an insurance adviser, must estimate the financial needs of survivors in case the person dies unexpectedly. Projections for expenses, income, taxes, funeral costs, and other financial factors lead to an understanding of the amount of insurance proceeds that would be needed to allow the survivors to continue in their present lifestyle. Once the optimal amount of insurance protection is determined, various kinds of TERM and CASH VALUE INSURANCE programs can be designed to meet these needs.

FINANCIAL PLANNER professional who analyzes personal financial circumstances and prepares a program to meet financial needs and objectives. Financial planners, who may be accountants, bankers, lawyers, insurance agents, real estate or securities brokers, or independent practitioners, should have knowledge in the areas of wills and estate planning, retirement planning, taxes, insurance, family budgeting, debt management, and investments.

Fee-only planners charge on the basis of service and time and have nothing to sell. *Commission-only planners* offer their services for free but sell commission-producing products such as MUTUAL FUNDS, LIMITED PARTNERSHIPS, insurance products, stocks, and bonds. *Fee-plus-commission planners* charge an upfront fee for consultation and their written plan, then charge commissions on the financial products they sell. *Fee-offset planners* charge fees against which they apply credits when they sell commission-producing products.

The Certified Financial Planner Board of Standards, Inc., in Denver, Colorado, issues the CERTIFIED FINANCIAL PLANNER (CFP) license, and the Institute of Certified Financial Planners, also in Denver, maintains a referral list. The International Association for Financial Planning (IAFP) in Atlanta, Georgia, provides a list of financial planners with CFA, CFP, ChFC, or CPA designation; a law or financial planning degree; or those who have completed its Practical Knowledge Examination. The American Institute of Certified Public Accountants in New York City provides a list of CPAs who offer financial planning services; The National Association of Personal Financial Advisors (NAPFA) in Buffalo Grove, Illinois, lists fee-only planners. The National Endowment for Financial Education, in Denver, offers a financial planning starter kit to consumers, on request.

FINANCIAL POSITION status of a firm's assets, liabilities, and equity accounts as of a certain time, as shown on its FINANCIAL STATEMENT. Also called *financial condition.*

FINANCIAL PUBLIC RELATIONS branch of public relations specializing in corporate disclosure responsibilities, stockholder relations, and relations with the professional investor community. Financial public relations is concerned not only with matters of corporate image and the cultivation of a favorable financial and investment environment but also with legal interpretation and adherence to Securities and Exchange Commission and other government regulations, as well as with the DISCLOSURE requirements of the securities exchanges. Its practitioners, therefore, include lawyers with expertise in such areas as tender offers and takeovers, public offerings, proxy solicitation, and insider trading. *See also* INVESTOR RELATIONS DEPARTMENT.

FINANCIAL PYRAMID
1. risk structure many investors aim for in spreading their investments between low-, medium-, and high-risk vehicles. In a financial pyramid, the largest part of the investor's assets is in safe, liquid investments that provide a decent return. Next, some money is invested in stocks and bonds that provide good income and the possibility for long-term growth of capital. Third, a smaller portion of one's capital is committed to speculative investments which may offer higher returns if they work out well. At the top of the financial pyramid, where only a small amount of money is committed, are high-risk ventures

that have a slight chance of success, but which will provide substantial rewards if they succeed.

2. acquisition of holding company assets through financial leverage. *See* PYRAMIDING.

Financial pyramid is not to be confused with fraudulent selling schemes, also sometimes called *pyramiding.*

FINANCIAL STATEMENT written record of the financial status of an individual, association, or business organization. The financial statement includes a BALANCE SHEET and an INCOME STATEMENT (or operating statement or profit and loss statement) and may also include a STATEMENT OF CASH FLOWS, a statement of changes in retained earnings, and other analyses.

FINANCIAL STRUCTURE makeup of the right-hand side of a company's BALANCE SHEET, which includes all the ways its assets are financed, such as trade accounts payable and short-term borrowings as well as long-term debt and ownership equity. Financial structure is distinguished from CAPITAL STRUCTURE, which includes only long-term debt and equity. A company's financial structure is influenced by a number of factors, including the growth rate and stability of its sales, its competitive situation (i.e., the stability of its profits), its asset structure, and the attitudes of its management and its lenders. It is the basic frame of reference for analyses concerned with financial leveraging decisions.

FINANCIAL SUPERMARKET company that offers a wide range of financial services under one roof. For example, some large retail organizations offer stock, insurance, and real estate brokerage, as well as banking services. For customers, having all their assets with one institution can make financial transactions and planning more convenient and efficient, since money does not constantly have to be shifted from one institution to another. For institutions, such all-inclusive relationships are more profitable than dealing with just one aspect of a customer's financial needs. Institutions often become financial supermarkets in order to capture all the business of their customers.

FINANCIAL TABLES tables found in newspapers listing prices, dividends, yields, price/earnings ratios, trading volume, and other important data on stocks, bonds, mutual funds, and futures contracts. While local newspapers may carry limited tables, more extensive listings are available in *Barron's, Investor's Business Daily,* the *Wall Street Journal,* and other publications.

FINANCING CORPORATION (FICO) agency set up by Congress in 1987 to issue bonds and bail out the FEDERAL SAVINGS AND LOAN INSURANCE CORPORATION (FSLIC). *See also* BAILOUT BOND.

FINDER'S FEE fee charged by a person or company acting as a finder (intermediary) in a transaction.

FINEX financial derivatives division of the NEW YORK COTTON EXCHANGE with a trading floor in Dublin, FINEX Europe, creating a 24-hour market in most FINEX contracts. FINEX/FINEX Europe trades futures and futures options on the U.S. Dollar Index, currencies, and cross-rate currencies. Futures and options on Treasury auction five-year U.S. Treasury note futures and Treasury auction two-year U.S. Treasury note futures are traded only in New York. *See also* SECURITIES AND COMMODITIES EXCHANGES.

FINITE LIFE REAL ESTATE INVESTMENT TRUST (FREIT) REAL ESTATE INVESTMENT TRUST (REIT) that promises to try to sell its holdings within a specified period to realize CAPITAL GAINS.

FIREWALL the legal separation of banking and broker/dealer operations within a financial institution. Under the GLASS-STEAGALL ACT OF 1933, banks are not allowed to own or control broker/dealers, though in recent years banks have offered many of the services traditionally provided by brokers. A firewall would prevent a bank from lending money to a securities affiliate, for example. To some extent, the separation is maintained to protect the FDIC insurance fund and insured bank deposits from the risks associated with the brokerage business.

FIRM
1. general term for a business, corporation, partnership, or proprietorship. Legally, a firm is not considered a corporation since it may not be incorporated and since the firm's principals are not recognized as separate from the identity of the firm itself. This might be true of a law or accounting firm, for instance.
2. solidity with which an agreement is made. For example, a firm order with a manufacturer or a firm bid for a stock at a particular price means that the order or bid is assured.

FIRM COMMITMENT
Lending: term used by lenders to refer to an agreement to make a loan to a specific borrower within a specific period of time and, if applicable, on a specific property. *See also* COMMITMENT FEE.

Securities underwriting: arrangement whereby investment bankers make outright purchases from the issuer of securities to be offered to the public; also called *firm commitment underwriting*. The underwriters, as the investment bankers are called in such an arrangement, make their profit on the difference between the purchase price—determined through either competitive bidding or negotiation—and the public offering price. Firm commitment underwriting is to be distinguished from conditional arrangements for distributing new securities, such as standby commitments and best efforts commitments. The word *underwriting* is frequently misused with respect to such conditional arrangements. It is used correctly only with respect to firm commitment underwritings or, as they are sometimes called, BOUGHT DEALS. *See also* BEST EFFORT; STANDBY COMMITMENT.

FIRM ORDER
Commercial transaction: written or verbal order that has been confirmed and is not subject to cancellation.

Securities: (1) order to buy or sell for the proprietary account of the broker-dealer firm; (2) buy or sell order not conditional upon the customer's confirmation.

FIRM QUOTE securities industry term referring to any round lot bid or offer price of a security stated by a market maker and not identified as a nominal (or subject) quote. Under National Association of Securities Dealers' (NASD) rules and practice, quotes requiring further negotiation or review must be identified as nominal quotes. *See also* NOMINAL QUOTATION.

FIRREA *see* FINANCIAL INSTITUTIONS REFORM, RECOVERY AND ENFORCEMENT ACT.

FIRST BOARD delivery dates for futures as established by the Chicago Board of Trade and other exchanges trading in futures.

FIRST CALL Boston-based global investment research service providing research opinion and data on over 7000 companies from more than 400 brokers. First Call delivers fully-integrated global equity and fixed income research notes and reports, consensus earnings estimates and related information, corporate news and broker buy/sell/hold/ recommendations. First Call Corporate Services provides investor relations services to companies. *See also* I/B/E/S/ INTERNATIONAL INC.; ZACKS ESTIMATE SYSTEM.

FIRST CALL DATE first date specified in the indenture of a corporate or municipal bond contract on which part or all of the bond may be redeemed at a set price. An XYZ bond due in 2030, for instance, may have a first call date of May 1, 2013. This means that, if XYZ wishes, bondholders may be paid off starting on that date in 2013. Bond brokers typically quote yields on such bonds with both yield to maturity (in this case, 2030) and yield to call (in this case, 2013). *See also* DURATION; YIELD TO CALL; YIELD TO MATURITY.

FIRST IN, FIRST OUT (FIFO) method of accounting for inventory whereby, quite literally, the inventory is assumed to be sold in the chronological order in which it was purchased. For example, the following formula is used in computing the cost of goods sold:
Under the FIFO method, inventory costs flow from the oldest purchases forward, with beginning inventory as the starting point and ending inventory representing the most recent purchases. The FIFO method contrasts with the LIFO or LAST IN, FIRST OUT method, which is FIFO in reverse. The significance of the difference becomes apparent when inflation or deflation affects inventory prices. In an inflationary period, the FIFO method produces a higher ending inventory, a lower cost of goods sold figure, and a higher gross profit. LIFO, on the other hand, produces a lower ending inventory, a higher cost of goods sold figure, and a lower reported profit.

In accounting for the purchase and sale of securities for tax purposes, FIFO is assumed by the IRS unless it is advised of the use of an alternative method.

FIRST MORTGAGE real estate loan that gives the mortgagee (lender) a primary lien against a specified piece of property. A primary lien has precedence over all other mortgages in case of default. *See also* JUNIOR MORTGAGE; SECOND MORTGAGE.

FIRST PREFERRED STOCK preferred stock that has preferential claim on dividends and assets over other preferred issues and common stock.

FISCAL AGENT
1. usually a bank or a trust company acting for a corporation under a corporate trust agreement. The fiscal agent handles such matters as disbursing funds for dividend payments, redeeming bonds and coupons, handling taxes related to the issue of bonds, and paying rents.
2. agent of the national government or its agencies or of a state or municipal government that performs functions relating to the issue and payment of bonds. For example, the Federal Reserve is the U.S. government's fiscal agent.

FISCAL POLICY federal taxation and spending policies designed to level out the business cycle and achieve full employment, price stability, and sustained growth in the economy. Fiscal policy basically follows the economic theory of the 20th-century English economist John Maynard Keynes that insufficient demand causes unemployment and excessive demand leads to inflation. It aims to stimulate demand and output in periods of business decline by increasing government purchases and cutting taxes, thereby releasing more disposable income into the spending stream, and to correct overexpansion by reversing the process. Working to balance these deliberate fiscal measures are the so-called built-in stabilizers, such as the progressive income tax and unemployment benefits, which automatically respond countercyclically. Fiscal policy is administered independently of MONETARY POLICY, by which the Federal Reserve Board attempts to regulate economic activity by controlling the money supply. The goals of fiscal and monetary policy are the same, but Keynesians and Monetarists disagree as to which of the two approaches works best. At the basis of their differences are questions dealing with the velocity (turnover) of money and the effect of changes in the money supply on the equilibrium rate of interest (the rate at which money demand equals money supply). *See also* KEYNESIAN ECONOMICS.

FISCAL YEAR (FY) accounting period covering 12 consecutive months, 52 consecutive weeks, 13 four-week periods, or 365 consecutive days, at the end of which the books are closed and profit or loss is determined. A company's fiscal year is often, but not necessarily, the same as the calendar year. A seasonal business will frequently select a fiscal rather than a calendar year, so that its year-end figures will show it in its most liquid condition, which also means having less inventory to verify physically. The FY of the U.S. government ends September 30.

FIT a situation where the features of a particular investment perfectly match the portfolio requirements of an investor.

FITCH INVESTORS SERVICE, INC. New York- and Denver-based RATING firm, which rates corporate and municipal bonds, preferred stock, commercial paper, and obligations of health-care and not-for-profit institutions.

FITCH SHEETS sheets indicating the successive trade prices of securities listed on the major exchanges. They are published by Francis Emory Fitch, Inc. in New York City.

FIVE HUNDRED DOLLAR RULE REGULATION T provision of the Federal Reserve that exempts deficiencies in margin requirements amounting to $500 or less from mandatory remedial action. Brokers are thus not forced to resort to the liquidation of an account to correct a trivial deficiency in a situation where, for example, a customer is temporarily out of town and cannot be reached. *See also* MARGIN CALL.

FIVE PERCENT RULE one of the Rules of Fair Practice of the National Association of Securities Dealers (NASD). It proposes an ethical guideline for spreads in dealer transactions and commissions in brokerage transactions, including PROCEEDS SALES and RISKLESS TRANSACTIONS.

FIXATION setting of a present or future price of a commodity, such as the twice-daily London GOLD FIXING. In other commodities, prices are fixed further into the future for the benefit of both buyers and sellers of that commodity.

FIXED ANNUITY investment contract sold by an insurance company that guarantees fixed payments, either for life or for a specified period, to an annuitant. In fixed annuities, the insurer takes both the investment and the mortality risks. A fixed annuity contrasts with a VARIABLE ANNUITY, where payments depend on an uncertain outcome, such as prices in the securities markets. See *also* ANNUITY.

FIXED ASSET tangible property used in the operations of a business, but not expected to be consumed or converted into cash in the ordinary course of events. Plant, machinery and equipment, furniture and fixtures, and leasehold improvements comprise the fixed assets of most companies. They are normally represented on the balance sheet at their net depreciated value.

FIXED BENEFITS payments to a BENEFICIARY that are fixed rather than variable.

FIXED-CHARGE COVERAGE ratio of profits before payment of interest and income taxes to interest on bonds and other contractual long-term debt. It indicates how many times interest charges have been earned by the corporation on a pretax basis. Since failure to meet interest payments would be a default under the terms of indenture agreements, the coverage ratio measures a margin of safety. The amount of safety desirable depends on the stability of a company's earnings. (Too much safety can be an indication of an undesirable lack of leverage.) In cyclical companies, the fixed-charge coverage in periods of recession is a telling ratio. Analysts also find it useful to calculate the number of times that a company's *cash flow*—i.e., *after*-tax earnings plus noncash expenses (for example, depreciation)—covers fixed charges. Also known as *times fixed charges.*

FIXED COST cost that remains constant regardless of sales volume. Fixed costs include salaries of executives, interest expense, rent, depreciation, and insurance expenses. They contrast with *variable costs* (direct labor, materials costs), which are distinguished from *semivariable costs.* Semivariable costs vary, but not necessarily in direct relation to sales. They may also remain fixed up to a level of sales, then increase when sales enter a higher range. For example, expenses associated with a delivery truck would be fixed up to the level of sales where a second truck was required. Obviously, no costs are purely fixed; the assumption, however, serves the purposes of cost accounting for limited planning periods. Cost accounting is also concerned with the allocation of portions of fixed costs to inventory costs, also called indirect costs, overhead, factory overhead, and supplemental overhead. *See also* DIRECT OVERHEAD; VARIABLE COST.

FIXED EXCHANGE RATE set rate of exchange between the currencies of countries. At the Bretton Woods international monetary conference in 1944, a system of fixed exchange rates was set up, which existed until the early 1970s, when a FLOATING EXCHANGE RATE system was adopted.

FIXED EXPENSES *see* FIXED COST.

FIXED-INCOME INVESTMENT security that pays a fixed rate of return. This usually refers to government, corporate, or municipal bonds, which pay a fixed rate of interest until the bonds mature, and to preferred stock, paying a fixed dividend. Such investments are advantageous in a time of low inflation, but do not protect holders against erosion of buying power in a time of rising inflation, since the bondholder or preferred shareholder gets the same amount of interest or dividends, even though consumer goods cost more.

FIXED PREMIUM equal installments payable to an insurance company for INSURANCE or an ANNUITY. *See also* SINGLE-PREMIUM DEFERRED ANNUITY (SPDA) and SINGLE-PREMIUM LIFE INSURANCE.

FIXED PRICE
Contracts: type of contract where the price is preset and invariable, regardless of the actual costs of production. *See also* COST-PLUS CONTRACT.
Investment: in a public offering of new securities, price at which investment bankers in the underwriting SYNDICATE agree to sell the issue to the public. The price remains fixed as long as the syndicate remains in effect. The proper term for this kind of system is *fixed price offering system.* In contrast, Eurobonds, which are also sold through underwriting syndicates, are offered on a basis that permits discrimination among customers; i.e., the underwriting spread may be adjusted to suit the particular buyer. *See also* EUROBOND.

FIXED RATE (LOAN) type of loan in which the interest rate does not fluctuate with general market conditions. There are fixed rate mortgage (also known as conventional mortgage) and consumer installment loans, as well as fixed rate business loans. Fixed rate loans tend to have higher original interest rates than flexible rate loans such as an ADJUSTABLE RATE MORTGAGE (ARM), because lenders are not protected against a rise in the cost of money when they make a fixed rate loan.
    The term fixed rate may also refer to fixed currency exchange rates. *See* FIXED EXCHANGE RATE.

FIXED TERM REVERSE MORTGAGE mortgage granted by a bank or other lending institution providing payments to a homeowner for a fixed number of years. A retired couple who have paid off their traditional mortgage might be interested in such a plan if they do not want to move out of their house, but want to be able to tap the equity in their house for current cash income.

FIXED TRUST UNIT INVESTMENT TRUST that has a fixed portfolio of previously agreed upon securities; also called *fixed investment trust*. The securities are usually of one type, such as corporate, government, or municipal bonds, in order to afford a regular income to holders of units. A fixed trust is distinguished from a PARTICIPATING TRUST.

FIXTURE attachment to real property that is not intended to be moved and would create damage to the property if it were moved—for example, a plumbing fixture. Fixtures are classified as part of real estate when they share the same useful life. Otherwise, they are considered equipment.

FLAG technical chart pattern resembling a flag shaped like a parallelogram with masts on either side, showing a consolidation within a trend. It results from price fluctuations within a narrow range, both preceded and followed by sharp rises or declines. If the flag—the consolidation period—is preceded by a rise, it will usually be followed by a rise; a fall will follow a fall.

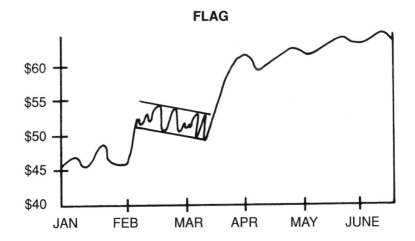

FLASH tape display designation used when volume on an exchange is so heavy that the tape runs more than five minutes behind. The flash interrupts the display to report the current price—called the *flash price*—of a heavily traded security. Current prices of two groups of 50 stocks are flashed at five-minute intervals as long as the tape is seriously behind.

FLAT
1. in bond trading, without accrued interest. This means that accrued interest will be received by the buyer if and when paid but that no accrued interest is payable to the seller. Issues in default and INCOME BONDS are normally quoted and traded flat. The opposite of a flat bond is an AND INTEREST bond. *See also* LOANED FLAT.
2. inventory of a market maker with a net zero position—i.e., neither long nor short.
3. position of an underwriter whose account is completely sold.

FLAT MARKET market characterized by HORIZONTAL PRICE MOVEMENT. It is usually the result of low activity. However, STABILIZATION, consolidation, and DISTRIBUTION are situations marked by both horizontal price movement and active trading.

FLAT SCALE
Industry: labor term denoting a uniform rate of pay that makes no allowance for volume, frequency, or other factors.
Municipal bonds: bond trader's term describing a situation where shorter and longer term yields show little difference over the maturity range of a new serial bond issue.

FLAT TAX tax applied at the same rate to all levels of income. It is often discussed as an alternative to the PROGRESSIVE TAX. Proponents of a flat tax argue that people able to retain larger portions of higher income would have an added incentive to earn, thus stimulating the economy. Advocates also note its simplicity. Opponents argue it is a REGRESSIVE TAX in effect, comparing it to the sales tax, a uniform tax that puts a greater burden on households with lower incomes. The TAX REFORM ACT OF 1986 instituted a modified flat tax system—a progressive tax with fewer tax brackets and lower rates. However, the trend towards a flat tax was reversed with the REVENUE RECONCILIATION ACT OF 1993, which added another tax bracket and a tax surcharge to the income tax system.

FLEXIBLE BUDGET statement of projected revenue and expenditure based on various levels of production. It shows how costs vary with different rates of output or at different levels of sales volume.

FLEXIBLE EXCHANGE RATE see FLOATING EXCHANGE RATE.

FLEXIBLE EXPENSES in personal finance, expenses that can be adjusted or eliminated, such as those for luxuries, as opposed to fixed expenses, such as rent or car payments.

FLEXIBLE MUTUAL FUND fund that can invest in stocks, bonds, and cash in whatever proportion the fund manager thinks will maximize returns to shareholders at the lowest level of risk. Flexible funds, also called ASSET ALLOCATION funds, can provide high returns if they are fully invested in stocks when stock prices soar, and they can also protect shareholders' assets by going largely to cash during a stock bear market. Flexible mutual funds are popular because the fund manager, not the shareholder, must make the difficult decisions on asset allocation and market timing. Some flexible funds allow managers to buy securities anywhere in the world in their quest to maximize shareholder returns.

FLIGHT OF CAPITAL see CAPITAL FLIGHT.

FLIGHT TO QUALITY moving capital to the safest possible investment to protect oneself from loss during an unsettling period in the market. For example, when a major bank fails, cautious money market investors may buy only government-backed money market securities instead of those issued by major banks. A flight to quality can be measured by the differing yields resulting from such a movement of capital. In the example just given, the yields on bank-issued money market paper will rise since there will be less demand for it, and the rates on government securities will fall, because there will be more demand for them.

FLIP-IN POISON PILL see POISON PILL.

FLIP-OVER POISON PILL see POISON PILL.

FLIPPING buying shares in an INITIAL PUBLIC OFFERING and selling them immediately for a profit. Brokerage firms underwriting new stock issues tend to discourage flipping, and will often try to allocate shares to investors who say they plan to hold on to the shares for some time. Still, the temptation to flip a new issue once it has risen in price sharply is too irresistible for many investors lucky enough to be allocated shares in a HOT ISSUE. An investor who flips stocks is called a *flipper.*

FLOAT

Banking: time between the deposit of a check in a bank and payment. Long floats are to the advantage of checkwriters, whose money may earn interest until a check clears. They are to the disadvantage of depositors, who must wait for a check to clear before they have access to the funds. As a rule, the further away the paying bank is from the deposit bank, the longer it will take for a check to clear. Some U.S. states limit the amount of float a bank can impose on the checks of its depositors. *See also* UNCOLLECTED FUNDS.

Investments: number of shares of a corporation that are outstanding and available for trading by the public. A small float means the stock will be more volatile, since a large order to buy or sell shares can influence the stock's price dramatically. A larger float means the stock will be less volatile.

FLOATER

Bonds: debt instrument with a variable interest rate tied to another interest rate, e.g., the rate paid by Treasury bills. A FLOATING RATE NOTE, for instance, provides a holder with additional interest if the applicable interest rate rises and less interest if the rate falls. It is generally best to buy floaters if it appears that interest rates will rise. If the outlook is for falling rates, investors typically favor fixed rate instruments. Floaters spread risk between issuers and debt-holders.

Insurance: endorsement to a homeowner's or renter's insurance policy, a form of property insurance for items that are moved from location to location. Typically, a floater is bought to cover jewelry, furs, and other items whose full value is not covered in standard homeowner's or renter's policies. A standard homeowner's policy typically covers $1000 to $2000 for jewelry, furs, and watches. Also called a *rider.*

FLOATING AN ISSUE *see* NEW ISSUE; UNDERWRITE.

FLOATING DEBT continuously renewed or refinanced short-term debt of companies or governments used to finance ongoing operating needs.

FLOATING EXCHANGE RATE movement of a foreign currency exchange rate in response to changes in the market forces of supply and demand; also known as *flexible exchange rate.* Currencies strengthen or weaken based on a nation's reserves of hard currency and gold, its international trade balance, its rate of inflation and interest rates, and the general strength of its economy. Nations generally do not want their currency to be too strong, because this makes the country's goods too expensive for foreigners to buy. A weak currency, on the other hand, may signify economic instability if it has been caused by high inflation or a weak economy. The opposite of the floating exchange rate is the FIXED EXCHANGE RATE system. *See also* PAR VALUE OF CURRENCY.

FLOATING RATE NOTE debt instrument with a variable interest rate. Interest adjustments are made periodically, often every six months, and are tied to a money-market index such as Treasury bill rates. Floating rate notes usually have a maturity of about five years. They provide holders with protection against rises in interest rates, but pay lower yields than fixed rate notes of the same maturity. Also known as a FLOATER.

FLOATING SECURITIES

1. securities bought for the purpose of making a quick profit on resale and held in a broker's name.
2. outstanding stock of a corporation that is traded on an exchange.
3. unsold units of a newly issued security.

FLOATING SUPPLY

Bonds: total dollar amount of municipal bonds in the hands of speculators and dealers that is for sale at any particular time as offered in the BLUE LIST. Someone might say, for instance, "There is $10 billion in floating supply available now in the municipal bond market."

Stocks: number of shares of a stock available for purchase. A dealer might say, "The floating supply in this stock is about 200,000 shares." Sometimes called simply the *float.*

FLOOR in general, the lower limit of something. In securities, the part of a stock exchange where active trading takes place or the price at which a STOP LOSS order is activated. *See also* FLOOR BROKER.

FLOOR BROKER member of an exchange who is an employee of a member firm and executes orders, as agent, on the floor of the exchange for clients. The floor broker receives an order via teletype machine from his firm's trading department, then proceeds to the appropriate trading post on the exchange floor. There he joins other brokers and the specialist in the security being bought or sold, and executes the trade at the best competitive price available. On completion of the transaction, the customer is notified through his registered representative back at the firm, and the trade is printed on the consolidated ticker tape, which is displayed electronically around the country. A floor broker should not be confused with a FLOOR TRADER, who trades as a principal for his or her own account, rather than as a broker.

FLOOR OFFICIAL securities exchange employee, who is present on the floor of the exchange to settle disputes in the auction procedure, such as questions about priority or precedence in the settling of an auction. The floor official makes rulings on the spot and his or her judgment is usually accepted.

FLOOR TICKET summary of the information entered on the ORDER TICKET by the registered representative on receipt of a buy or sell order from a client. The floor ticket gives the floor broker the information needed to execute a securities transaction. The information required on floor tickets is specified by securities industry rules.

FLOOR TRADER member of a stock or commodities exchange who trades on the floor of that exchange for his or her own account. The floor trader must abide by trading rules similar to those of the exchange specialists who trade on behalf of others. The term should not be confused with FLOOR BROKER. *See also* REGISTERED COMPETITIVE TRADER.

FLOTATION (FLOATATION) COST cost of issuing new stocks or bonds. It varies with the amount of underwriting risk and the job of physical distribution. It comprises two elements: (1) the compensation earned by the investment bankers (the underwriters) in the form of the spread between the price paid to the issuer (the corporation or government agency) and the offering price to the public, and (2) the expenses of the issuer (legal, accounting, printing, and other out-of-pocket expenses). Securities and Exchange Commission studies reveal that flotation costs are higher for stocks than for bonds, reflecting the generally wider distribution and greater volatility of common stock as opposed to bonds, which are usually sold in large blocks to relatively few investors. The SEC also found that flotation costs as a percentage of gross proceeds are greater for smaller issues than for larger ones. This occurs because the issuer's legal and other expenses tend to be relatively large and fixed; also, smaller issues tend to originate with less established issuers, requiring more information development and marketing expense. An issue involving a RIGHTS OFFERING can involve negligible underwriting risk and selling effort and therefore minimal flotation cost, especially if the underpricing is substantial.

The UNDERWRITING SPREAD is the key variable in flotation cost, historically ranging from 23.7% of the size of a small issue of common stock to as low as 1.25% of the par value of high-grade bonds. Spreads are determined by both negotiation and competitive bidding.

FLOWER BOND type of U.S. government bond that, regardless of its cost price, is acceptable at par value in payment of estate taxes if the decedent was the legal holder at the time of death; also called *estate tax anticipation bond*. Flower bonds were issued as recently as 1971, and the last of them, with a 3½% coupon, will mature in 1998.

FLOW OF FUNDS

Economics: in referring to the national economy, the way funds are transferred from savings surplus units to savings deficit units through financial intermediaries. *See also* FINANCIAL INTERMEDIARY.

Municipal bonds: statement found in the bond resolutions of municipal revenue issues showing the priorities by which municipal revenue will be applied. Typically, the flow of funds in decreasing order of priority is operation and maintenance, bond debt service, expansion of the facility, and sinking fund for retirement of debt prior to maturity. The flow of funds statement varies in detail from issue to issue.

Mutual funds: movement of money into or out of mutual funds or between various fund sectors. Heavy inflows and outflows are viewed respectively as bullish or bearish indicators for the stock market in general or for stock prices of the underlying companies in different sectors.

FLUCTUATION
1. change in prices or interest rates, either up or down. Fluctuation may refer to either slight or dramatic changes in the prices of stocks, bonds, or commodities. *See also* FLUCTUATION LIMIT.
2. the ups and downs in the economy.

FLUCTUATION LIMIT limits placed on the daily ups and downs of futures prices by the commodity exchanges. The limit protects traders from losing too much on a particular contract in one day. If a commodity reaches its limit, it may not trade any further that day. *See also* LIMIT UP, LIMIT DOWN.

FLURRY sudden increase in trading activity in a particular security. For example, there will be a flurry of trading in the stock of a company that was just the target of a surprise takeover bid. There are often trading flurries right after a company releases its quarterly earnings.

FNMA *see* FEDERAL NATIONAL MORTGAGE ASSOCIATION.

FOB *see* FREE ON BOARD.

FOCUS REPORT FOCUS is an acronym for the Financial and Operational Combined Uniform Single report, which broker-dealers are required to file monthly and quarterly with self-regulatory organizations (SROs). The SROs include exchanges, securities associations, and clearing organizations registered with the Securities and Exchange Commission and required by federal securities laws to be self-policing. The FOCUS report contains figures on capital, earnings, trade flow, and other required details.

FOOTSIE popular name for the *Financial Times'* FT-SE 100 Index (Financial Times-Stock Exchange 100 stock index), a market-value (capitalization)-weighted index of 100 blue chip stocks traded on the London Stock Exchange.

FORBES 500 annual listing by *Forbes* magazine of the largest U.S. publicly-owned corporations ranked four ways: by sales, assets, profits, and market value. *See also* FORTUNE 500.

FORCED CONVERSION when a CONVERTIBLE security is called in by its issuer. Convertible owners may find it to their financial advantage either to sell or to convert their holdings into common shares of the underlying company or to accept the call price. Such a conversion usually takes place when the convertible is selling above its CALL PRICE because the market value of the shares of the underlying stock has risen sharply. *See also* CONVERTIBLE.

FORECASTING projecting current trends using existing data.

Stock market forecasters predict the direction of the stock market by relying on technical data of trading activity and fundamental statistics on the direction of the economy.

Economic forecasters foretell the strength of the economy, often by utilizing complex econometric models as a tool to make specific predictions of future levels of inflation, interest rates, and employment. *See also* ECONOMETRICS.

Forecasting can also refer to various PROJECTIONS used in business and financial planning.

FORECLOSURE process by which a homeowner who has not made timely payments of principal and interest on a mortgage loses title to the home. The holder of the mortgage, whether it be a bank, a savings and loan, or an individual, must go to court to seize the property, which may then be sold to satisfy the claims of the mortgage.

FOREIGN CORPORATION
1. corporation chartered under the laws of a state other than the one in which it conducts business. Because of inevitable confusion with the term ALIEN CORPORATION, *out-of-state corporation* is preferred.
2. corporation organized under the laws of a foreign country; the term ALIEN CORPORATION is usually preferred.

FOREIGN CORRUPT PRACTICES SECURITIES EXCHANGE ACT OF 1934 amendment passed in 1977 providing internal controls and penalties aimed at curtailing bribery by publicly held companies of foreign government officials and personnel.

FOREIGN CROWD New York Stock Exchange members who trade on the floor in foreign bonds.

FOREIGN CURRENCY FUTURES AND OPTIONS futures and options contracts based on foreign currencies, such as the Japanese yen, Deutsche mark, British pound, and French franc. The buyer of a foreign currency futures contract acquires the right to buy a particular amount of that currency by a specific date at a fixed rate of exchange, and the seller agrees to sell that currency at the same fixed price. *Call options* give call buyers the right, but not the obligation, to buy the underlying currency at a particular price by a particular date. Call options on foreign currency futures give call buyers the right to a long underlying futures contracts. Those buying *put options* have the right to sell the underlying currencies at a specific price by a specific date. Most buyers and sellers of foreign currency futures and options do not exercise their rights to buy or sell, but trade out of their contracts at a profit or loss before they expire. SPECULATORS hope to profit by buying or selling a foreign currency futures or options contract before a currency rises or falls in value. HEDGERS buy or sell such contracts to protect their cash market position from fluctuations in currency values. These contracts are traded on SECURITIES AND COMMODITIES EXCHANGES throughout the world, including the CHICAGO MERCANTILE EXCHANGE (CME), FINEX, the Mid-America Commodity Exchange, and the PHILADELPHIA STOCK EXCHANGE (PHLX).

FOREIGN DIRECT INVESTMENT
1. investment in U.S. businesses by foreign citizens; usually involves majority stock ownership of the enterprise.
2. joint ventures between foreign and U.S. companies.

FOREIGN EXCHANGE instruments employed in making payments between countries—paper currency, notes, checks, bills of exchange, and electronic notifications of international debits and credits.

FOREIGN EXCHANGE RATE *see* EXCHANGE RATE. *See also* FOREIGN EXCHANGE.

FORFEITURE loss of rights or assets due to failure to fulfill a legal obligation or condition and as compensation for resulting losses or damages.

FORM 8-K Securities and Exchange Commission required form that a publicly held company must file, reporting on any material event that might affect its financial situation or the value of its shares, ranging from merger activity to amendment of the corporate charter or bylaws. The SEC considers as material all matters about which an average, prudent investor ought reasonably to be informed before deciding whether to buy, sell, or hold a registered security. Form 8-K must be filed within a month of the occurrence of the material event. Timely disclosure rules may require a corporation to issue a press release immediately concerning an event subsequently reported on Form 8-K.

FORM 4 document, filed with the Securities and Exchange Commission and the pertinent stock exchange, which is used to report changes in the holdings of (1) those who own at least 10% of a corporation's outstanding stock and (2) directors and officers, even if they own no stock. When there has been a major change in ownership, Form 4 must be filed within ten days of the end of the month in which the change took place. Form 4 filings must be constantly updated during a takeover attempt of a company when the acquirer buys more than 10% of the outstanding shares.

FORM T National Association of Securities Dealers (NASD) form for reporting equity transaction executed after the market's normal hours.

FORM 10-K annual report required by the Securities and Exchange Commission of every issuer of a registered security, every exchange-listed company, and any company with 500 or more shareholders or $1 million or more in gross assets. The form provides for disclosure of total sales, revenue, and pretax operating income, as well as sales by separate classes of products for each of a company's separate lines of business for each of the past five years. A source and application of funds statement presented on a comparative basis for the last two fiscal years is also required. Form 10-K becomes public information when filed with the SEC.

FORM 10-Q quarterly report required by the Securities and Exchange Commission of companies with listed securities. Form 10-Q is less comprehensive than the FORM 10-K annual report and does not require that figures be audited. It may cover the specific quarter or it may be cumulative. It should include comparative figures for the same period of the previous year.

FORM 13D form used to comply with SCHEDULE 13D.

FORM 13G short form of SCHEDULE 13D for positions acquired in the ordinary course of business and not to assume control or influence.

FORM 3 form filed with the Securities and Exchange Commission and the pertinent stock exchange by all holders of 10% or more of the stock of a company registered with the SEC and by all directors and officers, even if no shares are owned. Form 3 details the number of shares owned as well as the number of warrants, rights, convertible bonds, and options to purchase common stock. Individuals required to file Form 3 are considered insiders, and they are required to update their information whenever changes occur. Such changes are reported on FORM 4.

FORMULA INVESTING investment technique based on a predetermined timing or asset allocation model that eliminates emotional decisions. One type of formula investing, called dollar cost averaging, involves putting the same amount of money into a stock or mutual fund at regular intervals, so that more shares will be bought when the price is low and less when the price is high. Another formula investing method calls for shifting funds from stocks to bonds or vice versa as the stock market reaches particular price levels. If stocks rise to a particular point, a certain amount of the stock portfolio is sold and put in bonds. On the other hand, if stocks fall to a particular low price, money is brought out of bonds into stocks. *See also* CONSTANT DOLLAR PLAN; CONSTANT RATIO PLAN.

FORTUNE 500 listings of the top 500 U.S. corporations compiled by *Fortune* magazine. The companies are ranked by 12 indices, among them revenues; profits; assets; stockholders' equity; market value; profits as a percentage of revenues, assets, and stockholders' equity; earnings per share growth over a 10-year span; total return to investors in the year; and the 10-year annual rate of total return to investors. In separate listings, companies also are ranked by performance and within states. Headquarters city, phone number, and the name of the chief executive officer are included. In another listing 1,000 companies are ranked within 61 different industry groups.

FORWARD CONTRACT purchase or sale of a specific quantity of a commodity, government security, foreign currency, or other financial instrument at the current or SPOT PRICE, with delivery and settlement at a specified future date. Because it is a completed contract—as opposed to an options contract, where the owner has the choice of completing or not completing—a forward contract can be a COVER for the sale of a FUTURES CONTRACT. *See* HEDGE.

FORWARD EXCHANGE TRANSACTION purchase or sale of foreign currency at an exchange rate established now but with payment and delivery at a specified future time. Most forward exchange contracts have one-, three-, or six-month maturities, though contracts in major currencies can normally be arranged for delivery at any specified date up to a year, and sometimes up to three years.

FORWARD PRICING Securities and Exchange Commission requirement that open-end investment companies, whose share price is always determined by the NET ASSET VALUE of the outstanding shares, base all incoming buy and sell orders on the next net asset valuation of fund shares. *See also* INVESTMENT COMPANY.

FOR YOUR INFORMATION (FYI) prefix to a security price quote by a market maker that indicates the quote is "for your information" and is not a firm offer to trade at that price. FYI quotes are given as a courtesy for purposes of valuation. FVO (for valuation only) is sometimes used instead.

401(k) PLAN plan whereby employees may elect, as an alternative to receiving taxable cash in the form of compensation or a bonus, to contribute pretax dollars to a qualified tax-deferred retirement plan. Elective deferrals are limited to $10,000 a year (the amount is revised each year by the IRS based on inflation). Many companies, to encourage employee participation in the plan, match employee contributions anywhere from 10% to 100% annually. All employee contributions and employer matching funds can be invested in several options, usually including

The penalty requires that the customer's account be frozen for 90 days. *See also* FROZEN ACCOUNT.

FREE RIGHT OF EXCHANGE ability to transfer securities from one name to another without paying the charge associated with a sales transaction. The free right applies, for example, where stock in STREET NAME (that is, registered in the name of a broker-dealer) is transferred to the customer's name in order to be eligible for a dividend reinvestment plan. *See also* REGISTERED SECURITY.

FREE STOCK (1) stock that is fully paid for and is not assigned as collateral. (2) stock held by an issuer following a PRIVATE PLACEMENT but that can be traded free of the restrictions bearing on a LETTER SECURITY.

FREEZE OUT put pressure on minority shareholders after a takeover to sell their shares to the acquirer.

FREIT *see* FINITE LIFE REAL ESTATE INVESTMENT TRUST.

FRICTIONAL COST in an INDEX FUND, the amount by which the fund's return is less than that of the index it replicates. The difference, assuming it is not otherwise adjusted, represents the fund's management fees and transaction costs.

FRIENDLY TAKEOVER merger supported by the management and board of directors of the target company. The board will recommend to shareholders that they approve the takeover offer, because it represents fair value for the company's shares. In many cases, the acquiring company will retain many of the existing managers of the acquired company to continue to run the business. A friendly takeover is in contrast to a HOSTILE TAKEOVER, in which management actively resists the acquisition attempt by another company or RAIDER.

FRINGE BENEFITS compensation to employees in addition to salary. Some examples of fringe benefits are paid holidays, retirement plans, life and health insurance plans, subsidized cafeterias, company cars, stock options, and expense accounts. In many cases, fringe benefits can add significantly to an employee's total compensation, and are a key ingredient in attracting and retaining employees. For the most part, fringe benefits are not taxable to the employee, though they are generally tax-deductible for the employer.

FRONT-END LOAD sales charge applied to an investment at the time of initial purchase. There may be a front-end load on a mutual fund, for instance, which is sold by a broker. Annuities, life insurance policies, and limited partnerships can also have front-end loads. From the investor's point of view, the earnings from the investment should make up for this up-front fee within a relatively short period of time. *See also* INVESTMENT COMPANY.

FRONT OFFICE sales personnel in a brokerage, insurance, or other financial services operation. Front office workers produce revenue, in contrast to BACK OFFICE workers, who perform administrative and other support functions for the front office.

FRONT RUNNING practice whereby a securities or commodities trader takes a POSITION to capitalize on advance knowledge of a large upcoming transaction expected to influence the market price. In the stock market, this might be done by buying an OPTION on stock expected to benefit from a large BLOCK transaction. In commodities, DUAL TRADING is common practice and provides opportunities to profit from front running.

FROZEN ACCOUNT
Banking: bank account from which funds may not be withdrawn until a lien is satisfied and a court order is received freeing the balance.

A bank account may also be frozen by court order in a dispute over the ownership of property.

Investments: brokerage account under disciplinary action by the Federal Reserve Board for violation of REGULATION T. During the period an account is frozen (90 days), the customer may not sell securities until their purchase price has been fully paid and the certificates have been delivered. The penalty is invoked commonly in cases of FREERIDING.

FULL COUPON BOND bond with a coupon rate that is near or above current market interest rates. If interest rates are generally about 8%, for instance, a 7½% or 9% bond is considered a full coupon bond.

FULL DISCLOSURE
In general: requirement to disclose all material facts relevant to a transaction.
Securities industry: public information requirements established by the Securities Act of 1933, the Securities Exchange Act of 1934, and the major stock exchanges.
See also DISCLOSURE.

FULL FAITH AND CREDIT phrase meaning that the full taxing and borrowing power, *plus* revenue other than taxes, is pledged in payment of interest and repayment of principal of a bond issued by a government entity. U.S. government securities and general obligation bonds of states and local governments are backed by this pledge.

FULL REPLACEMENT COVERAGE *see* GUARANTEED REPLACEMENT COST COVERAGE INSURANCE.

FULL-SERVICE BROKER broker who provides a wide range of services to clients. Unlike a DISCOUNT BROKER, who just executes trades, a full-service broker offers advice on which stocks, bonds, commodities, and mutual funds to buy or sell. A full-service broker may also offer an ASSET MANAGEMENT ACCOUNT; advice on financial planning, tax shelters, and INCOME LIMITED PARTNERSHIPS; and new issues of stock. A full-service broker's commissions will be higher than those of a discount broker. The term *brokerage* is gradually being replaced by variations of the term *financial services* as the range of services offered by brokers expands.

FULL TRADING AUTHORIZATION freedom, even from broad guidelines, allowed a broker or adviser under a DISCRETIONARY ACCOUNT.

FULLY DEPRECIATED said of a fixed asset to which all the DEPRECIATION the tax law allows has been charged. Asset is carried on the books at its RESIDUAL VALUE, although its LIQUIDATING VALUE may be higher or lower.

FULLY DILUTED EARNINGS PER (COMMON) SHARE figure showing earnings per common share after assuming the exercise of warrants and stock options, and the conversion of convertible bonds and preferred stock (all potentially *dilutive* securities). Actually, it is more analytically correct to define the term as the smallest earnings per common share that can be obtained by computing EARNINGS PER SHARE (EPS) for all possible combinations of assumed exercise or conversion (because antidilutive securities—securities whose conversion would add to EPS—may not be assumed to be exercised or converted). Under accounting rules adopted in 1998, companies must report EPS on two bases: Basic EPS, which does not count stock options, warrants, and convertible securities, and (fully) Diluted EPS, which includes those securities. *See also* DILUTION; EARNINGS PER SHARE; PRIMARY EARNINGS PER (COMMON) SHARE.

FULLY DISTRIBUTED term describing a new securities issue that has been completely resold to the investing public (that is, to institutions and individuals and other investors rather than to dealers).

FULLY INVESTED said of an investor or a portfolio when funds in cash or CASH EQUIVALENTS are minimal and assets are totally committed to other investments, usually stock. To be fully invested is to have an optimistic view of the market.

FULLY VALUED said of a stock that has reached a price at which analysts think the underlying company's fundamental earnings power has been recognized by the market. If the stock goes up from that price, it is called OVERVALUED. If the stock goes down, it is termed UNDERVALUED.

FUND *see* FUND FAMILY; FUNDING; MUTUAL FUND.

FUNDAMENTAL ANALYSIS
Economics: research of such factors as interest rates, gross national product, inflation, unemployment, and inventories as tools to predict the direction of the economy.
Investment: analysis of the balance sheet and income statements of companies in order to forecast their future stock price movements. Fundamental analysts consider past records of assets, earnings, sales, products, management, and markets in predicting future trends in these indicators of a company's success or failure. By appraising a firm's prospects, these analysts assess whether a particular stock or group of stocks is UNDERVALUED or OVERVALUED at the current market price. The other major school of stock market analysis is TECHNICAL ANALYSIS, which relies on price and volume movements of stocks and does not concern itself with financial statistics.

FUNDED DEBT
1. debt that is due after one year and is formalized by the issuing of bonds or long-term notes.
2. bond issue whose retirement is provided for by a SINKING FUND.
   See also FLOATING DEBT.

FUNDED PENSION PLAN pension plan in which all liabilities are fully funded. A pension plan's administrator knows the potential payments necessary to make to pensioners over the coming years. In order to be funded, the plan must have enough capital contributions from the plan sponsor, plus returns from investments, to pay those claims. Employees are notified annually of the financial strength of their pension plans, and whether or not the plans are fully funded. If the plans are not funded, the PENSION BENEFIT GUARANTY CORPORATION (PBGC), which guarantees pension plans, will act to try to get the plan sponsor to contribute more money to the plan. If a company fails with an underfunded pension plan, the PBGC will step in to make the promised payments to pensioners.

FUND FAMILY mutual fund company offering funds with many investment objectives. A fund family may offer several types of stock, bond, and money market funds and allow free switching among their funds. Large no-load fund families include American Century, Fidelity, Dreyfus, T. Rowe Price, Scudder, Strong, and Vanguard. Most major brokerage houses such as Merrill Lynch, Smith Barney and PaineWebber also sponsor fund families of their own. Many independent firms such as American Funds, Loomis-Sayles, Putnam, and Pioneer distribute their funds with a sales charge through brokerage firms and financial planners. Many investors find it convenient to place most of their assets with one or two fund families because of the convenience offered by such switching privileges. In recent years, several discount brokerage firms have offered the ability to shift assets from one fund family to another, making it less important than it had been to consolidate assets in one fund family. *See also* INVESTMENT COMPANY.

FUNDING

1. refinancing a debt on or before its maturity; also called REFUNDING and, in certain instances, PREREFUNDING.

2. putting money into investments or another type of reserve fund, to provide for future pension or welfare plans.

3. in corporate finance, the word *funding* is preferred to *financing* when referring to bonds in contrast to stock. A company is said to be funding its operations if it floats bonds.

4. to provide funds to finance a project, such as a research study.

See also SINKING FUND.

FUND MANAGER manager of a pool of money such as a mutual fund, pension fund, insurance fund, or bank-pooled fund. Their job is to maximize the fund's returns at the least risk possible. Each fund manager tries his or her best to realize the fund's objectives, whether it be growth, income, or some combination of the two. Different fund managers use different styles to accomplish their objectives. For example, some stock fund managers use the value style of investing, while others concentrate on growth stocks. In picking a fund, it is important to know the fund manager's style, and how long he or she has been managing the fund. This information is generally available for publicly offered mutual funds from fund company literature or fund representatives.

FUND OF FUNDS mutual fund that invests in other mutual funds. The concept behind such funds is that they are able to move money between the best funds in the industry, and thereby increase shareholders' returns with more diversification than is offered by a single fund. The fund of funds has been criticized as adding another layer of management expenses on shareholders, however, because fees are paid to the fund's management company as well as to all the underlying fund management companies. The SEC limits the total amount of fees that shareholders can pay in such a fund. Funds of funds are usually organized in a fund family of their own, offering funds that will specialize in international stocks, aggressive growth, income, and other objectives. Funds of funds were extremely popular in the 1960s, but then faded in popularity in the 1970s because of a scandal involving Equity Funding, which was a fund of funds. They have enjoyed a modest comeback in recent years, however.

FUND SWITCHING moving money from one mutual fund to another, within the same FUND FAMILY. Purchases and sales of funds may be done to time the ups and downs of the stock and bond markets, or because investors' financial needs have changed. Several newsletters and fund managers specialize in advising clients on which funds to switch into and out of, based on market conditions. Switching among funds within a fund family is usually allowed without sales charges. Discount brokerages allow convenient switching of funds among fund families. Unless practiced inside a tax-deferred account such as an IRA or Keogh account, a fund switch creates a taxable event, since CAPITAL GAINS OR LOSSES are realized.

FUNGIBLES bearer instruments, securities, or goods that are equivalent, substitutable, and interchangeable. Commodities such as soybeans or wheat, common shares of the same company, and dollar bills are all familiar examples of fungibles.

Fungibility (interchangeability) of listed options, by virtue of their common expiration dates and strike prices, makes it possible for buyers and sellers to close out their positions by putting offsetting transactions through the OPTIONS CLEARING CORPORATION. *See also* OFFSET; STRIKE PRICE.

FUN MONEY money that is not necessary for everyday living expenses, and can therefore be risked in volatile, but potentially highly profitable, investments. If the investment pans out, the investor has had some fun speculating. If the investment turns sour, the investor's lifestyle has not been put at risk because he or she could afford to lose the money.

FURTHEST MONTH in commodities or options trading, the month that is furthest away from settlement of the contract. For example, Treasury bill futures may have outstanding contracts for three, six, or nine months. The six- and nine-month contracts would be the furthest months, and the three-month contract would be the NEAREST MONTH.

FUTA *see* FEDERAL UNEMPLOYMENT TAX ACT (FUTA).

FUTOP the screen-traded, Danish derivatives market which merged with the COPENHAGEN STOCK EXCHANGE in 1997. FUTOP offers futures and options on the KFX Stock Index, Danish government bonds, and Danish equities.

FUTURES CONTRACT agreement to buy or sell a specific amount of a commodity or financial instrument at a particular price on a stipulated future date. The price is established between buyer and seller on the floor of a commodity exchange, using the OPEN OUTCRY system. A futures contract obligates the buyer to purchase the underlying commodity and the seller to sell it, unless the contract is sold to another before settlement date, which may happen if a trader waits to take a profit or cut a loss. This contrasts with options trading, in which the option buyer may choose whether or not to exercise the option by the exercise date. *See also* FORWARD CONTRACT; FUTURES MARKET.

FUTURES MARKET exchange where futures contracts and options on futures contracts are traded. Different exchanges specialize in particular kinds of contracts. The major exchanges in the U.S. are the COFFEE, SUGAR AND COCOA EXCHANGE; COMEX; FINEX; NEW YORK COTTON EXCHANGE; NEW YORK MERCANTILE EXCHANGE; and the NEW YORK FUTURES EXCHANGE, all in New York; the CHICAGO BOARD OF TRADE; INTERNATIONAL MONETARY MARKET; CHICAGO MERCANTILE EXCHANGE; and the CHICAGO RICE AND COTTON EXCHANGE, all in Chicago; and the KANSAS CITY BOARD OF TRADE, in Kansas City, MO.

   Futures markets from around the world are also described elsewhere in this *Dictionary* including: DEUTSCHE TERMINBORSE; EUREX; INTERNATIONAL PETROLEUM EXCHANGE; LONDON INTERNATIONAL FINANCIAL FUTURES AND OPTIONS EXCHANGE (LIFFE); MARCHE A TERME INTERNATIONAL DE FRANCE (MATIF); MONTREAL EXCHANGE; SWISS OPTIONS AND FINANCIAL FUTURES EXCHANGE (SOFFEX); SYDNEY FUTURES EXCHANGE (SFE); TORONTO FUTURES EXCHANGE AND WINIPEG COMMODITY EXCHANGE. *See also* SECURITIES AND COMMODITIES EXCHANGES; SPOT MARKET.

FUTURES OPTION OPTION on a FUTURES CONTRACT.

FUTURE VALUE reverse of PRESENT VALUE.

FVO (FOR VALUATION ONLY) *see* FOR YOUR INFORMATION.

g

GAAP *see* GENERALLY ACCEPTED ACCOUNTING PRINCIPLES (GAAP).

GAIJIN non-Japanese investor in Japan. The Japanese refer to foreign competitors, on both the individual and institutional levels, as gaijin. In particular, the large, prestigious American and European brokerage firms that compete with the major Japanese brokerage firms, such as Nomura and Nikko, are called gaijin.

GAIN profit on a securities transaction. A gain is realized when a stock, bond, mutual fund, futures contract, or other financial instrument is sold for more than its purchase price. If the instrument was held for more than a year, the gain is taxable at more favorable capital gains tax rates. If held for under a year, the gain is taxed at regular income tax rates.

GAMMA STOCKS obsolete classification of stocks traded on the London Stock Exchange. Ranking third behind ALPHA and BETA stocks in capitalization and activity, gamma stocks are less regulated, requiring just two market makers quoting indicative share prices. *See also* NORMAL MARKET SIZE (NMS).

GAP

Finance: amount of a financing need for which provision has yet to be made. For example, ABC company might need $1.5 million to purchase and equip a new plant facility. It arranges a mortgage loan of $700,000, secures equipment financing of $400,000, and obtains new equity of $150,000. That leaves a gap of $250,000 for which it seeks gap financing. Such financing may be available from state and local governments concerned with promoting economic development.

Securities: securities industry term used to describe the price movement of a stock or commodity when one day's trading range for the stock or commodity does not overlap the next day's, causing a range, or gap, in which no trade has occurred. This usually takes place because of some extraordinary positive or negative news about the company or commodity. *See also* PRICE GAP.

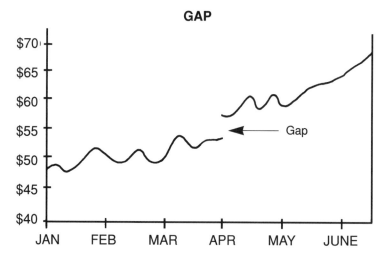

GAP

GAP OPENING opening price for a stock that is significantly higher or lower than the previous day's closing price. For example, if XYZ Company was the subject of a $50 takeover bid after the market closed with its shares trading at $30, its share price might open the next morning at $45 a share. There would therefore be a gap between the closing price of $30 and the opening price of $45. The same phenomenon can occur on the downside if a company reports disappointing earnings or a takeover bid falls through, for example. Stocks trading on the New York or American Stock Exchange may experience a delayed opening when such an event occurs as the specialist deals with the rush of buy or sell orders to find the stock's appropriate price level.

GARAGE annex floor on the north side of the main trading floor of the New York Stock Exchange.

GARBATRAGE stock traders' term, combining garbage and ARBITRAGE, for activity in stocks swept upward by the psychology surrounding a major takeover. For example, when two leading entertainment stocks, Time, Inc., and Warner Communications, Inc., were IN PLAY in 1989, stocks with insignificant involvement in the entertainment sector became active. Garbatrage would not apply to activity in bona fide entertainment stocks moving on speculation that other mergers would follow in the wake of Time-Warner. *See also* RUMORTRAGE.

GARNISHMENT court order to an employer to withhold all or part of an employee's wages and send the money to the court or to a person who has won a lawsuit against the employee. An employee's wages will be *garnished* until the court-ordered debt is paid. Garnishing may be used in a divorce settlement or for repayment of creditors.

GATHER IN THE STOPS stock-trading tactic that involves selling a sufficient amount of stock to drive down the price to a point where stop orders (orders to buy or sell at a given price) are known to exist. The stop orders are then activated to become market orders (orders to buy or sell at the best available price), in turn creating movement which touches off other stop orders in a process called SNOW-BALLING. Because this can cause sharp trading swings, floor officials on the exchanges have the authority to suspend stop orders in individual securities if that seems advisable. *See also* STOP ORDER.

GDP IMPLICIT PRICE DEFLATOR ratio of current-dollar GROSS DOMESTIC PRODUCT (GDP) to constant-dollar GDP. Changes in the implicit price deflator reflect both changes in prices of all goods and services that make up GDP and changes in the composite of GDP. Over time, the implicit price deflator understates inflation because people tend to shift consumption from goods that have high prices or rapidly increasing prices to goods that have less rapidly increasing prices. Therefore, theoretically, prices of all goods and service could increase and the implicit price deflator could decrease. *See also* PERSONAL INFLATION RATE.

G-8 FINANCE MINISTERS the finance ministers of the eight largest industrial countries: Canada, France, Germany, Great Britain, Italy, Japan, Russia and the United States. Meetings of the G-8 take place at least once a year and are important in coordinating economic policy among the major industrial countries. The political leaders of the G-8 countries also meet once a year, usually in July, at the Economic Summit, which is held in one of the eight countries. Before the admission of Russia in 1998, the group was called G-7 Finance Ministers and that designation was still being used in the late 1990s.

GENERAL ACCOUNT Federal Reserve Board term for brokerage customer margin accounts subject to REGULATION T, which covers extensions of credit by brokers for the purchase and short sale of securities. The Fed requires that all transactions in which the broker advances credit to the customer be made in this account. *See also* MARGIN ACCOUNT.

GENERAL AGREEMENT ON TARIFFS AND TRADE (GATT) United Nations-associated international treaty organization headquartered in Geneva that works to eliminate barriers to trade between nations. In December 1994 Congress approved a pact that reduced tariffs, enhanced international copyright protections, and generally liberalized trade. *See also* WORLD TRADE ORGANIZATION (WTO).

GENERAL LEDGER formal ledger containing all the financial statement accounts of a business. It contains offsetting debit and credit accounts, the totals of which are proved by a trial balance. Certain accounts in the general ledger, termed *control accounts,* summarize the detail booked on separate subsidiary ledgers.

GENERAL LIEN LIEN against an individual that excludes real property. The lien carries the right to seize personal property to satisfy a debt. The property seized need not be the property that gave rise to the debt.

GENERAL LOAN AND COLLATERAL AGREEMENT continuous agreement under which a securities broker-dealer borrows from a bank against listed securities to buy or carry inventory, finance the underwriting of new issues, or carry the margin accounts of clients. Synonymous with *broker's loan. See also* BROKER LOAN RATE; MARGIN ACCOUNT; UNDERWRITE.

GENERALLY ACCEPTED ACCOUNTING PRINCIPLES (GAAP) conventions, rules, and procedures that define accepted accounting practice, including broad guidelines as well as detailed procedures. The basic doctrine was set forth by the Accounting Principles Board of the American Institute of Certified Public Accountants, which was superseded in 1973 by the FINANCIAL ACCOUNTING STANDARDS BOARD (FASB), an independent self-regulatory organization.

GENERAL MORTGAGE mortgage covering all the mortgageable properties of a borrower and not restricted to any particular piece of property. Such a blanket mortgage can be lower in priority of claim in liquidation than one or more other mortgages on specific parcels.

GENERAL OBLIGATION BOND municipal bond backed by the FULL FAITH AND CREDIT (which includes the taxing and further borrowing power) of a municipality. A *GO bond,* as it is known, is repaid with general revenue and borrowings, in contrast to the revenue from a specific facility built with the borrowed funds, such as a tunnel or a sewer system. *See also* REVENUE BOND.

GENERAL PARTNER
1. one of two or more partners who are jointly and severally responsible for the debts of a partnership.
2. managing partner of a LIMITED PARTNERSHIP, who is responsible for the operations of the partnership and, ultimately, any debts taken on by the partnership. The general partner's liability is unlimited. In a real estate partnership, the general partner will pick the properties to be bought and will manage them. In an oil and gas partnership, the general partner will select drilling sites and oversee drilling activity. In return for these services, the general partner collects certain fees and often retains a percentage of ownership in the partnership.

GENERAL REVENUE when used in reference to state and local governments taken separately, the term refers to total revenue less revenue from utilities, sales of alcoholic beverages, and insurance trusts. When speaking of combined state and local total revenue, the term refers only to taxes, charges, and miscellaneous revenue, which avoids the distortion of overlapping intergovernmental revenue.

GENERAL REVENUE SHARING unrestricted funds (which can be used for any purpose) provided by the federal government until 1987 to the 50 states and to more than 38,000 cities, towns, counties, townships, Indian tribes, and Alaskan native villages under the State and Local Fiscal Assistance Act of 1972.

GENERATION-SKIPPING TRANSFER OR TRUST arrangement whereby your principal goes into a TRUST when you die, and transfers to your grandchildren when your children die, but which provides income to your children while they live. Once a major tax loophole for the wealthy because taxes were payable only at your death and your grandchildren's death, now only $1 million can be transferred tax-free to the grandchildren. Otherwise, a special generation-skipping tax—with rates equal to the maximum ESTATE TAX rate—applies to transfers to grandchildren, whether the gifts are direct or from a trust.

GHOSTING illegal manipulation of a company's stock price by two or more market makers. One firm will push a stock's price higher or lower, and the other firms will follow their lead in collusion to drive the stock's price up or down. The practice is called ghosting because the investing public is unaware of this coordinated activity among market makers who are supposed to be competing with each other.

GIC *see* GUARANTEED INVESTMENT CONTRACT.

GIFT INTER VIVOS gift of property from one living person to another, without consideration.

GIFT SPLITTING dividing a gift into $10,000 pieces to avoid GIFT TAX. For example, a husband and wife wanting to give $20,000 to their child will give $10,000 each instead of $20,000 from one parent, so that no gift tax is due.

GIFT TAX graduated tax, levied on the donor of a gift by the federal government and most state governments when assets are transferred from one person to another. The more money given as a gift, the higher the tax rate. The ECONOMIC RECOVERY TAX ACT OF 1981 allowed a $10,000 federal gift tax exemption per recipient. This means that individuals can gift $10,000 a year free of gift tax to another person ($20,000 from a married couple). The gift tax is computed on the fair market value of the asset being transferred above the $10,000 exemption level. According to the TAXPAYER RELIEF ACT OF 1997, this gift tax limit is indexed to inflation in $1,000 increments, starting on January 1, 1999. For those making gifts over the limit, a federal gift tax return using IRS Form 709 must be filed by April 15th of the year following the year of the gift. Gifts between spouses are not subject to gift tax. Many states match the $10,000 gift tax exemption, but some allow a smaller amount to be gifted free of tax. *See also* FEDERAL GIFT TAX; GIFT SPLITTING.

GILT-EDGED SECURITY stock or bond of a company that has demonstrated over a number of years that it is capable of earning sufficient profits to cover dividends on stocks and interest on bonds with great dependability. The term is used with corporate bonds more often than with stocks, where the term BLUE CHIP is more common.

GILTS bonds issued by the British government. Gilts are the equivalent of Treasury securities in the United States in that they are perceived to have no risk of default. Income earned from investing in gilts is therefore guaranteed. Gilt yields act as the benchmark against which all other British bond yields are measured. Gilt futures are traded on the LONDON INTERNATIONAL FINANCIAL FUTURES AND OPTIONS EXCHANGE (LIFFE). The name gilt is derived from the original British government certificates, which had gilded edges.

GINNIE MAE nickname for the GOVERNMENT NATIONAL MORTGAGE ASSOCIATION and the securities guaranteed by that agency. *See also* GINNIE MAE PASS-THROUGH.

GINNIE MAE PASS-THROUGH security, backed by a pool of mortgages and guaranteed by the GOVERNMENT NATIONAL MORTGAGE ASSOCIATION (Ginnie Mae), which passes through to investors the interest and principal payments of homeowners. Homeowners make their mortgage payments to the bank or savings and loan that originated their mortgage. After deducting a service charge (usually

½%), the bank forwards the mortgage payments to the pass-through buyers, who may be institutional investors or individuals. Ginnie Mae guarantees that investors will receive timely principal and interest payments even if homeowners do not make mortgage payments on time.

The introduction of Ginnie Mae pass-throughs has benefited the home mortgage market, since more capital has become available for lending. Investors, who are able to receive high, government-guaranteed interest payments, have also benefited. For investors, however, the rate of principal repayment on a Ginnie Mae pass-through is uncertain. If interest rates fall, principal will be repaid faster, since homeowners will refinance their mortgages. If rates rise, principal will be repaid more slowly, since homeowners will hold onto the underlying mortgages. *See also* HALF-LIFE.

GIVE UP
1. term used in a securities transaction involving three brokers, as illustrated by the following scenario: Broker A, a FLOOR BROKER, executes a buy order for Broker B, another member firm broker who has too much business at the time to execute the order. The broker with whom Broker A completes the transaction (the sell side broker) is Broker C. Broker A "gives up" the name of Broker B, so that the record shows a transaction between Broker B and Broker C even though the trade was actually executed between Broker A and Broker C.
2. another application of the term: A customer of brokerage firm ABC Co. travels out of town and, finding no branch office of ABC, places an order with DEF Co., saying he is an account of ABC. After confirming the account relationship, DEF completes a trade with GHI Co., advising GHI that DEF is acting for ABC ("giving up" ABC's name). ABC will then handle the clearing details of the transaction with GHI. Alternatively, DEF may simply send the customer's order directly to ABC for execution. Whichever method is used, the customer pays only one commission.

GLAMOR STOCK stock with a wide public and institutional following. Glamor stocks achieve this following by producing steadily rising sales and earnings over a long period of time. In bull (rising) markets, glamor stocks tend to rise faster than market averages. Although a glamor stock is often in the category of a BLUE CHIP stock, the glamor is characterized by a higher earnings growth rate.

GLASS-STEAGALL ACT OF 1933 legislation passed by Congress authorizing deposit insurance and prohibiting commercial banks from owning full-service brokerage firms. Under Glass-Steagall, these banks were prohibited from investment banking activities, such as underwriting corporate securities or municipal revenue bonds. The law was designed to insulate bank depositors from the risk involved when a bank deals in securities and to prevent a bank collapse like the one that occurred during the Great Depression. The original separation of commercial and investment banking has been significantly eroded in recent years, however, since banks now own discount brokerage operations, sell mutual funds and can perform some corporate and municipal underwriting operations, and can provide other investment services.

GLOBAL DEPOSITARY RECEIPT receipt for shares in a foreign-based corporation traded in capital markets around the world. While AMERICAN DEPOSITARY RECEIPTS permit foreign corporations to offer shares to American citizens, Global Depositary Receipts (GDRs) allow companies in Europe, Asia, the United States and Latin America to offer shares in many markets around the world. The advantage to the issuing company is that they can raise capital in many markets, as opposed to just their home market. The advantage of GDRs to local investors is that they do not have to buy shares through the issuing company's home exchange, which may be difficult and expensive. In addition, the share price and all dividends are converted into the shareholder's home currency. Many GDRs are issued by companies in emerging markets such as China, India, Brazil, and South Korea and are traded on major stock exchanges, particularly the London SEAQ International Trading system. Because the companies issuing GDRs are not as well established and do not use the same accounting systems as traditional Western corporations, their stocks tend to be more volatile and less liquid.

GLOBAL MUTUAL FUND mutual fund that can invest in stocks and bonds throughout the world. Such funds typically have a portion of their assets in American markets as well as Europe, Asia, and developing countries. Global funds differ from INTERNATIONAL MUTUAL FUNDS, which invest only in non-U.S. securities. The advantage of global funds is that the fund managers can buy stocks or bonds anywhere they think has the best opportunities for high returns. Thus if one market is underperforming, they can shift assets to markets with better potential. Though some global funds invest in both stocks and bonds, most funds specialize in either stocks or bonds.

GNOMES OF ZÜRICH term coined by Labour ministers of Great Britain, during the sterling crisis of 1964, to describe the financiers and bankers in Zürich, Switzerland, who were engaged in foreign exchange speculation.

GNP *see* GROSS NATIONAL PRODUCT.

GOAL financial objective set by an individual or institution. For example, an individual investor might set a goal to accumulate enough capital to finance a child's college education. A pension fund's goal is to build up enough money to pay pensioners their promised benefits. Investors may also set specific price objectives when buying a security. For example, an investor buying a stock at $30 may set a price goal of $50, at which point he or she will sell shares, or at least reevaluate whether or not to continue holding the stock. Also called *target price*.

GO AROUND term used to describe the process whereby the trading desk at the New York Federal Reserve Bank ("the DESK"), acting on behalf of the FEDERAL OPEN MARKET COMMITTEE, contacts primary dealers for bid and offer prices. Primary dealers are those banks and investment houses approved for direct purchase and sale transactions with the Federal Reserve System in its OPEN-MARKET OPERATIONS.

GODFATHER OFFER takeover offer that is so generous that management of the target company is unable to refuse it out of fear of shareholder lawsuits.

GO-GO FUND MUTUAL FUND that invests in highly risky but potentially rewarding stocks. During the 1960s many go-go funds shot up in value, only to fall dramatically later and, in some cases, to go out of business as their speculative investments fizzled.

GOING AHEAD unethical securities brokerage act whereby the broker trades first for his own account before filling his customers' orders. Brokers who go ahead violate the RULES OF FAIR PRACTICE of the National Association of Securities Dealers.

GOING AWAY bonds purchased by dealers for immediate resale to investors, as opposed to bonds purchased *for stock*—that is, to be held in inventory for resale at some future time. The significance of the difference is that bonds bought going away will not overhang the market and cause adverse pressure on prices.

  The term is also used in new offerings of serial bonds to describe large purchases, usually by institutional investors, of the bonds in a particular maturity grouping (or series).

GOING-CONCERN VALUE value of a company as an operating business to another company or individual. The excess of going-concern value over asset value, or LIQUIDATING VALUE, is the value of the operating organization as distinct from the value of its assets. In acquisition accounting, going-concern value in excess of asset value is treated as an intangible asset, termed *goodwill.* Goodwill is generally understood to represent the value of a well-respected business name, good customer relations, high employee morale, and other such factors expected to translate into greater than normal earning power. However, because this intangible asset has no independent market or liquidation value, accepted accounting principles require that goodwill be written off over a period of time. The Revenue Reconciliation Act of 1993 provides that goodwill and related intangible assets can be deducted ratably over a 15-year (180-month) period on a straight-line method.

GOING LONG purchasing a stock, bond, or commodity for investment or speculation. Such a security purchase is known as a LONG POSITION. The opposite of going long is GOING SHORT, when an investor sells a security he does not own and thereby creates a SHORT POSITION.

GOING PRIVATE movement from public ownership to private ownership of a company's shares either by the company's repurchase of shares or through purchases by an outside private investor. A company usually goes private when the market price of its shares is substantially below their BOOK VALUE and the opportunity thus exists to buy the assets cheaply. Another motive for going private is to ensure the tenure of existing management by removing the company as a takeover prospect.

GOING PUBLIC securities industry phrase used when a private company first offers its shares to the public. The firm's ownership thus shifts from the hands of a few private stockowners to a base that includes public shareholders. At the moment of going public, the stock is called an INITIAL PUBLIC OFFERING. From that point on, or until the company goes private again, its shares have a MARKET VALUE. *See also* NEW ISSUE; GOING PRIVATE.

GOING SHORT selling a stock or commodity that the seller does not have. An investor who goes short borrows stock from his or her broker, hoping to purchase other shares of it at a lower price. The investor will then replace the borrowed stock with the lower priced stock and keep the difference as profit. *See also* SELLING SHORT; GOING LONG.

GOLD BARS bars made out of 99.5% to 99.99% pure gold which can be traded for investment purposes or held by central banks. Gold bars range in size from 400 troy ounces to as little as 1 ounce of gold; an individual can either hold on to these bars or store them in a safe deposit box. Central banks store gold bars weighing 400 troy ounces in vaults. In the United States, gold is stored at a few Federal Reserve banks and Fort Knox, for example. In the past, this gold directly backed the American currency, but now it serves more as a symbolic backing for dollars issued by the Federal Reserve.

GOLD BOND bond backed by gold. Such debt obligations are issued by gold-mining companies, who peg interest payments to the level of gold prices. Investors who buy these bonds therefore anticipate a rising gold price. Silver mining firms similarly issue silver-backed bonds.

GOLDBUG analyst enamored of gold as an investment. Goldbugs usually are worried about possible disasters in the world economy, such as a depression or hyperinflation, and recommend gold as a HEDGE.

GOLD BULLION gold in its purest form. The metal may be smelted into GOLD COINS or GOLD BARS of different sizes. The price of gold bullion is set by market forces of supply and demand. Twice a day, the latest gold price is fixed at the

London GOLD FIXING. Gold bullion is traded in physical form, and also through futures and options contracts. Certain gold-oriented mutual funds also hold small amounts of gold bullion.

GOLD CERTIFICATE paper certificate providing evidence of ownership of gold bullion. An investor not wanting to hold the actual gold in his or her home because of lack of security, for example, may prefer to hold gold in certificate form; the physical gold backing the certificate is held in a secure bank vault. Certificate owners pay a small custodial charge each year to the custodian bank.

GOLD COIN coin minted in gold. Bullion coins are minted by governments and are traded mostly on the value of their gold content. Major gold bullion coins include the American Eagle, the Canadian Maple Leaf, the Mexican Peso, the Australian Kangaroo, and the South African Kruggerand. Other gold coins, called NUMISMATIC COINS, are minted in limited quantity and trade more on the basis of their aesthetic value and rarity, rather than on their gold content. Numismatic coins are sold at a hefty markup to their gold content, and are therefore not as pure a play on gold prices as bullion coins.

GOLDEN BOOT inducement, using maximum incentives and financial benefits, for an older worker to take "voluntary" early retirement, thus circumventing age discrimination laws.

GOLDEN HANDCUFFS contract that ties a broker to a brokerage firm. If the broker stays at the firm, he or she will earn lucrative commissions, bonuses, and other compensation. But if the broker leaves and tries to lure clients to another firm, the broker must promise to give back to the firm much of the compensation received while working there. Golden handcuffs are a response by the brokerage industry to the frequent movement of brokers from one firm to another.

GOLDEN HANDSHAKE generous payment by a company to a director, senior executive, or consultant who is let go before his or her contract expires because of a takeover or other development. *See also* GOLDEN PARACHUTE.

GOLDEN HELLO bonus paid by a securities firm, usually in England, to get a key employee away from a competing firm.

GOLDEN PARACHUTE lucrative contract given to a top executive to provide lavish benefits in case the company is taken over by another firm, resulting in the loss of the job. A golden parachute might include generous severance pay, stock options, or a bonus. The TAX REFORM ACT OF 1984 eliminated the deductibility of "excess compensation" and imposed an excise tax. The TAX REFORM ACT OF 1986 covered matters of clarification.

GOLD FIXING daily determination of the price of gold by selected gold specialists and bank officials in London, Paris, and Zürich. The price is fixed at 10:30 A.M. and 3:30 P.M. London time every business day, according to the prevailing market forces of supply and demand.

GOLDILOCKS ECONOMY term coined in the mid-90s to describe an economy that was "not too hot, not too cold, just right," as was the porridge in the children's story of "Goldilocks and the Three Bears." Adroit MONETARY POLICY was credited for an economy that enjoyed steady growth with a nominal rate of inflation. *See also* SOFT LANDING.

GOLD MUTUAL FUND mutual fund investing in gold mining shares. Some funds limit themselves to shares in North American mining companies, while others can buy shares anywhere in the world, including predominantly South Africa and Australia. Such mutual funds offer investors diversification among many gold mining companies, somewhat reducing risks. Still, such funds tend to be volatile, since the prices of gold mining shares tend to move up or down far more than the price of gold itself. Gold funds also tend to pay dividends, since many gold mining companies pay dividends based on gold sales.

GOLD STANDARD monetary system under which units of currency are convertible into fixed amounts of gold. Such a system is said to be anti-inflationary. The United States has been on the gold standard in the past but was taken off in 1971. *See also* HARD MONEY.

GOODBYE KISS *see* GREENMAIL.

GOOD DELIVERY securities industry designation meaning that a certificate has the necessary endorsements and meets all other requirements (signature guarantee, proper denomination, and other qualifications), so that title can be transferred by delivery to the buying broker, who is then obligated to accept it. Exceptions constitute *bad delivery. See also* DELIVERY DATE.

GOOD FAITH DEPOSIT
In general: token amount of money advanced to indicate intent to pursue a contract to completion.
Commodities: initial margin deposit required when buying or selling a futures contract. Such deposits generally range from 2% to 10% of the contract value.
Securities:
1. deposit, usually 25% of a transaction, required by securities firms of individuals who are not known to them but wish to enter orders with them.
2. deposit left with a municipal bond issuer by a firm competing for the underwriting business. The deposit typically equals 1% to 5% of the principal amount of the issue and is refundable to the unsuccessful bidders.

GOOD MONEY
Banking: federal funds, which are good the same day, in contrast to CLEARING HOUSE FUNDS. Clearing house funds are understood in two ways: (1) funds requiring three days to clear and (2) funds used to settle transactions on which there is a one-day FLOAT.
Gresham's Law: theory that money of superior intrinsic value, "good money," will eventually be driven out of circulation by money of lesser intrinsic value. *See also* GRESHAM'S LAW.

GOOD-THIS-MONTH ORDER (GTM) order to buy or sell securities (usually at a LIMIT PRICE or STOP PRICE set by the customer) that remains in effect until the end of the month. In the case of a limit price, the customer instructs the broker either to buy at the stipulated limit price or anything lower, or to sell at the limit price or anything higher. In the case of a stop price, the customer instructs the broker to enter a market order once a transaction in the security occurs at the stop price specified.
    A variation on the GTM order is the *good-this-week-order* (GTW), which expires at the end of the week if it is not executed.
    See also DAY ORDER; GOOD-TILL-CANCELED ORDER; LIMIT ORDER; OPEN ORDER; STOP ORDER.

GOOD THROUGH order to buy or sell securities or commodities at a stated price for a stated period of time, unless canceled, executed, or changed. It is a type of LIMIT ORDER and may be specified GTW (good this week), GTM (GOOD-THIS-MONTH ORDER), or for shorter or longer periods.

GOOD-TILL-CANCELED ORDER (GTC) brokerage customer's order to buy or sell a security, usually at a particular price, that remains in effect until executed or canceled. If the GTC order remains unfilled after a long period of time, a broker will usually periodically confirm that the customer still wants the transaction to occur if the stock reaches the target price. *See also* DAY ORDER; GOOD-THIS-MONTH ORDER; OPEN ORDER; TARGET PRICE.

GOODWILL *see* GOING-CONCERN VALUE.

GOVERNMENT NATIONAL MORTGAGE ASSOCIATION (GNMA) government-owned corporation, nicknamed Ginnie Mae, which is an agency of the U.S. Department of Housing and Urban Development. GNMA guarantees, with the full faith and credit of the U.S. Government, full and timely payment of all monthly principal and interest payments on the mortgage-backed PASS-THROUGH SECURITIES of registered holders. The securities, which are issued by private firms, such as MORTGAGE BANKERS and savings institutions, and typically marketed through security broker-dealers, represent pools of residential mortgages insured or guaranteed by the Federal Housing Administration (FHA), the Farmer's Home Administration (FmHA), or the Veterans Administration (VA). *See also* FEDERAL HOME LOAN MORTGAGE CORPORATION; FEDERAL NATIONAL MORTGAGE ASSOCIATION; GINNIE MAE PASS-THROUGH.

GOVERNMENT OBLIGATIONS U.S. government debt instruments (Treasury bonds, bills, notes, savings bonds) the government has pledged to repay. *See* GOVERNMENTS.

GOVERNMENTS
1. securities issued by the U.S. government, such as Treasury bills, bonds, notes, and savings bonds. Governments are the most creditworthy of all debt instruments since they are backed by the FULL FAITH AND CREDIT of the U.S. government, which if necessary can print money to make payments. Also called TREASURIES.
2. debt issues of federal agencies, which are not directly backed by the U.S. government. *See also* GOVERNMENT SECURITIES.

GOVERNMENT SECURITIES securities issued by U.S. government agencies, such as the RESOLUTION FUNDING CORPORATION (REFCORP) or the Federal Land Bank; also called *agency securities*. Although these securities have high credit ratings, they are not considered to be GOVERNMENT OBLIGATIONS and therefore are not directly backed by the FULL FAITH AND CREDIT of the government as TREASURIES are. *See also* AGENCY SECURITIES.

GRACE PERIOD period of time provided in most loan contracts and insurance policies during which default or cancellation will not occur even though payment is due.
Credit cards: number of days between when a credit card bill is sent and when the payment is due without incurring interest charges. Most banks offer credit card holders a 25-day grace period, though some offer more and others fewer days.
Insurance: number of days, typically 30, during which insurance coverage is in force and premiums have not been paid.
Loans: provision in some long-term loans, particularly EUROCURRENCY syndication loans to foreign governments and multinational firms by groups of banks, whereby repayment of principal does not begin until some point well into the lifetime of the loan. The grace period, which can be as long as five years for international transactions for corporations, is an important point of negotiation between a borrower and a lender; borrowers sometimes will accept a higher interest rate to obtain a longer grace period.

GRADUATED CALL WRITING strategy of writing (selling) covered CALL OPTIONS at gradually higher EXERCISE PRICES so that as the price of the underlying stock rises and the options are exercised, the seller winds up with a higher average price than the original exercise price. The premiums naturally rise as the underlying stock rises, representing income to the seller that helps offset the loss if the stock should decline.

GRADUATED LEASE longer-term lease in which payments, instead of being fixed, are adjusted periodically based on appraisals or a benchmark rate, such as increases in the CONSUMER PRICE INDEX.

GRADUATED-PAYMENT MORTGAGE (GPM) mortgage featuring lower monthly payments at first, which steadily rise until they level off after a few years. GPMs, also known as "jeeps," are designed for young couples whose income is expected to grow as their careers advance. A graduated-payment mortgage allows such a family to buy a house that would be unaffordable if mortgage payments started out at a high level. Persons planning to take on such a mortgage must be confident that their income will be able to keep pace with the rising payments. *See also* ADJUSTABLE RATE MORTGAGE; CONVENTIONAL MORTGAGE; REVERSE ANNUITY MORTGAGE; VARIABLE RATE MORTGAGE.

GRADUATED SECURITY security whose listing has been upgraded by moving from one exchange to another—for example, from the American Stock Exchange to the more prestigious New York Stock Exchange, or from a regional exchange to a national exchange. An advantage of such a transfer is to widen trading in the security.

GRAHAM AND DODD METHOD OF INVESTING investment approach outlined in Benjamin Graham and David Dodd's landmark book *Security Analysis,* published in the 1930s. Graham and Dodd founded the modern discipline of security analysis with their work. They believed that investors should buy stocks with undervalued assets and that eventually those assets would appreciate to their true value in the marketplace. Graham and Dodd advocated buying stocks in companies where current assets exceed current liabilities and all long-term debt, and where the stock is selling at a low PRICE/EARNINGS RATIO. They suggested that the stocks be sold after a profit objective of between 50% and 100% was reached, which they assumed would be three years or less from the time of purchase. Analysts today who call themselves Graham and Dodd investors hunt for stocks selling below their LIQUIDATING VALUE and do not necessarily concern themselves with the potential for earnings growth.

GRANDFATHER CLAUSE provision included in a new rule that exempts from the rule a person or business already engaged in the activity coming under regulation. For example, the Financial Accounting Standards Board might adopt a rule effective in 1998 relating, say, to depreciation that, under a grandfather clause, would exempt assets put in service before 1998.

GRANTOR
Investments: options trader who sells a CALL OPTION or a PUT OPTION and collects PREMIUM INCOME for doing so. The grantor sells the right to buy a security at a certain price in the case of a call, and the right to sell at a certain price in the case of a put.
Law: one who executes a deed conveying title to property or who creates a trust. Also called a *settlor.*

GRANTOR RETAINED INCOME TRUST (GRIT) type of TRUST designed to save estate taxes in the event the GRANTOR outlives the trust termination date. Under such a trust, which must be irrevocable and have a life of at least 15 years, the grantor transfers property immediately to the beneficiary but receives income until termination, at which time the beneficiary begins receiving it. At that point the grantor pays a GIFT TAX based on the original value of the gift. When the grantor dies, the gift is added back to the grantor's estate at the value as of the day of the gift, not its (presumably) higher current value.

GRAVEYARD MARKET bear market wherein investors who sell are faced with substantial losses, while potential investors prefer to stay liquid, that is, to keep their money in cash or cash equivalents until market conditions improve. Like a graveyard, those who are in can't get out and those who are out have no desire to get in.

GRAY KNIGHT acquiring company that, acting to advance its own interests, out-bids a WHITE KNIGHT but that, not being unfriendly, is preferable to a hostile bidder.

GRAY MARKET
Consumer goods: sale of products by unauthorized dealers, frequently at dis-counted prices. Consumers who buy gray market goods may find that the manu-facturer refuses to honor the product warranty. In some cases, gray market goods may be sold in a country they were not intended for, so, for example, instruc-tions may be in another language than the home market language.
Securities: sale of securities that have not officially been issued yet by a firm that is not a member of the underwriting syndicate. Such trading in the when-issued, or gray, market can provide a good indication of the amount of demand for an upcoming new stock or bond issue.

GREATER FOOL THEORY theory that even though a stock or the market as a whole is FULLY VALUED, speculation is justified because there are enough fools to push prices further upward.

GREENMAIL payment of a premium to a raider trying to take over a company through a proxy contest or other means. Also known as BON VOYAGE BONUS, it is designed to thwart the takeover. By accepting the payment, the raider agrees not to buy any more shares or pursue the takeover any further for a specified number of years. *See also* GOODBYE KISS.

GREEN SHOE clause in an underwriting agreement saying that, in the event of exceptional public demand, the issuer will authorize additional shares for distri-bution by the syndicate.

GRESHAM'S LAW theory in economics that bad money drives out good money. Specifically, people faced with a choice of two currencies of the same nominal value, one of which is preferable to the other because of metal content or because it resists mutilation, will hoard the good money and spend the bad money, there-by driving the good money out of circulation. The observation is named for Sir Thomas Gresham, master of the mint in the reign of Queen Elizabeth I.

GRIT *see* GRANTOR RETAINED INCOME TRUST (GRIT).

GROSS DOMESTIC PRODUCT (GDP) market value of the goods and services produced by labor and property in the United States. GDP is made up of con-sumer and government purchases, private domestic investments, and net exports of goods and services. Figures for GDP are released by the Commerce Department on a quarterly basis. Growth of the U.S. economy is measured by the change in inflation-adjusted GDP, or real GDP. Formerly called *Gross National Product.*

GROSS EARNINGS personal taxable income before adjustments made to arrive at ADJUSTED GROSS INCOME.

GROSS ESTATE total value of a person's assets before liabilities such as debts and taxes are deducted. After someone dies, the executor of the will makes an assessment of the stocks, bonds, real estate, and personal possessions that comprise the gross estate. Debts and taxes are paid, as are funeral expenses and estate administration costs. Beneficiaries of the will then receive their portion of the remainder, which is called the *net estate.*

GROSS INCOME total personal income before exclusions and deductions.

GROSS LEASE property lease under which the lessor (landlord) agrees to pay all the expenses normally associated with ownership (insurance, taxes, utilities, repairs). An exception might be that the lessee (tenant) would be required to pay real estate taxes above a stipulated amount or to pay for certain special operating expenses (snow removal, grounds care in the case of a shopping center, or institutional advertising, for example). Gross leases are the most common type of lease contract and are typical arrangements for short-term tenancy. They normally contain no provision for periodic rent adjustments, nor are there preestablished renewal arrangements. *See also* NET LEASE.

GROSS NATIONAL PRODUCT (GNP) *see* GROSS DOMESTIC PRODUCT.

GROSS PER BROKER gross amount of commission revenues attributable to a particular REGISTERED REPRESENTATIVE during a given period. Brokers, who typically keep one third of the commissions they generate, are often expected by their firms to meet productivity quotas based on their gross.

GROSS PROFIT net sales less the COST OF GOODS SOLD. Also called *gross margin. See also* NET PROFIT.

GROSS SALES total sales at invoice values, not reduced by customer discounts, returns or allowances, or other adjustments. *See also* NET SALES.

GROSS SPREAD difference (spread) between the public offering price of a security and the price paid by an underwriter to the issuer. The spread breaks down into the manager's fee, the dealer's (or underwriter's) discount, and the selling concession (i.e., the discount offered to a selling group). *See also* CONCESSION; FLOTATION (FLOATATION) COST.

GROUND LEASE lease on the land. Typically, the land will be under a building, which will have its own leases with tenants.

GROUP INSURANCE insurance coverage bought for and provided to a group instead of an individual. For example, an employer may buy disability, health, and term life insurance for its employees at a far better rate than the employees could obtain on their own. Credit unions, trade associations, and other groups may also offer their members preferential group insurance rates. Group insurance is not only advantageous to employees or group members because it is cheaper than they could obtain on their own, but some people may be able to get coverage under the group umbrella when they would be denied coverage individually because of preexisting conditions or other factors.

GROUP OF TEN ten major industrialized countries that try to coordinate monetary and fiscal policies to create a more stable world economic system. The ten are Belgium, Canada, France, Germany, Italy, Japan, the Netherlands, Sweden, the United Kingdom, and the United States. Also known as the *Paris Club.*

GROUP ROTATION tendency of stocks in one industry to outperform and then underperform other industries. This may be due to the economic cycle or what industry is popular or unpopular with investors at any particular time. For example, CYCLICAL stocks in the auto, paper, or steel industry may be group leaders when the economy is showing robust growth, while stocks of stable-demand firms such as drug or food companies may be market leaders in a recession. Alternatively, investor demand for stocks in certain industries, such as biotechnology, computer software, or real estate investment trusts may rise and fall because of enthusiasm or disappointment with the group, creating rotation into or out of such stocks. Market analysts watch which industry group is coming into and going out of vogue in recommending stocks that might lead or lag in coming months.

GROUP SALES term used in securities underwriting that refers to block sales made to institutional investors. The securities come out of a syndicate "pot" with credit for the sale prorated among the syndicate members in proportion to their original allotments.

GROUP UNIVERSAL LIFE POLICY (GULP) UNIVERSAL LIFE INSURANCE offered on a group basis, and therefore more cheaply than one could obtain it personally, to employees and, sometimes, their family members.

GROWING EQUITY MORTGAGE (GEM) mortgage with a fixed interest rate and growing payments. This technique allows the homeowner to build equity in the underlying home faster than if they made the same mortgage payment for the life of the loan. Borrowers who take on GEM loans should be confident in their ability to make higher payments over time based on their prospects for rising income.

GROWTH AND INCOME FUND MUTUAL FUND that seeks earnings growth as well as income. These funds invest mainly in the common stock of companies with a history of capital gains but that also have a record of consistent dividend payments.

GROWTH FUND mutual fund that invests in growth stocks. The goal is to provide capital appreciation for the fund's shareholders over the long term. Growth funds are more volatile than more conservative income or money market funds. They tend to rise faster than conservative funds in bull (advancing) markets and to drop more sharply in bear (falling) markets. *See also* GROWTH STOCK.

GROWTH RATE percentage rate at which the economy, stocks, or earnings are growing. The economic growth rate is normally determined by the growth of the GROSS DOMESTIC PRODUCT. Individual companies try to establish a rate at which their earnings grow over time. Firms with long-term earnings growth rates of more than 15% are considered fast-growing companies. Analysts also apply the term *growth rate* to specific financial aspects of a company's operations, such as dividends, sales, assets, and market share. Analysts use growth rates to compare one company to another within the same industry.

GROWTH STOCK stock of a corporation that has exhibited faster-than-average gains in earnings over the last few years and is expected to continue to show high levels of profit growth. Over the long run, growth stocks tend to outperform slower-growing or stagnant stocks. Growth stocks are riskier investments than average stocks, however, since they usually sport higher price/earnings ratios and make little or no dividend payments to shareholders. *See also* PRICE/EARNINGS RATIO.

GUARANTEE to take responsibility for payment of a debt or performance of some obligation if the person primarily liable fails to perform. A guarantee is a CONTINGENT LIABILITY of the guarantor—that is, it is a potential liability not recognized in accounts until the outcome becomes probable in the opinion of the company's accountant.

GUARANTEED BOND bond on which the principal and interest are guaranteed by a firm other than the issuer. Such bonds are nearly always railroad bonds, arising out of situations where one road has leased the road of another and the security holders of the leased road require assurance of income in exchange for giving up control of the property. Guaranteed securities involved in such situations may also include preferred or common stocks when dividends are guaranteed. Both guaranteed stock and guaranteed bonds become, in effect, DEBENTURE (unsecured) bonds of the guarantor, although the status of the stock may be questionable in the event of LIQUIDATION. In any event, if the guarantor enjoys stronger credit than the railroad whose securities are being guaranteed, the securities have greater value.

Guaranteed bonds may also arise out of parent-subsidiary relationships where bonds are issued by the subsidiary with the parent's guarantee.

GUARANTEED INSURABILITY feature offered as an option in life and health insurance policies that enables the insured to add coverage at specified future times and at standard rates without evidence of insurability.

GUARANTEED INVESTMENT CONTRACT contract between an insurance company and a corporate profit-sharing or pension plan that guarantees a specific rate of return on the invested capital over the life of the contract. Many defined contribution plans, such as 401(k) and 403(b) plans, offer guaranteed investment contracts as investment options to employees. Although the insurance company takes all market, credit, and interest rate risks on the investment portfolio, it can profit if its return exceeds the guaranteed amount. Only the insurance company backs the guarantee, not any governmental agency, so if the insurer fails, it is possible that there could be a default on the contract. For pension and profit-sharing plans, guaranteed investment contracts, also known as GICs, are a conservative way of assuring beneficiaries that their money will achieve a certain rate of return. *See also* BANK INVESTMENT CONTRACT.

GUARANTEED RENEWABLE POLICY INSURANCE policy that requires the insurer to renew the policy for a period specified in the contract provided premiums are paid in a timely fashion. The insurer cannot make any changes in the provisions of the policy other than a change in the premium rate for all insureds in the same class.

GUARANTEED REPLACEMENT COST COVERAGE INSURANCE policy that pays for the full cost of replacing damaged property without a deduction for depreciation and without a dollar limit. This policy is different from an actual cash value policy, which takes into account depreciation for lost and damaged items, if the damage resulted from an insured peril.

GUARANTEED STOCK *see* GUARANTEED BOND.

GUARANTEE LETTER letter by a commercial bank that guarantees payment of the EXERCISE PRICE of a client's PUT OPTION (the right to sell a given security at a particular price within a specified period) if or when a notice indicating its exercise, called an assignment notice, is presented to the option seller (writer).

GUARANTEE OF SIGNATURE certificate issued by a bank or brokerage firm vouching for the authenticity of a person's signature. Such a document may be necessary when stocks, bonds, or other registered securities are transferred from a seller to a buyer. Banks also require guarantees of signature before they will process certain transactions.

GUARDIAN individual who has the legal right to care for another person as a parent or to act as an administrator of the assets of a person declared incompetent for mental or physical reasons. Guardians can be *testamentary*, meaning appointed in a parent's will; *general*, meaning having the general responsibility to care for another person and that person's estate; or *special*, meaning the guardian has limited authority, such as half the responsibility of a general guardian but not the other.

GULP *see* GROUP UNIVERSAL LIFE POLICY (GULP).

GUN JUMPING
1. trading securities on information before it becomes publicly disclosed.
2. illegally soliciting buy orders in an underwriting, before a Securities and Exchange Commission REGISTRATION is complete.

GUNSLINGER aggressive portfolio manager who buys speculative stocks, often on margin. In the great bull market of the 1960s, several hot fund managers gained reputations and had huge followings as gunslingers by producing enormous returns while taking great risks. However, the bear market of the early 1970s caused many of these gunslingers to lose huge amounts of money, and in most cases, their followings. The term is still used when referring to popular managers who take big risks in search of high returns.

h

HAIRCUT securities industry term referring to the formulas used in the valuation of securities for the purpose of calculating a broker-dealer's net capital. The haircut varies according to the class of a security, its market risk, and the time to maturity. For example, cash equivalent GOVERNMENTS could have a 0% haircut, equities could have an average 30% haircut, and fail positions (securities with past due delivery) with little prospect of settlement could have a 100% haircut. *See also* CASH EQUIVALENTS; FAIL POSITION.

HALF-LIFE point in time in which half the principal has been repaid in a mortgage-backed security guaranteed or issued by the GOVERNMENT NATIONAL MORTGAGE ASSOCIATION, the FEDERAL NATIONAL MORTGAGE ASSOCIATION, or the FEDERAL HOME LOAN MORTGAGE CORPORATION. Normally, it is assumed that such a security has a half-life of 12 years. But specific mortgage pools can have vastly longer or shorter half-lives, depending on interest rate trends. If interest rates fall, more homeowners will refinance their mortgages, meaning that principal will be paid off more quickly, and half-lives will drop. If interest rates rise, homeowners will hold onto their mortgages longer than anticipated, and half-lives will rise.

HALF-STOCK common or preferred stock with a $50 PAR value instead of the more conventional $100 par value.

HAMMERING THE MARKET intense selling of stocks by those who think prices are inflated. Speculators who think the market is about to drop, and therefore sell short, are said to be hammering the market. *See also* SELLING SHORT.

HANDS-OFF INVESTOR investor willing to take a passive role in the management of a corporation. An individual or corporation with a large stake in another company may decide to adopt a "hands-off" policy if it is satisfied with the current performance of management. However, if management falters, it may become more actively involved in corporate strategy.

HANDS-ON INVESTOR investor who takes an active role in the management of the company whose stock he or she has bought.

HANG SENG INDEX the major indicator of stock market performance in Hong Kong. The index is comprised of 33 companies, divided into four sub-indices: financial (4), property (9), utilities (6), commerce and industry (14). It is computed on an arithmetic basis, weighted by market capitalization, and strongly

influenced by large capitalization stocks such as Hongkong Bank, Hang Seng
Bank, Hongkong Land and Cheung Kong.

HARD DOLLARS actual payments made by a customer for services, including
research, provided by a brokerage firm. For instance, if a broker puts together a
financial plan for a client, the fee might be $1000 in hard dollars. This contrasts
with SOFT DOLLARS, which refers to compensation by way of the commissions a
broker would receive if he were to carry out any trades called for in that financial plan. Brokerage house research is sold for either hard or soft dollars.

HARD MONEY (HARD CURRENCY)
1. currency in which there is widespread confidence. It is the currency of an
   economically and politically stable country, such as the U.S. or Switzerland.
   Countries that have taken out loans in hard money generally must repay them
   in hard money.
2. gold or coins, as contrasted with paper currency, which is considered *soft
   money*. Some hard-money enthusiasts advocate a return to the GOLD STAN-
   DARD as a method of reducing inflation and promoting economic growth.

HEAD AND SHOULDERS patterns resembling the head and shoulders outline of
a person, which is used to chart stock price trends. The pattern signals the reversal of a trend. As prices move down to the right shoulder, a head and shoulders
top is formed, meaning that prices should be falling. A reverse head and shoulders pattern has the head at the bottom of the chart, meaning that prices should
be rising.

HEAD AND SHOULDERS

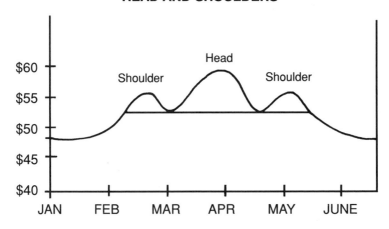

HEAD OF HOUSEHOLD tax filing status available in the tax code to individuals
who provide more than half of the financial support to their household during
the tax year. Heads of household can be married or single, as long as they support dependent children or grandchildren, parents, or other close relatives living
at home. Those qualifying for head-of-household status pay the same tax rates as
singles and married couples filing jointly, but the rates apply at different income
levels. For example, a head of household pays a 28% tax rate on taxable income
between $33,051 and $85,350, while a single pays the same tax rate on income
between $24,651 and $59,750, and a married couple filing jointly pays 28% on
$41,201 to $99,600.

HEALTH INSURANCE in popular usage, any insurance plan that covers medical expenses or health care services, including HMOs, insured plans, preferred provider organizations, etc. In insurance, protection against loss by sickness or bodily injury, in which sense it is synonymous with accident and health, accident and sickness, accident, or disability income insurance.

HEAVY MARKET stock, bond, or commodity market with falling prices resulting from a larger supply of offers to sell than bids to buy.

HEDGE/HEDGING strategy used to offset investment risk. A perfect hedge is one eliminating the possibility of future gain or loss.

A stockholder worried about declining stock prices, for instance, can hedge his or her holdings by buying a PUT OPTION on the stock or selling a CALL OPTION. Someone owning 100 shares of XYZ stock, selling at $70 per share, can hedge his position by buying a put option giving him the right to sell 100 shares at $70 at any time over the next few months. This investor must pay a certain amount of money, called a PREMIUM, for these rights. If XYZ stock falls during that time, the investor can exercise his option—that is, sell the stock at $70—thereby preserving the $70 value of the XYZ holdings. The same XYZ stockholder can also hedge his position by selling a call option. In such a transaction, he sells the right to buy XYZ stock at $70 per share for the next few months. In return, he receives a premium. If XYZ stock falls in price, that premium income will offset to some extent the drop in value of the stock.

SELLING SHORT is another widely used hedging technique.

Investors often try to hedge against inflation by purchasing assets that will rise in value faster than inflation, such as gold, real estate, or other tangible assets.

Large commercial firms that want to be assured of the price they will receive or pay for a commodity will hedge their position by buying and selling simultaneously in the FUTURES MARKET. For example, Hershey's, the chocolate company, will hedge its supplies of cocoa in the futures market to limit the risk of a rise in cocoa prices.

Managers of large pools of money such as pension and mutual funds frequently hedge their exposure to currency or interest rate risk by buying or selling futures or options contracts. For example, a GLOBAL MUTUAL FUND manager with a large position in Japanese stocks who thinks the Japanese yen is about to fall in value against the U.S. dollar may buy futures or options on the Japanese yen to offset the projected loss on the currency.

HEDGE CLAUSE disclaimer seen in market letters, security research reports, or other printed matter having to do with evaluating investments, which purports to absolve the writer from responsibility for the accuracy of information obtained from usually reliable sources. Despite such clauses, which may mitigate liability, writers may still be charged with negligence in their use of information. Typical language of a hedge clause: "The information furnished herein has been obtained from sources believed to be reliable, but its accuracy is not guaranteed."

HEDGED TENDER SELLING SHORT a portion of the shares being tendered to protect against a price drop in the event all shares tendered are not accepted. For example, ABC Company or another company wishing to acquire ABC Company announces a TENDER OFFER at $52 a share when ABC shares are selling at a market price of $40. The market price of ABC will now rise to near the tender price of $52. An investor wishing to sell all his or her 2000 shares at $52 will tender 2000 shares, but cannot be assured all shares will be accepted. To lock in the $52 price on the tendered shares the investor thinks might not be accepted—say half of them or 1000 shares—he or she will sell short that many shares.

Assuming the investor has guessed correctly and only 1000 shares are accepted, when the tender offer expires and the market price of ABC begins to drop, the investor will still have sold all 2000 shares for $52 or close to it—half to the tenderer and the other half when the short sale is consummated.

HEDGE FUND private investment partnership (for U.S. investors) or an off-shore investment corporation (for non-U.S. or tax-exempt investors) in which the general partner has made a substantial personal investment, and whose offering memorandum allows for the fund to take both long and short positions, use leverage and derivatives, and invest in many markets. Hedge funds often take large risks on speculative strategies, including PROGRAM TRADING, SELLING SHORT, SWAPS, and ARBITRAGE. A fund need not employ all of these tools all of the time; it must merely have them at its disposal. Since hedge funds are not limited to buying securities, they can potentially profit in any market environment, including one with sharply declining prices. Because they move billions of dollars in and out of markets quickly, hedge funds can have a significant impact on the day-to-day trading developments in the stock, bond, and futures markets.

Hedge funds entitle the general partner to an additional incentive management fee based upon positive returns—the higher the returns, the higher their fee. Hedge funds require that 65% of all investors be of the *accredited* type, defined as an individual or couple who have a net worth of at least $1 million, or an individual who had income in the previous year of at least $200,000, or a couple with at least $300,000 of income in the previous year. In reality, though, an investor needs much more than that.

The funds also require substantial minimum investments that can make it hard even for accredited investors to ante up. Minimums typically range from about $250,000 to $10 million. An investor gives up liquidity in hedge funds. They typically have a one-year lock-up for first-time investors.

HEDGE WRAPPER options strategy where the holder of a long position in an underlying stock buys an OUT OF THE MONEY put and sells an out of the money call. It defines a range where the stock will be sold at expiration of the option, whatever way the stock moves. The maximum profit is made if the call is exercised at expiration, since the holder gets the strike price plus any dividends. The maximum loss occurs if the put option is exercised, and represents the cost of the hedge wrapper less the strike price plus dividends received. The cost of the hedge wrapper less dividends received is the breakeven point. The strategy produces a loss whenever the breakeven price is higher than the strike price of the call.

HEIR one who inherits some or all of the estate of a deceased person by virtue of being in the direct line (*heir of the body*), or being designated in a will or by a legal authority (*heir at law*).

HEMLINE THEORY whimsical idea that stock prices move in the same general direction as the hemlines of women's dresses. Short skirts in the 1920s and 1960s were considered bullish signs that stock prices would rise, whereas longer dresses in the 1930s and 1940s were considered bearish (falling) indicators. Despite its sometimes uncanny way of being prophetic, the hemline theory has remained more in the area of wishful thinking than serious market analysis.

HEX LTD., HELSINKI STOCK AND DERIVATIVES EXCHANGE, clearing house formed in 1997 through the merger of the Helsinki Stock Exchange and SOM Ltd., Finnish Securities and Derivatives Exchange, Clearing House. HEX Ltd. is the parent company of two subsidiaries: EL-EX Electricity Exchange Ltd. and Somtel Ltd. Under an existing cooperation agreement between SOM and OM Stockholm AB, the Swedish exchange, SOM products can be traded in

Stockholm and at the market operated by OM's London-based exchange, OMLX. OM's products, in turn, are traded in Finland. The agreement also covers some cooperation on the equity market. The HEX Index includes all shares quoted on the exchange; share price indices are computed for industry groups. Futures and options are traded on the Finnish Options Index (FOX), currencies, and stocks. Futures are offered on the FIM government bond. Trading is fully automated through the HETI trading system, which is available in English. Clearing and settlement is through the Finnish Central Securities Depository's KATI clearing system. Trading hours: Monday through Friday, 9:30 A.M. to 5 P.M., with a pre-market session from 9 A.M. to 9:25 A.M., and an after-market session from 5:05 P.M. to 5:30 P.M.

HIBOR acronym for *Hong Kong Interbank Offered Rate,* the annualized offer rate paid by banks for Hong Kong dollar-denominated three-month deposits. It acts as a benchmark for many interest rates throughout the Far East.

HIDDEN LOAD sales charge which may not be immediately apparent to an investor. For example, a 12b-1 MUTUAL FUND assesses an annual asset base charge of up to 0.75% to cover marketing, distribution, and promotion expenses incurred by the fund. Even though it has been disclosed in the prospectus, many investors do not realize that they are paying this load. The sales charges levied on insurance policies are also hidden, because they are not explicitly disclosed to customers, and are instead subtracted from premiums paid by policyholders.

HIDDEN VALUES assets owned by a company but not yet reflected in its stock price. For example, a manufacturing firm may own valuable real estate that could be sold at a much higher price than it appears on the company's books, which is usually the price at which the real estate was purchased. Other undervalued assets that could have significant value include patents, trademarks, or exclusive contracts. Value-oriented money managers search for stocks with hidden values on their balance sheet in the hope that some day, those values will be realized through a higher stock price either by actions of the current management or by a takeover.

HIGH CREDIT
Banking: maximum amount of loans outstanding recorded for a particular customer.
Finance: the highest amount of TRADE CREDIT a particular company has received from a supplier at one time.

HIGH CURRENT INCOME MUTUAL FUND mutual fund with the objective of paying high income to shareholders. Such funds usually take higher risks than more conservative, but lower-yielding funds in order to provide an above-market rate of current yield. For example, JUNK BOND funds buy corporate bonds with below investment grade credit ratings in order to pay higher levels of income to shareholders than would be available from Treasury or high-quality corporate bonds. Another example of a high current income mutual fund is an international bond fund.

HIGH FLYER high-priced and highly speculative stock that moves up sharply over a short period. The stock of unproven high-technology companies might be high flyers, for instance.

HIGH-GRADE BOND bond rated triple-A or double-A by Standard & Poor's, Moody's, and other RATING services.

HIGHJACKING Japanese term for a TAKEOVER.

HIGHLY CONFIDENT LETTER letter from an investment banking firm that it is "highly confident" that it will be able to arrange financing for a securities deal.

This letter might be used to finance a leveraged buyout or multibillion-dollar takeover offer, for example. The board of directors of the target firm might request a highly confident letter in evaluating whether a proposed takeover can be financed. After the letter has been issued and the deal approved, the investment bankers will attempt to line up financing from banks, private investors, stock and bond offerings, and other sources. Though the investment banker professes to be highly confident he can arrange financing, the letter is not an ironclad guarantee of his ability to do so.

HIGHLY LEVERAGED TRANSACTION (HLT) loan, usually by a bank, to an already highly LEVERAGED COMPANY.

HIGH-PREMIUM CONVERTIBLE DEBENTURE bond with a long-term, high-premium, common stock conversion feature and also offering a fairly competitive interest rate. Premium refers in this case to the difference between the market value of the CONVERTIBLE security and the value at which it is convertible into common stock. Such bonds are designed for bond-oriented portfolios, with the "KICKER," the added feature of convertibility to stock, intended as an inflation hedge.

HIGHS stocks that have hit new high prices in daily trading for the current 52-week period. (They are listed as "highs" in daily newspapers.) Technical analysts consider the ratio between new highs and new LOWS in the stock market to be significant for pointing out stock market trends.

HIGH-TECH STOCK stock of companies involved in high-technology fields (computers, semiconductors, biotechnology, robotics, electronics). Successful high-tech stocks have above-average earnings growth and therefore typically very volatile stock prices.

HIGH-TICKET ITEMS items with a significant amount of value, such as jewelry and furs. Most standard homeowner's/renter's policies have limits on specific types of high-ticket items. Most policies have a limit of $1000–$2000 for all jewelry and furs. To provide appropriate coverage for these items, they should be scheduled separately in the form of a FLOATER or endorsement. Also called *valuables.*

HIGH-YIELD BOND bond that has RATING of BB or lower and that pays a higher yield to compensate for its greater risk. *See also* JUNK BOND.

HISTORICAL COST accounting principle requiring that all financial statement items be based on original cost or acquisition cost. The dollar is assumed to be stable for the period involved.

HISTORICAL TRADING RANGE price range within which a stock, bond, or commodity has traded since going public. A VOLATILE stock will have a wider trading range than a more conservative stock. Technical analysts see the top of a historical range as the RESISTANCE LEVEL and the bottom as the SUPPORT LEVEL. They consider it highly significant if a security breaks above the resistance level or below the support level. Usually such a move is interpreted to mean that the security will go onto new highs or new lows, thus expanding its historical trading range.

HISTORICAL YIELD yield provided by a mutual fund, typically a money market fund, over a particular period of time. For instance, a money market fund may advertise that its historical yield averaged 5% over the last year.

HISTORIC REHABILITATION LIMITED PARTNERSHIP partnership designed to take advantage of the historic rehabilitation tax credit available in the

Internal Revenue Code. These partnerships rehabilitate structures to their original condition, and limited partners receive credits that reduce partners' taxes dollar for dollar. For example, $5000 in tax credits reduces the amount of taxes due by $5000. Tax credits of 20% are available if the partnership rehabilitates a historic structure built before 1936. Tax credits of 10% are available for the restoration of buildings built before 1936 that are not certified as historic by the Department of the Interior. Historic rehabilitation limited partnerships can be assembled by local builders and investors, or by professional general partners specializing in such projects.

HIT informally, a significant securities loss or a development having a major impact on corporate profits, such as a large WRITE-OFF. Term is also used in the opposite sense to describe an investing success, similar to a "hit" in show business.

HIT THE BID to accept the highest price offered for a stock. For instance, if a stock's ask price is $50¼ and the current bid price is $50, a seller will hit the bid if he or she accepts $50 a share.

HOLD
Banking: retaining an asset in an account until the item has been collected. For example, a hold can be put on a certain amount of funds in a checking account if a certified check has been issued for that amount.
Securities: maintaining ownership of a stock, bond, mutual fund, or other security for a long period of time. Proponents of the BUY AND HOLD STRATEGY try to buy high-quality securities which they hope will grow in value over many years. By holding for a long time, the investor can delay capital gains taxes until the position is sold many years in the future.

Securities analysts also issue a HOLD recommendation if they are not enthusiastic enough about a security to recommend purchasing it, yet are not pessimistic enough to recommend selling it. However, many analysts who downgrade a stock from a buy to a hold rating are in fact saying that investors should sell the stock, since there are better opportunities to invest elsewhere.

HOLDER OF RECORD owner of a company's securities as recorded on the books of the issuing company or its TRANSFER AGENT as of a particular date. Dividend declarations, for example, always specify payability to holders of record as of a specific date.

HOLDING COMPANY corporation that owns enough voting stock in another corporation to influence its board of directors and therefore to control its policies and management. A holding company need not own a majority of the shares of its subsidiaries or be engaged in similar activities. However, to gain the benefits of tax consolidation, which include tax-free dividends to the parent and the ability to share operating losses, the holding company must own 80% or more of the subsidiary's voting stock.

Among the advantages of a holding company over a MERGER as an approach to expansion are the ability to control sizeable operations with fractional ownership and commensurately small investment; the somewhat theoretical ability to take risks through subsidiaries with liability limited to the subsidiary corporation; and the ability to expand through unobtrusive purchases of stock, in contrast to having to obtain the approval of another company's shareholders.

Among the disadvantages of a holding company are partial multiple taxation when less than 80% of a subsidiary is owned, plus other special state and local taxes; the risk of forced DIVESTITURE (it is easier to force dissolution of a holding company than to separate merged operations); and the risks of negative leverage effects in excessive PYRAMIDING.

The following types of holding companies are defined in special ways and subject to particular legislation: public utility holding company (*see* PUBLIC UTIL-ITY HOLDING COMPANY ACT), BANK HOLDING COMPANY, railroad holding company, and air transport holding company.

HOLDING PERIOD length of time an asset is held by its owner. Capital assets held for 12 months or more qualify for preferential capital gains tax treatment. Assets sold after being held for more than 12 months are subject to a maximum capital gains tax rate of 20%, while assets sold after being held for less than 12 months are taxed at regular income tax rates as high as 39.6%. *See also* ANTICI-PATED HOLDING PERIOD; CAPITAL GAIN; INVESTMENT LETTER.

HOLDING THE MARKET entering the market with sufficient buy orders to cre-ate price support for a security or commodity, for the purpose of stabilizing a downward trend. The Securities and Exchange Commission views "holding" as a form of illegal manipulation except in the case of stabilization of a new issue cleared with the SEC beforehand.

HOME BANKING service offered by banks allowing consumers and small busi-nesses to perform many banking functions at home through computers, tele-phones, and cable television links to the bank, thereby providing them with a num-ber of convenience services. Bank customers are able to shift money between accounts, apply for loans and make loan payments, pay bills, check balances, and buy and sell securities, among other services. As home banking becomes easier and more convenient to use, more and more consumers sign up for it. It offers the advantages of privacy, speed, accuracy and the ability to perform transactions at any time. Most banks charge an extra fee for access to home banking services. Home banking does not currently offer the ability to obtain cash, for which cus-tomers must still visit a bank teller or automatic teller machine.

HOMEOWNER'S EQUITY ACCOUNT credit line offered by banks, savings and loans, brokerage firms, credit unions and other mortgage lenders allowing a homeowner to tap the built-up equity in his or her home. Such an account is, in effect, a REVOLVING CREDIT second mortgage, which owners can access with the convenience of a check. Most lenders will provide a line of credit up to 70% or 80% of the appraised value of a home, minus any outstanding first mortgage debt. Some home equity lenders will lend as much as 125% of the home's value, although this is risky for both the lender and the borrower; if the borrower defaults, he must come up with 25% more equity than his home is worth to satis-fy the loan. When a homeowner receives the loan, a LIEN is automatically placed against the house and removed when the loan is repaid. A homeowner's equity account often carries a lower interest rate than a second mortgage; typically, the rate is tied to the PRIME RATE. Often, a lender will offer a below-market rate at or below the prime rate for some introductory period of six months to a year to entice the borrower. After that, many banks charge between the prime rate and two percentage points over prime for the long term. Most programs require an initial sign-up fee, an annual maintenance fee and payment of additional fees called POINTS when the credit line is tapped. Interest on such loans is tax deductible up to $100,000, no matter how loan proceeds are used. Interest on loans exceeding $100,000 may be deductible if the proceeds are used to purchase investments or for business purposes. Consult a tax specialist for the latest infor-mation on what qualifies as a deduction. *See also* SECOND MORTGAGE LENDING.

HOMEOWNER'S INSURANCE POLICY policy protecting a homeowner against property and casualty perils. A basic HO-3 policy (HO stands for homeowner's) is a standard policy and the most comprehensive. It will cover damage to the home from natural causes such as fire, lightning, windstorms, hail, rain, or volcanic eruption. In addition, man-made disasters such as riots, vandalism, damage from cars or airplanes, explosions, and theft will also be reimbursed. Damage caused by falling objects, the weight of ice, snow or sleet, freezing of plumbing, heating or air conditioning systems, electrical discharges, or the rupture of water heating or protective sprinkler systems also fall under the HO-3 policy. Flood, earthquake, war, and nuclear accident are not covered; flood and earthquake insurance can be purchased separately. Other types of homeowner's policies include HO-4 for renters (which also could include co-ops), HO-6 for condominium owners, and HO-8 for older homes. In general, homeowners should try to purchase coverage that will pay for the replacement of damaged or stolen items at current market prices, not at the prices for which those items may have been acquired years ago. There are dollar limits for high-ticket items such as jewelry. A FLOATER or an endorsement, purchased separately, can provide the additional coverage needed.

The average homeowner's or renter's policy provides approximately $100,000 of liability protection. A special policy is required for homeowner's business risk coverage. Home business owners need both property and liability insurance, since the homeowner's policy provides only limited coverage for business equipment, in most cases up to $2,500 for business equipment in the home and $250 away from the home.

Most mortgage lenders require homeowners to obtain adequate insurance coverage before they agree to provide a mortgage.

HOME RUN large gain by an investor in a short period of time. Someone who aims to hit an investment home run may be looking for a potential TAKEOVER target, for example, since takeover bids result in sudden price spurts. Such investing is inherently more risky than the strategy of holding for the long term.

HORIZON ANALYSIS method of measuring the discounted cash flow (time-adjusted return) from an investment, using time periods or series *(horizons)* that differ from the investment's contractual maturity. The horizon date might be the end of a BUSINESS CYCLE or some other date determined in the perspective of the investor's overall portfolio requirements. Horizon analysis calculations, which include reinvestment assumptions, permit comparison with alternative investments that is more realistic in terms of individual portfolio requirements than traditional YIELD-TO-MATURITY calculations.

HORIZONTAL MERGER *see* MERGER.

HORIZONTAL PRICE MOVEMENT movement within a narrow price range over an extended period of time. A stock would have a horizontal price movement if it traded between $47 and $51 for over six months, for instance. Also known as *sideways price movement. See* chart on next page. *See also* FLAT MARKET.

HORIZONTAL SPREAD options strategy that involves buying and selling the same number of options contracts with the same exercise price, but with different maturity dates; also called a CALENDAR SPREAD. For instance, an investor might buy ten XYZ call options with a striking price of $70 and a maturity date of October. At the same time, he would sell ten XYZ call options with the same striking price of $70 but a maturity date of July. The investor hopes to profit by moves in XYZ stock by this means.

HOSPITAL REVENUE BOND bond issued by a municipal or state agency to finance construction of a hospital or nursing home. The latter is then operated under lease by a not-for-profit organization or a for-profit corporation such as Columbia/HCA. A hospital revenue bond, which is a variation on the INDUSTRIAL DEVELOPMENT BOND, is tax exempt, but there may be limits to the exemption. *See also* REVENUE BOND.

HORIZONTAL PRICE MOVEMENT

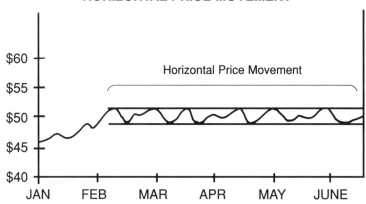

HOSTILE TAKEOVER takeover of a company against the wishes of current management and the board of directors. This takeover may be attempted by another company or by a well-financed RAIDER. If the price offered is high enough, shareholders may vote to accept the offer even if management resists and claims that the company is actually worth even more. If the acquirer raises the price high enough, management may change its attitude, converting the hostile takeover into a friendly one. Management has many weapons at its disposal to fend off a hostile takeover, such as GREENMAIL, POISON PILLS, the SCORCHED EARTH POLICY, and SUICIDE PILLS, among others. Also called *unfriendly takeover.* *See also* TAKEOVER.

HOT ISSUE newly issued stock that is in great public demand. Hot issue stocks usually shoot up in price at their initial offering, since there is more demand than there are shares available. Special National Association of Securities Dealers rules apply to the distribution of hot issues by the selling investment banking syndicate. *See also* UNDERWRITE.

HOT MONEY investment funds capriciously seeking high, short-term yields. Borrowers attracting hot money, such as banks issuing high-yielding CERTIFI-CATES OF DEPOSIT, should be prepared to lose it as soon as another borrower offers a higher rate.

HOT STOCK
  1. stock that has been stolen.
  2. newly issued stock that rises quickly in price. *See* HOT ISSUE.

HOUSE
  1. firm or individual engaged in business as a broker-dealer in securities and/or investment banking and related services.
  2. nickname for the London Stock Exchange.

HOUSE ACCOUNT account handled at the main office of a brokerage firm or managed by an executive of the firm; in other words, an account distinguished from one that is normally handled by a salesperson in the territory. Ordinarily, a salesperson does not receive a commission on a house account, even though the account may actually be in his or her territory.

HOUSE CALL brokerage house notification that the customer's EQUITY in a MAR-GIN ACCOUNT is below the maintenance level. If the equity declines below that point, a broker must call the client, asking for more cash or securities. If the client fails to deliver the required margin, his or her position will be liquidated. House call limits are usually higher than limits mandated by the National Association of Securities Dealers (NASD), a self-regulatory group, and the major exchanges with jurisdiction over these rules. Such a margin MAINTENANCE REQUIREMENT is in addition to the initial margin requirements set by REGULATION T of the Federal Reserve Board. *See also* HOUSE MAINTENANCE REQUIREMENT; MARGIN CALL.

HOUSE MAINTENANCE REQUIREMENT internally set and enforced rules of individual broker-dealers in securities with respect to a customer's MARGIN ACCOUNT. House maintenance requirements set levels of EQUITY that must be maintained to avoid putting up additional equity or having collateral sold out. These levels are normally higher than maintenance levels required by the NATIONAL ASSOCIATION OF SECURITIES DEALERS (NASD) and the stock exchange. *See also* HOUSE CALL; MINIMUM MAINTENANCE.

HOUSE OF ISSUE investment banking firm that underwrites a stock or bond issue and offers the securities to the public. *See also* UNDERWRITE.

HOUSE POOR short of cash because the bulk of your money is tied up in your house. Implication is that without the real estate investment and associated mortgage, you would be financially comfortable.

HOUSE RULES securities industry term for internal rules and policies of individual broker-dealer firms concerning the opening and handling of customers' accounts and the activities of the customers in such accounts. House rules are designed to assure that firms are in comfortable compliance with the requirements of outside regulatory authorities and in most cases are more stringent than the outside regulations. *See also* HOUSE CALL; HOUSE MAINTENANCE REQUIREMENT.

HOUSING AFFORDABILITY INDEX *see* AFFORDABILITY INDEX.

HOUSING AND URBAN DEVELOPMENT, DEPARTMENT OF (HUD) cabinet-level federal agency, founded in 1965, which is responsible for stimulating housing development in the United States. HUD has several programs to subsidize low- and moderate-income housing and urban renewal projects, often through loan guarantees. The GOVERNMENT NATIONAL MORTGAGE ASSOCIATION (Ginnie Mae), which fosters the growth of the secondary mortgage market, is within HUD.

HOUSING BOND short- or long-term bond issued by a local housing authority to finance short-term construction of (typically) low- or middle-income housing or long-term commitments for housing, plants, pollution control facilities, or similar projects. Such bonds are free from federal income taxes and from state and local taxes where applicable.

Shorter-term bonds sell in $5000 denominations and have maturities from 18 months to 4 years. They cannot be called (redeemed prior to maturity) and are paid at maturity with the proceeds from Federal Housing Administration-insured loans. Longer-term bonds are typically issued by local authorities under federal agency contracts, thus providing complete safety. Yields are competitive.

HOUSING STARTS category of residential construction monitored by the Department of Commerce. Housing starts represent the start of construction of a house or apartment building, which means the digging of the foundation. Other categories are housing permits, housing completions, and new home sales. In the aggregate, residential construction accounts for roughly 3% of GROSS DOMESTIC PRODUCT.

HULBERT RATING rating by *Hulbert Financial Digest* of Alexandria, Virginia, of how well the recommendations of various investment advisory newsletters have performed. The ratings cover performance as far back as 1980, if data are available. The *Digest* ranks over 150 investment advisory newsletters covering stocks, bonds, mutual funds, futures, and options by tabulating the profits and losses subscribers would have received had they followed the newsletter's advice exactly.

HUMAN CAPITAL skills acquired by a worker through formal education and experience that improve the worker's productivity and increase his or her income.

HUNG UP term used to describe the position of an investor whose stocks or bonds have dropped in value below their purchase price, presenting the problem of a substantial loss if the securities were sold.

HUNKERING DOWN trader's term for working to sell off a big position in a stock.

HURDLE RATE term used in the budgeting of capital expenditures, meaning the REQUIRED RATE OF RETURN in a DISCOUNTED CASH FLOW analysis. If the EXPECTED RATE OF RETURN on an investment is below the hurdle rate, the project is not undertaken. The hurdle rate should be equal to the INCREMENTAL COST OF CAPITAL.

HYBRID ANNUITY contract offered by an insurance company that allows an investor to mix the benefits of both fixed and variable annuities. Also called *combination annuity*. For instance, an annuity buyer may put a portion of his assets in a FIXED ANNUITY, which promises a certain rate of return, and the remainder in a stock or bond fund VARIABLE ANNUITY, which offers a chance for higher return but takes more risk.

HYBRID INVESTMENT OR SECURITY investment vehicle that combines two different kinds of underlying investments. For example, a structured note, which is a form of a bond, may have the interest rate it pays tied to the rise and fall of a commodity's price. Hybrid investments are also called *derivatives.*

HYPERINFLATION *see* INFLATION.

HYPOTHECATION
Banking: pledging property to secure a loan. Hypothecation does not transfer title, but it does transfer the right to sell the hypothecated property in the event of default.
Securities: pledging of securities to brokers as collateral for loans made to purchase securities or to cover short sales, called margin loans. When the same collateral is pledged by the broker to a bank to collateralize a broker's loan, the process is called *rehypothecation.*

I

IBC'S MONEY FUND REPORT AVERAGE average for all major taxable and tax-free money market mutual fund yields published weekly for 7- and 30-day simple and compound (assumes reinvested dividends) yields. IBC also tracks the average maturity of securities in money fund portfolios. A short maturity of about 30 days or less reflects the conviction of fund managers that interest rates will rise, and a long maturity of 60 days or more reflects a sentiment that rates will fall. Investors can compare the yield and average maturity against the industry average to ascertain if their money fund's return is competitive, and how their fund manager's views on the direction of interest rates compares to industry peers. IBC's Money Fund Report Average is published in major newspapers, including *The Wall Street Journal, The New York Times,* and *Barron's. Barron's* also publishes a list of the 7- and 30-day yields of most money market mutual funds, along with each fund's net assets and average maturity as compiled by the IBC Organization of Ashland, Massachusetts.

I/B/E/S INTERNATIONAL INC. provides the I/B/E/S data base, which comprises analysts' estimates of future earnings for thousands of publicly traded companies. These estimates are tabulated, and companies whose estimates have increased or decreased significantly are pinpointed. Reports also detail how many estimates are available on each company and the high, low, and average estimates for each. *See also* EARNINGS SURPRISE; FIRST CALL; ZACKS ESTIMATE SYSTEM.

I-BONDS inflation-indexed SAVINGS BONDS issued by the United States Treasury in eight denominations ranging from $50 to $10,000 with a 30-year maturity. Unlike other inflation-adjusted bonds, but like other savings bonds, the securities, which were introduced in 1998, offer special tax benefits. As long as investors hold their bonds, they may defer paying taxes on their earnings, which are automatically reinvested and added to the principal. Like other Treasury bonds, I-Bonds are exempt from state and local income taxes. If the bond is redeemed to pay for college tuition or other college fees, investors may exclude part or all of the income in calculating their taxes. The payout on the bonds is determined by two rates. A fixed rate, ranging from 3% to 3.5% when the bonds were first introduced, is set by the Treasury Department. The second rate, a rate of inflation, is determined every six months by the Bureau of Labor Statistics to reflect changes in a version of the Consumer Price Index. Some protection against deflation exists in that any decline in the CONSUMER PRICE INDEX (CPI) could eat into the fixed rate, but not affect the underlying principal. *See also* INFLATION INDEXED SECURITIES.

IDENTIFIED SHARES shares of stock or a mutual fund identified as having been bought at a particular price on a particular date. If a shareholder wishes to minimize his tax liability when selling shares, he must identify which shares were bought at what price in order to determine his cost basis. If he has acquired shares over a long period of time, through a CONSTANT DOLLAR PLAN or a DIVIDEND REINVESTMENT PLAN, for example, he will have many shares at many different prices. By identifying the shares with the highest cost basis, he will generally pay lower capital gains taxes than if he identified shares bought at a lower cost. If shares are sold at a loss, the shareholder can pick how large or small a loss he wants to take based on which shares he identifies. In addition, if the identified shares were held for 12 months or more, the investor qualifies for long-term capital gains tax rates. If the identified shares were held for less than 12 months, he will have to pay regular income tax rates on the gain.

ILLEGAL DIVIDEND dividend declared by a corporation's board of directors in violation of its charter or of state laws. Most states, for example, stipulate that dividends be paid out of current income or RETAINED EARNINGS; they prohibit dividend payments that come out of CAPITAL SURPLUS or that would make the corporation insolvent. Directors who authorize illegal dividends may be sued by stockholders and creditors and may also face civil and criminal penalties. Stockholders who receive such dividends may be required to return them in order to meet the claims of creditors.

ILLIQUID
Finance: firm that lacks sufficient CASH FLOW to meet current and maturing obligations.

Investments: not readily convertible into cash, such as a stock, bond, or commodity that is not traded actively and would be difficult to sell at once without taking a large loss. Other assets for which there is not a ready market, and which therefore may take some time to sell, include real estate and collectibles such as rare stamps, coins, or antique furniture.

IMBALANCE OF ORDERS too many orders of one kind—to buy or to sell—without matching orders of the opposite kind. An imbalance usually follows a dramatic event such as a takeover, the death of a key executive, or a government ruling that will significantly affect the company's business. If it occurs before the stock exchange opens, trading in the stock is delayed. If it occurs during the trading day, the specialist suspends trading until enough matching orders can be found to make for an orderly market.

IMF *see* INTERNATIONAL MONETARY FUND.

IMMEDIATE FAMILY parents, brothers, sisters, children, relatives supported financially, father-in-law, mother-in-law, sister-in-law, and brother-in-law. This definition is incorporated in the NATIONAL ASSOCIATION OF SECURITIES DEALERS RULES OF FAIR PRACTICE on abuses of *hot issues* through such practices as FREERIDING and WITHHOLDING. The ruling prohibits the sale of such securities to members of a broker-dealer's own family or to persons buying and selling for institutional accounts and their families.

IMMEDIATE OR CANCEL ORDER order requiring that all or part of the order be executed as soon as the broker enters a bid or offer; the portion not executed is automatically canceled. Such stipulations usually accompany large orders.

IMMEDIATE PAYMENT ANNUITY annuity contract bought with a single payment and with a specified payout plan that starts right away. Payments may be for a specified period or for the life of the annuitant and are usually on a monthly basis. *See also* ANNUITIZE.

IMMUNIZATION *see* DURATION.

IMPAIRED CAPITAL total capital that is less than the stated or par value of the company's CAPITAL STOCK. *See also* DEFICIT NET WORTH.

IMPAIRED CREDIT deterioration in the credit rating of a borrower, which may result in a reduction in the amount of credit made available by lenders. For example, a company may launch a product line that is a failure, and the resulting losses will seriously weaken the company's finances. Concerned lenders may reduce the firm's credit lines as a result. The same process can apply to an individual who has been late paying bills, or in an extreme case, has filed for bankruptcy protection. Also called *adverse credit.*

IMPORT DUTY *see* TARIFF.

IMPUTED INTEREST interest considered to have been paid in effect even though no interest was actually paid. For example, the Internal Revenue Service requires that annual interest be recognized on a ZERO-COUPON SECURITY.

IMPUTED VALUE logical or implicit value that is not recorded in any accounts. Examples: in projecting annual figures, values are imputed for months about which actual figures are not yet available; cash invested unproductively has an imputed value consisting of what it would have earned in a productive investment (OPPORTUNITY COST); in calculating national income, the U.S. Department of Commerce imputes a dollar value for wages and salaries paid in kind, such as food and lodging provided on ships at sea.

INACTIVE ASSET asset not continually used in a productive way, such as an auxiliary generator.

INACTIVE BOND CROWD *see* CABINET CROWD.

INACTIVE POST trading post on the New York Stock Exchange at which inactive stocks are traded in 10-share units rather than the regular 100-share lots. Known to traders as *Post 30. See also* ROUND LOT.

INACTIVE STOCK/BOND security traded relatively infrequently, either on an exchange or over the counter. The low volume makes the security ILLIQUID, and small investors tend to shy away from it.

IN-AND-OUT TRADER one who buys and sells the same security in one day, aiming to profit from sharp price moves. *See also* DAY TRADE.

INCENTIVE FEE compensation for producing above-average results. Incentive fees are common for commodities trading advisers who achieve or top a preset return, as well as for a GENERAL PARTNER in a real estate or oil and gas LIMITED PARTNERSHIP.

INCENTIVE STOCK OPTION plan created by the ECONOMIC RECOVERY TAX ACT OF 1981 (ERTA) under which qualifying options are free of tax at the date of grant and the date of exercise. Profits on shares sold after being held at least two years from the date of grant or one year from the date of transfer to the employee are subject to favorable CAPITAL GAINS TAX rates. *See also* QUALIFYING STOCK OPTION.

INCESTUOUS SHARE DEALING buying and selling of shares in each other's companies to create a tax or other financial advantage.

INCOME AVAILABLE FOR FIXED CHARGES *see* FIXED-CHARGE COVERAGE.

INCOME AVERAGING method of computing personal income tax whereby tax is figured on the average of the total of current year's income and that of the three preceding years. According to 1984 U.S. tax legislation, income averaging was used when a person's income for the current year exceeded 140% of the average taxable income in the preceding three years. The TAX REFORM ACT OF 1986 repealed income averaging.

INCOME BOND obligation on which the payment of interest is contingent on sufficient earnings from year to year. Such bonds are traded FLAT—that is, with no accrued interest—and are often an alternative to bankruptcy. *See also* ADJUSTMENT BOND.

INCOME DIVIDEND payout to shareholders of interest, dividends, or other income received by a mutual fund. By law, all such income must be distributed to shareholders, who may choose to take the money in cash or reinvest it in more shares of the fund. All income dividends are taxable to shareholders in the year they are received, unless the fund is held in a tax-deferred account such as an IRA or Keogh plan.

INCOME EXCLUSION RULE INCOME TAX rule excluding certain items from taxable income. Personal exclusions include interest on tax-exempt securities, returns of capital, life insurance death benefits, dividends on veterans' life insurance, child support, welfare payments, disability benefits paid by the Veterans Administration, and amounts received from an insurer because of the loss of use of a home. *See also* EXCLUSION.

INCOME INVESTMENT COMPANY management company that operates an income-oriented MUTUAL FUND for investors who value income over growth.

These funds may invest in bonds or high-dividend stocks or may write covered call options on stocks. *See also* INVESTMENT COMPANY.

INCOME LIMITED PARTNERSHIP real estate, oil and gas, or equipment leasing LIMITED PARTNERSHIP whose aim is high income, much of which may be taxable. Such a partnership may be designed for tax-sheltered accounts like Individual Retirement Accounts, Keogh plan accounts, or pension plans.

INCOME MUTUAL FUND mutual fund designed to produce current income for shareholders. Some examples of income funds are government, mortgage-backed security, municipal, international, and junk bond funds. Several kinds of equity-oriented funds also can have income as their primary investment objective, such as utilities income funds and equity income funds. All distributions from income funds are taxable in the year received by the shareholder unless the fund is held in a tax-deferred account such as an IRA or Keogh or the distributions come from tax-exempt bonds, such as with a municipal bond fund.

INCOME PROPERTY real estate bought for the income it produces. The property may be placed in an INCOME LIMITED PARTNERSHIP, or it may be owned by individuals or corporations. Buyers also hope to achieve capital gains when they sell the property.

INCOME SHARES one of two kinds or classes of capital stock issued by a DUAL-PURPOSE FUND or split investment company, the other kind being *capital shares.* Holders of income shares receive dividends from both classes of shares, generated from income (dividends and interest) produced by the portfolio, whereas holders of capital shares receive capital gains payouts on both classes. Income shares normally have a minimum income guarantee, which is cumulative.

INCOME STATEMENT *see* PROFIT AND LOSS STATEMENT.

INCOME STOCK stock paying high and regular dividends to shareholders. Some industries known for income stocks include gas, electric, and telephone utilities; real estate investment trusts; banks; and insurance companies. High-quality income stocks have established a long history of paying dividends, and in many cases have a track record of regularly increasing dividends. All dividends paid to shareholders of income stocks are taxable in the year received unless the stock is held in a tax-deferred account such as an IRA or Keogh plan.

INCOME TAX annual tax on income levied by the federal government and by certain state and local governments. There are two basic types: the personal income tax, levied on incomes of households and unincorporated businesses, and the corporate (or corporation) income tax, levied on net earnings of corporations.

The U.S. income tax was instituted in 1913 by the Sixteenth Amendment to the Constitution. Typically, it accounts for more than half the federal government's total annual revenue. Most states tax individual and corporate incomes, as do some cities, though sales and property taxes are the main sources of state and local revenue. The personal income tax, and to a lesser extent the corporate income tax, were designed to be progressive—that is, to take a larger percentage of higher incomes than lower incomes. The ranges of incomes to which progressively higher rates apply are called TAX BRACKETS, which also determine the value of DEDUCTIONS, such as business costs and expenses, state and local income taxes, or charitable contributions.

Under present tax law, there are effectively five tax brackets for individual taxpayers: 15%, 28%, 31%, 36% and 39.6%. The levels of TAXABLE INCOME for each bracket differs according to filing status (such as married filing jointly, singles, or heads of household) and is revised slightly every year. Long-term CAPITAL GAINS receive preferential tax treatment both for individuals and corporations. Assets held for more than 12 months are taxed at a top rate of 20%, versus a top rate of 39.6% for short-term gains on assets held for less than 12 months. Because capital gains rates rewarded taxpayers in a position to take risks, and since LOOPHOLES and TAX SHELTERS enabled the wealthiest corporations and individuals to escape the higher tax brackets, the progressiveness of the tax system has often been more theoretical than real. There have been many sweeping changes in the tax code, creating an enormous amount of complexity. In 1998, the INTERNAL REVENUE SERVICE RESTRUCTURING AND REFORM ACT OF 1998 instituted numerous changes in the way the Internal Revenue Service conducts business, including shifting the burden of proof from taxpayers to the IRS in court disputes over the amount of taxes owed by a taxpayer. The progression of changes in the tax code is described in great detail in other *Dictionary* entries, including: ECONOMIC RECOVERY TAX ACT OF 1981 (ERTA); INTERNAL REVENUE SERVICE RESTRUCTURING AND REFORM ACT OF 1998; REVENUE RECONCILIATION ACT OF 1993; TAX EQUITY AND FISCAL RESPONSIBILITY ACT OF 1982 (TEFRA); TAX REFORM ACT OF 1976; TAX REFORM ACT OF 1984; TAX REFORM ACT OF 1986; and the TAXPAYER RELIEF ACT OF 1997.

INCONTESTABILITY CLAUSE provision in a life insurance contract stating that the insurer cannot revoke the policy after it has been in force for one or two years if the policyholder concealed important facts from the company during the application process. For example, a policyholder who stated that he had never had a heart attack, but in fact had experienced one, would still be covered by the policy if the insurance company had not discovered this discrepancy within one or two years. However, if a policyholder lies about his age on the application, the policy's death benefit can be adjusted higher retroactively to account for the insured's true age.

INCORPORATION process by which a company receives a state charter allowing it to operate as a corporation. The fact of incorporation must be acknowledged in the company's legal name, using the word *incorporated,* the abbreviation *inc.,* or other acceptable variations. *See also* ARTICLES OF INCORPORATION.

INCREMENTAL CASH FLOW net of cash outflows and inflows attributable to a corporate investment project.

INCREMENTAL COST OF CAPITAL weighted cost of the additional capital raised in a given period. Weighted cost of capital, also called *composite cost of capital,* is the weighted average of costs applicable to the issues of debt and classes of equity that compose the firm's capital structure. Also called *marginal cost of capital.*

INDEMNIFY agree to compensate for damage or loss. The word is used in insurance policies promising that, in the event of a loss, the insured will be restored to the financial position that existed prior to the loss.

INDENTURE formal agreement, also called a deed of trust, between an issuer of bonds and the bondholder covering such considerations as: (1) form of the bond; (2) amount of the issue; (3) property pledged (if not a debenture issue); (4) protective COVENANTS including any provision for a sinking fund; (5) WORKING CAPITAL and CURRENT RATIO; and (6) redemption rights or call privileges. The indenture also provides for the appointment of a trustee to act on behalf of the bondholders, in accordance with the TRUST INDENTURE ACT OF 1939.

INDEPENDENT AGENT agent representing several insurance companies. The agent is independent from all the companies he or she sells for, and can therefore in theory evaluate different insurance policies objectively. Independent agents pay all their own expenses and keep their own records and earn their income from commissions on the policies they sell. The opposite of an independent agent is a CAPTIVE AGENT, who works exclusively for one company.

INDEPENDENT AUDITOR certified public accountant (CPA) who provides the ACCOUNTANT'S OPINION.

INDEPENDENT BROKER New York Stock Exchange member who executes orders for other floor brokers who have more volume than they can handle, or for firms whose exchange members are not on the floor. Formerly called $2 brokers because of their commission for a round lot trade, independent brokers are compensated by commission brokers with fees that once were fixed but are now negotiable. *See also* GIVE UP.

INDEX statistical composite that measures changes in the economy or in financial markets, often expressed in percentage changes from a base period or from the previous month. For instance, the CONSUMER PRICE INDEX uses 1982–84 as the base period. That index, made up of the prices for key consumer goods and services, moves up and down as the rate of inflation changes. By the late '90s the index climbed from 100 in 1982–84 to 160 and higher, meaning that the basket of goods the index was based on rose in price by more than 60%.

Indices also measure the ups and downs of stock, bond, and commodities markets, reflecting market prices and the number of shares outstanding for the companies in the index. Some well-known indices are the Dow Jones Averages, the New York Stock Exchange Composite Index, the American Stock Exchange Composite Index, the Standard & Poor's 500 Index, the NASDAQ Composite Index, the Russell 2000 Index and the Value Line Composite Index. Subindices for industry groups such as drugs, railroads, or computers are also tracked. Stock market indices form the basis for trading in INDEX OPTIONS. *See also* STOCK INDICES AND AVERAGES.

INDEX ARBITRAGE *see* ARBITRAGE.

INDEXATION *see* INDEXING, at meaning (2).

INDEX BOND bond whose cash flow is linked to the purchasing power of the dollar or a foreign currency. For example, a bond indexed to the CONSUMER PRICE INDEX (CPI) would ensure that the bondholder receives real value by making an upward adjustment in the interest rate to reflect higher prices.

INDEX FUND mutual fund that has a portfolio matching that of a broad-based portfolio. This may include the Dow Jones Industrial Average, Standard & Poor's 500 Index, indices of mid- and small-capitalization stocks, foreign stock indices, and bond indices, to name a few. Many institutional and individual investors, especially believers in the EFFICIENT MARKET theory, put money in index funds on the assumption that trying to beat the market averages over the long run is futile, and their investments in these funds will at least keep pace with the index being tracked. In addition, since the cost of managing an index fund is far cheaper than the cost of running an actively managed portfolio, index funds have a built-in cost advantage.

INDEXING
1. weighting one's portfolio to match a broad-based index such as Standard & Poor's so as to match its performance—or buying shares in an INDEX FUND.
2. tying wages, taxes, or other rates to an index. For example, a labor contract may call for indexing wages to the consumer price index to protect against loss of purchasing power in a time of rising inflation.

INDEX OF LEADING INDICATORS *see* LEADING INDICATORS.

INDEX OPTIONS calls and puts on indexes of stocks. These options are traded on the New York, American, and Chicago Board Options Exchanges, among others. Broad-based indexes cover a wide range of companies and industries, whereas narrow-based indexes consist of stocks in one industry or sector of the economy. Index options allow investors to trade in a particular market or industry group without having to buy all the stocks individually. For instance, someone who thought oil stocks were about to fall could buy a put on the oil index instead of selling short shares in half a dozen oil companies.

INDEX PARTICIPATION *see* BASKET.

INDICATED YIELD coupon or dividend rate as a percentage of the current market price. For fixed rate bonds it is the same as CURRENT YIELD. For common stocks, it is the market price divided into the annual dividend. For preferred stocks, it is the market price divided into the contractual dividend.

INDICATION approximation of what a security's TRADING RANGE (bid and offer prices) will be when trading resumes after a delayed opening or after being halted because of an IMBALANCE OF ORDERS or another reason. Also called *indicated market.*

INDICATION OF INTEREST securities underwriting term meaning a dealer's or investor's interest in purchasing securities that are still *in registration* (awaiting clearance by) the Securities and Exchange Commission. A broker who receives an indication of interest should send the client a preliminary prospectus on the securities. An indication of interest is not a commitment to buy, an important point because selling a security while it is in registration is illegal. *See also* CIRCLE.

INDICATOR technical measurement securities market analysts use to forecast the market's direction, such as investment advisory sentiment, volume of stock trading, direction of interest rates, and buying or selling by corporate insiders.

INDIRECT COST AND EXPENSE *see* DIRECT OVERHEAD; FIXED COST.

INDIRECT LABOR COSTS wages and related costs of factory employees, such as inspectors and maintenance crews, whose time is not charged to specific finished products.

INDIVIDUAL RETIREMENT ACCOUNT (IRA) personal, tax-deferred, retirement account that an employed person can set up with a deposit limited to $2,000 per year ($4,000 for a married couple filing jointly, whether or not both spouses work.) IRA contributions are deductible regardless of income if neither the taxpayer nor the taxpayer's spouse is covered by a QUALIFIED PLAN OR TRUST. If the taxpayer is covered by a qualified plan, they may deduct IRA contributions if ADJUSTED GROSS INCOME (AGI) is below $50,000 on a joint return, or $30,000 on a single return. Couples with incomes of $50,000 to $60,000 and single taxpayers with incomes of $30,000 to $40,000 are allowed partial deductions in amounts reduced proportionately over the $10,000 range with a minimum deduction of $200. Taxpayers with incomes over $60,000 (joint) and $40,000 (single) are not allowed deductions, but may make the same contributions (treated as a nontaxable RETURN OF CAPITAL upon withdrawal) and thus gain the benefit of tax-deferral. Under the TAXPAYER RELIEF ACT OF 1997, income limits gradually climb through the year 2007 to $80,000 for a couple and $50,000 for a single. Over those limits, the deduction phases out for the next $10,000 in income. For singles, the deduction is phased out completely once income tops $60,000 in 2005. For married couples filing jointly, the deduction is phased out once income exceeds $100,000 in 2007. Taxpayers who cannot make deductible contributions because of participation in qualified retirement plans may make nondeductible contributions.

Withdrawals from IRAs prior to age 59½ are generally subject to a 10% (of principal) penalty tax. Withdrawals after age 59½ are fully taxable if the original contributions generated deductions. If the original contributions were nondeductible, taxes need not be paid on the amount of those contributions. No IRA withdrawals are required until age 70½, when mandatory distributions must be made according to an IRS schedule based on life expectancy.

The 1997 tax law also created the ROTH IRA, named after Delaware Republican Senator William V. Roth, Jr. who championed the idea. Starting on January 1, 1998, individuals can invest up to $2,000 a year in earnings into a Roth IRA, even after reaching the age of 70½. As long as the assets have remained inside the account for five years, all earnings and principal can be withdrawn totally tax-free after age 59½. Unlike regular IRAs, participants do not have to take distributions from a Roth IRA starting at age 70½. In fact, they don't have to take distributions at all in their lifetimes, allowing them to pass the assets in the Roth to beneficiaries income-tax free. Contributors to Roth IRAs do not receive a tax deduction for making the contribution, but the value of tax-free withdrawals often exceeds the tax break from upfront deductions. Roth IRA rules also permit participants to withdraw assets without the usual 10% early withdrawal penalty if they use the money for the purchase of a first home (withdrawals are limited to up to $10,000), for college expenses, or if they become disabled. Only married couples with AGIs of $150,000 or less and singles with AGIs of $95,000 or less can contribute the full amount to Roth IRAs. The amount they can contribute is phased out for income between $150,000 and $160,000 for married couples, and between $95,000 and $110,000 for singles. No contributions are allowed over these income limits. For those with AGIs of $100,000 or less, the tax law allows ROLLOVERS of existing deductible and nondeductible IRA balances into a Roth IRA. Taxpayers who rollover, however, must pay income tax on all previously untaxed contributions and earnings. If they execute such a rollover before January 1, 1999, they can spread the resulting tax bill over 4 years. Starting in 1999, the rollover is fully taxable in the year it is completed.

The 1997 tax act also created another form of IRA called the EDUCATION IRA. It allows parents to contribute up to $500 per year for each child up to the age of 18. This $500 limit is reduced for married couples filing jointly with AGIs between $150,000 and $160,000, or singles reporting between $95,000 and $110,000 in income. Couples with incomes over $160,000 and singles with incomes over $110,000 may not contribute to Education IRAs. Contributions to Education IRAs do not generate tax deductions, however, assets inside the Education IRA grow tax-free and principal and earnings can be withdrawn tax-free as long as the proceeds are used to pay for education expenses at a postsecondary school, including tuition, fees, books, supplies and room and board. In a family with two or more children, Education IRA money not used by the first child can be used by the second or subsequent children if the first child does not attend college. The assets in the Education IRA must be spent on education before the child reaches age 30. If the assets are not used for college expenses, the account must be liquidated and taxes paid on the proceeds at regular income tax rates.

IRAs can be invested in almost every kind of instrument including stocks, bonds, mutual funds, certificates of deposit, annuities and precious metals. Physical real estate cannot be among an IRA's assets.

See also EDUCATION IRA; ROTH IRA; SIMPLIFIED EMPLOYEE PENSION (SEP) PLAN; SELF-DIRECTED IRA; SIMPLE IRA.

INDIVIDUAL RETIREMENT ACCOUNT (IRA) ROLLOVER provision of the IRA law that enables persons receiving LUMP-SUM payments from their company's pension, profit-sharing, or SALARY REDUCTION PLAN—due to retirement or other termination of employment—to roll over the amount into an IRA investment plan within 60 days. Also, current IRAs may be transferred to other investment options or financial institutions within a 60-day period. Through an IRA rollover, the capital continues to accumulate tax-deferred until time of withdrawal. In order to avoid a 20% withholding by the IRA trustee, assets should be rolled over from one place to another as a *direct transfer*, made by instructing the IRA trustee to transfer the assets directly to another IRA trustee. Tax-free rollovers may only occur once in a one-year period starting on the date of the first distribution. Otherwise, the distribution amount would be subject to regular income tax and a 10% premature distribution penalty. IRA account holders can also take advantage of the rollover rules to borrow funds from their IRAs for a 60-day loan. As long as the money is redeposited within 60 days, there is no tax on the withdrawal, which is considered a tax-free rollover. *See also* ROLLOVER.

INDIVIDUAL TAX RETURN tax return filed by an individual instead of a corporation. The 1040 tax form used by individuals comes in three basic varieties: the 1040EZ basic form, the 1040A short form, and the 1040 long form. Attached to the 1040 are several schedules, including Schedule A for itemized deductions, Schedule B for interest and dividend income, Schedule C for profits and losses from a business, Schedule D for reporting capital gains and losses, Schedule E for supplemental income and losses, Schedule F for profit or loss from farming, Schedule H for household employment taxes, Schedule K-1 for a limited partner's share of gains, losses, and credits, Schedule R for the credit for the elderly or the disabled and Schedule SE for self-employment tax. The 1040PC allows taxpayers to file their tax returns electronically through what is known as an *IRS e-file*. Form 1040X allows taxpayers to amend their return if they discover mistakes in their original filing. Form 1040 ES is designed for taxpayers making quarterly estimated tax payments.

INDUSTRIAL in stock market vernacular, general, catch-all category including firms producing or distributing goods and services that are not classified as utility, transportation, or financial companies. *See also* STOCK INDICES AND AVERAGES; FORBES 500; FORTUNE 500.

INDUSTRIAL DEVELOPMENT BOND (IDB) type of MUNICIPAL REVENUE BOND issued to finance FIXED ASSETS that are then leased to private firms, whose payments AMORTIZE the debt. IDBs were traditionally tax-exempt to buyers, but under the TAX REFORM ACT OF 1986, large IDB issues ($1 million plus) became taxable effective August 15, 1986, while tax-exempt small issues for commercial and manufacturing purposes were prohibited after 1986 and 1989 respectively. Also, effective August 7, 1986, banks lost their 80% interest deductibility on borrowings to buy IDBs.

INDUSTRIAL PRODUCTION monthly statistic released by the FEDERAL RESERVE BOARD on the total output of all U.S. factories and mines. These numbers are a key ECONOMIC INDICATOR.

INDUSTRIAL REVENUE BOND *see* INDUSTRIAL DEVELOPMENT BOND.

INEFFICIENCY IN THE MARKET failure of investors to recognize that a particular stock or bond has good prospects or may be headed for trouble. According to the EFFICIENT MARKET theory, current prices reflect all knowledge about securities. But some say that those who find out about securities first can profit by exploiting that information; stocks of small, little-known firms with a large growth potential most clearly reflect the market's inefficiency, they say.

INELASTIC DEMAND OR SUPPLY *see* ELASTICITY OF DEMAND OR SUPPLY.

IN ESCROW *see* ESCROW.

INFANT INDUSTRY ARGUMENT case made by developing sectors of the economy that their industries need protection against international competition while they establish themselves. In response to such pleas, the government may enact a TARIFF or import duty to stifle foreign competition. The infant industry argument is frequently made in developing nations that are trying to lessen their dependence on the industrialized world. In Brazil, for example, such infant industries as automobile production argue that they need protection until their technological capability and marketing prowess are sufficient to enable competition with well-established foreigners.

INFLATION rise in the prices of goods and services, as happens when spending increases relative to the supply of goods on the market—in other words, too much money chasing too few goods. Moderate inflation is a common result of economic growth. Hyperinflation, with prices rising at 100% a year or more, causes people to lose confidence in the currency and put their assets in hard assets like real estate or gold, which usually retain their value in inflationary times. *See also* COST-PUSH INFLATION; DEMAND-PULL INFLATION.

INFLATION ACCOUNTING showing the effects of inflation in financial statements. The Financial Accounting Standards Board (FASB) requires major companies to supplement their traditional financial reporting with information showing the effects of inflation. The ruling applies to public companies having inventories and fixed assets of more than $125 million or total assets of more than $1 billion.

INFLATION HEDGE investment designed to protect against the loss of purchasing power from inflation. Traditionally, gold and real estate have a reputation as good inflation hedges, though growth in stocks also can offset inflation in the long run. Money market funds, which pay higher yields as interest rates rise during inflationary times, can also be a good inflation hedge. In the case of hyperinflation, hard assets such as precious metals and real estate are normally viewed as inflation hedges, while the value of paper-based assets such as stocks, bonds, and currency erodes rapidly.

INFLATION-INDEXED SECURITIES bonds or notes that guarantee a return that beats INFLATION if held to maturity. Also applied to shares in mutual funds that hold such securities. Inflation-indexed Treasury securities were introduced in 1997 in 10-year maturities and were subsequently issued as 5-year notes. Similar offerings followed by issuers such as the Tennessee Valley Authority and the Federal Home Loan Bank. In April, 1998, the first 30-year inflation-indexed Treasury bonds were issued. Inflation-indexed Treasuries offer a fixed rate of return, as well as a fluctuating rate of return that matches inflation. The fixed portion is paid out as INTEREST, while the indexed portion is represented by an annual adjustment of PRINCIPAL. For example, a $1,000 inflation-indexed Treasury is issued at auction with a 3.5% INTEREST RATE and inflation that year turns out to be 3%. The 3.5% interest on $1,000 would be paid out and, at the end of the year, the inflation rate would adjust the principal, bringing it to $1,030. The following year, the fixed 3.5% interest rate would be applied to the new principal of $1,030 and the principal would again be adjusted according to that year's inflation rate. With low inflation prevailing in the late '90s, anti-inflation securities met a lackluster reception, although longer-term bonds were in somewhat greater demand. Chief drawbacks are the prospect of DEFLATION, a lack of LIQUIDITY, and the fact that the inflation adjustment is taxable annually but not paid out until maturity.

INFLATION RATE rate of change in prices. Two primary U.S. indicators of the inflation rate are the CONSUMER PRICE INDEX and the PRODUCER PRICE INDEX, which track changes in prices paid by consumers and by producers. The rate can be calculated on an annual, monthly, or other basis.

INFLATION RISK *see* RISK.

INFLEXIBLE EXPENSES *see* FLEXIBLE EXPENSES.

INFRASTRUCTURE a nation's basic system of transportation, communication, and other aspects of its physical plant. Building and maintaining road, bridge, sewage, and electrical systems provides millions of jobs nationwide. For developing countries, building an infrastructure is a first step in economic development.

INGOT bar of metal. The Federal Reserve System's gold reserves are stored in ingot form. Individual investors may take delivery of an ingot of a precious metal such as gold or silver or may buy a certificate entitling them to a share in an ingot.

INHERITANCE part of an estate acquired by an HEIR.

INHERITANCE TAX RETURN state counterpart to the federal ESTATE TAX return, required of the executor or administrator to determine the amount of state tax due on the inheritance.

INITIAL MARGIN amount of cash or eligible securities required to be deposited with a broker before engaging in margin transactions. A margin transaction is one in which the broker extends credit to the customer in a margin account. Under REGULATION T of the Federal Reserve Board, the initial margin is currently 50% of the purchase price when buying eligible stock or convertible bonds or 50% of the proceeds of a short sale. *See also* MAINTENANCE REQUIREMENT; MARGIN CALL; MARGIN REQUIREMENT; MARGIN SECURITY.

INITIAL PUBLIC OFFERING (IPO) corporation's first offering of stock to the public. IPO's are almost invariably an opportunity for the existing investors and participating venture capitalists to make big profits, since for the first time their shares will be given a market value reflecting expectations for the company's future growth. *See also* HOT ISSUE.

INJUNCTION court order instructing a defendant to refrain from doing something that would be injurious to the plaintiff, or face a penalty. The usual procedure is to issue a temporary restraining order, then hold hearings to determine whether a permanent injunction is warranted.

IN PLAY stock affected by TAKEOVER rumors or activities.

INSIDE INFORMATION corporate affairs that have not yet been made public. The officers of a firm would know in advance, for instance, if the company was about to be taken over, or if the latest earnings report was going to differ significantly from information released earlier. Under Securities and Exchange Commission rules, an INSIDER is not allowed to trade on the basis of such information.

INSIDE MARKET bid or asked quotes between dealers trading for their own inventories. Distinguished from the retail market, where quotes reflect the prices that customers pay to dealers. Also known as *inter-dealer market; wholesale market.*

INSIDER person with access to key information before it is announced to the public. Usually the term refers to directors, officers, and key employees, but the definition has been extended legally to include relatives and others in a position to capitalize on INSIDE INFORMATION. Insiders are prohibited from trading on their knowledge.

INSIDER TRADING practice of buying and selling shares in a company's stock by that company's management or board of directors, or by a holder of more than 10% of the company's shares. Managers may trade their company's stock as long as they disclose their activity within ten days of the close of the month within the time the transactions took place. However, it is illegal for insiders to trade based on their knowledge of material corporate developments that have not been announced publicly. Developments that would be considered *material* include news of an impending takeover, introduction of a new product line, a divestiture, a key executive appointment, or other news that could affect the company's stock positively or negatively. Insider trading laws have been extended to other people who have knowledge of these developments but who are not members of management, including investment bankers, lawyers, printers of financial disclosure documents, or relatives of managers and executives who learn of these material developments.

INSIDER TRADING SANCTIONS ACT OF 1984 amendment to the SECURITIES EXCHANGE ACT OF 1934 that outlined civil and criminal penalties for insider trading violations. Fines up to triple the amount of illegal gains can be levied. The amendment applies not only to people who buy or sell using material nonpublic information, but to anyone who gives them such information or aids and abets them.

INSOLVENCY inability to pay debts when due. *See also* BANKRUPTCY; CASH FLOW; SOLVENCY.

INSTALLMENT SALE
In general: sale made with the agreement that the purchased goods or services will be paid for in fractional amounts over a specified period of time.
Securities: transaction with a set contract price, paid in installments over a period of time. Gains or losses are generally taxable on a prorated basis.

INSTINET *see* FOURTH MARKET.

INSTITUTIONAL BROKER broker who buys and sells securities for banks, mutual funds, insurance companies, pension funds, or other institutional clients. Institutional brokers deal in large volumes of securities and generally charge their customers lower per-unit commission rates than individuals pay.

INSTITUTIONAL INVESTOR organization that trades large volumes of securities. Some examples are mutual funds, banks, insurance companies, pension funds, labor union funds, corporate profit-sharing plans, and college endowment funds. Typically, upwards of 70% of the daily trading on the New York Stock Exchange is on behalf of institutional investors.

INSTRUMENT legal document in which some contractual relationship is given formal expression or by which some right is granted—for example, notes, contracts, agreements. *See also* NEGOTIABLE INSTRUMENT.

INSTRUMENTALITY federal agency whose obligations, while not direct obligations of the U.S. Government, are sponsored or guaranteed by the government and backed by the FULL FAITH AND CREDIT of the government. Well over 100 series of notes, certificates, and bonds have been issued by such instrumentalities as Federal Home Loan Bank, and Student Loan Marketing Association.

INSURABILITY conditions under which an insurance company is willing to insure a risk. Each insurance company applies its own standards based on its own underwriting criteria. For example, some life insurance companies do not insure people with high-risk occupations such as stuntmen or firefighters, while other companies consider these people insurable, though the premiums they must pay are higher than for those in low-risk professions.

INSURABLE INTEREST relationship between an insured person or property and the potential beneficiary of the policy. For example, a wife has an insurable interest in her husband's life, because she would be financially harmed if he were to die. Therefore, she could receive the proceeds of the insurance policy if he were to die while the policy was in force. If there is no insurable interest, an insurance company will not issue a policy.

INSURANCE system whereby individuals and companies that are concerned about potential hazards pay premiums to an insurance company, which reimburses them in the event of loss. The insurer profits by investing the premiums it receives. Some common forms of insurance cover business risks, automobiles, homes, boats, workers' compensation, and health. Life insurance guarantees payment to the beneficiaries when the insured person dies. In a broad economic sense, insurance transfers risk from individuals to a larger group, which is better able to pay for losses.

INSURANCE AGENT representative of an insurance company who sells the firm's policies. CAPTIVE AGENTS sell the policies of only one company, while INDEPENDENT AGENTS sell the policies of many companies. Agents must be licensed to sell insurance in the states where they solicit customers.

INSURANCE BROKER independent broker who searches for the best insurance coverage at the lowest cost for the client. Insurance brokers do not work for insurance companies, but for the buyers of insurance products. They constantly are comparing the merits of competing insurance companies to find the best deal for their customers.

INSURANCE CLAIM request for payment from the insurance company by the insured. For example, a homeowner files a claim if he or she suffered damage because of a fire, theft, or other loss. In life insurance, survivors submit a claim when the insured dies. The insurance company investigates the claim and pays the appropriate amount if the claim is found to be legitimate, or denies the claim if it determines the loss was fraudulent or not covered by the policy.

INSURANCE DIVIDEND money paid to cash value life insurance policyholders with participating policies, usually once a year. Dividend rates are based on the insurance company's mortality experience, administrative expenses, and investment returns. Lower mortality experience (the number of policyholders dying) and expenses, combined with high investment returns, will increase dividends. Technically, dividends are considered a return of the policyholder's premiums, and are thus not considered taxable income by the IRS. Policyholders may choose to take these dividends in cash or may purchase additional life insurance.

INSURANCE POLICY insurance contract specifying what risks are insured and what premiums must be paid to keep the policy in force. Policies also spell out DEDUCTIBLES and other terms. Policies for life insurance specify whose life is insured and which beneficiaries will receive the insurance proceeds. HOMEOWNER'S INSURANCE POLICIES specify which property and casualty perils are covered. *Health insurance policies* detail which medical procedures, drugs, and devices are reimbursed. *Auto insurance policies* describe the conditions under which car owners will be covered in case of accidents, theft, or other damage to their cars. *Disability policies* specify the qualifying conditions of disability and how long payments will continue. *Business insurance policies* describe which liabilities are reimbursable. The policy is the written document that both insured and insurance company refer to when determining whether or not a claim is covered.

INSURANCE PREMIUM payment made by the insured in return for insurance protection. Premiums are set based on the probability of risk of loss and competitive pressures with other insurers. An insurance company's actuary will figure out the expected loss ratio on a particular class of customers, and then individual applicants will be evaluated based on whether they present higher or lower risks than the class as a whole. If a policyholder does not pay the premium, the insurance or policy may lapse. If the policy is a cash value policy, the policy-owner can choose to take a paid-up insurance policy with a lower face value amount or an extended term policy.

INSURANCE SETTLEMENT payment of proceeds from an insurance policy to the insured under the terms of an insurance contract. Insurance settlements may be either in the form of one lump-sum payment or a series of payments.

INSURED individual, group, or property that is covered by an INSURANCE POLICY. The policy specifies exactly which perils the insured is indemnified against. The insured may be a particular individual, such as someone covered by a life insurance policy. It may be a group of people, such as those covered by a group life insurance policy purchased by a company on behalf of its employees. The insured may also refer to property, such as a house and its possessions which are covered by a HOMEOWNER'S INSURANCE POLICY.

INSURED ACCOUNT account at a bank, savings and loan association, credit union, or brokerage firm that belongs to a federal or private insurance organization. Bank accounts are insured by the BANK INSURANCE FUND (BIF), and savings and loan deposits are insured by the SAVINGS ASSOCIATION INSURANCE FUND (SAIF); both programs are administered by the FEDERAL DEPOSIT INSURANCE COR-PORATION (FDIC). Credit union accounts are insured by the *National Credit Union Administration*. Brokerage accounts are insured by the SECURITIES INVESTOR PROTECTION CORPORATION. Such insurance protects depositors against loss in the event that the institution becomes insolvent. Federal insurance systems were set up in the 1930s, after bank failures threatened the banking system with collapse. Some money market funds are covered by private insurance companies.

INSURED BONDS municipal bonds that are insured against default by a MUNICI-PAL BOND INSURANCE company. The company pledges to make all interest and principal payments when due if the issuer of the bonds defaults on its obligations. In return, the bond's issuer pays a premium to the insurance company. Insured bonds usually trade based on the credit rating of the insurer rather than the rating of the underlying issuer, since the insurance company is ultimately at risk for the repayment of principal and interest. Insured bonds will pay slightly lower yields, because of the cost of the insurance protection, than comparable noninsured bonds. Some of the major municipal bond insurance firms include MBIA and AMBAC Indemnity Corporation.

INTANGIBLE ASSET right or nonphysical resource that is presumed to represent an advantage to the firm's position in the marketplace. Such assets include copyrights, patents, TRADEMARKS, goodwill, computer programs, capitalized advertising costs, organization costs, licenses, LEASES, FRANCHISES, exploration permits, and import and export permits.

INTANGIBLE COST tax-deductible cost. Such costs are incurred in drilling, testing, completing, and reworking oil and gas wells—labor, core analysis, fracturing, drill stem testing, engineering, fuel, geologists' expenses; also abandonment losses, management fees, delay rentals, and similar expenses.

INTERBANK RATE *see* LONDON INTERBANK OFFERED RATE (LIBOR).

INTERCOMMODITY SPREAD spread consisting of a long position and a short position in different but related commodities—for example, a long position in gold futures and a short position in silver futures. The investor hopes to profit from the changing price relationship between the commodities.

INTERDELIVERY SPREAD futures or options trading technique that entails buying one month of a contract and selling another month in the same contract—for instance, buying a June wheat contract and simultaneously selling a September wheat contract. The investor hopes to profit as the price difference between the two contracts widens or narrows.

INTEREST
1. cost of using money, expressed as a rate per period of time, usually one year, in which case it is called an annual rate of interest.
2. share, right, or title in property.

INTEREST COVERAGE *see* FIXED-CHARGE COVERAGE.

INTEREST DEDUCTION DEDUCTION allowable for certain types of interest expense, such as for interest on a home mortgage or interest on a MARGIN ACCOUNT.

INTEREST EQUALIZATION TAX (IET) tax of 15% on interest received by foreign borrowers in U.S. capital markets, imposed in 1963 and removed in 1974.

INTEREST-ONLY LOAN form of loan where the only current obligation is interest and where repayment of principal is deferred.

INTEREST OPTION insurance policyholder's choice to reinvest dividends with the insurer to earn a guaranteed rate of interest. A beneficiary may also reinvest proceeds to earn interest.

INTEREST RATE rate of interest charged for the use of money, usually expressed at an annual rate. The rate is derived by dividing the amount of interest by the amount of principal borrowed. For example, if a bank charged $10 per year in interest to borrow $100, they would be charging a 10% interest rate. Interest rates are quoted on bills, notes, bonds, credit cards, and many kinds of consumer and business loans.

INTEREST-RATE FUTURES CONTRACT futures contract based on a debt security or inter-bank deposit. In theory, the buyer of a bond futures contract agrees to take delivery of the underlying bonds when the contract expires, and the contract seller agrees to deliver the debt instrument. However, most contracts are not settled by delivery, but instead are traded out before expiration. The value of the contract rises and falls inversely to changes in interest rates. For example, if Treasury bond yields rise, futures contracts on Treasury bonds will fall in price. Conversely, when yields fall, Treasury bond futures prices rise. There are many kinds of interest rate futures contracts, including those on Treasury bills, notes, and bonds; Government National Mortgage Association (GNMA) mortgage-backed securities; municipal bonds; and inter-bank deposits such as Eurodollars. Speculators believing that interest rates are about to rise or fall trade these futures. Also, companies with exposure to fluctuations in interest rates, such as brokerage firms, banks, and insurance companies, may use these contracts to HEDGE their holdings of Treasury bonds and other debt instruments or their costs of future borrowings. For a list of interest rate futures contracts, *see* SECURITIES AND COMMODITIES EXCHANGES.

INTEREST-RATE OPTIONS CONTRACT options contract based on an underlying debt security. Options, unlike futures, give their buyers the right, but not the obligation, to buy the underlying bond at a fixed price before a specific date in the future. Option sellers promise to sell the bonds at a set price anytime until the contract expires. In return for granting this right, the option buyer pays a premium to the option seller. Yield-based calls become more valuable as yields rise, and puts become more valuable as yields decline. There are interest rate options on Treasury bills, notes, and bonds; GNMA mortgage-backed securities; certificates of deposit; municipal bonds; and other interest-sensitive instruments. For a complete list of these contracts, *see* SECURITIES AND COMMODITIES EXCHANGES.

INTEREST-RATE RISK RISK that changes in interest rates will adversely affect the value of an investor's securities portfolio. For example, an investor with large holdings in long-term bonds and utilities has assumed a significant interest-rate risk, because the value of those bonds and utility stocks will fall if interest rates rise. Investors can take various precautionary measures to HEDGE their interest-rate risk, such as buying INTEREST-RATE FUTURES or INTEREST-RATE OPTIONS CONTRACTS.

INTEREST-SENSITIVE INSURANCE POLICY cash value life insurance with dividend rates tied to the fluctuations in interest rates. For example, holders of UNIVERSAL LIFE INSURANCE policies will be credited with a greater increase in cash values when interest rates rise and a slower rate of increase in cash values when interest rates fall.

INTEREST-SENSITIVE STOCK stock of a firm whose earnings change when interest rates change, such as a bank or utility, and which therefore tends to go up or down on news of rate movements.

INTERIM DIVIDEND DIVIDEND declared and paid before annual earnings have been determined, generally quarterly. Most companies strive for consistency and plan quarterly dividends they are sure they can afford, reserving changes until fiscal year results are known.

INTERIM FINANCING temporary, short-term loan made conditional on a TAKE-OUT by intermediate or long-term financing. Also called *bridge loan* financing.

INTERIM LOAN *see* CONSTRUCTION LOAN.

INTERIM STATEMENT financial report covering only a portion of a fiscal year. Public corporations supplement the annual report with quarterly statements informing shareholders of changes in the balance sheet and income statement, as well as other newsworthy developments.

INTERLOCKING DIRECTORATE membership on more than one company's board of directors. This is legal so long as the companies are not competitors. Consumer activists often point to interlocking directorates as an element in corporate conspiracies. The most flagrant abuses were outlawed by the Clayton Antitrust Act of 1914.

INTERMARKET SPREAD *see* INTERDELIVERY SPREAD.

INTERMARKET SURVEILLANCE INFORMATION SYSTEM (ISIS) DATABASE sharing information provided by the major stock exchanges in the United States. It permits the identification of CONTRA BROKERS and aids in preventing violations.

INTERMARKET TRADING SYSTEM (ITS) video-computer display system that links the posts of specialists at the New York, American, Boston, Chicago, Philadelphia Stock Exchanges, and the Pacific Exchanges, as well as the NASD market makers who are trading the same securities. The quotes are displayed and are firm (good) for at least 100 shares. A broker at one exchange may direct an order to another exchange where the quote is better by sending the order through the electronic workstation. A transaction that is accepted by the broker at the other exchange is analogous to an electronic handshake and constitutes a contract.

INTERMEDIARY person or institution empowered to make investment decisions for others. Some examples are banks, savings and loan institutions, insurance companies, brokerage firms, mutual funds, and credit unions. These specialists are knowledgeable about investment alternatives and can achieve a higher return than the average investor can. Furthermore, they deal in large dollar volumes, have lower transaction costs, and can diversify their assets easily. Also called *financial intermediary.*

INTERMEDIATE TERM period between the short and long term, the length of time depending on the context. Stock analysts, for instance, mean 6 to 12 months, whereas bond analysts most often mean 3 to 10 years.

INTERMEDIATION placement of money with a financial INTERMEDIARY like a broker or bank, which invests it in bonds, stocks, mortgages, or other loans, money-market securities, or government obligations so as to achieve a targeted return. More formally called *financial intermediation.* The opposite is DISINTER-MEDIATION, the withdrawal of money from an intermediary.

INTERNAL AUDITOR employee of a company who examines records and procedures to ensure against fraud and to make certain board directives and management policies are being properly executed.

INTERNAL CONTROL method, procedure, or system designed to promote efficiency, assure the implementation of policy, and safeguard assets.

INTERNAL EXPANSION asset growth financed out of internally generated cash—usually termed INTERNAL FINANCING—or through ACCRETION or APPRECIA-TION. *See also* CASH EARNINGS.

INTERNAL FINANCING funds produced by the normal operations of a firm, as distinguished from external financing, which includes borrowings and new equity. *See also* INTERNAL EXPANSION.

INTERNAL RATE OF RETURN (IRR) discount rate at which the present value of the future cash flows of an investment equal the cost of the investment. It is found by a process of trial and error; when the net present values of cash outflows (the cost of the investment) and cash inflows (returns on the investment) equal zero, the rate of discount being used is the IRR. When IRR is greater than the required return—called the hurdle rate in capital budgeting—the investment is acceptable

INTERNAL REVENUE CODE blanket term for complexity of statutes comprising the federal TAX law.

INTERNAL REVENUE SERVICE (IRS) U.S. agency charged with collecting nearly all federal taxes, including personal and corporate income taxes, social security taxes, and excise and gift taxes. Major exceptions include taxes having to do with alcohol, tobacco, firearms, and explosives, and customs duties and tariffs. The IRS administers the rules and regulations that are the responsibility of the U.S. Department of the Treasury and investigates and prosecutes (through the U.S. Tax Court) tax illegalities.

INTERNAL REVENUE SERVICE RESTRUCTURING AND REFORM ACT OF 1998 legislation designed to reform the Internal Revenue Service, lower the holding period for CAPITAL GAINS, and make various technical corrections in the TAXPAYER RELIEF ACT OF 1997. Some of the major provisions of law, which was enacted in the summer of 1998, include:

1. **Reduction in the capital gains holding period:** Under the Taxpayer Relief Act of 1997, the holding period to qualify for preferential long-term 20% (10% for those in the 15% tax bracket) capital gains tax rates had been raised from 12 to 18 months. This law lowered the holding period back to 12 months, effective retroactively to January 1, 1998.
2. **Restructuring the Internal Revenue Service:** The IRS Commissioner was instructed to modify the organization and governance of the agency by

replacing the National-Regional-District structure with operating units to serve particular groups of taxpayers such as individuals, small businesses, big businesses, and tax-exempt organizations. In addition, the Act created an independent Oversight Board to supervise strategic IRS plans and modernization. The National Taxpayer Advocate was made independent of IRS control, now reporting directly to the Treasury Secretary. Local Taxpayer Advocates will help taxpayers resolve disputes separate from IRS examination, collection, and appeals functions.

3. **Taxpayer protections and rights:** Several sections of the law were designed to help taxpayers in disputes with the IRS during the audit and collection process:

   Shift in burden of proof: The burden of proof shifts from the taxpayer to the IRS in any court proceeding on income, gift, estate, or generation-skipping tax liability on factual issues. This applies only if the taxpayer introduces credible evidence on factual issues, maintains records and substantiates claims, and cooperates with reasonable IRS requests for meetings, interviews, witnesses, information, and documents. These rules apply to all court proceedings arising from audits after the Act was signed into law in July 1998. It does not apply to court proceedings started before that date. The burden of proof remains on corporations, trusts, and partnerships with a net worth over $7 million.

   Confidentiality privilege: The Act extends the existing attorney-client privilege of confidentiality to non-lawyers who are authorized to practice before the IRS, such as accountants or enrolled agents. This privilege may be asserted in any noncriminal tax proceeding before the IRS or federal courts.

   Innocent spouse relief: Spouses who become divorced, legally separated, or live apart for at least 12 months are entitled to relief from tax liabilities if their former mates made tax mistakes without their knowledge. Spouses may elect to make a separate-liability claim if the taxes paid were understated as late as two years after the IRS has initiated collection activities. The IRS also must inform taxpayers of their joint and several liability and innocent spouse rights.

   Liberalizes installment agreements and offers-in-compromise: The Act makes offers-in-compromise and installment agreements more flexible and accessible to taxpayers. The IRS is directed to try to negotiate deals with taxpayers instead of battling them in drawn-out court proceedings. If the taxpayer owes $10,000 or less, the IRS is required to allow the tax liability to be paid in installments.

   Increases safeguards against IRS collection abuses: The Act imposes a list of "due-process" procedures the IRS must follow as it attempts to collect taxes. For example, taxpayers can request a hearing before Tax Court before property is seized and they can appeal IRS liens more easily. Higher dollar amounts were instituted for property that is exempt from liens and levies. The IRS must follow fair debt collection practices imposed on private-sector collection agencies, such as the prohibition against late-night calls to taxpayers.

   Interest and penalty relief: The Act suspends interest and time-related penalties if the IRS does not provide appropriate notice of tax liability to a taxpayer within 18 months after a timely return is filed. In addition, taxpayers are entitled to a 0% interest rate when outstanding overpayments and underpayments of income and self-employment taxes are equal. The interest rate paid on refunds was raised to the same rate as the underpayment interest rate.

4. **Electronic filing incentives:** The Act encourages more filing of returns electronically, with the goal of limiting paper returns to 20% of all returns by the year 2007. By 2002, taxpayers who prepare their returns electronically but send a printout to the IRS will be required to file electronically. Those who

file information returns electronically after 1999 get an extra month to file, from February 28 under the old law to March 31 under the new rules.

5. **Limit the tax benefits of "paired-share" REITs:** A small number of Real Estate Investment Trusts, called "paired-share" REITs, had been taking advantage of a tax loophole allowing them to put the revenues from operating businesses through their tax-sheltered REIT structures. This practice was curtailed.

6. **Changes to Roth IRA rules:** Several changes were made to clarify regulations related to the Roth IRA, which was created in the TAXPAYER RELIEF ACT OF 1997. For example, those who convert to Roth IRAs from regular IRAs may elect to recognize all income in the year of conversion rather than over four years. In addition, taxpayers have until the due date of their return to change their minds about any Roth IRA conversion that took place at any time in the past tax year. This rule was designed to help taxpayers who incorrectly projected the size of their adjusted gross income as less than $100,000 when converting assets from a regular IRA to a Roth IRA.

7. **Pre-rata gains from sales of principal residences:** The Act settled the question of how to apply the capital gain exclusion to the sale of a residence that had been owned and occupied for less than two years. Such homeowners can now exclude the amount of the capital gain ($500,000 for couples and $250,000 for singles) that is equal to the fraction of the two years that the property was owned and occupied.

INTERNATIONAL BANK FOR RECONSTRUCTION AND DEVELOPMENT (IBRD) organization set up by the Bretton Woods Agreement of 1944 to help finance the reconstruction of Europe and Asia after World War II. That task accomplished, the *World Bank,* as IBRD is known, turned to financing commercial and infrastructure projects, mostly in developing nations. It does not compete with commercial banks, but it may participate in a loan set up by a commercial bank. World Bank loans must be backed by the government in the borrowing country.

INTERNATIONAL MARKET INDEX market-value weighted proprietary index of the American Stock Exchange which tracks the performance of 50 American Depositary Receipts traded on the American Stock Exchange, New York Stock Exchange and NASDAQ Market. Options are no longer traded on the index.

INTERNATIONAL MONETARY FUND (IMF) organization set up by the Bretton Woods Agreement in 1944. Unlike the World Bank, whose focus is on foreign exchange reserves and the balance of trade, the IMF focus is on lowering trade barriers and stabilizing currencies. While helping developing nations pay their debts, the IMF usually imposes tough guidelines aimed at lowering inflation, cutting imports, and raising exports. IMF funds come mostly from the treasuries of industrialized nations. *See also* INTERNATIONAL BANK FOR RECONSTRUCTION AND DEVELOPMENT.

INTERNATIONAL MONETARY MARKET (IMM) division of the Chicago Mercantile Exchange that trades futures in U.S. Treasury bills, foreign currency, certificates of deposit, and Eurodollar deposits.

INTERNATIONAL MUTUAL FUND mutual fund that invests in securities markets throughout the world so that if one market is in a slump, profits can still be earned in others. Fund managers must be alert to trends in foreign currencies as well as in world stock and bond markets. Otherwise, seemingly profitable investments in a rising market could lose money if the national currency is falling against the dollar. While international mutual funds tend to concentrate only on non-American securities, GLOBAL MUTUAL FUNDS buy both foreign and domestic stocks and bonds.

INTERNATIONAL PETROLEUM EXCHANGE (IPE) London-based energy futures and options exchange, trading Brent crude oil futures and options, gas oil futures and options, and natural gas futures. Brent crude futures are also traded through a mutual offset link on the SIMEX. There are three classes of IPE membership: floor members who are voting members, hold SEATS on the exchange and own a share of the exchange; trade associates, which are companies with direct interests in producing, refining, or trading oil and oil products; and local floor members, individuals who can trade on the exchange floor. Locals also have voting rights and a share of the exchange, while trade associates do not. Brent crude oil and gas oil are traded on the IPE floor through floor members; natural gas is traded electronically on the IPE's Energy Trading System (ETS). The IPE coordinates trading with the NEW YORK MERCANTILE EXCHANGE through the ETS 2/NYMEX ACCESS 2000 trading system. The IPE also trades electricity, carbon dioxide emissions, European natural gas and fuel oil. Anyone can trade through floor members. Locals can trade for their own accounts or for floor members and other locals, but not directly for clients. Trading hours are 9:27 A.M. to 8:12 P.M.

INTERNATIONAL STOCK EXCHANGE OF THE U.K. AND THE REPUBLIC OF IRELAND (ISE) organization formed after BIG BANG to replace the London Stock Exchange following its merger with the International Securities Regulatory Organization (ISRO). ISRO is a professional trade association of brokers and dealers in the United Kingdom that functions as a self-regulatory organization. The term *London Stock Exchange* persists in investment parlance despite the name change.

INTERPOLATION estimation of an unknown number intermediate between known numbers. Interpolation is a way of approximating price or yield using bond tables that do not give the net yield on every amount invested at every rate of interest and for every maturity. Interpolation is based on the assumption that a certain percentage change in yield will result in the same percentage change in price. The assumption is not altogether correct, but the variance is small enough to ignore.

INTERPOSITIONING placement of a second broker in a securities transaction between two principals or between a customer and a marketmaker. The practice is regulated by the Securities and Exchange Commission, and abuses such as interpositioning to create additional commission income are illegal.

INTERSTATE COMMERCE COMMISSION (ICC) federal agency created by the Interstate Commerce Act of 1887 to insure that the public receives fair and reasonable rates and services from carriers and transportation service firms involved in interstate commerce. Legislation enacted in the 1970s and 80s substantially curtailed the regulatory activities of the ICC, particularly in the rail, truck, and bus industries.

INTER VIVOS TRUST trust established between living persons—for instance, between father and child. In contrast, a TESTAMENTARY TRUST goes into effect when the person who establishes the trust dies. Also called *living trust.*

INTESTACY; INTESTATE a person who dies without a valid will is said to die *intestate* or *in intestacy.* State law determines who is entitled to inherit and who is entitled to manage the decedent's estate.

INTESTATE DISTRIBUTION distribution of assets to beneficiaries from the estate of a person who dies without a written will of instructions. This distribution is overseen by a PROBATE court and the appointed EXECUTOR of the estate. Each state has specific laws outlining how intestate distributions are to be made.

IN THE MONEY option contract on a stock whose current market price is above the striking price of a call option or below the striking price of a put option. A call option on XYZ at a striking price of 100 would be in the money if XYZ were selling for 102, for instance, and a put option with the same striking price would be in the money if XYZ were selling for 98. *See also* AT THE MONEY; OUT OF THE MONEY.

IN THE TANK slang expression meaning market prices are dropping rapidly. Stock market observers may say, "The market is in the tank" after a day in which stock prices fell.

INTRACOMMODITY SPREAD futures position in which a trader buys and sells contracts in the same commodity on the same exchange, but for different months. For instance, a trader would place an intracommodity spread if he bought a pork bellies contract expiring in December and at the same time sold a pork bellies contract expiring in April. His profit or loss would be determined by the price difference between the December and April contracts.

INTRADAY within the day; often used in connection with high and low prices of a stock, bond, or commodity. For instance, "The stock hit a new intraday high today" means that the stock reached an all-time high price during the day but fell back to a lower price by the end of the day. The listing of the high and low prices at which a stock is traded during a day is called the *intraday price range.*

INTRASTATE OFFERING securities offering limited to one state in the United States. *See also* BLUE-SKY LAW.

INTRINSIC VALUE
Financial analysis: valuation determined by applying data inputs to a valuation theory or model. The resulting value is comparable to the prevailing market price.
Options trading: difference between the EXERCISE PRICE or strike price of an option and the market value of the underlying security. For example, if the strike price is $53 on a call option to purchase a stock with a market price of $55, the option has an intrinsic value of $2. Or, in the case of a put option, if the strike price was $55 and the market price of the underlying stock was $53, the intrinsic value of the option would also be $2. Options AT THE MONEY or OUT OF THE MONEY have no intrinsic value.

INVENTORY
Corporate finance: value of a firm's raw materials, work in process, supplies used in operations, and finished goods. Since inventory value changes with price fluctuations, it is important to know the method of valuation. There are a number of inventory valuation methods; the most widely used are FIRST IN, FIRST OUT (FIFO) and LAST IN, FIRST OUT (LIFO). Financial statements normally indicate the basis of inventory valuation, generally the lower figure of either cost price or current market price, which precludes potentially overstated earnings and assets as the result of sharp increases in the price of raw materials.
Personal finance: list of all assets owned by an individual and the value of each, based on cost, market value, or both. Such inventories are usually required for property insurance purposes and are sometimes required with applications for credit.
Securities: net long or short position of a dealer or specialist. Also, securities bought and held by a dealer for later resale.

INVENTORY FINANCING
Factoring: sometimes used as a synonym for overadvances in FACTORING, where loans in excess of accounts receivable are made against inventory in anticipation of future sales.

Finance companies: financing by a bank or sales finance company of the inventory of a dealer in consumer or capital goods. Such loans, also called wholesale financing or *floorplanning*, are secured by the inventory and are usually made as part of a relationship in which retail installment paper generated by sales to the public is also financed by the lender. *See also* FINANCE COMPANY.

INVENTORY TURNOVER ratio of annual sales to inventory, which shows how many times the inventory of a firm is sold and replaced during an accounting period; sometimes called *inventory utilization ratio*. Compared with industry averages, a low turnover might indicate a company is carrying excess stocks of inventory, an unhealthy sign because excess inventory represents an investment with a low or zero rate of return and because it makes the company more vulnerable to falling prices. A steady drop in inventory turnover, in comparison with prior periods, can reveal lack of a sufficiently aggressive sales policy or ineffective buying.

Two points about the way inventory turnover may be calculated: (1) Because sales are recorded at market value and inventories are normally carried at cost, it is more realistic to obtain the turnover ratio by dividing inventory into cost of goods sold rather than into sales. However, it is conventional to use sales as the numerator because that is the practice of Dun & Bradstreet and other compilers of published financial ratios, and comparability is of overriding importance. (2) To minimize the seasonal factor affecting inventory levels, it is better to use an average inventory figure, obtained by adding yearly beginning and ending inventory figures and dividing by 2.

INVERSE FLOATER derivative instrument whose coupon rate is inversely related to some multiple of a specified market rate of interest. Typically a cap and floor are placed on the coupon. As interest rates go down, the amount of interest the inverse floater pays goes up. For example, if the inverse floater rate is 32% and the multiple is four times the London Interbank Offered Rate (LIBOR) of 7%, the coupon is valued at 4%. If the LIBOR goes to 6%, the new coupon is 8%. Many inverse floaters are based on pieces of mortgage-backed securities such as COLLATERALIZED MORTGAGE OBLIGATIONS which react inversely to movements in interest rates.

INVERTED SCALE serial bond offering where earlier maturities have higher yields than later maturities. *See also* SERIAL BOND.

INVERTED YIELD CURVE unusual situation where short-term interest rates are higher than long-term rates. Normally, lenders receive a higher yield when committing their money for a longer period of time; this situation is called a POSITIVE YIELD CURVE. An inverted YIELD CURVE occurs when a surge in demand for short-term credit drives up short-term rates on instruments like Treasury bills and money-market funds, while long-term rates move up more slowly, since borrowers are not willing to commit themselves to paying high interest rates for many years. This situation happened in the early 1980s, when short-term interest rates were around 20%, while long-term rates went up to only 16% or 17%. The existence of an inverted yield curve can be a sign of an unhealthy economy, marked by high inflation and low levels of confidence. Also called *negative yield curve*.

INVESTMENT use of capital to create more money, either through income-producing vehicles or through more risk-oriented ventures designed to result in capital gains. *Investment* can refer to a financial investment (where an investor puts money into a vehicle) or to an investment of effort and time on the part of an individual who wants to reap profits from the success of his labor. Investment connotes the idea that safety of principal is important. SPECULATION, on the other hand, is far riskier.

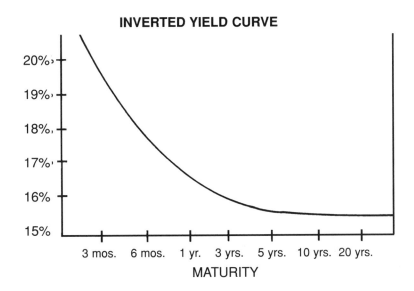

INVERTED YIELD CURVE

20%ʾ	
19%ʾ	
18%ᵢ	
17%ʾ	
16%	
15%	

3 mos.   6 mos.   1 yr.   3 yrs.   5 yrs.   10 yrs.   20 yrs.

MATURITY

INVESTMENT ADVISERS ACT legislation passed by Congress in 1940 that requires all investment advisers to register with the Securities and Exchange Commission. The Act is designed to protect the public from fraud or misrepresentation by investment advisers. One requirement, for example, is that advisers must disclose all potential *conflicts of interest* with any recommendations they make to those they advise. A potential conflict of interest might exist where the adviser had a position in a security he was recommending. *See also* INVESTMENT ADVISORY SERVICE.

INVESTMENT ADVISORY SERVICE service providing investment advice for a fee. Investment advisers must register with the Securities and Exchange Commission and abide by the rules of the INVESTMENT ADVISERS ACT. Investment advisory services usually specialize in a particular kind of investment—for example, emerging growth stocks, international stocks, mutual funds, or commodities. Some services only offer advice through a newsletter; others will manage a client's money. The performance of many investment advisory services is ranked by the *Hulbert Financial Digest. See* HULBERT RATING.

INVESTMENT BANKER firm, acting as underwriter or agent, that serves as intermediary between an issuer of securities and the investing public. In what is termed FIRM COMMITMENT underwriting, the investment banker, either as manager or participating member of an investment banking syndicate, makes outright purchases of new securities from the issuer and distributes them to dealers and investors, profiting on the spread between the purchase price and the selling (public offering) price. Under a conditional arrangement called BEST EFFORT, the investment banker markets a new issue without underwriting it, acting as agent rather than principal and taking a commission for whatever amount of securities the banker succeeds in marketing. Under another conditional arrangement, called STANDBY COMMITMENT, the investment banker serves clients issuing new securities by agreeing to purchase for resale any securities not taken by existing holders of RIGHTS.

Where a client relationship exists, the investment banker's role begins with pre-underwriting counseling and continues after the distribution of securities is completed, in the form of ongoing expert advice and guidance, often including a seat on the board of directors. The direct underwriting responsibilities include preparing the Securities and Exchange Commission registration statement; consulting on pricing of the securities; forming and managing the syndicate; establishing a selling group if desired; and PEGGING (stabilizing) the price of the issue during the offering and distribution period.

In addition to new securities offerings, investment bankers handle the distribution of blocks of previously issued securities, either through secondary offerings or through negotiations; maintain markets for securities already distributed; and act as finders in the private placement of securities.

Along with their investment banking functions, the majority of investment bankers also maintain broker-dealer operations, serving both wholesale and retail clients in brokerage and advisory capacities and offering a growing number of related financial services. *See also* FLOTATION COST; SECONDARY DISTRIBUTION; UNDERWRITE.

INVESTMENT CERTIFICATE certificate evidencing investment in a savings and loan association and showing the amount of money invested. Investment certificates do not have voting rights and do not involve stockholder responsibility. Also called *mutual capital certificate. See also* MUTUAL ASSOCIATION.

INVESTMENT CLIMATE economic, monetary, and other conditions affecting the performance of investments.

INVESTMENT CLUB group of people who pool their assets in order to make joint investment decisions. Each member of the club contributes a certain amount of capital, with additional money to be invested every month or quarter. Decisions on which stocks or bonds to buy are made by a vote of members. Besides helping each member become more knowledgeable about investing, these clubs allow people with small amounts of money to participate in larger investments, own part of a more diversified portfolio, and pay lower commission rates than would be possible for individual members on their own. The trade group for investment clubs is the National Association of Investors Corporation (NAIC) in Madison Heights, Michigan. The NAIC helps clubs get started and offers several programs, such as the Low-Cost Investment Plan allowing clubs to purchase an initial share of individual stocks at low commissions and reinvest dividends automatically at no charge.

INVESTMENT COMPANY firm that, for a management fee, invests the pooled funds of small investors in securities appropriate for its stated investment objectives. It offers participants more diversification, liquidity, and professional management service than would normally be available to them as individuals.

There are two basic types of investment companies: (1) *open-end,* better known as a MUTUAL FUND, which has a floating number of outstanding shares (hence the name *open-end*) and stands prepared to sell or redeem shares at their current NET ASSET VALUE; and (2) *closed-end,* also known as an *investment trust,* which, like a corporation, has a fixed number of outstanding shares that are traded like a stock, often on the New York and American Stock Exchanges.

Open-end management companies are basically divided into two categories, based on the way they distribute their funds to customers. The first category is *load funds,* which are sold in the over-the-counter market by broker-dealers, who do not receive a sales commission; instead a "loading charge" is added to the net asset value at time of purchase. For many years the charge was 8½%, but more recently it has been reduced to 4.5%–5%. Many load funds do not charge an upfront load, but instead impose a BACK-END LOAD which customers must pay if they sell fund shares within a certain number of years, usually five. The second category is *no-load funds,* which are bought directly from sponsoring fund companies. Such companies do not charge a loading fee, although some funds levy a redemption fee if shares are sold within a specified number of years.

Some funds, both load and no-load, are called 12b-1 MUTUAL FUNDS because they levy an annual 12b-1 charge of up to 0.75% of assets to pay for promotional and marketing expenses.

Dealers in closed-end investment companies obtain their revenue from regular brokerage commissions, just as they do in selling any individual stock.

Both open-end and closed-end investment companies charge annual management fees, typically ranging from 0.25% to 2% of the value of the assets in the fund.

Under the INVESTMENT COMPANY ACT OF 1940, the registration statement and prospectus of every investment company must state its specific investment objectives. Investment companies fall into many categories, including: diversified common stock funds (with growth of capital as the principal objective); balanced funds (mixing common and preferred stocks, bonds, and cash); bond and preferred stock funds (emphasizing current income); specialized funds (by industry, groups of industries, geography, or size of company); income funds buying high-yield stocks and bonds; dual-purpose funds (a form of closed-end investment company offering a choice of income shares or capital gains shares); and money market funds which invest in money market instruments.

INVESTMENT COMPANY ACT OF 1940 legislation passed by Congress requiring registration and regulation of investment companies by the Securities and Exchange Commission. The Act sets the standards by which mutual funds and other investment vehicles of investment companies operate, in such areas as promotion, reporting requirements, pricing of securities for sale to the public, and allocation of investments within a fund portfolio. *See also* INVESTMENT COMPANY.

INVESTMENT COUNSEL person with the responsibility for providing investment advice to clients and executing investment decisions. *See also* PORTFOLIO MANAGER.

INVESTMENT CREDIT reduction in income tax liability granted by the federal government over the years to firms making new investments in certain asset categories, primarily equipment; also called *investment tax credit.* The investment credit, designed to stimulate the economy by encouraging capital expenditure, has been a feature of tax legislation on and off, and in varying percentage amounts, since 1962; in 1985 it was 6% or 10% of the purchase price, depending on the life of the asset. As a credit, it has been deducted from the tax bill, not from pretax income, and it has been independent of DEPRECIATION. The TAX REFORM ACT OF 1986 generally repealed the investment credit retroactively for any property placed in service after January 1, 1986. The 1986 Act also provided for a 35% reduction of the value of credits carried over from previous years, which was later changed to 50%.

INVESTMENT GRADE bond with a RATING of AAA to BBB. *See also* JUNK BOND.

INVESTMENT HISTORY body of prior experience establishing "normal investment practice" with respect to the account relationship between a member firm and its customer. For example, the Rules of Fair Practice of the National Association of Securities Dealers (NASD) prohibit the sale of a new issue to members of a distributing dealer's immediate family, but if there was sufficient precedent in the investment history of this particular dealer-customer relationship, the sale would not be a violation.

INVESTMENT INCOME income from securities and other nonbusiness investments; such as DIVIDENDS, INTEREST, OPTION PREMIUMS, and income from a ROYALTY or ANNUITY. Under the TAX REFORM ACT OF 1986, interest on MARGIN ACCOUNTS may be used to offset investment income without limitation.

Investment income earned by passive activities must be treated separately from other PASSIVE income. The REVENUE RECONCILIATION ACT OF 1993 eliminated net gains from selling investment property from the definition of *investment income.* Expenses incurred to generate investment income can reduce investment income to the extent they exceed 2% of adjusted gross income. By excluding capital gains from the calculation, the 1993 Act, in effect, prevents a taxpayer from claiming an ordinary deduction for margin interest incurred to carry an investment that is taxable at the favorable capital gains rate. Also called UNEARNED INCOME and *portfolio income.*

INVESTMENT LETTER in the private placement of new securities, a letter of intent between the issuer of securities and the buyer establishing that the securities are being bought as an investment and are not for resale. This is necessary to avoid having to register the securities with the Securities and Exchange Commission. (Under provisions of SEC Rule 144, a purchaser of such securities may eventually resell them to the public if certain specific conditions are met, including a minimum holding period of at least two years.) Use of the investment letter gave rise to the terms *letter stock* and *letter bond* in referring to unregistered issues. *See also* LETTER SECURITY.

INVESTMENT MANAGEMENT in general, the activities of a portfolio manager. More specifically, it distinguishes between managed and unmanaged portfolios, examples of the latter being UNIT INVESTMENT TRUSTS and INDEX FUNDS, which are fixed portfolios not requiring ongoing decisions.

INVESTMENT OBJECTIVE financial objective that an investor uses to determine which kind of investment is appropriate. For example, if the investor's objective is growth of capital, he may opt for growth-oriented mutual funds or individual stocks. If he is more interested in income, he might purchase income-oriented mutual funds or individual bonds instead. Consideration of investment objectives, combined with the risk tolerance of investors, helps an investor narrow his search to an investment vehicle designed for his needs at a particular time.

INVESTMENT PHILOSOPHY style of investment practiced by an individual investor or money manager. For example, some investors follow the growth philosophy, concentrating on stocks with steadily rising earnings. Others are value investors, searching for stocks that have fallen out of favor, and are therefore cheap relative to the true value of their assets. Some managers favor small-capitalization stocks, while others stick with large blue-chip companies. Some managers have a philosophy of remaining fully invested at all times, while others believe in market timing, so that their portfolios can accumulate cash if the managers think stock or bond prices are about to fall.

INVESTMENT SOFTWARE software designed to aid investors' decision-making. Some software packages allow investors to perform TECHNICAL ANALYSIS, charting stock prices, volume, and other indicators. Other programs allow FUNDAMENTAL ANALYSIS, permitting investors to SCREEN STOCKS based on financial criteria such as earnings, price/earnings ratios, book value, and dividend yields. Some software offers recordkeeping, so that an investor can keep track of the value of his portfolio and the prices at which he bought or sold securities. Many software packages allow investors to tap into databases to update securities prices, scan news items, and execute trades. Specialty programs allow investors to value options, calculate yield analysis on bonds, and screen mutual funds.

INVESTMENT STRATEGY plan to allocate assets among such choices as stocks, bonds, CASH EQUIVALENTS, commodities, and real estate. An investment strategy should be formulated based on an investor's outlook on interest rates, inflation, and economic growth, among other factors, and also taking into account the investor's age, tolerance for risk, amount of capital available to invest, and future needs for capital, such as for financing children's college educations or buying a house. An investment adviser will help to devise such a strategy. *See also* INVESTMENT ADVISORY SERVICE.

INVESTMENT STRATEGY COMMITTEE committee in the research department of a brokerage firm that sets the overall investment strategy the firm recommends to clients. The director of research, the chief economist, and several top analysts typically sit on this committee. The group advises clients on the amount of money that should be placed into stocks, bonds, or CASH EQUIVALENTS, as well as the industry groups or individual stocks or bonds that look particularly attractive.

INVESTMENT TAX CREDIT *see* INVESTMENT CREDIT.

INVESTMENT TRUST *see* INVESTMENT COMPANY.

INVESTMENT VALUE OF A CONVERTIBLE SECURITY estimated price at which a CONVERTIBLE security (CV) would be valued by the marketplace if it had no stock conversion feature. The investment value for CVs of major companies is determined by investment advisory services and, theoretically, should never fall lower than the price of the related stock. It is arrived at by estimating the price at which a nonconvertible ("straight") bond or preferred share of the same issuing company would sell. The investment value reflects the interest rate; therefore, the market price of the security will go up when rates are down and vice versa. *See also* PREMIUM OVER BOND VALUE.

INVESTOR party who puts money at risk; may be an individual or an institutional investor.

INVESTOR RELATIONS DEPARTMENT in major listed companies, a staff position responsible for investor relations, reporting either to the chief financial officer or to the director of public relations. The actual duties will vary, depending on whether the company retains an outside financial public relations firm, but the general responsibilities are as follows:
- to see that the company is understood, in terms of its activities and objectives, and is favorably regarded in the financial and capital markets and the investment community; this means having input into the annual report and other published materials, coordinating senior management speeches and public statements with the FINANCIAL PUBLIC RELATIONS effort, and generally fostering a consistent and positive corporate image.
- to ensure full and timely public DISCLOSURE of material information, and to work with the legal staff in complying with the rules of the SEC, the securities exchanges, and other regulatory authorities.
- to respond to requests for reports and information from shareholders, professional investors, brokers, and the financial media.
- to maintain productive relations with the firm's investment bankers, the specialists in its stock, major broker-dealers, and institutional investors who follow the company or hold sizeable positions in its securities.
- to take direct measures, where necessary, to see that the company's shares are properly valued. This involves identifying the firm's particular investment audience and the professionals controlling its stock float, arranging analysts' meetings and other presentations, and generating appropriate publicity.

  The most successful investor relations professionals have been those who follow a policy of full and open dissemination of relevant information, favorable and unfavorable, on a consistent basis. The least successful, over the long run, have been the "touts"—those who emphasize promotion at the expense of credibility.

INVESTORS SERVICE BUREAU New York Stock Exchange public service that responds to written inquiries of all types concerning securities investments.

INVOICE bill prepared by a seller of goods or services and submitted to the purchaser. The invoice lists all the items bought, together with amounts.

INVOLUNTARY BANKRUPTCY *see* BANKRUPTCY.

IRA *see* INDIVIDUAL RETIREMENT ACCOUNT.

IRA ROLLOVER *see* INDIVIDUAL RETIREMENT ACCOUNT ROLLOVER.

IRREDEEMABLE BOND
1. bond without a CALL FEATURE (issuer's right to redeem the bond before maturity) or a REDEMPTION privilege (holder's right to sell the bond back to the issuer before maturity).
2. PERPETUAL BOND.

IRREVOCABLE something done that cannot legally be undone, such as an IRREVOCABLE TRUST.

IRREVOCABLE LIVING TRUST trust usually created to achieve some tax benefit, or to provide a vehicle for managing assets of a person the creator believes cannot or should not be managing his or her own property. This trust cannot be changed or reversed by the creator of the trust.

IRREVOCABLE TRUST trust that cannot be changed or terminated by the one who created it without the agreement of the BENEFICIARY.

IRS *see* INTERNAL REVENUE SERVICE.

IRS PRIVATE LETTER RULING *see* PRIVATE LETTER RULING.

ISIS *see* INTERMARKET SURVEILLANCE INFORMATION SYSTEM (ISIS).

ISRO acronym for *International Securities Regulatory Organization, see* INTERNATIONAL STOCK EXCHANGE OF THE UNITED KINGDOM AND THE REPUBLIC OF IRELAND (ISE).

ISSUE
1. stock or bonds sold by a corporation or a government entity at a particular time.
2. selling new securities by a corporation or government entity, either through an underwriter or by a private placement.
3. descendants, such as children and grandchildren. For instance, "This man's estate will be passed, at his death, to his issue."

ISSUED AND OUTSTANDING shares of a corporation, authorized in the corporate charter, which have been issued and are outstanding. These shares represent capital invested by the firm's shareholders and owners, and may be all or only a portion of the number of shares authorized. Shares that have been issued and subsequently repurchased by the company are called *treasury stock,* because they are held in the corporate treasury pending reissue or retirement. Treasury shares are legally issued but are not considered outstanding for purposes of voting, dividends, or earnings per share calculations. Shares authorized but not yet issued are called *unissued shares.* Most companies show the amount of authorized, issued and outstanding, and treasury shares in the capital section of their annual reports. *See also* TREASURY STOCK.

ISSUER legal entity that has the power to issue and distribute a security. Issuers include corporations, municipalities, foreign and domestic governments and their agencies, and investment trusts. Issuers of stock are responsible for reporting on corporate developments to shareholders and paying dividends once declared. Issuers of bonds are committed to making timely payments of interest and principal to bondholders.

ITALIAN DERIVATIVES MARKET (IDEM) operated by the Italian Stock Exchange Council, the IDEM trades on a national computerized system based on the Swedish OM system. The exchange began operations in November 1994. It trades futures and options on the MIB 30 Index and individual stock options.

ITALIAN STOCK EXCHANGE (ISE) based in Milan, ISE is the national computerized, order-driven trading system, resulting from a major reform program that united Italy's 10 national exchanges in 1991. Three institutions are responsible for market regulation and management: the Consiglio di Borsa (Consob), the market watchdog; the Bank of Italy; and the Italian Stock Exchange Council, which instituted computerized trading. Since 1994, all listed securities have been traded electronically. The electronic trading system is managed by the ISE Council and operated by CED Borsa, a private company. A network connects all authorized securities firms throughout Italy, enabling real-time trading in all securities. The main indices are the MIB and the MIBTEL, based on the prices of all listed shares, and the MIB 30, based on a sample of the 30 most liquid and highly capitalized shares. The Comit Index is calculated daily by the Banca Commerciale Italiana, and includes all ISE listed shares. Trading is conducted Monday through Friday. The main market offers an opening auction from 8 A.M. to 9:30 A.M., with continuous trading from 10 A.M. to 5 P.M. An electronic auction in the second market runs from 3 P.M. to 5 P.M. Trading on Italy's second market, Mercato Ristretto, is regulated and conducted by stockbrokers.

ITEMIZED DEDUCTION item that allows a taxpayer to reduce adjusted gross income on his or her tax return. For example, mortgage interest, charitable contributions, state and local income and property taxes, unreimbursed business expenses, IRA contributions, and other miscellaneous items are considered deductible under certain conditions, and are listed as itemized deductions on Schedule A of an individual's tax return. However, at certain income levels, deductions are phased out. For example, in the 1998 tax year, itemized deductions for married couples filing jointly were phased out by 3% of the excess of adjusted gross income over $121,200 (if married and filing separately, then $60,600) adjusted annually for inflation. Some deductions are not subject to the 3% reduction, including medical and dental expenses, investment interest, casualty and theft losses and gambling losses.

J

JANUARY BAROMETER market forecasting tool popularized by *The Stock Traders Almanac,* whose statistics show that with 88% consistency since 1950, the market has risen in years when the STANDARD & POOR'S INDEX of 500 stocks was up in January and dropped when the index for that month was down.

JANUARY EFFECT phenomenon that stocks (especially small stocks) have historically tended to rise markedly during the period starting on the last day of December and ending on the fourth trading day of January. The January Effect is owed to year-end selling to create tax losses, recognize capital gains, effect portfolio WINDOW DRESSING, or raise holiday cash; since such selling depresses the stocks but has nothing to do with their fundamental worth, bargain hunters quickly buy in, causing the January rally.

JEEP *see* GRADUATED PAYMENT MORTGAGE.

JOBBER
1. wholesaler, especially one who buys in small lots from manufacturers, importers, and/or other wholesalers and sells to retailers.
2. London Stock Exchange term for MARKET MAKER.

JOHANNESBURG STOCK EXCHANGE (JSE) largest stock exchange in Africa, established in 1886 to raise financing for the mining industry. In 1995, the JSE opened its doors to foreign and corporate members. The following year, the Johannesburg electronic trading system, JET, was introduced, moving stocks off the floor and into the system. A specialist manages an electronic order book for ODD LOTS, and market makers voluntarily quote prices. The mining sector dominates market capitalization of quoted companies, but financial services is a growing area. The JSE All Share Index tracks the overall ordinary share market. Shares are grouped in five sectors, each with a separate index: overall, mining producers, mining finance, financial and industrial. Two subsidiary markets are traded: the development capital market (DCM) aimed at smaller, developing companies that need to raise capital; and the venture capital market (VCM), to facilitate the listing of venture capital companies. Orders are matched electronically in the JET system and transferred electronically to the Equity Clearing House, a department in the exchange. The exchange has moved to a rolling settlement, ultimately three days after a trade. Trading hours: 8:30 A.M. to 6 P.M., Monday through Friday.

JOINT ACCOUNT bank or brokerage account owned jointly by two or more people. Joint accounts may be set up in two ways: (1) either all parties to the account must sign checks and approve all withdrawals or brokerage transactions or (2) any one party can take such actions on his or her own. *See also* JOINT TENANTS WITH RIGHT OF SURVIVORSHIP.

JOINT ACCOUNT AGREEMENT form needed to open a JOINT ACCOUNT at a bank or brokerage. It must be signed by all parties to the account regardless of the provisions it may contain concerning signatures required to authorize transactions.

JOINT AND SURVIVOR ANNUITY annuity that makes payments for the lifetime of two or more beneficiaries, often a husband and wife. When one of the annuitants dies, payments continue to the survivor annuitant in the same amount or in a reduced amount as specified in the contract.

JOINT BOND bond that has more than one obligator or that is guaranteed by a party other than the issuer; also called *joint and several bond*. Joint bonds are common where a parent corporation wishes to guarantee the bonds of a subsidiary. *See* GUARANTEED BOND.

JOINT LIABILITY mutual legal responsibility by two or more parties for claims on the assets of a company or individual. *See also* LIABILITY.

JOINTLY AND SEVERALLY
In general: legal phrase used in definitions of liability meaning that an obligation may be enforced against all obligators jointly or against any one of them separately.
Securities: term used to refer to municipal bond underwritings where the account is undivided and syndicate members are responsible for unsold bonds in proportion to their participations. In other words, a participant with 5% of the account would still be responsible for 5% of the unsold bonds, even though that member might already have sold 10%. *See also* SEVERALLY BUT NOT JOINTLY.

JOINT OWNERSHIP equal ownership by two or more people, who have right of survivorship.

JOINT STOCK COMPANY form of business organization that combines features of a corporation and a partnership. Under U.S. law, joint stock companies are recognized as corporations with unlimited liability for their stockholders. As in a conventional corporation, investors in joint stock companies receive shares of stock they are free to sell at will without ending the corporation; they also elect directors. Unlike in a limited liability corporation, however, each shareholder in a joint stock company is legally liable for all debts of the company.

There are some advantages to this form of organization compared with limited-liability corporations: fewer taxes, greater ease of formation under the common law, more security for creditors, mobility, and freedom from regulation, for example. However, the disadvantages—such as the fact that the joint stock company usually cannot hold title to real estate and, particularly, the company's unlimited liability—tend to outweigh the advantages, with the result that it is not a popular form of organization.

JOINT TAX RETURN tax return filed by two people, usually a married couple. Both parties must sign the return and they are equally responsible for paying the taxes due. Thus if one party does not pay the taxes, the IRS can come after the other party to make the required payment. Because of the way the tax tables are designed, it is frequently more advantageous for a married couple to file a joint return than for them to file separate returns. *See also* FILING STATUS; HEAD OF HOUSEHOLD.

JOINT TENANCY *see* TENANCY IN COMMON. *See also* JOINT TENANTS WITH RIGHT OF SURVIVORSHIP.

JOINT TENANTS WITH RIGHT OF SURVIVORSHIP when two or more people maintain a JOINT ACCOUNT with a brokerage firm or a bank, it is normally agreed that, upon the death of one account holder, ownership of the account assets passes to the remaining account holders. This transfer of assets escapes probate, but estate taxes may be due, depending on the amount of assets transferred.

JOINT VENTURE agreement by two or more parties to work on a project together. Frequently, a joint venture will be formed when companies with complementary technology wish to create a product or service that takes advantage of the strengths of the participants. A joint venture, which is usually limited to one project, differs from a partnership, which forms the basis for cooperation on many projects.

JOINT WILL single document setting forth the testamentary instructions of a husband and wife. The use of joint wills is not common in the United States, and it may create tax and other problems.

JONESTOWN DEFENSE tactics taken by management to ward off a hostile TAKEOVER that are so extreme that they appear suicidal for the company. For example, the company may try to sell its CROWN JEWELS or take on a huge amount of debt to make the company undesirable to the potential acquirer. The term refers to the mass suicide led by Jim Jones in Jonestown, Guyana, in the early 1980s. *See also* SCORCHED EARTH POLICY.

JUDGMENT decision by a court of law ordering someone to pay a certain amount of money. For instance, a court may order someone who illegally profited by trading on INSIDE INFORMATION to pay a judgment amounting to all the profits from the trade, plus damages. The term also refers to condemnation awards by government entities in payment for private property taken for public use.

JUMBO CERTIFICATE OF DEPOSIT certificate with a minimum denomination of $100,000. Jumbo CDs are usually bought and sold by large institutions such as banks, pension funds, money market funds, and insurance companies.

JUMBO LOANS loans in amounts exceeding the national guidelines of FREDDIE MAC and FANNIE MAE.

JUNIOR ISSUE issue of debt or equity that is subordinate in claim to another issue in terms of dividends, interest, principal, or security in the event of liquidation. *See also* JUNIOR SECURITY; PREFERRED STOCK; PRIORITY; PRIOR LIEN BOND: PRIOR PREFERRED STOCK.

JUNIOR MORTGAGE mortgage that is subordinate to other mortgages—for example, a second or a third mortgage. If a debtor defaults, the first mortgage will have to be satisfied before the junior mortgage.

JUNIOR REFUNDING refinancing government debt that matures in one to five years by issuing new securities that mature in five years or more.

JUNIOR SECURITY security with lower priority claim on assets and income than a SENIOR SECURITY. For example, a PREFERRED STOCK is junior to a DEBENTURE, but a debenture, being an unsecured bond, is junior to a MORTGAGE BOND. COMMON STOCK is junior to all corporate securities. Some companies—finance companies, for example—have senior SUBORDINATED and junior subordinated issues, the former having priority over the latter, but both ranking lower than senior (unsubordinated) debt.

JUNK BOND bond with a credit rating of BB or lower by RATING agencies. Although commonly used, the term has a pejorative connotation, and issuers and holders prefer the securities be called *high-yield bonds.* Junk bonds are issued by companies without long track records of sales and earnings, or by those with questionable credit strength. In the 1980s, they were a popular means of financing TAKEOVERS. Since they are more volatile and pay higher yields than INVEST-MENT GRADE bonds, many risk-oriented investors specialize in trading them. Institutions with FIDUCIARY responsibilities are regulated (*see* PRUDENT-MAN RULE). *See also* FALLEN ANGELS.

JURISDICTION defined by the American Bankers Association as "the legal right, power or authority to hear and determine a cause; as in the jurisdiction of a court." The term frequently comes up in finance and investment discussions in connection with the jurisdictions of the various regulatory authorities bearing on the field. For example, the Federal Reserve Board, not the Securities and Exchange Commission (as might be supposed), has jurisdiction in a case involving a brokerage MARGIN ACCOUNT (*see also* REGULATION T).

The term also is important with respect to EUROCURRENCY loan agreements, where it is possible for a loan to be funded in one country but made in another by a group of international banks each from different countries, to a borrower in still another country. The determination of jurisdiction, not to mention the willingness of courts in different countries to accept that jurisdiction, is a matter of obvious urgency in such cases.

JURY OF EXECUTIVE OPINION forecasting method whereby a panel of experts—perhaps senior corporate financial executives—prepare individual forecasts based on information made available to all of them. Each expert then reviews the others' work and modifies his or her own forecasts accordingly. The resulting composite forecast is supposed to be more realistic than any individual effort could be. Also known as *Delphi forecast.*

JUSTIFIED PRICE fair market price an informed buyer will pay for an asset, whether it be a stock, a bond, a commodity, or real estate. *See also* FAIR MARKET VALUE.

JUST TITLE title to property that is supportable against all legal claims. Also called *clear title, good title, proper title.*

k

KAFFIRS informal term for South African gold mining shares traded on the LONDON STOCK EXCHANGE. These shares are traded over the counter in the U.S. in the form of American Depositary Receipts, which are claims to share certificates deposited in a foreign bank. Under South African law, Kaffirs must pay out almost all their earnings to shareholders as dividends. These shares thus not only provide stockholders with a gold investment to hedge against inflation, but also afford substantial income in the form of high dividend payments. However, investors in Kaffirs must also consider the political risks of investing in South Africa, as well as the risk of fluctuations in the price of gold. *See also* AMERICAN DEPOSITARY RECEIPT.

KANGAROOS nickname for Australian stocks. The term normally refers to stocks in the ALL ORDINARIES INDEX, and refers to the animal most closely associated with Australia.

KANSAS CITY BOARD OF TRADE (KCBT) formed in 1856 as a chamber of commerce, it reorganized after the Civil War as an exchange. The KCBT trades red winter wheat futures and options; Western natural gas futures and options; Value Line Index futures; and Mini Value Line futures and options. Trading hours: 8:30 A.M. to 3:15 P.M., Monday to Friday. *See also* SECURITIES AND COMMODITIES EXCHANGES.

KEOGH PLAN tax-deferred pension account designated for employees of unincorporated businesses or for persons who are self-employed (either full-time or part-time). Eligible people can contribute up to 25% of earned income, up to a maximum of $30,000. Like the INDIVIDUAL RETIREMENT ACCOUNT (IRA), the Keogh plan allows all investment earnings to grow tax deferred until capital is withdrawn, as early as age 59½ and starting no later than age 70½. Almost any investment except precious metals or collectibles can be used for a Keogh account. Typically, people place Keogh assets in stocks, bonds, money-market funds, certificates of deposit, mutual funds, or limited partnerships. The Keogh plan, named after U.S. Representative Eugene James Keogh, was established by Congress in 1962 and was expanded in the ECONOMIC RECOVERY TAX ACT OF 1981 (ERTA).

KEY INDUSTRY industry of primary importance to a nation's economy. For instance, the defense industry is called a key industry since it is crucial to maintaining a country's safety. The automobile industry is also considered key since so many jobs are directly or indirectly dependent on it.

KEY MAN (OR WOMAN) INSURANCE life insurance policy bought by a company, usually a small business, on the life of a key executive, with the company as beneficiary.

KEYNESIAN ECONOMICS body of economic thought originated by the British economist and government adviser, John Maynard Keynes (1883–1946), whose landmark work, *The General Theory of Employment, Interest and Money,* was published in 1935. Writing during the Great Depression, Keynes took issue with the classical economists, like Adam Smith, who believed that the economy worked best when left alone. Keynes believed that active government intervention in the marketplace was the only method of ensuring economic growth and stability. He held essentially that insufficient demand causes unemployment and that excessive demand results in inflation; government should therefore manipulate the level of aggregate demand by adjusting levels of government expenditure and taxation. For example, to avoid depression Keynes advocated increased government spending and EASY MONEY, resulting in more investment, higher employment, and increased consumer spending.

Keynesian economics has had great influence on the public economic policies of industrial nations, including the United States. In the 1980s, however, after repeated recessions, slow growth, and high rates of inflation in the U.S., a contrasting outlook, uniting monetarists and "supply siders," blamed excessive government intervention for troubles in the economy.

See also AGGREGATE SUPPLY; LAISSEZ-FAIRE; MACROECONOMICS; MONETARIST; SUPPLY-SIDE ECONOMICS.

KICKBACK
Finance: practice whereby sales finance companies reward dealers who discount installment purchase paper through them with cash payments.
Government and private contracts: payment made secretly by a seller to someone instrumental in awarding a contract or making a sale—an illegal payoff.
Labor relations: illegal practice whereby employers require the return of a portion of wages established by law or union contract, in exchange for employment.

KICKER added feature of a debt obligation, usually designed to enhance marketability by offering the prospect of equity participation. For instance, a bond may be convertible to stock if the shares reach a certain price. This makes the bond more attractive to investors, since the bondholder potentially gets the benefit of an equity security in addition to interest payments. Other examples of equity kickers are RIGHTS and WARRANTS. Some mortgage loans also include kickers in the form of ownership participation or in the form of a percentage of gross rental receipts. Kickers are also called *sweeteners.*

KIDDIE TAX tax filed by parents on Form 8615 for the investment income of children under age 14 exceeding $1,400. Tax is at parent's top tax rate. In some cases, however, parents may elect to report such children's income on their own returns.

KILLER BEES those who aid a company in fending off a takeover bid. "Killer bees" are usually investment bankers who devise strategies to make the target less attractive or more difficult to acquire.

KITING
Commercial banking: (1) depositing and drawing checks between accounts at two or more banks and thereby taking advantage of the FLOAT—that is, the time it takes the bank of deposit to collect from the paying bank. (2) fraudently altering the figures on a check to increase its face value.
Securities: driving stock prices to high levels through manipulative trading methods, such as the creation of artificial trading activity by the buyer and the seller working together and using the same funds.

KNOCK-OUT OPTION form of derivative that gives the buyer the right, but not the obligation, to buy an underlying commodity, currency, or other position at a preset price. Unlike regular options, however, knock-out options expire worthless, or are "knocked out" if the underlying commodity or currency goes through a particular price level. For example, a knock-out option based on the value of the U.S. dollar against the German mark gets knocked out if the dollar falls below a specified exchange rate against the mark. Regular options can have unlimited moves up or down. Knock-out options are much cheaper to buy than regular options, allowing buyers to take larger positions with less money than regular options. Knock-out options are frequently used by hedge funds and other speculators.

KNOW YOUR CUSTOMER ethical concept in the securities industry either stated or implied by the rules of the exchanges and the other authorities regulating broker-dealer practices. Its meaning is expressed in the following paragraph from Article 3 of the NASD Rules of Fair Practice: "In recommending to a customer the purchase, sale or exchange of any security, a member shall have reasonable grounds for believing that the recommendation is suitable for such customer upon the basis of the facts, if any, disclosed by such customer as to his other security holdings and as to his financial situation and needs." Customers opening accounts at brokerage firms must supply financial information that satisfies the know your customer requirement for routine purposes.

KONDRATIEFF WAVE theory of the Soviet economist Nikolai Kondratieff in the 1920s that the economies of the Western capitalist world were prone to major up-and-down "supercycles" lasting 50 to 60 years. He claimed to have predicted the economic crash of 1929–30 based on the crash of 1870, 60 years earlier. The Kondratieff wave theory has adherents, but is controversial among economists. Also called *Kondratieff cycle.*

KRUGGERAND gold bullion coin minted by the Republic of South Africa which comes in one-ounce, half-ounce, quarter-ounce and one-tenth-ounce sizes. Kruggerands usually sell for slightly more than the current value of their gold content. Kruggerands, which had been the dominant gold coin in the world, were banned from being imported into the United States in 1985 because of the South African government's policy of apartheid. The ban was lifted on July 10, 1991. Other GOLD COINS traded in addition to the Kruggerand include the United States Eagle, Canadian Maple Leaf, Mexican Peso, Austrian Philharmonic, and Australian Kangaroo.

KUALA LUMPUR COMMODITY EXCHANGE exchange trading futures in crude palm oil by open outcry. Trading hours: 11 A.M. to 7 P.M., Monday to Friday.

KUALA LUMPUR OPTIONS & FINANCIAL FUTURES EXCHANGE BARHAD (KLOFFE) launched in December 1995, it trades the KLSE Composite Index, the benchmark of the KUALA LUMPUR STOCK EXCHANGE. Trading is electronic. Trading hours: 11 A.M. to 7 P.M., Monday to Friday.

KUALA LUMPUR STOCK EXCHANGE largest securities exchange in Malaysia, formerly affiliated with Singapore as the Stock Exchange of Malaysia. The KLSE Composite Index is the benchmark index, with 11 other sector indices traded. *SCORE,* the System on Computerized Order Routing and Execution, the exchange's semi-automated trading system, was introduced in 1989 and open outcry was discontinued. Settlement is through the Central Depository System (CDS), by book entry, with CDS accounts of buyers credited on the fifth day but held in lien until payment by the seventh market day; sellers are debited on the fifth market day. Trading hours: 9:30 A.M. to 12:30 P.M., and 2:30 P.M. to 5 P.M., Monday through Friday.

L

LABOR-INTENSIVE requiring large pools of workers. Said of an industry in which labor costs are more important than capital costs. Deep-shaft coal mining, for instance, is labor-intensive.

LADY MACBETH STRATEGY TAKEOVER tactic whereby a third party poses as a white knight then turns coat and joins an unfriendly bidder.

LAFFER CURVE curve named for U.S. economics professor Arthur Laffer, postulating that economic output will grow if marginal tax rates are cut. The curve is used in explaining SUPPLY-SIDE ECONOMICS, a theory that noninflationary growth is spurred when tax policies encourage productivity and investment.

LAGGING INDICATORS economic indicators that lag behind the overall pace of economic activity. The Conference Board publishes the Index of Lagging Indicators monthly along with the index of LEADING INDICATORS and the index of COINCIDENT INDICATORS. The six components of the lagging indicators are the unemployment rate, business spending, unit labor costs, bank loans outstanding, bank interest rates, and the book value of manufacturing and trade inventories.

LAISSEZ-FAIRE doctrine that interference of government in business and economic affairs should be minimal. Adam Smith's *The Wealth Of Nations* (1776) described laissez-faire economics in terms of an "invisible hand" that would provide for the maximum good for all, if businessmen were free to pursue profitable opportunities as they saw them. The growth of industry in England in the early 19th century and American industrial growth in the late 19th century both occurred in a laissez-faire capitalist environment. The laissez-faire period ended by the beginning of the 20th century, when large monopolies were broken up and government regulation of business became the norm. The Great Depression of the 1930s saw the birth of KEYNESIAN ECONOMICS, an influential approach advocating government intervention in economic affairs. The movement toward deregulation of business in the United States that began in the 1970s and 80s is to some extent a return to the laissez-faire philosophy. Laissez-faire is French for "allow to do."

LAND CONTRACT creative real estate financing method whereby a seller with a mortgage finances a buyer by taking a down payment and being paid installments but not yielding title until the mortgage is repaid. Also called *contract for deed* and *installment sales contract.*

LANDLORD owner of property who rents it to a TENANT.

LAPSE expiration of a right or privilege because one party did not live up to its obligations during the time allowed. For example, a life insurance policy will lapse if the policyholder does not make the required premium payments on time. This means that the policyholder is no longer protected by the policy.

LAPSED OPTION OPTION that reached its expiration date without being exercised and is thus without value.

LARGE CAP stock with a large capitalization (numbers of shares outstanding times the price of the shares). Large Cap stocks typically have at least $5 billion in outstanding MARKET VALUE. Numerous mutual funds specialize in Large Cap stocks, and many have the words Large Cap in their names.

LAST IN, FIRST OUT (LIFO) method of accounting for INVENTORY that ties the cost of goods sold to the cost of the most recent purchases. The formula for cost of goods sold is:

beginning inventory + purchases – ending inventory = cost of goods sold

In contrast to the FIRST IN, FIRST OUT (FIFO) method, in a period of rising prices LIFO produces a higher cost of goods sold and a lower gross profit and taxable income. The artificially low balance sheet inventories resulting from the use of LIFO in periods of inflation give rise to the term *LIFO cushion.*

LAST SALE most recent trade in a particular security. Not to be confused with the final transaction in a trading session, called the CLOSING SALE. The last sale is the point of reference for two Securities and Exchange Commission rules: (1) On a national exchange, no SHORT SALE may be made below the price of the last regular sale. (2) No short sale may be made at the same price as the last sale unless the last sale was at a price higher than the preceding different price. PLUS TICK, MINUS TICK, ZERO MINUS TICK, and ZERO PLUS TICK, used in this connection, refer to the last sale.

LAST TRADING DAY final day during which a futures contract may be settled. If the contract is not OFFSET, either an agreement between the buying and selling parties must be arranged or the physical commodity must be delivered from the seller to the buyer.

LATE CHARGE fee charged by a grantor of credit when the borrower fails to make timely payment.

LATE TAPE delay in displaying price changes because trading on a stock exchange is particularly heavy. If the tape is more than five minutes late, the first digit of a price is deleted. For instance, a trade at $62\frac{3}{4}$ is reported as $2\frac{3}{4}$. *See also* DIGITS DELETED.

LAUNDER to make illegally acquired cash look as if it were acquired legally. The usual practice is to transfer the money through foreign banks, thereby concealing its purpose. SEC Rule 17a-8 prohibits using broker-dealers for this purpose.

LAW OF LARGE NUMBERS statistical concept holding that the greater the number of units in a projection, the less important each unit becomes. Group insurance, which gets cheaper as the group gets larger, is an example of the principle in application; actuarial abnormalities have less influence on total claims.

LAY OFF
Investment banking: reduce the risk in a standby commitment, under which the bankers agree to purchase and resell to the public any portion of a stock issue not subscribed to by shareowners who hold rights. The risk is that the market value will fall during the two to four weeks when shareholders are deciding whether to exercise or sell their rights. To minimize the risk, investment bankers (1) buy up the rights as they are offered and, at the same time, sell the shares represented by these rights; and (2) sell short an amount of shares proportionate to the rights that can be expected to go unexercised—to $\frac{1}{2}\%$ of the issue, typically. Also called *laying off*.
Labor: temporarily or permanently remove an employee from a payroll because of an economic slowdown or a production cutback, not because of poor performance or an infraction of company rules.

LEADER
1. stock or group of stocks at the forefront of an upsurge or a downturn in a market. Typically, leaders are heavily bought and sold by institutions that want to demonstrate their own market leadership.
2. product that has a large market share.

LEADING INDICATORS components of indicators released monthly by the Conference Board, along with the Index of LAGGING INDICATORS and the Index of COINCIDENT INDICATORS. The 11 components are: the average workweek of production workers; average weekly claims for state unemployment insurance; manufacturers' new orders for consumer goods and materials; vendor performance (companies receiving slower deliveries from suppliers); contracts and orders for plant and equipment; building permits; change in manufacturers' unfilled orders for durable goods; changes in sensitive materials prices; stock prices; MONEY SUPPLY (M-2); and index of consumer expectations. The index of leading indicators, the components of which are adjusted for inflation, accurately forecasts the ups and downs of the business cycle.

LEAD REGULATOR leading self-regulatory organization (SRO) taking responsibility for investigation of a particular section of the law and all the cases that pertain to it. In the securities business, for example, the New York Stock Exchange may take the lead in investigating certain kinds of fraud or suspicious market activity, while the American Stock Exchange or NASDAQ may be the lead regulator in other areas. The lead regulator will report its findings to the other self-regulatory organizations, and ultimately to a government oversight agency, such as the Securities and Exchange Commission.

LEAPS acronym for Long-Term Equity AnticiPation Securities, LEAPS are long-term equity options traded on U.S. exchanges and over the counter. Instead of expiring in two near-term and two farther out months as most equity OPTIONS do, LEAPS expire in two to five years, giving the buyer a longer time for his strategy to come to fruition. LEAPS are traded on many individual stocks listed on the New York Stock Exchange, the American Stock Exchange, and NASDAQ.

LEARNING CURVE predictable improvements following the early part of the life of a production contract, when costly mistakes are made.

LEASE contract granting use of real estate, equipment, or other fixed assets for a specified time in exchange for payment, usually in the form of rent. The owner of the leased property is called the lessor, the user the lessee. *See also* CAPITAL LEASE; FINANCIAL LEASE; OPERATING LEASE; SALE AND LEASEBACK.

LEASE ACQUISITION COST price paid by a real estate LIMITED PARTNERSHIP, when acquiring a lease, including legal fees and related expenses. The charges are prorated to the limited partners.

LEASEBACK transaction in which one party sells property to another and agrees to lease the property back from the buyer for a fixed period of time. For example, a building owner wanting to get cash out of the building may decide to sell the building to a real estate or leasing company and sign a long-term lease to occupy the space. The original owner is thereby able to receive cash for the value of his property, which he can reinvest in his business, as well as remain in the property. The new owner is assured of the stability of a long-term tenant and a steady income. Leaseback deals (also called sale and leaseback deals) also are executed for business equipment such as computers, cars, trucks, and airplanes. Partial ownership interests in leasing deals are sold to investors in LIMITED PARTNERSHIP form, and are designed to produce a fixed level of income to limited partners for the lease term.

LEASEHOLD asset representing the right to use property under a LEASE.

LEASEHOLD IMPROVEMENT modification of leased property. The cost is added to fixed assets and then amortized.

LEASE-PURCHASE AGREEMENT agreement providing that portions of LEASE payments may be applied toward the purchase of the property under lease.

LEG
1. sustained trend in stock market prices. A prolonged bull or bear market may have first, second, and third legs.
2. one side of a spread transaction. For instance, a trader might buy a CALL OPTION that has a particular STRIKE PRICE and expiration date, then combine it with a PUT OPTION that has the same striking price and a different expiration date. The two options are called legs of the spread. Selling one of the options is termed LIFTING A LEG.

LEGACY gift under a WILL of cash or some other specific item of personal property, such as a stock certificate, a car, or a piece of jewelry. The legacy usually is conditioned, meaning the legatee is required to be employed by the TESTATOR—the person who makes the will—or related to the testator by marriage. In other cases, a legacy to a legatee who has not attained a particular age at the testator's death will be held in trust for the legatee, instead of being distributed outright.

LEGAL computerized data base maintained by the New York Stock Exchange to track enforcement actions against member firms, audits of member firms, and customer complaints. LEGAL is not an acronym, but is written in all capitals.

LEGAL AGE age at which a person can enter into binding contracts or agree to other legal acts without the consent of another adult. In most states, the legal age, also called the *age of majority,* is 18 years old.

LEGAL ENTITY person or organization that has the legal standing to enter into a contract and may be sued for failure to perform as agreed in the contract. A child under legal age is not a legal entity; a corporation is a legal entity since it is a person in the eyes of the law.

LEGAL INVESTMENT investment permissible for investors with FIDUCIARY responsibilities. INVESTMENT GRADE bonds, as rated by Standard & Poor's or Moody's, usually qualify as legal investments. Guidelines designed to protect investors are set by the state in which the fiduciary operates. *See also* LEGAL LIST.

LEGAL LIABILITY (1) monies owed, shown on a balance sheet. (2) individual's or company's obligation to act responsibly or face compensatory penalties. *See also* LIABILITY.

LEGAL LIST securities selected by a state agency, usually a banking department, as permissible holdings of mutual savings banks, pension funds, insurance companies, and other FIDUCIARY institutions. To protect the money that individuals place in such institutions, only high quality debt and equity securities are generally included. As an alternative to the legal list, some states apply the PRUDENT MAN RULE.

LEGAL MONOPOLY exclusive right to offer a particular service within a particular territory. In exchange, the company agrees to have its policies and rates regulated. Electric and water utilities are legal monopolies.

LEGAL OPINION
1. statement as to legality, written by an authorized official such as a city attorney or an attorney general.
2. statement as to the legality of a MUNICIPAL BOND issue, usually written by a law firm specializing in public borrowings. It is part of the *official statement,* the municipal equivalent of a PROSPECTUS. Unless the legality of an issue is established, an investor's contract is invalid at the time of issue and he cannot sue under it. The legal opinion is therefore required by a SYNDICATE MANAGER and customarily accompanies the transfer of municipal securities as long as they are outstanding.

LEGAL TRANSFER transaction that requires documentation other than the standard stock or bond power to validate the transfer of a stock certificate from a seller to a buyer—for example, securities registered to a corporation or to a deceased person. It is the selling broker's responsibility to supply proper documentation to the buying broker in a legal transfer.

LEGISLATIVE RISK risk that a change in legislation could have a major positive or negative effect on an investment. For instance, a company that is a large exporter may be a beneficiary of a trade agreement that lowers tariff barriers, and therefore may see its stock price rise. On the other hand, a company that is a major polluter may be harmed by laws that stiffen fines for polluting the air or water, thereby making its share price fall.

LEMON product or investment producing poor performance. A car that continually needs repairs is a lemon, and consumers are guaranteed a full refund in several states under so-called lemon laws. A promising stock that fails to live up to expectations is also called a lemon.

LENDER individual or firm that extends money to a borrower with the expectation of being repaid, usually with interest. Lenders create debt in the form of loans, and in the event of LIQUIDATION they are paid off before stockholders receive distributions. But the investor deals in both debt (bonds) and equity (stocks). It is useful to remember that investors in commercial paper, bonds, and other debt instruments are in fact lenders with the same rights and powers enjoyed by banks.

LENDER OF LAST RESORT
1. characterization of a central bank's role in bolstering a bank that faces large withdrawals of funds. The U.S. lender of last resort is the FEDERAL RESERVE BANK. Member banks may borrow from the DISCOUNT WINDOW to maintain reserve requirements or to meet large withdrawals. The Fed thereby maintains the stability of the banking system, which would be threatened if major banks were to fail.
2. government small business financing programs and municipal economic development organizations whose precondition to making loans to private enterprises is an inability to obtain financing elsewhere.

LENDING AGREEMENT contract between a lender and a borrower. *See also* INDENTURE; REVOLVING CREDIT; TERM LOAN.

LENDING AT A PREMIUM term used when one broker lends securities to another broker to cover customer's short position and imposes a charge for the loan. Such charges, which are passed on to the customer, are the exception rather than the rule, since securities are normally LOANED FLAT between brokers, that is, without interest. Lending at a premium might occur when the securities needed are in very heavy demand and are therefore difficult to borrow. The premium is in addition to any payments the customer might have to make to the lending broker to MARK TO THE MARKET or to cover dividends or interest payable on the borrowed securities.

LENDING AT A RATE paying interest to a customer on the credit balance created from the proceeds of a SHORT SALE. Such proceeds are held in ESCROW to secure the loan of securities, usually made by another broker, to cover the customer's short position. Lending at a rate is the exception rather than the rule.

LENDING SECURITIES securities borrowed from a broker's inventory, other MARGIN ACCOUNTS, or from other brokers, when a customer makes a SHORT SALE and the securities must be delivered to the buying customer's broker. As collateral, the borrowing broker deposits with the lending broker an amount of money equal to the market value of the securities. No interest or premium is ordinarily involved in the transaction. The Securities and Exchange Commission requires that brokerage customers give permission to have their securities used in loan transactions, and the point is routinely covered in the standard agreement signed by customers when they open general accounts.

LESS DEVELOPED COUNTRIES (LDC) countries that are not fully industrialized or do not have sophisticated financial or legal systems. These countries, also called members of the *Third World,* typically have low levels of per-capita income, high inflation and debt, and large trade deficits. The World Bank may be helping them by providing loan assistance. Loans to such countries are commonly called *LDC debt.*

LESSEE *see* LEASE.

LESSOR *see* LEASE.

LETTER BOND *see* LETTER SECURITY.

LETTER OF CREDIT (L/C) instrument or document issued by a bank guaranteeing the payment of a customer's drafts up to a stated amount for a specified period. It substitutes the bank's credit for the buyer's and eliminates the seller's risk. It is used extensively in international trade. A *commercial letter of credit* is normally drawn in favor of a third party, called the beneficiary. A *confirmed letter of credit* is provided by a correspondent bank and guaranteed by the issuing bank. A *revolving letter of credit* is issued for a specified amount and automatically renewed for the same amount for a specified period, permitting any number of drafts to be drawn so long as they do not exceed its overall limit. A *traveler's letter of credit* is issued for the convenience of a traveling customer and typically lists correspondent banks at which drafts will be honored. A *performance letter of credit* is issued to guarantee performance under a contract.

LETTER OF INTENT
1. any letter expressing an intention to take (or not take) an action, sometimes subject to other action being taken. For example, a bank might issue a letter of intent stating it will make a loan to a customer, subject to another lender's agreement to participate. The letter of intent, in this case, makes it possible for the customer to negotiate the participation loan.
2. preliminary agreement between two companies that intend to merge. Such a letter is issued after negotiations have been satisfactorily completed.
3. promise by a MUTUAL FUND shareholder to invest a specified sum of money monthly for about a year. In return, the shareholder is entitled to lower sales charges.
4. INVESTMENT LETTER for a LETTER SECURITY.

LETTER OF LAST INSTRUCTIONS letter placed with a WILL containing instructions on carrying out the provisions of the will. These letters generally are not binding on the executors, but many executors feel morally bound to follow the wishes of the TESTATORS who appointed them. Florida is one of several states where the law allows these letters to be incorporated by reference if the language of the will shows this intent and identifies the letter's purpose clearly.

LETTER SECURITY stock or bond that is not registered with the Securities and Exchange Commission and therefore cannot be sold in the public market. When an issue is sold directly by the issuer to the investor, registration with the SEC can be avoided if a LETTER OF INTENT, called an INVESTMENT LETTER, is signed by the purchaser establishing that the securities are being bought for investment and not for resale. The letter's integral association with the security gives rise to the terms *letter security, letter stock,* and *letter bond.*

LETTER STOCK *see* LETTER SECURITY.

LEVEL DEBT SERVICE provision in a municipal charter stipulating that payments on municipal debt be approximately equal every year. This makes it easier to project the amount of tax revenue needed to meet obligations.

LEVERAGE
Operating leverage: extent to which a company's costs of operating are fixed (rent, insurance, executive salaries) as opposed to variable (materials, direct labor).

In a totally automated company, whose costs are virtually all fixed, every dollar of increase in sales is a dollar of increase in operating income once the BREAKEVEN POINT has been reached, because costs remain the same at every level of production. In contrast, a company whose costs are largely variable would show relatively little increase in operating income when production and sales increased because costs and production would rise together. The leverage comes in because a small change in sales has a magnified percentage effect on operating income and losses. The *degree of operating leverage*—the ratio of the percentage change in operating income to the percentage change in sales or units sold—measures the sensitivity of a firm's profits to changes in sales volume. A firm using a high degree of operating leverage has a breakeven point at a relatively high sales level.

Financial leverage: debt in relation to equity in a firm's capital structure—its LONG-TERM DEBT (usually bonds), PREFERRED STOCK, and SHAREHOLDERS' EQUITY—measured by the DEBT-TO-EQUITY RATIO. The more long-term debt there is, the greater the financial leverage. Shareholders benefit from financial leverage to the extent that return on the borrowed money exceeds the interest costs and the market value of their shares rises. For this reason, financial leverage is popularly called *trading on the equity*. Because leverage also means required interest and principal payments and thus ultimately the risk of default, how much leverage is desirable is largely a question of stability of earnings. As a rule of thumb, an industrial company with a debt to equity ratio of more than 30% is highly leveraged, exceptions being firms with dependable earnings and cash flow, such as electric utilities.

Since long-term debt interest is a fixed cost, financial leverage tends to take over where operating leverage leaves off, further magnifying the effects on earnings per share of changes in sales levels. In general, high operating leverage should accompany low financial leverage, and vice versa.

Investments: means of enhancing return or value without increasing investment. Buying securities on margin is an example of leverage with borrowed money, and extra leverage may be possible if the leveraged security is convertible into common stock. RIGHTS, WARRANTS, and OPTION contracts provide leverage, not involving borrowings but offering the prospect of high return for little or no investment.

LEVERAGED BUYOUT takeover of a company, using borrowed funds. Most often, the target company's assets serve as security for the loans taken out by the acquiring firm, which repays the loan out of cash flow of the acquired company. Management may use this technique to retain control by converting a company from public to private. A group of investors may also borrow funds from banks, using their own assets as collateral, to take over another firm. In almost all leveraged buyouts, public shareholders receive a premium over the current market value for their shares. When a company that has gone private in a leveraged buyout offers shares to the public again, it is called a REVERSE LEVERAGED BUYOUT.

LEVEL LOAD sales charge that does not change over time. In mutual funds, level load shares are called *C class shares,* compared to *A class* for upfront loads and *B class* for back-end loads. A level load will typically be 1% to 2% of assets each year, which is lower than an upfront load of 4% to 5% or the back-end load, which starts at 5% and declines each year until it disappears if the fund shares are held for five years. Though the level load may be lower than an upfront or back-end load, an investor ends up paying a higher commission if he holds the fund for many years.

LEVEL PLAYING FIELD condition in which competitors operate under the same rules. For example, all banks must follow the same regulations set down by the Federal Reserve. In some situations, competitors complain to regulators or Congress that they are not playing on a level playing field. For example, banks contend that brokerage firms can offer certain banking services without the same rules imposed on banks. Companies wanting to export to a particular country may complain that domestic companies are protected by various trade barriers, creating an uneven playing field. Various sections of the tax code may favor some companies more than others, prompting cries from the disadvantaged firms to "level the playing field."

LEVEL TERM INSURANCE life insurance policy with a fixed face value and rising insurance premiums.

LEVERAGED COMPANY company with debt in addition to equity in its capital structure. In its popular connotation, the term is applied to companies that are highly leveraged. Although the judgment is relative, industrial companies with more than one third of their capitalization in the form of debt are considered highly leveraged. *See also* LEVERAGE.

LEVERAGED EMPLOYEE STOCK OWNERSHIP PLAN (LESOP) EMPLOYEE STOCK OWNERSHIP PLAN (ESOP) in which employee pension plans and profit-sharing plans borrow money to purchase stock in the company or issue CONVERTIBLES exchangeable for common stock. In addition to the usual advantages of employee ownership, the LESOP·is a way to ensure that majority ownership remains in friendly hands.

LEVERAGED INVESTMENT COMPANY
 1. open-end INVESTMENT COMPANY, or MUTUAL FUND, that is permitted by its charter to borrow capital from a bank or other lender.
 2. dual-purpose INVESTMENT COMPANY, which issues both income and capital shares. Holders of income shares receive dividends and interest on investments, whereas holders of capital shares receive all capital gains on investments. In effect each class of shareholder leverages the other.

LEVERAGED LEASE LEASE that involves a lender in addition to the lessor and lessee. The lender, usually a bank or insurance company, puts up a percentage of the cash required to purchase the asset, usually more than half. The balance is put up by the lessor, who is both the equity participant and the borrower. With the cash the lessor acquires the asset, giving the lender (1) a mortgage on the asset and (2) an assignment of the lease and lease payments. The lessee then makes periodic payments to the lessor, who in turn pays the lender. As owner of the asset, the lessor is entitled to tax deductions for DEPRECIATION on the asset and INTEREST on the loan.

LEVERAGED RECAPITALIZATION corporate strategy to fend off potential acquirers by taking on a large amount of debt and making a large cash distribution to shareholders. For example, XYZ Company, selling at $50 a share, may borrow $3 billion to make a one-time distribution of $20 a share to stockholders. After the distribution, the stock price will drop to $30. By replacing equity with $3 billion in debt, XYZ is a far less attractive takeover target for a raider or other company than it was before. Also called *leveraged recap* for short.

LEVERAGED STOCK stock financed with credit, as in a MARGIN ACCOUNT. Although not, strictly speaking, leveraged stock, securities that are convertible into common stock provide an extra degree of leverage when bought on margin. Assuming the purchase price is reasonably close to the INVESTMENT VALUE and CONVERSION VALUE, the downside risk is no greater than it would be with the same company's common stock, whereas the appreciation value is much greater.

LIABILITY claim on the assets of a company or individual—excluding ownership EQUITY. Characteristics: (1) It represents a transfer of assets or services at a specified or determinable date. (2) The firm or individual has little or no discretion to avoid the transfer. (3) The event causing the obligation has already occurred. *See also* BALANCE SHEET.

LIABILITY INSURANCE insurance for money the policyholder is legally obligated to pay because of bodily injury or property damage caused to another person and covered in the policy. Liabilities may result from property damage, bodily injury, libel, or any other damages caused by the insured. The insurance company agrees to pay for such damages if they are awarded by a court, up to the limitations specified in the insurance contract. The insurer may also cover legal expenses incurred in defending the suit.

LIBOR *see* LONDON INTERBANK OFFERED RATE.

LICENSE legal document issued by a regulatory agency permitting an individual to conduct a certain activity, usually because the person has passed a training course qualifying him. For example, a securities license is required for a broker to sell stocks, bonds, and mutual funds. An insurance license is required before someone can sell insurance products. Before a driver's license is granted, a driver must pass an examination proving that he knows how to drive safely. If the licensed individual violates the regulations, the license can be revoked.

LIEN creditor's claim against property. For example, a mortgage is a lien against a house; if the mortgage is not paid on time, the house can be seized to satisfy the lien. Similarly, a bond is a lien against a company's assets; if interest and principal are not paid when due, the assets may be seized to pay the bondholders. As soon as a debt is paid, the lien is removed. Liens may be granted by courts to satisfy judgments. *See also* MECHANIC'S LIEN.

LIFE ANNUITY ANNUITY that makes a guaranteed fixed payment for the rest of the life of the annuitant. After the annuitant dies, beneficiaries receive no further payments.

LIFE CYCLE most common usage refers to an individual's progression from cradle to grave and the assumption that the choice of appropriate investments changes. Term also applies to the life of a product or of a business, consisting of inception, development, growth, expansion, maturity, and decline (or change). Recently, the term has entered into the vocabulary of the family-owned business, referring to generations of management. The post-World War II baby boom produced entrepreneurs who built businesses that now approach a juncture where a second generation either takes over management or sells out.

LIFE CYCLE PLANNING planning contemplated by the concept of LIFE CYCLE.

LIFE EXPECTANCY age to which an average person can be expected to live, as calculated by an ACTUARY. Insurance companies base their projections of benefit payouts on actuarial studies of such factors as sex, heredity, and health habits and base their rates on actuarial analysis. Life expectancy can be calculated at birth or at some other age and generally varies according to age. Thus, all persons at birth might have an average life expectancy of 70 years and all persons aged 40 years might have an average life expectancy of 75 years.

Life expectancy projections determine such matters as the ages when an INDIVIDUAL RETIREMENT ACCOUNT may start and finish withdrawing funds. Annuities payable for lifetimes are usually based on separate male or female tables, except that a QUALIFIED PLAN OR TRUST must use unisex tables.

LIFE INSURANCE insurance policy that pays a death benefit to beneficiaries if the insured dies. In return for this protection, the insured pays a premium, usually on an annual basis. *Term insurance* pays off upon the insured's death but provides no buildup of cash value in the policy. Term premiums are cheaper than premiums for *cash value policies* such as whole life, variable life, and universal life, which pay death benefits and also provide for the buildup of cash values in the policy. The cash builds up tax-deferred in the policy and is invested in stocks, bonds, real estate, and other investments. Policyholders can take out loans against their policies, which reduce the death benefit if they are not repaid. Some life insurance provides benefits to policyholders while they are still living, including income payments. *See also* SINGLE PREMIUM LIFE INSURANCE.

LIFE INSURANCE IN FORCE amount of life insurance that a company has issued, including the face amount of all outstanding policies together with all dividends that have been paid to policyholders. Thus a life insurance policy for $500,000 on which dividends of $10,000 have been paid would count as life insurance in force of $510,000.

LIFE INSURANCE POLICY contract between an insurance company and the insured setting out the provisions of the life insurance coverage. These provisions include premiums, loan procedures, face amounts, and the designation of beneficiaries, among many other clauses. Policies may be for term or permanent cash value types of coverage.

LIFETIME REVERSE MORTGAGE type of reverse mortgage agreement whereby a homeowner borrows against the value of the home, retains title, and makes no payments while living in the home. When the home ceases to be the primary residence of the borrower, as when the borrower dies, the lender sells the property, repays the loan, and remits any surplus to the borrower's estate. Such arrangements may be appropriate for older people who need cash and are HOUSE POOR. *See also* REVERSE ANNUITY MORTGAGE (RAM).

LIFFE *see* LONDON INTERNATIONAL FINANCIAL FUTURES AND OPTIONS EXCHANGE.

LIFO *see* LAST IN, FIRST OUT.

LIFT rise in securities prices as measured by the Dow Jones Industrial Average or other market averages, usually caused by good business or economic news.

LIFTING A LEG closing one side of a HEDGE, leaving the other side as a long or short position. A leg, in Wall Street parlance, is one side of a hedged transaction. A trader might have a STRADDLE—that is, a call and a put on the same stock, at the same price, with the same expiration date. Making a closing sale of the put, thereby lifting a leg—or *taking off a leg,* as it is sometimes called—would leave the trader with the call, or the LONG LEG.

LIGHTEN UP to sell a portion of a stock or bond position in a portfolio. A money manager with a large profit in a stock may decide to realize some of the gains because he is unsure that the stock will continue to rise, or because he is concerned too much of the fund's assets are tied up in the stock. As a result, he will say that he is "lightening up" his position in the stock. However, some of the stock remains in the portfolio.

LIMIT *see* LIMIT ORDER; LIMIT UP, LIMIT DOWN.

LIMITED COMPANY form of business most common in Britain, where registration under the Companies Act is comparable to incorporation under state law in the United States. It is abbreviated Ltd. or PLC.

LIMITED DISCRETION agreement between broker and client allowing the broker to make certain trades without consulting the client—for instance, sell an option position that is near expiration or sell a stock on which there has just been adverse news.

LIMITED LIABILITY underlying principle of the CORPORATION and the LIMITED PARTNERSHIP in the United States and the LIMITED COMPANY in the United Kingdom that LIABILITY is limited to an investor's original investment. In contrast, a general partner or the owner of a PROPRIETORSHIP has unlimited liability.

LIMITED PARTNERSHIP organization made up of a GENERAL PARTNER, who manages a project, and limited partners, who invest money but have limited liability, are not involved in day-to-day management, and usually cannot lose more than their capital contribution. Usually limited partners receive income, capital gains, and tax benefits; the general partner collects fees and a percentage of capital gains and income. Typical limited partnerships are in real estate, oil and gas, and equipment leasing, but they also finance movies, research and development, and other projects. Typically, public limited partnerships are sold through brokerage firms, for minimum investments of $5000, whereas private limited partnerships are put together with fewer than 35 limited partners who invest more than $20,000 each. *See also* INCOME LIMITED PARTNERSHIP; MASTER LIMITED PARTNERSHIP; OIL AND GAS LIMITED PARTNERSHIP; PASSIVE; RESEARCH AND DEVELOPMENT LIMITED PARTNERSHIP; UNLEVERAGED PROGRAM.

LIMITED PAYMENT POLICY LIFE INSURANCE contract that provides protection for one's whole life but requires premiums for a lesser number of years.

LIMITED RISK risk in buying an options contract. For example, someone who pays a PREMIUM to buy a CALL OPTION on a stock will lose nothing more than the premium if the underlying stock does not rise during the life of the option. In contrast, a FUTURES CONTRACT entails *unlimited risk,* since the buyer may have to put up more money in the event of an adverse move. Thus options trading offers limited risk unavailable in futures trading.

Also, stock analysts may say of a stock that has recently fallen in price, that it now has limited risk, reasoning that the stock is unlikely to fall much further.

LIMITED TAX BOND MUNICIPAL BOND backed by the full faith of the issuing government but not by its full taxing power; rather it is secured by the pledge of a special tax or group of taxes, or a limited portion of the real estate tax.

LIMITED TRADING AUTHORIZATION *see* LIMITED DISCRETION.

LIMITED WARRANTY warranty that imposes certain limitations, and is therefore not a full warranty. For example, an automaker may issue a warranty that covers parts, but not labor, for a particular period of time.

LIMIT ON CLOSE ORDER order to buy or sell a stated amount of a stock at the closing price, to be executed only if the closing price is a specified price or better, e.g., an order to sell XYZ at the close, if the closing price is $30 or higher.

LIMIT ORDER order to buy or sell a security or commodity at a specific price or better. The broker will execute the trade only within the price restriction. For example, a customer puts in a limit order to buy XYZ Corp. at 30 when the stock is selling for 32. Even if the stock reached 30⅛ the broker will not execute the trade. Similarly, if the client put in a limit order to sell XYZ Corp. at 33 when the price is 31, the trade will not be executed until the stock price hits 33.

LIMIT ORDER INFORMATION SYSTEM electronic system that informs subscribers about securities traded on participating exchanges, showing the specialist, the exchange, the order quantities, and the bid and offer prices. This allows subscribers to shop for the most favorable prices.

LIMIT PRICE price set in a LIMIT ORDER. For example, a customer might put in a limit order to sell shares at 45 or to buy at 40. The broker executes the order at the limit price or better.

LIMIT UP, LIMIT DOWN maximum price movement allowed for a commodity FUTURES CONTRACT during one trading day. In the face of a particularly dramatic development, a future's price may move limit up or limit down for several consecutive days.

LINE category of insurance, such as the *liability line,* or the amount of insurance on a given property, such as a $500,000 line on the buildings of the XYZ Company. Term is also used generally, to refer to a product line. *See also* BANK LINE.

LINE OF CREDIT *see* BANK LINE.

LIPPER MUTUAL FUND INDUSTRY AVERAGE average performance level of all mutual funds, as reported by Lipper Analytical Services of New York. The performance of all mutual funds is ranked quarterly and annually, by type of fund—such as aggressive growth fund or income fund. Mutual fund managers try to beat the industry average as well as the other funds in their category. *See also* MUTUAL FUND.

LIQUID ASSET cash or easily convertible into cash. Some examples: money-market fund shares, U.S. Treasury bills, bank deposits. An investor in an ILLIQUID investment such as a real estate or oil and gas LIMITED PARTNERSHIP is required to have substantial liquid assets, which would serve as a cushion if the illiquid deal did not work out favorably.

In a corporation's financial statements, liquid assets are cash, marketable securities, and accounts receivable.

LIQUIDATING DIVIDEND distribution of assets in the form of a DIVIDEND from a corporation that is going out of business. Such a payment may come when a firm goes bankrupt or when management decides to sell off a company's assets and pass the proceeds on to shareholders.

LIQUIDATING VALUE projected price for an asset of a company that is going out of business—for instance, a real estate holding or office equipment. Liquidating value, also called *auction value,* assumes that assets are sold separately from the rest of the organization; it is distinguished from GOING-CONCERN VALUE, which may be higher because of what accountants term *organization value* or *goodwill.*

LIQUIDATION
1. dismantling of a business, paying off debts in order of priority, and distributing the remaining assets in cash to the owners. Involuntary liquidation is covered under Chapter 7 of the federal BANKRUPTCY law. *See also* JUNIOR SECURITY; PREFERRED STOCK.
2. forced sale of a brokerage client's securities or commodities after failure to meet a MARGIN CALL. *See also* SELL OUT.

LIQUIDITY ability to buy or sell an asset quickly and in large volume without substantially affecting the asset's price. Shares in large blue-chip stocks like General Motors or General Electric are liquid, because they are actively traded and therefore the stock price will not be dramatically moved by a few buy or sell orders. However, shares in small companies with few shares outstanding, or commodity markets with limited activity, generally are not considered liquid, because one or two big orders can move the price up or down sharply. A high level of liquidity is a key characteristic of a good market for a security or a commodity.

Liquidity also refers to the ability to convert to cash quickly. For example, a money market mutual fund provides instant liquidity since shareholders can write checks on the fund. Other examples of liquid accounts include checking accounts, bank money market deposit accounts, passbook accounts, and Treasury bills.

LIQUIDITY DIVERSIFICATION purchase of bonds whose maturities range from short to medium to long term, thus helping to protect against sharp fluctuations in interest rates.

LIQUIDITY FUND Emeryville, California, company that buys REAL ESTATE LIMITED PARTNERSHIP interests 25% to 35% below the current appraised value of the real estate assets. The company also buys REAL ESTATE INVESTMENT TRUSTS.

LIQUIDITY RATIO measure of a firm's ability to meet maturing short-term obligations. *See also* CASH ASSET RATIO; CURRENT RATIO; NET QUICK ASSETS; QUICK RATIO.

LISBON STOCK EXCHANGE (LSE) founded in January 1769, the exchange trades stocks, bonds, and unit trusts. The BVL General Index is the exchange's official index, and includes all listed shares on the LSE official market. Shares in the official market are traded through TRADIS, a computer-linked system. Physical settlement is three days after the trade; cash settlement is four days. Trading hours: Monday through Friday, 9 A.M to 10 A.M. pre-opening, 10 A.M. to 4 P.M. for continuous trading, and 10 A.M. to 4 P.M. for daily calls.

LISTED FIRM company whose stock trades on the New York Stock Exchange or American Stock Exchange. The company has to meet certain LISTING REQUIREMENTS or it will be delisted. Listed firms are distinguished from unlisted companies, whose stock trades over-the-counter on the NASDAQ market.

LISTED OPTION put or call OPTION that an exchange has authorized for trading, properly called an *exchange-traded option.*

LISTED SECURITY stock or bond that has been accepted for trading by one of the organized and registered securities exchanges in the United States, which list more than 6000 issues of securities of some 3500 corporations. Generally, the advantages of being listed are that the exchanges provide (1) an orderly marketplace; (2) liquidity; (3) fair price determination; (4) accurate and continuous reporting on sales and quotations; (5) information on listed companies; and (6) strict regulations for the protection of security holders. Each exchange has its own listing requirements, those of the New York Stock Exchange being most stringent. Listed securities include stocks, bonds, convertible bonds, preferred stocks, warrants, rights, and options, although not all forms of securities are accepted on all exchanges. Unlisted securities are traded in the OVER-THE-COUNTER market. *See also* LISTING REQUIREMENTS; STOCK EXCHANGE.

LISTING written employment agreement between a property owner and a real estate broker authorizing the broker to find a buyer or tenant for certain property. Oral listings, while not specifically illegal, are unenforceable under many state fraud statutes, and generally are not recommended. The most common form of listing is the exclusive-right-to-sell listing. Others include open listings, net listings and exclusive-agency listings. Listings are personal service contracts and cannot be assigned to another broker, but brokers can delegate the work to other members of the sales office. The listing usually states the amount of commission the seller will pay the broker and the time limit. In a buyer's listing, the buyer hires the broker to locate a property.

LISTING BROKER licensed real estate broker (agent) who secures a listing of a property for sale. A *listing* involves a contract authorizing the broker to perform services for the selling property owner. The listing broker may sell the property, but it may also be sold by the *selling broker,* a different agent, with the two sharing commissions, usually equally.

LISTING REQUIREMENTS rules that must be met before a stock is listed for trading on an exchange. Among the requirements of the New York Stock

Exchange: a corporation must have a minimum of one million publicly held shares with a minimum aggregate market value of $16 million as well as an annual net income topping $2.5 million before federal income tax.

LIST PRICE suggested retail price for a product according to the manufacturer. The list price is designed to guide retailers, though they remain free to sell products above or below list price.

LITTLE DRAGONS nickname for developing Asian nations such as Singapore, Hong Kong, South Korea, and Taiwan that pose a threat to Japan (the Big Dragon) because of their lower labor costs, high productivity, and pro-business attitudes. Also known as the *tigers.* Called an "economic miracle" for most of the 1990s, the so-called Pacific Rim region lost its economic underpinnings in 1997, causing currencies and securities markets to plunge.

LIVING BENEFITS life insurance benefits upon which the insured can draw cash while still alive. Some policies allow benefits to be paid to the insured in cases of terminal illness or illness involving certain long-term care costs. Beneficiaries receive any balance upon the insured's death. Also known as *accelerated benefits.*

LIVING DEAD *see* ZOMBIES.

LIVING TRUST *see* INTER VIVOS TRUST.

LLOYD'S OF LONDON a gathering place in London, England for insurance UNDERWRITERS. Lloyd's is a marketplace made up of hundreds of underwriting syndicates, each of them in effect a mini-insurer. Lloyd's sets standards for its members, but does not issue policies itself. Each syndicate is managed by an underwriter who decides which risks to accept. Typically, a risk underwritten at Lloyd's will be shared by many syndicates. The number of individual investors, known as "names," in a particular syndicate may vary from a few to hundreds. The Lloyd's market is also a major international reinsurer, allowing other insurance companies to limit their risks.

LOAD sales charge paid by an investor who buys shares in a load MUTUAL FUND or ANNUITY. Loads are usually charged when shares or units are purchased; a charge for withdrawing is called a BACK-END LOAD (or *rear-end load).* A fund that does not charge this fee is called a NO-LOAD FUND. *See also* INVESTMENT COMPANY.

LOAD FUND MUTUAL FUND that is sold for a sales charge by a brokerage firm or other sales representative. Such funds may be stock, bond, or commodity funds, with conservative or aggressive objectives. The stated advantage of a load fund is that the salesperson will explain the fund to the customer, and advise him or her when it is appropriate to sell the fund, as well as when to buy more shares. A NO-LOAD FUND, which is sold without a sales charge directly to investors by a fund company, does not give advice on when to buy or sell. Increasingly, traditional no-load funds are becoming *low-load funds,* imposing up-front charges of 3% or less with no change in services. *See also* INVESTMENT COMPANY.

LOAD SPREAD OPTION method of allocating the annual sales charge on some contractual mutual funds. In a CONTRACTUAL PLAN, the investor accumulates shares in the fund through periodic fixed payments. During the first four years of the contract, up to 20% of any single year's contributions to the fund may be credited against the sales charge, provided that the total charges for these four years do not exceed 64% of one year's contributions. The sales charge is limited to 9% of the entire contract.

LOAN transaction wherein an owner of property, called the LENDER, allows another party, the *borrower,* to use the property. The borrower customarily promises to return the property after a specified period with payment for its use, called INTEREST. The documentation of the promise is called a PROMISSORY NOTE when the property is cash.

LOAN AMORTIZATION reduction of debt by scheduled, regular payments of principal and interest sufficient to repay the loan at maturity.

LOAN COMMITMENT lender's agreement to make money available to a borrower in a specified amount, at a specified rate, and within a specified time. *See also* COMMITMENT FEE.

LOAN CROWD stock exchange members who lend or borrow securities required to cover the positions of brokerage customers who sell short—called a crowd because they congregate at a designated place on the floor of the exchange. *See also* LENDING SECURITIES.

LOANED FLAT loaned without interest, said of the arrangement whereby brokers lend securities to one another to cover customer SHORT SALE positions. *See also* LENDING AT A PREMIUM; LENDING AT A RATE; LENDING SECURITIES.

LOAN ORIGINATION FEE *see* POINT.

LOAN STOCK *see* LENDING SECURITIES.

LOAN-TO-VALUE RATIO (LTV) ratio of money borrowed to fair market value, usually in reference to real property. Residential mortgage loans conventionally have a maximum LTV of 80% (an $80,000 loan on a $100,0000 house).

LOAN VALUE
1. amount a lender is willing to lend against collateral. For example, at 50% of appraised value, a piece of property worth $800,000 has a loan value of $400,000.
2. with respect to REGULATION T of the FEDERAL RESERVE BOARD, the maximum percentage of the current market value of eligible securities that a broker can lend a margin account customer. Regulation T applies only to securities formally registered or having an unlisted trading privilege on a national securities exchange. For securities exempt from Regulation T, which comprise U.S. government securities, municipal bonds, and bonds of the International Bank for Reconstruction and Development, loan value is a matter of the individual firm's policy.

LOCAL member of a futures exchange who trades for his or her own account. The traders in a futures pit are composed of locals and employees of various brokerage firms. Locals initiate their own transactions on the floor of the exchange. Some, termed *dual traders,* also execute orders on behalf of customers.

LOCAL TAXES taxes paid by an individual to his or her locality. This includes city income, property, sewer, water, school, and other taxes. These taxes are usually deductible on the taxpayer's federal income tax return.

LOCK BOX
1. cash management system whereby a company's customers mail payments to a post office box near the company's bank. The bank collects checks from the lock box—sometimes several times a day—deposits them to the account of the firm, and informs the company's cash manager by telephone of the deposit. This reduces processing FLOAT and puts cash to work more quickly. The bank's fee for its services must be weighed against the savings from reduced float to determine whether this arrangement is cost-effective.
2. bank service that entails holding a customer's securities and, as agent, receiving and depositing income such as dividends on stock and interest on bonds.
3. box rented in a post office where mail is stored until collected.

LOCKED IN
1. unable to take advantage of preferential tax treatment on the sale of an asset because the required HOLDING PERIOD has not elapsed. *See also* CAPITAL GAIN.
2. commodities position in which the market has an up or down limit day, and investors cannot get in or out of the market.
3. said of a rate of return that has been assured for a length of time through an investment such as a certificate of deposit or a fixed rate bond; also said of profits or yields on securities or commodities that have been protected through HEDGING techniques.

LOCKED MARKET highly competitive market environment with identical bid and ask prices for a stock. The appearance of more buyers and sellers unlocks the market.

LOCK-UP OPTION privilege offered a WHITE KNIGHT (friendly acquirer) by a TARGET COMPANY of buying CROWN JEWELS or additional equity. The aim is to discourage a hostile TAKEOVER.

LONDON COMMODITY EXCHANGE (LCE) merged with the LONDON INTERNATIONAL FINANCIAL FUTURES & OPTIONS EXCHANGE (LIFFE) in September 1996.

LONDON INTERNATIONAL FINANCIAL FUTURES AND OPTIONS EXCHANGE (LIFFE) merged with the London Commodity Exchange in September 1996, adding futures and options on robust coffee, No. 7 cocoa, No. 5 white sugar, Baltic freight (Biffex), EU wheat, EU barley, and potatoes. The LCE conducts trade on its FAST electronic trading system from 9:30 A.M. to 5:30 P.M., Monday through Friday. LIFFE trades futures and options contracts on long-term and short-term interest rates, denominated in world currencies: three-month sterling (short sterling), three-month Eurodollar, three-month Euromark, three-month EuroSwiss franc (Euroswiss) and three-month Eurolira; three-month ECU and one-month Euromark futures; and long gilt futures and options. Bond trading includes German government bond (bund) futures and options, Italian government bond (BTP) futures and options, and Japanese government bond (JGB) futures. LIFFE trades futures and options on the FT-SE 100 Index and the FT-SE 250 Index, as well as equity options. Hours: 7:30 A.M. to 4:15 P.M., Monday through Friday. Short sterling, Euromarks, Euroswiss, Long Gilt, bund, BTP, and Bobl futures contracts are traded after hours on the exchange's Automated Pit Trading (APT) system, between 4:20 P.M. and 8 P.M.; the JGB trades from 7 A.M. to 4 P.M. The exchange has links with the TOKYO INTERNATIONAL FINANCIAL FUTURES EXCHANGE, the TOKYO STOCK EXCHANGE, the CHICAGO BOARD OF TRADE and the CHICAGO MERCANTILE EXCHANGE.

LONDON INTERBANK OFFERED RATE (LIBOR) rate that the most creditworthy international banks dealing in EURODOLLARS charge each other for large loans. The LIBOR rate is usually the base for other large Eurodollar loans to less creditworthy corporate and government borrowers. For instance, a Third World country may have to pay one point over LIBOR when it borrows money.

LONDON METAL EXCHANGE (LME) principal-to-principal market for base metals trading established in 1877. LME trades cash and three-month contracts on aluminum, copper, nickel, lead, zinc, tin and aluminum alloy. Traded options contracts are available against the underlying futures contracts. LME operates as a 24-hour market, with the majority of its business conducted outside of the twice-daily official floor trading sessions, or "rings." During the first ring, beginning at 11:45 A.M. Greenwich Mean Time (GMT), each contract trades in turn for five minutes; after a 10-minute break, the process is repeated. The second part of this session results in settlement and official prices, at or near 1:15 P.M. GMT.

After official prices are announced, a period of trading called "the kerb" begins, usually lasting around 15 minutes, with all contracts trading simultaneously. The second ring, or the afternoon session, begins at 3:20 P.M. GMT, following the structure of the first ring and ending with a 25-minute kerb period from 4:35 P.M. to 5 P.M. GMT. LME prices are used as reference prices in many world markets by metals producers and fabricators of metal products. LME contracts assume an eventual delivery of physical metal on the prompt date, but this generally does not occur, since the majority of LME business is for trade hedging. Both floor and interoffice trading are covered by a matching system run by the London Clearing House Ltd., which acts as a central counterpart to trades executed between clearing members of the exchange.

LONDON STOCK EXCHANGE (LSE) originated as New Jonathan's Coffee House in 1773. In 1973, it joined the United Kingdom's six regional exchanges to form the Stock Exchange of Great Britain and Ireland. Regional trading floors ceased in the late '80s, and in 1995 after the Dublin Stock Exchange left the alliance, the exchange became known as the London Stock Exchange. Six regional offices operate in the UK. The FT-SE 100 Index (known as the *Footsie*), based on the 100 largest listed companies by market capitalization, is the dominant index; it is calculated on a minute-by-minute basis. The Eurotrack 100 Index tracks the top Continental European and Irish shares using real-time prices through the exchange's Stock Exchange Automatic Quotation (SEAQ) and SEAQ International systems; this index is calculated once a minute in Deutschemarks. Traders can act as both market makers and agents as long as they are member firms of the LSE. The exchange introduced two major electronic systems in August 1996: Sequence, the electronic equity trading system, and Crest, the electronic share settlement system. Settlement is done on a five-day rolling basis. Trading hours: Monday to Friday, 8:30 A.M. to 4:30 P.M.

LONG BOND in general, bond that matures in more than 10 years. Since these bonds commit investors' money for a long time, they normally pay investors a higher yield. In Wall Street parlance, the "long bond" is the 30-year Treasury.

LONG COUPON
1. bond issue's first interest payment covering a longer period than the remaining payments, or the bond issue itself. Conventional schedules call for interest payments at six-month intervals. A long COUPON results when a bond is issued more than six months before the date of the first scheduled payment. *See also* SHORT COUPON.
2. interest-bearing bond maturing in more than 10 years.

LONG HEDGE
1. FUTURES CONTRACT bought to protect against a rise in the cost of honoring a future commitment. Also called a *buy hedge*. The hedger benefits from a narrowing of the BASIS (difference between cash price and future price) if the future is bought below the cash price, and from a widening of the basis if the future is bought above the cash price.
2. FUTURES CONTRACT or CALL OPTION bought in anticipation of a drop in interest rates, so as to lock in the present yield on a fixed-income security.

LONG LEG part of an OPTION SPREAD representing a commitment to buy the underlying security. For instance, if a spread consists of a long CALL OPTION and a short PUT OPTION, the long call is the long LEG.

LONG POSITION
1. ownership of a security, giving the investor the right to transfer ownership to someone else by sale or by gift; the right to receive any income paid by the security; and the right to any profits or losses as the security's value changes.
2. investor's ownership of securities held by a brokerage firm.

LONG TERM
1. holding period of 12 months or longer and applicable in calculating the CAPITAL GAINS TAX.
2. investment approach to the stock market in which an investor seeks appreciation by holding a stock for 12 months or more.
3. bond with a maturity of 10 years or longer.

See also CAPITAL GAIN; LONG BOND; LONG-TERM DEBT; LONG-TERM FINANCING; LONG-TERM GAIN; LONG-TERM INVESTOR; LONG-TERM LOSS; SHORT TERM.

LONG-TERM DEBT liability due in a year or more. Normally, interest is paid periodically over the term of the loan, and the principal amount is payable as notes or bonds mature. Also, a LONG BOND with a maturity of 10 years or more.

LONG-TERM DEBT RATIO *see* DEBT-TO-EQUITY RATIO (2). *See also* RATIO ANALYSIS.

LONG-TERM FINANCING liabilities not repayable in one year and all equity. *See also* LONG-TERM DEBT.

LONG-TERM GAIN gain on the sale of a CAPITAL ASSET where the HOLDING PERIOD was 12 months or more and the profit was subject to the long-term CAPITAL GAINS TAX.

LONG-TERM GOALS financial goals that an individual sets for five years or longer. Some examples of long-term goals include assembling a retirement fund, saving for a down payment on a house or for college tuition, buying a second home, or starting a business.

LONG-TERM INVESTOR someone who invests in stocks, bonds, mutual funds or other investment vehicles for a long time, typically at least five years, in order to fund long-term goals. A long-term investor looks for solid investments with a good long-term track record, such as a BLUE CHIP stock or a mutual fund with exemplary performance. As long as the investor holds his investments for 12 months, he will pay preferential CAPITAL GAINS TAXES at a top 20% tax rate instead of paying higher regular income tax rates, which are due when assets are sold after having been held for less than 12 months.

LONG-TERM LIABILITIES any monies owed that are not payable on demand or within one year. The *current portion of long-term debt* is a current liability, as distinguished from a long-term liability.

LONG-TERM LOSS negative counterpart to LONG-TERM GAIN as defined by the same legislation. A long-term loss is realized when an asset held for more than 12 months is sold at a lower price than its adjusted purchase price. A CAPITAL LOSS can be used to offset a CAPITAL GAIN plus $3000 of ORDINARY INCOME except that short-term losses exceeding short-term gains must first be applied to long-term gains, if any.

LONG-TERM PLANNING financial planning to accomplish LONG-TERM GOALS. A long-term plan will project how much money will be needed to fund retirement, pay college tuition, or buy a house in five years or more by designing an investment strategy to meet that goal.

LOOPHOLE technicality making it possible to circumvent a law's intent without violating its letter. For instance, a TAX SHELTER may exploit a loophole in the tax law, or a bank may take advantage of a loophole in the GLASS STEAGALL ACT to acquire a DISCOUNT BROKER.

LOOSE CREDIT policy by the Federal Reserve Board to make loans less expensive and thus widely available in the economy. The Fed implements a loose credit policy by reducing interest rates through OPEN-MARKET OPERATIONS by buying Treasury securities, which gives banks more funds they need to satisfy loan demand. The Fed initiates a loose credit policy when the economy is weak and inflation is low, in order to stimulate a faster pace of economic activity. Also called *easy money.* The opposite policy is called TIGHT MONEY, in which the Fed sells securities and makes it more difficult and expensive to borrow, and thereby hopes to slow down economic activity. Tight money policy is used to dampen inflation in an overheated economy.

LOSS opposite of PROFIT.

LOSS-CONTROL ACTIVITIES actions initiated by a company or individual at the urging of its insurance company to prevent accidents, losses or other insurance claims. For example, a home insurer may require smoke alarms. A commercial insurer may require certain safety procedures in a manufacturing plant.

LOSS LEADER concept, primarily in retailing, where an item is priced at a loss and widely advertised in order to draw trade into the store. The loss is considered a cost of promotion and is offset by the profits on other items sold. Concept is sometimes used by DISCOUNT BROKERS, who will advertise a particular transaction at a loss price to attract customers, who will enter into other transactions at a profit to the broker.

LOSS-OF-INCOME INSURANCE insurance coverage replacing income lost by a policyholder. For example, *business interruption insurance* will pay employee wages if a business is temporarily out of operation because of a fire, flood, or other disaster. *Disability insurance* will replace a portion of an insured disabled person's income while he or she is disabled due to injury or illness. *Worker's compensation insurance* will reimburse a worker who was injured on the job for lost wages during the disability period.

LOSS PREVENTION programs instituted by individuals or companies to prevent losses. Businesses implement safety programs to prevent workplace injuries. Individuals install fire detectors, burglar alarms, and other protective devices to prevent losses caused by fire and theft. Car owners install special locks to prevent auto theft. Insurance companies usually offer discounts to businesses or individuals taking loss prevention measures.

LOSS RATIO ratio of losses paid or accrued by an insurer to premiums earned, usually for a one-year period. *See also* BAD DEBT.

LOSS RESERVE *see* BAD DEBT.

LOT in a general business sense, a lot is any group of goods or services making up a transaction. *See also* ODD LOT; ROUND LOT.

LOW bottom price paid for a security over the past year or since trading in the security began; in the latter sense also called *historic low.*

LOW BALANCE METHOD interest computation method on savings accounts where interest is based on the lowest balance during the period.

LOW GRADE bond RATING of B or lower.

LOW-INCOME HOUSING LIMITED PARTNERSHIP limited partnership investment in housing complexes occupied by low- and moderate-income tenants paying rent that cannot exceed statutory limits. Such partnerships offer investors annual tax credits over a 10-year period that total approximately 130% to 150% of the amount invested. Due to the restricted rents as required under the tax law, anticipated cash flow during the holding period is minimal. Properties can be sold after a 15-year holding period, which may return some or all of the original investment. The primary investment motivation for limited partners is a predictable stream of annual tax benefits. Limited partners use IRS Form 8586 to claim the credit.

LOW-LOAD FUND *see* LOAD FUND.

LUMP SUM large payment of money received at one time instead of in periodic payments. People retiring from or leaving a company may receive a lump-sum distribution of the value of their pension, salary reduction or profit-sharing plan. (Special tax rules apply to such lump-sum distributions unless the money is rolled into an IRA rollover account.) Some annuities, called *single premium deferred annuities* (SPDAs) require one upfront lump sum which is invested. Beneficiaries of life insurance policies may receive a death benefit in a lump sum. A consumer making a large purchase such as a car or boat may decide to pay in one lump sum instead of financing the purchase over time.

LUXURY TAX tax on goods considered nonessential. For example, in the early '90s a 10% luxury tax was imposed on purchases of cars selling for $30,000 or more, airplanes, boats, furs and expensive jewelry. The result of the tax, however, was that purchases of these items dropped sharply, harming the producers and retailers of these goods severely. That luxury tax was repealed in the REVENUE RECONCILIATION ACT OF 1993.

m

MA BELL nickname for AT&T Corporation. Before the Bell System was broken up in 1984, AT&T controlled both local and long distance telephone service in the United States. After the breakup, local phone service was performed by the seven regional phone companies and AT&T concentrated on long distance, telecommunications research, equipment and computer manufacturing. Even though it no longer enjoys the monopoly it once had, people still refer to AT&T as Ma Bell. The stock is also a component of the Dow Jones Industrial Average, and is one of the most widely held and actively traded stocks on the New York Stock Exchange.

MACARONI DEFENSE defensive tactic used by a corporation trying to defeat a TAKEOVER attempt by a RAIDER or unfriendly bidder. The target corporation will issue a massive amount of bonds that must be redeemed at a mandatory higher redemption value if the company is taken over. The redemption value of these bonds therefore expands when the company is threatened—like macaroni when it is cooked—making the takeover prohibitively expensive to complete.

MACD *see* MOVING AVERAGE CONVERGENCE/DIVERGENCE.

MACROECONOMICS analysis of a nation's economy as a whole, using such aggregate data as price levels, unemployment, inflation, and industrial production. *See also* MICROECONOMICS.

MADRID STOCK EXCHANGE (BOLSA DE MADRID) largest and most international of Spain's four stock exchanges. More than 90% of trading is through the Spanish Stock Market Interconnection System (SIBE), linking the other exchanges in Barcelona, Bilbao, and Valencia. All fixed-income securities are traded through the on-line, fixed-income electronic system. Using SIBE, data can be displayed simultaneously on 72 different shares; trading can occur in any of the shares without interrupting the information flow. The Madrid Stock Exchange General Index is made up of 110 stocks and represents more than 90% of total market capitalization, excluding foreign stocks. Banks, utilities, and communications firms account for 70% of the index's capitalization. Settlement is three business days after the trade date. Trading on the continuous market owned by the four exchanges is Monday to Friday, from 10 A.M. to 5 P.M., with pre-opening trading from 9:30 A.M. to 10 A.M.

MACRS see MODIFIED ACCELERATED COST RECOVERY SYSTEM (MACRS).

MAINTENANCE BOND a bond that guarantees against defects in workmanship or materials for a specified period following completion of a contract.

MAINTENANCE CALL call for additional money or securities when a brokerage customer's margin account equity falls below the requirements of the National Association of Securities Dealers (NASD), of the exchanges, or of the brokerage firm. Unless the account is brought up to the levels complying with equity maintenance rules, some of the client's securities may be sold to remedy the deficiency. See also MAINTENANCE REQUIREMENT; MINIMUM MAINTENANCE; SELL OUT.

MAINTENANCE FEE annual charge to maintain certain types of brokerage accounts. Such a fee may be attached to an ASSET MANAGEMENT ACCOUNT, which combines securities and money market accounts. Banks and brokers may also charge a maintenance fee for an INDIVIDUAL RETIREMENT ACCOUNT (IRA).

MAINTENANCE REQUIREMENT see MINIMUM MAINTENANCE.

MAJORITY SHAREHOLDER one of the shareholders who together control more than half the outstanding shares of a corporation. If the ownership is widely scattered and there are no majority shareholders, effective control may be gained with far less than 51% of the outstanding shares. See also WORKING CONTROL.

MAKE A MARKET maintain firm bid and offer prices in a given security by standing ready to buy or sell ROUND LOTS at publicly quoted prices. The dealer is called a *market maker* in the over-the-counter market and a SPECIALIST on the exchanges. A dealer who makes a market over a long period is said to *maintain* a market. See *also* REGISTERED COMPETITIVE MARKET MAKER.

MAKE A PRICE see MAKE A MARKET.

MALAYSIA COMMODITY EXCHANGE trades interest rate futures on the three-month KIBOR (Kuala Lumpur Interbank Offered Rate). The exchange is a subsidiary of the KUALA LUMPUR COMMODITY EXCHANGE.

MALONEY ACT legislation, also called the Maloney Amendment, enacted in 1938 to amend the SECURITIES EXCHANGE ACT OF 1934 by adding Section 15A, which provides for the regulation of the OVER-THE-COUNTER market (OTC) through national securities associations registered with the Securities and Exchange Commission. See *also* NATIONAL ASSOCIATION OF SECURITIES DEALERS (NASD).

MANAGED ACCOUNT investment account consisting of money that one or more clients entrust to a manager, who decides when and where to invest it. Such an account may be handled by a bank trust department or by an investment advisory firm. Clients are charged a MANAGEMENT FEE And share in proportion to their participation in any losses and gains.

MANAGEMENT combined fields of policy and administration and the people who provide the decisions and supervision necessary to implement the owners' business objectives and achieve stability and growth. The formulation of policy requires analysis of all factors having an effect on short- and long-term profits.

The administration of policies is carried out by the CHIEF EXECUTIVE OFFICER, his or her immediate staff, and everybody else who possesses authority delegated by people with supervisory responsibility. Thus the size of management can range from one person in a small organization to multilayered management hierarchies in large, complex organizations. The top members of management, called senior management, report to the owners of a firm; in large corporations, the CHAIRMAN OF THE BOARD, the PRESIDENT, and sometimes other key senior officers report to the BOARD OF DIRECTORS, comprising elected representatives of the owning stockholders. The application of scientific principles to decision-making is called management science. *See also* ORGANIZATION CHART.

MANAGEMENT BUYIN purchase of a large, and often controlling, interest in a company by an outside investor group that chooses to retain existing management. In many cases, the outside investors are venture capitalists who believe the company's products, services, and management have bright prospects. The investor group will usually place its representatives on the company's board of directors to monitor the progress of the company.

MANAGEMENT BUYOUT purchase of all of a company's publicly held shares by the existing management, which takes the company private. Usually, management will have to pay a premium over the current market price to entice public shareholders to go along with the deal. If management has to borrow heavily to finance the transaction, it is called a LEVERAGED BUYOUT (LBO). Managers may want to buy their company for several reasons: They want to avoid being taken over by a raider who would bring in new management; they no longer want the scrutiny that comes with running a public company; or they believe they can make more money for themselves in the long run by owning a larger share of the company, and eventually reap substantial profits by going public again with a REVERSE LEVERAGED BUYOUT.

MANAGEMENT COMPANY same as INVESTMENT COMPANY.

MANAGEMENT FEE charge against investor assets for managing the portfolio of an open- or closed-end MUTUAL FUND as well as for such services as shareholder relations or administration. The fee, as disclosed in the PROSPECTUS, is a fixed percentage of the fund's net asset value, typically between 0.5% and 2% per year. The fee also applies to a MANAGED ACCOUNT. The management fee is deducted automatically from a shareholder's assets once a year.

MANAGING UNDERWRITER leading—and originating—investment banking firm of an UNDERWRITING GROUP organized for the purchase and distribution of a new issue of securities. The AGREEMENT AMONG UNDERWRITERS authorizes the managing underwriter, or syndicate manager, to act as agent for the group in purchasing, carrying, and distributing the issue as well as complying with all federal and state requirements; to form the selling group; to determine the allocation of securities to each member; to make sales to the selling group at a specified discount—or CONCESSION—from the public offering price; to engage in open market transactions during the underwriting period to stabilize the market price of the security; and to borrow for the syndicate account to cover costs. *See also* FLOTATION COST; INVESTMENT BANKER; UNDERWRITE.

MANDATORY CONVERTIBLES debt-equity hybrids that became popular in the 1980s to meet the strong demand by banks for the raising of capital. One type, *equity contract notes,* is exchangeable at maturity for common stock having a market value equal to the principal amount of the notes. If the holder of the notes does not choose to receive equities at maturity, the issuer will sell the equity on behalf of the holder. Another type, *equity commitment notes,* does not require the holder to purchase equity with the notes but rather commits the issuer to redeem the notes with the proceeds of an equity issue at some future date. The Federal Reserve requires issuers to fund a third of the equity in the first four years, another third in the second four years, and the balance by maturity in the third four years. CAPS are still another form of mandatory convertible.

MANIPULATION buying or selling a security to create a false appearance of active trading and thus influence other investors to buy or sell shares. This may be done by one person or by a group acting in concert. Those found guilty of manipulation are subject to criminal and civil penalties. *See also* MINI-MANIPU-LATION.

MAPLE LEAF bullion coin minted by the government of Canada in gold (99.99% pure), silver (99.99% pure) and platinum (99.95% pure). The gold and platinum coins are available in one ounce, one-half ounce, one-quarter ounce, one-tenth ounce, one-fifteenth ounce and one-twentieth ounce sizes. The silver coin is available only in the one-ounce size. The Maple Leaf is actively traded throughout the world along with the American Eagle, South African Kruggerand, and other coins. The Maple Leaf usually sells at a slight premium to the bullion value of the coin. *See also* GOLD COIN.

MARGIN

In general: amount a customer deposits with a broker when borrowing from the broker to buy securities. Under Federal Reserve Board regulation, the initial margin required since 1945 has ranged from 50 to 100 percent of the security's purchase price. In the mid-1990s the minimum was 50% of the purchase price or short sale price, in cash or eligible securities, with a minimum of $2000. Thereafter, MINIMUM MAINTENANCE requirements are imposed by the National Association of Securities Dealers (NASD) and the New York Stock Exchange, and by the individual brokerage firm, whose requirement is typically higher.

Banking: difference between the current market value of collateral backing a loan and the face value of the loan. For instance, if a $100,000 loan is backed by $50,000 in collateral, the margin is $50,000.

Corporate finance: difference between the price received by a company for its products and services and the cost of producing them. Also known as *gross profit margin.*

Futures trading: good-faith deposit an investor must put up when buying or selling a contract. If the futures price moves adversely, the investor must put up more money to meet margin requirements.

MARGINABLE SECURITIES see MARGIN SECURITY.

MARGIN ACCOUNT brokerage account allowing customers to buy securities with money borrowed from the broker. Margin accounts are governed by REGULATION T, by the National Association of Securities Dealers (NASD), by the New York Stock Exchange, and by individual brokerage house rules. Margin requirements can be met with cash or with eligible securities. In the case of securities sold short, an equal amount of the same securities is normally borrowed without interest from another broker to cover the sale, while the proceeds are kept in escrow as collateral for the lending broker. *See also* MINIMUM MAINTENANCE.

MARGIN AGREEMENT document that spells out the rules governing a MARGIN ACCOUNT, including the HYPOTHECATION of securities, how much equity the customer must keep in the account, and the interest rate on margin loans. Also known as a *hypothecation agreement.*

MARGINAL COST increase or decrease in the total costs of a business firm as the result of one more or one less unit of output. Also called *incremental cost* or *differential cost.* Determining marginal cost is important in deciding whether or not to vary a rate of production. In most manufacturing firms, marginal costs decrease as the volume of output increases due to economies of scale, which include factors such as bulk discounts on raw materials, specialization of labor, and more efficient use of machinery. At some point, however, diseconomies of scale enter in and marginal costs begin to rise; diseconomies include factors like more intense managerial supervision to control a larger work force, higher raw materials costs because local supplies have been exhausted, and generally less efficient input. The marginal cost curve is typically U-shaped on a graph.

A firm is operating at optimum output when marginal cost coincides with average total unit cost. Thus, at less than optimum output, an increase in the rate of production will result in a marginal unit cost lower than average total unit cost; production in excess of the optimum point will result in marginal cost higher than average total unit cost. In other words, a sale at a price higher than marginal unit cost will increase the net profit of the manufacturer even though the sales price does not cover average total unit cost; marginal cost is thus the lowest amount at which a sale can be made without adding to the producer's loss or subtracting from his profits.

MARGINAL COST

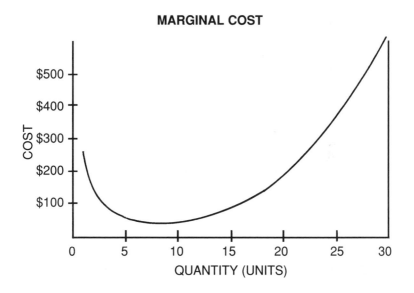

MARGINAL EFFICIENCY OF CAPITAL annual percentage yield earned by the last additional unit of capital. It is also known as *marginal productivity of capital, natural interest rate, net capital productivity,* and *rate of return over cost.* The significance of the concept to a business firm is that it represents the market rate of interest at which it begins to pay to undertake a capital investment. If the market rate is 10%, for example, it would not pay to undertake a project that has a return of 9½%, but any return over 10% would be acceptable. In a larger economic sense, marginal efficiency of capital influences long-term interest rates. This occurs because of the law of diminishing returns as it applies to the yield on capital. As the highest yielding projects are exhausted, available capital moves into lower yielding projects and interest rates decline. As market rates fall, investors are able to justify projects that were previously uneconomical. This process is called *diminishing marginal productivity* or *declining marginal efficiency of capital.*

MARGINAL REVENUE change in total revenue caused by one additional unit of output. It is calculated by determining the difference between the total revenues produced before and after a one-unit increase in the rate of production. As long as the price of a product is constant, price and marginal revenue are the same; for example, if baseball bats are being sold at a constant price of $10 apiece, a one-unit increase in sales (one baseball bat) translates into an increase in total revenue of $10. But it is often the case that additional output can be sold only if the price is reduced, and that leads to a consideration of MARGINAL COST—the added cost of producing one more unit. Further production is not advisable when marginal cost exceeds marginal revenue since to do so would result in a loss. Conversely, whenever marginal revenue exceeds marginal cost, it is advisable to produce an additional unit. Profits are maximized at the rate of output where marginal revenue equals marginal cost.

MARGINAL TAX RATE amount of tax imposed on an additional dollar of income. In the U.S. progressive income tax system, the marginal tax rate increases as income rises. Economists believing in SUPPLY-SIDE ECONOMICS hold that this reduces the incentive to be productive and discourages business investment. In urging that marginal tax rates be cut for individuals and businesses, they argue that the resulting increased work effort and business investment would reduce STAGFLATION. *See also* FLAT TAX.

MARGINAL UTILITY in economics, the addition to total satisfaction from goods or services (called *utility*) that is derived from consuming one more unit of that good or service.

MARGIN CALL demand that a customer deposit enough money or securities to bring a margin account up to the INITIAL MARGIN or MINIMUM MAINTENANCE requirements. If a customer fails to respond, securities in the account may be liquidated. *See also* FIVE HUNDRED DOLLAR RULE; SELL OUT.

MARGIN DEPARTMENT section within a brokerage firm that monitors customer compliance with margin regulations, keeping track of debits and credits, short sales, and purchases of stock on margin, and all other extensions of credit by the broker. Also known as the *credit department*. *See also* MARK TO THE MARKET.

MARGIN OF PROFIT relationship of gross profits to net sales. Returns and allowances are subtracted from gross sales to arrive at net sales. Cost of goods sold (sometimes including depreciation) is subtracted from net sales to arrive at gross profit. Gross profit is divided by net sales to get the profit margin, which is sometimes called the *gross margin*. The result is a ratio, and the term is also written as *margin of profit ratio.*

The term profit margin is less frequently used to mean the *net margin,* obtained by deducting operating expenses in addition to cost of goods sold and dividing the result by net sales. Operating expenses are usually shown on profit and loss statements as "selling, general and administrative (SG&A) expenses."

Both gross and net profit margins, when compared with prior periods and with industry statistics, can be revealing in terms of a firm's operating efficiency and pricing policies and its ability to compete successfully with other companies in its field.

MARGIN REQUIREMENT minimum amount that a client must deposit in the form of cash or eligible securities in a margin account as spelled out in REGULATION T of the Federal Reserve Board. Reg T requires a minimum of $2000 or 50% of the purchase price of eligible securities bought on margin or 50% of the proceeds of short sales. Also called INITIAL MARGIN. *See also* MARGIN; MARGIN SECURITY; MINIMUM MAINTENANCE; SELLING SHORT.

MARGIN SECURITY security that may be bought or sold in a margin account. REGULATION T defines margin securities as (1) any *registered security* (a LISTED SECURITY or a security having UNLISTED TRADING privileges); (2) any *OTC margin stock* or *OTC margin bond,* which are defined as any UNLISTED SECURITY that the Federal Reserve Board (FRB) periodically identifies as having the investor interest, marketability, disclosure, and solid financial position of a listed security; (3) any OTC security designated as qualified for trading in the NATIONAL MARKET SYSTEM under a plan approved by the Securities and Exchange Commission; (4) any mutual fund or unit investment trust registered under the Investment Company Act of 1940. Other securities that are not EXEMPT SECURITIES must be transacted in cash.

MARITAL DEDUCTION provision in the federal estate and gift tax law allowing spouses to transfer unlimited amounts of property to each other free of tax. Such transfers may be made during the life or at the death of the transferor, and are intended to treat a couple as an economic unit for transfer tax purposes. Although the deduction is unlimited, passing all assets to a spouse may create transfer tax problems in the surviving spouse's estate; planners should try to fully use each spouse's UNIFIED CREDIT, which offsets up to $625,000 in transfers in 1998, and equalize the rate of transfer taxes for both spouses to reduce taxes for the couple. According to the TAXPAYER RELIEF ACT OF 1997, the amount of assets that each person can exclude from federal estate taxes is $625,000 in 1998, rising to $1 million in 2006 and later years. This limit rises to $650,000 in 1999; $675,000 in 2000 and 2001; $700,000 in 2002 and 2003; $850,000 in 2004; $950,000 in 2005; and $1 million in 2006.

MARKDOWN
1. amount subtracted from the selling price, when a customer sells securities to a dealer in the OVER THE COUNTER market. Had the securities been purchased from the dealer, the customer would have paid a *markup,* or an amount added to the purchase price. The National Association of Securities Dealers (NASD) RULES OF FAIR PRACTICE established 5% as a reasonable guideline in markups and markdowns, though many factors enter into the question of fairness, and exceptions are common.
2. reduction in the price at which the underwriters offer municipal bonds after the market has shown a lack of interest at the original price.
3. downward adjustment of the value of securities by banks and investment firms, based on a decline in market quotations.
4. reduction in the original retail selling price, which was determined by adding a percentage factor, called a markon, to the cost of the merchandise. Anything added to the markon is called a markup, and the term markdown does not apply unless the price is dropped below the original selling price.

MARKET
1. public place where products or services are bought and sold, directly or through intermediaries. Also called *marketplace.*
2. aggregate of people with the present or potential ability and desire to purchase a product or service; equivalent to demand.
3. securities markets in the aggregate, or the New York Stock Exchange in particular.
4. short for *market value,* the value of an asset based on the price it would command on the open market, usually as determined by the MARKET PRICE at which similar assets have recently been bought and sold.
5. as a verb, to sell. *See also* MARKETING.

MARKETABILITY speed and ease with which a particular security may be bought and sold. A stock that has a large amount of shares outstanding and is actively traded is highly marketable and also liquid. In common use, marketability is interchangeable with LIQUIDITY, but liquidity implies the preservation of value when a security is bought or sold.

MARKETABLE SECURITIES securities that are easily sold. On a corporation's balance sheet, they are assets that can be readily converted into cash—for example, government securities, banker's acceptances, and commercial paper. In keeping with conservative accounting practice, these are carried at cost or market value, whichever is lower.

MARKETABLE TITLE title to a piece of real estate that is reasonably free from risk of litigation over possible defects, and while it may not be perfect, it is free from plausible or reasonable objections, and is one that a court of law would order the buyer to accept. A seller under a contract of sale is required to deliver marketable title at final closing; this requirement is implicit in law and does not need to be stated in the contract. Usually the property buyer will engage a title insurance company to ensure that the seller has CLEAR TITLE to the real estate before entering into a purchase contract. This search generally is not ordered until financing has been secured. Once the title company has researched the history of ownership of the property and feels sure that the seller owns it, it will issue a title insurance policy. The seller is thus assured that he has a marketable title, which allows him to transfer ownership to the buyer. *See also* BAD TITLE; CLOUD ON TITLE.

MARKET ANALYSIS
1. research aimed at predicting or anticipating the direction of stock, bond, or commodity markets, based on technical data about the movement of market prices or on fundamental data such as corporate earnings prospects or supply and demand.
2. study designed to define a company's markets, forecast their directions, and decide how to expand the company's share and exploit any new trends.

MARKET BASKET *see* BASKET.

MARKET BREAK any sudden drop (BREAK) in the stock market as measured by STOCK INDEXES AND AVERAGES. In SEC parlance, BLACK MONDAY, when the Dow Jones Industrial Average dropped 508 points.

MARKET BREADTH *see* BREADTH OF THE MARKET.

MARKET CAPITALIZATION value of a corporation as determined by the market price of its issued and outstanding common stock. It is calculated by multiplying the number of outstanding shares by the current market price of a share. Institutional investors often use market capitalization as one investment criterion, requiring, for example, that a company have a market capitalization of $100 million or more to qualify as an investment. Analysts look at market capitalization in relation to book, or accounting, value for an indication of how investors value a company's future prospects.

MARKET EYE financial information service that emanates from the British Broadcasting Company under the sponsorship of the INTERNATIONAL STOCK EXCHANGE OF THE UK AND THE REPUBLIC OF IRELAND (ISE). Market Eye supplies current market information plus statistical information on particular equity and debt issues and is a supplement to the Stock Exchange Automated Quotations System (SEAQ), which records trades.

MARKET IF TOUCHED ORDER (MIT) order to buy or sell a security or commodity as soon as a preset market price is reached, at which point it becomes a MARKET ORDER. When corn is selling for $4.75 a bushel, someone might enter a market if touched order to buy at $4.50. As soon as the price is dropped to $4.50, the contract would be bought on the customer's behalf at whatever market price prevails when the order is executed.

MARKET INDEX numbers representing weighted values of the components that make up the index. A stock market index, for example, is weighted according to the prices and number of outstanding shares of the various stocks. The Standard & Poor's 500 Stock Index is one of the most widely followed, but myriad other indexes track stocks in various industry groups.

MARKETING moving goods and services from the provider to consumer. This involves product origination and design, development, distribution, advertising, promotion, and publicity as well as market analysis to define the appropriate market.

MARKET JITTERS state of widespread fear among investors, which may cause them to sell stocks and bonds, pushing prices downward. Investors may fear lower corporate earnings, negative economic news, tightening of credit by the Federal Reserve, foreign currency fluctuations, or many other factors. In some cases, news may be good, but is interpreted as bad because investors are so fearful. For example, investors may think that positive economic or corporate earnings news is putting more pressure on the Federal Reserve to raise interest rates, which would hurt stock and bond prices.

MARKET LETTER newsletter provided to brokerage firm customers or written by an independent market analyst, registered as an investment adviser with the Securities and Exchange Commission, who sells the letter to subscribers. These letters assess the trends in interest rates, the economy, and the market in general. Brokerage letters typically reiterate the recommendations of their own research departments. Independent letters take on the personality of their writers—concentrating on growth stocks, for example, or basing their recommendations on technical analysis. A HULBERT RATING is an evaluation of such a letter's performance.

MARKET MAKER see MAKE A MARKET.

MARKET-ON-CLOSE (MOC) ORDER order to buy or sell stocks or futures and options contracts as near as possible to when the market closes for the day. Such an order may be a LIMIT ORDER which had not yet been executed during the trading day.

MARKET OPENING the start of formal trading on an exchange, usually referring to the New York Stock Exchange (NYSE) and marked by an opening bell. All stocks do not necessarily open trading at the bell, since there may be order imbalances causing a DELAYED OPENING. *See also* OPD; OPENING.

MARKET ORDER order to buy or sell a security at the best available price. Most orders executed on the exchanges are market orders.

MARKET OUT CLAUSE escape clause sometimes written into FIRM COMMITMENT underwriting agreements which essentially allows the underwriters to be released from their purchase commitment if material adverse developments affect the securities markets generally. It is not common practice for the larger investment banking houses to write "outs" into their agreements, since the value of their commitment is a matter of paramount concern. *See also* UNDERWRITE.

MARKET PERFORMANCE COMMITTEE (MPC) New York Stock Exchange (NYSE) SPECIALIST oversight group consisting of members and ALLIED MEMBERS. MOC monitors specialists' effectiveness in maintaining fair prices and orderly markets and is authorized to assign or reassign new or existing issues to specialist units based on their capability.

MARKETPLACE see MARKET.

MARKET PRICE last reported price at which a security was sold on an exchange. For stocks or bonds sold OVER THE COUNTER, the combined bid and offer prices available at any particular time from those making a market in the stock. For an inactively traded security, evaluators or other analysts may determine a market price if needed—to settle an estate, for example.

In the general business world, market price refers to the price agreed upon by buyers and sellers of a product or service, as determined by supply and demand.

MARKET RESEARCH exploration of the size, characteristics, and potential of a market to find out, before developing any new product or service, what people want and need. Market research is an early step in marketing—which stretches from the original conception of a product to its ultimate delivery to the consumer.

In the stock market, market research refers to TECHNICAL ANALYSIS of factors such as volume, price advances and declines, and market breadth, which analysts use to predict the direction of prices.

MARKET RISK *see* SYSTEMATIC RISK.

MARKET SHARE percentage of industry sales of a particular company or product.

MARKET SWEEP second offer to institutional investors, made following a public TENDER OFFER, aimed at increasing the buyer's position from a significant interest to a controlling interest. The second offering is usually at a slightly higher price than the original tender offer.

MARKET TIMING decisions on when to buy or sell securities, in light of economic factors such as the strength of the economy and the direction of interest rates, or technical indications such as the direction of stock prices and the volume of trading. Investors in mutual funds may implement their market timing decisions by switching from a stock fund to a bond fund to a money market fund and back again, as the market outlook changes.

MARKET TONE general health and vigor of a securities market. The market tone is good when dealers and market makers are trading actively on narrow bid and offer spreads; it is bad when trading is inactive and bid and offer spreads are wide.

MARKET VALUE

In general: market price—the price at which buyers and sellers trade similar items in an open marketplace. In the absence of a market price, it is the estimated highest price a buyer would be warranted in paying and a seller justified in accepting, provided both parties were fully informed and acted intelligently and voluntarily.

Investments: current market price of a security—as indicated by the latest trade recorded.

Accounting: technical definition used in valuing inventory or marketable securities in accordance with the conservative accounting principle of "lower of cost or market." While cost is simply acquisition cost, market value is estimated net selling price less estimated costs of carrying, selling, and delivery, and, in the case of an unfinished product, the costs to complete production. The market value arrived at this way cannot, however, be lower than the cost at which a normal profit can be made.

MARKET VALUE-WEIGHTED INDEX index whose components are weighted according to the total market value of their outstanding shares. Also called *capitalization-weighted index*. The impact of a component's price change is proportional to the issue's overall market value, which is the share price times the number of shares outstanding. For example, the AMEX Market Value Index (AMVI) has more than 800 component stocks. The weighting of each stock constantly shifts with changes in the stock's price and the number of shares outstanding. The index fluctuates in line with the price moves of the stocks.

MARKING UP OR DOWN increasing or decreasing the price of a security based on supply and demand forces. A securities dealer may mark up the price of a stock or bond if prices are rising, and may be forced to mark it down if demand is declining. The markup is the difference, or spread, between the price the dealer paid for the security and the price at which he sells it to the retail customer. *See also* MARKDOWN.

MARK TO THE MARKET
1. adjust the valuation of a security or portfolio to reflect current market values. For example, MARGIN ACCOUNTS are marked to the market to ensure compliance with maintenance requirements. OPTION and FUTURES CONTACTS are marked to the market at year end with PAPER PROFIT OR LOSS recognized for tax purposes.
2. in a MUTUAL FUND, the daily net asset value reported to shareholders is the result of marking the fund's current portfolio to current market prices.

MARKUP *see* MARKDOWN.

MARRIAGE PENALTY effect of a tax code that makes a married couple pay more than the same two people would pay if unmarried and filing singly. For example, the REVENUE RECONCILIATION ACT OF 1993 may penalize low-end taxpayers whose combined income disqualifies them for the EARNED INCOME CREDIT they would have received as single taxpayers. High-end married taxpayers, on the other hand, may find that, combined, their incomes become subject to the SURTAX on incomes over $250,000.

MARRIED PUT option to sell a certain number of securities at a particular price by a specified time, bought simultaneously with securities of the underlying company so as to hedge the price paid for the securities. *See also* OPTION; PUT OPTION.

MASTER LIMITED PARTNERSHIP (MLP) public LIMITED PARTNERSHIP composed of corporate assets spun off *(roll out)* or private limited partnerships *(roll up)* with income, capital gains, and/or TAX SHELTER orientations. Interests are represented by depositary receipts traded in the SECONDARY MARKET. Investors thus enjoy LIQUIDITY. Flow-through tax benefits, previously possible within PASSIVE income restrictions, were limited by tax legislation passed in 1987 that would treat most MLPs as corporations after a GRANDFATHER CLAUSE expired in 1998.

MATCHED AND LOST report of the results of flipping a coin by two securities brokers locked in competition to execute equal trades.

MATCHED BOOK term used for the accounts of securities dealers when their borrowing costs are equal to the interest earned on loans to customers and other brokers.

MATCHED MATURITIES coordination of the maturities of a financial institution's assets (such as loans) and liabilities (such as certificates of deposit and money-market accounts). For instance, a savings and loan might issue 10-year mortgages at 10%, funded with money received for 10-year CDs at 7% yields. The bank is thus positioned to make a three-percentage-point profit for 10 years. If a bank granted 20-year mortgages at a fixed 10%, on the other hand, using short-term funds from money-market accounts paying 7%, the bank would be vulnerable to a rapid rise in interest rates. If yields on the money-market accounts surged to 14%, the bank could lose a large amount of money, since it was earning only 10% from its assets. Such a situation, called a *maturity mismatch,* can cause tremendous problems for financial institutions if it persists, as it did in the early 1980s.

MATCHED ORDERS

1. illegal manipulative technique of offsetting buy and sell orders to create the impression of activity in a security, thereby causing upward price movement that benefits the participants in the scheme.
2. action by a SPECIALIST to create an opening price reasonably close to the previous close. When an accumulation of one kind of order—either buy or sell—causes a delay in the opening of trading on an exchange, the specialist tries to find counterbalancing orders or trades long or short from his own inventory in order to narrow the spread.

MATCHED SALE PURCHASE TRANSACTION FEDERAL OPEN MARKET COMMITTEE procedure whereby the Federal Reserve Bank of New York sells government securities to a nonbank dealer against payment in FEDERAL FUNDS. The agreement requires the dealer to sell the securities back by a specified date, which ranges from one to 15 days. The Fed pays the dealer a rate of interest equal to the discount rate. These transactions, also called reverse repurchase agreements, decrease the money supply for temporary periods by reducing dealer's bank balances and thus excess reserves. The Fed is thus able to adjust an abnormal monetary expansion due to seasonal or other factors. *See also* REPURCHASE AGREEMENT.

MATERIALITY characteristic of an event or information that is sufficiently important (or *material*) to have a large impact on a company's stock price. For example, if a company was about to report its earnings, or make a takeover bid for another company, that would be considered material information. Material information is information the reasonable investor needs to make an informed decision about an investment.

MATIF SA France's futures exchange, formally known as Marche a Terme International de France. MATIF uses a combination of open outcry (9 A.M. to 4:30 P.M.) and after-hours trading. MATIF participates in the French NCS electronic trading system developed by SB-Paris Bourse. MATIF also is linked with the CHICAGO MERCANTILE EXCHANGE so that its long-term interest rate products can be traded in Chicago. MATIF trades futures and options in the notional bond, ECU bond, three-month PIBOR (Paris Interbank Offered Rate) and white sugar; CAC 40 INDEX futures; potato, rapeseed and milling wheat futures; and currency options.

MATRIX TRADING bond swapping whereby traders seek to take advantage of temporary aberrations in YIELD SPREAD differentials between bonds of the same class but with different ratings or between bonds of different classes.

MATURE ECONOMY economy of a nation whose population has stabilized or is declining, and whose economic growth is no longer robust. Such an economy is characterized by a decrease in spending on roads or factories and a relative increase in consumer spending. Many of Western Europe's economies are considerably more mature than that of the United States and in marked contrast to the faster-growing economies of the Far East.

MATURITY

1. reaching the date at which a debt instrument is due and payable. A bond due to mature on January 1, 2010, will return the bondholder's principal and final interest payment when it reaches maturity on that date. Bond yields are frequently calculated on a YIELD-TO-MATURITY basis.
2. when referring to a company or economy, *maturity* means that it is well-established, and has little room for dynamic growth. For example, economists will

say that an aging industrial economy has reached maturity. Or stock analysts will refer to a company's market as mature, meaning that demand for the company's products is stagnant.

MATURITY DATE

1. date on which the principal amount of a note, draft, acceptance bond, or other debt instrument becomes due and payable. Also termination or due date on which an installment loan must be paid in full.

2. in FACTORING, average due date of factored receivables, when the factor remits to the seller for receivables sold each month.

MATURITY MATCHING *see* DURATION *(immunization).*

MAXIMUM CAPITAL GAINS MUTUAL FUND fund whose objective is to produce large capital gains for its shareholders. During a bull market it is likely to rise much faster than the general market or conservative mutual funds. But in a falling market, it is likely to drop much farther than the market averages. This increased volatility results from a policy of investing in small, fast-growing companies whose stocks characteristically are more volatile than those of large, well-established companies.

MAY DAY May 1, 1975, when fixed minimum brokerage commissions ended in the United States. Instead of a mandated rate to execute exchange trades, brokers were allowed to charge whatever they chose. The May Day changes ushered in the era of discount brokerage firms that execute buy and sell orders for low commissions, but give no investment advice. The end of fixed commissions also marked the beginning of diversification by the brokerage industry into a wide range of financial services utilizing computer technology and advanced communications systems.

McCARRAN-FERGUSON ACT OF 1945 federal law in which Congress declared that the states will continue to regulate the insurance business. As a result, insurers are granted a limited exemption to federal antitrust legislation.

MEALS AND ENTERTAINMENT EXPENSE expense for meals and entertainment that qualifies for a tax deduction. Under current tax law, employers may deduct 50% of meals and entertainment expenses that have a bona fide business purpose. For example, a business meal must include a discussion producing a direct business benefit.

MEAN RETURN in security analysis, expected value, or mean, of all the likely returns of investments comprising a portfolio; in capital budgeting, mean value of the probability distribution of possible returns. The portfolio approach to the analysis of investments aims at quantifying the relationship between risk and return. It assumes that while investors have different risk-value preferences, rational investors will always seek the maximum rate of return for every level of acceptable risk. It is the mean, or expected, return that an investor attempts to maximize at each level of risk. Also called *expected return. See also* CAPITAL ASSET PRICING MODEL, EFFICIENT PORTFOLIO, PORTFOLIO THEORY.

MECHANIC'S LIEN LIEN against buildings or other structures, allowed by some states to contractors, laborers, and suppliers of materials used in their construction or repair. The lien remains in effect until these people have been paid in full and may, in the event of a liquidation before they have been paid, give them priority over other creditors.

MEDIAN midway value between two points. There are an equal number of points above and below the median. For example, the number 5 is the median between the numbers 1 and 9, since there are 4 numbers above and below 5 in this sequence. Several important economic numbers use medians, including median household income and median home price.

MEDIUM-TERM BOND bond with a maturity of 2 to 10 years. *See also* INTER-MEDIATE TERM; LONG TERM; SHORT TERM.

MEFF RENTA FIJA Spain's screen-based derivatives exchange in Barcelona, listing futures and options on fixed-interest securities and on interest rates, including the 90-day MIBOR (Madrid Interbank Offered Rate) and 1-year MIBOR; and 3-year and 10-year government bond futures and options contracts. Trading hours: 9 A.M. to 5:15 P.M., Monday through Friday.

MEFF RENTA VARIABLE Spain's screen-based stock index and equity deriva-tives market, located in Madrid, trading futures and options on the Iberian Exchange (IBEX)-35 Index and on individual stocks: Fecsa, Iberdrola, Endesa, Telefonica, Repsol, Union Fenosa, Autopistas C.E.S.A., Argentaria, Banco Santander, Sevillana and BBV. The IBEX-35 is the official index of the continu-ous market of the Spanish Sociedad de Bolsas, owned by the four exchanges. It is composed of the 35 most liquid stocks on the SIBE electronic trading system. Trading hours: 10 A.M. to 5:15 P.M., Monday through Friday.

MELLO ROOS FINANCING financing of real estate developments in California authorized by legislation in 1982 sponsored by Henry Mello and Mike Roos of the California legislature. The bill allowed municipalities to float bonds to be repaid from the proceeds of tax revenues generated by real estate sales. The bonds financed construction of a community's infrastructure, such as sewers, roads, and electricity, which developers then finished with homes and businesses.

MEMBER BANK bank that is a member of the FEDERAL RESERVE SYSTEM, includ-ing all nationally chartered banks and any state-chartered banks that apply for membership and are accepted. Member banks are required to purchase stock in the FEDERAL RESERVE BANK in their districts. Half of that investment is carried as an asset of the member bank. The other half is callable by the Fed at any time. Member banks are also required to maintain a percentage of their deposits as reserves in the form of currency in their vaults and balances on deposit at their Fed district banks. These reserve balances make possible a range of money trans-fer and other services using the FED WIRE system to connect banks in different parts of the country.

MEMBER FIRM brokerage firm that has at least one membership on a major stock exchange, even though, by exchange rules, the membership is in the name of an employee and not of the firm itself. Such a firm enjoys the rights and priv-ileges of membership, such as voting on exchange policy, together with the obligations of membership, such as the commitment to settle disputes with cus-tomers through exchange arbitration procedures.

MEMBER SHORT-SALE RATIO ratio of the total shares sold short for the accounts of New York Stock Exchange members in one week divided by the total short sales for the same week. Because the specialists, floor traders, and off-the-floor traders who trade for members' accounts are generally considered the best minds in the business, the ratio is a valuable indicator of market trends. A ratio of 82% or higher is considered bearish; a ratio of 68% or lower is positive and bullish. The member short-sale ratio appears with other NYSE round lot statistics in the Monday edition of *The Wall Street Journal* and in *Barron's,* a weekly financial newspaper.

MERC nickname for the Chicago Mercantile Exchange. The exchange trades many types of futures, futures options, and foreign currency futures contracts. *See also* SECURITIES AND COMMODITIES EXCHANGES.

MERCANTILE AGENCY organization that supplies businesses with credit ratings and reports on other firms that are or might become customers. Such agencies may also collect past due accounts or trade collection statistics, and they tend to industry and geographical specialization. The largest of the agencies, DUN & BRADSTREET, was founded in 1841 under the name Mercantile Agency. It provides credit information on companies of all descriptions along with a wide range of other credit and financial reporting services.

MERCATO ITALIANO FUTURES (MIF) the Italian futures market, based in Rome. The MIF is a screen-based market, trading 10-year and 5-year Italian Treasury bond (BTP) futures. The market uses the same computer network that handles the underlying secondary market in Italian government securities.

MERCHANT BANK

1. European financial institution that engages in investment banking, counseling, and negotiating in mergers and acquisitions, and a variety of other services including securities portfolio management for customers, insurance, the acceptance of foreign bills of exchange, dealing in bullion, and participating in commercial ventures. Deposits in merchant banks are negligible, and the prominence of such names as Rothschild, Baring, Lazard, and Hambro attests to their role as counselors and negotiators in large-scale acquisitions, mergers, and the like.

2. part of an American bank that engages in investment banking functions, such as advising clients in mergers and acquisitions, underwriting securities, and taking debt or equity positions. The Federal Reserve permits commercial banks to underwrite corporate debt and common stock deals.

3. American bank that has entered into an agreement with a merchant to accept deposits generated by bank credit/charge card transactions.

MERGER combination of two or more companies, either through a POOLING OF INTERESTS, where the accounts are combined; a purchase, where the amount paid over and above the acquired company's book value is carried on the books of the purchaser as goodwill; or a consolidation, where a new company is formed to acquire the net assets of the combining companies. Strictly speaking, only combinations in which one of the companies survives as a legal entity are called mergers or, more formally, statutory mergers; thus consolidations, or statutory consolidations, are technically not mergers, though the term merger is commonly applied to them. Mergers meeting the legal criteria for pooling of interests, where common stock is exchanged for common stock, are nontaxable and are called tax-free mergers. Where an acquisition takes place by the purchase of assets or stock using cash or a debt instrument for payment, the merger is a taxable capital gain to the selling company or its stockholders. There is a potential benefit to such taxable purchase acquisitions, however, in that the acquiring company can write up the acquired company's assets by the amount by which the market value exceeds the book value; that difference can then be charged off to depreciation with resultant tax savings.

Mergers can also be classified in terms of their economic function. Thus a *horizontal merger* is one combining direct competitors in the same product lines and markets; a *vertical merger* combines customer and company or supplier and company; a *market extension merger* combines companies selling the same products in different markets; a *product extension merger* combines companies selling different but related products in the same market; a *conglomerate merger* combines companies with none of the above relationships or similarities. *See also* ACQUISITION.

MEXICAN STOCK EXCHANGE the only stock exchange in Mexico, formally known as the Bolsa Mexicana de Valores, and owned by the 33 casas de bolsa, or stock brokerage companies, five of which are foreign. The Indice de Precios y Cotizaciones, or IPC Index, consists of the 35 most representative stocks chosen every two months. The INMEX Index is an underlying index for derivative products, based on 20 companies and reviewed every six months so a single issuer cannot account for more than 10% of the index. Trading is conducted through a combination of open outcry and an automated system, BMV-SENTRA. The electronic system is used for trading debt instruments, warrants and about 50% of the stocks on the exchange. Trades are settled two days after the trade date. Trading hours: 8:30 A.M. to 3 P.M., Monday to Friday.

MEZZANINE BRACKET members of a securities underwriting group whose participations are of such a size as to place them in the tier second to the largest participants. In the newspaper TOMBSTONE advertisements that announce new securities offerings, the underwriters are listed in alphabetical groups, first the lead underwriters, then the mezzanine bracket, then the remaining participants.

MEZZANINE LEVEL stage of a company's development just prior to its going public, in VENTURE CAPITAL language. Venture capitalists entering at that point have a lower risk of loss than at previous stages and can look forward to early capital appreciation as a result of the MARKET VALUE gained by an INITIAL PUBLIC OFFERING.

MICROECONOMICS study of the behavior of basic economic units such as companies, industries, or households. Research on the companies in the airline industry would be a microeconomic concern, for instance. *See also* MACROECONOMICS.

MID CAP stock with a middle-level capitalization (numbers of shares outstanding times the price of the shares). Mid Cap stocks typically have between $1 billion and $5 billion in outstanding market value. Many mutual funds specializing in mid cap stocks will use the words mid cap in their names.

MIG-1 *see* MOODY'S INVESTMENT GRADE.

MILAN STOCK EXCHANGE largest of regional stock exchanges in Italy, accounting for more than 90% of trading volume. The MIB indices, based on the prices of all listed shares, and the COMIT Index, calculated by the Banca Commerciale Italiana, are the most widely used. Extensive reforms and reorganization in Italy created the Consiglio di Borsa, the Italian Stock Exchange Council, which instituted computerized trading and a block market. The regional exchanges are located in Rome, Turin, Genoa, Bologna, Florence, Naples, Palermo, Trieste, and Venice. Electronic trading is conducted Monday through Friday from 8:45 A.M. to 10 A.M. (order entry, automatic fixing of opening price), and from 10 A.M. to 4 P.M. (continuous trading with automatic matching of buy and sell orders). An open outcry system is used in the second market, from 9 A.M. to 10 A.M. Milan's second market, Mercato Ristretto, is the largest in the country. Trades are settled on a monthly basis, between 15 and 45 days after the trade date.

MILL one-tenth of a cent, the unit most often used in expressing property tax rates. For example, if a town's tax rate is 5 mills per dollar of assessed valuation, and the assessed valuation of a piece of property is $100,000, the tax is $500, or 0.005 times $100,000.

MINI-MANIPULATION trading in a security underlying an option contract so as to manipulate the stock's price, thus causing an increase in the value of the options. In this way the manipulator's profit can be multiplied many times, since a large position in options can be purchased with a relatively small amount of money.

MINIMUM FLUCTUATION smallest possible price movement of a security or options or futures contract. For example, most stocks on the New York Stock Exchange trade with a minimum fluctuation of one-eighth of a point. Some low-priced options contracts trade with a minimum fluctuation of one-sixteenth of a point. Minimum fluctuations are set by the securities, futures, or options exchanges regulating each security or contract. Also called MINIMUM TICK.

MINIMUM MAINTENANCE equity level that must be maintained in brokerage customers' margin accounts, as required by the New York Stock Exchange (NYSE), the National Association of Securities Dealers (NASD), and individual brokerage firms. Under REGULATION T, $2000 in cash or securities must be deposited with a broker before *any* credit can be extended; then an INITIAL MARGIN requirement must be met, currently 50% of the market value of eligible securities long or short in customers' accounts. The NYSE and NASD, going a step further, both require that a margin be *maintained* equal to 25% of the market value of securities in margin accounts. Brokerage firm requirements are typically a more conservative 30%. When the market value of margined securities falls below these minimums a MARGIN CALL goes out requesting additional equity. If the customer fails to comply, the broker may sell the margined stock and close the customer out. *See also* MARGIN REQUIREMENT; MARGIN SECURITY; MARK TO THE MARKET; SELL OUT.

MINIMUM PAYMENT minimum amount that a consumer is required to pay on a revolving charge account in order to keep the account in good standing. If the minimum payment is not made, late payment penalties are due. If the minimum is still not paid within a few months, credit privileges may be revoked. If a consumer pays just the minimum due, interest charges continue to accrue on all outstanding balances. In some cases, a credit card issuer will waive the minimum payment for a month or two, as long as the cardholder has demonstrated a good payment history. If the cardholder does not make any minimum payment in such a case, interest charges accrue on the entire outstanding balance.

MINIMUM TICK *see* MINIMUM FLUCTUATION.

MINI-WAREHOUSE LIMITED PARTNERSHIP partnership that invests in small warehouses where people can rent space to store belongings. Such partnerships offer tax benefits such as depreciation allowances, but mostly they provide income derived from rents. When the partnership is liquidated, the general partner may sell the warehouse for a profit, providing capital gains to limited partners.

MINORITY INTEREST interest of shareholders who, in the aggregate, own less than half the shares in a corporation. On the consolidated balance sheets of companies whose subsidiaries are not wholly owned, the minority interest is shown as a separate equity account or as a liability of indefinite term. On the income statement, the minority's share of income is subtracted to arrive at consolidated net income.

MINOR'S ACCOUNT bank savings account in the name of a minor, in which the minor has the power to deposit and withdraw. The minor must be able to sign for the account, but minimum deposit requirements and charges are waived until the child reaches majority (age 18 in most states).

MINUS symbol (–) preceding a fraction or number in the change column at the far right of newspaper stock tables designating a closing sale lower than that of the previous day.

MINUS TICK *see* DOWNTICK.

MISERY INDEX index that combines the unemployment and inflation rates. The index was devised in the 1970s when both inflation and unemployment rose sharply. The misery index is often credited with political significance, since it may be difficult for a president to be re-elected if there is a high misery index. The misery index is also linked to consumer confidence—the lower the index, in general, the more confident consumers tend to be.

MISSING THE MARKET failing to execute a transaction on terms favorable to a customer and thus being negligent as a broker. If the order is subsequently executed at a price demonstrably less favorable, the broker, as the customer's agent, may have to make up the loss.

MIXED ACCOUNT brokerage account in which some securities are owned (in long positions) and some borrowed (in short positions).

MLP *see* MASTER LIMITED PARTNERSHIP (MLP).

MOB SPREAD difference in yield between a tax-free MUNICIPAL BOND and a Treasury bond with the same maturity. Term is an acronym for *municipals-over-bonds* SPREAD, which will always exist because municipals involve different degrees of risk while Treasuries are risk-free as to principal. The spread between a "muni" of a given rating and a Treasury with the same maturity has significance in tax decisions and in transactions involving financial futures contracts.

MOBILE HOME CERTIFICATE mortgage-backed security guaranteed by the GOVERNMENT NATIONAL MORTGAGE ASSOCIATION consisting of mortgages on mobile homes. Although the maturity tends to be shorter on these securities than on single-family homes, they have all the other characteristics of regular Ginnie Maes, and the timely payment of interest and the repayment of principal are backed by the FULL FAITH AND CREDIT of the U.S. government.

MOCK TRADING simulated trading of stocks, bonds, commodities and mutual funds. Real money is not used. Students learning about investing in schools or brokerage training classes may go through exercises in mock trading, in which securities prices are tracked on a daily basis and fictional trades are made. With commodity futures and options, this may take the form of going through a simulated trading session on the trading floor or using computer programs to illustrate the futures and options strategies.

MODELING designing and manipulating a mathematical representation of an economic system or corporate financial application so that the effect of changes can be studied and forecast. For example, in ECONOMETRICS, a complex economic model can be drawn up, entered into a computer, and used to predict the effect of a rise in inflation or a cut in taxes on economic output.

MODERN PORTFOLIO THEORY *see* PORTFOLIO THEORY.

MODIFIED ACCELERATED COST RECOVERY SYSTEM (MACRS) provision, originally called the Accelerated Cost Recovery System (ACRS), instituted by the Economic Recovery Tax Act of 1981 (ERTA) and modified by the Tax Reform Act of 1986, which establishes rules for the DEPRECIATION (the recovery of cost through tax deductions) of qualifying assets. With certain exceptions, the 1986 Act modifications, which generally provide for greater acceleration over longer periods of time than ERTA rules, are effective for property placed in service after 1986.

    Under the modified rules, depreciable assets other than buildings fall within a 3-, 5-, 7-, 10-, 15-, or 20-year class life. The 3-, 5-, 7-, and 10-year classes use the DOUBLE-DECLINING-BALANCE DEPRECIATION METHOD, with a switch to STRAIGHT-LINE DEPRECIATION. Instead of the 200% rate, you may elect a 150% rate. For 15-

and 20-year property, the 150% declining-balance method is used with a switch to straight-line. The conversion to straight-line occurs when larger annual deductions may be claimed over the remaining life. Real estate uses the straight-line basis. Residential rental property placed in service after December 31, 1986 is depreciated over 27.5 years, while nonresidential property placed in service between December 1, 1986, and May 13, 1993 is depreciated over 31.5 years. A 39-year period applies to nonresidential property placed in service after May 12, 1993, although certain transition rules apply.

MOMENTUM rate of acceleration of an economic, price, or volume movement. An economy with strong growth that is likely to continue is said to have a lot of momentum. In the stock market, technical analysts study stock momentum by charting price and volume trends. *See also* EARNINGS MOMENTUM.

MOMENTUM INDICATORS indicators, called oscillators, used in technical analysis to measure the velocity of price movements (momentum), both up and down. In his book, *Introduction to Technical Analysis,* Martin Pring says, "All momentum series have the characteristics of an oscillator as they move from one extreme to the other. These extremes are known as OVERBOUGHT and OVERSOLD levels. An unruly dog taking a walk strains at the leash, moving from one side of the walk to the other. One moment the dog roams to the curb on his extreme left and the next he scampers back toward the lawns on his right, as far as the leash will allow him. Momentum works in a similar manner, so that when an oscillator is at an overextended reading on the upside, it is said to be overbought. When it reaches the opposite end of the spectrum on the downside, the condition is known as oversold. The horizontal line in between these extremes is called the equilibrium line."

Some of the most widely used momentum indicators are the RELATIVE STRENGTH INDICATOR (RSI), the MOVING AVERAGE CONVERGENCE/DIVERGENCE (MACD) and the STOCHASTICS INDEX. The basic characteristics of any momentum oscillator are illustrated below.

TYPICAL MOMENTUM OSCILLATOR

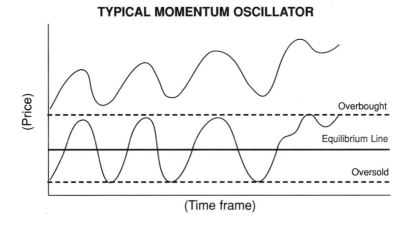

M-1, M-2 and M-3 three measures of the money supply as defined by the Federal Reserve Board:
M1 is the narrowest measure of money supply. It includes currency in circulation, checking account balances, NOW accounts and share draft accounts at credit unions, and travelers' checks. M1 represents all money that can be spent or readily converted to cash for immediate spending.

M2 includes everything in M1 plus savings accounts and time deposits such as CDs, money market deposit accounts, and repurchase agreements.

M3 includes everything in M2 plus large CDs and money market fund balances held by institutions. M3 is the broadest measure of money supply tracked by the Fed.

Federal Reserve policymakers carefully watch the growth rate of all three money supply measures, but especially M2, as key indicators of economic growth and the potential for inflation. Most economists maintain that most economic growth and inflation is determined by the rate of growth in the money supply.

MONEP (Marche des Options Negociables de Paris) subsidiary of the PARIS BOURSE, continuously trading stock and index options through open outcry and the STAMP electronic screen system. Two index classes and 50 stock classes are traded. The exchange trades CAC 40 INDEX short-term (American style) and long-term (European style) options, and equity options. The CAC 40 INDEX is the underlying index for derivative products traded on the MONEP and MATIF SA. Trading hours are 10 A.M. to 5 P.M., Monday through Friday.

MONETARIST economist who believes that the MONEY SUPPLY is the key to the ups and downs in the economy. Monetarists such as Milton Friedman think that the money supply has far more impact on the economy's future course than, say, the level of federal spending—a factor on which KEYNESIAN ECONOMICS puts great stress. Monetarists advocate slow but steady growth in the money supply.

MONETARY INDICATORS economic gauges of the effects of MONETARY POLICY, such as various measures of credit market conditions, U.S. Treasury BILL rates, and the Dow Jones Industrial Average (of common stocks).

MONETARY POLICY FEDERAL RESERVE BOARD decisions on the MONEY SUPPLY. To make the economy grow faster, the Fed can supply more credit to the banking system through its OPEN MARKET OPERATIONS, or it can lower the member bank reserve requirement or lower the DISCOUNT RATE—which is what banks pay to borrow additional reserves from the Fed. If, on the other hand, the economy is growing too fast and inflation is an increasing problem, the Fed might withdraw money from the banking system, raise the reserve requirement, or raise the discount rate, thereby putting a brake on economic growth. Other instruments of monetary policy range from selective credit controls to simple but often highly effective MORAL SUASION. Monetary policy differs from FISCAL POLICY, which is carried out through government spending and taxation. Both seek to control the level of economic activity as measured by such factors as industrial production, employment, and prices.

MONETIZE THE DEBT to finance the national debt by printing new money, causing inflation.

MONEY legal tender as defined by a government and consisting of currency and coin. In a more general sense, money is synonymous with CASH, which includes negotiable instruments, such as checks, based on bank balances.

MONEY CENTER BANK bank in one of the major financial centers of the world, among them New York, Chicago, San Francisco, Los Angeles, London, Paris, and Tokyo. These banks play a major national and international economic role because they are large lenders, depositories, and buyers of money market instruments and securities as well as large lenders to international governments and corporations. In the stock market, bank analysts usually categorize the money center banks as separate from regional banks—those that focus on one area of the country. Also known as *money market bank.*

MONEY MANAGEMENT financial planner's responsibility for the general management of monetary matters, including banking, credit management, budgeting, taxation, and borrowing. Term is also a synonym for PORTFOLIO MANAGEMENT.

MONEY MANAGER *see* PORTFOLIO MANAGER.

MONEY MARKET market for SHORT-TERM DEBT INSTRUMENTS—negotiable certificates of deposit, Eurodollar certificates of deposit, commercial paper, banker's acceptances, Treasury bills, and discount notes of the Federal Home Loan Bank, Federal National Mortgage Association, and Federal Farm Credit System, among others. Federal funds borrowings between banks, bank borrowings from the Federal Reserve Bank WINDOW, and various forms of repurchase agreements are also elements of the money market. What these instruments have in common are safety and LIQUIDITY. The money market operates through dealers, MONEY CENTER BANKS, and the Open Market Trading DESK at the New York Federal Reserve Bank. New York City is the leading money market, followed by London and Tokyo. The dealers in the important money markets are in constant communication with each other and with major borrowers and investors to take advantage of ARBITRAGE opportunities, a practice which helps keep prices uniform worldwide. *See also* MONEY MARKET FUND.

MONEY MARKET DEPOSIT ACCOUNT market-sensitive bank account that has been offered since December 1982. Under Depository Institutions Deregulatory Committee rules, such accounts had a minimum of $1000 (eliminated in 1986) and only three checks may be drawn per month, although unlimited transfers may be carried out at an automated teller machine. The funds are therefore liquid—that is, they are available to depositors at any time without penalty. The interest rate is generally comparable to rates on money market mutual funds, though any individual bank's rate may be higher or lower. These accounts are insured by the FEDERAL DEPOSIT INSURANCE CORPORATION.

MONEY MARKET FUND open-ended MUTUAL FUND that invests in commercial paper, banker's acceptances, repurchase agreements, government securities, certificates of deposit, and other highly liquid and safe securities, and pays money market rates of interest. Launched in the middle 1970s, these funds were especially popular in the early 1980s when interest rates and inflation soared. Management's fee is less than 1% of an investor's assets; interest over and above that amount is credited to shareholders monthly. The fund's net asset value remains a constant $1 a share—only the interest rate goes up or down. Such funds usually offer the convenience of checkwriting privileges.

Most funds are not federally insured, but some are covered by private insurance. Some funds invest only in government-backed securities, which give shareholders an extra degree of safety.

Many money market funds are part of fund families. This means that investors can switch their money from one fund to another and back again without charge. Money in an ASSET MANAGEMENT ACCOUNT usually is automatically swept into a money market fund until the accountholder decides where to invest it next. *See also* IBC'S MONEY FUND REPORT AVERAGE; FAMILY OF FUNDS; MONEY MARKET DEPOSIT ACCOUNT; TAX-EXEMPT MONEY MARKET FUND.

MONEY ORDER financial instrument that can be easily converted into cash by the payee named on the money order. The money order lists both the payee and the person who bought the instrument, known as the payor. Money orders are issued by banks, telephone companies, post offices, and traveler's check issuers to people presenting cash or other forms of acceptable payment. A personal money order from a bank can be considered a one-stop checking account, because the purchaser has the ability to stop payment on it; this does not hold true for money orders from other sources. Money orders often are used by people who do not have checking accounts. They can be used to pay bills or any outstanding debts.

MONEY PURCHASE PLAN program for buying a pension annuity that provides for specified, regular payments, usually based on salary.

MONEY SPREAD *see* VERTICAL SPREAD.

MONEY SUPPLY total stock of money in the economy, consisting primarily of (1) currency in circulation and (2) deposits in savings and checking accounts. Too much money in relation to the output of goods tends to push interest rates down and push prices and inflation up; too little money tends to push interest rates up, lower prices and output, and cause unemployment and idle plant capacity. The bulk of money is in demand deposits with commercial banks, which are regulated by the Federal Reserve Board. It manages the money supply by raising or lowering the reserves that banks are required to maintain and the DISCOUNT RATE at which they can borrow from the Fed, as well as by its OPEN MARKET OPERATIONS—trading government securities to take money out of the system or put it in.

Changes in the financial system, particularly since banking deregulation in the 1980s, have caused controversy among economists as to what really constitutes the money supply at a given time. In response to this, a more comprehensive analysis and breakdown of money was developed. Essentially, the various forms of money are now grouped into two broad divisions: M-1, M-2, and M-3, representing money and NEAR MONEY; and L, representing longer-term liquid funds. The table on the next page shows a detailed breakdown of all four categories. *See also* MONETARY POLICY.

MONEY SUPPLY

Classification	Components
M-1	currency in circulation
	commercial bank demand deposits
	NOW and ATS (automatic transfer
	from savings) accounts
	credit union share drafts
	mutual savings bank demand
	deposits
	nonbank travelers checks
M-2	M-1
	overnight repurchase agreements
	issued by commercial banks
	overnight Eurodollars
	savings accounts
	time deposits under $100,000
	money market mutual fund shares
M-3	M-2
	time deposits over $100,000
	term repurchase agreements
L	M-3 and other liquid assets such
	as:
	Treasury bills
	savings bonds
	commercial paper
	bankers' acceptances
	Eurodollar holdings of United
	States residents (nonbank)

MONOPOLY control of the production and distribution of a product or service by one firm or a group of firms acting in concert. In its pure form, monopoly, which is characterized by an absence of competition, leads to high prices and a general lack of responsiveness to the needs and desires of consumers. Although the most flagrant monopolistic practices in the United States were outlawed by ANTITRUST LAWS enacted in the late 19th century and early 20th century, monopolies persist in some degree as the result of such factors as patents, scarce essential materials, and high startup and production costs that discourage competition in certain industries. *Public monopolies*—those operated by the government, such as the post office, or closely regulated by the government, such as utilities—ensure the delivery of essential products and services at acceptable prices and generally avoid the disadvantages produced by private monopolies. MONOPSONY, the dominance of a market by one buyer or group of buyers acting together, is less prevalent than monopoly. *See also* CARTEL; OLIGOPOLY; PERFECT COMPETITION.

MONOPSONY situation in which one buyer dominates, forcing sellers to agree to the buyer's terms. For example, a tobacco grower may have no choice but to sell his tobacco to one cigarette company that is the only buyer for his product. The cigarette company therefore virtually controls the price at which it buys tobacco. The opposite of a monopsony is a MONOPOLY.

MONTHLY COMPOUNDING OF INTEREST *see* COMPOUND INTEREST.

MONTHLY INVESTMENT PLAN plan whereby an investor puts a fixed dollar amount into a particular investment every month, thus building a position at advantageous prices by means of *dollar cost averaging (see* CONSTANT DOLLAR PLAN).

MONTREAL EXCHANGE/BOURSE DE MONTREAL Canada's oldest stock exchange and second-largest in dollar value of trading. In 1996, the ME and its sister Canadian exchanges became the first in North America to introduce a decimal pricing system of trading and abandon the old "pieces of eight" system. Stocks, bonds, futures and options are traded through a specialist system combined with automated systems, including the Electronic Order Book for registering market and limit orders; MORRE, an electronic order execution system; and Montreal Direct Access, which provides access to the Electronic Order Board through existing terminals for the trading desks of member firms. Futures trading is conducted by traditional open outcry. A system-to-system link between the Montreal Exchange (ME) and the BOSTON STOCK EXCHANGE (BSE) enables ME member firms to electronically route retail orders for U.S. securities directly to BSE for automatic execution and confirmation at the best prevailing price in the Intermarket Trading System. The Canadian Market Portfolio Index (XXM) tracks the market performance of the 25 highest capitalized stocks traded on at least two Canadian exchanges, and is the ME's main index. Trading hours are 9:30 A.M. to 4 P.M. EST, Monday through Friday; extended sessions of 8:15 A.M. to 9:15 A.M., and 4:15 P.M. to 5:15 P.M., are offered. In addition, six sector indices track banking, forest products, industrial products, mining and minerals, oil and gas and utilities. In the derivatives market, the exchange trades 10-year Government of Canada bond futures (CGB) and options (OGB) and 3-month Canadian bankers' acceptance (BAX) futures and options (OBX); 1-month Canadian bankers' acceptance futures (BAR) and 5-year Government of Canada bond futures (CGF); equity options and long-term equity options; Canadian bond options; and LEAPS. Futures are traded from 8 A.M. to 3 P.M.; options, from 8:20 A.M. to 4 P.M. Settlement for securities is the third business day following the trade date; for futures and options, it is the day after a transaction by direct payment to the Canadian Derivatives Clearing Corporation.

MOODY'S INVESTMENT GRADE rating assigned by MOODY'S INVESTORS SERVICE to certain municipal short-term debt securities, classified as MIG-1, 2, 3, and

4 to signify best, high, favorable, and adequate quality, respectively. All four are investment grade or bank quality.

MOODY'S INVESTORS SERVICE headquartered with its parent company, Dun & Bradstreet, in downtown Manhattan, Moody's is one of the two best known bond rating agencies in the country, the other being Standard & Poor's. Moody's also rates commercial paper, preferred and common stocks, and municipal short-term issues. The six bound manuals it publishes annually, supplemented weekly or semiweekly, provide great detail on issuers and securities. The company also publishes the quarterly *Moody's Handbook of Common Stocks,* which charts more than 500 companies, showing industry group trends and company stock price performance. Also included are essential statistics for the past decade, an analysis of the company's financial background, recent financial developments, and the outlook. Moody's rates most of the publicly held corporate and municipal bonds and many Treasury and government agency issues, but does not usually rate privately placed bonds.

MORAL OBLIGATION BOND tax-exempt bond issued by a municipality or a state financial intermediary and backed by the moral obligation pledge of a state government. (State financial intermediaries are organized by states to pool local debt issues into single bond issues, which can be used to tap larger investment markets.) Under a moral obligation pledge, a state government indicates its intent to appropriate funds in the future if the primary OBLIGOR, the municipality or intermediary, defaults. The state's obligation to honor the pledge is moral rather than legal because future legislatures cannot be legally obligated to appropriate the funds required.

MORAL SUASION persuasion through influence rather than coercion, said of the efforts of the FEDERAL RESERVE BOARD to achieve member bank compliance with its general policy. From time to time, the Fed uses moral suasion to restrain credit or to expand it.

MORGAN STANLEY CAPITAL INTERNATIONAL INDICES indices maintained and calculated by Morgan Stanley's Capital International group (MSCI) which track more than 45 equity markets throughout the world. The MSCI indices are market capitalization weighted and cover both developed and emerging markets. In addition to the country indices, MSCI also calculates aggregate indices for the world, Europe, North America, Asia, and Latin America. Most international mutual funds and other international institutional investors measure their performance against MSCI indices.

MORNINGSTAR RATING SYSTEM system for rating open- and closed-end mutual funds and annuities by Morningstar Inc. of Chicago. The system rates funds from one to five stars, using a risk-adjusted performance rating in which performance equals total return of the fund. The system rates funds assessing down-side risk, which is linked to the three-month U.S. Treasury bill. If a fund underperforms the Treasury bill, it will lower the fund's rating. The score is plotted on a bell curve, and is applied to four distinct categories: all equities, fixed income, hybrids, municipals. The top 10% receive five stars; the top 22.5%, four stars; the top 35%, three stars; the bottom 22.5%, two stars; and the bottom 10%, one star. Morningstar is a subscription-based company, offering its ratings in binders, software, and CD-ROM form. It sells its data to America Online and Realities Telescan Analyzer and other databases, as well as metropolitan newspapers. Morningstar also sells information on U.S. equities and American Depositary Receipts (ADRs), but star ratings are not calculated for them.

MORTGAGE debt instrument by which the borrower (mortgagor) gives the lender (mortgagee) a lien on property as security for the repayment of a loan. The borrower has use of the property, and the lien is removed when the obligation is fully paid. A mortgage normally involves real estate. For personal property, such as machines, equipment, or tools, the lien is called a *chattel mortgage. See also* ADLUSTABLE RATE MORTGAGE; CLOSED-END MORTGAGE; CONSOLIDATED MORTGAGE BOND; MORTGAGE BOND; OPEN-END MORTGAGE; VARIABLE RATE MORTGAGE.

MORTGAGE-BACKED CERTIFICATE security backed by mortgages. Such certificates are issued by the FEDERAL HOME LOAN MORTGAGE CORPORATION, and the FEDERAL NATIONAL MORTGAGE ASSOCIATION. Others are guaranteed by the GOVERN-MENT NATIONAL MORTGAGE ASSOCIATION. Investors receive payments out of the interest and principal on the underlying mortgages. Sometimes banks issue certificates backed by CONVENTIONAL MORTGAGES, selling them to large institutional investors. The growth of mortgage-backed certificates and the secondary mortgage market in which they are traded has helped keep mortgage money available for home financing. *See also* PASS-THROUGH SECURITY.

MORTGAGE-BACKED SECURITY *see* MORTGAGE-BACKED CERTIFICATE.

MORTGAGE BANKER company, or individual, that originates mortgage loans, sells them to other investors, services the monthly payments, keeps related records, and acts as escrow agent to disperse funds for taxes and insurance. A mortgage banker's income derives from origination and servicing fees, profits on the resale of loans, and the spread between mortgage yields and the interest paid on borrowings while a particular mortgage is held before resale. To protect against negative spreads or mortgages that can't be resold, such companies seek commitments from institutional lenders or buy them from the FEDERAL NATIONAL MORTGAGE ASSOCIA-TION or the GOVERNMENT NATIONAL MORTGAGE ASSOCIATION. Mortgage bankers thus play an important role in the flow of mortgage funds even though they are not significant mortgage holders.

MORTGAGE BOND bond issue secured by a mortgage on the issuer's property, the lien on which is conveyed to the bondholders by a deed of trust. A mortgage bond may be designated senior, underlying, first, prior, overlying, junior, second, third, and so forth, depending on the priority of the lien. Most of those issued by corporations are first mortgage bonds secured by specific real property and also representing unsecured claims on the general assets of the firm. As such, these bonds enjoy a preferred position relative to unsecured bonds of the issuing corporation. *See also* CONSOLIDATED MORTGAGE BOND; MORTGAGE.

MORTGAGE BROKER one who places mortgage loans with lenders for a fee, but does not originate or service loans.

MORTGAGE INTEREST DEDUCTION federal tax deduction for mortgage interest paid in a taxable year. Interest on a mortgage to acquire, construct, or substantially improve a residence is deductible for indebtedness of up to $1 million. In addition, interest on a home equity loan of up to $100,000 is deductible. These amounts are halved for married taxpayers filing separately.

MORTGAGE LIFE INSURANCE policy that pays off the balance of a mortgage on the death of the insured.

MORTGAGE POOL group of mortgages sharing similar characteristics in terms of class of property, interest rate, and maturity. Investors buy participations and receive income derived from payments on the underlying mortgages. The principal attractions to the investor are DIVERSIFICATION and LIQUIDITY, along with a relatively attractive yield. Those backed by government-sponsored agencies such as the FEDERAL HOME LOAN MORTGAGE CORPORATION, FEDERAL NATIONAL MORTGAGE ASSOCIATION, and GOVERNMENT NATIONAL MORTGAGE ASSOCIATION have become popular not only with individual investors but with life insurance companies, pension funds, and even foreign investors.

MORTGAGE REIT invests in loans secured by real estate. These mortgages either may be originated and underwritten by the REAL ESTATE INVESTMENT TRUST or the REIT may purchase preexisting secondary mortgages. The funds the REIT invests may come from either shareholder equity capital or debt borrowed from other lenders. Mortgage REITs earn income from the interest they are paid and fees generated. This net income is generated from the excess of their interest and fee income and their interest expense and administrative fees. The other kind of real estate investment trust—called an EQUITY REIT—takes an ownership position in real estate, as opposed to acting as a lender. Some REITs, called *hybrid REITs,* take equity positions and make mortgage loans.

MORTGAGE SERVICING administration of a mortgage loan, including collecting monthly payments and penalties on late payments, keeping track of the amount of principal and interest that has been paid at any particular time, acting as escrow agent for funds to cover taxes and insurance, and, if necessary, curing defaults and foreclosing when a homeowner is seriously delinquent. For mortgage loans that are sold in the secondary market and packaged into a MORTGAGE-BACKED CERTIFICATE the local bank or savings and loan that originated the mortgage typically continues servicing the mortgages for a fee.

MOSCOW INTERBANK CURRENCY EXCHANGE (MICEX) the most liquid and best organized financial exchange in Russia. MICEX was established in 1992 to handle currency transactions from the former Gosbank of the USSR. It is a closed joint-stock company with ownership spread among major Russian commercial banks and the Central Bank of Russia. The Central Bank owns 6%, while less than 0.5% is held by the Association of Russian Banks, the Government of Moscow, and the Ministry of Finance of the Russian Federation. The rest of the shares are evenly split among 30 Russian and CIS banks. MICEX offers four market divisions which operate separately: electronic markets in foreign currencies, government securities, company shares and derivatives. Seven regional exchanges are linked to the MICEX trading and depositary system; some 1,000 remote terminals are connected to the MICEX government securities trading system either directly or through regional trading floors. The MICEX Settlement House provides settlement services for the four divisions. The exchange trades 10 foreign currencies, including the larger CIS currencies. The MICEX Derivatives Division, launched in 1996, trades cash-settled futures on the U.S. dollar, Russian T-bill (GKO), MICEX Composite Stock Index and deliverable futures on individual Russian stocks. Some 20 members trade derivatives in the trading hall. The exchange's trading system, developed by Computershare Systems of Australia, enables traders to trade GKOs and stocks alongside GKO futures, deliverable stock futures, and MICEX Composite Index futures. Trading hours are 11 A.M. to 3 P.M.

MOST ACTIVE LIST stocks with the most shares traded on a given day. Unusual VOLUME can be caused by TAKEOVER activity, earnings releases, institutional trading in a widely held issue, and other factors.

MOVING AVERAGE average of security or commodity prices constructed on a period as short as a few days or as long as several years and showing trends for the latest interval. For example, a 30-day moving average includes yesterday's figures; tomorrow the same average will include today's figures and will no longer show those for the earliest date included in yesterday's average. Thus every day it picks up figures for the latest day and drops those for the earliest day. *See* chart on the next page.

MOVING AVERAGE

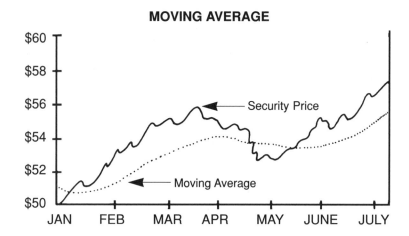

MOVING AVERAGE CONVERGENCE/DIVERGENCE (MACD) TECHNICAL ANALYSIS oscillator developed by Gerald Appel that measures OVERBOUGHT and OVERSOLD conditions. MACD, informally called "MacD," uses three exponential MOVING AVERAGES: a short one, a long one, and a third that plots the moving average of the difference between the other two and forms a signal line on an MACD graph. (MACD is usually shown as a histogram, which plots the difference between the signal line and the MACD line). Trend reversals are signaled by the convergence and divergence of these moving averages. A positive BREAKOUT occurs when the histogram crosses the zero line upward (a buy signal) and a negative breakout occurs when the histogram crosses the zero (equilibrium) line downward (a sell signal). One of the most popular MACDs is the 8/17/9 MACD. On a daily MACD, the short moving average would be 8 days, the long one 17 days, and the signal line 9 days. On a weekly MACD, the same numbers would refer to weeks instead of days. The weekly MACD overrides chatter (*see* WHIPSAWED) and is a better indicator of how strongly the market feels about a stock and how likely it is the current trend will continue. *See also* MOMENTUM INDICATORS.

MTN initials standing for *medium-term notes* that are issued by corporations and distributed by investment banks acting as agents, similar to shorter-term COMMERCIAL PAPER.

MUD acronym for *municipal utility district,* a political subdivision that provides utility-related services and may issue SPECIAL ASSESSMENT BONDS.

MULTINATIONAL CORPORATION corporation that has production facilities or other fixed assets in at least one foreign country and makes its major management decisions in a global context. In marketing, production, research and development, and labor relations, its decisions must be made in terms of host-country customs and traditions. In finance, many of its problems have no domestic counterpart—the payment of dividends in another currency, for example, or the need to shelter working capital from the risk of devaluation, or the choices between owning and licensing. Economic and legal questions must be dealt with in drastically different ways. In addition to foreign exchange risks and the special business risks of operating in unfamiliar environments, there is the specter of political risk—the risk that sovereign governments may interfere with operations or terminate them altogether.

MULTIPLE *see* PRICE/EARNINGS RATIO (P/E).

MULTIPLE LISTING listing agreement used by a broker who is a member of a multiple-listing organization that is an exclusive right to sell with an additional authority and obligation on the part of the listing broker to distribute the listing to other brokers in the organization. These listings then are distributed in a multiple-listing service publication. Generally, the listing broker and the selling broker will split the commission, but terms for division can vary. A multiple-listing agreement benefits the seller by exposing his property to a wider group of potential buyers than would be available from one exclusive broker, which should allow the sale to be completed more quickly, and for a higher price. The multiple-listing service, however, has come under close scrutiny by consumer groups and justice departments for alleged antitrust practices.

MULTIPLE PERIL INSURANCE policy that incorporates several different types of property insurance coverage, such as flood, fire, wind, etc. In its broadest application, the term is synonymous with *all-risks insurance,* which covers loss or damage to property from fortuitous circumstances not specifically excluded from coverage. Do not confuse multiple peril insurance with *multiple protection insurance,* which is a form of life insurance policy combining features of term and whole life insurance.

MULTIPLIER the multiplier has two major applications in finance and investments.

1. *investment multiplier* or *Keynesian multiplier:* multiplies the effects of investment spending in terms of total income. An investment in a small plant facility, for example, increases the incomes of the workers who built it, the merchants who provide supplies, the distributors who supply the merchants, the manufacturers who supply the distributors, and so on. Each recipient spends a portion of the income and saves the rest. By making an assumption as to the percentage each recipient saves, it is possible to calculate the total income produced by the investment.

2. *deposit multiplier* or *credit multiplier:* magnifies small changes in bank deposits into changes in the amount of outstanding credit and the money supply. For example, a bank receives a deposit of $100,000, and the RESERVE REQUIREMENT is 20%. The bank is thus required to keep $20,000 in the form of reserves. The remaining $80,000 becomes a loan, which is deposited in the borrower's bank. When the borrower's bank sets aside the $16,000 required reserve out of the $80,000, $64,000 is available for another loan and another deposit, and so on. Carried out to its theoretical limit, the original deposit of $100,000 could expand into a total of $500,000 in deposits and $400,000 in credit.

MUNICIPAL BOND debt obligation of a state or local government entity. The funds may support general governmental needs or special projects. Prior to the TAX REFORM ACT OF 1986, the terms *municipal* and *tax-exempt* were synonymous, since virtually all municipal obligations were exempt from federal income taxes and most from state and local income taxes, at least in the state of issue. The 1986 Act, however, divided municipals into two broad groups: (1) PUBLIC PURPOSE BONDS, which remain tax-exempt and can be issued without limitation, and (2) PRIVATE PURPOSE BONDS, which are taxable unless specifically exempted. The tax distinction between public and private purpose is based on the percentage extent to which the bonds benefit private parties; if a tax-exempt public purpose bond involves more than a 10% benefit to private parties, it is taxable. Permitted private purpose bonds (those specified as tax-exempt) are generally TAX PREFERENCE ITEMS in computing the ALTERNATIVE MINIMUM TAX, and effective August 15, 1986, are subject to volume caps. *See also* ADVANCE REFUNDING; GENERAL OBLIGATION BOND; HOSPITAL REVENUE BOND; INDUSTRIAL DEVELOPMENT BOND; LIMITED TAX BOND; MUNICIPAL INVEST-

MENT TRUST; MUNICIPAL REVENUE BOND; SINGLE-STATE MUNICIPAL BOND FUND; SPE-
CIAL ASSESSMENT BOND; TAXABLE MUNICIPAL BOND; TAX-EXEMPT SECURITY; UNDERLY-
ING DEBT; YIELD BURNING.

MUNICIPAL BOND INSURANCE policies underwritten by private insurers guaranteeing municipal bonds in the event of default. The insurance can be purchased
either by the issuing government entity or the investor; it provides that bonds will be
purchased from investors at par should default occur. Such insurance is available
from a number of large insurance companies, but a major portion is written by the
following "monoline" companies, so-called because their primary business is insuring municipal bonds: AMBAC Idemnity Corporation (AMBAC); Capital Guaranty
Insurance Company (CGIC); Connie Lee Insurance Company; Financial Guaranty
Insurance Company (FGIC); Financial Security Assurance, Inc. (FSA); and
Municipal Bond Investors Assurance Corporation (MBIA). Insured municipal bonds
generally enjoy the highest rating resulting in greater marketability and lower cost to
their issuers. From the investor's standpoint, however, their yield is typically lower
than similarly rated uninsured bonds because the cost of the insurance is passed on
by the issuer to the investor. Some unit investment trusts and mutual funds feature
insured municipal bonds for investors willing to trade marginally lower yield for the
extra degree of safety.

MUNICIPAL IMPROVEMENT CERTIFICATE certificate issued by a local
government in lieu of bonds to finance improvements or services, such as
widening a sidewalk, or installing a sewer, or repairing a street. Such an obligation is payable from a special tax assessment against those who benefit from the
improvement, and the payments may be collected by the contractor performing
the work. Interest on the certificate is usually free of federal, state, and local
taxes. *See also* GENERAL OBLIGATION BOND.

MUNICIPAL INVESTMENT TRUST (MIT) UNIT INVESTMENT TRUST that buys
municipal bonds and passes the tax-free income on to shareholders. Bonds in the
trust's portfolio are normally held until maturity, unlike the constant trading of
bonds in an open-ended municipal bond fund's portfolio. MITs are sold through
brokers, typically for a sales charge of about 3% of the principal paid, with a
minimum investment of $1000. The trust offers diversification, professional
management of the portfolio, and monthly interest, compared with the semiannual payments made by individual municipal bonds.

Many MITs invest in the securities of just one state. For California residents who buy a California-only MIT, for example, all the interest is free of federal, state, and local taxes. In contrast, a Californian who buys a national MIT
might have to pay state and local taxes on interest derived from out-of-state
bonds in the trust's portfolio.

MUNICIPAL NOTE in common usage, a municipal debt obligation with an original maturity of two years or less.

MUNICIPAL REVENUE BOND bond issued to finance public works such as
bridges or tunnels or sewer systems and supported directly by the revenues of
the project. For instance, if a municipal revenue bond is issued to build a bridge,
the tolls collected from motorists using the bridge are committed for paying off
the bond. Unless otherwise specified in the indenture, holders of these bonds
have no claims on the issuer's other resources.

MUNICIPAL SECURITIES RULEMAKING BOARD *see* SELF-REGULATORY
ORGANIZATION.

MUTILATED SECURITY certificate that cannot be read for the name of the
issue or the issuer, or for the detail necessary for identification and transfer, or

for the exercise of the holder's rights. It is then the seller's obligation to take corrective action, which usually means having the transfer agent guarantee the rights of ownership to the buyer.

MUTUAL ASSOCIATION SAVINGS AND LOAN ASSOCIATION organized as a cooperative owned by its members. Members' deposits represent shares; shareholders vote on association affairs and receive income in the form of dividends. Unlike state-chartered corporate S&Ls, which account for a minority of the industry, mutual associations are not permitted to issue stock, and they are usually chartered by the OFFICE OF THRIFT SUPERVISION (OTS) and belong to the SAVINGS ASSOCIATION INSURANCE FUND (SAIF). Deposits are technically subject to a waiting period before withdrawal, although in practice withdrawals are usually allowed on demand.

MUTUAL COMPANY corporation whose ownership and profits are distributed among members in proportion to the amount of business they do with the company. The most familiar examples are (1) mutual insurance companies, whose members are policy holders entitled to name the directors or trustees and to receive dividends or rebates on future premiums; (2) state-chartered MUTUAL SAVINGS BANKS, whose members are depositors sharing in net earnings but having nothing to do with management; and (3) federal savings and loan associations, MUTUAL ASSOCIATIONS whose members are depositors entitled to vote and receive dividends.

MUTUAL EXCLUSION DOCTRINE doctrine which established that interest from municipal bonds is exempt from federal taxation. In return for this federal tax exemption, states and localities are not allowed to tax interest generated by federal government securities, such as Treasury bills, notes, and bonds.

MUTUAL FUND fund operated by an INVESTMENT COMPANY that raises money from shareholders and invests it in stocks, bonds, options, futures, currencies, or money market securities. These funds offer investors the advantages of diversification and professional management. A management fee is charged for these services, typically between 0.5% and 2% of assets per year. Funds also levy other fees such as 12B-1 FEES, EXCHANGE FEES and other administrative charges. Funds that are sold through brokers are called LOAD FUNDS, and those sold to investors directly from the fund companies are called NO-LOAD FUNDS. Mutual fund shares are redeemable on demand at NET ASSET VALUE by shareholders. All shareholders share equally in the gains and losses generated by the fund.

   Mutual funds come in many varieties. Some invest aggressively for capital appreciation, while others are conservative and are designed to generate income for shareholders. Investors need to assess their tolerance for risk before they decide which fund would be appropriate for them. In addition, the timing of buying or selling depends on the outlook for the economy, the state of the stock and bond markets, interest rates, and other factors.

MUTUAL FUND CASH-TO-ASSETS RATIO amount of mutual fund assets held in cash instruments. A fund manager may choose to keep a large cash position if he is bearish on the stock or bond market, or if he cannot find securities he thinks are attractive to buy. A large cash position (10% or more of the fund's assets in liquid instruments) may also accumulate if many investors buy fund shares and the fund manager cannot put all the money to work at once. On the other hand, a low cash-to-assets ratio is an indication that the fund manager is bullish, because he is fully invested and expects stock or bond prices to rise. Some analysts consider this ratio to be an important indicator of bullish or bearish sentiment among sophisticated investment managers. If many fund managers are increasing their cash positions, the fund managers are becoming more bearish—though some analysts consider it bullish for the market because the managers will have more cash to buy securities. The ratio for the entire mutual fund industry is released on a monthly basis by the Investment Company Institute, the largest mutual fund trade group.

MUTUAL FUND CUSTODIAN commercial bank or trust company that provides safekeeping for the securities owned by a mutual fund and may also act as TRANSFER AGENT, making payments to and collecting investments from shareholders. Mutual fund custodians must comply with the rules set forth in the INVESTMENT COMPANY ACT OF 1940.

MUTUAL IMPROVEMENT CERTIFICATE certificate issued by a local government in lieu of bonds to finance improvements or services, such as widening a sidewalk, or installing a sewer, or repairing a street. Such an obligation is payable from a special tax assessment against those who benefit from the improvement, and the payments may be collected by the contractor performing the work. Interest on the certificate is free of federal, state, and local taxes. *See also* GENERAL OBLIGATION BOND.

MUTUAL SAVINGS BANK SAVINGS BANK organized under state charter for the ownership and benefit of its depositors. A local board of trustees makes major decisions as fiduciaries, independently of the legal owners. Traditionally, income is distributed to depositors after expenses are deducted and reserve funds are set aside as required. In recent times, many mutual savings banks have begun to issue stock and offer consumer services such as credit cards and checking accounts, as well as commercial services such as corporate checking accounts and commercial real estate loans.

n

NAKED OPTION OPTION for which the buyer or seller has no underlying security position. A writer of a naked CALL OPTION, therefore, does not own a LONG POSITION in the stock on which the call has been written. Similarly, the writer of a naked PUT OPTION does not have a SHORT POSITION in the stock on which the put has been written. Naked options are very risky—although potentially very rewarding. If the underlying stock or stock index moves in the direction sought by the investor, profits can be enormous, because the investor would only have had to put down a small amount of money to reap a large return. On the other hand, if the stock moved in the opposite direction, the writer of the naked option could be subject to huge losses.

For instance, if someone wrote a naked call option at $60 a share on XYZ stock without owning the shares, and if the stock rose to $70 a share, the writer of the option would have to deliver XYZ shares to the call buyer at $60 a share. In order to acquire those shares, he or she would have to go into the market and buy them for $70 a share, sustaining a $10-a-share loss on his or her position. If, on the other hand, the option writer already owned XYZ shares when writing the option, he or she could just turn those shares over to the option buyer. This latter strategy is known as writing a COVERED CALL.

NAKED POSITION securities position that is not hedged from market risk—for example, the position of someone who writes a CALL or PUT option without having the corresponding LONG POSITION or SHORT POSITION on the underlying security. The potential risk or reward of naked positions is greater than that of covered positions. *See* COVERED CALL; HEDGE; NAKED OPTION.

NAMED PERILS INSURANCE property insurance that covers risks specified in the policy. Contrasts with *all-risks insurance,* which specifies exclusions.

NARROWING THE SPREAD closing the SPREAD between the bid and asked prices of a security as a result of bidding and offering by market makers and specialists in a security. For example, a stock's bid price—the most anyone is willing to pay—may be $10 a share, and the asked price—the lowest price at which anyone will sell—may be $10¾. If a broker or market maker offers to buy shares at $10¼, while the asked price remains at $10¾, the spread has effectively been narrowed.

NARROW MARKET securities or commodities market characterized by light trading and greater fluctuations in prices relative to volume than would be the case if trading were active. The market in a particular stock is said to be narrow if the price falls more than a point between ROUND LOT trades without any apparent explanation, suggesting lack of interest and too few orders. The terms THIN MARKET and *inactive market* are used as synonyms for narrow market.

NASDAQ National Association of Securities Dealers Automated Quotations system, which is owned and operated by the NATIONAL ASSOCIATION OF SECURITIES DEALERS. NASDAQ is a computerized system that provides brokers and dealers with price quotations for securities traded OVER THE COUNTER as well as for many New York Stock Exchange listed securities. NASDAQ quotes are published in the financial pages of most newspapers. *See also* NATIONAL MARKET SYSTEM.

NASDAQ SMALL CAPITALIZATION COMPANIES separately listed group of some 2000 companies that have smaller capitalizations and are less actively traded than NASDAQ NATIONAL MARKET SYSTEM stocks, but that meet NASDAQ price and market value listing criteria and have at least two MARKET MAKERS.

NASDAQ STOCK MARKET the first electronic stock market listing nearly 5500 companies, operated by the NASDAQ Stock Market, Inc., a wholly owned subsidiary of the NATIONAL ASSOCIATION OF SECURITIES DEALERS (NASD). Some 530 market makers provide more than 60,000 competing bids to buy, offer, and sell NASDAQ stocks through an international computer network that displays the best quotations in 52 countries. The computer network is capable of trading more than 1 billion shares per day. Market makers use their own capital to buy and sell NASDAQ securities. The NASDAQ Stock Market is composed of two separate markets. The NASDAQ National Market, the market for NASDAQ'S largest and most actively traded securities, lists more than 4400 securities. This market comprises some of the best known companies in the world, among them Microsoft and Intel. The NASDAQ SmallCap Market lists nearly 1800 emerging growth companies. As these companies become established, they move up to the NASDAQ National Market. NASDAQ also operates NASDAQ International Ltd., a United Kingdom corporation based in London that helps non-U.S. companies list on the NASDAQ Stock Market directly through American Depositary Receipts. NASDAQ is developing a new communications infrastructure, called Enterprise Wide Network II (EWN II) that will handle 4 to 8 billion shares daily.

In 1998, the AMERICAN STOCK EXCHANGE and the PHILADELPHIA STOCK EXCHANGE (PHLX) merged with NASD, making the Amex and PHLX subsidiaries of NASD. Under the terms of the mergers, the Amex equity and options markets continue to operate separately from the NASDAQ Stock Market and NASDAQ International, both operated by the NASD. The Philadelphia Stock Exchange trading floor continues to operate separately for up to five years from the date of the merger.

NASD FORM FR-1 form required of foreign dealers in securities subscribing to new securities issues in the process of distribution, whereby they agree to abide by NATIONAL ASSOCIATION OF SECURITIES DEALERS rules concerning a HOT ISSUE.

Under NASD Rules of Fair Practice, firms participating in the distribution must make a bona fide public offering at the public offering price. Any sale designed to capitalize on a hot issue—one that on the first day of trading sells at a substantial premium over the public offering price—would be in violation of NASD rules. Violations include a sale to a member of the dealer's family or to an employee, assuming such sales could not be defended as "normal investment practice." Also called *blanket certification form.*

NATIONAL ASSOCIATION OF INVESTORS CORPORATION not-for-profit educational association that helps investment clubs become established. Investment clubs are formed by people who pool their money and make common decisions about how to invest those assets. The NAIC is located in Madison Heights, Michigan. *See also* INVESTMENT CLUB.

NATIONAL ASSOCIATION OF SECURITIES DEALERS (NASD) nonprofit organization formed under the joint sponsorship of the Investment Bankers' Conference and the Securities and Exchange Commission to comply with the MALONEY ACT. NASD members include virtually all investment banking houses and firms dealing in the OVER THE COUNTER market. Operating under the supervision of the SEC, the NASD's basic purposes are to (1) standardize practices in the field, (2) establish high moral and ethical standards in securities trading, (3) provide a representative body to consult with the government and investors on matters of common interest, (4) establish and enforce fair and equitable rules of securities trading, and (5) establish a disciplinary body capable of enforcing the above provisions. The NASD also requires members to maintain quick assets in excess of current liabilities at all times. Periodic examinations and audits are conducted to ensure a high level of solvency and financial integrity among members. A special Investment Companies Department is concerned with the problems of investment companies and has the responsibility of reviewing companies' sales literature in that segment of the securities industry. *See also* NASDAQ; NASDAQ SMALL CAPITALIZATION COMPANIES; NASDAQ STOCK MARKET.

NATIONAL BANK commercial bank whose charter is approved by the U.S. Comptroller of the Currency rather than by a state banking department. National banks are required to be members of the FEDERAL RESERVE SYSTEM and to purchase stock in the FEDERAL RESERVE BANK in their district *(see* MEMBER BANK). They must also belong to the FEDERAL DEPOSIT INSURANCE CORPORATION.

NATIONAL CREDIT UNION ADMINISTRATION independent federal agency based in Washington, D.C., established by Congress to oversee the federal credit union system. The NCUA is funded by credit unions and does not receive any tax dollars. The agency supervises nearly 7600 federal credit unions and federally insures member accounts in approximately 4600 state-chartered credit unions. The National Credit Union Share Insurance Fund is the agency's arm that insures member accounts up to $100,000. It is backed by the full faith and credit of the U.S. government and is managed by the NCUA Board, which is comprised of three members appointed by the President.

NATIONAL DEBT debt owed by the federal government. The national debt is made up of such debt obligations as Treasury bills, Treasury notes, and Treasury bonds. Congress imposes a ceiling on the national debt, which has been increased on occasion when accumulated deficits near the ceiling. By the late 1990s, the national debt stood at more than $5.5 trillion. The interest due on the national debt is one of the major expenses of the federal government. The national debt, which is the total debt accumulated by the government over many decades, should not be confused with the federal budget deficit, which is the excess of spending over income by the federal government in one fiscal year.

NATIONAL FOUNDATION FOR CONSUMER CREDIT a nonprofit national organization based in Silver Spring, Maryland, created in 1951 to help the increasing number of consumers who have taken on too much debt. The NFCC has more than 200 members operating 1100 locations providing consumers with money management, budget, and wise-credit-use education workshops and counseling sessions. While counselors work with creditors to work out a payment plan, the NFCC does not provide credit or financial assistance. Most members do not charge for counseling; however some members charge a low fee for services such as debt repayment or counseling. No one is turned away due to the inability to pay.

NATIONALIZATION takeover of a private company's assets or operations by a government. The company may or may not be compensated for the loss of assets. In developing nations, an operation is typically nationalized if the government feels the company is exploiting the host country and exporting too high a proportion of the profits. By nationalizing the firm, the government hopes to keep profits at home. In developed countries, industries are often nationalized when they need government subsidies to survive. For instance, the French government nationalized steel and chemical companies in the mid-1980s in order to preserve jobs that would have disappeared if free market forces had prevailed. In some developed countries, however, nationalization is carried out as a form of national policy, often by Socialist governments, and is not designed to rescue ailing industries.

NATIONAL MARKET ADVISORY BOARD board appointed by the Securities and Exchange Commission under provisions of the 1975 Securities Act to study and advise the commission on a national exchange market system (NEMS). NEMS is envisioned as a highly automated, national exchange with continuous auction markets and competing specialist or market makers, but one that would preserve the existing regional exchanges.

NATIONAL MARKET EXCHANGES formed by the BOSTON STOCK EXCHANGE, CHICAGO STOCK EXCHANGE, PACIFIC EXCHANGE and PHILADELPHIA STOCK EXCHANGE to help stock investors better understand the role of the NATIONAL MARKET SYSTEM and the Intermarket Trading System in the U.S. *See also* NATIONAL MARKET SYSTEM.

NATIONAL MARKET SYSTEM (NMS) developed in 1975 by the Securities and Exchange Commission following a mandate by the U.S. Congress to foster greater competition among the stock exchanges in the U.S. NMS consists of every major market center in the U.S.—the NEW YORK STOCK EXCHANGE, AMERICAN STOCK EXCHANGE, BOSTON STOCK EXCHANGE, CHICAGO STOCK EXCHANGE, CINCINNATI STOCK EXCHANGE, PACIFIC EXCHANGE, PHILADELPHIA STOCK EXCHANGE and the NATIONAL ASSOCIATION OF SECURITIES DEALERS. Its Intermarket Trading System (ITS) is an electronic linkage among all of the NMS exchanges that displays current bid and offer prices for all eligible stocks at a given exchange. It also displays the current bid and offer prices at all markets in the system and the best prices available nationwide. *See also* NATIONAL MARKET ADVISORY BOARD.

NATIONAL QUOTATION BUREAU daily service to subscribers that collects bid and offer quotes from MARKET MAKERS in stocks and bonds traded OVER THE COUNTER. Quotes are distributed on PINK SHEETS (for stocks) and YELLOW SHEETS (for corporate bonds). The Bureau is located in Cedar Grove, New Jersey. *See also* OTC BULLETIN BOARD.

NATIONAL SECURITIES CLEARING CORPORATION (NSCC) securities clearing organization formed in 1977 by merging subsidiaries of the New York and American Stock Exchanges with the National Clearing Corporation. It functions essentially as a medium through which brokerage firms, exchanges, and other clearing corporations reconcile accounts with each other. *See also* CONTINU-OUS NET SETTLEMENT.

NATIONAL STOCK EXCHANGE (NSE) established in India in 1994 to provide a more transparent alternative to the Bombay Stock Exchange. Creation of a wholesale debt market was concurrent with its establishment. NSE serves as a national exchange, integrating the country's stock markets through nationwide automated on-line screen operations and electronic clearing and settlement. NSE is India's second-largest stock exchange. Settlement, on an account period basis, takes one week. Trading hours: 10 A.M. to 2:30 P.M., Monday through Friday, with a carry-forward session on Saturday from 11 A.M. to 3:30 P.M.

NEARBYS months of futures or options contracts that are nearest to delivery (for futures) or expiration (for options). For example, in January, futures and options contracts settling in February and March would be considered nearbys. In general, nearby contracts are far more actively traded than contracts for more distant months. *See also* FURTHEST MONTH, NEAREST MONTH.

NEAREST MONTH in commodity futures or OPTION trading, the expiration dates, expressed as months, closest to the present. For a commodity or an option that had delivery or expiration dates available in September, December, March, and June, for instance, the nearest month would be September if a trade were being made in August. Nearest month contracts are always more heavily traded than FURTHEST MONTH contracts.

NEAR MONEY CASH EQUIVALENTS and other assets that are easily convertible into cash. Some examples are government securities, bank TIME DEPOSITS, and MONEY MARKET FUND shares. Bonds close to REDEMPTION date are also called near money.

NEGATIVE AMORTIZATION financing arrangement in which monthly payments are less than the true amortized amounts and the loan balance increases over the term of the loan rather than decreases; the interest shortage is added to the unpaid principal. In some cases, the interest shortage is added back to the loan and payable at maturity. For example, amortized payments for the first six months of a 30-year mortgage loan would be based on a 13% rate, but interest would be charged against equity at 18%; this rate charge would fluctuate every six-month period. In some loans, the negative amounts may be made up by applying such deficits against the borrower's down payment equity. Federal law requires mortgage lenders to make sure that borrowers understand the potential impact of negative amortization in several interest rate scenarios through a series of extensive disclosure documents.

NEGATIVE CARRY situation in which the cost of money borrowed to finance securities or financial futures positions is higher than the return on those positions. For example, if an investor borrowed at 10% to finance, or "carry," a bond yielding 8%, the bond position would have a negative carry. Negative carry does not necessarily mean a loss to the investor, however, and a positive yield can result on an aftertax basis. In this case, the yield from the 8% bond may be tax-exempt, whereas interest on the 10% loan is tax-deductible. In commodities, this would occur in any month in a BACKWARDATION where the price is higher than the spot month. With the negative carry, if the investor holds the physical position in copper, for example, it will continue to lose value.

NEGATIVE CASH FLOW situation in which a business spends more cash than it receives through earnings or other transactions in an accounting period. *See also* CASH FLOW.

NEGATIVE INCOME TAX proposed system of providing financial aid to poverty-level individuals and families, using the mechanisms already in place to collect income taxes. After filing a tax return showing income below subsistence levels, instead of paying an income tax, low-income people would receive a direct subsidy, called a negative income tax, sufficient to bring them up to the subsistence level.

NEGATIVE PLEDGE CLAUSE negative covenant or promise in an INDENTURE agreement that states the corporation will not pledge any of its assets if doing so would result in less security to the debtholders covered under the indenture agreement. Also called *covenant of equal coverage.*

NEGATIVE WORKING CAPITAL situation in which the current liabilities of a firm exceed its current assets. For example, if the total of cash, MARKETABLE SECURITIES, ACCOUNTS RECEIVABLE and notes receivable, inventory, and other current assets is less than the total of ACCOUNTS PAYABLE, short-term notes payable, long-term debt due in one year, and other current liabilities, the firm has a negative working capital. Unless the condition is corrected, the firm will not be able to pay debts when due, threatening its ability to keep operating and possibly resulting in bankruptcy.

To remedy a negative working capital position, a firm has these alternatives: (1) it can convert a long-term asset into a current asset—for example, by selling a piece of equipment or a building, by liquidating a long-term investment, or by renegotiating a long-term loan receivable; (2) it can convert short-term liabilities into long-term liabilities—for example, by negotiating the substitution of a current account payable with a long-term note payable; (3) it can borrow long term; (4) it can obtain additional equity through a stock issue or other sources of paid-in capital; (5) it can retain or "plow back" profits. *See also* WORKING CAPITAL.

NEGATIVE YIELD CURVE situation in which yields on short-term securities are higher than those on long-term securities of the same quality. Normally, short-term rates are lower than long-term rates because those who commit their money for longer periods are taking more risk. But if interest rates climb high enough, borrowers become unwilling to lock themselves into high rates for long periods and borrow short-term instead. Therefore, yields rise on short-term funds and fall or remain stable on long-term funds. Also called an INVERTED YIELD CURVE. *See also* YIELD CURVE.

NEGOTIABLE
In general:
1. something that can be sold or transferred to another party in exchange for money or as settlement of an obligation.
2. matter of mutual concern to one or more parties that involves conditions to be worked out to the satisfaction of the parties. As examples: In a lender-borrower arrangement, the interest rate may be negotiable; in securities sales, brokerage commissions are now negotiable, having historically been fixed; and in divorce cases involving children, the terms of visiting rights are usually negotiable.
Finance: instrument meeting the qualifications of the Uniform Commercial Code dealing with negotiable instruments. *See* NEGOTIABLE INSTRUMENT.
Investments: type of security the title to which is transferable by delivery. A stock certificate with the stock power properly signed is negotiable, for example.

NEGOTIABLE CERTIFICATE OF DEPOSIT large-dollar-amount, short-term certificate of deposit. Such certificates are issued by large banks and bought mainly by corporations and institutional investors. They are payable either to the bearer or to the order of the depositor, and, being NEGOTIABLE, they enjoy an active SECONDARY MARKET, where they trade in round lots of $5 million. Although they can be issued in any denomination from $100,000 up, the typical amount is $1 million.

They have a minimum original maturity of 14 days; most original maturities are under six months. Also called a JUMBO CERTIFICATE OF DEPOSIT.

NEGOTIABLE INSTRUMENT unconditional order or promise to pay an amount of money, easily transferable from one person to another. Examples: check, promissory note, draft (bill of exchange). The Uniform Commercial Code requires that for an instrument to be negotiable it must be signed by the maker or drawer, must contain an unconditional promise or order to pay a specific amount of money, must be payable on demand or at a specified future time, and must be payable to order or to the bearer.

NEGOTIABLE ORDER OF WITHDRAWAL a bank or savings and loan withdrawal ticket that is a NEGOTIABLE INSTRUMENT. The accounts from which such withdrawals can be made, called NOW accounts, are thus, in effect, interest-bearing checking accounts. They were first introduced in the late 1970s and became available nationally in January 1980. In the early and mid-1980s the interest rate on NOW accounts was capped at 5½%; the cap was phased out in the late 1980s. *See also* SUPER NEGOTIABLE ORDER OF WITHDRAWAL (NOW) ACCOUNT.

NEGOTIATED COMMISSION brokerage COMMISSION that is determined through negotiation. Prior to 1975, commissions were fixed. Since then, brokerage firms have been free to charge what they want and, although they have minimums and commission schedules, will negotiate commissions on large transactions.

NEGOTIATED UNDERWRITING underwriting of new securities issue in which the SPREAD between the purchase price paid to the issuer and the public offering price is determined through negotiation rather than multiple competitive bidding. The spread, which represents the compensation to the investment bankers participating in the underwriting (collectively called the *syndicate),* is negotiated between the issuing company and the MANAGING UNDERWRITER, with the consent of the group. Most corporate stock and bond issues and municipal revenue bond issues are priced through negotiation, whereas municipal general obligation bonds and new issues of public utilities are generally priced through competitive bidding. Competitive bidding is mandatory for new issues of public utilities holding companies. *See also* COMPETITIVE BID.

NEO abbreviation for *nonequity options.* This refers to options contracts on foreign currencies, bonds and other debt issues, commodities, metals, and stock indexes. In contrast, equity options have individual stocks as underlying values.

NEST EGG assets put aside for a person's retirement. Such assets are usually invested conservatively to provide the retiree with a secure standard of living for the rest of his or her life. Investment in an INDIVIDUAL RETIREMENT ACCOUNT would be considered part of a nest egg.

NET

In general: figure remaining after all relevant deductions have been made from the gross amount. For example: net sales are equal to gross sales minus discounts, returns, and allowances; net profit is gross profit less operating (sales, general, and administrative) expenses; net worth is assets (worth) less liabilities.

Investments: dollar difference between the proceeds from the sale of a security and the seller's adjusted cost of acquisition—that is, the gain or loss.

As a verb:

1. to arrive at the difference between additions and subtractions or plus amounts and minus amounts. For example, in filing tax returns, capital losses are netted against capital gains.

2. to realize a net profit, as in "last year we netted a million dollars after taxes."

NET AFTERTAX GAIN capital gain after income taxes.

NET ASSETS difference between a company's total assets and liabilities; another way of saying *owner's equity* or NET WORTH. *See* ASSET COVERAGE for a discussion of net asset value per unit of bonds, preferred stock, or common stock.

NET ASSET VALUE (NAV)
1. in mutual funds, the market value of a fund share, synonymous with *bid price*. In the case of no-load funds, the NAV, market price, and offering price are all the same figure, which the public pays to buy shares; load fund market or offer prices are quoted after adding the sales charge to the net asset value. NAV is calculated by most funds after the close of the exchanges each day by taking the closing market value of all securities owned plus all other assets such as cash, subtracting all liabilities, then dividing the result (total net assets) by the total number of shares outstanding. The number of shares outstanding can vary each day depending on the number of purchases and redemptions.
2. book value of a company's different classes of securities, usually stated as net asset value per bond, net asset value per share of preferred stock, and net book value per common share of common stock. The formula for computing net asset value is total assets less any INTANGIBLE ASSET less all liabilities and securities having a prior claim, divided by the number of units outstanding (i.e., bonds, preferred shares, or common shares). *See* BOOK VALUE for a discussion of how these values are calculated and what they mean. *See also* DEFINED ASSET FUNDS.

NET CAPITAL REQUIREMENT Securities and Exchange Commission requirement that member firms as well as nonmember broker-dealers in securities maintain a maximum ratio of indebtedness to liquid capital of 15 to 1; also called *net capital rule* and *net capital ratio*. Indebtedness covers all money owed to a firm, including MARGIN loans and commitments to purchase securities, one reason new public issues are spread among members of underwriting syndicates. Liquid capital includes cash and assets easily converted into cash.

NET CHANGE difference between the last trading price on a stock, bond, commodity, or mutual fund from one day to the next. The net change in individual stock prices is listed in newspaper financial pages. The designation +2½, for example, means that a stock's final price on that day was $2.50 higher than the final price on the previous trading day. The net changes in prices of NASDAQ STOCK MARKET stocks is usually the difference between bid prices from one day to the next.

NET CURRENT ASSETS difference between current assets and current liabilities; another name for WORKING CAPITAL. Some security analysts divide this figure (after subtracting preferred stock, if any) by the number of common shares outstanding to arrive at working capital per share. Believing working capital per share to be a conservative measure of LIQUIDATING VALUE (on the theory that fixed and other noncurrent assets would more than compensate for any shrinkage in current assets if assets were to be sold), they compare it with the MARKET VALUE of the company's shares. If the net current assets per share figure, or "minimum liquidating value," is higher than the market price, these analysts view the common shares as a bargain (assuming, of course, that the company is not losing money and that its assets are conservatively valued). Other analysts believe this theory ignores the efficiency of capital markets generally and, specifically, obligations such as pension plans, which are not reported as balance sheet liabilities under present accounting rules.

NET EARNINGS *see* NET INCOME.

NET ESTATE *see* GROSS ESTATE.

NET INCOME
In general: sum remaining after all expenses have been met or deducted; synonymous with *net earnings* and with *net profit* or *net loss* (depending on whether the figure is positive or negative).

For a business: difference between total sales and total costs and expenses. Total costs comprise cost of goods sold including depreciation; total expenses comprise selling, general, and administrative expenses, plus INCOME DEDUCTIONS. Net income is usually specified as to whether it is before income taxes or after income taxes. Net income after taxes is the *bottom line* referred to in popular vernacular. It is out of this figure that dividends are normally paid. See *also* OPERATING PROFIT (OR LOSS).

For an individual: gross income less expenses incurred to produce gross income. Those expenses are mostly deductible for tax purposes.

NET INCOME PER SHARE OF COMMON STOCK amount of profit or earnings allocated to each share of common stock after all costs, taxes, allowances for depreciation, and possible losses have been deducted. Net income per share is stated in dollars and cents and is usually compared with the corresponding period a year earlier. For example, XYZ might report that second-quarter net income per share was $1.20, up from 90 cents in the previous year's second quarter. Also known as *earnings per common share* (EPS).

NET INCOME TO NET WORTH RATIO *see* RETURN ON EQUITY.

NET INTEREST COST (NIC) total amount of interest that a corporate or municipal bond entity will end up paying when issuing a debt obligation. The net interest cost factors in the coupon rate, any premiums or discounts, and reduces this to an average annual rate for the number of years until the bond matures or is callable. Underwriters compete to offer issuers the lowest NIC when they bid for the deal. The underwriting syndicate with the lowest NIC is normally awarded the contract.

NET INVESTMENT INCOME PER SHARE income received by an investment company from dividends and interest on securities investments during an accounting period, less management fees and administrative expenses and divided by the number of outstanding shares. Short-term trading profits (net profits from securities held for less than six months) are considered dividend income. The dividend and interest income is received by the investment company, which in turn pays shareholders the net investment income in the form of dividends pro-rated according to each holder's share in the total PORTFOLIO.

NET LEASE financial lease stipulating that the user (rather than the owner) of the leased property shall pay all maintenance costs, taxes, insurance, and other expenses. Many real estate and oil and gas limited partnerships are structured as net leases with ESCALATOR CLAUSES, to provide limited partners with both depreciation tax benefits and appreciation of investment, minus cash expenses. *See also* GROSS LEASE.

NET OPERATING LOSS (NOL) tax term for the excess of business expenses over income in a tax year. Under TAX LOSS CARRYBACK, CARRYFORWARD provisions, NOLs can (if desired) be carried back three years and forward 15 years.

NET PRESENT VALUE (NPV) method used in evaluating investments whereby the net present value of all cash outflows (such as the cost of the investment) and cash inflows (returns) is calculated using a given discount rate, usually a REQUIRED RATE OF RETURN. An investment is acceptable if the NPV is positive. In capital budgeting, the discount rate used is called the HURDLE RATE and is usually equal to the INCREMENTAL COST OF CAPITAL.

NET PROCEEDS amount (usually cash) received from the sale or disposition of property, from a loan, or from the sale or issuance of securities after deduction of all costs incurred in the transaction. In computing the gain or loss on a securities transaction for tax purposes, the amount of the sale is the amount of the net proceeds.

NET PROFIT *see* NET INCOME.

NET PROFIT MARGIN   NET INCOME as a percentage of NET SALES. A measure of operating efficiency and pricing strategy, the ratio is usually computed using net profit before extraordinary items and taxes—that is, net sales less COST OF GOODS SOLD and SELLING, GENERAL, AND ADMINISTRATIVE (SG&A) EXPENSES.

NET QUICK ASSETS cash, MARKETABLE SECURITIES, and ACCOUNTS RECEIVABLE, minus current liabilities. *See also* QUICK RATIO.

NET REALIZED CAPITAL GAINS PER SHARE amount of CAPITAL GAINS that an investment company realized on the sale of securities, net of CAPITAL LOSSES, and divided by the number of outstanding shares. Such net gains are distributed annually to shareholders in proportion to their shares in the total portfolio. The distributions are eligible for favorable CAPITAL GAINS TAX rates if the positions were held for at least 12 months. If held for less than 12 months, the gains would be subject to regular income taxes at the shareholder's tax bracket. *See also* REGULATED INVESTMENT COMPANY.

NET SALES gross sales less returns and allowances, freight out, and cash discounts allowed. Cash discounts allowed is seen less frequently than in past years, since it has become conventional to report as net sales the amount finally received from the customer. Returns are merchandise returned for credit; allowances are deductions allowed by the seller for merchandise not received or received in damaged condition; freight out is shipping expense passed on to the customer.

NET TANGIBLE ASSETS PER SHARE total assets of a company, less any INTANGIBLE ASSET such as goodwill, patents, and trademarks, less all liabilities and the par value of preferred stock, divided by the number of common shares outstanding. *See* BOOK VALUE for a discussion of what this calculation means and how it can be varied to apply to bonds or preferred stock shares. *See also* NET ASSET VALUE.

NET TRANSACTION securities transaction in which the buyer and seller do not pay fees or commissions. For instance, when an investor buys a new issue, no commission is due. If the stock is initially offered at $15 a share, the buyer's total cost is $15 per share.

NETWORK A *see* CONSOLIDATED TAPE.

NETWORK B *see* CONSOLIDATED TAPE.

NET WORKING CAPITAL CURRENT ASSETS minus CURRENT LIABILITIES. Usually simply called WORKING CAPITAL.

NET WORTH amount by which assets exceed liabilities. For a corporation, net worth is also known as *stockholders' equity* or NET ASSETS. For an individual, net worth is the total value of all possessions, such as a house, stocks, bonds, and other securities, minus all outstanding debts, such as mortgage and revolving-credit loans. In order to qualify for certain high-risk investments, brokerage houses require that an individual's net worth must be at or above a certain dollar level.

NET YIELD RATE OF RETURN on a security net of out-of-pocket costs associated with its purchase, such as commissions or markups. *See also* MARKDOWN.

NEW ACCOUNT REPORT document filled out by a broker that details vital facts about a new client's financial circumstances and investment objectives. The report may be updated if there are material changes in a client's financial position. Based on the report, a client may or may not be deemed eligible for certain types of risky investments, such as commodity trading or highly leveraged LIMITED PARTNERSHIP deals. *See also* KNOW YOUR CUSTOMER.

NEW HIGH/NEW LOW stock prices that have hit the highest or lowest prices in the last year. Next to each stock's listing in a newspaper will be an indication of a new high with a letter "u" or a new low with the letter "d." Newspapers publish the total number of new highs and new lows each day on the New York and American Stock Exchanges and on the NASDAQ Stock Market. Technical analysts pay great attention to the trend of new highs and new lows. If the number of new highs is expanding, that is considered a bullish indicator. If the number of new lows is rising, that is considered bearish. Many analysts also track the ratio of new highs to new lows as a reflection of the general direction of the stock market.

NEW ISSUE stock or bond being offered to the public for the first time, the distribution of which is covered by Securities and Exchange Commission (SEC) rules. New issues may be initial public offerings by previously private companies or additional stock or bond issues by companies already public and often listed on the exchanges. New PUBLIC OFFERINGS must be registered with the SEC. PRIVATE PLACEMENTS avoid SEC registration if a LETTER OF INTENT establishes that the securities are purchased for investment and not for resale to the public. *See also* HOT ISSUE; LETTER SECURITY; UNDERWRITE.

NEW LISTING security that has just begun to trade on a stock or bond exchange. A new listing on the New York or American Stock Exchange must meet all LISTING REQUIREMENTS, and may either be an INITIAL PUBLIC OFFERING or a company whose shares have previously traded on the NASDAQ STOCK MARKET. New listings on the New York and American Stock Exchanges or a non-U.S. market carry the letter "n" next to their listing in newspaper tables for one year from the date they started trading on the exchange.

NEW MONEY amount of additional long-term financing provided by a new issue or issues in excess of the amount of a maturing issue or by issues that are being refunded.

NEW MONEY PREFERRED PREFERRED STOCK issued after October 1, 1942, when the tax exclusion for corporate investors receiving preferred stock dividends was raised from 60% to 85%, to equal the exclusion on common stock dividends. The change benefited financial institutions, such as insurance companies, which are limited in the amount of common stocks they can hold, typically 5% of assets. New money preferreds offer an opportunity to gain tax advantages over bond investments, which have fully taxable interest. The corporate tax exclusion on dividends is currently 70%.

NEW YORK COTTON EXCHANGE (NYCE) oldest commodity exchange in New York, founded in 1870 by a group of cotton brokers and merchants. The exchange trades futures and options on cotton, frozen concentrated orange juice and potatoes, as well as an array of interest rate, currency and index futures and options through two subsidiaries. NYCE and the COFFEE, SUGAR & COCOA EXCHANGE merged in 1998, with each exchange retaining its identity and derivative products but operating under a newly-created holding company, the Board of Trade of the City of New York. The FINEX division was created in 1985 as the exchange's financial futures and options division; FINEX Europe, a trading floor in Dublin, Ireland, was established in 1994 to trade FINEX products during European business hours. In December 1993, NYCE acquired the NEW YORK FUTURES EXCHANGE (NYFE) from the NEW YORK STOCK EXCHANGE, as a wholly-owned subsidiary. The exchange collaborates with Cantor Fitzgerald Co. on an electronic futures exchange, combining NYCE's supervision and clearing expertise and Cantor Fitzgerald's execution and brokerage services. NYCE trading hours: 9:45 A.M. to 2:15 P.M., Monday to Friday. *See also* SECURITIES AND COMMODITIES EXCHANGES.

NEW YORK CURB EXCHANGE *see* AMERICAN STOCK EXCHANGE.

NEW YORK FUTURES EXCHANGE (NYFE) wholly-owned subsidiary of the NEW YORK COTTON EXCHANGE, acquired from the NEW YORK STOCK EXCHANGE (NYSE) in December 1993. NYFE trades futures and futures options on the NYSE Composite Index, based on its approximately 2000 common stocks; the CRB/Bridge Index, based on the Commodity Research Bureau/Bridge Index of 21 commodity components; and the PSE (Pacific Stock Exchange) Technology Index, representing 100 listed and over-the-counter stocks from 15 different technology industries. NYSE Large Composite Index futures has a value of the NYSE Index times $1000, double the regular NYSE Composite Index future. Trading hours: Monday to Friday, 9:15 A.M. to 4:15 P.M. *See also* SECURITIES AND COMMODITIES EXCHANGES.

NEW YORK MERCANTILE EXCHANGE (NYMEX) world's largest physical commodity futures exchange, following its 1994 merger with COMEX (Commodity Exchange). The exchange operates as two divisions since the merger. The exchange and the INTERNATIONAL PETROLEUM EXCHANGE (IPE) cooperate in an advanced electronic trading system designed to serve as a standard for the oil, natural gas, electricity and coal industries, based on IPE's Energy Trading System (ETS). The NYMEX division trades light, sweet crude oil, heating oil, New York Harbor unleaded gasoline, natural gas, electricity and platinum futures and options; sour crude, Gulf Coast unleaded gasoline, propane and palladium futures; and crack spread options (intercommodity spreads) for heating oil-crude oil and New York Harbor unleaded gasoline-crude oil. The COMEX division trades futures and options in aluminum, coal, copper, gold, silver and the FTSE Eurotop 100 Index, and five-day gold, five-day copper, and five-day silver options. Trading is by open outcry, and is conducted on the ACCESS after hours electronic trading system: Monday through Thursday, 4 P.M. to 8 A.M., and Sunday, 7 P.M. to 8 A.M. for copper, gold, and silver futures; and Monday to Thursday, 4 P.M. to 8 A.M. and Sunday from 7 P.M. to 8 A.M., trading crude oil, heating oil, New York Harbor gasoline, propane, sour crude, natural gas and electricity futures. NYMEX division trading hours are Monday through Friday, from 8:10 A.M. to 3:30 P.M. COMEX division hours are Monday through Friday, from 8:10 A.M. to 3 P.M. (FTSE Eurotop trades from 5:30 A.M. to 11:30 A.M.). *See also* SECURITIES AND COMMODITIES EXCHANGES.

NEW YORK STOCK EXCHANGE (NYSE) founded in 1792, it is the oldest and largest stock exchange in the U.S., located at 11 Wall Street in New York City; also known as the *Big Board* and *The Exchange*. NYSE is an unincorporated association governed by a board of directors which is headed by a full-time paid chairman and is composed of 24 individuals representing the public and the exchange membership in about equal proportion. Staff groups handle specialized functions, such as legal issues, government relations, and economic research; certain operational functions are handled by affiliated corporations, such as Depository Trust Company, National Securities Clearing Corporation (NSCC), and Securities Industry Automation Corporation (SIAC). Total voting membership is currently fixed at 1366 "seats," which are owned by individuals, usually partners or officers of securities firms. The number of firms represented is over 400, more than 30 of which are specialists responsible for the maintenance of an orderly market in the securities they handle. Most members execute orders for the public, although a small number—called registered competitive market makers—deal exclusively for their own accounts. More than 3000 companies are listed on the NYSE, representing large firms meeting the exchange's stringent LISTING REQUIREMENTS. STOCKS, BONDS, WARRANTS, OPTIONS, and RIGHTS are traded on the floor of the exchange at 17 figure eight-shaped installations, called trading posts. Currently, NYSE-listed shares make up more than half of the total dollar volume in shares traded on all U.S. markets. Trading hours: 9:30 A.M. to 4:00 P.M., Monday through Friday. *See also* SECURITIES AND COMMODIITIES EXCHANGES.

NEW YORK STOCK EXCHANGE INDEX *see* STOCK INDEXES AND AVERAGES.

NEW ZEALAND FUTURES AND OPTIONS EXCHANGE electronic screen-trading exchange. A wholly owned subsidiary of the SYDNEY FUTURES EXCHANGE, the New Zealand Futures and Options Exchange allows SFE members access to the exchange's markets through SFE's Sycom trading system. The Forty Index Futures (FIF) contract is based on the NZSE 40 Capital Index; options are traded on the futures. Futures are traded on New Zealand Electricity; options are traded on equities. Futures and options are traded on the NZSE-10 Index, 90-day bank bills, New Zealand 3-year, and 10-year government stock.

NEW ZEALAND STOCK EXCHANGE automated, screen-based national trading system, based in Wellington. The principal index is the NZSE-40 Index of the 40 largest and most liquid stocks, weighted by total market capitalization. The NZSE-30 Selection Index includes the 30 stocks in the NZSE-40 with the largest float capital. Trading hours: 9:30 A.M. to 3:30 P.M., Monday through Friday, with a pre-opening session from 8:30 A.M. to 9:30 A.M. Clearing is through an automated broker-to-broker accounting system. Settlement is for cash on demand, unless otherwise stipulated. Maximum delivery time for a contract is five business days from the trade date.

NICHE particular specialty in which a firm has garnered a large market share. Often, the market will be small enough so that the firm will not attract very much competition. For example, a company that makes a line of specialty chemicals for use by only the petroleum industry is said to have a niche in the chemical industry. Stock analysts frequently favor such companies, since their profit margins can often be wider than those of firms facing more competition.

NICS acronym for *newly industrialized countries,* which are countries that have rapidly developing industrial economies. Some examples of NICS are Hong Kong, Singapore, Malaysia, South Korea, Mexico, Argentina, and Chile. NICS typically have instituted free-market policies which encourage exports to traditional Western industrialized countries and seek investment from Western corporations. Most NICS have increasingly been reducing trade barriers to imports from Western firms.

NIFTY FIFTY 50 stocks most favored by institutions. The membership of this group is constantly changing, although companies that continue to produce consistent earnings growth over a long time tend to remain institutional favorites. Nifty Fifty stocks also tend to have higher than market average price/earnings ratios, since their growth prospects are well recognized by institutional investors. The Nifty Fifty stocks were particularly famous in the bull markets of the 1960s and early 1970s, when many of the price/earnings ratios soared to 50 or more. *See also* PRICE/EARNINGS RATIO.

NIKKEI INDEX *See* NIKKEI STOCK AVERAGE.

NIKKEI STOCK AVERAGE index of 225 leading stocks traded on the Tokyo Stock Exchange. Called the Nikkei Dow Jones Stock Average until it was renamed in May 1985, it is similar to the Dow Jones Industrial Average because it is composed of representative BLUE CHIP companies (termed *first-section* companies in Japan) and is a PRICE-WEIGHTED INDEX. That means that the movement of each stock, in yen or dollars respectively, is weighed equally regardless of its market capitalization. The Nikkei Stock Average, informally called the Nikkei

Index and often still referred to as the Nikkei Dow, is published by the *Nihon Keizai Shimbun (Japan Economic Journal)* and is the most widely quoted Japanese stock index.

Also widely quoted is the Tokyo Stock Price Index (Topix) of all issues listed in the First Section.

NINE-BOND RULE New York Stock Exchange (NYSE) requirement that orders for nine bonds or less be sent to the floor for one hour to seek a market. Since bond trading tends to be inactive on the NYSE (because of large institutional holdings and because many of the listed bond trades are handled OVER THE COUNTER), Rule 396 is designed to obtain the most favorable price for small investors. Customers may request that the rule be waived, but the broker-dealer in such cases must then act only as a BROKER and not as a PRINCIPAL (dealer for his own account).

19c3 STOCK stock listed on a national securities exchange, such as the New York Stock Exchange or the American Stock Exchange, after April 26, 1979, and thus exempt from Securities and Exchange Commission rule 19c3 prohibiting exchange members from engaging in OFF-BOARD trading.

NO-ACTION LETTER letter requested from the Securities and Exchange Commission wherein the Commission agrees to take neither civil nor criminal action with respect to the specific activity and circumstances. LIMITED PARTNERSHIPS designed as TAX SHELTERS, which are frequently venturing in uncharted legal territory, often seek no-action letters to clear novel marketing or financing techniques.

NO-BRAINER term used to describe a market the direction of which has become obvious, and therefore requires little or no analysis. This means that most of the stocks will go up in a strong bull market and fall in a bear market, so that it does not matter very much which stock investors buy or sell.

NOB SPREAD acronym for *notes over bonds* spread. Traders buying or selling a NOB spread are trying to profit from changes in the relationship between yields in Treasury notes, which are intermediate-term instruments maturing in 2 to 10 years, and Treasury bonds, which are long-term instruments maturing in 15 or more years. Most people trade the NOB Spread by buying or selling futures contracts on Treasury notes and Treasury bonds. *See also* MOB SPREAD.

NO-FAULT concept used in divorce law and automobile insurance whereby the parties involved are not required to prove blame in an action. The concept recognizes irreconcilable differences as a basis for divorce. In automobile insurance, the accident victim collects directly from his or her own insurance company for medical and hospital expenses, regardless of who was at fault. No-fault statutes vary widely among states that have them. No-fault automobile insurance typically contains provisions aimed at discouraging frivolous lawsuits.

NOISE stock-market activity caused by PROGRAM TRADES and other phenomena not reflective of general sentiment.

NO-LOAD FUND MUTUAL FUND offered by an open-end investment company that imposes no sales charge (load) on its shareholders. Investors buy shares in no-load funds directly from the fund companies, rather than through a BROKER, as is done in load funds. Many no-load fund families (*see* FAMILY OF FUNDS) allow switching of assets between stock, bond, and money market funds. The listing of the price of a no-load fund in a newspaper is accompanied with the designation NL. The net asset value, market price, and offer prices of this type of fund are exactly the same, since there is no sales charge. *See also* LOAD FUND.

NO-LOAD STOCK shares available for DIRECT PURCHASE from the issuing companies, thus avoiding brokers and sales commissions. Such shares are typically offered as a part of a company's DIVIDEND REINVESTMENT PLAN to encourage long-term investment. Prices are based on an average of recent market prices and may not be as low as the current market price. Broker commissions are payable if and when the shares are sold.

NOMINAL DOLLARS dollars unadjusted for inflation. For example, economists will refer to a product that cost 100 nominal dollars several years ago, and now costs $150. However, adjusted for inflation, the product's current price may be much higher or lower. Most financial statements are reported in nominal dollars.

NOMINAL EXERCISE PRICE EXERCISE PRICE (strike price) of a GOVERNMENT NATIONAL MORTGAGE ASSOCIATION (GNMA or Ginnie Mae) option contract, obtained by multiplying the unpaid principal balance on a Ginnie Mae certificate by the ADJUSTED EXERCISE PRICE. For example, if the unpaid principal balance is $96,000 and the adjusted exercise price is 58, the nominal exercise price is $55,680.

NOMINAL INCOME income unadjusted for changes in the PURCHASING POWER OF THE DOLLAR. GENERALLY ACCEPTED ACCOUNTING PRINCIPLES (GAAP) require certain large, publicly held companies to provide supplementary information adjusting income from continuing operations for changing prices. FINANCIAL ACCOUNTING STANDARDS BOARD (FASB) Statement Number 89 removed the requirement to present general purchasing power and current cost/constant dollar supplement statements, however.

NOMINAL INTEREST RATE *see* NOMINAL YIELD.

NOMINAL QUOTATION bid and offer prices given by a market maker for the purpose of valuation, not as an invitation to trade. Securities industry rules require that nominal quotations be specifically identified as such; usually this is done by prefixing the quote with the letters FYI (FOR YOUR INFORMATION) or FVO (for valuation only).

NOMINAL RATE OF INTEREST rate of interest unadjusted for inflation. The actual interest rate charged by a bank on a loan is in nominal dollars. This is in contrast to interest rates that have been adjusted for either past or projected inflation, called REAL INTEREST RATES.

NOMINAL YIELD annual dollar amount of income received from a fixed-income security divided by the PAR VALUE of the security and stated as a percentage. Thus a bond that pays $90 a year and has a par value of $1000 has a nominal yield of 9%, called its *coupon rate*. Similarly, a preferred stock that pays a $9 annual dividend and has a par value of $100 has a nominal yield of 9%. Only when a stock or bond is bought exactly at par value is the nominal yield equal to the actual yield. Since market prices of fixed-income securities go down when market interest rates go up and vice versa, the actual yield, which is determined by the market price and coupon rate (nominal yield), will be higher when the purchase price is below par value and lower when the purchase price is above par value. *See also* RATE OF RETURN.

NOMINEE person or firm, such as a bank official or brokerage house, into whose name securities or other properties are transferred by agreement. Securities held in STREET NAME, for example, are registered in the name of a BROKER (nominee) to facilitate transactions, although the customer remains the true owner.

NONACCREDITED INVESTOR investor who does not meet the net worth requirements of SEC Regulation D. Under Rules 505 and 506 of Regulation D, an investment can be offered to a maximum of 35 nonaccredited investors. Such investors tend to be wealthy and sophisticated, and therefore the SEC feels they need less investor protection than smaller, less sophisticated investors.

NONCALLABLE preferred stock or bond that cannot be redeemed at the option of the issuer. A bond may offer CALL PROTECTION for a particular length of time, such as ten years. After that, the issuer may redeem the bond if it chooses and can justify doing so. U.S. government bond obligations are not callable until close to maturity. Provisions for noncallability are spelled out in detail in a bond's INDENTURE agreement or in the prospectus issued at the time a new preferred stock is floated. Bond yields are often quoted to the first date at which the bonds could be called. *See also* YIELD TO CALL.

NONCLEARING MEMBER member firm of the New York Stock Exchange or another organized exchange that does not have the operational facilities for clearing transactions and thus pays a fee to have the services performed by another member firm, called a *clearing member.* The clearing process involves comparison and verification of information between the buying and selling brokers and then the physical delivery of certificates in exchange for payment, called the *settlement.*

NONCOMPETITIVE BID method of buying Treasury bills without having to meet the high minimum purchase requirements of the regular DUTCH AUCTION; also called *noncompetitive tender.* The process of bidding for Treasury bills is split into two parts: competitive and noncompetitive bids.

COMPETITIVE BIDS are entered by large government securities dealers and brokers, who buy millions of dollars worth of bills. They offer the best price they can for the securities, and the highest bids are accepted by the Treasury in what is called the Dutch auction.

Noncompetitive bids are submitted by smaller investors through a Federal Reserve Bank, the Bureau of Federal Debt, or certain commercial banks. These bids will be executed at the average of the prices paid in all the competitive bids accepted by the Treasury. The minimum noncompetitive bid for a Treasury bill is $10,000. *See also* TREASURY DIRECT.

NONCONTESTABILITY CLAUSE provision found in insurance contracts stipulating that policyholders cannot be denied coverage after a specific period of time, usually two years, even if the policyholder provided inaccurate or even fraudulent information in his or her insurance application. In order to contest the policy, the insurer must find out about the incorrect information before the clause goes into effect. *See* INCONTESTABILITY CLAUSE.

NONCONTRIBUTORY PENSION PLAN pension plan that is totally funded by the employer, and to which employees are not expected to contribute. Most DEFINED BENEFIT PENSION PLANS are noncontributory. In contrast, DEFINED CONTRIBUTION PENSION PLANS offer employees the choice to contribute to a plan such as a 401(k) or 403(b).

NONCUMULATIVE term describing a preferred stock issue in which unpaid dividends do not accrue. Such issues contrast with CUMULATIVE PREFERRED issues, where unpaid dividends accumulate and must be paid before dividends on common shares. Most preferred issues are cumulative. On a noncumulative preferred, omitted dividends will, as a rule, never be paid. Some older railroad preferred stocks are of this type.

NONCURRENT ASSET asset not expected to be converted into cash, sold, or exchanged within the normal operating cycle of the firm, usually one year. Examples of noncurrent assets include FIXED ASSETS, such as real estate, machinery, and other equipment; LEASEHOLD IMPROVEMENTS; INTANGIBLE ASSETS, such as goodwill, patents, and trademarks; notes receivable after one year; other investments; miscellaneous assets not meeting the definition of a CURRENT ASSET. Prepaid expenses (also called DEFERRED CHARGES or *deferred expenses),* which include such items as rent paid in advance, prepaid insurance premiums, and subscriptions, are usually considered current assets by accountants. Credit analysts, however, prefer to classify these expenses as noncurrent assets, since prepayments do not represent asset strength and protection in the way that other current assets do, with their convertibility into cash during the normal operating cycle and their liquidation value should operations be terminated.

NONCURRENT LIABILITY LIABILITY due after one year.

NONDISCRETIONARY TRUST TRUST where the trustee has no power to determine the amount of distributions to the beneficiary. Contrast with DISCRETIONARY TRUST.

NONFINANCIAL ASSETS assets that are physical, such as REAL ESTATE and PERSONAL PROPERTY.

NON-INTEREST-BEARING NOTE note that makes no periodic interest payments. Instead, the note is sold at a discount and matures at face value. Also called a ZERO-COUPON BOND.

NONMEMBER FIRM brokerage firm that is not a member of an organized exchange. Such firms execute their trades either through member firms, on regional exchanges, or in the THIRD MARKET. *See* MEMBER FIRM; REGIONAL STOCK EXCHANGES.

NONPARTICIPATING LIFE INSURANCE POLICY life insurance policy that does not pay dividends. Policyholders thus do not participate in the interest, dividends, and capital gains earned by the insurer on premiums paid. In contrast, PARTICIPATING INSURANCE POLICIES pay dividends to policyholders from earnings on investments.

NONPARTICIPATING PREFERRED STOCK *see* PARTICIPATING PREFERRED STOCK.

NONPERFORMING ASSET ASSET not effectual in the production of income. In banking, commercial loans 90 days past due and consumer loans 180 days past due are classified as nonperforming.

NONPRODUCTIVE LOAN type of commercial bank loan that increases the amount of spending power in the economy but does not lead directly to increased output; for example, a loan to finance a LEVERAGED BUYOUT. The Federal Reserve has on occasion acted to curtail such lending as one of its early steps in implementing monetary restraint.

NONPUBLIC INFORMATION information about a company, either positive or negative, that will have a material effect on the stock price when it is released to the public. Insiders, such as corporate officers and members of the board of directors, are not allowed to trade on material nonpublic information until it has been released to the public, since they would have an unfair advantage over unsuspecting investors. Some examples of important nonpublic information are an imminent takeover announcement, a soon-to-be-released earnings report that is more favorable than most analysts expect, or the sudden resignation of a key corporate official. *See also* DISCLOSURE; INSIDER.

NONPURPOSE LOAN loan for which securities are pledged as collateral but which is not used to purchase or carry securities. Under Federal Reserve Board

REGULATION U, a borrower using securities as collateral must sign an affidavit called a PURPOSE STATEMENT, indicating the use to which the loan is to be put. Regulation U limits the amount of credit a bank may extend for purchasing and carrying margin securities, where the credit is secured directly or indirectly by stock.

NONQUALIFYING ANNUITY annuity purchased outside of an IRS-approved pension plan. The contributions to such an annuity are made with after-tax dollars. Just as with a QUALIFYING ANNUITY, however, the earnings from the nonqualifying annuity can accumulate tax deferred until withdrawn. Assets may be placed in either a FIXED ANNUITY, a VARIABLE ANNUITY, or a HYBRID ANNUITY.

NONQUALIFYING STOCK OPTION employee stock option not meeting the Internal Revenue Service criteria for QUALIFYING STOCK OPTIONS (INCENTIVE STOCK OPTIONS) and therefore triggering a tax upon EXERCISE. (The issuing employer, however, can deduct the nonqualifying option during the period when it is exercised, whereas it would not have a deduction when a qualifying option is exercised. A STOCK OPTION is a right issued by a corporation to an individual, normally an executive employee, to buy a given amount of shares at a stated price within a specified period of time. Gains realized on the exercise of nonqualifying options are treated as ordinary income in the tax year in which the options are exercised. Qualifying stock options, in contrast, are taxed neither at the time of granting or the time of exercise; only when the underlying stock is sold and a CAPITAL GAIN realized, does a tax event occur.

NONRATED bonds that have not been rated by one or more of the major rating agencies such as STANDARD & POOR'S, MOODY'S INVESTORS SERVICE or FITCH INVESTORS SERVICE. Issues are usually nonrated because they are too small to justify the expense of getting a rating. Nonrated bonds are not necessarily better or worse than rated bonds, though many institutions cannot buy them because they need to hold bonds with an investment-grade rating.

NONRECOURSE LOAN type of financial arrangement used by limited partners in a DIRECT PARTICIPATION PROGRAM, whereby the limited partners finance a portion of their participation with a loan secured by their ownership in the underlying venture. They benefit from the LEVERAGE provided by the loan. In case of default, the lender has no recourse to the assets of the partnership beyond those held by the limited partners who borrowed the money.

NONRECURRING CHARGE one-time expense or WRITE-OFF appearing in a company's financial statement; also called *extraordinary charge.* Nonrecurring charges would include, for example, a major fire or theft, the write-off of a division, and the effect of a change in accounting procedure.

NONREFUNDABLE provision in a bond INDENTURE that either prohibits or sets limits on the issuer's retiring the bonds with the proceeds of a subsequent issue, called REFUNDING. Such a provision often does not rule out refunding altogether but protects bondholders from REDEMPTION until a specified date. Other such provisions may preclude refunding unless new bonds can be issued at a specified lower rate. *See also* CALL PROTECTION.

NONVOTING STOCK corporate securities that do not empower a holder to vote on corporate resolutions or the election of directors. Such stock is sometimes issued in connection with a takeover attempt, when management creates nonvoting shares to dilute the target firm's equity and thereby discourage the merger attempt. Except in very special circumstances, the New York Stock Exchange does not list nonvoting stock. Preferred stock is normally nonvoting stock. *See also* VOTING STOCK; VOTING TRUST CERTIFICATE.

NO-PAR-VALUE STOCK stock with no set (par) value specified in the corporate charter or on the stock certificate; also called *no-par stock*. Companies issuing no-par value shares may carry whatever they receive for them either as part of the CAPITAL STOCK account or as part of the CAPITAL SURPLUS (paid-in capital) account, or both. Whatever amount is carried as capital stock has an implicit value, represented by the number of outstanding shares divided into the dollar amount of capital stock.

The main attraction of no-par stock to issuing corporations, historically, had to do with the fact that many states imposed taxes based on PAR VALUE, while other states, like Delaware, encouraged incorporations with no-par-value stock.

For the investor, there are two reservations: (1) that unwise or inept directors may reduce the value of outstanding shares by accepting bargain basement prices on new issues (shareholders are protected, to some extent, from this by PREEMPTIVE RIGHT—the right to purchase enough of a new issue to protect their power and equity) and (2) that too great an amount of shareholder contributions may be channeled into the capital surplus account, which is restricted by the law of many states from being a source of dividend payments. *See* ILLEGAL DIVIDEND.

Still, no-par stock, along with low-par stock, remains an appealing alternative, from the issuer's standpoint, to par-value shares because of investor confusion of par value and real value.

Most stock issued today is either no-par or low-par value.

NORMAL INVESTMENT PRACTICE history of investment in a customer account with a member of the National Association of Securities Dealers as defined in their rules of fair practice. It is used to test the bona fide PUBLIC OFFERINGS requirement that applies to the allocation of a HOT ISSUE. If the buying customer has a history of purchasing similar amounts in normal circumstances, the sale qualifies as a bona fide public offering and is not in violation of the Rules of Fair Practice. A record of buying only hot issues is not acceptable as normal investment practice. *See also* NASD FORM FR-1.

NORMALIZED EARNINGS earnings, either in the past or the future, that are adjusted for cyclical ups and downs in the economy. Earnings are normalized by analysts by generating a moving average over several years including up and down cycles. Analysts refer to normalized earnings when explaining whether a company's current profits are above or below its long-term trend.

NORMAL MARKET SIZE (NMS) share classification system that in 1991 replaced the alpha, beta, gamma, delta, system brought in with BIG BANG on the INTERNATIONAL STOCK EXCHANGE OF THE U.K. AND THE REPUBLIC OF IRELAND (ISE). The earlier system had unintentionally become a measure of corporate status, strength, and viability. The new system has 12 categories based on the size of the transactions that are normal for each security. The system fixes the size of transactions in which market makers are obligated to deal.

NORMAL RETIREMENT point at which a pension plan participant can retire and immediately receive unreduced benefits. Pension plans can specify age and length-of-service requirements that employees must meet to be eligible for retirement.

NORMAL TRADING UNIT standard minimum size of a trading unit for a particular security; also called a ROUND LOT. For instance, stocks have a normal trading unit of 100 shares, although inactive stocks trade in 10-share round lots. Any securities trade for less than a round lot is called an ODD LOT trade.

NOTE written promise to pay a specified amount to a certain entity on demand or on a specified date. See *also* MUNICIPAL NOTE; PROMISSORY NOTE; TREASURIES.

NOT-FOR-PROFIT type of incorporated organization in which no stockholder or trustee shares in profits or losses and which usually exists to accomplish some charitable, humanitarian, or educational purpose; also called *nonprofit*. Such groups are exempt from corporate income taxes but are subject to other taxes on income-producing property or enterprises. Donations to these groups are usually tax deductible for the donor. Some examples are hospitals, colleges and universities, foundations, and such familiar groups as the Red Cross and Girl Scouts.

NOT HELD instruction (abbreviated NH) on a market order to buy or sell securities, indicating that the customer has given the FLOOR BROKER time and price discretion in executing the best possible trade but will not hold the broker responsible if the best deal is not obtained. Such orders, which are usually for large blocks of securities, were originally designed for placement with specialists, who could hold an order back if they felt prices were going to rise. The Securities and Exchange Commission no longer allows specialists to handle NH orders, leaving floor brokers without any clear alternative except to persuade the customer to change the order to a LIMIT ORDER. The broker can then turn the order over to a SPECIALIST, who could sell pieces of the block to floor traders or buy it for his own account. *See* SPECIALIST BLOCK PURCHASE AND SALE. An older variation of NH is DRT, meaning disregard tape.

NOTICE OF SALE advertisement placed by an issuer of municipal securities announcing its intentions to sell a new issue and inviting underwriters to submit COMPETITIVE BIDS.

NOT RATED indication used by securities rating services (such as STANDARD & POOR'S, MOODY'S INVESTORS SERVICE, or FITCH INVESTORS SERVICE) and mercantile agencies (such as Dun & Bradstreet) to show that a security or a company has not been rated. It has neither negative nor positive implications. The abbreviation NR is used.

NOT-SUFFICIENT-FUNDS CHECK a bank check written against an inadequate balance. Also called *insufficient-funds check* and, informally, a *bounced check.*

NOUVEAU MARCHE equity market unit of the PARIS BOURSE dedicated to innovative, high-growth companies. Nouveau Marche, in turn, is linked to other European markets in EURO.NM, which is modeled on the NASDAQ market in the U.S.

NOVATION
1. agreement to replace one party to a contract with a new party. The novation transfers both rights and duties and requires the consent of both the original and the new party.
2. replacement of an older debt or obligation with a newer one.

NOW ACCOUNT *see* NEGOTIABLE ORDER OF WITHDRAWAL.

NUMISMATIC COIN coin that is valued based on its rarity, age, quantity originally produced, and condition. These coins are bought and sold as individual items within the coin collecting community. Most numismatic coins are legal tender coins that were produced in limited quantities to give them scarcity value. They are historic coins which also can be rare. The current price of gold is a minor factor when dealing with numismatic coins. Premiums are traditionally far higher than those of BULLION COINS, and values fluctuate to a much wider extent. For example, a $5 gold piece may contain $60 worth of gold and may sell for as much as $700. The minimum amount recovered from numismatic coin investments is always either its face value or its metal content. Most coins, however, sell substantially above these amounts. Since the markup over bullion value can vary widely from one dealer to another, investors need to shop around diligently to avoid paying exhorbitant markups.

O

OBLIGATION legal responsibility, as for a DEBT.

OBLIGATION BOND type of mortgage bond in which the face value is greater than the value of the underlying property. The difference compensates the lender for costs exceeding the mortgage value.

OBLIGOR one who has an obligation, such as an issuer of bonds, a borrower of money from a bank or another source, or a credit customer of a business supplier or retailer. The obligor *(obligator, debtor)* is legally bound to pay a debt, including interest, when due.

ODD LOT securities trade made for less than the NORMAL TRADING UNIT (termed a ROUND LOT). In stock trading, any purchase or sale of less than 100 shares is considered an odd lot, although inactive stocks generally trade in round lots of 10 shares. An investor buying or selling an odd lot pays a higher commission rate than someone making a round-lot trade. This odd-lot differential varies among brokers but for stocks is often ⅛ of a point (12½¢) per share. For instance, someone buying 100 shares of XYZ at $70 would pay $70 a share plus commission. At the same time, someone buying only 50 shares of XYZ would pay $70⅛ a share plus commission. *See also* ODD-LOT DEALER; ODD-LOT SHORT-SALE RATIO; ODD-LOT THEORY.

ODD-LOT DEALER originally a dealer who bought round lots of stock and resold it in odd lots to retail brokers who, in turn, accommodated their smaller customers at the regular commission rate plus an extra charge, called the odd-lot differential. The assembling of round lots from odd lots is now a service provided free by New York Stock Exchange specialists to member brokers, and odd-lot transactions can be executed through most brokers serving the retail public. Brokers handling odd lots do, however, receive extra compensation; it varies with the broker, but ⅛ of a point (12½¢) per share in addition to a regular commission is typical. *See also* ODD LOT.

ODD-LOT SHORT-SALE RATIO ratio obtained by dividing ODD LOT short sales by total odd-lot sales, using New York Stock Exchange (NYSE) statistics; also called the *odd-lot selling indicator.* Historically, odd-lot investors—those who buy and sell in less than 100-share round lots—react to market highs and lows; when the market reaches a low point, odd-lot short sales reach a high point, and vice versa. The odd-lot ratio has followed the opposite pattern of the NYSE MEMBER SHORT SALE RATIO. *See also* ODD-LOT THEORY.

ODD-LOT THEORY historical theory that the ODD LOT investor—the small personal investor who trades in less than 100-share quantities—is usually guilty of bad timing and that profits can be made by acting contrary to odd-lot trading patterns. Heavy odd-lot buying in a rising market is interpreted by proponents of this theory as a sign of technical weakness and the signal of a market reversal. Conversely, an increase of odd-lot selling in a declining market is seen as a sign of technical strength and a signal to buy. In fact, analyses of odd-lot trading over the years fail to bear out the theory with any real degree of consistency, and it has fallen into disfavor in recent years. It is also a fact that odd-lot customers generally, who tend to buy market leaders, have fared rather well in the upward market that has prevailed over the last fifty years or so. *See also* ODD-LOT SHORT-SALE RATIO.

OEX pronounced as three letters, Wall Street shorthand for the Standard & Poor's 100 stock index, which comprises stocks for which options are traded on the CHICAGO BOARD OPTIONS EXCHANGE (CBOE). OEX index options are traded on the CHICAGO BOARD OF TRADE (CBOT), and futures are traded on the CHICAGO MERCANTILE EXCHANGE (CME). *See also* STOCK INDICES AND AVERAGES.

OFF-BALANCE-SHEET FINANCING financing that does not add debt on a balance sheet and thus does not affect borrowing capacity as it would be determined by financial ratios. The most common example would be a lease structured as an OPERATING LEASE rather than a CAPITAL LEASE and where management's intent is, in fact, to acquire an asset and corresponding liability without reflecting either on its balance sheet. Other examples include the sale of receivables with recourse, TAKE-OR-PAY CONTRACTS, and bank financial instruments such as guarantees, letters of credit, and loan commitments. GENERALLY ACCEPTED ACCOUNTING PRINCIPLES (GAAP) require that information be provided in financial statements about off-balance-sheet financing involving credit, market, and liquidity risk.

OFF-BOARD off the exchange (the New York Stock Exchange is known as the Big Board, hence the term). The term is used either for a trade that is executed OVER THE COUNTER or for a transaction entailing listed securities that is not completed on a national exchange. Over-the-counter trading is handled by telephone, with competitive bidding carried on constantly by market makers in a particular stock. The other kind of off-board trade occurs when a block of stock is exchanged between customers of a brokerage firm, or between a customer and the firm itself if the brokerage house wants to buy or sell securities from its own inventory. *See also* THIRD MARKET.

OFFER price at which someone who owns a security offers to sell it; also known as the ASKED PRICE. This price is listed in newspapers for stocks traded OVER THE COUNTER. The bid price—the price at which someone is prepared to buy—is also shown. The bid price is always lower than the offer price. *See also* OFFERING PRICE.

OFFERING *see* PUBLIC OFFERING.

OFFERING CIRCULAR *see* PROSPECTUS.

OFFERING DATE date on which a distribution of stocks or bonds will first be available for sale to the public. *See also* DATED DATE; PUBLIC OFFERING.

OFFERING PRICE price per share at which a new or secondary distribution of securities is offered for sale to the public; also called PUBLIC OFFERING PRICE. For instance, if a new issue of XYZ stock is priced at $40 a share, the offering price is $40.

When mutual fund shares are made available to the public, they are sold at NET ASSET VALUE, also called the *offering price* or the ASKED PRICE, plus a sales charge, if any. In a NO-LOAD FUND, the offering price is the same as the net asset value. In a LOAD FUND, the sales charge is added to the net asset value, to arrive at the offering price. *See also* OFFER.

OFFERING SCALE prices at which different maturities of a SERIAL BOND issue are offered to the public by an underwriter. The offering scale may also be expressed in terms of YIELD TO MATURITY.

OFFER WANTED (OW) notice by a potential buyer of a security that he or she is looking for an offer by a potential seller of the security. The abbreviation OW is frequently seen in the PINK SHEETS (listing of stocks) and YELLOW SHEETS (listing of corporate bonds) published by the NATIONAL QUOTATION BUREAU for securities traded by OVER THE COUNTER dealers. *See also* BID WANTED.

OFF-FLOOR ORDER order to buy or sell a security that originates off the floor of an exchange. These are customer orders originating with brokers, as distinguished from orders of floor members trading for their own accounts (ON-FLOOR

ORDERS). Exchange rules require that off-floor orders be executed before orders initiated on the floor.

OFFICE OF MANAGEMENT AND BUDGET (OMB) at the federal level, an agency within the Office of the President responsible for (1) preparing and presenting to Congress the president's budget; (2) working with the Council of Economic Advisers and the Treasury Department in developing a fiscal program; (3) reviewing the administrative policies and performance of government agencies; and (4) advising the president on legislative matters.

OFFICE OF THRIFT SUPERVISION (OTS) agency of the U.S. Treasury Department created by the FINANCIAL INSTITUTIONS REFORM, RECOVERY AND ENFORCEMENT ACT OF 1989 (FIRREA), the bailout bill enacted to assist depositors that became law on August 9, 1989. The OTS replaced the disbanded FEDERAL HOME LOAN BANK BOARD and assumed responsibility for the nation's savings and loan industry. The legislation empowered OTS to institute new regulations, charter new federal savings and loan associations and federal savings banks, and supervise all savings institutions and their holding companies insured by the SAVINGS ASSOCIATION INSURANCE FUND (SAIF). *See also* BAILOUT BOND.

OFFICIAL NOTICE OF SALE notice published by a municipality inviting investment bankers to submit competitive bids for an upcoming bond issue. The notice provides the name of a municipal official from whom further details can be obtained and states certain basic information about the issue, such as its par value and important conditions. The *Bond Buyer* regularly carries such notices.

OFFICIAL STATEMENT *see* LEGAL OPINION.

OFFSET
Accounting: (1) amount equaling or counterbalancing another amount on the opposite side of the same ledger or the ledger of another account. *See also* ABSORBED. (2) amount that cancels or reduces a claim.
Banking: (1) bank's legal right to seize deposit funds to cover a loan in default—called *right of offset*. (2) number stored on a bank card that, when related to the code number remembered by the cardholder, represents the depositor's identification number, called *PAN-PIN pair*.
Securities, commodities, options: (1) closing transaction involving the purchase or sale of an OPTION having the same features as one already held. (2) HEDGE, such as the SHORT SALE of a stock to protect a capital gain or the purchase of a future to protect a commodity price, or a STRADDLE representing the purchase of offsetting put and call options on a security.

OFFSHORE term used in the United States for any financial organization with a headquarters outside the country. A MUTUAL FUND with a legal domicile in the Bahamas or the Cayman Islands, for instance, is called an *offshore fund*. To be sold in the United States, such funds must adhere to all pertinent federal and state regulations. Many banks have offshore subsidiaries that engage in activities that are either heavily regulated or taxed or not allowed under U.S. law.

OIL AND GAS LIMITED PARTNERSHIP partnership consisting of one or more limited partners and one or more general partners that is structured to find, extract, and market commercial quantities of oil and natural gas. The limited partners, who assume no liability beyond the funds they contribute, buy units in the partnership, typically for at least $5000 a unit, from a broker registered to sell that partnership. All the limited partners' money then goes to the GENERAL PARTNER, the partner with unlimited liability, who either searches for oil and gas (an exploratory or wildcat well), drills for oil and gas in a proven oil field (a DEVELOPMENTAL

DRILLING PROGRAM), or pumps petroleum and gas from an existing well (a COMPLETION PROGRAM). The riskier the chance of finding oil and gas, the higher the potential reward or loss to the limited partner. Conservative investors who mainly want to collect income from the sale of proven oil and gas reserves are safest with a developmental or completion program.

Subject to PASSIVE income rules, limited partners also receive tax breaks, such as depreciation deductions for equipment used for drilling and oil depletion allowances for the value of oil extracted from the fields. If the partnership borrows money for increased drilling, limited partners also can get deductions for the interest cost of the loans. *See also* EXPLORATORY DRILLING PROGRAM; INCOME LIMITED PARTNERSHIP; INTANGIBLE COSTS; LIMITED PARTNERSHIP; WILDCAT DRILLING.

OIL AND GAS LOTTERY program run by the Bureau of Land Management at the U.S. Department of the Interior that permits anyone filing an application to be selected for the right to drill for oil and gas on selected parcels of federal land. Both large oil companies and small speculators enter this lottery. An individual winning the drawing for a particularly desirable plot of land may sublet the property to an oil company, which will pay him or her royalties if the land yields commercial quantities of oil and gas.

OIL PATCH states in America that produce and refine oil and gas. This includes Texas, Oklahoma, Louisiana, California, and Alaska. Economists refer to oil patch states when assessing the strength or weakness of a region of the country tied to movements in oil prices.

OLIGOPOLY market situation in which a small number of selling firms control the market supply of a particular good or service and are therefore able to control the market price. An oligopoly can be *perfect*—where all firms produce an identical good or service (cement)—or *imperfect*—where each firm's product has a different identity but is essentially similar to the others (cigarettes). Because each firm in an oligopoly knows its share of the total market for the product or service it produces, and because any change in price or change in market share by one firm is reflected in the sales of the others, there tends to be a high degree of interdependence among firms; each firm must make its price and output decisions with regard to the responses of the other firms in the oligopoly, so that oligopoly prices, once established, are rigid. This encourages nonprice competition, through advertising, packaging, and service—a generally nonproductive form of resource allocation. Two examples of oligopoly in the United States are airlines serving the same routes and tobacco companies. *See also* OLIGOPSONY.

OLIGOPSONY market situation in which a few large buyers control the purchasing power and therefore the output and market price of a good or service; the buy-side counterpart of OLIGOPOLY. Oligopsony prices tend to be lower than the prices in a freely competitive market, just as oligopoly prices tend to be higher. For example, the large tobacco companies purchase all the output of a large number of small tobacco growers and therefore are able to control tobacco prices.

OMITTED DIVIDEND dividend that was scheduled to be declared by a corporation, but instead was not voted for the time being by the board of directors. Dividends are sometimes omitted when a company has run into financial difficulty and its board decides it is more important to conserve cash than to pay a dividend to shareholders. The announcement of an omitted dividend will typically cause the company's stock price to drop, particularly if the announcement is a surprise.

OM STOCKHOLM AB screen-based derivatives market of Sweden, trading a wide variety of interest rate and bond futures. The exchange trades futures and options on the OMX Equity Index. It offers a clearing service for interbank futures trading on notional bonds, Treasury bills and mortgage bonds. OMLX, the London Securities and Derivatives Exchange, is a wholly-owned subsidiary of OM Stockholm, and the two exchanges have a trading and clearing link. Under an existing cooperation agreement between SOM of Finland and OM Stockholm, SOM products also trade in Stockholm at the OMLX. OM's products, in turn, trade in Finland. Trading hours: 9 A.M. to 5 P.M.

ON ACCOUNT
In general: in partial payment of an obligation.
Finance: on credit terms. The term applies to a relationship between a seller and a buyer wherein payment is expected sometime after delivery and the obligation is not documented by a NOTE. Synonymous with *open account.*

ON A SCALE *see* SCALE ORDER.

ON-BALANCE VOLUME TECHNICAL ANALYSIS method that attempts to pinpoint when a stock, bond, or commodity is being accumulated by many buyers or is being distributed by many sellers. The on-balance volume line is superimposed on the stock price line on a chart, and it is considered significant when the two lines cross. The chart indicates a buy signal when accumulation is detected and a sell signal when distribution is spotted. The on-balance method can be used to diagnose an entire market or an individual stock, bond, or commodity.

ONE-CANCELS-THE-OTHER ORDER *see* ALTERNATIVE ORDER.

ONE DECISION STOCK stock with sufficient quality and growth potential to be suitable for a BUY AND HOLD STRATEGY.

ONE-SHARE, ONE-VOTE RULE the principle that public companies should not reduce shareholder voting rights. Originally, the New York Stock Exchange had a one-share, one-vote requirement for its listed companies. In 1988, the SEC adopted Rule 19c-4, which prohibited companies listed on a national securities exchange or quoted on the National Association of Securities Dealers Automated Quotation System (NASDAQ) from disenfranchising existing shareholders through, for example, issuances of super voting stock. The rule, however, was struck down by the Court of Appeals in *Business Roundtable v. SEC* in 1990. In December 1994, the SEC approved rules proposed by the New York Stock Exchange, American Stock Exchange, and National Association of Securities Dealers that establish a uniform voting standard. This new standard prohibits companies listed on the NYSE, the AMEX, or the NASDAQ system from taking any corporate action or issuing any stock that has the effect of disparately reducing or restricting the voting rights of existing common stock shareholders.

ON-FLOOR ORDER security order originating with a member on the floor of an exchange when dealing for his or her own account. The designation separates such orders from those for customers' accounts (OFF-FLOOR ORDERS), which are generally given precedence by exchange rules.

ON MARGIN *see* MARGIN.

ON THE CLOSE ORDER order to buy or sell a specified number of shares in a particular stock as close as possible to the closing price of the day. Brokers accepting on the close orders do not guarantee that the trade will be executed at the final closing price, or even that the trade can be completed at all. On an order ticket, on the close orders are abbreviated as "OTC" orders. *See also* AT THE CLOSE ORDER; MARKET-ON-CLOSE ORDER.

ON THE OPENING ORDER order to buy or sell a specified number of shares in a particular stock at the price of the first trade of the day. If the trader cannot buy or sell shares at that price, the order is immediately cancelled.

ON THE SIDELINES investors who refrain from investing because of market uncertainty are said to be on the sidelines. The analogy is to a football game, in which spectators on the sidelines do not actively participate in the game. Investors on the sidelines normally keep their money in short-term instruments such as money market mutual funds, which can be tapped instantly if the investor sees a good opportunity to reenter the stock or bond markets. Market commentators frequently say that trading activity was light "because investors stayed on the sidelines."

OPD ticker tape symbol designating (1) the first transaction of the day in a security after a DELAYED OPENING or (2) the opening transaction in a security whose price has changed significantly from the previous day's close—usually 2 or more points on stocks selling at $20 or higher, 1 or more points on stocks selling at less than $20.

OPEN
Securities:
1. status of an order to buy or sell securities that has still not been executed. A GOOD-TILL-CANCELED ORDER that remains pending is an example of an open order.
2. to establish an account with a broker.
Banking: to establish an account or a LETTER OF CREDIT.
Finance: unpaid balance.
   See also OPEN-END LEASE; OPEN-END MANAGEMENT COMPANY; OPEN-END MORTGAGE; OPEN INTEREST; OPEN ORDER; OPEN REPO.

OPEN-END CREDIT revolving line of credit offered by banks, savings and loans, and other lenders to consumers. The line of credit is set with a particular limit, after which consumers can borrow using a credit card, check, or cash advance. Every time a purchase or cash advance is made, credit is extended on behalf of the consumer. Consumers may pay off the entire balance each month, thereby avoiding interest charges. Or they may pay a minimum amount, with interest accruing on the outstanding balance.

OPEN-END LEASE lease agreement providing for an additional payment after the property is returned to the lessor, to adjust for any change in the value of the property.

OPEN-END MANAGEMENT COMPANY INVESTMENT COMPANY that sells MUTUAL FUNDS to the public. The term arises from the fact that the firm continually creates new shares on demand, although an open-end fund may close itself to new investors when its management decides that it is too large. Mutual fund shareholders buy the shares at NET ASSET VALUE and can redeem them at any time at the prevailing market price, which may be higher or lower than the price at which the investor bought. The shareholder's funds are invested in stocks, bonds, or money market instruments, depending on the type of mutual fund company. The opposite of an open-end management company is a CLOSED-END MANAGEMENT COMPANY, which issues a limited number of shares, which are then traded on a stock exchange.

OPEN-END MORTGAGE
Real estate finance: MORTGAGE that allows the issuance of additional bonds having equal status with the original issue, but that protects the original bondholders with specific restrictions governing subsequent borrowing under the original mortgage. For example, the terms of the original INDENTURE might permit additional mortgage-bond financing up to 75% of the value of the property acquired, but only if total fixed charges on all debt, including the proposed new bonds, have been earned a stated number of times over the previous five years. The open-end mortgage is a

more practical and acceptable (to the mortgage holder) version of the *open mortgage,* which allows a corporation to issue unlimited amounts of bonds under the original first mortgage, with no protection to the original bondholders. An even more conservative version is the *limited open-end mortgage,* which usually contains the same restrictions as the open-end, but places a limit on the amount of first mortgage bonds that can be issued, and typically provides that proceeds from new bond issues be used to retire outstanding bonds with the same or prior security.

Trust banking: corporate trust indenture that permits the trustee to authenticate and deliver bonds from time to time in addition to the original issue. *See also* AUTHENTICATION.

OPEN-END (MUTUAL) FUND *see* OPEN-END MANAGEMENT COMPANY.

OPENING
1. price at which a security or commodity starts a trading day. Investors who want to buy or sell as soon as the market opens will put in an order at the opening price.
2. short time frame of market opportunity. For instance, if interest rates have been rising for months, and for a few days or weeks they fall, a corporation that has wanted to FLOAT bonds at lower interest rates might seize the moment to issue the bonds. This short time frame would be called an *opening in the market* or a *window of opportunity. See also* WINDOW.

OPEN INTEREST total number of contracts in a commodity or options market that are still open; that is, they have not been exercised, closed out, or allowed to expire. The term also applies to a particular commodity or, in the case of options, to the number of contracts outstanding on a particular underlying security. The level of open interest is reported daily in newspaper commodity and options pages.

OPEN-MARKET COMMITTEE *see* FEDERAL OPEN MARKET COMMITTEE (FOMC).

OPEN-MARKET OPERATIONS activities by which the Securities Department of the Federal Reserve Bank of New York—popularly called the DESK—carries out instructions of the FEDERAL OPEN MARKET COMMITTEE designed to regulate the money supply. Such operations involve the purchase and sale of government securities, which effectively expands or contracts funds in the banking system. This, in turn, alters bank reserves, causing a MULTIPLIER effect on the supply of credit and, therefore, on economic activity generally. Open-market operations represent one of three basic ways the Federal Reserve implements MONETARY POLICY, the others being changes in the member bank RESERVE REQUIREMENTS and raising or lowering the DISCOUNT RATE charged to banks borrowing from the Fed to maintain reserves.

OPEN-MARKET RATES interest rates on various debt instruments bought and sold in the open market that are directly responsive to supply and demand. Such open, market rates are distinguished from the DISCOUNT RATE, set by the FEDERAL RESERVE BOARD as a deliberate measure to influence other rates, and from bank commercial loan rates, which are directly influenced by Federal Reserve policy. The rates on short-term instruments like COMMERCIAL PAPER and BANKER'S ACCEPTANCES are examples of open-market rates, as are yields on interest-bearing securities of all types traded in the SECONDARY MARKET.

OPEN ON THE PRINT BLOCK POSITIONER'S term for a BLOCK trade that has been completed with an institutional client and "printed" on the consolidated tape, but that leaves the block positioner open—that is, with a risk position to be covered. This usually happens when the block positioner is on the sell side of the transaction and sells SHORT what he lacks in inventory to complete the order.

OPEN ORDER buy or sell order for securities that has not yet been executed or canceled; a GOOD-TILL-CANCELED ORDER.

OPEN OUTCRY method of trading on a commodity exchange. The term derives from the fact that traders must shout out their buy or sell offers. When a trader shouts he wants to sell at a particular price and someone else shouts he wants to buy at that price, the two traders have made a contract that will be recorded.

OPEN REPO REPURCHASE AGREEMENT in which the repurchase date is unspecified and the agreement can be terminated by either party at any time. The agreement continues on a day-to-day basis with interest rate adjustments as the market changes.

OPERATING INCOME *see* OPERATING PROFIT (OR LOSS).

OPERATING IN THE RED operating at a loss. *See* OPERATING PROFIT (OR LOSS).

OPERATING LEASE type of LEASE, normally involving equipment, whereby the contract is written for considerably less than the life of the equipment and the lessor handles all maintenance and servicing; also called *service lease*. Operating leases are the opposite of capital leases, where the lessee acquires essentially all the economic benefits and risks of ownership. Common examples of equipment financed with operating leases are office copiers, computers, automobiles, and trucks. Most operating leases are cancelable, meaning the lessee can return the equipment if it becomes obsolete or is no longer needed.

OPERATING LEVERAGE *see* LEVERAGE.

OPERATING PROFIT MARGIN *see* NET PROFIT MARGIN.

OPERATING PROFIT (OR LOSS) the difference between the revenues of a business and the related costs and expenses, excluding income derived from sources other than its regular activities and before income deductions; synonymous with *net operating profit (or loss), operating income (or loss),* and *net operating income (or loss).* Income deductions are a class of items comprising the final section of a company's income statement, which, although necessarily incurred in the course of business and customarily charged before arriving at net income, are more in the nature of costs imposed from without than costs subject to the control of everyday operations. They include interest; amortized discount and expense on bonds; income taxes; losses from sales of plants, divisions, major items of property; prior-year adjustments; charges to contingency reserves; bonuses and other periodic profit distributions to officers and employees: write-offs of intangibles: adjustments arising from major changes in accounting methods, such as inventory valuation and other material and nonre-current items.

OPERATING RATE percentage of production capacity in use by a particular company, an industry, or the entire economy. While in theory a business can operate at 100% of its productive capacity, in practice the maximum output is less than that because machines need to be repaired, employees take vacations, etc. The operating rate is expressed as a percentage of the ideal 100% production output. For example, a company may be producing at an 85% operating rate, meaning its output is 85% of the maximum that could be produced with its existing resources. If a company has a low operating rate of under 50%, it usually is suffering meager profits or losses, though it has large potential for profit growth. A company operating at 80% of capacity or more is usually highly profitable, though it has less opportunity for improvement.

The Federal Reserve calculates the operating rate of U.S. industry on a monthly basis when its releases figures for industrial production. An operating rate of 85% or higher is generally considered to be full capacity by economists, who become concerned about inflationary pressures caused by production bottlenecks. An operating rate of less than 80% shows considerable slack in the economy, with few inflationary pressures.

OPERATING RATIO any of a group of ratios that measure a firm's operating efficiency and effectiveness by relating various income and expense figures from the profit and loss statement to each other and to balance sheet figures. Among the ratios used are sales to cost of goods sold, operating expenses to operating income, net profits to gross income, net income to net worth. Such ratios are most revealing when compared with those of prior periods and with industry averages.

OPERATIONS DEPARTMENT BACK OFFICE of a brokerage firm where all clerical functions having to do with clearance, settlement, and execution of trades are handled. This department keeps customer records and handles the day-to-day monitoring of margin positions.

OPINION *see* ACCOUNTANT'S OPINION.

OPINION SHOPPING dubious practice of changing outside auditors until one is found that will give an unqualified ACCOUNTANT'S OPINION.

OPM
1. other people's money; Wall Street slang for the use of borrowed funds by individuals or companies to increase the return on invested capital. *See also* FINANCIAL LEVERAGE.
2. options pricing model. *See* BLACK-SCHOLES OPTION PRICING MODEL.

OPORTO DERIVATIVES EXCHANGE (BOLSA DE DERIVADOS DO OPORTO) Portuguese exchange opened in June 1996 and similar in operation to the Spanish MEFF. The exchange trades futures on the 10-year government bond, Portuguese Stock Index, and three-month interbank deposit rate LISBOR (Lisbon Interbank Offered Rate). Trading hours: Monday through Friday, 9:45 A.M. to 4:45 P.M.

OPPORTUNITY COST
In general: highest price or rate of return an alternative course of action would provide.
Corporate finance: concept widely used in business planning; for example, in evaluating a CAPITAL INVESTMENT project, a company must measure the projected return against the return it would earn on the highest yielding alternative investment involving similar risk. *See also* COST OF CAPITAL.
Securities investments: cost of forgoing a safe return on an investment in hopes of making a larger profit. For instance, an investor might buy a stock that shows great promise but yields only 2%, even though a higher safe return is available in a money market fund yielding 5%. The 3% yield difference is called the opportunity cost.

OPTIMUM CAPACITY level of output of manufacturing operations that produces the lowest cost per unit. For example, a tire factory may produce tires at $30 apiece if it turns out 10,000 tires a month, but the tires can be made for $20 apiece if the plant operates at its optimum capacity of 100,000 tires a month. *See also* MARGINAL COST.

OPTION
In general: right to buy or sell property that is granted in exchange for an agreed upon sum. If the right is not exercised after a specified period, the option expires and the option buyer forfeits the money. *See also* EXERCISE.

Securities: securities transaction agreement tied to stocks, commodities, or stock indexes. Options are traded on many exchanges.

1. a CALL OPTION gives its buyer the right to buy 100 shares of the underlying security at a fixed price before a specified date in the future—usually three, six, or nine months. For this right, the call option buyer pays the call option seller, called the writer, a fee called a PREMIUM, which is forfeited if the buyer does not exercise the option before the agreed-upon date. A call buyer therefore speculates that the price of the underlying shares will rise within the specified time period. For example, a call option on 100 shares of XYZ stock may grant its buyer the right to buy those shares at $100 apiece anytime in the next three months. To buy that option, the buyer may have to pay a premium of $2 a share, or $200. If at the time of the option contract XYZ is selling for $95 a share, the option buyer will profit if XYZ's stock price rises. If XYZ shoots up to $120 a share in two months, for example, the option buyer can EXERCISE his or her option to buy 100 shares of the stock at $100 and then sell the shares for $120 each, keeping the difference as profit (minus the $2 premium per share). On the other hand, if XYZ drops below $95 and stays there for three months, at the end of that time the call option will expire and the call buyer will receive no return on the $2 a share investment premium of $200.

2. the opposite of a call option is a PUT OPTION, which gives its buyer the right to sell a specified number of shares of a stock at a particular price within a specified time period. Put buyers expect the price of the underlying stock to fall. Someone who thinks XYZ's stock price will fall might buy a three-month XYZ put for 100 shares at $100 apiece and pay a premium of $2. If XYZ falls to $80 a share, the put buyer can then exercise his or her right to sell 100 XYZ shares at $100. The buyer will first purchase 100 shares at $80 each and then sell them to the put option seller (writer) at $100 each, thereby making a profit of $18 a share (the $20 a share profit minus the $2 a share cost of the option premium).

In practice, most call and put options are rarely exercised. Instead, investors buy and sell options before expiration, trading on the rise and fall of premium prices. Because an option buyer must put up only a small amount of money (the premium) to control a large amount of stock, options trading provides a great deal of LEVERAGE and can prove immensely profitable. Options traders can write either covered options, in which they own the underlying security, or far riskier naked options, for which they do not own the underlying security. Often, options traders lose many premiums on unsuccessful trades before they make a very profitable trade. More sophisticated traders combine various call and put options in SPREAD and STRADDLE positions. Their profits or losses result from the narrowing or widening of spreads between option prices.

An *incentive stock option* is granted to corporate executives if the company achieves certain financial goals, such as a level of sales or profits. The executive is granted the option of buying company stock at a below-market price and selling the stock in the market for a profit. *See also* CALL; COVERED OPTION; DEEP IN (OUT OF) THE MONEY; IN THE MONEY; LEAPS; NAKED OPTION; OPTION WRITER; OUT OF THE MONEY.

OPTION ACCOUNT account at a brokerage firm that is approved to contain option positions or trades. Since certain option strategies require margin, an option account may be a margin account or a cash account. There are several prerequisites. The client must be given a copy of "Characteristics and Risks of Standardized Options Contracts," known as the Options Disclosure Documents, before the account can be approved. The client must complete an OPTION AGREEMENT in order to open the account. The client must show that he is suitable for options transactions, both in financial resources and investing experience, before the brokerage firm will approve the account for options trading.

OPTION AGREEMENT form filled out by a brokerage firm's customer when opening an option account. It details financial information about the customer, who agrees to follow the rules and regulations of options trading. This agreement, also called the *option information form,* assures the broker that the customer's financial resources are adequate to withstand any losses that may occur from options trading. The customer must receive a prospectus from the OPTIONS CLEARING CORPORATION before he or she can begin trading.

OPTION CYCLE cycle of months in which options contracts expire. These cycles are used for options on stocks and indices, as well as options on commodities, currencies, and debt instruments. The three most common cycles are: January, April, July, October (JAJO); February, May, August, November (FMAN); and March, June, September, December (MJSD). In addition to these expiration months, options on individual stocks and indices generally also expire in the current month and subsequent month. As an example, an option in the February cycle trading during May would have May, June and August expiration months listed at a minimum. Because of option cycles, there are four days a year—in March, June, September, and December, when TRIPLE WITCHING DAY takes place, as several options contracts expire on the same day.

OPTIONAL DIVIDEND dividend that can be paid either in cash or in stock. The shareholder entitled to the dividend makes the choice.

OPTIONAL PAYMENT BOND bond whose principal and/or interest are payable, at the option of the holder, in one or more foreign currencies as well as in domestic currency.

OPTION HOLDER someone who has bought a call or put OPTION but has not yet exercised or sold it. A call option holder wants the price of the underlying security to rise; a put option holder wants the price of the underlying security to fall.

OPTION MARGIN MARGIN REQUIREMENT applicable to OPTIONS, as set forth in REGULATION T and in the internal policies of individual brokers. Requirements vary with the type of option and the extent to which it is IN THE MONEY, but are strictest in the case of NAKED OPTIONS and narrow-based INDEX OPTIONS. There, Regulation T requires the option premium plus 20% of the underlying value as the maximum and the premium plus 10% of the underlying value as the minimum. Merrill Lynch, for example, would also require a minimum of $10,000 per account and $1,000 per position.

OPTION MUTUAL FUND MUTUAL FUND that either buys or sells options in order to increase the value of fund shares. OPTION mutual funds may be either conservative or aggressive. For instance, a conservative fund may buy stocks and increase shareholders' income through the PREMIUM earned by selling put and call options on the stocks in the fund's portfolio. This kind of fund would be called an *option income fund.* At the opposite extreme, an aggressive *option growth fund* may buy puts and calls in stocks that the fund manager thinks are about to fall or rise sharply; if the fund manager is right, large profits can be earned through EXERCISE of the options. The LEVERAGE that options provide makes it possible to multiply the return on invested funds many times over.

OPTION PREMIUM amount per share paid by an OPTION buyer to an option seller for the right to buy (call) or sell (put) the underlying security at a particular price within a specified period. Option premium prices are quoted in increments of eighths or sixteenths of 1% and are printed in the options tables of daily newspapers. A PREMIUM of $5 per share means an option buyer would pay $500 for an option on 100 shares. *See also* CALL OPTION; PUT OPTION.

OPTION PRICE market price at which an option contract is trading at any particular time. The price of an option on a stock reflects the fact that it covers 100 shares of a stock. So, for example, an option that is quoted at $7 would cost $700, because it would be an option for 100 shares of stock at a $7 cost per share covered. The option price is determined by many factors, including its INTRINSIC VALUE, time to expiration, volatility of the underlying stock, interest rates, dividends, and marketplace adjustments for supply and demand. Options on indices, debt instruments, currencies, and commodities also have prices determined by many of the same forces. Options prices are published daily in the business pages of many newspapers.

OPTIONS CLEARING CORPORATION (OCC) the largest clearing organization in the world for financial derivative instruments. OCC issues, guarantees, and clears options on underlying financial assets including common stocks, foreign exchange, stock indices, U.S. Treasury securities and interest rate composites. As the issuer and guarantor of every options contract executed on every securities options exchange in the U.S., OCC serves as the counterparty for all transactions. OCC's ability to meet its obligations arising from its options contracts earned it an AAA rating by STANDARD & POOR'S CORPORATION. OCC is the only securities clearinghouse in the world to receive this accreditation. Its options disclosure document, "Characteristics and Risks of Standardized Options," is required reading for all investors prior to trading options. OCC is owned by the four U.S. exchanges that trade options. *See also* OPTION.

OPTION SERIES options of the same class (puts or calls with the same underlying security) that also have the same EXERCISE PRICE and maturity month. For instance, all XYZ October 80 calls are a series, as are all ABC July 100 puts. *See also* OPTION.

OPTION SPREAD buying and selling of options within the same CLASS at the same time. The investor who uses the OPTION spread strategy hopes to profit from the widening or narrowing of the SPREAD between the various options. Option spreads can be designed to be profitable in either up or down markets.

Some examples:

(1) entering into two options at the same EXERCISE PRICE, but with different maturity dates. For instance, an investor could buy an XYZ April 60 call and sell an XYZ July 60 call.

(2) entering into two options at different STRIKE PRICES with the same expiration month. For example, an investor could buy an XYZ April 60 call and sell an XYZ April 70 call.

(3) entering into two options at different strike prices with different expiration months. For instance, an investor could buy an XYZ April 60 call and sell an XYZ July 70 call.

OPTION WRITER person or financial institution that sells put and call options. A writer of a PUT OPTION contracts to buy 100 shares of stock from the put option buyer by a certain date for a fixed price. For example, an option writer who sells XYZ April 50 put agrees to buy XYZ stock from the put buyer at $50 a share any time until the contract expires in April.

A writer of a CALL OPTION, on the other hand, guarantees to sell the call option buyer the underlying stock at a particular price before a certain date. For instance, a writer of an XYZ April 50 call agrees to sell stock at $50 a share to the call buyer any time before April.

In exchange for granting this right, the option writer receives a payment called an OPTION PREMIUM. For holders of large portfolios of the premiums from stocks, option writing therefore is a source of additional income.

ORAL CONTRACT contract between two parties that has been spoken, but not agreed to in writing or signed by both parties. Oral contracts are usually legally enforceable, though not in the case of real estate.

OR BETTER indication, abbreviated OB on the ORDER TICKET of a LIMIT ORDER to buy or sell securities, that the broker should transact the order at a price better than the specified LIMIT PRICE if a better price can be obtained.

ORDER

Investments: instruction to a broker or dealer to buy or sell securities or commodities. Securities orders fall into four basic categories: MARKET ORDER, LIMIT ORDER, time order, and STOP ORDER.

Law: direction from a court of jurisdiction, or a regulation.

Negotiable instruments: payee's request to the maker, as on a check stating, "Pay to the order of (when presented by) John Doe."

Trade: request to buy, sell, deliver, or receive goods or services which commits the issuer of the order to the terms specified.

ORDER IMBALANCE large number of buy or sell orders for a stock, causing an unusually wide spread between bid and offer prices. Stock exchanges frequently halt trading of a stock with a significant order imbalance until more buyers or sellers appear and an orderly market can be reestablished. A significant order imbalance on the buying side can occur when there is an announcement of an impending takeover of the company, better-than-expected earnings, or other unexpected positive news. A significant order imbalance on the selling side can occur when a takeover offer has fallen through, a key executive has left the company, earnings came in far worse than expected, or there is other unexpected negative news.

ORDER ROOM department in a brokerage firm that receives all orders to buy or sell securities. ORDER TICKETS are processed through the order room.

ORDER SPLITTING practice prohibited by rules of the National Association of Securities Dealers (NASD) whereby brokers might split orders in order to qualify them as small orders for purposes of automatic execution by the SMALL ORDER EXECUTION SYSTEM (SOES).

ORDER TICKET form completed by a registered representative (ACCOUNT EXECUTIVE) of a brokerage firm, upon receiving order instructions from a customer. It shows whether the order is to buy or to sell, the number of units, the name of the security, the kind of order (ORDER MARKET, LIMIT ORDER or STOP ORDER) and the customer's name or code number. After execution of the order on the exchange floor or in the firm's trading department (if over the counter), the price is written and circled on the order ticket, and the completing broker is indicated by number. The order ticket must be retained for a certain period in compliance with federal law.

ORDINARY INCOME income from the normal activities of an individual or business, as distinguished from CAPITAL GAINS from the sale of assets. Prior to the TAX REFORM ACT OF 1986, the long-term CAPITAL GAINS TAX was lower than that on ordinary income. The 1986 Act eliminated the preferential capital gains rate, but it kept the separate statutory language to allow for future increases in ordinary income rates. In 1991, capital gains rates were limited to 28%, and in the TAXPAYER RELIEF ACT OF 1997, capital gains tax rates were cut to 20%.

ORDINARY INTEREST simple interest based on a 360-day year rather than on a 365-day year (the latter is called *exact interest*). The difference between the two bases when calculating daily interest on large sums of money can be substantial. The ratio of ordinary interest to exact interest is 1.0139.

ORGANIZATION CHART chart showing the interrelationships of positions within an organization in terms of authority and responsibility. There are basically three patterns of organization: *line organization,* in which a single manager has final authority over a group of foremen or middle management supervisors; *functional organization,* in which a general manager supervises a number of managers identified by function; and *line and staff organization,* which is a combination of line and functional organization, with specialists in particular functions holding staff positions where they advise line officers concerned with actual production.

ORGANIZED SECURITIES EXCHANGE STOCK EXCHANGE as distinguished from an OVER THE COUNTER market. *See also* SECURITIES AND COMMODITIES EXCHANGES.

ORIGINAL COST
1. in accounting, all costs associated with the acquisition of an asset.
2. in public utilities accounting, the acquisition cost incurred by the entity that first devotes a property to public use; normally, the utility company's cost for the property. It is used to establish the rate to be charged customers in order to provide the utility company with a FAIR RATE OF RETURN on capital.

ORIGINAL ISSUE DISCOUNT (OID) discount from PAR VALUE at the time a bond or other debt instrument, such as a STRIP, is issued. (Although the par value of bonds is normally $1000, $100 is used when traders quote prices.) A bond may be issued at $50 ($500) per bond instead of $100 ($1000), for example. The bond will mature at $100 (1000), however, so that an investor has a built-in gain if the bond is held until maturity. The most extreme version of an original issue discount is a ZERO-COUPON BOND, which is originally sold at far below par value and pays no interest until it matures. The REVENUE RECONCILIATION ACT OF 1993 extended OID rules to include stripped preferred stock.

The tax treatment of original issue discount bonds is complex. The Internal Revenue Service assumes a certain rate of appreciation of the bond every year until maturity. No capital gain or loss will be incurred if the bond is sold for that estimated amount. But if the bond is sold for more than the assumed amount, a CAPITAL GAINS TAX or a tax at the ORDINARY INCOME rate is due.

SAVINGS BONDS are exempt from OID rules.

ORIGINAL MATURITY interval between the issue date and the maturity date of a bond, as distinguished from CURRENT MATURITY, which is the time difference between the present time and the maturity date. For example, in 2001 a bond issued in 1999 to mature in 2014 would have an original maturity of 15 years and a current maturity of 13 years.

ORIGINATOR
1. bank, savings and loan, or mortgage banker that initially made the mortgage loan comprising part of a pool of mortgages.
2. investment banking firm that worked with the issuer of a new securities offering from the early planning stages and that usually is appointed manager of the underwriting SYNDICATE; more formally called the *originating investment banker.*
3. in banking terminology, the initiator of money transfer instructions.

ORPHAN STOCK stock that has been neglected by research analysts. Since the company's story is rarely followed and the stock infrequently recommended, it is considered an orphan by investors. Orphan stocks may not attract much attention because they are too small, or because they have disappointed investors in the past. Because they are followed by so few investors, orphan stocks tend to trade at low price/earnings ratios. However, if the company assembles a solid record of rising profitability, it can be discovered again by research analysts, boosting the stock price and price/earnings ratio significantly. Investors who buy the stock when it is still a neglected orphan can thereby earn high returns. Also called a *wallflower.*

OSLO STOCK EXCHANGE founded in 1819 as a foreign exchange market, it later evolved as a commodity exchange; securities were launched in 1881. The stock exchanges in Bergen and Trondheim, Norway, are branches of the OSE. The OSE trades stocks, bonds, and stock options, and is considered the options market of Norway. Energy-related companies dominate the listings. The OSE General Price Index is made up of nearly 50 stocks. All trading is conducted electronically, and trades are settled three days from the transaction date. Pre-trading hours for stocks and options begins at 9:30 A.M., with continuous trading from 10 A.M. to 5 P.M., Monday through Friday.

OTC *see* OVER THE COUNTER.

OTC BULLETIN BOARD electronic listing of bid and asked quotations of over-the-counter stocks not meeting the minimum-net worth and other requirements of the NASDAQ stock-listing system. The new system, which was developed by the National Association of Securities Dealers (NASD) and approved by the Securities and Exchange Commission in 1990, provides continuously updated data on domestic stocks and twice-daily updates on foreign stocks. It was designed to facilitate trading and provide greater surveillance of stocks traditionally reported on once daily in the PINK SHEETS published by NATIONAL QUOTATION BUREAU.

OTC MARGIN STOCK shares of certain large firms traded OVER THE COUNTER that qualify as margin securities under REGULATION T of the Federal Reserve Board. Such stock must meet rigid criteria, and the list of eligible OTC shares is under constant review by the Fed. *See also* MARGIN SECURITY.

OTHER INCOME heading on a profit and loss statement for income from activities not in the normal course of business: sometimes called *other revenue*. Examples: interest on customers' notes, dividends and interest from investments, profit from the disposal of assets other than inventory, gain on foreign exchange, miscellaneous rent income. *See also* EXTRAORDINARY ITEM.

OTHER PEOPLE'S MONEY *see* OPM.

OUT-OF-FAVOR INDUSTRY OR STOCK industry or stock that is currently unpopular with investors. For example, the investing public may be disenchanted with an industry's poor earnings outlook. If interest rates were rising, interest-sensitive stocks such as banks and savings and loans would be out of favor because rising rates might harm these firms' profits. CONTRARIAN investors—those who consciously do the opposite of most other investors—tend to buy out-of-favor stocks because they can be bought cheaply. When the earnings of these stocks pick up, contrarians typically sell the stocks. Out-of-favor stocks tend to have a low PRICE/EARNINGS RATIO.

OUT OF LINE term describing a stock that is too high or too low in price in comparison with similar-quality stocks. A comparison of this sort is usually based on the PRICE/EARNINGS RATIO (PE), which measures how much investors are willing to pay for a firm's earnings prospects. If most computer industry stocks had PEs of 15, for instance, and XYZ Computers had a PE of only 10, analysts would say that XYZ's price is out of line with the rest of the industry.

OUT OF THE MONEY term used to describe an OPTION whose STRIKE PRICE for a stock is either higher than the current market value, in the case of a CALL, or lower, in the case of a PUT. For example, an XYZ December 60 CALL option would be out of the money when XYZ stock was selling for $55 a share. Similarly, an XYZ December 60 PUT OPTION would be out of the money when XYZ stock was selling for $65 a share.

Someone buying an out-of-the-money option hopes that the option will move IN THE MONEY, or at least in that direction. The buyer of the above XYZ call would want the stock to climb above $60 a share, whereas the put buyer would like the stock to drop below $60 a share.

OUTSIDE DIRECTOR member of a company's BOARD OF DIRECTORS who is not an employee of the company. Such directors are considered important because they are presumed to bring unbiased opinions to major corporate decisions and also can contribute diverse experience to the decision-making process. A retailing company may have outside directors with experience in finance and manufacturing, for instance. To avoid conflict of interest, outside directors never serve on the boards of two directly competing corporations. Directors receive fees from the company in return for their service, usually a set amount for each board meeting they attend.

OUTSTANDING
1. unpaid; used of ACCOUNTS RECEIVABLE and debt obligations of all types.
2. not yet presented for payment, as a check or draft.
3. stock held by shareholders, shown on corporate balance sheets under the heading of CAPITAL STOCK issued and outstanding.

OUT THE WINDOW term describing the rapid way a very successful NEW ISSUE of securities is marketed to investors. An issue that goes out the window is also called a BLOWOUT. *See also* HOT ISSUE.

OVER-AGE-55 HOME SALE EXEMPTION federal tax code regulation permitting an individual over the age of 55 a one-time exclusion up to $125,000 in capital gains on the sale of a home. The individual must have lived in the home as the primary residence for three of the past five years in order to qualify. The exclusion is allowed even if the proceeds from the home sale are not reinvested in another property. For example, if a 56-year-old person who bought a house for $100,000 sells the house for $300,000, he can choose to exclude $125,000 of the $200,000 gain and pay CAPITAL GAINS TAX on the remaining $75,000 profit. Congress enacted this rule to prevent older people from having to pay capital gains taxes on housing appreciation that was caused mainly by inflation. This exemption was superceded by a provision in the TAXPAYER RELIEF ACT OF 1997 allowing homeowners of any age who lived in their principal residence for at least two of the past five years to avoid capital gains taxes up to $500,000 for married couples filing jointly, and $250,000 for singles, when selling their home. Sellers do not have to reinvest the proceeds in another home.

OVERALL MARKET PRICE COVERAGE total assets less intangibles divided by the total of (1) the MARKET VALUE of the security issue in question and (2) the BOOK VALUE of liabilities and issues having a prior claim. The answer indicates the extent to which the market value of a particular CLASS of securities is covered in the event of a company's liquidation.

OVERBOOKED *see* OVERSUBSCRIBED.

OVERBOUGHT description of a security or a market that has recently experienced an unexpectedly sharp price rise and is therefore vulnerable to a price drop (called a CORRECTION by technical analysts). When a stock has been overbought, there are fewer buyers left to drive the price up further. *See also* MOMENTUM INDICATORS; OVERSOLD.

OVERDRAFT extension of credit by a lending institution. An overdraft check for which there are not sufficient funds (NSF) available may be rejected (bounced) by the bank. A bounced-check charge will be assessed on the check-writer's account. Alternatively, the bank customer may set up an overdraft loan account, which will cover NSF checks. While the customer's check will clear, the account will be charged overdraft check fees or interest on the outstanding balance of the loan starting immediately.

OVERHANG sizable block of securities or commodities contracts that, if released on the market, would put downward pressure on prices. Examples of overhang include shares held in a dealer's inventory, a large institutional holding, a secondary distribution still in registration, and a large commodity position about to be liquidated. Overhang inhibits buying activity that would otherwise translate into upward price movement.

OVERHEAD
1. costs of a business that are not directly associated with the production or sale of goods or services. Also called INDIRECT COSTS AND EXPENSES, *burden* and, in Great Britain, *on costs*.
2. sometimes used in a more limited sense, as in manufacturing or factory overhead.
   See also DIRECT OVERHEAD.

OVERHEATING term describing an economy that is expanding so rapidly that economists fear a rise in INFLATION. In an overheated economy, too much money is chasing too few goods, leading to price rises, and the productive capacity of a nation is usually nearing its limit. The remedies in the United States are usually a tightening of the money supply by the Federal Reserve and curbs in federal government spending. *See also* MONETARY POLICY; OPTIMUM CAPACITY.

OVERISSUE shares of CAPITAL STOCK issued in excess of those authorized. Preventing overissue is the function of a corporation's REGISTRAR (usually a bank acting as agent), which works closely with the TRANSFER AGENT in canceling and reissuing certificates presented for transfer and in issuing new shares.

OVERLAPPING DEBT municipal accounting term referring to a municipality's share of the debt of its political subdivisions or the special districts sharing its geographical area. It is usually determined by the ratio of ASSESSED VALUATION of taxable property lying within the corporate limits of the municipality to the assessed valuation of each overlapping district. Overlapping debt is often greater than the direct debt of a municipality, and both must be taken into account in determining the debt burden carried by taxable real estate within a municipality when evaluating MUNICIPAL BOND investments.

OVERNIGHT POSITION broker-dealer's LONG POSITION or SHORT POSITION in a security at the end of a trading day.

OVERNIGHT REPO overnight REPURCHASE AGREEMENT; an arrangement whereby securities dealers and banks finance their inventories of Treasury bills, notes, and bonds. The dealer or bank sells securities to an investor with a temporary surplus of cash, agreeing to buy them back the next day. Such transactions are settled in immediately available FEDERAL FUNDS, usually at a rate below the federal funds rate (the rate charged by banks lending funds to each other).

OVERSHOOT to exceed a target figure, such as an economic goal or an earnings projection.

OVERSOLD description of a stock or market that has experienced an unexpectedly sharp price decline and is therefore due, according to some proponents of TECHNICAL ANALYSIS, for an imminent price rise. If all those who wanted to sell a stock have done so, there are no sellers left, and so the price will rise. *See also* MOMENTUM INDICATORS; OVERBOUGHT.

OVERSUBSCRIBED underwriting term describing a new stock issue for which there are more buyers than available shares. An oversubscribed, or *overbooked,* issue often will jump in price as soon as its shares go on the market, since the buyers who could not get shares will want to buy once the stock starts trading. In some cases, an issuer will increase the number of shares available if the issue is oversubscribed. *See also* GREEN SHOE; HOT ISSUE.

OVER THE COUNTER (OTC)
  1. security that is not listed and traded on an organized exchange.
  2. market in which securities transactions are conducted through a telephone and computer network connecting dealers in stocks and bonds, rather than on the floor of an exchange.

  Over-the-counter stocks are traditionally those of smaller companies that do not meet the LISTING REQUIREMENTS of the New York Stock Exchange or the American Stock Exchange. In recent years, however, many companies that qualify for listing have chosen to remain with over-the-counter trading, because they feel that the system of multiple trading by many dealers is preferable to the centralized trading approach of the New York Stock Exchange, where all trading in a stock has to go through the exchange SPECIALIST in that stock. The rules of over-the-counter stock trading are written and enforced largely by the NATIONAL ASSOCIATION OF SECURITIES DEALERS (NASD), a self-regulatory group. Prices of over-the-counter stocks are published in daily newspapers, with the NATIONAL MARKET SYSTEM stocks listed separately from the rest of the over-the-counter market. Other over-the-counter markets include those for government and municipal bonds. *See also* NASDAQ.

OVERTRADING
Finance: practice of a firm that expands sales beyond levels that can be financed with normal WORKING CAPITAL. Continued overtrading leads to delinquent ACCOUNTS PAYABLE and ultimately to default on borrowings.
New issue underwriting: practice whereby a member of an underwriting group induces a brokerage client to buy a portion of a new issue by purchasing other securities from the client at a premium. The underwriter breaks even on the deal because the premium is offset by the UNDERWRITING SPREAD.
Securities: excessive buying and selling by a broker in a DISCRETIONARY ACCOUNT. *See also* CHURNING.

OVERVALUED description of a stock whose current price is not justified by the earnings outlook or the PRICE/EARNINGS RATIO. It is therefore expected that the stock will drop in price. Overvaluation may result from an emotional buying spurt, which inflates the market price of the stock, or from a deterioration of the company's financial strength. The opposite of overvalued is UNDERVALUED. *See also* FULLY VALUED.

OVERWITHHOLDING situation in which a taxpayer has too much federal, state, or local income tax withheld from salary. Because they have overwithheld, these taxpayers will usually be due income tax refunds after they file their tax returns by April 15. Overwithholding is not desirable for the taxpayer, because it is, in effect, granting the government an interest-free loan. To reduce overwithholding, a taxpayer must file a new W-4 form with his or her employer, increasing the number of dependents claimed, which will reduce the amount of tax withheld. *See also* UNDERWITHHOLDING.

OVERWRITING speculative practice by an OPTION WRITER who believes a security to be overpriced or underpriced and sells CALL OPTIONS or PUT OPTIONS on the security in quantity, assuming they will not be exercised. *See also* OPTION.

OWNER'S EQUITY PAID-IN CAPITAL, donated capital, and RETAINED EARNINGS less the LIABILITIES of a corporation.

P

PAC BOND acronym for *planned amortization class bond,* PAC is a TRANCHE class offered by some COLLATERIZED MORTGAGE OBLIGATIONS (CMOs), which is unlike other CMO classes in that (1) it has a sinking fund schedule that is observed as long as the prepayments on underlying mortgages remain within a broad range of speeds and (2) its ability to make principal payments is not subordinated to other classes. PAC bonds thus offer certainty of cash flow except in extreme prepayment situations, and because of this they trade at a premium to comparable traditional CMOs. *See also* TAC BONDS.

PACIFIC EXCHANGE (PCX) regional exchange founded in 1882, operating a trading floor in San Francisco. The Pacific Exchange changed its name from the Pacific Stock Exchange in 1997. In the following year, the PCX consolidated with the CHICAGO BOARD OPTIONS EXCHANGE (CBOE), combining the two exchange's product lines and operating under the CBOE name. In 1995, it joined the NATIONAL MARKET EXCHANGES—Boston, Chicago and Philadelphia—to establish a uniform definition and standard for measuring price improvement in the NATIONAL MARKET SYSTEM. The exchange trades more than 2700 stocks, bonds, and warrants, including almost all of the most active issues on the NEW YORK STOCK EXCHANGE and AMERICAN STOCK EXCHANGE. PCX also trades every Asian security listed on the NYSE and Amex. More than 700 equity and index options are traded by open outcry. PCX also offers contracts in LEAPS, which are extended term options contracts. The Pacific Exchange is an originating market for small, emerging companies before they reach sufficient size to list in New York; once they achieve this eligibility, they continue listing on the Pacific. Technology companies comprise a large part of its equity listings. The PSE Technology 100 Index is a benchmark for the technology sector, measuring the performance of 100 stocks in 15 technology industries. Other index options offered include the Morgan Stanley Emerging Growth Index and the Wilshire Small Cap Index. PCX formed a partnership with Dow Jones & Co. to list options on its global indices, beginning with the Dow Jones Taiwan Stock Index. The only U.S. exchange on the Pacific Rim, the PCX enjoys formal relationships with exchanges in Hong Kong, Kuala Lumpur, the Philippines, Shaghai, Taiwan, Seoul and Bangkok. In 1998, the PCX was the first U.S. exchange to inaugurate the OptiMark Trading System, a sophisticated electronic system for automatic order formulation, matching, and execution for equities and equity options. Nearly 95% of all equity trades are processed electronically through the P/COAST system. POETS, the exchange's options trading system, generates more than 85% of the exchange's option quotes. The Automated Credit Exchange trades emissions credits for air pollution on the Internet. Trading hours: Monday to Friday, 6:30 A.M. to 4:00 P.M. EST.

PACKAGE MORTGAGE mortgage on both a house and durable personal property in the house, such as appliances and furniture. The borrower therefore repays one mortgage loan instead of having to carry two loans. In construction lending, interim and takeout loans made by the same investor.

PAC-MAN STRATEGY technique used by a corporation that is the target of a takeover bid to defeat the acquirer's wishes. The TARGET COMPANY defends itself by threatening to take over the acquirer and begins buying its common shares. For instance, if company A moves to take over company B against the wishes of the management of company B, company B will begin buying shares in company A in order to thwart A's takeover attempt. The Pac-Man strategy is named after a popular video game of the early 1980s, in which each character that does not swallow its opponents is itself consumed. *See also* TAKEOVER; TENDER OFFER.

PAID-IN CAPITAL capital received from investors in exchange for stock, as distinguished from capital generated from earnings or donated. The paid-in capital account includes CAPITAL STOCK and contributions of stockholders credited to accounts other than capital stock, such as an excess over PAR value received from the sale or exchange of capital stock. It would also include surplus resulting from RECAPITALIZATION. Paid-in capital is sometimes classified more specifically as *additional paid-in capital, paid-in surplus,* or *capital surplus.* Such accounts are distinguished from RETAINED EARNINGS or its older variation, EARNED SURPLUS. *See also* DONATED STOCK.

PAID-IN SURPLUS *see* PAID-IN CAPITAL.

PAID UP a situation in which all payments due have been made. For example, if all premiums on a life insurance policy have been paid, it is known as a PAID-UP POLICY.

PAID-UP POLICY life insurance policy in which all premiums have been paid. Some policies require premium payments for a limited number of years, and if all premium payments have been made over those years, the policy is considered paid in full and requires no more premium payments. Such a policy remains in force until the insured person dies or cancels the policy.

PAINTING THE TAPE
1. illegal practice by manipulators who buy and sell a particular security among themselves to create artificial trading activity, causing a succession of trades to be reported on the CONSOLIDATED TAPE and luring unwary investors to the "action." After causing movement in the market price of the security, the manipulators hope to sell at a profit.
2. consecutive or frequent trading in a particular security, resulting in its repeated appearances on the ticker tape. Such activity is usually attributable to special investor interest in the security.

PAIRED SHARES common stocks of two companies under the same management that are sold as a unit, usually appearing as a single certificate printed front and back. Also called *Siamese shares* or *stapled stock.*

P & I abbreviations for *principal* and *interest* on bonds or mortgage-backed securities. A traditional debt instrument such as a bond makes periodic interest payments and returns bondholders' principal when the bond matures. But in many cases, the principal payment and each of the interest payments are separated from each other by brokerage firms and sold in pieces. When accomplished with Treasury bonds, each of the individual interest payments and the final principal payment is sold as a "stripped" zero-coupon bond known as a STRIP. In the case of a mortgage-backed security, each of the interest payments and principal repayments from mortgagees is packaged into a COLLATERALIZED MORTGAGE OBLIGATION. A security composed of only interest payments is known as an *interest-only* or *IO* security. A security composed of just principal repayments is known as a *principal-only* or PO security. Both IOs and POs are forms of DERIVATIVE SECURITIES.

P & L *see* PROFIT AND LOSS STATEMENT.

PANIC BUYING OR SELLING flurry of buying or selling accompanied by high volume done in anticipation of sharply rising or falling prices. A sudden news event will trigger panic buying or selling, leaving investors little time to evaluate the fundamentals of individual stocks or bonds. Panic buying may be caused by an unexpected cut in interest rates or outcome of a political election. Short sellers may also be forced into panic buying if stock prices start to rise quickly, and they have to cover their short positions to prevent further losses. Panic selling may be set off by an international crisis such as a war or currency devaluation, the assassination of a head of state, or other unforeseen event. If stock prices start to fall sharply, investors may start to panic sell because they fear prices will fall much farther. *See also* CIRCUIT BREAKERS.

PAPER shorthand for *short-term commercial paper,* which is an unsecured note issued by a corporation. The term is also more loosely used to refer to all debt issued by a company, as in "ABC has $100 million in short and long-term paper outstanding."

PAPER DEALER brokerage firm that buys COMMERCIAL PAPER at one rate of interest, usually discounted, and resells it at a lower rate to banks and other investors, making a profit on the difference.

PAPER PROFIT OR LOSS unrealized CAPITAL GAIN or CAPITAL LOSS in an investment or PORTFOLIO. Paper profits and losses are calculated by comparing the current market prices of all stocks, bonds, mutual funds, and commodities in a portfolio to the prices at which those assets were originally bought. These profits or losses become realized only when the securities are sold.

PAPER TRADING *see* MOCK TRADING.

PAR equal to the nominal or FACE VALUE of a security. A bond selling at par, for instance, is worth the same dollar amount it was issued for or at which it will be redeemed at maturity—typically, $1000 per bond.

With COMMON STOCK, par value is set by the company issuing the stock. At one time, par value represented the original investment behind each share of stock in goods, cash, and services, but today this is rarely the case. Instead, it is an assigned amount (such as $1 a share) used to compute the dollar accounting value of the common shares on a company's balance sheet. Par value has no relation to MARKET VALUE, which is determined by such considerations as NET ASSET VALUE, YIELD, and investors' expectations of future earnings. Some companies issue NO-PAR-VALUE STOCK. *See also* STATED VALUE.

Par value has more importance for bonds and PREFERRED STOCK. The interest paid on bonds is based on a percentage of a bond's par value—a 10% bond pays 10% of the bond's par value annually. Preferred dividends are normally stated as a percentage of the par value of the preferred stock issue.

PAR BOND bond that is selling at PAR, the amount equal to its nominal value or FACE VALUE. A corporate bond redeemable at maturity for $1000 is a par bond when it trades on the market for $1000.

PARENT COMPANY company that owns or controls subsidiaries through the ownership of voting stock. A parent company is usually an operating company in its own right; where it has no business of its own, the term HOLDING COMPANY is often preferred.

PARETO'S LAW theory that the pattern of income distribution is constant, historically and geographically, regardless of taxation or welfare policies; also called *law of the trivial many and the critical few* or *80-20 law.* Thus, if 80% of a nation's income will benefit only 20% of the population, the only way to improve the economic lot of the poor is to increase overall output and income levels.

Other applications of the law include the idea that in most business activities a small percentage of the work force produces the major portion of output or that 20% of the customers account for 80% of the dollar volume of sales. The law is attributed to Vilfredo Pareto, an Italian-Swiss engineer and economist (1848–1923).

Pareto is also credited with the concept called *Paretian optimum* (or *optimality*) that resources are optimally distributed when an individual cannot move into a better position without putting someone else into a worse position.

PARIS BOURSE national stock market of France, formed in 1991 when the computerized trading system in Paris was extended to the regional exchanges. It includes four markets: the official list of cash-settled securities; the second market of medium-sized companies; the Hors-Cote market of small companies that is subject to limited disclosure requirements; and NOUVEAU MARCHE, a stock market launched in February 1996, dedicated to innovative, high-growth companies and linked to EURO.NM. Through the Super CAC electronic system, member firms enter orders during an 8:30 A.M. to 10 A.M. pre-opening period. Trading is then continued from 10 A.M. to 5 P.M. Clearing and settlement is done through RELIT, a computerized system based on the simultaneous exchange of securities and cash on the same day, and on the standard time frame for trade comparisons and settlement. Automatic delivery and payment occur three days after a trade. The CAC 40 INDEX is the underlying index for derivative products traded on the MONEP, a subsidiary of the Paris Bourse. The SBF 250 Index is made up of 250 stocks that serve as an indicator of the wider French economy. Structured by sector, the SBF 250 replaced the CAC 240 and the INSEE Weekly Index. The SBF 120 Index is made up of the top 120 stocks based on liquidity and capitalization, and is a benchmark for indexed funds. The Mid-CAC is based on mid-cap securities listed on the Paris Bourse.

PARITY *see* CONVERSION PARITY.

PARITY PRICE price for a commodity or service that is pegged to another price or to a composite average of prices based on a selected prior period. As the two sets of prices vary, they are reflected in an index number on a scale of 100. For example, U.S. farm prices are pegged to prices based on the purchasing power of farmers in the period from 1910 to 1914. If the parity ratio is below 100, reflecting a reduction in purchasing power to the extent indicated, the government compensates the farmer by paying a certain percentage of parity, either in the form of a direct cash payment, in the purchase of surplus crops, or in a NONRECOURSE LOAN.

The concept of parity is also widely applied in industrial wage contracts as a means of preserving the real value of wages.

PARKING placing assets in a safe investment while other investment alternatives are under consideration. For instance, an investor will park the proceeds of a stock or bond sale in an interest-bearing money market fund while considering what other stocks or bonds to purchase. Term also refers to an illegal practice whereby ownership of stock is concealed, and DISCLOSURE requirements circumvented, by holding stock in the name of a conspiring party.

PARTIAL DELIVERY term used when a broker does not deliver the full amount of a security or commodity called for by a contract. If 10,000 shares were to be delivered, for example, and only 7000 shares are transferred, it is called a partial delivery.

PARTICIPATING DIVIDEND dividend paid from PARTICIPATING PREFERRED STOCK.

PARTICIPATING LIFE INSURANCE POLICIES life insurance that pays dividends to policyholders. The policyholders participate in the success or failure of the company's underwriting and investment performance by having their dividends rise or fall. The fewer claims the company experiences and the better its investment performance, the higher the dividends. Policyholders have many choices in what they can do with the dividends. They can have them paid in cash, in which case the income is taxable in the year received; they can use them to reduce policy premiums; they can buy more paid-up insurance, either cash value or term; or they can put them in an account with the insurance company that earns interest. The opposite of a participating policy is a NONPARTICIPATING LIFE INSURANCE POLICY.

PARTICIPATING PREFERRED STOCK PREFERRED STOCK that, in addition to paying a stipulated dividend, gives the holder the right to participate with the common stockholder in additional distributions of earnings under specified conditions. One example would be an arrangement whereby preferred shareholders are paid $5 per share, then common shareholders are paid $5 per share, and then preferred and common shareholders share equally in further dividends up to $1 per share in any one year.

Participating preferred issues are rare. They are used when special measures are necessary to attract investors. Most preferred stock is *nonparticipating preferred stock,* paying only the stipulated dividends.

PARTICIPATION CERTIFICATE certificate representing an interest in a POOL of funds or in other instruments, such as a MORTGAGE POOL. The following quasi-governmental agencies issue and/or guarantee such certificates (also called PASS-THROUGH SECURITIES): FEDERAL HOME LOAN MORTGAGE CORPORATION, FEDERAL NATIONAL MORTGAGE ASSOCIATION, GOVERNMENT NATIONAL MORTGAGE ASSOCIATION, SALLIE MAE.

PARTICIPATION LOAN
Commercial lending: loan made by more than one lender and serviced (administered) by one of the participants, called the *lead bank* or *lead lender.* Participation loans make it possible for large borrowers to obtain bank financing when the amount involved exceeds the legal lending limit of an individual bank (approximately 10% of a bank's capital).
Real estate: mortgage loan, made by a lead lender, in which other lenders own an interest.

PARTNERSHIP contract between two or more people in a joint business who agree to pool their funds and talent and share in the profits and losses of the enterprise. Those who are responsible for the day-to-day management of the partnership's activities, whose individual acts are binding on the other partners, and who are personally liable for the partnership's total liabilities are called *general partners.* Those who contribute only money and are not involved in management decisions are called *limited partners;* their liability is limited to their investment.

Partnerships are a common form of organization for service professions such as accounting and law. Each accountant or lawyer made a partner earns a percentage of the firm's profits.

Limited partnerships are also sold to investors by brokerage firms, financial planners, and other registered representatives. These partnerships may be either public (meaning that a large number of investors will participate and the partnership's plans must be filed with the Securities and Exchange Commission) or private (meaning that only a limited number of investors may participate and the plan need not be filed with the SEC). Both public and private limited partnerships invest in real estate, oil and gas, research and development, and equipment leasing. Some of these partnerships are oriented towards offering tax advantages and capital gains to limited partners, while others are designed to provide mostly income and some capital gains.

See also GENERAL PARTNER; LIMITED PARTNERSHIP; OIL AND GAS LIMITED PARTNERSHIP; PRIVATE LIMITED PARTNERSHIP; PUBLIC LIMITED PARTNERSHIP.

PARTNERSHIP AGREEMENT written agreement among partners specifying the conduct of the partnership, including the division of earnings, procedures for dividing up assets if the partnership is dissolved, and steps to be followed when a partner becomes disabled or dies. Investors in LIMITED PARTNERSHIPS also receive partnership agreements, detailing their rights and responsibilities.

PAR VALUE *see* PAR.

PAR VALUE OF CURRENCY ratio of one nation's currency unit to that of another country, as defined by the official exchange rates between the two countries; also called *par of exchange* or *par exchange rate.* Since 1971, exchange rates have been allowed to float; that is, instead of official rates of exchange, currency values are being determined by the forces of supply and demand in combination with the buying and selling by countries of their own currencies in order to stabilize the market value, a form of PEGGING.

PASSBOOK book issued by a bank to record deposits, withdrawals, and interest earned in a savings account, usually known as a passbook savings account. The passbook lists the depositor's name and account number as well as all transactions. Passbook savings accounts, though usually offering low yields, are safe because deposits in them are insured up to $100,000 by the Federal Deposit Insurance Corporation. There are many alternatives to passbooks today, including ATM machines, telephone banking services, and unlimited transfers.

PASSED DIVIDEND *see* OMITTED DIVIDEND; CUMULATIVE PREFERRED.

PASSIVE income or loss from activities in which a taxpayer does not materially participate, such as LIMITED PARTNERSHIPS, as distinguished from (1) income from wages and active trade or business or (2) *investment (or portfolio) income,* such as dividends and interest. Starting with the TAX REFORM ACT OF 1986, and after modification by the REVENUE RECONCILIATION ACT OF 1993, losses and credits from passive activities are deductible only against income and tax from passive activities, although one passive activity can offset another and unused passive losses can be carried forward until the earlier of (1) your realization of passive income to offset such losses; or (2) your sale of your entire interest in the activity, at which time suspended losses from that activity can be used without limitation. Under the 1986 Act, real estate rental activities were considered passive regardless of material participation. The 1993 Act liberalized that provision for tax years after 1993 by making an exception for professionals spending at least half their time or at least 750 hours involved in real property trade or services or for anyone, apparently including a landlord, meeting the same tests of material participation. Regular corporations (as opposed to S corporations) are exempt from passive activity rules unless they are closely held.

PASSIVE ACTIVITY LOSS (PAL) loss produced by PASSIVE investment activities. *See also* PASSIVE INCOME GENERATOR (PIG).

PASSIVE BOND BOND that yields no interest. Such bonds arise out of reorganizations or are used in NOT-FOR-PROFIT fund raising.

PASSIVE INCOME GENERATOR (PIG) investment whose main attraction is PASSIVE income. The most common example is an income-oriented real estate LIMITED PARTNERSHIP, especially an UNLEVERAGED PROGRAM. Since Tax Reform PASSIVE ACTIVITY LOSSES (PALs) are deductible to the limit of passive activity income, so an investor with excess PALs might buy a PIG as a source of tax-sheltered income.

PASSIVE INVESTING
1. putting money in an investment deemed *passive* by the Internal Revenue Service, such as a LIMITED PARTNERSHIP.
2. investing in a MUTUAL FUND that replicates a market index, such as the STANDARD & POOR'S INDEX, thus assuring investment performance no worse (or better) than the market as a whole. An INDEX FUND charges a much lower MANAGEMENT FEE than an ordinary mutual fund.

PASS THE BOOK system to transfer responsibility for a brokerage firm's trading account from one office to another around the world as trading ends in one place and begins in another. For example, a firm may start the day with the "book" of the firm's securities inventory controlled in London. As the London market closes, the book will be passed to New York, then Los Angeles, then Tokyo, then Singapore, and back to London. Passing the book is necessary because markets are now traded 24 hours a day. Customers wanting to trade at any time will often be referred to the office handling the book at that time.

PASS-THROUGH SECURITY security, representing pooled debt obligations repackaged as shares, that passes income from debtors through the intermediary to investors. The most common type of pass-through is a MORTGAGE-BACKED CERTIFICATE, usually government-guaranteed, where homeowners' principal and interest payments pass from the originating bank or savings and loan through a government agency or investment bank to investors, net of service charges. Pass-throughs representing other types of assets, such as auto loan paper or student loans, are also widely marketed. *See also* CERTIFICATE OF AUTOMOBILE RECEIVABLES (CARS); COLLATERALIZED MORTGAGE OBLIGATION; REMIC.

PATENT exclusive right to use a process or produce or sell a particular product for a designated period of time. In the United States the Patent and Trademarks Office issues design patents good for 14 years and plant and utility patents good for 17 years.

PATTERN technical chart formation made by price movements of stocks, bonds, commodities, or mutual funds. Analysts use patterns to predict future price movements. Some examples of patterns include ASCENDING TOPS; DOUBLE BOTTOM; FLAG; HEAD AND SHOULDERS; RISING BOTTOMS; SAUCER; and TRIANGLE. *See also* TECHNICAL ANALYSIS.

PAWNBROKER individual or employee of a pawn shop who lends money at a high rate of interest to a borrower leaving COLLATERAL such as jewelry, furs, appliances, or other valuable items. If the loan is repaid, the borrower gets the collateral back. If the loan is not repaid, the pawnbroker keeps the collateral, and in many cases, sells it to the public. Borrowers who turn to pawnbrokers and pawn shops typically do not have access to credit from banks or other financial institutions because they are in poor financial condition.

PAY-AS-YOU-GO BASIS INCOME TAX payment option, whereby an employer deducts and remits to the Internal Revenue Service a portion of an employee's monthly salary. Also refers generally to any service that is paid for as it is used.

PAYBACK PERIOD in capital budgeting; the length of time needed to recoup the cost of a CAPITAL INVESTMENT. The payback period is the ratio of the initial investment (cash outlay) to the annual cash inflows for the recovery period. The major shortcoming of the payback period method is that it does not take into account cash flows after the payback period and is therefore not a measure of the profitability of an investment project. For this reason, analysts generally prefer the DISCOUNTED CASH FLOW methods of capital budgeting—namely, the INTERNAL RATE OF RETURN and the NET PRESENT VALUE methods.

PAYDOWN
Bonds: refunding by a company of an outstanding bond issue through a smaller new bond issue, usually to cut interest costs. For instance, a company that issued $100 million of 12% bonds a few years ago will pay down (refund) that debt with a new $80 million issue with an 8% yield. The amount of the net deduction is called the paydown.
Lending: repayment of principal short of full payment. *See also* ON ACCOUNT.

PAYEE person receiving payment through a check, bill, money order, promissory note, credit card, cash, or other payment method.

PAYER person making a payment to a PAYEE through a check, bill, money order, promissory note, cash, credit card, or other form of payment.

PAYING AGENT agent, usually a bank, that receives funds from an issuer of bonds or stock and in turn pays principal and interest to bondholders and dividends to stockholders, usually charging a fee for the service. Sometimes called *disbursing agent.*

PAYMENT DATE date on which a declared stock dividend or a bond interest payment is scheduled to be paid.

PAYMENT IN KIND payment for goods and services made in the form of other goods and services, not cash or other forms of money. Usually, payment in kind is made when the payee returns with the same kind of good or service. For example, if someone's tire blows out, the payee will buy another tire to replace the first one. In the securities world, PAYMENT-IN-KIND SECURITIES pay bondholders in more bonds instead of cash interest. Payment in kind is different from BARTER because the payer gets the same goods and services in return, not other goods or services of equivalent value, as is the case in barter.

PAYMENT-IN-KIND SECURITIES *see* PIK (PAYMENT-IN-KIND) SECURITIES.

PAYOUT RATIO percentage of a firm's profits that is paid out to shareholders in the form of dividends. Young, fast-growing companies reinvest most of their earnings in their business and usually do not pay dividends. Regulated electric, gas, and telephone utility companies have historically paid out larger propor-tions of their highly dependable earnings in dividends than have other industrial corporations. Since these utilities are limited to a specified return on assets and are thus not able to generate from internal operations the cash flow needed for expansion, they pay large dividends to keep their stock attractive to investors desiring yield and are able to finance growth through new securities offerings. *See also* RETENTION RATE.

PAYROLL WITHHOLDING *see* WITHHOLDING (under Taxes: 1).

PAY-TO-PLAY practice in the municipal bond underwriting business in which underwriters feel compelled to contribute to the political campaigns of elected officials who decide which underwriters are awarded the municipality's business. Rules curtailing the practice were promulgated by the MUNICIPAL SECURITIES RULEMAKING BOARD (MSRB), though underwriters still seek to gain influence with elected officials through other means.

PAY UP
1. situation when an investor who wants to buy a stock at a particular price hes-itates and the stock begins to rise. Instead of letting the stock go, he "pays up" to buy the shares at the higher prevailing price.
2. when an investor buys shares in a high quality company at what is felt to be a high price. Such an investor will say "I realize that I am paying up for this stock, but it is worth it because it is such a fine company."

PBR abbreviation for price to BOOK VALUE ratio, which is the market value of a company's stock divided by its TANGIBLE NET WORTH. This ratio is especially significant to securities analysts where real estate not used in operations is a significant portion of assets, such as in the case of a typical Japanese company.

PC commonly used abbreviation for PARTICIPATION CERTIFICATE and, in brokerage parlance, for *plus commissions* (which are added to purchases and subtracted from sales).

PEACE DIVIDEND term used to describe the reallocation of spending from military purposes to peacetime priorities. After the end of World War II and at the end of the Cold War, government officials spoke of the peace dividend which could be spent on housing, education, social initiatives, deficit reduction, and other programs instead of on maintaining the military establishment.

PEGGING stabilizing the price of a security, commodity, or currency by intervening in a market. For example, until 1971 governments pegged the price of gold at certain levels to stabilize their currencies and would therefore buy it when the price dropped and sell when the price rose. Since 1971, a FLOATING EXCHANGE RATE system has prevailed, in which countries use pegging—the buying or selling of their own currencies—simply to offset fluctuations in the exchange rate. The U.S. government uses pegging in another way to support the prices of agricultural commodities, *see* PARITY PRICE.

In floating new stock issues, the managing underwriter is authorized to try to peg the market price and stabilize the market in the issuer's stock by buying shares in the open market. With this one exception, securities price pegging is illegal and is regulated by the Securities and Exchange Commission. *See also* STABILIZATION.

PENALTY CLAUSE clause found in contracts, borrowing agreements, and savings instruments providing for penalties in the event a contract is not kept, a loan payment is late, or a withdrawal is made prematurely. *See also* PREPAYMENT PENALTY.

PENNANT technical chart pattern resembling a pointed flag, with the point facing to the right. Unlike a FLAG pattern, in which rallies and peaks occur in a uniform range, it is formed as the rallies and peaks that give it its shape become less pronounced. A pennant is also characterized by diminishing trade volume. With these differences, this pattern has essentially the same significance as a flag; that is, prices will rise or fall sharply once the pattern is complete.

PENNANT

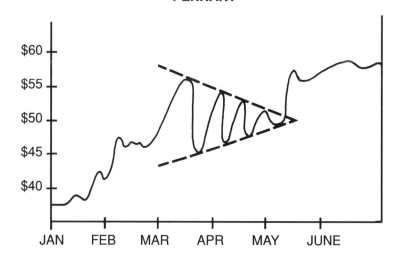

PENNY STOCK stock that typically sells for less than $1 a share, although it may rise to as much as $10 a share after the initial PUBLIC OFFERING, usually because of heavy promotion. Penny stocks are issued by companies with a short or erratic history of revenues and earnings, and therefore such stocks are more VOLATILE than those of large, well-established firms traded on the New York or American stock exchanges. Many brokerage houses therefore have special precautionary rules about trading in these stocks and the SECURITIES AND EXCHANGE COMMISSION (SEC) requires that brokers implement SUITABILITY RULES in writing and obtain written consent from investors.

All penny stocks are traded OVER THE COUNTER, many of them in the local markets of Denver, Vancouver, or Salt Lake City. These markets have had a history of boom and bust, with a speculative fervor for oil, gas, and gold-mining stocks in the Denver penny stock market in the late 1970s turning to bust by the early 1980s.

PENNY STOCK RULE *see* SECURITIES AND EXCHANGE COMMISSION RULES.

PENSION BENEFIT GUARANTY CORPORATION (PBGC) federal corporation established in 1974 under the EMPLOYEE RETIREMENT INCOME SECURITY ACT (ERISA) to guarantee basic pension benefits in covered plans by administering terminated plans and placing liens on corporate assets for certain unfunded pension liabilities. To be covered, a plan must promise clearly defined benefits to more than 25 employees. PBGC collects insurance premiums from pension plans to fund its operations.

When PBGC terminates a pension plan, it pays benefits to pensioners according to the provisions of the plan up to PBGC maximum guarantees. This includes early retirement, disability, and survivor benefits. Under the single employer program, the PBGC limit is adjusted annually based on changes in Social Security contributions and benefit bases. For plans with a 1998 termination date, the maximum annual guarantee is $34,568 for a single life annuity beginning at age 65. The PBGC also conducts a "Pension Search" program which locates people who are owed benefits from terminated fully funded, PBGC-insured defined benefit plans. The agency also offers an "Early Warning" program to target underfunded plans posing the greatest risk of pension fund termination. *See also* PENSION FUND, RETIREMENT PROTECTION ACT OF 1994.

PENSION FUND fund set up by a corporation, labor union, governmental entity, or other organization to pay the pension benefits of retired workers. Pension funds invest billions of dollars annually in the stock and bond markets, and are therefore a major factor in the supply-demand balance of the markets. Earnings on the investment portfolios of pension funds are TAX DEFERRED. Fund managers make actuarial assumptions about how much they will be required to pay out to pensioners and then try to ensure that the RATE OF RETURN on their portfolios equals or exceeds that anticipated payout need. *See also* APPROVED LIST; EMPLOYEE RETIREMENT INCOME SECURITY ACT (ERISA); PRUDENT-MAN RULE; VESTING.

PENSION PARACHUTE pension agreement that specifies that in the event of a hostile takeover attempt, any excess assets in a company pension plan can be used for the benefit of pension plan participants, such as increasing pension payments. This prevents the raiding firm or individual from using the pension assets to finance the takeover, and therefore acts as an additional deterrent to help the firm ward off the acquisition. A pension parachute is a form of POISON PILL.

PENSION PLAN provides replacement for salary when a person is no longer working. In the case of a DEFINED BENEFIT PENSION PLAN, the employer or union contributes to the plan, which pays a predetermined benefit for the rest of the employee's life based on length of service and salary. Payments may be made either directly or through an annuity. Pension payments are taxable income to recipients in the year received. The employer or union has fiduciary responsibility to invest the pension funds in stocks, bonds, real estate, and other assets; earn a satisfactory rate of return; and make payments to retired workers. Pension funds holding trillions of dollars are one of the largest investment forces in the stock, bond, and real estate markets. If the employer defaults, pension plan payments are usually guaranteed by the PENSION BENEFIT GUARANTY CORPORATION (PBGC).

In the case of a DEFINED CONTRIBUTION PENSION PLAN, such as a 401(k) or 403(b) plan, employees choose whether or not to contribute to the plan offered by the employer, who may or may not match employee contributions. Pension benefits are determined by the amount of assets built up by the employee during his or her years of contributions. Self-employed individuals can also set up pension plans such as KEOGH PLANS. An INDIVIDUAL RETIREMENT ACCOUNT (IRA) is a form of pension plan. *See also* VESTING.

PENSION REVERSION procedure initiated by a company with an overfunded DEFINED BENEFIT PENSION PLAN to terminate the plan and reclaim the surplus assets for itself. Pension beneficiaries continue to receive their benefits because the company replaces the pension plan with a life insurance company-sponsored fixed annuity plan. In some cases, the company will offer current employees a DEFINED CONTRIBUTION PENSION PLAN to replace the terminated defined benefit plan. Employees are usually not pleased when their company carries out a pension reversion plan for two reasons: By replacing the pension plan backed by the company with a fixed annuity backed by an insurance company, pensioners are no longer covered by the guarantee of the Pension Benefit Guaranty Corporation; and pensioners lose the prospect for increased pension benefits that they might have enjoyed under the company's pension plan if it had achieved superior investment performance.

PENULTIMATE PROFIT PROSPECT (PPP) second lowest-priced of the ten highest-yielding stocks in the Dow Jones Industrial Average, identified (by co-author's of *Beating the Dow,* Michael B. O'Higgins and John Downes) as the single Dow stock with the greatest probability of outperforming the average as a whole.

PEOPLE PILL defensive tactic to ward off a hostile TAKEOVER. Management threatens that, in the event of a successful takeover, the entire management team will resign at once, leaving the company without experienced leadership. This is a version of the POISON PILL defense.

PER CAPITA in Latin translation, *per head.* In other words, *per person.*

PER CAPITA DEBT total bonded debt of a municipality, divided by its population. A more refined version, called *net per capita debt,* divides the total bonded debt less applicable sinking funds by the total population. The result of either ratio, compared with ratios of prior periods, reveals trends in a municipality's debt burden, which bond analysts evaluate, bearing in mind that, historically, defaults in times of recession have generally followed overexpansion of debts in prior booms.

PERCENTAGE-OF-COMPLETION CAPITALIZED COST METHOD *see* COMPLETED CONTRACT METHOD.

PERCENTAGE ORDER order to a securities broker to buy or sell a specified number of shares of a stock after a fixed number of these shares have been traded. It can be a LIMIT ORDER or a MARKET ORDER and usually applies to one trading day.

PERCS acronym for *preferred equity—redemption cumulative stock.* A form of preferred stock that allows common shareholders to exchange common stock for preferred shares, thereby retaining a high dividend rate. PERCS usually have little appreciation potential, however.

PERFECT COMPETITION market condition wherein no buyer or seller has the power to alter the market price of a good or service. Characteristics of a perfectly competitive market are a large number of buyers and sellers, a homogeneous (similar) good or service, an equal awareness of prices and volume, an absence of discrimination in buying and selling, total mobility of productive resources, and complete freedom of entry. Perfect competition exists only as a theoretical ideal. Also called *pure competition.*

PERFECT HEDGE *see* HEDGE/HEDGING.

PERFORMANCE BOND surety bond given by one party to another, protecting the second party against loss in the event the terms of a contract are not fulfilled. The surety company is primarily liable with the principal (the contractor) for nonperformance. For example, a homeowner having a new kitchen put in may request a performance bond from the home improvement contractor so that the homeowner would receive cash compensation if the kitchen was not done satisfactorily within the agreed upon time.

PERFORMANCE FEE *see* INCENTIVE FEE.

PERFORMANCE FUND MUTUAL FUND designed for growth of capital. A performance fund invests in high-growth companies that do not pay dividends or that pay small dividends. Investors in such funds are willing to take higher-than-average risks in order to earn higher-than-average returns on their invested capital. *See also* GROWTH STOCK; PERFORMANCE STOCK.

PERFORMANCE STOCK high-growth stock that an investor feels will significantly rise in value. Also known as GROWTH STOCK, such a security tends to pay either a small dividend or no dividend at all. Companies whose stocks are in this category tend to retain earnings rather than pay dividends in order to finance their rapid growth. *See also* PERFORMANCE FUND.

PERIODIC PAYMENT PLAN plan to accumulate capital in a mutual fund by making regular investments on a monthly or quarterly basis. The plan has a set pay-in period, which may be 10 or 20 years, and a mechanism to withdraw funds from the plan after that time. Participants in periodic payment plans enjoy the advantages of DOLLAR COST AVERAGING and the diversification among stocks or bonds that is available through a mutual fund. Some plans also include completion insurance, which assures that all scheduled contributions to the plan will continue so that full benefits can be passed on to beneficiaries in the event the participant dies or is incapacitated.

PERIODIC PURCHASE DEFERRED CONTRACT ANNUITY contract for which fixed-amount payments, called *premiums,* are paid either monthly or quarterly and that does not begin paying out until a time elected by the holder (the *annuitant*). In some cases, premium payments may continue after payments from the annuity have begun. A periodic purchase deferred contract can be either fixed or variable. *See also* FIXED ANNUITY; VARIABLE ANNUITY.

PERIOD-CERTAIN ANNUITY annuity that guarantees payments to an ANNUITANT for a particular period of time. For example, a 10-year period-certain annuity will make annuity payments for 10 years and no more. If the annuitant dies before the 10 years have expired, the payments will continue to the policy's beneficiaries for the remaining term. The monthly payment rate for a period-certain annuity is generally higher than the rate for a LIFE ANNUITY because the insurance company knows its maximum liability in advance.

PERIOD OF DIGESTION time period after the release of a NEW ISSUE of stocks or bonds during which the trading price of the security is established in the marketplace. Particularly when an INITIAL PUBLIC OFFERING is released, the period of digestion may entail considerable VOLATILITY, as investors try to ascertain an appropriate price level for it.

PERLS acronym for *principal exchange-rate-linked securities.* Debt instrument that is denominated in U.S. dollars and pays interest in U.S. dollars, but with principal repayment linked to the performance of the U.S. dollar versus a foreign currency. For example, a PERLS offering by the STUDENT LOAN MARKETING ASSOCIATION (Sallie Mae), underwritten by Morgan Stanley Dean Witter, links the principal repayment to the exchange rate of the Australian dollar versus the U.S. dollar. If the Australian dollar gains value against the U.S. dollar when the bond matures, redemption will be at a premium to par value. If the Australian dollar is weaker, redemption will be at a discount.

PERMANENT FINANCING
Corporate finance: long-term financing by means of either debt (bonds or long-term notes) or equity (common or preferred stock).
Real estate: long-term mortgage loan or bond issue, usually with a 15-, 20-, or 30-year term, the proceeds of which are used to repay a CONSTRUCTION LOAN.

PERPENDICULAR SPREAD option strategy using options with similar expiration dates and different strike prices (the prices at which the options can be exercised). A perpendicular spread can be designed for either a bullish or a bearish outlook.

PERPETUAL BOND bond that has no maturity date, is not redeemable and pays a steady stream of interest indefinitely; also called *annuity bond.* The only notable perpetual bonds in existence are the consols first issued by the British Treasury to pay off smaller issues used to finance the Napoleonic Wars (1814). Some persons in the United States believe it would be more realistic to issue perpetual government bonds than constantly to refund portions of the national debt, as is the practice.

PERPETUAL INVENTORY inventory accounting system whereby book inventory is kept in continuous agreement with stock on hand; also called *continuous inventory.* A daily record is maintained of both the dollar amount and the physical quantity of inventory, and this is reconciled to actual physical counts at short intervals. Perpetual inventory contrasts with *periodic inventory.*

PERPETUAL WARRANT investment certificate giving the holder the right to buy a specified number of common shares of stock at a stipulated price with no expiration date. *See also* SUBSCRIPTION WARRANT.

PERQUISITE commonly known as a *perk.* A fringe benefit offered to an employee in addition to salary. Some examples of perquisites are reimbursement for educational expenses, legal services, vacation time, pension plans, life insurance coverage, company cars and aircraft, personal financial counseling, and employee assistance hotlines. In general, the higher an employee's position and the more valued he or she in a company, the more perks he or she receives.

PERSONAL ARTICLE FLOATER policy or an addition to a policy, used to cover personal valuables, such as jewelry and furs.

PERSONAL EXEMPTION amount of money a person can exclude from personal income in calculating federal and state income tax. Taxpayers can claim one exemption for every person in their household. The amount of the personal exemption is adjusted for inflation each year. In 1998, it was $2,650. Taxpayers also can claim additional exemptions for each dependent parent living with them, if the dependent is blind, or over age 65. Exemptions are phased out for certain high-income taxpayers. For a married couple filing jointly, exemptions begin to be phased out when adjusted gross income reaches $181,800 and are eliminated completely for those reporting more than $304,300 in income. For single people, phaseout starts at $121,200, and are eliminated for those reporting over $243,700. For heads of household, the phaseout begins at an income level of $151,500 and is complete at income over $274,000. For married couples filing separately, the phaseout begins at $90,900 and is complete at levels over $152,150.

PERSONAL INCOME income received by persons from all sources: from participation in production, from both government and business TRANSFER PAYMENTS and from government interest (which is treated like a transfer payment). "Persons" refers to individuals, nonprofit institutions that primarily serve individuals, private noninsured welfare funds, and private trust funds. Personal income is calculated as the sum of wages and salary disbursements, other labor income, proprietors' income with inventory valuation and capital consumption adjustment, rental income of persons, with capital consumption adjustment, personal dividend income, personal interest income, and transfer payments to persons, less personal contribution to Social Security.

PERSONAL INFLATION RATE rate of price increases as it affects a specific individual or couple. For example, a young couple with children who are buying and furnishing a home probably will have a much higher personal inflation rate than an elderly couple with their home paid off and self-supporting children, because the young couple needs to buy many more things that are likely to rise in price than the elderly couple. The personal inflation rate is far more relevant for most people than the general inflation rate tracked by the Labor Department's CONSUMER PRICE INDEX.

PERSONAL PROPERTY tangible and intangible assets other than real estate.

PER STIRPES formula for distributing the assets of a person who dies intestate (without a will) according to the "family tree." Under such a distribution, the estate is allocated according to the number of children the deceased had, and distributed accordingly to those surviving the decedent. If any children predeceased the decedent, the share allocated to them would be equally divided among their children and so on.

PETRODOLLARS dollars paid to oil-producing countries and deposited in Western banks. When the price of oil skyrocketed in the 1970s, Middle Eastern oil producers built up huge surpluses of petrodollars that the banks lent to oil-importing countries around the world. By the mid-1980s and 1990s, these surpluses had shrunk because consumption increased while oil exporters spent a good deal of the money on development projects. The flow of petrodollars, therefore, is very important in understanding the current world economic situation. Also called *petrocurrency* or *oil money*.

PHANTOM INCOME LIMITED PARTNERSHIP income that arises from debt restructuring and creates taxability without generating cash flow. Phantom income typically occurs in a tax shelter created prior to the TAX REFORM ACT OF 1986 where real estate properties, having declined in market value, are refinanced; income arises from portions of the debt that are forgiven and recaptured.

PHANTOM STOCK PLAN executive incentive concept whereby an executive receives a bonus based on the market appreciation of the company's stock over a fixed period of time. The hypothetical (hence phantom) amount of shares involved in the case of a particular executive is proportionate to his or her salary level. The plan works on the same principle as a CALL OPTION (a right to purchase a fixed amount of stock at a set price by a particular date). Unlike a call option, however, the executive pays nothing for the option and therefore has nothing to lose.

PHILADELPHIA BOARD OF TRADE (PBOT) subsidiary of the PHILADELPHIA STOCK EXCHANGE which trades currency futures on the Australian dollar, British pound, Canadian dollar, Deutsche mark, EURO, French franc, Japanese yen and Swiss franc. Options are traded on the PSE's United Currency Options Market.

PHILADELPHIA STOCK EXCHANGE (PHLX) founded in 1790 as the first organized stock exchange in the U.S. PHLX trades equities, equity options, sector index options and currency options. In 1998, the exchange became a charter member of the NASD/AMEX family of companies, formed with the merger of the AMERICAN STOCK EXCHANGE, (AMEX) and the NASDAQ STOCK MARKET. The alignment combines the best technology of the two entities and provides for operation of the PHLX trading floor in Philadelphia for up to five years. Trading is conducted through floor brokers or PACE (Philadelphia Automated Communication and Execution System), the exchange's electronic retail-oriented delivery and execution system. After the market officially closes at 4 P.M., PHLX's Post Primary Session (PPS) offers trading from 4:00 P.M. to 4:15 P.M. to allow institutional traders the ability to complete unfilled trades. PHLX also offers the VWAP (Volume Weighted Average Price) Trading System, which allows institutions to match equity orders before and after the market is open in an automated and electronic manner.

PHLX trades over 700 equity options, LEAPS (Long-Term Equity AnticiPation Securities) and FLEX (Flexible Exchange) options. LEAPS are options contracts with expiration dates as long as three years in the future. FLEX options allow users to tailor equity and index options to meet hedging and investment needs by allowing them to specify expiration dates, strike prices, and exercise styles. These options trades are executed by AUTOM (the Automated Options Market), which enables brokerage firms to electronically transmit retail customer orders directly to the trading floor for execution.

The exchange also trades several sector index options, covering both broad and industry specific market sectors. Some of the broad-based sectors include the National OTC Sector, SuperCap Sector, US TOP 100 Index, and Value Line Composite Index. Some of the industry-specific sectors include airlines, banking, forest and paper products, gold/silver, oil services, phones, semiconductors and utilities. Trading hours are 9:30 A.M. to 4:15 P.M.

PHLX, a leader in the trading of foreign currency options, offers the United Currency Options Market (UCOM) in such currencies as the Australian dollar, British pound, Canadian dollar, Deustsche mark, European Currency Unit, French franc, Italian lira, Japanese yen, Mexican peso, Spanish peseta, Swiss franc and U.S. dollar. UCOM offers trading in 3-D options, which are cash settled in U.S. dollars, and are also available in Japanese yen and Deutsche marks. Trading hours are 2:30 A.M. to 2:30 P.M. Monday through Friday. *See also* SECURITIES AND COMMODITIES EXCHANGES.

PHILIPPINE STOCK EXCHANGE operates two trading floors, Manila and Makati; Manila is the larger. Trading hours are from 9:30 A.M. to 12 noon, Monday through Friday, with a 15-minute extension at closing prices, and a 10-minute break at 10:50 A.M. Settlement takes place on the fourth business day after a trade.

PHYSICAL COMMODITY actual commodity that is delivered to the contract buyer at the completion of a commodity contract in either the SPOT MARKET or the FUTURES MARKET. Some examples of physical commodities are corn, cotton, gold, oil, soybeans, and wheat. The quality specifications and quantity of the commodity to be delivered are specified by the exchange on which it is traded.

PHYSICAL INVENTORY *see* PHYSICAL VERIFICATION.

PHYSICAL VERIFICATION procedure by which an auditor actually inspects the assets of a firm, particularly inventory, to confirm their existence and value, rather than relying on written records. The auditor may use statistical sampling in the verification process.

PICKUP value gained in a bond swap. For example, bonds with identical coupon rates and maturities may have different market values, mainly because of a difference in quality, and thus in yields. The higher yield of the lower-quality bond received in such a swap compared with the yield of the higher-quality bond that was exchanged for it results in a net gain for the trader, called his or her pickup on the transaction.

PICKUP BOND bond that has a relatively high coupon (interest) rate and is close to the date at which it is callable—that is, can be paid off prior to maturity—by the issuer. If interest rates fall, the investor can look forward to picking up a redemption PREMIUM, since the bond will in all likelihood be called.

PICTURE Wall Street jargon used to request bid and asked prices and quantity information from a specialist or from a dealer regarding a particular security. For example, the question "What's the picture on XYZ?" might be answered, "58⅜ [best bid] to ¾ [best offer is 58¾], 1000 either way [there are both a buyer and a seller for 1000 shares]."

PIG *see* PASSIVE INCOME GENERATOR.

PIGGYBACKING illegal practice by a broker who buys or sells stocks or bonds in his personal account after a customer buys or sells the same security. The broker assumes that the customer is making the trade because of access to material, nonpublic information that will make the stock or bond rise or fall sharply. Trading following customer orders is a conflict of interest, and may be disciplined by the broker's firm or regulatory authorities if discovered.

PIGGYBACK REGISTRATION situation when a securities underwriter allows existing holdings of shares in a corporation to be sold in combination with an offering of new public shares. The prospectus in a piggyback registration will reveal the nature of such a public/private share offering and name the sellers of the private shares. See also public offering.

PIK (PAYMENT-IN-KIND) SECURITIES bonds or preferred stock that pay interest/dividends in the form of additional bonds or preferred. PIK securities have been used in takeover financing in lieu of cash and are highly speculative.

PINK SHEETS daily publication of the national quotation bureau that details the bid and asked prices of over the counter (OTC) stocks not carried in daily newspaper listings of NASDAQ STOCK MARKET. Brokerage firms subscribe to the pink sheets—named for their color—because the sheets not only give current prices but list market makers who trade each stock. Debt securities are listed separately on YELLOW SHEETS. *See also* OTC BULLETIN BOARD.

PIN NUMBER acronym for *personal identification number.* Customers use PIN numbers to identify themselves, such as when performing transactions with a debit card at an automatic teller machine.

PIPELINE term referring to the underwriting process that involves securities being proposed for public distribution. The phrase used is "in the pipeline." The entire underwriting process, including registration with the Securities and

Exchange Commission, must be completed before a security can be offered for public sale. Underwriters attempt to have several securities issues waiting in the pipeline so that the issues can be sold as soon as market conditions become favorable. In the municipal bond market, the pipeline is called the "Thirty Day Visible Supply" in the *Bond Buyer* newspaper.

PIT location at a futures or options exchange in which trading takes place. Pits are usually shaped like rings, often with several levels of steps, so that a large number of traders can see and be seen by each other as they conduct business.

PITI acronym for *principal, interest, taxes and insurance,* the primary components of monthly mortgage payments. Many mortgage lenders, to ensure that property taxes and homeowner's insurance premiums are paid on schedule, require that borrowers include these amounts in their monthly payments. The funds are then placed in escrow until needed. When calculating how much a house will cost a borrower on a monthly basis, the payment is expressed for PITI.

PLACE to market new securities. The term applies to both public and private sales but is more often used with reference to direct sales to institutional investors, as in PRIVATE PLACEMENT. The terms FLOAT and *distribute* are preferred in the case of a PUBLIC OFFERING.

PLACEMENT RATIO ratio, compiled by the *Bond Buyer* as of the close of business every Thursday, indicating the percentage of the past week's new MUNICIPAL BOND offerings that have been bought from the underwriters. Only issues of $1 million or more are included.

PLANNED AMORTIZATION CLASS BONDS *see* PAC BONDS.

PLAN PARTICIPANTS employees or former employees of a company, members of an employee organization or beneficiaries who may become eligible to receive benefits from an employee benefit plan. Participants are legally entitled to certain information about the plan and the benefits, including a summary annual report and summary plan description.

PLAN SPONSOR entity that establishes and maintains a pension or insurance plan. This may be a corporation, labor union, government agency, or nonprofit organization. Plan sponsors must follow government guidelines in the establishment and administration of these plans, including informing plan participants about the financial health of the plan and the benefits available.

PLANT assets comprising land, buildings, machinery, natural resources, furniture and fixtures, and all other equipment permanently employed. Synonymous with FIXED ASSET.

In a limited sense, the term is used to mean only buildings or only land and buildings: "property, plant, and equipment" and "plant and equipment."

PLAYING THE MARKET unprofessional buying and selling of stocks, as distinguished from SPECULATION. Both players and speculators are seeking capital gains, but while playing the market is more akin to gambling, speculating is done by professionals taking calculated risks.

PLAZA ACCORD agreement in August of 1985 in which the finance ministers of the Group of 5—the United States, Great Britain, France, Germany, and Japan—met at the Plaza Hotel in New York City to mount a concerted effort to reduce the value of the U.S. dollar against other major currencies. Though the dollar had already begun its decline months earlier, the Plaza Accord accelerated the move. The action was necessary because the dollar had become so strong that it was difficult for U.S. exporters to sell their products abroad, weakening the American economy.

PLC *see* PUBLIC LIABILITY COMPANY.

PLEDGING transferring property, such as securities or the CASH SURRENDER VALUE of life insurance, to a lender or creditor as COLLATERAL for an obligation. *Pledge* and *hypothecate* are synonymous, as they do not involve transfer of title. ASSIGN, although commonly used interchangeably with *pledge* and *hypothecate,* implies transfer of ownership or of the right to transfer ownership at a later date. *See also* HYPOTHECATION.

PLOW BACK to reinvest a company's earnings in the business rather than pay out those profits as dividends. Smaller, fast-growing companies usually plow back most or all earnings in their businesses, whereas more established firms pay out more of their profits as dividends.

PLUS

1. plus sign (+) that follows a price quotation on a Treasury note or bond, indicating that the price (normally quoted as a percentage of PAR value refined to 32ds) is refined to 64ths. Thus 95.16 + (95$^{16}\!/_{32}$+ or 95$^{33}\!/_{64}$+) means 95$^{33}\!/_{64}$.
2. plus sign after a transaction price in a listed security (for example, 39½+), indicating that the trade was at a higher price than the previous REGULAR WAY transaction. *See also* PLUS TICK.
3. plus sign before the figure in the column labeled "Change" in the newspaper stock tables, meaning that the closing price of the stock was higher than the previous day's close by the amount stated in the "Change" column.

PLUS TICK expression used when a security has been traded at a higher price than the previous transaction in that security. A stock price listed as 28+ on the CONSOLIDATED TAPE has had a plus tick from 27$^{15}\!/_{16}$ or below on previous trades. It is a Securities and Exchange Commission rule that short sales can be executed only on plus ticks or ZERO-PLUS TICKS. Also called *uptick. See also* MINUS TICK; TICK; ZERO-MINUS TICK.

POINT

Bonds: percentage change of the face value of a bond expressed as a point. For example, a change of 1% is a move of one point. For a bond with a $1000 face value, each point is worth $10, and for a bond with a $5000 face value, each point is $50.

Bond yields are quoted in basis points: 100 basis points make up 1% of yield. *See* BASIS POINT.

Futures/options: measure of price change equal to one one-hundredth of one cent in most futures traded in decimal units. In grains, it is one quarter of one cent; in Treasury bonds, it is 1% of par. *See also* TICK.

Real estate and other commercial lending: upfront fee charged by a lender, separate from interest but designed to increase the overall yield to the lender. A point is 1% of the total principal amount of the loan. For example, on a $100,000 mortgage loan, a charge of 3 points would equal $3000. Since points are considered a form of prepaid mortgage interest, they are tax-deductible, usually over the term of the loan, but in some cases in a lump sum in the year they are paid.

Stocks: change of $1 in the market price of a stock. If a stock has risen 5 points, it has risen by $5 a share.

The movements of stock market averages, such as the Dow Jones Industrial Average, are also quoted in points. However, those points refer not to dollar amounts but to units of movement in the average, which is a composite of weighted dollar values. For example, a 20-point move in the Dow Jones Average from 8000 to 8020 does *not* mean the Dow now stands at $8020.

POINT AND FIGURE CHART graphic technique used in TECHNICAL ANALYSIS to follow the up or down momentum in the price moves of a security or sector.

Point and figure charting disregards the element of time and is solely used to record changes in price. Every time a price move is upward, an X is put on the graph above the previous point. Every time the price moves down, an O is placed one square down. When direction changes, the next column is used. The resulting lines of Xs and Os will indicate whether the security or sector being charted has maintained an up or a down momentum over a particular time period.

POINT AND FIGURE CHART

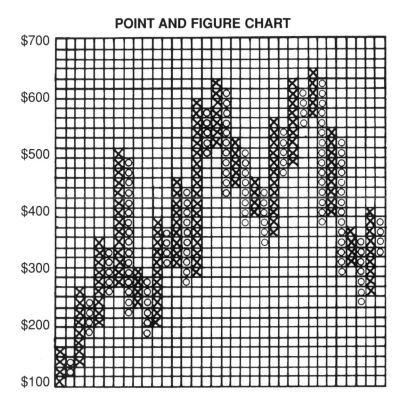

POISON PILL strategic move by a takeover-target company to make its stock less attractive to an acquirer. For instance, a firm may issue a new series of PREFERRED STOCK that gives shareholders the right to redeem it at a premium price after a TAKEOVER. Two variations: a *flip-in poison pill* allows all existing holders of target company shares except the acquirer to buy additional shares at a bargain price; a *flip-over poison pill* allows holders of common stock to buy (or holders of preferred stock to convert into) the acquirer's shares at a bargain price in the event of an unwelcome merger. Such measures raise the cost of an ACQUISITION, and cause DILUTION, hopefully deterring a takeover bid. A third type of poison pill, known as a PEOPLE PILL, is the threat that in the event of a successful takeover, the entire management team will resign at once, leaving the company without experienced leadership. *See also* PENSION PARACHUTE, POISON PUT, SUICIDE PILL.

POISON PUT provision in an INDENTURE giving bondholders the privilege of redemption at PAR if certain designated events occur, such as a hostile TAKEOVER, the purchase of a big block of shares, or an excessively large dividend payout. Poison puts, or *superpoison puts* as the more stringent variations are called, are popular antitakeover devices because they create an onerous cash obligation for the acquirer. They also protect the bondholder from the deterioration of credit quality and RATING that might result from a LEVERAGED BUYOUT that added to the issuer's debt. *See also* EVENT RISK.

POLICYHOLDER owner of an INSURANCE contract (policy). Term is commonly used synonymously with *insured,* although the two can be different parties and *insured* is the preferred designation for the person indemnified by the insurance company.

POLICYHOLDER LOAN BONDS packaged policyholder loans. Life insurance policyholders borrow against the CASH SURRENDER VALUE of their policies. The policyholder loan will be repaid either by the policyholder while alive or from the proceeds of the insurance policy if the policyholder dies before repayment. These loans are packaged by a broker/dealer that offers these asset-backed securities as policyholder loan bonds.

POLICY LIMIT limit of coverage provided by an insurance policy, known as a *maximum lifetime benefit.* For coverage of individuals, roughly two-thirds of existing policies have a limit of $1 million or more; 21% have no limit. Most employee plans are based on maximum lifetime coverage.

POLICY LOAN loan from an insurance company secured by the CASH SURRENDER VALUE of a life insurance policy. The amount available for such a loan depends on the number of years the policy has been in effect, the insured's age when the policy was issued, and the size of the death benefit. Such loans are often made at below-market interest rates to policyholders, although more recent policies usually only allow borrowing at rates that fluctuate in line with money market rates. If the loan is not repaid by the insured, the death benefit of the life insurance policy will be reduced by the amount of the loan plus accrued interest.

POOL
   Capital budgeting: as used in the phrase "pool of financing," the concept that investment projects are financed out of a pool of funds rather than out of bonds, preferred stock, and common stock individually. A weighted average cost of capital is thus used in analyses evaluating the return on investment projects. *See also* COST OF CAPITAL.
   Industry: joining of companies to improve profits by reducing competition. Such poolings are generally outlawed in the United States by various ANTITRUST LAWS.
   Insurance: association of insurers who share premiums and losses in order to spread risk and give small insurers an opportunity to compete with larger ones.
   Investments:
   1. combination of resources for a common purpose or benefit. For example, an INVESTMENT CLUB pools the funds of its members, giving them the opportunity to share in a PORTFOLIO offering greater diversification and the hope of a better return on their money than they could get individually. A *commodities pool* entrusts the funds of many investors to a trading professional and distributes profits and losses among participants in proportion to their interests.
   2. group of investors joined together to use their combined power to manipulate security or commodity prices or to obtain control of a corporation. Such pools are outlawed by regulations governing securities and commodities trading.
      See also MORTGAGE POOL.

POOLING OF INTERESTS accounting method used in the combining or merging of companies following an acquisition, whereby the balance sheets (assets and liabilities) of the two companies are simply added together, item by item. This tax-free method contrasts with the PURCHASE ACQUISITION method, in which the buying company treats the acquired company as an investment and any PREMIUM paid over the FAIR MARKET VALUE of the assets is reflected on the buyer's balance sheet as GOODWILL. Because reported earnings are higher under the pooling of interests method, most companies prefer it to the purchase acquisition method, particularly when the amount of goodwill is sizable.

The pooling of interests method can be elected only when the following conditions are met:

1. The two companies must have been autonomous for at least two years prior to the pooling and one must not have owned more than 10% of the stock of the other.
2. The combination must be consummated either in a single transaction or in accordance with a specific plan within one year after the plan is initiated; no contingent payments are permitted.
3. The acquiring company must issue its regular common stock in exchange for 90% or more of the common stock of the other company.
4. The surviving corporation must not later retire or reacquire common stock issued in the combination, must not enter into an arrangement for the benefit of former stockholders, and must not dispose of a significant portion of the assets of the combining companies for at least two years.

See also MERGER.

PORCUPINE PROVISIONS *see* SHARK REPELLENTS.

PORTABILITY ability of employees to retain benefits from one employer to the next when switching jobs. The term is most frequently used in connection with pension and insurance coverage. Credits earned towards pension benefits in a DEFINED BENEFIT PENSION PLAN are rarely portable from one company to another. Conversely, accumulated assets in a DEFINED CONTRIBUTION PENSION PLAN may be transferable to the defined contribution plan of another employer through a rollover. Under the CONSOLIDATED OMNIBUS BUDGET RECONCILIATION ACT (COBRA), employees have the right to carry their group health insurance coverage with them to a new job for up to 18 months. An employee may wish to do so if the new employer's health plan is inferior to the previous employer's plan. Employees choosing to continue coverage with a previous employer's group plan under the COBRA provision pay the full premium, which is subject to change. Generally, this continued coverage costs considerably less than a policy at individual rates.

PORTFOLIO combined holding of more than one stock, bond, commodity, real estate investment, CASH EQUIVALENT, or other asset by an individual or institutional investor. The purpose of a portfolio is to reduce risk by diversification. *See also* PORTFOLIO BETA SCORE; PORTFOLIO THEORY.

PORTFOLIO BETA SCORE relative VOLATILITY of an individual securities portfolio, taken as a whole, as measured by the BETA coefficients of the securities making it up. Beta measures the volatility of a stock relative to the market as a whole, as represented by an index such as Standard & Poor's 500 Stock Index. A beta of 1 means the stock has about the same volatility as the market.

PORTFOLIO INCOME *see* INVESTMENT INCOME.

PORTFOLIO INSURANCE the use, by a PORTFOLIO MANAGER, of STOCK INDEX FUTURES to protect stock portfolios against market declines. Instead of selling actual stocks as they lose value, managers sell the index futures; if the drop continues, they repurchase the futures at a lower price, using the profit to offset losses in the stock portfolio. The inability of the markets on BLACK MONDAY to process such massive quantities of stock efficiently and the subsequent instituting of CIRCUIT BREAKERS all but eliminated portfolio insurance. *See also* PROGRAM TRADING.

PORTFOLIO MANAGER professional responsible for the securities PORTFOLIO of an individual or INSTITUTIONAL INVESTOR. Also called a *money manager* or, especially when personalized service is involved, an INVESTMENT COUNSEL. A portfolio manager may work for a mutual fund, pension fund, profit-sharing plan, bank trust department, or insurance company. In return for a fee, the manager has the fiduciary responsibility to manage the assets prudently and choose whether stocks, bonds, CASH EQUIVALENTS, real estate, or some other assets present the best opportunities for profit at any particular time. *See also* PORTFOLIO THEORY; PRUDENT-MAN RULE.

PORTFOLIO THEORY sophisticated investment decision approach that permits an investor to classify, estimate, and control both the kind and the amount of expected risk and return; also called *portfolio management theory* or *modern portfolio theory.* Essential to portfolio theory are its quantification of the relationship between risk and return and the assumption that investors must be compensated for assuming risk. Portfolio theory departs from traditional security analysis in shifting emphasis from analyzing the characteristics of individual investments to determining the statistical relationships among the individual securities that comprise the overall portfolio. The portfolio theory approach has four basic steps: *security valuation*—describing a universe of assets in terms of expected return and expected risk; *asset allocation decision*—determining how assets are to be distributed among classes of investment, such as stocks or bonds; *portfolio optimization*—reconciling risk and return in selecting the securities to be included, such as determining which portfolio of stocks offers the best return for a given level of expected risk; and *performance measurement*—dividing each stock's performance (risk) into market-related (systematic) and industry/security-related (residual) classifications.

POSITION
Banking: bank's net balance in a foreign currency.
Finance: firm's financial condition.
Investments:
1. investor's stake in a particular security or market. A LONG POSITION equals the number of shares *owned;* a SHORT POSITION equals the number of shares *owed* by a dealer or an individual. The dealer's long positions are called his *inventory of securities.*
2. Used as a verb, to take on a long or a short position in a stock.

POSITION BUILDING process of buying shares to accumulate a LONG POSITION or of selling shares to accumulate a SHORT POSITION. Large institutional investors who want to build a large position in a particular security do so over time to avoid pushing up the price of the security.

POSITION LIMIT
Commodities trading: number of contracts that can be acquired in a specific commodity before a speculator is classified as a "large trader." Large traders are subject to special oversight by the COMMODITY FUTURES TRADING COMMISSION (CFTC) and the exchanges and are limited as to the number of contracts they can add to their positions. The position limit varies with the type of commodity.
Options trading: maximum number of exchange-listed OPTION contracts that can be owned or controlled by an individual holder, or by a group of holders acting jointly, in the same underlying security. The current limit is 2000 contracts on the same side of the market (for example, long calls and short puts are one side of the market); the limit applies to all expiration dates.

POSITION TRADER commodities trader who takes a long-term approach—six months to a year or more—to the market. Usually possessing more than average experience, information, and capital, these traders ride through the ups and downs of price fluctuations until close to the delivery date, unless drastic adverse developments threaten. More like insurance underwriters than gamblers, they hope to achieve long-term profits from calculated risks as distinguished from pure speculation.

POSITIVE CARRY situation in which the cost of money borrowed to finance securities is lower than the yield on the securities. For example, if a fixed-income bond yielding 10% is purchased with a loan bearing 8% interest, the bond has positive carry. The opposite situation is called NEGATIVE CARRY.

POSITIVE YIELD CURVE situation in which interest rates are higher on long-term debt securities than on short-term debt securities of the same quality. For example, a positive yield curve exists when 20-year Treasury bonds yield 10% and 3-month Treasury bills yield 6%. Such a situation is common, since an investor who ties up his money for a longer time is taking more risk and is usually compensated by a higher yield. When short-term interest rates rise above long-term rates, there is a NEGATIVE YIELD CURVE, also called an INVERTED YIELD CURVE.

POSITIVE YIELD CURVE

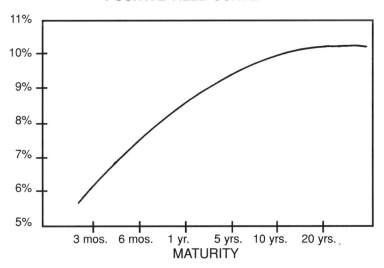

POST

Accounting: to transfer from a journal of original entry detailed financial data, in the chronological order in which it was generated, into a ledger book. Banks post checking account deposits and withdrawals in a ledger, then summarize these transactions on the monthly bank statement.

Investments: horseshoe-shaped structure on the floor of the New York Stock Exchange where specialists trade specific securities. Video screens surround the post, displaying the bid and offer prices available for stocks traded at that location. Also called *trading post.*

POSTDATED CHECK check dated in the future. It is not negotiable until the date becomes current.

POSTING in bookkeeping terminology, the transfer of data from a journal to a ledger.

POSTPONING INCOME technique to delay receipt of income into a later year to reduce current tax liability. For example, if it seems likely that Congress or the state legislature may reduce income tax rates in the upcoming year, it may be advantageous to receive income in that year instead of in the current year when tax rates are higher. Salespeople can appeal to their managers to pay their commissions in the next year, and small business owners can send invoices after the first of the year so that they are paid in the next year. In addition to qualifying for a lower tax rate, the full tax on the income may be delayed until April 15 of the following year, unless the taxpayer receiving the income is required to file quarterly estimated tax payments.

POT securities underwriting term meaning the portion of a stock or bond issue returned to the MANAGING UNDERWRITER by the participating investment bankers to facilitate sales to INSTITUTIONAL INVESTORS. Institutions buying from the pot designate the firms to be credited with pot sales. *See also* RETENTION.

POT IS CLEAN MANAGING UNDERWRITER'S announcement to members of the underwriting group that the POT—the portion of the stock or bond issue withheld to facilitate institutional sales—has been sold.

POWER OF ATTORNEY
In general: written document that authorizes a particular person to perform certain acts on behalf of the one signing the document. The document, which must be witnessed by a notary public or some other public officer, may bestow either *full power of attorney* or *limited power of attorney*. It becomes void upon the death of the signer.

Investments: *full power of attorney* might, for instance, allow assets to be moved from one brokerage or bank account to another. A *limited power of attorney,* on the other hand, would only permit transactions within an existing account. A broker given a limited power of attorney, for instance, may buy and sell securities in an account but may not remove them. Such an account is called a DISCRETIONARY ACCOUNT.

See also DISCRETIONARY ORDER; PROXY; STOCK POWER.

PREARRANGED TRADING questionable and probably fraudulent practice whereby commodities dealers arrange risk-free trades at predetermined prices, usually to gain tax advantages.

PREAUTHORIZED PAYMENT prearranged deductions from a bank account for the payment of a third party.

PRECEDENCE priority of one order over another on the floor of the exchanges, according to rules designed to protect the DOUBLE-AUCTION SYSTEM. The rules basically are that the highest bid and lowest offer have precedence over other bids and offers, that the first bid or first offer at a price has priority over other bids or offers at that price, and that the size of the order determines precedence thereafter, large orders having priority over smaller orders. Where two orders of equal size must compete for the same limited quantity after the first bid is filled, the impasse is resolved by a flip of the coin. *See also* MATCHED AND LOST. Exchange rules also require that public orders have precedence over trades for floor members' own accounts. *See also* OFF-FLOOR ORDER; ON-FLOOR ORDER.

PRECIOUS METALS gold, silver, platinum, and palladium. These metals are valued for their intrinsic value, backing world currencies, as well as their industrial applications. Fundamental issues of supply and demand are important factors in their prices, along with political and economic considerations, especially when producing countries are involved. Inflation fears will stimulate gold accumulation and higher prices, as will war and natural disaster, especially in major producing or consuming countries or regions. Precious metals are held by central banks and are considered a storehouse of value. While gold is often singled out, cultural factors assign different levels of significance to the metals. In the Far East, especially Japan, platinum traditionally is held in higher regard than gold, both in terms of physical metal and investment holdings, and for personal accumulation (e.g., jewelry and coins). Gold is favored in the West. In India and the Middle East, silver is highly prized, and the dowries of Indian women are replete with silver jewelry and coins. Investors can buy physical metal in bars, BULLION and NUMISMATIC COINS, and jewelry. There are numerous investment vehicles that do not involve physical delivery: futures and options contracts, mining company stocks, bonds, mutual funds, commodity indices, and commodity funds. The values of these investment vehicles are influenced by metal price volatility, with commodity funds and indices, and futures and options, more sensitive to daily price swings. Many metals analysts and advisors recommend that 5% to 15% of investor portfolios be held in some form of precious metals as a long-term hedge against inflation and political turmoil.

PRECOMPUTE in installment lending, methods of charging interest whereby the total amount of annual interest either is deducted from the face amount of the loan at the time the loan proceeds are disbursed or is added to the total amount to be repaid in equal installments. In both cases, the EFFECTIVE RATE to the borrower is higher than the stated annual rate used in the computation. "Truth in lending" laws require that the effective annual rate be expressed in SIMPLE INTEREST terms.

PREEMPTIVE RIGHT right giving existing stockholders the opportunity to purchase shares of a NEW ISSUE before it is offered to others. Its purpose is to protect shareholders from dilution of value and control when new shares are issued. Although 48 U.S. states have preemptive right statutes, most states also either permit corporations to pay stockholders to waive their preemptive rights or state in their statutes that the preemptive right is valid only if set forth in the corporate charter. As a result, preemptive rights are the exception rather than the rule. Where they do exist, the usual procedure is for each existing stockholder to receive, prior to a new issue, a SUBSCRIPTION WARRANT indicating how many new shares the holder is entitled to buy—normally, a proportion of the shares he or she already holds. Since the new shares would typically be priced below the market, a financial incentive exists to exercise the preemptive right. *See also* SUBSCRIPTION RIGHT.

PREFERENCE ITEM *see* TAX PREFERENCE ITEM.

PREFERENCE SHARES *see* PRIOR-PREFERRED STOCK.

PREFERRED DIVIDEND COVERAGE net income after interest and taxes (but before common stock dividends) divided by the dollar amount of preferred stock dividends. The result tells how many times over the preferred dividend requirement is covered by current earnings.

PREFERRED STOCK class of CAPITAL STOCK that pays dividends at a specified rate and that has preference over common stock in the payment of dividends and the liquidation of assets. Preferred stock does not ordinarily carry voting rights.

Most preferred stock is *cumulative;* if dividends are passed (not paid for any reason), they accumulate and must be paid before common dividends. A PASSED DIVIDEND on *noncumulative preferred* stock is generally gone forever. PARTICIPATING PREFERRED STOCK entitles its holders to share in profits above and beyond the declared dividend, along with common shareholders, as distinguished from *nonparticipating preferred,* which is limited to the stipulated dividend. *Adjustable-rate preferred* stock pays a dividend that is adjustable, usually quarterly, based on changes in the Treasury bill rate or other money market rates. *Convertible preferred stock* is exchangeable for a given number of common shares and thus tends to be more VOLATILE than *nonconvertible preferred,* which behaves more like a fixed-income bond. *See also* CONVERTIBLE; CUMULATIVE PREFERRED; PARTICIPATING PREFERRED; PIK (PAYMENT-IN-KIND) SECURITIES; PRIOR, PREFERRED STOCK.

PREFERRED STOCK RATIO PREFERRED STOCK at PAR value divided by total CAPITALIZATION; the result is the percentage of capitalization—bonds and net worth—represented by preferred stock.

PRELIMINARY PROSPECTUS first document released by an underwriter of a NEW ISSUE to prospective investors. The document offers financial details about the issue but does not contain all the information that will appear in the final or statutory prospectus, and parts of the document may be changed before the final prospectus is issued. Because portions of the cover page of the preliminary prospectus are printed in red ink, it is popularly called the *red herring.*

PREMIUM
In general: extra payment usually made as an incentive.
Bonds:
1. amount by which a bond sells above its face (PAR) value. For instance, a bond with a face value of $1000 would sell for a $100 premium when it cost $1100. The same meaning also applies to preferred stock. *See also* PREMIUM BOND; PREMIUM OVER BOND VALUE; PREMIUM OVER CONVERSION VALUE.
2. amount by which the REDEMPTION PRICE to the issuer exceeds the face value when a bond is called. *See also* CALL PREMIUM.
Insurance: fee paid to an insurance company for insurance protection. Also, the single or multiple payments made to build an ANNUITY fund.
Options: price a put or call buyer must pay to a put or call seller (writer) for an option contract. The premium is determined by market supply and demand forces. *See also* OPTION; PREMIUM INCOME.
Stocks:
1. charge occasionally paid by a short seller when stock is borrowed to make delivery on a SHORT SALE.
2. amount by which a stock's price exceeds that of other stocks to which it is comparable. For instance, securities analysts might say that XYZ Foods is selling at a 15% premium to other food company stocks—an indication that the stock is more highly valued by investors than its industry peers. It does not necessarily mean that the stock is overpriced, however. Indeed, it may indicate that the investment public has only begun to recognize the stock's market potential and that the price will continue to rise. Similarly, analysts might say that the food industry is selling for a 20% premium to Standard & Poor's 500 index, indicating the relative price strength of the industry group to the stock market as a whole.
3. in new issues, amount by which the trading price of the shares exceeds the OFFERING PRICE.
4. amount over market value paid in a *tender offer. See also* PREMIUM RAID.

PREMIUM BOND bond with a selling price above face or redemption value. A bond with a face value of $1000, for instance, would be called a premium bond if it sold for $1050. This price does not include any ACCRUED INTEREST due when the bond is bought. When a premium bond is called before scheduled maturity, bondholders are usually paid more than face value, though the amount may be less than the bond is selling for at the time of the CALL.

PREMIUM INCOME income received by an investor who sells a PUT OPTION or a CALL OPTION. An investor collects premium income by writing a COVERED

OPTION, if he or she owns the underlying stock, or a NAKED OPTION, if he or she does not own the stock. An investor who sells options to collect premium income hopes that the underlying stock will not rise very much (in the case of a call) or fall very much (in the case of a put).

PREMIUM OVER BOND VALUE upward difference between the market value of a CONVERTIBLE bond and the price at which a straight bond of the same company would sell in the same open market. A convertible bond, eventually convertible to common stock, will normally sell at a PREMIUM over its bond value because investors place a value on the conversion feature. The higher the market price of the issuer's stock is relative to the price at which the bond is convertible, the greater the premium will be, reflecting the investor's tendency to view it more as a stock than as a bond. When the stock price falls near or below the conversion price, investors then tend to view the convertible as a bond and the premium narrows or even disappears. Other factors affecting the prices of convertible bonds generally include lower transaction costs on the convertibles than would be incurred in buying the stock outright, an attraction that exerts some upward pressure on the premium; the demand from life insurance companies and other institutional investors that are limited by law as to the common stock investments they can have and that gain their equity participation through convertibles; the duration period of the option to convert—the longer it is, the more valuable the future and the higher the premium; high dividends on the issuer's common stock, a factor increasing demand for the common versus the convertible, and therefore a downward pressure. *See also* PREMIUM OVER CONVERSION VALUE.

PREMIUM OVER CONVERSION VALUE amount by which the MARKET PRICE of a CONVERTIBLE preferred stock or convertible bond exceeds the price at which it is convertible. Convertibles (CVs) usually sell at a PREMIUM for two basic reasons: (1) if the convertible is a bond, the bond value—defined as the price at which a straight bond of the same company would sell in the same open market—is the lowest value the CV will reach; it thus represents DOWNSIDE RISK protection, which is given a value in the marketplace, generally varying with the VOLATILITY of the common stock; (2) the conversion privilege is given a value by investors because they might find it profitable eventually to convert the securities.

At relatively high common-stock price levels, a convertible tends to sell for its common stock equivalent and the conversion value becomes negligible. This occurs because investors are viewing the security as a common stock, not as a bond, and because conversion would be preferable to redemption if the bond were called. On the other hand, when the market value of the convertible is close to its bond value, the conversion feature has little value and the security is valued more as a bond. It is here that the CONVERSION PREMIUM is highest. The conversion premium is also influenced to some extent by transaction costs, insurance company investment restrictions, the duration of the conversion OPTION, and the size of common dividends. *See also* PREMIUM OVER BOND VALUE.

PREMIUM RAID surprise attempt to acquire a position in a company's stock by offering holders an amount—or premium—over the market value of their shares. The term *raid* assumes that the motive is control and not simply investment. Attempts to acquire control are regulated by federal laws that require disclosure of the intentions of those seeking shares. *See also* TENDER OFFER; WILLIAMS ACT.

PRENUPTIAL CONTRACT agreement between a future husband and wife that details how the couple's financial affairs are to be handled both during the marriage and in the event of divorce. The agreement may cover insurance protection, ownership of housing and securities, and inheritance rights. Such contracts may not be accepted in a court of law.

PREPAID INTEREST asset account representing interest paid in advance. The interest is expensed, that is, charged to the borrower's profit and loss statement (P & L), as it is earned by the lender. Synonymous with UNEARNED INTEREST, which is the preferred term when DISCOUNT is involved.

PREPAYMENT

In general: paying a debt obligation before it comes due.

Accounting: expenditure for a future benefit, which is recorded in a BALANCE SHEET asset account called a DEFERRED CHARGE, then written off in the period when the benefit is enjoyed. For example, prepaid rent is first recorded as an asset, then charged to expense as the rent becomes due on a monthly basis.

Banking: paying a loan before maturity. Some loans (particularly mortgages) have a prepayment clause that allows prepayment at any time without penalty, while others charge a fee if a loan is paid off before due.

Installment credit: making payments before they are due. *See also* RULE OF THE 78s.

Securities: paying a seller for a security before the settlement date.

Taxes: prepaying taxes, for example, to have the benefit of deducting state and local taxes from one's federal income tax return in the current calendar year rather than in the next year.

PREPAYMENT PENALTY fee paid by a borrower to a bank when a loan or mortgage that does not have a prepayment clause is repaid before its scheduled maturity. Prepayment penalties are prohibited in many states, and by FANNIE MAE and FREDDIE MAC. Also called *prepayment fee.*

PREREFUNDING procedure, called a *pre-re* on Wall Street, in which a bond issuer floats a second bond in order to pay off the first bond at the first CALL date. The proceeds from the sale of the second bond are safely invested, usually in Treasury securities, that will mature at the first call date of the first bond issue. Those first bonds are said to be prerefunded after this operation has taken place. Bond issuers prerefund bonds during periods of lower interest rates in order to lower their interest costs. *See also* ADVANCE REFUNDING; REFUNDING; REFUNDING ESCROW DEPOSITS (REDS).

PRESALE ORDER order to purchase part of a new MUNICIPAL BOND issue that is accepted by an underwriting SYNDICATE MANAGER before an announcement of the price or COUPON rate and before the official PUBLIC OFFERING. Municipals are exempt from registration requirements and other rules of the Securities and Exchange Commission, which forbids preoffering sales of corporate bond issues. *See also* PRESOLD ISSUE.

PRESENT VALUE value today of a future payment, or stream of payments, discounted at some appropriate compound interest—or discount—rate. For example, the present value of $100 to be received 10 years from now is about $38.55, using a discount rate equal to 10% interest compounded annually.

The present value method, also called the DISCOUNTED CASH FLOW method, is widely used in corporate finance to measure the return on a CAPITAL INVESTMENT project. In security investments, the method is used to determine how much money should be invested today to result in a certain sum at a future time. Present value calculations are facilitated by present value tables, which are compound interest tables in reverse. Also called *time value of money.*

PRESIDENT highest-ranking officer in a corporation after the CHAIRMAN OF THE BOARD, unless the title CHIEF EXECUTIVE OFFICER (CEO) is used, in which case the president can outrank the chairman. The president is appointed by the BOARD OF DIRECTORS and usually reports directly to the board. In smaller companies the president is usually the CEO, having authority over all other officers in matters of day-to-day management and policy decision-making. In large corporations the CEO title is frequently held by the chairman of the board, leaving the president as CHIEF OPERATING OFFICER, responsible for personnel and administration on a daily basis.

PRESIDENTIAL ELECTION CYCLE THEORY hypothesis of investment advisers that major stock market moves can be predicted based on the four-year presidential election cycle. According to this theory, stocks decline soon after a president is elected, as the chief executive takes the harsh and unpopular steps necessary to bring inflation, government spending, and deficits under control. During the next two years or so, taxes may be raised and the economy may slip into a recession. About midway into the four-year cycle, stocks should start to rise in anticipation of the economic recovery that the incumbent president wants to be roaring at full steam by election day. The cycle then repeats itself with the election of a new president or the reelection of an incumbent.

PRESOLD ISSUE issue of MUNICIPAL BONDS or government bonds that is completely sold out before the price or yield is publicly announced. Corporate bond issues, which must be offered to the public with a Securities and Exchange Commission registration statement, cannot legally be presold. *See also* PRESALE ORDER.

PRETAX EARNINGS OR PROFITS NET INCOME (earnings or profits) before federal income taxes.

PRETAX RATE OF RETURN yield or capital gain on a particular security before taking into account an individual's tax situation. *See also* RATE OF RETURN.

PREVIOUS BALANCE METHOD method of charging credit card interest that uses the outstanding balance at the end of the previous month as the basis for the current month's interest computation. *See also* ADJUSTED BALANCE METHOD.

PRICE/BOOK RATIO ratio of a stock's price to its BOOK VALUE per share. This number is used by SECURITIES ANALYSTS and MONEY MANAGERS to judge whether a stock is undervalued or overvalued. A stock selling at a high price/book ratio, such as 3 or higher, may represent a popular GROWTH STOCK with minimal book value. A stock selling below its book value may attract value-oriented investors who think that the company's management may undertake steps, such as selling assets or restructuring the company, to unlock the hidden value on the company's BALANCE SHEET.

PRICE CHANGE net rise or fall of the price of a security at the close of a trading session, compared to the previous session's CLOSING PRICE. A stock that rose $2 in a day would have a + 2 after its final price in the newspaper stock listings. A stock that fell $2 would have a –2. The average of the price changes for groups of securities, in indicators such as the Dow Jones Industrial Average and Standard & Poor's 500 Stock Index, is calculated by taking into account all the price changes in the components of the average or index.

PRICE/EARNINGS RATIO (P/E) price of a stock divided by its earnings per share. The P/E ratio may either use the reported earnings from the latest year (called a *trailing P/E*) or employ an analyst's forecast of next year's earnings (called a *forward P/E*). The trailing P/E is listed along with a stock's price and trading activity in the daily newspapers. For instance, a stock selling for $20 a share that earned $1 last year has a trailing P/E of 20. If the same stock has projected earnings of $2 next year, it will have a forward P/E of 10.

The price/earnings ratio, also known as the *multiple,* gives investors an idea of how much they are paying for a company's earning power. The higher the P/E, the more investors are paying, and therefore the more earnings growth they are expecting. High P/E stocks—those with multiples over 20—are typically young, fast-growing companies. They are far riskier to trade than low P/E stocks, since it is easier to miss high-growth expectations than low-growth predictions. Low P/E stocks tend to be in low-growth or mature industries, in stock groups that have fallen out of favor, or in old, established, BLUE CHIP companies with long records of earnings stability and regular dividends. In general, low P/E stocks have higher yields than high P/E stocks, which often pay no dividends at all.

PRICE GAP term used when a stock's price either jumps or plummets from its last trading range without overlapping that trading range. For instance, a stock might shoot up from a closing price of $20 a share, marking the high point of an $18–$20 trading range for that day, and begin trading in a $22–$24 range the next day on the news of a takeover bid. Or a company that reports lower than expected earnings might drop from the $18–$20 range to the $13–$15 range without ever trading at intervening prices. Price gaps are considered significant movements by technical analysts, who note them on charts, because such gaps are often indications of an OVERBOUGHT or OVERSOLD position.

PRICE INDEXES indices that track levels of prices and rates of inflation. The two most common price indexes published by the government are the CONSUMER PRICE INDEX (CPI) and the PRODUCER PRICE INDEX (PPI).

PRICE LEADERSHIP establishment of a price by a leading producer of a product that becomes the price adopted by other producers.

PRICE LIMIT *see* LIMIT PRICE.

PRICE RANGE high/low range in which a stock has traded over a particular period of time. In the daily newspaper, a stock's 52-week price range is given. In most companies' annual reports, a stock's price range is shown for the FISCAL YEAR.

PRICE/SALES RATIO ratio of a stock's price to its per-share sales. This ratio is used by financial analysts to gauge whether a stock's current market price is expensive or cheap. Some analysts maintain that investors consistently buying stocks with low price/sales ratios will outperform those buying stocks with low price/book value, price/cash flow, or PRICE/EARNINGS RATIOS. Advocates of P/S ratio analysis say it works because it relates the popularity of a company's stock to the size of its business. Since sales are more difficult to manipulate than earnings, P/S ratios are less subject to accounting gimmickry. Sales are typically less volatile than earnings or cash flow, so P/S ratios work particularly well on companies that stumble temporarily. When profits decline, a stock's price/earnings ratio may increase, but the impact on the P/S ratio is usually dominated by the stock's price. Value investors will use this fact to identify good values among stocks with high P/E but low P/S ratios. Price/sales ratios vary widely among different industries. For instance, the P/S ratio of a retailer is usually much lower than the ratio of a high-technology company.

PRICE SPREAD OPTIONS strategy in which an investor simultaneously buys and sells two options covering the same security, with the same expiration months, but with different exercise prices. For example, an investor might buy an XYZ May 100 call and sell an XYZ May 90 call.

PRICE SUPPORT government-set price floor designed to aid farmers or other producers of goods. For instance, the government sets a minimum price for sugar that it guarantees to sugar growers. If the market price drops below that level, the government makes up the difference. *See also* PARITY PRICE.

PRICE-WEIGHTED INDEX index in which component stocks are weighted by their price. Higher-priced stocks therefore have a greater percentage impact on the index than lower-priced stocks. In recent years, the trend of using price-weighted indexes has given way to the use of MARKET VALUE-WEIGHTED INDEXES.

PRICEY term used of an unrealistically low bid price or unrealistically high offer price. If a stock is trading at $15, a pricey bid might be $10 a share, and a pricey offer $20 a share.

PRIMARY DEALER one of the three dozen or so banks and investment dealers authorized to buy and sell government securities in direct dealings with the FEDERAL RESERVE BANK of New York in its execution of Fed OPEN-MARKET OPERATIONS. Such dealers must be qualified in terms of reputation, capacity, and adequacy of staff and facilities.

PRIMARY DISTRIBUTION sale of a new issue of stocks or bonds, as distinguished from a SECONDARY DISTRIBUTION, which involves previously issued stock. All issuances of bonds are primary distributions. Also called *primary offering,* but not to be confused with *initial public offering,* which refers to a corporation's *first* distribution of stock to the public.

PRIMARY EARNINGS PER (COMMON) SHARE earnings available to common stock (which is usually net earnings after taxes and preferred dividends) divided by the number of common shares outstanding. This figure, called basic earnings per share after 1998, contrasts with earnings per share after DILUTION, which assumes warrants, rights, and options have been exercised and convertibles have been converted. *See also* CONVERTIBLE; EARNINGS PER SHARE; FULLY DILUTED EARNINGS PER (COMMON) SHARE; SUBSCRIPTION WARRANT.

PRIMARY MARKET market for new issues of securities, as distinguished from the SECONDARY MARKET, where previously issued securities are bought and sold. A market is primary if the proceeds of sales go to the issuer of the securities sold. The term also applies to government securities auctions and to opening option and futures contract sales.

PRIME

Banking: PRIME RATE.

Investments: acronym for Prescribed Right to Income and Maximum Equity. PRIME was a UNIT INVESTMENT TRUST, sponsored by the Americus Shareowner Service Corporation, which separated the income portion of a stock from its appreciation potential. The income-producing portion, called PRIME, and the appreciation potential, called SCORE (an acronym for Special Claim on Residual Equity) together made up a unit share investment trust, known by the acronym USIT. Both PRIME and SCORE were traded on the American Stock Exchange.

The first version of this unit came into existence with American Telephone and Telegraph stock in late 1983, as AT&T was undergoing divestiture. PRIME units entitled their holders to the dividend income that a holder of one common share of the old AT&T would have gotten plus a proportionate share of the dividends of the seven regional operating companies split off from AT&T. PRIME holders also received all price APPRECIATION in the stock up to the equivalent of $75 a share. The trusts expired in 1988. SCORE holders received all appreciation over $75, but no dividend income.

This form of unit trust allows investors who want income from a stock to maximize that income, and investors who want capital gains to have increased leverage in achieving those gains. *See also* CAPITAL GAIN.

PRIME PAPER highest quality COMMERCIAL PAPER, as rated by Moody's Investor's Service and other rating agencies. Prime paper is considered INVESTMENT GRADE,

and therefore institutions with FIDUCIARY responsibility can invest in it. Moody's has three ratings of prime paper:
P-1: Highest quality
P-2: Higher quality
P-3: High quality
Commercial paper below P-3 is not considered prime paper.

PRIME RATE base rate that banks use in pricing commercial loans to their best and most creditworthy customers. The rate is determined by the Federal Reserve's decision to raise or lower prevailing interest rates for short-term borrowing. Though some banks charge their best customers more and some less than the official prime rate, the rate tends to become standard across the banking industry when a major bank moves its prime up or down. The rate is a key interest rate, since loans to less-creditworthy customers are often tied to the prime rate. For example, a BLUE CHIP company may borrow at a prime rate of 8%, but a less-well-established small business may borrow from the same bank at prime plus 2, or 10%. Many consumer loans, such as home equity, automobile, mortgage, and credit card loans, are tied to the prime rate. Although the major bank prime rate is the definitive "best rate" reference point, many banks, particularly those in outlying regions, have a two-tier system, whereby smaller companies of top credit standing may borrow at an even lower rate.

PRIME RATE FUND *mutual fund* that buys portions of corporate loans from banks and passes along interest, which is designed to approximate the PRIME RATE, to shareholders, net of load charges and management fees. Although the bank loans are senior obligations and fully collateralized, they are subject to DEFAULT, particularly in recessions. Prime rate funds thus pay 2–3% more than the yield on one-year CERTIFICATES OF DEPOSIT (CDs), and management fees tend to be higher than those of other mutual funds. Another possible disadvantage is limited liquidity; the only way investors can get out is to sell back their shares to the funds once each quarter.

PRINCIPAL
In General:
1. major party to a transaction, acting as either a buyer or a seller. A principal buys and sells for his or her own account and risk.
2. owner of a privately held business.
Banking and Finance:
1. face amount of a debt instrument or deposit on which interest is either owed or earned.
2. balance of a debt, separate from interest. *See also* PRINCIPAL AMOUNT.
Investments: basic amount invested, exclusive of earnings.

PRINCIPAL AMOUNT FACE VALUE of an obligation (such as a bond or a loan) that must be repaid at maturity, as separate from the INTEREST.

PRINCIPAL STOCKHOLDER stockholder who owns a significant number of shares in a corporation. Under Securities and Exchange Commission (SEC) rules, a principal stockholder owns 10% or more of the voting stock of a REGISTERED COMPANY. These stockholders are often on the board of directors and are considered insiders by SEC rules, so that they must report buying and selling transactions in the company's stock. *See also* AFFILIATED PERSON; CONTROL STOCK; INSIDER.

PRINCIPAL SUM
Finance: also used as a synonym for PRINCIPAL, in the sense of the obligation due under a debt instrument exclusive of interest. Synonymous with CORPUS. *See also* TRUST.

Insurance: amount specified as payable to the beneficiary under a policy, such as the death benefit.

PRIORITY system used in an AUCTION MARKET, in which the first bid or offer price is executed before other bid and offer prices, even if subsequent orders are larger. Orders originating off the floor *(see* OFF-FLOOR ORDER) of an exchange also have priority over ON-FLOOR ORDERS. *See also* MATCHED AND LOST; PRECEDENCE.

PRIOR-LIEN BOND bond that has precedence over another bond of the same issuing company even though both classes of bonds are equally secured. Such bonds usually arise from REORGANIZATION. *See also* JUNIOR ISSUE.

PRIOR-PREFERRED STOCK PREFERRED STOCK that has a higher claim than other issues of preferred stock on dividends and assets in LIQUIDATION; also known as *preference shares.*

PRIVATE ACTIVITY BOND *see* PRIVATE PURPOSE BOND.

PRIVATE LETTER RULING Internal Revenue Service (IRS) response to a request for interpretation of the tax law with respect to a specific question or situation. Also called *letter ruling, revenue ruling.*

PRIVATE LIMITED PARTNERSHIP LIMITED PARTNERSHIP not registered with the Securities and Exchange Commission (SEC) and having a maximum of 35 limited partners. *See also* ACCREDITED INVESTOR.

PRIVATE MARKET VALUE (PMV) aggregate market value of a company if each of its parts operated independently and had its own stock price. Also called *breakup value* or *takeover value.* Analysts look for high PMV in relation to market value to identify bargains and potential TARGET COMPANIES. PMV differs from LIQUIDATING VALUE, which excludes GOING-CONCERN VALUE, and BOOK VALUE, which is an accounting concept.

PRIVATE MORTGAGE INSURANCE (PMI) type of insurance available from lenders that insures against loss resulting from a default on a mortgage loan and can substitute for down payment money.

PRIVATE PLACEMENT sale of stocks, bonds, or other investments directly to an institutional investor like an insurance company. A PRIVATE LIMITED PARTNERSHIP is also considered a private placement. A private placement does not have to be registered with the Securities and Exchange Commission, as a PUBLIC OFFERING does, if the securities are purchased for investment as opposed to resale. *See also* LETTER SECURITY.

PRIVATE PURPOSE BOND category of MUNICIPAL BOND distinguished from PUBLIC PURPOSE BOND in the TAX REFORM ACT OF 1986 because 10% or more of the bond's benefit goes to private activities or 5% of the proceeds (or $5 million if less) are used for loans to parties other than governmental units. Private purpose obligations, which are also called *private activity bonds* or *nonessential function bonds,* are taxable unless their use is specifically exempted. Even tax-exempt *permitted private activity bonds,* if issued after August 7, 1986, are TAX PREFERENCE ITEMS, except those issued for 501(c)(3) organizations (hospitals, colleges, universities). Private purpose bonds specifically *prohibited* from tax-exemption effective August 15, 1986, include those for sports, trade, and convention facilities and large-issue (over $1 million) INDUSTRIAL DEVELOPMENT BONDS. Permitted issues, except those for 501(c)(3) organizations, airports, docks, wharves, and government-owned solid-waste disposal facilities, are subject to volume caps. *See also* TAXABLE MUNICIPAL BOND.

PRIVATIZATION process of converting a publicly operated enterprise into a privately owned and operated entity. For example, many cities and states contract with private companies to run their prison facilities instead of managing them with municipal personnel. Many countries around the world have privatized formerly state-run enterprises such as banks, airlines, steel companies, utilities, phone systems, and large manufacturers. A wave of privatization swept through Russia and Eastern Europe after the fall of Communism in the 1990s, and through some Latin American countries such as Peru, as new, democratic governments were established. When a company is privatized, shares formerly owned by the government, as well as management control, are sold to the public. The theory behind privatization is that these enterprises run far more efficiently and offer better service to customers when owned by stockholders instead of the government.

PROBATE judicial process whereby the will of a deceased person is presented to a court and an EXECUTOR or ADMINISTRATOR is appointed to carry out the will's instructions.

PROCEEDS
1. funds given to a borrower after all costs and fees are deducted.
2. money received by the seller of an asset after commissions are deducted—for example, the amount a stockholder receives from the sale of shares, less broker's commission. *See also* PROCEEDS SALE.

PROCEEDS SALE OVER THE COUNTER securities sale where the PROCEEDS are used to purchase another security. Under the FIVE PERCENT RULE of the NATIONAL ASSOCIATION OF SECURITIES DEALERS (NASD), such a trade is considered one transaction and the NASD member's total markup or commission is subject to the 5% guideline.

PRODUCER PRICE INDEX (PPI) measure of change in wholesale prices (formerly called the *wholesale price index),* as released monthly by the U.S. Bureau of Labor Statistics. The index is broken down into components by commodity, industry sector, and stage of processing. The PPI tracks prices of foods, metals, lumber, oil and gas, and many other commodities, but does not measure the price of services. Economists look at trends in the PPI as an accurate precursor to changes in the CPI, since upward or downward pressure on wholesale prices is usually passed through to consumer prices over time. The PPI, published by the Bureau of Labor Statistics in the Department of Labor, is based at 100 in 1982 and is released monthly. Economists also look at the PPI excluding the volatile food and energy components, which they call the "core" PPI. The consumer equivalent of this index is the CONSUMER PRICE INDEX.

PRODUCTION RATE coupon (interest) rate at which a PASS-THROUGH SECURITY guaranteed by the GOVERNMENT NATIONAL MORTGAGE ASSOCIATION (GNMA), popularly known as a Ginnie Mae, is issued. The rate is set a half percentage point under the prevailing Federal Housing Administration (FHA) rate, the maximum rate allowed on residential mortgages insured and guaranteed by the FHA and the Veterans Administration.

PRODUCTIVITY in labor and other areas of economics, the amount of output per unit of input, for example, the quantity of a product produced per hour of labor.

PROFIT
Finance: positive difference that results from selling products and services for more than the cost of producing these goods. *See also* NET PROFIT.
Investments: difference between the selling price and the purchase price of commodities or securities when the selling price is higher.

PROFIT AND LOSS STATEMENT (P & L) summary of the revenues, costs, and expenses of a company during an accounting period; also called INCOME STATEMENT, *operating statement, statement of profit and loss, income and expense statement.* Together with the BALANCE SHEET as of the end of the accounting period, it constitutes a company's financial statement. *See also* COST OF GOODS SOLD; NET INCOME; NET SALES.

PROFIT CENTER segment of a business organization that is responsible for producing profits on its own. A conglomerate with interests in hotels, food processing, and paper may consider each of these three businesses separate profit centers, for instance.

PROFIT FORECAST prediction of future levels of profitability by analysts following a company, as well as company officials. Investors base their buy and sell decisions on such earnings projections. Stock prices typically reflect analysts' profit expectations—companies expected to produce rapidly growing profits often have high price/earnings ratios. Conversely, projections of meager earnings result in lower P/E ratios. The company will often guide analysts so that their profit forecasts are not too high or too low, preventing unwelcome surprises. Analyst profit forecasts are tracked by the INSTITUTIONAL BROKERS ESTIMATE SYSTEM (I/B/E/S) and ZACKS ESTIMATE SYSTEM.

PROFIT MARGIN *see* MARGIN OF PROFIT.

PROFIT-SHARING PLAN agreement between a corporation and its employees that allows the employees to share in company profits. Annual contributions are made by the company, when it has profits, to a profit-sharing account for each employee, either in cash or in a deferred plan, which may be invested in stocks, bonds, or cash equivalents. The funds in a profit-sharing account generally accumulate tax deferred until the employee retires or leaves the company. Many plans allow employees to borrow against profit-sharing accounts for major expenditures such as purchasing a home or financing children's education. Because corporate profit-sharing plans have custody over billions of dollars, they are major institutional investors in the stock and bond markets.

PROFIT TAKING action by short-term securities or commodities traders to cash in on gains earned on a sharp market rise. Profit taking pushes down prices, but only temporarily; the term implies an upward market trend.

PRO FORMA Latin for "as a matter of form"; refers to a presentation of data, such as a BALANCE SHEET or INCOME STATEMENT, where certain amounts are hypothetical. For example, a pro forma balance sheet might show a debt issue that has been proposed but has not yet been consummated.

PROGRAM TRADING computer-driven buying *(buy program)* or selling *(sell program)* of baskets of 15 or more stocks by *index* ARBITRAGE specialists or institutional traders. "Program" refers to computer programs that constantly monitor stock, futures, and options markets, giving buy and sell signals when opportunities for arbitrage profits occur or when market conditions warrant portfolio accumulation or liquidation transactions. Program trading has been blamed for excessive volatility in the markets, especially on Black Monday in 1987, when PORTFOLIO INSURANCE—the since discredited use of index options and futures to hedge stock portfolios—was an important contributing factor.

PROGRESSIVE TAX income tax system in which those with higher incomes pay taxes at higher rates than those with lower incomes; also called *graduated tax.* The U.S. income tax system is based on the concept of progressivity. There are several tax brackets, based on the taxpayer's income, which determine the tax rate that applies to each taxpayer. *See also* FLAT TAX; REGRESSIVE TAX.

PROGRESS PAYMENTS

1. periodic payments to a supplier, contractor, or subcontractor for work satisfactorily performed to date. Such schedules are provided in contracts and can significantly reduce the amount of WORKING CAPITAL required by the performing party.

2. disbursements by lenders to contractors under construction loan arrangements. As construction progresses, bills and LIEN waivers are presented to the bank or savings and loan, which advances additional funds.

PROJECTION estimate of future performance made by economists, corporate planners, and credit and securities analysts. Economists use econometric models to project GROSS DOMESTIC PRODUCT (GDP), inflation, unemployment, and many other economic factors. Corporate financial planners project a company's operating results and CASH FLOW, using historical trends and making assumptions where necessary, in order to make budget decisions and to plan financing. Credit analysts use projections to forecast DEBT SERVICE ability. Securities analysts tend to focus their projections on earnings trends and cash flow per share in order to predict market values and dividend coverage. *See also* ECONOMETRICS.

PROJECT LINK econometric model linking all the economies in the world and forecasting the effects of changes in different economies on other economies. The project is identified with 1980 Nobel Memorial Prize in Economics winner Lawrence R. Klein. *See also* ECONOMETRICS.

PROJECT NOTE short-term debt issue of a municipal agency, usually a housing authority, to finance the construction of public housing. When the housing is finished, the notes are redeemed and the project is financed with long-term bonds. Both project notes and bonds usually pay tax-exempt interest to note- and bondholders, and both are also guaranteed by the U.S. Department of Housing and Urban Development.

PROMISSORY NOTE written promise committing the maker to pay the payee a specified sum of money either on demand or at a fixed or determinable future date, with or without interest. Instruments meeting these criteria are NEGOTIABLE. Often called, simply, a NOTE.

PROPERTY AND EQUIPMENT *see* FIXED ASSET.

PROPERTY INVENTORY personal finance term meaning a list of PERSONAL PROPERTY with cost and market values. A property inventory, which should be accompanied by photographs, is used to substantiate insurance claims and tax losses.

PROPERTY TAX tax assessed on property such as real estate. The tax is determined by several factors, including the use of the land (residential, commercial, or industrial), the assessed valuation of the property, and the tax rate, expressed in MILLS. Property taxes are usually assessed by county and local governments, school districts, and other special authorities such as for water and sewer service. Property taxes are usually deductible on federal income tax returns. If a mortgage lender requires that it pay all property taxes, borrowers must remit their property taxes as part of their monthly mortgage payments and the lender keeps the money in escrow until property taxes are due. *See also* AD VALOREM, PITI.

PROPORTIONAL REPRESENTATION method of stockholder voting, giving individual shareholders more power over the election of directors than they have under statutory voting, which, by allowing one vote per share per director, makes it possible for a majority shareholder to elect all the directors. The most familiar example of proportional representation is cumulative voting, under which a shareholder has as many votes as he has shares of stock, multiplied by the number of vacancies on the board, all of which can be cast for one director. This makes it possible for a minority shareholder or a group of small shareholders to gain at least some representation on the board. Another variety provides for the holders of specified classes of stock to elect a number of directors in certain circumstances. For example, if the corporation failed to pay preferred dividends, the preferred holders might then be given the power to elect a certain proportion of the board. Despite the advocacy of stockholders' rights activists, proportional representation has made little headway in American corporations.

PROPRIETORSHIP unincorporated business owned by a single person. The individual proprietor has the right to all the profits from the business and also has responsibility for all the firm's liabilities. Since proprietors are considered self-employed, they are eligible for Keogh accounts for their retirement funds. *See also* KEOGH PLAN.

PRO RATA Latin for "according to the rate"; a method of proportionate allocation. For example, a pro rata property tax rebate might be divided proportionately (prorated) among taxpayers based on their original assessments, so that each gets the same percentage.

PROSPECTUS formal written offer to sell securities that sets forth the plan for a proposed business enterprise or the facts concerning an existing one that an investor needs to make an informed decision. Prospectuses are also issued by MUTUAL FUNDS, describing the history, background of managers, fund objectives, a financial statement, and other essential data. A prospectus for a PUBLIC OFFERING must be filed with the Securities and Exchange Commission and given to prospective buyers of the offering. The prospectus contains financial information and a description of a company's business history, officers, operations, pending litigation (if any), and plans (including the use of the proceeds from the issue).

Before investors receive the final copy of the prospectus, called the *statutory prospectus,* they may receive a PRELIMINARY PROSPECTUS, commonly called a *red herring*. This document is not complete in all details, though most of the major facts of the offering are usually included. The final prospectus is also called the *offering circular.*

Offerings of limited partnerships are also accompanied by prospectuses. Real estate, oil and gas, equipment leasing, and other types of limited partnerships are described in detail, and pertinent financial information, the background of the general partners, and supporting legal opinions are also given.

PROTECTIONISM practice of protecting domestic goods and service industries from foreign competition with tariff and non-tariff barriers. Protectionism causes higher prices for consumers because domestic producers are not exposed to foreign competition, and can therefore keep prices high. But domestic exporters also may suffer, because foreign countries tend to retaliate against protectionism with tariffs and barriers of their own. Many economists say that the Depression of the 1930s was precipitated by the protectionist trade barriers erected by the United States under the Smoot-Hawley Act, which led to retaliation by many countries throughout the world. In more recent years, many protectionist trade barriers have fallen through the passage of GATT, the General Agreement on Tariffs and Trade, which went into effect in 1995, and the creation of the WORLD TRADE ORGANIZATION (WTO).

PROTECTIVE COVENANT *see* COVENANT.

PROVISION *see* ALLOWANCE.

PROVISION FOR INCOME TAXES item on a company's profit and loss statement (P & L) representing its estimated income tax liability for the year.
Although taxes are actually paid according to a timetable determined by the
Internal Revenue Service and a certain portion of the liability may be accrued,
the provision gives an indication of the company's effective tax rate, which analysts compare to other companies as one measure of effective management and
profitability. EARNINGS BEFORE TAXES is the net earnings figure before provision
for income taxes.

PROXY
In general: person authorized to act or speak for another.
Business:
1. written POWER OF ATTORNEY given by shareholders of a corporation, authorizing a specific vote on their behalf at corporate meetings. Such proxies normally pertain to election of the BOARD OF DIRECTORS or to various resolutions
   submitted for shareholders' approval.
2. person authorized to vote on behalf of a stockholder of a corporation.

PROXY FIGHT technique used by an acquiring company to attempt to gain control of a TAKEOVER target. The acquirer tries to persuade the shareholders of the
TARGET COMPANY that the present management of the firm should be ousted in
favor of a slate of directors favorable to the acquirer. If the shareholders, through
their PROXY votes, agree, the acquiring company can gain control of the company
without paying a PREMIUM price for the firm.

PROXY STATEMENT information that the Securities and Exchange Commission
requires must be provided to shareholders before they vote by proxy on company
matters. The statement contains proposed members of the BOARD OF DIRECTORS,
inside directors' salaries, and pertinent information regarding their bonus and option
plans, as well as any resolutions of minority stockholders and of management.

PRUDENT-MAN RULE standard adopted by some U.S. states to guide those
with responsibility for investing the money of others. Such fiduciaries (executors of wills, trustees, bank trust departments, and administrators of estates)
must act as a prudent man or woman would be expected to act, with discretion
and intelligence, to seek reasonable income, preserve capital, and, in general,
avoid speculative investments. States not using the prudent-man system use the
LEGAL LIST system, allowing fiduciaries to invest only in a restricted list of securities, called the *legal list.*

PUBLIC DEBT borrowings by governments to finance expenditures not covered
by current tax revenues. *See also* AGENCY SECURITIES; MUNICIPAL BOND;
TREASURIES.

PUBLIC HOUSING AUTHORITY BOND obligation of local public housing
agencies, which is centrally marketed through competitive sealed-bid auctions
conducted by the U.S. Department of Housing and Urban Development (HUD).
These obligations are secured by an agreement between HUD and the local housing agency that provides that the federal government will loan the local authority
a sufficient amount of money to pay PRINCIPAL and INTEREST to maturity.
    The proceeds of such bonds provide low-rent housing through new construc-
tion, rehabilitation of existing buildings, purchases from private builders or developers, and leasing from private owners. Under special provisions, low income families may also purchase such housing.
    The interest on such bonds is exempt from federal income taxes and may
also be exempt from state and local income taxes.

PUBLIC LIMITED PARTNERSHIP real estate, oil and gas, equipment leasing, or other LIMITED PARTNERSHIP that is registered with the Securities and Exchange Commission and offered to the public through registered broker/dealers. Such partnerships may be oriented to producing income or capital gains, or, within PASSIVE income rules, to generating tax advantages for limited partners. The number of investors in such a partnership is limited only by the sponsor's desire to cap the funds raised. A public limited partnership, which does not have an active secondary market, is distinguished from a PRIVATE LIMITED PARTNERSHIP, which is limited to 35 limited partners plus ACCREDITED INVESTORS, and a MASTER LIMITED PARTNERSHIP (MLP) that is publicly traded, often on the major stock exchanges.

PUBLIC, THE term for individual investors, as opposed to professional investors. Wall Street analysts like to deride the public for constantly buying at the top of a bull market and selling at the bottom of a bear market. The public participates in stock and bond markets both by buying individual securities and through intermediaries such as mutual funds and insurance companies. The term *public* is also used to describe a security that is available to be bought and sold by individual investors (as opposed to just large institutions or wealthy people, in which case the offering is a private one). Stocks that offer shares to the public are known as *publicly held*, in contrast to *privately held* concerns in which shares are owned by founders, employees, and a few large investors.

PUBLICLY HELD company with shares outstanding that are held by public investors. A company converts from a privately held firm to a publicly held one through an INITIAL PUBLIC OFFERING (IPO) of stock.

PUBLIC OFFERING
1. offering to the investment public, after registration requirements of the Securities and Exchange Commission (SEC) have been complied with, of new securities, usually by an investment banker or a syndicate made up of several investment bankers, at a public offering price agreed upon between the issuer and the investment bankers.

   Public offering is distinguished from PRIVATE PLACEMENT of new securities, which is subject to different SEC regulations. *See also* REGISTERED NEW ISSUE; UNDERWRITE.
2. SECONDARY DISTRIBUTION of previously issued stock. *See also* SECONDARY OFFERING.

PUBLIC OFFERING PRICE price at which a NEW ISSUE of securities is offered to the public by underwriters. *See also* OFFERING PRICE; UNDERWRITE.

PUBLIC OWNERSHIP
Government: government ownership and operation of a productive facility for the purpose of providing some good or service to citizens. The government supplies the capital, controls management, sets prices, and generally absorbs all risks and reaps all profits—similar to a private enterprise. When public ownership displaces private ownership in a particular instance, it is called NATIONALIZATION.
Investments: publicly traded portion of a corporation's stock.

PUBLIC PURPOSE BOND category of MUNICIPAL BOND, as defined in the TAX REFORM ACT OF 1986, which is exempt from federal income taxes as long as it provides no more than 10% benefit to private parties and no more than 5% of the proceeds or $5 million are used for loans to private parties; also called *public activity, traditional government purpose,* and *essential purpose* bond. Public purpose bonds include purposes such as roads, libraries, and government buildings.

PUBLIC SYNDICATE *see* PURCHASE GROUP.

PUBLIC UTILITY HOLDING COMPANY ACT OF 1935 major landmark in legislation regulating the securities industry, which reorganized the financial structures of HOLDING COMPANIES in the gas and electric utility industries and regulated their debt and dividend policies. Prior to the Act, abuses by holding companies were rampant, including WATERED STOCK, top-heavy capital structures with excessive fixed-debt burdens, and manipulation of the securities markets. In summary:

1. It requires holding companies operating interstate and persons exercising a controlling influence on utilities and holding companies to register with the Securities and Exchange Commission (SEC) and to provide information on the organizational structure, finances, and means of control.

2. It provides for SEC control of the operation and performance of registered holding companies and SEC approval of all new securities offerings, resulting in such reforms as the elimination of NONVOTING STOCK, the prevention of the milking of subsidiaries, and the outlawing of the upstreaming of dividends (payment of dividends by operating companies to holding companies).

3. It provides for uniform accounting standards, periodic administrative and financial reports, and reports on holdings by officers and directors, and for the end of interlocking directorates with banks or investment bankers.

4. It began the elimination of complex organizational structures by allowing only one intermediate company between the top holding company and its operating companies (the GRANDFATHER CLAUSE).

PULLBACK reversal of an upward price trend when a stock or market rises in price for several trading sessions and then declines in price.

PULLING IN THEIR HORNS move to defensive strategies on the part of investors. If the stock or bond market has experienced a sharp rise, investors may want to lock in profits by selling part of their positions or instituting hedging techniques to guard against a downturn. If stock prices fall after a steep runup, commentators will frequently say that "investors are pulling in their horns" to describe the reason for the downturn.

PURCHASE ACQUISITION accounting method used in a business MERGER whereby the purchasing company treats the acquired company as an investment and adds the acquired company's assets to its own at their fair market value. Any premium paid over and above the FAIR MARKET VALUE of the acquired assets is reflected as GOODWILL on the buyer's BALANCE SHEET and must be written off against future earnings. Until 1993, goodwill amortization was not deductible for tax purposes, so the reduction of reported future earnings was a disadvantage of this method of merger accounting as compared with the alternative POOLING OF INTERESTS method. The purchase acquisition method is mandatory unless all the criteria for a pooling of interests combination are met.

PURCHASE FUND provision in some PREFERRED STOCK contracts and BOND indentures requiring the issuer to use its best efforts to purchase a specified number of shares or bonds annually at a price not to exceed par value. Unlike SINKING FUND provisions, which require that a certain number of bonds be retired annually, purchase funds require only that a tender offer be made; if no securities are tendered, none are retired. Purchase fund issues benefit the investor in a period of rising rates when the redemption price is higher than the market price and the proceeds can be put to work at a higher return.

PURCHASE GROUP group of investment bankers that, operating under the AGREEMENT AMONG UNDERWRITERS, agrees to purchase a NEW ISSUE of securities from the issuer for resale to the investment public; also called the UNDERWRITING

GROUP or *syndicate*. The purchase group is distinguished from the SELLING GROUP, which is organized by the purchase group and includes the members of the purchase group along with other investment bankers. The selling group's function is DISTRIBUTION.

The agreement among underwriters, also called the *purchase group agreement,* is distinguished from the underwriting or purchase agreement, which is between the underwriting group and the issuer. *See also* UNDERWRITE.

PURCHASE GROUP AGREEMENT *see* PURCHASE GROUP.

PURCHASE LOAN in consumer credit, a loan made at a rate of interest to finance a purchase.

PURCHASE-MONEY MORTGAGE MORTGAGE given by a buyer in lieu of cash for the purchase of property. Such mortgages make it possible to sell property when mortgage money is unavailable or when the only buyers are unqualified to borrow from commercial sources.

PURCHASE ORDER written authorization to a vendor to deliver specified goods or services at a stipulated price. Once accepted by the supplier, the purchase order becomes a legally binding purchase CONTRACT.

PURCHASING POWER
Economics: value of money as measured by the goods and services it can buy. For example, the PURCHASING POWER OF THE DOLLAR can be determined by comparing an index of consumer prices for a given base year to the present.
Investment: amount of credit available to a client in a brokerage account for the purchase of additional securities. Purchasing power is determined by the dollar amount of securities that can be margined. For instance, a client with purchasing power of $20,000 in his or her account could buy securities worth $40,000 under the Federal Reserve's currently effective 50% MARGIN REQUIREMENT. *See also* MARGIN SECURITY.

PURCHASING POWER OF THE DOLLAR measure of the amount of goods and services that a dollar can buy in a particular market, as compared with prior periods, assuming always an INFLATION or a DEFLATION factor and using an index of consumer prices. It might be reported, for instance, that one dollar in 1982 has 67 cents of purchasing power in the late 1990s because of the erosion caused by inflation. Deflation would increase the dollar's purchasing power.

PURE PLAY stock market jargon for a company that is virtually all devoted to one line of business. An investor who wants to invest in that line of business looks for such a pure play. For instance, Sears Roebuck may be considered a pure play in the retail business after spinning off its real estate and financial services businesses in the mid-1900s. Weyerhauser is a pure play in the forest products business. The opposite of a pure play is a widely diversified company, such as a CONGLOMERATE.

PURE MONOPOLY situation in which one firm controls the entire market for a product. This may occur because the firm has a patent on a product or a license from the government to be a monopoly. For example, an electric utility in a particular city may be a monopoly licensed by the city.

PURPOSE LOAN loan backed by securities and used to buy other securities under Federal Reserve Board MARGIN and credit regulations.

PURPOSE STATEMENT form filed by a borrower that details the purpose of a loan backed by securities. The borrower agrees not to use the loan proceeds to buy securities in violation of any Federal Reserve regulations. *See also* NONPURPOSE LOAN; REGULATION U.

PUT BOND bond that allows its holder to redeem the issue at specified intervals before maturity and receive full FACE VALUE. The bond-holders may be allowed to put bonds back to the issuer either only once during the lifetime of the issue or far more frequently. In return for this privilege, a bond buyer sacrifices some yield when choosing a put bond over a fixed-rate bond, which cannot be redeemed before maturity.

PUT-CALL RATIO ratio of trading volume in put options to the trading volume in call options. The ratio provides a quantitative measure of the bullishness or bearishness of investors. A high volume of puts relative to calls indicates investors are bearish, whereas a high ratio of calls to puts shows bullishness. Many market technicians find the put-call ratio to be a good contrary indicator, meaning that when the ratio is high, a market bottom is near and when the ratio is low, a market top is imminent. This reading assumes that the majority of options investors are making the wrong move.

PUT GUARANTEE LETTER letter from a bank certifying that the person writing a put option on an underlying security or index instrument has sufficient funds on deposit at the bank to cover the exercise price of the put if needed. On a short put, the obligation is to pay the aggregate exercise price. There are two forms, as required under New York Stock Exchange Rule 431: the *market index option deposit letter* for index options, and the *equity/Treasury option deposit letter* for security options.

PUT OPTION
Bonds: bondholder's right to redeem a bond before maturity. *See also* PUT BOND.
Options: contract that grants the right to sell at a specified price a specific number of shares by a certain date. The put option buyer gains this right in return for payment of an OPTION PREMIUM. The put option seller grants this right in return for receiving this premium. For instance, a buyer of an XYZ May 70 put has the right to sell 100 shares of XYZ at $70 to the put seller at any time until the contract expires in May. A put option buyer hopes the stock will drop in price, while the put option seller (called a *writer*) hopes the stock will remain stable, rise, or drop by an amount less than his or her profit on the premium.

PUT TO SELLER phrase used when a PUT OPTION is exercised. The OPTION WRITER is obligated to buy the underlying shares at the agreed upon price. If an XYZ June 40 put were "put to seller," for instance, the writer would have to buy 100 shares of XYZ at $40 a share from the put holder even though the current market price of XYZ may be far less than $40 a share.

PYRAMIDING
In general: form of business expansion that makes extensive use of financial LEVERAGE to build complex corporate structures.
Fraud: scheme that builds on nonexistent values, often in geometric progression, such as a chain letter, now outlawed by mail fraud legislation. A famous example was the Ponzi scheme, perpetrated by Charles Ponzi in the late 1920s. Investors were paid "earnings" out of money received from new investors until the scheme collapsed.
Investments: using unrealized profits from one securities or commodities POSITION as COLLATERAL to buy further positions with funds borrowed from a broker. This use of leverage creates increased profits in a BULL MARKET, and causes MARGIN CALLS and large losses in a BEAR MARKET.
Marketing: legal marketing strategy whereby additional distributorships are sold side-by-side with consumer products in order to multiply market reach and maximize profits to the sales organization.

q

Q-TIP TRUST qualified terminable interest property *trust,* which allows assets to be transferred between spouses. The grantor of a Q-tip trust directs income from the assets to his or her spouse for life but has the power to distribute the assets upon the death of the spouse. Such trusts qualify the grantor for the unlimited marital deduction if the spouse should die first.

A Q-tip trust is often used to provide for the welfare of a spouse while keeping the assets out of the estate of another (such as a future marriage partner) if the grantor dies first.

QUALIFICATION PERIOD period of time during which an insurance company will not reimburse a policyholder for a claim. The qualification period, which may be several weeks or months, gives the insurance company time to uncover fraud or deception in the policyholder's application for coverage. Such periods, which are stated in the insurance contract, are commonplace in health insurance plans.

QUALIFIED ENDORSEMENT endorsement (signature on the back of a check or other NEGOTIABLE INSTRUMENT transferring the amount to someone other than the one to whom it is payable) that contains wording designed to limit the endorser's liability. "Without recourse," the most frequently seen example, means that if the instrument is not honored, the endorser is not responsible. Where qualified endorsements are restrictive (such as "for deposit only") the term *restricted endorsement* is preferable.

QUALIFIED OPINION auditor's opinion accompanying financial statements that calls attention to limitations of the audit or exceptions the auditor takes to the statements. Typical reasons for qualified opinions: a pending lawsuit that, if lost, would materially affect the financial condition of the company; an indeterminable tax liability relating to an unusual transaction; inability to confirm a portion of the inventory because of inaccessible location. *See also* ACCOUNTANT'S OPINION.

QUALIFIED PLAN OR TRUST TAX DEFERRED plan set up by an employer for employees under 1954 Internal Revenue Service rules. Such plans usually provide for employer contributions—for example, a profit-sharing or pension plan—and may also allow employee contributions. They build up savings, which are paid out at retirement or on termination of employment. The employees pay taxes only when they draw the money out. When employers make payments to such plans, they receive certain deductions and other tax benefits. *See also* 401 (K) PLAN; SALARY REDUCTION PLAN.

QUALIFYING ANNUITY ANNUITY that is purchased under, and forms the investment program for, a QUALIFIED PLAN OR TRUST, including pension and profit sharing plans, INDIVIDUAL RETIREMENT ACCOUNTS (IRAs), 403(b)s, and 457s. *See also* KEOGH PLAN.

QUALIFYING SHARE share of COMMON STOCK owned in order to qualify as a director of the issuing corporation.

QUALIFYING STOCK OPTION privilege granted to an employee of a corporation that permits the purchase, for a special price, of shares of its CAPITAL STOCK, under conditions sustained in the Internal Revenue Code. The law states (1) that the OPTION plan must be approved by the stockholders, (2) that the option is not transferable, (3) that the EXERCISE PRICE must not be less than the MARKET PRICE of the shares at the time the option is issued, and (4) that the grantee may not own stock having more than 10% of the company's voting power unless the option price equals 110% of the market price and the option is not exercisable more than five years after the grant. No income tax is payable by the employee either at the time of the grant or at the time the option is exercised. If the market price falls below the option price, another option with a lower exercise price can be issued. There is a $100,000 per employee limit on the value of stock covered by options that are exercisable in any one calendar year. *See also* INCENTIVE STOCK OPTION.

QUALIFYING UTILITY utility in which shareholders were, until the end of 1985, able to defer taxes by reinvesting up to $750 in dividends ($1500 for a couple filing jointly) in the company's stock. Taxes were due when the stock was sold. This plan was enacted by the Economic Recovery Tax Act of 1981 as a means of helping utilities raise investment capital cheaply. Most of the utilities qualifying for the plan were electric utilities.

QUALITATIVE ANALYSIS
In general: analysis that evaluates important factors that cannot be precisely measured.
Securities and credit analysis: analysis that is concerned with such questions as the experience, character, and general caliber of management; employee morale; and the status of labor relations rather than with the actual financial data about a company. *See also* QUANTITATIVE ANALYSIS.

QUALITY CONTROL process of assuring that products are made to consistently high standards of quality. Inspection of goods at various points in their manufacture by either a person or a machine is usually an important part of the quality control process.

QUALITY OF EARNINGS phrase describing a corporation's earnings that are attributable to increased sales and cost controls, as distinguished from artificial profits created by inflated values in inventories or other assets. In a period of high inflation, the quality of earnings tends to suffer, since a large portion of a firm's profits is generated by the rising value of inventories. In a lower inflation period, a company that achieves higher sales and maintains lower costs produces a higher quality of earnings—a factor often appreciated by investors, who are frequently willing to pay more for a higher quality of earnings.

QUANT person with mathematical and computer skills who provides numerical and analytical support services in the securities industry.

QUANTISE to denominate an asset or liability in a currency other than the one in which it usually trades.

QUANTITATIVE ANALYSIS analysis dealing with measurable factors as distinguished from such qualitative considerations as the character of management or the state of employee morale. In credit and securities analysis, examples of quantitative considerations are the value of assets; the cost of capital; the historical and projected patterns of sales, costs, and profitability and a wide range of considerations in the areas of economics; the money market; and the securities markets. Although quantitative and qualitative factors are distinguishable, they must be combined to arrive at sound business and financial judgments. *See also* QUALITATIVE ANALYSIS.

QUANTO OPTION option in one currency or interest rate that pays out in another. A quanto option can be used when an investor favors a foreign index, but is bearish on the outlook for that country's currency.

QUARTERLY
In general: every three months (one quarter of a year).
Securities: basis on which earnings reports to shareholders are made; also, usual time frame of dividend payments.

QUARTER STOCK stock with a par value of $25 per share.

QUASI-PUBLIC CORPORATION corporation that is operated privately and often has its stock traded publicly, but that also has some sort of public mandate and often has the government's backing behind its direct debt obligations. Some examples: COMSAT (Communications Satellite Corporation), which was sponsored by the U.S. Congress to foster the development of space; the FEDERAL NATIONAL MORTGAGE ASSOCIATION (Fannie Mae), which was founded to encourage growth in the secondary mortgage market; and the STUDENT LOAN MARKETING ASSOCIATION (Sallie Mae), which was started to encourage the growth of a secondary market for student loans.

QUICK ASSETS cash, marketable securities, and accounts receivable. *See also* QUICK RATIO.

QUICK RATIO cash, MARKETABLE SECURITIES, and ACCOUNTS RECEIVABLE divided by current liabilities. By excluding inventory, this key LIQUIDITY ratio focuses on the firm's more LIQUID ASSETS, and helps answer the question "If sales stopped, could this firm meet its current obligations with the readily convertible assets on hand?" Assuming there is nothing happening to slow or prevent collections, a quick ratio of 1 to 1 or better is usually satisfactory. Also called *acid-test ratio, quick asset ratio.*

QUID PRO QUO
In general: from the Latin, meaning "something for something." By mutual agreement, one party provides a good or service for which he or she gets another good or service in return.
Securities industry: arrangement by a firm using institutional research that it will execute all trades based on that research with the firm providing it, instead of directly paying for the research. This is known as paying in SOFT DOLLARS.

QUIET PERIOD period an ISSUER is "in registration" and subject to an SEC embargo on promotional publicity. It dates from the preunderwriting decision to 40 or 90 days after the EFFECTIVE DATE.

QUORUM minimum number of people who must be present at a meeting in order to make certain decisions go into effect. A quorum may be required at a board of directors, committee, shareholder, legislative, or other meeting for any decisions to have legal standing. A quorum may be achieved by providing a PROXY as well as appearance in person.

QUOTATION
Business: price estimate on a commercial project or transaction.
Investments: highest bid and lowest offer (asked) price currently available on a security or a commodity. An investor who asks for a quotation ("quote") on XYZ might be told "60 to 60½," meaning that the best bid price (the highest price any buyer wants to pay) is currently $60 a share and that the best offer (the lowest price any seller is willing to accept) is $60½ at that time. Such quotes assume ROUND-LOT transactions—for example, 100 shares for stocks.

QUOTATION BOARD electronically controlled board at a brokerage firm that displays current price quotations and other financial data such as dividends, price ranges of stocks, and current volume of trading.

QUOTED PRICE price at which the last sale and purchase of a particular security or commodity took place.

r

RACKETEER INFLUENCED AND CORRUPT ORGANIZATIONS ACT *see* RICO.

RADAR ALERT close monitoring of trading patterns in a company's stock by senior managers to uncover unusual buying activity that might signal a TAKEOVER attempt. *See also* SHARK WATCHER.

RAIDER individual or corporate investor who intends to take control of a company by buying a controlling interest in its stock and installing new management. Raiders who accumulate 5% or more of the outstanding shares in the TARGET COMPANY must report their purchases to the Securities and Exchange Commission, the exchange of listing, and the target itself. *See also* BEAR RAID; WILLIAMS ACT.

RAINMAKER individual who brings significant amounts of new business to a financial services organization. The rainmaker may bring in wealthy brokerage customers who generate a large dollar volume of commissions. Or he or she may be an investment banker who attracts corporate or municipal finance underwritings or merger and acquisition business. Because they are so important to the firm, rainmakers are usually given special PERQUISITES and bonus compensation.

RALLY marked rise in the price of a security, commodity future, or market after a period of decline or sideways movement.

R & D *see* RESEARCH AND DEVELOPMENT.

RANDOM WALK theory about the movement of stock and commodity futures prices hypothesizing that past prices are of no use in forecasting future price movements. According to the theory, stock prices reflect reactions to information coming to the market in random fashion, so they are no more predictable than the walking pattern of a drunken person. The random walk theory was first espoused in 1900 by the French mathematician Louis Bachelier and revived in the 1960s. It is hotly disputed by advocates of TECHNICAL ANALYSIS, who say that charts of past price movements enable them to predict future price movements.

RANGE high and low end of a security, commodity future, or market's price fluctuations over a period of time. Daily newspapers publish the 52-week high and low price range of stocks traded on the New York Stock Exchange, American Stock Exchange, and over-the-counter markets. Advocates of TECHNICAL ANALYSIS attach great importance to trading ranges because they consider it of great significance if a security breaks out of its trading range by going higher or lower. *See also* BREAKOUT.

RATE BASE value established for a utility by a regulatory body such as a Public Utility Commission on which the company is allowed to earn a particular rate of return. Generally the rate base includes the utility's operating costs but not the cost of constructing new facilities. Whether modernization costs should be included in the rate base, and thus passed on to customers, is a subject of continuing controversy. *See also* FAIR RATE OF RETURN.

RATE CAP *see* CAP.

RATE COVENANT provision in MUNICIPAL REVENUE BOND agreements or resolutions covering the rates, or methods of establishing rates, to be charged users of the facility being financed. The rate covenant usually promises that rates will be adjusted when necessary to cover the cost of repairs and maintenance while continuing to provide for the payment of bond interest and principal.

RATE OF EXCHANGE *see* EXCHANGE RATE; PAR VALUE OF CURRENCY.

RATE OF INFLATION *see* CONSUMER PRICE INDEX; INFLATION RATE; PRODUCER PRICE INDEX.

RATE OF RETURN

Fixed-income securities (bonds and preferred stock): CURRENT YIELD, that is, the coupon or contractual dividend rate divided by the purchase price. *See also* YIELD TO AVERAGE LIFE; YIELD TO CALL; YIELD TO MATURITY.

Common stock: (1) dividend yield, which is the annual dividend divided by the purchase price. (2) TOTAL RETURN rate, which is the dividend plus capital appreciation.

Corporate finance: RETURN ON EQUITY or RETURN ON INVESTED CAPITAL.

Capital budgeting: INTERNAL RATE OF RETURN.

See also FAIR RATE OF RETURN; HORIZON ANALYSIS; MEAN RETURN; REAL INTEREST RATE; REQUIRED RATE OF RETURN; TOTAL RETURN; YIELD.

RATING

Credit and investments: evaluation of securities investment and credit risk by rating services such as Duff & Phelps/MCM, FITCH INVESTORS SERVICE INC., MOODY'S INVESTORS SERVICE, STANDARD & POOR'S CORPORATION, and VALUE LINE INVESTMENT SURVEY. *See also* CREDIT RATING; EVENT RISK; NOT RATED.

Insurance: using statistics, mortality tables, probability theory, experience, judgment, and mathematical analysis to establish the rates on which insurance premiums are based. There are three basic rating systems: *class rate,* applying to a homogeneous grouping of clients; *schedule system,* relating positive and negative factors in the case of a particular insured (for example, a smoker or nonsmoker in the case of a life policy) to a base figure; and *experience rating,* reflecting the historical loss experience of the particular insured. Also called *rate-making.*

Insurance companies are also rated. *See* BEST'S RATING.

LEADING BOND RATING SERVICES	RATING SERVICE			
Explanation of corporate/ municipal bond ratings	*Duff & Phelps/MCM*	*Fitch*	*Moody's*	*Standard & Poor's*
Highest quality, "gilt edged" High quality Upper medium grade	AAA AA A	AAA AA A	Aaa Aa A	AAA AA A
Medium grade Predominantly speculative Speculative, low grade	BBB BB B	BBB BB B	Baa Ba B	BBB BB B
Poor to default Highest speculation Lowest quality, no interest	CCC	CCC CC C	Caa Ca C	CCC CC C
In default, in arrears, questionable value		DDD DD D		DDD DD D

Fitch and Standard & Poor's may use + or − to modify some ratings. Moody's uses the numerical modifiers 1 (highest), 2, and 3 in the range from Aa1 through Ca3.

RATIO ANALYSIS method of analysis, used in making credit and investment judgments, which utilizes the relationship of figures found in financial statements to determine values and evaluate risks and compares such ratios to those of prior periods and other companies to reveal trends and identify eccentricities. Ratio analysis is only one tool among many used by analysts. *See also* ACCOUNTS RECEIVABLE TURNOVER; ACID TEST RATIO; BOND RATIO; CAPITALIZATION RATIO; CAPITAL TURNOVER; CASH RATIO; COLLECTION PERIOD; COMMON STOCK RATIO; CURRENT RATIO; DEBT-TO-EQUITY RATIO; DIVIDEND PAYOUT RATIO; EARNINGS/PRICE RATIO; FIXED-CHARGE COVERAGE; LEVERAGE; NET TANGIBLE ASSETS PER SHARE; OPERATING RATIO; PREFERRED STOCK RATIO; PRICE/EARNINGS RATIO; PROFIT MARGIN; QUICK RATIO; RETURN ON EQUITY; RETURN ON INVESTED CAPITAL; RETURN ON SALES.

RATIO WRITER OPTIONS writer who sells more CALL contracts than he has underlying shares. For example, an investor who writes (sells) 10 calls, 5 of them covered by 500 owned shares and the other 5 of them uncovered (or "naked"), has a 2 for 1 ratio write.

RAW LAND property in its natural state, prior to grading, construction, and subdividing. The property has no sewers, electricity, streets, buildings, water service, telephone service, or other amenities. Investors in raw land hope that the land's value will rise in the future if it is developed. While they wait, however, they must pay property taxes on the land's value.

RAW MATERIAL unfinished goods used in the manufacture of a product. For example, a steelmaker uses iron ore and other metals in producing steel. A publishing company uses paper and ink to create books, newspapers, and magazines. Raw materials are carried on a company's balance sheet as inventory in the current assets section.

REACHBACK ability of a LIMITED PARTNERSHIP or other tax shelter to offer deductions at the end of the year that reach back for the entire year. For instance, the investor who buys an OIL AND GAS LIMITED PARTNERSHIP in late December might be able to claim deductions for the entire year's drilling costs, depletion allowance, and interest expenses. Reachback on tax shelters was considered to be abusive by the Internal Revenue Service, and was substantially eliminated by 1984.

REACTION drop in securities prices after a sustained period of advancing prices, perhaps as the result of PROFIT TAKING or adverse developments. *See also* CORRECTION.

READING THE TAPE judging the performance of stocks by monitoring changes in price as they are displayed on the TICKER tape. An analyst reads the tape to determine whether a stock is acting strongly or weakly, and therefore is likely to go up or down. An investor reads the tape to determine whether a stock trade is going with or against the flow of market action. *See also* DON'T FIGHT THE TAPE.

REAGANOMICS economic program followed by the administration of President Ronald Reagan beginning in 1980. Reaganomics stressed lower taxes, higher defense spending, and curtailed spending for social services. After a reduction of growth in the money supply by the Federal Reserve Board combined with Reaganomics to produce a severe recession in 1981–82, the Reagan years were characterized by huge budget deficits, low interest and inflation rates, and continuous economic growth.

REAL ESTATE piece of land and all physical property related to it, including houses, fences, landscaping, and all rights to the air above and earth below the property. Assets not directly associated with the land are considered *personal property.*

REAL ESTATE AGENT licensed salesperson working for a licensed broker. The agent may hold an individual REAL ESTATE BROKER'S license.

REAL ESTATE APPRAISAL estimate of the value of property, usually required when a property is sold, financed, condemned, taxed, insured, or partitioned. An appraisal is not a determination of value. Three approaches are used. To produce an accurate resale price for a residence, appraisers compare the price of the property to the prices of similar nearby properties that have sold recently. For new construction and service properties such as churches and post offices, appraisers look at the reproduction or replacement cost of the improvements, less depreciation, plus the value of the land. For investment properties such as apartment buildings and shopping centers, an estimated value is based on the capitalization of net operating income from a property at an acceptable market rate.

REAL ESTATE BROKER person who arranges the purchase or sale of property for a buyer or seller in return for a commission. Brokers may help arrange financing of the purchase through contacts with banks, savings and loans, and mortgage bankers. Brokers must be licensed by the state to buy or sell real estate.

REAL ESTATE INVESTMENT TRUST (REIT) company, usually traded publicly, that manages a portfolio of real estate to earn profits for shareholders. Patterned after INVESTMENT COMPANIES, REITs make investments in a diverse array of real estate such as shopping centers, medical facilities, nursing homes, office buildings, apartment complexes, industrial warehouses, and hotels. Some REITs, called EQUITY REITS, take equity positions in real estate; shareholders receive income from the rents received and from the properties and receive capital gains as buildings are sold at a profit. Other REITs specialize in lending money to building developers; such MORTGAGE REITS pass interest income on to shareholders. Some REITs, called *hybrid REITs,* have a mix of equity and debt investments. To avoid taxation at the corporate level, 75% or more of the REIT's income must be from real property and 95% of its net earnings must be distributed to shareholders annually. Because REITs must distribute most of their earnings, they tend to pay high yields of 5% to 10% or more.

REAL ESTATE LIMITED PARTNERSHIP LIMITED PARTNERSHIP that invests in real estate. The partnership buys properties such as apartment or office buildings, shopping centers, industrial warehouses, and hotels and passes rental income through to limited partners. If the properties appreciate in value over time, they can be sold and the profit passed through to limited partners. A GENERAL PARTNER manages the partnership, deciding which properties to buy and sell and handling administrative duties, such as distributions to limited partners. In the early 1980s, many real estate partnerships were structured to reduce limited partners' tax liability, because operating losses, plus accelerated depreciation from real estate, could be used to offset other taxable income. But these deals were largely discontinued after the TAX REFORM ACT OF 1986 introduced the principle of PASSIVE LOSSES, meaning that investors could no longer use real estate partnership losses to offset their income from salaries and other investments. Since the mid-1980s, partnerships have been designed to produce high current income and long-term capital gains through appreciation in the underlying real estate, not tax benefits.

REAL ESTATE MORTGAGE INVESTMENT CONDUIT *see* REMIC.

REAL GAIN OR LOSS gain or loss adjusted for INFLATION. *See also* INFLATION ACCOUNTING.

REAL INCOME income of an individual, group, or country adjusted for changes in PURCHASING POWER caused by inflation. A price index is used to determine the difference between the purchasing power of a dollar in a base year and the purchasing power now. The resulting percentage factor, applied to total income, yields the value of that income in constant dollars, termed real income. For instance, if the cost of a market basket increases from $100 to $120 in ten years, reflecting a 20% decline in purchasing power, salaries must rise by 20% if real income is to be maintained.

REAL INTEREST RATE current interest rate minus inflation rate. The real interest rate may be calculated by comparing interest rates with present or, more frequently, with predicted inflation rates The real interest rate gives investors in bonds and other fixed-rate instruments a way to see whether their interest will allow them to keep up with or beat the erosion in dollar values caused by inflation. With a bond yielding 10% and inflation of 3%, for instance, the real interest rate of 7% would bring a return high enough to beat inflation. If inflation were at 15%, however, the investor would fall behind as prices rise.

REALIZED PROFIT (OR LOSS) profit or loss resulting from the sale or other disposal of a security. Capital gains taxes may be due when profits are realized: realized losses can be used to offset realized gains for tax purposes. Such profits and losses differ from a PAPER PROFIT OR LOSS, which (except for OPTION AND FUTURES CONTRACTS) has no tax consequences.

REAL PROPERTY land and all property attached to the land, such as houses, trees, fences, and all improvements.

REAL RATE OF RETURN RETURN on an investment adjusted for inflation.

REALTOR registered trade name that can be used only by members of state and local real estate boards affiliated with the National Association of Realtors (NAR). A realtor-associate is trained and licensed to help clients buy and sell real estate. Realtors must follow a strict code of ethics and receive ongoing training from the NAR. Any complaints about a particular realtor are dealt with at the local real estate board affiliated with the NAR.

REBATE
1. in lending, unearned interest refunded to a borrower if the loan is paid off before maturity.
2. in consumer marketing, payment made to a consumer after a purchase is completed, to induce purchase of a product. For instance, a customer who buys a television set for $500 may be entitled to a rebate of $50, which is received after sending a proof of purchase and a rebate form to the manufacturer. *See also* RULE OF THE 78s.

RECAPITALIZATION alteration of a corporation's CAPITAL STRUCTURE, such as an exchange of bonds for stock. BANKRUPTCY is a common reason for recapitalization; debentures might be exchanged for REORGANIZATION BONDS that pay interest only when earned. A healthy company might seek to save taxes by replacing preferred stock with bonds to gain interest deductibility. *See also* DEFEASANCE.

RECAPTURE
1. contract clause allowing one party to recover some degree of possession of an asset. In leases calling for a percentage of revenues, such as those for shopping centers, the recapture clause provides that the developer get a percentage of profits in addition to a fixed rent.
2. in the tax code, the reclamation by the government of tax benefits previously taken. For example, where a portion of the profit on the sale of a depreciable asset represented ACCELERATED DEPRECIATION or the INVESTMENT CREDIT, all or part of that gain would be "recaptured" and taxed as ORDINARY INCOME, with the balance subject to the favorable CAPITAL GAINS TAX. Recapture also has specialized applications in oil and other industries. Recapture assumed a new meaning under the 1986 Act whereby banks with assets of $500 million or

more were required to take into income the balance of their RESERVE for BAD DEBTS. The Act called for recapture of income at the rate of 10%, 20%, 30%, and 40% for the years 1987 through 1990, respectively.

RECEIVABLES *see* ACCOUNTS RECEIVABLE.

RECEIVER court-appointed person who takes possession of, but not title to, the assets and affairs of a business or estate that is in a form of BANKRUPTCY called *receivership* or is enmeshed in a legal dispute. The receiver collects rents and other income and generally manages the affairs of the entity for the benefit of its owners and creditors until a disposition is made by the court.

RECEIVER'S CERTIFICATE debt instrument issued by a RECEIVER, who uses the proceeds to finance continued operations or otherwise to protect assets in receivership. The certificates constitute a LIEN on the property, ranking ahead of all other secured or unsecured liabilities in LIQUIDATION.

RECEIVE VERSUS PAYMENT instruction accompanying sell orders by institutions that only cash will be accepted in exchange for delivery of the securities at the time of settlement. Institutions are generally required by law to accept only cash. Also called *receive against payment.*

RECESSION downturn in economic activity, defined by many economists as at least two consecutive quarters of decline in a country's GROSS DOMESTIC PRODUCT.

RECLAMATION
Banking: restoration or correction of a NEGOTIABLE INSTRUMENT—or the amount thereof—that has been incorrectly recorded by the *clearing house.*
Finance: restoration of an unproductive asset to productivity, such as by using landfill to make a swamp developable.
Securities: right of either party to a securities transaction to recover losses caused by *bad delivery* or other irregularities in the settlement process.

RECORD DATE *see* DATE OF RECORD; EX-DIVIDEND DATE; PAYMENT DATE.

RECOURSE legal ability the purchaser of a financial asset may have to fall back on the original creditor if the current debtor defaults. For example, an account receivable sold with recourse enables the buyer of the receivable to make claim on the seller if the account doesn't pay.

RECOURSE LOAN
1. loan for which an endorser or guarantor is liable for payment in the event the borrower defaults.
2. loan made to a DIRECT PARTICIPATION PROGRAM or LIMITED PARTNERSHIP whereby the lender, in addition to being secured by specific assets, has recourse against the general assets of the partnership. *See also* NONRECOURSE LOAN.

RECOVERY
Economics: period in a business cycle when economic activity picks up and the GROSS NATIONAL PRODUCT grows, leading into the expansion phase of the cycle.
Finance: (1) absorption of cost through the allocation of DEPRECIATION; (2) collection of an ACCOUNT RECEIVABLE that had been written off as a bad debt; (3) residual cost, or salvage value, of a fixed asset after all allowable depreciation.
Investment: period of rising prices in a securities or commodities market after a period of falling prices.

RECOVERY PERIOD
Economics: period of time in which the economy is emerging from a recession or depression. The recovery period is marked by rising sales and production, improved consumer confidence, and in many cases, rising interest rates.

Stocks: period of time in which a stock that has fallen sharply in price begins to rise again, thereby recovering some of its value.

Taxation: period over which property is subject to depreciation for tax purposes following the ACCELERATED COST RECOVERY SYSTEM (ACRS). Different classes of assets are assigned different periods in which costs can be recovered.

REDEEMABLE BOND *see* CALLABLE.

REDEMPTION repayment of a debt security or preferred stock issue, at or before maturity, at PAR or at a premium price.

Mutual fund shares are redeemed at NET ASSET VALUE when a shareholder's holdings are liquidated.

REDEMPTION DATE date on which a bond is scheduled to mature or be redeemed. If a bond is CALLED AWAY before scheduled maturity, the redemption date is the day that the bond will be taken back.

REDEMPTION FEES fees charged by a mutual fund on shareholders who sell fund shares within a short period of time. The time limit and size of the fee vary among funds, but the redemption fee usually is a relatively small percentage (1% or 2% of the amount withdrawn). Some mutual funds charge a small flat redemption fee of $5 or $10 to cover administrative charges. The intent of the redemption fee is to discourage rapid-fire shifts from one fund to another in an attempt to "time" swings in the stock or bond market. This fee often is confused with the contingent deferred sales charge, or back-end sales charge, typically a feature of the broker-sold fund.

REDEMPTION PRICE *see* CALL PRICE.

RED HERRING *see* PRELIMINARY PROSPECTUS.

REDISCOUNT DISCOUNT short-term negotiable debt instruments, such as banker's ACCEPTANCES and COMMERCIAL PAPER, that have been *discounted* with a bank—in other words, exchanged for an amount of cash adjusted to reflect the current interest rate. The bank then discounts the paper a second time for its own benefit with another bank or with a Federal Reserve bank. Rediscounting was once the primary means by which banks borrowed additional reserves from the Fed. Today most banks do this by discounting their own notes secured by GOVERNMENT SECURITIES or other ELIGIBLE PAPER. But *rediscount rate* is still used as a synonym for DISCOUNT RATE, the rate charged by the Fed for all bank borrowings.

REDLINING discrimination in the pattern of granting loans, insurance coverage, or other financial benefits. Lenders or insurers who practice redlining "draw a red line" around a troubled area of a city and vow not to lend or insure property in that neighborhood because of poor economic conditions and high default rates. Insurance companies withdraw from an area because of high claims experience and widespread fraud. With mortgage and business loans and insurance hard to obtain, redlining therefore tends to accelerate the decline of such neighborhoods. Redlining is illegal because it discriminates against residents of an area on the basis of where they live. Congress has enacted legislation such as the Community Reinvestment Act, which forces banks to lend to underprivileged areas, to combat redlining.

REDS *see* REFUNDING ESCROW DEPOSITS.

REDUCTION-OPTION LOAN (ROL) hybrid between a fixed-rate and adjustable mortgage and a cheaper alternative to refinancing, whereby the borrower has the one-time option from the second through the fifth year to match the current mortgage rate, which then becomes fixed for the rest of the term. The reduction is usually permitted if rates drop more than 2% in any one year.

REFCORP *see* RESOLUTION FUNDING CORPORATION (REFCORP).

REFINANCING
Banking: extending the maturity date, or increasing the amount of existing debt, or both.
Bonds: REFUNDING; retiring existing bonded debt by issuing new securities to reduce the interest rate, or to extend the maturity date, or both.
Personal finance: revising a payment schedule, usually to reduce the monthly payments and often to modify interest charges.

REFLATION reversal of DEFLATION by deliberate government monetary action.

REFUND
Bonds: retirement of an existing bond issue through the sale of a new bond issue. When interest rates have fallen, issuers may want to exercise the CALL FEATURE of a bond and replace it with another debt instrument paying a lower interest rate. *See also* PREREFUNDING.
Commerce: return of merchandise for money. For example, a consumer who is not happy with a product has the right to return it for a refund of his money.
Taxes: *see* TAX REFUND.

REFUNDING
1. replacing an old debt with a new one, usually in order to lower the interest cost of the issuer. For instance, a corporation or municipality that has issued 10% bonds may want to refund them by issuing 7% bonds if interest rates have dropped. *See also* PREREFUNDING; REFINANCING.
2. in merchandising, returning money to the purchaser, e.g., to a consumer who has paid for an appliance and is not happy with it.

REFUNDING ESCROW DEPOSITS (REDS) financial instruments used to circumvent 1984 tax restrictions on tax-exempt PREREFUNDINGS for certain kinds of state or local projects, such as airports, solid-waste disposal facilities, wharves, and convention centers. The object of prerefundings was to lock in a lower current rate in anticipation of maturing higher-rate issues. REDs accomplish this by way of a forward purchase contract obligating investors to buy bonds at a predetermined rate when they are issued at a future date. The future date coincides with the first optional call date on existing high-rate bonds. In the interim, investors' money is invested in Treasury bonds bought in the secondary market. The Treasuries are held in escrow, in effect securing the investor's deposit and paying taxable annual income. The Treasuries mature around the call date on the existing bonds, providing the money to buy the new issue and redeem the old one. Also called *municipal forwards.*

REGIONAL BANK bank that specializes in collecting deposits and making loans in one region of the country, as distinguished from a MONEY CENTER BANK, which operates nationally and internationally.

REGIONAL MUTUAL FUND mutual fund that buys securities from just one region of the country. There are regional mutual funds specializing in the Southwest, Southeast, Northwest, Midwest and other regions. Investors may be interested in such funds because they provide a PURE PLAY on the economic growth in a particular region. People living in these regions may also want to invest in nearby companies because of their firsthand experience with such firms.
   Regional mutual funds also specialize in different regions of the world. There are funds limited to investments in Latin America, Europe, Asia, and other regions. Regional funds, whether domestic or international, tend to be more volatile than funds with more geographically diversified holdings.

REGIONAL STOCK EXCHANGES organized national securities exchanges located outside of New York City and registered with the SECURITIES AND EXCHANGE COMMISSION. They include: the Boston, Cincinnati, Intermountain (Salt Lake City), Midwest (Chicago), Pacific (Los Angeles and San Francisco), Philadelphia (Philadelphia and Miami), and Spokane stock exchanges. These exchanges list both regional issues and many of the securities listed on the New York exchanges. Companies listed on the NEW YORK STOCK EXCHANGE and the AMERICAN STOCK EXCHANGE often are listed on regional exchanges to broaden the market for their securities. Using the INTERMARKET TRADING SYSTEM (ITS), a SPE-CIALIST on the floor of one of the New York or regional exchanges can see competing prices for the securities traded on video screens. Regional exchanges handle only a small percentage of the total volume of the New York exchanges, though most of the trading done on regional exchanges involves stocks listed on the New York exchanges. *See also* DUAL LISTING; GRADUATED SECURITY; SECURI-TIES AND COMMODITIES EXCHANGES.

REGISTERED BOND bond that is recorded in the name of the holder on the books of the issuer or the issuer's REGISTRAR and can be transferred to another owner only when ENDORSED by the registered owner. A bond registered for principal only, and not for interest, is called a *registered coupon bond.* One that is not registered is called a *bearer bond;* one issued with detachable coupons for presentation to the issuer or a paying agent when interest or principal payments are due is termed a COUPON BOND. Bearer bonds are NEGOTIABLE INSTRUMENTS payable to the holder and therefore do not legally require endorsement. Bearer bonds that may be changed to registered bonds are called *interchangeable bonds.*

REGISTERED CHECK check issued by a bank for a customer who places funds aside in a special register. The customer writes in his name and the name of the payee and the amount of money to be transferred. The bank, which collects a fee for the service, then puts on the bank's name and the amount of the check and gives the check a special number. The check has two stubs, one for the customer and one for the bank. The registered check is similar to a money order for someone who does not have a checking account at the bank.

REGISTERED COMPANY company that has filed a REGISTRATION STATEMENT with the Securities and Exchange Commission in connection with a PUBLIC OFFER-ING of securities and must therefore comply with SEC DISCLOSURE requirements.

REGISTERED COMPETITIVE MARKET MAKER
1. securities dealer registered with the NATIONAL ASSOCIATION OF SECURITIES DEAL-ERS (NASD) as a market maker in a particular OVER THE COUNTER stock—that is, one who maintains firm bid and offer prices in the stock by standing ready to buy or sell round lots. Such dealers must announce their quotes through NASDAQ, which requires that there be at least two market makers in each stock listed in the system; the bid and asked quotes are compared to ensure that the quote is a *representative spread. See also* MAKE A MARKET.
2. REGISTERED COMPETITIVE TRADER on the New York Stock Exchange. Such traders are sometimes called market makers because, in addition to trading for their own accounts, they are expected to help correct an IMBALANCE OF ORDERS. *See also* REGISTERED EQUITY MARKET MAKER.

REGISTERED COMPETITIVE TRADER one of a group of New York Stock Exchange members who buy and sell for their own accounts. Because these members pay no commissions, they are able to profit on small changes in market prices and thus tend to trade actively in stocks doing a high volume. Like SPE-CIALISTS, registered competitive traders must abide by exchange rules, including a requirement that 75% of their trades be *stabilizing.* This means they cannot sell unless the last trading price on a stock was up, or buy unless the last trading price was down. Orders from the general public take precedence over those of registered competitive traders, which account for less than 1% of volume. Also called *floor trader* or *competitive trader.*

REGISTERED COUPON BOND *see* REGISTERED BOND.

REGISTERED EQUITY MARKET MAKER AMERICAN STOCK EXCHANGE member firm registered as a trader for its own account. Such firms are expected to make stabilizing purchases and sales when necessary to correct imbalances in particular securities. *See also* REGISTERED COMPETITIVE MARKET MAKER.

REGISTERED INVESTMENT ADVISER investment adviser registered with the Securities and Exchange Commission. An RIA must fill out a form detailing educational and professional experience and pay an annual fee to the SEC. The Registered Investment Adviser (RIA) designation carries no endorsement from the SEC, which regulates RIAs' activities. RIAs may pick stocks, bonds, mutual funds, partnerships or other SEC-registered investments for clients. They may be paid on a fee-only or fee-plus-commission basis. Usually, fees are based on a fixed percentage of assets under management.

REGISTERED INVESTMENT COMPANY investment company, such as an open-end or closed-end MUTUAL FUND, which files a registration statement with the Securities and Exchange Commission and meets all the other requirements of the INVESTMENT COMPANY ACT OF 1940.

REGISTERED OPTIONS TRADER specialist on the floor of the AMERICAN STOCK EXCHANGE who is responsible for maintaining a fair and orderly market in an assigned group of options.

REGISTERED REPRESENTATIVE employee of a stock exchange member broker/dealer who acts as an ACCOUNT EXECUTIVE for clients. As such, the registered representative gives advice on which securities to buy and sell, and he collects a percentage of the commission income he generates as compensation. To qualify as a registered representative, a person must acquire a background in the securities business and pass a series of tests, including the General Securities Examination and state securities tests. "Registered" means licensed by the Securities and Exchange Commission and by the New York Stock Exchange.

REGISTERED RETIREMENT SAVINGS PLAN (RRSP) tax-deductible and tax-sheltered retirement plan for individuals in Canada, similar in concept to the INDIVIDUAL RETIREMENT PLAN (IRA) in the United States.

REGISTERED SECONDARY OFFERING offering, usually through investment bankers, of a large block of securities that were previously issued to the public, using the abbreviated Form S-16 of the Securities and Exchange Commission. Such offerings are usually made by major stockholders of mature companies who may be *control persons* or institutions who originally acquired the securities in a private placement. Form S-16 relies heavily on previously filed SEC documents such as the S-1, the 10-K, and quarterly filings. Where listed securities are concerned, permission to sell large blocks off the exchange must be obtained from the appropriate exchange. *See also* LETTER SECURITY; SECONDARY DISTRIBUTION; SECONDARY OFFERING; SHELF REGISTRATION.

REGISTERED SECURITY
1. security whose owner's name is recorded on the books of the issuer or the issuer's agent, called a *registrar*—for example, a REGISTERED BOND as opposed to a *bearer bond,* the former being transferable only by endorsement, the latter payable to the holder.

2. securities issue registered with the Securities and Exchange Commission as a new issue or as a SECONDARY OFFERING. *See also* REGISTERED SECONDARY OFFERING; REGISTRATION.

REGISTRAR agency responsible for keeping track of the owners of bonds and the issuance of stock. The registrar, working with the TRANSFER AGENT, keeps current files of the owners of a bond issue and the stockholders in a corporation. The registrar also makes sure that no more than the authorized amount of stock is in circulation. For bonds, the registrar certifies that a bond is a corporation's genuine debt obligation.

REGISTRATION process set up by the Securities Exchange Acts of 1933 and 1934 whereby securities that are to be sold to the public are reviewed by the Securities and Exchange Commission. The REGISTRATION STATEMENT details pertinent financial and operational information about the company, its management, and the purpose of the offering. Incorrect or incomplete information will delay the offering.

REGISTRATION FEE charge made by the Securities and Exchange Commission and paid by the issuer of a security when a public offering is recorded with the SEC.

REGISTRATION STATEMENT document detailing the purpose of a proposed public offering of securities. The statement outlines financial details, a history of the company's operations and management, and other facts of importance to potential buyers. *See also* REGISTRATION.

REGRESSION ANALYSIS statistical technique used to establish the relationship of a dependent variable, such as the sales of a company, and one or more independent variables, such as family formations, GROSS DOMESTIC PRODUCT, per capita income, and other ECONOMIC INDICATORS. By measuring exactly how large and significant each independent variable has historically been in its relation to the dependent variable, the future value of the dependent variable can be predicted. Essentially, regression analysis attempts to measure the degree of correlation between the dependent and independent variables, thereby establishing the latter's predictive value. For example, a manufacturer of baby food might want to determine the relationship between sales and housing starts as part of a sales forecast. Using a technique called a scatter graph, it might plot on the X and Y axes the historical sales for ten years and the historical annual housing starts for the same period. A line connecting the average dots, called the regression line, would reveal the degree of correlation between the two factors by showing the amount of unexplained variation—represented by the dots falling outside the line. Thus, if the regression line connected all the dots, it would demonstrate a direct relationship between baby food sales and housing starts, meaning that one could be predicted on the basis of the other. The proportion of dots scattered outside the regression line would indicate, on the other hand, the degree to which the relationship was less direct, a high enough degree of unexplained variation meaning there was no meaningful relationship and that housing starts have no predictive value in terms of baby food sales. This proportion of unexplained variations is termed the *coefficient of determination,* and its square root the CORRELATION COEFFICIENT. The correlation coefficient is the ultimate yardstick of regression analysis: a correlation coefficient of 1 means the relationship is direct—baby food and housing starts move together; –1 means there is a negative relationship—the more housing starts there are, the less baby food is sold; a coefficient of zero means there is no relationship between the two factors.

Regression analysis is also used in securities' markets analysis and in the risk-return analyses basic to PORTFOLIO THEORY.

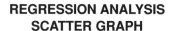

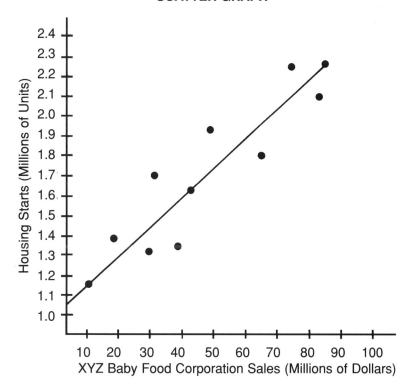

REGRESSION ANALYSIS
SCATTER GRAPH

Housing Starts (Millions of Units)

XYZ Baby Food Corporation Sales (Millions of Dollars)

REGRESSIVE TAX

1. system of taxation in which tax rates decline as the tax base rises. For example, a system that taxed values of $1000 to $5000 at 5%, $5000 to $10,000 at 4% and so on would be regressive. A regressive tax is the opposite of a PRO-GRESSIVE TAX.

2. tax system that results in a higher tax for the poor than for the rich, in terms of percentage of income. In this sense, a sales tax is regressive even though the same rate is applied to all sales, because people with lower incomes tend to spend most of their incomes on goods and services. Similarly, payroll taxes are regressive because they are borne largely by wage earners and not by higher income groups. Local property taxes also tend to be regressive because poorer people spend more of their incomes on housing costs, which are directly affected by property taxes. *See also* FLAT TAX.

REGULAR WAY DELIVERY (AND SETTLEMENT) completion of securities transaction at the office of the purchasing broker on (but not before) the third full business day following the date of the transaction, as required by the NEW YORK STOCK EXCHANGE. Government transactions are an exception; for them, regular way means delivery and settlement the next business day following a transaction.

REGULATED COMMODITIES all commodity futures and options contracts traded on organized U.S. futures exchanges. *See also* COMMODITY FUTURES TRADING COMMISSION.

REGULATED INVESTMENT COMPANY MUTUAL FUND or UNIT INVESTMENT TRUST eligible under *Regulation M* of the Internal Revenue Service to pass capital gains, dividends, and interest earned on fund investments directly to its shareholders to be taxed at the personal level. The process, designed to avoid double taxation, is called the *conduit theory.* To qualify as a regulated investment company, the fund must meet such requirements as 90% minimum distribution of interest and dividends received on investments less expenses and 90% distribution of capital gain net income. To avoid a 4% excise tax, however, a regulated investment company must pay out 98% of its net investment income and capital gains. Shareholders must pay taxes even if they reinvest their distributions.

REGULATION A
1. Securities and Exchange Commission provision for simplified REGISTRATION of small issues of securities. A Regulation A issue requires a shorter form of PROSPECTUS and carries lesser liability for officers and directors for false or misleading statements.
2. Federal Reserve Board statement of the means and conditions under which Federal Reserve banks make loans to member and other banks at what is called the DISCOUNT WINDOW. *See also* REDISCOUNT.

REGULATION D
1. FEDERAL RESERVE BOARD rule pertaining to the amount of reserves banks must maintain relative to deposits.
2. SECURITIES AND EXCHANGE COMMISSION (SEC) rules concerning PRIVATE PLACEMENTS and defining related concepts such as ACCREDITED INVESTOR.

REGULATION G Federal Reserve Board rule regulating lenders other than commercial banks, brokers or dealers who, in the ordinary course of business, extend credit to individuals to purchase or carry securities. Special provision is made for loans by corporations and credit unions to finance purchases under employee stock option and stock purchase plans.

REGULATION Q Federal Reserve Board ceiling on the rates that banks and other savings institutions can pay on savings and other time deposits. THE DEPOSITORY INSTITUTIONS DEREGULATION AND MONETARY CONTROL ACT OF 1980 provided for phasing out Regulation Q by 1986.

REGULATION T Federal Reserve Board regulation covering the extension of credit to customers by securities brokers, dealers, and members of the national securities exchanges. It establishes INITIAL MARGIN requirements and defines registered (eligible), unregistered (ineligible), and exempt securities. *See also* MARGIN REQUIREMENT; MARGIN SECURITIES.

REGULATION U Federal Reserve Board limit on the amount of credit a bank may extend a customer for purchasing and carrying MARGIN SECURITIES. *See also* NONPURPOSE LOAN.

REGULATION Z Federal Reserve Board regulation covering provisions of the CONSUMER CREDIT PROTECTION ACT OF 1968, known as the Truth-in-Lending Act.

REHYPOTHECATION pledging by brokers of securities in customers' MARGIN ACCOUNTS to banks as collateral for broker loans under a GENERAL LOAN AND COLLATERAL AGREEMENT. Broker loans cover the positions of brokers who have made margin loans to customers for margin purchases and SELLING SHORT. Margin loans are collateralized by the HYPOTHECATION of customers securities to the broker. Their rehypothecation is authorized when the customer originally signs a GENERAL ACCOUNT agreement.

REIMBURSEMENT paying someone back for out-of-pocket expenses. For example, a company reimburses employees for their out-of-pocket business-related expenses when employees file expense reports. Insurance companies reimburse policyholders for out-of-pocket expenses incurred paying medical bills (for health insurance) or for home repairs (homeowner's insurance).

REINSTATEMENT in INSURANCE, the restoration of coverage after a policy has lapsed because premium payments have not been made. Typically, life insurance can be reinstated within a three-year period if premiums are paid and subject to evidence of continued insurability.

REINSURANCE sharing of RISK among insurance companies. Part of the insurer's risk is assumed by other companies in return for a part of the premium fee paid by the insured. By spreading the risk, reinsurance allows an individual company to take on clients whose coverage would be too great a burden for one insurer to carry alone.

REINVESTMENT PRIVILEGE right of a shareholder to reinvest dividends in order to buy more shares in the company or MUTUAL FUND, usually at no additional sales charge.

REINVESTMENT RATE rate of return resulting from the reinvestment of the interest from a bond or other fixed-income security. The reinvestment rate on a ZERO-COUPON BOND is predictable and locked in, since no interest payments are ever made, and therefore all imputed interest is reinvested at the same rate. The reinvestment rate on coupon bonds is less predictable because it rises and falls with market interest rates.

REINVESTMENT RISK risk that rates will fall causing cash flows from an investment (dividends or interest), assuming reinvestment, to earn less than the original investment.

REIT *see* REAL ESTATE INVESTMENT TRUST.

REJECTION
Banking: refusal to grant credit to an applicant because of inadequate financial strength, a poor credit history, or some other reason.
Insurance: refusal to underwrite a risk, that is, to issue a policy.
Securities: refusal of a broker or a broker's customer to accept the security presented to complete a trade. This usually occurs because the security lacks the necessary endorsements. or because of other exceptions to the rules for GOOD DELIVERY.

RELATIVE STRENGTH rate at which a stock falls relative to other stocks in a falling market or rises relative to other stocks in a rising market. Analysts reason that a stock that holds value on the downside will be a strong performer on the upside and vice versa. Comparative relative strength, as the concept is more accurately called, compares a security's price performance with that of a "base security," which is often a market index. The security price is divided by the base security's price to get the ratio between the two, which is called the comparative relative strength indicator. When the indicator is moving up, the security is outperforming the base security and vice versa.

Comparative relative strength should not be confused with what technical analysts call the RELATIVE STRENGTH INDEX (RSI). The RSI is a MOMENTUM OSCILLATOR developed by J. Welles Wilder in the late 1970s and discussed in his book, *New Concepts in Technical Trading Systems.* The name relative strength index is somewhat misleading since it does not compare the relative strength of two securities, but rather the internal strength of a single security. The RSI measures the relative strength of the current price movement as increasing from 0 to 100. Although many variations are in use, Wilder favored the use of a 14-period measurement and set the significant levels of the indicator at 30 for oversold (signaling an imminent upturn) and 70 for overbought (signaling an imminent downturn). Thus the averages of up days and down days for 14-day periods would be plotted. If the security makes a new high but the RSI fails to surpass its previous high, this divergence is an indication of an impending reversal. When the RSI then turns down and falls below its most recent trough, it has completed a "failure swing" which confirms the impending reversal.

RELEASE CLAUSE provision in a MORTGAGE agreement allowing the freeing of pledged property after a proportionate amount of payment has been made.

REMAINDER remaining interest in a TRUST or ESTATE after expenses and after prior beneficiaries have been satisfied. *See also* CHARITABLE REMAINDER TRUST.

REMAINING MONTHLY BALANCE amount of debt remaining unpaid on a monthly statement. For example, a credit card customer may charge $300 worth of merchandise during a month, and pay $100, leaving a remaining monthly balance of $200, on which interest charges would accrue.

REMARGINING putting up additional cash or eligible securities to correct a deficiency in EQUITY deposited in a brokerage MARGIN ACCOUNT to meet MINIMUM MAINTENANCE REQUIREMENTS. Remargining usually is prompted by a MARGIN CALL.

REMIC acronym for *real estate mortgage investment conduit,* a pass-through vehicle created under the TAX REFORM ACT OF 1986 to issue multiclass mortgage-backed securities. REMICs may be organized as corporations, partnerships, or trusts, and those meeting qualifications are not subject to DOUBLE TAXATION. Interests in REMICs may be senior or junior, *regular* (debt instruments) or *residual* (equity interests). The practical meaning of REMICs has been that issuers have more flexibility than is afforded by the COLLATERALIZED MORTGAGE OBLIGATION (CMO) vehicle. Issuers can thus separate mortgage pools not only into different maturity classes but into different risk classes as well. Whereas CMOs normally have AAA bond ratings, REMICs represent a range of risk levels.

REMIT pay for purchased goods or services by cash, check, or electronic payment.

RENEWABLE TERM LIFE INSURANCE term life insurance policy offering the policyholder the option to renew for a specific period of time—frequently one year—for a particular length of time. Some term life policies stipulate a maximum age benefit. Some policies offer fixed premium rates for a certain number of years, usually ten, after which they are renewable at a higher premium rate. Other term policies are renewable every year, and charge escalating premium rates as the policyholder ages.

RENT payment from a tenant to a building owner for use of the specified property. For example, an apartment dweller must pay monthly rent to a landlord for the right to inhabit the apartment. A commercial tenant in an office or store must pay monthly rent to the building owner for the use of the commercial space.

RENT CONTROL state and local government regulation restricting the amount of rent landlords can charge their tenants. Rent control is used to regulate the quality of rental dwellings, with controls implemented only against those units that do not conform to building codes, as in New York City; or used across the board to deal with high rents resulting from a gross imbalance between housing supply and demand, as in Massachusetts and California. If a landlord violates rent control laws, the tenant may protest at the local housing authority charged with enforcing the law. While tenants may like rent control, landlords argue that it reduces their ability to earn a profit on their property, thereby discouraging them from investing any further to maintain or upgrade the property. In some cases, landlords argue that rent control encourages owners to abandon their property altogether since it will never be profitable to retain it.

REORGANIZATION financial restructuring of a firm in BANKRUPTCY. *See also* TRUSTEE IN BANKRUPTCY; VOTING TRUST CERTIFICATE.

REORGANIZATION BOND debt security issued by a company in REORGANIZA-TION proceedings. The bonds are generally issued to the company's creditors on a basis whereby interest is paid only if and when it is earned. *See also* ADJUST-MENT BOND; INCOME BOND.

REPATRIATION return of the financial assets of an organization or individual from a foreign country to the home country.

REPLACEMENT COST cost to replace an asset with another of similar utility at today's prices. Also called *current cost* and *replacement value. See also* BOOK VALUE, REPLACEMENT COST INSURANCE.

REPLACEMENT COST ACCOUNTING accounting method allowing additional DEPRECIATION on part of the difference between the original cost and current replacement cost of a depreciable asset.

REPLACEMENT COST INSURANCE property and casualty insurance that replaces damaged property. Replacement cost contents insurance pays the dollar amount needed to replace damaged personal property with items of like kind and quality, without deducting for depreciation. Replacement cost dwelling insurance pays the policyholder the cost of replacing the damaged property without deduction for depreciation, but limited by the maximum dollar amount indicated on the declarations page of the policy. *See also* REPLACEMENT COST.

REPURCHASE AGREEMENT (REPO; RP) agreement between a seller and a buyer, usually of U.S. government securities, whereby the seller agrees to repurchase the securities at an agreed upon price and, usually, at a stated time. Repos, also called RPs or buybacks, are widely used both as a money market investment vehicle and as an instrument of Federal Reserve MONETARY POLICY. Where a repurchase agreement is used as a short-term investment, a government securities dealer, usually a bank, borrows from an investor, typically a corporation with excess cash, to finance its inventory, using the securities as collateral. Such RPs may have a fixed maturity date or be OPEN REPOS, callable at any time. Rates are negotiated directly by the parties involved, but are generally lower than rates on collateralized loans made by New York banks. The attraction of repos to corporations, which also have the alternatives of COMMERCIAL PAPER, CERTIFICATES OF DEPOSIT, TREASURY BILLS and other short-term instruments, is the flexibility of maturities that makes them an ideal place to "park" funds on a very temporary basis. Dealers also arrange *reverse repurchase agreements,* whereby they agree to buy the securities and the investor agrees to repurchase them at a later date.

The FEDERAL RESERVE BANK also makes extensive use of repurchase agreements in its OPEN MARKET OPERATIONS as a method of fine tuning the MONEY SUPPLY. To temporarily expand the supply, the Fed arranges to buy securities from nonbank dealers who in turn deposit the proceeds in their commercial bank accounts thereby adding to reserves. Timed to coincide with whatever length of time the Fed needs to make the desired adjustment, usually 1 to 15 days, the dealer repurchases the securities. Such transactions are made at the Federal Reserve DISCOUNT RATE and accounts are credited in FEDERAL FUNDS. When it wishes to reduce the money supply temporarily, the Fed reverses the process. Using a procedure called the MATCHED SALE PURCHASE TRANSACTION, it sells securities to a nonbank dealer who either draws down bank balances directly or takes out a bank loan to make payment, thereby draining reserves.

In a third variation of the repurchase agreement, banks and thrift institutions can raise temporary capital funds with a device called the *retail repurchase agreement.* Using pooled government securities to secure loans from individuals, they agree to repurchase the securities at a specified time at a price including interest. Despite its appearance of being a deposit secured by government securities, the investor has neither a special claim on the securities nor protection by the FEDERAL DEPOSIT INSURANCE CORPORATION in the event the bank is forced to liquidate.

See also OVERNIGHT REPO.

REQUIRED RATE OF RETURN return required by investors before they will commit money to an investment at a given level of risk. Unless the expected return exceeds the required return, an investment is unacceptable. *See also* HURDLE RATE; INTERNAL RATE OF RETURN; MEAN RETURN.

REQUIRED RESERVE RATE factor used to determine the amount of reserves a bank must maintain on its deposits.

RESCHEDULED LOANS bank loans that, as an alternative to DEFAULT, were restructured, usually by lengthening the maturity to make it easier for the borrower to meet repayment terms.

RESCIND cancel a contract agreement. The Truth-in-Lending Act confers the RIGHT OF RESCISSION, which allows the signer of a contract to nullify it within three business days without penalty and have any deposits refunded. Contracts may also be rescinded in cases of fraud, failure to comply with legal procedures, or misrepresentation. For example, a contract signed by a child under legal age may be rescinded, since children do not have the right to take on contractual obligations.

RECISSION *see* RIGHT OF RESCISSION.

RESEARCH AND DEVELOPMENT (R&D) scientific and marketing evolution of a new product or service. Once such a product has been created in a laboratory or other research setting, marketing specialists attempt to define the market for the product. Then, steps are taken to manufacture the product to meet the needs of the market. Research and development spending is often listed as a separate item in a company's financial statements. In industries such as high-technology and pharmaceuticals, R&D spending is quite high, since products are outdated or attract competition quickly. Investors looking for companies in such fast-changing fields check on R&D spending as a percentage of sales because they consider this an important indicator of the company's prospects. *See also* RESEARCH AND DEVELOPMENT LIMITED PARTNERSHIP.

RESEARCH AND DEVELOPMENT LIMITED PARTNERSHIP plan whose investors put up money to finance new product RESEARCH AND DEVELOPMENT. In return, the investors get a percentage of the product's profits, if any, together with such benefits as DEPRECIATION of equipment. R&D partnerships may be offered publicly or privately, usually through brokerage firms. Those that are offered to the public must be registered with the Securities and Exchange Commission. *See also* LIMITED PARTNERSHIP.

RESEARCH DEPARTMENT division within a brokerage firm, investment company, bank trust department, insurance company, or other institutional investing organization that analyzes markets and securities. Research departments include analysts who focus on particular securities, commodities, and whole industries as well as generalists who forecast movements of the markets as a whole, using both FUNDAMENTAL ANALYSIS and TECHNICAL ANALYSIS. An analyst whose advice is followed by many investors can have a major impact on the prices of individual securities.

RESERVE
1. segregation of RETAINED EARNINGS to provide for such payouts as dividends, contingencies, improvements, or retirement of preferred stock.
2. VALUATION RESERVE, also called ALLOWANCE, for DEPRECIATION, BAD DEBT losses, shrinkage of receivables because of discounts taken, and other provisions created by charges to the PROFIT AND LOSS STATEMENT.
3. hidden reserves, represented by understatements of BALANCE SHEET values.
4. deposit maintained by a commercial bank in a FEDERAL RESERVE BANK to meet the Fed's RESERVE REQUIREMENT.

RESERVE REQUIREMENT FEDERAL RESERVE SYSTEM rule mandating the financial assets that member banks must keep in the form of cash and other liquid assets as a percentage of DEMAND DEPOSITS and TIME DEPOSITS. This money must be in the bank's own vaults or on deposit with the nearest regional FEDERAL RESERVE BANK. Reserve requirements, set by the Fed's Board of Governors, are one of the key tools in deciding how much money banks can lend, thus setting the pace at which the nation's money supply and economy grow. The higher the reserve requirement, the tighter the money—and therefore the slower the economic growth. *See also* MONETARY POLICY; MONEY SUPPLY; MULTIPLIER.

RESET BONDS bonds issued with a provision that on specified dates the initial interest rate must be adjusted so that the bonds trade at their original value. Although reset provisions can work in an issuer's favor by lowering rates should market rates fall or credit quality improve, they were designed as a protective feature for investors to enhance the marketability of JUNK BOND issues. Should market rates rise or credit quality decline (causing prices to decline), the interest rate would be increased to bring the bond price to PAR or above. The burden of increased interest payments on a weak issuer could prompt DEFAULT.

RESIDENTIAL ENERGY CREDIT tax credit granted to homeowners prior to 1986 by the federal government for improving the energy efficiency of their homes. Installation of storm windows and doors, insulation, or new fuel-saving heating systems before the end of 1985 meant a maximum federal credit on expenditures of $300. Equipping a home with renewable energy devices such as solar panels or windmills meant a maximum federal credit of $4000. Many states offer incentives for installing such devices.

RESIDENTIAL MORTGAGE mortgage on a residential property. Interest on such mortgages is deductible for federal and state income tax purposes up to $1 million; for home equity loans, interest up to $100,000 is deductible.

RESIDENTIAL PROPERTY property zoned for single-family homes, townhouses, multifamily apartments, condominiums, and coops. Residential property falls under different zoning and taxation regulations than commercial property.

RESIDUAL SECURITY
1. SECURITY that has a potentially dilutive effect on earnings per common share. Warrants, rights, convertible bonds, and preferred stock are potentially dilutive because exercising or converting them into common stock would increase the number of common shares competing for the same earnings, and earnings per share would be reduced. *See also* DILUTION: FULLY DILUTED EARNINGS PER (COMMON) SHARE.
2. the term *residual* is also used informally to describe investments based on the excess cash flow generated by collateral pools. CMO REITs and the bottom tier of most COLLATERALIZED BOND OBLIGATIONS (CBOs) are examples of "residuals."

RESIDUAL VALUE
1. realizable value of a FIXED ASSET after costs associated with the sale.
2. amount remaining after all allowable DEPRECIATION charges have been subtracted from the original cost of a depreciable asset.
3. scrap value, which is the value to a junk dealer. Also called *salvage value.*

RESISTANCE LEVEL price ceiling at which technical analysts note persistent
selling of a commodity or security. If XYZ's stock generally trades between a
low of $50 and a high of $60 a share, $50 is called the SUPPORT LEVEL and $60 is
called the resistance level. Technical analysts think it significant when the stock
breaks through the resistance level because that means it usually will go on to
new high prices. *See also* BREAKOUT; TECHNICAL ANALYSIS.

RESISTANCE LEVEL

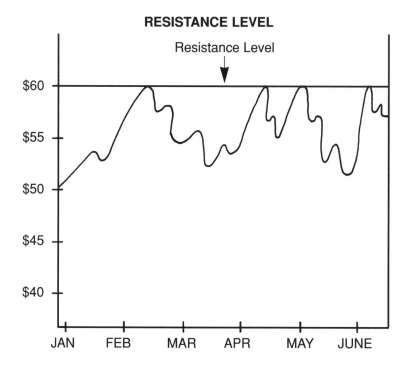

RESOLUTION
1. in general, expression of desire or intent.
2. formal document representing an action of a corporation's BOARD OF DIREC-
   TORS—perhaps a directive to management, such as in the declaration of a
   dividend, or a corporate expression of sentiment, such as acknowledging the
   services of a retiring officer. A *corporate resolution,* which defines the
   authority and powers of individual officers, is a document given to a bank.
3. legal order or contract by a government entity—called a *bond resolution*—
   authorizing a bond issue and spelling out the rights of bondholders and the
   obligations of the issuer.

RESOLUTION FUNDING CORPORATION (REFCORP) U.S. government
agency created by Congress in 1989 to (1) issue BAILOUT BONDS and raise industry funds to finance activities of the RESOLUTION TRUST CORPORATION (RTC) and

(2) merge or close sick institutions inherited from the disbanded FEDERAL SAVINGS AND LOAN INSURANCE CORPORATION (FSLIC). *See also* OFFICE OF THRIFT SUPERVISION (OTS).

RESOLUTION TRUST CORPORATION (RTC) U.S. government agency created by the 1989 bailout bill to merge or close savings and loan institutions becoming insolvent between 1989 and August 1992. The RTC was terminated in 1996 and its responsibilities were shifted to the SAVINGS ASSOCIATION INSURANCE FUND (SAIF), a unit of the FEDERAL DEPOSIT INSURANCE CORPORATION. The *Resolution Trust Corporation Oversight Board,* an arm of the executive branch, was charged with overseeing broad policy and the dispensing of funds to sick thrifts by RTC. *See also* OFFICE OF THRIFT SUPERVISION (OTS).

RESTRICTED ACCOUNT MARGIN ACCOUNT with a securities broker in which the EQUITY is less than the INITIAL MARGIN requirement set by the Federal Reserve Board's REGULATION T. A customer whose account is restricted may not make further purchases and must, in accordance with Regulation T's *retention requirement,* retain in the account a percentage of the proceeds of any sales so as to reduce the deficiency (debit balance). This retention requirement is currently set at 50%. *See also* MARGIN CALL.

RESTRICTED SURPLUS portion of RETAINED EARNINGS not legally available for the payment of dividends. Among the circumstances giving rise to such restriction: dividend arrearages in CUMULATIVE PREFERRED stock, a shortfall in the minimum WORKING CAPITAL ratio specified in an INDENTURE, or simply a vote by the BOARD OF DIRECTORS. Also called *restricted retained earnings.*

RESTRICTIVE COVENANT *see* COVENANT.

RESTRICTIVE ENDORSEMENT signature on the back of a check specifying the transfer of the amount of that check, under specific conditions. The most common type of restrictive endorsement is "for deposit only," meaning the check must be deposited in the payee's bank account and cannot be cashed.

RESTRUCTURING general term for major corporate changes aimed at greater efficiency and adaptation to changing markets. SPIN-OFFS, RECAPITALIZATIONS, STRATEGIC BUYOUTS, and major management realignments are all developments frequently associated with corporate restructurings. *See also* DOWNSIZING.

RESYNDICATION LIMITED PARTNERSHIP partnership in which existing properties are sold to new limited partners, who can gain tax advantages that had been exhausted by the old partnership. For instance, a partnership with government-subsidized housing may have given partners substantial tax benefits five years ago. Now the same housing development may be sold to a resyndication partnership, which will start the process of DEPRECIATION over again and claim additional tax benefits for its new limited partners. Resyndication partnerships are usually offered as PRIVATE PLACEMENTS through brokerage houses, although a few have been offered to the public.

RETAIL HOUSE brokerage firm that caters to retail investors instead of institutions. Such a firm may be a large national broker called a WIRE HOUSE, with a large RESEARCH DEPARTMENT and a wide variety of products and services for individuals, or it may be a small BOUTIQUE serving an exclusive clientele with specialized research or investment services.

RETAIL INVESTOR investor who buys securities and commodities futures on his own behalf, not for an organization. Retail investors typically buy shares of stock or commodity positions in much smaller quantities than institutions such as mutual funds, bank trust departments, and pension funds and therefore are usually charged commissions higher than those paid by the institutions. In recent years, market activity has increasingly been dominated by INSTITUTIONAL INVESTORS.

RETAIL PRICE price charged to retail customers for goods and services. Retailers buy goods from wholesalers, and increase the price to cover their costs, plus a profit. Manufacturers list suggested retail prices for their products; retailers may adhere to these prices or offer discounts from them.

RETAINED EARNINGS net profits kept to accumulate in a business after dividends are paid. Also called *undistributed profits* or *earned surplus.* Retained earnings are distinguished from *contributed capital*—capital received in exchange for stock, which is reflected in CAPITAL STOCK or CAPITAL SURPLUS and DONATED STOCK or DONATED SURPLUS. STOCK DIVIDENDS—the distribution of additional shares of capital stock with no cash payment—reduce retained earnings and increase capital stock. Retained earnings plus the total of all the capital accounts represent the NET WORTH of a firm. *See also* ACCUMULATED PROFITS TAX; PAID-IN CAPITAL.

RETAINED EARNINGS STATEMENT reconciliation of the beginning and ending balances in the RETAINED EARNINGS account on a company's BALANCE SHEET. It breaks down changes affecting the account, such as profits or losses from operations, dividends declared, and any other items charged or credited to retained earnings. A retained earnings statement is required by GENERALLY ACCEPTED ACCOUNTING PRINCIPLES whenever comparative balance sheets and income statements are presented. It may appear in the balance sheet, in a combined PROFIT AND LOSS STATEMENT and retained earnings statement, or as a separate schedule. It may also be called *statement of changes in earned surplus* (or *retained income*).

RETENTION in securities underwriting, the number of units allocated to a participating investment banker (SYNDICATE member) minus the units held back by the syndicate manager for facilitating institutional sales and for allocation to firms in the selling group that are not also members of the syndicate. *See also* UNDERWRITE.

RETENTION RATE percentage of after-tax profits credited to RETAINED EARNINGS. It is the opposite of the DIVIDEND PAYOUT RATIO.

RETENTION REQUIREMENT *see* RESTRICTED ACCOUNT.

RETIREMENT
1. cancellation of stock or bonds that have been reacquired or redeemed. *See also* CALLABLE; REDEMPTION.
2. removal from service after a fixed asset has reached the end of its useful life or has been sold and appropriate adjustments have been made to the asset and depreciation accounts.
3. repayment of a debt obligation.
4. permanent withdrawal of an employee from gainful employment in accordance with an employer's policies concerning length of service, age, or disability. A retired employee may have rights to a pension or other retirement provisions offered by the employer. Such benefits may in some circumstances supplement payments from an INDIVIDUAL RETIREMENT ACCOUNT (IRA) or KEOGH PLAN.

RETIREMENT AGE age at which employees no longer work. Though there is no longer any mandatory retirement age, many institutions do impose a retirement age. The federal government has a retirement age of 70. Many corporations have a retirement age of 65, although this has become more flexible and is no longer standard. Employees reaching age 62 may start to receive Social Security benefits, though the minimum age for receiving full Social Security benefits starts at age 65 and gradually increases to age 67 starting in the year 2000.

RETIREMENT PROTECTION ACT OF 1994 legislation designed to protect the pension benefits of American workers and retirees by increasing funding of underfunded pension plans and strengthening the pension insurance program administered by the PENSION BENEFIT GUARANTY CORPORATION (PBGC). Reinforcing the special requirement known as the Deficit Reduction Contribution (DRC) to fund underfunded pension plans, the act required severely underfunded plans to have enough cash and marketable securities to cover current benefit payments. The law also increased PBGC premiums for pension plans posing the greatest liquidation risk. It also required employers whose plans are less than 90% funded to provide a notice to their employees in simple language on the plan's funding and the limits of PBGC guarantees. The act also created the "Pension Search Program" which locates people who are owed benefits from fully funded, PBGC-insured defined benefit plans that terminate. *See also* PENSION BENEFIT GUARANTY CORPORATION (PBGC).

RETURN
Finance and investment: profit on a securities or capital investment, usually expressed as an annual percentage rate. *See also* RATE OF RETURN; RETURN ON EQUITY; RETURN ON INVESTED CAPITAL; RETURN ON SALES; TOTAL RETURN.
Retailing: exchange of previously sold merchandise for REFUND or CREDIT against future sales.
Taxes: form on which taxpayers submit information required by the government when they file with the INTERNAL REVENUE SERVICE. For example, Form 1040 is the tax return used by individual taxpayers.
Trade: physical return of merchandise for credit against an invoice.

RETURN OF CAPITAL distribution of cash resulting from DEPRECIATION tax savings, the sale of a CAPITAL ASSET or of securities in a portfolio, or any other transaction unrelated to RETAINED EARNINGS. Returns of capital are not directly taxable but may result in higher CAPITAL GAINS taxes later on if they reduce the acquisition cost base of the property involved. Also called *return of basis.*

RETURN ON COMMON EQUITY *see* RETURN ON EQUITY; RETURN ON INVESTED CAPITAL.

RETURN ON EQUITY amount, expressed as a percentage, earned on a company's common stock investment for a given period. It is calculated by dividing common stock equity (NET WORTH) at the beginning of the accounting period into NET INCOME for the period after preferred stock dividends but before common stock dividends. Return on equity tells common shareholders how effectually their money is being employed. Comparing percentages for current and prior periods reveals trends, and comparison with industry composites reveals how well a company is holding its own against its competitors.

RETURN ON INVESTED CAPITAL amount, expressed as a percentage, earned on a company's total capital—its common and preferred stock EQUITY plus its long-term FUNDED DEBT—calculated by dividing total capital into earnings before interest, taxes, and dividends. Return on invested capital, usually termed *return on investment,* or *ROI,* is a useful means of comparing companies, or corporate divisions, in terms of efficiency of management and viability of product lines.

RETURN ON SALES net pretax profits as a percentage of NET SALES—a useful measure of overall operational efficiency when compared with prior periods or with other companies in the same line of business. It is important to recognize, however, that return on sales varies widely from industry to industry. A supermarket chain with a 2% return on sales might be operating efficiently, for example, because it depends on high volume to generate an acceptable RETURN ON INVESTED CAPITAL. In contrast, a manufacturing enterprise is expected to average 4% to 5%, so a return on sales of 2% is likely to be considered highly inefficient.

REVALUATION change in the value of a country's currency relative to others that is based on the decision of authorities rather than on fluctuations in the market. Revaluation generally refers to an increase in the currency's value; DEVALUATION refers to a decrease. *See also* FLOATING EXCHANGE RATE; PAR VALUE OF CURRENCY.

REVENUE ANTICIPATION NOTE (RAN) short-term debt issue of a municipal entity that is to be repaid out of anticipated revenues such as sales taxes. When the taxes are collected, the RAN is paid off. Interest from the note is usually tax-free to RAN holders.

REVENUE BOND *see* MUNICIPAL REVENUE BOND.

REVENUE NEUTRAL guiding criterion in drafting the TAX REFORM ACT OF 1986 whereby provisions estimated to add revenue were offset by others estimated to reduce revenue, so that on paper the new bill would generate the same amount of revenue as the old tax laws. The concept, which has guided subsequent tax legislation, was theoretical rather than real, since estimates are subject to variation.

REVENUE RECONCILIATION ACT OF 1993 landmark legislation signed into law by President Clinton in August 1993 to reduce the federal budget deficit by curtailing spending and raising taxes. Among its major components:
Provisions Affecting Individuals
1. added a fourth tax bracket of 36% to the existing 15%, 28%, and 31% brackets. Single taxpayers earning over $115,000 and married taxpayers filing jointly earning over $140,000 pay at the 36% marginal rate.
2. added a 10% surtax on married couples filing jointly reporting more than $250,000 in taxable income, or on married couples filing separately with taxable incomes of more than $125,000, creating, in effect, a fifth tax bracket at 39.6%.
3. kept capital gains tax rate at 28% for assets held at least a year.
4. created special tax break for investing in small companies. Investors buying newly issued stock in a small company with less than $50 million in gross assets who hold the stock for at least five years may exclude 50% of the profit from capital gains taxes. For each subsequent year the investor holds the stock, the tax rate declines 10% until there is no capital gains tax after 10 years.
5. gasoline taxes were increased from 14.1 cents to 18.4 cents a gallon.
6. taxes on Social Security benefits were raised. Couples with provisional income plus half their Social Security benefits totaling more than $44,000 owe tax on up to 85% of their Social Security benefits. For singles, the equivalent level is $34,000. Provisional income is defined as adjusted gross income, interest on tax-exempt bonds, and certain income from foreign sources. Previously, couples with taxable income over $32,000 and singles with income over $25,000 had to pay taxes on 50% of their Social Security benefits.
7. Medicare tax cap was eliminated. Before this Act, the Medicare tax of 1.45% on wages applied to the first $135,000 of wages.
8. phaseout of personal exemptions, which had been temporary, was made permanent. Personal exemptions begin to phase out for singles reporting adjusted gross incomes of $108,450. For married couples filing jointly, exemptions begin to phase out when adjusted gross income reaches $167,700. (These amounts are adjusted for inflation annually).
9. investment interest deductions were limited. Interest paid to finance the purchase of securities remain deductible from interest income earned from investments, but that interest can no longer be deducted against realized capital gains.

10. pension contributions were limited. The income limit for contributions to pension plans such as Keoghs and SEPs was lowered from $235,840 to $150,000.
11. earned income credit was expanded. For taxpayers with more than one child, a credit of up to 18.5% can be claimed for the first $7750 of income, up to a maximum of $1511. The credit rose to 36% in 1995 and 40% in 1996.
12. moving deductions were limited. Under the law, unreimbursed moving expenses for house-hunting, closing fees, broker's commissions, and food costs while living in temporary quarters are no longer deductible as they had been previously. In addition, moves must be 50 miles, up from 35 miles, from the previous home in order to qualify for tax benefits. Moving expenses were converted from an itemized deduction—available only to those who filed an itemized return—to an above-the-line deduction, similar to alimony.
13. estimated tax rules were changed. For married taxpayers filing jointly reporting more than $150,000 in taxable income, quarterly estimated taxes must be paid at 110% of the previous year's tax liability.
14. alternative minimum tax (AMT) rates were raised. The AMT tax rate on income exceeding $175,000 was raised from 24% to 28%.
15. estate tax rates were raised. The top rate on inheritance taxes was raised from 50% to 55% on estates worth more than $3 million.
16. luxury taxes were repealed. The 10% luxury tax on airplanes, boats, cars, furs, and jewelry was repealed on all items except cars selling for more than $32,000.
17. rules governing donations of appreciated property were made permanent. Temporary rules allowing donors to deduct the full value of appreciated property such as art, real estate, and securities were made permanent. Such donations were also removed from calculations towards the alternative minimum tax (AMT).

Provisions Affecting Business

18. corporate tax rates were increased from 34% to 35%, for companies with taxable income of at least $10 million.
19. deductions for executive salaries exceeding $1 million were limited.
20. meal and entertainment deductions were lowered from 80% to 50% for business-related meal and entertainment expenses.
21. deductions were increased for small business purchases of equipment up to $17,500 a year, up from $10,000 previously.
22. tax breaks were reinstated for real estate professionals. Certified real estate professionals, defined as those working at least 750 hours a year in a real-estate-related line of work such as sales or construction, are allowed to deduct losses on rental property against any form of income. Previously, such passive losses could only be offset against passive income.
23. commercial real estate depreciation was lengthened from 31 years to 39 years.
24. club dues for country clubs; airline lounges; and social, athletic, and health clubs were made nondeductible.
25. standard period for depreciating goodwill when acquiring a business was set at 15 years.
26. expenses for lobbying Congress were made nondeductible.
27. restrictions on deductions for traveling spouses were imposed. Expenses for spouses traveling on a business trip were made non-deductible, unless the spouse is an employee of the company paying for the trip and has a business reason for going.
28. empowerment zones were created. Businesses that invest and create jobs in authorized empowerment zones in particular depressed communities qualify for tax incentives and special grants.

REVENUE SHARING

Limited partnerships: percentage split between the general partner and limited partners of profits, losses, cash distributions, and other income or losses which result from the operation of a real estate, oil and gas, equipment leasing, or other partnership. *See also* LIMITED PARTNERSHIP.

Taxes: return of tax revenue to a unit of government by a larger unit, such as from a state to one of its municipalities. GENERAL REVENUE SHARING between the federal government and states, localities, and other subunits existed between 1972 and 1987.

REVERSAL change in direction in the stock or commodity futures markets, as charted by technical analysts. If the Dow Jones Industrial Average has been climbing steadily from 7400 to 7900, for instance, chartists would speak of a reversal if the average started a sustained fall back toward 7400.

REVERSAL

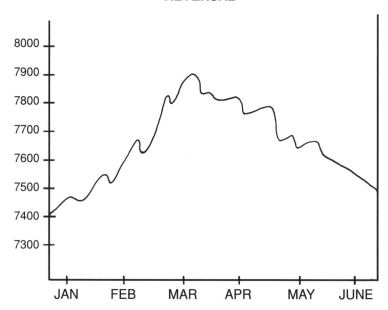

REVERSE ANNUITY MORTGAGE (RAM) MORTGAGE instrument that allows an elderly person to live off the equity in a fully paid-for house. Such a homeowner would enter into a reverse annuity mortgage agreement with a financial institution such as a bank, which would guarantee a lifelong fixed monthly income in return for gradually giving up ownership of the house. The longer the payments continue, the less equity the elderly owner would retain. At the owner's death the bank gains title to the real estate, which it can sell at a profit. The law also permits such arrangements between relatives, so that, for instance, a son or daughter might enter into a reverse annuity mortgage transaction with his or her retiring parents, thus providing the parents with cash to invest in income-yielding securities and the son or daughter with the depreciation and other tax benefits of real estate ownership. *See also* ARM'S LENGTH TRANSACTION.

REVERSE A SWAP restore a bond portfolio to its former position following a swap of one bond for another to gain the advantage of a YIELD SPREAD or a tax loss. The reversal may mean that the yield differential has disappeared or that the investor, content with a short-term profit, wishes to stay with the original bond for the advantages that may be gained in the future. *See also* BOND SWAP.

REVERSE CONVERSION technique whereby brokerage firms earn interest on their customers' stock holdings. A typical reverse conversion would work like this: A brokerage firm sells short the stocks it holds in customers' margin accounts, then invests this money in short-term money market instruments. To protect against a sharp rise in the markets, the firm hedges its short position by buying CALL options and selling PUT options. To unwind the reverse conversion, the firms buys back the stocks, sells the call, and buys the put. *See also* MARGIN ACCOUNT; OPTION.

REVERSE LEVERAGE situation, the opposite of FINANCIAL LEVERAGE, where the interest on money borrowed exceeds the return on investment of the borrowed funds.

REVERSE LEVERAGED BUYOUT process of bringing back into publicly traded status a company—or a division of a company—that had been publicly traded and taken private. In the 1980s, many public companies were taken private in LEVERAGED BUYOUTS by corporate raiders who borrowed against the companies' assets to finance the deal. When some or all of the debt incurred in the leveraged buyout was repaid, many of these companies were in sufficiently strong financial condition to go public again, enriching the private stockholders as well as the investment bankers who earned fees implementing these deals.

REVERSE MORTGAGE arrangement whereby a homeowner borrows against home equity and receives regular payments (tax-free) from the lender until the accumulated principal and interest reach the credit limit of equity; at that time, the lender either gets repayment in a lump sum or takes the house. Reverse mortgages are available privately and through the Federal Housing Administration (FHA). They are appropriate for cash-poor but house-rich older borrowers who want to stay in their homes and expect to live long enough to amortize high up-front fees but not so long that the lender winds up with the house. Lower income but greater security is provided by a variation, the REVERSE ANNUITY MORTGAGE (RAM).

REVERSE REPURCHASE AGREEMENT *see* REPURCHASE AGREEMENT.

REVERSE SPLIT procedure whereby a corporation reduces the number of shares outstanding. The total number of shares will have the same market value immediately after the reverse split as before it, but each share will be worth more. For example, if a firm with 10 million outstanding shares selling at $10 a share executes a reverse 1 for 10 split, the firm will end up with 1 million shares selling for $100 each. Such splits are usually initiated by companies wanting to raise the price of their outstanding shares because they think the price is too low to attract investors. Also called *split down. See also* SPLIT.

REVISIONARY TRUST IRREVOCABLE TRUST that becomes a REVOCABLE TRUST after a specified period, usually over 10 years or upon the death of the GRANTOR.

REVOCABLE TRUST agreement whereby income-producing property is deeded to heirs. The provisions of such a TRUST may be altered as many times as the GRANTOR pleases, or the entire trust agreement can be canceled, unlike irrevocable trusts. The grantor receives income from the assets, but the property passes directly to the beneficiaries at the grantor's death, without having to go through PROBATE court proceedings. Since the assets are still part of the grantor's estate, however, estate taxes must be paid on this transfer. This kind of trust differs from an IRREVOCABLE TRUST, which permanently transfers assets from the estate during the grantor's lifetime and therefore escapes estate taxes.

REVOLVING CREDIT
Commercial banking: contractual agreement between a bank and its customer, usually a company, whereby the bank agrees to make loans up to a specified maximum for a specified period, usually a year or more. As the borrower repays a portion of the loan, an amount equal to the repayment can be borrowed again under the terms of the agreement. In addition to interest borne by notes, the bank charges a fee for the commitment to hold the funds available. A COMPENSATING BALANCE may be required in addition.
Consumer banking: loan account requiring monthly payments of less than the full amount due, and the balance carried forward is subject to a financial charge. Also, an arrangement whereby borrowings are permitted up to a specified limit and for a specified period, usually a year, with a fee charged for the commitment. Also called *open-end credit* or *revolving line of credit.*

REVOLVING LINE OF CREDIT *see* REVOLVING CREDIT.

RICH
1. term for a security whose price seems too high in light of its price history. For bonds, the term may also imply that the yield is too low.
2. term for rate of interest that seems too high in relation to the borrower's risk.
3. synonym for *wealthy.*

RICO acronym for *Racketeer Influenced and Corrupt Organizations Act,* a federal law used to convict firms and individuals of INSIDER TRADING. Many critics have charged that the law was excessively enforced, and several indictments were dismissed for lack of evidence.

RIDER written form attached to an insurance policy that alters the policy's coverage, terms, or conditions. For example, after buying a diamond bracelet, a policyholder may want to add a rider to her homeowner's insurance policy to cover the jewelry. *See also* FLOATER.

RIEGLE-NEAL INTERSTATE BANKING AND BRANCHING EFFICIENCY ACT OF 1994 law allowing interstate banking in America. The legislation permitted banks to establish branches nationwide by eliminating all barriers to interstate banking at the state level. Before this legislation went into effect, banks had been required to set up separate subsidiaries in each state to conduct business and it was illegal for banks to accept deposits from customers out of their home states.

RIGGED MARKET situation in which the prices for a security are manipulated so as to lure unsuspecting buyers or sellers. *See also* MANIPULATION.

RIGHT *see* SUBSCRIPTION RIGHT.

RIGHT OF FIRST REFUSAL right of someone to be offered a right before it is offered to others. For example, a baseball team may have the right of first refusal on a ballplayer's contract, meaning that the club can make the first offer, or even match other offers, before the player plays for another team. A company may have the right of refusal to distribute or manufacture another company's product. A publishing company may have the right of refusal to publish a book proposed by one of its authors.

RIGHT OF REDEMPTION right to recover property transferred by a MORTGAGE or other LIEN by paying off the debt either before or after foreclosure. Also called *equity of redemption.*

RIGHT OF RESCISSION right granted by the federal CONSUMER CREDIT PROTECTION ACT OF 1968 to void a contract within three business days with full refund of any down payment and without penalty. The right is designed to protect consumers from high-pressure door-to-door sales tactics and hastily made credit commitments which involve their homes as COLLATERAL, such as loans secured by second mortgages.

RIGHT OF SURVIVORSHIP right entitling one owner of property held jointly to take title to it when the other owner dies. *See also* JOINT TENANTS WITH RIGHT OF SURVIVORSHIP; TENANTS IN COMMON.

RIGHTS OFFERING offering of COMMON STOCK to existing shareholders who hold rights that entitle them to buy newly issued shares at a discount from the price at which shares will later be offered to the public. Rights offerings are usually handled by INVESTMENT BANKERS under what is called a STANDBY COMMITMENT, whereby the investment bankers agree to purchase any shares not subscribed to by the holders of rights. *See also* PREEMPTIVE RIGHT; SUBSCRIPTION RIGHT.

RING location on the floor of an exchange where trades are executed. The circular arrangement where traders can make bid and offer prices is also called a *pit,* particularly when commodities are traded.

RISING BOTTOMS technical chart pattern showing a rising trend in the low prices of a security or commodity. As the range of prices is charted daily, the lows reveal an upward trend. Rising bottoms signify higher and higher basic SUPPORT LEVELS for a security or commodity. When combined with a series of ASCENDING TOPS, the pattern is one a follower of TECHNICAL ANALYSIS would call bullish.

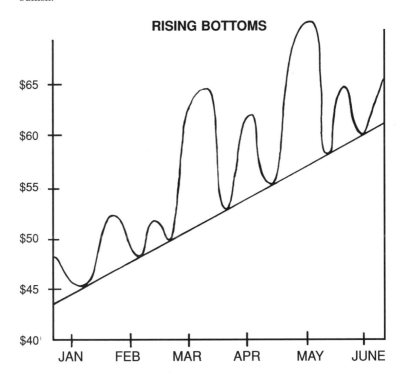

RISING BOTTOMS

RISK measurable possibility of losing or not gaining value. Risk is differentiated from uncertainty, which is not measurable. Among the commonly encountered types of risk are these:

Actuarial risk: risk an insurance underwriter covers in exchange for premiums, such as the risk of premature death.

Exchange risk: chance of loss on foreign currency exchange.

Inflation risk: chance that the value of assets or of income will be eroded as inflation shrinks the value of a country's currency.

Interest rate risk: possibility that a fixed-rate debt instrument will decline in value as a result of a rise in interest rates.

Inventory risk: possibility that price changes, obsolescence, or other factors will shrink the value of INVENTORY.

Liquidity risk: possibility that an investor will not be able to buy or sell a commodity or security quickly enough or in sufficient quantities because buying or selling opportunities are limited.

Political risk: possibility of NATIONALIZATION or other unfavorable government action.

Repayment (credit) risk: chance that a borrower or trade debtor will not repay an obligation as promised.

Risk of principal: chance that invested capital will drop in value.

Underwriting risk: risk taken by an INVESTMENT BANKER that a new issue of securities purchased outright will not be bought by the public and/or that the market price will drop during the offering period.

RISK-ADJUSTED DISCOUNT RATE in PORTFOLIO THEORY and CAPITAL BUD-GET analysis, the rate necessary to determine the PRESENT VALUE of an uncertain or risky stream of income; it is the risk-free rate (generally the return on short-term U.S. Treasury securities) plus a risk premium that is based on an analysis of the risk characteristics of the particular investment or project.

RISK ARBITRAGE ARBITRAGE involving risk, as in the simultaneous purchase of stock in a company being acquired and sale of stock in its proposed acquirer. Also called *takeover arbitrage*. Traders called *arbitrageurs* attempt to profit from TAKEOVERS by cashing in on the expected rise in the price of the target company's shares and drop in the price of the acquirer's shares. If the takeover plans fall through, the traders may be left with enormous losses. Risk arbitrage differs from riskless arbitrage, which entails locking in or profiting from the differences in the prices of two securities or commodities trading on different exchanges. *See also* RISKLESS TRANSACTION.

RISK AVERSE term referring to the assumption that, given the same return and different risk alternatives, a rational investor will seek the security offering the least risk—or, put another way, the higher the degree of risk, the greater the return that a rational investor will demand. *See also* CAPITAL ASSET PRICING MODEL; EFFICIENT PORTFOLIO; MEAN RETURN; PORTFOLIO THEORY.

RISK-BASED CAPITAL RATIO FIRREA-imposed requirement that banks maintain a minimum ratio of estimated total capital to estimated risk-weighted assets.

RISK CAPITAL *see* VENTURE CAPITAL.

RISK CATEGORY classification of risk elements used in analyzing MORTGAGES.

RISK-FREE RETURN YIELD on a risk-free investment. The 3-month Treasury bill is considered a riskless investment because it is a direct obligation of the U.S. government and its term is short enough to minimize the risks of inflation and market interest rate changes. The CAPITAL ASSET PRICING MODEL (CAPM) used in modern PORTFOLIO THEORY has the premise that the return on a security is equal to the risk-free return plus a RISK PREMIUM.

RISKLESS TRANSACTION

1. trade guaranteeing a profit to the trader that initiates it. An *arbitrageur* may lock in a profit by trading on the difference in prices for the same security or commodity in different markets. For instance, if gold were selling for $400 an ounce in New York and $398 in London, a trader who acts quickly could buy a contract in London and sell it in New York for a riskless profit.
2. concept used in evaluating whether dealer MARKUPS and MARKDOWNS in OVER THE COUNTER transactions with customers are reasonable or excessive. In what is known as the FIVE PERCENT RULE, the NATIONAL ASSOCIATION OF SECURITIES DEALERS (NASD) takes the position that markups (when the customer buys) and markdowns (when the customer sells) should not exceed 5%, the proper charge depending on the effort and risk of the dealer in completing a trade. The maximum would be considered excessive for a riskless transaction, in which a security has high marketability and the dealer does not simply act as a broker and take a commission but trades from or for inventory and charges a markup or markdown. Where a dealer satisfies a buy order by making a purchase in the open market for inventory, then sells the security to the customer, the trade is called a *simultaneous transaction*. To avoid NASD criticism, broker-dealers commonly disclose the markups and markdowns to customers in transactions where they act as dealers.

RISK PREMIUM in PORTFOLIO THEORY, the difference between the RISK-FREE RETURN and the TOTAL RETURN from a risky investment. In the CAPITAL ASSET PRICING MODEL (CAPM), the risk premium reflects market-related risk (SYSTEMATIC RISK) as measured by BETA. Other models also reflect specific risk as measured by ALPHA.

RISK-RETURN TRADE-OFF concept, basic in investment management, that RISK equals (varies with) RETURN; in other words, the higher the return the greater the risk and vice versa. In practice, it means that a speculative investment, such as stock in a newly formed company, can be expected to provide a higher potential return than a more conservative investment, such as BLUE CHIP or a BOND. Conversely, if you don't want the risk, don't expect the return. *See also* PORTFOLIO THEORY.

RISK TRANSFER shifting of risk, as with INSURANCE or the SECURITIZATION of debt.

ROAD SHOW presentation by an issuer of securities to potential buyers about the merits of the issue. Management of the company issuing stocks or bonds doing a road show travels around the country presenting financial information and an outlook for the company and answering the questions of analysts, fund managers, and other potential investors. Also known as a *dog and pony show.*

ROCKET SCIENTIST investment firm creator of innovative securities.

ROLL DOWN move from one OPTION position to another one having a lower EXERCISE PRICE. The term assumes that the position with the higher exercise price is closed out.

ROLL FORWARD move from one OPTION position to another with a later expiration date. The term assumes that the earlier position is closed out before the later one is established. If the new position involves a higher EXERCISE PRICE, it is called a *roll-up and forward;* if a lower exercise price, it is called a *roll-down and forward.* Also called *rolling over.*

ROLLING STOCK equipment that moves on wheels, used in the transportation industry. Examples include railroad cars and locomotives, tractor-trailers, and trucks.

ROLLOVER

1. movement of funds from one investment to another. For instance, an INDIVIDUAL RETIREMENT ACCOUNT may be rolled over when a person retires into an ANNUITY or other form of pension plan payout system. Balances in regular IRAs can be rolled over into ROTH IRAS, although income taxes will be due on untaxed earnings in the regular IRA account. When a BOND or CERTIFICATE OF DEPOSIT matures, the funds may be rolled over into another bond or certificate of deposit. A stock may be sold and the proceeds rolled over into the same stock, establishing a different cost basis for the shareholder. *See also* THIRTY-DAY WASH RULE.

2. term often used by banks when they allow a borrower to delay making a PRINCIPAL payment on a loan. Also, a country that has difficulty in meeting its debt payments may be granted a rollover by its creditors. With governments themselves, rollovers in the form of REFUNDINGS or REFINANCINGS are routine. *See also* CERTIFICATE OF DEPOSIT ROLLOVER.

ROLL UP move from one OPTION position to another having a higher EXERCISE PRICE. The term assumes that the earlier position is closed out before the new position is established. *See also* MASTER LIMITED PARTNERSHIP.

ROTH IRA INDIVIDUAL RETIREMENT ACCOUNT created by the TAXPAYER RELIEF ACT OF 1997 permitting account holders to allow their capital to accumulate tax free under certain conditions. The Roth IRA is named after Delaware Senator William V. Roth Jr., who championed the idea of expanded IRAs. Individuals can invest up to $2000 per year, and they can withdraw the principal and earnings totally tax free after age 59½, as long as the assets have remained in the IRA for at least five years after making the first contribution. If the account holder dies before they start withdrawing from a Roth, the proceeds go to their beneficiaries tax free. Unlike regular IRAs, participants do not have to take any distributions from a Roth IRA starting at age 70½, nor do they have to take any distributions at all during their lifetime. They can also continue to contribute after reaching age 70½.

Participants in Roth IRAs do not receive deductions for contributing to the account. However, the value of completely tax-free withdrawals usually outweighs the tax break from upfront deductions. The Roth IRA also permits participants to withdraw assets without the usual 10% early withdrawal penalty if the proceeds are used to purchase a first home (withdrawals are limited to $10,000), for college expenses, or if the participant becomes disabled.

There are income limitations governing who can open Roth IRAs. Married couples with an adjusted gross income of $150,000 or less or singles with adjusted gross incomes of $95,000 or less can contribute the full $2000. Contribution amounts are phased out for incomes between $150,000 and $160,000 for couples filing jointly and between $95,000 and $110,000 for singles. Those with income over these limits can not contribute to a Roth IRA.

Individuals with adjusted gross income of $100,000 or less can roll over existing and deductible IRA balances into a Roth without the usual 10% early distribution penalty, although regular income taxes are due on untaxed earnings in the account. For such ROLLOVERS completed before January 1, 1999, the resulting tax bill is spread over four years. After that, the rollover is fully taxable in the year it is completed. Figuring out whether or not it is advantageous to roll over assets from a regular IRA to a Roth IRA is a complex decision, and may require advice from a financial professional. *See* ROLLOVER.

ROUND LOT generally accepted unit of trading on a securities exchange. On the New York Stock Exchange, for example, a round lot is 100 shares for stock and $1000 or $5000 par value for bonds. In inactive stocks, the round lot is 10 shares. Increasingly, there seems to be recognition of a 500-share round lot for trading by institutions. Large denomination CERTIFICATES OF DEPOSIT trade on the

OVER THE COUNTER market in units of $1 million. Investors who trade in round lots do not have to pay the DIFFERENTIAL charged on ODD LOT trades.

ROUND TRIP TRADE purchase and sale of a security or commodity within a short time. For example, a trader who continually is making short-term trades in a particular commodity is making round trip or *round turn* trades. Commissions for such a trader are likely to be quoted in terms of the total for a purchase and sale—$100 for the round trip, for instance. Excessive round trip trading is called CHURNING.

ROYALTY payment to the holder for the right to use property such as a patent, copyrighted material, or natural resources. For instance, inventors may be paid royalties when their inventions are produced and marketed. Authors may get royalties when books they have written are sold. Land owners leasing their property to an oil or mining company may receive royalties based on the amount of oil or minerals extracted from their land. Royalties are set in advance as a percentage of income arising from the commercialization of the owner's rights or property.

ROYALTY TRUST oil or gas company *spin-off* of oil reserves to a trust, which avoids DOUBLE TAXATION, eliminates the expense and risk of new drilling, and provides DEPLETION tax benefits to shareholders. In the mid-1980s, Mesa Royalty Trust, which pioneered the idea, led other trusts in converting to a MASTER LIMITED PARTNERSHIP form of organization, offering tax advantages along with greater flexibility and liquidity.

RUBBER CHECK check for which insufficient funds are available. It is called a rubber check because it bounces. *See also* OVERDRAFT.

RULE 405 New York Stock Exchange codification of an ethical concept recognized industry wide by those dealing with the investment public. These KNOW YOUR CUSTOMER rules recognize that what is suitable for one investor may be less appropriate for another and require investment people to obtain pertinent facts about a customer's other security holdings, financial condition, and objectives. *See also* SUITABILITY RULES.

RULE OF 72 formula for approximating the time it will take for a given amount of money to double at a given COMPOUND INTEREST rate. The formula is simply 72 divided by the interest rate. In six years $100 will double at a compound annual rate of 12%, thus: 72 divided by 12 equals 6.

RULE OF THE 78s method of computing REBATES of interest on installment loans. It uses the SUM-OF-THE-YEAR'S-DIGITS basis in determining the interest earned by the FINANCE COMPANY for each month of a year, assuming equal monthly payments, and gets its name from the fact that the sum of the digits 1 through 12 is 78. Thus interest is equal to $^{12}/_{78}$ths of the total annual interest in the first month, $^{11}/_{78}$ths in the second month, and so on.

RULE 144 *see* INVESTMENT LETTER; SECURITIES AND EXCHANGE COMMISSION RULES.

RULES OF FAIR PRACTICE set of rules established by the Board of Governors of the NATIONAL ASSOCIATION OF SECURITIES DEALERS (NASD), a self-regulatory organization comprising investment banking houses and firms dealing in the OVER THE COUNTER securities market. As summarized in the NASD bylaws, the rules are designed to foster just and equitable principles of trade and business; high standards of commercial honor and integrity among members; the prevention of fraud and manipulative practices; safeguards against unreasonable profits, commissions, and other charges; and collaboration with governmental and other agencies to protect investors and the public interest in accordance with Section 15A of the MALONEY ACT. *See also* FIVE PERCENT RULE; IMMEDIATE FAMILY; KNOW YOUR CUSTOMER; MARKDOWN; RISKLESS TRANSACTION.

RUMORTRAGE stock traders' term, combining rumor and ARBITRAGE, for buying and selling based on rumor of a TAKEOVER. *See also* DEAL STOCK; GARBATRAGE.

RUN

Banking: demand for their money by many depositors all at once. If large enough, a run on a bank can cause it to fail, as hundreds of banks did in the Great Depression of the 1930s. Such a run is caused by a breach of confidence in the bank, perhaps as a result of large loan losses or fraud.

Securities:

1. list of available securities, along with current bid and asked prices, which a market maker is currently trading. For bonds the run may include the par value as well as current quotes.
2. when a security's price rises quickly, analysts say it had a quick run up, possibly because of a positive earnings report.

RUNDOWN

In general: status report or summary.

Municipal bonds: summary of the amounts available and the prices on units in a SERIAL BOND that has not yet been completely sold to the public.

RUNNING AHEAD illegal practice of buying or selling a security for a broker's personal account before placing a similar order for a customer, also called FRONT RUNNING. For example, when a firm's analyst issues a positive report on a company, the firm's brokers may not buy the stock for their own accounts before they have told their clients the news. Some firms prohibit brokers from making such trades for a specific period, such as two full days from the time of the recommendation.

RUNOFF printing of an exchange's closing prices on a TICKER tape after the market has closed. The runoff may take a long time when trading has been very heavy and the tape has fallen far behind the action.

RUSSELL INDICES MARKET CAPITALIZATION weighted U.S. equity indices published by Frank Russell Company of Tacoma, Washington. The Russell Indices are widely quoted on TV, radio and in newspapers, and are often used as benchmarks for institutional investors of mutual and pension funds. The *Russell 3000 Index*® measures the performance of the 3,000 largest U.S. companies based on market capitalization, which represents about 98% of the U.S. equity market. The stocks in the index have a market capitalization range of approximately $170 million to $200 billion, with an average of $2.8 billion. The *Russell 1000 Index*® represents the highest-ranking 1,000 stocks in the Russell 3000 Index, which represents about 90% of the total market capitalization of that index. The Russell 1000 Index has an average market capitalization of $7.6 billion; the median market capitalization is approximately $3 billion. The smallest company in the index has an average market capitalization of $1.1 billion. The *Russell 2000 Index*® consists of the 2000 smallest companies in the Russell 3000 Index, about 10% of its total market capitalization. The average capitalization is approximately $467 million; the median market capitalization is $395 million. The largest company in the index has an approximate market capitalization of $1 billion. The Russell 2000 is a popular measure of the stock price performance of small companies.

The *Russell Top 200 Index*® measures the performance of the 200 largest companies (65% of total market capitalization) in the Russell 1000, with average market capitalization of $26.4 billion. The median capitalization is approximately $15.5 billion; the smallest company in the index has an average capitalization of $8.1 billion. The *Russell Midcap Index*® measures performance of the 800 smallest companies (35% of total capitalization) in the Russell 1000, with average market capitalization of approximately $2.9 billion, median capitalization of

$15.5 billion and market capitalization of the largest company approximately $8 billion. The *Russell 2500 Index*® measures the performance of the 2,500 smallest companies in the Russell 3000 Index, or about 23% of its total capitalization. Average capitalization is approximately $733 million and median capitalization is $500 million. The largest company in the index is $2.9 billion.

Growth indices measure performance of the respective companies with higher PRICE/BOOK RATIOS and higher forecasted growth values. Value indices measure the performance of those companies with lower price/book ratios and lower forecasted growth values. *See also* STOCK INDICES AND AVERAGES.

RUSSIAN TRADING SYSTEM (RTS) electronic system operating in Russia since 1995, designed to emulate the NASDAQ system, on which the majority of Russian equities trading is conducted. The Russian securities market is principally an over-the-counter market in an informal dealer-to-dealer system. It is diverse: there are more than 60 officially registered stock and commodity exchanges. The Central Stock Exchange in Moscow and the St. Petersburg Stock Exchange specialize in securities trading.

RUST BELT geographical area of the United States, mainly in Pennsylvania, West Virginia, and the industrial Midwest, where iron and steel is produced and where there is a concentration of industries that manufacture products using iron and steel. Term is used broadly to mean traditional American manufacturing with its largely unmodernized plants and facilities.

S

SAFE HARBOR

1. financial or accounting step that avoids legal or tax consequences. Commonly used in reference to *safe harbor leasing,* as permitted by the ECONOMIC RECOVERY TAX ACT OF 1981 (ERTA). An unprofitable company unable to use the INVESTMENT CREDIT and ACCELERATED COST RECOVERY SYSTEM (ACRS) liberalized depreciation rules, could transfer those benefits to a profitable firm seeking to reduce its tax burden. Under such an arrangement, the profitable company would own an asset the unprofitable company would otherwise have purchased itself; the profitable company would then lease the asset to the unprofitable company, presumably passing on a portion of the tax benefits in the form of lower lease rental charges. Safe harbor leases were curtailed by provisions in the TAX EQUITY AND FISCAL RESPONSIBILITY ACT OF 1982 (TEFRA).
2. provision in a law that excuses liability if the attempt to comply in good faith can be demonstrated. For example, safe harbor provisions would protect management from liability under Securities and Exchange Commission rules for financial PROJECTIONS made in good faith.
3. form of SHARK REPELLENT whereby a TARGET COMPANY acquires a business so onerously regulated it makes the target less attractive, giving it, in effect, a safe harbor.

SAFEKEEPING storage and protection of a customer's financial assets, valuables, or documents, provided as a service by an institution serving as AGENT and, where control is delegated by the customer, also as custodian. An individual, corporate, or institutional investor might rely on a bank or a brokerage firm to hold stock certificates or bonds, keep track of trades, and provide periodic statements of changes in position. Investors who provide for their own safekeeping usually use a *safe deposit box,* provided by financial institutions for a fee. *See also* SELLING SHORT AGAINST THE BOX; STREET NAME.

SAIF *see* SAVINGS ASSOCIATION INSURANCE FUND (SAIF).

SALARY regular wages received by an employee from an employer on a weekly, biweekly, or monthly basis. Many salaries also include such employee benefits as health and life insurance, savings plans, and Social Security. Salary income is taxable by the federal, state, and local government, where applicable, through payroll withholding.

SALARY FREEZE cessation of increases in salary throughout a company for a period of time. Companies going through a business downturn will freeze salaries in order to reduce expenses. When business improves, salary increases are frequently reinstated.

SALARY REDUCTION PLAN plan allowing employees to contribute pretax compensation to a qualified TAX DEFERRED retirement plan. Until the TAX REFORM ACT OF 1986, the term was synonymous with 401(k) PLAN, but the 1986 Act prohibited employees of state and local governments and tax-exempt organizations from establishing new 401(k) plans and added restrictions to existing government and tax-exempt unfunded deferred compensation arrangements and tax-sheltered annuity arrangements creating, in effect, a broadened definition of salary reduction plan. Current law permits employees of tax-exempt religious, charitable, or educational organizations and public schools to take nontaxable reductions to a limit of 20% of salary multiplied by years of service less tax-free contributions made in prior years by the employer to a tax-sheltered annuity or qualified plan. The reduction, however, may not exceed the lower of 25% of salary or $9500, except that employees with at least 15 years of service may defer up to $12,500. Such contributions purchase a nonforfeitable tax-sheltered annuity.

Federal government employees are allowed salary deductions up to the limits for 401(k) plans. State and local governments and tax-exempt organizations other than churches may set up *Section 457* plans allowing employees to defer annually the lesser of $7500 or one-third of compensation.

Irrevocable alternative or "catch-up" formulae are also available with limitations.

SALE

In general: any exchange of goods or services for money. *Contrast with* BARTER.

Finance: income received in exchange for goods and services recorded for a given accounting period, either on a cash basis (as received) or on an accrual basis (as earned). *See also* GROSS SALES.

Securities: in securities trading, a sale is executed when a buyer and a seller have agreed on a price for the security.

SALE AND LEASEBACK form of LEASE arrangement in which a company sells an asset to another party—usually an insurance or finance company, a leasing company, a limited partnership, or an institutional investor—in exchange for cash, then contracts to lease the asset for a specified term. Typically, the asset is sold for its MARKET VALUE, so the lessee has really acquired capital that would otherwise have been tied up in a long-term asset. Such arrangements frequently have tax benefits for the lessee, although there is normally little difference in the effect on income between the lease payments and the interest payments that would have existed had the asset been purchased with borrowed money. A company generally opts for the sale and leaseback arrangement as an alternative to straight financing when the rate it would have to pay a lender is higher than the cost of rental or when it wishes to show less debt on its BALANCE SHEET (called *off-balance-sheet financing*). *See also* CAPITAL LEASE.

SALES CHARGE fee paid to a brokerage house by a buyer of shares in a load MUTUAL FUND or a LIMITED PARTNERSHIP. Normally, the sales charge for a mutual fund starts at 4.5% to 5% of the capital invested and decreases as the size of the investment increases. The sales charge for a limited partnership can be even higher—as much as 10%. In return for the sales charge, investors are entitled to investment advice from the broker on which fund or partnership is best for them. A fund that carries no sales charge is called a NO-LOAD FUND. *See also* BACK-END LOAD; FRONT-END LOAD; LETTER OF INTENT; LOAD FUND; REDEMPTION FEES; 12B-1 MUTUAL FUND.

SALES LITERATURE

In general: written material designed to help sell a product or a service.

Investments: written material issued by a securities brokerage firm, mutual fund, underwriter, or other institution selling a product that explains the advantages of the investment product. Such literature must be truthful and must comply with disclosure regulations issued by the Securities and Exchange Commission and state securities agencies.

SALES LOAD *see* SALES CHARGE.

SALES TAX tax based on a percentage of the selling price of goods and services. State and local governments assess sales tax and decide what percentage to charge. The retail buyer pays the sales tax to the retailer, who passes it on to the sales tax collection agency of the government. For an item costing $1000 in a state with a 5% sales tax, the buyer pays $50 in sales tax, for a total of $1050. Sales taxes are not deductible on federal or state income tax returns.

SALLIE MAE *see* STUDENT LOAN MARKETING ASSOCIATION.

SALOMON BROTHERS WORLD EQUITY INDEX (SBWEI) a comprehensive top-down, float capitalization-weighted index that includes shares of approximately 6000 companies in 22 countries. It is one member of a family of Salomon Smith Barney performance indexes that measure domestic and international fixed income and equity markets. The index includes all companies with available market capitalization greater than $100 million. Each issue is weighted by the proportion of its available equity capital, its float, rather than by its total equity capital. The index is the successor to the Salomon-Russell Global Equity Index. Other SBWEI equity products include GDP and weighted indexes, and emerging market indexes.

SALVAGE VALUE *see* RESIDUAL VALUE.

SAME-DAY FUNDS SETTLEMENT (SDFS) method of settlement in good-the-same-day FEDERAL FUNDS used by the DEPOSITORY TRUST COMPANY for transactions in U.S. government securities, short-term municipal notes, medium-term commercial paper notes, COLLATERALIZED MORTGAGE OBLIGATIONS (CMOs), DUTCH AUCTION PREFERRED STOCK, and other instruments when both parties to the trade are properly collateralized.

SAME-DAY SUBSTITUTION offsetting changes in a MARGIN ACCOUNT in the course of one day, resulting in neither a MARGIN CALL nor a credit to the SPECIAL MISCELLANEOUS ACCOUNT. Examples: a purchase and a sale of equal value; a decline in the MARKET VALUE of some margin securities offset by an equal rise in the market value of others.

SAMURAI BONDS bonds denominated in yen issued by non-Japanese companies for sale mostly in Japan. The bonds are not subject to Japanese withholding taxes, and therefore offer advantages to Japanese buyers.

SANDWICH GENERATION middle-aged working people who feel squeezed by the financial pressures of supporting their aging parents, the costs of raising and educating their children, and the need to save for their own retirement.

SANTA CLAUS RALLY rise in stock prices in the week between Christmas and New Year's Day. Also called the *year-end rally*. Some analysts attribute this rally to the anticipation of the JANUARY EFFECT, when stock prices rise in the first few days of the year as pension funds add new money to their accounts.

SAO PAULO STOCK EXCHANGE *see* BOLSA DE VALORES DE SAO PAULO (BOVESPA).

S&P PHENOMENON tendency of stocks newly added to the STANDARD & POOR'S COMPOSITE INDEX to rise temporarily in price as S&P-related INDEX FUNDS adjust their portfolios, creating heavy buying activity.

SATURDAY NIGHT SPECIAL sudden attempt by one company to take over another by making a public TENDER OFFER. The term was coined in the 1960s after a rash of such surprise maneuvers, which were often announced over weekends. The WILLIAMS ACT of 1968 placed severe restrictions on tender offers and required disclosure of direct or indirect ownership of 5% or more of any class of EQUITY. It thus marked the end of what, in its traditional form, was known as the "creeping tender."

SAUCER technical chart pattern (see below) signaling that the price of a security or a commodity has formed a bottom and is moving up. An inverse saucer shows a top in the security's price and signals a downturn. *See also* TECHNICAL ANALYSIS.

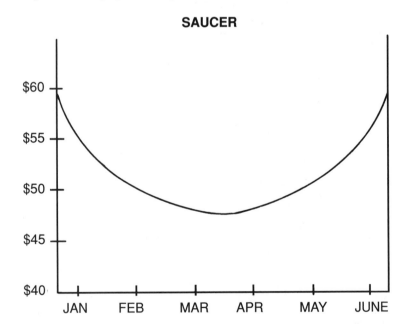

SAUCER

SAVING RATE ratio of personal saving to disposable personal income. Disposable personal income is personal income less personal tax and nontax payments. Personal saving is disposable personal income less personal outlays.

The U.S. Commerce Department's Bureau of Economic Analysis and the Federal Reserve each publish estimates of the saving rate on a quarterly basis.

SAVINGS ACCOUNT   deposit account at a commercial bank, savings bank, or savings and loan that pays interest, usually from a day-of-deposit to day-of-withdrawal basis. Financial institutions can pay whatever rate they like on savings accounts, but this rate tends to be in relation to the actions of the money center banks in repricing their PRIME RATE. Traditionally, savings accounts offered PASSBOOKS, but in recent years alternatives such as ATMs, monthly account statements and telephone banking services have been added to credit deposits and interest earned. Savings deposits are insured up to $100,000 per account if they are on deposit at banks insured by the FEDERAL DEPOSIT INSURANCE CORPORATION (FDIC) or a savings and loan insured by the SAVINGS ASSOCIATION INSURANCE FUND (SAIF).

SAVINGS AND LOAN ASSOCIATION depository financial institution, federally or state chartered, that obtains the bulk of its deposits from consumers and holds the majority of its assets as home mortgage loans. A few such specialized institutions were organized in the 19th century under state charters but with minimal regulation. Reacting to the crisis in the banking and home building industries precipitated by the Great Depression, Congress in 1932 passed the Federal Home Loan Bank Act, establishing the FEDERAL HOME LOAN BANK SYSTEM to supplement the lending resources of state-chartered savings and loans (S&Ls). The Home Owners' Loan Act of 1933 created a system for the federal chartering of S&Ls under the supervision of the Federal Home Loan Bank Board. Deposits in federal S&Ls were insured with the formation of the Federal Savings and Loan Insurance Corporation in 1934.

A second wave of restructuring occurred in the 1980s. The DEPOSITORY INSTITUTIONS DEREGULATION AND MONETARY CONTROL ACT of 1980 set a six-year timetable for the removal of interest rate ceilings, including the S&Ls' quarter-point rate advantage over the commercial bank limit on personal savings accounts. The act also allowed S&Ls limited entry into some markets previously open only to commercial banks (commercial lending, nonmortgage consumer lending, trust services) and, in addition, permitted MUTUAL ASSOCIATIONS to issue INVESTMENT CERTIFICATES. In actual effect, interest rate parity was achieved by the end of 1982.

The Garn-St Germain Depository Institutions Act of 1982 accelerated the pace of deregulation and gave the Federal Home Loan Bank Board wide latitude in shoring up the capital positions of S&Ls weakened by the impact of record-high interest rates on portfolios of old, fixed-rate mortgage loans. The 1982 Act also encouraged the formation of stock savings and loans or the conversion of existing mutual (depositor-owned) associations to the stock form, which gave the associations another way to tap the capital markets and thereby to bolster their net worth.

In 1989, responding to a massive wave of insolvencies caused by mismanagement, corruption, and economic factors, Congress passed the FINANCIAL INSTITUTIONS REFORM, RECOVERY AND ENFORCEMENT ACT OF 1989 (FIRREA) that revamped the regulatory structure of the industry under a newly created agency, the OFFICE OF THRIFT SUPERVISION (OTS). Disbanding the FEDERAL SAVINGS AND LOAN INSURANCE CORPORATION (FSLIC), it created the SAVINGS ASSOCIATION INSURANCE FUND (SAIF) to provide deposit insurance under the administration of the FEDERAL DEPOSIT INSURANCE CORPORATION (FDIC). It also created the RESOLUTION TRUST CORPORATION (RTC) and RESOLUTION FUNDING CORPORATION (REFCORP) to deal with insolvent institutions and scheduled the consolidation of their activities with SAIF after 1996. The Federal Home Loan Bank Board was replaced by the FEDERAL HOUSING FINANCE BOARD (FHFB), which now oversees the Federal Home Loan Bank System. *See also* SAVINGS BANK.

SAVINGS ASSOCIATION INSURANCE FUND (SAIF) U.S. government entity created by Congress in 1989 as part of its SAVINGS AND LOAN ASSOCIATION bailout bill to replace the FEDERAL SAVINGS AND LOAN INSURANCE CORPORATION (FSLIC) as the provider of deposit insurance for thrift institutions. SAIF, pronounced to rhyme with *safe,* is administered by the FEDERAL DEPOSIT INSURANCE CORPORATION (FDIC) separately from its bank insurance program, which was renamed *Bank Insurance Fund (BIF).* The new organization provides the same protection ($100,000 per depositor) as FSLIC. At the end of 1996, SAIF assumed responsibility for insolvent institutions from RESOLUTION TRUST CORPORATION (RTC). *See also* OFFICE OF THRIFT SUPERVISION (OTS).

SAVINGS BANK depository financial institution that primarily accepts consumer deposits and makes home mortgage loans. Historically, savings banks were of the mutual (depositor-owned) form and chartered in only 16 states; the majority of savings banks were located in the New England states, New York, and New Jersey. Prior to the passage of the Garn-St Germain Depository Institutions Act of 1982, state-chartered savings bank deposits were insured along with commercial bank deposits by the FEDERAL DEPOSIT INSURANCE CORPORATION (FDIC). The Garn-St Germain Act gave savings banks the options of a federal charter, mutual-to-stock conversion, supervision by the Federal Home Loan Bank Board, and insurance from the FEDERAL SAVINGS AND LOAN INSURANCE CORPORATION (FSLIC). In 1989, the Federal Home Loan Bank Board was replaced by the FEDERAL HOUSING FINANCE BOARD (FHFB), and the FSLIC by the newly created SAVINGS ASSOCIATION INSURANCE FUND (SAIF), a unit of the FDIC. *See also* MUTUAL SAVINGS BANK; SAVINGS AND LOAN ASSOCIATION.

SAVINGS BOND U.S. government bond issued in FACE VALUE denominations ranging from $50 to $10,000. From 1941 to 1979, the government issued SERIES E BONDS. Starting in 1980, Series EE and HH bonds were issued. Series EE bonds, issued at a discount of half their face value, range from $50 to $10,000; interest bearing Series HH bonds range from $500 to $10,000. Series EE bonds earn interest for 30 years; Series HH bonds earn interest for 20 years. Series EE bonds, if held for five years, pay 90% of the average yield on five-year Treasury securities based on the previous six months. Series HH bonds, available only through an exchange of at least $500 in Series E or EE bonds, pay a fixed 4% rate in two semiannual payments. For many years, the government guaranteed a minimum yield on savings bonds. This yield decreased from 7.5% to 6% and then 4%. The guaranteed minimum feature was dropped in May 1995, and bonds issued on May 1, 1997 or later and held for less than five years are now subject to a three-month interest penalty. For example, a bond cashed in after 18 months would receive 15 months' worth of interest. Savings bond yields are readjusted every six months, on May 1 and November 1.

   The interest from savings bonds is exempt from state and local taxes, and no federal tax on EE bonds is due until redemption. Bondholders wanting to defer the tax liability on their maturing Series EE bonds can exchange them for Series HH bonds. Taxpayers meeting income qualifications can buy EE bonds to save for higher educational expenses and enjoy total or partial federal tax exemption. This applies to individuals with modified ADJUSTED GROSS INCOMES between $50,850 and $65,850 and married couples filing jointly with incomes between $76,250 and $106,250. Income levels are adjusted for inflation annually. *See also* I-BONDS.

SAVINGS DEPOSITS interest-earning cash balances that can be withdrawn on demand, kept for the purpose of savings, in commercial banks, savings banks, credit unions, and savings and loans. Passbook savings, statement savings, and money market accounts are examples of savings deposits.

SAVINGS ELEMENT cash value accumulated inside a life insurance policy. A cash value policy has two components: a death benefit paid to beneficiaries if the insured dies, and a savings element, which is the amount of premium paid in excess of the cost of protection. This excess is invested by the insurance company in stocks, bonds, real estate, and other ventures and the returns build up tax-deferred inside the policy. A policyholder can borrow against this cash value or take it out of the policy, at which point it becomes taxable income. Once a policyholder reaches retirement age, he or she can ANNUITIZE the accumulated cash value and receive a regular payment from the insurance company for life. Insurance companies encourage people to buy policies with a savings element because it provides a disciplined way to save.

SCALE

Labor: wage rate for specific types of employees. For example: "Union scale for carpenters is $15.60 per hour."

Production economics: amount of production, as in "economy or diseconomy of scale." *See also* MARGINAL COST.

Serial bonds: vital data for each of the scheduled maturities in a new SERIAL BOND issue, including the number of bonds, the date they mature, the COUPON rate, and the offering price.

See also SCALE ORDER.

SCALE ORDER order for a specified number of shares that is to be executed in stages in order to average the price. Such an order might provide for the purchase of a total of 5000 shares to be executed in lots of 500 shares at each quarter-point interval as the market declines. Since scale orders are clerically cumbersome, not all brokers will accept them.

SCALPER

In general: speculator who enters into quasi-legal or illegal transactions to turn a quick and sometimes unreasonable profit. For example, a scalper buys tickets at regular prices for a major event and when the event becomes a sellout, resells the tickets at the highest price possible.

Securities:

1. investment adviser who takes a position in a security before recommending it, then sells out after the price has risen as a result of the recommendation. *See also* INVESTMENT ADVISERS ACT.

2. market maker who, in violation of the RULES OF FAIR PRACTICE of the NATIONAL ASSOCIATION OF SECURITIES DEALERS, adds an excessive markup or takes an excessive MARKDOWN on a transaction. *See also* FIVE PERCENT RULE.

3. commodity trader who trades for small gains, usually establishing and liquidating a position within one day.

SCHEDULE C common reference to a section of the bylaws of the NATIONAL ASSOCIATION OF SECURITIES DEALERS (NASD) concerned with membership requirements and procedures.

SCHEDULE 13d form required under Section 13d of the SECURITIES EXCHANGE ACT OF 1934 within ten business days of acquiring direct or BENEFICIAL OWNERSHIP of 5% or more of any class of equity securities in a PUBLICLY HELD corporation. In addition to filing with the Securities and Exchange Commission, the purchaser of such stock must also file the 13d with the stock exchange on which the shares are listed (if any) and with the company itself. Required information includes the way the shares were acquired, the purchaser's background, and future plans regarding the target company. The law is designed to protect against insidious TAKEOVER attempts and to keep the investing public aware of information that could affect the price of their stock. *See also* WILLIAMS ACT.

SCORCHED-EARTH POLICY technique used by a company that has become the target of a TAKEOVER attempt to make itself unattractive to the acquirer. For example, it may agree to sell off the most attractive parts of its business, called the CROWN JEWELS, or it may schedule all debt to become due immediately after a MERGER. *See also* JONESTOWN DEFENSE; POISON PILL; SHARK REPELLENT.

SCORE acronym for *Special Claim on Residual Equity,* a certificate issued by the Americus Shareowner Service Corporation, a privately held company formed to market the product. A SCORE gave its holder the right to all the appreciation on an underlying security above a specified price, but none of the dividend income from the security. Its counterpart, called PRIME, passed all dividend income to its holders, who got the benefit of price appreciation up to the limit where SCORE began. PRIME and SCORE together formed a unit share investment trust (USIT), and both were listed on the American Stock Exchange. A buyer of a SCORE unit hoped that the underlying stock would rise steeply in value.

The first USIT was formed with the shares of American Telephone and Telegraph. PRIME holders got all dividends and price appreciation in AT&T up to $75 a share; SCORE holders received all appreciation above $75. The trusts expired in 1988.

S CORPORATION *see* SUBCHAPTER S.

SCREEN (STOCKS) to look for stocks that meet certain predetermined investment and financial criteria. Often, stocks are screened using a computer and a data base containing financial statistics on thousands of companies. For instance, an investor may want to screen for all those companies that have a PRICE/EARNINGS RATIO of less than 10, an earnings growth rate of more than 15%, and a dividend yield of more than 4%.

SCRIP

In general: receipt, certificate, or other representation of value recognized by both payer and payee. Scrip is not currency, but may be convertible into currency.
Securities: temporary document that is issued by a corporation and that represents a fractional share of stock resulting from a SPLIT, exchange of stock, or SPIN-OFF. Scrip certificates may be aggregated or applied toward the purchase of full shares. Scrip dividends have historically been paid in lieu of cash dividends by companies short of cash.

SCRIPOPHILY practice of collecting stock and bond certificates for their scarcity value, rather than for their worth as securities. The certificate's price rises with the beauty of the illustration on it and the importance of the issuer in world finance and economic development. Many old certificates, such as those issued by railroads in the 19th century or by Standard Oil before it was broken up in the early 20th century, have risen greatly in value since their issue, even though the issuing companies no longer exist.

SDR *see* SPECIAL DRAWING RIGHTS.

SEASONALITY variations in business or economic activity that recur with regularity as the result of changes in climate, holidays, and vacations. The retail toy business, with its steep sales buildup between Thanksgiving and Christmas and pronounced dropoff thereafter, is an example of seasonality in a dramatic form, though nearly all businesses have some degree of seasonal variation. It is often necessary to make allowances for seasonality when interpreting or projecting financial or economic data, a process economists call *seasonal adjustment.*

SEASONED securities that have been trading in the secondary market for a lengthy period of time, and have established a track record of significant trading volume and price stability. Many investors prefer buying only seasoned issues instead of new securities that have not stood the test of time.

SEASONED ISSUE securities (usually from established companies) that have gained a reputation for quality with the investing public and enjoy LIQUIDITY in the SECONDARY MARKET.

SEAT figurative term for a membership on a securities or commodities exchange. Seats are bought and sold at prices set by supply and demand. A seat on the New York Stock Exchange, for example, traded for between $1 million and $2 million in the bull market of the late 1990s. *See also* ABC AGREEMENT; MEMBER FIRM.

SEC *see* SECURITIES AND EXCHANGE COMMISSION.

SEC FEE small (one cent per several hundred dollars) fee charged by the Securities and Exchange Commission (SEC) to sellers of EQUITY securities that are exchange traded.

SECONDARY DISTRIBUTION public sale of previously issued securities held by large investors, usually corporations, institutions, or other AFFILIATED PERSONS, as distinguished from a NEW ISSUE or PRIMARY DISTRIBUTION, where the seller is the issuing corporation. As with a primary offering, secondaries are usually handled by INVESTMENT BANKERS, acting alone or as a syndicate, who purchase the shares from the seller at an agreed price, then resell them, sometimes with the help of a SELLING GROUP, at a higher PUBLIC OFFERING PRICE, making their profit on the difference, called the SPREAD. Since the offering is registered with the Securities and Exchange Commission, the syndicate manager can legally stabilize—or peg—the market price by bidding for shares in the open market. Buyers of securities offered this way pay no commissions, since all costs are borne by the selling investor. If the securities involved are listed, the CONSOLIDATED TAPE will announce the offering during the trading day, although the offering is not made until after the market's close. Among the historically large secondary distributions were the Ford Foundation's offering of Ford Motor Company stock in 1956 (approximately $658 million) handled by seven firms under a joint management agreement and the sale of Howard Hughes' TWA shares ($566 million) through Merrill Lynch, Pierce, Fenner & Smith in 1966.

A similar form of secondary distribution, called the SPECIAL OFFERING, is limited to members of the New York Stock Exchange and is completed in the course of the trading day. *See also* EXCHANGE DISTRIBUTION; REGISTERED SECONDARY OFFERING; SECURITIES AND EXCHANGE COMMISSION RULES 144 and 237.

SECONDARY MARKET
1. exchanges and over-the-counter markets where securities are bought and sold subsequent to original issuance, which took place in the PRIMARY MARKET. Proceeds of secondary market sales accrue to the selling dealers and investors, not to the companies that originally issued the securities.
2. market in which money-market instruments are traded among investors.

SECONDARY MORTGAGE MARKET buying, selling, and trading of existing mortgage loans and mortgage-backed securities. Original lenders are thus able to sell loans in their portfolios in order to build LIQUIDITY to support additional lending. Mortgages originated by lenders are purchased by government agencies (such as the FEDERAL HOME LOAN MORTGAGE CORPORATION and the FEDERAL NATIONAL MORTGAGE ASSOCIATION) and by investment bankers. These agencies and bankers, in turn, create pools of mortgages, which they repackage as mortgage-backed securities, called PASS-THROUGH SECURITIES or PARTICIPATION CERTIFICATES, which are then sold to investors. The secondary mortgage market thus encompasses all activity beyond the PRIMARY MARKET, which is between the homebuyers and the originating mortgage lender.

SECONDARY OFFERING *see* SECONDARY DISTRIBUTION.

SECONDARY STOCKS used in a general way to mean stocks having smaller MARKET CAPITALIZATION, less quality, and more risk than BLUE CHIP issues represented by the Dow Jones Industrial Average. Secondary stocks, which often behave differently than blue chips, are tracked by the Amex Market Value Index, the NASDAQ Composite Index, and broad indexes, such as the Standard & Poor's Index. Also called *second-tier stocks.*

SECOND MORTGAGE LENDING advancing funds to a borrower that are secured by real estate previously pledged in a FIRST MORTGAGE loan. In the case of DEFAULT, the first mortgage has priority of claim over the second.

   A variation on the second mortgage is the *home equity loan,* in which the loan is secured by independent appraisal of the property value. A home equity loan may also be in the form of a line of credit, which may be drawn down on by using a check or even a credit card. *See also* HOMEOWNER'S EQUITY ACCOUNT; RIGHT OF RESCISSION.

SECOND-PREFERRED STOCK preferred stock issue that ranks below another preferred issue in terms of priority of claim on dividends and on assets in liquidation. Second-preferred shares are often issued with a CONVERTIBLE feature or with a warrant to make them more attractive to investors. *See also* JUNIOR SECURITY; PREFERRED STOCK; PRIOR-PREFERRED STOCK; SUBSCRIPTION WARRANT.

SECOND ROUND intermediate stage of VENTURE CAPITAL financing, coming after the SEED MONEY (or START-UP) and *first round* stages and before the MEZZANINE LEVEL, when the company has matured to the point where it might consider a LEVERAGED BUYOUT by management or an INITIAL PUBLIC OFFERING (IPO).

SECOND-TO-DIE INSURANCE insurance policy that pays a death benefit upon the death of the spouse who dies last. Such insurance typically is purchased by a couple wanting to pass a large estate on to their heirs. When the first spouse dies, the couple's assets are passed tax-free to the second spouse under the MARITAL DEDUCTION. When the second spouse dies, the remaining estate could be subject to large estate taxes. The proceeds from the second-to-die insurance are designed to pay the estate taxes, leaving the remaining estate for the heirs. Such insurance is appropriate only for those facing large estate tax liabilities. Because the policy is based on the joint life expectancy of both husband and wife, premiums typically cost less than those on traditional cash value policies on both lives insured separately. Also called *survivorship life insurance.*

SECTOR particular group of stocks, usually found in one industry. SECURITIES ANALYSTS often follow a particular sector of the stock market, such as airline or chemical stocks.

SECTOR FUND *see* SPECIALIZED MUTUAL FUND.

SECULAR long-term (10–50 years or more) as distinguished from seasonal or cyclical time frames.

SECURED BOND bond backed by the pledge of COLLATERAL, a MORTGAGE, or other LIEN. The exact nature of the security is spelled out in the INDENTURE. Secured bonds are distinguished from unsecured bonds, called DEBENTURES.

SECURED DEBT debt guaranteed by the pledge of assets or other COLLATERAL. *See also* ASSIGN; HYPOTHECATION.

SECURITIES ACT OF 1933 first law enacted by Congress to regulate the securities markets, approved May 26, 1933, as the Truth in Securities Act. It requires REGISTRATION of securities prior to public sale and adequate DISCLOSURE of pertinent financial and other data in a PROSPECTUS to permit informed analysis by potential investors. It also contains antifraud provisions prohibiting false representations and disclosures. Enforcement responsibilities were assigned to the SECURITIES AND EXCHANGE COMMISSION by the SECURITIES EXCHANGE ACT OF 1934. The 1933 Act did not supplant BLUE-SKY LAWS of the various states.

SECURITIES ACTS AMENDMENTS OF 1975 federal legislation enacted on June 4, 1975, to amend the SECURITIES EXCHANGE ACT OF 1934. The 1975 amendments directed the SECURITIES AND EXCHANGE COMMISSION to work with the industry toward establishing a NATIONAL MARKET SYSTEM together with a system for the nationwide clearance and settlement of securities transactions. Because of these provisions, the 1975 laws are sometimes called the *National Exchange Market System Act.* New regulations were also introduced to promote prompt and accurate securities handling, and clearing agencies were required to register with and report to the SEC. The 1975 amendments required TRANSFER AGENTS other than banks to register with the SEC and provided that authority with respect to bank transfer agents would be shared by the SEC and bank regulatory agencies. The Municipal Securities Rulemaking Board was created to regulate brokers, dealers, and banks dealing in municipal securities, with rules subject to SEC approval and enforcement shared by the NATIONAL ASSOCIATION OF SECURITIES DEALERS and bank regulatory agencies. The law also required the registration of broker-dealers in municipals, but preserved the exemption of issuers from REGISTRATION requirements. The amendments contained the prohibition of fixed commission rates, adopted earlier by the SEC in its Rule 19b-3.

SECURITIES ANALYST individual, usually employed by a stock brokerage house, bank, or investment institution, who performs investment research and examines the financial condition of a company or group of companies in an industry and in the context of the securities markets. Many analysts specialize in a single industry or SECTOR and make investment recommendations to buy, sell, or hold in that area. Among a corporation's financial indicators most closely followed by ANALYSTS are sales and earnings growth, CAPITAL STRUCTURE, stock price trend and PRICE/EARNINGS RATIO, DIVIDEND PAYOUTS, and RETURN ON INVESTED CAPITAL. Securities analysts promote corporate financial disclosure by sponsoring forums through local associations, the largest of which is the New York Society of Security Analysts, and through its national body, the Financial Analysts Federation. *See also* FORECASTING; FUNDAMENTAL ANALYSIS; QUALITATIVE ANALYSIS; QUANTITATIVE ANALYSIS; TECHNICAL ANALYSIS.

SECURITIES AND COMMODITIES EXCHANGES organized, national exchanges where securities, options, and futures contracts are traded by members for their own accounts and for the accounts of customers. In the U.S., the stock exchanges are registered with and regulated by the SECURITIES AND EXCHANGE COMMISSION (SEC); the commodities exchanges are registered with and regulated by the Commodity Futures Trading Commission (*see* REGULATED COMMODITIES); where options are traded on an exchange, such activity is regulated by the SEC.

STOCKS, BONDS, SUBSCRIPTION RIGHTS, SUBSCRIPTION WARRANTS, STOCK OPTIONS, INDEX OPTIONS, and other derivative products are traded on nine STOCK EXCHANGES in the U.S. COMMODITY FUTURES, FUTURES OPTIONS, and FINANCIAL FUTURES are traded on 13 leading commodities exchanges.

Exchanges listing basic securities—stocks, bonds, rights, warrants, and options on individual stocks—are described under the entries for the NEW YORK STOCK EXCHANGE, AMERICAN STOCK EXCHANGE, NASDAQ STOCK MARKET, BOSTON

STOCK EXCHANGE, and REGIONAL STOCK EXCHANGES. The exchanges listing futures and options contracts are:

American Stock Exchange (New York) *stock index options:* Airline Index, Amex Gold BUGS Index, Biotechnology Index, Computer Technology Index, de Jager Year 2000 Index, Disk Drive Index, Eurotop 100 Index, Hong Kong Option Index, Institutional Index, Inter@ctive Week Internet Index, Japan Index, Major Market Index, Mexico Index, Morgan Stanley Commodity Related Equity Index, Morgan Stanley Cyclical Index, Morgan Stanley Consumer Index, Morgan Stanley Healthcare Product Index, Morgan Stanley Healthcare Provider Index, Natural Gas Index, NatWest Energy Index, Networking Index, North American Telecommunications Index, Oil Index, Pharmaceutical Index, Pharmaceutical LEAPS Index, S&P MidCap 400 Index, Security Broker/Dealer Index, Tobacco Index.

Chicago Board of Trade (Chicago) *futures:* corn, oats, rough rice, soybeans, soybean oil, soybean meal, wheat, anhydrous ammonia, diammonium phosphate, corn yield insurance (Illinois, Indiana, Iowa, Nebraska, Ohio), silver (1,000 ounces, 5,000 ounces), gold (kilo, 100 ounces); CBOT Dow Jones Industrial Average Index, U.S. Treasury bonds, Treasury notes (10-year, 5-year, 2-year), Long-Term Municipal Bond Index, 10-year Canadian government bond, German government bond, 30-day Fed funds, yield curve spread. *options:* wheat, corn, oats, soybeans, soybean oil, soybean meal, rough rice, silver (1,000 ounces), U.S. Treasury bonds, Treasury notes (10-year, 5-year, 2-year), Municipal Bond Index, Canadian government bond, Long-term Municipal Bond Index, Flexible U.S. Treasury bonds, Flexible Treasury options (10-year, 5-year, 2-year), German government bond, quarterly catastrophe insurance (national, Eastern, Northeastern, Southeastern, Midwestern, Texas and Florida), annual catastrophe insurance.

Chicago Board Options Exchange (Chicago) *equity options: equity LEAPS, FLEX equity options; index options:* Standard & Poor's 100 Index and LEAPS, Standard & Poor's 500 Index and LEAPS, Standard & Poor's long-dated options, S&P SmallCap 600 Index, S&P/BARRA Growth and Value Indexes, Dow Jones Industrial Average and LEAPS, Dow Jones Transportation Average and LEAPS, Dow Jones Utility Average and LEAPS, FLEX index options (S&P 500, Russell 2000 and NASDAQ-100 Indexes), CBOE Isreal Index, Latin 15 Index, CBOE Mexico Index and LEAPS, Morgan Stanley Multinational Company Index, NASDAQ-100 Index, Nikkei 300 Index and LEAPS, Russell 2000 Index and LEAPS, IPC options. *sector index options:* CBOE Automotive Index, CBOE Computer Software Index, CBOE Environmental Index, CBOE Gaming Index, CBOE Gold Index, CBOE Internet Index and LEAPS, CBOE Oil Index and LEAPS, CBOE REIT Index, CBOE Technology Index and LEAPS, GSTI Composite Index, GSTI (Computer) Hardware Index, GSTI Internet Index, GSTI Multimedia Networking Index, GSTI Semiconductor Index, GSTI (Computer) Services Index, GSTI (Computer) Software Index, S&P Banks Index, S&P Chemical Index, S&P Health Care Index, S&P Insurance Index, S&P Retail Index, S&P Transportation Index. *interest rate options and LEAPS:* 13-week U.S. Treasury bill, 5-year Treasury note, 10-year Treasury note, 30-year Treasury bond.

Chicago Mercantile Exchange (Chicago) *agricultural futures and options:* live cattle, feeder cattle, boneless beef, boneless beef trimmings, lean hogs, frozen pork bellies, fresh pork bellies, BFP (basic formula price) milk, old butter, new butter, cheddar cheese, random-length lumber, oriented strand board. *foreign currency futures and options:* Australian dollar, Brazilian real, British pound, Canadian dollar, Deutsche mark, French franc, Japanese yen, Mexican peso, New Zealand dollar, South African rand, Swiss franc. *cross-rate futures and options:* British pound/Deutsche mark, Deutsche mark/Japanese yen, Deutsche mark/Swiss franc, Deutsche mark/French franc. *foreign currency-denominated interest rate futures and options:* Euroyen, 3-month Euromark, 91-day Mexican

Treasury bill, 28-day Mexican TIIE. *interest rate futures and options:* Eurodollar time deposit, 13-week U.S. Treasury bill, 1-year Treasury bill, 1-month LIBOR (London Interbank Offered Rate), Mexican Par Brady Bonds, Argentine FRB Bonds, Brazilian C Bonds, Brazilian EI Bonds, Federal Funds rate (futures only). *stock index futures and options:* Standard & Poor's 500, E-Mini S&P 500 Stock Price Index, Standard & Poor's MidCap 400, Nikkei 225 Stock Average, Goldman Sachs Commodity Index, Russell 2000 Stock Price Index, Major Market Index, S&P 500/BARRA Growth Index, S&P 500 BARRA Value Index, NASDAQ 100 Index, IPC Stock Index, Dow Jones Taiwan Stock Index.

Coffee, Sugar and Cocoa Exchange (New York) *futures and options:* coffee, cocoa, sugar #11, butter, cheddar cheese, milk, BFP (basic formula price) milk, nonfat dry milk. *futures:* sugar #14, white sugar. *flexible options:* sugar #11.

Kansas City Board of Trade (Kansas City) *futures and options:* wheat, Mini Value Line Index, Western natural gas. *futures:* Value Line Index.

FINEX *index/interest rate futures and options:* U.S. dollar index, U.S. Treasury auction notes (5-year, 2-year). *cross-rate currency futures and options:* Deutsche mark/French franc, Deutsche mark/lira, Deutsche mark/yen, Deutsche mark/Swedish krona, Deutsche mark/Swiss franc, Deutsche mark/Spanish peseta, British pound/Deutsche mark, British pound/yen, British pound/Swiss franc, British pound/U.S. dollar. *U.S. dollar currency pairs futures:* Deutsche mark, yen, Swiss franc, Canadian dollar, Australian dollar, New Zealand dollar, South African rand, Malaysian ringgit, Indonesian rupiah, Singapore dollar, Thai baht.

Mid-America Commodity Exchange (Chicago) *futures and options:* corn, wheat, soybeans, soybean oil, NY gold, U.S. Treasury bond. *futures:* oats, soybean meal, cattle, hogs, NY silver, platinum, Australian dollar, British pound, Canadian dollar, Deutsche mark, Japanese yen, Swiss franc, Eurodollar, U.S. Treasury bills, U.S. Treasury notes (10-year, 5-year).

Minneapolis Grain Exchange (Minneapolis) *futures and options:* hard red spring wheat, soft white wheat, barley, white shrimp, black tiger shrimp. *futures:* American spring wheat.

New York Cotton Exchange (New York) *agricultural futures and options:* cotton, frozen concentrated orange juice, potatoes.

New York Futures Exchange (New York) *futures and options:* NYSE Composite Index, NYSE Large Composite Index, CRB/Bridge Index, PSE Technology Index.

New York Mercantile Exchange (New York) *NYMEX division: futures and options:* light, sweet crude oil, New York Harbor unleaded gasoline, heating oil, Henry Hub natural gas, Permian Basin natural gas, Alberta natural gas, Palo Verde and California/Oregon Border (COB) electricity, Eastern electricity, coal, platinum. *futures:* sour crude, Gulf Coast unleaded gasoline, propane, palladium. COMEX *division: futures and options:* copper, gold, silver, FTSE Eurotop 100 Index. *options:* 5-day copper, 5-day gold, 5-day silver.

Pacific Exchange (San Francisco and Los Angeles) *index options:* Morgan Stanley Emerging Growth Index, Wilshire Small Cap Index, Dow Jones Taiwan Stock Index, PSE Technology 100 Index, LEAPS; FLEX options.

Philadelphia Stock Exchange (Philadelphia): *currency options:* Australian dollar, British pound, Canadian dollar, Deutsche mark, EURO, French franc, Italian lira, Japanese yen, Mexican peso, Spanish peseta, Swiss franc, U.S. dollar. *sector index options:* airline, KBW bank, forest and paper products, gold/silver, oil service, phone, semiconductor, utility, national over-the-counter, SuperCap, U.S. Top 100, Value Line Index, computer box maker.

SECURITIES AND EXCHANGE COMMISSION (SEC) federal agency created by the SECURITIES EXCHANGE ACT OF 1934 to administer that act and the SECURITIES ACT OF 1933, formerly carried out by the FEDERAL TRADE COMMISSION. The

SEC is made up of five commissioners, appointed by the President of the United States on a rotating basis for five-year terms. The chairman is designated by the President and, to insure its independence, no more than three members of the commission may be of the same political party. The statutes administered by the SEC are designed to promote full public DISCLOSURE and protect the investing public against malpractice in the securities markets. All issues of securities offered in interstate commerce or through the mails must be registered with the SEC; all national securities exchanges and associations are under its supervision, as are INVESTMENT COMPANIES, investment counselors and advisers, OVER THE COUNTER brokers and dealers, and virtually all other individuals and firms operating in the investment field. In addition to the 1933 and 1934 securities acts, responsibilities of the SEC include the PUBLIC UTILITY HOLDING COMPANY ACT of 1935, the TRUST INDENTURE ACT of 1939, the INVESTMENT COMPANY ACT of 1940 and the INVESTMENT ADVISERS ACT of 1940. It also administers the SECURITIES ACTS AMENDMENTS OF 1975, which directed the SEC to facilitate the establishment of a NATIONAL MARKET SYSTEM and a nationwide system for clearance and settlement of transactions and established the Municipal Securities Rulemaking Board, a self-regulatory organization whose rules are subject to SEC approval. *See also* SECURITIES AND EXCHANGE COMMISSION RULES.

SECURITIES AND EXCHANGE COMMISSION RULES The following are some of the more commonly encountered rules of the SEC. The list highlights the most prominent features of the rules and is not intended as a legal interpretation. The rules are listed in numerical order.

Rule 3b-3: Definition of Short Sale defines short sale as one in which the seller does not own the SECURITY sold or which is consummated by delivery of a borrowed security; ownership is defined in terms of securities, CONVERTIBLES, OPTIONS, and SUBSCRIPTION WARRANTS.

Rule 10a-1: Short sales known as the SHORT-SALE RULE, prohibits a short sale of securities below the price of the last regular trade and at that price unless it was higher than the last different price preceding it. In determining the price at which a short sale can be made after a security goes EX-DIVIDEND, EX-RIGHTS, or ex- any other distribution, all sales prices prior to the ex- date may be reduced by the amount of the distribution.

Rule 10b-2: Solicitation of purchases on an exchange to facilitate distribution of securities prohibits parties concerned with a PRIMARY DISTRIBUTION or a SECONDARY DISTRIBUTION of a security from soliciting orders for the issue other than through the offering circular or formal PROSPECTUS.

Rule 10b-4: Short tendering of securities prohibits a SHORT TENDER—the sale of borrowed securities (as in SELLING SHORT) to a person making a TENDER OFFER.

Rule 10b-6: Prohibitions against trading by persons interested in a distribution rule that prohibits issuers, underwriters, broker-dealers, or others involved in a DISTRIBUTION of securities from buying the issue, or rights to it, during the distribution. The section permits transactions between the issuer and the underwriters and among the participating underwriters as required to carry out a distribution. The law extends to a repurchase by the issuer or to a purchase by participants in a new issue of CONVERTIBLE securities already on the market and convertible into the securities being offered.

Rule 10b-7: Stabilizing to effect a distribution provisions governing market STABILIZATION activities by issuers or underwriters in securities offerings.

Rule 10b-8: Distributions through rights prohibits market price MANIPULATION by interested parties in a RIGHTS OFFERING.

Rule 10b-10: Confirmation of transactions sets minimum information and disclosure requirements for the written confirmations of sales or purchases that broker-dealers send to clients, including disclosure of whether a firm is acting as AGENT (broker) or as PRINCIPAL (dealer).

Rule 10b-13: Other purchases during tender offer or exchange offer prohibits a person making a cash tender offer or an offer to exchange one EQUITY security for another from taking a position in the security being tendered or in a security CONVERTIBLE into the security being tendered until the tender offer or exchange offer expires.

Rule 10b-16: Credit terms in margin transactions terms and conditions concerning the interest charges on MARGIN loans to brokerage customers and the broker's disclosure responsibilities to borrowers.

Rule 11A: Floor trading regulations rules governing floor trading by exchange members, including those concerning PRIORITY and PRECEDENCE of transactions, transactions for the accounts of persons associated with members, HEDGE transactions, exchange bond trading, transactions by REGISTERED COMPETITIVE MARKET MAKERS and REGISTERED EQUITY MARKET MAKERS, and transactions between members.

Rule 12b-1: *see* 12b-1 MUTUAL FUND.

Rule 13d: Acquisition of beneficial interest disclosures required by any person who directly or indirectly acquires a beneficial interest of 5% or more of any class of a registered equity security. *See also* WILLIAMS ACT.

Rule 13e: Repurchase of shares by issuers prohibits purchase by an issuer of its own shares during a TENDER OFFER for its shares and regulates GOING PRIVATE transactions by issuers or their affiliates.

Rule 14a: Solicitation of proxies sets forth the information and documentation required with PROXY materials distributed to shareholders of a public corporation.

Rule 14d: Tender offers regulations and restrictions covering public TENDER OFFERS and related disclosure requirements. *See also* WILLIAMS ACT.

Rule 15c2-1: Hypothecation of customers' securities regulates a broker-dealer's SAFEKEEPING of customers securities in a MARGIN ACCOUNT, prohibiting the COMMINGLING of customers accounts without the consent of the respective customers and the commingling of customers' accounts with the securities of non-customers, and limiting broker borrowings secured by customers' collateral to the aggregate amount of customers' indebtedness. *See also* HYPOTHECATION.

Rule 15c3-1: Net capital requirements for brokers or dealers covers NET CAPITAL REQUIREMENTS relative to the aggregate indebtedness of brokers and dealers of different types.

Rule 15c3-2: Customers' free credit balances requires a broker-dealer to notify customers with credit balances in their accounts that such balances may be withdrawn on demand.

Rule 15c3-3: Customer-protection reserves and custody of securities regulates the handling of customers' fully paid securities and excess MARGIN securities (security value in excess of MARGIN REQUIREMENTS) with broker-dealers. Fully paid securities must be segregated, and the broker must make weekly deposits to a Special Reserve Bank Account for the Exclusive Benefit of Customers.

Rule 17f-1: Missing, lost, counterfeit, or stolen securities requires exchanges, broker-dealers, clearing agencies, banks and transfer agents to report promptly to both the SEC and the appropriate law enforcement agency any knowledge of missing, lost, counterfeit, or stolen securities and to check with the SEC whenever a security comes into their possession to make sure it has not been reported at large.

Rule 19b-3: Prohibiting fixing of rates of commission by exchanges prohibits fixed commissions on stock exchange transactions pursuant to the SECURITIES ACT AMENDMENTS OF 1975.

Rule 19c-3: Off-board trading by exchange members permits securities listed on an exchange after April 26, 1979, to be traded off the exchange by member firms, a step toward an experimental NATIONAL MARKET SYSTEM in compliance with the SECURITIES ACT AMENDMENTS OF 1975.

Rule 19c-4: One share, one vote prohibits U.S. exchanges and the NASD from listing or providing quotes for any issuer of stock with more voting power than other common shares of the same issuer.

Rule 144: Public sale of unregistered securities sets forth the conditions under which a holder of unregistered securities may make a public sale without filing a formal REGISTRATION STATEMENT. No LETTER SECURITY purchased through a PRIVATE PLACEMENT may be sold for at least two years after the date of purchase. Thereafter, during any three-month period, the following amounts may be sold: if listed securities, the greater of 1% of the amount outstanding or the average trading volume within the four preceding weeks; if unlisted, 1% of outstandings. Securities may be sold only in broker's transactions.

Rule 145: Securities acquired in recapitalization persons who acquire securities as a result of reclassification, MERGER, consolidation, or transfer of corporate assets may sell such securities without REGISTRATION under stipulated conditions.

Rule 156: Mutual fund sales literature forbids false and misleading sales materials promoting INVESTMENT COMPANY securities.

Rule 237: Public sale of unregistered securities expanding on Rule 144, provides that five years after full payment for the purchase of privately placed securities, the lesser of $50,000 of such securities or 1% of the securities outstanding in a particular CLASS may be sold within a one year period.

Rule 254: Registration of small issues provides for simplified registration of small issues ($1.5 million or less in the mid-1980s) including a short-form REGISTRATION STATEMENT and PROSPECTUS. *See also* REGULATION A.

Rule 415: Shelf registration permits corporations to file a REGISTRATION for securities they intend to issue in the future when market conditions are favorable. *See also* SHELF REGISTRATION.

Rule 419: Blank-check companies (companies that issue penny stock before operations have begun or before engaging in an acquisition or merger with an unspecified business entity) must put investors' funds in an escrow account for the benefit of the purchaser.

SECURITIES EXCHANGE ACT OF 1934 law governing the securities markets, enacted June 6, 1934. The act outlaws misrepresentation, MANIPULATION, and other abusive practices in the issuance of securities. It created the SECURITIES AND EXCHANGE COMMISSION (SEC) to enforce both the SECURITIES ACT OF 1933 and the Securities Exchange Act of 1934.

Principal requirements of the 1934 act are as follows:

1. REGISTRATION of all securities listed on stock exchanges, and periodic DISCLOSURES by issuers of financial status and changes in condition.
2. regular disclosures of holdings and transactions of "INSIDERS"—the officers and directors of a corporation and those who control at least 10% of equity securities.
3. solicitation of PROXIES enabling shareholders to vote for or against policy proposals.
4. registration with the SEC of stock exchanges and brokers and dealers to ensure their adherence to SEC rules through self-regulation.
5. surveillance by the SEC of trading practices on stock exchanges and over-the-counter markets to minimize the possibility of insolvency among brokers and dealers.
6. regulation of MARGIN REQUIREMENTS for securities purchased on credit; the FEDERAL RESERVE BOARD sets those requirements.

7. SEC subpoena power in investigations of possible violations and in enforcement actions.

The SECURITIES ACT AMENDMENTS OF 1975 ratified the system of free-market determination of brokers' commissions and gave the SEC authority to oversee development of a NATIONAL MARKET SYSTEM.

SECURITIES EXCHANGE OF THAILAND (SET) only stock market in Thailand, based in Bangkok. The *SET Index,* calculated by the exchange, and the *Bangkok Book Club Price Index,* compiled by the Book Club Finance and Securities Co. Ltd., include all corporate stocks and mutual funds and are the most widely watched. Trading is conducted through the ASSET automated electronic trading system Monday through Friday from 10 A.M. to 12:30 P.M., and 2 P.M. to 4 P.M. Trades are settled on the third business day after the trade date.

SECURITIES INDUSTRY ASSOCIATION (SIA) trade group that represents broker-dealers. The SIA lobbies for legislation affecting the brokerage industry. It also educates its members and the public about industry trends and keeps statistics on revenues and profits of brokers. The SIA represents only the segment of broker-dealers that sells taxable securities. Tax-exempt bond, government bond, and mortgage-backed security dealers are represented by the BOND MARKET ASSOCIATION.

SECURITIES INDUSTRY AUTOMATION CORPORATION (SIAC) organization established in 1972 to provide communications and computer systems and services for the New York Stock Exchange (NYSE) and the American Stock Exchange (AMEX). It is two-thirds owned by NYSE and one-third owned by AMEX.

SECURITIES INDUSTRY COMMITTEE ON ARBITRATION (SICA) private body that applies its arbitration code in cases of customer complaints against securities firms.

SECURITIES INVESTOR PROTECTION CORPORATION (SIPC) nonprofit corporation, established by Congress under the Securities Investor Protection Act of 1970, that insures the securities and cash in the customer accounts of member brokerage firms against the failure of those firms. All brokers and dealers registered with the Securities and Exchange Commission and with national stock exchanges are required to be members of SIPC. The Corporation acts similarly to the FEDERAL DEPOSIT INSURANCE CORPORATION (FDIC), which insures banks, and the SAVINGS ASSOCIATION INSURANCE FUND (SAIF), which insures savings and loans. When a brokerage firm fails, SIPC will first try to merge it into another brokerage firm. If this fails, SIPC will liquidate the firm's assets and pay off account holders up to an overall maximum of $500,000 per customer, with a limit of $100,000 on cash or cash equivalents. SIPC does not protect investors against market risks. *See also* SEPARATE CUSTOMER.

SECURITIES LOAN
1. loan of securities by one broker to another, usually to cover a customer's short sale. The lending broker is secured by the cash proceeds of the sale.
2. in a more general sense, loan collateralized by MARKETABLE SECURITIES. These would include all customer loans made to purchase or carry securities by broker-dealers under Federal Reserve Board REGULATION T margin rules, as well as by banks under REGULATION U and other lenders under REGULATION G. Loans made by banks to brokers to cover customers' positions are also collateralized by securities, but such loans are called *broker's loans* or *call loans. See also* HYPOTHECATION; LENDING AT A PREMIUM; LENDING AT A RATE; LENDING SECURITIES; REHYPOTHECATION; SELLING SHORT.

SECURITIES MARKETS general term for markets in which securities are traded, including both ORGANIZED SECURITIES EXCHANGES and OVER THE COUNTER (OTC) markets.

SECURITIZATION process of distributing risk by aggregating debt instruments in a pool, then issuing new securities backed by the pool. *See also* ASSET-BACKED SECURITIES.

SECURITY
Finance: collateral offered by a debtor to a lender to secure a loan called *collateral security.* For instance, the security behind a mortgage loan is the real estate being purchased with the proceeds of the loan. If the debt is not repaid, the lender may seize the security and resell it.

Personal security refers to one person or firm's GUARANTEE of another's primary obligation.

Investment: instrument that signifies an ownership position in a corporation (a stock), a creditor relationship with a corporation or governmental body (a bond), or rights to ownership such as those represented by an OPTION, SUBSCRIPTION RIGHT, and SUBSCRIPTION WARRANT.

SECURITY DEPOSIT money paid in advance to protect the provider of a product or service against damage or nonpayment by the buyer. For example, landlords require a security deposit of one month's rent when a tenant signs a lease, to cover the possibility that the tenant will move out without paying the last month's rent, or that the tenant will inflict substantial damage on the property while living there. In such a case, the money from the security deposit is used to cover repairs. Similarly, car leasing companies typically demand security deposits for the last month's lease payment to protect the leasing company against damage to the car or nonpayment of the lease. If all payments are made on time and there is no damage, security deposits must be returned to those who paid them.

SECURITY MARKET LINE relationship between the REQUIRED RATE OF RETURN on an investment and its SYSTEMATIC RISK.

SECURITY RATINGS evaluations of the credit and investment risk of securities issues by commercial RATING agencies.

SEED MONEY venture capitalist's first contribution toward the financing or capital requirements of a START-UP business. It frequently takes the form of a loan, often SUBORDINATED, or an investment in convertible bonds or preferred stock. Seed money provides the basis for additional capitalization to accommodate growth. *See also* MEZZANINE LEVEL; SECOND ROUND; VENTURE CAPITAL.

SEEK A MARKET to look for a buyer (if a seller) or a seller (if a buyer) of securities.

SEGMENT REPORTING *see* BUSINESS SEGMENT REPORTING.

SEGREGATION OF SECURITIES Securities and Exchange Commission rules (8c and 15c2-1) designed to protect customers' securities used by broker-dealers to secure broker loans. Specifically, broker-dealers may not (1) commingle the securities of different customers without the written consent of each customer, (2) commingle a customer's securities with those of any person other than a bona-fide customer, or (3) borrow more against customers' securities than the customers, in the aggregate, owe the broker-dealer against the same securities. *See also* COMMINGLING; HYPOTHECATION; REHYPOTHECATION; SECURITIES AND EXCHANGE COMMISSION RULE 15c2-1.

SELECTED DEALER AGREEMENT agreement governing the SELLING GROUP in a securities underwriting and distribution. *See also* UNDERWRITE.

SELECT TEN PORTFOLIO UNIT INVESTMENT TRUST offered at various times each year as a subcategory of the DEFINED ASSET FUNDS sponsored by a group of brokers including Merrill Lynch, Paine Webber, Morgan Stanley Dean Witter, Salomon Smith Barney, and Prudential Securities. The majority of the select ten trusts buy and hold for one year the ten stocks in the Dow Jones Industrial Average (DJIA) with the highest dividend yields. Stocks thus selected have usually outperformed the DJIA. Other select ten portfolios comprise the highest yielding stocks in the blue chip indices of foreign markets such as the United Kingdom, Hong Kong, and until 1998, Japan. *See also* DOGS OF THE DOW.

SELF-AMORTIZING MORTGAGE mortgage in which all principal is paid off in a specified period of time through periodic interest and principal payments. The most common self-amortizing mortgages are for 15 and 30 years. Lenders will provide a table to borrowers showing how much principal and interest is being paid off each month until the loan is retired.

SELF-DIRECTED IRA INDIVIDUAL RETIREMENT ACCOUNT (IRA) that can be actively managed by the account holder, who designates a CUSTODIAN to carry out investment instructions. The account is subject to the same conditions and early withdrawal limitations as a regular IRA. Investors who withdraw money from a qualified IRA plan have 60 days in which to roll over the funds to another plan before they become liable for tax penalties. Most corporate and U.S. government securities, stocks, mutual funds, and metals such as gold, silver, platinum, and palladium are eligible to be held by a self-directed IRA. *See also* ROTH IRA.

SELF-EMPLOYED INCOME net taxable income of a self-employed person, as reported on Schedule C of IRS Form 1040. Self-employment income may be generated by freelance work, royalties, consulting, or income from sole proprietorship businesses. Social Security taxes must be paid on self-employment income.

SELF-EMPLOYED RETIREMENT PLAN *see* KEOGH PLAN.

SELF-EMPLOYMENT TAX tax paid by self-employed people to Social Security, qualifying them for receiving Social Security benefits at retirement. The tax is filed on Schedule SE of IRS Form 1040, which indicates the type of business generating self-employment income, net earnings, and the amount of self-employment tax.

SELF-REGULATORY ORGANIZATION (SRO) principal means contemplated by the federal securities laws for the enforcement of fair, ethical, and efficient practices in the securities and commodities futures industries. It is these organizations that are being referred to when "industry rules" are mentioned, as distinguished from the regulatory agencies such as the Securities and Exchange Commission or the Federal Reserve Board. The SROs include all the national SECURITIES AND COMMODITIES EXCHANGES as well as the NATIONAL ASSOCIATION OP SECURITIES DEALERS (NASD), which represents all the firms operating in the over-the-counter market, and the *Municipal Securities Rulemaking Board,* created under the Securities Acts Amendments of 1975 to regulate brokers, dealers and banks dealing in municipal securities. Rules made by the MSRB are subject to approval by the SEC and are enforced by the NASD and bank regulatory agencies.

SELF-SUPPORTING DEBT bonds sold for a project that will produce sufficient revenues to retire the debt. Such debt is usually issued by municipalities building a public structure (for example, a bridge or tunnel) that will be producing revenue through tolls or other charges. The bonds are not supported by the taxing power of the municipality issuing them. *See also* REVENUE BOND.

SELF-TENDER *see* SHARE REPURCHASE PLAN.

SELLER FINANCING financing provided by the owner/seller of real estate, who takes back a secured note. The buyer may be unable to qualify for a mortgage from a lending institution, or interest rates may have risen so high that the buyer is unwilling to take on a market-rate loan. In order to sell their property, sellers offer to lend the buyer the money needed, often at a below-market interest rate. The buyer takes full title to the property when the loan is fully repaid. If the buyer defaults on the loan, the seller can repossess the property. Also called *creative financing*.

SELLER'S MARKET situation in which there is more demand for a security or product than there is available supply. As a result, the prices tend to be rising, and the sellers can set both the prices and the terms of sale. It contrasts with a buyer's market, characterized by excess supply, low prices, and terms suited to the buyer's desires.

SELLER'S OPTION securities transaction in which the seller, instead of making REGULAR WAY DELIVERY, is given the right to deliver the security to the purchaser on the date the seller's option expires or before, provided written notification of the seller's intention to deliver is given to the buyer one full business day prior to delivery. Seller's option deliveries are normally not made before 6 business days following the transaction or after 60 days.

SELLING CLIMAX sudden plunge in security prices as those who hold stocks or bonds panic and decide to dump their holdings all at once. Technical analysts see a climax as both a dramatic increase in volume and a sharp drop in prices on a chart. To these analysts, such a pattern usually means that a short-term rally will soon follow since there are few sellers left after the climax. Sometimes, a selling climax can signal the bottom of a BEAR MARKET, meaning that after the climax the market will start to rise.

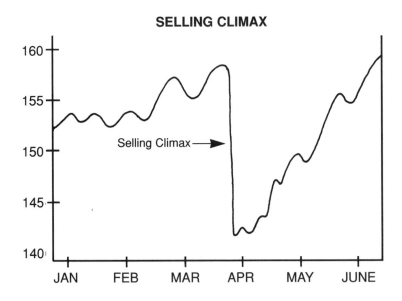

SELLING CLIMAX

SELLING CONCESSION discount at which securities in a NEW ISSUE offering (or a SECONDARY DISTRIBUTION) are allocated to the members of a SELLING GROUP by the underwriters. Since the selling group cannot sell to the public at a price higher than the PUBLIC OFFERING PRICE, its compensation comes out of the difference between the price paid to the issuer by the underwriters and the public offering price, called the SPREAD. The selling group's portion, called the CONCESSION, is normally one half or more of the gross spread, expressed as a discount off the public offering price. *See also* FLOTATION COST; UNDERWRITE; UNDERWRITING SPREAD.

SELLING DIVIDENDS questionable practice by sales personnel dealing in MUTUAL FUNDS whereby a customer is induced to buy shares in a fund in order to get the benefit of a dividend scheduled in the near future. Since the dividend is already part of the NET ASSET VALUE of the fund and therefore part of the share price, the customer derives no real benefit.

SELLING, GENERAL, AND ADMINISTRATIVE (SG&A) EXPENSES grouping of expenses reported on a company's PROFIT AND LOSS STATEMENT between COST OF GOODS SOLD and INCOME DEDUCTIONS. Included are such items as salespersons' salaries and commissions, advertising and promotion, travel and entertainment, office payroll and expenses, and executives' salaries. SG&A expenses do not include such items as interest or amortization of INTANGIBLE ASSETS, which would be listed as income deductions. *See also* OPERATING PROFIT (OR LOSS).

SELLING GROUP group of dealers appointed by the syndicate manager of an UNDERWRITING GROUP, as AGENT for the other underwriters, to market a new or secondary issue to the public; also called *selling syndicate.* The selling group typically includes members of the underwriting group but varies in size with the size of the issue, sometimes running into several hundred dealers. The selling group is governed by the selling group agreement, also called the SELECTED DEALER AGREEMENT. It sets forth the terms of the relationship, establishes the commission (or SELLING CONCESSION, as it is called), and provides for the termination of the group, usually in 30 days. The selling group may or may not be obligated to purchase unsold shares. *See also* UNDERWRITE.

SELLING OFF selling securities or commodities under pressure to avoid further declines in prices. Technical analysts call such action a *sell-off. See also* DUMPING.

SELLING ON THE GOOD NEWS practice of selling a stock soon after a positive news development is announced. Most investors, cheered by the news of a successful new product or higher earnings, buy a stock because they think it will go higher: this pushes up the price. Someone selling on this good news believes that the stock will have reached its top price once all those encouraged by the development have bought the stock. Therefore, it is better to sell at this point than to wait for more good news or to be holding the stock if the next announcement is disappointing. *Compare with* BUYING ON THE BAD NEWS.

SELLING SHORT sale of a security or commodity futures contract not owned by the seller; a technique used (1) to take advantage of an anticipated decline in the price or (2) to protect a profit in a LONG POSITION (*see* SELLING SHORT AGAINST THE BOX).

An investor borrows stock certificates for delivery at the time of short sale. If the seller can buy that stock later at a lower price, a profit results; if the price rises, however, a loss results.

A commodity sold short represents a promise to deliver the commodity at a set price on a future date. Most commodity short sales are COVERED before the DELIVERY DATE.

Example of a short sale involving stock: An investor, anticipating a decline in the price of XYZ shares, instructs his or her broker to sell short 100 XYZ when

XYZ is trading at $50. The broker then loans the investor 100 shares of XYZ, using either its own inventory, shares in the MARGIN ACCOUNT of another customer, or shares borrowed from another broker. These shares are used to make settlement with the buying broker within five days of the short sale transaction, and the proceeds are used to secure the loan. The investor now has what is known as a SHORT POSITION—that is, he or she still does not own the 100 XYZ and, at some point, must buy the shares to repay the lending broker. If the market price of XYZ drops to $40, the investor can buy the shares for $4000, repay the lending broker, thus covering the short sale, and claim a profit of $1000, or $10 a share.

Short selling is regulated by REGULATION T of the Federal Reserve Board. *See also* LENDING AT A RATE; LENDING AT A PREMIUM; LOANED FLAT; MARGIN REQUIREMENT; SHORT-SALE RULE.

SELLING SHORT AGAINST THE BOX SELLING SHORT stock actually owned by the seller but held in SAFEKEEPING, called the BOX in Wall Street jargon. The motive for the practice, which assumes that the securities needed to COVER are borrowed as with any short sale, may be simply inaccessibility of the box or that the seller does not wish to disclose ownership. The main motive is to protect a CAPITAL GAIN in the shares that are owned, while deferring a LONG-TERM GAIN into another tax year. This technique was curtailed as a way to defer taxes by the TAXPAYER RELIEF ACT OF 1997. Under the law, shorting against the box after June 8, 1997 is considered a "constructive sale," resulting in capital gains liability.

SELLING THE SPREAD spread where the sold option is trading at a higher premium than the purchased option. For example, purchasing a shorter term option and selling a longer term option (assuming both options have the same EXERCISE PRICE) would usually result in a net credit. *See* CALENDAR SPREAD. Another example would be purchasing a call with a higher exercise price and selling a call with a lower exercise price, assuming both options have the same expiration date. *See also* CREDIT SPREAD.

SELL-OFF massive selling of stocks or bonds after a steep decline in prices. Traders sell quickly in order to avoid further losses.

SELL ORDER order by an investor to a broker to sell a particular stock, bond, option, future, mutual fund, or other holding. There are several kinds of sell orders, including DAY ORDERS, GOOD-TILL-CANCELED ORDERS (GTC), LIMIT ORDERS, MARKET-ON-CLOSE ORDERS, MARKET ORDERS, ON THE CLOSE ORDERS, ON THE OPENING ORDERS, STOP-LIMIT ORDERS, STOP LOSS orders, and STOP ORDERS.

SELL OUT
1. liquidation of a MARGIN ACCOUNT by a broker after a MARGIN CALL has failed to produce additional equity to bring the margin to the required level. *See also* CLOSE A POSITION; MARGIN REQUIREMENT; MINIMUM MAINTENANCE.
2. action by a broker when a customer fails to pay for securities purchased and the securities received from the selling broker are sold to cover the transaction. Term also applies to commodities futures transactions.
3. expression used when all the securities in a NEW ISSUE underwriting have been distributed.

SELL PLUS sell order with instructions to execute only if the trading price in a security is higher than the last different preceding price. *See also* SHORT-SALE RULE.

SELL-STOP ORDER *see* STOP ORDER.

SELL THE BOOK order to a broker by the holder of a large quantity of shares of a security to sell all that can be ABSORBED at the current bid price. The term derives from the SPECIALIST'S BOOK—the record of all the buy and sell orders members have placed in the stock he or she handles. In this scenario, the buyers potentially include those in the specialist's book, the specialist for his or her own account, and the broker-dealer CROWD.

SENIOR DEBT loans or DEBT SECURITIES that have claim prior to junior obligations and EQUITY on a corporation's assets in the event of LIQUIDATION. Senior debt commonly includes funds borrowed from banks, insurance companies, or other financial institutions, as well as notes, bonds, or debentures not expressly defined as junior or subordinated.

SENIOR MORTGAGE BOND bond with the highest claim on the assets of the issuer in case of bankruptcy or liquidation. Senior mortgage bondholders are paid off in full before any payments are made to junior bondholders.

SENIOR REFUNDING replacement of securities maturing in 5 to 12 years with issues having original maturities of 15 years or longer. The objectives may be to reduce the bond issuer's interest costs, to consolidate several issues into one, or to extend the maturity date.

SENIOR SECURITY security that has claim prior to a junior obligation and EQUITY on a corporation's assets and earnings. Senior securities are repaid before JUNIOR SECURITIES in the event of LIQUIDATION. Debt, including notes, bonds, and debentures, is senior to stock; first mortgage bonds are senior to second mortgage bonds; and all mortgage bonds are senior to debentures, which are unsecured.

SENSITIVE MARKET market easily swayed by good or bad news.

SENSITIVITY ANALYSIS study measuring the effect of a change in a variable (such as sales) on the risk or profitability of an investment.

SENTIMENT INDICATORS measures of the bullish or bearish mood of investors. Many technical analysts look at these indicators as contrary indicators—that is, when most investors are bullish, the market is about to drop, and when most are bearish, the market is about to rise. Some financial newsletters measure swings in investor sentiment by tabulating the number of INVESTMENT ADVISORY SERVICES that are bullish or bearish.

SEP *see* SIMPLIFIED EMPLOYEE PENSION (SEP) PLAN.

SEPARATE CUSTOMER concept used by the SECURITIES INVESTOR PROTECTION CORPORATION (SIPC) in allocating insurance coverage. If there is a difference in the way investment accounts are owned, each account is viewed as a separate customer entitled to the maximum protection; thus two accounts, one in the name of John Jones and the other in the name of John Jones and his wife Mary Jones, would be treated as separate accounts and separate persons. On the other hand, a CASH ACCOUNT, a MARGIN ACCOUNT, and a special convertible bond account all owned by John Jones are not treated as separate customer accounts but as one.

SEPARATELY REPORTABLE SEGMENT *see* BUSINESS SEGMENT REPORTING.

SEPARATE TAX RETURNS tax returns filed by a married couple choosing the married, filing separately, status. Each person reports his or her own income, deductions, exemptions, and credits. Couples may choose to file separately instead of with a JOINT TAX RETURN for several reasons. A couple may choose to keep all of their financial affairs, including tax filing, separate. In some cases, a couple may find that the total amount of tax paid is less if they file separately than if they file jointly. This is usually the case when there is a wide disparity between the earnings of the husband and wife. However, because of the way the tax tables are designed, it is frequently more advantageous for a married couple to file a joint return than for them to file separate returns. *See also* FILING STATUS, HEAD OF HOUSEHOLD.

SERIAL BOND bond issue, usually of a municipality, with various MATURITY DATES scheduled at regular intervals until the entire issue is retired. Each bond certificate in the series has an indicated REDEMPTION DATE.

SERIAL REDEMPTION redemption of a SERIAL BOND.

SERIES E BOND savings bond issued by the U.S. government from 1941 to 1979. The bonds were then replaced by Series EE and Series HH bonds. Outstanding Series E bonds, which may be exchanged for Series HH bonds, continue to pay interest for between 30 and 40 years from their issue date. Those issued from 1941 to November 1965 accrue interest for 40 years; those issued from December 1965 and later, for 30 years. Their interest is exempt from state and local income and personal property taxes. *See also* SAVINGS BOND.

SERIES EE BOND *see* SAVINGS BOND.

SERIES HH BOND *see* SAVINGS BOND.

SERIES OF OPTION class of OPTION, either all CALL OPTIONS or all PUT OPTIONS, on the same underlying security, all of which have the same EXERCISE PRICE (strike price) and maturity date. For example, all XYZ May 50 calls would form a series of options.

SERIES 7 REGISTERED broker who has passed the General Securities Registered Representative Examination, commonly called the *Series 7,* and who is a REGISTERED REPRESENTATIVE. In addition to the Series 7, which is a six-hour multiple-choice test developed by the New York Stock Exchange (NYSE) and administered by the National Association of Securities Dealers (NASD), many states require that registered representatives pass a UNIFORM SECURITIES AGENT STATE LAW EXAMINATION.

SET-ASIDE percentage of a job set aside for bidding to minority contractors. In the securities business, many municipal and some corporate bond underwritings require that a certain percentage of the offering be handled by a minority-owned broker/ dealer underwriting firm. Other government and corporate contracts for products and services also stipulate that a certain percentage of the business must be handled by minority firms. Set-aside programs are designed to help minority firms become established more quickly than they might if they had to compete on an equal footing with entrenched competitors.

SETTLE
In general: to pay an obligation.
Estates: distribution of an estate's assets by an executor to beneficiaries after all legal procedures have been completed.
Law: (1) to resolve a legal dispute short of adjudication; (2) to arrange for disposition of property, such as between spouses or between parents and children, if there has been a dispute such as a divorce.
Securities: to complete a securities trade between brokers acting as AGENTS or between a broker and his customer. A trade is settled when the customer has paid the broker for securities bought or when the customer delivers securities that have been sold and the customer receives the proceeds from the sale. *See also* CONTINUOUS NET SETTLEMENT.

SETTLEMENT in general, a resolution of differences among various parties. For example, a labor dispute resulting in a strike may finally be settled by a new contract, or a conflict between a landlord and tenant may be settled in a housing court.

Securities: conclusion of a securities transaction in which a broker/dealer pays for securities bought for a customer or delivers securities sold and receives payment from the buyer's broker. REGULAR WAY DELIVERY (AND SETTLEMENT) is completed on the third full business day following the date of the transaction for stocks, called the SETTLEMENT DATE. Government bonds and options trades are settled the next business day. *See also* CONTINUOUS NET SETTLEMENT.

Futures/Options: the final price, established by exchange rule, for the prices prevailing during the closing period and upon which futures contracts are marked to market.

SETTLEMENT DATE date by which an executed order must be settled, either by a buyer paying for the securities with cash or by a seller delivering the securities and receiving the proceeds of the sale for them. In a REGULAR WAY DELIVERY of stocks and bonds, the settlement date is three business days after the trade was executed. For listed options and government securities, settlement is required by the next business day. *See also* SELLER'S OPTION.

SETTLEMENT OPTIONS options available to beneficiaries when a person insured by a life insurance policy dies. The DEATH BENEFIT may be paid in one lump sum, in several installments over a fixed period of time, or in the form of an ANNUITY for the rest of the beneficiary's life, among other options.

SETTLOR person who creates an INTER VIVOS TRUST as distinguished from a TESTAMENTARY TRUST. Also called *donor, grantor,* or *trustor.*

SEVERALLY BUT NOT JOINTLY form of agreement used to establish the responsibility for selling a portion of the securities in an underwriting. UNDERWRITING GROUP members agree to buy a certain portion of an issue (severally) but do not agree to joint liability for shares not sold by other members of the syndicate. In a less common form of underwriting arrangement, called a *several and joint agreement,* syndicate members agree to sell not only the shares allocated to them, but also any shares not sold by the rest of the group. *See also* UNDERWRITE.

SEVERANCE PAY money paid to an employee who has been laid off by an employer. The money may be paid in the form of a LUMP SUM, as an ANNUITY, or in the form of paychecks for a specified period of time. The size of the termination benefit is based on the length of service and job level of the employee, union contracts, and other factors. Also called *termination benefit.*

SG&A EXPENSES *see* SELLING, GENERAL, AND ADMINISTRATIVE EXPENSES.

SHADOW CALENDAR backlog of securities issues in REGISTRATION with the Securities and Exchange Commission for which no OFFERING DATE has been set pending clearance.

SHAKEOUT change in market conditions that results in the elimination of marginally financed participants in an industry. For example, if the market for microcomputers suddenly becomes glutted because there is more supply than demand, a shakeout will result, meaning that companies will fall by the wayside. In the securities markets, a shakeout occurs when speculators are forced by market events to sell their positions, usually at a loss.

SHAM transaction conducted for the purpose of avoiding taxation. Once discovered by tax authorities, it will be considered null and void, and the parties to the transaction will have to pay the taxes due. Some limited partnerships have been ruled to be "sham transactions" in the past, causing limited partners to owe back taxes, penalties, and interest to the Internal Revenue Service.

SHANGHAI SECURITIES EXCHANGE (SHSE) established in November 1990 as a non-profit organization, regulated by the China Securities Regulatory

Commission. B shares are restricted to foreign investors, and have the same rights and obligations as local A shares. Settlement is three days. Trading hours for B shares are 9:30 A.M. to 11:30 A.M. and 1 P.M. to 3 P.M., Monday through Friday.

SHARE
1. unit of equity ownership in a corporation. This ownership is represented by a stock certificate, which names the company and the shareowner. The number of shares a corporation is authorized to issue is detailed in its corporate charter. Corporations usually do not issue the full number of AUTHORIZED SHARES.
2. unit of ownership in a mutual fund. *See also* INVESTMENT COMPANY.
3. interest, normally represented by a certificate, in a general or LIMITED PARTNERSHIP.

SHARE BROKER DISCOUNT BROKER whose charges are based on the number of shares traded. The more shares in a trade, the lower the per-share cost will be. Trading with a share broker is usually advantageous for those trading at least 500 shares, or for those trading in high-priced shares, who would otherwise pay a percentage of the dollar amount. Those trading in small numbers of shares, or lower-priced ones, may pay lower commissions with a VALUE BROKER, the other kind of discount brokerage firm.

SHARED APPRECIATION MORTGAGE (SAM) mortgage in which the borrower receives a below-market rate of interest in return for agreeing to share part of the appreciation in the value of the underlying property with the lender in a specified number of years. If the borrower does not want to sell at that time, he or she must pay the lender its share of the appreciation in cash. If the borrower does not have that amount of cash on hand, the lender may force the borrower to sell the property to satisfy their claim.

SHARE DRAFT instrument similar to a bank check that is used by credit unions to withdraw from interest-bearing share draft accounts.

SHAREHOLDER
1. owner of one or more shares of STOCK in a corporation. A common shareholder is normally entitled to four basic rights of ownership: (1) claim on a share of the company's undivided assets in proportion to number of shares held; (2) proportionate voting power in the election of DIRECTORS and other business conducted at shareholder meetings or by PROXY; (3) DIVIDENDS when earned and declared by the BOARD OF DIRECTORS; and (4) PREEMPTIVE RIGHT to subscribe to additional stock offerings before they are available to the general public except when overruled by the ARTICLES OF INCORPORATION or in special circumstances, such as where stock is issued to effect a merger.
2. owner of one or more shares or units in a MUTUAL FUND. Mutual fund investors have voting rights similar to those of stock owners.
   Shareholders' rights can vary according to the articles of incorporation or BYLAWS of the particular company.
   See also PREFERRED STOCK.

SHAREHOLDER REPORT *see* STOCKHOLDER'S REPORT.

SHAREHOLDER'S EQUITY total ASSETS minus total LIABILITIES of a corporation. Also called *stockholder's equity,* EQUITY, and NET WORTH.

SHARE REPURCHASE PLAN program by which a corporation buys back its own shares in the open market. It is usually done when shares are UNDERVALUED. Since it reduces the number of shares outstanding and thus increases EARNINGS PER SHARE, it tends to elevate the market value of the remaining shares held by stockholders. *See also* GOING PRIVATE; TREASURY STOCK.

SHARES AUTHORIZED number of shares of stock provided for in the ARTICLES OF INCORPORATION of a company. This figure is ordinarily indicated in the capital accounts section of a company's BALANCE SHEET and is usually well in excess of the shares ISSUED AND OUTSTANDING. A corporation cannot legally issue more shares than authorized. The number of authorized shares can be changed only by amendment to the corporate charter, with the approval of the shareholders. The most common reason for increasing authorized shares in a public company is to accommodate a stock SPLIT.

SHARES OUTSTANDING *see* ISSUED AND OUTSTANDING.

SHARK REPELLENT measure undertaken by a corporation to discourage unwanted TAKEOVER attempts. Also called *porcupine provision.*
For example:
(1) fair price provision requiring a bidder to pay the same price to all shareholders. This raises the stakes and discourages TENDER OFFERS designed to attract only those shareholders most eager to replace management.
(2) GOLDEN PARACHUTE contract with top executives that makes it prohibitively expensive to get rid of existing management.
(3) defensive merger, in which a TARGET COMPANY combines with another organization that would create antitrust or other regulatory problems if the original, unwanted takeover proposal was consummated. *See also* SAFE HARBOR.
(4) STAGGERED BOARD OF DIRECTORS, a way to make it more difficult for a corporate RAIDER to install a majority of directors sympathetic to his or her views.
(5) supermajority provision, which might increase from a simple majority to two-thirds or three-fourths the shareholder vote required to ratify a takeover by an outsider.
See also POISON PILL; SCORCHED-EARTH POLICY.

SHARK WATCHER firm specializing in the early detection of TAKEOVER activity. Such a firm, whose primary business is usually the solicitation of proxies for client corporations, monitors trading patterns in a client's stock and attempts to determine the identity of parties accumulating shares.

SHARPE RATIO average return, less the RISK-FREE RETURN, divided by the STANDARD DEVIATION of return. The ratio measures the relationship of reward to risk in an investment strategy. The higher the ratio, the safer the strategy.

SHELF REGISTRATION term used for SECURITIES AND EXCHANGE COMMISSION RULE 415 adopted in the 1980s, which allows a corporation to comply with REGISTRATION requirements up to two years prior to a PUBLIC OFFERING of securities. With the registration on the shelf, the corporation, by simply updating regularly filed annual, quarterly, and related reports to the SEC, can go to the market as conditions become favorable with a minimum of administrative preparation. The flexibility corporate issuers enjoy as the result of shelf registration translates into substantial savings of time and expense.

SHELL CORPORATION company that is incorporated but has no significant assets or operations. Such corporations may be formed to obtain financing prior to starting operations, in which case an investment in them is highly risky. The term is also used of corporations set up by fraudulent operators as fronts to conceal tax evasion schemes.

SHENZHEN STOCK EXCHANGE (SZSE) opened in July 1991 in the Shenzhen province of China. The exchange levies a fee on new listings, which is set aside in a fund used by exchange officials to even out price fluctuations; organization and structure are similar to the SHANGHAI SECURITIES EXCHANGE (SHSE).

SHERMAN ANTITRUST ACT OF 1890 *see* ANTITRUST LAWS.

SHOCK ABSORBERS *see* CIRCUIT BREAKERS.

SHOGUN SECURITY security issued and distributed exclusively in Japan by a non-Japanese company and denominated in a currency other than yen.

SHOP
1. area of a business location where production takes place, as distinguished from the office or warehouse areas.
2. factory work force of an employer, as in a "union shop."
3. office of a broker-dealer in securities.
4. the act of canvassing dealers for the most favorable price, as in shopping securities dealers for the best bid or offer.
5. a small retail establishment.

SHORT AGAINST THE BOX *see* SELLING SHORT AGAINST THE BOX.

SHORT BOND
1. bond with a short maturity; a somewhat subjective concept, but generally meaning two years or less. *See also* SHORT TERM.
2. bond repayable in one year or less and thus classified as a CURRENT LIABILITY in accordance with the accounting definition of SHORT-TERM DEBT.
3. SHORT COUPON bond.

SHORT COUPON
1. bond interest payment covering less than the conventional six-month period. A short coupon payment occurs when the original issue date is less than a half year from the first scheduled interest payment date. Depending on how short the coupon is, the ACCRUED INTEREST makes a difference in the value of the bond at the time of issue, which is reflected in the offering price.
2. bond with a relatively short maturity, usually two years or less.
   See also LONG COUPON.

SHORT COVERING actual purchase of securities by a short seller to replace those borrowed at the time of a short sale. *See also* LENDING SECURITIES; SELLING SHORT.

SHORTFALL amount by which a financial objective has not been met. For example, a municipality expecting $100 million in tax revenue will say there is a $10 million shortfall if it collects only $90 million. For individual investors, a shortfall is the amount by which investment objectives have not been reached. For instance, investors execting to earn 15% a year will have a 5% shortfall if they earn 10% a year.

SHORT HEDGE transaction that limits or eliminates the risk of declining value in a security or commodity without entailing ownership.
Examples:
(1) SELLING SHORT AGAINST THE BOX leaves the owned securities untouched, possibly to gain in value, while protecting against a decline in value, since that would be offset by a profit on the short sale.
(2) purchasing a PUT OPTION to protect the value of a security that is owned limits loss to the cost of the option.
(3) buying a futures contract on raw materials at a specific price protects a manufacturer committed to sell a product at a certain price at a specified future time but who cannot buy the raw materials at the time of the commitment. Thus, if the price of the materials goes up, the manufacturer makes a profit on the contract; if the price goes down, he or she makes a profit on the product.
Compare with LONG HEDGE.

SHORT INTEREST total amount of shares of stock that have been sold short and have not yet been repurchased to close out SHORT POSITIONS. The short interest figure for the New York Stock Exchange, which is published monthly in newspapers, indicates how many investors think stock prices are about to fall. The Exchange reports all issues in which there are at least 5000 shares sold short, and in which the short interest position had changed by at least 2000 shares in the preceding month. The higher the short interest, the more people are expecting a downturn. Such short interest also represents potential buying pressure, however, since all short sales must eventually be covered by the purchase of shares. For this reason, a high short interest position is viewed as a bullish sign by many sophisticated market watchers. *See also* SELLING SHORT; SHORT INTEREST THEORY.

SHORT INTEREST THEORY theory that a large SHORT INTEREST in a stock presages a rise in the market price. It is based on the reasoning that even though short selling reflects a belief that prices will decline, the fact that short positions must eventually be covered is a source of upward price pressure. It is also called the CUSHION THEORY, since short sales can be viewed as a cushion of imminent buy orders. *See also* MEMBER SHORT-SALE RATIO; ODD-LOT SHORT-SALE RATIO; SELLING SHORT; SPECIALIST'S SHORT-SALE RATIO.

SHORT POSITION
Commodities: contract in which a trader has agreed to sell a commodity at a future date for a specific price.
Stocks: stock shares that an individual has sold short (by delivery of borrowed certificates) and has not covered as of a particular date. *See also* COVER; SELLING SHORT.

SHORT SALE *see* SELLING SHORT.

SHORT-SALE RULE Securities and Exchange Commission rule requiring that short sales be made only in a rising market; also called PLUS TICK rule. A short sale can be transacted only under these conditions: (1) if the last sale was at a higher price than the sale preceding it (called an UPTICK or PLUS TICK); (2) if the last sale price is unchanged but higher than the last preceding different sale (called a ZERO-PLUS TICK). The short-sale rule was designed to prevent abuses perpetuated by so-called pool operators, who would drive down the price of a stock by heavy short selling, then pick up the shares for a large profit.

SHORT-SHORT TEST Internal Revenue Service restriction on a regulated investment company limiting profits from short-term trading to 30% of gross income. Sometimes also called *short-3* test because the rule defines *short-term* as a holding period under three months. Excessive short-term trading could cause a mutual fund to lose its right not to pay taxes at the fund level. The short-short rule was repealed in the TAXPAYER RELIEF ACT OF 1997, freeing up managers of mutual funds to trade frequently without fear of losing their tax pass-through status.

SHORT SQUEEZE situation when prices of a stock or commodity futures contract start to move up sharply and many traders with short positions are forced to buy stocks or commodities in order to COVER their positions and prevent losses. This sudden surge of buying leads to even higher prices, further aggravating the losses of short sellers who have not covered their positions. *See also* SELLING SHORT.

SHORT TENDER using borrowed stock to respond to a TENDER OFFER. The practice is prohibited by SECURITIES AND EXCHANGE COMMISSION RULE 10b-4.

SHORT TERM
Accounting: assets expected to be converted into cash within the normal operating cycle (usually one year), or liabilities coming due in one year or less. *See also* CURRENT ASSETS; CURRENT LIABILITY.

Investment: investment with a maturity of one year or less. This includes bonds, although in differentiating between short-, medium-, and long-term bonds, short-term often is stretched to mean two years or less. *See also* SHORT-TERM BOND FUND; SHORT-TERM DEBT; SHORT-TERM GAIN (OR LOSS).

Taxes: HOLDING PERIOD of less than 12 months, used to differentiate SHORT-TERM GAIN (OR LOSS) from LONG-TERM GAIN or LONG-TERM LOSS. *See also* CAPITAL GAINS TAX.

SHORT-TERM BOND FUND bond mutual fund investing in short-to-intermediate term bonds. Such bonds, maturing in three to five years, typically pay higher yields than the shortest maturity bonds of one year or less, which are held by ULTRA-SHORT-TERM BOND FUND. Short-term bond funds also usually pay higher yields than money market mutual funds, which buy short-term commercial paper maturing in 90 days or less. However, short-term bond funds usually yield less than long-term bond funds holding bonds maturing in 10 to 30 years. Short-term bond funds, while yielding less than long-term bond funds, are also considerably less volatile, meaning that their value falls less when interest rates rise and rises less when interest rates fall. Many short-term bond funds offer checkwriting privileges, making them a source of easy liquidity. However, shareholders should remember than such checks will likely result in the realization of short- or long-term capital gains or losses.

SHORT-TERM DEBT all debt obligations coming due within one year; shown on a balance sheet as current liabilities. *See also* CURRENT LIABILITY.

SHORT-TERM GAIN (OR LOSS) for tax purposes, the profit or loss realized from the sale of securities or other capital assets held for less than 12 months. Short-term gains are taxable at ordinary income rates to the extent they are not reduced by offsetting capital losses. *See also* CAPITAL GAIN (OR LOSS).

SHORT-TERM INVESTMENT *see* SHORT TERM.

SHOW STOPPER legal barrier erected to prevent a takeover attempt from becoming successful. For example, a target company may appeal to the state legislature to pass laws preventing the takeover. Or the company may embark on a SCORCHED-EARTH POLICY, making the company unappealing to the suitor. *See also* SHARK REPELLENT.

SHRINKAGE difference between the amount of inventory recorded in a firm's books and the actual amount of inventory on hand. Shrinkage may occur because of theft, deterioration, loss, clerical error, and other factors.

SIDE-BY-SIDE TRADING trading of a security and an OPTION on that security on the same exchange.

SIDEWAYS MARKET period in which prices trade within a narrow range, showing only small changes up or down. Also called HORIZONTAL PRICE MOVEMENT. *See also* FLAT MARKET.

SIGNATURE GUARANTEE written confirmation by a financial institution such as a bank or brokerage firm that a customer's signature is valid. The institution will compare a new signature from a customer with the signature on file. Transfer agents require signature guarantees when transferring stocks, bonds, mutual funds, or other securities from one party to another to ensure that the transactions are legitimate.

SIGNATURE LOAN unsecured loan requiring only the borrower's signature on a loan application. The lender agrees to make the loan because the borrower has good credit standing. Collateral is not required. Also known as a *good-faith loan* or *character loan*.

SIGNIFICANT INFLUENCE holding of a large enough equity stake in a corporation to require accounting for it in financial statements. Usually, a company that holds at least 20% of the voting stock in another company is considered a holder of significant influence. A company with such a large holding is likely represented on the board of directors of the other firm. The company owning such a stake has to declare its equity holdings, and all dividends received from the position, in its financial reports.

SIGNIFICANT ORDER order to buy or sell securities that is significant enough to affect the price of the security. Many institutional investors, such as mutual funds, will try to spread out their significant buying or selling of a particular security over several days or weeks so they do not adversely affect the price at which they buy or sell.

SIGNIFICANT ORDER IMBALANCE large number of buy or sell orders for a stock, causing an unusually wide spread between bid and offer prices. Stock exchanges frequently halt trading of a stock with a significant order imbalance until more buyers or sellers appear and an orderly market can be reestablished. A significant order imbalance on the buying side can occur when there is an announcement of an impending takeover of the company, better-than-expected earnings, or other unexpected positive news. A significant order imbalance on the selling side can occur when a takeover offer has fallen through, a key executive has left the company, earnings came in far worse than expected, or there is other unexpected negative news.

SILENT PARTNER
1. limited partner in a DIRECT PARTICIPATION PROGRAM, such as real estate and oil and gas limited partnerships, in which CASH FLOW and tax benefits are passed directly through to shareholders. Such partners are called silent because, unlike general partners, they have no direct role in management and no liability beyond their individual investment.
2. general partner in a business who has no role in management but represents a sharing of the investment and liability. Silent partners of this type are often found in family businesses, where the intent is to distribute tax liability.
   See also LIMITED PARTNERSHIP.

SILVER THURSDAY the day—March 27, 1980—when the extremely wealthy Hunt brothers of Texas failed to meet a MARGIN CALL by the brokerage firm of Bache Halsey Stuart Shields (which later became Prudential-Bache Securities) for $100 million in silver futures contracts. Their position was later covered and Bache survived, but the effects on the commodities markets and the financial markets in general were traumatic.

SIMPLE INTEREST interest calculation based only on the original principal amount. Simple interest contrasts with COMPOUND INTEREST, which is applied to principal plus accumulated interest. For example, $100 on deposit at 12% simple interest would yield $12 per year (12% of $100). The same $100 at 12% interest compounded annually would yield $12 interest only in the first year. The second year's interest would be 12% of the first year's accumulated interest and principal of $112, or $13.44. The third year's payment would be 12% of $125.44—the second year's principal plus interest—or $15.05. For computing interest on loans, simple interest is distinguished from various methods of calculating interest on a precomputed basis. *See also* PRECOMPUTE; CONSUMER CREDIT PROTECTION ACT OF 1968.

SIMPLE IRA form of SALARY REDUCTION PLAN that qualifying small employers may offer to their employees. Employers with no more than 100 employees earning

$5,000 or more in a year who do not offer any other retirement plan can offer simple IRAs. Self-employed workers also are eligible to establish such accounts.

Workers offered a simple IRA may contribute up to $6,000 per year into the account. This $6,000 limit is adjusted for inflation by the IRS annually. Employee contributions are excluded from taxable pay on Form W-2 and are not subject to income tax withholding, although Social Security taxes are paid on those earnings. While the employer may pick the financial institution in which to deposit the simple IRA funds, employees have the right to transfer the funds to another financial institution of their choice without cost or penalty.

Employers must make either a matching contribution or a fixed "non-elective" contribution to their employees' accounts each year. If the employer chooses matching contributes, the employer must match the amount the employee contributes from a minimum of 1% to a maximum of 3%. There is no limit on the amount of compensation that can be matched, as long as the total amount of salary reduction in one year is no more than $6,000.

If the employer chooses to make a "non-elective" contribution instead, it must equal 2% of each employee's compensation per year. It must make the contribution for all employees, whether or not they contribute part of their pay to the plan. The maximum amount of compensation on which this 2% contribution can be made is $160,000, meaning a total contribution of $3,200 (2% of $160,000).

Distributions from simple IRAs follow the same rules as regular IRAs, with one exception. If premature distributions are taken before the employee reaches age 59½ and during the first two years after the employee starts participating in the plan, the penalty is 25%, not the usual 10%. After the first two years, the regular 10% penalty applies to pre-age 59½ withdrawals. Withdrawals taken after age 59½ are fully taxable at regular income tax rates, and mandatory withdrawals must begin at age 70½, according to IRS life expectancy tables.

Assets inside simple IRAs can be invested like any other IRAs, in stocks, bonds, mutual funds, bank deposits, annuities or precious metals.

The simple IRA replaced the Salary Reduction Simplified Employee Pension plan (known as SARSEP) in 1997. SARSEPs may be continued only by employers who established them before 1997. *See also* SIMPLIFIED EMPLOYEE PENSION (SEP) PLAN.

SIMPLE RATE OF RETURN rate of return that results from dividing the income and capital gains from an investment by the amount of capital invested. For example, if a $1000 investment produced $50 in income and $50 in capital appreciation in one year, the investment would have a 10% simple rate of return. This method of calculation does not factor in the effects of compounding.

SIMPLIFIED EMPLOYEE PENSION (SEP) PLAN pension plan in which both the employee and the employer contribute to an INDIVIDUAL RETIREMENT ACCOUNT (IRA). Under the TAX REFORM ACT OF 1986, employees (except those participating in SEPs of state or local governments) may elect to have employer contributions made to the SEP or paid to the employee in cash as with cash or deferred arrangements (401(k) PLANS). Elective contributions, which are excludable from earnings for income tax purposes but includable for employment tax (FICA and FUTA) purposes, are limited to 13.0435% of net wages up to a certain maximum, which was $160,000 in 1998. Employer contributions are limited to 15% of compensation, subject to the same limits. The total maximum contribution by employees and employers combined is $30,000 per year. SEPs are limited to small employers (25 or fewer employees) and at least 50% of employees must participate. Special provisions pertain to self-employed persons, the integration of SEP contributions and Social Security benefits and limitations on tax deferrals for highly compensated individuals.

SINGLE-COUNTRY MUTUAL FUNDS mutual funds investing in the securities of just one country. Such funds may be open-end, meaning they continue to create new shares as more money comes into the fund, or closed-end, meaning they issue a limited number of shares which then trade on the stock exchange at a premium or discount to net asset value. Single-country funds offer investors a PURE PLAY on the fortunes of securities in that country. This means that these funds typically are far more volatile than REGIONAL MUTUAL FUNDS holding securities in a wider region, or GLOBAL MUTUAL FUNDS investing in markets around the world. There are many single-country funds, including funds for Argentina, Australia, Canada, China, France, Germany, Israel, Japan, Korea, Mexico, Spain, Switzerland, and the United Kingdom.

SINGLE OPTION term used to distinguish a PUT OPTION or a CALL OPTION from a SPREAD or a STRADDLE, each of which involves two or more put or call options. *See also* OPTION.

SINGLE-PREMIUM DEFERRED ANNUITY (SPDA) tax-deferred investment similar to an INDIVIDUAL RETIREMENT ACCOUNT, without many of the IRA restrictions. An investor makes a lump-sum payment to an insurance company or mutual fund selling the annuity. That lump sum can be invested in either a fixed-return instrument like a CD or a variable-return portfolio that can be switched among stocks, bonds, and money-market accounts. Proceeds are taxed only when distributions are taken. In contrast to an IRA, there is no limit to the amount that may be invested in an SPDA. Like the IRA, the tax penalty for withdrawals before age 59½ is 10%.

SINGLE-PREMIUM LIFE INSURANCE WHOLE LIFE INSURANCE policy requiring one premium payment. Since this large, up-front payment begins accumulating cash value immediately, the policy holder will earn more than holders of policies paid up in installments. With its tax-free appreciation (assuming it remains in force); low or no net-cost; tax-free access to funds through POLICY LOANS; and tax-free proceeds to beneficiaries, this type of policy emerged as a popular TAX SHELTER under the TAX REFORM ACT OF 1986.

SINGLE-STATE MUNICIPAL BOND FUND MUTUAL FUND that invests entirely in tax-exempt obligations of governments and government agencies within a single state. Therefore, dividends paid on fund shares are not taxable to residents of that state when they file state tax returns although capital gains, if any, are taxable.

SINKER bond on which interest and principal payments are made from the proceeds of a SINKING FUND.

SINKING FUND money accumulated on a regular basis in a separate custodial account that is used to redeem debt securities or preferred stock issues. A bond indenture or preferred stock charter may specify that payments be made to a sinking fund, thus assuring investors that the issues are safer than bonds (or preferred stocks) for which the issuer must make payment all at once, without the benefit of a sinking fund. *See also* PURCHASE FUND.

SIZE
1. number of shares or bonds available for sale. A market maker will say, when asked for a quote, that a particular number of shares (the size) is available at a particular price.
2. term used when a large number of shares are for sale—a trader will say that "shares are available in size," for instance.

SKIP-PAYMENT PRIVILEGE
1. clause in some MORTGAGE contracts and installment loan agreements allowing borrowers to miss payments if ahead of schedule.

2. option offered some bank credit-card holders whereby they may defer the December payment on balances due.

SLD LAST SALE indication, meaning "sold last sale," that appears on the CON-SOLIDATED TAPE when a greater than normal change occurs between transactions in a security. The designation, which appears after the STOCK SYMBOL, is normally used when the change is a point or more on lower-priced issues (below $20) or two points or more on higher-priced issues.

SLEEPER stock in which there is little investor interest but which has significant potential to gain in price once its attractions are recognized. Sleepers are most easily recognized in retrospect, after they have already moved up in price.

SLEEPING BEAUTY potential TAKEOVER target that has not yet been approached by an acquirer. Such a company usually has particularly attractive features, such as a large amount of cash, or undervalued real estate or other assets.

SLUMP short-term drop in performance. The economy may enter a slump when it goes into a RECESSION. An individual stock or mutual fund may be in a slump if its price falls over several weeks or months. A normally productive employee may go into a slump and be less productive if he or she is having financial or emotional difficulties. A slump is considered to be a temporary phenomenon, from which the economy, investment or employee will soon recover.

SMALL BUSINESS ADMINISTRATION (SBA) federal agency created in 1953 to provide financial assistance (through direct loans and loan guarantees) as well as management assistance to businesses that lack the access to CAPITAL MARKETS enjoyed by larger more creditworthy corporations. Further legislation authorized the SBA to contribute to the VENTURE CAPITAL requirements of START-UP companies by licensing and funding small business investment companies (SBICs), to maintain a loan fund for rehabilitation of property damaged by natural disasters (floods, hurricanes, etc.), and to provide loans, counseling and training for small businesses owned by minorities, the economically disadvantaged, and the disabled.

The SBA finances its activities through direct grants approved by Congress.

SMALL CAP shorthand for *small capitalization stocks* or mutual funds holding such stocks. Small cap stocks usually have a market capitalization (number of shares outstanding multiplied by the stock price) of $500 million or less. Those under $50 million in market cap are known as *microcap issues.* Small capitalization stocks represent companies that are less well established, but in many cases faster-growing than *mid-cap stocks* (from $500 million to $3 billion–$5 billion) or *large cap stocks* ($1 billion or more). (Ranges vary somewhat and may overlap, depending on the funds or indexer defining them.) Since they are less established, small cap stocks are usually more volatile than BLUE CHIPS.

SMALL FIRM EFFECT tendency of stocks of smaller firms, defined by MARKET CAPITALIZATION, to outperform larger firms. Theories to explain this phenomenon vary, but include the following: (1) smaller companies tend to have more growth potential; (2) small capitalization groupings include more companies in financial difficulty; when fortunes recover, price gains are dramatic and lift the return of the group as a whole; (3) small firms are generally neglected by analysts and hence by institutions; once discovered, they become appropriately valued, registering dramatic gains in the process. The term is also used to describe the tendency of lower priced stocks to rise or fall in greater percentage increments than higher priced shares, market capitalization, and other factors being equal. *See also* ANKLE BITER.

SMALL INVESTOR individual investor who buys small amounts of stock or bonds, often in ODD LOT quantities; also called the RETAIL INVESTOR. Although there are millions of small investors, their total holdings are dwarfed by the share ownership of large institutions such as mutual funds and insurance companies. Together with the proliferation of mutual funds, recent developments in the brokerage industry and its diversification along full-service lines have brought new programs specifically designed to make investing more convenient for small investors. Thus, much cash traditionally kept in savings banks has found its way into the stock and bond markets. *See also* ODD-LOT SHORT-SALE RATIO; ODD-LOT THEORY.

SMALL ORDER ENTRY (OR EXECUTION) SYSTEM *see* SOES.

SMART MONEY investors who make profitable investment moves at the right time, no matter what the investing environment. In a bull market, such investors buy the stocks that go up the most. In bear markets, they sell stocks short that fall the most. Smart money investors also have access to information about companies, either positive or negative, in advance of when the typical small investor learns of it. The term is also used in a more general sense to convey what sophisticated investors are doing now. Analysts will say "the smart money is buying cyclical stocks now because the economy is improving," for example.

SMOKESTACK INDUSTRIES basic manufacturing industries, such as autos, chemicals, steel, paper, and rubber, which typically have smokestacks on their plants. The fate of these industries, when viewed by Wall Street analysts, is closely tied to the ups and downs of the economy—they are therefore called CYCLICAL stocks. Many smokestack industries are located in what is known as the RUST BELT.

SNOWBALLING process by which the activation of STOP ORDERS in a declining or advancing market causes further downward or upward pressure on prices, thus triggering more stop orders and more price pressure, and so on.

SOCIALLY CONSCIOUS MUTUAL FUND mutual fund that is managed for capital appreciation while at the same time investing in securities of companies that do not conflict with certain social priorities. As a product of the social consciousness movements of the 1960s and 1970s, this type of mutual fund might not invest in companies that derive significant profits from defense contracts or whose activities cause environmental pollution, nor in companies with significant interests in countries with repressive or racist governments.

SOCIAL SECURITY benefits provided under the Social Security Act (1935), financed by the SOCIAL SECURITY TAX authorized by the FEDERAL INSURANCE CONTRIBUTORS ACT (FICA), and administered by the Social Security Administration. Term usually refers to retirement income benefits, but other benefits include SOCIAL SECURITY DISABILITY INCOME INSURANCE; Aid to Families with Dependent Children (AFDC); the Food Stamp program; Unemployment Insurance; Medicare; Medicaid; Public Assistance for the Aged, Blind and Disabled; Veterans' Compensation and Pensions; Housing Subsidies and Public Housing; Nutritional Programs for Children; and Student Aid.

SOCIAL RESPONSIBILITY principle that businesses should actively contribute to the welfare of society and not only maximize profits. Most corporate annual reports will highlight what the company has done to further education, help minorities, give to the arts and social welfare agencies, and in general improve social conditions. The concept is also used by investors in picking companies that are fair to their employees, do not pollute or build weapons, and make beneficial products. *See also* SOCIALLY CONSCIOUS MUTUAL FUND.

SOCIAL SECURITY DISABILITY INCOME INSURANCE insurance financed by the SOCIAL SECURITY TAX that provides lost income to qualifying employees whose disabilities are expected to last at least one year. Benefits are payable until death.

SOCIAL SECURITY TAX federal tax created by the Social Security Act (1935) that is shared equally by employers and their employees, is levied on annual income up to a maximum level, and is invested in Social Security trust funds. Employees then qualify for retirement benefits based on years worked, amounts paid into the fund, and retirement age.

SOES acronym for the computerized *Small Order Entry (or Execution) System* used by NASDAQ, in which orders for under 1000 shares bypass brokers and are aggregated and executed against available firm quotes by market makers on the NASDAQ system. *See also* ORDER SPLITTING.

SOCIALISM political-economic doctrine that, unlike CAPITALISM, which is based on competition, seeks a cooperative society in which the means of production and distribution are owned by the government or collectively by the people.

SOFT CURRENCY funds of a country that are not acceptable in exchange for the hard currencies of other countries. Soft currencies, such as Russia's ruble, are fixed at unrealistic exchange rates and are not backed by gold, so that countries with hard currencies, like U.S. dollars or British pounds, are reluctant to convert assets into them. *See also* HARD MONEY (HARD CURRENCY).

SOFT DOLLARS means of paying brokerage firms for their services through commission revenue, rather than through direct payments, known as *hard-dollar fees.* For example, a mutual fund may offer to pay for the research of a brokerage firm by executing trades generated by that research through that brokerage firm. The broker might agree to this arrangement if the fund manager promises to spend at least $100,000 in commissions with the broker that year. Otherwise, the fund would have to pay a hard-dollar fee of $50,000 for the research. *Compare with* HARD DOLLARS.

SOFT LANDING term used to describe a rate of growth sufficient to avoid recession but slow enough to prevent high inflation and interest rates. When the economy is growing very strongly, the Federal Reserve typically tries to engineer a soft landing by raising interest rates to head off inflation. If the economy threatens to fall into a recession, the Fed may lower rates to stimulate growth.

SOFT MARKET market characterized by an excess of supply over demand. A soft market in securities is marked by inactive trading, wide bid-offer spreads, and pronounced price drops in response to minimal selling pressure. Also called *buyer's market.*

SOFTS term used to refer to tropical commodities—coffee, sugar, and cocoa—but in a broader sense could include grains, oilseeds, cotton, and orange juice. Metals, financial futures, and livestock generally are excluded from this category.

SOFT SPOT weakness in selected stocks or stock groups in the face of a generally strong and advancing market.

SOLD-OUT MARKET commodities market term meaning that futures contracts in a particular commodity or maturity range are largely unavailable because of contract liquidations and limited offerings.

SOLVENCY state of being able to meet maturing obligations as they come due. See *also* INSOLVENCY.

SOUR BOND bond in DEFAULT on its interest or principal payments. The issue will typically trade at a deep discount and have a low credit rating. Traders say that the bond has "gone sour" when it defaults.

SOURCES AND APPLICATIONS (or USES) OF FUNDS STATEMENT
financial statement section that analyzed changes affecting WORKING CAPITAL (or, optionally, cash) and that appeared as part of the annual reports of the publicly held companies prior to 1988. In that year, the Financial Accounting Standards Board (FASB) supplanted this statement with the STATEMENT OF CASH FLOWS, which analyzes all changes affecting cash in the categories of operations, investment, and financing.

SOUTH AFRICAN FUTURES EXCHANGE (SAFEX) trades futures and options on the Johannesburg Stock Exchange's All Share Index, All Gold Index, Financial Industrial Index and Industrial Index, as well as the KRUGGERAND, long-term bond, and short-term interest. Trading is electronic.

SOVEREIGN RISK risk that a foreign government will default on its loan or fail to honor other business commitments because of a change in national policy. A country asserting its prerogatives as an independent nation might prevent the REPATRIATION of a company or country's funds through limits on the flow of capital, tax impediments, or the nationalization of property. Sovereign risk became a factor in the growth of international debt that followed the oil price increases of the 1970s. Several developing countries that borrowed heavily from Western banks to finance trade deficits had difficulty later keeping to repayment schedules. Banks had to reschedule loans to such countries as Mexico and Argentina to keep them from defaulting. These loans ran the further risk of renunciation by political leaders, which also would have affected loans to private companies that had been guaranteed by previous governments. Beginning in the 1970s, banks and other multinational corporations developed sophisticated analytical tools to measure sovereign risk before committing to lend, invest, or begin operations in a given foreign country. Throughout periods of worldwide economic volatility, the United States has been able to attract foreign investment because of its perceived lack of sovereign risk. Also called *country risk* or *political risk.*

SPDR acronym for *Standard & Poor's Depositary Receipt,* traded on the American Stock Exchange under the ticker symbol "SPY." Called *spiders,* they are securities that represent ownership in a long-term UNIT INVESTMENT TRUST that holds a portfolio of common stocks designed to track the performance of the S&P 500 INDEX. A SPDR entitles a holder to receive proportionate quarterly cash distributions corresponding to the dividends that accrue to the S&P 500 stocks in the underlying portfolio, less trust expenses. Like a stock, SPDRs can be traded continuously throughout the trading day, or can be held for the long-term. In contrast, S&P 500 index mutual funds are priced only once, at the end of each trading day. Amex also trades MidCap SPDRs, which track the S&P MidCap 400 index. *See also* DIAMONDS.

SPECIAL ARBITRAGE ACCOUNT special MARGIN ACCOUNT with a broker reserved for transactions in which the customer's risk is hedged by an offsetting security transaction or position. The MARGIN REQUIREMENT on such a transaction is substantially less than in the case of stocks bought on credit and subject to price declines. *See also* HEDGE/HEDGING.

SPECIAL ASSESSMENT BOND municipal bond that is repaid from taxes imposed on those who benefit directly from the neighborhood-oriented public works project funded by the bond; also called *special assessment limited liability bond, special district bond, special purpose bond,* SPECIAL TAX BOND. For example, if a bond finances the construction of a sewer system, the homeowners and businesses hooked up to the sewer system pay a special levy that goes to repay the bonds. The interest from special assessment bonds is tax free to resident bondholders. These are not normally GENERAL OBLIGATION BONDS, and the

FULL FAITH AND CREDIT of the municipality is not usually behind them. Where the full faith and credit does back such bonds, they are called general obligation special assessment bonds.

SPECIAL BID infrequently used method of purchasing a large block of stock on the New York Stock Exchange whereby a MEMBER FIRM, acting as a broker, matches the buy order of one client, usually an institution, with sell orders solicited from a number of other customers. It is the reverse of an EXCHANGE DISTRIBUTION. The member broker makes a fixed price offer, which is announced in advance on the CONSOLIDATED TAPE. The bid cannot be lower than the last sale or the current regular market bid. Sellers of the stock pay no commissions; the buying customer pays both the selling and buying commissions. The transaction is completed during regular trading hours.

SPECIAL BOND ACCOUNT special MARGIN ACCOUNT with a broker that is reserved for transactions in U.S. government bonds, municipals, and eligible listed and unlisted nonconvertible corporate bonds. The restrictions under which brokers may extend credit with margin securities of these types are generally more liberal than in the case of stocks.

SPECIAL CASH ACCOUNT same as CASH ACCOUNT.

SPECIAL DISTRICT BOND *see* SPECIAL ASSESSMENT BOND.

SPECIAL DRAWING RIGHTS (SDR) measure of a nation's reserve assets in the international monetary system; known informally as "paper gold." First issued by the INTERNATIONAL MONETARY FUND (IMF) in 1970, SDRs are designed to supplement the reserves of gold and convertible currencies (or hard currencies) used to maintain stability in the foreign exchange market. For example, if the U.S. Treasury sees that the British pound's value has fallen precipitously in relation to the dollar, it can use its store of SDRs to buy excess pounds on the foreign exchange market, thereby raising the value of the remaining supply of pounds.

This neutral unit of account was made necessary by the rapid growth in world trade during the 1960s. International monetary officials feared that the supply of the two principal reserve assets—gold and U.S. dollars—would fall short of demand, causing the value of the U.S. currency to rise disproportionately in relation to other reserve assets. (At the time SDRs were introduced, the price of gold was fixed at about $35 per ounce.)

The IMF allocates to each of its more than 140 member countries an amount of SDRs proportional to its predetermined quota in the fund, which in turn is based on its GROSS NATIONAL PRODUCT (GNP). Each member agrees to back its SDRs with the full faith and credit of its government, and to accept them in exchange for gold or convertible currencies.

Originally, the value of one SDR was fixed at one dollar and at the dollar equivalent of other key currencies on January 1, 1970. As world governments adopted the current system of FLOATING EXCHANGE RATES, the SDR's value fluctuated relative to the "basket" of major currencies. Increasing reliance on SDRs in settling international accounts coincided with a decline in the importance of gold as a reserve asset.

Because of its inherent equilibrium relative to any one currency, the SDR has been used to denominate or calculate the value of private contracts, international treaties, and securities on the EUROBOND market.

See also EUROPEAN CURRENCY UNIT (ECU).

SPECIALIST member of a stock exchange who maintains a fair and orderly market in one or more securities. A specialist or SPECIALIST UNIT performs two main functions: executing LIMIT ORDERS on behalf of other exchange members for a portion of the FLOOR BROKER'S commission, and buying or selling—sometimes SELLING SHORT—for the specialist's own account to counteract temporary imbalances in supply and demand and thus prevent wide swings in stock prices. The specialist is prohibited by exchange rules from buying for his own account when there is an unexecuted order for the same security at the same price in the SPECIALIST'S BOOK, the record kept of limit orders in each price category in the sequence in which they are received. Specialists must meet strict minimum capital requirements before receiving formal approval by the New York Stock Exchange. *See also* SPECIALIST BLOCK PURCHASE AND SALE; SPECIALIST'S SHORT-SALE RATIO.

SPECIALIST BLOCK PURCHASE AND SALE transaction whereby a SPECIALIST on a stock exchange buys a large block of securities either to sell for his own account or to try and place with another block buyer and seller, such as a FLOOR TRADER. Exchange rules require that such transactions be executed only when the securities cannot be ABSORBED in the regular market. *See also* NOT HELD.

SPECIALIST'S BOOK record maintained by a SPECIALIST that includes the specialist's own inventory of securities, market orders to sell short, and LIMIT ORDERS and STOP ORDERS that other stock exchange members have placed with the specialist. The orders are listed in chronological sequence. For example, for a stock trading at 57 a broker might ask for 500 shares when the price falls to 55. If successful at placing this limit order, the specialist notifies the member broker who entered the request, and collects a commission. The specialist is prohibited from buying the stock for his own account at a price for which he has previously agreed to execute a limit order.

SPECIALIST'S SHORT-SALE RATIO ratio of the amount of stock sold short by specialists on the floor of the New York Stock Exchange to total short sales. The ratio signals whether specialists are more or less bearish (expecting prices to decline) on the outlook for stock prices than other NYSE members and the public. Since specialists must constantly be selling stock short in order to provide for an orderly market in the stocks they trade, their short sales cannot be entirely regarded as an indication of how they perceive trends. Still, their overall short sales activity reflects knowledge, and technical analysts watch the specialist's short-sale ratio carefully for a clue to imminent upturns or downturns in stock prices. Traditionally, when the ratio rises above 60%, it is considered a bearish signal. A drop below 45% is seen as bullish and below 35% is considered extremely bullish. *See also* ODD-LOT SHORT-SALE RATIO; SELLING SHORT; SPECIALIST.

SPECIALIST UNIT stock exchange SPECIALIST (individual, partnership, corporation, or group of two or three firms) authorized by an exchange to deal as PRINCIPAL and AGENT for other brokers in maintaining a stable market in one or more particular stocks. A specialist unit on the New York Stock Exchange is required to have enough capital to buy at least 5000 shares of the common stock of a company it handles and 1000 shares of the company's CONVERTIBLE preferred stock.

SPECIALIZED MUTUAL FUND mutual fund concentrating on one industry. By so doing, shareholders have a PURE PLAY on the fortunes of that industry, for better or worse. Some of the many industries with specialized mutual funds include banking, biotechnology, chemicals, energy, environmental services, natural resources, precious metals, technology, telecommunications, and utilities. These funds tend to be more volatile than funds holding a diversified portfolio of stocks in many industries. Also called *sector funds* or *specialty funds*.

SPECIAL MISCELLANEOUS ACCOUNT (SMA) memorandum account of the funds in excess of the MARGIN REQUIREMENT. Such excess funds may arise from the proceeds of sales, appreciation of market values, dividends, or cash or securities put up in response to a MARGIN CALL. An SMA is not under the jurisdiction of REGULATION T of the Federal Reserve Board, as is the INITIAL MARGIN requirement, but this does not mean the customer is free to withdraw balances from it. The account is maintained essentially so that the broker can gauge how far the customer might be from a margin call. Any withdrawals require the broker's permission.

SPECIAL OFFERING method of selling a large block of stock that is similar to a SECONDARY DISTRIBUTION but is limited to New York Stock Exchange members and takes place during normal trading hours. The selling member announces the impending sale on the CONSOLIDATED TAPE, indicating a fixed price, which is usually based on the last transaction price in the regular market. All costs and commissions are borne by the seller. The buyers are member firms that may be buying for customer accounts or for their own inventory. Such offerings must have approval from the Securities and Exchange Commission.

SPECIAL SITUATION
1. undervalued stock that should soon rise in value because of an imminent favorable turn of events. A special situation stock may be about to introduce a revolutionary new product or be undergoing a needed management change. Many securities analysts concentrate on looking for and analyzing special situation stocks.
2. stock that fluctuates widely in daily trading, often influencing market averages, because of a particular news development, such as the announcement of a TAKEOVER bid.

SPECIAL TAX BOND
1. MUNICIPAL REVENUE BOND that will be repaid through excise taxes on such purchases as gasoline, tobacco, and liquor. The bond is not backed by the ordinary taxing power of the municipality issuing it. The interest from these bonds is tax free to resident bondholders.
2. SPECIAL ASSESSMENT BOND.

SPECTAIL term for broker-dealer who is part retail broker but preponderantly dealer/speculator.

SPECULATION assumption of risk in anticipation of gain but recognizing a higher than average possibility of loss. Speculation is a necessary and productive activity. It can be profitable over the long term when engaged in by professionals, who often limit their losses through the use of various HEDGING techniques and devices, including OPTIONS trading, SELLING SHORT, STOP LOSS orders, and transactions in FUTURES CONTRACTS. The term speculation implies that a business or investment risk can be analyzed and measured, and its distinction from the term INVESTMENT is one of degree of risk. It differs from gambling, which is based on random outcomes.
   See also VENTURE CAPITAL.

SPECULATOR market participant who tries to profit from buying and selling futures and options contracts by anticipating future price movements. Speculators assume market price risk and add liquidity and capital to the futures markets. Speculators may purchase volatile stocks or mutual funds, and hold them for a short time in order to reap a profit. They may also sell stocks short and hope to cash in when the stock price drops quickly.

SPIDERS *see* SPDR.

SPIN-OFF form of corporate DIVESTITURE that results in a subsidiary or division becoming an independent company. In a traditional spin-off, shares in the new entity are distributed to the parent corporation's shareholders of record on a PRO RATA basis. Spin-offs can also be accomplished through a LEVERAGED BUYOUT by the subsidiary or division's management, or through an EMPLOYEE STOCK OWNERSHIP PLAN (ESOP).

SPINS acronym for *Standard & Poor's 500 Index Subordinated Notes,* as Salomon Brothers' product combining features of debt, equity, and options.

SPLIT increase in a corporation's number of outstanding shares of stock without any change in the shareholders' EQUITY or the aggregate MARKET VALUE at the time of the split. In a split, also called a *split up,* the share price declines. If a stock at $100 par value splits 2-for-1, the number of authorized shares doubles (for example, from 10 million to 20 million) and the price per share drops by half, to $50. A holder of 50 shares before the split now has 100 shares at the lower price. If the same stock splits 4-for-1, the number of shares quadruples to 40 million and the share price falls to $25. Dividends per share also fall proportionately. Directors of a corporation will authorize a split to make ownership more affordable to a broader base of investors. Where stock splits require an increase in AUTHORIZED SHARES and/or a change in PAR VALUE of the stock, shareholders must approve an amendment of the corporate charter.

    See also REVERSE SPLIT.

SPLIT COMMISSION commission divided between the securities broker who executes a trade and another person who brought the trade to the broker, such as an investment counselor or financial planner. Split commissions between brokers are also common in real estate transactions.

SPLIT COUPON BOND debt instrument that begins as a zero-coupon bond and converts to an interest-paying bond at a specified date in the future. These bonds, issued by corporations and municipalities, are advantageous to issuers because they do not have to pay out cash interest for several years. They are attractive to investors, particularly in tax-sheltered accounts like IRAs and Keoghs, because they have locked in a reinvestment rate for several years, and then can receive cash interest. For example, a 55-year-old investor may want a split coupon bond because it will appreciate in value for 10 years, and then pay interest when he is retired and needs regular income. Also known as ZERO-COUPON CONVERTIBLE SECURITY.

SPLIT DOWN *see* REVERSE SPLIT.

SPLIT OFFERING new municipal bond issue, part of which is represented by SERIAL BONDS and part by term maturity bonds.

SPLIT ORDER large transaction in securities that, to avoid unsettling the market and causing fluctuations in the market price, is broken down into smaller portions to be executed over a period of time.

SPLIT RATING situation in which two major rating agencies, such as Standard & Poor's and Moody's Investors Service, assign a different rating to the same security.

SPLIT UP *see* SPLIT.

SPONSOR

    Limited partnerships: GENERAL PARTNER who organizes and sells a LIMITED PARTNERSHIP. Sponsors (also called *promoters)* rely on their reputation in past real estate, oil and gas, or other deals to attract limited partners to their new deals.

Mutual funds: investment company that offers shares in its funds. Also called the *underwriter.*

Stocks: important investor—typically, an institution, mutual fund, or other big trader—whose favorable opinion of a particular security influences other investors and creates additional demand for the security. Institutional investors often want to make sure a stock has wide sponsorship before they invest in it, since this should ensure that the stock will not fall dramatically.

SPOT COMMODITY COMMODITY traded with the expectation that it will actually be delivered to the buyer, as contrasted to a FUTURES CONTRACT that will usually expire without any physical delivery taking place. Spot commodities are traded in the SPOT MARKET.

SPOT DELIVERY MONTH nearest month of those currently being traded in which a commodity could be delivered. In late January, therefore, the spot delivery month would be February for commodities with a February contract trade.

SPOT MARKET commodities market in which goods are sold for cash and delivered immediately. Trades that take place in FUTURES CONTRACTS expiring in the current month are also called *spot market trades.* The spot market tends to be conducted OVER THE COUNTER—that is, through telephone trading—rather than on the floor of an organized commodity exchange. Also called *actual market, cash market* or *physical market. See also* FUTURES MARKET.

SPOT PRICE current delivery price of a commodity traded in the SPOT MARKET. Also called *cash price.*

SPOUSAL IRA INDIVIDUAL RETIREMENT ACCOUNT that may be opened in the name of a nonworking spouse. The maximum annual IRA contribution for a married couple, only one of whom is employed, is $4000. The husband and wife can each contribute up to $2000, as long as their combined compensation is at least that much. Before 1997, the nonworking spouse could only contribute $250 to their IRA. The same rules apply ($2000 per person) when both spouses work. Contributions are deductible only if both husband and wife are not actively participating in a qualified retirement plan.

SPOUSAL REMAINDER TRUST means used prior to the TAX REFORM ACT OF 1986 to shift income to a person taxable at a lower rate. Income-producing property, such as securities, is transferred by the grantor to the trust for a specific time, typically five years. Trust income is distributed to the beneficiary (or to a minor's CUSTODIAL ACCOUNT) to be used for expenses such as a child's college education. The income is therefore taxed at the beneficiary's lower tax rate. When the trust term expires, the property passes irrevocably to the grantor's spouse. The TAX REFORM ACT OF 1986 provided that effective for trusts established or contributions to trusts made after March 1, 1986, income must be taxed at the grantor's tax rate if the beneficiary is under age 14 and the property can revert to the grantor or the grantor's spouse.

SPREAD

Commodities: in futures trading, the difference in price between delivery months in the same market, or between different or related contracts. *See also* MOB SPREAD; NOB SPREAD; TED SPREAD.

Fixed-income securities: (1) difference between yields on securities of the same quality but different maturities. For example, the spread between 6% short-term Treasury bills and 10% long-term Treasury bonds is 4 percentage points. (2) difference between yields on securities of the same maturity but different quality. For instance, the spread between a 10% long-term Treasury bond and a 14% long-term bond of a B-rated corporation is 4 percentage points, since an investor's risk of default is so much less with the Treasury bond. *See also* YIELD SPREAD.

Foreign exchange: spreading one currency versus another, or multiple spreads within various currencies. An example would be a long position in the U.S. dollar versus a short position in the Japanese yen or the Euro. An example of an intermonth spread would be a long March spot position in Swiss francs versus a short March position in the same currency. Spreads are frequently done in cash and futures markets. Interest rate differentials often have significant impact.

Options: position usually consisting of one long call and one short call option, or one long put and one short put option, with each option representing one "leg" of the spread. The two legs, if taken independently, would profit from opposite directional price movements. Spreads usually have lower cost and lower profit potential than an outright long option. They are entered into to reduce risk, or to profit from the change in the relative prices of the options. *See also* BEAR SPREAD; BULL SPREAD; BUTTERFLY SPREAD; CALENDAR SPREAD; CREDIT SPREAD; DEBIT SPREAD; DIAGONAL SPREAD; OPTION; PRICE SPREAD; SELLING THE SPREAD; VERTICAL SPREAD.

Stocks and bonds: (1) difference between the bid and offer price. If a stock is bid at $45 and offered at $46, the spread is $1. This spread narrows or widens according to supply and demand for the security being traded. *See also* BID-ASKED SPREAD; DEALER SPREAD. (2) difference between the high and low price of a particular security over a given period.

Underwriting: difference between the proceeds an issuer of a new security receives and the price paid by the public for the issue. This spread is taken by the underwriting syndicate as payment for its services. A security issued at $100 may entail a spread of $2 for the underwriter, so the issuer receives $98 from the offering. *See also* UNDERWRITING SPREAD.

SPREADING practice of buying and selling OPTION contracts of the same CLASS on the same underlying security in order to profit from moves in the price of that security. *See also* SPREAD.

SPREAD OPTION SPREAD position involving the purchase of an OPTION at one EXERCISE PRICE and the simultaneous sale of another option on the same underlying security at a different exercise price and/or expiration date. *See also* DIAGONAL SPREAD; HORIZONTAL SPREAD; VERTICAL SPREAD.

SPREAD ORDER OPTIONS market term for an order designating the SERIES of LISTED OPTIONS the customer wishes to buy and sell, together with the desired SPREAD—or difference in option premiums (prices)—shown as a net debit or net credit. The transaction is completed if the FLOOR BROKER can execute the order at the requested spread.

SPREAD POSITION status of an account in which a SPREAD has been executed.

SPREADSHEET ledger sheet on which a company's financial statements, such as BALANCE SHEETS, INCOME STATEMENTS, and sales reports, are laid out in columns and rows. Spreadsheets are used by securities and credit analysts in researching companies and industries. Since the advent of personal computers, spreadsheets have come into wide use, because software makes them easy to use. In an electronic spreadsheet on a computer, any time one number is changed, all the other numbers are automatically adjusted according to the relationships the computer operator sets up. For instance, in a spreadsheet of a sales report of a company's many divisions, the updating of a single division's sales figure will automatically change the total sales for the company, as well as the percentage of total sales that division produced.

SPRINKLING TRUST trust under which no beneficiary has a right to receive any trust income. Instead, the trustee is given discretion to divide, or "sprinkle," the trust's income as the trustee sees fit among a designated group of persons. Sprinkling trusts can be created both by LIVING TRUST agreements and by WILLS.

SPX ticker symbol for the Standard & Poor's 500 stock index options traded on the Chicago Board Options Exchange. The European-style index options contract is settled in cash, and can be exercised only on the last business day before expiration. The SPX is one of the most heavily traded of all index options contracts.

SQUEEZE
Finance: (1) tight money period, when loan money is scarce and interest rates are high, making borrowing difficult and expensive—also called a *credit crunch;* (2) any situation where increased costs cannot be passed on to customers in the form of higher prices.
Investments: situation when stocks or commodities futures start to move up in price, and investors who have sold short are forced to COVER their short positions in order to avoid large losses. When done by many short sellers, this action is called a SHORT SQUEEZE. *See also* SELLING SHORT; SHORT POSITION.

SRO *see* SELF-REGULATORY ORGANIZATION.

STABILIZATION
Currency: buying and selling of a country's own currency to protect its exchange value, also called PEGGING.
Economics: leveling out of the business cycle, unemployment, and prices through fiscal and monetary policies.
Market trading: action taken by REGISTERED COMPETITIVE TRADERS on the New York Stock Exchange in accordance with an exchange requirement that 75% of their trades be stabilizing—in other words, that their sell orders follow a PLUS TICK and their buy orders a MINUS TICK.
New issues underwriting: intervention in the market by a managing underwriter in order to keep the market price from falling below the PUBLIC OFFERING PRICE during the offering period. The underwriter places orders to buy at a specific price, an action called PEGGING that, in any other circumstance, is a violation of laws prohibiting MANIPULATION in the securities and commodities markets.

STAG speculator who makes it a practice to get in and out of stocks for a fast profit, rather than to hold securities for investment.

STAGFLATION term coined by economists in the 1970s to describe the previously unprecedented combination of slow economic growth and high unemployment (stagnation) with rising prices (inflation). The principal factor was the fourfold increase in oil prices imposed by the Organization of Petroleum Exporting Countries (OPEC) cartel in 1973–74, which raised price levels throughout the economy while further slowing economic growth. As is characteristic of stagflation, fiscal and monetary policies aimed at stimulating the economy and reducing unemployment only exacerbated the inflationary effects.

STAGGERED BOARD OF DIRECTORS board of directors of a company in which a portion of the directors are elected each year, instead of all at once. A board is often staggered in order to thwart unfriendly TAKEOVER attempts, since potential acquirers would have to wait a longer time before they could take control of a company's board through the normal voting procedure. Normally, all directors are elected at the annual meeting.

STAGGERING MATURITIES technique used to lower risk by a bond investor. Since long-term bonds are more volatile than short-term ones, an investor can

HEDGE against interest rate movements by buying short-, medium- and long-term bonds. If interest rates decline, the long-term bonds will rise faster in value than the shorter-term bonds. If rates rise, however, the shorter-term bonds will hold their value better than the long-term debt obligations, which could fall precipitously.

STAGNATION
Economics: period of no or slow economic growth or of economic decline, in real (inflation-adjusted) terms. Economic growth of 3% or less per year—as was the case in the late 1970s, measured according to increases in the U.S. gross national product—generally is taken to constitute stagnation.
Securities: period of low volume and inactivetrading.

STAGS acronym for *Sterling Transferable Accruing Government Securities.* A British version of U.S. government STRIPS, STAGS are deep discount zero-coupon bonds backed by British Treasury securities. *See also* ZERO-COUPON SECURITY.

STANDARD & POOR'S CORPORATION subsidiary of The McGraw-Hill Companies that provides a broad range of investment services, including RATING corporate and municipal bonds, common stocks, preferred stocks, and COMMERCIAL PAPER; compiling the STANDARD & POOR'S 500 COMPOSITE INDEX, the Standard & Poor's MidCap 400 Index, the Standard & Poor's SmallCap 600 Index, and the Standard & Poor's 100 Index, among other indices; publishing a wide variety of statistical materials, investment advisory reports, and other financial information, including: *Bond Guide,* a summary of data on corporate and municipal bonds; *Earnings Guide,* earnings-per-share estimates on more than 5,500 publicly traded stocks; *Emerging & Special Situations,* information and analysis on the new issue market; *Stock Guide,* investment data on listed and unlisted common and preferred stocks and mutual funds; *Analyst's Handbook,* per-share data on the stocks and industry groups making up industrial, transportation, financial and utility groups; *Corporation Records,* six alphabetical volumes and a daily news volume of information on more than 12,000 publicly held companies; and *Stock Reports,* analytical reports on listed and unlisted companies. A subsidiary publishes the daily BLUE LIST of municipal and corporate bonds. Standard & Poor's also publishes *Standard & Poor's Register,* a national directory of companies and their officers, and *Securities Dealers of North America,* a directory of investment banking and brokerage firms in North America. *See also* STANDARD & POOR'S RATING; STOCK INDICES AND AVERAGES.

STANDARD & POOR'S 500 COMPOSITE INDEX broad-based measurement of changes in stock market conditions based on the average performance of 500 widely held common stocks; commonly known as the *Standard & Poor's 500* (or *S&P 500*). The selection of stocks, their relative weightings to reflect differences in the number of outstanding shares, and publication of the index itself are services of STANDARD & POOR'S CORPORATION, a financial advisory, securities rating, and publishing firm. The index tracks industrial, transportation, financial, and utility stocks; it is a large cap index. The composition of the 500 stocks is flexible and the number of issues in each sector varies over time. Standard & Poor's also publishes several other important indices including the *S&P MidCap 400,* the *S&P SmallCap 600,* and the *S&P 1500 Super Composite Index,* which totals the S&P 500, 400 and 600 indices. These three indices represent approximately 82% of the total market capitalization of stocks traded in the U.S. equity market. S&P also maintains over 90 individual industry indices. *See also* S&P PHENOMENON, STANDARD & POOR'S CORPORATION; STOCK INDICES AND AVERAGES.

STANDARD & POOR'S RATING classification of stocks and bonds according to risk issued by STANDARD & POOR'S CORPORATION. S&P's top four debt grades—

called INVESTMENT GRADE AAA, AA, A, and BBB—indicate a minimal risk that a corporate or municipal bond issue will DEFAULT in its timely payment of interest and principal. Common stocks are ranked A+ through C on the basis of growth and stability, with a ranking of D signifying REORGANIZATION. *See also* EVENT RISK; LEGAL LIST; RATING.

STANDARD COST estimate, based on engineering and accounting studies, of what costs of production should be, assuming normal operating conditions. Standard costs differ from budgeted costs, which are forecasts based on expectations. Variances between standard costs and actual costs measure productive efficiency and are used in cost control.

STANDARD DEDUCTION individual taxpayer alternative to itemizing deductions. Current tax rules index the standard deduction to inflation, adjusting annually. They are:

	1998
Single Taxpayer	$4150
Head of Household	$6050
Married Filing Jointly	$6900
Married Filing Separately	$3450

STANDARD DEVIATION statistical measure of the degree to which an individual value in a probability distribution tends to vary from the mean of the distribution. It is widely applied in modern PORTFOLIO THEORY, for example, where the past performance of securities is used to determine the range of possible future performances and a probability is attached to each performance. The standard deviation of performance can then be calculated for each security and for the portfolio as a whole. The greater the degree of dispersion, the greater the risk. *See also* PORTFOLIO THEORY; REGRESSION ANALYSIS.

STANDARD INDUSTRIAL CLASSIFICATION (SIC) SYSTEM federally designed standard numbering system identifying companies by industry and providing other information. It is widely used by market researchers, securities analysts, and others. Computerized data bases frequently make use of this classification system.

STANDARD OF LIVING degree of prosperity in a nation, as measured by income levels, quality of housing and food, medical care, educational opportunities, transportation, communications, and other measures. The standard of living in different countries is frequently compared based on annual per capita income. On an individual level, the standard of living is a measure of the quality of life in such areas as housing, food, education, clothing, transportation, and employment opportunities.

STANDBY COMMITMENT
Securities: agreement between a corporation and an investment banking firm or group (the *standby underwriter)* whereby the latter contracts to purchase for resale, for a fee, any portion of a stock issue offered to current shareholders in a RIGHTS OFFERING that is not subscribed to during the two- to four-week standby period. A right, often issued to comply with laws guaranteeing the shareholder's PREEMPTIVE RIGHT, entitles its holder, either an existing shareholder or a person who has bought the right from a shareholder, to purchase a specified amount of shares before a PUBLIC OFFERING and usually at a price lower than the PUBLIC OFFERING PRICE.
    The risk to the investment banker in a standby commitment is that the market price of shares will fall during the standby period. *See also* LAY OFF for a discussion

of how standby underwriters protect themselves. *See also* FLOTATION COST; SUB-SCRIPTION RIGHT; UNDERWRITE.

Lending: a bank commitment to loan money up to a specified amount for a specific period, to be used only in a certain contingency. The most common example would be a commitment to repay a construction lender in the event a permanent mortgage lender cannot be found. A COMMITMENT FEE is normally charged.

STANDBY UNDERWRITER *see* STANDBY COMMITMENT.

STANDSTILL AGREEMENT accord by a RAIDER to abstain from buying shares of a company for a specified period. *See also* GREENMAIL.

START-UP new business venture. In VENTURE CAPITAL parlance, start-up is the earliest stage at which a venture capital investor or investment pool will provide funds to an enterprise, usually on the basis of a business plan detailing the background of the management group along with market and financial PROJECTIONS. Investments or loans made at this stage are also called SEED MONEY.

STATE BANK bank organized under a charter granted by a regulatory authority in one of the 50 U.S. states, as distinguished from a NATIONAL BANK, which is federally chartered. The powers of a state-chartered commercial bank are generally consistent with those of national banks, since state laws tend to conform to federal initiatives and vice versa. State banks deposits are insured by the FEDERAL DEPOSIT INSURANCE CORPORATION. State banks have the option of joining the FEDERAL RESERVE SYSTEM, and even if they reject membership, they may purchase support services from the Fed, including check-processing and coin and currency services.

STATED INTEREST RATE
Banking: rate paid on savings instruments, such as PASSBOOK savings accounts and certificates of deposit. The stated interest rate does not take into account any compounding of interest.
Bonds: interest rate stated on a bond coupon. A bond with a 7% coupon has a 7% stated interest rate. This rate is applied to the face value of the bond, normally $1000, so that bondholders will receive 7% annually for every $1000 in face value of bonds they own.

STATED VALUE assigned value given to a corporation's stock for accounting purposes in lieu of par value. For example, the stated value may be set at $1 a share, so that if a company issued 10 million shares, the stated value of its stock would be $10 million. The stated value of the stock has no relation to its market price. It is, however, the amount per share that is credited to the CAPITAL STOCK account for each share outstanding and is therefore the legal capital of the corporation. Since state law generally prohibits a corporation from paying dividends or repurchasing shares when doing so would impair its legal capital, stated value does offer stockholders a measure of protection against loss of value.

STATEMENT
1. summary for customers of the transactions that occurred over the preceding month. A bank statement lists all deposits and withdrawals, as well as the running account balances. A brokerage statement shows all stock, bond, commodity futures, or options trades, interest and dividends received, margin debt outstanding, and other transactions, as well as a summary of the worth of the accounts at month end. A trade supplier provides a summary of open account transactions. *See also* ASSET MANAGEMENT ACCOUNT.
2. statement drawn up by businesses to show the status of their ASSETS and LIABILITIES and the results of their operations as of a certain date. *See also* FINANCIAL STATEMENT.

STATEMENT OF CASH FLOWS analysis of CASH FLOW included as part of the financial statements in annual reports of publicly held companies as set forth in Statement 95 of the FINANCIAL ACCOUNTING STANDARDS BOARD (FASB). The statement shows how changes in balance sheet and income accounts affected cash and cash equivalents and breaks the analysis down according to operating, investing, and financing activities. As an analytical tool, the statement of cash flows reveals healthy or unhealthy trends and makes it possible to predict future cash requirements. It also shows how actual cash flow measured up to estimates and permits comparisons with other companies.

STATEMENT OF CONDITION
Banking: sworn accounting of a bank's resources, liabilities, and capital accounts as of a certain date, submitted in response to periodic "calls" by bank regulatory authorities.
Finance: summary of the status of assets, liabilities, and equity of a person or a business organization as of a certain date. *See also* BALANCE SHEET.

STATEMENT OF INCOME *see* PROFIT AND LOSS STATEMENT.

STATEMENT OF OPERATIONS *see* PROFIT AND LOSS STATEMENT.

STATUTE OF LIMITATIONS statute describing the limitations on how many years can pass before someone gives up their right to sue for a wrongful action. For example, the INTERNAL REVENUE SERVICE has up to three years to assess back taxes from the time the return is filed, unless tax fraud is charged. Most states impose a statute of limitations of six years to challenge the violation of a written contract. Therefore, a suit claiming damages filed seven years after the alleged contract violation would be thrown out of court because the statute of limitations had run out.

STATUTORY INVESTMENT investment specifically authorized by state law for use by a trustee administering a trust under that state's jurisdiction.

STATUTORY MERGER legal combination of two or more corporations in which only one survives as a LEGAL ENTITY. It differs from *statutory consolidation,* in which all the companies in a combination cease to exist as legal entities and a new corporate entity is created. *See also* MERGER.

STATUTORY PROSPECTUS *see* PROSPECTUS.

STATUTORY VOTING one-share, one-vote rule that governs voting procedures in most corporations. Shareholders may cast one vote per share either for or against each nominee for the board of directors, but may not give more than one vote to one nominee. The result of statutory voting is that, in effect, those who control over 50% of the shares control the company by ensuring that the majority of the board will represent their interests. *Compare with* CUMULATIVE VOTING. *See also* PROPORTIONAL REPRESENTATION.

STAYING POWER ability of an investor to stay with (not sell) an investment that has fallen in value. For example, a commodity trader with staying power is able to meet margin calls as the commodities FUTURES CONTRACTS he has bought fall in price. He can afford to wait until the trade ultimately becomes profitable. In real estate, an investor with staying power is able to meet mortgage and maintenance payments on his or her properties and is therefore not harmed as interest rates rise or fall, or as the properties become temporarily difficult to sell.

STEP DOWN NOTE type of FLOATING RATE whose interest rate declines at specified times in the course of the loan.

STICKY DEAL new securities issue that the underwriter fears will be difficult to sell. Adverse market conditions, bad news about the issuing entity, or other factors may lead underwriters to say, "This will be a sticky deal at the price we have set." As a result, the price may be lowered or the offering withdrawn from the market.

STOCHASTICS INDEX computerized TECHNICAL ANALYSIS tool, or oscillator, that measures OVERBOUGHT and OVERSOLD conditions in a stock, using MOVING AVERAGES and RELATIVE STRENGTH techniques. In its simplest form, the stochastics index is expressed as a percentage of the difference between the low and high stock price during the stochastics period. For example, if the stochastics period is 14 days and the high in that period was 50 and the low 40, the difference would be 10. On the day it is calculated, the stochastics is the percentage of the difference that the current price represents. If the price at the time of calculation was 40, the stochastics reading would be zero. At a price of 50, the stochastics reading would be 100. At 45, the stochastics reading would be 50.

In practice, the stochastics index typically plots a five-day moving average of the stochastics. Lines drawn at the 25% and 75% levels on the graph represent overbought and oversold conditions. When the stochastics index falls below the 25% line, it generally indicates an oversold condition, and when the stochastics index goes above the 75% line it indicates an overbought condition. An upward reversal that breaks the 25% line is a positive BREAKOUT and a downward reversal that breaks the 75% line is a negative breakout, signaling new uptrends and downtrends respectively. *See also* MOMENTUM INDICATOR; MOVING AVERAGE CONVERGENCE/DIVERGENCE (MACD).

STOCK
1. ownership of a CORPORATION represented by shares that are a claim on the corporation's earnings and assets. COMMON STOCK usually entitles the shareholder to vote in the election of directors and other matters taken up at shareholder meetings or by proxy. PREFERRED STOCK generally does not confer voting rights but it has a prior claim on assets and earnings—dividends must be paid on preferred stock before any can be paid on common stock. A corporation can authorize additional classes of stock, each with its own set of contractual rights. *See also* ARTICLES OF INCORPORATION; AUTHORIZED SHARES; BLUE CHIP; BOOK VALUE; CAPITAL STOCK; CERTIFICATE; CLASS; CLASSIFIED STOCK; CLOSELY HELD; COMMON STOCK; COMMON STOCK EQUIVALENT; CONVERTIBLES; CONTROL STOCK; CORPORATION; CUMULATIVE PREFERRED; DIVIDEND; EARNINGS PER SHARE; EQUITY; FLOAT; FRACTIONAL SHARES; GOING PUBLIC; GROWTH STOCK; INACTIVE STOCK; INITIAL PUBLIC OFFERING; ISSUED AND OUTSTANDING; JOINT STOCK COMPANY; LETTER SECURITY; LISTED SECURITY; MARKET VALUE; NONVOTING STOCK; NO-PAR-VALUE STOCK; OVER THE COUNTER; PAR VALUE; PARTICIPATING PREFERRED; PENNY STOCK; PREEMPTIVE RIGHT; PREFERENCE SHARES; PREFERRED STOCK; PRIOR PREFERRED STOCK; QUARTER STOCK; REGISTERED SECURITY; REGISTRAR; REVERSE SPLIT; SCRIP; SECURITY; SHARE; SHAREHOLDER; SPLIT; STATED VALUE; STOCK CERTIFICATE; STOCK DIVIDEND; STOCK EXCHANGE; STOCKHOLDER; STOCKHOLDER OF RECORD; STOCK MARKET; STOCK POWER; STOCK PURCHASE PLAN; STOCK SYMBOL; STOCK WATCHER; TRANSFER AGENT; TREASURY STOCK; VOTING STOCK; VOTING TRUST CERTIFICATE; WATERED STOCK.
2. inventories of accumulated goods in manufacturing and retailing businesses.
3. *see* ROLLING STOCK.

STOCK AHEAD situation in which two or more orders for a stock at a certain price arrive about the same time, and the exchange's PRIORITY rules take effect. New York Stock Exchange rules stipulate that the bid made first should be executed first or, if two bids came in at once, the bid for the larger number of shares receives priority. The bid that was not executed is then reported back to the broker, who informs the customer that the trade was not completed because there was stock ahead. *See also* MATCHED AND LOST.

STOCK BONUS PLAN plan established and maintained by an employer to provide benefits similar to those of a profit-sharing plan. Contributions by the employer, however, are not necessarily dependent on profits, and the benefits are distributed in shares of stock in the employer company. Stock bonus plans reward employee performance, and by giving employees a stake in the company they are used to help motivate them to perform at maximum efficiency.

STOCKBROKER *see* REGISTERED REPRESENTATIVE.

STOCK BUYBACK corporation's purchase of its own outstanding stock. A buyback may be financed by borrowings, sale of assets, or operating CASH FLOW. Its purpose is commonly to increase EARNINGS PER SHARE and thus the market price, often to discourage a TAKEOVER. When a buyback involves a PREMIUM paid to an acquirer in exchange for a promise to desist from takeover activity, the payment is called GREENMAIL. A buyback having a formula and schedule may also be called a SHARE REPURCHASE PLAN or SELF-TENDER. *See also* TREASURY STOCK.

STOCK CERTIFICATE documentation of a shareholder's ownership in a corporation. Stock certificates are engraved intricately on heavy paper to deter forgery. They indicate the number of shares owned by an individual, their PAR VALUE (if any), the CLASS of stock (for example, common or preferred), and attendant voting rights. To prevent theft, shareholders often store certificates in safe deposit boxes or take advantage of a broker's SAFEKEEPING service. Stock certificates become negotiable when endorsed.

STOCK DIVIDEND payment of a corporate dividend in the form of stock rather than cash. The stock dividend may be additional shares in the company, or it may be shares in a SUBSIDIARY being spun off to shareholders. The dividend is usually expressed as a percentage of the shares held by a shareholder. For instance, a shareholder with 100 shares would receive 5 shares as the result of a 5% stock dividend. From the corporate point of view, stock dividends conserve cash needed to operate the business. From the stockholder point of view, the advantage is that additional stock is not taxed until sold, unlike a cash dividend, which is declarable as income in the year it is received.

STOCK EXCHANGE organized marketplace in which stocks, COMMON STOCK EQUIVALENTS, and bonds are traded by members of the exchange, acting both as agents (brokers) and as principals (dealers or traders). Most exchanges have a physical location where brokers and dealers meet to execute orders from institutional and individual investors to buy and sell securities. Each exchange sets its own requirements for membership; the New York Stock Exchange has the most stringent requirements. *See also* AMERICAN STOCK EXCHANGE; LISTING REQUIREMENTS; NEW YORK STOCK EXCHANGE; REGIONAL STOCK EXCHANGES; SECURITIES AND COMMODITIES EXCHANGES.

THE STOCK EXCHANGE, MUMBAI (BSE) formerly known as the Bombay Stock Exchange, accounts for more than one-third of Indian trading volume, over 70% of listed capital and 90% of market capitalization. It is a voluntary, nonprofit association of brokers. BSE is the largest of 23 stock exchanges in India. Market capitalization has decreased, however, since the establishment of the NATIONAL STOCK EXCHANGE (NSE) in 1994. BSE's on-line trading system, BOLT replaced open outcry. Settlement is in one week. Trading Hours: 10 A.M. to 2:30 P.M., Monday through Friday, and 11 A.M. to 3:30 P.M. on alternate Saturdays (exclusively for carry-over sessions).

STOCK EXCHANGE OF SINGAPORE (SES) only stock exchange in Singapore, trading through the Central Limit Order Book (CLOB) system, a fully computerized system. There is no trading floor. A direct link between SES and the NASDAQ Stock Market was established in 1988, with all prices quoted in U.S. currency. The *Straits Times Industrial Index* and the *SES Share Indices* are the most widely followed indicators of share performance. Trades are settled on a seven-day settlement. Trading hours are 9:00 A.M. to 12:30 P.M. and 2 P.M. to 5 P.M., Monday through Friday.

STOCK EXCHANGE OF THAILAND (SET) only stock market in Thailand, based in Bangkok. The SET Index includes all corporate securities and mutual funds. The SET 50 Index is composed of the 50 largest capitalized and most liquid stocks in the market. Both are calculated by the exchange. Trading is conducted through the asset automated electronic trading system Monday through Friday from 10 A.M. to 12:30 P.M., and 2 P.M. to 4:30 P.M. Trades are settled on the third business day after the trade date.

STOCKHOLDER individual or organization with an ownership position in a corporation; also called a SHAREHOLDER or *shareowner.* Stockholders must own at least one share, and their ownership is confirmed by either a stock certificate or a record by their broker, if shares are in the broker's custody.

STOCKHOLDER OF RECORD common or preferred stockholder whose name is registered on the books of a corporation as owning shares as of a particular date. Dividends and other distributions are made only to shareholders of record. Common stockholders are usually the only ones entitled to vote for candidates for the board of directors or on other matters requiring shareholder approval.

STOCKHOLDER'S EQUITY *see* OWNER'S EQUITY.

STOCKHOLDER'S REPORT company's ANNUAL REPORT and supplementary quarterly reports giving financial results and usually containing an ACCOUNTANT'S OPINION. Special stockholder's reports are sometimes issued covering major corporate developments. Also called *shareholder's report. See also* DISCLOSURE.

STOCKHOLM STOCK EXCHANGE only market in Sweden for official equity trading. The Stockholm Automatic Exchange (SAX) electronic trading system, introduced in 1989, includes all traded shares. A parallel system, called SOX, operates for fixed-interest securities. Clearing and settlement occur on the third business day following the trade. Trading is conducted Monday through Friday from 10 A.M. to 4 P.M.

STOCK INDICES AND AVERAGES indicators used to measure and report value changes in representative stock groupings. Strictly speaking, an AVERAGE is simply the ARITHMETIC MEAN of a group of prices, whereas an INDEX is an average expressed in relation to an earlier established BASE MARKET VALUE. (In practice, the distinction between indices and averages is not always clear; the AMEX Major Market Index is an average, for example.) Indices and averages may be broad based—comprised of many stocks representative of the overall market—or narrowly based, meaning they are composed of a smaller number of stocks reflecting a particular industry or market SECTOR. Selected indices and averages are also used as the underlying value of stock index futures, index options, or options on index futures; these derivative instruments enable investors to hedge a position against general market movement at relatively low cost. An extensive number and variety of indices and averages exist. Among the best known and most widely used are:

AMEX Composite Index (XAX): introduced in January 1997, it is a market capitalization-weighted, price appreciation index with a base level of 550 as of December 29, 1995. It replaces the AMEX Market Value Index (XAM), which had been in use since 1973, and was calculated on a total return basis to include reinvestment of dividends paid by AMEX companies. XAX reflects the aggregate market value of all of its components relative to their aggregate value on December 29, 1995. The index includes common stocks or AMERICAN DEPOSITARY RECEIPTS, AMEX-listed companies, REITs, master limited partnerships and closed-end investment funds. Each component's market value is determined by multiplying its price by the number of shares outstanding. The day-to-day price change in each issue is weighted by its market value at the start of the day as a percent of the total market value for all components. The level of the index is not altered by stock splits, stock dividends, trading halts, new listings, additional issuances, delistings or suspensions. Accompanying the AMEX Composite Index are five subindices that track the performance of companies in major industry sectors, and are measured against a base level of 100 as of December 29, 1995. These subindices are Technologies, Financial, Healthcare, Natural Resources and Industrials.

AMEX Major Market Index (XMI): AMERICAN STOCK EXCHANGE'S price-weighted (high-priced issues have more influence than low-priced issues) average of 20 BLUE CHIP industrial stocks listed on the NEW YORK STOCK EXCHANGE (NYSE), 17 of which are components of the DOW JONES INDUSTRIAL AVERAGE (DJIA). The index is designed to closely track the DJIA in measuring representative performance in the stocks of major industrial corporations. Futures on the XMI are traded on the CHICAGO BOARD OF TRADE. Options on the index are traded on Amex, and are traded under license on the Amsterdam Exchanges.

Dow Jones Global Industry Group and Economic Sector Indices: comprised of companies in the Dow Jones World Stock Index, classified on the basis of their business type, which then are sorted into more than 100 industry groups and nine broad economic sectors. The indices are computed to measure the movement of stock prices by industry groups and broad economic sectors on a global, regional, and national basis. These indices are tracked in real time. Country indices are calculated in each country's own currency, plus the U.S. dollar, British pound, German mark, and Japanese yen. The regional and world indices are calculated in these four global currencies, although all indices can be converted to any currency.

Dow Jones Global–U.S. Index: a broad-based, capitalization-weighted (price times the shares outstanding for each company) index (June 30, 1982 = 100) of more than 700 stocks traded on the NYSE, AMEX, and NASDAQ Stock Market, representing approximately 80% of the U.S. equity market. It is the U.S. portion of the Dow Jones World Stock Index.

Dow Jones Industrial Average (DJIA): price-weighted average of 30 actively traded BLUE CHIP stocks, primarily industrials like Alcoa, General Motors, and IBM but including American Express, Coca-Cola, McDonald's, J.P. Morgan, Walt Disney and other service-oriented firms. Prepared and published by Dow Jones & Co., it is the oldest and most widely quoted of all the market indicators. The components, which change from time to time, represent between 15% and 20% of the market value of NYSE stocks. The DJIA is calculated by adding the trading prices of the component stocks and using a divisor adjusted for STOCK DIVIDENDS and SPLITS, cash equivalent distributions equal to 10% or more of the closing prices of an issue, and substitutions and mergers. The average is quoted in points, not dollars. Futures are traded on the DJIA on the CHICAGO BOARD OF TRADE and index options on the DJIA are traded on the CHICAGO BOARD OPTIONS EXCHANGE. Other averages similarly prepared by Dow Jones & Co. are the *Dow Jones Transportation Average*—20 stocks representative of the airline, trucking, railroad, and shipping businesses (*see also* DOW THEORY); and the *Dow Jones Utility Average* (DJUA)—15 geographically representative gas and electric utilities. Index options on the DJTA and DJUA are traded on the CHICAGO BOARD OPTIONS EXCHANGE. The combination of the Dow Industrials, Transportation, and Utility Averages encompasses 65 stocks and is known as the *Dow Jones Composite Average* or the *65 Stock Average.*

Dow Jones Stoxx Indices: four "pan-European" index products, calculated on a real-time basis. Dow Jones Stoxx includes 666 companies across Europe; Dow Jones Euro Stoxx is limited to 326 companies in countries participating in the European Monetary Union; Dow Jones Stoxx 50 includes shares of 50 European companies; and Dow Jones Euro Stoxx 50 is limited to 50 companies in countries that adopted the EURO. The Stoxx 50 indices include only a country's leading company in each key sector; pharmaceuticals, energy companies, banks, insurance and telecommunications companies dominate the Stoxx 50. The indices are traded on the SBF-Paris Bourse, Deutsche Borse AG, and Swiss Exchange; the three exchanges are partners with Dow Jones & Co. in these products.

Dow Jones World Stock Index: a broad-based, capitalization-weighted index (December 31, 1991 = 100) tracking approximately 3,000 companies in a growing list of countries and representing about 80% of the equity capital on stock markets around the globe.The index includes 34 countries in North America, Europe, and Asia/Pacific regions.

NASDAQ Composite Index: market value-weighted index that measures all domestic and non-U.S.-based securities—more than 5,400 companies—listed on the NASDAQ Stock Market. The index was introduced on February 5, 1971, with a base value of 100. The market value—the last-sale price multiplied by total shares outstanding—is calculated through the trading day, and is related to the total value of the index. Each security in the index is assigned to a NASDAQ sub-index: Bank, Biotechnology, Computer, Industrial, Insurance, Other Finance, Transportation, Telecommunications. Values for the sub-indices began in February 1971, except for Biotechnology, Computer, and Telecommunications, which started November 1993.

NASDAQ-100 Index: a capitalization-weighted index, begun in January 1985, representing the largest and most active non-financial U.S. and foreign equities listed on the NASDAQ Stock Market. All securities in the index come from the top 125 eligible securities in terms of market value. Unless the security was in the top 100 during the previous year's ranking, larger eligible securities will replace issues ranked 101 to 125. To be eligible, a security must have a minimum average daily trading volume of 100,000 shares and be listed on NASDAQ for at least two years. Market value is determined annually on October 31. A foreign security must have a worldwide market value of at least $10 billion, a U.S. market value of at least $4 billion, and an average daily trading volume of at least 200,000 shares. Foreign securities must be eligible for listed-options trading. NASDAQ-100 futures and options on futures trade on the CHICAGO MERCANTILE EXCHANGE. The NASDAQ-100 option is a European-style option, and can be exercised on its expiration date only.

New York Stock Exchange Composite Index: market value-weighted index which relates all NYSE stocks to an aggregate market value as of December 31, 1965, adjusted for capitalization changes. The base value of the index is $50 and point changes are expressed in dollars and cents. NYSE sub-indices include the *NYSE Finance, NYSE Industrials, NYSE Transportation*, and *NYSE Utilities* indices.

PSE Technology 100 Index: price-weighted, broad-based index representing 100 listed and over-the-counter stocks from 15 different industries on the PACIFIC EXCHANGE. The index measures the performance of the technology sector of the U.S. equities market, and is considered the industry benchmark. Options are traded on the PACIFIC EXCHANGE and the NEW YORK FUTURES EXCHANGE.

Russell Indices: market capitalization-weighted U.S. equity indices published by Frank Russell Company of Tacoma, Washington. The *Russell 3000 Index*® measures the performance of the 3,000 largest U.S. companies based on market capitalization, representing about 98% of the investable U.S. equities market. The highest-ranking 1,000 stocks in this index comprise the *Russell 1000 Index®*. The *Russell 2000 Index®* consists of the 2,000 smallest companies in the Russell 3000 Index. The *Russell Top 200 Index®* measures performance of the largest 200 companies in the Russell 1000, while the *Russell 2500 Index®* measures performance of the 2,500 smallest companies in the Russell 3000 Index. Growth indices on the Russell Indices measure performance of the respective companies with higher price/book ratios and higher forecasted growth values. Value indices on the Russell Indices measure performance of those companies with lower price/book ratios and lower forecasted growth values. *See also* RUSSELL INDICES.

Standard & Poor's 500 Composite Index: market value-weighted index showing the change in the aggregate market value of 500 stocks relative to the base period 1941-43. Mostly NYSE-listed companies with some AMEX and NASDAQ Stock Market stocks, it is comprised of 379 industrial stocks, 37 utilities, 74 financials, and 10 transportation issues representing about 74% of the market value of all issues traded on the NYSE. Index options are traded on the CHICAGO BOARD OPTIONS EXCHANGE and futures and options are traded on the CHICAGO MERCANTILE EXCHANGE. Other indices maintained by Standard & Poor's include the *Industrials, Utilities, 400 MidCap, 600 SmallCap* and *1500 Index.*

Standard & Poor's 100 Index (OEX): calculated on the same basis as the 500 Stock Index, is made up of stocks for which options are listed on the CHICAGO BOARD OPTIONS EXCHANGE. Its components are mainly NYSE industrials, with some transportation, utility, and financial stocks. Options on the S&P 100 Index are listed on the CHICAGO BOARD OPTIONS EXCHANGE.

Value Line Composite Average: equally weighted geometric average of approximately 1,700 NYSE, AMEX, and over-the-counter stocks tracked by the VALUE LINE INVESTMENT SURVEY. The index uses a base value of 100, established June 30, 1961; changes are expressed in index numbers rather than dollars and cents. Designed to reflect price changes of typical stocks (industrials, transportation, and utilities) without being price-weighted or market value-weighted, the index largely succeeds. Futures on the index are traded on the KANSAS CITY BOARD OF TRADE and futures options are traded on the PHILADELPHIA STOCK EXCHANGE.

Wilshire Indices: performance measurement indices created by Wilshire Associates Inc., of Santa Monica, California. The Wilshire 5000 Equity Index is the most widely followed and the broadest of all the averages and indices. It is market value-weighted and measures the performance of all U.S.-headquartered equity securities with readily available price data, or more than 7,000 security returns. Its capitalization is approximately 81% NYSE, 2% AMEX, and 17% NASDAQ Stock Market. Changes are measured against a base value established December 31, 1980. Other indices maintained by Wilshire include the *Wilshire 4500 Equity Index, Wilshire Small Cap Index*, four *Wilshire Asset Management Indexes* derived from the Wilshire 5000; six individual style indices and three *Real Estate Securities Indexes. Wilshire Small Cap Index* options are traded on the PACIFIC EXCHANGE, which helped develop the index.

Many indices and averages track the performance of stock markets around the world. The major indices include the: ALL ORDINARIES INDEX; AMSTERDAM EXCHANGES; ATHENS STOCK EXCHANGE; BOLSA DE COMMERCIO DE SANTIAGO; BOLSA DE VALORES DE SAO PAULO; BOLSA DE VALORES DO RIO DE JANIERO; CAC 40 INDEX; EAFE INDEX; EMERGING MARKET FREE (EMF) INDEX; HANG SENG INDEX; INTERNATIONAL MARKET INDEX; ITALIAN STOCK EXCHANGE; JOHANNESBURG STOCK EXCHANGE; KUALA LUMPUR STOCK EXCHANGE; LISBON STOCK EXCHANGE; LONDON STOCK EXCHANGE; MADRID STOCK EXCHANGE (BOLSO DE MADRID); MEXICAN STOCK EXCHANGE; MONTREAL EXCHANGE/BOURSE DE MONTREAL; MORGAN STANLEY CAPITAL INTERNATIONAL INDICES; NEW ZEALAND STOCK EXCHANGE; OSLO STOCK EXCHANGE;

STOCK EXCHANGE OF SINGAPORE (SES); STOCK EXCHANGE OF THAILAND (SET); STOCKHOLM STOCK EXCHANGE; SWISS ELECTONIC BOURSE (EBS); TAIWAN STOCK EXCHANGE; TEL AVIV STOCK EXCHANGE; TOKYO STOCK EXCHANGE; TORONTO STOCK EXCHAGNE (TSE); VANCOUVER STOCK EXCHANGE; and VIENNA STOCK EXCHANGE.

See also BARRON'S CONFIDENCE INDEX; BOND BUYER'S INDEX; COMMODITY INDICES; ELVES; LIPPER MUTUAL FUND INDUSTRY AVERAGE; SECURITIES AND COMMODITIES EXCHANGES.

STOCK INDEX FUTURE security that combines features of traditional commodity futures trading with securities trading using composite stock indices. Investors can speculate on general market performance or buy an index future contract to hedge a LONG POSITION or SHORT POSITION against a decline in value. Settlement is in cash, since it is obviously impossible to deliver an index of stocks to a futures buyer. Among the most popular stock index futures traded are the Dow Jones Industrial Average on the CHICAGO BOARD OF TRADE, the NASDAQ 100 on the CHICAGO MERCANTILE EXCHANGE, New York Stock Exchange Composite Index on the New York Futures Exchange (NYFE), the Standard & Poor's 500 Composite, Mini Index, the S&P Mini Index, and the S&P MidCap Index on the CHICAGO MERCANTILE EXCHANGE (CME), and the Value Line Composite Index on the KANSAS CITY BOARD OF TRADE (KCBT). It is also possible to buy options on stock index futures; the Dow Jones Industrials futures options trade on the Chicago Board of Trade and the Standard & Poor's 500 Stock Index futures options are traded on the Chicago Mercantile Exchange, for example. Unlike stock index futures or index options, however, futures options are not settled in cash; they are settled by delivery of the underlying stock index futures contracts. See also FUTURES CONTRACT; HEDGE/HEDGING; SECURITIES AND COMMODITIES EXCHANGES.

STOCK INSURANCE COMPANY insurance company that is owned by stockholders, as distinguished from a MUTUAL COMPANY that is owned by POLICYHOLDERS. Even in a stock company, however, policyholders interests are ahead of shareholder's dividends.

STOCK JOCKEY stockbroker who actively follows individual stocks and frequently buys and sells shares in his client's portfolios. If the broker does too much short-term trading in accounts over which he has discretion, he may be accused of CHURNING.

STOCK LIST function of the organized stock exchanges that is concerned with LISTING REQUIREMENTS and related investigations, the eligibility of unlisted companies for trading privileges, and the delisting of companies that have not complied with exchange regulations and listing requirements. The New York Stock Exchange department dealing with listing of securities is called the Department of Stock List.

STOCK MARKET general term referring to the organized trading of securities through the various exchanges and the OVER THE COUNTER market. The securities involved include COMMON STOCK, PREFERRED STOCK, BONDS, CONVERTIBLES, OPTIONS, rights, and warrants. The term may also encompass commodities when used in its most general sense, but more often than not the stock market and the commodities (or futures) market are distinguished. The query "How did the market do today?" is usually answered by a reference to the Dow Jones Industrial Average, comprised of stocks listed on the New York Stock Exchange. See also SECURITIES AND COMMODITIES EXCHANGES.

STOCK OPTION
1. right to purchase or sell a stock at a specified price within a stated period. OPTIONS are a popular investment medium, offering an opportunity to hedge

positions in other securities, to speculate in stocks with relatively little investment, and to capitalize on changes in the MARKET VALUE of options contracts themselves through a variety of options strategies.

See also CALL OPTION; PUT OPTION.

2. widely used form of employee incentive and compensation, usually for the executives of a corporation. The employee is given an OPTION to purchase its shares at a certain price (at or below the market price at the time the option is granted) for a specified period of years.

See also INCENTIVE STOCK OPTION; QUALIFIED STOCK OPTION.

STOCK POWER power of attorney form transferring ownership of a REGISTERED SECURITY from the owner to another party. A separate piece of paper from the CERTIFICATE, it is attached to the latter when the security is sold or pledged to a brokerage firm, bank, or other lender as loan COLLATERAL. Technically, the stock power gives the owner's permission to another party (the TRANSFER AGENT) to transfer ownership of the certificate to a third party. Also called *stock/bond power.*

STOCK PURCHASE PLAN organized program for employees of a company to buy shares of its stock. The plan could take the form of compensation if the employer matches employee stock purchases. In some companies, employees are offered the chance to buy stock in the company at a discount. Also, a corporation can offer to reinvest dividends in additional shares as a service to shareholders, or it can set up a program of regular additional share purchases for participating shareholders who authorize periodic, automatic payments from their wages for this purpose. *See also* AUTOMATIC INVESTMENT PROGRAM.

Another form of stock purchase plan is the EMPLOYEE STOCK OWNERSHIP PLAN (ESOP), whereby employees regularly accumulate shares and may ultimately assume control of the company.

STOCK RATING evaluation by rating agencies of common stocks, usually in terms of expected price performance or safety. Standard & Poor's and Value Line's respective quality and timeliness ratings are among the most widely consulted.

STOCK RECORD control, usually in the form of a ledger card or computer report, used by brokerage films to keep track of securities held in inventory and their precise location within the firm. Securities are recorded by name and owner.

STOCK RIGHT *see* SUBSCRIPTION RIGHT.

STOCK SPLIT *see* SPLIT.

STOCK SYMBOL letters used to identify listed companies on the securities exchanges on which they trade. These symbols, also called *trading symbols,* identify trades on the CONSOLIDATED TAPE and are used in other reports and documents whenever such shorthand is convenient. Some examples: ABT (Abbott Laboratories), AA (Aluminum Company of America), XON (Exxon), KO (Coca Cola). Stock symbols are not necessarily the same as abbreviations used to identify the same companies in the stock tables of newspapers. *See also* COMMITTEE ON UNIFORM SECURITIES IDENTIFICATION PROCEDURES (CUSIP).

STOCK-TRANSFER AGENT *see* TRANSFER AGENT.

STOCK WARRANT *see* SUBSCRIPTION WARRANT.

STOCK WATCHER (NYSE) computerized service that monitors all trading activity and movement in stocks listed on the New York Stock Exchange. The system is set up to identify any unusual activity due to rumors or MANIPULATION or other illegal practices. The stock watch department of the NYSE is prepared to conduct investigations and to take appropriate action, such as issuing clarifying information or turning questions of legality over to the Securities and Exchange Commission. *See also* SURVEILLANCE DEPARTMENT OF EXCHANGES.

STOP-LIMIT ORDER order to a securities broker with instructions to buy or sell at a specified price or better (called the *stop-limit price)* but only after a given *stop price* has been reached or passed. It is a combination of a STOP ORDER and a LIMIT ORDER. For example, the instruction to the broker might be "buy 100 XYZ 55 STOP 56 LIMIT" meaning that if the MARKET PRICE reaches $55, the broker enters a limit order to be executed at $56 or a better (lower) price. A stop-limit order avoids some of the risks of a stop order, which becomes a MARKET ORDER when the stop price is reached; like all price-limit orders, however, it carries the risk of missing the market altogether, since the specified limit price or better may never occur. The American Stock Exchange prohibits stop-limit orders unless the stop and limit prices are equal.

STOP LOSS
Insurance: promise by a reinsurance company that it will cover losses incurred by the company it reinsures over and above an agreed-upon amount.
Stocks: customer order to a broker that sets the sell price of a stock below the current MARKET PRICE. A stop-loss order therefore will protect profits that have already been made or prevent further losses if the stock drops.

STOP ORDER order to a securities broker to buy or sell at the MARKET PRICE once the security has traded at a specified price called the *stop price.* A stop order may be a DAY ORDER, a GOOD-TILL-CANCELED ORDER, or any other form of time-limit order. A stop order to buy, always at a stop price above the current market price, is usually designed to protect a profit or to limit a loss on a short sale *(see* SELLING SHORT). A stop order to sell, always at a price below the current market price, is usually designed to protect a profit or to limit a loss on a security already purchased at a higher price. The risk of stop orders is that they may be triggered by temporary market movements or that they may be executed at prices several points higher or lower than the stop price because of market orders placed ahead of them. Also called *stop-loss order. See also* GATHER IN THE STOPS; STOP-LIMIT ORDER; STOP LOSS (stocks).

STOP-OUT PRICE lowest dollar price at which Treasury bills are sold at a particular auction. This price and the beginning auction price are averaged to establish the price at which smaller purchasers may purchase bills under the NONCOMPETITIVE BID system. *See also* BILL; DUTCH AUCTION.

STOP PAYMENT revocation of payment on a check after the check has been sent or delivered to the payee. So long as the check has not been cashed, the writer has up to six months in which to request a stop payment. The stop payment right does not carry over to electronic funds transfers.

STOPPED OUT term used when a customer's order is executed under a STOP ORDER at the price predetermined by the customer, called the *stop price.* For instance, if a customer has entered a stop-loss order to sell XYZ at $30 when the stock is selling at $33, and the stock then falls to $30, his or her position will be stopped out. A customer may also be stopped out if the order is executed at a guaranteed price offered by a SPECIALIST. *See also* GATHER IN THE STOPS; STOPPED STOCK.

STOPPED STOCK guarantee by a SPECIALIST that an order placed by a FLOOR BROKER will be executed at the best bid or offer price then in the SPECIALIST'S BOOK unless it can be executed at a better price within a specified period of time.

STOP PRICE *see* STOP ORDER.

STORY STOCK/BOND security with values or features so complex that a "story" is required to persuade investors of its merits. Story stocks are frequently from companies with some unique product or service that is difficult for competitors to copy. In a less formal sense, term is used by news organizations to mean stocks most actively traded.

STRADDLE strategy consisting of an equal number of PUT OPTIONS and CALL OPTIONS on the same underlying stock, stock index, or commodity future at the same STRIKE PRICE and maturity date. Each OPTION may be exercised separately, although the combination of options is usually bought and sold as a unit.

STRAIGHT-LINE DEPRECIATION method of depreciating a fixed asset whereby the asset's useful life is divided into the total cost less the estimated salvage value. The procedure is used to arrive at a uniform annual DEPRECIATION expense to be charged against income before figuring income taxes. Thus, if a new machine purchased for $1200 was estimated to have a useful life of ten years and a salvage value of $200, annual depreciation under the straight-line method would be $100, charged at $100 a year. This is the oldest and simplest method of depreciation and is used by many companies for financial reporting purposes, although faster depreciation of some assets with greater tax benefits in the early years is allowed under the MODIFIED ACCELERATED COST RECOVERY SYSTEM (MACRS).

STRAIGHT TERM INSURANCE POLICY term life insurance policy for a specific number of years in which the death benefit remains unchanged. A level premium policy will charge the same premium for a number of years, usually ten, and then increase. An annual renewable term policy will charge slightly higher premiums each year.

STRANGLE sale or purchase of a put option and a call option on the same underlying instrument, with the same expiration, but at strike prices equally OUT OF THE MONEY. A strangle costs less than a STRADDLE because both options are out of the money, but profits are made only if the underlying instrument moves dramatically.

STRAP OPTION contract combining one PUT OPTION and two CALL OPTIONS of the same SERIES, which can be bought at a lower total premium than that of the three options bought individually. The put has the same features as the calls—same underlying security, exercise price, and maturity. Also called *triple option. Compare with* STRIP.

STRATEGIC BUYOUT ACQUISITION based on analysis of the operational benefits of consolidation. Implicitly contrasts with the type of TAKEOVER based on "paper values" that characterized the "merger mania" of the 1980s—undervalued stock bought using JUNK BONDS ultimately repayable from the liquidation of acquired assets and activities. A strategic buyout focuses on how companies fit together and anticipates enhanced long-term earning power. *See also* SYNERGY.

STREET short for Wall Street, referring to the financial community in New York City and elsewhere. It is common to hear "The Street likes XYZ." This means there is a national consensus among securities analysts that XYZ's prospects are favorable. *See also* STREET NAME.

STREET NAME phrase describing securities held in the name of a broker or another nominee instead of a customer. Since the securities are in the broker's custody, transfer of the shares at the time of sale is easier than if the stock were registered in the customer's name and physical certificates had to be transferred.

STRIKE PRICE *see* EXERCISE PRICE.

STRIP

Bonds: brokerage-house practice of separating a bond into its CORPUS and COUPONS, which are then sold separately as ZERO-COUPON SECURITIES. The 1986 Tax Act permitted MUNICIPAL BOND strips. Some, such as Salomon Brothers' tax-exempt M-CATS, represent PREREFUNDINGS backed by U.S. Treasury securities held in escrow. Other strips include Treasuries stripped by brokers, such as TIGERS, and stripped mortgage-backed securities of government-sponsored issuers like Fannie Mae. A variation known by the acronym STRIPS (Separate Trading of Registered Interest and Principal of Securities) is a prestripped zero-coupon bond that is a direct obligation of the U.S. Treasury.

Options: OPTION contract consisting of two PUT OPTIONS and one CALL OPTION on the same underlying stock or stock index with the same strike and expiration date. *Compare with* STRAP.

Stocks: to buy stocks with the intention of collecting their dividends. Also called *dividend stripping. See also* DIVIDEND ROLLOVER PLAN.

STRIPPED BOND

bond separated into its two components: periodic interest payments and principal repayment. Each of the interest payments and the principal repayment are stripped apart by a brokerage firm and sold individually as ZERO-COUPON SECURITIES. Investors therefore have a wide choice of maturities to pick from when shopping for a zero-coupon bond. When a U.S. government bond is stripped, it is often called a STRIP, which stands for *separate trading of registered interest and principal of securities.* Such bonds are also called CATS and TIGERS.

STRONG DOLLAR

dollar that can be exchanged for a large amount of a foreign currency. The dollar can gain strength in currency markets because the United States is considered a haven of political and economic stability, or because yields on American securities are attractive. A strong dollar is a blessing for American travelers going abroad, because they get more pounds, francs, marks, and yen and other currencies for their greenbacks. However, a strong dollar makes it difficult for American firms to export their goods to foreign countries because it raises the cost to foreigners of purchasing American products. In 1985, the dollar became so strong that the PLAZA ACCORD was signed to bring the dollar down. *See also* EXCHANGE RATE; WEAK DOLLAR.

STRUCTURED NOTE

1. derivative instrument based on the movement of an underlying index. For example, a structured note issued by a corporation may pay interest to note-holders based on the rise and fall of oil prices. This gives investors the opportunity to earn interest and profit from the change in price of a commodity at the same time.
2. complex debt instrument, usually a medium-term note, in which the issuer enters into one or more SWAP arrangements to change the cash flows it is required to make. A simple form utilizing interest-rate swaps might be, for example, a three-year FLOATING RATE NOTE paying the London Interbank Offered Rate (LIBOR) plus a premium semiannually. The issuer arranges a swap transaction whereby it agrees to pay a fixed semiannual rate for three years in exchange for the LIBOR. Since the floating rate payments (cash flows) offset each other, the issuer has synthetically created a fixed-rate note.

STRUCTURED SETTLEMENT

agreement to pay a designated person a specified sum of money in periodic payments, usually for his or her lifetime, instead of in a single LUMP SUM payment. Structured settlements typically are used to pay court-ordered or privately-agreed upon damages to injured claimants or their survivors. Structured settlements are also used to pay lottery winners. In both cases, the settlement is funded with an ANNUITY.

STUB STOCK common stocks or instruments convertible to equity in a company that is overleveraged as the result of a BUYOUT or RECAPITALIZATION and may have DEFICIT NET WORTH. Stub stock is highly speculative and highly volatile but, unlike JUNK BONDS, has unlimited potential for gain if the company succeeds in restoring financial balance.

STUDENT LOAN MARKETING ASSOCIATION (SLMA) publicly traded stock corporation that guarantees student loans traded in the SECONDARY MARKET. It was established by federal decree in 1972 to increase the availability of education loans to college and university students made under the federally sponsored Guaranteed Student Loan Program and the Health, Education Assistance Loan Program. Known as *Sallie Mae,* it purchases student loans from originating financial institutions and provides financing to state student loan agencies. It also sells short- and medium-term notes, some FLOATING RATE NOTES.

SUBCHAPTER M Internal Revenue Service regulation dealing with what is commonly called the *conduit theory,* in which qualifying investment companies and real estate investment trusts avoid double taxation by passing interest and dividend income and capital gains directly through, without taxation, to shareholders, who are taxed as individuals. *See also* REAL ESTATE INVESTMENT TRUST; REGULATED INVESTMENT COMPANY.

SUBCHAPTER S section of the Internal Revenue Code giving a corporation that has 35 or fewer shareholders and meets certain other requirements the option of being taxed as if it were a PARTNERSHIP. Thus a small corporation can distribute its income directly to shareholders and avoid the corporate income tax while enjoying the other advantages of the corporate form. These companies are known as *Subchapter S corporations, tax-option corporations,* or *small business corporations.*

SUBJECT Wall Street term referring to a bid and/or offer that is negotiable—that is, a QUOTATION that is not firm. For example, a broker looking to place a sizable order might call several dealers with the question, "Can you give me a *subject quote* on 20,000 shares of XYZ?"

SUBJECT QUOTE *see* SUBJECT.

SUBORDINATED junior in claim on assets to other debt, that is, repayable only after other debts with a higher claim have been satisfied. Some subordinated debt may have less claim on assets than other subordinated debt; a *junior subordinated debenture* ranks below a subordinated DEBENTURE, for example.

It is also possible for unsubordinated (senior) debt to become subordinated at the request of a lender by means of a subordination agreement. For example, if an officer of a small company has made loans to the company instead of making a permanent investment in it, a bank might request the officer's loan be subordinated to its own loan as long as the latter is outstanding. This is accomplished by the company officer's signing a subordination agreement. *See also* EFFECTIVE NET WORTH; JUNIOR SECURITY.

SUBORDINATION CLAUSE clause in a MORTGAGE loan agreement that permits a mortgage recorded at a subsequent date to have preference over the original mortgage.

SUBROGATION legal process by which an insurance company, after paying for a loss, seeks to recover the amount of the loss from another party who is legally liable for it.

SUBSCRIPTION agreement of intent to buy newly issued securities. *See also* NEW ISSUE; SUBSCRIPTION RIGHT; SUBSCRIPTION WARRANT.

SUBSCRIPTION AGREEMENT application submitted by an investor seeking to join a limited partnership. All prospective limited partners must be approved by the general partner before they are allowed to become limited partners.

SUBSCRIPTION PRICE price at which existing shareholders of a corporation are entitled to purchase common shares in a RIGHTS OFFERING or at which subscription warrants are exercisable. *See also* SUBSCRIPTION RIGHT; SUBSCRIPTION WARRANT.

SUBSCRIPTION PRIVILEGE right of existing shareholders of a corporation, or their transferees, to buy shares of a new issue of common stock before it is offered to the public. *See also* PREEMPTIVE RIGHT; SUBSCRIPTION RIGHT.

SUBSCRIPTION RATIO *see* SUBSCRIPTION RIGHT.

SUBSCRIPTION RIGHT privilege granted to existing shareholders of a corporation to subscribe to shares of a new issue of common stock before it is offered to the public; better known simply as a *right*. Such a right, which normally has a life of two to four weeks, is freely transferable and entitles the holder to buy the new common stock below the PUBLIC OFFERING PRICE. While in most cases one existing share entitles the stockholder to one right, the number of rights needed to buy a share of a new issue (called the *subscription ratio)* varies and is determined by a company in advance of an offering. To subscribe, the holder sends or delivers to the company or its agent the required number of rights plus the dollar price of the new shares.

Rights are sometimes granted to comply with state laws that guarantee the shareholders' PREEMPTIVE RIGHT—their right to maintain a proportionate share of ownership. It is common practice, however, for corporations to grant rights even when not required by law; protecting shareholders from the effects of DILUTION is seen simply as good business.

The actual certificate representing the subscription is technically called a SUBSCRIPTION WARRANT, giving rise to some confusion. The term *subscription warrant,* or simply *warrant,* is commonly understood in a related but different sense—as a separate entity with a longer life than a right—maybe 5, 10, or 20 years or even perpetual—and with a SUBSCRIPTION PRICE higher at the time of issue than the MARKET VALUE of the common stock.

Subscription rights are offered to shareholders in what is called a RIGHTS OFFERING, usually handled by underwriters under a STANDBY COMMITMENT.

SUBSCRIPTION WARRANT type of security, usually issued together with a BOND or PREFERRED STOCK, that entitles the holder to buy a proportionate amount of common stock at a specified price, usually higher than the market price at the time of issuance, for a period of years or to perpetuity; better known simply as a *warrant*. In contrast, rights, which also represent the right to buy common shares, normally have a subscription price lower than the current market value of the common stock and a life of two to four weeks. A warrant is usually issued as a SWEETENER, to enhance the marketability of the accompanying fixed income securities. Warrants are freely transferable and are traded on the major exchanges. They are also called *stock-purchase warrants. See also* PERPETUAL WARRANT; SUBSCRIPTION RIGHT.

SUBSIDIARY company of which more than 50% of the voting shares are owned by another corporation, called the PARENT COMPANY. *See also* AFFILIATE.

SUBSTITUTION
Banking: replacement of COLLATERAL by other collateral.
Contracts: replacement of one party to a contract by another. *See also* NOVATION.

Economics: concept that, if one product or service can be replaced by another, their prices should be similar.
Law: replacement of one attorney by another in the exercise of stock powers relating to the purchase and sale of securities. *See also* STOCK POWER.
Securities:
1. exchange or SWAP of one security for another in a client's PORTFOLIO. Securities analysts often advise substituting a stock they currently favor for a stock in the same industry that they believe has less favorable prospects.
2. substitution of another security of equal value for a security acting as COLLATERAL for a MARGIN ACCOUNT. *See also* SAME-DAY SUBSTITUTION.

SUICIDE PILL POISON PILL with potentially catastrophic implications for the company it is designed to protect. An example might be a poison pill providing for an exchange of stock for debt in the event of a *hostile takeover;* that would discourage an acquirer by making the TAKEOVER prohibitively expensive, but its implementation could put the TARGET COMPANY in danger of bankruptcy.

SUITABILITY RULES guidelines that those selling sophisticated and potentially risky financial products, such as limited partnerships or commodities futures contracts, must follow to ensure that investors have the financial means to assume the risks involved. Such rules are enforced through self-regulation administered by such organizations as the NATIONAL ASSOCIATION OF SECURITIES DEALERS, the SECURITIES AND COMMODITIES EXCHANGES, and other groups operating in the securities industry. Individual brokerage firms selling the products have their own guidelines and policies. They typically require the investor to have a certain level of NET WORTH and LIQUID ASSETS, so that he or she will not be irreparably harmed if the investment sours. A brokerage firm may be sued if it has allowed an unsuitable investor to buy an investment that goes sour. *See also* KNOW YOUR CUSTOMER.

SUM-OF-THE-YEARS'-DIGITS METHOD (SOYD) method of ACCELERATED DEPRECIATION that results in higher DEPRECIATION charges and greater tax savings in the earlier years of a FIXED ASSET'S useful life than the STRAIGHT-LINE DEPRECIATION method, where charges are uniform throughout. Sometimes called just *sum-of-digits method,* it allows depreciation based on an inverted scale of the total of digits for the years of useful life. Thus, for four years of life, the digits 4, 3, 2, and 1 are added to produce 10. The first year's rate becomes $\frac{4}{10}$ths of the depreciable cost of the asset (cost less salvage value), the second year's rate $\frac{3}{10}$ths, and so on. The effects of this method of accelerated depreciation are compared with the straight-line method in the following illustration, which assumes an asset with a total cost of $1000, a useful life of four years, and no salvage value:

YEAR	STRAIGHT-LINE		SUM-OF-YEARS' DIGITS	
	Expense	Cumulative	Expense	Cumulative
1	$250	$250	$400	$400
2	$250	$500	$300	$700
3	$250	$750	$200	$900
4	$250	$1000	$100	$1000
	$1000		$1000	

See also MODIFIED ACCELERATED COST RECOVERY SYSTEM (MACRS).

SUNK COSTS costs already incurred in a project that cannot be changed by present or future actions. For example, if a company bought a piece of machinery five years ago, that amount of money has already been spent and cannot be recovered. It should also not affect the company's decision on whether or not to buy a new piece of machinery if the five-year old machinery has worn out.

SUNRISE INDUSTRIES figurative term for the emerging growth sectors that some believe will be the mainstays of the future economy, taking the place of declining *sunset industries*. Although the latter, including such mature industries as the automobile, steel, and other heavy manufacturing industries, will continue to be important, their lead role as employers of massive numbers of workers is expected to be superseded by the electronics and other computer-related high-technology, biotechnology, and genetic engineering sectors and by service industries.

SUNSET PROVISION condition in a law or regulation that specifies an expiration date unless reinstated by legislation. For examples a sunset provision in the TAX REFORM ACT OF 1986 prohibits tax-exempt single-family mortgage bonds after 1988.

SUNSHINE LAWS state or federal laws (also called *government in the sunshine laws)* that require most meetings of regulatory bodies to be held in public and most of their decisions and records to be disclosed. Many of these statutes were enacted in the 1970s because of concern about government abuses during the Watergate period. Most prominent is the federal Freedom of Information (FOI) Act, which makes it possible to obtain documents relating to most federal enforcement and rule-making agencies.

SUPER BOWL INDICATOR technical indicator that holds that if a team from the old American Football League pre-1970 wins the Super Bowl, the stock market will decline during the coming year. If a team from the old pre-1990 National Football League wins the Super Bowl, the stock market will end the coming year higher. The indicator has been a remarkably accurate predictor of stock market performance for many years.

SUPER DOT *see* DESIGNATED ORDER TURNAROUND (DOT).

SUPERMAJORITY AMENDMENT corporate AMENDMENT requiring that a substantial majority (usually 67% to 90%) of stockholders approve important transactions, such as mergers.

SUPER NOW ACCOUNT deregulated transaction account authorized for depository institutions in 1982. It paid interest higher than on a conventional NOW (NEGOTIABLE ORDER OF WITHDRAWAL) account but slightly lower than that on the MONEY MARKET DEPOSIT ACCOUNT (MMDA). With the deregulation of banking deposit accounts in 1986, however, banks are free to pay whatever rates they feel cost considerations and competitive conditions warrant. Although some banks continue to offer MMDA accounts which pay a slightly higher rate to compensate for the fact that checkwriting is limited to three checks a month, most banks now offer one transaction account with unlimited checkwriting.

SUPER SINKER BOND bond with long-term coupons (which might equal a 20-year-bond's yield) but with short maturity. Typically, super sinkers are HOUSING BONDS, which provide home financing. If homeowners move from their homes and prepay their mortgages, bondholders receive their principal back right away. Super sinkers may therefore have an actual life of as little as three to five years, even though their yield is about the same as bonds of much longer maturities. *See also* COUPON BOND.

SUPERVISORY ANALYST member firm research analyst who has passed a special New York Stock Exchange examination and is deemed qualified to approve publicly distributed research reports.

SUPPLEMENTAL AGREEMENT agreement that amends a previous agreement and contains additional conditions.

SUPPLEMENTAL SECURITY INCOME SOCIAL SECURITY program benefiting the blind, disabled, and indigent.

SUPPLY-SIDE ECONOMICS theory of economics contending that drastic reductions in tax rates will stimulate productive investment by corporations and wealthy individuals to the benefit of the entire society. Championed in the late 1970s by Professor Arthur Laffer *(see* LAFFER CURVE) and others, the theory held that MARGINAL TAX RATES had become so high (primarily as a result of big government) that major new private spending on plant, equipment, and other "engines of growth" was discouraged. Therefore, reducing the size of government, and hence its claim on earned income, would fuel economic expansion.

Supporters of the supply-side theory claimed they were vindicated in the first years of the administration of President Ronald W. Reagan, when marginal tax rates were cut just prior to a sustained economic recovery. However, members of the opposing KEYNESIAN ECONOMICS school maintained that the recovery was a classic example of "demand-side" economics—growth was stimulated not by increasing the supply of goods, but by increasing consumer demand as disposable incomes rose. Also clashing with the supply-side theory were MONETARIST economists, who contended that the most effective way of regulating aggregate demand is for the Federal Reserve to control growth in the money supply. *See also* AGGREGATE SUPPLY.

SUPPORT LEVEL price level at which a security tends to stop falling because there is more demand than supply. Technical analysts identify support levels as prices at which a particular security or market has bottomed in the past. When a stock is falling towards its support level, these analysts say it is "testing its support," meaning that the stock should rebound as soon as it hits the support price. If the stock continues to drop through the support level, its outlook is considered very bearish. The opposite of a support level is a RESISTANCE LEVEL. *See* chart on next page.

SURCHARGE charge added to a charge, cost added to a cost, or tax added to a tax. *See also* SURTAX.

SURETY individual or corporation, usually an insurance company, that guarantees the performance or faith of another. Term is also used to mean *surety bond,* which is a bond that backs the performance of the person bonded, such as a contractor, or that pays an employer if a bonded employee commits theft.

SURRENDER VALUE *see* CASH SURRENDER VALUE.

SURPLUS connotes either CAPITAL SURPLUS or EARNED SURPLUS. *See also* FEDERAL DEFICIT (SURPLUS); PAID-IN CAPITAL; RETAINED EARNINGS.

SURTAX tax applied to corporations or individuals who have earned a certain level of income. For example, the REVENUE RECONCILIATION ACT OF 1993 provided for a 10% surtax on adjusted gross incomes over $250,000.

SURVEILLANCE DEPARTMENT OF EXCHANGES division of a stock exchange that is constantly watching to detect unusual trading activity in stocks, which may be a tipoff to an illegal practice. These departments cooperate with the Securities and Exchange Commission in investigating misconduct. *See also* STOCK WATCHER.

SURVIVING SPOUSE spouse remaining alive when his or her spouse dies (in other words, the spouse who lives longer). In most states, the surviving spouse cannot be totally disinherited, but has a right to receive a share of the deceased spouse's estate, with the size of that share determined by state law.

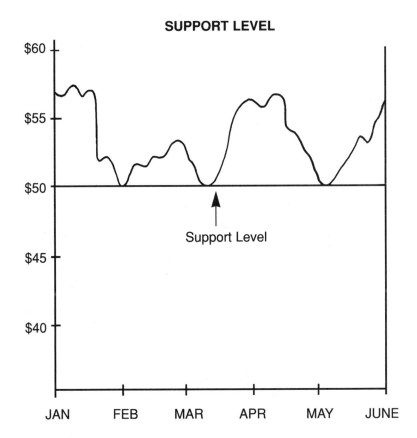

SUPPORT LEVEL

Support Level ↑

$60
$55
$50
$45
$40

JAN   FEB   MAR   APR   MAY   JUNE

SURVIVORSHIP ACCOUNT *see* JOINT TENANTS WITH RIGHT OF SURVIVORSHIP.

SURVIVORSHIP LIFE INSURANCE *see* SECOND-TO-DIE INSURANCE.

SUSPENDED TRADING temporary halt in trading in a particular security, in advance of a major news announcement or to correct an imbalance of orders to buy and sell. Using telephone alert procedures, listed companies with material developments to announce can give advance notice to the New York Stock Exchange Department of Stock List or the American Stock Exchange Securities Division. The exchanges can then determine if trading in the securities affected should be suspended temporarily to allow for orderly dissemination of the news to the public. Where advance notice is not possible, a *floor governor* may halt trading to stabilize the price of a security affected by a rumor or news development. Destabilizing developments might include a MERGER announcement, an unfavorable earnings report, or a major resource discovery. *See also* CIRCUIT BREAKER; DISCLOSURE; FORM 8-K; INVESTOR RELATIONS DEPARTMENT.

SUSPENSE ACCOUNT in accounting, an account used temporarily to carry receipts, disbursements, or discrepancies, pending their analysis and permanent classification.

SWAP traditionally, an exchange of one security for another to change the maturities of a bond PORTFOLIO or the quality of the issues in a stock or bond portfolio, or because investment objectives have shifted. Investors with bond portfolio losses often swap for other higher-yielding bonds to be able to increase the return on their portfolio and realize tax losses. Recent years have seen explosive growth in more complex *currency swaps,* used to link increasingly global capital markets, and in *interest-rate swaps,* used to reduce risk by synthetically matching the DURATION of assets and liabilities of financial institutions as interest rates got higher and more volatile. In a simple currency swap (swaps can be done with varying degrees of complexity), two parties sell each other a currency with a commitment to re-exchange the principal amount at the maturity of the deal. Originally done to get around the problems of exchange controls, currency swaps are widely used to tap new capital markets, in effect to borrow funds irrespective of whether the borrower requires funds within that market. The INTERNATIONAL BANK FOR RECONSTRUCTION AND DEVELOPMENT (WORLD BANK) has been an active participant in currency swaps with U.S. corporations.

An interest-rate swap is an arrangement whereby two parties (called counter-parties) enter into an agreement to exchange periodic interest payments. The dollar amount the counterparties pay each other is an agreed-upon periodic interest rate multiplied by some predetermined dollar principal, called the *notational principal amount.* No principal (no notational amount) is exchanged between parties to the transaction; only interest is exchanged. In its most common and simplest variation, one party agrees to pay the other a fixed rate of interest in exchange for a floating rate. The benefit of interest-rate swaps, which can be used to synthetically extend or shorten the duration characteristics of an asset or liability, is that direct changes in the contractual characteristics of the assets or the liabilities become matters affecting only administrative, legal, and investment banking costs.

See also BOND SWAP; SUBSTITUTION.

SWAP ORDER *see* CONTINGENT ORDER.

SWAPTION option to enter an interest rate swap. A *payer swaption* gives its purchaser the right, but not the obligation, to enter into an interest-rate swap at a pre-set rate within a specific period of time. The swaption buyer pays a premium to the seller for this right. A *receiver swaption* gives the purchaser the right to receive fixed payments. The seller agrees to provide the specified swap if called upon, though it is possible for him to hedge that risk with other offsetting transactions.

SWEAT EQUITY equity created in a property by the hard work of the owner. For example, a small business may be built up more on the efforts of its founders than on the capital raised to finance it. Homeowners who renovate a house with their own labor create rising value with the sweat of their own brows, not the general increase in housing prices from inflation.

SWEETENER feature added to a securities offering to make it more attractive to purchasers. A bond may have the sweetener of convertibility into common stock added, for instance. *See also* KICKER.

SWISS ELECTRONIC BOURSE (EBS) formed in 1996, incorporating the former stock exchange trading floors in Zurich, Geneva, and Basel. The three exchanges operate simultaneously and are linked by computers, enabling orders to be executed on any of the three exchanges regardless of origin. Trading is by open outcry, although an electronic system is under development. The Swiss Performance Index, the official and most widely used index, is computed on 3-minute intervals using real-time prices at all three exchanges. There are three different market segments: the official market, official parallel market, and unofficial market. The official market is open from 10 A.M. to 1 P.M. and 2 P.M. to 4 P.M., while the official parallel market is open from 9:15 A.M. to 10 A.M., Monday through Friday. Trades are settled on the third business day after the trade.

SWISS OPTIONS AND FINANCIAL FUTURES EXCHANGE (SOFFEX)
first fully electronic trading system in the world, with a completely integrated and automated clearing system. SOFFEX, the Swiss derivatives market, changed its name to EUREX ZURICH AG in keeping with the 1998 launch of EUREX, the joint German-Swiss electronic derivatives market. Contracts traded include: futures and options on the DAX Index (the German stock index) and the Swiss Market Index (SMI); futures and future options on the DAX future, BOBL national government bonds (3.3 to 5 years), BUND naional government bonds (8.5 to 10 years), Swiss government bonds (Conf), Dow Jones STOXX 50 and Dow Jones Euro STOXX 50; futures on the one-month Euromark, three-month Euromark, Mid-Cap DAX and Jumbo Pfandbrief; stock options on German and Swiss blue chip equities; and U.S. dollar/Deutschemark options.

SWITCHING
Mutual funds: moving assets from one mutual fund to another, either within a FUND FAMILY or between different fund families. There is no charge for switching within a no-load family of mutual funds, which offer a variety of stock, bond, and money market funds. A sales charge might have to be paid when switching from one LOAD FUND to another. Customers of many discount brokerage firms can switch among fund families, sometimes at no fee and sometimes by paying a brokerage commission. Switching usually occurs at the shareholder's initiative, as a result of changes in market conditions or investment objectives. Some investment advisers and investment advisory newsletters recommend when to switch into or out of different mutual funds. See also NO-LOAD FUND.

Securities: selling stocks or bonds to replace them with other stocks and bonds with better prospects for gain or higher yields. See also SWAP.

SWITCH ORDER see CONTINGENT ORDER.

SYDNEY FUTURES EXCHANGE (SFE) Australia's derivatives market, trading through a combination of open outcry and Sycom, its electronic trading system for overnight trading. The exchange operates a link between Sycom and the NEW YORK MERCANTILE EXCHANGE'S ACCESS electronic trading system, allowing SFE members to trade NYMEX energy contracts. SFE also trades futures and futures options on wool and wheat. Financial futures and futures options are traded on Treasury bonds, bank bills, and the All Ordinaries Share Price Index; share futures are traded on some of the top Australian equities, including BHP and CRA. Trading hours are Monday to Friday, 9:50 A.M. to 4:30 P.M.

SYNDICATE see PURCHASE GROUP.

SYNDICATE MANAGER see MANAGING UNDERWRITER.

SYNERGY ideal sought in corporate mergers and acquisitions that the performance of a combined enterprise will exceed that of its previously separate parts. For example, a MERGER of two oil companies, one with a superior distribution network and the other with more reserves, would have synergy and would be expected to result in higher earnings per share than previously. See also STRATEGIC BUYOUT.

SYNTHETIC ASSET value that is artificially created by using other assets, such as securities, in combination. For example, the simultaneous purchase of a CALL OPTION and sale of a PUT OPTION on the same stock creates synthetic stock having the same value, in terms of CAPITAL GAIN potential, as the underlying stock itself.

SYNTHETIC SECURITIES see STRUCTURED NOTE; SYNTHETIC ASSET.

SYSTEMATIC INVESTMENT PLAN plan in which investors make regular payments into a stock, bond, mutual fund, or other investment. This may be accomplished through an AUTOMATIC INVESTMENT PROGRAM, such as a salary reduction plan with an employer, a dividend reinvestment plan with a company or mutual fund, or an automatic investment plan in which a mutual fund withdraws a set amount from a bank checking or savings account on a regular basis. By investing systematically, investors are benefiting from the advantages of DOLLAR-COST AVERAGING.

SYSTEMATIC WITHDRAWAL PLAN MUTUAL FUND option whereby the shareholder receives specified amounts at specified intervals.

SYSTEMATIC RISK that part of a security's risk that is common to all securities of the same general class (stocks and bonds) and thus cannot be eliminated by DIVERSIFICATION; also known as *market risk*. The measure of systematic risk in stocks is the BETA COEFFICIENT. *See also* PORTFOLIO BETA SCORE, PORTFOLIO THEORY.

t

TAC BONDS *see* TARGETED AMORTIZATION CLASS (TAC) BONDS.

TACTICAL ASSET ALLOCATION shifting percentages of portfolios among stocks, bonds, or cash, depending on the relative attractiveness of the respective markets. *See also* ASSET ALLOCATION.

TAFT-HARTLEY ACT federal law (in full, Labor Management Relations Act) enacted in 1947, which restored to management in unionized industries some of the bargaining power it had lost in prounion legislation prior to World War II. Taft-Hartley prohibited a union from
• refusing to bargain in good faith
• coercing employees to join a union
• imposing excessive or discriminatory dues and initiation fees
• forcing employers to hire union workers to perform unneeded or non-existent tasks (a practice known as *featherbedding)*
• striking to influence a bargaining unit's choice between two contesting unions (called a *jurisdictional strike)*
• engaging in secondary boycotts against businesses selling or handling nonunion goods
• engaging in sympathy strikes in support of other unions
Taft-Hartley also
• imposed disclosure requirements to regulate union business dealings and uncover fraud and racketeering
• prohibited unions from directly making contributions to candidates running for federal offices
• authorized the President of the United States to postpone strikes in industries deemed essential to national economic health or national security by declaring an 80-day "cooling-off period"
• permitted states to enact right-to-work laws, which outlaw compulsory unionization.

TAIL
Insurance: interval between receipt of premium income and payment of claims. For example, REINSURANCE companies have a long tail as compared to CASUALTY INSURANCE companies.
Treasury auctions: spread in price between the lowest COMPETITIVE BID accepted by the U.S. Treasury for bills, bonds, and notes and the average bid by all those offering to buy such Treasury securities. *See also* TREASURIES.

Underwriting: decimal places following the round-dollar amount of a bid by a potential UNDERWRITER in a COMPETITIVE BID underwriting. For instance, in a bid of $97.3347 for a particular bond issue, the tail is .3347.

TAILGATING unethical practice of a broker who, after a customer has placed an order to buy or sell a certain security, places an order for the same security for his or her own account. The broker hopes to profit either because of information the customer is known or presumed to have or because the customer's purchase is of sufficient size to put pressure on the security price.

TAIWAN STOCK EXCHANGE exchange of the Republic of China, located in Taipei. The *Taiwan Stock Exchange Capitalization Weighted Stock Index* is the oldest and most widely quoted of three leading indices, and is comparable to the STANDARD & POOR'S 500 INDEX in terms of its construction. Trading hours are Monday through Friday from 9 A.M. to noon, and Saturday from 9 A.M. to 11 A.M. Settlement by delivery of stock or cash payment must be made to the commissioning broker by the next business day.

TAKE
In general:
1. profit realized from a transaction.
2. gross receipts of a lottery or gambling enterprise.
3. open to bribery, as in *being on the take*.
Law: to seize possession of property. When a debtor defaults on a debt backed by COLLATERAL, that property is taken back by the creditor.
Securities: act of accepting an OFFER price in a transaction between brokers or dealers.

TAKE A BATH to suffer a large loss on a SPECULATION or investment, as in "I took a bath on my XYZ stock when the market dropped last week."

TAKE A FLIER to speculate, that is, to buy securities with the knowledge that the investment is highly risky.

TAKE A POSITION
1. to buy stock in a company with the intent of holding for the long term or, possibly, of taking control of the company. An acquirer who takes a position of 5% or more of a company's outstanding stock must file information with the Securities and Exchange Commission, the exchange the TARGET COMPANY is listed on, and the target company itself.
2. phrase used when a broker/dealer holds stocks or bonds in inventory. A position may be either long or short. *See also* LONG POSITION; SHORT POSITION.

TAKEDOWN
1. each participating INVESTMENT BANKER'S proportionate share of the securities to be distributed in a new or a secondary offering.
2. price at which the securities are allocated to members of the UNDERWRITING GROUP, particularly in municipal offerings.
   See also UNDERWRITE.

TAKE-HOME PAY amount of salary remaining after all deductions have been taken out. Some of the most common deductions are for federal, state, and local income tax withholding; Social Security tax withholding; health care premiums; flexible spending account contributions; and contributions to salary reduction or other retirement savings plans.

TAKE OFF to rise sharply. For example, when positive news about a company's earnings is released, traders say that the stock takes off. The term is also used referring to the overall movement of stock prices, as in "When the Federal Reserve lowered interest rates, the stock market took off."

TAKE-OR-PAY CONTRACT agreement between a buyer and a seller that obligates the buyer to pay a minimum amount of money for a product or a service, even if the product or service is not delivered. These contracts are most often used in the utility industry to back bonds to finance new power plants. A take-or-pay contract stipulates that the prospective purchaser of the power will take the power from the bond issuer or, if construction is not completed, will repay bondholders the amount of their investment. Take-or-pay contracts are a common way to protect bondholders. In a precedent-setting case in 1983, however, the Washington State Supreme Court voided take-or-pay contracts that many utilities had signed to support the building of the Washington Public Power Supply System (known as WHOOPS) nuclear plants. This action caused WHOOPS to default on some of its bonds, putting a cloud over the validity of the take-or-pay concept.

TAKEOUT
Real estate finance: long-term mortgage loan made to refinance a short-term construction loan (INTERIM LOAN). *See also* STANDBY COMMITMENT.
Securities: withdrawal of cash from a brokerage account, usually after a sale and purchase has resulted in a net CREDIT BALANCE.

TAKEOVER change in the controlling interest of a corporation. A takeover may be a friendly acquisition or an unfriendly bid that the TARGET COMPANY may fight with SHARK REPELLENT techniques. A hostile takeover (aiming to replace existing management) is usually attempted through a public TENDER OFFER. Other approaches might be unsolicited merger proposals to directors, accumulations of shares in the open market, or PROXY FIGHTS that seek to install new directors. *See also* ANY-AND-ALL BID; ARBITRAGEUR; ASSET STRIPPER; BEAR HUG; BLITZKREIG TENDER OFFER; BUST-UP TAKEOVER; CRAM-DOWN DEAL; CROWN JEWELS; DAWN RAID; DEAL STOCK; FAIR-PRICE AMENDMENT; GAP OPENING; GARBATRAGE; GODFATHER OFFER; GOLDEN PARACHUTE; GOODBYE KISS; GREENMAIL; GREY KNIGHT; HIGHLY CONFIDENT LETTER; HIGHJACKING; HOSTILE TAKEOVER; IN PLAY; INSIDER TRADING; KILLER BEES; LADY MACBETH STRATEGY; LEVERAGED BUYOUT; LEVERAGED RECAPITALIZATION; LOCK-UP OPTION; MACARONI DEFENSE; MANAGEMENT BUYOUT; MATERIALITY; MERGER; PAC-MAN STRATEGY; PEOPLE PILL; POISON PILL; POISON PUT; RADAR ALERT; RAIDER; RISK ARBITRAGE; REVERSE LEVERAGED BUYOUT; RUMORTRAGE; SAFE HARBOR; SATURDAY NIGHT SPECIAL; SCHEDULE 13D; SCORCHED-EARTH POLICY; SHARK WATCHER; SHOW STOPPER; SLEEPING BEAUTY; STAGGERED BOARD OF DIRECTORS; STANDSTILL AGREEMENT; STOCK BUYBACK; STRATEGIC BUYOUT; SUICIDE PILL; SUPERMAJORITY AMENDMENT; TAKEOVER TARGET; TWO-TIER BID; WAR CHEST; WHITE KNIGHT; WHITEMAIL; WHITE SQUIRE; WILLIAMS ACT.

TAKEOVER ARBITRAGE *See* RISK ARBITRAGE.

TAKEOVER TARGET company that is the object of a takeover offer, whether the offer is friendly or unfriendly. In a HOSTILE TAKEOVER attempt, management tries to use various defensive strategies to repel the acquirer. In a friendly takeover situation, management cooperates with the acquirer, negotiating the best possible price, and recommends that shareholders vote to accept the final offer. *See also* TAKEOVER.

TAKING DELIVERY
In general: accepting receipt of goods from a common carrier or other shipper, usually documented by signing a bill of lading or other form of receipt.
Commodities: accepting physical delivery of a commodity under a FUTURES CONTRACT or SPOT MARKET contract. Delivery requirements, such as the size of

the contract and the necessary quality of the commodity, are established by the exchange on which the commodity is traded.

Securities: accepting receipt of stock or bond certificates that have recently been purchased or transferred from another account.

TANGIBLE ASSET any asset not meeting the definition of an INTANGIBLE ASSET, which is a nonphysical right to something presumed to represent an advantage in the marketplace, such as a trademark or patent. Thus tangible assets are clearly those having physical existence, like cash, real estate, or machinery. Yet in accounting, assets such as ACCOUNTS RECEIVABLE are considered tangible, even though they are no more physical than a license or a lease, both of which are considered intangible. In summary: if an asset has physical form it is tangible; if it doesn't, consult a list of what accountants have decided are intangible assets.

TANGIBLE COST oil and gas drilling term meaning the cost of items that can be used over a period of time, such as casings, well fittings, land, and tankage, as distinguished from intangible costs such as drilling, testing, and geologist's expenses. In the most widely used LIMITED PARTNERSHIP sharing arrangements, tangible costs are borne by the GENERAL PARTNER (manager) while intangible costs are borne by the limited partners (investors), usually to be taken as tax deductions. In the event of a dry hole, however, all costs become intangibles. *See also* INTANGIBLE COST.

TANGIBLE NET WORTH total ASSETS less INTANGIBLE ASSETS and total LIABILITIES; also called *net tangible assets.* Intangible assets include nonmaterial benefits such as goodwill, patents, copyrights, and trademarks.

TAPE
1. service that reports prices and size of transactions on major exchanges. Also called *composite tape* and *ticker tape* (because of the sound made by the machine that printed the tape before the process was computerized).
2. tape of Dow Jones and other news wires, usually called the BROAD TAPE.
   See also CONSOLIDATED TAPE.

TAPE IS LATE situation in which trading volume is so heavy that the consolidated tape is running more than a minute behind when the actual trades are taking place on the floor of the exchange. The tape will not run faster than 900 characters a minute because the human eye cannot take in information any faster. When trading volume is heavy and the tape is running late, some price digits will first be deleted, and then volume digits will be deleted.

TARGET COMPANY firm that has been chosen as attractive for TAKEOVER by a potential acquirer. The acquirer may buy up to 5% of the target's stock without public disclosure, but it must report all transactions and supply other information to the Securities and Exchange Commission, the exchange the target company is listed on, and the target company itself once 5% or more of the stock is acquired. *See also* TOEHOLD PURCHASE; SCHEDULE 13D; SLEEPING BEAUTY; TENDER OFFER; WILLIAMS ACT.

TARGETED AMORTIZATION CLASS (TAC) BONDS bonds offered as a tranche class of some COLLATERALIZED MORTGAGE OBLIGATIONS (CMOs). TACs are similar to PAC BONDS in that, unlike conventional CMO classes, they are based on a SINKING FUND schedule. They differ from PAC bonds, however, in that whereas a PAC's amortization is guaranteed as long as prepayments on the underlying mortgages do not exceed certain limits, a TAC's schedule will be met at only one prepayment rate. At other prepayment rates, the TAC will experience either excesses or shortfalls. A TAC bond provides more cash flow stability than a regular CMO class but less than a PAC, and trades accordingly.

TARGET PRICE
Finance: price at which an acquirer aims to buy a company in a TAKEOVER.
Options: price of the underlying security after which a certain OPTION will become profitable to its buyer. For example, someone buying an XYZ 50 call for a PREMIUM of $200 could have a target price of 52, after which point the premium will be recouped and the CALL OPTION will result in a profit when exercised.
Stocks: price that an investor is hoping a stock he or she has just bought will rise to within a specified period of time. An investor may buy XYZ at $20, with a target price of $40 in one year's time, for instance.

TARIFF
1. federal tax on imports or exports usually imposed either to raise revenue (called a *revenue tariff*) or to protect domestic firms from import competition (called a *protective tariff*). A tariff may also be designed to correct an imbalance of payments. The money collected under tariffs is called DUTY or *customs duty.*
2. schedule of rates or charges, usually for freight.

TAXABLE ESTATE portion of an estate subject to the unified transfer tax of the federal government and to state taxes where applicable. The estate, not the recipients, is taxed on what remains after all expenses, contributions, transfers to a surviving spouse, debts, taxes, and losses. There is a federal EXCLUSION on property transferred by the person who died. According to the TAXPAYER RELIEF ACT OF 1997, the amount of assets that each person can exclude from federal estate taxes is $625,000 in 1998, rising to $1 million in 2006 and later years. This limit rises to $650,000 in 1999, $675,000 in 2000 and 2001, $700,000 in 2002 and 2003, $850,000 in 2004, $950,000 in 2005 and $1 million in 2006. The law created a special $1.3 million exclusion for qualifying farmers and small business owners starting January 1, 1998.

TAXABLE EVENT occurrence with tax consequences. For example, if a stock or mutual fund is sold at a profit, CAPITAL GAINS TAXES may be due. Withdrawal of assets from a tax-deferred retirement account like an IRA, KEOGH, or SALARY REDUCTION PLAN is a taxable event because some or all of the proceeds may be considered TAXABLE INCOME in the year withdrawn. Proper TAX PLANNING can help taxpayers time taxable events to maximum advantage.

TAXABLE INCOME amount of income (after all allowable deductions and adjustments to income) subject to tax. On an individual's federal income tax return, taxable income is ADJUSTED GROSS INCOME (the sum of wages, salaries, dividends, interest, capital gains, business income, etc., less allowable adjustments that, in part, include INDIVIDUAL RETIREMENT ACCOUNT contributions, alimony payments, unreimbursed business expenses and CAPITAL LOSSES up to $3000) less itemized or standard deductions and the total of personal exemptions. Once taxable income is known, the individual taxpayer finds the total income tax obligation for his or her TAX BRACKET by checking the Internal Revenue Service tax tables or by calculating the tax according to a rate schedule. TAX CREDITS reduce the tax liability dollar-for-dollar.

NET INCOME of a self-employed person (self-proprietorship) and distributions to members of a partnership are included in adjusted gross income, and hence taxable income, on an individual tax return.

Taxable income of an incorporated business, also called *net income before taxes,* consists of total revenues less cost of goods sold, selling and administrative expenses, interest, and extraordinary items.

TAXABLE MUNICIPAL BOND taxable debt obligation of a state or local government entity, an outgrowth of the TAX REFORM ACT OF 1986 (which restricted the issuance of traditional TAX-EXEMPT SECURITIES). Taxable MUNICIPAL BONDS are issued as PRIVATE PURPOSE BONDS to finance such prohibited projects as a sports stadium; as MUNICIPAL REVENUE BONDS where caps apply; or as PUBLIC PURPOSE BONDS where the 10% private use limitation has been exceeded.

TAX AND LOAN ACCOUNT account in a private-sector depository institution, held in the name of the district Federal Reserve Bank as fiscal agent of the United States, that serves as a repository for operating cash available to the U.S. Treasury. Withheld income taxes, employers' contributions to the Social Security fund, and payments for U.S. government securities routinely go into a tax and loan account.

TAX ANTICIPATION BILL (TAB) short-term obligation issued by the U.S. Treasury in competitive bidding at maturities ranging from 23 to 273 days. TABs typically come due within 5 to 7 days after the quarterly due dates for corporate tax payments, but corporations can tender them at PAR value on those tax deadlines in payment of taxes without forfeiting interest income. Since 1975, TABs have been supplemented by cash management bills, due in 30 days or less, and issued in minimum $10 million blocks. These instruments, which are timed to coincide with the maturity of existing issues, provide the Treasury with additional cash management flexibility while giving large investors a safe place to park temporary funds.

TAX ANTICIPATION NOTE (TAN) short-term obligation of a state or municipal government to finance current expenditures pending receipt of expected tax payments. TAN debt evens out the cash flow and is retired once corporate and individual tax revenues are received.

TAX AUDIT audit by the INTERNAL REVENUE SERVICE (IRS), or state or local tax collecting agency, to determine if a taxpayer paid the correct amount of tax. Returns will be chosen for audits if they have suspiciously high claims for deductions or credits, or if reported income is suspiciously low, or if computer matching of income uncovers discrepancies. Audits may be done on a relatively superficial level, or in great depth. If the auditor finds a tax deficiency, the taxpayer may have to pay back-taxes, as well as interest and penalties. The taxpayer does have the right of appeal through the IRS appeals process and, if warranted, to the U.S. Tax Court and even the U.S. Supreme Court.

TAX AVOIDANCE strategy to pay the least amount of tax possible through legal means. For example, taxpayers may buy tax-free municipal bonds; shelter gains inside tax-deferred IRA, KEOGH accounts, SALARY REDUCTION PLANS or tax-free ROTH IRA accounts; shift assets to children who need not pay taxes on part of their income; make legitimate charitable contributions to generate tax deductions; and establish trusts to avoid ESTATE TAXES. Illegal strategies to avoid paying taxes are called TAX EVASION.

TAX BASE total amount of taxable property, assets, and income that can be taxed within a specific jurisdiction. A town's tax base is the assessed value of the homes and apartments (minus exempted property), income from businesses, and other sources of taxable activity. If a business moves out of the town, the tax base shrinks, shifting the tax burden onto remaining homeowners and businesses.

TAX BASIS
Finance: original cost of an ASSET, less accumulated DEPRECIATION, that goes into the calculation of a gain or loss for tax purposes. Thus, a property acquired for $100,000 that has been depreciated by $40,000 has a tax basis of $60,000 assuming no other adjustments; sale of that property for $120,000 results in a taxable CAPITAL GAIN of $60,000.

Investments: price at which a stock or bond was purchased, plus brokerage commission. The law requires that a PREMIUM paid on the purchase of an investment be amortized.

TAX BRACKET point on the income-tax rate schedules where TAXABLE INCOME falls; also called *marginal tax bracket.* It is expressed as a percentage applied to each additional dollar earned over the base amount for that bracket. Under a PROGRESSIVE TAX SYSTEM, increases in taxable income lead to higher marginal rates in the form of higher brackets. Under current tax law, there are five tax brackets for individuals: 15%, 28%, 31%, 36% and 39.6%. The final bracket is created by applying a 10% surtax on taxable income greater than $271,050. A DEDUCTION comes off the last marginal dollar earned; thus the 31% taxpayer would save $31 in taxes with each additional $100 of deductions until he worked his way back into the 28% bracket where each $100 deduction would save $28. (A deduction should not be confused with a tax credit.)

For corporations, there are four effective tax brackets. Firms with taxable income of $50,000 or less are subject to a 15% rate; incomes from $50,000 to $75,000 are taxed at 25%; and incomes from $75,000 and up are taxed at 35%.

TAX CREDIT direct, dollar-for-dollar reduction in tax liability, as distinguished from a tax DEDUCTION, which reduces taxes only by the percentage of a taxpayer's TAX BRACKET. (A taxpayer in the 31% tax bracket would get a 31 cent benefit from each $1.00 deduction, for example.) In the case of a tax credit, a taxpayer owing $10,000 in tax would owe $9,000 if he took advantage of a $1,000 tax credit. Under certain conditions, tax credits are allowed for low-income people over age 65, people with disabilities, income tax paid to a foreign country, child care expenses ($400 per child supported under age 17 in 1998 and $500 in 1999 and thereafter), costs of adopting a child (up to $6,000), rehabilitation of historic properties, conducting research and development, building low-income housing, and providing jobs for economically disadvantaged people. THE TAXPAYER RELIEF ACT OF 1997 also created the Hope Scholarship Credit, which can offset college tuition and related educational expenses for the first two years of postsecondary education, up to a maximum of $1,500. The Act also created the Lifetime Learning Credit, which applies to tuition costs for undergraduates, graduates, and those improving their skills through a training program. The credit is worth up to 20% of up to $5,000 of qualified expenses, or $1,000 starting June 30, 1998. Starting in the year 2002, this credit increases to a maximum of 20% of $10,000, or $2,000.

TAX DEDUCTIBLE expense that generates a tax deduction. For individuals, some tax deductible items include charitable contributions, mortgage interest, state, local and foreign taxes, casualty and theft losses, medical expenses and unreimbursed business expenses. In some cases, taxpayers must meet a minimum threshold before an expense is deductible. For example, unreimbursed medical expenses are deductible if they exceed 7.5% of ADJUSTED GROSS INCOME (AGI) in a tax year, and casualty and theft losses must exceed 10% of AGI before they are deductible. In order to deduct miscellaneous expenses, they must total at least 2% of adjusted gross income. If that threshold is reached, such expenses as professional dues and subscriptions, employer-required equipment or uniforms, unreimbursed business travel and entertainment expenses, investment and tax advice, moving expenses and some home office expenses are deductible. For businesses, the costs of doing business are generally tax deductible.

TAX DEDUCTION deductible expense that reduces taxable income for individuals or businesses. *See* TAX DEDUCTIBLE for examples of legal tax deductions.

TAX DEFERRED term describing an investment whose accumulated earnings are free from taxation until the investor takes possession of them. For example, the holder of an INDIVIDUAL RETIREMENT ACCOUNT postpones paying taxes on interest, dividends, or capital appreciation if he or she waits until after age 59½ to cash in those gains. Other examples of tax-deferred investment vehicles include KEOGH PLANS; ANNUITIES; VARIABLE LIFE INSURANCE, WHOLE LIFE INSURANCE, AND UNIVERSAL LIFE INSURANCE; STOCK PURCHASE or DIVIDEND REINVESTMENT PLANS; SIMPLE IRAS; SALARY REDUCTION PLANS and SERIES EE and SERIES HH U.S. SAVINGS BONDS.

TAX STATUS ELECTION selection of filing status. Individuals may choose single, married filing jointly, married filing separately, or head of household. Businesses may elect C corporation, S corporation, limited partnership, or sole proprietorship status, among others. Taxpayers may choose to figure their tax return under two filing status categories to find out which status is most advantageous.

TAX EQUITY AND FISCAL RESPONSIBILITY ACT OF 1982 (TEFRA) federal legislation to raise tax revenue, mainly through closing various loopholes and instituting tougher enforcement procedures. Among its major components:

1. penalties for noncompliance with tax laws were increased, and various steps were taken to facilitate the collection of taxes by the Internal Revenue Service (IRS).
2. ten percent of interest and dividends earned was required to be withheld from all bank and brokerage accounts and forwarded directly to the IRS. (This provision was later canceled by Congress after a major lobbying campaign to overturn it.)
3. TAX PREFERENCE ITEMS were added to the old add-on minimum tax to strengthen the ALTERNATIVE MINIMUM TAX.
4. the floor for medical expense deductions was raised from 3% to 5% of ADJUSTED GROSS INCOME (AGI).
5. casualty and theft losses were made deductible only if each loss exceeds $100 and the total excess losses exceed 10% of AGI.
6. deductions for original issue discount bonds were limited to the amount the issuer would deduct as interest if it issued bonds with a face amount equivalent to the actual proceeds and paying the market rate of interest. This amount must be reduced by the amount of the deductions for any actual interest.
7. more rapid rates for recovering costs under the ACCELERATED COST RECOVERY SYSTEM (ACRS), which had been scheduled to go into effect in 1985 and 1986, were repealed.
8. most of the rules providing for SAFE HARBOR leasing transactions authorized under ERTA were repealed.
9. excise taxes were raised to 3% on telephone use, to 16 cents a pack on cigarettes, and to 8% on airline tickets.
10. the Federal Unemployment Tax Act wage base and tax rate were increased.
11. numerous tax incentives for corporate mergers were reduced.
12. net extraction losses in foreign oil and gas operations in one country were allowed to offset net extraction income from such operations in other countries in the computation of oil and gas extraction taxes.
13. most bonds were required to be registered so that the government could ensure that bondholders are reporting interest.
14. as long as they are not prohibited by a Foreign Corrupt Practices Act, payments to foreign officials were authorized to be deducted as legitimate business expenses.
15. the basis of assets that generate tax INVESTMENT CREDITS was reduced by one-half the amount of the credit.
16. pension and profit-sharing qualified plans were curtailed with a series of new rules that restricted plan loans, required withholding on plan distributions, limited estate-tax exclusions on certain plan distributions, and restricted

"top-heavy" plans, those tilted to benefit mostly the top-earning employees of a company.

17. changes were made in the way life insurance companies were taxed.

TAX-EQUIVALENT YIELD pretax yield that a taxable bond would have to pay to equal the tax-free yield of a municipal bond in an investor's tax bracket. To figure out the tax-equivalent yield, an investor must subtract his or her marginal tax bracket from 100, which results in the *tax bracket reciprocal.* This figure must then be divided by the yield of the tax-free municipal bond. The result is the yield which a taxable bond would have to pay to give the investor the same dollars in his or her pocket after all taxes were paid. For example, an investor in the 31% tax bracket would first take 31 from 100, producing 69 (the tax bracket reciprocal). To evaluate a 7% tax-free bond, the investor would divide 7% by 69, resulting in a 10.1% yield. Therefore, the investor would have to find a taxable bond paying 10.1% to end up with the same after-tax return as the 7% tax-free bond is offering. In general, the higher tax rates become, the more attractive tax-free income becomes, because it allows investors to escape more taxes than if tax rates were lower. *See also* YIELD EQUIVALENCE.

TAX EVASION illegal practice of intentionally evading taxes. Taxpayers who evade their true tax liability may underreport income, overstate deductions and exemptions, or participate in fraudulent tax shelters. If the taxpayer is caught, tax evasion is subject to criminal penalties, as well as payment of back taxes with interest, and civil penalties. Tax evasion is different from TAX AVOIDANCE, which is the legal use of the tax code to reduce tax liability.

TAX-EXEMPT free from tax liability. This status is granted to most municipal bonds, which pay interest that is totally free from federal taxes. Municipal bond interest is also usually tax-exempt to Londholders who are residents of the issuing state. However, other states may impose taxes on interest earned from out-of-state bonds. Certain organizations, such as registered charities, religious organizations, educational institutions, and nonprofit groups, also hold tax-exempt status, meaning they are exempt from federal, state, or local government taxes. Earnings on assets held for at least five years inside a ROTH IRA also accumulate tax-free, as long as they are withdrawn after the account holder reaches age 59½.

TAX-EXEMPT MONEY MARKET FUND MONEY MARKET FUND invested in short-term municipal securities that are tax-exempt and that thus distributes income tax-free to shareholders. Such funds pay lower income than taxable funds and should be evaluated on an AFTERTAX BASIS.

TAX-EXEMPT SECURITY obligation whose interest is exempt from taxation by federal, state, and/or local authorities. It is frequently called a MUNICIPAL BOND (or simply a *municipal),* even though it may have been issued by a state government or agency or by a county, town, or other political district or subdivision. The security is backed by the FULL FAITH AND CREDIT or by anticipated revenues of the issuing authority. Interest income from tax-exempt municipals is free from federal income taxation as well as from taxation in the jurisdiction where the securities have been issued. Thus, New York City obligations are TRIPLE TAX-EXEMPT to city residents whose income is taxed on the federal, state, and local levels. (A very few municipalities tax residents for their own otherwise tax-exempt issues.)

MUTUAL FUNDS that invest exclusively in tax-exempt securities confer the same tax advantages on their shareholders. However, while a fund's dividends would be entirely tax-exempt on a shareholder's federal tax return, they would be free from state income tax only in proportion to the amount of interest income derived from the taxpayer's home state, assuming no interstate reciprocity arrangements pertain.

The return to investors from a tax-exempt bond is less than that from a corporate bond, because the tax exemption provides extra compensation; the higher the TAX BRACKET of the investor, the more attractive the tax-free alternative becomes. Municipal bond yields vary according to local economic factors, the issuer's perceived ability to repay, and the security's quality RATING assigned by one of the bond-rating agencies. *See also* MORAL OBLIGATION BOND.

TAX-FREE EXCHANGE *see* 1031 TAX-FREE EXCHANGE.

TAX LIABILITY income, property, sales, or other taxes owed to a government entity. *See also* PROVISION FOR INCOME TAXES.

TAX HAVEN country offering outside businesses and individuals an environment with little or no taxation. Several Caribbean islands, such as the Cayman Islands, have attracted billions of dollars in bank deposits by creating a tax haven. Depositors and businesses not only lower the tax burdens in their home countries, but also are subject to less regulation and increased privacy for their financial affairs.

TAX LIEN statutory right obtained by a government to enforce a claim against the property of a person owing taxes until the debt is paid.

TAX LOSS CARRYBACK, CARRYFORWARD tax benefit that allows a company or individual to apply losses to reduce tax liability. A company may OFFSET the current year's capital or NET OPERATING LOSSES against profits in the three immediately preceding years, with the earliest year first. After the carryback, it may carry forward (also called a *carryover*) capital losses five years and net operating losses up to 15 years. By then it will presumably have regained financial health.

Individuals may carry over capital losses until they are used up for an unlimited number of years to offset capital gains. Unlike corporations, however, individuals generally cannot carry back losses to apply to prior years' tax returns. The 1986 tax act curbed tax-motivated BUYOUTS by limiting the use of NOLs where a loss corporation has had a 50% or more ownership change in a three-year period. A special set of complex rules pertains to carryback of losses for trading in commodity futures contracts.

The Revenue Reconciliation Act of 1993 introduced a provision requiring that short-term loss be first applied to reduce any long-term gain. Since previously the short-term loss would have been deductible against ordinary income up to $3000 per year, the provision effectively reduces the long-term gain available for the favorable long-term capital gains rate.

TAXPAYER RELIEF ACT OF 1997 landmark legislation signed into law by President Clinton in August 1997 as part of a larger act designed to balance the federal budget. Some of the major provisions of the law:

1. **Tax credits for children:** Parents or grandparents supporting children under the age of 17 are allowed to claim a TAX CREDIT of $400 per child in 1998 and $500 per child in 1999 and every year thereafter. The credit can be used in addition to the existing deduction for each dependent. This tax credit is phased out for families reporting an ADJUSTED GROSS INCOME of $110,000 on a joint return, $55,000 for those married filing separately, and $75,000 for a single filer. The credit is reduced by $50 for each $1,000 of the threshold, and it disappears altogether for couples with incomes of $119,000 or more and singles with incomes of $85,000 or higher. A tax credit of $5,000 was also added for taxpayers who adopt children, with up to $6,000 for adoptions of "special needs" children.

2. **Estate tax exclusion raised:** The amount of ASSETS that individuals can exclude from estate taxes was boosted from $600,000 to $1 million, and up to $1.3 million for small businessmen and farmers. The increase in the universal

estate tax exclusion is phased in over a nine-year period, with the limit rising to $625,000 in 1998, $650,000 in 1999, $675,000 in 2000 and 2001, $700,000 in 2002 and 2003, $850,000 in 2004, $950,000 in 2005, and topping out at $1 million in 2006 and later years. However, the $1.3 million limit for farms and other small businesses went into effect fully on January 1, 1998. To qualify as a small business, an estate's business assets must represent at least 50% of its total assets. To preserve the tax break, heirs must also "materially participate" in running the business for at least five of the eight years within ten years of the owner's death. If heirs sell the business to nonfamily members within ten years after the owner's death, they must pay some of the taxes from which they were originally exempt.

In the Tax Act, three other estate tax limits were indexed to inflation, rounded to the next lowest multiple of $10,000:
• the $1 million exemption from the generation-skipping transfer (GST) tax.
• the $750,000 maximum reduction in value on special use valuation of real property used in farming or a closely held business.
• the $1 million maximum value of a closely held business eligible for a special 4% interest rate on estate tax installment payments.

3. **Gift tax limit indexed to inflation:** The $10,000 a year GIFT TAX limit was tied to the rate of inflation, and is adjustable in $1,000 increments starting on January 1, 1999.

4. **Lower capital gains tax rates:** The top tax rate on profits from the sale of assets like stocks, bonds, mutual funds and real estate was lowered from 28% to 20%. Before this law, those in the 15% and 28% income tax brackets paid the same tax rate on CAPITAL GAINS as on regular income. Only those in higher tax brackets benefited from the 28% capital gains tax rate cap. Under the 1997 law, those in the 28% bracket pay a maximum rate of 20%, while those in the 15% tax bracket pay a maximum of just 10% when they realize capital gains. The new rules apply to anyone selling assets after May 6, 1997, but do not apply to sales of hard assets like art, antiques, stamps, coins, gems and collectibles, for which the top capital gains tax rate remains 28%. These capital gains tax rates apply for ALTERNATIVE MINIMUM TAX (AMT) purposes as well as for regular federal taxes.

5. **New tax rate for property that received accelerated depreciation:** For those selling a business or investment real estate on which they took accelerated depreciation, the portion of the capital gain representing depreciation is eligible for a maximum tax rate of 25% if the asset is sold after May 6, 1997.

6. **Longer-term capital gains rates created:** For assets like stocks, bonds, and mutual funds purchased after January 1, 2000 and held for at least five years, the top capital gains rate was lowered to 18% for those in the 28% tax bracket or higher. The tax rate for holding assets for five years was lowered to 8% for those in the 15% tax bracket.

7. **Changed holding period for capital gains:** Previous law stated that assets had to be held for at least 12 months to qualify for long-term CAPITAL GAINS rates. Under the 1997 law, assets must be held for at least 18 months to qualify for the advantageous capital gains tax rates. Subsequently, the INTERNAL REVENUE SERVICE RESTRUCTURING AND REFORM ACT OF 1998, enacted into law in the summer of 1998, reduced the holding period back to 12 months.

8. **Expanded tax deductibility for individual retirement account contributions:** Under previous law, taxpayers could not fully deduct their contributions to INDIVIDUAL RETIREMENT ACCOUNTS if their adjusted gross income exceeded $40,000 on a joint tax return or $25,000 for a single tax return. The law raised those income caps to $50,000 for a joint return and $30,000 for a

single, starting in 1998. The caps gradually climb over ten years (by 2007) to $80,000 for a couple and $50,000 for a single. Over those limits, the deduction phases out for the next $10,000 in income. For singles, the deduction is phased out completely once income tops $40,000 in 1998, climbing to $60,000 in 2005. For married couples filing jointly, the deduction is phased out once income exceeds $60,000 in 1998, rising to $100,000 in 2007.

9. **Introduction of the Roth IRA:** A new kind of INDIVIDUAL RETIREMENT ACCOUNT was created called the ROTH IRA, which allows individuals to invest up to $2,000 in earnings a year, even after they reach age 70½. They can withdraw all the principal and earnings totally tax free after age 59½, as long as the assets have remained in the IRA for at least five years. Unlike regular IRAs, participants do not have to take distributions from a Roth IRA starting at age 70½. In fact, they do not have to take distributions at all in their lifetime if they prefer, allowing them to pass the assets in the Roth to their beneficiaries income-tax free. Contributions to Roth IRAs do not generate tax deductions.

   Roth IRA rules also permit account holders to withdraw assets without the usual 10% early withdrawal penalty if they use the money for the purchase of a first home (withdrawals are limited to up to $10,000), for college expenses or if they become disabled.

   Only married couples with adjusted gross incomes of $150,000 or less and singles with adjusted gross incomes of $95,000 or less can contribute the full amount to Roth IRAs. The amount they can contribute is phased out for incomes between $150,000 and $160,000 for married couples, and between $95,000 and $110,000 for singles. No contributions are allowed over those income limits.

   For those with adjusted gross incomes of $100,000 or less, the law allows people to roll over existing deductible and nondeductible IRA balances into a Roth IRA without the normal 10% premature distribution penalty. When they do so, however, they must pay income tax on all previously untaxed contributions and earnings. For rollovers executed before January 1, 1999, the resulting tax bill is spread over four years. Starting in 1999, the rollover is fully taxable in the year it is completed.

10. **"Cash-out" threshold for 401(k) plans raised:** Under previous law, an employer could "cash out" any departing employee whose 401(k) balance was $3,500 or less. The employee could either take the money and pay taxes on it or roll it over into an IRA ROLLOVER ACCOUNT. The new tax law raised that limit to $5,000, meaning that more workers will be "cashed out" of their 401(k) plans than before.

11. **More investments allowed in IRAs:** Starting in 1998, IRA account holders can invest in metals such as gold, silver, platinum and palladium. Previously, such IRA investments were banned.

12. **Repeal of the "short-short" rule:** Under previous law, mutual funds lost their tax pass-through status if more than 30% of their gross income was generated from short-term investment gains under what was known as the "short-short" rule. As a result, fund managers were afraid to use trading strategies such as the use of options contracts, hedging, and short-selling that would generate short-term profits on holdings, even though the fund manager wanted to do so for investment reasons. The tax bill repealed the "short-short" rule, freeing up managers to trade frequently without fear of losing their tax pass-through status. *See also* SHORT-SHORT RULE.

13. **Eliminated "short against the box" as a tax delay technique:** A popular way for some investors to delay paying taxes was "SELL SHORT AGAINST THE BOX." In this technique, an investor who owns a particular stock would sell borrowed shares of the stock rather than shares already owned. This tactic is

similar to selling because the investor no longer owns an economic interest in the stock, but previous tax law did not treat it as a sale. Under the 1997 law, shorting against the box after June 8, 1997 is considered a "constructive sale," and will result in a CAPITAL GAINS TAX liability. In effect, this law change means it no longer makes sense to use this technique to delay paying taxes.

14. **Simplifies reporting of taxes on foreign investments:** Starting with 1998 tax-year returns, investors with holdings in foreign stocks, bonds, or mutual funds no longer need to fill out the complicated IRS Form 116 to claim the foreign tax credit. This applies to single investors who pay up to $300 a year in foreign taxes and for married couples filing jointly up to $600 a year. The amount of foreign earned income that taxpayers can exclude from taxation increases from $72,000 in 1998 to $74,000 in 1999, $76,000 in 2000, $78,000 in 2001 and $80,000 in 2002 and later years.

15. **Repeal of excess accumulation and excess distributions tax:** In earlier legislation, Congress imposed a 15% "excess accumulation tax" on LUMP SUM payouts of more than $800,000 from pension plans and a 15% "excess distributions tax" on payouts from INDIVIDUAL RETIREMENT ACCOUNTS of more than $160,000. All of these taxes were repealed for distributions made after December 31, 1996.

16. **New capital gains rules for home sales:** Under previous law, homeowners could avoid CAPITAL GAINS TAXES on the sale of their home only if they bought another home within two years and reinvested the proceeds into a home of the same or greater value. Those over age 55 could escape capital gains tax when selling their homes up to $125,000 once in their lifetime. The 1997 tax law allows people to avoid all capital gains taxes on profits up to $500,000 for married couples filing jointly and up to $250,000 for those filing singly. The rule which benefits anyone selling their home after May 6, 1997, only applies to a person's primary residence, defined as a home occupied for at least two of the five years prior to the sale. Individuals can claim the $500,000 capital gains tax exemption every two years. The old $125,000 exemption for those over 55 was superceded by the new law. In the past, someone with gains of more than $500,000 could avoid taxes by rolling the profits into a larger home. The 1997 law eliminates such a rollover. Capital gains taxes of up to 20% are due upon the sale of a home with profits over $500,000. One other twist affects real-estate investors who depreciate their property over time. When these investors sell the property, they must pay a maximum 25% capital gains tax for the part of their gain due to depreciation.

17. **Tax credits for college education:** The law created the "Hope Scholarship," a tax credit to help pay for the first two years of tuition and fees for students attending college or vocational school. The tax credit started at $1,500 in 1998 and rises to $2,000 in 2003. Starting on July 1, 1998, a yearly "Lifetime Learning Credit" of up to $1,000 for 20% of tuition and school fees up to $5,000 is available for third- and fourth-year college students, graduate students, and people returning to school to sharpen job skills. This credit rises to 20% of $10,000, or a maximum of $2,000, in 2002. These tax credits are available only to married couples filing jointly with adjusted gross incomes of $80,000 or less, or singles with $40,000 or less. The credit is phased out for couples with incomes of $100,000 and singles earning over $50,000.

18. **Deductible education-related interest:** Starting in 1998, up to $1,000 in interest on student loans is deductible for taxpayers repaying loans for their own or a dependent's college or vocational school expenses. The interest is deductible only for the first 60 months (5 years) that the loan is outstanding. The $1,000 cap increases by $500 annually until it reaches a maximum of $2,500 in 2001. Taxpayers can get this deduction even if they don't file an itemized return. This deductible interest is fully available to married taxpay-

ers with $60,000 or less in income if filing jointly or $40,000 or less for singles. The deduction phases out for couples with incomes between $60,000 and $75,000 and for singles with incomes between $40,000 and $55,000, and is not available for those with incomes over those thresholds. Income levels will be adjusted for inflation starting in 2003.

19. **Tax-free employer-paid education:** Employees are entitled to receive up to $5,250 per year from their employers for undergraduate classes without having to declare that money as taxable income. This rule applies to classes not directly related to their job. The tax break remains in effect for courses beginning before June 1, 2000. Reimbursement for schooling that is job-related remains tax-free without limitation.

20. **Creation of Education IRA:** A new type of account, similar to an INDIVIDUAL RETIREMENT ACCOUNT, called the EDUCATION IRA, was created to allow parents to save up to $500 per year per child under age 18 to help pay educational expenses. The money invested does not generate a deduction when placed in the Education IRA, but the principal, income, and CAPITAL GAINS are completely tax-free when withdrawn to pay for college expenses such as tuition, fees, books and room and board. *See also* EDUCATION IRA.

21. **Tax relief for children:** In the past, children earning more than $650 a year in wages could not use their standard deduction to shelter investment income from taxes. Beginning in 1998, children can use the standard deduction to shelter both their job earnings plus up to $250 in investment income.

22. **Bigger deductions for health insurance premiums for the self-employed:** Under previous law, only a portion of health insurance premiums paid by the self-employed were deductible, while all premiums paid by larger companies were deductible. This inequity was phased out by the law. In 1997, 40% of the premium paid by the self-employed were deductible. In 1998 and 1999, it rose to 45%. In 2000 and 2001, it rises to 50%. In 2002 it is 60%. From 2003 through 2005, the deduction rises to 80%. In 2006 it is 90%. From 2007 and future years, the deduction is 100%.

23. **Creation of the Medical Savings Account (MSA):** People with high-deductible health plans may participate in a Medical Savings Account. They can deduct MSA contributions even if they do not itemize deductions. MSAs are generally available for the self-employed and small employers with fewer than 50 workers.

24. **Social Security and Medicare taxes:** The maximum wages subject to Social Security tax (6.2%) was raised to $65,400. All wages are subject to the Medicare tax of 1.45%.

25. **Liberalization of the home office deduction:** For many years, the IRS rules and court decisions greatly restricted home office deductions. The 1997 tax law eased the rules and home office deductions are allowed starting in 1999 if the space used is essential to running or administering the business. No longer does the space have to be the only place where the taxpayer meets clients or conducts their work. However, taxpayers must use the home office space exclusively and regularly for business purposes.

26. **Higher exemption from filing quarterly estimated taxes:** Starting in 1998, the law exempts those expecting to pay less than $1,000 in taxes from having to make quarterly estimated tax payments. This doubles the previous limit of $500. In figuring estimated tax, however, taxpayers must include any expected employment taxes for household workers.

27. **Higher deduction for charitable use of your car:** The deduction for using an automobile to benefit a charity rose from 12 cents to 14 cents a mile, starting in 1998.

28. **Repeal of motorboat gas tax:** The 24.3 cent a gallon tax on diesel fuel for recreational motorboats was repealed.

29. **Paying taxes by credit card:** The bill authorized the Internal Revenue Service to accept payment of taxes by credit or debit card or electronic funds transfer, though the IRS is prohibited from paying fees to card issuers.

30. **Higher cigarette taxes:** The excise tax on cigarettes rises by 10 cents a pack to 34 cents in 2000 and by an additional 5 cents to 39 cents in 2002.

31. **Higher airline ticket taxes:** The excise tax on airline tickets rose from $6 to $12 on departures to international destinations, and a $12 per ticket fee was added on international arrivals. A $3 airport-to-airport segment tax was also added on all domestic flights. The airline ticket tax was gradually scaled back from 10% to 7.5%.

See also INTERNAL REVENUE SERVICE RESTRUCTURING AND REFORM ACT OF 1998.

TAX PLANNING strategy of minimizing tax liability for an individual or company by analyzing the tax implications of various options throughout a tax year. Tax planning involves choosing a FILING STATUS, figuring out the most advantageous time to realize capital gains and losses, knowing when to accelerate deductions and postpone income or vice versa, setting up a proper estate plan to reduce estate taxes, and other legitimate tax-saving moves.

TAX PREFERENCE ITEM item specified by the tax law that a taxpayer must include when calculating the ALTERNATIVE MINIMUM TAX (AMT). Preference items include: the (adjusted) excess of MODIFIED ACCELERATED COST RECOVERY SYSTEM (MACRS) deductions over alternative depreciation system (ADS) deductions (ADS is an alternative depreciation system with longer deduction periods) on real property placed into service before 1987; and tax-exempt interest on nonessential PRIVATE PURPOSE BONDS of municipalities issued after August 7, 1986.

Corporate preferences are generally the same as for individuals, but also include an adjustment for current earnings (ACE) aimed at profits reported to shareholders but not regularly taxed. The ACE adjustment is based on 75% of the difference between a corporation's alternative minimum taxable income (AMTI) for the tax year and its adjusted earnings and profits. The depreciation deduction for PERSONAL PROPERTY, a large part of AMTI, requires use of the 150% declining-balance method. *See also* TAX EQUITY AND FISCAL RESPONSIBILITY ACT OF 1982, TAX REFORM ACT OF 1976, TAX REFORM ACT OF 1986.

TAX PREPARATION SERVICES businesses that specialize in preparing tax returns. Such services may range from national tax preparation chains such as H&R Block to local tax preparers, enrolled agents, CPAs, and tax lawyers. Services normally charge based on the complexity of the tax return and the amount of time needed to fill it out correctly. Many services can arrange to file a tax return with the Internal Revenue Service electronically, which can result in a faster TAX REFUND.

TAX RATE percentage of tax paid on a certain level of income. The U.S. uses a system of marginal tax rates, meaning that the rates rise with taxable income. The top rate is paid only on the portion of income over the threshold. Currently, the federal government imposes four tax rates—15%, 28%, 31%, and 36%. There is also a 10% surtax on married couples filing jointly or singles reporting taxable incomes of more than $271,050 or married couples filing separately with taxable incomes of more than $135,525. This creates an effective fifth tax rate of 39.6%.

TAX REFORM ACT OF 1976 federal legislation that tightened several provisions and benefits relating to taxation, beginning in the 1976 tax year. Among its major provisions:

1. extended the long-term CAPITAL GAINS holding period from six months to nine months in 1977 and to 12 months beginning in 1978.

2. instituted new rules on determining the TAX BASIS of inherited property.

3. set a new minimum capital gains tax on the sale of a house.

4. established, for homeowners over age 65, a once-in-a-lifetime exclusion of up to $35,000 in capital gains tax on the sale of a principal residence. (This amount was later raised by other tax bills, until it stood at $125,000 in the mid-1980s.)

5. increased the maximum net CAPITAL LOSS deduction from ordinary income on a personal income tax return to $3000 beginning in 1978.

6. extended the period of tax loss carryforward from five years to seven; gave companies the option of carrying losses forward without having first to carry them back; and prohibited acquiring corporations from taking advantage of an acquired firm's loss carryovers unless it gave the acquired firm's stockholders continuing ownership in the combined company.

7. limited deductions for home-office expenses to cases where homes are used as principal business locations, or for meeting with clients.

8. disallowed owners who rent their vacation homes from reporting losses, deducting maintenance costs or taking depreciation on those rentals unless the owners themselves used the homes less than two weeks per year, or less than 10% of total rental time.

9. instituted a deduction up to $3000 for "indirect" moving costs if a new job is more than 35 miles from a previous job.

10. established a child-care tax credit of up to $400 for one child and up to $800 for more than one child.

11. allowed a divorced parent, if contributing at least $1200 in child support, to claim a child as a dependent deduction.

12. instituted a spousal INDIVIDUAL RETIREMENT ACCOUNT, which allowed non-working spouses to contribute up to $250.

13. disallowed losses on tax shelters financed through loans made without any obligation to pay, or where taxpayer's risk is limited by a form of guarantee, except for real estate investments.

14. treated the exercise of a STOCK OPTION as ordinary income rather than as a CAPITAL GAIN.

TAX REFORM ACT OF 1984 legislation enacted by Congress as part of the Deficit Reduction Act of 1984 to reduce the federal budget deficit. The following are highlights from the more than 100 provisions in the Act:

1. shortened the minimum holding period for assets to qualify for long-term capital gains treatment from one year to six months.

2. allowed contributions to be made to an INDIVIDUAL RETIREMENT ACCOUNT no later than April 15 after the tax year for which an IRA benefit is sought; previously the cut-off was the following October 15th.

3. allowed the Internal Revenue Service to tax the benefits of loans made on below-market, interest-free, or "gift" terms.

4. tightened INCOME AVERAGING requirements.

5. set a $150 per capita limit on the amount of INDUSTRIAL DEVELOPMENT BONDS that a state could issue in a year, and permitted interest to be tax-exempt only for certain "small issues."

6. retained the 15% minimum tax on corporate TAX PREFERENCE ITEMS as in the TAX REFORM ACT OF 1976, but increased from 15% to 20% the deduction allowed for a tax preference item.

7. restricted GOLDEN PARACHUTE payments to executives by eliminating the corporate tax deductibility of these payments and subjecting them to a nondeductible 20% excise tax.

8. required registration of TAX SHELTERS with the Internal Revenue Service and set penalties for failure to comply. Also set penalties for overvaluing assets used for depreciation in a tax shelter.

9. expanded rules in ERTA to cover additional types of stock and options transactions that make up TAX STRADDLES.

10. repealed the 30% withholding tax on interest, dividends, rents, and royalties paid to foreign investors by U.S. corporations and government agencies.

11. raised the liquor tax, reduced the cigarette tax, and extended the 3% telephone excise tax.

12. delayed to 1987 the scheduled decline in estate and gift taxes.

13. granted a specific tax exemption for many fringe benefits.

14. extended mortgage subsidy bonds through 1988.

15. required ALTERNATIVE MINIMUM TAX quarterly estimated payments.

16. changed the rules affecting taxation of life insurance companies.

17. disqualified from eligibility for long-term capital gains tax the appreciation of market discounts on newly issued ORIGINAL ISSUE DISCOUNT bonds.

18. real estate depreciation was lengthened from 15 to 18 years.

19. delayed implementation of new finance leasing rules until 1988.

20. restricted the sale of unused depreciation tax deductions by tax-exempt entities to companies that can use the deductions.

21. phased out the graduated corporate income tax on the first $100,000 of income for corporations with income over $1 million.

22. created Foreign Sales Corporations (FSCs) to provide American companies with tax deferral advantages to encourage exports.

23. limited tax breaks for luxury automobiles to a maximum write-off of $16,000 in the first three years of ownership.

24. increased the earned income tax credit for lower-income taxpayers from 10% to a maximum of 11% of the first $5000 of income.

25. eliminated the tax on property transfers in a divorce.

26. increased the standard automobile mileage rate from 9 cents a mile to 12 cents a mile for expenses incurred in volunteer charity work.

27. tightened rules and increased penalties for those who try to inflate deductions by overvaluing property donated to charity.

TAX REFORM ACT OF 1986 landmark federal legislation enacted that made comprehensive changes in the system of U.S. taxation. Among the law's major provisions:

Provisions Affecting Individuals

1. lowered maximum marginal tax rates from 50% to 28% beginning in 1988 and reduced the number of basic TAX BRACKETS from 15 to 2—28% and 15%. Also instituted a 5% rate surcharge for high-income taxpayers.

2. eliminated the preferential tax treatment of CAPITAL GAINS. Starting in 1988, all gains realized on asset sales were taxed at ordinary income rates, no matter how long the asset was held.

3. increased the personal exemption to $1900 in 1987, $1950 in 1988, and $2000 in 1989. Phased out exemption for high-income taxpayers.

4. increased the STANDARD DEDUCTION, and indexed it to inflation starting in 1989.

5. repealed the deduction for two-earner married couples.

6. repealed income averaging for all taxpayers.

7. repealed the $100 ($200 for couples) dividend exclusion.

8. restricted the deductibility of IRA contributions.

9. mandated the phaseout of consumer interest deductibility by 1991.

10. allowed investment interest expense to be offset against investment income, dollar-for-dollar, without limitation.

11. limited unreimbursed medical expenses that could be deducted to amounts in excess of 7.5% of adjusted gross income.

12. limited the tax deductibility of interest on a first or second home mortgage to the purchase price of the house plus the cost of improvements and amounts used for medical or educational purposes.
13. repealed the deductibility of state and local sales taxes.
14. limited miscellaneous deductions to expenses exceeding 2% of adjusted gross income.
15. limited the deductibility of itemized charitable contributions.
16. strengthened the ALTERNATIVE MINIMUM TAX, and raised the rate to 21%.
17. tightened home office deductions.
18. lowered the deductibility of business entertainment and meal expenses from 100% to 80%.
19. eliminated the benefits of CLIFFORD TRUSTS and other income-shifting devices by taxing unearned income over $1000 on gifts to children under 14 years old at the grantor's tax rate.
20. repealed the tax credit for political contributions.
21. limited the use of losses from PASSIVE activity to offsetting income from passive activity.
22. lowered the top rehabilitation tax credit from 25% to 20%.
23. made all unemployment compensation benefits taxable.
24. repealed the deduction for attending investment seminars.
25. eased the rules for exercise of INCENTIVE STOCK OPTIONS.
26. imposed new limitations on SALARY REDUCTION PLANS and SIMPLIFIED EMPLOYEE PENSION (SEP) PLANS.

Provisions Affecting Business
27. lowered the top corporate tax rate to 34% from 46%, and lowered the number of corporate tax brackets from five to three.
28. applied the ALTERNATIVE MINIMUM TAX (AMT) to corporations, and set a 20% rate.
29. repealed the investment tax credit for property placed in service after 1985.
30. altered the method of calculating DEPRECIATION.
31. limited the deductibility of charges to BAD DEBT reserves to financial institutions with less than $500 million in assets.
32. extended the research and development tax credit, but lowered the rate from 25% to 20%.
33. eliminated the deductibility of interest that banks pay to finance tax-exempt securities holdings.
34. eliminated the deductibility of GREENMAIL payments by companies warding off hostile takeover attempts.
35. restricted COMPLETED CONTRACT METHOD accounting for tax purposes.
36. limited the ability of a company acquiring more than 50% of another firm to use NET OPERATING LOSSES to offset taxes.
37. reduced the corporate DIVIDEND EXCLUSION from 85% to 80%.
38. limited cash and installment method accounting for tax purposes.
39. restricted tax-exemption on MUNICIPAL BONDS to PUBLIC PURPOSE BONDS and specified PRIVATE PURPOSE BONDS. Imposed caps on the dollar amount of permitted private purpose bonds. Limited PREREFUNDING. Made interest on certain private purpose bonds subject to the AMT.
40. amended the rules for qualifying as a REAL ESTATE INVESTMENT TRUST and the taxation of REITs.
41. set up tax rules for real estate mortgage investment conduits (REMICs).
42. changed many rules relating to taxation of foreign operations of U.S. multinational companies.
43. liberalized the requirements for employee VESTING rules in a company's qualified pension plan, and changed other rules affecting employee benefit plans.
44. enhanced benefit of SUBCHAPTER S corporation status.

TAX REFORM ACT OF 1993 *see* REVENUE RECONCILIATION ACT OF 1993.

TAX REFUND refund of overpaid taxes from the government to the taxpayer. Refunds are due when the taxpayer has been OVERWITHHOLDING, or has overestimated income or underestimated deductions, exemptions, and credits. Though taxpayers may like the fact that they are getting a tax refund, in fact they are granting the government an interest-free loan for most of the year, which is not astute TAX PLANNING.

TAX SCHEDULES tax forms used in addition to the Form 1040 to report itemized deductions (Schedule A); dividend and interest income (Schedule B); profit or loss from business (Schedule C); capital gains and losses (Schedule D); supplemental income and loss (Schedule E); and Social Security Self-employment tax (Schedule SE).

TAX SELLING selling of securities, usually at year end, to realize losses in a PORTFOLIO, which can be used to OFFSET capital gains and thereby lower an investor's tax liability. *See also* LONG-TERM GAIN; LONG-TERM LOSS; SELLING SHORT AGAINST THE BOX; SHORT-TERM GAIN (OR LOSS); SWAP; THIRTY-DAY WASH RULE.

TAX SHIELD deductions that reduce tax liabilities. For example, mortgage interest, charitable contributions, unreimbursed business expenses, and medical expenses can be considered tax shields if a taxpayer qualifies for the deduction. The higher the marginal tax rate, the more the deduction is worth.

TAX SHELTER method used by investors to legally avoid or reduce tax liabilities. Legal shelters include those using DEPRECIATION of assets like real estate or equipment, or DEPLETION allowances for oil and gas exploration. LIMITED PARTNERSHIPS traditionally offered investors limited liability and tax benefits including "flow through" operating losses which offset income from other sources. The TAX REFORM ACT OF 1986 dealt a severe blow to such tax shelters by ruling that passive losses could only offset passive income, lengthening depreciation schedules, and extending AT RISK rules to include real estate investments. Vehicles that allow tax-deferred capital growth, such as INDIVIDUAL RETIREMENT ACCOUNTS (IRAs) and KEOGH PLANS (which also provide current tax deductions for qualified taxpayers), SALARY REDUCTION PLANS, SIMPLE IRAS, and LIFE INSURANCE, are also popular tax shelters as are tax-exempt MUNICIPAL BONDS. The ROTH IRA, created in the TAXPAYER RELIEF ACT OF1997, allows tax free accumulation of earnings on assets held in the account for at least five years.

TAX SOFTWARE software that helps taxpayers plan for and prepare their tax returns. Software such as TurboTax and TaxCut helps taxpayers analyze their tax situation and take actions to minimize tax liability. Different versions of tax software are appropriate for large and small businesses, partnerships, individuals, and estates. The software also comes in state-specific versions to aid in preparation and planning for state taxes. When integrated with a personal finance software package, a taxpayer does not have to reenter data, which can easily be exchanged from the personal finance side into the tax preparation side of the package.

TAX STRADDLE technique whereby OPTION or FUTURES CONTRACTS are used to eliminate economic risk while creating an advantageous tax position. In its most common use, an investor with a CAPITAL GAIN would take a position creating an offsetting "artificial" loss in the current tax year and postponing the gain until the next tax year. The ECONOMIC RECOVERY TAX ACT OF 1981 curtailed this practice by requiring traders to MARK TO THE MARKET at year-end and include unrealized gains in taxable income. The TAX REFORM ACT OF 1986 introduced a change whereby an exception for COVERED WRITERS of calls is denied if the taxpayer fails to hold the covered CALL OPTION for 30 days after the related stock is disposed of at a loss, if gain on the termination or disposition of the option is included in the next year.

TAX UMBRELLA tax loss carryforwards stemming from losses of a firm in past years, which shield profits earned in current and future years from taxes. *See also* TAX LOSS CARRYBACK, CARRYFORWARD.

TEAR SHEET sheet from one of a dozen loose-leaf books comprising Standard & Poor's Stock Reports, which provide essential background and financial data on several thousand companies. Brokers often tear and mail these sheets to customers (hence the name).

TEASER RATE introductory interest rate on an adjustable rate mortgage (ARM) designed to entice borrowers. The teaser rate may last for a few months, or as long as a year, before the rate returns to a market level. In a competitive mortgage market, some mortgage lenders may offer competing teaser rates to try to win over potential borrowers. In addition to the marketing rationale for teaser rates, lenders maintain that having a low initial rate makes it easier for homeowners to settle into a new home, with all the expenses entailed in moving in. Only portfolio lenders can offer teaser rates. Mortgage bankers cannot because they must comply with investor guidelines.

TECHNICAL ANALYSIS research into the demand and supply for securities, options, mutual funds, and commodities based on trading volume and price studies. Technical analysts use charts or computer programs to identify and project price trends in a market, security, fund, or futures contract. Most analysis is done for the short- or intermediate-term, but some technicians also predict long-term cycles based on charts and other data. Unlike FUNDAMENTAL ANALYSIS, technical analysis is not concerned with the financial position of a company. *See also* ADVANCE/DECLINE (A/D); ASCENDING TOPS; BREAKOUT; CORRECTION; DEAD CAT BOUNCE; DESCENDING TOPS; DIP; DOUBLE BOTTOM; ELVES; FALL OUT OF BED; FLAG; FLURRY; GAP; GAP OPENING; HEAD AND SHOULDERS; HORIZONTAL PRICE MOVEMENT; MOMENTUM INDICATORS; MOVING AVERAGE; MOVING AVERAGE CONVERGENCE/DIVERGENCE (MACD); NEW HIGH/NEW LOW; PENNANT; POINT AND FIGURE CHART; PUT-CALL RATIO; RELATIVE STRENGTH; RESISTANCE LEVEL; REVERSAL; RISING BOTTOMS; SAUCER; SELLING CLIMAX; STOCHASTICS INDEX; SUPPORT LEVEL; TRADING PATTERN; TRIANGLE; V FORMATION; VERTICAL LINE CHARTING; W FORMATION.

TECHNICAL RALLY short rise in securities or commodities futures prices within a general declining trend. Such a rally may result because investors are bargain-hunting or because analysts have noticed a particular SUPPORT LEVEL at which securities usually bounce up. Technical rallies do not last long, however, and soon after prices resume their declining pattern.

TECHNICAL SIGN short-term trend that technical analysts can identify as significant in the price movement of a security or a commodity. *See also* TECHNICAL ANALYSIS.

TED SPREAD difference between interest rates on U.S. Treasury bills and Eurodollars. The term *Ted* refers to *Treasuries over Eurodollars*. Many traders in the futures markets actively trade the Ted spread, speculating that the difference between U.S. Treasuries and Eurodollars will widen or narrow. The Ted spread also is used as an indicator of confidence in the U.S. government and the general level of fear or confidence in the markets for private financing. A narrow spread indicates confidence in financial markets in general and the U.S. Government in particular. When the spread is wide, confidence is diminished. *See also* FLIGHT TO QUALITY.

TEFRA *see* TAX EQUITY AND FISCAL RESPONSIBILITY ACT OF 1982.

TEL AVIV STOCK EXCHANGE only stock exchange in Israel. Trading hours for stocks, warrants, and convertible bonds are 10:30 A.M. to 3:30 P.M., Sunday through Thursday. Options are traded on the 25 companies with highest market value that are part of the *Maof Index*. All other derivatives and all shares are reflected in the *General Share Index*. Trades are settled on the day following the trade.

TELEPHONE SWITCHING process of shifting assets from one MUTUAL FUND or VARIABLE ANNUITY portfolio to another by telephone. Such a switch may be among the stock, bond, or money-market funds of a single FAMILY OF FUNDS, or it may be from a fund in one family to a fund in another. Transfers involving portfolios in annuity contracts do not trigger taxation of gains as do mutual fund switches.

TEMPORARY INVESTMENT investment designed to be held for a short period of time, typically a year or less. Some examples of temporary investments are money market mutual funds, money market deposit accounts, NOW checking accounts, Treasury bills, and short-term CDs. Investors shifting money into such investments may have sold stocks, bonds, or mutual funds, and are keeping their assets liquid while they decide which investments to buy next. They also may be fearful that securities prices are about to fall, and they want to keep their assets in temporary investments to sidestep such a downdraft. While their money is in temporary investments, it continues to earn interest at prevailing market interest rates. *See also* PARKING.

TENANCY AT WILL tenancy where a person holds or occupies real estate with the permission of the owner, for an unspecified term. A tenancy at will could occur when a lease is being negotiated, or under a valid oral lease or contract of sale. All the duties and obligations of a landlord-tenant relationship exist. Notice of termination is required by either party. The tenancy is not assignable.

TENANCY BY THE ENTIRETY (TBE) form of individual (versus corporate or partnership) co-ownership in which ownership passes automatically at the death of one co-owner to the surviving co-owner. The person with a TBE co-ownership interest lacks the power to freely dispose of that interest by WILL. In this respect, it is similar to JOINT TENANCY WITH RIGHT OF SURVIVORSHIP (JTWROS). Unlike JTWROS, however, the TBE ownership interests are limited to ownership by two persons who are husband and wife at the time the property is acquired. If the married couple then divorces, the form of ownership automatically changes to TENANCY IN COMMON (TIC). Generally, TBE ownership is limited to real estate, although about a dozen states permit TBE ownership of personal property.

TENANCY IN COMMON (TIC) ownership of real or personal property by two or more persons in which ownership at the death of one co-owner is part of the owner's disposable ESTATE, and does not pass to the co-owner(s). There is no limit to the number of persons who can acquire property as TIC, and those persons could be, but need not be married to each other.

TENANT
Real Estate: (1) holder or possessor of real property; (2) lessee.
Securities: part owner of a security.
    See also JOINT TENANTS WITH RIGHT OF SURVIVORSHIP; TENANCY IN COMMON.

TENBAGGER stock that grows in value by ten times. The term comes from baseball lingo, since a double is called a two-bagger because it earns the hitter the right to two bases, or bags. Similarly, a triple is a three-bagger and a home run a four-bagger. The term, as applied to investing, is also used in larger multiples, such as a twenty-bagger, for a stock that grows twenty-fold.

TENDER
1. act of surrendering one's shares in a corporation in response to an offer to buy them at a set price. *See also* TENDER OFFER.
2. to submit a formal bid to buy a security, as in a U.S. Treasury bill auction. *See also* DUTCH AUCTION.
3. offer of money or goods in settlement of a prior debt or claim, as in the delivery of goods on the due date of a FUTURES CONTRACT.
4. agreed-upon medium for the settlement of financial transactions, such as U.S. currency, which is labeled "legal tender for all debts, public and private."

TENDER OFFER offer to buy shares of a corporation, usually at a PREMIUM above the shares' market price, for cash, securities, or both, often with the objective of taking control of the TARGET COMPANY. A tender offer may arise from friendly negotiations between the company and a corporate suitor or may be unsolicited and possibly unfriendly, resulting in countermeasures being taken by the target firm. The Securities and Exchange Commission requires any corporate suitor accumulating 5% or more of a target company to make disclosures to the SEC, the target company, and the relevant exchange. *See also* SCHEDULE 13D; TAKEOVER; TREASURY STOCK.

1040 EZ FORM simplified alternative to the 1040 FORM for taxpayers who (1) have single or "married filing jointly" status; (2) are under age 65; (3) are not blind; (4) claim no dependents; (5) have taxable income under $50,000; (6) have income only from salaries, wages, tips, taxable scholarship or fellowship grants, unemployment compensation and taxable interest income below $400; and (7) did not receive any advance EARNED INCOME CREDIT payments.

1040 FORM basic form issued by the INTERNAL REVENUE SERVICE for individual tax returns. *See also* TAX SCHEDULES.

10-K REPORT *see* FORM 10-K.

1099 annual statement sent to the Internal Revenue Service and to taxpayers by the payers of dividends (1099-DIV) and interest (1099-INT) and by issuers of taxable ORIGINAL ISSUE DISCOUNT securities (1099-OID).

TEN PERCENT GUIDELINE MUNICIPAL BOND analysts' guideline that funded debt over 10% of the ASSESSED VALUATION of taxable property in a municipality is excessive.

1031 TAX-FREE EXCHANGE "like-kind" exchange of business or investment property that is free of capital gain taxation under Section 1031 of the Internal Revenue Code. Properties held for rental income, for business purposes, as investment property, or as vacation homes may be exchanged for qualifying like-kind property (a piece of land and a building can be traded because both are real estate), provided certain conditions are met: (1) the seller must identify the replacement property within 45 days after escrow on the old property and (2) the seller must take title to the new property within the earlier of 180 days of the old property's close of escrow or the seller's tax deadline. To the extent *boot,* meaning cash or additional property, is part of the exchange, the transaction is taxable. *See also* POOLING OF INTERESTS.

TERM
1. period of time during which the conditions of a contract will be carried out. This may refer to the time in which loan payments must be made, or the time when interest payments will be made on a certificate of deposit or a bond. It also may refer to the length of time a life insurance policy is in force. *See also* TERM LIFE INSURANCE.

2. provision specifying the nature of an agreement or contract, as in *terms and conditions.*
3. period of time an official or board member is elected or appointed to serve. For example, Federal Reserve governors are appointed for 14-year terms.

TERM CERTIFICATE CERTIFICATE OF DEPOSIT with a longer-term maturity date. Such CDs can range in length from one year to ten years, though the most popular term certificates are those for one or two years. Certificate holders usually receive a fixed rate of interest, payable semiannually during the term, and are subject to costly EARLY WITHDRAWAL PENALTIES if the certificate is cashed in before the scheduled maturity.

TERMINATION BENEFIT *see* SEVERANCE PAY.

TERM LIFE INSURANCE form of life insurance, written for a specified period, that requires the policyholder to pay only for the cost of protection against death; that is, no cash value is built up as in WHOLE LIFE INSURANCE. Every time the policy is renewed, the premium is higher, since the insured is older and therefore statistically more likely to die. Term insurance is far cheaper than whole life, giving policyholders the alternative of using the savings to invest on their own.

TERM LOAN intermediate- to long-term (typically, two to ten years) secured credit granted to a company by a commercial bank, insurance company, or commercial finance company usually to finance capital equipment or provide working capital. The loan is amortized over a fixed period, sometimes ending with a BALLOON payment. Borrowers under term loan agreements are normally required to meet minimum WORKING CAPITAL and debt to net worth tests, to limit dividends, and to maintain continuity of management.

TEST
In general: examination to determine knowledge, competence, or qualifications.
Finance: criterion used to measure compliance with financial ratio requirements of indentures and other loan agreements (e.g., a current asset to current liability test or a debt to net worth test). *See also* QUICK RATIO.
Securities: term used in reference to a price movement that approaches a SUPPORT LEVEL or a RESISTANCE LEVEL established earlier by a commodity future, security, or market. A test is passed if the levels are not penetrated and is failed if prices go on to new lows or highs. Technical analysts say, for instance, that if the Dow Jones Industrials last formed a solid base at 7000, and prices have been falling from 7400, a period of testing is approaching. If prices rebound once the Dow hits 7000 and go up further, the test is passed. If prices continue to drop below 7000, however, the test is failed. *See also* TECHNICAL ANALYSIS.

TESTAMENT synonym for a WILL, a document that will dispose of property a person owns at his or her death. The testament is created by the TESTATOR or TESTATRIX, usually with the aid of an estate planning lawyer or will-writing software.

TESTAMENTARY TRUST trust created by a will, as distinguished from an INTER VIVOS TRUST created during the lifetime of the GRANTOR.

TESTATE having made and left a valid WILL; a person who dies with a will is said to die testate. A person who dies without a will is said to die INTESTATE.

TESTATOR/TESTATRIX a man/woman who has made and left a valid WILL at his/her death.

THEORETICAL VALUE (OF A RIGHT) mathematically determined MARKET VALUE of a SUBSCRIPTION RIGHT after the offering is announced but before the stock goes EX-RIGHTS. The formula includes the current market value of the common stock, the subscription price, and the number of rights required to purchase a share of stock:

theoretical value of a right

$$= \frac{\text{market value of common stock} - \text{subscription price per share}}{\text{number of rights needed to buy 1 share} + 1}$$

Thus, if the common stock market price is $50 per share, the subscription price is $45 per share, and the subscription ratio is 4 to 1, the value of one right would be $1:

$$\frac{50 - 45}{4 + 1} = \frac{5}{5} = 1$$

THIN MARKET market in which there are few bids to buy and few offers to sell. A thin market may apply to an entire class of securities or commodities futures such as small OVER THE COUNTER stocks or the platinum market—or it may refer to a particular stock, whether exchange-listed or over-the-counter. Prices in thin markets are more volatile than in markets with great LIQUIDITY, since the few trades that take place can affect prices significantly. Institutional investors who buy and sell large blocks of stock tend to avoid thin markets, because it is difficult for them to get in or out of a POSITION without materially affecting the stock's price.

THIRD MARKET nonexchange-member broker/dealers and institutional investors trading OVER THE COUNTER in exchange-listed securities. The third market rose to importance in the 1950s when institutional investors began buying common stocks as an inflation hedge and fixed commission rates still prevailed on the exchanges. By trading large blocks with nonmember firms, they both saved commissions and avoided the unsettling effects on prices that large trades on the exchanges produced. After commission rates were deregulated in May 1975, a number of the firms active in the third market became member firms so they could deal with members as well as nonmembers. At the same time, member firms began increasingly to move large blocks of stock off the floor of the exchanges, in effect becoming participants in the third market. Before selling securities off the exchange to a nonmember, however, a member firm must satisfy all LIMIT ORDERS on the SPECIALIST'S BOOK at the same price or higher. *See also* OFF-FLOOR ORDER.

THIRD-PARTY CHECK
1. check negotiated through a bank, except one payable to the writer of the check (that is, a check written for cash). The *primary party* to a transaction is the bank on which a check is drawn. The *secondary party* is the drawer of the check against funds on deposit in the bank. The *third party* is the payee who endorses the check.
2. double-endorsed check. In this instance, the payee endorses the check by signing the back, then passes the check to a subsequent holder, who endorses it prior to cashing it. Recipients of checks with multiple endorsers are reluctant to accept them unless they can verify each endorser's signature.
3. payable-through drafts and other negotiable orders not directly serviced by the providing company. For example, a check written against a money market mutual fund is processed not by the mutual fund company but typically by a commercial bank that provides a "third-party" or "payable-through" service. Money orders, credit union share drafts, and checks drawn against a brokerage account are other examples of payable-through or third-party items.

THIRD WORLD name for the less developed countries of Africa, Asia, and Latin America.

THIRTY-DAY VISIBLE SUPPLY total dollar volume of new MUNICIPAL BONDS carrying maturities of 13 months or more that are scheduled to reach the market within 30 days. The figure is supplied on Thursdays in the *BOND BUYER*.

THIRTY-DAY WASH RULE Internal Revenue Service rule stating that losses on a sale of stock may not be used as losses for tax purposes (that is, used to OFFSET gains) if equivalent stock is purchased within 30 days before or 30 after the date of sale.

THREE STEPS AND A STUMBLE RULE rule holding that stock and bond prices will fall if the Federal Reserve raises the DISCOUNT RATE three times in a row. By raising interest rates, the Federal Reserve both raises the cost of borrowing for companies and makes alternative investments such as money market funds and CDs relatively more attractive than stocks and bonds. Many market historians have tracked this rule, and found it to be a good predictor of drops in stock and bond prices.

THRIFT INSTITUTION organization formed primarily as a depository for consumer savings, the most common varieties of which are the SAVINGS AND LOAN ASSOCIATION and the SAVINGS BANK. Traditionally, savings institutions have loaned most of their deposit funds in the residential mortgage market. Deregulation in the early 1980s expanded their range of depository services and allowed them to make commercial and consumer loans. Deregulation led to widespread abuse by savings and loans that used insured deposits to engage in speculative real estate lending. This resulted in the OFFICE OF THRIFT SUPERVISION (OTS), established in 1989 by the FINANCIAL INSTITUTIONS REFORM, RECOVERY AND ENFORCEMENT ACT (FIRREA), popularly known as the "bailout bill." CREDIT UNIONS are sometimes included in the thrift institution category, since their principal source of deposits is also personal savings, though they have traditionally made small consumer loans, not mortgage loans. *See also* DEPOSITORY INSTITUTIONS DEREGULATION AND MONETARY CONTROL ACT; MUTUAL ASSOCIATION; MUTUAL SAVINGS BANK.

TICK
1. upward or downward price movement in a security's trades. Technical analysts watch the tick of a stock's successive up or down moves to get a feel of the stock's trend. The term also applies to the overall market. In futures and options trading, a minimum change in price up or down.
2. market indicator representing the difference between the number of stocks whose last sale was on an uptick and the number of stocks whose last sale was on a downtick. A negative low tick, for example, would be a short-term technical signal of a weak market.
   See also CLOSING TICK; DOWNTICK; MINUS TICK; PLUS TICK; SHORT-SALE RULE; TECHNICAL ANALYSIS; TRIN; UPTICK; ZERO-MINUS TICK; ZERO-PLUS TICK.

TICKER system that produces a running report of trading activity on the stock exchanges, called the TICKER TAPE. The name derives from machines that, in times past, printed information by punching holes in a paper tape, making an audible ticking sound as the tape was fed forth. Today's ticker tape is a computer screen and the term is used to refer both to the CONSOLIDATED TAPE, which shows the STOCK SYMBOL, latest price, and volume of trades on the exchanges, and to news ticker services. *See also* QUOTATION BOARD; TICKER TAPE.

TICKER SYMBOL letters that identify a security for trading purposes on the CONSOLIDATED TAPE, such as XON for Exxon Corporation. *See also* STOCK SYMBOL; TICKER TAPE.

TICKER TAPE device that relays the STOCK SYMBOL and the latest price and volume on securities as they are traded to investors around the world. Prior to the advent of computers, this machine had a loud printing device that made a ticking sound. Since 1975, the New York Stock Exchange and the American Stock Exchange have used a CONSOLIDATED TAPE that indicates the New York or REGIONAL STOCK EXCHANGE on which a trade originated. Other systems, known as news tickers, pass along the latest economic, financial and market news developments. See also TAPE. *See* illustration of consolidated tape, below.

TWX	MMM&P	IBM&T	XON&C
3S41⅝	83½	4S124¼	2S41

Sample section of the consolidated tape.

Trades in Time Warner, Minnesota Mining and Manufacturing, IBM, and Exxon are shown. Letters following the ampersands in the upper line indicate the marketplace in which the trade took place: P signifies the Pacific Exchange, T the THIRD MARKET, C the Chicago Stock Exchange; no indication means the New York Stock Exchange. Other codes not illustrated are X for Philadelphia Stock Exchange, B for Boston Stock Exchange, O for other markets, including INSTINET. In the lower line, where a number precedes the letter S, a multiple of 100 shares is indicated. Thus, 300 shares of Time Warner were transacted at a price of 41⅝ on the New York Stock Exchange; 100 shares of Minnesota Mining were traded on the Pacific Exchange at 83½, and so on.

TICKET short for ORDER TICKET.

TIER 1 AND TIER 2 in computing the capital adequacy of banks, Tier 1 refers to core capital, the sum of equity capital and disclosed reserves as adjusted, while Tier 2 refers to undisclosed reserves, revaluation reserves, general provisions and loan loss reserves, hybrid debt-equity instruments, and subordinated long-term debt.

TIGER acronym for Treasury Investors Growth Receipt, a form of ZERO-COUPON SECURITY first created by the brokerage firm of Merrill Lynch, Pierce, Fenner & Smith. TIGERS are U.S. government-backed bonds that have been stripped of their COUPONS. Both the CORPUS (principal) of the bonds and the individual coupons are sold separately at a deep discount from their face value. Investors receive FACE VALUE for the TIGERS when the bonds mature but do not receive periodic interest payments. Under Internal Revenue Service rules, however, TIGER holders owe income taxes on the imputed interest they would have earned had the bond been a FULL COUPON BOND. To avoid having to pay taxes without having the benefit of the income to pay them from, most investors put TIGERS in Individual Retirement or Keogh accounts, or in other TAX DEFERRED plans. Also called *TIGR.*

TIGHT MARKET market in general or market for a particular security marked by active trading and narrow bid-offer price spreads. In contrast, inactive trading and wide spreads characterize a *slack market. See also* SPREAD.

TIGHT MONEY economic condition in which credit is difficult to secure, usually as the result of Federal Reserve action to restrict the MONEY SUPPLY. The opposite is *easy money. See also* MONETARY POLICY.

TIME DEPOSIT savings account or CERTIFICATE OF DEPOSIT held in a financial institution for a fixed term or with the understanding that the depositor can withdraw only by giving notice. While a bank is authorized to require 30 days' notice of withdrawal from savings accounts, passbook accounts are generally regarded as readily available funds. Certificates of deposit, on the other hand, are issued for a specified term of 30 days or more, and provide penalties for early withdrawal. Financial institutions are free to negotiate any maturity term a customer might desire on a time deposit or certificate, as long as the term is at least 30 days, and to pay interest rates as high or low as the market will bear. *See also* DEPOSITORY INSTITUTIONS DEREGULATION AND MONETARY CONTROL ACT; REGULATION Q.

TIME DRAFT DRAFT payable at a specified or determinable time in the future, as distinguished from a *sight draft,* which is payable on presentation and delivery.

TIMES FIXED CHARGES *see* FIXED-CHARGE COVERAGE.

TIME SHARING
Computers: practice of renting time on a central computer through a smaller computer, frequently through modems and phone lines. The user can upload or download files, access electronic mail, use computer programs on the central computer, and perform other tasks, for a fee based on usage.
Real estate: practice of sharing a piece of real estate, such as a condominium, apartment, or house, with other owners. Typically, a buyer will purchase a particular block of time for a vacation, such as the second week of February, during which the buyer will have exclusive use of the property. In return, the buyer must pay his share of annual maintenance charges, whether he uses the property or not. One condominium may therefore be sold to 52 different parties, each for one week per year. Time share owners have the benefit of changing their weeks with other owners around the world through one of the worldwide exchange companies. Time shares should be viewed as a purchase of one's vacation, and not as a real estate investment.

TIMES INTEREST EARNED *see* FIXED-CHARGE COVERAGE.

TIME SPREAD OPTION strategy in which an investor buys and sells PUT OPTION and CALL OPTION contracts with the same EXERCISE PRICE but with different expiration dates. The purpose of this and other option strategies is to profit from the difference in OPTION PREMIUMS—the prices paid to buy the options. *See also* CALENDAR SPREAD; HORIZONTAL SPREAD; SPREAD.

TIME VALUE
In general: price put on the time an investor has to wait until an investment matures, as determined by calculating the PRESENT VALUE of the investment at maturity. *See also* YIELD TO MATURITY.
Options: that part of a stock option PREMIUM that reflects the time remaining on an option contract before expiration. The premium is composed of this time value and the INTRINSIC VALUE of the option.
Stocks: difference between the price at which a company is taken over and the price before the TAKEOVER occurs. For example, if XYZ Company is to be taken over at $30 a share in two months, XYZ shares might presently sell for $28.50. The $1.50 per share difference is the cost of the time value those owning XYZ must bear if they want to wait two months to get $30 a share. As the two months pass, the time value will shrink, until it disappears on the day of the takeover. The time that investors hold XYZ has a price because it could be used to invest in something else providing a higher return. *See also* OPPORTUNITY COST.

TIME-WEIGHTED RETURN portfolio accounting method that measures investment performance (income and price changes) as a percentage of capital "at work," effectively eliminating the effects of additions and withdrawals of capital and their timing that distort DOLLAR-WEIGHTED RETURN accounting. Since exact timing-weighting is impractical, the industry accepts an approximation that assumes all additions and withdrawals occur simultaneously at the midpoint of a reporting period. Performance thus equals the return on the value of assets at the beginning of the measuring period plus the return on the net amount of additions and withdrawals during the period divided in half. The periods, usually quarters, are then linked to produce a compound average TOTAL RETURN.

TIMING trying to pick the best time to make a decision. For example, MARKET TIMING involves the analysis of fundamental and technical data to decide when to buy or sell stocks, bonds, mutual funds or futures contracts. Timing is also important in making consumer decisions, such as when to make a major purchase. Consumers might want to time their purchase of real estate when prices and mortgage rates are especially attractive, or their purchase of a car when dealers are offering particularly good prices.

TIP
In general: payment over and above a formal cost or charge, ostensibly given in appreciation for extra service, to a waiter, bellhop, cabdriver, or other person engaged in service. Also called a *gratuity*.
Investments: information passed by one person to another as a basis for buy or sell action in a security. Such information is presumed to be of material value and not available to the general public. The Securities and Exchange Commission regulates the use of such information by so-called insiders, and court cases have established the liability of persons receiving and using or passing on such information (called tippees) in certain circumstances. *See also* INSIDER; INSIDE INFORMATION.

TITLE INSURANCE insurance policies, written by title insurance companies, protecting lenders against challenges to the title claim to a property. Title insurance protects a policyholder against loss from some occurrence that already has happened, such as a forged deed somewhere in the chain of title. If, for example, someone came along claiming that her parents formerly owned the house in question, and that, as beneficiary of her parents' estate, she now deserved to take possession of the property, the title insurance company would defend the present owner's title claim in court. Title insurance premiums are usually paid in one lump sum at the time the policy is issued, and the policy remains in force until the property is sold. Mortgage lenders normally require that borrowers obtain title insurance to protect the lenders' interest in the property. Property buyers also may purchase an owner's policy to protect their interest in the property.

TOEHOLD PURCHASE accumulation by an acquirer of less than 5% of the shares of a TARGET COMPANY. Once 5% is acquired, the acquirer is required to file with the Securities and Exchange Commission, the appropriate stock exchange, and the target company, explaining what is happening and what can be expected. *See also* SCHEDULE 13D; WILLIAMS ACT.

TOKYO COMMODITY EXCHANGE (TOCOM) trades futures on gold, silver, platinum, palladium, rubber, cotton yarn, and woolen yarn. Metal contracts are traded from 9 A.M. to 11 A.M. and 1 P.M. to 3:30 P.M.; rubber is traded from 9:45 A.M. to 3:30 P.M.; and yarns are traded from 8:50 A.M. to 3:10 P.M.

TOKYO INTERNATIONAL FINANCIAL FUTURES EXCHANGE screen-traded market for three-month Euroyen futures and options, and futures on the one-year Euroyen, three-month Eurodollar and U.S. dollar/Japanese yen currency.

TOKYO STOCK EXCHANGE (TSE) largest of eight stock exchanges in Japan and one of the largest, most important, and most active stock markets in the world. TSE is a continuous auction market, similar to open outcry. It uses the

Floor Order-Routing and Execution System (FORES), an electronic system, for trading the 150 most active domestic stocks. Less-active stocks are traded through the Computer-Assisted Order-Routing and Execution System (CORES). The *Tokyo Stock Price Index* (TOPIX) is a composite of all stocks on the first section of the exchange, supplemented by size groups that classify first section companies as small, medium, and large and by sub-indices for each of the 33 industry groups. The NIKKEI STOCK AVERAGE known as the Nikkei 225, and the Nikkei 500 are the principal indices and are calculated by a formula similar to the DOW JONES INDUSTRIAL AVERAGE (as simple averages of the component stock's prices). The Nikkei 300 on the Osaka Securities Exchange is weighted by market capitalization and includes 300 listed companies on the first section of the TSE. The majority of shares are settled on the third business day following the trade. Trading takes place Monday through Friday in two daily sessions: 9 A.M. to 11 A.M., and 12:30 P.M. to 3 P.M. The TSE derivatives market trades futures and options on the TOPIX, the Nikkei 225, Nikkei 300 and 10-year government bond, and futures on the 20-year government bond and U.S. Treasury bond.

TOKYO STOCK PRICE INDEX (TOPIX) *see* NIKKEI STOCK AVERAGE.

TOLL REVENUE BOND MUNICIPAL BOND supported by revenues from tolls paid by users of the public project built with the bond proceeds. Toll revenue bonds frequently are floated to build bridges, tunnels, and roads. *See also* REVENUE BOND.

TOMBSTONE advertisement placed in newspapers by investment bankers in a PUBLIC OFFERING of securities. It gives basic details about the issue and lists the UNDERWRITING GROUP members involved in the offering in alphabetically organized groupings according to the size of their participations. It is not "an offer to sell or a solicitation of an offer to buy," but rather it calls attention to the PROSPECTUS, sometimes called the *offering circular.* A tombstone may also be placed by an investment banking firm to announce its role in a PRIVATE PLACEMENT, corporate MERGER, or ACQUISITION; by a corporation to announce a major business or real estate deal; or by a firm in the financial community to announce a personnel development or a principal's death. *See also* MEZZANINE BRACKET.

TON bond traders' jargon for $100 million.

TOP-DOWN APPROACH TO INVESTING method in which an investor first looks at trends in the general economy, and next selects industries and then companies that should benefit from those trends. For example, an investor who thinks inflation will stay low might be attracted to the retailing industry, since consumers' spending power will be enhanced by low inflation. The investor then might look at Sears, Wal-Mart, Federated Department Stores, Dayton Hudson, and other retailers to see which company has the best earnings prospects in the near term. Or, an investor who thinks there will be rapid inflation may identify the mining industry as attractive, and then look at particular gold, copper, and other mining companies to see which would benefit most from a trend of rising prices. The opposite method is called the BOTTOM-UP APPROACH TO INVESTING.

TOPIX *see* NIKKEI STOCK AVERAGE.

TOPPING OUT term denoting a market or a security that is at the end of a period of rising prices and can now be expected to stay on a plateau or even to decline.

TORONTO FUTURES EXCHANGE wholly owned subsidiary of the TORONTO STOCK EXCHANGE (TSE), trading Toronto 35 Index and TSE 100 Index futures, TSE 100 Index and Toronto 35 Index options, and Toronto 35 Index Participation (TIPs) options. Options are traded on the TSE. Trading is by open outcry.

TORONTO STOCK EXCHANGE (TSE) largest stock exchange in Canada, listing some 1,200 company stocks and 33 options. The exchange uses both open outcry and the Computer Assisted Trading System (CATS). TSE is home to many resource-based companies in the mining, paper, timber, and other natural resource industries, but also trades manufacturing, biotechnology, and telecommunications equities. The *TSE Composite Index*, known as the TSE 300, is the most widely-quoted index tracking this marketplace. The *Toronto 35 Index*, composed of a cross-section of major Canadian stocks, is the base for derivative products such as the Toronto 35 Index option (TXO) and future (TXF). The *TSE 100 Index* is a performance benchmark for institutional investors, and is the base for the TSE 100 Index option and TSE 100 Index future contract. The *TSE 200 Index* is a small- to mid-cap index composed of 200 stocks in the TSE 300 that are not represented in the TSE 100. Toronto 35 Index Participation Units, or TIPs, and TIPs options, are proprietary products. Each TIPs unit represents an interest in a trust that holds BASKETS of stocks in the Toronto 35 Index. TIPs options are American exercise and physically settled, while TXO options are European exercise and cash settled. TSE Index 35 options, TSE Index 100 options, and TIPs products trade on the TSE. Trading hours are 9:30 A.M. to 4 P.M., Monday through Friday, with an extended afternoon session from 4:15 P.M. to 5 P.M. Settlement is the third day following the trade.

TOTAL CAPITALIZATION CAPITAL STRUCTURE of a company, including LONG-TERM DEBT and all forms of EQUITY.

TOTAL COST
Accounting: (usually pl.) sum of FIXED COSTS, semivariable costs, and VARIABLE COSTS.
Investments: contract price paid for a security plus the brokerage commission plus any ACCRUED INTEREST due the seller (if the security is a bond). The figure is not to be confused with the COST BASIS for the purpose of figuring the CAPITAL GAINS TAX, which may involve other factors such as amortization of bond premiums.

TOTAL DISABILITY injury or illness that is so serious that it prevents a worker from performing any functions for which he or she is educated and trained. Workers with total disability may qualify for DISABILITY INCOME INSURANCE, either though a private employer's plan or through Social Security's disability insurance program. There is normally a waiting period before disability insurance payments begin, to determine if the disability is long-term. Waiting periods vary, from a month to several months, and are determined by the plan and premium structure of the employer.

TOTAL RETURN annual return on an investment including appreciation and dividends or interest. For bonds held to maturity, total return is YIELD TO MATURITY. For stocks, future appreciation is projected using the current PRICE/EARNINGS RATIO. In options trading, total return means dividends plus capital gains plus premium income.

TOTAL VOLUME total number of shares or contracts traded in a stock, bond, commodity future, or option on a particular day. For stocks and bonds, this is the aggregate of trades on national exchanges like the New York and American stock exchanges and on regional exchanges. For commodities futures and options, it represents the volume of trades executed around the world in one day. For over-the-counter securities, total volume is measured by the NASDAQ index.

TOUT to promote a particular security aggressively, usually done by a corporate spokesman, public relations firm, broker, or analyst with a vested interest in promoting the stock. Touting a stock is unethical if it misleads investors. *See also* INVESTMENT ADVISERS ACT; INVESTOR RELATIONS DEPARTMENT.

T-PLUS-THREE *see* DELIVERY DATE.

TRACKING STOCK category of common stock that pays a dividend based on the operating performance of a particular corporate segment. Tracking stock, which is sometimes informally called "designer stock," exists alongside the issuer's regular common shares, but, unlike the latter, usually has limited or no voting power and does not represent a legal claim on assets of the corporation. When identified with a letter, such as General Motors "H" shares, the stock is also called ALPHABET STOCK, but differs from CLASSIFIED STOCK.

TRADE
In general:
1. buying or selling of goods and services among companies, states, or countries, called *commerce*. The amount of goods and services imported minus the amount exported makes up a country's BALANCE OF TRADE. *See also* TARIFF; TRADE DEFICIT.
2. those in the business of selling products are called *members of the trade*. As such, they receive DISCOUNTS from the price the public has to pay.
3. group of manufacturers who compete in the same market. These companies form trade associations and publish trade journals.
4. commercial companies that do business with each other. For example, ACCOUNTS PAYABLE to suppliers are called *trade accounts payable;* the term TRADE CREDIT is used to describe accounts payable as a source of WORKING CAPITAL financing. Companies paying their bills promptly receive *trade discounts* when available.
5. synonymous with BARTER, the exchange of goods and services without the use of money.

Securities: to carry out a transaction of buying or selling a stock, a bond, or a commodity future contract. A trade is consummated when a buyer and seller agree on a price at which the trade will be executed. A TRADER frequently buys and sells for his or her own account securities for short-term profits, as contrasted with an investor who holds his positions in hopes of long-term gains.

TRADE BALANCE *see* BALANCE OF TRADE.

TRADE CREDIT open account arrangements with suppliers of goods and services, and a firm's record of payment with the suppliers. Trade liabilities comprise a company's ACCOUNTS PAYABLE. DUN & BRADSTREET is the largest compiler of trade credit information, rating commercial firms and supplying published reports. Trade credit data is also processed by MERCANTILE AGENCIES specializing in different industries.

Trade credit is an important external source of WORKING CAPITAL for a company, although such credit can be highly expensive. Terms of 2% 10 days, net 30 days (2% discount if paid in 10 days, the net [full] amount due in 30 days) translate into a 36% annual interest rate if not taken advantage of. On the other hand, the same terms translate into a borrowing rate of slightly over 15% if payment is made in 60 days instead of 30.

TRADE DATE day on which a security or a commodity future trade actually takes place. The SETTLEMENT DATE usually follows the trade date by five business days, but varies depending on the transaction and method of delivery used. *See also* DELAYED DELIVERY; DELIVERY DATE; REGULAR WAY DELIVERY (AND SETTLEMENT); SELLER'S OPTION.

TRADE DEFICIT OR SURPLUS excess of imports over exports *(trade deficit)* or of exports over imports *(trade surplus),* resulting in a negative or positive

BALANCE OF TRADE. The balance of trade is made up of transactions in merchandise and other movable goods and is only one factor comprising the larger *current account* (which includes services and tourism, transportation, and other *invisible items,* such as interest and profits earned abroad) in the overall BALANCE OF PAYMENTS. Factors influencing a country's balance of trade include the strength or weakness of its currency in relation to those of the countries with which it trades (a strong U.S. dollar, for example, makes goods produced in other countries relatively cheap for Americans), production advantages in key manufacturing areas (Japanese automobiles, for instance), or the domestic economy of a trading country where production may or may not be meeting demand.

TRADEMARK distinctive name, symbol, motto, or emblem that identifies a product, service, or firm. In the United States, trademark rights—the right to prevent competitors from using similar marks in selling or advertising—arise out of use; that is, registration is not essential to establish the legal existence of a mark. A trademark registered with the U.S. Patent and Trademark Office is good for 20 years, renewable as long as used. Products may be both patented and protected by trademark, the advantage being that when the patent runs out, exclusivity can be continued indefinitely with the trademark. A trademark is classified on a BALANCE SHEET as an INTANGIBLE ASSET.

Although, like land, trademarks have an indefinite life and cannot technically be amortized, in practice accountants do amortize trademarks over their estimated life, not to exceed 40 years.

TRADER

In general: anyone who buys and sells goods or services for profit; a DEALER or *merchant. See also* BARTER; TRADE.

Investments:

1. individual who buys and sells securities, such as STOCKS, BONDS, OPTIONS, or commodities, such as wheat, gold, or FOREIGN EXCHANGE, for his or her own account—that is, as a dealer or PRINCIPAL—rather than as a BROKER or AGENT.

2. individual who buys and sells securities or commodities for his or her own account on a short-term basis in anticipation of quick profits; a *speculator. See also* DAY TRADE; COMPETITIVE TRADER; FLOOR TRADER; REGISTERED COMPETITIVE MARKET MAKER; REGISTERED COMPETITIVE TRADER; SPECULATION.

TRADING AUTHORIZATION document giving a brokerage firm employee acting as AGENT (BROKER) the POWER OF ATTORNEY in buy-sell transactions for a customer.

TRADING DIVIDENDS technique of buying and selling stocks in other firms by a corporation in order to maximize the number of DIVIDENDS it can collect. This action is advantageous, because 70% of the dividend income it receives from the stocks of other companies is not taxed, according to Internal Revenue Service regulations. *See also* DIVIDEND EXCLUSION.

TRADING HALT *see* SUSPENDED TRADING.

TRADING LIMIT *see* DAILY TRADING LIMIT; LIMIT UP, LIMIT DOWN.

TRADING PATTERN long-range direction of a security or commodity future price. This pattern is charted by drawing a line connecting the highest prices the security has reached and another line connecting the lowest prices the security has traded at over the same time frame. These two lines will be pointing either up or down, indicating the security's long-term trading pattern. *See also* TECHNICAL ANALYSIS, TRENDLINE. *See* chart on next page.

TRADING PATTERN

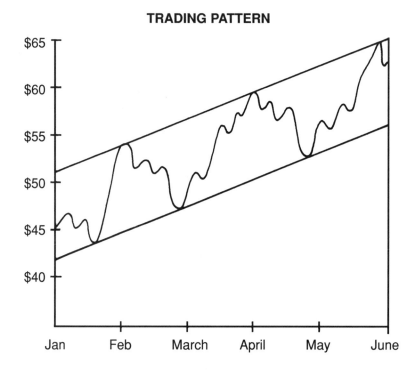

TRADING POST physical location on a stock exchange floor where particular securities are bought and sold. It is here that the SPECIALIST in a particular security performs his market-making functions and that the CROWD (floor brokers with orders in that security) congregates. The New York Stock Exchange, for example, has 17 trading posts. *See also* FLOOR BROKER; FLOOR TRADER; MAKE A MARKET.

TRADING PROFIT profit earned based on short-term trades. For assets such as stocks, bonds, futures contracts, and mutual funds held under a year, such trading profits are taxed at regular income tax rates. In general commerce, *trading profit* refers to the difference between what a product is sold for by a retailer and what it costs to buy or produce at the wholesale or producer level.

TRADING RANGE
    Commodities: trading limit set by a COMMODITIES futures exchange for a particular commodity. The price of a commodity future contract may not go higher or lower than that limit during one day's trading. *See also* LIMIT UP, LIMIT DOWN.
    Securities: range between the highest and lowest prices at which a security or a market has traded. The trading range for XYZ Corporation might be $40 to $60 over the last two years, for example. If a security or a market seems to be stuck in a narrow price range, analysts say that it is a trading range market, which will eventually be followed by a significant up or down move. *See also* FLAG; PENNANT; TRIANGLE; WEDGE.

TRADING UNIT number of SHARES, BONDS, or other securities that is generally accepted for ordinary trading purposes on the exchanges, *See also* ODD LOT; ROUND LOT; UNIT OF TRADING.

TRADING VARIATION increments in which securities transaction prices are rounded. For example, stocks are rounded up or down to the nearest eighth of a point. Over the next several years, though, DECIMAL TRADING, in which stock prices are quoted in decimals, will gradually replace quotations in eighths. Options over $3 are also rounded to an eighth, but options under $3 are rounded to ⅟₁₆. Corporate and municipal bonds are rounded to ⅛, medium- and long-term government notes and bonds to ⅟₃₂, and shorter-term government bonds to ⅟₆₄. *See also* PLUS.

TRANCH CD *see* TRANCHES.

TRANCHES

1. risk maturity or other classes into which a multi-class security, such as a COL-LATERALIZED MORTGAGE OBLIGATION (CMO) or a REMIC is split. For example, the typical CMO has A, B, C, and Z tranches, representing fast pay, medium pay, and slow pay bonds plus an issue (tranch) that bears no coupon but receives the cash flow from the collateral remaining after the other tranches are satisfied. More sophisticated CMO versions have multiple Z tranches and a Y tranch incorporating a sinking fund schedule.

2. in the United Kingdom, fixed-rate security issues are often prearranged by governments, local authorities, or corporations, then brought out in successive rounds, termed tranches. One thus speaks of new tranches of existing securities. A variation of the term, *tranchettes,* refers to small tranches of gilt-edged securities (government bonds) sold by the government to the Bank of England, which then sells them into the market at times it deems appropriate.

3. subunits of a large ($10–$30 million) Eurodollar certificate of deposit that are marketed to smaller investors in $10,000 denominations. Tranches are represented by separate certificates and have the same interest rate, issue date, interest payment date, and maturity of the original instrument, which is called a *tranch CD.*

TRANCHETTES *see* TRANCHES.

TRANSACTION
Accounting: event or condition recognized by an entry in the books of account.
Securities: execution of an order to buy or sell a security or commodity futures contract. After the buyer and seller have agreed on a price, the seller is obligated to deliver the security or commodity involved, and the buyer is obligated to accept it. *See also* TRADE.

TRANSACTION COSTS cost of buying or selling a security, which consists mainly of the *brokerage commission,* the dealer MARKDOWN or markup, or fee (as would be charged by a bank or broker-dealer to transact Treasuries, for example) but also includes direct taxes, such as the SEC FEE, any state-imposed TRANSFER TAXES, or other direct taxes.

TRANSFER exchange of ownership of property from one party to another. For example, a piece of real estate may be transferred from seller to buyer through the execution of a sales contract. Securities and mutual funds are typically transferred through a transfer agent, who electronically switches ownership of the securities. In banking, *transfer* refers to the movement of funds from one account to another, such as from a passbook account to a checking account.

TRANSFER AGENT agent, usually a commercial bank, appointed by a corporation, to maintain records of stock and bond owners, to cancel and issue certificates, and to resolve problems arising from lost, destroyed, or stolen certificates. (Preventing OVERISSUE of shares is the function of the REGISTRAR.) A corporation may also serve as its own transfer agent.

TRANSFER PAYMENTS money transferred to people from the government. Many payments under government benefit programs are considered transfer payments, including Social Security, disability payments, unemployment compensation, welfare, and veterans' benefits. A large portion of the federal government's yearly budget goes to make transfer payments.

TRANSFER PRICE price charged by individual entities in a multi-entity corporation on transactions among themselves; also termed *transfer cost*. This concept is used where each entity is managed as a PROFIT CENTER—that is, held responsible for its own RETURN ON INVESTED CAPITAL—and must therefore deal with the other internal parts of the corporation on an arm's-length (or market) basis. *See also* ARM'S LENGTH TRANSACTION.

TRANSFER TAX
1. combined federal tax on gifts and estates. *See* ESTATE TAX; GIFT TAX.
2. federal tax on the sale of all bonds (except obligations of the United States, foreign governments, states, and municipalities) and all stocks. The tax is paid by the seller at the time ownership is transferred and involves a few pennies per $100 of value.
3. tax levied by some state and local governments on the transfer of such documents as deeds to property, securities, or licenses. Such taxes are paid, usually with stamps, by the seller or donor and are determined by the location of the transfer agent. States with transfer taxes on stock transactions include New York, Florida, South Carolina, and Texas. New York bases its tax on selling price; the other states apply the tax to PAR value (giving NO-PAR-VALUE STOCK a value of $100). Bonds are not taxed at the state level.

TRANSMITTAL LETTER letter sent with a document, security, or shipment describing the contents and the purpose of the transaction.

TRAVEL AND ENTERTAINMENT ACCOUNT separate account set up by an employer to track and reimburse employees' travel and entertainment expenses. Many employers give special credit cards to employees so that all travel and entertainment expenses can be tracked separately from personal expenses. Employers need to track travel and entertainment expenses carefully if they are to claim the appropriate tax deductions for these business expenses.

TRAVEL AND ENTERTAINMENT EXPENSE expense for travel and entertainment that may qualify for a tax deduction. Under current tax law, employers may deduct 50% of legitimate travel and entertainment expenses. Expenses are deductible if they are directly related to business. For example, a business meal must include a discussion that produces a direct business benefit.

TRAVELER'S CHECK check issued by a financial institution such as American Express, Visa, or Mastercard that allows travelers to carry travel funds in a more convenient way than cash. The traveler buys the checks, often for a nominal fee, with cash, a credit card, or a regular check at a bank or travel service office and then signs each traveler's check. The check can then be used virtually anywhere in the world once it has been countersigned with the same signature. The advantage to the traveler is that the traveler's check cannot be used by someone else if it is lost or stolen, and can be replaced usually anywhere in the world. Traveler's checks are also issued in many foreign currencies, allowing a traveler to lock in at a particular exchange rate before the trip begins. Many issuers of traveler's checks offer a type of check that enables two travelers to share the same travel funds. American Express was the first issuer to introduce this form of check. Institutions issuing traveler's checks profit from the FLOAT, earning interest on the money from the time the customer buys the check to the time they use the check.

TREASURER company officer responsible for the receipt, custody, investment, and disbursement of funds, for borrowings, and, if it is a public company, for the maintenance of a market for its securities. Depending on the size of the organization, the treasurer may also function as the CONTROLLER, with accounting and audit responsibilities. The laws of many states require that a corporation have a treasurer. *See also* CHIEF FINANCIAL OFFICER (CFO).

TREASURIES NEGOTIABLE debt obligations of the U.S. government, secured by its FULL FAITH AND CREDIT and issued at various schedules and maturities. The income from Treasury securities is exempt from state and local, but not federal, taxes.

1. *Treasury bills*—short-term securities with maturities of one year or less issued at a discount from FACE VALUE. Auctions of 91-day and 182-day BILLS take place weekly, and the yields are watched closely in the money markets for signs of interest rate trends. Many floating rate loans and variable rate mortgages have interest rates tied to these bills. The Treasury also auctions 52-week bills once every four weeks. At times it also issues very short-term cash management bills, TAX ANTICIPATION BILLS, and treasury certificates of indebtedness. Treasury bills are issued in minimum denominations of $10,000, with $5000 increments above $10,000 (except for cash management bills, which are sold in minimum $10 million blocks). Individual investors who do not submit a COMPETITIVE BID are sold bills at the average price of the winning competitive bids. Treasury bills are the primary instrument used by the Federal Reserve in its regulation of MONEY SUPPLY through OPEN-MARKET OPERATIONS. *See also* DUTCH AUCTION; REPURCHASE AGREEMENT.

2. *Treasury bonds*—long-term debt instruments with maturities of 10 years or longer issued in minimum denominations of $1000.

3. *Treasury notes*—intermediate securities with maturities of 1 to 10 years. Denominations range from $1000 to $1 million or more. The notes are sold by cash subscription, in exchange for outstanding or maturing government issues, or at auction.

TREASURY BILL *see* BILL; TREASURIES.

TREASURY BOND *see* TREASURIES.

TREASURY DIRECT system through which an individual investor can make a NONCOMPETITIVE BID on U.S. Treasury securities (TREASURIES), thus bypassing middlemen like banks or broker-dealers and avoiding their fees. The system works through FEDERAL RESERVE BANKS and branches, and the minimum purchase is $10,000.

TREASURY STOCK stock reacquired by the issuing company and available for RETIREMENT or resale. It is issued but not outstanding. It cannot be voted and it pays or accrues no dividends. It is not included in any of the ratios measuring values per common share. Among the reasons treasury stock is created are (1) to provide an alternative to paying taxable dividends, since the decreased amount of outstanding shares increases the per share value and often the market price; (2) to provide for the exercise of stock options and warrants and the conversion of convertible securities; (3) in countering a TENDER OFFER by a potential acquirer; (4) to alter the DEBT-TO-EQUITY RATIO by issuing bonds to finance the reacquisition of shares; (5) as a result of the STABILIZATION of the market price during a NEW ISSUE. Also called *reacquired stock* and *treasury shares*. *See also* ISSUED AND OUTSTANDING; UNISSUED STOCK.

TREND

In general: any general direction of movement. For example: "There is an upward (downward, level) trend in XYZ sales," or "There is a trend toward increased computerization of trading on Wall Street."

Securities: long-term price or trading volume movements either up, down, or sideways, which characterize a particular market, commodity or security. Also applies to interest rates and yields.

TRENDLINE line used by technical analysts to chart the past direction of a security or commodity future in order to help predict future price movements. The trendline is made by connecting the highest or lowest prices to which a security or commodity has risen or fallen within a particular time period. The angle of the resulting line will indicate if the security or commodity is in a downtrend or uptrend. If the price rises above a downward sloping trendline or drops below a rising uptrend line, technical analysts say that a new direction may be emerging. *See also* TECHNICAL ANALYSIS; TRADING PATTERN.

TRENDLINE

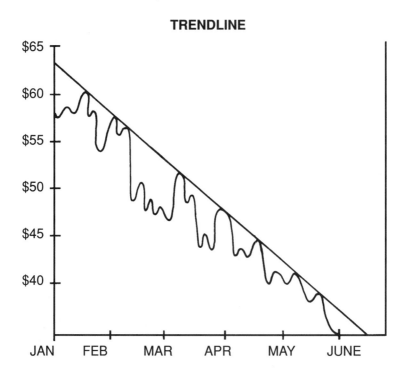

TRIANGLE technical chart pattern that has two base points and a top point, formed by connecting a stock's price movements with a line. In a typical triangle pattern, the apex points to the right, although in reverse triangles the apex points to the left. In a typical triangle, there are a series of two or more rallies and price drops where each succeeding peak is lower than the preceding peak, and each bottom is higher than the preceding bottom. In a right-angled triangle, the sloping part of the formation often points in the direction of the breakout. Technical analysts find it significant when a security's price breaks out of the triangle formation, either up or down, because that usually means the security's price will continue in that direction. *See* chart on next page. *See also* PENNANT; TECHNICAL ANALYSIS; WEDGE.

TRICKLE DOWN theory that economic growth can best be achieved by letting businesses flourish, since their prosperity will ultimately trickle down to middle- and lower-income people, who will benefit by increased economic activity. Proponents say that it produces more long-term growth than direct welfare grants to the middle- and lower-income sectors. *See also* SUPPLY-SIDE ECONOMICS.

TRIANGLE

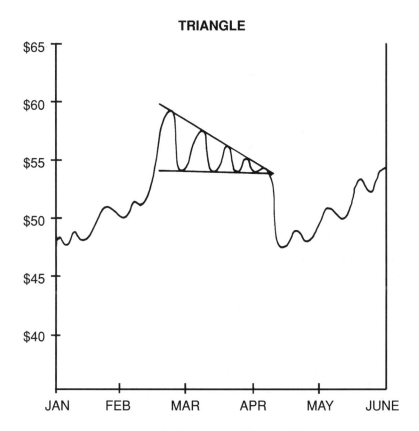

TRIN measure of stock market strength that relates the ADVANCE-DECLINE ratio (the number of issues that advanced in price divided by the number of issues that declined in price) to the advance volume-decline volume ratio (the total number of shares that advanced divided by the total number of shares that declined). For example, if 800 stocks advanced and 750 issues declined while a total of 68 million shares advanced and 56 million shares declined, the trin would be calculated as follows:

$$\frac{\text{Advances } 800 \div \text{Declines } 750}{\text{Advance volume } 68{,}000{,}000 \div \text{Decline volume } 56{,}000{,}000} = \frac{1.067}{1.214}$$

$$= 0.88$$

A trin of under 1.00 is considered bullish while a trin over 1.00 is considered bearish. The above trin of 0.88 is thus a bullish sign. A trin based on closing figures is called a *closing trin. See also* CLOSING TICK.

TRIPLE NET LEASE lease requiring tenants to pay all ongoing maintenance expenses such as utilities, taxes, insurance, and upkeep of the property. There are many LIMITED PARTNERSHIPS investing in triple net lease real estate deals. In such a deal, the limited partnership owns the property and collects rent, but the tenants pay most of the operating expenses. This results in higher returns for limited partners with lower risks, because tenants bear any increased costs for utilities, insurance, or taxes.

TRIPLE TAX EXEMPT feature of MUNICIPAL BONDS in which interest is exempt from federal, state, and local taxation for residents of the states and localities that issue them. Such bonds are particularly attractive in states with high income tax rates. Many municipal bond funds buy only triple tax exempt bonds and market them to residents of the state and city of the issuer. *See also* SINGLE-STATE MUNICIPAL BOND FUND.

TRIPLE WITCHING DAY third Friday in March, June, September, and December when OPTIONS, INDEX OPTIONS, AND FUTURES CONTRACTS all expire simultaneously. At times there may be massive trades in index futures, options, and the underlying stocks by hedge strategists, arbitrageurs, and other investors, resulting in volatile markets on those days. In the past, all contracts expired in the same hour, but steps were taken so that contracts now expire at the open as well as the close of the day instead of all at once. Smaller-scale witching days occur in the other eight months, usually on the third Friday, when other options, index options, and futures contracts expire concurrently. *See also* DOUBLE WITCHING DAY.

TRUNCATION shortening of processing steps, in an effort to reduce paperwork and operating costs. For example, check truncation, or check SAFEKEEPING, where the bank holds the checks or microfilm records of them in a central file.

TRUST

Business: type of corporate combination that engaged in monopolies and restraint of trade and that operated freely until the ANTITRUST LAWS of the late 19th century and early 20th century. The name derived from the use of the voting trust, in which a small number of trustees vote a majority of the shares of a corporation. The voting trust survives as a means of facilitating the reorganization of firms in difficulty. *See also* INVESTMENT COMPANY; VOTING TRUST CERTIFICATE.

Law: FIDUCIARY relationship in which a person, called a *trustee,* holds title to property for the benefit of another person, called a BENEFICIARY. The agreement that establishes the trust, contains its provisions, and sets forth the powers of the trustee is called the *trust indenture.* The person creating the trust is the *creator, settlor,* GRANTOR, or *donor;* the property itself is called the CORPUS, *trust res, trust fund,* or *trust estate,* which is distinguished from any income earned by it. If the trust is created while the donor is living, it is called a *living trust* or INTER VIVOS TRUST. A trust created by a will is called a TESTAMENTARY TRUST. The trustee is usually charged with investing trust property productively and, unless specifically limited, can sell, mortgage, or lease the property as he or she deems warranted. *See also* CHARITABLE REMAINDER TRUST; CLIFFORD TRUST; INVESTMENT TRUST; REVISIONARY TRUST; TRUST COMPANY; TRUSTEE IN BANKRUPTCY; TRUST INDENTURE ACT OF 1939.

TRUST COMPANY organization, usually combined with a commercial bank, which is engaged as a trustee, FIDUCIARY, or AGENT for individuals or businesses in the administration of TRUST funds, estates, custodial arrangements, stock transfer and registration, and other related services. Trust companies also engage in fiduciary investment management functions and estate planning. They are regulated by state law.

TRUSTEE *see* TRUST.

TRUSTEE IN BANKRUPTCY trustee appointed by a U.S. district court or by creditors to administer the affairs of a bankrupt company or individual. Under Chapter 7 of the U.S. BANKRUPTCY Code, the trustee has the responsibility for liquidating the property of the company and making distributions of liquidating dividends to creditors. Under the Chapter 11 provision, which provides for REORGANIZATION, a trustee may or may not be appointed. If one is, the trustee is responsible for seeing that a reorganization plan is filed and often assumes responsibility for the company.

TRUST FUND *see* TRUST.

TRUST INDENTURE ACT OF 1939 federal law requiring all corporate bonds and other debt securities to be issued under an INDENTURE agreement approved by the SECURITIES AND EXCHANGE COMMISSION (SEC) and providing for the appointment of a qualified trustee free of conflict of interest with the issuer. The Act provides that indentures contain protective clauses for bondholders, that bondholders receive semiannual financial reports, that periodic filings be made with the SEC showing compliance with indenture provisions, and that the issuer be liable for misleading statements. Securities exempted from regulation under the SECURITIES ACT OF 1933 are also exempted from the Trust Indenture Act, but some securities not requiring registration under the 1933 Act do fall under the provisions of the Trust Indenture Act, such as bonds issued in REORGANIZATION or RECAPITALIZATION.

TRUTH-IN-LENDING LAW legislation stipulating that lenders must disclose to borrowers the true cost of loans and make the interest rate and terms of the loan simple to understand. *See also* CONSUMER CREDIT PROTECTION ACT OF 1968; RIGHT OF RESCISSION.

TURKEY disappointing investment. The term may be used with reference to a business deal that went awry, or to the purchase of a stock or bond that dropped in value sharply, or to a new securities issue that did not sell well or had to be sold at a loss.

TURNAROUND favorable reversal in the fortunes of a company, a market, or the economy at large. Stock market investors speculating that a poorly performing company is about to show a marked improvement in earnings might profit handsomely from its turnaround.

TURNKEY any project constructed or manufactured by a company that ultimately turns it over in finished form to the company that will use it, so that all the user has to do is turn the key, so to speak, and the project is underway. The term is used of housing projects that, after construction, are turned over to property managers. There are also turnkey computer systems, for which the user needs no special computer knowledge and which can therefore be put right to work once they are installed.

TURNOVER
Finance:
1. number of times a given asset is replaced during an accounting period, usually a year. *See also* ACCOUNTS RECEIVABLE TURNOVER; INVENTORY TAKEOVER.
2. ratio of annual sales of a company to its NET WORTH, measuring the extent to which a company can grow without additional capital investment when compared over a period. *See also* CAPITAL TURNOVER.

Great Britain: annual sales volume.

Industrial relations: total employment divided by the number of employees replaced during a given period.

Securities: volume of shares traded as a percentage of total shares listed on an exchange during a period, usually either a day or a year. The same ratio is applied to individual securities and the portfolios of individual or institutional investors.

12b-1 MUTUAL FUND MUTUAL FUND that assesses shareholders for some of its promotion expenses. Adopted by the Securities and Exchange Commission in 1980, Rule 12b-1 provides mutual funds and their shareholders with an asset-based alternative method of covering sales and marketing expenses. At least half of the more than 10,000 mutual funds in existence today have a 12b-1 fee typically ranging from .25%, in the case of "no-load" funds that use it to cover advertising and marketing costs, to as high as 8.5%, the maximum "front-end load" allowed under National

Association of Securities Dealers (NASD) rules, in cases where annual 12b-1 "spread loads" replaced traditional front-end loads. The predominant use of 12b-1 fees is in funds sold through brokers, insurance agents, and financial planners.

Changes to 12b-1 that became effective July 7, 1993, aim to limit fees paid by most fund investors to the 8.5% limit on front-end loads. This is achieved by an annual limit and by a rolling cap placed on new sales. The annual limit is .85% of assets, with an additional .25% permitted as a service fee. The rolling cap on the total of all sales charges is 6.25% of new sales, plus interest, for funds that charge the service fee, and 7.25%, plus interest, for funds that do not. The new regulation also prohibits funds with front-end, deferred, and/or 12b-1 fees in excess of .25% from being called "no-load." *See also* NO-LOAD FUND.

TWENTY BOND INDEX index tracking the yields on 20 general obligation municipal bonds with 20-year maturities and an average rating equivalent to A1. The index, published weekly by *The Bond Buyer* in the newspaper's Friday edition, serves as a benchmark for the general level of municipal bond yields. *See also* BOND BUYER'S INDEX; ELEVEN BOND INDEX.

TWENTY-DAY PERIOD period required by the Securities and Exchange Commission (SEC) after filing of the REGISTRATION STATEMENT and PRELIMINARY PROSPECTUS in a NEW ISSUE or SECONDARY DISTRIBUTION during which they are reviewed and, if necessary, modified. The end of the 20-day period—also called the COOLING-OFF PERIOD—marks the EFFECTIVE DATE when the issue may be offered to the public. The period may be extended by the SEC if more time is needed to respond to a DEFICIENCY LETTER.

TWENTY-FIVE PERCENT RULE MUNICIPAL BOND analyst's guideline that bonded debt over 25% of a municipality's annual budget is excessive.

TWENTY-PERCENT CUSHION RULE guideline used by analysts of MUNICIPAL REVENUE BONDS that estimated revenues from the financed facility should exceed the operating budget plus maintenance costs and DEBT SERVICE by a 20% margin or "cushion" to allow for unanticipated expenses or error in estimating revenues.

TWISTING unethical practice of convincing a customer to trade unnecessarily, thereby generating a commission for the broker or salesperson. Examples: A broker may induce a customer to sell one mutual fund with a sales charge in order to buy another fund, also with a sales charge, thereby generating a commission. A life insurance salesperson may persuade a policyholder to cancel his or her policy or allow it to lapse, in order to sell the insured a new policy, which would be more costly but which would produce sizable commissions for the salesperson. Also called CHURNING.

TWO-DOLLAR BROKER FLOOR BROKER who executes orders for other brokers too busy to do it themselves; a "broker's broker." Such brokers once were paid two dollars for a ROUND LOT trade, hence the name. Today they receive a negotiated commission rate varying with the dollar value of the transaction. *See also* INDEPENDENT BROKER.

200 PERCENT DECLINING-BALANCE METHOD *see* DOUBLE-DECLINING-BALANCE DEPRECIATION METHOD (DDB).

TWO-SIDED MARKET market in which both the BID AND ASKED sides are firm, such as that which a SPECIALIST and others who MAKE A MARKET are required to maintain. Both buyers and sellers are thus assured of their ability to complete transactions. Also called *two-way market.*

TWO-TIER BID TAKEOVER bid where the acquirer offers to pay more for the shares needed to gain control than for the remaining shares; contrasts with ANY-AND-ALL BID.

u

ULTRA-SHORT-TERM BOND FUND mutual fund buying bonds with maturities typically of one year or less. Such funds usually pay higher yields than money market mutual funds, but lower yields than SHORT-TERM BOND FUNDS. Their advantage to investors is that they offer more price stability than short-term bond funds, along with a yield that beats money funds. The NET ASSET VALUE of ultra-short-term bond funds does fluctuate, however, unlike the net asset value for money market mutual funds, which remains fixed at $1 a share. It is therefore possible to realize capital gains and losses with ultra-short-term bond funds.

ULTRA VIRES ACTIVITIES actions of a corporation that are not authorized by its charter and that may therefore lead to shareholder or third-party suits. *See also* ARTICLES OF INCORPORATION.

UMBRELLA PERSONAL LIABILITY POLICY liability insurance policy providing excess coverage beyond regular liability policies. For example, typical homeowner's policies offer $300,000 in liability coverage against lawsuits and other negligence claims. An umbrella policy may provide $1 million in liability coverage. An umbrella policy will begin to pay claims only after the underlying liability policy's coverage limits have been exceeded. People usually buy umbrella policies to protect themselves against the possibility of a large jury award in a lawsuit. An umbrella policy also protects in situations not covered by a standard liability policy found in homeowner's and automobile insurance, like slander and libel. An umbrella policy also links policies, raising the limits on underlying policies in a cost-effective manner.

UNAMORTIZED BOND DISCOUNT difference between the FACE VALUE (par value) of a bond and the proceeds received from the sale of the bond by the issuing company, less whatever portion has been amortized, that is, written off to expense as recorded periodically on the PROFIT AND LOSS STATEMENT. At the time of issue, a company has two alternatives: (1) it can immediately absorb as an expense the amount of discount plus costs related to the issue, such as legal, printing, REGISTRATION, and other similar expenses, or (2) it can decide to treat the total discount and expenses as a DEFERRED CHARGE, recorded as an ASSET to be written off over the life of the bonds or by any other schedule the company finds desirable. The amount still to be expensed at any point is the unamortized bond discount.

UNAMORTIZED PREMIUMS ON INVESTMENTS unexpensed portion of the amount by which the price paid for a security exceeded its PAR value (if a BOND or PREFERRED STOCK) or MARKET VALUE (if common stock). A PREMIUM paid in acquiring an investment is in the nature of an INTANGIBLE ASSET, and conservative accounting practice dictates it be written off to expense over an appropriate period. *See also* GOING-CONCERN VALUE.

UNCOLLECTED FUNDS portion of bank deposit made up of checks that have not yet been collected by the depository bank—that is, payment has not yet been acknowledged by the bank on which a check was drawn. A bank will usually not let a depositor draw on uncollected funds. *See also* FLOAT.

UNCOLLECTIBLE ACCOUNT customer account that cannot be collected because of the customer's unwillingness or inability to pay. A business normally writes off such a receivable as worthless after several attempts at collecting the funds.

UNCOVERED OPTION short option that is not fully collateralized. A short call position is uncovered if the writer does not have long stock to deliver or does not own another call on the same security with a lower or same strike price, and with a longer or same time of expiration. Also called NAKED OPTION. *See also* NAKED POSITION; COVERED OPTION; COVERED WRITER.

UNDERBANKED said of a NEW ISSUE underwriting when the originating INVESTMENT BANKER is having difficulty getting other firms to become members of the UNDERWRITING GROUP, or syndicate. *See also* UNDERWRITE.

UNDERBOOKED said of a NEW ISSUE of securities during the preoffering REGISTRATION period when brokers canvassing lists of prospective buyers report limited INDICATIONS OF INTEREST. The opposite of underbooked would be *fully circled. See also* CIRCLE.

UNDERCAPITALIZATION situation in which a business does not have enough capital to carry out its normal business functions. *See also* CAPITALIZATION; WORKING CAPITAL.

UNDERLYING DEBT MUNICIPAL BOND term referring to the debt of government entities within the jurisdiction of larger government entities and for which the larger entity has partial credit responsibility. For example, a township might share responsibility for the general obligations of a village within the township, the debt of the village being underlying debt from the township's standpoint. The term OVERLAPPING DEBT is also used to describe underlying debt, but overlapping debt can also exist with entities of equal rank where, for example, a school district crosses boundaries of two or more townships.

UNDERLYING FUTURES CONTRACT FUTURES CONTRACT that underlies an OPTION on that future. For example, the Chicago Board of Trade offers a U.S. Treasury bond futures option. The underlying future is the Treasury bond futures contract traded on the Board of Trade. If the option contract were exercised, delivery would be made in the underlying futures contract.

UNDERLYING SECURITY
Options: security that must be delivered if a PUT OPTION or CALL OPTION contract is exercised. Stock INDEX OPTIONS and STOCK INDEX FUTURES, however, are settled in cash, since it is not possible to deliver an index of stocks.
Securities: common stock that underlies certain types of securities issued by corporations. This stock must be delivered if a SUBSCRIPTION WARRANT or SUBSCRIPTION RIGHT is exercised, if a CONVERTIBLE bond or PREFERRED STOCK is converted into common shares, or if an INCENTIVE STOCK OPTION is exercised.

UNDERMARGINED ACCOUNT MARGIN ACCOUNT that has fallen below MARGIN REQUIREMENTS or MINIMUM MAINTENANCE requirements. As a result, the broker must make a MARGIN CALL to the customer.

UNDERVALUED security selling below its LIQUIDATION value or the MARKET VALUE analysts believe it deserves. A company's stock may be undervalued because the industry is out of favor, because the company is not well known or has an erratic history of earnings, or for many other reasons. Fundamental analysts try to spot companies that are undervalued so their clients can buy before the stocks become FULLY VALUED. Undervalued companies are also frequently targets of TAKEOVER attempts, since acquirers can buy assets cheaply this way. *See also* FUNDAMENTAL ANALYSIS.

UNDERWATER OPTION OUT OF THE MONEY option. Being out of the money indicates the option has no intrinsic value; all of its value consists of time value. A call option is out of the money if its exercise price is higher than the current price of the underlying contract. A put option is out of the money if its exercise price is lower than the current price of the underlying contract.

UNDERWITHHOLDING situation in which taxpayers have too little federal, state, or local income tax withheld from their salaries. Because they have under-withheld, these taxpayers may owe income taxes when they file their tax returns. If the underwithholding is large enough, penalties and interest also may be due. To correct underwithholding, taxpayers must file a new W-4 form with their employers, decreasing the number of dependents claimed. *See also* OVERWITHHOLDING.

UNDERWRITE

Insurance: to assume risk in exchange for a PREMIUM.

Investments: to assume the risk of buying a NEW ISSUE of securities from the issuing corporation or government entity and reselling them to the public, either directly or through dealers. The UNDERWRITER makes a profit on the difference between the price paid to the issuer and the PUBLIC OFFERING PRICE, called the UNDERWRITING SPREAD.

Underwriting is the business of investment bankers, who usually form an UNDERWRITING GROUP (also called a PURCHASE GROUP or syndicate) to pool the risk and assure successful distribution of the issue. The syndicate operates under an AGREEMENT AMONG UNDERWRITERS, also termed a *syndicate contract* or PURCHASE GROUP contract.

The underwriting group appoints a MANAGING UNDERWRITER, also known as *lead underwriter, syndicate manager,* or simply *manager,* that is usually the *originating investment banker*—the firm that began working with the issuer months before to plan details of the issue and prepare the REGISTRATION materials to be filed with the SECURITIES AND EXCHANGE COMMISSION. The manager, acting as agent for the group, signs the UNDERWRITING AGREEMENT (or *purchase contract)* with the issuer. This agreement sets forth the terms and conditions of the arrangement and the responsibilities of both issuer and underwriter. During the offering period, it is the manager's responsibility to stabilize the MARKET PRICE of the issuer's shares by bidding in the open market, a process called PEGGING. The manager may also appoint a SELLING GROUP, comprised of dealers and the underwriters themselves, to assist in DISTRIBUTION of the issue.

Strictly speaking, *underwrite* is properly used only in a FIRM COMMITMENT underwriting, also known as a BOUGHT DEAL, where the securities are purchased outright from the issuer.

Other investment banking arrangements to which the term is sometimes loosely applied are BEST EFFORT, ALL OR NONE, and STANDBY COMMITMENTS; in each of these, the risk is shared between the issuer and the INVESTMENT BANKER.

The term is also sometimes used in connection with a REGISTERED SECONDARY OFFERING, which involves essentially the same process as a new issue, except that the proceeds go to the selling investor, not to the issuer. For these arrangements, the term *secondary offering* or SECONDARY DISTRIBUTION is preferable to *underwriting,* which is usually reserved for new, or primary, distributions.

There are two basic methods by which underwriters are chosen by issuers and underwriting spreads are determined: NEGOTIATED UNDERWRITINGS and COMPETITIVE BID underwritings. Generally, the negotiated method is used in corporate equity (stock) issues and most corporate debt (bond) issues, whereas the competitive bidding method is used by municipalities and public utilities. *See also* ALLOTMENT; BLOWOUT; FLOATING AN ISSUE; FLOTATION COST; HOT ISSUE; INITIAL PUBLIC OFFERING; PRESOLD ISSUE; PRIMARY MARKET; PUBLIC OFFERING; STANDBY UNDERWRITER.

UNDERWRITER

Insurance: company that assumes the cost risk of death, fire, theft, illness, etc., in exchange for payments, called *premiums.*

Securities: INVESTMENT BANKER who, singly or as a member of an UNDERWRITING GROUP or syndicate, agrees to purchase a NEW ISSUE of securities from an issuer and distribute it to investors, making a profit on the UNDERWRITING SPREAD. *See also* UNDERWRITE.

UNDERWRITING AGREEMENT agreement between a corporation issuing new securities to be offered to the public and the MANAGING UNDERWRITER as agent for the UNDERWRITING GROUP. Also termed the *purchase agreement* or *purchase contract,* it represents the underwriters' commitment to purchase the securities, and it details the PUBLIC OFFERING PRICE, the UNDERWRITING SPREAD (including all discounts and commissions), the net proceeds to the issuer, and the SETTLEMENT DATE.

The issuer agrees to pay all expenses incurred in preparing the issue for resale, including the costs of REGISTRATION with the SECURITIES AND EXCHANGE COMMISSION (SEC) and of the PROSPECTUS, and agrees to supply the managing underwriter with sufficient copies of both the PRELIMINARY PROSPECTUS (red herring) and the final, statutory prospectus. The issuer guarantees (1) to make all required SEC filings and to comply fully with the provisions of the SECURITIES ACT OF 1933; (2) to assume responsibility for the completeness, accuracy, and proper certification of all information in the registration statement and prospectus; (3) to disclose all pending litigation; (4) to use the proceeds for the purposes stated; (5) to comply with state securities laws; (6) to work to get listed on the exchange agreed upon; and (7) to indemnify the underwriters for liability arising out of omissions or misrepresentations for which the issuer had responsibility.

The underwriters agree to proceed with the offering as soon as the registration is cleared by the SEC or at a specified date thereafter. The underwriters are authorized to make sales to members of a SELLING GROUP.

The underwriting agreement is not to be confused with the AGREEMENT AMONG UNDERWRITERS. *See also* BEST EFFORT; FIRM COMMITMENT; STANDBY COMMITMENT; UNDERWRITE.

UNDERWRITING GROUP temporary association of investment bankers, organized by the originating INVESTMENT BANKER in a NEW ISSUE of securities. Operating under an AGREEMENT AMONG UNDERWRITERS, it agrees to purchase securities from the issuing corporation at an agreed-upon price and to resell them at a PUBLIC OFFERING PRICE, the difference representing the UNDERWRITING SPREAD. The purpose of the underwriting group is to spread the risk and assure successful distribution of the offering. Most underwriting groups operate under a *divided syndicate contract,* meaning that the liability of members is limited to their individual participations. Also called DISTRIBUTING SYNDICATE, PURCHASE GROUP, *investment banking group,* or *syndicate. See also* FIRM COMMITMENT; UNDERWRITE; UNDERWRITING AGREEMENT.

UNDERWRITING SPREAD difference between the amount paid to an issuer of securities in a PRIMARY DISTRIBUTION and the PUBLIC OFFERING PRICE. The amount of SPREAD varies widely, depending on the size of the issue, the financial strength of the issuer, the type of security involved (stock, bonds, rights), the status of the security (senior, junior, secured, unsecured), and the type of commitment made by the investment bankers. The range may be from a fraction of 1% for a bond issue of a big utility company to 25% for the INITIAL PUBLIC OFFERING of a small company. The division of the spread between the MANAGING UNDERWRITER, the SELLING GROUP, and the participating underwriters also varies, but in a two-point spread the manager might typically get 0.25%, the selling group 1%, and the underwriters 0.75%. It is usual, though, for the underwriters also to be members of the selling group, thus picking up 1.75% of the spread, and for the manager to be in all three categories, thus picking up the full 2%. *See also* COMPETITIVE BID; FLOTATION COST; GROSS SPREAD; NEGOTIATED UNDERWRITING; SELLING CONCESSION; UNDERWRITE.

UNDIGESTED SECURITIES newly issued stocks and bonds that remain undistributed because there is insufficient public demand at the OFFERING PRICE. *See also* UNDERWRITE.

UNDISTRIBUTED PROFITS (EARNINGS, NET INCOME) *see* RETAINED EARNINGS.

UNDIVIDED PROFITS account shown on a bank's BALANCE SHEET representing profits that have neither been paid out as DIVIDENDS nor transferred to the bank's SURPLUS account. Current earnings are credited to the undivided profits account and are then either paid out in dividends or retained to build up total EQUITY. As the account grows, round amounts may be periodically transferred to the surplus account.

UNEARNED DISCOUNT account on the books of a lending institution recognizing interest deducted in advance and which will be taken into income as earned over the life of the loan. In accordance with accounting principles, such interest is initially recorded as a LIABILITY. Then, as months pass and it is gradually "earned," it is recognized as income, thus increasing the lender's profit and decreasing the corresponding liability. *See also* UNEARNED INCOME.

UNEARNED INCOME (REVENUE)
Accounting: income received but not yet earned, such as rent received in advance or other advances from customers. Unearned income is usually classified as a CURRENT LIABILITY on a company's BALANCE SHEET, assuming that it will be credited to income within the normal accounting cycle. *See also* DEFERRED CHARGE.
Income taxes: income from sources other than wages, salaries, tips, and other employee compensation—for example, DIVIDENDS, INTEREST, rent.

UNEARNED INTEREST interest that has already been collected on a loan by a financial institution, but that cannot yet be counted as part of earnings because the principal of the loan has not been outstanding long enough. Also called DISCOUNT and UNEARNED DISCOUNT.

UNEMPLOYED OR UNEMPLOYMENT condition of being out of work involuntarily. The federal-state unemployment insurance system makes cash payments directly to laid-off workers. Most states now pay a maximum of 26 weeks; a few extend duration somewhat farther. In periods of very high unemployment in individual states, benefits are payable for as many as 13 additional weeks. These "extended benefits" are funded on a shared basis, approximately half from state funds and half from federal sources. In general, to collect unemployment benefits a person must have previously held a job and must be actively seeking employment. Unemployed people apply for and collect unemployment compensation from their state's Department of Labor. Except in states where there are small employee payments, the system is financed by a payroll tax on employers.

UNEMPLOYMENT RATE percentage of the civilian labor force actively looking for work but unable to find jobs. The rate is compiled by the U.S. Department of Labor, in cooperation with the Labor Departments in all the states, and released to the public on the first Friday of every month. The unemployment rate is affected by the number of people entering the workforce as well as the number of unemployed people. An important part of the Labor Department's report is "Payroll Employment," which covers data on hours, earnings, and employment for nonfarm industries nationally, by state and for major metropolitan areas. The unemployment report is one of the most closely watched of all government reports, because it gives the clearest indication of the direction of the economy. A rising unemployment rate will be seen by analysts and the Federal Reserve as a sign of a weakening economy, which might call for an easing of monetary policy by the Fed. On the other hand, a drop in the unemployment rate shows that the economy is growing, which may spark fears of higher inflation on the part of the Fed, which may raise interest rates as a result.

UNENCUMBERED property free and clear of all liens (creditors' claims). When a homeowner pays off his mortgage, for example, the house becomes unencumbered property. Securities bought with cash instead of on MARGIN are unencumbered.

UNFUNDED PENSION PLAN pension plan that is funded by the employer out of current income as funds are required by retirees or beneficiaries. Also known as a *pay-as-you-go* pension plan, or a plan using the *current disbursement funding approach.* This contrasts with an ADVANCE FUNDED PENSION PLAN, under which the employer puts aside money on a regular basis into a separate fund that is invested in stocks, bonds, real estate, and other assets.

UNIFIED CREDIT federal TAX CREDIT that may be applied against the gift tax, the estate tax, and, under specified conditions, the generation-skipping transfer tax.

UNIFORM COMMERCIAL CODE (UCC) legal code adopted by most states that codifies various laws dealing with commercial transactions, primarily those involving the sale of goods, both tangible and intangible, and secured transactions. It was drafted by the National Conference of Commissioners of Uniform State Laws and covers bank deposits, bankruptcy, commercial letters of credit, commercial paper, warranties, and other commercial activities. Article 8 of the UCC applies to transactions in investment securities.

UNIFORM GIFTS TO MINORS ACT (UGMA) enacted to provide a simple way to transfer property to a minor without the complications of a formal trust, and without the restrictions applicable to the guardianship of a minor's property. In many states, gifts under the UGMA can be made both by lifetime gift and by the donor's WILL. Lifetime UGMA gifts qualify for the $10,000 annual GIFT TAX exclusion. Under the TAXPAYER RELIEF ACT OF 1997, the $10,000 limit on gifts free of the gift tax will be adjusted for inflation in $1,000 increments. An UGMA property is managed by a CUSTODIAN appointed by the donor. If the donor names him/herself as custodian and dies before the property is turned over to the minor, the value of the custodial property at the donor-custodian's death is included in the donor-custodian's taxable estate even though the property belongs to the minor from the instant the UGMA gift is made. The custodial property must be turned over to the minor when the minor attains the age specified in the UGMA law of the state in which the gift is made. In most states, the age is 18, but in some states it is 21. In New York State it is 18 unless the donor, at the time the UGMA gift is made, specifies age 21. All 50 states also enacted a UNIFORM TRANSFER TO MINORS ACT (UTMA), which in some case supplements the UGMA, and in others replaces it.

UNIFORM PRACTICE CODE rules of the NATIONAL ASSOCIATION OF SECURITIES DEALERS (NASD) concerned with standards and procedures for the operational handling of OVER THE COUNTER securities transactions, such as delivery, SETTLEMENT DATE, EX-DIVIDEND DATE, and other ex-dates (such as EX-RIGHTS and EX-WARRANTS), and providing for the arbitration of disputes through Uniform Practice committees.

UNIFORM SECURITIES AGENT STATE LAW EXAMINATION test required of prospective REGISTERED REPRESENTATIVES in many U.S. states. In addition to the examination requirements of states, all registered representatives, whether employees of member firms or OVER THE COUNTER brokers, must pass the General Securities Representative Examination (also known as the Series 7 Examination), administered by the National Association of Securities Dealers (NASD).

UNIFORM TRANSFERS TO MINORS ACT (UTMA) law adopted by all 50 states that is similar to the UNIFORM GIFTS TO MINORS ACT (UGMA) but different in that it extends the definition of GIFTS beyond cash and securities to include real estate, paintings, royalties, and patents. UTMA also prohibits the minor from taking control of the assets until age 21 (25 in California).

UNINSURED MOTORIST INSURANCE form of insurance that covers the policyholder and family members if injured by a hit-and-run motorist or driver who carries no liability insurance, assuming the driver is at fault. In most instances, reimbursements of costs of property damage and medical expenses resulting from the accident will be rewarded. The premiums for uninsured motorist coverage are usually rather modest, and are included as part of a regular auto insurance policy.

UNISSUED STOCK shares of a corporation's stock authorized in its charter but not issued. They are shown on the BALANCE SHEET along with shares ISSUED AND OUTSTANDING. Unissued stock may be issued by action of the board of directors, although shares needed for unexercised employee STOCK OPTIONS, rights, warrants, or convertible securities must not be issued while such obligations are outstanding. Unissued shares cannot pay dividends and cannot be voted. They are not to be confused with TREASURY STOCK, which is issued but not outstanding.

UNIT
In general: any division of quantity accepted as a standard of measurement or of exchange. For example, in the commodities markets, a unit of wheat is a bushel, a unit of coffee a pound, and a unit of shell eggs a dozen. The unit of U.S. currency is the dollar.
Banking: bank operating out of only one office, and with no branches, as required by states having unit banking laws.
Finance:
1. segment or subdivision (division or subsidiary, product line, or plant) of a company.
2. in sales or production, quantity rather than dollars. One might say, for example, "Unit volume declined but dollar volume increased after prices were raised."
Securities:
1. minimum amount of stocks, bonds, commodities, or other securities accepted for trading on an exchange. *See also* ODD LOT; ROUND LOT; UNIT OF TRADING.
2. group of specialists on a stock exchange, who maintain fair and orderly markets in particular securities. *See also* SPECIALIST; SPECIALIST UNIT.
3. more than one class of securities traded together; one common share and one SUBSCRIPTION WARRANT might sell as a unit, for example.
4. in primary and secondary distributions of securities, one share of stock or one bond.

UNITED STATES GOVERNMENT SECURITIES direct GOVERNMENT OBLIGATIONS—that is, debt issues of the U.S. government, such as Treasury bills, notes, and bonds and SERIES EE and SERIES HH SAVINGS BONDS as distinguished from government-sponsored AGENCY issues. *See also* GOVERNMENT SECURITIES; TREASURIES.

UNIT INVESTMENT TRUST (UIT) investment vehicle registered with the SECURITIES AND EXCHANGE COMMISSION under the INVESTMENT COMPANY ACT OF 1940, that purchases a fixed PORTFOLIO of securities, such as corporate, municipal or government bonds, mortgage-backed securities, COMMON STOCK, or PREFERRED STOCK. Units in the trust, which usually cost at least $1,000, are sold to investors by brokers for a sales charge that is typically 4% for traditional municipal bond trusts and 1%-2% for equity trusts, which feature reduced sales charges when the trusts are rolled over. The trust expires when bonds mature or, in the case of equity funds, at a specified future date. Unit holders receive an undivided interest in both the principal and the income portion of the portfolio in proportion to the amount of captial they invest.

Traditionally, the majority of UITs held municipal bonds. In the late 1990s, however, equity UITs became predominant. Among the most popular variations were those holding high-yield stocks in the DOW JONES INDUSTRIAL AVERAGE (DOGS OF THE DOW) or the Standard & Poor's 500 Index and their counterparts on foreign exchanges. A large proportion of equity trust money was invested in such DEFINED ASSET FUNDS offered by Merrill Lynch, Salomon Smith Barney Inc., Prudential Securities, Morgan Stanley Dean Witter and Paine Webber, as the Select 10 Portfolios based on the Dow, the S&P, and indices in Japan, Hong Kong, and the United Kingdom. *See also* DIAMONDS; SPDR; UNIT SHARE INVESTMENT TRUST (USIT).

UNIT OF TRADING normal number of shares, bonds, or commodities comprising the minimum unit of trading on an exchange. For stocks, this is usually 100 shares, although inactive shares trade in 10-share units. For corporate bonds on the NYSE, the unit for exchange trading is $1000 or $5000 par value. Commodities futures units vary widely, according to the COMMODITY involved. *See also* FUTURES CONTRACT; ODD LOT; ROUND LOT.

UNIT SHARE INVESTMENT TRUST (USIT) specialized form of UNIT INVESTMENT TRUST comprising one unit of PRIME and one unit of SCORE.

UNIVERSAL LIFE INSURANCE form of life insurance, first marketed in the early 1980s, that combines the low-cost protection of TERM LIFE INSURANCE with a savings portion, which is invested in a tax-deferred account earning money-market rates of interest. The policy is flexible; that is, as age and income change, a policyholder can increase or decrease premium payments and coverage, or shift a certain portion of premiums into the savings account, without additional sales charges or complications. A new form of the policy; called *universal variable life insurance,* combines the flexibility of universal life with the growth potential of variable life. *See also* VARIABLE LIFE INSURANCE; WHOLE LIFE INSURANCE.

UNIVERSE OF SECURITIES group of stocks sharing a common characteristic. For example, one analyst may define a universe of securities as those with $100 to $500 million in outstanding market capitalization. Another may define it as stocks in a particular industry, such as communications, paper, or airlines. A mutual fund will often define itself to investors as limiting itself to a particular universe of securities, allowing investors to know in advance which kinds of securities that fund will buy and hold.

UNLEVERAGED PROGRAM LIMITED PARTNERSHIP whose use of borrowed funds to finance the acquisition of properties is 50% or less of the purchase price. In contrast, a *leveraged program* borrows 50% or more. Investors seeking to maximize income tend to favor unleveraged partnerships, where interest expense and other deductions from income are at a minimum. Investors looking for TAX SHELTERS might favor leveraged programs despite the higher risk because of the greater amount of property acquired with the borrowed money and the greater amount of tax deductible interest but the longer depreciation periods required by tax legislation have substantially reduced the tax benefits from real estate.

UNLIMITED MARITAL DEDUCTION *see* MARITAL DEDUCTION.

UNLIMITED TAX BOND MUNICIPAL BOND secured by the pledge to levy taxes at an unlimited rate until the bond is repaid.

UNLISTED SECURITY security that is not listed on an organized exchange, such as the NEW YORK STOCK EXCHANGE, the AMERICAN STOCK EXCHANGE, or the REGIONAL STOCK EXCHANGES, and is traded in the OVER THE COUNTER market.

UNLISTED TRADING trading of securities not listed on an organized exchange but traded on that exchange as an accommodation to its members. An exchange wishing to trade unlisted securities must file an application with the SECURITIES

AND EXCHANGE COMMISSION and make the necessary information available to the investing public. The New York Stock Exchange does not allow unlisted trading privileges, and the practice has declined at the American Stock Exchange and other organized exchanges.

UNLOADING
Finance: selling off large quantities of merchandise inventory at below-market prices either to raise cash quickly or to depress the market in a particular product.
Investments: selling securities or commodities when prices are declining to preclude further loss.
See also PUMP; PROFIT TAKING; SELLING OFF.

UNMARGINED ACCOUNT brokerage CASH ACCOUNT.

UNPAID DIVIDEND dividend that has been declared by a corporation but has still not been paid. A company may declare a dividend on July 1, for example, payable on August 1. During July, the declared dividend is called an unpaid dividend. *See also* EX-DIVIDEND.

UNQUALIFIED OPINION independent auditor's opinion that a company's financial statements are fairly presented, in all material respects, in conformity with generally accepted accounting principles. The justification for the expression of the auditor's opinion rests on the conformity of his or her audit with generally accepted auditing standards and on his or her feelings. Materiality and audit risk underly the application of auditing standards. *See also* ACCOUNTANT'S OPINION; ADVERSE OPINION; QUALIFIED OPINION.

UNREALIZED PROFIT (OR LOSS) profit or loss that has not become actual. It becomes a REALIZED PROFIT (OR LOSS) when the security or commodity future contract in which there is a gain or loss is actually sold. Also called a *paper profit or loss.*

UNREGISTERED STOCK *see* LETTER SECURITY.

UNSECURED DEBT obligation not backed by the pledge of specific COLLATERAL.

UNSECURED LOAN loan without COLLATERAL.

UNWIND A TRADE to reverse a securities transaction through an offsetting transaction. *See also* OFFSET.

UPGRADING increase in the quality rating of a security. An analyst may upgrade a company's bond or stock rating if its finances improve, profitability is enhanced, and its debt level is reduced. For municipal bond issues, upgrading will occur if tax revenues increase and expenses are reduced. The upgrading of a stock or bond issue may in itself raise the price of the security because investors will feel more confident in the financial soundness of the issuer. The credit rating of issuers is constantly being evaluated, which may lead to further upgradings, or, if conditions deteriorate, downgradings. The term *upgrading* is also applied to an entire portfolio of securities. For example, a mutual fund manager who wants to improve the quality of his bond holdings will say that he is in the process of upgrading his portfolio.

UPSET PRICE term used in auctions that represents the minimum price at which a seller of property will entertain bids.

UPSIDE POTENTIAL amount of upward price movement an investor or an analyst expects of a particular stock, bond, or commodity. This opinion may result from either FUNDAMENTAL ANALYSIS or TECHNICAL ANALYSIS.

UPSTAIRS MARKET transaction completed within the broker-dealer's firm and without using the stock exchange. Securities and Exchange Commission and stock exchange rules exist to ensure that such trades do not occur at prices less favorable to the customer than those prevailing in the general market. *See also* OFF BOARD.

UPSWING upward movement in the price of a security or commodity after a period of falling prices. Analysts will say "that stock has bottomed out and now has started an upswing which should carry it to new highs." The term is also used to refer to the general condition of the economy. An economy that is recovering from a prolonged downturn or recession is said to be in an upswing.

UPTICK transaction executed at a price higher than the preceding transaction in that security; also called PLUS TICK. A plus sign is displayed throughout the day next to the last price of each stock that showed a higher price than the preceding transaction in that stock at the TRADING POST of the SPECIALIST on the floor of the New York Stock Exchange. Short sales may only be executed on upticks or ZERO-PLUS TICKS. *See* also MINUS TICK; SELLING SHORT; TICK.

UPTICK RULE Securities and Exchange Commission rule that selling short may only be done on an UPTICK. In 1990, interpretation of the rule was extended to cover PROGRAM TRADING.

UPTREND upward direction in the price of a stock, bond, or commodity future contract or overall market. *See also* TRENDLINE.

USEFUL LIFE estimated period of time during which an asset subject to DEPRECIATION is judged to be productive in a business. Also called *depreciable life.* The MODIFIED ACCELERATED COST RECOVERY SYSTEM (MACRS) established useful lives for different property classes. *See also* RESIDUAL VALUE.

USES OF FUNDS *see* SOURCES AND APPLICATIONS (OR USES) OF FUNDS STATEMENT.

U.S. SAVINGS BOND *see* SAVINGS BOND.

USURY LAWS state laws limiting excessive interest rates on loans.

UTILITY power company that owns or operates facilities used for the generation, transmission, or distribution of electric energy. Utilities provide electric, gas, and water to their customers. In the United States, utilities are regulated at the state and federal level. State public service and public utility commissions regulate retail rates. The Federal Energy Regulatory Commission (FERC) regulates wholesale rates, the sale, resale, and interstate commerce for approximately 200 investor-owned utilities. On a percentage and revenue basis, however, the states regulate most of the trade. Rates for the sale of power and its transmission to retail customers, as well as approval for the construction of new plants, are regulated at the state level. The electric utility industry came under government regulation in the 1920s because it was a virtual MONOPOLY, vertically integrated, producing energy and transmitting it to customers. The industry has evolved to include public power agencies and electricity cooperatives. DEREGULATION of the natural gas industry in recent years has served to open that market to more competition, although transmission pipelines still come under FERC jurisdiction. The electric utility industry is also undertaking a similar deregulation process.

Utility stocks usually offer above-average dividend yields to investors, but less capital appreciation potential than growth stocks. Utility stocks are also very sensitive to the direction of interest rates. Rising interest rates tend to harm the value of utility shares because higher rates provide a more attractive alternative to investors. In addition, utilities tend to be heavy borrowers, so higher interest rates add to their borrowing costs. Conversely, falling interest rates tend to buoy the value of utility stocks because utility dividends look more attractive and because the companies' borrowing costs will be reduced.

UTILITY REVENUE BOND MUNICIPAL BOND issued to finance the construction of electric generating plants, gas, water and sewer systems, among other types of public utility services. These bonds are repaid from the revenues the project produces once it is operating. Such bonds usually have a reserve fund that contains an amount equal to one year's DEBT SERVICE, which protects bondholders in case there is a temporary cash shortage or revenues are less than anticipated. *See also* REVENUE BOND.

V

VALUABLES *see* HIGH-TICKET ITEMS.

VALUATION placing a value or worth on an asset. Stock analysts determine the value of a company's stock based on the outlook for earnings and the market value of assets on the balance sheet. Stock valuation is normally expressed in terms of price/earnings (P/E) ratios. A company with a high P/E is said to have a high valuation, and a low P/E stock has a low valuation. Other assets, such as real estate and bonds, are given valuations by analysts who recommend whether the asset is worth buying or selling at the current price. Estates also go through the valuation process after someone has died.

VALUATION RESERVE reserve or allowance, created by a charge to expenses (and therefore, in effect, taken out of profits) in order to provide for changes in the value of a company's assets. Accumulated DEPRECIATION, allowance for BAD DEBTS, and UNAMORTIZED BOND DISCOUNT are three familiar examples of valuation reserves. Also called *valuation account.*

VALUE-ADDED TAX (VAT) consumption tax levied on the value added to a product at each stage of its manufacturing cycle as well as at the time of purchase by the ultimate consumer. The value-added tax is a fixture in European countries and a major source of revenue for the EUROPEAN UNION (EU). Advocates of a value-added tax for the U.S. contend that it would be the most efficient method of raising revenue and that the size of its receipts would permit a reduction in income tax rates. Opponents argue that in its pure form it would be the equivalent of a national sales tax and therefore unfair and regressive, putting the greatest burden on those who can least afford it. As an example, for each part that goes into the assembling of an automobile, the auto manufacturer would pay a value-added tax to the supplier, probably a percentage of the purchase price, as is the case with a sales tax. When the finished car is sold, the consumer pays a value-added tax on the cost of the finished product less the material and supply costs that were taxed at earlier stages. This avoids double taxation and thus differs from a flat sales tax based on the total cost of purchase.

VALUE BROKER DISCOUNT BROKER whose rates are based on a percentage of the dollar value of each transaction. It is usually advantageous to place orders through a value broker for trades of low-priced shares or small numbers of shares, since commissions will be relatively smaller than if a shareholder used a SHARE BROKER, another type of discount broker, who charges according to the number and the price of the shares traded.

VALUE CHANGE change in a stock price adjusted for the number of outstanding shares of that stock, so that a group of stocks adjusted this way are equally weighted. A unit of movement of the group—called an INDEX—is thus representative of the average performance.

VALUE DATE

Banking: official date when money is transferred, that is, becomes good funds to the depositor. The value date differs from the *entry date* when items are received from the depositor, since the items must then be forwarded to the paying bank or otherwise collected. The term is used mainly with reference to foreign accounts, either maintained in a domestic bank or maintained by a domestic bank in foreign banks. *See also* FLOAT.

Eurodollar and foreign currency transactions: synonymous with SETTLEMENT DATE or DELIVERY DATE, which on spot transactions involving North American currencies (U.S. dollar, Canadian dollar, and Mexican peso) is one business day and on spot transactions involving other currencies, two business days. In the forward exchange market, value date is the maturity date of the contract plus one business day for North American currencies, two business days for other currencies. *See also* FORWARD EXCHANGE TRANSACTION; SPOT MARKET.

VALUE LINE INVESTMENT SURVEY investment advisory service that ranks about 1,700 stocks for "timeliness" and safety. Using a computerized model based on earnings momentum, Value Line projects which stocks will have the best or worst relative price performance over the next 6 to 12 months. In addition, each stock is assigned a risk rating, which identifies the VOLATILITY of a stock's price behavior relative to the market average. The service also ranks all major industry groups for timeliness. Value Line's ranking system for both timeliness and safety of an individual stock is as follows:

    1—highest rank
    2—above average rank
    3—average rank
    4—below average rank
    5—lowest rank

The weekly writeups of companies that Value Line subscribers receive include detailed financial information about a company, as well as such data as corporate INSIDER buying and selling decisions and the percentage of a company's shares held by institutions.

Value Line offers several specialized financial surveys. The *Value Line Convertibles Survey* is a subscription service that evaluates convertible securities. The *Value Line Mutual Fund Survey* offers details on fund holdings and performance and ranks funds on expected returns. Value Line also sponsors its own family of mutual funds. Value Line also produces several stock indices and averages, the most important of which is the *Value Line Composite Average,* which tracks the stocks followed by the *Value Line Investment Survey.*

VA MORTGAGE *see* VETERANS ADMINISTRATION (VA) MORTGAGE.

VANCOUVER STOCK EXCHANGE (VSE) securities and options exchange in Vancouver, British Columbia, Canada, specializing since 1907 in venture capital companies. VSE's securities market trades stocks, rights, warrants and units, while its options market focuses on equity and gold options. Mining stocks account for most of the trading, with junior mining companies making up the largest single group. Natural resource companies have raised billions of dollars on the exchange. The number of technology, entertainment, real estate and financial services companies listed on the exchange is increasing. Traditionally between 10% and 20% of the financings originate in the U.S., with 20% to 25% from Europe and Asia. The *VSE Composite Index* is capital-weighted and is a composite of three sub-indices: Commercial/Industrial, Resource, and Venture. In 1990, with the introduction of Vancouver Computerized Trading (VCT), VSE became the first North American exchange to convert from open outcry to a completely automated trading system. VISTA, an evening trading session that corresponds with the start of the business day in the Asia Pacific region, was introduced in 1996. Computerized clearing is conducted through the West Canada Clearing Corp. Settlement is on the third business day following a trade. Trading hours are 9 A.M. to 5 P.M., Monday through Friday.

VARIABLE ANNUITY life insurance ANNUITY contract whose value fluctuates with that of an underlying securities PORTFOLIO or other INDEX of performance. The variable annuity contrasts with a conventional or FIXED ANNUITY, whose rate of return is constant and therefore vulnerable to the effects of inflation. Income on a variable annuity may be taken periodically, beginning immediately or at any future time. The annuity may be a single-premium or multiple-premium contract. The return to investors may be in the form of a periodic payment that varies with the MARKET VALUE of the portfolio or a fixed minimum payment with add-ons based on the rate of portfolio appreciation. *See also* SINGLE-PREMIUM DEFERRED ANNUITY.

VARIABLE COST cost that changes directly with the amount of production—for example, direct material or direct labor needed to complete a product. *See also* FIXED COST.

VARIABLE INTEREST RATE interest rate on a loan that rises and falls based on the movement of an underlying index of interest rates. For example, many credit cards charge variable interest rates, based on a specific spread over the prime rate. Most home equity loans charge variable rates tied to the prime rate. Also called *adjustable interest rate.*

VARIABLE LIFE INSURANCE innovation in LIFE INSURANCE that allows policyholders to invest the cash value of the policy in stock, bond, or money market portfolios. Investors can elect to move from one portfolio to another or rely on the company's professional money managers to make such decisions for them. As in WHOLE LIFE INSURANCE, the annual premium is fixed, but part of it is earmarked for the investment PORTFOLIO. The policyholder bears the risk of securities investments, meaning that cash values and death benefits will rise if the underlying investments do well, and fall if the investments drop in value. Some insurance companies guarantee a minimum death benefit for an extra premium. When portfolio investments rise substantially, policyholders can use a portion of the increased cash value to buy additional insurance coverage. Policyholders can borrow against the accumulated cash value or cash in the policy. As in an INDIVIDUAL RETIREMENT ACCOUNT, earnings from variable life policies are tax deferred until distributed. Income is then taxed only to the extent it exceeds the total premiums paid into the policy. Death benefits are not taxed as individual income but as taxable estate income, which carries an exclusion of $625,000. This ESTATE TAX exclusion is scheduled to rise to $1 million in 2006, according to the TAXPAYER RELIEF ACT OF 1997.

Variable life insurance is different from UNIVERSAL LIFE INSURANCE. Universal life allows policyholders to increase or decrease premiums and change the death benefit. It also accrues interest at market-related rates on premiums over and above insurance charges and expenses.

VARIABLE RATE CERTIFICATE a CERTIFICATE OF DEPOSIT (CD) whose rate of interest is periodically adjusted in relation to some benchmark, such as the prime rate or a stock index.

VARIABLE RATE DEMAND NOTE note representing borrowings (usually from a commercial bank) that is payable on demand and that bears interest tied to a money market rate, usually the bank PRIME RATE. The rate on the note is adjusted upward or downward each time the base rate changes.

VARIABLE RATE MORTGAGE (VRM) *see* ADJUSTABLE RATE MORTGAGE (ARM).

VARIABLE RATE PREFERRED STOCK *see* ADJUSTABLE RATE PREFERRED STOCK (ARP).

VARIANCE
Accounting: difference between actual cost and STANDARD COST in the categories of direct material, direct labor, and DIRECT OVERHEAD. A positive variation (when the actual cost is lower than the standard or anticipated cost) would translate into a higher profit unless offset by negative variances elsewhere.
Finance: (1) difference between corresponding items on a comparative BALANCE SHEET and PROFIT AND LOSS STATEMENT. (2) difference between actual experience and budgeted or projected experience in any financial category. For example, if sales were projected to be $2 million for a period and were actually $2.5 million, there would be a positive variance of $500,000 or 25%.
Real estate: allowed exception to zoning rules. If a particular neighborhood were zoned for residential use only, a person wanting to open a store would need to be granted a variance from the zoning board in order to proceed.
Statistics: measure of the dispersion of a distribution. It is the sum of the squares of the deviation from the mean. *See also* STANDARD DEVIATION.

VELDA SUE acronym for *Venture Enhancement & Loan Development Administration for Smaller Undercapitalized Enterprises,* a federal agency that buys small business loans made by banks, pools them, then issues securities that are bought as investments by large institutions.

VELOCITY rate of spending, or turnover of money—in other words, how many times a dollar is spent in a given period of time. The more money turns over, the faster velocity is said to be. The concept of "income velocity of money" was first explained by the economist Irving Fisher in the 1920s as bearing a direct relationship to GROSS DOMESTIC PRODUCT (GDP). Velocity usually is measured as the ratio of GDP to the money supply. Velocity affects the amount of economic activity generated by a given money supply, which includes bank deposits and cash in circulation. Velocity is a factor in the Federal Reserve Board's management of MONETARY POLICY, because an increase in velocity may obviate the need for a stimulative increase in the money supply. Conversely, a decline in velocity might reflect dampened economic growth, even if the money supply holds steady. *See also* FISCAL POLICY.

VENDOR
1. supplier of goods or services of a commercial nature; may be a manufacturer, importer, or wholesale distributor. For example, one component of the Index of LEADING INDICATORS is vendor performance, meaning the rate at which suppliers of goods are making delivery to their commercial customers.
2. retailer of merchandise, especially one without an established place of business, as in *sidewalk vendor.*

VENTURE CAPITAL important source of financing for START-UP companies or others embarking on new or TURNAROUND ventures that entail some investment risk but offer the potential for above average future profits; also called *risk capital.* Sources of venture capital include wealthy individual investors; subsidiaries of banks and other corporations organized as small business investment companies (SBICs); groups of investment banks and other financing sources who pool investments in venture capital funds or VENTURE CAPITAL LIMITED PARTNERSHIPS. The SMALL BUSINESS ADMINISTRATION (SBA) promotes venture capital programs through the licensing and financing of SBICs. Venture capital financing supplements other personal or external funds that an ENTREPRENEUR is able to tap, or takes the place of loans of other funds that conventional financial institutions are unable or unwilling to risk. Some venture capital sources invest only at a certain stage of entrepreneurship, such as the start-up or SEED MONEY stage, the *first round* or SECOND ROUND phases that follow, or at the MEZZANINE LEVEL immediately preceding an INITIAL PUBLIC OFFERING. In return for taking an investment risk, venture capitalists are usually rewarded with some combination of PROFITS, PREFERRED STOCK, ROYALTIES on sales, and capital appreciation of common shares.

VENTURE CAPITAL LIMITED PARTNERSHIP investment vehicle organized by a brokerage firm or entrepreneurial company to raise capital for START-UP companies or those in the early processes of developing products and services. The partnership will usually take shares of stock in the company in return for capital supplied. Limited partners receive income from profits the company may earn. If the company is successful and goes public, limited partners' profits could be realized from the sale of formerly private stock to the public. This type of partnership differs from a RESEARCH AND DEVELOPMENT LIMITED PARTNERSHIP in that R&D deals receive revenue only from the particular products they UNDERWRITE, whereas a venture capital partnership participates in the profits of the company, no matter what product or service is sold. *See also* ENTREPRENEUR; LIMITED PARTNERSHIP.

VERTICAL LINE CHARTING form of technical charting on which the high, low, and closing prices of a stock or a market are shown on one vertical line with the closing price indicated by a short horizontal mark. Each vertical line represents another day, and the chart shows the trend of a stock or a market over a period of days, weeks, months, or years. Technical analysts discern from these charts whether a stock or a market is continually closing at the high or low end of its trading range during a day. This is useful in understanding whether the market's action is strong or weak, and therefore whether prices will advance or decline in the near future. *See also* TECHNICAL ANALYSIS.

VERTICAL LINE CHARTING

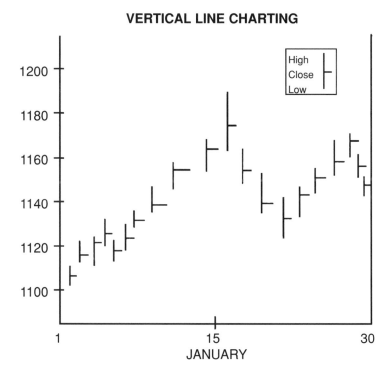

VERTICAL MERGER merger between a company that supplies goods and services and a company that buys those goods and services. For example, if a publishing company buys a paper producer, it is considered a vertical merger because the publisher buys large amounts of paper. In some cases, vertical mergers may be challenged by the government if they are found to violate ANTITRUST LAWS. *See also* MERGER.

VERTICAL SPREAD OPTION strategy that involves purchasing an option at one STRIKE PRICE while simultaneously selling another option of the same class at the next higher or lower strike price. Both options have the same expiration date. For example, a vertical spread is created by buying an XYZ May 30 call and selling an XYZ May 40 call. The investor who buys a vertical spread hopes to profit as the difference between the option premium on the two option positions widens or narrows. Also called a PRICE SPREAD. *See also* OPTION PREMIUM.

VESTED INTEREST in law, an interest in something that is certain to occur as opposed to being dependent on an event that might not happen. In general usage, an involvement having the element of personal gain. *See also* VESTING.

VESTING right an employee gradually acquires by length of service at a company to receive employer-contributed benefits, such as payments from a PENSION FUND, PROFIT-SHARING PLAN, or other QUALIFIED PLAN OR TRUST. Under the TAX REFORM ACT OF 1986, employees must be vested 100% after five years of service or at 20% a year starting in the third year and becoming 100% vested after seven years.

VETERANS ADMINISTRATION (VA) independent agency under the president that operates various programs for veterans and their families, including hospital services and guarantees of home mortgage loans made by financial institutions at rates set by the VA.

VETERANS ADMINISTRATION (VA) MORTGAGE home mortgage loan granted by a lending institution to qualified veterans of the U.S. armed forces or to their surviving spouses and guaranteed by the VA. The guarantee reduces risk to the lender for all or part of the purchase price on conventional homes, mobile homes, and condominiums. Because of this federal guarantee, banks and thrift institutions can afford to provide 30-year VA mortgages on favorable terms with a relatively low down payment even during periods of TIGHT MONEY. Interest rates on VA mortgages, formerly fixed by the Department of Housing and Urban Development together with those on Federal Housing Administration (FHA) mortgages, are now set by the VA.

    VA mortgages comprise an important part of the mortgage pools packaged and sold as securities by such quasi-governmental organizations as the FEDERAL HOME MORTGAGE CORPORATION (Freddie Mac) and the GOVERNMENT NATIONAL MORTGAGE ASSOCIATION (Ginnie Mae).

V FORMATION technical chart pattern that forms a V. The V pattern indicates that the stock, bond, or commodity being charted has bottomed out and is now in a bullish (rising) trend. An upside-down (inverse) V is considered bearish (indicative of a falling market). *See also* BOTTOM; TECHNICAL ANALYSIS. *See* chart on next page.

VIENNA STOCK EXCHANGE (VSX) founded in 1771 as a state institution to provide a market for state-issued bonds, it is one of the world's oldest exchanges. VSX represents approximately 50% of Austrian stock transactions, with the balance traded over-the-counter. The *WBI Index* is made up of all domestic shares listed on the official market, while the *Austrian Traded Index* (ATX) measures the most liquid stocks and is favored by institutional investors who use it as a benchmark for their equity positions. All trading is conducted electronically through

EQOS (Electronic Quote and Order-Driven System). Trades are settled three days after execution. Trading is conducted from 9:30 A.M. to 1:30 P.M., Monday through Friday. Futures and options are traded on the Osterreichische Termin-und Optionenborse (OTOB). Products include ATX futures, Austrian government bond futures, American-style stock options, and European-style ATX options.

V FORMATION

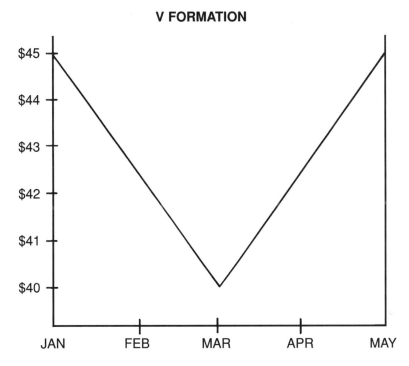

VISIBLE SUPPLY dollar volume of municipal bonds scheduled to be issued over the coming month. Municipal bond investors, analysts, traders, and investment bankers watch the visible supply to determine whether the coming month might provide a good opportunity to buy bonds, sell bonds, or float a new bond issue. A large amount of new issues might depress bond prices and make it difficult to float a new issue. Conversely, a small amount of new issues may help bond prices and make it easier to float a new issue. The visible supply, also known as the calendar or the *30-day visible supply*, is compiled by *The Bond Buyer.*

VOID deprived of legal force or effect, as a CONTRACT.

VOIDABLE contract that can be annulled by either party after it is signed because fraud, incompetence, or another illegality exists or because a RIGHT OF RESCISSION applies.

VOLATILE tending to rapid and extreme fluctuations. The term is used to describe the size and frequency of the fluctuations in the price of a particular stock, bond, or commodity. A stock may be volatile because the outlook for the company is particularly uncertain, because there are only a few shares outstanding (*see also* THIN MARKET), or because of various other reasons. Where the reasons for the variation have to do with the particular security as distinguished from market conditions, return is measured by a concept called ALPHA. A stock with an alpha factor of 1.25 is projected to rise in price by 25% in a year on the strength of its inherent values such as growth in earnings per share and regardless of the performance of the market as a whole. Market-related volatility, also called SYSTEMATIC RISK, is measured by BETA. *See also* DURATION.

VOLATILITY characteristic of a security, commodity, or market to rise or fall sharply in price within a short-term period. A measure of the relative volatility of a stock to the overall market is its BETA. *See also* VOLATILE.

VOLUME total number of stock shares, bonds, or commodities futures contracts traded in a particular period. Volume figures are reported daily by exchanges, both for individual issues trading and for the total amount of trading executed on the exchange. Technical analysts place great emphasis on the amount of volume that occurs in the trading of a security or a commodity futures contract. A sharp rise in volume is believed to signify future sharp rises or falls in price, because it reflects increased investor interest in a security, commodity, or market. *See also* TECHNICAL ANALYSIS; TURNOVER.

VOLUME DELETED note appearing on the CONSOLIDATED TAPE, usually when the tape is running behind by two minutes or more because of heavy trading, that only the STOCK SYMBOL and the trading price will be displayed for transactions of less than 5000 shares.

VOLUME DISCOUNT any reduction in price based on the purchase of a large quantity.

VOLUNTARY ACCUMULATION PLAN plan subscribed to by a MUTUAL FUND shareholder to accumulate shares in that fund on a regular basis over time. The amount of money to be put into the fund and the intervals at which it is to be invested are at the discretion of the shareholder. A plan that invests a set amount on a regular schedule is called a dollar cost averaging plan or CONSTANT DOLLAR PLAN.

VOLUNTARY BANKRUPTCY legal proceeding that follows a petition of BANK-RUPTCY filed by a debtor in the appropriate U.S. district court under the Bankruptcy Act. Petitions for voluntary bankruptcy can be filed by any insolvent business or individual except a building and loan association or a municipal, railroad, insurance, or banking corporation.

VOLUNTARY LIQUIDATION LIQUIDATION approved by a company's shareholders, as opposed to involuntary liquidation under Chapter 7 BANKRUPTCY. In the United Kingdom, a distinction is made between creditors' voluntary liquidation (or winding-up), which requires insolvency, and members' voluntary liquidation (or winding-up), which requires a declaration of solvency. *See also* VOLUNTARY BANKRUPTCY.

VOLUNTARY PLAN short for *voluntary deductible employee contribution plan,* a type of pension plan where the employee elects to have contributions (which, depending on the plan, may be before- or after-tax) deducted from each paycheck.

VOTING RIGHT right attending the ownership of most common stock to vote in person or by PROXY on corporate resolutions and the election of directors. *See also* NONVOTING STOCK.

VOTING STOCK shares in a corporation that entitle the shareholder to voting and PROXY rights. When a shareholder deposits such stock with a CUSTODIAN that acts as a voting TRUST, the shareholder retains rights to earnings and dividends but delegates voting rights to the trustee. *See also* COMMON STOCK; PROPORTIONAL REPRESENTATION; VOTING TRUST CERTIFICATE.

VOTING TRUST CERTIFICATE transferable certificate of beneficial interest in a *voting trust,* a limited-life trust set up to center control of a corporation in the hands of a few individuals, called *voting trustees*. The certificates, which are issued by the voting trust to stockholders in exchange for their common stock, represent all the rights of common stock except voting rights. The common stock is then registered on the books of the corporation in the names of the trustees. The usual purpose for such an arrangement is to facilitate REORGANIZA-TION of a corporation in financial difficulty by preventing interference with management. Voting trust certificates are limited to the five-year life of a TRUST but can be extended with the mutual consent of the holders and trustees.

VULTURE FUND type of LIMITED PARTNERSHIP that invests in depressed property, usually real estate, aiming to profit when prices rebound.

W

WAGE ASSIGNMENT loan agreement provision, prohibited in some states, that authorizes the lender to deduct payments from an employee's wages in the event of DEFAULT.

WAGE GARNISHMENT *see* GARNISHMENT.

WAGE-PUSH INFLATION inflationary spiral caused by rapid increases in wages. *See also* COST-PUSH INFLATION; DEMAND-PULL INFLATION; INFLATION.

WAITING PERIOD period of time before something goes into effect. In securities, there is a waiting period between the filing of registration statements and the time when securities may be offered for sale to the public. This waiting period may be extended if the Securities and Exchange Commission requires revisions to the registration statement. In DISABILITY INCOME INSURANCE, there is a waiting period of several months from the time the disability occurs to the time when disability benefits are paid. For insurance claims, the waiting period is also known as the *elimination period.*

WAIVER OF PREMIUM clause in an insurance policy providing that all policy premiums will be waived if the policyholder becomes seriously ill or disabled, either permanently or temporarily, and therefore is unable to pay the premiums. Some policies include a waiver-of-premium clause automatically, while in other cases it is an optional feature that must be paid with additional premiums. During the waiver period, all policy benefits remain in force.

WALLFLOWER *see* ORPHAN STOCK.

WALLPAPER worthless securities. The implication of the term is that certificates of stocks and bonds that have gone bankrupt or defaulted have no other use than as wallpaper. However, there may be value in the worthless certificates themselves by collectors of such certificates, who prize rare or historically significant certificates. The practice of collecting such certificates is known as SCRIPOPHILY.

WALL STREET
1. common name for the financial district at the lower end of Manhattan in New York City, where the New York and American Stock Exchanges and numerous brokerage firms are headquartered. The New York Stock Exchange is actually located at the corner of Wall and Broad Streets.
2. investment community, such as in "Wall Street really likes the prospects for that company" or "Wall Street law firm," meaning a firm specializing in securities law and mergers. Also referred to as "the Street."

WANTED FOR CASH TICKER tape announcement that a bidder will pay cash the same day for a specified block of securities. Cash trades are executed for delivery and settlement at the time the transaction is made.

WAR BABIES jargon for the stocks and bonds of corporations engaged primarily as defense contractors. Also called *war brides*.

WAR CHEST fund of liquid assets (cash) set aside by a corporation to pay for a takeover or to defend against a takeover. Traders will say that a company has a war chest that it plans to use to take over another company. Or traders might say that a particular company will be difficult to take over because it has a large war chest that it can use to defend itself by buying back its stock, making an acquisition of its own, paying for legal fees to mount defenses, or taking other defensive measures. *See also* TAKEOVER.

WAREHOUSE RECEIPT document listing goods or commodities kept for SAFE-KEEPING in a warehouse. The receipt can be used to transfer ownership of that commodity, instead of having to deliver the physical commodity. Warehouse receipts are used with many commodities, particularly precious metals like gold, silver, and platinum, which must be safeguarded against theft.

WARRANT *see* SUBSCRIPTION WARRANT.

WARRANTY contract between the seller and the buyer of a product specifying the conditions under which the seller will make repairs or remedy other problems that may arise, at no additional cost to the buyer. The warranty document describes how long the warranty remains in effect, and which specific repairs will be performed at no extra charge. Warranties usually cover workmanship or the failure of the product if used normally, but not negligence on the part of the user if the product is used in ways for which it was not designed. Warranties are commonly issued for automobiles, appliances, electronic gear, and most other products. In some cases, manufacturers will offer extended warranties for several years beyond the original warranty period, at an extra charge. Consumers should consult federal and state laws for more extensive applications or interpretations of warranties.

WASH SALE purchase and sale of a security either simultaneously or within a short period of time. It may be done by a single investor or (where MANIPULATION is involved) by two or more parties conspiring to create artificial market activity in order to profit from a rise in the security's price. Wash sales taking place within 30 days of the underlying purchase do not qualify as tax losses under Internal Revenue Service rules.

Under the TAX REFORM ACT OF 1984, wash sale rules were extended to all taxpayers except those trading in securities in the normal course of business, such as securities dealers. Prior to the 1984 Act, noncorporate taxpayers engaged in a trade or business were exempt from wash sale rules. The Act also extended the wash sale prohibition to closing short sales of substantially identical securities, or to instances where short sales are made within 30 days of closing. *See also* THIRTY-DAY WASH RULE.

WASTING ASSET
1. fixed asset, other than land, that has a limited useful life and is therefore subject to DEPRECIATION.
2. natural resource that diminishes in value because of extractions of oil, ores, or gas, or the removal of timber, or similar depletion and that is therefore subject to AMORTIZATION.
3. security with a value that expires at a particular time in the future. An OPTION contract, for instance, is a wasting asset, because the chances of a favorable

move in the underlying stock diminish as the contract approaches expiration, thus reducing the value of the option.

WATCH LIST list of securities singled out for special surveillance by a brokerage firm or an exchange or other self-regulatory organization to spot irregularities. Firms on the watch list may be TAKEOVER candidates, companies about to issue new securities, or others that seem to have attracted an unusually heavy volume of trading activity. *See also* STOCK WATCHER; SURVEILLANCE DEPARTMENT OF EXCHANGES.

WATERED STOCK stock representing ownership of OVERVALUED assets, a condition of overcapitalized corporations, whose total worth is less than their invested capital. The condition may result from inflated accounting values, gifts of stock, operating losses, or excessive stock dividends. Among the negative features of watered stock from the shareholder's standpoint are inability to recoup full investment in LIQUIDATION, inadequate return on investment, possible liability exceeding the PAR value of shares, low MARKET VALUE because of poor dividends and possible adverse publicity, reduced ability of the firm to issue new stock or debt securities to capitalize on growth opportunity, and loss of competitive position because of the need to raise prices to provide a return acceptable to investors. To remedy the situation, a company must either increase its assets without increasing its OUTSTANDING shares or reduce outstanding shares without reducing assets. The alternatives are to increase RETAINED EARNINGS or to adjust the accounting values of assets or of stock.

WEAK DOLLAR dollar that has fallen in value against foreign currencies. This means that those holding dollars will get fewer pounds, yen, marks, francs, or other currencies in exchange for their dollars. A weak dollar makes it easier for U.S. companies to export their goods to other countries because foreigners' buying power is enhanced. The dollar may weaken because of loose U.S. monetary policy (creating too many dollars) and lack of confidence in the U.S. government, large trade and budget deficits, unattractive interest rates on dollar-denominated investments compared to investments denominated in other currencies, or other reasons.

WEAK MARKET market characterized by a preponderance of sellers over buyers and a general declining trend in prices.

WEBS (WORLD EQUITY BENCHMARK SHARES) shares traded on the AMERICAN STOCK EXCHANGE (ASE) enabling investors to gain exposure to selected international equity markets. Introduced in March 1996, WEBS are issued in a number of country-specific Index Series by WEBS Index Fund, Inc., a registered investment company. The fund's objective is to track the price and yield performance of the underlying countries' stock markets, as defined by the securities contained in the Morgan Stanley Capital International (MSCI) Index. Currently 17 countries trade WEBS: Australia, Austria, Belgium, Canada, France, Germany, Hong Kong, Italy, Japan, Malaysia, Mexico, Netherlands, Singapore, Spain, Sweden, Switzerland and the United Kingdom.

Unlike index open-ended mutual funds, WEBS trade continuously on the secondary market at AMEX like any other publicly-traded stock. Mutual funds do not trade in the secondary market and are priced only at the end of each trading day. There are also no LOADS to buy or sell WEBS, though normal brokerage commissions do apply as they would on the purchase or sale of any individual stock. WEBS charge management fees, but they are lower than those charged by actively-managed mutual funds because, as index funds, WEBS involve very little investment, research, or trading decisions. WEBS prices reflect the reinvestment of net dividends, and the fund distributes CASH DIVIDENDS and CAPITAL GAINS DISTRIBUTIONS once a year.

Unlike closed-end mutual funds, WEBS do not trade at large discounts or premiums to their NET ASSET VALUE (NAV), because, unlike closed-end shares, of which only a limited number are issued investors can create or redeem WEBS every day. The NAV of WEBS fluctuate based on changes in the market value of the underlying portfolio securities and in the exchange rates between the relevant country's currency and the U.S. Dollar, and the income and expenses of each WEBS Index fund.

WEBS offer investors wanting to invest internationally several advantages. They allow exposure to an entire country's market in one trade which is executed in U.S. dollars on the ASE. This frees investors from the difficult process of stock selection and other complexities involved in direct foreign stock ownership.

WEDGE technical chart pattern similar to but varying slightly from a TRIANGLE. Two converging lines connect a series of peaks and troughs to form a wedge. These converging lines move in the same direction, unlike a triangle, in which one rises while the other falls or one rises or falls while the other line stays horizontal. Falling wedges usually occur as temporary interruptions of upward price rallies, rising wedges as interruptions of a falling price trend. *See also* TECHNICAL ANALYSIS.

WEDGE

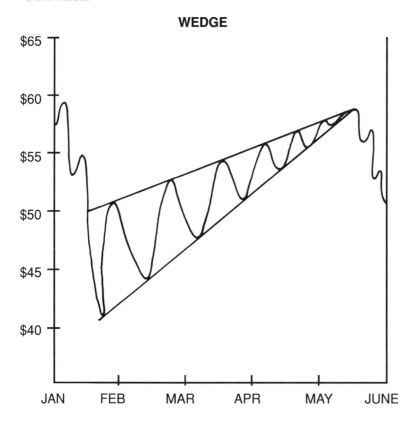

WEIGHTED AVERAGE MATURITY also called *average life* or *weighted average life* and used in mortgage-backed PASS-THROUGH SECURITIES meaning the weighted-average time to the return of a dollar of principal. It is arrived at by multiplying each portion of principal received by the time at which it is received, and then summing and dividing by the total amount of principal. Fabozzi's *Handbook of Fixed Income Securities* uses this example: Consider a simple annual-pay, four-year bond with a face value of $100 and principal payments of $40 the first year, $30 the second year, $20 the third year, and $10 the fourth year. The average life would be calculated as: Average life = .4 × 1 year + .3 × 2 years + .2 × 3 years + .1 × 4 years = 2 years. An alternative measure of investment life is DURATION.

W FORMATION technical chart pattern of the price of a stock, bond, or commodity that shows the price has hit a SUPPORT LEVEL two times and is moving up; also called a *double bottom.*

A reverse W is just the opposite; the price has hit a resistance level and is headed down. This is called a DOUBLE TOP.

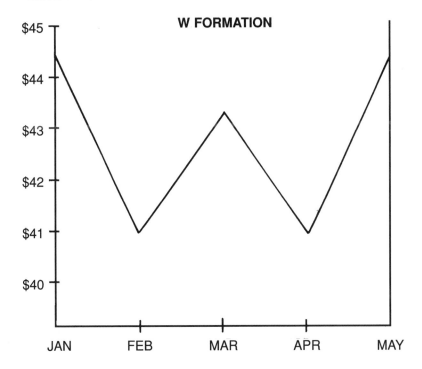

W-4 FORM tax form prepared by an employee for an employer indicating the employee's exemptions and Social Security number and enabling the employer to determine the amount of taxes to be withheld.

WHEN DISTRIBUTED transactions conditional on the SECONDARY DISTRIBUTION of shares ISSUED AND OUTSTANDING but CLOSELY HELD, as those of a wholly owned subsidiary, for example. *See also* WHEN ISSUED.

WHEN ISSUED short form of "when, as, and if issued." Term refers to a transaction made conditionally because a security, although authorized, has not yet been issued. NEW ISSUES of stocks and bonds, stocks that have SPLIT, and Treasury securities are all traded on a when issued basis. In a newspaper listing, a "WI" is placed next to the price of such a security. *See also* WHEN DISTRIBUTED.

WHIPSAWED caught in VOLATILE price movements while making losing trades as prices rise and fall. A trader is whipsawed if he or she buys just before prices fall and sells just before prices rise. A variation of this term is also used in TECH-NICAL ANALYSIS referring to misleading signals, called *whipsaws* or *chatter,* in the chart trends of markets or particular securities.

WHISPER NUMBER unofficial earnings estimates made by security analysts. If an analyst is more optimistic about a company's earnings prospects than his official profit estimate reveals, he may speak of a "whisper number" to his clients that is higher than his published numbers. The opposite can be true on the downside. Investors and the media sometimes start to count on "whisper numbers" when earnings are announced. While a company may report profits in line with official estimates, those companies that do not meet their "whisper numbers," disappoint investors, which drives stock prices down.

WHISPER STOCK stock that is rumored to be a takeover target. Speculators, arbitrageurs, and other investors may buy shares in the company hoping that the "whispers" they have heard are true, allowing them to reap huge profits when the takeover is officially announced. Whisper stocks may trade in heavier-than-usual volume once the rumors about the takeover spread widely. Investing in whisper stocks is risky, however, because the takeover rumors may prove to be inaccurate.

WHISTLE BLOWER employee or other person with inside knowledge of wrongdoing inside a company or government agency. The employee is supposed to be protected from retribution by the employer by several federal laws protecting whistle blowers, though whistle blowers frequently are punished for revealing wrongdoing by their employer. Several employees who disclosed illegal billing practices by defense contractors were demoted or fired, for example. In securities, under the Insider Trading and Securities Fraud Enforcement Act of 1988, whistle blowers who provide the SEC with information about illegal insider trading or other illegal activity that leads to a conviction may qualify for bounties.

WHITE COLLAR WORKER office worker in professional, managerial, or administrative position. Such workers typically wear shirts with white collars. Those working in factories or doing manual labor typically wear blue collars, and are therefore called *blue collar workers.*

WHITE KNIGHT friendly acquirer sought by the target of an unfriendly TAKEOVER.

WHITEMAIL anti-TAKEOVER device whereby a vulnerable company sells a large amount of stock to a friendly party at below-market prices. This puts a potential raider in a position where it must buy a sizable amount of stock at inflated prices to get control and thus helps perpetuate existing management.

WHITE SHEETS list of prices published by the NATIONAL QUOTATION BUREAU for market makers in OVER THE COUNTER stocks traded in Chicago, Los Angeles, and San Francisco.

WHITE-SHOE FIRM anachronistic characterization of certain broker-dealers as venerable, "upper-crust" and "above" such practices as participating in hostile takeovers. Derives from the '50s culture of Ivy League colleges, where white buck shoes were *de rigueur* in elite fraternities and clubs.

WHITE SQUIRE WHITE KNIGHT who buys less than a majority interest.

WHITE'S RATING White's Tax-Exempt Bond Rating Service's classification of municipal securities, which is based on market factors rather than credit considerations and which attempts to determine appropriate yields. *See also* MUNICIPAL BOND.

WHOLE LIFE INSURANCE form of life insurance policy that offers protection in case the insured dies and also builds up cash value. The policy stays in force for the lifetime of the insured, unless the policy is canceled or lapses. The policyholder usually pays a level PREMIUM for whole life, which does not rise as the person grows older (as in the case of TERM INSURANCE). The earnings on the cash value in the policy accumulate tax-deferred, and can be borrowed against in the form of a POLICY LOAN. The death benefit is reduced by the amount of the loan, plus interest, if the loan is not repaid.

Traditionally, life insurance companies invest insurance premiums conservatively in bonds, stocks, and real estate in order to generate increases in cash value for policyholders. Policyholders have no input into the investment decision-making process in a whole life insurance policy. Other forms of cash value policies, such as UNIVERSAL LIFE INSURANCE and VARIABLE LIFE INSURANCE give policyholders more options, such as stock, bond, and money market accounts, to choose from in investing their premiums. Whole life insurance is also known as *ordinary life, permanent life, or straight life insurance. See also* ADEQUACY OF COVERAGE; ANNUAL EXCLUSION; CASH VALUE INSURANCE; CONTINGENT BENEFICIARY; CONVERTIBILITY; DEATH BENEFIT; EXPERIENCE RATING; FINANCIAL NEEDS APPROACH; FIXED PREMIUM; FULLY PAID POLICY; GUARANTEED INSURABILITY; HIDDEN LOAD; INCOME EXCLUSION RULE; INSURABILITY; INSURABLE INTEREST; INSURANCE AGENT; INSURANCE CLAIM; INSURANCE DIVIDEND; INSURANCE POLICY; INSURANCE PREMIUM; INSURANCE SETTLEMENT; INSURED; LAPSE; LIFE INSURANCE; LIFE INSURANCE POLICY; LIVING BENEFITS; LUMP SUM; MORTALITY RISK; NONCONTESTABILITY CLAUSE; NONPARTICIPATING LIFE INSURANCE POLICY; PAID UP; PAID-UP POLICY; PARTICIPATING DIVIDENDS; PARTICIPATING INSURANCE; SAVINGS ELEMENT; SECOND-TO-DIE INSURANCE; SETTLEMENT OPTIONS; SINGLE-PREMIUM LIFE INSURANCE; SURRENDER VALUE.

WHOLE LOAN SECONDARY MORTGAGE MARKET term that distinguishes an investment representing an original residential mortgage loan (whole loan) from a loan representing a participation with one or more lenders or a PASS-THROUGH SECURITY representing a pool of mortgages.

WHOLESALE PRICE INDEX *see* PRODUCER PRICE INDEX.

WHOLESALER
In general: middleman or DISTRIBUTOR who sells mainly to retailers, JOBBERS, other merchants, and industrial, commercial, and institutional users as distinguished from consumers. *See also* VENDOR.
Securities:
1. INVESTMENT BANKER acting as an UNDERWRITER in a NEW ISSUE or as a distributor in a secondary offering of securities. *See also* SECONDARY DISTRIBUTION.
2. broker-dealer who trades with other broker-dealers, rather than with the retail investor, and receives discounts and selling commissions.
3. SPONSOR of a MUTUAL FUND.

WHOLLY OWNED SUBSIDIARY SUBSIDIARY whose common stock is virtually 100%-owned by the PARENT COMPANY.

WHOOPS nickname for the Washington Public Power Supply System. In the late 1970s and early 1980s, WHOOPS raised billions of dollars through MUNICIPAL BOND offerings to finance construction of five nuclear plants in the state of Washington. Because of cost overruns, bad management, and numerous delays, two of the plants were canceled, and it was doubtful that two others would ever be completed. WHOOPS defaulted on the payments to bondholders on the two canceled plants after the Washington Supreme Court ruled that the TAKE-OR-PAY

CONTRACTS with the many utilities in the Northwest that had backed the bonds were invalid. This was the largest municipal bond default in history.

WIDE OPENING abnormally large SPREAD between the BID AND ASKED prices of a security at the OPENING of a trading session.

WIDGET symbolic American gadget, used wherever a hypothetical product is needed to illustrate a manufacturing or selling concept.

WIDOW-AND-ORPHAN STOCK stock that pays high dividends and is very safe. It usually has a low BETA COEFFICIENT and is involved in a noncyclical business. For years American Telephone and Telegraph was considered a widow-and-orphan stock, but it lost that status after the breakup of the Bell System in 1984. High-quality electric utility stocks are still considered widow-and-orphan stocks by and large.

WILDCAT DRILLING exploring for oil or gas in an unproven area. A wildcat OIL AND GAS LIMITED PARTNERSHIP is structured so that investors take high risks but can reap substantial rewards if oil or gas is found in commercial quantities.

WILL document, also called a *testament,* that, when signed and witnessed, gives legal effect to the wishes of a person, called a *testator,* with respect to disposal of property upon death.

WILLIAMS ACT federal legislation enacted in 1968 that imposes requirements with respect to public TENDER OFFERS. It was inspired by a wave of unannounced TAKEOVERS in the 1960s, which caught managers unawares and confronted stockholders with decisions they were ill prepared to make, The Williams Act and amendments now comprise Sections 13(d) and 14(d) of the SECURITIES EXCHANGE ACT OF 1934. The law requires the bidder opening a tender to file with both the SECURITIES AND EXCHANGE COMMISSION and the TARGET COMPANY a statement detailing the terms of the offer, the bidder's background, the cash source, and his or her plans for the company if there is a takeover. The same information is required within 10 days from any person or company acquiring 5% or more of another company. The law mandates a minimum offering period of 20 days and gives tendering shareholders 15 days to change their minds. If only a limited number of shares are accepted, they must be prorated among the tendering stockholders. *See also* SATURDAY NIGHT SPECIAL.

WILSHIRE INDICES performance measurement indices created by Wilshire Associates, Inc. of Santa Monica, California. The Wilshire 5000 Equity Index is the most widely followed index; it is published in national daily newspapers and is carried by the *Associated Press*. It measures the performance of all U.S.-head-quartered equity securities with readily available price data; more than 7,000 capitalization-weighted security returns are used to adjust the index. The Wilshire 5000 base is its December 31, 1980 capitalization of $1,404.596; its capitalization is approximately 81% New York Stock Exchange (NYSE), 2% American Stock Exchange (AMEX), and 17% National Association of Dealers Automated Quotations (NASDAQ). Equity issues include common stocks, REITs, and master limited partnerships. Additions to the index are made monthly, after the month-end close. Initial public offerings (IPOs) are generally added at the end of the month. The Wilshire 4500 Equity Index is the Wilshire 5000 less the STANDARD & POOR'S 500 COMPOSITE INDEX; current capitalization is about 60% NYSE , 3% AMEX, and 37% NASDAQ. The Wilshire Small Cap Index consists of 250 companies with an average market capitalization of $933 million, and is designed to meet the need for derivative trading instruments reflecting the true character of the small cap market. Wilshire Small Cap Index options are traded on the PACIFIC EXCHANGE (PCX), which helped develop the index. Four Wilshire asset management indices are derived from the Wilshire 5000; six individual style indices (such as growth and value) and three real estate securities indices. *See also* STOCK INDICES AND AVERAGES.

WINDFALL PROFIT profit that occurs suddenly as a result of an event not controlled by the person or company profiting from the event. For example, oil companies profited in the 1970s from an explosion in the price of oil brought about by the Arab oil embargo and the price increases demanded by the Organization of Petroleum Exporting Countries. *See also* WINDFALL PROFITS TAX.

WINDFALL PROFITS TAX tax on profits that result from a sudden windfall to a particular company or industry. In 1980, federal legislation was passed that levied such a tax on oil companies because of the profits they earned as a result of the sharp increase in oil prices in the 1970s. Since then, the tax has not been reenacted.

WINDOW
1. limited time during which an opportunity should be seized, or it will be lost. For example, a period when new stock issues are welcomed by the public only lasts for a few months, or maybe as long as a year—that time is called the *window of opportunity.*
2. DISCOUNT WINDOW of a Federal Reserve bank.
3. cashier department of a brokerage firm, where delivery and settlement of securities transactions takes place.

WINDOW DRESSING
1. trading activity near the end of a quarter or fiscal year that is designed to dress up a PORTFOLIO to be presented to clients or shareholders. For example, a fund manager may sell losing positions in his portfolio so he can display only positions that have gained in value.
2. accounting gimmickry designed to make a FINANCIAL STATEMENT show a more favorable condition than actually exists—for example by omitting certain expenses, by concealing liabilities, by delaying WRITE-OFFS, by anticipating sales, or by other such actions, which may or may not be fraudulent.

WINNEPEG COMMODITY EXCHANGE Canada's only agricultural futures and options exchange, opened in 1887 as the Winnipeg Grain and Produce Exchange. It trades futures and options on canola and flaxseed, as well as Western domestic feed grades of barley and wheat, and feed pea futures. Trading is conducted Monday through Friday, from 9:30 A.M. to 1:15 P.M. for futures, and 9:30 A.M. to 1:20 P.M. for options.

WIRE HOUSE national or international brokerage firm whose branch offices are linked by a communications system that permits the rapid dissemination of prices, information, and research relating to financial markets and individual securities. Although smaller retail and regional brokers currently have access to similar data, the designation of a firm as a wire house dates back to the time when only the largest organizations had access to high-speed communications. Therefore, *wire house* still is used to refer to the biggest brokerage houses.

WIRE ROOM operating department of a brokerage firm that receives customers' orders from the REGISTERED REPRESENTATIVE and transmits the vital data to the exchange floor, where a FLOOR TICKET is prepared, or to the firm's trading department for execution. The wire room also receives notices of executed trades and relays them to the appropriate registered representatives. Also called *order department, order room,* or *wire and order.*

WITCHING HOUR *see* TRIPLE WITCHING HOUR.

WITHDRAWAL PLAN program available through most open-end MUTUAL FUND companies in which shareholders can receive fixed payments of income or CAPITAL GAINS (or both) on a regular basis, usually monthly or quarterly.

WITHHOLDING

Securities: violation of the RULES OF FAIR PRACTICE of the NATIONAL ASSOCIATION OF SECURITIES DEALERS whereby a participant in a PUBLIC OFFERING fails to make a bona fide public offering at the PUBLIC OFFERING PRICE—for example, by withholding shares for his or her own account or selling shares to a family member, an employee of the dealer firm, or another broker-dealer—in order to profit from the higher market price of a HOT ISSUE. *See also* IMMEDIATE FAMILY; INVESTMENT HISTORY.

Taxes:

1. deduction from salary payments and other compensation to provide for an individual's tax liability. Federal income taxes and Social Security contributions are withheld from paychecks and are deposited in a Treasury TAX AND LOAN ACCOUNT with a bank. The yearly amount of withholding is reported on an income statement (form W-2), which must be submitted with the federal, state, and local tax returns. Liability not provided for by withholding must be paid in four ESTIMATED TAX payments.
2. withholding by corporations and financial institutions of a flat 10% of interest and dividend payments due securities holders, as required under the TAX EQUITY AND FISCAL RESPONSIBILITY ACT OF 1982. The purpose was to levy a tax on people whose earnings escaped tracking by the Internal Revenue Service. The 10% withholding requirement was repealed in 1983. As a compromise, "backup withholding" was instituted, whereby, using Social Security numbers, payments can be reported to the IRS and matched against the actual income reported.
3. withholdings from pension and annuity distributions, sick pay, tips, and sizeable gambling winnings, as stipulated by law.
4. 30% withholding requirement on income from U.S. securities owned by foreigners—repealed by the TAX REFORM ACT OF 1984.

WORKERS COMPENSATION INSURANCE INSURANCE that pays benefits on behalf of an insured employer to employees or their families in the case of injury, disability, or death resulting from occupational hazards.

WORKING CAPITAL funds invested in a company's cash, ACCOUNTS RECEIVABLE, INVENTORY, and other CURRENT ASSETS *(gross working capital);* usually refers to *net working capital*—that is, current assets minus CURRENT LIABILITIES. Working capital finances the CASH CONVERSION CYCLE of a business—the time required to convert raw materials into finished goods, finished goods into sales, and accounts receivable into cash. These factors vary with the type of industry and the scale of production, which varies in turn with seasonality and with sales expansion and contraction. Internal sources of working capital include RETAINED EARNINGS, savings achieved through operating efficiencies and the allocation of CASH FLOW from sources like DEPRECIATION or deferred taxes to working capital. External sources include bank and other short-term borrowings, TRADE CREDIT, and term debt and EQUITY FINANCING not channeled into long-term assets. *See also* CURRENT RATIO; NET CURRENT ASSETS.

WORKING CONTROL effective control of a corporation by a shareholder or shareholders with less than 51% voting interest. Working control by a minority holder, or by two or more minority holders working in concert, is possible when share ownership of a firm is otherwise widely dispersed. *See also* MINORITY INTEREST.

WORKING INTEREST direct participation with unlimited liability, as distinguished from passive LIMITED PARTNERSHIP shares. The TAX REFORM ACT OF 1986 let investors with working interests in drilling ventures, such as GENERAL PARTNERS, offset losses against all types of income.

WORK-IN-PROCESS *see* INVENTORY.

WORKOUT situation, such as a bad loan or troubled firm, where remedial measures are being taken.

WORKSHEET computerized page allowing the user to manipulate many columns and rows of numbers. The worksheet can contain formulas so that if one number is changed, the entire worksheet is automatically updated, based on those formulas. Analysts, investors, and accountants track a company's financial statements, balance sheets, and other data on worksheets.

WORLD BANK *see* INTERNATIONAL BANK FOR RECONSTRUCTION AND DEVELOPMENT.

WORLD TRADE ORGANIZATION (WTO) independent multilateral agency administering world trade agreements. WTO, headquartered in Geneva, Switzerland, resulted from the Uruguay round of GENERAL AGREEMENT ON TRADE AND TARIFFS (GATT) concluded in 1995. WTO's tasks include fostering trade relations among its members, resolving disputes, and serving as a forum for future multilateral trade negotiations.

WRAP ACCOUNT investment consulting relationship in which a client's funds are placed with one or more money managers, and all administrative and management fees, along with commissions, are wrapped into one comprehensive fee, which is paid quarterly. The wrap fee varies, but usually ranges from 1% to 3% of the value of the assets in the account. Wrap accounts usually require a minimum initial investment of anywhere from $25,000 to $10 million for individual accounts. The term *wrap* has been expanded to involve mutual fund asset allocation programs. Technically, these are not wrap programs because they are not "all inclusive." Transaction commissions in these programs on mutual funds are still a variable and they are pooled accounts as distinguished from individual accounts. From the customer's point of view, a wrap account provides access to top investment managers. The broker overseeing the account is paid an ongoing fee to monitor the performance of the money managers. Although brokers may switch assets to other managers within the program if one manager consistently starts to underperform, most sponsors of wrap programs suggest a three- to five-year time horizon to reach investment goals.

WRAPAROUND ANNUITY ANNUITY contract allowing an annuitant discretion in the choice of underlying investments. Wraparound refers to the protection the annuity vehicle provides through its TAX DEFERRED status, which becomes precarious when the annuity vehicle is being used as a technical way to avoid tax payment. The tax courts have ruled against tax deferment where money can be allocated by an annuity owner to a portfolio managed by an annuitant and where the annuitant can switch among funds of the sponsoring insurance company that are also marketed independently of annuities. On the other hand, the IRS has upheld tax deferral where an individual could not buy such funds without also buying the annuity. In any event, the insurer must legally own the annuity money.

WRAPAROUND MORTGAGE second mortgage that increases a borrower's indebtedness while leaving the original mortgage contract in force. The wraparound mortgage becomes the JUNIOR MORTGAGE and is held by the lending institution as security for the total mortgage debt. The borrower makes payments on both loans to the wraparound lender, who in turn makes scheduled installment payments on the original *senior mortgage.* It is a convenient way for a property owner to obtain additional credit without having first to pay off an existing mortgage.

WRINKLE novel feature that may attract a buyer for a new product or a security. For example, ZERO-COUPON SECURITIES were a new wrinkle when they were introduced but soon thereafter became quite commonplace.

WRITE-OFF charging an ASSET amount to expense or loss. The effect of a write-off is to reduce or eliminate the value of the asset and reduce profits. Write-offs are systematically taken in accordance with allowable tax DEPRECIATION of a FIXED ASSET, and with the AMORTIZATION of certain other assets, such as an INTANGIBLE ASSET and a capitalized cost (like premiums paid on investments). Write-offs are also taken when assets are, for whatever reason, deemed worthless, the most common example being uncollectible ACCOUNTS RECEIVABLE. Where such write-offs can be anticipated and therefore estimated, the usual practice has been to charge income regularly in amounts needed to maintain a RESERVE, the actual losses then being charged to the reserve. The TAX REFORM ACT OF 1986 required that BAD DEBT write-offs be charged directly to income by taxpayers other than small banks and thrift institutions. *See also* EXTRAORDINARY ITEM: NONRECURRING CHARGE.

WRITE OUT procedure followed when a SPECIALIST on an exchange makes a trade involving his own inventory, on one hand, and an order he is holding for a FLOOR BROKER, on the other. Exchange rules require a two-part transaction: the broker first completes a trade with the specialist, who then completes the transaction by a separate trade with the customer. The write out involves no charge other than the normal broker's commission.

WRITER
1. person who sells PUT OPTION and CALL OPTION contracts, and therefore collects PREMIUM INCOME. The writer of a put option is obligated to buy (and the writer of a call option is obligated to sell) the UNDERLYING SECURITY at a predetermined price by a particular date if the OPTION is exercised. *See also* COVERED CALL; NAKED OPTION; WRITING NAKED.
2. insurance UNDERWRITER.

WRITE UP/WRITE DOWN upward or downward adjustment of the accounting value of an asset according to GENERALLY ACCEPTED ACCOUNTING PRINCIPLES GAAP. *See also* WRITE-OFF.

WRITING CASH-SECURED PUTS OPTION strategy that a trader who wants to sell PUT OPTIONS uses to avoid having to use a MARGIN ACCOUNT. Rather than depositing MARGIN with a broker, a put WRITER can deposit cash equal to the option EXERCISE PRICE. With this strategy, the put option writer is not subject to additional margin requirements in the event of changes in the underlying stock's price. The put writer can also be earning money by investing the PREMIUM he or she receives in MONEY MARKET instruments.

WRITING NAKED strategy used by an OPTION seller in which the trader does not own the UNDERLYING SECURITY. This strategy can lead to large profits if the stock moves in the hoped-for direction, but it can lead to large losses if the stock moves in the other direction, since the trader will have to go into the marketplace to buy the stock in order to deliver it to the option buyer. *See also* NAKED OPTION.

WRITING PUTS TO ACQUIRE STOCK strategy used by an OPTION writer (seller) who believes a stock is going to decline and that its purchase at a given price would represent a good investment. By writing a PUT OPTION exercisable at that price, the writer cannot lose. If the stock, contrary to his expectation, goes up, the option will not be exercised and he is at least ahead the amount of the PREMIUM he received. If, as expected, the stock goes down and the option is exercised, he has bought the stock at what he had earlier decided was a good buy, and he has the premium income in addition.

WRITTEN-DOWN VALUE BOOK VALUE of an asset after DEPRECIATION or other AMORTIZATION; also called *net book value.* For example, if the original cost of a piece of equipment was $1000 and accumulated depreciation charges totaled $400, the written-down value would be $600. *See also* INTANGIBLE ASSET.

WT abbreviation for *warrant. See also* SUBSCRIPTION WARRANT.

W-2 FORM tax form prepared by an employer for an employee to enclose with the 1040 FORM, summarizing wages earned for the year, federal and state taxes withheld, and SOCIAL SECURITY tax information.

X

X or XD symbol used in newspapers to signify that a stock is trading EX-DIVIDEND, that is, without dividend. The symbol X is also used in bond tables to signify without interest.

XR symbol used in newspapers to signify that a stock is trading EX-RIGHTS, that is, without rights attached. *See also* SUBSCRIPTION RIGHT.

XW symbol used in newspapers to signify that a stock is trading EX-WARRANTS, that is, without warrants attached. *See also* SUBSCRIPTION WARRANT.

Y

YANKEE BOND MARKET dollar-denominated bonds issued in the U.S. by foreign banks and corporations. The bonds are issued in the U.S. when market conditions there are more favorable than on the EUROBOND market or in domestic markets overseas. Similarly, Yankee CERTIFICATES OF DEPOSIT are negotiable CDs issued in the U.S. by branches and agencies of foreign banks.

YEAR-END BONUS bonus payment given to employees at the end of a year, based on the employee's performance and the performance of the company. Most securities firms operate on a bonus system, providing employees with huge bonuses in highly profitable years and little or no bonuses in lean years. Many salespeople also operate on a year-end bonus system, in which they receive bonuses if they met or exceeded certain sales goals during the year.

YEAR-END DIVIDEND an additional or special DIVIDEND declared based on a company's profits during the fiscal year.

YEAR-TO-DATE (YTD) period from the beginning of the calendar year (or FISCAL YEAR (FY) if so indicated) to the reporting date. For example third-quarterly results of a company would be reported for the quarter alone and for the year-to-date, which would be nine months.

YELLOW SHEETS daily publication of the NATIONAL QUOTATION BUREAU that details the BID AND ASKED prices and firms that MAKE A MARKET in CORPORATE

BONDS traded in the OVER THE COUNTER (OTC) market. Much of this information is not available in the daily OTC newspaper listings. The sheets are named for their color. OTC equity issues are covered separately on PINK SHEETS and regional OTC issues of both classes are listed on white sheets.

YEN BOND in general terms, any bond issue denominated in Japanese yen. International bankers using the term are usually referring to yen-denominated bonds issued or held outside Japan.

YIELD

In general: RETURN on an investor's CAPITAL INVESTMENT. A piece of real estate may yield a certain return, or a business deal may offer a particular yield. *See also* RETURN ON INVESTED CAPITAL.

Agriculture: agricultural output in terms of quantity of a crop.

Bonds:

1. COUPON rate of interest divided by the purchase price, called CURRENT YIELD. For example, a bond selling for $1000 with a 10% coupon offers a 10% current yield. If that same bond were selling for $500, however, it would offer a 20% yield to an investor who bought it for $500. (As a bond's price falls, its yield rises and vice versa.)

2. rate of return on a bond, taking into account the total of annual interest payments, the purchase price, the redemption value, and the amount of time remaining until maturity; called *maturity yield* or YIELD TO MATURITY. *See also* DURATION; YIELD TO AVERAGE LIFE; YIELD TO CALL.

Lending: total money earned on a loan—that is, the ANNUAL PERCENTAGE RATE of interest multiplied by the term of the loan.

Stocks: percentage rate of return paid on a common or preferred stock in dividends. For example, a stock that sells for $20 and pays an annual dividend of $2 per share has a yield, also called a *dividend yield,* of 10%.

Taxes: amount of revenue received by a governmental entity as a result of a tax.

YIELD ADVANTAGE extra amount of return an investor will earn if he or she purchases a CONVERTIBLE security instead of the common stock of the same issuing corporation. If an XYZ Corporation convertible yields 10% and an XYZ common share yields 5%, the yield advantage is 5%. *See also* YIELD SPREAD.

YIELD BURNING MUNICIPAL BOND financing practice whereby underwriters in ADVANCE REFUNDINGS (PREREFUNDING) slap excessive MARKUPS on U.S. Treasury bonds bought and held in escrow to compensate investors during the time between issuance of the new bonds and repayment of the old ones. Since bond prices and yields move in opposite directions, when underwriters mark up the bonds, they "burn down" the yield, violating federal tax rules and costing the government tax revenues. Under IRS regulations, municipalities, not the underwriters, incur the tax liability. The SEC, which was conducting a wide-ranging probe of alleged yield-burning abuses by Wall Street firms in the late 1990s, favors making the underwriters responsible, not the municipalities.

YIELD CURVE graph showing the term structure of interest rates by plotting the yields of all bonds of the same quality with maturities ranging from the shortest to the longest available. The resulting curve shows if short-term interest rates are higher or lower than long-term rates. If short-term rates are lower, it is called a POSITIVE YIELD CURVE. If short-term rates are higher, it is called a NEGATIVE (or INVERTED) YIELD CURVE. If there is little difference between short-term and long-term rates, it is called a *flat yield* curve. For the most part, the yield curve is positive, since investors who are willing to tie up their money for a longer period of time usually are compensated for the extra risk they are taking by receiving a higher yield. The most common version of the yield curve graph plots Treasury securities, showing the range of yields from a three-month TREASURY BILL to a 20- or 30-year TREASURY BOND.

Fixed-income analysts study the yield curve carefully in order to make judgments about the direction of interest rates. *See also* DURATION.

YIELD EQUIVALENCE the rate of interest at which a tax-exempt bond and a taxable security of similar quality provide the same return. In the day of the 50% TAX BRACKET, for example, a tax-exempt bond paying 10% was the equivalent of a taxable corporate bond of 20%. To calculate the yield that must be provided by a taxable security to equal that of a tax-exempt bond for investors in different tax brackets, the tax exempt yield is divided by the reciprocal of the tax bracket (100 less 28%, for example) to arrive at the taxable yield. Thus, a person in the 28% tax bracket who wished to figure the taxable equivalent of a 10% tax free municipal bond would divide 10% by 72% (100 minus 28%) to get 13.9%—the yield a corporate taxable bond would have to provide to be equivalent, after taxes, to the 10% municipal bond. To convert a taxable yield to a tax-exempt yield, the formula is reversed—that is, the tax exempt yield is equal to the taxable yield multiplied by the reciprocal of the tax bracket.

YIELD SPREAD difference in YIELD between various issues of securities. In comparing bonds, it usually refers to issues of different credit quality since issues of the same maturity and quality would normally have the same yields, as with Treasury securities, for example. Yield spread also refers to the differential between dividend yield on stocks and the CURRENT YIELD on bonds. The comparison might be made, for example, between the STANDARD & POOR'S INDEX (of 500 stocks) dividend yield and the current yield of an index of corporate bonds. A significant difference in bond and stock yields, assuming similar quality, is known as a *yield gap.*

YIELD TO AVERAGE LIFE yield calculation used, in lieu of YIELD TO MATURITY or YIELD TO CALL, where bonds are retired systematically during the life of the issue, as in the case of a SINKING FUND with contractual requirements. Because the issuer will buy its own bonds on the open market to satisfy its sinking fund requirements if the bonds are trading below PAR, there is to that extent automatic price support for such bonds; they therefore tend to trade on a yield-to-average-life basis.

YIELD TO CALL yield on a bond assuming the bond will be redeemed by the issuer at the first CALL date specified in the INDENTURE agreement. The same calculations are used to calculate yield to call as YIELD TO MATURITY except that the principal value at maturity is replaced by the first CALL PRICE and the maturity date is replaced by the first call date. Assuming the issuer will put the interest of the company before the interest of the investor and will call the bonds if it is favorable to do so, the lower of the yield to call and the yield to maturity can be viewed as the more realistic rate of return to the investor. *See also* DURATION.

YIELD TO MATURITY (YTM) concept used to determine the rate of return an investor will receive if a long-term, interest-bearing investment, such as a bond, is held to its MATURITY DATE. It takes into account purchase price, REDEMPTION value, time to maturity, COUPON yield, and the time between interest payments. Recognizing time value of money, it is the DISCOUNT RATE at which the PRESENT VALUE of all future payments would equal the present price of the bond, also known as INTERNAL RATE OF RETURN. It is implicitly assumed that coupons are reinvested at the YTM rate. YTM can be approximated using a bond value table (also called a bond yield table) or can be determined using a programmable calculator equipped for bond mathematics calculations. *See also* DURATION; HORIZON ANALYSIS; YIELD TO AVERAGE LIFE, YIELD TO CALL.

YO-YO STOCK stock that fluctuates in a VOLATILE manner, rising and falling quickly like a yo-yo.

Z

ZACKS ESTIMATE SYSTEM service offer by Zacks Investment Research of Chicago compiling earnings estimates and brokerage buy/hold/sell recommendations from more than 200 Wall Street research firms, covering more than 4500 stocks. Zacks tracks the number of analysts following each stock, how many analysts have raised or lowered their estimates, and the high, low and average earnings estimate for each quarter and fiscal year. Zacks offers a multiple selection of data bases, of print reports, and software for institutional and individual investors. *See also* FIRST CALL, I/B/E/S INTERNATIONAL INC.

Z-BOND the fourth (Z) TRANCHE of bonds in the structure of a typical COLLATERALIZED MORTGAGE OBLIGATION (CMO). Combining features of ZERO-COUPON SECURITIES and mortgage PASS-THROUGH SECURITIES, Z bonds receive no coupon payments until the earlier A (fast-pay), B (medium-pay), and C (slow-pay) classes have been paid off. Z holders then receive all the remaining cash flow, although interest has been added to principal as cash was used to repay earlier tranches. Some CMOs have been issued with multiple Z and Y tranches, incorporating SINKING FUND schedules.

ZERO-BASE BUDGETING (ZBB) method of setting budgets for corporations and government agencies that requires a justification of all expenditures, not only those that exceed the prior year's allocations. Thus all budget lines are said to begin at a zero base and are funded according to merit rather than according to the level approved for the preceding year, when circumstances probably differed.

ZERO-BRACKET AMOUNT until the TAX REFORM ACT OF 1986, the STANDARD DEDUCTION, that is, the income automatically not subject to federal income tax for taxpayers choosing not to itemize deductions. The zero-bracket amount was built into the tax tables and schedules used to compute tax. The 1986 Act replaced the zero-bracket amount with an increased standard deduction, which was subtracted from income before computing taxes rather than being part of the rate tables. Current (*see* REVENUE RECONCILIATION ACT OF 1993) law indexes the standard deduction to inflation and contains special provisions for the blind and elderly.

ZERO-COUPON CONVERTIBLE SECURITY
1. Zero-coupon BOND convertible into the common stock of the issuing company when the stock reaches a predetermined price. Introduced as Liquid Yield Option Notes (LYONS), these securities have a PUT OPTION that permits holders to redeem the bonds within three years after the initial offering. They tend to trade at a small PREMIUM OVER CONVERSION VALUE and provide a lower YIELD TO MATURITY than their nonconvertible counterparts.
2. Zero-coupon bond, usually a MUNICIPAL BOND, convertible into an interest bearing bond at some time before maturity. For example, a zero-coupon (tax-free) municipal bond would automatically accumulate and compound interest for its first 15 years at which time it would convert to a regular income-paying bond. Thus, an investor is able to lock in a current interest rate with a small initial investment. Varieties are marketed under the acronyms GAINS (Growth and Income Securities) and FIGS (Future Income and Growth Securities).

ZERO-COUPON SECURITY security that makes no periodic interest payments but instead is sold at a deep discount from its face value. The buyer of such a bond receives the rate of return by the gradual APPRECIATION of the security, which is redeemed at FACE VALUE on a specified maturity date. For tax purposes, the Internal Revenue Service maintains that the holder of a zero-coupon bond owes income tax on the interest that has accrued each year, even though the bondholder does not actually receive the cash until maturity. The IRS calls this interest *imputed interest.* Because of this interpretation, many financial advisers recommend that zero-coupon securities be used in INDIVIDUAL RETIREMENT ACCOUNTS or KEOGH ACCOUNTS, where they remain tax-sheltered.

There are many kinds of zero-coupon securities. The most commonly known is the zero-coupon bond, which either may be issued at a deep discount by a corporation or government entity or may be created by a brokerage firm when it strips the coupons off a bond and sells the CORPUS and the coupons separately. This technique is used frequently with Treasury bonds, and the zero-coupon issue is marketed under such names as CATS (CERTIFICATE OF ACCRUAL ON TREASURY SECURITIES), TIGER (Treasury Investors Growth Receipt) or STRIPS (separate trading of registered interest and principal of securities). Zero-coupon bonds are also issued by municipalities. Buying a municipal zero frees its purchaser of the worry about paying taxes on imputed interest, since the interest is tax-exempt. Zero-coupon certificates of deposit and zero mortgages also exist; they work on the same principle as zero-coupon bonds—the CD holder or mortgage holder receives face value at maturity, and no payments until then. Zero-coupon securities based on COLLATER-ALIZED MORTGAGE OBLIGATION bonds are called *Z-tranche bonds.* Some mutual funds buy exclusively zero-coupon securities, offering shareholders a diversified portfolio that will mature in a particular year.

Zero-coupon securities are frequently used to plan for a specific investment goal. For example, parents knowing their child will enter college in 10 years can buy a zero that will mature in 10 years, and thus be assured of having money available for tuition. People planning for retirement in 20 years can buy 20-year zeros, assuring them that they will get the money when they need it.

Because zero-coupon securities bear no interest, they are the most VOLATILE of all fixed-income securities. Since zero-coupon bondholders do not receive interest payments, zeros fall more dramatically than bonds paying out interest on a current basis when interest rates rise. However, when interest rates fall, zero-coupon securities rise more rapidly in value than full-coupon bonds, because the bonds have locked in a particular rate of reinvestment that becomes more attractive the further rates fall. The greater the number of years that a zero-coupon security has until maturity, the less an investor has to pay for it, and the more LEVERAGE is at work for him. For instance, a bond maturing in 5 years may double, but one maturing in 25 years may increase in value ten times, depending on the interest rate of the bond. *See also* ACCRUAL BONDS; COUPON BOND; DEEP DIS-COUNT BOND, SPLIT COUPON BONDS; STAGS; STRIPPED BOND; ZERO-COUPON CONVERT-IBLE SECURITY.

ZERO-MINUS TICK sale that takes place at the same price as the previous sale, but at a lower price than the last different price; also called a *zero downtick.* For instance, stock trades may be executed consecutively at prices of $52, $51, and $51. The final trade at $51 was made at a zero-minus tick, because it was made at the same price as the previous trade, but at a lower price than the last different price.

ZERO-PLUS TICK securities trade that takes place at the same price as the previous transaction but at a higher price than the last different price; also called *zero uptick.* For instance, with trades executed consecutively at $51, $52, and $52, the last trade at $52 was made at a zero-plus tick—the same price as the previous trade but a higher price than the last different price. Short sales must be executed only on zero-plus ticks or on PLUS TICKS. *See also* SHORT-SALE RULE.

ZERO-SUM GAME situation in which the gains of the winners are matched by the losses of the losers. For example, futures and options trading are zero-sum games because for every investor holding a profitable contract, there is another investor on the other side of the trade who is losing money. The total amount of wealth held by all the traders in a zero-sum game remains the same, but the wealth is shifted from some traders to others.

ZOMBIES companies that continue to operate even though they are insolvent and bankrupt. For example, during the savings and loan industry bailout, many savings and loans that had lost millions of dollars in bad real estate loans continued to function, awaiting merger into another financial institution or closure by the RESO-LUTION TRUST CORPORATION. Such companies, in addition to being called zombies, are called *brain dead* or *living dead.*

ZONING LAWS municipal ordinances that authorize the establishment of zoning boards to administer regulations concerning the use of property and buildings in designated areas.

ZURICH STOCK EXCHANGE *see* SWISS ELECTRONIC BOURSE (EBS).

PART V

Finance and Investment
Ready Reference

INTRODUCTION

In today's complex world of finance and investment, it's crucial not only to know *how* different investments work, but also *where* to find the information essential to making wise decisions about those investments.

In the following pages you will find an enormous wealth of information concerning finance and investment. In some cases, the data presented is designed mainly to help you tap the many sophisticated sources available to investors. In other cases, we present well-organized data that can offer important insight into the workings of finance and investment. *In all cases, you are given information you can use.* The address, telephone number, and, if available, web site address is given for just about every institution, organization, and firm listed, and you are encouraged to make direct contact in order to obtain the data required to make a well-informed investment decision.

The section is divided into the following principal parts:

Sources of Information and Assistance Public and private agencies, associations that help investors and consumers, and major financial publications, software programs, online databases, and web sites are listed.

Major Financial Institutions In this part are listed the names, addresses, and phone numbers of commercial banks, thrift institutions, life insurance companies, brokerage firms, accounting firms, and major stock and futures exchanges around the world.

Mutual Funds Both open-end and closed-end funds are presented.

Futures and Options Contracts Detailed specifications of each contract are presented in tabular form, along with a list of where each contract is traded.

Historical Data This section provides graphs and tabular matter showing important longer-term financial and economic trends. Dow Jones and other indexes are included.

Publicly Traded Companies About 6000 corporations are listed, according to the place where the shares trade: NYSE, AMEX, NASDAQ, and Toronto Stock Exchange. Listings include name, stock symbol, address, phone number, line of business, option availability, and whether the firm offers a dividend reinvestment plan. These listings are followed by a compilation of important American Depositary Receipts (ADRs) and a listing of benefits some companies offer shareholders such as free merchandise or services.

1. SOURCES OF INFORMATION AND ASSISTANCE

When trying to make decisions and keep up-to-date in the increasingly complex world of finance and investment, it is often necessary to turn to others. This section of the *Handbook* is designed to guide you to the organizations that can help you.

Since the financial markets are so heavily regulated by the government today, it is important to know which federal and state regulators can be of assistance. The first part of this section gives a brief description of major federal, state and provincial regulatory agencies in the United States and Canada, and how to contact them.

A government agency sometimes is not the best place to turn. Private associations, trade groups and self-regulatory organizations are often well equipped to deal with problems or questions related to finance and investment. The second part of this section lists many of these private groups.

For advice on where to invest and how to manage your financial affairs, there is an enormous pool of advice available in finance and investment publications. The third part of this section gives you the information you need to contact a great number of worthy publications that contain such advice.

To tap information about financial markets in an even speedier fashion, you can use computer databases and web sites, which are listed in the fourth section. In addition, we have selected some of the best software that can make sense of the massive amounts of information these databases and web sites contain.

FEDERAL REGULATORY ORGANIZATIONS IN THE UNITED STATES AND CANADA

This is a list of the major governmental agencies that regulate the finance and investment markets in the United States and Canada. Each agency's address and telephone number is accompanied by a brief description of its major responsibilities. These agencies primarily oversee the fairness and efficiency of finance and investment markets. In that role, consumers and investors can complain to them about perceived abuses or illegality in the marketplace. Many of the agencies are discussed in more detail in the Dictionary section of the Handbook, along with the legislation that created the agency. The regulatory aspect of some of the agencies is less important than other functions.

Agencies of the United States Government

Bureau of Economic Analysis
1441 L Street, N.W.
Washington, D.C. 20230
(202) 606-9900

Compiles, analyzes and publishes data on economic activity, including gross national product, personal income, corporate profits and leading economic indicators.

Bureau of Labor Statistics
2 Massachusetts Avenue, N.E.
Washington, D.C. 20212
(202) 606-7800

Compiles, analyzes and publishes data on labor activity such as unemployment, consumer price index, producer price index and wages.

Commerce Department
14th and Constitution Ave., N.W.
Washington, D.C. 20230
(202) 482-2000

Regulates international trade and helps American businesses expand in a variety of ways. Publishes a large amount of data about the U.S. economy.

Commodity Futures Trading Commission
1155 21st Street, N.W.
Washington, D.C. 20581
(202) 418-5000

Regulates U.S. futures and options markets. Investigates charges of fraud against commodity dealers and approves all new contracts that exchanges want to trade.

Comptroller of the Currency
250 E Street, S.W.
Washington, D.C. 20219
(202) 622-2000   (202) 874-5280

Regulates all national banks in the United States and handles consumer complaints against those banks.

Consumer Product Safety Commission
5401 Westbard Avenue
Bethesda, Maryland 20207
(301) 504-0621

Regulates and monitors the safety of consumer products. Provides information to the public on, and develops manufacturing standards for, consumer goods.

Council of Economic Advisers
17th Street and Pennsylvania Avenue, N.W.
Washington, D.C. 20502
(202) 395-5084

Monitors and analyzes the economy and advises the president on economic developments, trends and policies. Also prepares the economic reports of the President to Congress.

Farm Credit Administration
1501 Farm Credit Drive
McLean, Virginia 22102-5090
(703) 883-4000

Supervises and regulates lending activities of the Farm Credit System, which provides funding for agricultural, aquatic and rural electric enterprises.

Federal Deposit Insurance Corporation
550 17th Street, N.W.
Washington, D.C. 20429
(202) 393-8400   (800) 424-5488

Insures deposits in member institutions up to $100,000 per depositor. Also regularly examines banks and replies to consumer complaints about federally insured state banks. Helps arrange the merger of weak banks into stronger ones.

Federal Home Loan Mortgage Corporation
8200 Jones Branch Drive
McLean, Virginia 22102
(703) 903-2000

Freddie Mac, as it is known, encourages the growth of the secondary mortgage market by buying mortgages from lenders, packaging and guaranteeing them, and reselling them as mortgage-backed securities.

Federal Housing Finance Board
1777 F Street, N.W.
Washington, D.C. 20006
(202) 408-2000

Supervises the 12 regional Federal Home Loan Banks. Replaced the Federal Home Loan Bank Board, which was dismantled in 1989.

Federal National Mortgage Association
3900 Wisconsin Ave., N.W.
Washington, D.C. 20016
(202) 752-7000

Creates a secondary market in mortgage-backed securities. Called "Fannie Mae," the agency offers a wide variety of brochures about real estate.

Federal Reserve Board
20th Street and C Street, N.W.
Washington, D.C. 20551
(202) 452-3946

Regulates national money supply, oversees activities of, and supplies credit to, member banks, and supervises the printing of money at the U.S. Mint. Investors can also buy Treasury securities directly from the Fed or any of its district banks or branches.

Federal Trade Commission
Sixth Street and Pennsylvania Avenue, N.W.
Washington, D.C. 20580
(202) 326-2000

Enforces antitrust laws and consumer protection legislation. For instance, the FTC oversees the Truth-in-Lending laws, and seeks to curtail unfair sales practices and deceptive advertising.

Health Care Financing Administration
7500 Security Blvd.
Baltimore, MD 21244-1850
(410) 786-3000

Federal agency that oversees the Medicare and Medicaid health insurance system.

Internal Revenue Service
1111 Constitution Avenue, N.W.
Washington, D.C. 20224
(202) 622-5000

Collects personal and corporate taxes for the Federal Government and administers rules and regulations of the Treasury Department.

International Monetary Fund
700 19th Street, N.W.
Washington, D.C. 20431
(202) 623-7900

An intergovernmental organization that maintains funds contributed by, and available to, member nations. Payments are designed to promote world trade and aid members with temporary problems.

International Trade Administration
14th Street and Constitution Avenue, N.W.
Washington, D.C. 20230
(202) 482-5023

Regulates and promotes non-agricultural trade between the U.S. and its trading partners. Also develops global policies to expand U.S. exports.

National Credit Union Administration
1775 Duke St.
Alexandria, VA 22314-3428
(703) 518-6300

Regulates federally chartered credit unions and handles consumer complaints.

Office of Thrift Supervision
1700 G Street, N.W.
Washington, D.C. 20552
(202) 906-6000

Charters federal savings and loan associations, supervises and examines federally and state chartered thrifts, handles public complaints.

Pension Benefit Guaranty Corporation
2020 K Street, N.W.
Washington, D.C. 20006
(202) 778-8800

Insures corporate pension plans to make sure that covered pensioners receive the money due them.

Securities and Exchange Commission
450 Fifth Street, N.W.
Washington, D.C. 20549
(202) 942-8088

Regulates the securities industry. Registers issues of securities, investigates fraud and insider trading, supervises investment companies, investment advisers, accounting firms and self-regulatory organizations like the stock exchanges and the National Association of Securities Dealers.

Securities Investor Protection Corporation
805 15th Street, N.W., Suite 800
Washington, D.C. 20005-2207
(202) 371-8300

Insures brokerage customers' holdings up to $500,000 per customer, with a limit of $100,000 in cash or cash equivalents against losses due to financial failure of a firm. SIPC does not cover losses due to market fluctuations or default by the issuers of securities. Helps arrange mergers of failing brokerage firms into stronger firms.

Small Business Administration
409 3rd Street, S.W.
Washington, D.C. 20416
(202) 205-6740   (800) UASK-SBA

Offers advice and guarantees market rate loans through a separate lending institution or intermediary to qualifying small businesses, with special programs for veterans and women, among other groups. Also licenses and funds Small Business Investment Companies (SBICs).

Social Security Administration
6401 Security Boulevard
Baltimore, Maryland 21235
(401) 965-7700   (800) 772-1213

Regulates eligibility and payments of social security benefits to workers after they retire or become disabled. Also administers supplemental income programs for the aged, blind and dependents.

Student Loan Marketing Association
1050 Thomas Jefferson St. N.W.
Washington, DC 20007
(202) 333-8000   (800) 831-5626

Known as Sallie Mae, the agency makes a secondary market in student loans.

Treasury Department
Main Treasury Building
15th Street and Pennsylvania Avenue, N.W.
Washington, D.C. 20220
(202) 622-2000

Regulates the issuance of government debt (Treasury bills, bonds and notes) in coordination with the Federal Reserve and issues savings bonds. Plays a large role in coordinating economic and financial issues with foreign governments.

United State International Trade Commission
500 E Street, S.W.
Washington, D.C. 20436
(202) 205-2000

Studies factors relating to U.S. foreign trade and its relation to domestic production, employment and competitiveness. Also provides technical advice for government and private policy-makers.

United States Tax Court
400 Second Street, N.W.
Washington, D.C. 20217
(202) 606-8754

Hears cases involving disputes between the IRS and taxpayers.

Federal Government Agencies of Canada

Bank of Canada
234 Wellington Street
Ottawa, Ontario K1A OG9
(613) 782-8111

Regulates the money supply of Canada. It also acts as fiscal agent for the Government of Canada in managing the public debt. The Bank of Canada also has the sole right to issue Canadian paper money.

Canada Deposit Insurance Corporation
50 O'Connor Street, 17th floor
P.O. Box 2340, Station D
Ottawa, Ontario K1P 5W5
(613) 996-2081

Insures deposits up to $60,000 per depositor in member institutions. Membership in the Corporation is restricted to banks, trust companies and mortgage loan companies.

Canada Mortgage and Housing Corporation
700 Montreal Road
Ottawa, Ontario K1A OP7
(613) 748-2000

Administers the National Housing Act and is responsible for delivering housing assistance to increase the supply of housing. The Corporation also insures mortgage loans made by approved lenders on the open market, and makes direct loans to areas not served by approved lenders.

Department of Finance, Canada
140 O'Connor Street
Ottawa, Ontario K1A OG5
(613) 992-1573

Conducts the financial affairs and economic planning for the Canadian government.

Export Development Corporation EDC/SEE
151 O'Connor Street
Ottawa, Ontario K1A 1K3
(613) 598-2500

Assists Canadian companies to export their products and services.

External Affairs Department
125 Sussex Drive
Ottawa, Ontario K1A OG2
(613) 995-1851

Coordinates international trade policy, and helps Canadian companies export their products and services.

Federal Business Development Bank
BDC Building, Suite 400
5 Place Ville Marie
Montreal, Quebec H3B 5E7
(514) 283-5904

Provides capital and equity financing and management services to Canadian businesses.

Office of Superintendent of Financial
  Institutions, Canada
255 Albert Street, 16th floor
Ottawa, Ontario K1A OH2
(613) 990-7788

Regulates all banking, trust companies, loan companies, investment companies, life insurance companies, property and casualty insurance companies, and federally regulated pension plans.

Ministry of National Revenue
Connaught Building, 7th floor
555 MacKenzie Avenue
Ottawa, Ontario K1A OL5
(613) 995-2960

Collects corporate and individual taxes from Canadians.

Statistics Canada
Holland Avenue
Tunney's Pasture
RH Coats Building
Ottawa, Ontario K1A OT6
(613) 951-8116

Compiles many of the economic and financial statistics for the government of Canada.

Treasury Board of Canada
140 O'Connor Street, East Tower,
L'esplanade Laurier
Ottawa, Ontario K1A 0R5
(613) 957-2400

A Cabinet committee, brought into existence by the Financial Administration Act, which advises the rest of the Cabinet on the optimum allocation of public funds among government programs to permit the most efficient use of the government's manpower, financial and material resources.

U.S. STATE ATTORNEY GENERAL'S OFFICES

The attorney general's office is the place to go for a wide variety of consumer complaints. The attorney general is particularly concerned with stopping fraud, and frequently several attorneys general will coordinate their efforts to stop a multistate fraudulent business. Those who suspect a solicitation to be fraudulent should contact their state's attorney general on this list before handing over any money.

Besides taking consumer complaints, the attorney general's office promulgates rules and regulations which promote fair business practices. Areas in their jurisdiction include deceptive advertising and contract law, for example. When appropriate, attorneys general also appeal to legislative bodies to pass new consumer protection laws. To enforce these laws, attorneys general pursue both civil and criminal prosecution of violators.

Your state attorney general's offices may also be a source of help when considering a purchase decision. These offices usually publish helpful publications giving tips on what to avoid in entering certain kinds of sales contracts, for instance. Even if one is not sure where to turn for help for a particular consumer problem, the attorney general is often a good place to start.

ALABAMA
Attorney General
115 Union Street
Montgomery, Alabama 36130
(205) 242-7300

ALASKA
Attorney General
P.O. Box 110300
Juneau, Alaska 99811
(907) 465-3600

ARIZONA
Attorney General
1275 W. Washington Street
Phoenix, Arizona 85007
(602) 542-4266

ARKANSAS
Attorney General
200 Catlett-Prien Building
323 Center Street
Little Rock, Arkansas 72201
(501) 682-2007

CALIFORNIA
Attorney General
1300 I Street
Sacramento, California 95814
(916) 324-5437

COLORADO
Attorney General
1525 Sherman Street
Denver, Colorado 80203-1525
(303) 866-3611

CONNECTICUT
Attorney General
55 Elm Street
Hartford, Connecticut 06106
(203) 566-2026

DELAWARE
Attorney General
820 North French Street, 7th and 8th Floors
Wilmington, Delaware 19801
(302) 577-3838

DISTRICT OF COLUMBIA
Office of the Corporation Counsel
441 4th Street, N.W., Suite 1060N
Washington, D.C. 20001
(202) 727-6248

FLORIDA
Attorney General
State Capitol Building, PL01
Tallahassee, Florida 32399-1050
(904) 487-1963

GEORGIA
Attorney General
40 Capitol Square SW
Atlanta, Georgia 30334-1300
(404) 656-4585

HAWAII
Attorney General
425 Queen Street
Honolulu, Hawaii 96813
(808) 586-1282

IDAHO
Attorney General
P.O. Box 83720
Boise, Idaho 83720-0010
(208) 334-2400

ILLINOIS
Attorney General
State of Illinois Center
100 West Randolph Street, 11th Floor
Chicago, Illinois 60601
(312) 814-3000

INDIANA
Attorney General
Indiana State Government Center
South Building
402 W. Washington Street, 5th floor
Indianapolis, Indiana 46204
(317) 232-6201, (800) 382-5516

IOWA
Attorney General
Hoover State Office Building, 2nd Floor
Des Moines, Iowa 50319
(515) 281-5164

KANSAS
Attorney General
301 Southwest 10th Avenue
Topeka, Kansas 66612
(913) 296-2215

KENTUCKY
Attorney General
P.O. Box 2000
Frankfort, Kentucky 40602
(502) 564-7600

LOUISIANA
Attorney General
Department of Justice
P.O. Box 94005
Baton Rouge, Louisiana 70804-9005
(504) 342-7013

MAINE
Attorney General
State House, Station 6
Augusta, Maine 04333
(207) 626-8800

MARYLAND
Attorney General
200 St. Paul Place
Baltimore, Maryland 21202
(410) 576-6300

MASSACHUSETTS
Attorney General
One Ashburton Place
Boston, Massachusetts 02108
(617) 727-2200

MICHIGAN
Attorney General
Law Building
P.O. Box 30212
525 W. Ottawa
Lansing, Michigan 48909
(517) 373-1110

MINNESOTA
Attorney General
102 State Capitol
St. Paul, Minnesota 55155
(612) 296-6196

MISSISSIPPI
Attorney General
Carroll Gartin Justice Building
P.O. Box 220
Jackson, Mississippi 39205
(601) 359-3680

MISSOURI
Attorney General
P.O. Box 899
207 W. High Street
Jefferson City, Missouri 65102
(573) 751-3321

MONTANA
Attorney General
Justice Building
215 N. Sanders Street, 3rd floor
Helena, Montana 59620-1401
(406) 444-2026

NEBRASKA
Attorney General
2115 State Capitol
P.O. Box 98920
Lincoln, Nebraska 68509-8920
(402) 471-2682

NEVADA
Attorney General
Heroes Memorial Building
Capitol Complex
198 S. Carson Street
Carson City, Nevada 89710
(702) 687-4170

NEW HAMPSHIRE
Attorney General
33 Capitol Street
Concord, New Hampshire 03301-6397
(603) 271-3658

NEW JERSEY
Office of the Attorney General
Dept. of Law & Public Safety, CN 080
25 Market Street
Trenton, New Jersey 08625
(609) 292-4925

NEW MEXICO
Attorney General
Bataan Memorial Building
P.O. Drawer 1508
Santa Fe, New Mexico 87504-1508
(505) 827-6000

NEW YORK
Attorney General
120 Broadway, 25th Floor
New York, New York 10271
(212) 416-8519

NORTH CAROLINA
Attorney General
P.O. Box 629
2 E. Morgan Street
Raleigh, North Carolina 27602-0629
(919) 733-3377

NORTH DAKOTA
Attorney General
State Capitol
600 E. Boulevard Avenue
Bismarck, North Dakota 58505
(701) 328-2210

OHIO
Attorney General
30 E. Broad Street, 17th floor
Columbus, Ohio 43215
(614) 466-3376

OKLAHOMA
Attorney General
State Capitol Building
2300 N. Lincoln Boulevard, Suite 112
Oklahoma City, Oklahoma 73105
(405) 521-3921

OREGON
Attorney General
1162 Court Street NE
Salem, Oregon 97310
(503) 378-6002

PENNSYLVANIA
Attorney General
Strawberry Square, 16th Floor
Harrisburg, Pennsylvania 17120
(717) 787-3391

PUERTO RICO
Department of Justice
P.O. Box 192
Old San Juan, Puerto Rico 00902
(809) 721-7700

RHODE ISLAND
Attorney General
150 S. Main Street
Providence, Rhode Island 02903
(401) 274-4400

SOUTH CAROLINA
Attorney General
Rembert C. Dennis Building
P.O. Box 11549
Columbia, South Carolina 29211
(803) 734-3970

SOUTH DAKOTA
Attorney General
500 E. Capitol
Pierre, South Dakota 57501-5070
(605) 773-3215

TENNESSEE
Attorney General
500 Charlotte Avenue
Nashville, Tennessee 37243-0497
(615) 741-3491

TEXAS
Attorney General
Capitol Station
P.O. Box 12548
Austin, Texas 78711-2548
(512) 463-2191

UTAH
Attorney General
236 State Capitol
Salt Lake City, Utah 84114
(801) 538-1326

VERMONT
Attorney General
109 State Street, 2nd floor
Montpelier, Vermont 05609
(802) 828-3171

VIRGINIA
Attorney General
900 E. Main Street
Richmond, Virginia 23219
(804) 786-2071

VIRGIN ISLANDS OF THE UNITED
  STATES
Department of Justice
G.E.R.S. Complex, 2nd Floor
St. Thomas
U.S. Virgin Islands 00802
(809) 774-5566

WASHINGTON
Attorney General
1125 Washington Street, SE
P.O. Box 40100
Olympia, Washington 98504-0100
(360) 753-6200

WEST VIRGINIA
Attorney General
State Capitol, Room 26, East Wing
Charleston, West Virginia 25305-0220
(304) 558-2021

WISCONSIN
Attorney General
114 East State Capitol
P.O. Box 7857
Madison, Wisconsin 53707-7857
(608) 266-1221

WYOMING
Attorney General
123 State Capitol Building
Cheyenne, Wyoming 82002
(307) 777-7841

U.S. STATE BANKING REGULATORS

The regulators listed here are charged with supervising the activities of state-chartered banks. These are banks not regulated at the national level, where the Comptroller of the Currency and Federal Reserve Board do the supervision. Depending on the state, state chartered banks may have more or fewer powers than federally regulated banks. For example, the amount of money state banks can lend to customers as a percent of deposits varies widely from state to state. State banking regulators also oversee the financial soundness of the banks in their jurisdictions, and help to merge failing banks into healthy ones. These regulators do not insure state bank deposits, however; that is usually done by the Federal Deposit Insurance Corporation.

State bank regulators also pursue consumer complaints against banks in their state. For example, it would be appropriate to contact a regulator if a state bank was preventing checks from clearing within a reasonable time or if fees were excessive. Complaints about deceptive advertising or promotional materials by banks can also be addressed to these agencies. Questions about credit, and the denial of credit privileges, are also handled by the agencies in this list.

State banking agencies are also helpful when shopping for a bank. They will usually publish helpful literature about banks and bank services. Do not expect these agencies to do comparisons of yields paid on bank accounts or interest rates charged on loans—these numbers change too frequently for the agencies to track them.

ALABAMA
101 South Union Street
Montgomery, Alabama 36130
(334) 242-3452

ALASKA
P.O. Box 110807
Juneau, Alaska 99811-0807
(907) 465-2521

ARIZONA
2910 North 44th Street, Suite 310
Phoenix, Arizona 85018
(602) 255-4421

ARKANSAS
Tower Building
323 Center Street, Suite 500
Little Rock, Arkansas 72201-2613
(501) 324-9019

CALIFORNIA
111 Pine Street, Suite 1100
San Francisco, California 94111-5613
(415) 263-8555

COLORADO
1560 Broadway, Suite 1175
Denver, Colorado 80202
(303) 894-7575

CONNECTICUT
260 Constitution Plaza
Hartford, Connecticut 06103
(203) 240-8299

DELAWARE
555 East Loockerman Street, Suite 210
Dover, Delaware 19901
(302) 739-4235

DISTRICT OF COLUMBIA
Comptroller of the Currency
250 E Street, S.W.
Washington D.C. 20219
(202) 622-2000

FLORIDA
State Capitol Building
Tallahassee, Florida 32399-0350
(904) 488-0370

GEORGIA
2990 Brandywine Road, Suite 200
Atlanta, Georgia 30341-5565
(770) 986-1633

HAWAII
Division of Financial Institutions
P.O. Box 2054
Honolulu, Hawaii 96805
(808) 586-2820

IDAHO
P.O. Box 83720
700 West State Street
Boise, Idaho 83720-0031
(208) 334-3678

ILLINOIS
Office of Banks and Real Estate
500 East Munroe Street
Springfield, Illinois 62701
(217) 782-3000

INDIANA
402 West Washington Street, Room W066
Indianapolis, Indiana 46204-2759
(317) 232-3955

IOWA
Iowa Division of Banking
200 East Grand Avenue
Des Moines, Iowa 50309
(515) 281-4014

KANSAS
700 Jackson Street S.W., Suite 300
Topeka, Kansas 66603
(913) 296-2266

KENTUCKY
Department of Financial Institutions
477 Versailles Road
Frankfort, Kentucky 40601
(502) 573-3390

LOUISIANA
Office of Financial Institutions
P.O. Box 94095
Baton Rouge 70804-9095
(504) 925-4661

MAINE
State of Maine Bureau of Banking
36 State House Station
Augusta, Maine 04333
(207) 624-8570

MARYLAND
Commissioner of Financial Regulations
501 St. Paul Place
Baltimore, Maryland 21202-2272
(410) 333-6808

MASSACHUSETTS
100 Cambridge Street, Room 2004
Boston, Massachusetts 02202
(617) 727-3145, ext. 349

MICHIGAN
Financial Institutions Bureau
P.O. Box 30224
Lansing, Michigan 48909
(517) 373-3460

MINNESOTA
Financial Examinations Divisions
133 East 7th Street, 4th floor
St. Paul, Minnesota 55101
(612) 296-2715

MISSISSIPPI
P.O. Box 23729
Jackson, Mississippi 39225-3729
(601) 359-1031

MISSOURI
Division of Finance
P.O. Box 716
Jefferson City, Missouri 65102
(573) 751-3242

MONTANA
846 Front Street
Helena, Montana 59620-0546
(406) 444-2091

NEBRASKA
The Atrium
1200 N Street, Suite 311
Lincoln, Nebraska 68508
(402) 471-2171

NEVADA
Financial Institutions Division of the
  Department of Business & Industry
406 E. Second Street
Carson City, Nevada 89710
(702) 687-4259

NEW HAMPSHIRE
169 Manchester Street
Concord, New Hampshire 03301
(603) 271-3561

NEW JERSEY
20 West State Street, CN040
Trenton, New Jersey 08625
(609) 292-3420

NEW MEXICO
FInancial Institutions Division
P.O. Box 25101
Santa Fe, New Mexico 87504
(505) 827-7100

NEW YORK
2 Rector Street
New York, New York 10006
(212) 618-6557

NORTH CAROLINA
702 Oberlin Road, Suite 400
Raleigh, North Carolina 27605
(919) 733-3016

NORTH DAKOTA
700 East Main Avenue
Bismark, North Dakota 58502
(701) 328-5600

OHIO
Office of Financial Institutions
77 South High Street, 21st Floor
Columbus, Ohio 43266-0121
(614) 466-2932

OKLAHOMA
4545 North Lincoln Boulevard, Suite 164
Oklahoma City, Oklahoma 73105
(405) 521-2782

OREGON
350 Winter Street NE, Room 21
Salem, Oregon 97310
(503) 378-4140

PENNSYLVANIA
333 Market Street, 16th Floor
Harrisburg, Pennsylvania 17101-2290
(717) 787-6991

RHODE ISLAND
233 Richmond Street, Suite 231
Providence, Rhode Island 02903-4231
(401) 277-2405

SOUTH CAROLINA
1015 Sumter Street, Room 309
Columbia, South Carolina 29201
(803) 734-2001

SOUTH DAKOTA
State Capitol
500 East Capitol Avenue
Pierre, South Dakota 57501-5070
(605) 773-3421

TENNESSEE
John Sevier Building, 4th Floor
Nashville, Tennessee 37243-0705
(615) 741-2236

TEXAS
2601 North Lamar Boulevard
Austin, Texas 78705
(512) 475-1300

UTAH
324 South State, Suite 201
Salt Lake City, Utah 84111
(801) 538-8830

VERMONT
89 Main Street, Drawer #20
Montpelier, Vermont 05620-3101
(802) 828-3301

VIRGINIA
1300 East Main Street, Suite 800
P.O. Box 640
Richmond, Virginia 23218-0640
(804) 371-9657

WASHINGTON
P.O. Box 41200
Olympia, Washington 98504-1200
(360) 902-8704

WEST VIRGINIA
State Capitol Complex, Building 3, Suite 311
Charleston, West Virginia 25305-0240
(304) 558-2294

WISCONSIN
Department of Financial Institutions
P.O. Box 7876
Madison, Wisconsin 53707-7876
(608) 266-1621

WYOMING
Herschler Building, East Wing, 3rd Floor
122 West 25th Street
Cheyenne 82002
(307) 777-7797

U.S. STATE INSURANCE REGULATORS

Every state has its own laws and regulations which govern all types of insurance. Unlike most other areas in the financial services field, there is very little regulation of the insurance industry at the federal level. The state agencies listed here enforce all state insurance laws. Insurance commissioners must approve of the sale of all life, health, automobile and homeowners insurance products in their states. Some states, such as New York and California, are particularly rigorous in approving any new product for sale to state residents. If a product has been approved for sale in one of those states, it is often approved elsewhere as well.

When there are problems with an insurance company, these regulators step in. For example, they oversee the process of merging failing insurance companies into strong ones. They also protect policyholders by assuring that insurance companies keep adequate reserves. In the case of an insurance company failure, they see to it that policyholders' interests are protected as much as possible. State insurance offices also respond to consumer complaints against insurance companies on such issues as unfair pricing, denial of insurance claims, and deceptive advertising practices. Before bringing a complaint to one of these agencies, however, it is important to complain to the insurance company first. If the problem has not been resolved at that level, then these agencies should be consulted.

These insurance regulators also offer assistance to those looking to purchase insurance coverage. They may provide helpful literature about the kinds of insurance policies being offered, and also be able to inform buyers about patterns of complaints against particular companies.

ALABAMA
Insurance Commissioner
P.O. Box 303351
Montgomery, Alabama 36130-3551
(334) 269-3550

ALASKA
Director of Insurance
3601 C Street, Suite 1324
Anchorage, Alaska 99503-5948
(907) 269-7900

ARIZONA
Director of Insurance
3030 N. 3rd Street, Suite 1100
Phoenix, Arizona 85012
(602) 255-5400

ARKANSAS
Insurance Commissioner
1200 West 3rd Street
Little Rock, Arkansas 72201
(501) 371-2750

CALIFORNIA
Insurance Commissioner
320 Capital Mall
Sacramento, California 95814
(916) 322-3555

COLORADO
Commissioner of Insurance Division
1560 Broadway, Suite 850
Denver, Colorado 80202
(303) 894-7499

CONNECTICUT
Insurance Commissioner
P.O. Box 816
Hartford, Connecticut 06142-0816
(203) 297-3800

DELAWARE
Insurance Commissioner
P.O. Box 7007
Dover, Delaware 19903-1507
(302) 739-4251

DISTRICT OF COLUMBIA
Insurance Commissioner
P.O. Box 37378
Washington D.C. 20013
(202) 727-8000

FLORIDA
Bureau of Consumer Assistance
200 E. Gaines Street
Tallahassee, Florida 32399-0322
(904) 922-3131   (800) 342-2762

GEORGIA
Insurance Commissioner
2 Martin L. King, Jr. Drive
West Tower, 7th Floor
Atlanta, Georgia 30334
(404) 656-2056

HAWAII
Insurance Commissioner
P.O. Box 3614
Honolulu, Hawaii 96811
(808) 586-2790

IDAHO
Director of Insurance
700 West State Street
Boise, Idaho 83720
(208) 334-2250

ILLINOIS
Director of Insurance
320 West Washington Street
Springfield, Illinois 62767
(312) 782-4515

INDIANA
Insurance Commissioner
311 West Washington Street, Suite 300
Indianapolis, Indiana 46204
(317) 232-2385   (800) 622-4461

IOWA
Insurance Commissioner
Lucas State Office Building
Des Moines, Iowa 50319
(515) 281-5705

KANSAS
Insurance Commissioner
420 SW Ninth Street
Topeka, Kansas 66612-1678
(913) 296-3071   (800) 432-2484

KENTUCKY
Insurance Commissioner
P.O. Box 517
Frankfort, Kentucky 40602
(502) 564-3630

LOUISIANA
Insurance Commissioner
P.O. Box 94214
Baton Rouge, Louisiana 70804-9214
(504) 342-5900

MAINE
Insurance Bureau Chief
State House Station 34
Augusta, Maine 04333
(207) 624-8475

MARYLAND
Maryland Insurance Administration
501 St. Paul Place
Baltimore, Maryland 21202
(410) 333-6500   (800) 492-6116

MASSACHUSETTS
Commonwealth Division of Insurance
470 Atlantic Avenue
Boston, Massachusetts 02210-2223
(617) 521-7794

MICHIGAN
Insurance Commissioner
P.O. Box 30220
Lansing, Michigan 48909
(517) 373-0240

MINNESOTA
Deputy Commissioner of Commerce
133 East Seventh Street
St. Paul, Minnesota 55101
(612) 296-2488   (800) 657-3602

MISSISSIPPI
Insurance Commissioner
1804 Walter Sillers Building
Jackson, Mississippi 39201
(601) 359-3569   (800) 562-2957

MISSOURI
Director of Insurance
Truman Building
301 West High Street, Suite 630
Jefferson City, Missouri 65101
(573) 751-4126

MONTANA
Deputy Commissioner of Insurance
126 N. Sanders Street
P.O. Box 4009
Helena, Montana 59604-4009
(406) 444-2040

NEBRASKA
Director of Insurance
941 O Street, Suite 400
Lincoln, Nebraska 68508
(402) 471-2201

NEVADA
Insurance Commissioner
1665 Hot Springs Road, Suite 152
Carson City, Nevada 89710
(702) 687-4270   (800) 992-0900, ext. 4270

NEW HAMPSHIRE
Insurance Commissioner
169 Manchester Street
Concord, New Hampshire 03301-5151
(603) 271-2261   (800) 852-3416

NEW JERSEY
Insurance Commissioner
20 West State Street, CN 325
Trenton, New Jersey 08625
(609) 292-5360

NEW MEXICO
State Corporation Commission, Department
 of Insurance
P.O. Drawer 1269
Santa Fe, New Mexico 87504-1269
(505) 827-4500

NEW YORK
Superintendent of Insurance
Empire State Plaza, Building One, 8th floor
Albany, New York 12257
(800) 342-3736

NORTH CAROLINA
Insurance Commissioner
P.O. Box 26387
Raleigh, North Carolina 27611
(919) 733-7343   (800) 662-7777

NORTH DAKOTA
Insurance Commissioner
State Capitol Building
600 East Boulevard Avenue
Bismark, North Dakota 58505
(701) 328-2440

OHIO
Director of Insurance
2100 Stella Court
Columbus, Ohio 43215-1067
(614) 644-2658   (800) 686-1526

OKLAHOMA
Insurance Commissioner
P.O. Box 53408
Oklahoma City, Oklahoma 73152-3408
(405) 521-2828

OREGON
Insurance Administrator
350 Winter Street, NE
Salem, Oregon 97310
(503) 378-4271

PENNSYLVANIA
Insurance Commissioner
132 Strawberry Square
Harrisburg, Pennsylvania 17120
(717) 787-5173

RHODE ISLAND
Superintendent of Insurance
233 Richmond Street, Suite 233
Providence, Rhode Island 02903-4233
(401) 277-2223

SOUTH CAROLINA
Insurance Commissioner
P.O. Box 100105
Columbia, South Carolina 29202
(803) 737-6160   (800) 768-3467

SOUTH DAKOTA
Director of Insurance
500 E. Capitol Avenue
Pierre, South Dakota 57501-5070
(605) 773-3563

TENNESSEE
Assistant Commissioner of
 Insurance
500 James Robertson Parkway
Nashville, Tennessee 37243
(615) 741-2241   (800) 342-4029

TEXAS
Insurance Commissioner
P.O. Box 149104
Austin, Texas 78714-9104
(512) 463-6169

UTAH
Insurance Commissioner
3110 State Office Building
Salt Lake City, Utah 84114
(801) 538-3800

VERMONT
Deputy Commissioner of Insurance
89 Main Street, Drawer 20
Montpelier, Vermont 05620-3101
(802) 828-3301

VIRGINIA
Insurance Commissioner
1300 East Main Street
Richmond, Virginia 23219
(804) 371-9741

WASHINGTON
Insurance Commissioner
Insurance Building
AQ-21
Olympia, Washington 98504
(206) 753-7300   (800) 562-6900

WEST VIRGINIA
Insurance Commissioner
P.O. Box 50540
Charleston, West Virginia 25305
(304) 558-3386   (800) 642-9004

WISCONSIN
Office of the Commission of Insurance
P.O. Box 7873
Madison, Wisconsin 53707-7873
(608) 266-3585   (800) 236-8517

WYOMING
Wyoming Insurance Department
Herschler Building, 3rd Floor East
122 West 25th Street
Cheyenne, Wyoming 82002-0440
(307) 777-7401

U.S. STATE SECURITIES REGULATORS

Anyone dealing with the potential purchase or sale of securities might want to consult with the state regulators listed here. Brokerage firms and financial planners selling securities must pass tests adminstered by state securities departments. In the event of any malfeasance on the part of those with a license to sell securities, the state securities department will look into the complaint, and possibly revoke the license, if such action is called for.

These regulators protect buyers of securities sold in their states in another way: They screen all securities offering documents such as prospectuses to ensure that adequate information has been disclosed and that the deal is not fraudulent. The securities office will not judge each deal on its investment potential, but it will reject offerings which it deems abusive. This prescreening process is commonly called the blue-sky process, because a judge once asserted that a particular offering had as much value as a patch of blue sky. It is important to ask these state securities regulators, therefore, if a particular security, such as a mutual fund or limited partnership, has passed the blue-sky process in one's state. If it has not, state residents are not allowed to buy it.

Besides watching over the securities industry in their states and screening new securities offerings, state securities offices can be helpful in explaining the pros and cons of various kinds of securities. They often have helpful literature describing what investors should watch for in making good investments and avoiding bad ones. In general, these offices will be one of the best places to contact about any question that might come up regarding a security sold in one's state.

ALABAMA
770 Washington Street,
Suite 570
Montgomery, Alabama 36130-4700
(334) 242-2984

ALASKA
P.O. Box 110807
Juneau, Alaska 99811-0807
(907) 465-2521

ARIZONA
1300 West Washington,
3rd Floor
Phoenix, Arizona 85007
(602) 542-4242

ARKANSAS
Heritage West Building
201 East Markham
Little Rock, Arkansas 72201-1692
(501) 324-9260

CALIFORNIA
3700 Wilshire Boulevard
Suite 600
Los Angeles, California 90010-3001
(213) 736-2741

COLORADO
Division of Securities
1580 Lincoln Street, Suite 420
Denver, Colorado 80203-1506
(303) 894-2320

CONNECTICUT
260 Constitution Plaza
Hartford, Connecticut 06103
(203) 240-8299

DELAWARE
State Office Building
820 North French Street, 8th Floor
Wilmington, Delaware 19801
(302) 577-2515

DISTRICT OF COLUMBIA
450 5th Street, N.W., Suite 821
Washington, D.C. 20001
(202) 626-5105

FLORIDA
State Capitol Building
Suite LL-22
Tallahassee, Florida 32399-0350
(904) 488-9805

GEORGIA
2 Martin Luther King Drive
West Tower, Suite 802
Atlanta, Georgia 30334
(404) 656-2894

HAWAII
P.O. Box 40
Honolulu, Hawaii 96810
(808) 586-2730

IDAHO
P.O. Box 83720
Boise, Idaho 83720-0031
(208) 334-3684

ILLINOIS
520 South 2nd Street
Springfield, Illinois 62701
(217) 782-2256

INDIANA
302 West Washington, Room E-111
Indianapolis, Indiana 46204
(317) 232-6690

IOWA
Securities Bureau
Lucas State Office Building, 2nd Floor
Des Moines, Iowa 50319
(515) 281-4441

KANSAS
618 South Kansas Avenue, 2nd Floor
Topeka, Kansas 66603
(913) 296-3307

KENTUCKY
Department of Financial Institutions
477 Versailles Road
Frankfort, Kentucky 40601-3868
(502) 573-3390

LOUISIANA
1100 Poydras Street, Suite 2250
New Orleans, Louisiana 70163
(504) 568-5515

MAINE
121 State House Station
Augusta, Maine 04333
(207) 624-8551

MARYLAND
200 St. Paul Place, 20th Floor
Baltimore, Maryland 21202-2020
(410) 576-6360

MASSACHUSETTS
One Ashburton Place, Room 1701
Boston, Massachusetts 02108
(617) 727-3548

MICHIGAN
The Michigan Department of Commerce
6546 Mercantile Way
Lansing, Michigan 48910
(517) 334-6200

MINNESOTA
133 E. 7th Street
St. Paul, Minnesota 55101
(612) 296-6848

MISSISSIPPI
202 No. Congress Street, Suite 601
Jackson, Mississippi 39201
(601) 359-6364

MISSOURI
600 West Main Street
Jefferson City, Missouri 65101
(573) 751-4136

MONTANA
Mitchell Building
126 N. Sanders, Suite 270
Helena, Montana 59620
(406) 444-2040

NEBRASKA
The Atrium
1200 N Street, Suite 311
Lincoln, Nebraska 68508
(402) 471-3445

NEVADA
555 E. Washington Avenue, Suite 5200
Las Vegas, Nevada 89101
(702) 486-2440

NEW HAMPSHIRE
State House, Room 204
Concord, New Hampshire 03301-4989
(603) 271-1463

NEW JERSEY
153 Halsey Street
Newark, New Jersey 07102
(201) 504-3600

NEW MEXICO
P.O. Box 25101
725 St. Michael's Drive
Santa Fe, New Mexico 87501
(505) 827-7140

NEW YORK
Securities Bureau
120 Broadway, 23rd Floor
New York, New York 10271
(212) 416-8200

NORTH CAROLINA
Secretary of State
Securities Division
300 North Salisbury Street, Room 100
Raleigh, North Carolina 27603
(919) 733-3924

NORTH DAKOTA
Securities Commissioner
600 E. Boulevard Avenue
5th floor, State Capitol
Bismarck, North Dakota 58505
(701) 328-2910

OHIO
77 South High Street, 22nd Floor
Columbus, Ohio 43215
(614) 644-7381

OKLAHOMA
First National Center
120 No. Robinson, Suite 860
Oklahoma City, Oklahoma 73102
(405) 235-0230

OREGON
Department of Consumer and Business
  Services
Division of Finance and Corporate Securities
350 Winter Street NE, Room 21
Salem, Oregon 97310
(503) 378-4387

PENNSYLVANIA
2nd Floor, 1010 North 7th Street
Harrisburg, Pennsylvania 17102-1410
(717) 787-8061

PUERTO RICO
Securities Commissioner's Office
Department of the Treasury
P.O. Box 3508
San Juan, Puerto Rico 00904
(809) 723-1122

RHODE ISLAND
233 Richmond Street, Suite 232
Providence, Rhode Island 02903-4232
(401) 277-3048

SOUTH CAROLINA
Office of the Attorney General
Securities Section
P.O. Box 11549
Columbia, South Carolina 29211-1549
(803) 734-1087

SOUTH DAKOTA
118 West Capitol Avenue
Pierre, South Dakota 57501-2017
(605) 773-4823

TENNESSEE
Davy Crockett Building
500 James Robertson Parkway, Suite 680
Nashville, Tennessee 37243-0575
(615) 741-2947

TEXAS
P.O. Box 13167
Austin, Texas 78711
(512) 305-8300

UTAH
P.O. Box 146760
160 E. 300 South, 2nd floor
Salt Lake City, Utah 84114-6760
(801) 530-6600

VERMONT
89 Main Street, Drawer 20
Montpelier, Vermont 05620-3101
(802) 828-3420

VIRGINIA
1300 E. Main Street, 9th floor
Richmond, Virginia 23219
(804) 371-9051

VIRGIN ISLANDS
Corporations & Trade Names Division
Office of Lieutenant Governor
P.O. Box 450
St. Thomas, Virgin Islands 00801
(809) 774-2991

WASHINGTON
405 Black Lake Boulevard SW, 2nd floor
Olympia, Washington 98502
(206) 753-6928

WEST VIRGINIA
State Capitol Building
Room W-118
Charleston, West Virginia 25305
(304) 558-2257

WISCONSIN
Division of Securities
101 E. Wilson Street, 4th floor
Madison, Wisconsin 53703
(608) 266-3431

WYOMING
State Capitol Building
Cheyenne, Wyoming 82002-0020
(307) 777-7370

CANADIAN PROVINCIAL AGENCIES

The provincial and territorial agencies listed here have many of the same powers as state regulators in the United States. We have listed the two major finance and investment agencies in each province. The Consumer and Corporate Affairs Agencies and Departments regulate such areas as consumer protection, mortgages, insurance, credit, and securities, among other areas. The Finance Departments of each province run the financial affairs of government and collect taxes.

ALBERTA
Alberta Municipal Affairs, Consumer
  Services Division
22nd Floor, 10025 Jasper Avenue
Edmonton, Alberta T5J 3Z5
(403) 422-0199

Deputy Provincial Treasurer, Finance, and
  Revenue
443 Terrace Building
9515 107th Street
Edmonton, Alberta T5K 2C3
(403) 427-3076

BRITISH COLUMBIA
Ministry of Municipal Affairs and Housing
800 Johnson Street
Victoria, British Columbia V8V 1X4
(604) 387-3126

Ministry of Finance & Corporate Relations
617 Government Street
Victoria, British Columbia V8V 1X4
(604) 387-9286

MANITOBA
Consumer & Corporate Affairs Department
317 Legislative Building
Winnipeg, Manitoba R3C 0V8
(204) 945-4256

Manitoba Finance
109 Legislative Building
Winnipeg, Manitoba R3C OV8
(204) 945-3754

NEW BRUNSWICK
Consumer Affairs Branch
Department of Justice
P.O. Box 6000, Centennial Building
Fredericton, New Brunswick E3B 5H1
(506) 453-2719

Department of Finance
P.O. Box 6000, 607 King Street
Fredericton, New Brunswick E3B 5H1
(506) 453-2286

NEWFOUNDLAND
Department of Justice, Consumer Affairs
  Division
P.O. Box 8700
St. John's, Newfoundland A1B 4J6
(709) 729-2869

Department of Finance
P.O. Box 8700
St. John's, Newfoundland A1B 4J6
(709) 729-6297

NORTHWEST TERRITORIES
Department of Finance
P.O. Box 1320
Yellowknife, Northwest Territories X1A 2L9
(403) 873-7117

NOVA SCOTIA
Department of Business and Consumer
  Services
Maritime Center, 8 South
1505 Barrington Street
P.O. Box 1003
Halifax, Nova Scotia B3J 2X1
(902) 424-7777

Department of Finance
1723 Hollis Street
P.O. Box 187
Halifax, Nova Scotia B3J 2N3
(902) 424-5554

ONTARIO
Ministry of Consumer & Commercial
  Relations
250 Yonge Street, 35th floor
Toronto, Ontario M5B 2N5
(416) 326-8500

Ministry of Finance
Frost Building South, 7th floor
7 Queen's Park Crescent
Toronto, Ontario M7A 1Y7
(800) 263-7965

PRINCE EDWARD ISLAND
Department of Community Affairs &
  Attorney General
P.O. Box 2000
95 Rochford Street, 4th floor
Charlottetown, Prince Edward Island
  C1A 7N8
(902) 368-4580

Department of Provincial Treasury
95 Rochford Street, 2nd floor
P.O. Box 2000
Charlottetown, Prince Edward Island
  C1A 7N8
(902) 368-4053

QUEBEC
Ministère des Finances
12 rue St. Louis
Quebec, P.Q. G1R 5L3
(418) 691-2233

Ministère de la Protection du Consommateur
400 Bout Jean-Lesage, #450
Quebec, P.Q. G1K 8W4
(418) 643-1484

SASKATCHEWAN
Saskatchewan Justice, Consumer Protection
  Branch
1871 Smith Street
Regina, Saskatchewan S4P 3V7
(306) 787-5550

Saskatchewan Department of Finance
2350 Albert Street
Regina, Saskatchewan S4P 4A6
(306) 787-6768

YUKON TERRITORY
Department of Finance
P.O. Box 2703
Whitehorse, Yukon Territory Y1A 2C6
(403) 667-5343

FINANCE AND INVESTMENT ORGANIZATIONS

This is a list of the most important organizations in the finance and investment field. Included are trade associations, which educate the public about their industries and lobby for their political positions in Congress; self-regulatory organizations, which regulate the conduct of the marketplace under the supervision of a federal regulatory agency; and consumer and investor organizations, which educate consumers and investors and help them resolve problems.

American Arbitration Association
335 Madison Avenue, 10th floor
New York, New York 10013
(212) 484-4000
Sets the rules for arbitration proceedings and supplies arbitrators to resolve disputes.

American Association of Individual
  Investors
625 North Michigan Avenue
Chicago, Illinois 60611
(312) 280-0170
Educates individual investors about opportunities in stocks, bonds and mutual funds and investment computer software. Conducts seminars, workshops, offers home study courses and education on its web site (www.aaii.org).

American Bankers Association
1120 Connecticut Avenue, N.W.
Washington, D.C. 20036
(202) 663-5000
Represents commercial banks in legislative and regulatory activities and legal action. Also educates the public about banking.

American College of Trust & Estate
  Counsel
3415 S. Sepulveda Blvd., Suite 330
Los Angeles, California 90034

(310) 398-1888
Professional organization of trust and estate lawyers that provides written referrals upon request.

American Council of Life Insurance
1001 Pennsylvania Avenue, N.W.
5th Floor S.
Washington, D.C. 20004-2599
(202) 624-2000
Represents life insurance companies in lobbying on life insurance-related issues and educates the public about insurance.

American Financial Services Association
919 18th Street, N.W., Suite 300
Washington, D.C. 20006
(202) 296-5544
Represents companies that lend to consumers, mostly finance companies. Lobbies on issues related to consumer lending, and also educates the public about credit and budgeting issues.

American Institute of Certified Public
  Accountants
Harborside Financial Center
201 Plaza 3
Jersey City, New Jersey 07311-3881
(201) 938-3000   (800) 862-4272

Professional society of certified public accountants that establishes auditing and reporting standards and prepares the Uniform CPA Examination for state licensing bodies.

American Insurance Association
1130 Connecticut Avenue, N.W.,
Suite 1000
Washington, D.C. 20036
(202) 828-7100
Represents property and liability insurance companies in lobbying on insurance-related issues. Educates the public about safety issues and suggests codes to governments on such areas as industrial safety and fire prevention.

American League of Financial Institutions
900 19th Street, N.W., Suite 400
Washington, D.C. 20006
(202) 857-3176
Represents minority savings and loan associations. Provides counseling, consulting, and technical assistance to member associations.

American Management Association
International
1601 Broadway
New York, New York 10019
(212) 586-8100
Non-profit educational organization working to improve management skills in government and industry.

American Numismatic Association
818 N. Cascade Avenue
Colorado Springs, Colorado 80903-3279
(719) 632-2646   (800) 367-9723
Educates collectors of coins, paper money, and metals.

American Society of Chartered Life
Underwriters (CLU) and Chartered
Financial Consultants (ChFC)
270 S. Bryn Mawr Avenue
Bryn Mawr, Pennsylvania 19010-2194
(610) 526-2500
Professional society of chartered life underwriters specializing in life and health insurance, education funding, and estate planning. Chartered financial consultants provide overall financial planning.

Appraisers Association of America
60 East 42nd Street, Suite 2505
New York, New York 10165
(212) 867-9775
Professional association that sets standards for appraisers of personal property.

Associated Credit Bureaus
1090 Vermont Avenue N.W., Suite 200
Washington, D.C. 20005-4905
(202) 371-0910
Represents consumer credit bureaus, which maintain files on credit histories of individuals. Consumers can take complaints about a local credit bureau to the Associated Credit Bureaus for resolution.

Association for Investment Management
and Research
5 Boar's Head Lane
Charlottesville, Virginia 22903-0668
(804) 980-3668
Certifies and educates investment management professionals who are known as Chartered Financial Analysts once they are admitted to membership.

Association of Financial Guaranty Insurors
52 Vanderbilt Avenue, 21st Floor
New York, New York 10017
(212) 953-2550
Represents issuance companies that insure municipal bonds against default.

Association of Publicly Traded Companies
1200 19th Street, N.W., Suite 300
Washington, D.C. 20036
(202) 857-1114
Represents the interests of publicly traded companies on issues these companies have in common, such as securities law, corporate governance, and accounting.

Bank Administration Institute
1 N. Franklin Street, Suite 1000
Chicago, Illinois 60606
(312) 553-4600
Conducts research, sponsors developmental programs and serves as the banking industry's major resource in management, administrative, and technical specialties.

Bond Investors Association
P.O. Box 4427
6175 N.W. 153rd Street, Suite 221
Miami Lakes, Florida 33014
(305) 557-1832
A non-profit organization that educates and informs members and the general public about bonds and keeps statistics on defaulted bonds.

Bond Market Association
40 Broad Street, 12th Floor
New York, New York 10004-2373
(212) 809-7000

International trade association of banks and broker/dealers in U.S. government and federal agency securities, municipal securities, mortgage-backed securities and money-market securities.

Bond & Share Society
15 Dyatt Place
P.O. Box 4306
Hackensack, New Jersey 07602
(201) 529-4126
Society for promoting the hobby of scripopholy, that is, the collection and study of antique stock and bond certificates.

Canadian Securities Institute
33 Yonge Street, Suite 360
Toronto, Ontario M5E 1G4 Canada
(416) 364-9130
Provides education on investments to Canadian brokerage firms and the general public.

Certified Financial Planner Board of Standards
1700 Broadway, Suite 2100
Denver, Colorado 80290
(303) 830-7500   (888) 237-6275
Administers the Certified Financial Planner examinations and licenses individuals to use the CFP designation.

Chartered Property Casualty Underwriters (CPCU) Society
720 Providence Road
Malvern, Pennsylvania 19355-0709
(610) 644-2100   (800) 932-2728
Professional association of agents selling property and casualty insurance and risk management services.

Closed End Fund Association
P.O. Box 28037
Kansas City, Missouri 64188
(816) 413-8900
Represents closed end mutual funds to the public, providing education about the nature and benefits of closed end funds and investing in them.

College for Financial Planning
919 18th Street, N.W., Suite 300
Denver, Colorado 80237-3403
(303) 220-1200   (800) 553-5343
Provides mail-order educational material and administers tests for financial planners. A person passing the College's multi-part test becomes a certified financial planner, and is entitled to use the CFP designation.

Commercial Investment Real Estate Institute
430 North Michigan Avenue, Suite 600
Chicago, Illinois 60611
(312) 321-4460
Represents real estate brokers, developers, and mortgage bankers involved in commercial investment.

Consumer Bankers Association
1000 Wilson Boulevard, Suite 3012
Arlington, Virginia 22209
(703) 276-1750
Represents commercial banks, savings and loans, and credit unions and educates the public about banking.

Consumer Federation of America
1424 16th St. N.W.
Washington, D.C. 20036
(202) 387-6121
Organization representing consumer interests in several fields, including banking, insurance, and government regulation. CFA also educates consumers about how to make the most of their money.

Council of Better Business Bureaus
4200 Wilson Boulevard
Arlington, Virginia 22203
(703) 276-0100
Mediates disputes between consumers and businesses and promotes ethical business standards.

Council of Institutional Investors
1730 Rhode Island Avenue, N.W., Suite 512
Washington, D.C. 20036
(202) 822-0800
Represents trustees from public and union pension funds, non-profit foundations and endowment funds. Educates members about corporate actions and ways to boost returns on investments.

Credit Union National Association, Inc.
5710 Mineral Point Road
Madison, Wisconsin 53705
(608) 231-4000
Represents credit unions in lobbying on issues related to credit unions. Promotes credit union membership and the formation of new credit unions, and educates the public about credit unions.

Electronic Funds Transfer Association
950 Herndon Parkway, Suite 390
Herndon, Virginia 22070
(703) 435-9800

Provides a forum for financial institutions, retailers, telecommunications companies and other businesses involved in the transfer of funds by computer.

Employee Benefit Research Institute
2121 K Street, Suite 600
Washington, D.C. 20037
(202) 659-0670

A group of corporations, banks, insurance companies, unions and other organizations concerned with employee benefit programs.

ESOP Association
1726 M St., Suite 501
Washington, D.C. 20036
(202) 293-2971

Association of companies offering Employee Stock Ownership Plans that promotes wider use of these plans.

Financial Accounting Standards Board
401 Merritt 7
Norwalk, Connecticut 06856-5116
(203) 847-0700

Sets financial reporting standards for private-sector organizations. Its sister organization, the Governmental Accounting Standards Board, sets standards for state and local governments.

Financial Executives Institute
10 Madison Avenue
Morristown, New Jersey 07960
(973) 898-4600

Organization of senior financial corporate executives (such as controllers, treasurers, vice presidents of finance and chief financial officers).

Futures Industry Association
2001 Pennsylvania Avenue, N.W.,
   Suite 600
Washington, D.C. 20006
(202) 466-5460

Represents brokerage firms and brokers that deal in futures and options and lobbies on issues related to the futures industry.

Gold Institute/Silver Institute
1112 16th Street, N.W., Suite 240
Washington, D.C. 20036
(202) 835-0185

Represents gold/silver mining, refining, manufacturing and retailing firms, conducts research on technology and industrial uses. Compiles statistics on production, distribution and sales of gold and silver and lobbies on issues affecting the industries. Offers

variety of publications at nominal charge on metals, their uses, and investment vehicles.

Health Insurance Association of America
555 13th Street, N.W.
Suite 600 East
Washington, D.C. 20004
(202) 824-1600

Represents accident and health insurance companies in lobbying and educating the public about health insurance.

Independent Bankers Association of
   America
1 Thomas Circle, N.W., Suite 400
Washington, D.C. 20005
(202) 659-8111

Represents small- and medium-sized commercial banks in lobbying on banking issues. Provides its members with income-producing and cost-saving programs in areas such as credit cards, equipment purchasing, advertising, loan participations and insurance.

Industry Council For Tangible Assets
P.O. Box 11365
Severra Park, Maryland 2146-8365
(410) 626-7005

Monitors regulations and legislation concerning the precious metals and rare coin businesses.

Institute of Certified Financial Planners
3801 E. Florida Avenue, Suite 708
Denver, Colorado 80231-4397
(303) 759-4900   (800) 282-PLAN

Represents financial planners who have earned the CFP (Certified Financial Planner) designation. Provides continuing education for planners, and refers consumers who inquire about CFPs in their area.

Insurance Information Institute
110 William Street, 24th Floor
New York, New York 10038
(212) 669-9200   (800) 942-4242

Represents property and liability insurance companies. Maintains a consumer insurance hotline.

Insurance Institute of America
720 Providence Road
Malvern, Pennsylvania 19355-0716
(610) 644-2100

The educational arm of the American Institute for Chartered Property Casualty Underwriters.

Insurance Services Office
7 World Trade Center
New York, New York 10048
(212) 898-6000

Establishes rate guidelines for property and liability insurance companies.

International Association for Financial
  Planning
5775 Glenridge Drive N.W., Suite B300
Atlanta, Georgia 30328-5364
(404) 845-0011   (800) 945-4237

Represents those in the financial services industry who are involved with financial planning. Promotes education of financial planners and offers assistance to the public in finding planners in their area.

International Credit Association
243 North Lindbergh Boulevard
St. Louis, Missouri 63141
(314) 991-3030

Represents members of the credit industry. Conducts continuing education programs on credit issues.

International Franchise Association
1350 New York Avenue, N.W., Suite 900
Washington, D.C. 20005-4709
(202) 628-8000

Represents franchisors and franchisees of many different kinds of businesses by lobbying Congress on issues of concern to the industry. Gives advice to those wanting to evaluate franchise opportunities.

International Precious Metals Institute
4905 Tilghman Street, Suite 160
Allentown, Pennsylvania 18104
(215) 395-9700

Represents international producers and fabricators of platinum and platinum group metals.

Investment Company Institute
4201 H Street, N.W., Suite 1200
Washington, D.C. 20005
(202) 326-5800

Represents load and no-load mutual fund companies, open-end and closed-end funds and unit investment trusts. Lobbies on mutual fund issues in Congress and educates the public about the uses of mutual funds.

Investment Counsel Association of
  America
1050 17th Street, Suite 725
Washington, D.C. 20036
(202) 293-4222

Association of independent investment counsel firms that manage assets of individuals, pension plans, trusts and non-profits.

Investment Management Consultants
  Association
9101 E. Kenyon Avenue, Suite 3000
Denver, Colorado 80237-8015
(303) 770-3377

Represents consultants who find and supervise the performance of money managers on behalf of individual and institutional investors.

Investment Program Association
607 14th Street N.W., Suite 1000
Washington, D.C. 20005
(202) 775-9750

Trade association for limited partnerships, many of which are real estate partnerships sold by brokerage firms.

Investor Responsibility Research Center
1755 Massachusetts Avenue, N.W.,
  Suite 600
Washington, D.C. 20036
(202) 234-7500

Publishes impartial reports and analyses on contemporary business and public policy issues for corporations and institutional investors that vote proxies independently.

LIMRA International
300 Dayhill Road
Windsor, Connecticut 06095-4761
(860) 688-3358

Formerly known as the Life Insurance Marketing and Research Association, LIMRA conducts research, and operates seminars and schools for the life insurance industry.

Managed Futures Association
471 Emerson Street, Suite 200
Palo Alto, California 94301
(415) 325-4533

Represents and educates trading advisors, brokers, and individuals in the area of managed futures.

MicroComputer Investors Association
902 Anderson Drive
Fredricksburg, Virginia 22405
(540) 371-5474

Represents and educates professional investors who use personal computers. Also operates hardware and software library and compiles investing statistics.

Mortgage Bankers Association of America
125 15th Street, N.W.
Washington, D.C. 20005-2766
(202) 861-6500

Represents mortgage lenders such as mortgage bankers, commercial banks, savings and loans and insurance companies. The MBAA lobbies on housing finance issues before Congress and conducts continuing education seminars for members of the industry.

Municipal Securities Rulemaking Board
1818 N Street, N.W., Suite 800
Washington, D.C. 20036
(202) 223-9347

A self-regulatory agency for brokers and dealers in the municipal securities industry.

Mutual Fund Education Alliance
100 N.W. Englewood Road, Suite 130
Kansas City, Missouri 64118
(816) 454-9422

Represents mostly no-load mutual funds and provides information to consumers on the name, telephone number and kinds of funds available.

National Association of Business
   Economists
1233 20th Street, N.W., Suite 505
Washington, D.C. 20036
(202) 463-6223

Society composed of corporate and governmental economists and those with an active interest in applied, practical economics.

National Association of Investment
   Companies
111 14th Street, N.W., Suite 700
Washington, D.C. 20005
(202) 289-4336

Provides technical assistance and monitors legislation for investment companies supplying capital to minority-owned businesses.

National Association of Investors
   Corporation
711 West Thirteen Mile Road
Madison Heights, Michigan 48071
(801) 583-6242

Represents investment clubs. Helps people set up such clubs, and monitors performance of the clubs.

National Association of Life Underwriters
1922 F Street, N.W.
Washington, D.C. 20006-4387
(202) 331-6000

Association of health and life insurance agents and brokers. Educates the public on how to work with insurance agents and brokers.

National Association of Manufacturers
1331 Pennsylvania Avenue, N.W.
Washington, D.C. 20004
(202) 637-3000

Represents industry views to government on national and international issues. Also reviews legislation, administrative rulings, and judicial decisions affecting industry.

National Association of Personal Financial
   Advisors
355 West Dundee Road, Suite 107
Buffalo Grove, Illinois 60089
(847) 537-7722   (800) 366-2732

Represents financial planners who work for a consulting fee only, and do not take commissions for selling products.

National Association of Real Estate
   Investment Trusts
1129 20th Street, N.W., Suite 305
Washington, D.C. 20036
(202) 785-8717

Represents real estate investment trusts before Congress in lobbying on REIT-related issues, and educates the public about REITs.

National Association of Realtors
430 North Michigan Avenue
Chicago, Illinois 60611-4087
(312) 329-8200

Trade group representing real estate agents.

National Association of Securities Dealers,
   Inc.
1735 K Street, N.W.
Washington, D.C. 20006
(202) 728-8000

Organization created in 1939 by amendments to the Securities Exchange Act of 1934. NASD is the largest securities industry self-regulatory organization (SRO) in the United States. It operates subject to the oversight of the Securities and Exchange Commission. NASD is responsible for the regulation of the Nasdaq Stock Market Inc. as well as the products traded on it. Through its subsidiaries, the Nasdaq Stock Market and NASD Regulation Inc., NASD designs, operates, and regulates securities markets, develops rules and regulations, provides a dispute resolution forum and conducts regulatory reviews of member activities, all for the benefit and protection of the investor.

National Association of Small Business
Investment Companies
1199 N. Fairfax Street, Suite 200
Alexandria, Virginia 22314-1437
(703) 683-1601

Represents small business investment companies (SBICs) that are publicly traded or private companies that invest in private small businesses. The Association lobbies Congress on issues related to the industry and educates the public about SBICs.

National Association of Women Business
Owners
1100 Wayne Avenue, Suite 830
Silver Spring, Maryland 20910
(301) 608-2590   (800) 556-2926

Provides technical assistance, management training, and business and economic information to women business owners through national meetings and local chapters, and represents members in legislative and lobbying efforts.

National Foundation for Consumer Credit
8611 2nd Avenue, Suite 100
Silver Spring, Maryland 20910
(301) 589-5600   (800) 388-2227

Aids consumers who have taken on too much debt. Helps consumers restructure their debt through local consumer credit counseling service centers throughout the United States.

National Futures Association
200 West Madison Street, Suite 1600
Chicago, Illinois 60606
(312) 781-1300

Represents firms that trade futures and options. Resolves disputes between its members and customers with complaints against those members.

National Investor Relations Institute
8045 Leesburg Pike, Suite 600
Vienna, Virginia 22182
(703) 506-3570

Represents executives in the investor relations and financial communications fields. Conducts continuing education programs for members.

National Venture Capital Association
1655 North Fort Meyer Drive, Suite 850
Arlington, Virginia 22209
(703) 524-2549

Represents venture capitalists seeking to invest money in growing enterprises. Lobbies in Congress for programs to improve the environment for venture capital investing.

New York Society of Security Analysts
One World Trade Center, Suite 4447
New York, New York 10048
(212) 912-9249

Affiliate of the Financial Analysts Federation which conducts regular meetings between securities analysts and managements of companies followed by those analysts. This is the largest society in the country, though there are similar societies in most major American cities as well.

North American Securities Administrators
Association
10 G Street, N.E. Suite 710
Washington, D.C. 20002
(202) 737-0900

Represents the securities regulators of the United States, the District of Columbia, Puerto Rico, Canada, and Mexico. Provides grass-roots investor protection and efficient capital formation and enforces "blue sky" laws in the sale of securities.

100% No-Load Mutual Fund Council
1346 S. Third Street
Louisville, Kentucky 40208
(502) 636-5282

Represents mutual funds that charge no sales commissions of any type.

Options Industry Council
440 S. LaSalle St., Suite 2400
Chicago, Illinois 60605
(800) 566-9642

The Council provides educational material to investors interested in trading options.

Overseas Private Investment Corporation
1100 New York Avenue, N.W.
Washington, D.C. 20527
(202) 336-8404

Supports and assists qualified U.S. investors in private ventures in less developed countries.

Pension Rights Center
918 16th St. N.W., Suite 704
Washington, D.C. 20006
(202) 296-3778

Educates the public about pension issues. Offers a legal referral service for pension-related problems.

Platinum Guild International
150 E. 58th St., 25th floor
New York, NY 10155
(212) 758-6767

Represents producers and marketers of platinum and palladium and informs investors about investing in these metals.

Professional Numismatists Guild
3950 Concordia Lane
Fallbrook, California 92028
(760) 728-1300

Organization of professional coin dealers. The Guild offers binding arbitration services for consumer disputes with coin dealers.

Profit-Sharing/401(k) Council of America
10 S. Riverside, Suite 1610
Chicago, Illinois 60606
(312) 441-8550

Devoted to explaining and promoting the use of profit-sharing and 401(k) plans.

Savings & Community Bankers of
America
900 19th Street N.W., Suite 400
Washington, D.C. 20006
(202) 857-3100

Trade association for savings banks and savings and loans. The group educates the public about the role of savings and loans in the American financial system, and lobbies the government on issues of concern to the thrift industry.

Securities Industry Association
120 Broadway
New York, New York 10271
(212) 608-1500

Represents securities broker/dealers, underwriters, and investment bankers in lobbying Congress on issues of concern to the securities industry. Educates the public about the securities industry.

United States Chamber of Commerce
1615 H Street, N.W.
Washington, D.C. 20062
(202) 659-6000

Represents the business community's views on business, the economy, and other issues at the federal, state and local level. Sponsors educational programs and maintains a business forecast and survey center.

World Gold Council
900 Third Avenue, 26th floor
New York, New York 10022
(212) 688-0005

Represents gold-mining companies and offers investors information about investing in gold.

FINANCE AND INVESTMENT PUBLICATIONS

The following is a list of the major publications that can help keep you informed about the fast-changing world of finance and investment. The list encompasses the full spectrum of publications, from mass circulation business magazines to investment newsletters that reach only a handful of subscribers. The publications also cover a wide variety of topics, from investment advice about stocks, bonds, futures, options, money market instruments, and commodities to mutual funds, taxation, entrepreneurship, and corporate finance. Other subjects covered include international investing, banking, precious metals, collectibles, management trends, economic forecasting, socially conscious investing, estate planning, venture capital, insider trading, and real estate. The title of each newsletter will often give you a clue to its subject matter.

Almost all the publications are available for a subscription charge; some also require that you join the organization that puts out the publication. Many will send you a sample either free or for a nominal charge.

Before subscribing to a newsletter or magazine, you must assess your needs and level of sophistication. Some letters listed here are designed for the novice investor with a relatively small amount of money to put into stocks or mutual funds. Other publications are aimed at a highly sophisticated audience that is knowledgeable about technical analysis, commodity trading, or some other specialty. In general, the more complex the publication, the higher the subscription fee.

Whichever publications you read, employ an appropriate amount of caution before following specific investment recommendations. Despite many advisors' claims, no one calls every move in the complex financial markets right every time. You should be satisfied if you find a few letters that offer a style you are comfortable with and have a good long-term track record at spotting unfolding investment trends.

AAII Journal
Computerized Investing
Individual Investor
Quarterly Low Load Mutual Fund Update
625 North Michigan Avenue, Suite 1900
Chicago, Illinois 60611
(312) 280-0170   (800) 428-2244

Addison Report, The
P.O. Box 402
Franklin, Massachusetts 02038
(508) 528-8678

Aden Forecast, The
P.O. Box 68710
St. Louis, Missouri 63166-9526
(888) ADE-NMKT   (888) 233-6658

Adrian Day's Investment Analyst
1217 Saint Paul Street
Baltimore, Maryland 21202
(800) 433-1528

AgBiotech Stock Letter
P.O. Box 40460
Berkeley, California 94704
(510) 843-1842

Agora Inc. Publications:
Adrian Day's Investment Analyst
Bob Czechin's World Investor
Crisis Investing
Insightful Investor
Investing with Barry Ziskin
Scientific Investment
Strategic Investment
Taipan
Tax Wise Money
Agora Inc.
824 E. Baltimore Street
Baltimore, Maryland 21202
(800) 433-1528

Alan Shawn Feinstein Insiders Report
37-41 Alhambra Circle
Cranston, Rhode Island 02905
(401) 467-5155

All Star Funds
P.O. Box 203427
Austin, Texas 78720-3427
(800) 299-4223

American Banker Bond Buyer Publications:
American Banker
American Banker Online
American Banker CD-ROM
FutureBanker Magazine
Turning Points
American Banker/Bond Buyer Reference
  Books:
Consumer Survey

Mergers & Acquisitions Yearbook
Ranking the Banks
Small Business Banking Survey
Strategic Technology Investment Report
American Banker/Bond Buyer
One State Street Plaza
New York, New York 10004
(212) 803-8200

American Stock Exchange Publications:
Amex Story, The
Directory of Exchange Listed Options
Increasing Your Income with Options
Invest Wisely
New on the Amex
Protecting Your Investments with
  Options
Shareholder's Glossary, The
Stock Market Specialist Game
Taxes & Investing
Understanding Stock Options
Weekly Bulletin
American Stock Exchange
86 Trinity Place
New York, New York 10006
(800) AMEX-LIT   (800) THE-AMEX
                  (for derivatives)

Analyst Watch
155 N. Wacker Drive
Chicago, Illinois 60606-4301
(800) 399-6659

Annuity and Life Insurance Shopper
8 Talmadge Road
Monroe Township, New Jersey 08831
(908) 521-5110   (800) 872-6684

Banking Safety Digest, The
Veribanc
P.O. Box 461
Wakefield, Massachusetts 01880
(617) 245-8370   (800) 442-2657

Bankruptcy Data Source, The
Troubled Company Prospector (fax)
Turnaround Letter, The
225 Friend Street, Suite 801
Boston, Massachusetts 02114
(617) 573-9550 (800) 468-3810

Barron's National Business and Financial
  Weekly
200 Liberty Street
New York 10281
(212) 416-2700

Baxter Bulletin
1030 East Putnam Avenue
Greenwich, Connecticut 06836
(203) 637-4559

BCA (Bank Credit Analyst) Publications:
Credit Analyst, The
China Analyst, The
Emerging Markets Analyst, The
Interest Rate Forecast, The
International Bank Credit Analyst, The
3463 Peel Street
Montreal, Quebec H3A 1W7
(514) 398-0653

Beating the Dow
P.O. Box 2069
Riverdale, New Jersey 07675
(800) 477-3400

Better Investing
NAIC
711 West 13 Mile Road
Madison Heights, Michigan 48071
(810) 583-6242

B.I. Research
P.O. Box 133
Redding, Connecticut 06875
(203) 270-9244

Bloomberg Personal Finance Magazine
P.O. Box 888
Princeton, New Jersey 08542-0888
(609) 279-3000   (888) 432-5820

Blue Chip Investor
575 Antone Boulevard, Suite 570
Costa Mesa, California 92626
(714) 641-3579

Boardroom Reports
Bottom Line Personal
Personal Advantage Financial
Boardroom Classics
330 West 42nd Street
New York, New York 10036
(212) 239-9000   (201) 379-4642

Bob Brinker's Marketimer
P.O. Box 7005
Princeton, New Jersey 08543
(908) 359-8838

Bob Nurock's Advisory
P.O. Box 460
Santa Fe, New Mexico 87504-0460
(800) 227-8883

Bond Fund Advisor, The
IBC Financial Data
290 Eliot Street
P.O. Box 9104
Ashland, Massachusetts 01721-9104
(508) 881-2800   (800) 343-5413

Bowser Directory of Small Stocks
Bowser Report
Bowser Warrant Register
P.O. Box 6278
Newport News, Virginia 23606
(804) 877-5979

Bullish Review of Commodity Futures
  Markets
14600 Blaine Avenue
East Rosemount, Minnesota 55068
(612) 423-4949

Business Week Magazine
McGraw-Hill, Inc.
1221 Avenue of the Americas
New York, New York 10020
(212) 512-2000

Cabot's Mutual Fund Navigator
Cabot's Market Letter
P.O. Box 3067
176 North Street
Salem, Massachusetts 01970
(508) 745-5532   (800) 777-2658

California Technology Stock Letter
P.O. Box 308
Half Moon Bay, California 94019
(415) 726-8495

Candlelight
MBH Weekly Commodity Letter
MBH Commodities
P.O. Box 353
Winnetka, Illinois 60093
(847) 291-1870   (800) 678-5253

CardTrak
RAM Research Corporation
P.O. Box 1700
Frederick, Maryland 21702
(301) 695-4660   (800) 344-7714

CCH Incorporated Publications:
Business Strategies Bulletin
  (newsletter)
Capital Changes Reports
Congressional Index
Consumer Credit Guide
Estate Planning Review
Financial and Estate Planning
Guide to Computer Law
Individual Retirement Plans Guide
Mutual Funds Guide
CCH Incorporated
4025 West Peterson Avenue
Chicago, Illinois 60646
(800) TELL-CCH
(800) 835-5224

CDA/Spectrum Research:
CDA Mutual Fund Report
CDA/Spectrum Convertibles
CDA/Spectrum International:
Directory of Buy-Side Traders
Five Percent Owner Portfolios
Five Percent Stock Holdings
Insider Holdings
Institutional Portfolios
Investment Company Portfolios
Investment Company Stock Holdings
Stock Holdings
13(f) Institutional Portfolios
13(f) Institutional Stock Holdings
CDA Investment Technologies, Inc.
1355 Piccard Drive
Rockville, Maryland 20850
(800) 232-6362

Certified Coin Dealer
Coin Dealer Newsletter
Currency Dealer Newsletter
CDN Publications Inc.
P.O. Box 7939
Torrance, California 90504
(310) 515-7369

CFP Today
The Institute of Certified Financial
   Planners
7600 East Eastman Avenue, Suite 301
Denver, Colorado 80231-4397
(303) 751-7600

Chartcraft Publications:
Annual Long Term P&F Chartbook
Bi-Monthly Over-the-Counter P&F
   Chartbook
Bi-Weekly Investors Intelligence
Bi-Weekly Technical Indicator
Charcraft by Fax
Monthly P&F Chartbook on NYSE/ASE
Quarterly Mutual Funds P&F Chartbook
Quarterly Options P&F Chartbook
Quarterly Options Chartbook
Weekly ASE-OTC Breakout Service
Weekly Breakout Service
Weekly Futures Service
Weekly Mutual Funds Breakouts
Weekly Options Service
Weekly Service on NYSE/ASE
Chartcraft, Inc.
30 Church Street/P.O. Box 2046
New Rochelle, New York 10801
(914) 632-0422

Chartist, The
Chartist Mutual Fund Timer, The
P.O. Box 758
Seal Beach, California 90740
(310) 596-2385

Cheap Investor, The
Mathews and Associates
2549 West Golf Road, Suite 350
Hoffman Estates, Illinois 60194
(847) 697-5666

Clean Yield, The
Garvin Hill Road
P.O. Box 117
Greensboro, Vermont 05841
(802) 533-7178

Closed-End Country Fund Report
725 15th Street, N.W., Suite 501
Washington, D.C. 20005
(202) 783-7051

Closed End Fund Digest and Real Estate
   Securities
C.E.F.D. Inc.
415 Chapala Street, Suite 206
Santa Barbara, California 93109
(805) 884-1150

CMI Stock and Index Options Trader
P.O. Box 3289
Newport Beach, California 92659
(714) 851-9079

COINage Magazine
James Miller Publications
4880 Market Street
Ventura, California 93003
(805) 644-3824

Coin World
911 Vandemark Road
Sidney, Ohio 45365
(513) 498-0800

Commodex
Commodity Futures Forecast
Commodex
The Mall at the Galaxy
7000 Boulevard East
Guttenberg, New Jersey 07093
(201) 868-2600   (800) 336-1818

Commodity Closeup
Oster Communications
P.O. Box 6, 219 Parkade
Cedar Falls, Iowa 50613
(319) 277-1271   (800) 635-3936

Commodity Traders Consumer Report
P.O. Box 7603, FDR Station
New York, New York 10150-7603
(800) 832-6065

Comparative Annuity Reports
P.O. Box 1268
Fair Oaks, California 95628
(916) 487-7863

Complete Strategist, The
Wall Street On-Line Publishing Co.,
  Inc.
P.O. Box 6
Riverdale, New York 10471
(718) 884-5408

Contrarian's View, The
132 Moreland Street
Worcester, Massachusetts 01609
(508) 757-2881

Contrary Investor
Contrary Investor Follow-up
Fraser Opinion Letter
Fraser Management Associates,
  Inc.
P.O. Box 494
Burlington, Vermont 05402
(802) 658-0322

Crain Communications Publications:
Advertising Age
AutoWeek
Automotive News
Business Insurance
Business Marketing
Crain's Chicago Business
Crain's Cleveland Business
Crain's Detroit Business
Crain's New York Business
Electronic Media
Franchise Buyer
Modern Healthcare
Pensions & Investments
RCR Radio Communications Report
Crain Communications Inc.
740 Rush Street
Chicago, Illinois 60611-2590
(312) 649-5200

Crawford Perspectives
1382 Third Avenue, Suite 403
New York, New York 10021-0403
(212) 744-6973

CRB Commodity Yearbook
CRB Futures Perspective
Commodity Index Report
Futures Market Service
Bridge/CRB
30 S. Wacker Drive, Suite 1810
Chicago, Illinois 60606
(800) 621-5271

Creative Real Estate Magazine
Drawer L
Rancho Santa Fe, California 92067
(619) 756-1441

Czeschin's Mutual Fund Outlook &
  Recommendations
P.O. Box 1423
Baltimore, Maryland 21203-1423
(410) 235-0983

Daily Trader, The
Investment Research Institute
P.O. Box 46709
Cincinnati, Ohio 45246
(800) 448-2080

Danbell Energy Alert
Danbell Energy Letter
Daniells & Bell
99 Wall Street
New York, New York 10005
(212) 422-1710   (800) 427-9446

Defaulted Bonds Newsletter
Income Securities Advisor
Bond Investors Association
P.O. Box 4427
Miami Lakes, Florida 33014
(305) 557-1832

Deliberations: The Ian McAvity Market
  Letter
P.O. Box, Adelaide Street Station
Toronto, Ontario M5C 2J1, Canada
(416) 867-1100

John Dessauer's Investor's World: Your
  Passport to Profits
7811 Montrose Road
Potomac, Maryland 20854
(301) 424-3700

Dick Davis Digest
Dick Davis Publishing
P.O. Box 350630
Fort Lauderdale, Florida 33335-0630
(800) 654-1514

Dick Young's Intelligence Report
Young Research & Publishing, Inc.
98 William Street
Newport, Rhode Island 02840
(401) 849-2131

Digest for Financial Planning
College for Financial Planning
4095 S. Monaco Street
Denver, Colorado 80237-3403
(303) 220-1200

Dines Letter, The
P.O. Box 22
Belvedere, California 94920
(800) 84LUCKY   (800) 845-8259

Directory of Mutual Funds
Investment Company Institute
1401 H Street, N.W., Suite 1200
Washington D.C. 20005-2148
(202) 326-5800

Donoghue's Wealth Letter
Money Market Square East
P.O. Box 309
Milford, Massachusetts 01757
(800) 982-2455

Dow Theory Forecasts
7412 Calumet Avenue
Hammond, Indiana 46324
(219) 931-6480

Dow Theory Letters
P.O. Box 1759
La Jolla, California 92038
(619) 454-0481

Dunn & Hargitt Commodity Service
P.O. Box 1100
22 North Second Street
Lafayette, Indiana 47902
(317) 423-2624   (800) 922-7289

Economist, The
111 West 57th Street
New York, New York 10019
(212) 541-5730

Elderlaw News
Ampersand Solutions
40 Beerborn Street
Newton, Massachusetts 02165
(617) 951-4550

Elliott Wave Theorist
P.O. Box 1618
Gainesville, Georgia 30503
(404) 563-0309

Emerging and Special Situations
Standard & Poor's Corp.
25 Broadway
New York, New York 10004
(212) 208-8000   (800) 852-1641

Equities Special Situations
160 Madison Avenue, 3rd Floor
New York, New York 10016
(212) 213-1300   (800) 237-8400

Equity Fund Outlook
P.O. Box 76
Boston, Massachusetts 02117
(617) 397-6844

Estates, Gifts and Trusts Journal
Tax Management, Inc.
Bureau of National Affairs
1250 23rd Street, N.W.
Washington, D.C. 20037
(202) 833-7261

Fabians Investment Resources
2100 Main Street, Suite 300
Huntington Beach, California 92648
(800) 950-8765

Family Money
Meredith Corproation
1716 Locust Street
Des Moines, Iowa 50309-3023
(515) 284-3450   (800) 642-9607

Fidelity Insight
Mutual Fund Investors Association
20 William Street
P.O. Box 9135
Wellesley Hills, Massachusetts 02180
(800) 444-6342

Fidelity Monitor
P.O. Box 1270
Rocklin, California 95677
(800) 397-3094

Financial Executive Magazine
Financial Executives Institute
P.O. Box 1938, 10 Madison Avenue
Morristown, New Jersey 07962-1938
(973) 898-4600

Financial Freedom Report Quarterly
2450 Fort Union Boulevard
Salt Lake City, Utah 84121
(801) 272-3500   (800) 289-9715

Financial Planning Magazine
Securities Data Publishing
40 West 57th Street, Suite 114
New York, New York 10019
(212) 765-5311

The Financial Post Datagroup
    Publications:
Annual Dividend Record
Canadian Bond Prices (annual)
Canadian Markets (book/CD-ROM)
Complete Dividend Service
Corporate Bond Record (annual)
Corporate Surveys: Industrial/Mines &
    Energy Resources/Predecessor &
    Defunct Companies
Data Speed
Directory of Directors

Financial Post Investment Reports, The
Government Bond Record (annual)
Mastering Management
Monthly Dividend Service
Preferred Shares & Warrants (annual)
Record of New Issues
   (weekly/monthly/quarterly, annual)
Survey of Mutual Funds
The Financial Post Datagroup
333 King Street East
Toronto, Ontario M5A 4N2, Canada
(416) 350-6500

Financial Rates Inc. Publications:
100 Highest Yields
Bank Advertising News
Bank Rate Monitor
Best Ads of the Month
Jumbo Flash Report
Financial Rates Inc.
P.O. Box 088888
North Palm Beach, Florida 33408
(407) 627-7330   (800) 327-7717

Financial Times
14 East 60th Street
New York, New York 10022
(212) 752-4500

Financial World
1328 Broadway
New York, New York 10001
(212) 594-5030

Forbes Magazine
60 Fifth Avenue
New York, New York 10011
(212) 620-2200   (800) 888-9896

Ford Value Report
11722 Sorrento Valley Road, Suite "I"
San Diego, California 92121
(619) 755-1327

Forecaster, The
Forecaster Publishing Company
19623 Ventura Boulevard
Tarzana, California 91356
(818) 345-4421

Fortune Magazine
1271 Avenue of the Americas
New York, New York 10020
(212) 522-1212   (800) 541-1000

Fund Exchange
1200 Westlake Avenue North,
   Suite 700
Seattle, Washington 98109
(800) 423-4893

Fund Kinetics
2841 23rd Avenue West
Seattle, Washington 98199
(800) 634-6790

Fundline
P.O. Box 663
Woodland Hills, California 91365
(818) 346-5637

Fund Profit Alert
P.O. Box 46709
Cincinnati, Ohio 45246
(513) 589-3800

Futures Hotline/Mutual Funds Timer
P.O. Box 6275
Jacksonville, Florida 32236
(904) 693-0355

Futures Industry
Futures Industry Association
2001 Pennsylvania Avenue N.W.,
   Suite 600
Washington D.C. 20006
(202) 466-5460

Futures Magazine
219 Parkade
P.O. Box 6
Cedar Falls, Iowa 50613
(319) 277-6341   (800) 635-3936

FXC Newsletter, The
FXC Investors Corporation
62-19 Cooper Avenue
Glendale, New York 11385
(718) 417-1330

Gann Angles
495 Trinity Avenue, Suite A
Seaside, California 93955
(408) 393-2000

Garzarelli Outlook
7811 Montrose Road
Potomac, Maryland 20854
(800) 804-0939

Georgeson Report
Georgeson & Company Inc.
Wall Street Plaza/88 Pine Street
New York, New York 10005
(212) 440-9800   (800) 445-1790

Ken Gerbino's Smart Investing
Phillips Publishing
7811 Montrose Road
Potomac, Maryland 20854
(301) 340-2100   (800) 777-5015

Gold Monitor
M. Murenbeeld & Associates
P.O. Box 6187
Victoria, British Columbia V8P 5L5,
  Canada
(604) 477-7579

Gold News
Gold Facts
Silver Facts
Silver News
U.S. Gold Industry, The (annual)
World Silver Survey (annual)
*Your Introduction to Investing in
  Gold*
*Your Introduction to Investing in
  Silver*
The Gold Institute/The Silver Institute
1112 16th Street N.W., Suite 240
Washington D.C. 20036
(202) 835-0185

Gold Newsletter
Jefferson Financial
2400 Jefferson Highway, Suite 600
Jefferson, Louisiana 70121
(800) 877-8847

Good Money
Netback
Good Money Publications
P.O. Box 363
Worcester, Vermont 05682
(802) 223-8911   (800) 535-3551

Grants Interest Rate Observer
30 Wall Street, 6th Floor
New York, New York 10005-2201
(212) 809-7994

Granville Market Letter, The
P.O. Drawer 413006
Kansas City, Missouri 64141
(816) 474-5353

Graphic Fund Forecaster
6 Pioneer Circle
P.O. Box 673
Andover, Massachusetts 01810
(508) 470-3511

Growth Fund Guide
P.O. Box 6600
Rapid City, South Dakota 57709
(605) 341-1971

Growth Stock Outlook
4405 E. West Highway, Suite 305
Bethesda, Maryland 20814
(301) 654-5205

Harmonic Research
50 Fifth Avenue, 5th Floor
New York, New York 10019
(212) 484-2065

Hirsch Publications:
Beating the Dow
Ground Floor
Mutual Fund Digest
Smart Money
Stock Trader's Almanac
Turov on Timing
The Hirsch Organization
184 Central Avenue
Old Tappan, New Jersey 07675
(201) 767-4100   (800) 477-3400

Hulbert Financial Digest
316 Commerce Street
Alexandria, Virginia 22314
(703) 683-5905

Hussman Econometrics
34119 Twelve Mile Road, Suite 350
Farmington Hills, Michigan 48331
(248) 553-8383

IBC's Money Fund Report
IBC USA Inc.
290 Eliot Street
Ashland, Massachusetts 01721-9104
(508) 881-2800   (800) 343-5413

In Business
JG Press
419 State Avenue
Emmaus, Pennsylvania 18049
(215) 967-4135

Inc. Magazine
488 Madison Avenue
New York, New York 10022
(212) 326-2600

*Individual Investor Special Situations
  Report*
38 E. 29th Street, 4th Floor
New York, New York 10016
(212) 689-2777

Industries in Transition
Business Communication Co.
25 Van Zant Street, Suite 13
Norwalk, Connecticut 06855
(203) 853-4266

Industry Forecast
Levy Economic Forecasts
P.O. Box 26
Chappaqua, New York 10514
(914) 238-3665

Insight: Investing for a Better World
Insight: The Advisory Letter for Concerned
  Investors
Franklin Research and Development
  Corp.
711 Atlantic Avenue
Boston, Massachusetts 02111
(617) 423-6655   (800) 548-5684

Institute for Econometric Research
  Publications:
Fidelity Forecaster
Hot Funds
Income Fund Outlook
Investors Digest
Market Logic
Mutual Fund Buyer's Guide
Mutual Fund Forecaster
Mutual Funds Magazine
New Issues
The Institute for Econometric
  Research
2200 Southwest 10th Street
Deerfield Beach, Florida 33442
(954) 421-1000   (800) 442-9000

Institutional Investor, Inc. Publications:
Bank Accounting and Finance
Bank Letter
Bond Week
Commercial Lending Review
Corporate Finance
Defined Contribution News
Derivatives Week
Emerging Markets Week
Euromoney Magazine
Euroweek
Fund Action
Global Investor
Global Money Management
Institutional Investor Magazine
International Bond Investor
Journal of Fixed Income, The
Journal of Investing, The
Journal of Private Porfolio Management,
  The
Journal of Portfolio Management,
  The
Money Management Letter
Private Asset Management
Portfolio Letter
Wall Street Letter
Institutional Investor, Inc.
488 Madison Avenue
New York, New York 10022
(212) 224-3570   (800) 437-9997

Insurance Forum
P.O. Box 245
Ellettsville, Indiana 47429
(812) 876-6502

Interactive Multimedia Communications
21st Century Research
8200 Boulevard East
North Bergen, New Jersey 07047
(201) 868-0881

Intermarket Review, The
International Institute for Economic
  Research Inc.
P.O. Box 624
Gloucester, Virginia 23061
(804) 694-0415   (800) 221-7514

International Bank Credit Analyst
BCA Publications
1002 Sherbrooke Street West, Suite 1600
Montreal, Quebec, H3A 3L6 Canada
(514) 499-9550

International Harry Schultz Letter
FERC
P.O. Box 622
CH-1001
Lausanne, Switzerland

InvesTech Market Analyst
InvesTech Mutual Fund Advisor
2472 Birch Glen
Whitefish, Montana 59937
(406) 862-7777   (800) 955-8500

Investment Advisor Magazine
Realty Stock Review
Dow Jones Financial Publishing
  Company
170 Avenue at the Commons
Shrewsbury, New Jersey 07702
(732) 389-8700

Investment Blue Book, The
Investment and Tax Shelter Blue Book
Securities Investigations, Inc.
P.O. Box 888
Woodstock, New York 12498
(914) 679-2300

Investment Quality Trends
7440 Girard Avenue, Suite 4
La Jolla, California 92037
(619) 459-3818

Investment Reporter, The
133 Richmond Street West, Suite 700
Toronto, Ontario, Canada M5H 3M8
(416) 869-1177

Investment Strategy Letter, The
Birkelback Management Corp.
208 South La Salle Street, Suite 1700
Chicago, Illinois 60604
(312) 853-2820   (800) 458-2358

Investor News
Kemper Securities, Inc.
1300 North Point Tower
1001 Lakeside Avenue
Cleveland, Ohio 44114
(216) 574-7300

Investor Relations Update
National Investor Relations Institute
2000 L Street, N.W., Suite 701
Washington D.C. 20036
(202) 861-0630

Investors Business Daily
12655 Beatrice Street
Los Angeles, California 90066
(310) 448-6000   (800) 831-2525

Investors Guide to Closed-End Funds
Thomas J. Herzfeld Advisors
P.O. Box 161465
Miami, Florida 33116
(305) 271-1900

Investors Hotline
Valuetrac
10616 Beaver Dam Road, Suite S-6
Hunt Valley, Maryland 21030
(410) 771-0064   (800) 345-8112

Investors Intelligence
P.O. Box 2046
30 Church Street
New Rochelle, New York 10801
(914) 632-0422

Investor, U.S.A.
Seahorse Financial Advisers
15 Seatuck Lane, P.O. Box 370
Remsenburg, New York 11960
(516) 423-1118

*Jay Schabacker's Mutual Fund
   Investing*
Phillips Publishing
7811 Montrose Road
Potomac, Maryland 20854
(301) 340-2100   (800) 777-5005

John Bollinger's Capital Growth Letter
Group Power
Bollinger Capital Management
P.O. Box 3358
Manhattan Beach, California 90266
(310) 798-8855   (800) 888-8400

*John T. Reed's Real Estate Investors
   Monthly*
342 Bryan Drive
Danville, California 94526
(510) 820-6292   (800) 635-5425

Journal of Financial Planning, The
Institute of Certified Financial Planners
7600 East Eastman Avenue, Suite 301
Denver, Colorado 80231
(303) 759-4900

Journal of Futures Markets
John Wiley & Sons, Inc.
605 Third Avenue
New York, New York 10158-0012
(212) 850-6000

Jumbo Rate News
Rate Watch
Bauer Communications
P.O. Drawer 145510
Coral Gables, Florida 33114-5510
(305) 441-2062   (800) 388-6686

Kagan World Media Ltd. Publications:
Broadcast Banker/Broker
Broadcast Investor
B-Stats
*Business of Movie Production &
   Distribution, The*
Cable Network Investor
Cable TV Advertising
Cable TV Finance
Cable TV Financial Databook, The
Cable TV Investor
Cable TV Law Reporter
Cable TV Programming
Cable TV Regulation
Cable TV Technology
Consumer Media Tech
DBS Report, The
Digital Television
Economics of Basic Cable Networks, The
Interactive Multimedia Investor
Interactive Television
Kagan Box Office Report, The
Kagan Media Index, The
Kagan's MediaCast 2006
Media Mergers and Acquisitions
Media Sports Business
Motion Picture Investor
Newspaper Investor
Pay TV Newsletter, The
Private Cable Investor
State of Home Video, The
TV Program Investor
TV Program Stats
Video Investor
Wireless Cable Investor
Wireless Data & Messaging
Wireless Market Stats
Wireless Telecom Investor
Paul Kagan Associates
126 Clock Tower Place
Carmel, California 93923-8734
(408) 624-1536

KCI Communications Publications:
Big Picture, The
Global Investing
Personal Finance Letter
Special Alert Bulletin
Utilities Forecaster
Wall Street Bargains
Winning with Options
KCI Communications
1101 King Street, Suite 400
Alexandria, Virginia 22314
(703) 548-2400

Ken Gerbino's Smart Investing
Phillips Publishing
7811 Montrose Road
Potomac, Maryland 20854
(301) 340-2100   (800) 777-5015

Key Volume Strategies
P.O. Box 407
White Plains, New York 10602
(914) 997-1276

Kinsman's Telephone Growth & Income
    Service
P.O. Box 2107
Sonoma, California 95476
(707) 935-6504

Kiplinger's Personal Finance Magazine
Kiplinger Washington Letter, The
Kiplinger Tax Letter, The
1729 H Street, N.W.
Washington D.C. 20006
(202) 887-6400   (800) 544-0155

Kon-Lin Letter, The
Kon-Lin Research and Analysis
    Corporation
5 Water Road
Rocky Point, New York 11778
(516) 744-8536

LaLoggia's Special Situation Report
P.O. Box 167
Rochester, New York 14601
(716) 232-1240

Laser Report
Medical Report
10 Tara Boulevard, 5th Floor
Nashua, New Hampshire 03062-2801
(603) 891-0123

Louis Rukeyser's Mutual Funds
Louis Rukeyser's Wall Street
Financial Service Associates
1750 Old Meadow Road, Suite 300
McLean, Virginia 22102
(703) 905-8000   (800) 892-9702

Lynch Municipal Bond Advisory
P.O. Box 20476
New York, New York 10025
(212) 663-5552

Margo's Market Monitor
P.O. Box 642
Lexington, Massachusetts 02173
(617) 861-0302

Market Alert Newsletter
Blanchard & Co.
110 Veterans Highway, Suite 200
Metairie, Louisiana 70003
(800) 880-4653

Market Beat Inc.
1436 Granada
Ann Arbor, Michigan 48103
(313) 426-2146

Market Charts Inc.: Point and Figure Charts
10 Hanover Square, 20th Floor
New York, New York 10005
(212) 509-0944   (800) 431-6082

Market Cycle Investing
995 Oak Park Drive
Morgan Hill, California 95037

Market Express
1801 Lee Road, Suite 301
Winterpark, Florida 32789
(407) 628-5200   (800) 333-5697

Market Guide
Market Guide, Inc.
49 Glen Head Road
Glen Head, New York 11545
(516) 759-1253

Market Insider Bulletin
Evasona Company
P.O. Box 541
Thornhill, Ontario L3T 2CO Canada
(905) 883-4843

Market Maneuvers
305 Madison Avenue, #1166
New York, New York 10165

Marketarian Letter, The
P.O. Box 9803
Grand Island, Nebraska 68802
(800) 658-4325

Mark Skousen's Forecasts & Strategies
Phillips Publishing
7811 Montrose Road
Potomac, Maryland 20854
(301) 340-2100   (800) 770-5015

Marples Business Newsletter
Newsletter Publishing Corporation
117 West Mercer Street, Suite 200
Seattle, Washington 98119-3960
(206) 281-9609

Martin Weiss' Safe Money Report
Weiss Research
P.O. Box 109665
Palm Beach Gardens, Florida 33402
(800) 289-9222

Master Indicator of the Stock Market
11371 Torchwood Court
West Palm Beach, Florida 33414-6040
(561) 793-8316

McShane Letter
155 East 55th Street
New York, New York 10022
(212) 688-2387

Medical Technology Stock Letter
P.O. Box 40460
Berkeley, California 94704
(510) 843-1857

Metal Bulletin Publications:
Financial Products
Futures & OTC World
F+O Week
Managed Account Reports
Metal Bulletin
Metal Bulletin/MAR Inc.
220 Fifth Avenue
New York, New York 10001
(212) 213-6202   (800) 638-2525

Middle/Fixed Income Letter
MASTCA Publishing Corp.
P.O. Box 55
Loch Sheldrake, New York 12759
(914) 794-5792

MMA Cycles Report
Merriman Market Analyst
P.O. Box 250012
West Bloomfield, Michigan 48325
(313) 626-3034

Money Fund Report
290 Elliot Street
Ashland, Massachusetts 01721-9104
(508) 881-2800   (800) 343-5413

Money Letter, The
4100 Yonge Street, Suite 515
Willowdale, Ontario
Canada M2P 2B9
(416) 221-4596

Moneyletter, The
Agora Publishing
1217 Saint Paul Street
Baltimore, Maryland 21202
(410) 223-2400   (800) 433-1528

Money Magazine
1271 Avenue of the Americas
New York, New York 10020
(212) 522-1212   (800) 541-1000

Moneypaper, The
Moneypaper Guide to Dividend Program
  Reinvestment
1010 Mamaroneck Avenue
Mamaroneck, New York 10543
(914) 381-5400   (800) 388-9993

Monthly Tax Update
1046 North Council Hills Drive
Meguon, Wisconsin 53097-3303
(414) 238-1150

Moody's Financial Information Services
  Publications:
Bank & Finance Manual & News
  Report
Bond Record
Dividend Record
Handbook of Common Stocks
Handbook of Nasdaq Stocks
Handbook of Dividend Achievers
Industrial Manual & News Reports
Industry Review
International Manual & News Reports
Moody's Company Data (CD-ROM)
Moody's International Company Data
  (CD-ROM)
Municipal and Government Manuals &
  News Reports
Municipal and Government Manuals
  (CD-ROM)
OTC Industrial Manual & News Reports
OTC Unlisted Manual & News Reports
Public Utility Manual & News Reports
Transportation Manual & News Reports
Unit Investment Trusts Manual
Moody's Investors Service
99 Church Street
New York, New York 10007
(212) 553-0435
(800) 342-5647 Ext 0546 (Print)
(800) 955-8080 (CD-ROM)

Morningstar Mutual Funds
Morningstar Mutual Fund 500
Morningstar No-Load Funds
Morningstar Variable Annuity/Life
  Performance Report
Morningstar Investor

Morningstar
225 West Wacker Drive, Suite 400
Chicago, Illinois 60606
(800) 735-0700

MPL Communications Publications:
Best U.S. Stocks for Canadian Investors
Blue Book of CBS Stock Reports
Canadian Mutual Fund Advisor
Canadian News Facts
Canadian Resources & Pennymines
  Analyst
Investment Reporter, The
Investors Digest of Canada
Money Reporter
MPL Communications, Inc.
133 Richmond Street West
Toronto, Ontario, M5H 3M8 Canada
(416) 869-1177

MPT Review
1 East Liberty, 3rd Floor
Reno, Nevada 89501
(702) 785-2300   (800) 454-1395

Mutual Fund Advisor, The
One Sarasota Tower, Suite 602
Two North Tamiami Trail
Sarasota, Florida 34236
(813) 954-5500

Mutual Fund Guide
Commerce Clearing House
4025 W. Peterson Avenue
Chicago, Illinois 60646
(312) 583-8500

Mutual Fund Letter
12514 Starkey Road
Largo, Florida 34643
(813) 585-3801   (800) 326-6941

Mutual Fund Specialist
Royal R. LeMier & Company
P.O. Box 1025
Eau Claire, Wisconsin 54702
(715) 834-7425

Mutual Fund Strategist
P.O. Box 446
Burlington, Vermont 05402
(802) 658-3513

Mutual Fund Technical Trader
1971 Spear Street, P.O. Box 4560
Burlington, Vermont 05406
(802) 343-9133

Mutual Fund Timer
P.O. Box 6275
Jacksonville, Florida 32236
(904) 693-0355

Mutual Fund Values
Morningstar
225 W. Wacker Drive
Chicago, Illinois 60606
(312) 424-4288   (800) 876-5005

Mutual Funds Magazine
Institute for Econometric Research
2200 S.W. 10th Street
Deerfield Beach, Florida 33442-8799
(954) 421-1000   (800) 442-9000

National Mortgage News
11 Penn Plaza
New York, New York 10001
(212) 564-8782

National Trendlines
National Investment Advisors
14001 Berryville Road
North Potomac, Maryland 20874
(800) 521-1585

Nation's Business
1615 H Street N.W.
Washington, D.C. 20062
(202) 463-5650

Nelson Publications:
Catalog of Institutional Research Reports
  (Global Edition)
Directory of Institutional Real Estate
Directory of Investment Managers
Directory of Investment Research
Directory of Pension Fund
  Consultants
Directory of Plan Sponsors
World's Best Money Managers
Nelson Publications
One Gateway Plaza, P.O. Box 591
Port Chester, New York 10573
(914) 937-8400   (800) 333-6357

Neurovest Journal
P.O. Box 764
Haymarket, Virginia 22069-0764
(703) 754-0696

New York Mercantile Exchange
  Publications:
Barrels, Bars and BTUs
Energy in the News
Metals in the News
Comex Division Daily Market Report
Nymex Division Daily Market Report
New York Mercantile Exchange
One North End Avenue
World Financial Center
New York, New York 10282-1101
(212) 299-2000

New York Times, The
229 West 43rd Street
New York, New York 10036
(212) 556-1234   (800) 631-2580

Next Superstock, The
15779 Columbia Pike, Suite 275
Burtonsville, Maryland 20866
(301) 890-3523

Ney Report, The
P.O. Box 92223
Pasadena, California 91109
(818) 441-2222

*Nielsen's International Investment
   Letter*
P.O. Box 7532
Olympia, Washington 98507

No-Load Fund Analyst
4 Orinda Way, Suite 230D
Orinda, California 94563
(510) 254-9017

NoLoad Fund*X
235 Montgomery Street, Suite 662
San Francisco, California 94104
(415) 986-7979   (800) 763-8639

No Load Fund Investor
P.O. Box 318
Irvington-on-Hudson, New York 10533
(914) 693-7420   (800) 252-2042

*No Load Mutual Fund Selections and
   Timing Newsletter*
100 North Central Expressway,
   Suite 1112
Richardson, Texas 75080-5328
(800) 800-6563

No-Load Portfolios
8635 West Sahara, Suite 420
The Lakes, Nevada 89117
(702) 871-4710

Numismatic News
World Coin News
Bank Note Reporter
Coin Price News
Coins Magazine
Krause Publications
700 East State Street
Iola, Wisconsin 54990
(715) 445-2214

Oberweis Report, The
951 Ice Cream Drive
North Aurora, Illinois 60542
(708) 801-6000

Oil and Gas Finance Source Book
Oil and Gas Investor
Oil and Gas Interests Newsletter
Hart Publications, Inc.
4545 Post Oak Place
Houston, Texas 77027
(800) 874-2544

Oil/Energy Statistics Bulletin
P.O. Box 189
Whitman, Massachusetts 02382
(617) 447-6407

On Markets
31 Melkhout Crescent
Hout Bay 7800
South Africa
2721-790-4259

Opportunities in Options
Options Advisor, The
Option Tactician, The
Optionetics
Select Information Exchange
244 West 54th Street
New York, New York 10019
(800) 743-9346

Opportunities in Options Newsletter
Option Volatility Chartbook
Options Advantage Trading Manual
Option Secret Book
300 Esplanade Drive, Suite 200
Oxnard, California 93030
(310) 456-9699   (800) 456-9699

Option Advisor, The
Fund Profit Alert
Investment Research Institute, Inc.
P.O. Box 46709
Cincinnati, Ohio 45246
(513) 589-3838   (800) 327-8833

Option Pro
Essex Press
107 North Hale
Wheaton, Illinois 60187
(630) 682-5780   (800) 726-2140

OTC Growth Stock Watch
OTC Communications
1040 Great Plain Avenue, Suite 2
Needham, Massachusetts 02192-2517
(781) 444-6100

OTC Insight
P.O. Box 5759
Walnut Creek, California 94596
(800) 955-9566

Outlook, The
Standard & Poor's Corporation
25 Broadway
New York, New York 10004
(800) 852-1641

Outstanding Investor Digest
Portfolio Reports
Outstanding Investor Digest Inc.
295 Greenwich Street
P.O. Box 282
New York, New York 10007
(212) 925-3885

Overpriced Stock Service
P.O. Box 308
Half Moon Bay, California 94019
(415) 726-8495

PAD System Report, The
Patience & Discipline Inc.
P.O. Box 554
Oxford, Ohio 45056
(513) 523-3042

Patient Investor
Ariel Capital Management
307 North Michigan Avenue,
 Suite 500
Chicago, Illinois 60601
(312) 726-0140   (800) 292-7435

Pension World
6151 Powers Ferry Road
Atlanta, Georgia 30339
(404) 955-2500

Personal Finance
1101 King Street, Suite 400
Alexandria, Virginia 22314
(703) 905-8000

Peter Dag Portfolio Strategy and
 Management
65 Lakefront Drive
Akron, Ohio 44319
(330) 644-2782   (800) 833-2782

Phillips Publishing Publications:
Bert Dohmen's Mutual Fund Strategies
Ken Gerbino's Investment Letter
Independent Advisor for Vanguard
 Investors
Jay Schabacker's Mutual Fund Investing
John Dessauer's Investors World
Ken and Daria Dolan's Straight Talk on
 Your Money
Mark Skousen's Forecasts and Strategies
Pete Dickinson's Retirement Letter
Richard E. Band's Profitable Investing
Richard C. Young's Intelligence Report

Phillips Publishing Inc.
7811 Montrose Road
Potomac, Maryland 20854
(301) 340-2100   (800) 777-5015

Portfolio Monitor, The
Rutledge Report, The
Rutledge & Company, Inc.
One East Putman Avenue
Greenwich, Connecticut 06830
(203) 869-8866

Portfolios Investment Advisory
P.O. Box 997
Lynchburg, Virginia 24505
(804) 845-1335

Powell Gold Industry Guide and The
 International Mining Analyst
Powell Monetary Analyst
Reserve Research Ltd.
P.O. Box 4135, Station A
Portland, Maine 04101
(207) 774-4971

P.Q. Wall Forecast
P.O. Box 15558
New Orleans, Louisiana 70175-5558
(504) 895-4891

Precision Timing
Precision Timing Fax
P.O. Box 11722
Atlanta, Georgia 30355
(404) 355-0447

Primary Trend, The
Arnold Investment Counsel
700 North Water Street
Milwaukee, Wisconsin 53202
(414) 271-2726   (800) 443-6544

Prime Investment Alert
P.O. Box 701
Bangor, Maine 04401
(207) 945-0241

Professional Investor
P.O. Box 2144
Pompano Beach, Florida 33061

Professional Tape Reader, The
P.O. Box 2407
Hollywood, Florida 33022
(800) 868-7857

Professional Timing Service
P.O. Box 7483
Missoula, Montana 59807
(406) 543-4131

Prudent Speculator, The
P.O. Box 1438
Laguna Beach, California 92652
(714) 497-7657

Public Investor
Government Finance Officers Association
180 North Michigan Avenue, Suite 800
Chicago, Illinois 60601
(312) 977-9700

Publishers Management Corporation
  Publications:
Larry Abraham's Insider Report
McAlvany Intelligence Advisor
Reaper, The
Publishers Management Corporation
P.O. Box 84902
Phoenix, Arizona 85071
(602) 252-4477   (800) 528-0559

Real Estate Investing Letter
861 Lafayette Road, Number 5
Hampton, New Hampshire 03842-1232
(603) 929-1600

Real Estate Weekly
1 Madison Avenue
New York, New York 10010
(212) 679-1234

Realty Stock Review
Dow Jones Financial Publishing
170 Avenue at the Commons
Shrewsbury, New Jersey 07702
(732) 389-8700

Reaper, The
Publisher's Management Corporation
P.O. Box 84901
Phoenix, Arizona 85071
(800) 528-0559

Red Book, The
Western Publishing Company
1220 Mound Avenue
Racine, Wisconsin 53404
(414) 633-2431

REITLine
REITWatch
National Association of Real Estate
  Investment Trusts, Inc.
1129 20th Street, N.W., Suite 305
Washington D.C. 20036
(202) 785-8717

Research Institute of America Group
  Publications:
All States Tax Guide
Corbel Pension Forms

Cumulative Changes
Employee Benefits Alert
Estate Planner's Alert
Estate Planning and Taxation Coordinator
Executive Compensation & Taxation
  Coordinator
Federal Taxation of Insurance Companies
Federal Tax Coordinator
Income Taxation of Natural Resources
Internal Revenue Code & Regulations
Pension Coordinator
RIA's Analysis of Federal Taxes
RIA's Analysis: Income
RIA's Analysis: Estate & Gift Tax
RIA's Analysis: Excise Sales & Use Taxes
State & Local Sales & Use Taxes
  (CD-ROM)
State & Local Taxes (CD-ROM
State & Local Income Taxes
Tax Action Coordinator
Tax Advisors Planning Series
Tax Court
Tax Guide
Tax Guide Plus
United States Tax Reporter
United States Tax Reporter: Estate & Gift
  Taxes
United States Tax Reporter: Excise Taxes
Wills & Trust Forms
Warren Gorham Lamont Tax Publications:
  Corporate Tax Digest
Consolidated Tax Return, The
Charitable Giving and Solicitation
Depreciation and Capital Planning
Divorce Taxation
Estate and Gift Tax Digest
Estate Planning
Estate Planning Law and Taxation
Federal Estate and Gift Taxation
Federal Income Taxation of Banks and
  Financial Institutions
Federal Income Taxation of Corporations
  and Shareholders
Federal Income Taxation of Estates and
  Trusts
Federal Income Taxation of Individuals
Federal Income Taxation of Passive
  Activities
Federal Income Taxation of Real Estate
Federal Income Taxation of S
  Corporations, Third Edition
Federal Tax Accounting
Federal Tax Collections, Liens and Levies
Federal Taxation of Income, Estates and
  Gifts
Federal Taxation of Partnerships and
  Partners
Federal Taxation of Trusts, Grantors and
  Beneficiaries
IRS Practice Alert
IRS Practice and Procedure

Journal of Taxation of Investments, The
Real Estate Tax Digest
Real Estate Tax Ideas
State Taxation/Tax Ideas
Tax Fraud and Evasion
Tax Planning for Highly Compensated
  Individuals
Tax Planning for Retirement
Tax Planning with Life Insurance: Analysis
  with Forms
Tax Planning for Family Wealth Transfers:
  Analysis with Forms
Tax Planning for Dispositions of Business
  Interests
Tax Procedure Digest
Tax Treaties
Taxation for Accountants
Taxation of the Closely Held Corporation
Taxation of Distributions from Qualified
  Plans
Taxation for Lawyers
U.S. International Taxation
U.S.Taxation of International
  Operations
Research Institute of America Group
117 E. Stevens Avenue
Valhalla, New York 10595
(800) 431-9025

RHM Convertible Survey
RHM Survey of Warrants, Options and
  Low-Priced Stocks
172 Forest Avenue
Glen Cove, New York 11542
(516) 759-2904

Richard E. Bard's Profitable
  Investing
Phillips Publishing
7811 Montrose Road
Potomac, Maryland 20854
(301) 424-3370   (800) 777-5005

Richland Report
P.O. Box 222
La Jolla, California 92038
(619) 459-2611

Ripples in the Wave
918 N.E. 16th Avenue
Gainesville, Florida 32601

Ronald Sadoff's Major Trends
250 West Coventry Court
Milwaukee, Wisconsin 53217
(414) 352-8460

Ruff Times, The
757 Main Street
Springville, Utah 84663
(801) 489-8681

Scientific Investing
1521 Alton Street, Suite 368
Miami Beach, Florida 33139
(800) 232-8197

Scott Letter: Closed End Fund Report,
  The
P.O. Box 17800
Richmond, Virginia 23226
(407) 684-8100   (800) 356-3508

Securities and Federal Corporate Law
  Report
West Group
610 Opperman Drive
Eagan, Minnesota 55123-1396
(800) 328-4880

Securities Data Publishing Publications:
Bank Loan Report
Bank Investment Marketing
Buyouts
Buyouts Yearbook
Corporate Syndicate Personnel
  Directory
Directory of Private Equity
  Investors
European Venture Capital Journal
Financial Planning Magazine
Investment Dealers' Digest
Investment Management Weekly
IPO Reporter, The
Mergers & Acquisitions Journal
Mergers & Acquisitions Report
Merger Yearbook, The
On Wall Street Magazine
Private Equity Week
Private Placement Letter
Retail Brokerage-Dealer
  Directory
Traders Magazine
UK Venture Capital Journal
Venture Capital Journal
Venture Capital Yearbook
Securities Data Publishing
40 West 57th Street, 11th Floor
New York, New York 10019
(212) 765-5311

Securities Industry Management
Registered Representative
Plaza Communications Inc.
18818 Teller Avenue, Suite 280
Irvine, California 92715
(714) 851-2220

Securities Week
McGraw-Hill Publications
1221 Avenue of the Americas
New York, New York 10020
(212) 512-3144

Sentinel Investment Letter
Hanover Investment Management
  Corporation
P.O. Box 189
52 South Main Street
New Hope, Pennsylvania 18938
(215) 862-5454

Silver Magazine
P.O. Box 9690
Rancho Santa Fe, California 92067
(619) 756-1054

Sindlinger Fax Service
405 Osborne Lane
Wallingford, Pennsylvania 19086
(215) 565-0247

Small Cap Opportunities Report
13F Opportunities Report
100 Executive Drive
Southeast Executive Park
Brewster, New York 10509
(914) 278-6500

Smart Money Magazine
1790 Broadway
New York, New York 10019
(212) 492-1300   (800) 444-4204

Sound Advice
319 Diablo Road, #102
Danville, California 94526
(510) 838-6710

Special Investment Situations
P.O. Box 4254
Chattanooga, Tennessee 37405
(423) 886-1628

Special Situation Report
P.O. Box 167
Rochester, New York 14601
(716) 232-1240

Spidell's California Tax Letter
Spidell Publishing Inc.
1110 North Gilbert Street
Anaheim, California 92801
(714) 776-7850

Spread Scope Commodity Spread
  Charts
Spread Scope Long-Term Weekly
  Charts
Spread Scope Spread Letter
Spread Scope Inc.
P.O. Box 950841
Mission Hills, California 91345
(818) 782-0774   (800) 232-7285

Standard and Poor's Publications:
Analyst's Handbook
Bond Guide
Chart Guide
Compmark
Compustat Services (Electronic, CD-ROM)
Comstock (Electronic)
Corporate Descriptions Online
  (Electronic)
Corporations CD-ROM
Corporation Records
Current Market Perspectives
Daily Action Stock Charts
Daily News Online (Electronic)
Daily Stock Price Record
Directory of Dividend Reinvestment Plans
Earnings Guide
Emerging and Special Situations
FundScope
Index Alert
Index Services
Industry Reports
Industry Services
Institutional Equity Research
Market Month
MarketScope
MarketScope Europe
Money Market Directory
Mutual Fund Reports
Mutual Fund Reports CD-ROM
New Issues Research
OTC Chart Manual
OUTLOOK, The
Register of Corporations, Directors &
  Executives
Research Reports
S&P 500 Directory
S&P Midcap 400 Directory
S&P Information Bulletins
Standard & Poor's Advantage
Standard & Poor's DRI
Standard & Poor's Platt's
Standard & Poor's Register Online
Statistical Service
Stock Guide/Bond Guide Database
Stock Guide
Stock Market Encyclopedia
Stock Reports CD-ROM
Stock Reports
Your Financial Future
Personalwealth.com
Standard & Poor's Corporation
25 Broadway
New York, New York 10004
(212) 208-8786

Stanger Report, The
Robert Stanger and Company
1129 Broad Street
Shrewsbury, New Jersey 07702
(732) 389-3600

Steve Puetz Letter
1105 Sunset Court
West Lafayette, Indiana 47906
(765) 884-0600

Stock Market Cycles
P.O. Box 6873
Santa Rosa, California 95406
(707) 579-8444

Strategic Investment
1217 Saint Paul Street
Baltimore, Maryland 21201
(410) 234-0515   (800) 433-1528

Street Smart Investing
13D Research
Southeast Executive Park
100 Executive Drive
Brewster, New York 10509
(914) 278-6500

Switch Fund Timing
P.O. Box 25430
Rochester, New York 14625
(716) 385-3122

Sy Harding Hotline by fax
169 Daniel Webster Highway
Suite 7
Meredith, New Hampshire 03253
(603) 279-4783

Systems & Forecasts
150 Great Neck Road
Great Neck, New York 11021
(516) 829-6444

Taurus Publications:
Crude Oil Trader
Grand Cayman System
Taurus Top 16 System
Taurus Corporation
133 West Boscawen Street
Winchester, Virginia 22601
(540) 662-8032

J. Taylor's Gold & Gold Stocks
P.O. Box 770871
Woodside, New York 11377
(718) 457-1426

*Technical Analysis of Stocks and
   Commodities Magazine*
3517 S.W. Alaska Street
Seattle, Washington 98126
(206) 938-0570   (800) 832-4642

Technical Trends
P.O. Box 792
Wilton, Connecticut 06897
(203) 762-0229   (800) 736-0229

Telephone Switch Newsletter
2100 Main Street, Suite 300
Huntington Beach, Caifornia 92648-2489
(800) 950-8765

Timer Digest
P.O. Box 1688
Greenwich, Connecticut 06836
(203) 629-3503

Todd Market Timer
26861 Trabuco Road, Suite E182
Mission Viejo, California 92691
(714) 581-2457

Tomorrow's Commodities
Tomorrow's Options
Tomorrow's Stocks
Techno-Fundamental Investments
P.O. Box 14111
Scottsdale, Arizona 85267-1411
(602) 996-2908

Top Performing Stock Outlook
P.O. Box 725
Corona Del Mar, California 92625
(714) 721-0822   (800) 522-5155

Toronto Stock Exchange Daily Record
TSE Review
Toronto Stock Exchange
2 First Canadian Place,
   Exchange Tower
Toronto, Ontario M5X 1J2, Canada
(416) 947-4200

Trends in Mutual Fund Activity
Investment Company Institute
1401 H Street N.W., Suite 1200
Washington D.C. 20005
(202) 326-5800

Turnaround Letter, The
225 Friend Street, Suite 801
Boston, Massachusetts 02114
(617) 573-9550

Turtle Talk
Russell J. Sands
1800 N.E. 114th Street, Suite 401
Miami, Florida 33181
(800) 532-1563

*United & Babson Investment
   Report*
United Mutual Fund Selector
United Retirement Bulletin
101 Prescott Street
Wellesley Hills, Massachusetts 02181
(617) 235-0900

USA Today
1000 Wilson Boulevard
Arlington, Virginia 22229
(703) 276-3400   (800) 872-8632

U.S. Banker
Faulkner & Gray
11 Penn Plaza
New York, New York 10001
(212) 967-7000

U.S. Investment Report
25 Fifth Avenue, Suite 4-C
New York, New York 10003
(212) 995-2963

Value Income Advisor, The
Income Investment Advisory
1040 W. Upas Street
San Diego, California 92103
(619) 291-4901

Value Line Publications:
Value Line Convertibles
Value Line Investment Survey
Value Line Mutual Fund Survey
Value Line Options
Value Line OTC Special Situations
Value Line
220 E. 42nd Street
New York, New York 10017
(800) 634-3583

Vards Report, The
Financial Planning Resources, Inc.
P.O. Box 1927
Roswell, Georgia 30077-1927
(404) 998-5186

Vector Vest Stock Advisory
286 N. Cleveland Massillon Road
Akron, Ohio 44333
(800) 533-3923

Volume Reversal Survey
P.O. Box 1451
Sedona, Arizona 86339
(520) 282-1275

Wall Street Companion, The
175 Fifth Avenue, Suite 2503
New York, New York 10010
(800) 966-6567

Wall Street Digest, The
One Sarasota Tower
Two North Tamiami Trail, Suite 602
Sarasota, Florida 34236
(941) 954-5500

Wall Street Generalist
Market Metrics Inc.
630 S. Orange Avenue, Suite 104
Sarasota, Florida 34236
(941) 366-5645

Wall Street Journal
200 Liberty Street
New York, New York 10281
(212) 416-2000

Wall Street Transcript
100 Wall Street, 9th Floor
New York, New York 10005
(212) 747-9500

Washington Bond & Money Market Report
Newsletter Services, Inc.
9700 Philadelphia Court
Lanham, Maryland 20706-4405
(301) 731-5202   (800) 345-2611

Washington International Business Report
818 Connecticut Avenue, N.W., 12th Floor
Washington, D.C. 20006
(202) 872-8181

Winning Edge, The
Ellesmere Numismatics
P.O. Box 915
Danbury, Connecticut 06813
(203) 794-1232   (800) 426-3343

Worth, Financial Intelligence
575 Lexington Avenue, 33rd Floor
New York, New York 10022
(212) 751-4550   (800) 777-1851

Wright Investors Service Publications:
Approved Wright Investment List
International Investment Advice and Analysis
Wright Bankers' Service
Wright Newsletter
Wright Monthly Report
Wright Investors Service
1000 Lafayette Boulevard
Bridgeport, Connecticut 06604
(203) 330-5000   (800) 232-0013

Your Money Magazine
5705 North Lincoln Avenue
Chicago, Illinois 60659
(312) 275-3590

Zweig Forecast
Zweig Performance Ratings Report
P.O. Box 360
Bellmore, New York 11710
(516) 223-3800   (800) 633-2252

DATABASES AND ONLINE SERVICES FOR INVESTORS

The following firms offer online services and software databases that enable investors to follow price movements in investment markets with up-to-the-second accuracy. Investors can tap into these data banks to download both current and historical price and volume information as well as news about investment markets. Some of these databases also allow investors to execute trades through their computers. Web sites, where available, are included, which provide more information about products and services.

We wish to thank the American Association of Individual Investors (625 North Michigan Avenue, Chicago, Illinois 60611, 312-280-0170) and *Wall Street & Technology Magazine* (One Penn Plaza, New York, New York, 10119-1198, 212-714-1300) for their assistance in preparing these listings.

America Online:
America Online
22000 AOL Way
Dulles, Virginia 20166
(703) 448-8700   (800) 827-6364
www.aol.com

Bloomberg L.P.:
Bloomberg Financial
499 Park Avenue
New York, New York 10022
(212) 318-2000
www.bloomberg.com

Bond Buyer, The:
Bond Buyer Online
One State Street Plaza
New York, New York 10004-1549
(212) 803-8367   (800) 660-5184
www.bondbuyer.com

Charles Schwab & Co., Inc.:
Schwab Online
101 Montgomery Street
San Francisco, California 94104
(415) 627-7000   (800) 435-4000
www.schwab.com

CompuServe Interactive Services Inc.:
Compuserve
5000 Arlington Center Boulevard
Columbus, Ohio 43220
(614) 723-4000   (800) 848-8990
www.compuserve.com

Dow Jones & Co. Inc.:
Dow Jones Interactive
Info Globe-Dow Jones Interactive
Report on Business Corporate Data
(The Globe and Mail)
P.O. Box 300
Princeton, New Jersey 08543-0300
(609) 452-1511   (800) 369-7466
http://djinteractive.com

Dow Jones & Co. Inc.:
Wall Street Journal Interactive
  Edition
P.O. Box 300
Princeton, New Jersey 08543-0300
(609) 452-1511   (800) 369-2834
http://wsj.com

E*Trade Group Inc.:
E*Trade
4 Embarcadero Place
2400 Geng Road
Palo Alto, California 94303
(650) 842-2500
www.etrade.com

Fidelity Investments:
Fidelity On-Line Xpress+
82 Devonshire Street
Boston, Massachusetts 02109
(800) 544-7272   (800) 544-5555
                [TouchToneXpress]
www.fidelity.com

Financial Post Data Group, The:
Canadian Corporate Database
Canadian Dividend Database
Financial Post Online
Historical Earnings Database
Mutual Funds Database
Record of New Issues
333 King Street East
Toronto, Ontario M5A 4N2
Canada
(416) 350-6500

Micro Trading Software Inc.:
Stock Watcher
Wall Street Watcher
Box 175
Wilton, Connecticut 06897
(203) 762-7820
www.marketwatcher.com

Morningstar Inc.:
Morningstar
Morningstar Mutual Funds
225 West Wacker Drive
Chicago, Illinois 60606
(312) 696-6000   (800) 735-0700
www.morningstar.net

Nihon Keizai Shimbun America, Inc.:
Nikkei/DJ Japan Report
Nikkei Telecom
NEEDS Fundamental & Pricing Data
NEEDS-Net
1325 Avenue of the Americas, Suite 2500
New York, New York 10019
(212) 261-6245
www.nikkei.co.jp

Quick & Reilly Inc.:
Q&R Online
QuickWay Net
QuickWay Plus
26 Broadway
New York, New York 10004
(800) 837-7220
www.qronline.com
www.quick-reilly.com

Reality Online Inc.:
Reuters Money Network
Reuters Money Network for Quicken
1000 Madison Avenue
Norristown, Pennsylvania 19403
(610) 650-8600   (800) 521-2471
www.moneynet.com

Stock Data Corporation:
Stock Market Data
905 Bywater Road
Annapolis, Maryland 21401
(410) 280-5533
www.stockdata.com

SOFTWARE AND ONLINE SERVICES FOR INVESTING AND FINANCIAL PLANNING

The following lists contain a sampling of software packages and online services that can help investors to make better investment decisions and to improve record-keeping, as well as to perform personal financial planning. There are, of course, hundreds of software packages and services on the market to perform these tasks. Those listed here are all marketed by established companies in the software business.

Web sites are provided where available.

The programs and services in group one perform asset allocation functions. These programs evaluate the potential risks and returns on different classes of assets, such as stocks, bonds and cash. This allows investors to allocate their money among assets for maximum returns at acceptable levels of risk.

The group two programs and services are designed for fixed income analysis. These programs analyze the quality and maturity structures of bond portfolios. They also allow investors to maximize returns on the bond portion of their portfolios based on different interest rate assumptions.

The programs and services in group three are designed to help an individual do financial planning. This means that investments can be tracked, tax strategy formulated, real estate decisions examined, and retirement and estate planning options explored. One particular advantage of these programs is that once data has been entered into the computer for one part of a program, it is stored for use in other parts of the program. For instance, when a stock sale that generates a taxable capital gain is entered in the investment records section, it is also recorded in the income tax preparation part of the program.

The programs and services in group four allow users to screen lists of stocks to isolate the companies that meet certain fundamental investment criteria. The information on companies comes either from a disk that is updated monthly or from a continuously updated online database. Usually these disks or online databases are available for an annual fee. There are many kinds of screens that investors can perform with this software, depending on what kinds of stocks they want to find. For example, an investor looking for high income could find the highest-yielding stocks in the database. Someone looking for growth stocks could find the companies with fast earnings growth records.

Programs and services in the fifth group enable users to keep track of their investment portfolios. Once stocks, bonds and other instruments are entered into the computer, the value of the portfolio can be updated easily by tapping into a database. These programs also reveal the tax implications of potential investment moves.

Programs and services in the sixth group are designed to pick stocks, derivatives, and mutual funds based on technical considerations, such as price movements and volume. These programs usually display data in chart form, allowing investors to isolate financial products with technical indicators thought to point to a good buying or selling opportunity.

Programs and services in the seventh group help investors pick the best mutual funds for their portfolios. These programs and online services and databases allow sorting and screening of fund track records and portfolio holdings, permitting investors to isolate funds meeting their investment criteria.

Finally, some of the most active Web sites have been compiled in a separate listing for quick and ready reference. Most of these sites are free, but some require a fee or subscription.

Our thanks to the American Association of Individual Investors (625 North Michigan Avenue, Chicago, Illinois 60611, 312-280-0170) and *Wall Street & Technology Magazine* (One Penn Plaza, New York, New York, 10119-1198, 212-714-1300) for their assistance in preparing these listings.

1. Asset Allocation Software

Ibbotson Associates:
EnCorr
225 North Michigan Avenue, Suite 700
Chicago, Illinois 60601
(312) 616-0404
www.ibbotson.com

Macro*World Research:
Macro*World Online
4265 Brownsboro Road
Winston-Salem, North Carolina 27106
(336) 759-0600
www.mworld.com

Wilson Associates International:
RAMCAP-The Intelligent Asset Allocator
21300 Victory Boulevard, Suite 920
Woodland Hills, California 91367
(818) 999-0015
www.wilsonintl.com

2. Fixed Income Analysis Software

Bond-Tech, Inc.:
Bond Calculator
P.O. Box 192
Englewood, Ohio 45322
(937) 836-3991

3. Financial Planning Software

CD Titles:
Kiplinger's Simply Money 2.1
411 Waverley Oaks Road, Suite 165
Waltham, Massachusetts 02154
(617) 642-1700
www.cdtitles.com

Dow Jones & Co.:
Wall Street Journal Interactive
  Edition
P.O. Box 300
Princeton, New Jersey 08543-0300
(609) 452-1511   (800) 369-2834
www.barrons.com

Dynacomp, Inc.:
Calcugram Stock Options List
Family Budget
Finance Master
Money Decisions
Personal Balance Sheet
Personal Finance Manager
Personal Finance Planner
Personal Finance System
Portview 2020
4560 East Lake Road
Livonia, New York 14487
(716) 346-9788   (800) 828-6772
www.dynacorpsoftware.com

Financial Navigator International:
Financial Navigator
254 Polaris Avenue
Mountain View, California 94043
(650) 962-0300   (800) 468-3636
www.finnav.com

Intuit Inc.:
Quicken Deluxe
2535 Garcia Avenue
Mountain View, California 94043
(520) 295-3220   (800) 446-8848
www.quicken.com

Microsoft, Inc.:
Money Financial Suite
One Microsoft Way, Building 8
Redmond, Washington 98052
(206) 635-7131   (800) 426-9400
www.microsoft.com/money

OptionVue Systems International, Inc.:
OptionVue V
1117 Milwaukee Avenue, Suite C10
Libertyville, Illinois 60048
(800) 733-6610
www.optionvue.com

Quant IX Software, Inc.:
Quant IX Portfolio Evaluator
Quant IX Stock Analyst
5900 North Port Washington Road,
  Suite 142-A
Thiensville, Wisconsin 53217
(414) 241-3990   (800) 247-6354

Reality Technologies, Inc.:
Reality Online
Reuters Internet-Quotron
(www.quotron.com)
Wealth Builder
1000 Madison Avenue
Norristown, Pennsylvania 19403
(610) 277-7600   (800) 521-2471
www.moneynet.com

4. Securities Selection Software

American Association of Individual Investors:
Stock Investor
Stock Investor Professional
625 North Michigan Avenue, Suite 1900
Chicago, Illinois 60611
(312) 280-0170
www.aaii.com

Charles Schwab & Co., Inc.:
Schwab Online
101 Montgomery Street
San Francisco, California 94104
(415) 627-7000   (800) 435-4000
www.schwab.com
www.schwab500.com

CompuServe:
Company Screen on CompuServe
5000 Arlington Centre Boulevard
Columbus, Ohio 43220
(800) 848-8990
world.compuserve.com

Dynacomp, Inc.:
Business Pack
Calcugram Stock Options System
Financial Management System
MicroBJ Box-Jenkins Forecasting
Nuametrics
Ratios
Stock Market Bargains

4560 East Lake Road
Livonia, New York 14487
(716) 346-9788   (800) 828-6772
www.dynacompsoftware.com

Hoover's, Inc.:
Stockscreener On-Line
1033 LaPosada Drive, Suite 250
Austin, Texas 78752-3812
(512) 374-4500
www.stockscreener.com

Market Guide Inc.:
Market Guide
NetScreen on marketguide.com
StockQuest on marketguide.com
2001 Marcus Avenue South, Suite 2000
Lake Success, New York 11042-1011
(516) 327-2400
www.marktguide.com

Microsoft, Inc.:
Microsoft Investor on investor.msn.com
One Microsoft Way, Building 8,
   N. Office 2211
Redmond, Washington 98052
(206) 635-7131   (800) 373-3676
investor.msn.com

Omega Research:
SuperCharts
8700 West Flagler, Suite 250
Miami, Florida 33174
(305) 551-9991   (800) 556-2022
www.omegaresearch.com

Prodigy Services Corp.:
Prodigy Strategic Investor
445 Hamilton Avenue
White Plains, New York 10601

(800) 776-3449
www.prodigy.com

Reality Online Inc.:
Reuters Money Network 2.5
1000 Madison Avenue
Norristown, Pennsylvania 19403
(610) 650-8600
www.moneynet.com

Research Inc.:
Stock Screens on researchmag.com
2201 Third Street
San Francisco, California 94107
(800) 438-1032
www.researchmag.com

Thomson Financial Services:
Thomson Investors Network
1355 Piccard Drive
Rockville, Maryland 20850
(301) 548-5880
www.thomsoninvest.net

Value Line, Inc.:
Value Line Investment Survey
220 East 42nd Street
New York, New York 10017
(212) 687-3965   (800) 535-8760
www.valueline.com

Zacks Investment Research:
Research Wizard
Zacks Company Screening on zacks.com
155 North Wacker Drive
Chicago, Illinois 60606
(312) 630-9880   (800) 399-6659
www.zacks.com

5. Portfolio Management Software

CD Titles:
Kiplinger's Simply Money 2.1
411 Waverley Oaks Road, Suite 165
Waltham, Massachusetts 02154
(617) 642-1700
www.cdtitles.com

Charles Schwab & Co., Inc.:
Schwab Online
Streetsmart
101 Montgomery Street
San Francisco, California 94104
(415) 627-7000   (800) 435-4000
www.schwab.com

Dow Jones & Co.:
Wall Street Journal Interactive Edition
P.O. Box 300
Princeton, New Jersey 08543-0300
(609) 452-1511   (800) 369-2834
www.barrons.com
www.smartmoney.com

Dynacorp, Inc.:
Portfolio Decisions
4560 East Lake Road
Livonia, New York 14487
(716) 346-9788   (800) 828-6772
www.dynacorpsoftware.com

Fidelity Investments:
Fidelity On-Line Xpress+
82 Devonshire Street
Boston, Massachusetts 02109
(800) 544-7272   (800) 544-5555
                        [TouchToneXpress]

Financial Navigator International:
Financial Navigator
254 Polaris Avenue
Mountain View, California 94043
(650) 962-0300   (800) 468-3636
www.finnav.com

Intuit Inc.:
Quicken Deluxe
2535 Garcia Avenue
Mountain View, California 94043
(520) 295-3220   (800) 446-8848
www.quicken.com

ITS Associates, Inc.:
Portfolio Management Information System
Query2
Query2/Trader
36 Washington Street
Wellesley, Massachusetts 02481
(617) 528-7800
www.itsww.com

Lotus Development Corp.:
Lotus 1-2-3
55 Cambridge Parkway
Cambridge, Massachusetts 02142
(617) 577-8500   (800) 635-6887
www.lotus.com

Micro Trading Software, Inc.:
Market Watcher
P.O. Box 175
Wilton, Connecticut 06897
(203) 762-7820
www.marketwatcher.com

Performance Technologies, Inc.:
Centerpiece 4.1
1008 Bullard Court, Suite 100
Raleigh, North Carolina 27615
(919) 876-2187
www.centerpiece.com

Quant IX Software, Inc.:
Quant IX Portfolio Manager
5900 North Port Washington Road,
   Suite 142-A
Thiensville, Wisconsin 53217
(414) 241-3990   (800) 247-6354

Reality Technologies, Inc.:
Reality Online
Wealthbuilder
1000 Madison Avenue
Norristown, Pennsylvania 19403
(610) 650-8600   (800) 521-2471
www.moneynet.com

Stratagem Software International, Inc.:
SMARTrader
SMARTrader Professional
520 Transcontinental Drive, Suite B
Metairie, Louisiana 70001
(504) 885-7353   (800) 779-7353
http//:members.aol.com/strategem1

6. Technical Analysis Software

AIQ Systems:
TradingExpert
916 Southwood Boulevard
P.O. Drawer 7530
Incline Village, Nevada 89450
(702) 831-2999   (800) 332-2999
www.aiq.com

American River Software:
FundScope
Mutual Fund Investor
1523 Kingsford Drive
Carmichael, California 95608
(916) 483-1600
www.americanriver.com

Charles Schwab & Co, Inc.:
100 Montgomery Street
San Francisco, California 94104
(415) 627-7000   (800) 435-4000
www.schwab500.com

ComOp Publishing Inc.:
Bookmaker 2.0
300 Esplanade Drive, Suite 200
Oxnard, California 93030
(800) 926-0926

Dynacomp, Inc.:
Buysel
Fourier Analysis Forecaster
FundWatch

Hansen-Predict
Interactive Multiple Prediction
Microcomputer Stock Program
Stockaid 4.0
4560 East Lake Road
Livonia, New York 14487
(716) 346-9788   (800) 828-6772
www.dynacompsoftware.com

Gannsoft Publishing Company:
Ganntrader
806A Gillette Road
Colville, Washington 99114
(509) 684-7637

Kasanjian Research:
Nature's Pulse
Pattern Smasher
P.O. Box 4608
Blue Jay, California 92317
(909) 337-0816   (888) 220-9789
www.kasanjianresearch.com

Linn Software, Inc.:
Investor RT 2.3
1776 Peachtree Road, N.W., Suite 701
Atlanta, Georgia 30309
(800) 546-6842
www.linnsoft.com

Macro*World Research:
Macro*World Online
4265 Brownsboro Road
Winston-Salem, North Carolina 27106
(336) 759-0600
www.mworld.com

MarketSoft, Inc.:
VectorVest ProGraphics 4.0
2167 Wehrle Drive
Williamsville, New York 14221
(888) 658-7638
www.vectorvest.com

Omega Research, Inc.:
OptionStation
Supercharts
Supercharts Real Time
Tradestation
8700 West Flagler, Suite 250
Miami, Florida 33174
(305) 551-9911   (800) 556-2022
www.omegaresearch.com

PC Quote Inc.:
PC Quote
300 South Wacker Drive, Suite 300
Chicago, Illinois 60606-6688
(312) 913-2800   (800) 225-5657
www.pcquote.com

Ret-Tech Software:
MegaTech Chart System
26185 Twin Pond
Lake Barrington, Illinois 60010
(847) 382-3903
www.rettech.com

SPSS, Inc.:
Invest @ SPSS.com
SPSS for Windows
SPSS Trends
233 South Wacker Drive, Suite 1100
Chicago, Illinois 60606
(312) 651-3000   (800) 543-2185
www.spss.com

Stock Blocks, Inc.:
Insider TA3.03
89 Auburn Street
Portland, Maine 04103
(800) 697-1617
www.stockblocks.com

Stratagem Software International, Inc.:
SMARTrader
SMARTrader Professional
520 Transcontinental Drive, Suite B
Metairie, Louisiana 70001
(504) 885-7353   (800) 779-7353
http//:members.aol.com/strategem1

Tiger Investment Software:
Peerless Intermediate-Term Market Timing
   Package
Peerless Short-Term Market Timing
   Package
Tiger-Power-Stock-Ranker
631 La Jolla Boulevard
La Jolla, California 92037
(619) 459-8577
www.tigersoft.com

Trendsetter Software:
Personal Analyst
Personal Analyst Lite
Personal Hotline
Professional Analyst
2024 North Broadway, Suite 310
Santa Ana, California 92706
(714) 547-5005   (800) 825-1852
www.trendsoft.com

7. Mutual Funds Software

American Association of Individual
  Investors:
Quarterly Low-Load Mutual Fund Update
625 North Michigan Avenue, Suite 1900
Chicago, Illinois 60611
(312) 280-0170
www.aaii.com

CompuServe:
Fundwatch Online on CompuServe
5000 Arlington Centre Boulevard
Columbus, Ohio 43220
(800) 848-8990
world.compuserve.com

Intuit, Inc.:
Fund Search on networth.quicken.com
2535 Garcia Avenue
Mountain View, California 94043
(800) 446-8848
networth.quicken.com

Microsoft, Inc.:
Mutual Fund Investor on investor.msn.com
One Microsoft Way, Building 8
Redmond, Washington 98052
(800) 373-3676
investor.msn.com

Morningstar Inc.:
Ascent
Principia for Mutual Funds
225 W. Wacker Drive
Chicago, Illinois 60606
(800) 735-0700
www.morningstar.net

Prodigy:
Mutual Fund Analyst on Prodigy
445 Hamilton Avenue
White Plains, New York 10601
(800) 776-3449
www.prodigy.com

Quote.com, Inc.:
Mutual Fund Center on quote.com
850 North Shoreline Boulevard
Mountain View, California 94043-1931
(650) 930-1000
www.quote.com

Reality Online, Inc.:
Reuters Money Network
1000 Madison Avenue
Norristown, Pennsylvania 19403
(610) 650-8600
www.moneynet.com

Research, Inc.:
Mutual Fund Screens on
  researchmag.com
2201 Third Street
San Francisco, California 94107
(800) 438-1032
www.researchmag.com

Steele Systems, Inc.:
Mutual Fund Expert-Personal
Mutual Fund Expert-Pro Plus
12021 Wilshire Boulevard,
  Suite 407
Los Angeles, California 90025-1200
(310) 478-4213
www.steelesystems.com

Value Line, Inc.:
No-Load Analyzer
220 East 42nd Street
New York, New York 10017
(800) 230-1138 ext. 5970
www.valuline.com

INVESTMENT WEB SITES

Following is a list of investment Web sites that provide investment data and information. The list includes real-time news and price information providers, like Dow Jones, Reuters, and Bloomberg News; financial news and analysis from Barron's and The New York Times; and historical information from investment trade organizations like the American Association of Individual Investors and the Primary Investment Research Center. Other sites offer specific information on stocks, bonds, mutual funds, futures and options, and technical analysis; many offer multiple services and are defined by their primary focus. Broad general information on the economy, taxes, and portfolio management are offered at other sites. Sites offering online trading or sales of products and services are not included. Web sites of securities, futures, and options exchanges are listed in Chapter 2. Fee-based sites are marked with an asterisk (*). This information is courtesy of *The Individual Investor's Guide to Computerized Investing,* published by the American Association of Individual Investors, 625 North Michigan Avenue, Chicago, Illinois, 60611, (312) 280-0170, (800) 428-2244.

Site Address	Site Name	Primary Focus
www.xis.com(*)	.xis	stock data
www.1040.com	10.40.com	tax information
aarp.scudder.com	AARP Investment Program	mutual funds
www.wanger.com	Acorn Funds	mutual funds
www.osterman.com/alert-ipo(*)	Alert-IPO	IPOs
mma.dowjones.com	AlertNET	mutual funds
www.amcore.com	Amcore Funds	mutual funds
www.aaii.com(*)	American Association of Individual Investors	educational, fund data
www.americancentury.com	American Century Funds	mutual funds
www.aicpa.com	American Institute of CPAs	regulations
aw.zacks.com(*)	Analyst Watch on the Internet	analyst estimates
www.report gallery.com	Annual Report Gallery	company reports
www.asc.gov.au	Australian Securities Commission	foreign investing
www.bankrate.com	Bank Rate Monitor	mortgage calculator
www.barrons.com(*)	Barron's	financial news, analysis
www.bigcharts.com	BigCharts	stock charts, analysis
www.bloomberg.com(*)	Bloomberg Financial	financial news, analysis
www.bradynet.com	Bradynet, Inc.	bonds
www.briefing.com(*)	Briefing.com	financial news
www.businessweek.com	Business Week	financial news, analysis
cgmfunds.com	CGM Realty Fund	mutual funds
www.caltrust.com	California Investment Trust	mutual funds
www.columbiafunds.com	Columbia Funds	mutual funds
www.cftc.com	Commodity Futures Trading Commission	futures/options
www.contrarian.com	Crabbe Huson	mutual funds
www.dailystocks.com	Daily Stocks	stock/fund quotes
www.dbc.com	Data Broadcasting Corp.	stock/fund data
www.dickdavis.com	Dick Davis Online Financial Newsletter	advisory service
www.djmarkets.com	Dow Jones Markets	stock data
www.dreyfus.com/funds	Dreyfus Funds	mutual funds
www.dupree-funds.com	Dupree Funds	mutual funds
www.equis.com	Equis International	technical analysis
www.eclipsefund.com	Eclipse Fund	mutual funds
www.economist.com	Economist	financial news, analysis
www.emgmkts.com	Emerging Markets Companies	foreign investing
www.e-analytics.com	Equity Analytics	stock data, analysis

sso.org/fta/fta.html	Federation of Tax Administrators	tax information
www.fidelity.com	Fidelity Investments	mutual funds
finnav.com	Financial Navigator International	investment Web links
www.fponline.com	Financial Planning Magazine Online Edition	financial planning
www.ft.com	Financial Times	financial news, analysis
www.financialworld.com	Financial World magazine	financial news, analysis
www.firstcall.com(*)	First Call Corporation	analyst estimates
www.flexfunds.com	Flex Funds	mutual funds
www.pathfinder.com/fortune	Fortune magazine	finance news, analysis
www.founders.com	Founders Funds	mutual funds
www.tresor.finances.fr/oat	France-French Government Securities	foreign investing
www.futurestrading.com	Futures Trading Group	futures/options
www.gabelli.com	Gabelli Funds	mutual funds
www.galaxyfunds.com	Galaxy Funds	mutual funds
www.globalfindata.com	Global Financial Data	market data (historical)
www.greenjungle.com	Green Jungle	mutual funds
www.hrblock.com	H&R Block	tax information
www.hoovers.com	Hoover's Online	company profiles
www.stockscreener.com	Hoover's Stockscreener	stock data
www.iaifunds.com	IAI Funds	mutual funds
www.ibcdata.com	IBC Financial Data, Inc.	mutual funds (money-market)
www.ici.org	ICI Mutual Fund Connection	mutual funds
nestegg.iddis.com	IDD Information Services (Online)	financial planning
www.invesco.com	INVESCO Funds	mutual funds
www.ipocentral.com	IPO Central	IPOs
www.ipodata.com(*)	IPO Data Systems	IPOs
www.infofund.com	InfoFund	portfolio tracking
www.insure.com	Insurance News Network	life insurance
www.interquote.com(*)	InterQuote	stock quotes
www.irs.ustreas.gov	Internal Revenue Service	tax information
www.icefi.com(*)	Internet Closed-End Fund Investor	closed-end funds
www.investlink.com	InvestLink	portfolio tracking
members.ici.org	Investment Company Institute	mutual funds
www.options-iri.com	Investment Research Institute	futures/options
www.investools.com(*)	InvesTools	portfolio tracking
www.investorguide.com	Investor Guide	investment Web links
www.investorhome.com	Investor Home	investment Web links
www.investorsquare.com	Investor Square	mutual funds
www.investors.com	Investor's Business Daily Web Edition	financial news, analysis
www.investorweb.com	InvestorWEB	investment Web links
www.investorama.com	Investorama	investment Web links
www.investorsedge.com	Investors Edge	portfolio tracking
www.mgr.com/mgr/lasser	J.K. Lasser	tax information
www.janusfunds.com	Janus Funds	mutual funds
www.jbfunds.com	Jones and Babson Funds	mutual funds
www.kaufmann.com	Kaufmann Funds	mutual funds
www.kiplinger.com	Kiplinger Online	financial news, analysis
www.life-line.com	LIFE-Line	life insurance
www.investorsleague.com	League of American Investors	portfolio tracking
www.lindnerfunds.com	Lindner Funds	mutual funds
www.marketguide.com	Market Guide	stock data
www.markman.com	Markman Funds	mutual funds
www.mgfs.com	Media General Financial Services	stock data
www.merc.com	Mercury Mail	e-mail service
www.investor.msn.com(*)	Microsoft Investor	stock/fund data
www.moneypages.com	Moneypages	investment Web links
www.montgomeryfunds.com	Montgomery Funds	mutual funds
www.moodys.com	Moody's Investors Service	bond ratings

www.morningstar.net	Morningstar Net	stock/fund data
www.gitfunds.com	Mosaic Funds	mutual funds
www.fool.com	Motley Fool	stock data, analysis
www.muhlenkamp.com	Muhlenkamp Funds	mutual funds
www.municipal.com	Municipal.Com	municipal bonds
www.mfea.com	Mutual Fund Education Alliance	mutual funds
www.dasnet.com	Mutual Fund Encyclopedia	mutual funds
www.fundmaster.com	Mutual Fund Investors Resource Center	mutual funds
www.brill.com	Mutual Funds Interactive	mutual funds
www.mfmag.com(*)	Mutual Funds Magazine Online	mutual funds
www.nareit.com	NAREIT Online	real estate investment trusts
www.nasdr.com	NASD Regulation Inc.	securities regulations
networth.quicken.com	NETworth	mutual funds
quotes.quicken.com	Networth Quotes	stock/fund quotes
www.natcorp.com/ir	National Corporate Services	investment Web links
www.fraud.org	National Fraud Information Center	investment fraud
www.net-gold.com	Net Chart	stock charts, analysis
www.nbfunds.com	Neuberger & Berman Funds	mutual funds
www.nikkei.co.jp/enews	Nikkei News (English version)	foreign investing
www.nri.co.jp/QR	Nomura Research Institute	foreign investing
investorsleague.com	nVestor	portfolio tracking
www.otcfn.com	OTC Financial Network	small stock profiles
www.oakmark.com	Oakmark Funds	mutual funds
pawws.com(*)	PAWWS Financial Network	stock/fund data, analysis
www.pbhgfunds.com	PBHG Funds	mutual funds
prnewswire.com	PR Newswire	finance news
www.countrydata.com(*)	PRS Online	foreign investing
www.paxfund.com	Pax World Funds	mutual funds
www.payden.com	Payden & Rygel	mutual funds
www.netrunner.net/philfund	Philadelphia Funds	mutual funds
www.pirc.com(*)	Primark Investment Research Center	stock data, analysis
www.prars.com	Public Register's Annual Report Service (PRARS)	company reports
www.quickquote.com	QuickQuote	life insurance
www.qfn.com	Quicken Financial Network	personal finance
www.quote.com(*)	Quote.Com	stock data, analysis
www.raging bull.com	Raging Bull	newsgroups
www.moneynet.com	Reality Online, Inc.	financial news, analysis
www.researchmag.com	Research Magazine On-Line	educational
www.reuter.com	Reuters	financial news
www.rsim.com	Robertson Stephens Funds	mutual funds
www.rouycefunds.com	Royce Funds	mutual funds
www.fe.msk.ru	Russian Institute for Commercial Engineering	foreign investing
www.seclaw.com	SEC Law.com	regulations
www.sitfunds.com	SIT Funds	mutual funds
www.safecofunds.com	Safeco Funds	mutual funds
www.scudder.com	Scudder Funds	mutual funds
www.securitieslaw.com	Securities Fraud & Investor Protection	securities fraud
www.sia.com	Securities Industry Association	securities industry
www.techstocks.com	Silicon Investor	technology stocks
www.smithbreeden.com	Smith Breeden Funds	mutual funds
www.stockinfo.standard-poor.com	Standard & Poor's Investor Services	stock data
www.stat-usa.gov(*)	Stat-USA	economic data
www.steinroe.com	SteinRoe Funds	mutual funds
www.stockbrokerfraud.com	Stock Investors Fraud Resource	securities fraud
www.stocksmart.com	Stock Smart	portfolio tracking

www.stockmaster.com	StockMaster	stock/fund data
www.stockwiz.com	StockWiz	stock data
www.stockguide.com	StockGuide	small stock profiles
www.effrontier.com	StreetEYE	investment Web links
www.strong-funds.com	Strong Funds	mutual funds
www.troweprice.com	T. Rowe Price	mutual funds
www.alphachart.com	Technical Analysis Charting	technical analysis
www.thestreet.com(*)	TheStreet.com	stock/fund quotes, analysis
www.mjwhitman.com	Third Avenue Value	mutual funds
www.thomsoninvest.net	Thomson Investors Network	stock/fund data
www.publicdebt.treas.gov	U.S. Bureau of the Public Debt	bonds
www.sec.gov	U.S. Securities & Exchange Commission (SEC)	securities regulations
www.usfunds.com	United Services Funds	mutual funds
www.vanwagoner.com	Van Wagoner Funds	mutual funds
www.vanguard.com	Vanguard Funds	mutual funds
www.vusa.com	Vontobel Funds	mutual funds
www.websontheweb.com	WEBS	index fund products
www.wwquote.com	WWQuote	stock quotes
www.wsdinc.com	Wall St. Directory	financial service clearinghouse
www.wallstreetcity.com	Wall Street City	stock screening
wsj.com(*)	Wall Street Journal Interactive Edition	financial news, analysis
www.netresource.com/wsn	Wall Street Net	IPOs
www.wsn.com	Wall Street Research Net	investment Web links
www.wallst.com(*)	WallSt.com	stock data
www.oakassociates.com	White Oak Growth funds	mutual funds
www.wmblair.com	William Blair Funds	mutual funds
www-sharpe.stanford.edu	William F. Sharpe's Home Page	educational, options
quote.yahoo.com	Yahoo! Finance	stock/fund data, analysis
www.younginvestor.com	Young Investor	educational for children
www.zacks.com(*)	Zacks Investment Research	analyst estimates
www.myagent.com	Zacks Portfolio Alert	e-mail service

2. MAJOR FINANCIAL INSTITUTIONS

This section of the *Finance and Investment Handbook* provides listings of major financial institutions, such as banks, life insurance companies, brokerages, limited partnership sponsors, and securities and commodities exchanges. All provide vital financial services. Personal investors deal directly with most of the institutions, and at least indirectly with all. Introductions to the lists provide background information on the types of institutions covered; for additional information it is best to contact an institution directly.

The first part of this section provides lists of the major institutions of the banking system. The 12 banks and the 25 branches that make up the Federal Reserve System and the 12 banks that comprise the Federal Home Loan Bank System are listed. Then follows a list of the primary dealers in government securities, which interact with the Federal Reserve banks. Next is a compilation of the 100 largest commercial banks in the United States and the commercial banks of Canada, followed by a listing of the 100 largest thrift institutions (savings and loans and savings banks) in the United States and the trust and loans of Canada.

The second part of this section provides a listing of the top 100 life-insurance companies in the U.S. and Canada. Insurance companies are important not only because of the protection they provide to policyholders, but also because they are major institutional investors.

A listing of the top 100 full-service brokerage firms and a listing of major discount brokers follow. Full-service brokers play a key role in raising capital for corporations and government bodies, and distributing securities and a wide array of financial services to individual and institutional investors. Investors can save on commissions by dealing with discount brokers.

Next is a listing of the 25 leading accounting firms. These firms, which in the past generally restricted their activities to auditing and accounting, have diversified recently into a variety of financial services. The final part of this section presents stock and commodity exchanges around the world. As financial markets have grown and become more interdependent, foreign exchanges have become more important to North Americans looking for investment opportunities.

FEDERAL RESERVE BANKS

The following is a list of the names, addresses and telephone numbers of the 12 banks and 25 branch banks that make up the Federal Reserve System. These banks supervise the activities of commercial banks and savings banks in their regions. Each branch is associated with one of the 12 Federal Reserve banks—on the list of branches, the parent bank is shown in parentheses. Nationally chartered banks must join the Federal Reserve system; state-chartered banks join on a voluntary basis. The Fed banks ensure that the banks they supervise follow Federal Reserve rules and provide member banks with access to emergency funds through the discount window. Each regional bank is owned by the member banks in its region.

The Federal Reserve System was set up by Congress in 1913 to regulate the U.S. monetary and banking system. The System regulates the nation's money supply by buying and selling government securities on the open market, setting reserve requirements for member banks, setting the discount rate at which it lends funds to member banks, supervising printing of the currency at the mint, acting as a clearinghouse for the transfer of funds throughout the banking system, and examining member banks to ensure that they meet Federal Reserve regulations.

Members of the top policy-making body of the Federal Reserve—the Board of Governors—are appointed by the President of the United States with the consent of the Senate. However, in conducting monetary policy, the Fed is designed to operate independently, so that the rate of growth of the money supply is not directly controlled by Congress or the President. To assure independence, members of the Board of Governors of the Federal Reserve are appointed to 14-year terms. Statements by members of the Board of Governors—especially the Chairman— often have much influence in the finance and investment community.

Depositors and borrowers can complain to the Federal Reserve about practices of member banks considered unfair or abusive. The Fed has jurisdiction over consumer credit, for instance, so consumers can bring complaints about problems with bank lending policies, credit cards, or advertising. In addition, consumers wanting to buy U.S. Treasury and government agency securities without the fees that banks and brokers usually charge can buy them directly through any of the Federal Reserve banks or branches on this list. Several years ago the Federal Reserve reorganized its U.S. Savings Bond sales operation. Now, only the Kansas City bank actually issues savings bonds. Private banks, which used to keep a supply of bonds for sale to customers, only process applications. An application is forwarded to the Kansas City Federal Reserve with a check for the appropriate amount, and the bond is sent to the purchaser within several weeks. Investors may also directly contact the Kansas City Fed to buy savings bonds. Also, Federal Reserve banks publish a variety of economic reports and studies that can be helpful to an investor.

Board of Governors

Board of Governors of the Federal Reserve
  System
21st and Constitution Avenue, N.W.
Washington, D.C. 20551
(202) 452-3000

Federal Reserve Banks

ATLANTA
Federal Reserve Bank of Atlanta
104 Marietta Street, N.W.
Atlanta, Georgia 30303
(404) 521-8653

BOSTON
Federal Reserve Bank of Boston
600 Atlantic Avenue
Boston, Massachusetts 02106
(617) 973-3805

CHICAGO
Federal Reserve Bank of Chicago
230 South LaSalle Street
Chicago, Illinois 60604
(312) 322-5369

CLEVELAND
Federal Reserve Bank of Cleveland
1455 East Sixth Street, P.O. Box 6387
Cleveland, Ohio 44114
(216) 579-2000

DALLAS
Federal Reserve Bank of Dallas
2200 N. Pearl Street
Dallas, Texas 75201
(214) 922-6000

KANSAS CITY
Federal Reserve Bank of Kansas City
925 Grand Boulevard
Kansas City, Missouri 64198
(816) 881-2000

MINNEAPOLIS
Federal Reserve Bank of Minneapolis
P.O. Box 291
Minneapolis, Minnesota 55480-0291
(612) 340-2345

NEW YORK
Federal Reserve Bank of New York
33 Liberty Street
New York, New York 10045
(212) 720-5000

PHILADELPHIA
Federal Reserve Bank of Philadelphia
Ten Independence Mall
Philadelphia, Pennsylvania 19106
(215) 574-6680

RICHMOND
Federal Reserve Bank of Richmond
701 East Byrd Street
Richmond, Virginia 23219
(804) 697-8000

ST. LOUIS
Federal Reserve Bank of St. Louis
P.O. Box 14935
St. Louis, Missouri 63178-4935
(314) 444-8703

SAN FRANCISCO
Federal Reserve Bank of San Francisco
101 Market Street
San Francisco, California 94120
(415) 974-2330

Federal Reserve Branch Banks

BALTIMORE (Richmond)
502 South Sharp Street
Baltimore, Maryland 21201
(410) 576-3300

BIRMINGHAM (Atlanta)
P.O. Box 830447
Birmingham, Alabama 35283-0447
(205) 731-8500

BUFFALO (New York)
160 Delaware Avenue
Buffalo, New York 14202
(716) 849-5000

CHARLOTTE (Richmond)
530 E. Trade Street
Charlotte, North Carolina 28202
(704) 358-2100

CINCINNATI (Cleveland)
150 East Fourth Street
Cincinnati, Ohio 45202
(513) 721-4787

DENVER (Kansas City)
P.O. Box 5228
Denver, Colorado 80217-5228
(303) 572-2473

DETROIT (Chicago)
160 West Fort Street
Detroit, Michigan 48231
(313) 961-6880

EL PASO (Dallas)
301 East Main Street
El Paso, Texas 79901
(915) 544-4730

HELENA (Minneapolis)
100 Neill Avenue
Helena, Montana 59601
(406) 447-3800

HOUSTON (Dallas)
1701 San Jacinto Street
Houston, Texas 77001
(713) 659-4433

JACKSONVILLE (Atlanta)
P.O. Box 929
Jacksonville, Florida 32231-0044
(904) 632-1000

LITTLE ROCK (St. Louis)
325 West Capitol Avenue
Little Rock, Arkansas 72203
(501) 324-8275

LOS ANGELES (San Francisco)
950 South Grand Avenue
Los Angeles, California 90015
(213) 683-2300

LOUISVILLE (St. Louis)
P.O. Box 32710
Louisville, Kentucky 40232
(502) 568-9236

MEMPHIS (St. Louis)
200 North Main Street
Memphis, Tennessee 38103
(901) 523-7171

MIAMI (Atlanta)
P.O. Box 520847
Miami, Florida 33152-0847
(305) 591-2065

NASHVILLE (Atlanta)
301 Eighth Avenue North
Nashville, Tennessee 37203-4407
(615) 251-7100

NEW ORLEANS (Atlanta)
525 St. Charles Avenue
New Orleans, Louisiana 70130
(504) 593-3200

OKLAHOMA CITY (Kansas City)
226 Dean McGee Avenue
Oklahoma City, Oklahoma 73125
(405) 270-8652

OMAHA (Kansas City)
2201 Farnam Street
Omaha, Nebraska 68102
(402) 221-5500

PITTSBURGH (Cleveland)
717 Grant Street
Pittsburgh, Pennsylvania 15230
(412) 261-7802

PORTLAND (San Francisco)
915 S.W. Stark Street
Portland, Oregon 97208
(503) 221-5932

SALT LAKE CITY (San Francisco)
120 South State Street
Salt Lake City, Utah 84130
(801) 322-7844

SAN ANTONIO (Dallas)
126 East Nueva Street
San Antonio, Texas 78295
(512) 224-2141

SEATTLE (San Francisco)
1015 Second Avenue
Seattle, Washington 98104
(206) 343-3600

PRIMARY GOVERNMENT SECURITIES DEALERS

The following is a list of banks and brokerage firms that act as primary government securities dealers, reporting to the Federal Reserve Bank of New York. In this
role, they facilitate the Fed's open market operations by buying and selling Treasury
securities directly through the New York Fed's Securities Department, commonly
called The Desk. These dealers are therefore key players in the execution of Federal
Reserve policy, as set down by the Federal Open Market Committee, which decides
to tighten or loosen the money supply to combat inflation or to ease the money supply to stimulate economic growth. When the Fed wants to tighten money supply, it
sells government securities to the primary dealers—the dollars the dealers pay for
the securities are thus taken out of circulation, and the money supply contracts.
When the Fed, on the other hand, wants to expand the money supply, it buys government securities from the dealers—the proceeds from these sales then go into the
economy, and the money supply increases.

When the government issues new Treasury securities, these primary dealers also
play a key role, because they are among other large dealers and investors making
competitive bids for the securities. Under the competitive bid system, also known
as a Dutch auction, bidders offer higher prices for the securities, and the highest
prices are accepted. Most individual investors do not participate in this auction.
Rather than risk losing out to a higher bidder, they buy Treasury securities with noncompetitive bids, for which the investor accepts whatever price is determined by the
competitive auction.

In order to become a primary dealer, a firm must show the Federal Reserve that
the company has an excellent reputation, large capacity for trading in government
securities, and adequate staff and facilities. It is considered to be very prestigious to
be accepted into the inner circle of primary government securities dealers.

Aubrey G. Lanston & Co., Inc.
One Chase Manhattan Plaza
New York, New York 10005
(212) 612-1600

BancAmerica Robertson Stephens
1455 Market Street, 5th Floor
San Francisco, California 94103
(415) 622-2708

Barclay's Capital
222 Broadway
New York, New York 10038
(212) 412-4000

Bear, Stearns & Co. Inc.
245 Park Avenue
New York, New York 10167
(212) 272-2000

BT Alex. Brown, Incorporated
One Bankers Trust Plaza
New York, New York 10006
(212) 250-2500

Chase Securities, Inc.
270 Park Avenue
New York, New York 10017
(212) 834-4500

CIBC Oppenheimer Corporation
CIBC Oppenheimer Tower
World Financial Center
New York, New York 10281
(212) 667-7000

Citicorp Securities, Inc.
399 Park Avenue, 7th Floor
New York, New York 10043
(212) 291-1000

Credit Suisse First Boston
Corporation
12 East 49th Street
New York, New York 10017
(212) 909-2000

Daiwa Securities America Inc.
Financial Square
32 Old Slip
New York, New York 10005
(212) 612-7000

Deutsche Bank Securities Inc.
31 West 52nd Street, 3rd Floor
New York, New York 10019
(212) 468-5000

Donaldson, Lufkin & Jenrette Securities
Corporation
277 Park Avenue
New York, New York 10172
(212) 892-3000

Dresdner Kleinwort Benson North America
LLC
75 Wall Street
New York, New York 10005
(212) 429-2800

First Chicago Capital Markets, Inc.
One First National Plaza, Suite 0030
Chicago, Illinois 60670
(312) 732-5600

Fuji Securities Inc.
311 S. Wacker Drive, 20th Floor
Chicago, Illinois 60606
(312) 294-8898

Goldman, Sachs & Co.
85 Broad Street
New York, New York 10004
(212) 902-1000

Greenwich Capital Markets, Inc.
600 Steamboat Road
Greenwich, Connecticut 06830
(203) 625-2818

HSBC Securities, Inc.
140 Broadway, 17th Floor
New York, New York 10005
(212) 825-6780

J.P. Morgan Securities Inc.
60 Wall Street, 3rd Floor
New York, New York 10260
(212) 483-2323

Lehman Brothers Inc.
Three World Financial Center, 9th Floor
New York, New York 10285
(212) 526-6430

Merrill Lynch Government Securities Inc.
250 Vesey Street, World Financial Center,
North Tower
New York, New York 10281
(212) 449-1000

Morgan Stanley Dean Witter Inc.
1585 Broadway
New York, New York 10036
(212) 761-4000

Nationsbanc Montgomery Securities LLC
100 North Tryon Street
Charlotte, North Carolina 28255
(704) 386-5073

Nesbitt Burns Securities Inc.
115 S. LaSalle Street, 20th Floor
Chicago, Illinois 60603
(312) 461-6220

The Nikko Securities Co. International, Inc.
200 Liberty Street, One World Financial
   Center
New York, New York 10281
(212) 986-1600

Nomura Securities International, Inc.
Two World Financial Center, Building B
New York, New York 10281
(212) 667-9300

Paine Webber Incorporated
1285 Avenue of the Americas
New York, New York 10019
(212) 713-2000

Paribas Corporation
787 Seventh Avenue
New York, New York 10019
(212) 841-3000

Prudential Securities Incorporated
One Seaport Plaza
New York, New York 10292
(212) 214-1000

Salomon Smith Barney Inc.
388 Greenwich Street
New York, New York 10013
(212) 816-6000

Warburg Dillon Read LLC
222 Broadway
New York, New York 10038
(212) 335-1186

Zions First National Bank
One South Main Street
Salt Lake City, Utah 84111
(801) 974-8800

FEDERAL HOME LOAN BANKS

The following are the names, addresses and telephone numbers of the 12 banks of the Federal Home Loan Bank System. The Federal Home Loan Bank System, established by Congress in 1932 after the collapse of the banking system during the Great Depression, raises money by issuing notes and bonds and lends money to savings and loans and other mortgage lenders based on the amount of collateral the borrowing institution can provide. The Federal Home Loan Banks supply credit reserves to federally and state-chartered savings and loans, cooperative banks and other mortgage lenders in their regions. Each Home Loan Bank is owned by the member financial institutions in its region.

Prior to the Thrift Bailout Bill of 1989, the Federal Home Loan Banks were supervised by the Federal Home Loan Bank Board. With the bailout, however, the FHLBB was eliminated and was replaced by two organizations: the Office of Thrift Supervision and the Federal Housing Finance Board. The Office of Thrift Supervision regulates federal- and state-chartered thrifts. The Federal Housing Finance Board supervises the 12 Federal Home Loan Banks.

National Headquarters

Federal Housing Finance Board
1777 F Street, N.W.
Washington, D.C. 20006
(202) 408-2500

Office of Thrift Supervision
1700 G Street, N.W.
Washington, D.C. 20552
(202) 906-6000

Federal Home Loan Banks

ATLANTA
Federal Home Loan Bank of Atlanta
1475 Peachtree Street, N.E.
Atlanta, Georgia 30309
(404) 888-8097

BOSTON
Federal Home Loan Bank of Boston
One Financial Center, 20th Floor
Boston, Massachusetts 02111
(617) 292-9610

CHICAGO
Federal Home Loan Bank of Chicago
111 E. Wacker Drive, Suite 700
Chicago, Illinois 60601
(312) 565-5701

CINCINNATI
Federal Home Loan Bank of Cincinnati
Atrium Two, Suite 1000
221 E. Fourth Street
Cincinnati, Ohio 45202
(513) 852-7511

DALLAS
Federal Home Loan Bank of Dallas
5605 N. MacArthur Boulevard
Irving, Texas 75038
(214) 944-8800

DES MOINES
Federal Home Loan Bank of Des Moines
907 Walnut Street
Des Moines, Iowa 50309
(515) 281-1099

INDIANAPOLIS
Federal Home Loan Bank of Indianapolis
8250 Woodfield Crossing Boulevard
Indianapolis, Indiana 46240
(317) 465-0510

NEW YORK
Federal Home Loan Bank of New York
7 World Trade Center, Floor 22
New York, New York 10048-1185
(212) 441-6601

PITTSBURGH
Federal Home Loan Bank of Pittsburgh
601 Grant Street
Pittsburgh, Pennsylvania 15219-4455
(412) 288-3434

SAN FRANCISCO
Federal Home Loan Bank of San Francisco
600 California Street
San Francisco, California 94108
(415) 616-2680

SEATTLE
Federal Home Loan Bank of Seattle
1501 4th Avenue, 19th Floor
Seattle, Washington 98101-1693
(206) 340-8690

TOPEKA
Federal Home Loan Bank of Topeka
2 Townsite Plaza
120 E. 6th Street
Topeka, Kansas 66603
(913) 233-0507

COMMERCIAL BANKS

The following is an alphabetical list of the names, addresses and telephone numbers of the headquarters of the 100 largest commercial banks in the United States. The institutions listed here are the largest based on their total deposits, the criterion generally used for comparing the size of banks. These deposits are made up of deposits by corporations, individuals, correspondent banks, government agencies, not-for-profit organizations and many other groups. They are in such forms as checking accounts and certificates of deposit and other time deposits. Another way of ranking banks is by the amount of permanent capital. This capital has been built over the years by offerings of stock to the public and retained earnings. The top 100 institutions would basically be the same using either method of ranking.

Most banks listed here are national banks, because they are chartered by the federal government. Any bank with the initial N (meaning National) or with national in its name is a national bank. Although there are about 14,000 banks in the United

States, there is a high amount of concentration of deposits and capital in the largest banks. The two largest banks, Citibank N.A. and Bank of America N.T. & S.A., have $179 billion and $165 billion in deposits respectively. Each of the top one-third banks have deposits in excess of $16 billion. The banks that rank near number 100, in contrast, have about $4 billion in deposits.

In the 1980s and 1990s there were many bank mergers, as banks sought to compete better in the new, less regulated environment brought about largely by the Depository Institutions Deregulation and Monetary Control Act in 1980. Some large banks operate newly acquired banks as separate subsidiaries. In cases where they are run independently, though still under the corporate umbrella, they are listed separately.

This list of the largest commercial banks (current as of mid-1997) is courtesy of the American Banker newspaper [1 State Street Plaza, New York, New York 10004 (212) 943-8200].

American Express Centurion Bank
6985 Union Park Center
Midvale, Utah 84047-4177
(801) 565-5000

American National Bank & Trust Company
33 No. LaSalle Street
Chicago, Illinois 60690
(312) 661-5000

AmSouth Bank
1900 5th Avenue North
Birmingham, Alabama 35203-2610
(205) 326-5163

Banco Popular de Puerto Rico
209 Munoz Rivera Avenue
San Juan, Puerto Rico 00918
(787) 765-9800

BankBoston, NA
100 Federal Street
Boston, Massachusetts 02110
(617) 434-2200

Bank of America, NT and SA
555 California Street
San Francisco, California 94104-1502
(415) 622-3456

Bank of America, NT and SA
2727 South 48th Street
Tempe, Arizona 85282-7620
(602) 594-6305

Bank of America Texas, NA
1925 W. John Carpenter Freeway
Irving, Texas 75063-3297
(972) 444-5555

Bank of Hawaii
P.O. Box 2900
Honolulu, Hawaii 96846
(808) 537-8111

Bank of New York
48 Wall Street
New York, New York 10286
(212) 495-1784

Bank of Tokyo-Mitsubishi Trust Company
1251 Avenue of the Americas
New York, New York 10020
(212) 667-2500

Bank of the West
180 Montgomery Street
San Francisco, California 94104-4205
(415) 765-4800

Bank One Arizona, NA
241 N. Central Avenue
Phoenix, Arizona 85004-2267
(602) 221-2900

Bank One Indiana, NA
111 Monoment Circle, Tower 801
Indianapolis, Indiana 46277-0108
(317) 321-3000

Bank One Kentucky, NA
416 West Jefferson
Louisville, Kentucky 40202-3244
(502) 566-2000

Bank One Ohio, NA
100 E. Broad Street
Columbus, Ohio 43215
(614) 248-5800

Bank One Texas, NA
1717 Main Street
Dallas, Texas 75201-4605
(214) 290-2000

Bank One, Wisconsin
111 E. Wisconsin Avenue
Milwaukee, Wisconsin 53202-4803
(414) 765-3000

Bankers Trust Company
280 Park Avenue
New York, New York 10017-1216
(212) 250-2500

Barnett Bank, NA
50 N. Laura Street
Jacksonville, Florida 32202-3609
(904) 464-7000

Boston Safe Deposit & Trust Company
1 Boston Place
Boston, Massachusetts 02108
(617) 722-7000

Branch Banking & Trust Company
200 W. 2nd Street
Winston-Salem, North Carolina 27101
(910) 733-2000

Central Carolina Bank & Trust Company
111 Corcoran Street
Durham, North Carolina 27701-3231
(919) 683-7777

Central Fidelity National Bank
Central Fidelity Bank Building,
 James Center
Richmond Virginia 23219
(804) 782-4000

Centura Bank
131 N. Church Street
Rocky Mount, North Carolina 27804-5402
(919) 977-4400

Chase Manhattan Bank
1 Chase Manhattan Plaza
New York, New York 10081
(212) 552-2222

Chase Manhattan Bank USA, NA
1 Chase Manhattan Plaza
802 Delaware Avenue
Wilmington, Delaware 19801-1398
(302) 575-5024

Citibank, NA
399 Park Avenue
New York, New York 10043
(212) 559-1000

Citibank Nevada
8725 West Sahara Avenue
Las Vegas, Nevada 89117
(702) 797-4444

Citibank South Dakota
701 East 60th Street North
Sioux Falls, South Dakota 57104-0493
(605) 331-2626

Comerica Bank
One Detroit Center
500 Woodward Avenue
Detroit, Michigan 48243
(313) 222-3300

Commerce Bank, NA
1000 Walnut Street
Kansas City, Missouri 64106-2123
(816) 234-2000

Compass Bank
15 S. 20th Street
Birmingham, Alabama 35233-2035
(205) 933-3000

Compass Bank-Houston
24 Greenway Plaza, Suite 1402
Houston, Texas 77046-2401
(713) 621-3336

CoreStates Bank, NA
Broad & Chestnut Streets
Philadelphia, Pennsylvania 19101
(215) 973-3100

Deposit Guaranty National Bank
One Deposit Guaranty Plaza
Jackson, Mississippi 39201
(601) 354-8211

European American Bank
120 Broadway
New York, New York 10005
(212) 296-5000

FCC National Bank
One Gateway Center
300 King Street
Wilmington, Delaware 19801
(302) 594-8682

Fifth Third Bank
38 Fountain Square Plaza
Cincinnati, Ohio 45263-0001
(513) 579-5300

First American National Bank
First American Center
Nashville, Tennessee 37237
(615) 748-2000

First-Citizens Bank & Trust Company
239 Fayetteville Street
Raleigh, North Carolina 27604
(919) 755-7000

First Hawaiian Bank
P.O. Box 3200
Honolulu, Hawaii 96847
(808) 525-7000

First National Bank of Chicago
1 First National Plaza
Chicago, Illinois 60670-0002
(312) 732-4000

First National Bank of Commerce
210 Baronne Street
New Orleans, Louisiana 70112-1721
(504) 561-1371

First National Bank of Maryland
25 S. Charles Street
Baltimore, Maryland 21201-3330
(410) 244-4000

First of America Bank-Illinois, NA
2595 Waukegan Road
Bannockburn, Illinois 60015-5506
(847) 317-2350

First of America Bank, NA
1700 Bronson Way
Kalamazoo, Michigan 49009
(616) 376-9525

First Security Bank, NA
2040 South 2300 East
Salt Lake City, Utah 84108
(435) 846-4955

First Tennessee Bank, NA
165 Madison Avenue
Memphis, Tennessee 38103-2723
(901) 523-4444

First Union National Bank
102 Pennsylvania Avenue
Avondale, Pennsylvania 19311
(610) 268-2201

First Union National Bank
201 S. Jefferson Street
Roanoke, Virginia 24011-1701
(540) 563-7787

First Union National Bank
Two First Union Plaza
301 So. Tryon Street
Charlotte, North Carolina 28288
(704) 374-6161

Firstar Bank Milwaukee, NA
777 E. Wisconsin Avenue
Milwaukee, Wisconsin 53202-5302
(414) 765-4321

Fleet Bank of New York
120 Washington Avenue
Albany, New York 12203-5366
(518) 456-1143

Fleet National Bank
One Monarch Place
Springfield, Massachusetts 01102
(800) 833-6623

Greenwood Trust Company
12 Read's Way
New Castle, Delaware 19720-1601
(302) 323-7110

Harris Trust and Savings Bank
111 W. Monroe Street
Chicago, Illinois 60603-4003
(312) 461-2121

Hibernia National Bank
313 Carondelet Street
New Orleans, Louisiana 70130
(504) 533-3333

Huntington National Bank
41 S. High Street
Columbus, Ohio 43215-6101
(614) 480-8300

KeyBank, NA
127 Public Square
Cleveland, Ohio 44114-2601
(216) 689-3000

LaSalle National Bank
515 N. LaSalle Street
Chicago, Illinois 60603-3499
(312) 904-2000

Magma Bank, NA
1401 S. Brentwood Boulevard
Brentwood, Missouri 63144
(314) 963-2600

MBNA America Bank, NA
1100 N. King Street
Wilmington, Delaware 19801
(302) 453-9930

Manufacturers & Traders Trust Company
1 M&T Plaza
Buffalo, New York 14240
(716) 842-4200

Marine Midland Bank
1 Marine Midland Center, 22nd Floor
Buffalo, New York 14203
(716) 841-2424

Mellon Bank, NA
1 Mellon Bank Center
500 Grant Street
Pittsburgh, Pennsylvania 15219
(412) 234-5000

Mercantile Bank, NA
8820 Ladue Road
St. Louis, Missouri 63124-2096
(314) 746-2652

Michigan National Bank
27777 Inkster Road
Farmington Hills, Michigan 48334
(248) 473-3000

Morgan Guaranty Trust Company
of New York
60 Wall Street
New York, New York 10260-0060
(212) 483-2323

NBD Bank
611 Woodward Avenue
Detroit, Michigan 48231-0116
(313) 225-1000

National City Bank
1900 E. 9th Street
Cleveland, Ohio 44114
(216) 575-2000

National City Bank of Columbus
155 E. Broad Street
Columbus, Ohio 43251-3609
(614) 463-7100

National City Bank of Kentucky
101 S. 5th Street
Louisville, Kentucky 40202
(502) 581-4200

National City Bank of Pennsylvania
20 Stanwix Street
Pittsburgh, Pennsylvania 15222-4802
(412) 644-8111

NationsBank, NA
101 S. Tryon Street
Charlotte, North Carolina 28255
(704) 386-5000

NationsBank of Texas, NA
904 E. Main Street
Dallas, Texas 75201
(214) 508-6262

NBD Bank, NA
One Indiana Square
Indianapolis, Indiana 46266-0100
(317) 266-6000

Northern Trust Company
50 South LaSalle Street
Chicago, Illinois 60675-0002
(312) 630-6000

North Fork Bank
245 Love Lane
Mattituck, New York 11952-8607
(516) 844-1004

Norwest Bank of Minnesota, NA
6th Street and Marquette Avenue
Minneapolis, Minnesota 55479
(612) 667-0764

Old Kent Bank
One Vandenberg Center
Grand Rapids, Michigan 49503
(616) 771-5000

PNC Bank, NA
5th Avenue and Wood Street
Pittsburgh, Pennsylvania 15222
(412) 762-2000

Provident Bank
1 East 4th Street
Cincinnati, Ohio 45202
(513) 579-2000

Regions Bank
417 20th Street North
Birmingham, Alabama 35203-3203
(205) 326-7884

Republic National Bank of New York
452 Fifth Avenue
New York, New York 10018-2706
(212) 525-5000

Sanwa Bank California
444 Market Street
San Francisco, California 94111-5325
(415) 597-5000

Southtrust Bank, NA
420 N. 20th Street
Birmingham, Alabama 35203-3204
(205) 254-5989

Star Bank, NA
425 Walnut Street
Cincinnati, Ohio 45202-3912
(513) 632-4000

State Street Bank and Trust Company
225 Franklin Street
Boston, Massachusetts 02110-2801
(617) 786-3000

Summit Bank
301 Carnegie Center
Princeton, New Jersey 08543-3516
(609) 987-3670

SunTrust Bank, Atlanta
25 Park Place N.E.
Atlanta, Georgia 30303
(404) 588-7929

Texas Commerce Bank, NA
712 Main Street
Houston, Texas 77002-3206
(713) 216-4865

U.S. Bank, NA
321 SW 6th
Portland, Oregon 97204
(503) 275-5250

Union Bank of California, NA
400 California Street
San Francisco, California 94104-1302
(415) 765-0400

Valley National Bank
615 Main Avenue
Passaic, New Jersey 07055-4900
(973) 777-1800

Wachovia Bank, NA
100 No. Main Street
Winston-Salem, North Carolina 27101-0001
(910) 770-5000

Wells Fargo Bank, NA
420 Montgomery Street
San Francisco, California 94104-1205
(800) 411-4932

Wells Fargo Bank (Texas), NA
1000 Louisiana Street
Houston, Texas 77002-5008
(713) 224-6611

Wilmington Trust Company
Rodney Square North
1100 North Market Street
Wilmington, Delaware 19890
(302) 651-1000

Zions First National Bank
One South Main Street
Salt Lake City, Utah 84111
(801) 974-8800

CANADIAN BANKS

The following is a list of the 9 major banks of Canada. Unlike the United States, Canadian banking is highly concentrated into a few large institutions that provide the full range of banking services to consumers and institutions. These banks are regulated at the federal and provincial levels in a similar way to American banks. Deposits are insured to $60,000.

Bank of Montreal
1 First Canadian Place
Toronto, Ontario M5X 1A1
(416) 867-5000

Manulife Bank of Canada
2 Mississaga Street East
Orillia, Ontario L3V 6H9
(705) 325-2328

Bank of Nova Scotia
Scotia Plaza
44 King Street West
Toronto, Ontario M5H 1H1
(416) 866-6161

National Bank of Canada
Tour de la Banque Nationale
600 de La Gauchetiere ouest
Montreal, Quebec H3B 4L2
(514) 394-4000

Canadian Imperial Bank of Commerce
Commerce Court
Commerce Court Postal Station
Toronto, Ontario M5L 1A2
(416) 980-2211

Royal Bank of Canada
Royal Bank Plaza
200 Bay Street
Toronto, Ontario M5J 2J5
(416) 974-5151

Canadian Western Bank
Suite 2300
10303 Jasper Avenue
Edmonton, Alberta T5J 3X6
(403) 423-8888

Toronto-Dominion Bank
1 Toronto-Dominion Centre
King Street West and Bay Street
Toronto, Ontario M5K 1A2
(416) 982-8222

Laurentian Bank of Canada
Tour Banque Laurentienne
1981 McGill College Avenue
Montreal, Quebec H3A 3K3
(514) 284-5996

THRIFT INSTITUTIONS

The following is an alphabetical listing of the names, addresses and telephone numbers of the headquarters of the 100 largest savings and loans and savings banks in the United States, ranked by total deposits, as tabulated by the *American Bankers Association Financial Institutions Directory,* published by Thomson Financial Publishing [4709 West Golf Road, Skokie, IL 60076-1253; (800) 280-5450]. Total deposits, made up mostly of certificates of deposit and money-market accounts from individual and institutional investors, are the best measure of thrift institution size, and they are therefore commonly used in ranking savings and loans and savings banks. Some tabulations compare thrifts by the amount of their total assets—mostly mortgage loans. In either case, the list of the top 100 institutions would be similar.

Savings and loans were initially founded predominantly in the western states, particularly California, as a mechanism for pioneer settlers in the 19th century to finance the construction of homes. They were largely regulated by state authorities until 1932, when the Federal Home Loan Bank Board was set up in reaction to the crisis of the banking and home-building industries during the Great Depression. Savings and loans are now regulated at both the federal and state levels and most deposits are insured by the Savings Association Insurance Fund.

Savings banks were initially found mainly on the East Coast, where, like savings and loans, they catered to consumers and made home loans. They are chartered and regulated by both state authorities and the Federal Reserve Board, as well as the Office of Thrift Supervision in some cases. Most deposits are insured by the Federal Deposit Insurance Corporation (FDIC). Over the years, the few distinctions between savings banks and savings and loans have largely faded away.

Historically, both types of thrifts have been distinguished from commercial banks in that they obtained most of their deposits from consumers, and lent that money out in the form of fixed-rate mortgages to homebuyers. To give them an edge in attracting deposits, they were allowed (under Regulation Q) to pay 1/4% more interest on passbook savings accounts than commercial banks. Starting in the late 1970s, when the general level of interest rates started to rise dramatically, many thrifts ran into financial trouble, because their income from mortgages was fixed at low rates, while they had to pay out higher rates on unregulated certificates of deposit to retain depositors. The pressure from this predicament ultimately led to the Depository Institutions Deregulation and Monetary Control Act of 1980 and the Garn-St Germain Act of 1982, which mandated the gradual phase-out of control on interest rates on all deposits, and permitted thrifts to offer adjustable-rate mortgages. They were also allowed to enter businesses from which they had previously been banned, such as commercial lending, issuing credit cards and providing trust services.

By the mid-1980s, thrifts played a prominent and highly competitive role in providing financial services. Many institutions went after consumer dollars by paying among the highest interest rates in the country on money-market deposits and certificates of deposit. These savings and loans and savings banks often arranged to take deposits over the phone. They sometimes brought in millions of dollars by allying with a securities brokerage firm that sells certificates of deposit. With the ability to bring in large amounts of money quickly, many thrifts became aggressive lenders as well.

By the late 1980s and early 1990s, many thrifts had gotten into severe financial trouble because they had taken excessive risks or because of fraud. A federal bailout had to be arranged to merge failed institutions into healthy ones. The bailout bill created a new regulatory structure for the industry by replacing the Federal Savings and Loan Insurance Corporation with the Savings Association Insurance Fund. The Federal Home Loan Bank Board became the Office of Thrift Supervision, and a new agency, the Resolution Trust Corporation, was formed to dispose of thrift assets. The RTC was dissolved in 1996 and its responsibilities were shifted to the Savings Association Insurance Fund. By the end of the 1990s, the thrifts that remained were generally financially healthy and operating profitably.

Albank, FSB
10 N. Pearl Street
Albany, New York 12207-2774
(518) 432-2200

American Savings Bank, FSB
Financial Plaza of the Pacific
Honolulu, Hawaii 96813-4408
(808) 531-6262

American Savings Bank, FA
400 E. Main Street
Stockton, California 92590
(714) 252-7200

AnchorBank, SSB
25 W. Main Street
Madison, Wisconsin 53703-3329
(608) 252-8700

Apple Bank for Savings
277 Park Avenue, 40th Floor
New York, New York 10172
(212) 224-6400

Astoria Federal Savings & Loan
  Association
1 Astoria Federal Plaza
Lake Success, New York 11042-1085
(516) 327-3000

BankAtlantic, A Federal Savings Bank
1750 E. Sunrise Boulevard
Fort Lauderdale, Florida 33304-3098
(954) 760-5000

Bank of America, FSB
121 SW Morrison, Suite 1700
Portland, Oregon 97204
(415) 953-2249

Bank of Boston, Connecticut
100 Pearl Street
Hartford, Connecticut 06103-1696
(860) 727-5000

Bank United
3200 Southwest Freeway, Drop 1940
Houston, Texas 77027-7596
(713) 543-6500

Bank United, FSB
255 Alhambra Circle, 2nd Floor
Coral Gables, Florida 33134-7411
(305) 569-2000

Bay View Bank
2121 South El Camino Real
San Mateo, California 94403-1897
(415) 573-7300

Bluebonnet Savings Bank, FSB
P.O. Box 8400
Dallas, Texas 75205
(214) 443-9000

California Federal Bank, FSB
135 Main Street
San Francisco, California 94105
(415) 904-1100

Capitol Federal Savings & Loan Association
700 Kansas Avenue
Topeka, Kansas 66603-3809
(785) 235-1341

CenFed Bank, Federal Savings Bank
199 N. Lake Avenue
Pasadena, California 91101-1859
(626) 585-2400

Charter One Bank, FSB
1215 Superior Avenue
Cleveland, Ohio 44114-3249
(216) 566-5300

Chevy Chase Bank, FSB
8251 Greensboro Drive
Suite 100
McLean, Virginia 22102
(301) 986-7000

Citibank, Federal Savings Bank
260 California Street
San Francisco, California 94111-4303
(415) 981-3180

Citizens Bank of Massachusetts
55 Summer Street, 3rd Floor
Boston, Massachusetts 02110
(617) 482-2600

Citizens Bank of New Hampshire
875 Elm Street
Manchester, New Hampshire 03101
(603) 634-7000

Citizens Federal Bank, FSB
One Citizens Federal Center
Dayton, Ohio 45402
(937) 223-4234

Coast Federal Bank, FSB
1000 Wilshire Boulevard
Los Angeles, California 90017-2457
(213) 362-2222

Coastal Bank, SSB
5718 Westheimer, Suite 600
Houston, Texas 77057
(713) 435-5000

Collective Bank
158 Philadelphia Avenue
Egg Harbor City, New Jersey 08215-1393
(609) 625-1110

Columbia Federal Savings Bank
93-22 Jamaica Avenue
Woodhaven, New York 11421-2294
(718) 847-7041

Columbia Savings Bank
25-00 Broadway
Fair Lawn, New Jersey 07410-3831
(201) 796-3600

Commercial Federal Bank, FSB
2120 S. 72nd Street
Omaha, Nebraska 68124-2341
(402) 554-5690

Commonwealth Bank
70 Valley Stream Parkway
Malvern, Pennsylvania 19355
(610) 251-1600

D&N Bank
400 Quincy Street
Hancock, Michigan 49930-1829
(906) 482-2700

Dime Savings Bank of New York, FSB
589 Fifth Avenue
New York, New York 10017-6904
(212) 326-6170

Dollar Bank
3 Gateway Center
Pittsburgh, Pennsylvania 15222
(412) 261-4900

Downey Savings & Loan Association, F.A.
3501 Jamboree Road
Newport Beach, California 92660-2939
(714) 854-3100

Eagle Bank
222 Main Street
Bristol, Connecticut 06010-6375
(860) 584-6300

Eastern Bank
270 Union Street
Lynn, Massachusetts 01901
(781) 599-2100

Emigrant Savings Bank
5 E. 42nd Street
New York, New York 10017-6904
(212) 850-4000

EurekaBank, FSB
950 Tower Lane
Foster City, California 94404
(650) 637-2350

Fidelity Federal Bank, FSB
600 North Brand Boulevard
Glendale, California 91203-1241
(800) 434-3354

Fidelity New York, FSB
1000 Franklin Avenue
Garden City, New York 11530
(516) 746-8500

First American Bank Texas, SSB
2800 S. Texas Avenue
Bryan, Texas 77802
(409) 361-6200

First Bank of Florida
450 S. Australian Avenue
West Palm Beach, Florida 33401-5685
(561) 655-8511

First Federal Bank of California, FSB
401 Wilshire Boulevard
Santa Monica, California 90401-1490
(310) 319-6000

First Federal Savings Bank La Crosse-
    Madison
605 State Street
La Crosse, Wisconsin 54601
(608) 784-8000

First Financial Bank
1305 Main Street
Stevens Point, Wisconsin 54481
(715) 341-0400

First Indiana Bank
135 N. Pennsylvania Street
Indianapolis, Indiana 46204-2400
(317) 269-1200

Flagstar Bank, FSB
2600 Telegraph Road
Bloomfield Hills, Michigan 48302
(248) 338-7700

Glendale Federal Bank
700 North Brand Boulevard
Glendale, California 91203
(818) 500-2000

Great Financial Bank, FSB
1 Financial Square
Louisville, Kentucky 40202-3322
(502) 562-6000

Greater New York Savings Bank
1 Penn Plaza
New York, New York 10119
(212) 643-4000

GreenPoint Bank
90 Park Avenue
New York, New York 10016
(212) 834-1000

Guaranty Federal Bank, FSB
8333 Douglas Avenue
Dallas, Texas 75225-5806
(214) 360-3360

Guardian Savings & Loan Association
1220 Augusta
Houston, Texas 77057-2212
(713) 787-3100

Harris Savings Bank
235 N. Second Street
Harrisburg, Pennsylvania 17101
(717) 236-4041

Home Federal Savings Bank
241-02 Northern Boulevard
Queens, New York 11362
(718) 631-8100

Home Savings of America, FSB
4900 Rivergrade Road
Irwindale, California, 91706
(626) 960-6311

Household Bank, FSB
700 Wood Dale Road
Prospect Heights, Illinois 60191
(847) 564-5000

Hudson City Savings Bank
West 80 Century Road
Paramus, New Jersey 07652
(201) 967-1900

Independence Savings Bank
195 Montague Street
Brooklyn, New York 11201
(718) 722-5300

Interwest Bank
275 SE Pioneer Way
Oak Harbor, Washington 98277
(360) 679-4181

Investors Savings Bank
243 Milburn Avenue
Milburn, New Jersey 07041-1718
(973) 376-5100

LaSalle Bank, FSB
5501 S. Kedzie Avenue
Chicago, Illinois 60629-2489
(773) 434-3322

Local Federal Bank, FSB
P.O. Box 26020
Oklahoma City, Oklahoma 73126
(405) 841-2100

The Long Island Savings Bank, FSB
201 Old Country Road
Mellville, New York 11747
(516) 547-2000

Main Line Bank
Two Aldwyn Center
Villanova, Pennsylvania 19085-1431
(800) 233-4653

Mid America Federal Savings Bank
55th & Holmes
Clarendon Hills, Illinois 60514
(630) 325-7300

MidFirst Bank
501 W. I-44 Service Road
Oklahoma City, Oklahoma 73118
(405) 840-7600

Middlesex Savings Bank
6 Main Street
Natick, Massachusetts 01760-4506
(508) 653-0300

Mutual Savings Bank
4949 W. Brown Deer Road
Milwaukee, Wisconsin 53223
(414) 354-1500

New Haven Savings Bank
195 Church Street
New Haven, Connecticut 06510-2009
(203) 787-1111

Northwest Savings Bank
Liberty & Second Streets
Warren, Pennsylvania 16365-2353
(814) 726-2140

Ocwen Federal Bank, FSB
2400 Lemoine Avenue
Fort Lee, New Jersey 07024-2099
(201) 947-1637

Ohio Savings Bank, FSB
1801 E. 9th Street
Cleveland, Ohio 44114-3103
(216) 696-2222

People's Bank
850 Main Street
Bridgeport, Connecticut 06604-4913
(203) 338-7001

Peoples Bank of California
5900 Wilshire Boulevard
Los Angeles, California 90036
(213) 938-6300

Peoples Heritage Savings Bank
P.O. Box 9540
Portland, Maine 04112
(207) 761-8500

PFF Bank & Trust
350 S. Garey Avenue
Pomona, California 91767
(909) 623-2323

Provident Savings Bank
830 Bergen Avenue
Jersey City, New Jersey 07306-4599
(201) 333-1000

Regency Savings Bank, FSB
1804 N. Naper Boulevard
Naperville, Illinois 60563-8803
(630) 357-4500

Reliance Federal Savings Bank
585 Stewart Avenue
Garden City, New York 11530-4701
(516) 222-9300

Ridgewood Savings Bank
71-02 Forest Avenue
Ridgewood, New York 11385-5697
(718) 240-4800

Rochester Community Savings Bank
40 Franklin Street
Rochester, New York 14604-1495
(716) 258-3000

Roosevelt Savings Bank
1122 Franklin Avenue
Garden City, New York 11530-1602
(516) 742-9300

The Roslyn Savings Bank
1400 Old Northern Boulevard
Roslyn, New York 11576-2154
(516) 621-6000

St. Paul Federal Bank for Savings
6700 West North Avenue
Chicago, Illinois 60607-3964
(773) 622-5000

Security Bank, SSB
184 W. Wisconsin Avenue
Milwaukee, Wisconsin 53201-3082
(414) 273-1900

Sovereign Bank
1130 Berkshire Boulevard
Wyomissing, Pennsylvania 19610-1200
(610) 320-8400

Standard Federal Bank
2600 West Big Beaver Road
Troy, Michigan 48084-3306
(248) 643-9600

State Savings Bank
20 E. Broad Street
Columbus, Ohio 43215-3465
(614) 460-6100

Staten Island Savings Bank
15 Beach Street
Stapleton, New York 10304-2713
(718) 447-7900

Sterling Savings Association
111 N. Wall Street
Spokane, Washington 99201
(509) 624-4114

Third Federal Savings & Loan Association of
  Cleveland
7007 Broadway Avenue
Cleveland, Ohio 44105-1490
(216) 441-6000

Union Federal Savings Bank of
  Indianapolis
45 N. Pennsylvania Avenue
Indianapolis, Indiana 46204
(317) 269-4700

United Savings Bank, FSB
711 Van Ness Avenue
San Francisco, California 94102-3224
(415) 928-0700

USAA Federal Savings Bank
10750 McDermott Freeway
San Antonio, Texas 78288-0544
(210) 498-2265

Washington Federal Savings & Loan
  Association
425 Pike Street
Seattle, Washington 98101-2334
(206) 624-7930

Washington Mutual Bank
1201 Third Avenue
Seattle, Washington 98101
(206) 461-2000

Webster Bank
145 Bank Street
Webster Plaza
Waterbury, Connecticut 06702
(203) 755-1422

Western Financial Bank, FSB
16485 Laguna Canyon Road
Irvine, California 92618-3820
(714) 727-1000

World Savings & Loan Association,
  FSLA
1970 Broadway
Oakland, California 94612-2212
(510) 446-3300

World Savings Bank, FSB
1970 Broadway
Oakland, California 94612-2212
(510) 446-3300

CANADIAN TRUST AND LOANS

The equivalent of the U.S. savings and loan in Canada is called a trust and loan. These trust and loans act as executors, trustees and administrators of wills and trust agreements; serve as transfer agents, registrars and bond trustees for corporations; take deposits that are invested in fixed-term instruments; offer unit investment trusts; manage profit-sharing and pension plans for companies; and offer mortgage loans, mostly to residential home buyers. The following is an alphabetical list of Canadian Trust and Loans.

Aetna Trust Company
2230 Park Place
666 Burrard Street
Vancouver, B.C. V6C 2X8
(604) 685-1208

AGF Trust Company
77 King Street West
Royal Trust Tower, Suite 2006
Toronto, Ontario M5K 1B9
(416) 216-5353

Bank of Nova Scotia Trust Company (The)
Scotia Plaza, 44 King Street West
Toronto, Ontario M5H 1H1
(416) 866-6832

Bayshore Trust Company
825 Eglinton Avenue West, 4th Floor
Toronto, Ontario M5N 1E7
(416) 256-0888

Bonaventure Trust Inc.
1245 Sherbrooke Street West, Room 200
Montreal, Quebec H3G 1G3
(514) 879-9257

Canada Trust
Canada Trust Tower, BCE Place
161 Bay Street
Toronto, Ontario M5J 2T2
(416) 361-8000

Canadian Italian Trust Company
6999 St. Laurent Boulevard
Montreal, Quebec H2S 3E1
(514) 270-4124

CanWest Trust
31st Floor - TD Centre
201 Portage Avenue
Winnipeg, Manitoba R3B 3L7
(204) 956-2025

Capital Trust Corporation
600 René Levesque Boulevard
Montreal, Quebec H3B 1N4
(514) 393-8877

CIBC Trust Corporation
55 Yonge Street, Suite 900
Toronto, Ontario M5E 1J4
(416) 861-7000

Citizens Trust Company
815 West Hastings Street, Suite 401
Vancouver, B.C. V6C 1B4
(604) 682-7171

Co-Operative Trust Company of
   Canada
333 3rd Avenue North
Saskatoon, Saskatchewan S7K 2M2
(306) 956-1800

Community Trust Company Ltd.
2271 Bloor Street West
Toronto, Ontario M6S 1P1
(416) 763-2291

Effort Trust Company (The)
240 Main Street East
Hamilton, Ontario L8N 1H5
(905) 528-8956

Equitable Trust Company (The)
30 St. Clair Avenue West, Suite 700
Toronto, Ontario M4V 3A1
(416) 515-7000

Evangeline Trust Company
535 Albert Street
Windsor, N.S. B0N 2T0
(902) 798-8326

Family Trust Corporation
5954 Highway 7
Markham, Ontario L3P 1A2
(416) 471-1111

Fiducle Desjardins Inc.
1 Complexe Desjardins
Tour Sud 16e étage
Montréal, Québec H5B 1E4
(514) 286-9441

FirstLine Trust Company
33 Yonge Street, Suite 700
Toronto, Ontario M5E 1G4
(416) 865-1511

Fortis Trust Corporation
The Fortis Building
139 Water Street, P.O. Box 7067
St. John's, Newfoundland A1E 3Y3
(709) 726-7992

Granville Savings & Mortgage
  Corporation
Grosvenor Bldg.
Suite 290, 1040 West Georgia Street
Vancouver, B.C. V6E 4H1
(604) 682-2694

Home Savings & Loan Corporation
15 Church Street, Suite 100
St. Catherines, Ontario L2R 7JP
(905) 688-3131

Household Trust Company
101 Duncan Mill Road
Don Mills, Ontario M3B 1Z3
(416) 443-3600

Income Trust Company
181 Main Street West
Hamilton, Ontario L8P 4S1
(416) 528-9811

Inland Trust and Savings Corp. Ltd.
201 - One Forks Market Road
Winnipeg, Manitoba R3C 4L9
(204) 949-4800

Investors Group Trust Co. Ltd.
One Canada Centre
447 Portage Avenue
Winnipeg, Manitoba R3C 3B6
(204) 943-0361

League Savings & Mortgage Company
6074 Lady Hammond Road
P.O. Box 8900, Station A
Halifax, N.S. B3K 5M5
(902) 453-4220

London Trust & Savings Corporation
4950 Yonge Street, Suite 200
Toronto, Ontario M2N 6K1
(416) 229-6700

Merchant Private Trust Company (The)
Scotia Plaza, Suite 4714
40 King Street West
Toronto, Ontario M5H 3Y2
(416) 867-1716

Metropolitan Trust Company of
  Canada
2700-10303 Jasper Avenue
Edmonton, Alberta T5J 3N6
(403) 421-2020

Montreal Trust Company
Place Montreal Trust
1800 McGill College Avenue
Montreal, Quebec H3A 3K9
(514) 982-7000

MRS Trust Company
150 Bloor Street West, Suite 305
Toronto, Ontario M5S 2X9
(416) 926-0221

Municipal Trust Company
The Municipal Tower
70 Collier Street, P.O. Box 147
Barrie, Ontario L4M 4S9
(705) 734-7500

Mutual Trust Company
Suite 400, 70 University Avenue
Toronto, Ontario M5J 2M4
(416) 598-7837

Natcan Trust Company
National Bank Building
600 Rue de la Gauchetière West
Montréal, Québec H3B 4L2
(514) 394-4000

National Trust Company
1 Ontario Street
P.O. Box 128
Stratford, Ontario N5A 6S9
(519) 271-2050

North American Trust Company
18th Floor, 151 Yonge Street
Toronto, Ontario M5C 2W7
(416) 362-7211

NAL Mortgage Company
151 Yonge Street, Suite 1800
Toronto, Ontario M5C 2W7
(416) 867-8858

North West Trust Company
1800 TD Tower
Edmonton Centre, 10205 - 101 Street
Edmonton, Alberta T5J 4G1
(403) 429-9300

Northern Trust Company Canada
BCE Place
161 Bay Street, Suite 4540
Toronto, Ontario M5J 2S1
(416) 365-7161

Pacific and Western Trust Corporation
Suite 950, 410 - 22nd Street East
Saskatoon, Saskatchewan S7K 5T6
(306) 244-1868

Peace Hills Trust Company
10th Floor, Peace Hills Trust Tower
10011 - 109 Street
Edmonton, Alberta T5J 3S8
(403) 421-1606

Peoples Trust Company
14th Floor, 888 Dunsmuir Street
Vancouver, B.C. V6C 3K4
(604) 683-2881

RBC Trust
14th Floor, North Tower
Royal Bank Plaza
Toronto, Ontario M5J 2J2
(416) 865-0515

Royal Trust
Royal Trust Tower
3rd Floor
Toronto, Ontario M5W 1P9
(416) 955-2700

Security Home Mortgage Investment
Suite 1510
25 Adelaide Street East
Toronto, Ontario
M5C 1Y2
(416) 366-2254

Sherbrooke Trust
75 Wellington North
P.O. Box 250
Sherbrooke, P.Q. J1H 5J2
(819) 563-4011

Sun Life Trust Company
225 King Street West
Toronto, Ontario M5V 3C5
(416) 408-7283

TD Trust Company
Toronto Dominion Centre, P.O. Box 1
Commercial Union Tower, 4th Floor
Toronto, Ontario M5K 1A2
(416) 982-8222

Trust Company of Bank of Montreal (The)
302 Bay Street
Toronto, Ontario M5X 1A1
(416) 867-5688

Trust Général du Canada
1100 University Street, 12th Floor
Montréal, Québec H3B 2G7
(514) 871-7200

Trust La Laurentienne du Canada Inc.
425 de Maisonneuve Blvd. West
Montréal, Québec H3A 3G5

Trust Prêt et Revenu
Suite 700, 850 Place d'Youville
Quebec, Quebec G1K 7P3
(418) 692-1221

Victoria & Grey Mortgage Corporation
1 Adelaide Street East
Toronto, Ontario M5C 2W8
(416) 361-3661

LIFE INSURANCE COMPANIES

The following is an alphabetical list of the headquarters addresses and telephone numbers of the 100 largest life insurance companies in the United States and Canada. The list is provided courtesy of A.M. Best Company of Oldwick, New Jersey 08858 (tel. 908-439-2200), which rates the financial stability of life insurance companies.

Life insurance companies are normally ranked in one of three ways: by admitted assets, by life insurance in force, or by total premium income. Although any of these rankings would include most of the same companies, this particular list is based on admitted assets. Such assets include all the assets a life insurance company has accumulated over the years, including investments in real estate, mortgages, stocks, and bonds. Because of the enormous size of these assets, insurance companies have become extremely important institutional investors. The other two methods of ranking these companies, by life insurance in force and by total premium income, show the amount of coverage insurance companies are providing and the dollar amount of their sales. These are also important figures to judge a company by, but they do not provide as direct an indication of a company's importance in the finance and investment markets.

The life insurance industry is characterized by a few giant firms with a high percentage of the industry's total assets and a large number of smaller companies. The top two firms, Prudential Insurance Co. of America and Metropolitan Life Insurance Company, had assets at the end of 1996 of $178.6 billion and $162.5 billion, respectively. The third-ranking firm, Teachers Insurance & Annuity Association of America, had assets of $86.4 billion. The 25th ranked company, State Farm Life Insurance Co., had assets of $21.9 billion, while the 50th, SAFECO Life Insurance Co., posted assets of $11.5 billion. The 100th ranked firm, Provident Mutual Life Insurance Co., reported $5.2 billion.

The companies on this list represent two distinct types of insurance company. One is owned by stockholders, and its or its parent company's shares are traded on the New York or American Stock Exchange or over the counter. This type of company is in business to write life insurance policies, invest premiums, and a portion of the difference between investment income and insurance claims and expenses ultimately reaches shareholders as dividends or increases in shareholder's equity. The other type of company, called a mutual life insurance company (the word mutual is usually in the name), is owned by policyholders, who receive a portion of the profits the company may earn through policyholder dividends. Mutual companies have no outstanding stock traded on an exchange, since the company is owned solely by its policyholders.

As in other areas of the financial services industry, competition has been increasing among life insurers. The advent in the early 1980s of universal life insurance, which ties cash value buildup to money-market rates, put additional pressure on all insurers to make policies more competitive. By the 1990s, the life insurance industry had produced a panoply of products which allow policyholders a wide range of flexibility in paying premiums, building cash value and buying insurance protection. In addition to traditional whole life and term policies, companies now offer universal life, variable life (where the policyholder chooses between stock, bond, and money-market investments), variable universal life, and a wide range of annuity and Individual Retirement Account products. Many insurers also offer financial planning services.

In addition to their role as insurers of lives, life insurance companies have become an important source of capital for world capital markets. Insurance companies are a major force in the stock market; the municipal, corporate, and government bond markets; in real estate (both as owners and lenders); and as providers of venture capital. Some insurance companies have expanded their offerings by acquiring brokerage and money management firms.

Aetna Life Insurance and Annuity
Company
151 Farmington Avenue
Hartford, Connecticut 06156
(860) 273-0123

Aid Association for Lutherans
4321 North Ballard Road
Appleton, Wisconsin 54919-0001
(414) 734-5721

AIG Life Insurance Co.
One ALICO Plaza
Wilmington, Delaware 19801
(302) 594-2000

Alexander Hamilton Life Insurance
Company of America
32991 Hamilton Court
Farmington Hills, Michigan 48334-3358
(810) 553-2000

Allianz Life Insurance Company of North
America
1750 Hennepin Avenue
Minneapolis, Minnesota 55403-2195
(612) 347-6500

Allmerica Financial Life Insurance &
Annuity Co.
440 Lincoln Street
Worcester, Massachusetts 01653
(508) 855-1000

Allstate Life Insurance Company
3100 Sanders Road, Suite M5B
Northbrook, Illinois 60062-7154
(847) 402-5000

American Family Life Assurance Company
of Columbus
1932 Wynnton Road
Columbus, Georgia 31999
(306) 323-3431

American General Life and Accident
Insurance Co.
American General Center
Nashville, Tennessee 37250
(615) 749-1000

American General Life Insurance Co.
P.O. Box 1591
Houston, Texas 77251-1591
(713) 522-1111

American International Life Assurance Co.
of New York
70 Pine Street
New York, New York 10270
(212) 770-7000

American Life & Casualty Insurance Co.
11815 N. Pennsylvania Street
Carmel, Indiana 46032
(317) 817-4000

American Life Insurance Company of
Delaware
P.O. Box 2226
Wilmington, Delaware 19899
(302) 594-2000

American National Insurance Company
One Moody Plaza
Galveston, Texas 77550-7999
(409) 763-4661

American Skandia Life Assurance Corp.
P.O. Box 883
Shelton, Connecticut 06484-0883
(203) 926-1888

American United Life Insurance Company
P.O. Box 368
Indianapolis, Indiana 46206-0368
(317) 263-1877

Anchor National Life Insurance Company
1 SunAmerica Center
Los Angeles, California 90067-6022
(310) 772-6000

AUSA Life Insurance Co.
666 Fifth Avenue, 25th Floor
New York, New York 10103-0001
(212) 246-5234

Canada Life Assurance Company
330 University Avenue
Toronto, Ontario, Canada M5G 1R8
(416) 597-1456

Connecticut General Life Insurance
Company
900 Cottage Grove Road
Bloomfield, Connecticut 06002
(203) 726-6000

Continental Assurance Company
CNA Plaza, 22 South
Chicago, Illinois 60685
(312) 822-5000

Crown Life Insurance Company
1901 Scarth Street
Regina, Saskatchewan, Canada S4P 4L4
(306) 751-6000

Equitable Life Assurance Society of the
United States
787 Seventh Avenue, 49th Floor
New York, New York 10019
(212) 554-1234

Equitable Variable Life Insurance
Company
787 Seventh Avenue, 49th Floor
New York, New York 10019-6082
(212) 554-1234

Fidelity Investments Life Insurance Co.
82 Devonshire Street, R25B
Boston, Massachusetts 02109
(617) 663-9106

First Allmerica Financial Life Insurance
Co.
440 Lincoln Street
Worcester, Massachusetts 01653
(508) 855-1000

First Colony Life Insurance Company
P.O. Box 1280
Lynchburg, Virginia 24505
(804) 845-0911

Fortis Benefits Insurance Co.
P.O. Box 64271
St. Paul, Minnesota 55164
(612) 538-4000

The Franklin Life Insurance Company
Franklin Square
Springfield, Illinois 62713
(217) 528-2011

General American Life Insurance
Company
P.O. Box 396
St. Louis, Missouri 63166
(314) 843-8700

General Electric Capital Assurance Co.
P.O. Box 490
Seattle, Washington 98111-0490
(206) 625-1755

Great American Life Insurance Co.
250 East Fifth Street
Cincinnati, Ohio 45202
(513) 357-3350

Great Northern Insured Annuities Corp.
P.O. Box 490
Seattle, Washington 98111-0490
(206) 625-1755

Great-West Life & Annuity Insurance Co.
8515 East Archard Road
Englewood, Colorado 80111
(303) 689-3000

Great-West Life Assurance Company
100 Osborne Street North
Winnipeg, Manitoba, Canada R3C 3A5
(204) 946-1190

Guardian Insurance & Annuity Co. Inc.
201 Park Avenue South
New York, New York 10003
(212) 598-8000

Guardian Life Insurance Company of America
201 Park Avenue South
New York, New York 10003
(212) 598-8000

Hartford Life Insurance Company
200 Hopmeadow Street
Simsbury, Connecticut 06089
(860) 843-8291

IDS Life Insurance Company
IDS Tower 10
Minneapolis, Minnesota 55440-0010
(612) 671-3131

Industrial Alliance Life Insurance Co.
1080 Saint Louis Road
Sillcry, Quebec, Canada G1K 7M3
(418) 684-5275

Jackson National Life Insurance Company
5901 Executive Drive
Lansing, Michigan 48911
(517) 394-3400

Jefferson-Pilot Life Insurance Company
P.O. Box 21008
Greensboro, North Carolina 27420
(910) 691-3000

John Alden Life Insurance Company
P.O. Box 020270
Miami, Florida 33102-0270
(305) 470-3100

John Hancock Mutual Life Insurance
  Company
P.O. Box 111
Boston, Massachusetts 02117
(617) 572-6000

Kemper Investors Life Insurance Company
1 Kemper Drive T-1
Long Grove, Illinois 60049-0001
(847) 550-5500

Keyport Life Insurance Company
125 High Street
Boston, Massachusetts 02110-2712
(617) 526-1400

Knights of Columbus
P.O. Box 1670
New Haven, Connecticut 06507-0901
(203) 772-2130

Liberty National Life Insurance Company
P.O. Box 2612
Birmingham, Alabama 35202
(205) 325-2722

Life Investors Insurance Co. of America
4333 Edgewood Road, N.E.
Cedar Rapids, Iowa 52499
(319) 398-8511

Life Insurance Company of Virginia
6610 West Broad Street
Richmond, Virginia 23230-1702
(804) 281-6000

Lincoln National Life Insurance Company
1300 South Clinton Street
Fort Wayne, Indiana 46802
(219) 455-2000

London Life Insurance Co. of Canada
255 Dufferin Avenue
London, Ontario, Canada N6A 4K1
(519) 432-2000

Lutheran Brotherhood
625 Fourth Avenue South
Minneapolis, Minnesota 55415
(612) 340-7000

Manufacturers Life Insurance Company
200 Bloor Street East
Toronto, Ontario, Canada M4W 1E5
(416) 926-0100

Manufacturers Life Insurance Co. (USA)
73 Tremont Street, Suite 1300
Boston, Massachusetts 02108-3915
(617) 854-4300

Manulife Financial
116 Huntington Avenue
Boston, Massachusetts 02116
(617) 266-6004

Massachusetts Mutual Life Insurance
  Company
1295 State Street
Springfield, Massachusetts 01111
(413) 788-8411

MBL Life Assurance Corp.
520 Broad Street
Newark, New Jersey 07102-3111
(201) 481-8000

Merrill Lynch Life Insurance Company
P.O. Box 9061
Princeton, New Jersey 08543-9061
(609) 282-1405

Metropolitan Insurance and Annuity
  Company
One Madison Avenue, Area 6C
New York, New York 10010
(212) 578-2211

Metropolitan Life Insurance Company
One Madison Avenue, Area 9H
New York, New York 10010-3690
(212) 578-2211

Minnesota Mutual Life Insurance Company
400 Robert Street North
St. Paul, Minnesota 55101
(612) 665-3500

Mutual Life Assurance Co. of Canada
227 King Street South
Waterloo, Ontario, Canda N2J 4C5
(519) 888-2290

The Mutual Life Insurance Company of
New York
1740 Broadway at 55th Street
New York, New York 10019
(212) 708-2000

Mutual of America Life Insurance Company
320 Park Avenue
New York, New York 10022
(212) 224-1600

National Life Insurance Co. of Vermont
National Life Drive
Montpelier, Vermont 05604
(802) 229-3333

Nationwide Life Insurance Company
One Nationwide Plaza
Columbus, Ohio 43216
(614) 249-7111

New York Life Insurance Company
51 Madison Avenue
New York, New York 10010
(212) 576-7000

Northern Life Insurance Co.
1110 Third Avenue
Seattle, Washington 98101
(206) 292-1111

Northwestern Mutual Life Insurance
Company
720 East Wisconsin Avenue
Milwaukee, Wisconsin 53202
(414) 271-1444

PFL Life Insurance Company
4333 Edgewood Road N.E.
Cedar Rapids, Iowa 52499
(319) 398-8511

Pacific Mutual Life Insurance Company
700 Newport Center Drive
Newport Beach, California 92660
(714) 640-3011

Penn Mutual Life Insurance Company
600 Dresher Road
Horsham, Pennsylvania 19044
(215) 956-8000

Peoples Security Life Insurance Company
300 West Morgan Street
Durham, North Carolina 27701
(919) 687-8200

Phoenix Home Life Mutual Life Insurance
Company
100 Bright Meadow Boulevard
Enfield, Connecticut 06083-1900
(518) 479-8000

Principal Mutual Life Insurance Company
711 High Street
Des Moines, Iowa 50392-0120
(515) 247-5111

Protective Life Insurance Company
P.O. Box 2606
Birmingham, Alabama 35202
(705) 879-9230

Provident Life and Accident Insurance
Company
One Fountain Square
Chattanooga, Tennessee 37402-1330
(423) 755-1011

Provident Mutual Life Insurance Company
P.O. Box 1717
Valley Forge, Pennsylvania 19482-1717
(610) 407-1717

Providian Life & Health Insurance Co.
20 Moores Road
Frazer, Pennsylvania 19355
(610) 648-5000

Pruco Life Insurance Company
213 Washington Street
Newark, New Jersey 07102
(201) 802-6000

The Prudential Insurance Company of
America
Prudential Plaza
Newark, New Jersey 07102-2992
(201) 802-6000

ReliaStar Life Insurance Co.
20 Washington Avenue South
Minneapolis, Minnesota 55401
(612) 372-5432

SAFECO Life Insurance Company
P.O. Box 34690
Seattle, Washington 98124-1690
(425) 867-8000

Security Benefit Life Insurance Co.
700 Harrison Street
Topeka, Kansas 66636
(913) 295-3000

State Farm Life Insurance Company
One State Farm Plaza
Bloomington, Illinois 61710
(309) 766-2311

SunAmerica Life Insurance Co.
1 SunAmerica Center
Los Angeles, California 90067-6022
(310) 772-6000

Sun Life Assurance Company
of Canada
150 King Street West
Toronto, Ontario, Canada M5H 1J9
(416) 979-9966

Sun Life Assurance Company of Canada
(U.S.)
One Sun Life Executive Park
Wellesley Hills, Massachusetts 02181
(617) 237-6030

Teachers Insurance and Annuity Association
of America
730 Third Avenue
New York, New York 10017
(212) 490-9000

Transamerica Life Insurance and Annuity
Company
1150 South Olive Street
Los Angeles, California 90015
(213) 742-3111

Transamerica Occidental Life Insurance
Company
1150 South Olive Street
Los Angeles, California 90015
(213) 742-2111

The Travelers Insurance Company
One Tower Square
Hartford, Connecticut 06183
(860) 277-0111

UNUM Life Insurance Company of
America
2211 Congress Street
Portland, Maine 04122
(207) 770-2211

United of Omaha Life Insurance
Company
Mutual of Omaha Plaza
Omaha, Nebraska 68175
(402) 342-7600

USAA Life Insurance Company
9800 Fredericksburg Road
San Antonio, Texas 78288
(210) 498-8000

USG Annuity and Life Company
604 Locust Street
Des Moines, Iowa 50309
(515) 282-3230

The Variable Annuity Life Insurance
Company
P.O. Box 3206
Houston, Texas 77019
(713) 526-5251

Western National Life Insurance
Company
5555 San Felipe, Suite 900
Houston, Texas 77056
(713) 888-7800

Western and Southern Life Insurance
Company
400 Broadway
Cincinnati, Ohio 45202
(513) 629-1800

BROKERAGE FIRMS

Traditionally, brokers sold mostly stocks and bonds to their customers, who were primarily persons of substantial means. Today, these firms allow customers to buy and sell stocks, bonds, commodities, options, mutual funds, bank certificates of deposit, limited partnerships and many other financial products. Brokers also offer asset management accounts, which combine holdings of assets like stocks and bonds with a money-market fund which provides checkwriting and credit card features. Most brokers in addition offer individualized financial planning services. As a result of this wide range of products, brokers today have a much more diverse clientele, ranging from young persons just starting to invest to wealthy retired people who are experienced investors.

On May 1, 1975, known as May Day in the brokerage industry, the era of fixed commissions ended. This move brought much more competition within the industry and ushered in a new breed of broker—the discounter. These brokers specialize in executing buy and sell orders for stocks, bonds and options. As a rule, they charge commissions far lower than full-service brokers. Discounters do not give advice about which securities to buy or sell, however, so investors who use them generally are more experienced and knowledgeable. Some discount brokers were acquired in the 1980s by commercial banks, who under the Glass-Steagall Act of 1933 are not allowed to act as full-service brokers. Banks were allowed to make such acquisitions because discount brokers do not give advice or underwrite securities. Full-service firms offer far more guidance on what investments are appropriate for each client. For this guidance, however, clients must pay significantly higher charges.

Within the full-service brokerage firm category, two varieties exist. The largest firms are known as wire houses, because they have a large network of offices nationally linked by advanced communications equipment. National wire house firms also tend to have an important presence overseas. In contrast, regional brokerage firms concentrate on serving customers in a particular area of the country. Such firms typically do not offer as wide an array of financial products, although they usually provide all the basics. Regional firms tend to concentrate on finding investment opportunities not yet discovered by large national firms.

In addition to providing services to individuals, brokers who also engage in investment banking play an important role in raising capital for federal, state and local governments and for corporations. Such firms underwrite new issues of debt securities for governments and equity and debt issues for corporations and distribute them to both institutional and individual investors. In addition, brokers act as advisers to corporations involved in merger and acquisition activity and other areas of corporate finance. Increasingly, brokerage firms are expanding their operations internationally, to facilitate trading of foreign currencies, and foreign debt and equity securities.

This alphabetical list contains the top 100 brokerage firms as measured by the amount of capital. (Capital is the sum of long-term borrowings and ownership equity.) Capital is crucial to a brokerage firm because it must constantly be put at risk in underwriting and trading securities.

Most of these brokerage firms were originally formed as partnerships, but in recent years, many incorporated and a number offered shares of stock in their companies to the public. Such public offerings are often the best way for a brokerage firm to raise the additional capital it needs to be competitive.

Today, the lines are blurring in the full-service sector. Many brokerage firms, such as The Charles Schwab Corporation, which made its reputation as a discount broker, offer many of the services of full-service brokers. The discount brokerage business has also expanded dramatically, and most discounters offer websites. The listing of the top 100 full-service brokerage firms is courtesy of the Securities

Industry Association [120 Broadway, New York, NY 10271-0080; (212) 608-1500]. The listing of top discount brokers is courtesy of Mercer & Co. [379 West Broadway, Suite 400, New York, NY 10012; (212) 334 -6212; (800) 582-9854].

Full-Service Brokerage Firms

ABN AMRO Chicago Corp.
208 South LaSalle Street
Chicago, Illinois 60604
(312) 855-7600

Advest Group, Inc.
280 Trumbull Street
Hartford, Connecticut 06103
(203) 525-1421

Allen & Company Incorporated
711 Fifth Avenue
New York, New York 10022
(212) 832-7057

Alliance Capital Management L.P.
1345 Avenue of the Americas
New York, New York 10105
(212) 969-1000

American Express Financial
    Advisors Inc.
IDS Tower 10
Minneapolis, Minnesota 55440
(612) 671-3142

Arnhold and S. Bleichroeder, Inc.
45 Broadway
New York, New York 10006
(212) 943-9200

BA Investment Services, Inc.
2000 Broadway, 3rd Floor
Oakland, California 94612
(510) 287-3230

Robert W. Baird & Co. Incorporated
777 East Wisconsin Avenue
Milwaukee, Wisconsin 53202
(414) 765-3500

The Bank of Tokyo-Mitsubishi Trust
    Company
1251 Avenue of the Americas
New York, New York 10116-3138
(212) 782-4000

The Bear Stearns Companies Inc.
245 Park Avenue
New York, New York 10167
(212) 272-2000

BHC Securities, Inc.
One Commerce Square
2005 Market Street, 12th Floor
Philadelphia, Pennsylvania 19103-3212
(215) 636-3000

William Blair & Company, L.L.C.
222 West Adams Street
Chicago, Illinois 60606
(312) 236-1600

Brown & Company Securities Corporation
One Beacon Street
Boston, Massachusetts 02108-3102
(617) 357-4410

Brown Brothers Harriman & Co.
59 Wall Street
New York, New York 10005
(212) 483-1818

J.C. Bradford & Co. LLC
330 Commerce Street
Nashville, Tennessee 37201-1809
(615) 748-9000

BT Alex. Brown Inc.
One Bankers Trust Plaza
New York, New York 10167
(212) 250-2500

Chase Securities Inc.
One Chase Manhattan Plaza, 35th Floor
New York, New York 10081
(212) 552-1776

CIBC Oppenheimer Corp.
CIBC Oppenheimer Tower
World Financial Center
New York, New York 10281
(212) 856-4000

Citicorp Securities, Inc.
399 Park Avenue, 2nd Floor
New York, New York 10043
(212) 559-1000

Commerzbank Capital Markets Corporation
Two World Financial Center, 34th Floor
New York, New York 10281-1050
(212) 266-7700

Cowen & Co.
Financial Square
New York, New York 10005-3597
(212) 495-6000

Credit Lyonnais Securities (USA) Inc.
1301 Avenue of the Americas, 37th Floor
New York, New York 10019
(212) 408-5700

Credit Suisse First Boston
11 Madison Avenue
New York, New York 10010-3629
(212) 325-2000

Crowell, Weedon & Co.
One Wilshire Boulevard
Los Angeles, California 90017
(213) 620-1850

Daiwa Securities America, Inc.
32 Old Slip, One Financial Square
New York, New York 10005
(212) 612-7000

Deutsche Bank Securities Inc.
31 West 52nd Street
New York, New York 10019
(212) 468-5000

Donaldson, Lufkin & Jenrette, Inc.
140 Broadway
New York, New York 10005
(212) 504-3000

E.D. & F. Man International Inc.
440 South LaSalle Street, 20th Floor
Chicago, Illinois 60605
(312) 663-7500

A.G. Edwards, Inc.
One North Jefferson
St. Louis, Missouri 63103
(314) 955-3000

EVEREN Securities Inc.
77 West Wacker Drive
Chicago, Illinois 60601
(312) 574-6000

Fahnestock & Co. Inc.
110 Wall Street
New York, New York 10005-3878
(212) 668-8000

Ferris, Baker, Watts, Inc.
1720 Eye Street, N.W.
Washington, D.C. 20006
(202) 429-3500

Fidelity Brokerage
82 Devonshire Street, L15A
Boston, Massachusetts 02109
(617) 563-7000

First Marathon Inc.
2 First Canadian Place, Suite 3200
Toronto, Ontario M5X 1J9, Canada
(416) 869-3707

First Union Brokerage Services, Inc.
201 S. College Street, 4th Floor
Charlotte, North Carolina 28288
(800) 326-4434 (704) 374-6927

Furman Selz LLC
230 Park Avenue
New York, New York 10169
(212) 309-8200

The Goldman Sachs Group, L.P.
85 Broad Street
New York, New York 10004
(212) 902-1000

Greenwich Capital Markets, Inc.
600 Steamboat Road
Greenwich, Connecticut 06830
(203) 625-2700

Gruntal Financial L.L.C.
14 Wall Street
New York, New York 10005
(212) 267-8800

GT Global, Inc.
50 California Street, 27th Floor
San Francisco, California 94111
(415) 392-6181

Hambrecht & Quist LLC
One Bush Street
San Francisco, California 94104
(415) 439-3000

John Hancock Funds, Inc.
101 Huntington Avenue
Boston, Massachusetts 02199
(617) 375-1500

Herzog, Heine, Geduld, Inc.
26 Broadway
New York, New York 10004-1763
(212) 908-4000

J.J.B. Hilliard, W.L. Lyons, Inc.
Hilliard Lyons Center
501 S. 4th Avenue
Louisville, Kentucky 40232-2760
(502) 588-8400

HSBC Securities, Inc.
140 Broadway
New York, New York 10005-1101
(212) 825-6780

ING Baring (U.S.) Securities, Inc.
667 Madison Avenue
New York, New York 10021
(212) 409-7700

Interra Financial Incorporated
Dain Bosworth Plaza
60 South Sixth Street
Minneapolis, Minnesota 55402-4402
(612) 371-7750

Interstate/Johnson Lane Corporation
Interstate Tower
121 W. Trade Street
Charlotte, North Carolina 28202
(704) 379-9000

Janney Montgomery Scott Inc.
1801 Market Street, 10th Floor
Philadelphia, Pennsylvania 19103
(215) 665-6000

Jeffries Group, Inc.
11100 Santa Monica Boulevard, Suite 1100
Los Angeles, California 90025
(310) 445-1199

Edward Jones
12555 Manchester Road
St. Louis, Missouri 63131
(314) 515-2000

Keefe, Bruyette & Woods, Inc.
Two World Trade Center, Suite 8566
New York, New York 10048
(212) 323-8300

Lazard Freres & Co. LLC
1 Rockefeller Plaza
New York, New York 10020
(212) 632-6000

Legg Mason, Inc.
Legg Mason Tower
111 South Calvert Street
Baltimore, Maryland 21202
(410) 539-0000

Lehman Brothers Holdings Inc.
Three World Financial Center
New York, New York 10285
(212) 526-7000

Levesque Beaubien Geoffrion Inc.
1155 Metcalfe Street, 5th Floor
Montreal, Quebec H3B 4S9, Canada
(514) 879-2222

Bernard L. Madoff Investment Securities
885 Third Avenue
New York, New York 10022
(212) 230-2424

McDonald & Company Securities, Inc.
800 Superior Avenue, Suite 2100
Cleveland, Ohio 44114-2603
(216) 443-2300

Merrill Lynch & Co., Inc.
250 Vesey Street
North Tower, World Financial Center
New York, New York 10281-1332
(212) 449-1000

Midland Walwyn Capital Inc.
BCE Place, 181 Bay Street, Suite 400
Toronto, Ontario M5J 2V8, Canada
(416) 369-7400

Morgan Keegan, Inc.
Morgan Keegan Tower
Fifty Front Street
Memphis, Tennessee 38103
(901) 524-4100

J.P. Morgan Securities Inc.
60 Wall Street
New York, New York 10260
(212) 483-2323

Morgan Stanley Dean Witter
1585 Broadway
New York, New York 10036
(212) 761-4000

Nesbitt Burns Inc.
1 First Canadian Plaza, 5th Floor
P.O. Box 150
Toronto, Ontario M5X 1H3 Canada
(416) 359-4000

Nesbitt Burns Securities Inc.
115 S. LaSalle Street, 20th Floor
Chicago, Illinois 60603
(312) 461-6220

Neuberger & Berman, LLC
605 Third Avenue
New York, New York 10158-3698
(212) 476-9000

Nikko Securities Co. International, Inc.
200 Liberty Street
New York, New York 10281
(212) 416-5400

Nomura Securities International, Inc.
2 World Financial Center, Building B
New York, New York 10281
(212) 667-9300

The John Nuveen Company
333 West Wacker Drive
Chicago, Illinois 60606
(312) 917-7700

Oppenheimer & Co., Inc.
Oppenheimer Tower
World Financial Center
New York, New York 10281
(212) 667-7000

Oppenheimer Funds Distributor,
  Inc.
Two World Trade Center, Suite 3400
New York, New York 10048-0203
(212) 323-0200

PaineWebber Group Inc.
1285 Avenue of the Americas
New York, New York 10019
(212) 713-2000

Paloma Securities L.L.C.
2 American Lane, Box 2571
Greenwich American Centre
Greenwich, Connecticut 06836-2571
(203) 861-3200

Paribas Corporation
787 Seventh Avenue
New York, New York 10019
(212) 841-3000

Piper Jaffray Companies Inc.
Piper Jaffray Tower
222 South 9th Street
Minneapolis, Minnesota 55402
(612) 342-6000

Prudential Securities Incorporated
One Seaport Plaza
199 Water Street
New York, New York 10292
(212) 214-1000

Putnam Mutual Funds Corporation
One Post Office Square
Boston, Massachusetts 02109
(617) 292-1000

Ragen MacKenzie Inc.
999 Third Avenue, Suite 4300
Seattle, Washington 98104
(206) 343-5000

Raymond James Financial, Inc.
880 Carillon Parkway
St. Petersburg, Florida 33716
(813) 573-3800

Republic New York Securities Corp.
425 Fifth Avenue, 12th Floor
New York, New York 10018
(212) 525-6600 (800) 487-2346

The Robinson-Humphrey Company,
  Inc.
Atlanta Financial Center
3333 Peachtree Road, N.E.
Atlanta, Georgia 30326
(404) 266-6000

Santander Investment Securities Inc.
45 East 53rd Street
New York, New York 10022
(212) 350-3950

Salomon Smith Barney Inc.
388 Greenwich Street
New York, New York 10013
(212) 816-6000

Sanford C. Bernstein & Co., Inc.
767 Fifth Avenue
New York, New York 10153
(212) 486-5800

M.A. Schapiro & Co., Inc.
One Chase Manhattan Plaza
New York, New York 10005
(212) 530-7500

Schroder & Co. Inc.
Equitable Center
787 Seventh Avenue
New York, New York 10019-6016

The Charles Schwab Corporation
101 Montgomery Street
San Francisco, California 94101
(415) 627-7000

D.E. Shaw & Co.
39th Floor Tower 45
120 West Forty-Fifth Street
New York, New York 10036
(212) 478-0000

Societe Generale Securities
  Corporation
50 Rockefeller Plaza, 2nd Floor
New York, New York 10020
(212) 957-3800

Southwest Securities Group, Inc.
1201 Elm Street, 43rd Floor
Dallas, Texas 75270
(214) 651-1800

Spear, Leeds & Kellogg
120 Broadway
New York, New York 10271
(212) 433-7000

Stephens Inc.
111 Center Street
Little Rock, Arkansas 72203
(501) 374-4361

TD Securities (USA) Inc.
31 West 52nd Street
New York, New York 10019
(212) 468-0600

Tucker Anthony Incorporated
One Beacon Street
Boston, Massachusetts 02108
(617) 725-2000

UBS Securities LLC
10 East 50th Street
New York, New York 10022
(212) 335-1000

Waterhouse Investor Services, Inc.
100 Wall Street
New York, New York 10005
(212) 806-3500

Weiss, Peck & Greer, L.L.C.
One New York Plaza
New York, New York 10004
(212) 908-9500

Wheat First Butcher Singer
901 East Byrd Street
Richmond, Virginia 23219
(804) 649-2311

Yamaichi International (America), Inc.
Two World Trade Center, Suite 9650
New York, New York 10048
(212) 912-6400

Zurich Kemper Investments, Inc.
222 Riverside Plaza
Chicago, Illinois 60606
(312) 537-7000

Discount Brokerage Firms

Accutrade
4211 South 102nd Street
Omaha, Nebraska 68127
(402) 330-7605   (800) 882-4887

The Advisors Group Corp.
51 Louisiana Avenue, N.W.
Washington, DC 20001
(202) 783-0759   (800) 321-1640

Andrew Peck Associates
111 Pavonia Avenue
Jersey City, New Jersey 07310-1755
(201) 217-9500   (800) 221-5873

Arnold Securities
830 Second Avenue South
Minneapolis, Minnesota 55402
(612) 339-7040   (800) 292-4135
(800) 328-4076

Aufhauser & Company
53 Wall Street, 5th Floor
New York, New York 10005
(800) 368-3668

Baker & Co.,
1940 East Sixth Street
Cleveland, Ohio 44114
(216) 696-0167   (800) 321-1640

Barry Murphy & Co., Inc.
77 Summer Street
Boston, Massachusetts 02110
(617) 426-1770   (800) 221-2111

Berlind Securities
One North Broadway
White Plains, New York 10601
(914) 761-6665

Bidwell & Company
209 S.W. Oak Street
Portland, Oregon 97204
(503) 790-9000   (800) 547-6337

Brown & Company
20 Winthrop Square
Boston, Massachusetts 02110
(617) 426-8241

Bruno, Stolze & Company
Manchester/270 Office Center
12444 Powerscourt Drive, Suite 230
St. Louis, Missouri 63131
(314) 821-1990   (800) 899-6878

Bull & Bear Securities, Inc.
11 Hanover Square
New York, New York 10005
(212) 742-1300   (800) 262-5800

Burke, Christensen & Lewis
303 West Madison
Chicago, Illinois 60606
(800) 621-0392

Ceres Securities Inc.
P.O. Box 2209
Omaha Nebraska 68103-2209
(800) 628-6100

Charles Schwab
101 Montgomery Street
San Francisco, California 94104
(415) 627-7000   (800) 435-4000

Computel Securities, a division of
   Thomas F. White & Co.
1 Second Street, 5th Floor
San Francisco, 94105
(800) 432-0327

Consolidated Financial Investments
287 North Lindbergh, Suite 201
St. Louis, Missouri 63141
(314) 991-4030   (800) 292-6637

Cutter & Company Brokerage, Inc.
130 E. Jefferson, 2nd Floor
Kirkwood, Missouri 63122
(314) 965-6337   (800) 218-4625

Downstate Discount Brokers
259 Indian Rocks Road, North
Belleair Bluffs, Florida 34640
(813) 586-3541   (800) 780-3543

E*Trade Securities, Inc.
4 Embarcadero Place
2400 Geng Road
Palo Alto, California 94303
(800) 786-2575

Empire Financial
220 Crown Oak Centre
Longwood, Florida 32779
(407) 260-0084   (800) 900-8101

Fidelity Investments
161 Devonshire Street
Boston, Massachusetts 02110
(617) 737-6075   (800) 544-8666

First Union Brokerage Services
301 South College Street, 5th Floor
Charlotte, North Carolina 28288
(704) 383-0915   (800) 326-4434

Fleet Brokerage Securities
67 Wall Street, 9th Floor
New York, New York 10005
(212) 806-2888   (800) 221-8210

Freedom Investments
555 Madison Avenue
New York, New York 10022
(800) 221-1660 [national];
(800) 427-9503 [NY State]

Freeman Welwood & Company
1501 Fourth Avenue
Seattle, Washington 98101
(206) 382-5353   (800) 729-7585

Investors National Corporation
1300 North State Street
Bellingham, Washington 98225
(360) 734-1266   (800) 728-1266

Jack White & Company
9191 Town Centre Drive, Suite 220
San Diego, California 92122
(619) 587-2000   (800) 233-3411

J.D. Seibert & Company
20 West Ninth Street
Cincinnati, Ohio 45202-2024
(513) 241-8888   (800) 247-3396

JB Oxford & Company
665 Wilshire Boulevard, 3rd Floor
Beverly Hills, California 90212
(310) 275-7745   (800) 500-5007

John Finn & Company, Inc.
205 Dixie Terminal Building
Cincinnati, Ohio 45202
(513) 579-0066   (800) 743-7059

Kashner Davidson Securities Corporation
77 South Palm Avenue
Sarasota, Florida 34236
(941) 951-2626   (800) 678-2626

Kennedy, Cabot & Company
9470 Wilshire Boulevard
Beverly Hills, California 90212
(310) 550-0711   (800) 252-0090

Levitt & Levitt
135 S. LaSalle Street, Suite 1945
Chicago, Illinois 60603-4303
(312) 263-8500   (800) 671-8505

Lombard Institutional
598 Market Street, Suite 780
San Francisco, California 94105
(415) 597-6829   (800) 688-6896
(800) 688-3462 (Calfiornia only)

Marquette de Bary Company, Inc.
477 Madison Avenue
New York, New York 10022
(212) 644-5300   (800) 221-3305

Max Ule
26 Broadway, Suite 200
New York, New York 10004
(212) 809-1160   (800) 223-6642

Midwest Discount Brokers, Inc.
5945 Mission Gorge Road
San Diego, Calfiornia 92160
(619) 563-1131

Mongerson & Company
135 LaSalle Street, Suite 1000
Chicago, Illinois 60603-4109
(312) 263-3100   (800) 621-2627

Muriel Siebert & Company
885 Third Avenue, 17th Floor
New York, New York 10022-4802
(212) 644-2400   (800) 872-0711

National Discount Brokers
7 Hanover Square, 4th Floor
New York, New York 10004
(212) 248-2310   (800) 888-3999

Olde Discount Stockbrokers
751 Griswold Street
Detroit, Michigan 48226
(313) 961-6666   (800) 823-5400

Pacific Brokerage Services, Inc.
5757 Wilshire Boulevard, Suite 3
Los Angeles, California 90036
(213) 939-1101 (800) 421-8395

PC Financial Network
One Pershing Plaza
Jersey City, New Jersey 07399
(800) 825-5723

Peremel & Company, Inc.
1829 Reisterstown Road, Suite 120
Baltimore, Maryland 21208
(410) 486-4700   (800) 666-1440

Prestige Status, Inc.
271-603 Grand Central Parkway
Floral Park, New York 11005
(718) 229-4500   (800) 782-8871

Principal Financial Securities
North LaSalle Street
Chicago, Illinois 60602-3702
(312) 444-2110   (800) 621-4480 [national]
(800) 642-3105 [Illinois]

PT Discount Brokerage
11 S. LaSalle Street, 15th Floor
Chicago, Illinois 60603
(800) 248-5008

Quick & Reilly Inc.
26 Broadway
New York, New York 10004-1899
(212) 747-1200   (800) 672-7220

Recom Securities, Inc.
619 Marquette Avenue S., Suite 142
Minneapolis, Minnesota 55402
(612) 339-5566   (800) 328-8600

Regal Discount Securities
209 W. Jackson Boulevard, 4th Floor
Chicago, Illinois 60606
(312) 554-2240   (800) 786-9000

R.F. Lafferty & Company
50 Broad Street
New York, New York 10004
(212) 293-9000   (800) 221-8514

R.J. Forbes Group
150 Broad Hollow Road
Melville, New York 11747
(516) 549-7000   (800) 488-0090

Rodecker & Company
4000 Town Center
Southfield, Michigan 48075
(810) 358-2282   (800) 676-1848

Russo Securities
128 Sand Lane
Staten Island, New York 10305
(718) 448-2900   (800) 451-7877

S.C. Costa Company
320 South Boston Avenue, West Lobby
Tulsa, Oklahoma 74103
(918) 481-7090

Savoy Discount Brokerage
823 3rd Avenue, Suite 206
Seattle, Washington 98104-1617
(800) 961-1500

Scottsdale Securities
12855 Flushing Meadow Drive
St. Louis, Missouri 63131
(314) 965-1555 (800) 619-7283

Seaport Securities Corporation
19 Rector Street
New York, New York 10006
(212) 482-8689   (800) 732-7678

Shearman Ralston Inc.
17 Battery Place, Suite 604
New York, New York 10004-1102
(212) 248-1160   (800) 221-4242

Shochet Securities, Inc.
2351 East Hallandale Beach Boulevard
Hallandale, Florida 33009
(954) 454-0304   (800) 327-1536
(800) 940-4567 (Florida Only)

Spectrum Securities
21800 Burbank Boulevard, Suite 100
Woodland Hills, California 91367
(818) 715-1776   (800) 400-1776

St. Louis Discount Securities, Inc.
200 South Hanley, Lobby Suite 103
Clayton, Missouri 63105
(314) 721-7400   (800) 726-7401

State Discount Brokers
27600 Chagrin Boulevard
Cleveland, Ohio 44122
(216) 765-8500   (800) 222-5520

Sterling Investment Securities
135 S. LaSalle Street, Suite 2100
Chicago, Illinois 60603
(312) 236-0676   (800) 782-1522

StockCross
One Washington Mall
Boston, Massachusetts 02108
(617) 367-5700   (800) 225-6196
(800) 392-6104 (Mass. Only)

The Stock Mart
12655 Beatrice Street
Los Angeles, California 90066
(310) 577-7460 (800) 421-6563

Summit Discount Brokerage
305 Route 17 South
Paramus, NJ 07652
(201) 262-8400   (800) 631-1635

Sunlogic Securities Inc.
5333 Thornton Avenue
Newark, California 94560
(800) 556-4600

T. Rowe Price Discount Brokerage
100 East Pratt Street
Baltimore, Maryland 21202
(410) 547-2308   (800) 225-7720

Tradewell Discount Investing
25 Broadway, 7th Floor
New York, New York 10004
(212) 514-4000   (800) 289-7355

Tradex Brokerage Service
20 Vesey Street, Suite 800
New York, New York 10007
(212) 233-2000 (800) 522-3000

Tuttle Securities
307 South Townsend Street
Syracuse, New York 13202
(315) 422-2515   (800) 962-5489

USAA Brokerage Services
9800 Fredericksburg Road
San Antonio, Texas 78288
(210) 456-7215   (800) 531-8343

Vanguard Group
Vanguard Financial Center
Valley Forge, Pennsylvania 19482
(800) 992-8327

Voss & Company
6225 Brandon Avenue, Suite 120
Springfield, Virginia 22150
(703) 569-9300   (800) 426-8106

W.J. Gallagher & Company
2920 Garfield, Suite 303
Missoula, Montana 59801
(406) 721-1777   (800) 935-6633

Wall Street Access
17 Battery Place
New York, New York 10004
(212) 709-9518   (800) 925-5781

Wall Street Discount Corp.
100 Wall Street
New York, New York 10005
(212) 747-5100   (800) 221-7990

Wall Street Equities
40 Exchange Place
New York, New York 10005
(212) 425-4768
(800) 447-8625 [national]
(800) 499-9144 [New York State]

Wall Street Electronica
247 E. 28th Street, Suite 11A
New York, New York 10016
(212) 213-8743   (800) 925-5783

Washington Discount Brokerage
100 Wall Street
New York, New York 10005
(212) 425-0228   (800) 843-9601

Waterhouse Securities, Inc.
100 Wall Street
New York, New York 10005
(212) 334-7500   (800) 934-4430

Wilshire Capital Management
120 Broadway, Suite 960
New York, New York 10271
(212) 433-6490   (800) 926-9991

Wisconsin Discount Securities
7161 North Port Washington Road
Milwaukee, Wisconsin 53217
(414) 352-5050   (800) 537-0239

York Securities
160 Broadway, East Building,
   7th Floor
New York, New York 10038
(212) 349-9700 (800) 221-3154

Young, Stovall & Company
9627 South Dixie Highway,
   Suite 101
Miami, Florida 33156
(305) 666-2511 (800) 433-5132

Your Discount Broker
855 South Federal Highway
Boca Raton, Florida 33432
(407) 367-9836   (800) 800-3215

Ziegler Thrift Trading, Inc.
733 Marquette Avenue, Suite 106
Mineapolis, Minnesota 55402-2340
(612) 333-4206   (800) 328-4854

ACCOUNTING FIRMS

Following is a list of the names, addresses and telephone numbers of the head-quarters of the 26 largest U.S. certified public accounting firms, based on revenues generated in 1996. These firms are organized as partnerships of the certified public accountants who work in them. CPAs, who must pass examinations to earn their licenses, mainly do corporate accounting and auditing and prepare tax returns.

Mergers have reduced the Big Six to the Big Five. Andersen Worldwide, with 1997 revenues of $4.511 billion, remains the largest U.S. firm. The merger of Coopers & Lybrand and Price Waterhouse created the second-largest firm with revenues of $4.135 billion. Ernst & Young ranked third at $3.571 billion, followed by Deloitte & Touche with revenues of $2.925 billion. The fifth-ranked firm was KPMG Peat Marwick at $2.53 billion. Most major corporations do business with the Big Five, and their revenues far outpace other accounting firms. The sixth-ranked firm, Grant Thornton, had revenues of $266 million. The 25th ranked firm, Mayer Hoffman McCann LC, had revenues of $24 million.

Diversification has played a key role in the consolidation trend. Accounting firms are branching out beyond traditional auditing and accounting functions into business services like management counsulting. A number of these firms offer specialized advice for clients in financial services, health care, and telecommunications industries.

This list is provided courtesy of *Accounting Today* [11 Penn Plaza, New York, NY 10001, (212) 967-7000].

Altschuler, Melvoin and Glasser
30 South Wacker Drive, Suite 2600
Chicago, Illinois 60606
(312) 207-2837

Anchin, Block & Anchin
1375 Broadway, 18th Floor
New York, New York 10018
(212) 840-3456

Andersen Worldwide
33 W. Monroe, 12-177
Chicago, Illinois 60603
(312) 580-0069

Baird, Kurtz & Dobson
P.O. Box 1900
Springfield, Missouri 65801
(417) 831-7283

BDO Seidman
Two Prudential Plaza
180 N. Stetson Avenue, Suite 4300
Chicago, Illinois 60601
(312) 240-1236

Clifton Gunderson & Co.
301 Southwest Adams, Suite 600
Peoria, Illinois 61602
(309) 671-4560

Crowe, Chizek & Co.
P.O. Box 7
South Bend, Indiana 46624
(317) 632-8989

David Berdon & Co.
415 Madison Avenue
New York, New York 10017
(212) 832-0400

Deloitte & Touche
Ten Westport Road
Wilton, Connecticut 06897
(203) 761-3000

Ernst & Young
787 Seventh Avenue
New York, New York 10019
(212) 773-3131

Friedman Eisenstein Raemer & Schwartz
401 North Michigan Avenue,
  Suite 2600
Chicago, Illinois 60611
(312) 644-6000

George S. Olive & Co.
201 North Illinois Street, Suite 700
Indianapolis, Indiana 46204
(317) 383-4052

Goldstein Golub Kessler & Co.
1185 Avenue of the Americas
New York, New York 10036
(212) 372-1234

Grant Thornton
130 East Randolph Drive, Suite 800
Chicago, Illinois 60601-6144
(312) 856-0001

J.H. Cohn & Co.
75 Eisenhower Parkway
Roseland, New Jersey 07068
(201) 228-3500

KPMG Peat Marwick
767 Fifth Avenue
New York, New York 10153-0194
(212) 909-5000

Larson Allen Weishair & Co.
220 South Sixth Street,
  Suite 1000
Minneapolis, Minnesota 55440
(612) 376-4500

Mayer Hoffman McCann LC
420 Nichols Road
Kansas City, Missouri 64112
(816) 968-1000

McGladrey & Pullen
102 W. Second Street,
  2nd Floor
Davenport, Iowa 52801
(319) 324-0447

Moss Adams
1001 Fourth Avenue, Suite 2900
Seattle, Washington 98154
(206) 223-1820

M.R. Weiser & Co.
135 W. 50th Street
New York, New York 10020
(212) 641-6700

Plante & Moran
27400 Northwestern Highway
P.O. Box 307
Southfield, Michigan 48037
(248) 352-2500

PricewaterhouseCoopers
1251 Avenue of the Americas
New York, New York 10020
(212) 259-1000   (212) 819-5000

Reznick Fedder & Silverman
4520 East West Highway, Suite 300
Bethesda, Maryland 20814
(301) 652-9100

Richard A. Eisner & Co.
575 Madison Avenue
New York, New York 10022
(212) 355-1700

Wipfli Ullrich Bertelson
500 Third Street
P.O. Box 8010
Wausau, Wisconsin 54402
(715) 845-3111

SECURITIES AND FUTURES EXCHANGES
AROUND THE WORLD

The following is a list of the name and address of major securities and futures exchanges around the world. Telephone numbers are provided for American, Canadian and several other major exchanges. The list is arranged alphabetically by country.

The most active financial markets are those in the industrialized countries of North America, Western Europe and Japan. In these countries, there is more regulation of securities markets, and companies have to disclose more about their financial status; the regulation and disclosure requirements of U.S. exchanges are by far the strictest. The more active markets are more competitive and therefore are characterized by narrower spreads between bid and asked prices.

The stock markets of the less industrialized countries offer both greater rewards and greater risks to investors. Regulation of these markets tends to be looser and financial disclosure rules less stringent. With less trading activity, the spreads between bid and asked prices tend to be wide. In some cases, investment by non-nationals of the country is banned or strictly limited. Many of these markets provide rich opportunities to participate in some of the world's fastest growing economies, such as Taiwan and Singapore.

The shares of some prominent companies listed on these and other exchanges are also traded in the United States as American Depositary Receipts (ADRs). For investors who are interested in participating in these foreign markets, but do not have the time or expertise to do so directly, there are a number of mutual funds, both closed-end and open-end, specializing in buying securities in markets around the world.

Argentina

Bolsa de Comercio de Buenos Aires
Sarmiento 299, 2nd Floor
1353 Buenos Aires
(54) 1 313 7218

Australia

Adelaide
55 Exchange Place
Adelaide, S.A. 5000
(61) 8 261 5000

Australian Stock Exchange Ltd.
20 Bond Street
Sydney NSW 2000
(61) 2 227 0400

Brisbane
Riverside Centre
123 Eagle Street
Brisbane, QLD 4000
(61) 7 3 835 4000

Hobart
86 Collins Street
Hobart, Tasmania 7000
(61) 02 34 7333

Melbourne
530 Collins Street
Melbourne, Vic 3000
(61) 3 9 617 8611

Perth
2, the Esplanade
Perth, WA 6000

Sydney Futures Exchange
Grouner Street
Sydney, NSW 2000
(61) 2 256 0555

Sydney
Exchange Centre
20 Bond Street
Sydney, N.S.W. 2000
(61) 2 227 0000

Austria

Wiener Borse
Wipplingerstrasse 34
A-1013 Vienna
(43) 1 534 990

Bahrain

Bahrain Stock Exchange
P.O. Box 3203
Manama
(973) 261260

Bangladesh

Dhaka Stock Exchange Ltd.
Stock Exchange Building
9F Motijheel Commercial Area
Dhaka 1000
(880) 2 231 935

Chittagong Stock Exchange
Kashfia Plaza (First Floor), 923/A
Sk. Mujib Road
Chittagong

Belgium

Effectenbeursvennootschap Van Antwerpen
Korte Klarenstraat 1
2600 Antwerp
(32) 3 233 8016

Bourse de Bruxelles, Beurs Van Brussel
Palais de la Bourse
1000 Brussels
(32) 2 509 1211

Bermuda

Bermuda Stock Exchange
3rd Floor Washington Mall
Church Street
Hamilton
(1-441) 292 7212

Botswana

Botswana Stock Exchange
5th Floor, Barclays House
Khama Crescent
P.O. Box 51015
Gabarone
(267) 357900

Brazil

Bolsa Brasileira de Futuros
Praca XV de novembro 20
6th Floor
Rio de Janeiro 20010-010
(55) 21 271 1086

Bolsa de Mercadorias & Futuros
Praca Antonio Prado, 48
Sao Paulo SP, 01010-901
(55 11) 232 5454

Bolsa de Valores do Rio de Janeiro
Praca XV Novembro 20
20010 010 Rio de Janeiro/RJ

Bolsa de Valores de Sao Paulo
Rue XV de Novembro 275
01013 011 Sao Paulo SP
(55) 21 532 4616

Bolsa Mercantil and de Futuros
Praca Antonio Prado, 48
Sao Paulo/SP 01010
(5511) 239-5511

Bulgaria

Bulgarian Stock Exchange
1 Macedonia Square
1040 Sofia
(359) 2 815 711

Canada

Alberta Stock Exchange
300 5th Avenue, S.W., 21st Floor
Calgary, Alberta T2P 3C4
(403) 262-7791

Montreal Exchange
Tour de la Bourse, P.O. Box 61
800 Victoria Square
Montreal, Quebec H4Z 1A9
(514) 871-3585

Toronto Futures Exchange
Toronto Stock Exchange
The Exchange Tower
2 First Canadian Place
Toronto, Ontario M5X 1J2
(416) 947-4325   (416) 947-4700

Vancouver Stock Exchange
609 Granville Street
Vancouver, British Columbia V7Y 1H1
(604) 689-3334

Winnipeg Commodity Exchange
500 Commodity Exchange Tower
360 Main Street
Winnipeg, Manitoba R3C 3Z4
(204) 925-5000

Winnipeg Stock Exchange
2901-One Lombard Place
Winnipeg, Manitoba R3B 0Y2
(204) 942-8431

Chile

Bolsa de Comercio de Santiago
Casilla 123-D
Santiago
(56) 2 698 2001

Bolsa Electronica
Huerfanos 770, piso 14
Santiago
(56) 2 639 4699

Bolsa de Valparaiso
PRAT 798
Valparaiso
(56) 3 225 6955

China

Shanghai Metal Exchange
No. 430, Caoyang Road
Putuo District
Shanghai 200063
(86) 021 6 2445566

Shanghai Securities Exchange
15 Huang Pu Road
Shanghai
(86) 21 306 3291

Shenzhen Metal Exchange
1-3f, Block B
Zhongjian Overseas Decoration Building
Hua Fu Road
518031 Shenzhen Special Economic Zone
(86) 755 3343473 (information)

Shenzhen Stock Exchange
203 Honglixi Road
Shenzhen 518028
(86) 755 320 3431

Colombia

Bolsa de Bogota
Carrera 8, #13-82, 7th Floor
Apdo. Aereo 3584
Santafe de Bogota, D.C.
(57) 1 243 6501

Bolsa de Medellin
Carrera 50, #50-48, 2nd Floor
Apdo. Aereo 3535
Medellin
(57) 4 260 3000

Bolsa de Occidente
Calle 8, #3-14, 17th Floor
Cali
(57) 4 260 3000

Congo

Congo Stock Exchange
5th Floor, Southhampton House
P.O. Box UA 234
Union Avenue/1st Street
Harare
(263) 4 736 861

Costa Rica

BolsaNacional de Valores
P.O. Box 1736-1000
San Jose
(506) 256 1180

Croatia

Zagrebacka Burza
Ksaver 208
Zagreb 10000
(385) 1 42 8455

Czech Republic

Prague Stock Exchange
Rybna 14
110 00 Prague 1
(420) 2 2183 2126

Denmark

Kobenhavns Fondsbors
2 Nikolaj Plads 2
1067 Copenhagen K
(45) 33 93 33 66

Ecuador

Bolsa de Valores de Guayaquil (BVG)
Baquerizo Moreno 1112
Guayaquil
(593) 4 307 710

Bolsa de Valores de Quito (BVQ)
Av. Rio Amazonas 540 y Jeronimo Carrion
Quito
(593) 2 526 805

Bolsa de Valores de Cuenca (SATI)
Presidente Cordova 785 y Luis Cordero
Cuenca
(593) 7 841 600

Egypt

Cairo Stock Exchange
4a Sherifen Street
Cairo
(20) 2 392 1447/8968

Alexandria Stock Exchange
11Talat Harb Street
Menshia
Alexandria
(20) 3 483 5432

Finland

Helsingin Arvopapereriporssi Oy
Fabianinkatu 14
001310 Helsinki
(358) 9 1733 0399

France

MATIF SA
115 Rue Reaumur
75083 Paris CEDEX 02
(33) 1 40 28 82 82

MONEP (Marche des Options Negociables
  de Paris)
Societe de Compensation des Marches
  Conditionnels—SCMC
39 Rue Cambon
75001 Paris
(33) (1) 49 27 18 00

SBF-Paris Bourse
39 Rue Cambon
75001 Paris
(33) 1 49 27 10 00

Germany

Baden-Wurttembergische
  Wertpapierborse zu Stuttgart
Konigstrasse 28
Postfach 100441
D-70003 Stuttgart
(49) 711 29 01 83

Bayerische Borse
Lenbachplatz 2 a
D-80333 Munich
(49) 89 5990-0

Berliner Borse
Fasanenstrasse 3
D-10623 Berlin
(49) 30 31 1091-0

Bremen Wertpapierborse
Oberstrasse 2-12
Postfach 10 07 26
D-28007 Bremen
(49) 421 32 1282

Deutsche Borse AG
Borsenplatz 7-11
D-60313 Frankfurt/Main 1
(49) 69 2101 5371

Deutsche Terminborse (DTB)
60284 Frankfurt
(49) 69 2101-0

Frankfurter Wertpapierborse
Borsenplatz 7-11
D-60284 Frankfurt 4
(49) 69 2101-0

Hanseatische Wertpapierborse Hamburg
Schauenburgerstrasse 47
20415 Hamburg
(49) 40 36 1302-0

Niedersachsische Borse zu Hannover
Rathenstrasse 2
Postfach 4427
D-30044 Hanover
(49) 511 32 76 61

Rheinisch-Westfalische Borse zu Dusseldorf
Ernst-Schneider-Platz 1, Postfach 104262
D-40033 Dusseldorf 1
(49) 211 13890

Greece

Athens Stock Exchange
10 Sophocleous Street
Athens 10559
(30) 1 321 1301

Hong Kong

Stock Exchange of Hong Kong Ltd.
Hong Kong
852 5 22 11 22

The Stock Exchange of Hong Kong Ltd.
First Floor, 1&2 Exchange Square
P.O. Box 8888
Hong Kong
(852) 2522 1122

Hungary

Budapest Commodity Exchange
H-1373 P.O. Box
H-1134 Budapest
(36) 1 269 8571

Budapest Stock Exchange
Deak Ferenc u.5
H-1364 Bp., Pf.24
H-1052 Budapest
(36) 1 117 5226

India

The Stock Exchange, Mumbai
25th Floor, Phiroze Jeejeebhoy Towers
Dalal Street
Mumbai 400 001
(91) 22 265 5581

Calcutta Stock Exchange
7 Lyons Range
Calcutta 700
(91) 33 22 93 66

Delhi Stock Exchange
3 & 4/4B Asaf Ali Road
New Delhi 110 002
(91) 11 27 13 02

National Stock Exchange
Mahindra Towers, 1st Floor
Mumbai 400 018
A-Wing, RBC, Worli
(91) 22 496 1525

Over-the-Counter Exchange of India
Sir Vithaldas Thackersey Marg.
New Marine Lines
Mumbai 400 020
(91) 22 204 3389

Indonesia

Jakarta Stock Exchange
Jln Jendral Sudirman Kav. 52-53
Jakarta 12190
(62) 21 515 0515

Surabaya Stock Exchange
Gedung Medan Pemuda
Jalan Permuda 2731
(62) 31 510 646

Ireland

Irish Stock Exchange
28 Anglesea Street
Dublin 2
(353) 1 677 8808

Israel

Tel Aviv Stock Exchange
54 Ahad Haam Street
Tel-Aviv 65202
(972) 3567 7411

Italy

Italian Stock Exchange
Piazza Degli Affari 6
20123 Milan
(39) 2 853 44636

Jamaica

Jamaica Stock Exchange
40 Harbour Street
P.O. Box 1084
Kingston
(1 809) 922 0806

Japan

Chubu Commodity Exchange
3-2-15
Nisiki Naka-ku
Nagoya 460
(81) 52 951 2170

Fukuoka Stock Exchange
14-2, Tenjin 2-chome
Chuo-ku
Fukuoka 810
(81) 92 741 8231

Hiroshima Stock Exchange
14-18, Kanayama-cho
Naka-ku
Hiroshima 730
(81) 82 541 1121

Kanmon Commodity Exchange
1-5 Nabe-cho, Shimonoseki
Yamaguchi Pref 20750
(81) 832 31 1313

Kansai Agricultural Commondities
  Exchange
1-10-14 Awaza
Osaka 550
(81) 6 531 7931

Kobe Raw Silk Exchange
126 Higashimachi
Chuo-ku
Kobe 650
(81) 78 331 7141

Kyoto Stock Exchange
66- Tachiurinishi-machi
  Higashinotoin-higashiiru
Shijo-dori Simogyo-ku
Kyoto 600
(81) 75 221 1171

Maebashi Dried Cocoon Exchange
1-49-1 Furuichi-machi
Maebashi 371
(81) 272 521401

Nagoya Stock Exchange
3-17, Sakae 3-chome
Naka-ku
Nagoya 460
(81) 52 262 3171

Niigata Stock Exchange
1245, Hachiban-cho
Kamiohkawamae-dori
Niigata 951
(81) 25 222 4181

Osaka Mercantile Exchange
2-5-28 Kyutaro-machi
Chuo-ku
Osaka 541
(81) 6 244 2191

Osaka Securities Exchange
8-16 Kitahama 1-Chome
Chuo-ku
Osaka 541
(81) 6 229 8607

Sapporo Stock Exchange
14-1, Nishi 5-chome
Minami 1-jo
Chuo-ku
Sapporo 060
(81) 11 241 6171

Tokyo Commodity Exchange
36-2 Nihonbashi-Hakozakicho
Chuo-ku
Tokyo 103
(81) 3 3661 9191

Tokyo Grain Exchange
1-12-5 Nihonbashi kakigara-cho
Chuo-ku
Tokyo 103
(81) 3 3668 9321

Tokyo International Financial Futures
  Exchange
1-3-1 Marunouchi
Chiyoda ku
Tokyo 100
(81) 3 5223 2400

Tokyo Stock Exchange
2-1, Nihombashi-Kabuto
Chuo-ku
Tokyo 103
(81) 3 3666 0141

Yokohama Raw Silk Exchange
Silk Center
1 Yamashita-cho
Naka-ku
Yokohama 231
(81) 45 641 1341

Jordan

Amman Financial Market
Housing Bank Centre, 6th Floor
Amman
(962) 6 607 171

Kenya

Nairobi Stock Exchange Ltd.
Nation Centre
P.O. Box 43633
Nairobi
(254) 2 230 2692

Korea

Korea Stock Exchange
33 Yoido-dong
Youngdungpo-ku
Seoul 150-010
(82) 2 780 2271

Lebanon

Bourse de Beyrouth
Sadat Tower, 2nd Floor
Sadat Street
Beirut
(961) 1 807 552

Luxembourg

Societe de la Bourse de Luxembourg SA
Avenue de la Porte-Neuve, BP 165
L-2011 Luxembourg
(352) 47 79 36-1

Malaysia

Kuala Lumpur Commodity Exchange
  (KLCE)
4th Floor, Dayabumi Complex
Jalan Sultan Hishamuddin
P.O. Box 11260
50750 Kuala Lumpur
60 (3) 293-6822

Kuala Lumpur Stock Exchange
3rd, 4th, & 5th Floors, Exchange Square
Damansara Heights
Kuala Lumpur 50490
(60) 3 254 6433/6662

Mexico

Bolsa Mexicana de Valores
Paseo de la Reforma 255
Col. Cuauhtemoc
06500, Mexico D.F.
(52) 5 726 6735

Morocco

Casablanca Stock Exchange
Avenue de L'Armeé Royale
Casablanca
(212) 2 45 2626

Netherlands

Agricultural Futures Market Amsterdam
Postbus 529
1000 AM Amsterdam
(31) 20 638 2258

Amsterdam Exchanges
Beursplein 5
1012 JW Amsterdam
(31) 20 550 4444

New Zealand

New Zealand Stock Exchange
8th Floor, Caltex Tower
282 Lambton Quay
Wellington
(64) 4 472 7599

New Zealand Futures & Options Exchange
 (NZFE)
P.O. Box 6734, Wellesley Street
Auckland
64 (9) 309 8308

Nigeria

Nigerian Stock Exchange
24 Customs Street
P.O. Box 2457
Lagos
(234) 1 266 0287

Norway

Bergen Branch
Olav Kyrresgt 11
5000 Bergen
(47) 55 32 30 50

Oslo Bors
P.O. Box 460 Sentrum
0105 Oslo 1
(47) 2 34 17 00

Trondheim Branch
Dronningens gt 12
7011, Trondheim
(47) 73 88 31 15

Oman

Muscat Securities Market
P.O. Box 3265
Ruwi, Postal Code 112
(968) 702 665

Pakistan

Karachi Stock Exchange
Stock Exchange Building
Stock Exchange Road
Karachi
(92) 21 242 5502/3/4/8

Lahore Stock Exchange
19 Khayaban-e-Iqbal
Egerton Road
Lahore
(92) 42 636 8111/8555

Islamabad Stock Exchange
Anees Plaza
Fazal-ul-Haq Road
Islamabad
(92) 51 216 040/41

Panama

Bolsa de Valores de Panama SA
Calle Elvira Mendez y Calle 52
Edif. Vallarino
Planta Baja
Panama City
(5070 269 1966

Peru

Bolsa de Valores de Lima
Pasaje Acuna 191
Lima
(51) 1 426 7939

Philippines

Manila International Futures Exchange
 (MIFE)
PDCP Bank Centre, 7th Floor
Paseo de Roxas
Makati, Metro Manila
63 (2) 818 54 96

PSE (Makati trading floor)
Ayala Tower
Ayala Avenue and Paseo de Roxas
Makati, Metro Manila
(63) 2 891 9001

PSE (Pasig trading floor)
Philippine Stock Exchange Centre
Exchange Road
Ortigas Centre
Pasig, Metro Manila
(63) 2 636 0122

Poland

Warsaw Stock Exchange
6/12 Nowy Swiat
00-400 Warsaw
(48) 22 628 3232

Portugal

Bolsa de Derivados do Oporto
Av da Boavista 3,433
4100 Oporto
(351) 2 618 5858

Bolsa de Valores de Lisboa
Edificio de Bolsa
Rua SoeiroPereira Gomes
1600 Lisboa
(351) 1 790 9904

Russia

Moscow Interbank Currency Exchange
119021 Moscow
4 Zubovsky Boulevard
(7) 095 201 2817

Moscow International Stock Exchange
103084 Moscow
4, bld.2, Slavyanska pl.
(7) 095 924 8259

Russian Exchange
101000 Moscow
26 Myasnitskaya Street
(7) 095 262 2352

St. Petersburg Stock Exchange
St. Petersburg
274 Ligovsky pr.
(7) 812 296 0523

Yekaterinburg Stock Exchange
620 Yekaterinburg
109 Furmanova Street
(7) 3432 221 225

Vladivostok Stock Exchange
Vladivisotok
62A Partizansky Prospect
(7) 4232 228 009

Sibirskaya Stock Exchange
630194 Novosibirsk
5 Frounze Street
(7) 3832 216 951

Singapore

Singapore Commodity Exchange
111 North Bridge Road #23-04/05
Peninsula Plaza
Singapore 179098
(65) 338 5600

Stock Exchange of Singapore Ltd.
20 Cecil Street #26-01/08
The Exchange
Singapore 049705
(65) 535-3788

Singapore International Monetary Exchange
(SIMEX)
1 Raffles Place
07-00 OUB Centre
Singapore 048616
(65) 535 7382

Slovakia

Bratislava Stock Exchange
Vyosoka 17
P.O. Box 151
SK 814 99 Bratislava
(421) 7 5036 103

Slovenia

Ljubljana Stock Exchange
Slovenska 56
61000 Ljubljana
(386) 61 171 02 11

South Africa

Johannesburg Stock Exchange
17 Diagonal Street
P.O. Box 1174
Johannesburg 2000
(27) 11 377 2200

South African Futures Exchange
105 Central Street
Houghton Estate, 2198
P.O. Box 4406
Johannesburg 2000
(27) 11 728 5960

South Korea

Korea Stock Exchange
33, Yoido-Dong
Youngdeungpo-Ku
Seoul 150-010

Spain

Bolsa de Barcelona
Paseo Isabel II, 1
08003 Barcelona
(34) 3 401 3555

Bolsa de Bilbao
Olavarri 1
48001 Bilbao (Vizcaya)
(34) 4 423 6818

Bolsa de Madrid
Plaza de la Lealtad 1
Madrid 28014
(34) 1 589 2600

Bolsa de Valencia
San Vincente 23
46002 Valencia
(34) 6 387 0100

MEFF Renta Fija
Via Layetana 58
08003 Barcelona
(34) 3 412 1128

MEFF Renta Variable
Torre Pcasso pl 26
28020 Madrid
(34) 1 585 0800

Sri Lanka

Colombo Stock Exchange
#04-01 West Block
World Trade Centre
Echelon Square
Colombo 1

Sweden

Stockholms Fondbors AB
Box 1256
SE-111 82 Stockholm
(46) 8 613 8800

OM Stockholm AB
Box 16305
S-103 26, Stockholm
46 (8) 700 06 00

Switzerland

Swiss Exchange and SOFFEX
Selnaustrasse 32
CH-8021 Zurich
(41) 1 229 2111

Swiss Exchange Geneva
8 Rue de la Confederation
CH-1204 Geneva 11
(41) 22 818 5830

Taiwan

Taiwan Stock Exchange Corporation
7-10th Floors, City Building
85 Yen-Ping Road
Taipei
(886) 2 311 4020

ROC (OTC) Exchange
3F, No. 51 Sec 2 Chung Ching
  South Road
Taipei
(886) 2 322 5555

Thailand

Stock Exchange of Thailand
132 Sintorn Building, 2nd Floor
Wireless Road
Bangkok, 10330
(66) 2 254 0960

Trinidad and Tobago

Trinidad and Tobago Stock
  Exchange
65 Independence Square
Port of Spain
Trinidad
(1 809) 625 5107

Tunisia

Bourse des Valeurs Mobilieres de
  Tunis
19 bis
Rue Kamal Ataturk
1001 Tunis
(216) 1 259 411

Turkey

Istanbul Stock Exchange
Istinye 80860
Istanbul
(90) 212 298 2100

United Kingdom

International Petroleum Exchange
1 St. Katharine's Way
London E1 9UN
44 171 481 0643

London International Financial Futures
  Exchange (LIFFE)
Cannon Bridge
London EC4R 3XX
44 171 623 0444

London Metal Exchange (LME)
56 Leadenhall Street
London EC3A 2BJ
44 171 264 5555

London Securities and Derivatives
  Exchange—OMLX
Milestone House, 6th Floor
107 Cannon Street
London EC4N 5AD
(44) 171 283 0678

London Stock Exchange
Old Broad Street
London EC2N 1HP
(44) 171 797 1000

Regional Offices/London Stock Exchange
MIDLANDS & WEST
The Stock Exchange
Margaret Street
Birmingham B3 3JL
(44) 121 236 9181

NORTH WEST
The Stock Exchange
76 King Street
Manchester M2 4NH
(44) 161 833 0931

NORTH EAST
The Stock Exchange
Enterprise House
12 St. Paul's Street
Leeds LS1 2LQ
(44) 113 243 0738

NORTHERN IRELAND
The Stock Exchange
Northern Bank House
10 High Street
Belfast BT1 2BP
(44) 1232 321 094

SCOTLAND
The Stock Exchange
Stock Exchange House
P.O. Box 141
7 Nelson Mandela Place
Glasgow G2 1BU
(44) 141 221 7060

United States

American Stock Exchange (AMEX)
86 Trinity Place
New York, New York 10006-1881
(212) 306-1841

Boston Stock Exchange (BSE)
One Boston Place
Boston, Massachusetts 02108
(617) 723-9500

Chicago Board of Trade (CBOT)
141 West Jackson Boulevard
Chicago, Illinois 60604-2994
(312) 435-3500

Chicago Board Options Exchange (CBOE)
400 South LaSalle Street
Chicago, Illinois 60605
(312) 786-5600

Chicago Mercantile Exchange (CME)
30 South Wacker Drive
Chicago, Illinois 60606
(312) 930-1000

Chicago Stock Exchange (CHX)
440 S. LaSalle Street
Chicago, Illinois 60605
(312) 663-2222

Cincinnati Stock Exchange (CSE)
400 South LaSalle Street
Chicago, Illinois 60605
(312) 786-8803

Coffee, Sugar & Cocoa Exchange (CSCE)
4 World Trade Center
New York, New York 10048
(212) 742-6000

FINEX
4 World Trade Center
New York, New York 10048
(212) 938-2629

Kansas City Board of Trade (KCBT)
4800 Main Street, Suite 303
Kansas City, Missouri 64112
(816) 753-7500

MidAmerica Commodity Exchange
  (MIDAM)
141 West Jackson Boulevard
Chicago, Illinois 60604
(312) 341-3000

Midwest Stock Exchange (MSE)
440 South LaSalle Street
Chicago, Illinois 60605
(312) 663-2222

Minneapolis Grain Exchange (MGE)
130 Grain Exchange Building
400 South Fourth Street
Minneapolis, Minnesota 55415
(612) 321-7101

New York Cotton Exchange (NYCE)
4 World Trade Center
New York, New York 10048
(212) 742-5050

New York Futures Exchange (NYFE)
20 Broad Street
New York, New York 10005
(212) 748-1248

New York Mercantile Exchange (NYMEX)
One North End Avenue
New York, New York 10282
(212) 292-2000

New York Stock Exchange (NYSE)
11 Wall Street
New York, New York 10005
(212) 656-2065

Pacific Exchange (PCX)
301 Pine Street
San Francisco, California 94104
(415) 393-4000

Philadelphia Stock Exchange (PHLX)
Philadelphia Board of Trade (PBOT)
1900 Market Street
Philadelphia, Pennsylvania 19103
(215) 496-5000, 496-5165

Uruguay

Bolsa de Valores de Montevideo
Misiones 1400
Montevideo
(598) 2 965 051

Venezuela

Bolsa de Valores de Caracas
Apartado Postal 62724-A Chacao
(58) 2 905 5511

Bolsa de Valores de Maracaibo
Edif. Banco Central de Venezuela
Ave 5 de Julio y Las Delicias
Piso 9
Maracaibo, Edo. Zulia
(58) 61 226 833

Bolsa Electronica de Valores de Venezuela
Ave. Bolivar
Camara de Comercio de Valencia
Valencia, Edo. Carabobo
(58) 41 575 109/115

Zambia

Lusaka Stock Exchange
1st Floor, Stock Exchange Building
Cairo Road
Lusaka
(260) 1 228391

3. MUTUAL FUNDS

OPEN-END MUTUAL FUNDS

The following is a list of the names, addresses and telephone numbers of American open-end mutual funds. Most organizations offer more than one fund, and the funds in this list are grouped under the name of the firm to which they belong. In order to obtain information about a fund you may be interested in, look first for the name of its management group. Newspaper listings also usually group mutual funds by family.

The funds on this list are both load and no-load. Load funds are sold through brokers and financial planners for commissions that generally range from about 3% (this is called a low-load fund) to as much as 8$^1/_2$%. In return for this sales charge, customers should expect expert advice on which fund is most appropriate for their investment needs and goals. A broker should also tell the customer when to get out of the fund, as well as when to get in. No-load funds, on the other hand, charge no commissions. Investors buy shares directly from the management companies over the phone, by mail or in person. The management company representative will offer information on the funds the firm offers, but they may not advise investors on which fund to buy. No one will call when the time comes to switch from one fund to another—that is left totally up to the individual shareholder.

The funds on this list are each categorized by the investment objective of the fund manager. The following is a brief characterization of each objective, the abbreviation of which is given in parentheses after each fund's name in the list of funds.

Aggressive Growth (AgGr) Aggressive-growth funds seek maximum capital gains; current income is not a consideration. Fund managers may use several strategies, such as buying high-technology stocks, emerging growth stocks, or companies that have fallen on hard times or are out of favor. Some aggressive funds make use of options and futures, and/or borrow against funds shares to buy stock. Aggressive-growth funds typically provide dramatic gains and losses for shareholders, and should therefore be monitored closely.

Balanced (Bal) Balanced mutual funds generally invest in both stocks and bonds, with the intent of providing capital gains and income. Preservation of principal is a primary objective of balanced fund managers. These funds are for conservative investors who are looking for some growth of capital.

Corporate Bond (CorB) Corporate-bond funds seek to pay a high level of income to shareholders by buying corporate bonds. Some conservative bond funds buy only the debt of highly rated corporations. The yield on this kind of fund would be lower than on that of a fund buying bonds from lower-rated corporations—frequently called junk bonds or high-yield bonds. Although income, not capital gains, is the primary objective of most corporate bond shareholders, gains can be significant if the country's general level of interest rates falls. On the other hand, losses can also be substantial if interest rates rise.

Flexible Portfolio (Flex) Flexible portfolio funds give the fund manager great flexibility in deciding which asset offers the best risk-return tradeoff at any particular time. Therefore, such funds may invest in stocks, bonds, money-market instruments, options, futures, or foreign securities at various times. Such funds are sometimes called asset-allocation funds. Shareholders of flexible funds desire some current income, but also are expecting superior long-term capital gains.

Global Bond (GloB) Global bond funds invest in fixed-income securities from anywhere in the world. Such funds may purchase bonds issued by foreign corporations or by U.S. corporations. Global bond funds also invest in bonds issued by foreign governments or their agencies. Investors in global funds expect a high level of current income and capital gains, if the direction of interest rates and currency rates is favorable.

Global Equity (GloE) Global equity funds invest in securities anywhere in the world. They buy stocks, bonds, and money-market instruments in both the United States and foreign countries, depending on where the fund manager sees the best opportunity for growth. Global equity funds' main objective is long-term capital appreciation, although they may provide some current income.

Government National Mortgage Association (GNMA) These funds buy Government National Mortgage Association (GNMA or Ginnie Mae) certificates, which are securities backed by home mortgages. GNMA funds are designed to provide a high level of current income to shareholders and to minimize risk to capital. These funds are subject to fluctuation because of the ups and downs of interest rates, however. They are also affected by the rate at which homeowners refinance their mortgages. When interest rates fall, more mortgages are refinanced, and therefore shareholders in GNMA funds see their yields fall. When rates rise, on the other hand, fewer mortgages are refinanced, and so the fund maintains its yield, but it does not grow very quickly. GNMA funds are designed for conservative, income-oriented investors.

Growth (Gr) Growth funds invest in the common stock of growth companies. The primary aim is to achieve capital gains, and income is of little concern. Growth funds vary widely in the amount of risk they are willing to take, but in general they take less risk than aggressive growth funds because the stocks they buy are those of more seasoned companies.

Growth and Income (Gr&I) Growth and income funds seek to provide both capital gains and a steady stream of income by buying the shares of high-yielding, conservative stocks. Growth and income fund managers look for companies with solid records of increasing their dividend payments as well as earnings gains. These funds are more conservative than pure growth funds.

High-Yield Bond (HiYB) High-yield bond funds buy the debt securities issued by non-investment-grade corporations and municipalities. Because these securities offer higher risks than investment-grade bonds, high-yield bonds pay higher yields. Because the companies and municipalities that issue high-yield bonds are more highly leveraged than top-quality issuers, their bonds are more subject to default, particularly if there is an economic downturn in the issuer's industry or region. Such defaults would not only cut the yield on high-yield bond funds but also erode the capital value of the shares. Investors in high-yield bond funds, therefore, should be well aware that they are taking an extra degree of default risk in exchange for a higher level of current income than is available from more conservative bond funds.

Income Bond (IncB)   Income bond funds invest in a variety of bonds to produce high taxable current income for shareholders. Such funds usually invest in corporate or government bonds, but they may also buy foreign bonds. They are usually managed more conservatively than bond funds that buy high-yield bonds and therefore offer lower current yields.

Income Equity (IncE)   Income equity funds invest in bonds and high-yielding stocks with the objective of providing shareholders with a moderate level of current income and a moderate level of long-term capital appreciation. Income equity funds are slightly more conservatively managed and usually have a higher percentage of their assets in bonds than growth and income funds.

Income Mixed (IncM)   Income mixed funds seek to provide a high level of current income by buying government and corporate bonds as well as high-yielding common and preferred stocks. Income mixed funds are not designed to provide major capital gains, but their shares do rise when interest rates fall. (Conversely, the shares fall in value when interest rates rise.) Income funds are designed for conservative, income-oriented investors.

International (Intl)   International funds invest in stocks of companies outside the United States as well as in bonds issued by foreign companies and governments. International funds provide investors with diversification among countries as well as industries. Such funds are strongly influenced by the rise and fall of foreign exchange rates—a factor important to consider before buying shares. For Americans it generally would be beneficial to buy an international fund when the outlook is for the dollar to fall against other currencies. Conversely, international-fund performance usually suffers when the dollar strengthens. International funds are for those who are willing to take some risk; understanding the effect of currency changes on holdings is essential.

Money Market (MM)   Money-market mutual funds buy short-term securities sold in the money markets to provide current income to shareholders. Because of the short-term nature of their holdings, these funds reflect changes in short-term interest rates rather quickly. The principal in money-market funds is extremely safe. Some money funds buy commercial instruments like commercial paper, banker's acceptances, and repurchase agreements, while others restrict themselves to buying U.S. Treasury obligations like Treasury bills. The portfolios of some money-market funds are insured by private insurance companies. Most money funds allow check writing, often with a minimum check size of $250 or $500. Money-market funds are frequently included in asset management accounts offered by brokerage firms and are used as parking places for funds while shareholders decide where the best place to invest long-term might be. Otherwise, money-market funds are for extremely conservative investors, who want virtually no risk of capital loss.

National Municipal Bond, Long Term (NMuB)   These funds aim to provide a high level of tax-exempt income to shareholders, by buying the debt obligations of cities, states, and other municipal government agencies. Depending on the state in which a shareholder resides, interest earned is either totally or partially free of federal, state, and local income taxes. While such funds are designed to provide current income, their value also rises and falls inversely with the country's general level of interest rates. The municipal bonds these funds usually buy tend to mature anywhere from 10 to 20 years in the future.

National Tax-Exempt Money Market (NMMX) These funds invest in municipal securities with relatively short maturities, which range from as little as a few days to as much as 5 years. National money-market funds buy short term obligations of cities, states and municipal government agencies. Investors who use these funds seek tax-free investments with minimum risk. Portions of income from these securities may be subject to the federal alternative minimum tax. These funds generally allow shareholders to write checks, typically with a minimum withdrawal of $250 to $500 per check.

Precious Metals—Gold (PM/G) Such funds invest in the shares of gold and silver mining companies. These shares often pay high dividends, and therefore the funds often can pay high yields. As with all precious-metal investments, these funds reflect the ups and downs of investor psychology as it relates to the outlook for inflation as well as political upheaval. These funds tend to perform better when inflation is high and rising and there is considerable political turmoil in the world. Some funds invest largely in South African mines, while others restrict themselves to shares in North American mining companies.

State Municipal Bond, Long Term (SMuB) These funds buy debt obligations of cities and municipal authorities in one state only. The interest from these bonds is usually tax exempt to residents of the particular state. Thus, shareholders can have a higher after-tax yield than if they bought shares in an out-of-state fund on which they had to pay taxes. These funds typically buy longer-term bonds maturing in 10 to 20 years. As a result, they fluctuate considerably with the ups and downs of the general level of interest rates.

State Tax-Exempt Money Market (SMMX) These funds invest in municipal securities with relatively short maturities, which range from as little as a few days to as much as 5 years. State money-market funds buy the debt obligations of cities and municipal authorities in one state only, and a resident of that state has the advantage of receiving income free of both federal and state tax. Investors who use these funds seek tax-free investments with minimum risk. Portions of income from these securities may be subject to the federal alternative minimum tax. These funds generally allow shareholders to write checks, typically with a minimum withdrawal of $250 to $500 per check.

U.S. Government Income (USGI) U.S. government income funds invest only in direct obligations of the U.S. Treasury. The funds therefore buy U.S. Treasury bills, bonds, and notes and federally backed mortgage securities. Shareholders of such funds want a high level of current income as well as maximum safety against default. Some funds have short maturities, while others buy bonds with maturities as long as 20 or 30 years. The longer the portfolio's overall maturity, the more the fund will fluctuate with general interest-rate movements.

This listing of mutual funds was made possible through the generous cooperation of the Investment Company Institute. The Investment Company Institute (1401
H Street, N.W., Suite 1200, Washington, D.C. 20005-2148 (202) 326-5800) has
both load and no-load members and regularly keeps track of new fund groups and
funds. It publishes an annual directory of members.

Abbreviations of Fund Objectives

AgGr	Aggressive Growth
Bal	Balanced
CorB	Corporate Bond
Flex	Flexible Portfolio
GloB	Global Bond
GloE	Global Equity
GNMA	Government National Mortgage Association
Gr	Growth
Gr&I	Growth and Income
HiYB	High-Yield Bond
IncB	Income Bond
IncE	Income Equity
IncM	Income Mixed
Intl	International
MM	Money Market
NMuB	National Municipal Bond
NMMX	National Tax-Exempt Money Market
PM/G	Precious Metals—Gold
SMMX	State Tax-Exempt Money Market
SMuB	State Municipal Bond
USGI	U.S. Government Income

AAL Mutual Funds
222 W. College Ave.
Appleton, WI 54919-0007
800/553-6319
AAL Mutual Funds (The)
  AAL Bond Fund (The) (IncB)
  AAL Capital Growth Fund (The) (Gr)
  AAL High Yield Bond Fund (The) (HiYB)
  AAL International Fund (The) (Intl)
  AAL Mid Cap Stock Fund (The) (Gr)
  AAL Money Market Fund (The) (MM)
  AAL Municipal Bond Fund (The) (NMuB)
  AAL Small Cap Stock Fund (The) (AgGr)
  AAL Utilities Fund (The) (IncE)

Achievement Funds Trust
One Freedom Valley Drive
Oaks, PA 19456
800/472-0577
Achievement Funds Trust (The)
  Balanced Fund (Gr&I)
  Equity Fund (Gr&I)
  Idaho Municipal Bond Fund (SMuB)
  Intermediate Term Bond Fund (IncB)
  Municipal Bond Fund (NMuB)
  Short Term Bond Fund (IncB)
  Short Term Municipal Bond Fund (NMuB)

Acorn Funds
227 W. Monroe St.
Ste. 3000
Chicago, IL 60606-5016
800/922-6769
Acorn Investment Trust
  Acorn Fund (Gr)
  Acorn International (Intl)
  Acorn USA Fund (AgGr)

Advantus Funds
400 Robert St. North
St. Paul, MN 55101-2015
800/443-3677
Advantus Bond Fund, Inc. (IncB)
Advantus Cornerstone Fund, Inc. (Gr&I)
Advantus Enterprise Fund, Inc. (Gr)
Advantus Horizon Fund, Inc. (Gr&I)
Advantus Index 500 Fund, Inc. (Gr)
Advantus International Balanced Fund, Inc.
  (Intl)
Advantus Money Market Fund, Inc. (MM)
Advantus Mortgage Securities Fund, Inc.
  (GNMA)
Advantus Spectrum Fund, Inc. (Bal)
Advantus Venture Fund, Inc. (AgGr)

Advisors' Inner Circle Fund
One Freedom Valley Drive
Oaks, PA 19456
800/342-5734
Advisors' Inner Circle Fund
  Clover Capital Equity Value Fund (Gr)

Clover Capital Fixed Income Fund (IncB)
Clover Capital Small Cap Value Fund
  (AgGr)
CRA Realty Shares Portfolio (IncE)
FMC Select Fund (Bal)
HGK Fixed Income Fund (IncM)
Pin Oak Aggressive Stock Fund (Gr)
White Oak Growth Stock Fund (Gr)

Advisors Series Trust
4455 E. Camelback Rd.
Ste. 261-E
Phoenix, AZ 85018
602/952-1100
Advisors Series Trust
  American Trust Allegiance Fund (Gr)
  InformationTech 100 Fund (AgGr)

Aetna Funds
151 Farmington Ave.
Hartford, CT 06156
800/367-7732
Aetna Generation Portfolios, Inc.
  Aetna Ascent Variable Fund (Bal)
  Aetna Crossroads Variable Fund (Bal)
  Aetna Legacy Variable Fund (Bal)
  Aetna Income Shares (IncB)
Aetna Series Fund
  Aetna Ascent Fund (Bal)
  Aetna Bond Fund (CorB)
  Aetna Crossroads Fund (Bal)
  Aetna Fund (Flex)
  Aetna Government Fund (USGI)
  Aetna Growth and Income Fund (Gr&I)
  Aetna Growth Fund (Gr)
  Aetna International Growth Fund (Intl)
  Aetna Legacy Fund (Bal)
  Aetna Money Market Fund (MM)
  Aetna Small Company Growth Fund
    (AgGr)
  Aetna Variable Fund (Gr&I)

AIG Fund Group
70 Pine St.
58th Fl.
New York, NY 10270-0002
800/862-3984
Advisors' Inner Circle Fund
  AIG Money Market Fund (MM)
AIG All Ages Funds, Inc.
  AIG Children's World Fund—2005
    (IncM)
  AIG Retiree Fund 2003 (IncM)

AIM Family of Funds
P.O. Box 4333
Houston, TX 77210-4333
800/347-1919
AIM Equity Funds, Inc.
  AIM Aggressive Growth Fund (AgGr)
  AIM Blue Chip Fund (Gr)

AIM Capital Development Fund (Gr)
AIM Charter Fund (Gr&I)
AIM Constellation Fund (AgGr)
AIM Weingartern Fund (Gr)
AIM Funds Group
  AIM Balanced Fund (Bal)
  AIM Global Utilities Fund (IncE)
  AIM Growth Fund (Gr)
  AIM High Yield Fund (HiYB)
  AIM Income Fund (IncB)
  AIM Intermediate Government Fund
    (USGv)
  AIM Money Market Fund (MM)
  AIM Municipal Bond Fund (NMuB)
  AIM Value Fund (Gr&I)
AIM International Funds, Inc.
  AIM Global Aggressive Growth Fund
    (GloE)
  AIM Global Growth Fund (GloE)
  AIM Global Income Fund (GloB)
  AIM International Equity Fund (Intl)
AIM Investment Securities Funds
  Limited Maturity Treasury Shares (USGv)
AIM Summit Fund, Inc. (Gr)
AIM Tax-Exempt Funds, Inc.
  AIM Tax-Exempt Bond Fund of
    Connecticut (SMuB)
  AIM Tax-Exempt Cash Fund (NMMX)
  AIM Tax-Free Intermediate Shares
    (NMuB)
AIM Variable Insurance Funds, Inc.
  AIM V.I. Capital Appreciation Fund
    (AgGr)
  AIM V.I. Diversified Income Fund
    (IncB)
  AIM V.I. Global Utilities Fund (GloE)
  AIM V.I. Government Securities Fund
    (USGv)
  AIM V.I. Growth and Income Fund
    (Gr&I)
  AIM V.I. Growth Fund (Gr)
  AIM V.I. International Equity Fund
    (Intl)
  AIM V.I. Money Market Fund (MM)
  AIM V.I. Value Fund (Bal)
Short-Term Investments Company
  Liquid Asset Portfolio (MM)
  Prime Portfolio (MM)
Short-Term Investments Trust
Treasury Portfolio (MM)
Treasury Tax Advantage Portfolio
  (MM)
Tax-Free Investments Company
  Cash Reserve Portfolio (NMMX)

Alamo Fund
1777 N.E. Loop 410
Ste. 1512
San Antonio, TX 78217-5290
210/829-1800
Alamo Growth Fund, Inc. (Gr)

Albemarle Investment Trust
105 N. Washington St.
P.O. Drawer 69
Rocky Mount, NC 27801-5436
800/525-FUND
Albemarle Investment Trust (The)
  North Carolina Tax Free Bond Fund (The)
  (SMuB)

Alger Funds
75 Maiden Lane
New York, NY 10038
800/992-3863
Alger American Fund (The)
  Alger American Balanced Portfolio (Bal)
  Alger American Growth Portfolio (Gr)
  Alger American Income and Growth
    Portfolio (IncE)
  Alger American Leveraged AllCap
    Portfolio (Gr)
  Alger American MidCap Growth Portfolio
    (Gr)
  Alger American Small Capitalization
    Portfolio (AgGr)
Alger Fund (The)
  Alger Balanced Portfolio (Bal)
  Alger Capital Appreciation Portfolio (Gr)
  Alger Growth Portfolio (Gr)
  Alger MidCap Growth Portfolio (Gr)
  Alger Money Market Portfolio (MM)
  Alger Small Capitalization Portfolio
    (AgGr)
Alger Retirement Fund (The)
  Alger Capital Appreciation Retirement
    Portfolio (Gr)
  Alger Growth Retirement Portfolio (Gr)
  Alger MidCap Growth Retirement
    Portfolio (Gr)
  Alger Small Cap Retirement Portfolio
    (AgGr)
Spectra Fund, Inc. (Gr)

Alliance Funds
1345 Avenue of the Americas
New York, NY 10105-0302
800/221-5672
ACM Institutional Reserves, Inc.
  Government Portfolio (MM)
  Prime Portfolio (MM)
  Tax-Free Portfolio (NMMX)
  Trust Portfolio (MM)
AFD Exchange Reserves (MM)
Alliance All-Asia Investment Fund, Inc.
  (Intl)
Alliance Balanced Shares, Inc. (Bal)
Alliance Bond Fund, Inc.
  Corporate Bond Portfolio (CorB)
  U.S. Government Portfolio (USGv)
Alliance Capital Reserves
  Alliance Capital Reserves Portfolio (MM)
  Alliance Money Reserves Portfolio (MM)

Alliance Developing Markets Fund (GloE)
Alliance Fund, Inc. (The) (Gr)
Alliance Global Dollar Government Fund,
  Inc. (GloB)
Alliance Global Small Cap Fund, Inc.
  (GloE)
Alliance Global Strategic Income Trust, Inc.
  (GloB)
Alliance Government Reserves
  Alliance Government Reserves Portfolio
  (MM)
  Alliance Treasury Reserves Portfolio
  (MM)
Alliance Growth & Income Fund, Inc.
  (Gr&I)
Alliance High Yield Fund, Inc. (HiYB)
Alliance Income Builder Fund, Inc. (IncM)
Alliance International Fund (Intl)
Alliance Limited Maturity Government
  Fund, Inc. (GNMA)
Alliance Money Market Fund
  General Municipal Portfolio (NMMX)
  Government Portfolio (MM)
  Prime Portfolio (MM)
Alliance Mortgage Securities Income Fund,
  Inc. (GNMA)
Alliance Multi-Market Strategy Trust, Inc.
  (GloB)
Alliance Municipal Income Fund, Inc.
  California Portfolio (SMuB)
  Insured California Portfolio (SMuB)
  Insured National Portfolio (NMuB)
  National Portfolio (NMuB)
  New York Portfolio (SMuB)
Alliance Municipal Income Fund II
  Arizona Portfolio (SMuB)
  Florida Portfolio (SMuB)
  Massachusetts Portfolio (SMuB)
  Michigan Portfolio (SMuB)
  Minnesota Portfolio (SMuB)
  New Jersey Portfolio (SMuB)
  Ohio Portfolio (SMuB)
  Pennsylvania Portfolio (SMuB)
  Virginia Portfolio (SMuB)
Alliance Municipal Trust
  California Portfolio (SMMX)
  Connecticut Portfolio (SMMX)
  Florida Portfolio (SMMX)
  General Portfolio (NMMX)
  Massachusetts Portfolio (SMuB)
  New Jersey Portfolio (SMMX)
  New York Portfolio (SMMX)
  Virginia Portfolio (SMMX)
Alliance New Europe Fund, Inc. (Intl)
Alliance North American Government
  Income Trust, Inc. (GloB)
Alliance Portfolios (The)
  Alliance Conservative Investors Fund
  (Bal)
  Alliance Growth Fund (Gr)
  Alliance Growth Investors Fund (Bal)

Alliance Short-Term U.S. Government
  Fund (USGv)
Alliance Strategic Balanced Fund (Bal)
Alliance Premier Growth Fund, Inc. (Gr)
Alliance Quasar Fund, Inc. (AgGr)
Alliance Real Estate Investment Fund, Inc.
  (Gr&I)
Alliance/Regent Sector Opportunity Fund,
  Inc. (Gr)
Alliance Short-Term Multi-Market Trust,
  Inc. (GloB)
Alliance Technology Fund, Inc. (Gr)
Alliance Utility Income Fund, Inc. (IncE)
Alliance World Income Trust, Inc. (GloB)
Alliance Worldwide Privatization Fund, Inc.
  (Intl)
Fiduciary Management Associates
  Growth Portfolio (AgGr)
  Large Cap Portfolio (Gr&I)

Alliance Variable Products Funds
P.O. Box 1520
Secaucus, NJ 07096-1520
800/221-5672
Alliance Variable Products Series Fund, Inc.
  Conservative Investors Portfolio (Bal)
  Global Bond Portfolio (GloB)
  Global Dollar Government Portfolio
  (GloB)
  Growth and Income Portfolio (Gr&I)
  Growth Investors Portfolio (Flex)
  Growth Portfolio (Gr)
  International Portfolio (Intl)
  Money Market Portfolio (MM)
  North American Government Income
  Portfolio (GloB)
  Premier Growth Portfolio (Gr)
  Quasar Portfolio (AgGr)
  Real Estate Investment Portfolio (Gr&I)
  Short-Term Multi-Market Portfolio (GloB)
  Technology Portfolio (Gr)
  Total Return Portfolio (IncM)
  U.S. Government/High Grade Securities
  Portfolio (IncB)
  Utility Income Portfolio (IncM)
  Worldwide Privatization Portfolio (GloE)

Allmerica Funds
4400 Computer Dr.
Westboro, MA 01581
508/855-1000
Allmerica Funds
  Investment Grade Income Fund (IncM)
Allmerica Investment Trust
  Equity Index Fund (Gr&I)
  Government Bond Fund (IncB)
  Growth Fund (Gr&I)
  Investment Grade Income Fund (IncB)
  Money Market Fund (MM)
  Select Aggressive Growth Fund (AgGr)
  Select Growth & Income Fund (Gr&I)

Select Growth Fund (Gr)
Select Income Fund (CorB)
Select International Equity Fund (The)
(Intl)

AMBAC Treasurer's Trust
300 Nyala Farms Rd.
Westport, CT 06880
203/341-2300
AMBAC Treasurer's Trust
  AMBAC Short-Term U.S. Government
  Income Fund (USGv)
  AMBAC U.S. Government Money
  Market Fund (MM)
  AMBAC U.S. Treasury Money Market
  Fund (MM)

Amelia Earhart Fund
26100 Northwestern Hwy.
Ste. 1913, One Towne Sq.
Southfield, MI 48076-3719
800/326-6580
Amelia Earhart: Eagle Equity Fund (Gr)

American Century Family of Funds
4500 Main St.
P.O. Box 419200
Kansas City, MO 64141
800/345-2021
American Century Capital Portfolios, Inc.
  American Century Equity Income Fund
  (IncE)
  American Century Value Fund (Gr&I)
American Century Mutual Funds, Inc.
  American Century Balanced Fund (Bal)
  American Century-Benham Bond Fund
  (IncB)
  American Century-Benham Cash Reserve
  Fund (MM)
  American Century-Benham Intermediate-
  Term Bond Fund (IncB)
  American Century-Benham Intermediate-
  Term Government Fund (USGv)
  American Century-Benham Intermediate-
  Term Tax-Exempt Fund (NMuB)
  American Century-Benham Limited-Term
  Bond Fund (IncB)
  American Century-Benham Limited-Term
  Tax-Exempt Fund (NMuB)
  American Century-Benham Long-Term
  Tax-Exempt Fund (NMuB)
  American Century-Benham Short-Term
  Government Fund (USGv)
  American Century-Twentieth Century
  Giftrust (AgGr)
  American Century-Twentieth Century
  Growth Fund (Gr)
  American Century-Twentieth Century
  Heritage Fund (Gr)
  American Century-Twentieth Century
  Select Fund (Gr)

American Century-Twentieth Century
  Ultra Fund (AgGr)
American Century-Twentieth Century
  Vista Fund (AgGr)
American Century Premium Reserves, Inc.
  American Century-Benham Premium
  Bond Fund (CorB)
  American Century-Benham Premium
  Capital Reserve Fund (MM)
  American Century-Benham Premium
  Government Reserve Fund (MM)
American Century Strategic Asset
  Allocations, Inc.
  American Century Strategic Allocation:
  Aggressive (Bal)
  American Century Strategic Allocation:
  Conservative (Bal)
  American Century Strategic Allocation:
  Moderate (Bal)
American Century Variable Portfolios, Inc.
  American Century VP Balanced (Bal)
  American Century VP Capital
  Appreciation (Gr)
  American Century VP International (Intl)
  American Century VP Value (Bal)
American Century World Mutual Funds,
  Inc.
  American Century-Twentieth Century
  International Discovery Fund (Intl)
  American Century-Twentieth Century
  International Growth Fund (Intl)
American Century California Tax-Free and
  Municipal Funds
  American Century-Benham California
  High Yield Municipal Fund (SMuB)
  American Century-Benham California
  Insured Tax-Free Fund (SMuB)
  American Century-Benham California
  Intermediate-Term Tax-Free Fund
  (SMuB)
  American Century-Benham California
  Limited-Term Tax-Free Fund (SMuB)
  American Century-Benham California
  Long-Term Tax-Free Fund (SMuB)
  American Century-Benham California
  Municipal Money Market Fund (SMMX)
  American Century-Benham California
  Tax-Free Money Market Fund (SMMX)
American Century Capital Preservation
  Fund, Inc.
  American Century-Benham Capital
  Preservation Fund (MM)
American Century Capital Preservation
  Fund II, Inc.
  American Century-Benham Capital
  Preservation Fund II (MM)
American Century Government Income
  Trust
  American Century-Benham Adjustable
  Rate Government Securities Fund
  (USGv)

American Century-Benham GNMA Fund (GNMA)
American Century-Benham Government Agency Money Market Fund (MM)
American Century-Benham Intermediate-Term Treasury Fund (USGv)
American Century-Benham Long-Term Treasury Fund (USGv)
American Century-Benham Short-Term Treasury Fund (USGv)
American Century International Bond Funds
American Century-Benham European Government Bond Fund (GloB)
American Century Investment Trust
American Century Prime Money Market Fund (MM)
American Century Manager Funds
American Century Capital Manager Fund (Bal)
American Century Municipal Trust
American Century-Benham Arizona Intermediate-Term Municipal Fund (SMuB)
American Century-Benham Florida Intermediate-Term Municipal Fund (SMuB)
American Century-Benham Florida Municipal Money Market Fund (SMMX)
American Century-Benham Intermediate-Term Tax-Free Fund (NMuB)
American Century-Benham Long-Term Tax-Free Fund (NMuB)
American Century-Benham Tax-Free Money Market Fund (NMMX)
American Century Quantitative Equity Funds
American Century Equity Growth Fund (Gr)
American Century Global Gold Fund (PM/G)
American Century Global Natural Resources Fund (GloE)
American Century Income & Growth Fund (Gr&I)
American Century Utilities Fund (IncE)
American Century Target Maturities Trust
American Century-Benham Target Maturities Trust: 2000 (USGv)
American Century-Benham Target Maturities Trust: 2005 (USGv)
American Century-Benham Target Maturities Trust: 2010 (USGv)
American Century-Benham Target Maturities Trust: 2015 (USGv)
American Century-Benham Target Maturities Trust: 2020 (USGv)
American Century-Benham Target Maturities Trust: 2025 (USGv)

American Funds
333 S. Hope St.
Los Angeles, CA 90071-1406
800/421-0180
AMCAP Fund, Inc. (Gr)
American Balanced Fund, Inc. (Bal)
American Funds Income Series (The)
U.S. Government Securities Fund (USGv)
American Funds Tax-Exempt Series I (The)
Tax-Exempt Fund of Maryland (SMuB)
Tax-Exempt Fund of Virginia (SMuB)
American Funds Tax-Exempt Series II (The)
Tax-Exempt Fund of California (SMuB)
American High Income Municipal Bond Fund (NMuB)
American High-Income Trust (HiYB)
American Mutual Fund, Inc. (Gr&I)
American Variable Insurance Series
Asset Allocation Fund (Bal)
Bond Fund (IncB)
Cash Management Fund (MM)
Global Growth Fund (GloE)
Growth Fund (Gr)
Growth-Income Fund (Gr&I)
High-Yield Bond Fund (HiYB)
International Fund (Intl)
U.S. Government Guaranteed/AAA-Rated Securities Fund (USGv)
Bond Fund of America, Inc. (The) (IncB)
Bond Portfolio for Endowments, Inc. (IncB)
Capital Income Builder, Inc. (IncE)
Capital World Bond Fund, Inc. (GloB)
Capital World Growth & Income Fund (GloE)
Cash Management Trust of America (The) (MM)
Endowments, Inc. (Gr&I)
EuroPacific Growth Fund (Intl)
Fundamental Investors, Inc. (Gr&I)
Growth Fund of America, Inc. (The) (Gr)
Income Fund of America, Inc. (The) (IncM)
Intermediate Bond Fund of America (IncB)
Investment Company of America (The) (Gr&I)
Limited Term Tax-Exempt Bond Fund of America (NMuB)
New Economy Fund (The) (Gr)
New Perspective Fund, Inc. (GloE)
SMALLCAP World Fund, Inc. (GloE)
Tax-Exempt Bond Fund of America, Inc. (The) (NMuB)
Tax-Exempt Money Fund of America (The) (NMMX)
U.S. Treasury Money Fund of America (The) (MM)
Washington Mutual Investors Fund, Inc. (Gr&I)

American Growth Fund
110 16th St.
Ste. 1400
Denver, CO 80202
800/525-2406
American Growth Fund, Inc. (Gr)

American National Funds
One Moody Plaza
Galveston, TX 77550-7948
800/231-4639
American National Government Income
   Fund Series (USGv)
American National Growth Fund, Inc. (Gr)
American National Income Fund, Inc.
   (IncE)
American National Investment Accounts,
   Inc.
   Balanced Portfolio (Bal)
   Growth Portfolio (Gr)
   Managed Portfolio (Gr&I)
   Money Market Portfolio (MM)
American National Primary Fund Series
   (MM)
American National Tax Free Fund Series
   (NMuB)
Triflex Fund, Inc. (Bal)

American Odyssey Funds
Two Tower Ctr.
E. Brunswick, NJ 08816-1063
908/214-2000
American Odyssey Funds, Inc.
   American Odyssey Core Equity Fund
      (Gr&I)
   American Odyssey Emerging
      Opportunities Fund (AgGr)
   American Odyssey Intermediate Term
      Bond Fund (IncB)
   American Odyssey International Equity
      Fund (Intl)
   American Odyssey Long-Term Bond
      Fund (IncB)
   American Odyssey Short-Term Bond
      Fund (IncB)

American Performance Funds
3435 Stelzer Rd.
Columbus, OH 43219-3035
800/762-7085
American Performance Funds
   American Performance Aggressive
      Growth Fund (AgGr)
   American Performance Balanced Fund
      (Bal)
   American Performance Bond Fund
      (IncB)
   American Performance Cash Management
      Fund (MM)
   American Performance Equity Fund
      (Gr&I)

American Performance Intermediate Bond
   Fund (IncB)
American Performance Intermediate Tax
   Free Bond Fund (NMuB)
American Performance Short-Term
   Income Fund (IncB)
American Performance U.S. Treasury
   Fund (MM)

American Skandia Trust
One Corporate Dr.
P.O. Box 883
Shelton, CT 06484-0883
800/628-6039
American Skandia Trust
   AST Janus Overseas Growth Portfolio
      (GloE)
   AST Money Market Portfolio (MM)
   AST Putnam Balanced Portfolio (Bal)
   AST Putnam International Equity
      Portfolio (Intl)
   AST Putnam Value Growth & Income
      Portfolio (Gr&I)
   Berger Capital Growth Portfolio (Gr)
   Federated High Yield Portfolio (HiYB)
   Federated Utility Income Portfolio
      (IncE)
   Founders Capital Appreciation Portfolio
      (Gr)
   Founders Passport Portfolio (Intl)
   INVESCO Equity Income Portfolio (IncE)
   JanCap Growth Portfolio (Gr)
   Lord Abbett Growth and Income Portfolio
      (Gr&I)
   PIMCO Limited Maturity Bond Portfolio
      (Gr&I)
   PIMCO Total Return Bond Portfolio
      (IncB)
   Robertson Stephens Value + Growth
      Portfolio (AgGr)
   T. Rowe Price Asset Allocation Portfolio
      (IncM)
   T. Rowe Price International Bond
      Portfolio (GloB)
   T. Rowe Price International Equity
      Portfolio (Intl)
   T. Rowe Price Natural Resources Portfolio
      (Gr)
   T. Rowe Price Small Company Value
      Portfolio (AgGr)
   Twentieth Century International Growth
      Portfolio (Intl)
   Twentieth Century Strategic Balanced
      Portfolio (Bal)

Amerindo Funds Inc.
399 Park Ave., 18th Fl.
New York, NY 10022
888/TECHFUND
Amerindo Funds, Inc.
   Amerindo Technology Fund (AgGr)

AmeriPrime Funds
1793 Kingswood Dr.
Ste. 200
Southlake, TX 76092
800/298-1995
AmeriPrime Funds
  AIT Vision U.S. Equity Fund (Gr)
  Carl Domino Equity Income Fund (Gr&I)
  Fountainhead Special Value Fund (Gr&I)
  GLOBALT Growth Fund (Gr)
  IMS Capital Value Fund (Gr)
  MAXIM Contrarian Fund (GloE)

AmSouth Mutual Funds
3435 Stelzer Rd.
Columbus, OH 43219-3035
800/451-8382
AmSouth Mutual Funds
  Balanced Fund (Bal)
  Bond Fund (IncB)
  Equity Fund (Gr)
  Florida Tax-Free Fund (SMuB)
  Government Income Fund (USGv)
  Limited Maturity Fund (IncB)
  Prime Obligations Fund (MM)
  Regional Equity Fund (Gr)
  Tax Exempt Fund (NMMX)
  U.S. Treasury Fund (MM)

AmTrust Fund
P.O. Box 3467
Victoria, TX 77903-3467
800/532-1146
AmTrust Value Fund (Gr)

Amway Funds
7575 Fulton St. East
Ada, MI 49355-0001
800/346-2670
Amway Mutual Fund, Inc. (Gr)

Analytic Funds
700 S. Flower St.
Ste. 2400
Los Angeles, CA 90017
800/374-2633
Analytic Optioned Equity Fund, Inc. (Gr&I)
Analytic Series Fund (The)
  Enhanced Equity Portfolio (Gr&I)
  Master Fixed Income Portfolio (IncM)
  Short-Term Government Portfolio (USGv)

Anchor Funds
2717 Furlong Rd.
Doylestown, PA 18901
215/794-2980
Anchor Capital Accumulation Trust (Gr)
Anchor International Bond Trust (GloB)
Anchor Resource and Commodity Trust
  (Gr)
Anchor Strategic Assets Trust (PM/G)

Anchor Pathway Funds
733 Third Ave.
New York, NY 10017-3204
800/858-8850
Anchor Pathway Fund
  Asset Allocation Series (Flex)
  Cash Management Series (MM)
  Growth-Income Series (Gr&I)
  Growth Series (Gr)
  High-Yield Bond Series (HiYB)
  International Series (Intl)
  U.S. Government/AAA-Rated Securities
    Series (USGv)
Anchor Series Trust
  Capital Appreciation Portfolio (AgGr)
  Fixed Income Portfolio (IncB)
  Foreign Securities Portfolio (Intl)
  Government and Quality Bond Portfolio
    (USGv)
  Growth and Income Portfolio (Gr&I)
  Growth Portfolio (Gr)
  High Yield Portfolio (HiYB)
  Money Market Portfolio (MM)
  Multi-Asset Portfolio (Flex)
  Natural Resources Portfolio (Gr&I)
  Strategic Multi-Asset Portfolio (GloB)
  Target '98 Portfolio (USGv)

API Trust
2303 Yorktown Ave.
P.O. Box 2529
Lynchburg, VA 24501-2529
800/544-6060
American Pension Investors Trust
  Capital Income Fund (IncM)
  Growth Fund (Gr)
  T-1 Treasury Trust (USGv)
  Yorktown Classic Value Trust (AgGr)

Aquila Funds
380 Madison Ave.
Ste. 2300
New York, NY 10017
800/762-5955
Aquila Cascadia Equity Fund (Gr)
Aquila Rocky Mountain Equity Fund (Gr)
Cascades Trust (The)
  Tax-Free Trust of Oregon (SMuB)
Capital Cash Management Trust (MM)
Cash Assets Trust
  Pacific Capital Tax-Free Cash Assets Trust
    (NMMX)
  Pacific Capital U.S. Treasuries Cash
    Assets Trust (MM)
Churchill Cash Reserves Trust (MM)
Churchill Tax-Free Trust
  Churchill Tax-Free Fund of Kentucky
    (SMuB)
Hawaiian Tax-Free Trust (SMuB)
Narragansett Insured Tax-Free Income Fund
  (SMuB)

Tax-Free Trust of Arizona (SMuB)
Tax-Free Fund of Colorado (SMuB)
Tax-Free Fund for Utah (SMuB)

Aquinas Funds
5310 Harvest Hill Rd.
Ste. 248
Dallas, TX 75230-5800
800/423-6369
Aquinas Funds, Inc.
  Aquinas Balanced Fund (Bal)
  Aquinas Equity Growth Fund (Gr)
  Aquinas Equity Income Fund (IncE)
  Aquinas Fixed Income Fund (IncB)

Arbor Fund
One Freedom Valley Drive
Oaks, PA 19456
800/342-5734
Arbor Fund (The)
  Arbor California Tax Exempt Portfolio
  (SMMX)
  Arbor Institutional Tax-Free Portfolio
  (NMMX)
  Crestar Prime Obligation Fund (MM)
  Crestar U.S. Government Securities
  Money Fund (MM)
  OVB Capital Appreciation Portfolio (Gr)
  OVB Emerging Growth Portfolio (AgGr)
  OVB Equity Income Portfolio (IncE)
  OVB Government Securities Portfolio
  (USGv)
  OVB Prime Obligations Money Market
  Fund (MM)
  OVB West Virginia Tax-Exempt Income
  Portfolio (SMuB)

ARCH Funds
3435 Stelzer Rd.
Columbus, OH 43219-3035
800/551-3731
ARCH Fund, Inc. (The)
  ARCH Balanced Portfolio (Bal)
  ARCH Bond Index Portfolio (IncB)
  ARCH Equity Income Portfolio (IncE)
  ARCH Equity Index Portfolio (Gr)
  ARCH Government & Corporate Bond
  Portfolio (IncB)
  ARCH Growth and Income Equity
  Portfolio (Gr&I)
  ARCH Intermediate Corporate Bond
  Portfolio (IncB)
  ARCH International Fund (Intl)
  ARCH Money Market Portfolio (MM)
  ARCH Treasury Money Market Portfolio
  (MM)
  ARCH U.S. Government Securities
  Portfolio (USGv)
ARCH Tax-Exempt Trust
  ARCH Missouri Tax-Exempt Bond
  Portfolio (SMuB)

  ARCH Tax-Exempt Money Market
  Portfolio (NMMX)
  Money Market Portfolio (NMMX)

Ariel Mutual Funds
307 N. Michigan Ave.
Ste. 500
Chicago, IL 60601-5305
800/292-7435
Ariel Growth Fund
  Ariel Appreciation Fund (Gr)
  Ariel Growth Fund (Gr)
  Ariel Premier Bond Fund (IncB)

Ark Funds
One Freedom Valley Drive
Oaks, PA 19456
800/624-4116
Ark Funds
  Balanced Portfolio (Gr&I)
  Blue Chip Equity Portfolio (Gr)
  Capital Growth Portfolio (Gr)
  Income Portfolio (IncB)
  International Equity Portfolio (Intl)
  Maryland Tax-Free Bond Portfolio
  (SMuB)
  Money Market Portfolio (MM)
  Pennsylvania Tax-Free Portfolio (SMuB)
  Short-Term Treasury Portfolio (USGv)
  Special Equity Portfolio (Gr)
  Tax-Free Money Market Portfolio
  (NMMX)
  U.S. Government Money Market Portfolio
  (MM)
  U.S. Treasury Money Market Portfolio
  (MM)

Armstrong Associates, Inc.
750 North St. Paul
Ste. 1300, LB 13
Dallas, TX 75201-7105
214/720-9101
Armstrong Associates, Inc. (Gr)

Arrow Funds
Federated Investors Twr.
1001 Liberty Ave.
Pittsburgh, PA 15222-3779
800/341-7400
Arrow Funds
  Arrow Equity Portfolio (Gr)
  Arrow Fixed Income Portfolio (IncB)
  Arrow Government Money Market
  Portfolio (MM)
  Arrow Municipal Income Portfolio (NMuB)

Artisan Funds, Inc.
1000 N. Water St.
Ste. 1770
Milwaukee, WI 53202
800/399-1770

Artisan Funds, Inc.
  Artisan International Fund (Intl)
  Artisan Small Cap Fund (Gr)

ASM Fund
15438 N. Florida
Ste. 107
Tampa, FL 33613-1221
800/445-2763
ASM Fund, Inc. (Gr&I)

Astra Funds
11400 W. Olympic Blvd.
Ste. 200
Los Angeles, CA 90064
800/441-7267
Astra All-American Government Income
  Trust (GloB)
Astra Global Investment Series
  Short-Term Multi-Market Income Fund I
    (GloB)
  Short-Term Multi-Market Income Fund II
    (GloB)
Astra Strategic Investment Series
  Adjustable Rate Securities Trust I
    (GNMA)
  Adjustable Rate Securities Trust I-A
    (GNMA)
  Adjustable Rate Securities Trust IV
    (GNMA)
  Adjustable U.S. Government Securities
    Trust I (GNMA)
  Adjustable U.S. Government Securities
    Trust I-A (GNMA)
  Adjustable U.S. Government Securities
    Trust II (GNMA)
  Adjustable U.S. Government Securities
    Trust IV (GNMA)

Atlas Funds
794 Davis St.
P.O. Box 1894
San Leandro, CA 94577
800/933-2852
Atlas Assets, Inc.
  Atlas Balanced Fund (Bal)
  Atlas California Insured Intermediate
    Municipal Fund (SMuB)
  Atlas California Municipal Bond Fund
    (SMuB)
  Atlas California Municipal Money Fund
    (SMMX)
  Atlas Emerging Growth Fund (Intl)
  Atlas Global Growth Fund (GloE)
  Atlas Growth and Income Fund (Gr&I)
  Atlas National Insured Intermediate
    Municipal Fund (NMuB)
  Atlas National Municipal Bond Fund
    (NMuB)
  Atlas National Municipal Money Fund
    (NMMX)

Atlas Strategic Growth Fund (Gr)
Atlas Strategic Income Fund (IncB)
Atlas U.S. Government and Mortgage
  Securities Fund (USGv)
Atlas U.S. Treasury Intermediate Fund
  (USGv)
Atlas U.S. Treasury Money Fund (MM)

AVESTA Funds
P.O. Box 2558
26-TCBE-45
Houston, TX 77252-8045
713/216-6433
AVESTA Trust
  Balanced Fund (Bal)
  Core Equity Fund (Gr&I)
  Equity Growth Fund (Gr)
  Equity Income Fund (IncE)
  Income Fund (IncB)
  Intermediate Term Bond Fund (IncB)
  Money Market Fund (MM)
  Risk Manager-Balanced Fund (Bal)
  Risk Manager-Growth Fund (Gr)
  Risk Manager-Income Fund (Bal)
  Short-Intermediate Term U.S. Government
    Securities Fund (USGv)
  Small Capitalization Fund (IncE)
  U.S. Government Securities Fund
    (USGv)

Bankers Trust Family of Funds
4 Albany St.
2nd Fl.
New York, NY 10006
800/422-6577
BT Advisor Funds
  EAFE Equity Index Fund (Intl)
  Small Cap Index Fund (AgGr)
BT Institutional Funds
  Equity 500 Index Fund (Gr&I)
  Institutional Cash Management Fund
    (MM)
  Institutional Cash Reserves (MM)
  Institutional Liquid Assets Fund (MM)
  Institutional Treasury Money Fund
    (MM)
  International Equity Fund (Intl)
BT Investment Funds
  BT Investment Lifecycle Long Range
    Fund (Bal)
  BT Investment Lifecycle Mid Range Fund
    (Bal)
  BT Investment Lifecycle Short Range
    Fund (IncM)
  Capital Appreciation Fund (Gr)
  Cash Management Fund (MM)
  Global High Yield Securities Fund
    (GloB)
  Intermediate Tax Free Fund (NMuB)
  International Equity Fund (Intl)
  Latin American Equity Fund (Intl)

Limited Term US Government Securities
Fund (USGv)
NY Tax Free Money Fund (SMMX)
Pacific Basin Equity Fund (Intl)
Small Cap Fund (AgGr)
Tax Free Money Fund (NMMX)
Treasury Money Fund (MM)
Utility Fund (IncE)
BT Pyramid Mutual Funds
BT Institutional Asset Management Fund
(Bal)
BT Investment Equity Appreciation Fund
(Gr)
BT Investment Equity 500 Index Fund
(Gr&I)
BT Investment Money Market Fund
(MM)

Baron Funds
767 Fifth Ave.
24th Fl.
New York, NY 10153
800/99-BARON
Baron Funds (The)
Baron Asset Fund (AgGr)
Baron Growth and Income Fund (Gr&I)

Barr Rosenberg Series Trust
Four Orinda Way
Ste. 300E
Orinda, CA 94563-2523
800/447-3332
Barr Rosenberg Series Trust
International Small Capitalization Fund
(Intl)
Japan Fund (Intl)
U.S. Small Capitalization Fund (AgGr)

Battery Park Funds
2 World Trade Ctr.
Bldg. B
New York, NY 10281-1198
888/848-7800
Battery Park Funds, Inc.
High Yield Fund (HiYB)

Baupost Fund Group
44 Brattle St.
P.O. Box 381288
Cambridge, MA 02238
617/497-6680
Baupost Fund (The)
Baupost Fund (Gr&I)

Baxter Financial Funds
1200 N. Federal Hwy.
Ste. 424
Boca Raton, FL 33432-2847
800/749-9933
Eagle Growth Shares, Inc. (Gr)
Philadelphia Fund, Inc. (Gr&I)

BB&K Funds
950 Tower Lane
Ste. 1900
Foster City, CA 94404-2131
800/882-8383
Bailard, Biehl & Kaiser Fund Group
Bailard, Biehl & Kaiser Diversa Fund
(Gr&I)
Bailard, Biehl & Kaiser International Fund
Group, Inc.
Bailard, Biehl & Kaiser International
Bond Fund (GloB)
Bailard, Biehl & Kaiser International
Equity Fund (Intl)

BB&T Mutual Funds Group
3435 Stelzer Rd.
Columbus, OH 43219-3035
800/228-1872
BB&T Mutual Funds Group
Balanced Fund (Bal)
Growth and Income Stock Fund (Gr&I)
Intermediate U.S. Government Bond Fund
(USGv)
North Carolina Intermediate Tax-Free
Fund (SMuB)
Short/Intermediate U.S. Government
Income Fund (USGv)
Small Company Growth Fund (Gr)
U.S. Treasury Money Market Fund (MM)

BEA Advisor Funds
153 E. 53rd St.
58th Fl.
New York, NY 10022-4611
800/293-1232
BEA Advisor Funds
Emerging Markets Equity Fund (Intl)
Global Telecommunications Fund (GloE)
High Yield Fund (HiYB)
International Equity Fund (Intl)

Bear Stearns Funds
245 Park Ave.
15th Fl.
New York, NY 10167
800/766-4111
Bear Stearns Funds (The)
Insiders Select Fund (Gr)
Large Cap Value Portfolio (Gr)
S&P STARS Portfolio (Gr&I)
Small Cap Value Portfolio (AgGr)
Total Return Bond Portfolio (IncB)

Bear Stearns Investment Trust
245 Park Ave.
15th Fl.
New York, NY 10167
800/766-4111
Bear Stearns Investment Trust (The)
Emerging Markets Debt Portfolio (GloB)

Benchmark Funds
50 S. LaSalle St.
Chicago, IL 60675
800/621-2550
Benchmark Funds (The)
  Balanced Portfolio (Bal)
  Bond Portfolio (CorB)
  Diversified Assets Portfolio (MM)
  Diversified Growth Portfolio (Gr)
  Equity Index Portfolio (Gr&I)
  Focused Growth Portfolio (Gr)
  Government Portfolio (MM)
  Government Select Portfolio (MM)
  International Bond Portfolio (Intl)
  International Growth Portfolio (Intl)
  Short Duration Portfolio (CorB)
  Short/Intermediate Bond Portfolio (CorB)
  Small Company Index Portfolio (AgGr)
  Tax-Exempt Portfolio (NMMX)
  U.S. Government Securities Portfolio
  (USGv)
  U.S. Treasury Index Portfolio (USGv)

Berger Funds
210 University Blvd., Ste. 900
Denver, CO 80206-4626
800/333-1001
Berger/BIAM Worldwide Funds Trust (The)
  Berger/BIAM International CORE Fund
  (Gr)
  Berger/BIAM International Fund (Intl)
  Berger/BIAM International Institutional
  Fund (Gr)
Berger Institutional Products Trust (The)
  Berger/BIAM IPT-International Fund (Gr)
Berger Growth and Income Fund (The)
  (Gr&I)
Berger Investment Portfolio Trust (The)
  Berger New Generation Fund (AgGr)
  Berger Small Company Growth Fund
  (AgGr)
  Berger One Hundred Fund, Inc. (The) (Gr)
  Berger Small Cap Value Fund (Gr)

Bernstein Funds Group
767 Fifth Ave.
New York, NY 10153-0002
212/756-4097
Sanford C. Bernstein Fund, Inc.
  Bernstein California Municipal Portfolio
  (SMuB)
  Bernstein Diversified Municipal Portfolio
  (NMuB)
  Bernstein Emerging Markets Value
  Portfolio (Intl)
  Bernstein Government Short Duration
  Portfolio (USGv)
  Bernstein Intermediate Duration Portfolio
  (IncM)
  Bernstein International Value Portfolio
  (Intl)

Bernstein New York Municipal Portfolio
  (SMuB)
Bernstein Short Duration California
  Municipal Portfolio (SMuB)
Bernstein Short Duration Diversified
  Municipal Portfolio (NMuB)
Bernstein Short Duration New York
  Municipal Portfolio (SMuB)
Bernstein Short Duration Plus Portfolio
  (IncM)

Biltmore Funds
Federated Investors Twr.
1001 Liberty Ave.
Pittsburgh, PA 15222-3779
800/341-7400
Biltmore Funds (The)
  Biltmore Balanced Fund (Bal)
  Biltmore Emerging Markets Fund (Intl)
  Biltmore Equity Fund (Gr)
  Biltmore Equity Index Fund (Gr)
  Biltmore Fixed Income Fund (IncB)
  Biltmore Georgia Municipal Bond Fund
  (SMuB)
  Biltmore Money Market Fund (MM)
  Biltmore North Carolina Municipal Bond
  Fund (SMuB)
  Biltmore Prime Cash Management Fund
  (MM)
  Biltmore Quantitative Equity Fund (Gr&I)
  Biltmore Short Term Fixed Income Fund
  (IncB)
  Biltmore South Carolina Municipal Bond
  Fund (SMuB)
  Biltmore Special Values Fund (Gr)
  Biltmore Tax-Free Money Market Fund
  (NMMX)
  Biltmore U.S. Treasury Money Market
  Fund (MM)

Bishop Street Funds
One Freedom Valley Drive
Oaks, PA 19456
800/262-9565
Bishop Street Funds
  Bishop Street Equity Fund (Gr)
  Bishop Street Hawaii Municipal Bond
  Fund (SMuB)
  Bishop Street High Grade Income Fund
  (Gr&I)
  Bishop Street Money Market Fund
  (MM)
  Treasury Money Market Fund (MM)

BNY Hamilton Funds, Inc.
125 W. 55th St.
New York, NY 10019-3800
800/426-9363
BNY Hamilton Funds, Inc.
  BNY Hamilton Equity Income Fund
  (Gr&I)

BNY Hamilton Intermediate Investment Grade Fund (IncB)
BNY Hamilton Intermediate Investment Grade Fund (USGv)
BNY Hamilton Intermediate New York Tax-Exempt Fund (SMuB)
BNY Hamilton Intermediate Tax-Exempt Fund (NMuB)
BNY Hamilton International Equity Fund (Intl)
BNY Hamilton Large Cap Growth Fund (Gr)
BNY Hamilton Money Fund (MM)
BNY Hamilton Small Cap Growth Fund (AgGr)
BNY Hamilton Treasury Money Fund (MM)

Bramwell Funds
745 Fifth Ave.
New York, NY 10151
800/272-6227
Bramwell Funds, Inc. (The)
　Bramwell Growth Fund (The) (Gr)

Brandes Investment Trust
12750 High Bluff Dr.
San Diego, CA 92130-2018
619/755-0239
Brandes Investment Trust
　Brandes Institutional International Equity Fund (Intl)

Bridges Investment Fund
8401 W. Dodge Rd.
256 Durham Plaza
Omaha, NE 68114-3493
402/397-4700
Bridges Investment Fund, Inc. (Gr&I)

Bridgeway Funds
5650 Kirby Dr., Ste. 141
Houston, TX 77005
800/661-3550
Bridgeway Fund, Inc.
　Aggressive Growth Portfolio (AgGr)
　Social Responsibility Portfolio (Gr)
　Ultra-Small Company Portfolio (AgGr)

Brinson Funds
209 S. LaSalle St.
Chicago, IL 60604-1295
800/448-2430
Brinson Funds (The)
　Global Bond Fund (GloB)
　Global Equity Fund (GloE)
　Global Fund (GloB)
　Non-U.S. Equity Fund (Intl)
　U.S. Balanced Fund (Bal)
　U.S. Bond Fund (IncB)
　U.S. Equity Fund (Gr&I)

Brundage, Story & Rose Investment Trust
312 Walnut St.
21st Fl.
Cincinnati, OH 45202-4024
800/545-0103
Brundage, Story and Rose Investment Trust
　Equity Fund (Gr&I)
　Short/Intermediate Term Fixed-Income Fund (IncB)

Bull & Bear Funds
11 Hanover Square
New York, NY 10005-3452
800/847-4200
Bull & Bear Funds I, Inc.
　Bull & Bear U.S. and Overseas Fund (GloE)
Bull & Bear Funds II, Inc.
　Bull & Bear Dollar Reserves (MM)
Bull & Bear Gold Investors Ltd. (PM/G)
Bull & Bear Special Equities Fund, Inc. (AgGr)
Midas Fund, Inc. (PM/G)
Rockwood Fund, Inc. (Gr)

Burnham Fund
1325 Avenue of the Americas
17th Fl.
New York, NY 10019-6026
800/874-FUND
Burnham Fund, Inc. (The) (Gr&I)

Calamos Funds
1111 E. Warrenville Rd.
Naperville, IL 60563-1493
800/823-7386
CFS Investment Trust
　Calamos Convertible Fund (Bal)
　Calamos Global Growth and Income Fund (GloB)
　Calamos Growth and Income Fund (Gr&I)
　Calamos Growth Fund (Gr)
　Calamos Strategic Income Fund (IncM)

Caldwell & Orkin Funds
2050 Tower Place
3340 Peachtree Rd.
Atlanta, GA 30326
800/237-7073
Caldwell & Orkin Funds, Inc.
　Caldwell & Orkin Market Opportunity Fund (Flex)

Calvert Funds
4550 Montgomery Ave.
Ste. 1000-N
Bethesda, MD 20814-3343
800/368-2748
Calvert Fund (The)
　Calvert Income Fund (IncB)

Calvert New Vision Small Cap Fund
  (AgGr)
Calvert Strategic Growth Fund (Gr)
Calvert Municipal Fund, Inc.
  Calvert Arizona Municipal Intermediate
    Fund (SMuB)
  Calvert California Municipal Intermediate
    Fund (SMuB)
  Calvert Maryland Municipal Intermediate
    Fund (SMuB)
  Calvert Michigan Municipal Intermediate
    Fund (SMuB)
  Calvert National Municipal Intermediate
    Fund (NMuB)
  Calvert New York Municipal Intermediate
    Fund (SMuB)
  Calvert Pennsylvania Municipal
    Intermediate Fund (SMuB)
  Calvert Virginia Municipal Intermediate
    Fund (SMuB)
Calvert Social Investment Fund
  Bond Portfolio (CorB)
  Equity Portfolio (Gr)
  Managed Growth Portfolio (Bal)
  Money Market Portfolio (MM)
Calvert Tax-Free Reserves
  California Money Market Portfolio
    (SMMX)
  Limited-Term Portfolio (NMuB)
  Long-Term Portfolio (NMuB)
  Money Market Portfolio (NMMX)
  Vermont Municipal Portfolio (SMuB)
Calvert World Values Fund, Inc.
  Capital Accumulation Fund (Gr)
  International Equity Fund (GloE)
First Variable Rate Fund
  Calvert First Government Money Market
    Fund (MM)
  Calvert Florida Municipal Intermediate
    Fund (SMuB)
Money Management Plus
  Institutional Prime Fund (MM)
Calvert New World Fund, Inc.
  Calvert New Africa Fund (GloE)

Canada Life Funds
330 University Ave.
Toronto, Ont., M5G 1R8
416/597-1456
Canada Life of America Series Fund, Inc.
  Bond Series (IncB)
  Capital Series (Gr)
  International Equity Series (GloE)
  Managed Series (IncM)
  Money Market Series (MM)
  Value Equity Series (Gr)

Capital Management Funds
105 N. Washington St.
P.O. Box 69
Rocky Mount, NC 27870

800/773-3863
Capital Management Investment Trust
  Capital Management Equity Fund (Gr)

Capital Management Investment Trust
140 Broadway
New York, NY 10005
888/626-3863
Capital Management Investment Trust
  Capital Management Mid-Cap Fund (Gr)

Capital Value Funds
2203 Grand Ave.
Des Moines, IA 50312-5338
800/798-1819
Capital Value Fund, Inc.
  Equity Portfolio (Gr)
  Fixed Income Portfolio (CorB)
  Prime Money Market Portfolio (MM)
  Short-Term Government Portfolio (USGv)
  Total Return Portfolio (Gr&I)

Capstone Group of Mutual Funds
5847 San Felipe Dr.
Ste. 4100
Houston, TX 77057-3011
800/262-6631
Capstone Fixed Income Series, Inc.
  Capstone Government Income Fund
    (USGv)
Capstone Growth Fund, Inc. (Gr)
Capstone International Series Trust
  Capstone New Zealand Fund (Intl)
Capstone International Series Trust
  Capstone Nikko Japan Fund (Intl)

Cardinal Family of Funds
155 E. Broad St.
Columbus, OH 43215-3609
800/848-7734
Cardinal Aggressive Growth Fund (AgGr)
Cardinal Balanced Fund (Bal)
Cardinal Fund (The) (Gr&I)
Cardinal Government Obligations Fund
  (USGv)
Cardinal Government Securities Money
  Market Fund (MM)
Cardinal Tax Exempt Money Market Fund
  (NMMX)

Carillon Funds
1876 Waycross Rd.
Cincinnati, OH 45240-2825
800/999-1840
Carillon Fund, Inc.
  Bond Portfolio (CorB)
  Capital Portfolio (Flex)
  Equity Portfolio (Gr)
  S&P 500 Portfolio (Gr&I)
Carillon Investment Trust
  Carillon Capital Fund (Flex)

Cash Resource Trust
P.O. Box 1357
Richmond, VA 23211-1357
800/382-0016
Cash Resource Trust
  Cash Resource Money Market Fund
    (MM)
  Cash Resource New York Tax-Exempt
    Money Market Fund (SMMX)
  Cash Resource Tax-Exempt Money
    Market Fund (NMMX)
  Cash Resource U.S. Government Money
    Market Fund (MM)

Centura Funds
3435 Stelzer Rd.
Columbus, OH 43219-3035
800/442-3688
Centura Funds
  Equity Growth Fund (Gr)
  Federal Securities Income Fund (USGv)
  North Carolina Tax-Free Bond Fund
    (SMuB)

Centurion T.A.A. Fund
11545 W. Bernardo Ct. #100
San Diego, CA 92127
800/878-8536
Centurion T.A.A. Fund, Inc. (Gr)

Century Shares Trust
One Liberty Sq.
Boston, MA 02109-4825
800/321-1928
Century Shares Trust (Gr&I)

CGM Funds
222 Berkeley St.
10th Fl.
Boston, MA 02116-3748
800/345-4048
CGM Capital Development Fund (Gr)
CGM Trust
  CGM American Tax-Free Fund (NMuB)
  CGM Fixed Income Fund (IncB)
  CGM Mutual Fund (Bal)
  CGM Realty Fund (Gr&I)

Chaconia Fund
24 W. Carver St.
Huntington, NY 11743
800/368-3332
Chaconia Income and Growth Fund, Inc.
  (The) (Gr&I)

Chapman Funds, Inc.
World Trade Center
401 East Pratt St., 28th Fl.
Baltimore, MD 21202-3117
800/752-1013
Chapman Funds, Inc. (The)

Chapman Institutional Cash Management
  Fund (MM)
Chapman U.S. Treasury Money Fund
  (MM)

Chicago Trust Funds
171 N. Clark St.
Chicago, IL 60601-3203
800/992-8151
Chicago Trust Funds
  Chicago Trust Asset Allocation Fund
    (IncM)
  Chicago Trust Bond Fund (IncB)
  Chicago Trust Growth and Income Fund
    (Gr&I)
  Chicago Trust Money Market Fund
    (MM)
  Chicago Trust Municipal Bond Fund
    (NMuB)
  Chicago Trust Talon Fund (Gr)
  Montag & Caldwell Balanced Fund
    (Bal)
  Montag & Caldwell Growth Fund
    (Gr)

Chubb America Fund, Inc.
One Granite Place
Concord, NH 03301-3258
800/258-3648
Chubb America Fund, Inc.
  Balanced Portfolio (Bal)
  Bond Portfolio (IncB)
  Capital Growth Portfolio (Gr)
  Domestic Growth Portfolio (Gr&I)
  Gold Stock Portfolio (PM/G)
  Growth & Income Portfolio (Gr&I)
  Money Market Portfolio (MM)
  World Growth Stock Portfolio (GloE)

Chubb Investment Fund, Inc.
One Granite Place
Concord, NH 03301-3258
800/258-3648
Chubb Investment Funds, Inc.
  Capital Appreciation Fund (Gr)
  Chubb Government Securities Fund
    (USGv)
  Chubb Growth and Income Fund
    (Gr&I)
  Chubb Money Market Fund (MM)
  Chubb Tax-Exempt Fund (NMuB)
  Chubb Total Return Fund (Bal)
  Global Income Fund (GloB)

CIGNA Funds
900 Cottage Grove Rd.
S-210
Hartford, CT 06152-2210
860/726-3700
CIGNA Institutional Funds Group
  CIGNA International Stock Fund (Intl)

CitiSelect Funds
153 E. 53rd St.
6th Fl., Zone 6
New York, NY 10022-4611
800/625-4554
Landmark Funds I
  CitiSelect Asset Allocation Portfolio 200
  (Bal)
  CitiSelect Asset Allocation Portfolio 300
  (Bal)
  CitiSelect Asset Allocation Portfolio 400
  (Bal)
  CitiSelect Asset Allocation Portfolio 500
  (Bal)

Citizens Trust
One Harbour Pl., Ste. 525
Portsmouth, NH 03801
800/223-7010
Citizens Trust
  Citizens Emerging Growth Portfolio
  (AgGr)
  Citizens Global Equity Portfolio (GloE)
  Citizens Income Portfolio (IncM)
  Citizens Index Portfolio (Gr)
  EFund (MM)
  Muir California Tax-Free Income
  Portfolio (SMuB)
  Working Assets Money Market Fund
  (MM)

Cohen & Steers Funds
757 Third Ave.
27th Fl.
New York, NY 10017-2013
800/437-9912
Cohen & Steers Realty Shares, Inc. (Gr&I)

College Retirement Equities Fund
730 Third Ave.
New York, NY 10017-3206
800/842-2733
College Retirement Equities Fund
  Bond Market Account (IncB)
  Equity Index Account (Gr&I)
  Global Equities Account (GloE)
  Growth Account (Gr)
  Money Market Account (MM)
  Social Choice Account (Bal)
  Stock Account (Gr&I)
  Stock Index Account (Gr)

Colonial Family of Funds
One Financial Ctr.
Boston, MA 02111-2621
800/225-2365
Colonial California Tax-Exempt Fund
  (SMuB)
Colonial Connecticut Tax-Exempt Fund
  (SMuB)
Colonial Federal Securities Fund (USGv)

Colonial Florida Tax-Exempt Fund (SMuB)
Colonial Fund (The) (Gr&I)
Colonial Global Equity Fund (GloE)
Colonial High Yield Municipal Fund
  (NMuB)
Colonial High Yield Securities Fund
  (HiYB)
Colonial Income Fund (IncB)
Colonial Intermediate Tax-Exempt Fund
  (NMuB)
Colonial International Fund For Growth
  (Intl)
Colonial International Horizons Fund (Gr)
Colonial Massachusetts Tax-Exempt Fund
  (SMuB)
Colonial Michigan Tax-Exempt Fund
  (SMuB)
Colonial Minnesota Tax-Exempt Fund
  (SMuB)
Colonial Money Market Fund (MM)
Colonial Municipal Money Market Fund
  (NMMX)
Colonial New York Tax-Exempt Fund
  (SMuB)
Colonial North Carolina Tax-Exempt Fund
  (SMuB)
Colonial Ohio Tax-Exempt Fund (SMuB)
Colonial Select Value Fund (Gr)
Colonial Short Duration U.S. Government
  Fund (GNMA)
Colonial Small Cap Value Fund (Gr&I)
Colonial Strategic Balanced Fund (Bal)
Colonial Strategic Income Fund (IncM)
Colonial Tax-Exempt Fund (NMuB)
Colonial Tax-Exempt Insured Fund
  (NMuB)
Colonial U.S. Government Fund (USGv)
Colonial U.S. Stock Fund (Gr)
Colonial Utilities Fund (IncE)
Colonial Newport Tiger Fund (Intl)
Colonial Trust II
  Colonial Newport Japan Fund (Intl)
  Colonial Newport Tiger Cub Fund (Intl)
Colonial Global Utilities Fund (GloE)
Colonial Trust I
  Colonial Tax-Managed Growth Fund (Gr)

Columbia Family of Funds
P.O. Box 1350
Portland, OR 97207-1350
800/547-1707
Columbia Balanced Fund, Inc. (Bal)
Columbia Common Stock Fund, Inc.
  (Gr&I)
Columbia Daily Income Company (MM)
Columbia Fixed Income Securities Fund,
  Inc. (IncB)
Columbia Growth Fund, Inc. (Gr)
Columbia High Yield Fund, Inc. (HiYB)
Columbia International Stock Fund, Inc.
  (Intl)

Columbia Municipal Bond Fund, Inc.
(SMuB)
Columbia Real Estate Equity Fund, Inc.
(Gr&I)
Columbia Small Cap Fund, Inc. (AgGr)
Columbia Special Fund, Inc. (AgGr)
Columbia U.S. Government Securities
Fund, Inc. (USGv)

Commerce Funds
922 Walnut St.
P.O. Box 13686
Kansas City, MO 64199-3686
800/993-6365
Commerce Funds
  Balanced Fund (Bal)
  Bond Fund (IncB)
  Growth & Income Fund (IncE)
  Growth Fund (Gr&I)
  International Equity Fund (Intl)
  MidCap Fund (AgGr)
  Missouri Tax-Free Bond Fund (SMuB)
  National Tax-Free Bond Fund (NMuB)
  Short-Term Government Fund (USGv)

Common Sense Trust
2800 Post Oak Blvd.
P.O. Box 3121
Houston, TX 77056-6106
800/421-5666
Common Sense Trust
  Common Sense Emerging Growth Fund
  (Intl)
  Common Sense Government Fund
  (USGv)
  Common Sense Growth and Income Fund
  (Gr&I)
  Common Sense Growth Fund (Gr)
  Common Sense International Equity Fund
  (Intl)
  Common Sense Money Market Fund
  (MM)
  Common Sense Municipal Bond Fund
  (NMuB)

Compass Capital Funds
400 Bellevue Pkwy.
Wilmington, DE 19809-3748
800/422-6538
Compass Capital Funds (The)
  Balanced Portfolio (Bal)
  Core Bond Portfolio (IncB)
  Government Income Portfolio (USGv)
  Growth Equity Portfolio (Gr)
  Index Equity Portfolio (Gr&I)
  Intermediate Government Portfolio
  (USGv)
  Intermediate-Term Bond Portfolio (IncB)
  International Bond Portfolio (GloB)
  International Emerging Markets Portfolio
  (Intl)

International Equity Portfolio (Intl)
  Low Duration Portfolio (IncB)
  Managed Income Portfolio (IncB)
  Mid-Cap Growth Portfolio (Gr)
  Mid-Cap Value Portfolio (Gr)
  Money Market Portfolio (MM)
  Municipal Money Market Portfolio
  (NMMX)
  New Jersey Municipal Money Market
  Portfolio (SMMX)
  New Jersey Tax-Free Income Portfolio
  (SMuB)
  North Carolina Municipal Money Market
  Portfolio (SMMX)
  Ohio Municipal Money Market Portfolio
  (SMMX)
  Ohio Tax-Free Income Portfolio (SMuB)
  Pennsylvania Municipal Money Market
  Portfolio (SMMX)
  Pennsylvania Tax-Free Income Portfolio
  (SMuB)
  Select Equity Portfolio (Gr&I)
  Small Cap Growth Equity Portfolio
  (AgGr)
  Small Cap Value Equity Portfolio (AgGr)
  Tax-Free Income Portfolio (NMuB)
  U.S. Treasury Portfolio (MM)
  Value Equity Portfolio (Gr)
  Virginia Municipal Money Market
  Portfolio (SMMX)

Composite Group of Funds
1201 Third Ave.
Ste. 1400
Seattle, WA 98101
800/543-8072
Composite Bond and Stock Fund, Inc. (Bal)
Composite Cash Management Company
  Money Market Portfolio (MM)
  Tax-Exempt Money Market Portfolio
  (NMMX)
Composite Deferred Series, Inc.
  Growth Portfolio (Gr&I)
  Income Portfolio (CorB)
  Northwest 50 Portfolio (Gr)
Composite Growth and Income Fund, Inc.
  (Gr&I)
Composite Income Fund, Inc. (CorB)
Composite Northwest Fund, Inc. (Gr)
Composite Tax-Exempt Bond Fund, Inc.
  (NMuB)
Composite U.S. Government Securities,
  Inc. (USGv)

Concorde Funds
5430 LBJ Freeway
Ste. 1500
Dallas, TX 75240-2387
800/338-1579
Concorde Income Fund, Inc. (IncM)
Concorde Value Fund, Inc. (Gr)

Conseco Mutual Funds
11815 N. Pennsylvania St.
P.O. Box 1911
Carmel, IN 46032-4911
800/888-4918
Conseco Fund Group
  Asset Allocation Fund (Bal)
  Equity Fund (Gr)
  Fixed Income Fund (IncB)
Conseco Series Trust
  Asset Allocation Portfolio (Bal)
  Common Stock Portfolio (Gr)
  Corporate Bond Portfolio (CorB)
  Government Securities Portfolio (USGv)
  Money Market Portfolio (MM)

CoreFunds, Inc.
One Freedom Valley Drive
Oaks, PA 19456
800/355-CORE
CoreFund Inc. (The)
  CoreFund Balanced Fund (Bal)
  CoreFund Bond Fund (IncB)
  CoreFund Cash Reserve (MM)
  CoreFund Elite Reserve (MM)
  CoreFund Elite Tax-Free Reserve
    (NMMX)
  CoreFund Elite Treasury Reserve (MM)
  CoreFund Equity Fund (Gr)
  CoreFund Equity Index Fund (Gr&I)
  CoreFund Global Bond Fund (GloB)
  CoreFund Government Income Fund
    (USGv)
  CoreFund Growth Equity Fund (Gr&I)
  CoreFund Intermediate Municipal Bond
    Fund (NMuB)
  CoreFund International Growth Fund (Intl)
  CoreFund New Jersey Municipal Bond
    Fund (SMuB)
  CoreFund Pennsylvania Municipal Bond
    Fund (SMuB)
  CoreFund Short-Intermediate Bond Fund
    (CorB)
  CoreFund Short-Term Income Fund
    (IncB)
  CoreFund Special Equity Fund (Gr)
  CoreFund Tax-Free Reserve (NMMX)
  CoreFund Treasury Reserve (MM)

CornerCap Group of Funds
The Peachtree
1355 Peachtree St., NE, Ste. 1700
Atlanta, GA 30305
800/848-9555
CornerCap Balanced Fund (Bal)
CornerCap Growth Fund (Gr)

Countrywide Funds
312 Walnut St.
21st Fl.
Cincinnati, OH 45202-4024

800/543-8721
Countrywide Investment Trust
  Adjustable Rate U.S. Government
    Securities Fund (GNMA)
  Global Bond Fund (GloB)
  Institutional Government Income Fund
    (MM)
  Intermediate Term Government Income
    Fund (USGv)
  Short Term Government Income Fund
    (MM)
Countrywide Strategic Trust
  Equity Fund (Gr)
  Treasury Total Return Fund (USGv)
  U.S. Government Securities Fund
    (GNMA)
  Utility Fund (IncE)
Countrywide Tax-Free Trust
  California Tax-Free Money Fund
    (SMMX)
  Florida Tax-Free Money Fund (SMMX)
  Ohio Insured Tax-Free Fund (SMuB)
  Ohio Tax-Free Money Fund (SMMX)
  Tax-Free Intermediate Term Fund
    (NMuB)
  Tax-Free Money Fund (NMMX)

Coventry Group
3435 Stelzer Rd.
Columbus, OH 43219-3035
800/438-6375
Coventry Group (The)
  Amcore Vintage Aggressive Growth Fund
    (Gr)
  Amcore Vintage Balanced Fund (Bal)
  Amcore Vintage Equity Fund (Gr)
  Amcore Vintage Fixed Income Fund
    (IncB)
  Amcore Vintage Fixed Total Return Fund
    (IncB)
  Amcore Vintage Intermediate Tax-Free
    Fund (NMuB)
  Amcore Vintage U.S. Government
    Obligations Fund (MM)
  Brenton Intermediate U.S. Government
    Securities Fund (USGv)
  Brenton U.S. Government Money Market
    Fund (MM)
  Brenton Value Equity Fund (Gr)
  Shelby Fund (Gr)

Cowen Funds
One Financial Sq.
New York, NY 10005-3500
800/262-7116
Cowen Funds, Inc.
  Cowen Government Securities Fund
    (USGv)
  Cowen Intermediate Fixed Income Fund
    (IncM)
  Cowen Opportunity Fund (AgGr)

Cowen Income + Growth Fund, Inc. (IncE)
Cowen Standby Reserve Fund, Inc. (MM)
Cowen Standby Tax-Exempt Reserve Fund,
Inc. (NMMX)

Crabbe Huson Funds
121 S.W. Morrison
Ste. 1400
Portland, OR 97204-3144
800/541-9732
Crabbe Huson Funds (The)
Crabbe Huson Asset Allocation Fund
(Bal)
Crabbe Huson Equity Fund (Gr)
Crabbe Huson Income Fund (IncB)
Crabbe Huson Oregon Tax-Free Fund
(SMuB)
Crabbe Huson Real Estate Investment
Fund (Gr)
Crabbe Huson Small Cap Fund (AgGr)
Crabbe Huson U.S. Government Income
Fund (USGv)
Crabbe Huson U.S. Government Money
Market Fund (MM)
Crabbe Huson Special Fund, Inc. (AgGr)

CrestFunds
One Freedom Valley Drive
Oaks, PA 19456
800/342-5734
CrestFunds, Inc.
Capital Appreciation Fund (AgGr)
Cash Reserve Fund (MM)
Government Bond Fund (USGv)
Intermediate Bond Fund (CorB)
Limited Term Bond Fund (CorB)
Maryland Municipal Bond Fund (SMuB)
Municipal Bond Fund (NMuB)
Special Equity Fund (AgGr)
Tax Free Money Fund (NMMX)
U.S. Treasury Money Fund (MM)
Value Fund (Bal)
Virginia Intermediate Municipal Bond
Fund (SMuB)
Virginia Municipal Bond Fund (SMuB)

Crowley Funds
1813 Marsh Rd.
Ste. H
Wilmington, DE 19810-4544
302/529-1717
Crowley Portfolio Group, Inc. (The)
Crowley Diversified Management
Portfolio (IncM)
Crowley Growth and Income Portfolio
(Gr&I)
Crowley Income Portfolio (IncM)

CU Funds
One Freedom Valley Drive
Oaks, PA 19456

800/538-9683
CU Fund
Adjustable Rate Portfolio (GNMA)
Short Term Maturity Portfolio (GNMA)

Cutler Trust
503 Airport Rd.
Medford, OR 97504-4159
800/228-8537
Cutler Trust (The)
Approved List Equity Fund (Gr&I)
Equity Income Fund (IncE)

Daruma Funds, Inc.
237 Park Ave.
Ste. 801
New York, NY 10017
800/435-5076
Daruma Funds, Inc.
Daruma Mid-Cap Value Fund (Gr)

Davis Funds
124 E. Marcy St.
P.O. Box 1688
Santa Fe, NM 87504-1688
800/279-0279
Davis High Income Fund, Inc. (HiYB)
Davis International Series, Inc.
Davis International Total Return Fund
(Intl)
Davis New York Venture Fund, Inc. (Gr)
Davis Series, Inc.
Davis Convertible Securities Fund (Gr&I)
Davis Financial Fund (Gr)
Davis Government Bond Fund (USGv)
Davis Government Money Market Fund
(MM)
Davis Growth Opportunity Fund (AgGr)
Davis Real Estate Fund (Gr&I)
Davis Tax-Free High Income Fund, Inc.
(NMuB)

Dean Witter Funds Family
Two World Trade Ctr.
72nd Fl.
New York, NY 10048-0203
800/869-NEWS
Active Assets California Tax-Free Trust
(SMMX)
Active Assets Government Securities Trust
(MM)
Active Assets Money Trust (MM)
Active Assets Tax-Free Trust (NMMX)
Dean Witter American Value Fund (Gr)
Dean Witter Balanced Growth Fund (Bal)
Dean Witter Balanced Income Fund
(IncM)
Dean Witter California Tax-Free Daily
Income Trust (SMMX)
Dean Witter California Tax-Free Income
Fund (SMuB)

Dean Witter Capital Appreciation Fund
(AgGr)
Dean Witter Capital Growth Securities (Gr)
Dean Witter Convertible Securities Trust
(Gr&I)
Dean Witter Developing Growth Securities
Trust (AgGr)
Dean Witter Diversified Income Trust
(IncB)
Dean Witter Dividend Growth Securities
Inc. (Gr&I)
Dean Witter European Growth Fund Inc.
(Intl)
Dean Witter Federal Securities Trust
(USGv)
Dean Witter Financial Services Trust
(AgGr)
Dean Witter Global Asset Allocation Fund
(GloE)
Dean Witter Global Dividend Growth
Securities (GloE)
Dean Witter Global Short-Term Income
Fund Inc. (GloB)
Dean Witter Global Utilities Fund (Intl)
Dean Witter Hawaii Municipal Trust
(SMuB)
Dean Witter Health Sciences Trust (Gr)
Dean Witter High Income Securities
(HiYB)
Dean Witter High Yield Securities Inc.
(HiYB)
Dean Witter Income Builder Fund (IncE)
Dean Witter Information Fund (Gr)
Dean Witter Intermediate Income Securities
(IncB)
Dean Witter Intermediate-Term U.S.
Treasury Trust (USGv)
Dean Witter International SmallCap Fund
(Intl)
Dean Witter Japan Fund (Intl)
Dean Witter Limited Term Municipal Trust
(NMuB)
Dean Witter Liquid Asset Fund Inc. (MM)
Dean Witter Market Leader Trust (Gr)
Dean Witter Mid-Cap Growth Fund (Gr)
Dean Witter Multi-State Municipal Series
Trust
 Arizona Series (SMuB)
 California Series (SMuB)
 Florida Series (SMuB)
 Massachusetts Series (SMuB)
 Michigan Series (SMuB)
 Minnesota Series (SMuB)
 New Jersey Series (SMuB)
 New York Series (SMuB)
 Ohio Series (SMuB)
 Pennsylvania Series (SMuB)
Dean Witter National Municipal Trust
(NMuB)
Dean Witter Natural Resource Development
Securities Inc. (Gr)

Dean Witter New York Municipal Money
Market Trust (SMMX)
Dean Witter New York Tax-Free Income
Fund (SMuB)
Dean Witter Pacific Growth Fund Inc. (Intl)
Dean Witter Precious Metals and Minerals
Trust (PM/G)
Dean Witter Retirement Series
 American Value Series (Gr)
 Capital Growth Series (Gr)
 Dividend Growth Series (IncE)
 Global Equity Series (GloE)
 Intermediate Income Securities Series
 (IncB)
 Liquid Asset Series (MM)
 Strategist Series (Flex)
 U.S. Government Money Market Series
 (MM)
 U.S. Government Securities Series
 (USGv)
 Utilities Series (Gr&I)
 Value-Added Market Series (Gr&I)
Dean Witter Select Dimensions Investment
 Series
 American Value Portfolio (Gr)
 Balanced Portfolio (Bal)
 Core Equity Portfolio (Gr)
 Developing Growth Portfolio (AgGr)
 Diversified Income Portfolio (IncB)
 Dividend Growth Portfolio (Gr&I)
 Emerging Markets Portfolio (AgGr)
 Global Equity Portfolio (GloE)
 Mid-Cap Growth Portfolio (Gr)
 Money Market Portfolio (MM)
 North American Government Securities
 Portfolio (GloB)
 Utilities Portfolio (Gr&I)
 Value-Added Market Portfolio (Gr&I)
Dean Witter Select Municipal Reinvestment
 Fund (NMuB)
Dean Witter Short-Term Bond Fund (IncM)
Dean Witter Short-Term U.S. Treasury
 Trust (USGv)
Dean Witter Special Value Fund (Gr)
Dean Witter Strategist Fund (Flex)
Dean Witter Tax-Exempt Securities Trust
 (NMuB)
Dean Witter Tax-Free Daily Income Trust
 (NMMX)
Dean Witter U.S. Government Money
 Market Trust (MM)
Dean Witter U.S. Government Securities
 Trust (USGv)
Dean Witter Utilities Fund (Gr&I)
Dean Witter Value-Added Market Series
 Equity Portfolio (Gr&I)
Dean Witter Variable Investment Series
 Capital Appreciation Portfolio (AgGr)
 Capital Growth Portfolio (Gr)
 Dividend Growth Portfolio (Gr&I)
 Equity Portfolio (Gr)

European Growth Portfolio (Intl)
Global Dividend Growth Portfolio (GloE)
High Yield Portfolio (HiYB)
Income Builder Portfolio (IncE)
Money Market Portfolio (MM)
Pacific Growth Portfolio (Intl)
Quality Income Plus Portfolio (IncB)
Strategist Portfolio (Flex)
Utilities Portfolio (Gr&I)
Dean Witter World Wide Income Trust
   (GloB)
Dean Witter World Wide Investment Trust
   (GloE)
TCW/DW Balanced Fund (Bal)
TCW/DW Core Equity Trust (Gr)
TCW/DW Global Telecom Trust (GloE)
TCW/DW Income and Growth Fund
   (Gr&I)
TCW/DW Latin American Growth Fund
   (Intl)
TCW/DW Mid-Cap Equity Trust (Gr)
TCW/DW North American Government
   Income Trust (GloB)
TCW/DW Small Cap Growth Fund
   (AgGr)
TCW/DW Strategic Income Trust (IncB)
TCW/DW Total Return Trust (IncM)

Declaration Investment Funds
555 North Lane
Ste. 6160
Conshohocken, PA 19428-2233
800/423-2345
Declaration Cash Account (MM)
Pauze Funds
   Pauze Tombstone Fund (AgGr)
   Pauze U.S. Government Intermediate
   Bond Fund (USGv)
   Pauze U.S. Government Short Bond Fund
   (USGv)
   Pauze U.S. Government Total Return
   Bond Fund (USGv)

Delaware-Voyageur Group of Funds
1818 Market St.
Philadelphia, PA 19103-3682
800/523-4640
Delaware Pooled Trust, Inc.
   Aggressive Growth Portfolio (AgGr)
   Defensive Equity Portfolio (Gr&I)
   Defensive Equity Utility Portfolio (Gr&I)
   Defensive Small/Mid-Cap Portfolio
   (AgGr)
   Fixed Income Portfolio (IncB)
   Global Fixed Income Portfolio (GloB)
   High-Yield Bond Portfolio (HiYB)
   International Equity Portfolio (Intl)
   International Fixed Income Portfolio (The)
   (GloB)
   Labor Select International Equity Portfolio
   (The) (GloE)

Limited-Term Maturity Portfolio (IncB)
Real Estate Investment Trust Portfolio
   (IncE)
Delaware Group Cash Reserve, Inc. (MM)
Delaware Group Decatur Fund, Inc.
   Decatur Income Fund (IncE)
   Decatur Total Return Fund (IncE)
Delaware Group Delaware Fund, Inc. (Bal)
Delaware Group DelCap Fund, Inc. (Gr)
Delaware Group Delchester High-Yield
   Bond Fund, Inc. (HiYB)
Delaware Group Devon Fund, Inc. (Gr&I)
Delaware Group Global & International
   Funds, Inc.
   Global Assets Fund (GloE)
   Global Bond Fund (GloB)
   International Equity Series (Intl)
Delaware Group Government Fund, Inc.
   U.S. Government Fund (USGv)
Delaware Group Limited-Term Government
   Funds, Inc.
   Limited-Term Government Fund
   (USGv)
   U.S. Government Money Series (MM)
Delaware Group Tax-Free Fund, Inc.
   Tax-Free Insured Fund (NMuB)
   Tax-Free USA Fund (NMuB)
   Tax-Free USA Intermediate Fund (NMuB)
Delaware Group Tax-Free Money Fund,
   Inc. (NMMX)
Delaware Group Tax-Free Pennsylvania
   Fund (SMuB)
Delaware Group Trend Fund, Inc. (AgGr)
Delaware Group Value Fund, Inc. (AgGr)
Delaware Group Advisor Funds, Inc.
   Delaware Group Corporate Income
   Portfolio (CorB)
   Delaware Group Enterprise Portfolio
   (Gr)
   Delaware Group Federal Bond Portfolio
   (USGv)
   Delaware Group New Pacific Portfolio
   (Intl)
   Delaware Group U.S. Growth Portfolio
   (Gr)
   Delaware Group World Growth Portfolio
   (Intl)

DG Investor Series
Federated Investors Twr.
1001 Liberty Ave.
Pittsburgh, PA 15222-3779
800/341-7400
DG Investor Series
   DG Equity Fund (Gr&I)
   DG Government Income Fund (USGv)
   DG International Equity Fund (GloE)
   DG Limited Term Government Income
   Fund (USGv)
   DG Municipal Income Fund (NMuB)
   DG Opportunity Fund (Gr)

DG Prime Money Market Fund (MM)
DG U.S. Government Money Market
Fund (MM)

Diversified Investor's Fund Group
4 Manhattanville Rd.
MD 53-31
Purchase, NY 10577-2119
800/666-9800
Diversified Investor's Fund Group
  Diversified Investor's Balanced Fund
  (Bal)
  Diversified Investor's Equity Growth
  Fund (Gr)
  Diversified Investor's Equity Income
  Fund (IncE)
  Diversified Investor's Government/
  Corporate Bond Fund (IncB)
  Diversified Investor's Growth & Income
  Fund (Gr&I)
  Diversified Investor's High Quality Bond
  Fund (CorB)
  Diversified Investor's Money Market
  Fund (MM)
  Diversified Investor's Special Equity Fund
  (AgGr)

DLB Fund Group
One Memorial Drive
Cambridge, MA 02142-1300
888/7-BABSON
DLB Fund Group (The)
  DLB Fixed Income Fund (IncB)
  DLB Global Small Capitalization Fund
  (GloE)
  DLB Mid Capitalization Fund (AgGr)
  DLB Value Fund (Gr)

Dodge & Cox Funds
One Sansome St.
35th Fl.
San Francisco, CA 94104-4448
800/621-3979
Dodge & Cox Balanced Fund (Bal)
Dodge & Cox Income Fund (IncB)
Dodge & Cox Stock Fund (Gr&I)

Dreyfus Funds
200 Park Ave.
New York, NY 10166
800/645-6561
Dreyfus A Bonds Plus, Inc. (CorB)
Dreyfus Appreciation Fund, Inc. (Gr)
Dreyfus Asset Allocation Fund, Inc. (Flex)
Dreyfus Balanced Fund, Inc. (Bal)
Dreyfus BASIC GNMA Fund (GNMA)
Dreyfus BASIC Money Market Fund, Inc.
  (MM)
Dreyfus BASIC Municipal Fund, Inc.
  Dreyfus BASIC Intermediate Municipal
  Bond Portfolio (NMuB)

Dreyfus BASIC Municipal Bond Portfolio
  (NMuB)
Dreyfus BASIC Municipal Money Market
  Portfolio (NMMX)
Dreyfus BASIC New Jersey Municipal
  Money Market Portfolio (SMMX)
Dreyfus BASIC U.S. Government Money
  Market Fund (MM)
Dreyfus California Intermediate Municipal
  Bond Fund (SMuB)
Dreyfus California Tax Exempt Bond Fund,
  Inc. (SMuB)
Dreyfus California Tax Exempt Money
  Market Fund (SMMX)
Dreyfus Cash Management (MM)
Dreyfus Cash Management Plus, Inc. (MM)
Dreyfus Connecticut Intermediate
  Municipal Bond Fund (SMuB)
Dreyfus Connecticut Municipal Money
  Market Fund, Inc. (SMMX)
Dreyfus Florida Intermediate Municipal
  Bond Fund (SMuB)
Dreyfus Florida Municipal Money Market
  Fund (SMMX)
Dreyfus Fund Incorporated (The) (Gr&I)
Dreyfus Global Bond Fund, Inc. (GloB)
Dreyfus Global Growth Fund (GloE)
Dreyfus GNMA Fund, Inc. (GNMA)
Dreyfus Government Cash Management
  (MM)
Dreyfus Growth and Income Fund, Inc.
  (Gr&I)
Dreyfus Growth and Value Funds, Inc.
  Dreyfus Aggressive Growth Fund (AgGr)
  Dreyfus Aggressive Value Fund (AgGr)
  Dreyfus Emerging Leaders Fund (AgGr)
  Dreyfus International Value Fund (Intl)
  Dreyfus Large Company Growth Fund
  (Gr)
  Dreyfus Large Company Value Fund (Gr)
  Dreyfus Midcap Value Fund (Gr)
  Dreyfus Small Company Value Fund
  (AgGr)
Dreyfus Growth Opportunity Fund, Inc.
  (Gr)
Dreyfus Income Funds
  Dreyfus Equity Dividend Fund (IncE)
  Dreyfus High Yield Securities Fund
  (HiYB)
  Dreyfus Short Term High Yield Fund
  (HiYB)
  Dreyfus Strategic Income Fund (IncM)
Dreyfus Institutional Money Market Fund
  Government Securities Series (MM)
  Money Market Series (MM)
Dreyfus Institutional Short Term Treasury
  Fund (IncB)
Dreyfus Insured Municipal Bond Fund, Inc.
  (NMuB)
Dreyfus Intermediate Municipal Bond
  Fund, Inc. (NMuB)

Dreyfus International Funds, Inc.
  Dreyfus Emerging Markets Fund (Intl)
  Dreyfus International Growth Fund (Intl)
Dreyfus Investment Grade Bond Funds, Inc.
  Dreyfus Intermediate Term Income Fund
    (IncB)
  Dreyfus Short Term Income Fund (IncB)
Dreyfus/Laurel Funds, Inc. (The)
  Dreyfus Bond Market Index Fund
    (USGv)
  Dreyfus Disciplined Equity Income Fund
    (IncE)
  Dreyfus Disciplined Intermediate Bond
    Fund (IncB)
  Dreyfus Disciplined MidCap Stock Fund
    (Gr)
  Dreyfus Disciplined Stock Fund (Gr&I)
  Dreyfus Institutional Government Money
    Market Fund (MM)
  Dreyfus Institutional Prime Money Market
    Fund (The) (MM)
  Dreyfus Institutional S&P 500 Index Fund
    (Gr&I)
  Dreyfus Institutional U.S. Treasury Money
    Market Fund (MM)
  Dreyfus International Equity Allocation
    Fund (Intl)
  Dreyfus Money Market Reserves (MM)
  Dreyfus Municipal Reserves (NMMX)
  Dreyfus U.S. Treasury Reserves (MM)
Dreyfus/Laurel Funds Trust (The)
  Dreyfus Core Value Fund (Gr)
Dreyfus/Laurel Tax-Free Municipal Funds
    (The)
  Dreyfus BASIC CA Municipal Money
    Market Fund (SMMX)
  Dreyfus BASIC Massachusetts Municipal
    Money Market Fund (SMMX)
  Dreyfus BASIC New York Municipal
    Money Market Fund (SMMX)
Dreyfus Lifetime Portfolios, Inc.
  Growth and Income Portfolio (Gr&I)
  Growth Portfolio (Gr)
  Income Portfolio (IncM)
Dreyfus Liquid Assets, Inc. (MM)
Dreyfus Massachusetts Intermediate
    Municipal Bond Fund (SMuB)
Dreyfus Massachusetts Municipal Money
    Market Fund (SMMX)
Dreyfus Massachusetts Tax Exempt Bond
    Fund (SMuB)
Dreyfus MidCap Index Fund, Inc. (Gr&I)
Dreyfus Money Market Instruments, Inc.
  Government Securities Series (MM)
  Money Market Series (MM)
Dreyfus Municipal Bond Fund, Inc.
    (NMuB)
Dreyfus Municipal Cash Management Plus
    (NMMX)
Dreyfus Municipal Money Market Fund,
    Inc. (NMMX)

Dreyfus New Jersey Intermediate Municipal
    Bond Fund (SMuB)
Dreyfus New Jersey Municipal Bond Fund,
    Inc. (SMuB)
Dreyfus New Jersey Municipal Money
    Market Fund, Inc. (SMMX)
Dreyfus New Leaders Fund, Inc. (Gr)
Dreyfus New York Insured Tax Exempt
    Bond Fund (SMuB)
Dreyfus New York Municipal Cash
    Management (SMMX)
Dreyfus New York Tax Exempt Bond Fund,
    Inc. (SMuB)
Dreyfus New York Tax Exempt
    Intermediate Bond Fund (SMuB)
Dreyfus New York Tax Exempt Money
    Market Fund (SMMX)
Dreyfus 100% U.S. Treasury Intermediate
    Term Fund (USGv)
Dreyfus 100% U.S. Treasury Long Term
    Fund (USGv)
Dreyfus 100% U.S. Treasury Money
    Market Fund (MM)
Dreyfus 100% U.S. Treasury Short Term
    Fund (USGv)
Dreyfus Pennsylvania Intermediate
    Municipal Bond Fund (SMuB)
Dreyfus Pennsylvania Municipal Money
    Market Fund (SMMX)
Dreyfus S&P 500 Index Fund, Inc. (Gr&I)
Dreyfus Short-Intermediate Government
    Fund (USGv)
Dreyfus Short-Intermediate Municipal Bond
    Fund (NMuB)
Dreyfus Socially Responsible Growth Fund,
    Inc. (The) (Gr)
Dreyfus Stock Index Fund (Gr&I)
Dreyfus Tax Exempt Cash Management
    (NMMX)
Dreyfus Third Century Fund, Inc. (The)
    (Gr)
Dreyfus Treasury Cash Management (MM)
Dreyfus Treasury Prime Cash Management
    (MM)
Dreyfus Variable Investment Fund
  Balanced Portfolio (Bal)
  Capital Appreciation Portfolio (Gr)
  Disciplined Stock Portfolio (Gr&I)
  Growth and Income Portfolio (Gr&I)
  International Equity Portfolio (Intl)
  International Value Portfolio (Intl)
  Limited Term High Income Portfolio
    (HiYB)
  Managed Assets Portfolio (Flex)
  Money Market Portfolio (MM)
  Quality Bond Portfolio (IncB)
  Small Cap Portfolio (AgGr)
  Small Company Stock Portfolio (AgGr)
  Zero Coupon 2000 Portfolio (USGv)
Dreyfus Worldwide Dollar Money Market
    Fund, Inc. (MM)

General California Municipal Bond Fund,
Inc. (SMuB)
General California Municipal Money
Market Fund (SMMX)
General Government Securities Money
Market Fund, Inc. (MM)
General Money Market Fund, Inc. (MM)
General Municipal Bond Fund, Inc.
(NMuB)
General Municipal Money Market Fund,
Inc. (NMMX)
General New York Municipal Bond Fund,
Inc. (SMuB)
General New York Municipal Money
Market Fund (SMMX)

Dreyfus Premier Funds
200 Park Ave.
New York, NY 10166
800/554-4611
Dreyfus/Laurel Funds, Inc. (The)
Dreyfus Premier Balanced Fund (Bal)
Dreyfus Premier Limited Term Income
Fund (CorB)
Dreyfus Premier Small Company Stock
Fund (AgGr)
Dreyfus/Laurel Funds Trust (The)
Dreyfus Premier Limited Term High
Income Fund (HiYB)
Dreyfus Premier Managed Income Fund
(CorB)
Dreyfus/Laurel Tax-Free Municipal Funds
(The)
Dreyfus Premier Limited Term California
Municipal Fund (SMuB)
Dreyfus Premier Limited Term
Massachusetts Municipal Fund (SMuB)
Dreyfus Premier Limited Term Municipal
Fund (NMuB)
Dreyfus Premier Limited Term New York
Municipal Fund (SMuB)
Dreyfus Premier California Municipal Bond
Fund (SMuB)
Dreyfus Premier Equity Funds, Inc.
Dreyfus Premier Aggressive Growth Fund
(AgGr)
Dreyfus Premier Growth and Income
Fund (Bal)
Dreyfus Premier Global Investing Fund,
Inc. (GloE)
Dreyfus Premier GNMA Fund (GNMA)
Dreyfus Premier Insured Municipal Bond
Fund (NMuB)
Dreyfus Premier Value Fund (AgGr)
Dreyfus Premier Worldwide Growth Fund,
Inc. (Gr)
Premier Municipal Bond Fund (NMuB)
Premier New York Municipal Bond Fund
(SMuB)
Premier State Municipal Bond Fund
Connecticut Series (SMuB)

Florida Series (SMuB)
Georgia Series (SMuB)
Maryland Series (SMuB)
Massachusetts Series (SMuB)
Michigan Series (SMuB)
Minnesota Series (SMuB)
New Jersey Series (SMuB)
North Carolina Series (SMuB)
Ohio Series (SMuB)
Pennsylvania Series (SMuB)
Texas Series (SMuB)
Virginia Series (SMuB)

Driehaus Mutual Funds
25 E. Erie St.
Chicago, IL 60611
800/688-8819
Driehaus Mutual Funds
Driehaus International Growth Fund (Intl)

Eastcliff Funds
900 Second Ave.
South 300
International Centre
Minneapolis, MN 55402
800/595-5519
Eastcliff Funds
Eastcliff Growth Fund (Gr)
Eastcliff Regional Small Cap Value Fund
(AgGr)
Eastcliff Total Return Fund (Flex)

Eaton Vance Funds
24 Federal St.
Boston, MA 02110-2507
800/225-6265
Capital Exchange Fund, Inc. (Gr&I)
Depositors Fund of Boston, Inc.
(Gr&I)
Diversification Fund, Inc. (Gr&I)
Eaton Vance Growth Trust
EV Classic Growth Fund (Gr)
EV Marathon Growth Fund (Gr)
EV Marathon Worldwide Development
Resources Fund (PM/G)
EV Traditional Growth Fund (Gr)
Eaton Vance Income Fund of Boston
(HiYB)
Eaton Vance Investment Trust
EV Classic Florida Limited Maturity
Municipals Fund (SMuB)
EV Classic Greater China Growth Fund
(Intl)
EV Classic Information Age Fund
(GloE)
EV Classic Massachusetts Limited
Maturity Municipals Fund (SMuB)
EV Classic National Limited Maturity
Municipals Fund (NMuB)
EV Classic New York Limited Maturity
Municipals Fund (SMuB)

EV Classic Pennsylvania Limited Maturity Municipals Fund (SMuB)

EV Marathon California Limited Maturity Municipals Fund (SMuB)

EV Marathon Connecticut Limited Maturity Municipals Fund (SMuB)

EV Marathon Florida Limited Maturity Municipals Fund (SMuB)

EV Marathon Greater China Growth Fund (Intl)

EV Marathon Information Age Fund (GloE)

EV Marathon Massachusetts Limited Maturity Municipals Fund (SMuB)

EV Marathon Michigan Limited Maturity Municipals Fund (SMuB)

EV Marathon National Limited Maturity Municipals Fund (NMuB)

EV Marathon New Jersey Limited Maturity Municipals Fund (SMuB)

EV Marathon New York Limited Maturity Municipals Fund (SMuB)

EV Marathon Ohio Limited Maturity Municipals Fund (SMuB)

EV Marathon Pennsylvania Limited Maturity Municipals Fund (SMuB)

EV Marathon Worldwide Health Sciences Fund, Inc. (Intl)

EV Traditional California Limited Maturity Municipals Fund (SMuB)

EV Traditional Connecticut Limited Maturity Municipals Fund (SMuB)

EV Traditional Florida Limited Maturity Municipals Fund (SMuB)

EV Traditional Greater China Growth Fund (Intl)

EV Traditional Information Age Fund (GloE)

EV Traditional Michigan Limited Maturity Municipals Fund (SMuB)

EV Traditional National Limited Maturity Municipals Fund (NMuB)

EV Traditional New Jersey Limited Maturity Municipals Fund (SMuB)

EV Traditional New York Limited Maturity Municipals Fund (SMuB)

EV Traditional Ohio Limited Maturity Municipals Fund (SMuB)

Eaton Vance Municipal Bond Fund L.P. (NMuB)

Eaton Vance Municipals Trust

EV Classic National Municipals Fund (NMuB)

EV Marathon Alabama Municipals Fund (SMuB)

EV Marathon Arizona Municipals Fund (SMuB)

EV Marathon Arkansas Municipals Fund (SMuB)

EV Marathon California Municipals Fund (SMuB)

EV Marathon Colorado Municipals Fund (SMuB)

EV Marathon Connecticut Municipals Fund (SMuB)

EV Marathon Florida Insured Municipals Fund (SMuB)

EV Marathon Florida Municipals Fund (SMuB)

EV Marathon Georgia Municipals Fund (SMuB)

EV Marathon Hawaii Municipals Fund (SMuB)

EV Marathon Kansas Municipals Fund (SMuB)

EV Marathon Kentucky Municipals Fund (SMuB)

EV Marathon Louisiana Municipals Fund (SMuB)

EV Marathon Maryland Municipals Fund (SMuB)

EV Marathon Massachusetts Municipals Fund (SMuB)

EV Marathon Michigan Municipals Fund (SMuB)

EV Marathon Minnesota Municipals Fund (SMuB)

EV Marathon Mississippi Municipals Fund (SMuB)

EV Marathon Missouri Municipals Fund (SMuB)

EV Marathon National Municipals Fund (NMuB)

EV Marathon New Jersey Municipals Fund (SMuB)

EV Marathon New York Municipals Fund (SMuB)

EV Marathon North Carolina Municipals Fund (SMuB)

EV Marathon Ohio Municipals Fund (SMuB)

EV Marathon Oregon Municipals Fund (SMuB)

EV Marathon Pennsylvania Municipals Fund (SMuB)

EV Marathon Rhode Island Municipals Fund (SMuB)

EV Marathon South Carolina Municipals Fund (SMuB)

EV Marathon Tennessee Municipals Fund (SMuB)

EV Marathon Texas Municipals Fund (SMuB)

EV Marathon Virginia Municipals Fund (SMuB)

EV Marathon West Virginia Municipals Fund (SMuB)

EV Traditional Alabama Municipals Fund (SMuB)

EV Traditional Arizona Municipals Fund (SMuB)

EV Traditional Arkansas Municipals Fund (SMuB)

EV Traditional California Municipals
Fund (SMuB)
EV Traditional Colorado Municipals Fund
(SMuB)
EV Traditional Connecticut Municipals
Fund (SMuB)
EV Traditional Florida Insured Municipals
Fund (SMuB)
EV Traditional Florida Municipals Fund
(SMuB)
EV Traditional Georgia Municipals Fund
(SMuB)
EV Traditional Hawaii Municipals Fund
(SMuB)
EV Traditional Kansas Municipals Fund
(SMuB)
EV Traditional Kentucky Municipals Fund
(SMuB)
EV Traditional Louisiana Municipals
Fund (SMuB)
EV Traditional Maryland Municipals Fund
(SMuB)
EV Traditional Massachusetts Municipals
Fund (SMuB)
EV Traditional Michigan Municipals Fund
(SMuB)
EV Traditional Minnesota Municipals
Fund (SMuB)
EV Traditional Mississippi Municipals
Fund (SMuB)
EV Traditional Missouri Municipals Fund
(SMuB)
EV Traditional National Municipals Fund
(NMuB)
EV Traditional New Jersey Municipals
Fund (SMuB)
EV Traditional New York Municipals
Fund (SMuB)
EV Traditional North Carolina Municipals
Fund (SMuB)
EV Traditional Ohio Municipals Fund
(SMuB)
EV Traditional Oregon Municipals Fund
(SMuB)
EV Traditional Pennsylvania Municipals
Fund (SMuB)
EV Traditional Rhode Island Municipals
Fund (SMuB)
EV Traditional South Carolina Municipals
Fund (SMuB)
EV Traditional Tennessee Municipals
Fund (SMuB)
EV Traditional Texas Municipals Fund
(SMuB)
EV Traditional Virginia Municipals Fund
(SMuB)
EV Traditional West Virginia Municipals
Fund (SMuB)
Massachusetts Municipal Bond Portfolio
(SMuB)
Eaton Vance Municipals Trust II

EV Marathon High Yield Municipals
Fund (NMuB)
EV Traditional High Yield Municipals
Fund (NMuB)
Eaton Vance Mutual Funds Trust
Eaton Vance Cash Management Fund
(MM)
Eaton Vance Liquid Assets Trust (MM)
Eaton Vance Money Market Fund
(MM)
Eaton Vance Short-Term Treasury Fund
(USGv)
Eaton Vance Tax-Free Reserves (NMMX)
EV Classic Government Obligations Fund
(USGv)
EV Classic High Income Fund (HiYB)
EV Classic Strategic Income Fund
(GloB)
EV Classic Tax-Managed Growth Fund
(Gr)
EV Marathon Government Obligations
Fund (USGv)
EV Marathon High Income Fund (HiYB)
EV Marathon Strategic Income Fund (GloB)
EV Marathon Tax-Managed Growth Fund
(Gr)
EV Traditional Government Obligations
Fund (USGv)
EV Traditional Tax-Managed Growth
Fund (Gr)
Eaton Vance Series Trust
Vance, Sanders Exchange Fund (Gr&I)
Eaton Vance Special Investment Trust
EV Classic Investors Fund (Bal)
EV Classic Special Equities Fund (Gr)
EV Classic Stock Fund (Gr&I)
EV Classic Total Return Fund (IncB)
EV Marathon Emerging Markets Fund
(Intl)
EV Marathon Greater India Fund (Intl)
EV Marathon Investors Fund (Bal)
EV Marathon Special Equities Fund (Gr)
EV Marathon Stock Fund (Gr&I)
EV Marathon Total Return Fund (IncB)
EV Traditional Emerging Growth Fund
(AgGr)
EV Traditional Emerging Markets Fund
(Intl)
EV Traditional Greater India Fund (Intl)
EV Traditional Investors Fund (Bal)
EV Traditional Special Equities Fund
(Gr)
EV Traditional Stock Fund (Gr&I)
EV Traditional Total Return Fund (Gr&I)
EV Traditional Worldwide Health Sciences
Fund, Inc. (GloE)
Exchange Fund of Boston, Inc. (The)
(Gr&I)
Fiduciary Exchange Fund, Inc. (Gr&I)
Second Fiduciary Exchange Fund, Inc. (Gr&I)

Eclipse Funds
144 E. 30th St.
New York, NY 10016-7365
800/872-2710
Eclipse Financial Asset Trust
Eclipse Balanced Fund (Bal)
Eclipse Equity Fund (AgGr)
Eclipse Growth and Income Fund (Gr&I)
Eclipse Ultra Short Term Income Fund
(IncB)

Elfun Funds
3003 Summer St.
P.O. Box 120074
Stamford, CT 06905-4316
800/242-0134
Elfun Diversified Fund (Flex)
Elfun Global Fund (GloE)
Elfun Income Fund (IncB)
Elfun Money Market Fund (MM)
Elfun Tax-Exempt Income Fund (NMuB)
Elfun Trusts (Gr)

Elite Funds Group
1325 Fourth St.
Ste. 2144
Seattle, WA 98101-2509
800/423-1068
Elite Group (The)
Elite Growth & Income Fund (Gr&I)
Elite Income Fund (IncB)

Emerald Funds
3435 Stelzer Rd.
Columbus, OH 43219
800/637-3759
Emerald Funds
Emerald Balanced Fund (Bal)
Emerald Equity Fund (Gr)
Emerald Equity Value Fund (Gr&I)
Emerald Florida Tax-Exempt Fund (SMuB)
Emerald International Equity Fund (Intl)
Emerald Managed Bond Fund (IncM)
Emerald Prime Advantage Fund (MM)
Emerald Prime Fund (MM)
Emerald Short-Term Bond Fund (IncB)
Emerald Small Cap Fund (AgGr)
Emerald Tax-Exempt Fund (NMMX)
Emerald Treasury Advantage Fund (MM)
Emerald Treasury Fund (MM)
Emerald U.S. Government Securities
Fund (USGv)

Endeavor Series Trust
2101 E. Coast Hwy.
#300
Corona Del Mar, CA 92625-1900
800/854-8393
Endeavor Series Trust
Dreyfus Small Cap Portfolio (AgGr)
Dreyfus U.S. Government Securities

Portfolio (USGv)
Opportunity Value Portfolio (Bal)
TCW Managed Asset Allocation Portfolio
(Flex)
TCW Money Market Portfolio (MM)
TRP Equity Income Portfolio (IncE)
TRP Growth Stock Portfolio (Gr)
TRP International Stock Portfolio (Intl)
Value Equity Portfolio (Gr)
Endeavor Series Trust
Enhanced Index Portfolio (Gr&I)

Enterprise Group of Funds
3343 Peachtree Rd., Ste. 450
Atlanta, GA 30326-1022
800/432-4320
Enterprise Accumulation Trust Funds
Equity Portfolio (Gr)
High-Yield Bond Portfolio (HiYB)
International Growth Portfolio (Intl)
Managed Portfolio (Flex)
Small Cap Portfolio (AgGr)
Enterprise Group of Funds, Inc.
Capital Appreciation Portfolio (AgGr)
Equity Income Portfolio (IncE)
Equity Portfolio (Gr)
Government Securities Portfolio (USGv)
Growth & Income Portfolio (Gr)
Growth Portfolio (Gr)
High-Yield Bond Portfolio (HiYB)
International Growth Portfolio (Intl)
Managed Portfolio (Flex)
Money Market Portfolio (MM)
Small Company Growth Portfolio (AgGr)
Small Company Value Portfolio (AgGr)
Tax-Exempt Income Portfolio (NMuB)

Equi-Select Series Trust
699 Walnut St.
Des Moines, IA 50309
800/344-6864
Equi-Select Series Trust
Advantage Portfolio (IncM)
Growth & Income Portfolio (Gr&I)
International Fixed Income Portfolio (Intl)
Money Market Portfolio (MM)
Mortgage-Backed Securities Portfolio
(GNMA)
OTC Portfolio (Gr)
Research Portfolio (Gr&I)
Total Return Portfolio (IncE)
Value+Growth Portfolio (Gr)

Evergreen Funds
2500 Westchester Ave.
Purchase, NY 10577-2515
800/807-2940
Evergreen American Retirement Trust (The)
Evergreen American Retirement Fund (Bal)
Evergreen Small Cap Equity Income Fund
(IncE)

Evergreen Equity Trust (The)
 Evergreen Global Leaders Fund (GloE)
 Evergreen Global Real Estate Equity Fund
  (GloE)
 Evergreen U.S. Real Estate Equity Fund
  (AgGr)
Evergreen Foundation Trust (The)
 Evergreen Foundation Fund (Bal)
 Evergreen Tax Strategic Foundation Fund
  (Gr&I)
Evergreen Growth and Income Fund (The)
  (Gr&I)
Evergreen Income and Growth Fund (The)
  (Gr&I)
Evergreen Investment Trust (The)
 Evergreen Balanced Fund (Bal)
 Evergreen Emerging Markets Growth
  Fund (Intl)
 Evergreen Florida Municipal Bond Fund
  (SMuB)
 Evergreen Georgia Municipal Bond Fund
  (SMuB)
 Evergreen High Grade Tax Fee Fund
  (NMuB)
 Evergreen International Equity Fund
  (Intl)
 Evergreen North Carolina Municipal Bond
  Fund (SMuB)
 Evergreen Short-Intermediate Bond Fund
  (CorB)
 Evergreen South Carolina Municipal Bond
  Fund (SMuB)
 Evergreen Treasury Money Market Fund
  (MM)
 Evergreen U.S. Government Fund (USGv)
 Evergreen Utility Fund (IncE)
 Evergreen Value Fund (Gr)
 Evergreen Virginia Municipal Bond Fund
  (SMuB)
Evergreen Lexicon Fund
 Intermediate-Term Bond Fund (IncB)
 Intermediate-Term Government Securities
  Fund (The) (USGv)
Evergreen Limited Market Fund, Inc. (The)
  (AgGr)
Evergreen Money Market Fund (The)
  (MM)
Evergreen Money Market Trust
 Evergreen Institutional Money Market
  Fund (MM)
 Evergreen Institutional Treasury Money
  Market Fund (MM)
Evergreen Municipal Trust (The)
 Evergreen Florida High Income Municipal
  Bond Fund (SMuB)
 Evergreen Institutional Tax-Exempt
  Money Market Fund (NMMX)
 Evergreen Short-Intermediate Municipal
  Fund (NMuB)
 Evergreen Short-Intermediate Municipal
  Fund—California (SMuB)

Evergreen Tax Exempt Money Market
 Fund (NMMX)
Evergreen Tax-Free Trust
 New Jersey Tax-Free Income Fund
  (SMuB)
 Pennsylvania Tax-Free Money Market
  Fund (SMMX)
Evergreen Trust (The)
 Evergreen Aggressive Growth Fund
  (AgGr)
 Evergreen Fund (Gr)
Evergreen Variable Trust
 Evergreen VA Aggressive Growth Fund
  (AgGr)
 Evergreen VA Foundation Fund (Bal)
 Evergreen VA Fund (AgGr)
 Evergreen VA Global Leaders Fund
  (GloE)
 Evergreen VA Growth & Income Fund
  (Gr&I)
 Evergreen VA Strategic Income Fund
  (IncB)

Excelsior Funds
114 W. 47th St.
New York, NY 10036-1510
800/446-1012
Excelsior Funds, Inc.
 Aging of America Fund (Gr)
 Business & Industrial Fund (Gr)
 Communication and Entertainment Fund
  (Gr)
 Early Life Cycle Fund (Gr)
 Emerging Americas Fund (Intl)
 Environmentally Related Products &
  Services Fund (Gr)
 Equity Fund (Gr)
 Global Competitors Fund (Gr)
 Government Money Fund (MM)
 Income and Growth Fund (Gr&I)
 Intermediate-Term Managed Income Fund
  (IncB)
 International Fund (Intl)
 Long-Term Supply of Energy Fund (Gr)
 Managed Income Fund (IncB)
 Money Fund (MM)
 Pacific/Asia Fund (Intl)
 Pan European Fund (Intl)
 Productivity Enhancers Fund (Gr)
 Short-Term Government Securities Fund
  (USGv)
 Treasury Money Fund (MM)

Excelsior Institutional Funds
114 W. 47th St.
New York, NY 10036-1510
800/446-1012
Excelsior Institutional Trust Fund, Inc.
 Institutional Bond Index Fund (IncB)
Excelsior Institutional Trust Fund, Inc.
 Institutional Balanced Fund (Bal)

Institutional Equity Fund (Gr)
Institutional Income Fund (IncM)
Institutional International Equity Fund
(Intl)
Institutional Optimum Growth Fund
(Gr&I)
Institutional Total Return Bond Fund
(IncB)
Institutional Value Equity Fund (Gr)

Excelsior Tax-Exempt Funds
114 W. 47th St.
New York, NY 10036-1510
800/446-1012
Excelsior Tax-Exempt Funds, Inc.
Intermediate-Term Tax-Exempt Fund
(NMuB)
Long-Term Tax-Exempt Fund (NMuB)
New York Intermediate-Term Tax-Exempt
Fund (SMuB)
Short-Term Tax-Exempt Securities Fund
(NMuB)
Tax-Exempt Money Fund (NMMX)

Expedition Funds
One Freedom Valley Rd.
Oaks, PA 19456
800/992-2085
Expedition Funds
Expedition Bond Fund (IncB)
Expedition Equity Fund (IncB)

Fairport Funds
4000 Chester Ave.
Cleveland, OH 44103-3612
800/3FAMILY
Fairport Funds
Fairport Government Securities Fund
(USGv)
Fairport Growth and Income Fund (Gr&I)
Fairport Midwest Growth Fund (Gr)

FAM Value Fund
Box 399
Cobleskill, NY 12043-0399
800/932-3271
Fenimore Asset Management Trust
FAM Value Fund (Gr&I)

Fasciano Fund, Inc.
190 S. LaSalle St.
Ste. 2800
Chicago, IL 60603-3412
800/848-6050
Fasciano Fund, Inc. (Gr)

FBL Fund Family
5400 University Ave. W.
Des Moines, IA 50266-5997
800/247-4170
FBL Money Market Fund, Inc. (MM)

FBL Series Fund, Inc.
Blue Chip Portfolio (Gr&I)
High Grade Bond Portfolio (IncB)
High Yield Bond Portfolio (HiYB)
Managed Portfolio (Flex)
Money Market Portfolio (MM)
Value Growth Portfolio (Gr)

FBR Funds
1001 Nineteenth St.
North Arlington, VA 22209
888/888-0025
FBR Family of Funds (The)
Financial Services Fund (AgGr)
Small Cap Financial Fund (AgGr)
Small Cap Growth/Value Fund (AgGr)

Federated Investors
Federated Investors Twr.
1001 Liberty Ave.
Pittsburgh, PA 15222-3779
800/341-7400
Automated Government Money Trust
(MM)
Cash Trust Series, Inc.
Government Cash Series (MM)
Municipal Cash Series (NMMX)
Prime Cash Series (MM)
Treasury Cash Series (MM)
Cash Trust Series II
Municipal Cash Series II (NMMX)
Treasury Cash Series II (MM)
Edward D. Jones & Co. Daily Passport
Cash Trust (MM)
Federated Adjustable Rate U.S.
Government Fund, Inc.—F Shares
(GNMA)
Federated American Leaders Fund, Inc.
(Gr&I)
Federated ARMS Fund (GNMA)
Federated Equity Funds
Federated Aggressive Growth Fund
(AgGr)
Federated Growth Strategies Fund (Gr)
Federated Small Cap Strategies Fund
(Gr)
Federated Equity Income Fund, Inc.
(Gr&I)
Federated Fund for U.S. Government
Securities, Inc. (USGv)
Federated GNMA Trust (GNMA)
Federated Government Income Securities
Fund, Inc. (USGv)
Federated Government Trust
Automated Government Cash Reserves
(MM)
Automated Treasury Cash Reserves (MM)
U.S. Treasury Cash Reserves (MM)
Federated High Income Bond Fund, Inc.
(HiYB)
Federated High Yield Trust (HiYB)

Federated Limited Term Fund (CorB)
Federated Limited Term Municipal Fund
(NMuB)
Federated Strategic Income Fund (IncM)
Federated Income Securities Trust
Federated Short-Term Income Fund
(IncB)
Intermediate Income Fund (IncM)
Federated Income Trust (USGv)
Federated Index Trust
Max-Cap Fund (Gr&I)
Mid-Cap Fund (Gr&I)
Mini-Cap Fund (Gr&I)
Federated Institutional Trust
Federated Institutional Short-Term
Government Fund (USGv)
Federated Insurance Series
Federated American Leaders Fund II
(Gr&I)
Federated Equity Income Fund II (Gr)
Federated Growth Strategies Fund II
(Gr)
Federated High Income Bond Fund II
(CorB)
Federated International Equity Fund II
(Intl)
Federated Prime Money Fund II (MM)
Federated U.S. Government Securities II
(USGv)
Federated Utility Fund II (IncE)
Federated Investment Trust
Federated Bond Index Fund (IncB)
Federated Master Trust (MM)
Federated Municipal Opportunities Fund,
Inc. (NMuB)
Federated Municipal Securities Fund, Inc.
(NMuB)
Federated Municipal Trust
Alabama Municipal Cash Trust (SMMX)
California Municipal Cash Trust (SMMX)
Connecticut Municipal Cash Trust
(SMMX)
Florida Municipal Cash Trust (SMMX)
Georgia Municipal Cash Trust (SMMX)
Maryland Municipal Cash Trust (SMMX)
Massachusetts Municipal Cash Trust
(SMMX)
Michigan Municipal Cash Trust (SMMX)
Minnesota Municipal Cash Trust (SMMX)
New Jersey Municipal Cash Trust
(SMMX)
New York Municipal Cash Trust (SMMX)
North Carolina Municipal Cash Trust
(SMMX)
Ohio Municipal Cash Trust (SMMX)
Pennsylvania Municipal Cash Trust
(SMMX)
Tennessee Municipal Cash Trust (SMMX)
Virginia Municipal Cash Trust (SMMX)
Federated Short-Term Municipal Trust
(NMuB)

Federated Short Term U.S. Government
Trust (MM)
Federated Stock and Bond Fund, Inc. (Bal)
Federated Stock Trust (Gr&I)
Federated Total Return Bond Fund (USGv)
Federated Tax Free Trust (NMMX)
Federated Total Return Series, Inc.
Federated Total Return Limited Duration
Fund (IncB)
Federated U.S. Government Bond Fund
(IncB)
Federated U.S. Government Fund: 1-3
Years (USGv)
Federated U.S. Government Securities
Fund: 2-5 Years (USGv)
Federated U.S. Government Securites Fund:
5-10 Years (USGv)
Federated Utility Fund, Inc. (IncE)
Fixed Income Securities, Inc.
Intermediate Municipal Trust
Federated Intermediate Municipal Trust
(NMuB)
Federated Ohio Intermediate Municipal
Trust (SMuB)
Federated Pennsylvania Intermediate
Municipal Trust (SMuB)
International Series, Inc.
Federated International Equity Fund (Intl)
Federated International Income Fund
(GloB)
Investment Series Funds, Inc.
Federated Bond Fund (CorB)
Liberty U.S. Government Money Market
Trust (MM)
Liquid Cash Trust (MM)
Managed Series Trust
Federated Managed Aggressive Growth
Fund (AgGr)
Federated Managed Growth and Income
Fund (Gr&I)
Federated Managed Growth Fund (Gr)
Federated Managed Income Fund (IncM)
Money Market Management, Inc. (MM)
Money Market Obligations Trust
Government Obligations Tax Managed
Fund (MM)
Tax-Free Obligations Fund (NMMX)
Money Market Obligations Trust II
Municipal Obligations Fund (NMMX)
Prime Cash Obligations Fund (MM)
Prime Value Obligations Fund (MM)
Money Market Trust (MM)
Municipal Securities Income Trust
Federated California Municipal Income
Fund (SMuB)
Federated Michigan Intermediate
Municipal Trust (SMuB)
Federated New York Municipal Income
Fund (SMuB)
Federated Ohio Municipal Income Fund
(SMuB)

Federated Pennsylvania Municipal Income
Fund (SMuB)
Tax-Free Instruments Trust (NMMX)
Trust for Government Cash Reserves (MM)
Trust for Short-Term U.S. Government
Securities (MM)
Trust for U.S. Treasury Obligations (MM)
World Investment Series, Inc.
  Federated Asia Pacific Growth Fund (Intl)
  Federated Emerging Markets Fund (Intl)
  Federated European Growth Fund (Intl)
  Federated International High Income Fund
  (GloB)
  Federated International Small Company
  Fund (Intl)
  Federated Latin American Growth Fund
  (Intl)
  Federated World Utility Fund (GloB)

FFTW Funds, Inc.
200 Park Avenue, 46th Fl.
New York, NY 10166
800/762-4848
FFTW Funds, Inc.
  International Portfolio (GloB)
  Stable Return Portfolio (IncB)
  U.S. Short-Term Portfolio (IncB)
  Worldwide Hedged Portfolio (GloB)
  Worldwide Portfolio (GloB)

Fidelity Advisor Funds
82 Devonshire St.
Boston, MA 02109-3605
800/526-0084
Fidelity Advisor Series I
  Fidelity Advisor Equity Growth Fund
  (AgGr)
  Fidelity Advisor Growth & Income Fund
  (Gr&I)
  Fidelity Advisor Large Cap Fund (Gr)
  Fidelity Advisor Mid Cap Fund (Gr)
  Fidelity Advisor TechnoQuant Growth
  Fund (Gr)
Fidelity Advisor Series II
  Fidelity Advisor Balanced Fund (IncM)
  Fidelity Advisor Government Investment
  Fund (USGv)
  Fidelity Advisor Growth Opportunities
  Fund (Gr)
  Fidelity Advisor High Yield Fund (HiYB)
  Fidelity Advisor Short Fixed-Income Fund
  (IncB)
Fidelity Advisor Series III
  Fidelity Advisor Equity Income Fund
  (Gr&I)
Fidelity Advisor Series IV
  Fidelity Advisor Intermediate Bond Fund
  (IncB)
  Fidelity Institutional Short-Intermediate
  Government Fund (USGv)
Fidelity Advisor Series V

Fidelity Advisor California Municipal
Income Fund (SMuB)
Fidelity Advisor High Income Municipal
Fund (NMuB)
Fidelity Advisor Natural Resources Fund
(GloE)
Fidelity Advisor New York Municipal
Income Fund (SMuB)
Fidelity Advisor Series VI
  Fidelity Advisor Intermediate Municipal
  Income Fund (NMuB)
  Fidelity Advisor Short-Intermediate
  Municipal Income Fund (NMuB)
Fidelity Advisor Series VII
  Fidelity Advisor Consumer Industries
  Fund (AgGr)
  Fidelity Advisor Cyclical Industries Fund
  (AgGr)
  Fidelity Advisor Financial Services Fund
  (AgGr)
  Fidelity Advisor Health Care Fund (AgGr)
  Fidelity Advisor Overseas Fund (Intl)
  Fidelity Advisor Technology Fund (AgGr)
  Fidelity Advisor Utilities Growth Fund
  (AgGr)
Fidelity Advisor Series VIII
  Fidelity Advisor Emerging Markets
  Income Fund (GloB)
  Fidelity Advisor Strategic Income Fund
  (IncB)
  Fidelity Advisor Strategic Opportunities
  Fund (AgGr)

Fidelity Funds
82 Devonshire St.
Boston, MA 02109-3605
800/544-8888
Fidelity Aberdeen Street Trust
  Fidelity Freedom Income Fund (IncM)
  Fidelity Freedom 2000 Fund (Bal)
  Fidelity Freedom 2010 Fund (Gr&I)
  Fidelity Freedom 2020 Fund (Gr)
  Fidelity Freedom 2030 Fund (Gr)
Fidelity Beacon Street Trust
  Fidelity Municipal Money Market Fund
  (NMMX)
  Spartan New Jersey Municipal Money
  Market Fund (SMMX)
Fidelity Boston Street Trust
  Fidelity Target Timeline 1999 Fund (IncB)
  Fidelity Target Timeline 2001 Fund (IncB)
  Fidelity Target Timeline 2003 Fund (IncB)
Fidelity California Municipal Trust
  Fidelity California Insured Municipal
  Income Fund (SMuB)
  Fidelity California Municipal Income
  Fund (SMuB)
  Spartan California Intermediate Municipal
  Income Fund (SMuB)
  Spartan California Municipal Income
  Fund (SMuB)

Fidelity California Municipal Trust II
  Fidelity California Municipal Money
    Market Fund (SMMX)
  Spartan California Municipal Money
    Market Fund (SMMX)
Fidelity Capital Trust
  Fidelity Capital Appreciation Fund (Gr)
  Fidelity Disciplined Equity Fund (Gr)
  Fidelity Stock Selector (Gr)
  Fidelity TechnoQuant Growth Fund (Gr)
  Fidelity Value Fund (Gr)
Fidelity Charles Street Trust
  Fidelity Asset Manager (Flex)
  Fidelity Asset Manager: Growth Fund
    (Flex)
  Fidelity Asset Manager: Income Fund
    (IncM)
  Fidelity Short-Intermediate Government
    Fund (USGv)
  Spartan Investment Grade Bond Fund
    (CorB)
  Spartan Short-Term Bond Fund (IncB)
Fidelity Commonwealth Trust
  Fidelity Intermediate Bond Fund (IncB)
  Fidelity Large Cap Stock Fund (Gr)
  Fidelity Market Index Fund (Gr&I)
  Fidelity Small Cap Stock Fund (AgGr)
Fidelity Concord Street Trust
  Spartan U.S. Equity Index Fund (Gr&I)
Fidelity Contrafund (AgGr)
Fidelity Court Street Trust
  Fidelity Municipal Income Fund (NMuB)
  Spartan Connecticut Municipal Income
    Fund (SMuB)
  Spartan Florida Municipal Income Fund
    (SMuB)
  Spartan New Jersey Municipal Income
    Fund (SMuB)
Fidelity Court Street Trust II
  Fidelity Connecticut Municipal Money
    Market Fund (SMMX)
  Fidelity New Jersey Municipal Money
    Market Fund (SMMX)
  Spartan Connecticut Municipal Money
    Market Fund (SMMX)
  Spartan Florida Municipal Money Market
    Fund (SMMX)
Fidelity Destiny Portfolios
  Destiny I (Gr)
  Destiny II (Gr)
Fidelity Deutsche Mark Performance
  Portfolio, L.P. (GloB)
Fidelity Devonshire Trust
  Fidelity Equity-Income Fund (IncE)
  Fidelity Mid-Cap Stock Fund (Gr)
  Fidelity Real Estate Investment Portfolio
    (Gr&I)
  Fidelity Utilities Fund (IncE)
Fidelity Financial Trust
  Fidelity Convertible Securities Fund
    (Gr&I)

Fidelity Equity-Income II Fund (IncE)
Fidelity Retirement Growth Fund (Gr)
Fidelity Fixed-Income Trust
  Fidelity Investment Grade Bond Fund
    (IncB)
  Fidelity Short-Term Bond Fund (IncB)
  Spartan Government Income Fund
    (USGv)
  Spartan High Income Fund (HiYB)
  Spartan Short-Intermediate Government
    Fund (USGv)
Fidelity Government Securities Fund
  (USGv)
Fidelity Hastings Street Trust
  Fidelity Fifty (Gr)
  Fidelity Fund (Gr&I)
Fidelity Hereford Street Trust
  Spartan Money Market Fund (MM)
  Spartan U.S. Government Money Market
    Fund (MM)
  Spartan U.S. Treasury Money Market
    Fund (MM)
Fidelity Income Fund
  Fidelity Advisor Mortgage Securities Fund
    (GNMA)
  Fidelity Ginnie Mae Fund (GNMA)
  Spartan Limited Maturity Government
    Fund (USGv)
Fidelity Institutional Cash Portfolios
  Domestic (MM)
  Government (MM)
  Money Market (MM)
  Treasury (MM)
Fidelity Institutional Tax-Exempt Cash
  Portfolios
  Tax-Exempt (NMMX)
Fidelity Institutional Trust
  Fidelity U.S. Bond Index Portfolio
    (USGv)
Fidelity Investment Trust
  Fidelity Canada Fund (Intl)
  Fidelity Diversified International Fund
    (Intl)
  Fidelity Emerging Markets Fund (Intl)
  Fidelity Europe Capital Appreciation Fund
    (Intl)
  Fidelity Europe Fund (Intl)
  Fidelity France Fund (Intl)
  Fidelity Germany Fund (Intl)
  Fidelity Global Bond Fund (GloB)
  Fidelity Hong Kong and China Fund (Intl)
  Fidelity International Growth & Income
    Fund (Intl)
  Fidelity International Value Fund (Intl)
  Fidelity Japan Fund (Intl)
  Fidelity Japan Small Companies Fund
    (Intl)
  Fidelity Latin America Fund (Intl)
  Fidelity New Markets Income Fund
    (GloB)
  Fidelity Nordic Fund (Intl)

Fidelity Overseas Fund (Intl)
Fidelity Pacific Basin Fund (Intl)
Fidelity Southeast Asia Fund L.C.
  (Intl)
Fidelity United Kingdom Fund (Intl)
Fidelity Worldwide Fund (GloE)
Fidelity Magellan Fund (Gr)
Fidelity Massachusetts Municipal Trust
  Fidelity Massachusetts Municipal Money
    Market Fund (SMMX)
  Spartan Massachusetts Municipal Income
    Fund (SMuB)
  Spartan Massachusetts Municipal Money
    Market Fund (SMMX)
Fidelity Money Market Trust
  Rated Money Market (MM)
  Retirement Government Money Market
    Portfolio (MM)
  Retirement Money Market Portfolio
    (MM)
Fidelity Mt. Vernon Street Trust
  Fidelity Emerging Growth Fund (AgGr)
  Fidelity Growth Company Fund (AgGr)
  Fidelity New Millennium Fund (AgGr)
Fidelity Municipal Trust
  Fidelity Advisor Municipal Bond Fund
    (NMuB)
  Fidelity Aggressive Municipal Fund
    (NMuB)
  Fidelity Insured Municipal Income Fund
    (NMuB)
  Spartan Michigan Municipal Income Fund
    (SMuB)
  Spartan Minnesota Municipal Income
    Fund (SMuB)
  Spartan Ohio Municipal Income Fund
    (SMuB)
  Spartan Pennsylvania Municipal Income
    Fund (SMuB)
Fidelity Municipal Trust II
  Fidelity Michigan Municipal Money
    Market Fund (SMMX)
  Fidelity Ohio Municipal Money Market
    Fund (SMMX)
  Spartan Pennsylvania Municipal Money
    Market Fund (SMMX)
Fidelity Newbury Street Trust
  Capital Reserves: Money Market Portfolio
    (MM)
  Capital Reserves: Municipal Money
    Market Portfolio (NMMX)
  Capital Reserves: U.S. Government
    Portfolio (MM)
  Prime Fund-Daily Money Class (MM)
  Tax-Exempt Fund-Daily Money Class
    (NMMX)
  Treasury Fund (MM)
  Treasury Only (MM)
Fidelity New York Municipal Trust
  Fidelity New York Insured Municipal
    Income Fund (SMuB)

Fidelity New York Municipal Income
  Fund (SMuB)
Spartan New York Intermediate Municipal
  Income Fund (SMuB)
Spartan New York Municipal Income
  Fund (SMuB)
Fidelity New York Municipal Trust II
  Fidelity New York Municipal Money
    Market Fund (SMMX)
  Spartan New York Municipal Money
    Market Fund (SMMX)
Fidelity Phillips Street Trust
  Fidelity Cash Reserves (MM)
  Fidelity U.S. Government Reserves (MM)
Fidelity Puritan Trust
  Fidelity Balanced Fund (Bal)
  Fidelity Global Balanced Fund (GloB)
  Fidelity Low-Priced Stock Fund (AgGr)
  Fidelity Puritan Fund (IncE)
Fidelity School Street Trust
  Fidelity Limited Term Municipal Income
    Fund (NMuB)
Fidelity Securities Fund
  Fidelity Blue Chip Growth Fund (Gr)
  Fidelity Dividend Growth Fund (Gr)
  Fidelity Growth & Income Portfolio
    (Gr&I)
  Fidelity OTC Portfolio (AgGr)
Fidelity Select Portfolios
  Air Transportation Portfolio (AgGr)
  American Gold Portfolio (PM/G)
  Automotive Portfolio (AgGr)
  Biotechnology Portfolio (AgGr)
  Brokerage and Investment Management
    Portfolio (AgGr)
  Chemicals Portfolio (AgGr)
  Computers Portfolio (AgGr)
  Construction and Housing Portfolio
    (AgGr)
  Consumer Industries Portfolio (AgGr)
  Cyclical Industries Portfolio (AgGr)
  Defense and Aerospace Portfolio
    (AgGr)
  Developing Communications Portfolio
    (AgGr)
  Electronics Portfolio (AgGr)
  Energy Portfolio (AgGr)
  Energy Service Portfolio (AgGr)
  Environmental Services Portfolio
    (AgGr)
  Financial Services Portfolio (AgGr)
  Food and Agriculture Portfolio (AgGr)
  Health Care Portfolio (AgGr)
  Home Finance Portfolio (AgGr)
  Industrial Equipment Portfolio (AgGr)
  Industrial Materials Portfolio (AgGr)
  Insurance Portfolio (AgGr)
  Leisure Portfolio (AgGr)
  Medical Delivery Portfolio (AgGr)
  Money Market Portfolio (MM)
  Multimedia Portfolio (AgGr)

Natural Gas Portfolio (AgGr)
Natural Resources Portfolio (AgGr)
Paper and Forest Products Portfolio
 (AgGr)
Precious Metals and Minerals Portfolio
 (PM/G)
Regional Banks Portfolio (AgGr)
Retailing Portfolio (AgGr)
Software and Computer Services Portfolio
 (AgGr)
Technology Portfolio (AgGr)
Telecommunications Portfolio (AgGr)
Transportation Portfolio (AgGr)
Utilities Growth Portfolio (AgGr)
Fidelity Sterling Performance Portfolio, L.P.
 (GloB)
Fidelity Summer Street Trust
 Fidelity Capital & Income Fund (HiYB)
Fidelity Trend Fund (Gr)
Fidelity Union Street Trust
 Fidelity Export and Multinational Fund
  (Gr)
 Spartan Aggressive Municipal Fund
  (NMuB)
 Spartan Arizona Municipal Income Fund
  (SMuB)
 Spartan Ginne Mae Fund (GNMA)
 Spartan Intermediate Municipal Income
  Fund (NMuB)
 Spartan Maryland Municipal Income Fund
  (SMuB)
 Spartan Municipal Income Fund (NMuB)
 Spartan Short-Intermediate Municipal
  Income Fund (NMuB)
Fidelity Yen Performance Portfolio, L.P.
 (GloB)
First Union Street Trust II
 Fidelity Daily Income Trust (MM)
 Spartan Arizona Municipal Money Market
  Fund (SMMX)
 Spartan Municipal Money Fund (NMMX)
North Carolina Capital Management Trust
 (The)
 Cash Portfolio (MM)
 Term Portfolio (USGv)
Variable Insurance Products Fund
 Equity-Income Portfolio (IncE)
 Growth Portfolio (AgGr)
 High Income Portfolio (HiYB)
 Money Market Portfolio (MM)
 Overseas Portfolio (Intl)
Variable Insurance Products Fund II
 Asset Manager: Growth Portfolio (Gr&I)
 Asset Manager Portfolio (Flex)
 Contrafund Portfolio (Gr)
 Index 500 Portfolio (Gr)
 Investment Grade Bond Portfolio (IncB)
Variable Insurance Products Fund III
 Balanced Fund (Gr&I)
 Growth Opportunities Fund (Gr)
 Money Market Fund (MM)

59 Wall Street Funds
40 Water St.
Boston, MA 02109
800/625-5759
59 Wall Street Fund, Inc. (The)
 European Equity Fund (Intl)
 Inflation Index Securities Fund (IncM)
 Pacific Basin Equity Fund (Intl)
 Small Company Fund (AgGr)
 U.S. Equity Fund (Gr)
59 Wall Street Trust (The)
 Money Market Fund (MM)
 Tax Free Short/Intermediate Fixed Income
  Fund (NMuB)
 U.S. Treasury Money Market Fund
  (MM)

First American Funds
One Freedom Valley Drive
Oaks, PA 19456
800/637-2548
First American Funds Inc.
 Government Obligations Fund (MM)
 Prime Obligations Fund (MM)
 Treasury Obligations Fund (MM)
First American Investment Funds, Inc.
 Asset Allocation Fund (Flex)
 Balanced Fund (Bal)
 Colorado Intermediate Tax Free Fund
  (SMuB)
 Diversified Growth Fund (Gr)
 Emerging Growth Fund (AgGr)
 Equity Income Fund (Gr&I)
 Equity Index Fund (Gr&I)
 Fixed Income Fund (IncB)
 Health Sciences Fund (Gr)
 Intermediate Government Bond Fund
  (USGv)
 Intermediate Tax-Free Fund (NMuB)
 Intermediate Term Income Fund (IncB)
 International Fund (Intl)
 Limited Term Income Fund (IncB)
 Minnesota Insured Intermediate Tax Free
  Fund (SMuB)
 Real Estate Securities Fund (IncE)
 Regional Equity Fund (AgGr)
 Special Equity Fund (AgGr)
 Stock Fund (Gr&I)
 Technology Fund (AgGr)
First American Strategy Funds, Inc.
 Aggressive Growth Fund (AgGr)
 Growth and Income Fund (Bal)
 Growth Fund (Gr&I)
 Income Fund (IncM)

First Eagle Funds
1345 Ave. of the Americas
New York, NY 10105-4300
800/451-3623
First Eagle Fund of America, Inc. (Gr)
First Eagle International Fund, Inc. (Intl)

First Investors Funds
95 Wall St.
23rd Fl.
New York, NY 10005-4201
800/423-4026
Executive Investors Trust
  Executive Investors Blue Chip Fund (IncE)
  Executive Investors High Yield Fund
    (HiYB)
  Executive Investors Insured Tax Exempt
    Fund (NMuB)
First Investors Cash Management Fund,
  Inc. (MM)
First Investors Fund For Income, Inc.
  (HiYB)
First Investors Global Fund, Inc. (GloE)
First Investors Government Fund, Inc.
  (USGv)
First Investors High Yield Fund, Inc.
  (HiYB)
First Investors Insured Tax Exempt Fund,
  Inc. (NMuB)
First Investors Life Series Fund
  Blue Chip Fund (IncE)
  Cash Management Fund (MM)
  Discovery Fund (AgGr)
  Government Fund (USGv)
  Growth Fund (Gr)
  High Yield Fund (HiYB)
  International Securities Fund (GloE)
  Investment Grade Fund (IncM)
  Target Maturity 2007 Fund (USGv)
  Target Maturity 2010 Fund (IncB)
  Utility Income Fund (Gr&I)
First Investors Multi-State Insured Tax Free
  Fund
  Arizona Fund (SMuB)
  California Fund (SMuB)
  Colorado Fund (SMuB)
  Connecticut Fund (SMuB)
  Florida Fund (SMuB)
  Georgia Fund (SMuB)
  Maryland Fund (SMuB)
  Massachusetts Fund (SMuB)
  Michigan Fund (SMuB)
  Minnesota Fund (SMuB)
  Missouri Fund (SMuB)
  New Jersey Fund (SMuB)
  North Carolina Fund (SMuB)
  Ohio Fund (SMuB)
  Oregon Fund (SMuB)
  Pennsylvania Fund (SMuB)
  Virginia Fund (SMuB)
First Investors New York Insured Tax Free
  Fund, Inc. (SMuB)
First Investors Series Fund
  First Investors Blue Chip Fund (IncE)
  First Investors Insured Intermediate Tax
    Exempt Fund (NMuB)
  First Investors Investment Grade Fund
    (IncB)

First Investors Special Situations Fund
  (Gr)
First Investors Total Return Fund (Flex)
First Investors Series Fund II, Inc.
  Growth and Income Fund (Gr&I)
  U.S.A. Mid-Cap Opportunity Fund (Gr)
  Utilities Income Fund (IncE)
First Investors Special Bond Fund, Inc.
  (HiYB)
First Investors Tax-Exempt Money Market
  Fund, Inc. (NMMX)
First Investors U.S. Government Plus Fund
  1st Fund (USGv)
First Investors U.S. Government Plus Fund
  2nd Fund (USGv)
First Investors U.S. Government Plus Fund
  3rd Fund (USGv)

First Pacific Mutual Fund, Inc.
2756 Woodlawn Dr.
#6-201
Honolulu, HI 96822
808/988-8088
First Pacific Mutual Fund, Inc.
  First Hawaii Intermediate Municipal Fund
    (SMuB)
  First Hawaii Municipal Bond Fund
    (SMuB)
  First Idaho Tax-Free Fund (SMuB)

First Priority Funds
Federated Investors Twr.
1001 Liberty Ave.
Pittsburgh, PA 15222-3779
800/341-7400
First Priority Funds
  First Priority Balanced Fund (Bal)
  First Priority Fixed Income Fund
    (IncB)
  First Priority Growth Fund (Gr&I)
  First Priority Limited Maturity
    Government Fund (USGv)
  First Priority Treasury Money Market
    Fund (MM)
  First Priority Value Fund (Gr&I)

Flag Investors Funds
One South St.
Baltimore, MD 21202
800/767-3524
Alex. Brown Cash Reserve Fund, Inc.
  Prime Series (MM)
  Tax-Free Series (NMMX)
  Treasury Series (MM)
Flag Investors Emerging Growth Fund, Inc.
  (AgGr)
Flag Investors Equity Partners Fund, Inc.
  (Gr&I)
Flag Investors International Fund (Intl)
Flag Investors Maryland Intermediate Tax
  Free Income Fund (SMuB)

Flag Investors Real Estate Securities Fund
  (Gr&I)
Flag Investors Short Intermediate Income
  Fund, Inc. (IncB)
Flag Investors Telephone Income Fund, Inc.
  (IncM)
Flag Investors Value Builder Fund, Inc.
  (Bal)
Managed Municipal Fund, Inc. (NMuB)
North American Government Bond Fund,
  Inc. (GloB)
Total Return U.S. Treasury Fund, Inc.
  (USGv)

Flex Funds
6000 Memorial Dr.
P.O. Box 7177
Dublin, OH 43017-9767
800/325-FLEX
Flex-Funds (The)
  Highlands Growth Fund (Gr)
  Institutional Fund (MM)
  Money Market Fund (MM)
  Muirfield Fund (Flex)
  Total Return Utilities Fund (Flex)
  U.S. Government Bond Fund (USGv)
Flex-Partners Trust
  BTB Fund (Flex)
  TAA Fund (Gr)

FMB Funds
One Freedom Valley Drive
Oaks, PA 19456
800/342-5734
FMB Funds, Inc.
  FMB Diversified Equity Fund (Gr)
  FMB Intermediate Government Income
    Fund (USGv)
  FMB Michigan Tax-Free Bond Fund
    (SMuB)
  FMB Money Market Fund (MM)

Focus Trust, Inc.
230 Sugartown Rd.
Ste. 150
Wayne, PA 19087-3029
800/665-2550
Focus Trust, Inc. (Gr)

Fortis Financial Group of Funds
P.O. Box 64284
St. Paul, MN 55164-0284
800/800-2638
Fortis Advantage Portfolios, Inc.
  Asset Allocation Portfolio (Flex)
  Capital Appreciation Portfolio (AgGr)
  High Yield Portfolio (HiYB)
Fortis Equity Portfolios
  Fortis Capital Fund (Gr&I)
Fortis Fiduciary Fund, Inc. (Gr)
Fortis Growth Fund, Inc. (Gr)

Fortis Income Portfolios, Inc.
  Fortis U.S. Government Securities Fund
    (USGv)
Fortis Money Portfolios, Inc.
  Fortis Money Fund (MM)
Fortis Stock Funds, Inc.
  Fortis Growth and Income Fund (Gr&I)
  Fortis Value Fund (Gr)
Fortis Tax-Free Portfolios, Inc.
  Minnesota Portfolio (SMuB)
  National Portfolio (NMuB)
Fortis Worldwide Portfolios, Inc.
  Fortis Global Growth Portfolio (GloE)

Forum Funds
Two Portland Sq.
Portland, ME 04101
800/94-FORUM
Forum Funds
  Austin Global Equity Fund (GloE)
  Daily Assets Cash Fund (MM)
  Daily Assets Government Fund (MM)
  Daily Assets Treasury Fund (MM)
  Investors Bond Fund (CorB)
  Maine Municipal Bond Fund (SMuB)
  New Hampshire Bond Fund (SMuB)
  Oak Hall Equity Fund (Gr)
  Payson Balanced Fund (Bal)
  Payson Value Fund (Gr&I)
  QUADRA International Equity Fund
    (Intl)
  QUADRA Limited Maturity Treasury
    Fund (USGv)
  QUADRA Opportunistic Bond Fund
    (IncB)
  QUADRA Value Equity Fund (Gr)
  TaxSaver Bond Fund (NMuB)
Highland Family of Funds
  Highland Aggressive Growth Fund
    (AgGr)
  Highland Growth Fund (Gr)

Founders Funds, Inc.
2930 E. Third Ave.
Denver, CO 80206-5002
800/525-2440
Founders Funds, Inc.
  Founders Balanced Fund (Bal)
  Founders Blue Chip Fund (Gr&I)
  Founders Discovery Fund (AgGr)
  Founders Frontier Fund (AgGr)
  Founders Government Securities Fund
    (USGv)
  Founders Growth Fund (Gr)
  Founders International Equity Fund
    (Intl)
  Founders Money Market Fund (MM)
  Founders Passport Fund (Intl)
  Founders Special Fund (AgGr)
  Founders Worldwide Growth Fund
    (GloE)

Fountain Square Funds
3435 Stelzer Rd.
Columbus, OH 43219-3035
800/554-3862
Fountain Square Funds
  Balanced Fund (Bal)
  Bond Fund for Income (IncB)
  Commercial Paper Fund (MM)
  Equity Income Fund (IncE)
  Government Cash Reserves Fund (MM)
  International Equity Fund (Intl)
  Mid Cap Fund (Gr&I)
  Municipal Bond Fund (NMuB)
  Ohio Tax Free Bond Fund (SMuB)
  Quality Bond Fund (CorB)
  Quality Growth Fund (Gr)
  U.S. Government Securities Fund (USGv)
  U.S. Treasury Obligations Fund (MM)

FPA Funds
11400 W. Olympic Blvd.
Ste. 1200
Los Angeles, CA 90064-1568
800/982-4372
FPA Capital Fund, Inc. (Gr)
FPA Crescent Portfolio (Bal)
FPA New Income, Inc. (IncB)
FPA Paramount Fund, Inc. (Gr&I)
FPA Perennial Fund, Inc. (Gr&I)

Franklin Group of Funds
777 Mariners Island Blvd.
San Mateo, CA 94404-1584
800/632-2180
AGE High Income Fund, Inc. (HiYB)
Franklin Asset Allocation Fund (Flex)
Franklin California Tax-Free Income Fund,
  Inc. (SMuB)
Franklin California Tax-Free Trust
  Franklin California Insured Tax-Free
  Income Fund (SMuB)
  Franklin California Intermediate-Term
  Tax-Free Income Fund (SMuB)
  Franklin California Tax-Exempt Money
  Fund (SMMX)
Franklin Custodian Funds, Inc.
  DynaTech Series (AgGr)
  Growth Fund (Gr)
  Income Fund (IncM)
  U.S. Government Securities Series
  (GNMA)
  Utilities Fund (Gr&I)
Franklin Federal Money Fund (MM)
Franklin Federal Tax-Free Income Fund
  (NMuB)
Franklin Gold Fund (PM/G)
Franklin International Trust
  Templeton Foreign Smaller Companies
  Fund (Intl)
  Templeton Pacific Growth Fund (Intl)
Franklin Investors Securities Trust

Franklin Adjustable Rate Securities Fund
  (GNMA)
Franklin Adjustable U.S. Government
  Securities Fund (GNMA)
Franklin Convertible Securities Fund
  (Gr&I)
Franklin Equity Income Fund (IncE)
Franklin Global Government Income
  Fund (GloB)
Franklin Short-Intermediate U.S.
  Government Securities Fund (USGv)
Franklin Managed Trust
  Franklin Corporate Qualified Dividend
  Fund (IncM)
  Franklin Investment Grade Income Fund
  (CorB)
  Franklin Rising Dividends Fund (Gr)
Franklin Money Fund (MM)
Franklin Municipal Securities Trust
  Franklin Arkansas Municipal Bond Fund
  (SMuB)
  Franklin California High Yield Municipal
  Fund (SMuB)
  Franklin Hawaii Municipal Bond Fund
  (SMuB)
  Franklin Tennessee Municipal Bond Fund
  (SMuB)
  Franklin Washington Municipal Bond
  Fund (SMuB)
Franklin New York Tax-Free Income Fund,
  Inc. (SMuB)
Franklin New York Tax-Free Trust
  Franklin New York Insured Tax-Free
  Income Fund (SMuB)
  Franklin New York Intermediate-Term
  Tax-Free Income Fund (SMuB)
  Franklin New York Tax-Exempt Money
  Fund (SMMX)
Franklin Partners Funds
  Franklin Tax-Advantaged High Yield
  Securities Fund (HiYB)
  Franklin Tax-Advantaged International
  Bond Fund (GloB)
  Franklin Tax-Advantaged U.S.
  Government Securities Fund (GNMA)
Franklin Real Estate Securities Trust
  Franklin Real Estate Securities Fund (Gr)
Franklin Strategic Mortgage Portfolio
  (GNMA)
Franklin Strategic Series
  Franklin California Growth Fund (Gr)
  Franklin Global Health Care Fund (GloE)
  Franklin Global Utilities Fund (GloE)
  Franklin Institutional MidCap Growth
  Fund (Gr)
  Franklin Natural Resources Fund (Gr)
  Franklin Small Cap Growth Fund (Gr)
  Franklin Strategic Income Fund (IncM)
Franklin Tax-Exempt Money Fund
  (NMMX)
Franklin Tax-Free Trust

Franklin Alabama Tax Free Income Fund
(SMuB)
Franklin Arizona Insured Tax-Free Income
Fund (SMuB)
Franklin Arizona Tax-Free Income Fund
(SMuB)
Franklin Colorado Tax-Free Income Fund
(SMuB)
Franklin Connecticut Tax-Free Income
Fund (SMuB)
Franklin Federal Intermediate-Term
Tax-Free Income Fund (NMuB)
Franklin Florida Insured Tax-Free Income
Fund (SMuB)
Franklin Florida Tax-Free Income Fund
(SMuB)
Franklin Georgia Tax-Free Income Fund
(SMuB)
Franklin High Yield Tax-Free Income
Fund (NMuB)
Franklin Indiana Tax-Free Income Fund
(SMuB)
Franklin Insured Tax-Free Income Fund
(NMuB)
Franklin Kentucky Tax-Free Income Fund
(SMuB)
Franklin Louisiana Tax-Free Income Fund
(SMuB)
Franklin Maryland Tax-Free Income Fund
(SMuB)
Franklin Massachusetts Insured Tax-Free
Income Fund (SMuB)
Franklin Michigan Insured Tax-Free
Income Fund (SMuB)
Franklin Minnesota Insured Tax-Free
Income Fund (SMuB)
Franklin Missouri Tax-Free Income Fund
(SMuB)
Franklin New Jersey Tax-Free Income
Fund (SMuB)
Franklin North Carolina Tax-Free Income
Fund (SMuB)
Franklin Ohio Insured Tax-Free Income
Fund (SMuB)
Franklin Oregon Tax-Free Income Fund
(SMuB)
Franklin Pennsylvania Tax-Free Income
Fund (SMuB)
Franklin Puerto Rico Tax-Free Income
Fund (SMuB)
Franklin Texas Tax-Free Income Fund
(SMuB)
Franklin Virginia Tax-Free Income Fund
(SMuB)
Franklin/Templeton Global Trust (The)
Franklin/Templeton German Government
Bond Fund (GloB)
Franklin/Templeton Global Currency Fund
(GloB)
Franklin/Templeton Hard Currency Fund
(GloB)

Franklin/Templeton High Income
Currency Fund (GloB)
Franklin/Templeton Japan Fund (Intl)
Franklin/Templeton Money Fund Trust
Franklin/Templeton Money Fund II (MM)
Franklin Value Investors Trust
Franklin Balance Sheet Investment Fund
(Gr&I)
Franklin MicroCap Value Fund (AgGr)
Franklin Value Fund (Gr)
Institutional Fiduciary Trust
Franklin Cash Reserves Fund (MM)
Franklin Institutional Adjustable Rate
Securities Fund (GNMA)
Franklin Institutional Adjustable U.S.
Government Securities Fund (GNMA)
Franklin U.S. Government Agency Money
Market Portfolio (MM)
Franklin U.S. Government Securities
Money Market Portfolio (MM)
Franklin U.S. Treasury Money Market
Portfolio (MM)
Money Market Portfolio (MM)
Money Market Portfolios (The)
U.S. Government Securities Money
Market Portfolio (The) (MM)
Templeton American Trust, Inc. (Gr&I)
Templeton Capital Accumulator Fund, Inc.
(GloE)
Templeton Developing Markets Trust (Intl)
Templeton Global Opportunities Trust
(GloE)
Templeton Global Real Estate Fund (GloE)
Templeton Global Small Companies Fund,
Inc. (GloE)
Templeton Growth Fund, Inc. (GloE)

Franklin Mutual Series Fund
51 J.F. Kennedy Pkwy.
Short Hills, NJ 07078-2702
800/448-3863
Franklin Mutual Series Fund Inc.
Franklin Mutual Beacon Fund (Gr&I)
Franklin Mutual Discovery Fund (AgGr)
Franklin Mutual European Fund (Intl)
Franklin Mutual Qualified Fund (Gr&I)
Franklin Mutual Shares Fund (Gr&I)

Frank Russell Mutual Funds
909 A St.
P.O. Box 1591
Tacoma, WA 98402-5111
800/972-0700
Frank Russell Investment Company
Aggressive Strategy Fund (Bal)
Balanced Strategy Fund (Bal)
Conservative Strategy Fund (IncM)
Diversified Bond Fund (IncB)
Diversified Equity Fund (Gr&I)
Emerging Markets Fund (Intl)
Equity Balanced Strategy Fund (Gr)

Equity Income Fund (IncE)
Equity I Fund (Gr&I)
Equity II Fund (AgGr)
Equity III Fund (IncE)
Equity Q Fund (Gr&I)
Equity T Fund (Gr)
Fixed Income I Fund (IncB)
Fixed Income II Fund (IncB)
Fixed Income III Fund (IncB)
International Fund (Intl)
International Securities Fund (Intl)
Limited Volatility Tax Free Fund (NMuB)
Moderate Strategy Fund (Incm)
MultiStrategy Bond Fund (IncB)
Quantitative Equity Fund (Gr&I)
Real Estate Securities Fund (Gr&I)
Special Growth Fund (AgGr)
Tax Free Money Market Fund (NMMX)
U.S. Government Money Market Fund
(MM)
Volatility Constrained Bond Fund (IncB)
Russell Insurance Funds
Aggressive Equity Fund (AgGr)
Core Bond Fund (IncB)
Multi-Style Equity Fund (Gr&I)
Non-U.S. Fund (GloB)

Fremont Mutual Funds
50 Beale St.
Ste. 100
San Francisco, CA 94105-1813
800/548-4539
Fremont Mutual Funds, Inc.
Fremont Bond Fund (IncB)
Fremont California Intermediate Tax-Free
Fund (SMuB)
Fremont Emerging Markets Fund (Intl)
Fremont Global Fund (GloB)
Fremont Growth Fund (Gr)
Fremont International Growth Fund (Intl)
Fremont International Small Cap Fund (Intl)
Fremont Money Market Fund (MM)
Fremont U.S. Micro-Cap Fund (AgGr)

Frontier Funds, Inc.
101 W. Wisconsin Ave.
P.O. Box 68
Pewaukee, WI 53072-3457
800/231-2901
Frontier Funds, Inc.
Equity Fund Portfolio (Gr)

FTI Funds
Federated Investors Twr.
Pittsburgh, PA 15222-3779
800/341-7400
FTI Funds
FTI Global Bond Fund (GloB)
FTI International Bond Fund (GloB)
FTI International Equity Fund (Intl)
FTI Small Cap Equity Fund (AgGr)

Fundamental Family of Funds
90 Washington St.
19th Fl.
New York, NY 10006-2214
800/225-6864
Fundamental California Muni Fund (The)
(SMuB)
Fundamental Fixed-Income Fund
High Yield Municipal Bond Series
(HiYB)
Tax-Free Money Market Series (NMMX)
U.S. Government Strategic Income Series
(USGv)
Fundamental New York Muni Fund (The)
(SMuB)

FundManager Portfolios
One Beacon St.
Boston, MA 02108
800/638-1896
Freedom Group of Tax-Exempt Funds
Freedom California Tax Exempt Money
Fund (SMMX)
Freedom Tax Exempt Money Fund
(NMMX)
Freedom Mutual Fund
Freedom Cash Management Fund (MM)
Freedom Government Securities Fund
(MM)
Freedom U.S. Treasury Money Market
Fund (MM)
FundManager Portfolios
FundManager Aggressive Growth
Portfolio (AgGr)
FundManager Bond Portfolio (IncB)
FundManager Growth & Income Portfolio
(Gr&I)
FundManager Growth Portfolio (Gr)
FundManager Managed Total Return
Portfolio (Gr&I)

Gabelli Funds
One Corporate Ctr.
Rye, NY 10580-1434
800/422-3554
Gabelli Asset Fund (The) (Gr)
Gabelli Capital Series Funds, Inc.
Gabelli Capital Asset Fund (Gr)
Gabelli Equity Series Funds, Inc.
Gabelli Equity Income Fund (IncE)
Gabelli Small Cap Growth Fund
(AgGr)
Gabelli Global Series Funds, Inc.
Gabelli Global Convertible Securities
Fund (GloB)
Gabelli Global Interactive Couch Potato
Fund (GloE)
Gabelli Global Telecommunications Fund
(GloE)
Gabelli Gold Fund, Inc. (The) (PM/G)
Gabelli Growth Fund (The) (Gr)

Gabelli International Growth Fund, Inc.
  (Intl)
Gabelli Investor Funds, Inc.
  Gabelli ABC Fund (Gr)
Gabelli Money Market Funds (The)
  Gabelli U.S. Treasury Money Market
  Fund (NMMX)
Gabelli Value Fund Inc. (The) (Gr)

Galaxy Funds
4400 Computer Drive
Westboro, MA 01581
800/628-0414
Galaxy Fund (The)
  Asset Allocation Fund (IncM)
  Connecticut Municipal Bond Fund
  (SMuB)
  Connecticut Municipal Money Market
  Fund (SMMX)
  Corporate Bond Fund (CorB)
  Equity Growth Fund (Gr)
  Equity Income Fund (Gr&I)
  Equity Value Fund (Gr&I)
  Government Money Market Fund (MM)
  Growth and Income Fund (Gr&I)
  High Quality Bond Fund (IncB)
  Institutional Treasury Fund (MM)
  Intermediate Government Income Fund
  (USGv)
  International Equity Fund (Intl)
  Massachusetts Municipal Bond Fund
  (SMuB)
  Massachusetts Municipal Money Market
  Fund (SMMX)
  Money Market Fund (MM)
  New York Municipal Bond Fund (SMuB)
  Rhode Island Municipal Bond Fund
  (SMuB)
  Short Term Bond Fund (IncB)
  Small Capitalization Value Fund (AgGr)
  Small Company Equity Fund (AgGr)
  Tax-Exempt Bond Fund (NMuB)
  Tax-Exempt Money Market Fund
  (NMMX)
  U.S. Treasury Money Market Fund (MM)
Galaxy II Fund (The)
  Galaxy II Large Company Index Fund
  (Gr&I)
  Galaxy II Municipal Bond Fund (NMuB)
  Galaxy II Small Company Index Fund
  (Gr)
  Galaxy II U.S. Treasury Index Fund
  (USGv)
  Galaxy II Utility Index Fund (IncE)

GAM Funds
135 East 57th St.
New York, NY 10022-2009
800/GAM-INTL
GAM Funds, Inc.
  GAM Asian Capital Fund (Intl)

GAMerica Capital Fund (Gr)
GAM Europe Fund (Intl)
GAM Global Fund (GloE)
GAM International Fund (Intl)
GAM Japan Capital Fund (Intl)
GAM North America Fund (GloE)
GAM Pacific Basin Fund (Intl)

Gannett Welsh & Kotler Funds
222 Berkeley St.
Boston, MA 02116
888/495-3863
Gannett Welsh & Kotler Funds
  GW&K Equity Fund (Gr&I)
  GW&K Government Securities Fund
  (USGv)

Gardner Lewis Trust
105 N. Washington St.
P.O. Drawer 69
Rocky Mount, NC 27802-0069
800/525-FUND
Gardner Lewis Investment Trust
  Chesapeake Fund (Gr)
  Chesapeake Growth Fund (Gr)

Gateway Funds
400 TechneCenter Dr.
Ste. 220
Milford, OH 45150-2746
800/354-6339
Gateway Trust (The)
  Cincinnati Fund (Gr)
  Gateway Index Plus Fund (Gr&I)
  Gateway Mid Cap Index Fund (Gr)
  Gateway Small Cap Index Fund
  (Gr)

GCG Funds
280 Park Ave.
14th Fl. West
New York, NY 10017-1216
800/243-3706
GCG Trust (The)
  All-Growth Series (Gr)
  Capital Appreciation Series (AgGr)
  Emerging Markets Series (Intl)
  Fully Managed Series (Flex)
  Fund For Life Series (Gr)
  Hard Assets Series (IncE)
  Limited Maturity Bond Series
  (IncB)
  Liquid Asset Series (MM)
  Managed Global Series (GloE)
  Market Manager Series (Gr&I)
  Multiple Allocation Series (Bal)
  Real Estate Series (Gr&I)
  Rising Dividends Series (IncE)
  Small Cap Series (AgGr)
  Strategic Equity Series (Gr)
  Value Equity Series (Gr)

GE Funds
3003 Summer St.
Stamford, CT 06905-4316
800/242-0134
GE Funds
  GE Fixed Income Fund (IncB)
  GE Global Equity Fund (GloE)
  GE International Equity Fund (Intl)
  GE Money Market Fund (MM)
  GE Premier Growth Equity Fund (Gr)
  GE Short-Term Government Bond Fund
    (USGv)
  GE Strategic Investment Fund (Flex)
  GE Tax-Exempt Income Fund (NMuB)
  GE U.S. Equity Fund (Gr&I)
GE Investments Funds, Inc.
  General Investments Global Income
    Portfolio (GloB)
  General Investments Government
    Securities Portfolio (USGv)
  General Investments International Equities
    Portfolio (Intl)
  General Investments Money Market
    Portfolio (MM)
  General Investments Real Estate
    Securities Portfolio (IncE)
  General Investments S&P 500 Index
    Portfolio (Gr&I)
  General Investments Total Return
    Portfolio (Gr&I)
  General Investments Value Equity
    Portfolio (AgGr)
General Electric S&S Long Term Interest
  Fund (IncB)
General Electric S&S Program Mutual
  Fund (Gr&I)

General Securities Fund
5100 Eden Ave. So., Ste. 204
Edina, MN 55436
800/577-9217
General Securities, Incorporated (Gr&I)

Golden Oak Family of Funds
One Freedom Valley Drive
Oaks, PA 19456
800/545-6331
Golden Oak Family of Funds
  Golden Oak Growth Portfolio (Gr&I)
  Intermediate-Term Income Portfolio
    (IncB)
  Prime Obligation Money Market Portfolio
    (MM)

Goldman Sachs Funds
4900 Sears Twr.
Chicago, IL 60606-6391
800/621-2550
Goldman Sachs Equity Portfolios, Inc.
  GS Asia Growth Fund (Intl)
  GS Balanced Fund (Bal)

  GS Capital Growth Fund (Gr)
  GS CORE U.S. Equity Fund (Gr)
  GS Growth and Income Fund (Gr&I)
  GS International Equity Fund (Intl)
  GS Small Cap Equity Fund (AgGr)
Goldman Sachs Trust GS Adjustable Rate
  Government Fund (GNMA)
  GS CORE Fixed Income Fund (IncM)
  GS Global Income Fund (GloB)
  GS Government Income Fund (USGv)
  GS Mid Cap Fund (Gr&I)
  GS Municipal Income Fund (NMuB)
  GS Short Duration Government Fund
    (USGv)
  GS Short Duration Tax-Free Fund
    (NMuB)

Goldman Sachs Money Market Trust
32 Old Slip
New York, NY 10005
212/902-0800
Goldman Sachs—Institutional Liquid Assets
  Federal Portfolio (MM)
  Government Portfolio (MM)
  Money Market Portfolio (MM)
  Prime Obligations Portfolio (MM)
  Tax-Exempt California Money Market
    Portfolio (SMMX)
  Tax-Exempt Diversified Portfolio
    (NMMX)
  Tax-Exempt New York Portfolio
    (SMMX)
  Treasury Instruments Portfolio (MM)
  Treasury Obligations Portfolio (MM)

Govett Funds
250 Montgomery St.
Ste. 1200
San Francisco, CA 94104
800/634-6838
Govett Funds, Inc. (The)
  Govett Emerging Markets Fund (Intl)
  Govett Global Income Fund (GloB)
  Govett International Equity Fund (Intl)
  Govett Latin America Fund (Intl)
  Govett Pacific Strategy Fund (Intl)
  Govett Smaller Companies Fund (AgGr)

Gradison Mutual Funds
580 Walnut St.
Cincinnati, OH 45202-3110
800/869-5999
Gradison Custodian Trust
  Gradison Government Income Fund
    (USGv)
Gradison Growth Trust
  Gradison Established Value Fund (Gr)
  Gradison Growth and Income Fund
    (Gr&I)
  Gradison International Fund (Intl)
  Gradison Opportunity Value Fund (Gr)

Gradison-McDonald Cash Reserves Trust
  Gradison U.S. Government Reserves
  (MM)
Gradison-McDonald Municipal Custodian
  Trust
  Gradison Ohio Tax-Free Income Fund
  (SMuB)

GrandView Trust
105 N. Washington St.
P.O. Drawer 69
Rocky Mount, NC 27802-0069
800/525-FUND
GrandView Trust
  GrandView Realty Growth Fund (AgGr)
  GrandView REIT Index Fund (GNMA)

Great Hall Investment Funds
60 S. Sixth St.
Ste. 2000
Minneapolis, MN 55402-4400
800/934-6674
Great Hall Investment Funds, Inc.
  Prime Money Market Fund (MM)
  Tax-Free Money Market Fund (NMMX)
  U.S. Government Money Market Fund
  (MM)

Green Century Funds
29 Temple Pl.
Ste. 200
Boston, MA 02111-1350
800/93-GREEN
Green Century Funds
  Balanced Fund (Bal)
  Growth Fund (Gr&I)

Greenspring Fund
2330 Joppa Rd.
Ste. 110
Lutherville, MD 21093-4609
800/366-3863
Greenspring Fund, Incorporated (Bal)

Griffin Funds
5000 Rivergrade Rd.
Irwindale, CA 91706
800/676-4450
Griffin Funds (The)
  Griffin Bond Fund (CorB)
  Griffin California Tax-Free Fund
  (SMuB)
  Griffin Growth & Income Fund (Gr&I)
  Griffin Growth Fund (Gr)
  Griffin Money Market Fund (MM)
  Griffin Municipal Bond Fund (NMuB)
  Griffin Short-Term Bond Fund (IncB)
  Griffin Tax-Free Money Market Fund
  (NMMX)
  Griffin U.S. Government Income Fund
  (USGv)

Growth Fund of Washington
1101 Vermont Ave., NW
Ste. 600
Washington, DC 20005-3521
800/972-9274
Growth Fund of Washington, Inc. (The)
  (Gr)

GT Global Group of Funds
50 California St.
27th Fl.
San Francisco, CA 94111-4624
800/824-1580
GT Global Consumer Products and Services
  Fund (GloB)
GT Global Dollar Fund (MM)
GT Global Emerging Markets Fund (GloE)
GT Global Financial Services Fund (Intl)
GT Global Government Income Fund
  (GloB)
GT Global Growth & Income Fund (Bal)
GT Global Growth Series
  GT Global America Mid Cap Fund
  (GloB)
  GT Global America Small Cap Growth
  Fund (AgGr)
  GT Global America Value Fund (Gr)
  GT Global Europe Growth Fund (Intl)
  GT Global International Growth Fund
  (Intl)
  GT Global Japan Growth Fund (Intl)
  GT Global New Pacific Growth Fund
  (Intl)
  GT Global Worldwide Growth Fund
  (GloE)
GT Global Health Care Fund (GloE)
GT Global High Income Fund (GloB)
GT Global Infrastructure Fund (GloE)
GT Global Latin America Growth Fund
  (Intl)
GT Global Money Market Fund (MM)
GT Global Natural Resources Fund (GloE)
GT Global Strategic Income Fund (GloB)
GT Global Telecommunications Fund
  (GloE)
GT Global Variable America Fund (Gr)
GT Global Variable Emerging Markets
  Fund (GloE)
GT Global Variable Europe Fund (Intl)
GT Global Variable Global Government
  Income Fund (GloB)
GT Global Variable Growth and Income
  Fund (Bal)
GT Global Variable Infrastructure Fund
  (GloE)
GT Global Variable International Fund
  (Intl)
GT Global Variable Latin America Fund
  (Intl)
GT Global Variable Natural Resources Fund
  (GloE)

GT Global Variable New Pacific Fund (Intl)
GT Global Variable Strategic Income Fund
  (GloB)
GT Global Variable Telecommunications
  Fund (Gr)
GT Global Variable U.S. Government
  Income Fund (IncB)

Guinness Flight Investment Funds
225 S. Lake Ave., Ste. 777
Pasadena, CA 91101-3016
800/434-5623
Guinness Flight Investment Funds, Inc.
  Guinness Flight Asia Blue Chip Fund
    (Intl)
  Guinness Flight Asia Small Cap Fund
    (Intl)
  Guinness Flight China & Hong Kong
    Fund (Intl)
  Guinness Flight Global Government Bond
    Fund (GloB)

Hansberger Institutional Series
515 East Las Olas Blvd.
Ste. 1300
Fort Lauderdale, FL 33301
954/922-5150
Hansberger Institutional Series
  All Countries Fund (GloB)
  Emerging Markets Fund (Intl)
  Foreign Small Cap Fund (Intl)
  International Fund (GloB)

Harbor Funds
One SeaGate
Toledo, OH 43666-1000
800/422-1050
Harbor Fund
  Harbor Bond Fund (IncB)
  Harbor Capital Appreciation Fund (Gr)
  Harbor Growth Fund (Gr)
  Harbor International Fund (Intl)
  Harbor International Fund II (Intl)
  Harbor International Growth Fund (Intl)
  Harbor Money Market Fund (MM)
  Harbor Short Duration Fund (IncB)
  Harbor Value Fund (Gr&I)

Harris Insight Funds
One Exchange Pl.
Boston, MA 02109
800/982-8782
Harris Insight Funds
  Balanced Blended Fund (Bal)
  Bond Fund (IncB)
  Convertible Securities Fund (Gr&I)
  Equity Fund (Gr)
  Equity Income Fund (IncE)
  Government Money Market Fund (MM)
  Growth Fund (Gr)
  Index Fund (Gr)

Intermediate Government Bond Fund
  (USGv)
Intermediate Tax-Exempt Bond Fund
  (NMuB)
International Fund (Intl)
Money Market Fund (MM)
Short/Intermediate Bond Fund (IncB)
Small Cap Opportunity Fund (AgGr)
Small Cap Value Fund (AgGr)
Tax-Exempt Bond Fund (NMuB)
Tax-Exempt Money Market Fund
  (NMMX)

Hartford Funds
200 Hopmeadow St.
P.O. Box 2999
Hartford, CT 06104-2999
800/862-6668
Hartford Advisers Fund, Inc. (Flex)
Hartford Bond Fund, Inc. (IncB)
Hartford Capital Appreciation Fund, Inc.
  (Gr)
Hartford Dividend and Growth Fund, Inc.
  (Gr&I)
Hartford Index Fund, Inc. (Gr&I)
Hartford International Advisers Fund, Inc.
  (GloE)
Hartford International Opportunities Fund,
  Inc. (Intl)
Hartford Mortgage Securities Fund, Inc.
  (GNMA)
Hartford Stock Fund, Inc. (Gr)
Hartford U.S. Government Money Market
  Fund, Inc. (MM)
HVA Money Market Fund, Inc. (MM)

Hawthorne Investment Trust
One Lewis Wharf
Boston, MA 02110-3902
800/272-4548
Hawthorne Investment Trust
  Hawthorne Bond Fund (IncB)
  Hawthorne Sea Fund (Gr)

Heartland Group
790 N. Milwaukee St.
Milwaukee, WI 53202-3712
800/432-7856
Heartland Group
  Heartland High Yield Municipal Bond
    Fund (HiYB)
  Heartland Large Cap Value Fund
    (Gr&I)
  Heartland Mid Cap Value Fund (Gr&I)
  Hearland Short Duration High Yield
    Municipal Bond Fund (HiYB)
  Heartland Small Cap Contrarian Fund
    (AgGr)
  Heartland U.S. Government Securities
    Fund (USGv)
  Heartland Value Fund (AgGr)

Heartland Value Plus Fund (Gr&I)
Heartland Wisconsin Tax Free Fund
(SMuB)

Heitman Funds
180 N. LaSalle St.
Ste. 3600
Chicago, IL 60601
800/435-1405
Heitman Securities Trust
  Heitman Real Estate Fund (Gr&I)

Henlopen Fund
415 McFarlan Rd.
Ste. 213
Kennett Square, PA 19348
610/925-0400
Henlopen Fund (The) (Gr)

Heritage Funds
880 Carillon Pkwy.
St. Petersburg, FL 33716-1102
800/421-4184
Heritage Capital Appreciation Trust (Gr)
Heritage Cash Trust
  Money Market Fund (MM)
  Municipal Money Market Fund (NMMX)
Heritage Income-Growth Trust (Gr&I)
  Heritage Income Trust
  High Yield Bond Portfolio (HiYB)
  Intermediate Government Fund (USGv)
Heritage Series Trust
  Heritage Eagle International Equity Fund
    (Intl)
  Heritage Growth Equity Fund (Gr)
  Heritage Value Equity Fund (Gr)
  Small Cap Stock Fund (AgGr)

HighMark Group of Funds
One Freedom Valley Drive
Oaks, PA 19456
800/433-6884
HighMark Funds
  HighMark Balanced Fund (Bal)
  HighMark Blue Chip Growth Fund (Gr)
  HighMark Bond Fund (IncB)
  HighMark California Tax-Free Money
    Market Fund (SMMX)
  HighMark Convertible Securities Fund
    (CorB)
  HighMark Diversified Money Market
    Fund (MM)
  HighMark Emerging Growth Fund (Gr)
  HighMark Government Securities Fund
    (USGv)
  HighMark Growth Fund (Gr)
  HighMark Income Equity Fund (IncE)
  HighMark Intermediate California Tax
    Free Bond Fund (SMuB)
  HighMark Intermediate Term Bond Fund
    (CorB)

HighMark International Equity Fund
  (GloE)
HighMark 100% U.S. Treasury Money
  Market Fund (MM)
HighMark U.S. Government Money
  Market Fund (MM)
HighMark Value Momentum Fund (Gr&I)

Hilliard-Lyons Funds
55 E. Monroe St.
Ste. 3800
Chicago, IL 60603-5802
800/338-8214
Hilliard-Lyons Government Fund Inc. (MM)
Hilliard Lyons Growth Fund, Inc. (Gr)

HomeState Group Trust
1857 William Penn Way
P.O.Box 10666
Lancaster, PA 17601-6741
800/232-0224
HomeState Group Trust (The)
  HomeState Pennsylvania Growth Fund
    (Gr)
  HomeState Select Opportunities Fund
    (AgGr)

Homestead Funds, Inc.
4301 Wilson Blvd.
RSI8-305
Arlington, VA 22203-1860
800/258-3030
Homestead Funds, Inc.
  Daily Income Fund (MM)
  Short Term Bond Fund (IncB)
  Short-Term Government Securities Fund
    (USGv)
  Value Fund (Gr&I)

Horace Mann Mutual Funds
One Horace Mann Plaza
P.O. Box 4657
Springfield, IL 62708-4657
800/999-1030
Horace Mann Balanced Fund (Bal)
Horace Mann Growth Fund (Gr&I)
Horace Mann Income Fund (IncB)
Horace Mann International Equity Fund
  (Intl)
Horace Mann Short-Term Investment Fund
  (GNMA)
Horace Mann Small Cap Growth Fund
  (AgGr)

Hospital & Health Facilities Trust
905 Marconi Ave.
Ronkonkoma, NY 11779-7211
800/221-4524
Hospital & Health Facilities Trust
  California Hospital & Health Facilities
    Liquid Asset Fund (MM)

Hotchkis and Wiley Funds
800 W. Sixth St.
5th Fl.
Los Angeles, CA 90017-2704
800/236-4479
Hotchkis and Wiley Funds
  Balanced Income Fund (Bal)
  Equity Income Fund (IncE)
  Global Equity Fund (GloE)
  International Fund (Intl)
  Low Duration Fund (IncB)
  Mid-Cap Fund (Gr&I)
  Short Term Investment Fund (IncB)
  Small Cap Fund (AgGr)
  Total Return Bond Fund (IncM)

Hough Group of Funds
100 Second Ave. South
Ste. 800
St. Petersburg, FL 33701-4337
800/557-7555
Hough Group of Funds (The)
  Florida TaxFree Money Market Fund
  (SMMX)
  Florida TaxFree ShortTerm Fund (SMuB)

HSBC Funds
3435 Stelzer Rd.
Columbus, OH 43219
800/634-2536
HSBC Funds Trust
  HSBC Cash Management Fund (MM)
  HSBC Government Money Market Fund
  (MM)
  HSBC New York Tax-Free Money Market
  Fund (SMMX)
  HSBC U.S. Treasury Money Market Fund
  (MM)
HSBC Mutual Funds Trust
  HSBC Fixed Income Fund (CorB)
  HSBC Growth & Income Fund (Gr&I)
  HSBC International Equity Fund (Intl)
  HSBC New York Tax Free Bond Fund
  (SMuB)
  HSBC Small Cap Fund (AgGr)

Hudson Investors Fund, Inc.
50 Mt. Prospect Ave.
P.O. Box 2070
Clifton, NJ 07013
800/HUDSON-4
Hudson Investors Fund Inc. (Gr)

Hudson River Trust
1345 Avenue of the Americas
New York, NY 10105-0302
800/221-5672
Hudson River Trust (The)
  Alliance Aggressive Stock Portfolio
  (AgGr)
  Alliance Balanced Portfolio (Bal)

Alliance Common Stock Portfolio
  (Gr)
Alliance Conservative Investors Portfolio
  (IncM)
Alliance Equity Index Portfolio (Gr&I)
Alliance Global Portfolio (GloE)
Alliance Growth and Income Portfolio
  (Gr&I)
Alliance Growth Investors Portfolio
  (IncM)
Alliance High Yield Portfolio (HiYB)
Alliance Intermediate Government
  Securities Portfolio (USGv)
Alliance International Portfolio (Intl)
Alliance Money Market Portfolio
  (MM)
Alliance Quality Bond Portfolio (CorB)
Alliance Small Cap Growth Portfolio
  (AgGr)

IAA Trust Mutual Funds
808 IAA Dr.
Bloomington, IL 61701-2220
800/245-2100
IAA Trust Asset Allocations Fund, Inc.
  (Gr&I)
IAA Trust Growth, Inc. (Gr)
IAA Trust Taxable Fixed Income Series
  Fund, Inc. (MM)
IAA Trust Tax Exempt Bond Fund, Inc.
  (NMuB)

IAI Family of Funds
601 Second Ave. S.
P.O. Box 357
Minneapolis, MN 55402-4303
800/945-3863
IAI Investment Funds I, Inc.
  IAI Bond Fund (IncB)
  IAI Institutional Bond Fund (IncB)
IAI Investment Funds II, Inc.
  IAI Growth Fund (Gr)
IAI Investment Funds III, Inc.
  IAI Developing Countries Fund (Intl)
  IAI International Fund (Intl)
  IAI Latin American Fund (Intl)
IAI Investment Funds IV, Inc.
  IAI Regional Fund (Gr)
IAI Investment Funds V, Inc.
  IAI Reserve Fund (IncB)
IAI Investment Funds VI, Inc.
  IAI Balanced Fund (Bal)
  IAI Capital Appreciation Fund (AgGr)
  IAI Emerging Growth Fund (AgGr)
  IAI Government Fund (USGv)
  IAI MidCap Growth Fund (Gr)
  IAI Money Market Fund (MM)
IAI Investment Funds VII, Inc.
  IAI Growth & Income Fund (Gr&I)
IAI Investment Funds VIII, Inc.
  IAI Value Fund (Gr)

ICON Funds
12835 E. Arapahoe Rd.
Tower II—Penthouse
Englewood, CO 80112
800/828-4881
ICON Funds
  ICON Basic Materials Fund (AgGr)
  ICON Capital Goods Fund (AgGr)
  ICON Consumer Cyclicals Fund (AgGr)
  ICON Consumer Staples Fund (AgGr)
  ICON Energy Fund (AgGr)
  ICON Financial Services Fund (AgGr)
  ICON Healthcare Fund (AgGr)
  ICON Leisure Fund (AgGr)
  ICON North Asia Region Fund (Intl)
  ICON North Europe Region Fund (Intl)
  ICON Short-Term Fixed Income Fund
    (IncB)
  ICON South Asia Region Fund (Intl)
  ICON South Europe Region Fund (Intl)
  ICON Technology Fund (AgGr)
  ICON Telecommunication & Utilities
    Fund (AgGr)
  ICON Transportation Fund (AgGr)
  ICON Western Hemisphere Fund (Intl)

IDEX Mutual Funds
201 Highland Ave.
Largo, FL 34640-2512
800/851-9777
IDEX Series Fund
  Aggressive Growth Portfolio (Gr)
  Balanced Portfolio (Gr&I)
  Capital Appreciation Portfolio (Gr)
  C.A.S.E Portfolio (Gr)
  Flexible Income Portfolio (IncB)
  Global Portfolio (GloE)
  IDEX Growth Portfolio (Gr)
  Income Plus Portfolio (HiYB)
  International Equity Portfolio (Intl)
  Strategic Total Return Portfolio (IncE)
  Tactical Asset Allocation Fund (Bal)
  Tax-Exempt Portfolio (NMuB)
  Value Equity Portfolio (Gr)

IDS Mutual Fund Group
901 Marquette Ave. S.
Ste. 2810
Minneapolis, MN 55402-3268
800/328-8300
IDS Bond Fund, Inc. (CorB)
IDS California Tax-Exempt Trust
  IDS California Tax-Exempt Fund (SMuB)
IDS Discovery Fund, Inc. (AgGr)
IDS Equity Select Fund, Inc. (Gr&I)
IDS Extra Income Fund, Inc. (HiYB)
IDS Federal Income Fund, Inc. (USGv)
IDS Global Series, Inc.
  IDS Global Bond Fund (GloB)
  IDS Global Growth Fund (GloE)
IDS Growth Fund, Inc.

IDS Growth Fund (Gr)
IDS Research Opportunities Fund (Gr)
IDS High Yield Tax-Exempt Fund, Inc.
  (NMuB)
IDS International Fund, Inc. (Intl)
IDS Investment Series, Inc.
  IDS Diversified Equity Income Fund
    (IncE)
  IDS Mutual (Bal)
IDS Life Investment Series, Inc.
  IDS Life Aggressive Growth Fund (AgGr)
  IDS Life Capital Resource Fund (Gr)
  IDS Life Growth Dimensions Fund (Gr)
  IDS Life International Equity Fund (Intl)
IDS Life Managed Fund, Inc. (Gr&I)
IDS Life Moneyshare Fund, Inc. (MM)
IDS Life Special Income Fund, Inc.
  IDS Life Global Yield Fund (GloB)
  IDS Life Income Advantage Fund (HiYB)
  IDS Life Special Income Fund (IncB)
IDS Managed Retirement Fund, Inc. (Flex)
IDS Market Advantage Series, Inc.
  IDS Blue Chip Advantage Fund (Gr&I)
  IDS Small Company Index Fund (AgGr)
IDS MoneyMarket Series, Inc.
  IDS Cash Management Fund (MM)
IDS New Dimensions Fund, Inc. (Gr)
IDS Precious Metals Fund, Inc. (PM/G)
IDS Progressive Fund, Inc. (AgGr)
IDS Selective Fund, Inc. (CorB)
IDS Special Tax-Exempt Series Trust
  IDS Insured Tax-Exempt Fund (NMuB)
  IDS Massachusetts Tax-Exempt Fund
    (SMuB)
  IDS Michigan Tax-Exempt Fund (SMuB)
  IDS Minnesota Tax-Exempt Fund (SMuB)
  IDS New York Tax-Exempt Fund (SMuB)
  IDS Ohio Tax-Exempt Fund (SMuB)
IDS Stock Fund, Inc. (Gr&I)
IDS Strategy Fund, Inc.
  IDS Equity Value Fund (Gr&I)
  IDS Strategy Aggressive Fund (AgGr)
IDS Tax-Exempt Bond Fund, Inc. (NMuB)
IDS Tax-Free Money Fund, Inc. (NMMX)
IDS Utilities Income Fund, Inc. (IncE)

Independence Capital Group of Funds
600 Dresher Rd.
Horsham, PA 19044
800/818-8184
Penn Series Funds, Inc.
  Emerging Growth Fund (AgGr)
  Growth Equity Fund (Gr)
  Money Market Fund (MM)
  Quality Bond Fund (IncB)
Penn Series Funds, Inc.
  Small Capitalization Fund (AgGr)
  Value Equity Fund (Gr&I)
Penn Series Funds, Inc.
  Flexibly Managed Fund (Bal)
  High Yield Bond Fund (HiYB)

Penn Series Funds, Inc.
  International Equity Fund (GloE)

Independence One Funds
Federated Investors Twr.
1001 Liberty Ave.
Pittsburgh, PA 15222-3779
800/341-7400
Independence One Mutual Funds
  Independence One Equity Plus Fund
  (Gr&I)
  Independence One Fixed Income Fund
  (IncB)
  Independence One Michigan Municipal
  Bond Fund (SMuB)
  Independence One Michigan Municipal
  Cash Fund (SMMX)
  Independence One Prime Money Market
  Fund (MM)
  Independence One U.S. Government
  Securities Fund (USGv)
  Independence One U.S. Treasury Money
  Market Fund (MM)

Infinity Mutual Funds
3435 Stelzer Rd.
Columbus, OH 43219-3035
800/852-0045
Infinity Mutual Funds, Inc. (The)
  Alpha Government Securities Portfolio
  (MM)
Infinity Mutual Funds, Inc. (The)
  Correspondent Cash Reserves Money
  Market Portfolio (MM)
Infinity Mutual Funds, Inc. (The)
  AmeriStar Capital Growth Portfolio (Gr)
  AmeriStar Core Income Portfolio (IncB)
  AmeriStar Dividend Growth Portfolio
  (Gr&I)
  AmeriStar Limited Duration Income
  Portfolio (IncB)
  AmeriStar Limited Duration Tennessee
  Tax Free Portfolio (SMuB)
  AmeriStar Limited Duration U.S.
  Government Portfolio (USGv)
  AmeriStar Prime Money Market Portfolio
  (MM)
  AmeriStar Tennessee Tax-Exempt Bond
  Portfolio (SMuB)
  AmeriStar U.S. Treasury Money Market
  Portfolio (MM)

Integrity Mutual Funds
1 North Main St.
Minot, ND 58703
800/56-BONDS
Integrity Fund of Funds, Inc. (Gr)
Montana Tax Free Fund, Inc. (SMuB)
ND Insured Income Fund, Inc. (IncB)
ND Tax-Free Fund, Inc. (SMuB)
Ranson Managed Portfolios

Kansas Insured Intermediate Fund
  (SMuB)
Kansas Municipal Fund (SMuB)
Nebraska Municipal Fund (SMuB)
Oklahoma Municipal Fund (SMuB)
South Dakota Tax-Free Fund, Inc. (SMuB)

Interactive Investments
446 Martil Way
Milpitas, CA 95035
888/883-3863
Interactive Investments Trust
  Technology Value Fund (Gr)

INVESCO Funds Group
7800 E. Union Ave.
Denver, CO 80237-2752
800/525-8085
INVESCO Advisor Funds, Inc.
  Cash Management Fund (MM)
  Equity Fund (Gr&I)
  Flex Fund (Flex)
  Income Fund (IncB)
  International Value Fund (Intl)
  MultiFlex Fund (Flex)
  Real Estate Fund (Gr&I)
INVESCO Diversified Funds
  INVESCO Small Company Value Fund
  (AgGr)
INVESCO Dynamics Fund (AgGr)
INVESCO Emerging Opportunity Funds
  INVESCO Small Company Growth Fund
  (AgGr)
INVESCO Growth Fund (Gr)
INVESCO Income Funds
  High Yield Fund (HiYB)
  Select Income Fund (IncB)
  Short-Term Bond Fund (IncB)
  U.S. Government Fund (USGv)
INVESCO Industrial Income Fund (Bal)
INVESCO International Fund
  European Fund (Intl)
  International Growth Fund (Intl)
  Pacific Basin Fund (Intl)
INVESCO Money Market Funds
  Cash Reserves Fund (MM)
  Tax Free Money Fund (NMMX)
  U.S. Government Money Fund (MM)
INVESCO Multiple Asset Funds
  INVESCO Balanced Fund (Bal)
  INVESCO Multi-Asset Allocation Fund
  (Bal)
INVESCO Specialty Funds, Inc.
  Asian Growth Fund (Intl)
  Euro Small Company Fund (Intl)
  Latin American Growth Fund (Intl)
  Realty Fund (IncE)
  Worldwide Capital Goods Fund (Intl)
  Worldwide Communications Fund (Intl)
INVESCO Strategic Portfolios
  Energy Portfolio (AgGr)

Environmental Services Portfolio (AgGr)
Financial Services Portfolio (AgGr)
Gold Portfolio (PM/G)
Health Sciences Portfolio (AgGr)
Leisure Portfolio (AgGr)
Technology Portfolio (AgGr)
Utilities Portfolio (Gr&I)
INVESCO Tax Free Income Funds
Tax-Free Intermediate Bond Fund
(NMuB)
Tax Free Long Term Bond Fund (NMuB)
INVESCO Treasurers Series Trust
Money Market Reserve Fund (MM)
Tax-Exempt Fund (NMMX)
INVESCO Value Trust
Intermediate Government Bond Fund
(USGv)
Total Return Fund (Flex)
Value Equity Fund (IncE)

Investors Research Fund, Inc.
3757 State St.
Ste. 204
Santa Barbara, CA 93105
800/473-8631
Investors Research Fund, Inc. (Gr)

Investors Trust
601 Union St.
Ste. 5600
Seattle, WA 98101-2336
800/426-5520
Investors Trust
Adjustable Rate Fund (GNMA)
Government Fund (USGv)
Growth Fund (Gr)
Tax Free Fund (NMuB)
Value Fund (Gr&I)

IPS Funds
625 S. Gay St.
Ste. 630
Knoxville, TN 37902
800/232-9142
IPS Funds
IPS Millennium Fund (Gr&I)

Ivy Mackenzie Group of Funds
700 S. Federal Hwy., Ste. 300
P.O. Box 5007
Boca Raton, FL 33432
800/456-5111
Ivy Fund
Ivy Asia Pacific Fund (Intl)
Ivy Bond Fund (CorB)
Ivy Canada Fund (Intl)
Ivy China Region Fund (Intl)
Ivy Emerging Growth Fund (AgGr)
Ivy Global Fund (GloE)
Ivy Global Natural Resources Fund
(GloE)

Ivy Global Science & Technology Fund
(GloE)
Ivy Growth Fund (Gr)
Ivy Growth with Income Fund (Gr)
Ivy International Fund (Intl)
Ivy International Fund II (Intl)
Ivy International Small Companies Fund
(Intl)
Ivy Latin America Strategy Fund (Intl)
Ivy Money Market Fund (MM)
Ivy New Century Fund (Intl)
Ivy Pan-Europe Fund (Intl)
Mackenzie Series Trust
Mackenzie California Municipal Fund
(SMuB)
Mackenzie Limited Term Municipal Fund
(NMuB)
Mackenzie National Municipal Fund
(NMuB)
Mackenzie New York Municipal Fund
(SMuB)

Janus
100 Fillmore St.
Ste. 300
Denver, CO 80206-4923
800/525-8983
Janus Investment Fund
Janus Balanced Fund (Bal)
Janus Enterprise Fund (Gr)
Janus Equity Income Fund (IncE)
Janus Federal Tax Exempt Fund (NMuB)
Janus Flexible Income Fund (IncB)
Janus Fund (Gr)
Janus Government Money Market Fund
(MM)
Janus Growth and Income Fund (Gr&I)
Janus High-Yield Fund (HiYB)
Janus Mercury Fund (AgGr)
Janus Money Market Fund (MM)
Janus Olympus Fund (AgGr)
Janus Overseas Fund (Intl)
Janus Short-Term Bond Fund (IncB)
Janus Special Situations Fund (Gr)
Janus Tax-Exempt Money Market Fund
(NMMX)
Janus Twenty Fund (Gr)
Janus Venture Fund (AgGr)
Janus Worldwide Fund (GloE)

Jefferson Fund Group Trust
839 N. Jefferson St., Ste. 200
Milwaukee, WI 53202
800/871-3863
Jefferson Fund Group Trust
Jefferson Growth and Income Fund (Flex)

Jensen Portfolio, Inc.
430 Pioneer Twr.
888 SW Fifth Ave.
Portland, OR 97204-2018

800/221-4384
Jensen Portfolio, Inc. (The) (Gr&I)

JNL Series Trust
5901 Executive Dr.
P.O. Box 25127
Lansing, MI 48909-9979
800/322-8257
JNL Series Trust
  JNL Aggressive Growth Series (AgGr)
  JNL/Alger Growth Series (Gr)
  JNL Capital Growth Series (Gr)
  JNL/Eagle Core Equity Series (Gr)
  JNL/Eagle SmallCap Equity Series
  (AgGr)
  JNL Global Equities Series (GloE)
  JNL/Phoenix Investment Counsel
  Balanced Series (Bal)
  JNL/Putnam Growth Series (Gr)
  PPM America/JNL High Yield Bond
  Series (HiYB)
  PPM America/JNL Money Market Series
  (MM)
  PPM America/JNL Value Equity Series
  (Gr&I)
  Salomon Brothers/JNL Global Bond
  Series (GloB)
  Salomon Brothers/JNL U.S. Government
  & Quality Bond Series (USGv)
  T. Rowe Price/JNL Established Growth
  Series (Gr&I)
  T. Rowe Price/JNL International Equity
  Investment Series (Intl)
  T. Rowe Price/JNL Mid-Cap Growth
  Series (Gr)

John Hancock Funds
101 Huntington Ave.
Boston, MA 02199-7603
800/225-5291
Freedom Investment Trust
  John Hancock Disciplined Growth Fund
  (Gr)
  John Hancock Regional Bank Fund (Gr)
  John Hancock Sovereign U.S.
  Government Income Fund (USGv)
Freedom Investment Trust II
  John Hancock Global Fund (GloE)
  John Hancock International Fund (Intl)
  John Hancock Short-Term Strategic
  Income Fund (GloB)
  John Hancock Special Opportunities Fund
  (Gr)
  John Hancock World Bond Fund (GloB)
Freedom Investment Trust III
  John Hancock Discovery Fund (Gr)
John Hancock Bond Fund
  John Hancock Intermediate Maturity
  Government Trust (GNMA)
John Hancock California Tax-Free Income
  Fund (SMuB)

John Hancock Capital Series
  John Hancock Growth Fund (Gr)
  John Hancock Special Value Fund (Gr&I)
John Hancock Cash Management Fund
  (MM)
John Hancock Cash Reserve, Inc. (MM)
John Hancock Current Interest
  John Hancock U.S. Government Cash
  Reserve (MM)
John Hancock Institutional Series Trust
  John Hancock Active Bond Fund (IncB)
  John Hancock Dividend Performers Fund
  (Gr)
  John Hancock Fundamental Value Fund
  (Gr&I)
  John Hancock Global Bond Fund (GloB)
  John Hancock Independence Balanced
  Fund (Bal)
  John Hancock Independence Diversified
  Core Equity Fund II (Gr&I)
  John Hancock Independence Growth Fund
  (Gr)
  John Hancock Independence Medium
  Capitalization Fund (Gr)
  John Hancock Independence Value Fund
  (Gr&I)
  John Hancock International Growth Fund
  (Intl)
  John Hancock Multi-Sector Opportunity
  Fund (AgGr)
John Hancock Investment Trust
  John Hancock Growth and Income Fund
  (Gr&I)
John Hancock Investment Trust II
  John Hancock Financial Industries Fund
  (AgGr)
  John Hancock Limited Term Government
  Fund (USGv)
John Hancock Series, Inc.
  John Hancock Emerging Growth Fund
  (AgGr)
  John Hancock Government Income Fund
  (USGv)
  John Hancock High Yield Bond Fund
  (HiYB)
  John Hancock High Yield Tax Free Fund
  (NMuB)
  John Hancock Money Market Fund (MM)
John Hancock Sovereign Bond Fund
  (CorB)
John Hancock Sovereign Investors Fund,
  Inc.
  John Hancock Sovereign Balanced Fund
  (Bal)
  John Hancock Sovereign Investors Fund,
  Inc. (Gr&I)
John Hancock Special Equities Fund
  (AgGr)
John Hancock Strategic Series
  John Hancock Independence Equity Fund
  (Gr&I)

John Hancock Strategic Income Fund
(IncB)
John Hancock Utilities Fund (IncE)
John Hancock Tax-Exempt Series Fund
  Massachusetts Portfolio (SMuB)
  New York Portfolio (SMuB)
John Hancock Tax-Free Bond Fund
(NMuB)
John Hancock Technology Series, Inc.
  John Hancock Global Technology Fund
  (GloE)
John Hancock World Fund
  John Hancock Global Marketplace Fund
  (GloE)
  John Hancock Global RX Fund (GloE)
  John Hancock Pacific Basin Equities Fund
  (GloE)

Johnson Mutual Funds
5556 Cheviot Rd.
Cincinnati, OH 45247-7094
800/541-0170
Johnson Mutual Funds Trust
  Fixed Income Fund (IncM)
  Growth Fund (Gr)
  Municipal Income Fund (NMuB)
  Opportunity Fund (AgGr)

JPM Institutional Funds
522 Fifth Ave.
11th Fl.
New York, NY 10036
800/766-7722
JPM Institutional Funds (The)
  JPM Institutional Asia Growth Fund
  (Intl)
  JPM Institutional Bond Fund (IncB)
  JPM Institutional Disciplined Equity Fund
  (Gr)
  JPM Institutional Diversified Fund (Bal)
  JPM Institutional Emerging Markets
  Equity Fund (Intl)
  JPM Institutional European Equity Fund
  (Intl)
  JPM Institutional Federal Money Market
  Fund (MM)
  JPM Institutional Global Strategic Income
  Fund (GloB)
  JPM Institutional International Bond Fund
  (Intl)
  JPM Institutional International
  Opportunities Fund (Intl)
  JPM Institutional Japan Equity Fund (Intl)
  JPM Institutional Money Market Fund
  (MM)
  JPM Institutional New York Total Return
  Bond Fund (SMuB)
  JPM Institutional Non-U.S. Equity Fund
  (Intl)
  JPM Institutional Selected U.S. Equity
  Fund (Gr)

JPM Institutional Short Term Bond Fund
(IncB)
JPM Institutional Tax Exempt Bond Fund
(NMuB)
JPM Institutional Tax Exempt Money
  Market Fund (NMMX)
JPM Institutional U.S. Small Company
  Fund (Gr)

JPM Pierpont Funds
522 Fifth Ave.
11th Fl.
New York, NY 10036
800/766-7722
JPM Pierpont Funds (The)
  JPM Pierpont Asia Growth Fund (Intl)
  JPM Pierpont Bond Fund (IncB)
  JPM Pierpont Capital Appreciation Fund
  (AgGr)
  JPM Pierpont Diversified Fund (Bal)
  JPM Pierpont Emerging Markets Debt
  Fund (GloB)
  JPM Pierpont Emerging Markets Equity
  Fund (Intl)
  JPM Pierpont Equity Fund (Gr)
  JPM Pierpont European Equity Fund (Intl)
  JPM Pierpont Federal Money Market
  Fund (MM)
  JPM Pierpont International Opportunities
  Fund (Intl)
  JPM Pierpont Japan Equity Fund (Intl)
  JPM Pierpont Money Market Fund (MM)
  JPM Pierpont New York Total Return
  Bond Fund (SMuB)
  JPM Pierpont Non-U.S. Equity Fund
  (Intl)
  JPM Pierpont Short Term Bond Fund
  (IncB)
  JPM Pierpont Tax Exempt Bond Fund
  (NMuB)
  JPM Pierpont Tax Exempt Money Market
  Fund (NMMX)

JPM Series Trust
522 Fifth Ave.
11th Fl.
New York, NY 10036
800/766-7722
JPM Series Trust
  JPM Institutional Shares: California Bond
  Fund (SMuB)
  JPM Pierpont Shares: Tax Aware
  Disciplined Equity Fund (Gr&I)
  JPM Pierpont Shares: Tax Aware Equity
  Fund (Gr&I)

JPM Series Trust II
522 Fifth Ave.
11th Fl.
New York, NY 10036
800/766-7722

JPM Series Trust II
JPM Bond Portfolio (IncB)
JPM Equity Portfolio (Gr)
JPM International Equity Portfolio (Intl)
JPM Small Company Portfolio (AgGr)
JPM Treasury Money Market Portfolio
(MM)

Jurika & Voyles Fund Group
1999 Harrison
Ste. 700
Oakland, CA 94612-3517
800/852-1991
Jurika & Voyles Fund Group
Jurika & Voyles Balanced Fund (Bal)
Jurika & Voyles Mini-Cap Fund (Gr&I)
Jurika & Voyles Value + Growth Fund
(Gr)

Kaufmann Fund
140 East 45th St.
43rd Fl.
New York, NY 10017
212/922-0123
Kaufmann Fund, Inc. (The) (AgGr)

Kenilworth Fund, Inc.
One First National Plaza
Ste. 2594
Chicago, IL 60603
312/236-5388
Kenilworth Fund, Inc. (Flex)

Kent Funds
P.O. Box 182201
Columbus, OH 43218-2201
800/633-KENT
Kent Funds (The)
Kent Growth and Income Fund (Gr&I)
Kent Income Fund (IncB)
Kent Index Equity Fund (Gr)
Kent Intermediate Bond Fund (IncB)
Kent Intermediate Tax-Free Fund (NMuB)
Kent International Growth Fund (Intl)
Kent Limited Term Tax-Free Fund
(NMuB)
Kent Michigan Municipal Bond Fund
(SMuB)
Kent Michigan Municipal Money Market
Fund (SMMX)
Kent Money Market Fund (MM)
Kent Short-Term Bond Fund (IncB)
Kent Small Company Growth Fund
(AgGr)
Kent Tax-Free Income Fund (NMuB)

Kenwood Funds
c/o Firstar Trust Co.
615 E. Michigan St.
Milwaukee, WI 53202
800/536-3863

Kenwood Funds (The)
Kenwood Growth and Income Fund
(Gr&I)

Key Funds
3435 Stelzer Rd.
Columbus, OH 43219-3035
800/539-3863
Key Mutual Funds
Key Capital Growth Fund (Gr)
Key Convertible Securities Fund (Gr&I)
Key International Index Fund (Intl)
Key Money Market Mutual Fund (MM)
Key SBSF Fund (Gr)
Key Stock Index Fund (Gr&I)

Keystone Family of Funds
200 Berkeley St.
Boston, MA 02116-5034
800/343-2898
Hartwell Emerging Growth Fund (AgGr)
Keystone America California Tax-Free
Fund (SMuB)
Keystone America Capital Preservation and
Income Fund (USGv)
Keystone America Florida Tax Free Fund
(SMuB)
Keystone America Fund for Total Return
(IncE)
Keystone America Fund of the Americas
(Intl)
Keystone America Global Opportunities
Fund (GloE)
Keystone America Global Resources and
Development Fund (GloE)
Keystone America Government Securities
Fund (USGv)
Keystone America Intermediate Term Bond
Fund (CorB)
Keystone America Massachusetts Tax Free
Fund (SMuB)
Keystone America Missouri Tax Free Fund
(SMuB)
Keystone America New York Tax-Free
Fund (SMuB)
Keystone America Omega Fund (AgGr)
Keystone America Pennsylvania Tax Free
Fund (SMuB)
Keystone America Strategic Income Fund
(HiYB)
Keystone America Tax Free Income Fund
(NMuB)
Keystone America World Bond Fund
(GloB)
Keystone Balanced Fund (K-1) (IncE)
Keystone Balanced Fund II (AgGr)
Keystone Diversified Bond Fund (B-2)
(CorB)
Keystone Growth and Income Fund (S-1)
(Gr&I)
Keystone High Income Fund (B-4) (HiYB)

Keystone Institutional Adjustable Rate Fund
  (GNMA)
Keystone Institutional Small Cap Growth
  Fund (AgGr)
Keystone International Fund (Intl)
Keystone Liquid Trust (MM)
Keystone Mid-Cap Growth Fund (S-3) (Gr)
Keystone Precious Metals Holdings, Inc.
  (PM/G)
Keystone Quality Bond Fund (B-1) (IncB)
Keystone Small Company Growth Fund
  (S-4) (AgGr)
Keystone Small Company Growth Fund II
  (AgGr)
Keystone Strategic Growth Fund (K-2) (Gr)
Keystone Tax Free Fund (NMuB)

Kobren Insight Funds
20 William St.
Ste. 310
Wellesley Hills, MA 02181
800/456-2736 ·
Kobren Insight Funds
  Kobren Conservative Allocation Fund
    (Gr&I)
  Kobren Growth Fund (Gr)
  Kobren Moderate Growth Fund (Gr)

KPM Funds, Inc.
10250 Regency Circle
Ste. 500
Omaha, NE68114-3723
800/776-5782
KPM Funds, Inc.
  KPM Equity Portfolio (Gr)
  KPM Fixed Income Portfolio (IncB)

Lake Forest Funds
One Westminister Place
Lake Forest, IL 60045-1821
888/295-5707
Lake Forest Funds (The)
  Lake Forest Core Equity Fund (Gr&I)
  Lake Forest Money Market Fund (MM)

Lancaster Funds
1225 L St.
200 Centre Terrace
Lincoln, NE 68501-3000
800/279-7437
SMITH HAYES Trust, Inc.
  Capital Builder Fund (Gr&I)
  Convertible Fund (IncM)
  Government/Quality Bond Fund (USGv)
  Nebraska Tax-Free Fund (SMuB)
  Small Cap Fund (Gr)

Landmark Family of Funds
153 E. 53rd St
6th Fl., Zone 6
New York, NY 10022-4611

800/625-4554
Landmark Fixed Income Funds
  Landmark Intermediate Income Fund
    (IncB)
  Landmark U.S. Government Income Fund
    (USGv)
Landmark Funds I
  Landmark Balanced Fund (Bal)
Landmark Funds II
  Landmark Equity Fund (Gr)
  Landmark Small Cap Equity Fund
    (AgGr)
Landmark Funds III
  Landmark Cash Reserves (MM)
  Landmark U.S. Treasury Reserves (MM)
Landmark Institutional Trust
  Landmark Institutional Liquid Reserves
    (MM)
  Landmark Institutional U.S. Treasury
    Reserves (MM)
Landmark International Funds
  Landmark Emerging Asian Markets
    Equity Fund (Intl)
  Landmark International Equity Fund
    (Intl)
Landmark Multi-State Tax Free Funds
  Landmark California Tax Free Reserves
    (SMMX)
  Landmark Connecticut Tax Free Reserves
    (SMMX)
  Landmark New York Tax Free Reserves
    (SMMX)
Landmark Premium Funds
  Premium Liquid Reserves (MM)
  Premium U.S. Treasury Reserves (MM)
Landmark Tax Free Income Funds
  Landmark National Tax Free Income Fund
    (NMuB)
  Landmark New York Tax Free Income
    Fund (SMuB)
  Landmark Tax Free Reserves (NMMX)

Lazard Freres Funds
30 Rockefeller Plaza
New York, NY 10020
800/823-6300
Lazard Funds, Inc. (The)
  Lazard Bantam Value Portfolio (AgGr)
  Lazard Bond Portfolio (IncB)
  Lazard Emerging Markets Portfolio
    (Intl)
  Lazard Equity Portfolio (Gr)
  Lazard Global Equity Fund (GloE)
  Lazard International Equity Portfolio
    (Intl)
  Lazard International Fixed-Income
    Portfolio (GloB)
  Lazard International Small Cap Portfolio
    (Intl)
  Lazard Small Cap Portfolio (AgGr)
  Lazard Strategic Yield Portfolio (HiYB)

Lebenthal
120 Broadway
12th Fl.
New York, NY 10271
800/221-5822
Lebenthal Funds, Inc.
Lebenthal New Jersey Municipal Bond
Fund (SMuB)
Lebenthal New York Municipal Bond
Fund (SMuB)
Lebenthal Taxable Municipal Bond Fund
(NMuB)

Legends Fund, Inc.
515 W. Market St.
8th Fl.
Louisville, KY 40202-3319
800/634-0142
Legends Fund, Inc. (The)
ARM Capital Advisers Money Market
Portfolio (MM)
Dreman Value Portfolio (Gr)
Harris Bretall Sullivan & Smith Equity
Growth Portfolio (Gr)
Morgan Stanley Asian Growth Portfolio
(Intl)
Morgan Stanley Worldwide High Income
Portfolio (GloB)
Nicholas-Applegate Balanced Portfolio
(Bal)
Pinnacle Fixed Income Portfolio (IncM)
Renaissance Balanced Portfolio (Bal)
Zweig Asset Allocation Portfolio (Gr)
Zweig Equity (AgGr)

Legg Mason Funds
111 S. Calvert St.
P.O. Box 1476
Baltimore, MD 21203-1476
800/822-5544
Bartlett Capital Trust
Bartlett Basic Value Fund (Gr&I)
Bartlett Value International Fund (Intl)
Legg Mason Cash Reserve Trust (MM)
Legg Mason Global Trust, Inc.
Emerging Markets Trust (Intl)
Global Government Trust (GloB)
International Equity Trust (Intl)
Legg Mason Income Trust, Inc. (The)
High Yield Portfolio (HiYB)
Investment Grade Income Portfolio (IncB)
U.S. Government Intermediate Portfolio
(USGv)
U.S. Government Money Market Portfolio
(MM)
Legg Mason Investors Trust, Inc.
American Leading Companies Trust
(Gr&I)
Balanced Trust (Bal)
Legg Mason Special Investment Trust, Inc.
(AgGr)

Legg Mason Tax-Exempt Trust, Inc.
(NMMX)
Legg Mason Tax-Free Income Fund
Intermediate-Term Income Trust
(NMuB)
Maryland Tax-Free Income Trust
(SMuB)
Pennsylvania Tax-Free Income Trust
(SMuB)
Legg Mason Total Return Trust, Inc. (Gr&I)
Legg Mason Value Trust, Inc. (Gr)
Western Asset Trust, Inc.
Limited Duration Portfolio (IncB)
Western Core Portfolio (IncB)
Western Intermediate Portfolio (IncB)
Western International Securities Portfolio
(GloB)

Lepercq-Istel Fund
1675 Broadway, 16th Fl.
New York, NY 10019-5820
800/497-1411
Lepercq-Istel Trust
Lepercq-Istel Fund (Gr&I)

Lexington Funds
Park 80 W., Plaza Two
P.O. Box 1515
Saddle Brook, NJ 07663-1515
800/526-0056
Lexington Convertible Securities Fund
(Gr&I)
Lexington Corporate Leaders Trust Fund
(Gr&I)
Lexington Crosby Small Cap Asia Growth
Fund, Inc. (Intl)
Lexington Emerging Markets Fund, Inc.
(Intl)
Lexington Global Fund, Inc. (GloE)
Lexington GNMA Income Fund, Inc.
(GNMA)
Lexington Goldfund, Inc. (PM/G)
Lexington Growth and Income Fund, Inc.
(Gr&I)
Lexington International Fund (Intl)
Lexington Money Market Trust (MM)
Lexington Natural Resources Trust (PM/G)
Lexington Ramirez Global Income Fund
(GloB)
Lexington SmallCap Value Fund, Inc.
(AgGr)
Lexington Strategic Investments Fund
(PM/G)
Lexington Strategic Silver Fund, Inc.
(PM/G)
Lexington Tax Free Money Fund, Inc.
(NMMX)
Lexington Troika Dialog Russia Fund, Inc.
(Intl)
Lexington Worldwide Emerging Markets
Fund, Inc. (Intl)

Life and Annuity Trust
111 Center St.
Little Rock, AR 72201-4402
800/222-8222
Life And Annuity Trust
  Asset Allocation Fund (Flex)
  Growth and Income Fund (Gr&I)
  Money Market Fund (MM)
  U.S. Government Allocation Fund (USGv)

LKCM Funds
301 Commerce
Ste. 1600
Fort Worth, TX 76102-4116
800/688-5526
LKCM Funds
  LKCM Equity Portfolio (Gr)
  LKCM Small Capitalization Equity
  Portfolio (AgGr)

Longleaf Partners Funds
6075 Poplar Ave.
Ste. 900
Memphis, TN 38119-4717
800/445-9469
Longleaf Partners Funds Trust
  Longleaf Partners Fund (Gr)
  Longleaf Partners Realty Fund (Gr&I)
  Longleaf Partners Small-Cap Fund (Gr)

Loomis Sayles Funds
600 Fifth Ave.
New York, NY 10020-2302
800/676-6779
Loomis Sayles Funds
  Loomis Sayles Bond Fund (IncB)
  Loomis Sayles Core Value Fund (Gr&I)
  Loomis Sayles Global Bond Fund (GloB)
  Loomis Sayles Growth Fund (Gr)
  Loomis Sayles High Yield Fund (HiYB)
  Loomis Sayles Intermediate Maturity
  Bond Fund (IncB)
  Loomis Sayles International Equity Fund
  (Intl)
  Loomis Sayles Investment Grade Bond
  Fund (IncB)
  Loomis Sayles Mid Cap Growth Fund
  (Gr)
  Loomis Sayles Municipal Bond Fund
  (NMuB)
  Loomis Sayles Short-Term Bond Fund
  (CorB)
  Loomis Sayles Small Cap Growth Fund
  (AgGr)
  Loomis Sayles Small Cap Value Fund
  (AgGr)
  Loomis Sayles Strategic Value Fund
  (AgGr)
  Loomis Sayles U.S. Government
  Securities Fund (USGv)
  Loomis Sayles Worldwide Fund (GloE)

Lord Abbett Funds
The General Motors Bldg.
767 Fifth Ave.
New York, NY 10153-0002
800/223-4224
Lord Abbett Affiliated Fund, Inc. (Gr&I)
Lord Abbett Bond-Debenture Fund, Inc.
  (HiYB)
Lord Abbett Developing Growth Fund, Inc.
  (AgGr)
Lord Abbett Equity Fund—1990 Series (Gr)
Lord Abbett Global Fund, Inc.
  Equity Series (GloE)
  Income Series (GloB)
Lord Abbett Investment Trust
  Balanced Series (Bal)
  Limited Duration U.S. Government Series
  (USGv)
  U.S. Government Securities Series
  (USGv)
Lord Abbett Mid-Cap Value Fund (Gr)
Lord Abbett Research Fund, Inc.
  Large-Cap Series (Gr&I)
  Small-Cap Series (AgGr)
Lord Abbett Securities Trust
  Growth and Income Trust (Gr&I)
  International Series (Intl)
Lord Abbett Tax-Free Income Fund, Inc.
  California Series (SMuB)
  Connecticut Series (SMuB)
  Hawaii Series (SMuB)
  Minnesota Series (SMuB)
  Missouri Series (SMuB)
  National Series (NMuB)
  New Jersey Series (SMuB)
  New York Series (SMuB)
  Texas Series (SMuB)
  Washington Series (SMuB)
Lord Abbett Tax-Free Income Trust
  Florida Series (SMuB)
  Georgia Series (SMuB)
  Michigan Series (SMuB)
  Pennsylvania Series (SMuB)
Lord Abbett U.S. Government Money
  Market Fund, Inc. (MM)

Lou Holland Trust
35 W. Wacker Dr.
Ste. 3260
Chicago, IL 60601
800/295-9779
Lou Holland Trust (The)
  Lou Holland Growth Fund (Gr)

Lutheran Brotherhood Fund Family
625 Fourth Ave. South
Minneapolis, MN 55415-1624
800/328-4552
LB Series Fund, Inc.
  Growth Series (Gr)
  High Yield Series (HiYB)

Income Series (IncM)
Money Market Series (MM)
Opportunity Growth Series (AgGr)
World Growth Series (Intl)
Lutheran Brotherhood Family of Funds
Lutheran Brotherhood Fund (Gr&I)
Lutheran Brotherhood High Yield Fund
(HiYB)
Lutheran Brotherhood Income Fund
(IncB)
Lutheran Brotherhood Mid Cap Growth
Fund (AgGr)
Lutheran Brotherhood Money Market
Fund (MM)
Lutheran Brotherhood Municipal Bond
Fund (NMuB)
Lutheran Brotherhood Opportunity
Growth Fund (AgGr)
Lutheran Brotherhood World Growth
Fund (Intl)

MainStay Funds
260 Cherry Hill Rd.
Parsippany, NJ 07054-1108
800/624-6782
MainStay Funds
California Tax Free Fund (SMuB)
Capital Appreciation Fund (AgGr)
Convertible Fund (Gr&I)
Equity Index Fund (Gr&I)
Government Fund (USGv)
High Yield Corporate Bond Fund (HiYB)
International Bond Fund (GloB)
International Equity Fund (Intl)
Money Market Fund (MM)
New York Tax Free Fund (SMuB)
Strategic Income Fund (GloB)
Tax Free Bond Fund (NMuB)
Total Return Fund (Bal)
Value Fund (Gr)
MainStay Institutional Funds Inc.
Bond Fund (IncB)
EAFE Index Fund (Intl)
Growth Equity Fund (Gr)
Indexed Bond Fund (IncB)
Indexed Equity Fund (Gr&I)
International Bond Fund (GloB)
International Equity Fund (Intl)
Money Market Fund (MM)
Multi-Asset Fund (Bal)
Short-Term Bond Fund (IncM)
Value Equity Fund (AgGr)
MainStay VP Series Fund, Inc.
Bond Portfolio (IncB)
Capital Appreciation Portfolio (Gr)
Cash Management Portfolio (MM)
Government Portfolio (USGv)
Growth Equity Portfolio (Gr)
High Yield Corporate Bond Portfolio
(CorB)
Indexed Equity Portfolio (Gr&I)

International Equity Portfolio (Intl)
Total Return Portfolio (Flex)
Value Portfolio (Gr&I)

Mairs and Power Growth Fund, Inc.
W-2062 First Natl Bank Bldg.
332 Minnesota St.
St. Paul, MN 55101
800/304-7404
Mairs and Power Growth Fund, Inc. (Gr)

Mairs and Power Income Fund, Inc.
W-2062 First Natl Bank Bldg.
332 Minnesota St.
St. Paul, MN 55101
612/222-8478
Mairs and Power Balanced Fund, Inc. (Bal)

Managers Funds
40 Richards Ave.
Norwalk, CT 06854-2319
800/835-3879
Managers Funds (The)
Bond Fund (IncB)
Capital Appreciation Fund (Gr)
Global Bond Fund (GloB)
Income Equity Fund (IncE)
Intermediate Mortgage Fund (GNMA)
International Equity Fund (Intl)
Money Market Fund (MM)
Short and Intermediate Bond Fund
(IncB)
Short Government Fund (IncB)
Special Equity Fund (AgGr)

Manning & Napier Funds
P.O. Box 41118
Rochester, NY 14604
800/466-3863
Manning & Napier Fund, Inc.
Blended Asset Series I (Gr)
Blended Asset Series II (Gr)
Defensive Series (Flex)
Diversified Tax Exempt Series (NMuB)
Flexible Yield Series I (USGv)
Flexible Yield Series II (USGv)
Flexible Yield Series III (USGv)
International Series (Intl)
Maximum Horizon Series (Bal)
New York Tax Exempt Series (SMuB)
Ohio Tax Exempt Series (SMuB)
Small Cap Series (AgGr)
Tax Managed Series (Gr)
World Opportunities Series (GloE)
Manning & Napier Insurance Fund, Inc.
Bond Portfolio (IncB)
Equity Portfolio (Gr)
Growth Portfolio (Flex)
Maximum Horizon Portfolio (AgGr)
Moderate Growth Portfolio (Flex)
Small Cap Portfolio (AgGr)

MAP Funds
c/o First Priority Investment Corp.
520 Broad St., A16N
Newark, NJ 07102
800/559-5535
MAP-Government Fund, Inc. (MM)
MAP-Equity Fund (Gr)
MBL Growth Fund, Inc. (Gr)

Market Street Fund, Inc.
P.O. Box 1717
Valley Forge, PA 19482-1717
215/636-5000
Market Street Fund, Inc. (The)
  International Portfolio (Intl)

Marketvest Funds
Federated Investors Twr.
1001 Liberty Ave.
Pittsburgh, PA 15222
800/MKT-VEST
Marketvest Funds
  Marketvest International Equity Fund
  (Intl)
  Marketvest Pennsylvania Intermediate
  Municipal Bond Fund (SMuB)
Marketvest Funds, Inc.
  Marketvest Equity Fund (Gr)
  Marketvest Intermediate U.S. Government
  Bond Fund (USGv)
  Marketvest Short-Term Bond Fund (IncB)

MarketWatch Funds
3435 Stelzer Rd.
Columbus, OH 43219-3035
800/497-9433
MarketWatch Funds
  Equity Fund (Gr&I)
  Intermediate Fixed Income Fund (IncB)
  Treasury Money Market Fund (MM)
  Virginia Municipal Bond Fund (SMuB)

Markman MultiFund Trust
6600 France Ave. South
Ste. 565
Edina, MN 55435
800/395-4848
Markman MultiFund Trust
  Markman Aggressive Allocation Porfolio
  (Gr)
  Markman Conservative Allocation
  Portfolio (IncM)
  Markman Moderate Allocation Portfolio
  (Gr&I)

Marquis Funds
One Freedom Valley Drive
Oaks, PA 19456
800/342-5734
Marquis Funds
  Balanced Fund (Bal)

Government Securities Fund (USGv)
Growth Equity Fund (Gr)
Institutional Money Market Fund (MM)
International Equity Fund (Intl)
Louisiana Tax-Free Income Fund (SMuB)
Small Cap Equity Fund (AgGr)
Strategic Income Bond Fund (IncB)
Tax-Exempt Money Market Fund
  (NMMX)
Treasury Securities Money Market Fund
  (MM)
Value Equity Fund (Gr)

Marshall Funds
Federated Investors Twr.
1001 Liberty Ave.
Pittsburgh, PA 15222-3779
800/236-3863
Marshall Funds, Inc.
  Marshall Equity Income Fund (IncE)
  Marshall Government Income Fund
  (USGv)
  Marshall Intermediate Bond Fund (IncB)
  Marshall Intermediate Tax-Free Fund
  (NMuB)
  Marshall International Stock Fund (Intl)
  Marshall Large-Cap Growth & Income
  Fund (Gr&I)
  Marshall Mid-Cap Growth Fund (Gr)
  Marshall Mid-Cap Value Fund (Gr&I)
  Marshall Money Market Fund (MM)
  Marshall Short-Term Income Fund (IncB)

MAS Funds
One Tower Bridge
West Conshohocken, PA 19428
800/354-8185
MAS Funds
  Advisory Foreign Fixed Income Portfolio
  (GloB)
  Advisory Mortgage Portfolio (GNMA)
  Balanced Portfolio (Bal)
  Cash Reserves Portfolio (MM)
  Domestic Fixed Income Portfolio (IncB)
  Emerging Markets Portfolio (Intl)
  Equity Portfolio (Gr&I)
  Fixed Income Portfolio (IncB)
  Fixed Income Portfolio II (IncB)
  Global Fixed Income Portfolio (GloB)
  Growth Portfolio (Gr)
  High Yield Portfolio (HiYB)
  Intermediate Duration Portfolio (IncB)
  International Equity Portfolio (Intl)
  International Fixed Income Portfolio (Intl)
  Limited Duration Portfolio (CorB)
  Mid Cap Growth Portfolio (AgGr)
  Mid Cap Value Portfolio (IncM)
  Mortgage-Backed Securities Portfolio
  (GNMA)
  Multi-Asset-Class Portfolio (IncM)
  Municipal Portfolio (NMuB)

PA Municipal Portfolio (SMuB)
Small Cap Value Portfolio (Gr&I)
Special Purpose Fixed Income Portfolio
(IncB)
Value Portfolio (Gr&I)

MassFinancial Funds
500 Boylston St.
Boston, MA 02116-3740
800/343-2829
Compass Money Market Variable Account
(MM)
Compass II Capital Appreciation Variable
Account (AgGr)
Compass II Government Securities Variable
Account (GNMA)
Compass II High Yield Variable Account
(HiYB)
Compass II Managed Sectors Variable
Account (IncE)
Compass II Total Return Variable Account
(Gr&I)
Compass II World Government Variable
Account (GloE)
MFS Government Limited Maturity Fund
(USGv)
MFS Government Securities Fund (USGv)
MFS Growth Opportunities Fund (Gr)
MFS Institutional Trust
  International Equity Fund (Intl)
  MFS Core Plus Fixed Income Fund
  (IncM)
  MFS Emerging Equities Fund (AgGr)
  MFS Emerging Markets Fixed Income
  Fund (GloB)
  MFS Mid-Cap Growth Equity Fund (Gr)
  MFS Research Fund (Gr&I)
  MFS Worldwide Fixed Income Fund
  (GloB)
MFS Massachusetts Investors Growth Stock
Fund (Gr)
MFS Massachusetts Investors Trust
(Gr&I)
MFS Municipal Series Trust
  MFS Alabama Municipal Bond Fund
  (SMuB)
  MFS Arkansas Municipal Bond Fund
  (SMuB)
  MFS California Municipal Bond Fund
  (SMuB)
  MFS Florida Municipal Bond Fund
  (SMuB)
  MFS Georgia Municipal Bond Fund
  (SMuB)
  MFS Maryland Municipal Bond Fund
  (SMuB)
  MFS Massachusetts Municipal Bond Fund
  (SMuB)
  MFS Mississippi Municipal Bond Fund
  (SMuB)
  MFS Municipal Income Fund (NMuB)

  MFS New York Municipal Bond Fund
  (SMuB)
  MFS North Carolina Municipal Bond
  Fund (SMuB)
  MFS Pennsylvania Municipal Bond Fund
  (SMuB)
  MFS South Carolina Municipal Bond
  Fund (SMuB)
  MFS Tennessee Municipal Bond Fund
  (SMuB)
  MFS Virginia Municipal Bond Fund
  (SMuB)
  MFS West Virginia Municipal Bond Fund
  (SMuB)
MFS Series Trust I
  MFS Blue Chip Fund (Gr)
  MFS Cash Reserve Fund (MM)
  MFS Convertible Securities Fund (Gr&I)
  MFS Core Growth Fund (Gr)
  MFS Equity Income Fund (IncE)
  MFS Managed Sectors Fund (AgGr)
  MFS New Discovery Fund (AgGr)
  MFS Research Growth & Income Fund
  (Gr&I)
  MFS Research International Fund (Intl)
  MFS Science & Technology Fund (AgGr)
  MFS Special Opportunities Fund (Flex)
  MFS Strategic Growth Fund (AgGr)
  MFS World Asset Allocation Fund
  (GloE)
MFS Series Trust II
  MFS Capital Growth Fund (Gr)
  MFS Emerging Growth Fund (AgGr)
  MFS Gold & Natural Resources Fund
  (PM/G)
  MFS Intermediate Income Fund (IncM)
MFS Series Trust III
  MFS High Income Fund (HiYB)
  MFS Municipal High Income Fund
  (NMuB)
MFS Series Trust IV
  MFS Government Money Market Fund
  (MM)
  MFS Money Market Fund (MM)
  MFS Municipal Bond Fund (NMuB)
  MFS OTC Fund (AgGr)
MFS Series Trust V
  MFS Research Fund (Gr&I)
  MFS Total Return Fund (IncM)
MFS Series Trust VI
  MFS Utilities Fund (IncM)
  MFS World Equity Fund (GloE)
  MFS World Total Return Fund (GloE)
MFS Series Trust VII
  MFS Value Fund (Gr)
  MFS World Governments Fund (GloB)
MFS Series Trust VIII
  MFS Strategic Income Fund (IncB)
  MFS World Growth Fund (GloE)
MFS Series Trust IX
  MFS Bond Fund (CorB)

MFS Limited Maturity Fund (IncB)
MFS Municipal Limited Maturity Fund
(NMuB)
MFS Series Trust X
  MFS/Foreign & Colonial Emerging
  Markets Equity Fund (Intl)
  MFS/Foreign & Colonial International
  Growth and Income Fund (Intl)
  MFS/Foreign & Colonial International
  Growth Fund (Intl)
  MFS Government Mortgage Fund
  (GNMA)
MFS/SunLife Series Trust
  Capital Appreciation Series (AgGr)
  Conservative Growth Series (Gr)
  Emerging Growth Series (AgGr)
  Government Securities Series (GNMA)
  High Yield Series (CorB)
  Managed Sectors Series (AgGr)
  Money Market Series (MM)
  Research Series (Gr&I)
  Utilities Series (IncB)
  Value Series (Gr)
  World Government Series (GloB)
  World Growth Series (GloB)
  World Total Return Series (GloB)
MFS SunLife Total Return Fund (Gr&I)
MFS Union Standard Trust
  Equity Fund (Gr)

MassMutual Funds
1295 State St.
Springfield, MA 01111-0001
413/788-8411
MassMutual Institutional Funds
  MassMutual Balanced Fund (Bal)
  MassMutual Core Bond Fund (IncB)
  MassMutual International Equity Fund
  (Intl)
  MassMutual Prime Fund (IncB)
  MassMutual Short-Term Bond Fund
  (IncB)
  MassMutual Small Cap Value Equity
  Fund (Gr)
  MassMutual Value Equity Fund (Gr&I)

Masterworks Funds, Inc.
111 Center St.
Little Rock, AR 72201
800/458-6589
Masterworks Funds, Inc.
  Asset Allocation Fund (Flex)
  Bond Index Fund (CorB)
  Growth Stock Fund (AgGr)
  LifePath 2000 Fund (Flex)
  LifePath 2010 Fund (Flex)
  LifePath 2020 Fund (Flex)
  LifePath 2030 Fund (Flex)
  LifePath 2040 Fund (Flex)
  Money Market Fund (MM)
  S&P 500 Fund (Gr)

  Short Intermediate Term Fund (Flex)
  U.S. Treasury Fund (USGv)

Matthews International Funds
655 Montgomery St.
Ste. 1438
San Francisco, CA 94111
800/789-ASIA
Matthews International Funds
  Matthews Asian Convertible Securities
  Fund (Intl)
  Matthews Korea Fund (Intl)
  Matthews Pacific Tiger Fund (Intl)

Matthew 25 Fund
605 Cloverly Ave.
Jenkintown, PA 19046
800/M25-FUND
Matthew 25 Fund Inc. (Gr)

Maxus Funds
28601 Chagrin Blvd.
Ste. 500
Cleveland, OH 44122-4500
800/44-MAXUS
Maxus Equity Fund (Flex)
Maxus Income Fund (IncM)
Maxus Laureate Fund (Gr&I)

Mentor Funds
901 E. Byrd St.
Riverfront Plaza
Richmond, VA 23219-4069
800/382-0016
America's Utility Fund, Inc. (Gr&I)
Mentor Funds
  Mentor Capital Growth Portfolio (Gr)
  Mentor Growth Fund (Gr)
  Mentor Income and Growth Portfolio
  (Gr&I)
  Mentor Municipal Income Portfolio
  (NMuB)
  Mentor Perpetual Global Portfolio
  (GloE)
  Mentor Quality Income Portfolio (USGv)
  Mentor Short Duration Income Portfolio
  (IncB)
  Mentor Strategy Portfolio (Flex)

Mentor Institutional Funds
901 E. Byrd St.
Richmond, VA 23219
800/869-6042
Mentor Institutional Trust
  Mentor Fixed Income Portfolio (IncB)
  Mentor Intermediate Duration Portfolio
  (IncB)
  Mentor International Portfolio (Intl)
  Mentor SNAP Portfolio (IncB)
  Mentor U.S. Government Cash
  Management Portfolio (MM)

Meridian Funds
60 E. Sir Francis Drake Blvd.
Ste. 306
Larkspur, CA 94939-1714
800/446-6662
Meridian Fund, Inc.
  Meridian Fund (Gr)
  Meridian Value Fund (Gr)

Merrill Lynch Funds
P.O. Box 9011
Princeton, NJ 08543-9011
800/637-3863
CBA Money Fund (MM)
CMA Government Securities Fund (MM)
CMA Money Fund (MM)
CMA Multi-State Municipal Series Trust
  CMA Arizona Municipal Money Fund
  (SMMX)
  CMA California Municipal Money Fund
  (SMMX)
  CMA Connecticut Municipal Money Fund
  (SMMX)
  CMA Massachusetts Municipal Money
  Fund (SMMX)
  CMA Michigan Municipal Money Fund
  (SMMX)
  CMA New Jersey Municipal Money Fund
  (SMMX)
  CMA New York Municipal Money Fund
  (SMMX)
  CMA North Carolina Municipal Money
  Fund (SMMX)
  CMA Ohio Municipal Money Fund
  (SMMX)
  CMA Pennylvania Municipal Money
  Fund (SMMX)
CMA Tax-Exempt Fund (NMMX)
CMA Treasury Fund (MM)
Corporate Fund Investment Accumulation
  Program, Inc. (The) (CorB)
Emerging Tigers Fund, Inc. (Intl)
Merrill Lynch Adjustable Rate Securities
  Fund (GNMA)
Merrill Lynch Americas Income Fund
  (GloB)
Merrill Lynch Asset Growth Fund, Inc.
  (IncM)
Merrill Lynch Asset Income Fund, Inc.
  (IncM)
Merrill Lynch Basic Value Fund, Inc.
  (Gr&I)
Merrill Lynch California Municipal Series
  Trust
  California Insured Municipal Bond Fund
  (SMuB)
  California Municipal Bond Fund (SMuB)
Merrill Lynch Capital Fund, Inc. (Gr&I)
Merrill Lynch Consults International (Intl)
Merrill Lynch Corporate Bond Fund, Inc.
  High Income Portfolio (HiYB)

Intermediate Term Portfolio (CorB)
Investment Grade Portfolio (CorB)
Merrill Lynch Developing Capital Markets
  Fund, Inc. (Intl)
Merrill Lynch Dragon Fund, Inc. (Intl)
Merrill Lynch EuroFund (Intl)
Merrill Lynch Federal Securities Trust
  (USGv)
Merrill Lynch Fundamental Growth Fund
  Inc. (Gr)
Merrill Lynch Funds for Institutions Series
  Merrill Lynch Government Fund (MM)
  Merrill Lynch Institutional Fund (MM)
  Merrill Lynch Institutional Tax-Exempt
  Fund (NMMX)
  Merrill Lynch Premier Institutional Fund
  (MM)
  Merrill Lynch Treasury Fund (MM)
Merrill Lynch Fund For Tomorrow, Inc.
  (Gr)
Merrill Lynch Global Allocation Fund, Inc.
  (GloB)
Merrill Lynch Global Bond Fund For
  Investment and Retirement (GloB)
Merrill Lynch Global Convertible Fund,
  Inc. (GloE)
Merrill Lynch Global Holdings, Inc. (GloE)
Merrill Lynch Global Resources Trust
  (GloE)
Merrill Lynch Global SmallCap Fund, Inc.
  (GloE)
Merrill Lynch Global Utility Fund (GloE)
Merrill Lynch Global Value Fund, Inc.
  (GloE)
Merrill Lynch Growth Fund (Gr&I)
Merrill Lynch Index Funds
  Merrill Lynch Aggregate Bond Index
  Fund (IncB)
  Merrill Lynch International Index Fund
  (Intl)
  Merrill Lynch S&P 500 Index Fund (Gr)
  Merrill Lynch Small Company Index
  Fund (AgGr)
Merrill Lynch Intermediate Government
  Bond Fund (USGv)
Merrill Lynch International Equity Fund
  (Intl)
Merrill Lynch Latin America Fund, Inc.
  (Intl)
Merrill Lynch Middle East/Africa Fund,
  Inc. (Intl)
Merrill Lynch Multi-State Limited Maturity
  Municipal Series Trust
  Arizona Limited Maturity Fund (SMuB)
  California Limited Maturity Fund (SMuB)
  Florida Limited Maturity Fund (SMuB)
  Massachusetts Limited Maturity Fund
  (SMuB)
  Michigan Limited Maturity Fund (SMuB)
  New Jersey Limited Maturity Fund
  (SMuB)

New York Limited Maturity Fund (SMuB)
Pennsylvania Limited Maturity Fund
(SMuB)
Merrill Lynch Multi-State Municipal Series
Trust
Arizona Municipal Bond Fund (SMuB)
Arkansas Municipal Bond Fund (SMuB)
Colorado Municipal Bond Fund (SMuB)
Connecticut Municipal Bond Fund
(SMuB)
Florida Municipal Bond Fund (SMuB)
Maryland Municipal Bond Fund (SMuB)
Massachusetts Municipal Bond Fund
(SMuB)
Michigan Municipal Bond Fund (SMuB)
Minnesota Municipal Bond Fund (SMuB)
New Jersey Municipal Bond Fund
(SMuB)
New Mexico Municipal Bond Fund
(SMuB)
New York Municipal Bond Fund (SMuB)
North Carolina Municipal Bond Fund
(SMuB)
Ohio Municipal Bond Fund (SMuB)
Oregon Municipal Bond Fund (SMuB)
Pennsylvania Municipal Bond Fund
(SMuB)
Texas Municipal Bond Fund (SMuB)
Merrill Lynch Municipal Bond Fund, Inc.
Insured Portfolio (NMuB)
Limited Maturity Portfolio (NMuB)
National Portfolio (NMuB)
Merrill Lynch Municipal Series Trust
Municipal Intermediate Term Fund
(NMuB)
Merrill Lynch Phoenix Fund, Inc. (AgGr)
Merrill Lynch Pacific Fund, Inc. (Intl)
Merrill Lynch Ready Assets Trust (MM)
Merrill Lynch Retirement Asset Builder
Program, Inc.
Fundamental Value Portfolio (AgGr)
Global Opportunity Portfolio (GloB)
Growth Opporunities Portfolio (Gr)
Quality Bond Portfolio (CorB)
U.S. Government Securities Portfolio
(USGv)
Merrill Lynch Retirement Reserves Money
Fund (MM)
Merrill Lynch Series Fund
Balanced Portfolio (Bal)
Capital Stock Portfolio (Gr&I)
Global Strategy Portfolio (GloB)
Growth Stock Portfolio (Gr)
High Yield Portfolio (HiYB)
Intermediate Government Bond Portfolio
(USGv)
Long Term Corporate Bond Portfolio
(CorB)
Money Reserve Portfolio (MM)
Multiple Strategy Portfolio (Bal)
Natural Resources Portfolio (Gr)

Merrill Lynch Short-Term Global Income
Fund, Inc. (GloB)
Merrill Lynch Special Value Fund, Inc. (Gr)
Merrill Lynch Strategic Dividend Fund
(Gr&I)
Merrill Lynch Technology Fund, Inc. (Gr)
Merrill Lynch U.S. Treasury Money Fund
(MM)
Merrill Lynch U.S.A. Government Reserves
(MM)
Merrill Lynch Utility Income Fund (IncM)
Merrill Lynch Variable Series Funds
American Balanced Fund (Bal)
Basic Value Focus Fund (AgGr)
Developing Capital Markets Focus Fund
(Intl)
Domestic Money Market Fund (MM)
Equity Growth Fund (Gr)
Global Bond Focus Fund (GloB)
Global Strategy Fund (GloB)
Global Utility Focus Fund (GloE)
High Current Income Fund (HiYB)
Index 500 Fund (Gr&I)
Intermediate Government Bond Fund
(USGv)
International Equity Focus Fund (Intl)
Natural Resources Focus Fund (Gr)
Prime Bond Fund (CorB)
Quality Equity Fund (Gr&I)
Reserve Assets Fund (MM)
ML Healthcare Fund, Inc. (GloE)
Municipal Fund Investment Accumulation
Program, Inc. (The) (NMuB)
Summit Cash Reserve Fund (MM)
World Income Fund, Inc. (GloB)

Merriman Funds
1200 Westlake Ave. North
Ste. 700
Seattle, WA 98109-3529
800/423-4893
Merriman Investment Trust
Merriman Asset Allocation Fund (GloB)
Merriman Capital Appreciation Fund (Gr)
Merriman Flexible Bond Fund (GloB)
Merriman Growth and Income Fund
(Gr&I)
Merriman Leveraged Growth Fund (Gr)

Minerva Fund
3435 Stelzer Rd.
Columbus, OH 43219-3035
800/393-4998
Minerva Fund, Inc.
Equity Portfolio (IncE)

Monetta Funds
1776-A S. Naperville Rd.
Ste. 207
Wheaton, IL 60187-8143
800/MONETTA

Monetta Fund, Inc. (Gr&I)
Monetta Trust
Balanced Fund (Bal)
Government Money Market Fund (MM)
Intermediate Bond Fund (IncB)
Large-Cap Equity Fund (Gr)
MidCap Equity Fund (Gr)
Small-Cap Equity Fund (AgGr)

Monitor Funds
One Freedom Valley Drive
Oaks, PA 19456
800/342-5734
Monitor Funds (The)
Monitor Fixed Income Securities Fund
(IncB)
Monitor Growth Fund (Gr)
Monitor Income Equity Fund (IncE)
Monitor Money Market Fund (MM)
Monitor Mortgage Securities Fund
(GNMA)
Monitor Ohio Municipal Money Market
Fund (SMMX)
Monitor Ohio Tax Free Fund (SMuB)
Monitor Short/Intermediate Fixed Income
Securities (IncB)
Monitor U.S. Treasury Money Market
Fund (MM)

Monitrend Mutual Fund
2000 Richard Jones Rd.
Ste. 123
Nashville, TN 37215-2885
800/251-1970
Monitrend Mutual Fund
Gaming and Leisure Series (Gr)
Gold Series (PM/G)
Government Income Series (USGv)
Growth and Income Fund (Gr&I)
Growth Series (Gr)
PIA Adjustable Rate Government
Securities Fund (GNMA)
Technology Series (Gr)

Montgomery Funds
101 California St.
35th Fl.
San Francisco, CA 94111-2701
800/572-3863
Montgomery Funds (The)
Montgomery California Tax-Free
Intermediate Bond Fund (SMuB)
Montgomery California Tax-Free Money
Market Fund (SMMX)
Montgomery Emerging Asia Fund
(Intl)
Montgomery Emerging Markets Fund
(Intl)
Montgomery Equity Income Fund (IncE)
Montgomery Federal Tax-Free Money
Fund (NMMX)

Montgomery Global Asset Allocation
Fund (GloE)
Montgomery Global Communications
Fund (GloE)
Montgomery Global Opportunities Fund
(GloE)
Montgomery Government Reserve Fund
(MM)
Montgomery Growth Fund (Gr)
Montgomery International Growth Fund
(Intl)
Montgomery International SmallCap Fund
(Intl)
Montgomery MicroCap Fund (Gr)
Montgomery Select 50 Fund (Gr)
Montgomery Short Government Bond
Fund (USGv)
Montgomery Small Cap Fund (AgGr)
Montgomery Small Cap Opportunities
Fund (AgGr)
Montgomery Funds II (The)
Montgomery Asset Allocation Fund (Bal)
Montgomery Institutional Series:
Emerging Markets Portfolio (Intl)

MONY Series Fund, Inc.
1740 Broadway
Mail Drop 9-30
New York, NY 10019
800/786-6244
MONY Series Fund, Inc.
Diversified Portfolio (Bal)
Equity Growth Portfolio (Gr)
Equity Income Portfolio (IncE)
Government Securities Portfolio (IncB)
Intermediate Term Bond Portfolio (IncB)
Long Term Bond Portfolio (IncB)
Money Market Portfolio (MM)

Morgan Keegan Funds
50 Front St.
21st Fl.
Memphis, TN 38103
800/238-7127
Morgan Keegan Southern Capital Fund (Gr)

Morgan Stanley Funds
c/o Chase Global Funds Srvcs. Co.
P.O. Box 2798
Boston, MA 02208-2798
800/548-7786
Morgan Stanley Institutional Fund, Inc.
Active Country Allocation Portfolio (Intl)
Aggressive Equity Portfolio (Gr)
Asian Equity Portfolio (Intl)
Balanced Portfolio (IncM)
Emerging Growth Portfolio (AgGr)
Emerging Markets Debt Portfolio (GloB)
Emerging Markets Portfolio (Intl)
Equity Growth Portfolio (Gr)
European Equity Portfolio (Intl)

Fixed Income Portfolio (IncB)
Global Equity Portfolio (GloE)
Global Fixed Income Portfolio (GloB)
Gold Portfolio (PM/G)
High Yield Portfolio (HiYB)
International Equity Portfolio (Intl)
International Magnum Portfolio (Intl)
International Small Cap Portfolio (Intl)
Japanese Equity Portfolio (Intl)
Latin American Portfolio (Intl)
Money Market Portfolio (MM)
Municipal Bond Portfolio (NMuB)
Municipal Money Market Portfolio
(NMMX)
Small Cap Value Equity Portfolio (AgGr)
Technology Portfolio (AgGr)
U.S. Real Estate Portfolio (GNMA)
Value Equity Portfolio (Gr&I)

Morgan Stanley Retail Funds
c/o Chase Global Funds Srvcs. Co.
P.O. Box 2798
Boston, MA 02208-2798
800/548-7786
Morgan Stanley Fund, Inc.
Morgan Stanley Aggressive Equity Fund
(AgGr)
Morgan Stanley American Value Fund
(AgGr)
Morgan Stanley Asian Growth Fund (Intl)
Morgan Stanley Emerging Markets Fund
(Intl)
Morgan Stanley Global Equity Allocation
Fund (GloE)
Morgan Stanley Global Fixed Income
Fund (GloB)
Morgan Stanley Government Obligations
Money Market Fund (MM)
Morgan Stanley Growth and Income Fund
(Gr&I)
Morgan Stanley High Yield Fund (HiYB)
Morgan Stanley International Magnum
Fund (Intl)
Morgan Stanley Latin American Fund
(Intl)
Morgan Stanley Money Market Fund
(MM)
Morgan Stanley U.S. Real Estate Fund
(IncE)
Morgan Stanley Worldwide High Income
Fund (GloB)

Mosaic Funds
1655 Fort Myer Dr.
Arlington, VA 22209-3108
800/336-3063
Mosaic Equity Trust
Mosaic Balanced Fund (IncE)
Mosaic Investors Fund (Gr)
Mosaic Mid-Cap Growth Fund (AgGr)
Mosiac Worldwide Growth Fund (Intl)

Mosaic Government Money Market Trust
(MM)
Mosaic Income Trust
Mosaic Bond Fund (IncB)
Mosaic High Yield Fund (HiYB)
Mosiac Government Fund (IncB)
Mosaic Tax-Free Trust
Mosaic Tax-Free Arizona Fund (SMuB)
Mosaic Tax-Free Maryland Fund (SMuB)
Mosaic Tax-Free Missouri Fund (SMuB)
Mosaic Tax-Free Money Market
(NMMX)
Mosaic Tax-Free National Fund (NMuB)
Mosaic Tax-Free Virginia Fund (SMuB)

M.S.D.&T. Funds
3435 Stelzer Rd.
Columbus, OH 43219-3035
800/551-2145
M.S.D.&T. Funds, Inc.
Government Money Market Fund (MM)
Intermediate Fixed Income Fund (IncB)
International Equity Fund (Intl)
Maryland Tax-Exempt Bond Fund
(SMuB)
Prime Money Market Fund (MM)
Tax-Exempt Money Market Fund
(NMMX)
Tax-Exempt Money Market Fund (Tru)
(NMMX)
Value Equity Fund (Gr&I)

Muhlenkamp Fund
12300 Perry Hwy.
Ste. 306
Wexford, PA 15090-8318
800/860-3863
Wexford Trust
Muhlenkamp Fund (Gr&I)

Munder Funds, Inc.
P.O. Box 9755
Providence, RI 02940-9755
800/239-3334
Munder Framlington Funds Trust
Munder Framlington Emerging Markets
Fund (Intl)
Munder Framlington Healthcare Fund
(AgGr)
Munder Framlington International Growth
Fund (Intl)
Munder Funds, Inc.
Munder International Bond Fund (GloB)
Munder Micro-Cap Equity Fund (AgGr)
Munder Mid-Cap Growth Fund (Gr)
Munder Money Market Fund (MM)
Munder Multi-Season Growth Fund (Gr)
Munder Real Estate Equity Investment
Fund (Gr&I)
Munder Short Term Treasury Fund (USGv)
Munder Small-Cap Value Fund (AgGr)

Munder Value Fund (Gr)
NetNet Fund (AgGr)
Munder Lifestyle Funds
  Munder All-Season Accumulation Fund
    (Bal)
  Munder All-Season Development Fund
    (Bal)
  Munder All-Season Maintenance Fund
    (Bal)
St. Clair Funds, Inc.
  Liquidity Plus Money Market Fund (MM)

Munder Funds Trust
P.O. Box 9755
Providence, RI 02940-9755
800/239-3334
Munder Funds Trust
  Munder Accelerating Growth Fund (Gr)
  Munder Balanced Fund (Bal)
  Munder Bond Fund (CorB)
  Munder Cash Investment Fund (MM)
  Munder Equity Selection Fund (Gr)
  Munder Growth and Income Fund (Gr&I)
  Munder Index 500 Fund (Gr&I)
  Munder Intermediate Bond Fund (CorB)
  Munder International Equity Fund (Intl)
  Munder Michigan Triple Tax-Free Bond
    Fund (SMuB)
  Munder Small Company Growth Fund
    (AgGr)
  Munder Tax Free Bond Fund (NMuB)
  Munder Tax-Free Intermediate Bond Fund
    (NMuB)
  Munder Tax-Free Money Market Fund
    (NMMX)
  Munder U.S. Government Income Fund
    (USGv)
  Munder U.S. Treasury Money Market
    Fund (MM)

Mutual of America Funds
320 Park Ave.
New York, NY 10022-6839
800/468-3785
Mutual of America Institutional Funds, Inc.
  All America Fund (Gr&I)
  Bond Fund (IncB)
Mutual of America Investment Corporation
  Aggressive Equity Fund (AgGr)
  All America Fund (Gr&I Bond Fund
    (IncB)
  Composite Fund (Bal)
  Equity Index Fund (Gr)
  Mid-Term Bond Fund (IncB)
  Money Market Fund (MM)
  Short-Term Bond Fund (IncB)

Mutual Selection Fund
2610 Park Ave.
P.O. Box 209
Muscatine, IA 52761-5639

800/334-8920
Mutual Selection Fund, Inc. (Gr)

NASL Funds
116 Huntington Ave.
Boston, MA 02116-5749
800/344-1029
NASL Series Trust
  Aggressive Asset Allocation Trust (Flex)
  Balanced Trust (Bal)
  Blue Chip Growth Trust (Gr)
  Capital Growth Bond Trust (CorB)
  Conservative Asset Allocation Trust (Flex)
  Emerging Growth Trust (AgGr)
  Equity Income Trust (Gr&I)
  Equity Index Trust (Gr)
  Equity Trust (Gr)
  Global Equity Trust (GloE)
  Global Government Bond Trust (GloB)
  Growth and Income Trust (Gr&I)
  Growth Trust (Gr)
  High Yield Trust (HiYB)
  International Growth and Income Trust
    (Intl)
  International Small Cap Trust (GloE)
  International Stock Trust (Intl)
  Investment Quality Bond Trust (CorB)
  Lifestyle Aggressive 1000 Trust (AgGr)
  Lifestyle Balanced 640 Trust (Bal)
  Lifestyle Conservative 280 Trust (Bal)
  Lifestyle Growth 820 Trust (Bal)
  Lifestyle Moderate 460 Trust (Bal)
  Moderate Asset Allocation Trust (Flex)
  Money Market Trust (MM)
  Pacific Rim Emerging Markets Trust
    (Intl)
  Pilgrim Baxter Growth Trust (AgGr)
  Quantitative Equity Trust (Gr&I)
  Real Estate Securities Trust (Gr&I)
  Science and Technology Trust (AgGr)
  Small/Mid Cap Trust (AgGr)
  Strategic Bond Trust (IncB)
  U.S. Government Securities Trust (USGv)
  Value Trust (Gr)
  Worldwide Growth Trust (GloE)
North American Funds
  Balanced Fund (Bal)
  Equity-Income Fund (Gr)
  Global Equity Fund (GloE)
  Growth & Income Fund (Gr&I)
  Growth Equity Fund (Gr)
  International Growth and Income Trust
    (Intl)
  International Small Cap Fund (Intl)
  Investment Quality Bond Fund (CorB)
  Money Market Fund (MM)
  National Municipal Bond Fund (NMuB)
  Small/Mid Cap Fund (Gr)
  Strategic Income Fund (IncM)
  U.S. Government Securities Fund
    (USGv)

Nations Funds
111 Center St.
Ste. 300
Little Rock, AR 72201-4402
800/321-7854
Nations Fund, Inc.
  Nations Equity Income Fund (IncE)
  Nations Government Securities Fund
  (USGv)
  Nations International Equity Fund (Intl)
  Nations International Growth Fund (Intl)
  Nations Managed SmallCap Index Fund
  (AgGr)
  Nations Prime Fund (MM)
  Nations Small Company Growth Fund
  (AgGr)
  Nations Treasury Fund (MM)
  Nations U.S. Government Bond Fund
  (USGv)
Nations Fund Portfolios, Inc.
  Nations Emerging Markets Fund (Intl)
  Nations Global Government Income Fund
  (GloB)
  Nations Pacific Growth Fund (Intl)
Nations Fund Trust
  Nations Balanced Assets Fund (Bal)
  Nations Capital Growth Fund (Gr)
  Nations Disciplined Equity Fund (Gr)
  Nations Diversified Income Fund (IncB)
  Nations Emerging Growth Fund (AgGr)
  Nations Equity Index Fund (Gr)
  Nations Florida Intermediate Municipal
  Bond Fund (SMuB)
  Nations Florida Municipal Bond Fund
  (SMuB)
  Nations Georgia Intermediate Municipal
  Bond Fund (SMuB)
  Nations Georgia Municipal Bond Fund
  (SMuB)
  Nations Government Money Market Fund
  (MM)
  Nations Intermediate Municipal Bond
  Fund (NMuB)
  Nations Managed Index Fund (Gr&I)
  Nations Maryland Intermediate Municipal
  Bond Fund (SMuB)
  Nations Maryland Municipal Bond Fund
  (SMuB)
  Nations Municipal Income Fund (NMuB)
  Nations North Carolina Intermediate
  Municipal Bond Fund (SMuB)
  Nations North Carolina Municipal Bond
  Fund (SMuB)
  Nations Short-Intermediate Government
  Fund (USGv)
  Nations Short Term Municipal Income
  Fund (NMuB)
  Nations Short-Term Income Fund
  (IncB)
  Nations South Carolina Intermediate
  Municipal Bond Fund (SMuB)

Nations South Carolina Municipal Bond
  Fund (SMuB)
Nations Strategic Fixed Income Fund
  (IncB)
Nations Tax Exempt Fund (NMMX)
Nations Tennessee Intermediate Municipal
  Bond Fund (SMuB)
Nations Tennessee Municipal Bond Fund
  (SMuB)
Nations Texas Intermediate Municipal
  Bond Fund (SMuB)
Nations Texas Municipal Bond Fund
  (SMuB)
Nations Value Fund (Gr&I)
Nations Virginia Intermediate Municipal
  Bond Fund (SMuB)
Nations Virginia Municipal Bond Fund
  (SMuB)
Nations Institutional Reserves
  Nations Cash Reserves (MM)
  Nations Government Reserves (MM)
  Nations Municipal Reserves (NMMX)
  Nations Treasury Reserves (MM)

Nations LifeGoal Funds, Inc.
One NationsBank Plaza
33rd Fl.
Charlotte, NC 28255
800/321-7854
Nations LifeGoal Funds, Inc.
  LifeGoal Balanced Growth Portfolio (Bal)
  LifeGoal Growth Portfolio (Gr)
  LifeGoal Income and Growth Portfolio
  (Gr&I)

Nationwide Advisory Funds
Three Nationwide Plaza
P.O. Box 1492
Columbus, OH 43215-2423
800/848-0920
Financial Horizons Investment Trust
  Cash Reserve Fund (MM)
  Government Bond Fund (USGv)
  Growth Fund (Gr)
  Municipal Bond Fund (NMuB)
Nationwide Investing Foundation
  Bond Fund (CorB)
  Growth Fund (Gr)
  Money Market Fund (MM)
  Nationwide Fund (Gr&I)
Nationwide Investing Foundation II
  Tax-Free Income Fund (NMuB)
  U.S. Government Income Fund (USGv)

Navellier Funds
1 East Liberty
3rd Fl.
Reno, NV 89501
800/887-8671
Navellier Performance Funds
  Aggressive Growth Portfolio (AgGr)

Aggressive Small Cap Portfolio (AgGr)
Mid Cap Growth Portfolio (AgGr)
Navellier Series Fund
Aggressive Small Cap Equity Portfolio
(AgGr)

Neuberger & Berman Funds
605 Third Ave., 2nd Fl.
New York, NY 10158-0001
800/877-9700
Neuberger & Berman Advisers
Management Trust
Balanced Portfolio (Bal)
Government Income Portfolio (IncB)
Growth Portfolio (Gr)
Limited Maturity Bond Portfolio (IncB)
Liquid Asset Portfolio (MM)
Partners Portfolio (Gr)
Neuberger & Berman Equity Assets
Neuberger & Berman Focus Assets (Gr)
Neuberger & Berman Guardian Assets
(Gr&I)
Neuberger & Berman Manhattan Assets
(Gr)
Neuberger & Berman Partners Assets (Gr)
Neuberger & Berman Socially
Responsible Trust (Gr)
Neuberger & Berman Equity Funds
Focus Fund (Gr)
Genesis Fund (Gr)
Guardian Fund (Gr&I)
International Fund (Intl)
Manhattan Fund (Gr)
Partners Fund (Gr)
Socially Responsive Fund (Gr)
Neuberger & Berman Focus Trust (Gr)
Neuberger & Berman Genesis Trust (Gr)
Neuberger & Berman Guardian Trust (Gr&I)
Neuberger & Berman Income Funds
Cash Reserves (MM)
Government Money Fund (MM)
Limited Maturity Bond Fund (IncB)
Municipal Money Fund (NMMX)
Municipal Securities Trust (NMuB)
New York Insured Tax-Free Fund (SMuB)
Ultra Short Bond Fund (IncB)
Neuberger & Berman Limited Maturity
Bond Trust (IncB)
Neuberger & Berman Manhattan Trust (Gr)
Neuberger & Berman NYCDC Socially
Responsive Trust (Gr)
Neuberger & Berman Partners Trust (Gr)
Neuberger & Berman Ultra Short Bond
Trust (IncB)

New Alternatives Fund, Inc.
150 Broadhollow Rd.
Ste. 306
Melville, NY 11747-4901
800/423-8383
New Alternatives Fund, Inc. (Gr)

New Century Funds
20 William St.
Wellesley, MA 02181-4102
617/239-0445
Weston Portfolios, Inc.
New Century Capital Portfolio (Flex)
New Century I Portfolio (IncM)

New England Funds
399 Boylston St.
Boston, MA 02116-3305
800/225-7670
New England Funds
New England Growth Fund (Gr)
New England Cash Management Trust
Money Market Series (MM)
U.S. Government Series (MM)
New England Funds
New England Adjustable Rate U.S.
Government Fund (GNMA)
New England Balanced Fund (Bal)
New England Bond Income Fund (IncB)
New England Capital Growth Fund (Gr)
New England Equity Income Fund
(IncE)
New England Government Securities
Fund (USGv)
New England Growth Opportunities Fund
(Gr&I)
New England High Income Fund (HiYB)
New England Intermediate Term Tax Free
Fund of California (SMuB)
New England Intermediate Term Tax Free
Fund of New York (SMuB)
New England International Equity Fund
(Intl)
New England Limited Term U.S.
Government Fund (USGv)
New England Massachusetts Tax Free
Income Fund (SMuB)
New England Municipal Income Fund
(NMuB)
New England Star Advisors Fund (AgGr)
New England Star Small Cap Fund
(AgGr)
New England Star Worldwide Fund
(GloE)
New England Strategic Income Fund
(IncM)
New England Value Fund (Gr&I)
New England Tax Exempt Money Market
Trust (NMMX)

New England Zenith Funds
399 Boylston St.
Boston, MA 02116-3305
800/225-7670
New England Zenith Fund
Capital Growth Series (AgGr)
New England Zenith Fund
Alger Equity Growth Series (Gr)

Avanti Growth Series (Gr)
Balanced Series (Bal)
Bond Income Series (IncB)
International Equity Series (Intl)
Managed Series (Gr&I)
Money Market Series (MM)
Small Cap Series (AgGr)
Stock Index Series (Gr)
Strategic Bond Series (IncB)
U.S. Government Series (USGv)
Value Growth Series (Gr&I)
Venture Value Series (Gr)

Newpoint Funds
Federated Investors Twr.
1001 Liberty Ave.
Pittsburgh, PA 15222-3779
800/341-7400
Newpoint Funds
  Newpoint Equity Fund (Gr&I)
  Newpoint Government Money Market
  Fund (MM)

Nicholas-Applegate Mutual Funds
600 W. Broadway
29th Fl.
San Diego, CA 92101-3311
800/551-8643
Nicholas-Applegate Mutual Funds
  Balanced Growth Fund (Bal)
  Core Growth Fund (Gr)
  Emerging Countries Fund (GloE)
  Emerging Growth Fund (AgGr)
  Fully Discretionary Fixed Income Fund
  (IncB)
  Government Income Fund (USGv)
  High Yield Bond Fund (HiYB)
  Income and Growth Fund (Gr&I)
  International Core Growth Institutional
  Fund (Intl)
  International Small Cap Growth Fund
  (Intl)
  Large Cap Growth Institutional Fund
  (Gr)
  Mini-Cap Fund (AgGr)
  Money Market Fund (MM)
  Short/Intermediate Fixed Income Fund
  (IncB)
  Strategic Income Fund (IncM)
  Value Fund (Gr&I)
  Worldwide Growth Fund (Intl)

Ni Family of Mutual Funds
One Memorial Dr.
4th Fl.
Cambridge, MA 02142
800/686-3742
Ni Family of Mutual Funds
  Ni Growth & Value Fund (Gr)
  Ni Growth Fund (Gr)
  Ni Micro Cap Fund (AgGr)

Nomura Capital Funds
180 Maiden Lane
26th Fl.
New York, NY 10038-4925
800/833-0018
Nomura Pacific Basin Fund, Inc. (Intl)

Northern Trust Mutual Funds
50 S. LaSalle St.
Chicago, IL 60675
800/595-9111
Northern Funds (The)
  California Municipal Money Market Fund
  (SMMX)
  Fixed Income Fund (IncM)
  Florida Intermediate Tax-Exempt Fund
  (SMuB)
  Growth Equity Fund (Gr)
  Income Equity Fund (IncE)
  Intermediate Tax-Exempt Fund (NMuB)
  International Fixed Income Fund (GloE)
  International Growth Equity Fund (Intl)
  International Select Equity Fund (Intl)
  Money Market Fund (MM)
  Municipal Money Market Fund (NMMX)
  Select Equity Fund (Gr)
  Small Cap Fund (AgGr)
  Stock Index Fund (Gr&I)
  Tax-Exempt Fund (NMuB)
  Technology Fund (Gr)
  U.S. Government Fund (USGv)
  U.S. Government Money Market Fund
  (MM)
  U.S. Government Select Money Market
  Fund (MM)

Northstar Funds
Two Pickwick Plaza
Greenwich, CT 06830-5530
800/595-7827
Northstar Series Trust
  Northstar Balance Sheet Opportunities
  Fund (IncM)
  Northstar Government Securities Fund
  (USGv)
  Northstar Growth Fund (Gr)
  Northstar Growth + Value Fund (Gr)
  Northstar High Total Return Fund
  (HiYB)
  Northstar High Yield Fund (HiYB)
  Northstar Income and Growth Fund
  (Gr&I)
  Northstar Special Fund (Gr)
  Northstar Strategic Income Fund
  (IncB)

Nottingham Investment Trust II
105 N. Washington St.
P.O. Drawer 69
Rocky Mount, NC 27802-0069
800/525-FUND

Nottingham Investment Trust II (The)
  Brown Capital Management Balanced
  Fund (Bal)
  Brown Capital Management Equity Fund
  (Gr)
  Brown Capital Management Small
  Company Fund (AgGr)
  Capital Value Fund (The) (Gr&I)
  Investek Fixed Income Trust (IncM)
  ZSA Asset Allocation Fund (Gr&I)

Nuveen Flagship Funds
333 W. Wacker Dr.
Chicago, IL 60606-1218
800/621-7227
Flagship Admiral Funds, Inc.
  Flagship Utility Income Fund (IncM)
  Golden Rainbow Fund, A James Advised
  Mutual Fund (The) (Bal)
Nuveen California Tax-Free Fund, Inc.
  Nuveen California Tax-Free Money
  Market Fund (SMMX)
Nuveen Flagship Multistate Trust I
  Nuveen Flagship Arizona Municipal Bond
  Fund (SMuB)
  Nuveen Flagship Colorado Municipal
  Bond Fund (SMuB)
  Nuveen Flagship Florida Intermediate
  Municipal Bond Fund (SMuB)
  Nuveen Flagship Florida Municipal Bond
  Fund (SMuB)
  Nuveen Flagship New Mexico Municipal
  Bond Fund (SMuB)
  Nuveen Flagship Pennsylvania Municipal
  Bond Fund (SMuB)
  Nuveen Flagship Virginia Municipal Bond
  Fund (SMuB)
  Nuveen Maryland Municipal Bond Fund
  (SMuB)
Nuveen Flagship Multistate Trust II
  Nuveen California Insured Municipal
  Bond Fund (SMuB)
  Nuveen California Municipal Bond Fund
  (SMuB)
  Nuveen Flagship Connecticut Municipal
  Bond Fund (SMuB)
  Nuveen Flagship New Jersey Intermediate
  Municipal Bond Fund (SMuB)
  Nuveen Flagship New Jersey Municipal
  Bond Fund (SMuB)
  Nuveen Flagship New York Municipal
  Bond Fund (SMuB)
  Nuveen Massachusetts Insured Municipal
  Bond Fund (SMuB)
  Nuveen Massachusetts Municipal Bond
  Fund (SMuB)
  Nuveen New York Insured Municipal
  Bond Fund (SMuB)
Nuveen Flagship Multistate Trust III
  Nuveen Flagship Alabama Municipal
  Bond Fund (SMuB)

Nuveen Flagship Georgia Municipal Bond
  Fund (SMuB)
  Nuveen Flagship Lousiana Municipal
  Bond Fund (SMuB)
  Nuveen Flagship North Carolina
  Municipal Bond Fund (SMuB)
  Nuveen Flagship South Carolina
  Municipal Bond Fund (SMuB)
  Nuveen Flagship Tennessee Municipal
  Bond Fund (SMuB)
Nuveen Flagship Multistate Trust IV
  Nuveen Flagship Kansas Municipal Bond
  Fund (SMuB)
  Nuveen Flagship Kentucky Limited
  Term Municipal Bond Fund
  (SMuB)
  Nuveen Flagship Kentucky Municipal
  Bond Fund (SMuB)
  Nuveen Flagship Michigan Municipal
  Bond Fund (SMuB)
  Nuveen Flagship Missouri Municipal
  Bond Fund (SMuB)
  Nuveen Flagship Ohio Municipal Bond
  Fund (SMuB)
  Nuveen Flagship Wisconsin Municipal
  Bond Fund (SMuB)
Nuveen Flagship Municipal Trust
  Nuveen Flagship All-American Municipal
  Bond Fund (NMuB)
  Nuveen Flagship Intermediate Municipal
  Bond Fund (NMuB)
  Nuveen Flagship Limited Term Municipal
  Bond Fund (NMuB)
  Nuveen Insured Municipal Bond Fund
  (NMuB)
  Nuveen Municipal Bond Fund
  (NMuB)
Nuveen Investment Trust (The)
  Nuveen Balanced Municipal and Stock
  Fund (Bal)
  Nuveen Balanced Stock and Bond Fund
  (Bal)
  Nuveen Growth and Income Stock Fund
  (Gr&I)
Nuveen Tax-Exempt Money Market Fund,
  Inc. (NMMX)
Nuveen Tax-Free Money Market Fund,
  Inc.
  Nuveen Massachusetts Tax-Free Money
  Market Fund (SMMX)
  Nuveen New York Tax-Free Money
  Market Fund (SMMX)
Nuveen Tax-Free Reserves, Inc.
  (NMMX)

Oak Value Fund
3100 Tower Blvd.
Ste. 800
Durham, NC 27707
800/680-4199
Oak Value Fund (Gr)

Oberweis Funds
951 Ice Cream Dr.
Suite 200
N. Aurora, IL 60542
800/323-6166
Oberweis Emerging Growth Portfolio
  (AgGr)
Oberweis Micro Cap Portfolio (AgGr)
Oberweis Mid-Cap Portfolio (AgGr)

OFFITBANK Investment Funds
125 W. 55th St.
New York, NY 10019
800/618-9510
OFFITBANK Investment Fund, Inc.
  Emerging Markets Fund (GloB)
  High Yield Fund (HiYB)
  Latin America Fund (Intl)
  New York Municipal Fund (SMuB)

Ohio National Funds
One Financial Way
Cincinnati, OH 45242
800/578-8078
Ohio National Fund, Inc.
  Aggressive Growth Portfolio (AgGr)
  Bond Portfolio (CorB)
  Capital Appreciation Portfolio (Gr)
  Core Growth Portfolio (Gr)
  Equity Portfolio (Gr)
  Global Contrarian Portfolio (GloE)
  Growth & Income Portfolio (Gr&I)
  International Portfolio (Intl)
  Money Market Portfolio (MM)
  Omni Portfolio (Flex)
  Relative Value Portfolio (AgGr)
  S&P 500 Index Portfolio (Gr)
  Small Cap Portfolio (Gr)
  Social Awareness Portfolio (Gr)
  Stellar Portfolio (GloB)
  Strategic Income Portfolio (IncB)
ONE Fund, Inc.
  Core Growth Portfolio (AgGr)
  Global Contrarian Portfolio (GloE)
  Growth Portfolio (Gr)
  Income & Growth Portfolio (Gr&I)
  Income Portfolio (IncM)
  International Portfolio (Intl)
  Money Market Portfolio (MM)
  Small Cap Portfolio (AgGr)
  Tax-Free Income Portfolio (IncB)

Old Westbury Funds, Inc.
Federated Investors Tower
Pittsburgh, PA 15222-3779
800/607-2200
Old Westbury Funds, Inc.
  Old Westbury Growth Opportunity Fund
    (IncE)
  Old Westbury International Fund
    (Intl)

Olstein Funds
4 Manhattanville Rd.
Purchase, NY 10577
800/799-2113
Olstein Funds
  Olstein Financial Alert Fund (Gr&I)

111 Corcoran Funds
Federated Investors Twr.
1001 Liberty Ave.
Pittsburgh, PA 15222-3779
800/341-7400
111 Corcoran Funds
  111 Corcoran Bond Fund (IncB)
  111 Corcoran Equity Fund (IncE)
  111 Corcoran North Carolina Municipal
    Securities Fund (SMuB)

One Group Family of Mutual Funds
1111 Polaris Pkwy.
P.O. Box 710211
Columbus, OH 43271-0211
800/480-4111
One Group (The)
  Arizona Municipal Bond Fund (SMuB)
  Asset Allocation Fund (Bal)
  Disciplined Value Fund (IncE)
  Equity Index Fund (Gr&I)
  Government Bond Fund (USGv)
  Government Money Market Fund (MM)
  Growth Opportunities Fund (AgGr)
  Gulf South Growth Fund (Gr)
  Income Bond Fund (IncM)
  Income Equity Fund (IncE)
  Intermediate Bond Fund (IncB)
  Intermediate Tax-Free Bond Fund (NMuB)
  International Equity Index Fund (Intl)
  Kentucky Municipal Bond Fund (SMuB)
  Large Company Growth Fund (Gr)
  Large Company Value Fund (Gr&I)
  Limited Volatility Bond Fund (IncM)
  Louisiana Municipal Bond Fund (SMuB)
  Municipal Income Fund (NMuB)
  Municipal Money Market Fund (NMMX)
  Ohio Municipal Bond Fund (SMuB)
  Ohio Municipal Money Market Fund
    (SMMX)
  One Group Investor Balanced Fund (Bal)
  One Group Investor Conservative Growth
    Fund (IncM)
  One Group Investor Growth and Income
    Fund (Gr&I)
  One Group Investor Growth Fund (Gr)
  Prime Money Market Fund (MM)
  Treasury & Agency Bond Fund (USGv)
  Treasury Only Money Market Fund (MM)
  Ultra Short-Term Income Fund (GNMA)
  U.S. Treasury Money Market Fund (MM)
  Value Growth Fund (Gr)
  West Virginia Municipal Bond Fund
    (SMuB)

OpCap Advisors Funds
One World Financial Ctr.
New York, NY 10281-1098
800/207-6909
OCC Cash Reserves, Inc.
  California Municipal Portfolio (SMMX)
  General Municipal Portfolio (NMMX)
  Government Portfolio (MM)
  New York Municipal Portfolio (SMMX)
  Primary Portfolio (MM)

OppenheimerFunds Family (Denver)
6803 S. Tucson Way
Englewood, CO 80112
800/525-7048
Centennial America Fund L.P. (MM)
Centennial California Tax-Exempt Trust
  (SMMX)
Centennial Government Trust (MM)
Centennial Money Market Trust (MM)
Centennial New York Tax-Exempt Trust
  (SMMX)
Centennial Tax-Exempt Trust (NMMX)
Daily Cash Accumulation Fund, Inc. (MM)
Oppenheimer Champion Income Fund
  (HiYB)
Oppenheimer Equity Income Fund (IncE)
Oppenheimer High Yield Fund (HiYB)
Oppenheimer Integrity Funds
  Oppenheimer Bond Fund (IncB)
  Oppenheimer Value Stock Fund (Gr&I)
Oppenheimer International Bond Fund
  (GloB)
Oppenheimer Limited-Term Government
  Fund (USGv)
Oppenheimer Main Street Funds, Inc.
  California Municipal Fund (SMuB)
  Income & Growth Fund (Gr&I)
Oppenheimer Real Asset Fund (IncM)
Oppenheimer Strategic Income & Growth
  Fund (IncM)
Oppenheimer Strategic Income Fund
  (IncM)
Oppenheimer Total Return Fund, Inc.
  (Gr&I)
Oppenheimer Variable Account Funds
  Oppenheimer Bond Fund (IncB)
  Oppenheimer Capital Appreciation Fund
    (AgGr)
  Oppenheimer Global Securities Fund
    (GloE)
  Oppenheimer Growth & Income Fund
    (Gr&I)
  Oppenheimer Growth Fund (Gr)
  Oppenheimer High Income Fund (HiYB)
  Oppenheimer Money Fund (MM)
  Oppenheimer Multiple Strategies Fund
    (Flex)
  Oppenheimer Strategic Bond Fund (IncB)
Panorama Series Fund, Inc.
  Growth Portfolio (Gr)

International Equity Portfolio (Intl)
LifeSpan Balanced Portfolio (Bal)
LifeSpan Capital Appreciation Portfolio
  (Flex)
Panorama Life Span Diversified Income
  Portfolio (IncM)
Total Return Portfolio (Bal)

OppenheimerFunds Family (New York)
Two World Trade Ctr.
New York, NY 10048-0203
800/525-7048
Oppenheimer California Municipal Fund
  (SMuB)
Oppenheimer Capital Appreciation Fund
  (AgGr)
Oppenheimer Developing Markets Fund
  (Intl)
Oppenheimer Discovery Fund (AgGr)
Oppenheimer Enterprise Fund (AgGr)
Oppenheimer Fund (Gr)
Oppenheimer Global Emerging Growth
  Fund (GloE)
Oppenheimer Global Fund (GloE)
Oppenheimer Global Growth & Income
  Fund (GloE)
Oppenheimer Gold & Special Minerals
  Fund (PM/G)
Oppenheimer Growth Fund (Gr)
Oppenheimer International Growth Fund
  (Intl)
Oppenheimer Money Market Fund, Inc.
  (MM)
Oppenheimer Multiple Strategies Fund
  (Flex)
Oppenheimer Multi-State Municipal Trust
  Oppenheimer Florida Municipal Fund
    (SMuB)
  Oppenheimer New Jersey Municipal Fund
    (SMuB)
  Oppenheimer Pennsylvania Municipal
    Fund (SMuB)
Oppenheimer Municipal Bond Fund
  (NMuB)
Oppenheimer Municipal Fund
  Oppenheimer Insured Municipal Fund
    (NMuB)
  Oppenheimer Intermediate Fund (NMuB)
Oppenheimer New York Municipal Fund
  (SMuB)
Oppenheimer Series Fund, Inc.
  Oppenheimer Disciplined Allocation Fund
    (Bal)
  Oppenheimer Disciplined Value Fund (Gr)
  Oppenheimer LifeSpan Balanced Fund
    (Bal)
  Oppenheimer LifeSpan Growth Fund (Flex)
  Oppenheimer LifeSpan Income Fund
    (IncM)
Oppenheimer U.S. Government Trust
  (USGv)

**OppenheimerFunds Family
(Quest Funds)**
Two World Trade Center
New York, NY 10048-0203
800/525-7048
Oppenheimer Quest for Value Funds
  Oppenheimer Quest Growth & Income
  Value Fund (Gr&I)
  Oppenheimer Quest Officers Value Fund
  (Gr)
  Oppenheimer Quest Opportunity Value
  Fund (Flex)
  Oppenheimer Quest Small Cap Value
  Fund (AgGr)
  Oppenheimer Quest Capital Value Fund,
  Inc. (Gr)
  Oppenheimer Quest Global Value Fund,
  Inc. (GloE)
  Oppenheimer Quest Value Fund, Inc. (Gr)

**OppenheimerFunds Family
(Rochester Funds)**
350 Linden Oaks
Rochester, NY 14625-2807
800/552-1149
Bond Fund Series
  Oppenheimer Bond Fund for Growth
  (Gr&I)
Rochester Fund Municipals (SMuB)
Rochester Portfolio Series
  Limited Term New York Municipal Fund
  (SMuB)

ORI Funds
P.O. Box 419032
Kansas City, MO 64141-6032
800/407-7298
ORI Funds, Inc.
  ORI Growth Fund (Gr)

O'Shaughnessy Funds, Inc.
60 Arch St.
Greenwich, CT 06830
800/797-0773
O'Shaughnessey Funds, Inc.
  O'Shaughnessy Aggressive Growth Fund
  (AgGr)
  O'Shaughnessy Cornerstone Growth Fund
  (Gr)
  O'Shaughnessy Cornerstone Value Fund
  (Gr&I)
  O'Shaughnessy Dogs of the Market Fund
  (Gr&I)

Overland Express Funds, Inc.
111 Center St.
Ste. 300
Stephens Bldg.
Little Rock, AR 72201-4402
800/458-6589
Overland Express Funds, Inc.

California Tax-Free Bond Fund (SMuB)
California Tax-Free Money Market Fund
  (SMMX)
Index Allocation Fund (Flex)
Money Market Fund (MM)
Municipal Income Fund (NMuB)
National Tax Free Money Market Fund
  (NMMX)
Short-Term Government/Corporate
  Income Fund (USGv)
Short-Term Municipal Income Fund
  (NMuB)
Small Cap Strategy Fund (AgGr)
Strategic Growth Fund (AgGr)
Sweep Fund (MM)
U.S. Government Income Fund (USGv)
U.S. Treasury Money Market Fund (MM)
Variable Rate Government Fund (GNMA)

Pacific Advisors Funds
206 N. Jackson St.
Ste. 201
Glendale, CA 91206
800/989-6693
Pacific Advisors Fund Inc.
  Balanced Fund (Bal)
  Government Securities Fund (USGv)
  Income Fund (IncE)
  Small Cap Fund (AgGr)

Pacific Capital Funds
3435 Stelzer Rd.
Columbus, OH 43219-3035
800/451-8377
Pacific Capital Funds
  Pacific Capital Diversified Fixed Income
  Fund (IncM)
  Pacific Capital Growth Stock Fund (Gr)
  Pacific Capital Income Stock Fund (IncE)
  Pacific Capital New Asia Growth Fund
  (Intl)
  Pacific Capital Short/Intermediate
  Treasury Securities Fund (USGv)
  Pacific Capital Tax-Free Securities Fund
  (NMuB)
  Pacific Capital Tax-Free Short
  Intermediate Securities Fund (NMuB)
  Pacific Capital U.S. Treasury Securities
  Fund (USGv)

Pacific Financial Research Funds
9601 Wilshire Blvd.
Ste. 800
Beverly Hills, CA 90210-5210
800/776-5033
Clipper Fund, Inc. (Gr)

Pacific Horizon Funds
3435 Stelzer Rd.
Columbus, OH 43219
800/332-3863

Pacific Horizon Funds, Inc. (The)
Aggressive Growth Fund (AgGr)
Asset Allocation Fund (Flex)
Blue Chip Fund (Gr)
California Tax-Exempt Bond Fund
(SMuB)
California Tax-Exempt Money Market
Fund (SMMX)
Capital Income Fund (Gr&I)
Corporate Bond Fund (CorB)
Corporate Bond Fund (IncM)
Government Fund (MM)
Intermediate Grade Fund (IncB)
International Equity Fund (Intl)
National Municipal Bond Fund (NMuB)
Prime Fund (MM)
Short-Term Government Fund (USGv)
Tax-Exempt Money Fund (NMMX)
Treasury Fund (MM)
Treasury Only Fund (MM)
U.S. Government Securities Fund
(USGv)

PaineWebber Funds
1285 Avenue of the Americas
PaineWebber Bldg.
New York, NY 10019-6028
800/647-1568
Liquid Institutional Reserves
Government Securities Fund (MM)
Money Market Fund (MM)
Treasury Securities Fund (MM)
Managed Accounts Services Portfolio Trust
PACE Global Fixed Income Investments
(GloB)
PACE Government Securities Fixed
Income Investments (USGv)
PACE Intermediate Fixed Income
Investments (IncB)
PACE International Emerging Markets
Equity Investments (GloE)
PACE International Equity Investments
(Intl)
PACE Large Company Growth Equity
Investments (Gr)
PACE Large Company Value Equity
Investments (Gr&I)
PACE Money Market Investments
(NMMX)
PACE Municipal Fixed Income
Investments (NMuB)
PACE Small/Medium Company Growth
Equity Investments (AgGr)
PACE Small/Medium Company Value
Equity Investments (Gr)
PACE Strategic Fixed Income Investments
(IncB)
PaineWebber America Fund
PaineWebber Growth and Income Fund
(Gr&I)
PaineWebber Cashfund, Inc. (MM)

PaineWebber Financial Services Growth
Fund, Inc. (Gr)
PaineWebber Investment Series
PaineWebber Global Income Fund (GloB)
PaineWebber Investment Trust I
PaineWebber Global Equity Fund (GloE)
PaineWebber Tactical Allocation Fund
(Flex)
PaineWebber Investment Trust II
PaineWebber Emerging Markets Equity
Fund (Intl)
PaineWebber Managed Assets Trust
PaineWebber Capital Appreciation Fund
(Gr)
PaineWebber Managed Investments Trust
PaineWebber Asia Pacific Growth Fund
(Intl)
PaineWebber High Income Fund (HiYB)
PaineWebber Investment Grade Income
Fund (CorB)
PaineWebber Low Duration U.S.
Government Income Fund (USGv)
PaineWebber U.S. Government Income
Fund (GNMA)
PaineWebber Utility Income Fund
(IncB)
PaineWebber Managed Municipal Trust
PaineWebber RMA California Municipal
Money Fund (SMMX)
PaineWebber RMA New Jersey Municipal
Money Fund (SMMX)
PaineWebber RMA New York Municipal
Money Fund (SMMX)
PaineWebber Master Series, Inc.
PaineWebber Balanced Fund (Flex)
PaineWebber Money Market Fund (MM)
PaineWebber Municipal Series
PaineWebber Municipal High Income
Fund (NMuB)
PaineWebber New York Tax-Free Income
Fund (SMuB)
PaineWebber Mutual Fund Trust
PaineWebber California Tax-Free Income
Fund (SMuB)
PaineWebber National Tax-Free Income
Fund (NMuB)
PaineWebber Olympus Fund
PaineWebber Growth Fund (Gr)
PaineWebber RMA Money Fund, Inc.
PaineWebber Retirement Money Fund
(MM)
PaineWebber RMA Money Market
Portfolio (MM)
PaineWebber RMA New Jersey Portfolio
(SMMX)
PaineWebber RMA U.S. Government
Portfolio (MM)
PaineWebber RMA Tax-Free Fund, Inc.
(NMMX)
PaineWebber Securities Trust
PaineWebber Small Cap Fund (AgGr)

PaineWebber Strategic Income Fund
  (IncM)
PaineWebber Series Trust
  Aggressive Growth Portfolio (AgGr)
  Balanced Portfolio (Flex)
  Global Growth Portfolio (GloE)
  Global Income Portfolio (GloB)
  Growth and Income Portfolio (Gr&I)
  Growth Portfolio (Gr)
  High Grade Fixed Income Portfolio (IncB)
  Money Market Portfolio (MM)
  Strategic Fixed Income Portfolio (USGv)

Palladian Trust
4225 Executive Sq.
Ste. 270
La Jolla, CA 92037
619/677-5917
Palladian Trust
  Global Interactive/Telecomm Portfolio
    (GloE)
  Global Strategic Income Portfolio (GloB)
  Growth Portfolio (Gr)
  International Growth Portfolio (Intl)
  Value Portfolio (AgGr)

PanAgora Institutional Funds
260 Franklin St.
Boston, MA 02110-3112
800/423-6041
PanAgora Institutional Funds (The)
  PanAgora Asset Allocation Fund (Flex)
  PanAgora International Equity Fund (Intl)

Papp & Associates Funds
4400 N. 32nd St.
Ste. 280
Phoenix, AZ 85018-3965
800/421-4004
Papp America-Abroad Fund, Inc. (Gr)
Papp America-Pacific Rim Fund, Inc. (GloE)
Papp (The L. Roy) Stock Fund, Inc. (Gr)

Park Avenue Portfolio
201 Park Ave. South
New York, NY 10003-1605
800/221-3253
Park Avenue Portfolio (The)
  Guardian Baillie Gifford Emerging
    Markets Fund (Intl)
  Guardian Baillie Gifford International
    Fund (Intl)
Park Avenue Portfolio (The)
  Guardian Asset Allocation Fund (Flex)
  Guardian Cash Management Fund (MM)
  Guardian Investment Quality Bond Fund
    (CorB)
  Guardian Park Avenue Fund (Gr)
  Guardian Park Avenue Small Cap Fund
    (AgGr)
  Guardian Tax-Exempt Fund (NMuB)

Parkstone Group of Funds
3435 Stelzer Rd.
Columbus, OH 43219-3035
800/451-8377
Parkstone Group of Funds (The)
  Balanced Fund (Bal)
  Bond Fund (IncB)
  Equity Fund (Gr)
  High Income Equity Fund (IncE)
  Intermediate Government Obligations
    Fund (USGv)
  International Discovery Fund (Intl)
  Large Capitalization Fund (Gr)
  Limited Maturity Bond Fund (IncB)
  Michigan Municipal Bond Fund (SMuB)
  Municipal Bond Fund (NMuB)
  Prime Obligation Fund (MM)
  Small Capitalization Fund (AgGr)
  Tax-Free Obligation Fund (NMMX)
  Treasury Fund (MM)
  U.S. Government Income Fund (USGv)
  U.S. Government Obligations Fund
    (MM)

Parnassus Funds
One Market St.
Steuart Twr. #1600
San Francisco, CA 94105
800/999-3505
Parnassus Fund (The) (Gr)
Parnassus Income Fund (The)
  Balanced Portfolio (Bal)
  California Tax-Exempt Portfolio
    (SMuB)
  Fixed-Income Portfolio (IncB)

Pasadena Group of Mutual Funds
P.O. Box 8505
Boston, MA 02266-8505
800/648-8050
Pasadena Investment Trust
  Pasadena Balanced Return Fund (Bal)
  Pasadena Global Growth Fund (GloE)
  Pasadena Growth Fund (Gr)
  Pasadena Nifty-Fifty Fund (Gr)
  Pasadena Small and Mid-Cap Growth
    Fund (AgGr)
  Pasadena Value 25 Fund (Gr&I)

Pathfinder Fund
4023 W. Sixth St.
Los Angeles, CA 90020-4403
800/444-4778
Pathfinder Fund (The)
  Pathfinder Fund (AgGr)

Pax World Fund
222 State St.
Portsmouth, NH 03801-3828
800/767-1729
Pax World Fund, Inc. (Bal)

Payden & Rygel Investment Group
333 S. Grand Ave., 32nd Fl.
Los Angeles, CA 90071-1504
800/5PAYDEN
Payden & Rygel Investment Group
  Global Balanced Fund (GloB)
  Global Fixed Income Fund (GloB)
  Global Short Bond Fund (GloB)
  Growth and Income Fund (Gr&I)
  Intermediate Bond Fund (CorB)
  International Bond Fund (GloB)
  International Equity Fund (Intl)
  Investment Quality Bond Fund (IncB)
  Limited Maturity Fund (IncB)
  Market Return Fund (IncM)
  Short Bond Fund (IncB)
  Short Duration Tax-Exempt Fund (NMuB)
  Tax Exempt Bond Fund (NMuB)
  Total Return Fund (IncB)
  U.S. Treasury Fund (USGv)

PBHG Funds
One Freedom Valley Drive
Oaks, PA 19456
800/809-8008
PBHG Funds, Inc.
  PBHG Cash Reserve Fund (MM)
  PBHG Core Growth Fund (Gr)
  PBHG Emerging Growth Fund (AgGr)
  PBHG Growth Fund (AgGr)
  PBHG International Fund (Intl)
  PBHG Large Cap Growth Fund (Gr)
  PBHG Large Cap 20 Fund (Gr)
  PBHG Large Cap Value Fund (Gr)
  PBHG Limited Fund (AgGr)
  PBHG Small-Cap Value Fund (AgGr)
  PBHG Select Equity Fund (Gr)
  PBHG Mid-Cap Value Fund (Gr)
  PBHG Strategic Small Company Fund
    (AgGr)
  PBHG Technology &
    Telecommunications Fund (Gr)
PBHG Insurance Series
  PBHG Growth II Portfolio (Gr)
  PBHG Large Cap Growth Portfolio (Gr)
  PBHG Technology & Communications
    Portfolio (Gr)

Pegasus Funds
3435 Stelzer Road
Columbus, OH 43219-3035
800/688-3350
Pegasus Funds (The)
  Pegasus Bond Fund (CorB)
  Pegasus Cash Management Fund (MM)
  Pegasus Equity Income Fund (IncE)
  Pegasus Equity Index Fund (Gr&I)
  Pegasus Growth and Value Fund (Gr&I)
  Pegasus Growth Fund (Gr)
  Pegasus Income Fund (IncB)
  Pegasus Intermediate Bond Fund (CorB)

Pegasus Intermediate Municipal Bond
  Fund (NMuB)
Pegasus International Bond Fund (GloB)
Pegasus International Equity Fund (Intl)
Pegasus Intrinsic Value Fund (Gr)
Pegasus Managed Assets Balanced Fund
  (Bal)
Pegasus Managed Assets Conservative
  Fund (IncM)
Pegasus Michigan Municipal Bond Fund
  (SMuB)
Pegasus Michigan Municipal Money
  Market Fund (SMMX)
Pegasus Mid-Cap Opportunity Fund
  (AgGr)
Pegasus Money Market Fund (MM)
Pegasus Municipal Bond Fund (NMuB)
Pegasus Municipal Money Market Fund
  (NMMX)
Pegasus Short Bond Fund (CorB)
Pegasus Small Cap Opportunity Fund
  (Gr)
Pegasus Treasury Money Market Fund
  (MM)
Pegasus Treasury Prime Cash
  Management Fund (MM)
Pegasus U.S. Government Securities Cash
  Management Fund (MM)

Peregrine Funds
4 Embarcadero Ctr.
San Francisco, CA 94111
888/352-6938
Peregrine Funds
  Asia Pacific Growth Fund (Intl)

Performance Funds
3435 Stelzer Rd.
Columbus, OH 43219-3035
800/762-7085
Performance Funds Trust
  Equity Fund (Gr)
  Intermediate Term Fixed Income Fund
    (IncB)
  MidCap Growth Fund (Gr)
  Money Market Fund (MM)
  Short-Term Fixed Income Fund (IncB)

Perritt Capital Growth Fund, Inc.
120 S. Riverside Plaza
Ste. 1745
Chicago, IL 60606-3911
800/331-8936
Perritt Capital Growth Fund, Inc. (AgGr)

Phillips Capital Investments, Inc.
15400 Knoll Trail-Ste. 100
P.O. Box 796787
Dallas, TX 75379-6787
972/458-2448
Phillips Capital Investments, Inc. (Gr)

Phoenix Duff & Phelps Family of Funds
101 Munson St.
Greenfield, MA 01301-9659
800/243-1574
Phoenix-Aberdeen Series Fund
 Phoenix-Aberdeen Global Small Cap
  Fund (GloE)
 Phoenix-Aberdeen New Asia Fund (Intl)
Phoenix California Tax-Exempt Bonds, Inc.
 (SMuB)
Phoenix Income & Growth Fund (Bal)
Phoenix Institutional Mutual Funds
 Balanced Portfolio (Bal)
 Enhanced Reserves Portfolio (IncB)
 Growth Stock Portfolio (Gr)
 Managed Bond Portfolio (IncB)
 Money Market Portfolio (MM)
 Real Estate Equity Securities Portfolio
  (Gr&I)
 U.S. Government Securities Portfolio
  (USGv)
Phoenix Multi-Portfolio Fund
 Phoenix Diversified Income Fund Series
  (IncM)
 Phoenix Emerging Market Bond Portfolio
  (GloB)
 Phoenix International Portfolio (Intl)
 Phoenix Mid-Cap Portfolio (Gr)
 Phoenix Real Estate Securities Portfolio
  (Gr&I)
 Phoenix Tax-Exempt Bond Portfolio
  (NMuB)
Phoenix Multi-Sector Fixed Income Fund,
 Inc. (IncB)
Phoenix Multi-Sector Short-Term Bond
 Fund (IncB)
Phoenix Series Fund
 Phoenix Aggressive Growth Fund (AgGr)
 Phoenix Balanced Fund Series (Bal)
 Phoenix Convertible Fund Series (Gr&I)
 Phoenix Growth Fund Series (Gr)
 Phoenix High Yield Fund Series (HiYB)
 Phoenix Money Market Fund Series
  (MM)
 Phoenix U.S. Government Securities Fund
  Series (USGv)
Phoenix Strategic Allocation Fund (Flex)
Phoenix Strategic Equity Series Fund
 Phoenix Equity Opportunities Fund
  (Gr&I)
 Phoenix Small Cap Fund (Gr)
 Phoenix Strategic Theme Fund (Gr)
Phoenix Worldwide Opportunities Fund
 (GloE)

Pilgrim America Funds
Two Renaissance Sq.
40 N. Central Ave.,
Ste. 1200
Phoenix, AZ 85004-4424
800/331-1080

Pilgrim America Investment Funds, Inc.
 Pilgrim America High Yield Fund (HiYB)
 Pilgrim America MagnaCap Fund (Gr&I)
Pilgrim America Masters Series, Inc.
 Pilgrim America Masters Asia-Pacific
  Equity Fund (Intl)
 Pilgrim America Masters LargeCap Value
  Fund (Gr)
 Pilgrim America Masters MidCap Value
  Fund (Gr)
Pilgrim Government Securities Income
 Fund, Inc. (USGv)

Pillar Funds
One Freedom Valley Drive
Oaks, PA 19456
800/342-5734
Pillar Funds (The)
 Pillar Balanced Growth Fund (Bal)
 Pillar Equity Growth Fund (Gr&I)
 Pillar Equity Income Fund (Gr&I)
 Pillar Equity Value Fund (Gr&I)
 Pillar Fixed Income Fund (IncM)
 Pillar GNMA Fund (GNMA)
 Pillar Intermediate Term Government
  Securities Fund (USGv)
 Pillar International Growth Fund (Intl)
 Pillar Mid Cap Value Fund (AgGr)
 Pillar New Jersey Municipal Securities
  Fund (SMuB)
 Pillar Pennsylvania Municipal Securities
  Fund (SMuB)
 Pillar Prime Obligations Fund (MM)
 Pillar Short Term Investment Fund (CorB)
 Pillar Tax Exempt Money Market Fund
  (NMMX)
 Pillar U.S. Treasury Money Market Fund
  (MM)
 Pillar U.S. Treasury Securities Plus
  Money Market Fund (MM)

PIMCO Funds
840 Newport Ctr. Dr.
Ste. 360
Newport Beach, CA 92660-6322
800/927-4648
PIMCO Funds: Pacific Investment
 Management Series
 Foreign Bond Fund (GloB)
 Global Bond Fund (GloB)
 Global Bond Fund II (GloB)
 High Yield Fund (HiYB)
 International Bond Fund (GloB)
 Long-Term U.S. Government Fund
  (USGv)
 Low Duration Fund (IncB)
 Low Duration Fund II (IncB)
 Low Duration Fund III (IncB)
 Moderate Duration Fund (IncB)
 Money Market Fund (MM)
 Real Return Bond Fund (IncB)

Short-Term Fund (IncB)
StocksPLUS Fund (Gr&I)
Strategic Balanced Fund (Bal)
Total Return Fund (IncB)
Total Return Fund II (IncB)
Total Return Fund III (IncB)
Cash Accumulation Trust
National Money Market Fund (MM)
PIMCO Funds: Multi-Manager Series
Balanced Fund (Bal)
Capital Appreciation Fund (Gr)
Core Equity Fund (Gr&I)
Emerging Markets Fund (Intl)
Enhanced Equity Fund (Gr)
Equity Income Fund (IncE)
Growth Fund (Gr)
Innovation Fund (Gr)
International Developed Fund (Intl)
International Fund (Intl)
Micro Cap Growth Fund (AgGr)
Mid Cap Equity Fund (Gr)
MidCap Growth Fund (Gr)
Opportunity Fund (AgGr)
Precious Metals Fund (PM/G)
Renaissance Fund (Gr&I)
Small Cap Growth Fund (AgGr)
Small Cap Value Fund (Gr&I)
Target Fund (AgGr)
Tax Exempt Fund (NMuB)
Value Fund (Gr&I)

Pioneer Funds
60 State St.
Boston, MA 02109-1803
800/225-6292
Pioneer America Income Trust (USGv)
Pioneer Balanced Fund, Inc. (Bal)
Pioneer Bond Fund (CorB)
Pioneer Emerging Markets Fund (Intl)
Pioneer Europe Fund (Intl)
Pioneer Fund (Gr&I)
Pioneer Growth Shares, Inc. (Gr)
Pioneer Growth Trust
Pioneer Capital Growth Fund (Gr)
Pioneer Equity-Income Fund (IncE)
Pioneer Gold Shares (PM/G)
Pioneer India Fund (Intl)
Pioneer Intermediate Tax Free Fund (NMuB)
Pioneer International Growth Fund (Intl)
Pioneer Micro-Cap Fund (AgGr)
Pioneer Mid-Cap Fund (Gr&I)
Pioneer Money Market Trust
Pioneer Cash Reserves Fund (MM)
Pioneer Real Estates Shares (IncE)
Pioneer Short-Term Income Trust (IncM)
Pioneer Small Company Fund (Gr)
Pioneer Tax-Free Income Fund (NMuB)
Pioneer II (Gr&I)
Pioneer Variable Contracts Trust
Pioneer America Income Portfolio (IncM)
Pioneer Balanced Portfolio (Bal)

Pioneer Capital Growth Portfolio (Gr)
Pioneer Equity Income Portfolio (IncE)
Pioneer International Growth Portfolio
(Intl)
Pioneer Money Market Portfolio (MM)
Pioneer Real Estate Growth Portfolio (Gr)
Pioneer Swiss Franc Bond Portfolio
(GloB)
Pioneer World Equity Fund (GloE)

Piper Capital Funds
222 S. Ninth St.
Piper Jaffray Twr.
Minneapolis, MN 55402-3804
800/866-7778
Piper Funds Inc.
Balanced Fund (Bal)
Emerging Growth Fund (AgGr)
Government Income Fund (GNMA)
Growth and Income Fund (Gr&I)
Growth Fund (Gr)
Intermediate Bond Fund (IncB)
Minnesota Tax-Exempt Fund (SMuB)
Money Market Fund (MM)
National Tax-Exempt Fund (NMuB)
Small Company Growth Fund (AgGr)
Tax-Exempt Money Market Fund
(NMMX)
U.S. Government Money Market Fund
(MM)
Piper Funds Inc. II
Piper Adjustable Rate Mortgage Securities
Fund (GNMA)
Piper Global Funds, Inc.
Emerging Markets Growth Fund (Intl)
Pacific-European Growth Fund (Intl)
Piper Institutional Funds, Inc.
Institutional Money Market Fund (MM)

Planters Funds
Federated Investors Twr.
1001 Liberty Ave.
Pittsburgh, PA 15222-3779
800/341-7400
Planters Funds (The)
Tennessee Tax-Free Bond Fund (SMuB)

Portico Funds
615 E. Michigan St.
P.O. Box 3011
Milwaukee, WI 53201-3011
800/982-8909
Portico Funds, Inc. (The)
Balanced Fund (Bal)
Bond IMMDEX Fund (CorB)
Equity Index Fund (Gr&I)
Growth and Income Fund (Gr&I)
Institutional Money Market Fund (MM)
Intermediate Bond Market Fund (IncB)
International Equity Fund (Intl)
MicroCap Fund (AgGr)

MidCore Growth Fund (Gr)
Money Market Fund (MM)
Short-Term Bond Market Fund (IncB)
Special Growth Fund (AgGr)
Tax-Exempt Intermediate Bond Fund
 (NMuB)
Tax Exempt Money Market Fund
 (NMMX)
U.S. Government Money Market Fund
 (MM)
U.S. Treasury Money Market Fund (MM)

PRAGMA Investment Trust
7150 Greenville Ave.
Ste. 101, LB 340
Dallas, TX 75231-7900
800/738-2065
PRAGMA Investment Trust
 PRAGMA Providence Fund (AgGr)

Praxis Mutual Funds
3435 Stelzer Rd.
Columbus, OH 43219-3035
800/9-PRAXIS
MMA Praxis Mutual Funds
 Growth Fund (Gr&I)
 Intermediate Income Fund (IncM)
 International Fund (Intl)

Preferred Group of Funds
100 NE Adams St.
Peoria, IL 61629-7310
800/662-GROW
Preferred Group of Mutual Funds (The)
 Preferred Asset Allocation Fund (Flex)
 Preferred Balanced Fund (Bal)
 Preferred Fixed Income Fund (IncM)
 Preferred Growth Fund (Gr)
 Preferred International Fund (Intl)
 Preferred Money Market Fund (MM)
 Preferred Short-Term Government
 Securities Fund (USGv)
 Preferred Small Cap Fund (AgGr)
 Preferred Value Fund (Gr&I)

Primary Trend Funds
First Financial Centre
700 N. Water St.
Milwaukee, WI 53202-4226
800/443-6544
Primary Income Funds, Inc. (The)
 Primary Income Fund (IncM)
 Primary U.S. Government Fund (USGv)
Primary Trend Fund, Inc. (The) (Flex)

Principal Preservation Funds
215 N. Main St.
West Bend, WI 53095-3317
800/826-4600
Principal Preservation Portfolios, Inc.
 Cash Reserve Portfolio (MM)

 Dividend Achievers Portfolio (Gr&I)
 Government Portfolio (USGv)
 PE Tech 100 Index Portfolio (AgGr)
 S&P 100 Plus Portfolio (Gr&I)
 Select Value Portfolio (Gr)
 Tax-Exempt Portfolio (NMuB)
 Wisconsin Tax-Exempt Portfolio (SMuB)

Princor Funds
The Principal Financial Group
Des Moines, IA 50392-0200
800/247-4123
Principal Aggressive Growth Fund (Gr)
Principal Asset Allocation Fund (Flex)
Principal Balanced Fund, Inc. (Bal)
Principal Bond Fund, Inc. (CorB)
Principal Capital Accumulation Fund, Inc.
 (Gr&I)
Principal Emerging Growth Fund, Inc.
 (AgGr)
Principal Government Securities Fund, Inc.
 (GNMA)
Principal Growth Fund (Gr)
Principal High Yield Fund, Inc. (HiYB)
Principal Money Market Fund, Inc. (MM)
Principal Special Markets Fund, Inc.
 International Securities Portfolio (Intl)
 Mortgage-Backed Securities Portfolio
 (GNMA)
Principal World Fund (Intl)
Princor Balanced Fund, Inc. (Bal)
Princor Blue Chip Fund, Inc. (Gr&I)
Princor Bond Fund, Inc. (CorB)
Princor Capital Accumulation Fund, Inc.
 (Gr&I)
Princor Cash Management Fund, Inc. (MM)
Princor Emerging Growth Fund, Inc.
 (AgGr)
Princor Government Securities Income
 Fund, Inc. (GNMA)
Princor Growth Fund, Inc. (Gr)
Princor High Yield Fund, Inc. (HiYB)
Princor Limited Term Bond Fund, Inc.
 (IncB)
Princor Tax-Exempt Bond Fund, Inc.
 (NMuB)
Princor Tax-Exempt Cash Management
 Fund, Inc. (NMMX)
Princor Utilities Fund, Inc. (IncM)
Princor World Fund, Inc. (GloE)

Professionally Managed Portfolios
479 W. 22nd St.
New York, NY 10011
800/385-7003
Professionally Managed Portfolios
 Academy Value Fund (Gr)
 Avondale Total Return Fund (Bal)
 Boston Managed Growth Fund (IncM)
 Harris Bretall Sullivan & Smith Growth
 Equity Fund (Gr)

Hodges Fund (Gr)
Insightful Investor Growth Fund (Gr)
Leonetti Balanced Fund (Bal)
Lighthouse Growth Fund (Gr)
Matrix Emerging Growth Fund (AgGr)
Matrix Growth Fund (Gr)
Osterweis Fund (Gr&I)
Perkins Opportunity Fund (AgGr)
Pro-Conscience Women's Equity Mutual
  Fund (Gr)
Pzena Focused Value Fund (Gr)
Titan Financial Services Fund (Gr)
Trent Equity Fund (Gr)
U.S. Global Leaders Growth Fund (Gr)

Profit Funds Investment Trust
8720 Georgia Ave.
Ste. 808
Silver Spring, MD 20910
888/335-6629
Profit Funds Investment Trust
  Profit Lomax Value Fund (Gr)

Protective Investment Funds
2801 Hwy. 280 South
Birmingham, AL 35223-2407
800/627-0220
Protective Investment Company
  Protective Capital Growth Fund (Gr)
  Protective Core U.S. Equity Fund (Gr&I)
  Protective Global Income Fund (GloB)
  Protective Growth and Income Fund
    (Gr&I)
  Protective International Equity Fund (Intl)
  Protective Money Market Fund (MM)
  Protective Small Cap Equity Fund (AgGr)

Provident Funds
300 N. Lake Ave.
Pasadena, CA 91101-4106
800/618-7643
PIC Investment Trust
  PIC Balanced Portfolio (Bal)
  PIC Growth Fund (Gr)
  PIC Growth Portfolio (Gr)
  PIC Pinnacle Balanced Fund (Bal)
  PIC Pinnacle Growth Fund (Gr)
  PIC Pinnacle Small Company Growth
    Fund (AgGr)
  PIC Small Cap Growth Fund (AgGr)
  PIC Small Company Growth Fund (AgGr)

Provident Institutional Funds Group
400 Bellevue Pkwy.
Wilmington, DE 19809-3748
800/422-6538
Provident Institutional Funds Group
  California Intermediate Municipal Fund
    (SMuB)
  California Money Fund (SMMX)
  Federal Trust Fund Portfolio (MM)

FedFund Portfolio (MM)
Intermediate Municipal Fund (NMuB)
MuniCash Portfolio (NMMX)
Municipal Fund for New York Investors
  (SMMX)
Municipal Fund for Temporary
  Investments (NMMX)
TempCash Portfolio (MM)
TempFund Portfolio (MM)
T-Fund Portfolio (MM)
Treasury Trust Fund Portfolio (MM)

Prudential Mutual Funds
One Seaport Plaza
New York, NY 10292
800/225-1852
BlackRock Government Income Trust (The)
  (USGv)
Command Government Fund (MM)
Command Money Fund (MM)
Command Tax-Free Fund (NMMX)
Global Government Plus Fund, Inc. (The)
  (GloB)
Global Total Return Fund, Inc. (The)
  (GloB)
Global Utility Fund, Inc. (GloE)
Nicholas-Applegate Fund, Inc.
  Nicholas-Applegate Growth Equity Fund
    (Gr)
Prudential Allocation Fund
  Balanced Portfolio (Flex)
  Strategy Portfolio (Flex)
Prudential California Municipal Fund
  California Income Series (SMuB)
  California Money Market Series (SMMX)
  California Series (SMuB)
Prudential Distressed Securities Fund
  (AgGr)
Prudential Diversified Bond Fund, Inc.
  (IncB)
Prudential Dryden Fund
  Prudential Dryden Active Balanced Fund
    (Bal)
  Prudential Stock Index Fund (Gr&I)
Prudential Emerging Growth Fund, Inc.
  (AgGr)
Prudential Equity Fund (Gr)
Prudential Equity Income Fund (IncE)
Prudential Europe Growth Fund (GloE)
Prudential Global Genesis Fund (GloE)
Prudential Global Limited Maturity Fund,
  Inc.
  Limited Maturity Series (GloB)
Prudential Government Income Fund
  (USGv)
Prudential Government Securities Trust
  Money Market Series (MM)
  Short-Intermediate Term Series (USGv)
  U.S. Treasury Money Market Series
    (MM)
Prudential High Yield Fund (HiYB)

Prudential Institutional Liquidity Portfolio,
Inc.
 Institutional Money Market Series (MM)
Prudential Intermediate Global Income
Fund (GloB)
Prudential Jennison Series Fund
 Prudential Jennison Growth and Income
 Fund (Gr&I)
 Prudential Jennison Growth Fund, Inc.
 (Gr)
Prudential MoneyMart Assets (MM)
Prudential Mortgage Income Fund
 (GNMA)
Prudential Multi-Sector Fund (AgGr)
Prudential Municipal Bond Fund
 High Yield Series (NMuB)
 Insured Series (NMuB)
 Intermediate Series (NMuB)
Prudential Municipal Series Fund
 Connecticut Money Market Series
 (SMMX)
 Florida Series (SMuB)
 Hawaii Series (SMuB)
 Maryland Series (SMuB)
 Massachusetts Money Market Series
 (SMMX)
 Massachusetts Series (SMuB)
 Michigan Series (SMuB)
 New Jersey Money Market Series
 (SMMX)
 New Jersey Series (SMuB)
 New York Money Market Series (SMMX)
 New York Series (SMuB)
 North Carolina Series (SMuB)
 Ohio Series (SMuB)
 Pennsylvania Series (SMuB)
Prudential National Municipals Fund
 (NMuB)
Prudential Natural Resources Fund (GloE)
Prudential Pacific Growth Fund (Intl)
Prudential Small Companies Fund (AgGr)
Prudential Special Money Market Fund
 Special Money Market Series (MM)
Prudential Structured Maturity Fund (IncB)
Prudential Tax-Free Money Fund (NMMX)
Prudential Utility Fund (IncE)
Prudential World Fund
 Global Series (GloE)
 International Stock Series (Intl)
Target Portfolio Trust (The)
 Intermediate-Term Bond Portfolio (IncB)
 International Bond Portfolio (Intl)
 International Equity Portfolio (Intl)
 Large Capitalization Growth Portfolio
 (Gr)
 Large Capitalization Value Portfolio
 (Gr&I)
 Mortgage Backed Securities Portfolio
 (GNMA)
 Small Capitalization Growth Portfolio
 (AgGr)

 Small Capitalization Value Portfolio
 (AgGr)
 Total Return Bond Portfolio (IncB)
 U.S. Government Money Market Portfolio
 (MM)

Public Employees Retirement Trust
P.O. Box 1138
St. Michaels, MD 21663
410/822-4456
Public Employees Retirement Trust (Gr&I)

Purisima Funds
13100 Skyline
Woodside, CA 94062
800/841-2858
Purisima Funds (The)
 Purisima Total Return Fund (Gr&I)

Putnam Family of Funds
One Post Office Sq.
Boston, MA 02109-2103
800/225-2465
George Putnam Fund (The) (Bal)
Putnam American Government Income
 Fund (USGv)
Putnam American Renaissance Fund
 (AgGr)
Putnam Arizona Tax-Exempt Income Fund
 (SMuB)
Putnam Asia Pacific Fund (Intl)
Putnam Asset Allocation Funds
 Balanced Portfolio (Bal)
 Conservative Portfolio (Gr&I)
 Growth Portfolio (Gr)
Putnam Balanced Fund (Gr&I)
Putnam Balanced Retirement Fund (IncE)
Putnam California Tax Exempt Income
 Fund (SMuB)
Putnam California Tax Exempt Money
 Market Fund (SMMX)
Putnam Capital Appreciation Fund (AgGr)
Putnam Convertible Income-Growth Trust
 (Gr&I)
Putnam Diversified Equity Trust (GloE)
Putnam Diversified Income Trust (IncM)
Putnam Diversified Income Trust II (IncB)
Putnam Equity Income Fund (Gr&I)
Putnam Europe Growth Fund (Intl)
Putnam Federal Income Trust (GNMA)
Putnam Florida Tax Exempt Income Fund
 (SMuB)
Putnam Fund for Growth and Income (The)
 (Gr&I)
Putnam Funds Trust
 Putnam High Yield Total Return Fund
 (HiYB)
 Putnam International Growth and Income
 Fund (Intl)
Putnam Global Governmental Income Trust
 (GloB)

Putnam Global Growth & Income Fund
(GloB)
Putnam Global Growth Fund (GloE)
Putnam Global Natural Resources Trust
(Gr)
Putnam Growth and Income Fund II (Gr&I)
Putnam Health Sciences Trust (AgGr)
Putnam High Yield Advantage Fund
(HiYB)
Putnam High Yield Trust (HiYB)
Putnam Income Fund (IncM)
Putnam Intermediate U.S. Government
Fund (USGv)
Putnam International Fund (Intl)
Putnam International Growth Fund (Intl)
Putnam Investment Funds
  Putnam International New Opportunities
  Fund (Intl)
  Putnam New Value Fund (Gr)
Putnam Investors Fund (Gr)
Putnam Japan Fund (Intl)
Putnam Massachusetts Tax Exempt Income
Fund II (SMuB)
Putnam Michigan Tax Exempt Income
Fund II (SMuB)
Putnam Minnesota Tax Exempt Income
Fund II (SMuB)
Putnam Money Market Fund (MM)
Putnam Municipal Income Fund (NMuB)
Putnam New Jersey Tax Exempt Income
Fund (SMuB)
Putnam New Opportunities Fund (Gr)
Putnam New York Tax Exempt Income
Fund (SMuB)
Putnam New York Tax Exempt Money
Market Fund (SMMX)
Putnam New York Tax Exempt
Opportunities Fund (SMuB)
Putnam Ohio Tax Exempt Income Fund II
(SMuB)
Putnam OTC and Emerging Growth Fund
(AgGr)
Putnam Pennsylvania Tax Exempt Income
Fund (SMuB)
Putnam Preferred Income Fund (IncM)
Putnam Real Estate Opportunity Fund
(Gr&I)
Putnam Research Fund (Gr)
Putnam Tax Exempt Income Fund (NMuB)
Putnam Tax Exempt Money Market Fund
(NMMX)
Putnam Tax-Free Income Trust
  Tax Free High Yield Fund (NMuB)
  Tax Free Insured Fund (NMuB)
Putnam U.S. Government Income Trust
(GNMA)
Putnam Utilities Growth and Income Fund
(Gr&I)
Putnam Variable Trust
  PVT Asia Pacific Growth Fund (Intl)
  PVT Diversified Income Fund (IncM)

PVT Global Asset Allocation Fund (GloB)
PVT Global Growth Fund (GloE)
PVT Growth and Income Fund (Gr&I)
PVT High Yield Fund (HiYB)
PVT International Growth and Income
Fund (Intl)
PVT International New Opportunities
Fund (Intl)
PVT Money Market Fund (MM)
PVT New Opportuniites Fund (Gr)
PVT New Value Fund (Gr)
PVT U.S. Government and High Quality
Bond Fund (IncB)
PVT Utilities Growth and Income Fund
(Gr&I)
PVT Vista Fund (AgGr)
PVT Voyager Fund (AgGr)
Putnam Vista Fund (AgGr)
Putnam Voyager Fund (AgGr)
Putnam Voyager II Fund (Gr)

Qualivest Funds
3435 Stelzer Rd.
Columbus, OH 43219-3035
800/743-8637
Qualivest Funds
  Diversified Bond Fund (IncB)
  Intermediate Bond Fund (IncB)
  International Opportunities Fund (Intl)
  Large Company Value Fund (Gr&I)
  Money Market Fund (MM)
  Optimized Stock Fund (Gr)
  Small Company Value Fund (AgGr)
  Tax Free Money Market Fund (NMMX)
  U.S. Treasury Money Market Fund
  (MM)

Quantitative Group of Funds
55 Old Bedford Rd.
Lincoln, MA 01773
800/331-1244
Quantitative Group of Funds
  Quantitative Foreign Frontier Fund (Intl)
  Quantitative Growth and Income Fund
  (Gr&I)
  Quantitative International Equity Fund
  (Intl)
  Quantitative Numeric Fund (AgGr)
  Quantitative Numeric II Fund (AgGr)

Rainier Mutual Funds
601 Union St.
Ste. 2801 Seattle, WA 98101
800/280-6111
Rainier Investment Management Mutual
Funds
  Balanced Fund (Bal)
  Core Equity Portfolio (Gr)
  Intermediate Fixed Income Portfolio
  (IncB)
  Small/MidCap Equity Portfolio (Gr)

Rea-Graham Funds
10966 Chalon Rd.
Los Angeles, CA 90077-3208
800/433-1998
Rea-Graham Funds, Inc.
  Rea-Graham Balanced Fund (Bal)

Reich & Tang Mutual Funds
600 Fifth Ave.
New York, NY 10020-2302
800/676-6779
California Daily Tax Free Income Fund,
  Inc. (SMMX)
Connecticut Daily Tax Free Income Fund,
  Inc. (SMMX)
Cortland Trust, Inc.
  General Money Market Fund (MM)
  Municipal Money Market Fund (NMMX)
  U.S. Government Money Market Fund
  (MM)
Daily Tax Free Income Fund, Inc. (NMMX)
Delafield Fund, Inc. (Gr)
Florida Daily Municipal Income Fund
  (SMMX)
Institutional Daily Income Fund
  Money Market Portfolio (MM)
  U.S. Government Portfolio (MM)
Michigan Daily Income Fund, Inc.
  (SMMX)
New Jersey Daily Municipal Income Fund,
  Inc. (SMMX)
New York Daily Tax Free Income Fund,
  Inc. (SMMX)
North Carolina Daily Municipal Income
  Fund, Inc. (SMMX)
Pennsylvania Daily Municipal Income Fund
  (SMMX)
Reich & Tang Equity Fund (Gr)
Short Term Income Fund, Inc.
  Money Market Portfolio (MM)
  U.S. Government Portfolio (MM)

Rembrandt Funds
One Freedom Valley Drive
Oaks, PA 19456
800/443-4725
Rembrandt Funds
  Asian Tigers Fund (Intl)
  Balanced Fund (Bal)
  Fixed Income Fund (IncB)
  Government Money Market Fund (MM)
  Growth Fund (Gr)
  Intermediate Government Fixed Income
  Fund (USGv)
  International Equity Fund (Intl)
  International Fixed Income Fund (GloB)
  Latin America Equity Fund (Intl)
  Limited Volatility Fixed Income Fund
  (IncB)
  Money Market Fund (MM)
  Small Cap Fund (AgGr)

Tax-Exempt Fixed Income Fund (NMuB)
Tax-Exempt Money Market Fund
  (NMMX)
TransEurope Fund (Intl)
Treasury Money Market Fund (MM)
Value Fund (Gr)

Republic Funds
Six St. James Ave.
9th Fl.
Boston, MA 02116
800/782-8183
Republic Funds
  Equity Fund (Gr)
  Fixed Income Fund (IncM)
  International Equity Fund (Intl)
  New York Tax Free Bond Fund (SMuB)
  New York Tax Free Money Market Fund
  (SMMX)
  U.S. Government Money Market Fund
  (MM)

Rightime Family of Funds
218 Glenside Ave.
Wyncote, PA 19095-1534
800/866-9393
Rightime Fund, Inc. (The)
  Rightime Blue Chip Fund (Gr&I)
  Rightime Fund (Gr&I)
  Rightime Government Securities Fund
  (USGv)
  Rightime MidCap Fund (Gr&I)
  Rightime Social Awareness Fund (Gr)

Rimco Funds
Federated Investors Twr.
1001 Liberty Ave.
Pittsburgh, PA 15222-3779
800/341-7400
RIMCO Monument Funds
  RIMCO Monument Bond Fund (IncB)
  RIMCO Monument Prime Money Market
  Fund (MM)
  RIMCO Monument Small Cap Equity
  Fund (Gr)
  RIMCO Monument Stock Fund (Gr&I)
  RIMCO Monument U.S. Treasury Money
  Market Fund (MM)

Riverfront Funds, Inc.
3435 Stelzer Rd.
Columbus, OH 43219-3035
800/344-2716
Riverfront Funds (The)
  Riverfront Balanced Fund (Bal)
  Riverfront Income Equity Fund (IncM)
  Riverfront Ohio Tax Free Fund (NMuB)
  Riverfront U.S. Government Income Fund
  (USGv)
  Riverfront U.S. Government Securities
  Money Market Fund (MM)

RNC Mutual Fund Group
11601 Wilshire Blvd.
Penthouse
Los Angeles, CA 90025-1770
800/431-7249
RNC Mutual Fund Group, Inc.
  RNC Equity Fund (Gr&I)
  RNC Money Market Fund (MM)

Robertson, Stephens Funds
555 California St.
Ste. 2600
San Francisco, CA 94104
800/766-FUND
Robertson Stephens Investment Trust
  Robertson Stephens Contrarian Fund (Gr)
  Robertson Stephens Developing Countries
  Fund (Intl)
  Robertson Stephens Diversified Growth
  Fund (Gr)
  Robertson Stephens Emerging Growth
  Fund (AgGr)
  Robertson Stephens Global Low-Priced
  Stock Fund (GloE)
  Robertson Stephens Global Natural
  Resources Fund (GloE)
  Robertson Stephens Global Value Fund
  (GloE)
  Robertson Stephens Growth & Income
  Fund (Gr&I)
  Robertson Stephens Information Age
  Fund (Gr)
  Robertson Stephens MicroCap Growth
  Fund (AgGr)
  Robertson Stephens Partners Fund (Gr)
  Robertson Stephens Value + Growth Fund
  (AgGr)

Rodney Square Funds
Rodney Sq. North
1100 N. Market St.
Wilmington, DE 19801-1246
800/336-9970
Rodney Square Fund (The)
  Money Market Portfolio (MM)
  U.S. Government Portfolio (MM)
Rodney Square Multi-Manager Fund (The)
  Growth Portfolio (The) (Gr)
Rodney Square Strategic Fixed-Income
  Fund
  Diversified Income Portfolio (IncB)
  Municipal Income Portfolio (NMuB)
Rodney Square Tax-Exempt Fund (The)
  (NMMX)

Royce Family of Funds
1414 Avenue of the Americas
New York, NY 10019-2514
800/221-4268
Royce Fund (The)
  Pennsylvania Mutual Fund (Gr)

  PMF II (Gr)
  Royce Equity Income Fund (IncE)
  Royce GiftShares Fund (Gr)
  Royce Global Services Fund (GloE)
  Royce Low-Priced Stock Fund (AgGr)
  Royce Micro-Cap Fund (AgGr)
  Royce Premier Fund (Gr)
  Royce Total Return Fund (Gr&I)
Royce Fund (The)
  REvest Growth and Income Fund (The)
  (Gr&I)

RREEF Real Estate Securites Fund, Inc.
875 N. Michigan Ave., 41st Fl.
Chicago, IL 60611
312/266-9300
RREEF Securities Fund, Inc.
  RREEF Real Estate Securities Fund
  (IncE)

Rydex Series Trust
6116 Executive Blvd.
Ste. 400
Rockville, MD 20852
800/820-0888
Rydex Series Trust
  High Yield Fund (HiYB)
  Institutional Money Market Fund (MM)
  Juno Fund (USGv)
  Nova Fund (AgGr)
  Over-The-Counter Fund (AgGr)
  Precious Metals Fund (PM/G)
  U.S. Government Bond Fund (USGv)
  U.S. Government Money Market Fund
  (NMMX)
  URSA Fund (AgGr)

SAFECO Family of Funds
SAFECO Plaza
Seattle, WA 98185-0001
800/426-6730
SAFECO Common Stock Trust
  SAFECO Balanced Fund (Bal)
  SAFECO Equity Fund (Gr&I)
  SAFECO Growth Fund (Gr)
  SAFECO Income Fund (IncE)
  SAFECO International Fund (Intl)
  SAFECO Northwest Fund (Gr)
  SAFECO Small Company Stock Fund
  (AgGr)
  SAFECO U.S. Value Fund (Gr&I)
SAFECO Managed Bond Trust
  SAFECO Managed Bond Fund (IncB)
SAFECO Money Market Trust
  SAFECO Money Market Fund (MM)
  SAFECO Tax-Free Money Market Fund
  (NMMX)
SAFECO Taxable Bond Trust
  SAFECO GNMA Fund (GNMA)
  SAFECO High-Yield Bond Fund
  (HiYB)

SAFECO Intermediate-Term U.S.
Treasury Fund (USGv)
SAFECO Tax-Exempt Bond Trust
SAFECO California Tax-Free Income
Fund (SMuB)
SAFECO Insured Municipal Bond Fund
(NMuB)
SAFECO Intermediate-Term Municipal
Bond Fund (NMuB)
SAFECO Municipal Bond Fund (NMuB)
SAFECO Washington State Municipal
Bond Fund (SMuB)

Salomon Brothers Funds
Seven World Trade Ctr.
New York, NY 10048-1102
800/725-6666
Salomon Brothers Capital Fund Inc. (AgGr)
Salomon Brothers Institutional Investment
Series
Institutional Asia Growth Fund (Intl)
Institutional Emerging Markets Debt Fund
(GloB)
Institutional High Yield Bond Fund
(HiYB)
Institutional Money Market Fund (MM)
Salomon Brothers Opportunity Fund Inc.
(Gr)
Salomon Brothers Series Funds Inc.
Asia Growth Fund (Intl)
Cash Management Fund (MM)
High Yield Bond Fund (HiYB)Investors
Fund (Gr&I)
National Intermediate Municipal Fund
(NMuB)
New York Municipal Money Market Fund
(SMMX)
Strategic Bond Fund (GloB)
Total Return Fund (Bal)
U.S. Government Income Fund (USGv)

Saturna Capital
1300 N. State
P.O. Box 2969
Bellingham, WA 98227-2969
800/728-8762
Amana Mutual Funds Trust
Growth Fund (Gr)
Income Fund (IncE)
Saturna Investment Trust
Idaho Tax-Exempt Fund (SMuB)
Sextant Bond Income Fund (SMuB)
Sextant Growth Fund (Gr)
Sextant International Fund (Intl)
Sextant Short-Term Bond Fund (IncB)

Schroder Fund Advisers, Inc.
787 Seventh Ave.
34th Fl.
New York, NY 10019-6018
800/344-8332

Schroder Capital Funds, Inc.
Schroder Emerging Markets Fund (Intl)
Schroder International Bond Fund (GloB)
Schroder International Equity Fund (Intl)
Schroder International Smaller Companies
Fund (Intl)
Schroder U.S. Equity Fund (Gr)
Schroder Series Trust
Schroder Equities Small Capitalization
Value Fund (AgGr)
Schroder High Yield Income Fund (HiYB)
Schroder Investment Grade Income Fund
(IncE)
Schroder Short-Term Income Fund (IncB)
Scroder Equity Value Fund (Gr)
Schroder U.S. Smaller Companies Fund
(AgGr)

Schwab Annuity Funds
101 Montgomery St., MKT-8th
San Francisco, CA 94104-4122
800/526-8600
Schwab Annuity Portfolios
Schwab Asset Director-High Growth
Portfolio (Bal)
Schwab Money Market Portfolio (MM)
Schwab S&P 500 Portfolio (AgGr)

SchwabFunds Family
101 Montgomery St.
MKT-8th
San Francisco, CA 94104-4122
800/526-8600
Charles Schwab Family of Funds (The)
Schwab California Municipal Money
Fund (SMMX)
Schwab Government Money Fund (MM)
Schwab Institutional Advantage Money
Fund (MM)
Schwab Money Market Fund (MM)
Schwab Municipal Money Fund (NMMX)
Schwab New York Municipal Money
Fund (SMMX)
Schwab Retirement Money Fund (MM)
Schwab U.S. Treasury Money Fund
(MM)
Schwab Value Advantage Money Fund
(MM)
Schwab Capital Trust
Schwab Analytics Fund (Gr)
Schwab Asset Director—Balanced
Growth Fund (Bal)
Schwab Asset Director—Conservative
Growth Fund (IncM)
Schwab Asset Director—High Growth
Fund (Gr)
Schwab International Index Fund (Intl)
Schwab OneSource Portfolio: Balanced
Allocation (Bal)
Schwab OneSource Portfolio: Growth
Allocation (Gr)

Schwab OneSource Portfolio:
  International (Intl)
Schwab S&P 500 Fund (Gr&I)
Schwab Small-Cap Index Fund (AgGr)
Schwab Investments
  Schwab California Long-Term Tax-Free
    Bond Fund (SMuB)
  Schwab California Short/Intermediate
    Tax-Free Bond Fund (SMuB)
  Schwab Long-Term Government Bond
    Fund (USGv)
  Schwab Long-Term Tax-Free Bond Fund
    (NMuB)
  Schwab 1000 Fund (Gr&I)
  Schwab Short/Intermediate Government
    Bond Fund (USGv)
  Schwab Short/Intermediate Tax-Free Bond
    Fund (NMuB)

Schwartz Investment Trust
3707 W. Maple Rd.
Bloomfield Hills, MI 48301-3212
810/644-8500
Schwartz Investment Trust
  Schwartz Value Fund (AgGr)

SCM Portfolio Fund, Inc.
100 SMI Building
119 Maple St.
Carrollton, GA 30117
770/834-5839
SCM Portfolio Fund, Inc. (Flex)

Scudder Family of Funds
Two International Place
Boston, MA 02110-4101
800/225-2470
AARP Cash Investment Funds
  AARP High Quality Money Fund (MM)
AARP Growth Trust
  AARP Balanced Stock and Bond Fund
    (Bal)
  AARP Capital Growth Fund (Gr)
  AARP Global Growth Fund (GloE)
  AARP Growth and Income Fund (Gr&I)
  AARP International Stock Fund (Intl)
  AARP Small Company Stock Fund
    (AgGr)
  AARP U.S. Stock Index Fund (Gr&I)
AARP Income Trust
  AARP Bond Fund for Income (IncB)
  AARP GNMA and U.S. Treasury Fund
    (GNMA)
  AARP High Quality Bond Fund (CorB)
AARP Managed Investment Portfolios
  Trust
  AARP Diversified Growth Portfolio (Bal)
  AARP Diversified Income Portfolio (Bal)
AARP Tax Free Income Trust
  AARP High Quality Tax-Free Money
    Fund (NMMX)

AARP Insured Tax Free General Bond
  Fund (NMuB)
Japan Fund, Inc. (The) (Intl)
Scudder California Tax Free Trust
  Scudder California Tax Free Fund
    (SMuB)
  Scudder California Tax Free Money Fund
    (SMMX)
Scudder Cash Investment Trust (MM)
Scudder Equity Trust
  Scudder Large Company Value Fund (Gr)
  Scudder Value Fund (Gr)
Scudder Fund, Inc.
  Managed Cash Fund (MM)
  Managed Government Securities Fund
    (MM)
  Managed Tax-Free Fund (NMMX)
Scudder Funds Trust
  Scudder Short Term Bond Fund (IncB)
  Scudder Zero Coupon 2000 Fund (USGv)
Scudder Global Fund, Inc.
  Scudder Emerging Markets Income Fund
    (GloB)
  Scudder Global Bond Fund (GloB)
  Scudder Global Discovery Fund (GloE)
  Scudder Global Fund (GloE)
  Scudder International Bond Fund (GloB)
Scudder GNMA Fund (GNMA)
Scudder Institutional Fund, Inc.
  Institutional Cash Portfolio (MM)
  Institutional Government Portfolio (MM)
  Institutional International Equity Portfolio
    (Intl)
  Institutional Tax-Free Portfolio (NMMX)
Scudder International Fund, Inc.
  Scudder Emerging Markets Growth Fund
    (Intl)
  Scudder Greater Europe Growth Fund
    (Intl)
  Scudder International Fund (Intl)
  Scudder Latin America Fund (Intl)
  Scudder Pacific Opportunities Fund (Intl)
Scudder Investment Trust
  Scudder Classic Growth Fund (AgGr)
  Scudder Growth and Income Fund (Gr&I)
  Scudder Large Company Growth Fund
    (Gr)
Scudder Municipal Trust
  Scudder High Yield Tax Free Fund
    (NMuB)
  Scudder Managed Municipal Bonds
    (NMuB)
Scudder Mutual Funds, Inc.
  Scudder Gold Fund (PM/G)
Scudder Pathway Series
  Balanced Portfolio (Gr&I)
  Conservative Portfolio (Gr&I)
  Growth Portfolio (AgGr)
  International Portfolio (Intl)
Scudder Portfolio Trust
  Scudder Balanced Fund (Bal)

Scudder High Yield Bond Fund (HiYB)
Scudder Income Fund (IncM)
Scudder Securities Trust
  Scudder Development Fund (AgGr)
  Scudder Micro Cap Fund (AgGr)
  Scudder Small Company Value Fund
    (AgGr)
  Scudder 21st Century Growth Fund
    (AgGr)
Scudder State Tax Free Trust
  Scudder Massachusetts Limited Term Tax
    Free Fund (SMuB)
  Scudder Massachusetts Tax Free Fund
    (SMuB)
  Scudder New York Tax Free Fund
    (SMuB)
  Scudder New York Tax Free Money Fund
    (SMMX)
  Scudder Ohio Tax Free Fund (SMuB)
  Scudder Pennsylvania Tax Free Fund
    (SMuB)
Scudder Tax Free Money Fund (NMMX)
Scudder Tax Free Trust
  Scudder Limited Term Tax Free Fund
    (NMuB)
  Scudder Medium Term Tax Free Fund
    (NMuB)
Scudder U.S. Treasury Money Fund (MM)

Seafirst Retirement Funds
1230 Columbia St.
Suite 500
San Diego, CA 92101
800/332-3863
Seafirst Retirement Funds
  Asset Allocation Fund (Flex)
  Blue Chip Fund (Gr)
  Bond Fund (IncB)

Security Benefit Funds Group
700 Harrison St.
Topeka, KS 66636-0001
800/888-2461
SBL Fund
  Emerging Growth Series (AgGr)
  Equity Income Series (Gr&I)
  Global Aggressive Bond Series (GloB)
  Growth Series (Gr)
  High Grade Income Series (IncB)
  Income & Growth Series (Gr&I)
  Managed Asset Allocation Series (Bal)
  Money Market Series (MM)
  Social Awareness Series (Gr)
  Specialized Asset Allocation Series (Bal)
  Worldwide Equity Series (GloE)
Security Cash Fund (MM)
Security Equity Funds
  Asset Allocation Series (Bal)
  Equity Series (Gr)
  Global Series (GloE)
  Security Social Awareness Fund (Gr)

Security Growth & Income Fund (Gr&I)
Security Income Fund
  Corporate Bond Series (CorB)
  High Yield Fund (HiYB)
  Limited Maturity Bond Fund (IncB)
  MFR Emerging Markets Total Return
    Series (Glob)
  MFR Global Asset Allocation Series
    (Glob)
  MFR Global High Yield Series (Glob)
  U.S. Government Series (USGv)
Security Tax-Exempt Fund (NMuB)
Security Ultra Fund (AgGr)

SEI Funds
One Freedom Valley Drive
Oaks, PA 19456
800/342-5734
SEI Asset Allocation Trust
  Diversified Conservative Fund (Bal)
  Diversified Conservative Income Fund
    (IncB)
  Diversified Global Growth Fund (GloE)
  Diversified Global Moderate Growth
    Fund (GloE)
  Diversified Moderate Growth Fund (Bal)
  Diversified U.S. Stock Fund (Gr)
SEI Daily Income Trust
  Corporate Daily Portfolio (IncB)
  GNMA Portfolio (GNMA)
  Government Portfolio (MM)
  Government II Portfolio (MM)
  Intermediate Term Government Portfolio
    (USGv)
  Money Market Portfolio (MM)
  Prime Obligation Portfolio (MM)
  Short-Term Government Portfolio
    (USGv)
  Treasury Portfolio (MM)
  Treasury II Portfolio (MM)
SEI Index Funds
  Bond Index Portfolio (IncB)
  S&P 500 Index Portfolio (Gr&I)
SEI Institutional Investment Trust
  Core Fixed Income Fund (IncB)
  Emerging Markets Equity Fund (Intl)
  High Yield Bond Fund (HiYB)
  International Equity Fund (Intl)
  International Fixed Income Fund (GloB)
  Large Cap Fund (Gr&I)
  Small Cap Fund (AgGr)
SEI Institutional Managed Trust
  Bond Portfolio (IncB)
  Capital Appreciation Portfolio (Gr)
  Core Fixed Income Portfolio (IncB)
  Equity Income Portfolio (IncE)
  High Yield Bond Fund (HiYB)
  Large Cap Growth Portfolio (Gr)
  Large Cap Value Portfolio (Gr&I)
  Mid-Cap Growth Portfolio (AgGr)
  Real Estate Securities Portfolio (Gr&I)

Small Cap Growth Portfolio (AgGr)
Small Cap Value Portfolio (Gr)
SEI Liquid Asset Trust
  Government Portfolio (MM)
  Institutional Cash Portfolio (MM)
  Prime Obligation Portfolio (MM)
  Treasury Portfolio (MM)
SEI Tax Exempt Trust
  California Tax Exempt Portfolio (SMMX)
  Institutional Tax Free Portfolio (NMMX)
  Intermediate Term Municipal Portfolio
    (NMuB)
  Pennsylvania Municipal Portfolio (SMuB)
  Pennsylvania Tax Free Portfolio (SMMX)
  Tax Free Portfolio (NMMX)

Select Advisors Funds
311 Pike St.
Cincinnati, OH 45202
800/669-2796
Select Advisors Trust A
  Touchstone Balanced Fund A (Bal)
  Touchstone Bond Fund A (IncB)
  Touchstone Emerging Growth Fund A
    (Gr)
  Touchstone Growth and Income Fund A
    (Gr&I)
  Touchstone Income Opportunity Fund A
    (IncM)
  Touchstone International Equity Fund A
    (Intl)
  Touchstone Standby Income Fund (IncM)
Select Advisors Trust C
  Touchstone Balanced Fund C (Bal)
  Touchstone Bond Fund C (IncB)
  Touchstone Emerging Growth Fund C
    (Gr)
  Touchstone Growth and Income Fund C
    (Gr&I)
  Touchstone Income Opportunity Fund B
    (IncM)
  Touchstone International Equity Fund C
    (Intl)

Selected Funds
124 E. Marcy St.
P.O. Box 1688
Santa Fe, NM 87504-1688
800/279-0279
Selected American Shares, Inc. (Gr&I)
Selected Capital Preservation Trust
  Selected Daily Government Fund (MM)
  Selected U.S. Government Income Fund
    (USGv)
Selected Special Shares, Inc. (Gr)

Seligman Funds
100 Park Ave.
New York, NY 10017-5516
800/221-7844
Seligman Capital Fund, Inc. (AgGr)

Seligman Cash Management Fund, Inc.
  (MM)
Seligman Common Stock Fund, Inc. (Gr&I)
Seligman Communications and Information
  Fund, Inc. (AgGr)
Seligman Frontier Fund, Inc. (AgGr)
Seligman Growth Fund, Inc. (Gr)
Seligman Henderson Global Fund Series,
  Inc.
  Seligman Henderson Emerging Markets
    Growth Fund (Intl)
  Seligman Henderson Global Growth
    Opportunities Fund (GloE)
  Seligman Henderson Global Smaller
    Companies Fund (GloE)
  Seligman Henderson Global Technology
    Fund (GloE)
  Seligman Henderson International Fund
    (Intl)
Seligman High Income Fund Series
  High-Yield Bond Series (HiYB)
  U.S. Government Securities Series
    (USGv)
Seligman Income Fund, Inc. (Bal)
Seligman Municipal Fund Series, Inc.
  Colorado Muncipal Series (SMuB)
  Georgia Municipal Series (SMuB)
  Louisiana Municipal Series (SMuB)
  Maryland Municipal Series (SMuB)
  Massachusetts Municipal Series (SMuB)
  Michigan Municipal Series (SMuB)
  Minnesota Municipal Series (SMuB)
  Missouri Municipal Series (SMuB)
  National Municipal Series (NMuB)
  New York Municipal Series (SMuB)
  Ohio Municipal Series (SMuB)
  Oregon Municipal Series (SMuB)
  South Carolina Municipal Series
    (SMuB)
Seligman Municipal Series Trust
  California Municipal High Yield Series
    (SMuB)
  California Municipal Quality Series
    (SMuB)
  Florida Municipal Series (SMuB)
  North Carolina Municipal Series (SMuB)
Seligman New Jersey Municipal Fund, Inc.
  (SMuB)
Seligman Pennsylvania Municipal Fund
  Series (SMuB)
Seligman Portfolios, Inc.
  Seligman Bond Portfolio (IncB)
  Seligman Capital Portfolio (AgGr)
  Seligman Cash Management Portfolio
    (MM)
  Seligman Common Stock Portfolio (Gr&I)
  Seligman Communications and
    Information Portfolio (AgGr)
  Seligman Frontier Portfolio (AgGr)
  Seligman Henderson Global Growth
    Opportunities Portfolio (GloE)

Seligman Henderson Global Smaller
Companies Portfolio (GloE)
Seligman Henderson Global Technology
Portfolio (GloE)
Seligman Henderson International
Portfolio (GloE)
Seligman High-Yield Bond Portfolio
(HiYB)
Seligman Income Portfolio (IncM)
Seligman Value Series, Inc.
Seligman Large-Cap Value Fund (Gr)
Seligman Small-Cap Value Fund (AgGr)

Seneca Funds
909 Montgomery St.
Ste. 600
San Francisco, CA 94133
800/828-1212
Seneca Funds
Seneca Bond Fund (IncB)
Seneca Growth Fund (Gr)
Seneca Mid-Cap "EDGE" Fund (Gr)
Seneca Real Estate Securities Fund
(Gr&I)

Sentinel Funds
National Life Dr.
P.O. Box 1499
Montpelier, VT 05601-1499
800/282-3863
Sentinel Group Funds, Inc.
Sentinel Balanced Fund Series (Bal)
Sentinel Bond Fund Series (IncB)
Sentinel Common Stock Fund Series
(Gr&I)
Sentinel Government Securities Fund
Series (USGv)
Sentinel Growth Fund Series (Gr)
Sentinel New York Tax-Free Income Fund
(SMuB)
Sentinel Short Maturity Government Fund
(USGv)
Sentinel Small Company Fund Series
(AgGr)
Sentinel Tax-Free Income Fund Series
(NMuB)
Sentinel U.S. Treasury Money Market
Fund Series (MM)
Sentinel World Fund Series (GloE)
Sentinel Pennsylvania Tax-Free Trust
(SMuB)

Sentry Fund
1800 N. Point Dr.
Stevens Point, WI 54481-1283
800/533-7827
Sentry Fund, Inc. (Gr)

Sessions Group
3435 Stelzer Rd.
Columbus, OH 43219-3035

800/874-8376
Sessions Group (The)
1st Source Monogram Diversified Equity
Fund (Gr)
1st Source Monogram Income Equity
Fund (IncE)
1st Source Monogram Income Fund
(IncB)
1st Source Monogram Intermediate Tax-
Free Bond Fund (NMuB)
1st Source Monogram Special Equity
Fund (AgGr)
1st Source Monogram U.S. Treasury
Obligations Money Market Fund (MM)
KeyPremier Aggressive Growth Fund
(AgGr)
KeyPremier Established Growth Fund
(Gr&I)
KeyPremier Intermediate Term Income
Fund (IncB)
KeyPremier Limited Duration
Government Securities Fund (USGv)
KeyPremier Pennsylvania Municipal
Bond Fund (SMuB)
KeyPremier Prime Money Market Fund
(MM)
KeyPremier U.S. Treasury Obligations
Money Market Fund (MM)
Riverside Capital Equity Fund (Gr)
Riverside Capital Fixed Income Fund
(IncB)
Riverside Capital Growth Fund (Gr)
Riverside Capital Low Duration
Government Fund (USGv)
Riverside Capital Money Market Fund
(MM)
Riverside Capital Tennessee Municipal
Obligations Fund (SMuB)

1784 Funds
1 Freedom Valley Rd.
Oaks, PA 19456
800/252-1784
1784 Funds
Asset Allocation Fund (Flex)
Connecticut Tax-Exempt Income Fund
(SMuB)
Growth & Income Fund (Gr&I)
Growth Fund (Gr)
Income Fund (IncB)
Institutional U.S. Treasury Money Market
Fund (MM)
International Equity Fund (Intl)
Massachusetts Tax-Exempt Income Fund
(SMuB)
Prime Money Market Fund (MM)
Rhode Island Tax-Exempt Income Fund
(SMuB)
Short-Term Income Fund (IncB)
Tax-Exempt Medium-Term Income Fund
(NMuB)

Tax-Free Money Market Fund (NMMX)
U.S. Government Medium-Term Income
Fund (USGv)
U.S. Treasury Money Market Fund (MM)

Sheffield Funds
900 Circle 75 Pkwy.
Ste. 750
Atlanta, GA 30339-3084
404/953-1597
Sheffield Funds, Inc. (The)
Sheffield Intermediate Term Bond Fund
(CorB)
Sheffield Total Return Fund (Gr&I)

Sierra Trust Funds
9301 Corbin Ave.
NO321
Northridge, CA 91324-2431
800/221-9876
Sierra Asset Management Portfolios
Balanced Portfolio (Bal)
Capital Growth Portfolio (Gr)
Growth Portfolio (Gr&I)
Income Portfolio (IncB)
Value Portfolio (IncM)
Sierra Trust Funds
California Insured Intermediate Municipal
Fund (SMuB)
California Money Fund (SMMX)
California Municipal Fund (SMuB)
Corporate Income Fund (CorB)
Emerging Growth Fund (AgGr)
Florida Insured Municipal Fund (SMuB)
Global Money Fund (MM)
Growth and Income Fund (Gr&I)
Growth Fund (Gr)
International Growth Fund (Intl)
National Municipal Fund (NMuB)
Short-Term Global Government Fund
(GloB)
Short-Term High Quality Bond Fund
(IncB)
Target Maturity Fund 2002 (USGv)
U.S. Government Fund (USGv)
U.S. Government Money Fund (MM)
Sierra Variable Trust
Balanced Portfolio (Bal)
Capital Growth (AgGr)
Corporate Income Fund (CorB)
Emerging Growth Fund (GloE)
Global Money Market Fund (MM)
Growth and Income Fund (Gr&I)
Growth Fund (Gr)
Growth Portfolio (Gr)
International Growth Fund (Intl)
Short-Term Global Government Fund
(GloB)
Short-Term High Quality Bond Fund
(IncB)
U.S. Government Securities Fund (USGv)

Sit Mutual Funds
4600 Norwest Ctr.
90 S. Seventh St.
Minneapolis, MN 55402-4130
800/332-5580
Sit Balanced Fund (Bal)
Sit Bond Fund (IncB)
Sit Developing Markets Growth Fund (Intl)
Sit International Growth Fund (Intl)
Sit Large Cap Growth Fund, Inc. (Gr&I)
Sit Mid Cap Growth Fund, Inc. (Gr)
Sit Minnesota Tax-Free Income Fund
(SMuB)
Sit Money Market Fund, Inc. (MM)
Sit Small Cap Growth Fund (AgGr)
Sit Tax-Free Income Fund (NMuB)
Sit U.S. Government Securities Fund, Inc.
(USGv)

Skyline Funds
311 S. Wacker Dr.
Ste. 4500
Chicago, IL 60606
800/458-5222
Skyline Fund
Special Equities Portfolio (AgGr)
Special Equities II (AgGr)

Smith Barney Funds
Two World Trade Ctr.
100th Fl.
New York, NY 10048-0203
212/464-6000
Consulting Group Capital Markets Funds
Balanced Fund (Bal)
Emerging Markets Fund (Intl)
Government Money Investments Funds
(MM)
International Equity Investments Fund
(Intl)
International Fixed Income Investments
Fund (GloB)
Intermediate Fixed Income Investments
Fund (IncM)
Large Capitalization Growth Investments
Fund (Gr)
Large Capitalization Value Equity
Investments Fund (Gr&I)
Long-Term Bond Fund (IncM)
Mortgage Backed Investments Fund
(GNMA)
Municipal Bond Investments Fund
(NMuB)
Small Capitalization Growth Investments
Fund (AgGr)
Small Capitalization Value Equity
Investments Fund (AgGr)
Shearson Series Funds
Appreciation Portfolio (AgGr)
Diversified Strategic Income Portfolio
(IncM)

Emerging Growth Portfolio (Gr)
Equity Income Portfolio (IncE)
Equity Index Portfolio (Gr&I)
Growth & Income Portfolio (Gr&I)
Intermediate High Grade Portfolio (CorB)
International Equity Portfolio (Intl)
Money Market Portfolio (MM)
Total Return Portfolio (IncM)

Smith Barney Adjustable Rate Government
  Income Fund (GNMA)
Smith Barney Aggressive Growth Fund Inc.
  (AgGr)
Smith Barney Appreciation Fund Inc. (Gr)
Smith Barney Arizona Municipals Fund Inc.
  (SMuB)
Smith Barney California Municipal Money
  Market Fund (SMMX)
Smith Barney California Municipals Fund
  Inc. (SMuB)
Smith Barney Daily Dividend Fund Inc.
  (MM)
Smith Barney Disciplined Small Cap Fund
  (Gr)
Smith Barney Equity Funds
  SB Concert Social Awareness Fund (Flex)
Smith Barney Equity Funds SB Growth and
  Income Fund (Gr&I)
Smith Barney Exchange Reserve Fund
  (MM)
Smith Barney Fundamental Value Fund Inc.
  (Gr)
Smith Barney Funds, Inc.
  Equity-Income Portfolio (Gr&I)
  Income Return Account Portfolio (IncB)
  Short-Term U.S. Treasury Securities
    Portfolio (USGv)
  U.S. Government Securities Portfolio
    (GNMA)
Smith Barney Government and Agencies
  Fund, Inc. (MM)
Smith Barney Income Funds
  SB Convertible Fund (Gr&I)
  SB Diversified Strategic Income Fund
    (CorB)
  SB High Income Fund (HiYB)
  SB Tax Exempt Income Fund (NMuB)
  SB Utilities Fund (IncM)
  SB Money Market Fund (MM)
  SB Premium Total Return Fund (IncE)
Smith Barney Income Trust
  SB Intermediate Maturity California
    Municipals Fund (SMuB)
  SB Intermediate Maturity New York
    Municipals Fund (SMuB)
Smith Barney Institutional Cash
  Management Fund
  Cash Portfolio (MM)
  Government Portfolio (MM)
  Municipal Portfolio (MM)
Smith Barney Investment Funds Inc.

SB Government Securities Fund (USGv)
SB Growth Opportunity Fund (Gr)
SB Investment Grade Bond Fund (IncB)
SB Managed Growth Fund (Gr)
SB Special Equities Fund (AgGr)
Smith Barney Managed Government Fund
  Inc. (GNMA)
Smith Barney Managed Municipals Fund
  Inc. (NMuB)
Smith Barney Massachusetts Municipals
  Fund (SMuB)
Smith Barney Money Fund, Inc.
  Cash Portfolio (MM)
  Government Portfolio (MM)
  Municipal Portfolio (NMMX)
  Retirement Portfolio (MM)
Smith Barney Muni Bond Funds
  California Money Market Portfolio
    (SMMX)
  Florida Portfolio (SMuB)
  Georgia Portfolio (SMuB)
  Limited Term Portfolio (NMuB)
  National Portfolio (NMuB)
  New York Money Market Portfolio
    (SMMX)
  New York Portfolio (SMuB)
  Ohio Portfolio (SMuB)
  Oregon Portfolio (SMuB)
  Pennsylvania Portfolio (SMuB)
Smith Barney Municipal Money Market
  Fund, Inc. (NMMX)
Smith Barney Natural Resources Funds Inc.
  (PM/G)
Smith Barney New Jersey Municipals Fund
  Inc. (SMuB)
Smith Barney New York Municipal Money
  Market Fund (SMMX)
Smith Barney Principal Return Fund
  SB Safe 1998 (Gr)
  SB Safe 2000 (Gr)
  Security and Growth Fund (Bal)
Smith Barney Telecommunications Trust
  SB Telecommunications Income Fund
    (Gr&I)
Smith Barney/Travelers Series Fund, Inc.
  AIM Appreciation Portfolio (Gr)
  Alliance Growth Portfolio (Gr)
  American Capital Enterprise Portfolio
    (Gr)
  G.T. Global Strategic Income Portfolio
    (GloB)
  MFS Total Return Portfolio (IncM)
  Putnam Diversified Income Portfolio (Bal)
  Smith Barney High Income Portfolio
    (CorB)
  Smith Barney Income and Growth
    Portfolio (Gr&I)
  Smith Barney International Equity
    Portfolio (Intl)
  Smith Barney Money Market Portfolio
    (MM)

Smith Barney Pacific Basin Portfolio
(Intl)
TBC Managed Income Portfolio (IncM)
Smith Barney Variable Account Funds, Inc.
Income and Growth Portfolio (Gr&I)
Reserve Account Portfolio (IncB)
U.S. Government/High Quality Portfolio
(GNMA)
Smith Barney World Funds, Inc.
Emerging Markets Portfolio (Intl)
European Portfolio (Intl)
Global Government Bond Portfolio
(GloB)
International Balanced Portfolio (Intl)
International Equity Portfolio (Intl)
Pacific Portfolio (Intl)

Smith Breeden Mutual Funds
100 Europa Dr.
Ste. 200
Chapel Hill, NC 27514-2310
800/221-3138
Smith Breeden Equity Plus Fund (Gr&I)
Smith Breeden Series Fund
Smith Breeden Intermediate Duration U.S.
Government Series (USGv)
Smith Breeden Short Duration U.S.
Government Series (USGv)

SoGen Funds
1221 Avenue of the Americas
8th Fl.
New York, NY 10020-1605
212/278-5800
SoGen Funds, Inc.
SoGen Gold Fund (PM/G)
SoGen Money Fund (MM)
SoGen Overseas Fund (Intl)
SoGen International Fund, Inc. (GloE)

Solon Funds
1981 N. Broadway
Ste. 325
Walnut Creek, CA 94596-3852
800/467-6566
Solon Funds (The)
Solon Short Duration Government Funds:
One Year Portfolio (USGv)
Solon Short Duration Government Funds:
Three Year Portfolio (USGv)

SSgA Funds
2 International Place
35th Fl.
Boston, MA 02110
800/647-7327
SSgA Funds (The)
SSgA Active International Fund (Intl)
SSgA Emerging Markets Fund (Intl)
SSgA Growth and Income Fund (Gr&I)
SSgA Intermediate Bond Fund (IncB)

SSgA Matrix Equity Fund (Gr)
SSgA Money Market Fund (MM)
SSgA Prime Money Market Fund (MM)
SSgA S&P 500 Index Fund (Gr)
SSgA Small Cap Fund (Gr)
SSgA Tax Free Money Market Fund
(NMMX)
SSgA U.S. Government Money Market
Fund (MM)
SSgA U.S. Treasury Money Market Fund
(MM)
SSgA Yield Plus Fund (IncB)

Stagecoach Funds, Inc.
111 Center St.
Little Rock, AR 72201-4402
800/222-8222
Stagecoach Funds, Inc. (The)
Aggressive Growth Fund (AgGr)
Arizona Tax-Free Fund (SMuB)
Asset Allocation Fund (Flex)
Balanced Fund (Bal)
California Tax-Free Bond Fund (SMuB)
California Tax-Free Income Fund (SMuB)
California Tax-Free Money Market Fund
(SMMX)
Corporate Stock Fund (Gr&I)
Diversified Income Fund (IncM)
Equity Value Fund (Gr)
Ginnie Mae Fund (GNMA)
Government Money Market Fund (MM)
Growth and Income Fund (Gr&I)
Intermediate Bond Fund (IncB)
Money Market Fund (MM)
Money Market Trust (MM)
National Tax-Free Fund (NMuB)
Oregon Tax-Free Fund (SMuB)
Prime Money Market Fund (MM)
Short/Intermediate U.S. Government
Income Fund (USGv)
Small Cap Fund (AgGr)
Tax-Free Money Market Fund (NMMX)
U.S. Government Allocation Fund
(USGv)
U.S. Treasury Money Market Fund (MM)

Stagecoach Trust
111 Center St., Ste. 300
Stephens Bldg.
Little Rock, AR 72201-4402
800/458-6589
Stagecoach Trust
LifePath 2000 Fund (Flex)
LifePath 2010 Fund (Flex)
LifePath 2020 Fund (Flex)
LifePath 2030 Fund (Flex)
LifePath 2040 Fund (Flex)

Standish, Ayer & Wood Investment Trust
One Financial Center
Boston, MA 02111-2621

800/221-4795

Standish, Ayer & Wood Investment Trust
Standish Global Fixed Income Fund
(GloB)
Standish International Equity Fund (Intl)
Standish International Fixed Income Fund
(GloB)
Standish, Ayer & Wood Investment Trust
Standish Controlled Maturity Fund (IncB)
Standish Equity Fund (Gr)
Standish Fixed Income Fund (IncB)
Standish Fixed Income Fund II (IncB)
Standish Intermediate Tax Exempt Bond
Fund (NMuB)
Standish Massachusetts Intermediate Tax
Exempt Bond Fund (SMuB)
Standish Securitized Fund (GNMA)
Standish Short-Term Asset Reserve Fund
(IncM)
Standish Small Capitalization Equity Fund
(AgGr)
Standish Small Capitalization Equity Fund
II (AgGr)
Standish Small Cap Tax-Sensitive Equity
Fund (AgGr)
Standish Tax-Sensitive Equity Fund (Gr)

Star Funds
Federated Investors Twr.
1001 Liberty Ave.
Pittsburgh, PA 15222-3779
800/341-7400
Star Funds
Star Capital Appreciation Fund (Bal)
Star Growth Equity Fund (Gr)
Star Relative Value Fund (Gr&I)
Star Strategic Income Fund (IncM)
Star Tax-Free Money Market Fund Fund
(NMMX)
Star Treasury Fund (MM)
Star U.S. Government Income Fund
(USGv)
Stellar Fund (The)
Stellar Insured Tax-Free Bond Fund
(IncB)

State Farm Funds
One State Farm Plaza
Bloomington, IL 61710-0001
309/766-2029
State Farm Balanced Fund, Inc. (Bal)
State Farm Growth Fund, Inc. (Gr)
State Farm Interim Fund, Inc. (USGv)
State Farm Municipal Bond Fund, Inc.
(NMuB)

State Street Research Funds
One Financial Ctr.
31st Fl.
Boston, MA 02111-2621
800/562-0032

State Street Research Capital Trust
State Street Research Aurora Fund (AgGr)
State Street Research Capital Fund (AgGr)
State Street Research Emerging Growth
Fund (AgGr)
State Street Research Equity Trust
State Street Research Capital Appreciation
Fund (AgGr)
State Street Research Equity Income Fund
(IncE)
State Street Research Equity Investment
Fund (Gr&I)
State Street Research Global Resources
Fund (GloE)
State Street Research Exchange Trust
State Street Research Exchange Fund
(Gr&I)
State Street Research Financial Trust
State Street Research Government Income
Fund (USGv)
State Street Research Strategic Portfolios:
Aggressive (Bal)
State Street Research Strategic Portfolios:
Conservative (IncB)
State Street Research Strategic Portfolios:
Moderate (Bal)
State Street Research Growth Trust
State Street Research Growth Fund
(Gr&I)
State Street Research Income Trust
State Street Research High Income Fund
(HiYB)
State Street Research Managed Assets
(Flex)
State Street Research Master Investment
Trust
State Street Research Investment Trust
(Gr&I)
State Street Research Money Market Trust
State Street Research Money Market Fund
(MM)
State Street Research Portfolios, Inc.
State Street Research International Equity
Fund (Intl)
State Street Research International Fixed
Income Fund (GloB)
State Street Research Securities Trust
State Street Research Intermediate Bond
Fund (IncB)
State Street Research Strategic Income
Fund (IncB)
State Street Research Tax-Exempt Trust
State Street Research New York Tax- Free
Fund (SMuB)
State Street Research Tax-Exempt Fund
(NMuB)

Stein Roe Mutual Funds
One S. Wacker Dr.
Chicago, IL 60606-4614
800/338-2550

Stein Roe Advisor Trust
  Stein Roe Advisor Balanced Fund (Bal)
  Stein Roe Advisor Growth & Income
    Fund (Gr&I)
  Stein Roe Advisor Growth Stock Fund
    (Gr)
  Stein Roe Advisor International Fund
    (Intl)
  Stein Roe Advisor Special Venture Fund
    (AgGr)
  Stein Roe Advisor Young Investor Fund
    (AgGr)
Stein Roe Income Trust
  Stein Roe Cash Reserves Fund (MM)
  Stein Roe Government Income Fund
    (USGv)
  Stein Roe Government Reserves Fund
    (MM)
  Stein Roe Income Fund (CorB)
  Stein Roe Intermediate Bond Fund (IncB)
Stein Roe Institutional Trust
  Stein Roe Institutional High Yield Fund
    (GloE)
Stein Roe Investment Trust
  Stein Roe Balanced Fund (Bal)
  Stein Roe Capital Opportunities Fund
    (Gr)
  Stein Roe Emerging Markets Fund (Intl)
  Stein Roe Growth and Income Fund
    (Gr&I)
  Stein Roe Growth Opportunities Fund
    (Gr)
  Stein Roe Growth Stock Fund (Gr)
  Stein Roe International Fund (Intl)
  Stein Roe Special Fund (Gr)
  Stein Roe Special Venture Fund (Gr)
  Stein Roe Young Investor Fund (Gr)
Stein Roe Municipal Trust
  Stein Roe High-Yield Municipals Fund
    (NMuB)
  Stein Roe Intermediate Municipals Fund
    (NMuB)
  Stein Roe Managed Municipals Fund
    (NMuB)
  Stein Roe Municipal Money Market Fund
    (NMMX)
Stein Roe Trust
  Stein Roe Institutional Client High Yield
    Fund (HiYB)

SteinRoe Variable Funds
600 Atlantic Ave.
Boston, MA 02210-2214
800/367-3653
SteinRoe Variable Investment Trust
  Capital Appreciation Fund (AgGr)
  Cash Income Fund (MM)
  Managed Assets Fund (Flex)
  Managed Growth Stock Fund (Gr)
  Mortgage Securities Income Fund
    (GNMA)

STI Classic Funds
One Freedom Valley Drive
Oaks, PA 19456
800/342-5734
STI Classic Funds
  Balanced Fund (Bal)
  Capital Growth Fund (Gr)
  Classic Institutional Cash Management
    Money Market Fund (MM)
  Classic Institutional U.S. Treasury
    Securities Money Market Fund (MM)
  Emerging Markets Equity Fund (Intl)
  Florida Tax-Exempt Bond Fund (SMuB)
  Georgia Tax-Exempt Bond Fund (SMuB)
  International Equity Fund (Intl)
  International Equity Index Fund (Intl)
  Investment Grade Bond Fund (CorB)
  Investment Grade Tax-Exempt Bond Fund
    (NMuB)
  Limited-Term Federal Mortgage Securities
    Fund (GNMA)
  Mid-Cap Equity Fund (Gr)
  Prime Quality Money Market Fund
    (MM)
  Short-Term Bond Fund (IncB)
  Short-Term U.S. Treasury Securities Fund
    (USGv)
  Small Cap Equity Fund (AgGr)
  Sunbelt Equity Fund (Gr)
  Tax-Exempt Money Market Fund
    (NMMX)
  Tennessee Tax-Exempt Bond Fund
    (SMuB)
  U.S. Government Securities Fund (USGv)
  U.S. Government Securities Money
    Market Fund (MM)
  Value Income Stock Fund (IncM)
STI Classic Variable Trust (The)
  Capital Growth Fund (Gr)
  International Equity Fund (Intl)
  Investment Grade Bond Fund (CorB)
  Mid-Cap Equity Fund (Gr)
  Value Income Stock Fund (IncM)

Strategist Mutual Fund Group
IDS Tower
10 Minneapolis, MN 55440
800/297-7378
Strategist Growth & Income Fund, Inc.
  Strategist Balanced Fund (Bal)
  Strategist Equity Fund (Gr&I)
  Strategist Equity Income Fund (IncE)
  Strategist Total Return Fund (Flex)
Strategist Growth Fund, Inc.
  Strategist Growth Fund (Gr)
  Strategist Growth Trends Fund (Gr)
  Strategist Special Growth Fund (Gr)
Strategist Income Fund, Inc.
  Strategist Government Income Fund
    (USGv)
  Strategist High Yield Fund (HiYB)

Strategist Quality Income Fund (CorB)
Strategist Tax-Free Income Fund, Inc.
  Strategist Tax-Free High Yield Fund
  (NMuB)
Strategist World Fund, Inc.
  Strategist World Growth Fund (GloE)
  Strategist World Income Fund (GloB)

Stratton Mutual Funds
610 W. Germantown Pike
Ste. 300
Plymouth Meeting, PA 19462-1050
800/634-5726
Stratton Growth Fund, Inc. (Gr&I)
Stratton Monthly Dividend Shares, Inc.
  (IncE)
Stratton Small-Cap Yield Fund (Gr&I)

Strong Funds
P.O. Box 2936 Milwaukee, WI 53201
800/368-3863
Strong Advantage Fund (IncB)
Strong Advantage II Fund (IncB)
Strong American Utilities Fund (Gr&I)
Strong Asia Pacific Fund (GloE)
Strong Asset Allocation Fund (Bal)
Strong Asset Allocation II Fund (Bal)
Strong Common Stock Fund (Gr)
Strong Corporate Bond Fund (IncM)
Strong Discovery Fund (AgGr)
Strong Discovery Fund II (AgGr)
Strong Equity Income Fund (IncE)
Strong Government Securities Fund
  (USGv)
Strong Growth & Income Fund (Gr&I)
Strong Growth Fund (Gr)
Strong Heritage Money Fund (MM)
Strong High-Yield Bond Fund (HiYB)
Strong High-Yield Municipal Bond Fund
  (NMuB)
Strong Index 500 Fund (Gr)
Strong Institutional Money Fund (MM)
Strong International Bond Fund (Intl)
Strong International Stock Fund (Intl)
Strong International Stock II Fund (Intl)
Strong Money Market Fund (MM)
Strong Municipal Advantage Fund (IncB)
Strong Municipal Bond Fund (NMuB)
Strong Municipal Money Market Fund
  (NMMX)
Strong Opportunity Fund (AgGr)
Strong Short-Term Bond Fund (IncB)
Strong Short-Term Bond II Fund (IncB)
Strong Short-Term Global Bond Fund
  (GloB)
Strong Short-Term Municipal Bond Fund
  (NMuB)
Strong Small Cap Fund (AgGr)
Strong Special Fund II (Gr)
Strong Total Return Fund (Flex)
Strong Value Fund (Gr)

Strong Schafer Value Fund
645 Fifth Ave.
New York, NY 10022-5910
800/368-1030
Strong Schafer Value Fund, Inc. (Gr&I)

Style Select Series
733 Third Ave.
New York, NY 10017-3204
800/858-8850
Style Select Series, Inc.
  Aggressive Growth Portfolio (AgGr)
  International Equity Portfolio (Intl)
  Mid-Cap Growth Portfolio (Gr)
  Value Portfolio (Gr)

Summit Investment Trust
3435 Stelzer Rd.
Columbus, OH 43219-3035
800/554-3862
Summit Investment Trust
  Summit High Yield Fund (HiYB)

SunAmerica Funds Group
733 Third Ave.
New York, NY 10017-3204
800/858-8850
Seasons Series Trust
  Asset Allocation: Diversified Growth
    Portfolio (Bal)
  Multi-Managed Growth Portfolio (Bal)
  Multi-Managed Income/Equity Portfolio
    (Bal)
  Multi-Managed Income Portfolio (Bal)
  Multi-Managed Market Growth Portfolio
    (Bal)
  Stock Portfolio (Gr&I)
SunAmerica Equity Funds
  SunAmerica Balanced Assets Fund (Bal)
  SunAmerica Blue Chip Growth Fund (Gr)
  SunAmerica Global Balanced Fund
    (GloE)
  SunAmerica Growth and Income Fund
    (Gr&I)
  SunAmerica Midcap Growth Fund (Gr)
  SunAmerica Small Company Growth
    Fund (AgGr)
SunAmerica Income Funds
  SunAmerica Diversified Income Fund
    (IncM)
  SunAmerica Federal Securities Fund
    (GNMA)
  SunAmerica High Income Fund (HiYB)
  SunAmerica Tax-Exempt Insured Fund
    (NMuB)
  SunAmerica U.S. Government Securities
    Fund (USGv)
SunAmerica Money Market Funds, Inc.
  SunAmerica Money Market Fund (MM)
SunAmerica Series Trust
  Aggressive Growth Portfolio (AgGr)

Alliance Growth Portfolio (Gr)
Asset Allocation Portfolio (Flex)
Balanced Phoenix Investment Counsel
  Portfolio (Bal)
Cash Management Portfolio (MM)
Corporate Bond Portfolio (CorB)
Federated Value Portfolio (Gr&I)
Global Bond Portfolio (GloB)
Global Equities Portfolio (GloE)
Growth-Income Portfolio (Gr&I)
Growth/Phoenix Investment Counsel
  Portfolio (Gr)
High-Yield Bond Portfolio (HiYB)
International Diversified Equities Portfolio
  (Intl)
Putnam Growth Portfolio (Gr)
SunAmerica Balanced Portfolio (Bal)
Utility Portfolio (IncM)
Venture Value Portfolio (Gr)
Worldwide High Income Portfolio (GloB)

Sun Growth Fund
One Sun Life Exec. Park
Wellesley Hills, MA 02181
800/225-3950
Sun Growth Variable Annuity Fund, Inc.
  (Gr)

Tax-Free Fund of Vermont
128 Merchants Row
Rutland, VT 05701-5917
800/675-3333
Tax Free Fund of Vermont, Inc. (SMuB)

TCW Funds
865 S. Figueroa St.
Ste. 1800
Los Angeles, CA 90017-2543
800/386-3829
TCW Money Market Portfolio (MM)

Templeton Group of Funds
700 Central Ave.
St. Petersburg, FL 33701-3628
800/342-5236
Templeton Funds, Inc.
  Templeton Foreign Fund (Intl)
  Templeton World Fund (GloE)
Templeton Global Investment Trust
Templeton Americas Government
  Securities Fund (USGv)
Templeton Global Infrastructure Fund
  (GloE)
Templeton Greater European Fund (GloB)
Templeton Growth and Income Fund
  (GloE)
Templeton Latin American Fund (Intl)
Templeton Income Trust
  Templeton Global Bond Fund (GloB)
Templeton Institutional Funds, Inc.
  Templeton Emerging Markets Series (Intl)

Templeton Foreign Equity Series (GloE)
Templeton Growth Series (Intl)
Templeton Variable Annuity Fund (Gr)

Texas Capital Value Funds, Inc.
1600 W. 38th St.
Ste. 412
Austin, TX 78731-6407
800/628-4077
Texas Capital Value Funds, Inc.
  Value and Growth Portfolio (Gr)

Third Avenue Value Fund
767 Third Ave.
5th Fl.
New York, NY 10017-2023
800/443-1021
Third Avenue Trust
  Third Avenue Small Cap Value Fund
    (AgGr)
  Third Avenue Value Fund, Inc. (Gr)

Thomas White Funds Family
440 S. LaSalle St.
Ste. 3900
Chicago, IL 60605-1028
800/811-0535
Thomas White World Fund (GloE)

Thompson Plumb Funds
8201 Excelsior Dr.
Ste. 200
Madison, WI 53717-1944
800/999-0887
Thompson Plumb Funds, Inc.
  Thompson Plumb Balanced Fund
    (Bal)
  Thompson Plumb Bond Fund (IncB)
  Thompson Plumb Growth Fund (Gr)

Time Horizon Funds
3435 Stelzer Rd.
Columbus, OH 43219
800/737-5438
Time Horizon Series of Funds
  Time Horizon Portfolio 1 (IncM)
  Time Horizon Portfolio 2 (Bal)
  Time Horizon Portfolio 3 (Gr&I)

Timothy Plan Fund
1304 W. Fairbanks Ave.
Winter Park, FL 32789-4804
800/441-6580
Timothy Plan (The) (Gr)

TMK/United Funds
6300 Lamar
P.O. Box 29217
Shawnee Mission, KS 66202-4247
800/366-5465
TMK/United Funds, Inc.

TMK/United Asset Strategy Portfolio
(Flex)
TMK/United Balanced Portfolio (Bal)
TMK/United Bond Portfolio (CorB)
TMK/United Growth Portfolio (Gr)
TMK/United High Income Portfolio
(HiYB)
TMK/United Income Portfolio (IncM)
TMK/United International Portfolio (Intl)
TMK/United Limited Term Bond
Portfolio (IncB)
TMK/United Money Market Portfolio
(MM)
TMK/United Science and Technology
Portfolio (AgGr)
TMK/United Small Cap Portfolio (AgGr)

Tocqueville Fund
1675 Broadway
16th Fl.
New York, NY 10019-5820
212/698-0800
Tocqueville Trust (The)
Tocqueville Fund (Gr)
Tocqueville Government Fund (USGv)
Tocqueville International Value Fund (Intl)
Tocqueville Small Cap Value Fund (AgGr)

Torray Fund
6610 Rockledge Dr.
Ste. 450
Bethesda, MD 20817-1811
800/443-3036
Torray Fund (The) (Flex)

Tower Funds
Federated Investors Twr.
1001 Liberty Ave.
Pittsburgh, PA 15222-3779
800/999-0124
Tower Mutual Funds
Tower Capital Appreciation Fund (Gr&I)
Tower Cash Reserve Fund (MM)
Tower Louisiana Municipal Income Fund
(SMuB)
Tower Total Return Bond Fund (IncB)
Tower U.S. Government Income Fund
(USGv)

Transamerica Premier Funds
1150 S. Olive St.
Los Angeles, CA 90015
800/892-7587
Transamerica Premier Funds
Transamerica Premier Aggressive Growth
Fund (AgGr)
Transamerica Premier Balanced Fund
(Bal)
Transamerica Premier Bond Fund (IncB)
Transamerica Premier Cash Reserve Fund
(MM)

Transamerica Premier Equity Fund (Gr)
Transamerica Premier Index Fund (Gr&I)
Transamerica Premier Small Company
Fund (AgGr)

T. Rowe Price Family of Funds
100 E. Pratt St.
Baltimore, MD 21202-1009
800/638-5660
Institutional International Funds, Inc.
Foreign Equity Fund (Intl)
T. Rowe Price International Funds, Inc.
T. Rowe Price Emerging Markets Bond
Fund (Intl)
T. Rowe Price Emerging Markets Stock
Fund (Intl)
T. Rowe Price European Stock Fund (Intl)
T. Rowe Price Global Government Bond
Fund (GloB)
T. Rowe Price Global Stock Fund (GloE)
T. Rowe Price International Bond Fund
(GloB)
T. Rowe Price International Discovery
Fund (Intl)
T. Rowe Price International Stock Fund
(Intl)
T. Rowe Price Japan Fund (Intl)
T. Rowe Price Latin America Fund
(Intl)
T. Rowe Price New Asia Fund (Intl)
T. Rowe Price International Series, Inc.
T. Rowe Price International Stock
Portfolio (Intl)
T. Rowe Price Spectrum Fund, Inc.
Spectrum International Fund (Intl)
Institutional Equity Funds, Inc.
Mid-Cap Equity Growth Fund (Gr)
T. Rowe Price Balanced Fund, Inc. (Bal)
T. Rowe Price Blue Chip Growth Fund, Inc.
(Gr)
T. Rowe Price California Tax-Free Income
Trust
California Tax-Free Bond Fund (SMuB)
California Tax-Free Money Fund
(SMMX)
T. Rowe Price Capital Appreciation Fund
(Gr)
T. Rowe Price Capital Opportunity Fund,
Inc. (Flex)
T. Rowe Price Corporate Income Fund, Inc.
(CorB)
T. Rowe Price Dividend Growth Fund, Inc.
(IncE)
T. Rowe Price Equity Income Fund (IncE)
T. Rowe Price Equity Series, Inc.
T. Rowe Price Equity Income Portfolio
(IncE)
T. Rowe Price Mid-Cap Growth Portfolio
(Gr)
T. Rowe Price New America Growth
Portfolio (AgGr)

T. Rowe Price Personal Strategy Balanced
Portfolio (Bal)
T. Rowe Price Financial Services Fund, Inc.
(Gr&I)
T. Rowe Price Fixed Income Series, Inc.
T. Rowe Price Limited-Term Bond
Portfolio (IncB)
T. Rowe Price Prime Reserve Portfolio
(MM)
T. Rowe Price GNMA Fund (GNMA)
T. Rowe Price Growth & Income Fund, Inc.
(Gr&I)
T. Rowe Price Growth Stock Fund, Inc.
(Gr)
T. Rowe Price Health Sciences Fund, Inc.
(AgGr)
T. Rowe Price High Yield Fund, Inc.
(HiYB)
T. Rowe Price Index Trust, Inc.
Equity Index Fund (Gr)
T. Rowe Price Mid-Cap Growth Fund, Inc.
(Gr)
T. Rowe Price Mid-Cap Value Fund, Inc.
(Gr)
T. Rowe Price New America Growth Fund
(AgGr)
T. Rowe Price New Era Fund, Inc. (Gr)
T. Rowe Price New Horizons Fund, Inc.
(AgGr)
T. Rowe Price New Income Fund, Inc.
(IncB)
T. Rowe Price OTC Fund, Inc.
T. Rowe Price OTC Fund (AgGr)
T. Rowe Price Personal Strategy Funds, Inc.
T. Rowe Price Personal Strategy Balanced
Fund (Flex)
T. Rowe Price Personal Strategy Growth
Fund (Flex)
T. Rowe Price Personal Strategy Income
Fund (Flex)
T. Rowe Price Prime Reserve Fund, Inc.
(MM)
T. Rowe Price Science & Technology Fund,
Inc. (AgGr)
T. Rowe Price Short-Term Bond Fund, Inc.
(IncB)
T. Rowe Price Short-Term U.S.
Government Fund, Inc. (USGv)
T. Rowe Price Small-Cap Value Fund, Inc.
(AgGr)
T. Rowe Price Spectrum Fund, Inc.
Spectrum Growth Fund (Gr)
Spectrum Income Fund (IncM)
T. Rowe Price State Tax-Free Income Trust
Florida Insured Intermediate Tax-Free
Fund (SMuB)
Georgia Tax-Free Bond Fund (SMuB)
Maryland Short-Term Tax-Free Bond
Fund (SMuB)
Maryland Tax-Free Bond Fund (SMuB)
New Jersey Tax-Free Bond Fund (SMuB)

New York Tax-Free Bond Fund (SMuB)
New York Tax-Free Money Fund (SMMX)
Virginia Short-Term Tax-Free Bond Fund
(SMuB)
Virginia Tax-Free Bond Fund (SMuB)
T. Rowe Price Summit Funds, Inc.
T. Rowe Price Summit Cash Reserves
Fund (MM)
T. Rowe Price Summit GNMA Fund
(GNMA)
T. Rowe Price Summit Limited-Term
Bond Fund (IncB)
T. Rowe Price Summit Municipal Funds,
Inc.
T. Rowe Price Summit Municipal Income
Fund (NMuB)
T. Rowe Price Summit Municipal
Intermediate Fund (NMuB)
T. Rowe Price Summit Municipal Money
Market Fund (NMMX)
T. Rowe Price Tax-Exempt Money Fund,
Inc. (NMMX)
T. Rowe Price Tax-Free High Yield Fund,
Inc. (NMuB)
T. Rowe Price Tax-Free Income Fund, Inc.
(NMuB)
T. Rowe Price Tax-Free Insured
Intermediate Bond Fund, Inc. (NMuB)
T. Rowe Price Tax-Free Short-Intermediate
Fund, Inc. (NMuB)
T. Rowe Price U.S. Treasury Funds, Inc.
U.S. Treasury Intermediate Fund (USGv)
U.S. Treasury Long-Term Fund (USGv)
U.S. Treasury Money Fund (MM)
T. Rowe Price Value Fund, Inc. (Gr&I)

Trust for Credit Unions
P.O. Box 16931
St. Louis, MO 63105
800/305-2140
Trust for Credit Unions
Government Securities Portfolio (GNMA)
Money Market Portfolio (MM)
Mortgage Securities Portfolio (GNMA)

Tweedy, Browne Fund Inc.
52 Vanderbilt Ave.
8th Fl.
New York, NY 10017-3808
800/432-4789
Tweedy, Browne American Value Fund (Gr)
Tweedy, Browne Global Value Fund (GloE)

UAM Funds
211 Congress St.
Boston, MA 02110
800/638-7983
UAM Funds, Inc.
Acadian Emerging Markets Portfolio (Intl)
Acadian International Equity Portfolio
(Intl)

UAM Funds Trust
  BHM&S Total Return Bond Portfolio
    (IncB)
  C&B Mid Cap Equity Portfolio (AgGr)
  Chicago Asset Management Intermediate
    Bond Portfolio (IncB)
  Chicago Asset Management Value/
    Contrarian Portfolio (Gr&I)
  IRC Enhanced Index Portfolio (Gr&I)
  Jacobs International Octagon Portfolio
    (Intl)
  MJI International Equity Portfolio (Intl)
  Newbold's Equity Portfolio (Gr&I)
  TJ Core Equity Portfolio (Gr&I)
UAM Funds, Inc.
  C&B Balanced Portfolio (Bal)
  C&B Equity Portfolio (Gr)
  C&B Equity Portfolio for Taxable
    Investors (Gr&I)
  DSI Disciplined Value Portfolio (Gr&I)
  DSI Limited Maturity Bond Portfolio
    (IncB)
  DSI Money Market Portfolio (MM)
  FMA Small Company Portfolio (AgGr)
  ICM Equity Portfolio (Gr&I)
  ICM Fixed Income Portfolio (IncB)
  ICM Small Company Portfolio (AgGr)
  McKee Domestic Equity Portfolio
    (Gr&I)
  McKee International Equity Portfolio
    (Intl)
  McKee Small Cap Equity Portfolio
    (AgGr)
  McKee U.S. Government Portfolio
    (USGv)
  NWQ Balanced Portfolio (Bal)
  NWQ Value Equity Portfolio (Gr&I)
  Rice Hall James Small Cap Portfolio
    (AgGr)
  Rice Hall James Small/Mid Cap Portfolio
    (Gr)
  SAMI Preferred Stock Income Portfolio
    (IncE)
  Sirach Equity Portfolio (Gr)
  Sirach Fixed Income Portfolio (IncB)
  Sirach Growth Portfolio (Gr)
  Sirach Short-Term Reserves Portfolio
    (IncB)
  Sirach Special Equity Portfolio (Gr)
  Sirach Strategic Balanced Portfolio (Bal)
  Sterling Partners' Balanced Portfolio
    (Bal)
  Sterling Partners' Equity Portfolio (Gr)
  Sterling Partners' Short-Term Fixed
    Income Portfolio (IncB)
  Sterling Partners' Small Cap Value
    Portfolio (AgGr)
  TS&W Equity Portfolio (Gr)
  TS&W Fixed Income Portfolio (IncB)
  TS&W International Equity Portfolio
    (Intl)

UBS Private Investor Funds, Inc.
200 Clarendon St.
Boston, MA 02116
888/UBS-FUND
UBS Private Investor Funds, Inc.
  UBS Bond Fund (CorB)
  UBS International Equity Fund (Intl)
  UBS Tax Exempt Bond Fund (NMuB)
  UBS U.S. Equity Fund (Gr&I)

Ultra Series Fund
2000 Heritage Way
Waverly, IA 50677-9208
800/798-5500
Ultra Series Fund
  Balanced Fund (Bal)
  Bond Fund (IncB)
  Capital Appreciation Stock Fund (Gr)
  Growth and Income Stock Fund (Gr&I)
  Money Market Fund (MM)
  Treasury 2000 Fund (USGv)

United Funds
6300 Lamar
P.O. Box 29217
Shawnee Mission, KS 66202-4247
800/366-5465
United Asset Strategy Fund, Inc. (IncM)
United Cash Management Fund, Inc. (MM)
United Continental Income Fund, Inc. (Bal)
United Funds, Inc.
  United Accumulative Fund (Gr)
  United Bond Fund (IncB)
  United Income Fund (IncE)
  United Science and Technology Fund (Gr)
United Gold & Government Fund, Inc.
  (PM/G)
United Government Securities Fund, Inc.
  (USGv)
United High Income Fund II, Inc. (HiYB)
United High Income Fund, Inc. (HiYB)
United International Growth Fund, Inc.
  (Intl)
United Municipal Bond Fund, Inc. (NMuB)
United Municipal High Income Fund, Inc.
  (NMuB)
United New Concepts Fund, Inc. (AgGr)
United Retirement Shares, Inc. (Gr&I)
United Vanguard Fund, Inc. (AgGr)
Waddell Reed Fund, Inc.
  Asset Strategy Fund (Gr&I)
  Growth Fund (AgGr)
  International Growth Fund (Intl)
  Limited Term Bond Fund (IncB)
  Municipal Bond Fund (NMuB)
  Total Return Fund (Gr&I)

Universal Capital Fund
One Oakbrook Ter.
Ste. 708
Oakbrook Terrace, IL 60181-4728

888/255-2437
Universal Capital Investment Trust
  Universal Capital Growth Fund (Gr)

USAA Funds
9800 Fredericksburg Rd.
San Antonio, TX 78288-0001
800/382-8722
USAA Investment Trust
  Balanced Strategy Fund (Bal)
  Cornerstone Strategy Fund (Bal)
  Emerging Markets Fund (Intl)
  GNMA Trust (GNMA)
  Gold Fund (PM/G)
  Growth and Tax Strategy Fund (Bal)
  Growth Strategy Fund (Bal)
  Income Strategy Fund (Bal)
  International Fund (Intl)
  Treasury Money Market Trust (MM)
  World Growth Fund (GloE)
USAA Life Investment Trust
  USAA Life Variable Annuity Diversified
    Assets Fund (Gr&I)
  USAA Life Variable Annuity Growth and
    Income Fund (Gr&I)
  USAA Life Variable Annuity Income
    Fund (IncM)
  USAA Life Variable Annuity Money
    Market Fund (MM)
  USAA Life Variable Annuity World
    Growth Fund (GloE)
USAA Mutual Fund, Inc.
  Aggressive Growth Fund (AgGr)
  Growth & Income Fund (Gr&I)
  Growth Fund (Gr)
  Income Fund (IncM)
  Income Stock Fund (IncE)
  Money Market Fund (MM)
  S&P 500 Index Fund (Gr&I)
  Short-Term Bond Fund (IncB)
USAA State Tax-Free Trust
  Florida Tax-Free Income Fund (SMuB)
  Florida Tax-Free Money Market Fund
    (SMMX)
  Texas Tax-Free Income Fund (SMuB)
  Texas Tax-Free Money Market Fund
    (SMMX)
USAA Tax Exempt Fund, Inc.
  California Bond Fund (SMuB)
  California Money Market Fund
    (SMMX)
  Intermediate-Term Fund (NMuB)
  Long-Term Fund (NMuB)
  New York Bond Fund (SMuB)
  New York Money Market Fund
    (SMMX)
  Short-Term Fund (NMuB)
  Tax Exempt Money Market Fund
    (NMMX)
  Virginia Bond Fund (SMuB)
  Virginia Money Market Fund (SMMX)

U.S. Global Investors Funds
7900 Callaghan Rd.
San Antonio, TX 78229-2327
800/873-8637
U.S. Global Accolade Funds
  Adrian Day Global Opportunity Fund
    (Intl)
  Bonnel Growth Fund (Gr)
  MegaTrends Fund (The) (Gr)
  Regent Eastern European Fund (Intl)
U.S. Global Investors Funds
  China Region Opportunity Fund (Intl)
  United Services Near Term Tax Free Fund
    (NMuB)
  U.S. All American Equity Fund (Gr&I)
  U.S. Global Resources Fund (GloE)
  U.S. Gold Shares Fund (PM/G)
  U.S. Government Securities Savings Fund
    (MM)
  U.S. Income Fund (IncE)
  U.S. Real Estate Fund (Gr)
  U.S. Tax Free Fund (NMuB)
  U.S. Treasury Securities Cash Fund (MM)
  U.S. World Gold Fund (PM/G)

VALIC Funds
2929 Allen Pkwy.
P.O. Box 3206
Houston, TX 77019-2142
713/526-5251
American General Series Portfolio
  Company
  Capital Conservation Fund (CorB)
  Government Securities Fund (USGv)
  Growth and Income Fund (Gr&I)
  Growth Fund (Gr)
  International Equities Fund (Intl)
  International Government Bond Fund
    (GloB)
  MidCap Index Fund (Gr)
  Money Market Fund (MM)
  Science and Technology Fund (AgGr)
  Small Cap Index Fund (AgGr)
  Social Awareness Fund (Gr&I)
  Stock Index Fund (Gr&I)
  Timed Opportunity Fund (Bal)

Value Line Funds
220 E. 42nd St.
New York, NY 10017-5806
800/223-0818
Value Line Aggressive Income Trust (The)
  (HiYB)
Value Line Asset Allocation Fund (The)
  (Flex)
Value Line Cash Fund, Inc. (The) (MM)
Value Line Centurion Fund, Inc. (The) (Gr)
Value Line Convertible Fund, Inc. (The)
  (Gr&I)
Value Line Fund, Inc. (The) (Gr)
Value Line Income Fund, Inc. (The) (IncM)

Value Line Intermediate Bond Fund (The)
  (GNMA)
Value Line Leveraged Growth Investors,
  Inc. (The) (AgGr)
Value Line New York Tax Exempt Trust
  (The) (SMuB)
Value Line Small Cap Fund (The) (AgGr)
Value Line Special Situations Fund, Inc.
  (The) (AgGr)
Value Line Strategic Asset Management
  Trust (The) (Flex)
Value Line Tax Exempt Fund, Inc. (The)
  High Yield Portfolio (NMuB)
  Money Market Portfolio (NMMX)
Value Line U.S. Government Securities
  Fund, Inc. (The) (USGv)
Value Line U.S. Multinational Company
  Fund, Inc. (Gr&I)

Van Eck
99 Park Ave.
New York, NY 10016
800/221-2220
Van Eck Funds Asia Dynasty Fund (Intl)
  Asia Infrastructure Fund (Intl)
  Emerging Markets Growth Fund (Intl)
  Global Balanced Fund (GloB)
  Global Hard Assets Fund (GloE)
  Global Income Fund (GloB)
  Gold Opportunity Fund (PM/G)
  Gold/Resources Fund (PM/G)
  International Investors Gold Fund (PM/G)
Van Eck Worldwide Insurance Trust
  Gold and Natural Resources Fund (PM/G)
  Worldwide Balanced Fund (Intl)
  Worldwide Bond Fund (GloB)
  Worldwide Emerging Markets Fund (Intl)

Vanguard Group of Funds
Vanguard Financial Ctr.
P.O. Box 2600
Valley Forge, PA 19482-2600
800/662-7447
Gemini II (Gr&I)
PRIMECAP Fund, Inc. (Gr)
Vanguard Admiral Funds, Inc.
  Admiral Intermediate-Term U.S. Treasury
    Portfolio (USGv)
  Admiral Long-Term U.S. Treasury
    Portfolio (USGv)
  Admiral Short-Term U.S. Treasury
    Portfolio (USGv)
  Admiral U.S. Treasury Money Market
    Portfolio (MM)
Vanguard Asset Allocation Fund, Inc. (Flex)
Vanguard Balanced Index Fund (Bal)
Vanguard Bond Index Fund
  Intermediate-Term Bond Portfolio (IncB)
  Long-Term Bond Portfolio (IncB)
  Short-Term Bond Portfolio (IncB)
  Total Bond Market Portfolio (IncB)

Vanguard California Tax-Free Fund
  Insured Intermediate-Term Portfolio
    (SMuB)
  Insured Long-Term Portfolio (SMuB)
  Money Market Portfolio (SMMX)
Vanguard Convertible Securities Fund, Inc.
  (Bal)
Vanguard Equity Income Fund, Inc. (IncE)
Vanguard Explorer Fund, Inc. (AgGr)
Vanguard Fixed Income Securities Fund,
  Inc.
  GNMA Portfolio (GNMA)
  High Yield Corporate Portfolio (HiYB)
  Intermediate-Term Corporate Portfolio
    (CorB)
  Intermediate-Term U.S. Treasury Portfolio
    (USGv)
  Long-Term Corporate Portfolio (CorB)
  Long-Term U.S. Treasury Portfolio
    (USGv)
  Short-Term Corporate Portfolio (CorB)
  Short-Term Federal Portfolio (USGv)
  Short-Term U.S. Treasury Portfolio
    (USGv)
Vanguard Florida Insured Tax-Free Fund
  (SMuB)
Vanguard Horizon Fund
  Aggressive Growth Portfolio (AgGr)
  Capital Opportunity Portfolio (Gr)
  Global Asset Allocation Portfolio (Intl)
  Global Equity Portfolio (GloE)
Vanguard Index Trust
  Extended Market Portfolio (Gr)
  500 Portfolio (Gr&I)
  Growth Portfolio (Gr)
  Small Capitalization Stock Portfolio
    (AgGr)
  Total Stock Market Portfolio (Gr&I)
  Value Portfolio (Gr&I)
Vanguard Institutional Index Fund (Gr&I)
Vanguard International Equity Index Fund,
  Inc.
  Emerging Markets Portfolio (Intl)
  European Portfolio (Intl)
  Pacific Portfolio (Intl)
Vanguard International Growth Portfolio
  (Intl)
Vanguard LIFEStrategy Funds
  Conservative Growth Portfolio (Bal)
  Growth Portfolio (Gr)
  Income Portfolio (IncM)
  Moderate Growth Portfolio (Gr&I)
  Total International Portfolio (Intl)
Vanguard Money Market Reserves, Inc.
  Federal Portfolio (MM)
  Prime Portfolio (MM)
  Treasury Money Market Portfolio (MM)
Vanguard/Morgan Growth Fund, Inc. (Gr)
Vanguard Municipal Bond Fund, Inc.
  High-Yield Portfolio (NMuB)
  Insured Long-Term Portfolio (NMuB)

Intermediate-Term Portfolio (NMuB)
Limited-Term Portfolio (NMuB)
Long-Term Portfolio (NMuB)
Money Market Portfolio (NMMX)
Short-Term Portfolio (NMuB)
Vanguard New Jersey Tax-Free Fund
Insured Long-Term Portfolio (SMuB)
Money Market Portfolio (SMMX)
Vanguard New York Insured Tax-Free Fund
(SMuB)
Vanguard Ohio Tax-Free Fund
Insured Long-Term Portfolio (SMuB)
Money Market Portfolio (SMMX)
Vanguard Pennsylvania Tax-Free Fund
Insured Long-Term Portfolio (SMuB)
Money Market Portfolio (SMMX)
Vanguard Preferred Stock Fund (IncE)
Vanguard Quantitative Portfolios, Inc.
(Gr&I)
Vanguard Specialized Portfolio, Inc.
Energy Portfolio (AgGr)
Health Care Portfolio (AgGr)
REIT Index Portfolio (IncE)
Utilities Income Portfolio (Gr&I)
Vanguard STAR Fund (Bal)
Vanguard Tax-Managed Fund
Balanced Portfolio (Bal)
Capital Appreciation Portfolio (Gr)
Growth and Income Portfolio (Gr&I)
Vanguard/Trustees' Equity Fund
U.S. Portfolio (Gr&I)
Vanguard U.S. Growth Portfolio (Gr)
Vanguard Variable Insurance Fund (The)
Balanced Portfolio (Bal)
Equity Income Portfolio (IncE)
Equity Index Portfolio (Gr&I)
Growth Portfolio (Gr)
High-Grade Bond Portfolio (CorB)
High Yield Bond Portfolio (HiYB)
International Portfolio (Intl)
Money Market Portfolio (MM)
Small Company Growth Portfolio
(AgGr)
Vanguard Specialized Portfolio, Inc.
Gold & Precious Metals Portfolio (PM/G)
Vanguard/Trustees' Equity Fund
International Portfolio (Intl)
Vanguard/Wellesley Income Fund (IncM)
Vanguard/Wellington Fund, Inc. (Bal)
Vanguard Whitehall Funds, Inc.
Vanguard Selected Value Portfolio (Gr)
Vanguard/Windsor Fund (Gr&I)
Vanguard/Windsor II (Gr&I)

Van Kampen American Capital Mutual Funds
One Parkview Plaza
Oakbrook Terrace, IL 60181-4400
800/225-2222
Van Kampen American Capital Comstock
Fund, Inc. (Gr&I)

Van Kampen American Capital Corporate
Bond Fund (CorB)
Van Kampen American Capital Emerging
Growth Fund (AgGr)
Van Kampen American Capital Enterprise
Fund (Gr)
Van Kampen American Capital Equity
Income Fund (IncE)
Van Kampen American Capital Equity Trust
Great American Companies Fund (Gr)
Growth Fund (AgGr)
Prospector Fund (Gr&I)
Utility Fund (IncE)
Value Fund (Gr)
Van Kampen American Capital
Aggressive Growth Fund (AgGr)
Van Kampen American Capital Exchange
Fund (Gr)
Van Kampen American Capital Global
Managed Assets Fund (GloE)
Van Kampen American Capital Government
Securities Fund (USGv)
Van Kampen American Capital Growth and
Income Fund (Gr&I)
Van Kampen American Capital Harbor
Fund (Gr&I)
Van Kampen American Capital High
Income Corporate Bond Fund (HiYB)
Van Kampen American Capital Life
Investment Trust
Asset Allocation Fund (Flex)
Domestic Income Fund (CorB)
Emerging Growth Fund (AgGr)
Enterprise Fund (Gr)
Global Equity Fund (GloE)
Government Fund (USGv)
Money Market Fund (MM)
Real Estate Securities Fund (Gr&I)
Van Kampen American Capital Limited
Maturity Government Fund (GNMA)
Van Kampen American Capital Pace Fund
(Gr)
Van Kampen American Capital
Pennsylvania Tax Free Income (SMuB)
Van Kampen American Capital Real Estate
Securities Fund (Gr&I)
Van Kampen American Capital Reserve
Fund (MM)
Van Kampen American Capital Small
Capitalization Fund (AgGr)
Van Kampen American Capital Tax-Exempt
Trust
High Yield Municipal Fund (NMuB)
Van Kampen American Capital Tax Free
Fund
Van Kampen American Capital California
Insured Tax Free Fund (SMuB)
Van Kampen American Capital Florida
Insured Tax Free Income Fund (SMuB)
Van Kampen American Capital Insured
Tax Free Income Fund (NMuB)

Van Kampen American Capital
Intermediate Term Municipal Income
Fund (NMuB)
Van Kampen American Capital Municipal
Income Fund (NMuB)
Van Kampen American Capital New
Jersey Tax Free Income Fund (SMuB)
Van Kampen American Capital New York
Tax Free Income Fund (SMuB)
Van Kampen American Capital Tax Free
High Income Fund (NMuB)
Van Kampen American Capital Tax Free
Money Fund (NMMX)
Van Kampen American Capital Trust
Van Kampen American Capital High Yield
Fund (HiYB)
Van Kampen American Capital Short
Term Global Income Fund (GloB)
Van Kampen American Capital Strategic
Income Fund (IncM)
Van Kampen American Capital U.S.
Government Trust
Van Kampen Merritt U.S. Government
Fund (USGv)
Van Kampen American Capital U.S.
Government Trust for Income (USGv)
Van Kampen American Capital World
Portfolio Series Trust
Global Equity Fund (GloE)
Global Government Securities Fund
(GloB)

Variable Investors Series Trust
10 Post Office Square
Boston, MA 02109
617/457-6700
Variable Investors Series Trust
Cash Management Portfolio (MM)
Growth and Income Portfolio (Gr&I)
Growth Portfolio (Gr)
High Income Bond Portfolio (HiYB)
Multiple Strategies Portfolio (Flex)
Small Cap Growth Portfolio (AgGr)
Tilt Utility Fund (Gr&I)
U.S. Government Bond Portfolio (IncB)
World Equity Portfolio (GloE)

Victory Portfolios
3435 Stelzer Rd.
Columbus, OH 43219-3035
800/539-3863
Victory Portfolios (The)
Lakefront Fund (The) (Gr&I)
Victory Portfolios (The)
Balanced Fund (Bal)
Diversified Stock Fund (Gr)
Financial Reserves Portfolio (MM)
Fund for Income Portfolio (IncM)
Government Bond Fund (USGv)
Government Mortgage Fund (USGv)
Growth Fund (Gr)

Institutional Money Market Fund (MM)
Intermediate Income Fund (IncM)
International Growth Fund (Intl)
Investment Quality Bond Fund (IncB)
Limited Term Income Fund (IncM)
National Municipal Bond Fund (NMuB)
New York Daily Tax-Free Income Fund
(SMMX)
New York Tax-Free Bond Fund (SMuB)
Ohio Municipal Bond Fund (SMuB)
Ohio Municipal Money Market Portfolio
(SMMX)
Ohio Regional Stock Fund (Gr)
Prime Obligations Fund (MM)
Special Growth Fund (AgGr)
Special Value Fund (Gr)
Stock Index Fund (Gr)
Tax-Free Money Market Fund (NMMX)
U.S. Government Obligations Fund (MM)
Value Fund (Gr)

Virtus/Blanchard Funds
Federated Investors Twr.
1001 Liberty Ave.
Pittsburgh, PA 15222-3779
800/356-2805
Blanchard Funds
Blanchard Asset Allocation Fund (Flex)
Blanchard Capital Growth Fund (Gr)
Blanchard Flexible Income Fund (IncM)
Blanchard Flexible Tax-Free Bond Fund
(NMuB)
Blanchard Global Growth Fund (GloE)
Blanchard Growth & Income Fund (Gr&I)
Blanchard Precious Metals Fund (PM/G)
Blanchard Short-Term Flexible Income
Fund (IncB)
Virtus Funds (The)
Maryland Municipal Bond Fund (SMuB)
Money Market Fund (MM)
Style Manager Fund (Gr)
Style Manager: Large Cap Fund (Gr&I)
Tax-Free Money Market Fund (NMMX)
Treasury Money Market Fund (MM)
U.S. Government Securities Fund (USGv)
Virginia Municipal Bond Fund (SMuB)

Vision Funds
Federated Investors Twr.
1001 Liberty Ave.
Pittsburgh, PA 15222-3779
800/341-7400
Vision Group of Funds, Inc.
Vision Capital Appreciation Fund (Gr)
Vision Growth and Income Fund (Gr&I)
Vision Money Market Fund (MM)
Vision New York Tax-Free Fund (SMuB)
Vision New York Tax-Free Money Market
Fund (SMMX)
Vision Treasury Money Market Fund
(MM)

Vision U.S. Government Securities Fund (USGv)

Vista Mutual Funds
125 W. 55th St.
11th Fl.
New York, NY 10019-3800
800/367-6075
Mutual Fund Select Group
  Vista Select Balanced Fund (Bal)
  Vista Select Bond Fund (IncB)
  Vista Select Equity Income Fund (IncE)
  Vista Select Intermediate Bond Fund (IncB)
  Vista Select International Equity Fund (Intl)
  Vista Select Large Cap Equity Fund (Gr)
  Vista Select Large Cap Growth Fund (Gr)
  Vista Select New Growth Opportunities Fund (AgGr)
  Vista Select Short-Term Bond Fund (IncB)
  Vista Select Small Cap Value Fund (AgGr)
Mutual Fund Select Trust
  Vista Select Intermediate Tax Free Income Fund (NMuB)
  Vista Select New Jersey Tax Free Income Fund (SMuB)
  Vista Select New York Tax Free Income Fund (SMuB)
  Vista Select Tax Free Income Fund (NMuB)
Vista Mutual Funds
  Vista Balanced Fund (Bal)
  Vista Bond Fund (IncB)
  Vista California Intermediate Tax-Free Fund (SMuB)
  Vista California Tax Free Money Market Fund (SMMX)
  Vista Capital Growth Fund (Gr)
  Vista Cash Management Money Market Fund (MM)
  Vista Equity Income Fund (Gr&I)
  Vista European Fund (Intl)
  Vista Federal Money Market Fund (NMMX)
  Vista Growth and Income Fund (Gr&I)
  Vista International Equity Fund (Intl)
  Vista Japan Fund (Intl)
  Vista Large Cap Equity Fund (Gr)
  Vista New York Tax Free Income Fund (SMuB)
  Vista New York Tax Free Money Market Fund (SMMX)
  Vista Prime Money Market Fund (MM)
  Vista Short-Term Bond Fund (CorB)
  Vista Small Cap Equity Fund (AgGr)
  Vista Small Cap Opportunities Fund (AgGr)
  Vista Southeast Asian Fund (Intl)

Vista Tax Free Income Fund (NMuB)
Vista Tax Free Money Market Fund (NMMX)
Vista Treasury Plus Money Market Fund (MM)
Vista U.S. Government Income Fund (USGv)
Vista U.S. Government Money Market Fund (MM)
Vista 100% U.S. Treasury Money Market Fund (MM)
Vista U.S. Government Securities Fund (USGv)

Volumetric Fund, Inc.
87 Violet Dr.
Pearl River, NY 10965-1212
800/541-3863
Volumetric Fund, Inc. (Gr)

Vontobel Funds
1500 Forest Ave.
Ste. 223
Richmond, VA 23229-5104
800/527-9500
Vontobel Funds, Inc. (The)
  Sand Hill Portfolio Manager Fund (IncM)
Vontobel Funds, Inc. (The)
  Vontobel Eastern European Equity Fund (Intl)
  Vontobel International Bond Fund (GloB)
  Vontobel International Equity Fund (Intl)
  Vontobel U.S. Value Fund (Gr)

Voyageur Funds
90 S. Seventh St.
Ste. 4400
Minneapolis, MN 55402-4115
800/553-2143
Voyageur Funds, Inc.
  Voyageur National Tax-Free Fund (NMuB)
  Voyageur U.S. Government Securities Fund (USGv)
Voyageur Insured Funds, Inc.
  Voyageur Arizona Insured Tax-Free Fund (SMuB)
  Voyageur Minnesota Insured Fund (SMuB)
  Voyageur National Insured Tax-Free Fund (NMuB)
Voyageur Intermediate Tax-Free Funds, Inc.
  Voyageur Arizona Limited Term Tax Free Fund (SmuB)
  Voyageur Minnesota Limited Term Tax-Free Fund (SMuB)
  Voyageur National Limited Term Tax-Free Fund (NMuB)
Voyageur Investment Trust
  Voyageur California Insured Tax Free Fund (SMuB)

Voyageur Florida Insured Tax Free Fund
(SMuB)
Voyageur Idaho Tax Free Fund (SMuB)
Voyageur Kansas Tax-Free Fund (SMuB)
Voyageur Missouri Insured Tax Free Fund
(SMuB)
Voyageur New Mexico Tax Free Fund
(SMuB)
Voyageur Oregon Insured Tax Free Fund
(SMuB)
Voyageur Utah Tax Free Fund (SMuB)
Voyageur Washington Insured Tax-Free
Fund (SMuB)
Voyageur Investment Trust II
Florida Limited Term Tax Free Fund
(SMuB)
Voyageur Mutual Funds, Inc.
Voyageur Iowa Tax Free Fund (SMuB)
Voyageur Minnesota High Yield
Municipal Bond Fund (SMuB)
Voyageur National High Yield Municipal
Bond Fund (NMuB)
Voyageur Wisconsin Tax-Free Fund
(SMuB)
Voyageur Mutual Funds II, Inc.
Voyageur Colorado Tax-Free Fund
(SMuB)
Voyageur Mutual Funds III, Inc.
Voyageur Aggressive Growth Fund
(AgGr)
Voyageur Growth and Income Fund
(Gr&I)
Voyageur Growth Stock Fund (Gr)
Voyageur Tax-Free Funds, Inc.
Voyageur Arizona Tax-Free Fund (SMuB)
Voyageur California Tax-Free Fund
(SMuB)
Voyageur Florida Tax-Free Fund (SMuB)
Voyageur Minnesota Tax-Free Fund
(SMuB)
Voyageur New York Tax Free Fund (SmuB)
Voyageur North Dakota Tax-Free Fund
(SMuB)

Vulcan Funds
Federated Investors Twr.
1001 Liberty Ave.
Pittsburgh, PA 15222-3779
800/341-7400
SouthTrust Vulcan Funds
Vulcan Bond Fund (IncB)
Vulcan Stock Fund (Gr&I)
Vulcan Treasury Obligations Money
Market Fund (MM)

Wade Fund
5100 Poplar Ave.
Ste. 2224
Memphis, TN 38137-2201
901/682-4613
Wade Fund, Inc. (Gr)

Walnut Street Funds
670 Mason Ridge Center Dr.
Ste. 300
St. Louis, MO 63141
800/862-6363
Walnut Street Funds, Inc.
Walnut Street Prime Reserve Fund (MM)

Wanger Funds
227 W. Monroe St.
Ste. 3000
Chicago, IL 60606-5016
800/592-6437
Wanger Advisors Trust
Wanger International Small Cap Advisor
Portfolio (Intl)
Wanger U.S. Small Cap Advisor (Gr)

Warburg Pincus Funds
466 Lexington Ave.
New York, NY 10017-3147
800/927-2874
Warburg Pincus Balanced Fund (Bal)
Warburg Pincus Capital Appreciation Fund
(Gr)
Warburg Pincus Cash Reserve Fund (MM)
Warburg Pincus Emerging Growth Fund
(AgGr)
Warburg Pincus Emerging Markets Fund
(Intl)
Warburg Pincus Fixed Income Fund (IncB)
Warburg Pincus Global Fixed Income Fund
(GloB)
Warburg Pincus Global Post-Venture
Capital Fund (GloE)
Warburg Pincus Growth & Income Fund
(Gr&I)
Warburg Pincus Health Sciences Fund
(AgGr)
Warburg Pincus Institutional Fund, Inc.
Emerging Markets Portfolio (Intl)
Global Fixed Income Portfolio (GloB)
International Equity Portfolio (Intl)
Managed EAFE Countries Portfolio (Intl)
Small Company Growth Portfolio (AgGr)
Warburg Pincus Intermediate Maturity
Government Fund (USGv)
Warburg Pincus International Equity Fund
(Intl)
Warburg Pincus Japan Growth Fund (Intl)
Warburg Pincus Japan OTC Fund (Intl)
Warburg Pincus New York Intermediate
Municipal Fund (SMuB)
Warburg Pincus New York Tax Exempt
Fund (SMMX)
Warburg Pincus Post-Venture Capital Fund
(Gr)
Warburg Pincus Small Company Growth
Fund (AgGr)
Warburg Pincus Small Company Value
Fund (AgGr)

Warburg Pincus Strategic Value Fund (Gr)
Warburg Pincus Tax Free Fund (NMuB)
Warburg Pincus Trust
  Emerging Markets Portfolio (Intl)
  International Equity Portfolio (Intl)
  Post-Venture Capital Portfolio (AgGr)
  Small Company Growth Portfolio (AgGr)
Warburg Pincus Trust II
  Fixed Income Portfolio (IncB)
  Global Fixed Income Portfolio (GloB)

Wasatch Funds
68 S. Main St.
Ste. 400
Salt Lake City, UT 84101-1523
800/551-1700
Wasatch Advisors Funds, Inc.
  Wasatch Aggressive Equity Fund
  (AgGr)
  Wasatch Growth Fund (Gr)
  Wasatch-Hoisington U.S. Treasury Fund
  (USGv)
  Wasatch MicroCap Fund (Gr)
  Wasatch Mid-Cap Fund (Gr&I)

**Waterhouse Investors Cash Management
Fund, Inc.**
50 Main St.
White Plains, NY 10606
800/934-4410
Waterhouse Investors Cash Management
  Fund, Inc.
  Money Market Portfolio (MM)
  Municipal Portfolio (NMMX)
  U.S. Government Portfolio (MM)

Wayne Hummer Funds
300 S. Wacker Dr.
Chicago, IL 60606-6610
800/621-4477
Wayne Hummer Investment Trust
  Growth Fund (Gr&I)
  Income Fund (CorB)
Wayne Hummer Money Fund Trust
  Money Market Fund (MM)

Weiss Peck & Greer Funds
One New York Plaza
31st Fl.
New York, NY 10004-1902
800/223-3332
RWB/WPG U.S. Large Stock Fund (Gr&I)
Tomorrow Long-Term Retirement Fund
  (Flex)
Tomorrow Medium-Term Retirement Fund
  (Gr&I)
Tomorrow Short-Term Retirement Fund
  (Bal)
Weiss Peck & Greer Funds Trust
  WPG Government Money Market Fund
  (MM)

WPG Government Securities Fund
  (USGv)
WPG Intermediate Municipal Bond Fund
  (NMuB)
WPG Quantitative Equity Fund
  (Gr&I)
WPG Tax Free Money Market Fund
  (NMMX)
Weiss Peck & Greer International Fund
  (Intl)
WPG Growth and Income Fund (Gr&I)
WPG Growth Fund (AgGr)
WPG Tudor Fund (The) (AgGr)

Weitz Funds
One Pacific Place, Ste. 600
1125 South 103 St.
Omaha, NE 68124-6008
800/232-4161
Weitz Partners, Inc.
  Partners Value Fund (Gr)
Weitz Series Fund, Inc.
  Fixed Income Portfolio (IncB)
  Government Money Market Portfolio
  (MM)
  Hickory Portfolio (AgGr)
  Value Portfolio (Gr)

WesMark Funds
Federated Investors Tower
Pittsburgh, PA 15222-3779
800/341-7400
WesMark Funds
  Growth Fund (AgGr)
  West Virginia Municipal Bond Fund
  (SMuB)

Westcore Funds
370 Seventeenth St.
Ste. 2700
Denver, CO 80202
800/392-2673
Westcore Trust
  Westcore Blue Chip Fund (Gr&I)
  Westcore Colorado Tax-Exempt Fund
  (SMuB)
  Westcore Growth & Income Fund
  (Gr&I)
  Westcore Intermediate-Term Bond Fund
  (CorB)
  Westcore Long-Term Bond Fund
  (CorB)
  Westcore Midco Growth Fund (Gr)
  Westcore Small-Cap Opportunity Fund
  (AgGr)

West University Fund, Inc.
3030 University Blvd.
Houston, TX 77005
800/465-5657
West University Fund, Inc. (IncE)

William Blair Mutual Funds
222 West Adams St.
Chicago, IL 60606
312/236-1600
William Blair Mutual Funds, Inc.
  William Blair Growth Fund (Gr)
  William Blair Income Fund (IncB)
  William Blair International Growth Fund
  (Intl)
  William Blair Ready Reserves Fund
  (MM)
  William Blair Value Discovery Fund (Gr)

Williamsburg Investment Trust
312 Walnut St.
P.O. Box 5354
Cincinnati, OH 45201-5354
800/443-4249
Williamsburg Investment Trust
  Alabama Tax Free Bond Fund (SMuB)
  FBP Contrarian Balanced Fund (Bal)
  FBP Contrarian Equity Fund (Gr)
  Government Street Bond Fund (IncB)
  Government Street Equity Fund (Gr)
  Jamestown Balanced Fund (Bal)
  Jamestown Bond Fund (IncB)
  Jamestown Equity Fund (Gr)
  Jamestown International Equity Fund
  (Intl)
  Jamestown Short Term Bond Fund (IncB)
  Jamestown Tax-Exempt Virginia Fund
  (SMuB)

WNL Series Trust
5555 San Felipe
Ste. 900
Houston, TX 77056
800/262-4764
WNL Series Trust
  American Capital Emerging Growth Fund
  (Gr)
  BEA Growth and Income Fund (Gr&I)
  Black Rock Managed Bond Fund (IncB)
  Credit Suisse International Equity Fund
  (Intl)
  Global Advisors Growth Equity Fund (Gr)
  Global Advisors Money Market Fund
  (MM)
  Quest for Value Asset Allocation Fund
  (Flex)
  Salomon Brothers U.S. Government
  Securities Fund (USGv)

Wood Struthers & Winthrop Funds
277 Park Ave.
24th Fl.
New York, NY 10172
800/922-9004
Winthrop Focus Funds
  Winthrop Fixed Income Fund (CorB)
  Winthrop Growth & Income Fund (Gr&I)

Winthrop Growth Fund (Gr)
Winthrop Municipal Fund (NMuB)
Winthrop Small Company Value Fund
  (AgGr)
Winthrop Opportunity Funds
Winthrop Developing Markets Fund
  (Intl)
Winthrop International Equity Fund
  (Intl)
Winthrop Opportunity Government
  Money Market Fund (MM)
Winthrop Opportunity Municipal Money
  Market Fund (NMMX)

Wright Funds
24 Federal St.
Boston, MA 02110-2507
800/225-6265
Wright EquiFund Equity Trust
  Wright EquiFund—Australasian (Intl)
  Wright EquiFund—Austrian (Intl)
  Wright EquiFund—Belgium/Luxembourg
  (Intl)
  Wright EquiFund—Britain (Intl)
  Wright EquiFund—Canada (Intl)
  Wright EquiFund—France (Intl)
  Wright EquiFund—Germany (Intl)
  Wright EquiFund—Global (GloE)
  Wright EquiFund—Hong Kong (Intl)
  Wright EquiFund—International (Intl)
  Wright EquiFund—Ireland (Intl)
  Wright EquiFund—Japan (Intl)
  Wright EquiFund—Mexico (Intl)
  Wright EquiFund—Netherlands (Intl)
  Wright EquiFund—Nordic (Intl)
  Wright EquiFund—Switzerland (Intl)
  Wright EquiFund—United States
  (Gr&I)
Wright Managed Blue Chip Series Trust
  Wright International Blue Chip Portfolio
  (Intl)
  Wright Near Term Bond Portfolio (IncB)
  Wright Selected Blue Chip Portfolio
  (Gr&I)
  Wright Total Return Bond Portfolio
  (CorB)
Wright Managed Equity Trust
  Wright International Blue Chip Equities
  Fund (Intl)
  Wright Junior Blue Chip Equities Fund
  (Gr&I)
  Wright Quality Major Blue Chip Fund
  (Gr&I)
  Wright Selected Blue Chip Equities Fund
  (Gr&I)
Wright Managed Income Trust
  Wright Current Income Fund (IncB)
  Wright Insured Tax Free Bond Fund
  (NMuB)
  Wright Total Return Bond Fund (CorB)
  Wright U.S. Treasury Fund (USGv)

Wright U.S. Treasury Money Market Fund (MM)
Wright U.S. Treasury Near Term Fund (IncB)

Yamaichi Funds
Two World Trade Ctr.
Ste. 9828
New York, NY 10048-0203
212/466-6800
Yamaichi Funds, Inc.
  Yamaichi Global Fund (GloE)

Zurich Kemper Funds
200 S. Riverside Plaza
Chicago, IL 60606
800/621-1048
Cash Account Trust
  Government Securities Portfolio (MM)
  Money Market Portfolio (MM)
  Tax-Exempt Portfolio (NMMX)
Cash Equivalent Fund
  Government Securities Portfolio (MM)
  Money Market Portfolio (MM)
  Tax-Exempt Portfolio (NMMX)
Investors Cash Trust
  Government Securities Portfolio (MM)
  Treasury Portfolio (MM)
Kemper Adjustable Rate U.S. Government Fund (USGv)
Kemper Aggressive Growth Fund (AgGr)
Kemper Asian Growth Fund (Intl)
Kemper Blue Chip Fund (Gr&I)
Kemper Cash Reserves Fund (MM)
Kemper Diversified Income Fund (IncB)
Kemper-Dreman Funds
  Kemper-Dreman Contrarian Fund (Gr&I)
  Kemper-Dreman High Return Equity Fund (IncE)
  Kemper-Dreman Small Cap Value Fund (AgGr)
Kemper Europe Fund (Intl)
Kemper Global Income Fund (GloB)
Kemper Growth Fund (Gr)
Kemper High Yield Fund (HiYB)
Kemper Horizon Fund
  Horizon 5 Portfolio (Bal)
  Horizon 10+ Portfolio (Bal)
  Horizon 20+ Portfolio (Bal)
Kemper Income & Capital Preservation Fund (IncB)
Kemper International Bond Fund (Intl)
Kemper International Fund (Intl)
Kemper Quantitative Equity Fund (Gr)

Kemper Short-Intermediate Government Fund (USGv)
Kemper Small Capitalization Equity Fund (AgGr)
Kemper Target Equity Fund
  Kemper Retirement Fund I (Bal)
  Kemper Retirement Fund II (Bal)
  Kemper Retirement Fund III (Bal)
  Kemper Retirement Fund IV (Bal)
  Kemper Retirement Fund V (Bal)
  Kemper Retirement Fund VI (Bal)
  Kemper Retirement Fund VII (Bal)
  Kemper Worldwide 2004 Fund (Bal)
Kemper Tax-Free Income Funds
  California Tax-Free Income Fund (SMuB)
  Florida Tax-Free Income Fund (SMuB)
  Intermediate Municipal Bond Fund (NMuB)
  Michigan Tax-Free Income Fund (SMuB)
  Municipal Bond Fund (NMuB)
  New Jersey Tax-Free Income Fund (SMuB)
  New York Tax-Free Income Fund (SMuB)
  Ohio Tax-Free Income Fund (SMuB)
  Pennsylvania Tax-Free Income Fund (SMuB)
  Texas Tax-Free Income Fund (SMuB)
Kemper Technology Fund (Gr)
Kemper Total Return Fund (Bal)
Kemper U.S. Government Securities Fund (GNMA)
Kemper U.S. Mortgage Fund (GNMA)
Kemper Value + Growth Fund (Gr)
Tax-Exempt California Money Market Fund (SMMX)
Tax-Exempt New York Money Market Fund (SMMX)
Zurich Money Funds
  Zurich Government Money Fund (MM)
  Zurich Money Market Fund (MM)
  Zurich Tax-Free Money Fund (NMMX)

Zweig Fund Group
900 Third Ave.
New York, NY 10022-4728
800/272-2700
Zweig Series Trust
  Zweig Appreciation Fund (Gr)
  Zweig Cash Fund (MM)
  Zweig Government Securities Series (USGv)
  Zweig Growth and Income Fund (Gr&I)
  Zweig Managed Assets (Flex)
  Zweig Strategy Fund (Gr)

CLOSED-END MUTUAL FUNDS

The following is a compilation of the names, ticker symbols and addresses of American closed-end mutual funds, with the types of investments made by each. The notation *bond* means the fund buys only bonds, and is therefore likely to pay a high yield. The notation *convertible* means that the fund mainly buys convertible bonds, which pay a higher yield than stocks, but also have more potential to rise in value than bonds. The notation *dual purpose* means that the fund is split into two, with one part of the fund designed for investors who want income, and the other part designed for shareholders intent upon capital gains. The notation *equity* means the fund buys stocks, mostly for capital gains purposes. The notation *gold* means the fund exclusively buys shares of gold-mining companies, which usually have a high yield, but are subject to the ups and downs of gold prices. The notation *specialized equity* means that the fund buys only particular kinds of stocks for the purpose of capital appreciation. Some funds, for instance, only buy stocks of medical companies, while others concentrate on the stocks of a particular foreign country like Japan.

Closed-end mutual funds issue a fixed number of shares, which are then traded either on exchanges or over-the-counter. Funds traded on the New York Stock Exchange are notated with an NYSE, those on the American Stock Exchange, with an ASE, and those traded over the counter, with an OTC. Closed-end funds contrast with open-ended mutual funds, which create new shares whenever additional funds are received from customers. But closed-end fund managers buy and sell stocks, bonds and convertible securities just like open-end mutual fund managers.

Open-end funds sell at the net asset value (NAV) of their holdings on a particular day (plus a charge, or load, in some cases) and always stand ready to redeem shares at the NAV. In contrast, closed-end funds usually sell above or below their net asset value. The price of the shares is determined by the same forces of supply and demand that affect the value of any publicly traded security. Therefore, those buying shares in a closed-end fund when it is selling below net asset value are, in effect, buying a dollar's worth of securities for less than a dollar, and those buying such a fund when it is trading at a premium to its (NAV) receive less than a dollar's worth of securities for each dollar invested.

This list is provided courtesy of Thomas J. Herzfeld, author of *The Investor's Guide To Closed-End Funds* (McGraw-Hill) and *The Thomas J. Herzfeld Encyclopedia of Closed-End Funds*. Mr. Herzfeld, who can be reached at P.O. Box 161465, Miami, Florida 33116 (305) 271-1900, is an investment advisor specializing in closed-end funds.

Adams Express Co.
7 St. Paul St.
Ste. 1140
Baltimore, MD 21202-1626
800/638-2479
Adams Express Company

Alger Closed-End Funds
75 Maiden Lane
New York, NY 10038
800/992-3863
Castle Convertible Fund, Inc.

Alliance Closed-End Funds
1345 Avenue of the Americas
New York, NY 10105-0302
800/221-5672
ACM Government Income Fund, Inc.
ACM Government Opportunity Fund,
   Inc.
ACM Government Securities Fund, Inc.
ACM Government Spectrum Fund, Inc.
ACM Managed Dollar Income Fund
ACM Managed Income Fund, Inc.
ACM Municipal Securities Income Fund,
   Inc.
Alliance All-Market Advantage Fund
Alliance Global Environment Fund, Inc.
Alliance World Dollar Government Fund,
   Inc.
Alliance World Dollar Government Fund II,
   Inc.
Austria Fund, Inc.
Korean Investment Fund, Inc. (The)
Southern Africa Fund (The)
Spain Fund, Inc. (The)

Allied Capital Funds
1666 K St. NW
9th Fl.
Washington, DC 20006
202/331-1112
Allied Capital Corporation
Allied Capital Corporation II
Allied Capital Lending Corporation

Allmerica Closed-End Funds
4400 Computer Dr.
Westboro, MA 01581 508/855-1000
Allmerica Securities Trust

American Closed-End Funds
333 S. Hope St.
Los Angeles, CA 90071-1406
800/421-0180
Emerging Markets Growth Fund, Inc.

**American Express Closed-End
Fund Group**
IDS Tower 10
Minneapolis, MN 55440

800/328-8300
Latin American Growth Fund Inc.

Anchor Closed-End Funds
2717 Furlong Rd.
Doylestown, PA 18901
215/794-2980
Anchor Gold and Currency Trust

Baker, Fentress & Co.
200 W. Madison St.
Ste. 3510
Chicago, IL 60606-3417
800/BKF-1891
Baker, Fentress & Company

Bancroft Convertible Fund, Inc.
65 Madison Ave.
Ste. 550
Morristown, NJ 07960-6078
201/631-1177
Bancroft Convertible Fund, Inc.

BEA Closed-End Funds
153 E. 53rd St.
58th Fl.
New York, NY 10022-4611
800/293-1232
BEA Income Fund, Inc.
BEA Strategic Income Fund
Brazilian Equity Fund, Inc. Chile Fund, Inc.
Emerging Markets Infrastructure Fund, Inc.
   (The)
Emerging Markets Telecommunications
   Fund, Inc.
First Israel Fund, Inc. Indonesia Fund, Inc.
Latin America Equity Fund, Inc. (The)
Latin America Investment Fund, Inc. (The)
Portugal Fund, Inc. (The)

Bergstrom Capital Corp.
505 Madison St.
Ste. 220
Seattle, WA 98104-1138
206/623-7302
Bergstrom Capital Corporation

Bull & Bear Closed-End Funds
11 Hanover Sq.
New York, NY 10005-3452
800/847-4200
Bull & Bear Global Income Fund, Inc.
Bull & Bear Municipal Income Fund, Inc.
Bull & Bear U.S. Government Securities
   Fund, Inc.

Central Securities Corp.
375 Park Ave.
New York, NY 10152-0002
212/688-3011
Central Securities Corporation

CIGNA Closed-End Funds
900 Cottage Grove Rd.
S-210
Hartford, CT 06152-2210
860/726-3700
CIGNA High Income Shares
INA Investment Securities, Inc.

Clemente Closed-End Funds
152 W. 57th St.
25th Fl.
New York, NY 10019-3310
800/524-4458
Clemente Global Growth Fund, Inc.
First Philippine Fund, Inc. (The)

Cohen & Steers Closed-End Funds
757 Third Ave.
27th Fl.
New York, NY 10017-2013
800/437-9912
Cohen & Steers Realty Income Fund, Inc.
Cohen & Steers Total Return Realty Fund

Colonial Closed-End Funds
One Financial Ctr.
Boston, MA 02111-2621
800/225-2365
Colonial High Income Municipal Trust
Colonial InterMarket Income Trust I
Colonial Intermediate High Income Fund
Colonial Investment Grade Municipal Trust
Colonial Municipal Income Trust

Dean Witter Closed-End Funds
Two World Trade Ctr.
72nd Fl.
New York, NY 10048-0203
800/869-NEWS
Dean Witter Government Income Trust
High Income Advantage Trust
High Income Advantage Trust II
High Income Advantage Trust III
InterCapital California Insured Municipal
    Income Trust
InterCapital California Quality Municipal
    Securities
InterCapital Income Securities Inc.
InterCapital Insured California Municipal
    Securities
InterCapital Insured Municipal Bond Trust
InterCapital Insured Municipal Income
    Trust
InterCapital Insured Municipal Securities
InterCapital Insured Municipal Trust
    InterCapital
New York Quality Municipal Securities
InterCapital Quality Municipal Income
    Trust
InterCapital Quality Municipal Investment
    Trust

InterCapital Quality Municipal Securities
Municipal Income Opportunities Trust
Municipal Income Opportunities Trust II
Municipal Income Opportunities Trust III
Municipal Income Trust
Municipal Income Trust II
Municipal Income Trust III
Municipal Premium Income Trust
Prime Income Trust
TCW/DW Emerging Markets Opportunities
    Trust
TCW/DW Term Trust 2000
TCW/DW Term Trust 2002
TCW/DW Term Trust 2003

Delaware-Voyageur Closed-End Funds
1818 Market St.
Philadelphia, PA 19103-3682
800/523-4640
Delaware Group Dividend & Income Fund
    Inc.
Delaware Group Global Dividend and
    Income Fund
Voyageur Arizona Municipal Income Fund,
    Inc.
Voyageur Colorado Insured Municipal
    Income Fund
Voyageur Florida Insured Municipal
    Income Fund
Voyageur Minnesota Municipal Income
    Fund, Inc.
Voyageur Minnesota Municipal Income
    Fund II, Inc.
Voyageur Minnesota Municipal Income
    Fund III, Inc.

Dessauer Global Equity Fund
P.O. Box 1689
Orleans Brewster Office Park, Unit #5
Orleans, MA 06253-1689
508/225-1651
Dessaur Global Equity Fund

Deutsche Morgan Grenfell Funds
31 W. 52nd St.
5th Fl.
New York, NY 10019-6118
800/GERMANY
Central European Equity Fund, Inc. (The)
Germany Fund, Inc. (The)
New Germany Fund, Inc. (The)

Dreyfus Closed-End Funds
200 Park Ave.
New York, NY 10166
800/645-6561
Dreyfus California Municipal Income, Inc.
Dreyfus Municipal Income, Inc.
Dreyfus New York Municipal Income, Inc.
Dreyfus Strategic Governments Income,
    Inc.

Dreyfus Strategic Municipal Bond Fund, Inc.
Dreyfus Strategic Municipals, Inc.

Duff & Phelps Closed-End Funds
55 E. Monroe St.
Ste. 3800
Chicago, IL 60603-5802
800/338-8214
Duff & Phelps Utilities Income Inc.

Eaton Vance Closed-End Funds
24 Federal St.
Boston, MA 02110-2507
800/225-6265
Eaton Vance Prime Rate Reserves Fund
EV Classic Senior Floating-Rate Fund

Ellsworth Convertible Growth & Income Fund, Inc.
65 Madison Ave.
Ste. 550
Morristown, NJ 07960-6078
201/631-1177
Ellsworth Convertible Growth & Income
    Fund, Inc.

Emerging Markets Income Fund
Seven World Trade Ctr.
38th Fl.
New York, NY 10048-1102
800/725-6666
Emerging Markets Income Fund Inc.
    (The)

Fidelity Advisor Closed-End Funds
82 Devonshire St.
Boston, MA 02109-3605
800/526-0084
Fidelity Advisor Emerging Asia Fund,
    Inc.
Fidelity Advisor Korea Fund, Inc.

Fort Dearborn Income Securities, Inc.
209 S. LaSalle St.
Chicago, IL 60604-1295
800/448-2430
Fort Dearborn Income Securities, Inc.

Fortis Financial Closed-End Funds
P.O. Box 64284
St. Paul, MN 55164-0284
800/800-2638
Fortis Securities, Inc.

France Growth Fund
1211 Avenue of the Americas
c/o Banque Indosuez, 7th Fl.
New York, NY 10036-8701
212/278-2000
France Growth Fund, Inc. (The)

Franklin Group of Closed-End Funds
777 Mariners Island Blvd.
San Mateo, CA 94404-1584
800/632-2180
Franklin Multi-Income Trust
Franklin Principal Maturity Trust
Franklin Universal Trust

Gabelli Closed-End Funds
One Corporate Ctr.
Rye, NY 10580-1434
800/422-3554
Gabelli Convertible Securities Fund, Inc.
    (The)
Gabelli Equity Trust Inc. (The)
Gabelli Global Multimedia Trust Inc.
    (The)

General American Investors
450 Lexington Ave.
Ste. 3300
New York, NY 10017-3911
800/436-8401
General American Investors Company, Inc.

GT Global Closed-End Funds
50 California St.
27th Fl.
San Francisco, CA 94111-4624
800/824-1580
GT Global Developing Markets Fund, Inc.
GT Global Eastern Europe Fund

H & Q Closed-End Funds
50 Rowes Wharf
4th Fl.
Boston, MA 02110-3328
800/327-6679
H&Q Healthcare Investors
H&Q Life Sciences Investors

Harris & Harris Group, Inc.
One Rockefeller Plaza
Rockefeller Center
New York, NY 10020-2001
212/332-3600
Harris & Harris Group, Inc.

Heritage Closed-End Funds
880 Carillon Pkwy.
St. Petersburg, FL 33716-1102
800/421-4184
Heritage U.S. Government Income Fund

Herzfeld Caribbean Basin Fund, Inc.
The Herzfeld Bldg.
P.O. Box 161465
Miami, FL 33116-1465
800/854-3863
Herzfeld Caribbean Basin Fund, Inc.
    (The)

Horace Mann Mutual Funds
One Horace Mann Plaza
P.O. Box 4657
Springfield, IL 62708-4657
800/999-1030
Horace Mann Socially Responsible Fund

Hyperion Closed-End Funds
165 Broadway
36th Fl.
New York, NY 10006
800/HYPERION
Hyperion 1997 Term Trust, Inc.
Hyperion 1999 Term Trust, Inc.
Hyperion 2002 Term Trust, Inc.
Hyperion 2005 Investment Grade
   Opportunity Term Trust, Inc.
Hyperion Total Return Fund, Inc.

INVESCO Closed-End Funds
7800 E. Union Ave.
Denver, CO 80237-2752
800/525-8085
Global Health Sciences Fund, Inc.

Irish Investment Fund
c/o Shareholder Services Group
One Exchange Pl.
Boston, MA 02109-2809
800/468-6475
Irish Investment Fund, Inc. (The)

John Hancock Closed-End Funds
101 Huntington Ave.
Boston, MA 02199-7603
800/225-5291
John Hancock Bank and Thrift Opportunity
   Fund
John Hancock Income Securities Trust
John Hancock Investors Trust
John Hancock Patriot Global Dividend Fund
John Hancock Patriot Preferred Dividend
   Fund
John Hancock Patriot Premium Dividend
   Fund I
John Hancock Patriot Premium Dividend
   Fund II
John Hancock Patriot Select Dividend Trust
Southeastern Thrift and Bank Fund, Inc. (The)

Kleinwort Benson Closed-End Fund
75 Wall St.
New York, NY 10005
800/237-4218
Kleinwort Benson Australian Income Fund,
   Inc.

Legg Mason Closed-End Funds
111 S. Calvert St.
P.O. Box 1476
Baltimore, MD 21203-1476

800/822-5544
Worldwide Value Fund, Inc.
Pacific American Income Shares,
   Inc.

Liberty Closed-End Funds
One Financial Ctr.
Boston, MA 02111-2621
800/225-2365
Liberty ALL-STAR Equity Fund
Liberty ALL-STAR Growth Fund

Liberty Term Trust
Federated Investors Tower
1001 Liberty Ave.
Pittsburgh, PA 15222-3779
800/245-0242
Liberty Term Trust, Inc.—1999

Lincoln National Group of Funds
200 E. Berry St.
Ft. Wayne, IN 46802-3506
800/923-8476
Lincoln National Convertible Securities
   Fund, Inc.
Lincoln National Income Fund, Inc.

MassFinancial Closed-End Funds
500 Boylston St.
Boston, MA 02116-3740
800/343-2829
MFS Charter Income Trust
MFS Government Markets Income
   Trust
MFS Intermediate Income Trust
MFS Multimarket Income Trust
MFS Municipal Income Trust
MFS Special Value Trust

MassMutual Closed-End Funds
1295 State St.
Springfield, MA 01111-0001
413/788-8411
MassMutual Corporate Investors
MassMutual Participation Investors

Mentor Closed-End Funds
901 E. Byrd St.
Riverfront Plaza
Richmond, VA 23219-4069
800/382-0016
Mentor Income Fund, Inc.

Mercury Investment Closed-End
   Funds
780 Third Ave.
Ste. 3401
New York, NY 10017-2024
800/543-6217
Europe Fund, Inc. (The)
United Kingdom Fund, Inc. (The)

Merrill Lynch Closed-End Funds
P.O. Box 9011
Princeton, NJ 08543-9011
800/637-3863
Apex Municipal Fund, Inc.
Convertible Holdings, Inc.
Corporate High Yield Fund, Inc.
Corporate High Yield Fund II, Inc.
Income Opportunities Fund 1999
Income Opportunities Fund 2000, Inc.
Merrill Lynch High Income Municipal
  Bond Fund, Inc.
MuniAssets Fund, Inc.
MuniEnhanced Fund, Inc.
MuniInsured Fund, Inc.
MuniVest Florida Fund, Inc.
MuniVest Fund, Inc.
MuniVest Fund II, Inc.
MuniVest Michigan Insured Fund, Inc.
MuniVest New Jersey Fund, Inc.
MuniVest Pennsylvania Insured Fund, Inc.
MuniYield Arizona Fund, Inc.
MuniYield California Fund, Inc.
MuniYield California Insured Fund, Inc.
MuniYield California Insured Fund II
MuniYield Florida Fund, Inc.
MuniYield Florida Insured Fund
MuniYield Fund, Inc.
MuniYield Insured Fund
MuniYield Michigan Fund, Inc.
MuniYield Michigan Insured Fund, Inc.
MuniYield New Jersey Fund, Inc.
MuniYield New Jersey Insured Fund, Inc.
MuniYield New York Insured Fund, Inc.
MuniYield New York Insured Fund II, Inc.
MuniYield Pennsylvania Fund, Inc.
MuniYield Quality Fund, Inc.
MuniYield Quality Fund II, Inc.
Senior High Income Portfolio, Inc.
Taurus Muni California Holdings, Inc.
Taurus Muni New York Holdings, Inc.
WorldWide DollarVest Fund, Inc.

Mexico Fund, Inc.
Aristoteles 77
3er Piso
D.F., 11560
MEXICO
800/224-4134
Mexico Fund, Inc. (The)

Morgan Stanley Closed-End Funds
c/o Chase Global Funds Srvcs. Co.
P.O. Box 2798
Boston, MA 02208-2798
800/548-7786
Brazilian Investment Fund, Inc. (The)
Latin American Discovery Fund, Inc. (The)
Malaysia Fund, Inc. (The)
Morgan Stanley Africa Investment Fund,
  Inc.

Morgan Stanley Asia Pacific Fund, Inc.
Morgan Stanley Emerging Markets Debt
  Fund, Inc.
Morgan Stanley Emerging Markets Fund
Morgan Stanley Global Opportunity Fund,
  Inc.
Morgan Stanley High Yield Fund, Inc.
Morgan Stanley India Investment Fund, Inc.
Pakistan Investment Fund, Inc. (The)
Thai Fund, Inc. (The)
Turkish Investment Fund, Inc. (The)

Nations Closed-End Funds
111 Center St.
Ste. 300
Little Rock, AR 72201-4402
800/321-7854
Hatteras Income Securities, Inc.
Nations Balanced Target Maturity Fund,
  Inc.
Nations Government Income Term Trust
  2003, Inc.
Nations Government Income Term Trust
  2004, Inc.

New South Africa Fund
101 Carnegie Ctr.
c/o Custodial Trust Co.
Princeton, NJ 08540-6231
609/951-2300
New South Africa Fund Inc. (The)

Nomura Capital Closed-End Funds
180 Maiden Lane
26th Fl.
New York, NY 10038-4925
800/833-0018
Jakarta Growth Fund, Inc.
Japan OTC Equity Fund, Inc.
Korea Equity Fund, Inc.

Nuveen Closed-End Funds
333 W. Wacker Dr.
Chicago, IL 60606-1218
800/257-8787
Nuveen Arizona Premium Income
  Municipal Fund, Inc.
Nuveen California Investment Quality
  Municipal Fund, Inc.
Nuveen California Municipal Market
  Opportunity Fund, Inc.
Nuveen California Municipal Value Fund,
  Inc.
Nuveen California Performance Plus
  Municipal Fund, Inc.
Nuveen California Premium Income
  Municipal Fund
Nuveen California Quality Income
  Municipal Fund, Inc.
Nuveen California Select Quality Municipal
  Fund, Inc.

Nuveen Connecticut Premium Income
Municipal Fund
Nuveen Florida Investment Quality
Municipal Fund
Nuveen Florida Quality Income Municipal
Fund
Nuveen Georgia Premium Income
Municipal Fund
Nuveen Insured California Premium
Income Municipal Fund, Inc.
Nuveen Insured California Premium
Income Municipal Fund 2, Inc.
Nuveen Insured California Select Tax Free
Income Portfolio
Nuveen Insured Florida Premium Income
Municipal Fund
Nuveen Insured Municipal Opportunity
Fund, Inc.
Nuveen Insured New York Premium
Income Municipal Fund, Inc.
Nuveen Insured New York Select Tax Free
Income Portfolio
Nuveen Insured Premium Income
Municipal Fund 2
Nuveen Insured Quality Municipal Fund,
Inc.
Nuveen Investment Quality Municipal
Fund, Inc.
Nuveen Maryland Premium Municipal
Fund
Nuveen Massachusetts Premium Municipal
Fund
Nuveen Michigan Premium Income
Municipal Fund, Inc.
Nuveen Michigan Quality Income
Municipal Fund, Inc.
Nuveen Missouri Premium Income
Municipal Fund
Nuveen Municipal Advantage Fund, Inc.
Nuveen Municipal Income Fund, Inc.
Nuveen Municipal Market Opportunity
Fund, Inc.
Nuveen Municipal Value Fund, Inc.
Nuveen New Jersey Investment Quality
Municipal Fund, Inc.
Nuveen New Jersey Premium Income
Municipal Fund, Inc.
Nuveen New York Investment Quality
Municipal Fund, Inc.
Nuveen New York Municipal Value Fund,
Inc.
Nuveen New York Performance Plus
Municipal Fund, Inc.
Nuveen New York Quality Income
Municipal Fund, Inc.
Nuveen New York Select Quality Municipal
Fund, Inc.
Nuveen North Carolina Premium Income
Municipal Fund
Nuveen Ohio Quality Income Municipal
Fund, Inc.

Nuveen Pennsylvania Investment Quality
Municipal Fund
Nuveen Pennsylvania Premium Income
Municipal Fund 2
Nuveen Performance Plus Municipal Fund,
Inc.
Nuveen Premier Insured Municipal Income
Fund, Inc.
Nuveen Premier Municipal Income Fund,
Inc.
Nuveen Premium Income Municipal Fund,
Inc.
Nuveen Premium Income Municipal Fund
2, Inc.
Nuveen Premium Income Municipal Fund
4, Inc.
Nuveen Quality Income Municipal Fund,
Inc.
Nuveen Select Maturities Municipal Fund
Nuveen Select Tax Free Income Portfolio
Nuveen Select Tax Free Income Portfolio 2
Nuveen Select Tax Free Income Portfolio 3
Nuveen Select Quality Municipal Fund, Inc.
Nuveen Texas Quality Income Municipal
Fund
Nuveen Virginia Premium Income
Municipal Fund
Nuveen Washington Premium Income
Municipal Fund

OpCap Advisors Closed-End Funds
One World Financial Ctr.
New York, NY 10281-1098
800/421-4777
Czech Republic Fund, Inc.
Municipal Advantage Fund, Inc.

**OppenheimerFunds Closed-End Funds
(Denver)**
6803 S. Tucson Way
Englewood, CO 80112
800/525-7048
New York Tax-Exempt Income Fund, Inc.
(The)

**OppenheimerFunds Closed-End Funds
(New York)**
Two World Trade Ctr.
New York, NY 10048-0203
800/525-7048
Oppenheimer Multi-Sector Income Trust
Oppenheimer World Bond Fund

PaineWebber Closed-End Funds
1285 Avenue of the Americas
PaineWebber Bldg.
New York, NY 10019-6028
800/647-1568
Emerging Mexico Fund, Inc. (The)
Global High Income Dollar Fund Inc.
Global Small Cap Fund Inc.

Greater China Fund, Inc. (The)
India Growth Fund Inc. (The)
Insured Municipal Income Fund Inc.
Investment Grade Municipal Income Fund Inc.
Jardine Fleming India Fund, Inc.
Managed High Yield Fund Inc.
Strategic Global Income Fund, Inc.
Triple A and Government Series—1997, Inc.
2002 Target Term Trust Inc.

Petroleum & Resources Corporation
Seven St. Paul St.
Ste. 1140
Baltimore, MD 21202-1626
800/638-2479
Petroleum & Resources Corporation

Pilgrim America Closed-End Funds
Two Renaissance Sq.
40 N. Central Ave., Ste. 1200
Phoenix, AZ 85004-4424
800/331-1080
Pilgrim America Bank and Thrift Fund, Inc.
Pilgrim America Prime Rate Trust

PIMCO Closed-End Funds
840 Newport Ctr. Dr.
Ste. 360
Newport Beach, CA 92660-6322
800/213-3606
PIMCO Commercial Mortgage Securities Trust, Inc.

Pioneer Closed-End Funds
60 State St.
Boston, MA 02109-1803
800/225-6292
Pioneer Interest Shares, Inc.

Piper Capital Closed-End Funds
222 S. Ninth St.
Piper Jaffray Twr.
Minneapolis, MN 55402-3804
800/866-7778
American Government Income Fund Inc.
American Government Income Portfolio Inc.
American Municipal Income Portfolio Inc.
American Municipal Term Trust Inc.
American Municipal Term Trust Inc.—II
American Municipal Term Trust Inc.—III
American Opportunity Income Fund Inc.
American Select Portfolio Inc.
American Strategic Income Portfolio Inc.
American Strategic Income Portfolio Inc.—II
American Strategic Income Portfolio Inc.—III
Americas Income Trust Inc. (The)

Highlander Income Fund Inc.
Minnesota Municipal Income Portfolio Inc.
Minnesota Municipal Term Trust Inc.
Minnesota Municipal Term Trust Inc.—II

Prudential Closed-End Funds
One Seaport Plaza
New York, NY 10292
800/225-1852
Asia Pacific Fund, Inc. (The)
First Australia Fund, Inc. (The)
First Australia Prime Income Fund, Inc. (The)
First Financial Fund, Inc.
High Yield Income Fund, Inc. (The)
High Yield Plus Fund, Inc. (The)

Putnam Closed-End Funds
One Post Office Sq.
Boston, MA 02109-2103
800/225-2465
Putnam California Investment Grade Municipal Trust
Putnam Convertible Opportunities and Income Trust
Putnam Dividend Income Fund
Putnam High Income Convertible and Bond Fund
Putnam High Yield Municipal Trust
Putnam Intermediate Government Income Trust
Putnam Investment Grade Municipal Trust
Putnam Investment Grade Municipal Trust II
Putnam Investment Grade Municipal Trust III
Putnam Managed High Yield Trust
Putnam Managed Municipal Income Trust
Putnam Master Income Trust
Putnam Master Intermediate Income Trust
Putnam Municipal Opportunities Trust
Putnam New York Investment Grade Municipal Trust
Putnam Premier Income Trust
Putnam Tax Free Health Care Fund

R.O.C. Taiwan Fund
c/o Dewe, Rogerson Inc.
850 Third Ave.
New York, NY 10022
212/688-6840
R.O.C. Taiwan Fund

Royce Closed-End Funds
1414 Avenue of the Americas
New York, NY 10019-2514
800/221-4268
Royce Global Trust, Inc.
Royce Micro-Cap Trust, Inc.
Royce Value Trust, Inc.

Salomon Brothers Closed-End Funds
Seven World Trade Ctr.
New York, NY 10048-1102
800/725-6666
Emerging Markets Floating Rate Fund Inc.
 (The)
Emerging Markets Income Fund II, Inc.
 (The)
Global Partners Income Fund Inc.
Municipal Partners I
Municipal Partners II
Salomon Brothers Fund Inc. (The)
Salomon Brothers High Income Fund, Inc.
Salomon Brothers 2008 Worldwide Dollar
 Government Term Trust
Salomon Brothers Worldwide Income Fund
 Inc.

Schroder Closed-End Funds
787 Seventh Ave.
34th Fl.
New York, NY 10019-6018
800/344-8332
Schroder Asian Growth Fund

Scudder Closed-End Funds
Two International Place
Boston, MA 02110-4101
800/225-2470
Argentina Fund, Inc. (The)
Brazil Fund, Inc. (The)
First Iberian Fund, Inc. (The)
Korea Fund, Inc. (The)
Latin America Dollar Income Fund, Inc.
 (The)
Montgomery Street Income Securities, Inc.
Scudder New Asia Fund, Inc.
Scudder New Europe Fund, Inc.
Scudder World Income Opportunities Fund,
 Inc.

Seligman Closed-End Funds
100 Park Ave.
New York, NY 10017-5516
800/221-7844
Seligman Quality Municipal Fund, Inc.
Seligman Select Municipal Fund, Inc.
Tri-Continental Corporation

Sierra Trust Closed-End Funds
9301 Corbin Ave.
NO321
Northridge, CA 91324-2431
800/221-9876
Sierra Prime Income Fund

Smith Barney Closed-End Funds
Two World Trade Ctr.
100th Fl.
New York, NY 10048-0203
212/464-6000

Italy Fund (The)
Managed High Income Fund, Inc.
Managed Municipals Portfolio, Inc.
Managed Municipals Portfolio II, Inc.
Municipal High Income Fund, Inc.
Smith Barney Disciplined Small Cap Fund
 (The)
Smith Barney High Income Opportunity
 Fund, Inc.
Smith Barney Intermediate Municipal Fund,
 Inc.
Smith Barney Municipal Fund, Inc.
Zenix Income Fund, Inc.

Source Capital, Inc.
11400 W. Olympic Blvd.
Ste. 1200
Los Angeles, CA 90064-1568
800/982-4372
Source Capital, Inc.

Swiss Helvetia Fund, Inc.
630 Fifth Ave.
Ste. 915
New York, NY 10111-0001
888/794-7700
Swiss Helvetia Fund, Inc. (The)

TCW Closed-End Funds
865 S. Figueroa St.
Ste. 1800
Los Angeles, CA 90017-2543
800/386-3829
TCW Convertible Securities Fund, Inc.

**Templeton Group of Closed-End
 Funds**
700 Central Ave.
St. Petersburg, FL 33701-3628
800/342-5236
Templeton China World Fund
Templeton Dragon Fund, Inc.
Templeton Emerging Markets Appreciation
 Fund
Templeton Emerging Markets Fund, Inc.
Templeton Emerging Markets Income Fund,
 Inc.
Templeton Global Governments Income
 Trust
Templeton Global Income Fund, Inc.
Templeton Global Utilities, Inc.
Templeton Russia Fund, Inc.
Templeton Vietnam Opportunities Fund,
 Inc.

Thermo Opportunity Fund
312 Walnut St.
21st Fl.
Cincinnati, OH 45202-4024
800/320-2212
Thermo Opportunity Fund (The)

Transamerica Income Shares
1150 S. Olive St.
P.O. Box 2438
Los Angeles, CA 90015-2211
213/742-2222
Transamerica Income Shares, Inc.

T. Rowe Price Closed-End Funds
100 E. Pratt St.
Baltimore, MD 21202-1009
800/638-5660
Jardine Fleming China Region Fund, Inc.
New Age Media Fund, Inc.

USF&G Pacholder Fund
8044 Montgomery Rd.
Ste. 382
Cincinnati, OH 45236-2922
513/985-3200
USF&G Pacholder Fund, Inc.

U.S. Global Investors Funds
7900 Callaghan Rd.
San Antonio, TX 78229-2327
800/873-8637
U.S. Global Investors Funds
  United Services Intermediate Treasury
  Fund

**Van Kampen American Capital
Closed-End Funds**
One Parkview Plaza
Oakbrook Terrace, IL 60181-4400
800/225-2222
Mosher, Inc.
Van Kampen American Capital Advantage
  Municipal Income Trust
Van Kampen American Capital Advantage
  Municipal Income Trust II
Van Kampen American Capital Advantage
  Pennsylvania Municipal Income Trust
Van Kampen American Capital Bond Fund,
  Inc.
Van Kampen American Capital California
  Municipal Trust
Van Kampen American Capital California
  Quality Municipal Trust
Van Kampen American Capital California
  Value Municipal Income Trust
Van Kampen American Capital Convertible
  Securities, Inc.
Van Kampen American Capital Florida
  Municipal Opportunity Trust
Van Kampen American Capital Florida
  Quality Municipal Trust
Van Kampen American Capital Income Trust
Van Kampen American Capital Intermediate
  Term High Income Trust
Van Kampen American Capital Investment
  Grade Municipal Trust
Van Kampen American Capital Limited

Term High Income Trust
Van Kampen American Capital
  Massachusetts Value Municipal Trust
Van Kampen American Capital Municipal
  Income Trust
Van Kampen American Capital Municipal
  Opportunity Trust
Van Kampen American Capital Municipal
  Opportunity Trust II
Van Kampen American Capital Municipal
  Trust
Van Kampen American Capital New Jersey
  Value Municipal Income Trust
Van Kampen American Capital New York
  Quality Municipal Trust
Van Kampen American Capital New York
  Value Municipal Income Trust
Van Kampen American Capital Ohio
  Quality Municipal Trust
Van Kampen American Capital Ohio Value
  Municipal Income Trust
Van Kampen American Capital
  Pennsylvania Quality Municipal Trust
Van Kampen American Capital
  Pennsylvania Value Municipal Trust
Van Kampen American Capital Select
  Sector Municipal Trust
Van Kampen American Capital Strategic
  Sector Municipal Trust
Van Kampen American Capital Trust For
  Insured Municipals
Van Kampen American Capital Trust For
  Invest. Grade Florida Municipals
Van Kampen American Capital Trust For
  Investment Grade New Jersey
  Municipals
Van Kampen American Capital Trust For
  Investment Grade New York Municipals
Van Kampen American Capital Trust For
  Investment Grade Pennsylvania
  Municipals
Van Kampen American Capital Trust For
  Investment Grade Municipals
Van Kampen American Capital Value
  Municipal Income Trust
Van Kampen Merritt Trust For Investment
  Grade California Municipals

**Van Kampen American Capital Interval
Funds**
2800 Post Oak Blvd.
P.O. Box 3121
Houston, TX 77056-6106
800/421-5666
Van Kampen American Capital Prime Rate
  Income Trust

Venture Lending & Leasing, Inc.
Rockefeller Center
630 Fifth Ave., 16th Fl.
New York, NY 10111

212/332-5100
Venture Lending & Leasing, Inc.

Westcore Closed-End Funds
370 Seventeenth St.
Ste. 2700
Denver, CO 80202
800/392-2673
Blue Chip Value Fund

Z-Seven Fund
2651 W. Guadalupe Rd.
Suite B-233
Mesa, AZ 85202-7253
602/897-6214
Z-Seven Fund, Inc.

Zurich Kemper Closed-End Funds
222 S. Riverside Plaza
Chicago, IL 60606
800/621-1048
Growth Fund of Spain, Inc. (The)
Kemper High Income Trust
Kemper Intermediate Government Trust
Kemper Multi-Market Income Trust
Kemper Municipal Income Trust
Kemper Strategic Income Fund
Kemper Strategic Municipal Income Trust

Zweig Closed-End Fund Group
900 Third Ave.
New York, NY 10022-4728
800/272-2700
Zweig Fund, Inc. (The)
Zweig Total Return Fund, Inc. (The)

4. FUTURES AND OPTIONS CONTRACTS

On the following pages, you will find a listing of futures and options contracts being traded in the United States, Canada, and major foreign markets, according to the exchanges on which they are traded. Each exchange listing is divided into two sections: futures and options. Each section, in turn, is divided into product categories: agricultural, metals, financial, currency, index, interest rate, and so forth. Each contract is listed alphabetically within its category, with complete contract specifications.

Contract specifications include:

Trading Unit: The underlying commodity, stock or group of stocks, and the quantity.

Price Quote: The unit of value, such as cents per pound, dollars per barrel.

Tick Size: The smallest move, up or down, the contract can make, indicated by the increments in which the contract can move, and as a monetary valuation.

Daily Price Limit: Many exchanges do not allow prices to rise or fall beyond certain limits within a day. Such limits, if any, are shown first in the increment of the contract, and then as a dollar figure.

Settlement: The way contracts are settled when they expire. Some contracts provide for the physical delivery of a commodity. Specific rules must be followed on how and where commodities are delivered from seller to buyer. Other contracts involve no physical delivery. These contracts are settled in cash.

Last Trading Day: The last day trading can occur in a contract.

Contract Months: Most contracts are traded in all 12 months, but only a group of "active months" are featured in many categories, especially commodities. Although all of these contracts trade constantly, most expire in only certain months of the year. This column presents the active months in those cases, using standard exchange abbreviations.

Trading Hours: The hours during which a contract is traded, in local time. CST means Central Standard Time, EST means Eastern Standard Time, GMT means Greenwich Mean Time and PST means Pacific Standard Time. Trading hours for contracts traded on foreign exchanges are expressed in local time.

Ticker Symbol: The symbol by which a contract's current price and trading activity can be checked through an electronic price quote service.

For options contracts and options on futures contracts, the following additional information is provided:

Strike Price: This is set both above and below the current market price of the future or index, so puts and calls can be traded in both directions. This column also gives the intervals at which strike prices are set, and when new strike prices are added.

Expiration Day: If options are not exercised, they expire. This column details when options expire.

Expiration Month: The month the option expires.

The following is an index to the listings, by name of traded instrument. Exchanges on which the instrument is traded are in parentheses.

Index to Contract Listing (U.S.)

Airline Sector (PHLX)
Alberta Natural Gas (NYMEX)
Annual Catastrophe Insurance (CBOT)
Australian Dollar (CME, MIDAM, PHLX)
BFP Milk (CME, CSCE)
Big Cap Index (PHLX)
Biotechnology Index (AMEX)
Black Tiger Shrimp (MGE)
Boneless Beef (CME)
Boneless Beef Trimmings (CME)
Brazilian Real (CME)
British Pound (CME, MIDAM, PHLX)
Butter (CME, CSCE)
California/Oregon Border (COB) Electricity (NYMEX)
Canadian Dollar (CME, MIDAM, PHLX)
CBOE Automotive Index (CBOE)
CBOE Computer Software Index (CBOE)
CBOE Environmental Index (CBOE)
CBOE Gaming Index (CBOE)
CBOE Gold Index (CBOE)
CBOE Internet Index (CBOE)
CBOE Internet Index (Reduced-Value) LEAPS (CBOE)
CBOE Israel Index: Index Options (CBOE)
CBOE Mexico Index (CBOE)
CBOE Mexico Index (Reduced-Value) LEAPS (CBOE)
CBOE Oil Index (CBOE)
CBOE Oil Index (Reduced-Value) LEAPS (CBOE)
CBOE REIT Index (CBOE)
CBOE Technology Index (CBOE)
CBOE Technology Index (Reduced-Value) LEAPS (CBOE)
Cheddar Cheese (CME, CSCE)
Coal (NYMEX)
Cocoa (CSCE)
Coffee "C" (CSCE)
Computer Box Maker Sector (PHLX)
Computer Technology Index (AMEX)
Copper (COMEX)
Corn (CBOT, MIDAM)
Corn Yield Insurance (CBOT)
Cotton (NYCE)

CRB/Bridge Index (NYFE)
Cross-Rate Currencies (CME, FINEX, PHLX)
Crude Oil (Light Sweet) (NYMEX)
Currency Forwards (CME)
Deutsche Mark (CME, MIDAM, PHLX)
Dow Jones Industrial Average (CBOE, CBOT)
Dow Jones Taiwan Stock Index (PE)
Dow Jones Transportation Average (CBOE)
Dow Jones Utility Average (CBOE)
E-Mini S&P 500 Stock Price Index (CME)
Equity LEAPS (CBOE)
Equity Options (CBOE)
Euro Canada (CME)
Eurodollar/3-Month (CME)
Eurodollar Bundle/5-Year (CME)
European Currency Unit (PHLX)
Euromark/3-Month (CME)
Euroyen (CME)
FT-SE Eurotop 100 Index (AMEX, COMEX)
Feeder Cattle (CME)
FLEX Options (CBOE)
Forest & Paper Products Sector (PHLX)
French Franc (CME, PHLX)
Fresh Pork Bellies (CME)
Frozen Concentrated Orange Juice (NYCE)
Frozen Pork Bellies (CME)
FT-SE 100 Index: Index Options (CBOE), Futures, Futures Options (CME)
German Government Bond [Bund] (CBOT)
Gold (COMEX division, NYMEX), (CBOT, MIDAM)
Gold/Silver Sector (PHLX)
Goldman-Sachs Commodity Index (CME)
Gulf Coast Unleaded Gasoline (NYMEX)
Hard Red Spring Wheat (MGE)
Hard Red Winter Wheat (KCBT)
Heating Oil (NYMEX)
Heating Oil/Crude Oil Crack Spread (NYMEX)
Henry Hub Natural Gas (NYMEX)
Hong Kong Index (AMEX)
Inflation-Indexed U.S. Treasury Bond (CBOT)
Institutional Index: Index Options (AMEX)
IPC Stock Index (CBOE, CME)
Japan Index: Index Options (AMEX)
Japanese Yen (CME, MIDAM, PHLX)
Keefe Bruyette & Woods, Inc. Bank Sector (PHLX)
Latin 15 Index (CBOE)
Lipper Analytical/Salomon Brothers Growth Funds Index (CBOE)
Lipper Analytical/Salomon Brothers Income Funds Index (CBOE)
Live Cattle (CME, MIDAM)
Lean Hogs (CME, MIDAM)
Long-Term Inflation-Indexed U.S. Treasury Note (CBOT)
Long-Term Municipal Bond Index (CBOT)
Major Market Index (AMEX, CME)
Medium-Term Inflation Indexed U.S. Treasury Note (CBOT)
Mexico Index (AMEX)
Mexican Peso (CME)

Mexican TIIE/28-Day (CME)
Mexican Treasury Bill/91-Day (CME)
Milk (CSCE)
Mini BFP Milk (CME)
Mini Value Line Stock Index (KCBT)
Morgan Stanley Emerging Growth Index (PE)
Morgan Stanley Multinational Company Index (CBOE)
Morgan Stanley Consumer Index: Index Options (AMEX)
Morgan Stanley Cyclical Index: Index Options (AMEX)
Nasdaq-100 Index (CBOE, CME)
National Over-the-Counter Sector (PHLX)
Natural Gas (NYMEX)
Natural Gas Index (AMEX)
New York Harbor Unleaded Gasoline (NYMEX)
New York Harbor Unleaded Gasoline/Crude Oil Crack Spread (NYMEX)
New Zealand Dollar (CME)
Nikkei 225 Stock Average (CME)
Nikkei 300 Index (CBOE)
Nonfat Dry Milk (CSCE)
NYSE Composite Index (NYFE)
NYSE Large Composite Index (NYFE)
NYSE Small Composite Index (NYFE)
Oats (CBOT, MIDAM)
OEX CAPS (CBOE)
OEX LEAPS (CBOE)
OEX S&P 100 Index (CBOE)
Oil Index (AMEX)
Oil Service Sector (PHLX)
One-Month Libor (AMEX, CME)
Oriented Strand Board (CME)
Palladium (NYMEX)
Palo Verde Electricity (NYMEX)
Permian Basin Natural Gas (NYMEX)
Pharmaceutical Index (AMEX)
Phone Sector (PHLX)
Platinum (NYMEX, MIDAM)
Potatoes (NYCE)
Propane (NYMEX)
PSE Technology Index (NYFE, PE)
Quarterly Bankruptcy Index (CME)
Quarterly Catastrophe Insurance (CBOT)
Random Length Lumber (CME)
Rough Rice (CBOT)
Russell 2000 Index (CBOE, CME)
Russian Ruble (CME)
S&P Banks Index (CBOE)
S&P Chemical Index (CBOE)
S&P 500/BARRA Growth Index (CBOE, CME)
S&P 500/BARRA Value Index (CBOE, CME)
S&P 500 Stock Index (CME)
S&P Healthcare Index (CBOE)
S&P Insurance Index (CBOE)
S&P MidCap 400 (CME)
S&P Retail Index (CBOE)
S&P Small Cap 600 Index (CBOE)

S&P Transportation Index (CBOE)
Securities Broker/Dealer Index (AMEX)
Semiconductor Sector (PHLX)
S&P MidCap 400 Index (AMEX, CME)
Silver (CBOT, COMEX, MIDAM)
Soft White Wheat (MGE)
Sour Crude Oil (NYMEX)
South African Rand (CME)
Soybeans (CBOT, MIDAM)
Soybean Meal (CBOT, MIDAM)
Soybean Oil (CBOT, MIDAM)
SPL S&P 500 Index Long Dated Options (CBOE)
SPX (Reduced-Value) LEAPS (CBOE)
Sugar (CSCE)
Sugar No. 11 (CSCE)
Sugar No. 14 (CSCE)
SuperCap Sector (PHLX)
Swiss Franc (CME, MIDAM, PHLX)
30-Day Fed Funds (CBOT)
Twin Cities Electricity (MGE)
U.S. Dollar Currencies Paired (FINEX)
U.S. Dollar Index (FINEX)
U.S. TOP 100 Index (PHLX)
U.S. Treasury Bill (CBOE, CME, MIDAM)
U.S. Treasury Bill/1-Year (AMEX, CME)
U.S. Treasury Bill/13-Week (CME)
U.S. Treasury Bond (CBOT, CBOE, CFFE, MIDAM)
U.S. Treasury Note/5-year (CBOT, CBOE, CFFE)
U.S. Treasury Note/10-year (CBOT, CBOE, CFFE)
U.S. Treasury Note/2-year (CBOT, CFFE)
Utility Sector (PHLX)
Value Line Composite Index (PHLX)
Value Line Stock Index (KCBT)
Value Line Mini Index (KCBT)
Western Natural Gas (KCBT)
Wheat (CBOT, KCBT, MIDAM)
White Shrimp (MGE)
White Sugar (CSCE)
Wilshire Small Cap Index (PE)

Key to Abbreviations of U.S. Exchanges:

AMEX: American Stock Exchange
CBOE: Chicago Board Options Exchange
CBOT: Chicago Board of Trade
CME: Chicago Mercantile Exchange
COMEX division, New York Mercantile Exchange: formerly Commodity
   Exchange, Inc.
CSCE: Coffee, Sugar, and Cocoa Exchange
CFFE: Cantor Financial Futures Exchange
FINEX: financial futures division of New York Cotton Exchange
KCBT: Kansas City Board of Trade
MGE: Minneapolis Grain Exchange
MIDAM: MidAmerica Commodity Exchange
NYBOT: Board of Trade of the City of New York
NYCE: New York Cotton Exchange

NYFE: New York Futures Exchange
NYMEX: New York Mercantile Exchange
PHLX: Philadelphia Stock Exchange
PE: Pacific Exchange

Index to Contract Listing (International)

All Ordinaries Share Price Index (SFE)
Aluminum (LME)
ANZ Bank Shares (SFE)
Bank Accepted Bills/90-day (SFE)
Barley (LIFFE)
BIFFEX (LIFFE)
Brent Crude Oil (IPE)
Broken Hill Proprietary Shares (SFE)
CAC 40 Stock Index (MATIF)
Canadian Bankers Acceptance/3-month (ME)
Canadian Bankers Acceptance/1-month (ME)
Canola (WCE)
Cocoa No. 7 (LIFFE)
Commonwealth Treasury Bond/10-year (SFE)
Commonwealth Treasury Bond/3-year (SFE)
Copper (LME)
CRA Limited Shares (SFE)
ECU/3-month (LIFFE)
Euribor/3-month (MATIF)
Euro Bond/5-year (MATIF)
Euro Notional Bond (MATIF)
Eurodollar/3-month (SIMEX)
Eurolira/3-month (LIFFE)
Euromark/3-month (LIFFE, SIMEX)
Euromark/1-month (LIFFE)
European Rapeseed (MATIF)
Euroswiss/3-month (LIFFE)
Euroyen/3-month (LIFFE, SIMEX)
Feed Peas (WCE)
Feed Wheat (WCE)
Flaxseed (WCE)
Fosters Brewing Group Shares (SFE)
FTSE 100 (LIFFE)
Gas Oil (IPE)
German Government Bond [Bund] (LIFFE)
German Government Bond [Bobl] (LIFFE)
Gilt/10-year (MATIF)
Gilt/5-year (MATIF)
Gold (SIMEX)
Government of Canada Bonds/10-year (ME)
Government of Canada Bonds/5-year (ME)
Hong Kong Index (SIMEX)
Italian Government Bond (LIFFE)
Japanese Government Bond/10-year (LIFFE, SIMEX, TSE)
Japanese Government Bond/5-year, 20-year (TSE)
Lead (LME)
Long Gilt (LIFFE)

Milling Wheat (MATIF)
MIM Holdings Shares (SFE)
Major Market Index: futures options (EOE)
Matif E-Bond/30-Year (MATIF)
Matif 5-Year (MATIF)
National Australia Bank Shares (SFE)
Natural Gas (IPE)
New South Wales Electricity (SFE)
News Corporation Shares (SFE)
Nickel (LME)
Nikkei 225 Stock Index (SIMEX)
Nikkei 300 Stock Index (SIMEX)
Notional Bond (MATIF)
Oats (WCE)
Overnight Options (SFE)
Pacific Dunlop Shares (SFE)
Pibor/3-month (MATIF)
Potatoes (LIFFE)
Robusta Coffee (LIFFE)
Silver (LME)
Simex MSCI Taiwan Index (SIMEX)
Sterling/3-month (LIFFE)
TIPS 35 (TSEX)
Tokyo Stock Price Index (TSE)
Tokyo Stock Price Sector Index (TSE)
Toronto 35 Index (TFE, TSEX)
TSE 100 Index (TFE)
U.S. Treasury Bond (LIFFE, TSE)
Victorian Electricity (SFE)
Western Barley (WCE)
Western Mining Corporation Shares (SFE)
Westpac Banking Corporation Shares (SFE)
Wheat (LIFFE, SFE)
White Sugar No. 5 (LIFFE)
White Sugar 45 (MATIF)
White Sugar 100 (MATIF)
Wool (SFE)
Zinc (LME)

Key to Abbreviations of International Exchanges

PE: International Petroleum Exchange (U.K.)
IFFE: London International Financial Futures Exchange (U.K.)
LME: London Metal Exchange (U.K.)
MATIF: Matif SA (France)
ME: Montreal Exchange (Canada)
SFE: Sydney Futures Exchange (Australia)
SIMEX: Singapore International Monetary Exchange (Singapore)
TFE: Toronto Futures Exchange (Canada)
TSE: Tokyo Stock Exchange (Japan)
TSEX: Toronto Stock Exchange (Canada)
WCE: Winnipeg Commodity Exchange (Canada)

UNITED STATES SECURITIES,
FUTURES AND OPTIONS EXCHANGES
American Stock Exchange (AMEX)

Index Options

Contract	Underlying Index	Trading Unit	Prices Quoted In	Minimum Price Fluctuation
● Airline Index	top 10 representative U.S., foreign stocks and American Depositary Receipts, equal dollar weighted	$100 × index	index points	¹⁄₁₆ up to 3 ⅛ over 3
● AMEX Gold BUGS Index	portfolio of major gold mining company stocks with low hedging ratios (under 1.5 years' production), modified equal-dollar weighted	$100 × index	index points	¹⁄₁₆ up to 3 ⅛ over 3
● Biotechnology Index	15 biotechnology stocks developing new products, services	$100 × index	index points	¹⁄₁₆ up to 3 ⅛ over 3
● Computer Hardware Index	Stocks of 10 designers and producers of commerical and consumer PCs and systems	$100 × index	index points	¹⁄₁₆ up to 3 ⅛ over 3
● Computer Technology Index	26 U.S. computer stocks	$100 × index	index points	¹⁄₁₆ up to 3 ⅛ over 3
● deJager Year 2000 Index	portfolio of 18 companies involved in Year 2000 software solutions; price-weighted	$100 × index	index points	¹⁄₁₆ up to 3 ⅛ over 3
● Disk Drive Index	designers and manufacturers of disk drives and interacting software, equal dollar weighted	$100 × index	index points	¹⁄₁₆ up to 3 ⅛ over 3
● Eurotop 100 Index	most actively traded, highly capitalized stocks on Europe's top 9 stock exchanges	$100 × index	index points	¹⁄₁₆ up to 3 ⅛ over 3

Strike Price Intervals	Settlement	Contract Months	Trading Hours (EST)	Ticker Symbol
5 points (200 up) 2½ points (under 200)	in cash	3 consecutive near-term months + 2 successive from the January cycle	9:30 A.M.– 4:02 P.M.	XAL
5 points (over 200) 2½ points (under 200)	in cash	3 consecutive near-term months + 2 successive from the March cycle	9:30 A.M.- 4:02 P.M.	HUI
5 points	in cash	3 consecutive near-term months + 2 successive from the January cycle	9:30 A.M.– 4:10 P.M.	BTK
5 points	in cash	3 consecutive near-term months + 2 successive from the February cycle	9:30 A.M.– 4:02 P.M.	HWI
5 points	in cash	3 consecutive near-term months +2 successive from the January cycle	9:30 A.M.– 4:02 P.M.	XCI
5 points (over 200) 2½ points (under 200)	in cash	3 consecutive near-term months +2 successive from the February cycle	9:30 A.M.– 4:02 P.M.	YTK
5 points (over 200) 2½ points (under 200)	in cash	3 consecutive near-term months +2 successive from the February cycle	9:30 A.M.– 4:02 P.M.	DDX
5 points	in cash	3 consecutive near-term months + 1 successive from the March cycle	8:30 A.M.– 11:30 A.M.	EUR

Contract	Underlying Index	Trading Unit	Prices Quoted In	Minimum Price Fluctuation
• Hong Kong Index	broad market index tracking performance of the Hong Kong stock market through 30 highly capitalized stocks on the Stock Exchange of Hong Kong Ltd.	$100 × index	index points	1/16 up to 3 1/8 over 3
• Institutional Index	75 stocks held in the greatest dollar amount each quarter among all publicly traded issues in institutional portfolios	$100 × index	index points	1/16 up to 3 1/8 over 3
• Inter@ctive Week Internet Index	aggregate performance of 37 companies providing digital interactive services, software and hardware	$100 × index	index points	1/16 up to 3 1/8 over 3
• Japan Index	aggregate performance of 210 common stocks actively traded on Tokyo Stock Exchange	$100 × index	index points	1/16 up to 3 1/8 over 3
• Major Market Index	20 Blue Chip Stocks, price weighted	$100 × index	index points	1/16 up to 3 1/8 over 3
• Mexico Index	American Depositary Receipts or U.S. shares of companies reflecting Mexico Stock Market	$100 × index	index points	1/16 up to 3 1/8 over 3
• Morgan Stanley Commodity Related Equity Index	20 companies, each represented as 5% of the Index's initial dollar value	$100 × index	index points	1/16 up to 3 1/8 over 3
• Morgan Stanley Consumer Index	measures performance of 30 stocks in consumer oriented stable growth industries	$100 × index	index points	1/16 up to 3 1/8 over 3

Strike Price Intervals	Settlement	Contract Months	Trading Hours (EST)	Ticker Symbol
5 points	in cash	3 consecutive near-term months + 2 successive from the March cycle	9:30 A.M.– 4:30 P.M.	HKO
5 points	in cash	3 consecutive near-term months + 2 further-term months from the March cycle	9:30 A.M.– 4:15 P.M.	XII
5 points (over 200) 2½ points (under 200)	in cash	3 consecutive near-term months + 2 successive from the January cycle	9:30 A.M.– 4:02 P.M.	IIX
5 points	in cash	3 consecutive near-term months + 2 further-term months from the March cycle	9:30 A.M.– 4:15 P.M.	JPN
5 points	in cash	3 consecutive near-term months + 2 successive from the March cycle	9:30 A.M.– 4:15 P.M.	XMI
5 points	in cash	3 consecutive near-term months + 2 successive from the March cycle	9:30 A.M.– 4:15 P.M.	MXY
5 points (over 200) 2½ points (under 200)	in cash	3 consecutive near-term months + 2 further-term months from the March cycle	9:30 A.M.– 4:02 P.M.	CRX
5 points	in cash	3 consecutive near-term months + 2 successive from the March cycle	9:30 A.M.– 4:15 P.M	CMR

Contract	Underlying Index	Trading Unit	Prices Quoted In	Minimum Price Fluctuation
• Morgan Stanley Cyclical Index	measures performance of 30 stocks in economically sensitive industries	$100 × index	index points	1/16 up to 3 1/8 over 3
• Morgan Stanley Healthcare Payor Index	12 managed health care services companies	$100 × index	index points	1/16 up to 3 1/8 over 3
• Morgan Stanley Healthcare Product Index	26 companies, primarily drugs and medical/ biotechnology	$100 × index	index points	1/16 up to 3 1/8 over 3
• Morgan Stanley Healthcare Provider Index	15 companies, hospitals, and nursing homes	$100 × index	index points	1/16 up to 3 1/8 over 3
• Morgan Stanley High Technology 35 Index	35 bellwether stocks across technology spectrum	$100 × index	index points	1/16 up to 3 1/8 over 3
• Natural Gas Index	15 highly capitalized natural gas companies	$100 × index	index points	1/16 up to 3 1/8 over 3
• NatWest Energy Index	30 stocks and actively traded ADRs of global energy producers and service providers	$100 × index	index points	1/16 up to 3 1/8 over 3
• Networking Index	measures composite price performance of large, actively traded computer and telecommu- nication networking stocks	$100 × index	index points	1/16 up to 3 1/8 over 3
• North American Telecommuni- cations Index	15 U.S., Canadian, and Mexican companies	$100 × index	index points	1/16 up to 3 1/8 over 3
• Oil Index	16 oil stocks or American Depositary Receipts	$100 × index	index points	1/16 up to 3 1/8 over 3

Strike Price Intervals	Settlement	Contract Months	Trading Hours (EST)	Ticker Symbol
5 points	in cash	3 consecutive near-term months + 2 successive from the March cycle	9:30 A.M.– 4:15 P.M.	CYC
5 points (over 200) 2½ points (under 200)	in cash	3 consecutive near-term months + 2 successive from the March cycle	9:30 A.M.– 4:02 P.M.	HMO
5 points (over 200) 2½ points (under 200)	in cash	3 consecutive near-term months + 2 successive from the March cycle	9:30 A.M.– 4:02 P.M.	RXP
5 points (over 200) 2½ points (under 200)	in cash	3 consecutive near-term months + 2 successive from the March cycle	9:30 A.M.– 4:02 P.M.	RXH
5 points (over 200) 2½ points (under 200)	in cash	3 consecutive near-term months + 2 further-term months from the March cycle	9:30 A.M.– 4:02 P.M.	MSH
5 points	in cash	3 consecutive near-term months + 2 further-term months from the January cycle	9:30 A.M.– 4:02 P.M.	XNG
5 points (over 200) 2½ points (under 200)	in cash	3 consecutive near-term months + 2 further-term months from the March cycle; long-term options up to 36 months	9:30 A.M.– 4:02 P.M.	NEX
5 points (over 200) 2½ points (under 200)	in cash	3 consecutive near-term months + 2 further-term months from the January cycle	9:30 A.M.– 4:02 P.M.	NWX
5 points	in cash	3 consecutive near-term months + 2 further-term months from the January cycle	9:30 A.M.– 4:02 P.M.	XTC
5 points	in cash	3 consecutive near-term months + 2 further-term months from the January cycle	9:30 A.M.– 4:10 P.M.	XOI

Contract	Underlying Index	Trading Unit	Prices Quoted In	Minimum Price Fluctuation
• Pharmaceutical Index	15 widely held, highly capitalized U.S. and European companies	$100 × index	index points	¹⁄₁₆ up to 3 ⅛ over 3
• Securities Broker/Dealer Index	highly capitalized companies in the U.S. securities brokerage industry	$100 × index	index points	¹⁄₁₆ up to 3 ⅛ over 3
• S&P MidCap 400 Index	measures prices of 400 middle-capitalization companies	$100 × index	index points	¹⁄₁₆ up to 3 ⅛ over 3
• Tobacco Index	measures composite performance of 9 large, actively traded stocks	$100 × index	index points	¹⁄₁₆ up to 3 ⅛ over 3

Cantor Financial Futures Exchange (CFFE)
(A subsidiary of the Board of Trade of the City of New York [NYBOT])

Futures

Contract	Trading Unit	Price Quote	Tick Size	Daily Price Limit
• U.S. Treasury Bond	1 U.S. T-bond with face value at maturity of $100,000	Points and ¹⁄₃₂ of a point	¹⁄₃₂ of point ($31.25/contract)	None
• U.S. Treasury Note (10-Year)	1 U.S. T-note with face value at maturity of $100,000	Points and ¹⁄₃₂ of a point	¹⁄₃₂ of point ($31.25/contract)	None
• U.S. Treasury Note (5-Year)	1 U.S. T-note with face value at maturity of $100,000	Points and ½ of ¹⁄₃₂ of a point	½ of ¹⁄₃₂ of point ($15.625/contract)	None
• U.S. Treasury Note (2-Year)	1 U.S. T-note with face value at maturity of $200,000	Points and ¼ of ¹⁄₃₂ of a point	¼ of ¹⁄₃₂ of point ($15.625/contract)	None

Strike Price Intervals	Settlement	Contract Months	Trading Hours (EST)	Ticker Symbol
5 points	in cash	3 consecutive near-term months + 2 further-term months from the January cycle	9:30 A.M.–4:02 P.M.	DRG
5 points	in cash	3 consecutive near-term months + 2 further-term months from the January cycle	9:30 A.M.–4:02 P.M.	XBD
5 points	in cash	up to 4 consecutive near-term months + 2 further-term months from the March cycle	9:30 A.M.–4:15 P.M.	MID
5 points (over 200) 2½ points (under 200)	in cash	3 consecutive near-term months +2 further-term months from the February cycle	9:30 A.M.–4:15 P.M.	TOB

Last Trading Day	Contract Months	Trading Hours (EST)	Ticker Symbol
8th business day of month	Mar, June, Sept, Dec	7:30 A.M.–5:30 P.M.	UT
8th business day of month	Mar, June, Sept, Dec	7:30 A.M.–5:30 P.M.	TZ
8th business day of month	Mar, June, Sept, Dec	7:30 A.M.–5:30 P.M.	TV
8th business day of month	Mar, June, Sept, Dec	7:30 A.M.–5:30 P.M.	UT

Chicago Board of Trade (CBOT)

Agricultural Futures

Contract	Trading Unit	Price Quote	Tick Size
● Corn	5,000 bushels	cents and ¼ cent per bushel	¼ cent per bushel ($12.50/contract)
● Oats	5,000 bushels	cents and ¼ cent per bushel	¼ cent per bushel ($12.50/contract)
● Rough Rice	2,000 hundred-weight	cents per hundredweight	½ cent per hundredweight ($10/contract)
● Soybeans	5,000 bushels	cents and ¼ cent per bushel	½ cent per bushel ($12.50/contract)
● Soybean Meal	100 tons	dollars and cents per ton	10 cents per ton ($10/contract)
● Soybean Oil	60,000 pounds	cents per pound	1/100 cent per pound ($6/contract)
● Wheat	5,000 bushels	cents and ¼ cent per bushel	¼ cent per bushel ($12.50/contract)
● Iowa, Illinois, Indiana, Nebraska, Ohio, and U.S. Corn Yield Insurance	USDA state and U.S. yield estimates released during growing/harvest season	corn yield estimate × $100 reflected in each monthly underlying futures contract	¹⁄₁₀ bushel per acre harvested ($10/contract)

Equity Index Futures

Contract	Trading Unit	Price Quote	Tick Size
● CBOT Dow Jones Industrial Average	$10 × Dow Jones Industrial Average	Points ($10)	1 point ($10)

Financial Futures

Contract	Trading Unit	Price Quote	Tick Size
● German Government Bond (Bund)	250,000 Deutsche marks	¹⁄₁₀₀ point	¹⁄₁₀₀ point (DM25/contract)

Daily Price Limit	Contract Months	Trading Hours (CST)	Ticker Symbol
12 cents per bushel ($600/contract)	Dec, Mar, May, July, Sept	9:30 A.M.–1:15 P.M.	C
10 cents per bushel ($500/contract)	Mar, May, July, Sept, Dec	9:30A.M.–1:15 P.M.	O
30 cents per hundredweight ($600/contract)	Sept, Nov, Jan, Mar, May, July	9:15 A.M.–1:30 P.M.	RR
30 cents per bushel ($1500/contract)	Sept, Nov, Jan, Mar, May, July, Aug	9:30 A.M.–1:15 P.M.	S
$10 per ton ($1,000/contract)	Oct, Dec, Jan, Mar, May, July, Aug, Sept	9:30 A.M.–1:15 P.M.	SM
1 cent per pound ($600/contract)	Oct, Dec, Jan, Mar, May, July, Aug, Sept	9:30 A.M.–1:15 P.M.	BO
20 cents per bushel ($1,000/contract)	July, Sept, Dec, Mar, May	9:30 A.M.–1:15 P.M.	W
15 bushel per acre harvested ($1,500/contract)	Sept, Oct, Nov, Jan	10:30 A.M.–12:45 P.M.	CA (Iowa) YG (Illinois) YH (Indiana) YI (Nebraska) YJ (Ohio) YC (U.S.)

Daily Price Limit	Contract Months	Trading Hours (CST)	Ticker Symbol
Successive price limits of 350, 550, 700 index points below settlement price of previous regular trading session	Mar, June, Sept, Dec	8:15 A.M.–3:15 P.M.	DJ

Daily Price Limit	Contract Months	Trading Hours (CST)	Ticker Symbol
None	Mar, June, Sept, Dec	10:20 A.M.–2:00 P.M.	BU

Contract	Trading Unit	Price Quote	Tick Size
• Long-Term Municipal Bond Index	$1,000 × closing value of *The Bond Buyer* 40 Index	points and $\frac{1}{32}$ point ($31.25/contract)	$\frac{1}{32}$ point
• 30-Day Federal Funds	$5 million	Based on 100 minus monthly average over-night federal effective rate for delivery month	$41.67 per basis point
• U.S.Treasury Bonds	1 U.S. T-bond at $100,000	points ($1,000) and $\frac{1}{32}$ point	$\frac{1}{32}$ point ($31.25/contract)
• U.S. Treasury Notes (10-Year)	1 U.S. T-Note at $100,000	points ($1,000) and $\frac{1}{32}$ point	$\frac{1}{32}$ point ($31.25/contract)
• U.S. Treasury Notes (5-Year)	1 U.S. T-Note at $100,000	points ($1,000) and $\frac{1}{2}$ of $\frac{1}{32}$ point	$\frac{1}{2}$ of $\frac{1}{32}$ point ($15.625/contract)
• U.S. Treasury Notes (2-Year)	1 U.S. T-Note at $200,000	points ($2,000) and $\frac{1}{4}$ of $\frac{1}{32}$ point	$\frac{1}{4}$ of $\frac{1}{32}$ point ($15.625/contract)
• Inflation-Indexed U.S. Treasury Bonds	1 Inflation-Indexed U.S. T-Bond at $100,000	points ($1,000) and $\frac{1}{32}$ point	$\frac{1}{32}$ point ($31.25/contract)
• Long-Term Inflation-Indexed U.S. Treasury Notes	1 Inflation-Indexed U.S. T-Note at $100,000	points ($1,000) and $\frac{1}{32}$ point	$\frac{1}{32}$ point ($31.25/contract)
• Medium-Term Inflation-Indexed U.S. Treasury Notes	1 Inflation-Indexed U.S. T-Note at $100,000	points ($1,000) and $\frac{1}{64}$ point	$\frac{1}{64}$ point ($15.625/contract)

Metals Futures

Contract	Trading Unit	Price Quote	Tick Size
• Gold (Kilo)	1 kilogram (32.15 troy ounces)	dollars and cents per troy ounce	10 cents per fine troy ounce ($3.22/contract)

Daily Price Limit	Contract Months	Trading Hours (CST)	Ticker Symbol
3 points ($3,000/contract)	Mar, June, Sept, Dec	7:20 A.M.-2:00 P.M.	MB
150 basis points	First 25 calendar months (and next 2 months in Mar, June, Sept, Dec cycle thereafter)	7:20 A.M.-2:00 P.M.; (Project A sessions: 2:30 P.M.–4:30 P.M., 10:00 P.M.–6:45 A.M.)	FF
3 points ($3,000/contract)	Mar, June, Sept, Dec	7:20 A.M.-2:00 P.M., 5:20 P.M.–8:05 P.M. (Project A sessions: 2:30 P.M.–4:30 P.M., 10:00 P.M.–6:45 A.M.)	US
3 points ($3,000/contract)	Mar, June, Sept, Dec	7:20 A.M.-2:00 P.M., 5:20 P.M.–8:05 P.M. (Project A sessions: 2:30 P.M.–4:30 P.M., 10:00 P.M.–6:45 A.M.)	TY
3 points ($3,000/contract)	Mar, June, Sept, Dec	7:20 A.M.-2:00 P.M. 5:20 P.M.–8:05 P.M. (Project A sessions: 2:30 P.M.–4:30 P.M., 10:00 P.M.–6:45 A.M.)	FV
1 point ($2,000/contract)	Mar, June, Sept, Dec	7:20 A.M.-2:00 P.M. 5:20 P.M.–8:05 P.M. (Project A sessions: 2:30 P.M.–4:30 P.M., 10:00 P.M.–6:45 A.M.)	TU
3 points ($3,000/contract)	Mar, June, Sept, Dec	7:20 A.M.-2:00 P.M.	BX
3 points ($3,000/contract)	Mar, June, Sept, Dec	7:20 A.M.-2:00 P.M.	II
3 points ($3,000/contract)	Mar, June, Sept, Dec	7:20 A.M.-2:00 P.M.	BI

Daily Price Limit	Contract Months	Trading Hours (CST)	Ticker Symbol
$50 per troy ounce ($1,607.50/ contract)	3 nearest months and Feb, Apr, June, Aug, Oct, Dec	7:20 A.M.–1:40 P.M.	KI

Contract	Trading Unit	Price Quote	Tick Size
● Gold (100 Ounce)	100 troy ounces	dollars and cents per troy ounce	10 cents per fine troy ounce ($10/contract)
● Silver (1,000 Ounces)	1000 troy ounces	dollars and cents to last $\frac{1}{10}$ cent per troy ounce	$\frac{1}{10}$ cent per troy ounce ($1/contract)
● Silver (5,000 Ounces)	5000 troy ounces	dollars and cents to last $\frac{1}{10}$ cent per troy ounce	$\frac{1}{10}$ cent per troy ounce ($5/contract)

Agricultural Options on Futures

Contract	Trading Unit	Tick Size	Daily Price Limit	Strike Price
● Corn	1 CBOT corn futures contract	$\frac{1}{8}$ cent per bushel ($6.25)	12 cents per bushel ($600)	10 cents apart
● Oats	1 CBOT oat futures contract	$\frac{1}{8}$ cent per bushel ($6.25)	10 cents per bushel ($500)	10 cents apart
● Rough Rice	1 CBOT rough rice futures contract	$\frac{1}{4}$ cent per hundredweight ($5/contract)	30 cents	20 cents apart
● Soybeans	1 CBOT soybean futures contract	$\frac{1}{8}$ cent per bushel ($6.25)	30 cents per bushel ($1,500)	25 cents apart
● Soybean Meal	1 CBOT soybean mean futures contract	5 cents per ton ($5/contract)	$10 per ton ($1,000)	$5 to $10 to $20 apart
● Soybean Oil	1 CBOT soybean oil futures contract	$\frac{5}{1000}$ cent per pound ($3/contract)	1 cent per lb. ($600/contract)	$\frac{1}{2}$ cent to 1 cent apart

Daily Price Limit	Contract Months	Trading Hours (CST)	Ticker Symbol
$50 per troy ounce ($5,000/contract)	3 nearest months and Feb, Apr, June, Aug, Oct, Dec	7:20 A.M.–1:40 P.M. 5:00 P.M.–9:30 P.M.	GH
$1 per troy ounce ($1,000/contract)	3 nearest months and Feb, Apr, June, Aug, Oct, Dec	7:25 A.M.–1:25 P.M.	AG
$1 per troy ounce ($5,000/contract)	3 nearest months and Feb, Apr, June, Aug, Oct, Dec	7:25 A.M.–1:25 P.M. 5:00 P.M.–9:30 P.M.	SV

Expiration Day	Last Trading Day	Contract Months	Trading Hours (CST)	Ticker Symbol
Saturday after last trading day	Last Friday preceding 1st notice day of corresponding futures contract by at least 5 business days	Dec, Mar, May, July, Sept	9:30 A.M.– 1:15 P.M. (Project A session: 10:30 P.M.– 4:30 A.M.)	CY (call) PY (put)
Saturday after last trading day	Last Friday preceding 1st notice day of corresponding futures contract by at least 5 business days	Dec, Mar, May, July, Sept	9:30 A.M.– 1:15 P.M. (Project A session: 10:30 P.M.– 4:30 A.M.)	OO (call) OV (put)
Saturday after last trading day	Last Friday preceding 1st notice day of corresponding futures contract by at least 5 business days	Sept, Nov, Jan, Mar, May, July, Aug	9:15 A.M.– 1:15 P.M. (Project A session: 10:30 P.M.– 4:30 A.M.)	RRC (call) RRP (put)
Saturday after last trading day	Last Friday preceding 1st notice day of corresponding futures contract by at least 5 business days	Oct, Dec, Jan, Mar, May, July, Aug, Sept	9:30 A.M.– 1:15 P.M. (Project A session: 10:30 P.M.– 4:30 A.M.)	CZ (call) PZ (put)
Saturday after last trading day	Last Friday preceding 1st notice day of corresponding futures contract by at least 5 business days	Oct, Dec, Jan, Mar, May, July, Aug, Sept	9:30 A.M.– 1:15 P.M. (Project A session: 10:30 P.M.– 4:30 A.M.)	MY (call) MZ (put)
Saturday after last trading day	Last Friday preceding 1st notice day of corresponding futures contract by at least 5 business days	July, Sept, Dec, Mar, May	9:15 A.M.– 1:30 P.M. (Project A session: 10:30 P.M.– 4:30 A.M.)	OY (call) OZ (put)

Contract	Trading Unit	Tick Size	Daily Price Limit	Strike Price
• Wheat	1 CBOT wheat futures contract	⅛ cent per bushel ($6.25)	20 cents per bushel ($1,000)	10 cents apart

Equity Index Options on Futures

Contract	Trading Unit	Tick Size	Daily Price Limit	Strike Price
• CBOT Dow Jones Industrial Average	1 CBOT Dow Jones Industrial Average futures contract	.05 ($5)	Successive price limits of 350, 550, 700 index points below settlement price of previous regular trading session	100 index points ($1,000)

Financial Options on Futures

Contract	Trading Unit	Tick Size	Daily Price Limit	Strike Price
• German Government Bond (Bund)	1 German Government Bond (Bund) futures contract of a specified contract month on LIFFE	Multiples of ¹⁄₁₀₀ of a point (DM25)	None	Multiples of DM 0.50
• Long-Term Municipal Bond Index	1 CBOT Long-Term Municipal Bond Index futures contract	¹⁄₆₄ point ($15.625)	3 points ($3,000)	1 point ($1,000)
• U.S. Treasury Bonds	1 CBOT T-Bond futures contract	¹⁄₆₄ point ($15.625)	3 points ($3,000)	1 point, 2 points

Expiration Day	Last Trading Day	Contract Months	Trading Hours (CST)	Ticker Symbol
Saturday after last trading day	Last Friday preceding 1st notice day of corresponding futures contract by at least 5 business days	July, Sept, Dec, Mar, May	9:30 A.M.– 1:15 P.M. (Project A session: 10:30 P.M.– 4:30 A.M.)	WY (call) WZ (put)

Expiration Day	Last Trading Day	Contract Months	Trading Hours (CST)	Ticker Symbol
Quarterly: business day following last trading day; Serial: last trading day	Quarterly: trading day preceding futures contract's final settlement day; Serial: 3rd Friday of option contract month	Front month of current quarter plus next 3 contract months of quarterly cycle (Mar, June, Sept, Dec)	8:15 A.M.– 3:15 P.M.	DJC (call) DJP (put)

Expiration Day	Last Trading Day	Contract Months	Trading Hours (CST)	Ticker Symbol
Last trading day, 11:30 A.M. London time	2 CBOT business days prior to LIFFE's last trading day	Mar, June, Sept, Dec quarterly months and 2 most current calendar months	10:20 A.M.– 2:00 P.M.; 5:20– 8:05 P.M.	BUC (call) BUP (put)
Last trading day	Quarterly: last trading day of futures contract's corresponding delivery month; All others: last Friday preceding last business day of expiring month by 5 days	1st 3 months + 2 in quarterly cycle	7:20 A.M.– 2:00 P.M. (Project A session: 2:30– 4:30 P.M., 10:00 P.M.– 6:45 A.M.)	QC (call) QP (put)
Saturday after last trading day	Last Friday preceding last business day of month by at least 5 business days	Front month of current quarter + next 3 contract months of quarterly cycle (Mar, June, Sept, Dec)	7:20 A.M.– 2:00 P.M., 5:20– 8:05 P.M. (Project A session: 2:30–4:30 P.M., 10:00 P.M.– 6:45 A.M.)	CG (call) PG (put)

Contract	Trading Unit	Tick Size	Daily Price Limit	Strike Price
• U.S. Treasury Notes (10-Year)	1 CBOT 10-Yr. U.S. T-Note futures contract	1/64 point ($15.625)	3 points ($3,000)	1 point apart
• U.S. Treasury Notes (5-Year)	1 CBOT 5-Year U.S. T-Note futures contract	1/64 point ($15.625)	3 points ($3,000)	1/2 point apart
• U.S. Treasury Notes (2-Year)	1 CBOT 2-Year U.S. T-Note futures contract	1/2 of 1/64 point ($15.625)	1 point ($2,000)	1/4 point apart
• Inflation-Indexed U.S. Treasury Bonds	1 Inflation-Indexed U.S. T-Bond	1/64 point ($15.625)	None	2 points, 1 point
• Long-Term Inflation-Indexed U.S. Treasury Notes	1 Long-Term Inflation-Indexed U.S. T-Note	1/64 point ($15.625)	None	1 point apart
• Medium-Term Inflation-Indexed U.S. Treasury Notes	1 Medium-Term Inflation-Indexed U.S. T-Note	1/64 point ($15.625)	None	1/2 point

Expiration Day	Last Trading Day	Contract Months	Trading Hours (CST)	Ticker Symbol
Saturday after last trading day	Last Friday preceding by at least 5 business days the last business day of the month preceding the option contract month	Front month of current quarter + next 3 contract months of quarterly cycle (Mar, June, Sept, Dec)	7:20 A.M.– 2:00 P.M.; 5:20– 8:05 P.M. (Project A session: 2:30–4:30 P.M., 10:00 P.M.– 6:45 A.M.)	TC (call) TP (put)
Saturday after last trading day	Last Friday preceding by at least 5 business days the last business day of the month preceding the option contract month	Front month of current quarter + next 3 contract months of quarterly cycle (Mar, June, Sept, Dec)	7:20 A.M.– 2:00 P.M.; 5:20– 8:05 P.M. (Project A session: 2:30–4:30 P.M., 10:00 P.M.– 6:45 A.M.)	FL (call) FP (put)
Saturday after last trading day	Last Friday preceding by at least 5 business days the last business day of the month preceding the option contract month	Front month of current quarter + next 3 contract months of quarterly cycle (Mar, June, Sept, Dec)	7:20 A.M.– 2:00 P.M.; 5:20– 8:05 P.M. (Project A session: 2:30–4:30 P.M., 10:00 P.M.– 6:45 A.M.)	TUC (call) TUP (put)
Saturday after last trading day	Last Friday preceding by at least 5 business days the last business day of the month preceding the option contract month	Front month of current quarter + next 3 contract months of quarterly cycle (Mar, June, Sept, Dec)	7:20 A.M.– 2:00 P.M.	BXC (call) BXP (put)
Saturday after last trading day	Last Friday preceding by at least 5 business days the last business day of the month preceding the option month	Front month of current quarter + next 3 contract months of quarterly cycle (Mar, June, Sept, Dec)	7:20 A.M.– 2:00 P.M.	IIC (call) IIP (put)
Saturday after last trading day	Last Friday preceding by at least 5 business days the last business day of the month preceding the option month	Front month of current quarter + next 3 contract months of quarterly cycle (Mar, June, Sept, Dec)	7:20 A.M.– 2:00 P.M.	BIC (call) BIP (put)

Contract	Trading Unit	Tick Size	Daily Price Limit	Strike Price
● Quarterly Catastrophe Insurance Options	National, Eastern, Northeastern, Southeastern, Midwestern, Texas, and Florida PCS loss indices	⅒ index point ($20/contract)	10 points, 20 points	5 points apart
● Annual Catastrophe Insurance Options	National, Western, and California PCS loss indices	⅒ index point ($20/contract)	10 points, 20 points	5 points apart

Metals Options on Futures

Contract	Trading Unit	Tick Size	Daily Price Limit	Strike Price
● Silver (1,000 ounces)	1 CBT silver futures contract	⅒ cent per troy ounce ($1/contract)	$1 per troy ounce ($1,000)	25 cents, 50 cents, $1 per troy ounce

Chicago Board Options Exchange (CBOE)

Equity Options

Contract	Trading Unit	Price Quote	Tick Size
● Equity Options	100 shares of common stock or ADRs listed on securities exchanges or traded OTC	points and fractions 1 point = $100	1/16 up to 3 ⅛ all others
● Equity LEAPS	100 shares of common stock or ADRs listed on securities exchanges or traded OTC	points and fractions 1 point = $100	1/16 up to 3 ⅛ all others

Expiration Day	Last Trading Day	Contract Months	Trading Hours (CST)	Ticker Symbol
Last business day of 12th month following loss periods	Same day as expiration	Mar, June, Sept, Dec	8:30 A.M.–12:30 P.M.	QN, HN, DN, KN; QE, HE, DE, KE; QR, HR, DR, KR; QS, HS, DS, KS QD, HD, DD, KD; QF, HF, DF, KF; QT, HT, DT, KT
Last business day of 12th month following loss periods	Same day as expiration	Listed on annual basis	8:30 A.M.–12:30 P.M.	QH, HH, DH, KH; QW, HW, DW, KW; QQ, HQ, DQ, KQ

Expiration Day	Last Trading Day	Contract Months	Trading Hours (CST)	Ticker Symbol
Saturday after last trading day	Last Friday preceding 1st notice day for corresponding silver futures contract by at least 5 business days	Feb, Apr, June, Aug, Oct, Dec	7:25 A.M.–1:25 P.M.	AC (call) AP (put)

Strike Price	Settlement	Last Trading Day	Expiration Months	Trading Hours (CST)	Ticker Symbol
2.5 points apart ($5–$25); 10 points apart ($200+)	delivery of underlying stock	Business day before expiration (usually Friday)	2 near-term months + 2 additional months from the Jan, Feb or Mar quarterly cycles	8:30 A.M.–3:02 P.M.	Underlying stock
2.5 points apart ($5–$25); 10 points apart ($200+)	delivery of underlying stock	Business day before expiration (usually Friday)	Up to 39 months from date of initial Jan expiration only	8:30 A.M.–3:02 P.M.	Underlying stock; modified by L,V,W or Z

FLEX Options
FLexible EXchange (FLEX) Equity Options [Customized]

Classes Available	Minimum Size	Premium Price
• S&P 100 Index, S&P 500 Index, Nasdaq 100 Index, Russell 2000 Index, Dow Jones Industrial Average	$10 million underlying value for transactions that open a new FLEX series; $1 million underlying value for subsequent transactions in opened FLEX accounts	Percentage of value of underlying index, rounded to nearest $\frac{1}{100}$; may be expressed as specific dollar amount per contract, or may be contingent on specific factors in other related markets

Index Options

Contract	Underlying Index	Trading Unit	Price Quote	Tick Size
• CBOE Automotive Index	Modified equal-dollar weighted index of 10 companies that design and manufacture automobiles and automotive parts	$100 × index	points and fractions 1 point = $100	$\frac{1}{16}$ up to 3 $\frac{1}{8}$ all others
• CBOE Computer Software Index	Computer stocks	index × $100	points and fractions 1 point = $100	$\frac{1}{16}$ up to 3 $\frac{1}{8}$ all others
• CBOE Environmental Index	Environmental stocks	index × $100	points and fractions 1 point = $100	$\frac{1}{16}$ up to 3 $\frac{1}{8}$ all others
• CBOE Gaming Index	Gaming stocks	index × $100	points and fractions 1 point = $100	$\frac{1}{16}$ up to 3 $\frac{1}{8}$ all others

Customized Strike Price	Customized Expiration	Customized Position Limit	Hours (CST)	Ticker Symbol
Any reference price that rounds to 1 decimal place when converted to an index level	Business day up to 5 years from trade date, excluding 3rd Friday or 2 days on either side	200,000 contracts on same side of market on a given index	9:00 A.M.– 3:15 P.M.	OEX, SPX, NDX, RUT

Strike Price	Settlement	Last Trading Day	Expiration Months	Trading Hours (CST)	Ticker Symbol
5-point intervals	cash	Business day before day exercise-settlement value is calculated (usually a Thursday)	Up to 3 near-term months + up to 3 additional months from Mar quarterly cycle	8:30 A.M.– 3:02 P.M.	AUX
5-point intervals	cash	Business day before day exercise-settlement value is calculated (usually a Thursday)	2 near-term months + 2 additional months from Mar quarterly cycle	8:30 A.M.– 3:02 P.M.	CWX
5-point intervals	cash	Business day before day exercise-settlement value is calculated (usually a Thursday)	Up to 3 near-term months + up to 3 additional months from Mar quarterly cycle	8:30 A.M.– 3:02 P.M.	EVX
5-point intervals	cash	Business day before day exercise-settlement value is calculated (usually a Thursday)	Up to 3 near-term months + up to 3 additional months from Mar quarterly cycle	8:30 A.M.– 3:02 P.M.	GAX

Contract	Underlying Index	Trading Unit	Price Quote	Tick Size
• CBOE Gold Index	Equal-dollar weighted index, 10 gold mining companies	$100 × index	points and fractions 1 point = $100	$\frac{1}{16}$ up to 3 $\frac{1}{8}$ all others
• CBOE Internet Index	Equal-dollar weighted index of 15 Internet access service companies and software and hardware designers and manufacturers	$100 × index	points and fractions 1 point = $100	$\frac{1}{16}$ up to 3 $\frac{1}{8}$ all others
• CBOE Internet Index (Reduced-Value) LEAPS	$\frac{1}{10}$ of CBOE Internet Index	$100 × index	points and fractions 1 point = $100	$\frac{1}{16}$ up to 3 $\frac{1}{8}$ all others
• CBOE Israel Index	15 U.S.-listed Israeli stocks	index × $100	points and fractions 1 point = $100	$\frac{1}{16}$ up to 3 $\frac{1}{8}$ all others
• CBOE Mexico Index	Equal-dollar-weighted index of 10 U.S.-listed Mexican ADRs and ADSs	index × $100	points and fractions 1 point = $100	$\frac{1}{16}$ up to 3 $\frac{1}{8}$ all others
• CBOE Mexico Index (LEAPS)	$\frac{1}{10}$ of CBOE Mexico Index	index × $100	points and fractions 1 point = $100	$\frac{1}{16}$ up to 3 $\frac{1}{8}$ all others
• CBOE Oil Index	Price-weighted index of 15 large, widely held integrated oil companies	$100 × index	points and fractions 1 point = $100	$\frac{1}{16}$ up to 3 $\frac{1}{8}$ all others

Strike Price	Settlement	Last Trading Day	Expiration Months	Trading Hours (CST)	Ticker Symbol
5-point intervals	cash	Business day before day exercise-settlement value is calculated (usually a Thursday)	Up to 3 near-term months + up to 3 additional months from Mar quarterly cycle	8:30 A.M.– 3:02 P.M.	GOX
5-point intervals	cash	Business day before day exercise-settlement value is calculated	Up to 3 near-term months + up to 3 additional months from Mar quarterly cycle	8:30 A.M.– 3:02 P.M.	INX
2.5-point intervals	cash	Business day before day exercise-settlement value is calculated	Jan	8:30 A.M.– 3:02 P.M.	WXI
5-point intervals	cash	Business day before day exercise-settlement value is calculated (usually a Thursday)	2 near-term months + 2 months from Mar quarterly cycle	8:30 A.M.– 3:15 A.M.	ISX
5-point intervals	cash	Business day before day exercise-settlement value is calculated (usually a Thursday)	Up to 3 near-term months + up to 3 additional months from Mar quarterly cycle	8:30 A.M.– 3:15 P.M.	MEX
2.5-point intervals	cash	Business day before day exercise-settlement value is calculated (usually a Thursday)	Jan	8:30 A.M.– 3:15 P.M.	VEX LEX
5-point intervals	cash	Business day before day exercise-settlement value is calculated	Up to 3 near-term months + up to 3 additional months from Mar quarterly cycle	8:30 A.M.– 3:02 P.M.	OIX

Contract	Underlying Index	Trading Unit	Price Quote	Tick Size
• CBOE Oil Index (Reduced Value) LEAPS	¹⁄₁₀ of CBOE Oil Index	$100 × index	points and fractions 1 point = $100	¹⁄₁₆ up to 3 ¹⁄₈ all others
• CBOE REIT Index	Price-weighted index of equity securities of large real estate investment trusts	$100 × index	points and fractions 1 point = $100	¹⁄₁₆ up to 3 ¹⁄₈ all others
• CBOE Technology Index	Price-weighted index of 30 high technology stocks trading on the NYSE and NASDAQ	$100 × index	points and fractions 1 point = $100	¹⁄₁₆ up to 3 ¹⁄₈ all others
• CBOE Technology Index (Reduced Value) LEAPS	¹⁄₁₀ of CBOE Technology Index	$100 × index	points and fractions 1 point = $100	¹⁄₁₆ up to 3 ¹⁄₈ over 3
• Dow Jones Industrial Average (options)	Price-weighted index of 30 largest, most liquid NYSE listed stocks	¹⁄₁₀₀ of DJIA level	points and fractions 1 point = $100	¹⁄₁₆ up to 3 ¹⁄₈ over 3
• Dow Jones Industrial Average (LEAPS)	Price-weighted index of 30 largest, most liquid NYSE listed stocks	¹⁄₁₀₀ of DJIA level	points and fractions 1 point = $100	¹⁄₁₆ up to 3 ¹⁄₈ over 3
• Dow Jones Transportation Average (options)	Price-weighted index of 20 largest, most liquid NYSE and NASDAQ listed transportation stocks	¹⁄₁₀₀ of DJIA level	points and fractions 1 point = $100	¹⁄₁₆ up to 3 ¹⁄₈ over 3

Strike Price	Settlement	Last Trading Day	Expiration Months	Trading Hours (CST)	Ticker Symbol
2.5-point intervals	cash	Business day before day exercise-settlement value is calculated	Jan of expiration year	8:30 A.M.– 3:10 P.M.	WOO
5-point intervals	cash	Business day before day exercise-settlement value is calculated	Up to 3 near-term months + up to 3 additional months from Mar quarterly cycle	8:30 A.M.– 3:02 P.M.	RIX
5-point intervals	cash	Business day before day exercise-settlement value is calculated	Up to 3 near-term months + up to 3 additional months from Mar quarterly cycle	8:30 A.M.– 3:02 P.M.	TXX
2.5-point intervals	cash	Business day before day exercise-settlement value is calculated	Jan of expiration year	8:30 A.M.– 3:10 P.M.	WXC
1 point minimum interval	cash	Business day before day the exercise-settlement value is calculated (usually a Thursday)	3 near-term months + 3 months on Mar quarterly cycle	8:30 A.M.– 3:15 P.M.	DJX
5-point minimum interval	cash	Business day before day the exercise-settlement value is calculated (usually a Thursday)	3 years from date of initial listing	8:30 A.M.– 3:15 P.M.	WDJ VDJ LDJ
5-point minimum interval	cash	Business day before day the exercise-settlement value is calculated (usually a Thursday)	2 near-term months and 2 cycle months	8:30 A.M.– 3:02 P.M.	DTX

Contract	Underlying Index	Trading Unit	Price Quote	Tick Size
• Dow Jones Transportation Average (LEAPS)	Price-weighted index of 20 largest, most liquid NYSE and NASDAQ listed transportation stocks	¹⁄₁₀₀ of DJIA level	points and fractions 1 point = $100	¹⁄₁₆ up to 3 ⅛ over 3
• Dow Jones Utility Average (option)	Price-weighted index of 15 largest, most liquid NYSE listed utility stocks	¹⁄₁₀₀ of DJIA level	points and fractions 1 point = $100	¹⁄₁₆ up to 3 ⅛ over 3
• Dow Jones Utility Average (LEAPS)	Price-weighted index of 15 largest, most liquid NYSE listed utility stocks	¹⁄₁₀₀ of DJIA level	points and fractions 1 point = $100	¹⁄₁₆ up to 3 ⅛ over 3
• GSTI Composite Index	Modified capitalization-weighted index of 178 technology industry companies		points and fractions	¹⁄₁₆ up to 3 ⅛ over 3
• GSTI Hardware Index	Modified capitalization-weighted index of companies in the computer hardware sector of the technology industry		points and fractions	¹⁄₁₆ up to 3 ⅛ over 3
• GSTI Internet Index	Modified capitalization-weighted index of companies in the Internet-related sector of the technology industry		points and fractions	¹⁄₁₆ up to 3 ⅛ over 3
• GSTI Multimedia Networking Index	Modified capitalization-weighted index of companies in the multimedia networking sector of the technology industry		points and fractions	¹⁄₁₆ up to 3 ⅛ over 3

Strike Price	Settlement	Last Trading Day	Expiration Months	Trading Hours (CST)	Ticker Symbol
2.5-point minimum interval	cash	Business day before day the exercise-value is calculated (usually a Thursday)	3 years from date of initial listing settlement	8:30 A.M.– 3:02 P.M.	WDX VDN LDN
5-point minimum interval	cash	Business day before day the exercise-settlement value is calculated (usually a Thursday)	2 near-term months and 2 cycle months	8:30 A.M.– 3:02 P.M.	DUX
2.5-point minimum interval	cash	Business day before day the exercise-settlement value is calculated (usually a Thursday)	3 years fron date of initial listing	8:30 A.M.– 3:02 P.M.	WDU VDU LDU
2.5 or 5-point increments above and below index level	cash	Business day before day the exercise-settlement value is calculated (usually a Thursday)	Up to 3 near-term months + 3 months on Mar quarterly cycle	8:30 A.M.– 3:02 P.M.	GTC
2.5 or 5-point increments above and below index level	cash	Business day before day the exercise-settlement value is calculated (usually a Thursday)	Up to 3 near-term months + 3 months on Mar quarterly cycle	8:30 A.M.– 3:02 P.M.	GHA
2.5 or 5-point increments above and below index level	cash	Business day before day the exercise-settlement value is calculated (usually a Thursday)	Up to 3 near-term months + 3 months on Mar quarterly cycle	8:30 A.M.– 3:02 P.M.	GIN
2.5 or 5-point increments above and below index level	cash	Business day before day the exercise-settlement value is calculated (usually a Thursday)	Up to 3 near-term months + 3 months on Mar quarterly cycle	8:30 A.M.– 3:02 P.M.	GIP

Contract	Underlying Index	Trading Unit	Price Quote	Tick Size
• GSTI Semiconductor Index	Modified capitalization-weighted index of companies in the semiconductor sector of the technology industry		points and fractions	$\frac{1}{16}$ up to 3 $\frac{1}{8}$ over 3
• GSTI Services Index	Modified capitalization-weighted index of companies in the computer services sector of the technology industry		points and fractions	$\frac{1}{16}$ up to 3 $\frac{1}{8}$ over 3
• GSTI Software Index	Modified capitalization-weighted index of companies in the computer software sector of the technology industry		points and fractions	$\frac{1}{16}$ up to 3 $\frac{1}{8}$ over 3
• IPC Options	$\frac{1}{10}$ level of the Indice de Precios y Cotizaciones, a total return capitalization-weighted index of 35 major equity securities listed on the Bolsa Mexicana de Valores	$100 × index	points and fractions 1 point = $100	$\frac{1}{16}$ up to 3 $\frac{1}{8}$ all others
• Latin 15 Index Index	Modified equal-dollar weighted index of ADRs, ADSs and closed-end country funds from 4 Latin American countries	$100 × index	points and fractions 1 point = $100	$\frac{1}{16}$ up to 3 $\frac{1}{8}$ all others
• Lipper Analytical/ Salomon Brothers Growth Funds Index	30 largest mutual funds with a "growth" investment objective	$100 × index	points and fractions 1 point = $100	$\frac{1}{16}$ up to 3 $\frac{1}{8}$ over 3

Strike Price	Settlement	Last Trading Day	Expiration Months	Trading Hours (CST)	Ticker Symbol
2.5 or 5-point increments above and below index level	cash	Business day before day the exercise-settlement value is calculated (usually a Thursday)	Up to 3 near-term months + 3 months on Mar quarterly cycle	8:30 A.M.–3:02 P.M.	GSM
2.5 or 5-point increments above and below index level	cash	Business day before day the exercise-settlement value is calculated (usually a Thursday)	Up to 3 near-term months + 3 months on Mar quarterly cycle	8:30 A.M.–3:02 P.M.	GSV
2.5 or 5-point increments above and below index level	cash	Business day before day the exercise-settlement value is calculated (usually a Thursday)	Up to 3 near-term months + 3 months on Mar quarterly cycle	8:30 A.M.–3:02 P.M.	GSO
5- or 10-point intervals, above and below index	cash	Business day preceding expiration date (usually a Friday)	Up to 3 months from Mar quarterly cycle	8:30 A.M.–3:15 P.M.	MXX
5-point intervals	cash	Business day before day exercise-settlement value is calculated (usually a Thursday)	Up to 3 near-term months + up to 3 additional months from Mar quarterly cycle	8:30 A.M.–3:15 P.M.	LTX
5-point intervals	cash	2 business days before expiration date (usually a Thursday)	Up to 3 near-term months + up to 3 additional months from quarterly cycle	8:30 A.M.–3:15 P.M.	LGO

Contract	Underlying Index	Trading Unit	Price Quote	Tick Size
• Lipper Analytical/ Salomon Brothers Growth and Income Funds Index	30 largest mutual funds with a "growth and income" investment objective	$100 × index	points and fractions 1 point = $100	⅟₁₆ up to 3 ⅛ over 3
• Morgan Stanley Multinational Company Index	Capitalization-weighted index of stocks of 50 U.S. listed companies that derive a substantial portion of earnings from foreign operations and have cash flows denominated in multiple currencies	$100 × index	points and fractions 1 point = $100	⅟₁₆ up to 3 ⅛ all others
• Nasdaq-100 Index	Capitalization weighted 100 largest non-financial securities listed on Nasdaq Stock Market	index × $100	points and fractions 1 point = $100	⅟₁₆ up to 3 ⅛ all others
• NYSE Composite Index	Capitalization-weighted index of all common stocks listed on the New York Stock Exchange	$100 × index	points and fractions 1 point = $100	⅟₁₆ up to 3 ⅛ all others
• Nikkei 300 Index	Capitalization-weighted index of major equity securities traded on first section of Tokyo Stock Exchange	index × $100	points and fractions 1 point = $100	⅟₁₆ up to 3 ⅛ all others
• OEX S&P 100 Index	Capitalization-weighted index of 100 stocks from a broad range of industries	index × $100	points and fractions 1 point = $100	⅟₁₆ up to 3 ⅛ all others
• OEX (Reduced-Value) LEAPS	⅟₁₀ of S&P 100 Index	index × $100	points and fractions 1 point = $100	⅟₁₆ up to 3 ⅛ all others

Strike Price	Settlement	Last Trading Day	Expiration Months	Trading Hours (CST)	Ticker Symbol
5-point intervals	cash	2 business days before expiration date (usually a Thursday)	Up to 3 near-term months + up to 3 additional months from quarterly cycle	8:30 A.M.– 3:15 P.M.	LIO
5-point intervals above 200; 2-point intervals below 200	cash	Business day before day exercise settlement value is calculated (usually a Thursday)	Up to 3 near-term months + up to 3 additional months from Mar quarterly cycle	8:30 A.M.– 3:15 P.M.	NFT
5-point intervals	cash	Business day before day exercise settlement value is calculated (usually a Thursday)	Up to 3 near-term months + up to 3 additional months in Mar quarterly cycle	8:30 A.M.– 3:15 P.M.	NDX
5-point intervals	cash	Business day before expiration day (usually a Thursday)	3 consecutive near-term months +2 additional months in the Mar quarterly cycle	8:30 A.M.– 3:15 P.M.	NYA
5-point intervals	cash	Business day before day exercise-settlement value is calculated (usually a Thursday)	2 near-term months + 2 additional months from Mar quarterly cycle	8:00 A.M.– 3:15 P.M.	NIK
5-point intervals, 10 points in far-term month	cash	Business day preceding expiration date (usually a Friday)	4 near-term months	8:30 A.M.– 3:15 P.M.	OEX
2.5-point intervals	cash	Business day preceding expiration date (usually a Friday)	Jan	8:30 A.M.– 3:15 P.M.	OBX

Contract	Underlying Index	Trading Unit	Price Quote	Tick Size
• Russell 2000 Index	Capitalization-weighted index of domestic equities traded on NYSE, AMEX, and NASDAQ	index × $100	points and fractions 1 point = $100	¹⁄₁₆ up to 3 ⅛ all others
• Russell 2000 Index (Reduced Value) LEAPS	¹⁄₁₀ of Russell 2000 Index	index × $100	points and fractions 1 point = $100	¹⁄₁₆ up to 3 ⅛ all others
• S&P Banks Index	Capitalization-weighted index of bank industry equities on NYSE and NASDAQ	index × $100	points and fractions 1 point = $100	¹⁄₁₆ up to 3 ⅛ all others
• S&P Chemical Index	Capitalization-weighted index of chemical industry equities on NYSE	index × $100	points and fractions 1 point = $100	¹⁄₁₆ up to 3 ⅛ all others
• S&P Health Care Index	Capitalization-weighted index of domestic health care industry equities	index × $100	points and fractions 1 point = $100	¹⁄₁₆ up to 3 ⅛ all others
• S&P Insurance Index	Capitalization-weighted index of domestic insurance industry equities	index × $100	points and fractions 1 point = $100	¹⁄₁₆ up to 3 ⅛ all others
• S&P Retail Index	Capitalization-weighted index of domestic equities traded on NYSE, AMEX, and NASDAQ (Sector of S&P 500)	index × $100	points and fractions 1 point = $100	¹⁄₁₆ up to 3 ⅛ all others

Strike Price	Settlement	Last Trading Day	Expiration Months	Trading Hours (CST)	Ticker Symbol
5-point intervals	cash	Business day before day exercise-settlement value is calculated (usually a Thursday)	3 near-term months + 3 additional months from Mar quarterly cycle	8:30 A.M.–3:15 P.M.	RUT
2.5-point intervals	cash	Business day before day exercise-settlement value is calculated	Jan of expiration year	8:30 A.M.–3:15 P.M.	VRU
5-point intervals	cash	Business day before day exercise-settlement value is calculated	Up to 3 near-term months + up to 3 additional months from Mar quarterly cycle	8:30 A.M.–3:02 P.M.	BIX
5-point intervals	cash	Business day before day exercise-settlement value is calculated	Up to 3 near-term months + up to 3 additional months from Mar quarterly cycle	8:30 A.M.–3:02 P.M.	CEX
5-point intervals	cash	Business day before day exercise-settlement value is calculated	Up to 3 near-term months + up to 3 additional months from Mar quarterly cycle	8:30 A.M.–3:02 P.M.	HCX
5-point intervals	cash	Business day before day exercise-settlement value is calculated	Up to 3 near-term months + up to 3 additional months from Mar quarterly cycle	8:30 A.M.–3:02 P.M.	IUX
5-point intervals	cash	Business day before day exercise-settlement value is calculated	Up to 3 near-term months + up to 3 additional months from Mar quarterly cycle	8:30 A.M.–3:02 P.M.	RLX

Contract	Underlying Index	Trading Unit	Price Quote	Tick Size
• S&P Transportation Index	Capitalization-weighted index of domestic transportation industry equities	index × $100	points and fractions 1 point = $100	1/16 up to 3 1/8 all others
• S&P 500 Index (SPX)	S&P 500 Index, capitalization-weighted index of 500 stocks from broad range of industries	$100 × index	points and fractions 1 point = $100	1/16 up to 3 1/8 over 3
• SPX (Reduced-Value) LEAPS	S&P 500 Index	$100 × index	points and fractions 1 point = $100	1/16 up to 3 1/8 over 3
• S&P 500 Index Long Dated Options (SPL)	S&P 500 Index	index × $100	points and fractions 1 point = $100	1/16 up to 3 1/8 all others
• S&P 500/BARRA Growth Index	Bottom 50% of S&P 500 market capitalization, sorted by book-to-price ratios	$100 × index	points and fractions 1 point = $100	1/16 up to 3 1/8 all others
• S&P 500/BARRA Value Index	Top 50% of S&P 500 market capitalization, sorted by book-to-price ratios	$100 × index	points and fractions 1 point = $100	1/16 up to 3 1/8 all others
• S&P Small Cap 600 Index	Capitalization-weighted index of 600 U.S. stocks chosen for market size, liquidity, and industry representation	$100 × index	points and fractions 1 point = $100	1/16 up to 3 1/8 all others

Strike Price	Settlement	Last Trading Day	Expiration Months	Trading Hours (CST)	Ticker Symbol
5-point intervals	cash	Business day before day exercise-settlement value is calculated	Up to 3 near-term months + up to 3 additional months from Mar quarterly cycle	8:30 A.M.–3:02 P.M.	TRX
5-point intervals; 25 points for far months	cash	Business day before day exercise-settlement value is calculated	Up to 3 near-term months + up to 3 additional months from Mar quarterly cycle	8:30 A.M.–3:15 P.M.	SPX
2.5-point intervals	cash	Business day before day exercise-settlement value is calculated	Jan of expiration year	8:30 A.M.–3:15 P.M.	LSX
25-point intervals	cash	Business day before day exercise-settlement value is calculated	Jun and Dec, up to 24 months	8:30 A.M.–3:15 P.M.	SPL
5-point intervals	cash	Business day before day exercise-settlement value is calculated	Up to 3 near-term months + up to 3 additional months from Mar quarterly cycle	8:30 A.M.–3:15 P.M.	SGX
5-point intervals	cash	Business day before day exercise-settlement value is calculated	Up to 3 near-term months + up to 3 additional months from Mar quarterly cycle	8:30 A.M.–3:15 P.M.	SVX
2.55-point intervals	cash	Business day before day exercise-settlement value is calculated	Up to 3 near-term months + up to 3 additional months from Mar quarterly cycle	8:30 A.M.–3:15 P.M.	SML

Interest Rate Options

Contract	Underlying Instrument	Trading Unit	Price Quote	Tick Size
● Treasury Bill	13-week U.S. Treasury Bill	composite × $100	points and fractions 1 point = $100	1/16 up to 3 1/8 all others
● Treasury Bond	30-year Treasury Note	composite × $100	points and fractions 1 point = $100	1/16 up to 3 1/8 all others
● Treasury Note	5-year Treasury Note	composite × $100	points and fractions 1 point = $100	1/16 up to 3 1/8 all others
● Treasury Note	10-year Treasury Note	composite × $100	points and fractions 1 point = $100	1/16 up to 3 1/8 all others

Chicago Mercantile Exchange (CME)

Agricultural Futures

Contract	Trading Unit	Price Quote	Tick Size
● Basic Formula Price (BFP) Fluid Milk	20,000 pounds of Grade A cow's milk	cents per pound	1/100 cent per pound ($20/contract)
● Boneless Beef	20,000 pounds of fresh 90% chemical lean boneless beef	cents per pound	$.10 per pound ($20/contract)

Strike Prices	Settlement	Last Trading Day	Contract Months	Trading Hours (EST)	Ticker Symbol
2.5-point intervals	cash	Business day preceding expiration date (usually a Friday)	3 near-term months + 2 additional months from Mar quarterly cycle	7:20 A.M.– 2:00 P.M.	IRX
2.5-point intervals	cash	Business day preceding expiration date (usually a Friday)	3 near-term months + 3 additional months from Mar quarterly cycle	7:20 A.M.– 2:00 P.M.	TYX
2.5-point intervals	cash	Business day preceding expiration date (usually a Friday)	3 near-term months + 3 additional months from Mar quarterly cycle	7:20 A.M.– 2:00 P.M.	FVX
2.5-point intervals	cash	Business day preceding expiration date (usually a Friday)	3 near-term months + 3 additional months from Mar quarterly cycle	7:20 A.M.– 2:00 P.M.	TNX

Daily Price Limit	Contract Months	Trading Hours (CST)	Ticker Symbol
1.5 cents per pound ($3,000/contract)	All months	8:00 A.M.–1:10 P.M.	DA
3 cents per pound ($600/contract); expandable to 4.5 cents per pound ($900/contract) after 2-day limit move up or down; removed after of trading last 5 days	Feb, Apr, June, Aug, Oct, Dec	8:50 A.M.–1:00 P.M.	BB

Contract	Trading Unit	Price Quote	Tick Size
● Boneless Beef Trimmings	20,000 pounds of fresh 90% chemical lean boneless beef trimmings	cents per pound	$.10 per pound ($20/contract)
● Cheddar Cheese	40,000 pounds	cents per pound	$.025 to $2.5 per pound ($10 to $1,000/contract)
● Feeder Cattle	50,000 pounds feeder steers	cents per pound	$.25 per pound ($12.50/contract)
● Fresh Pork Bellies	40,000 pounds	cents per pound	$.025 per pound ($10/contract)
● Lean Hogs	40,000 pounds	cents per pound	$.025 per pound ($10/contract)
● Live Cattle	40,000 pounds	cents per pound	$.025 per pound ($10/contract)
● New Butter	40,000 pounds	cents per pound	$.025 per pound ($10/contract)

Forest Products Futures

Contract	Trading Unit	Price Quote	Tick Size
● Oriented Strand Board	100,000 square feet of 4 feet by 8 feet panels	dollars per 1,000 sq. feet	10 cents per msf ($10/contract)
● Random Length Lumber	160,000 board feet	dollars per thousand board feet	10 cents per MBF ($16/contract)

Currency Futures

Contract	Trading Unit	Price Quote	Tick Size
● Australian Dollar	100,000 Australian dollars	U.S. dollars per Australian dollar	$.0001 (1 point) ($10)
● Brazilian Real	100,000 Brazilian reals	U.S. dollars per Brazilian real	$.0001 (1 point) ($10)

Daily Price Limit	Contract Months	Trading Hours (CST)	Ticker Symbol
3 cents per pound ($600/contract); expandable to 4.5 cents per pound ($900/contract) after 2-day limit move up or down; removed after last 5 days of trading	Feb, Apr, June, Aug, Oct, Dec	8:50 A.M.–1:00 P.M.	TR
2.5 cents per pound ($1,000/contract)	Jan, Mar, May, July, Sept, Nov	8:00 A.M.–1:00 P.M.	DC
1.5 cents per pound ($750/contract)	Jan, Mar, Apr, May, Aug, Sept, Oct, Nov	9:05 A.M.–1:00 P.M.	FC
2 cents per pound ($800/contract)	Feb, Mar, May, July, Aug	9:10 A.M.–1:00 P.M.	PB
1.5 cents per pound ($600/contract)	Feb, Apr, June, July, Aug, Oct, Dec	9:10 A.M.–1:00 P.M.	LH
1.5 cents per pound ($600/contract)	Feb, Apr, June, Aug, Oct, Dec	9:05 A.M.–1:00 P.M.	LC
2.5 cents per pound ($1,000/contract)	Feb, Apr, June, July, Sept, Nov	8:00 A.M.–1:10 P.M.	DB

Daily Price Limit	Contract Months	Trading Hours (CST)	Ticker Symbol
10 dollars per msf ($1,000/contract)	Jan, Mar, May July, Sept, Nov	9:00 A.M.–1:05 P.M.	BD
10 dollars per MBF $1,600/contract)	Jan, Mar, May, July, Sept, Oct	9:00 A.M.–1:05 P.M.	LB

Daily Price Limit	Last Trading Day	Contract Months	Trading Hours (CST)	Ticker Symbol
Call CME	2nd business day before 3rd Wednesday of month	Mar, June, Sept, Dec	7:20 A.M.–2:00 P.M. Globex: M-Th, 2:30 P.M.– 7:05 A.M.; Sun/hol, 5:30 P.M.–7:05 A.M.	AD
Call CME	Last business day of month preceding contract month	All months	7:20 A.M.–2:00 P.M. Globex: M-Th, 2:30 P.M.– 7:05 A.M.; Sun/hol, 5:30 P.M.–7:05 A.M.	BR

Contract	Trading Unit	Price Quote	Tick Size
• British Pound	62,500 British pounds	U.S. dollars per British pound	$.0002 (2 points) ($12.50)
• Canadian Dollar	100,000 Canadian dollars	U.S. dollars per Canadian dollar	$.0001 (1 point) ($10)
• Deutsche mark	125,000 Deutsche marks	U.S. dollars per Deutsche mark	$.0001 (1 point) ($12.50)
• Euro Currency	125,000 Euros	U.S. dollars per Euro	$.0001 (1 point) ($12.50)
• French Franc	500,000 French francs	U.S. dollars per French franc	$.00002 (2 points) ($10)
• Japanese Yen	12,500,000 yen	U.S. dollars per yen	$.000001 (1 point) ($12.50)
• Mexican Peso	500,000 pesos	U.S. dollars per peso	$.000025 (2.5 points) ($12.50)
• New Zealand Dollar	100,000 New Zealand dollars	U.S. dollars per NZ dollars	$.0001 (1 point) ($10)
• Russian Ruble	500,000 rubles	U.S. dollars per rubles	$.000025 (2.5 points) ($12.50)
• South African Rand	500,0000 rand	U.S. dollars per rand	$.000025 (2.5 points) ($12.50)

Daily Price Limit	Last Trading Day	Contract Months	Trading Hours (CST)	Ticker Symbol
Call CME	2nd business day before 3rd Wednesday of month	Mar, June, Sept, Dec	7:20 A.M.–2:00 P.M. Globex: M-Th, 2:30 P.M.– 7:05 A.M.; Sun/hol 5:30 P.M.–7:05 A.M.	BP
Call CME	1st business day before 3rd Wednesday of contract month	Mar, June, Sept, Dec	7:20 A.M.–2:00 P.M. Globex: M-Th, 2:30 P.M.– 7:05 A.M.; Sun/hol, 5:30 P.M.–7:05 A.M.	CD
Call CME	2nd business day before 3rd Wednesday of contract month	Mar, June, Sept, Dec	7:20 A.M.–2:00 P.M. Globex: M-Th, 2:30 P.M.– 7:05 A.M.; Sun/hol, 5:30 P.M.–7:05 A.M.	DM
Call CME	2nd business day before 3rd Wednesday of contract month	Jan, Mar, Apr, June, July, Sept, Dec	7:20 A.M.–2:00 P.M. Globex: M-Th, 2:30 P.M.– 7:05 A.M.; Sun/hol, 5:30 P.M.–7:05 A.M.	EC
Call CME	2nd business day before 3rd Wednesday of contract month	Mar, June, Sept, Dec	7:20 A.M.–2:00 P.M. Globex: M-Th, 2:30 P.M.– 7:05 A.M.; Sun/hol, 5:30 P.M.–7:05 A.M.	FR
Call CME	2nd business day before 3rd Wednesday of contract month	Mar, June, Sept, Dec	7:20 A.M.–2:00 P.M. Globex: M-Th, 2:30 P.M.– 7:05 A.M.; Sun/hol, 5:30 P.M.–7:05 A.M.	JY
Call CME	2nd business day before 3rd Wednesday of contract month	Mar, June, Sept, Dec	7:20 A.M.–2:00 P.M. Globex: M-Th, 2:30 P.M.– 7:05 A.M.; Sun/hol, 5:30 P.M.–7:05 A.M.	MP
Call CME	2nd business day before 3rd Wednesday of contract month	Mar, June, Sept, Dec	7:20 A.M.–2:00 P.M. Globex: M-Th, 2:30 P.M.– 7:05 A.M.; Sun/hol, 5:30 P.M.–7:05 A.M.	NZ
Call CME	10 A.M. Moscow time, 15th calendar day of contract month (usually 1 A.M. (CST)	Mar, June, Sept, Dec	7:20 A.M.–2:00 P.M. Globex: M-Th, 2:32 P.M.– 7:05 A.M.; Sun/hol, 5:30 P.M.–7:05 A.M.	RR
Call CME	2nd business day before 3rd Wednesday of contract month	Mar, Jun Sept, Dec	7:20 A.M.–2:00 P.M. Globex: M-Th, 2:30 P.M.– 7:05 A.M.; Sun/hol, 5:30 P.M.–7:05 A.M.	RA

Contract	Trading Unit	Price Quote	Tick Size
• Swiss Franc	125,000 Swiss francs	U.S. dollars per Swiss franc	$.0001 (1 point) ($12.50)

Foreign Currency Denominated (Cross Rate) Futures

Contract	Trading Unit	Price Quote	Tick Size
• British Pound/ Deutsche Mark	125,000 pounds	Deutsche marks per pound	.0001 Deutsche mark (DM12.50)
• Deutsche Mark/ Japanese Yen	125,000 Deutsche marks	Yen per Deutsche marks	.001 yen (¥1,250)
• Deutsche Mark Swiss Franc	250,000 Deutsche marks	Swiss francs per Deutsche mark	.005 Swiss franc (SF12.50)
• Deutsche Mark/ French Franc	250,000 Deutsche marks	French francs per Deutsche mark	.001 French franc (FF25)
• Eurocurrency/ British Pound	125,000 Euros	Pounds per Euro	.00005 pound (6.25 pounds)
• Eurocurrency/ Canadian Dollar	125,000 Euros	Canadian dollars per Euro	.0001 Canadian dollars (CD12.50)
• Eurocurrency/ Deutsche Mark	125,000 Euros	Deutsche marks per Euro	.0001 Deutsche marks (DM1.25)
• Eurocurrency/ Japanese Yen	125,000 Euros	Yen per Euro	.01 yen (¥1,250)

Daily Price Limit	Last Trading Day	Contract Months	Trading Hours (CST)	Ticker Symbol
Call CME	2nd business day before 3rd Wednesday of contract month	Mar, June, Sept, Dec	7:20 A.M.–2:00 P.M. Globex: M-Th, 2:30 P.M.– 7:05 P.M.; Sun/hol, 5:30 P.M.–7:05 A.M.	SF

Last Trading Day	Contract Months	Trading Hours (CST)	Ticker Symbol
2nd business day before 3rd Wednesday of month	Mar, June, Sept, Dec	7:20 A.M.–2:00 P.M.; Globex: M-Th, 2:30 P.M.– 7:05 A.M.; Sun/hols, 5:30 P.M.–7:05 A.M.	IP
2nd business day before 3rd Wednesday of month	Mar, June, Sept, Dec	7:20 A.M.–2:00 P.M.; Globex: M-Th, 2:30 P.M.– 7:05 A.M.; Sun/hols, 5:30 P.M.–7:05 A.M.	DJ
2nd business day before 3rd Wednesday of month	Mar, June, Sept, Dec	7:20 A.M.–2:00 P.M.; Globex: M-Th, 2:30 P.M.– 7:05 A.M.; Sun/hols, 5:30 P.M.–7:05 A.M.	IS
2nd business day before 3rd Wednesday of month	Mar, June, Sept, Dec	7:20 A.M.–2:00 P.M.; Globex: M-Th, 2:30 P.M.– 7:05 A.M.; Sun/hols, 5:30 P.M.–7:05 A.M.	IF
2nd business day before 3rd Wednesday of month	Mar, June, Sept, Dec	7:20 A.M.–2:00 P.M.; Globex: M-Th, 2:30 P.M.– 7:05 A.M.; Sun/hols, 5:30 P.M.–7:05 A.M.	RE
2nd business day before 3rd Wednesday of month	Mar, June, Sept, Dec	7:20 A.M.–2:00 P.M.; Globex: M-Th, 2:30 P.M.– 7:05 A.M.; Sun/hols, 5:30 P.M.–7:05 A.M.	RK
2nd business day before 3rd Wednesday of month	Mar, June, Sept, Dec	7:20 A.M.–2:00 P.M.; Globex: M-Th, 2:30 P.M.– 7:05 A.M.; Sun/hols, 5:30 P.M.–7:05 A.M.	RD
2nd business day before 3rd Wednesday of month	Mar, June, Sept, Dec	7:20 A.M.–2:00 P.M.; Globex: M-Th, 2:30 P.M.– 7:05 A.M.; Sun/hols, 5:30 P.M.–7:05 A.M.	RJ

Contract	Trading Unit	Price Quote	Tick Size
• Eurocurrency/ Swiss Franc	125,000 Euros	Swiss francs per Euro	.0001 Swiss franc (SF12.50)

Foreign Currency-Denominated Interest Rate Futures

Contract	Trading Unit	Price Quote	Tick Size
• EuroCanada (3-month)	$1,000,000 Canadian dollars	index points	.01 Canadian dollar (C$25)
• Euroyen	100,000,000 yen	index points	.01 yen (¥2,500)
• 91-Day Mexican Treasury Bill (CETES)	2,000,000 pesos	index points	.01 peso (MP50)
• 28-Day Mexican TIIE	6,000,000 pesos	index points	.01 peso (MP50)

Interest Rate Futures

Contract	Trading Unit	Price Quote	Tick Size
• Eurodollar Time Deposit 3-month)	$1,000,000	index point	.01 point ($25)
• LIBOR (1-Month)	$3,000,000	index point	.005 point ($12.50)
• U.S. Treasury Bill (13-Week)	$1,000,000	index point	.005 point ($12.50)
• U.S. Treasury Bill (1-Year)	$500,000	index point	.005 point ($25)

Daily Price Limit	Contract Months	Trading Hours (CST)	Ticker Symbol
2nd business day before 3rd Wednesday of month	Mar, June, Sept, Dec	7:20 A.M.–2:00 P.M.; Globex: M-Th, 2:30 P.M.–7:05 A.M.; Sun/hols, 5:30 P.M.–7:05 A.M.	RF

Last Trading Day	Contract Months	Trading Hours (CST)	Ticker Symbol
2 business days before 3rd Wednesday of contract month	Mar, June, Sept, Dec	7:20 A.M.–2:00 P.M.; Globex: M-Th, 2:45 P.M.–7:05 A.M.; Sun/hol, 5:30 P.M.–7:05 A.M.	KJ
3rd business day before 3rd Wednesday of contract month	Mar, June, Sept, Dec	7:20 A.M.–2:00 P.M.	EY
Tuesday before 3rd Wednesday of contract month	Mar, June, Sept, Dec	8:00 A.M.–2:00 P.M.; Globex: 2:45 P.M.–7:05 P.M.	TS
3rd Wednesday of contract month	All 12 months	8:00 A.M.–2:00 P.M.; Globex: 2:30 P.M.–7:05 P.M.	TE

Last Trading Day	Contract Months	Trading Hours (CST)	Ticker Symbol
11 A.M. London time on 2nd London bank business day before 3rd Wednesday of contract month	Mar, June, Sept, Dec	7:20 A.M.–2:00 P.M.; Globex: M-Th; 2:30 P.M.–7:05 A.M.; Sun/hol, 5:30 P.M.–7:05 A.M.	ED
11 A.M. London time on 2nd London bank business day before 3rd Wednesday of contract month	All months	7:20 A.M.–2:00 P.M.; Globex: M-Th; 2:30 P.M.–7:05 A.M.; Sun/hol, 5:30 P.M.–7:05 A.M.	EM
12 P.M. (CST) on day of 91-day T-bill auction in week of 3rd Wednesday of contract month	Mar, June, Sept, Dec	7:20 A.M.–2:00 P.M.; Globex: M-Th; 2:30 P.M.–7:05 A.M.; Sun/hol, 5:30 P.M.–7:05 A.M.	TB
None	Mar, June, Sept, Dec	7:20 A.M.–2:00 P.M.; Globex: M-Th; 2:30 P.M.–7:05 A.M.; Sun/hol, 5:30 P.M.–7:05 A.M.	YR

Stock Index Futures

Contract	Trading Unit	Price Quote	Tick Size
● Goldman-Sachs Commodity Index	$250 × Goldman-Sachs Commodity Index	index points	.10 index point ($25)
● IPC Stock Index	$25 × index	index points	1 index point ($25)
● Major Market Index	$500 × index	index points	.05 index point ($25)
● Nasdaq 100 Index	$100 × index	index points	.05 index point ($5)
● Nikkei 225 Stock Average	$5 × Nikkei Stock Average	index points	5 points ($25)
● Quarterly Bankruptcy Index	$1,000 × CME Quarterly Bankruptcy Index	index points	.025 index point ($10)
● Russell 2000 Index	$500 × Russell 2000 Stock Price Index	index points	.05 index point ($25)
● S&P 500 Index	$250 × S&P 500 Stock Index	index points	.10 points ($25)
● E-Mini S&P 500 Stock Price Index	$50 × S&P 500 Stock Index	index points	.25 index point ($12.50)
● S&P MidCap 400 Index	$500 × MidCap Index	index points	.05 index point ($25)
● S&P 500/ BARRA Growth Index	$250 × index	index points	.10 index point ($25)
● S&P 500/ BARRA Value Index	$250 × index	index points	.10 index point ($25)

Last Trading Day	Contract Months	Trading Hours (CST)	Ticker Symbol
3rd Friday of contract month	Mar, June, Sept, Dec	8:30 A.M.–3:15 P.M. Globex: 3:45 P.M.–8:15 P.M.	GI
3rd Friday of contract month	Mar, June, Sept, Dec	8:30 A.M.–3:15 P.M. Globex: 3:45 P.M.–8:15 A.M.	MX
3rd Friday of contract month	Mar, June, Sept, Dec	8:30 A.M.–3:15 P.M. Globex: 3:45 P.M.–8:15 A.M.	BC
Thursday before 3rd Friday of contract month	Mar, June, Sept, Dec	8:30 A.M.–3:15 P.M. Globex: 3:45 P.M.–8:15 A.M.	ND
Thursday before 2nd Friday of contract month	Mar, June, Sep Dec	8:00 A.M.–3:15 P.M.	NK
Business day before final settlement: 2 bank business days before 15th day of month following the contract month	Mar, June, Sept, Dec	7:20 A.M.–2:00 P.M. Globex: 2:10 P.M.–7:05 P.M.	QB
Thursday before 3rd Friday of contract month	Mar, June, Sept, Dec	8:30 A.M.–3:15 P.M. Globex: 3:45 P.M.–8:15 P.M.	RL
Thursday before 3rd Friday of contract month	Mar, June, Sept, Dec	8:30 A.M.–3:15 P.M. Globex: 3:45 P.M.–8:15 A.M.	SP
Thursday before 3rd Friday of contract month	Mar, June, Sept, Dec	24-hour trading except: M-Th, 3:15 P.M.– 3:30 P.M.; Fri-Sun, 3:15 P.M.–5:30 P.M.	ES
Thursday before 3rd Friday of contract month	Mar, June, Sept, Dec	8:30 A.M.–3:15 P.M. Globex: 8:30 A.M.–3:15 P.M.	MD
Thursday before 3rd Friday of contract month	Mar, June, Sept, Dec	8:30 A.M.–3:15 P.M. Globex: 3:45 P.M.–8:15 A.M.	SG
Thursday before 3rd Friday of contract month	Mar, June, Sept, Dec	8:30 A.M.–3:15 P.M. Globex: 3:45 P.M.–8:15 A.M.	SU

Agricultural Options on Futures

Contract	Trading Unit	Price Quote	Tick Size	Strike Price
● Basic Formula Price (BFP) Fluid Milk	1 BFP fluid milk futures contract	cents per pound	$\frac{1}{100}$ cent per pound ($20/contract)	25-cent intervals
● Boneless Beef	1 boneless beef futures contract	cents per pound	.10 cent per pound ($20/contract)	2-cent intervals
● Boneless Beef Trimmings	1 boneless beef trimmings futures contract	cents per pound	.10 cent per pound ($20/contract)	2-cent intervals
● Cheddar Cheese	1 cheddar cheese futures contract	cents per pound	2.5 cents per hundred pounds	2-cent intervals
● Feeder Cattle	1 feeder cattle futures contract	cents per pound	2.5 cents per hundred pounds ($12.50)	2-cent intervals except front month which is 1 cent apart
● Fresh Pork Bellies	1 pork belly futures contract	cents per pound	.025 cent per pound ($10/contract)	2-cent intervals
● Lean Hogs	1 lean hog futures contract	cents per pound	.025 cent per pound ($7.50)	2-cent intervals, 2 nearby contracts at 1-cent intervals
● Live Cattle	1 cattle futures contract	cents per pound	.025 cent per pound ($10/contract)	2-cent intervals, 1 cent apart for 1st 2 months listed

Expiration Day	Last Trading Day	Contract Months	Trading Hours (CST)	Ticker Symbol
Last trading day	Business day prior to USDA BFP announcement on 5th day of the following month or preceding business day if 5th is not a business day	All months	8:00 A.M.–12:10 P.M.	DA (call) DA (put)
Last trading day	6th to last business day of contract month; Dec ends on 10th business day	Feb, Apr, June, Aug, Oct, Dec	8:50 A.M.–1:00 P.M.	BB (call) BB (put)
Last trading day	6th to last business day of contract month; Dec ends on 10th business day	Feb, Apr, June, Aug, Oct, Dec	8:50 A.M.–1:00 P.M.	TR (call) TR (put)
Last trading day	Business day prior to USDA release of weekly average for week ending on last Friday of contract month	Jan, Mar, May, July, Sept, Nov	8:00 A.M.–1:00 P.M.	DC (call) DC (put)
Last trading day	Last Thursday of month	Jan, Mar, Apr, May, Aug, Sept, Oct, Nov	9:05 A.M.–1:00 P.M.	KF (call) JF (put)
Last trading day	1st Friday of delivery month; Nov/Feb option terminates on 3rd Friday	Feb, Mar, May, July, Aug, Nov	9:10 A.M.–1:00 P.M.	KP (call) JP (put)
Last trading day	Non-serial options: 10th business day of contract month; Serial options: 10th business day of month prior to underlying futures contract month	Feb, Apr, June, Aug, Oct, Dec	9:10 A.M.–1:00 P.M.	CH (call) PH (put)
Last trading day	Non-serial options: 1st Friday of futures contract delivery month; Serial options: 1st Friday of contract month that is a business day	Feb, Apr, June, Aug, Sept, Oct, Dec and serial delivery months (Jan, Mar, May, July, Sept, Nov)	9:05 A.M.–1:00 P.M.	CK (call) PK (put)

Contract	Trading Unit	Price Quote	Tick Size	Strike Price
• New Butter	1 new butter futures contract	cents per pound	.025 cent per pound ($10/contract)	2-cent intervals

Forest Products Options on Futures

Contract	Trading Unit	Price Quote	Tick Size	Strike Price
• Oriented Strand Board	1 oriented strand board futures contract	dollars per 1,000 square feet	10 cents per msf ($10/contract)	$5 intervals
• Random Length Lumber	1 random length lumber futures contract	cents per thousand board foot	10 cents per MBF	$5 intervals

Currency Options on Futures

Contract	Trading Unit	Price Quote	Tick Size	Strike Price
• Australian Dollar	1 Australian dollar futures contract	cents per Australian dollar	$.0001 ($10)	.0100 intervals; ½ strikes for 1st 7 months
• Brazilian Real	1 Brazilian real futures contract	dollars per Brazilian real	$.00005 ($5)	.0100 intervals; ½ strikes for 1st 7 months
• British Pound	1 British pound futures contract	dollars per pound sterling	$.0002 ($12.50)	.0200 intervals; ½ strikes for 1st 7 months
• Canadian Dollar	1 Canadian dollar futures contract	dollars per Canadian dollar	$.0001 ($10)	0.050 intervals
• Deutsche Mark	1 Deutsche mark futures contract	dollars per Deutsche mark	$.0001 ($12.50)	.0100 intervals; ½ strikes for 1st 7 months
• Euro Currency	1 Euro futures contract	dollars per Euro	$.0001 ($12.50)	.0100 intervals
• French Francs	1 French franc futures contract	dollars per French franc	$.00002 ($10)	.0025 intervals

Expiration Day	Last Trading Day	Contract Months	Trading Hours (CST)	Ticker Symbol
Last trading day	1st Friday of delivery month	Feb, Apr, June, July, Sept, Nov	8:00 A.M.–1:10 P.M.	DB (call) DB (put)

Expiration Day	Last Trading Day	Contract Months	Trading Hours (CST)	Ticker Symbol
Last trading day	Last Friday of month preceding delivery	Jan, Mar, May, July, Sept, Nov	9:00 A.M.–1:05 P.M.	BD (call) BD (put)
Last trading day	Last Friday before 1st day of month	Jan, Mar, May, July, Sept, Nov	9:00 A.M.–1:05 P.M.	KL (call) KL (put)

Last Trading Day	Contract Months	Trading Hours (CST)	Ticker Symbol
2nd Friday before 3rd Wednesday of contract month	All months + weekly expiration	7:20 A.M.–2:00 P.M. Globex: M-F, 2:30 P.M.–7:05 A.M.; Sun, 5:30 P.M.–7:05 A.M.	KA (call) JA (put)
Same date as underlying futures contract	All months + weekly expiration	7:20 A.M.–2:00 P.M. Globex: M-F, 2:30 P.M.–7:05 A.M.; Sun, 5:30 P.M.–7:05 A.M.	BRC (call) BRP (put)
2nd Friday before 3rd Wednesday of contract month	All months + weekly expiration	7:20 A.M.–2:00 P.M. Globex: M-F, 2:30 P.M.–7:05 A.M.; Sun, 5:30 P.M.–7:05 A.M.	CP (call) PP (put)
2nd Friday before 3rd Wednesday of contract month	All months + weekly expiration	7:20 A.M.–2:00 P.M. Globex: M-F, 2:30 P.M.–7:05 A.M.; Sun, 5:30 P.M.–7:05 A.M.	CV (call) PV (put)
2nd Friday before 3rd Wednesday of contract month	All months + weekly expiration	7:20 A.M.–2:00 P.M. Globex: M-F, 2:30 P.M.–7:05 A.M.; Sun, 5:30 P.M.–7:05 A.M.	CM (call) PM (put)
2nd Friday before 3rd Wednesday of contract month	Mar, June, Sept, Dec + serial months	7:20 A.M.–2:00 P.M. Globex: M-F, 2:30 P.M.–7:05 A.M.; Sun, 5:30 P.M.–7:05 A.M.	EC (call) EC (put)
2nd Friday before 3rd Wednesday of contract month	All months + weekly expiration	7:20 A.M.–2:00 P.M.	FR (call) FR (put)

Contract	Trading Unit	Price Quote	Tick Size	Strike Price
• Japanese Yen	1 yen futures contract	dollars per yen	$.000001 ($12.50)	.0001 intervals; ½ strikes for 1st 7 months
• Mexican Peso	1 peso futures contract	dollars per peso	$.000025 ($12.50)	.00125 intervals
• New Zealand Dollar	1 NZ dollar futures contract	dollars per NZ dollar	$.0001 ($10)	.0100 intervals; ½ strikes for 1st 7 months
• Russian Ruble	1 ruble futures contract	dollars per ruble	$.000025 ($12.50)	.0100 intervals; ½ strikes for 1st 7 months
• South African Rand	1 rand futures contract	dollars per rand	$.000025 ($12.50)	.00500 intervals; ½ strikes for 1st 7 months
• Swiss Franc	1 Swiss franc futures contract	dollars per Swiss franc	$.0001 ($12.50)	.0100 intervals; ½ strikes for 1st 7 months

Foreign Currency-Denominated (Cross-Rate) Options on Futures

Contract	Trading Unit	Price Quote	Tick Size	Strike Price
• British Pound/ Deutsche Mark	1 futures contract	Deutsche marks per British pound	1 point	.025 intervals
• Deutsche Mark/Yen	1 futures contract	Yen per Deutsche mark	1 point	1.0/.5 intervals
• Deutsche Mark/ Swiss Franc	1 futures contract	Swiss francs per Deutsche mark	.1 point	.01 intervals
• Deutsche Mark/ French Franc	1 futures contract	French francs per Deutsche mark	1 point	.01 intervals
• Eurocurrency/ British Pound	1 futures contract	British pounds per Euro	.5 point	.005 intervals

Last Trading Day	Contract Months	Trading Hours (CST)	Ticker Symbol
2nd Friday before 3rd Wednesday of contract month	All months + weekly expiration	7:20 A.M.–2:00 P.M. Globex:. M-F, 2:30 P.M.–7:05 A.M.; Sun, 5:30 P.M.–7:05 A.M.	CJ (call) PJ (put)
2nd Friday before 3rd Wednesday of contract month	All months + weekly expiration	7:20 A.M.–2:00 P.M. Globex: M-F, 2:30 P.M.–7:05 A.M.; Sun, 5:30 P.M.–7:05 A.M.	MPC (call) PP (put)
2nd Friday before 3rd Wednesday of contract month	All months + weekly expiration	7:20 A.M.–2:00 P.M. Globex: M-F, 2:30 P.M.–7:05 A.M.; Sun, 5:30 P.M.–7:05 A.M.	NE (call) NE (put)
2nd Friday before 3rd Wednesday of contract month	All months + weekly expiration	7:20 A.M.–2:00 P.M. Globex: M-F, 2:30 P.M.–7:05 A.M.; Sun, 5:30 P.M.–7:05 A.M.	CM (call) PM (put)
2nd Friday before 3rd Wednesday of contract month	Mar, June, Dec and 2 serial months + 4 weekly	7:20 A.M.–2:00 P.M. Globex: M-F, 2:30 P.M.–7:05 A.M.; Sun, 5:30 P.M.–7:05 A.M.	RU (call) RU (put)
2nd Friday before 3rd Wednesday of contract month	All months + weekly expiration	7:20 A.M.–2:00 P.M. Globex: M-F, 2:30 P.M.–7:05 A.M.; Sun, 5:30 P.M.–7:05 A.M.	RA (call) RA (put)

Expiration Day	Contract Months	Trading Hours (CST)	Ticker Symbol
Every week	Quarterly, serial months	7:20 A.M.–2:00 P.M. Globex: M-Th, 2:30 P.M.–7:05 A.M.; Sun/hol, 5:30 P.M.–7:05 A.M.	IP
Every week	Quarterly, serial months	7:20 A.M.–2:00 P.M. Globex: M-Th, 2:30 P.M.–7:05 A.M.; Sun/hol, 5:30 P.M.–7:05 A.M.	DJ
Every week	Quarterly, serial months	7:20 A.M.–2:00 P.M. Globex: M-Th, 2:30 P.M.–7:05 A.M.; Sun/hol, 5:30 P.M.–7:05 A.M.	IS
Every week	Quarterly, serial months	7:20 A.M.–2:00 P.M. Globex: M-Th, 2:30 P.M.–7:05 A.M.; Sun/hol, 5:30 P.M.–7:05 A.M.	IF
Every week	Quarterly, serial months	7:20 A.M.–2:00 P.M. Globex: M-Th, 2:30 P.M.–7:05 A.M.; Sun/hol, 5:30 P.M.–7:05 A.M.	RE

Contract	Trading Unit	Price Quote	Tick Size	Strike Price
● Eurocurrency/ Canadian Dollar	1 futures contract	Canadian dollar per Euro	1 point	.01 intervals
● Eurocurrency/ Deutsche Mark	1 futures contract	Deutsche mark per Euro	1 point	.002 intervals
● Eurocurrency/ Japanese Yen	1 futures contract	Yen per Euro	1 point	1 intervals
● Eurocurrency/ Swiss Franc	1 futures contract	Swiss franc per Euro	1 point	.005 intervals

Foreign Currency Denominated Interest Rate Options on Futures

Contract	Trading Unit	Price Quote	Tick Size	Strike Price
● EuroCanada	1 EuroCanada futures contract	index points	1 point	.25-point intervals
● Euroyen	1 Euroyen futures contract	index points	1 point	.25-point intervals
● 91-Day Mexican Treasury Bill (CETES)	1 CETES futures contract	index points	1 point	.50-point intervals
● 28-Day Mexican TIIE	1 TIIE futures contract	index points	1 point	.50-point intervals

Interest Rate Options on Futures

Contract	Trading Unit	Price Quote	Tick Size	Strike Price
● Eurodollar Time Deposit (3-month)	1 Eurodollars futures contract	index points	point	25-point intervals

Expiration Day	Contract Months	Trading Hours (CST)	Ticker Symbol
Every week	Quarterly, serial months	7:20 A.M.–2:00 P.M. Globex: M-Th, 2:30 P.M.–7:05 A.M.; Sun/hol, 5:30 P.M.–7:05 A.M.	RK
Every week	Quarterly, serial months	7:20 A.M.–2:00 P.M. Globex: M-Th, 2:30 P.M.–7:05 A.M.; Sun/hol, 5:30 P.M.–7:05 A.M.	RD
Every week	Quarterly, serial months	7:20 A.M.–2:00 P.M. Globex: M-Th, 2:30 P.M.–7:05 A.M.; Sun/hol, 5:30 P.M.–7:05 A.M.	RJ
Every week	Quarterly, serial months	7:20 A.M.–2:00 P.M. Globex: M-Th, 2:30 P.M.–7:05 A.M.; Sun/hol, 5:30 P.M.–7:05 A.M.	RF

Last Trading Day	Contract Months	Trading Hours (CST)	Ticker Symbol
3rd business day before 3rd Wednesday of contract month	Mar, June, Sept, Dec and serial months	7:20 A.M.–2:00 P.M. Globex: 2:45 P.M.–7:05 A.M.	KJ
3rd business day before 3rd Wednesday of contract month	Mar, June, Sept, Dec	7:20 A.M.–2:00 P.M.	EY
Tuesday before 3rd Wednesday of contract month	Mar, June, Sept, Dec	7:20 A.M.–2:00 P.M. Globex: 2:45 P.M.–7:05 A.M.	TS
3rd Wednesday of contract month	All months	8:00 A.M.–2:00 P.M. Globex: 2:45 P.M.–7:05 A.M.	TE

Last Trading Day	Contract Months	Trading Hours (CST)	Ticker Symbol
Quarterly options: 2nd London bank business day before 3rd Wednesday of contract month Serial options: Friday before 3rd Wednesday of contract month	Mar, June, Sept, Dec + serial and quarterly months	7:20 A.M.–2:00 P.M. Globex: M-F, 2:45 P.M.–7:05 A.M.; Sun., 5:30 P.M.–7:05 A.M.	CE (Call) PE (Put)

Contract	Trading Unit	Price Quote	Tick Size	Strike Price
• LIBOR (1-month)	1 LIBOR futures contract	Total IMM index points	.005 index points ($12.50)	25-point intervals
• U.S. Treasury Bill (13-Week)	1 13-week T-bill futures contract	index points	½ index point	.25-point intervals
• U.S. Treasury Bill (1-Year)	1 1-year T-bill futures contract	IMM 1-Year Treasury Bill Index	.005 index points ($25)	.25-point intervals

Stock Index Options on Futures

Contract	Trading Unit	Price Quote	Tick Size	Strike Price
• Goldman-Sachs Commodity Index	1 Goldman-Sachs Commodity Index	index points	.10 index point ($25)	1-point intervals
• IPC Stock Index	1 IPC futures contract	index points	1 index point ($25)	50-points intervals for 2 nearest contracts, 100 points for deferreds
• Major Market Index	1 Major Market Index futures contract	index points	.05 index point ($25)	5-point intervals
• Nasdaq 100 Index	1 futures contract	index points	.05 index point ($5)	10-point intervals
• Nikkei 225 Stock Average	1 Nikkei Stock Average futures contract	index points	5 index points ($25)	500-point intervals
• Quarterly Bankruptcy Index	1 futures contract	index points	.025 index point ($10)	2.5 point intervals
• Russell 2000 Stock Price Index	1 Russell 2000 Stock Price	index points	.05 index point ($25)	2.5 point intervals for 2 nearest months; 5 points for deferreds

Last Trading Day	Contract Months	Trading Hours (CST)	Ticker Symbol
2nd London bank business day before 3rd Wednesday of contract month	All months	7:20 A.M.–2:00 P.M. Globex: M-F, 2:45 P.M.–7:05 A.M.; Sun., 5:30 P.M.–7:05 A.M.	EM
Call CME	Mar, June, Sept, Dec and serial months	7:20 A.M.–2:00 P.M. Globex: 2:45 P.M.–7:05 A.M.	CQ (call) PQ (put)
Call CME	Mar, June, Sept, Dec and serial months	7:20 A.M.–2:00 P.M. Globex: 2:45 P.M.–7:05 A.M.	YR (call) YR (put)

Last Trading Day	Contract Months	Trading Hours (CST)	Ticker Symbol
Call CME	All months	8:15 A.M.–2:15 P.M.	GI (call) GI (put)
3rd Friday of contract month	All months	8:30 A.M.–3:15 P.M. Globex: 3:45 P.M.–8:15 A.M.	MX (call) MX (put)
3rd Friday of contract month	All months	8:30 A.M.–3:15 P.M. Globex: 3:45 P.M.–8:15 A.M.	BC (call) BC (put)
Mar, June, Sept, Dec: same date as futures contract; other 8 months: 3rd Friday of contract month	All months	8:30 A.M.–3:15 P.M. Globex: 3:45 P.M.–8:15 A.M.	ND (call) ND (put)
Mar, June, Sept, Dec: same date as futures contract; other 8 months: 3rd Friday of contract month	All months	8:30 A.M.–3:15 P.M. Globex: 3:45 P.M.–8:15 A.M.	KN (call) JN (put)
Business day prior to final settlement day (2 bank business days prior to 15th of month following contract month)	Mar, June Sept, Dec	7:20 A.M.–2:00 P.M. Globex: 2:10 P.M.–7:05 A.M.	QB (call) QB (put)
Mar, June, Sept, Dec: same date as futures contract; other 8 months: 3rd Friday of contract month	All months	8:30 A.M.–3:15 P.M. Globex: 3:45 P.M.–8:15 A.M.	RL (call) RL (put)

Contract	Trading Unit	Price Quote	Tick Size	Strike Price
● S&P 500 Stock Index	1 S&P 500 futures contract	index points	.10 index point ($25)	5-point intervals for 2 nearest contracts; 10 points for defereds
● E-Mini S&P Stock Price Index	1 E-Mini S&P futures contract	index points	.25 index point ($12.50)	5-point intervals for 2 nearest contracts; 10 points for deferreds
● S&P MidCap 400 Stock Index	1 S&P Mid-Cap 400 futures contract	index points	.05 index point ($25)	2.5-point intervals for 2 nearest contracts; 5 points for deferrreds
● S&P 500/ BARRA Growth Index	1 S&P 500/ BARRA Growth Index	index points	.10 index point	2.5-point intervals for 2 nearest contracts; 5 points for deferreds
● S&P 500/ BARRA Value Index	1 S&P 500/ BARRA Value Index	index points	.10 index point	2.5-point intervals for 2 nearest contracts; 5 points for deferreds

Coffee, Sugar and Cocoa Exchange (CSCE)

Futures

Contract	Trading Unit	Price Quote	Tick Size
● Basic Formula Price (BFP) Milk	1,000 times the BFP (100,000 pounds of milk)	dollars and cents per hundredweight	1 cent per hundredweight ($10)
● Butter	10,000 pounds	cents per pound	10/100 of a cent per pound ($10)
● Cheddar Cheese	10,500 pounds	cents per pound	10/100 of a cent per pound ($10.50)
● Cocoa	10 metric tons	dollars per metric ton ($10)	1 dollar per metric ton

Last Trading Day	Contract Months	Trading Hours (CST)	Ticker Symbol
Mar, June, Sept, Dec: same date as futures contract; other 8 months: 3rd Friday of contract month	All months	8:30 A.M.–3:15 P.M. Globex: 3:45 P.M.–8:15 A.M.	CS (call) PS (put)
Mar, June, Sept, Dec: same date as futures contract; other 8 months: 3rd Friday of contract month	All months	24-hour trading except: M-Th, 3:15 P.M.–3:30 P.M.; Fri-Sun, 3:15 P.M.– 5:30 P.M.	ES (call) ES (put)
Mar, June, Sept, Dec: same date as futures contract; other 8 months: 3rd Friday of contract month	All months	8:30 A.M.–3:15 P.M. Globex: 3:45 P.M.–8:15 A.M.	MD (call) MD (put)
Mar, June, Sept, Dec: same date as futures contract; other 8 months: 3rd Friday of contract month	All months	8:30 A.M.–3:15 P.M. Globex: 3:45 P.M.–8:15 A.M.	SG (call) SG (put)
Mar, June, Sept, Dec: same date as futures contract; other 8 months: 3rd Friday of contract month	All months	8:30 A.M.–3:15 P.M. Globex: 3:45 P.M.–8:15 A.M.	SU (call) SU (put)

Daily Price Limit	Contract Months	Trading Hours (CST)	Ticker Symbol
50 cents	All months in 13-month calendar cycle (for delivery)	9:00 A.M.–2:00 P.M.	MJ
6 cents	Current calendar month, next 2 months and each Feb, Apr, June, Aug, Oct, Dec in ensuing 12 months (for delivery)	9:00 A.M.–2:00 P.M.	BW
6 cents	Current calendar month, next 2 months and each Feb, Apr, June, Aug, Oct, Dec in ensuing 12 months (for delivery)	9:00 A.M.–2:00 P.M.	EZ
88 dollars per metric ton	Mar, May, July, Sept, Dec	9:00 A.M.–2:00 P.M.	CC

Contract	Trading Unit	Price Quote	Tick Size
● Coffee "C"	37,500 pounds	cents per pound	5/100 of a cent per pound ($18.75)
● Milk	1 tank load (50,000 pounds)	dollars and cents per hundredweight	1 cent per hundredweight ($5)
● Nonfat Dry Milk	11,000 pounds	cents per pound	10/100 of a cent per pound ($11)
● Sugar No. 11 (World)	112,000 pounds	cents per pound	1/100 of a cent per pound ($11.20)
● Sugar No. 14	112,000 pounds	cents per pound	1/100 of a cent per pound ($11.20)
● White Sugar	50 metric tons	dollars per metric ton	20 cents per metric ton ($10)

Options on Futures

Contract	Trading Unit	Tick Size	Daily Price Limit	Strike Price
● Basic Formula Price (BFP) Milk	1 CSCE BFP milk futures contract	1 cent per hundredweight	None	$.25 to $.50
● Butter	1 butter futures contract	1/100 of a cent per pound ($1)	None	$.025 to $.10
● Cheddar Cheese	1 cheddar cheese futures contract	1/100 of a cent per pound	None	$0.25 to $.10
● Cocoa	1 cocoa futures contract	1 dollar per metric ton ($10)	None	$50 to $200

Daily Price Limit	Contract Months	Trading Hours (CST)	Ticker Symbol
6 cents	Mar, May, July, Sept, Dec	9:15 A.M.–1:32 P.M.	KC
50 cents	Current calendar month, next 2 months and each Feb, Apr, June, Aug, Oct, Dec in ensuing 12 months (for delivery)	9:00 A.M.–2:00 P.M.	MI
6 cents	Current calendar month, next 2 months and each Feb, Apr, June, Aug, Oct, Dec in ensuing 12 months (for delivery)	9:00 A.M.–2:00 P.M.	MU
1/2 of a cent	Mar, May, July, Oct	9:30 A.M.–1:20 P.M.	SB
1/2 of a cent	Jan, Mar, May, July, Sept, Nov	9:00 A.M.–1:18 P.M.	SE
10 dollars per metric ton	Mar, May, July, Oct, Dec	9:15 A.M.–1:20 P.M.	WS

Expiration Day	Last Trading Day	Contract Months	Trading Hours (EST)	Ticker Symbol
Last trading day at 9:00 P.M.	CSCE business day prior to day USDA announces BFP	All months in 13-month cycle	9:00 A.M. until completion of closing period, beginning at 2:00 P.M.	MJ
Last trading day at 9:00 P.M.	1st Friday of contract month	Current calendar month, next 2 months and each Feb, Apr, June, Aug, Oct, Dec in ensuing 12 months (for delivery)	9:00 A.M. until completion of closing period, beginning at 2:00 P.M.	BW
Last trading day at 9:00 P.M.	1st Friday of contract month	Current calendar month, next 2 months and each Feb, Apr, June, Aug, Oct, Dec in ensuing 12 months (for delivery)	9:00 A.M. until completion of closing period, beginning at 2:00 P.M.	EZ
Last trading day at 9:00 P.M.	1st Friday of month before contract month	Regular Options: Mar, May, July, Sept, Dec Serial Options: Jan, Feb, Apr, June, Aug, Oct, Nov	9:00 A.M. until completion of closing period, beginning at 2:00 P.M.	CC

Contract	Trading Unit	Tick Size	Daily Price Limit	Strike Price
• Coffee "C"	1 coffee "C" futures contract	1/100 of a cent per pound ($3.75)	None	$.025 to $.10
• Milk	1 CSCE milk futures contract	1 cent per hundredweight	None	$.025 to $1
• Nonfat Dry Milk	1 nonfat dry milk futures contract	1/100 of a cent per pound ($1.10)	None	$.025 to $.10
• Sugar No. 11	1 sugar no. 11 futures contract	1/100 of a cent per pound ($11.20)	None	$.005 to $.02

New York Mercantile Exchange (COMEX division)

Futures

Contract	Trading Unit	Price Quote	Tick Size	Daily Price Limit
• Copper	25,000 pounds	cents per pound	$.0005 cent per pound ($12.50)	20 cents per pound
• Gold	100 troy ounces	dollars per troy ounce	$.10 cent per troy ounce ($10)	$75 per troy ounce
• Silver	5,000 troy ounces	cents per troy ounce	$.005 cent per troy ounce ($5)	$.50 per troy ounce
• FTSE Eurotop 100 Index	$100 × index value	hundreds of dollars per index point	.1 index point ($10)	none

Expiration Day	Last Trading Day	Contract Months	Trading Hours (EST)	Ticker Symbol
Last trading day at 9:00 P.M.	1st Friday of month before contract month	Regular Options: Mar, May, July, Sept, Dec Serial Options: Jan, Feb, Apr, June, Aug, Oct, Nov	9:15 A.M. until completion of closing period, beginning at 2:00 P.M.	KC
Last trading day at 9:00 P.M.	1st Friday of contract month	Current calendar month, next 2 months and each Feb, Apr, June, Aug, Oct, Dec in ensuing 12 months (for delivery)	9:00 A.M. until completion of closing period, at 2:00 P.M.	MI
Last trading day at 9:00 P.M.	1st Friday of contract month	Current calendar month, next 2 months and each Feb, Apr, June, Aug, Oct, Dec in ensuing 12 months (for delivery)	9:00 A.M. until completion of closing period, at 2:00 P.M.	MU
Last trading day at 9:00 P.M.	2nd Friday of month before contract month	Regular Options: Mar, May, July, Oct, plus Jan option on Mar futures; Serial Options: Feb, Apr, June, Aug, Sept, Nov, Dec	10:00 A.M.– 1:50 P.M.	SB

Last Trading Day	Contract Months	Trading Hours (EST)	Ticker Symbol
3rd to last business day of contract month	Mar, May, July, Sept, Dec	8:10 A.M.–2:35 P.M. ACCESS: M–Th, 4:00 P.M.–8:00 A.M.; Sun, 7:00 P.M.	HG
3rd to last business day of contract month	Feb, Apr, June, Aug, Oct	8:20 A.M.–2:30 P.M. ACCESS: M–Th, 4:00 P.M.–8:00 A.M.; Sun, 7:00 P.M.	GC
3rd to last day of contract month	Mar, May, July, Sept, Dec	8:25 A.M.–2:25 P.M. ACCESS: M–Th, 4:00 P.M.–8:00 A.M.; Sun, 7:00 P.M.	SI
3rd Friday of delivery month until 7:00 A.M. (EST)	Mar, June, Sept, Dec	5:30 A.M.–11:30 A.M.	ER

Metals Options on Futures

Contract	Trading Unit	Price Quote	Tick Size	Strike Price
● Copper	1 futures contract	cents per pound	.0005 cent per pound	1 to 5 cent intervals
● Gold	1 futures contract	dollars per troy ounce	10 cents per troy ounce	$10 to $50 intervals
● Silver	1 futures contract	cents per troy ounce	½ cent per troy ounce	25 cent to $1 intervals
● FTSE Eurotop 100 Index	1 futures contract	dollars and cents	.05 index point ($5)	10 index point intervals

New York Mercantile Exchange (NYMEX Division)

Energy Futures

Contract	Trading Unit	Price Quote	Tick Size
● Alberta Natural Gas	10,000 million British thermal units (MMBtu)	dollars and cents per MMBtu	$1.50 per MMBtu ($15,000)
● California/Oregon Border (COB) Electricity	736 megawatt hours (MWh)	dollars and cents per MWh	1 cent per MWh ($7.36)
● Gulf Coast Unleaded Gasoline	42,000 gallons	dollars and cents per gallon	.01 cent per gallon ($4.20)
● Heating Oil	42,000 gallons	cents per gallon	.01 cent per gallon ($4.20)
● Henry Hub Natural Gas	10,000 million MMBtu	dollars and cents per MMBtu	.1 cent per MMBtu ($10)
● Light, Sweet Crude Oil	1,000 barrels	dollars and cents per barrel	1 cent per barrel ($10)

Last Trading Day	Contract Months	Trading Hours (EST)	Ticker Symbol
4th to last business day of month before futures delivery month	Mar, May, July, Sept, Dec	8:10 A.M.–2:35 P.M.	HX
2nd Friday of month before futures contract delivery month	Feb, Apr, June, Aug, Oct, Dec	8:20 A.M.–2:30 P.M.	OG
2nd Friday of month before futures contract delivery month	Mar, May, July, Sept, Dec	8:25 A.M.–2:25 P.M.	SO
Mar, June, Sept and Dec: 3rd Friday of delivery month until 7:00 A.M. (EST); all other months: Thursday before 3rd Friday	Nearest 2 futures months and next 2 nearest non-regular trading months	5:30 A.M.–11:30 A.M.	EQ

Last Trading Day	Contract Months	Trading Hours (EST)	Ticker Symbol
3rd business day before 1st day of delivery month	18 consecutive months	10:00 A.M.–3:10 P.M. ACCESS: M–Th, 4:00–7:00 P.M.	NC
4th business day before 1st day of delivery month	18 consecutive months	10:30 A.M.–3:30 P.M. ACCESS: M–Th, 4:15–7:15 P.M.	MW
Last business day of month before delivery month	18 consecutive months	9:40 A.M.–3:10 P.M.	GU
Last business day of month before delivery month	18 consecutive months	9:50 A.M.–3:10 P.M. ACCESS: M–Th, 4:00 P.M.–8:00 A.M.; Sun., 7 P.M.–8 A.M.	HO
3 business days prior to 1st day of delivery month	36 consecutive months	10 A.M.–3:10 P.M. ACCESS: M–Th 4:00 P.M.–7:00 P.M.	NG
3rd business day before 25th day of month preceding delivery month	18 consecutive months + long-dated futures out to 36 months	9:45 A.M.–3:10 P.M. ACCESS: M–Th, 4:00 P.M.–8:00 A.M.; Sun, 7:00 P.M.–8:00 A.M.	CL

Contract	Trading Unit	Price Quote	Tick Size
• New York Harbor Unleaded Gasoline	42,000 gallons	dollars and cents per gallon	.01 cent per gallon ($4.20)
• Palo Verde Electricity	736 megawatt hours	dollars and cents per MWh	1 cent per MWh ($7.36)
• Permian Basin Natural Gas	10,000 MMBtu	dollars and cents per MMBtu	.1 cent per MMBtu ($10)
• Propane	42,000 gallons	dollars and cents per gallon	.01 cent per gallon ($4.20)
• Sour Crude Oil	1,000 barrels	dollars and cents per barrel	1 cent per barrel ($10/contract)

Metals Futures

Contract	Trading Unit	Price Quote	Tick Size	Daily Price Limit
• Palladium	100 troy ounces	dollars and cents per troy ounce	5 cent per troy ounce ($5)	$6 per troy ounce ($600)
• Platinum	50 troy ounces	dollars and cents per troy ounce	10 cent per troy ounce ($5)	$25 per troy ounce ($1,250)

Energy Options on Futures

Contract	Trading Unit	Price Quote	Tick Size	Strike Price
• Alberta Natural Gas	1 futures contract	dollars and cents per MMBtu	.1 cent per MMBtu ($10)	2 cent intervals
• California/ Oregon Border (COB) Electricity	1 futures contract	dollars and cents per MWh	1 cent per MWh ($7.36)	½-cent intervals
• Heating Oil	1 futures contract	cents per gallon	.01 cent ($4.20)	1-cent and 2-cent intervals

Last Trading Day	Contract Months	Trading Hours (EST)	Ticker Symbol
Last business day of month preceding delivery month	18 consecutive months	9:50 A.M.–3:10 P.M. ACCESS: M–Th, 4:00 P.M.–8:00 A.M.; Sun., 7:00 P.M.–8:00 A.M.	HU
4th business day before 1st day of delivery month	18 consecutive months	10:30 A.M.–3:25 P.M. ACCESS: M–Th, 4:15 P.M.–7:15 P.M.	KV
3rd business day before 1st day of delivery month	18 consecutive months	10:10 A.M.–3:10 P.M. ACCESS: M–Th, 4:00 P.M.–7:00 P.M.	NP
Last business day of month preceding delivery month	15 consecutive months	9:55 A.M.–3:00 P.M. ACCESS: M–Th, 5:00 P.M.–7:00 P.M.	PN
3rd business day before 25th day of preceding delivery month	18 consecutive months	9:35 A.M.–3:20 P.M.	SC

Last Trading Day	Contract Months	Trading Hours (EST)	Ticker Symbol
4th business day before end of delivery month	Mar, June, Sept, Dec	8:10 A.M.–2:20 P.M.	PA
2nd Friday of month before end of delivery month	Jan, Apr, July, Oct	8:20 A.M.–2:30 P.M. ACCESS: M–Th, 4:00 P.M.–8:00 A.M.; Sun., 7:00 P.M.–8:00 A.M.	PL

Last Trading Day	Contract Months	Trading Hours (EST)	Ticker Symbol
Close of business on business day immediately before futures contract expiration	12 consecutive months	10:00 A.M.–3:10 P.M. ACCESS: M–Th, 4:00 P.M.–7:00 P.M.	OC
Day before expiration of underlying futures contract	12 consecutive months	10:30 A.M.–3:30 P.M. ACCESS: M–Th, 4:15 P.M.–7:15 P.M.	WO
Close of business on business day immediately before futures contract expiration	12 consecutive months	10:00 A.M.–3:10 P.M. ACCESS: M–Th, 4:00 P.M.–7:00 P.M.	ON

Contract	Trading Unit	Price Quote	Tick Size	Strike Price
• Henry Hub Natural Gas	1 futures contract	dollars and cents per MMBtu	0.1 cent per MMBtu ($10)	5 cent intervals
• Light, Sweet Crude Oil	1 futures contract	dollars and cents per barrel	1 cent per per barrel ($10)	50 cent, $1, $5 intervals
• New York Harbor Unleaded Gasoline	1 futures contract	dollars and cents per gallon	.01 cent per gallon	1 cent and 2 cent intervals
• Palo Verde Electricity	1 futures contract	dollars and cents per MWh	1 cent per MWh ($7.36)	½ cent intervals
• Permian Basin Natural Gas	1 futures contract	dollars and cents per MMBtu	.1 cent per MMBtu ($10)	5 cent intervals

Energy Crack Spread Options

Contract	Trading Unit	Price Quote	Tick Size	Strike Price
• Heating Oil/ Crude Oil	1:1 option on price differential between heating oil and crude oil futures	dollars and cents per barrel	1 cent per barrel ($10)	25 cent intervals
• New York Harbor Unleaded Gasoline/ Crude Oil	1:1 option on price differential between New York Harbor unleaded gasoline and crude oil futures	dollars and cents per barrel	1 cent per barrel ($10)	25 cent intervals

Crack Spread Options on Futures

Expiration Day	Contract Months	Trading Hours (EST)	Ticker Symbol
• Day immediately before crude oil futures expiration	6 months plus 2 quarterly months on Mar, June, Sept, Dec cycle	9:50 A.M.–3:10 P.M.	CH

Last Trading Day	Contract Months	Trading Hours (EST)	Ticker Symbol
Close of business on business day immediately before futures contract expiration	12 consecutive months	10:00 A.M.–3:10 P.M. ACCESS: M–Th, 4:00 P.M.–7:00 P.M.	HH
3 business days before underlying futures contract	12 consecutive months + 3 long-dated options at 18, 24, 36 months	9:45 A.M.–3:10 P.M. ACCESS: M–Th, 4:00 P.M.–8:00 A.M.; Sun., 7:00 P.M.–8:00 A.M.	LO
3 business days before underlying futures contract	12 consecutive months	9:50 A.M.–3:10 P.M. ACCESS: M–Th, 4:00 P.M.–8:00 A.M.; Sun., 7:00 P.M.–8:00 A.M.	GO
Day before expiration of underlying futures contract	12 consecutive months	10:30 A.M.–3:25 P.M. ACCESS: M–Th, 4:15 P.M.–7:15 P.M.	VO
Close of business on business day immediately before futures contract expiration	12 consecutive months	10:10 A.M.–3:10 P.M. ACCESS: M–Th, 4:00 P.M.–7:00 P.M.	OP

Expiration Day	Contract Months	Trading Hours (EST)	Ticker Symbol
• Day immediately before crude oil futures expiration	6 months plus 2 quarterly months on Mar, June, Sept, Dec cycle	9:50 A.M.–3:10 P.M.	CG

Metal Options on Futures

Contract	Trading Unit	Price Quote	Tick Size	Strike Price
• Platinum	1 futures contract	dollars and cents per troy ounce	10 cents per troy ounce	$10 intervals

Kansas City Board of Trade (KCBT)

Commodity Futures

Contract	Trading Unit	Price Quote	Tick Size
• Hard Red Winter Wheat	5,000 bushels	dollars, cents and 1/4 cent per bushel	1/4 cent per bushel ($12.50)
• Western Natural Gas	10,000 MMBtu	dollars and cents per MMBtu	$0.001 per MMBtu ($10)

Index Futures

Contract	Underlying Cash Index	Trading Unit	Price Quote	Tick Size
• Value Line Stock Index	Value Line Arithmetic	$250 × futures price	index points	$.05 ($12.50)
• Mini Value Line Stock Index	Value Line Arithmetic	$100 × futures price	index points	$.05 ($5)

Commodity Options on Futures

Contract	Trading Unit	Price Quote	Tick Size
• Hard Red Winter Wheat	1 futures contract	dollars, cents and 1/8 cent per bushel	1/8 cent per bushel ($6.25)

Last Trading Day	Contract Months	Trading Hours (EST)	Ticker Symbol
2nd Friday of month before delivery month of options contract	Nearest 3 contract months + two quarterly months of Jan, April, July, Oct quarterly cycle	8:20 A.M.–2:30 P.M. ACCESS: M–Th, 4:00 P.M.–8:00 A.M.; Sun., 7:00 P.M.–8:00 A.M.	PO

Last Trading Day	Contract Months	Trading Hours (CST)	Ticker Symbol
8th day before end of month	July, Sept, Dec, Mar, May	9:30 A.M.–1:15 P.M.	KW
2nd business day before 1st day of delivery month	36 consecutive months	8:50 A.M.–2:30 P.M.	KG

Last Trading Day	Contract Months	Trading Hours (CST)	Ticker Symbol
3rd Friday of month	Mar, June, Sept, Dec	8:30 A.M.–3:15 P.M.	KV
3rd Friday of month	Mar, June, Sept, Dec	8:30 A.M.–3:15 P.M.	MV

Strike Prices	Last Trading Day	Contract Months	Trading Hours (CST)	Ticker Symbol
10 cent intervals	Friday at least 5 trading days before first notice day for futures	July, Sept, Dec, Mar, May	9:30 A.M.–1:20 P.M.	WC (call) WP (put)

Contract	Trading Unit	Price Quote	Tick Size
• Western Natural Gas	1 futures contract	dollars and cents per MMBtu	$0.001 per MMBtu

Index Options on Futures

Contract	Trading Unit	Price Quote	Tick Size
• Mini Value Line Index	1 futures contract	index points	$.05 ($5)

MidAmerica Commodity Exchange (MIDAM)
[An Affiliate of the Chicago Board of Trade]

Agricultural Futures

Contract	Trading Unit	Price Quote	Tick Size
• Corn	1,000 bushels	cents per bushel	⅛ cent per bushel ($1.25/contract)
• Oats	1,000 bushels	cents per bushel	⅛ cent per bushel ($1.25/contract)
• Soybeans	1,000 bushels	cents per bushel	⅛ cent per bushel ($1.25/contract)
• Soybean Meal	50 tons	cents per ton	10 cents per ton ($5/contract)
• Soybean Oil	30,000 pounds	cents per pound	¹⁄₁₀₀ cent per pound ($3/contract)
• Wheat	1,000 bushels	cents per bushel	⅛ cent per bushel ($1.25/contract)

Currency Futures

Contract	Trading Unit	Price Quote	Tick Size
• Australian Dollars	50,000 Australian dollars	U.S. dollars per Australian dollar	$.0001 ($5)
• British Pound	12,500 British pounds	U.S. dollars per British pound	$.0002 ($2.50)

Strike Prices	Last Trading Day	Contract Months	Trading Hours (CST)	Ticker Symbol
5-cent intervals	Business day before last trading day in underlying futures contract month	36 consecutive months	8:50 A.M.– 2:35 P.M.	KGC (call) KGP (put)

Strike Prices	Last Trading Day	Contract Months	Trading Hours (CST)	Ticker Symbol
5 points	3rd Friday of contract	2 nearest serial months and 3 nearest quarterly months	8:30 A.M– 3:15 P.M.	MVC (call) MVP (put)

Daily Price Limit	Contract Months	Trading Hours (CST)	Ticker Symbol
12 cents per bushel ($120/contract)	Mar, May, July, Sept, Dec	9:30 A.M.–1:45 P.M.	XC
10 cents per bushel ($100/contract)	Mar, May, July, Sept, Dec	9:30 A.M.–1:45 P.M.	XO
30 cents per bushel ($300/contract)	Jan, Mar, May, July, Aug, Sept, Nov	9:30 A.M.–1:45 P.M.	XS
$10 per ton ($500/contract)	Jan, Mar, May, July, Aug, Sept, Oct, Dec	9:30 A.M.–1:45 P.M.	XE
$0.01 per pound ($300/contract)	Jan, Mar, May, July, Aug, Sept, Oct, Dec	9:30 A.M.–1:45 P.M.	XR
20 cents per bushel ($200/contract)	Mar, May, July, Sept, Dec	9:30 A.M.–1:45 P.M.	XW

Last Trading Day	Contract Months	Trading Hours (CST)	Ticker Symbol
2nd business day before 3rd Wednesday of contract month	Mar, June, Sept, Dec	7:20 A.M.–2:15 P.M.	XA
2nd business day before 3rd Wednesday of contract month	Mar, June, Sept, Dec	7:20 A.M.–2:15 P.M.	XP

Contract	Trading Unit	Price Quote	Tick Size
● Canadian Dollar	50,000 Canadian dollars	U.S. dollars per Canadian dollars	$.0001 ($5)
● Deutsche Mark	62,500 Deutsche marks	U.S. dollars per Deutsche mark	$.0001 ($6.25)
● Japanese Yen	6,250,000 yen	U.S. dollars per yen	$.000001 ($6.25)
● Swiss Franc	62,500 Swiss francs	U.S. dollars per Swiss franc	$.0001 ($6.25)

Financial Futures

Contract	Trading Unit	Price Quote	Tick Size
● Eurodollar	$500,000	100 minus 3-month Eurodollar rate	1 basis point ($12.50)
● Treasury Note (5-year)	$50,000 face value	points and ½ of $\frac{1}{32}$ point par=100	½ of $\frac{1}{32}$ point ($7.81)
● Treasury Note (10-year)	$50,000 face value	points and ½ of $\frac{1}{32}$ point par=100	$\frac{1}{32}$ point ($16.62)
● U.S. Treasury Bill	$500,000 face value	100 minus T-bill yield	1 basis point ($12.50)
● U.S. Treasury Bonds	$50,000 face value	points and $\frac{1}{32}$ point	$\frac{1}{32}$ point ($15.62)

Livestock Futures

Contract	Trading Unit	Price Quote	Tick Size
● Live Cattle	20,000 pounds	cents per pound	$.00025 per pound ($5/contract)
● Lean Hogs	15,000 pounds	cents per pound	$.00025 per pound ($5/contract)

Last Trading Day	Contract Months	Trading Hours (CST)	Ticker Symbol
Business day before 3rd Wednesday of contract month	Mar, June, Sept, Dec	7:20 A.M.–2:15 P.M.	XD
2nd business day before 3rd Wednesday of contract month	Mar, June, Sept, Dec	7:20 A.M.–2:15 P.M.	XM
2nd business day before 3rd Wednesday of contract month	Mar, June, Sept, Dec	7:20 A.M.–2:15 P.M.	XJ
2nd business day before 3rd Wednesday of contract month	Mar, June, Sept, Dec	7:20 A.M.–2:15 P.M.	XF

Last Trading Day	Contract Months	Trading Hours (CST)	Ticker Symbol
3rd business day before 3rd Wednesday of contract month	Mar, June, Sept, Dec	7:20 A.M.–2:15 P.M.	UD
8th to last business day of contract month	Mar, June, Sept, Dec	7:20 A.M.–3:15 P.M.	XV
8th to last business day of contract month	Mar, June, Sept, Dec	7:20 A.M.–3:15 P.M.	XN
2nd business day before 3rd Wednesday of contract month	Mar, June, Sept, Dec	7:20 A.M.–3:15 P.M.	XB
8th to last business day of contract	Mar, June, Sept, Dec	7:20 A.M.–2:15 P.M.	XT

Daily Price Limit	Contract Months	Trading Hours (CST)	Ticker Symbol
$.015 per pound ($300/contract)	Feb, Apr, Jun, Aug, Oct, Dec	9:05 A.M.–1:15 P.M.	XL
$.015 per pound ($300/contract)	Feb, Apr, June, July, Aug, Sept, Oct, Dec	9:10 A.M.–1:15 P.M.	XH

Metals Futures

Contract	Trading Unit	Price Quote	Tick Size
• New York Gold	33.2 troy ounces	dollars and cents	10 cents per troy ounce ($3.32/contract)
• New York Silver	1,000 troy ounces	cents per troy ounce	$\frac{10}{100}$ cent per troy ounce ($1/ contract)
• Platinum	25 troy ounces	cents per troy ounce	10 cents per troy ounce ($2.50/contract)

Agricultural Options on Futures

Contract	Trading Unit	Price Quote	Tick Size
• Corn	1 futures contract	cents per bushel	$\frac{1}{8}$ cent per bushel ($1.25)
• Soybeans	1 futures contract	cents per bushel	$\frac{1}{8}$ cent per bushel ($1.25)
• Soybean Oil	1 futures contract	cents per pound	$\frac{1}{100}$ cent per bushel ($3)
• Wheat	1 futures contract	cents per bushel	$\frac{1}{8}$ cent per bushel ($1.25)

Financial Options on Futures

Contract	Trading Unit	Price Quote	Tick Size
• U.S. Treasury Bond	1 futures contract	points and $\frac{1}{64}$ point	$\frac{1}{64}$ point ($7.81)

Daily Price Limit	Contract Months	Trading Hours (CST)	Ticker Symbol
None	All months	7:20 A.M.–1:40 P.M.	XK
None	All months	7:25 A.M.–1:40 P.M.	XY
$25 per troy ounce	Jan, Apr, July, Aug	7:20 A.M.–1:40 P.M.	XU

Expiration Day	Last Trading Day	Contract Months	Trading Hours (CST)	Ticker Symbol
Saturday after last trading day	1st Friday preceding by at least 5 business days the last business day of month preceding option month	Mar, May, July, Sept, Dec	9:30 A.M.– 1:45 P.M.	XCC (call) XCP (put)
Saturday after last trading day	1st Friday preceding by at least 5 business days the last business day of month preceding option month	Jan, Mar, May, July, Aug, Sep, Nov	9:30 A.M.– 1:45 P.M.	SC (call) SP (put)
Saturday after last trading day	1st Friday preceding by at least 5 business days the last business day of month preceding option month	Jan, Mar, May, July, Aug, Sep, Nov	9:30 A.M.– 1:45 P.M.	XRC (call) XRP (put)
Saturday after last trading day	1st Friday preceding by at least 5 business days the last business day of month preceding option month	Mar, May, July, Sept, Dec	9:30 A.M.– 1:45 P.M.	WC (call) WP (put)

Expiration Day	Last Trading Day	Contract Months	Trading Hours (CST)	Ticker Symbol
Saturday after last trading day	1st Friday preceding by at least 5 business days the last business day of month before options month	Front month of current quarter and next 3 contracts of regular quarterly cycle	7:20 A.M.– 3:15 P.M.	XBC (call) XBP (put)

Metals Options on Futures

Contract	Trading Unit	Price Quote	Tick Size
● New York Gold	1 futures contract	cents per troy ounce	10 cents per troy ounce ($3.32)

Minneapolis Grain Exchange (MGE)

Futures

Contract	Trading Unit	Price Quote	Tick Size	Daily Price Limit
● Black Tiger Shrimp	5,000 pounds	cents per pound	¼ cent per pound ($12.50)	20 cents per pound ($1,000/contract)
● Durham Wheat	5,000 bushels	cents per bushel	¼ cent per bushel ($12.50)	20 cents per bushel ($1,000/contract)
● Hard Red Spring Wheat	5,000 bushels	cents per bushel	¼ cent per bushel ($12.50)	20 cents per bushel ($1,000)
● Soft White Wheat	5,000 bushels	cents per bushel	¼ cent per bushel ($12.50)	20 cents per bushel ($1000)
● Twin Cities Electricity (On-Peak)	736 megawatt hours	megawatt hours	1 cent per megawatt hour ($7.36)	$3 per megawatt hours
● Twin Cities Electricity (Off-Peak)	736 megawatt hours	megawatt hours	1 cent per megawatt hour ($7.36)	$3 per megawatt hours
● White Shrimp	5,000 pounds	cents per pound	¼ cent per pound ($12.50)	20 cents per pound ($1000/contract)

Options on Futures

Contract	Trading Unit	Price Quote	Tick Size	Strike Prices
● Black Tiger Shrimp	1 futures contract	cents per pound	⅛ cent per pound ($6.25)	n/a

Expiration Day	Last Trading Day	Contract Months	Trading Hours (CST)	Ticker Symbol
Saturday after last trading day	1st Friday preceding by at least 5 business days the last business day of month preceding contract month	All months	7:20 A.M.–1:40 P.M.	KC (call) KP (put)

Last Trading Day	Contract Months	Trading Hours (CST)	Ticker Symbol
10th to last business day of delivery month	Mar, June, Sept, Dec	9:40 A.M.–1:30 P.M.	BT
8th business day of contract month	Mar, May, July, Sept, Dec	9:40 A.M.–1:25 P.M.	DW
8th business day of contract month	Mar, May, July, Sept, Dec	8:30 A.M.–1:15 P.M.	MW
8th business day of contract month	Mar, May, July, Sept, Dec	8:30 A.M.–1:15 P.M.	NW
6th business day before 1st delivery day	17 months + nearby month	8:30 A.M.–12:30 P.M.	BG
6th business day before 1st delivery day	17 months + nearby month	8:30 A.M.–12:30 P.M.	BS
10th to last business day of delivery month	Mar, June, Sept, Dec	9:40 A.M.–1:30 P.M.	SH

Last Trading Day	Contract Months	Trading Hours (CST)	Ticker Symbol
Last Friday 5 business days before 1st notice day	All months	9:45 A.M.–1:40 P.M.	BT (c) (call) BT (p) (put)

Contract	Trading Unit	Price Quote	Tick Size	Strike Prices
• Durham Wheat	1 futures contract	cents per hundredweight	⅛ cent per hundredweight ($6.25)	n/a
• Hard Red Spring Wheat	1 futures contract	cents per bushel	⅛ cent per bushel ($6.25)	n/a
• Soft White Wheat	1 futures contract	cents per bushel	⅛ cent per bushel ($6.25)	n/a
• Twin Cities Electricity (On-Peak)	1 futures contract	megawatt hours	1 cent per megawatt hour	50-cent intervals
• Twin Cities Electricity (Off-Peak)	1 futures contract	megawatt hours	1 cent per megawatt hour	50-cent intervals
• White Shrimp	1 futures contract	cents per pound	⅛ cent per pound ($6.25)	n/a

New York Cotton Exchange (NYCE)
[A Subsidiary of the Board of Trade of the City of New York (NYBOT)]

Futures

Contract	Trading Unit	Price Quote	Tick Size
• Cotton	50,000 pounds	cents and ¹⁄₁₀₀ of a cent per pound	¹⁄₁₀₀ of a cent per pound ($5) below 95 cents per pound; 5/100 of a cent per pound above 95 cents per pound
• Frozen Concentrated Orange Juice	15,000 pounds	cents and ¹⁄₁₀₀ of a cent per pound	⁵⁄₁₀₀ of a cent per pound ($7.50)
• Potato	85,000 pounds	dollars per hundredweight to 2 decimal points	1 cent per hundredweight ($8.50)

Last Trading Day	Contract Months	Trading Hours (CST)	Ticker Symbol
Last Friday 5 business days before 1st notice day	Mar, May, July, Sept, Dec	9:45 A.M.–1:30 P.M.	DC (call) DP (put)
Last Friday 5 business days before 1st notice day	Mar, May, July, Sept, Dec	9:35 A.M.–1:25 P.M.	WC (call) WP (put)
Last Friday 5 business days before 1st notice day	Mar, May, July, Sept, Dec	9:35 A.M.–1:25 P.M.	NC (call) NP (put)
Friday before product placement day of underlying futures contract	17 months + nearby month	8:35 A.M.–12:35 P.M.	TC (call) TP (put)
Friday before product placement day of underlying futures contract	17 months + nearby month	8:35 A.M.–12:35 P.M.	EC (call) EP (put)
Last Friday 5 business days before 1st notice day	All months	9:45 A.M.–1:40 P.M.	SH (c) (call) SH (p) (put)

Futures Daily Price Limit	Contract Months	Trading Hours (EST)	Ticker Symbol
3 cents unless contract settles at $1.10 or higher; price limit for all months is 4 cents	Mar, May, July, Oct, Dec	10:30 A.M.–2:40 P.M.	CT
5 cents ($750 per contract)	Jan, Mar, May, July, Sept, Nov	10:15 A.M.–2:15 P.M.	JO
$2	Jan, Mar, May, July, Sept, Nov	9:45 A.M.–2:00 P.M.	PT

Options on Futures

Contract	Trading Unit	Price Quote	Tick Size	Daily Price Limit	Strike Price
• Cotton	1 cotton futures contract	cents and $\frac{1}{100}$ of a cent per pound	$\frac{1}{100}$ of a cent ($5) below 95 cents per pound; $\frac{5}{100}$ of a cent at and above 95 cents	None	1-cent intervals
• Frozen Concentrated Orange Juice	1 frozen concentrated orange juice futures contract	cents and $\frac{1}{100}$ of a cent	$\frac{5}{100}$ of a cent ($7.50)	None	5-cent intervals
• Potato	1 potato futures contract	dollars per hundredweight to 2 decimals	1 cent per hundredweight ($8.50)	None	50-cent intervals

FINEX (A division of the New York Cotton Exchange)

Cross-Rate Currency Futures

Contract	Trading Unit	Price Quote	Tick Size
• British Pound/ Deutsche Mark	125,000 British pounds	Marks per pound to 4 decimal places	.0001 mark (DM12.50/contract)
• British Pound/ Japanese Yen	125,000 British pounds	Yen per pound to 2 decimal places	.01 yen (¥1,250/contract)
• British Pound/ Swiss Franc	125,000 British pounds	Swiss francs per pound to 4 decimal places	.0001 Swiss franc (SF12.50/contract)

Expiration Day	Last Trading Day	Contract Months	Trading Hours (EST)	Ticker Symbol
Last trading day	Last Friday before 1st notice for underlying future by at least 5 business days	Mar, May, July, Oct, Dec	10:30 A.M.–2:40 P.M.	CO
Last trading day	3rd Friday of month before option month	Jan, Mar, May, July, Sept, Nov	10:15 A.M.–2:15 P.M.	OJ
Last trading day	2nd Friday of month before option month	Jan, Mar, May, July, Sept, Nov plus nearest calendar month that is not a futures month	9:45 A.M.–2:00 P.M.	PT

Last Trading Day	Settlement/ Delivery	Contract Months	Trading Hours	Ticker Symbol
2 business days before 3rd Wednesday of expiring month at 10:16 A.M. (EST), 3:16 P.M. (GMT)	Physical delivery 3rd Wednesday of expiring month	Mar, June, Sept, Dec	U.S. (EST): 7:00 P.M.–10:00 P.M. 9:05 A.M.–3:00 P.M.; Europe (GMT): 12:00 A.M.–3:00 A.M. 2:05 P.M.–8:00 P.M.; Dublin trading floor: 3:00 A.M.–9:00 P.M. (EST) 8:00 A.M.–2:00 P.M. (GMT)	MP
2 business days before 3rd Wednesday of expiring month at 10:16 A.M. (EST), 3:16 P.M. (GMT)	Physical delivery 3rd Wednesday of expiring month	Mar, June, Sept, Dec	U.S. (EST): 7:00 P.M.–10:00 P.M. 9:05 A.M.–3:00 P.M.; Europe (GMT): 12:00 A.M.–3:00 A.M. 2:05 P.M.–8:00 P.M.; Dublin trading floor: 3:00 A.M.–9:00 P.M. (EST) 8:00 A.M.–2:00 P.M. (GMT)	SY
2 business days before 3rd Wednesday of expiring month at 10:16 A.M. (EST), 3:16 P.M. (GMT)	Physical delivery 3rd Wednesday of expiring month	Mar, June, Sept, Dec	U.S. (EST): 7:00 P.M.–10:00 P.M. 9:05 A.M.–3:00 P.M.; Europe (GMT): 12:00 A.M.–3:00 A.M. 2:05 P.M.–8:00 P.M.; Dublin trading floor: 3:00 A.M.–9:00 P.M. (EST) 8:00 A.M.–2:00 P.M. (GMT)	SS

Contract	Trading Unit	Price Quote	Tick Size
● Deutsche Mark/ French Franc	500,000 Deutsche marks	French francs per mark to 4 decimal places	.0001 franc (FF50/contract)
● Deutsche Mark/ Italian Lira	250,000 Deutsche marks	Lira per mark to 2 decimal places	.05 lira (ITL12,500/contract)
● Deutsche Mark/ Japanese Yen	125,000 Deutsche marks	Yen per mark to 2 decimal places	.01 yen (¥1,250/ contract)
● Deutsche Mark/ Spanish Peseta	250,000 Deutsche marks	Pesetas per mark to 2 decimal places	.01 pesetas (2,500 ptas/contract)
● Deutsche Mark/ Swedish Krona	125,000 Deutsche marks	Krona per mark to 4 decimal places	.0005 krona (SEK62.50/contract)
● Deutsche Mark/ Swiss Franc	125,000 Deutsche marks	Swiss francs per mark to 4 decimal places	.0001 Swiss francs (SF12.50/contract)

Last Trading Day	Settlement/ Delivery	Contract Month	Trading Hours	Ticker Symbol
2 business days before 3rd Wednesday of expiring month at 10:16 A.M. (EST), 3:16 P.M. (GMT)	Physical delivery 3rd Wednesday of expiring month	Mar, June, Sept, Dec	U.S. (EST): 7:00 P.M.–10:00 P.M. 9:05 A.M.–3:00 P.M.; Europe (GMT): 12:00 A.M.–3:00 A.M. 2:05 P.M.–8:00 P.M.; Dublin trading floor: 3:00 A.M.–9:00 P.M. (EST) 8:00 A.M.–2:00 P.M. (GMT)	MF
2 business days before 3rd Wednesday of expiring month at 10:16 A.M. (EST), 3:16 P.M. (GMT)	Physical delivery 3rd Wednesday of expiring month	Mar, June, Sept, Dec	U.S. (EST): 7:00 P.M.–10:00 P.M. 9:05 A.M.–3:00 P.M.; Europe (GMT): 12:00 A.M.–3:00 A.M. 2:05 P.M.–8:00 P.M.; Dublin trading floor: 3:00 A.M.–9:00 P.M. (EST) 8:00 A.M.–2:00 P.M. (GMT)	ML
2 business days before 3rd Wednesday of expiring month at 10:16 A.M. (EST), 3:16 P.M. (GMT)	Physical delivery 3rd Wednesday of expiring month	Mar, June, Sept, Dec	U.S. (EST): 7:00 P.M.–10:00 P.M. 9:05 A.M.–3:00 P.M.; Europe (GMT): 12:00 A.M.–3:00 A.M. 2:05 P.M.–8:00 P.M.; Dublin trading floor: 3:00 A.M.–9:00 P.M. (EST) 8:00 A.M.–2:00 P.M. (GMT)	MY
2 business days before 3rd Wednesday of expiring month at 10:16 A.M. (EST), 3:16 P.M. (GMT)	Physical delivery 3rd Wednesday of expiring month	Mar, June, Sept, Dec	U.S. (EST): 7:00 P.M.–10:00 P.M. 9:05 A.M.–3:00 P.M.; Europe (GMT): 12:00 A.M.–3:00 A.M. 2:05 P.M.–8:00 P.M.; Dublin trading floor: 3:00 A.M.–9:00 P.M. (EST) 8:00 A.M.–2:00 P.M. (GMT)	MT
2 business days before 3rd Wednesday of expiring month at 10:16 A.M. (EST), 3:16 P.M. (GMT)	Physical delivery 3rd Wednesday of expiring month	Mar, June, Sept, Dec	U.S. (EST): 7:00 P.M.–10:00 P.M. 9:05 A.M.–3:00 P.M.; Europe (GMT): 12:00 A.M.–3:00 A.M. 2:05 P.M.–8:00 P.M.; Dublin trading floor: 3:00 A.M.–9:00 P.M. (EST) 8:00 A.M.–2:00 P.M. (GMT)	MK
2 business days before 3rd Wednesday of expiring month at 10:16 A.M. (EST), 3:16 P.M. (GMT)	Physical delivery 3rd Wednesday of expiring month	Mar, June, Sept, Dec	U.S. (EST): 7:00 P.M.–10:00 P.M. 9:05 A.M.–3:00 P.M.; Europe (GMT): 12:00 A.M.–3:00 A.M. 2:05 P.M.–8:00 P.M.; Dublin trading floor: 3:00 A.M.–9:00 P.M. (EST) 8:00 A.M.–2:00 P.M. (GMT)	MH

Emerging Asian Currency Futures

Contract	Trading Unit	Price Quote	Tick Size
• Indonesian Rupiah/ U.S. Dollar	700,000,000 rupiah	U.S. dollars per 1,000 rupiah to 5 decimal places	$.00001 U.S. dollars ($7/contract)
• Malaysian Ringgit/ U.S. Dollar	700,000 ringgit	U.S. dollars per ringgit to 5 decimal places	$.00001 U.S. dollars ($7/contract)
• Singapore Dollar/ U.S. Dollar	350,000 Singapore dollars	U.S. dollars per Singapore dollar to 5 decimal places	$.00001 U.S. dollars ($7/contract)
• Thai Baht/ U.S. Dollar	7,000,000 baht	U.S. dollars per 100 Thai baht to 4 decimal places	$.0001 U.S. dollars ($3.50/contract)

Euro Currency Futures

Contract	Trading Unit	Price Quote	Tick Size
• Euro Currency	200,000 Euros	U.S. dollars per Euro	$.0001 U.S. dollars ($20/contract)

Last Trading Day	Settlement/ Delivery	Contract Month	Trading Hours	Ticker Symbol
2 business days before 3rd Wednesday of expiring month at 4:00 A.M. (EST), 9:00 A.M. (GMT)	Cash on last trading day	Mar, June, Sept, Dec	U.S. (EST): 7:00 P.M.–10:00 P.M. 8:05 A.M.–3:00 P.M.; Europe (GMT): 12:00 A.M.–3:00 A.M. 1:05 P.M.–8:00 P.M.; Dublin trading floor: 3:00 A.M.–8:00 P.M. (EST) 8:00 A.M.–1:00 P.M. (GMT)	RH
2 business days before 3rd Wednesday of expiring month at 4:00 A.M. (EST), 9:00 A.M. (GMT)	Cash on last trading day	Mar, June, Sept, Dec	U.S. (EST): 7:00 P.M.–10:00 P.M. 8:05 A.M.–3:00 P.M.; Europe (GMT): 12:00 A.M.–3:00 A.M. 1:05 P.M.–8:00 P.M.; Dublin trading floor: 3:00 A.M.–8:00 P.M. (EST) 8:00 A.M.–1:00 P.M. (GMT)	RM
2 business days before 3rd Wednesday of expiring month at 4:00 A.M. (EST), 9:00 A.M. (GMT)	Physical delivery 3rd Wednesday of expiring month	Mar, June, Sept, Dec	U.S. (EST): 7:00 P.M.–10:00 P.M. 8:05 A.M.–3:00 P.M.; Europe (GMT): 12:00 A.M.–3:00 A.M. 1:05 P.M.–8:00 P.M.; Dublin trading floor: 3:00 A.M.–8:00 P.M. (EST) 8:00 A.M.–1:00 P.M. (GMT)	DG
2 business days before 3rd Wednesday of expiring month at 4:00 A.M. (EST), 9:00 A.M. (GMT)	Physical delivery 3rd Wednesday of expiring month	Mar, June, Sept, Dec	U.S. (EST): 7:00 P.M.–10:00 P.M. 8:05 A.M.–3:00 P.M.; Europe (GMT): 12:00 A.M.–3:00 A.M. 1:05 P.M.–8:00 P.M.; Dublin trading floor: 3:00 A.M.–8:00 P.M. (EST) 8:00 A.M.–1:00 P.M. (GMT)	TH

Last Trading Day	Settlement/ Delivery	Contract Month	Trading Hours	Ticker Symbol
2 business days before 3rd Wednesday of expiring month at 10:16 A.M. (EST), 3:16 P.M. (GMT)	Physical delivery 3rd Wednesday of expiring month	Mar, June, Sept, Dec	U.S. (EST): 7:00 P.M.–10:00 P.M. 8:05 A.M.–3:00 P.M.; Europe (GMT): 12:00 A.M.–3:00 A.M. 1:05 P.M.–8:00 P.M.; Dublin trading floor: 3:00 A.M.–8:00 P.M. (EST) 8:00 A.M.–1:00 P.M. (GMT)	UU

Cross-Rate Currency Futures Options

Contract	Trading Unit	Price Quote	Tick Size	Strike Price
● British Pound/ Deutsche Mark	1 futures contract	Marks per pound to 4 decimal places	.0001 marks (DM50/ contract)	.005 mark intervals
● Deutsche Mark/ French Franc	1 futures contract	French francs per mark to 4 decimal places	.0001 French francs (FF50/contract)	.005 French franc intervals
● Deutsche Mark/ Italian Lira	1 futures contract	Lira per marks to 2 decimal places	.05 lira (ITL12,500/ contract)	5 lira intervals
● Deutsche Mark/ Japanese Yen	1 futures contract	Yen per marks to 2 decimal places	.01 yen (¥1,250/ contract)	.5 yen intervals
● Deutsche Mark/ Swedish Krona	1 futures contract	Krona per mark to 4 decimal places	.0005 krona (SEK62.50/ contract)	.02 krona intervals
● Deutsche Mark/ Swiss Franc	1 futures contract	Swiss francs per mark to 4 decimal places	.0001 Swiss francs (SF12.50/ contract)	SF.002 intervals

Last Trading Day	Exercise Day	Contract Months	Trading Hours	Ticker Symbol
2 Fridays before 3rd Wednesday of month	Until 10:00 A.M. (EST) 3:00 P.M. (GMT) on last trading day; automatic exercise if at least 1 tick in-the-money	Mar, June, Sept, Dec and 2 nearest months	U.S. (EST): 7:00 P.M.–10:00 P.M. 9:05 A.M.–3:00 P.M.; Europe (GMT): 12:00 A.M.–3:00 A.M. 2:05 P.M.–8:00 P.M.; Dublin trading floor: 3:00 A.M.–9:00 P.M. (EST) 8:00 A.M.–2:00 P.M. (GMT)	MP
2 Fridays before 3rd Wednesday of month	Until 10:00 A.M. (EST) 3:00 P.M. (GMT) on last trading day; automatic exercise if at least 1 tick in-the-money	Mar, June, Sept, Dec and 2 nearest months	U.S. (EST): 7:00 P.M.–10:00 P.M. 9:05 A.M.–3:00 P.M.; Europe (GMT): 12:00 A.M.–3:00 A.M. 2:05 P.M.–8:00 P.M.; Dublin trading floor: 3:00 A.M.–9:00 P.M. (EST) 8:00 A.M.–2:00 P.M. (GMT)	MF
2 Fridays before 3rd Wednesday of month	Until 10:00 A.M. (EST) 3:00 P.M. (GMT) on last trading day; automatic exercise if at least 1 tick in-the-money	Mar, June, Sept, Dec and 2 nearest months	U.S. (EST): 7:00 P.M.–10:00 P.M. 9:05 A.M.–3:00 P.M.; Europe (GMT): 12:00 A.M.–3:00 A.M. 2:05 P.M.–8:00 P.M.; Dublin trading floor: 3:00 A.M.–9:00 P.M. (EST) 8:00 A.M.–2:00 P.M. (GMT)	ML
2 Fridays before 3rd Wednesday of month	Until 10:00 A.M. (EST) 3:00 P.M. (GMT) on last trading day; automatic exercise if at least 1 tick in-the-money	Mar, June, Sept, Dec and 2 nearest months	U.S. (EST): 7:00 P.M.–10:00 P.M. 9:05 A.M.–3:00 P.M.; Europe (GMT): 12:00 A.M.–3:00 A.M. 2:05 P.M.–8:00 P.M.; Dublin trading floor: 3:00 A.M.–9:00 P.M. (EST) 8:00 A.M.–2:00 P.M. (GMT)	MY
2 Fridays before 3rd Wednesday of month	Until 10:00 A.M. (EST) 3:00 P.M. (GMT) on last trading day; automatic exercise if at least 1 tick in-the-money	Mar, June, Sept, Dec and 2 nearest months	U.S. (EST): 7:00 P.M.–10:00 P.M. 9:05 A.M.–3:00 P.M.; Europe (GMT): 12:00 A.M.–3:00 A.M. 2:05 P.M.–8:00 P.M.; Dublin trading floor: 3:00 A.M.–9:00 P.M. (EST) 8:00 A.M.–2:00 P.M. (GMT)	MK
2 Fridays before 3rd Wednesday of month	Until 10:00 A.M. (EST) 3:00 P.M. (GMT) on last trading day; automatic exercise if at least 1 tick in-the-money	Mar, June, Sept, Dec and 2 nearest months	U.S. (EST): 7:00 P.M.–10:00 P.M. 9:05:00 A.M.–3:00 P.M.; Europe (GMT): 12:00 A.M.–3:00 A.M. 2:05 P.M.–8:00 P.M.; Dublin trading floor: 3:00 A.M.–9:00 P.M. (EST) 8:00 A.M.–2:00 P.M. (GMT)	MH

U.S. Dollar Currency Paired Futures

Contract	Trading Unit	Price Quote	Tick Size
• Australian Dollar/ U.S. Dollar	$200,000 Australian dollars	U.S. dollars per Australian dollar to 4 decimal places	.001 U.S. dollars ($20/contract)
• British Pound/ U.S. Dollar	125,000 British pounds	U.S. dollars per pound to 4 decimal places	.0001 U.S. dollars ($12.50/contract)
• New Zealand Dollar/U.S. Dollar	200,000 New Zealand dollars	U.S. dollars per New Zealand dollar to 4 decimal places	.0001 U.S. dollars ($20/contract)
• U.S. Dollar/ Canadian Dollar	200,000 U.S. dollars	Canadian dollars per U.S. dollar to 4 decimal places	.0001 Canadian dollars (CD20/contract)
• U.S. Dollar/ Deutsche Mark	200,000 U.S. dollars	Marks per U.S. dollar to 4 decimal places	.0001 marks (DM20/contract)

Last Trading Day	Settlement/ Delivery	Contract Months	Trading Hours	Ticker Symbol
2 business days before 3rd Wednesday of expiring month at 4:00 A.M. (EST), 9:00 A.M. (GMT) for cash settled; 10:16 A.M. (EST), 3:16 P.M. (GMT) for all other contracts	Physical delivery on 3rd Wednesday of expiring month	Mar, June, Sept, Dec	U.S. (EST): 7:00 P.M.–10:00 P.M. 8:05 A.M.–3:00 P.M.; Europe (GMT): 12:00 A.M.–3:00 A.M. 1:05 P.M.–8:00 P.M.; Dublin trading floor: 3:00 A.M.–8:00 P.M. (EST) 8:00 A.M.–1:00 P.M. (GMT)	AU
2 business days before 3rd Wednesday of expiring month at 4:00 A.M. (EST), 9:00 A.M. (GMT) for cash settled; 10:16 A.M. (EST), 3:16 P.M. (GMT) for all other contracts	Physical delivery on 3rd Wednesday of expiring month	Mar, June, Sept, Dec	U.S. (EST): 7:00 P.M.–10:00 P.M. 8:05 A.M.–3:00 P.M.; Europe (GMT): 12:00 A.M.–3:00 A.M. 1:05 P.M.–8:00 P.M.; Dublin trading floor: 3:00 A.M.–8:00 P.M. (EST) 8:00 A.M.–1:00 P.M. (GMT)	YP
2 business days before 3rd Wednesday of expiring month at 4:00 A.M. (EST), 9:00 A.M. (GMT) for cash settled; 10:16 A.M. (EST), 3:16 P.M. (GMT) for all other contracts	Physical delivery on 3rd Wednesday of expiring month	Mar, June, Sept, Dec	U.S. (EST): 7:00 P.M.–10:00 P.M. 8:05 A.M.–3:00 P.M.; Europe (GMT): 12:00 A.M.–3:00 A.M. 1:05 P.M.–8:00 P.M.; Dublin trading floor: 3:00 A.M.–8:00 P.M. (EST) 8:00 A.M.–1:00 P.M. (GMT)	ZX
1 business day before 3rd Wednesday of expiring month at 4:00 A.M. (EST), 9:00 A.M. (GMT) for cash settled; 10:16 A.M. (EST), 3:16 P.M. (GMT) for all other contracts	Physical delivery on 3rd Wednesday of expiring month	Mar, June, Sept, Dec	U.S. (EST): 7:00 P.M.–10:00 P.M. 8:05 A.M.–3:00 P.M.; Europe (GMT): 12:00 A.M.–3:00 A.M. 1:05 P.M.–8:00 P.M.; Dublin trading floor: 3:00 A.M.–8:00 P.M. (EST) 8:00 A.M.–1:00 P.M. (GMT)	YD
2 business days before 3rd Wednesday of expiring month at 4:00 A.M. (EST), 9:00 A.M. (GMT) for cash settled; 10:16 A.M. (EST), 3:16 P.M. (GMT) for all other contracts	Physical delivery on 3rd Wednesday of expiring month	Mar, June, Sept, Dec	U.S. (EST): 7:00 P.M.–10:00 P.M. 8:05 A.M.–3:00 P.M.; Europe (GMT): 12:00 A.M.–3:00 A.M. 1:05 P.M.–8:00 P.M.; Dublin trading floor: 3:00 A.M.–8:00 P.M. (EST) 8:00 A.M.–1:00 P.M. (GMT)	YM

Contract	Trading Unit	Price Quote	Tick Size
• U.S. Dollar/ Japanese Yen	200,000 U.S. dollars	Yen per U.S. dollar to 4 decimal places	.01 yen (¥2,000/contract)
• U.S. Dollar/ South African Rand	100,000 U.S. dollars	Rands per U.S. dollar to 4 decimal points	.005 rands (R50/contract)
• U.S. Dollar/ Swiss.Franc	200,000 U.S. dollars	Swiss francs per U.S. dollar to 4 decimal places	.0001 Swiss francs (SF20/contract)

U.S. Dollar Currency Paired Futures Options

Contract	Trading Unit	Price Quote	Tick Size	Strike Price
• British Pound/ U.S. Dollar	1 futures contract	U.S. dollars per pound to 4 decimal places	.0001 U.S. dollars ($12.50/contract)	.0050 U.S. dollars intervals

Last Trading Day	Settlement/ Delivery	Contract Month	Trading Hours)	Ticker Symbol
2 business days before 3rd Wednesday of expiring month at 4:00 A.M. (EST), 9:00 A.M. (GMT) for cash settled; 10:16 A.M. (EST), 3:16 P.M. (GMT) for all other contracts	Physical delivery on 3rd Wednesday of expiring month	Mar, June, Sept, Dec	U.S. (EST): 7:00 P.M.–10:00 P.M. 8:05 A.M.–3:00 P.M.; Europe (GMT): 12:00 A.M.–3:00 A.M. 1:05 P.M.–8:00 P.M.; Dublin trading floor: 3:00 A.M.–8:00 P.M. (EST) 8:00 A.M.–1:00 P.M. (GMT)	YY
2 business days before 3rd Wednesday of expiring month at 4:00 A.M. (EST), 9:00 A.M. (GMT) for cash settled; 10:16 A.M. (EST), 3:16 P.M. (GMT) for all other contracts	Physical delivery on 3rd Wednesday of expiring month	Mar, June, Sept, Dec	U.S. (EST): 7:00 P.M.–10:00 P.M. 8:05 A.M.–3:00 P.M.; Europe (GMT): 12:00 A.M.–3:00 A.M. 1:05 P.M.–8:00 P.M.; Dublin trading floor: 3:00 A.M.–8:00 P.M. (EST) 8:00 A.M.–1:00 P.M. (GMT)	ZR
2 business days before 3rd Wednesday of expiring month at 4:00 A.M. (EST), 9:00 A.M. (GMT) for cash settled; 10:16 A.M. (EST), 3:16 P.M. (GMT) for all other contracts	Physical delivery on 3rd Wednesday of expiring month	Mar, June, Sept, Dec	U.S. (EST): 7:00 P.M.–10:00 P.M. 8:05 A.M.–3:00 P.M.; Europe (GMT): 12:00 A.M.–3:00 A.M. 1:05 P.M.–8:00 P.M.; Dublin trading floor: 3:00 A.M.–8:00 P.M. (EST) 8:00 A.M.–1:00 P.M. (GMT)	YF

Last Trading Day	Exercise Day	Contract Months	Trading Hours	Ticker Symbol
2 Fridays before 3rd Wednesday of month	Until 10:00 A.M. (EST) 3:00 P.M. (GMT) on last trading day; automatic exercise if at least 1 tick in-the-money	Mar, June, Sept, Dec and 2 nearest months	U.S. (EST): 7:00 P.M.–10:00 P.M. 8:05 A.M.–3:00 P.M.; Europe (GMT): 12:00 A.M.–3:00 A.M. 1:05 P.M.–8:00 P.M.; Dublin trading floor: 3:00 A.M.–8:00 P.M. (EST) 8:00 A.M.–1:00 P.M. (GMT)	YP

Contract	Trading Unit	Price Quote	Tick Size	Strike Price
• U.S. Dollar/ Deutsche Mark	1 futures contract	Marks per U.S. dollar to 4 decimal places	.0001 mark (DM20/contract)	.0050 mark intervals
• U.S. Dollar/ Japanese Yen	1 futures contract	Yen to U.S. dollars to 4 decimal places	.01 yen (¥2,000/contract)	.50 yen intervals
• U.S. Dollar/ Swiss Franc	1 futures contract	Swiss francs to U.S. dollars to 4 decimal places	.0001 Swiss franc (SF20/contract)	.0050 Swiss franc intervals

U.S. Dollar Index Futures

Contract	Underlying Index	Trading Unit	Price Quote	Tick Size
• U.S. Dollar Index	Trade–weighted geometric average of 10 currencies	$1,000 × U.S. Dollar Index	Index = 100	.01 of Index point ($10)

Last Trading Day	Exercise Day	Contract Months	Trading Hours	Ticker Symbol
2 Fridays before 3rd Wednesday of month	Until 10:00 A.M. (EST) 3:00 P.M. (GMT) on last trading day; automatic exercise if at least 1 tick in-the-money	Mar, June, Sept, Dec and 2 nearest months	U.S. (EST): 7:00 P.M.–10:00 P.M. 8:05 A.M.–3:00 P.M.; Europe (GMT): 12:00 A.M.–3:00 A.M. 1:05 P.M.–8:00 P.M.; Dublin trading floor: 3:00 A.M.–8:00 P.M. (EST) 8:00 A.M.–1:00 P.M. (GMT)	YM
2 Fridays before 3rd Wednesday of month	Until 10:00 A.M. (EST) 3:00 P.M. (GMT) on last trading day; automatic exercise if at least 1 tick in-the-money	Mar, June, Sept, Dec and 2 nearest months	U.S. (EST): 7:00 P.M.–10:00 P.M. 8:05 A.M.–3:00 P.M.; Europe (GMT): 12:00 A.M.–3:00 A.M. 1:05 P.M.–8:00 P.M.; Dublin trading floor: 3:00 A.M.–8:00 P.M. (EST) 8:00 A.M.–1:00 P.M. (GMT)	YY
2 Fridays before 3rd Wednesday of month	Until 10:00 A.M. (EST) 3:00 P.M. (GMT) on last trading day; automatic exercise if at least 1 tick in-the-money	Mar, June, Sept, Dec and 2 nearest months	U.S. (EST): 7:00 P.M.–10:00 P.M. 8:05 A.M.–3:00 P.M.; Europe (GMT): 12:00 A.M.–3:00 A.M. 1:05 P.M.–8:00 P.M.; Dublin trading floor: 3:00 A.M.–8:00 P.M. (EST) 8:00 A.M.–1:00 P.M. (GMT)	YF

Last Trading Day	Settlement	Contract Months	Trading Hours	Ticker Symbol
3rd Wednesday of expiring contract month	Cash	Mar, June, Sept, Dec	U.S. (EST): 7:00 P.M.–10:00 P.M., 8:05 A.M.–3:00 P.M.; Europe (GMT): 12:00 A.M.–3:00 A.M., 1:05 A.M.–8:00 P.M.; Dublin trading floor: 3:00 A.M.–8:00 A.M. (EST), 8:00 A.M.–1:00 P.M. (GMT)	DX

U.S. Dollar Index Options on Futures

Contract	Trading Unit	Price Quote	Tick Size	Strike Price
• U.S. Dollar Index	1 U.S. Dollar Index futures contract	U.S. Dollar Index points and ⅟₁₀₀ths-point	.01 Index point ($10/contract) ($10)	1 point intervals

New York Futures Exchange (NYFE)
[A subsidiary of the New York Cotton Exchange)

Futures

Contract	Trading Unit	Price Quote	Tick Size
• CRB/Bridge Index	$500 × commodity index	index points	5 basis points ($25)
• NYSE Composite Index	$500 × index	index points	5 basis points ($25)
• NYSE Large Composite Index	$1,000 × NYSE Composite Index	index points	5 basis points ($50)

Last Trading Day	Exercise Day	Trading Months	Trading Hours	Ticker Symbol
2nd Friday before 3rd Wednesday of expiring contract month	Until 5 P.M. (EST), 10:00 P.M. (GMT) on last trading day	Mar, June, Sept, Dec and nearest 2 months	U.S. (EST): 7:00 P.M.–10:00 P.M., 8:05 A.M.–3:00 P.M.; Europe (GMT): 12:00 A.M.–3:00 A.M., 1:05 A.M.–8:00 P.M.; Dublin trading floor: 3:00 A.M.–8:00 A.M. (EST), 8:00 A.M.–1:00 P.M. (GMT)	DO

Daily Price Limit	Contract Months	Trading Hours	Ticker Symbol
None	Jan, Feb, Apr, June, Aug, Nov	9:40 A.M.–2:45 P.M. (EST)	CRB
Calculated each calendar quarter, based on average settlement price of nearest primary futures contract, during month prior to beginning of the quarter (Average Price). 10% Price Limit: 10% of Average Price rounded down to nearest integral multiple of 10 index points; 20% Price Limit: 2 times the 10% limit; 30% Price Limit: 3 times the 10% limit	Mar, June, Sep, Dec	In U.S.(EST): 4:45 P.M.–10:00 P.M., 3:00 A.M.–9:15 A.M., 9:30 A.M.–4:15 P.M., 7:00 P.M.–10:00 P.M. (Sun.); In Europe (GMT): 9:45 A.M.–3:00 A.M., 8:00 A.M.–2:15 P.M., 2:30 P.M.–9:15 P.M., 12:00 A.M.–3:00 A.M. (Sun.)	YX
Calculated each calendar quarter, based on average settlement price of nearest primary futures contract, during month prior to beginning of the quarter (Average Price). 10% Price Limit: 10% of Average Price rounded down to nearest integral multiple of 10 index points; 20% Price Limit: 2 times the 10% limit; 30% Price Limit: 3 times the 10% limit	Mar, June, Sept, Dec	In U.S.(EST): 4:45 P.M.–10:00 P.M., 3:00 A.M.–9:15 A.M., 9:30 A.M.–4:15 P.M., 7:00 P.M.–10:00 P.M. (Sun.); In Europe (GMT): 9:45 A.M.–3:00 A.M., 8:00 A.M.–2:15 P.M., 2:30 P.M.–9:15 P.M., 12:00 A.M.–3:00 A.M. (Sun.)	YL

Contract	Trading Unit	Price Quote	Tick Size
• NYSE Small Composite Index	$250 × NYSE Composite Index	index points	5 basis points ($12.50)
• PSE Technology Index	$100 × index	index points	5 basis points ($25)

Options on Futures

Contract	Underlying Index	Price Quote	Tick Size	Strike Price
• CRB/Bridge Index	CRB/Bridge Index	index points 1 point = $5	5 points ($25)	numbers divisible by 2
• NYSE Composite Index Contract	NYSE Composite Index futures contract	index points 1 point = $5	5 points ($25)	numbers divisible by 2
• PSE Technology Index	PSE Technology Index futures contract	index points	5 points	numbers divisible by 2

Daily Price Limit	Contract Months	Trading Hours (EST)	Ticker Symbol
Calculated each calendar quarter, based on average settlement price of nearest primary futures contract, during month prior to beginning of the quarter (Average Price). 10% Price Limit: 10% of Average Price rounded down to nearest integral multiple of 10 index points; 20% Price Limit: 2 times the 10% limit; 30% Price Limit: 3 times the 10% limit	Mar, June, Sept, Dec	In U.S. (EST): 4:45 P.M.–10:00 P.M., 3:00 A.M.–9:15 A.M., 9:30 A.M.–4:15 P.M., 7:00 P.M.–10:00 P.M. (Sun.); In Europe (GMT): 9:45 A.M.–3:00 A.M., 8:00 A.M.–2:15 P.M., 2:30 P.M.–9:15 P.M., 12:00 A.M.–3:00 A.M. (Sun.)	YS
Calculated each calendar quarter, based on average settlement price of nearest primary futures contract, during month prior to beginning of the quarter (Average Price). 10% Price Limit: 10% of Average Price rounded down to nearest integral multiple of 10 index points; 20% Price Limit: 2 times the 10% limit; 30% Price Limit: 3 times the 10% limit	Mar, June, Sept, Dec	9:15 A.M.–4:15 P.M. (EST)	TK

Expiration Day	Last Trading Day	Contract Months	Trading Hours (EST)	Ticker Symbol
Last trading day	2nd Friday of expiration month	Jan, Feb, Apr, June, Aug, Nov	9:00 A.M.–3:15 P.M.	CR
Last trading day	Calendar quarterly cycle months: Last trading day of underlying futures contract; non-calendar months: 3rd Friday of expiration month	1st 3 calendar months & next 3 months in the calendar quartlerly cycle (Mar, June, Sept, Dec)	In U.S. (EST): 4:45 P.M.–10:00 P.M., 3:00 A.M.–9:15 A.M., 9:30 A.M.–4:15 P.M 7:00 P. M.–10:00 P.M. (Sun.); In Europe: (GMT) 9:45 P.M.–3:00 A.M., 8:00 A.M.–2:15 P.M., 2:30 P.M.–9:15 P.M., 12:00 A.M.–3:00 A.M. (Sun.)	YX
Last trading day	Calendar quarterly cycle months: Last trading day of underlying futures contract; non-calendar months: 3rd Friday of expiration month	1st 3 calendar months & next 3 months in the calendar quarterly cycle (Mar, June, Sept, Dec)	9:15 A.M.–4:15 P.M.	TK

Pacific Exchange (PE)

Index Options

Contract	Underlying Index	Trading Unit	Price Quote	Tick Size
• Dow Jones Taiwan Stock Index	Broad-based, capitalization-weighted average of largest, most liquid stocks traded on Taiwan Stock Exchange	index × $100	dollars and fractions	1/16 up to $3 1/8 over $3
• Morgan Stanley Emerging Growth Index	Broad-based, capitalization-weighted index of 50 most rapidly growing U.S. traded companies	index × $100	dollars and fractions	1/16 up to $3 1/8 over $3
• PSE Technology Index	Price-weighted, broad-based index of 100 listed & over-the-counter stocks from 15 different industries	index × $100	dollars and fractions	1/16 up to $3 1/8 over $3
• Wilshire Small Cap Index	Market-weighted index of 250 small cap stocks chosen on basis of market capitalization, liquidity and industry group representation, picked from Wilshire Next 1750 Index	index × $100	dollars and fractions	1/16 up to $3 1/8 over $3

Philadelphia Stock Exchange (PHLX)

Currency Options: U.S. Dollar Based

Contract	Trading Unit	Price Quote	Tick Size	Strike Price Intervals
• Australian Dollar	50,000 Australian dollars	cents per Australian dollars	$.(00)01 per unit ($5)	3 nearest months = 1 cent 6, 9, and 12 months = 1 cent over 12 months = 2 cents

Strike Price	Last Trading Day	Expiration Months	Trading Hours (PST)	Ticker Symbol
5-point intervals	2 business days before expiration (usually Thursday)	3 consecutive near-term months + 2 successive months from March quarterly cycle	6:30 A.M.–1:15 P.M.	XDT
5-point intervals	2 business days before expiration (usually Thursday)	2 consecutive near-term months + 2 successive months from March quarterly cycle	6:30 A.M.–1:15 P.M.	EGI
5-point intervals	2 business days before expiration (usually Thursday)	2 consecutive near-term months + 2 successive months from March quarterly cycle	6:30 A.M.–1:15 P.M.	PSE
5-point intervals	2 business days before expiration (usually Thursday)	3 consecutive near-term months + 3 successive months from March quarterly cycle	6:30 A.M.–1:15 P.M.	WSX

Expiration Day	Contract Months	Trading Hours (EST)	Ticker Symbol
Mid-month options: Friday before 3rd Wednesday of expiring month	Mid-month options: Mar, June, Sept, Dec + 2 near-term months	2:30 A.M.–2:30 P.M.	XAD (American-style) CAD (European style)
Month-end options: Last Friday of month	Month-end options: 3 nearest months Long-term options: 18 and 24 months (June and Dec)		ADW (American) EDA (European) n.a. (American) n.a. (European)

Contract	Trading Unit	Price Quote	Tick Size	Strike Price Intervals
• British Pound	31,250 British pounds	cents per British pound	$.(00)01 per unit ($3.125)	3 nearest months = 1 cent 6, 9, and 12 months = 2 cents over 12 months = 4 cents
• Canadian Dollar	50,000 Canadian dollars	cents per Canadian dollar	$.(00)01 per unit ($5)	3 nearest months = .5 cent 6, 9, and 12 months =.5 cent over 12 months = 1 cent
• Deutsche Mark	62,500 marks	cents per Deutsche mark	$.(00)01 per unit ($6.25)	3 nearest months = .5 cent 6, 9, and 12 months = 1 cent over 12 months = 2 cents
• Euro Currency	62,500 Euro	cents per Euro	$.(00)01 per unit ($6.25)	3 nearest months = .5 cent 6, 9, and 12 months = 1 cent over 12 months = 2 cents
• French Franc	250,000 French francs	cents per French franc	$.(000)02 per unit ($5)	3 nearest months = .25 cents 6, 9, and 12 months = .25 cents over 12 months = .50 cents
• Japanese Yen	6,250,000 yen	cents per yen	$.(000)001 per unit ($6.25)	3 nearest months = .005 cent 6, 9, and 12 months = .01 cent over 12 months = .02 cent

Expiration Day	Contract Months	Trading Hours (EST)	Ticker Symbol
Mid-month options: Friday before 3rd Wednesday of expiring month Month-end options: Last Friday of month	Mid-month options: Mar, June, Sept, Dec + 2 near-term months Month-end options: 3 nearest months Long-term options: 18 and 24 months (June and Dec)	2:30 A.M.– 2:30 P.M.	XBP (American-style CBP (European style) BPW (American) EPO (European) n.a. (American) YPX (European)
Mid-month options: Friday before 3rd Wednesday of expiring month Month-end options: Last Friday of month	Mid-month options: Mar, June, Sept, Dec + 2 near-term months Month-end options: 3 nearest months Long-term options: 18 and 24 months (June and Dec)	7:00 A.M.– 2:30 P.M.	XCD (American-style) CCD (European style) CDW (American) ECD (European) n.a. (American) n.a. (European)
Mid-month options: Friday before 3rd Wednesday of expiring month Month-end options: Last Friday of month	Mid-month options: Mar, June, Sept, Dec + 2 near-term months Month-end options: 3 nearest months Long-term options: 18 and 24 months (June and Dec)	7:00 A.M.– 2:30 P.M.	XDM (American-style) CDM (European style) DMW (American) EDM (European) n.a. (American) n.a. (European)
Mid-month options: Friday before 3rd Wednesday of expiring month Month-end options: Last Friday of month	Mid-month options: Mar, June, Sept, Dec + 2 near-term months Month-end options: 3 nearest months Long-term options: 18 and 24 months (June and Dec)	2:30 A.M.– 2:30 P.M.	XDM (American-style) CDM (European style) DMW (American) EDM (European) n.a. (American) YDM (European)
Mid-month options: Friday before 3rd Wednesday of expiring month Month-end options: Last Friday of month	Mid-month options: Mar, June, Sept, Dec + 2 near-term months Month-end options: 3 nearest months Long-term options: 18 and 24 months (June and Dec)	2:30 A.M.– 2:30 P.M.	XFF (American-style) CFF (European style) FFW (American) EFF (European) n.a. (American) YFF (European)
Mid-month options: Friday before 3rd Wednesday of expiring month Month-end options: Last Friday of month	Mid-month options: Mar, June, Sept, Dec + 2 near-term months Month-end options: 3 nearest months Long-term options: 18 and 24 months (June and Dec)	2:30 A.M.– 2:30 P.M.	XJY (American-style) CJY (European style) JYW (American) EJY (European) n.a. (American) YJY(European)

Contract	Trading Unit	Price Quote	Tick Size	Strike Price Intervals
• Swiss Franc	62,500 Swiss francs	cents per Swiss franc	$.(00)01 per unit ($6.25)	3 nearest months = .5 cent 6, 9, and 12 months = 1 cent over 12 months = 2 cents

Currency Cross Rate Options

Contract	Trading Unit	Price Quote	Tick Size	Strike Price Intervals
• British Pound/ Deutsche Mark	31,250 British pounds	Deutsche marks per British pound	.0002 Deutsche mark per unit (DM6.25)	3 nearest months = DM.02 6, 9 and 12 months = DM.02 over 12 months = DM.04
• Deutsche Mark/ Japanese Yen	62,500 British pounds	Yen per Deutsche marks	.01 yen per unit (¥625)	3 nearest months = ¥.5 6, 9 and 12 months = ¥1 over 12 months = ¥2

3-D (dollar-denominated delivery) Options

Contract	Trading Unit	Price Quote	Tick Size	Strike Price Intervals
• Deutsche Mark	62,500 Deutsche marks	cents per Deutsche mark	$.01 ($6.25)	.5 cent or $.005
• Japanese Yen	6,250,000 yen	dollars per yen	$.000001 ($6.25)	3 months = .005 cent or $.00005 6 and 9 months = .01 cent or $.0001

Expiration Day	Contract Months	Trading Hours (EST)	Ticker Symbol
Mid-month options: Friday before 3rd Wednesday of expiring month Month-end options: Last Friday of month	Mid-month options: Mar, June, Sept, Dec + 2 near-term months Month-end options: 3 nearest months Long-term options: 18 and 24 months (June and Dec)	2:30 A.M.– 2:30 P.M.	XSF (American-style) CSF (European style) SFW (American) ESW (European) n.a. (American) n.a. (European)

Expiration Day	Contract Months	Trading Hours (EST)	Ticker Symbol
Mid-month options: Friday before 3rd Wednesday of expiring month Month-end options: Last Friday of month	Mid-month options: Mar, June, Sept, Dec + 2 near-term months Month-end options: 3 nearest months	2:30 A.M.– 2:30 P.M.	PMX (European-style) PMW (European)
Mid-month options: Friday before 3rd Wednesday of expiring month Month-end options: Last Friday of month	Mid-month options: Mar, June, Sept, Dec + 2 near-term months Month-end options: 3 nearest months	2:30 A.M.– 2:30 P.M.	MYX (European) MYW (European)

Expiration Day	Exercise Settlement	Trading Hours (EST)	Ticker Symbol
1 and 2-week options: every Monday; Mid-month options: Monday before 3rd Wednesday of expiring month	Cash in U.S. dollars based on PHLX calculated settlement value for spot	2:30 A.M.– 2:30 P.M.	XDA/1st Monday XDB/2nd Monday XDC/3rd Monday XDD/4th Monday XDE/5th Monday
1 and 2-week options: every Monday; Mid-month options: Monday before 3rd Wednesday of expiring month	Cash in U.S. dollars based on PHLX calculated settlement value for spot	2:30 A.M.– 2:30 P.M.	XJA/1st Monday XJB/2nd Monday XJC/3rd Monday XJD/4th Monday XJE/5th Monday

Sector Index Options

Contract	Underlying Index	Trading Unit	Price Quote	Tick Size
• Airline Sector	12 U.S. airline stocks	index × $100	index points (1 point = $100)	$\frac{1}{16}$ under 3 $\frac{1}{8}$ over 3
• Keefe, Bruyette and Woods, Inc. Bank Sector	24 geographically diverse stocks of U.S. money center banks and regional institutions	index × $100	index points (1 point = $100)	$\frac{1}{16}$ under 3 $\frac{1}{8}$ over 3
• Computer Box Maker Sector	9 personal computer and notebook stocks	index × $100	index points (1 point = $100)	$\frac{1}{16}$ under 3 $\frac{1}{8}$ over 3
• Forest and Paper Products Sector	13 timber company stocks	index × $100	index points (1 point = $100)	$\frac{1}{16}$ under 3 $\frac{1}{8}$ over 3
• Gold/Silver Sector	11 mining company stocks	index × $100	index points (1 point = $100)	$\frac{1}{16}$ under 3 $\frac{1}{8}$ over 3
• National Over-the-Counter Sector	100 largest capitalized OTC-traded companies	index × $100	index points (1 point = $100)	$\frac{1}{16}$ under 3 $\frac{1}{8}$ over 3
• Oil Service Sector	15 oil drilling and service companies	index × $100	index points (1 point = $100)	$\frac{1}{16}$ under 3 $\frac{1}{8}$ over 3
• Phone Sector	stocks of AT & T and Baby Bells	index × $100	index points (1 point = $100)	$\frac{1}{16}$ under 3 $\frac{1}{8}$ over 3
• Semiconductor Sector	16 U.S. semiconductor designers, distributors and manufacturers	index × $100	index points (1 point = $100)	$\frac{1}{16}$ under 3 $\frac{1}{8}$ over 3
• SuperCap Sector	5 most highly capitalized U.S. corporations listed on the New York Stock Exchange	index × $100	index points (1 point = $100)	$\frac{1}{16}$ under 3 $\frac{1}{8}$ over 3

Strike Prices	Settlement/ Expiration	Expiration Months	Trading Hours (EST)	Ticker Symbol
5 points	Cash; Saturday after 3rd Friday of expiration month	3 months from Mar, June, Sept, Dec cycle + 2 additional near-term months	9:30 A.M.– 4:02 P.M.	PLN
5 points	Cash; Saturday after 3rd Friday of expiration month	3 months from Mar, June, Sept, Dec cycle + 2 additional near-term months	9:30 A.M.– 4:02 P.M.	BKX
5 points	Cash; Saturday after 3rd Friday of expiration month	3 months from Mar, June, Sept, Dec cycle + 2 additional near-term months	9:30 A.M.– 4:02 P.M.	BMX
5 points	Cash; Saturday after 3rd Friday of expiration month	3 months from Mar, June, Sept, Dec cycle + 2 additional near-term months	9:30 A.M.– 4:02 P.M.	FPP
5 points	Cash; Saturday after 3rd Friday of expiration month	3 months from Mar, June, Sept, Dec cycle + 2 additional near-term months	9:30 A.M.– 4:02 P.M.	XAU
5 points	Cash; Saturday after 3rd Friday of expiration month	3 months from Mar, June, Sept, Dec cycle + 2 additional near-term months	9:30 A.M.– 4:15 P.M.	XOC
5 points	Cash; Saturday after 3rd Friday of expiration month	3 months from Mar, June, Sept, Dec cycle + 2 additional near-term months	9:30 A.M.– 4:02 P.M.	OSX
5 points	Cash; Saturday after 3rd Friday of expiration month	3 months from Mar, June, Sept, Dec cycle + 2 additional near-term months	9:30 A.M.– 4:02 P.M.	PNX
5 points	Cash; Saturday after 3rd Friday of expiration month	3 months from Mar, June, Sept, Dec cycle + 2 additional near-term months	9:30 A.M.– 4:02 P.M.	SOX
5 points	Cash; Saturday after 3rd Friday of expiration month	3 months from Mar, June, Sept, Dec cycle + 2 additional near-term months	9:30 A.M.– 4:15 P.M.	HFX

Contract	Underlying Index	Trading Unit	Price Quote	Tick Size
● U.S. Top 100 Index	100 most highly capitalized U.S. corporations	index × $100	index points (1 point = $100)	1/16 under 3 1/8 over 3
● Utility Sector	20 public utility stocks listed on the New York Stock Exchange	index × $100	index points (1 point = $100)	1/16 under 3 1/8 over 3
● Value Line Composite Index	1,700 listed and OTC stocks, equal weighted	index × $100	index points (1 point = $100)	1/16 under 3 1/8 over 3

Philadelphia Board of Trade
(Subsidiary of Philadelphia Stock Exchange)

Futures

Contract	Trading Unit	Price Quote	Tick Size
● Australian Dollar	100,000 Australian dollars	cents per unit	$.(00)01 ($10)
● British Pound	62,500 British pounds	cents per unit	$.(00)01 ($6.25)
● Canadian Dollar	100,000 Canadian dollars	cents per unit	$.(00)01 ($10)
● Deutsche Mark	125,000 Deutsche marks	cents per unit	$.(00)01 ($12.50)
● Euro Currency	125,000 Euro	cents per unit	$.(00)01 ($12.50)
● French Franc	500,000 French francs	1/10 cent per unit	$.(000)02 ($10)
● Japanese Yen	12,500,000 yen	1/100 cent per unit	$.(0000)01 ($10)
● Swiss Francs	125,000 Swiss francs	cents per unit	$.(00)01 ($12.50)

Strike Prices	Settlement/ Expiration	Expiration Months	Trading Hours (EST)	Ticker Symbol
5 points	Cash; Saturday after 3rd Friday of expiration month	3 months from Mar, June, Sept, Dec cycle + 2 additional near-term months	9:30 A.M.– 4:15 P.M.	TPX
5 points	Cash; Saturday after 3rd Friday of expiration month	3 months from Mar, June, Sept, Dec cycle + 2 additional near-term months	9:30 A.M.– 4:02 P.M.	UTY
5 points	Cash; Saturday after 3rd Friday of expiration month	3 months from Mar, June, Sept, Dec cycle + 2 additional near-term months	9:30 A.M.– 4:15 P.M.	VLE

Last Trading Day	Contract Months	Trading Hours (EST)	Ticker Symbol
Friday before 3rd Wednesday of month	Mar, June, Sept, Dec + 2 additional near-term months	2:30 A.M.–2:30 P.M.	ZA
Friday before 3rd Wednesday of month	Mar, June, Sept, Dec + 2 additional near-term months	2:30 A.M.–2:30 P.M.	ZB
Friday before 3rd Wednesday of month	Mar, June, Sept, Dec + 2 additional near-term months	2:30 A.M.–2:30 P.M.	ZC
Friday before 3rd Wednesday of month	Mar, June, Sept, Dec + 2 additional near-term months	2:30 A.M.–2:30 P.M.	ZD
Friday before 3rd Wednesday of month	Mar, June, Sept, Dec + 2 additional near-term months	2:30 A.M.–2:30 P.M.	ZE
Friday before 3rd Wednesday of month	Mar, June, Sept, Dec + 2 additional near-term months	2:30 A.M.–2:30 P.M.	ZF
Friday before 3rd Wednesday of month	Mar, June, Sept, Dec + 2 additional near-term months	2:30 A.M.–2:30 P.M.	ZJ
Friday before 3rd Wednesday of month	Mar, June, Sept, Dec + 2 additional near-term months	2:30 A.M.–2:30 P.M.	ZS

CANADIAN SECURITIES, FUTURES AND OPTIONS EXCHANGES

Montreal Exchange (ME)

Futures

Contract	Trading Unit	Price Quote	Tick Size
• Canadian Bankers' Acceptance (1-Month)	C$3 million in Bankers' Acceptances	Index: 100 minus yield	.01 (C$25/contract)
• Canadian Bankers' Acceptance (3-Month)	C$1 million in Bankers' Acceptances	Index: 100 minus yield	.01 (C$25/contract)
• Government of Canada Bonds (5-Year)	1 C$100,000 Government of Canada bond	per C$100 nominal value	.01 (C$10/contract)
• Government of Canada Bonds (10-Year)	1 C$100,000 Government of Canada bond	per C$100 nominal value	.01 (C$10/contract)

Options on Futures

Contract	Trading Unit	Price Quote	Tick Size	Strike Price
• Canadian Bankers' Acceptance (3-month)	1 futures contract	points	.01 (C$25)	.50 point intervals; .25 point on nearest contract month
• Government of Canada Bonds (10-Year)	1 futures contract	points and 1/100 point per $100 nominal value of underlying futures contract	.01 (C$10)	2 point intervals

Daily Price Limit	Expiration Day	Exercise Settlement	Trading Hours (EST)	Ticker Symbol
None	10 A.M. on 2nd London banking day before 3rd Wednesday of contract month	1st 6 consecutive months	8:00 A.M.– 3:00 P.M.	BAR
None	10 A.M. on 2nd London banking day before 3rd Wednesday of contract month	Mar, June, Sept, Dec + 2 additional near months	8:00 A.M.– 3:00 P.M.	BAX
3 points (C$3,000)	7th business day before last business day of delivery month	Mar, Jun, Sept, Dec	8:20 A.M.– 3:00 P.M.	CGF
3 points (C$3,000)	7th business day before last business day of delivery month	Mar, Jun, Sept, Dec	8:20 A.M.– 3:00 P.M.	CGB

Expiration Day	Last Trading Day	Contract Months	Trading Hours (EST)	Ticker Symbol
Last trading day	Call Montreal Exchange	4 nearest months in 3-month Canadian Bankers' Acceptance futures quarterly cycle	8:20 A.M.– 3:00 P.M.	OBX
Last trading day	3rd Friday of month before option contract month	Mar, June, Sept, Dec plus monthly option contracts based on next quarterly futures contract nearest to option contract	8:20 A.M.– 3:00 P.M.	OGB

Toronto Stock Exchange (TSE)

Equity Options

Contract	Trading Unit	Price Quote	Tick Size	Strike Price Intervals
• Long-Term Equity Anticipation Securities (LEAPS)	shares of TSE stocks	dollars and cents	$.01 up to $.10 $.05 over $.10	$2 up to $15 $5 over $15
• TSE Equity Options	shares of TSE stocks	dollars and cents	$.01 up to $.10 $.05 over $.10	$1 to $10 intervals

Index Options

Contract	Underlying Product	Trading Unit	Tick Size	Strike Price
• Toronto 35 Index	Index of 35 larger, more liquid stocks in Canada	index × $500	$.01 up to $.10 $.05 over $.10	5 point intervals
• TIPS 35	100 Toronto 35 Index Participation Units	100 units per contract	$.01 up to $.10, $.05 over $.10	$.50 intervals

Winnipeg Commodity Exchange (WCE)

Futures

Contract	Trading Unit	Price Quote	Tick Size
• Canola	20 metric tons	dollars and cents	10 cents per metric ton
• Feed Peas	20 gross metric tons	U.S. dollars and cents	10 cents per metric ton
• Feed Wheat	20 metric tons	dollars and cents	10 cents per metric ton
• Flaxseed	20 metric tons	dollars and cents	10 cents per metric ton

Expiration Day	Last Trading Day	Contract Months	Trading Hours (EST)	Ticker Symbol
Saturday after 3rd Friday of expiration month	3rd Friday of expiration month	Jan of expiration year	9:30 A.M.–4:00 P.M.	Varies with stock; preceded by V for 1999, L for 2000, Z for 2001, W for 2002 as 1st character
Saturday after 3rd Friday of expiration month	3rd Friday of expiration month	Cycle 5 [1,2,3] (call TSE)	9:30 A.M.–4:00 P.M.	Varies with underlying stock

Expiration Day	Last Trading Day	Contract Months	Trading Hours (EST)	Ticker Symbol
3rd Friday of expiration month	Thursday before 3rd Friday of expiration	Cycle 5[3] (call TSE)	9:30 A.M.–4:15 P.M.	TXO
Saturday after 3rd Friday of expiration month	3rd Friday of expiration month	Cycle 5[3] (call TSE)	9:30 A.M.–4:00 P.M.	TIP

Daily Price Limit	Last Trading Day	Contract Months	Trading Hours (EST)	Ticker Symbol
$5 per metric ton	7 business days before end of delivery month	Jan, Mar, May, July, Aug, Sept, Nov	9:30 A.M.–1:15 P.M.	RS
$5 per metric ton	7 business days before end of delivery month	Feb, May, July, Oct, Dec	9:30 A.M.–1:15 P.M.	WP
$5 per metric ton	7 business days before end of delivery month	Mar, May, July, Oct, Dec	9:30 A.M.–1:15 P.M.	WW
$10 per metric ton	7 business days before end of delivery month	Jan, Mar, May, July, Sept, Nov	9:30 A.M.–1:15 P.M.	WF

Contract	Trading Unit	Price Quote	Tick Size
• Oats	20 metric tons	U.S. dollars and cents	10 cents per metric ton
• Western Barley	20 metric tons	dollars and cents	10 cents per metric ton

Options on Futures

Contract	Trading Unit	Price Quote	Tick Size	Strike Price Intervals
• Canola	1 futures contract	C$ dollars and cents	C$10 per metric ton	C$10 per metric ton
• Feed Wheat	1 futures contract	C$ dollars and cents	C$ 5 per metric ton	C$5 per metric ton
• Flaxseed	1 futures contract	C$ dollars and cents	C$ 10 per metric ton	C$10 per metric ton
• Western Barley	1 futures contract	C$ dollars and cents	C$ 5 per metric ton	C$5 per metric ton

EUROPEAN SECURITIES, FUTURES AND OPTIONS EXCHANGES

FRANCE

MATIF SA

Agricultural Futures

Contract	Trading Unit	Price Quote	Tick Size
• European Rapeseed	50 metric tons	Deutsche marks per metric ton	Deutsche mark per metric ton (DM50)
• Milling Wheat	50 metric tons	French francs per metric ton	1 French franc per metric ton (FF50)
• White Sugar 45	50 metric tons	dollars and cents per metric ton	10 cents per metric ton
• White Sugar 100	50 metric tons	dollars and cents per metric ton	10 cents per metric ton

Daily Price Limit	Last Trading Day	Contract Months	Trading Hours	Ticker Symbol
$5 per metric ton	7 business days before end of delivery month	Mar, May, July, Oct, Dec	9:30 A.M.–1:15 P.M.	WO
$5 per metric ton	7 business days before end of delivery month	Mar, May, July, Oct, Dec	9:30 A.M.–1:15 P.M.	AB

Expiration Day	Last Trading Day	Contract Months	Trading Hours (EST)	Ticker Symbol
last trading day	7 business days before end of delivery month	Jan, Mar, May, July, Aug, Sept, Nov	9:30 A.M.–1:15 P.M.	RS
last trading day	7 business days before end of delivery month	Mar, May, July, Oct, Dec	9:30 A.M.–1:15 P.M.	WW
last trading day	7 business days before end of delivery month	Jan, Mar, May, July, Sept, Nov	9:30 A.M.–1:15 P.M.	WF
last trading day	7 business days before end of delivery month	Mar, May, July, Oct, Dec	9:30 A.M.–1:15 P.M.	AB

Last Trading Day	Contract Months	Trading Hours	Ticker Symbol
Last business day of month before delivery month	Aug, Nov, Feb, May	10:45 A.M.–1:00 P.M. 3:00–6:30 P.M.	COM
10th day of delivery month	Sept, Nov, Jan, Mar, May	10:45 A.M.–1 P.M. 3:00–6:30 P.M.	BL2
15th of month before delivery month	7 delivery months from Mar, May, Aug, Oct, Dec	10:45 A.M.–7:30 P.M.	SUD
15 calendar days before 1st calendar day of delivery month	7 delivery months from Mar, May, Aug, Oct, Dec	10:45 A.M.–7:30 P.M.	SUB

Currency Futures

Contract	Trading Unit	Price Quote	Tick Size
● Matif Gilt (10-Year)	£100,000	% of nominal, to 2 decimal points	.01% (£10)
● Matif Gilt (5-Year)	£100,000	% of nominal, to 2 decimal points	.01% (£10)

Financial Futures

Contract	Underlying Instrument	Trading Unit	Price Quote	Tick Size
● Matif E-Bond (30-Year)	25 to 35-year notional Treasury bond denominated in euros, with 5.5% coupon	100,000 Euros	% of nominal value, to 2nd decimal point	1 basis point = 10 Euros
● Matif 5-Year	4 to 5½-year notional French government bond, 4.5% coupon	500,000 French francs	% of nominal value, with 2 decimals	.01% nominal value (FF50)
● 5-Year Euro Bond	4 to 5½-year notional government bond, 4.5% coupon	100,000 Euros	% of nominal value, with 2 decimals	.01% nominal value (10 Euros)
● Notional Bond	8½–10½ year notional French government bond with 5.5% coupon	500,000 French francs	% of nominal value, with 2 decimals	.1% nominal value (FF50)
● Euro Notional Bond	8½–10½ year notional government bond, 5.5% coupon	100,000 Euros	% of nominal value, with 2 decimals	.1% nominal value (10 Euros)

Index Futures

Contract	Underlying Index	Trading Unit	Price Quote	Tick Size
● CAC 40 Stock Index	40 French stocks	index × 25 French francs	index with 1 decimal	0.5 index point (FF25)

Last Trading Day	Contract Months	Trading Hours	Ticker Symbol
2nd business day preceding 3rd Wednesday of delivery month	1st 2 from Mar, June, Sept, Dec cycle	8:30 A.M.–6:30 P.M.	GLT
2nd business day preceding 3rd Wednesday of delivery month	1st 2 from Mar, June, Sept, Dec cycle	8:30 A.M.–6:30 P.M.	GMT

Last Trading Day	Contract Months	Trading Hours	Ticker Symbol
2nd trading day before 3rd Wednesday of delivery month	2 successive quarterly maturities out of Mar, June, Sept, Dec	8:00 A.M.–10:00 P.M.	XVL
2nd trading day before 3rd Wednesday of delivery month	2 successive quarterly delivery contract months out of Mar, June, Sept, Dec	8:00 A.M.–10:00 P.M.	YR5
2nd trading day before 3rd Wednesday of delivery month	2 successive quarterly delivery contract months out of Mar, June, Sept, Dec	8:00 A.M.–10:00 P.M.	XMT
2nd trading day before 3rd. Wednesday of contract month	4 successive quarterly cycle of Mar, June, Sept, Dec	8:00 A.M.–10:00 P.M.	NNN
2nd trading day before 3rd. Wednesday of contract month	3 successive quarterly cycle of Mar, June, Sept, Dec	8:00 A.M.–10:00 P.M.	XUT

Last Trading Day	Contract Months	Trading Hours	Ticker Symbol
Last trading day of delivery month	3 spot months, 3 quarterly months and 2 half-year months in Mar, June, Sept, Dec cycle	8:00 A.M.–9:55 A.M. 10:00 A.M.–5:00 P.M. 5:05–10:00 P.M.	CAC

Interest Rate Futures

Contract	Underlying Instrument	Trading Unit	Price Quote	Tick Size
• Pibor (3-Month)	Paris InterBank Offered Rate on 3-month deposits	5 million French francs	index to 3rd decimal point corresponding to 100 minus 3-month Pibor	1/2 basis pt. (FF62.50)
• Euribor (3-Month)	European InterBank Offered Rate on 3-month deposits, calculated by the Banking Federation of the European Union	1 million Euros	index to 3rd decimal point corresponding to 100 minus 3-month Euribor	1/2 basis pt. (12.5 Euros)

Agricultural Options on Futures

Contract	Trading Unit	Price Quote	Tick Size	Strike Price Interval
• White Sugar 45	1 futures contract	dollars and cents per metric ton	$0.5 per metric ton	$5

Financial Options on Futures

Contract	Trading Unit	Price Quote	Tick Size	Strike Price Interval
• Matif 5-Year	1 futures contract	% nominal value to 2nd decimal point	.01% nominal value (FF50)	25 basis points
• 5-Year Euro Bond	1 futures contract	% nominal value to 2nd decimal point	.01% nominal value (FF50)	25 basis points
• Notional Bond	1 futures contract	Premium as % of nominal value to 2nd decimal point	.01% of nominal value (FF50)	50 basis points multiples
• Euro Notional Bond	1 futures contract	Premium as % of nominal value to 2nd decimal point	.01% of nominal value (FF50)	50 basis points multiples

Last Trading Day	Contract Months	Trading Hours	Ticker Symbol
2nd trading day before 3rd Wednesday of contract month	2 monthly and 20 successive quarterly contract cycles out of Mar, June, Sept, Dec	8:00 A.M.–10:00 P.M.	PIB
2nd trading day before 3rd Wednesday of contract month	2 monthly and 20 successive quarterly contract cycles out of Mar, June, Sept, Dec	8:00 A.M.–10:00 P.M.	XST

Last Trading Day	Contract Months	Trading Hours	Ticker Symbol
Last trading day of month before month in which an expiration closes on the futures contract	7 delivery months from Mar, May, Aug, Oct, Dec	10:45 A.M.–1:00 P.M. 3:00–7:30 P.M.	SUD

Last Trading Day	Contract Months	Trading Hours	Ticker Symbol
Last Thursday of month before option expiration month	2 serial options + 2 quarterly contract cycles out of Mar, June, Sept, Dec	8:00–8:30 A.M. 4:30–10:00 P.M.	OY5
Last Thursday of month before option expiration month	2 serial options + 2 quarterly contract cycles out of Mar, June, Sept, Dec	8:00–8:30 A.M. 4:30 P.M.–10:00 P.M.	OXM
Last Thursday of month before Notional option delivery month	2 serial options + 3 or 4 successive quarterly delivery months of Mar, June, Sept, Dec cycle	8:00–8:30 A.M. 4:30–10:00 P.M.	ONN
Last Thursday of month before Notional option delivery month	2 serial (monthly) and 3 quarterly option maturities out of Mar, June, Sept, Dec cycle	8:00–8:30 A.M. 4:30–10:00 P.M.	OXL

Interest Rate Options on Futures

Contract	Trading Unit	Price Quote	Tick Size	Strike Price Interval
● Pibor (3-Month)	1 futures contract	% of nominal value to 3rd decimal point	½ basis point (FF62.50)	10 basis points
● Euribor (3-Month)	1 futures contract	% of nominal value to 3rd decimal point	½ basis point (12.5 Euros)	10 basis points

UNITED KINGDOM

International Petroleum Exchange (IPE)

Futures

Contract	Trading Unit	Price Quote	Tick Size
● Brent Crude	1,000 net barrels (42,000 U.S. gallons)	dollars and cents per barrel	1cent per barrel ($10)
● Gas Oil	100 metric tons	dollars and cents per metric ton	25 cents per metric ton ($25)
● Natural Gas	minimum 5 lots of 1,000 therms	British pounds and pence	.01 pence per therm

Options on Futures

Contract	Trading Unit	Price Quote	Tick Size	Strike Price Intervals
● Brent Crude	1 futures contract	dollars and cents per barrel	1 cent per barrel	50 cents per barrel
● Gas Oil	1 futures contract	dollars and cents per metric ton	5 cents per metric ton	$5 per metric ton

Last Trading Day	Contract Months	Trading Hours	Ticker Symbol
2nd day before 3rd Wednesday of delivery month	2 serial monthly and 4 quarterly contract cycles out of Mar, June, Sept, Dec	8:00–8:30 A.M. 4:30–10:00 P.M.	OPI
2nd day before 3rd Wednesday of delivery month	2 serial monthly and 4 quarterly contract cycles out of Mar, June, Sept, Dec	8:00–8:30 A.M. 4:30–10:00 P.M.	OXS

Last Trading Day	Contract Months	Trading Hours (GMT)
Business day preceding 15th day prior to 1st day of delivery month	12 months, then quarterly to maximum 24 months, then half-yearly to maximum 36 months	10:02 A.M.–8:13 P.M.
2 business days before 14th day of delivery month	Up to 12 consecutive months forward, then quarterly to 18 months forward	9:15 A.M.–5:27 P.M.
2 business days before 1st calendar day of delivery month	Balance of Month contract listed for any unexpired days remaining in current month; complete months listed 15 consecutive months into future, beginning with next whole month	10:00 A.M.–5:00 P.M., 10:00 A.M.–4:00 P.M. (daily contracts)

Last Trading Day	Contract Months	Trading Hours
3rd business day prior to end of trading in underlying futures contract	1st 6 quoted months of underlying futures contract	10:00 A.M.–8:13 P.M.
5th busines day prior to end of trading in underlying futures contract	1st 6 quoted months of underlying futures contract	9:15 A.M.–5:27 P.M.

London International Financial Futures Exchange (LIFFE)

Commodity Futures

Contract	Trading Unit	Price Quote	Tick Size
• Baltic Freight Index (BIFFEX)	$10 per index point	dollars per index point	1 index point ($10)
• Barley	100 metric tons	British pounds and pence per metric ton	5 pence per metric ton (5 pounds)
• Cocoa No. 7	10 metric tons	British pounds per metric ton	1 pound per metric ton (10 pounds)
• Potato	20 metric tons	British pounds and pence per metric ton	10 pence per metric ton (2 pounds)
• Robusta Coffee	5 metric tons	dollars per metric ton	1 dollar per metric ton ($5)
• Wheat	100 metric tons	British pounds and pence per metric ton	5 pence (5 pounds)
• White Sugar No. 5	50 metric tons	dollars and cents	10 cents per metric ton ($5)

Commodity Options on Futures

Contract	Trading Unit	Price Quote	Tick Size
• Baltic Freight Index (BIFFEX)	1BIFFEX futures contract	dollars per index point	1 index point ($10)
• Barley	1 barley futures contract	British pounds and and pence per metric ton	5 pence per metric ton (5 pounds)
• Cocoa No. 7	1 cocoa futures contract	British pounds per metric ton	1 pound per metric ton
• Potato	1 potato futures contract	pence per metric ton	10 pence per metric ton (2 pounds)

Last Trading Day	Contract Months	Trading Hours (GMT)
Last business day of expiration month	Jan, Apr, July, Oct	10:15 A.M.–12:30 P.M. 2:30–4:40 P.M.
23rd day of delivery month	Jan, Mar, May, Sept, Nov	10:00 A.M.–12:30 P.M. 2:30–4:15 P.M.
Last business day of delivery month	Mar, May, July, Sept, Dec	9:30 A.M.–12:25 P.M. 2:00–4:55 P.M.
Close of business on 4th calendar day of delivery month	Mar, Apr, May, June, Nov	10:00 A.M.–12.30 P.M. 2:30–4:15 P.M.
Last business day of delivery month	Jan, Mar, May, July, Sept, Nov	9:45 A.M.–12:30 P.M. 2:15–5:00 P.M.
16 days before 1st day of tender period	Mar, May, Aug, Oct, Dec	9:45 A.M.–6:30 P.M. on FAST electronic system
23rd day of delivery month	Jan, Mar, May, July, Sept, Nov	10:00 A.M.–12.30 P.M. 2:30–4:15 P.M.

Strike Prices	Expiration Day	Expiration Months	Trading Hours (GMT)
50 index point intervals	Futures expiration day	Current month, followed by 2 consecutive months and Jan, Apr, July, Oct for up to 18 months forward	10:15 A.M.–12:30 P.M. 2:30–4:40 P.M.
1 pound per metric ton interval	2nd Thursday of month preceding expiration month	Jan, Mar, May, Sept, Nov	10:00 A.M.–12:30 P.M. 2:30–4:15 P.M.
25 pounds per metric ton intervals	3rd Wednesday of month preceding expiration month	Mar, May, July, Sept, Dec	9:30 A.M.–12:25 P.M. 2:00–4:55 P.M.
5 pounds per metric ton intervals	15th business day of month before expiration month	Apr, Nov	11:00 A.M.–12:30 P.M. 2:30–4:00 P.M.

Contract	Trading Unit	Price Quote	Tick Size
• Robusta Coffee	1 robusta coffee futures contract	dollars per metric ton	1 dollar per metric ton ($5)
• Wheat	1 wheat futures contract	British pounds and pence per metric ton	5 pence per metric ton (5 pounds)
• White Sugar No. 5	1 No. 5 white sugar futures contract	dollars and cents per metric ton	5 cents per metric ton ($2.50)

Government Bond Futures

Contract	Trading Unit	Price Quote	Tick Size
• German Government Bond (Bund)	250,000 Deutsche marks nominal value notional bond with 6% coupon	per 100 Deutsche marks	.01 Deutsche mark (DM25)
• German Government Bond (Bobl)	250,000 Deutsche marks nominal value notional bond with 6% coupon	per 100 Deutsche marks	.01 Deutsche mark (DM25)
• Italian Government Bond (BTP)	200,000 lira nominal value notional bond with 8% coupon	per 100 lira	.01 lira (ITL20,000)
• Japanese Government Bond (JGB)	100,000,000 yen face value notional long-term bond with 6% coupon	per 100 yen	.01 yen (¥10,000)
• Long Gilt	50,000 British pounds nominal value notional Gilt with 9% coupon	per 100 British pounds	¹⁄₃₂ pound (15.625 pounds)
• U.S. Treasury Bond	$100,000 U.S. dollars nominal value bond with with 8% coupon	per 100 U.S. dollars	¹⁄₃₂ dollar ($31.25)

Government Bond Options on Futures

Contract	Trading Unit	Price Quote	Tick Size
• German Government Bond (Bund)	1 Bund futures contract	Multiples of .01 Deutsche mark	.01 Deutsche mark (DM25)

Strike Prices	Expiration Day	Expiration Months	Trading Hours (GMT)
50 dollars per metric ton intervals	3rd Wednesday of month preceding expiration month	Jan, Mar, May, July, Sept, Nov	9:45 A.M.–12:30 P.M. 2:15–5:00 P.M.
1 pound per metric ton intervals	2nd Thursday of month preceding expiration month	Jan, Mar, May, July, Sept, Nov	10:00 A.M.–12:30 P.M. 2:30–6:15 P.M.
10 dollars per metric ton intervals	1st business day of month before expiration month	Mar, May, Aug, Oct, Dec	10:00 A.M.–6:30 P.M. on FAST electronic system

Last Trading Day	Contract Months	Trading Hours (GMT)
3 Frankfurt working days before delivery	Mar, June, Sept, Dec	7:00 A.M.–4:15 P.M.; APT electronic system; 4:20–5:55 P.M.
10th calendar day of delivery month	Mar, June, Sept, Dec	7:30 A.M.–4:15 P.M.; APT: 4:20–5:55 P.M.
10th calendar day of delivery month	Mar, June, Sept, Dec	8:00 A.M.–4:10 P.M.; APT: 4:21–5:58 P.M.
1 business day prior to Tokyo Stock Exchange last trading day	Mar, June, Sept, Dec	APT: 7:00 P.M.–4:00 P.M.
2 business days before last business day of delivery month	Mar, June, Sept, Dec	8:00 A.M.–4:15 P.M.; APT: 4:22–6:00 P.M.
LIFFE business with CBOT business day	Mar, June, Sept, Dec	7:30 A.M.–1:00 P.M.

Strike Prices	Expiration Day	Expiration Months	Trading Hours (GMT)
.50 Deutsche mark intervals	Last trading day	Mar, June, Sept, Dec plus additional serial months	7:02 A.M.–4:15 P.M.; APT: 4:28–5:53 P.M.

Contract	Trading Unit	Price Quote	Tick Size
• German Government Bond (Bobl)	1 Bobl futures contract	Multiples of .01 Deutsche mark	.01 Deutsche mark (DM25)
• Italian Government Bond (BTP)	1 BTP futures contract	Multiples of .01 lira	.01 lira (ITL20,000)
• Long Gilt	1 long gilt futures contract	Multiples of ¹⁄₆₄ pound	¹⁄₆₄ pound (7.8125 pounds)
• U.S. Treasury Bond	1 T-Bond futures contract	Multiples of ¹⁄₆₄ dollar	¹⁄₆₄ dollar ($15.625)

Short Term Interest Rate Futures

Contract	Trading Unit	Price Quote	Tick Size
• Euro (3-month)	1,000,000 Euro	100 minus rate of interest	.01 Euro (Euro 25)
• Eurolira (3-month)	1,000,000,000 lira	100 minus rate of interest	.01 lira (ITL25,000)
• Euromark (1-month)	3,000,000 Deutsche marks	100 minus rate of interest	.01 Deutsche mark (DM25)
• Euromark (3-month)	1,000,000 Deutsche marks	100 minus rate of interest	.01 Deutsche mark (DM25)
• Euroswiss (3-month)	1,000,000 Swiss francs	100 minus rate of interest	.01 Swiss franc (SF25)
• Euroyen (3-month)	1,000,000 yen	100 minus rate of interest	.01 yen (¥2,500)
• Sterling (3-month)	500,000 British pounds	100 minus rate of interest	.01 pound (12.50 pounds)

Strike Prices	Expiration Day	Expiration Months	Trading Hours (GMT)
.25 Deutsche mark intervals	Last trading day	Mar, June, Sept, Dec plus additional serial months	7:32 A.M.–4:15 P.M.
.50 lira intervals	7 business days before 1st day of delivery month	Mar, June, Sept, Dec	8:02 A.M.–4:10 P.M.
2 pound intervals	6 business days before 1st day of delivery month	Mar, June, Sept, Dec plus additional serial months	8:02 A.M.–4:15 P.M.
2-point intervals	LIFFE business day coinciding with CBOT last trading day	Mar, June, Sept, Dec	7:32 A.M.–1:00 P.M.

Last Trading Day	Contract Months	Trading Hours (GMT)
2 business days before 3rd Wednesday of delivery month	Mar, June, Sept, Dec	8:05 A.M.–4:05 P.M.
2 business days before 3rd Wednesday of delivery month	Mar, June, Sept, Dec	7:55 A.M.–4:10 P.M. APT: 4:23–5:58 P.M.
2 business days before 3rd Wednesday of delivery month	All calendar months	7:30 A.M.–4:10 P.M. APT: 4:25–5:59 P.M.
2 business days before 3rd Wednesday of delivery month	Mar, June, Sept, Dec plus 2 additional months	7:30 A.M.–4:10 P.M. APT: 4:25–5:59 P.M.
2 business days before 3rd Wednesday of delivery month	Mar, June, Sept, Dec	8:10 A.M.–4:05 P.M. APT: 4:24–5:55 P.M.
2 LIFFE business days before TIFFE last trading day for equivalent Euroyen contract	Mar, June, Sept, Dec contracts listed on 3-year cycle	9:00 A.M.–4:00 P.M.
3rd Wednesday of delivery month	Mar, June, Sept, Dec	8:05 A.M.–4:05 P.M. APT: 4:22–5:57 P.M.

Short Term Interest Rate Options on Futures

Contract	Trading Unit	Price Quote	Tick Size
• Eurolira (3-month)	1 3-month Eurolira futures contract	Multiples of .01 lira	.01 lira (ITL25,000)
• Euromark (3-month)	1 3-month Euromark futures contract	Multiples of .01 Deutsche mark	.01 Deutsche mark (DM25,000)
• Euroswiss (3-month)	1 3-month Euroswiss futures contract	Multiples of .01 Swiss franc	.01 Swiss franc (SF25)
• Sterling (3-month)	1 3-month Sterling futures contract	Multiples of .01 British pound	.01 pound (12.50 pounds)

UK Stock Index Futures

Contract	Trading Unit	Price Quote	Tick Size
• FTSE 100 Index	25 British pounds per index point	index points	.5 pound (12.50 pounds)

UK Stock Index Options on Futures

Contract	Trading Unit	Price Quote	Tick Size
• FTSE 100 Index (American Sytle Exercise)	10 British pounds per index point	index points	.5 pound (5 pounds)

Strike Prices	Expiration Day	Contract Months	Trading Hours (GMT)
.25 intervals	Last trading day	Mar, June, Sept, Dec	7:57 A.M.–4:10 P.M.
.25 intervals	Last trading day	Mar, June, Sept, Dec plus additional serial months	7:32 A.M.–4:10 P.M.
.25 intervals	Last trading day	Mar, June, Sept, Dec	8:12 A.M.–4:05 P.M.
.25 intervals	Last trading day	Mar, June, Sept, Dec	8:07 A.M.–4:05 P.M.

Last Trading Day	Contract Months	Trading Hours (GMT)
3rd Friday in delivery month	Mar, June, Sept, Dec	8:35 A.M.–4:10 P.M.; APT: 4:32–5:30 P.M.

Strike Prices	Expiration Day	Contract Months	Trading Hours (GMT)
50 or 100 index points	Any business day	June and Dec plus additional months so 4 nearest calendar months are always available	8:35 A.M.–4:10 P.M.

London Metal Exchange (LME)

Futures

Contract	Trading Unit	Price Quote	Tick Size
● Aluminium Alloy	20 metric tons	dollars and cents	50 cents per metric ton
● Copper	25 metric tons	dollars and cents	50 cents per metric ton
● Nickel	6 metric tons	dollars and cents	$1 per metric ton
● Primary Aluminium	25 metric tons	dollars and cents	50 cents per metric ton
● Special High Grade Zinc	25 metric tons	dollars and cents	50 cents per metric ton
● Standard Lead	25 metric tons	dollars and cents	50 cents per metric ton
● Tin	5 metric tons	dollars and cents	$1 per metric ton

Delivery Dates	Contract Type	Trading Hours
Daily for 3 months forward, then every Wednesday for 3 months and every 3rd Wednesday of month for next 9 months	Cash and 3 months forward	11:45–11:50 P.M. 1:05–1:10 P.M. 3:50–3:55 P.M. 4:30–4:35 P.M.
Daily for 3 months forward, then every 3rd Wednesday of month for next 21 months	Cash and 3 months forward	12:00–12:05 P.M. 12:30–12:35 P.M. 3:30–3:35 P.M. 4:10–4:15 P.M.
Daily for 3 months forward, then every Wednesday for 3 months and every 3rd Wednesday of month for next 21 months	Cash and 3 months forward	12:15–12:20 P.M. 1:00–1:05 P.M. 3:45–3:50 P.M. 4:25–4:30 P.M.
Daily for 3 months forward, then every Wednesday for 3 months and every 3rd Wednesday of month for next 21 months	Cash and 3 months forward	11:55–12:00 P.M. 12:55–1:00 P.M. 3:35–3:40 P.M. 4:15–4:20 P.M.
Daily for 3 months forward, then every Wednesday for 3 months and every 3rd Wednesday of month for next 21 months	Cash and 3 months forward	12:10–12:15 P.M. 12:50–12:55 P.M. 3:25–3:30 P.M. 4:05–4:10 P.M.
Daily for 3 months forward, then every Wednesday of month for next 6 months and every 3rd Wednesday for next 9 months	Cash and 3 months forward	12:05–12:10 P.M. 12:40–12:45 P.M. 3:20–3:25 P.M. 4:00–4:05 P.M.
Daily for 3 months forward, then every Wednesday for 3 months and every 3rd Wednesday of month for next 9 months	Cash and 3 months forward	11:50 P.M.-11:55 P.M. 12:40 P.M.-12:45 P.M. 3:40 P.M.-3:45 P.M. 4:20 P.M.-4:25 P.M.

Traded Options

Contract	Trading Unit	Price Quote	Tick Size	Strike Price Intervals
• Aluminium Alloy	1 futures contract	U.S. dollars, sterling, yen, Deutsche marks	$.01, £.01, ¥10, DM.10	$25, $50, $100; £25; ¥10,000 and ¥20,000; DM50 and DM200
• Copper	1 futures contract	U.S. dollars, sterling, yen, Deutsche marks	$.01, £.01, ¥10, DM.10	$25, $50, $100; £25; ¥10,000 and ¥20,000; DM50 and DM200
• Nickel	1 futures contract	U.S. dollars, sterling, yen, Deutsche marks	$.01, £.01, ¥10, DM.10	$100; £50; ¥20,000; DM200
• Primary Aluminium	1 futures contract	U.S. dollars, sterling, yen, Deutsche marks	$.01, £.01, ¥10, DM.10	$25, $50, $100; £25; ¥10,000 and ¥20,000; DM50 and DM200
• Special High Grade Zinc	1 futures contract	U.S. dollars, sterling, yen, Deutsche marks	$.01, £.01, ¥10, DM.10	$25, $50, $100; £20; ¥10,000 and ¥20,000; DM100 and DM200
• Standard Lead	1 futures contract	U.S. dollars, sterling, yen, Deutsche marks	$.01, £.01, ¥10, DM.10	$25; £20; ¥5,000 and ¥10,000; DM50 and DM100
• Tin	1 futures contract	U.S. dollars, sterling, yen, Deutsche marks	$.01, £.01, ¥10, DM.10	$100; £50; ¥20,000; DM200

ASIA/PACIFIC SECURITIES, FUTURES AND OPTIONS EXCHANGES

AUSTRALIA

Sydney Futures Exchange (SFE)

Commodity Futures

Contract	Trading Unit	Price Quote	Tick Size
• New South Wales Electricity	500 megawatt hours	Australian dollars and cents	A$.05 per Mwh (A$25)

Declaration Day	Prompt Months	Prompt Date
1st Wednesday of prompt month	Any of 15 months	3rd Wednesday of prompt month
1st Wednesday of prompt month	Any of 27 months	3rd Wednesday of prompt month
1st Wednesday of prompt month	Any of 27 months	3rd Wednesday of prompt month
1st Wednesday of prompt month	Any of 27 months	3rd Wednesday of prompt month
1st Wednesday of prompt month	Any of 27 months	3rd Wednesday of prompt month
1st Wednesday of prompt month	Any of 15 months	3rd Wednesday of prompt month
1st Wednesday of prompt month	Any of 15 months	3rd Wednesday of prompt month

Last Trading Day	Contract Months	Trading Hours	Ticker Symbol
Last business day of contract month	Up to 12 months	Sycom: 10:00 A.M.– 12:30 P.M. 2:00–4:00 P.M.	NE (Sycom)

Contract	Trading Unit	Price Quote	Tick Size
● Victorian Electricity	500 megawatt hours	Australian dollars and cents	A$0.05 per Mwh (A$25)
● Wheat	50 metric tons	Australian dollar per metric ton	A$0.50 per metric ton (A$25)
● Wool	2,500 kilograms	cents per kilogram	1 cent per kilogram (A$25)

Financial Futures

Contract	Trading Unit	Price Quote	Tick Size
● Bank Accepted Bills (90-Day)	A$1 million face value bank acceptance bills of exchange	100 minus annual percentage yield, to 2 decimals	.01% ($24)
● Commonwealth Treasury Bond (10-year)	Bonds with face value of A$100,000 with 12% per year coupon	yield minus index of 100	.0005% (A$44)
● Commonwealth Treasury Bond (3-year)	Bonds with face value of A$100,000 with 12% per year coupon	yield minus index of 100	.01% (A$28)

Index Futures

Contract	Trading Unit	Price Quote	Tick Size
● All Ordinaries Share Price Index	25 × index in Australian dollars	1 full index point	1 index point (A$25)

Share Futures

Contract	Trading Unit	Price Quote	Tick Size
● ANZ Bank Share	1,000 ANZ Bank shares	cents per share	1cent = A$10
● Broken Hill Proprietary Share	1,000 BHP shares	cents per share	1cent = A$10
● CRA Ltd. Share	1,000 CRA Ltd. shares	cents per share	1cent = A$10

Last Trading Day	Contract Months	Trading Hours	Ticker Symbol
Last business day of contract month	Up to 12 months	Sycom:10:00 A.M.–12:30 P.M. 2:00–4:00 P.M.	VE (Sycom)
3rd Tuesday of contract month	Jan, Mar, May, July, Sept, Nov	Floor: 10:00 A.M.–12:30 P.M. Sycom: 4:40 P.M.–6:00 A.M.	WH (Floor) SW (Sycom)
3rd Thursday of contract month	Feb, Apr, June, Aug, Oct, Dec	Floor: 10:30 A.M.–12:30 P.M. 2:00–4:00 P.M. Sycom: 4:40 P.M.–6:00 A.M.	GW (Floor) SG (Sycom)

Last Trading Day	Contract Months	Trading Hours	Ticker Symbol
2nd Friday of delivery month	Mar, June, Sept, Dec	Floor: 8:30 A.M.–12:30 P.M. 2:00–4:30 P.M. Sycom: 4:40 P.M.–6:00 A.M.	IR (Floor) SR (Sycom)
15th day of contract month	Mar, June, Sept, Dec	Floor: 8:30 A.M.–12:30 P.M. 2:00–4:30 P.M. Sycom: 4:40 P.M.–6:00 A.M.	XB (Floor) SX (Sycom)
15th day of contract month	Mar, June, Sept, Dec	Floor: 8:30 A.M.–12:30 P.M. 2:00–4:30 P.M. Sycom: 4:40 P.M.–6:00 A.M.	YB (Floor) SY (Sycom)

Last Trading Day	Contract Months	Trading Hours	Ticker Symbol
Last business day of contract month	Mar, June, Sept, Dec	9:50 A.M.–12:30 P.M. 2:00–4:10 P.M. Sycom: 4:40 P.M.–6:00 A.M.	AO (Floor) SA (Sycom)

Last Trading Day	Contract Months	Trading Hours	Ticker Symbol
Thursday before last Friday of settlement month	Jan, Apr, July, Oct	Floor: 9:50 A.M.–12:30 P.M. 2:00– 4:15 P.M. Sycom: 4:40 P.M.–6:00 A.M.	AN (Floor) NA (Sycom)
Thursday before last Friday of settlement month	Mar, Jun, Sept, Dec	Floor: 9:50 A.M.–12:30 P.M. 2:00– 4:15 P.M. Sycom: 4:40 P.M.–6:00 A.M.	BH (Floor) SH (Sycom)
Thursday before last Friday of settlement month	Mar, June, Sept, Dec	Floor: 9:50 A.M.–12:30 P.M. 2:00– 4:15 P.M. Sycom: 4:40 P.M.–6:00 A.M.	CA (Floor) RS (Sycom)

Contract	Trading Unit	Price Quote	Tick Size
● Fosters Brewing Group Share	1,000 Fosters Brewing shares	cents per share	1cent = A$10
● MIM Holdings Shares	1,000 MIM Holdings shares	cents per share	1cent = A$10
● National Australia Bank Share	1,000 NAB shares	cents per share	1cent = A$10
● News Corporation Share	1,000 News Corp. shares	cents per share	1cent = A$10
● Pacific Dunlop Share	1,000 Pacific Dunlop shares	cents per share	1cent = A$10
● Western Mining Corporation Share	1,000 Western Mining Corp. shares	cents per share	1cent = A$10
● Westpac Banking Corporation Share	1,000 Westpac Banking shares	cents per share	1cent = A$10

Commodity Options on Futures

Contract	Trading Unit	Price Quote	Tick Size	Strike Price Intervals
● Wheat	1 futures contract	cents per metric ton	10 cent multiples	A$5 per metric ton
● Wool	1 futures contract	cents per kilogram	$1/10$ cent multiples	25 cents per kilogram

Financial Options on Futures

Contract	Trading Unit	Price Quote	Tick Size	Strike Price Intervals
● Bank Accepted Bills (90-Day)	1 futures contract	100 minus annual yield	.01%	.25%
● Commonwealth Treasury Bond (10-Year)	1 futures contract	yield minus index of 100	.005%	.25%

Last Trading Day	Contract Months	Trading Hours	Ticker Symbol
Thursday before last Friday of settlement month	Jan, Apr, July, Oct	Floor: 9:50 A.M.–12:30 P.M. 2:00– 4:15 P.M. Sycom: 4:40 P.M.–6:00 A.M.	FB (Floor) OF (Sycom)
Thursday before last Friday of settlement month	Jan, Apr, July, Oct	Floor: 9:50 A.M.–12:30 P.M. 2:00– 4:15 P.M. Sycom: 4:40 P.M.–6:00 A.M.	IM (Floor) SM (Sycom)
Thursday before last Friday of settlement month	Jan, Apr, July, Oct	Floor: 9:50 A.M.–12:30 P.M. 2:00–4:15 P.M. Sycom: 4:40 P.M.–6:00 A.M.	NB (Floor) SN (Sycom)
Thursday before last Friday of settlement month	Feb, May, Aug, Nov	Floor: 9:50 A.M.–12:30 P.M. 2:00–4:15 P.M. Sycom: 4:40 P.M.–6:00 A.M.	NU (Floor) UN (Sycom)
Thursday before last Friday of settlement month	Feb, May, Aug, Nov	Floor: 9:50 A.M.–12:30 P.M. 2:00–4:15 P.M. Sycom: 4:40 P.M.–6:00 A.M.	PC (Floor) DP (Sycom)
Thursday before last Friday of settlement month	Mar, Jun, Sept, Dec	Floor: 9:50 A.M.–12:30 P.M. 2:00–4:15 P.M. Sycom: 4:40 P.M.–6:00 A.M.	WM (Floor) MC (Sycom)
Thursday before last Friday of settlement month	Jan, Apr, July, Oct	Floor: 9:50 A.M.–12:30 P.M. 2:00–4:15 P.M. Sycom: 4:40 P.M.–6:00 A.M.	BC (Floor) SC (Sycom)

Last Trading Day	Contract Months	Trading Hours	Ticker Symbol
Business day 7 days before end of delivery period for underlying futures contract	Jan, Mar, May, July, Sept, Nov	Floor: 10:00 A.M.–12:30 P.M. Sycom: 4:40 P.M.–6:00 A.M.	WH (Floor) SW (Sycom)
Friday before end of delivery period for underlying futures contract	Jan, Mar, May, July, Sept, Nov	Floor: 10:00 A.M.–12:30 P.M. Sycom: 4:40 P.M.–6:00 A.M.	GW (Floor) SG (Sycom)

Expiration Day	Contract Months	Trading Hours	Ticker Symbol
Friday 1 week before underlying future's settlement day	Mar, June, Sept, Dec	Floor: 8:30 A.M.–12:30 P.M. 2:00–4:30 P.M. Sycom: 4:40 P.M.–6:00 A.M.	IR (Floor) SR (Sycom)
Last day of trading in underlying futures contract	Mar, June, Sept, Dec	Floor: 8:30 A.M.–12:30 P.M. 2:00–4:30 P.M. Sycom: 4:40 P.M.–6:00 A.M.	XB (Floor) SX (Sycom)

Contract	Trading Unit	Price Quote	Tick Size	Strike Price Intervals
• Commonwealth Treasury Bond (3-Year)	1 futures contract	yield minus index of 100	.01%	.25%

Index Options on Futures

Contract	Trading Unit	Price Quote	Tick Size	Strike Price Intervals
• All Ordinaries Share Price Index	1 futures contract	index points	.1 index point	25 points

JAPAN

Tokyo Stock Exchange

Financial Futures

Contract	Trading Unit	Price Quote	Tick Size
• Japanese Government Bond (5-Year)	bond = ¥100 million face value	Yen and points	$\frac{1}{100}$ point/100 points (¥10,000/contract)
• Japanese Government Bond (10-Year)	bond = ¥100 million face value	Yen and points	$\frac{1}{100}$ point/100 points (¥10,000/contract)
• Japanese Government Bond (20-Year)	bond = ¥100 million face value	Yen and points	$\frac{1}{100}$ point/100 points (¥10,000/contract)
• U.S. Treasury Bond (20-Year)	bond = $100,000 face value	Dollars and points	$\frac{1}{32}$ point/100 points ($31.25/contract)

Index Futures

Contract	Trading Unit	Price Quote	Tick Size
• Tokyo Stock Price Index (TOPIX)	¥10,000 × index	Yen and points	.5 point of TOPIX
• TOPIX Bank Index	¥10,000 × index	Yen and points	.1 point of index

Expiration Day	Contract Months	Trading Hours	Ticker Symbol
Last day of trading in underlying futures contract	Mar, June, Sept, Dec	Floor: 8:30 A.M.–12:30 P.M. 2:00–4:30 P.M. Sycom: 4:40 P.M.–6:00 A.M.	YB (Floor) SY (Sycom)

Expiration Day	Contract Months	Trading Hours	Ticker Symbol
Last trading day of underlying futures contract	Mar, June, Sept, Dec	9:50 A.M.–12:30 P.M. 2:00–4:10 P.M. Sycom: 4:40 P.M.–6:00 A.M.	AO (Floor) SA (Sycom)

Last Trading Day	Delivery Date	Contract Months	Trading Hours
7th business day before delivery date	20th day of contract month	Mar, June, Sept, Dec (5 contract months always traded)	9:00–11:00 A.M. 12:30–3:00 P.M.
7th business day before delivery date	20th day of contract month	Mar, June, Sept, Dec (5 contract months always traded)	9:00–11:00 A.M. 12:30–3:00 P.M.
7th business day before delivery date	20th day of contract month	Mar, June, Sept, Dec (5 contract months always traded)	9:00–11:00 A.M. 12:30–3:00 P.M.
7th Chicago Board of Trade business day prior to CBOT's last business day of month	Last business day of each contract month	Mar, June, Sept, Dec (5 contract months always traded)	9:00–11:00 A.M. 12:30–3:00 P.M.

Last Trading Day	Settlement Date	Contract Months	Trading Hours
Business day before 2nd Friday of month	3rd business day after 2nd Friday of month	Mar, June, Sept, Dec (5 contract months always traded)	9:00–11:00 A.M. 12:30–3:10 P.M.
Business day before 2nd Friday of month	3rd business day after 2nd Friday of month	Mar, June, Sept, Dec (5 contract months always traded)	9:00–11:00 A.M. 12:30–3:10 P.M.

Contract	Trading Unit	Price Quote	Tick Size
• TOPIX Electric Appliances Index	¥10,000 × index	Yen and points	.5 point of index
• TOPIX Transportation Equipment Index	¥10,000 × index	Yen and points	.5 point of index

Options

Contract	Trading Unit	Tick Size	Strike Price
• Equity Options	Corresponding to minimum trading lot of underlying stock	¥.5 under ¥1,000, ¥5 under ¥10,000, ¥50 under ¥100,000, ¥500 under ¥1,000,000, ¥5,000 over ¥1,000,000	¥25 to ¥1 million
• Japanese Government Bond (10-Year)	1 futures contract	$\frac{1}{100}$ point/100 points (¥10,000/contract)	1 yen intervals
• Tokyo Stock Price Index (TOPIX)	¥10,000 × TOPIX	.5 point (¥5,000 in value)	25 point intervals

SINGAPORE

Singapore International Monetary Exchange (SIMEX)

Commodity Futures

Contract	Trading Unit	Price Quote	Tick Size
• Brent Crude Oil	1,000 barrels	dollars and cents	1 cent per barrel ($10)
• Gold	100 troy ounces	dollars and cents	$.05 per troy ounce ($5)

Last Trading Day	Settlement Date	Contract Months	Trading Hours
Business day before 2nd Friday of month	3rd business day after 2nd Friday of month	Mar, June, Sept, Dec (5 contract months always traded)	9:00–11:00 A.M. 12:30 P.M.–3:10 P.M.
Business day before 2nd Friday of month	3rd business day after 2nd Friday of month	Mar, June, Sept, Dec (5 contract months always traded)	9:00–11:00 A.M. 12:30 P.M.–3:10 P.M.

Last Trading Day	Expiration Date	Contract Months	Trading Hours
Business day before 2nd Friday of month	Last trading day	2 closest quarterly months and 2 serial months	9:00–11:00 A.M. 12:30 A.M.–3:10 P.M.
Expiration date	Last business day of month before delivery month of under-lying futures	2 closest quarterly months and 1 or 2 serial months	9:00–11:00 A.M. 12:30 P.M.–3:00 P.M.
Business day before 2nd Friday of month	Business day before 2nd Friday of month; 2nd Friday for Mar, June, Sept, Dec contracts	4 near-term months	9:00–11:00 A.M. 12:30 A.M.–3:10 P.M.

Last Trading Day	Contract Months	Trading Hours	Ticker Symbol
IPE business day preceding 15th calendar day before 1st day of contract month	12 months	9:25 A.M.–12:30 P.M. IPE mutual offset: 2:00–5:58 P.M.	BC
2nd last business day of month before 1st business day of contract month	Feb, Apr, June, Aug, Oct, Dec	9:00 A.M.–5:15 P.M. electronic trading: 7:35 P.M.–1:00 A.M.	GD

Financial Futures

Contract	Trading Unit	Price Quote	Tick Size
• Eurodollar (3-Month)	$1 million	basis points	½ basis point = $12.50 (front year months) 1 basis point = $25 (all other months)
• Euromark (3-Month)	1 million Deutsche marks	basis points	1 basis point (DM25)
• Euroyen (3-Month)	100 million yen	basis points	1 basis point (¥2,500)
• Japanese Government Bond	50 million yen	yen face value notional long-term 10-year JGB with 6% coupon	¥.01/Y100 face value (¥100)

Options on Financial Futures

Contract	Trading Unit	Price Quote	Tick Size	Strike Price Intervals
• Eurodollar (3-Month)	1 futures contract	index points	.0005 point ($12.50)	.50 point below 88 .25 point above 88
• Euroyen (3-Month)	1 futures contract	index points	.01 point (¥2,500)	.25 points
• Japanese Government Bond	1 futures contract	yen	¥.001/¥100 face value (¥5,000)	¥.05

Index Futures

Contract	Trading Unit	Price Quote	Tick Size
• Hong Kong Index	HK$100 × index	HK$	1 index point (HK$100)
• Nikkei 225 Stock Index	¥500 × index	index points	5 points (¥2,500)

Last Trading Day	Contract Months	Trading Hours	Ticker Symbol
2nd London business day before 3rd Wednesday of contract month	2 serial months and Mar, June, Sept, Dec	7:45 A.M.–7:00 P.M. CME mutual offset: 9:20 P.M.–4:00 A.M.	ED
2nd London business day before 3rd Wednesday of contract month	Mar, June, Sept, Dec	10:00 A.M.–7:10 P.M. CME mutual offset: 7:35 P.M.–1:00 A.M.	EM
2nd business day before 3rd Wednesday of contract month	Mar, June, Sept, Dec	7:58 A.M.–8:05 P.M. CME mutual offset: 7:35 P.M.–1:00 A.M.	EY
1 business day before Tokyo Stock Exchange JGB future's last trading day	5 quarterly contract months on Mar, June, Sept, Dec cycle	7:45 A.M.–7:10 P.M. CME mutual offset: 7:35 P.M.–1:00 A.M.	JB

Last Trading Day	Contract Months	Trading Hours	Ticker Symbol
2nd London business day before 3rd Wednesday of contract month	Mar, June, Sept, Dec	7:45 A.M.–7:00 P.M.	CE (call) PE (put)
2nd business day before 3rd Wednesday of contract month	Mar, June, Sept, Dec	7:58 A.M.–8:05 P.M.	CEY (call) PEY (put)
Last TSE business day of calendar month before expiring contract month	2 nearest serial months + 2 nearest quarterly months in Mar, June, Sept, Dec cycle	7:45 A.M.–7:10 P.M.	CJB (call) PJB (put)

Last Trading Day	Contract Months	Trading Hours	Ticker Symbol
2nd last business day of contract month	2 serial months and Mar, June, Sept, Dec contracts listed on a 5 quarterly month cycle	10:00 A.M.–12:30 P.M. 2:30–4:00 P.M.	HI
Day before 2nd Friday of contract month	Mar, June, Sept, Dec contracts listed on a 5 quarterly month cycle	7:55 A.M.–10:15 P.M. 11:15 A.M.–2:15 P.M.	NK

Contract	Trading Unit	Price Quote	Tick Size
• Nikkei 300 Stock Index	¥10,000 × index	index points	.1 point (¥1,000)
• Simex MSCI Taiwan Index	$100 × index	index points	.1 point ($10)

Options on Index Futures

Contract	Trading Unit	Price Quote	Tick Size	Strike Price Intervals
• Nikkei 225 Stock Index	1 futures contract	index points	5 points (¥2,500)	500 points
• Nikkei 300 Stock Index	1 futures contract	index points	.1 point (¥1,000)	5 points
• Simex MSCI Taiwan Index	1 futures contract	index points	.1 point ($10)	5 points

Last Trading Day	Contract Months	Trading Hours	Ticker Symbol
Day before 2nd Friday of contract month	Mar, June, Sept, Dec contracts listed on a 5 quarterly month cycle	8:00 A.M.–10:15 P.M. 11:15 A.M.–2:15 P.M.	N3
2nd last business day of contract month	Nearest 4 Mar quarterly contract months with 2 nearest serial months	M–F, 8:45 A.M.– 12:15 P.M.; Sat, 8:45– 11:15 A.M.	TW

Last Trading Day	Contract Months	Trading Hours	Ticker Symbol
Day before 2nd Friday of contract month	5 serial months and 5 quarterly months in Mar, June, Sept, Dec cycle	7:55 A.M.–10:15 P.M. 11:15 A.M.–2:15 P.M.	CNK (call) PNK (put)
Day before 2nd Friday of contract month	5 serial months and 5 quarterly months in Mar, June, Sept, Dec cycle	8:00 A.M.–10:15 P.M. 11:15 A.M.–2:15 P.M.	CN3 (call) PN3 (put)
2nd last business day of contract month	Nearest 4 Mar quarterly contract months with 2 nearest serial months	M–F, 8:45 A.M.– 12:15 P.M.; Sat, 8:45– 11:15 A.M.	CTW (call) PTW (put)

5. HISTORICAL DATA

This section of the *Handbook* allows you to follow the major ups and downs of the financial markets and the United States economy during the 20th century. Although history never repeats itself exactly, it is important to understand historical market cycles if you are to understand where the markets and economy stand today, as well as where they might be going in the future.

The historical section is presented with graphs accompanied by tabular data and explanations of what the information signifies to you as an investor. Graphs are based on end-of-month closing stock index values; municipal bond yields compiled the first week of each month; month-end London afternoon fix prices of gold; monthly average discount, prime, and federal funds rates; and monthly or monthly average government economic statistics.

The tabular data show annual highs, lows, and year-end figures on the same monthly bases as the above with these exceptions: stock indexes are based on daily closing figures; the consumer and producer price indexes and money supply (M-1) statistics are annual percentage changes (for instance, December 1997 vs. December 1996); gold prices are daily London afternoon fixings; and the discount and prime rates are day-end figures.

Note that the month-end data points on which the stock index graphs are based may reflect different highs and lows than the daily closing data. The month-end data plot long-term trends with a minimum of aberrations caused by PROGRAM TRADES and other NOISE, while the daily data are more subject to short-term fluctuations. The graphs showing trends of the discount and prime rates, because they are based on monthly averages, will also differ from the accompanying tables, which are based on day-end rates.

Much of the securities data and related charts have been provided courtesy of EQUIS International, an investment analysis and charting service. EQUIS International has its headquarters at 3950 South 700 East, Suite 100, Salt Lake City, Utah 84107 [(800) 882-3040, (801) 265-9996; http://www.equis.com]. DIAL/DATA provided much of the data utilized by EQUIS in producing the tables and charts. The table data used were taken from as far back as the data banks went. In the case of the Dow Jones 30 Industrials Stock Average the data went as far back as 1897.

The economic data and charts have been provided courtesy of the WEFA Group, with headquarters at 800 Baldwin Tower, Eddystone, Pennsylvania 19022 [(610) 490-4000; http://www.wefa.com]. If data were received from another source, such as the Federal Reserve Board, the U.S. Bureau of Labor Statistics, Dow Jones & Co., or Standard & Poor's Corporation, either EQUIS or WEFA and that source have been credited.

AMEX COMPOSITE INDEX

Source: American Stock Exchange, DIAL/DATA Data
Chart by MetaStock, EQUIS International

This graph shows the movement of the American Stock Exchange Composite Index. The AMEX Composite (symbol XAX) is a capitalization-weighted, price appreciation index that measures the performance of about 800 issues, representing all major industry groups, including shares, American Depositary Receipts and warrants. The companies listed on the AMEX tend to be medium-sized and smaller growth firms. The AMEX Composite Index replaced the AMEX Market Value Index (XAM) on January 2, 1997. The Market Value Index had been calculated on a total return basis to include reinvestment of dividends and price change. The AMEX Composite's capitalization method is the same as most other major market indices.

Year	High	Low	Close
1970	58.60	36.10	49.21
1971	60.86	49.09	58.49
1972	69.18	58.55	64.53
1973	65.24	42.61	45.17
1974	51.46	29.13	30.16
1975	48.43	31.10	41.74
1976	54.92	42.16	54.92
1977	63.95	54.81	63.95
1978	88.44	59.87	75.28
1979	123.54	76.02	123.54
1980	185.38	107.85	174.50
1981	190.18	138.38	160.32
1982	170.93	118.65	170.30
1983	254.33	169.61	223.01
1984	227.73	187.16	203.24
1985	246.13	201.93	246.13
1986	285.19	240.30	263.27
1987	365.01	231.90	260.35
1988	309.59	262.76	306.00
1989	397.29	304.60	377.72
1990	383.32	286.93	308.11
1991	395.06	295.80	395.05
1992	419.18	361.72	399.23

Year	High	Low	Close
1993	484.59	394.97	477.15
1994	488.00	419.43	433.67
1995	553.96	432.20	548.23
1996	616.32	510.98	583.28
1997	723.03	541.02	684.61

BOND BUYER INDEX (11 BONDS)

Source: Bond Buyer, DIAL/DATA
Chart by MetaStock, EQUIS International

This graph shows the movement of the *Bond Buyer* Index of 11 bonds. The *Bond Buyer* is a daily newspaper covering the municipal bond market. This index is made up of the yields of 11 newly issued general obligation municipal bonds averaging 20 years to maturity rated Aa and selling at par. The issuers of these bonds, whose average rating is second only to Aaa, are among the most creditworthy of all those issuing bonds in the municipal market. The yield offered by these bonds, therefore, is lower than that of less creditworthy municipalities, but it acts as a benchmark against which market participants compare other municipal bond yields.

Year	High	Low	Close
1917	4.55	3.88	4.60
1918	4.65	4.39	4.42
1919	4.53	4.42	4.53
1920	5.25	4.53	5.03
1921	5.16	4.48	4.35
1922	4.37	4.05	4.14
1923	4.38	4.10	4.35
1924	4.35	4.07	4.15
1925	4.23	3.98	4.19
1926	4.19	4.05	4.10
1927	4.10	3.89	3.83
1928	4.15	3.83	4.13
1929	4.47	4.13	4.19
1930	4.25	3.92	4.05
1931	4.23	3.60	4.66

Year	High	Low	Close
1932	4.66	4.02	3.81
1933	4.90	3.81	4.50
1934	4.50	3.38	3.30
1935	3.30	2.79	2.84
1936	2.84	2.35	2.35
1937	2.90	2.35	2.75
1938	2.75	2.42	2.36
1939	2.94	2.26	2.24
1940	2.66	1.82	1.80
1941	2.13	1.57	1.91
1942	2.79	1.72	1.80
1943	1.80	1.35	1.44
1944	1.44	1.30	1.32
1945	1.43	1.06	1.14
1946	1.66	1.04	1.62
1947	2.13	1.53	2.11
1948	2.25	1.98	1.97
1949	2.00	1.84	1.86
1950	1.87	1.54	1.50
1951	2.04	1.43	1.92
1952	2.20	1.84	2.21
1953	2.88	2.21	2.37
1954	2.37	2.10	2.24
1955	2.50	2.22	2.41
1956	3.10	2.29	3.08
1957	3.43	2.81	2.85
1958	3.51	2.70	3.26
1959	3.70	3.17	3.65
1960	3.65	3.12	3.26
1961	3.44	3.16	3.28
1962	3.28	2.92	2.97
1963	3.24	2.95	3.19
1964	3.25	3.06	3.01
1965	3.47	2.99	3.45
1966	4.14	3.43	3.66
1967	4.37	3.32	4.27
1968	4.72	3.96	4.72
1969	6.74	4.68	6.42
1970	7.00	5.02	5.47
1971	6.04	4.75	4.82
1972	5.35	4.78	4.98
1973	5.45	4.87	5.05
1974	6.71	5.04	6.62
1975	7.23	5.94	6.45
1976	6.57	5.36	5.36
1977	5.57	5.18	5.37
1978	6.28	5.32	6.22
1979	7.02	5.77	6.85

Year	High	Low	Close
1980	10.08	6.63	9.27
1981	12.89	9.04	12.89
1982	13.05	8.90	9.18
1983	9.86	8.54	9.57
1984	10.95	9.34	9.78
1985	9.74	8.25	8.26
1986	8.24	6.64	6.70
1987	9.05	6.40	7.72
1988	7.85	7.22	7.40
1989	7.78	6.75	6.84
1990	7.38	6.92	6.98
1991	6.98	6.44	6.44
1992	6.65	5.80	6.09
1993	6.01	5.19	5.19
1994	6.92	5.18	6.62
1995	6.56	5.25	5.35
1996	6.02	5.23	5.56
1997	5.79	5.10	5.10

BOND BUYER INDEX (20 BONDS)

Source: Bond Buyer, DIAL/DATA
Chart by MetaStock, EQUIS International

This graph shows the movement of the *Bond Buyer* Index of 20 bonds. The *Bond Buyer* is a daily newspaper covering the municipal bond market. This index is made up of the yields of 20 newly issued general obligation municipal bonds with an average maturity of 20 years, rated from Baa to AAA (thus including all those of investment grade, and selling at par. The issuers of these bonds are among the most creditworthy of all those issuing bonds in the municipal market.

Year	High	Low	Close
1917	4.56	3.92	4.62
1918	4.72	4.40	4.44
1919	4.55	4.44	4.56

Year	High	Low	Close
1920	5.27	4.56	5.06
1921	5.26	4.50	5.06
1922	4.41	4.09	4.16
1923	4.40	4.11	4.37
1924	4.37	4.11	4.16
1925	4.26	3.99	4.23
1926	4.23	4.10	4.13
1927	4.13	3.93	3.87
1928	4.18	3.87	4.17
1929	4.49	4.17	4.23
1930	4.29	3.97	4.12
1931	4.45	3.74	4.87
1932	5.09	4.57	4.61
1933	5.69	4.48	5.48
1934	5.48	3.89	3.81
1935	3.81	3.23	3.25
1936	3.25	2.69	2.62
1937	3.17	2.62	3.16
1938	3.19	2.83	2.78
1939	3.30	2.66	2.59
1940	3.00	2.18	2.14
1941	2.43	1.90	2.24
1942	2.51	2.13	2.17
1943	2.17	1.69	1.77
1944	1.77	1.59	1.62
1945	1.72	1.35	1.42
1946	1.91	1.29	1.85
1947	2.35	1.78	2.36
1948	2.48	2.20	2.19
1949	2.21	2.08	2.07
1950	2.07	1.70	1.06
1951	2.23	1.58	2.11
1952	2.39	2.03	2.40
1953	3.09	2.40	2.54
1954	2.54	2.26	2.38
1955	2.63	2.37	2.56
1956	3.24	2.42	3.23
1957	3.57	2.96	2.97
1958	3.59	2.85	3.40
1959	3.81	3.26	3.78
1960	3.78	3.27	3.39
1961	3.55	3.26	3.37
1962	3.37	2.98	3.05
1963	3.31	3.01	3.26
1964	3.32	3.12	3.07
1965	3.56	3.04	3.53
1966	4.24	3.51	3.76
1967	4.45	3.40	4.38

Year	High	Low	Close
1968	4.85	4.07	4.85
1969	6.90	4.82	6.61
1970	7.12	5.33	5.74
1971	6.23	4.97	5.03
1972	5.54	4.96	5.08
1973	5.59	4.99	5.18
1974	7.15	5.16	7.08
1975	7.67	6.27	7.13
1976	7.13	5.83	5.83
1977	5.93	5.45	5.66
1978	6.67	5.58	6.61
1979	7.38	6.08	7.23
1980	10.56	7.11	9.76
1981	13.30	9.49	13.30
1982	13.44	9.25	9.56
1983	10.04	8.78	9.76
1984	11.07	9.51	9.91
1985	9.87	8.36	8.36
1986	8.33	6.77	6.83
1987	9.17	6.54	7.86
1988	7.97	7.33	7.50
1989	7.72	6.86	6.97
1990	7.53	7.08	7.14
1991	7.14	6.58	6.58
1992	6.77	5.89	6.17
1993	6.10	5.28	5.28
1994	7.03	5.28	6.71
1995	6.66	5.35	5.44
1996	6.12	5.33	5.66
1997	5.88	5.17	5.17

DOW JONES 30 INDUSTRIALS STOCK AVERAGE

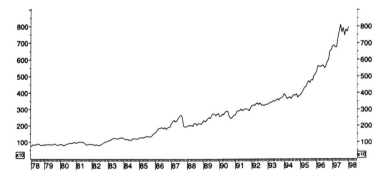

Source: Dow Jones and Company, DIAL/DATA
Chart by MetaStock, EQUIS International

The graph above shows the movement of the Dow Jones 30 Industrials Stock Average, the oldest and most widely used of all stock market indicators. When people ask "What did the market do today?" they usually expect to hear whether this average was up or down for the day. The price-weighted average is comprised of the stocks of 30 blue-chip firms, primarily manufacturing companies but also service companies like American Express. The components, which change from time to time, represent between 15% and 20% of the market value of all NYSE stocks. The Dow, as it is known, is calculated by adding the closing prices of the component stocks and using a divisor that adjusts for splits and stock dividends equal to 10% or more of the market issue as well as for mergers and changes in the components of the list. The Dow Jones 65 Composite Stock Average is composed of the Dow Jones 30 industrials, the Dow Jones 20 transportations and the Dow Jones 15 utilities.

The components of the Dow Jones Industrial Average (DJIA) are:

Allied-Signal Company
Aluminum Company of America
American Express Company
AT&T Corporation
The Boeing Company
Caterpillar, Inc.
Chevron Corporation
Coca-Cola Company
E.I. Dupont de Nemours and Company
Eastman Kodak Company
Exxon Corporation
General Electric Company
General Motors Corporation
Goodyear Tire & Rubber Company
Hewlett-Packard Company
International Business Machines Corporation
International Paper Company
Johnson & Johnson Company
J. P. Morgan & Company, Incorporated
McDonald's Corporation
Merck & Company
Minnesota Mining & Manufacturing Company
Philip Morris Company
Procter & Gamble Corporation
Sears, Roebuck and Company
Travelers Group
Union Carbide Corporation
United Technologies Company
The Walt Disney Company
Wal-Mart Stores

Year	High	Low	Close
1897	55.82	38.49	49.41
1898	60.97	42.00	60.52
1899	77.61	58.27	66.08
1900	71.04	52.96	70.71
1901	78.26	61.52	64.56
1902	68.44	59.57	64.29
1903	67.70	42.15	49.11

Year	High	Low	Close
1904	73.23	46.41	69.61
1905	96.56	68.76	96.20
1906	103.00	85.18	93.63
1907	96.37	53.00	58.75
1908	88.38	58.62	86.15
1909	100.53	79.91	99.05
1910	98.34	73.62	81.36
1911	87.06	72.94	81.68
1912	94.15	80.15	87.87
1913	88.57	72.11	78.78
1914	83.43	53.17	53.17
1915	99.21	54.22	99.15
1916	110.15	84.96	95.00
1917	99.18	65.95	74.38
1918	89.07	73.38	82.20
1919	119.62	79.15	107.23
1920	109.88	66.75	71.95
1921	81.50	63.90	81.10
1922	103.43	78.59	98.73
1923	105.38	85.76	95.52
1924	120.51	88.33	120.51
1925	159.39	115.00	156.66
1926	166.64	135.20	157.20
1927	202.40	152.73	202.40
1928	300.00	191.33	300.00
1929	381.17	198.69	248.48
1930	294.07	157.51	164.58
1931	194.36	73.79	77.90
1932	88.78	41.22	59.93
1933	108.67	50.16	99.90
1934	110.74	85.51	104.04
1935	148.44	96.71	144.13
1936	184.90	143.11	179.90
1937	194.40	113.64	120.85
1938	158.41	98.95	154.76
1939	155.92	121.44	150.24
1940	152.80	111.84	131.13
1941	133.59	106.34	110.96
1942	119.71	92.92	119.40
1943	145.82	119.26	135.89
1944	152.53	134.22	152.32
1945	195.82	151.35	192.91
1946	212.50	163.12	177.20
1947	186.85	163.21	181.16
1948	193.16	165.39	177.30

Year	High	Low	Close
1949	200.52	161.60	200.13
1950	235.47	196.81	235.41
1951	276.37	238.99	269.23
1952	292.00	256.35	291.90
1953	293.79	255.49	280.90
1954	404.39	279.87	404.39
1955	488.40	388.20	488.40
1956	521.05	462.35	499.47
1957	520.77	419.79	435.69
1958	583.65	436.89	583.65
1959	679.36	574.46	679.36
1960	685.47	566.05	615.89
1961	734.91	610.25	731.14
1962	726.01	535.76	652.10
1963	767.21	646.79	762.95
1964	891.71	766.08	874.13
1965	969.26	840.59	969.26
1966	995.15	744.32	785.69
1967	943.08	786.41	905.11
1968	985.21	825.13	943.75
1969	968.85	769.93	800.36
1970	842.00	631.16	838.92
1971	950.82	797.97	890.20
1972	1036.27	889.15	1020.02
1973	1051.70	788.31	850.86
1974	891.66	577.60	616.24
1975	881.81	632.04	852.41
1976	1014.79	858.71	1004.65
1977	999.75	800.85	831.17
1978	907.74	742.12	805.01
1979	897.61	796.67	838.74
1980	1000.17	759.13	963.99
1981	1024.05	824.01	875.00
1982	1070.55	776.92	1046.55
1983	1287.20	1027.04	1258.64
1984	1286.64	1086.57	1211.57
1985	1553.10	1184.96	1546.67
1986	1955.57	1502.29	1895.95
1987	2722.42	1738.74	1938.83
1988	2183.50	1879.14	2168.57
1989	2791.41	2144.64	2753.20
1990	3024.26	2344.31	2633.66
1991	3204.61	2447.03	3168.83
1992	3435.24	3087.41	3301.11
1993	3818.92	3219.25	3754.09

Year	High	Low	Close
1994	4002.84	3520.80	3834.44
1995	5266.69	3794.40	5117.12
1996	6607.81	5000.07	6560.91
1997	8340.14	6315.84	7679.31

DOW JONES 20 TRANSPORTATION STOCK AVERAGE

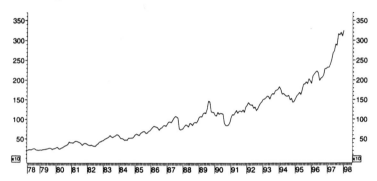

Source: Dow Jones and Company, DIAL/DATA
Chart by MetaStock, EQUIS International

This graph shows the movement of the Dow Jones 20 Transportation Stock Average. This price-weighted average consists of the stocks of the 20 large companies in the transportation business, which includes airlines, railroads and trucking. The Transportation Average is important not only in that it tracks the movement of a major segment of American industry, but also because it is watched by the proponents of the Dow Theory, which maintains that a significant trend is not confirmed until both the Dow Jones Industrial Average and Transportation Average reach new highs or lows; if they don't, the market will fall back to its former trading range, according to this theory. From 1897 to 1969, this average was called the Dow Jones Railroad Average. The Dow Jones 65 Composite Average is composed of the Dow Jones 20 Transportation Stock Average, as well as the Dow Jones 30 Industrials and the Dow Jones 15 Utilities.

The components of the Dow Jones Transportation Average are:

Airborne Freight Company
Alaska Air Group, Inc.
Alexander & Baldwin Inc.
AMR Corporation
Burlington Northern Santa Fe Corporation
CNF Transportation, Inc.
CSX Corporation
Delta Air Lines, Inc.
FDX Corporation
GATX Corporation
Norfolk Southern Corporation
Roadway Express, Inc.
Ryder System Incorporated
Southwest Airlines Company

UAL Corporation
Union Pacific Corporation
USAirways Group, Inc.
US Freightways Corporation
XTRA Corporation
Yellow Corporation

Year	High	Low	Close
1897	67.23	48.12	62.29
1898	74.99	55.89	74.99
1899	87.04	72.48	77.73
1900	94.99	72.99	94.99
1901	117.86	92.66	114.85
1902	129.36	111.73	118.98
1903	121.28	88.80	98.33
1904	119.46	91.31	117.43
1905	133.51	114.52	133.26
1906	138.36	120.30	129.80
1907	131.95	81.41	88.77
1908	120.05	86.04	120.05
1909	134.46	113.90	130.41
1910	129.90	105.59	114.06
1911	123.86	109.80	116.83
1912	124.35	114.92	116.84
1913	118.10	100.50	103.72
1914	109.43	87.40	88.53
1915	108.28	87.85	108.05
1916	112.28	99.11	105.15
1917	105.76	70.75	79.73
1918	92.91	77.21	84.32
1919	91.13	73.63	75.30
1920	85.37	67.83	75.96
1921	77.56	65.52	74.27
1922	93.99	73.43	86.11
1923	90.63	76.78	80.86
1924	99.50	80.23	98.33
1925	112.93	92.98	112.93
1926	123.33	102.41	120.86
1927	144.82	119.29	140.30
1928	152.70	132.60	151.14
1929	189.11	128.07	144.72
1930	157.94	91.65	96.58
1931	111.58	31.42	33.63
1932	41.30	13.23	25.90
1933	56.53	23.43	40.80
1934	52.97	33.19	36.44
1935	41.84	27.31	40.48

Year	High	Low	Close
1936	59.89	40.66	53.63
1937	64.46	28.91	29.46
1938	33.98	19.00	33.98
1939	35.90	24.14	31.83
1940	32.67	22.14	28.13
1941	30.88	24.25	25.42
1942	29.28	23.31	27.39
1943	38.30	27.59	33.56
1944	48.40	33.45	48.40
1945	64.89	47.03	62.80
1946	68.31	44.69	51.13
1947	53.42	41.16	52.48
1948	64.95	48.13	52.86
1949	54.29	41.03	52.76
1950	77.89	51.24	77.64
1951	90.08	72.39	81.70
1952	112.53	82.03	111.27
1953	112.21	90.56	94.03
1954	146.23	94.84	145.86
1955	167.83	137.84	163.29
1956	181.23	150.44	153.23
1957	157.67	95.67	96.96
1958	157.91	99.89	157.65
1959	173.56	146.65	154.05
1960	160.43	123.37	130.85
1961	152.93	131.06	143.84
1962	149.83	114.86	141.04
1963	179.46	142.03	178.54
1964	224.91	178.81	205.34
1965	249.55	187.29	247.48
1966	271.72	184.34	202.97
1967	274.49	205.16	233.24
1968	279.48	214.58	271.60
1969	279.88	169.03	176.34
1970	183.31	116.69	171.52
1971	248.33	169.70	243.72
1972	275.71	212.24	227.17
1973	228.10	151.97	196.19
1974	202.45	125.93	143.44
1975	174.57	146.47	172.65
1976	237.03	175.69	237.03
1977	246.64	199.60	217.18
1978	261.49	199.31	206.56
1979	271.77	205.78	252.39
1980	425.68	233.69	398.10
1981	447.38	335.48	380.30
1982	464.55	292.12	448.38

Year	High	Low	Close
1983	612.57	434.24	598.59
1984	612.63	444.03	558.13
1985	723.31	553.03	708.21
1986	866.74	686.97	807.17
1987	1101.16	661.00	748.86
1988	973.61	737.57	969.84
1989	1532.01	959.95	1177.81
1990	1225.18	809.73	910.23
1991	1368.27	882.22	1358.00
1992	1481.88	1196.35	1449.21
1993	1789.47	1441.15	1762.32
1994	1874.87	1353.96	1455.03
1995	2105.19	1443.62	1981.00
1996	2336.43	1858.88	2287.69
1997	3391.26	2203.27	3101.69

DOW JONES 15 UTILITIES STOCK AVERAGE

Source: Dow Jones and Company, DIAL/DATA
Chart by MetaStock, EQUIS International

This graph shows the movement of the Dow Jones 15 Utilities Stock Average. This price-weighted average is composed of 15 geographically representative and well-established gas and electric utility companies. Since utilities are heavy borrowers, their stock prices are inversely affected by the ups and downs of interest rates. The Dow Jones 65 Composite Stock Average is composed of the Dow Jones 15 Utilities Stock Average, the Dow Jones 30 industrials and the Dow Jones 20 transportations.

The components of the Dow Jones Utilities Average are:

American Electric Power Company
Columbia Energy Group
Consolidated Edison Company
Consolidated Natural Gas Company
Duke Energy
Edison International
Enron Corporation
Houston Industries

PECO Energy Company
PG&E Corporation
Public Service Enterprise Group Incorporated
Southern Company
Texas Utilities Company
Unicom Corporation
Williams Companies

Year	High	Low	Close
1929	144.61	64.72	88.27
1930	108.62	55.14	60.80
1931	73.40	30.55	31.41
1932	36.11	16.53	27.50
1933	37.73	19.33	23.29
1934	31.03	16.83	17.80
1935	29.78	14.46	29.55
1936	36.08	28.63	34.83
1937	37.54	19.65	20.35
1938	25.19	15.14	23.02
1939	27.10	20.71	25.58
1940	26.45	18.03	19.85
1941	20.65	13.51	14.02
1942	14.94	10.58	14.54
1943	22.30	14.69	21.87
1944	26.37	21.74	26.37
1945	39.15	26.15	38.13
1946	43.74	33.20	37.27
1947	37.55	32.28	33.40
1948	36.04	31.65	33.55
1949	41.31	33.36	41.29
1950	44.26	37.40	40.98
1951	47.22	41.47	47.22
1952	52.64	47.53	52.60
1953	53.88	47.87	52.04
1954	62.47	52.22	62.47
1955	66.68	61.39	64.16
1956	71.17	63.03	68.54
1957	74.61	62.10	68.58
1958	91.00	68.94	91.00
1959	94.70	85.05	87.83
1960	100.07	85.02	100.02
1961	135.90	99.75	129.16
1962	130.85	103.11	129.23
1963	144.37	129.19	138.99
1964	155.71	137.30	155.17
1965	163.32	149.84	152.63
1966	152.39	118.96	136.18
1967	140.43	120.97	127.91
1968	141.30	119.79	137.17

Year	High	Low	Close
1969	139.95	106.31	110.08
1970	121.84	95.86	121.84
1971	128.39	108.03	117.75
1972	124.14	105.06	119.50
1973	120.72	84.42	89.37
1974	95.09	57.93	68.76
1975	87.07	72.02	83.65
1976	108.38	84.52	108.38
1977	118.67	104.97	111.28
1978	110.98	96.35	98.24
1979	109.74	98.24	106.60
1980	117.34	96.04	114.42
1981	117.81	101.28	109.02
1982	122.83	103.22	119.46
1983	140.70	119.51	131.84
1984	149.93	122.25	149.52
1985	174.96	146.54	174.81
1986	219.15	169.47	206.01
1987	227.83	160.98	175.08
1988	190.02	167.08	186.28
1989	235.98	181.84	235.04
1990	236.98	187.94	209.70
1991	226.53	194.54	226.15
1992	226.46	199.67	221.02
1993	257.58	215.82	229.30
1994	229.77	172.03	181.52
1995	226.66	180.79	225.40
1996	239.59	202.84	235.95
1997	270.81	207.80	267.60

DOW JONES 65 COMPOSITE STOCK AVERAGE

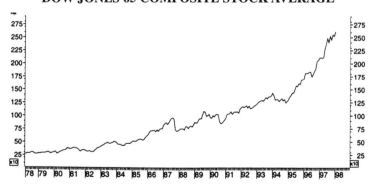

Source: Dow Jones and Company, DIAL/DATA
Chart by MetaStock, EQUIS International

This graph shows the movement of the Dow Jones 65 Composite Stock Average.
This average is made up of the 30 stocks in the Dow Jones Industrial Average, the

20 stocks in the Dow Jones Transportation Average and the 15 stocks in the Dow Jones Utility Average. The average therefore is significant because it combines the three blue-chip averages and thus gives a good indication of the overall direction of the largest, most established companies.

Year	High	Low	Close
1939	53.0	40.4	50.6
1940	51.7	37.2	44.0
1941	44.9	35.5	39.4
1942	39.6	31.5	39.6
1943	50.9	39.8	47.1
1944	56.6	47.0	56.6
1945	73.5	55.9	73.5
1946	79.4	58.5	65.4
1947	67.1	57.3	65.1
1948	71.9	59.9	64.7
1949	71.9	57.8	71.9
1950	87.2	70.3	87.2
1951	100.0	86.9	97.4
1952	113.6	96.1	113.6
1953	114.0	98.2	108.0
1954	150.2	106.0	150.2
1955	174.2	137.8	174.2
1956	184.1	164.3	174.2
1957	179.9	142.8	149.4
1958	202.4	147.4	202.4
1959	233.5	200.1	219.5
1960	222.6	190.4	206.1
1961	251.4	204.8	249.6
1962	245.8	187.4	228.9
1963	269.1	228.7	269.1
1964	314.2	269.1	307.5
1965	340.9	290.4	340.9
1966	352.4	261.3	290.3
1967	337.3	282.7	314.1
1968	353.1	290.1	352.7
1969	346.2	253.0	268.3
1970	273.2	208.7	273.2
1971	318.4	270.2	310.1
1972	338.5	302.1	338.5
1973	334.1	247.7	272.5
1974	282.5	184.2	199.7
1975	268.2	205.3	261.7
1976	325.5	264.5	325.5
1977	324.9	274.3	287.2
1978	315.3	260.7	272.2
1979	315.1	274.3	298.3
1980	388.9	271.7	373.4
1981	394.6	320.6	347.8
1982	416.3	299.4	409.2

Year	High	Low	Close
1983	515.1	401.0	502.9
1984	514.0	421.4	489.9
1985	619.4	480.9	616.5
1986	767.9	602.8	736.8
1987	992.2	653.7	714.2
1988	830.2	700.7	825.9
1989	1115.1	816.9	1035.1
1990	1073.82	830.62	920.61
1991	1167.02	869.42	1156.82
1992	1222.29	1092.09	1204.55
1993	1402.07	1188.85	1381.03
1994	1457.25	1207.50	1274.41
1995	1748.95	1265.28	1693.21
1996	2078.55	1642.43	2058.78
1997	2669.31	1984.65	2520.94

GOLD (London Afternoon Fix Price)

Source: World Gold Council
Chart by MetaStock, EQUIS International

This graph shows the movement of the per troy ounce gold price, according to the month-end afternoon fixings in London. Twice each business day (at 10:30 a.m. and 3:30 p.m.), five major metals dealers meet in London to fix a benchmark price for gold, after assessing supply and demand at that time. Gold has traditionally been considered a store of value against both the erosion through inflation of a currency's purchasing power and political instability or turmoil. From the 1930s until the early 70s, gold was fixed at $35 an ounce in the United States. When trading in the metal resumed, gold at first rose to about $200 an ounce, then fell to about $100, then rose again modestly in the mid-1970s. In the late 1970s and early 80s, with inflation driven by rising oil prices, compounded by Middle East tensions, the gold price soared. It then dropped precipitously and after a period of relative stability in the mid-1980s began falling as a reflection of disinflation. Gold prices have been falling for the most part in the 1990s.

Year	High	Low	Close
1975	185.25	128.75	140.25
1976	140.35	103.50	134.50
1977	167.95	121.00	164.95
1978	242.75	160.90	226.00
1979	512.00	216.85	512.00
1980	850.00	481.50	598.75
1981	599.25	391.25	397.50
1982	481.00	296.75	456.90
1983	509.25	374.50	382.40
1984	405.85	307.50	309.00
1985	340.90	284.25	326.80
1986	415.80	355.75	398.60
1987	499.75	390.00	484.10
1988	483.90	395.30	410.25
1989	415.80	355.75	398.60
1990	423.75	345.85	392.75
1991	403.00	344.25	353.20
1992	359.60	330.25	332.90
1993	405.60	326.10	391.75
1994	396.25	369.65	383.25
1995	392.00	374.90	387.00
1996	414.80	367.40	369.25
1997	366.55	283.00	290.20

NASDAQ NATIONAL MARKET SYSTEM COMPOSITE INDEX

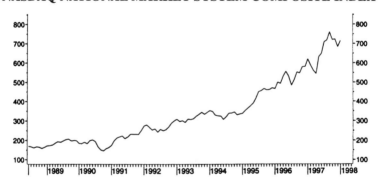

Source: National Association of Securities Dealers, DIAL/DATA
Chart by MetaStock, EQUIS International

This graph shows the movement of the National Association of Securities Dealers Automated Quotations (NASDAQ) National Market System Composite Index. This market-value weighted index is composed of all the stocks traded on the National Market System of the over-the-counter market, which is supervised by the National Association of Securities Dealers. The companies in this index are smaller growth companies, many of them in high technology and financial services. The direction of the index is used by analysts to gauge investor interest in more speculative stocks. In times of enthusiasm for small stocks, this index will rise dramatically, and it will fall just as much when investors opt for safety instead of risk.

Year	High	Low	Close
1989	206.75	173.20	199.18
1990	202.69	144.62	165.17
1991	259.74	183.63	259.74
1992	300.56	249.44	300.56
1993	344.26	292.36	343.61
1994	354.43	313.06	335.24
1995	481.66	329.93	471.17
1996	597.44	436.87	580.65
1997	791.40	516.13	683.00

NEW YORK STOCK EXCHANGE COMPOSITE INDEX

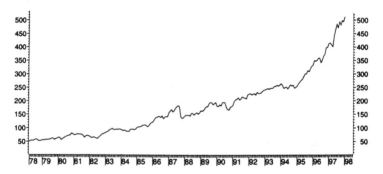

Source: New York Stock Exchange, DIAL/DATA
Chart by MetaStock, EQUIS International

This graph shows the movement of the New York Stock Exchange Composite Index. This market-value weighted index is composed of four subindexes—the NYSE Industrial, Transportation, Utilities, and Finance indexes. As such, the Composite Index provides a broader measure of the performance of the New York Stock Exchange than the more widely quoted Dow Jones Industrial Average. Stock index futures and options on the NYSE Composite are traded on the New York Futures Exchange.

Year	High	Low	Close
1968	61.27	48.70	58.90
1969	59.32	49.31	51.53
1970	52.36	37.69	50.23
1971	57.76	49.60	56.43
1972	65.14	56.23	64.48
1973	65.48	49.05	51.82
1974	53.37	32.89	36.13

Year	High	Low	Close
1975	51.24	37.06	47.64
1976	57.88	48.04	57.88
1977	57.69	49.78	52.50
1978	60.38	48.37	53.62
1979	63.39	53.88	61.95
1980	81.02	55.30	77.86
1981	79.14	64.96	71.41
1982	82.35	58.80	81.03
1983	99.63	79.79	95.18
1984	98.12	85.13	96.38
1985	121.90	94.60	121.58
1986	145.75	117.75	138.58
1987	187.99	125.91	138.23
1988	159.42	136.72	156.26
1989	199.34	154.98	195.04
1990	201.55	161.76	180.49
1991	229.85	169.74	229.44
1992	242.76	216.86	240.21
1993	261.16	235.15	259.08
1994	267.78	241.79	250.94
1995	331.73	249.86	329.51
1996	401.08	320.90	398.10
1997	515.24	386.36	493.60

STANDARD & POOR'S 40 STOCK FINANCIAL INDEX

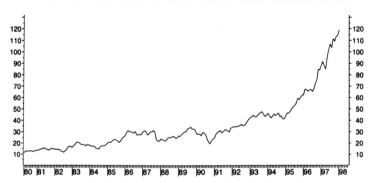

Source: Standard & Poor's Corporation, DIAL/DATA
Chart by MetaStock, EQUIS International

This graph shows the movement of the Standard & Poor's Financial Index. This market-value weighted index is composed of 40 large financial institutions such as banks and insurance companies. As such, the stocks in the index tend to move inversely with interest rates. The S&P Financial Index is combined with the S&P 400 Industrials, 20 Transportations and 40 Utilities to form the Standard and Poor's 500, one of the main benchmarks of performance of the stock market.

Year	High	Low	Close
1976	12.79	11.25	12.79
1977	12.67	10.57	11.15
1978	13.18	10.14	11.22
1979	13.90	11.05	12.57
1980	13.76	10.39	13.70
1981	16.56	13.15	14.47
1982	18.05	11.55	16.58
1983	20.99	15.77	18.13
1984	18.88	14.09	18.80
1985	25.87	18.37	25.72
1986	31.13	25.19	26.92
1987	32.56	20.39	21.63
1988	24.63	24.46	24.49
1989	35.24	24.30	31.30
1990	31.94	18.54	23.43
1991	34.41	21.74	34.10
1992	41.31	32.17	40.89
1993	48.48	39.74	44.27
1994	47.10	39.64	41.41
1995	63.79	41.28	61.97
1996	85.39	58.47	84.13
1997	121.46	79.89	114.06

STANDARD & POOR'S 500 STOCK INDEX

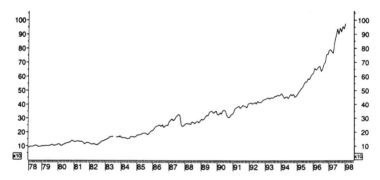

Source: Standard & Poor's Corporation, DIAL/DATA
Chart by MetaStock, EQUIS International

This graph shows the movement of Standard & Poor's 500 Stock Index. This market-value weighted index is composed of the S&P 400 Industrials, the S&P 20 Transportations, the S&P 40 Financials and the S&P 40 Utilities. Most of the stocks in the S&P 500 are found on the New York Stock Exchange, though there are a few from the American Stock Exchange and the NASDAQ market. The index represents about 80 percent of the market value of all the issues traded on the NYSE. The S&P is commonly considered the benchmark against which the performance of individual stocks or stock groups is measured. It is a far broader measure of market activity than the Dow Jones Industrial Average, even though the DJIA is quoted more widely. There are mutual funds, called index funds, which aim to mirror the performance of the S&P 500. Such funds appeal to investors who wish to match the general performance of the stock market. Stock index futures and options are also traded on the S&P 500 and its smaller version, the S&P 100, on the Chicago Mercantile Exchange and the Chicago Board Options Exchange.

Year	High	Low	Close
1930	25.92	14.44	15.34
1931	18.17	7.72	8.12
1932	9.31	4.40	6.89
1933	12.20	5.53	10.10
1934	11.82	8.36	9.50
1935	13.46	8.06	13.43
1936	17.69	13.40	17.18
1937	18.68	10.17	10.55
1938	13.79	8.50	13.21
1939	13.23	10.18	12.49
1940	12.77	8.99	10.58
1941	10.86	8.37	8.69
1942	9.77	7.47	9.77
1943	12.64	9.84	11.67
1944	13.29	11.56	13.28
1945	17.68	13.21	17.36
1946	19.25	14.12	15.30
1947	16.20	13.71	15.30
1948	17.06	13.84	15.20
1949	16.79	13.55	16.76
1950	20.43	16.65	20.41
1951	23.85	20.69	23.77
1952	26.59	23.09	26.57
1953	26.66	22.71	24.81
1954	35.98	24.80	35.98
1955	46.41	34.58	45.48
1956	49.74	43.11	46.67
1957	49.13	38.98	39.99
1958	55.21	40.33	55.21
1959	60.71	53.58	59.89
1960	60.39	52.30	58.11
1961	72.64	57.57	71.55
1962	71.13	52.32	63.10
1963	75.02	62.69	75.02
1964	86.28	75.43	84.75
1965	92.63	81.60	92.43
1966	94.06	73.20	80.33
1967	97.59	80.38	96.47
1968	108.37	87.72	103.86
1969	106.16	89.20	92.06
1970	93.46	69.29	92.15
1971	104.77	90.16	102.09

Year	High	Low	Close
1972	119.12	101.67	118.05
1973	120.24	92.16	97.55
1974	99.80	62.28	68.56
1975	95.61	70.04	90.19
1976	107.83	90.90	107.46
1977	107.97	90.71	95.10
1978	106.99	86.90	96.11
1979	111.27	96.13	107.94
1980	140.52	98.22	135.76
1981	138.12	112.77	122.55
1982	143.02	102.42	140.64
1983	172.65	138.34	164.93
1984	170.41	147.82	167.24
1985	212.02	163.68	211.28
1986	254.00	203.49	242.17
1987	336.77	223.92	247.08
1988	283.66	276.83	277.72
1989	359.80	275.31	353.40
1990	369.78	294.51	330.22
1991	418.32	309.35	417.09
1992	442.65	392.41	435.71
1993	471.29	426.88	466.45
1994	482.85	435.86	459.27
1995	622.88	457.20	615.93
1996	762.12	597.29	756.80
1997	986.24	729.56	936.46

STANDARD & POOR'S 400 INDUSTRIAL STOCK INDEX

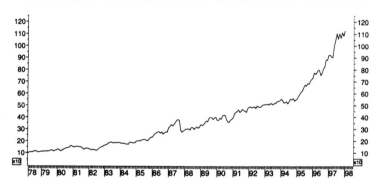

Source: Standard & Poor's Corporation, DIAL/DATA
Chart by MetaStock, EQUIS International

This graph shows the movement of Standard & Poor's 400 Industrial Stock Index, commonly known as the S&P 400. This market-value weighted index is made up of 400 large, established industrial companies, most of which are traded on the New York Stock Exchange. The stocks in the Dow Jones Industrial Average are also included in the S&P 400, but the S&P index provides a much broader picture of the performance of industrial stocks. Standard & Poor's 500 index is comprised of the S&P 400 plus the S&P 40 Utilities, 20 Transportations and 40 Financials Indexes.

Year	High	Low	Close
1930	20.32	11.33	11.90
1931	14.07	6.02	6.32
1932	7.26	3.52	5.18
1933	10.25	4.24	9.26
1934	10.54	7.63	9.12
1935	12.84	7.90	12.77
1936	17.02	12.67	16.50
1937	18.10	9.73	10.26
1938	13.66	8.39	13.07
1939	13.08	9.92	12.17
1940	12.42	8.70	10.37
1941	10.62	8.47	8.78
1942	9.94	7.54	9.93
1943	12.58	10.00	11.61
1944	13.18	11.43	13.05
1945	17.06	12.97	16.79
1946	18.53	13.64	14.75
1947	15.83	13.40	15.18
1948	16.93	13.58	15.12
1949	16.52	13.23	16.49
1950	20.60	16.34	20.57
1951	24.33	20.85	24.24
1952	26.92	23.30	26.89
1953	26.99	22.70	24.87
1954	37.24	24.84	37.24
1955	49.54	35.66	48.44
1956	53.28	45.71	50.08
1957	53.25	41.98	42.86
1958	58.97	43.20	58.97
1959	65.32	57.02	64.50
1960	65.02	55.34	61.49
1961	76.69	60.87	75.72
1962	75.22	54.80	66.00
1963	79.25	65.48	79.25
1964	91.29	79.74	89.62
1965	98.55	86.43	98.47
1966	100.60	77.89	85.24
1967	106.15	85.31	105.11
1968	118.03	95.05	113.02
1969	116.24	97.75	101.49
1970	102.87	75.58	100.90
1971	115.84	99.36	112.72
1972	132.95	112.19	131.87
1973	134.54	103.37	109.14

Year	High	Low	Close
1974	111.65	69.53	76.47
1975	107.40	77.71	100.88
1976	120.89	101.64	119.46
1977	118.92	99.88	104.71
1978	118.71	95.52	107.21
1979	124.99	107.08	121.02
1980	160.96	111.09	154.45
1981	157.02	125.93	137.12
1982	159.66	114.08	157.62
1983	194.84	154.95	186.24
1984	191.48	167.75	186.36
1985	235.75	182.24	234.56
1986	282.77	224.88	269.93
1987	393.17	255.43	285.86
1988	326.84	320.18	321.26
1989	410.49	318.66	403.49
1990	438.56	345.79	387.42
1991	494.62	362.88	492.72
1992	516.38	464.29	507.46
1993	544.68	493.09	540.19
1994	564.50	507.30	547.51
1995	733.52	544.26	721.19
1996	893.40	699.98	881.21
1997	1146.82	857.73	1082.63

STANDARD & POOR'S 20 TRANSPORTATION STOCK INDEX

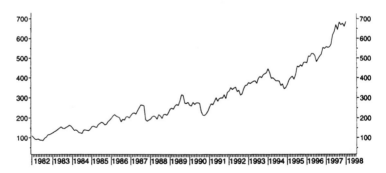

Source: Standard & Poor's Corporation, DIAL/DATA
Chart by MetaStock, EQUIS International

This graph shows the movement of the Standard & Poor's 20 Transportation Stock Index. This market-value weighted index is made up of 20 large transportation companies in the airline, trucking and railroad businesses. It is combined with the S&P 400 Industrials, S&P 40 Utilities and S&P 40 Financials to make up the Standard & Poor's 500 Index.

Year	High	Low	Close
1930	46.34	28.27	30.20
1931	34.75	10.08	10.57
1932	13.02	4.32	8.72
1933	18.97	7.69	13.89
1934	17.77	11.15	12.25
1935	14.81	9.36	14.32
1936	20.95	14.40	18.90
1937	22.07	9.76	9.89
1938	11.23	6.58	11.23
1939	12.04	7.80	10.47
1940	10.78	7.25	9.47
1941	10.22	7.77	8.21
1942	10.12	7.75	9.43
1943	13.34	9.52	11.65
1944	15.85	11.57	15.85
1945	21.33	15.45	20.83
1946	22.74	13.86	15.61
1947	16.46	11.95	14.46
1948	17.26	13.34	13.92
1949	14.49	11.24	13.86
1950	19.39	13.34	19.34
1951	21.93	17.59	20.08
1952	25.41	20.16	24.90
1953	25.13	19.79	20.33
1954	30.48	20.42	30.38
1955	35.78	28.54	34.17
1956	37.57	30.45	31.36
1957	32.48	20.82	20.95
1958	34.39	21.57	34.39
1959	38.03	31.98	33.82
1960	34.92	27.17	29.55
1961	35.30	29.64	33.25
1962	34.48	26.81	32.73
1963	40.70	32.88	40.65
1964	49.87	40.54	45.82
1965	51.56	41.06	51.28
1966	56.32	37.91	41.04
1967	51.46	41.35	43.71
1968	56.08	40.82	54.15
1969	56.96	35.26	37.16
1970	38.94	24.65	35.40
1971	48.32	35.03	44.61
1972	48.31	40.40	44.26
1973	45.80	32.50	45.80
1974	47.36	29.38	35.59
1975	40.18	34.02	38.12

Year	High	Low	Close
1976	78.11	67.57	78.11
1977	78.72	63.29	69.50
1978	82.48	63.14	65.12
1979	84.11	65.33	76.73
1980	136.71	70.72	126.22
1981	135.29	96.13	110.44
1982	126.93	81.77	123.12
1983	164.97	119.45	158.81
1984	161.46	117.21	143.91
1985	192.35	141.56	188.72
1986	217.28	176.16	197.27
1987	274.20	167.59	190.17
1988	229.61	228.10	228.17
1989	331.07	226.42	278.48
1990	292.62	206.97	234.67
1991	364.58	223.45	341.46
1992	369.97	304.98	363.75
1993	430.36	362.17	425.60
1994	454.73	331.09	350.11
1995	492.57	336.54	479.01
1996	558.04	460.12	548.20
1997	715.61	529.19	659.94

STANDARD & POOR'S 40 UTILITIES STOCK INDEX

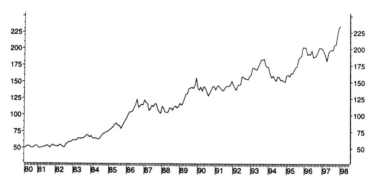

Source: Standard & Poor's Corporation, DIAL/DATA
Chart by MetaStock, EQUIS International

This graph shows the movement of Standard & Poor's 40 Utilities Stock Index. This market-value weighted index is made up of 40 large and geographically representative electric and gas utilities. It is combined with the S&P 400 Industrials, S&P 20 Transportations, and S&P 40 Financials to make up Standard & Poor's 500 Index.

Year	High	Low	Close
1930	67.83	35.33	38.75
1931	49.17	22.38	23.66
1932	26.77	12.49	21.97
1933	27.41	14.73	16.21
1934	21.78	11.35	12.13
1935	20.46	9.52	20.25
1936	24.61	19.36	23.46
1937	25.26	13.47	13.96
1938	17.04	10.90	15.97
1939	17.77	14.23	16.81
1940	17.36	12.65	13.08
1941	13.48	7.77	8.21
1942	8.88	6.65	8.69
1943	12.72	8.79	12.07
1944	13.72	11.98	13.51
1945	20.61	13.63	19.96
1946	23.54	16.95	19.58
1947	19.83	15.89	16.28
1948	18.01	15.56	16.04
1949	19.94	15.90	19.93
1950	21.45	18.35	19.42
1951	21.72	19.61	21.72
1952	24.55	21.73	24.55
1953	25.30	22.25	25.10
1954	29.82	25.16	29.82
1955	32.87	29.53	31.70
1956	33.93	31.15	31.76
1957	34.29	28.96	32.14
1958	43.28	32.32	43.28
1959	45.45	41.87	44.74
1960	51.76	43.74	51.76
1961	67.97	51.42	64.83
1962	65.11	50.21	61.09
1963	67.99	61.26	66.42
1964	74.97	66.36	74.52
1965	78.20	72.03	75.51
1966	75.37	59.03	69.35
1967	72.59	62.21	66.08
1968	72.30	61.06	69.69
1969	70.74	54.33	56.09
1970	61.71	47.67	61.71
1971	64.81	54.48	59.83
1972	62.99	52.02	61.05
1973	61.57	43.51	46.91
1974	49.44	29.37	33.54
1975	45.61	35.31	44.45
1976	54.24	44.70	54.24
1977	57.56	51.60	54.73

Year	High	Low	Close
1978	54.47	48.23	48.47
1979	52.85	47.14	50.24
1980	53.97	43.29	52.45
1981	55.75	48.96	52.98
1982	61.69	50.31	60.45
1983	70.30	60.22	66.17
1984	76.47	62.90	75.89
1985	93.26	74.70	93.17
1986	123.74	90.33	112.29
1987	124.04	91.80	102.12
1988	112.94	112.21	112.64
1989	155.29	111.15	156.04
1990	157.86	123.35	143.59
1991	155.22	133.34	155.16
1992	162.64	135.48	158.46
1993	189.49	156.25	172.58
1994	173.55	147.29	150.12
1995	202.58	149.82	202.58
1996	214.75	182.81	201.37
1997	232.58	180.46	231.47

TORONTO 300 COMPOSITE STOCK INDEX

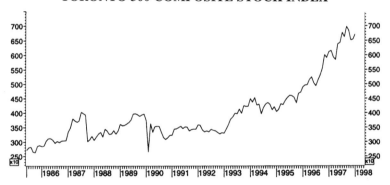

Source: Toronto Stock Exchange, Compuserve
Chart by MetaStock, EQUIS International

This graph shows the movement of the Toronto 300 Composite Stock Index. This is the major index for Canadian stocks, since most of the stock market trading in Canada takes place in Toronto. The index is composed of the Industrial, Transportation, Utilities and Financial Indexes maintained by the Toronto Stock Exchange. Stock index futures on the Composite 300 are traded on the Toronto Futures Exchange.

Year	High	Low	Close
1971	1036.09	879.80	990.54
1972	1226.58	990.54	1226.58

Year	High	Low	Close
1973	1319.26	1122.34	1187.78
1974	1276.81	821.10	835.42
1975	1081.96	862.74	942.94
1976	1100.55	931.17	1011.52
1977	1067.35	961.04	1059.59
1978	1332.71	998.19	1309.99
1979	1813.17	1315.82	1813.17
1980	2402.23	1702.51	2268.70
1981	2390.50	1812.48	1954.24
1982	1958.08	1346.35	1958.08
1983	2598.26	1949.81	2552.35
1984	2585.73	2079.69	2400.33
1985	2900.60	2348.55	2900.60
1986	3129.20	2754.06	3066.18
1987	4112.89	2837.90	3160.10
1988	3465.40	2978.00	3390.00
1989	3985.11	3350.50	3969.79
1990	4020.86	3007.80	3256.75
1991	3604.09	3150.88	3512.36
1992	3672.58	3149.97	3350.44
1993	4330.01	3263.19	4321.43
1994	4609.93	3935.66	4213.61
1995	4740.56	4042.82	4713.54
1996	6016.64	4753.00	5902.60
1997	7110.40	5683.64	6539.48
1995	4740.56	4042.82	4713.54
1996	6016.64	4753.00	5902.60
1997	7110.40	5683.64	6539.48

TREASURY BILL (3-MONTH) YIELDS

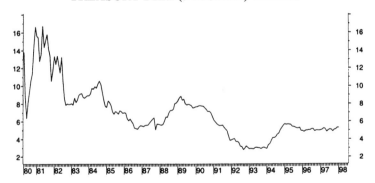

Source: Federal Reserve Bulletin, DIAL/DATA
Chart by MetaStock, EQUIS International

This graph shows the movement of the yields of 3-month U.S. Treasury bills. These yields are considered the most important yardsticks of short-term interest rates, and they are therefore watched closely by credit market analysts for signs that rates might be rising or falling. Many floating-rate loans and variable-rate mortgages are tied to the Treasury bill rate. The minimum purchase amount of a Treasury bill is $10,000. Auctions for Treasury bills are held weekly. Individual investors who do not submit a competitive bid are sold bills at the average price of the winning competitive bids. Treasury bills are the primary instrument used by the Federal Reserve in its regulation of the money supply through open market operations. Futures on Treasury bills are traded on the International Monetary Market and the MidAmerica Commodity Exchange. Futures and futures options on Treasury bills are traded on the Chicago Mercantile Exchange, and futures on T-bills are traded on the Mid-America Commodity Exchange.

Year	Average Rates	Year	Average Rates
1965	4.37%	1982	10.68%
1966	4.96%	1983	8.63%
1967	4.96%	1984	9.58%
1968	5.94%	1985	7.49%
1969	7.81%	1986	5.97%
1970	4.87%	1987	5.82%
1971	4.01%	1988	6.68%
1972	5.07%	1989	8.11%
1973	7.45%	1990	7.50%
1974	7.15%	1991	5.39%
1975	5.44%	1992	3.44%
1976	4.35%	1993	3.00%
1977	6.07%	1994	4.26%
1978	9.08%	1995	5.52%
1979	12.04%	1996	5.01%
1980	11.50%	1997	5.05%
1981	14.07%		

TREASURY BOND (30-YEAR) YIELDS

Source: Federal Reserve Bulletin, Interactive Data Corporation
Chart by MetaStock, EQUIS International

This graph shows the movement of the yields of 30-year Treasury bonds. Treasury-bond yields are considered the most important yardsticks of long-term interest rates, and they are therefore watched closely by credit market analysts for signs that rates might be rising or falling. The minimum denomination of a Treasury bond is $1000 and maturities range from 10 to 30 years. The 20-year T-bond represented a large percentage of the bonds traded until the late 1980s. In the 1990s the 30-year Treasury bond became more widely used. Futures on Treasury bonds are traded on the Chicago Board of Trade and the MidAmerica Commodity Exchange. Futures options on T-bonds are traded on the Chicago Board of Trade, and interest rate options and LEAPS on T-bonds are traded on the Chicago Board Options Exchange.

Year	Average Rates
1988	8.96%
1989	8.47%
1990	8.61%
1991	8.07%
1992	7.67%
1993	6.57%
1994	7.40%
1995	6.86%
1996	6.70%
1997	6.60%

VALUE LINE COMPOSITE INDEX

Source: Value Line, Inc., DIAL/DATA
Chart by MetaStock, EQUIS International

This graph shows the movement of the Value Line Composite Index. This equally weighted geometric average is composed of the approximately 1700 stocks traded on the New York Stock Exchange, American Stock Exchange, and NASDAQ that are tracked by the Value Line Investment Survey. This index is particularly broad in scope, since Value Line covers both large industrial companies and smaller growth firms. Futures on the Value Line Composite Index are traded on the Kansas City Board of Trade, and index options on the index are traded on the Philadelphia Stock Exchange.

Year	High	Low	Close
1968	188.64	138.92	183.18
1969	183.67	127.40	130.56
1970	135.46	84.23	103.60
1971	125.76	97.36	112.94
1972	125.98	107.11	114.05
1973	116.20	70.50	73.61
1974	83.41	47.03	48.97
1975	80.88	51.12	70.69
1976	93.47	71.62	93.47
1977	96.34	86.53	93.92
1978	119.77	88.67	97.97
1979	125.25	98.88	121.91
1980	149.76	100.60	144.20
1981	159.03	125.66	137.81
1982	161.37	112.32	158.94
1983	208.51	156.70	194.35
1984	200.32	162.46	177.98
1985	214.86	176.61	214.86
1986	246.80	210.84	225.62
1987	289.36	180.14	201.62
1988	241.35	200.70	232.68
1989	278.98	231.46	258.78
1990	262.78	178.42	195.99
1991	249.36	185.54	249.34
1992	267.08	235.06	266.68
1993	295.47	263.62	295.28
1994	305.91	265.28	277.52
1995	335.06	276.10	331.04
1996	379.10	319.87	375.88
1997	477.14	362.65	439.14

WILSHIRE 5000 EQUITY INDEX

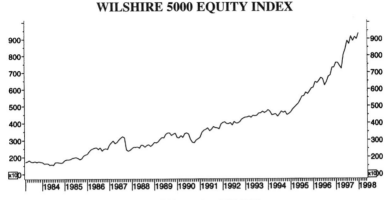

Source: Wilshire Associates, DIAL/DATA
Chart by MetaStock, EQUIS International

This graph shows the movement of the Wilshire 5000 Equity Index. This market-value weighted index of 5000 stocks is the broadest of all the indexes and averages, and represents the value, in billions of dollars, of all New York Stock Exchange, American Stock Exchange and NASDAQ stocks for which quotes are available. The index is used as a measure of how all stocks are doing as a group, as opposed to a particular segment of the market.

Year	High	Low	Close
1971	955	871	949
1972	1090	976	1090
1973	1059	854	861
1974	863	550	590
1975	840	675	784
1976	954	879	954
1977	919	851	887
1978	1004	822	922
1979	1101	935	1100
1980	1466	1026	1404
1981	1415	1208	1286
1982	1451	1099	1451
1983	1791	1508	1723
1984	1702	1536	1702
1985	2164	1845	2164
1986	2598	2109	2434
1987	3299	2188	2434
1988	2794	2398	2738
1989	3523	2718	3419
1990	3448	2834	3101
1991	4041	3245	4041
1992	4290	3930	4290
1993	4673	4316	4658
1994	4798	4395	4541
1995	6057	4546	6057
1996	7292	5897	7288
1997	9407	7059	8976

CONSUMER PRICE INDEX

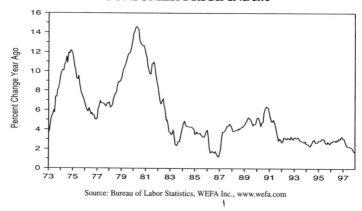

Source: Bureau of Labor Statistics, WEFA Inc., www.wefa.com

This graph shows the movement of the Consumer Price Index. The line represents the rolling 12-month average of changes in consumer prices—a method which best shows the ups and downs of the inflation rate. Each month, the U.S. Bureau of Labor Statistics shops a fixed market basket of goods and services available to an average urban wage earner. The market basket of goods is updated every few years. The major groups included in the CPI are food, shelter, fuel oil and coal, gas and electricity, apparel, private transportation, public transportation, medical care, entertainment, services and commodities. The CPI is important because many pension and employment contracts are tied to changes in it. The inflationary spike of the 1970s did much damage to the world economy and had profound consequences, including the strongly anti-inflationary monetary policies from the middle 1980s to the present.

Year	Annual Change in CPI	Year	Annual Change in CPI	Year	Annual Change in CPI
1948	7.7%	1965	1.6%	1982	6.2%
1949	−1.0%	1966	3.0%	1983	3.2%
1950	1.1%	1967	2.7%	1984	4.4%
1951	8.0%	1968	4.2%	1985	3.6%
1952	2.3%	1969	5.4%	1986	1.9%
1953	0.8%	1970	5.9%	1987	3.7%
1954	0.3%	1971	4.2%	1988	4.1%
1955	−0.2%	1972	3.3%	1989	4.8%
1956	1.4%	1973	6.3%	1990	5.4%
1957	3.4%	1974	11.0%	1991	4.2%
1958	2.7%	1975	9.1%	1992	3.0%
1959	1.0%	1976	5.8%	1993	3.0%
1960	1.5%	1977	6.5%	1994	2.6%
1961	1.0%	1978	7.6%	1995	2.8%
1962	1.2%	1979	11.3%	1996	2.9%
1963	1.3%	1980	13.5%	1997	2.4%
1964	1.3%	1981	10.4%		

DISCOUNT RATE

Source: The Federal Reserve Board, WEFA Inc., www.wefa.com

This graph shows the movement of the discount rate, which is the rate the Federal Reserve charges its member banks for loans from the discount window. Credit market analysts watch the Fed's discount rate moves very carefully, since changes in the rate are a major indication of whether the Fed wants to ease or tighten the money supply. When the Fed wants to ease the money supply to stimulate the economy, it cuts the discount rate. When the Fed wants to tighten the money supply to slow the economy and thereby to try to lower the inflation rate, it raises the discount rate. The discount rate acts as a floor on interest rates, since banks set their loan rates, such as the prime rate, a notch above the disount rate.

Year	High	Low	Close
1914	6.00%	5.00%	6.00%
1915	5.00%	4.00%	4.00%
1916	4.00%	3.00%	3.00%
1917	3.50%	3.00%	3.00%
1918	3.50%	4.00%	4.00%
1919	4.75%	4.00%	4.75%
1920	7.00%	4.75%	7.00%
1921	7.00%	4.50%	4.50%
1922	4.50%	4.00%	4.00%
1923	4.50%	4.00%	4.50%
1924	4.50%	3.00%	3.00%
1925	3.50%	3.00%	3.50%
1926	4.00%	3.50%	4.00%
1927	4.00%	3.50%	4.00%
1928	5.00%	3.50%	5.00%
1929	6.00%	4.50%	4.50%
1930	4.50%	2.00%	2.00%
1931	3.50%	1.50%	3.50%
1932	3.50%	2.50%	2.50%
1933	3.50%	2.00%	2.00%
1934	2.00%	1.50%	1.50%
1935	1.50%	1.50%	1.50%

Year	High	Low	Close
1936	1.50%	1.50%	1.50%
1937	1.50%	1.00%	1.00%
1938	1.00%	1.00%	1.00%
1939	1.00%	1.00%	1.00%
1940	1.00%	1.00%	1.00%
1941	1.00%	1.00%	1.00%
1942	1.00%	0.50%	0.50%
1943	1.00%	0.50%	0.50%
1944	1.00%	0.50%	0.50%
1945	1.00%	0.50%	0.50%
1946	1.00%	0.50%	0.50%
1947	1.00%	1.00%	1.00%
1948	1.50%	1.00%	1.50%
1949	1.50%	1.50%	1.50%
1950	1.75%	1.50%	1.75%
1951	1.75%	1.75%	1.75%
1952	1.75%	1.75%	1.75%
1953	2.00%	1.75%	2.00%
1954	2.00%	1.50%	2.00%
1955	2.50%	1.50%	2.50%
1956	3.00%	2.50%	3.00%
1957	3.50%	3.00%	3.00%
1958	3.00%	1.75%	3.00%
1959	4.00%	2.50%	4.00%
1960	4.00%	3.00%	3.00%
1961	3.00%	3.00%	3.00%
1962	3.00%	3.00%	3.00%
1963	3.50%	3.00%	3.50%
1964	4.00%	3.50%	4.00%
1965	4.50%	4.00%	4.50%
1966	4.50%	4.50%	4.50%
1967	4.50%	4.00%	4.50%
1968	5.50%	4.50%	5.50%
1969	6.00%	5.50%	6.00%
1970	6.00%	5.50%	5.50%
1971	5.00%	4.50%	4.50%
1972	4.50%	4.50%	4.50%
1973	7.50%	4.50%	7.50%
1974	8.00%	7.75%	7.75%
1975	7.75%	6.00%	6.00%
1976	6.00%	5.25%	5.25%
1977	6.00%	5.25%	6.00%
1978	9.50%	6.00%	9.50%
1979	12.00%	9.50%	12.00%
1980	10.00%	13.00%	13.00%
1981	14.00%	12.00%	12.00%
1982	12.00%	8.50%	8.50%

Year	High	Low	Close
1983	8.50%	8.50%	8.50%
1984	9.00%	8.00%	8.00%
1985	8.00%	7.50%	7.50%
1986	7.50%	5.50%	5.50%
1987	7.00%	5.50%	6.00%
1988	6.50%	6.00%	6.50%
1989	7.00%	6.50%	7.00%
1990	7.00%	6.80%	6.80%
1991	6.50%	4.10%	4.10%
1992	3.50%	3.00%	3.00%
1993	3.00%	3.00%	3.00%
1994	4.75%	3.00%	4.75%
1995	5.25%	4.75%	5.25%
1996	5.25%	5.00%	5.00%
1997	5.00%	5.00%	5.00%

FEDERAL FUNDS RATE

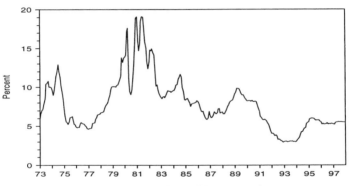

Source: The Federal Reserve Board, WEFA Inc., www.wefa.com

This graph shows the movement of the federal funds rate, which is the rate at which banks with excess reserves lend to banks needing overnight loans to meet reserve requirements. The fed funds rate is the most sensitive of all short-term interest rates, and therefore it is carefully watched by credit market analysts as a precursor of moves in other interest rates. For instance, when the fed funds rate consistently stays below the discount rate, analysts often anticipate that the Federal Reserve will cut the discount rate.

Year	High	Low	Close
1968	6.12%	4.6%	6.02%
1969	9.19%	6.3%	8.97%
1970	8.98%	4.9%	4.9%
1971	5.57%	3.71%	4.14%

Year	High	Low	Close
1972	5.33%	3.29%	5.33%
1973	10.78%	5.94%	9.95%
1974	12.92%	8.53%	8.53%
1975	7.13%	5.20%	5.20%
1976	5.48%	4.65%	4.65%
1977	6.56%	4.61%	7.75%
1978	10.03%	6.70%	10.03%
1979	13.78%	10.01%	13.78%
1980	18.90%	9.03%	18.90%
1981	19.08%	12.37%	12.37%
1982	14.94%	8.95%	8.95%
1983	9.56%	8.51%	9.47%
1984	11.64%	8.38%	8.38%
1985	8.58%	7.53%	8.27%
1986	8.14%	5.85%	6.91%
1987	7.29%	6.10%	6.77%
1988	8.76%	6.58%	8.76%
1989	9.95%	8.46%	8.52%
1990	8.29%	7.31%	7.31%
1991	6.91%	4.43%	4.43%
1992	4.06%	2.92%	2.92%
1993	3.09%	2.96%	2.96%
1994	5.50%	3.05%	5.50%
1995	6.05%	5.53%	5.60%
1996	5.56%	5.22%	5.29%
1997	5.56%	5.19%	5.50%

INDEX OF LEADING ECONOMIC INDICATORS

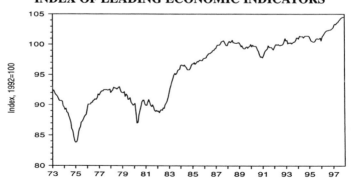

Source: Bureau of Economic Analysis, WEFA Inc., www.wefa.com

This graph shows the movement of the Index of Leading Economic Indicators. This composite of 12 economic indicators (adjusted for inflation) is designed to forecast whether the economy will gain or lose strength, and is therefore an important tool for economists and others doing business planning. On the whole, it has been an

accurate barometer of future economic activity. The 12 components of the Index
are: average workweek of production workers; average weekly claims for unemployment insurance; new orders for consumer goods and materials; vendor performance (companies receiving slower deliveries from suppliers); contracts for plant
and equipment; new building permits; durable goods order backlog; sensitive materials prices; stock prices; money supply as measured by M-2; and consumer expectations. The index is released monthly and is based at 100 in 1992.

Year	High	Low	Last
1970	85.30	83.90	85.30
1971	88.70	85.80	88.70
1972	92.30	89.10	92.30
1973	92.40	89.80	89.80
1974	89.60	84.00	84.00
1975	88.40	83.80	88.40
1976	91.80	89.40	91.80
1977	92.60	91.60	92.60
1978	93.00	92.00	92.10
1979	92.20	89.90	89.90
1980	90.80	87.00	90.10
1981	90.90	88.90	89.10
1982	91.20	88.70	91.20
1983	95.90	92.10	95.90
1984	96.60	95.80	96.50
1985	97.60	96.70	97.60
1986	99.30	97.70	99.30
1987	100.60	99.30	99.80
1988	100.70	99.80	100.30
1989	100.30	99.30	99.80
1990	100.00	97.90	98.00
1991	99.80	97.80	99.10
1992	101.00	99.40	101.00
1993	101.10	100.10	101.10
1994	101.40	100.90	101.40
1995	101.30	100.40	101.10
1996	102.60	100.60	102.60
1997	104.50	102.80	104.50

MONEY SUPPLY (M-1)

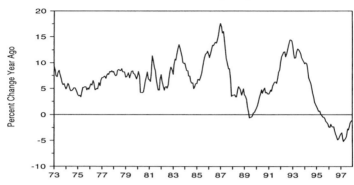

Source: The Federal Reserve Board, WEFA Inc., www.wefa.com

This graph shows the movement of changes in the money supply in the United States, as measured by M-1. The line represents the rolling 12-month change in the money supply. The percentage change is calculated by comparing, for example, the December 1997 figure with the December 1996 figure. This method best shows the ups and downs of the growth of the amount of money circulating in the economy. The rate of change in the money supply is important because it has an important bearing on how quickly or slowly the economy will be growing in the future. Monetarist economists believe changes in the money supply are the key to economic ups and downs. When the Federal Reserve, which strongly influences the money supply through its conduct of open market operations and by setting bank reserve requirements and the discount rate, wants the economy to expand, it eases the money supply. When the Fed is concerned that inflation may be accelerating, it will slow the economy by tightening the money supply. The components of the M-1 measure of the money supply are: currency in circulation; commercial and mutual savings bank demand deposits; NOW and ATS (automatic transfer from savings) accounts; credit union share drafts; and nonbank travelers checks.

Year	High	Low	Last
1970	5.15	2.85	5.15
1971	8.13	4.56	6.48
1972	9.15	5.91	9.15
1973	9.30	5.46	5.46
1974	5.96	4.34	4.34
1975	5.33	3.37	4.81
1976	6.58	4.75	6.58
1977	8.43	6.93	8.13
1978	8.85	7.43	8.21
1979	8.39	6.84	6.84
1980	8.28	4.19	6.79
1981	11.36	4.70	6.82
1982	9.13	4.67	8.65
1983	13.54	7.74	9.82
1984	9.90	4.98	5.95
1985	12.26	5.94	12.26

Year	High	Low	Last
1986	16.86	10.99	16.86
1987	17.59	3.49	3.49
1988	5.37	3.37	4.98
1989	3.82	−0.66	0.91
1990	5.12	1.18	3.98
1991	8.66	3.95	8.66
1992	14.42	10.08	14.23
1993	13.41	10.22	10.22
1994	9.99	1.85	1.85
1995	1.54	−1.89	−1.89
1996	−1.82	−4.88	−4.24
1997	−1.15	−5.19	−1.15

PRIME RATE

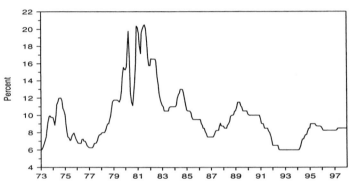

Source: The Federal Reserve Board, WEFA Inc., www.wefa.com

This graph shows the movement of the prime rate, which is the interest rate banks charge their most creditworthy customers. The rate is determined by market forces affecting a bank's cost of funds and the rates borrowers will accept. The prime often moves up or down in concert with the Federal Reserve discount rate. The prime rate tends to become standard across the banking industry when a major bank moves its rate up or down. The rate is a key interest rate, since loans to less creditworthy customers are often tied to the prime.

Year	High	Low	Close
1968	6.75%	6%	6.75%
1969	8.5%	6.75%	8.5%
1970	8.5%	6.75%	6.75%
1971	6.75%	5.25%	5.25%
1972	6%	5%	6%
1973	10%	6%	10%
1974	12%	8.75%	10.5%
1975	10.5%	7%	7%

Year	High	Low	Close
1976	7.25%	6.25%	6.25%
1977	7.75%	6.5%	7.75%
1978	11.75%	7.75%	11.75%
1979	15.75%	11.5%	15%
1980	21.50%	10.75%	21.50%
1981	20.5%	15.75%	15.75%
1982	17%	11.5%	11.5%
1983	11.5%	10.5%	11%
1984	13%	10.75%	10.75
1985	10.75%	9.5%	9.5%
1986	9.5%	7.5%	7.5%
1987	9.25%	7.5%	8.75%
1988	10.5%	8.5%	10.5%
1989	11.5%	10.5%	10.5%
1990	10.1%	10.0%	10.0%
1991	9.5%	7.2%	7.2%
1992	6.5%	6.0%	6.0%
1993	6.0%	6.0%	6.0%
1994	8.5%	6.0%	8.5%
1995	9.00%	8.50%	8.65%
1996	8.50%	8.25%	8.25%
1997	8.50%	8.25%	8.50%

PRODUCER PRICE INDEX

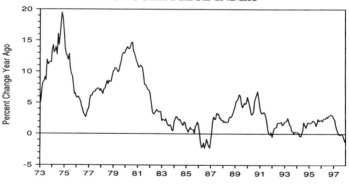

Source: Bureau of Labor Statistics, WEFA Inc., www.wefa.com

This graph shows the movement of the Producer Price Index. The line represents the rolling 12-month average of changes in producer prices—a method that best shows the ups and downs of the wholesale inflation rate. Each month, the U.S. Bureau of Labor Statistics measures changes in the prices of all commodities, at all stages of processing, produced for sale in primary markets in the United States. Approximately 3400 commodity prices are collected by the Bureau from sellers. The prices are generally the first significant large-volume commercial transaction for each commodity—either the manufacturer's selling price or the selling price from an organized commodity exchange. The major commodity groups that are represented in the PPI are: farm products; processed food and feed; textiles and apparel; hides, skins and leather; fuels; chemicals; rubber and plastic products; lumber and wood products; pulp and paper products; metals and metal products; machinery and equipment; furniture and household durables; nonmetallic mineral products; and transportation equipment. The PPI is important not only because it is a good gauge of what is happening in the industrial economy but also because it gives an indication of the future trend in consumer prices.

Year	Annual Percent Change	Year	Annual Percent Change
1955	0.3%	1977	6.4%
1956	2.6%	1978	7.9%
1957	3.8%	1979	11.2%
1958	2.2%	1980	13.4%
1959	−0.3%	1981	9.2%
1960	0.9%	1982	4.1%
1961	−0.0%	1983	1.6%
1962	0.3%	1984	2.1%
1963	−0.3%	1985	1.0%
1964	0.3%	1986	−1.4%
1965	1.8%	1987	2.1%
1966	3.2%	1988	2.5%
1967	1.1%	1989	4.9%
1968	2.8%	1990	4.9%
1969	3.8%	1991	2.2%
1970	3.4%	1992	1.2%
1971	3.1%	1993	1.2%.
1972	3.2%	1994	0.7%
1973	9.1%	1995	1.9%
1974	15.4%	1996	2.6%
1975	10.6%	1997	0.4%
1976	4.5%		

UNEMPLOYMENT RATE (CIVILIAN)

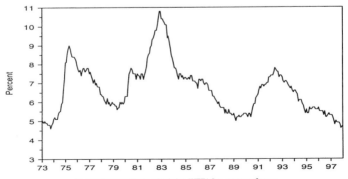

Source: Bureau of Labor Statistics, WEFA Inc., www.wefa.com

This graph shows the movement of the unemployment rate. This is the rate of civilians, 16 years of age and older, who were not employed, and who made specific efforts to find a job within the previous four weeks and who were available for work. Persons on layoff from a job or waiting to report to a new job within 30 days are also classified as unemployed. The unemployment rate is a lagging indicator—that is, it rises months after business has already slowed down, and it falls months after business has picked up.

MONTHLY RATE

Year	High	Low	Last
1970	6.10	3.90	6.10
1971	6.10	5.80	6.00
1972	5.80	5.20	5.20
1973	5.00	4.60	4.90
1974	7.20	5.10	7.20
1975	9.00	8.10	8.20
1976	7.90	7.40	7.80
1977	7.60	6.40	6.40
1978	6.40	5.80	6.00
1979	6.00	5.60	6.00
1980	7.80	6.30	7.20
1981	8.50	7.20	8.50
1982	10.80	8.60	10.80
1983	10.40	8.30	8.30
1984	8.00	7.20	7.30
1985	7.40	7.00	7.00
1986	7.20	6.60	6.60
1987	6.60	5.70	5.70
1988	5.70	5.30	5.30
1989	5.40	5.00	5.40
1990	6.30	5.20	6.30
1991	7.30	6.40	7.30
1992	7.80	7.30	7.40
1993	7.30	6.50	6.50
1994	6.60	5.40	5.40
1995	5.70	5.40	5.60
1996	5.70	5.20	5.30
1997	5.30	4.60	4.70

6. PUBLICLY TRADED COMPANIES

On the following pages, you will find a comprehensive list of the companies whose common stock is traded on the New York Stock Exchange, the American Stock Exchange, and the NASDAQ (National Association of Securities Dealers Automated Quotation) system. In addition, there is a listing of the 300 largest capitalization stocks traded on the Toronto Stock Exchange. In the case of the New York Stock Exchange, the list is complete. The American Stock Exchange listing is also complete. The NASDAQ list includes those approximately 1,600 companies which are reported on by the Standard & Poors Stock Reports Service.

Following the overall company lists are two lists of special interest: the first presents companies offering free or reduced-price goods or services to shareholders; the second, foreign companies whose American Depositary Receipts (ADRs) are traded in the United States.

The New York Stock Exchange is the home of many of the largest, most established public companies, though many smaller growth companies are traded there as well. The NYSE operates with a specialist system of trading, where buyers and sellers are brought together by a specialist on the floor of the Exchange. The specialist steps in to buy or sell shares if there is an imbalance of orders on one side of the market or the other. The requirements the NYSE imposes for being listed on the exchange are the most stringent of all the places where stocks are traded in the United States. Two of the most important requirements are that a corporation must have (1) a minimum aggregate market value of $40 million and (2) annual net income topping $2.5 million before federal income taxes.

The American Stock Exchange is where medium and smaller-sized companies are traded. In addition, many foreign companies are listed on the AMEX. The American Stock Exchange uses the same specialist trading system employed by the New York Stock Exchange. The AMEX's listing requirements at a minimum value of stockholder's equity of $4 million, and pre-tax income of $750,000 are less stringent than those of the NYSE.

The NASDAQ Stock Market is home to many of the nations's largest high-technology companies as well as a majority of its emerging growth companies. Many of these growth companies don't pay dividends since they plow their earnings back into their businesses. Unlike the two exchanges, trading on The NASDAQ Stock Market is executed by hundreds of competing market makers who are linked by a network of NASDAQ computer terminals. The screen-based electronic market is owned and operated by the National Association of Securities Dealers and is headquartered in Washington, D.C. The NASDAQ Stock Market has two tiers, the SmallCap market, for smaller emerging companies, and the National Market, where the larger issues trade. Listing standards vary for NASDAQ's two tiers, but they are more stringent for NASDAQ's National Market, and to be accepted a company must have either $6 million in tangible assets with pre-tax income of $1 million and a public share float value of $8 million, or tangible assets of $18 million, a public share float value of $18 million with no income requirement.

Each listing includes up to eight elements: the company's name, stock symbol, address, telephone number, fax number (if available), line of business, if it has a dividend reinvestment plan and whether options are traded on the stock.

Company Name: We have used each company's full corporate name, though words such as Incorporated, Company and Corporation are abbreviated to become Inc., Co. and Corp. The lists are arranged alphabetically, by company name.

Stock Symbol: The stock symbol—usually three or four capital letters—follows each company's name. When asking a broker to look up the price or other information about a stock, it is usually necessary to provide the stock symbol. The symbol is then entered into a computer terminal, which retrieves data about the company. The stock symbol is not the same abbreviation as one sees in newspaper stock tables, however.

Address: The street address or post office box listed refers to the executive office at the headquarters of the company. In the case of foreign companies, the home address of the company usually is listed, though the address of a contact office in the U.S. may be given.

Telephone Number: The phone number is that of the executive offices at the company's headquarters. If you require further information about the company because you are considering whether to invest in it, you should ask for the investor relations department, which will send annual and quarterly financial reports and other data about the firm.

Fax Number: The fax number, when listed, is the fax number at company headquarters.

Line Of Business: This is a brief description of the main business of the company. Some companies specialize in a narrow field—in this case, the description is quite specific to its line of business. Other companies engage in diverse activities, and for them, we have listed the largest segments of their business, or when no business is dominant, we have labeled the company a conglomerate. To find out each company's exact product line, you must call or write the firm's investor relations department.

Dividend Reinvestment Plan: If the letters DRP are in brackets on the final line of an entry for a company, this means that shareholders can use a company plan to reinvest cash dividends into more of the company's stock, instead of receiving a cash payment. Usually, there will be little or no commission cost to the shareholder who participates in a plan. Many companies also allow shareholders to make cash payments in addition to reinvesting dividends to buy more shares, usually at no commission charge.

Some companies offer an extra bonus in their dividend reinvestment plan. Companies on the list with a 5% following the DRP listing offer a 5% discount on the purchase price of newly issued stock for the amount of reinvested dividends. Thus, a shareholder who reinvested $100 of dividends would be credited with purchasing $105 worth of stock. Some companies allow the 5% discount on both dividends reinvested as well as additional cash put up by the shareholder.

Most companies allow shareholders to participate in a dividend reinvestment plan while owning as little as one share. If the dividend is not sufficient to purchase a full share, a shareholder's account is credited with the appropriate fractional share.

The information on dividend reinvestment plans was compiled by Suzanne Mitchell, who publishes a list tracking company plans. A sample copy of this list is available for $19.95 from Suzanne Mitchell at P.O. Box 7969, 3226 Pain Place, Tyler, Texas 75711, or by calling her at (903) 592-5465.

Options: Also on the final line of a company entry is a notation of whether options are traded on the company's stock. This is signified with the letter O. Stock options may be traded on the American Stock Exchange, the Chicago Board

Options Exchange, the Pacific Stock Exchange or the Philadelphia Stock Exchange. Options of larger companies may trade on more than one of these exchanges simultaneously. Stock options can be used by an investor to make a speculative bet on a stock going up or down. Other investors use options to increase their income or hedge the value of their stock holdings.

In today's fast-moving world of finance and investment, a company may merge with another, add or drop a line of business, change its address or telephone number, move from one exchange to another, or even go out of business. Despite such changes, this list will remain an indispensable resource for investors and others in the finance and investment community.

NEW YORK STOCK EXCHANGE

A. G. Edwards, Inc. AGE
One N. Jefferson Ave.
St. Louis, MO 63103
314-289-3000
Financial - investment bankers

A. H. Belo Corp. BLC
400 S. Record St.
Dallas, TX 75202
214-977-6606
Broadcasting - radio & TV

A. O. Smith Corp. SMC
PO Box 23972
Milwaukee, WI 53223
414-359-4000   Fax 414-359-4198
Automotive & trucking - original
  equipment

Aames Financial AAM
3731 Wilshire Blvd
Los Angeles, CA 90010
213-351-6100
Consumer finance - mortgage loans

AAR Corp. AIR
1111 Nicholas Blvd.
Elk Grove Village, IL 60007
708-439-3939   Fax 708-439-3955
Aerospace - aircraft equipment O DRP

Abbott Laboratories ABT
One Abbott Park Rd.
Abbott Park, IL 60064
708-937-6100   Fax 847-937-1511
Drugs O DRP

Abercrombie & Fitch Co. ANF
Four Limited Pkwy.
Reynoldsburg, OH 43068
614-577-6500
Retail - apparel & shoes O

Acceptance Insurance Cos AIF
222 South 15th St., Suite 600N
Omaha, NE 68102
402-344-8800
Property & casualty insurance holding
  company

AccuStaff Inc. ASI
6440 Atlantic Blvd.
Jacksonville, FL 32211
904-725-5574
Provider of strategic staffing, consulting
  services

ACM Government Income Fund, Inc. ACG
1345 Avenue of the Americas
New York, NY 10105
212-969-1000
Financial - investment management

ACM Government Opportunity Fund, Inc.
  AOF
1345 Avenue of the Americas
New York, NY 10105
212-969-1000
Financial - investment management

ACM Government Securities Fund, Inc. GSF
1345 Avenue of the Americas
New York, NY 10105
212-969-1000
Financial - investment management

ACM Government Spectrum Fund, Inc. SI
1345 Avenue of the Americas
New York, NY 10105
212-969-1000
Financial - investment management

ACM Managed Dollar Income Fund, Inc.
  ADF
1345 Avenue of the Americas
New York, NY 10105
212-969-1000
Financial - investment management

ACM Managed Income Fund, Inc. AMF
1345 Avenue of the Americas
New York, NY 10105
212-969-1000
Financial - investment management

ACM Managed Multi-Market Trust, Inc.
  MMF
1345 Avenue of the Americas
New York, NY 10105
212-969-1000
Financial - investment management

ACM Municipal Securities Income, Inc.
  AMU
1345 Avenue of the Americas
New York, NY 10105
212-969-1000
Financial - investment management

Acme Electric Corp. ACE
400 Quaker Rd.
East Aurora, NY 14052
716-655-3800
Electrical products - misc.

Acme Metals, Inc. AMI
13500 S. Perry Ave.
Riverdale, IL 60627
708-849-2500
Metal processing & fabrication

ACNielsen Corp. ART
177 Broad St.
Stamford, CT 06901
203-961-3000
Business services O

Acuson Corp. ACN
1220 Charleston Rd.
Mountain View, CA 94043
415-969-9112   Fax 415-952-8018
Medical instruments O

ACX Technologies, Inc. ACX
16000 Table Mountain Pkwy.
Golden, CO 80403
303-271-7000
Diversified operations

Adams Express Co. ADX
Seven St. Paul St., Ste. 1140
Baltimore, MD 21202
410-752-5900
Financial - investment management

Administaff, Inc. ASF
19001 Crescent Springs Dr.
Kingwood, TX 77339
281-358-8986
Business services

Advanced Micro Devices, Inc. AMD
One AMD Place, PO Box 3453
Sunnyvale, CA 94088
408-732-2400   Fax 408-774-7010
Electrical components - semiconductors O

Advest Group ADV
90 State House Square
Hartford, CT 06103
860-509-1000
Investment banking/brokerage, consumer
  lending

ADVO, Inc. AD
One Univac Ln., PO Box 755
Windsor, CT 06095
860-285-6100
Business services

Advocat Inc. AVC
277 Mallory Station Rd.
Franklin, TN 37067
615-771-7575
Nursing homes

Aeroflex Inc. ARX
35 South Services Rd.
Plainview, NY 11803
516-694-6700
Electronics - defense, control systems

Aeroquip-Vickers, Inc. ANV
3000 Strayer
Maumee, OH 43537
419-867-2200
Machinery - general industrial O DRP

AES Corp., (The) AES
1001 N. 19th Street
Arlington, VA 22209
703-522-1315   Fax 703-528-4510
Utility - electric power O

Aetna Inc. AET
151 Farmington Ave.
Hartford, CT 06156
860-273-0123   Fax 860-273-3971
Insurance - multi line & misc. O DRP

Affiliated Computer Services, Inc. AFA
2828 N. Haskell Ave.
Dallas, TX 75204
214-841-6111
Data collection & systems DRP

AFLAC, Inc. AFL
1932 Wynnton Rd.
Columbus, GA 31999
706-323-3431   Fax 706-324-6330
Insurance - life O DRP

Ag Services of America, Inc. ASV
Thunder Ridge Ct., PO Box 688
Cedar Falls, IA 50613
319-277-0261   Fax 319-277-0144
Agricultural operations

AGCO Corp. AG
5295 Triangle Parkway
Norcross, GA 30092
404-447-5546   Fax 404-246-6158
Machinery - farm O

AGL Resources, Inc. ATG
303 Peachtree St., N.E.
Atlanta, GA 30308
404-584-4000
Utility - gas distribution O DRP

Agree Realty Corp. ADC
31850 Northwestern Hwy.
Farmington Hills, MI 48334
810-737-4190   Fax 810-737-9110
Real estate investment trust

Agrium Inc. AGU
10333 Southport Rd. S.W.
Calgary, AB T2W3X6
403-258-4600
Produces & markets fertilizers

Air Products and Chemicals, Inc. APD
7201 Hamilton Blvd.
Allentown, PA 18195
610-481-4911   Fax 610-481-5900
Chemicals - specialty O DRP

Airborne Freight Corp. ABF
3101 Western Ave., PO Box 662
Seattle, WA 98111
206-285-4600
Transportation - air freight O

Airgas, Inc. ARG
259 Radnor-Chester Rd.
Radnor, PA 19087
610-687-5253   Fax 610-687-1052
Chemicals - specialty O

Airlease Ltd. FLY
733 Front St.
San Francisco, CA 94119
415-627-9289   Fax 415-627-9241
Leasing

AirNet Systems, Inc. ANS
3939 International Gateway
Columbus, OH 43219
614-237-9777
Transportation - air freight

AirTouch Communications ATI
425 Market St.
San Francisco, CA 94105
415-658-2000
Telecommunications services O DRP

AK Steel Holding Corp. AKS
703 Curtis St.
Middletown, OH 45043
513-425-5000   Fax 513-425-5613
Steel - production O

Alamo Group Inc. ALG
1502 E. Walnut
Seguin, TX 78155
210-379-1480   Fax 210-372-9679
Miscellaneous - not elsewhere classified

Alaska Air Group, Inc. ALK
19300 Pacific Highway South
Seattle, WA 98188
206-431-7040
Transportation - airline O

Albany International Corp. AIN
1373 Broadway
Albany, NY 12204
518-445-2200   Fax 518-445-2265
Paper & paper products DRP

Albemarle Corp. ALB
330 S. Fourth St.
Richmond, VA 23219
804-788-6000   Fax 804-788-6008
Chemicals - specialty O DRP

Alberto-Culver Co. ACV
2525 Armitage Ave.
Melrose Park, IL 60160
708-450-3000
Cosmetics & toiletries O

Albertson's, Inc. ABS
250 Parkcenter Blvd.
Boise, ID 83726
208-385-6200   Fax 208-385-6349
Retail - supermarkets O DRP

Alcan Aluminium Ltd. AL
1188 Sherbrooke St. West
Montreal, QC H3A3G2
514-848-8000
Aluminum smelter & producer DRP

Alexander's, Inc. ALX
31 W. 34th St.
New York, NY 10001
212-560-2121
Retail - discount & variety

Alexandria R.E., Equities ARE
251 South Lake Ave., Suite 700
Pasadena, CA 91101
626-578-0777
Real estate investment trust

Alleghany Corp. Y
375 Park Avenue
New York, NY 10152
212-752-1356   Fax 212-759-8149
Financial - business services

Allegheny Energy System, Inc. AYE
12 E. 49th St.
New York, NY 10017
212-752-2121   Fax 212-836-4340
Utility - electric power O DRP

Allegheny Teledyne Inc. ALT
1000 Six PPG Pl.
Pittsburgh, PA 15222
412-394-2800
Diversified operations O

Allegiance Corp. AEH
1430 Waukegan Rd.
McGraw Park, IL 60085
847-689-8410
Medical products O

Allen Telecom Inc. ALN
25101 Chagrin Blvd., Ste. 350
Beachwood, OH 44122
216-765-5800
Automotive & trucking - original
equipment O

Alliance Capital Management L.P. AC
1345 Avenue of the Americas
New York, NY 10105
212-969-1000
Financial - investment management O

Alliance World Dollar Government Fund
  II, Inc. AWF
1345 Avenue of the Americas
New York, NY 10105
212-969-1000
Financial - investment management

Alliance World Dollar Government Fund,
  Inc. AWG
1345 Avenue of the Americas
New York, NY 10105
212-969-1000
Financial - investment management

Alliant Techsystems Inc. ATK
600 Second St. NE
Hopkins, MN 55343
612-931-6000   Fax 612-931-5423
Weapons & weapon systems O

ALLIED Group, Inc. GRP
701 Fifth Ave.
Des Moines, IA 50391
515-280-4211
Insurance - multi line & misc. DRP

Allied Products Corp. ADP
10 S. Riverside Plaza
Chicago, IL 60606
312-454-1020
Diversified operations

Allied Signal Inc. ALD
101 Columbia Rd., PO Box 2245
Morristown, NJ 07962
201-455-2000   Fax 201-455-4807
Diversified operations O DRP

Allmerica Financial Corp. AFC
440 Lincoln St.
Worcester, MA 01653
508-855-1000   Fax 508-853-6332
Insurance - multi line & misc. O

Allmerica Securities Trust ALM
440 Lincoln St.
Worcester, MA 01653
508-855-1000
Financial - investment management

Allstate Corp. ALL
2775 Sanders Rd.
Northbrook, IL 60062
847-402-5000
Property & casualty insurance DRP

ALLTEL Corp. AT
One Allied Dr.
Little Rock, AR 72202
501-661-8000   Fax 501-651-5444
Utility - telephone O DRP

Alpine Group Inc. (The) AGI
1790 Broadway
New York, NY 10019
212-757-3333   Fax 212-757-3423
Chemicals - specialty O

Alpharma, Inc. ALO
One Executive Dr., PO Box 1399
Fort Lee, NJ 07024
201-947-7774
Drugs - generic O

Aluminum Company of America AA
425 6th Ave., Alcoa Building
Pittsburgh, PA 15219
412-553-4545   Fax 412-553-4498
Metals - nonferrous O DRP

ALZA Corp. AZA
950 Page Mill Rd.
Palo Alto, CA 94303
415-494-5000   Fax 415-494-5151
Drugs O

Amax Gold Inc. AU
9100 E. Mineral Circle
Englewood, CO 80112
303-643-5500   Fax 303-643-5507
Gold mining & processing O DRP

AMBAC Inc. ABK
One State St. Plaza
New York, NY 10004
212-668-0340   Fax 212-509-9190
Insurance - multi line & misc. O

Amcast Industrial Corp. AIZ
7887 Washington Village Dr.
Dayton, OH 45459
513-291-7000
Metal processing & fabrication DRP

Amerada Hess Corp. AHC
1185 Avenue of the Americas
New York, NY 10036
212-997-8500
Oil & gas - US integrated O DRP

America Online, Inc. AOL
8619 Westwood Center Dr.
Vienna, VA 22182
703-448-8700
Telecommunications services O

America West Holdings Corp. AWA
4000 E. Sky Harbor Blvd.
Phoenix, AZ 85034
602-693-0800
Transportation - airline O

American Annuity Group, Inc. AAG
580 Walnut
Cincinnati, OH 45202
513-333-5300
Insurance - life

American Bankers Insurance Group, Inc.
 ABI
11222 Quail Roost Dr.
Miami, FL 33157
305-253-2244
Insurance - life O

American Banknote Corp. ABN
51 W. 52nd St., 14th Fl.
New York, NY 10019
212-582-9200
Financial - business services

American Business Products, Inc. ABP
2100 RiverEdge Pkwy.
Atlanta, GA 30328
404-953-8300
Office equipment & supplies DRP

American Electric Power Co., Inc. AEP
1 Riverside Plaza
Columbus, OH 43215
614-223-1000
Utility - electric power O DRP

American Express Co. AXP
World Financial Center
New York, NY 10285
212-640-2000   Fax 212-640-3370
Financial - business services O DRP

American Financial Group AFG
One East Fourth St.
Cincinnati, OH 45202
513-579-2121
Property & casualty insurance

American General Corp. AGC
2929 Allen Parkway
Houston, TX 77019
713-522-1111
Insurance - life O DRP

American Government Income Fund Inc.
 AGF
222 S. Ninth St.
Minneapolis, MN 55402
800-333-6000
Financial - investment management

American Government Income Portfolio
 Inc. AAF
222 S. Ninth St.
Minneapolis, MN 55402
800-866-7778
Financial - investment management

American Health Properties, Inc. AHE
6400 S. Fiddler's Green Circle
Englewood, CO 80111
303-796-9793   Fax 303-796-9708
Real estate investment trust O DRP

American Heritage Life Investment Corp.
 AHL
1776 American Heritage Life Dr.
Jacksonville, FL 32224
904-354-1776
Insurance - life DRP

American Home Products Corp. AHP
Five Giralda Farms
Madison, NJ 07940
201-660-5000
Drugs O DRP

American Income Holding, Inc. AIH
1200 Wooded Acres Dr.
Waco, TX 76710
817-772-3050
Insurance - multi line & misc.

American Industrial Properties REIT IND
6220 N. Beltline, Ste. 205
Irving, TX 75063
972-550-6053
Real estate investment trust DRP

American International Group, Inc. AIG
70 Pine St.
New York, NY 10270
212-770-7000
Insurance - property & casualty O

American Media, Inc. ENQ
600 S. East Coast Ave.
Lantana, FL 33462
561-540-1000
Publishing - periodicals

American Municipal Income Portfolio, Inc.
 XAA
222 S. Ninth St.
Minneapolis, MN 55402
800-866-7778
Financial - investment management

American Municipal Term Trust - II BXT
222 S. Ninth St.
Minneapolis, MN 55402
800-866-7778
Financial - investment management

American Municipal Term Trust - III CXT
222 S. Ninth St.
Minneapolis, MN 55402
800-866-7778
Financial - investment management

American Municipal Term Trust Inc. AXT
222 S. Ninth St.
Minneapolis, MN 55402
800-886-7778
Financial - investment management

American Opportunity Income Fund, Inc.
 OIF
222 S. Ninth St.
Minneapolis, MN 55402
800-866-7778
Financial - investment management

American Pad & Paper Co. AGP
17304 Preston Rd.
Dallas, TX 75252
214-733-6200
Office & art materials O

American Precision Industries Inc. APR
2777 Walden Ave.
Buffalo, NY 14225
716-684-9700
Electrical products - misc.

American Real Estate Partners, L.P. ACP
90 S. Bedford Rd.
Mt. Kisco, NY 10549
914-242-7700
Real estate operations DRP

American Realty Trust, Inc. ARB
10670 N. Central Expwy.
Dallas, TX 75231
214-692-4700
Real estate investment trust

American Residential Services ARS
5051 Westheimer Rd., Suite 725
Houston, TX 77056
713-599-0100
Heating & air conditioning repair & maint.
 services

American Select Portfolio, Inc. SLA
222 S. Ninth St.
Minneapolis, MN 55402
800-333-6000
Financial - investment management

American Standard Companies Inc. ASD
One Centennial Ave.
Piscataway, NJ 08855
908-980-6000
Diversified operations O

American Strategic Income Portfolio, Inc.
 ASP
222 S. Ninth St.
Minneapolis, MN 55402
800-866-7778
Financial - investment management

American Strategic Income Portfolio, Inc. -
 II BSP
222 S. Ninth St.
Minneapolis, MN 55402
800-866-7778
Financial - investment management

American Strategic Income Portfolio, Inc. -
 III CSP
222 S. Ninth St.
Minneapolis, MN 55402
800-866-7778
Financial - investment management

American Water Works Co., Inc. AWK
1025 Laurel Oak Rd.
Voorhees, NJ 08043
609-346-8200
Utility - water supply DRP

Americas Income Trust, (The) XUS
222 S. Ninth St.
Minneapolis, MN 55402
800-866-7778
Financial - investment management

AmeriCredit Corp. ACF
200 Bailey Ave.
Fort Worth, TX 76107
817-332-7000
Financial - business services O

AmeriGas Partners, L.P. APU
460 N. Guelph Rd.
Valley Forge, PA 19406
610-337-7000
Retail - misc.

AmeriSource Health Corp. AAS
300 Chester Field Pkwy.
Malvern, PA 19355
610-296-4480
Wholesale distribution - consumer products

Ameritech Corp. AIT
30 S. Wacker Dr.
Chicago, IL 60606
312-750-5000   Fax 312-207-0016
Utility - telephone O DRP

Ameron International Corp. AMN
4700 Ramona Blvd.
Monterey Park, CA 91754
818-683-4000   Fax 818-683-4060
Building products - misc.

Amli Residential Properties, Inc. AML
125 S. Wacker Dr., Ste. 3100
Chicago, IL 60606
312-984-5037
Real estate investment trust

AMP Inc. AMP
PO Box 3608
Harrisburg, PA 17105
717-564-0100   Fax 717-780-6130
Electrical connectors O DRP

Ampco-Pittsburgh Corp. AP
600 Grant St., Ste. 4600
Pittsburgh, PA 15219
412-456-4400
Metal processing & fabrication

Amphenol Corp. APH
358 Hall Ave.
Wallingford, CT 06492
203-265-8900
Fiber optics O

AMR Corp. AMR
Dallas/Ft. Worth Airport
Dallas, TX 76155
817-963-1234
Transportation - airline O

AMREP Corp. AXR
641 Lexington Ave.
New York, NY 10022
212-705-4700
Building - residential & commercial

AmSouth Bancorporation ASO
1900 Fifth Ave. North
Birmingham, AL 35203
205-320-7151   Fax 205-326-4072
Banks - southeast O DRP

AmVestors Financial Corp. AMV
415 S.W. 8th Ave.
Topeka, KS 66603
913-232-6945   Fax 913-232-3534
Insurance - life DRP

Anadarko Petroleum Corp. APC
17001 Northchase Dr.
Houston, TX 77060
713-875-1101
Oil & gas - US exploration & production O

Analog Devices, Inc. ADI
One Technology Way
Norwood, MA 02062
617-329-4700
Electrical components - semiconductors O

Angelica Corp. AGL
424 S. Woods Mill Rd.
Chesterfield, MO 63017
314-854-3800
Linen supply & related DRP

Anheuser-Busch Companies, Inc. BUD
One Busch Place
St. Louis, MO 63118
314-577-2000   Fax 314-577-2900
Alcoholic beverages - brewer O DRP

Anixter International, Inc. AXE
2 N. Riverside Plaza
Chicago, IL 60606
312-902-1515
Diversified operations O

AnnTaylor Stores Corp. ANN
142 W. 57th St.
New York, NY 10019
212-541-3300
Retail - apparel & shoes O

Aon Corp. AOC
123 N. Wacker Dr.
Chicago, IL 60606
312-701-3000
Insurance - accident & health O DRP

Apache Corp. APA
2000 Post Oak Blvd., Ste. 100
Houston, TX 77056
713-296-6000
Oil & gas - US exploration & production
O DRP

Apartment Investment and Management
Co. AIV
1873 S. Bellaire St.
Denver, CO 80222
303-757-8101
Real estate investment trust

Apex Municipal Fund, Inc. APX
PO Box 9011
Princeton, NJ 08543
609-282-2800
Financial - investment management

Appalachian Power Co. AEWpB
40 Franklin Rd., S.W.
Roanoke, VA 24011
540-985-2300
Utility - electric power

Applied Industrial Technologies, Inc. APZ
3600 Euclid Ave.
Cleveland, OH 44115
216-881-8900
Metal products - distribution DRP

Applied Magnetics Corp. APM
75 Robin Hill Rd.
Goleta, CA 93117
805-683-5353   Fax 805-967-8227
Computers - peripheral equipment O

Applied Power Inc. APW
13000 W. Silver Spring Dr.
Butler, WI 53007
414-781-6600   Fax 414-781-0629
Machine tools & related products

Apria Healthcare Group Inc. AHG
3560 Hyland Ave.
Costa Mesa, CA 92626
714-427-2000   Fax 714-540-2482
Healthcare - outpatient & home O

AptarGroup, Inc. ATR
475 W. Terra Cotta Ave.
Crystal Lake, IL 60014
815-477-0424   Fax 815-477-0481
Pumps and seals

Aquarion Co. WTR
835 Main St.
Bridgeport, CT 06601
203-335-2333
Utility - water supply DRP 5%

Aquila Gas Pipeline Corp. AQP
100 N.E. Loop, Ste. 1000
San Antonio, TX 78216
210-342-0685
Oil & gas - production & pipeline

Arbor Property Trust ABR
10 E. Sixth Ave., Ste. 310
Conshohocken, PA 19428
610-941-9511
Real estate investment trust DRP

Arcadia Financial Ltd. AAC
7825 Washington Ave. South
Minneapolis, MN 55439
612-942-9880   Fax 612-942-0015
Financial - consumer loans O

Arch Coal ACI
City Place One, Suite 300
St. Louis, MO 63141
314-994-2700
Mines coal for electric utilities

Archer Daniels Midland Co. ADM
4666 Faries Pkwy, PO Box 1470
Decatur, IL 62525
217-424-5200
Food - flour & grain O

ARCO Chemical Co. RCM
3801 W. Chester Pike
Newtown Square, PA 19073
610-359-2000   Fax 610-359-2722
Chemicals - specialty O DRP

Arden Realty ARI
9100 Wilshire Blvd., Suite 700
Beverley Hills, CA 90212
310-271-8600
Real estate investment trust

Argentina Fund, (The) AF
345 Park Ave.
New York, NY 10154
212-326-6200
Financial - investment management

Argosy Gaming Co. AGY
219 Piasa St.
Alton, IL 62002
618-474-7500   Fax 618-474-7636
Leisure & recreational services O

Armco Inc. AS
301 Grant St., 15th Fl.
Pittsburgh, PA 15219
412-255-9800
Steel - production O

Armstrong World Industries, Inc. ACK
313 W. Liberty St.
Lancaster, PA 17603
717-397-0611
Building products - misc. O DRP

Arrow Electronics, Inc. ARW
25 Hub Dr.
Melville, NY 11747
516-391-1300
Electronics - parts distribution O

Arthur J. Gallagher & Co. AJG
Two Pierce Place
Itasca, IL 60143
630-773-3800   Fax 630-285-4000
Insurance - brokerage

ARTRA GROUP Inc. ATA
500 Central Ave.
Northfield, IL 60093
708-441-6650
Diversified operations

Arvin Industries, Inc. ARV
One Noblitt Plaza, PO Box 3000
Columbus, IN 47202
812-379-3000
Automotive & trucking - original
   equipment DRP

ASARCO Inc. AR
180 Maiden Lane
New York, NY 10038
212-510-2000   Fax 212-510-1855
Metal ores - misc. O DRP

Ashland Inc. ASH
1000 Ashland Dr.
Russell, KY 41169
606-329-3333
Oil refining & marketing O DRP

Asia Pacific Fund, Inc. APB
One Seaport Plaza
New York, NY 10292
212-214-3334
Financial - investment management

Asia Tigers GRR
200 Liberty St
New York, NY 10281
212-667-4302
Closed-end fund - Asia equities

Asset Investors Corp. AIC
3600 S. Yosemite St., Ste. 900
Denver, CO 80237
303-793-2703
Real estate investment trust DRP

Associated Estates Realty Corp. AEC
5025 Swetland Ct.
Richmond Heights, OH 44143
216-461-1111   Fax 216-449-3387
Real estate investment trust DRP

Associates First Capital AFS
250 East Carpenter Freeway
Irving, TX 75062
972-652-4000
Consumer & commercial finance, leasing

AT&T Corp. T
32 Avenue of the Americas
New York, NY 10013
212-387-5400   Fax 212-387-5347
Telecommunications services O DRP

Atchison Casting Corp. FDY
400 S. Fourth St.
Atchison, KS 66002
913-367-2121
Steel - production

Atlantic Energy, Inc. ATE
6801 Black Horse Pike
Egg Harbor Township, NJ 08234
609-645-4500
Utility - electric power DRP

Atlantic Richfield Co. ARC
515 S. Flower St.
Los Angeles, CA 90071
213-486-3511
Oil & gas - US integrated O DRP

Atmos Energy Corp. ATO
5430 LBJ Freeway
Dallas, TX 75240
214-934-9227
Utility - gas distribution 3% DRP

Atwood Oceanics ATW
15835 Park Ten Place Dr.
Houston, TX 77218
281-492-2929
International oil & gas drilling &
   equipment

Austria Fund, (The) OST
1345 Avenue of the Americas
New York, NY 10105
800-247-4154
Financial - investment management

Authentic Fitness Corp. ASM
7911 Haskell Ave.
Van Nuys, CA 91410
818-376-0300
Apparel

Automatic Data Processing, Inc. AUD
One ADP Blvd.
Roseland, NJ 07068
201-994-5000
Business services O

AutoZone, Inc. AZO
3030 Poplar Ave.
Memphis, TN 38111
901-325-4600
Auto parts - retail & wholesale O

Avalon Bay Communities AVB
11 Burtis Ave.
New Canaan, CT 06840
203-972-4000   Fax 203-966-6823
Real estate investment trust

Avatex Corp. AAV
1220 Senlac Dr.
Carrollton, TX 75006
972-446-4800
Diversified operations

Avery Dennison Corp. AVY
150 N. Orange Grove Blvd.
Pasadena, CA 91103
818-304-2000   Fax 818-792-7312
Office & art materials O DRP

Aviall Inc. AVL
9311 Reeves St.
Dallas, TX 75235
214-956-5356
Aerospace - aircraft equipment O

Aviation Sales Co. AVS
6905 N.W. 25th St.
Miami, FL 33122
305-592-4055
Aerospace - aircraft equipment

Avnet, Inc. AVT
80 Cutter Mill Rd.
Great Neck, NY 11021
516-466-7000   Fax 516-466-1203
Electronics - parts distribution O DRP

Avon Products, Inc. AVP
1345 Avenue of the Americas
New York, NY 10105
212-282-5000
Cosmetics & toiletries O DRP

AVX Corp. AVX
801 12th Ave. South
Myrtle Beach, SC 29577
803-448-9411
Electronics - components & systems
  O DRP

Aydin Corp. AYD
700 Dresher Rd., PO Box 349
Horsham, PA 19044
215-657-7510   Fax 215-657-3830
Electronics - military

Aztar Corp. AZR
2390 E. Camelback Rd.
Phoenix, AZ 85016
602-381-4100   Fax 602-381-4107
Leisure & recreational services O

Aztec Manufacturing Co. AZZ
400 N. Tarrant, PO Box 668
Crowley, TX 76036
817-297-4361   Fax 817-297-4621
Building products - lighting fixtures

BA Merchant Services, Inc. BPI
One South Van Ness Ave.
San Francisco, CA 94103
415-241-3390
Financial - business services O

Bairnco Corp. BZ
2251 Lucien Way, Ste. 300
Maitland, FL 32751
407-875-2222
Diversified operations

Baker Hughes, Inc. BHI
3900 Essex Ln.
Houston, TX 77027
713-439-8699   Fax 713-439-8699
Oil field machinery & equipment O DRP

Baker, Fentress & Co. BKF
200 W. Madison St., Ste. 3510
Chicago, IL 60606
312-236-9190
Financial - investment management

Baldor Electric Co. BEZ
5711 R. S. Boreham, Jr. St.
Fort Smith, AR 72902
501-646-4711
Machinery - electrical DRP

Ball Corp. BLL
345 S. High St., PO Box 2407
Muncie, IN 47307
765-747-6100   Fax 765-747-6813
Glass products O DRP 5%

Ballard Medical Products BMP
12050 Lone Peak Pkwy.
Draper, UT 84020
801-572-6800
Medical & dental supplies O

Baltimore Gas and Electric Co. BGE
39 W. Lexington St.
Baltimore, MD 21201
410-783-5920
Utility - electric power O DRP

Banc One Corp. ONE
100 E. Broad St.
Columbus, OH 43271
614-248-5944
Banks - midwest O DRP

BancorpSouth, Inc. BXS
One Mississippi Plaza
Tupelo, MS 38801
601-680-2000
Banks - southeast DRP

BancTec, Inc. BTC
4435 Spring Valley Rd.
Dallas, TX 75244
214-450-7700
Optical character recognition O

Bandag, Inc. BDG
2905 N. Highway 61
Muscatine, IA 52761
319-262-1400
Rubber tires DRP

Bangor Hydro-Electric Co. BGR
33 State St.
Bangor, ME 04401
207-945-5621
Utility - electric power DRP

Bank of New York Co., Inc. BK
48 Wall St.
New York, NY 10286
212-495-1784
Banks - northeast O DRP

BankAmerica Corp. BAC
Bank of America Center
San Francisco, CA 94104
415-622-3530
Banks - money center O DRP

BankBoston Corp. BKB
100 Federal St.
Boston, MA 02110
617-434-2200 Fax 617-434-6802
Banks - northeast O DRP 3%

Bankers Trust New York Corp. BT
280 Park Ave.
New York, NY 10017
212-250-2500
Banks - money center O DRP

Banner Aerospace, Inc. BAR
300 W. Service Rd.
Washington, DC 20041
703-478-5790
Aerospace - aircraft equipment

Bard (C.R.) BCR
730 Central Ave.
Murray Hill, NJ 07974
908-277-8000
Manufactures disposable medical devices
  DRP

Barnes & Noble, Inc. BKS
122 Fifth Ave.
New York, NY 10011
212-633-3300
Retail - misc. O

Barnes Group Inc. B
123 Main St., PO Box 489
Bristol, CT 06011
203-583-7070
Wire & cable products DRP

Barrett Resources Corp. BRR
1125 Seventeenth St.
Denver, CO 80202
303-297-3900 Fax 303-297-0807
Oil & gas - US exploration & production
  O

Barrick Gold ABX
200 Bay St., Suite 2700
Toronto, ON M5J2J3
416-861-9911 Fax 416-861-0727
Gold mining & production

Barry (R.G.) RGB
13405 Yarmouth Rd. N.W.
Pickerington, OH 43147
614-864-6400
Footwear production/sells microwave
  technology

Battle Mountain Gold Co. BMG
333 Clay St., 42nd Fl.
Houston, TX 77002
713-650-6400 Fax 713-650-3636
Gold mining & processing O

Bausch & Lomb Inc. BOL
One Lincoln First Square
Rochester, NY 14601
716-338-6000
Medical products O DRP

Baxter International Inc. BAX
One Baxter Parkway
Deerfield, IL 60015
708-948-2000 Fax 708-948-3080
Medical products O DRP

Bay Networks, Inc. BAY
4401 Great America Pkwy.
Santa Clara, CA 95052
408-988-2400 Fax 408-988-5525
Telecommunications equipment O

Bay State Gas Co. BGC
300 Friberg Parkway
Westborough, MA 01581
508-836-7000
Utility - gas distribution DRP

BB&T Corp. BBK
500 N. Chestnut St.
Lumberton, NC 28358
910-671-2000
Banks - southeast O DRP 5%

BCE Inc. BCE
1000 Rue de la Gauchetieve Ouest
Montreal, Quebec H3B 4Y7
Canada
514-397-7310
Telecommunications DRP

BEA Income Fund, Inc. FBF
Vanguard Financial Center
Valley Forge, PA 19482
610-648-6000
Financial - investment management

BEA Strategic Global Income Fund, Inc.
  FBI
Vanguard Financial Center
Valley Forge, PA 19482
610-648-6000
Financial - investment management

Bear Stearns Cos. BSC
245 Park Ave.
New York, NY 10167
212-272-2000
Investment banking/brokerage

Beazer Homes USA, Inc. BZH
1927 Lakeside Pkwy., Ste. 602
Tucker, GA 30084
404-934-2888   Fax 404-938-5524
Building - residential & commercial

Beckman Instruments, Inc. BEC
2500 Harbor Blvd.
Fullerton, CA 92634
714-871-4848   Fax 714-773-8283
Medical instruments O DRP

Becton, Dickinson and Co. BDX
1 Becton Dr.
Franklin Lakes, NJ 07417
201-847-6800
Medical & dental supplies O DRP

Bedford Property Investors, Inc. BED
270 Lafayette Circle
Lafayette, CA 94549
510-283-8910   Fax 510-283-5697
Real estate investment trust DRP

Belco Oil & Gas Corp. BOG
767 Fifth Ave.
New York, NY 10153
212-644-2200
Oil & gas - US exploration & production

Belden Inc. BWC
7701 Forsyth Blvd., Ste. 800
St. Louis, MO 63105
314-854-8000
Electrical products - misc. O

Bell & Howell Co. BHW
5215 Old Orchard Rd.
Skokie, IL 60077
708-470-7100   Fax 708-470-9825
Business services O

Bell Atlantic Corp. BEL
1717 Arch St.
Philadelphia, PA 19103
215-963-6000   Fax 215-963-9029
Utility - telephone DRP

Bell Industries, Inc. BI
11812 San Vicente Blvd.
Los Angeles, CA 90049
310-826-2355   Fax 310-447-3265
Electronics - parts distribution

BellSouth Corp. BLS
1155 Peachtree St., N.E.
Atlanta, GA 30309
404-249-2000   Fax 404-249-5597
Utility - telephone O DRP

Belo (A.H.) BLC
400 South Record St.
Dallas, TX 75202
214-977-6606   Fax 214-977-6603
Publishing newspapers, broadcasting TV

Bemis Co., Inc. BMS
222 S. Ninth St., Ste. 2300
Minneapolis, MN 55402
612-376-3000
Containers - paper & plastic O DRP

Benchmark Electronics, Inc. BHE
3000 Technology Dr.
Angleton, TX 77515
409-849-6550
Electrical components - misc.

Benton Oil and Gas Co. BNO
1145 Eugenia Pl., Ste. 200
Carpinteria, CA 93013
805-566-5600
Oil & gas - US exploration & production
  O

Berg Electronics Corp. BEI
101 S. Hanley Rd., Ste. 400
St. Louis, MO 63105
314-726-1323
Electronics - components & systems

Bergen Brunswig Corp. BBC
4000 Metropolitan Dr.
Orange, CA 92668
714-385-4000
Drugs & sundries - wholesale

Berkshire Hathaway Inc. BRK
1440 Kiewit Plaza
Omaha, NE 68131
402-346-1400
Diversified operations

Berkshire Realty Co. BRI
470 Atlantic Ave.
Boston, MA 02210
617-423-2233
Real estate investment trust   DRP

Berlitz International, Inc. BTZ
293 Wall St.
Princeton, NJ 08540
609-924-8500
Schools

Berry Petroleum Co. BRY
28700 Hovey Hills Rd.
Taft, CA 93268
805-769-8811
Oil & gas - US exploration & production

Best Buy Co., Inc. BBY
7075 Flying Cloud Dr.
Eden Prairie, MN 55344
612-947-2000
Retail - consumer electronics O

Bethlehem Steel Corp. BS
1170 Eighth Ave.
Bethlehem, PA 18016
610-694-2424   Fax 810-694-5743
Steel - production O DRP

Beverly Enterprises, Inc. BEV
5111 Rogers Ave., Ste. 40-A
Fort Smith, AR 72919
501-452-6712   Fax 501-452-5131
Nursing homes O

Big Flower Press Holdings, Inc. BGF
3 E. 54th St., 19th Fl.
New York, NY 10022
212-521-1600   Fax 212-521-1697
Publishing - newspapers O

Bindley Western Industries, Inc. BDY
10333 N. Meridian St.
Indianapolis, IN 46290
317-298-9900
Drugs & sundries - wholesale O

Biovail Corp International BVF
2488 Dunwin Dr.
Mississauga, ON L5L1J9
416-285-6000   Fax 416-285-6499
Manufacture & testing medicinal drugs

Birmingham Steel Corp. BIR
1000 Urban Center Pkwy.
Birmingham, AL 35242
205-970-1200
Steel - production O DRP

BJ Services Co. BJS
5500 N.W. Central Dr.
Houston, TX 77092
713-462-4239
Oil & gas - field services O

Black & Decker Corp. BDK
701 E. Joppa Rd.
Towson, MD 21286
410-716-3900
Producer power tools & household
  products O DRP

Black Hills Corp. BKH
625 Ninth St., PO Box 1400
Rapid City, SD 57709
605-348-1700
Utility - electric power DRP

BlackRock Advantage Term Trust Inc.
  BAT
One Seaport Plaza
New York, NY 10292
800-227-7236
Financial - investment management

BlackRock California Ins. Municipal
  2008 Term Trust BFC
One Seaport Plaza
New York, NY 10292
800-227-7236
Financial - investment management

BlackRock Florida Municipal 2008 Term
  Trust BRF
One Seaport Plaza
New York, NY 10292
800-227-7236
Financial - investment management

BlackRock Income Trust Inc. BKT
One Seaport Plaza
New York, NY 10292
800-227-7236
Financial - investment management

BlackRock Insured Municipal 2008 Term
  Trust BRM
One Seaport Plaza
New York, NY 10292
800-227-7236
Financial - investment management

BlackRock Insured Municipal Term Trust
  Inc. BMT
One Seaport Plaza
New York, NY 10292
800-227-7236
Financial - investment management

BlackRock Investment Quality Municipal
Trust Inc. BKN
One Seaport Plaza
New York, NY 10292
800-227-7236
Financial - investment management

BlackRock Investment Quality Term Trust
  Inc. BQT
One Seaport Plaza
New York, NY 10292
800-227-7236
Financial - investment management

BlackRock Mun. Target Term Trust Inc.
  BMN
One Seaport Plaza
New York, NY 10292
800-227-7236
Financial - investment management

BlackRock New York Ins. Municipal
  2008 Term Trust BLN
One Seaport Plaza
New York, NY 10292
800-227-7236
Financial - investment management

BlackRock North American Government
  Trust Inc. BNA
One Seaport Plaza
New York, NY 10292
800-227-7236
Financial - investment management

BlackRock Strategic Term Trust Inc. BGT
One Seaport Plaza
New York, NY 10292
800-227-7236
Financial - investment management

BlackRock Target Term Trust Inc. BTT
One Seaport Plaza
New York, NY 10292
800-227-7266
Financial - investment management

Block (H & R) HRB
4410 Main St.
Kansas City, MO 64111
816-753-6900
Income tax services DRP

Blount International, Inc. BLT
4520 Executive Park Dr.
Montgomery, AL 36116
334-244-4000
Machinery - general industrial DRP 5%

Blue Chip Value Fund, Inc. BLU
633 17th St., Ste. 1800
Denver, CO 80202
303-293-5999
Financial - investment management

Bluegreen Corp. BXG
5295 Town Center Rd.
Boca Raton, FL 33486
561-391-6336   Fax 561-391-6337
Real estate development

Blyth Industries, Inc. BTH
100 Field Point Rd.
Greenwich, CT 06830
203-661-1926
Miscellaneous - not elsewhere classified O

BMC Industries, Inc. BMC
Two Appletree Square, Ste. 400
Minneapolis, MN 55425
612-851-6000   Fax 612-851-6050
Medical & dental supplies O

Boeing BA
7755 East Marginal Way South
Seattle, WA 98108
206-655-2121
Air and space craft manufacturer DRP

Boise Cascade Corp. BCC
One Jefferson Square
Boise, ID 83728
208-384-6161   Fax 208-384-7298
Paper & paper products O DRP

Boise Cascade Office Products Corp. BOP
800 W. Bryn Mawr Rd.
Itasca, IL 60143
630-773-5000
Wholesale distribution - consumer products
  O

Bombay Company BBA
550 Bailey Ave.
Fort Worth, TX 76107
817-347-8200
Furniture retailer

Borden Chemicals and Plastics L.P. BCU
Highway 73
Geismar, LA 70734
504-387-5101
Chemicals - diversified O

Borders Group, Inc. BGP
500 E. Washington St.
Ann Arbor, MI 48104
313-913-2333
Retail - books, music & video O

Borg-Warner Automotive, Inc. BWA
200 S. Michigan Ave.
Chicago, IL 60604
312-322-8500
Automotive & trucking - original
equipment O DRP

Borg-Warner Security Corp. BOR
200 S. Michigan Ave.
Chicago, IL 60604
312-322-8500
Protection - safety equipment & services

Boston Beer SAM
75 Arlington St
Boston, MA 02116
617-368-5000
Alcoholic beverages - brewer DRP

Boston Celtics L.P. BOS
151 Merrimac St.
Boston, MA 02114
617-523-6050
Leisure & recreational services

Boston Edison Co. BSE
800 Boylston St.
Boston, MA 02199
617-424-2000
Utility - electric power DRP

Boston Scientific Corp. BSX
480 Pleasant St.
Watertown, MA 02172
617-923-1720
Medical products O

Bowater Inc. BOW
55 E. Camperdown Way
Greenville, SC 29602
864-271-7733   Fax 864-282-9482
Paper & paper products O DRP

Boyd Gaming Corp. BYD
2950 S. Industrial Rd.
Las Vegas, NV 89109
702-792-7200   Fax 702-792-7229
Leisure & recreational services O

Boykin Lodging Co. BOY
50 Public Square
Cleveland, OH 44113
216-241-6375
Real estate investment trust

BP Amoco BP
200 Public Square
Cleveland, OH 44114
800-428-4237
International oil DRP

Bradley Real Estate Trust BTR
250 Boylston St.
Boston, MA 02116
617-421-0741
Real estate investment trust DRP 3%

Brazil Fund, (The) BZF
345 Park Ave.
New York, NY 10154
800-349-4281
Financial - investment management

Brazilian Equity Fund, (The) BZL
153 E. 53rd Street, 58th Floor
New York, NY 10022
212-832-2626
Financial - investment management

BRE Properties, Inc. BRE
One Montgomery St., Ste. 2500
San Francisco, CA 94104
415-445-6530   Fax 415-445-6505
Real estate investment trust DRP

Breed Technologies, Inc. BDT
5300 Old Tampa Highway
Lakeland, FL 33811
813-284-6000
Automotive & trucking - original
equipment O

Briggs & Stratton Corp. BGG
12301 W. Wirth St.
Wauwatosa, WI 53222
414-259-5333   Fax 414-259-5338
Engines - internal combustion O DRP

Brinker International, Inc. EAT
6820 LBJ Freeway
Dallas, TX 75240
214-980-9917
Retail - food & restaurants O

Bristol Hotel Co. BH
14285 Midway Rd., Ste. 300
Dallas, TX 75244
972-788-0001   Fax 972-687-0357
Hotels & motels

Bristol-Myers Squibb Co. BMY
345 Park Ave.
New York, NY 10154
212-546-4000   Fax 212-546-4020
Drugs O DRP

British Airways PLC BAB
P.O. Box 8205
Boston, MA 02266
800-711-6475
International airline DRP

Brooke Group Ltd. BGL
65 E. 55th St.
New York, NY 10022
305-579-8000
Tobacco

Brown & Sharpe Manufacturing Co. BNS
200 Frenchtown Rd.
North Kingstown, RI 02852
401-886-2000   Fax 401-886-2762
Electronics - measuring instruments O

Brown Group, Inc. BG
8300 Maryland Ave.
St. Louis, MO 63105
314-854-4000   Fax 314-854-4274
Shoes & related apparel O DRP

Brown-Forman Corp. BFB
850 Dixie Hwy.
Louisville, KY 40210
502-585-1100   Fax 502-774-7876
Beverages - alcoholic DRP

Browning-Ferris Industries, Inc. BFI
757 N. Eldridge, PO Box 3151
Houston, TX 77253
713-870-8100   Fax 713-870-7844
Pollution control equipment & services
  DRP

BRT Realty Trust BRT
60 Cutter Mill Rd.
Great Neck, NY 11021
516-466-3100
Real estate investment trust

Brunswick Corp. BC
1 N. Field Ct.
Lake Forest, IL 60045
708-375-4700
Leisure & recreational products O DRP

Brush Wellman Inc. BW
17876 St. Clair Ave.
Cleveland, OH 44110
216-486-4200   Fax 216-383-4091
Metals - nonferrous DRP

Brylane Inc. BYL
463 Seventh Ave., 21st Floor
New York, NY 10018
212-613-9500
Apparel catalog retailer

BT Office Products International, Inc.
  BTF
2150 E. Lake Cook Rd.
Buffalo Grove, IL 60089
847-793-7500   Fax 847-808-3001
Retail - misc.

Buckeye Partners, L.P. BPL
3900 Hamilton Blvd.
Allentown, PA 18103
610-770-4400
Oil & gas - production & pipeline DRP

Buckle Co., (The) BKE
2407 W. 24th Street
Kearney, NE 68847
308-236-8491
Retail - apparel & shoes

Budget Group, Inc. BD
1028 Dr. Mary M. Bethune Blvd.
Daytona Beach, FL 32114
904-238-7035
Transportation - equipment & leasing

Burlington Coat Factory Warehouse Corp.
  BCF
1830 Route 130 North
Burlington, NJ 08016
609-387-7800
Retail - apparel & shoes O

Burlington Industries, Inc. BUR
3330 W. Friendly Ave.
Greensboro, NC 27410
910-379-2000
Textiles - mill products O

Burlington Northern Sante Fe Corp. BNI
777 Main St.
Fort Worth, TX 76102
817-333-2000
Transportation - rail O DRP

Burlington Resources Coal Seam Gas
  Royalty Trust BRU
700 Louisiana St., Ste. 3100
Houston, TX 77002
713-247-7508
Oil & gas - US royalty trust

Burlington Resources Inc. BR
5051 Westheimer, Ste. 1400
Houston, TX 77056
713-624-9500
Oil & gas - US exploration & production
  O

Burnham Pacific Properties, Inc. BPP
610 W. Ash St.
San Diego, CA 92101
619-232-2001   Fax 619-237-8019
Real estate investment trust DRP

Bush Boake Allen Inc. BOA
7 Mercedes Dr.
Montvale, NJ 07645
201-391-9870   Fax 201-391-0860
Chemicals - specialty

Bush Industries, Inc. BSH
One Mason Dr.
Jamestown, NY 14702
716-665-2000
Furniture

Butler Manufacturing Co. BBR
BMA Tower, Penn Valley Park
Kansas City, MO 64141
816-968-3000
Building products - misc.

BWAY Corp. BY
8607 Roberts Dr., Ste. 250
Atlanta, GA 30350
404-587-0888
Metal products - fabrication

Cable Design Technologies Corp. CDT
661 Andersen Dr.
Pittsburgh, PA 15220
412-937-2300   Fax 412-937-9690
Telecommunications equipment O

Cabletron Systems, Inc. CS
35 Industrial Way
Rochester, NH 03867
603-332-9400
Computers - peripheral equipment O

Cabot Corp. CBT
75 State St.
Boston, MA 02109
617-345-0100
Chemicals - specialty O DRP

Cabot Oil & Gas Corp. COG
15375 Memorial Dr.
Houston, TX 77079
713-589-4600
Oil & gas - US exploration & production

Cadence Design Systems, Inc. CDN
555 River Oaks Pkwy.
San Jose, CA 95134
408-943-1234   Fax 408-943-0513
Computers - software

CalEnergy Co. CE
10831 Old Mill Rd.
Omaha, NE 68154
402-330-8900   Fax 402-330-9888
Energy - alternate sources O

Calgon Carbon Corp. CCC
400 Calgon Carbon Dr.
Pittsburgh, PA 15205
412-787-6700
Pollution control equipment & services O

Caliber System, Inc. CBB
3925 Embassy Pkwy.
Akron, OH 44334
330-665-5646
Transportation - truck O DRP

California Water Service Co. CWT
1720 N. First St.
San Jose, CA 95112
408-451-8200
Utility - water supply DRP

Callaway Golf Co. ELY
2285 Rutherford Rd.
Carlsbad, CA 92008
760-931-1771   Fax 760-931-9539
Leisure & recreational products O DRP

CalMat Co. CZM
3200 San Fernando Rd.
Los Angeles, CA 90065
213-258-2777
Construction - cement & concrete O

Calpine Corp. CPN
50 W. San Fernando St.
San Jose, CA 05113
408-995-5115   Fax 408-995-0505
Utility - electric power

Camco International, Inc. CAM
7030 Ardmore
Houston, TX 77054
713-747-4000
Oil & gas - field services O

Camden Property Trust CPT
3200 Southwest Freeway
Houston, TX 77027
713-964-3555   Fax 713-964-3599
Real estate investment trust

Cameco Corp. CCJ
2121 11th Street West
Saskatoon, SK S7M1J3
306-956-6200   Fax 306-956-6201
Uranium & gold mining

Campbell Resources CCH
120 Adelaide Street West, Suite 1910
Toronto, ON M5H1T1
416-366-5201
Gold & precious metals mining

Campbell Soup Co. CPB
Campbell Place
Camden, NJ 08103
609-342-4800   Fax 609-342-3878
Food - canned O DRP

Canada Pacific CP
910 Peel St.
Montreal, Quebec H3C 3E4
Canada
514-395-5151
Railroad DRP

Capital One Financial Corp. COF
8330 Boone Blvd.
Vienna, VA 22182
703-734-7495
Financial - business services O DRP

Capital Re Corp. KRE
1325 Avenue of the Americas
New York, NY 10019
212-974-0100   Fax 212-581-3268
Insurance - property & casualty

Capital Trust CT
885 Third Ave., Suite 1240
New York, NY 10022
212-593-5400
Investments - commercial real estate
 DRP 5%

Capstar Hotels CHO
1010 Wisconsin Ave. N.W., Suite 650
Washington, DC 20007
202-965-4455
Hotels - owns, renovates & manages

Capstead Mortgage Corp. CMO
2711 N. Haskell Ave., LB 12
Dallas, TX 75204
214-874-2323
Real estate investment trust

Capstone Capital Corp. CCT
1 Perimeter Park South
Birmingham, AL 35243
205-967-2092
Real estate investment trust DRP 2%

Cardinal Health, Inc. CAH
655 Metro Place South
Dublin, OH 43017
614-761-8700
Drugs & sundries - wholesale O

Caribiner International, Inc. CWC
24 W. 61st St.
New York, NY 10023
212-541-5300
Business services

Carlisle Companies Inc. CSL
250 S. Clinton St., Ste. 201
Syracuse, NY 13202
315-474-2500
Diversified operations DRP

Carlyle Industries, Inc. CRL
1430 Broadway
New York, NY 10018
212-556-4700   Fax 212-869-1002
Textiles - mill products

Carmike Cinemas, Inc. CKE
1301 First Ave.
Columbus, GA 31901
706-576-3400
Motion pictures & services

Carnival Corp. CCL
3655 N.W. 87th Ave.
Miami, FL 33178
305-599-2600
Leisure & recreational services O DRP

Carolina Power & Light Co. CPL
411 Fayetteville St.
Raleigh, NC 27601
919-546-6111
Utility - electric power O DRP

Carpenter Technology Corp. CRS
101 W. Bern St.
Reading, PA 19612
610-208-2000
Steel - specialty alloys O DRP

Carr Gottstein Foods Co. CGF
6411 A St.
Anchorage, AK 99518
907-561-1944
Retail - convenience stores

CarrAmerica Realty Corp. CRE
1700 Pennsylvania Ave., N.W.
Washington, DC 20006
202-624-7500   Fax 202-638-0102
Real estate investment trust

Carson CIC
64 Ross Rd.
Savannah, GA 31405
912-651-3400
African-American hair products

Carter-Wallace, Inc. CAR
1345 Avenue of the Americas
New York, NY 10105
212-339-5000
Drugs O

Cascade Corp. CAE
2020 S.W. 4th Ave., Ste. 600
Portland, OR 97201
503-227-0024 Fax 503-274-1705
Machinery - material handling O

Cascade Natural Gas Corp. CGC
222 Fairview Ave. North
Seattle, WA 98109
206-624-3900 Fax 206-624-7215
Utility - gas distribution DRP

Case Corp. CSE
700 State St.
Racine, WI 53404
414-636-6011
Machinery - farm O DRP

Cash America International, Inc. PWN
1600 W. 7th St.
Fort Worth, TX 76102
817-335-1100
Retail - misc. DRP

Castle & Cooke, Inc. CCS
10900 Wilshire Blvd.
Los Angeles, CA 90024
310-208-3636 Fax 310-824-7770
Real estate development DRP

Catalina Lighting, Inc. LTG
6073 NW 167th St. #16
Miami, FL 33015
305-558-4777
Building products - lighting fixtures DRP

Catalina Marketing Corp. POS
11300 Ninth St. North
St. Petersburg, FL 33716
813-579-5000
Business services - marketing O DRP

Catellus Development Corp. CDX
201 Mission St.
San Francisco, CA 94105
415-974-4500
Real estate development O DRP

Caterpillar Inc. CAT
100 N.E. Adams St.
Peoria, IL 61629
309-675-1000
Machinery - construction & mining
  O DRP

Cavalier Homes, Inc. CAV
Highway 41 N. and Cavalier Rd.
Addison, AL 35540
205-747-1575 Fax 205-747-1605
Building - residential & commercial

CBL & Associates Properties, Inc. CBL
6148 Lee Highway
Chattanooga, TN 37421
615-855-0001 Fax 615-490-8662
Real estate investment trust DRP 5%

CCB Financial Corp. CCB
111 Corcoran St.
Durham, NC 27702
919-683-7777
Banks - southeast DRP

CDI Corp. CDI
1717 Arch St., 35th Fl.
Philadelphia, PA 19103
215-569-2200
Engineering - R & D services

Cedar Fair, L.P. FUN
PO Box 5006
Sandusky, OH 44871
419-626-0830
Leisure & recreational services DRP

Centerior Energy Corp. CX
6200 Oak Tree Blvd.
Independence, OH 44131
216-447-3100 Fax 216-447-3240
Utility - electric power O DRP

CenterPoint Properties Corp. CNT
401 N. Michigan Ave.
Chicago, IL 60611
312-346-5600
Real estate investment trust

Centex Construction Products, Inc. CXP
3710 Rawlins, Ste. 1600
Dallas, TX 75219
214-559-6500
Building products - misc.

Centex Corp. CTX
3333 Lee Pkwy., Ste. 1200
Dallas, TX 75219
214-559-6500
Building - residential & commercial O

Central and South West Corp. CSR
1616 Woodall Rodgers Freeway
Dallas, TX 75202
214-777-1000
Utility - electric power O DRP

Central Hudson Gas & Electric Corp.
CNH
284 South Ave.
Poughkeepsie, NY 12601
914-452-2000
Utility - electric power DRP

Central Louisiana Electric Co., Inc. CNL
2030 Donahue Ferry Rd.
Pineville, LA 71360
318-484-7400
Utility - electric power DRP

Central Maine Power Co. CTP
83 Edison Dr.
Augusta, ME 04336
207-623-3521
Utility - electric power DRP

Central Newspapers, Inc. ECP
135 N. Pennsylvania St.
Indianapolis, IN 46204
317-231-9200
Publishing - newspapers

Central Parking Corp. PK
2401 21st Ave. South, Ste. 200
Nashville, TN 37212
615-297-4255
Miscellaneous - not elsewhere classified

Central Vermont Public Service Corp. CV
77 Grove St.
Rutland, VT 05701
802-773-2711
Utility - electric power DRP

Centris Group, Inc. CGE
650 Town Center Dr., Ste. 1600
Costa Mesa, CA 92626
714-549-1600
Insurance - multi line & misc.

Centura Banks, Inc. CBC
134 N. Church St., PO Box 1220
Rocky Mount, NC 27802
919-977-4400 Fax 919-977-4800
Banks - southeast DRP

Century Telephone Enterprises, Inc. CTL
100 Century Park Dr.
Monroe, LA 71203
318-388-9500
Utility - telephone O DRP

Ceridian Corp. CEN
8100 34th Ave. South
Minneapolis, MN 55425
612-853-8100
Computers - mainframe O

Champion Enterprises, Inc. CHB
2701 University Dr., Ste. 320
Auburn Hills, MI 48326
810-340-9090
Building - mobile homes & RV O

Champion International Corp. CHA
One Champion Plaza
Stamford, CT 06921
203-358-7000
Paper & paper products O DRP

Chart House Enterprises, Inc. CHT
115 S. Acacia Ave.
Solana Beach, CA 92075
619-755-8281 Fax 619-481-2579
Retail - food & restaurants

Chart Industries, Inc. CTI
35555 Curtis Blvd.
Eastlake, OH 44095
216-946-2525
Machinery - general industrial

Chartwell Re Corp. CWL
Four Stamford Plaza
Stamford, CT 06912
203-705-2500 Fax 203-705-2710
Insurance - multi line & misc.

Chase Industries, Inc. CSI
State Route 15
Montpelier, OH 43543
419-485-3193 Fax 419-485-8150
Metals - nonferrous

Chase Manhattan Bank CMB
270 Park Ave.
New York, NY 10017
212-270-6000
Bank DRP 5%

Chateau Communities, Inc. CPJ
19500 Hall Rd.
Clinton Township, MI 48038
313-286-3600
Real estate investment trust

Chaus (Bernard) Inc. CHS
1410 Broadway
New York, NY 10018
212-354-1280
Producer women's clothing

Checkpoint Systems, Inc. CKP
550 Grove Rd., PO Box 188
Thorofare, NJ 08086
609-848-1800 Fax 609-848-0937
Protection - safety equipment & services
  O

Chelsea GCA Realty, Inc. CCG
103 Eisenhower Parkway
Roseland, NJ 07068
201-228-6111
Real estate investment trust

Chemed Corp. CHE
255 E. Fifth St.
Cincinnati, OH 45202
513-762-6900
Diversified operations DRP

Chemfab Corp. CFA
701 Daniel Webster Hwy.
Merrimack, NH 03054
603-424-9000 Fax 603-424-9028
Chemicals - fibers

ChemFirst Inc. CEM
700 North St., PO Box 1249
Jackson, MS 39215
601-948-7550 Fax 601-949-1228
Non-fertilizer chemicals, producer

Chesapeake Corp. CSK
1021 E. Cary St., PO Box 2350
Richmond, VA 23218
804-697-1000
Paper & paper products DRP

Chesapeake Energy Corp. CHK
6104 N. Western Ave.
Oklahoma City, OK 73118
405-848-8000 Fax 405-843-0573
Oil & gas - US exploration & production
O

Chesapeake Utilities Corp. CPK
909 Silver Lake Blvd.
Dover, DE 19904
302-734-6713
Utility - gas distribution O DRP

Chevron Corp. CHV
225 Bush St.
San Francisco, CA 94104
415-894-7700 Fax 415-894-7000
Oil & gas - international integrated O DRP

Chic by H.I.S., Inc. JNS
1372 Broadway
New York, NY 10018
212-302-6400
Apparel

Chile Fund, (The) CH
153 E. 53rd Street
New York, NY 10022
212-832-2626
Financial - investment management

China Fund, (The) CHN
250 Park Ave.
New York, NY 10177
800-421-4777
Financial - investment management

Chiquita Brands International, Inc. CQB
250 E. Fifth St.
Cincinnati, OH 45202
513-784-8000 Fax 513-784-8030
Food - misc. O DRP

Chock Full O'Nuts Corp. CHF
370 Lexington Ave.
New York, NY 10017
212-532-0300
Food - misc. DRP

Chris-Craft Industries, Inc. CCN
767 Fifth Ave.
New York, NY 10153
212-421-0200
Broadcasting - radio & TV O

Christiana Companies, Inc. CST
777 E. Wisconsin Ave.
Milwaukee, WI 53202
414-291-9000 Fax 414-291-9061
Real estate development

Chromcraft Revington, Inc. CRC
1100 N. Washington St.
Delphi, IN 46923
317-564-3500
Furniture

Chrysler Corp. C
1000 Chrysler Dr.
Auburn Hills, MI 48326
810-575-5741 Fax 810-512-1756
Automotive manufacturing O DRP

Chubb CB
15 Mountain View Rd.
Warren, NJ 07061
908-903-2000
Property/casualty insurance O DRP

Church & Dwight Co., Inc. CHD
469 N. Harrison St.
Princeton, NJ 08543
609-683-5900
Soap & cleaning preparations DRP

Chyron Corp. CHY
265 Spagnoli Rd.
Melville, NY 11747
516-845-2000
Video equipment

CIBER CBR
5251 DTC Parkway, Suite 1400
Englewood, CO 80111
303-220-0100
Information technology consulting services

CIGNA Corp. CI
One Liberty Place
Philadelphia, PA 19192
215-761-1000
Insurance - multi line & misc. O DRP

CIGNA High Income Shares HIS
1380 Main St.
Springfield, MA 01103
413-781-7776
Financial - investment management

CILCORP Inc. CER
300 Hamilton Blvd., Ste. 300
Peoria, IL 61602
309-675-8810   Fax 309-675-8800
Electric & gas utility holding company
  DRP

Cincinnati Bell Inc. CSN
201 E. Fourth St.
Cincinnati, OH 45202
513-397-9900
Utility - telephone O DRP

Cincinnati Milacron Inc. CMZ
4701 Marburg Ave.
Cincinnati, OH 45209
513-841-8100   Fax 513-841-8991
Machine tools & related products O DRP

CINergy Corp. CIN
139 E. Fourth St.
Cincinnati, OH 45202
513-381-2000
Utility - electric power O DRP

Circuit City - CarMax Group KMX
9950 Mayland Dr.
Richmond, VA 23233
804-527-4000
Retailer used cars & trucks

Circuit City Group, Inc. CC
9950 Mayland Dr.
Richmond, VA 23233
804-527-4000
Retail - consumer electronics O

Circus Circus Enterprises, Inc. CIR
2880 Las Vegas Blvd. South
Las Vegas, NV 89109
702-734-0410
Leisure & recreational services O

Citicorp CCI
399 Park Ave.
New York, NY 10043
212-559-1000
Banks - money center O DRP

Citizens Corp DE CZC
645 W. Grand River
Howell, MI 48843
517-546-2160
Insurance - multi line & misc.

Citizens Utilities Co. CZNA
High Ridge Park, PO Box 3801
Stamford, CT 06905
203-329-8800   Fax 203-329-4602
Utility - telephone DRP

City National Corp. CYN
400 N. Roxbury Dr.
Beverly Hills, CA 90210
310-888-6000
Banks - west O

Claire's Stores, Inc. CLE
3 S.W. 129th Ave.
Pembrook Pines, FL 33027
954-433-3900
Retail - jewelry stores O

CLARCOR Inc. CLC
2323 Sixth St., PO Box 7007
Rockford, IL 61125
815-962-8867   Fax 815-962-0417
Diversified operations DRP

Clayton Homes, Inc. CMH
623 Market St.
Knoxville, TN 37902
615-970-7200
Building - mobile homes & RV O DRP

Clear Channel Communications, Inc. CCU
200 Concord Plaza, Ste. 600
San Antonio, TX 78216
210-822-2828   Fax 210-822-2299
Broadcasting - radio & TV O

Clemente Global Growth Fund, Inc. CLM
152 W. 57th St.
New York, NY 10019
212-765-0700
Financial - investment management

Cleveland-Cliffs Inc. CLF
1100 Superior Ave.
Cleveland, OH 44114
216-694-5700   Fax 216-694-4880
Iron ores DRP

Cliffs Drilling Co. CDG
1200 Smith St., Ste. 300
Houston, TX 77002
713-651-9426
Oil & gas - offshore drilling O

Clorox Co. CLX
1221 Broadway
Oakland, CA 94612
510-271-7000
Producer of household cleaning products
  O DRP

CMAC Investment Corp. CMT
1601 Market St.
Philadelphia, PA 19103
215-564-6600   Fax 215-496-0346
Insurance - multi line & misc.

CMI Corp. CMX
I-40 and Morgan Rd.
Oklahoma City, OK 73101
405-787-6020   Fax 405-491-2417
Machinery - material handling

CML Group, Inc. CML
524 Main St.
Acton, MA 01720
508-264-4155
Retail - apparel & shoes O DRP

CMS Energy Corp. CMS
330 Town Center Dr.
Dearborn, MI 48126
313-436-9200
Utility - electric power O DRP

CNA Financial Corp. CNA
CNA Plaza
Chicago, IL 60685
312-822-5000
Insurance - property & casualty O

CNA Income Shares, Inc. CNN
CNA Plaza
Chicago, IL 60685
312-822-4181
Financial - investment management

CNB Bancshares, Inc. BNK
20 N.W. Third Street
Evansville, IN 47739
812-464-3400   Fax 812-464-3496
Banks - midwest DRP 3%

CNF Transportation, Inc. CNF
3240 Hillview Ave.
Palo Alto, CA 94304
415-494-2900   Fax 415-813-0160
Transportation - truck O

Coach USA, Inc. CUI
4801 Woodway Dr.
Houston, TX 77056
713-964-2779

Coachmen Industries, Inc. COA
601 E. Beardsley Ave.
Elkhart, IN 46514
219-262-0123   Fax 219-262-8823
Building - mobile homes & RV O

Coastal Corp. CGP
Coastal Tower, 9 Greenway Plaza
Houston, TX 77046
713-877-1400
Operates natural gas pipeline systems
  O DRP

Coastal Physician Group, Inc. DR
2828 Croasdaile Dr.
Durham, NC 27705
919-383-0355
Medical services O

Coastcast Corporation PAR
3025 E. Victoria St.
Rancho Dominguez, CA 90221
310-638-0595
Manufactures investment-cast golf
  clubheads

Coca-Cola Company KO
1 Coca-Cola Plaza NW
Atlanta, GA 30313
404-676-02121
Soft drink & fruit juice producer O DRP

Coca-Cola Enterprises Inc. CCE
2500 Windy Ridge Pkwy.
Atlanta, GA 30339
770-989-3000
Beverages - soft drinks O DRP

Coeur d'Alene Mines Corp. CDE
505 Front Ave., PO Box 1
Coeur d'Alene, ID 83816
208-667-3511   Fax 208-765-0324
Silver mining & processing O

Cohen & Steers Total Return Realty Fund,
  Inc. RFI
757 Third Ave.
New York, NY 10017
212-832-3232
Financial - investment management

Cold Metal Products, Inc. CLQ
8526 South Ave.
Youngstown, OH 44514
216-758-1194
Metal products - fabrication

Cole National Corp. CNJ
5915 Landerbrook Dr.
Mayfield Heights, OH 44124
216-449-4100   Fax 216-461-3489
Retail - misc.

Coleman Co. CLN
250 N. St. Francis
Wichita, KS 67202
316-261-3211
Leisure & recreational products

Colgate-Palmolive Co. CL
300 Park Ave.
New York, NY 10022
212-310-2000   Fax 212-310-3284
Soap & cleaning preparations O DRP

Collins & Aikman Corp. CKC
701 McCullough Dr.
Charlotte, NC 28262
704-548-2382
Diversified operations

Colonial Gas CGES
40 Market St.
Lowell, MA 01852
508-332-3000
Retail pipeline distributor of natural gas
  DRP 5%

Colonial High Income Municipal Trust
  CXE
One Financial Center
Boston, MA 02111
617-426-3750
Financial - investment management

Colonial High Yield Securities Trust CIF
One Financial Center
Boston, MA 02111
617-426-3750
Financial - investment management

Colonial InterMarket Income Trust 1
  CMK
One Financial Center
Boston, MA 02111
617-426-3750
Financial - investment management

Colonial Investment Grade Municipal Trust
  CXH
One Financial Center
Boston, MA 02111
617-426-3750
Financial - investment management

Colonial Municipal Income Trust CMU
One Financial Center
Boston, MA 02111
617-426-3750
Financial - investment management

Colonial Properties Trust CLP
120 University Park Dr.
Orlando, FL 32792
407-677-1112
Real estate investment trust

Coltec Industries Inc. COT
430 Park Ave.
New York, NY 10022
212-940-0400
Diversified operations O

Columbia Energy Group, Inc. CG
20 Montchanin Rd.
Wilmington, DE 19807
800-441-3551   Fax 302-429-5596
Oil & gas - production & pipeline O DRP

Columbia/HCA Healthcare Corp. COL
One Park Plaza
Nashville, TN 37203
615-327-9551   Fax 615-320-2570
Hospitals O

Columbus Realty Trust CLB
15851 N. Dallas Parkway
Dallas, TX 75248
214-387-1492   Fax 214-770-5192
Real estate investment trust DRP 5%

Comdisco, Inc. CDO
6111 N. River Rd.
Rosemont, IL 60018
847-698-3000   Fax 847-518-5060
Leasing O

Comerica Inc. CMA
100 Renaissance Center
Detroit, MI 48243
313-222-3300   Fax 313-964-0638
Banks - midwest O DRP

Commerce Bancorp, Inc. CBH
1701 Route 70 East
Cherry Hill, NJ 08034
609-751-9000
Banks - northeast DRP 3%

Commerce Group Inc. CGI
211 Main St.
Webster, MA 01570
508-943-9000
Property/casualty insurance

Commercial Federal Corp. CFB
2120 S. 72nd St.
Omaha, NE 68124
402-554-9200
Financial - savings and loans

Commercial Intertech Corp. TEC
1775 Logan Ave.
Youngstown, OH 44505
216-746-8011
Machinery - construction & mining

Commercial Metals Co. CMC
7800 Stemmons Fwy.
Dallas, TX 75247
214-689-4300   Fax 214-689-4320
Metal processing & fabrication

Commercial Net Lease Realty, Inc. NNN
400 E. South St., Ste. 500
Orlando, FL 32801
407-422-1574
Real estate investment trust DRP 3%

Commonwealth Energy System CES
One Main St.
Cambridge, MA 02142
617-225-4000
Utility - electric power DRP

Compaq Computer CPQ
20555 SH 249
Houston, TX 77070
713-370-0670
Computer Manufacturer O DRP

Complete Management CMI
254 West 31st St.
New York, NY 10001
212-868-1188
Provides support services to medical
  community

Comprehensive Care CMP
1111 Bayside Dr., Suite 100
Corona del Mar, CA 92625
800-678-2273
Provides care for chronic/catastrophic
  diseases

CompUSA Inc. CPU
14951 N. Dallas Parkway
Dallas, TX 75240
214-980-4000   Fax 214-982-4276
Computers - retail & wholesale O

Computer Associates International, Inc.
  CA
One Computer Associates Plaza
Islandia, NY 11788
516-342-5224   Fax 516-342-5329
Computers - software DRP

Computer Sciences Corp. CSC
2100 E. Grand Ave.
El Segundo, CA 90245
310-615-0311   Fax 310-322-9805
Computers - services

Computer Task Group, Inc. TSK
800 Delaware Ave.
Buffalo, NY 14209
716-882-8000   Fax 716-887-7456
Computers - services

COMSAT Corp CQ
6560 Rock Spring Drive
Bethesda, MD 20817
301-214-3200
Telecommunications - cellular & wireless
  O DRP

Comstock Resources, Inc. CRK
5005 LBJ Fwy., Ste. 1000
Dallas, TX 75244
214-701-2000
Oil & gas - US exploration & production

ConAgra, Inc. CAG
One ConAgra Dr.
Omaha, NE 68102
402-595-4000
Food - meat products O DRP

Cone Mills Corp. COE
1201 Maple St.
Greensboro, NC 27405
910-379-6220
Textiles - mill products

Congoleum Corp. CGM
3705 Quakerville Rd.
Mercerville, NJ 08619
609-584-3000
Miscellaneous - not elsewhere classified

Connecticut Energy Corp. CNE
855 Main St.
Bridgeport, CT 06604
203-579-1732
Utility - gas distribution DRP

Conseco, Inc. CNC
11825 N. Pennsylvania St.
Carmel, IN 46032
317-817-6100   Fax 317-817-6327
Insurance - life O

Consolidated Cigar Holdings Inc. CIG
5900 N. Andrews Ave.
Fort Lauderdale, FL 33309
954-772-9000
Tobacco

Consolidated Edison Co. of New York, Inc.
  ED
4 Irving Pl.
New York, NY 10003
212-460-4600
Utility - electric power O DRP

Consolidated Graphics, Inc. CGX
2210 W. Dallas St.
Houston, TX 77019
713-529-4200   Fax 713-525-4305
Printing - commercial O

Consolidated Natural Gas Co. CNG
625 Liberty Ave.
Pittsburgh, PA 15222
412-227-1000
Utility - gas distribution O DRP

Consolidated Papers, Inc. CDP
PO Box 8050
Wisconsin Rapids, WI 54495
715-422-3111
Paper & paper products O

Consolidated Products, Inc. COP
36 S. Pennsylvania St.
Indianapolis, IN 46204
317-633-4100
Retail - food & restaurants

Consolidated Stores Corp. CNS
1105 N. Market St., Ste. 1300
Wilmington, DE 19899
302-478-4896
Retail - discount & variety O

ContiFinancial Corp. CFN
277 Park Ave., 38th Fl.
New York, NY 10172
212-207-2800
Financial - mortgages & related services

Continental Airlines CAI
2929 Allen Parkway, Suite 2010
Houston, TX 77019
713-834-5000
Airline

Converse, Inc. CVE
1 Fordham Rd.
North Reading, MA 01864
508-664-1100
Leisure & recreational products

Cooker Restaurant Corp. CGR
1530 Bethel Rd.
Columbus, OH 43220
614-457-8500   Fax 614-442-2120
Retail - food & restaurants

Cooper Cameron Corp. RON
515 Post Oak Blvd., Ste. 1200
Houston, TX 77027
713-513-3300   Fax 713-513-3320
Oil field machinery & equipment

Cooper Cos. COO
6140 Stoneridge Mall Rd., Suite 590
Pleasanton, CA 94588
510-460-3600
Produces eyecare, gynecological products
O

Cooper Industries, Inc. CBE
1001 Fannin, Ste. 4000
Houston, TX 77210
713-739-5400
Diversified operations DRP

Cooper Tire & Rubber Co. CTB
Lima and Western Aves.
Findlay, OH 45840
419-423-1321
Rubber tires O

Coram Healthcare Corp. CRH
1125 Seventeenth St., 15th Fl.
Denver, CO 80202
303-292-4973
Medical services O

Cornerstone Properties, Inc. CPP
126 E. 56th St., Tower 56
New York, NY 10022
212-605-7100   Fax 212-605-7199
Real estate investment trust

Cornerstone Realty Income Trust, Inc. TC
306 E. Main St.
Richmond, VA 23219
804-643-1761   Fax 804-782-9302
Real estate investment trust

Corning Inc. GLW
One Riverfront Plaza
Corning, NY 14831
607-974-9000   Fax 607-974-8830
Glass products O DRP

Corporate High Yield Fund II, Inc. KYT
PO Box 9011
Princeton, NJ 08543
609-282-2000
Financial - investment management

Corporate High Yield Fund, Inc. COY
PO Box 9011
Princeton, NJ 08543
609-282-2800
Financial - investment management

Corrections Corporation of America CXC
102 Woodmont Blvd.
Nashville, TN 37205
615-292-3100   Fax 615-269-8635
Prison services O

Corrpro Companies, Inc. CO
1055 W. Smith Rd.
Medina, OH 44256
216-723-5082   Fax 216-722-7654
Industrial maintenance

CORT Business Services Corp. CBS
4401 Fair Lakes Ct.
Fairfax, VA 22033
703-968-8500
Leasing

Countrywide Credit Industries, Inc. CCR
155 N. Lake Ave.
Pasadena, CA 91101
818-304-8400
Financial - mortgages & related services O
 DRP 2%

Cousins Properties Inc. CUZ
2500 Windy Ridge Parkway
Marietta, GA 30339
770-955-2200   Fax 770-857-2360
Real estate investment trust DRP 5%

Covance Inc. CVD
210 Carnegie Ctr.
Princeton, NJ 08540
609-452-4440
Health care research - biotech.,
 pharmaceutical

Cox Communications, Inc. COX
1400 Lake Hearn Dr., NE
Atlanta, GA 30319
404-843-5000   Fax 404-843-5777
Cable TV O

CPC International Inc. CPC
International Plaza
Englewood Cliffs, NJ 07632
201-894-4000   Fax 201-894-2186
Food - misc. O DRP

CPI Corp. CPY
1706 Washington Ave.
St. Louis, MO 63103
314-231-1575
Photographic equipment & supplies DRP

Craig Corp. CRG
116 N. Robertson Blvd.
Los Angeles, CA 90048
310-659-6641
Retail - supermarkets

Crane Co. CR
100 First Stamford Place
Stamford, CT 06902
203-363-7300
Diversified operations O DRP

Crawford & Co. Risk Management
 Services CRDB
5620 Glenridge Dr., NE
Atlanta, GA 30342
404-256-0830
Insurance - property & casualty

Crescent Real Estate Equities, Inc. CEI
9 West 57th St., 47th Fl.
New York, NY 10019
212-888-2399
Real estate investment trust O

Crompton & Knowles Corp. CNK
One Station Place
Stamford, CT 06902
203-353-5400
Chemicals - specialty O DRP

Cross-Continent Auto Retailers XC
1201 South Taylor St.
Amarillo, TX 79101
806-374-8653
Retails new & used cars in Texas &
 California

Cross Timbers Oil Co. XTO
810 Houston St., Ste. 2000
Fort Worth, TX 76102
817-870-2800   Fax 817-870-1671
Oil & gas - US exploration & production
 O

Cross Timbers Royalty Trust CRT
PO Box 1317
Fort Worth, TX 76101
817-390-6592
Oil & gas - US royalty trust DRP

Crown American Realty Trust CWN
Pasquerilla Plaza
Johnstown, PA 15901
814-536-4441   Fax 814-535-9343
Real estate investment trust DRP

Crown Cork & Seal Co., Inc. CCK
9300 Ashton Rd.
Philadelphia, PA 19136
215-698-5100
Containers - metal O

Crown Crafts, Inc. CRW
1600 River Edge Pkwy., Ste. 200
Atlanta, GA 30328
404-644-6400   Fax 404-644-6410
Textiles - home furnishings

Crown Pacific Partners, L.P. CRO
121 S.W. Morrison, Ste. 1500
Portland, OR 97204
503-274-2300   Fax 503-221-2490
Miscellaneous - not elsewhere classified

CryoLife Inc. CRY
1655 Roberts Blvd., N.W.
Kennesaw, GA 30144
770-419-3355
Technology for preservation of organs for
  transplant

CSS Industries, Inc. CSS
1845 Walnut St.
Philadelphia, PA 19103
215-569-9900
Paper - business forms

CSX Corp. CSX
901 E. Cary St.
Richmond, VA 23219
804-782-1400   Fax 804-782-1409
Transportation - rail O DRP

CTG Resources, Inc. CTG
100 Columbus Blvd.
Hartford, CT 06103
860-727-3459
Utility - gas distribution DRP

CTS Corp. CTS
905 West Blvd. North
Elkhart, IN 46514
219-293-7511   Fax 219-293-6146
Electrical components - misc.

Cullen/Frost Bankers, Inc. CFR
100 W. Houston St.
San Antonio, TX 78205
210-220-4011
Banks - southwest

Culp, Inc. CFI
101 S. Main St.
High Point, NC 27261
910-889-5161
Textiles - home furnishings O

Cummins Engine Co., Inc. CUM
500 Jackson St., PO Box 3005
Columbus, IN 47202
812-377-5000   Fax 812-377-3334
Engines - internal combustion O DRP

Current Income Shares, Inc. CUR
445 S. Figueroa St.
Los Angeles, CA 90071
213-236-4056
Financial - investment management

Curtiss-Wright Corp. CW
1200 Wall St. West
Lyndhurst, NJ 07071
201-896-8400   Fax 201-438-5680
Aerospace - aircraft equipment DRP

CV REIT, Inc. CVI
100 Century Blvd.
West Palm Beach, FL 33417
407-640-3155
Real estate investment trust

CVS Corp. CVS
One Theall Rd.
Rye, NY 10580
914-925-4000
Retail - apparel & shoes O

Cypress Semiconductor Corp. CY
3901 N. First St.
San Jose, CA 95134
408-943-2600   Fax 408-943-2796
Electrical components - semiconductors O

Cyprus Amax Minerals Co. CYM
9100 E. Mineral Circle
Englewood, CO 80112
303-643-5000
Metal ores - misc. O DRP

Cytec Industries, Inc. CYT
Five Garret Mountain Plaza
West Patterson, NJ 07424
201-357-3100
Chemicals - specialty O

Czech Republic Fund, (The) CRF
200 Liberty Street, 38th Floor
New York, NY 10281
800-421-4777
Financial - investment management

D.R. Horton, Inc. DHI
1901 Ascension Blvd., Ste. 100
Arlington, TX 76006
817-856-8200
Building - residential & commercial

Dal-Tile International Inc. DTL
7834 C.F. Hawn Fwy.
Dallas, TX 75217
214-398-1411
Ceramics & ceramic products

Dallas Semiconductor Corp. DS
4401 S. Beltwood Pkwy.
Dallas, TX 75244
214-450-0400
Electrical components - semiconductors O

Dames & Moore, Inc. DM
911 Wilshire Blvd., Ste. 700
Los Angeles, CA 90017
213-683-1560
Engineering - R & D services

Dana Corp. DCN
4500 Dorr St.
Toledo, OH 43615
419-535-4500   Fax 419-535-4544
Automotive & trucking - original
  equipment O DRP

Danaher Corp. DHR
1250 24th St., N.W., Ste. 800
Washington, DC 20037
202-828-0850
Automotive & trucking - original
  equipment O

Daniel Industries, Inc. DAN
9753 Pine Lake Dr.
Houston, TX 77055
713-467-6000
Oil field machinery & equipment

Darden Restaurants, Inc. DRI
5900 Lake Ellenor Dr.
Orlando, FL 32809
407-245-4000
Retail - food & restaurants O

Data General Corp. DGN
4400 Computer Dr.
Westboro, MA 01580
508-898-5000
Computers - mini & micro O

Datapoint Corp. DPT
8400 Datapoint Dr.
San Antonio, TX 78229
210-593-7000
Computers - mini & micro

Dayton Hudson Corp. DH
777 Nicollet Mall
Minneapolis, MN 55402
612-370-6948
Retail - major department stores O DRP

Dayton Superior Corp. DSD
721 Richard St.
Miamisburg, OH 45342
513-866-0711
Building products - misc.

DDL Electronics, Inc. DDL
1270 NW 167th Place
Beaverton, OR 97006
503-645-3807
Electronics - components & systems

Dean Foods Co. DF
3600 N. River Rd.
Franklin Park, IL 60131
847-678-1680
Food - dairy products DRP

Dean Witter Government Income Trust
  GVT
Two World Trade Center
New York, NY 10048
212-392-1600
Financial - investment management

Deere & Co. DE
John Deere Rd.
Moline, IL 61265
309-765-8000   Fax 309-765-5682
Machinery - farm O DRP

DEKALB Genetics Corp. DKB
3100 Sycamore Rd.
DeKalb, IL 60115
815-758-3461   Fax 815-758-3711
Agricultural operations O

Delaware Group Dividend and Income
  Fund, Inc. DDF
1818 Market St.
Philadelphia, PA 19103
800-523-4640
Financial - investment management

Delaware Group Global Div. and Inc.
  Fund, Inc. DGF
1818 Market St.
Philadelphia, PA 19103
800-523-4640
Financial - investment management

Delmarva Power & Light Co. DEW
800 King St., PO Box 231
Wilmington, DE 19899
302-429-3089
Utility - electric power DRP

Delphi Financial Group, Inc. DFG
1105 N. Market St., Ste. 1230
Wilmington, DE 19899
302-478-5142
Insurance - multi line & misc.

Delta Air Lines, Inc. DAL
Hartsfield Atlanta Airport
Atlanta, GA 30320
404-765-2600
Transportation - airline O DRP

Delta Financial Corp. DFC
1000 Woodbury Rd., Suite 200
Woodbury, NY 11797
516-364-8500
Consumer finance - home equity

Delta Woodside Industries, Inc. DLW
233 N. Main St., Ste. 200
Greenville, SC 29601
864-232-8301
Textiles - apparel O

Deltic Timber Corp. DEL
210 E. Elm, PO Box 7200
El Dorado, AR 71731
870-881-6634
Building products - wood

Deluxe Corp. DLX
1080 W. County Rd. F
St. Paul, MN 55126
612-483-7111
Paper - business forms O

Denbury Resources DNR
17304 Preston Rd., Suite 200
Dallas, TX 75252
972-380-6967
Oil & gas exploration & production -
  Gulf coast

Department 56, Inc. DFS
6436 City West Parkway
Eden Prairie, MN 55344
612-944-5600
Housewares

Designer Holdings Ltd. DSH
1385 Broadway
New York, NY 10018
212-556-9600
Apparel O

Detroit Diesel DDC
13400 Outer Dr., West
Detroit, MI 48239
313-592-5000
Engines - internal combustion O

Developers Diversified Realty Corp. DDR
34555 Chagrin Blvd.
Moreland Hills, OH 44022
216-247-4700
Real estate operations

DeVry DV
One Tower Lane
Oakbrook Terrace, IL 60181
630-571-7700
Schools

Dexter Corp. DEX
One Elm St.
Windsor Locks, CT 06096
860-292-7675
Chemicals for packaging, medical,
  electronics O DRP

Diagnostic Products Corp. DP
5700 W. 96th St.
Los Angeles, CA 90045
213-776-0180
Biomedical & genetic products O

Dial Corp. DL
1850 N. Central Ave.
Phoenix, AZ 85077
602-207-2800
Soap & cleaning preparations O

Diamond Offshore Drilling, Inc. DO
15415 Katy Fwy.
Houston, TX 77094
713-492-5300
Oil & gas - offshore drilling O

Diebold, Inc. DBD
PO Box 8230
Canton, OH 44711
330-489-4000
Protection - safety equipment & services
  O DRP

Dillard's, Inc. DDS
1600 Cantrell Rd.
Little Rock, AR 72201
501-376-5200   Fax 501-376-5917
Retail - regional department stores O

Dime Bancorp, Inc. DME
589 Fifth Ave.
New York, NY 10017
212-326-6170
Financial - savings and loans O

DIMON, Inc. DMN
512 Bridge St.
Danville, VA 24541
804-792-7511
Tobacco

Discount Auto Parts, Inc. DAP
4900 Frontage Rd. South
Lakeland, FL 33801
941-687-9226
Auto parts - retail & wholesale

Disney (Walt) Co. DIS
500 S. Buena Vista St.
Burbank, CA 91521
818-560-1000
Film entertainment & theme parks O DRP

Dole Food Co., Inc. DOL
31365 Oak Crest Dr.
Westlake Village, CA 91361
818-879-6600 Fax 818-879-6618
Food - canned O

Dollar General Corp. DG
104 Woodmont Blvd., Ste. 500
Nashville, TN 37205
615-783-2000
Retail - discount & variety O

Dominick's Supermarkets, Inc. DFF
505 Railroad Ave.
Northlake, IL 60164
708-562-1000
Retail - supermarkets

Dominion Resources Black Warrior Trust
 DOM
901 E. Byrd St.
Richmond, VA 23219
804-775-5700
Oil & gas - US royalty trust

Dominion Resources, Inc. D
901 E. Byrd St., PO Box 26532
Richmond, VA 23261
804-775-5700 Fax 804-775-5819
Utility - electric power O DRP

Domtar Inc. DTC
395 de Maisonneuve Blvd. W.
Montreal, QC H3A1L6
514-848-5400
Manufactures paper & forest products O

Donaldson Co., Inc. DCI
1400 W. 94th St.
Minneapolis, MN 55431
612-887-3131
Pollution control equipment & services
 DRP

Donaldson, Lufkin & Jenrette, Inc. DLJ
140 Broadway, 27th Fl.
New York, NY 10005
212-504-3000
Financial - investment bankers O DRP

Donna Karan International, Inc. DK
550 Seventh Ave.
New York, NY 10018
212-789-1500
Apparel O DRP

Donelley (RR) & Sons DNY
77 West Wacker Dr.
Chicago, IL 60601
312-326-8000
Specialty printer O DRP

Donnelly Corp. DON
414 E. Fortieth St.
Holland, MI 49423
616-786-7000 Fax 616-786-6034
Automotive & trucking - original
 equipment

Dover Corp. DOV
280 Park Ave.
New York, NY 10017
212-922-1640 Fax 212-922-1656
Machinery - general industrial O

Dover Downs Entertainment, Inc. DVD
1131 N. DuPont Hwy.
Dover, DE 19901
302-674-4600
Leisure & recreational services

Dow Chemical Co. DOW
2030 Dow Center
Midland, MI 48674
517-636-1000
Chemicals, plastics, household products
 O DRP

Dow Jones & Co., Inc. DJ
200 Liberty St.
New York, NY 10281
212-416-2000
Publishing - newspapers O DRP

Downey Financial Corp. DSL
3501 Jamboree Rd.
Newport Beach, CA 92660
714-854-3100
Financial - savings and loans DRP

DPL Inc. DPL
Courthouse Plaza S.W.
Dayton, OH 45402
937-224-6000
Utility - electric power O DRP

DQE, Inc. DQE
500 Cherrington Pky.
Coraopolis, PA 15108
412-262-4700
Utility - electric power DRP

Dravo Corp. DRV
3600 One Oliver Plaza
Pittsburgh, PA 15222
412-566-3000 Fax 412-566-3116
Construction - cement & concrete

Dresser Industries, Inc. DI
2001 Ross Ave.
Dallas, TX 75201
214-740-6000 Fax 214-740-6584
Oil field machinery & equipment O DRP

Dreyfus Strategic Governments Income,
 Inc. DSI
144 Glenn Curtiss Blvd.
Uniondale, NY 11556
516-794-5200
Financial - investment management

Dreyfus Strategic Municipal Bond Fund,
 Inc. DSM
144 Glenn Curtiss Blvd.
Uniondale, NY 11556
516-794-5200
Financial - investment management

Dreyfus Strategic Municipals, Inc. LEO
144 Glenn Curtiss Blvd.
Uniondale, NY 11556
516-794-5200
Financial - investment management

DST Systems, Inc. DST
1055 Broadway
Kansas City, MO 64105
816-435-1000
Computers - services O

DTE Energy Co. DTE
2000 Second Ave.
Detroit, MI 48226
313-237-8000
Utility - electric power O DRP

Ducommon DCO
23301 S. Wilmington Ave.
Carson, CA 90745
310-513-7200
Components for aerospace &
  telecommunications

Duff & Phelps Credit Rating Co. DCR
55 E. Monroe St., Ste. 3500
Chicago, IL 60603
312-368-3100   Fax 312-368-3155
Business services

Duff & Phelps Utilities Income Inc. DNP
55 E. Monroe St.
Chicago, IL 60603
312-368-5510
Financial - investment management

Duff & Phelps Utilities Tax-Free Income
  Inc. DTF
55 E. Monroe St.
Chicago, IL 60603
312-368-5510
Financial - investment management

Duff & Phelps Utility and Corporate Bond
  Trust DUC
55 E. Monroe St.
Chicago, IL 60603
312-368-5510
Financial - investment management

Duke Energy DUK
422 S. Church St.
Charlotte, NC 28242
704-594-0887   Fax 704-382-8375
Utility - electric power O DRP

Duke Realty Investments, Inc. DRE
8888 Keystone Crossing
Indianapolis, IN 46240
317-846-4700
Real estate investment trust DRP 4%

Dun & Bradstreet DNB
One Diamond Hill Rd.
Murray Hill, NJ 07974
908-665-5000
Provider of commercial credit & business
  information O

duPont de Nemours DD
1007 Market St.
Wilmington, DE 19898
302-774-1000
Diversified operations O DRP

DVI, Inc. DVI
One Park Plaza, Ste. 800
Irvine, CA 92714
714-474-5800
Leasing

Dycom Industries, Inc. DY
450 Australian Ave. South
West Palm Beach, FL 33401
407-659-6301
Telecommunications equipment

Dyersburg Corp. DBG
1315 Philips St.
Dyersburg, TN 38024
901-285-2323
Textiles - apparel

Dynatech Corp. DYT
3 New England Executive Park
Burlington, MA 01803
617-272-6100   Fax 617-272-2304
Instruments - scientific O

Dynex Capital, Inc. DX
2800 E. Parham Rd.
Richmond, VA 23228
804-967-5800
Real estate investment trust

EA Industries EA
185 Monmouth Pkwy.
West Long Branch, NJ 07764
908-229-1100
Computers - mini & micro

Earthgrains Co. EGR
8400 Maryland Ave.
St Louis, MO 63105
314-259-7000
Produces and distributes fresh baked goods

EastGroup Properties EGP
188 E. Capitol St.
Jackson, MS 39201
601-354-3555   Fax 601-949-4077
Real estate investment trust

Eastern American Natural Gas Trust NGT
311 W. Monroe St., 12th Fl.
Chicago, IL 60606
312-461-6676
Oil & gas - US royalty trust

Eastern Enterprises EFU
9 Riverside Rd.
Weston, MA 02193
617-647-2300
Utility - gas distribution O DRP

Eastern Utilities Associates EUA
One Liberty Square
Boston, MA 02109
617-357-9590
Utility - electric power DRP

Eastman Chemical Co. EMN
100 N. Eastman Rd.
Kingsport, TN 37660
423-229-2000 Fax 423-229-1008
Chemicals - diversified O DRP

Eastman Kodak Co. EK
343 State St.
Rochester, NY 14650
716-724-4000
Photographic equipment & supplies
  O DRP

Eaton Corp. ETN
Eaton Center
Cleveland, OH 44114
216-523-5000
Automotive & trucking - original
  equipment O DRP

Eaton Vance Corp. EV
24 Federal St.
Boston, MA 02110
617-482-8260
Financial - investment management

ECC International Corp. ECC
175 Strafford Ave.
Wayne, PA 19087
610-687-2600
Electronics - military

Echelon International Corp. EIN
One Progress Plaza, Ste. 2400
St. Petersburg, FL 33701
813-824-6767 Fax 813-824-6536
Real estate development

Ecolab Inc. ECL
370 Wabasha St. North
St. Paul, MN 55102
612-293-2233
Building - maintenance & services
  O DRP

Edison International EIX
2244 Walnut Grove Ave.
Rosemead, CA 91770
818-302-2222
Utility - electric power O DRP

EDO Corp. EDO
14-04 111th St.
College Point, NY 11356
718-321-4000
Electronics - military

EG&G, Inc. EGG
45 William St.
Wellesley, MA 02181
617-237-5100 Fax 617-431-4255
Instruments - scientific O DRP

1838 Bond-Debenture Trading Fund BDF
100 Matsonford Rd., Ste. 320
Radnor, PA 19087
610-293-4300
Financial - investment management

Ekco Group, Inc. EKO
98 Split Brook Rd., Ste. 102
Nashua, NH 03062
603-888-1212 Fax 603-888-1427
Appliances - household

Eli Lilly and Co. LLY
Lilly Corporate Center
Indianapolis, IN 46285
317-276-2000
Health care (drugs - major
  pharmaceuticals) O DRP

El Paso Energy Co. EPG
304 Texas Ave.
El Paso, TX 79901
915-541-2600
Utility - gas distribution O

Elcor Corp. ELK
14643 Dallas Pkwy.
Dallas, TX 75240
214-851-0500
Machinery - general industrial DRP

EMC Corp. EMC
171 South St.
Hopkinton, MA 01748
508-435-1000 Fax 508-435-7954
Computers - peripheral equipment O

Emerging Markets Income Fund, (The)
  EDF
7 World Trade Center
New York, NY 10048
212-783-1301
Financial - investment management

Emerging Markets Telecommunications
  Fund, Inc. ETF
153 E. 53rd St.
New York, NY 10022
212-832-2626
Financial - investment management

Emerging Mexico Fund, (The) MEF
1285 Avenue of the Americas
New York, NY 10019
212-713-2000
Financial - investment management

Emerson Electric Co. EMR
8000 W. Florissant Ave.
St. Louis, MO 63136
314-553-2000
Machinery - electrical O DRP

Empire District Electric EDE
602 Joplin St.
Joplin, MO 64801
417-625-5100
Electric utility - Missouri DRP 5%

Energen Corp. EGN
2101 Sixth Ave. North
Birmingham, AL 35203
205-326-2700
Utility - gas distribution DRP

EnergyNorth, Inc. EI
1260 Elm St., PO Box 329
Manchester, NH 03105
603-625-4000
Utility - gas distribution DRP 5%

Engelhard Corp. EC
101 Wood Ave.
Iselin, NJ 08830
908-205-5000
Chemicals - specialty O DRP

Enhance Financial Services Group Inc.
  EFS
335 Madison Ave.
New York, NY 10017
212-983-3100   Fax 212-682-5377
Insurance - multi line & misc.

Ennis Business Forms, Inc. EBF
107 N. Sherman St.
Ennis, TX 75119
214-875-6581
Paper - business forms

Enron Corp. ENE
1400 Smith St.
Houston, TX 77002
713-853-6161
Oil & gas - production & pipeline O DRP

Enron Global Power & Pipelines L.L.C.
  EPP
333 Clay St., Ste. 1700
Houston, TX 77002
713-646-6100
Oil & gas - production & pipeline

Enron Oil & Gas Co. EOG
1400 Smith St.
Houston, TX 77002
713-853-6161
Oil & gas - US exploration & production
  O

ENSCO International Inc. ESV
1445 Ross Ave.
Dallas, TX 75202
214-922-1500   Fax 214-855-0080
Oil & gas - offshore drilling O

Entergy Corp. ETR
639 Loyola Ave.
New Orleans, LA 70113
504-529-5262
Utility - electric power O DRP

Environmental Elements Corp. EEC
3700 Koppers St.
Baltimore, MD 21227
410-368-7000
Pollution control equipment & services

EOTT Energy Partners, L.P. EOT
1330 Post Oak Blvd.
Houston, TX 77056
713-993-5200
Oil & gas - US exploration & production

Equifax Inc. EFX
1600 Peachtree St. NW
Atlanta, GA 30302
404-885-8000   Fax 404-888-5452
Business services O DRP

Equitable Companies EQ
787 Seventh Ave.
New York, NY 10019
212-554-1234
Life & health insurance O DRP

Equitable Resources, Inc. EQT
420 Boulevard of the Allies
Pittsburgh, PA 15219
412-261-3000
Utility - gas distribution DRP

Equity Corporation International EQU
415 S. First St., Ste. 210
Lufkin, TX 75901
409-634-1033   Fax 409-634-1041
Funeral services & related O

Equity Inns, Inc. ENN
4735 Spottswood Ave., Ste. 102
Memphis, TN 38117
901-761-9651
Real estate investment trust

Equity Office Properties Trust EOP
Two North Riverside Plaza
Chicago, IL 60606
312-466-3300
Real estate investment trust

Equity Residential Properties Trust EQR
Two North Riverside Plaza
Chicago, IL 60606
312-474-1300
Real estate investment trust DRP

ESCO Electronics Corp. ESE
8888 Ladue Rd., STE. 200
St. Louis, MO 61124
314-213-7200
Electronics - military

Essex International SXC
1601 Wall St.
Fort Wayne, IN 46802
219-461-4000
Manufacturer copper electrical wire/cable

Essex Property Trust, Inc. ESS
777 California Ave.
Palo Alto, CA 94304
415-494-3700   Fax 415-494-8743
Real estate investment trust

Estee Lauder EL
767 Fifth Ave.
New York, NY 10153
212-572-4200
Producer of skin care, makeup, fragrance
  products

Esterline Technologies Corp. ESL
10800 NE 8th St.
Bellevue, WA 98004
206-453-9400
Instruments - control

Ethan Allen Interiors, Inc. ETH
Ethan Allen Dr.
Danbury, CT 06811
203-743-8000
Retail - home furnishings O

Ethyl Corp. EY
330 S. Fourth St., PO Box 2189
Richmond, VA 23218
804-788-5000
Chemicals - specialty O DRP

E'town Corp. ETW
600 South Ave.
Westfield, NJ 07090
908-654-1234
Utility - water supply DRP 5%

Europe Fund, (The) EF
780 Third Ave.
New York, NY 10017
212-751-8340
Financial - investment management

European Warrant Fund, Inc. EWF
330 Madison Ave.
New York, NY 10017
212-949-9055
Financial - investment management

EVEREN Capital EVR
77 W. Wacker Dr.
Chicago, IL 60601
312-574-6000
Brokerage services

Everest Reinsurance Holdings, Inc. RE
3 Gateway Center
Newark, NJ 07102
201-802-8000   Fax 201-802-4793
Insurance - property & casualty

EVI, Inc. EVI
5 Post Oak Park, Ste. 1760
Houston, TX 77027
713-297-8400
Oil & gas - field services O

E.W. Blanch Holdings, Inc. EWB
3500 W. 80th St.
Minneapolis, MN 55431
612-835-3310
Insurance brokers

EXCEL Communications, Inc. ECI
8750 N. Central Expy.
Dallas, TX 75231
972-705-5500
Telecommunications services O

Excel Industries, Inc. EXC
1120 N. Main St.
Elkhart, IN 46514
219-264-2131
Automotive & trucking - original
  equipment

Excel Realty Trust, Inc. XEL
16955 Via Del Campo, Ste. 110
San Diego, CA 92127
619-485-9400   Fax 619-485-8530
Real estate investment trust DRP 5%

Excelsior Income Shares, Inc. EIS
114 W. 47th St., 9th Fl.
New York, NY 10036
212-852-3732
Financial - investment management

Executive Risk Inc. ER
82 Hopmeadow St., PO Box 2002
Simsbury, CT 06070
203-244-8900
Insurance - multi line & misc.

Exide Corp. EX
645 Penn St., PO Box 14205
Reading, PA 19612
610-378-0500
Automotive & trucking - original
  equipment O

Extended Stay America, Inc. ESA
200 S. Andrews Ave.
Fort Lauderdale, FL 33301
954-627-5002
Hotels & motels O

Extendicare Inc. EXE
3000 Steeles Ave. East
Markham, ON L3R9W2
905-470-4000   Fax 905-470-5588
Operator - long-term care facilities

Exxon Corp. XON
225 E. John W. Carpenter Fwy.
Irving, TX 75062
972-444-1000
Oil & gas - international integrated
  O DRP

F&M National Corp. FMN
38 Rouss Ave.
Winchester, VA 22601
703-665-4200
Banks - southeast DRP 5%

Fabri-Centers of America, Inc. FCA
5555 Darrow Rd.
Hudson, OH 44236
216-656-2600
Retail - misc.

FactSet Research Systems, Inc. FDS
One Greenwich Plaza
Greenwich, CT 06830
203-863-1500
Computers - services

Fair, Isaac and Co., Inc. FIC
120 N. Redwood Dr.
San Rafael, CA 94903
415-472-2211   Fax 415-492-9381
Business services

Fairchild Corp. FA
110 E. 59th St.
New York, NY 10022
212-308-6700
Aerospace - aircraft equipment

Fairfield Communities, Inc. FFD
2800 Cantrell Rd., PO Box 3375
Little Rock, AR 72202
501-664-6000
Building - residential & commercial

Falcon Products, Inc. FCP
9387 Dielman Industrial Dr.
St. Louis, MO 63132
314-991-9200
Furniture

Family Dollar Stores, Inc. FDO
10401 Old Monroe Rd.
Matthews, NC 28205
704-847-6961
Retail - discount & variety O

Fannie Mae FNM
3900 Wisconsin Ave., NW
Washington, DC 20016
202-752-7000   Fax 202-752-3808
Financial - mortgages & related services
  DRP

Fansteel Inc. FNL
Number One Tantalum Place
North Chicago, IL 60064
708-689-4900
Metal processing & fabrication

Farm Family Holdings, Inc. FFH
344 Route 9W
Glenmont, NY 12077
518-431-5000
Insurance - property & casualty

FBL Financial Group FFG
5400 University Ave.
Des Moines, IA 50266
515-225-5400
Insurance - life, annuity, property/casualty

FDX Corp. FDX
2005 Corporate Ave.
Memphis, TN 38132
901-369-3600
Transportation - air freight O

Fedders Corp. FJQ
158 Highway 206
Peapack, NJ 07977
908-234-2100   Fax 908-234-0906
Appliances - household O

Federal Realty Investment Trust FRT
4800 Hampden Ln., Ste. 500
Bethesda, MD 20814
301-652-3360
Real estate investment trust DRP

Federal Signal Corp. FSS
1415 W. 22nd St.
Oak Brook, IL 60521
708-954-2000
Diversified operations O DRP

Federal-Mogul Corp. FMO
26555 Northwestern Highway
Southfield, MI 48034
810-354-7700
Automotive & trucking - replacement parts
  O DRP

Federated Department Stores, Inc. FD
7 W. Seventh St.
Cincinnati, OH 45202
513-579-7000
Retail - major department stores O

FelCor Suite Hotels, Inc. FCH
545 E. John Carpenter Fwy.
Irving, TX 75062
972-869-0013   Fax 972-869-0001
Real estate investment trust

Ferrellgas Partners, LP FGP
One Liberty Plaza
Liberty, MO 64068
816-792-1600
Retail - misc.

Ferro Corp. FOE
1000 Lakeside Ave.
Cleveland, OH 44144
216-641-8580
Paints & allied products O DRP

FiberMark, Inc. FMK
Brudies Rd., PO Box 498
Brattleboro, VT 05301
802-257-0365
Paper & paper products

Fidelity Advisor Emerging Asia Fund, Inc.
  FAE
82 Devonshire St.
Boston, MA 02109
800-426-5523
Financial - investment management

Fidelity Advisor Korea Fund, Inc. FAK
82 Devonshire St.
Boston, MA 02109
800-426-5523
Financial - investment management

Fidelity National Financial, Inc. FNF
17911 Von Kaman Ave.
Irvine, CA 92614
714-622-5000
Insurance - multi line & misc.

Financial Security Assurance Holdings Ltd.
  FSA
350 Park Avenue, 13th Fl.
New York, NY 10022
212-826-0100   Fax 212-688-3101
Insurance - brokerage

Fingerhut Companies, Inc. FHT
4400 Baker Rd.
Minnetonka, MN 55343
612-932-3100
Retail - mail order & direct O

Finova Group, Inc. FNV
1850 N. Central Ave.
Phoenix, AZ 85004
602-207-4900   Fax 602-207-4099
Financial - business services O DRP

First American Financial FAF
114 East 5th St.
Santa Ana, CA 92701
714-558-3211
Insurance - title, home warranty

First Banks America, Inc. FBA
8820 Westheimer
Houston, TX 77263
713-954-2400
Banks - midwest

First Brands Corp. FBR
83 Wooster Heights Rd.
Danbury, CT 06813
203-731-2300
Containers - paper & plastic O

First Chicago NBD Corp. FCN
One First National Plaza
Chicago, IL 60670
312-732-4000   Fax 312-732-6092
Banks - money center O DRP

First Commonwealth Financial Corp.
  FCF
22 N. Sixth St.
Indiana, PA 15701
412-349-7220
Banks - midwest DRP 5%

First Commonwealth Fund, (The) FCO
PO Box 9011
Princeton, NJ 08543
609-282-4600
Financial - investment management

First Data Corp. FDC
401 Hackensack Ave.
Hackensack, NJ 07601
201-525-4700
Financial - business services O

First Energy FE
76 South Main St.
Akron, OH 44308
216-384-5100
Utility - electric DRP

First Financial Fund, Inc. FF
One Seaport Plaza
New York, NY 10292
212-214-3334
Financial - investment management

First Industrial Realty Trust, Inc. FR
150 N. Wacker Dr., Ste. 150
Chicago, IL 60606
312-704-9000
Real estate investment trust

First Israel Fund, (The) ISL
153 E. 53rd St.
New York, NY 10022
212-832-2626
Financial - investment management

First Phillipine Fund FPF
152 West 57th St.
New York, NY 10019
212-765-0700
Closed-end management investment
company

First Republic Bancorp Inc. FRC
388 Market St., 2nd Fl.
San Francisco, CA 94111
415-392-1400   Fax 415-392-1413
Banks - west

First Union Corp. FTU
One First Union Center
Charlotte, NC 28288
704-374-6161   Fax 704-374-3425
Banks - southeast O DRP 3%

First Union Real Estate Eq. & Mort.
 Investments FUR
55 Public Square, Ste. 1900
Cleveland, OH 44113
216-781-4030   Fax 216-781-7364
Real estate investment trust DRP

First Virginia Banks, Inc. FVB
6400 Arlington Blvd.
Falls Church, VA 22042
703-241-4000
Banks - southeast DRP

First Washington Realty Trust FRW
4350 East-West Hwy., Ste. 400
Bethesda, MD 20814
301-907-7800
Real estate investment trust

Firstar Corp. FSR
777 E. Wisconsin Ave.
Milwaukee, WI 53202
414-765-4321   Fax 414-765-6040
Banks - midwest O DRP

FirstFed Financial Corp. FED
401 Wilshire Blvd.
Santa Monica, CA 90401
310-319-6000
Financial - savings and loans

Fisher Scientific International Inc. FSH
Liberty Ln.
Hampton, NH 03842
603-929-2650
Instruments - scientific O

Fleet Financial Group, Inc. FLT
One Federal St.
Boston, MA 02110
617-292-2000
Banks - northeast DRP 3%

Fleetwood Enterprises, Inc. FLE
3125 Myers St., PO Box 7638
Riverside, CA 92513
909-351-3500
Building - mobile homes & RV O DRP

Fleming Companies, Inc. FLM
6301 Waterford Blvd.
Oklahoma City, OK 73126
405-840-7200   Fax 405-841-8149
Food - wholesale O DRP 5%

Florida East Coast Industries, Inc. FLA
1650 Prudential Dr.
Jacksonville, FL 32201
904-396-6600
Transportation - rail

Florida Panthers Holdings, Inc. PAW
100 N.E. Third Ave., 2nd Fl.
Fort Lauderdale, FL 33301
954-768-1900   Fax 954-768-1920
Leisure & recreational services

Florida Progress Corp. FPC
One Progress Plaza
St. Petersburg, FL 33701
813-824-6400
Utility - electric power O DRP

Flowers Industries, Inc. FLO
PO Box 1338
Thomasville, GA 31799
912-226-9110
Food - misc. O DRP

Flowserve Corp. FLS
3100 Research Blvd.
Dayton, OH 45420
937-476-6100
Industrial pumps for oil/gas & power
 industries O

Fluor Corp. FLR
3333 Michelson Dr.
Irvine, CA 92730
714-975-2000
Construction - heavy O DRP

FMC Corp. FMC
200 E. Randolph Dr.
Chicago, IL 60601
312-861-6000
Chemicals - diversified O

Foodmaker, Inc. FM
9330 Balboa Ave.
San Diego, CA 92123
619-571-2121
Retail - food & restaurants O

Footstar, Inc. FTS
933 MacArthur Blvd.
Mahwah, NJ 07430
201-934-2000
Retail - apparel & shoes

Forcenergy Inc. FEN
2730 S.W. Third Ave., Ste. 800
Miami, FL 33129
305-856-8500 Fax 305-856-4300
Oil & gas - US exploration & production

Ford Motor Co. F
The American Road
Dearborn, MI 48121
313-322-3000 Fax 313-845-0570
Automotive manufacturing O DRP

Foremost Corporation of America FOM
5600 Beach Tree Lane
Caledonia, MI 49316
616-942-3000
Insurance - property & casualty

Forest City Enterprises FCE
10800 Brookpark Rd.
Cleveland, OH 44130
216-267-1200
Real Estate - develops, constructs, manages

Fort Dearborn Income Securities, Inc.
 FTD
209 S. LaSalle St., 11th Fl.
Chicago, IL 60604
312-346-0676
Financial - investment management

Fort James Paper Co. FJ
120 Tredegar St.
Richmond, VA 23219
804-644-5411
Producer consumer & commercial tissue
 products O DRP

Fortis Securities, Inc. FOR
PO Box 64284
St. Paul, MN 55164
612-738-4000
Financial - investment management

Fortune Brands, Inc. FO
1700 E. Putnam Ave.
Old Greenwich, CT 06870
203-698-5000 Fax 203-637-2580
Tobacco O DRP

Foster Wheeler Corp. FWC
Perryville Corporate Park
Clinton, NJ 08809
908-730-4000
Machinery - electric utility O DRP

Foundation Health Systems, Inc. FHS
321600 Oxnrd St.
Woodland Hills, CA 91367
818-719-6978
Health maintenance organization O

Four Seasons Hotels FS
1165 Leslie St.
Toronto, ON M3C2K8
416-449-1750 Fax 416-441-4374
Lodging - hotels

FPL Group Inc. FPL
700 Universe Blvd.
Juno Beach, FL 33408
407-694-3509
Utility - electric power O DRP

France Growth Fund, (The) FRF
1285 Avenue of the Americas
New York, NY 10019
212-713-2000
Financial - investment management

Franchise Finance Corporation of America
 FFA
17207 N. Perimeter Dr.
Scottsdale, AZ 85255
602-585-4500 Fax 602-585-2225
Real estate investment trust DRP

Franklin Covey FC
2200 West Parkway Blvd
Salt Lake City, UT 84119
801-975-1776
Time management/training seminars

Franklin Electronic Publishers, Inc. FEP
One Franklin Plaza
Burlington, NJ 08016
609-386-2500
Publishing - books

Franklin Multi-Income Trust FMI
777 Mariners Island Blvd.
San Mateo, CA 94404
415-312-2000
Financial - investment management

Franklin Principal Maturity Trust FPT
777 Mariners Island Blvd.
San Mateo, CA 94404
415-570-3000
Financial - investment management

Franklin Resources, Inc. BEN
777 Mariners Island Blvd.
San Mateo, CA 94404
415-312-2000
Financial - investment management
  O DRP

Franklin Universal Trust FT
777 Mariners Island Blvd.
San Mateo, CA 94404
415-378-2200
Financial - investment management

Fred Meyer, Inc. FMY
3800 S.E. 22nd Ave.
Portland, OR 97202
503-232-8844
Retail - regional department stores

Freddie Mac Corp. FRE
8200 Jones Branch Dr.
McLean, VA 22102
703-903-2000
Financial - mortgages & related services O

Freeport-McMoRan Copper & Gold Inc.
  FCX
1615 Poydras St.
New Orleans, LA 70112
504-582-4000
Metals - nonferrous O

Freeport-McMoRan Inc. FTX
1615 Poydras St.
New Orleans, LA 70112
504-582-4000
Fertilizers O

Freeport-McMoRan Oil and Gas Royalty
  Trust FMR
712 Main St.
Houston, TX 77002
713-216-5447
Oil & gas - US royalty trust

Freeport-McMoRan Resource Partners,
  L.P. FRP
1615 Poydras St.
New Orleans, LA 70112
504-582-4000
Fertilizers O

Fremont General Corp. FMT
2020 Santa Monica Blvd.
Santa Monica, CA 90404
310-315-5500   Fax 310-315-5594
Insurance - property & casualty

Frontier Corp. FRO
180 S. Clinton Ave.
Rochester, NY 14646
716-777-7100   Fax 716-325-4624
Utility - telephone O DRP

Frontier Insurance Group, Inc. FTR
195 Lake Louise Marie Rd.
Rock Hill, NY 12775
914-796-2100
Insurance - property & casualty O DRP

Fruit of the Loom, Inc. FTL
233 S. Wacker Dr.
Chicago, IL 60606
312-876-1724
Apparel O

Fund American Enterprises Holdings FFC
80 South Main St.
Hanover, NH 03755
603-643-0567
Property/casualty insurance & mortgage
  banking

Furniture Brands International, Inc. FBN
101 S. Hanley Rd.
St. Louis, MO 63105
314-863-1100
Diversified operations

Furon Co. FCY
29982 Ivy Glenn Dr.
Laguna Niguel, CA 92677
714-831-5350
Rubber & plastic products O

Furr's/Bishop's Cafeterias, L.P. CHI
6901 Quaker Ave.
Lubbock, TX 79493
806-792-7151
Retail - food & restaurants

G&L Realty Corp. GLR
439 N. Bedford Dr.
Beverly Hills, CA 90210
310-273-9930   Fax 310-859-9032
Real estate operations

Gabelli Equity Trust Inc., (The) GAB
One Corporate Center
Rye, NY 10580
914-921-5100   Fax 914-921-5118
Financial - investment management

Gabelli Global Multimedia Trust Inc.,
(The) GGT
One Corporate Center
Rye, NY 10580
914-921-5100   Fax 914-921-5118
Financial - investment management

Gables Residential Trust GBP
2859 Paces Ferry Rd.
Atlanta, GA 30339
770-436-4600
Real estate investment trust

GAINSCO, INC. GNA
500 Commerce St.
Fort Worth, TX 76102
817-336-2500
Insurance - property & casualty

Galey & Lord, Inc. GNL
980 Avenue of the Americas
New York, NY 10018
212-465-3000   Fax 212-465-3025
Textiles - mill products

Gallaher (Arthur J.) AJG
Two Pierce Place
Itasca, IL 60143
630-773-3800
Insurance brokers - commercial &
individual

Galoob Toys GAL
500 Forbes Blvd.
San Francisco, CA 94080
415-952-1678   Fax 415-952-7084
Designs & markets toys

Gannett Co., Inc. GCI
1100 Wilson Blvd.
Arlington, VA 22234
703-284-6000   Fax 703-276-5540
Publishing - newspapers O DRP

The Gap Inc. GPS
One Harrison St.
San Francisco, CA 94105
415-952-4400
Specialty apparel retailer

Gateway Inc. GTW
610 Gateway Dr., PO Box 2000
North Sioux City, SD 57049
605-232-2000   Fax 605-232-2465
Computers - mini & micro O

GATX Corp. GMT
500 W. Monroe St.
Chicago, IL 60661
312-621-6200   Fax 312-621-6646
Transportation - equipment & leasing
O DRP

Gaylord Entertainment Co. GET
One Gaylord Dr.
Nashville, TN 37214
615-316-6000
Leisure & recreational services O

GC Companies, Inc. GCX
27 Boylston St.
Chestnut Hill, MA 02167
617-278-5600
Motion pictures & services

GenCorp Inc. GY
175 Ghent Rd.
Fairlawn, OH 44333
216-869-4200   Fax 216-869-4211
Diversified operations O DRP

GenRad, Inc. GEN
300 Baker Ave.
Concord, MA 01742
508-287-7000
Electronics - measuring instruments

Genentech, Inc. GNE
460 Point San Bruno Blvd.
South San Francisco, CA 94080
415-225-1000
Biomedical & genetic products O

General American Investors Co., Inc.
GAM
450 Lexington Ave.
New York, NY 10017
212-916-8400
Financial - investment management

General Cable Corp. GCN
4 Tesseneer Dr.
Highland, KY 41076
606-572-8000
Wire & cable products O

General Chemical Group GCG
Liberty Lane
Hampton, NH 03842
603-926-5911   Fax 603-929-2404
Chemicals - specialty

General Cigar MPP
387 Park Ave.
New York, NY 10016
212-448-3800
Manufacturer, marketer of premium cigars

General DataComm Industries, Inc. GDC
1579 Straits Turnpike
Middlebury, CT 06762
203-574-1118
Computers - peripheral equipment O

General Dynamics Corp. GD
3190 Fairview Park Dr.
Falls Church, VA 22042
703-876-3000
Weapons & weapon systems O

General Electric Co. GE
3135 Easton Tnpk.
Fairfield, CT 06431
203-373-2211   Fax 203-373-2884
Diversified operations O DRP

General Growth Properties, Inc. GGP
55 W. Monroe, Ste. 3100
Chicago, IL 60603
312-551-5000   Fax 312-551-5475
Real estate investment trust DRP

General Housewares Corp. GHW
1536 Beech St., PO Box 4066
Terre Haute, IN 47804
812-232-1000   Fax 812-232-7016
Housewares DRP

General Mills, Inc. GIS
One General Mills Blvd.
Minneapolis, MN 55440
612-540-2311
Food - misc. O DRP

General Motors Corp. GM
3044 W. Grand Blvd.
Detroit, MI 48202
313-556-2044
Automotive manufacturing O DRP

General Signal Corp. GSX
High Ridge Park, PO Box 10010
Stamford, CT 06904
203-329-4100
Instruments - control O DRP

Genesco Inc. GCO
1415 Murfreesboro Rd.
Nashville, TN 37217
615-367-7000   Fax 615-367-8278
Shoes & related apparel

Genesis Energy, L.P. GEL
500 Dallas, Ste. 3200
Houston, TX 77002
713-646-1200
Oil & gas - US exploration & production

Genesis Health Ventures, Inc. GHV
148 W. State St.
Kennett Square, PA 19348
215-444-6350   Fax 215-444-3365
Healthcare - outpatient & home O

Geneva Steel Co. GNV
10 S. Geneva Rd.
Vineyard, UT 84058
801-227-9000
Steel - production O

Genuine Parts Co. GPC
2999 Circle 75 Parkway
Atlanta, GA 30339
770-953-1700
Auto parts - retail & wholesale O DRP

Geon Co GON
One Geon Center
Avon Lake, OH 44012
216-930-1221
Producer of PVC resins & compounds

Georgia Gulf Corp. GGC
400 Perimeter Center Terrace
Atlanta, GA 30346
770-395-4500
Chemicals - specialty O

Georgia Power Co. GPEp
333 Piedmont Ave., N.E.
Atlanta, GA 30308
404-526-6526
Utility - electric power

Georgia-Pacific Corp. GP
133 Peachtree St. NE
Atlanta, GA 30303
404-521-4000
Building products - wood O DRP

Gerber Scientific, Inc. GRB
83 Gerber Road West
South Windsor, CT 06074
203-644-1551   Fax 860-643-7039
Industrial automation & robotics O DRP

Germany Fund Inc., (The) GER
31 W. 52nd Street
New York, NY 10019
800-437-6269
Financial - investment management

Getty Realty GTY
125 Jericho Turnpike
Jericho, NY 11753
516-338-6000   Fax 516-338-6062
Oil refining & marketing

GIANT GROUP, LTD. GPO
150 El Camino Dr., Ste. 303
Beverly Hills, CA 90212
310-273-5678
Construction - cement & concrete

Giant Industries, Inc. GI
23733 N. Scottsdale Rd.
Scottsdale, AZ 85255
602-585-8888
Oil refining & marketing

Gillette Co. G
Prudential Tower Building
Boston, MA 02199
617-421-7000
Manufacturer razors, toiletries O DRP

Glamis Gold GLG
1055 Dunsmuir St.
Vancouver, BC V7X1L3
604-681-3541   Fax 604-681-9306
Operates gold mines in California

Gleason Corp. GLE
1000 University Ave.
Rochester, NY 14692
716-473-1000
Machine tools & related products

Glenborough Realty Trust, Inc. GLB
400 S. El Camino Real
San Mateo, CA 94402
415-343-9300   Fax 415-343-9690
Real estate investment trust DRP

Glimcher Realty Trust GRT
20 S. 3rd St.
Columbus, OH 43215
614-621-9000   Fax 614-621-9311
Real estate investment trust

Global Direct Mail Corp. GML
11 Harbor Park Dr.
Port Washington, NY 11050
516-625-4300
Business services - marketing

Global High Income Dollar Fund, Inc.
  GHI
1285 Avenue of the Americas
New York, NY 10019
212-713-2000
Financial - investment management

Global Industrial Technologies, Inc. GIX
2121 San Jacinto St.
Dallas, TX 75201
214-953-4500   Fax 214-953-4596
Machinery - construction & mining

Global Marine Inc. GLM
777 N. Eldridge Rd.
Houston, TX 77079
713-596-5100
Oil & gas - offshore drilling O

Global Partners Income Fund, Inc. GDF
7 World Trade Center, 38th Fl.
New York, NY 10048
212-783-1301
Financial - investment management

Golden State Bancorp GSB
700 North Brand Blvd.
Glendale, CA 91203
818-500-2000
Regional banks

Golden West Financial Corp. GDW
1901 Harrison St.
Oakland, CA 94612
510-446-3420
Financial - savings and loans O

Goodrich (B.F.) GR
4020 Kinross Lakes Parkway
Richfield, OH 44286
216-659-7789
Provides aircraft systems/components -
  chemicals O DRP

Goodrich Petroleum Corp. GDP
5847 San Felipe, Ste. 700
Houston, TX 77057
713-780-9494   Fax 713-780-9254
Oil & gas - US exploration & production

Goodyear Tire and Rubber Co. GT
1144 E. Market St.
Akron, OH 44316
330-796-2121
Tire manufacturer O DRP

Gottschalks Inc. GOT
7 River Park Place East
Fresno, CA 93720
209-434-8000   Fax 209-434-4804
Retail - apparel & shoes

GPU, Inc. GPU
100 Interpace Pkwy.
Parsippany, NJ 07054
201-263-6500
Utility - electric power O DRP

Grace (W.R.) & Co. GRA
One Town Center Rd.
Boca Raton, FL 33486
561-362-2000
Specialty chemicals DRP

Graco Inc. GGG
4050 Olson Memorial Hwy.
Golden Valley, MN 55422
612-623-6000   Fax 612-623-6777
Machinery - general industrial DRP

Graham-Field Health Products, Inc. GFI
400 Rabro Dr., East
Hauppauge, NY 11788
516-582-5900   Fax 516-582-5608
Medical products

Grainger (W.W.) GWW
455 Knightsbridge Way
Lincolnshire, IL 60069
847-793-9030
Distributor of electronic equipment

Grand Casinos, Inc. GND
13705 First Ave. North
Plymouth, MN 55441
612-449-9092
Leisure & recreational services O

Granite Construction Inc. GVA
585 W. Beach St.
Watsonville, CA 95076
408-724-1011
Construction - heavy

Gray Communications Systems, Inc. GCS
126 N. Washington St.
Albany, GA 31701
912-888-9390   Fax 912-888-9374
Broadcasting - radio & TV

GRC International, Inc. GRH
1900 Gallows Rd.
Vienna, VA 22182
703-506-5000   Fax 703-448-6890
Electronics - military

Great Atlantic & Pacific Tea GAP
2 Paragon Dr.
Montvale, NJ 07645
201-573-9700
Operates supermarkets

Great Lakes Chemical Corp. GLK
PO Box 2200
West Lafayette, IN 47906
317-497-6100
Chemicals - specialty O

Great Lakes REIT, Inc. GL
823 Commerce Dr., Ste. 300
Oak Brook, IL 60521
630-368-2900
Real estate investment trust

Great Northern Iron Ore Properties GNI
332 Minnesota St.
St. Paul, MN 55101
612-224-2385   Fax 612-224-2387
Iron ores

Greater China Fund, Inc. GCH
1285 Avenue of the Americas
New York, NY 10019
212-713-2000
Financial - investment management

Green (AP) APK
Green Blvd
Mexico, MO 65265
573-473-3626
Mines, processes specialty minerals

Green Mountain Power Corp. GMP
25 Green Mountain Dr.
South Burlington, VT 05403
802-864-5731
Utility - electric power DRP 5%

Greenbrier Cos GBX
One Centerpointe Dr.
Lake Oswego, OR 97035
503-684-7000
Supplies equipment & services to railroads

GreenPoint Financial Corp. GPT
41-60 Main St.
Flushing, NY 11355
718-670-4355
Financial - savings and loans O

Griffon Corp. GFF
100 Jericho Quadrangle
Jericho, NY 11753
516-938-5544
Diversified operations O

Growth Fund of Spain, Inc. (The) GSP
120 S. LaSalle St.
Chicago, IL 60603
800-422-2848
Financial - investment management

Grubb & Ellis Co. GBE
One Montgomery St.
San Francisco, CA 94104
415-956-1990
Real estate operations

GTE Corp. GTE
One Stamford Forum
Stamford, CT 06904
203-965-2000 Fax 203-965-3496
Utility - telephone O DRP

GTECH Corp. GTK
55 Technology Way
West Greenwich, RI 02817
401-392-1000 Fax 401-392-1234
Telecommunications services O

Guardsman Products Inc. GPI
3033 Orchard Vista Drive S.E.
Grand Rapids, MI 49501
616-957-2600
Paint and chemicals products DRP

Guess?, Inc. GES
1444 S. Alameda St.
Los Angeles, CA 90021
213-765-3100
Apparel O

Guest Supply, Inc. GSY
4301 U.S. Highway One
Monmouth Junction, NJ 08852
609-514-9696 Fax 609-514-2692
Cosmetics & toiletries

Guidant Corp. GDT
307 E. McCarty St.
Indianapolis, IN 46225
317-971-2000 Fax 317-971-2040
Medical instruments O DRP

Guilford Mills, Inc. GFD
4925 W. Market St.
Greensboro, NC 27407
910-316-4000
Textiles - mill products

Gulf Canada Resources GOU
401 9th Ave. S.W., PO Box 130
Calgary, AB T2P2H7
403-233-4000
Producer of crude oil, natural gas O

Gulfstream Aerospace GAC
PO Box 2206, 500 Gulfstream Rd.
Savannah, GA 31402
912-965-3000
Designer, developer of business jet aircraft
O

Gundle/SLT Environmental, Inc. GSE
19103 Gundle Rd.
Houston, TX 77073
713-443-8564
Pollution control equipment & services

H&Q Healthcare Investors HQH
50 Rowes Wharf, 4th Fl.
Boston, MA 02110
617-574-0567
Financial - investment management

H&Q Life Science Investors HQL
50 Rowes Wharf, 4th Fl.
Boston, MA 02110
617-574-0567
Financial - investment management

H. J. Heinz Co. HNZ
600 Grant St.
Pittsburgh, PA 15219
412-456-5700
Food - canned O

Haemonetics Corp. HAE
400 Wood Rd.
Braintree, MA 02184
617-848-7100 Fax 617-848-9923
Medical products O

Halliburton Co. HAL
3600 Lincoln Plaza
Dallas, TX 75201
214-978-2600
Diversified operations O

Hallwood HWG
3710 Rawlins, Suite 1500
Dallas, TX 75219
214-528-5588
Diversified holding company

Hambrecht & Quist Group HMQ
One Bush St.
San Francisco, CA 94104
415-439-3000
Financial - business services O

Hancock Fabrics, Inc. HKF
3406 W. Main St.
Tupelo, MS 38801
601-842-2834
Retail - misc.

Handleman Co. HDL
500 Kirts Blvd.
Troy, MI 48084
810-362-4400
Wholesale distribution - consumer products
O DRP

Handy & Harman HNH
250 Park Ave.
New York, NY 10177
212-661-2400
Precious metals & jewelry O DRP

Hanna, M.A. MAH
200 Public Square, Suite 36-5000
Cleveland, OH 44114
216-589-4000
Chemicals DRP

Hannaford Bros. Co. HRD
145 Pleasant Hill Rd.
Scarborough, ME 04074
207-883-2911
Retail - supermarkets DRP

Harcourt General, Inc. H
27 Boylston St.
Chestnut Hill, MA 02167
617-232-8200
Publishing, movies O DRP

Harland, John H. Co. JH
2939 Miller Rd., PO Box 105250
Decatur, GA 30035
800-723-3690
Specialty Printing DRP

Harley-Davidson, Inc. HDI
3700 W. Juneau Ave.
Milwaukee, WI 53208
414-342-4680
Leisure & recreational products O DRP

Harman International Industries, Inc. HAR
1101 Pennsylvania Ave., N.W.
Washington, DC 20004
202-393-1101
Audio & video home products O

Harnischfeger Industries, Inc. HPH
13400 Bishops Lane
Brookfield, WI 53005
414-671-4400
Machinery - construction & mining O

Harrah's Entertainment, Inc. HET
1023 Cherry Rd.
Memphis, TN 38117
901-762-8600
Leisure & recreational services O

Harris Corp. HRS
1025 W. NASA Blvd.
Melbourne, FL 32919
407-727-9100   Fax 407-727-9846
Telecommunications equipment O DRP

Harsco Corp. HSC
350 Poplar Church Rd.
Camp Hill, PA 17001
717-763-7064   Fax 717-763-6424
Metal processing & fabrication DRP

Harte-Hanks Communications, Inc. HHS
PO Box 269
San Antonio, TX 78291
210-829-9000
Diversified operations

Hartford Financial HIG
Hartford Plaza
Hartford, CT 06115
860-547-5000
Insurance (multiline) O DRP

Hartford Life, Inc. HLI
200 Hopmeadow St.
Simsbury, CT 06089
860-843-7716
Insurance - multi line & misc. O

Hartmarx Corp. HMX
101 N. Wacker Dr.
Chicago, IL 60606
312-372-6300
Apparel DRP

Harveys Casino Resorts HVY
Highway 50 and Stateline Ave.
Lake Tahoe, NV 89449
702-588-2411
Leisure & recreational services DRP

Hatteras Income Securities, Inc. HAT
One Nations Bank Plaza T39-5
Charlotte, NC 28255
704-386-5000
Financial - investment management

Hawaiian Electric Industries, Inc. HE
900 Richards St.
Honolulu, HI 98813
808-543-5662   Fax 808-543-7966
Utility - electric power O DRP 5%

HCC Insurance Holdings, Inc. HCC
13403 Northwest Fwy.
Houston, TX 77040
713-690-7300   Fax 713-462-2401
Insurance - property & casualty

Health & Retirement Properties Trust HRP
400 Centre St.
Newton, MA 02158
617-332-3990
Real estate investment trust DRP

Health Care Property Investors, Inc. HCP
10990 Wilshire Blvd.
Los Angeles, CA 90024
310-473-1990   Fax 310-444-7817
Real estate investment trust DRP

Health Care REIT, Inc. HCN
One SeaGate, Ste. 1950
Toledo, OH 43604
419-247-2800   Fax 419-247-2826
Real estate investment trust DRP 4%

Health Care and Retirement Corp. HCR
One SeaGate
Toledo, OH 43604
419-247-5000
Healthcare - outpatient & home

Health Management Associates, Inc. HMA
5811 Pelican Bay Blvd.
Naples, FL 33963
813-598-3131
Hospitals O

Healthcare Realty Trust Inc. HR
3310 West End Ave., Ste. 400
Nashville, TN 37203
615-269-8175   Fax 615-269-8122
Real estate investment trust

HealthPlan Services HPS
3501 Frontage Rd.
Tampa, FL 33607
813-289-1000   Fax 813-287-6629
Managed health care

Healthsouth Corp. HRC
2 Perimeter Park South
Birmingham, AL 35243
205-967-7116
Hospitals O

Hecla Mining Co. HL
6500 Mineral Dr.
Coeur d'Alene, ID 83814
208-769-4100   Fax 208-769-4159
Gold mining & processing O

Heilig-Meyers Co. HMY
2235 Staples Mill Rd.
Richmond, VA 23230
804-359-9171
Retail - home furnishings O DRP

Heinz, H.J. Co. HNZ
600 Grant St.
Pittsburgh, PA 15219
412-456-5700
Foods DRP

Helmerich & Payne, Inc. HP
Utica at Twenty-first St.
Tulsa, OK 74114
918-742-5531
Oil & gas - US exploration & production
  O

Hercules Inc. HPC
Hercules Plaza
Wilmington, DE 19894
302-594-5000   Fax 302-594-5400
Chemicals - specialty O DRP

Heritage Propane Partners, L.P. HPG
8801 S. Yale Ave., Ste. 310
Tulsa, OK 74137
918-492-7272
Oil & gas - US integrated

Heritage U.S. Government Income Fund
  HGA
800 Carillon Parkway
St. Petersburg, FL 33716
800-421-4184
Financial - investment management

Hershey Foods Corp. HSY
100 Crystal A Dr., PO Box 810
Hershey, PA 17033
717-534-6799   Fax 717-534-7873
Food - confectionery O DRP

Hertz Corp. HRZ
225 Brae Blvd.
Park Ridge, NJ 07656
201-307-2000   Fax 201-307-2644
Transportation - services O

Hewlett-Packard Co. HWP
3000 Hanover St.
Palo Alto, CA 94304
415-857-2030   Fax 415-857-7299
Computers - mini & micro O

Hexcel Corp. HXL
5794 W. Las Positas Blvd.
Pleasanton, CA 94588
510-847-9500
Chemicals - specialty

Hi-Lo Automotive, Inc. HLO
2575 W. Bellfort
Houston, TX 77054
713-663-6700
Auto parts - retail & wholesale

Hibernia Corp. HIB
313 Carondelet St.
New Orleans, LA 70130
504-586-5361
Banks - southeast O DRP 5%

High Income Advantage Trust YLD
Two World Trade Center
New York, NY 10048
212-392-1600
Financial - investment management

High Income Advantage Trust II YLT
Two World Trade Center
New York, NY 10048
212-392-1600
Financial - investment management

High Income Advantage Trust III YLH
Two World Trade Center
New York, NY 10048
212-392-1600
Financial - investment management

High Income Opportunity Fund, Inc. HIO
1345 Avenue of the Americas
New York, NY 10105
212-698-5349
Financial - investment management

High Yield Income Fund, Inc. HYI
One Seaport Plaza
New York, NY 10292
212-214-3332
Financial - investment management

High Yield Plus Fund, Inc. HYP
One Seaport Plaza
New York, NY 10292
212-214-3332
Financial - investment management

Highlands Insurance Group, Inc. HIC
10370 Richmond Ave.
Houston, TX 77042
713-952-9555
Insurance - property & casualty

Highwoods Properties, Inc. HIW
3100 Smoke Tree Court
Raleigh, NC 27604
919-872-4924
Real estate investment trust

Hilb, Rogal and Hamilton Co. HRH
4235 Innslake Dr.
Glen Allen, VA 23060
804-747-6500   Fax 804-747-6046
Insurance - brokerage

Hillenbrand Industries, Inc. HB
700 State Route 46 East
Batesville, IN 47006
812-934-7000
Medical & dental supplies O DRP

Hills Stores Co. HDS
15 Dan Rd.
Canton, MA 02021
617-821-1000
Retail - discount & variety

Hilton Hotels Corp. HLT
9336 Civic Center Dr.
Beverly Hills, CA 90210
310-278-4321
Hotels & motels O

Hollinger International Inc. HLR
721 Fifth Ave.
New York, NY 10019
212-586-5666   Fax 212-586-0100
Publishing - newspapers O

HomeBase Inc. HBI
3345 Michelson Dr
Irvine, CA 92715
714-442-5000
Retail (specialty)

Home Depot, Inc. HD
2727 Paces Ferry Rd.
Atlanta, GA 30339
770-433-8211
Retail (building supplies) O DRP

Home Properties of New York, Inc. HME
850 Clinton Square
Rochester, NY 14604
716-546-4900   Fax 716-546-5433
Real estate investment trust DRP

Homestake Mining Co. HM
650 California St.
San Francisco, CA 94108
415-981-8150
Gold mining & processing O DRP

Honeywell Inc. HON
Honeywell Plaza
Minneapolis, MN 55408
612-951-1000   Fax 612-951-2294
Diversified operations O DRP

Horace Mann Educators Corp. HMN
1 Horace Mann Plaza
Springfield, IL 62715
217-789-2500
Insurance - multi line & misc.

Hormel Foods Corp. HRL
1 Hormel Place
Austin, MN 55912
507-437-5611
Food - meat products O DRP

Hospitality Properties Trust HPT
400 Center St.
Newton, MA 02158
617-964-8389   Fax 617-969-5730
Real estate investment trust

Host Marriott Corp. HMT
10400 Fernwood Rd.
Bethesda, MD 20817
301-380-9000
Hotels & motels O

Houghton Mifflin Co. HTN
222 Berkley St.
Boston, MA 02116
617-351-5000
Publishing - books O DRP

Household International, Inc. HI
2700 Sanders Rd.
Prospect Heights, IL 60070
847-564-5000
Financial - consumer loans O DRP

Houston Exploration THX
1331 Lamar, Suite 1065
Houston, TX 77010
713-652-2847
Oil & gas exploration

Houston Industries Inc. HOU
1111 Louisiana
Houston, TX 77002
713-207-3000   Fax 713-207-0206
Utility - electric power O DRP

Howell Corp. HWL
1111 Fanin St., Ste. 1500
Houston, TX 77002
713-658-4000   Fax 713-658-4007
Oil & gas - US integrated

HRE Properties HRE
530 Fifth Ave.
New York, NY 10036
212-642-4800
Real estate investment trust DRP

HS Resources, Inc. HSE
One Maritime Plaza, 15th Fl.
San Francisco, CA 94111
415-433-5795
Oil & gas - US exploration & production

Hubbell Inc. HUBA
584 Derby Milford Rd.
Orange, CT 06477
203-799-4100
Electrical products - misc. DRP

Huffy Corp. HUF
225 Byers Rd.
Miamisburg, OH 45342
513-866-6251
Leisure & recreational products DRP

Hughes Supply, Inc. HUG
20 N. Orange Ave.
Orlando, FL 32801
407-841-4755
Building products - retail & wholesale

Humana Inc. HUM
500 W. Main St.
Louisville, KY 40202
502-580-1000   Fax 502-580-3615
Health maintenance organization O

Hunt Manufacturing Co. HUN
2005 Market St.
Philadelphia, PA 19103
215-656-0300   Fax 215-656-3700
Office & art materials

Huntco Inc. HCO
14323 S. Outer Forty
Town & Country, MO 63017
314-878-0155   Fax 314-878-4537
Steel - production

Huntway Partners, L.P. HWY
25129 The Old Rd., Ste. 322
Newhall, CA 91381
805-286-1582
Oil refining & marketing

Hyperion 1999 Term Trust, Inc. HTT
520 Madison Ave.
New York, NY 10022
212-980-8400
Financial - investment management

Hyperion 2002 Term Trust, Inc. HTB
520 Madison Ave.
New York, NY 10022
212-980-8400
Financial - investment management

Hyperion 2005 Inv. Grade Opp. Term
 Trust, Inc. HTO
520 Madison Ave.
New York, NY 10022
212-980-8400
Financial - investment management

Hyperion Total Return Fund, Inc. HTR
520 Madison Ave.
New York, NY 10022
212-980-8400
Financial - investment management

IBP, Inc. IBP
IBP Ave., PO Box 515
Dakota City, NE 68731
402-494-2061
Food - meat products O

ICF Kaiser International, Inc. ICF
9300 Lee Highway
Fairfax, VA 22031
703-934-3600   Fax 703-934-9740
Engineering - R & D services

ICN Pharmaceuticals, Inc. ICN
3300 Hyland Ave.
Costa Mesa, CA 92626
714-545-0100
Drugs O

Idaho Power Co. IDA
1221 W. Idaho St.
Boise, ID 83702
208-383-2200   Fax 208-383-6911
Utility - electric power O DRP

IDEX Corp. IEX
630 Dundee Rd., Ste. 400
Northbrook, IL 60062
708-498-7070
Machinery - general industrial

IKON Office Solutions, Inc. IKN
825 Duportail Rd.
Wayne, PA 19087
610-296-8000   Fax 610-296-8419
Wholesale distribution - consumer
  products O

Illinois Central Corp. IC
455 N. Cityfront Plaza Dr.
Chicago, IL 60611
312-755-7500
Transportation - rail O DRP

Illinois Tool Works Inc. ITW
3600 W. Lake Ave.
Glenview, IL 60025
708-724-7500
Metal products - fasteners O DRP

Illinova Corp. ILN
500 S. 27th St., PO Box 511
Decatur, IL 62525
217-424-6600   Fax 217-424-7390
Utility - electric power O DRP

Imation Corp. IMN
1 Imation Place
Oakdale, MN 55128
612-704-4000
Photography/imaging O

IMC Global, Inc. IGL
2100 Sanders Rd.
Northbrook, IL 60062
708-272-9200
Fertilizers O

IMCO Recycling Inc. IMR
5215 N. O'Connor Blvd.
Irving, TX 75039
972-869-6575   Fax 972-869-6585
Recycling - metal & plastic

IMO Industries Inc. IMD
1009 Lenox Dr.
Lawrenceville, NJ 08648
609-896-7600   Fax 609-896-7688
Instruments - control DRP

Imperial Bancorp IMP
9920 S. La Cienega Blvd.
Inglewood, CA 90301
310-417-5600
Banks - west O DRP

INA Investment Securities, Inc. IIS
900 Cottage Grove Rd.
Hartford, CT 06152
203-726-3700
Financial - investment management

INCO Ltd. N
Royal Trust Tower
Toronto, ON M5K1N4
416-361-7511
Metals mining O DRP

Income Opportunities Fund 1999, Inc. IOF
PO Box 9011
Princeton, NJ 08543
609-282-2800
Financial - investment management

Income Opportunities Fund 2000, Inc. IFT
PO Box 9011
Princeton, NJ 08543
609-282-2800
Financial - investment management

India Fund IFN
200 Liberty St.
New York, NY 10281
800-421-4777
Closed-end mutual fund

India Growth Fund IGF
1285 Ave. of the Americas
New York, NY 10019
800-852-4750
Closed-end mutual fund

Indiana Energy, Inc. IEI
1630 N. Meridian St.
Indianapolis, IN 46202
317-926-3351
Utility - gas distribution DRP

Indiana Michigan Power Co. IMEpB
One Summit Square, PO Box 60
Fort Wayne, IN 46801
219-425-2111
Utility - electric power

Indonesia Fund Inc., (The) IF
153 E. 53rd Street, 58th Floor
New York, NY 10022
212-832-2626
Financial - investment management

Ingersoll-Rand Co. IR
200 Chestnut Ridge Rd.
Woodcliff Lake, NJ 07675
201-573-0123
Machinery - general industrial DRP

Inland Steel Industries, Inc. IAD
30 W. Monroe St.
Chicago, IL 60603
312-346-0300   Fax 312-899-3964
Steel - production O DRP

Innkeepers USA Trust KPA
5255 N. Federal Hwy., Ste. 300
Boca Raton, FL 33487
561-994-1701   Fax 561-994-5999
Real estate investment trust

Input/Output, Inc. IO
12300 Parc Crest Dr.
Stafford, TX 77477
713-933-3339   Fax 713-879-3600
Electronics - measuring instruments O

Insignia Financial Group, Inc. IFS
PO Box 1089
Greenville, SC 29602
803-239-1000
Real estate operations O

Insteel Industries, Inc. III
1373 Boggs Dr.
Mt. Airy, NC 27030
910-786-2141   Fax 910-786-2144
Wire & cable products DRP

Integrated Health Services, Inc. IHS
10065 Red Run Blvd.
Owings Mill, MD 21117
410-998-8400
Medical services O

Intellicall, Inc. ICL
2155 Chenault, Ste. 410
Carrollton, TX 75006
972-416-0022   Fax 972-416-7213
Telecommunications equipment

InterCapital California Ins. Municipal
   Income Trust IIC
Two World Trade Center
New York, NY 10048
212-392-1600
Financial - investment management

InterCapital California Quality Municipal
   Securities IQC
Two World Trade Center
New York, NY 10048
212-392-1600
Financial - investment management

InterCapital Income Securities Inc. ICB
Two World Trade Center
New York, NY 10048
212-392-1600
Financial - investment management

InterCapital Insured California Municipal
   Securities ICS
Two World Trade Center
New York, NY 10048
212-392-1600
Financial - investment management

InterCapital Insured Municipal Bond Trust
   IMB
Two World Trade Center
New York, NY 10048
212-392-1600
Financial - investment management

InterCapital Insured Municipal Income
   Trust IIM
Two World Trade Center
New York, NY 10048
212-392-1600
Financial - investment management

InterCapital Insured Municipal Securities
   IMS
Two World Trade Center
New York, NY 10048
212-392-1600
Financial - investment management

InterCapital Municipal Trust IMT
Two World Trade Center
New York, NY 10048
212-392-1600
Financial - investment management

InterCapital New York Quality Municipal
   Securities IQN
Two World Trade Center
New York, NY 10048
212-392-1600
Financial - investment management

InterCapital Quality Municipal Income
  Trust IQI
Two World Trade Center
New York, NY 10048
212-392-1600
Financial - investment management

InterCapital Quality Municipal Investment
  Trust IQT
Two World Trade Center
New York, NY 10048
212-392-1600
Financial - investment management

InterCapital Quality Municipal Securities
  IQM
Two World Trade Center
New York, NY 10048
212-392-1600
Financial - investment management

Interim Services, Inc. IS
2050 Spectrum Blvd.
Fort Lauderdale, FL 33309
954-938-7600
Business services O

Interlake Corp IK
550 Warrenville Rd.
Lisle, IL 60532
630-852-8800
Manufacturing (diversified)

International Aluminum Corp. IAL
767 Monterey Pass Rd.
Monterey Park, CA 91754
213-264-1670
Building products - doors & trim

International Business Machines Corp.
  IBM
One Old Orchard Rd.
Armonk, NY 10504
914-765-1900
Computers - mainframe O DRP

International Flavors & Fragrances Inc.
  IFF
521 W. 57th St.
New York, NY 10019
212-765-5500
Cosmetics & toiletries O DRP

International Game Technology IGT
5270 Neil Rd.
Reno, NV 89502
702-686-1200   Fax 702-688-0777
Leisure & recreational products O

International Multifoods Corp. IMC
33 S. 6th St., PO Box 2942
Minneapolis, MN 55402
612-340-3300
Food - flour & grain O DRP

International Paper Co. IP
2 Manhattanville Rd.
Purchase, NY 10577
914-397-1500
Paper & paper products O DRP

International Rectifier Corp. IRF
233 Kansas St.
El Segundo, CA 90245
310-322-3331 Fax 310-322-3332
Electrical components - semiconductors O

International Shipholding Corp. ISH
650 Poydras St., Ste. 1700
New Orleans, LA 70130
504-529-5461
Transportation - shipping

International Specialty Products Inc. ISP
818 Washington St.
Wilmington, DE 19801
302-429-8554
Chemicals - specialty O

International Technology Corp. ITX
23456 Hawthorne Blvd.
Torrance, CA 90505
310-378-9933   Fax 310-791-2586
Pollution control equipment & services

Interpool, Inc. IPX
211 College Rd. East
Princeton, NJ 08540
609-452-8900   Fax 609-452-8211
Leasing

Interpublic Group Companies IPG
1271 Avenue of the Americas
New York, NY 10020
212-399-8000
Services (advertising & marketing) O
  DRP

Interstate Bakeries Corp. IBC
12 E. Armour Blvd.
Kansas City, MO 64141
816-502-4000
Food - misc. O

Interstate/Johnson Lane, Inc. IJL
121 W. Trade St., Ste. 1500
Charlotte, NC 28201
704-379-9000
Financial - investment bankers

InterTAN Inc. ITN
201 Main St., Suite 1805
Fort Worth, TX 76102
817-348-9701
Retail (computers & electronics)

Intimate Brands, Inc. IBI
3 Limited Pkwy.
Columbus, OH 43230
614-479-7101
Apparel O

Intrawest Corp. IDR
200 Burrard St., Suite 800
Vancouver, BC V6C3L6
604-669-9777
Lodging, hotels

Invesco Global Health Sciences Fund
 GHS
7800 E. Union Ave., Suite 800
Denver, CO 80237
800-528-8765
Closed-end fund

Iomega Corp. IOM
1821 W. Iomega Way
Roy, UT 84067
801-778-1000
Computers - peripheral equipment O

Ionics, Inc. ION
65 Grove St.
Watertown, MA 02172
617-926-2500   Fax 617-926-4304
Filtration products O

IPALCO Enterprises, Inc. IPL
One Monument Circle
Indianapolis, IN 46204
317-261-8261
Electric companies O DRP

IPSCO Inc. IPS
PO Box 1670
Regina, SK S4P3C7
306-924-7700
Steel recycler/manufacturer

Irish Investment Fund, Inc. IRL
Vanguard Financial Center
Valley Forge, PA 19482
800-468-6475
Financial - investment management

IRT Property Co. IRT
200 Galleria Pkwy., Ste. 1400
Atlanta, GA 30339
770-955-4406   Fax 770-988-8773
Real estate investment trust DRP 5%

Irvine Apartment Communities, Inc. IAC
550 Newport Center Dr.
Newport Beach, CA 92660
714-720-5500   Fax 714-720-5550
Real estate development   DRP 2%

Italy Fund Inc. ITA
Two World Trade Center
New York, NY 10048
212-298-7350
Financial - investment management

ITT Educational Services, Inc. ESI
5975 Castle Creek Pkwy. N. Dr.
Indianapolis, IN 46250
317-594-9499   Fax 317-594-4284
Schools

ITT Industries IIN
4 West Red Oak Lane
White Plains, NY 10604
914-696-2950
Auto parts & equipment

J&L Specialty Steel, Inc. JL
One PPG Place, PO Box 3373
Pittsburgh, PA 15230
412-338-1600
Steel - specialty alloys O

J. Alexander's Corp. JAX
3401 West End Ave.
Nashville, TN 37202
615-269-1900
Retail - food & restaurants DRP

J.C. Penney Co., Inc. JCP
6501 Legacy Dr.
Plano, TX 75024
214-431-1000   Fax 214-431-4944
Retail - major department stores O DRP

J. Ray McDermott, S.A. JRM
1450 Poydras St.
New Orleans, LA 70112
504-587-5300
Oil field machinery & equipment DRP

Jackpot Enterprises, Inc. J
1110 Palms Airport Dr.
Las Vegas, NV 89119
702-263-5555   Fax 702-263-5500
Leisure & recreational services O

Jacobs Engineering Group Inc. JEC
251 S. Lake Ave.
Pasadena, CA 91101
818-449-2171
Construction - heavy

Jakarta Growth Fund, Inc. JGF
180 Maiden Lane
New York, NY 10038
800-833-0018
Financial - investment management

Japan Equity Fund, Inc. JEQ
One Evertrust Plaza, 9th Fl.
Jersey City, NJ 07302
800-933-3440
Financial - investment management

Japan OTC Equity Fund, Inc. JOF
180 Maiden Lane
New York, NY 10038
800-833-0018
Financial - investment management

Jardine Fleming China Region Fund, Inc.
 JFC
PO Box 89000
Baltimore, MD 21289
800-638-8540
Financial - investment management

Jardine Fleming India Fund, Inc. JFI
1285 Avenue of the Americas
New York, NY 10019
212-713-2848
Financial - investment management

JDN Realty Corp. JDN
3340 Peachtree Rd., N.E.
Atlanta, GA 30326
404-262-3252
Real estate investment trust DRP

Jefferies Group, Inc. JEF
11100 Santa Monica Blvd.
Los Angeles, CA 90025
310-445-1199
Financial - investment bankers

Jefferson-Pilot Corp. JP
100 N. Greene St.
Greensboro, NC 27401
910-691-3000   Fax 910-691-3311
Insurance - life O DRP

JLG Industries, Inc. JLG
One JLG Dr.
McConnellsburg, PA 17233
717-485-5161   Fax 717-485-6417
Machinery - construction & mining O

Jenny Craig, Inc. JC
445 Marine View Ave., Ste. 300
Del Mar, CA 92014
619-259-7000   Fax 619-259-2812
Retail - misc.

John Alden Financial Corp. JA
7300 Corporate Center Dr.
Miami, FL 33126
305-470-3767
Insurance - multi line & misc. O

John Hancock Bank & Thrift Opportunity
 Fund   BTO
101 Huntington Ave.
Boston, MA 02199
800-843-0090
Financial - investment management

John Hancock Income Securities Trust
 JHS
101 Huntington Ave.
Boston, MA 02199
800-843-0090
Financial - investment management

John Hancock Investors Trust JHI
101 Huntington Ave.
Boston, MA 02199
800-843-0090
Financial - investment management

John Hancock Patriot Global Dividend
 Fund PGD
101 Huntington Ave.
Boston, MA 02199
800-843-0090
Financial - investment management

John Hancock Patriot Preferred Dividend
 Fund PPF
101 Huntington Ave.
Boston, MA 02199
800-843-0090
Financial - investment management

John Hancock Patriot Premium Dividend
 Fund I PDF
101 Huntington Ave.
Boston, MA 02199
800-843-0090
Financial - investment management

John Hancock Patriot Premium Dividend
 Fund II PDT
101 Huntington Ave.
Boston, MA 02199
800-843-0090
Financial - investment management

John Hancock Patriot Select Dividend
 Trust DIV
101 Huntington Ave.
Boston, MA 02199
800-843-0090
Financial - investment management

John Nuveen JNC
333 W. Wacker Dr.
Chicago, IL 60606
312-917-7700
Investment Management O

John Q. Hammons Hotels, Inc. JQH
300 John Q. Hammons Pkwy.
Springfield, MO 65806
417-864-4300
Hotels & motels

John Wiley & Sons, Inc. JWA
605 Third Ave.
New York, NY 10158
212-850-6000   Fax 212-850-6088
Publishing - books

Johns Manville Corp. JM
717 17th St.
Denver, CO 80202
303-978-2000
Building products - misc. O

Johnson & Johnson JNJ
One Johnson & Johnson Plaza
New Brunswick, NJ 08933
908-524-0400
Medical & dental supplies O DRP

Johnson Controls, Inc. JCI
5757 N. Green Bay Ave.
Milwaukee, WI 53201
414-228-1200
Diversified operations O DRP

Johnston Industries, Inc. JII
105 13th St.
Columbus, GA 31901
706-641-3140
Textiles - mill products

Jones Apparel Group, Inc. JNY
250 Rittenhouse Circle
Bristol, PA 19007
215-785-4000
Textiles - apparel O

Jostens, Inc. JOS
5501 Norman Center Dr.
Minneapolis, MN 55437
612-830-3300
Diversified operations O DRP

Journal Register JRC
50 West State Square
Trenton, NJ 8608
609-396-2200
Publishing

JP Realty, Inc. JPR
35 Century Park Way
Salt Lake City, UT 84115
801-486-3911   Fax 801-486-7653
Financial - investment management

Jumbo Sports, Inc. JSI
4701 W. Hillsborough Ave.
Tampa, FL 33614
813-886-9688
Retail - misc. O

Kaiser Aluminum Corp. KLU
5847 San Felipe, Ste. 2600
Houston, TX 77057
713-267-3777
Metals - nonferrous O

Kaneb Pipe Line Partners, L.P. KPP
2435 North Central Expressway
Richardson, TX 75080
972-699-4000
Natural gas

Kaneb Services, Inc. KAB
2435 North Central Expressway
Richardson, TX 75080
214-699-4000
Oil & gas - production & pipeline

Kansas City Power & Light Co. KLT
1201 Walnut St.
Kansas City, MO 64106
816-556-2200
Utility - electric power DRP

Kansas City Southern Industries, Inc. KSU
114 W. 11th St.
Kansas City, MO 64105
816-556-0303
Transportation - rail O DRP

Katy Industries, Inc. KT
6300 S. Syracuse Way, Ste. 300
Englewood, CO 80111
303-290-9300
Diversified operations

Kaufman and Broad Home Corp. KBH
10990 Wilshire Blvd.
Los Angeles, CA 90024
310-231-4000   Fax 310-231-4222
Building - residential & commercial O

Kaydon Corp. KDN
19329 US 19 North
Clearwater, FL 34624
813-531-1101   Fax 813-530-9247
Metal processing & fabrication

KCS Energy, Inc. KCS
379 Thornall St.
Edison, NJ 08837
732-632-1770   Fax 732-603-8960
Oil & gas - production & pipeline

Keithley Instruments, Inc. KEI
28775 Aurora Rd.
Cleveland, OH 44139
216-248-0400   Fax 216-248-6168
Instruments - scientific DRP

Kellogg Co. K
One Kellogg Square
Battle Creek, MI 49016
616-961-2000
Food - misc. O DRP

Kellwood Co. KWD
600 Kellwood Pkwy.
St. Louis, MO 63178
314-576-3100
Textiles - apparel DRP

Kemper High Income Trust KHI
120 S. LaSalle St.
Chicago, IL 60603
800-422-2848
Financial - investment management

Kemper Intermediate Government Trust
  KGT
120 S. LaSalle St.
Chicago, IL 60603
800-422-2848
Financial - investment management

Kemper Multi-Market Income Trust KMM
120 S. LaSalle St.
Chicago, IL 60603
800-422-2848
Financial - investment management

Kemper Municipal Income Trust KTF
120 S. LaSalle St.
Chicago, IL 60603
800-422-2848
Financial - investment management

Kemper Strategic Income Fund KST
120 S. LaSalle St.
Chicago, IL 60603
800-422-2848
Financial - investment management

Kemper Strategic Municipal Income Trust
  KSM
120 S. LaSalle St.
Chicago, IL 60603
800-422-2848
Financial - investment management

Kennametal Inc. KMT
PO Box 231
Latrobe, PA 15650
412-539-5000   Fax 412-539-4710
Machine tools & related products O
  DRP 5%

Kenneth Cole Productions, Inc. KCP
152 W. 57th St.
New York, NY 10019
212-265-1500
Leather & related products

Kent Electronics Corp. KNT
7433 Harwin Dr.
Houston, TX 77036
713-780-7770
Electrical components - misc. O

Kerr-McGee Corp. KMG
123 Robert S. Kerr Ave.
Oklahoma City, OK 73102
405-270-1313
Oil & gas - US integrated O DRP

Key Production Co. KP
1700 Lincoln St., Ste. 2050
Denver, CO 80203
303-837-0779   Fax 303-830-7158
Oil & gas - US exploration & production
  DRP

KeyCorp, Inc. KEY
127 Public Square
Cleveland, OH 44114
216-689-3000
Banks - northeast O DRP

Keyspan Energy Corp. KSE
One Metrotech Center
Brooklyn, NY 11201
718-403-2000
Utility - electric & gas DRP

Keystone Consolidated Industries, Inc.
  KES
5430 LBJ Freeway, Ste. 1740
Dallas, TX 75240
214-458-0028
Wire & cable products

Kimberly-Clark Corp. KMB
PO Box 619100
Dallas, TX 75261
214-281-1200
Paper & paper products O DRP

Kimco Realty Corp. KIM
1044 Northern Blvd.
Roslyn, NY 11576
516-484-5858   Fax 516-484-5637
Real estate operations DRP

Kimmins Corp. KVN
1501 Second Ave.
Tampa, FL 33605
813-248-3878
Pollution control equipment & services

Kinder Morgan Energy Partners, L.P. ENP
1400 Smith St.
Houston, TX 77002
713-853-6161   Fax 713-646-3750
Oil & gas - production & pipeline

King World Productions, Inc. KWP
1700 Broadway
New York, NY 10019
212-315-4000
Broadcasting - radio & TV O

Kinross Gold KGC
40 King St. W., 57th Floor
Toronto, ON M5H3Y2
416-365-5123
Gold & precious metals mining

Kirby Corp. KEX
1775 St. James Place, Ste. 300
Houston, TX 77056
713-629-9370   Fax 713-964-2200
Diversified operations O

Kleinwort Benson Australian Income Fund,
   Inc. KBA
200 Park Ave., 24th Floor
New York, NY 10166
212-687-2515
Financial - investment management

KLM Royal Dutch Airlines KLM
565 Taxter Rd.
Elmsford, NY 10523
914-784-2000
Airline O

Kmart Corp. KM
3100 W. Big Beaver Rd.
Troy, MI 48084
313-643-1000
Retail - major department stores DRP

KN Energy, Inc. KNE
370 Van Gordon St.
Lakewood, CO 80228
303-989-1740
Utility - gas distribution O DRP

Knight-Ridder, Inc. KRI
One Herald Plaza
Miami, FL 33132
305-376-3800
Publishing - newspapers O DRP

Knoll, Inc. KNL
1235 Water St.
East Greenville, PA 18041
215-679-7991   Fax 215-679-1755
Office equipment & supplies O

Kohl's Corp. KSS
N. 56 W 17000 Ridgewood Drive
Menomenee Falls, WI 53051
414-703-7000
Retail - supermarkets O

Kollmorgen Corp. KOL
1601 Trapelo Rd.
Waltham, MA 02154
617-890-5655   Fax 617-890-7150
Electrical products - misc. DRP

Korea Equity Fund, Inc. KEF
180 Maiden Lane
New York, NY 10038
800-833-0018
Financial - investment management

Korea Fund KF
345 Park Ave.
New York, NY 10154
212-326-6200
Closed-end fund

Korean Investment Fund, Inc. KIF
1345 Avenue of the Americas
New York, NY 10105
212-969-1000
Financial - investment management

Kranzco Realty Trust KRT
128 Fayette St.
Conshohocken, PA 19428
610-941-9292
Real estate investment trust DRP

Kroger Co. KR
1014 Vine St.
Cincinnati, OH 45202
513-762-4000
Retail - supermarkets O

K2 Inc. KTO
4900 S. Eastern Ave.
Los Angeles, CA 90040
213-724-2800
Leisure & recreational products

Kuhlman Corp. KUH
101 Kuhlman Ave.
Versailles, KY 40383
606-879-2999
Electrical products - misc. DRP

Kysor Industrial Corp. KZ
One Madison Ave.
Cadillac, MI 49601
616-779-2200
Auto parts DRP

Laboratory Corporation of America
 Holdings LH
1447 York Ct.
Burlington, NC 27215
910-584-5171   Fax 910-222-1568
Medical & dental supplies O

Laclede Gas Co. LG
720 Olive St.
St. Louis, MO 63101
314-342-0500
Utility - gas distribution DRP

Lafarge Corp. LAF
11130 Sunrise Valley Dr.
Reston, VA 22091
703-264-3600   Fax 703-264-0634
Construction - cement & concrete O
 DRP 5%

Laidlaw Environmental Services, Inc. LLE
PO Box 2349
Wilmington, DE 19899
302-479-2757
Pollution control equipment & services

Laidlaw Inc. LDW
3221 N. Service Rd.
Burlington, ON L7R3Y8
905-336-1800   Fax 416-336-3976
School & health transportation services O

Lakehead Pipe Line Partners, L.P. LHP
21 West Superior St.
Duluth, MN 55802
218-725-0100
Oil & gas - production & pipeline

Lamson & Sessions LMS
25701 Science Park Dr.
Cleveland, OH 44122
216-464-3400
Building materials

Lands' End, Inc. LE
Lands' End Lane
Dodgeville, WI 53595
608-935-9341
Retail - mail order & direct O

Latin America Investment Fund, Inc. LAM
153 E. 53rd St.
New York, NY 10022
212-832-2626
Financial - investment management

Latin American Discovery Fund,
 Inc. LDF
1221 Ave. of the Americas, 21st Fl.
New York, NY 10020
212-296-7000
Financial - investment management

Lawter International, Inc. LAW
990 Skokie Blvd.
Northbrook, IL 60062
708-498-4700   Fax 708-498-0066
Chemicals - specialty O

Lawyers Title Corp. LTI
6630 W. Broad St.
Richmond, VA 23230
804-281-6700   Fax 804-282-5453
Business services O

La-Z-Boy, Inc. LZB
1284 N. Telegraph Rd.
Monroe, MI 48162
313-242-1444
Furniture DRP

LeaRonal, Inc. LRI
272 Buffalo Ave.
Freeport, NY 11520
516-868-8800   Fax 516-868-8824
Chemicals - specialty

Lear Corp. LEA
21557 Telegraph Rd.
Southfield, MI 48034
810-746-1500
Automotive & trucking - original
 equipment O DRP

Learning Co TLC
One Anathaeum St.
Cambridge, MA 02142
617-494-1200
Computer software & services O

Lee Enterprises, Inc. LEE
215 N. Main St.
Davenport, IA 52801
319-383-2100
Publishing - newspapers

Legg Mason, Inc. LM
111 S. Calvert St.
Baltimore, MD 21202
410-539-0000
Financial - investment bankers O

Leggett & Platt, Inc. LEG
No. 1 Leggett Rd.
Carthage, MO 64836
417-358-8131
Furniture O

Lehman Brothers Holdings, Inc. L
EH
3 World Financial Center
New York, NY 10285
212-526-7000
Financial - investment bankers O

Lennar Corp. LEN
700 N.W. 107th Ave.
Miami, FL 33172
305-559-4000
Building - residential & commercial
O

Leucadia National Corp. LUK
315 Park Avenue South
New York, NY 10010
212-460-1900
Diversified operations

Leviathan Gas Pipeline Partners, L.P.
LEV
600 Travis St., Ste. 7200
Houston, TX 77002
713-224-7400
Utility - gas distribution

Lexington Corporate Properties, Inc.
LXP
355 Lexington Ave.
New York, NY 10017
212-692-7260   Fax 212-986-6972
Real estate investment trust

Lexmark International Group, Inc.
LXK
55 Railroad Ave.
Greenwich, CT 06836
203-629-6700
Computers - peripheral equipment O

LG&E Energy Corp. LGE
220 W. Main St., PO Box 32030
Louisville, KY 40232
502-627-2000
Utility - electric power DRP

Libbey Inc. LBY
420 Madison Ave.
Toledo, OH 43604
419-727-2100
Glass products DRP

Liberte Investors LBI
1420 Viceroy Dr.
Dallas, TX 75235
214-879-5800
Financial - mortgages & related
  services

Liberty ALL-STAR Equity Fund USA
Federal Reserve Plaza
Boston, MA 02210
800-542-3863
Financial - investment management

Liberty All-Star Growth Fund, Inc. GSO
4405 East-West Hwy.
Bethesda, MD 20814
301-986-5866
Financial - investment management

Liberty Corp LC
PO Box 789, Wade Hampton Blvd.
Greenville, SC 29602
864-609-8435
Life & health insurance

Liberty Financial Cos. L
600 Atlantic Ave.
Boston, MA 02210
617-722-6000   Fax 617-742-8386
Financial - investment management

Liberty Property Trust LRY
65 Valley Stream Parkway
Malvern, PA 19355
610-648-1700
Real estate investment trust DRP

Liberty Term Trust, Inc. - 1999 LTT
Federated Investors Tower
Pittsburgh, PA 15222
412-288-1900
Financial - investment management

Life Re Corp. LRE
969 High Ridge Rd.
Stamford, CT 06905
203-321-3000
Insurance - life

Lilly Industries, Inc. LI
733 S. West St.
Indianapolis, IN 46225
317-687-6700
Chemicals - specialty DRP

Limited Inc., (The) LTD
Two Limited Parkway
Columbus, OH 43216
614-479-7000
Retail - apparel & shoes

Lincoln National Convert. Securities Fund,
  Inc. LNV
200 E. Berry St.
Fort Wayne, IN 46802
219-455-2210
Financial - investment management

Lincoln National Corp. LNC
200 E. Berry St.
Fort Wayne, IN 46802
219-455-2000
Insurance - property & casualty O DRP

Lincoln National Income Fund, Inc. LND
200 E. Berry St.
Fort Wayne, IN 46802
219-455-2210
Financial - investment management DRP

Linens n Things LIN
6 Brighton Rd.
Clifton, NJ 07015
201-778-1300
Retail (specialty) O

Litton Industries, Inc. LIT
21240 Burbank Blvd.
Woodland Hills, CA 91367
818-598-5000   Fax 818-598-5940
Diversified operations O

Liz Claiborne, Inc. LIZ
1441 Broadway
New York, NY 10018
212-354-4900
Textiles - apparel O DRP

LL&E Royalty Trust LRT
712 Main St.
Houston, TX 77002
713-216-4424
Oil & gas - US royalty trust

Lockheed Martin Corp. LMT
6801 Rockledge Dr.
Bestheda, MD 20817
301-897-6000   Fax 301-897-6083
Diversified operations O DRP

Loews Corp. LTR
667 Madison Ave.
New York, NY 10021
212-545-2000
Diversified operations O

Lomak Petroleum, Inc. LOM
500 Throckmorton St.
Fort Worth, TX 76102
817-870-2601
Oil & gas - US exploration & production

Lone Star Industries, Inc. LCE
300 First Stamford Place
Stamford, CT 06912
203-969-8600   Fax 203-969-8546
Construction - cement & concrete

Lone Star Technologies, Inc. LSS
5501 LBJ Fwy., Ste. 1200
Dallas, TX 75240
214-386-3981
Steel - production O

Longs Drug Stores Corp. LDG
141 N. Civic Dr.
Walnut Creek, CA 94596
510-937-1170
Retail - drug stores O DRP

Longview Fibre Co. LFB
PO Box 639
Longview, WA 98632
206-425-1550
Paper & paper products O

Loral Space and Communications Ltd.
  LOR
600 Third Ave.
New York, NY 10016
212-697-1105
Telecommunications equipment O

Louis Dreyfus Natural Gas Corp. LD
14000 Quail Springs Pkwy.
Oklahoma City, OK 73134
405-749-1300   Fax 405-749-9385
Oil & gas - US exploration & production

Louisiana-Pacific Corp. LPX
111 S.W. Fifth Ave.
Portland, OR 97204
503-221-0800   Fax 503-796-0204
Building products - wood O DRP

Lowe's Companies, Inc. LOW
State Highway 268 East
North Wilkesboro, NC 28659
910-651-4000   Fax 919-851-4766
Building products - retail & wholesale O
  DRP

LSB Industries, Inc. LSB
16 S. Pennsylvania Ave.
Oklahoma City, OK 73107
405-235-4546   Fax 405-235-5067
Diversified operations

LSI Logic Corp. LSI
1551 McCarthy Blvd.
Milpitas, CA 95035
408-433-8000   Fax 408-433-7715
Electrical components - semiconductors O

LTC Properties, Inc. LTC
300 Esplanade Dr., Ste. 1860
Oxnard, CA 93030
805-981-8655   Fax 805-981-8663
Real estate investment trust DRP

LTV Corp LTV
25 W. Prospect Ave.
Cleveland, OH 44115
216-622-5000
Iron & Steel O

Lubrizol LZ
29400 Lakeland Blvd.
Wickliffe, OH 44092
216-943-4200
Chemicals (specialty) O DRP

Luby's Cafeterias, Inc. LUB
2211 Northeast Loop 410
San Antonio, TX 78265
210-654-9000
Retail - food & restaurants DRP

Lucent Technologies Inc. LU
600 Mountain Ave.
Murray Hill, NJ 07974
908-582-8500
Telecommunications services O DRP

Lydall, Inc. LDL
One Colonial Rd.
Manchester, CT 06045
860-646-1233 Fax 860-646-4917
Paper & paper products

Lyondell Petrochemical Co. LYO
1221 McKinney Ave., Ste. 1600
Houston, TX 77010
713-652-7200
Chemicals - plastics O DRP

M & F Worldwide Corp. MFW
2220 Palmer Ave.
Kalamazoo, MI 49001
616-384-3400
Aerospace - aircraft equipment

Mac Frugal's Bargains - Close-outs, Inc.
 MFI
2430 E. Del Amo Blvd.
Dominguez, CA 90220
310-537-9220 Fax 310-632-4477
Retail - discount & variety O

Macerich Co. MAC
233 Wilshire Blvd.
Santa Monica, CA 90401
310-394-5333
Real estate investment trust DRP

MacNeal-Schwendler MNS
815 Colorado Blvd.
Los Angeles, CA 90041
213-258-9111
Computer, software & services

Magellan Health Services, Inc. MGL
3414 Peachtree Rd. NE
Atlanta, GA 30326
404-841-9200
Medical services O

Magna Group, Inc. MGR
1401 S. Brentwood Blvd.
St. Louis, MO 63144
314-963-2500
Banks - midwest DRP

MagneTek, Inc. MAG
26 Century Blvd.
Nashville, TN 37214
615-316-5100
Electrical products - misc. O

Mail-Well, Inc. MWL
23 Inverness Way East, Ste. 160
Inglewood, CO 80112
303-790-8023
Paper & paper products

Malan Realty Investors, Inc. MAL
30200 Telegraph Rd., Ste. 105
Birmingham, MI 48025
810-644-7110 Fax 810-644-7880
Real estate investment trust

Malaysia Fund, Inc. MF
Vanguard Financial Center
Valley Forge, PA 19482
610-648-6000
Financial - investment management

Mallinckrodt, Inc. MKG
7733 Forsyth Blvd.
St. Louis, MO 63105
314-854-5200
Diversified operations O DRP

Managed High Income Portfolio, Inc.
 MHY
Two World Trade Center
New York, NY 10048
212-720-9218
Financial - investment management

Managed Municipals Portfolio Inc. MMU
2 World Trade Ctr., 101st Fl.
New York, NY 10048
212-720-9218
Financial - investment management

Manitowoc Co., Inc. MTW
500 South 16th St., PO Box 66
Manitowoc, WI 54220
414-684-4410
Machinery DRP

Manor Care, Inc. MNR
11555 Darnestown Rd.
Gaithersburg, MD 20878
301-979-4000
Nursing homes O

Manpower, Inc. MAN
5301 N. Ironwood Rd.
Milwaukee, WI 53217
414-961-1000
Business services O DRP

Manufactured Home Communities, Inc.
  MHC
2 N. Riverside Plaza
Chicago, IL 60606
312-454-0100
Real estate investment trust

Marcus Corp MCS
250 E. Wisconsin Ave., Ste. 1700
Milwaukee, WI 53202
414-272-6020
Lodging - hotels DRP

Maritrans Inc. TUG
One Logan Square
Philadelphia, PA 19103
215-864-1200
Transportation - shipping

Mark IV Industries, Inc. IV
501 John James Audubon Parkway
Amherst, NY 14228
716-689-4972
Diversified operations O

Markel Corp. MKL
4551 Cox Rd.
Glen Allen, VA 23060
804-747-0136   Fax 804-965-1600
Insurance - property & casualty

Marriott International, Inc. MAR
10400 Fernwood Rd.
Bethesda, MD 20817
301-380-3000
Hotels & motels O DRP

Marsh & McLennan Companies, Inc.
  MMC
1166 Avenue of the Americas
New York, NY 10036
212-345-5000
Insurance - brokerage O DRP

Marshall Industries MI
9320 Telstar Ave.
El Monte, CA 91731
818-307-6000
Electronics - parts distribution O

Martin Marietta Materials, Inc. MLM
2710 Wycliff Rd.
Raleigh, NC 27607
919-781-4550
Construction - cement & concrete

MasTec, Inc. MTZ
8600 NW 36th St., 8th Fl.
Miami, FL 33166
305-587-4512
Telecommunications equipment O

Masco Corp. MAS
21001 Van Born Rd.
Taylor, MI 48180
313-274-7400   Fax 313-374-6666
Building products - misc. O

Mascotech, Inc. MSX
21001 Van Born Rd.
Taylor, MI 48180
313-274-7405
Miscellaneous - not elsewhere classified O

MassMutual Corporate Investors Inc. MCI
1295 State St.
Springfield, MA 01111
413-788-8411
Financial - investment management

MassMutual Participation Investors MPV
1295 State St.
Springfield, MA 01111
413-788-8411
Financial - investment management

Material Sciences Corp. MSC
2300 E. Pratt Blvd.
Elk Grove Village, IL 60007
847-439-8270   Fax 847-439-0737
Steel - specialty alloys O

Matlack Systems, Inc. MLK
One Rollins Plaza
Wilmington, DE 19803
302-426-2700
Transportation - truck

Mattel, Inc. MAT
333 Continental Blvd.
El Segundo, CA 90245
310-252-2000
Toys - games & hobby products O DRP

Mauna Loa Macadamia Partners, L.P.
  NUT
827 Fort St.
Honolulu, HI 96813
808-544-6112
Agricultural operations

Maxim Group, Inc. MXG
1035 Cobb Industrial Dr.
Marietta, GA 30066
770-590-9369
Retail - misc.

MAXIMUS MMS
1356 Beverley Rd.
McLean, VA 22101
703-434-4200
Health Care (specialized services)

MAXXIM Medical, Inc. MAM
104 Industrial Blvd.
Sugarland, TX 77478
281-240-5588
Medical products

May Dept. Stores 35551
611 Olive St.
St. Louis, MO 63101
314-342-6300
Retail department stores DRP

Maytag Corp. MYG
403 W. Fourth St. North
Newton, IA 50208
515-792-8000
Appliances - household O DRP

MBIA Inc. MBI
113 King St.
Armonk, NY 10504
914-273-4545   Fax 914-765-3163
Insurance - multiline & misc. O

MBNA Corp. KRB
400 Christiana Rd.
Newark, DE 19713
302-453-9930
Financial - business services O

MCN Energy Group MCN
500 Ginswold St.
Detroit, MI 48226
313-256-5500
Utility - gas distribution O DRP

McClatchy Newspapers, Inc. MNI
2100 "Q" St.
Sacramento, CA 95816
916-321-1846
Publishing - newspapers

McDermott International, Inc. MDR
1450 Poydras Rd.
New Orleans, LA 70112
504-587-5400
Machinery - electric utility O DRP

McDermott (J. Ray) JRM
1450 Poydras St.
New Orleans, LA 70012
504-587-5300
Oil & Gas drilling and equipment

McDonald's Corp. MCD
McDonald's Plaza
Oak Brook, IL 60521
708-575-3000
Retail - food & restaurants O DRP

McDonalds Investment MOD
800 Superior Ave.
Cleveland, OH 44114
216-443-2300
Investment banking - brokerage

McGraw-Hill Companies MHP
1221 Avenue of the Americas
New York, NY 10020
212-512-2000
Publishing O DRP

McKesson Corp. MCK
One Post St.
San Francisco, CA 94104
415-983-8300
Drugs & sundries - wholesale O DRP

McWhorter Technologies, Inc. MWT
400 E. Cottage Place
Carpentersville, IL 60110
708-428-2657
Paints & allied products

M.D.C. Holdings, Inc. MDC
3600 S. Yosemite St., Ste. 900
Denver, CO 80237
303-773-1100
Financial - investment management

MDU Resources Group, Inc. MDU
400 N. Fourth St.
Bismarck, ND 58501
701-222-7900
Utility - electric power DRP

Mead Corp., (The) MEA
Courthouse Plaza Northeast
Dayton, OH 45463
937-495-6323
Paper & paper products O DRP

Meadowbrook Insurance Group, Inc. MIG
26600 Telegraph Rd.
Southfield, MI 48034
810-358-1100
Insurance - brokerage DRP

Medical Assurance MAI
100 Brookwood Place
Birmingham, AL 35209
205-877-4400
Insurance - property & casualty

MedPartners, Inc. MDM
3000 Galleria Tower, Ste. 1000
Birmingham, AL 35244
205-733-8996
Business services O

Meditrust MT
197 First Ave.
Needham, MA 02194
617-433-6000   Fax 617-433-1290
Real estate investment trust DRP

Medtronic, Inc. MDT
7000 Central Ave. NE
Minneapolis, MN 55432
612-574-4000   Fax 612-574-4879
Medical instruments O DRP

Mellon Bank Corp. MEL
One Mellon Bank Center
Pittsburgh, PA 15258
412-234-5000   Fax 412-236-1662
Banks - northeast O DRP

MEMC Electronic Materials, Inc. WFR
501 Pearl Dr.
St. Peters, MO 63376
314-279-5000
Electrical components - misc. O

Mentor Income Fund, Inc. MRF
10221 Wincopin Circle
Columbia, MD 21044
410-964-8260
Financial - investment management

Mercantile Bancorporation Inc. MTL
PO Box 524
St. Louis, MO 63166
314-425-2525
Banks - midwest O DRP

Mercantile Stores Co., Inc. MST
9450 Seward Rd.
Fairfield, OH 45014
513-881-8000
Retail - regional department stores O

Merck & Co., Inc. MRK
One Merck Dr.
Whitehouse Station, NJ 08889
908-423-1000
Drugs O DRP

Mercury General Corp. MCY
4484 Wilshire Blvd.
Los Angeles, CA 90010
213-937-1060
Insurance - property & casualty

Meredith Corp. MDP
1716 Locust St.
Des Moines, IA 50309
515-284-3000
Publishing - periodicals

Meridian Gold MDG
5011 Meadowood Way
Reno, NV 89502
702-827-3777
Gold & precious metals mining

Meridian Industrial Trust, Inc. MDN
455 Market St., 17th Fl.
San Francisco, CA 94105
415-956-3031
Real estate investment trust

Meridian Resource TMR
15995 N. Barkers Landing, Ste. 300
Houston, TX 77079
281-558-8080
Oil & gas - exploration and production O

Merrill Lynch & Co., Inc. MER
World Financial Center
New York, NY 10281
212-449-1000
Financial - investment bankers O DRP

Merry Land & Investment Co., Inc. MRY
PO Box 1417
Augusta, GA 30903
706-722-6756
Real estate investment trust DRP 5%

Mesa Royalty Trust MTR
712 Main St.
Houston, TX 77002
713-216-5100
Oil & gas - US royalty trust

Mesabi Trust MSB
PO Box 318, Church St. Station
New York, NY 10015
212-250-6519
Oil & gas - US royalty trust

Mestek, Inc. MCC
260 N. Elm St.
Westfield, MA 01085
413-568-9571
Building products - a/c & heating

Metals USA MUI
4801 Woodway, Suite 300E
Houston, TX 77056
888-871-8701
Metal fabricators

Mexico Equity and Income Fund, Inc.
 MXE
200 Liberty St.
New York, NY 10281
212-667-5000
Financial - investment management

Mexico Fund, (The) MXF
Wall Street Plaza
New York, NY 10005
800-224-4134
Financial - investment management

MFS Charter Income Trust MCR
500 Boylston St.
Boston, MA 02116
617-954-5000
Financial - investment management

MFS Government Markets Income Trust
 MGF
500 Boylston St.
Boston, MA 02116
617-954-5000
Financial - investment management

MFS Intermediate Income Trust MIN
500 Boylston St.
Boston, MA 02116
617-954-5000
Financial - investment management

MFS Multimarket Income Trust MMT
500 Boylston St.
Boston, MA 02116
617-954-5000
Financial - investment management

MFS Municipal Income Trust MFM
500 Boylston St.
Boston, MA 02116
617-954-5000
Financial - investment management

MFS Special Value Trust MFV
500 Boylston St.
Boston, MA 02116
617-954-5000
Financial - investment management

MGI Properties MGI
30 Rowes Wharf
Boston, MA 02110
617-330-5335   Fax 617-330-5046
Real estate investment trust

MGIC Investment Corp. MTG
250 E. Kilbourn Ave.
Milwaukee, WI 53202
414-347-6480   Fax 414-347-6802
Financial - mortgages & related services O

MGM Grand, Inc. MGG
3799 Las Vegas Blvd. South
Las Vegas, NV 89109
702-891-1111
Hotels & motels O

M/I Schottenstein Homes, Inc. MHO
41 S. High St., Ste. 2410
Columbus, OH 43215
614-221-5700
Building - residential & commercial

Micron Technology, Inc. MU
2805 E. Columbia Rd.
Boise, ID 83706
208-383-4000
Electrical components - semiconductors O

Mid Atlantic Medical Services, Inc. MME
4 Taft Court
Rockville, MD 20850
301-294-5140
Healthcare - outpatient & home O

Mid Atlantic Realty Trust MRR
1302 Concourse Dr., Suite 204
Linthicum, MD 21090
410-684-2000
Real estate investment trust

Mid-America Apartment Communities,
 Inc. MAA
6584 Poplar Ave., Ste. 340
Memphis, TN 38138
901-682-6600   Fax 901-682-6667
Real estate investment trust

Mid-America Realty Investments, Inc.
 MDI
11506 Nicholas St., Ste. 100
Omaha, NE 68154
402-496-3300   Fax 402-496-9210
Real estate operations DRP

MidAmerican Energy Co. MEC
666 Grand Ave., PO Box 9244
Des Moines, IA 50306
515-242-4300
Utility - gas DRP

Midwest Express Holdings, Inc. MEH
6744 S. Howell Ave.
Oak Creek, WI 53154
414-570-4000
Transportation - airline

Mikasa, Inc. MKS
20633 S. Fordyce Ave.
Long Beach, CA 90810
310-886-3700   Fax 310-635-1546
Glass products

Millenium Chemicals, Inc. MCH
99 Wood Ave. South
Iselin, NJ 08830
908-603-6600
Chemicals - specialty O

Miller Industries, Inc. MLR
900 Circle 75 Pkwy.
Atlanta, GA 30339
770-988-0797
Automotive & trucking - original
   equipment O

Millipore Corp. MIL
80 Ashby Rd.
Bedford, MA 01730
617-275-9200   Fax 617-275-5550
Filtration products O DRP

Mills Corp MLS
1300 Wilson Blvd.
Arlington, VA 22209
703-526-5000
Real estate investment trust DRP 3%

Minerals Technologies Inc. MTX
405 Lexington Ave.
New York, NY 10174
212-878-1800
Chemicals - specialty O

Minnesota Mining and Manufacturing Co.
   MMM
3M Center
St. Paul, MN 55144
612-733-1110   Fax 612-733-9973
Diversified operations O DRP

Minnesota Municipal Term Trust, Inc.
   MNA
222 S. Ninth St.
Minneapolis, MN 55402
800-333-6000
Financial - investment management

Minnesota Power & Light Co. MPL
30 W. Superior St.
Duluth, MN 55802
218-722-2641
Utility - electric power DRP

Mirage Resorts, Inc. MIR
3400 Las Vegas Blvd. South
Las Vegas, NV 89109
702-791-7111
Leisure & recreational services O

Mississippi Chemical Corp. GRO
PO Box 388
Yazoo City, MS 39194
601-746-4131   Fax 601-746-9158
Chemicals - specialty O

Mitchell Energy & Development Corp.
   MNDA
2001 Timberloch Place
The Woodlands, TX 77380
281-377-5500
Oil & gas - US exploration & production
   O

Mitel Corp MLT
350 Legget Dr., PO Box 13089
Kanata, ON K2K1X3
613-592-2122
Communications equipment

MMI Companies, Inc. MMI
540 Lake Cook Rd.
Deerfield, IL 60015
708-940-7550
Insurance - multi line & misc.

Mobil Corp. MOB
3225 Gallows Rd.
Fairfax, VA 22037
703-846-3000   Fax 703-846-6002
Oil & gas - international integrated O
   DRP

Molecular Biosystems, Inc. MB
10030 Barnes Canyon Rd.
San Diego, CA 92121
619-452-0681   Fax 619-452-6187
Biomedical & genetic products O

Monarch Machine Tool MMO
615 North Oak St.
Sidney, OH 45365
513-492-4111
Machinery - diversified

Monsanto Co. MTC
800 N. Lindbergh Blvd.
St. Louis, MO 63167
314-694-1000   Fax 314-694-7625
Chemicals - diversified O DRP

Montana Power MTP
40 E. Broadway
Butte, MT 59701
406-723-5421
Electric & gas company DRP

Monterey Homes Corp. MTH
5333 N. Seventh St., Ste. 219
Phoenix, AZ 85014
602-265-8541   Fax 602-230-1690
Real estate investment trust

Montgomery Street Income Securities Inc.
  MTS
101 California St., Ste. 4100
San Francisco, CA 94111
415-981-8191
Financial - investment management

Morgan Grenfell SMALLCap Fund, Inc.
  MGC
885 Third Ave., 32nd Fl.
New York, NY 10022
212-230-2600   Fax 212-755-9132
Financial - investment management

Morgan (J.P.) and Co. JPM
23 Wall St.
New York, NY 10015
212-483-2323
Banking DRP

Morgan Keegan, Inc. MOR
Fifty Front St.
Memphis, TN 38103
901-524-4100
Financial - investment bankers

Morgan Products Ltd. MGN
25 Tri-State International
Lincolnshire, IL 60069
708-317-2400   Fax 708-317-1900
Building products - doors & trim

Morgan Stanley Africa Investment Fund,
  Inc. AFF
1221 Avenue of the Americas
New York, NY 10020
212-296-7100
Financial - investment management

Morgan Stanley Asia-Pacific Fund, Inc.
  APF
1221 Avenue of the Americas
New York, NY 10020
212-296-7100
Financial - investment management

Morgan Stanley Dean Witter MWD
1585 Broadway
New York, NY 10036
212-761-3000
Securities brokerage DRP

Morgan Stanley Emerging Markets Debt
  Fund, Inc. MSD
1221 Avenue of the Americas
New York, NY 10020
212-296-7100
Financial - investment management

Morgan Stanley Emerging Markets Fund,
  Inc. MSF
1221 Avenue of the Americas
New York, NY 10020
212-296-7100
Financial - investment management

Morgan Stanley Global Opportunity Bd.
  Fd., Inc. MGB
1221 Avenue of the Americas
New York, NY 10020
212-296-7100
Financial - investment management

Morgan Stanley High Yield Fund, Inc.
  MSY
1221 Avenue of the Americas
New York, NY 10020
212-296-7100
Financial - investment management

Morgan Stanley India Investment Fund IIF
1221 Ave. of the Americas
New York, NY 10020
212-296-7100
Financial - investment management

Morgan Stanley Russia RNE
1221 Ave. of the Americas
New York, NY 10020
212-296-7100
Financial - investment management

Morrison Health Care, Inc. MHI
1955 Lake Park Dr., Ste. 400
Smyrna, GA 30080
770-437-3300
Food - misc.

Morrison Knudsen Corp. MK
27400 E. Fifth St.
Highland, CA 92346
909-382-0125
Construction - heavy

Morrison Restaurants MRN
4893 Riverdale Rd.
Atlanta, GA 30337
770-991-0351
Owns, operates cafeterias, buffets

Morton International, Inc. MII
100 N. Riverside Plaza
Chicago, IL 60606
312-807-2000
Chemicals - specialty O DRP

Mossimo, Inc. MGX
15320 Barranca Pkwy.
Irvine, CA 92718
714-453-1300
Apparel

Motive Power Industries MPO
1200 Reedsdale St.
Pittsburgh, PA 15233
412-237-2250
Provides railroad components O

Motorola, Inc. MOT
1303 E. Algonquin Rd.
Schaumburg, IL 60196
847-576-5000
Telecommunications equipment O DRP

MSC Industrial Direct Co., Inc. MSM
151 Sunnyside Blvd.
Plainview, NY 11803
516-349-7100
Business services - marketing

Mueller Industries, Inc. MLI
6799 Great Oaks Rd., Ste. 200
Memphis, TN 38138
901-753-3200
Steel - production

MuniAssets Fund, Inc. MUA
PO Box 9011
Princeton, NJ 08543
609-282-2800
Financial - investment management

MuniVest Florida Fund MVS
PO Box 9011
Princeton, NJ 08543
609-282-2800
Financial - investment management

MuniVest Fund II, Inc. MVT
PO Box 9011
Princeton, NJ 08543
609-282-2800
Financial - investment management

MuniVest Michigan Insured Fund, Inc.
MVM
PO Box 9011
Princeton, NJ 08543
609-282-2800
Financial - investment management

MuniVest New Jersey Fund, Inc. MVJ
PO Box 9011
Princeton, NJ 08543
609-282-2800
Financial - investment management

MuniVest Pennyslvania Insured Fund
MVP
PO Box 9011
Princeton, NJ 08543
609-282-2800
Financial - investment management

MuniYield California Fund, Inc. MYC
PO Box 9011
Princeton, NJ 08543
609-282-2800
Financial - investment management

MuniYield California Insured Fund II, Inc.
MCA
PO Box 9011
Princeton, NJ 08543
609-282-2800
Financial - investment management

MuniYield California Insured Fund, Inc.
MIC
PO Box 9011
Princeton, NJ 08543
609-282-2800
Financial - investment management

MuniYield Florida Fund MYF
PO Box 9011
Princeton, NJ 08543
609-282-2800
Financial - investment management

MuniYield Florida Insured Fund, Inc.
MFT
PO Box 9011
Princeton, NJ 08543
609-282-2800
Financial - investment management

MuniYield Fund, Inc. MYD
PO Box 9011
Princeton, NJ 08543
609-282-2800
Financial - investment management

MuniYield Insured Fund, Inc. MYI
PO Box 9011
Princeton, NJ 08543
609-282-2800
Financial - investment management

MuniYield Michigan Fund, Inc. MYM
PO Box 9011
Princeton, NJ 08543
609-282-2800
Financial - investment management

MuniYield Michigan Insured Fund, Inc.
MIY
PO Box 9011
Princeton, NJ 08543
609-282-2800
Financial - investment management

MuniYield New Jersey Fund, Inc. MYJ
PO Box 9011
Princeton, NJ 08543
609-282-2800
Financial - investment management

MuniYield New Jersey Insured Fund, Inc.
 MJI
PO Box 9011
Princeton, NJ 08543
609-282-2800
Financial - investment management

MuniYield New York Insured Fund II, Inc.
 MYT
PO Box 9011
Princeton, NJ 08543
609-282-2800
Financial - investment management

MuniYield New York Insured Fund, Inc.
 MYN
PO Box 9011
Princeton, NJ 08543
609-282-2800
Financial - investment management

MuniYield Pennsylvania Fund, Inc. MPA
PO Box 9011
Princeton, NJ 08543
609-282-2800
Financial - investment management

MuniYield Quality Fund II, Inc. MQT
PO Box 9011
Princeton, NJ 08543
609-282-2800
Financial - investment management

MuniYield Quality Fund, Inc. MQY
PO Box 9011
Princeton, NJ 08543
609-282-2800
Financial - investment management

Municipal Income Opportunities Trust
 OIA
Two World Trade Center
New York, NY 10048
212-392-2222
Financial - investment management

Municipal Income Opportunities Trust II
 OIB
Two World Trade Center
New York, NY 10048
212-392-2222
Financial - investment management

Municipal Income Opportunities Trust III
 OIC
Two World Trade Center
New York, NY 10048
212-392-2222
Financial - investment management

Municipal Income Trust TFA
Two World Trade Center
New York, NY 10048
212-392-2222
Financial - investment management

Municipal Income Trust II TFB
Two World Trade Center
New York, NY 10048
212-392-2222
Financial - investment management

Municipal Income Trust III TFC
Two World Trade Center
New York, NY 10048
212-392-2222
Financial - investment management

Municipal Partners Fund II, Inc. MPT
Seven World Trade Center
New York, NY 10048
212-783-1301
Financial - investment management

Municipal Partners Fund, Inc. MNP
Seven World Trade Center
New York, NY 10048
212-783-1301
Financial - investment management

Municipal Premium Income Trust PIA
Two World Trade Center
New York, NY 10048
212-392-2222
Financial - investment management

Murphy Oil Corp. MUR
200 Peach St., PO Box 7000
El Dorado, AR 71731
501-862-6411
Oil & gas - international specialty O

Musicland Stores Corp. MLG
10400 Yellow Circle Dr.
Minnetonka, MN 55343
612-931-8000
Retail - misc. O

Mutual Risk Management MM
44 Church St.
Hamilton, BM
441-295-5688
Risk management insurance

Mylan Laboratories Inc. MYL
1030 Century Bldg.
Pittsburgh, PA 15222
412-232-0100
Drugs - generic O DRP

MYR Group, Inc. MYR
2550 W. Golf Rd., Ste. 200
Rolling Meadows, IL 60008
708-290-1891
Construction - heavy

Nabisco, Inc. NA
1301 Avenue of the Americas
New York, NY 10019
201-682-5000
Food - misc. O

NAC Re Corp. NRC
One Greenwich Plaza
Greenwich, CT 06836
203-622-5200   Fax 203-622-1494
Insurance - property & casualty

NACCO Industries, Inc. NC
5875 Landerbrook Dr., Ste. 300
Mayfield Heights, OH 44124
216-449-9600
Diversified operations

Nalco Chemical Co. NLC
One Nalco Center
Naperville, IL 60563
708-305-1000   Fax 708-305-2900
Chemicals - specialty O DRP

Nashua Corp. NSH
44 Franklin St., PO Box 2002
Nashua, NH 03061
603-880-2323   Fax 603-880-5671
Office equipment O DRP

National City Corp. NCC
1900 E. Ninth St.
Cleveland, OH 44114
216-575-2000
Banks - midwest O DRP 3%

National Data Corp. NDC
National Data Plaza
Atlanta, GA 30329
404-728-2000   Fax 404-728-2551
Data collection & systems O DRP

National Fuel Gas Co. NFG
30 Rockefeller Plaza
New York, NY 10112
212-541-7533
Utility - gas distribution DRP

National Golf Properties, Inc. TEE
1448 15th St., Ste. 200
Santa Monica, CA 90404
310-260-5500
Real estate investment trust

National Health Investors, Inc. NHI
100 Vine St., Ste. 1402
Murfreesboro, TN 37130
615-890-9100
Real estate investment trust DRP 3%

National Media Corp. NM
1700 Walnut St.
Philadelphia, PA 19103
215-772-5000
Retail - mail order & direct O

National-Oilwell Inc. NOI
5555 San Felipe
Houston, TX 77056
713-960-5100
Manufactures oil & gas drilling equipment

National Presto Industries, Inc. NPK
3925 N. Hastings Way
Eau Claire, WI 54703
715-839-2121
Appliances - household

National Processing NAP
191 Bullitt Lane, Suite 450
Louisville, KY 40222
502-326-7000
Data processing services

National Propane Partners, L.P. NPL
200 1st St. S.E.
Cedar Rapids, IA 52401
319-365-1550   Fax 319-365-6084
Oil & gas - US integrated

National Semiconductor Corp. NSM
2900 Semiconductor Dr.
Santa Clara, CA 95052
408-721-5000   Fax 408-739-9803
Electrical components - semiconductors O

National Service Industries, Inc. NSI
1420 Peachtree St., N.E.
Atlanta, GA 30309
404-853-1000
Diversified operations O DRP

National-Standard NSD
1618 Terminal Rd.
Niles, MI 49120
616-683-8100
Wire manufacturers DRP

National Steel Corp. NS
4100 Edison Lakes Parkway
Mishawaka, IN 46545
219-273-7000   Fax 219-273-7869
Steel - production O

NationsBank Corp. NB
NationsBank Corporate Center
Charlotte, NC 28255
704-386-5000   Fax 704-386-4579
Banks - money center O DRP

Nationwide Financial Services NFX
One Nationwide Plaza
Columbus, OH 43215
614-249-7111
Insurance DRP

Nationwide Health Properties, Inc. NHP
4675 McArthur Court, Ste. 1170
Newport Beach, CA 92660
714-251-1211   Fax 714-251-9644
Real estate investment trust DRP

Navistar International Corp. NAV
455 N. Cityfront Plaza Dr.
Chicago, IL 60611
312-836-2000
Automotive & trucking - original
  equipment O

NCH Corp. NCH
2727 Chemsearch Blvd.
Irving, TX 75062
972-438-0211
Soap & cleaning preparations

NCR Corp. NCR
1700 S. Patterson Blvd.
Dayton, OH 45479
937-445-5000
Electronics - components & systems O

Neiman Marcus Group NMG
27 Boylston St.
Chestnut Hill, MA 02167
617-232-0760
Upscale retail stores O DRP

Nelson (Thomas), Inc. TNM
Nelson Place at Elm Hill Pike
Nashville, TN 37214
615-889-9000
Publishing - books

Network Equipment Technologies, Inc.
  NWK
800 Saginaw Dr.
Redwood City, CA 94063
415-366-4400   Fax 415-366-5675
Telecommunications equipment O

New America High Income Fund, Inc.
  HYB
Ten Winthrop Square, Fifth Fl.
Boston, MA 02110
617-350-8610
Financial - investment management

New Century Energy NCE
1225 17th St.
Denver, CO 80202
303-571-7511
Holding company - electric companies
  DRP

New England Business Service, Inc. NEB
500 Main St.
Groton, MA 01471
508-448-6111
Paper - business forms

New England Electric System NES
25 Research Dr.
Westborough, MA 01582
508-366-9011
Utility - electric power DRP

New England Investment Companies, L.P.
  NEW
399 Boylston St.
Boston, MA 02116
617-578-3500
Financial - investment management

New Jersey Resources Corp. NJR
1415 Wycoff Rd.
Wall, NJ 07719
908-938-1480
Utility - gas distribution DRP

New Plan Realty Trust NPR
1120 Avenue of the Americas
New York, NY 10036
212-869-3000
Real estate investment trust O DRP 5%

New South Africa Fund, (The) NSA
245 Park Ave., 13th Floor
New York, NY 10167
212-272-9027
Financial - investment management

New York State Electric & Gas Corp.
  NGE
PO Box 3287
Ithaca, NY 14852
607-347-4131   Fax 607-347-2560
Utility - electric power O DRP

New York Times NYT
229 W. 43rd St.
New York, NY 10036
212-556-1234
Publishing DRP

Newbridge Networks NN
600 March Rd.
Kanata, ON K2K2E6
613-591-3600
Digital network products O

Newell Co. NWL
29 E. Stephenson St.
Freeport, IL 61032
815-235-4171
Building products - misc. O DRP

Newfield Exploration Co. NFX
363 N. Sam Houston Pkwy. East
Houston, TX 77060
713-847-6000   Fax 713-847-6006
Oil & gas - US exploration & production
   O

Newhall Land & Farming NHL
23823 Valencia Blvd.
Valencia, CA 91355
805-255-4000
Land development - residential & comm'l

Newmont Gold Co. NGC
1700 Lincoln St.
Denver, CO 80203
303-863-7414
Gold mining & processing O

Newmont Mining Corp. NEM
1700 Lincoln St.
Denver, CO 80203
303-863-7414
Gold mining & processing O

Newpark Resources, Inc. NR
3850 W. Causeway Blvd.
Metairie, LA 70002
504-838-8222   Fax 504-833-9506
Oil & gas - field services

Newport News Shipbuilding NNS
4101 Washington Ave.
Newport News, VA 23607
757-380-2000
Ship design & construction O DRP

Niagara Mohawk Power Corp. NMK
300 Erie Blvd. West
Syracuse, NY 13202
315-474-1511
Utility - electric power O DRP

NICOR Inc. GAS
1844 Ferry Rd.
Naperville, IL 60563
708-305-9500   Fax 708-983-9328
Utility - gas distribution O DRP

NIKE, Inc. NKE
One Bowerman Dr.
Beaverton, OR 97005
503-671-6453
Shoes & related apparel O

NIPSCO Industries, Inc. NI
5265 Hohman Ave.
Hammond, IN 46320
219-853-5200
Utility - electric power O DRP

Nine West Group Inc. NIN
9 W. Broad St.
Stamford, CT 06902
203-324-7567
Shoes & related apparel O

99 Cents Only Stores NDN
4000 Union Pacific Ave.
City of Commerce, CA 90023
213-980-8145
Retail discounters

NL Industries, Inc. NL
16825 Northchase Dr.
Houston, TX 77060
281-423-3300
Chemicals - specialty O

Noble Affiliates, Inc. NBL
110 W. Broadway
Ardmore, OK 73401
405-223-4110
Oil & gas - US exploration & production
   O

Noble Drilling Corp. NE
10370 Richmond Ave., Ste. 400
Houston, TX 77042
713-974-3131
Oil & gas - field services O

Nord Resources Corp. NRd.
8150 Washington Village Dr.
Dayton, OH 45458
937-433-6307   Fax 937-435-7285
Metal ores - misc. O

Norfolk Southern Corp. NSC
Three Commercial Place
Norfolk, VA 23510
804-629-2680
Transportation - rail O DRP

Norrell Corp. NRL
3535 Piedmont Rd. NE
Atlanta, GA 30305
404-240-3000
Personnel O

Nortek, Inc. NTK
50 Kennedy Plaza
Providence, RI 02903
401-751-1600
Diversified operations

North Carolina Natural Gas Corp. NCG
150 Rowan St., PO Box 909
Fayetteville, NC 28302
910-483-0315
Utility - gas distribution DRP 5%

North European Oil Royalty Trust NET
43 W. Front St., Ste. 19A
Red Bank, NJ 07701
908-741-4008   Fax 908-741-3140
Oil & gas - US royalty trust

North Fork Bancorporation, Inc. NFB
275 Broad Hollow Rd.
Melville, NY 11747
516-844-1004
Banks - northeast O DRP 5%

Northeast Utilities NU
174 Brush Hill Ave.
West Springfield, MA 01090
413-785-5871
Utility - electric power O DRP

Northern Border Partners L.P. NBP
1400 Smith St.
Houston, TX 77002
713-853-6161
Oil & gas - US exploration & production

Northern States Power Co. NSP
414 Nicollet Mall
Minneapolis, MN 55401
612-330-5500   Fax 612-330-7558
Utility - electric power O DRP

Northern Telecom NT
2920 Matheson Blvd. East
Mississauga, ON L4W4M7
905-238-7000
Telecommunications euipment O DRP

Northgate Exploration NGX
1 First Canadian Pl., Ste. 2630
Toronto, ON M5X1C7
416-362-6683
Mines precious metals

Northrop Grumman Corp. NOC
1840 Century Park East
Los Angeles, CA 90067
310-553-6262
Aerospace - aircraft equipment O DRP

Northwestern Public Service Co. NPS
33 Third St. S.E.
Huron, SD 57350
605-352-8411
Utility - electric power DRP

Norwest Corp. NOB
Sixth and Marquette
Minneapolis, MN 55479
612-667-1234
Banks - midwest O DRP

Nova Corp NIS
Five Concourse Pkwy.
Atlanta, GA 30328
770-396-1456
Business services DRP

NovaCare, Inc. NOV
1016 W. Ninth Ave.
King of Prussia, PA 19406
610-992-7200
Medical services O

NOVA Corp. NVA
801 Seventh Ave.
Calgary, AB T2P2N6
403-290-6000
Transmission, marketing natural gas
  O DRP

NS Group, Inc. NSS
Ninth & Lowell Sts.
Newport, KY 41072
606-292-6809   Fax 606-292-0593
Steel - pipes & tubes

Nu Skin Asia Pacific, Inc. NUS
75 W. Center St.
Provo, UT 84601
801-345-6100
Cosmetics & toiletries O

Nucor Corp. NUE
2100 Rexford Rd.
Charlotte, NC 28211
704-366-7000   Fax 704-362-4208
Steel - production O DRP

Nuevo Energy Co. NEV
1221 Lamar, Ste. 1600
Houston, TX 77010
713-652-0706
Oil & gas - US exploration & production

NUI Corp. NUI
550 Route 202-206, PO Box 760
Bedminster, NJ 07921
908-781-0500   Fax 908-781-0718
Utility - gas distribution DRP

Nuveen Arizona Premium Income
  Municipal Fund, Inc. NAZ
333 W. Wacker Dr.
Chicago, IL 60606
312-917-7700
Financial - investment management

Nuveen California Inv. Quality Municipal
Fund, Inc. NQC
333 W. Wacker Dr.
Chicago, IL 60606
312-917-7700
Financial - investment management

Nuveen California Municipal Mkt. Opp.
Fd., Inc. NCO
333 W. Wacker Dr.
Chicago, IL 60606
312-917-7700
Financial - investment management

Nuveen California Municipal Value Fund,
Inc. NCA
333 W. Wacker Dr.
Chicago, IL 60606
312-917-7700
Financial - investment management

Nuveen California Perform. Plus
Municipal Fd., Inc. NCP
333 W. Wacker Dr.
Chicago, IL 60606
312-917-7700
Financial - investment management

Nuveen California Qual. Income Municipal
Fund, Inc. NUC
333 W. Wacker Dr.
Chicago, IL 60606
312-917-7700
Financial - investment management

Nuveen California Select Qual. Municipal
Fund, Inc. NVC
333 W. Wacker Dr.
Chicago, IL 60606
312-917-7700
Financial - investment management

Nuveen California Select Tax-Free Income
Port. NXC
333 W. Wacker Dr.
Chicago, IL 60606
312-917-7700
Financial - investment management

Nuveen Connecticut Premium Income
Municipal Fund NTC
333 W. Wacker Dr.
Chicago, IL 60606
312-917-7700
Financial - investment management

Nuveen Florida Investment Quality
Municipal Fund NQF
333 W. Wacker Dr.
Chicago, IL 60606
312-917-7700
Financial - investment management

Nuveen Florida Quality Income Municipal
Fund NUF
333 W. Wacker Dr.
Chicago, IL 60606
312-917-7700
Financial - investment management

Nuveen Insured CA Premium Inc.
Municipal Fd. 2, Inc. NCL
333 W. Wacker Dr.
Chicago, IL 60606
312-917-7700
Financial - investment management

Nuveen Insured CA Premium Inc.
Municipal Fd., Inc. NPC
333 W. Wacker Dr.
Chicago, IL 60606
312-917-7700
Financial - investment management

Nuveen Insured Florida Premium Inc.
Municipal Fd. NFL
333 W. Wacker Dr.
Chicago, IL 60606
312-917-7700
Financial - investment management

Nuveen Insured Municipal Opportunity
Fund, Inc. NIO
333 W. Wacker Dr.
Chicago, IL 60606
312-917-7700
Financial - investment management

Nuveen Insured NY Premium Inc.
Municipal Fund, Inc. NNF
333 W. Wacker Dr.
Chicago, IL 60606
312-917-7700
Financial - investment management

Nuveen Insured Premium Income
Municipal Fund 2 NPX
333 W. Wacker Dr.
Chicago, IL 60606
312-917-7700
Financial - investment management

Nuveen Insured Quality Municipal Fund,
Inc. NQI
333 W. Wacker Dr.
Chicago, IL 60606
312-917-7700
Financial - investment management

Nuveen Investment Quality Municipal
Fund, Inc. NQM
333 W. Wacker Dr.
Chicago, IL 60606
312-917-7700
Financial - investment management

Nuveen Maryland Premium Income
Municipal Fund NMY
333 W. Wacker Dr.
Chicago, IL 60606
312-917-7700
Financial - investment management

Nuveen Mass. Premium Income Municipal
Fund NMT
333 W. Wacker Dr.
Chicago, IL 60606
312-917-7700
Financial - investment management

Nuveen Michigan Premium Income
Municipal Fund, Inc. NMP
333 W. Wacker Dr.
Chicago, IL 60606
312-917-7700
Financial - investment management

Nuveen Michigan Quality Income
Municipal Fund, Inc. NUM
333 W. Wacker Dr.
Chicago, IL 60606
312-917-7700
Financial - investment management

Nuveen Municipal Advantage Fund, Inc.
NMA
333 W. Wacker Dr.
Chicago, IL 60606
312-917-7700
Financial - investment management

Nuveen Municipal Income Fund, Inc. NMI
333 W. Wacker Dr.
Chicago, IL 60606
312-917-7700
Financial - investment management

Nuveen Municipal Market Opportunity
Fund, Inc. NMO
333 W. Wacker Dr.
Chicago, IL 60606
312-917-7700
Financial - investment management

Nuveen Municipal Value Fund, Inc. NUV
333 W. Wacker Dr.
Chicago, IL 60606
312-917-7700
Financial - investment management

Nuveen N. Carolina Premium Inc.
Municipal Fund NNC
333 W. Wacker Dr.
Chicago, IL 60606
312-917-7700
Financial - investment management

Nuveen New Jersey Inv. Qual. Municipal
Fd., Inc. NQJ
333 W. Wacker Dr.
Chicago, IL 60606
312-917-7700
Financial - investment management

Nuveen New Jersey Premium Inc.
Municipal Fd., Inc. NNJ
333 W. Wacker Dr.
Chicago, IL 60606
312-917-7700
Financial - investment management

Nuveen New York Investment Qual.
Municipal Fd., Inc. NQN
333 W. Wacker Dr.
Chicago, IL 60606
312-917-7700
Financial - investment management

Nuveen New York Municipal Value Fund,
Inc. NNY
333 W. Wacker Dr.
Chicago, IL 60606
312-917-7700
Financial - investment management

Nuveen New York Performance Plus
Municipal Fd., Inc. NNP
333 W. Wacker Dr.
Chicago, IL 60606
312-917-7700
Financial - investment management

Nuveen New York Quality Income
Municipal Fund, Inc. NUN
333 W. Wacker Dr.
Chicago, IL 60606
312-917-7700
Financial - investment management

Nuveen New York Select Quality
Municipal Fund, Inc. NVN
333 W. Wacker Dr.
Chicago, IL 60606
312-917-7700
Financial - investment management

Nuveen Ohio Quality Inc. Municipal Fund,
Inc. NUO
333 W. Wacker Dr.
Chicago, IL 60606
312-917-7700
Financial - investment management

Nuveen Pennsylvania Investment Qual.
Mun. Fund NQP
333 W. Wacker Dr.
Chicago, IL 60606
312-917-7700
Financial - investment management

Nuveen Pennsylvania Premium Income
Mun. Fd. 2 NPY
333 W. Wacker Dr.
Chicago, IL 60606
312-917-7700
Financial - investment management

Nuveen Performance Plus Municipal Fund,
Inc. NPP
333 W. Wacker Dr.
Chicago, IL 60606
312-917-7700
Financial - investment management

Nuveen Premier Insured Municipal Inc.
Fd., Inc. NIF
333 W. Wacker Dr.
Chicago, IL 60606
312-917-7700
Financial - investment management

Nuveen Premier Municipal Fund, Inc.
NPF
333 W. Wacker Dr.
Chicago, IL 60606
312-917-7700
Financial - investment management

Nuveen Premium Income Municipal
Fund 2, Inc. NPM
333 W. Wacker Dr.
Chicago, IL 60606
312-917-7700
Financial - investment management

Nuveen Premium Income Municipal
Fund 4, Inc. NPT
333 W. Wacker Dr.
Chicago, IL 60606
312-917-7700
Financial - investment management

Nuveen Premium Income Municipal Fund,
Inc. NPI
333 W. Wacker Dr.
Chicago, IL 60606
312-917-7700
Financial - investment management

Nuveen Quality Income Municipal Fund,
Inc. NQU
333 W. Wacker Dr.
Chicago, IL 60606
312-917-7700
Financial - investment management

Nuveen Select Maturities Municipal Fund
NIM
333 W. Wacker Dr.
Chicago, IL 60606
312-917-7700
Financial - investment management

Nuveen Select Quality Municipal Fund,
Inc. NQS
333 W. Wacker Dr.
Chicago, IL 60606
312-917-7700
Financial - investment management

Nuveen Select Tax-Free Income Portfolio
NXP
333 W. Wacker Dr.
Chicago, IL 60606
312-917-7700
Financial - investment management

Nuveen Select Tax-Free Income Portfolio 2
NXQ
333 W. Wacker Dr.
Chicago, IL 60606
312-917-7700
Financial - investment management

Nuveen Select Tax-Free Income Portfolio 3
NXR
333 W. Wacker Dr.
Chicago, IL 60606
312-917-7700
Financial - investment management

Nuveen Texas Quality Income Municipal
Fund NTX
333 W. Wacker Dr.
Chicago, IL 60606
312-917-7700
Financial - investment management

Nuveen Virginia Premium Income
Municipal Fund NPV
333 W. Wacker Dr.
Chicago, IL 60606
312-917-7700
Financial - investment management

NYMAGIC, INC. NYM
330 Madison Ave.
New York, NY 10017
212-551-0600
Insurance - property & casualty

Oak Industries Inc. OAK
1000 Winter St.
Waltham, MA 02154
617-890-0400
Electrical products - misc. O

Oakley, Inc. OO
10 Holland Dr.
Irvine, CA 92718
714-951-0991
Retail - misc. O

Oakwood Homes Corp. OH
2225 S. Holden Rd.
Greensboro, NC 27417
910-855-2400
Building - mobile homes & RV O

Occidental Petroleum Corp. OXY
10889 Wilshire Blvd.
Los Angeles, CA 90024
310-208-8800
Oil & gas - US integrated O DRP

Oceaneering International, Inc. OII
16001 Park Ten Place, Ste. 600
Houston, TX 77084
713-578-8868   Fax 713-578-5243
Oil & gas - field services O

Ocean Energy OEI
8440 Jefferson Highway, Ste. 420
Baton Rouge, LA 70809
504-927-1450
Produces oil & gas - Louisiana Gulf O

OEA, Inc. OEA
34501 E. Quincy Ave.
Denver, CO 80250
303-693-1248   Fax 303-699-6991
Electronics - military O

OEC Medical Systems, Inc. OXE
384 Wright Brothers Dr.
Salt Lake City, UT 84116
801-328-9300   Fax 801-328-4300
Medical products O

Office Depot, Inc. ODP
2200 Old Germantown Rd.
Delray Beach, FL 33445
561-278-4800
Retail - misc. O

Office Max, Inc. OMX
3605 Warrensville Center Rd.
Shaker Heights, OH 44122
216-921-6900   Fax 216-491-4040
Retail - misc. O

Ogden Corp. OG
2 Pennsylvania Plaza
New York, NY 10121
212-868-6100
Diversified operations O

OGE Energy Corp. OGE
321 N. Robinson, PO Box 321
Oklahoma City, OK 73101
405-272-3000
Utility - electric power DRP

Ohio Edison Co. OEC
76 S. Main St.
Akron, OH 44308
216-384-5100   Fax 800-633-4766
Utility - electric power O DRP

Oil-Dri Corporation of America ODC
410 N. Michigan Ave.
Chicago, IL 60611
312-321-1515   Fax 312-321-1271
Chemicals - specialty

Old Republic International Corp. ORI
307 N. Michigan Ave.
Chicago, IL 60601
312-346-8100
Insurance - property & casualty O DRP

Olin Corp. OLN
120 Long Ridge Rd.
Stamford, CT 06904
203-356-2000
Diversified operations O DRP

Olsten Corp. OLS
175 Broad Hollow Rd.
Melville, NY 11747
516-844-7800   Fax 516-844-7022
Business services O

OM Group, Inc. OMP
3800 Terminal Tower
Cleveland, OH 44113
216-781-0083   Fax 216-781-1502
Chemicals - specialty DRP

Omega Healthcare Investors, Inc. OHI
905 W. Eisenhower Circle
Ann Arbor, MI 48103
313-747-9790   Fax 313-996-0020
Financial - mortgages & related services

OMI Corp. OMM
90 Park Ave.
New York, NY 10016
212-986-1960
Transportation - shipping

Omnicare, Inc. OCR
255 E. Fifth St.
Cincinnati, OH 45202
513-762-6666   Fax 513-762-6678
Medical & dental supplies O DRP

Omnicom Group Inc. OMC
437 Madison Ave.
New York, NY 10022
212-415-3600   Fax 212-415-3530
Advertising O

One Valley Bancorp, Inc. OV
PO Box 1793
Charleston, WV 25326
304-348-7000
Banks - southeast

Oneida Ltd. OCQ
Oneida, NY 13421
315-361-3636
Appliances - household DRP

ONEOK Inc. OKE
100 W. Fifth St.
Tulsa, OK 74103
918-588-7000
Utility - gas distribution O DRP 3%

Oppenheimer Multi-Sector Income Trust
  OMS
Two World Trade Center
New York, NY 10048
212-323-0200
Financial - investment management

Orange-co, Inc. OJ
2022 U.S. Highway 17 South
Bartow, FL 33830
941-533-0551 Fax 941-533-6357
Agricultural operations

Oregon Steel Mills, Inc. OS
1000 S.W. Broadway, Ste. 2200
Portland, OR 97205
503-223-9228
Steel - specialty alloys O

Oriental Financial Group OFG
268 Munoz Rivera Ave., 5th Fl.
Hato Rey, PR 00918
787-766-1986
Savings & loan companies

Orion Capital Corp. OC
30 Rockefeller Plaza
New York, NY 10112
212-332-8080
Insurance - property & casualty

Oryx Energy Co. ORX
13155 Noel Rd.
Dallas, TX 75240
214-715-4000
Oil & gas - US exploration & production
  O

Osmonics, Inc. OSM
5951 Clearwater Dr.
Minnetonka, MN 55343
612-933-2277 Fax 612-933-0141
Pollution control equipment & services

O'Sullivan Industries Holdings, Inc. OSU
1900 Gulf St.
Lamar, MO 64759
417-682-3322
Furniture O

Outboard Marine Corp. OM
100 Sea-horse Drive
Waukegan, IL 60085
708-689-6200
Recreational products DRP

Overseas Shipholding Group, Inc. OSG
1114 Avenue of the Americas
New York, NY 10036
212-869-1222
Transportation - shipping

Owens & Minor, Inc. OMI
4800 Cox Rd.
Glen Allen, VA 23060
804-747-9794
Drugs & sundries - wholesale DRP

Owens-Corning OCF
One Owens Corning Pkwy.
Toledo, OH 43659
419-248-8000 Fax 419-248-8445
Building products - misc. O DRP

Owens-Illinois, Inc. OI
One SeaGate
Toledo, OH 43666
419-247-5000
Glass products O

Oxford Industries, Inc. OXM
222 Piedmont Ave., N.E.
Atlanta, GA 30308
404-659-2424 Fax 404-653-1545
Textiles - apparel

PacifiCorp PPW
700 N.E. Multnomah
Portland, OR 97232
503-731-2000
Utility - electric power O DRP

Pacific American Income Shares, Inc. PAI
PO Box 983
Pasadena, CA 91102
818-449-0309
Financial - investment management

Pacific Century Financial Corp. BOH
130 Merchant St.
Honolulu, HI 96813
808-847-3888
Banks - west O DRP

Pacific Gulf Properties Inc. PAG
4220 Von Karman, Second Fl.
Newport Beach, CA 92660
714-223-5000   Fax 714-223-5032
Real estate investment trust

PaineWebber Group Inc. PWJ
1285 Avenue of the Americas
New York, NY 10019
212-713-2000
Financial - investment bankers O DRP

Pakistan Investment Fund PKF
1221 Ave. of the Americas
New York, NY 10020
617-557-8742
Closed-end fund

Pall Corp. PLL
2200 Northern Blvd.
East Hills, NY 11548
516-484-5400   Fax 516-484-3529
Filtration products O DRP

Pameco Corp. PCN
1000 Center Place
Norcross, GA 30093
770-798-0700
Distributor heating, ventilating, a/c
  equipment

Panavision Inc. PVI
6219 De Soto Ave.
Woodland Hills, CA 91367
818-316-1000
Motion pictures & services

PAR Technology Corp. PTC
8383 Seneca Turnpike
New Hartford, NY 13413
315-738-0600
Advanced technology software

Paracelsus Healthcare Corp. PLS
515 W. Greens Rd., Ste. 800
Houston, TX 77067
713-873-6623
Hospitals

Paragon Trade Brands, Inc. PTB
180 Technology Pkwy.
Norcross, GA 30092
770-300-4000
Miscellaneous - not elsewhere classified O

Park Electrochemical Corp. PKE
5 Dakota Dr.
Lake Success, NY 11042
516-354-4100
Electrical components - misc. O

Parker Drilling Co. PKD
Eight E. Third St.
Tulsa, OK 74103
918-585-8221   Fax 918-585-1058
Oil & gas - field services O

Parker Hannifin Corp. PH
17325 Euclid Ave.
Cleveland, OH 44112
216-531-3000   Fax 216-383-9414
Instruments - control O DRP

Parkway Properties, Inc. PKY
188 E. Capitol St.
Jackson, MS 39201
601-948-4091
Real estate investment trust

PartnerRe Ltd. PRE
106 Pitts Bay Rd.
Pembroke, BA HM08
441-292-0888   Fax 441-292-6080
Catastrophe insurance

Patina Oil & Gas Corp. POG
4100 E. Mississippi Ave.
Denver, CO 80222
303-757-1110   Fax 303-757-1197
Oil & gas - US exploration & production

Patriot American Hospitality, Inc. PAH
3030 LBJ Fwy., Ste. 1500
Dallas, TX 75234
214-888-8000   Fax 214-888-8029
Real estate investment trust

Paxar Corp. PXR
275 N. Middletown Rd.
Pearl River, NY 10965
914-735-9200   Fax 914-735-9037
Machinery - general industrial

Payless Shoesource, Inc. PSS
3232 E. Sixth St.
Topeka, KS 66607
913-233-5171
Retail - apparel & shoes O

PEC Israel Economic Corp. IEC
511 Fifth Ave.
New York, NY 10017
212-687-2400
Financial - investment management

PECO Energy Co. PE
2301 Market St., PO Box 8699
Philadelphia, PA 19101
215-841-4000
Utility - electric power O DRP

Pediatrix Medical Group, Inc. PDX
1455 North Park Dr.
Fort Lauderdale, FL 33326
954-384-0175   Fax 954-384-7657
Business services

Penn Engineering & Manufacturing Co.
 PNN
PO Box 1000
Danboro, PA 18916
215-766-8853   Fax 215-766-7366
Metal products - fasteners

PennCorp Financial Group, Inc. PFG
745 Fifth Ave., Ste. 500
New York, NY 10151
212-832-0700
Insurance - accident & health

Penney (J.C.) Co., Inc. JCP
6501 Legacy Dr.
Plano, TX 75024
214-431-1000
Department stores O DRP

Pennsylvania Enterprises, Inc. PNT
One PEI Center
Wilkes-Barre, PA 18711
717-829-8843
Utility - gas distribution DRP

Penn Traffic PNF
1200 State Fair Blvd.
Syracuse, NY 13221
315-453-7284
Operates supermarkets

Penn Virginia Corp. PVA
100 Matsonford Rd, Suite 200
Radnor, PA 19807
610-687-8900
Coal, oil & gas props in WV, VA

Pennzoil Co. PZL
Pennzoil Place, PO Box 2967
Houston, TX 77252
713-546-4000
Oil & gas - US integrated O DRP

Pentair, Inc. PNR
1500 County Rd., Ste. B2 West
St. Paul, MN 55113
612-636-7920
Paper & paper products DRP

Peoples Energy Corp. PGL
122 S. Michigan Ave.
Chicago, IL 60603
312-431-4000   Fax 312-431-4082
Utility - gas distribution DRP

Pep Boys Manny, Moe, and Jack (The)
 PBY
3111 W. Allegheny Ave.
Philadelphia, PA 19132
215-229-9000
Auto parts & accessories retailer O DRP

PepsiCo, Inc. PEP
700 Anderson Hill Rd.
Purchase, NY 10577
914-253-2000
Beverages - soft drinks O DRP

Pepsi-Cola Puerto Rico Bottling PPO
KM 19.4, Barrio Candeleria
Toa Baja, PR 00949
787-251-2000
Sells, distributes soft drinks in PR

Perkin-Elmer PKN
761 Main Ave.
Norwalk, CT 06859
203-762-1000
Produces analytical instruments O DRP

Permian Basin Royalty Trust PBT
PO Box 1317
Fort Worth, TX 76101
817-390-6905
Oil & gas - US royalty trust

Personnel Group of America, Inc. PGA
6302 Fairview Rd., Ste. 201
Charlotte, NC 28210
704-442-5100
Personnel

Petro-Canada PCZ
150 6th Ave. S.W.
Calgary, AB T2P3E3
403-296-8000
Canadian oil & gas company

Petroleum & Resources Corp. PEO
Seven St. Paul St., Ste. 1140
Baltimore, MD 21202
410-752-5900
Financial - investment management

Petroleum Geo-Services PGO
16010 Barkers Point Lane, Ste. 600
Houston, TX 77079
713-589-7935   Fax 713-589-1482
Oilfield service co. - Norway O

Pfizer Inc. PFE
235 E. 42nd St.
New York, NY 10017
212-573-2323   Fax 212-573-7851
Drugs O DRP

PG&E Corp. PCG
77 Beale St., PO Box 770000
San Francisco, CA 94177
415-973-7000
Utility - electric power O DRP

Pharmaceutical Resources, Inc. PRX
One Ram Ridge Rd.
Spring Valley, NY 10977
914-425-7100   Fax 914-425-7907
Drugs - generic O

Pharmacia & Upjohn, Inc. PNU
7000 Portage Rd.
Kalamazoo, MI 49001
616-833-4000
Drugs O DRP

Phelps Dodge Corp. PD
2600 N. Central Ave.
Phoenix, AZ 85004
602-234-8100
Metals - nonferrous O DRP

Philadelphia Suburban Corp. PSC
762 Lancaster Ave.
Bryn Mawr, PA 19010
610-527-8000   Fax 610-645-1061
Utility - water supply DRP 5%

Philip Morris Companies Inc. MO
120 Park Ave.
New York, NY 10017
212-880-5000
Tobacco O DRP

Philip Services PHV
100 King St. West
Hamilton, ON L8N4J6
905-521-1600   Fax 905-521-9160
Waste management O

Phillips Petroleum Co. P
Phillips Bldg.
Bartlesville, OK 74004
918-661-6600
Oil & gas - US integrated O DRP

Phillips-Van Heusen Corp. PVH
1290 Avenue of the Americas
New York, NY 10104
212-541-5200
Textiles - apparel O

PHP Healthcare Corp. PPH
4900 Seminary Rd., 12th Fl.
Alexandria, VA 22311
703-998-7808
Healthcare - outpatient & home O

Physicians Resource Group, Inc. PRG
5430 LBJ Fwy.
Dallas, TX 75240
214-982-8200
Medical services O

Piccadilly Cafeterias, Inc. PIC
3232 Sherwood Forest Blvd.
Baton Rouge, LA 70816
504-293-9440
Retail - food & restaurants DRP 5%

Piedmont Natural Gas Co., Inc. PNY
1915 Rexford Rd.
Charlotte, NC 28211
704-364-3120
Utility - gas distribution DRP 5%

Pier 1 Imports, Inc. PIR
301 Commerce St., Ste. 600
Fort Worth, TX 76102
817-878-8000
Retail - discount & variety O

Pierce Leahy PLH
631 Park Ave.
King of Prussia, PA 19406
610-992-8200
Archive records management

Pilgrim America Bank & Thrift Fund, Inc.
 PBS
40 N. Central Ave., Ste. 1200
Phoenix, AZ 85004
800-334-3444
Financial - investment management

Pilgrim America Prime Rate Trust PPR
40 N. Central Ave., Ste. 1200
Phoenix, AZ 85004
800-336-3436
Financial - investment management

Pilgrim's Pride Corp. CHX
110 S. Texas St.
Pittsburg, TX 75686
903-855-1000   Fax 903-856-7505
Food - meat products

Pillowtex Corp. PTX
4111 Mint Way
Dallas, TX 75237
214-333-3225   Fax 214-330-6016
Textiles - home furnishings

PIMCO Advisors L.P. PA
One Station Place, 7 South
Stamford, CT 06902
203-352-4900
Financial - investment management

PIMCO Commercial Mortgage Securities
Tr., Inc. PCM
840 Newport Center Dr.
Newport Beach, CA 92660
800-213-3606
Financial - investment management

Pinkerton's, Inc. PKT
15910 Ventura Blvd., Ste. 900
Encino, CA 91436
818-380-8800
Business services

Pinnacle West Capital Corp. PNW
400 E. Van Buren St., Ste. 700
Phoenix, AZ 85004
602-379-2500
Utility - electric power O DRP

Pioneer Hi-Bred International, Inc. PHB
400 Locust St.
Des Moines, IA 50309
515-248-4800
Agricultural operations O DRP

Pioneer Interest Shares, Inc. MUO
60 State St.
Boston, MA 02109
617-742-7825
Financial - investment management

Pioneer Natural Resources PXD
5205 North O'Connor Blvd.
Irving, TX 75039
972-444-9001
Oil & gas exploration & production O

Pitney Bowes Inc. PBI
1 Elmcroft Rd.
Stamford, CT 06926
203-356-5000   Fax 203-351-6303
Office equipment & supplies O DRP

Pittston Brink's Group PZB
1000 Virginia Center Pkwy.
Glen Allen, VA 23060
804-553-3600
Business services O

Pittston Burlington Group PZX
1000 Virginia Center Pkwy.
Glen Allen, VA 23060
804-553-3600
Transportation - air freight

Pittston Minerals Group PZM
1000 Virginia Center Pkwy.
Glen Allen, VA 23060
804-553-3600
Coal

Pittway Corp. PRY
200 S. Wacker Dr., Ste. 700
Chicago, IL 60606
312-831-1070
Diversified operations

Placer Dome PDG
1055 Dunsmuir St., Suite 1600
Vancouver, BC V7X1V1
604-682-7082
Gold & precious metals mining O

Plantronics, Inc. PLT
337 Encinal St., PO Box 1802
Santa Cruz, CA 95061
408-426-6060
Telecommunications equipment

Playboy Enterprises, Inc. PLA
680 N. Lake Shore Dr.
Chicago, IL 60611
312-751-8000
Publishing - periodicals

Playtex Products, Inc. PYX
300 Nyala Farms
Westport, CT 06880
203-341-4000
Cosmetics & toiletries O

Plum Creek Timber Co., L.P. PCL
999 Third Ave., Ste. 2300
Seattle, WA 98104
206-467-3600
Building products - wood O

PMI Group PMA
601 Montgomery St.
San Francisco, CA 94111
415-788-7878
Provides insurance to mortgage lenders O

PNC Bank Corp. PNC
249 Fifth Ave.
Pittsburgh, PA 15222
412-762-2666
Banks - northeast O DRP

Pogo Producing Co. PPP
5 Greenway Plaza, PO Box 2504
Houston, TX 77252
713-297-5000
Oil & gas - US exploration & production
O

Polaris Industries, Inc. PII
2424 S. 130th Circle
Omaha, NE 68144
800-255-1345
Leisure & recreational products

Polaroid Corp. PRd.
549 Technology Square
Cambridge, MA 02139
617-577-2000
Photographic equipment & supplies O
DRP

Policy Management Systems Corp. PMS
One PMS Center
Blythewood, SC 29016
803-735-4000
Computers - software O

Polo Ralph Lauren Corp. RL
650 Madison Ave.
New York, NY 10022
212-318-7000
Men's & women's clothes retailer

Polymer Group, Inc. PGH
4838 Jenkins Ave.
North Charleston, SC 29405
803-744-5174
Textiles - mill products

Pope & Talbot, Inc. POP
1500 S.W. First Ave.
Portland, OR 97201
503-228-9161
Paper & paper products

Portugal Fund, (The) PGF
153 E. 53rd Street, 58th Floor
New York, NY 10022
212-832-2626
Financial - investment management

Post Properties, Inc. PPS
3350 Cumberland Circle
Atlanta, GA 30339
770-850-4400
Real estate operations

Potash Corp. of Saskatchewan POT
122 1st Ave. South
Saskatoon, SK 7K7G3
306-933-8500
Fertilizer producer O

Potlatch Corp. PCH
One Maritime Plaza
San Francisco, CA 94111
415-576-8800
Paper & paper products O DRP

Potomac Electric Power Co. POM
1900 Pennsylvania Ave., N.W.
Washington, DC 20068
202-872-2456
Utility - electric power O DRP

PP&L Resources, Inc. PPL
Two N. Ninth St.
Allentown, PA 18101
610-774-5151   Fax 610-774-5281
Utility - electric power O DRP

PPG Industries, Inc. PPG
One PPG Place
Pittsburgh, PA 15272
412-434-3131
Chemicals - diversified O DRP

Praxair, Inc. PX
39 Old Ridgebury Rd.
Danbury, CT 06810
203-837-2000   Fax 203-837-2454
Miscellaneous - not elsewhere classified
O DRP

Precision Castparts Corp. PCP
4600 S.E. Harney Dr.
Portland, OR 97206
503-777-3881
Aerospace - aircraft equipment

Preferred Income Fund Inc. PFD
301 E. Colorado Blvd.
Pasadena, CA 91101
818-795-7300
Financial - investment management

Preferred Income Management Fund Inc.
PFM
301 E. Colorado Blvd.
Pasadena, CA 91101
818-795-7300
Financial - investment management

Preferred Income Opportunity Fund Inc.
PFO
301 E. Colorado Blvd.
Pasadena, CA 91101
818-795-7300
Financial - investment management

Premdor Inc. PI
1600 Britannia East
Mississauga, ON L4W1J2
905-670-6500
Mnaufactures doors & moldings

Premium Wear, Inc. PWA
8000 W. 78th St., Ste. 400
Edina, MN 55439
612-943-5000
Apparel

Prentiss Properties Trust PP
3890 W. Northwest Hwy.
Dallas, TX 75220
214-654-0886   Fax 214-654-5818
Real estate invesment trust

Presley Companies PDC
19 Corporate Plaza
Newport Beach, CA 92660
714-640-6400
Homebuilding

Pride Companies, L.P. PRF
500 Chestnut, Ste. 1300
Abilene, TX 79602
915-674-8000
Oil & gas - production & pipeline

Primark Corp. PMK
1000 Winter St., Ste. 4300N
Waltham, MA 02154
617-466-6611
Diversified operations

Prime Hospitality Corp. PDQ
700 Route 46 East
Fairfield, NJ 07004
201-882-1010   Fax 201-882-8577
Hotels & motels

Prime Retail PRT
100 E. Pratt St.
Baltimore, MD 21202
410-234-0782
Real estate investment trust

Procter & Gamble PG
1 Procter & Gamble Plaza
Cincinnati, OH 45202
513-983-1100
Household & personal care products
 O DRP

Proffitt's, Inc. PFT
115 N. Calderwood
Alcoa, TN 37701
615-983-7000   Fax 615-981-6336
Retail - regional department stores DRP

Progressive Corp. PGR
6300 Wilson Mills Rd.
Mayfield Village, OH 44143
216-461-5000
Specialty insurance - property/casualty O

Promus Hotel Corp. PRH
850 Ridge Lake Blvd., Ste. 400
Memphis, TN 38120
901-680-7200   Fax 901-680-7220
Hotels & motels O DRP

Prospect Street High Income Portfolio Inc.
 PHY
One Exchange Place, 37th Fl.
Boston, MA 02109
617-742-3800
Financial - investment management DRP

Protective Life Corp. PL
2801 Highway 280 South
Birmingham, AL 35223
205-879-9230
Insurance - life DRP

Providence Energy Corp. PVY
100 Weybosset St.
Providence, RI 02903
401-272-9191
Utility - gas distribution DRP

Provident Cos. PVT
One Fountain Square
Chattanooga, TN 37402
615-755-1011
Insurance - accident & health O DRP

Providian Financial PVN
201 Mission St.
San Francisco, CA 94105
415-543-0404
Consumer finance O

PS Group, Inc. PSG
4370 La Jolla Village Dr.
San Diego, CA 92122
619-642-2999
Leasing DRP

Public Service Company of New Mexico
 PNM
Alvarado Square
Albuquerque, NM 87158
505-241-2700
Utility - electric power DRP

Public Service Company of North
 Carolina, Inc. PGS
400 Cox Rd., PO Box 1398
Gastonia, NC 28053
704-864-6731
Utility - gas distribution DRP 5%

Public Service Enterprise Group Inc. PEG
80 Park Plaza, PO Box 1171
Newark, NJ 07101
201-430-7000
Utility - electric power O DRP

Public Storage, Inc. PSA
600 N. Brand Blvd.
Glendale, CA 91203
818-244-8080
Real estate investment trust O

Puerto Rican Cement PRN
PO Box 3644087
San Juan, PR 00936
787-783-3000
Manufacturer of cement

Puget Sound Energy, Inc. PSD
PO Box 97034
Bellevue, WA 98009
206-454-6363
Utility - electric power O DRP

Pulitzer Publishing Co. PTZ
900 N. Tucker Blvd.
St. Louis, MO 63101
314-340-8000
Broadcasting - radio & TV

Pulte Corp. PHM
33 Bloomfield Hills Parkway
Bloomfield Hills, MI 48304
810-647-2750
Building - residential & commercial O

Putnam Convertible Opportunities &
  Income Trust PCV
One Post Office Square
Boston, MA 02109
617-292-1000
Financial - investment management

Putnam Dividend Income Trust PDI
One Post Office Square
Boston, MA 02109
617-292-1000
Financial - investment management

Putnam High Income Convertible Bond
  Fund PCF
One Post Office Square
Boston, MA 02109
617-292-1000
Financial - investment management

Putnam High Yield Municipal Trust PYM
One Post Office Square
Boston, MA 02109
617-292-1000
Financial - investment management

Putnam Intermediate Government Income
  Trust PGT
One Post Office Square
Boston, MA 02109
617-292-1000
Financial - investment management

Putnam Investment Grade Municipal Trust
  PGM
One Post Office Square
Boston, MA 02109
617-292-1000
Financial - investment management

Putnam Investment Grade Municipal Trust
  II PMG
One Post Office Square
Boston, MA 02109
617-292-1000
Financial - investment management

Putnam Managed High Yield Trust PTM
One Post Office Square
Boston, MA 02109
617-292-1000
Financial - investment management

Putnam Managed Municipal Income Trust
  PMM
One Post Office Square
Boston, MA 02109
617-292-1000
Financial - investment management

Putnam Master Income Trust PMT
One Post Office Square
Boston, MA 02109
617-292-1000
Financial - investment management

Putnam Master Intermediate Income
  Trust PIM
One Post Office Square
Boston, MA 02109
617-292-1000
Financial - investment management

Putnam Municipal Opportunities Trust
  PMO
One Post Office Square
Boston, MA 02109
617-292-1000
Financial - investment management

Putnam Premier Income Trust PPT
One Post Office Square
Boston, MA 02109
617-292-1000
Financial - investment management

Putnam Tax-Free Health Care Fund PMH
One Post Office Square
Boston, MA 02109
617-292-1000
Financial - investment management

PXRE Corp. PXT
399 Thornall St., 14th Fl.
Edison, NJ 08837
732-906-8100   Fax 732-906-9157
Insurance - property & casualty

QMS, Inc. AQM
One Magnum Pass, PO Box 81250
Mobile, AL 36618
334-633-4300   Fax 334-633-2523
Computers - peripheral equipment O

Quaker Chemical Corp. KWR
Elm and Lee Sts.
Conshohocken, PA 19428
610-832-4000
Chemicals - specialty

Quaker Oats OAT
321 N. Clark St.
Chicago, IL 60610
312-222-7111
Producer packaged food & beverages
  O DRP

Quaker State Corp. KSF
225 Elm St.
Oil City, PA 16301
814-676-7676
Oil refining & marketing O DRP

Quanex Corp. NX
1900 W. Loop South, Ste. 1500
Houston, TX 77027
713-961-4600
Steel - pipes & tubes O DRP

Quebecor Printing PRW
612 Saint-Jacques St.
Montreal, ON H3C4M8
514-954-0101   Fax 514-954-9624
Specialty printing

Quest Diagnostics Inc. DGX
One Malcolm Ave.
Teterboro, NJ 07608
201-393-5000
Medical services O

Questar Corp. STR
180 E. First South
Salt Lake City, UT 84145
801-534-5000
Utility - gas distribution O DRP

R. G. Barry Corp. RGB
13405 Yarmouth Rd., N.W.
Pickerington, OH 43147
614-864-6400
Shoes & related apparel

R.R. Donnelley & Sons Co. DNY
77 W. Wacker Dr.
Chicago, IL 60601
312-326-8000
Printing - commercial

Ralcorp Holdings, Inc. RAH
800 Market St.
St. Louis, MO 63101
314-877-7000
Food - misc.

Ralston Purina Co. RAL
Checkerboard Square
St. Louis, MO 63164
314-982-1000
Food - misc. O DRP

Ramco-Gershenson Property Trust RPT
733 Third Ave.
New York, NY 10017
212-370-8585   Fax 212-972-0423
Real estate investment trust

Ranger Oil RGO
321 6th Ave. S.W.
Calgary, AB T2P3H3
403-232-5200
Oil & gas exploration & production O

Raychem Corp. RYC
300 Constitution Dr.
Menlo Park, CA 94025
415-361-3333
Electrical products - misc. O

Raymond James Financial, Inc. RJF
880 Carillon Parkway
St. Petersburg, FL 33716
813-578-3800
Financial - investment bankers O

Rayonier Timberlands, L.P. LOG
1177 Summer St.
Stamford, CT 06905
203-348-7000
Building products - wood O

Rayonier, Inc. RYN
1177 Summer St.
Stamford, CT 06905
203-348-7000
Paper & paper products

Raytech Corp. RAY
One Corporate Dr., Ste. 512
Shelton, CT 06484
203-925-8023
Automotive & trucking - original
  equipment

Raytheon Corp. RTN
141 Spring St.
Lexington, MA 01273
617-862-6600   Fax 617-860-2172
Diversified operations O DRP

RCM Strategic Global Government Fund,
Inc. RCS
4 Embarcadero Center, 30th Fl.
San Francisco, CA 94111
415-954-5400   Fax 415-954-8200
Financial - investment management

Reader's Digest Association RDA
Pleasantville, NY 10570
914-238-1000
Publishing O DRP

Realty Income Corp. O
220 W. Crest St.
Escondido, CA 92025
760-741-2111   Fax 760-741-2235
Real estate investment trust

Realty ReFund Trust RRF
1385 Eaton Center
Cleveland, OH 44114
216-771-7663
Real estate investment trust

Reckson Associates Realty Corp. RA
225 Broadhollow Rd.
Melville, NY 11747
516-694-6900
Real estate investment trust

Red Roof Inns, Inc. RRI
4355 Davidson Rd.
Hilliard, OH 43026
614-876-3200
Hotels & motels

Reebok International Ltd. RBK
100 Technology Center Dr.
Stoughton, MA 02072
617-341-5000
Shoes & related apparel O

Regency Realty Corp. REG
121 W. Forsyth St., Ste. 200
Jacksonville, FL 32202
904-356-7000
Real estate investment trust

Reinsurance Group of America, Inc. RGA
666 Mason Ridge Center Dr.
St. Louis, MO 63141
314-453-7300
Insurance - multi line & misc.

ReliaStar Financial Corp. RLR
20 Washington Ave. South
Minneapolis, MN 55401
612-372-5432   Fax 612-342-3966
Insurance - life O DRP 4%

Reliance Group Holdings, Inc. REL
55 E. 52nd St.
New York, NY 10055
212-909-1100   Fax 212-909-1864
Insurance - multi line & misc. O

Reliance Steel and Aluminum Co. RS
2550 E. 25th St.
Los Angeles, CA 90058
213-582-2272
Metal processing & fabrication

Rental Service Corp. RSV
14505 N. Hayden Rd., Ste. 322
Scottsdale, AZ 85260
602-905-3300
Leasing

Republic Group, Inc. RGC
811 E. 30th Ave.
Hutchinson, KS 67502
316-727-2700   Fax 316-727-2727
Building products - misc.

Republic Industries, Inc. RII
2849 Paces Ferry Rd. N.W.
Atlanta, GA 30339
770-431-7140
Pollution control equipment & services O

Republic New York Corp. RNB
452 Fifth Ave.
New York, NY 10018
212-525-6100   Fax 212-525-5678
Banks - northeast O

Resource Mortgage Capital RMR
230 South Tryon St.
Charlotte, NC 28288
800-829-8432
Reatl estate investment trust DRP 3%

Revlon, Inc. REV
625 Madison Ave.
New York, NY 10022
212-527-4000
Cosmetics & toiletries O

REX Stores Corp. RSC
2875 Needmore Rd.
Dayton, OH 45414
937-276-3931
Retail - misc.

Reynolds Metals Co. RLM
6601 W. Broad St.
Richmond, VA 23261
804-281-2000   Fax 804-281-4160
Metals - nonferrous O DRP

Reynolds and Reynolds Co. REY
115 S. Ludlow St.
Dayton, OH 45402
937-443-2000
Paper - business forms O DRP

RFS Hotel Investors, Inc. RFS
1213 Park Place Center
Memphis, TN 38119
901-767-5154
Real estate investment trust O

Rhone-Poulenc Rorer Inc. RPR
500 Arcola Rd.
Collegeville, PA 19426
610-454-8000
Drugs O

Richfood Holdings, Inc. RFH
PO Box 26967
Richmond, VA 23261
804-746-6000
Food - wholesale O

RightChoice Managed Care, Inc. RIT
1831 Chestnut St.
St. Louis, MO 63103
314-923-4444
Business services

Rio Hotel and Casino, Inc. RHC
3700 W. Flamingo Rd.
Las Vegas, NV 89103
702-252-7733
Leisure & recreational services O

Rite Aid Corp. RAD
30 Hunter Ln.
Camp Hill, PA 17011
717-761-2633   Fax 717-731-3870
Retail - drug stores O DRP

RJR Nabisco, Inc. RN
1301 Avenue of the Americas
New York, NY 10019
212-258-5600
Tobacco O DRP

RLI Corp. RLI
9025 N. Lindbergh Dr.
Peoria, IL 61615
309-692-1000
Insurance - accident & health DRP

RMI Titanium Co. RTI
1000 Warren Ave., PO Box 269
Niles, OH 44446
303-544-7700
Metals - nonferrous O

Robert Half International Inc. RHI
2884 Sand Hill Rd., Ste. 200
Menlo Park, CA 94025
415-854-9700
Business services

Robertson-Ceco Corp. RHH
222 Berkeley St.
Boston, MA 02116
617-424-5500
Diversified operations

Rochester Gas and Electric Corp. RGS
89 East Ave.
Rochester, NY 14649
716-546-2700
Utility - electric power DRP

Rock-Tenn Co. RKT
504 Thrasher St.
Norcross, GA 30071
770-448-2193
Paper & paper products

Rockwell International Corp. ROK
2201 Seal Beach Blvd.
Seal Beach, CA 90740
310-797-3311   Fax 310-797-5049
Aerospace - aircraft equipment O DRP

Rogers Cantel Mobile Communications
  RCN
40 King St., West
Toronto, ON M5H3Y2
416-864-2348   Fax 416-864-2365
Telecommunications services O

Rohm and Haas Co. ROH
Independence Mall West
Philadelphia, PA 19106
215-592-3000   Fax 215-592-3377
Chemicals - diversified O

Rollins Truck Leasing Corp. RLC
One Rollins Plaza, PO Box 1791
Wilmington, DE 19899
302-479-2700
Leasing O DRP

Rollins, Inc. ROL
2170 Piedmont Rd., N.E.
Atlanta, GA 30324
404-888-2000
Building - maintenance & services DRP

Roper Industries, Inc. ROP
160 Ben Burton Rd.
Bogart, GA 30622
706-369-7170
Instruments - control

Rouge Industries Co. ROU
3001 Miller Rd.
Dearborn, MI 48121
313-390-6877
Steel - production O

Rouse Co. RSE
10275 Little Patuxent Pkwy.
Columbia, MD 21044
410-992-6000
Land development DRP

Rowan Companies, Inc. RDC
2800 Post Oak Blvd.
Houston, TX 77056
713-621-7800
Oil & gas - offshore drilling O

Rowe Furniture Corp. ROW
239 Rowan St.
Salem, VA 24153
703-389-8671
Furniture

Royal Appliance Mfg. Co. RAM
650 Alpha Dr.
Cleveland, OH 44143
216-449-6150
Appliances - household O

Royce Value Trust, Inc. RVT
1414 Avenue of the Americas
New York, NY 10019
800-221-4268
Financial - investment management

RPC, Inc. RES
2170 Piedmont Rd. N.E.
Atlanta, GA 30324
404-888-2950
Oil & gas - field services

Rubbermaid Inc. RBD
1147 Akron Rd.
Wooster, OH 44691
216-264-6464   Fax 216-287-2982
Rubber & plastic products O DRP

Ruby Tuesday's, Inc. RI
4721 Morrison Dr.
Mobile, AL 36609
334-344-3000   Fax 334-344-3066
Retail - food & restaurants O

Ruddick Corp. RDK
2000 Two First Union Center
Charlotte, NC 28282
704-372-5404
Retail - supermarkets DRP

Russ Berrie & Co., Inc. RUS
111 Bauer Dr.
Oakland, NJ 07436
201-337-9000
Drugs & sundries - wholesale O

Russell Corp. RML
1 Lee St.
Alexander City, AL 35010
205-329-4000
Textiles - apparel O DRP

Ryder System, Inc. R
3600 N.W. 82nd Ave.
Miami, FL 33166
305-593-3726   Fax 305-593-4196
Leasing O DRP

Ryerson Tull, Inc. RT
2621 W. 15th Pl.
Chicago, IL 60608
312-762-2121
Metal products - distribution

Ryland Group RYL
1000 Broken Land Parkway
Columbia, MD 21044
410-715-7000
Homebuilder & mortgage lender O

Sabine Royalty Trust SBR
901 Main St., 12th Fl.
Dallas, TX 75202
214-508-2400
Oil & gas - US royalty trust

SABRE Group Holdings TSG
4255 Amon Carter Blvd.
Fort Worth, TX 76155
817-931-7300
Information technology for travel industry
O

Safeguard Scientifics, Inc. SFE
435 Devon Park Dr.
Wayne, PA 19087
610-293-0600   Fax 610-293-0601
Financial - investment bankers O

Safeway Inc. SWY
Fourth and Jackson Sts.
Oakland, CA 94660
510-891-3000
Retail - supermarkets O

Saks Holdings, Inc. SKS
12 E. 49th St.
New York, NY 10017
212-599-4700
Retail - major department stores O

Salant Corp. SLT
1114 Avenue of the Americas
New York, NY 10036
212-221-7500
Textiles - apparel

Salomon Brothers Fund SBF
7 World Trade Center
New York, NY 10048
800-825-6666
Closed-end investment company

Salomon Brothers High Income Fund Inc.
  HIF
Seven World Trade Center
New York, NY 10048
800-221-7065
Financial - investment management

Salomon Brothers Worldwide Income
  Fund, Inc. SBW
Seven World Trade Center
New York, NY 10048
800-221-7065
Financial - investment management

San Juan Basin Royalty Trust SJT
PO Box 2604
Fort Worth, TX 76113
817-884-4630
Oil & gas - US royalty trust

Santa Fe Energy Resources, Inc. SFR
1616 S. Voss, Ste. 1000
Houston, TX 77057
713-783-2401
Oil & gas - US exploration & production
  O

Santa Fe Energy Trust SFF
600 Travis St., Ste. 1150
Houston, TX 77002
713-216-5100
Oil & gas - US royalty trust

Santa Fe International SDC
5420 LBJ Freeway
Dallas, TX 75240
972-701-7300
Oil & gas, offshore & land driller

Santa Fe Pacific Pipeline Partners, L.P.
  SFL
1100 Town & Country Rd.
Orange, CA 92868
714-560-4400
Oil & gas - production & pipeline DRP

Sara Lee Corp. SLE
Three First National Plaza
Chicago, IL 60602
312-726-2600
Diversified operations O DRP

Saul Centers, Inc. BFS
8401 Connecticut Ave.
Chevy Chase, MD 20815
301-986-6000   Fax 301-986-6079
Real estate investment trust DRP 3%

Sbarro, Inc. SBA
763 Larkfield Rd.
Commack, NY 11725
516-864-0200
Retail - food & restaurants O

SBC Communications Inc. SBC
175 E. Houston, PO Box 2933
San Antonio, TX 78299
210-821-4105
Utility - telephone DRP

SCANA Corp. SCG
1426 Main St.
Columbia, SC 29201
803-748-3000
Electrical/natural gas utility operations O
  DRP

Schawk, Inc. SGK
1695 River Rd.
Des Plaines, IL 60018
847-827-9494   Fax 847-827-1264
Imaging systems & products

Schering-Plough Corp. SGP
One Giralda Farms
Madison, NJ 07940
201-822-7000   Fax 201-822-7048
Drugs O DRP

Schlumberger Ltd. SLB
277 Park Ave.
New York, NY 10172
212-350-9400
Oil & gas - field services O

Schwab (Charles) Corp. SCH
101 Montgomery St.
San Francisco, CA 94104
415-627-7000
Financial - investment brokerage firm O
  DRP

Schweitzer-Mauduit International, Inc.
  SWM
100 N. Point East
Alpharetta, GA 30202
800-514-0186
Paper & paper products

SCI Systems, Inc. SCI
2101 Clinton Ave.
Huntsville, AL 35805
205-882-4800
Electronics - components & systems

Scientific Games Holding Corp, SG
1500 Blue Grass Lakes Pkwy.
Alpharetta, GA 30201
404-664-3700
Leisure & recreational products O

Scientific-Atlanta, Inc. SFA
One Technology Pkwy., South
Atlanta, GA 30092
404-903-5000
Telecommunications equipment O DRP

Scotsman Industries, Inc. SCT
775 Corporate Woods Parkway
Vernon Hills, IL 60061
847-215-4500
Building products - a/c & heating

Scotts Co. SMG
14111 Scottslawn Rd.
Marysville, OH 43041
513-644-0011
Garden hardware & tools O

Scott's Liquid Gold Inc. SGD
4880 Havana St.
Denver, CO 80239
303-373-4860
Diversified operations

SCPIE Holdings Inc. SKP
9441 W. Olympic Blvd.
Beverly Hills, CA 90213
310-551-5900 Fax 800-870-6622
Insurance - multi line & misc.

Scripps (E.W.) Co. SSP
312 Walnut St.
Ciccinnati, OH 45201
513-977-3000
Publishing

Scudder New Asia Fund, Inc. SAF
345 Park Ave.
New York, NY 10154
800-349-4281
Financial - investment management

Scudder New Europe Fund, Inc. NEF
345 Park Ave.
New York, NY 10154
800-349-4281
Financial - investment management

Scudder Spain & Portugal IBF
345 Park Ave.
New York, NY 10154
800-349-4281
Closed-end fund

Scudder World Income Opportunities
Fund, Inc. SWI
345 Park Ave.
New York, NY 10154
800-349-4281
Financial - investment management

SEACOR Smit, Inc. CKH
5000 Railroad Ave.
Morgan City, LA 70380
504-385-3475
Oil & gas - field services

Seagate Technology, Inc. SEG
920 Disc Dr.
Scotts Valley, CA 95066
408-438-6550 Fax 408-438-4127
Computers - peripheral equipment O

Seagram Co. VO
1430 Peel St.
Montreal, QC H3A1S9
514-849-5271
Alcoholic beverages - producer O

Seagull Energy Corp. SGO
1001 Fannin St., Ste. 1700
Houston, TX 77002
713-951-4700
Oil & gas - production & pipeline O

Sealed Air Corp. SEE
Park 80 East
Saddle Brook, NJ 07662
201-791-7600 Fax 201-703-4205
Containers - paper & plastic O

Sears, Roebuck and Co. S
3333 Beverly Rd.
Hoffman Estates, IL 60179
847-286-2500
Diversified operations O DRP

Security Capital Pacific Trust PTR
7777 Market Center Ave.
El Paso, TX 79912
915-877-3900
Real estate investment trust DRP 2%

Seitel, Inc. SEI
50 Briar Hollow Lane West
Houston, TX 77027
713-627-1990
Oil & gas - field services O

Seligman Quality Municipal Fund, Inc.
 SQF
100 Park Ave.
New York, NY 10017
212-850-1864
Financial - investment management

Seligman Select Municipal Fund, Inc. SEL
100 Park Ave.
New York, NY 10017
800-622-4597
Financial - investment management

Sempra Energy SRA
101 Ash St.
San Diego, CA 92101
619-696-2000
Utility - electric power DRP

Senior High Income Portfolio, Inc. ARK
800 Scudders Mill Rd.
Plainsboro, NJ 08536
609-282-2800
Financial - investment management

Sensormatic Electronics Corp. SRM
500 N.W. 12th Ave.
Deerfield Beach, FL 33442
305-420-2000   Fax 305-420-2017
Protection - safety equipment & services
 O

Sequa Corp. SQAA
200 Park Ave.
New York, NY 10166
212-986-5500   Fax 212-370-1969
Chemicals - specialty

Service Corporation International SRV
1929 Allen Parkway
Houston, TX 77019
713-522-5141
Funeral & services related O

Service Experts, Inc. SVE
1134 Murfreesboro Rd.
Nashville, TN 37217
615-391-4600
Building products - a/c & heating O

Service Merchandise Co., Inc. SME
7100 Service Merchandise Dr.
Brentwood, TN 37027
615-660-6000
Retail - catalog showrooms O

ServiceMaster SVM
One ServiceMaster Way
Downers Grove, IL 60515
630-271-1300   Fax 630-271-2710
Building - maintenance & services DRP

Servico, Inc. SER
1601 Belvedere Rd.
West Palm Beach, FL 33406
561-689-9970   Fax 561-689-0321
Hotels & motels

Shared Medical Systems SMS
51 Valley Stream Parkway
Malvern, PA 19355
610-219-6300
Computer-based information systems

Shaw Group SGR
11100 Mead Rd., 2nd Fl.
Baton Rouge, LA 70816
504-296-1140
Industrial piping for utility & refining O

Shaw Industries, Inc. SHX
PO Drawer 2128
Dalton, GA 30722
706-278-3812
Textiles - home furnishings DRP

Shelby Williams Industries, Inc. SY
1348 Merchandise Mart
Chicago, IL 60654
312-527-3593   Fax 312-527-3597
Furniture

Shell Transport & Trading SC
Shell Centre
London, EN SE17NA
071-934-3856
Integrated petroleum company

Sherwin-Williams SHW
101 Prospect Ave., N.W.
Cleveland, OH 44115
216-566-2000
Cotings, paints and varnishes O DRP

Shoney's, Inc. SHN
1727 Elm Hill Pike
Nashville, TN 37210
615-391-5201
Retail - food & restaurants O

ShopKo Stores, Inc. SKO
700 Pilgrim Way
Green Bay, WI 54304
414-497-2211
Retail - regional department stores O

Shurgard Storage Centers, Inc. SHU
1201 Third Ave., Ste. 2200
Seattle, WA 98101
206-624-8100
Real estate investment trust DRP

Sierra Health Services, Inc. SIE
2724 N. Tenaya Way
Las Vegas, NV 89128
702-242-7000
Health maintenance organization O

Sierra Pacific Resources SRP
6100 Neil Rd., PO Box 30150
Reno, NV 89520
702-689-3600
Utility - electric power DRP

SIGCORP, Inc. SIG
20 N.W. Fourth St.
Evansville, IN 47741
812-465-5300
Utility - electric power DRP

Signal Apparel Co., Inc. SIA
537 Market St., Ste. 403
Chattanooga, TN 37402
615-752-2032
Textiles - apparel

Silicon Graphics, Inc. SGI
2011 N. Shoreline Blvd.
Mountain View, CA 94043
415-933-1980 Fax 415-969-6289
Computers - graphics O

Simon DeBartolo Group, Inc. SPG
115 W. Washington St.
Indianapolis, IN 46204
317-636-1600
Real estate investment trust O DRP

Simula, Inc. SMU
401 W. Baseline, Ste. 204
Tempe, AZ 85283
602-752-8918 Fax 602-491-0566
Aerospace - aircraft equipment

Singapore Fund SGF
One Evertrust Plaza
Jersey City, NJ 07302
201-915-3026
Closed-end fund

SITEL Corp. SWW
13215 Birch St.
Omaha, NE 68134
402-498-6810
Business services - marketing

Sizeler Property Investors, Inc. SIZ
2542 Williams Blvd.
Kenner, LA 70062
504-466-5363
Real estate investment trust DRP

Sizzler International, Inc. SZ
12655 W. Jefferson Blvd.
Los Angeles, CA 90066
310-827-2300
Retail - food & restaurants

Skyline Corp. SKY
2520 By-Pass Rd., PO Box 743
Elkhart, IN 46515
219-294-6521
Building - mobile homes & RV O

SL Green Realty Corp. SLG
70 West 36th St.
New York, NY 10018
212-594-2700
Real estate investment trust

SL Industries, Inc. SL
520 Fellowship Rd., Ste. 306
Mt. Laurel, NJ 08054
609-727-1500 Fax 609-727-1683
Electrical products - misc.

SLM Holding SLM
1050 Thomas Jefferson St. N.W.
Washington, DC 20007
202-333-8000
Education finance company

Smart & Final Inc. SMF
4700 S. Boyle Ave.
Los Angeles, CA 90058
213-589-1054
Retail - supermarkets

Smith (A.O.) AOS
11270 W. Park Place
Milwaukee, WI 53224
414-359-4000 Fax 414-359-4198
Electric motors, water heaters DRP

Smith (Charles E.) Residential SRW
2345 Crystal Dr.
Crystal City, VA 22202
703-920-8500
Real estate investment trust

Smith International, Inc. SII
16740 Hardy St.
Houston, TX 77032
713-443-3370
Oil field machinery & equipment O

Smucker (J.M.) SJM
Strawberry Lane
Orrville, OH 44667
330-682-3000
Preserves, jams DRP

Snap-on Tools, Inc. SNA
2801 80th St.
Kenosha, WI 53141
414-656-5200
Tools - handheld O DRP

Snyder Communications, Inc. SNC
6903 Rockledge Dr.
Bethesda, MD 20817
301-468-1010
Business sevices

Snyder Oil Corp. SNY
777 Main St.
Fort Worth, TX 76102
817-338-4043
Oil & gas - US exploration & production
  O

Sofamor Danek Group, Inc. SDG
3092 Directors Row
Memphis, TN 38131
901-396-2695   Fax 901-396-2699
Medical products O

Sola Inernational Inc. SCL
2420 Sand Hill Rd., Ste.200
Menlo Park, CA 94025
415-324-6868
Miscellaneous - not elsewhere classified O

Solectron Corp. SLR
777 Gibraltar Dr.
Milpitas, CA 95035
408-957-8500
Electrical components - misc. O

Solutia Inc. SCI
10300 Olive Blvd.
St. Louis, MO 63166
314-674-1000
High performance chemical materials

Sonat Inc. SNT
AmSouth-Sonat Tower
Birmingham, AL 35203
205-325-3800
Oil & gas - production & pipeline O DRP

Sonoco Products Co. SON
N. Second St.
Hartsville, SC 29550
803-383-7000   Fax 803-339-6078
Containers - paper & plastic O DRP

Sony Corporation SNE
550 Madison Ave., 33rd Flr.
New York, NY 10022
212-833-6800
Consumer electronics/entertainment O

Sotheby's Holdings, Inc. BID
500 N. Woodward Ave., Ste. 100
Bloomfield Hills, MI 48304
810-646-2400
Retail - misc. O DRP

Source Capital, Inc. SOR
11400 W. Olympic Blvd.
Los Angeles, CA 90064
310-473-0225
Financial - investment management

South Jersey Industries, Inc. SJI
Number One South Jersey Plaza
Folsom, NJ 08037
609-561-9000
Utility - gas distribution DRP

Southdown, Inc. SDW
1200 Smith St., Ste. 2400
Houston, TX 77002
713-650-6200
Construction - cement & concrete

Southern Africa Fund, Inc. (The) SOA
1345 Avenue of the Americas
New York, NY 10105
800-247-4154
Financial - investment management

Southern Co. SO
270 Peachtree St. N.W.
Atlanta, GA 30330
770-393-0650
Electric holding co. O DRP

Southern Pacific Funding Corp. SFC
One Centerpoint Dr.
Lake Oswego, OR 97035
503-684-4700
Financial - mortgages & related services

Southern Peru Copper Corp. PCU
180 Maiden Lane
New York, NY 10038
212-510-2000
Metal ores - misc.

Southern Union Co. SUG
504 Lavaca St., Ste. 800
Austin, TX 78701
512-477-5852
Utility - gas distribution O DRP

Southwest Airlines Co. LUV
PO Box 36611
Dallas, TX 75235
214-904-4000   Fax 214-904-4011
Transportation - airline O

Southwest Gas Corp. SWX
5241 Spring Mountain Rd.
Las Vegas, NV 89102
702-876-7237
Utility - gas distribution DRP

Southwestern Energy Co. SWN
1083 Sain St., PO Box 1408
Fayetteville, AR 72702
501-521-1141
Utility - gas distribution DRP

Southwestern Property Trust, Inc. SWP
5949 Sherry Lane
Dallas, TX 75225
214-369-1995
Real estate investment trust DRP

Sovran Self Storage, Inc. SSS
5166 Main St.
Williamsville, NY 14221
716-633-1850
Real estate investment trust

Spaghetti Warehouse, Inc. SWH
402 West I-30
Garland, TX 75043
214-226-6000
Retail - food & restaurants

Spain Fund SNF
1345 Avenue of the Americas
New York, NY 10105
212-969-1000
Financial - investment management

SPARTECH Corp. SEH
7733 Forsyth, Ste. 1450
Clayton, MO 63105
314-721-4242
Rubber & plastic products

Sparton Corp. SPA
2400 E. Ganson St.
Jackson, MI 49202
517-787-8600
Electronics - military

Speedway Motorsports, Inc. TRK
U.S. Highway 29 North
Concord, NC 28026
704-455-3239
Leisure & recreational services O

Spelling Entertainment Group Inc. SP
5700 Wilshire Blvd.
Los Angeles, CA 90036
213-965-5700
Leisure & recreational products O

Spieker Properties, Inc. SPK
2180 Sand Hill Rd.
Menlo Park, CA 94025
415-854-5600
Real estate investment trust

Sport Supply Group, Inc. GYM
1901 Diplomat
Dallas, TX 75234
214-484-9484
Leisure & recreational products

Sports Authority, Inc. TSA
3383 N. State Rd. 7
Fort Lauderdale, FL 33319
954-735-1701
Retail - misc. O

Springs Industries, Inc. SMI
205 N. White St., PO Box 70
Fort Mill, SC 29715
803-547-1500
Textiles - home furnishings

Sprint Corp. FON
PO Box 11315
Kansas City, KS 64112
913-624-3000   Fax 913-624-3496
Utility - telephone O DRP

SPS Technologies, Inc. ST
101 Greenwood Ave., Ste. 470
Jenkintown, PA 19046
215-517-2000
Metal products - fasteners

SPS Transaction Services, Inc. PAY
2500 Lake Cook Rd.
Riverwoods, IL 60015
708-405-3400
Business services

SPX Corp. SPW
700 Terrace Point Dr.
Muskegon, MI 49443
616-724-5000   Fax 616-724-5720
Automotive & trucking - original
  equipment DRP

St. Joe Corp. SJP
1650 Prudential Dr., Suite 400
Jacksonville, FL 32207
904-396-6600
Paper & paper products

St. John's Knits, Inc. SJK
17422 Derian Ave.
Irvine, CA 92614
714-261-9585   Fax 714-261-9585
Apparel

St. Joseph Light & Power Co. SAJ
520 Francis St., PO Box 998
St. Joseph, MO 64502
816-233-8888
Utility - electric power DRP

St. Jude Medical STJ
One Lillehei Plaza
St. Paul, MN 55117
612-483-2000
Heart valves, pacemakers

St. Paul Companies SPC
385 Washington St.
St. Paul, MN 55102
612-221-7911
Insurance - property & casualty DRP

Standard Commercial Corp. STW
2201 Miller Rd.
Wilson, NC 27893
919-291-5507   Fax 919-237-0018
Tobacco DRP

Standard Motor Products, Inc. SMP
37-18 Northern Blvd.
Long Island City, NY 11101
718-392-0200
Automotive & trucking - replacement parts

Standard Pacific Corp. SPF
1565 W. MacArthur Blvd.
Costa Mesa, CA 92626
714-668-4300
Building - residential & commercial

Standard Products Co. SPD
2401 S. Gulley Rd.
Dearborn, MI 48124
313-561-1100
Automotive parts - rubber & plastic DRP

Standard Register SR
600 Albany St.
Dayton, OH 45401
937-443-1000
Office equipment & supplies

Standex International Corp. SXI
6 Manor Pkwy.
Salem, NH 03079
603-893-9701   Fax 603-893-7324
Diversified operations

Stanhome Inc. STH
333 Western Ave.
Westfield, MA 01085
413-562-3631   Fax 413-568-2820
Retail - mail order & direct O DRP

Stanley Works SWK
1000 Stanley Dr.
New Britain, CT 06053
860-225-5111
Hardware & tools - consumer/industrial O
DRP

Star Banc Corp. STB
425 Walnut St.
Cincinnati, OH 45202
513-632-4000
Banks - midwest O DRP

Starrett (L.S.) SCX
121 Crescent St.
Athol, MA 01331
508-249-3551
High grade tools for industry

StarTek, Inc. SRT
111 Havana St.
Denver, CO 80010
303-361-6000
Advertising/marketing services

Starter Corp. STA
370 James St.
New Haven, CT 06513
203-781-4000
Apparel O

Starwood Lodging Trust HOT
11845 W. Olympic Blvd.
Los Angeles, CA 90064
310-575-3900
Real estate investment trust

State Street Corp. STT
225 Franklin St.
Boston, MA 02110
617-786-3000   Fax 617-654-3386
Banks - northeast O DRP

Station Casinos, Inc. STN
2411 W. Sahara Ave.
Las Vegas, NV 89102
702-367-2411
Leisure & recreational services O

Steinway Musical Instruments, Inc. LVB
600 Industrial Blvd.
Elkhart, IN 46516
219-522-1675
Leisure & recreational products

Stepan Co. SCL
22 West Frontage Rd.
Northfield, IL 60093
847-446-7500
Chemicals - specialty

Sterling Bancorp STL
540 Madison Ave.
New York, NY 10022
212-826-8000
Banks - northeast O

Sterling Commerce, Inc. SE
300 Crescent Ct., Ste. 1200
Dallas, TX 75201
214-981-1100   Fax 214-981-1215
Telecommunications services O

Sterling Software, Inc. SSW
300 Crescent Ct., Ste. 1200
Dallas, TX 75201
214-981-1000   Fax 214-981-1255
Computers - software O

Stewart Information Services Corp. STC
1980 Post Oak Blvd.
Houston, TX 77056
713-625-8100   Fax 713-552-9523
Financial - business services

Stifel Financial Corp. SF
500 N. Broadway
St. Louis, MO 63102
314-342-2000
Financial - business services

Stone & Webster, Inc. SW
250 W. 34th St.
New York, NY 10119
212-290-7500
Construction - heavy DRP

Stone Container Corp. STO
150 N. Michigan Ave.
Chicago, IL 60601
312-346-6600
Containers - paper & plastic O

Stone Energy Corp. SGY
625 E. Kaliste Saloom Rd.
Lafayette, LA 70508
318-237-0410
Oil & gas - US exploration & production

Storage Technology Corp. STK
2270 S. 88th St.
Louisville, CO 80028
303-661-4800   Fax 303-673-2296
Computers - peripheral equipment O

Storage Trust Realty SEA
2407 Rangeline
Columbia, MO 65202
573-499-4799   Fax 573-442-5554
Real estate investment trust

Storage USA, Inc. SUS
10440 Little Patuxent Pkwy.
Columbia, MD 21044
410-730-9500
Real estate investment trust

Strategic Global Income Fund, Inc. SGL
1285 Avenue of the Americas
New York, NY 10019
212-713-2000
Financial - investment management

Stratus Computer, Inc. SRA
55 Fairbanks Blvd.
Marlborough, MA 01752
508-460-2000
Computers - mini & micro O

Stride Rite SRR
191 Spring St.
Lexington, MA 02173
617-824-6000
Footwear O DRP

Stryker Corporation SYK
2725 Fairfield Rd.
Kalamazoo, MI 49003
616-385-2600
Specialty surgical & medical products O

Student Loan Corp. STU
99 Gamsey Rd.
Pittsford, NY 14534
716-248-7187
Consumer finance

Sturm, Ruger & Co., Inc. RGR
Lacey Place
Southport, CT 06490
203-259-7843
Leisure & recreational products O

Suburban Propane Partners, L.P. SPH
240 Route 10 West
Whippany, NJ 07981
201-887-5300
Retail - misc.

Suiza Foods Corp. SZA
3811 Turtle Creek Blvd.
Dallas, TX 75219
214-528-0939
Food - dairy products

Summit Bancorp. SUB
301 Carnegie Ctr., PO Box 2066
Princeton, NJ 08543
609-987-3200
Banks - northeast O DRP 3%

Summit Properties, Inc. SMT
212 S. Tryon St., Ste. 500
Charlotte, NC 28281
704-334-9905
Real estate investment trust DRP

Sun Communities, Inc. SUI
31700 Middlebelt Rd., Ste. 145
Farmington Hills, MI 48334
313-932-3100
Real estate development

Sun Company, Inc. SUN
1801 Market St.
Philadelphia, PA 19103
215-977-3000
Oil refining & marketing O DRP

Sun Energy Partners, L.P. SLP
13155 Noel Rd.
Dallas, TX 75240
214-715-4000
Oil & gas - US exploration & production

Sun Healthcare Group, Inc. SHG
5131 Masthead St. NE
Albuquerque, NM 87109
505-821-3355   Fax 505-821-9440
Insurance - accident & health O

SunGard Data Systems, Inc. SDS
1285 Drummers Lane
Wayne, PA 19087
610-341-8700
Computers - services O

SunSource L.P. SDP
2600 One Logan Square
Philadelphia, PA 19103
215-665-3650
Auto parts - retail & wholesale

SunTrust Banks, Inc. STI
25 Park Place, N.E.
Atlanta, GA 30303
404-588-7711
Banks - southeast DRP

Sunbeam Corp. SOC
1615 S. Congress Ave.
Delray Beach, FL 33445
561-243-2100
Appliances - household O

Suncor Energy SU
112 4th Ave., S.W.
Calgary, AB T2P2V5
403-269-8100
Produces, markets, refines crude oil

Sundstrand Corp. SNS
4949 Harrison Ave.
Rockford, IL 61125
815-226-6000   Fax 815-226-2699
Aerospace - aircraft equipment O DRP

Sunrise Medical Inc. SMD
2355 Crenshaw Blvd., Ste. 150
Torrance, CA 90501
310-328-8018   Fax 310-328-8184
Medical & dental supplies O

Sunshine Mining and Refining Co. SSC
877 W. Main St., Ste. 600
Boise, ID 83702
208-345-0660   Fax 208-342-0004
Silver mining & processing

Sunstone Hotel Investors, Inc. SSI
300 S. El Camino Real
San Clemente, CA 92672
714-361-3900
Real estate investment trust DRP

Superior Industries International, Inc. SUP
7800 Woodley Ave.
Van Nuys, CA 91406
818-781-4973   Fax 818-780-3500
Automotive & trucking - original
  equipment O DRP

Superior TeleCom Inc. SUT
1790 Broadway
New York, NY 10019
212-757-3333
Wine & cable products

Supervalu Stores Inc. SVU
11840 Valley View Rd.
Eden Prairie, MN 55344
612-828-4000
Operates supermarkets O DRP

Swift Energy Co. SFY
16825 Northchase Dr., Ste. 400
Houston, TX 77060
713-874-2700
Oil & gas - US exploration & production
  O

Swiss Helvetia Fund SWZ
630 Fifth Ave., Suite 915
New York, NY 10111
212-486-4990
Closed-end fund

Sybron International Corp. SYB
411 E. Wisconsin Ave.
Milwaukee, WI 53202
414-274-6600   Fax 414-274-6561
Medical & dental supplies O

Symbol Technologies, Inc. SBL
116 Wilbur Place
Bohemia, NY 11716
516-563-2400
Optical character recognition O

Syms Corp. SYM
Syms Way
Secaucus, NJ 07094
201-902-9600
Retail - apparel & shoes

Synovus Financial Corp. SNV
901 Front Ave., Ste. 301
Columbus, GA 31901
706-649-2311
Banks - southeast O DRP

Sysco Corp. SYY
1390 Enclave Pkwy.
Houston, TX 77077
713-584-1390
Food - wholesale O DRP

TB Woods Corp. TBW
440 N. Fifth Ave.
Chambersburg, PA 17201
717-264-7161   Fax 717-264-6420
Electrical products - misc.

Taiwan Equity Fund TYW
One Evertrust Plaza
Jersey City, NJ 07302
800-933-3440
Closed-end fund

Taiwan Fund, Inc. TWN
82 Devonshire St.
Boston, MA 02109
800-334-9393
Financial - investment management

Talbots Inc. TLB
175 Beal St.
Hingham, MA 02043
617-749-7600
Specialty apparel retail stores O

Tandy Corp. TAN
1800 One Tandy Center
Fort Worth, TX 76102
817-390-3700   Fax 817-390-2647
Computers - retail & wholesale O DRP

Tandycrafts, Inc. TAC
1400 Everman Parkway
Fort Worth, TX 76140
817-551-9600
Retail - misc.

Tanger Factory Outlet Centers, Inc. SKT
1400 W. Northwood St.
Greensboro, NC 27408
910-274-1666   Fax 910-274-6632
Retail - misc.

Tasty Baking Co. TBC
2801 Hunting Park Ave.
Philadelphia, PA 19129
215-221-8500
Food - misc.

Taubman Centers, Inc. TCO
200 E. Long Lake Rd.
Bloomfield Hills, MI 48303
810-258-6800
Real estate operations O DRP

TCBY Enterprises, Inc. TBY
425 W. Capitol Ave., Ste. 1100
Little Rock, AR 72201
501-688-8229
Retail - food & restaurants O

TCC Industries, Inc. TEL
1545 W. Mockingbird Ln.
Dallas, TX 75235
214-638-0638
Diversified operations

TCF Financial Corp. TCB
801 Marquette Ave., Ste. 302
Minneapolis, MN 55402
612-661-6500
Banks - midwest O DRP

TCW Convertible Securities Fund, Inc.
  CVT
865 S. Figueroa St.
Los Angeles, CA 90017
213-244-0000
Financial - investment management

TCW/DW Emerging Markets
  Opportunities Trust EMO
Two World Trade Center
New York, NY 10048
212-392-1600
Financial - investment management

TCW/DW Term Trust 2000 TDT
Two World Trade Center
New York, NY 10048
212-392-1600
Financial - investment management

TCW/DW Term Trust 2002 TRM
Two World Trade Center
New York, NY 10048
212-392-1600
Financial - investment management

TCW/DW Term Trust 2003 TMT
Two World Trade Center
New York, NY 10048
212-392-1600
Financial - investment management

Tech-Sym Corp. TSY
10500 Westoffice Dr., Ste. 200
Houston, TX 77042
713-785-7790   Fax 713-780-3524
Electronics - military

Technitrol, Inc. TNL
1210 Northbrook Dr., Ste. 385
Trevose, PA 19053
215-355-2900
Electrical products - misc. O

TECO Energy, Inc. TE
702 N. Franklin St.
Tampa, FL 33602
813-228-4111   Fax 813-228-1670
Utility - electric power O DRP

Teekay Shipping TK
Tradewinds Bldg., Bay St., 6th Fl.
Nassau, BA
809-322-8020
Crude oil & petroleum shipping

Tektronix, Inc. TEK
26600 SW Pkwy., PO Box 1000
Wilsonville, OR 97070
503-627-7111
Electronics - measuring instruments O

Teleflex Inc. TFX
630 W. Germantown Pike
Plymouth Meeting, PA 19462
610-834-6301   Fax 610-834-8228
Instruments - control O

Temple-Inland Inc. TIN
303 S. Temple Dr.
Diboll, TX 75941
409-829-2211
Paper & paper products O DRP

Templeton China World Fund, Inc. TCH
700 Central Ave.
St. Petersburg, FL 33701
813-823-8712
Financial - investment management

Templeton Dragon Fund, Inc. TDF
700 Central Ave.
St. Petersburg, FL 33701
813-823-8712
Financial - investment management

Templeton Emerging Markets Appreciation
  Fund TEA
700 Central Ave.
St. Petersburg, FL 33701
813-342-5236
Financial - investment management

Templeton Emerging Markets Fund, Inc.
  EMF
700 Central Ave.
St. Petersburg, FL 33701
813-823-8712
Financial - investment management

Templeton Emerging Markets Income
  Fund, Inc. TEI
700 Central Ave.
St. Petersburg, FL 33701
813-823-8712
Financial - investment management

Templeton Global Governments Income
  Trust TGG
700 Central Ave.
St. Petersburg, FL 33701
813-823-8712
Financial - investment management

Templeton Global Income Fund, Inc. GIM
700 Central Ave.
St. Petersburg, FL 33701
813-823-8712
Financial - investment management

Templeton Russia Fund, Inc. TRF
700 Central Ave.
St. Petersburg, FL 33701
813-823-8712
Financial - investment management

Templeton Vietnam Opportunities Fund,
  Inc. TVF
700 Central Ave.
St. Petersburg, FL 33701
813-823-8712
Financial - investment management

Tenet Healthcare Corp. THC
2700 Colorado Ave.
Santa Monica, Ca 90404
310-998-8000
Hospitals O DRP

Tenneco Inc. TEN
1275 King Street
Greenwich, CT 06831
203-863-1000
Diversified operations O DRP

TEPPCO Partners, L.P. TPP
2929 Allen Pkwy., PO Box 2521
Houston, TX 77252
713-759-3131
Miscellaneous - not elsewhere classified

Teradyne, Inc. TER
321 Harrison Ave.
Boston, MA 02118
617-482-2700 Fax 617-422-2910
Electronics - measuring instruments O

Terex Corp. TEX
500 Post Rd. East, Ste. 320
Westport, CT 06880
203-222-7170 Fax 203-222-7976
Machinery - construction & mining O

Terra Industries Inc. TRA
600 Fourth St., PO Box 6000
Sioux City, IA 51102
712-277-1340
Diversified operations O

Terra Nitrogen Co., L.P TNH
5100 E. Skelly Dr., Ste. 800
Tulsa, OK 74135
918-660-0050
Fertilizers

Terra Nova (Bermuda) Holdings TNA
Richmond Hse, 12 Par-la-Ville Rd.
Hamilton, BA HM08
441-292-7731
Property/casualty insurance

Tesoro Petroleum Corp. TSO
8700 Tesoro Dr.
San Antonio, TX 78217
210-828-8484 Fax 210-828-8600
Oil refining & marketing O

Texaco Inc. TX
2000 Westchester Ave.
White Plains, NY 10650
914-253-4000 Fax 914-253-7753
Oil & gas - international integrated O
  DRP

Texas Industries, Inc. TXI
7610 Stemmons Freeway
Dallas, TX 75247
214-647-6700 Fax 214-647-3878
Diversified operations O

Texas Instruments Inc. TXN
13500 N. Central Expressway
Dallas, TX 75265
214-995-2551 Fax 214-995-4360
Electrical components - semiconductors O
  DRP

Texas Pacific Land Trust TPL
80 Broad St.
New York, NY 10004
212-269-2266
Real estate operations

Texas Utilities Co. TXU
2001 Bryan Tower
Dallas, TX 75201
214-812-4600
Utility - electric power O DRP

Texfi Industries, Inc. TXF
5400 Glenwood Ave., Ste. 318
Raleigh, NC 27612
919-783-4736
Textiles - mill products

Textron Inc. TXT
40 Westminster St.
Providence, RI 02903
401-421-2800 Fax 401-457-2220
Diversified operations O DRP

Thai Capital Fund, Inc. TC
800 Scudders Mill Rd.
Plainsboro, NJ 08536
212-449-4600
Financial - investment management

Thermo Electron Corp. TMO
81 Wyman St., PO Box 9046
Waltham, MA 02254
617-622-1000
Machinery - general industrial O

Thomas & Betts Corp. TNB
1555 Lynnfield Rd.
Memphis, TN 38119
901-682-7766
Electrical connectors O DRP

Thomas Industries Inc. TII
4360 Brownsboro Rd.
Louisville, KY 40207
502-893-4600
Building products - lighting fixtures DRP

Thor Industries, Inc. THO
419 W. Pike St.
Jackson Center, OH 45334
937-596-6849
Building - mobile homes & RV

Thornburg Mortgage Asset Corp. TMA
119 E. Marcy St., Ste. 201
Santa Fe, NM 87501
505-989-1900
Real estate investment trust DRP 3%

Three-Five Systems, Inc. TFS
1600 N. Desert Dr.
Tempe, AZ 85281
602-389-8600
Electronics - components & systems

360° Communications XO
8725 W. Higgins Rd.
Chicago, IL 60631
773-399-2500
Telecommunications, cellular/wireless O

Tidewater Inc. TDW
1440 Canal St.
New Orleans, LA 70112
504-568-1010
Oil & gas - offshore drilling O DRP

Tiffany & Co. TIF
727 Fifth Ave.
New York, NY 10022
212-755-8000
Retail - jewelry stores O

TIG Holdings, Inc. TIG
65 E. 55th St.
New York, NY 10022
212-446-2700
Insurance - multi line & misc. O

Timberland Co. TBL
200 Domain Dr.
Stratham, NH 03885
603-772-9500
Footwear

Time Warner Inc. TWX
75 Rockefeller Plaza
New York, NY 10019
212-484-8000   Fax 212-489-6183
Publishing - periodicals O DRP 5%

Times Mirror Co. TMC
Times Mirror Square
Los Angeles, CA 90053
213-237-3700
Publishing O DRP

Timken Co. TKR
1835 Dueber Ave., S.W.
Canton, OH 44706
330-438-3000
Bearings & steels - auto, aerospace,
 railroads O DRP 5%

TIS Mortgage Investment Co. TIS
655 Montgomery St., Ste. 800
San Francisco, CA 94111
415-393-8000
Real estate investment trust

Titan Corp. TTN
3033 Science Park Rd.
San Diego, CA 92121
619-453-9500
Electronics - military

Titan International, Inc. TWI
2701 Spruce St.
Quincy, IL 62301
217-228-6011
Metal products - fabrication O

TJX Companies TJX
770 Cochituate Rd.
Framingham Rd., MA 01701
508-390-1000
Specialty apparel retail stores O

TNP Enterprises, Inc. TNP
4100 International Plaza
Fort Worth, TX 76109
817-731-0099
Utility - electric power DRP

Toastmaster Inc. TM
1801 N. Stadium Blvd.
Columbia, MO 65202
573-445-8666
Appliances - household

Todd Shipyards Corp. TOD
1801 16th Ave., S.W.
Seattle, WA 98134
206-623-1635
Boat building

Tokheim Corp. TOK
10501 Corporate Dr.
Fort Wayne, IN 46801
219-423-2552   Fax 219-484-1110
Oil refining & marketing

Toll Brothers, Inc. TOL
3103 Philmont Ave.
Huntingdon Valley, PA 19006
215-938-8000
Building - residential & commercial O

Tommy Hilfiger TOM
25 W. 39th St.
New York, NY 10018
212-840-8888
Men's & boys' apparel O

Tootsie Roll Industries, Inc. TR
7401 S. Cicero Ave.
Chicago, IL 60629
312-838-3400   Fax 312-838-3534
Food - confectionery

Torch Energy Royalty Trust TRU
1100 N. Market St.
Wilmington, DE 19890
302-651-8775
Oil & gas - US royalty trust

Torchmark Corp. TMK
2001 Third Ave. South
Birmingham, AL 35233
205-325-4200
Insurance - life O DRP

Toro Co. TTC
8111 Lyndale Ave. South
Bloomington, MN 55420
612-888-8801
Consumer/comm'l lawn/turf equipment
  DRP

Toronto-Dominium Bank TD
PO Box 1, Toronto-Dominium Ctr.
Toronto, ON M5K1A2
416-982-8222
Regional banks O

Tosco Corp. TOS
72 Cummings Point Rd.
Stamford, CT 06902
203-977-1000
Oil refining & marketing O

Total Rental Care Holdings, Inc. TRL
21250 Hawthorne Blvd.
Torrance, CA 90503
310-792-2600   Fax 310-792-8929
Medical services

Total System Services, Inc. TSS
1200 Sixth Ave.
Columbus, GA 31901
706-649-2204
Financial - business services O DRP

Tower Automotive, Inc. TWR
4508 IDS Center
Minneapolis, MN 55402
612-342-2310   Fax 612-332-2012
Automotive & trucking - original
  equipment

Town & Country Trust TCT
100 S. Charles St.
Baltimore, MD 21201
410-539-7600
Real estate investment trust

Toy Biz, Inc. TBZ
333 E. 38th St., 4th Fl.
New York, NY 10016
212-682-4700
Toys - games & hobby products

Toys "R" Us, Inc. TOY
461 From Rd.
Paramus, NJ 07652
201-262-7800
Retail - misc. O

TransTechnology Corp. TT
150 Allen Rd.
Liberty Corner, NJ 07938
908-903-1600   Fax 908-903-1616
Electronics - military

Transamerica Corp. TA
600 Montgomery St.
San Francisco, CA 94111
415-983-4000
Insurance - multi line & misc. O DRP

Transamerica Income Shares, Inc. TAI
PO Box 2438
Los Angeles, CA 90051
213-742-4141
Financial - investment management

Transatlantic Holdings, Inc. TRH
80 Pine St.
New York, NY 10005
212-770-2000   Fax 212-269-6801
Insurance - property & casualty

TransCanada Pipelines TRP
111 Fifth Ave., S.W.
Calgary, AB T2P3Y6
403-267-6100   Fax 403-267-5444
Operates natural gas pipeline system
  O DRP 5%

Transcontinental Realty Investors, Inc.
  TCI
10670 N. Central Expressway
Dallas, TX 75231
214-692-4700
Real estate investment trust

Transmedia Network, Inc. TMN
11900 Biscayne Blvd.
Miami, FL 33181
305-892-3300
Business services O

Transocean Offshore RIG
4 Greenway Plaza
Houston, TX 77046
713-871-7500
Worldwide contract offshore driller O

TransPro TPR
100 Gando Dr.
New Haven, CT 06513
203-401-6450
Fabricated metal products for trucks, vans

Travelers Group TRV
388 Greenwich St.
New York, NY 10013
212-816-8000
Consumer finance, investment, insurance
 O

Travelers Property Casualty Corp. TAP
One Tower Sq.
Hartford, CT 06183
860-277-0111
Insurance - property & casualty O

TRC Companies, Inc. TRR
Five Waterside Crossing
Windsor, CT 06095
860-289-8631   Fax 860-298-6399
Pollution control equipment & services

Tredegar Industries, Inc. TG
1100 Boulders Pkwy.
Richmond, VA 23225
804-330-1000
Diversified operations

Tremont Corp. TRE
1999 Broadway, Ste. 4300
Denver, CO 80202
303-296-5652
Metal ores - misc.

Tri-Continental Corp. TY
100 Park Ave.
New York, NY 10017
212-850-1864
Financial - investment management

TriNet Corporate Realty Trust, Inc. TRI
4 Embarcadero Center
San Francisco, CA 94111
415-391-4300   Fax 415-391-6259
Real estate investment trust

Triarc Cos., Inc. TRY
900 Third Ave.
New York, NY 10022
212-230-3000
Diversified operations O

Tribune Co. TRB
435 N. Michigan Ave.
Chicago, IL 60611
312-222-9100   Fax 312-222-9670
Publishing - newspapers O DRP

Tricon Global Restaurants YUM
1441 Gardiner Lane
Louisville, KY 40213
502-456-8300
Restaurants DRP

Trigen Energy Corp. TGN
One Water St.
White Plains, NY 10601
914-286-6600   Fax 914-948-9157
Energy - cogeneration

Trigon Healthcare Inc. TGH
2015 Staples Mill Rd.
Richmond, VA 23230
804-354-7000
Managed healthcare provider

Trinity Industries, Inc. TRN
2525 Stemmons Fwy.
Dallas, TX 75207
214-631-4420
Transportation - equipment & leasing O

Triton Energy Corp. OIL
6688 N. Central Expwy.
Dallas, TX 75206
214-691-5200   Fax 214-987-0571
Oil & gas - US exploration & production
 O

Triumph Group, Inc. TGI
1255 Drummers Lane, Ste. 200
Wayne, PA 19087
610-975-0420
Industrial maintenance

TrizecHahn Group TZH
181 Bay St., Suite 3900
Toronto, ON M5J2T3
416-361-7200   Fax 416-361-7201
Land development, office bldgs, malls O

True North Communications Inc. TNO
101 E. Erie St.
Chicago, IL 60611
312-751-7227   Fax 312-751-3501
Advertising DRP

Trump Hotels & Casino Resorts, Inc. DJT
725 Fifth Ave., 26th Fl.
New York, NY 10022
212-832-2000
Hotels & motels

TRW Inc. TRW
1900 Richmond Rd.
Cleveland, OH 44124
216-291-7000   Fax 216-291-0620
Diversified operations O DRP

Tuboscope Inc. TBI
2835 Holmes Rd.
Houston, TX 77051
713-799-5100
Services & equipment - oil & gas ind.

Tultex Corp. TTX
101 Commonwealth Blvd.
Martinsville, VA 24115
540-632-2961   Fax 540-632-5446
Textiles - apparel

Tupperware Corp. TUP
PO Box 2353
Orlando, FL 32802
407-826-5050
Plastic food storage products O

Turkish Investment Fund, Inc. TKF
1221 Avenue of the Americas
New York, NY 10020
212-703-4000
Financial - investment management

TVX Gold TVX
161 Bay St.
Toronto, ON M5J2S1
416-366-8160   Fax 416-366-8163
Gold & precious metals mining O

20th Century Industries TW
6301 Owensmouth Ave.
Woodland Hills, CA 91367
818-704-3700
Automotive insurance - direct O

Twin Disc, Inc. TDI
1328 Racine St.
Racine, WI 53403
414-638-4000
Machinery - general industrial DRP

2002 Target Team Trust, Inc. TTR
1285 Avenue of the Americas
New York, NY 10019
212-713-2000
Financial - investment management

Tyco International Ltd. TYC
One Tyco Park
Exeter, NH 03833
603-778-9700
Diversified operations DRP

Tyler Corp. TYL
3200 San Jacinto Tower
Dallas, TX 75201
214-754-7800
Diversified operations

Tyson Foods, Inc. TSN
2210 West Oaklawn Drive
Springvale, AR 72762
800-822-7096
Poultry processing DRP

UAL Corp. UAL
1200 E. Algonquin Rd.
Elk Grove Township, IL 60007
847-700-4000
Transportation - airline O

UCAR International Inc. UCR
39 Old Ridgebury Rd.
Danbury, CT 06817
203-207-7700
Electrical components - semiconductors O

UGI Corp. UGI
PO Box 858
Valley Forge, PA 19482
610-337-1000
Utility - gas distribution DRP 3%

Ultramar Diamond Shamrock Corp. UDS
9830 Colonnade Blvd.
San Antonio, TX 78230
210-641-6800
Oil refining & marketing O

Unicom Corp. UCM
10 S. Dearborn St., 37th Floor
Chicago, IL 60690
312-394-7399
Electric utility holding co. O DRP

UniFirst Corp. UNF
68 Jonspin Rd.
Wilmington, MA 01887
508-658-8888
Linen supply & related

Unifi, Inc. UFI
7201 W. Friendly Rd.
Greensboro, NC 27410
910-294-4410
Textiles - mill products O

Unilever N.V. UN
390 Park Ave.
New York, NY 10022
212-906-4694
Foods, detergents, toiletries O

Union Camp Corp. UCC
1600 Valley Rd.
Wayne, NJ 07470
201-628-2000
Container & packaging materials O DRP

Union Carbide Corp. UK
39 Old Ridgebury Rd.
Danbury, CT 06817
203-794-2000
Chemicals - diversified O DRP

Union Electric Co. UEP
1901 Chouteau Ave.
St. Louis, MO 63103
314-621-3222
Utility - electric power O DRP

Union Pacific Corp. UNP
Eighth and Eaton Aves.
Bethlehem, PA 18018
610-861-3200
Transportation - rail O DRP

Union Pacific Resources Group Inc. UPR
801 Cherry St., PO Box 7
Fort Worth, TX 76101
817-877-6000
Oil & gas - US exploration & production
  O

Union Planters Corp. UPC
7130 Goodlett Farms Pkwy.
Cordova, TN 38018
901-383-6000
Banks - southeast O DRP 5%

Unisource Worldwide, Inc. UWW
825 Duportail Rd.
Wayne, PA 19087
610-296-4470   Fax 610-644-1574
Wholesale distribution - consumer products
  O

Unisys Corp. UIS
PO Box 500
Blue Bell, PA 19424
215-986-4011   Fax 215-986-2312
Computers - mainframe O

Unit Corp. UNT
7130 S. Lewis
Tulsa, OK 74136
918-493-7700
Oil & gas - field services

United American Healthcare Corp. UAH
1155 Brewery Park Blvd.
Detroit, MI 48207
313-393-0200
Medical services

United Asset Management Corp. UAM
One International Pl.
Boston, MA 02110
617-330-8900
Financial - investment management O

United Auto Group, Inc. UAG
375 Park Ave.
New York, NY 10152
212-223-3300
Retail - new & used cars

United Companies Financial Corp. UC
4041 Essen Lane
Baton Rouge, LA 70809
504-924-6007
Insurance - life O

United Dominion Industries Ltd. UDI
2300 One First Union Center
Charlotte, NC 28202
704-347-6800
Building - residential & commercial

United Dominion Realty Trust, Inc. UDR
10 S. Sixth St., Ste. 203
Richmond, VA 23219
804-780-2691   Fax 804-343-1912
Real estate investment trust DRP 5%

United HealthCare Corp. UNH
9900 Bren Rd. East
Minnetonka, MN 55343
612-936-1300
Health maintenance organization O

United Illuminating UIL
157 Church St.
New Haven, CT 06506
203-499-2000
Electric utility companies DRP

United Industrial Corp. UIC
18 E. 48th St.
New York, NY 10017
212-752-8787
Electronics - military

United Kingdom Fund Inc. UKM
245 Park Ave., 10th Fl.
New York, NY 10167
800-524-4458
Financial - investment management

United Park City Mines Co. UPK
PO Box 1450
Park City, UT 84060
801-649-8011
Real estate operations

United Technologies Corp. UTX
United Technologies Bldg.
1 Financial Plaza
Hartford, CT 06101
860-728-7000   Fax 860-728-7979
Diversified operations O

United Water Resources Inc. UWR
200 Old Hook Rd.
Harrington Park, NJ 07640
201-784-9434
Utility - water supply DRP

United Wisconsin Services, Inc. UWZ
401 W. Michigan St.
Milwaukee, WI 53203
414-226-6900
Insurance - accident & health DRP

Unitrode Corp. UTR
7 Continental Blvd.
Merimack, NH 03054
603-424-2410
Electrical components - semiconductors O

Universal Corp. UVV
Hamilton St. at Broad
Richmond, VA 23230
804-359-9311
Tobacco DRP

Universal Foods Corp. UFC
433 E. Michigan St.
Milwaukee, WI 53202
414-271-6755   Fax 414-347-3785
Food - misc. O DRP

Universal Health Realty Income Trust
  UHT
367 S. Gulph Rd.
King of Prussia, PA 19406
610-265-0688
Real estate investment trust DRP

Universal Health Services, Inc. UHS
367 S. Gulph Rd.
King of Prussia, PA 19406
610-768-3300
Hospitals O

Univision Communications Inc. UVN
1999 Avenue of the Stars
Los Angeles, CA 90067
310-656-7676
Broadcasting - radio & TV

Uno Restaurant Corp. UNO
100 Charles Park Rd.
West Roxbury, MA 02132
617-323-9200
Retail - food & restaurants

Unocal Corp. UCL
2141 Rosecrans Ave., Ste. 4000
El Segundo, CA 90245
310-726-7600
Oil & gas - US integrated O DRP 3%

UNUM Corp. UNM
2211 Congress St.
Portland, ME 04122
207-770-2211
Insurance - multi line & misc. O DRP

Urban Shopping Centers, Inc. URB
900 N. Michigan Ave.
Chicago, IL 60611
312-915-2000   Fax 312-915-2001
Real estate investment trust DRP

URS Corp. URS
100 California St., Ste. 500
San Francisco, CA 94111
415-774-2700   Fax 415-398-1905
Engineering - R & D services

US Airways Group, Inc. U
2345 Crystal Dr.
Arlington, VA 22227
703-418-5306
Transportation - airline O

U.S. Bancorp USB
601 2nd Ave. South
Minneapolis, MN 55402
612-973-1111
Banking DRP

U.S. Can Corp. USE
900 Commerce Dr., Ste. 302
Oak Brook, IL 60521
708-571-2500
Containers - metal

U.S. Filter USF
40-004 Cook St.
Palm Desert, CA 92211
619-340-0098   Fax 619-341-9368
Water treatment systems O

USG Corp. USG
125 S. Franklin St.
Chicago, IL 60606
312-606-4000
Building products - misc.

U.S. Home Corp. UH
1800 W. Loop South
Houston, TX 77027
713-877-2311
Building - residential & commercial

U.S. Industries, Inc. USN
101 Wood Ave. South
Iselin, NJ 08830
908-767-0700
Diversified operations O

USLIFE Income Fund, Inc. UF
125 Maiden Lane
New York, NY 10038
212-709-6000
Financial - investment management DRP

US 1 Industries USO
1000 Colfax
Gary, IN 46406
219-944-6116
Truck load carrier - commodities

U.S. Rentals USR
1581 Cummins Dr., Suite 155
Modesto, CA 95358
209-544-9000
Equipment rental

U.S. Restaurant Properties Master USV
1342 Grand Ave.
St. Paul, MN 55105
612-690-1946
Real estate operations

U.S. Surgical USS
150 Glover Ave.
Norwalk, CT 06856
203-845-1000
Manufacturer surgical products O

UST Inc. UST
100 W. Putnam Ave.
Greenwich, CT 06830
203-661-1100
Tobacco O DRP

U S WEST Comm. Group USW
7800 E. Orchard Rd.
Englewood, CO 80111
303-793-6500
Utility - telephone O DRP

U S WEST Media Group UMG
7800 E. Orchard Rd.
Englewood, CO 80111
303-793-6500   Fax 303-793-6309
Publishing - periodicals O DRP

USX Corp. - Delhi Group DGP
600 Grant St.
Pittsburgh, PA 15219
412-433-1121
Oil & gas - production & pipeline O

USX Corp. - Marathon Group MRO
600 Grant St.
Pittsburgh, PA 15219
412-433-1121
Oil & gas - US integrated O DRP

USX Corp. - U.S. Steel Group X
600 Grant St.
Pittsburgh, PA 15219
412-433-1121
Steel - production O DRP

Utah Medical Products, Inc. UM
7043 S. 300 West
Midvale, UT 84047
801-566-1200
Medical products O

UtiliCorp United Inc. UCU
911 Main
Kansas City, MO 64105
816-421-6600
Utility - electric power DRP 5%

Vail Resorts, Inc. MTN
137 Benchmark Rd.
Avon, CO 81620
970-476-5601
Leisure & recreational services O

Valassis Communications, Inc. VCI
19975 Victor Pkwy.
Livonia, MI 48152
313-591-3000
Business services O

Valero Energy Corp. VLO
530 McCullough Ave.
San Antonio, TX 78215
210-246-2000
Oil & gas - production & pipeline

Valhi, Inc. VHI
5430 LBJ Freeway, Ste. 1700
Dallas, TX 75240
972-233-1700   Fax 972-385-0586
Diversified operations

Valley National Bancorp VLY
1445 Valley Rd.
Wayne, NJ 07470
201-305-8800
Banks - northeast DRP

Valspar Corp. VAL
1101 Third St. South
Minneapolis, MN 55415
612-332-7371   Fax 612-375-7723
Distributor of paints & coatings DRP

Value City Department Stores, Inc. VCD
3241 Westerville Rd.
Columbus, OH 43224
614-471-4722
Retail - regional department stores

Van Kampen American Advantage
  Municipal Inc. Trust VKA
One Parkview Plaza
Oakbrook Terrace, IL 60181
708-684-6000
Financial - investment management

Van Kampen American Advantage PA
  Municipal Inc. Tr. VAP
One Parkview Plaza
Oakbrook Terrace, IL 60181
708-684-6000
Financial - investment management

Van Kampen American CA Value
  Municipal Inc. Trust VCV
One Parkview Plaza
Oakbrook Terrace, IL 60181
708-684-6000
Financial - investment management

Van Kampen American California Qual.
  Municipal Trust VQC
One Parkview Plaza
Oakbrook Terrace, IL 60181
708-684-6000
Financial - investment management

Van Kampen American Capital Income
  Trust ACD
One Parkview Plaza
Oakbrook Terrace, IL 60181
708-684-6000
Financial - investment management

Van Kampen American Florida Qual.
  Municipal Trust VFM
One Parkview Plaza
Oakbrook Terrace, IL 60181
708-684-6000
Financial - investment management

Van Kampen American Int. Term High
  Income Trust VIT
One Parkview Plaza
Oakbrook Terrace, IL 60181
708-684-6000
Financial - investment management

Van Kampen American Investment Grade
  Municipal VIG
One Parkview Plaza
Oakbrook Terrace, IL 60181
708-684-6000
Financial - investment management

Van Kampen American Ltd. Term High
  Income Trust VLT
One Parkview Plaza
Oakbrook Terrace, IL 60181
708-684-6000
Financial - investment management

Van Kampen American Municipal
  Opportunity Trust II VOT
One Parkview Plaza
Oakbrook Terrace, IL 60181
708-684-6000
Financial - investment management

Van Kampen American Municipal Income
  Trust VMT
One Parkview Plaza
Oakbrook Terrace, IL 60181
708-684-6000
Financial - investment management

Van Kampen American Municipal
  Opportunity Tr. VMO
One Parkview Plaza
Oakbrook Terrace, IL 60181
708-684-6000
Financial - investment management

Van Kampen American Municipal Trust
  VKQ
One Parkview Plaza
Oakbrook Terrace, IL 60181
708-684-6000
Financial - investment management

Van Kampen American NY Value
  Municipal Income Trust VNV
One Parkview Plaza
Oakbrook Terrace, Il 60181
708-684-6000
Financial - investment management

Van Kampen American New York Qual.
  Municipal Trust VNM
One Parkview Plaza
Oakbrook Terrace, IL 60181
708-684-6000
Financial - investment management

Van Kampen American Ohio Qual.
  Municipal Trust VOQ
One Parkview Plaza
Oakbrook Terrace, IL 60181
708-684-6000
Financial - investment management

Van Kampen American PA Quality
  Municipal Trust VPQ
One Parkview Plaza
Oakbrook Terrace, IL 60181
708-684-6000
Financial - investment management

Van Kampen American PA Value
  Municipal Inc. TrustVPV
One Parkview Plaza
Oakbrook Terrace, IL 60181
708-684-6000
Financial - investment management

Van Kampen American Strategic Sector
  Municipal Trust VKS
One Parkview Plaza
Oakbrook Terrace, IL 60181
708-684-6000
Financial - investment management

Van Kampen American Tr. For Insured
  Municipals VIM
One Parkview Plaza
Oakbrook Terrace, IL 60181
708-684-6000
Financial - investment management

Van Kampen American Tr. For Inv. Grade
  CA Municipal VIC
One Parkview Plaza
Oakbrook Terrace, IL 60181
708-684-6000
Financial - investment management

Van Kampen American Tr. For Inv. Grade
  FL Municipal VTF
One Parkview Plaza
Oakbrook Terrace, IL 60181
708-684-6000
Financial - investment management

Van Kampen American Tr. For Inv. Grade
  Municipal VGM
One Parkview Plaza
Oakbrook Terrace, IL 60181
708-684-6000
Financial - investment management

Van Kampen American Tr. For Inv. Grade
  NJ Municipal VTJ
One Parkview Plaza
Oakbrook Terrace, IL 60181
708-684-6000
Financial - investment management

Van Kampen American Tr. For Inv. Grade
  NY Municipal VTN
One Parkview Plaza
Oakbrook Terrace, IL 60181
708-684-6000
Financial - investment management

Van Kampen American Tr. For Inv. Grade
  PA Municipal VTP
One Parkview Plaza
Oakbrook Terrace, IL 60181
708-684-6000
Financial - investment management

Van Kampen American Value Municipal
  Income Tr. VKV
One Parkview Plaza
Oakbrook Terrace, IL 60181
708-684-6000
Financial - investment management

Van Kampen Capital Bond Fund ACB
One Parkview Plaza
Oakbrook Terrace, IL 60181
708-684-6000
Financial - investment management

Van Kampen Capital Convertible
  Securities, Inc. ACS
One Parkview Plaza
Oakbrook Terrace, IL 60181
708-684-6000
Financial - investment management

Vanstar Corp. VST
5964 W. Las Positas Blvd.
Pleasanton, CA 94588
510-734-4000
Computers - services O

Varco International, Inc. VRC
743 N. Eckhoff St.
Orange, CA 92668
714-978-1900
Oil field machinery & equipment O

Varian Associates, Inc. VAR
3050 Hansen Way
Palo Alto, CA 94304
415-493-4000
Instruments - scientific O DRP

Vastar Resources, Inc. VRI
15375 Memorial Dr.
Houston, TX 77079
713-584-6000
Oil & gas - US exploration & production

Vencor, Inc. VC
400 W. Market St.
Louisville, KY 40202
502-569-7300 Fax 502-569-7499
Hospitals O

Veritas DGC, Inc. VTS
3701 Kirby Dr., Ste. 112
Houston, TX 77098
713-512-8300 Fax 713-512-8701
Oil & gas - field services O

Vesta Insurance Group, Inc. VTA
3760 River Run Rd.
Birmingham, AL 35243
205-970-7000 Fax 205-970-7007
Insurance - multi line & misc.

Vestaur Securities, Inc. VES
Centre Square West
Philadelphia, PA 19101
215-567-3969
Financial - investment management

V.F. Corp. VFC
1047 N. Park Rd.
Wyomissing, PA 19610
610-378-1151 Fax 610-375-9371
Textiles - apparel O DRP

Viad Corp. VVI
1850 N. Central Ave.
Phoenix, AZ 85077
602-207-4000
Diversified operations O DRP

Vintage Petroleum, Inc. VPI
4200 One Williams Center
Tulsa, OK 74172
918-592-0101
Oil & gas - US exploration & production
O

Vishay Intertechnology, Inc. VSH
63 Lincoln Highway
Malvern, PA 19355
610-644-1300   Fax 610-296-0657
Electronics - measuring instruments O

Vitalink Pharmacy Services, Inc. VTK
1250 E. Diehl Rd., Ste. 208
Naperville, IL 60563
708-505-1320   Fax 708-505-1319
Medical services O

Volt Information Sciences, Inc. VOL
1221 Avenue of the Americas
New York, NY 10020
212-704-2400
Diversified operations

Vornado Realty Trust VNO
Park 80 West, Plaza II
Saddle Brook, NJ 07662
201-587-1000
Real estate investment trust O

Vulcan Materials Co. VMC
One Metroplex Dr.
Birmingham, AL 35209
205-877-3000   Fax 205-877-3094
Construction - cement & concrete DRP

Wabash National Corp. WNC
1000 Sagamore Pkwy. South
Lafayette, IN 47905
765-448-1591
Automotive & trucking - original
  equipment O

Wachovia Corp. WB
301 N. Main St.
Winston-Salem, NC 27101
910-770-5000
Banks - southeast O DRP

Wackenhut Corp. WAK
4200 Wackenhut Dr.
Palm Beach Gardens, FL 33410
561-622-5656
Developer correctional/detention facilities

Wackenhut Corrections Corp. WCH
1500 San Remo Ave.
Coral Gables, FL 33146
305-662-7396
Business services O

Wal-Mart Stores, Inc. WMT
702 S.W. 8th St.
Bentonville, AR 72716
501-273-4000
Retail - discount & variety O DRP

Walden Residential Properties, Inc. WDN
13601 Preston Rd., Ste. 800W
Dallas, TX 75240
214-788-0510
Real estate investment trust DRP 5%

Walgreen Co. WAG
200 Wilmot Rd.
Deerfield, IL 60015
708-940-2500
Retail - drug stores O DRP

Wallace Computer Services, Inc. WCS
2275 Cabot Dr.
Hillside, IL 60532
630-588-5000
Paper - business forms O

Warnaco Group WAC
90 Park Ave.
New York, NY 10016
212-661-1300
Textiles (apparel) O

Warner-Lambert Co. WLA
201 Tabor Rd.
Morris Plains, NJ 07950
201-540-2000
Drugs O DRP

Washington Gas Light Co. WGL
1100 H St., N.W.
Washington, DC 20080
703-750-4440
Utility - gas distribution DRP

Washington Homes, Inc. WHI
1802 Brightseat Rd.
Landover, MD 20785
301-772-8900
Building - residential & commercial

Washington National Corp. WNT
300 Tower Pkwy.
Lincolnshire, IL 60069
847-793-3000
Insurance - life DRP 5%

Washington Post WPO
1150 15th St.
Washington, DC 20071
202-334-6000
Publishing

Washington Water Power Co. WWP
1411 E. Mission Ave.
Spokane, WA 99202
509-489-0500
Utility companies DRP

Waste Management, Inc. WMX
3003 Butterfield Rd.
Oak Brook, IL 60521
708-572-8800
Pollution control equipment & services O

Waters Corp. WAT
34 Maple St.
Milford, MA 01757
508-478-2000   Fax 508-872-1990
Instruments - scientific

Watkins-Johnson Co. WJ
3333 Hillview Ave.
Palo Alto, CA 93404
415-493-4141
Electronics - military O

Watsco, Inc. WSO
2665 S. Bayshore Dr.
Coconut Grove, FL 33133
305-858-0828
Diversified operations

Watson Pharmaceuticals WPI
311 Bonnie Circle
Corona, CA 91720
909-270-1400
Drugs

Watts Industries, Inc. WTS
815 Chestnut St.
North Andover, MA 01845
508-688-1811
Instruments - control

Waxman Industries, Inc. WAX
24460 Aurora Rd.
Bedford Heights, OH 44146
216-439-1830
Building products - misc.

Webb (Del) Corp WBB
6001 N. 24th St.
Phoenix, AZ 85016
602-808-8000
Land development O

Weeks Corp. WKS
4497 Park Dr.
Norcross, GA 30093
404-923-4076
Real estate investment trust

Weider Nutrition International, Inc. WNI
1960 S. 4250 West
Salt Lake City, UT 84104
801-975-5000   Fax 801-972-2223
Vitamins & nutritional products

Weingarten Realty Investors WRI
2600 Citadel Plaza Dr.
Houston, TX 77292
713-866-6000   Fax 713-866-6049
Real estate investment trust DRP

Weirton Steel Corp. WS
400 Three Springs Dr.
Weirton, WV 26062
304-797-2000
Steel - production O

Weis Markets, Inc. WMK
1000 S. Second St.
Sunbury, PA 17801
717-286-4571
Retail - supermarkets DRP

Wellman, Inc. WLM
1040 Broad St., Ste. 302
Shrewsbury, NJ 07702
908-542-7300
Chemicals - plastics O

WellPoint Health Networks Inc. WLP
21555 Oxnard St.
Woodland Hills, CA 91367
818-703-4000
Medical services O

Wells Fargo & Co. WFC
420 Montgomery St.
San Francisco, CA 94163
415-477-1000
Banks - west O DRP

Wendy's International, Inc. WEN
4288 W. Dublin-Granville Rd.
Dublin, OH 43017
614-764-3100
Retail - food & restaurants O DRP

West Co., Inc. WST
101 Gordon Dr.
Lionville, PA 19341
215-594-2900
Medical & dental supplies DRP

West Penn Power Co. WSPp
800 Cabin Hill Dr.
Greensburg, PA 15601
412-837-3000
Utility - electric power

Westbridge Capital Corp. WBC
777 Main St.
Fort Worth, TX 76102
817-878-3300
Insurance - accident & health

Westcoast Energy WE
666 Burrard St., Suite 3400
Vancouver, BC V6C3M8
604-488-8000   Fax 604-488-8500
Operates natural gas pipeline DRP 5%

Westcorp WES
23 Pasteur
Irvine, CA 92718
714-727-1000
Financial - savings and loans

Western Digital Corp. WDC
8105 Irvine Center Dr.
Irvine, CA 92718
714-932-5000
Computers - peripheral equipment O

Western Gas Resources, Inc. WGR
12200 N. Pecos St.
Denver, CO 80234
303-452-5603
Oil & gas - production & pipeline

Westinghouse Air Brake Co. WAB
1001 Air Brake Ave.
Wilmerding, PA 15148
412-825-1000
Diversified operations

Westvaco Corp. W
299 Park Ave.
New York, NY 10171
212-688-5000
Paper & paper products O DRP

Weyerhaeuser Co. WY
P.O. Box 2999
Tacoma, WA 98477
253-924-2345
Building products - wood O DRP

Whirlpool Corp. WHR
2000 M-63
Benton Harbor, MI 49022
616-926-5000
Appliances - household O DRP

Whitman Corp. WH
3501 Algonquin Rd.
Rolling Meadows, IL 60008
708-818-5000
Diversified operations O DRP

Whittaker Corp. WKR
1955 N. Surveyor Ave.
Simi Valley, CA 93063
805-526-5700   Fax 805-526-4369
Aerospace - aircraft equipment O

WHX Corp. WHX
110 E. 59th St.
New York, NY 10022
212-355-5200
Steel - production O

WICOR, Inc. WIC
626 E. Wisconsin Ave.
Milwaukee, WI 53202
414-291-7026
Utility - gas distribution DRP

Willamette Industries, Inc. WLL
1300 S.W. Fifth Ave.
Portland, OR 97201
503-227-5581
Paper & paper products O

Willbros Group WG
2431 E. 61st St.
Tulsa, OK 74136
918-748-7000
Oil & gas drilling & equipment

Williams Coal Seam Gas Royalty Trust
 WTU
One Williams Center
Tulsa, OK 74172
918-588-2000
Oil & gas - US royalty trust

Williams Companies WMB
One Williams Center
Tulsa, OK 74172
918-588-2000
Natural gas pipeline systems O

Wilshire Oil Company of Texas WOC
921 Bergen Ave.
Jersey City, NJ 07306
201-420-2796
Oil & gas - US exploration & production

Windmere-Durable Holdings WND
5980 Miami Lakes Dr.
Miami Lakes, FL 33014
305-362-2611
Drugs & sundries - wholesale O

Winn-Dixie Stores, Inc. WIN
5050 Edgewood Ct.
Jacksonville, FL 32254
904-783-5000
Retail - supermarkets O DRP

Winnebago Industries, Inc. WGO
PO Box 152
Forest City, IA 50436
515-582-3535   Fax 515-582-6966
Building - mobile homes & RV O

Winston Hotels, Inc. WXH
2209 Century Dr., Ste. 300
Raleigh, NC 27612
919-510-6010   Fax 919-787-4633
Real estate investment trust

Wisconsin Energy Corp. WEC
231 W. Michigan St.
Milwaukee, WI 53201
414-221-2345
Utility - electric power O DRP

Wiser Oil WZR
8115 Preston Rd., Suite 400
Dallas, TX 75225
214-265-0080
Oil & gas exploration & production

Witco Corp. WIT
One American Lane
Greenwich, CT 06831
203-552-2000   Fax 203-552-2870
Chemicals - diversified O DRP

WMS Industries Inc. WMS
3401 N. California Ave.
Chicago, IL 60618
773-961-1111
Leisure & recreational products O

Wm. Wrigley Jr. Co. WWY
410 N. Michigan Ave.
Chicago, IL 60611
312-644-2121
Food - confectionery O DRP

Wolverine Tube, Inc. WLV
2100 Market St., N.E.
Decatur, AL 35602
205-353-1310
Miscellaneous - not elsewhere classified O

Wolverine World Wide, Inc. WWW
9341 Courtland Dr.
Rockford, MI 49351
616-866-5500
Shoes & related apparel O

World Color Press, Inc. WRC
101 Park Ave., 19th Fl.
New York, NY 10178
212-986-2440
Food - confectionery

World Fuel Services Corp. INT
700 S. Royal Poinciana Blvd.
Miami Springs, FL 33166
305-884-2001
Oil refining & marketing

WorldCorp, Inc. WOA
13873 Park Center Rd.
Herndon, VA 22071
703-834-9200
Transportation - airline O

Worldtex, Inc. WTX
212 12th Ave. N.E.
Hickory, NC 28601
704-328-5381
Textiles - mill products

Worldwide DollarVest Fund, Inc. WDV
PO Box 9011
Princeton, NJ 08543
609-282-2800
Financial - investment management

WPL Holdings, Inc. WPH
222 W. Washington Ave.
Madison, WI 53703
608-252-3311
Utility - electric power DRP

WPS Resources Corp. WPS
700 N. Adams St., PO Box 19001
Green Bay, WI 54307
414-433-1445
Utility - electric power DRP

Wynn's International, Inc. WN
500 N. State College Blvd.
Orange, CA 92668
714-938-3700
Automotive & trucking - replacement parts

Xerox Corp. XRX
800 Long Ridge Rd.
Stamford, CT 06904
203-968-3000
Office equipment & supplies O DRP

XTRA Corp. XTR
60 State St.
Boston, MA 02109
617-367-5000
Transportation - equipment & leasing O
DRP

Yankee Energy System, Inc. YES
599 Research Pkwy.
Meriden, CT 06450
203-639-4000
Utility - gas distribution DRP

York International Corp. YRK
631 S. Richland Ave.
York, PA 17403
717-771-7890   Fax 717-771-7440
Building products - a/c & heating O DRP

Zale Corp. ZLC
901 W. Walnut Hill Lane
Irving, TX 75038
972-580-4000
Retail - jewelry stores O

Zapata Corp. ZOS
One Riverway, PO Box 4240
Houston, TX 77210
713-940-6100
Oil & gas - offshore drilling

Zeigler Coal Holding Co. ZEI
50 Jerome Lane
Fairview Heights, IL 62208
618-394-2400
Coal O

Zemex Corp. ZMX
161 Bay St., Suite 3750
Toronto, ON M5J2S1
416-365-8080   Fax 416-365-8094
Metals mining

Zenith National Insurance Corp. ZNT
21255 Califa St.
Woodland Hills, CA 91367
818-713-1000
Insurance - property & casualty

Zenix Income Fund Inc. ZIF
Two World Trade Center
New York, NY 10048
212-298-7350
Financial - investment management

Zweig Fund F
900 Third Ave.
New York, NY 10022
800-272-2700
Closed-end fund

Zweig Total Return Fund, Inc. (The) ZTR
900 Third Avenue
New York, NY 10022
212-755-9860
Financial - investment management

AMERICAN STOCK EXCHANGE

Acadiana Bancshares, Inc. ANA
107 W. Vermilion St.
Lafayette, LA 70501
318-232-4631
Financial - savings and loans

Acme United Corp. ACU
75 Kings Highway Cutoff
Fairfield, CT 06430
203-332-7330
Medical instruments

Adams Resources & Energy, Inc. AE
6910 Fannin
Houston, TX 77030
713-797-9966
Oil & gas - production & pipeline

Advanced Magnetics, Inc. AVM
61 Mooney St.
Cambridge, MA 02138
617-497-2070   Fax 617-547-2445
Medical products

Advanced Photonix, Inc. API
1240 Avenida Acaso
Camarillo, CA 93012
805-987-0146   Fax 805-484-9935
Electronics - measuring instruments

Aerosonic Corp. AIM
1212 N. Hercules Rd.
Clearwater, FL 34625
813-461-3000
Instruments - control

Air & Water Technologies Corp. AWT
US Hwy. 22 West & Station Rd.
Branchburg, NJ 08876
908-685-4600   Fax 908-685-4587
Pollution control equipment & services

Alarmguard Holdings AGD
125 Frontage Rd.
Orange, CT 06477
203-795-9000
Provides electronic security systems

Alba-Waldensian, Inc. AWS
201 St. Germain Ave., S.W.
Valdese, NC 28690
704-874-2191
Textiles - apparel

Alexander Haagen Properties, Inc. ACH
3500 Sepulveda Blvd.
Manhattan Beach, CA 90266
310-546-4520   Fax 310-545-8455
Real estate investment trust

Allied Digital Technologies Corp. ADK
15 Gilpin Ave.
Hauppauge, NY 11788
516-234-0200
Miscellaneous - not elsewhere classified

Allied Research Corp. ALR
8000 Towers Cresent Dr.
Vienna, VA 22182
703-847-5268   Fax 703-847-5334
Weapons & weapon systems

Allou Health & Beauty Care, Inc. ALU
50 Emjay Blvd.
Brentwood, NY 11717
516-273-4000
Cosmetics & toiletries

Alternative Living Services, Inc. ALI
450 N. Sunnyslope Rd.
Brookfield, WI 53005
414-789-9565   Fax 414-789-9592
Nursing homes

AMC Entertainment Inc. AEN
106 W. 14th St.
Kansas City, MO 64105
816-221-4000   Fax 816-421-5744
Motion pictures & services

American Bank of Connecticut BKC
Two W. Main St.
Waterbury, CT 06723
203-757-9401
Financial - savings and loans

American Biltrite Inc. ABL
57 River St.
Wellesley Hills, MA 02181
617-237-6655
Building products - misc.

American Insured Mortgage Inv. L.P. -
  Series 85 AII
11200 Rockville Pike
Rockville, MD 20852
301-468-9200
Financial - investment management

American Insured Mortgage Inv. L.P. -
  Series 86 AIJ
11200 Rockville Pike
Rockville, MD 20852
301-468-9200
Financial - investment management

American Insured Mortgage Inv. L.P. -
 Series 88AIK
11200 Rockville Pike
Rockville, MD 20852
301-468-9200
Financial - investment management

American Insured Mortgage Investors AIA
11200 Rockville Pike
Rockville, MD 20852
301-468-9200
Financial - investment management

American Real Estate Investment REA
1670 Broadway, Suite 3350
Denver, CO 80202
303-869-4700
Real Estate Investment Trust

American Science and Engineering, Inc.
 ASE
40 Erie St.
Cambridge, MA 02139
617-868-1600   Fax 617-354-1054
Electronics - measuring instruments

American Shared Hospital Services AMS
4 Embarcadero Ctr., Ste. 3620
San Francisco, CA 94111
415-788-5300   Fax 415-788-5660
Medical services

American Technical Ceramics Corp. AMK
17 Stepar Place
Huntington Station, NY 11746
516-547-5700   Fax 516-547-5748
Electrical components - misc.

Ampal-American Israel Corp. AISA
1177 Avenue of the Americas
New York, NY 10036
212-782-2100   Fax 212-782-2114
Financial - SBIC & commercial

Ampex, Inc. AXC
401 Broadway
Redwood City, CA 94063
415-367-4111   Fax 415-367-4669
Miscellaneous - not elsewhere classified O

Amwest Insurance Group, Inc. AMW
6320 Canoga Ave.
Woodland Hills, CA 91367
818-704-1111   Fax 818-592-3660
Insurance - property & casualty

Andrea Electronics Corp. AND
11-40 45th Rd.
Long Island City, NY 11101
718-729-8500
Telecommunications equipment

Angeles Mortgage Investment Trust ANM
340 N. Westlake Blvd.
Westlake Village, CA 91362
805-449-1335   Fax 805-449-1336
Real estate investment trust DRP

Angeles Participating Mortgage Trust APT
340 N. Westlake Blvd.
Westlake Village, CA 91362
805-449-1335   Fax 805-449-1336
Real estate investment trust DRP

Apple Orthodontix AOI
2777 Allen Parkway
Houston, TX 77019
281-698-2500
Orthodontic practice management firm

ARC International ATV
4000 Chesswood Dr.
Downsview, ON M3J2B9
461-630-0200
Leisure, entertainment & communications

Arizona Land Income Corp. AZL
2999 N. 44th St., Ste. 100
Phoenix, AZ 85018
602-952-6800
Real estate investment trust

ARM Financial Group, Inc. ARM
239 S. Fifth St., 12th Fl.
Louisville, KY40202
502-582-7900
Insurance - multi line & misc.

Armor Holdings, Inc. ABE
85 Nassau Place
Yulee, FL 32097
904-261-4035
Protection - safety equipment & services

Arrhythmia Research Technology, Inc.
 HRT
5910 Courtyard Dr., Ste. 300
Austin, TX 78731
512-343-6912
Medical products

Arrow Automotive Industries, Inc. AI
3 Speen St.
Framingham, MA 01701
508-872-3711
Automotive & trucking - replacement parts

Assisted Living Concepts, Inc. ALF
10570 S.E. Washington
Portland, OR 97216
503-255-4647
Miscellaneous - not elsewhere classified

AT Plastics ATJ
134 Kennedy Rd. South
Brampton, ON L6W3G5
905-451-1630   Fax 905-451-7650
Makes specialty plastic new materials

Atlantic Tele-Network ANK
P.O. Box 1730
St. Croix, VI 00821
809-777-8000
Telephone service - U.S. Virgin Islands

Atlantis Plastics, Inc. AGH
2665 S. Bayshore Dr., 8th Fl.
Miami, FL 33133
305-858-2200   Fax 305-285-0102
Diversified operations

Audiovox Corp. VOX
150 Marcus Blvd.
Hauppauge, NY 11788
516-231-7750
Auto parts - retail & wholesale

Audits and Surveys Worldwide, Inc. ASW
62 Southfield Ave.
Stamford, CT 06902
203-327-9050
Tools - hand held

Autotote Corp. TTE
100 Bellevue Rd., PO Box 6009
Newark, DE 19714
302-737-4300
Leisure & recreational products

Aviva Petroleum Inc. AVV
8235 Douglas Ave., Ste. 400
Dallas, TX75225
214-691-3464   Fax 214-361-0010
Oil & gas - international integrated

AZCO Mining, Inc. AZC
30 S. Bowie
Solomon, AZ 85551
602-428-6881   Fax 602-428-5865
Metal ores - misc.

B+H Ocean Carriers BHO
14 Par-La-Ville Rd., 3rd Floor
Hamilton, BA HMJX
809-295-6875
Owns & operates shipping vessels

Badger Meter, Inc. BMI
4545 W. Brown Deer Rd.
Milwaukee, WI 53223
414-355-0400
Electronics - measuring instruments

Baker (Michael) BKR
420 Rouser Rd., Building 3
Coraopolis, PA 15108
412-269-6300
Engineering, construction, operations
 services

Balchem Corp. BCP
PO Box 175
Slate Hill, NY 10973
914-355-2861   Fax 914-355-6314
Chemicals - specialty

Baldwin Technology Co., Inc. BLD
65 Rowayton Ave.
Rowayton, CT 06853
203-838-7470   Fax 203-852-7040
Machinery - printing DRP

Bancroft Convertible Fund, Inc. BCV
65 Madison Ave.
Morristown, NJ 07960
201-631-1177
Financial - investment management

Bank of Southington BSO
130 N. Main St.
Southington, CT 06489
203-276-0155   Fax 203-276-9950
Banks - northeast

Barnwell Industries, Inc. BRN
1100 Alakea St., Ste. 2900
Honolulu, HI 96813
808-531-8400   Fax 808-531-7181
Oil & gas - international specialty

Barrister Information Systems Corp. BIS
45 Oak St.
Buffalo, NY 14203
716-845-5010   Fax 716-845-0077
Business services

BayCorp Holdings, Ltd. MWH
100 Main St., Ste. 201
Dover, NH 03820
603-742-3388   Fax 603-742-3223
Utility - electric power

Bayou Steel Corp. BYX
River Rd., PO Box 5000
LaPlace, LA 70069
504-652-4900
Steel - production

Beard Co. BOC
5600 North May Ave., Suite 320
Oklahoma City, OK 73112
405-842-2333
Dry ice manufacturing

Bema Gold BGO
595 Burrard St., Suite 3113
Vancouver, BC V7X1G4
604-681-8371   Fax 604-681-6209
Develops precious metal properties in the
  Americas

Bentley Pharmaceuticals, Inc. BNT
4830 W. Kennedy Blvd.
Tampa, FL 33609
813-286-4401
Drugs

Bergstrom Capital Corp. BEM
505 Madison St., Ste. 220
Seattle, WA 98104
206-623-7302
Financial - investment management

Besicorp Group, Inc. BGI
1151 Flatbush Rd.
Kingston, NY 12401
914-336-7700   Fax 914-336-7172
Energy - alternate sources

Bethlehem Corp. BET
25th and Lennox Sts.
Easton, PA 18044
610-258-7111
Machinery - general industrial

BFC Construction BNC
3660 Midland Ave.
Scarborough, ON M1V4V3
416-754-8735   Fax 416-754-8736
Civil, pipeline, building, utility engineering

BFX Hospitality Group BFX
226 Bailey Ave., Suite 101
Fort Worth, TX 76107
817-332-4761
Operates restaurants

BHC Communications, Inc. BHC
600 Madison Ave.
New York, NY 10022
212-421-0200
Broadcasting - radio & TV

Binks Sames Corp. BIN
9201 W. Belmont Ave.
Franklin Park, IL 60131
708-671-3000
Machinery - material handling

Bio-Rad Laboratories, Inc. BIOA
1000 Alfred Nobel Dr.
Hercules, CA 94547
510-724-7000   Fax 510-724-3167
Biomedical & genetic products

Biscayne Apparel, Inc. BHA
1373 Broad St.
Clifton, NJ 07013
201-473-3240   Fax 201-473-5401
Textiles - apparel

Blair Corp. BL
220 Hickory St.
Warren, PA 16366
814-723-3600
Retail - mail order & direct

Blonder Tongue Laboratories, Inc. BDR
One Jake Brown Rd.
Old Bridge, NJ 08857
908-679-4000   Fax 908-679-4353
Electronics - components & systems

Boddie-Noell Properties, Inc. BNP
3710 One First Union Center
Charlotte, NC 28202
704-333-1367   Fax 704-334-3507
Real estate investment trust DRP

BostonFed Bancorp, Inc. BFD
17 New England Executive Park
Burlington, MA 01803
617-273-0300
Banks - northeast

Bowl America Inc. BWLA
6446 Edsall Rd.
Alexandria, VA 22312
703-941-6300
Leisure & recreational services

Bowmar Instrument Corp. BOM
5080 N. 40th St., Ste. 475
Phoenix, AZ 85018
602-957-0271
Electrical products - misc.

Bowne & Co., Inc. BNE
345 Hudson St.
New York, NY 10014
212-924-5500
Printing - commercial

Bridge View Bancorp BVB
457 Sylvan Ave.
Englewood Cliffs, NJ 07632
201-871-7800
Regional banks

Brilliant Digital Entertainment, Inc. BDE
6355 Topanga Canyon Blvd.
Woodland Hills, CA 91367
818-346-3653
Motion pictures & services

Cablevision Systems Corp. CVC
One Media Crossways
Woodbury, NY 11797
516-364-8450
Cable TV

Cagle's, Inc. CGLA
2000 Hills Ave., N.W.
Atlanta, GA 30318
404-355-2820
Food - meat products

Calton, Inc. CN
500 Craig Rd.
Manalapan, NJ 07726
908-780-1800   Fax 908-780-7257
Real estate development

Cambior, Inc. CBJ
800 Renee-Levesque Blvd., Ste. 650
Montreal, QC H3B1X9
514-878-3166
Gold mining in North & South America

Canadian Marconi CMW
600 Frederik Phillips Blvd.
Quebec, QC H4M2S9
514-748-3113   Fax 514-748-3184
Hi-tech electronic products - a'space &
   comm.

Canadian Occidental CXY
1500, 635-8th Ave. S.W.
Calgary, AB T2P3Z1
403-324-6700
Explores, produces crude oil, natural gas

Canyon Resources Corp. CAU
141-42 Denver West Pkwy.
Golden, CO 80401
303-278-8464   Fax 303-279-3772
Metals - non ferrous

Capital Pacific Holdings, Inc. CPH
3501 Jamboree Rd., Ste. 200
Newport Beach, CA 92660
714-854-2500   Fax 714-854-0514
Building - residential & commercial

Capital Properties CPI
One Hospital Trust Plaza
Providence, RI 02903
401-331-0100   Fax 401-331-2965
Land developer

CareMatrix Corp. CMD
197 First Ave.
Needham, MA 02194
617-433-1000
Nursing homes

Carver Bancorp CNY
75 West 125th St.
New York, NY 10027
212-876-4747
Regional bank

Castle (A.M.) & Co. CAS
3400 N. Wolf Rd.
Franklin Park, IL 60131
708-455-7111
Metal products - distribution

Castle Convertible Fund, Inc. CVF
75 Maiden Lane
New York, NY 10038
212-806-8800
Financial - investment management

CEL-SCI Corp. HIV
55 Canal Center Plaza
Alexandria, VA 22314
703-549-5293   Fax 703-549-6269
Drugs

Central Securities Corp. CET
375 Park Ave.
New York, NY 10152
212-688-3011
Financial - investment management

CET Environmental Services, Inc. ENV
14761 Bentley Circle
Tustin, CA 92680
714-505-1800   Fax 714-505-0987
Pollution control equipment & services

Chad Therapeutics, Inc. CTU
9445 De Soto Ave.
Chatsworth, CA 91311
818-882-0883   Fax 818-882-1809
Medical products

Chase Corp. CCF
50 Braintree Hill Park
Braintree, MA 02184
617-848-2810   Fax 617-843-9639
Miscellaneous - not elsewhere classified

Chicago Rivet & Machine Co. CVR
901 Frontenac Rd., PO Box 3061
Naperville, IL 60566
708-357-8500
Metal products - fasteners

CIM High Yield Securities CIM
PO Box 1376
Boston, MA 02104
800-331-1710
Financial - investment management

Citadel Holding Corp. CDL
600 N. Brand Blvd.
Glendale, CA 91203
818-956-7100
Financial - savings and loans

Citizens First Financial Corp. CBK
301 Broadway
Normal, IL 61761
309-452-1102
Banks - midwest

Citizens, Inc. CIA
400 E. Anderson Lane
Austin, TX 78752
512-837-7100
Insurance - life

Cirvw Cinema CLV
7 Waverley Place
Madison, NJ 07940
201-377-4646
Operates multiplex theaters -
  New York/New Jersey

Coast Distribution System CRV
1982 Zanker Rd.
San Jose, CA 95112
408-436-8611
Auto parts - retail & wholesale

Cognitronics Corp. CGN
3 Corporate Dr.
Danbury, CT 06810
203-830-3400   Fax 203-830-3554
Computers - peripheral equipment

Cohen & Steers Realty Income Fund,
  Inc. RIF
757 Third Ave.
New York, NY 10017
212-832-3232
Financial - investment management

Columbia Laboratories, Inc. COB
2665 S. Bayshore Dr., PH II-B
Miami, FL 33133
305-860-1670   Fax 305-860-1671
Drugs O

Columbus Energy Corp. EGY
1660 Lincoln St., Ste. 2400
Denver, CO 80264
303-861-5252   Fax 303-831-0135
Oil & gas - US exploration & production

Comforce CFS
2001 Marcus Ave.
Lake success, NY 11042
516-352-3200
Provides staffing, consulting services to
  telecom ind.

Cominco CLT
200 Burrad St., Suite 500
Vancouver, BC V6C3L7
604-682-0611   Fax 604-685-3019
Mines & produces zinc & lead

Commercial Assets, Inc. CAX
3600 S. Yosemite St., Ste. 900
Denver, CO 80237
303-793-2703
Real estate investment trust DRP

Commodore Applied Technologies, Inc.
  CXI
150 E. 58th St., Ste. 3400
New York, NY 10155
212-308-5800
Pollution control equipment & services

Community Banks, Inc. CTY
150 Market St.
Millersburg, PA 17061
717-692-4781
Banks - northeast

Community Capital CYL
109 Montague Ave.
Greenwood, SC 29646
864-941-8200
Regional bank holding company

Competitive Technologies, Inc. CTT
1465 Post Rd. East, PO Box 901
Westport, CT 06881
203-255-6044   Fax 203-254-1102
Diversified operations

Comptek Research, Inc. CTK
2732 Transit Rd.
Buffalo, NY 14224
716-677-0014
Computers - software

CompuTrac, Inc. LLB
222 Municipal Dr.
Richardson, TX 75080
214-234-4241 Lfax 214-234-6280
Computers - software

ComSouth Bankshares, Inc. CSB
1136 Washington St., Ste. 200
Columbia, SC 29201
803-343-2100
Banks - southeast

Concord Fabrics Inc. CIS
1359 Broadway
New York, NY 10018
212-760-0300
Textiles - mill products

Consolidated-Tomoka Land Co. CTO
149 S. Ridgewood Ave.
Daytona Beach, FL 32114
904-255-7558
Real estate development

Continental Materials Corp. CUO
325 N. Wells St.
Chicago, IL 60610
312-661-7200
Building products - a/c & heating

Continucare Corp. CNU
100 Southeast Second St.
Miami, FL 33131
305-350-7515   Fax 305-350-9833
Medical services

Core Materials Corp. CME
100 N. Fourth St.
Steubenville, OH 43952
800-666-6960
Rubber & plastic products

Cornell Corrections, Inc. CRN
4801 Woodway, Ste. 400W
Houston, TX 77056
713-623-0790
Protection - safety equipment & services

Cornerstone Bank CBN
550 Summer St.
Stamford, CT 06901
203-356-0111   Fax 203-348-3576
Banks - northeast

Courtalds COU
50 George St.
London, EN W1A2BB
171-612-1000   Fax 171-612-1500
Manufactures coatings, sealants, fibers &
  chemicals

Creative Computer Applications, Inc. CAP
26115-A Mureau Rd.
Calabasas, CA 91302
818-880-6700   Fax 818-880-4398
Computers - software

Cross (AT) ATXA
One Albion Rd.
Lincoln, RI 02865
401-333-1200   Fax 401-334-2861
Manufacturer office writing instruments

Crowley, Milner and Co. COM
2301 W. Lafayette Blvd.
Detroit, MI 48216
313-962-2400
Retail - regional department stores

Crown Central Petroleum Corp. CNPA
One N. Charles St.
Baltimore, MD 21201
410-539-7400
Oil refining & marketing

Crystal Oil Co. COR
229 Milam St.
Shreveport, LA 71101
318-222-7791
Oil & gas - US exploration & production

Crystlxint KRY
700 West Pender St.
Vancouver, BC V6C1G8
604-683-0672
Metals mining/exploration - Venezuela &
  Brazil

Cubic Corp. CUB
9333 Balboa Ave.
San Diego, CA 92123
619-277-6780   Fax 619-277-1878
Electronics - military

CVB Financial Corp. CVB
701 N. Haven Ave., Ste. 350
Ontario, CA 91764
909-980-4030   Fax 909-980-5232
Banks - west

Cybex International, Inc. CYB
81 Spence St.
Bay Shore, NY 11706
516-273-2200   Fax 516-273-1706
Medical & dental supplies

Dairy Mart Convenience Stores, Inc.
  DMCA
One Vision Dr.
Enfield, CT 06082
860-741-4444
Retail - convenience stores

Dallas Gold and Silver Exchange, Inc.
  DLS
2817 Forest Lane
Dallas, TX 75234
214-484-3662   Fax 214-241-0646
Precious metals & jewelry

Danielson Holding Corp. DHC
767 Third Ave., Fifth Fl.
New York, NY 10017
212-888-0347
Diversified operations

Datametrics Corp. DC
21135 Erwin St.
Woodland Hills, CA 91367
818-598-6200
Electronics - military

Dataram Corp. DTM
PO Box 7528
Princeton, NJ 08543
609-799-0071   Fax 609-799-6734
Electrical components - semiconductors

Daxor Corp. DXR
350 Fifth Ave., Ste. 7120
New York, NY 10118
212-244-0555   Fax 212-244-0806
Medical services

Dayton Mining DAY
200 Burrard St., Suite 1610
Vancouver, BC V6C 3L6
604-662-8383   Fax 604-684-1329
Precious metals mining, exploration

Decorator Industries, Inc. DII
10011 Pines Blvd.
Pembroke Pines, FL 33024
305-436-8909
Textiles - home furnishings

Del Laboratories, Inc. DLI
565 Broad Hollow Rd.
Farmingdale, NY 11735
516-293-7070
Cosmetics & toiletries

DenAmerica Corp. DEN
3000 Northwoods Pkwy.
Norcross, GA 30071
404-729-1300   Fax 404-729-0772
Retail - food & restaurants

Devon Energy Corp. DVN
20 N. Broadway, Ste. 1500
Oklahoma City, OK 73102
405-235-3611   Fax 405-552-4667
Oil & gas - US exploration & production

DeWolfe DWL
80 Hayden Ave.
Lexington, MA 02173
617-863-5858
Real estate brokerage, mortgage banking,
  insurance

Dia Met Minerals DMMB
1695 Powick Rd.
Kelowna, BC V1X4L1
250-861-8660   Fax 250-861-3649
Diamond mining/exploration

Digital Power DPW
41920 Christy St.
Fremont, CA 94538
510-657-2635
Switches power supplies—computers

Diodes Inc. DIO
3050 E. Hillcrest Dr.
Westlake Village, CA 91362
805-446-4800
Electrical components - semiconductors

Dixon Ticonderoga Co. DXT
2600 Maitland Center Pkwy.
Maitland, FL 32751
407-875-9000
Office & art materials

Drew Industries, Inc. DW
200 Mamaroneck Ave.
White Plains, NY 10601
914-428-9098   Fax 914-428-4581
Building products - misc.

Dreyfus California Municipal Income, Inc.
  DCM
144 Glenn Curtiss Blvd.
Uniondale, NY 11556
516-794-5200
Financial - investment management

Dreyfus Municipal Income, Inc. DMF
144 Glenn Curtiss Blvd.
Uniondale, NY 11556
516-794-5200
Financial - investment management

Dreyfus New York Municipal Income,
  Inc. DNM
144 Glenn Curtiss Blvd.
Uniondale, NY 11556
516-794-5200
Financial - investment management

Driver-Harris Co. DRH
308 Middlesex St.
Harrison, NJ 07029
201-483-4802
Metals - non ferrous

E-Z Serve Corp. EZS
2550 North Loop West, Ste. 600
Houston, TX 77092
713-684-4300
Oil refining & marketing

E-Z-EM, Inc. EZMA
717 Main St.
Westbury, NY 11590
516-333-8230   Fax 516-333-8278
Medical instruments

Eastern Co. EML
112 Bridge St.
Naugatuck, CT 06770
203-729-2255   Fax 203-723-8653
Security products for industrial,
  transportation mkts.

Echo Bay Mines MECO
6400 S. Fiddlers Green Circle, Ste. 1000
Englewood, CO 80111
303-714-8600   Fax 303-714-8999
Gold, precious metals mining

Ecology and Environment, Inc. EEI
368 Pleasant View Dr.
Lancaster, NY 14086
716-684-8060   Fax 716-684-0844
Pollution control equipment & services

El Paso Electric Co. EE
303 N. Oregon St.
El Paso, TX 79901
915-543-5711
Utility - electric power

Ellsworth Convertible Growth and Income
  Fund ECF
65 Madison Ave.
Morristown, NJ 07960
201-631-1177
Financial - investment management

Emeritus Corp. ESC
2003 Western Ave., Ste. 660
Seattle, WA 98121
206-443-4313   Fax 206-443-5432
Medical services

Emerson Radio Corp. MSN
9 Entin Rd., PO Box 430
Parsippany, NJ 07054
201-884-5800
Audio & video home products

Empire of Carolina, Inc. EMP
441 S. Federal Hwy.
Deerfield Beach, FL 33441
305-428-9001
Diversified operations

Energy Research Corp. ERC
3 Great Pasture Rd.
Danbury, CT 06813
203-792-1460
Engineering - R & D services

Engex, Inc. EGX
44 Wall St.
New York, NY 10005
212-495-4200
Financial - investment management

Environmental Tectonics Corp. ETC
County Line Industrial Park
Southampton, PA 18966
215-355-9100
Instruments - control

Envirotest Systems Corp. ENR
2002 N. Forbes Blvd.
Tucson, AZ 85745
602-620-1500
Miscellaneous - not elsewhere classified

Enzo Biochem, Inc. ENZ
60 Executive Blvd.
Farmingdale, NY 11735
516-755-5500
Biomedical & genetic products

Espey Mfg. & Electronics Corp. ESP
Congress & Ballston Aves.
Saratoga Springs, NY 12866
518-584-4100
Electronics - components & systems

Essex Bancorp, Inc. ESX
370 17th St., Ste. 4125
Denver, CO 80202
800-477-8209
Financial - savings and loans

EXX, Inc. EXXA
250 W. 57th St., Ste. 713
New York, NY 10107
212-757-1717
Machinery - electrical

Fab Industries, Inc. FIT
200 Madison Ave.
New York, NY 10016
212-592-2700
Textiles - mill products

Falmouth Co-operative Bank FCB
20 Davis Straits
Falmouth, MA 02540
508-548-3500
Banks - northeast

Farmstead Telephone Group, Inc. FTG
22 Prestige Park Circle
East Hartford, CT 06108
860-610-6000
Telecommunications equipment

Female Health FHC
919 N. Michigan Ave., Suite 2208
Chicago, IL 60611
312-280-2281
Feminine personal care products

FFP Partners, L.P. FFP
2801 Glenda Ave.
Fort Worth, TX 76117
817-838-4700
Retail - convenience stores

First Australia Fund, Inc. IAF
One Seaport Plaza
New York, NY 10292
212-214-3334
Financial - investment management

First Australia Prime Income Fund,
  Inc. FAX
One Seaport Plaza
New York, NY 10292
212-214-3334
Financial - investment management

First Central Financial Corp. FCC
266 Merrick Rd.
Lynbrook, NY 11563
516-593-7070
Insurance - property & casualty DRP

First Empire State Corp. FES
One M&T Plaza
Buffalo, NY 14240
716-842-5445
Banks - northeast DRP

First National Corp. FNC
950 John C. Calhoun Dr., S.E.
Orangeburg, SC 29115
803-534-2175
Regional banks holding company -
  So. Carolina

First West Virginia Bancorp, Inc. FWV
1701 Warwood Ave.
Wheeling, WV 26003
304-277-1100
Banks - southeast

Flanigan's Enterprises, Inc. BDL
2841 Cypress Creek Rd.
Fort Lauderdale, FL 33309
954-974-9003   Fax 954-974-2940
Retail - food & restaurants

Florida Public Utilities Co. FPU
401 S. Dixie Hwy.
West Palm Beach, FL 33401
407-832-2461
Utility - gas distribution DRP

Foodarama Supermarkets, Inc. FSM
303 W. Main St.
Freehold, NJ 07728
908-462-4700
Retail - supermarkets

Forest Laboratories, Inc. FRX
150 E. 58th St.
New York, NY 10155
212-421-7850   Fax 212-750-9152
Drugs

Fortune Petroleum Corp. FPX
30101 Agoura Court, Ste. 110
Agoura Hills, CA 91301
818-991-0526
Oil & gas - US exploration & production

Forum Retirement Partners, L.P. FRL
8900 Keystone Crossing
Indianapolis, IN 46240
317-846-0700
Real estate operations

Franklin Capital Corp., (The) FKL
450 Park Ave.
New York, NY 10022
212-486-2323   Fax 212-755-5451
Financial - SBIC & commercial

Franklin Select Realty Trust FSN
PO Box 7777
San Mateo, CA 94403
415-312-2000
Real estate investment trust

Frequency Electronics, Inc. FEI
55 Charles Lindbergh Blvd.
Mitchell Field, NY 11553
516-794-4500   Fax 516-794-4340
Electronics - military

Friedman Industries, Inc. FRD
4001 Homestead Rd.
Houston, TX 77028
713-672-9433
Steel - production

Frisch's Restaurants, Inc. FRS
2800 Gilbert Ave.
Cincinnati, OH 45206
513-961-2660
Retail - food & restaurants

Frontier Adjusters of America, Inc. FAJ
45 E. Monterey Way
Phoenix, AZ 85012
602-264-1061   Fax 602-279-5813
Insurance - brokerage

GA Financial, Inc. GAF
4750 Clairton Blvd.
Pittsburgh, PA 15236
412-882-9946
Financial - savings and loans

Gamma Biologicals, Inc. GBL
3700 Mangum Rd.
Houston, TX 77092
713-681-8481   Fax 713-956-3333
Biomedical & genetic products

Garan, Inc. GAN
350 Fifth Ave.
New York, NY 10118
212-563-2000
Textiles - apparel

Gaylord Container Corp. GCR
500 Lake Cook Rd., Suite 400
Deerfield, IL 60015
708-405-5500
Paper & paper products

Gencor Industries, Inc. GX
5201 N. Orange Blossom Trail
Orlando, FL 32810
407-290-6000   Fax 407-578-0577
Diversified operations

General Automation, Inc. GA
1045 S. East St., PO Box 4883
Anaheim, CA 92803
714-778-4800
Computers - mini & micro

General Employment Enterprises, Inc.
 JOB
One Tower Lane, Ste. 2100
Oakbrook Terrace, IL 60181
708-954-0400
Business services

General Microwave Corp. GMW
5500 New Horizons Blvd.
Amityville, NY 11701
516-226-8900   Fax 516-226-8966
Electrical components - misc.

Genovese Drug Stores GDXA
80 Marcus Dr.
Melville, NY 11747
516-420-1900   Fax 516-845-8487
Retail - drug stores

Getschell Gold Corp. GGO
5460 S. Quebec St., Ste. 240
Englewood, CO 80411
303-771-9000
Gold mining & processing

Giant Food Inc. GFSA
6300 Sheriff Rd.
Landover, MD 20785
301-341-4100
Retail - supermarkets DRP

Glacier Water Services, Inc. HOO
2261 Cosmos Court
Carlsbad, CA 92009
760-930-2420   Fax 760-930-1206
Retail - misc.

Glatfelter (P.H.) Co. GLT
228 So. Main St.
Spring Grove, PA 17362
717-225-4711
Produces printing, writing, specialty papers

Global Small Cap Fund Inc. GSG
1285 Avenue of the Americas
New York, NY 10019
800-852-4750
Financial - investment management

Globalink, Inc. GNK
9302 Lee Hwy., 12th Fl.
Fairfax, VA 22031
703-273-5600
Computers - software

Go-Video, Inc. VCR
14455 N. Hayden Rd., Ste. 219
Scottsdale, AZ 85260
602-998-3400
Audio & video home products

Golden Star Resources Ltd. GSR
1700 Lincoln St., Ste. 1950
Denver, CO 80203
303-830-9000   Fax 303-830-9022
Gold mining & processing

Goldfield Corp. GV
100 Rialto Place, Suite 500
Melbourne, FL 32901
407-724-1700
Electrical construction & mining

Golf Trust of America, Inc. GTA
190 King St.
Charleston, SC 29401
803-768-8300
Real estate investment trust

Gorman-Rupp GRC
305 Bowman St.
Mansfield, OH 44901
419-755-1011
Produces pumps & equipment for
  construction ind. DRP

Graham Corp. GHM
20 Florence Ave.
Batavia, NY 14020
716-343-2216
Machinery - general industrial

Greenbriar Corp. GBR
4265 Kellway Circle
Addison, TX 75244
214-407-8400   Fax 214-407-8421
Operates full-service residential retirement
  facilities

Greyhound Lines, Inc. BUS
15110 N. Dallas Pkwy.
Dallas, TX 75248
214-789-7000
Transportation - bus

GreyWolf Inc. GW
10370 Richmond Ave., Suite 600
Houston, TX 77042
713-435-6100
Oil, gas, geothermal drilling services

Grove Property Trust GVE
598 Asylum Ave.
Hartford, CT 06105
203-523-3960
Real estate investment trust

Gull Laboratories, Inc. GUL
1011 E. 4800 South
Salt Lake City, UT 84117
801-263-3524   Fax 801-265-9268
Medical products

HEARx, Ltd. EAR
1250 Northpoint Pkwy.
West Palm Beach, FL 33407
561-478-8770   Fax 561-478-9603
Medical services

HEICO Corp. HEI
3000 Taft St.
Hollywood, FL 33021
954-987-6101   Fax 954-987-8228
Aerospace - aircraft equipment

HMG/Courtland Properties, Inc. HMG
2701 S. Bayshore Dr.
Coconut Grove, FL 33133
305-854-6803
Real estate investment trust

Halifax Corp. HX
5250 Cherokee Ave.
Alexandria, VA 22312
703-750-2202
Engineering - R & D services

Hallmark Financial Services, Inc. HAF
14651 Dallas Pkwy., Ste. 900
Dallas, TX 75240
214-404-1637
Insurance - property & casualty

Hallwood Energy Partners, L.P. HEP
4582 S. Ulster St. Pkwy.
Denver, CO 80237
303-850-7373
Oil & gas - US exploration & production

Hallwood Realty Partners, L.P. HRY
3710 Rawlins St., Ste. 1500
Dallas, TX 75219
214-528-5588   Fax 214-528-8855
Real estate investment trust

Halsey Drug Co., Inc. HDG
1827 Pacific St.
Brooklyn, NY 11233
718-467-7500   Fax 718-493-1575
Drugs - generic

Halter Marine Group, Inc. HLX
13085 Seaway Rd.
Gulfport, MS 39503
601-896-0029   Fax 601-897-4828
Boat building O

Hampton Industries, Inc. HAI
2000 Greenville Hwy.
Kinston, NC 28502
919-527-8011   Fax 919-527-3538
Textiles - apparel

Hanger Orthopedic Group, Inc. HGR
8200 Wisconsin Ave.
Bethesda, MD 20814
301-986-0701
Medical products

Hanover Direct Inc. HNV
1500 Harbor Blvd.
Weehawken, NJ 07087
201-863-7300
Retail - mail order & direct

Harken Energy Corp. HEC
2505 N. Highway 360, Ste. 800
Grand Prairie, TX 75050
817-695-4900
Oil & gas - US exploration & production

Harold's Stores, Inc. HLD
765 Asp Ave.
Norman, OK 73069
405-329-4045   Fax 405-366-2588
Retail - apparel & shoes

Hasbro, Inc. HAS
1027 Newport Ave.
Pawtucket, RI 02861
401-431-8697
Toys - games & hobby products O DRP

Hastings Manufacturing Co. HMF
325 N. Hanover St.
Hastings, MI 49058
616-945-2491
Automotive & trucking - replacement parts

Hawaiian Airlines, Inc. HA
3375 Koapaka St., Ste. G350
Honolulu, HI 96819
808-835-3700   Fax 808-835-3690
Transportation - airline

Haywood Bancshares, Inc. HBS
505 N. Main St.
Waynesville, NC 28786
704-456-9092
Financial - savings and loans

Health-Chem Corp. HCH
1212 Avenue of the Americas
New York, NY 10036
212-398-0700
Medical products

Healthy Planet Products, Inc. HPP
1129 N. McDowell Blvd.
Petaluma, CA 47404
707-778-2280   Fax 707-778-7518
Paper & paper products

Heartland Partners, L.P. HTL
547 W. Jackson Blvd.
Chicago, IL 60606
312-822-0400
Real estate operations

Heist (C.H.) Corp. HST
810 N. Belcher Rd.
Clearwater, FL 34625
813-461-5656
Furnishes industrial maintenance services

Helm Capital Inc. HHH
66 Field Point Rd.
Greenwich, CT 06830
203-629-1400
Diversified operations

Helmstar Group, Inc. HLM
2 World Trade Ctr., Ste. 2112
New York, NY 10048
212-775-0400
Financial - investment bankers

Hi-Shear Technology Corp. HSR
24225 Garnier St.
Torrance, CA 90505
310-784-2100
Aerospace - aircraft equipment

Holly Corp. HOC
100 Crescent Court, Ste. 1600
Dallas, TX 75201
214-871-3555   Fax 214-871-3566
Oil refining & marketing

Hooper Holmes, Inc. HH
170 Mt. Airy Rd.
Basking Ridge, NJ 07920
908-766-5000
Business services

Host Funding, Inc. HFD
7825 Fay Ave., Ste. 250
La Jolla, CA 92037
619-456-6070
Real estate investment trust

Hovnanian Enterprises, Inc. HOV
10 Highway 35, PO Box 500
Red Bank, NJ 07701
908-747-7800
Building - residential & commercial

Hudson General Corp. HGC
111 Great Neck Rd.
Great Neck, NY 11021
516-487-8610
Transportation - services

Hungarian Telephone & Cable Corp. HTC
90 West St.
New York, NY 10007
212-571-7400
Telecommunications services

Identix Inc. IDX
510 N. Pastoria Ave.
Sunnyvale, CA 94086
408-739-2000   Fax 408-739-3308
Electronics - measuring instruments O

IGI, Inc. IG
Wheat Rd. and Lincoln Ave.
Buena, NJ 08310
609-697-1441
Drugs

Imperial Credit Mortgage Holdings Inc.
 IMH
20371 Irvine Ave.
Santa Ana Heights, CA 92707
714-556-0122
Real estate investment trust O DRP 3%

Imperial Holly Corp. IHK
One Imperial Square, Ste. 200
Sugar Land, TX 77487
281-491-9181   Fax 281-491-9198
Food - sugar & refining DRP

Imperial Oil IMO
111 St. Clair Ave. W.
Toronto, Ont., M5W1K3
416-968-4111
Integrated petroleum & natural gas co.

Income Opportunity Realty Investors, Inc.
  IOT
10670 N. Central Expwy.
Dallas, TX 75231
214-692-4700
Real estate investment trust

Independent Bankshares, Inc. IBK
547 Chestnut St.
Abilene, TX 79602
915-677-5550
Banks - midwest

Instron Corp. ISN
100 Royall St.
Canton, MA 02021
617-828-2500   Fax 617-575-5750
Electronics - measuring instruments

Integrated Orthopedics, Inc. IOI
Three Riverway, Ste. 1430
Houston, TX 77056
713-439-7511   Fax 713-439-0826
Medical services

Intelligent Controls, Inc. ITC
74 Industrial Park Rd.
Saco, ME 04072
207-283-0156   Fax 207-283-0158
Electronics - components & systems

Intelligent Systems Corp. INS
4355 Shackleford Rd.
Norcross, GA 30093
404-381-2900   Fax 404-381-2808
Computers - peripheral equipment

Interchange Financial Services Corp. ISB
Park 80 West/Plaza Two
Saddle Brook, NJ 07662
201-703-2265
Banks - northeast DRP

Interdigital Communications Corp. IDC
2200 Renaissance Blvd.
King of Prussia, PA 19406
610-278-7800   Fax 610-278-6801
Telecommunications equipment O

Interlott Technologies Inc. ILI
6665 Creek Rd.
Cincinnati, OH 45242
513-792-7000
Leisure & recreational products

Intermagnetics General Corp. IMG
450 Old Niskayuna Rd.
Latham, NY 12110
518-782-1122   Fax 518-783-2601
Miscellaneous - not elsewhere classified O

International Air Support Group YLF
1954 Airport Rd., Suite 200
Atlanta, GA 30341
770-455-7575
Supplier aircraft spare parts

International Comfort Products ICP
201 Fourth Ave., Suite 1700
Nashville, GA 37219
615-726-5200
Residential heating/cooling products

International Remote Imaging Systems,
  Inc. IRI
9162 Eton Ave.
Chatsworth, CA 91311
818-709-1244
Medical instruments

Interstate General Co. L.P. IGC
222 Smallwood Village Center
St. Charles, MD 20602
301-843-8600   Fax 301-870-8481
Real estate development

InterSystems Inc. II
8790 Wallisville Rd.
Houston, TX 77029
713-675-0307
Machinery - material handling

Intertape Polymer Group Inc. ITP
110 E. Montee de Liesse
St. Laurent, QC H4T1N4
514-731-7591

Ion Laser Technology, Inc. ILT
3828 S. Main St.
Salt Lake City, UT 84115
801-262-5555   Fax 801-262-5770
Lasers - systems & components

IVAX Corp. IVX
8800 N.W. 36th St.
Miami, FL 33178
305-590-2200   Fax 305-590-2252
Medical products O

Jaclyn, Inc. JLN
635 59th St.
West New York, NJ 07093
201-868-9400
Shoes & related apparel

Jalate Ltd. JLT
1675 S. Alameda St.
Los Angeles, CA 90021
213-765-5000
Apparel

Jan Bell Marketing, Inc. JBM
13801 N.W. 14th St.
Sunrise, FL 33323
305-846-2705
Precious metals & jewelry O

Jetronic Industries, Inc. JET
4200 Mitchell St.
Philadelphia, PA 19128
215-482-7660
Diversified operations

JOULE Inc. JOL
1245 U.S. Route 1 South
Edison, NJ 08837
732-494-6500
Business services

Kankakee Bancorp, Inc. KNK
310 S. Schuyler Ave.
Kankakee, IL 60901
815-937-4440   Fax 815-937-3674
Banks - midwest

KBK Capital Corp. KBK
301 Commerce Street
Fort Worth, TX 76102
817-335-7557
Financial - business services

Keane, Inc. KEA
Ten City Square
Boston, MA 02129
617-241-9200
Computers - services

Kentucky First Bancorp, Inc. KYF
306 N. Main St.
Cynthiana, KY 41031
606-234-1440
Banks - southeast

KFX, Inc. KFX
1999 Broadway, Ste. 3200
Denver, CO 80202
303-293-2992   Fax 303-293-8430
Miscellaneous - not elsewhere classified

Killearn Properties of Georgia, Inc. KPI
100 Eagle Landing Way
Atlanta, GA 30281
404-389-2020
Real estate development

Kinark Corp. KIN
7060 S. Yale Ave.
Tulsa, OK 74136
918-494-0964   Fax 918-494-3999
Chemicals - specialty

KIT Manufacturing Co. KIT
530 E. Wardlow Rd.
Long Beach, CA 90807
310-595-7451
Building - mobile homes & RV

Koger Equity, Inc. KE
3986 Boulevard Center Dr.
Jacksonville, FL 32207
904-398-3403
Real estate investment trust

KRUG International Corp. KRG
6 N. Main St., Ste. 500
Dayton, OH 45402
937-224-9066   Fax 937-224-3654
Diversified operations

KV Pharmaceutical Co. KVA
2503 S. Hanley Rd.
St. Louis, MO 63144
314-645-6600   Fax 314-645-6732
Medical products

LaBarge, Inc. LB
707 N. Second St.
St. Louis, MO 63102
314-231-5960
Electronics - military

Lancer Corp. LAN
235 W. Turbo
San Antonio, TX 78216
210-344-3071   Fax 210-344-8174
Machinery - material handling

Landauer, Inc. LDR
2 Science Rd.
Glenwood, IL 60425
708-755-7000   Fax 708-755-7016
Engineering - R & D services

Laser Technology, Inc. LSR
7070 S. Tucson Way
Englewood, CO 80112
303-649-1000   Fax 303-649-9710
Lasers - systems & components

Lazare Kaplan International Inc. LKI
529 Fifth Ave.
New York, NY 10017
212-972-9700   Fax 212-972-8561
Precious metals & jewelry

Leather Factory TLF
3847 E. Loop 820 South
Ft. Worth, TX 76119
817-496-4414
Leather & leatherworking tools/footwear

Lillian Vernon Corp. LVC
543 Main St.
New Rochelle, NY 10801
914-576-6400
Retail - mail order & direct

Luxtec Corp. LXU
326 Clark St.
Worcester, MA 01606
508-856-9454   Fax 508-856-9462
Fiber optics

LXR Biotechnology Inc. LXR
1401 Marina Way South
Richmond, CA 94804
510-412-9100
Drugs

Lynch Corp. LGL
8 Sound Shore Dr., Ste. 290
Greenwich, CT 06830
203-629-3333
Diversified operations

Magic Works Entertainment MJK
930 Washington Ave.
Miami Beach, FL 33139
305-532-1566   Fax 305-532-4014
Produces, manages & books live
 entertainment

Magnum Hunter Resources, Inc. MHR
42-500 Cook St., Ste. 160
Palm Desert, CA 92211
619-341-1520   Fax 619-341-2391
Oil & gas - field services

Maine Public Service Co. MAP
209 State St.
Presque Isle, ME 04769
207-768-5811
Utility - electric power

MAI Systems Corp. NOW
9600 Jeronimo Rd.
Irvine, CA 92718
714-580-0700   Fax 714-598-6391
Computers - software

Malibu Entertainment Worldwide,
 Inc. MBE
5895 Windward Pkwy., Ste. 220
Alpharetta, GA 30202
404-442-6640
Leisure & recreational services

Marlton Technologies, Inc. MTY
111 Presidential Blvd.
Bala Cynwyd, PA 19004
215-664-6900
Business services

MATEC Corp. MXC
75 South St.
Hopkinton, MA 01748
508-435-9039   Fax 508-435-4469
Diversified operations

Maxim Pharmaceuticals, Inc. MMP
4350 Executive Dr., Ste. 310
San Diego, CA 92121
619-453-4040
Drugs

MAXXAM Inc. MXM
5847 San Felipe, Ste. 2600
Houston, TX 77257
713-975-7600
Diversified operations

McRae Industries, Inc. MRIA
402 N. Main St.
Mt. Gilead, NC 27306
910-439-6147   Fax 910-439-9596
Shoes & related apparel

Measurement Specialities, Inc. MSS
80 Little Falls Rd.
Fairfield, NJ 07004
201-808-1819
Electronics - measuring instruments

Medco Research, Inc. MRE
85 J. T. Alexander Dr.
Research Triangle, NC 27709
919-549-8117
Medical services O

Media General, Inc. MEGA
333 E. Grace St.
Richmond, VA 23219
804-649-6000
Publishing - newspapers DRP

Media Logic, Inc. TST
310 South St.
Plainville, MA 02762
508-695-2006
Electronics - measuring instruments

Medtox Scientific, Inc. TOX
1238 Anthony Rd.
Burlington, NC 27215
910-226-6311   Fax 910-229-4471
Medical products

Merchants Group, Inc. MGP
250 Main St.
Buffalo, NY 14202
716-849-3101
Insurance - property & casualty

Mercury Air Group, Inc. MAX
6851 W. Imperial Highway
Los Angeles, CA 90045
310-646-2994   Fax 310-215-5794
Transportation - services

Meridian Point Realty Trust VIII MPH
50 California St., Ste. 1600
San Francisco, CA 94111
415-956-3031
Real estate investment trust

Merrimac Industries, Inc. MRM
PO Box 986
West Caldwell, NJ 07007
201-575-1300   Fax 201-575-0531
Electronics - military

Meteor Industries MTE
216 Sixteenth St.
Denver, CO 80202
303-572-1137
Markets & distributes refined petroleum

Metromedia International Group, Inc.
 MMG
945 E. Paces Ferry Rd.
Atlanta, GA 30326
404-261-6190
Diversified operations O

Michael Anthony Jewelers, Inc. MAJ
115 S. MacQuesten Parkway
Mt. Vernon, NY 10550
914-699-0000
Precious metals & jewelry

Michael Baker Corp. BKR
420 Rouser Rd., Bldg. 3
Coraopolis, PA 15108
412-269-6300
Engineering - R & D services

Mid-America Bancorp MAB
500 W. Broadway
Louisville, KY 40202
502-589-3351
Banks - southeast

Midcoast Energy Resources Inc. MRS
1100 Louisiana, Ste. 2950
Houston, TX 77002
713-650-8900   Fax 713-650-3232
Oil & gas - production & pipeline

The Midland Company MLA
7000 Midland Blvd.
Amelia, OH 45102
513-943-7100
Insurance - manufactured housing

Midland Resources MLD
16701 Greenpoint Park Dr., Ste. 200
Houston, TX 77060
281-873-4828
Exploration, production of oil & gas -
 Texas

MidSouth Bancorp, Inc. MSL
102 Versailles Blvd.
Lafayette, LA 70501
318-237-8343
Banks - southeast

Minnesota Municipal Income Portfolio,
 Inc. MXA
222 S. Ninth St.
Minneapolis, MN 55402
800-333-6000
Financial - investment management

Minnesota Municipal Term Trust, Inc.
 II MNB
222 S. Ninth St.
Minneapolis, MN 55402
800-333-6000
Financial - investment management

Mission West Properties MSW
6815 Flanders Dr., Ste. 250
San Diego, CA 92121
619-450-3135   Fax 619-450-1618
Real estate operations

Monongahela Power Co. MPNpA
1310 Fairmont Ave.
Fairmont, WV 26554
304-366-3000
Utility - electric power

Moog Inc. MOGA
East Aurora, NY 14052
716-652-2000   Fax 716-687-4457
Aerospace - aircraft equipment

Moore Medical Corp. MMD
389 John Downey Dr.
New Britain, CT 06050
860-826-3600   Fax 860-223-2382
Drugs & sundries - wholesale

Morgan Group, Inc. MG
28651 U.S. 20 West
Elkhart, IN 46514
219-295-2200
Transportation - truck

Morgan's Foods, Inc. MR
25201 Chargin Blvd., Ste. 126
Beachwood, OH 44122
216-360-7500   Fax 216-360-0299
Retail - food & restaurants

Movie Star, Inc. MSI
136 Madison Ave.
New York, NY 10016
212-679-7260
Textiles - apparel

MSR Exploration Ltd. MSR
CBM Building, PO Box 250
Cut Bank, MT 59427
406-873-2235   Fax 406-873-4731
Oil & gas - US exploration & production

Multigraphics, Inc. MTI
1800 W. Central Rd.
Mt. Prospect, IL 60056
708-818-1294   Fax 708-818-3499
Office equipment & supplies

MuniVest Fund, Inc. MVF
PO Box 9011
Princeton, NJ 08543
609-282-2800
Financial - investment management

MuniYield Arizona Fund II, Inc. MZA
PO Box 9011
Princeton, NJ 08543
609-282-2800
Financial - investment management

Myers Industries, Inc. MYE
1293 S. Main St.
Akron, OH 44301
216-253-5592   Fax 216-253-1882
Rubber & plastic products

Nabors Industries, Inc. NBR
515 W. Greens Rd., Ste. 1200
Houston, TX 77067
713-874-0035   Fax 713-872-5205
Oil & gas - field services O

National Bancshares (Texas) NBT
104 E. Mann Rd.
Laredo, Tx 78042
210-724-2424
Banks - midwest

National Beverage Corp. FIZ
One N. University Dr.
Fort Lauderdale, FL 33324
954-581-0922
Beverages - soft drinks

National Gas & Oil Co. NLG
1500 Granville Rd.
Newark, OH 43058
614-344-2102
Utility - gas distribution

National Healthcare, L.P. NHC
100 Vine St.
Murfreesboro, TN 37130
615-890-2020
Nursing homes

National Realty, L.P. NLP
10670 N. Central Expressway
Dallas, TX 75231
214-692-4700
Real estate operations

NeoPharm Inc. NEO
225 E. Deerpath, Suite 250
Lake Forest, IL 60045
847-295-8678
Biotechnology

NetMed, Inc. NMD
425 Metro Pl. North, Ste. 140
Dublin, OH 43017
614-793-9356   Fax 614-793-9376
Medical products

New Mexico and Arizona Land Co. NZ
3033 N. 44th St.
Phoenix, AZ 85018
602-952-8836
Real estate operations

New York Tax-Exempt Income Fund,
   Inc. XTX
500 W. Madison St., Ste. 3000
Chicago, IL 60606
312-559-3000
Financial - investment management

North American Vaccine NVX
12103 Indian Creek Court
Beltsville, MD 20705
301-470-6100
Research development vaccines

Northeast Bancorp NBN
489 Congress St., Ste. 200
Portland, ME 04101
207-772-8587   Fax 207-828-5768
Financial - savings and loans

Northern Technologies International Corp.
   NTI
6680 North Highway 59
Lino Lakes, MN 55014
612-784-1250
Instruments - control

Novavax Inc. NOX
8320 Guilford Rd.
Columbia, MD 21046
301-854-3900
Topical & oral drug delivery system

Novavax, Inc. NOX
12601 Twinbrook Pkwy.
Rockville, MD 20852
301-231-9250
Biomedical & genetic products

nStor Technologies NSO
100 Century Blvd.
West Palm Beach, FL 33147
561-640-3103
Computer disk products

NTN Communications, Inc. NTN
2121 Palomar Airport Rd.
Carlsbad, CA 92009
760-438-7400   Fax 760-438-3505
Broadcasting - radio & TV O

Numac Energy Inc. NMC
Cadillac Fairview Bldg., 321-6 Ave. S.W.
Calgary, AB T2P3H3
403-260-9400
Oil & gas exploration & production

Nuveen California Premium Income
  Municipal Fund NCU
333 W. Wacker Dr.
Chicago, IL 60606
312-917-7700
Financial - investment management

Nuveen Georgia Premium Income
  Municipal Fund NPG
333 W. Wacker Dr.
Chicago, IL 60606
312-917-7700
Financial - investment management

Nuveen Missouri Premium Income
  Municipal Fund NOM
333 W. Wacker Dr.
Chicago, IL 60606
312-917-7700
Financial - investment management

Nuveen Washington Premium Income
Municipal Fd. NPW
333 W. Wacker Dr.
Chicago, IL 60606
312-917-7700
Financial - investment management

NVR, Inc. NVR
7601 Lewinsville Rd., Ste. 300
McLean, VA 22102
703-761-2000   Fax 703-761-2030
Building - residential & commercial

Ohio Art Co. OAR
One Toy St., P.O. Box 111
Bryan, OH 43506
419-636-3141   Fax 419-638-7614
Manufactures toys

ONCOR, Inc. ONC
209 Perry Pkwy.
Gaithersburg, MD 20877
301-963-3500   Fax 301-926-6129
Biomedical & genetic products

OncorMed, Inc. ONM
205 Perry Pkwy.
Gaithersburg, MD 20877
301-208-1888
Biomedical & genetic products

One Liberty Properties, Inc. OLP
60 Cutter Mill Rd.
Great Neck, NY 11021
516-466-3100
Real estate investment trust

Organogenesis Inc. ORG
83 Rogers St.
Cambridge, MA 02142
617-575-0775
Medical products O

Oriole Homes Corp. OHCA
1690 S. Congress Ave.
Delray Beach, FL 33445
561-274-2000   Fax 561-274-0068
Building - residential & commercial

Oshman's Sporting Goods, Inc. OSH
2302 Maxwell Lane
Houston, TX 77023
713-928-3171
Retail - misc.

O'Sullivan Corp. OSL
1944 Valley Ave., PO Box 3510
Winchester, VA 22604
703-667-6666   Fax 703-722-2695
Rubber & plastic products

PAB Bankshares, Inc. PAB
3102 N. Oak St. Extension
Valdosta, GA 31602
912-242-7758
Banks - southeast

Pacific Gateway Properties, Inc. PGP
101 Spear St., Ste. 215
San Francisco, CA 94105
415-543-8600
Real estate operations

Pacific Pharmaceuticals PHA
6730 Mesa Ridge Rd., Suite A
San Diego, CA 92121
619-550-3900   Fax 619-550-3929
Biotechnology

Pacific Research & Engineering Corp.
 PXE
2070 Las Palmas Dr.
Carlsbad, CA 92009
760-438-3911
Electronics - components & systems

Pamida Holdings Corp. PAM
8800 F St.
Omaha, NE 68127
402-339-2400
Retail - discount & variety

Park National Corp. PRK
50 N. Third St., PO Box 850
Newark, OH 43058
614-349-8451
Financial - savings and loans DRP

Paxson Communications Corp. PXN
601 Clearwater Park Rd.
West Palm Beach, FL 33401
407-859-4122
Broadcasting - radio & TV O

PC Quote, Inc. PQT
300 S. Wacker Dr.
Chicago, IL 60606
312-913-2800   Fax 312-913-2900
Business services

Penobscot Shoe Co. PSO
450 N. Main St., PO Box 545
Old Town, ME 04468
207-827-4431   Fax 207-827-4834
Shoes & related apparel

Peoples Telephone Co., Inc. PHO
8041 NW 14th St.
Miami, FL 33126
305-593-9667
Telecommunications services

Perini Corp. PCR
73 Mt. Wayte Ave., PO Box 9160
Framingham, MA 01701
508-628-2000
Construction - heavy

PhoneTel Technologies PHN
1127 Euclid Ave.
Cleveland, OH 44115
216-241-2555
Telecommunications

Pico Products, Inc. PPI
12500 Foothill Blvd.
Lakeview Terrace, CA 91342
818-897-0028
Telecommunications equipment

Piedmont Bancorp, Inc. PDB
260 S. Churton St.
Hillsborough, NC 27278
919-732-2143   Fax 919-732-6001
Banks - southeast

Pinnacle Bancshares PLE
1811 Second Ave., PO Box 1388
Jasper, AL 35502
205-221-4111
Financial - savings and loans

Pitt-Des Moines, Inc. PDM
3400 Grand Ave.
Pittsburgh, PA 15225
412-331-3000   Fax 412-331-7403
Construction - heavy

Pittsburgh & West Virginia Railroad PW
3 PPG Place, Ste. 410
Pittsburgh, PA 15222
412-687-4956
Real estate investment trust

Plains Resources Inc. PLX
1600 Smith St.
Houston, TX 77002
713-654-1414
Oil & gas - US exploration & production O

PLC Systems Inc. PLC
113 Cedar St., Ste. S-2
Milford, MA 01757
508-478-6046   Fax 508-478-5844
Lasers - systems & components O

PLM International, Inc. PLM
One Market, Steuart St. Tower
San Francisco, CA 94105
415-974-1399
Leasing

Plymouth Rubber Co., Inc. PLRA
104 Revere St.
Canton, MA 02021
617-828-0220   Fax 617-828-6041
Rubber & plastic products

PMC Capital, Inc. PMC
18301 Biscayne Blvd.
North Miami Beach, FL 33160
305-933-5858
Financial - business services DRP 2%

PMC Commercial Trust PCC
17290 Preston Rd.
Dallas, TX 75252
214-380-0044
Real estate investment trust DRP

Polk Audio, Inc. PKA
5601 Metro Dr.
Baltimore, MD 21215
410-358-3600   Fax 410-764-5266
Audio & video home products

PolyMedica Industries, Inc. PM
2 Constitution Way
Woburn, MA 01801
617-933-2020   Fax 617-933-7992
Medical products

Polyphase Corp. PLY
175 Commerce Dr.
Fort Washington, PA 19034
215-643-6950   Fax 215-643-5237
Electrical products - misc.

Polyvision Corporation PLI
1305 Grandview Ave.
Pittsburgh, PA 15211
412-381-2600
Video equipment

Porta Systems Corp. PSI
575 Underhill Blvd.
Syosset, NY 11791
516-364-9300   Fax 516-682-4655
Telecommunications equipment

Premier Bancshares PMB
950 East Paces Ferry Rd.
Atlanta, GA 30326
404-814-3090
Regional banks

Pre-Paid Legal Services, Inc. PPD
321 E. Main
Ada, OK 74820
405-436-1234
Business services

Presidential Realty Corp. PDLB
180 S. Broadway
White Plains, NY 10605
914-948-1300   Fax 914-948-1327
Real estate investment trust   DRP 5%

Price Communications Corp. PR
45 Rockefeller Plaza
New York, NY 10020
212-757-5600
Broadcasting - radio & TV

Prime Resources Group PRU
1065 West Georgia St.
Vancouver, BC V6E3P3
604-684-2345   Fax 604-684-9831
Gold & precious metals mining

Proactive Technologies, Inc. PTE
7118 Beech Ridge Trail
Tallahassee, FL 32312
904-668-8500
Real estate development

Professional Bancorp, Inc. MDB
606 Broadway
Santa Monica, CA 90401
310-458-1521
Banks - west

Professional Dental Technologies, Inc.
 PRO
633 Lawrence St.
Batesville, AR 72501
501-698-2300
Medical & dental supplies

Property Capital Trust PCT
One Post Office Sq., 21st Fl.
Boston, MA 02109
617-451-2400   Fax 617-451-2499
Real estate investment trust

Provena Foods Inc. PZA
5010 Eucalyptus Ave.
Chino, CA 91710
909-627-1082
Food - meat products

Providence and Worcester Railroad Co.
 PWX
75 Hammond St.
Worcester, MA 01610
508-755-4000
Transportation - rail

Psychemedics Corp. PMD
1280 Mass Ave., Ste. 200
Cambridge, MA 02138
617-868-7455   Fax 617-864-1639
Medical services

Putnam California Investment Grade
 Municipal Trust PCA
One Post Office Square
Boston, MA 02109
617-292-1000
Financial - investment management

Putnam Investment Grade Municipal Trust
  IIIP ML
One Post Office Square
Boston, MA 02109
617-292-1000
Financial - investment management

Putnam New York Investment Grade
  Municipal Trust PMN
One Post Office Square
Boston, MA 02109
617-292-1000
Financial - investment management

QC Optics, Inc. OPC
154 Middlesex Turnpike
Burlington, MA 01803
617-272-4949
Instruments - control

Quebecor PQB
612 Saint Jacques St.
Montreal, QCH3C4M8
514-877-9777   Fax 514-877-9757
Specialty printing - holding company O

Ragan (Brad) BRD
4404-G Stuart Andrew Blvd.
Charlotte, NC 28217
704-521-2100   Fax 704-521-2171
Retail - automotive tires & service

Randers Group RGI
570 Seminole Rd.
Norton Shores, MI 49444
616-733-0036
Engineering, contracting services

Redwood Empire Bancorp REB
111 Santa Rosa Ave.
Santa Rosa, CA 95404
707-545-9611
Banks - west DRP

REFAC Technology Development REF
122 E. 42nd St.
New York, NY 10168
212-687-4741
International technology transfer

Regal-Beloit Corp. RBC
200 State St.
Beloit, WI 53511
608-364-8800
Machinery - general industrial

RF Power Products RFP
502 Gibbsboro-Marlton Rd.
Voorhees, NJ 08043
609-751-0033   Fax 609-751-2960
Electronics - components & systems

Richmont Mines RIC
100 Ave. Principale
Rouyn-Noranda, QC J9X4P2
819-797-2465   Fax 819-797-0166
Gold & precious metals mining

Richton International Corp. RHT
340 Main St.
Madison, NJ 07940
201-966-0104   Fax 201-966-7892
Financial - investment bankers

Rio Algom Ltd. ROM
120 Adelaide St. W., Suite 2600
Toronto, ON M5H1W5
416-367-4000
Metals mining

Riviera Holdings Corp. RIV
2901 Las Vegas Blvd. South
Las Vegas, NV 89109
702-734-5110
Leisure & recreational services

Riviera Tool RTC
5460 Executive Parkway
Grand Rapids, MI 49512
616-698-2100
Sheet metal stamping dies

Roberts Pharmaceutical Corp. RPC
6 Industrial Way West
Eatontown, NJ 07724
908-389-1182   Fax 908-389-1014
Drugs O

Rogers Corp. ROG
One Technology Dr., PO Box 188
Rogers, CT 06263
860-774-9605
Electrical components - misc.

Rotonics Manufacturing Inc. RMI
17022 S. Figueroa St.
Gardena, CA 90248
310-538-4932
Rubber & plastic products

Royal Oak Mines RYO
5501 Lakeview Dr.
Kirkland, WA 98033
206-822-8992   Fax 206-822-3552
Gold & precious metals mining

Saba Petroleum Co. SAP
17512 Von Karman Ave.
Irvine, CA 92714
714-724-1112   Fax 714-724-1555
Oil & gas - production & pipeline

Saga Communications, Inc. SGA
73 Kercheval Ave.
Grosse Pointe Farms, MI 48236
313-886-7070   Fax 313-886-7150
Broadcasting - radio & TV

Santa Fe Gaming Corp. SGM
4949 N. Rancho Dr.
Las Vegas, NV 89130
702-658-4900
Leisure & recreational services

SBM Industries, Inc. SBM
Two Madison Ave.
Larchmont, NY 10538
914-833-0649   Fax 914-833-1068
Office equipment & supplies

Scheib (Earl), Inc. ESH
8737 Wilshire Blvd.
Beverly Hills, CA 90211
310-652-4880   Fax 310-659-4827
Auto parts - retail & wholesale

Schulte Homes Corp. SHC
221 U.S. Highway 20 West
Middlebury, IN 46540
219-825-5881
Building - residential & commercial

Scope Industries SCP
233 Wilshire Blvd., Ste. 310
Santa Monica, CA 90401
310-458-1574
Agricultural operations

Scotland Bancorp SSB
505 South Main St.
Luarinburg, NC 28352
910-276-2703
Savings & loan companies

Seaboard Corp. SEB
9000 W. 67th St.
Shawnee Mission, KS 66202
913-676-8800   Fax 913-676-8872
Food - meat products

Selas Corporation of America SLS
PO Box 200
Dresher, PA 19025
215-646-6600   Fax 215-646-3536
Diversified operations

Selfcare, Inc. SLF
200 Prospect St.
Waltham, MA 02154
617-647-3900   Fax 617-647-3939
Medical products

Sentry Technology SKV
350 Wireless Blvd.
Hauppauge, NY 11788
516-232-2100
Electronic surveillance systems

Servotronics, Inc. SVT
3901 Union Rd.
Buffalo, NY 14225
716-633-5990   Fax 716-633-8278
Diversified operations

Sheffield Pharmaceuticals SHM
666 Fifth Ave., 13th Fl.
New York, NY 10103
212-957-6600
Medical services

SIFCO Industries, Inc. SIF
970 E. 64th St.
Cleveland, OH 44103
216-881-8600   Fax 216-881-1828
Metal processing & fabrication DRP

Signal Technology Corp. STZ
955 Benecia Ave.
Sunnyvale, CA 94086
408-730-6318   Fax 408-245-3396
Electrical components - misc.

Silverado Foods, Inc. SLV
7313 E. 38th St.
Tulsa, OK 74145
918-627-7783   Fax 918-627-7784
Food - misc.

SJW Corp. SJW
374 W. Santa Clara St.
San Jose, CA 95196
408-279-7810
Utility - water supply

Smith Barney Intermediate Municipal
  Fund, Inc. SBI
1345 Avenue of the Americas
New York, NY 10105
212-698-5349
Financial - investment management

Smith Barney Municipal Fund SBT
1345 Avenue of the Americas
New York, NY 10105
212-464-6000
Financial - investment management

Softnet Systems, Inc. SOF
1425 E. Bush Pkwy.
Buffalo Grove, IL 60089
708-793-2000
Miscellaneous - not elsewhere classified

Soligen Technologies, Inc. SGT
19408 Londelius St.
Northridge, CA 91324
818-718-1221   Fax 818-718-0760
Miscellaneous - not elsewhere classified

Southern Banc Co. SRN
221 S. 6th St.
Gladsden, AL 35901
205-543-3860
Savings & loan companies

Southfirst Bancshares, Inc. SZB
126 N. Norton Ave., PO Box 167
Sylacauga, AL 35150
205-245-4365
Financial - savings and loans

Southwest Georgia Financial SGB
201 First St. S.E.
Moultie, GA 31768
912-985-1120
Regional banks

Spatial Technology Inc. STY
2425 55th St., Bldg. A
Boulder, CO 80301
303-449-0549
Computers - software

Specialty Chemical Resources, Inc. CHM
9100 Valley View Rd.
Macedonia, OH 44056
216-468-1380   Fax 216-468-0287
Chemicals - specialty

Sports Club Co. SCY
11100 Santa Monica Blvd., Ste. 300
Los Angeles, CA 90025
310-479-5200   Fax 310-479-8350
Operator of sports & fitness clubs

Stage 1 Apparel Corp. SA
350 Fifth Ave.
New York, NY 10118
212-564-5865   Fax 212-239-0377
Textiles - apparel

Standard and Poor's (SPDR) SPY
25 Broadway
New York, NY 10004
212-208-8000
Financial - business services

Stephan Co. TSC
1850 W. McNab Rd.
Ft. Lauderdale, FL 33309
954-971-0600
Personal grooming products

Sterling Capital Corp. SPR
635 Madison Ave.
New York, NY 10022
212-980-3360
Financial - investment management

Stevens International, Inc. SVGA
5500 Airport Fwy.
Fort Worth, TX 76113
817-831-3911
Machinery - printing

Stillwater Mining Co. SWC
717 17th St., Ste. 1480
Denver, CO 80202
303-978-2525   Fax 303-978-2590
Metal ores - misc.

Stone Street Bancorp, Inc. SSM
232 S. Main St.
Mocksville, NC 27028
704-634-5936
Banks - southeast

Storage Computer Corp. SOS
Precision Park
North Springfield, VT 05150
802-886-2256   Fax 802-886-2682
Computers - peripheral equipment

Sulcas Hospitality Technologies SUL
41 N. Main St.
Greensburg, PA 15601
412-836-2000   Fax 412-846-1440
Computers - software O

Sunair Electronics, Inc. SNR
3101 S.W. Third Ave.
Fort Lauderdale, FL 33315
954-525-1505   Fax 954-765-1322
Telecommunications equipment

Supreme Industries, Inc. STS
65140 U.S. 33 East, PO Box 237
Goshen, IN 46526
219-642-3070
Automotive & trucking - original
  equipment

Surety Capital Corp. SRY
1845 Precinct Line Rd.
Hurst, TX 76054
817-498-8154
Banks - southwest

Sybron Chemicals Inc. SYC
Birmingham Rd., PO Box 66
Birmingham, NJ 08011
609-893-1100   Fax 609-893-2063
Chemicals - specialty

Tab Products Co. TBP
1400 Page Mill Rd.
Palo Alto, CA 94304
415-852-2400
Office equipment & supplies

Team, Inc. TMI
1001 Fannin, Ste. 4656
Houston, TX 77002
713-659-3600   Fax 713-659-3420
Construction - heavy

Teche Holding TSH
211 Willow St.
Franklin, LA 70538
318-828-3212   Fax 318-828-0110
Savings & loan companies

Tech/Ops Sevcon, Inc. TO
One Beacon St.
Boston, MA 02108
617-523-2030   Fax 617-523-0073
Electrical products - misc.

Tejon Ranch Co. TRC
PO Box 1000
Lebec, CA 93243
805-327-8481
Agricultural operations

Telephone and Data Systems, Inc. TDS
30 N. LaSalle St.
Chicago, IL 60602
312-630-1900   Fax 312-630-1908
Utility - telephone O DRP 5%

TENERA, Inc. TNR
One Market, Spear Tower
San Francisco, CA 94105
415-536-4744   Fax 415-536-4714
Computers - services

Texarkana First Financial Corp. FTF
3rd and Olive Streets
Texarkana, TX 75504
501-773-1103   Fax 501-773-2673
Banks - southeast

Texas Biotechnology Corp. TXB
7000 Fannin St., Ste. 1920
Houston, TX 77030
713-796-8822
Drugs

Thermedics Detection TDX
220 Mill Rd.
Chelmsford, MA 01824
617-622-1000
Electronics instrumentation

Thermedics Inc. TMD
470 Wildwood St., PO Box 2999
Woburn, MA 01888
617-938-3786   Fax 617-933-4476
Medical products O

Thermo BioAnalysis TBA
504 Airport Rd.
Santa Fe, NM 87504
505-471-3232
Specialized instrumentation

Thermo Cardiosystems Inc. TCA
470 Wildwood St., PO Box 2697
Woburn, MA 01888
617-622-1000
Medical products

Thermo Ecotek Corp. TCK
81 Wyman St.
Waltham, MA 02254
617-622-1500
Energy - cogeneration

Thermo Fibergen Inc. TFG
8 Alfred Circle
Bedford, MA 01730
617-275-3600
Miscellaneous - not elsewhere classified

Thermo Fibertek, Inc. TFT
81 Wyman St.
Waltham, MA 02254
617-622-1000
Industrial processing - misc.

Thermo Instrument Systems Inc. THI
1275 Hammerwood Ave.
Sunnyvale, CA 94089
617-622-1000
Instruments - scientific O

Thermo Optek Corp. TOC
8-E. Forge Pkwy.
Franklin, MA 02038
508-541-7111   Fax 508-541-0140
Instruments - scientific

Thermo Power Corp. THP
81 Wyman St., PO Box 9046
Waltham, MA 02254
617-622-1000   Fax 617-622-1207
Energy - alternate sources

Thermo Remediation Inc. THN
1964 S. Orange Blossom Trail
Apopka, FL 32703
617-622-1000
Pollution control equipment & services
DRP

Thermo Sentron Inc. TSR
501 Ninetieth Ave., NW
Minneapolis, MN 55433
612-783-2500
Electronics - measuring instruments

Thermo TerraTech Inc. TTT
81 Wyman St.
Waltham, MA 02254
617-622-1000
Machinery - general industrial

Thermo Voltek Corp. TVL
470 Wildwood St., PO Box 2878
Woburn, MA 01888
617-622-1000
Electronics - measuring instruments

ThermoLase Corp. TLZ
9550 Distribution Ave.
San Diego, CA 92121
619-578-5885
Miscellaneous - not elsewhere classified

ThermoQuest Corp. TMQ
355 River Oaks Pkwy.
San Jose, CA 95134
617-622-1000
Instruments - scientific

ThermoSpectra Corp. THS
Eight E. Forge Pkwy.
Franklin, MA 02038
617-622-1000
Electronics - measuring instruments

ThermoTrex Corp. TKN
10455 Pacific Center Ct.
San Diego, CA 92121
619-622-1000
Engineering - R & D services

Thermwood Corp. THM
PO Box 436
Dale, IN 47523
812-937-4476
Instruments - control

Three Rivers Financial Corp. THR
123 Portage Ave.
Three Rivers, MI 49093
616-279-5117   Fax 616-279-7974
Banks - midwest

Tipperary Corp. TPY
633 17th St., Ste. 1550
Denver, CO 80202
303-293-9379
Oil & gas - US exploration & production

Tofutti Brands Inc. TOF
50 Jackson Dr.
Cranford, NJ 07016
908-272-2400
Food - misc.

Tompkins County Trustco, Inc. TMP
The Commons, PO Box 460
Ithaca, NY 14851
607-273-3210
Banks - northeast DRP

Top Source Technologies TPS
2000 PGA Blvd., Ste. 3200
Palm Beach Gardens, FL 33408
407-775-5756
Automotive & trucking - original
    equipment O

Torotel, Inc. TTL
13402 S. 71 Highway
Grandview, MO 64030
816-761-6314
Electronics - military

Trans World Airlines, Inc. TWA
515 N. Sixth St.
St. Louis, MO 63101
314-589-3000
Transportation - airline O

Transfinancial Holdings TFH
8245 Nieman Rd., Suite 100
Lenaxa, KS 66214
913-859-0055
Trucking - common carrier

Trans-Lux Corp. TLX
110 Richards Ave.
Norwalk, CT 06856
203-853-4321
Electrical products - misc.

TransMontagne Oil Co. TMG
1801 Broadway, Ste. 600
Denver, CO 80202
303-296-0231
Oil & gas - US exploration & production

Trex Medical TXM
36 Apple Ridge Rd.
Danbury, CT 06810
203-425-8000   Fax 203-790-1188
Medical equipment

Trinitech Systems, Inc. TSI
333 Ludlow St.
Stamford, CT 06902
203-425-8000 Fax 203-425-8100
Data collection & systems

Turner Corp. TUR
375 Hudson St.
New York, NY 10014
212-229-6000
Engineering & construction

Unapix Entertainment, Inc. UPX
500 Fifth Ave.
New York, NY 10110
212-575-7070
Motion pictures & services

Uni-Marts, Inc. UNI
477 E. Beaver Ave.
State College, PA 16801
814-234-6000
Retail - convenience stores

Uniflex, Inc. UFX
383 W. John St.
Hicksville, NY 11802
516-932-2000
Miscellaneous - not elsewhere classified

Unilab Corp. ULB
18448 Oxnard St.
Tarzana, CA 91356
818-757-0601   Fax 818-757-3809
Medical services

Unimar Co. UMR
1221 McKinley, Ste. 600
Houston, TX 77010
713-654-8550   Fax 713-654-8569
Oil & gas - international integrated

Unique Mobility, Inc. UQM
425 Corporate Circle
Golden, CO 80401
303-278-2002
Automotive & trucking - original
equipment

United Capital Corp. AFP
111 Great Neck Rd.
Great Neck, NY 11021
516-466-6464
Real estate operations

United Foods, Inc. UFDA
Ten Pictsweet Dr.
Bells, TN 38006
901-422-7600
Food - misc.

United-Guardian UG
230 Marcus Blvd.
Hauppauge, NY 11788
516-273-0900
Personal & healthcare products

United Mobile Homes, Inc. UMH
125 Wyckoff Rd.
Eatontown, NJ 07724
908-389-3890
Real estate investment trust DRP 5%

United States Cellular Corp. USM
8410 W. Bryn Mawr, Ste. 700
Chicago, IL 60631
773-399-8900   Fax 773-399-8936
Telecommunications, cellular/wireless O

Unitel Video, Inc. UNV
515 W. 57th St.
New York, NY 10019
212-265-3600
Motion pictures & services

UNITIL Corp. UTL
216 Epping Rd.
Exeter, NH 03833
603-772-0775   Fax 603-772-4651
Real estate development DRP 5%

Unity Bancorp, Inc. UBI
64 Old Hwy. 22
Clinton, NJ 08809
908-730-7630
Banks - northeast

U.S. Bioscience, Inc. UBS
100 Front St.
West Conshohacken, PA 19428
215-832-0570   Fax 610-832-4500
Drugs O

U.S. Liquids USL
411 N. San Houston Pkwy. E., Ste. 400
Houston, TX 77060
281-272-4500
Waste management

UTI Energy Corp. UTI
485 Devon Park Dr., Ste. 112
Wayne, PA 19087
610-971-9600
Oil & gas - field services

Valley Forge Corp. VF
100 Smith Ranch Rd., Ste. 326
San Raphael, CA 94903
415-492-1500
Leisure & recreational products

Valley Resources, Inc. VR
1595 Mendon Rd., PO Box 7900
Cumberland, RI 02864
401-334-1188
Utility - gas distribution DRP 5%

Van Kampen American Advantage
  Municipal Inc. Tr. II VKI
One Parkview Plaza
Oakbrook Terrace, IL 60181
708-684-6000
Financial - investment management

Van Kampen American California
  Municipal Trust VKC
One Parkview Plaza
Oakbrook Terrace, IL 60181
708-684-6000
Financial - investment management

Van Kampen American Florida Municipal
  Opp. Trust VOF
One Parkview Plaza
Oakbrook Terrace, IL 60181
708-684-6000
Financial - investment management

Van Kampen American MA Value
  Municipal Income Trust VMV
One Parkview Plaza
Oakbrook Terrace, IL 60181
708-684-6000
Financial - investment management

Van Kampen American NJ Value
  Municipal Income Trust VJV
One Parkview Plaza
Oakbrook Terrace, IL 60181
708-684-6000
Financial - investment management

Van Kampen American Ohio Value
  Municipal Income Tr. VOV
One Parkview Plaza
Oakbrook Terrace, IL 60181
708-684-6000
Financial - investment management

Van Kampen American Select Sector
  Municipal Trust VKL
One Parkview Plaza
Oakbrook Terrace, IL 60181
708-684-6000
Financial - investment management

Versar, Inc. VSR
6850 Versar Center
Springfield, VA 22151
703-750-3000   Fax 703-642-6807
Pollution control equipment & services

Viacom Inc. VIA
1515 Broadway
New York, NY 10036
212-258-6000
Diversified operations O

Vicon Industries, Inc. VII
89 Arkay Dr.
Hauppauge, NY 11788
516-952-2288   Fax 516-951-2288
Video equipment

Virco Manufacturing Corp. VIR
2027 Harpers Way
Torrance, CA 90501
310-533-0474   Fax 310-533-1906
Furniture

Vita Food Products, Inc. VSF
2222 W. Lake St.
Chicago, IL 60612
312-738-4500
Food - misc.

Voyageur Arizona Municipal Income Fund,
  Inc. VAZ
90 S. Seventh St., Ste. 4400
Minneapolis, MN 55402
612-376-7000
Financial - investment management

Voyageur Colorado Insured Municipal
  Income Fund, Inc. VCF
90 S. Seventh St., Ste. 4400
Minneapolis, MN 55402
612-376-7000
Financial - investment management

Voyageur Florida Insured Municipal
  Income Fund VFL
90 S. Seventh St., Ste. 4400
Minneapolis, MN 55402
612-376-7000
Financial - investment management

Voyageur Minnesota Municipal Income
  Fund II, Inc. VMM
90 S. Seventh St., Ste. 4400
Minneapolis, MN 55402
612-376-7000
Financial - investment management

Voyageur Minnesota Municipal Income
  Fund III, Inc. VYM
90 S. Seventh St., Ste. 4400
Minneapolis, MN 55402
612-376-7000
Financial - investment management

Voyageur Minnesota Municipal Income
  Fund, Inc. VMN
90 S. Seventh St., Ste. 4400
Minneapolis, MN 55402
612-376-7000
Financial - investment management

VSI Holdings, Inc. VIS
4900 Highlands Pkwy.
Smyrna, GA 30082
770-432-0636
Retail - apparel & shoes

Vulcan International Corp. VUL
30 Garfield Place, Ste. 1000
Cincinnati, OH 45202
513-621-2850
Shoes & related apparel

Washington Real Estate Investment Trust
  WRE
10400 Connecticut Ave.
Kensington, MD 20895
301-929-5900   Fax 301-929-5910
Real estate investment trust DRP

Washington Savings Bank WSB
Route 301
Waldorf, MD 20603
301-843-7200
Financial - savings and loans

Webco Industries WEB
200 Woodland Dr.
Sand Springs, OK 74063
918-241-1000
High quality carbon & stainless steel
  tubing

Wellco Enterprises, Inc. WLC
PO Box 188
Waynesville, NC 28786
704-456-3545   Fax 704-456-3547
Military equipment

Wellsford Real Properties WRP
610 Fifth Ave.
New York, NY 10020
212-233-2300
Land development

Wells-Gardner Electronics Corp. WGA
2701 N. Kildare Ave.
Chicago, IL 60639
312-252-8220   Fax 312-252-8072
Electrical products - misc.

Wendt-Bristol Health Services Corp. WMD
Two Nationwide Plaza
Columbus, OH 43215
614-221-6000
Nursing homes

Wesco Financial Corp. WSC
315 E. Colorado Blvd.
Pasadena, CA 91101
818-585-6700
Financial - savings and loans

Western Investment Real Estate Trust WIR
3450 California St.
San Francisco, CA 94118
415-929-0211   Fax 415-929-0905
Real estate investment trust DRP

Western Star Trucks Holdings WSH
2076 Enterprise Way
Kelowna, BC V19 6H8
250-860-3319   Fax 250-860-1252
Manufactures trucks, buses & parts

Whitman Education Group, Inc. WIX
4400 Biscayne Blvd.
Miami, FL 33137
305-575-6510
Schools

Winston Resources, Inc. WRS
535 Fifth Ave.
New York, NY 10017
212-557-5000
Temporary and permanent staffing services

Wireless Telecom Group, Inc. WTT
49 E. Midland Ave.
Paramus, NJ 07652
201-261-8797
Electronics - measuring instruments O

Wolf (Howard B.) Inc. HBW
3809 Parry Ave.
Dallas, TX 75226
214-823-9941
Makes, markets women's fashion apparel

XCL Ltd. XCL
110 Rue Jean Lafitte
Lafayette, LA 70508
318-237-0325   Fax 318-237-3316
Oil & gas - US exploration & production

Zevex International ZVX
4314 Zevex Park Lane
Salt Lake City, UT 84123
801-264-1001
Medical electronic equipment

Ziegler Cos. ZCO
215 N. Main St.
West Bend, WI 53095
414-334-5521
Investment banking, financing

NASDAQ NATIONAL MARKET SYSTEM

Abaxis, Inc. ABAX
1320 Chesapeake Terrace
Sunnyvale, CA 94089
408-734-0200 Fax 408-734-2874
Medical instruments

ABC Rail Products Corp. ABCR
200 S. Michigan Ave.
Chicago, IL 60604
312-322-0360
Transportation - equipment & leasing

ABIOMED, Inc. ABMD
33 Cherry Hill Dr.
Danvers, MA 01923
508-777-5410
Medical instruments

Able Telcom Holding Corp. ABTE
1601 Forum Place
West Palm Beach, FL 33401
561-688-0400
Telecommunications equipment

ABR Information Services, Inc. ABRX
34125 US Highway 19 North
Palm Harbor, FL 34684
813-785-2819 Fax 813-789-3854
Miscellaneous - not elsewhere classified

Abrams Industries, Inc. ABRI
5775-A Glenridge Dr., N.E.
Atlanta, GA 30328
404-256-9785 Fax 404-252-3891
Diversified operations

ACCEL International Corp. ACLE
475 Metro Place North
Dublin, OH 43017
614-764-7000
Insurance - multi line & misc.

Access Health, Inc. ACCS
11020 White Rock Rd.
Rancho Cordova, CA 95670
916-851-4000 Fax 916-852-3890
Medical services O

Acclaim Entertainment, Inc. AKLM
71 Audrey Ave.
Oyster Bay, NY 11771
516-624-8888
Toys - games & hobby products O

Aceto Corp. ACET
One Hollow Ln., Ste. 201
Lake Success, NY 11042
516-627-6000
Chemicals - specialty

Actel Corp. ACTL
955 E. Arques Ave.
Sunnyvale, CA 94086
408-739-1010 Fax 408-739-1540
Electrical components - semiconductors O

Action Performance Companies, Inc.
 ACTN
2401 W. First St.
Tempe, AZ 85281
602-894-0100 Fax 602-894-6316
Toys - games & hobby products

Acxiom Corp. ACXM
301 Industrial Blvd.
Conway, AR 72033
501-336-1000
Computers - services

ADAC Laboratories ADAC
540 Alder Dr.
Milpitas, CA 95035
408-321-9100
Medical instruments O DRP 5%

Adaptec, Inc. ADPT
691 S. Milpitas Blvd.
Milpitas, CA 95035
408-945-8600 Fax 408-262-2533
Computers - peripheral equipment O

ADC Telecommunications, Inc. ADCT
4900 W. 78th St.
Minneapolis, MN 55435
612-938-8080 Fax 612-946-3292
Telecommunications equipment O

ADFlex Solutions, Inc. AFLX
2001 W. Chandler Blvd.
Chandler, AZ 85224
602-963-4584 Fax 602-786-8280
Electronics - components & systems

Adobe Systems Inc. ADBE
1585 Charleston Rd.
Mountain View, CA 94043
415-961-4400 Fax 415-961-3769
Computers - software O

ADTRAN, Inc. ADTN
901 Explorer Blvd.
Huntsville, AL 35806
205-971-8000
Telecommunications equipment

Advanced Energy Industries, Inc. AEIS
1625 Sharp Point Dr.
Fort Collins, CO 80525
970-221-4670
Miscellaneous - not elsewhere classified

Advanced Marketing Services, Inc. ADMS
5880 Oberlin Dr., Ste. 400
San Diego, CA 92121
619-457-2500 Fax 619-452-2237
Wholesale distribution - consumer products

Advanced Polymer Systems, Inc. APOS
3696 Haven Ave.
Redwood City, CA 94063
415-366-2626
Medical products

Advanced Tissue Sciences, Inc. ATIS
10933 N. Torrey Pines Rd.
La Jolla, CA 92037
619-450-5730
Biomedical & genetic products O

ADVANTA Corp. ADVNA
300 Welsh Rd.
Horsham, PA 19044
215-784-5335
Financial - business services DRP 5%

AEP Industries Inc. AEPI
125 Phillips Ave.
South Hackensack, NJ 07606
201-641-6600 Fax 201-807-2490
Chemicals - plastics

Aerovox Inc. ARVX
740 Belleville Ave.
New Bedford, MA 02745
508-994-9661
Electrical components - misc.

Affymetrix, Inc. AFFX
3380 Central Expwy.
Santa Clara, CA 95051
408-522-6000
Instruments - scientific

Agouron Pharmaceuticals, Inc. AGPH
10350 N. Torrey Pines Rd.
La Jolla, CA 92037
619-622-3000
Drugs O

Air Express International Corp. AEIC
120 Tokeneke Rd.
Darien, CT 06820
203-655-7900 Fax 203-655-5779
Transportation - air freight

Akorn, Inc. AKRN
100 Akorn Dr.
Abita Springs, LA 70420
504-893-9300 Fax 504-893-1257
Medical products

ALARIS Medical, Inc. ALRS
9775 Businesspark Ave.
San Diego, CA 92131
619-566-0426
Drugs

Alcide Corp. ALCD
One Willard Rd.
Norwalk, CT 06851
203-847-2555 Fax 203-846-3331
Chemicals - specialty

Alexander & Baldwin, Inc. ALEX
822 Bishop St., PO Box 3440
Honolulu, HI 96801
808-525-6611
Transportation - shipping

Aliant Communications, Inc. ALNT
1440 M St.
Lincoln, NE 68508
402-474-2211
Utility - telephone O

Allen Organ Co. AORGB
150 Locust St.
Macungie, PA 18062
610-966-2202 Fax 610-965-3098
Leisure & recreational products

Alliance Gaming Corp. ALLY
4380 Boulder Hwy.
Las Vegas, NV 89121
702-435-4200
Leisure & recreational services

Alliance Pharmaceutical Corp. ALLP
3040 Science Park Rd.
San Diego, CA 92121
619-558-4300 Fax 619-558-3825
Biomedical & genetic products O

Alliance Semiconductor Corp. ALSC
3099 N. First St.
San Jose, CA 95134
408-383-4900 Fax 408-383-4599
Electrical components - semiconductors O

Allied Capital Commercial Corp. ALCC
1666 K St., NW, 9th Fl.
Washington, DC 20006
202-331-1112
Real estate investment trust DRP

Allied Capital Corp. ALLC
1666 K St., NW, 9th Fl.
Washington, DC 20006
202-331-1112 Fax 202-659-2053
Real estate investment trust DRP

Allied Capital Corp. II ALII
1666 K St., NW, 9th Fl.
Washington, DC 20006
202-331-1112 Fax 202-659-2053
Financial - SBIC & commercial DRP

Allied Capital Lending Corp. ALCL
1666 K St., NW, 9th Fl.
Washington, DC 20006
202-331-1112 Fax 202-659-2053
Financial - SBIC & commercial DRP

Allied Healthcare Products, Inc. AHPI
1720 Sublette Ave.
St. Louis, MO 63110
314-771-2400
Medical products

Alpha Technologies Group, Inc. ATGI
2500 City West Blvd.
Houston, TX 77042
713-954-7000
Computers - software

Alta Gold Co. ALTA
601 Whitney Ranch Dr., Ste. 10
Henderson, NV 89014
702-433-8525 Fax 702-433-1547
Gold mining & processing

Altera Corp. ALTR
2610 Orchard Pkwy.
San Jose, CA 95134
408-894-7000 Fax 408-428-0463
Electrical components - semiconductors O

Altron Inc. ALRN
One Jewel Dr.
Wilmington, MA 01887
508-658-5800 Fax 508-988-0900
Electrical connectors O

AMBI, Inc. AMBI
771 Old Saw Mill River Rd.
Tarrytown, NY 10591
914-347-5767 Fax 914-347-6370
Biomedical & genetic products

AMCOL International Corp. ACOL
1500 W. Shure Dr., Ste. 500
Arlington Heights, IL 60004
708-392-4600 Fax 708-508-6199
Metal ores - misc. O DRP

AMCORE Financial, Inc. AMCRY
501 Seventh St.
Rockford, IL 61104
815-968-2241
Banks - midwest DRP

America First Prt./Pfd. Eqty. Mtg. Fnd. L.P.
 AFPFZ
1004 Farnam St., Ste. 400
Omaha, NE 68102
402-444-1630
Financial - investment management

America First Tax Exempt Mtg. Fund L.P.
 AFTXZ
1004 Farnam St., Ste. 400
Omaha, NE 68102
402-444-1630
Financial - investment management

American Biogenetic Sciences, Inc.
 MABXA
PO Box 1001
Notre Dame, IN 46556
219-631-7755 Fax 219-239-7595
Biomedical & genetic products

American Classic Voyages Co. AMCV
Two N. Riverside Plaza
Chicago, IL 60606
312-258-1890
Leisure & recreational services

American Ecology Corp. ECOL
5333 Westheimer, Ste. 1000
Houston, TX 77056
713-624-1900 Fax 713-624-1999
Pollution control equipment & services

American Freightways Corp. AFWY
2200 Forward Dr.
Harrison, AR 72601
501-741-9000
Transportation - truck

American Healthcorp, Inc. AMHC
One Burton Hills Blvd.
Nashville, TN 37215
615-665-1122
Healthcare - outpatient & home

American HomePatient, Inc. AHOM
105 Reynolds Dr., Ste. 400
Brentwood, TN 37027
615-221-8884
Healthcare - outpatient & home

American International Petroleum Co.
 AIPN
444 Madison Ave.
New York, NY 10022
212-688-3333
Oil & gas - US exploration & production

American Management Systems, Inc.
 AMSY
4050 Legato Rd.
Fairfax, VA 22033
703-267-8000
Computers - services O

American National Insurance Co. ANAT
One Moody Plaza
Galveston, TX 77550
409-763-4661
Insurance - life

American Pacific Corp. APFC
3770 Howard Hughes Parkway
Las Vegas, NV 89109
702-735-2200 Fax 702-735-4876
Chemicals - specialty

American Power Conversion Corp. APCC
132 Fairgrounds Rd.
West Kingston, RI 02892
401-789-5735 Fax 401-789-3710
Electrical products - misc. O

American Safety Razor Co. RAZR
Razor Blade Lane
Verona, VA 24482
703-248-8000
Cosmetics & toiletries

American Software, Inc. AMSWA
470 E. Paces Ferry Rd. NE
Atlanta, GA 30305
404-261-4381
Computers - software

American Woodmark Corp. AMWD
3102 Shawnee Dr.
Winchester, VA 22601
540-665-9100
Building products - doors & trim

Ames Department Stores, Inc. AMES
2418 Main St.
Rocky Hill, CT 06067
203-257-2000
Retail - discount & variety O

Amgen Inc. AMGN
1840 DeHavilland Dr.
Thousand Oaks, CA 91320
805-447-1000
Biomedical & genetic products O

Amplicon, Inc. AMPI
5 Hutton Centre Dr.
Santa Ana, CA 92707
714-751-7551 Fax 714-751-7557
Leasing

AMRESCO, INC. AMMB
700 N. Pearl St., Ste. 2400
Dallas, TX 75201
214-953-7700
Business services

Amtech Corp. AMTC
17304 Preston Rd., Bldg. E-100
Dallas, TX 75252
214-733-6600 Fax 214-733-6699
Computers - services

Analogic Corp. ALOG
8 Centennial Dr.
Peabody, MA 01960
508-977-3000 Fax 508-977-6811
Computers - peripheral equipment

Analysis & Technology, Inc. AATI
Route 2, PO Box 220
North Stonington, CT 06359
860-599-3910
Engineering - R & D services

Analysts International Corp. ANLY
7615 Metro Blvd.
Minneapolis, MN 55439
612-835-5900
Computers - services

Andersen Group, Inc. ANDR
Ney Industrial Park
Bloomfield, CT 06002
860-242-0761 Fax 860-242-7426
Diversified operations

Andrew Corp. ANDW
10500 W. 153rd St.
Orland Park, IL 60462
708-349-3300 Fax 708-349-5943
Telecommunications equipment O

Apogee Enterprises, Inc. APOG
7900 Xerxes Ave. South
Minneapolis, MN 55431
612-835-1874
Glass products O

Apple Computer, Inc. AAPL
1 Infinite Loop
Cupertino, CA 95014
408-996-1010 Fax 408-974-4507
Computers - mini & micro O

Apple South, Inc. APSO
Hancock at Washington
Madison, GA 30650
706-342-4552
Retail - food & restaurants O

Applebee's International, Inc. APPB
4551 W. 107th St., Ste. 100
Overland Park, KS 66207
913-967-4000 Fax 913-341-1694
Retail - food & restaurants O

Applied Digital Access, Inc. ADAX
9855 Scranton Rd.
San Diego, CA 92121
619-623-2200 Fax 619-623-2208
Instruments - control

Applied Extrusion Technologies, Inc.
 AETC
96 Swampscott Rd.
Salem, MA 01970
508-744-8000 Fax 508-744-4464
Rubber & plastic products

Applied Innovation, Inc. AINN
651 C Lakeview Plaza Blvd.
Columbus, OH 43085
614-798-2000
Telecommunications equipment

Applied Materials, Inc. AMAT
3050 Bowers Ave.
Santa Clara, CA 95054
408-727-5555 Fax 408-748-5119
Electrical components - semiconductors O

Applied Signal Technology, Inc. APSG
400 W. California Ave.
Sunnyvale, CA 94086
408-749-1888 Fax 408-738-1928
Telecommunications equipment

Arch Communications Group, Inc. APGR
110 Turnpike Rd. Ste. 210
Westborough, MA 01581
508-898-0962
Telecommunications services O

Arch Petroleum, Inc. ARCH
777 Taylor St., Ste. II
Fort Worth, TX 76102
817-332-9209 Fax 817-332-9249
Oil & gas - US exploration & production

Arctic Cat, Inc. ACAT
600 Brooks Ave. South
Thief River Falls, MN 56701
218-681-8558
Leisure & recreational products O

Arkansas Best Corp. ABFS
3801 Old Greenwood Rd.
Fort Smith, AR 72903
501-785-6000 Fax 501-785-6004
Transportation - truck

Arnold Industries Inc. AIND
625 S. Fifth Ave.
Lebanon, PA 17042
717-274-2521
Transportation - truck

Artisoft, Inc. ASFT
2202 N. Forbes Blvd.
Tucson, AZ 85745
602-670-7100 Fax 602-670-7101
Computers - software

ASA Holdings, Inc. ASAI
100 Hartsfield Centre Pkwy.
Atlanta, GA 30354
404-766-1400
Transportation - airline O

Ascend Communications, Inc. ASND
1275 Harbor Bay Pkwy.
Alameda, CA 94502
510-769-6001 Fax 510-814-2300
Computers - peripheral equipment O

Ashworth, Inc. ASHW
2791 Loker Ave. West
Carlsbad, CA 92008
760-438-6610 Fax 760-438-6657
Apparel O

Aspect Telecommunications Corp. ASPT
1730 Fox Dr.
San Jose, CA 95131
408-441-2200 Fax 408-441-2260
Telecommunications equipment O

Astec Industries, Inc. ASTE
4101 Jerome Ave., PO Box 72787
Chattanooga, TN 37407
423-867-4210 Fax 423-867-4127
Machinery - material handling

Astoria Financial Corp. ASFC
One Astoria Federal Plaza
Lake Success, NY 11042
516-327-3000
Financial - savings and loans O

Astro-Med, Inc. ALOT
600 E. Greenwich Ave.
West Warwick, RI 02893
401-828-4000 Fax 401-822-2430
Medical products

Astronics Corp. ATRO
1801 Elmwood Ave.
Buffalo, NY 14207
716-447-9013 Fax 716-449-9201
Diversified operations

Atlantic American Corp. AAME
4370 Peachtree Rd., N.E.
Atlanta, GA 30319
404-266-5500 Fax 404-266-5596
Insurance - accident & health

Atlantic Gulf Communities Corp. AGLF
2601 S. Bayshore Dr.
Miami, FL 33133
305-859-4000 Fax 305-859-4623
Real estate development

Atmel Corp. ATML
2325 Orchard Pkwy.
San Jose, CA 95131
408-441-0311 Fax 408-436-4200
Electrical components - misc.

Atria Communities, Inc. ATRC
515 W. Market St.
Louisville, KY 40202
502-596-7540
Nursing homes

ATRION Corporation ATRI
PO Box 918
Florence, AL 35631
205-383-3631
Oil & gas - production & pipeline

Atrix Laboratories, Inc. ATRX
1625 Midpoint Dr.
Fort Collins, CO 80525
303-482-5868
Medical services

Au Bon Pain Co., Inc. ABPCA
19 Fid Kennedy Ave.
Boston, MA 02210
617-423-2100
Retail - food & restaurants

Aura Systems, Inc. AURA
2335 Alaska Ave.
El Segundo, CA 90245
310-643-5300
Electrical products - misc.

Auspex Systems, Inc. ASPX
5200 Great America Pkwy.
Santa Clara, CA 95054
408-986-2000 Fax 408-986-2020
Computers - mini & micro O

Autocam Corp. ACAM
4070 E. Paris Ave.
Kentwood, MI 49512
616-698-0707 Fax 616-698-6876
Metal products - fabrication

Autodesk, Inc. ACAD
111 McInnis Pkwy.
San Rafael, CA 94903
415-507-5000
Computers - software O

Avert, Inc. AVRT
119 E. Mountain Ave.
Fort Collins, CO 80524
303-484-7722 Fax 800-237-4011
Business services

Avid Technology, Inc. AVID
One Park West
Tewksbury, MA 01876
508-640-6789
Video equipment O

Avigen, Inc. AVGN
1201 Harbor Bay Pkwy.
Alameda, CA 94502
510-748-7150
Biomedical & genetic products

Avondale Industries, Inc. AVDL
5100 River Rd.
Avondale, LA 70094
504-436-2121
Transportation - equipment & leasing O

Baldwin & Lyons, Inc. BWINA
1099 N. Meridian St.
Indianapolis, IN 46204
317-636-9800 Fax 317-632-9444
Insurance - property & casualty

Baldwin Piano & Organ Co. BPAO
422 Wards Corner Rd.
Loveland, OH 45140
513-576-4500
Leisure & recreational products

Baltek Corp. BTEK
10 Fairway Court, PO Box 195
Northvale, NJ 07647
201-767-1400 Fax 201-387-6631
Building products - wood

Bancorp Connecticut, Inc. BKCT
121 Main St.
Southington, CT 06489
203-628-0351
Financial - savings and loans

Bando McGlocklin Capital Corp. BMCC
13555 Bishops Court, Ste. 205
Brookfield, WI 53005
414-784-9010 Fax 414-784-3426
Financial - investment bankers DRP

BankUnited Financial Corp. BKUNA
2334 Ponce de Leon Blvd.
Coral Gables, FL 33134
305-447-0200
Financial - savings and loans

Banta Corp. BNTA
225 Main St., PO Box 8003
Menasha, WI 54952
414-751-7777
Printing - commercial O DRP

Banyan Systems, Inc. BNYN
120 Flanders Rd.
Westboro, MA 01581
508-898-1000 Fax 508-898-1755
Computers - software

Barnett Inc. BNTT
3333 Lenox Ave.
Jacksonville, FL 32254
904-384-6530
Wholesale distribution - consumer products

BARRA, Inc. BARZ
1995 University Ave., Ste. 400
Berkeley, CA 94704
510-548-5442 Fax 510-548-4374
Computers - software

Barrett Business Services Inc. BBSI
4724 SW Macadam Ave.
Portland, OR 97201
503-220-0988
Personnel

Base Ten Systems, Inc. BASEA
One Electronics Dr.
Trenton, NJ 08619
609-586-7010 Fax 609-586-1593
Computers - mini & micro

Bassett Furniture Industries, Inc. BSET
PO Box 626
Bassett, VA 24055
703-629-7511
Furniture

BCT International, Inc. BCTI
3000 NE 30th Place, 5th Fl.
Fort Lauderdale, FL 33306
954-563-1224
Printing - commercial

BE Aerospace, Inc. BEAV
1300 Corporate Center Way
Wellington, FL 33414
561-791-5000 Fax 561-791-7900
Aerospace - aircraft equipment O

BeautiControl Cosmetics, Inc. BUTI
2121 Midway Rd.
Carrollton, TX 75006
972-458-0601
Cosmetics & toiletries

Bed Bath & Beyond Inc. BBBY
650 Liberty Ave.
Union, NJ 07083
908-688-0988
Retail - home furnishings O

Bedford Bancshares, Inc. BFSB
125 W. Main St.
Bedford, VA 24523
540-586-2590
Financial - savings and loans

Bel Fuse Inc. BELF
198 Van Vorst St.
Jersey City, NJ 07302
201-432-0463 Fax 201-432-9542
Electrical components - misc.

Bell Microproducts Inc. BELM
1941 Ringwood Ave.
San Jose, CA 95131
408-451-9400
Electronics - parts distribution

Bell Sports Corp. BSPT
10601 N. Hayden Rd.
Scottsdale, AZ 85260
602-951-0033
Leisure & recreational products O

Benihana, Inc. BNHN
8685 N.W. 53rd Terrace
Miami, FL 33166
305-593-0770
Retail - food & restaurants

Berkshire Gas Co. BGAS
115 Cheshire Rd.
Pittsfield, MA 01201
413-442-1511
Utility - gas distribution DRP 3%

BioCryst Pharmaceuticals, Inc. BCRX
2190 Parkway Lane Dr.
Birmingham, AL 35244
205-444-4600
Drugs

Biogen, Inc. BGEN
14 Cambridge Center
Cambridge, MA 02142
617-679-2000 Fax 617-679-2617
Biomedical & genetic products O

Bioject Medical Technologies, Inc. BJCT
7620 S.W. Bridgeport Rd.
Portland, OR 97224
503-639-7221 Fax 503-624-9002
Medical products

Biomet, Inc. BMET
Airport Industrial Park
Warsaw, IN 46581
219-267-6639 Fax 219-267-8137
Medical products O

Biospherics Inc. BINC
12051 Indian Creek Court
Beltsville, MD 20705
301-419-3900 Fax 301-725-4908
Pollution control equipment & services

BISYS Group, Inc., (The) BSYS
150 Clove Rd.
Little Falls, NJ 07424
201-812-8600
Business services O

BMC Software, Inc. BMCS
2101 Citywest Blvd.
Houston, TX 77042
713-918-8800 Fax 713-918-8000
Computers - software

Bob Evans Farms, Inc. BOBE
3776 S. High St.
Columbus, OH 43207
614-491-2225
Retail - food & restaurants O DRP

Boca Research Inc. BOCI
1377 Clint Moore Rd.
Boca Raton, FL 33487
561-997-6227 Fax 561-997-0918
Computers - software O

Bon-Ton Stores, Inc., (The) BONT
2801 E. Market St.
York, PA 17402
717-757-7660
Retail - regional department stores

Books-A-Million, Inc. BAMM
402 Industrial Lane
Birmingham, AL 35211
205-942-3737
Retail - miscellaneous

Boole & Babbage, Inc. BOOK
3131 Zanker Rd.
San Jose, CA 95134
408-526-3000 Fax 408-526-3055
Computers - software

Boston Chicken, Inc. BOST
14103 Denver West Pkwy.
Golden, CO 80401
303-278-9500
Retail - food & restaurants O

BRC Holding, Inc. BRCP
1111 W. Mockingbird, Ste. 1400
Dallas, TX 75247
214-688-1800
Office automation

Brenton Banks, Inc. BRBK
400 Locust, Ste. 300
Des Moines, IA 50309
515-237-5100
Banks - midwest

Brite Voice Systems, Inc. BVSI
7309 E. 21st St. North
Wichita, KS 67206
316-652-6500 Fax 316-652-6800
Telecommunications equipment O

BroadBand Technologies, Inc. BBTK
PO Box 13737
Research Triangle, NC 27704
919-544-0015
Telecommunications equipment O

Broderbund Software, Inc. BROD
500 Redwood Blvd.
Novato, CA 94948
415-382-4400 Fax 415-382-4582
Computers - software O

Brooks Automation, Inc. BRKS
15 Elizabeth Dr.
Chelmsford, MA 01824
508-262-2400 Fax 508-262-2500
Miscellaneous - not elsewhere classified

Brunswick Technologies, Inc. BTIC
43 Bibber Pkwy.
Brunswick, ME 04011
207-729-7792
Textiles - mill products

BTU International BTUI
23 Esquire Rd.
North Billerica, MA 01862
508-667-4111 Fax 508-667-9068
Electrical components - semiconductors

Buffets, Inc. BOCB
10260 Viking Dr.
Eden Prairie, MN 55344
612-942-9760
Retail - food & restaurants O

Burr-Brown Corp. BBRC
6730 S. Tucson Blvd.
Tucson, AZ 85706
602-746-1111 Fax 602-746-7752
Electrical components - semiconductors O

Cache, Inc. CACH
1460 Broadway
New York, NY 10036
212-840-4242
Retail - apparel & shoes

CACI International Inc. CACI
1100 N. Glebe Rd.
Arlington, VA 22201
703-841-7800 Fax 703-841-7882
Business services

Cade Industries, Inc. CADE
5640 Enterprise Dr.
Lansing, MI 48911
517-394-1333 Fax 517-394-1404
Aerospace - aircraft equipment

Cadmus Communications Corp. CDMS
6620 W. Broad St., Ste. 500
Richmond, VA 23230
804-287-5680 Fax 804-287-6267
Printing - commercial DRP

Cadus Pharmaceutical Corp. KDUS
777 Old Saw Mill Rd.
Tarrytown, NY 10591
914-345-3344
Drugs

Caere Corp. CAER
100 Cooper Court
Los Gatos, CA 95030
408-395-7000 Fax 408-354-2743
Computers - software O

California Culinary Academy, Inc. COOK
625 Polk St.
San Francisco, CA 94102
415-771-3536 Fax 415-771-0606
Schools

California Independent Bancorp CIBN
1005 Stafford Way
Yuba City, CA 95991
916-674-4444
Banks - west

California Microwave, Inc. CMIC
985 Almanor Ave.
Sunnyvale, CA 94086
408-732-4000 Fax 408-732-4244
Telecommunications equipment O

Cape Cod Bank and Trust Co. CCBT
307 Main St.
Hyannis, MA 02601
508-394-1300
Banks - northeast

Capital Southwest Corp. CSWC
12900 Preston Rd., Ste. 700
Dallas, TX 75230
214-233-8242 Fax 214-233-7362
Financial - investment bankers DRP

Capitol Transamerica Corp. CATA
4610 University Ave.
Madison, WI 53705
608-231-4450 Fax 608-231-2053
Insurance - property & casualty

Carolina First Corp. CAFC
102 S. Main St.
Greenville, SC 29601
803-255-7900
Banks - southeast DRP 5%

Carrington Laboratories, Inc. CARN
2001 Walnut Hill Lane
Irving, TX 75038
972-518-1300
Biomedical & genetic products

Casey's General Stores, Inc. CASY
One Convenience Blvd.
Ankeny, IA 50021
515-965-6100
Retail - convenience stores O

Casino America, Inc. CSNO
711 Washington Loop
Biloxi, MS 39530
601-436-7000
Leisure & recreational services

Casino Magic Corp. CMAG
711 Casino Magic Dr.
Bay St. Louis, MS 39520
601-467-9257
Leisure & recreational services

Castle Energy Corp. CECX
100 Matsonford Rd., Ste. 250
Radnor, PA 19087
610-995-9400
Oil & gas - US exploration & production

Catalytica, Inc. CTAL
430 Ferguson Dr.
Mountain View, CA 94043
415-960-3000 Fax 415-960-0127
Pollution control equipment & services O

Catherines Stores Corp. CATH
3742 Lamar Ave.
Memphis, TN 38118
901-363-3900
Retail - apparel & shoes

Cato Corp., (The) CACOA
8100 Denmark Rd.
Charlotte, NC 28273
704-554-8510
Retail - apparel & shoes

CCA Industries, Inc. CCAM
200 Murray Hill Parkway
East Rutherford, NJ 07073
201-330-1400 Fax 201-935-0675
Wholesale distribution - consumer products

C-COR Electronics, Inc. CCBL
60 Decibel Rd.
State College, PA 16801
814-238-2461 Fax 814-238-4065
Telecommunications equipment

Celgene Corp. CELG
7 Powder Horn Dr.
Warren, NJ 07059
908-271-1001 Fax 908-271-4184
Chemicals - specialty

Cell Genesys, Inc. CEGE
322 Lakeside Dr.
Foster City, CA 94404
415-358-9600 Fax 415-358-0803
Medical products

CellPro, Inc. CPRO
22215 26th Ave. S.E.
Bothell, WA 98021
206-485-7644 Fax 206-485-4787
Medical services O

CellStar Corp. CLST
1730 Briercroft Dr.
Carrollton, TX 75006
972-323-0600
Wholesale distribution - consumer products

Cellular Technical Services Co. CTSC
2401 Fourth Ave.
Seattle, WA 98121
206-443-6400
Computers - software

CEM Corp. CEMX
3100 Smith Farm Rd.
Matthews, NC 28105
704-821-7015 Fax 704-821-4369
Instruments - scientific

Centigram Communications Corp. CGRM
91 E. Tasman Dr.
San Jose, CA 95134
408-944-0250 Fax 408-428-3732
Telecommunications equipment

Centocor, Inc. CNTO
200 Great Valley Parkway
Malvern, PA 19355
610-651-6000 Fax 610-651-6100
Biomedical & genetic products O

Central Reserve Life Corp. CRLC
17800 Royalton Rd.
Strongsville, OH 44136
216-572-2400
Insurance - accident & health

Cephalon, Inc. CEPH
145 Brandywine Parkway
West Chester, PA 19380
610-344-0200
Medical products O

Ceradyne, Inc. CRDN
3169 Red Hill Ave.
Costa Mesa, CA 92626
714-549-0421 Fax 714-549-5787
Ceramics & ceramic products

Cerner Corp. CERN
2800 Rockcreek Pkwy.
Kansas City, MO 64117
816-221-1024 Fax 816-474-1742
Computers - software O

CFI ProServices, Inc. PROI
220 N.W. Second Ave.
Portland, OR 97209
503-274-7280
Computers - software

CFM Technologies, Inc. CFMT
1336 Enterprise Dr.
West Chester, PA 19380
610-696-8300
Miscellaneous - not elsewhere classified

Champion Industries, Inc. CHMP
PO Box 2968
Huntington, WV 25728
304-528-2791
Diversified operations

Charming Shoppes, Inc. CHRS
450 Winks Lane
Bensalem, PA 19020
215-245-9100
Retail - apparel & shoes O

Charter One Financial, Inc. COFI
1215 Superior Ave.
Cleveland, OH 44114
216-566-5300 Fax 216-566-1465
Financial - savings and loans O DRP

Chattem, Inc. CHTT
1715 W. 38th St.
Chattanooga, TN 37409
615-821-4571 Fax 615-821-6132
Cosmetics & toiletries

Cheesecake Factory, Inc. (The) CAKE
26635 Agoura Rd., Ste. 101
Calabasas, CA 91302
818-880-9323 Fax 818-880-6501
Retail - food & restaurants

Cherry Corp. (The) CHER
3600 Sunset Ave.
Waukegan, IL 60087
847-662-9200
Electrical components - miscellaneous

Chesapeake Biological Laboratories CBLI
11412 Cronridge Drive
Ownings Mills, MD 21117
410-998-9800
Medical products

Chico's FAS, Inc. CHCS
11215 Metro Pkwy.
Fort Myers, FL 33912
941-277-6200
Retail - apparel & shoes

Children's Comprehensive Services, Inc.
 KIDS
805 S. Church St., PO Box 8
Murfreesboro, TN 37133
615-896-3100 Fax 615-896-5068
Protection - safety equipment & services

Childtime Learning Centers, Inc. CTIM
38345 W. Ten Mile Rd.
Farmington Hills, MI 48335
810-476-3200
Schools

Chiron Corp. CHIR
4560 Horton St.
Emeryville, CA 94608
510-655-8730 Fax 510-655-9910
Biomedical & genetic products O

Chronimed Inc. CHMD
13911 Ridgedale Dr.
Minnetonka, MN 55305
612-541-0239
Medical products

Chrysalis International Corp. CRLS
303B College Rd. East
Princeton, NJ 08540
609-520-0300 Fax 609-520-9864
Medical products

Cincinnati Financial Corp. CINF
PO Box 145496
Cincinnati, OH 45250
513-870-2000
Insurance - property & casualty O DRP

Cintas Corp. CTAS
6800 Cintas Blvd.
Cincinnati, OH 45262
513-459-1200
Linen supply & related O

Ciprico Inc. CPCI
2800 Campus Dr.
Plymouth, MN 55441
612-551-4000
Computers - peripheral equipment

Circle International, Inc. CRCL
260 Townsend St.
San Francisco, CA 94107
415-978-0600 Fax 415-978-0699
Transportation - air freight

Circon Corp. CCON
460 Ward Dr.
Santa Barbara, CA 93111
805-967-0404 Fax 805-967-5035
Medical instruments O

Circuit Systems, Inc. CSYI
2350 E. Lunt Ave.
Elk Grove Village, IL 60007
847-439-1999 Fax 847-437-5910
Electrical components - misc.

Cirrus Logic, Inc. CRUS
3100 W. Warren Ave.
Fremont, CA 94538
510-623-8300 Fax 510-226-2240
Electrical components - misc. O

CITATION Computer Systems, Inc. CITA
424 S. Woods Mill Rd.
Chesterfield, MO 63017
314-579-7900 Fax 314-579-7990
Computers - software

Citation Corp. CAST
2 Office Park Circle, Ste. 204
Birmingham, AL 35223
205-871-5731 Fax 205-870-8211
Steel - production

CNS, Inc. CNXS
1250 Park Rd.
Chanhassen, MN 55317
612-474-7600
Medical instruments

Cobra Electronics, Inc. COBR
6500 W. Cortland St.
Chicago, IL 60635
312-889-8870 Fax 312-889-1678
Electronics - components & systems

Coca-Cola Bottling Co. Consolidated
 COKE
1900 Rexford Rd.
Charlotte, NC 28211
704-551-4400
Beverages - soft drinks DRP

Cognex Corp. CGNX
15 Crawford St.
Needham, MA 02194
617-449-6030
Machinery - general industrial O

Coherent, Inc. COHR
5100 Patrick Henry Dr.
Santa Clara, CA 95054
408-764-4000
Lasers - systems & components O

Cohu, Inc. COHU
5755 Kearny Villa Rd.
San Diego, CA 92123
619-277-6700 Fax 619-277-9412
Diversified operations

Collagen Corp. CGEN
2500 Faber Place
Palo Alto, CA 94303
415-856-0200 Fax 415-856-1430
Biomedical & genetic products

Columbus McKinnon Corp. CMCO
140 John James Aubudon Pkwy.
Amherst, NY 14228
716-689-5400
Machinery - material handling

Comair Holdings, Inc. COMR
PO Box 75021
Cincinnati, OH 45275
606-525-2550
Transportation - airline O

COMARCO, Inc. CMRO
22800 Savi Ranch Parkway
Yorba Linda, CA 92687
714-282-3832 Fax 714-283-0604
Engineering - R & D services

Comcast Corp. CMCSA
1234 Market St.
Philadelphia, PA 19102
215-665-1700 Fax 215-981-7790
Cable TV O

Comdial Corp. CMDL
1180 Seminole Trail
Charlottesville, VA 22901
804-978-2200
Telecommunications equipment

Commerce Bancshares, Inc. CBSH
1000 Walnut St.
Kansas City, MO 64106
816-234-2000
Banks - midwest

CommNet Cellular, Inc. CELS
8350 E. Crescent Pkwy.
Englewood, CO 80111
303-694-3234 Fax 303-694-3293
Telecommunications services O

Commodore Holdings CCLNF
4000 Hollywood Blvd., #385
Hollywood, FL 33021
954-967-2100
Water transportation

Communications Systems, Inc. CSII
213 Main St. South, PO Box 777
Hector, MN 55342
612-848-6231 Fax 612-848-2702
Telecommunications equipment

CompDent Corp. CPDN
8800 Roswell Rd., Ste. 244
Atlanta, GA 30350
770-998-8936 Fax 770-992-4349
Miscellaneous - not elsewhere classified

Computer Network Technology Corp.
 CMNT
6600 Wedgwood Rd.
Maple Grove, MN 55311
612-550-8000 Fax 612-550-8800
Computers - services O

Compuware Corp. CPWR
31440 Northwestern Highway
Farmington Hills, MI 48334
810-737-7300
Computers - software O

Comtech Telecommunications Corp.
 CMTL
105 Baylis Rd.
Melville, NY 11747
516-777-8900
Telecommunications equipment

Comverse Technology, Inc. CMVT
170 Crossways Park Dr.
Woodbury, NY 11797
516-677-7200
Computers - mini & micro O

Concord Camera Corp. LENS
35 Mileed Way
Avenel, NJ 07001
908-499-8280 Fax 908-499-0697
Photographic equipment & supplies

Connecticut Water Service, Inc. CTWS
93 W. Main St.
Clinton, CT 06413
203-669-8636
Utility - water supply DRP 5%

Consilium, Inc. CSIM
640 Clyde Court
Mountain View, CA 94043
415-691-6100 Fax 415-691-6130
Computers - software

Conso Products Co. CNSO
513 N. Duncan Bypass
Union, SC 29379
803-427-9004 Fax 803-427-8820
Textiles - home furnishings

Consumers Water Co. CONW
Three Canal Plaza
Portland, ME 04112
207-773-6438
Utility - water supply DRP

Continental Circuits Corp. CCIR
3502 E. Roeser Rd.
Phoenix, AZ 85040
602-258-3461
Electronics - components & systems

Coors, Adolph ACCOB
311 10th St., NH470, PO Box 4030
Golden, CO 80401
303-279-6565
Beverages O

Copart, Inc. CPRT
282 Fifth St.
Vallejo, CA 94590
707-644-4468 Fax 707-644-7355
Business services

Cornerstone Imaging, Inc. CRNR
1990 Concourse Dr.
San Jose, CA 95131
408-435-8900 Fax 408-435-8998
Computers - graphics

Corporate Express, Inc. CEXP
325 Interlocken Pkwy.
Broomfield, CO 80021
303-373-2800 Fax 303-438-5181
Office equipment & supplies O

CorVel Corp. CRVL
1920 Main St., Ste. 1090
Irvine, CA 92714
714-851-1473 Fax 714-851-1469
Medical services

Costco Cos., Inc. COST
999 Lake Dr.
Issaquah, WA 98027
206-313-8100 Fax 208-313-6593
Retail - misc. O

Coventry Corp. CVTY
53 Century Blvd., Ste. 250
Nashville, TN 37214
615-391-2440
Health maintenance organization O

CPAC, Inc. CPAK
2364 Leicester Rd., PO Box 175
Leicester, NY 14481
716-382-3223 Fax 716-382-3031
Chemicals - specialty

Cracker Barrel Old Country Store, Inc.
CBRL
Hartmann Dr., PO Box 787
Lebanon, TN 37088
615-444-5533
Retail - food & restaurants O DRP

Creative Technology CREAF
1901 McCarthy Blvd.
Milpitas, CA 95035
408-428-6600
Office & computing machines O

Credence Systems Corp. CMOS
3500 W. Warren Ave.
Fremont, CA 94538
510-657-7400 Fax 510-623-2560
Electronics - measuring instruments O

Credit Acceptance Corp. CACC
25505 W. Twelve Mile Rd.
Southfield, MI 48034
810-353-2700
Financial - business services

Criticare Systems, Inc. CXIM
20925 Crossroads Circle
Waukesha, WI 53186
414-798-8282 Fax 414-798-8290
Medical instruments

Crown Resources Corp. CRRS
1225 17th St., Ste. 1500
Denver, CO 80202
303-295-2171 Fax 303-295-2249
Gold mining & processing

Crown Vantage Inc. CVAN
300 Lakeside Dr.
Oakland, CA 94612
510-874-3400 Fax 510-874-3531
Paper & paper products

CSP Inc. CSPI
40 Linnell Circle
Billerica, MA 01821
508-663-7598 Fax 508-663-0150
Computers - peripheral equipment

Curative Health Services CURE
14 Research Way, PO Box 9052
East Setauket, NY 11733
516-689-7000
Drugs

CyberCash, Inc. CYCH
2100 Reston Pkwy.
Reston, VA 22091
703-620-4200
Computers - software

Cygnus, Inc. CYGN
400 Penobscot Dr.
Redwood City, CA 94063
415-369-4300
Medical products O

Cyrk, Inc. CYRK
3 Pond Rd.
Gloucester, MA 01930
508-283-5800
Apparel

Cytel Corp. CYTL
3525 John Hopkins Court
San Diego, CA 92121
619-552-3000 Fax 619-552-8801
Drugs

CYTOGEN Corp. CYTO
600 College Rd. East - CN 5308
Princeton, NJ 08540
609-987-8200 Fax 609-452-2975
Biomedical & genetic products

CytRx Corp. CYTR
150 Technology Parkway
Norcross, GA 30092
404-368-9500 Fax 404-368-0622
Miscellaneous - not elsewhere classified

D & N Financial Corp. DNFC
400 Quincy St.
Hancock, MI 49930
906-482-2700
Financial - savings and loans DRP

Daisytek International Corp. DZTK
500 N. Central Expwy.
Plano, TX 75074
214-881-4700
Office equipment & supplies

Damark International DMRK
7101 Winnetka Ave. N.
Minneapolis, MN 55428
612-531-0066
Misc. retail stores

Data Broadcasting DBCC
1900 S. Norfolk St., #150
San Mateo, CA 94403
415-377-3525
Security & commodity services

Data Research Associates, Inc. DRAI
1276 N. Warson Rd.
St. Louis, MO 63132
314-432-1100 Fax 314-993-8927
Computers - software

Datascope Corp. DSCP
14 Philips Parkway
Montvale, NJ 07645
201-391-8100 Fax 201-307-5400
Medical instruments O

Datron Systems, Inc. DTSI
200 W. Los Angeles Ave.
Simi Valley, CA 93065
805-584-1717
Telecommunications equipment

Datum Inc. DATM
1363 S. State College Blvd.
Anaheim, CA 92806
714-533-6333 Fax 714-533-6345
Fiber optics

Dave & Buster's, Inc. DANB
2751 Electronic Lane
Dallas, TX 75220
214-357-9588
Retail - food & restaurants

Davox Corp. DAVX
6 Technology Park Dr.
Westboro, MA 01886
508-667-4455
Telecommunications equipment

Daw Technologies DAWK
2700 South, 900 W.
Salt Lake City, UT 84119
801-977-3100
Fabricated structural metal product

Dawson Geophysical Co. DWSN
208 S. Marienfeld St.
Midland, TX 79701
915-682-7356 Fax 915-683-4298
Oil & gas - field services

Day Runner, Inc. DAYR
2750 W. Moore Avenue
Fullerton, CA 92633
714-680-3500 Fax 714-680-0542
Paper & paper products

Deckers Outdoor Corp. DECK
1140 Mark Ave.
Carpintera, CA 93013
805-684-7722
Shoes & related apparel

Defiance, Inc. DEFI
1111 Chester Ave., Ste. 750
Cleveland, OH 44114
216-861-6300
Automotive & trucking - original
  equipment

Del Global Technologies DGTC
1 Commerce Pk.
Valhalla, NY 10595
914-686-3600
Electronic components & accessories

Dell Computer Corp. DELL
2214 W. Braker Lane
Austin, TX 78758
512-338-4400 Fax 512-338-3653
Computers - mini & micro

Delta Natural Gas Co., Inc. DGAS
3617 Lexington Rd.
Winchester, KY 40391
606-744-6171
Utility - gas distribution DRP

Dense-Pac Microsystems DPAC
7321 Lincoln Way
Garden Grove, CA 92641
714-898-0007
Electronic components & accessories

DENTSPLY International Inc. XRAY
570 W. College Ave.
York, PA 17405
717-845-7511
Medical & dental supplies O

Designs, Inc. DESI
1244 Boylston St.
Chestnut Hill, MA 01267
617-739-6722 Fax 617-277-3516
Retail - apparel & shoes

Detection Systems, Inc. DETC
130 Perinton Parkway
Fairport, NY 14450
716-223-4060
Protection - safety equipment & services

Detrex Corp. DTRX
4000 Town Center, Ste. 1100
Southfield, MI 48075
810-358-5800
Chemicals - specialty

Devcon International Corp. DEVC
1350 E. Newport Center Dr.
Deerfield Beach, FL 33442
305-429-1500 Fax 305-429-1506
Construction - cement & concrete

Dialogic Corp. DLGC
300 Littleton Rd.
Parsippany, NJ 07054
201-334-8450
Computers - peripheral equipment

DIANON Systems, Inc. DIAN
200 Watson Blvd.
Stratford, CT 06497
203-381-4000 Fax 203-381-4079
Medical services

Dick Clark Productions, Inc. DCPI
3003 W. Olive Ave.
Burbank, CA 91505
818-841-3003
Producers, orchestras, entertainers

Digi International, Inc. DGII
6400 Flying Cloud Dr.
Eden Prairie, MN 55344
612-943-9020 Fax 612-943-5398
Computers - peripheral equipment O

Digital Link Corp. DLNK
217 Humboldt Court
Sunnyvale, CA 94089
408-745-6200
Telecommunications equipment

Digital Microwave Corp. DMIC
170 Rose Orchard Way
San Jose, CA 95134
408-943-0777 Fax 408-954-9014
Fiber optics O

Dionex Corp. DNEX
1228 Titan Way, PO Box 3603
Sunnyvale, CA 94088
408-737-0700 Fax 408-737-0700
Instruments - scientific O

Dixie Group DXYN
100 S. Watkins St.
Chattanooga, TN 37404
423-698-2501
Textile finishing

Dorchester Hugoton, Ltd. DHULZ
9696 Skillman St.
Dallas, TX 75243
214-340-3443
Miscellaneous - not elsewhere classified

Draxis Health DRAX
6870 Goreway Dr.
Mississauga, ON L4V1P1
905-677-5500
Drugs, proprietaries & sundries

Drexler Technology Corp. DRXR
1077 Independence Ave.
Mountain View, CA 94043
415-969-7277 Fax 415-969-6121
Computers - peripheral equipment O

Dreyer's Grand Ice Cream, Inc. DRYR
5929 College Ave.
Oakland, CA 94618
510-652-8187
Food - dairy products O

Drug Emporium, Inc. DEMP
155 Hidden Ravines Dr.
Powell, OH 43065
614-548-7080 Fax 614-548-6541
Retail - drug stores

DSC Communications Corp. DIGI
1000 Coit Rd.
Plano, TX 75075
214-519-3000
Telecommunications equipment O

DSP Technology, Inc. DSPT
48500 Kato Rd.
Fremont, CA 94538
510-657-7555 Fax 510-657-7576
Electronics - measuring instruments

Durakon Industries, Inc. DRKN
2101 N. Lapeer Rd.
Lapeer, MI 48446
810-664-0850
Automotive & trucking - replacement parts

DUSA Pharmaceuticals DUSA
181 University Ave.
Toronto, ON M5H3M7
416-363-5059
Drugs

Dynamic Healthcare Technologies DHTI
101 Southhall Lane, #210
Maitland, FL 32751
407-875-9991
Computer & data processing services

Dynamics Research Corp. DRCO
60 Frontage Rd.
Andover, MA 01810
508-475-9090 Fax 508-475-8205
Engineering - R & D services

Eagle Financial Corp. EGFC
222 Main St.
Bristol, CT 06010
860-314-6400 Fax 203-584-8052
Financial - savings and loans DRP

Eagle Hardware & Garden, Inc. EAGL
101 Andover Park East
Tukwila, WA 98188
208-431-5740
Building products - retail & wholesale O

Easco, Inc. ESCO
706 S. State St.
Girard, OH 44420
330-545-4311 Fax 330-545-3119
Metal products - fabrication

Edelbrock Corp. EDEL
2700 California St.
Torrance, CA 90503
310-781-2222 Fax 310-320-1187
Auto parts - retail & wholesale

Egghead.com EGGS
22705 E. Mission
Liberty Lake, WA 99019
509-922-7031 Fax 800-773-9359
Computers - retail & wholesale

Einstein/Noah Bagel Corp. ENBX
14123 Denver West Pkwy.
Golden, CO 80401
303-215-9300
Retail - food & restaurants O

Electro Rent Corp. ELRC
6060 Sepulveda Blvd.
Van Nuys, CA 91411
818-786-2525
Leasing

Electro Scientific Industries, Inc. ESIO
13900 N.W. Science Park Dr.
Portland, OR 97229
503-641-4141 Fax 503-643-4873
Lasers - systems & components O

Electroglas, Inc. EGLS
2901 Coronado Dr.
Santa Clara, CA 95054
408-727-6500 Fax 408-982-8011
Electronics - measuring instruments O

Electromagnetic Sciences, Inc. ELMG
660 Engineering Dr.
Norcross, GA 30091
404-263-9200 Fax 404-263-9207
Telecommunications services

Electronic Arts Inc. ERTS
1450 Fashion Island Blvd.
San Mateo, CA 94404
415-571-7171
Computers - software O

Eltron International, Inc. ELTN
21617 Nordhoff St.
Chatsworth, CA 91311
818-885-6484 Fax 818-882-5315
Computers - software

ELXSI Corp. ELXS
4209 Vineland Rd., Suite J-1
Orlando, FL 32811
407-849-1090
Eating & Drinking Places

EMCON MCON
400 S. El Camino Real
San Mateo, CA 94402
415-375-1522 Fax 415-375-0763
Pollution control equipment & services

Empi, Inc. EMPI
1275 Grey Fox Rd.
St. Paul, MN 55112
612-636-6600 Fax 612-636-2405
Medical products

Employee Solutions ESOL
2929 E. Camelback Rd., #220
Phoenix, AZ 85016
602-955-5556
Personnel supply services

Enamelon, Inc. ENML
15 Kimball Ave.
Yonkers, NY 10704
914-237-1308
Medical & dental supplies

Encore Wire Corp. WIRE
1410 Millwood Rd., PO Box 1149
McKinney, TX 75069
214-548-9473
Wire & cable products

EntreMed, Inc. ENMD
9610 Medical Center Dr.
Rockville, MD 20850
301-217-9858
Biomedical & genetic products

EnviroSource, Inc. ENSO
Five High Ridge Park
Stamford, CT 06904
203-322-8333 Fax 203-968-1039
Pollution control equipment & services

Enzon, Inc. ENZN
40 Kingsbridge Rd.
Piscataway, NJ 08854
908-980-4500 Fax 908-980-5911
Biomedical & genetic products

Equitrac Corp. ETRC
836 Ponce de Leon Blvd.
Coral Gables, FL 33134
305-442-2060 Fax 305-442-0687
Computers - services

Equity Oil Co. EQTY
10 W. Broadway, Ste. 806
Salt Lake City, UT 84101
801-521-3515 Fax 801-521-3534
Oil & gas - US exploration & production

ESSEF Corp. ESSF
220 Park Dr.
Chardon, OH 44024
216-286-2200 Fax 216-286-2206
Machinery - general industrial

Essex County Gas Co. ECGC
7 N. Hunt Rd.
Amesbury, MA 01913
508-388-4000
Utility - gas distribution DRP 5%

Etec Systems, Inc. ETEC
26460 Corporate Ave.
Hayward, CA 94545
510-783-9210
Electrical components - misc. O

Evans & Sutherland Computer Corp.
  ESCC
600 Komas Dr.
Salt Lake City, UT 84108
801-588-1000 Fax 801-588-4500
Computers - graphics

Exabyte Corp. EXBT
1685 38th St.
Boulder, CO 80301
303-442-4333 Fax 303-447-7170
Computers - peripheral equipment O

Exar Corp. EXAR
48720 Kato Rd.
Freemont, CA 94538
510-668-7000 Fax 510-668-7001
Electrical components - semiconductors

Excel Technology, Inc. XLTC
45 Adams Ave.
Hauppauge, NY 11788
516-273-6900 Fax 516-273-6958
Lasers - systems & components

Executive TeleCard, Ltd. EXTL
8 Avenue C
Nanuet, NY 10954
914-627-2060
Telecommunications services

Executone Information Systems, Inc.
  XTON
478 Wheelers Farm Rd.
Milford, CT 06460
203-876-7600 Fax 203-882-5749
Telecommunications equipment

Expeditors International of Washington,
  Inc. EXPD
19119 16th Ave. South
Seattle, WA 98188
206-246-3711 Fax 206-246-3197
Transportation - services

Express Scripts, Inc. ESRX
1400 Riverport Dr.
Maryland Heights, MO 63043
314-770-1666
Medical services

EZCORP, Inc. EZPW
1901 Capital Parkway
Austin, TX 78746
512-314-3400
Financial - consumer loans

F&M Bancorp FMBN
110 Thomas Johnson Dr.
Frederick, MD 21702
301-694-4000
Banks - northeast DRP 5%

Farr Co. FARC
2221 Park Place
El Segundo, CA 90245
310-536-6300
Filtration products

Fastenal Co. FAST
2001 Theurer Blvd.
Winona, MN 55987
507-454-5374 Fax 507-454-6542
Building products - retail & wholesale O

Fidelity Bancorp, Inc. FSBI
1009 Perry Hwy.
Pittsburgh, PA 15237
412-367-3300
Financial - savings and loans

Fifth Third Bancorp FITB
38 Fountain Square Plaza
Cincinnati, OH 45263
513-579-5300 Fax 513-579-5226
Banks - midwest O DRP

FileNet Corp. FILE
3565 Harbor Blvd.
Costa Mesa, CA 92626
714-966-3400
Computers - services O

Filene's Basement Corp. BSMT
40 Walnut St.
Wellesley, MA 02181
617-348-7000
Retail - discount & variety

First American Corp. FATN
First American Center
Nashville, TN 37237
615-748-2000
Banks - southeast O DRP 5%

First Cash, Inc. PAWN
600 Six Flags Dr., Ste. 518
Arlington, TX 76011
817-633-7296 Fax 817-840-4335
Financial - consumer loans

First Charter Corp. FCTR
22 Union St. North
Concord, NC 28026
704-786-3300
Banks - southeast

First Commercial Corp. FCLR
400 W. Capitol Ave.
Little Rock, AR 72201
501-371-7000
Banks - southeast DRP 5%

First Federal Capital Corp. FTFC
605 State St.
LaCrosse, WI 54601
608-784-8000
Financial - savings and loans DRP

First Financial Corp. FFHC
1305 Main St.
Stevens Point, WI 54481
715-341-0400
Financial - savings and loans   O   DRP

First Financial Holdings, Inc. FFCH
34 Broad St.
Charleston, SC 29401
803-529-5800
Financial - savings and loans   DRP

First Hawaiian, Inc. FHWN
1132 Bishop St.
Honolulu, HI 96813
808-525-7000   Fax 808-533-7844
Banks - west   O   DRP

First Indiana Corp. FISB
135 N. Pennsylvania St.
Indianapolis, IN 46204
317-269-1200
Financial - savings and loans

First Merchants Corp. FRME
200 E. Jackson St.
Muncie, IN 47305
317-747-1500
Banks - midwest

First Midwest Bancorp, Inc. FMBI
50 E. Shuman Blvd., Ste. 310
Naperville, IL 60566
708-778-8700
Banks - midwest   DRP

First Northern Capital Corp. FNGB
201 N. Monroe Ave.
Green Bay, WI 54301
414-437-7101
Financial - savings and loans   DRP

First Security Corp. FSCO
79 S. Main St., PO Box 30006
Salt Lake City, UT 84130
801-246-5706
Banks - west   O   DRP

1st Source Corp. SRCE
100 N. Michigan St.
South Bend, IN 46601
219-236-2000
Banks - midwest

First Team Sports, Inc. FTSP
2274 Woodale Dr.
Mounds View, MN 55112
612-780-4454   Fax 612-780-8908
Leisure & recreational products

First Tennessee National Corp. FTEN
165 Madison Ave.
Memphis, TN 38103
901-523-5630
Banks - southeast   O   DRP

FirstMerit Corp. FMER
800 First National Tower
Akron, OH 44308
216-384-8000
Banks - midwest   DRP

Fiserv, Inc. FISV
255 Fiserv Dr.
Brookfield, WI 53045
847-956-5098
Computer & data processing services

Flow International Corp. FLOW
23500 64th Ave. South
Kent, WA 98032
206-813-3286   Fax 206-813-3311
Machine tools & related products

Fluor Daniel GTI, Inc. FDGT
100 River Ridge Dr.
Norwood, MA 02062
617-769-7600
Pollution control equipment & services

Foamex International Inc. FMXI
1000 Columbia Ave.
Lynnwood, PA 19061
610-859-3000
Miscellaneous - not elsewhere classified   O

Food Lion, Inc. FDLNA
2110 Executive Dr.
Salisbury, NC 28145
704-633-8250   Fax 704-636-5024
Retail - supermarkets   O   DRP

Foothill Independent Bancorp FOOT
510 S. Grand Ave.
Glendora, CA 91740
818-963-8551
Banks - west

FORE Systems, Inc. FORE
174 Thorn Hill Rd.
Warrendale, PA 15086
412-772-6600   Fax 412-772-6500
Computers - services   O

Foster (LB) Co. FSTR
415 Holiday Dr.
Pittsburgh, PA 15220
412-928-3400
Steel

Franklin Bank, National Associates FSVB
26400 W. Twelve Mile Rd.
Southfield, MI 48086
248-358-4710
Commercial banks

Franklin Electric FELE
400 E. Spring St.
Bluffton, IN 46714
219-824-2900
Electrical industrial apparatus

Fresh Choice, Inc. SALD
2901 Tasman Dr., Ste. 109
Santa Clara, CA 95054
408-986-8661
Retail - food & restaurants

Fritz Companies, Inc. FRTZ
706 Mission St., Ste. 900
San Francisco, CA 94103
415-904-8360
Business services O

Frozen Food Express Industries, Inc.
FFEX
318 Cadiz St.
Dallas, TX 75207
214-630-8090
Transportation - truck

FSI International, Inc. FSII
322 Lake Hazeltine Dr.
Chaska, MN 55318
612-448-5440 Fax 612-448-2825
Machinery - material handling

Fuller (H.B.) FULL
1200 W. County Rd. E.
Arden Hills, MN 55112
612-481-4730
Miscellaneous chemical products DRP

G&K Services, Inc. GKSRA
505 Waterford Park, Ste. 455
Minneapolis, MN 55441
612-546-7440
Linen supply & related

G-III Apparel Group, Ltd. GIII
345 W. 37th St.
New York, NY 10018
212-629-8830
Leather & related products

Galileo Corp. GAEO
Galileo Park, PO Box 550
Sturbridge, MA 01566
508-347-9191 Fax 508-347-3849
Fiber optics

Gaming Lottery Corp. GLCC
160 Nashdene Rd.
Scarborough, ON M1V4C4
416-292-5963
Commercial printing

Gantos, Inc. GTOS
3260 Patterson, S.E.
Grand Rapids, MI 49512
616-949-7000
Retail - apparel & shoes

Gartner Group, Inc. GART
56 Top Gallant Rd.
Stamford, CT 06904
203-964-0096
Business services O

GaSonics International Corp. GSNX
2730 Junction Ave.
San Jose, CA 95134
408-944-0212 Fax 408-473-9509
Electronics - components & systems O

Gehl Co. GEHL
143 Water St.
West Bend, WI 53095
414-334-9461 Fax 414-334-1565
Machinery - farm

General Communications, Inc. GNCMA
2550 Denali St., Ste. 1000
Anchorage, AK 99503
907-265-5600
Telecommunications services

General Magnaplate Corp. GMCC
1331 U.S. Route 1
Linden, NJ 07036
908-862-6200 Fax 908-862-6110
Metal processing & fabrication

General Nutrition Companies, Inc. GNCI
921 Penn Ave.
Pittsburgh, PA 15222
412-288-4600
Retail - misc. O

GENICOM Corp. GECM
14800 Conference Center Dr.
Chantilly, VA 22021
703-802-9200
Computers - peripheral equipment

Genome Therapeutics Corp. GENE
100 Beaver St.
Waltham, MA 02154
617-487-7979 Fax 617-487-7960
Biomedical & genetic products

Gensia Sicor, Inc. GNSA
9360 Towne Center Dr.
San Diego, CA 92121
619-546-8300 Fax 619-453-0095
Drugs

Gentex Corp. GNTX
600 N. Centennial St.
Zeeland, MI 49464
616-772-1800 Fax 616-772-7348
Automotive & trucking - original
  equipment O

Genzyme Corp. GENZ
One Kendall Square
Cambridge, MA 02139
617-252-7500
Biomedical & genetic products O

Giant Cement Holding, Inc. GCHI
320-D Midland Pkwy.
Summerville, SC 29485
803-851-9898
Building products - misc.

Gibson Greetings, Inc. GIBG
2100 Section Rd.
Cincinnati, OH 45237
513-841-6600
Printing - commercial O

Glacier Bancorp, Inc. GBCI
202 Main St., PO Box 27
Kalispell, MT 59903
406-756-4200
Financial - savings and loans

Glenayre Technologies, Inc. GEMS
5935 Carnegie Blvd.
Charlotte, NC 28209
704-553-0038
Real estate operations O

Global Village Communications, Inc.
  GVIL
685 E. Middlefield Rd.
Mountain View, CA 94043
415-390-8200 Fax 415-390-8282
Computers - peripheral equipment

Golden Books Family Entertainment Inc.
  GBFE
850 Third Ave.
New York, NY 10022
212-583-6700 Fax 212-371-1091
Publishing - books

Golden Enterprises, Inc. GLDC
2101 Magnolia Ave. South
Birmingham, AL 35205
205-326-6101
Diversified operations DRP

Good Guys GGUY
7000 Marina Blvd.
Brisbane, CA 94005
415-615-5000
Radio, television & music stores O

Government Technology Services, Inc.
  GTSI
4100 Lafayette Center Dr.
Chantilly, VA 22021
703-631-3333
Computers - services

Grande Tel Technologies GTTIF
135-13500 Maycrest Way
Richmond, BC V6V 2N8
604-278-8788
Radio & TV receiving equipment

Granite Broadcasting Corp. GBTVK
767 Third Ave., 28th Fl.
New York, NY 10017
212-826-2530 Fax 212-826-2858
Broadcasting - radio & TV

Green Industries (A. P.), Inc. APGI
Green Blvd.
Mexico, MO 65265
573-473-3626
Building products - misc.

GSE Systems, Inc. GSES
8930 Stanford Blvd.
Columbia, MD 21045
410-312-3500
Computers - software

GST Telecom GSTX
4317 NE Thurston Way
Vancouver, WA 98662
360-254-4700 Fax 360-260-2075
Manufactures communications equipment

GTS Duratec DRTK
10100 Old Columbia Rd.
Columbia, MD 21046
410-312-5100
Sanitary services

Gymboree Corp. GYMB
700 Airport Blvd., #200
Burlingame, CA 94010
415-579-0600
Children's & infants' wear stores O

Hach Co. HACH
5600 Lindbergh Dr., PO Box 389
Loveland, CO 80537
970-669-3050
Instruments - scientific

Haggar Corp. HGGR
6113 Lemmon Ave.
Dallas, TX 75209
214-352-8481
Apparel

Hahn Automotive Warehouse, Inc. HAHN
415 W. Main St.
Rochester, NY 14608
716-235-1595 Fax 716-235-3108
Auto parts - retail & wholesale

Hancock Holding Co. HBHC
One Hancock Plaza
Gulfport, MS 39501
601-868-4715
Banks - southeast DRP

Harbinger Corp. HRBC
1055 Lennox Park Blvd.
Atlanta, GA 30319
404-841-4334
Computers - software O

Harding Lawson Associates Group, Inc.
 HRDG
7655 Redwood Blvd.
Novato, CA 94948
415-892-0821 Fax 415-892-0831
Engineering - R & D services

Harleysville Group Inc. HGIC
355 Maple Ave.
Harleysville, PA 19438
215-256-5000
Insurance - property & casualty DRP

Harmon Industries, Inc. HRMN
1300 Jefferson Court
Blue Springs, MO 64015
816-229-3345 Fax 816-229-0556
Transportation - equipment & leasing

Harris & Harris Group, Inc. HHGP
One Rockefeller Plaza
New York, NY 10020
212-332-3600 Fax 212-332-3601
Financial - investment management

Haskel International, Inc. HSKL
100 E. Graham Place
Burbank, CA 91502
818-843-4000 Fax 818-841-4291
Pumps and seals

Hathaway Corp. HATH
8228 Park Meadows Dr.
Littleton, CO 80124
303-799-8200 Fax 303-799-8880
Computers - software

Hauser Chemical Research, Inc. HAUS
5555 Airport Blvd.
Boulder, CO 80301
303-443-4662 Fax 303-441-5800
Chemicals - specialty O

Haven Bancorp, Inc. HAVN
93-22 Jamaica Ave.
Woodhaven, NY 11421
718-847-7041
Financial - savings and loans

Haverty Furniture Companies, Inc. HAVT
866 W. Peachtree St., N.W.
Atlanta, GA 30308
404-881-1911
Retail - home furnishings

HBO & Co. HBOC
301 Perimeter Center North
Atlanta, GA 30346
770-393-6000 Fax 770-393-6092
Computers - services

Health Management Systems, Inc. HMSY
401 Park Ave. South
New York, NY 10016
212-685-4545 Fax 212-889-8776
Business services

Health Risk Management, Inc. HRMI
8000 W. 78th St.
Minneapolis, MN 55439
612-829-3500
Medical services

Healthcare Services Group HCSG
2643 Huntingdon Pike
Huntingdon Valley, PA 19006
215-938-1661
Services to buildings

HEI, Inc. HEII
1495 Steiger Lake Ln.
Victoria, MN 55386
612-443-2500
Electrical components - misc.

Helen of Troy Ltd. HELED
6827 Market Ave.
El Paso, TX 79915
915-779-6363
Cosmetics & toiletries O

Helix Technology Corp. HELX
Nine Hampshire St.
Mansfield, MA 02048
508-337-5500
Instruments - scientific O

Henry Schein, Inc. HSIC
135 Duryea Rd.
Melville, NY 11747
516-843-5500
Retail - mail order & direct

Herbalife International, Inc. HERBA
9800 La Cienega Blvd.
Inglewood, CA 90301
310-410-9600
Retail - mail order & direct O

Heritage Financial Services, Inc. HFWA
17500 S. Oak Park Ave.
Tinley Park, IL 60477
708-532-8000
Banks - midwest

Herley Industries, Inc. HRLY
10 Industry Dr.
Lancaster, PA 17603
717-397-2777
Electronics - military

Hirsch International Corp. HRSH
355 Marcus Blvd.
Hauppauge, NY 11788
516-436-7100
Machinery - general industrial

HNC Software, Inc. HNCS
5930 Cornerstone Court West
San Diego, CA 92121
619-546-8877 Fax 619-452-6524
Computers - softwaare

Hollywood Casino Corp. HWCC
13455 Noel Rd., LB 48
Dallas, TX 75240
972-392-7777 Fax 972-386-7411
Leisure & recreational services O

Hollywood Entertainment Corp. HLYW
10300 S.W. Allen Blvd.
Beaverton, OR 97005
503-677-1600
Retail - misc. O

Hologic, Inc. HOLX
590 Lincoln St.
Waltham, MA 02154
617-890-2300 Fax 617-890-8031
Medical instruments

Horizon Financial Corp. HRZB
1500 Cornwall Ave.
Bellingham, WA 98225
360-733-3050 Fax 360-733-7019
Financial - savings and loans

HUBCO, Inc. HUBC
1000 MacArthur Blvd.
Mahwah, NH 07430
201-236-2600
Banks - northeast O DRP

Hunt (J.B.) Transport Services, Inc. JBHT
615 J.B. Hunt Corporate Dr.
Lowell, AR 72745
501-820-0000
Transportation - truck

Huntington Bancshares Inc. HBAN
Huntington Center
Columbus, OH 43287
614-480-8300
Banks - midwest O DRP 5%

Hutchinson Technology, Inc. HTCH
40 W. Highland Park
Hutchinson, MN 55350
612-587-3797
Computers - peripheral equipment O

Hycor Biomedical Inc. HYBD
7272 Chapman Ave.
Garden Grove, CA 92641
714-895-9558 Fax 714-891-4153
Medical products

Hyperion Software Corp. HYSW
900 Long Ridge Rd.
Stamford, CT 06902
203-703-3000 Fax 203-595-8500
Computers - software O

ICOS Corp. ICOS
22021 20th Ave. S.E.
Bothell, WA 98021
206-485-1900
Drugs O

IDEXX Laboratories, Inc. IDXX
One IDEXX Dr.
Westbrook, ME 04092
207-856-0300 Fax 207-856-0346
Biomedical & genetic products O

IFR Systems, Inc. IFRS
10200 W. York St.
Wichita, KS 67215
316-522-4981 Fax 316-524-2623
Electronics - measuring instruments

IHOP Corp. IHOP
525 N. Brand Blvd.
Glendale, CA 91203
818-240-6055
Retail - food & restaurants O

II-VI Inc. IIVI
375 Saxonburg Blvd.
Saxonburg, PA 16056
412-352-4455 Fax 412-352-4980
Electrical components - misc.

Image Entertainment, Inc. DISK
9333 Oso Ave.
Chatsworth, CA 91311
818-407-9100 Fax 818-407-9151
Leisure & recreational products

Imatron Inc. IMAT
389 Oyster Point Blvd.
South San Francisco, CA 94080
415-583-9964 Fax 415-871-0418
Medical instruments

Imax Corp. IMAX
38 Isabella St.
Toronto, ON M4Y1N1
416-960-8509
Mis. amusement recreational services O

ImmuLogic Pharmaceutical Corp. IMUL
610 Lincoln St.
Waltham, MA 02154
617-466-6000 Fax 617-466-6010
Biomedical & genetic products

Immucor, Inc. BLUD
3130 Gateway Dr.
Norcross, GA 30071
770-441-2051
Medical & dental supplies

Immune Response IMNR
5935 Darwin Ct.
Carlsbad, CA 92008
760-431-7080
Drugs O

Immunex Corp. IMNX
51 University St.
Seattle, WA 98101
206-587-0430 Fax 206-587-0606
Biomedical & genetic products O

IMP, Inc. IMPX
2830 N. First St.
San Jose, CA 95134
408-432-9100 Fax 408-434-0335
Electronics - components & systems

In Focus Systems, Inc. INFS
27700B SW Parkway Ave.
Wilsonville, OR 97070
503-685-8888
Computers - peripheral equipment O

In Home Health, Inc. IHHI
601 Lakeshore Parkway
Minnetonka, MN 55305
612-449-7500
Healthcare - outpatient & home

InControl, Inc. INCL
6675 185th Ave. N.E.
Redmond, WA 98052
206-861-9800 Fax 206-861-9301
Medical products

Independent Bank Corp. IBCP
230 W. Main St., PO Box 491
Ionia, MI 48846
616-527-9450
Banks - midwest DRP 5%

Individual Investor Group INDI
1633 Broadway, 38th Floor
New York, NY 10019
212-843-2777
Periodicals

Information Resources, Inc. IRIC
150 N. Clinton St.
Chicago, IL 60661
312-726-1221
Data collection & systems O

Informix Corp. IFMX
4100 Bohannon Dr.
Menlo Park, CA 94025
415-926-6300 Fax 415-926-6593
Computers - software O

InnerDyne, Inc. IDYN
1244 Reamwood Ave.
Sunnyvale, CA 94089
408-745-6010 Fax 408-745-6570
Medical products

InnoServ Technologies, Inc. ISER
1611 Pomona Rd.
Corona, CA 91720
909-736-4570 Fax 909-736-3753
Medical services

Innovex, Inc. INVX
1313 5th St. South
Hopkins, MN 55343
612-938-4155 Fax 612-938-7718
Photographic equipment & supplies O

Insilco Corp. INSL
425 Metro Place North
Dublin, OH 43017
614-792-0468
Diversified operations

Insituform Technologies, Inc. INSUA
1770 Kirby Pkwy., Ste. 300
Memphis, TN 38138
901-759-7473 Fax 901-759-7500
Building products - misc. O

Insurance Auto Auctions, Inc. IAAI
1270 W. Northwest Hwy.
Palatine, IL 60067
847-705-9550
Insurance - property & casualty

Integrated Circuit Systems, Inc. ICST
2435 Blvd. of the Generals
Norristown, PA 19403
610-630-5300
Electrical components - misc.

Integrated Device Technology, Inc. IDTI
2975 Stender Way
Santa Clara, CA 95054
408-727-6116 Fax 408-492-8674
Electrical components - semiconductors O

Integrated Process Equipment IPEC
911 Bern Ct., Suite 100
San Jose, CA 95112
408-436-2170
Misc. electrical equipment & supplies O

Integrated Silicon Solution, Inc. ISSI
680 Almanor Ave.
Sunnyvale, CA 94086
408-733-4774
Computers - peripheral equipment O

Integrated Systems, Inc. INTS
3260 Jay St.
Santa Clara, CA 95054
408-980-1500 Fax 408-980-0400
Computers - software

Intel Corp. INTC
2200 Mission College Blvd.
Santa Clara, CA 95052
408-765-8080 Fax 408-765-1774
Electrical components - semiconductors O
  DRP

InteliData INTD
13100 Worldgate Dr., #600
Herndon, VA 20170
703-834-8500
Computer & data processing services

Intelect Communications Systems Ltd.
  ICOM
100 Executive Drive
Richardson, TX 75081
972-437-1888
Misc. durable goods O

Inter-Tel, Inc. INTL
4909 E. McDowell Rd., Ste. 106
Phoenix, AZ 85008
602-231-5151
Telecommunications services

Intercargo Corp. ICAR
1450 American Lane, 20th Fl.
Schaumburg, IL 60173
708-517-2510
Insurance - property & casualty

Interface Systems, Inc. INTF
5855 Interface Dr.
Ann Arbor, MI 48103
313-769-5900 Fax 313-769-1047
Computers - peripheral equipment

Interface, Inc. IFSIA
Orchard Hill Rd., PO Box 1503
LaGrange, GA 30241
404-882-1891
Textiles - home furnishings

Intergraph Corp. INGR
1 Madison Industrial Park
Huntsville, AL 35894
205-730-2000
Computers - graphics O

Interleaf, Inc. LEAF
9 Hillside Ave.
Waltham, MA 02154
617-290-0710
Computers - software

Interlink Electronics LINK
546 Flynn Rd.
Camarillo, CA 93012
510-657-9800
Electronic components & accessories

Interlinq Software Corp. INLQ
11255 Kirkland Way
Kirkland, WA 98033
206-827-1112
Computers - software

Intermedia communications, Inc. ICIX
9280 Bay Plaza Blvd., Ste. 720
Tampa, FL 33619
813-621-0011 Fax 813-620-3195
Telecommunications services

Intermet Corp. INMT
2859 Paces Ferry Rd.
Atlanta, GA 30339
770-431-6000 Fax 770-431-6001
Automotive & trucking - original
  equipment O

Interneuron Pharmaceuticals, Inc. IPIC
99 Hayden Ave., Ste. 340
Lexington, MA 02173
617-861-8444
Drugs

Interphase Corp. INPH
13800 Senlac
Dallas, TX 75234
214-919-9000 Fax 214-919-9200
Computers - peripheral equipment

Intuit, Inc. INTU
2535 Garcia Ave.
Mountain View, CA 94043
415-944-6000
Computers - software O

Invacare Corp. IVCR
899 Cleveland St., PO Box 4028
Elyria, OH 44036
216-329-6000
Medical & dental supplies O DRP

Investment Technology Group, Inc. ITGI
900 Third Ave.
New York, NY 10022
212-755-6800
Computers - services

Investors Title Co. ITIC
121 N. Columbia St.
Chapel Hill, NC 27514
919-968-2200 Fax 919-968-2223
Insurance - multi line & misc.

Invivo Corp. SAFE
49050 Milmont Dr.
Fremont, CA 94538
510-226-9600
Instruments - control

IPC Information Systems, Inc. IPCI
88 Pine St.
New York, NY 10005
212-825-9060
Telecommunications equipment

Isis Pharmaceuticals, Inc. ISIP
2292 Faraday Ave.
Carlsbad, CA 92008
760-931-9200
Drugs

ITLA Capital Corp. ITLA
700 N. Central Ave., Ste. 600
Glendale, CA 91203
818-551-0600
Financial - savings and loans

Itron, Inc. ITRI
2818 N. Sullivan Rd.
Spokane, WA 99216
509-924-9900 Fax 509-928-1465
Electronics - measuring instruments O

Iwerks Entertainment, Inc. IWRK
4540 W. Valerio St.
Burbank, CA 91505
818-841-7766 Fax 818-841-7847
Motion pictures & services O

J & J Snack Foods Corp. JJSF
6000 Central Hwy.
Pennsauken, NJ 08109
609-665-9533
Food - misc.

J. Baker, Inc. JBAK
555 Turnpike St.
Canton, MA 02021
617-828-9300
Retail - apparel & shoes

Jack Henry & Associates, Inc. JKHY
663 Highway 60, PO Box 807
Monett, MO 65708
417-235-6652 Fax 417-235-8406
Computers - software DRP

Jaco Electronics, Inc. JACO
145 Oser Ave.
Hauppauge, NY 11788
516-273-5500 Fax 515-273-5640
Electronics - parts distribution

Jacobson Stores Inc. JCBS
3333 Sargent Rd.
Jackson, MI 49201
517-764-6400
Retail - regional department stores DRP

Jameson Inns, Inc. JAMS
1950 Century Blvd., N.E.
Atlanta, GA 30345
770-636-2973
Hotels DRP 5%

Jean Philippe Fragrances, Inc. JEAN
551 Fifth Ave.
New York, NY 10176
212-983-2640 Fax 212-983-4197
Cosmetics & toiletries

Jefferson Bankshares, Inc. JEFF
123 E. Main St.
Charlottesville, VA 22902
804-972-1100
Banks - southeast

Jefferson Smurfit JJSC
8182 Maryland
St. Louis, MO 63105
314-746-1100
Paperboard containers and boxes O

JMAR Technologies, Inc. JMAR
3956 Sorrento Valley Blvd.
San Diego, CA 92121
619-535-1706
Lasers - systems & components

JMC Group, Inc. JMCG
9710 Scranton Rd., Ste. 100
San Diego, CA 92121
619-450-0055
Financial - business services

Johnson Worldwide Associates, Inc.
 JWAIA
1326 Willow Rd.
Sturtevant, WI 53177
414-884-1500
Leisure & recreational products

Jones Intercable, Inc. JOIN
9697 E. Mineral Ave.
Englewood, CO 80112
303-792-3111
Cable TV

Juno Lighting, Inc. JUNO
2001 S. Mt. Prospect Rd.
Des Plaines, IL 60017
847-827-9880
Building products - lighting fixtures

Just For Feet, Inc. FEET
153 Cahaba Valley Pkwy. North
Birmingham, AL 35124
205-403-8000
Shoes & related apparel O

Justin Industries, Inc. JSTN
2821 W. 7th St.
Fort Worth, TX 76101
817-336-5125
Shoes & related apparel DRP

Kaiser Ventures KRSC
8300 Utica Ave., Ste. 301
Rancho Cucamonga, CA 91730
909-944-4155
Miscellaneous - not elsewhere classified

Kaman Corp. KAMNA
Blue Hills Ave.
Bloomfield, CT 06002
203-243-7100
Aerospace - aircraft equipment DRP

Kelley Oil & Gas Corp. KOGC
601 Jefferson St., Ste. 1100
Houston, TX 77002
713-652-5200
Oil & gas - US exploration & production

Kelly Services, Inc. KELYA
999 W. Big Beaver Rd.
Troy, MI 48084
810-362-4444 Fax 810-244-4154
Personnel O

KEMET Corp. KMET
2835 KEMET Way
Simpsonville, SC 29681
864-963-6300
Electronics - components & systems O

Kewaunee Scientific Corp. KEQU
1144 Wilmette Ave.
Wilmette, IL 60091
704-873-7202
Furniture

KeyTronic Corp. KTCC
N. 4424 Sullivan Rd.
Spokane, WA 99216
509-928-8000
Computers - peripheral equipment

Keystone Financial, Inc. KSTN
One Keystone Plaza
Harrisburg, PA 17105
717-233-1555
Banks - northeast O DRP

Kimball International, Inc. KBALB
1600 Royal St.
Jasper, IN 47549
812-482-1600
Furniture

Kinnard Investments, Inc. KINN
1700 Northstar Center
Minneapolis, MN 55402
612-370-2700
Financial - business services

KLA-Tencor Corp. KLAC
160 Rio Robles
San Jose, CA 95134
408-468-4200
Machinery - general industrial O

KLLM Transport Services, Inc. KLLM
3475 Lakeland Dr.
Jackson, MS 39208
601-939-2545
Transportation - truck

Knape & Vogt Manufacturing Co. KNAP
2700 Oak Industrial Dr., N.E.
Grand Rapids, MI 49505
616-459-3311
Furniture DRP

Knickerbocker (L.L.) KNIC
30055 Comercio
Rancho Santa Margari, CA 92688
714-858-3661
Toys and sporting goods

Komag, Inc. KMAG
275 S. Hillview Dr.
Milpitas, CA 95035
408-946-2300
Computers - peripheral equipment O

Kronos, Inc. KRON
62 Fourth Ave.
Waltham, MA 02154
617-890-3232
Miscellaneous - not elsewhere classified

K-Swiss, Inc. KSWS
12300 Montague St.
Pacoima, CA 91331
818-998-3388
Shoes & related apparel

K-Tron International, Inc. KTII
1810 Chapel Ave. West
Cherry Hill, NJ 08002
609-661-6240
Instruments - control

Kulicke & Soffa Industries, Inc. KLIC
2101 Blair Mill Rd.
Willow Grove, PA 19090
215-784-6000 Fax 215-659-7588
Electrical components - semiconductors O

Kushner-Locke Co. KLOC
11601 Wilshire Blvd., 21st Fl.
Los Angeles, CA 90025
310-445-1111 Fax 310-445-1191
Leisure & recreational products

LabOne, Inc. LABS
10310 W. 84th Terrace
Lenaxa, KS 66214
913-888-8397 Fax 913-888-8343
Medical & dental supplies

Laclede Steel Co. LCLD
One Metropolitan Square
St. Louis, MO 63102
314-425-1400
Steel - specialty alloys

LADD Furniture, Inc. LADF
One Plaza Center, Box HP-3
High Point, NC 27261
910-889-0333 Fax 910-888-6446
Furniture

Lakeland Industries, Inc. LAKE
1 Comac Loop
Ronkonkoma, NY 11779
516-981-9700 Fax 516-981-9751
Textiles - apparel

Lam Research Corp. LRCX
4650 Cushing Parkway
Fremont, CA 94538
510-659-0200 Fax 510-490-5026
Electrical components - semiconductors O

Lancaster Colony Corp. LANC
37 W. Broad St.
Columbus, OH 43215
614-224-7141
Household products and appliances
  O DRP

Lance, Inc. LNCE
8600 S. Boulevard
Charlotte, NC 28232
704-554-1421 Fax 704-554-5586
Food - misc. DRP

Landry's Seafood Restaurants, Inc. LDRY
1400 Post Oak Blvd., Ste. 1010
Houston, TX 77056
713-850-1010
Retail - food & restaurants O

Landstar Systems, Inc. LSTR
1000 Bridgeport Ave.
Shelton, CT 06484
203-925-2900 Fax 203-925-2916
Transportation - truck O

Laserscope LSCP
3052 Orchard Dr.
San Jose, CA 95134
408-943-0636 Fax 408-943-9630
Lasers - systems & components

Lattice Semiconductor Corp. LSCC
5555 Northeast Moore Court
Hillsboro, OR 97124
503-681-0118 Fax 503-681-0347
Electrical components - semiconductors O

Lawson Products, Inc. LAWS
1666 E. Touhy Ave.
Des Plaines, IL 60018
847-827-9666
Metal products - distribution

LCS Industries, Inc. LCSI
120 Brighton Rd.
Clifton, NJ 07012
201-778-5588
Retail - mail order & direct

Lechters, Inc. LECH
1 Cape May St.
Harrison, NJ 07029
201-481-1100 Fax 201-481-5493
Retail - discount & variety

Lidak Pharmaceuticals LDAKA
11077 Torrey Pines Rd.
La Jolla, CA 92037
619-558-0364
Drugs

Life Technologies, Inc. LTEK
8717 Grovemont Circle
Gaithersburg, MD 20877
301-840-8000 Fax 301-670-1394
Biomedical & genetic products

Life USA Holding, Inc. LUSA
300 S. Highway 169
Minneapolis, MN 55426
612-546-7386
Insurance - life

LifeCore Biomedical, Inc. LCBM
3515 Lyman Blvd.
Chaska, MN 55318
612-368-4300 Fax 612-368-3411
Biomedical & genetic products

LifeQuest Medical, Inc. LQMD
9601 McAllister Fwy.
San Antonio, TX 78216
210-366-2100 Fax 210-349-0500
Medical products

Lifeline Systems, Inc. LIFE
640 Memorial Dr.
Cambridge, MA 02139
617-679-1000 Fax 617-679-1384
Healthcare - outpatient & home

Lifetime Hoan Corp. LCUT
One Merrick Ave.
Westbury, NY 11590
516-683-6000
Housewares

Lincare Holdings, Inc. LNCR
19337 US 19 North, Ste. 500
Clearwater, FL 34624
813-530-7700 Fax 813-532-9692
Medical services

Lindal Cedar Homes, Inc. LNDL
4300 S. 104th Place
Seattle, WA 98178
206-725-0900
Building - residential & commercial

Lindberg Corp. LIND
6133 N. River Rd., Ste. 700
Rosemont, IL 60018
708-823-2021 Fax 708-823-0795
Metal processing & fabrication

Linear Technology Corp. LLTC
1630 McCarthy Blvd.
Milpitas, CA 95035
408-432-1900
Electrical components - semiconductors O

Liposome Co. LIPO
1 Research Way
Princeton, NJ 08540
609-951-4304
Drugs O

Liqui-Box Corp. LIQB
6950 Worthington-Galena Rd.
Worthington, OH 43085
614-888-9280 Fax 614-880-0982
Containers - paper & plastic

Little Switzerland LSVI
161B Crown Bay, PO Box 930
St. Thomas, VI
809-776-2010
Misc. shopping goods stores

Liuski International, Inc. LSKI
6585 Crescent Dr.
Norcross, GA 30071
404-447-9454
Computers - peripheral equipment

LoJack Corp. LOJN
333 Elm St.
Dedham, MA 02026
617-326-4700
Data collection & systems O

Lone Star Steakhouse & Saloon, Inc.
 STAR
224 E. Douglas, Ste. 700
Wichita, KS 67202
316-264-8899
Retail - food & restaurants O

Long Island Bancorp LISB
201 Old Country Rd.
Melville, NY 11747
516-547-2000
Banks - northeast O

Lowrance Electronics, Inc. LEIX
12000 E. Skelly Dr.
Tulsa, OK 74128
918-437-6881
Leisure & recreational products

LSI Industries Inc. LYTS
10000 Alliance Rd.
Cincinnati, OH 45242
513-793-3200 Fax 513-984-1335
Building products - lighting fixtures

Lufkin Industries, Inc. LUFK
601 S. Raguet
Lufkin, TX 75901
409-634-2211
Oil field machinery & equipment

MacDermid, Inc. MACD
245 Freight St.
Waterbury, CT 06702
203-575-5700
Chemicals - specialty DRP

Macromedia, Inc. MACR
600 Townsend St.
San Francisco, CA 94103
415-252-2000
Computers - software O

Madge Networks MADGE
2310 N. First St.
San Jose, CA 95131
408-383-1335
Office & computing machines O

Madison Gas and Electric MDSN
133 S. Blair St., PO Box 1231
Madison, WI 53701
608-252-7923
Combination utility services DRP

MAF Bancorp, Inc. MAFB
55th St. & Holmes Ave.
Clarendon Hills, IL 60514
708-325-7300
Banks - midwest

Mallon Resources Corp. MLRC
999 18th St., Ste. 1700
Denver, CO 80202
303-293-2333 Fax 303-293-3601
Oil & gas - US exploration & production

Mark VII, Inc. MVII
5310 St. Joseph Ave.
St. Joseph, MO 64505
816-233-3158 Fax 816-387-4201
Transportation - truck

Marsh Supermarkets, Inc. MARSA
9800 Crosspoint Blvd.
Indianapolis, IN 46256
317-594-2100
Retail - supermarkets DRP

Marshall & Ilsley Corp. MRIS
770 N. Water St.
Milwaukee, WI 53202
414-765-7801
Banks - midwest O DRP

Matthews Studio Equipment Group MATT
2405 Empire Ave.
Burbank, CA 91504
818-843-6715
Motion pictures & services

Maverick Tube Corp. MAVK
400 Chesterfield Center
Chesterfield, MO 63017
314-537-1314 Fax 314-537-1316
Oil field machinery & equipment

Maxco, Inc. MAXC
1118 Centennial Way
Lansing, MI 48909
517-321-3130
Lumber & construction materials

Maxicare Health Plans, Inc. MAXI
1149 S. Broadway St.
Los Angeles, CA 90015
213-765-2000
Health maintenance organization O

Maxim Integrated Products, Inc. MXIM
120 San Gabriel Dr.
Sunnyvale, CA 94086
408-737-7600
Electrical components - misc. O

Maynard Oil Co. MOIL
8080 N. Central Expwy.
Dallas, TX 75206
214-891-8880 Fax 214-891-8827
Oil & gas - US exploration & production

McCormick & Co., Inc. MCCRK
18 Loveton Circle
Sparks, MD 21152
410-771-7301
Food - spices O DRP

McGrath RentCorp MGRC
2500 Grant Ave.
San Lorenzo, CA 94580
510-276-2626
Leasing

Meade Instruments Corp. MEAD
16542 Millikan Ave.
Irvine, CA 92606
714-756-2291 Fax 714-756-1450
Instruments - scientific

Medaphis Corp. MEDA
2700 Cumberland Pkwy.
Atlanta, GA 30339
404-319-3300
Medical services O

Medar, Inc. MDXR
38700 Grand River Ave.
Farmington Hills, MI 48335
810-477-3900 Fax 810-477-8897
Industrial automation & robotics

Medarex, Inc. MEDX
22 Chambers St.
Princeton, NJ 08542
609-921-7121 Fax 609-921-7450
Drugs

Medford Bancorp MDBK
29 High St.
Medford, MA 02155
617-395-7700
Financial - savings and loans DRP

Media 100 MDEA
100 Locke Dr.
Marlboro, MA 91752
508-481-3700
Office & computing machines

Media Arts Group, Inc. ARTS
Ten Almadin Blvd., Ste. 900
San Jose, CA 95113
408-947-4680
Ceramics & ceramic products

Medicis Pharmaceutical Corp. MDRXA
100 E. 42nd St., 15th Fl.
New York, NY 10017
212-599-2000 Fax 212-599-2429
Drugs O

MedImmune, Inc. MEDI
19 Firstfield Rd.
Gaithersburg, MD 20878
301-417-0770
Medical products

Medstone International, Inc. MEDS
100 Columbia, Ste. 100
Aliso Viejo, CA 92656
714-448-7700
Medical services

Mego Financial Corp. MEGO
4310 Paradise Rd.
Las Vegas, NV 89109
702-737-3700 Fax 702-369-4398
Real estate development

Men's Wearhouse, Inc. SUIT
5803 Glenmont Dr.
Houston, TX 77081
713-664-3692
Retail - apparel & shoes

Mentor Corp. MNTR
5425 Hollister Ave.
Santa Barbara, CA 93111
805-681-6000
Medical & dental supplies O

Mentor Graphics Corp. MENT
8005 S.W. Boeckman Rd.
Wilsonville, OR 97070
503-685-7000
Computers - graphics O

Mercantile Bankshares Corp. MRBK
Two Hopkins Plaza
Baltimore, MD 21203
410-237-5900
Banks - southeast O DRP 5%

Mercer International MERCS
400 Burrard St. #1250
Vancouver, BC V6C 386
604-683-8286
Investment offices O

Merchants New York Bancorp MBNY
275 Madison Ave.
New York, NY 10016
212-973-6600
Commercial banks

Mercury Interactive Corp. MERQ
3333 Octavius Dr.
Santa Clara, CA 95054
408-987-0100
Computers - software O

Meridian Data, Inc. MDCD
1310 Villa St.
Mountain View, CA 94041
415-960-0288
Computers - peripheral equipment O

Meridian Diagnostics, Inc. KITS
3471 River Hills Dr.
Cincinnati, OH 45244
513-271-3700 Fax 513-271-3762
Medical products DRP

Meridian Medical Technologies, Inc.
 MTEC
2275 Research Blvd.
Rockville, MD 20850
301-926-1800 Fax 301-926-6186
Medical products

Merisel, Inc. MSEL
200 Continental Blvd.
El Segundo, CA 90245
310-615-3080 Fax 310-615-1234
Computers - retail & wholesale

Merit Medical Systems, Inc. MMSI
1600 W. Merit Pkwy.
South Jordan, UT 84095
801-253-1600
Medical products

Merrill Corp. MRLL
One Merrill Circle
St. Paul, MN 55108
612-646-4501
Printing - commercial

Mesa Air Group, Inc. MESA
2325 E. 30th St.
Farmington, NM 87401
505-327-0271
Transportation - airline O

MetaCreations Corp. MCRE
6303 Carpinteria Ave.
Carpinteria, CA 93013
805-566-6200
Computers - software

META Group, Inc. METG
208 Harbor Dr., PO Box 120061
Stamford, CT 06912
203-973-6700
Business services

Methanex Corp. MEOH
200 Burrard St.
Vancouver, BC V6C3M1
604-661-2600
Industrial organic chemicals

Methode Electronics, Inc. METHA
7447 W. Wilson Ave.
Chicago, IL 60656
708-867-9600
Electrical connectors

Metro One Telecommunications, Inc.
 MTON
8405 S.W. Nimbus Ave.
Beaverton, OR 97008
503-643-9500
Telecommunications services

Metrocall, Inc. MCLL
6677 Richmond Highway
Alexandria, VA 23306
703-660-6677
Telecommunications services

MGI PHARMA, Inc. MOGN
9900 Bren Rd. East, Ste. 300E
Minneapolis, MN 55343
612-935-7335 Fax 612-935-0468
Drugs O

Miami Subs Corp. SUBS
6300 N.W. 31st Ave.
Fort Lauderdale, FL 33309
954-973-0000 Fax 954-973-7616
Retail - food & restaurants

Michael Foods, Inc. MIKL
5353 Wayzata Blvd.
Minneapolis, MN 55416
612-546-1500
Food - misc.

Michaels Stores, Inc. MIKE
5931 Campus Circle Dr.
Irving, TX 75063
972-714-7000
Retail - craft supplies O DRP

Micro Warehouse, Inc. MWHS
535 Connecticut Ave.
Norwalk, CT 06854
203-899-4000
Computers - retail & wholesale O

MicroAge, Inc. MICA
2400 S. MicroAge Way
Tempe, AZ 85282
602-804-2000 Fax 602-966-7339
Computers - retail & wholesale O

MICROS Systems, Inc. MCRS
12000 Baltimore Ave.
Beltsville, MD 20705
301-210-6000
Office automation

Microchip Technology Inc. MCHP
2355 W. Chandler Blvd.
Chandler, AZ 85224
602-786-7200
Electronics - components & systems O

Microcide Pharmaceuticals, Inc. MCDE
850 Maude Ave.
Mountain View, CA 94043
415-428-1550
Biomedical & genetic products

Microdyne Corp. MCDY
3601 Eisenhower Ave.
Alexandria, VA 22304
703-739-0500 Fax 703-739-0558
Telecommunications equipment

Micron Electronics, Inc. MUEI
900 E. Karcher Rd.
Nampa, ID 83687
208-465-3434 Fax 208-465-8995
Computers - mini & micro O

Microsemi Corp. MSCC
2830 S. Fairview St.
Santa Ana, CA 92704
714-979-8220
Electrical components - semiconductors O

Microsoft Corp. MSFT
One Microsoft Way
Redmond, WA 98052
206-882-8080 Fax 206-936-7329
Computers - software O

MicroTouch Systems, Inc. MTSI
300 Griffin Brook Park Dr.
Methuen, MA 01844
508-659-9000 Fax 508-659-9100
Computers - peripheral equipment

Middlesex Water Co. MSEX
1500 Ronson Rd.
Iselin, NJ 08830
908-634-1500
Utility - water supply DRP

Miller Building Systems, Inc. MBSI
58120 County Rd. 3 South
Elkhart, IN 46517
219-295-1214 Fax 219-295-2232
Building - residential & commercial

Miller (Herman), Inc. MLHR
855 E. Main Ave.
Zeeland, MI 49464
616-772-3300
Furniture O

Miltope Group Inc. MILT
1770 Walt Whitman Rd.
Melville, NY 11747
516-420-0200 Fax 516-756-7606
Computers - mini & micro

Mine Safety Appliances Co. MNES
121 Gamma Dr.
Pittsburgh, PA 15238
412-967-3000
Protection - safety equipment & services

MiniMed, Inc. MNMD
12744 San Fernando Rd.
Sylmar, CA 91342
818-362-5958
Medical products

Miramar Mining MAENE
311 W. First St.
Vancouver, BC V7M1B5
604-985-2572
Gold & silver ores

Mobile Gas Service Corp. MBLE
2828 Dauphin St.
Mobile, AL 36606
334-476-2720
Utility - gas distribution DRP

Modern Controls, Inc. MOCO
7500 Boone Ave. North
Minneapolis, MN 55428
612-493-6370 Fax 612-493-6358
Instruments - control

Modine Manufacturing Co. MODI
1500 DeKoven Ave.
Racine, WI 53403
414-636-1200 Fax 414-636-1424
Automotive & trucking - original
  equipment O DRP

Molex Inc. MOLX
2222 Wellington Court
Lisle, IL 60532
708-969-4550 Fax 708-969-1352
Electrical connectors O

Monmouth Real Estate Investment Corp.
  MNRTA
125 Wycoff Rd., PO Box 335
Eatontown, NJ 07724
908-542-4927
Real estate investment trust DRP 5%

Monro Muffler Brake, Inc. MNRO
2340 Brighton-Henrietta TL Rd.
Rochester, NY 14623
716-427-2280
Auto parts - retail & wholesale

Moore Products Co. MORP
Sumneytown Pike
Spring House, PA 19477
215-646-7400 Fax 215-283-6358
Instruments - control

Moore-Handley, Inc. MHCO
3140 Pelham Pkwy.
Pelham, AL 35124
205-663-8011
Building products - retail & wholesale

Mosaix, Inc. MOSX
6464 185th Ave. N.E.
Redmond, WA 98052
206-881-7544 Fax 206-869-4530
Telecommunications equipment

Motor Club of America MOTR
95 Route 17 South
Paramus, NJ 07553
201-291-2000
Insurance - property & casualty

Movado Group MOVA
125 Chubb Ave.
Lyndhurst, NJ 07071
201-460-4800
Precious metals & jewelry

Multi-Color Corp. LABL
4575 Eastern Ave.
Cincinnati, OH 45226
513-321-5381 Fax 513-321-6138
Printing - commercial

Mutual Savings Bank, f.s.b. MSBK
623 Washington Ave.
Bay City, MI 48707
517-892-3511
Financial - savings and loans

Mycogen Corporation MYCO
5501 Oberlin Dr.
San Diego, CA 92121
619-453-8030
Biomedical & genetic products O DRP

NABI, Inc. NABI
1111 Park Centre Blvd.
Miami, FL 33169
305-628-5303 Fax 305-624-1646
Biomedical & genetic products O

NAI Technologies NATL
282 New York Ave.
Huntington, NY 11743
516-271-5685
Office & computing machines

Nam Tai Electronics NTAI
999 W. Hastings St., Suite 350
Vancouver, BC V6C2W2
604-669-7800
Office & computing machines

Nash Finch Co. NAFC
7600 France Ave. South
Minneapolis, MN 55440
612-929-0371
Food - wholesale DRP

National Computer Systems, Inc. NLCS
11000 Prairie Lakes Dr.
Minneapolis, MN 55344
612-829-3000
Optical character recognition

National Home Centers, Inc. NHCI
Highway 265 North, PO Box 789
Springdale, AR 72765
501-756-1700 Fax 501-756-9122
Retail - misc.

National Technical Systems, Inc. NTSC
24007 Ventura Blvd.
Calabasas, CA 91302
818-591-0776 Fax 818-591-0899
Engineering - R & D services

Natural Alternatives International, Inc.
 NAII
1185 Linda Vista Dr.
San Marcos, CA 92069
619-744-7340
Vitamins & nutritional products

Nature's Sunshine Products, Inc. NATR
75 E. 1700 South
Provo, UT 84606
801-342-4300
Medical products

Nautica Enterprises, Inc. NAUT
40 W. 57th St., 3rd Fl.
New York, NY 10019
212-541-5990
Textiles - apparel O

Navigators Group NAVG
123 Williams St., 25th Floor
New York, NY 10038
212-346-6751
Fire, marine & casualty insurance

Navarre Corp. NAVR
7400 49th Ave. North
New Hope, MN 55428
612-535-8333 Fax 612-533-2156
Wholesale distribution - consumer products

NBTY, Inc. NBTY
90 Orville Dr.
Bohemia, NY 11716
516-567-9500
Vitamins & nutritional products O

NeoMagic Corp. NMGC
3260 Jay St.
Santa Clara, CA 95054
408-988-7020 Fax 408-988-5196
Electronics - components & systems

NeoRx Corp. NERX
410 W. Harrison St.
Seattle, WA 98119
206-281-7001 Fax 206-284-7112
Biomedical & genetic products

Neoprobe Corp. NEOP
425 Metro Place North
Dublin, OH 43017
614-793-7500
Biomedical & genetic products O

Neose Technologies, Inc. NTEC
102 Witner Rd.
Horsham, PA 19044
215-441-5890
Biomedical & genetic products

NETCOM On-Line Communications
  Services, Inc. NETC
3031 Tisch Way
San Jose, CA 95128
408-345-2600
Telecommunications services O

NetManage, Inc. NETM
10725 N. De Anza Blvd.
Cupertino, CA 95014
408-973-7171 Fax 408-257-6405
Computers - software O

Netscape Communications Copr. NSCP
501 E. Middlefield Rd.
Mountain View, CA 94043
415-254-1900 Fax 415-528-4124
Computers - software O

Network Computing Devices, Inc. NCDI
350 N. Bernardo Ave.
Mountain View, CA 94043
415-694-0650 Fax 415-961-7711
Computers - peripheral equipment O

Neurex Corp. NXCO
3760 Haven Ave.
Menlo Park, CA 94025
415-853-1500 Fax 415-853-1538
Biomedical & genetic products

Newport Corp. NEWP
1791 Deere Ave.
Irvine, CA 92714
714-863-3144 Fax 714-253-1671
Instruments - scientific DRP

NeXstar Pharmaceuticals, Inc. NXTR
2860 Wilderness Place
Boulder, CO 80301
303-444-5893
Drugs

Nobility Homes, Inc. NOBH
3741 S.W. 7th St.
Ocala, FL 32674
904-732-5157
Building - residential & commercial

Nordson Corp. NDSN
28601 Clemens Rd.
Westlake, OH 44145
216-892-1580 Fax 216-892-9507
Machinery - general industrial DRP

Nordstrom, Inc. NOBE
1501 Fifth Ave.
Seattle, WA 98101
206-628-2111
Retail - major department stores O

Norstan, Inc. NRRD
6900 Wedgwood Rd., Ste. 150
Maple Grove, MN 55311
612-420-1100
Telecommunications equipment

Northern Trust Co. NTRS
50 S. La Salle St.
Chicago, IL 60675
312-630-6000 Fax 312-630-6739
Banks - midwest O DRP

Northwest Airlines Corp. NWAC
2700 Lone Oak Pkwy.
Eagan, MN 55121
612-726-2111
Transportation - airline O

Northwest Natural Gas Co. NWNG
220 N.W. Second Ave.
Portland, OR 97209
503-226-4211
Utility - gas distribution DRP

Northwestern Steel and Wire Co. NWSW
121 Wallace St.
Sterling, IL 61081
815-625-2500
Wire & cable products

Norwood Promotional Products Inc. NPPI
817 N. Frio St.
San Antonio, TX 78207
210-227-7629
Business services

Novell, Inc. NOVL
122 E. 1700 South
Provo, UT 84606
801-429-7000
Computers - peripheral equipment O

Novellus Systems, Inc. NVLS
81 Vista Montana
San Jose, CA 95134
408-943-9700 Fax 408-943-3422
Electrical components - semiconductors O

Noven Pharmaceuticals, Inc. NOVN
11960 S.W. 144th St.
Miami, FL 33186
305-253-5099
Drugs O

Novoste Corp. NOVT
4350-C International Blvd.
Norcross, GA 30093
770-717-0904
Medical instruments

NVIEW Corp. NVUE
860 Omni Blvd.
Newport News, VA 23606
757-873-1354
Manufacturer

Oak Technology, Inc. OAKT
139 Kifer Court
Sunnyvale, CA 94086
408-737-0888
Computers - peripheral equipment O

Objective Systems Integrators, Inc. OSII
100 Blue Ravine Rd.
Folsom Junction, CA 95630
916-353-2400
Computers - software O

Ocal, Inc. OCAL
14538 Keswick St.
Van Nuys, CA 91405
818-782-0711
Building products - misc.

O'Charley's Inc. CHUX
3038 Sidco Dr.
Nashville, TN 37204
615-256-8500
Retail - food & restaurants

Odetics, Inc. ODETA
1515 S. Manchester Ave.
Anaheim, CA 92802
714-774-5000 Fax 714-774-9432
Electronics - measuring instruments

Offshore Logistics, Inc. OLOG
224 Rue de Jean, PO Box 5-C
Lafayette, LA 70505
318-233-1221 Fax 318-235-6678
Oil & gas - field services

Oglebay Norton Co. OGLE
1100 Superior Ave.
Cleveland, OH 44114
216-861-3300 Fax 216-861-2863
Diversified operations

Ohio Casualty Corp. OCAS
136 N. Third St.
Hamilton, OH 45025
513-867-3000
Insurance - property & casualty DRP

OHSL Financial OHSL
5889 Bridgetown Rd.
Cincinnati, OH 45248
513-574-3322
Savings institution

Old Kent Financial Corp. OKEN
One Vandenberg Center
Grand Rapids, MI 49503
616-771-5000
Banks - midwest O DRP

Old National Bancorp OLDB
420 Main St.
Evansville, IN 47708
812-464-1434
Banks - midwest DRP 3%

On Assignment Inc. ASGN
21515 Vanowen St., Ste. 204
Canoga Park, CA 91303
818-878-7900
Personnel

One Price Clothing Stores, Inc. ONPR
Highway 290, Commerce Park
Duncan, SC 29334
803-439-6666 Fax 803-439-9584
Retail - apparel & shoes

OPTi, Inc. OPTI
2525 Walsh Ave.
Santa Clara, CA 95051
408-980-8178
Electrical components - misc.

Optical Cable Corp. OCCF
5290 Concourse Dr.
Roanoke, VA 24019
540-265-0690
Nonferrous rolling & drawing

Optical Coating Laboratory, Inc. OCLI
2789 Northpoint Parkway
Santa Rosa, CA 95407
707-545-6440 Fax 707-525-7410
Instruments - scientific

Optima Petroleum Corporation OPPCF
600-595 Howe St.
Vancouver, BC V6C 2T5
604-684-6886
Crude petroleum & natural gas

Oracle Corporation ORCL
500 Oracle Pkwy.
Redwood Shores, CA 94065
415-506-7000 Fax 415-506-7200
Computers - software

Ortel Corp. ORTL
2015 W. Chestnut St.
Alhambra, CA 91803
818-281-3636
Fiber optics

Oshkosh B'Gosh, Inc. GOSHA
112 Otter Ave.
Oshkosh, WI 54901
414-231-8800
Apparel

Oshkosh Truck Corp. OTRKB
2307 Oregon St.
Oshkosh, WI 54901
414-235-9151
Automotive & trucking - original equipment

Otter Tail Power Co. OTTR
215 S. Cascade St., PO Box 496
Fergus Falls, MN 56538
218-739-8200
Utility - electric power DRP

Outback Steakhouse, Inc. OSSI
550 N. Reo St., Ste. 204
Tampa, FL 33609
813-282-1225
Retail - food & restaurants O

Oxford Health Plans, Inc. OXHP
800 Connecticut Ave.
Norwalk, CT 06854
203-852-1442
Health maintenance organization O

OXIS International, Inc. OXIS
6040 N. Cutter Cir., Ste. 317
Portland, OR 97217
503-283-3911 Fax 503-283-4058
Drugs

P & F Industries, Inc. PFINA
300 Smith St.
Farmingdale, NY 11735
516-694-1800
Metal products - fabrication

PACCAR Inc. PCAR
777 106th Ave. N.E.
Bellevue, WA 98004
206-455-7400 Fax 206-453-4900
Automotive & trucking - original
  equipment

PacifiCare Health Systems, Inc. PHSYA
5995 Plaza Dr.
Cypress, CA 90630
714-952-1121 Fax 714-220-3725
Health maintenance organization O

Pacific Bank PBSF
351 California St.
San Francisco, CA 94104
415-576-2746
Commercial bank

Paging Network, Inc. PAGE
4965 Preston Park Blvd.
Plano, TX 75093
214-985-4100
Telecommunications services O

PairGain Technologies, Inc. PAIR
12921 E. 166th St.
Cerritos, CA 90701
310-404-8811
Telecommunications equipment O

Pancho's Mexican Buffet, Inc. PAMX
3500 Noble Ave., PO Box 7407
Fort Worth, TX 76111
817-831-0081
Retail - food & restaurants

Panda Project PNDA
901 Yamato Rd.
Boca Raton, FL 33431
561-994-2300
Office & computing machines

Papa John's International, Inc. PZZA
11492 Bluegrass Parkway
Louisville, KY 40299
502-266-5200
Retail - food & restaurants O

Parallel Petroleum PLLL
1 Marienfield Pl., #465
Midland, TX 79701
915-684-3727
Oil & gas, service & exploration

Park-Ohio Industries, Inc. PKOH
20600 Chagrin Blvd.
Cleveland, OH 44122
216-991-9700
Metal products - fabrication

ParkerVision, Inc. PRKR
8493 Baymeadows Way
Jacksonville, FL 32256
904-737-1367
Video equipment

Parlex Corp. PRLX
145 Milk St.
Methuen, MA 01844
508-685-4341
Electrical connectors

Parlux Fragrances PARL
3725 S.W. 30th Ave.
Ft. Lauderdale, FL 33312
954-316-9008
Apparel & notions O

Patrick Industries, Inc. PATK
1800 S. 14th St., PO Box 638
Elkhart, IN 46515
219-294-7511 Fax 219-522-5213
Building products - retail & wholesale

Patterson Dental Co. PDCO
1031 Mendota Heights Rd.
St. Paul, MN 55120
612-686-1600
Medical & dental supplies

Paul Harris Stores, Inc. PAUH
6003 Guion Rd.
Indianapolis, IN 46254
317-293-3900
Retail - apparel & shoes O

Paychex, Inc. PAYX
911 Panorama Trail South
Rochester, NY 14625
716-385-7522
Financial - business services O DRP

PCA International, Inc. PCAI
815 Matthews-Mint Hill Rd.
Matthews, NC 28105
704-847-8011
Retail - misc.

PCD Inc. PCDI
2 Technology Dr.
Peabody, MA 01960
508-532-8800
Electronics - components & systems

PDS Financial Corp. PDSF
6442 City West Pkwy., Ste. 300
Eden Prairie, MN 55344
612-941-9500 Fax 612-941-9320
Financial - business services

Peerless Mfg. Co. PMFG
2819 Walnut Hill Ln.
Dallas, TX 75229
214-357-6181 Fax 214-351-0194
Filtration products

People's Bank PBCT
850 Main St.
Bridgeport, CT 06604
203-579-7171 Fax 203-338-3600
Banks - northeast O

PeopleSoft, Inc. PSFT
4440 Rosewood Dr.
Pleasanton, CA 94588
510-225-3000 Fax 510-225-3341
Computers - software O

Peoples Heritage Financial Group, Inc.
PHBK
One Portland Square
Portland, ME 04112
207-761-8500
Financial - savings and loans

Perceptron, Inc. PRCP
23855 Research Dr.
Farmington Hills, MI 48335
810-478-7710 Fax 810-478-7059
Machinery - general industrial

Perrigo Co. PRGO
117 Water St.
Allegan, MI 49010
616-673-8451
Cosmetics & toiletries O

Personnel Management, Inc. TPMI
16 Public Square, Ste. A
Shelbyville, IN 46176
317-392-7400
Business services

PETCO Animal Supplies, Inc. PETC
9151 Rehco Rd.
San Diego, CA 92121
619-453-7845 Fax 619-453-6585
Retail - misc.

Petroleum Heat and Power, Inc. HEAT
2187 Atlantic St.
Stamford, CT 06902
203-325-5400
Oil refining & marketing DRP 5%

PETsMART, Inc. PETM
10000 N. 31st Ave., C-100
Phoenix, AZ 85051
602-944-7070
Retail - misc. O

Pharmos Corp. PARS
101 E. 52nd St., 36th Fl.
New York, NY 10022
212-838-0087 Fax 212-223-4669
Drugs

Photronics, Inc. PLAB
15 Secor Rd., PO Box 5226
Brookfield, CT 06804
203-775-9000
Electrical components & accessories

PhyCor, Inc. PHYC
30 Burton Hills Blvd.
Nashville, TN 37215
615-665-9066
Hospitals O

Physician Reliance Network, Inc. PHYN
3320 Live Oak, Ste. 700
Dallas, TX 75204
214-828-0377 Fax 214-826-8109
Medical services

PictureTel Corp. PCTL
222 Rosewood Dr.
Danvers, MA 01923
508-762-5000 Fax 508-762-5245
Telecommunications services O

Pinnacle Systems, Inc. PCLE
870 W. Maude Ave.
Sunnyvale, CA 94086
408-720-9669 Fax 408-720-9674
Video equipment

Pioneer Companies, Inc. PIONA
700 Louisiana St.
Houston, TX 77002
713-225-3831 Fax 713-225-4426
Chemicals - specialty

Pioneer Group, Inc. (The) PIOG
60 State Street
Boston, MA 02109
617-742-7825 Fax 617-742-5470
Financial - investment management

Pioneer-Standard Electronics, Inc. PIOS
4800 E. 131st St.
Cleveland, OH 44105
216-587-3600 Fax 216-587-3563
Electronics - parts distribution O DRP

Platinum Software Corp. PSQL
15615 Alton Pkwy., Ste. 300
Irvine, CA 92718
714-727-1250 Fax 714-727-1255
Computers - software O

PLATINUM Technology, Inc. PLAT
1815 S. Meyers Rd.
Oakbrook Terrace, IL 60181
708-620-5000 Fax 708-691-0710
Computers - software

Players International, Inc. PLAY
1300 Atlantic Ave., Ste. 800
Atlantic City, NJ 08401
609-449-7777
Leisure & recreational services

Plexus Corp. PLXS
55 Jewelers Park Dr.
Neenah, WI 54956
414-722-3451
Electrical products - misc.

Pool Energy Services Co. PESC
10375 Richmond Ave.
Houston, TX 77042
713-954-3000
Oil & gas - field services

Possis Medical, Inc. POSS
2905 Northwest Blvd.
Minneapolis, MN 55441
612-550-1010 Fax 612-550-1020
Medical products

Powell Industries, Inc. POWL
8550 Mosley Dr.
Houston, TX 77075
713-944-6900 Fax 713-947-4435
Machinery - electrical

Praegitzer Industries, Inc. PGTZ
1270 S.E. Monmouth Cut-Off Rd.
Dallas, OR 97338
503-623-9273 Fax 503-623-3403
Electrical components - misc.

President Casinos, Inc. PREZ
802 N. First St.
St. Louis, MO 63102
314-622-3000
Leisure & recreational services

Presstek, Inc. PRST
8 Commercial St.
Hudson, NH 03051
603-595-7000
Miscellaneous - not elsewhere classified O

Prime Retail, Inc. PRME
100 E. Pratt St., 19th Fl.
Baltimore, MD 21202
410-234-0782
Real estate investment trust

Printronix, Inc. PTNX
17500 Cartwright Rd.
Irvine, CA 92713
714-863-1900 Fax 714-660-8682
Computers - peripheral equipment

ProCyte Corp. PRCY
12040 115th Ave. N.E.
Kirkland, WA 98034
206-820-4548 Fax 206-820-4111
Drugs

Progress Software Corp. PRGS
14 Oak Park
Bedford, MA 01730
617-280-4000 Fax 617-280-4095
Computers - software O

Protein Design Labs, Inc. PDLI
2375 Garcia Ave.
Mountain View, CA 94043
415-903-3700 Fax 415-903-3730
Biomedical & genetic products O

Provident American PAMC
2500 DeKalb Pike
Norristown, PA 19404
610-279-2500
Life insurance

Provident Bankshares Corp. PBKS
114 E. Lexington St.
Baltimore, MD 21202
410-281-7000
Banks - southeast DRP

PSC Inc. PSCX
770 Basket Rd.
Webster, NY 14580
716-265-1600 Fax 716-265-1689
Data collection & systems

Pulaski Furniture Corp. PLFC
PO Box 1371
Pulaski, VA 24301
703-980-7330 Fax 703-980-0425
Furniture

QUALCOMM Inc. QCOM
6455 Lusk Blvd.
San Diego, CA 92121
619-587-1121
Telecommunications equipment O

Quality Systems, Inc. QSII
17822 E. 17th St.
Tustin, CA 92780
714-731-7171 Fax 714-731-9494
Computers - software

Quantum Corp. QNTM
500 McCarthy Blvd.
Milpitas, CA 95035
408-894-4000 Fax 408-894-3218
Computers - peripheral equipment

Quidel Corp. QDEL
10165 McKellar Court
San Diego, CA 92121
619-552-1100 Fax 619-453-4338
Medical products

Quintel Entertainment, Inc. QTEL
One Blue Hill Plaza, Ste. 650
Pearl River, NY 10965
914-620-1212 Fax 914-620-1717
Leisure & recreational services

Quintiles Transnational Corp. QTRN
1007 Slater Rd.
Morrisville, NC 27560
919-941-2888 Fax 919-941-9113
Medical services O

Quixote Corp. QUIX
One E. Wacker Dr.
Chicago, IL 60601
312-467-6755 Fax 312-467-1356
Protection - safety equipment & services

Quorum Health Group, Inc. QHGI
155 Franklin Rd., Ste. 401
Brentwood, TN 37027
615-320-7979
Hospitals O

R&B, Inc. RBIN
3400 E. Walnut St.
Colmar, PA 18915
215-997-1800
Automotive & trucking - replacement parts

RailTex, Inc. RTEX
4040 Broadway, Ste. 200
San Antonio, TX 78209
210-841-7600
Transportation - rail

Ramsay Health Care, Inc. RHCI
639 Loyola Ave., Ste. 1700
New Orleans, LA 70113
504-525-2505 Fax 504-525-5812
Hospitals

Rational Software Corp. RATL
2800 San Tomas Expwy.
Santa Clara, CA 95051
408-496-3600
Computers - software O

Raven Industries, Inc. RAVN
PO Box 1007
Sioux Falls, SD 57117
605-336-2750
Diversified operations

Read-Rite Corp. RDRT
345 Los Coches St.
Milpitas, CA 95035
408-262-6700 Fax 408-956-3205
Computers - peripheral equipment O

Recoton Corp. RCOT
145 E. 57th St.
New York, NY 10022
212-644-0220 Fax 212-644-8205
Audio & video home products O

Redhook Ale Brewery, Inc. HOOK
3400 Finney North
Seattle, WA 98103
206-483-3232
Beverages - alcoholic

Regeneron Pharmaceuticals, Inc. REGN
777 Old Sawmill River Rd.
Tarrytown, NY 10591
914-347-7000
Biomedical & genetic products O

Regions Financial Corp. RGBK
417 N. 20th St., PO Box 10247
Birmingham, AL 35202
205-326-7100
Banks - southeast O DRP

Regis Corp. RGIS
7201 Metro Blvd.
Minneapolis, MN 55439
612-947-7777 Fax 612-947-7600
Retail - misc. O

Reliv' International Inc. RELV
136 Chesterfield Industrial Blvd.
Chesterfield, MO 63005
314-537-9715
Foods

Rentrak Corp. RENT
7227 N.E. 55th Ave.
Portland, OR 97218
503-284-7581
Leisure & recreational services

Repligen Corp. RGEN
One Kendall Square, Bldg. 700
Cambridge, MA 02139
617-225-6000 Fax 617-494-1786
Biomedical & genetic products

Res-Care, Inc. RSCR
10140 Linn Station Rd.
Louisville, KY 40223
502-394-2100
Healthcare - outpatient & home

Research, Inc. RESR
6425 Flying Cloud Dr.
Eden Prairie, MN 55344
612-941-3300 Fax 612-941-3628
Electrical components - misc.

Resource Bancshares Mortgage Group Inc.
 REMG
7909 Parklane Rd.
Columbia, SC 29223
803-741-3000
Financial - mortgages & related services
 DRP 5%

Resound Corp. RSND
220 Saginaw Dr.
Redwood City, CA 94063
415-780-7800 Fax 415-367-0675
Medical products

Respironics, Inc. RESP
1001 Murry Ridge Dr.
Murrysville, PA 15668
412-733-0200 Fax 412-733-0299
Medical products ·O

Revenue Properties Co. Ltd. RPCLF
131 Bloor St. W., Suite 300
Toronto, ON M5S1R1
416-963-8100
Real estate operations & lessors

Rexall Sundown, Inc. RXSD
851 Broken Sound Pkwy. NW
Boca Raton, FL 33487
561-241-9400
Vitamins & nutritional products

Ribi ImmunoChem Research, Inc. RIBI
553 Old Corvallis Rd.
Hamilton, MT 59840
406-363-6214 Fax 406-363-6129
Biomedical & genetic products O

Riggs National Corp. RIGS
1503 Pennsylvania Ave., N.W.
Washington, DC 20005
202-835-6000
Banks - southeast O

Right Management Consultants, Inc.
 RMCI
1818 Market St.
Philadelphia, PA 19103
215-988-1588
Business services

Right Start Inc. RTST
5334 Sterling Center Dr.
Westgate Village, CA 91361
818-707-7100
Catalog retailes

Rival Company RIVL
800 E. 101 Terrace, Suite 100
Kansas City, MO 64131
816-943-4100
Holding office

Roadway Express, Inc. ROAD
1077 Gorge Blvd.
Akron, OH 44310
216-384-1717 Fax 216-258-6082
Transportation - truck DRP

Robert Mondavi Corporation MOND
841 Latour Ct.
Napa, CA 94558
707-226-1395
Alcoholic beverages

Robinson Nugent, Inc. RNIC
800 E. Eighth St., PO Box 1208
New Albany, IN 47151
937-945-0211 Fax 812-945-0804
Electrical connectors

Robotic Vision Systems, Inc. ROBV
425 Rabro Dr. East
Hauppauge, NY 11788
516-273-9700 Fax 516-273-1167
Video equipment O

Ross Stores, Inc. ROST
8333 Central Ave.
Newark, CA 94560
510-505-4400
Retail - apparel & shoes O

RPM, Inc. RPOW
2628 Pearl Rd., PO Box 777
Medina, OH 44258
216-273-5090 Fax 216-225-8743
Paints & allied products O DRP

Ryan's Family Steak Houses, Inc. RYAN
405 Lancaster Ave.
Greer, SC 29650
854-879-1000
Retail - food & restaurants

S3, Inc. SIII
2770 San Tomas Expressway
Santa Clara, CA 95051
408-980-5400 Fax 408-980-5444
Computers - software O

SAFECO Corp. SAFC
SAFECO Plaza
Seattle, WA 98185
206-545-5000
Insurance - property & casualty O

Safeskin Corp. SFSK
5100 Town Center Circle
Boca Raton, FL 33486
561-395-9988
Medical & dental supplies O

Safety Components International, Inc.
  ABAG
3190 Pullman St.
Costa Mesa, CA 92626
714-662-7756
Automotive & trucking - original
  equipment

Salient 3 Communications, Inc. STCIA
PO Box 1498
Reading, PA 19603
610-775-5900
Engineering - R & D services

Sanderson Farms, Inc. SAFM
225 N. 13th Ave., PO Box 988
Laurel, MS 39441
601-649-4030
Food - meat products

Sands Regent, (The) SNDS
345 N. Arlington Ave.
Reno, NV 89501
702-348-2200 Fax 702-348-2226
Hotels & motels

Sanmina Corp. SANM
355 Trimble Rd.
San Jose, CA 95131
408-435-8444 Fax 408-943-1401
Electrical components - misc.

SBE, Inc. SBEI
4550 Norris Canyon Rd.
San Ramon, CA 94583
510-355-2000 Fax 510-355-2020
Computers - peripheral equipment

Scherer Healthcare, Inc. SCHR
2859 Paces Ferry Rd., Ste. 300
Atlanta, GA 30339
770-333-0066
Diversified operations

Scholastic Corp. SCHL
555 Broadway
New York, NY 10012
212-343-6100
Publishing - periodicals O

Schuler Homes, Inc. SHLR
828 Fort Street Mall, 4th Fl.
Honolulu, HI 96813
808-521-5661 Fax 808-538-1476
Building - residential & commercial

Schulman (A.), Inc. SHLM
3550 W. Market St.
Akron, OH 44313
216-666-3751
Chemicals - plastics

Schultz Sav-O Stores, Inc. SAVO
2215 Union Ave.
Sheboygan, WI 53081
414-457-4433
Retail - supermarkets

SciClone Pharmaceuticals, Inc. SCLN
901 Mariner's Island Blvd.
San Mateo, CA 94404
415-358-3456 Fax 415-358-3469
Drugs

Scientific Technologies Inc. STIZ
31069 Genstar Rd.
Hayward, CA 94544
510-471-9717 Fax 415-471-9752
Instruments - control

Scios, Inc. SCIO
2450 Bayshore Pkwy.
Mountain View, CA 94043
415-966-1550 Fax 415-968-2438
Biomedical & genetic products

Scott & Stringfellow Financial, Inc. SCOT
909 E. Main St.
Richmond, VA 23219
804-643-1811 Fax 804-643-3718
Financial - investment management

SCP Pool Corp. POOL
128 Northpark Blvd.
Covington, LA 70433
504-892-5521
Wholesale distribution - consumer products

SeaMED Corp. SEMD
14500 N.E. 87th St.
Redmond, WA 98052
206-867-1818 Fax 206-867-0622
Medical instruments

Seattle FilmWorks, Inc. FOTO
1260 16th Ave. West
Seattle, WA 98119
206-281-1390 Fax 206-284-5357
Retail - mail order & direct

Seaway Food Town, Inc. SEWY
1020 Ford St.
Maumee, OH 43537
419-893-9401
Retail - supermarkets

Secom General Corp. SECM
37650 Professional Center Dr.
Livonia, MI 48154
313-953-3990
Machine tools & related products

Second Bancorp, Inc. SECD
108 Main Ave., S.W.
Warren, OH 44482
216-841-0123
Banks - midwest DRP

Secure Computing Corp. SCUR
2675 Long Lake Rd.
Roseville, MN 55113
612-628-2700 Fax 612-628-2701
Computers - peripheral equipment O

SEI Investments Co. SEQU
1 Freedom Valley Rd.
Oaks, PA 19456
610-676-1932
Computer & data processing services

Seibels Bruce Group Inc. (The) SBIG
1501 Lady St.
Columbia, SC 29201
803-748-2000
Insurance - property & casualty

Selective Insurance Group, Inc. SIGI
40 Wantage Ave.
Branchville, NJ 07890
201-948-3000
Insurance - property & casualty DRP

Sepracor Inc. SEPR
33 Locke Dr.
Marlborough, MA 01752
508-481-6700 Fax 508-481-7683
Drugs O

Sequent Computer Systems, Inc. SQNT
15450 SW Koll Pkwy.
Beaverton, OR 97006
503-626-5700
Computers - mainframe O

SEQUUS Pharmaceuticals, Inc. SEQU
960 Hamilton Court
Menlo Park, CA 94025
415-323-9011 Fax 415-323-9106
Drugs

Shaman Pharmaceuticals, Inc. SHMN
213 E. Grand Ave.
South San Francisco, CA 94080
415-952-7070 Fax 415-873-1463
Drugs

Sharper Image Corp. SHRP
650 Davis St.
San Francisco, CA 94111
415-445-6000 Fax 415-445-1574
Retail - mail order & direct

Sheldahl, Inc. SHEL
1150 Sheldahl Rd.
Northfield, MN 55057
507-663-8000 Fax 507-663-8545
Electrical components - misc. O

Shiva Corp. SHVA
28 Crosby Dr.
Bedford, MA 01730
617-270-8300 Fax 617-270-8599
Telecommunications equipment O

Sigma-Aldrich Corp. SIAL
3050 Spruce St.
St. Louis, MO 63103
314-771-5765 Fax 314-652-9115
Chemicals - specialty O

Sigma Circuits, Inc. SIGA
393 Mathew St.
Santa Clara, CA 95050
408-727-9169
Electrical connectors

Sigma Designs, Inc. SIGM
46501 Landing Pkwy.
Fremont, CA 94538
510-770-0100 Fax 510-770-2640
Computers - peripheral equipment O

SigmaTron International, Inc. SGMA
2201 Landmeier Rd.
Elk Grove Village, IL 60007
708-956-8000 Fax 708-956-8082
Electrical components - misc.

Silicon Valley Group, Inc. SVGI
2240 Ringwood Ave.
San Jose, CA 95131
408-434-0500
Electrical components - semiconductors

Silicon Valley Research, Inc. SVRI
300 Ferguson Dr., Ste. 300
Mountain View, CA 94043
415-962-3000 Fax 415-962-3001
Computers - software

Siliconix Inc. SILI
2201 Laurelwood Rd.
Santa Clara, CA 95054
408-988-8000 Fax 408-567-8950
Electrical components - semiconductors

Simpson Industries, Inc. SMPS
32100 Telegraph Rd., Ste. 120
Birmingham Farms, MI 48025
313-540-6200 Fax 313-540-7484
Automotive & trucking - original
   equipment DRP

SkyWest, Inc. SKYW
444 S. River Rd.
St. George, UT 84770
801-634-3000
Transportation - airline

Smartflex Systems, Inc. SFLX
14312 Franklin Ave.
Tustin, CA 92680
714-838-8737 Fax 714-573-6918
Electronics - components & systems

Smithfield Foods, Inc. SFDS
501 N. Church St.
Smithfield, VA 23430
804-357-4321
Food - meat products O

SofTech, Inc. SOFT
3260 Eagle Park Dr., N.E.
Grand Rapids, MI 49505
616-957-2330
Computers - services

Software Spectrum, Inc. SSPE
2140 Merritt Dr.
Garland, TX 75041
214-840-6600 Fax 214-864-7878
Computers - software

Somerset Group, Inc. (The) SOMR
135 N. Pennsylvania St.
Indianapolis, IN 46204
317-269-1285
Diversified operations

Sonic Corp. SONC
120 Robert S. Kerr Ave.
Oklahoma City, OK 73102
405-232-4334
Retail - food & restaurants O

Southam Inc. STM
1450 Don Mills Rd.
Don Mills, ON M3B2X7
416-445-6641 Fax 416-442-2077
Publishing

Southern Energy Homes, Inc. SEHI
Highway 41 North, PO Box 269
Addison, AL 35540
205-747-1544 Fax 205-747-2963
Building - residential & commercial

SouthTrust Corp. SOTR
420 N. 20th St.
Birmingham, AL 35203
205-254-5009 Fax 205-254-5404
Banks - southeast O DRP

Southwall Technologies Inc. SWTX
1029 Corporation Way
Palo Alto, CA 94303
415-962-9111 Fax 415-967-8713
Chemicals - plastics

Southwest Water Systems SWWC
225 N. Barranca Ave., Ste. 200
West Covina, CA 91791
818-915-1551
Utility - water supply DRP 5%

Sovereign Bancorp, Inc. SVRN
1130 Berkshire Blvd.
Wyomissing, PA 19610
610-320-8400
Financial - savings and loans

SpaceLabs Medical, Inc. SLMD
15220 N.E. 40th St.
Redmond, WA 98052
206-882-3700 Fax 206-885-4877
Medical services

Spartan Motors, Inc. SPAR
1000 Reynolds Rd.
Charlotte, MI 48813
517-543-6400
Automotive & trucking - original equipment

Spectral Diagnostics DIAGF
135-2 The West Mall
Toronto, ON M9C1C2
416-626-3233 Fax 416-626-7383
Develops cardiac diagnostic tests

SpecTran SPTR
50 Hall Rd.
Sturbridge, MA 01566
508-347-2261
Data transmission fiber optic products

Spectrian Corp. SPCT
550 Ellis St.
Mountain View, CA 94043
415-961-1473 Fax 415-967-9322
Electronics - components & systems

Spectrum Control, Inc. SPEC
6000 W. Ridge Rd.
Erie, PA 16506
814-835-4000 Fax 814-835-9000
Electronics - components & systems

Spiegel, Inc. SPGLA
3500 Lacey Rd.
Downers Grove, IL 60515
708-986-8800
Retail - mail order & direct O

SPSS, Inc. SPSS
444 N. Michigan Ave.
Chicago, IL 60611
312-329-2400
Computers - software

St. Paul Bancorp, Inc. SPBC
6700 W. North Ave.
Chicago, IL 60707
773-622-5000
Financial - savings and loans DRP

STAAR Surgical Co. STAA
1911 Walker Ave.
Monrovia, CA 91016
818-303-7902 Fax 818-303-2962
Medical products

Staff Builders Inc. SBLI
1981 Marcus Ave.
Lake Success, NY 11042
516-358-1000
Business services

Standard Microsystems Corp. SMSC
80 Arkay Dr.
Hauppauge, NY 11788
516-435-6000
Computers - peripheral equipment O

Stanford Telecommunications, Inc. STII
1221 Crossman Ave.
Sunnyvale, CA 94089
408-745-0818
Electronics - military

Staples, Inc. SPLS
100 Pennsylvania Ave.
Framingham, MA 01701
508-370-8500 Fax 508-370-8956
Retail - misc. O

Starbucks Corp. SBUX
2203 Airport Way South
Seattle, WA 98134
206-447-1575
Retail - food & restaurants O

Steel Technologies Inc. STTX
15415 Shelbyville Rd.
Louisville, KY 40245
502-245-2110
Steel - production

Stein Mart, Inc. SMRT
1200 Riverplace Blvd.
Jacksonville, FL 32207
904-346-1500
Retail - apparel & shoes

STERIS Corp. STRL
5960 Heisley Rd.
Mentor, OH 44060
216-354-2600
Medical products

Steven Madden SHOO
15-16 Barnett Ave.
Long Island City, NY 11104
718-446-1800 Fax 718-446-5599
Footwear

STM Wireless, Inc. STMI
3530 Hyland Ave.
Costa Mesa, CA 92626
714-557-2400
Telecommunications equipment

Structural Dynamics Research Corp.
 SDRC
2000 Eastman Dr.
Milford, OH 45150
513-576-2400
Computers - software

Summa Four, Inc. SUMA
25 Sundial Ave.
Manchester, NH 03103
603-625-4050
Telecommunications equipment

Summa Industries SUMX
1600 W. Commonwealth Ave.
Fullerton, CA 92633
714-738-5000 Fax 714-738-5960
Machinery - general industrial

Summit Technology, Inc. BEAM
21 Hickory Dr.
Waltham, MA 02154
617-890-1234
Lasers - systems & components O

Sun Microsystems, Inc. SUNW
2550 Garcia Ave.
Mountain View, CA 94043
415-960-1300 Fax 415-969-9131
Computers - mini & micro

Sunglass Hut International, Inc. RAYS
255 Alhambra Circle
Coral Gables, FL 33134
305-461-6100 Fax 305-461-6282
Retail - misc. O

Superior Energy Services, Inc. SESI
1001 E. FM 700
Big Spring, TX 79720
915-267-3188
Oil & gas - field services

Supreme International Corp. SUPI
7495 N.W. 48th St.
Miami, FL 33166
305-592-2760
Apparel

Susquehanna Bancshares, Inc. SUSQ
26 N. Cedar St.
Lititz, PA 17543
717-626-4721 Fax 717-626-1874
Banks - northeast DRP

Swiss Army Brands, Inc. SABI
151 Long Hill Cross Rds.
Shelton, CT 06484
203-929-6391
Leisure & recreational products

Sybase, Inc. SYBS
6475 Christie Ave.
Emeryville, CA 94608
510-596-3500
Computers - software O

Sykes Enterprises, Inc. SYKE
100 N. Tampa St., Ste. 3900
Tampa, FL 33602
813-274-1000
Miscellaneous - not elsewhere classified O

Symantec Corp. SYMC
10201 Torre Ave.
Cupertino, CA 95014
408-253-9600
Computers - software O

SymmetriCom, Inc. SYMM
85 W. Tasman Dr.
San Jose, CA 95134
408-943-9403 Fax 408-428-7896
Diversified operations O

Synalloy Corp. SYNC
Croft Industrial Park
Spartanburg, SC 29304
864-585-3605
Steel - pipes & tubes

Synbiotics Corp. SBIO
11011 Via Frontera
San Diego, CA 92127
619-451-3771 Fax 619-451-5719
Biomedical & genetic products

Syncor International Corp. SCOR
6464 Canoga Ave.
Woodland, CA 91311
818-737-4000 Fax 818-737-4898
Drugs & sundries - wholesale

Synetic, Inc. SNTC
100 Summit Ave.
Montvale, NJ 07645
201-358-5300
Medical products

Synopsys, Inc. SNPS
700 E. Middlefield Rd.
Mountain View, CA 94043
415-962-5000
Computers - software

Synthetic Industries, Inc. SIND
309 LaFayette Rd.
Chickamauga, GA 30707
706-375-3121
Textiles - mill products

System Software Associates, Inc. SSAX
500 W. Madison St.
Chicago, IL 60606
312-641-2900 Fax 312-641-3737
Computers - software

Taco Cabana, Inc. TACO
262 Losoya, Ste. 330
San Antonio, TX 78205
210-231-8226
Retail - food & restaurants

Tandy Brands, Inc. TBAC
690 E. Lamar Blvd., Ste. 200
Arlington, TX 76011
817-548-0090
Leather & related products

TBC Corp. TBCC
4770 Hickory Hill Rd.
Memphis, TN 38115
901-363-8030
Auto parts - retail & wholesale

TCA Cable TV, Inc. TCAT
3015 SSE Loop 323
Tyler, TX 75713
214-595-3701
Cable TV O

T Cell Sciences, Inc. TCEL
115 Fourth Ave.
Needham, MA 02194
617-433-0771 Fax 617-433-0262
Biomedical & genetic products

TCI International, Inc. TCII
222 Caspian Dr.
Sunnyvale, CA 94089
408-747-6100
Telecommunications equipment

Tech Data Corp. TECD
5350 Tech Data Dr.
Clearwater, FL 34620
813-539-7429 Fax 813-538-5860
Computers - retail & wholesale O

Technology Solutions Co. TSCC
205 N. Michigan Ave.
Chicago, IL 60601
312-819-2250 Fax 312-819-2299
Computers - services O

Tecumseh Products Co. TECUA
100 E. Patterson St.
Tecumseh, MI 49286
517-423-8411
Automotive & trucking - original
  equipment O

Tel-Save Holdings, Inc. TALK
22 Village Sq.
New Hope, PA 18938
215-862-1500
Telecommunications services O

Telco Systems, Inc. TELC
63 Nahatan St.
Norwood, MA 02062
617-551-0300 Fax 617-551-0534
Telecommunications equipment

Tele-Communications International, Inc.
  TINTA
5619 DTC Pkwy.
Denver, CO 80111
303-287-5500
Broadcasting - radio & TV O

Tele-Communications, Inc. TCOMA
5619 DTC Pkwy.
Englewood, CO 80111
303-267-5500
Cable TV O

TeleVideo, Inc. TELV
550 E. Brokaw Rd.
San Jose, CA 95161
408-954-8333 Fax 408-954-0622
Computers - peripheral equipment

Tellabs, Inc. TLAB
4951 Indiana Ave.
Lisle, IL 60532
708-969-8800 Fax 708-852-7346
Telecommunications equipment O

Telxon Corp. TLXN
3330 W. Market St.
Akron, OH 44334
216-867-3700
Computers - mini & micro O

Tennant Co. TANT
701 N. Lilac Dr., PO Box 1452
Minneapolis, MN 55440
612-540-1208
Machinery - general industrial

TETRA Technologies, Inc. WATR
25025 I-45 North
The Woodlands, TX 77380
281-367-1983
Pollution control equipment & services

TheraTech, Inc. THRT
417 Wakara Way
Salt Lake City, UT 84108
801-583-6028 Fax 801-583-6042
Medical products O

Thomas Group, Inc. TGIS
5215 N. O'Connor Blvd.
Irving, TX 75039
972-869-3400 Fax 972-869-6501
Business services

Thomaston Mills, Inc. TMSTA
115 E. Main St.
Thomaston, GA 30286
706-647-7131
Textiles - mill products

Thorn Apple Valley, Inc. TAVI
26999 Central Park Blvd.
Southfield, MI 48076
810-213-1000
Food - meat products

THQ, Inc. TOYH
5016 N. Parkway Calabasas
Calabasas, CA 91302
818-591-1310 Fax 818-591-1615
Toys - games & hobby products

3COM Corp. COMS
5400 Bayfront Plaza
Santa Clara, CA 95052
408-764-5000 Fax 408-764-5001
Computers - peripheral equipment

3D Systems Corp. TDSC
26081 Avenue Hall
Valencia, CA 91355
805-295-5600 Fax 805-295-0249
Instruments - control

Timberline Software Corp. TMBS
9600 S.W. Nimbus Ave.
Beaverton, OR 97005
503-626-6775 Fax 503-526-8299
Computers - software

TJ International, Inc. TJCO
380 E. ParkCenter Blvd.
Boise, ID 83706
208-345-8500
Building products - misc.

Today's Man, Inc. TMAN
835 Lancer Dr.
Moorestown, NJ 08057
609-235-5656
Retail - apparel & shoes

Topps Co., Inc., (The) TOPP
One Whitehall Street
New York, NY 10004
212-376-0300
Food - confectionary

Tractor Supply Co. TSCO
320 Plus Park Blvd.
Nashville, TN 37217
615-366-4600
Retail - misc.

Trenwick Group Inc. TREN
One Station Pl.
Stamford, CT 06902
203-353-5500 Fax 203-353-5550
Insurance - property & casualty

Trident Microsystems, Inc. TRID
189 N. Bernardo Ave.
Mountain View, CA 94043
415-691-9211 Fax 415-691-9260
Computers - peripheral equipment O

Trimble Navigation Ltd. TRMB
645 N. Mary Ave., PO Box 3642
Sunnyvale, CA 94088
408-481-8000 Fax 408-481-2000
Electronics - measuring instruments O

Trion, Inc. TRON
101 McNeill Rd., PO Box 760
Sanford, NC 27331
919-775-2201 Fax 919-774-8771
Machinery - general industrial

TriQuint Semiconductor, Inc. TQNT
3625A S.W. Murray Blvd.
Beaverton, OR 97005
503-644-3535 Fax 503-644-3198
Electrical components - semiconductors

Tseng Labs, Inc. TSNG
6 Terry Dr.
Newtown, PA 18940
215-968-0502
Computers - peripheral equipment

TSI Inc. TSII
500 Cardigan Rd.
Shoreview, MN 55126
612-483-0900 Fax 612-481-1220
Instruments - control

Ugly Duckling Corp. UGLY
2525 E. Camelback Rd.
Phoenix, AZ 85016
602-852-6600
Retail - new & used cars O

UICI, Inc. UICI
4001 McEwen Dr., Ste. 200
Dallas, TX 75244
214-960-8497 Fax 214-851-9097
Insurance - accident & health

Ultrak, Inc. ULTK
1220 Champion Circle
Carrollton, TX 75006
972-233-7171
Video equipment O

Ultratech Stepper, Inc. UTEK
3050 Zanker Rd.
San Jose, CA 95134
408-321-8835 Fax 408-577-3379
Electronics - components & systems O

Unico American Corp. UNAM
23251 Mulholland Dr.
Woodland Hills, CA 91364
818-591-9800 Fax 818-591-9822
Insurance - multi line & misc.

Unimed Pharmaceuticals, Inc. UMED
2150 E. Lake Cook Rd.
Buffalo Grove, IL 60089
708-541-2525 Fax 708-541-2569
Drugs

Union Bankshares Corp. UBSH
211 N. Main St., PO Box 446
Bowling Green, VA 22427
804-633-5031
Financial - SBIC & commercial

Union Bankshares, Ltd. UBSC
1825 Lawrence St., Ste. 444
Denver, CO 80202
303-298-5352 Fax 303-298-5380
Banks - west

Uniroyal Technology Corp. UTCI
Two N. Tamiami Trail, Ste. 900
Sarasota, FL 34236
941-361-2100
Chemicals - specialty

Unit Instruments, Inc. UNII
22600 Savi Ranch Pkwy.
Yoba Linda, CA 92687
714-921-2640
Instruments - control

United Retail Group, Inc. URGI
365 W. Passaic St.
Rochelle Park, NJ 07662
201-845-0880
Retail - apparel & shoes

United Stationers Inc. USTR
2200 E. Golf Rd.
Des Plaines, IL 60016
708-699-5000
Office equipment & supplies

Unitog Co. UTOG
101 W. 11th St.
Kansas City, MO 64105
816-474-7000
Linen supply & related

Universal Forest Products, Inc. UFPI
2801 E. Beltline N.E.
Grand Rapids, MI 49505
616-364-6161 Fax 616-361-7534
Building products - wood

Upper Peninsula Energy Corp. UPEN
600 Lakeshore Dr.
Houghton, MI 49931
906-487-5000
Utility - electric power DRP

Uranium Resources, Inc. URIX
12750 Merit Dr., Ste. 1210
Dallas, TX 75251
972-387-7777 Fax 972-387-7779
Metal ores - misc.

USA Detergents, Inc. USAD
1735 Jersey Ave.
North Brunswick, NJ 08902
908-828-1800
Soap & cleaning preparations

USANA, Inc. ISNA
3838 Parkway Blvd.
Salt Lake City, UT 84107
801-288-2290
Cosmetics & toiletries

U.S. Bancorp USBC
111 S.W. Fifth Ave.
Portland, OR 97204
503-275-6111 Fax 503-275-3452
Banks - west

USBANCORP, Inc. UBAN
Main and Franklin Sts.
Johnstown, PA 15901
814-533-5300
Banks - northeast

U.S. Energy Corp. USEG
877 N. 8th West
Riverton, WY 82501
307-856-9271 Fax 307-857-3050
Metal ores - misc.

US Freightways Corp. USFC
9700 Higgins Rd., Ste. 570
Rosemont, IL 60018
708-696-0200 Fax 708-696-2080
Transportation - truck O

UST Corp. USTB
40 Court Street
Boston, MA 02108
617-726-7000
Banks - northeast DRP

UTILX Corp. UTLX
22404 66th Ave. South
Kent, WA 98064
206-395-0200 Fax 206-395-1040
Telecommunications services

Valence Technology, Inc. VLNC
6781 Via Del Ora
San Jose, CA 95119
408-365-6125
Engineering - R & D services

Vallen Corp. VALN
13333 Northwest Fwy.
Houston, TX 77040
713-462-8700 Fax 713-462-7634
Protection - safety equipment & services

Valmont Industries, Inc. VALM
PO Box 358
Valley, NE 68064
402-359-2201 Fax 402-343-0668
Diversified operations O

Value Line, Inc. VALU
220 E. 42nd St.
New York, NY 10017
212-907-1500
Financial - investment management

Vanguard Cellular Systems, Inc. VCELA
2002 Pisgah Church Rd.
Greensboro, NC 27455
910-282-3690 Fax 919-545-2500
Telecommunications services O

Vans, Inc. VANS
2095 N. Batavia
Orange, CA 92665
714-974-7414 Fax 714-998-6564
Shoes & related apparel

Vantive Corp. (The) VNTV
2455 Augustine Dr.
Santa Clara, CA 95054
408-982-5700 Fax 408-982-5710
Computers - software O

Varlen Corp. VRLN
55 E. Shuman Blvd., Ste. 500
Naperville, IL 60566
708-420-0400
Transportation - equipment & leasing

Venturian Corp. VENT
1600 Second St. South
Hopkins, MN 55343
612-931-2500
Computers - mini & micro

Vertex Communications Corp. VTEX
2600 N. Longview St.
Kilgore, TX 75662
214-984-0555
Telecommunications equipment

Vertex Pharmaceuticals, Inc. VRTX
130 Waverly St.
Cambridge, MA 02139
617-576-6000 Fax 617-577-6680
Drugs

Veterinary Centers of America, Inc. VCAI
1725 Cloverfield Ave.
Santa Monica, CA 90404
310-829-7533 Fax 310-829-2087
Veterinary products & services O

VIASOFT, Inc. VIAS
3033 N. 44th St.
Phoenix, AZ 85018
602-952-0050
Computers- software

Vicor Corp. VICR
23 Frontage Rd.
Andover, MA 01810
508-470-2900 Fax 508-475-6715
Electrical components - misc. O

VICORP Restaurants, Inc. VRES
400 W. 48th Ave., PO Box 16601
Denver, CO 80216
303-296-2121
Retail - food & restaurants

Video Display Corp. VIDE
1868 Tucker Industrial Dr.
Tucker, GA 30084
404-938-2080 Fax 404-493-3903
Miscellaneous - not elsewhere classified

Viking Office Products, Inc. VKNG
13809 S. Figueroa St.
Los Angeles, CA 90061
213-321-4493
Retail - mail order & direct O

VISX, Inc. VISX
3400 Central Expressway
Santa Clara, CA 95051
408-733-2020 Fax 408-773-7300
Lasers - systems & components

Vital Signs, Inc. VITL
20 Campus Rd.
Totowa, NJ 07512
201-790-1330 Fax 201-790-3307
Medical products

Vitesse Semiconductor Corp. VTSS
741 Calle Plano
Camarillo, CA 93012
805-388-3700 Fax 805-987-5896
Electrical components - semiconductors O

VLSI Technology, Inc. VLSI
1109 McKay Dr.
San Jose, CA 95131
408-434-3000 Fax 408-263-2511
Electrical components - semiconductors

Voice Control Systems, Inc. VCSI
14140 Midway Rd., Ste. 100
Dallas, TX 75244
214-386-0300
Miscellaneous - not elsewhere classified

VTEL Corp. VTEL
108 Wild Basin Rd.
Austin, TX 78746
512-314-2700
Telecommunications equipment

VWR Scientific Products Corp. VWRX
1310 Goshen Pkwy.
West Chester, PA 19380
610-431-1700
Instruments - scientific

Walbro Corp. WALB
6242 Garfield St.
Cass City, MI 48726
517-872-2131 Fax 517-872-2301
Automotive & trucking - original equipment

Wall Data, Inc. WALL
11332 N.E. 122nd Way
Kirkland, WA 98034
206-814-9255
Computers - software

Wall Street Deli, Inc. WSDI
400 Century Park South
Birmingham, AL 35226
205-822-3960
Retail - food & restaurants

Wang Laboratories, Inc. WANG
One Industrial Ave.
Lowell, MA 01851
508-459-5000
Computers - mini & micro O

Washington Federal, Inc. WFSL
425 Pike St.
Seattle, WA 98101
206-624-7930
Financial - savings and loans O

Washington Mutual Bank, Inc. WAMU
1201 Third Ave.
Seattle, WA 98101
206-461-2000
Financial - savings and loans O DRP

Wausau-Mosinee Paper Co. WSAU
One Clark's Island
Wausau, WI 54402
715-845-5266
Paper & paper products O DRP

WavePhore, Inc. WAVO
3311 N. 44th St.
Phoenix, AZ 85018
602-952-5500 Fax 602-952-5517
Miscellaneous - not elsewhere classified

WD-40 Co. WDFC
1061 Cudahy Place
San Diego, CA 92110
619-275-1400 Fax 619-275-5823
Paints & allied products

Werner Enterprises, Inc. WERN
Interstate 80 & Highway 50
Omaha, NE 68137
402-895-6640
Transportation - truck O

Westamerica Bancorporation WABC
1108 Fifth Ave.
San Rafael, CA 94901
415-257-8000
Regional banks DRP

Western Beef, Inc. BEEF
47-05 Metropolitan Ave.
Ridgewood, NY 11385
718-417-3770 Fax 718-366-6148
Food - wholesale

Western Staff Services, Inc. WSTF
301 Lennon Lane
Walnut Creek, CA 94598
510-930-5300
Personnel

Weston (Roy F.) WSTNA
1 Weston Way
West Chester, PA 19380
215-692-3030
Environmental engineering & consulting
  company

WestPoint Stevens, Inc. WPSN
400 W. Tenth St.
West Point, GA 31833
706-645-4000
Textiles - home furnishings O

Westwood One, Inc. WONE
9540 Washington Blvd.
Culver City, CA 90232
310-205-5000
Broadcasting - radio & TV

Wet Seal WTSL
64 Fairbanks
Irvine, CA 92718
714-583-9029
Specialty apparel retailer O

WFS Financial Inc. WFSI
16485 Laguna Canyon Rd.
Irvine, Ca 92713
714-753-3000
Financial - consumer loans

Whitney Holding Corp. WTNY
228 St. Charles Ave.
New Orleans, LA 70130
504-586-7272
Banks - southeast

Whole Foods Market, Inc. WFMI
1705 Capital of Texas Hwy.
Austin, TX 78746
512-328-7541
Retail - supermarkets O

Williams Controls WMCO
7001 Orchard Lake Rd., Suite 420-C
West Bloomfield, MI 48322
248-851-5651
Motor vehicles & equipment

Wilmington Trust Corp. WILM
1100 N. Market St.
Wilmington, DE 19890
302-651-1000
Banks - northeast DRP

Winstar Communications WCII
230 Park Ave., 31st Floor
New York, NY 10169
212-687-7577
Telephone communication O

Wisconsin Central Transportation Corp.
  WCLX
6250 N. River Rd., Ste. 9000
Rosemont, IL 60018
708-318-4600
Transportation - rail O

Wolohan Lumber Co. WLHN
1740 Midland Rd.
Saginaw, MI 48603
517-793-4532
Building products - retail & wholesale

Woodhead Industries, Inc. WDHD
2150 E. Lake Cook Rd.
Buffalo Grove, IL 60089
847-465-8300 Fax 847-465-8310
Electrical products - misc.

World Acceptance Corp. WRLD
1251 S. Pleasantburg Dr.
Greenville, SC 29605
803-277-4570
Financial - business services

World Access, Inc. WAXS
945 E. Paces Ferry Rd.
Atlanta, GA 30326
404-231-2025 Fax 404-262-2598
Electronics - components & systems

WorldCom, Inc. WCOM
515 E. Amite St.
Jackson, MS 39201
601-360-8600
Telecommunications services O

Worthington Industries, Inc. WTHG
1205 Dearborn Dr.
Columbus, OH 43085
614-438-3210
Metal processing & fabrication O DRP

WTD Industries, Inc. WTDI
10260 S.W. Greenburg Rd.
Portland, OR 97223
503-246-3440
Building products - wood

Wyman-Gordon Co. WYMN
244 Worcester St.
North Grafton, MA 01536
508-839-4441 Fax 508-839-7500
Aerospace - aircraft equipment O

Xicor, Inc. XICO
1511 Buckeye Dr.
Milpitas, CA 95035
408-432-8888 Fax 408-432-0640
Electrical components - semiconductors O

Xilinx, Inc. XLNX
2100 Logic Dr.
San Jose, CA 95124
408-559-7778
Computers - software O

Xircom, Inc. XIRC
2300 Corporate Center Dr.
Thousand Oaks, CA 91320
805-376-9300
Computers - peripheral equipment O

XOMA Corp. XOMA
2910 Seventh St.
Berkeley, CA 94710
510-644-1170 Fax 510-644-0539
Biomedical & genetic products

X-Rite, Inc. XRIT
3100 44th St. SW
Grandville, MI 49418
616-534-7663 Fax 616-534-9212
Instruments - control

Yahoo! Inc. YHOO
635 Vaqueros Ave.
Sunnyvale, CA 94086
408-328-3300
Computers - services

Yellow Corp. YELL
10777 Barkley Ave.
Overland Park, KS 66207
913-967-4300
Transportation - truck O

York Research Corp. YORK
280 Park Ave., Ste. 2700 West
New York, NY 10017
212-557-6200
Energy - cogeneration

Zebra Technologies Corp. ZBRA
333 Corporate Woods Parkway
Vernon Hills, IL 60061
708-634-6700 Fax 708-634-1830
Optical character recognition O

Zions Bancorporation ZION
1380 Kennecott Building
Salt Lake City, UT 84133
801-524-4787
Banks - west DRP

Zitel Corp. ZITL
47211 Bayside Pkwy.
Fremont, CA 94538
510-440-9600
Computers - peripheral equipment O

Zoll Medical Corp. ZOLL
32 Second Ave., Ste. 40
Burlington, MA 10803
617-229-0020
Medical products

Zoltek Companies, Inc. ZOLT
3101 McKelvey Rd.
St. Louis, MO 63044
314-291-5110 Fax 314-291-8536
Diversified operations O

Zoom Telephonics, Inc. ZOOM
207 South St.
Boston, MA 02111
617-423-1072
Computers - peripheral equipment

Z-Seven Fund, Inc. ZSEV
2651 W. Guadalupe, Ste. B-233
Mesa, AZ 85202
602-897-6214 Fax 602-345-9227
Financial - investment management

TORONTO STOCK EXCHANGE

Abacan Resource Corporation ABC
1100, 800-5th Avenue S.W.
Calgary, AB T2P 3T6
403-237-9050 Fax 403-269-3944
Oil & gas exploration O

Aber Resources Ltd ABZ
930-355 Burrard Street
Vancouver, BC V6C 2G8
604-682-8555 Fax 604-685-8359
Resource exploration & development O

Abitibi-Consolidated, Inc. A
207 Queen's Quay West, Suite 680,
 Box 102
Toronto, Ontario M5J 2P5
416-203-5060 Fax 514-875-6284
Newsprint & paper

AGF Management Ltd. AGF
PO Box 50, T.D. Bank Centre
Toronto, ON M5K 1E9
416-367-1900 Fax 416-368-5244
Mutual funds

Agnico-Eagle Mines Ltd. AGE
401 Bay Street, Suite 2302
Toronto, ON M5H 2Y4
416-947-1212 Fax 416-367-4681
Gold & silver, exploration & development

AGRA Inc. AGR
355-8th Ave. S.W., Suite 1900
Calgary, BC T2P 1C9
403-263-9606 Fax 403-263-9676
Diversified manufacturing

Agrium Inc. AGU
426 - 10333 Southport Road S.W.
Calgary, AB T2W 3X6
403-258-4600 Fax 403-258-8331
Fertilizers O

Air Canada AC
7373 Cote Vertu Blvd. West
Saint-Laurent, QB H4Y 1H4
514-422-5000 Fax 514-422-5789
Airline O

Alberta Energy Co. Ltd. AEC
3900 421, 7th Ave. S.W.
Calgary, AB T2P 4K9
403-266-8113 Fax 403-266-8154
Oil & gas exploration & development

Alcan Aluminum AL
1188 Sherbrooke Street West
Montreal, QB H3A 3G2
514-848-8402 Fax 514-848-8115
Aluminum production O

Algoma Steel Inc. ALG
PO Box 1400
Sault Ste. Marie, ON P6A 5P2
705-945-2351 Fax 705-945-2203
Steel Production

Allelix Biopharmaceuticals AXB
6850 Goreway Drive
Mississauga, ON L4V 1V7
905-677-0831 Fax 905-677-9595
Biopharmaceuticals

Alliance Forest Products ALP
1000 De La Gauchetiere W., Suite 2820
Montreal, QB H3B 4W5
514-954-2118 Fax 514-954-2167
Forest products

Amber Energy Inc. AMB
1100, 321 6th Ave. S.W.
Calgary, AB T2P 3H3
403-237-9977 Fax 403-237-9970
Oil & gas exploration and development

Anderson Exploration Ltd. AXL
324 8th Ave. S.W., Suite 1600
Calgary, AB T2P 2Z5
403-232-5572 Fax 403-232-7657
Oil & gas exploration and development O

AT Plastics Inc. APP
134 Kennedy Road South
Brampton, ON L6W 3G5
905-452-6738 Fax 905-451-7650
Film & packaging products

Atco, Ltd. ACO
1600 Canadian Western Centre
909 11th Ave. S.W.
Calgary, AB T2R 1N6
403-292-7546 Fax 403-292-7643
Diversified operations

ATI Technologies Inc. ATY
33 Commerce Valley Drive East
Thornhill, ON L3T 7N6
905-882-2600 Fax 905-882-2620
Software development, marketing

ATS Automation Tooling System ATA
250 Royal Oak Rd.
Cambridge, ON N3H 4R6
519-653-6500 Fax 519-653-6533
Automated manufacturing systems

Aur Resources Inc. AUR
1 Adelaide St. West, Suite 2501
Toronto, ON M5C 2V9
416-362-2614 Fax 416-367-0427
Mineral exploration & development

Avenor, Inc. AVR
1250 Rene-Levesque Blvd. West
Montreal, QB H3B 4V3
514-846-5052 Fax 514-846-5181
Pulp & paper

BC Gas Utility Ltd. BCG
1111 West Georgia St.
Vancouver, BC V6E 4M4
604-443-6559 Fax 604-443-6904
Natural gas transportation

BC Telecom Inc. BCT
3777 Kingsway
Burnaby, BC V5H 3Z7
604-432-2151 Fax 604-434-6616
Telecommunications

BCE Inc. BCE
1000 Rue De La Gauchetiere Ouest
  Bureau 3700
Montreal, QB H3B 4Y7
514-397-7278 Fax 514-397-7321
Telecommunications O

BCE Mobile Communications Inc. BCX
8501 Transcanada Highway
St. Laurent, QB H4S 1Z1
514-956-4800 Fax 514-333-4468
Mobile communications

Ballard Power Systems Inc. BLD
9000 Glenlyon Parkway
Burnaby, BC V5J 5J9
604-454-0900 Fax 604-412-4700
Energy research & development

Bank of Montreal BMO
129 St Jacques St.
Montreal, QB H2Y 1L6
514-877-6835 Fax 514-877-1805
Banking

Bank of Nova Scotia (The) BNS
44 King Street West
Toronto, ON M5H 1H1
416-866-5090 Fax 416-866-5090
Banking O

Barrick Gold Corp. ABX
200 Bay St. Suite 2700
Toronto, ON M5J 2J3
416-861-9911 Fax 416-861-2492
Gold exploration & development O

Barrington Petroleum Ltd. BPL
400-3rd Ave. S.W., Suite 2700
Calgary, AB T2P 4H2
403-263-9464 Fax 403-266-5794
Oil & gas exploration & development

Battle Mountain Canada Ltd. BMC
1 Adelaide Street East, Suite 2902
Toronto, ON M5C 2Z9
416-367-2560 Fax 416-367-5535
Gold exploration & development

Beau Canada Exploration Ltd. BAU
150 6th Ave. S.W., 47th Floor
Calgary, AB T2P 3Y7
403-266-2400 Fax 403-233-2565
Oil & gas exploration & development

Bema Gold Corp. BGO
595 Burrard St., Suite 3113
Vancouver, BC V7X 1G4
604-681-6209 Fax 604-681-6209
Mineral exploration & development

Berkley Petroleum Corp. BKP
202 6th Ave. S.W., Suite 1250
Calgary, AB T2P 2R9
403-571-3600 Fax 403-269-6510
Oil & gas development & exploration

BioChem Pharma Inc. BCH
275 Armand-Frappier Blvd.
Laval, QB H7V 4A7
514-681-1744 Fax 514-978-7755
Pharmaceuticals production

Biomira Inc. BRA
Edmonton Research Par 2011-94 Street
Edmonton, AB T6N 1H1
403-450-3761 Fax 403-463-0871
Biotechnology O

Biovail Corporation International BVF
2488 Dunwin Drive
Mississauga, ON L5L 1J9
906-285-6000 Fax 416-285-6499
Pharmaceutical production

Blue Range Resources Corporation BBR
1300 Trimac House, 800-5th Avenue S.W.
Calgary, AB T2P 3T6
403-264-7422 Fax 403-231-6367
Oil & gas producer

Bombardier Inc. BBD
800 Rene-Levesque Blvd. W, Suite 2900
Montreal, QB H3B 1Y8
514-861-9481 Fax 514-861-7053
Aerospace & heavy equipment

Brookfield Properties Corp. BPC
BCE Place, 181 Bay St., Suite 4500,
  Box 770
Toronto, ON M5J 2T3
416-359-8600 Fax 416-865-1288
Holding company

Bruncor Inc. BRR
1 Brunswick Square, Box 5030
Saint John, NB E2L 4L4
506-694-6330 Fax 506-694-2028
Telecommunications

Cabre Exploration Ltd. CBE
PO Box 630, Station M
Calgary, AB T2P 2J3
403-231-8800 Fax 403-263-4865
Oil & gas exploration & development

CAE Inc. CAE
Royal Bank Plaza, Suite 3060, PO Box 30
Toronto, ON M5J 2J1
416-865-0070 Fax 416-865-0337
Holding company

Caledonia Mining Corp. CAL
2150 Winston Park Drive, Suite 16
Oakville, ON L6H 5V1
905-829-4848 Fax 905-829-4238
Mineral exploration & development

Call-Net Enterprises Inc. CN
2550 Victoria Park Avenue, Suite 400
North York, ON M2J 5E6
416-496-1644 Fax 416-718-6410
Telecommunications

Cambior Inc. CBJ
800 Rene-Levesque West, Suite 850
Montreal, QB H3B 1X9
514-878-3166 Fax 514-878-4608
Gold exploration & development

Cambridge Shopping Centers Ltd. CBG
95 Wellington Street, Suite 300
Toronto, ON M5J 2R2
416-369-1260 Fax 416-369-1327
Real estate

Cameco Corp CCO
2121 11th Street West
Saskatoon, SK S7M 1J3
306-956-6312 Fax 306-956-6201
Uranium exploration & development

Campbell Resources Inc. CCH
120 Adelaide Street West, Suite 1910
Toronto, ON M5H 1T1
416-366-5201 Fax 416-367-3294
Mineral exploration & development

Canadian 88 Energy Corp. EEE
700 400-3rd Avenue S.W.
Calgary, AB T2P 4H2
403-974-8800 Fax 403-974-8811
Oil & gas exploration & development

Canadian Fracmaster Ltd. CFC
1700 Fracmaster Tower, 355-4th Ave. S.W.
Calgary, AB T2P 0J1
403-262-2222 Fax 403-266-0505
Oil & gas wells service

Canadian Imperial Bank of Commerce
  CM
Commerce Court West
Toronto, ON M5L 1T4
416-980-3043 Fax 416-980-7012
Banking O

Canadian Marconi Company CMW
600 Dr. Frederick Phillips Blvd.
St. Laurent, QB H4M 2S9
514-748-3000 Fax 514-748-3100
Electronic components

Canadian National Railway Co. CNR
935 De La Gauchetiere Street West,
  16th Floor
Montreal, QB H3B 2M9
514-399-4743 Fax 514-399-3779
Railroad

Canadian Natural Resources Ltd. CNQ
Esso Plaza, 425 1st Street S.W., Suite 2000
Calgary, AB T2P 3L8
403-221-2100 Fax 403-233-8941
Oil & gas exploration & development

Canadian Occidental Petroleum CXY
635 8th Ave., S.W., Suite 1500
Calgary, AB T2P 3Z1
403-234-6729 Fax 403-234-6971
Resource exploration & development

Canadian Pacific Ltd. CP
901 Peel St., PO Box 6042, Station Centre-
Ville
Montreal, QB H3C 3E4
514-395-6592 Fax 403-205-9005
Transportation O

Canadian Tire Corp. CTR
2180 Yonge St., PO Box 770, Station K
Toronto, ON M4P 2V8
416-480-8398
Retail stores

Canadian Utilities Ltd. CU
10035-105 Street, Room 1927
Edmonton, AB T5J 2V6
403-420-7757 Fax 403-292-7643
Holding company

Canfor Corp CFP
2800-1055 Dunsmuir St., PO Box 49420
Vancouver, BC V7X 1B5
604-661-5241 Fax 604-661-5472
Forest products

Canwest Global Communications CGS
TD Centre, 201 Portage Ave., 31st Floor
Winnipeg, Manitoba R3B 3L7
204-956-2025 Fax 204-947-9841
Broadcasting

Cascades Inc. CAS
404 Marie Victoria St.
Kingsey Falls, QB J0A 1B0
819-363-2245 Fax 819-363-5155
Paper & packaging

CCL Industries Inc. CCQ
105 Gordon-Baker Rd., Suite 800
Willowdale, ON M2H 3P8
416-756-8500 Fax 416-756-8555
Diversified operations

Celanese Canada Inc. CCL
800 Rene-Levesque Blvd. W.
Montreal, QB H3B 1Z1
514-871-5506 Fax 514-871-5635
Chemical manufacturing

Centurion Energy International CUX
205 5th Ave. S.W., Suite 800
Calgary, AB T2P 2V7
403-264-1400 Fax 403-263-5998
Oil & gas exploration & development

CFM Majestic Inc. CFM
475 Admiral Boulevard
Mississauga, ON L5T 2N1
905-670-7777 Fax 905-670-7915
Gas fireplaces

Chauvco Resources Ltd. CHA
255 5th Ave. S.W., Suite 2900
Calgary, AB T2P 3G6
403-231-3100 Fax 403-269-9497
Oil & gas exploration & development

Chieftan International Inc. CID
1201 Toronto-Dominion Tower,
  Edmonton Centre
Edmonton, AB T5J 2Z1
403-425-1950 Fax 403-429-4681
Oil & gas exploration

CHUM Ltd. CHM
1331 Yonge Street
Toronto, ON M4T 1Y1
416-925-6666 Fax 416-926-0279
Broadcasting

C.I. Fund Management Inc. CIX
151 Yonge Street, Eighth Floor
Toronto, ON M5C 2V1
416-364-1145 Fax 416-365-0501
Mutual funds

Cinar Films Inc. CIF
1055 Rene-Levesque Blvd. East
Montreal, QB H2L 4S5
514-843-7070 Fax 514-843-7080
Film production

Cinram International Inc. CRW
2255 Markham Road
Scarborough, ON M1B 2W3
416-298-8190 Fax 416-298-0612
Audio products

Clearnet Communications Inc. NET
1305 Pickering Parkway, Suite 300
Pickering, ON L1V 3P2
905-831-6222 Fax 905-831-7389
Communications

C-MAC Industries Inc. CMS
3000 Industrial Boulevard
Sherbrooke, QB J1H 1V8
819-821-4524 Fax 819-563-1167
Microelectronics

Cognos Incorporated CSN
3755 Riverside Drive, PO Box 9707,
  Station "T"
Ottawa, ON K1G 4K9
613-738-1440 Fax 613-738-7442
Computer developer O

Com Dev International Ltd. CDV
155 Sheldon Drive
Cambridge, ON N1R 7H6
519-622-2300 Fax 519-622-1691
Communication systems

Cominco Ltd CLT
500-200 Burrard Street
Vancouver, BC V6C 3L7
604-682-0611 Fax 604-685-3019
Mining & smelting O

Corel Corporation COS
1600 Carling Avenue
Ottawa, ON K1Z 8R7
613-728-8200 Fax 613-761-9176
Mineral exploration and development O

Co-Steel Inc. CEI
Scotia Plaza, 40 King St. W., Box 130
Toronto, ON M5H 3V2
416-366-4500 Fax 416-366-4616
Steel production

Cott Corporation BCB
207 Queen's Quay West, Suite 800
Toronto, ON M5J 1A7
416-203-3898 Fax 416-203-5609
Beverage production

Counsel Corporation CXS
2 First Con Place, Suite 1300, Box 435
Toronto, ON M5X 1E3
416-866-3058 Fax 416-866-3061
Financial services

Crestar Energy Inc. CRS
700 Fourth Ave., Suite 500
Calgary, AB T2P 3J4
403-266-4422 Fax 403-264-1028
Oil & gas exploration and development

Dayton Mining Corporation DAY
1610-200 Burrard Street
Vancouver, BC V6C 3L6
604-662-8383 Fax 604-684-1329
Mineral exploration & development

Delrina Corporation DE
895 Don Mills Rd., 500-2 Park Centre
Toronto, ON M3C 1W3
416-441-3676 Fax 416-446-8233
Computer development

Dia Met Minerals Ltd. DMM
1695 Powick Rd.
Kelowna, BC V1X 4L1
604-861-8660 Fax 250-861-3649
Mineral exploration & development

Dofasco Inc. DFS
PO Box 2460, 1330 Burlington St. E.
Hamilton, ON L8N 3J5
905-544-3761 Fax 905-548-4249
Steel

Doman Industries Ltd. DOM
435 Trunk Rd.
Duncan, BC V9L 2P9
604-746-5155 Fax 604-748-6045
Forest products

Dominion Textile Inc. DTX
1950 Sherbrooke Street West
Montreal, QC H3H 1E7
514-989-6087 Fax 514-989-6073
Textiles

Domtar Inc. DTC
395 De Maisonneuve Blvd. West,
 Box 7210
Montreal, QC H3A 1L6
514-848-5535 Fax 514-848-6850
Pulp and paper

Donohue Inc. DHC
500 Sherbrooke Street, W. 8th Floor
Montreal, QC H3A 3C6
418-684-7700 Fax 514-847-7707
Forest products

Dreco Energy Services Ltd. DRE
Weber Centre, #1340, 5555 Calgary Trail
Edmonton, AB T6H 5P9
403-944-3900 Fax 403-438-8256
Diversified manufacturing

Dundee Bancorp Inc. DBC
40 King Street W., Scotia Plaza, 55th Floor
Toronto, ON M5H 4A9
416-863-6990 Fax 416-383-4536
Management company

Dupont Canada Inc. DUP
PO Box 2200, 7070 Mississauga Rd.
Mississauga, ON L5M 2H3
905-821-5101
Chemical manufacturing

Echo Bay Mines Ltd. ECO
6400 S. Fiddlers Green Circle, Suite 1000
Englewood, CO 80111
303-423-7218 Fax 303-714-8994
Mineral exploration and development O

EdperBrascan Corporation EBC
181 Bay Street, Suite 4440, PO Box 770
Toronto, ON M5J 2T3
416-359-8619 Fax 416-865-1288
Financial services

Eldorado Gold Corporation ELD
1920 Guiness Tower
1055 West Hastings Street
Vancouver, BC V6E 2E9
604-687-4018 Fax 604-687-4026
Mineral exploration and development

E-L Financial ELF
165 University Avenue, 10th Floor
Toronto, ON M5H 3B8
416-947-2578 Fax 416-868-6199
Insurance

Empire Company Ltd. EMP
115 King Street
Stellarton, Nova Scotia B0K 1S0
902-755-4440 Fax 902-755-6477
Holding company

Encal Energy Ltd. ENL
1800, 421 7th Ave. S.W.
Calgary, AB T2P 4K9
403-750-3300 Fax 403-266-2337
Oil & gas exploration and development

Enerflex systems Ltd. EFX
4949 76 Ave. S.E.
Calgary, AB T2C 2C6
403-236-6800 Fax 403-236-6816
Gas equipment, manufacturing/leasing

Ensign Resource Service Group ESI
400 5th Avenue S.W., Suite 900
Calgary, AB T2P 0L6
403-262-1361 Fax 403-266-3596
Oil & gas wells service

Euro-Nevada Mining Corp. EN
20 Eglinton Ave. W., Suite 1900
Toronto, ON M4R 1K8
416-480-6490 Fax 416-488-6598
Mineral exploration and development

Extendicare Inc. EXE
3000 Steeles Avenue East, Suite 300
Markham, ON L3R 9W3
905-470-5515 Fax 905-470-5588
Health services

Fahnestock Viner Holdings, Inc. FHV
181 University Avenue, Suite 1204,
  PO Box 16
Toronto, ON M5H 3M7
416-367-6247 Fax 416-322-7007
Holding company

Fairfax Financial Holdings Ltd. FFH
95 Wellington Street West, Suite 800
Toronto, ON M5J 2N7
416-367-4944 Fax 416-367-4946
Holding Company

Falconbridge Limited FL
95 Wellington Street West, Suite 1200
Toronto, ON M5J 2V4
416-956-5700 Fax 416-956-5757
Mineral exploration and development O

Finning International Inc. FTT
555 Great Northern Way
Vancouver, BC V5T 1E2
604-691-6250 Fax 604-331-4899
Heavy equipment

First Marathon Inc. FMS
The Exchange Tower
2 First Canadian Place, Suite 3100
Toronto, ON M5X 1J9
416-869-3707 Fax 416-869-0089
Holding company

Fletcher Challenge Canada Ltd. FCC
700 West Georgia St., 9th Floor,
  Box 10058
Vancouver, BC V7Y 1J7
604-654-4000 Fax 604-654-4132
Forest products

Fonorola Inc. FON
500 Rene-Levesque Blvd. W., Suite 305
Montreal, QB H2Z 1W7
514-954-3666 Fax 514-954-4329
Telecommunications

Fortis, Inc. FTS
The Fortis Building, 139 Water St.,
  Suite 1201
St. John's, Newfoundland A1B 3T2
709-737-5614 Fax 709-737-5307
Management company

Four Seasons Hotels Inc. FSH
1165 Leslie Street
Don Mills, ON M3C 2K8
416-449-4339 Fax 416-441-4374
Hotels, lodging

Franco-Nevada Mining Corporation FN
20 Eglinton Avenue W., Box 2005,
  Suite 1900
Toronto, ON M4R 1K8
416-480-6490 Fax 416-488-6598
Gold exploration and development

Geac Computer Corporation Ltd GAC
11 Allstate Parkway, Suite 300
Markham, ON L3R 9T8
416-475-0525 Fax 905-475-3847
Computer development O

Gennum Corporation GND
970 Fraser Dr., PO Box 489, Station A
Burlington, ON L7R 3Y3
905-632-2996 Fax 905-632-2055
Circuits manufacturing

Gentra Inc. GTA
70 York Street, Suite 1400
Toronto, ON M5J 1S9
416-359-8555 Fax 416-359-8599
Trust company

Glamis Gold Ltd GLG
1055 Dunsmuir St., Box 49287
Vancouver, BC V7X 1L3
604-681-3541 Fax 604-681-9306
Gold exploration & development

Goldcorp Inc. G
145 King Street West, Suite 2700
Toronto, ON M5H 1J8
416-865-0326 Fax 416-865-9636
Gold producer

Golden Star Resources Ltd GSC
One Norwest Center, 1700 Lincoln Street,
  Suite 1950
Denver, CO 80203
303-830-9000 Fax 303-830-9092
Gold exploration & development

Great West Lifeco Inc. GWO
100 Osborne Street North
Winnipeg, Manitoba R3C 3A5
204-946-1190 Fax 204-946-4129
Holding company

Greenstone Resources Ltd. GRE
26 Wellington Street East, Suite 910
Toronto, ON M5E 1S2
416-862-7300 Fax 416-862-7604
Mineral exploration & development O

G.T.C. Transcontinental Group GRT
1 Place Ville Marie, Suite 3315
Montreal, QB H3B 3N2
514-954-4000 Fax 514-954-4016
Printing & publishing

Gulf Canada Resources Ltd. GOU
401-9th Avenue S.W., PO Box 130,
  Station M
Calgary, AB T2P 2H7
403-233-4480 Fax 403-233-5143
Oil and gas producer

Gulfstream Resources Canada Ltd. GUR
3465, 855-2nd Street, S.W.
Calgary, AB T2P 4J8
403-264-8288 Fax 403-264-8265
Oil & gas exploration & development O

Harmac Pacific Inc. HRC
2650-666 Burrard Street, Park Place
Vancouver, V6C 2X8
604-895-7700 Fax 604-687-8469
Pulp & paper

Hollinger Inc. HLG
10 Toronto Street
Toronto, ON M5C 2B7
416-363-8721 Fax 416-364-2088
Publishing, printing

Hudson's Bay Company HBC
401 Bay Street
Toronto, ON M5H 2Y4
416-861-4593 Fax 416-861-4720
Department stores

Hummingbird Communications Ltd. HUM
1 Sparks Avenue
North York, ON M2H 2W1
416-496-2200 Fax 416-496-2207
Computer systems O

Hyal Pharmaceutical Corporation HPC
2425 Skymark Avenue
Mississauga, ON L4W 4Y6
905-625-8181 Fax 905-625-1884
Pharmaceuticals

Imasco Ltd IMS
600 De Maisonneuve Blvd. West,
  20th Floor
Montreal, QB H3A 3K7
514-982-9111 Fax 514-982-9369
Tobacco

Imax Corporation IMX
45 Charles St. East
Toronto, ON M4Y 1N1
416-960-8509 Fax 905-403-6450
Film distributor

Imperial Oil Ltd. IMO
111 St. Clair Avenue W.
Toronto, ON M5W 1K3
416-968-5387 Fax 416-968-5345
Integrated oil O

Inco Ltd N
145 King Street West, Suite 1500
Toronto, ON M5H 4B7
416-361-7664 Fax 416-361-7788
Mining & smelting O

Indochina Goldfields Ltd. ING
200 Burrard Street, 9th Floor
Vancouver, BC V6C 3L6
604-688-5755 Fax 604-687-7121
Mineral exploration & development

Inmet Mining Corporation IMN
Aetna Tower, Suite 3400, PO Box 19
Toronto, ON M5K 1A1
416-361-6400 Fax 416-368-4692
Mining & smelting

International Comfort Products ICP
1 Queen Street East, Suite 1820, Box 68
Toronto, ON M5C 2W5
416-955-9789 Fax 416-955-4665
Heating & air conditioning manufacturing

International Curator Resources IC
203-409 Granville Street
Vancouver, BC V6C 1T2
604-688-4450 Fax 604-688-0313
Mineral exploration & development

International Forest Products IFP
1055 Dunsmuir Street, Suite 3500,
 Box 49114
Vancouver, BC V7X 1H7
604-689-6800 Fax 604-688-0313
Forest products

Intertape Polymer Group Inc. ITP
110E Montee De Liesse
St. Laurent, QB H4T 1N4
514-731-7591 Fax 514-397-3222
Plastic products

Intrawest Corporation ITW
200 Burrad Street, Suite 800
Vancouver, BC V6C 3L6
604-669-9777 Fax 604-669-0605
Real estate

Investors Group Inc. IGI
447 Portage Avenue
Winnipeg, Manitoba R3C 3B6
204-956-8514 Fax 204-942-5350
Financial services

IPL Energy Inc. IPL
421 Seventh Avenue S., Suite 2900
Calgary, AB T2P 4K9
403-231-3900 Fax 403-231-4844
Oil pipeline

Ipsco Inc. IPS
PO Box 1670
Regina, Saskatchewan S4P 3C7
306-924-7230 Fax 306-924-7500
Steel

Jannock Ltd. JN
Scotia Plaza, 40 King St., Suite 5205,
 Box 1012
Toronto, ON M5H 3Y2
416-364-8586 Fax 416-364-9342
Building products

JDS FITEL Inc. JDS
570 West Hunt Club Rd.
Nepeam, ON K2G 5W8
613-727-1303 Fax 613-727-8284
Fibre optic communications

Jean Coutu Group, Inc. PJC
530 Rue Beriault
Longueuil, QB J4G 1S8
514-646-9760 Fax 514-646-5649
Retail stores

Jordan Petroleum Ltd. JDN
850 Bow Valley Square 3,
 255 5th Ave. S.W.
Calgary, AB T2P 3G6
403-260-1024 Fax 403-266-4325
Oil & gas exploration & development

Kingsway Financial Services Inc. KFS
200-5310 Explorer Drive
Mississauga, ON L4W 5H8
905-629-7888 Fax 905-629-5008
Insurance

Kinross Gold Corporation K
40 King Street West, 57th Floor
Toronto, ON M5H 3Y2
416-365-5123 Fax 416-363-6622
Natural Resources O

KWG Resources Inc. KWG
630 Rene-Levesque Blvd. West, Suite 3200
Montreal, QB H3B 1S6
514-866-6001 Fax 416-869-0727
Diamonds exploration & development O

Lafarge Canada Inc LCI
606 Cathcart Street, Suite 900
Montreal, QB H3B 1L7
514-861-1411 Fax 514-861-1123
Cement manufacturing

Lafarge Corporation LAF
Box 4600
Reston, VA 22090
703-264-3670 Fax 703-264-0634
Holding company

Laidlaw Inc LDM
3221 North Service Rd., PO Box 5028
Burlington, ON L7R 3Y8
905-336-1800 Fax 905-336-3976
Transportation, waste management

Leitch Technology Corporation LTV
25 Dyas Road
North York, ON M3B 1V7
416-445-9640 Fax 416-445-4308
TV equipment design & manufacturing

Linamar Machine Corporation LNR
301 Massey Rd.
Guelph, ON N1K 1B2
519-836-7550 Fax 519-824-8479
Machine equipment & manufacturing

LionOre Mining International Ltd. LIM
602 West Hastings Street, Suite 801
Vancouver, BC V6B 1P2
604-681-9696 Fax 416-777-1320
Iron ore exploration & development

Loblaw Companies Ltd. L
22 St. Clair Avenue E, Suite 1500
Toronto, ON M4T 2S8
416-922-2500 Fax 416-922-7791
Retail food chain

Loewen Group Inc. (The) LWN
4126 Norland Avenue
Burnaby, BC V5G 3S8
604-299-9321 Fax 604-473-7333
Funeral services O

London Insurance Group LON
255 Dufferin Avenue
London, ON N6A 4K1
519-432-2000 Fax 519-432-4822
Insurance

Lytton Minerals Ltd. LTL
700 West Pender Street, Suite 501
Vancouver, BC V6C 1G8
604-689-7401 Fax 604-689-7406
Mineral exploration and development

MacKenzie Financial Corporation MKF
150 Bloor Street W, 4th Floor
Toronto, ON M5S 3B5
416-922-5322 Fax 416-922-7062
Investment management

MacMillan Bloedel Ltd. MB
925 West Georgia Street
Vancouver, BC V6C 3L2
604-661-8302 Fax 604-681-5908
Forest products O

Magna International Inc. MG
36 Apple Creek Blvd.
Markham, ON L3R 4Y4
905-477-7766 Fax 905-726-7172
Auto components O

Manitoba Telecom Services, Inc. MBT
489 Empress St.
Winnipeg, Manitoba R3C 3V6
204-941-4111 Fax 204-775-9255
Telecommunications

Maple Leaf Foods MFI
30 St. Clair Avenue West
Toronto, ON M4V 3A2
416-926-2000 Fax 416-926-2033
Food producer & distributor

Maritime Telegraph & Telephone MTT
1505 Barrington Street, PO Box 880
Halifax, NS B3J 2W3
800-565-7168 Fax 902-429-8755
Telecommunications

MDS, Inc. MHG
100 International Blvd.
Etobicoke, ON M9W 6J6
416-213-4213 Fax 416-675-4095
Health services

Meridian Gold MNG
5011 Meadowood Way
Reno, NV 89502
702-827-3777
Gold mining

Methanex Corporation MX
1800 Waterford Centre, 200 Burrard St.
Vancouver, BC V6C 3M1
604-661-2600 Fax 604-661-2676
Oil & gas exploration & development

Metro-Richelieu Inc. MRU
11011 Maurice-Duplessis Blvd.
Montreal, QB H1C 1V6
514-643-1207 Fax 514-643-1290
Food service

Midland Walwyn Inc. MWI
181 Bay Street, Suite 400
Toronto, ON M5L 2V8
416-369-7483 Fax 416-369-7766
Investment management O

Milltronics Ltd. MLS
730 The Kingsway
Peterborough, ON K9J 7B1
705-745-2431 Fax 705-745-7464
Measurement instruments

Mitel Corporation MLT
350 Legget Drive, PO Box 13089
Kanata, ON K2K 1X3
613-592-2122 Fax 613-592-4170
Telecommunications O

Molson Companies Ltd. MOL
Scotia Plaza, 40 King St. West, Suite 3600
Toronto, ON M5H 3Z5
416-360-1786 Fax 416-360-4345
Brewery/diverse manufacturing

Moore Corporation Ltd. MCL
1 First Canadian Place, PO Box 78
Toronto, ON M5X 1G5
416-364-2600 Fax 416-364-1667
Business information services O

Muramar Mining Corporation MAE
311 West First Street
North Vancouver, BC V7M 1B5
604-985-2572 Fax 604-980-0731
Gold/copper exploration & mining

National Bank of Canada NA
600 De La Gauchetiere Ouest, 4th Floor
Montreal, QB H3B 4L2
514-394-6080 Fax 514-394-8434
Banking

Newbridge Networks Corporation NNC
600 March Road
Kanata, ON K2K 2E6
613-591-3600 Fax 613-591-3680
Digital electronics O

Newcourt Credit Group NCT
BCE Place, 181 Bay St., Suite 3500
Toronto, ON M5J 2T3
416-594-2400 Fax 416-594-5248
Financial services O

Newport Petroleum Corporation NPP
Bow Valley Sq. II, 205 5th Ave. S.W.,
   Suite 3300
Calgary, AB T2P 2V7
403-531-1530 Fax 403-531-1539
Oil & gas exploration & development

Newtel Enterprises Ltd. NEL
PO Box 12110, Fort William Building
St. John's, Newfoundland A1C 6J7
709-739-2108 Fax 709-739-3155
Telecommunications

Noranda Forest, Inc. NF
T.D. Bank Tower, Suite 4414, PO Box 7
Toronto, ON M5K 1A1
416-982-7363 Fax 403-531-1539
Forest products

Noranda Inc. NOR
181 Bay St., Suite 4100, Box 755
Toronto, ON M5J 2T3
416-982-7111 Fax 416-982-7490
Mining & smelting

Norcen Energy Resources Ltd. NCN
715 5th Ave. S.W.
Calgary, AB T2P 2X7
403-231-0097 Fax 403-231-0011
Oil & gas exploration & development

Northern Telecom Ltd. NTL
8200 Dixie Rd., Suite 100
Brampton, ON L6T 5P6
905-863-1191 Fax 905-863-8423
Telecommunications O

Northrock Resources Ltd. NRK
700 Second Street S.W., Suite 3500
Calgary, AB T2P 2W2
403-269-3100 Fax 403-232-4650
Oil & gas development

Northstar Energy Corp. NEN
535 7th Avenue S.W., Suite 300
Calgary, AB T2P 0Y4
403-298-0500 Fax 403-213-8100
Oil & gas exploration & development

Nova Scotia Power NSI
Scotia Square, 1894 Barrington Street,
   PO Box 910
Halifax, Nova Scotia B3J 2W5
902-428-6494 Fax 902-428-6171
Hydro-electric utility

Numac Energy Inc. NMC
321-6th Avenue S.W.
Edmonton, AB T2P 3H3
403-260-4728 Fax 403-260-9457
Oil & gas exploration & development

Ocelot Energy Inc. OCE
150-6th Avenue, 30th Floor
Calgary, AB T2P 3V7
403-299-5700 Fax 403-299-5750
Oil & gas development

Onex Corporation OCX
161 Bay St., Box 700
Toronto, ON M5J 2S1
416-362-7711 Fax 416-362-5765
Investment company

Orvana Minerals Corp. ORV
710-1177 West Hastings Street
Vancouver, BC V6E 2K3
604-682-4929 Fax 604-682-3888
Gold exploration & development

Oshawa Group Ltd. (The) OSH
302 The East Mall
Islington, ON M9B 6B8
416-236-1971 Fax 416-234-1420
Wholesale grocers

Oxford Properties Group Inc. OXG
120 Adelaide Street West, Suite 1700
Toronto, ON M5H 1T1
416-362-2111 Fax 416-868-0701
Real estate

Pacalta Resources Ltd. PAZ
633-6th Avenue S.W., Suite 1850
Calgary, AB T2P 2Y5
403-266-0085 Fax 403-266-1965
Oil & gas exploration & development

Pacific Forest Products Ltd. PFF
1040 West Georgia Street, Suite 1000
Vancouver, BC V6E 4K4
604-640-3400 Fax 604-640-3480
Acquisitions

Pan American Silver Corporation PAA
625 Howe Street, Suite 1500
Vancouver, BC V6C 2T6
604-684-1175 Fax 604-684-0147
Mineral exploration & development

PanCanadian Petroleum Ltd. PCP
150-9th Ave. S.W., PanCanadian Plaza,
  Box 2850
Calgary, AB T2P 2S5
403-290-2000 Fax 403-290-3499
Mineral exploration & development

Pan East Petroleum Corp. PEC
839-5th Avenue S.W., Suite 405
Calgary, AB T2P 3C8
403-234-7477 Fax 403-234-7540
Oil & gas exploration & development

PC DOCS Group International Inc. DXX
2005 Sheppard Avenue East, Suite 800
Toronto, ON M2J 5B4
416-497-7700 Fax 416-499-7777
Computer systems

Pegasus Gold Inc. PGU
601 West First Avenue, Suite 1500
Spokane, WA 99204
509-624-4653 Fax 509-838-8317
Mineral exploration & development

Penn West Petroleum Ltd. PWT
111 5th Avenue, Suite 800
Calgary, AB T2P 3Y6
403-237-0120 Fax 403-777-2601
Oil & gas exploration & development

Petro-Canada PCA
150 6th Avenue S.W.
Calgary, AB T2P 3E3
403-296-8000 Fax 403-296-3061
Oil & gas exploration & development O

Philip Services Corporation PHV
651 Burlington St., PO Box 423 Depot 1
Hamilton, ON L8L 7W2
905-544-6687
Waste management services O

Phoenix International Life Sciences PHX
4625 Dobrin Street
Saint-Laurent, AB H4R 2P7
514-333-0033 Fax 514-333-8861
Biotechnology

Pinnacle Resources PNN
400 4th Avenue S.W., Suite 3300
Calgary, AB T2P 0J4
403-232-9100 Fax 403-232-9200
Oil & gas exploration & development

Placer Dome Inc. PDG
1055 Dunsmuir Street, Suite 3500,
  Box 49330
Vancouver, BC V7X 1P1
604-682-7082 Fax 604-682-7092
Minerals exploration & development O

Poco Petroleum Ltd. POC
250-6th Avenue S.W., Suite 3500
Calgary, AB T2P 3H7
403-260-8025 Fax 403-263-2708
Oil & gas exploration & development

Potash Corporation of Saskatchewan POT
122-1st Avenue South, Suite 500
Saskatoon, Saskatchewan S7K 7G3
306-933-8521 Fax 306-933-8877
Potash mining & production

Power Corporation of Canada POW
751 Victoria Square
Montreal, QB H2Y 2J3
514-286-7400 Fax 514-286-7424
Holding company

Power Financial Corporation PWF
751 Victoria Square
Montreal, QB H2Y 2J3
514-286-7430 Fax 514-286-7424
Holding company

Precision Drilling Corporation PD
112 4th Avenue S.W., Suite 700
Calgary, AB T2P O3H
403-264-4882 Fax 403-266-1480
Oil & gas wells service

Premdor Inc PDI
1600 Britannia Road East
Mississauga, ON L4W 1J2
416-670-6500 Fax 905-670-6520
Doors manufacturing and distribution

Prime Resources Group Inc PRU
700 West Pender Street, Suite 1000
Vancouver, BC V6C 1G8
604-684-2345 Fax 604-684-9831
Minerals exploration & development

Provigo, Inc PGV
1611 Cremazie Blvd. E., 9th Floor
Montreal, QB H2M 2R9
514-383-2802 Fax 514-383-2836
Wholesale grocery

Prudential Steel Ltd. PTS
1800 Sunlife Plaza, 140 4th Avenue S.W.
Calgary, AB T2P 3N3
403-267-0300 Fax 403-265-3426
Metal fabrication

QLT Phototherapeutics Inc. QLT
520 West Sixth Avenue, Suite 400
Vancouver, BC V5C 4H5
604-872-7881 Fax 604-875-0001
Biopharmaceutical

Quebec Telephone QT
6 Jules-A Brillant Street
Rimouski, QB G5L 7E4
418-722-5883 Fax 418-722-5949
Telecommunications

Quebecor Inc QBR
612 Rue St. Jacques Ouest
Montreal, QB H3C 4M8
514-877-9777 Fax 514-877-9790
Holding company

Quebecor Printing Inc IQI
612 St. Jacques Street
Montreal, QB H3C 4M8
514-954-0101 Fax 514-954-1426
Printing

Rand A Technology Corporation RND
5285 Solar Drive
Mississauga, ON L4W 5B8
905-625-2000 Fax 905-625-2035
Computer systems

Ranger Oil Ltd. RGO
321 6th Avenue S.W., Suite 1600
Calgary, AB T2P 3H3
403-232-5202 Fax 403-263-0090
Oil & gas exploration & development O

Rayrock Yellowknife Resources RAY
30 Soudan Avenue, Suite 500
Toronto, ONM4S 1V6
416-49-0022 Fax 416-489-0096
Resource exploration & development

Remington Energy Ltd. REL
550 6th Avenue S.W., Suite 750
Calgary, AB T2P 0S2
403-269-9309 Fax 403-269-5592
Oil & gas exploration & development

Renaissance Energy Ltd. RES
425 First Street S.W., Suite 3000
Calgary, AB T2P 3L8
403-750-1400 Fax 403-750-1440
Oil & gas exploration & development

Repap Enterprises Inc. RPP
1250 Rene Levesque Blvd. West,
 Suite 3800
Montreal, QB H3B 4W8
514-846-1316 Fax 514-846-1313
Forest products O

Rigel Energy Corporation RJL
225 5th Ave., Bow Valley Square III,
 Suite 1900
Calgary, AB T2P 2G6
403-267-3000 Fax 403-267-3006
Oil & gas exploration & development

Rio Algom Ltd. ROM
120 Adelaide Street West, Suite 2600
Toronto, ON M5H 1W5
416-367-4000 Fax 416-365-6870
Mineral exploration & development

Rio Alto Exploration Ltd. RAX
111-5th Avenue S.W., Suite 1600
Calgary, AB T2P 3Y6
403-264-8780 Fax 403-261-7626
Oil & gas exploration & development

Rio Narcea Gold Mines Ltd. RNG
1543 Champa Street, Suite 400-A
Denver, CO 80202
303-893-6918 Fax 303-296-0896
Mineral exploration & development

Rogers Cantel Mobile Communications
 RCM
10 York Mills Road
North York, ON M2P 2C9
416-229-1400
Mobile communications O

Rogers Communications Inc. RCI
40 King St. W., Scotia Plaza, Suite 6400,
Box 1007
Toronto, ON M5H 3Y2
416-864-2373 Fax 416-864-2385
Broadcasting/telecommunications

Rothmans Inc. ROC
1500 Don Mills Rd.
Don Mills, ON M3B 3L1
416-449-5525 Fax 416-449-9601
Tobacco

Royal Bank of Canada RY
1 Place Ville Marie, PO Box 6001
Montreal, QB H3C 3A9
514-874-5012/416-974-4227
Fax 416-955-7800
Banking O

Royal Group Technologies Ltd. RYG
4945 Steeles Avenue West
Weston, ON M9L 1R4
416-749-5131 Fax 905-264-0702
Building products

Royal Oak Mines Inc. RYO
5501 Lakeview Drive, 2nd Floor
Kirkland, WA 98033
206-822-8992 Fax 425-822-3552
Gold exploration & mining O

Russel Metals Inc. RUS
One Lombard Place, Suite 600
Winnipeg, Manitoba R3B 0X3
204-942-8161 Fax 905-819-7409
Metal processing/distribution

Saskatchewan Wheat Pool SWP
2625 Victoria Avenue
Regina, Saskatchewan S4T 7T9
306-569-4411 Fax 306-569-4708
Grain handling & marketing

Sceptre Investment Counsel Ltd. SZ
26 Wellington St. East, Suite 1200
Toronto, ON M5E 1W4
416-360-4804 Fax 416-367-8716
Investment company

Seagram Company Ltd. (The) VO
1430 Peel Street
Montreal, QB H3A 1S9
514-849-5271 Fax 514-987-5221
Distillery O

Sears Canada Inc. SCC
222 Jarvis Street, D766
Toronto, ON M5B 2B8
416-941-4793 Fax 416-941-2321
Retail stores

Semi-Tech Corporation SEM
131 McNabb Street
Markham, ON L3R 5V7
905-475-2670 Fax 905-475-2321
Diverse electronics

Shaw Communications Inc. SCL
630 3rd Avenue S.W., Suite 900
Calgary, AB T2P 4L4
403-750-4573 Fax 403-750-4501
Telecommunications

Shaw Industries Ltd. SHL
25 Bethridge Road
Rexdale, ON M9W 1M7
416-743-7111 Fax 416-743-4501
Holding company

Shell Canada Ltd. SHC
400 4th Avenue S.W.
Calgary, AB T2P 0J4
403-691-3404 Fax 403-691-3696
Integrated oil

Sherritt International Corporation S
1133 Yonge Street
Toronto, ON M4T 2Y7
416-924-4551 Fax 416-924-5015
Holding company

Slocan Forest Products Ltd. SFF
240-10451 Shellbridge Way,
  Airport Executive Park
Richmond, BC V6X 2W8
604-278-7311 Fax 604-278-7316
Forest products

SNC-Lavalin Group Inc. SNC
2 Place Felix Martin
Montreal, QB H2Z 1Z3
514-393-1000 Fax 514-866-5057
Engineering & construction

Southam Inc. STM
1450 Don Mills Rd.
Don Mills, ON M3B 2X7
416-442-2929 Fax 416-442-3388
Printing & publishing

Southwestern Gold Corporation SWG
701 West Georgia Street, Suite 1650
Vancouver, BC V7Y 1C6
604-669-2528 Fax 604-688-5175
Mineral exploration and development

Spar Aerospace Ltd. SPZ
121 King Street West, Suite 1800
Toronto, ON M5H 4C2
416-682-7600 Fax 416-682-7601
Aerospace & development

SR Telecom Inc. SRX
8150 Trans Canada Highway
St. Laurent, QB H4S 1M5
514-335-1210 Fax 514-334-7783
Radio systems manufacturing

St. Laurent Paperboard Inc. SPI
630 Rene-Levesque Blvd. West, Suite 3000
Montreal, QB H3B 5C7
514-861-2204 Fax 514-861-2208
Forest products

Stelco Inc. STE
Stelco Tower, Box 2030
Hamilton, ON L8N 3T1
905-528-2511 Fax 905-577-4401
Steel

Suncor Energy Inc. SU
112 4th Avenue, PO Box 38
Calgary, AB T2P 2V5
403-269-8100 Fax 403-269-6217
Integrated oil

Talisman Energy Inc. TLM
855 2nd Street S.W., Suite 2100
Calgary, AB T2P 4J9
403-237-1234 Fax 403-237-1210
Resource exploration & development

Tarragon Oil & Gas Ltd. TN
500 4th Avenue S.W., Suite 2500
Calgary, AB T2P 2V6
403-974-7500 Fax 403-262-5324
Oil & gas exploration & development

Teck Corporation TEK
200 Burrard Street, Suite 600
Vancouver, BC V6C 3L9
604-687-1117 Fax 604-687-6100
Mineral exploration & development

Teleglobe Inc. TGO
1000 Rue De La Gauchetiere Ouest
Montreal, QB H3B 4X5
514-868-7722 Fax 514-868-7719
Data communications

Telus Corporation T
10020 100th Street, 31st Floor
Edmonton, AB T5J 0N5
403-493-3110
Telecommunications

Tembec Inc. TBC
800 Rene-Levesque Blvd. West, Suite 2790
Montreal, QB H3B 1X9
514-871-0137 Fax 514-397-0896
Pulp & paper

Tesco Corporation TEO
6204-6A Street S.W.
Calgary, AB T2H 2B7
403-233-0757 Fax 403-252-3362
Oil & gas exploration & development

Thomson Corporation (The) TOC
T.D. Bank Tower, PO Box 24, Suite 2706
Toronto, ON M5K 1A1
416-360-8700 Fax 416-360-8812
Holding company

Toromont Industries Ltd. TIH
1 Crothers Drive, PO Box 20011
Concord, ON L4K 4T1
416-667-5511 Fax 416-667-5555
Holding company

Toronto-Dominion Bank (The) TD
PO Box 1,Toronto Dominion Centre
Toronto, ON M5K 1A2
416-944-5741 Fax 416-982-6166
Banking O

Torstar Corporation TS
1 Yonge Street
Toronto, ON M5E 1P9
416-869-4545 Fax 416-869-4813
Newspaper publishing

Transat A.T. Inc. TRZ
400 Leo Parisau, Suite 300
Montreal, QB H2W 2P4
514-987-1660 Fax 514-987-8029
Air transportation

TransAlta Utilities Corporation TAU
110 12th Avenue S.W. Box 1900
Calgary, AB T2P 2M1
403-267-7110 Fax 403-267-2559
Public utility

TransCanada Pipelines Ltd. TRP
111 5th Avenue S.W., 29th Floor
Calgary, AB T2P 3Y6
403-267-8514 Fax 403-267-8884
Gas pipeline

Tri Link Resources Ltd. TLR
550-6th Avenue S.W., 10th Floor
Calgary, AB T2P 0S2
403-262-4601 Fax 403-265-0892
Oil & gas exploration & development

Trilon Financial Corporation TFC
181 Bay Street, 1 First Canadian Place,
 Suite 4420
Toronto, ON M5J 2T3
416-663-0061 Fax 416-365-9642
Investment management/public utility

Trimac Corporation TMA
PO Box 3500
Calgary, AB T2P 2P9
403-298-5119 Fax 403-298-5258
Transportation

Trimark Financial Corporation TMF
1 First Canadian Place, Suite 5600,
 Box 487
Toronto, ON M5X 1E5
416-594-2929 Fax 416-362-8515
Mutual Funds

Trizec Hahn Corporation TZH
181 Bay Street, Suite 3900, Box 768
Toronto, ON M5J 2T3
416-682-8600 Fax 416-361-7203
Oil & gas exploration & development

TVX Gold TVX
181 Bay Street, Suite 4300
Toronto, ON M5J 2S1
416-366-8160 Fax 416-366-8163
Mineral exploration & development O

Ulster Petroleums Ltd. ULP
1400 Sun Life Plaza 1, 144 4th Ave. S.W.
Calgary, AB T2P 3N4
403-269-6911 Fax 403-264-5835
Oil & gas exploration & development

Unican Security systems Ltd. UCS
7301 Decarie Blvd.
Montreal, QB H4P 2G7
514-735-5411 Fax 514-735-0428
Security systems

United Dominion Industries Ltd. UDI
2300 One First Union Center
301 S. College St.
Charlotte, NC 28202
704-347-6911 Fax 704-347-6539
Structural steel fabrication

Viceroy Resource Corporation EOY
1066 West Hastings Street, Suite 2200
Vancouver, BC V6E 3X2
604-688-9780 Fax 604-682-3941
Gold exploration & development

Westaim Corp. (The) WED
10102-114 Melville Street
Vancouver, BC V6E 4A6
403-992-5231 Fax 403-237-6565
Diversified manufacturing

Westburne Inc. WBI
505 Locke Street, Suite 200
St. Laurent, QB H4T 1X7
514-342-3027 Fax 514-342-9838
Plumbing & electrical supplies

Westcoast Energy Inc. W
666 Burrard Street, Suite 3400
Vancouver, BC V6C 3M8
604-488-8015 Fax 604-488-8500
Gas pipeline

Western Star Truck Holdings Ltd. WS
2076 Enterprise Way
Kelowna, BC V1Y 6H8
604-868-6401 Fax 250-860-1252
Truck manufacturing

West Fraser Timber Co Ltd. WFT
1000-1100 Melville Street
Vancouver, BC V6E 4A6
604-895-2700 Fax 604-681-6061
Forest products

Westmin Resources Ltd. WMI
904-1055 Dunsmuir Street, Box 49066
Vancouver, BC V7X 1C4
604-895-8400 Fax 604-681-0357
Integrated mining O

Weston, George Ltd. WN
22 St. Clair Avenue East, Suite 1500
Toronto, ON M4T 2S7
416-922-2500 Fax 416-922-4395
Food production & distribution

WIC Western International
 Communications WIC
1960-505 Burrard Street
Vancouver, BC V7X 1M6
604-661-4305 Fax 604-687-4118
Communications

William Resources Inc. WIM
390 Bay Street, Suite 2008
Toronto, ON M5H 2Y2
416-861-9500 Fax 416-861-8165
Mining services

YBM Magnex International Inc. YBM
110 Terry Drive
Newtown, PA 18940
215-579-0400 Fax 215-579-3444
Magnetic products

AMERICAN DEPOSITARY RECEIPTS (ADRs)

Investors wishing to buy shares in some companies headquartered outside the United States can avoid dealing directly with foreign exchanges by purchasing American Depositary Receipts in U.S. markets. ADRs are traded on the New York Stock Exchange, the American Stock Exchange and NASDAQ.

ADRs are receipts for foreign-based corporation's shares, which are held in American bank vaults. A buyer of an ADR in America is entitled to the same dividends and capital gains accruing to a shareholder purchasing shares on an exchange in the home country of the company. ADRs are denominated in dollars, so quoted prices reflect the latest currency exchange rates. ADR prices are listed in the *Wall Street Journal* and other newspapers, as well as in electronic databases.

The companies with ADRs generally are well-established, financially stable corporations with worldwide operations. In many cases, Americans would be familiar with their products and services because they are offered in the United States. A total of about 700 ADRs are traded. Most of the trading activity, however, is limited to some 100 issues. It is these actively traded issues that are presented here in alphabetical order, courtesy of Wilshire Associates (1299 Ocean Avenue, Santa Monica, California 90401 (310) 451-3051.] The entry for each company includes (1) the firm's name, (2) its stock symbol, (3) the exchange where it trades (NYSE for New York Stock Exchange, AMEX for American Stock Exchange and OTC for NAS-DAQ), (4) its main line of business, and (5) the country where it is headquartered.

Akzo NV [AKZO.Y], NASD, Chemicals, Netherlands
Alcatel Althsom [ALA], NYSE, Telecomm. Equipment, France
Aracruz Celulose [ARA], NYSE, Pulp and paper, Brazil
Ashanti Goldfields [ASL], NYSE, Gold mining, Ghana
Asia Pulp & Paper [PAP], NYSE, Manufacturer pulp & paper products, Indonesia
Astra [A], NYSE, Pharmaceutical R&D, Sweden
Banco Galicia-Buenos Aires [BGAL.Y], NYSE, Commercial banking, Argentina
Banco De Santander [STD], NYSE, General banking, Chile
Banco Frances Del Rio [BFR], NYSE, Commercial bank, Argentina
Banco Santander Chile [BSB], NYSE, Banking, Chile
Bank Tokyo-Mitsubishi [MBK], NYSE, Banking, Japan
B.A.T. Industries [BTI], AMEX, Tobacco producer, financial & insurance services, United Kingdom
British Petroleum [BP], NYSE, Petroleum products, United Kingdom
British Steel [BST], NYSE, Steel production, United Kingdom
British Telecommunications [BTY], NYSE, Telecommunications, United Kingdom
Cable & Wireless [CWP], NYSE, Telecomm. Equipment, United Kingdom
Chilgener [CHR], NYSE, Electricity generation, Chile
Coca-Cola Femsa [KOF], NYSE, Beverages, Mexico
Coflexip [CXIP.Y], NASD, Offshore flexible pipe/robots, France
Compania Anonimia [VNT], NYSE, Telecommunication services, Venezuela
Compania Cervecerias Unidas [CCUU.Y], NASD, Beverages, Chile
Compania De Telecommunications [CTC], NYSE, Telecommunication services, Chile
Consorcio G Grupo Dina [DIN], NYSE, Automobiles, Mexico
Danka Business Systems [DANK.Y], NASD, Computers, United Kingdom
De Beers Consolidated Mines [DBRS.Y], NASD, Mining, South Africa
Desc S A De C V [DES], NYSE, Auto parts, chemicals, Finland
Deutsche Telecom [DT], NYSE, Telecommunications, Germany
Driefontein Consolidated [DRFN.Y], NASD, Gold mining, South Africa
Elan [ELN], NYSE, Drugs, Ireland
Elf Aquitaine [ELF], NYSE, Oil refining & marketing, France
Empresas Ica Socieda [ICA], NYSE, Construction, Mexico

Endesa [ELE], NYSE, Electricity supplier, Spain
Enersis [ENI], NYSE, Energy, Chile
Ericsson L M Telecommunications [ERIC.Y], NASD, Telecom. equipment, Sweden
Esperito Santo Financial [ESF], NYSE, Banks, Portugal
Free State Consolidated Gold Mines [FSCN.Y], NASD, Gold Mining, South Africa
Fresenius Medical AG [FMS], NYSE, Manufacturer, distributor, pharmaceutical products, Germany
Glaxo [GLX], NYSE, Drugs, United Kingdom
Grand Metropolitan [GRM], NYSE, Food, United Kingdom
Grupo Financiero Serfin [SFN], NYSE, Finance, Mexico
Grupo Industrial Maseca [MSK], NYSE, Corn flour production, Mexico
Grupo Mexicana de Desarrollo [GMD], NYSE, Construction, Mexico
Grupo Radio Centro [RC], NYSE, Radio broadcasting, Mexico
Grupo Televisa [TV], NYSE, Broadcasting, Mexico
Grupo Tribasa [GTR], NYSE, Construction, Mexico
Hanson [HAN], NYSE, Multi-industry, United Kingdom
Hong Kong Telecommunications [HKT], NYSE, Telecommunication Services, Hong Kong
Imperial Chemical Industries [ICI], NYSE, Chemicals, United Kingdom
Kloof Gold Mining [KLOF.Y], NASD, Gold Mining, South Africa
Koor Industries [KOR], NYSE, Telecommunications systems & equipment, Israel
Korea Electric Power [KEP], NYSE, Utility, South Korea
Maderas y Sinteticos [MYS], NYSE, Building materials, Chile
Multicanal Participacoes [MPAR.Y], NASD, Cable TV operations, Brazil
News Corp [NWS], NYSE, Publishing, Australia
Nice Systems [NICE.Y], NASD, Telecommunication specialty systems, Israel
Nokia [NOK.A], NYSE, Telecommunications systems & equipment, Finland
Norsk Hydro [NMY], NYSE, Chemicals, Norway
Orbital Engine [OE], NYSE, Automobiles, Australia
Perusahaan P.T. Indosat [IIT], NYSE, International telecommunications services, Indonesia
Philippine Long Distance [PHI], NYSE, Telecommunications, Philippines
Philips N V [PHG], NYSE, Electrical machinery, Netherlands
Pohang Iron & Steel [PKX], NYSE, Steel production, South Korea
P.T. Telekomunikasi [TLK], NYSE, Telecommunication services, Indonesia
Quilmes Industrial Quinsa [LQU], NYSE, Beer producer, Argentina
Repsol [REP], NYSE, Energy-integration, Spain
Reuters Holding [RTRS.Y], NASD, Publishing, United Kingdom
Rhone-Poulenc [RP], NYSE, Chemicals, France
Royal Dutch Petroleum [RD], NYSE, Energy-integration, Netherlands
Santa Isabel [ISA], NYSE, Supermarket chain, Chile & Peru
Senetek [SNTK.Y], NASD, Biotechnology, United Kingdom
Shell Transport & Trading [SC], NYSE, Oil refining & marketing, United Kingdom
Smithkline Beecham [SBH], NYSE, Drugs, United Kingdom
Sony [SNE], NYSE, Consumer electronics, Japan
Southern Pacific Petroleum [SPPT.Y], NASD, Shale oil development, Australia
Telecom Argentina [TEO], NYSE, Telecommunications, Argentina
Telecommunicados Brasil [TBR], NYSE, Telecommunications, Brazil
Telecom Corp of New Zealand [NZT], NYSE, Telecommunications equipment, New Zealand
Tele Denmark [TLD], NYSE, Telecommunications, Denmark
Telefonica De Argentina [TAR], NYSE, Telecommunications equipment, Argentina
Telefonica De Espana [TEF], NYSE, Telecommunications equipment, Spain
Telefonica De Peru [TDP], NYSE, Telecommunications equipment, Peru
Telefonos De Mexico [TMX], NYSE, Telecommunications equipment, Mexico
Telefonos De Mexico [TFON.Y], NASD, Telecommunications equipment, Mexico
Teva Pharmaceutical [TEVI.Y], NASD, Drugs, Israel
Total [TOT], NYSE, Oil refining & marketing, France
Transportacion Maritima Mexico [TMM], NYSE, Marine transportation, Mexico
Transportatdora De Ca [TGS], NYSE, Natural gas transportation, Argentina
Tranz Rail Holdings [TNZE.Y], NASD, Freight transportation railroad, New Zealand

Tubos de Acero De Mexico [TAM], AMEX, Steel, Mexico
Tyco International [TYC], NYSE, Fire protection and security systems, Bermuda
Unilever [UL], NYSE, Food, Netherlands
Vaal Reefs Exploration & Mining [VAAL.Y], NASD, Mining, South Africa
Vitro Sociedad Anoni [VTO], NYSE, Building materials, Mexico
Vodafone Group [VOD], NYSE, Telecommunications equipment, United Kingdom
Volvo Aktiebolaget [VOLV.Y], NASD, Automobiles, Sweden
Waste Management International [WME], NYSE, Environmental, United Kingdom
Willis Corroon [WCG], NYSE, Insurance, United Kingdom
Ypf Sociedad Anonima [YPF], NYSE, Energy integration, Argentina

FREE AND DISCOUNTED GOODS FOR SHAREHOLDERS

The following is a list of American corporations that give free or discounted merchandise or services to their shareholders. In order to make a claim, shareholders usually must write or call the company, since most companies do not know the names of their shareholders (shares are often held in a street name by a brokerage firm). These freebies usually are not taxed as income to shareholders—if they are, the company will so inform their shareholders.

This list is provided courtesy of Gene Walden, who has written a book, *The 100 Best Stocks To Own In America*, 5th edition, Dearborn Publishing, 1998. The book describes some of these shareholder perks in more detail.

Abbott Laboratories: Shareholders attending the annual meeting receive a sampling of Abbott's consumer products such as Selsun Blue, Murine, an ice pack and a bottle of vitamins.

Albertson's, Inc.: Discount coupons with values ranging from $20 to $30 for shareholders who attend the annual meeting.

American Home Products: American Home occasionally sends out coupons for some of its foods and health care products along with the dividend check.

Anheuser-Busch Companies, Inc.: The company makes a point of moving its annual meetings around the country. Those who attend the annual meeting get an opportunity to sample all of the company's brews. Shareholders are also entitled to a discount on admission to the company's amusement parks.

Bristol-Myers Squibb Company: The company sends all of its new shareholders of record a welcome packet of its consumer products, including, for example, small bottles of Excedrin, Bufferin, Nuprin, Clairol and Ban deodorant.

Campbell Soup Company: The company hands out bags of freebies at the annual meeting, including coupons, soup, cookies, chicken nuggets and some new product samples.

ConAgra, Inc.: Shareholders attending the annual meeting receive a gift pack of some of ConAgra's foods. Sometimes sends discount offers along with its quarterly earnings reports.

Gillette Company (The): Shareholders who attend the annual meeting receive an excellent selection of products including shaving accessories, Right Guard deodorant, Oral B toothbrushes, Papermate pens and Duracell batteries.

Hershey Foods Corporation: Shareholders who attend the annual meeting receive gift certificates for 30%–50% discounts on the company's products. Also, a Christmas gift catalog exclusively for shareholders who want gifts wrapped and mailed directly from the chocolate factory.

Kellogg Company: All new shareholders receive a welcome kit with brochures and reports on the company along with coupons for free grocery products such as cereal, frozen waffles or one of Kellogg's newer products. Those attending the annual meetings in Battle Creek also receive product samples and discount coupons.

Kimberley-Clark Corporation: Share-holders who attend the annual meeting receive sample packages of the company's products.

Newell Company: Special gift to shareholders at the annual meeting.

Sara Lee Corporation: Gift box of Sara Lee products, including such items as coupons, bath soaps, coffee samples, Chicago Bull T-shirts and key chains.

Schering-Plough Corporation: Schering-Plough hands out a sample packet of products to shareholders at its annual meetings. The packets include such products as Coppertone suntan lotion, Afrin nasal spray, Gyne-Lotramin and other over-the-counter remedies.

Walgreen Company: Shareholders who attend the annual meeting usually receive one or two Walgreen products.

Walt Disney: Sometimes sends discount coupons for its amusement parks to shareholders.

Warner Lambert: Sends coupons for some of its products in its quarterly report to shareholders.

William Wrigley Jr. Company: Gift package to all shareholders each Christmas that includes several packs of Wrigley's gum, personally selected by company chairman and president, William Wrigley.

Appendix

SELECTED FURTHER READING

Overall Bibliography

Books in Print 1998–1999, New York: R.R. Bowker

Daniells, Lorna M. *Business Information Sources.* 3rd ed. Berkeley: University of California Press.

Economics

Keynes, John Maynard. *The General Theory of Employment, Interest and Money.* Amherst, New York: Promethius Books.

The definitive work of the British economist and government advisor, whose influential theories advocating government intervention (fiscal policy) as a solution to economic problems have become known as Keynesian economics.

McConnell, Campbell R. Economics: *Principles, Problems, and Policies.* 13th ed. New York: McGraw-Hill.

A highly regarded introduction to the fundamental problems and principles of economics and the policy alternatives available to countries, both from a national and international perspective.

Nelson, Charles R. *The Investor's Guide to Economic Indicators.* New York: Wiley.

Using plain language and simple charts, a prominent economist provides a guide to reading, interpreting, and using economic and financial news to make better investment decisions.

Samuelson, Paul A. and W. Nordhaus. *Economics,* 16th ed. New York: McGraw-Hill.

This famous and widely used introductory economics text has been thoroughly revised and updated. It takes students from fundamental to sophisticated levels of understanding of income and production factors including international trade and finance and current economic problems.

Smith, Adam. *An Inquiry into the Nature and Causes of the Wealth of Nations.* New York: Oxford University Press.

The definitive work, first published in 1776, of the most famous of the classical economists, who held that economies function best under a laissez-faire system in which market forces are free to operate without government interference.

International Economics, Finance, and Investment

Brandes, Charles H. and Glenn R. Carlson. *International Value Investing.* New York: McGraw-Hill.

A step-by-step guide to value investing in markets outside the United States.

Lindert, Peter H. *International Economics.* 9th ed. Burr Ridge, Illinois: Irwin Professional Publishing.

A classic text covering aspects of international economics and finance on theoretical and practical levels, plus an examination of larger problems concerning international mobility of people and factors of production.

Root, Franklin R. *International Trade and Investment,* 7th ed. Cincinnati: South-Western.

Covers theory, policy, and the marketplace of international trade, including international payments, development financing, and international investments and multinational enterprises.

Walmsley, Julian. *The New Financial Instruments.* New York: Wiley.

An explanation of sophisticated modern financial instruments used in international finance and investment.

Money and Banking

The Bank Rating Service by Veribanc (Wakefield, Massachusetts)

Veribanc is a service that rates the financial strength of most U.S. banks, savings and loans, credit unions, and bank holding companies and provides short-form or in-depth reports for a fee. Also provides lists of safe financial institutions by state, region, or financial condition. Veribanc also offers default insurance up to $5 million through a program called DEPOSITSURE.

Kaufman, George G. *The U.S. Financial System: Money Markets and Institutions.* 6th ed. Englewood Cliffs: Prentice-Hall.

Assuming a basic knowledge of economics, this text covers in terms of theory and practice the evolution and operations of the national and international financial markets as well as instruments, institutions, and regulators. The Federal Reserve System and other aspects of the economic macrostructure are also examined.

Ritter, Lawrence S. and William L Silber. *Principles of Money, Banking and Financial Markets.* 8th ed. New York: Basic Books

A comprehensive introductory text that covers money and banking fundamentals; banks and other intermediaries; central banking; monetary theory; financial markets and interest rates; and international finance.

Updegrave, Walter. *How to Keep Your Savings Safe: Protecting the Money You Can't Afford to Lose.* New York: Crown Publishers.

How to find the strongest banks, insurance companies, and money market mutual funds. Lists of safe U.S. banks, insurers, savings and loan institutions, and money funds are provided.

Bond and Money Markets

Douglas, Livingston G. *The Fixed-Income Almanac: The Bond Investor's Compendium of Key Market, Product and Performance Data.* New York: McGraw-Hill.

Provides a cornucopia of historical performance data for the bond markets, including yield levels, measures of bond volatility, information on ratings upgrades and downgrades, and levels of new bond issuance.

Fabozzi, Frank J. and Irving M. Pollock, eds. *The Handbook of Fixed Income Securities,* 5th ed. Burr Ridge, Illinois: Irwin Professional Publishing.

Includes 47 chapters, each by an expert, covering general investment information; securities and instruments; bond investment management; interest rates and rate forecasting.

Faerber, Esme. *All About Bonds from the Inside Out.* New York: McGraw-Hill.

As the title suggests, a discussion of bond basics, including types of bonds, different risk characteristics, methods of valuation, calculating rates and returns, and understanding the yield curve.

Kerzner, Harold. *Understanding Corporate Bonds.* New York: McGraw-Hill.

Excellent primer on the complex world of corporate bonds.

Lederman, Jess and Michael P. Sullivan. *The New High-Yield Bond Market.* New York: McGraw-Hill.

How the high-yield (junk) bond market works and how to reduce risk without compromising return. Buying bonds of bankrupt companies.

Stigum, Marcia. *Money Market Derivatives and Structured Notes.* Burr Ridge, Illinois: Irwin Professional Publishing.

Like her book, *The Money Market,* an excellent and comprehensive guide, in this case to the more exotic financial derivatives and complex debt instruments invested for modern worldwide money markets.

Stigum, Marcia. *The Money Market,* 3rd ed. Burr Ridge, Illinois: Irwin Professional Publishing.

A comprehensive guide, by a working professional, to the U.S. money market. It covers the various instruments traded, how yields are calculated, and the role of the Federal Reserve; the major participants, including Eurobanks; and particular markets, such as those for commercial paper, Treasury bills, and CDs. Includes financial futures.

Corporate Finance

Altman, Edward I., ed. *Handbook of Corporate Finance.* 6th ed./ *Handbook of Financial Markets & Institutions.* 6th ed. New York: Wiley.

Volume one, the *Handbook of Corporate Finance,* includes chapters by different authorities on financial forecasting, planning, and control; sources of funds; capital budgeting; pensions and profit sharing; and modern finance, including multinationals, international cash management, bankruptcies and reorganizations, mergers and acquisitions, and small business.

The second volume, *Handbook of Financial Markets & Institutions,* covers the domestic and international marketplace, investment analysis strategies, securities and portfolio management, and related subjects.

Brigham, Eugene F. and Louis C. Gapenski. *Financial Management: Theory and Practice.* 8th ed. Orlando, Florida: Dryden Press.

A well-written discussion of basic concepts in financial management and their use in maximizing the value of a firm. Using real-life examples, the text covers financial forecasting, working capital management, capital budgeting, and other relevant subjects, including international financial management and mergers and acquisitions.

Van Horne, James C. *Financial Management & Policy.* 11th ed., Englewood Cliffs: Prentice-Hall.

Replaces *Fundamentals of Financial Management,* an excellent introductory text with sections on principles of financial returns, tools of financial analysis and planning, working capital management, investing in capital assets, capital structure and dividend policies, long-term financing and markets, and special areas including cash management models and options pricing.

Weston, J. Fred and Eugene F. Brigham. *Essentials of Managerial Finance.* 19th ed., Orlando, Florida: Dryden Press.

A fine introductory text emphasizing decision rather than theory, with sections on fundamental concepts; financial analysis, planning and control; working capital management; investment decisions; cost of capital and valuation; long-term financing decisions; and integrated topics in managerial finance.

Mutual Funds

Brouwer, Kurt. *Kurt Brouwer's Guide to Mutual Funds: How to Invest with the Pros.* New York: Wiley.

A fine book that explains how mutual funds work and discusses the best strategies for buying and selling them.

Coleman, Aaron H. and David H. Coleman. *How to Select Top-Performing Mutual Fund Investments.* New York: McGraw-Hill.

A guide to profitable mutual fund investing, with extensive performance data.

Herzfeld, Thomas J. *Herzfeld's Guide to Closed-End Funds.* New York: McGraw-Hill.

Everything you need to know about closed-end funds. Profiles more than 300 fund portfolios with analyses and rankings.

Jacobs, Sheldon. *The Handbook for No-Load Fund Investors.* New York: McGraw-Hill.

The definitive book on no-load mutual funds.

Taylor, John H. *Building Wealth with Mutual Funds.* New York: McGraw-Hill.

A step-by-step guide to investing in mutual funds, including international investing, index funds, variable annuity funds, and socially responsible funds.

Securities Markets, Securities Analysis, and Portfolio Management

Amling, Frederick. *Investments, An Introduction to Analysis and Management.* 6th ed. Englewood Cliffs: Prentice-Hall.

A text for the beginning investor or aspiring investment professional. Using practical cases to illustrate principles, the book deals with various aspects of fundamental analysis, modern portfolio theory, and technical analysis.

Brown, David L. and Kassandra Bentley. *Cyber-Investing, Cracking Wall Street with Your Personal Computer.* New York: Wiley.

Using computer programs and data bases to sort for stock opportunities and to time purchases and sales.

Cohen, Jerome B., Edward D. Zinbarg, and Arthur Zeikel. *Investment Analysis and Portfolio Management.* 5th ed. Burr Ridge, Illinois: Irwin Professional Publishing.

An introductory text, notable because it is comprehensive and discusses modern portfolio theory and security valuation techniques in a nonmathematical, readable way. It also covers the current investment scene and industry and company analysis.

Dreman, David. *The New Contrarian Investment Strategy.* New York: Random House.

An established title and modern classic on contrarian investment strategy by a noted contrarian and Forbes columnist.

Engel, Louis and Henry L. Hecht. *How to Buy Stocks.* 8th ed. New York: Little, Brown.

A highly readable, clear, and informative introduction to investing in the stock market, this book has been a deserved fixture in the literature of investing for several decades.

Graham, Benjamin. *The Intelligent Investor.* 4th rev. ed. New York: Harper Collins.

In The Money Masters (below), John Train says this book is "More useful for most readers [than Security Analysis:) and indeed the best book ever written for the stockholder. One is ill-advised to buy a bond or a share of stock without having read its pages."

Graham, Benjamin, David L. Dodd, and Sidney Cottle. *Securities Analysis: The Original 1934 Edition.* New York: McGraw-Hill.

This classic work remains the bible for students of the fundamentalist approach to securities analysis. It comprises six parts: survey and approach; analysis of financial statements; fixed-income securities; the valuation of common stocks; senior securities with speculative features; and other aspects of security analysis.

Little, Jeffrey and Lucian Rhodes. *Understanding Wall Street.* New York: Tab Books/McGraw-Hill.

The ubiquitous little green book that provides an education on how to evaluate stocks and bonds and how the brokerage industry works.

Lynch, Peter. *One Up on Wall Street.* New York: Simon & Schuster.

Down-to-earth investment advice from the legendary manager of Fidelity's Magellan Fund.

O'Higgins, Michael B. with John Downes. *Beating the Dow, A High-Return, Low-Risk Method for Investing in the Dow Jones Industrial Stocks with As Little As $5000.* New York: HarperPerennial.

One of the most influential investment books of the 1990s, this is a clearly written investment primer and discussion of the simple, highly successful and widely used investment strategy using high-yield Dow Jones industrials.

O'Shaughnessy, James P. *What Works on Wall Street.* New York: McGraw-Hill.

Investment tools and stock selection strategies are quantitatively tested over a 40-year period and the results discussed in a clear and readable fashion.

Pring, Martin. *Introduction to Technical Analysis.* New York: McGraw-Hill.

An introduction to the basics of technical analysis by the author of the classic *Technical Analysis Explained,* this chart-filled book explains traditional techniques as well as new analytical tools, such as momentum indicators, made possible by computers.

Schwager, Jack D. *The New Market Wizards; Conversations with America's Top Traders.* New York: Wiley.

A distinguished group of money managers discuss their secrets and methodologies.

Teweles, Richard J. and Edward S. Bradley. *The Stock Market.* 6th ed. New York: Wiley.

A revision of a work originally authored by George L. Leffler in 1951. It examines the stock market in five sections dealing with fundamental information, the exchanges, securities houses, regulations, investing practices, and special instruments.

Train, John. *The Money Masters.* New York: Harper Business.

Interesting stories, by an investment counselor, about the investment strategies of nine distinguished portfolio managers, such as T. Rowe Price, Benjamin Graham, and John Templeton, with commentary on their methods and personalities.

Train, John. *The New Money Masters.* New York: Harper Business.

A sequel to *The Money Masters* that profiles ten great contemporary investors, including Peter Lynch, John Neff, and George Soros.

Commodity and Financial Futures Markets

Frost, Ronald, J. *Options on Futures: A Hands-on Workbook of Market-Proven Trading Strategies.* Cedar Falls, Iowa: Oster Communications.

A clearly written explanation of the complex world of options on futures.

Kaufman, Perry J. *The New Commodity Trading Systems & Methods.* New York: Wiley.

An extensive reference guide dealing with individual commodities, including financial futures, and covering markets, forecasting, hedging, risk and money management, along with other technical aspects.

Lass, John P. and Sol Waksman. *Managed Futures Portfolio Strategies; Investment Analysis and the Evaluation and Selection of Commodity Trading Advisors.* New York: McGraw-Hill.

How to evaluate, select, and track the performance of a commodity trading advisor.

Powers, Mark J. *Starting Out in Futures Trading.* 5th ed. New York: McGraw-Hill.

A combination of theory and practical information for the beginner; includes history, exchanges, choosing a broker, trading programs, hedging, and forecasting. Covers financial futures.

Schwager, Jack D. *A Complete Guide to the Futures Markets: Fundamental Analysis, Technical Analysis, Trading, Spreads and Options.* New York: Wiley.

Assumes a basic familiarity with futures trading, but otherwise provides a non-technical discussion of various analytical techniques, including regression analysis and chart analysis. Has sample charts and a section on trading guidelines.

Siegel, Diane F. *The Futures Markets.* Orlando, Florida: Dryden Press.

A comprehensive study of the futures markets. Emphasizing the mechanics of futures trading; the theory of futures pricing; futures trading stretegies used for arbitrage, hedging, and speculation; and descriptions of all the major futures contracts.

Options Markets

Ansbacher, Max G. *The New Options Market.* rev. and enlarged ed. New York: Walker & Co.

An easy-to-read, yet comprehensive rundown, by a professional trader, of options and option strategies. For the speculator as well as the conservative investor.

Fabozzi, Frank J. and Gregory M. Kipnis, eds. *The Handbook of Stock Index Futures and Options.* Burr Ridge, Illinois: Irwin Professional Publishing.

Twenty-six chapters by recognized authorities cover strategies for using index futures and options in equity portfolio management and trading the market.

Gastineau, Gary L. *The Options Manual.* 3rd ed. New York: McGraw-Hill.

Assuming a basic knowledge of options and how they are used, Gastineau discusses option valuation methods and their applications in portfolio analysis and management. The book also covers option investment and trading strategies and tax implications.

McMillan, Lawrence G. *Options as a Strategic Investment.* Englewood Cliffs: Prentice-Hall.

An advanced discussion of option strategies, focusing on which ones work where and why. Includes chapters on arbitrage, mathematical applications, and tax ramifications.

Roth, Harrison. *LEAPS (Long-Term Equity AnticiPation Securities),* Burr Ridge, Illinois: Irwin Professional Publishing.

Written in easy-to-understand English with examples and summaries, this book covers the history, the risks, and the strategies possible with long-term options, a 1990s innovation.

Other Securities and General Investor Information

Amerman, Daniel R. *Mortgage Securities: The High-Yield Alternative to CDs, the Low-Risk Alternative to Stocks.* New York: McGraw-Hill.

How to invest in mortgage securities, which are the highest yielding of all government-issued securities. Covers mortgage-backed securities mutual funds, buying and selling individual mortgage-backed bonds; how prepayment risk is factored into bond prices, differences among Fannie Mae, Ginnie Mae, and other issuers of mortgage-backed securities.

Calamos, John P. *Investing in Convertible Securities: Your Complete Guide to the Risk and Rewards.* Chicago: Dearborn Financial Publishing.

A clearly written guide through the sometimes bewildering world of convertible securities.

Goodman, Jordan E. *Everyone's Money Book.* Chicago: Dearborn Financial Publishing, Inc.

A friendly, readable reference covering virtually every aspect of personal finance, with illustrations and recommended resources.

Lederman, Jess. *The Handbook of Asset-Backed Securities.* New York: New York Institute of Finance.

Mechanics and economics of asset-backed securities, including those backed by mortgages, credit cards, and auto loans.

CURRENCIES OF THE WORLD

This is a list of the currencies of most of the countries on earth. The countries are listed alphabetically, with the name of the currency, the symbol used to look up the currency on computerized foreign exchange systems, and the denomination that currency is broken down into. For example, one dollar is made up of 100 cents. This listing should be useful to anyone traveling or doing business in any of these countries.

Of course, the value of these currencies is constantly changing in relation to the amount of dollars necessary to buy them. For current exchange rates of the currencies of most major countries, one must consult the financial tables of newspapers such as the *Wall Street Journal* or London's *Financial Times*.

For the nations in Europe that are in the process of changing over their national currencies to the Euro, both currencies are listed. This changeover also affects the former colonies and dependencies of European states that had been using national currencies such as francs, marks, and pesetas. On January 1, 1999, the Euro will be introduced at the institutional level, such as for the issuance of public debt issues, for trade among corporations, and for stock market trading. On January 1, 2002, Euro banknotes and coins go into circulation and by July 1, 2002, all national notes and coins are scheduled to be withdrawn from circulation and replaced by Euros. The Euro will be denominated in cents, with 8 different coins from 1 cent to 2 Euros. Euronotes will be issued in denominations of 5, 10, 20, 50, 100, 200, and 500 Euros.

Afghanistan 1 afghani (Af) = 100 puls
Albania 1 lek (L) = 100 qintars
Algeria 1 Algerian dinar (DA) = 100 centimes
American Samoa 1 U.S. dollar (US$) = 100 cents
Andorra 1 Androran franc (F) = 100 centimes; (1/1 to French franc); 1 Andorran peseta (pta) = 100 centimos (1/1 to Spanish peseta); Euro
Angola 1 new kwanza (Kz) = 100 lwei
Anguilla 1 EC dollar (EC$) = 100 cents
Antarctica Each Antarctic base uses the currency of its home country
Antigua and Barbuda 1 EC dollar (EC$) = 100 cents
Argentina 1 austral (AA) = 100 centavos
Armenia 1 dram (Ar) = 100 luma

Aruba 1 Aruban guilder (also known as florin or gulden) (Af.) = 100 cents
Australia 1 Australian dollar (A$) = 100 cents
Austria 1 Austrian schilling (S) = 100 groschen; Euro
Azerbaijan 1 manat = 100 gopik
Bahamas 1 Bahamian dollar (B$) = 100 cents
Bahrain 1 Bahraini dinar (BD) = 1,000 fils
Bangladesh 1 taka (Tk) = 100 paisa (poisha)
Barbados 1 Barbadian dollar (Bds$) = 100 cents
Belarus Balarusian rubel (BR)
Belgium 1 Belgian franc (BF) = 100 centimes; Euro
Belize 1 Belizean dollar (BZ$) = 100 cents

Benin 1 CFA franc (CFAF) = 100 centimes; Euro

Bermuda 1 Bermudian dollar (Bd$) = 100 cents

Bhutan 1 ngultrum (Nu) = 100 chetrum; Indian currency also legal tender

Bolivia 1 boliviano (Bs) = 100 centavos

Bosnia 1 B.H. dinar = 100 para

Botswana 1 pula (P) = 100 thebe

Brazil 1 real (R$) = 100 centavos

British Virgin Islands 1 U.S. dollar (US$) = 100 cents

Brunei 1 ringgit, also known as Bruneian dollar (B$) = 100 sen or cents

Bulgaria 1 leva (Lv) = 100 stotinki

Burkina Faso 1 CFA franc (CFAF) = 100 centimes; Euro

Burma (see Myanmar)

Burundi 1 Burundi franc (FBu) = 100 centimes

Cambodia 1 new riel (CR) = 100 sen

Cameroon 1 CFA franc (CFAF) = 100 centimes; Euro

Canada 1 Canadian dollar (Can$) = 100 cents

Cape Verde Islands 1 Cape Verdean escudo (CVEsc) = 100 centavos

Cayman Islands 1 Caymanian dollar (CI$) = 100 cents

Central African Republic 1 CFA franc (CFAF) = 100 centimes; Euro

Chad 1 CFA franc (CFAF) = 100 centimes; Euro

Chile 1 Chilean peso (Ch$) = 100 centavos

China 1 yuan renminbi (Y) = 10 jiao = 100 fen

Christmas Island 1 Australian dollar (A$) = 100 cents

Cocos (Keeling) Islands 1 Australian dollar (A$) = 100 cents

Colombia 1 Colombian peso (Col$) = 100 centavos

Comoros 1 Comoran franc (CF) = 100 centimes; Euro

Congo, Democratic Republic of, 1 CFA franc (CFAF) = 100 centimes; Euro

Cook Islands 1 New Zealand dollar (NZ$) = 100 cents

Costa Rica 1 Costa Rican colon (C) = 100 centimos

Côte d'Ivoire 1 CFA franc (CFAF) = 100 centimes; Euro

Croatia 1 Croatian kuna (HRK) = 100 lipas

Cuba 1 Cuban peso (Cu$) = 100 centavos

Cyprus 1 Cypriot pound (£C) = 100 cents; Northern Cyprus = 1 Turkish lira (TL) = 100 kurus

Czech Republic 1 koruna (Kc) = 100 haleru

Denmark 1 Danish krone (DKr) = 100 øre

Djibouti 1 Djibouti franc (DF) = 100 centimes

Dominica 1 EC dollar (EC$) = 100 cents

Dominican Republic 1 Dominican peso (RD$) = 100 centavos

Ecuador 1 sucre (S/) = 100 centavos

Egypt 1 Egyptian pound (£E) = 100 piasters or 1,000 milliemes

El Salvador 1 Salvadoran colon (c) = 100 centavos

Equatorial Guinea 1 CFA franc (CFAF) = 100 centimes; Euro

Eritrea 1 birr (Br) = 100 cents

Estonia 1 Estonian kroon (KR) = 100 senti

Ethiopia 1 birr (Br) = 100 cents

European Union 1 Euro = 100 cents

Faeroe Islands 1 Danish krone (DKr) = 100 ore

Falkland Islands 1 Falkland pound (£F) = 100 pence

Fiji 1 Fijian dollar (F$) = 100 cents

Finland 1 markka (Mk) = 100 penniä; Euro

France 1 French franc (F) = 100 centimes; Euro

French Guiana 1 French franc (F) = 100 centimes; Euro

French Polynesia 1 CFP franc (CFPF) = 100 centimes; Euro

Gabon 1 CFA franc (CFAF) = 100 centimes; Euro

Gambia 1 dalasi (D) = 100 butut

Gaza 1 new Israeli shekel (NIS) = 100 new agorot; 1 Jordanian dinar (JD) = 1,000 fils

Georgia 1 lari (Gl) = 100 tetri

Germany 1 deutsche mark (DM) = 100 pfennig; Euro

Ghana 1 new cedi (c) = 100 psewas

Gibraltar 1 Gibraltar pound (£G) = 100 pence
Great Britain 1 pound (£) = 100 pence
Greece 1 drachma (Dr) = 100 lepta
Greenland 1 Danish krone (DKr) = 100 ore
Grenada 1 EC dollar (EC$) = 100 cents
Guadeloupe 1 French franc (F) = 100 centimes; Euro
Guam 1 U.S. dollar (US$) = 100 cents
Guatemala 1 quetzal (Q) = 100 centavos
Guernsey 1 pound (£) = 100 pence
Guinea 1 Guinean franc (FG) = 10 francs; 1 franc = 100 centimes
Guinea-Bissau 1 Guinea-Bissau franc (CFAF) = 100 centimes; Euro
Guyana 1 Guyanese dollar (G$) = 100 cents
Haiti 1 gourde (G) = 100 centimes
Honduras 1 lempira (L) = 100 centavos
Hong Kong 1 Hong Kong dollar (HK$) = 100 cents
Hungary 1 forint (Ft)
Iceland 1 Icelandic krona (IKr) = 100 aurar
India 1 rupee (Rs) = 100 paise
Indonesia 1 rupiah (Rp) = 100 sen
Iran 1 rial (Rls) = 100 dinars = 0.1 toman
Iraq 1 dinar (ID) = 1,000 fils
Ireland 1 Irish pound or punt (IR£) = 100 pence or pingin; Euro
Israel 1 new shekel (NIS) = 100 new agorot
Italy 1 lira (Lit) = 100 centesimi; Euro
Jamaica 1 Jamaican dollar (J$) = 100 cents
Japan 1 yen (¥) = 100 sen
Jersey 1 pound (£) = 100 pence
Jordan 1 Jordanian dinar (JD) = 1,000 fils
Kazakhstan 1 tenge (KZT) = 100 tiyn
Kenya 1 Kenyan shilling (KSh) = 100 cents
Kiribati 1 Australian dollar (A$) = 100 cents
Korea, North 1 North Korean won (Wn) = 100 chon
Korea, South 1 South Korean won (W) = 100 chon
Kuwait 1 Kuwaiti dinar (KD) = 1,000 fils

Kyrgyzstan 1 som = 100 tyyn
Laos 1 new kip (NK) = 100 at
Latvia 1 lat (Ls) = 100 santims
Lebanon 1 Lebanese pound (£L) = 100 piastres
Lesotho 1 loti (L) = 100 lisente
Liberia 1 Liberian dollar (L$) = 100 cents
Libya 1 Libyan dinar (LD) = 1,000 dirhams
Liechtenstein 1 Swiss franc (SwF) = 100 centimes
Lithuania 1 litas (L) = 100 centu
Luxembourg 1 Luxembourg franc (LuxF) = 100 centimes; Euro
Macau 1 pataca (P) = 100 avos
Macedonia, the Former Yugoslav Republic of denar
Madagascar 1 Malagasy franc (FMG) = 100 centimes
Malawi 1 Malawian kwacha (MK) = 100 tambala
Malaysia 1 ringgit (RM) = 100 sen
Maldives 1 rufiyaa (Rf) = 100 lari
Mali 1 CFA franc (CFAF) = 100 centimes; Euro
Malta 1 Maltese lira (£M) = 100 cents
Man, Isle of 1 pound (£M) = 100 pence
Marshall Islands 1 U.S. dollar (US$) = 100 cents
Martinique 1 French franc (F) = 100 centimes; Euro
Mauritania 1 ouguiya (UM) = 5 khoums
Mauritius 1 Mauritian rupee (MauR) = 100 cents
Mayotte 1 French franc (F) = 100 centimes
Mexico 1 New Mexican peso (MEX$) = 100 centavos
Micronesia, Federated States of, 1 U.S. dollar (US$) = 100 cents
Moldova leu, plural = lei
Monaco 1 French franc (F) = 100 centimes
Mongolia 1 tughrik (Tug) = 100 mongos
Montserrat 1 EC dollar (EC$) = 100 cents
Morocco 1 Moroccan dirham (DH) = 100 centimes
Mozambique 1 metical (Mt) = 100 centavos

Myanmar 1 kyat (K) = 100 pyas

Namibia 1 Namibian dollar (N$) = 100 cents

Nauru 1 Australian dollar (A$) = 100 cents

Nepal 1 Nepalese rupee (NRs) = 100 paise

Netherlands 1 Netherlands guilder, gulden, or florin = 100 cents; Euro

Netherlands Antilles 1 Netherlands Antillean guilder, gulden, or florin (NAf. or Ant.f) = 100 cents

New Caledonia 1 CFP franc (CFPF) = 100 centimes; Euro

New Zealand 1 New Zealand dollar (NZ$) = 100 cents

Nicaragua 1 gold cordoba (C$) = 100 centavos

Niger 1 CFA franc (CFAF) = 100 centimes; Euro

Nigeria 1 naira (N) = 100 kobo

Niue 1 New Zealand dollar (NZ$) = 100 cents

Norfolk Island 1 Australian dollar (A$) = 100 cents

Northern Mariana Islands 1 U.S. dollar (US$) = 100 cents

Norway 1 Norwegian krone (NKr) = 100 øre

Oman 1 Omani rial (RO) = 1,000 baizas

Pacific Islands, Trust Territory of the, 1 U.S. dollar (US$) = 100 cents

Pakistan 1 Pakistani rupee (Rs) = 100 paisa

Panama 1 balboa (B) = 100 centesimos

Papua New Guinea 1 kina (K) = 100 toeas

Paraguay 1 guarani (G) = 100 centimos

Peru 1 nuevo sol (S/.) = 100 centimos

Philippines 1 Philippine peso (P) = 100 centavos

Pitcairn Islands 1 New Zealand dollar (NZ$) = 100 cents

Poland 1 zloty (Zl) = 100 groszy

Portugal 1 Portuguese escudo (Esc) = 100 centavos; Euro

Puerto Rico 1 U.S. dollar (US$) = 100 cents

Qatar 1 Qatari riyal (QR) = 100 dirhams

Réunion 1 French franc (F) = 100 centimes

Romania 1 leu (L) = 100 bani

Russia 1 ruble (R) = 100 kopeks

Rwanda 1 Rwandan franc (RF) = 100 centimes; Euro

Saint Helena 1 Saint Helenian pound (£S) = 100 pence

Saint Kitts-Nevis 1 EC dollar (EC$) = 100 cents

Saint Lucia 1 EC dollar (EC$) = 100 cents

Saint Pierre and Miquelon 1 French franc (F) = 100 centimes; Euro

Saint Vincent and the Grenadines 1 EC dollar (EC$) = 100 cents

Samoa (Western) 1 tola (WS$) = sene

San Marino 1 Italian lire (Lit) = 100 centesimi; Euro

Saõ Tomé and Principe 1 dobra (Db) = 100 centimos

Saudi Arabia 1 Saudi riyal (SRls) = 100 halalas

Senegal 1 CFA franc (CFAF) = 100 centimes; Euro

Serbia 1 Yugoslav New Dinar (YD) = 100 paras

Seychelles 1 Seychelles rupee (SR) = 100 cents

Sierra Leone 1 leone (Le) = 100 cents

Singapore 1 Singapore dollar (S$) = 100 cents

Slovakia 1 koruna (Sk) = 100 haliers

Slovenia 1 tolar (SIT) = 100 stotinov

Solomon Islands 1 Solomon Islands dollar (SI$) = 100 cents

Somalia 1 Somali shilling (So.Sh.) = 100 centesimi

South Africa 1 rand (R) = 100 cents

Spain 1 peseta (Ptas) = 100 centimos; Euro

Sri Lanka 1 Sri Lankan rupee (SLRs) = 100 cents

Sudan 1 Sudanese pound (£Sd) = 100 piastres

Suriname 1 Surinamese guilder, gulden, or florin (Sf. or Sur.f.) = 100 cents; Euro

Svalbard 1 Norwegian krone (NKr) = 100 ore; Euro

Swaziland 1 lilangeni (L) = 100 cents

Sweden 1 Swedish krona (SK) = 100 ore

Switzerland 1 Swiss franc (SwF) = 100 centimes or rappen

Syria 1 Syrian pound (£S) = 100 piasters

Taiwan 1 New Taiwan dollar (NT$) = 100 cents

Tajikistan 1 ruble (R) = 100 kopeks

Tanzania 1 Tanzanian shilling (TSh) = 100 cents

Thailand 1 baht (Bht) = 100 sastangs

Togo 1 CFA franc (CFAF) = 100 centimes; Euro

Tokelau 1 New Zealand dollar (NZ$) = 100 cents

Tonga 1 pa'anga (T$) = 100 sentini

Trinidad and Tobago 1 Trinidad and Tobago dollar (TT$) = 100 cents

Tunisia 1 Tunisian dinar (TD) = 1,000 millimes

Turkey 1 Turkish lira (TL) = 100 kurus

Turkmenistan 1 manat (Tm) = tenga

Turks and Caicos Islands 1 U.S. dollar (US$) = 100 cents

Tuvalu 1 Tuvaluan dollar ($T) or 1 Australian dollar (A$) = 100 cents

Uganda 1 Ugandan shilling (USh) = 100 cents

Ukraine 1 Hryvnia (H) = 100 kopiykas

United Arab Emirates 1 Emirian dirham (Dh) = 100 fils

United Kingdom 1 British pound (£) = 100 pence

United States of America 1 U.S. dollar (US$) = 100 cents

Uruguay 1 Uraguayan peso ($U) = 100 centésimos

Uzbekistan 1 som (Us) = 100 tiyin

Vanuatu 1 vatu (VT) = 100 centimes

Vatican 1 lira (Lit) = 100 centesimi; Euro

Venezuela 1 bolivar (Bs) = 100 centimos

Vietnam 1 new dong (D) = 100 xu or 100 hao

Virgin Islands 1 U.S. dollar (US$) = 100 cents

Wake Island 1 U.S. dollar (US$) = 100 cents

Wallis and Futuna Islands 1 CFP franc (CFPF) = 100 centimes; Euro

Western Sahara 1 Moroccan dirham (DH) = 100 centimes

Western Samoa 1 tala (WS$) = 100 sene

Yemen 1 Yemeni rial (YRls) = 100 fils

Yugoslavia 1 new dinar (Din) = 100 paras

Zaire See Congo, Democratic Republic of

Zambia 1 Zambian kwacha (ZK) = 100 ngwee

Zimbabwe 1 Zimbabwean dollar (Z$) = 100 cents

ABBREVIATIONS AND ACRONYMS

A

A Includes Extra (or Extras) (in stock listings of newspapers)

AAII American Association of Individual Investors

AB Aktiebolag (Swedish stock company)

ABA American Bankers Association

ABA American Bar Association

ABLA American Business Law Association

ABS Automated Bond System

ABWA American Business Women's Association

ACE AMEX Commodities Exchange

ACRS Accelerated Cost Recovery System

A-D Advance-Decline Line

ADB Adjusted Debit Balance

ADR American Depositary Receipt

ADR Automatic Dividend Reinvestment

ADRS Asset Depreciation Range System

ADS American Depositary Shares

AE Account Executive

AFL-CIO American Federation of Labor-Congress of Industrial Organizations

AICPA American Institute of Certified Public Accountants

AID Agency for International Development

AIM American Institute for Management

AG Aktiengesellschaft (German stock company)

AGI Adjusted Gross Income

AIP Automatic Investment Program

AMA American Management Association

AMA Asset Management Account

AMBAC American Municipal Bond Assurance Corporation

AMEX American Stock Exchange

AMPS Auction Market Preferred Stock

AMT Alternative Minimum Tax

AON All or None

APB Accounting Principles Board

APR Annual Percentage Rate

APS Auction Preferred Stock

ARB Airport Revenue Bond

Arb Arbitrageur

ARF American Retail Federation

ARM Adjustable Rate Mortgage

ARPS Adjustable Rate Preferred Stock

ART Annual Renewable Term (insurance)

ASAP As Soon as Possible

ASE American Stock Exchange

ASE Amsterdam Stock Exchange

ASPIRIN Australian Stock Price Riskless Indexed Notes

ASX Australia Stock Exchange

ATM Automatic Teller Machine

ATP Arbitrage Trading Program

B

B Annual Rate Plus Stock Dividend (in stock listings of newspapers)

BAC Business Advisory Council

BAN Bond Anticipation Note

BBB Better Business Bureau

BD Bank Draft

BD Bills Discontinued

B/D Broker-Dealer

BE Bill of Exchange

BEACON Boston Exchange Automated Communication Order-routing Network

BEARS Bond Enabling Annual Retirement Savings

BF Brought Forward
BFP Basic Formula Price (milk)
BIC Bank Investment Contract
BIF Bank Insurance Fund
BL Bill of Lading
BLS Bureau of Labor Statistics
BMA Bond Market Association
BO Branch Office
BO Buyer's Option
BOM Beginning of the Month
BOP Balance of Payments
BOT Balance of Trade
BOT Bought
BOT Board of Trustees
BOVESPA Bolsa de Valores de Sao Paulo
BPW Business and Professional Women's Foundation
BR Bills Receivable
BS Balance Sheet
BS Bill of Sale
BS Bureau of Standards
BSE Boston Stock Exchange
BSE Brussels Stock Exchange
BTCI Bankers Trust Commodity Index
BVRJ Bolsa de Valores de Rio de Janiero
BW Bid Wanted

C

C Liquidating Dividend (in stock listings of newspapers)
CA Capital Account
CA Chartered Accountant
CA Commercial Agent
CA Credit Account
CA Current Account
CACM Central American Common Market
CAD Cash against Documents
CAF Cost Assurance and Freight
CAMPS Cumulative Auction Market Preferred Stocks
C&F Cost and Freight
CAPM Capital Asset Pricing Model
CAPS Convertible Adjustable Preferred Stock
CARDS Certificates for Amortizing Revolving Debts
CARs Certificate for Automobile Receivables
CATS Certificate of Accrual on Treasury Securities

CATV Community Antenna Television
CBA Capital Builder Account
CBA Cost Benefit Analysis
CBD Cash Before Delivery
CBO Collateralized Bond Obligation
CBOE Chicago Board Options Exchange
CBT Chicago Board of Trade
CC Chamber of Commerce
CCH Commerce Clearing House
CD Certificate of Deposit
CD Commercial Dock
CDN Canadian Dealing Network
CEA Council of Economic Advisors
CEO Chief Executive Officer
CF Certificates (in bond listings of newspapers)
CF Carried Forward
CFA Chartered Financial Analyst
CFC Chartered Financial Counselor
CFC Consolidated Freight Classification
CFI Cost, Freight, and Insurance
CFO Chief Financial Officer
CFP Certified Financial Planner
CFTC Commodities Futures Trading Commission
CH Clearing House
CH Custom House
ChFC Chartered Financial Consultant
CHX Chicago Stock Exchange
Cía Compañía (Spanish company)
Cie Compagnie (French company)
CIF Corporate Income Fund
CIF Cost, Insurance, and Freight
CIPs Cash Index Participations
CLD Called (in stock listings of newspapers)
CLN Construction Loan Note
CLU Chartered Life Underwriter
CME Chicago Mercantile Exchange
CMO Collateralized Mortgage Obligation
CMV Current Market Value
CN Consignment Note
CN Credit Note
CNS Continuous Net Settlement
CO Cash Order
CO Certificate of Origin
Co. Company
COB Close of Business (with date)
COBRA Consolidated Omnibus Budget Reconciliation Act

COD Cash on Delivery
COD Collect on Delivery
CODA Cash or Deferred Arrangement
COFI Cost of Funds Index
COLA Cost-of-Living Adjustment
COLTS Continuously Offered Longer-Term Securities
COMEX Commodity Exchange (New York)
COMSAT Communications Satellite Corporation
CONNIE LEE College Construction Loan Insurance Association
COO Chief Operating Officer
CPA Certified Public Accountant
CPCI Chase Physical Commodity Index
CPD Commissioner of Public Debt
CPPF Cost Plus Fixed Fee
CPI Consumer Price Index
CPM Cost per Thousand
CPPC Cost plus a Percentage of Cost
CR Carrier's Risk
CR Class Rate
CR Company's Risk
CR Current Rate
CRB Commodity Research Bureau
CRT Charitable Remainder Trust
CSCE Coffee, Sugar and Cocoa Exchange
CSE Cincinnati Stock Exchange
CSE Copenhagen Stock Exchange
CSVLI Cash Surrender Value of Life Insurance
CUBS Calls Underwritten by Swanbrook
CUNA Credit Union National Association
CUSIP Committee on Uniform Securities Identification Procedures
CV Convertible Security (in bond and stock listings of newspapers)
CWO Cash with Order

D

DA Deposit Account
DA Documents against Acceptance
DAC Delivery against Cost
DAF Defined Asset Fund
D&B Dun and Bradstreet
DAPS Dutch Auction Preferred Stock
DBA Doing Business As

DC Deep Discount Issue (in bond listings of newspapers)
DCFM Discounted Cash Flow Method
DDB Double-Declining-Balance Depreciation Method
DENKS Dual-Employed, No Kids
DEWKS Dual Employed, With Kids
DF Damage Free
DIDC Depository Institutions Deregulatory Committee
DINKS Dual-Income, No Kids
DISC Domestic International Sales Corporation
DJIA Dow Jones Industrial Average
DJTA Dow Jones Transportation Average
DJUA Dow Jones Utility Average
DK Don't Know
DN Debit Note
DNI Do Not Increase
DNR Do Not Reduce
D/O Delivery Order
DOT Designated Order Turnaround
DP Documents against Payment
DPI Disposable Personal Income
DS Days After Sight
DTB Deutsche Terminbourse
DTC Depository Trust Company
DUNS Data Universal Numbering System (Dun's Number)
DVP Delivery Versus Payment

E

E Declared or Paid in the Preceding 12 Months (in stock listings of newspapers)
EAFE Europe and Australasia, Far East Equity Index
E&OE Errors and Omissions Excepted
EBIT Earnings Before Interest and Taxes
EBITA Earnings Before Interest, Taxes, Depreciation, and Amortization
EBS Swiss Electronic Bourse
EC European Community
ECB European Central Bank
ECM Emerging Company Marketplace
ECM European Common Market
ECOA Equal Credit Opportunity Act
ECT Estimated Completion Time

ECU European Currency Unit
EDD Estimated Delivery Date
EEC European Economic Community
EEOC Equal Employment Opportunity Commission
EMF INDEX Emerging Market Free Index
EMP End-of-Month Payment
EMS European Monetary System
ENMET Energy and Metals Index
EOA Effective On or About
EOD Every Other Day (advertising)
EOE European Options Exchange
EOM End of Month
EPR Earnings Price Ratio
EPS Earnings Per Share
ERISA Employee Retirement Income Security Act of 1974
ERM Exchange Rate Mechanism
ERTA Economic Recovery Tax Act of 1981
ESOP Employee Stock Ownership Plan
ESP Exchange Stock Portfolio
ETA Estimated Time of Arrival
ETD Estimated Time of Departure
ETLT Equal To or Less Than
ETM Escrowed to Maturity
ETS Energy Trading System (on the International Petroleum Exchange)
EU European Union
EXIMBANK Export-Import Bank

F

F Dealt in Flat (in bond listings in newspapers)
FA Free Alongside
FACT Factor Analysis Chart Technique
F&F Furniture and Fixtures
FAS Free Alongside
FASB Financial Accounting Standards Board
FAT Fixed Asset Transfer
FAX Facsimile
FB Freight Bill
FCA Fellow of the Institute of Chartered Accountants
FCBA Fair Credit Billing Act
FCC Federal Communications Commission
FCFAC Federal Credit Financial Assistance Corporation

FCRA Fair Credit Reporting Act
FCUA Federal Credit Union Administration
FDIC Federal Deposit Insurance Corporation
Fed Federal Reserve System
FET Federal Excise Tax
FFB Federal Financing Bank
FFCS Federal Farm Credit System
FGIC Financial Guaranty Insurance Corporation
FHA Farmers Home Administration
FHA Federal Housing Administration
FHFB Federal Housing Finance Board
FHLBB Federal Home Loan Bank Board
FHLMC Federal Home Loan Mortgage Corporation (Freddie Mac)
FIBOR Frankfurt Interbank Offered Rate
FICA Federal Insurance Contributions Act
FICB Federal Intermediate Credit Bank
FICO Financing Corporation
FIFO First In, First Out
FINEX Financial Derivatives Division of New York Cotton Exchange
FIRREA Financial Institutions Reform and Recovery Act
FIT Federal Income Tax
FITW Federal Income Tax Withholding
FLB Federal Land Bank
FLEX Flexible Exchange Options
FMAN February, May, August, November Cycle
FMC Federal Maritime Commission
FNMA Federal National Mortgage Association (Fannie Mae)
FOB Free on Board
FOC Free of Charge
FOCUS Financial and Operations Combined Uniform Single Report
FOI Freedom of Information Act
FOK Fill or Kill
FOMC Federal Open Market Committee
FOOTSIE Financial Times-SE 100 Index of U.K. Stocks
FOR Free on Rail (or Road)

FOT Free on Truck
FOX Finnish Options Index
FP Floating Policy
FP Fully Paid
FPM Fixed-Payment Mortgage
FRA Federal Reserve Act
FRB Federal Reserve Bank
FRB Federal Reserve Board
FRD Federal Reserve District
FREDDIE MAC Federal Home Loan Mortgage Corporation
FREIT Finite Life REIT
FRS Federal Reserve System
FS Final Settlement
FSC Foreign Sales Corporation
FSLIC Federal Savings and Loan Insurance Corporation
FTC Federal Trade Commission
FTI Federal Tax Included
FUTA Federal Unemployment Tax Act
FVO For Valuation Only
FX Foreign Exchange
FY Fiscal Year
FYA For Your Attention
FYI For Your Information

G

G Dividends and Earnings in Canadian Dollars (in stock listings of newspapers)
GAAP Generally Accepted Accounting Principles
GAAS Generally Accepted Auditing Standards
GAI Guaranteed Annual Income
GAO General Accounting Office
GATT General Agreement on Tariffs and Trade
GDP Gross Domestic Product
GDR Global Depositary Receipt
G-8 Group of Eight Finance Ministers
GEM Growing Equity Mortgage
GIC Guaranteed Investment Contract
GINNIE MAE Government National Mortgage Association
GIT Guaranteed Income (or Investment) Contract
GM General Manager
GmbH Gesellschaft mit beschränkter Haftung (German limited liability company)
GNMA Government National Mortgage Association

GNP Gross National Product
GO General Obligation Bond
GPM Graduated Payment Mortgage
GRIT Grantor Retained Income Trust
GSA General Services Administration
GSCI Goldman Sachs Commodity Index
GSE Government Sponsored Entity
GTC Good Till Canceled
GTM Good This Month
GTW Good This Week
GULP Group Universal Life Policy

H

H Declared or Paid After Stock Dividend or Split-Up (in stock listings of newspapers)
HEL Home Equity Loan
HEX Helsinki Stock and Derivatives Exchange
H/F Held For
HFR Hold for Release
HIBOR Hong Kong Interbank Offered Rate
HLT Highly Leveraged Transaction
HO Home Owner's Insurance Policy
HQ Headquarters
HR U.S. House of Representatives
HR U.S. House of Representatives Bill (with number)
HUD Department of Housing and Urban Development

I

I Paid This Year, Dividend Omitted, Deferred, or No Action Taken at Last Dividend Meeting (in stock listings of newspapers)
IAFP International Association for Financial Planning
I/B/E/S Institutional Broker's Estimate System
I-Bonds Inflation-indexed Savings Bonds
IBRD International Bank for Reconstruction and Development (World Bank)
ICC Interstate Commerce Commission
ICFP Institute of Certified Financial Planners
ICFTU International Confederation of Free Trade Unions

ICI Investable Commodity Index
ICI Investment Company Institute
ICMA Institute of Cost and Management Accountants
IDB Industrial Development Bond
IDEM Italian Derivatives Market
IET Interest Equalization Tax
IFC International Finance Corporation
ILA International Longshoremen's Association
ILGWU International Ladies' Garment Workers' Union
ILO International Labor Organization
IMF International Monetary Fund
IMM International Monetary Market of the Chicago Mercantile Exchange
Inc. Incorporated
INSTINET Institutional Networks Corporation
IO Interest Only
IOC Immediate-or-Cancel Order
IOU I Owe You
IPE International Petroleum Exchange
IPO Initial Public Offering
IR Investor Relations
IRA Individual Retirement Account
IRB Industrial Revenue Bond
IRC Internal Revenue Code
IRR Internal Rate of Return
IRS Internal Revenue Service
ISBN International Standard Book Number
ISE International Stock Exchange of the U.K. and the Republic of Ireland
ISE Italian Stock Exchange
ISIS Intermarket Surveillance Information System
ISO Incentive Stock Option
ISRO International Securities Regulatory Organization
ISSN International Standard Serial Number
ITC Investment Tax Credit
ITS Intermarket Trading System

J

JA Joint Account
JAJO January, April, July, October Cycle
Jeep Graduated Payment Mortgage

JPMCI J.P. Morgan Commodity Index
JSE Johannesburg Stock Exchange
JTWROS Joint Tenancy With Right of Survivorship

K

K Declared or Paid This Year on a Cumulative Issue with Dividends in Arrears (in stock listings of newspapers)
K Kilo- (prefix meaning multiplied by one thousand)
KCBT Kansas City Board of Trade
KD Knocked Down (disassembled)
KIBOR Kuala Lumpur Interbank Offered Rate
KK Kabushiki-Kaisha (Japanese stock company)
KLOFFE Kuala Lumpur Options & Financial Futures Exchange (Barhad)
KLSE Kuala Lumpur Stock Exchange
KW Kilowatt
KWH Kilowatt-hour
KYC Know Your Customer Rule

L

L Listed (securities)
LBO Leveraged Buyout
L/C Letter of Credit
LCL Less-Than-Carload Lot
LCM Least Common Multiple (mathematics)
LDC Less Developed Country
LEAPS Long-Term Equity Anticipation Securities
LEI Leading Economic Indicators
LESOP Leveraged Employee Stock Ownership Plan
L/I Letter of Intent
LIBOR London Interbank Offered Rate
LIFFE London International Financial Futures and Options Exchange
LIFO Last In, First Out
LISBOR Lisbon Interbank Offered Rate
LME London Metal Exchange
LMRA Labor-Management Relations Act
LP Limited Partnership

LSE Lisbon Stock Exchange
LSE London Stock Exchange
Ltd Limited (British corporation)
LTV Loan to Value

M

M Matured Bonds (in bond listings in newspapers)
M Milli- (prefix meaning divided by one thousand)
M Mega- (prefix meaning multiplied by one million)
M One Thousand (Roman numeral)
MACD Moving Average Convergence/Divergence
MACRS Modified Accelerated Cost Recovery System
M&L Matched and Lost
MATIF Marche a Terme International de France
Max Maximum
MBA Master of Business Administration
MBIA Municipal Bond Insurance Association
MBO Management by Objective
MBS Mortgage-Backed Security
MC Marginal Credit
M-CATS Municipal Certificates of Accrual on Tax-exempt Securities
MCE Malaysia Commodity Exchange
MD Months After Date
ME Montreal Exchange/Bourse de Montreal
MFN Most Favored Nation (tariff regulations)
MGE Minneapolis Grain Exchange
MGM Milligram
MHR Member of the U.S. House of Representatives
MIBOR Madrid Interbank Offered Rate
MICEX Moscow Interbank Currency
MIF Mercato Italiano Futures Exchange
MIG-1 Moody's Investment Grade
MIMC Member of the Institute of Management Consultants
Min Minimum
MIS Management Information System
Misc Miscellaneous
MIT Market if Touched

MIT Municipal Investment Trust
MJSD March, June, September, December Cycle
MLP Master Limited Partnership
MLR Minimum Lending Rate
MM Millimeter (metric unit)
MMDA Money Market Deposit Account
MO Money Order
MOB Municipals Over Bonds
MOC Market-on-Close Order
MONEP Marche des Options Negociables de Paris
MPC Market Performance Committee
MSA Medical Savings Account
MSB Mutual Savings Bank
MSCI Morgan Stanley Capital International
MSE Madrid Stock Exchange (Bolsa de Madrid)
MSE Mexican Stock Exchange
MSRB Municipal Securities Rulemaking Board
MTN Medium-term Note
MTU Metric Units
MUD Municipal Utility District

N

N New Issue (in stock listings of newspapers)
NA National Association (National Bank)
NAFTA North American Free Trade Agreement
NAIC National Association of Investors Corporation
NAM National Association of Manufacturers
NAPA National Association of Purchasing Agents
NAPFA National Association of Personal Financial Advisors
NAPM National Association of Purchasing Management
NAR National Association of Realtors
NASA National Aeronautics and Space Administration
NASD National Association of Securities Dealers
NASDAQ National Association of Securities Dealers Automated Quotation

NATO North Atlantic Treaty Organization
NAV Net Asset Value
NBS National Bureau of Standards
NC No Charge
NCUA National Credit Union Administration
NCV No Commercial Value
ND Next Day Delivery (in stock listings of newspapers)
NEMS National Exchange Market System
NEO Nonequity Options
NFCC National Foundation for Consumer Credit
NH Not Held
NIC Net Interest Cost
NICS Newly Industrialized Countries
NIP Normal Investment Practice
NIT Negative Income Tax
NL No Load
NLRA National Labor Relations Act
NLRB National Labor Relations Board
NMAB National Market Advisory Board
NMB National Mediation Board
NMS National Market System
NMS Normal Market Size
NNP Net National Product
NOB Notes Over Bonds
NOL Net Operating Loss
NOW National Organization for Women
NOW Negotiable Order of Withdrawal
NP No Protest (banking)
NP Notary Public
N/P Notes Payable
NPV Net Present Value
NPV No Par Value
NQB National Quotation Bureau
NQB No Qualified Bidders
NR Not Rated
NSBA National Small Business Association
NSCC National Securities Clearing Corporation
NSE National Stock Exchange (India)
NSF Not Sufficient Funds (banking)
NSTS National Securities Trading System
NTU Normal Trading Unit

NV Naamloze Vennootschap (Dutch corporation)
NYCE New York Cotton Exchange
NYCSCE New York Coffee, Sugar and Cocoa Exchange
NYFE New York Futures Exchange
NYMEX New York Mercantile Exchange
NYSE New York Stock Exchange
NYZE New Zealand Stock Exchange
NZFOE New Zealand Futures and Options Exchange

O

O Old (in options listing of newspapers)
OAPEC Organization of Arab Petroleum Exporting Countries
OB Or Better
OBV On-Balance Volume
OCC Option Clearing Corporation
OD Overdraft, overdrawn
ODE Oporto Derivatives Exchange (Bolsa de Derivados de Oporto) in Portugal
OECD Organization for Economic Cooperation and Development
OEX Standard & Poor's 100 Stock Index
OID Original Issue Discount
OMB Office of Management and Budget
OMLX London Securities and Derivatives Exchange
OPD Delayed Opening
OPEC Organization of Petroleum Exporting Countries
OPM Options Pricing Model
OPM Other People's Money
OSE Oslo Stock Exchange
O/T Overtime
OTC Over the Counter
OTS Office of Thrift Supervision
OW Offer Wanted

P

P Paid this Year (in stock listings of newspapers)
P Put (in options listings of newspapers)
PA Power of Attorney
PA Public Accountant
PA Purchasing Agent

PAC Planned Amortization Class
PAC Put and Call (options market)
PACE Philadelphia Automated Communication and Execution System
PAL Passive Activity Loss
P&I Principal and Interest
P&L Profit and Loss Statement
PAYE Pay as You Earn
PBGC Pension Benefit Guaranty Corporation
PBOT Philadelphia Board of Trade
PBR Price-to-Book Value Ratio
PC Participation Certificates
PCX Pacific Exchange
PE Price Earnings Ratio (in stock listings of newspapers)
PEFC Private Export Funding Corporation
PER Price Earnings Ratio
PERCS Preferred Equity Redemption Cumulative Stock
PERLS Principal Exchange-Rate-Linked Securities
PFD Preferred Stock
PHLX Philadelphia Stock Exchange
PIG Passive Income Generator
PIK Securities Payment-in-Kind Securities
PIN Personal Identification Number
PITI Principal, Interest, Taxes, and Insurance
PL Price List
PLC Public Liability Company
PLC (British) Public Limited Company
PMI Private Mortgage Insurance
PMV Private Market Value
PN Project Note
PN Promissory Note
PO Principal Only
POA Power of Attorney
POD Pay on Delivery
POE Port of Embarkation
POE Port of Entry
POR Pay on Return
PPI Producer Price Index
PPP Penultimate Profit Prospect
PPS Prior Preferred Stock
PR Public Relations
PRE-RE Pre-refunded Municipal Note
PRIME Prescribed Right to Income and Maximum Equity
Prop Proprietor

PSE Philippine Stock Exchange
PSR Price/Sales Ratio
PUC Public Utilities Commission
PUHCA Public Utility Holding Company Act of 1935
PVR Profit/Volume Ratio

Q

QB Qualified Buyers
QC Quality Control
QI Quarterly Index
QT Questioned Trade
QTIP Qualified Terminable Interest Property Trust

R

R Declared or Paid in the Preceding 12 Months plus Stock Dividend (in stock listings of newspapers)
R Option Not Traded (in option listings in newspapers)
RAM Reverse Annuity Mortgage
RAN Revenue Anticipation Note
R&D Research and Development
RCIA Retail Credit Institute of America
RCMM Registered Competitive Market Maker
REA Rural Electrification Administration
REDs Refunding Escrow Deposits
REFCORP Resolution Funding Corporation
REIT Real Estate Investment Trust
RELP Real Estate Limited Partnership
REMIC Real Estate Mortgage Investment Conduit
Repo Repurchase Agreement
RIA Registered Investment Adviser
RICO Racketeer Influenced and Corrupt Organization Act
ROC Return on Capital
ROE Return on Equity
ROI Return on Investment (Return on Invested Capital)
ROL Reduction-Option Loan
ROP Registered Options Principal
ROS Return on Sales
RP Repurchase Agreement
RPA Retirement Protection Act of 1994
RRP Reverse Repurchase Agreement

RRSP Registered Retirement Savings Plan
RT Royalty Trust
RTC Resolution Trust Corporation
RTS Russian Trading System
RTW Right to Work

S

S No Option Offered (in option listings of newspapers)
S Signed (before signature on typed copy of a document, original of which was signed)
S Split or Stock Dividend (in stock listings of newspapers)
SA Sociedad Anónima (Spanish corporation)
SA Société Anonyme (French corporation)
SAA Special Arbitrage Account
SAB Special Assessment Bond
SAFEX South African Futures Exchange
SAIF Savings Association Insurance Fund
SALLIE MAE Student Loan Marketing Association
SAM Shared Appreciation Mortgage
S&L Savings and Loan
S&L Sale and Leaseback
S&P Standard & Poor's
SAX Stockholm Automatic Exchange
SB Savings Bond
SB U.S. Senate Bill (with number)
SB Short Bill
SBA Small Business Administration
SBIC Small Business Investment Corporation
SBLI Savings Bank Life Insurance
SBWEI Salomon Brothers World Equity Index
SCORE Special Claim on Residual Equity
SD Standard Deduction
SDB Special District Bond
SDBL Sight Draft, Bill of Lading Attached
SDRs Special Drawing Rights
SE Shareholders' Equity
SEAQ Stock Exchange Automated Quotations
SEC Securities and Exchange Commission
Sen Senator

SEP Simplified Employee Pension Plan
SES Stock Exchange of Singapore
SET Securities Exchange of Thailand
SET Stock Exchange of Thailand
SF Sinking Fund
SFE Sydney Futures Exchange
SG&A Selling, General and Administrative Expenses
SHSE Shanghai Securities Exchange
SIA Securities Industry Association
SIAC Securities Industry Automation Corporation
SIBE Spanish Stock Market Interconnection System
SIC Standard Industrial Classification
SICA Securities Industry Committee on Arbitration
SIMPLE IRA Savings Incentive Match Plan for Employees Individual Retirement Account
SIPC Securities Investor Protection Corporation
SL Sold
SLMA Student Loan Marketing Association (Sallie Mae)
SLO Stop-Limit Order, Stop-Loss Order
SMA Society of Management Accountants
SMA Special Miscellaneous Account
SN Stock Number
SOES Small Order Entry (or Execution) System
SOFFEX Swiss Options and Financial Futures Exchange
SOP Standard Operating Procedure
SOYD Sum of the Years' Digits Method
SpA Società per Azioni (Italian corporation)
SPDA Single Premium Deferred Annuity
SPDR Standard & Poor's Depository Receipt
SPLI Single Premium Life Insurance
SPQR Small Profits, Quick Returns
SPRI Société de Personnes a Responsabilité Limitée (Belgian corporation)
SPX Standard & Poor's 500 Stock Index
Sr Senior
SRO Self-Regulatory Organization

SRP Salary Reduction Plan
SRT Spousal Remainder Trust
SS Social Security
SSA Social Security Administration
SSE Stockholm Stock Exchange
STAGS Sterling Transferable Accruing Government Securities
STB Special Tax Bond
STRIPS Separate Trading of Registered Interest and Principal of Securities
SU Set Up (freight)
SZSE Shenzhen Stock Exchange

T

T- Treasury (as in T-bill, T-bond, T-note)
TA Trade Acceptance
TA Transfer Agent
TAB Tax Anticipation Bill
TAC Targeted Amortization Class
TAN Tax Anticipation Note
T&E Travel and Entertainment Expenses
TASE Tel Aviv Stock Exchange
TBA To Be Announced
TBE Tenancy by the Entirety
TC Tax Court of the United States
TD Time Deposit
TED Spread Treasury Bills versus Eurodollar Futures
TEFRA Tax Equity and Fiscal Responsibility Act of 1982
TFE Toronto Futures Exchange
TIC Tenancy in Common
TIFFE Tokyo International Financial Futures Exchange
TIGER Treasury Investors Growth Receipt
TIP To Insure Promptness
TL Trade-Last
TM Trademark
TOCOM Tokyo Commodity Exchange
TOPIX Tokyo Stock Price Index
TRA Taxpayer Relief Act of 1997
TSE Taiwan Stock Exchange
TSE Toronto Stock Exchange
TT Testamentary Trust
TVA Tennessee Valley Authority

U

UAW United Automobile Workers
UCC Uniform Commercial Code

UCOM United Currency Options Market
UGMA Uniform Gifts to Minors Act
UIT Unit Investment Trust
UL Underwriters' Laboratories
ULC Underwriter's Laboratories of Canada
ULI Underwriter's Laboratories, Inc.
UMW United Mine Workers
UN United Nations
UPC Uniform Practice Code
US United States (of America)
USA United States of America
USBS United States Bureau of Standards
USC United States Code
USCC United States Chamber of Commerce
USIT Unit Share Investment Trust
USJCC United States Junior Chamber of Commerce (JAYCEES)
USS United States Senate
USS United States Ship
UTMA Uniform Transfer to Minors Act
UW Underwriter

V

VA Veterans Administration
VAT Value Added Tax
VD Volume Deleted
Veep Vice President
VELDA SUE Venture Enhancement & Loan Development Administration for Smaller Undercapitalized Enterprises
VI In bankruptcy or receivership; being reorganized under the Bankruptcy Act; securities assumed by such companies (in bond and stock listings of newspapers)
VIP Very Important Person
VL Value Line Investment Survey
VOL Volume
VP Vice President
VRM Variable Rate Mortgage
VSE Vancouver Stock Exchange
VSE Vienna Stock Exchange
VTC Voting Trust Certificate

W

WAM Weighted Average Maturity
WB Waybill
WCA Workmen's Compensation Act

WCE Winnipeg Commodity Exchange

WD When Distributed (in stock listings of newspapers)

WEBS World Equity Benchmark Shares

WHOOPS Washington Public Power Supply System

WI When Issued (in stock listings of newspapers)

WR Warehouse Receipt

WSJ Wall Street Journal

WT Warrant (in stock listings of newspapers)

W/Tax Withholding Tax

WTO World Trade Organization

WW With Warrants (in bond and stock listings of newspapers)

X

X Ex-Interest (in bond listings of newspapers)

XAM AMEX Market Value Index

XD Ex-Dividend (in stock listings of newspapers)

X-Dis Ex-Distribution (in stock listings of newspapers)

XMI AMEX Major Market Index

XR Ex-Rights (in stock listings of newspapers)

XW Ex-Warrants (in bond and stock listings of newspapers)

Y

Y Ex-Dividend and Sales in Full (in stock listings of newspapers)

YLD Yield (in stock listings of newspapers)

YTB Yield to Broker

YTC Yield to Call

YTD Year to Date

YTM Yield to Maturity

Z

Z Zero

ZBA Zero Bracket Amount

ZBB Zero-Based Budgeting

ZR Zero Coupon Issue (Security) (in bond listings of newspapers)

INDEX